# Zulu Identities

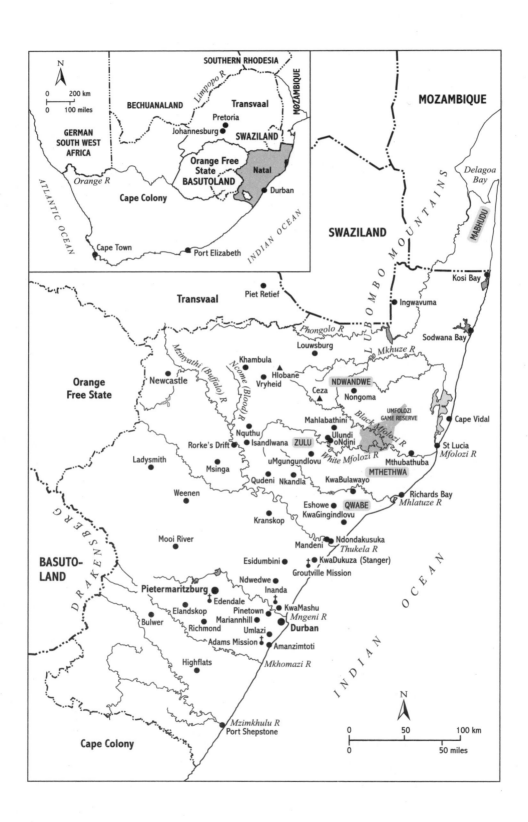

**Inset map labels:**

N
0   200 km
0   100 miles

SOUTHERN RHODESIA
BECHUANALAND
*Limpopo R*
MOZAMBIQUE
Transvaal
Pretoria
Johannesburg
SWAZILAND
GERMAN SOUTH WEST AFRICA
Orange Free State
BASUTOLAND
Natal
*Orange R*
Cape Colony
Durban
ATLANTIC OCEAN
Cape Town
Port Elizabeth
*INDIAN OCEAN*

**Main map labels:**

MOZAMBIQUE
Delagoa Bay
MABHUDU
SWAZILAND
Kosi Bay
Transvaal
Piet Retief
Ingwavuma
LUBOMBO MOUNTAINS
*Phongolo R*
Sodwana Bay
Louwsburg
*Mkhuze R*
*Mzinyathi (Buffalo) R*
Khambula
Hlobane
Vryheid
NDWANDWE
Orange Free State
Newcastle
*Ncome (Blood) R*
Ceza
Nongoma
*Black Mfolozi R*
UMFOLOZI GAME RESERVE
Cape Vidal
Mahlabathini
Ulundi
oNdini
Nquthu
Rorke's Drift
Isandlwana
ZULU
*White Mfolozi R*
St Lucia
*Mfolozi R*
Ladysmith
Msinga
uMgungundlovu
KwaBulawayo
Mthubathuba
MTHETHWA
Qudeni
Nkandla
Weenen
Richards Bay
QWABE
*Mhlatuze R*
Eshowe
KwaGingindlovu
Kranskop
Mooi River
Ndondakusuka
Mandeni
*Thukela R*
BASUTO-LAND
DRAKENSBERG
Esidumbini
KwaDukuza (Stanger)
Groutville Mission
Ndwedwe
Inanda
Pietermaritzburg
Edendale
KwaMashu
Elandskop
Pinetown
*Mngeni R*
Bulwer
Mariannhill
Richmond
Umlazi
Durban
Adams Mission
Amanzimtoti
Highflats
*Mkhomazi R*
INDIAN OCEAN
N
0   50   100 km
0   50 miles
*Mzimkhulu R*
Port Shepstone
Cape Colony

# Zulu Identities
## Being Zulu, Past and Present

*Edited by*
*Benedict Carton, John Laband and Jabulani Sithole*

Columbia University Press
New York

Columbia University Press
Publishers Since 1893
New York / Chichester, West Sussex

Copyright © 2009 The University of Kwa-Zulu Natal
First published in South Africa in 2008 by the
University of Kwa-Zulu Natal Press

Library of Congress Cataloging-in-Publication Data

Zulu identities : being Zulu, past and present / edited by Benedict Carton, John Laband
and Jabulani Sithole.
     p. cm.
 Includes index.
 ISBN 978-0-231-70058-0 (cloth : alk. paper)
 ISBN 978-0-231-70059-7 (pbk. : alk. paper)
 1. Zulu (African people)--Ethnic identity. 2. Zulu (African people)--History. 3. Zulu
(African people)--Politics and government. 4.  Chiefdoms--South Africa--KwaZulu-Natal--
History. 5. Shaka, Zulu Chief, 1787?-1828. 6.  KwaZulu-Natal (South Africa) 7.  KwaZulu-
Natal (South Africa) 8.  KwaZulu-Natal (South Africa)  I. Carton, Benedict. II. Laband,
John, 1947- III. Sithole, Jabulani. IV. Title.

DT1768.Z95Z85 2009
 305.896'3986--dc22

                                    2009004468

Columbia University Press books are printed on permanent and durable acid-free paper.
This book is printed on paper with recycled content.
Printed in India

c 10 9 8 7 6 5 4 3 2 1
p 10 9 8 7 6 5 4 3 2 1

For my friend, colleague and mentor, the late Larry Levine.
*Benedict Carton*


For Fenella, as ever.
*John Laband*


For Zanele and the children and all those who subscribe to
ethnic and racial tolerance in South Africa.
*Jabulani Sithole*

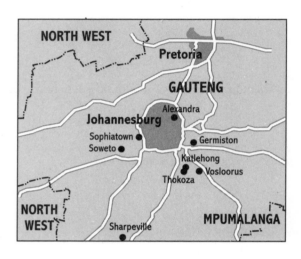

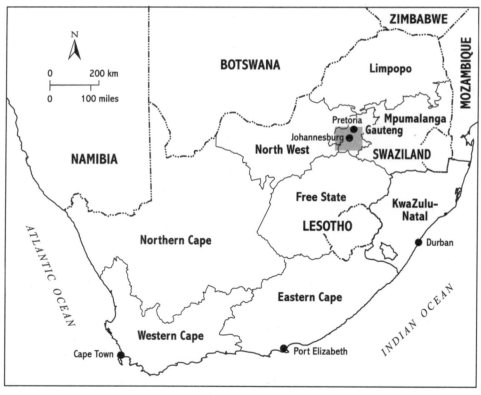

# Contents

# Preface

## Zuluness in South Africa: From 'Struggle' Debate to Democratic Transformation

JABULANI SITHOLE

Individual historians are conditioned by the assumptions and prejudices of their own community, whether it is a community of religion, class, language, race or some combination of two or more of these factors. That is why their historical account, despite some indisputable breakthrough achievements, cannot be free from the limitations set on the authors by their environment.[1]

THESE WORDS SPURRED the making of *Zulu Identities*. While the chapters vary as much in style as in content and analysis, all seek to engage a central aim of our project: to represent different voices. What we bring together are diverse interpretations, which we hope will initiate an interdisciplinary dialogue. The three editors are historians who conceived of *Zulu Identities* in 2001, when the transition to democracy was beginning to open educational institutions, as never before, to the aspirations of scholars who think, speak and write in African languages, among them isiZulu.

It is notable that the presence of more black intellectuals in South African universities has not signalled an end to the politics that circumscribed activist scholarship during the recent decades of mass opposition to white minority rule. Although there has been a shift to 'postmodern' and 'postcolonial' interests, a clash of ideas that once drove anti-apartheid scholarship, the debate between Marxists and liberals, remains relevant today. In fact this crucial disagreement, as many chapters in *Zulu Identities* illustrate, still shapes studies of race, class, gender and ethnicity. In the 1970s and 1980s, when liberal academics charged that Afrikaner and African nationalisms (including Zulu nationalism) were stumbling blocks to the emergence of a 'free' capitalist South Africa, they were criticised by neo-Marxists for being apologists of the economic system that underpinned apartheid.[2] Needless to say, the neo-Marxist school similarly discounted 'backward-looking' racial and tribal categories, even assailing the homeland-based black businessmen, who espoused a mixture of chauvinistic Zulu ethnicity and African nationalism, for maintaining 'social exploitation of, or social control over, their own people'.[3] In this regard the rival liberal and Marxist camps shared a common belief in the 'static' nature of precolonial social relations. Most important, by rejecting nationalism in general and the profiling of ethnicity in particular, they effectively discouraged in-depth investigations of cultural identity.[4]

Harold Wolpe, Bernard Magubane and Jabulani 'Mzala' Nxumalo were among the first scholars influenced by historical materialism to move beyond the Marxist-liberal debate.[5] Wolpe pointed to one major shortcoming of the neo-Marxist anti-nationalist view, economic reductionism, which mistakenly emptied the South African class structure of its racial and ethnic content.[6] Instead, he sought to examine the trajectories of African nationalism, probing the contradictory motives of African middle classes working within the bantustans who were violently opposed to the radical liberation movements and who preferred to opt for greater local autonomy. Wolpe maintained that in the South African apartheid context nationalism could be both reactionary and progressive.[7] Magubane added that in South Africa linkages between the national and class struggles would remain an 'indispensable' reality for as long as apartheid conditions prevailed. He went on to challenge both the neo-Marxist and liberal academics to learn more about the African areas they wrote about but hardly, if ever, visited by venturing outside their comfortable existence and experiencing daily black realities. He further faulted the neo-Marxists for romanticising the working class as a progressive force that was impervious to prejudices that drew on contested ideological, racial and cultural realities in their own societies.[8] 'Mzala' Nxumalo called on liberal and neo-Marxist writers to consider critically the importance of African ethnic identities,[9] not as a fiction of the 'civilising mission' or product of 'divide-and-rule', but rather as a 'lived' entity with linguistic and customary norms that pre-dated the advent of European colonialism.[10]

A group of scholars in the late 1970s, who had recently come under the influence of Shula Marks and Anthony Atmore through their Southern African Societies seminar series at the University of London (Henry Slater, David Hedges, Philip Bonner and Jeff Guy), were the first to apply the historical materialist approach to studies of precolonial southeast African societies.[11] Building on these materialist insights during the 1980s, John Wright and Carolyn Hamilton pioneered studies of Zulu ethnicity in which they argued that Shaka, the founder of the Zulu kingdom, presided over a highly stratified and hierarchal society with the king and the royal aristocracy at the apex.[12] Underneath was a three-tiered society whose social status was determined by the stages at which its members were incorporated into the emerging Zulu state. They included the *amakhosi* and *iziphakanyiswa* (the more important chiefs and notables) who were subjugated in the ensuing stages of Zulu expansion. They were encouraged to align themselves politically with the established Zulu aristocracy and were made to believe that they had a shared interest in maintaining the existing social hierarchy.

The next two tiers consisted of the *amantungwa* and the *amalala*. The former supplied the necessary labour to the state, and the Zulu aristocracy encouraged them to adopt the *ntungwa* ethnic identity as a means of fostering a sense of belonging. In time they came to think of themselves as sharing a common origin and culture as the Zulu aristocracy. The last tier was made up of the majority of people who were viewed as ethnically inferior and referred to in derogatory terms by members of the other tiers. They were either known as *amalala* (the menials), the *amanhlwenga* (the destitutes), or *iziyendane* (those with strange hairstyles). These people lived on the peripheries of the Zulu kingdom and their subjugation was only effected in the final stages of Shaka's Zulu expansion.[13] Hamilton and Wright, therefore, saw Zulu ethnicity as a shifting historical force with rational, as opposed to mechanical or manufactured, components that could be manipulated by African and colonial actors alike.

Gerhard Maré followed this line of inquiry by exploring how a civil conflict in Natal and KwaZulu in the 1980s revealed, among other things, the consequences of the Inkatha Freedom Party's (Inkatha or IFP) enforced monopolisation of the construction of patriarchal Zulu culture, which extended the life of a moribund homeland system while nurturing embryonic violence that threatened political transition to an inclusive democracy in South Africa.[14] Indeed, two decades ago the mere mention of Zulu politics conjured fears of catastrophic turmoil. Such turmoil had its origins in one of the most closely observed events at the end of the last millennium, the escalating apartheid state-sponsored internecine violence between the IFP, on the one hand, and the United Democratic Front (UDF), the Congress of South African Trade Unions (COSATU) and, by the early 1990s, their recently unbanned ally, the African National Congress (ANC)), on the other hand. Wright, in particular, noted that Western reporters, who ignored the role of ethnicity in their own societies while reflexively hyping it in South Africa, analysed these clashes as manifestations of the timeless Zulu warrior spirit, without understanding relations of power historically. These relations of power reflected multiple Zulu identities, which in the past and present defied stereotypical characteristics associated with 'Shaka's martial nation'.[15] Wright's view found resonance in Hamilton's publication on Shaka in the late 1990s.[16]

For too many reasons to cite here, the imagined racial and/or tribal apocalypse never occurred. Since the relatively peaceful elections in April 1994, the idea of national citizenship has gained more and more supporters. In fact, it is enshrined in a new Constitution that recognises the importance of ethnic identities in the context of each citizen's protection against the abuses of 'tribalism' and sexism. Yet, in spite of these legal provisions, some sections of the South African population are still searching for a way to understand how to reconcile individual human rights with collective cultural belonging. This is best illustrated in the unfolding drama around issues of Zulu culture, history and identities that is a direct consequence of recent legislation, the Traditional Leadership and Governance Framework Act, No. 41 of 2003, which has not only generated fresh political tensions but has also deepened interest in what it means to be Zulu in early twenty-first-century South Africa.[17]

In October 2004 President Thabo Mbeki appointed a twelve-member Commission on Traditional Leadership Disputes and Claims under the leadership of Professor Thandabantu Nhlapo of the University of Cape Town (hereafter the Nhlapo Commission) to perform two important tasks.[18] They were to investigate the position of all paramountcies and paramount chiefs that had been in existence and recognised, and which were still in existence and recognised before the commencement of the Traditional Leadership and Governance Framework Act; and to hear more than five kinds of cases. These were cases where there was doubt whether traditional leadership was established in accordance with the customary law; cases where the title of an incumbent traditional leader was challenged; claims by communities to be recognised as traditional communities; cases questioning whether any establishment of 'tribes' was legitimate; disputes around traditional authority boundaries and the resultant division or merging of 'tribes'; and other relevant matters.[19] The Commission had received more than 705 countrywide claims and applications by the end of June 2007. Eleven of these were from the KwaZulu-Natal-based *amakhosi* and their councils.[20]

Some of the applicants took advantage of the provisions of the new legislation and denied ever being subjects of any of the Zulu kings.[21] The Hlubi, for example, went so far as to announce that they were on the verge of developing and codifying their own distinct 'isiHlubi' language.[22] *Inkosi* Melizwe Dlamini also hinted that the Nhlangwini, too, were in the process of reviving their own language, 'isiNhlangwini'. He alleged that it had existed in precolonial southern KwaZulu-Natal before the missionaries mistook it for a regional variation of isiZulu when they codified the languages spoken in southeast Africa.[23] Other applicants simply maintained that all they wanted was to rectify the historical distortions that denied that their great-grandparents were paramount rulers during the precolonial period.[24] A few of the applicants had longstanding disputes with the former homeland 'elites', which dated back to the 1970s and 1980s. They were, therefore, using the provisions of the Traditional Leadership and Governance Framework Act to try to put right the wrongs of the apartheid state and the KwaZulu homeland administration.[25]

There were mixed reactions to the KwaZulu-Natal applications to the Nhlapo Commission. Goodwill Zwelithini publicly condemned the submissions, dismissing them as mischievous challenges, not only to his authority as the Zulu king, but also to the Zulu nation as a whole. In a show of force, he presided over gatherings at

Donnybrook, in the vicinity of the Nhlangwini chiefdom, and at Ingwavuma among the people of *Inkosi* Mabhudu Israel Tembe. At these gatherings he vowed to deal with the alleged 'impostors'.[26] He returned to the Ingwavuma area to preside over the reed dance ceremony within weeks after the first visit.[27] Cracks began to show within the ruling families of both the Nhlangwini and Thonga polities when some members publicly pledged loyalty to the Zulu monarch shortly after his visits to their areas.[28]

The IFP-dominated Provincial House of Traditional Leaders convened two meetings to mount a campaign to defend the Zulu kingdom on 5 and 11 July 2007.[29] These gatherings brought together the former KwaZulu homeland-based allies in the person of the IFP president, *Inkosi* Mangosuthu Buthelezi, more than 300 IFP-aligned *amakhosi* and their subjects, senior Zulu princes and the Zulu monarch. They also revived 'war talk', which was last witnessed during the peak of violence in the late 1980s and early 1990s. The king told the meeting at kwaNongoma on 5 July 2007 that he had received numerous calls from his subjects, urging him to let them have a go at those who were undermining the Zulu kingdom.[30] The print media also reported that senior Prince Reggie suggested that, in order to resolve this matter once and for all, the king and the Zulu nation should pay a visit to Bergville and Nhlangwini and to the chiefdoms of the other applicants. He said, to great applause from the *amakhosi* present, that he betted that they would all take to the mountains.[31] The meeting echoed the king's view that the applicants were traitors and rebels who threatened the very existence of the Zulu nation.[32]

The KwaZulu-Natal government, which had expediently positioned itself as the new champions of Zulu nationalism when the ANC took control of the province from the IFP in 2004, also rallied behind the Zulu monarch. On 5 July 2007, Dr Zweli Mkhize, the ANC's deputy provincial chairperson, assured the gathering at kwaNongoma that the laws which the provincial government had passed since 2004 protected the rights of and recognised Goodwill Zwelithini as the only king in the KwaZulu-Natal province.[33] On 19 July 2007, the provincial cabinet issued a statement in which it reiterated that it recognised Goodwill Zwelithini as the only king in KwaZulu-Natal.[34] Shortly thereafter, the then ANC's deputy president, Jacob Zuma, also acknowledged Goodwill Zwelithini as the only recognised monarch in the province.[35] Faced with such powerful forces, six of the eleven *amakhosi* developed cold feet and withdrew their applications. Meanwhile four of the five remaining applicants, Mabhudu Tembe, Melizwe Dlamini, Mboneni Mavuso and Mzondeni Hlongwane, asked the Nhlapo Commission for 'personal protection'. They alleged that they were receiving death threats.[36] Just over a month later Professor Nhlapo and two of his senior commissioners, Professors Jeff Peires and Jan Bekker, resigned. Nhlapo cited work pressures, as a member of the University of Cape Town's Executive, as reasons for his resignation from the Commission.[37]

Most of the arguments that the various applicants submitted to the Nhlapo Commission were not entirely new. When scholars highlighted existing tensions and contradictions in various parts of the province in the past, the Zulu nationalist politicians, leaders and activists either ignored them, intimidated authors, or simply dismissed their views with contempt. Now that the same set of issues has been raised by fellow *amakhosi* and their traditional councils, they are deemed subversive. This is evident in the recent angry responses of both the Zulu monarch and various Zulu nationalist groups. Patrick Harries, for example, published a journal article shortly after the beginning of the Ingwavuma land controversy in the early 1980s in which he highlighted the long-standing contestations over Zulu over-lordship among Tembe chiefdoms to the north of the Hluhluwe and Mkhuze Rivers.[38] Shortly before David Webster was assassinated, he too wrote a chapter that was published posthumously in which he mentioned that there were competing Zulu and Thonga ethnic identities in the Ingwavuma area.[39] His chapter drew sharp criticism from Harriet Ngubane who accused him of political bias because he had alleged that the IFP was imposing Zuluness on the local population through a campaign of forced recruitment. She also dismissed his arguments on the grounds of insider knowledge as a person who was born and raised in the area and on the basis of her vast research experience and her linguistic abilities and expertise.[40]

Two of our authors in this volume, Dingani Mthethwa and Mbongiseni Buthelezi, talk to the same set of issues. Mthethwa, who was born and raised in the Ingwavuma area like Ngubane, also recounts the dynamic struggles between one of the rival *amakhosi* within the Tembe polity and the apartheid state and the KwaZulu homeland authorities. He concludes that these struggles highlighted the existence of competing Thonga and Zulu ethnic identities in the area. Buthelezi appears to have anticipated submissions to the Nhlapo Commission because he, too, questions the simplistic assumptions that all black people in KwaZulu-Natal are voluntary subjects of the Zulu king. He uses *izibongo* to show that the Buthelezi people were forcibly integrated into the Zulu state against their will and that during this process their history and heritage were deliberately suppressed and silenced. He therefore argues that the Buthelezi people should strive for South African citizenship as a more accurate and collective designation and identity than the Zulu ethnic classification. Fierce contestation over Zulu history and culture, which speaks directly to the subjects of the chapters by authors such as Michael Lambert and Suzanne Leclerc-Madlala in this volume, also unfolded alongside the above disputes over Zuluness and Zulu identities.

Even a cursory review of the dynamics of Zulu history and identities show that there is an urgent need for established academic scholars to rejuvenate their intellectual engagement with Zuluness and for younger scholars to accord this subject new treatment and nuanced understanding. The three editors ensured that an unprecedented number of Zulu-speaking intellectuals contributed to this volume because we share the view that they are in a position to hear things that used to go unheard and, in this way, they will be able to engage their non-Zulu-speaking counterparts in ways that were not possible in the past. *Zulu Identities* has benefited from both the recent political transformation, as well as the challenges that continue to confront the South African nation-building exercise. The editors also share the view that the greatest value of the radical-liberal debate of the past few decades was its ability to foreground both the political and intellectual concerns in the context of the struggle against apartheid. However, its tendency to discourage serious enquiry into issues of national and ethnic identities was one of its major weaknesses. We therefore think that the defeat of apartheid and the emerging democracy have created openings for scholars to venture into these fields of enquiry without fearing possible stigmatisation that such work could have provoked in the past. This, we believe, will free South African history from its past constraints and prejudices.

## Notes

1. M. Wilson and L. Thompson, *The Oxford History of South Africa, Volume 1* (Oxford: Clarendon Press, 1969), p. vi. It is also cited in J. Nxumalo, 'The National Question in the Writing of South African History: A Critical Survey of Some Major Tendencies', Working Paper 22, Faculty of Technology, The Open University, undated, p. 29.
2. For a brief representation of these views, see M. Legassick, 'Legislation, Ideology and Economy in Post-1948 South Africa', *Journal of Southern African Studies (JSAS)* 1:1 (October 1974): 5.
3. Ibid.: 7. For similar views on the African middle classes, see also T. Couzens, *The New African: A Study of the Life and Work of H.I.E. Dhlomo* (Johannesburg: Ravan Press, 1985), Chapter One.
4. Saul Dubow has recently made a similar point about the liberal and radical scholars. See S. Dubow, 'Thoughts on South Africa: Some Preliminary Points', in *History Making and Present Day Politics: The Meaning of Collective Memory in South Africa*, ed. Hans Erik Stolten (Uppsalla: Nordic Africa Institute, 2007), pp. 70 and 72.
5. Harold Wolpe and Bernard Magubane were United States and England based exiled South African academics who doubled up as political activists. Mzala Nxumalo was a cadre of Umkhonto weSizwe, and a member of both the ANC and the South African Communist Party. At the time of his death in 1991 he was studying towards a doctoral qualification with the Open University.
6. H. Wolpe, 'Race and Class and the National Struggle in South Africa', in *The National Question in South Africa*, ed. M. van Diepen (London and New Jersey: Zed Books, 1988), p. 62; H. Wolpe, *Race, Class and the Apartheid State* (London and Paris: James Currey and UNESCO Press, 1988), p. 33.
7. Wolpe, 'Race and Class and the National Struggle in South Africa', p. 57.
8. B. Magubane, 'Mounting Class and National Struggles in South Africa', in *South Africa: From Uitenhage to Soweto*, ed. B. Magubane (Trenton, NJ: Africa World Press, 1989), p. 86.
9. Nxumalo, 'The National Question in the Writing of South African History', pp. 3, 30–31.
10. The contours of 'tribal' community could be clarified further through comparative studies of neighbouring polities, as in the case of the nineteenth-century Zulu and Swazi kingdoms; see Nxumalo, 'The National Question in the Writing of South African History', p. 33.
11. See H. Slater, 'Transitions in the Political Economy of South-East Africa before 1840' (D.Phil. thesis, University of Sussex, 1976); D.W. Hedges, 'Trade and Politics in Southern Mozambique and Zululand in the Eighteenth and Nineteenth Centuries' (Ph.D. thesis, University of London, 1978); P. Bonner, 'Classes, the Mode of Production and the State in Pre-colonial Swaziland', in *Economy*

*and Society in Pre-Industrial South Africa*, eds. S. Marks and A. Atmore (London: Longman, 1980); and J. Guy, *The Destruction of the Zulu Kingdom: The Civil War in Zululand, 1879–1884* (London: Longman, 1979).

12. C.A. Hamilton, 'Ideology, Oral Tradition and the Struggle for Power in the Early Zulu Kingdom' (Masters thesis, University of the Witwatersrand, 1986); J.B. Wright, 'The Dynamics of Power and Conflict in the Thukela-Mzimkhulu Region in the Late 18th and Early 19th Centuries: A Critical Reconstruction' (Ph.D. thesis, University of the Witwatersrand, 1989).

13. See C. Hamilton and J. Wright, 'The Making of the Lala: Ethnicity, Ideology and Class-Formation in a Pre-colonial Context', unpublished paper presented to the History Workshop, University of the Witwatersrand, 1984; C. Hamilton and J. Wright, 'The Making of the Amalala: Ethnicity, Ideology and Relations of Subordination in a Precolonial Context', *South African Historical Journal* 22 (May 1990): 1–32. For a more refined account of the origins and the making of an ideology that underpinned precolonial Zulu ethnicity, see J. Wright and C. Hamilton, 'Traditions and Transformations: The Pongolo-Mzimkhulu Region in the Late Eighteenth and Early Nineteenth Centuries', in *Natal and Zululand: From Earliest Times to 1910: A New History*, eds. A. Duminy and B. Guest (Pietermaritzburg: University of Natal Press and Shuter & Shooter, 1989), pp. 72–73.

14. G. Maré, *Brothers Born of Warrior Blood: Politics and Ethnicity in South Africa* (Johannesburg: Ravan Press, 1992), pp. vii, viii and ix.

15. J. Wright, 'Reconstituting Shaka Zulu for the Twentieth-Century', *Southern African Humanities* 18: 2 (2006): 139–153. See also J. Wright, 'Reflections on the Politics of Being Zulu', Chapter 3 in this volume.

16. C.A. Hamilton, *Terrific Majesty: The Powers of Shaka Zulu and the Limits of Historical Invention* (Cape Town and Johannesburg: David Philip, 1998), p. 3.

17. Republic of South Africa (hereafter RSA), *Government Gazette No. 25855*, Volume 462, Traditional Leadership and Governance Framework Act No. 41 of 2003, 19 December 2003.

18. See Department of Provincial and Local Government (hereafter DPLG), 'Press Statement on the Occasion of the Announcement of a "Commission on Traditional Leadership", Saturday, 16 October 2004', http://www.thedplg.gov.za (accessed 16 August 2007).

19. RSA, *Government Gazette No. 25855*, Volume 462, 19 December 2003, Chapter 6, Section 25, sub-sections (i)–(vi).

20. These applicants were the amaHlubi under the leadership of M.J. Hadebe (Langalibalele Hadebe II), the amaNgwane of Mzondeni Alfred Hlongwane, the amaNgwane of Mboneni Absolom Mavuso, the Nhlangwini under Melizwe Zeluxolo Dlamini, the amaThonga under Mabhudu Israel Tembe, the amaNguni under Mbhekeni Shadrack Ndwandwe, the amaZizi of Mfanafuthi Miya, the Mngomezulu under S.D. Mngomezulu; and the two Madlala polities under the leadership of Elias Msomi and Vusimuzi Andries Madlala respectively. See *Sunday Tribune*, 1 July 2007; *Sunday Times*, 8 July 2007; see also 'Minutes of the AmaHlubi National Committee held in Pietermaritzburg on 24 April 2004', http://www.mkhangelingoma.co.za./heritage/national (accessed 13 October 2007); and '*ISIZWE SAMAHLUBI*, Submission to the Commission on Traditional Disputes and Claims, July 2004', http://www.mkhangelingoma.co.za./heritage/historypdf (accessed 16 August 2007).

21. *The Mercury,*13 July 2007 and *Sowetan*, 3 August 2007.

22. *Isolezwe*, 8 August 2007.

23. Author's conversation with the *Inkosi* Melizwe Dlamini at Killie Campbell Africana Library (KCAL), University of KwaZulu-Natal, 19 October 2007.

24. *Um-Africa*, 13–19 July 2007.

25. Langalibalele II, for instance, who refused to accept the homeland system if it meant inclusion into KwaZulu put the Hlubi on a collision course with the KwaZulu homeland authorities, which worsened at the beginning of the 1980s. The KwaZulu homeland government also deposed the *inkosi* of the Mngomezulu people named Ntunja (Zondiwe II) because of his opposition to the apartheid and homeland systems. He was exiled to Swaziland where he died. Other chiefs who clashed with the KwaZulu homeland authorities were *Inkosi* Hlongwane of the Amangwane in Bergville, and the *Nkosi* Molefe of the Ba Tlokoa in the Nquthu and Mhlabunzima Maphumulo of the Mkhambathini area. S. Dlamini, '*Kodwa uShenge wayizondani kangaka inkosi uNtunja?*', *Umafrika*, 24–30 August 2007; University of KwaZulu-Natal (UKZN), KCAL, Buthelezi Speeches (BS), 'Opening Address by the Chief Executive Officer: The Honourable Umntwana Mangosuthu G. Buthelezi, Special Session of the Second KwaZulu Legislative Assembly, Bhekuzulu College, Nongoma, 16 January 1976'; University of Fort Hare (UFH), ANC Archives, Oliver Reginald

Tambo (ORT) Papers, Series C, Box 75, C4.22.1.2b, 'Speech at the KwaZulu Elections Rally, Umlazi, 19 February 1978'; *Post*, 23 March 1978; *Sunday Times*, 8 July 1979; and J. Sithole, 'Neither Communists nor Saboteurs: KwaZulu Bantustan Politics', in South African Democracy Education Trust, *The Road to Democracy in South Africa (1970–1980)* (Pretoria: University of South Africa Press, 2006), pp. 813 and 831–832.

26. *Sowetan*, 5 and 6 August 2007 and *Sunday Times*, 5 August 2007.
27. *The Mercury*, 1 October 2007.
28. Letters to the Editor by *Inkosi* A. Makhoba, Spokesperson of the Nhlangwini Royal Council, *Um-Afrika*, 27 July–2 August 2007; and Mr Noxhaka Dlamini, the head *induna* of the *Nkosi* Melizwe Dlamini, *Um-Afrika*, 27 July–2 August 2007. See also *The Mercury*, 23 August 2007 and *Isolezwe*, 23 Agasti 2007.
29. *Sunday Tribune*, 8 July 2007; *The Mercury*, 5 and 13 July 2007 and *Sowetan*, 11 July 2007.
30. *The Mercury*, 6 July 2007.
31. Ibid. and *Sunday Tribune*, 8 July 2007.
32. *The Mercury*, 5 and 13 July 2007 and *Sowetan*, 11 July 2007.
33. See *The Mercury*, 6 July 2007.
34. *Sowetan*, 20 July 2007.
35. *Sunday Tribune*, 29 July 2007.
36. *Sowetan*, 11 October 2007. More groups are pursuing research initiatives which have also grown out of the desire to make submissions to the Nhlapo Commission. See for example, Siyabonga Mkhize, 'Isizwe sabaMbo', unpublished draft document, September–October 2007.
37. See *Daily Dispatch*, 29 November 2007.
38. P. Harries, 'History, Ethnicity and the Ngwavuma Land Deal: The Zulu Northern Frontier in the Nineteenth-Century', *Journal of Natal and Zulu History* (1983): 19.
39. D. Webster, '*Abafazi baThonga Bafihlakala*: Ethnicity and Gender in a KwaZulu Border Community', in eds. A.D. Spiegel and P.A. McAllister, *Tradition and Transition in Southern Africa: Festschrift for Philip and Iona Mayer* (Johannesburg: Witwatersrand University Press, 1991), pp. 243–271.
40. H. Ngubane, 'A Review of David Webster's: *Abafazi baThonga Bafihlakala*' in *Agenda: A Journal about Women and Gender* 13 (1992): 70–74.

# Note on Orthography, Translation and Terminology

ISIZULU ORTHOGRAPHY IS a subject of ongoing debate. Since there is no equivalent language institution, like the French Académie Française, overseeing the uniformity of isiZulu, the reader should expect some fluidity in the linguistic dimensions of 'Zuluness'. In this book we have endeavoured to use recent spellings of isiZulu terms, though different renderings of place names, for example, Umfolozi and Mfolozi, may appear in chapters. Where there are quoted archival sources using an older orthography, we have not changed the original words. Some authors' isiZulu-to-English translations may not accord with readers' understandings of isiZulu. We have checked all translations, particularly idiomatic expressions, with a number of expert mother-tongue speakers and writers of isiZulu. At the same time, we feel that slightly variant translations are inevitable; they reflect how a predominantly 'oral' language embodies long-standing performance traditions such as praise poetry that shift over time and adjust to new audiences. Finally, the reader may note that authors use a range of terms to describe 'Zulu' people (i.e., amaZulu, isiZulu-speaking Africans, isiZulu speakers, and so forth). There is considerable disagreement over what defines a Zulu person and Zulu polity. Indeed, one of the organising themes of this volume probes that very question.

# Acknowledgments

THIS VOLUME WOULD not have been possible without the vision and commitment of our contributors. We, the editors, thank them. Our families and colleagues have supported us during the long journey that culminated in *Zulu Identities*. To them, we express our deepest appreciation. Along the way, Mike Kirkwood intervened with crucial conceptual advice. From start to finish, we were fortunate to work with publisher Glenn Cowley and the superb professionals of the University of KwaZulu-Natal Press. In particular, Trish Comrie and Alison Lockhart moulded a huge manuscript into a beautiful book. Finally, we owe an especial debt of gratitude to editor Sally Hines, whose insight and perseverance made *Zulu Identities* a reality.

# Abbreviations

| | |
|---|---|
| ABM | American Board Mission or American Board of Commissioners for Foreign Missions |
| ACC | African Congregational Church |
| ACLA | Advisory Committee on Land Allocation |
| ACU | African Christian Union |
| AICs | African Independent Churches |
| AME | African Methodist Episcopal (Church) |
| ANC | African National Congress |
| AZM | American Zulu Mission |
| BC | black consciousness |
| BEE | black economic empowerment |
| BMSC | Bantu Men's Social Centre |
| CCP | Central Cattle Pattern |
| CMS | Christian Missionary Society (British) |
| COSAS | Congress of South African Students |
| COSATU | Congress of South African Trade Unions |
| CRLR | Commission on Restitution of Land Rights |
| DACST | Department of Arts, Culture, Science and Technology |
| DDAFA | Durban and District African Football Association |
| DDNFA | Durban and District Native Football Association |
| DLA | Department of Land Affairs |
| DRLA | Department of Regional and Land Affairs |
| EIA | Environmental Impact Assessment |
| FOSATU | Federation of South African Trade Unions |
| GDTA | Germiston and District Taxi Association |
| GPS | Global Positioning Satellite |
| GSLWP | Greater St Lucia Wetland Park |
| ICU | Industrial and Commercial Workers' Union |
| IEC | Independent Electoral Commission |
| IFP | Inkatha Freedom Party |

| | |
|---|---|
| Inkatha | Inkatha Yenkululedo Yesiwe |
| IYB | Inkatha Youth Brigade |
| KATO | Katlehong Taxi Association |
| KBNR | KwaZulu Bureau of Natural Resources |
| KLA | KwaZulu Legislative Assembly |
| KMC | KwaZulu Monuments Council |
| KZN | KwaZulu-Natal |
| LAPC | Land and Agricultural Policy Centre |
| LSDI | Lubombo Spatial Development Initiative |
| MAWU | Metal and Allied Workers' Union |
| MK | Umkhonto weSizwe |
| NAA | Native Administration Act |
| NAC | Native Appeals Court |
| NAD | Native Affairs Department |
| NC | Native Commissioner |
| NEC | National Executive Committee (of the ANC) |
| NGO | non-governmental organisation |
| NNC | Natal Native Congress |
| NP | National Party |
| NPA | Natal Provincial Administration |
| NPB | Natal Parks Board |
| NSCA | Native Service Contract Act |
| NUMSA | National Union of Metalworkers of South Africa |
| PAC | Pan-Africanist Congress |
| PLAAS | Programme for Land and Agrarian Studies |
| RBM | Richards Bay Minerals |
| RLCC | Regional Land Claims Commissioner |
| RTV | Rural Television Network |
| SABC | South African Broadcasting Company |
| SACP | South African Communist Party |
| SADF | South African Defence Force |
| SANNC | South African Native National Congress |
| SASA | South African Scout Association |
| SASCO | South African Students Congress |
| SNA | Secretary for Native Affairs |
| TNC | Transvaal Native Congress |
| TRC | Truth and Reconciliation Commission |
| UDF | United Democratic Front |
| UNNACI | United Native National Association of Commerce and Industry |
| UWUSA | United Workers' Union of South Africa |
| WDAFA | Witwatersrand and District African Football Association |

| | |
|---|---|
| ZCC | Zulu Congregational Church |
| ZEAL | Zululand Environmental Alliance |
| ZNA | Zulu National Association |

# Frames of Debate

*Chapter 1*

# Introduction
## Zuluness in the Post- and Neo-worlds

BENEDICT CARTON

IN JUNE 2005 the queen of talk-television, Oprah Winfrey, visited KwaZulu-Natal and treated schoolchildren to lunch, one of her many gifts to a country that makes her 'feel so at home'. She has funded various development projects in South Africa, often introducing her philanthropic endeavours with salutes to Nelson Mandela, father of the rainbow nation. After a goodwill stop in Pietermaritzburg, Oprah lauded efforts to accelerate black economic advancement. She also confided to an audience that she 'always wondered what it would be like if it turned out I am a South African'. She then continued: 'Do you know that I actually am one? I went in search of my roots and had my DNA tested, and I am a Zulu.' This revelation made headlines, with daily newspapers from South Africa and the United States running the caption, 'Oprah: I'm a Zulu and Proud of It'.[1] In KwaZulu-Natal, where Zulu pride once stoked internecine conflict, her affirmation barely stirred comment.

Although it faded quickly, the story of 'Oprah Zulu' signals a decisive moment. Only fifteen years earlier, during South Africa's transition from apartheid, her disclosure might have unleashed a flood of articles sensationalising her devotion to Mangosuthu Buthelezi's Inkatha Freedom Party (IFP or Inkatha). As F.W. de Klerk's National Party joined Mandela's African National Congress (ANC) in multiparty talks, Buthelezi urged Zulus to pursue self-determination, fuelling a civil war between the IFP and ANC and its allies. Yet invoking the context of this violent interregnum tends to obscure contemporary dimensions of Oprah's bond, in the words of one *New York Post* journalist, to the 'famous Zulu tribe'.[2] Her admission might be more fully understood in relation to the fate of Inkatha's platform, which proclaimed that Shaka's great nation would rise again. Buthelezi acknowledged the abrupt diminution of this heroic belief in an address in January 2005, when he beseeched 'Zulus . . . not [to] let our Zuluness be destroyed'. He envisaged the 'collapse of our nation into . . . South Africa',[3] a trend confirmed in Chapter 33 of this book – Lawrence Piper's meticulous appraisal of voting patterns in KwaZulu-Natal, where loyalty to the IFP is fast eroding.

How then do we make sense of Buthelezi's plaintive message and Oprah's lineage-hunting?[4] One answer could hinge on the accomplishments of populist nation-building and rising black elites in South Africa.[5] Contrary to Buthelezi's lament, Oprah's revelation suggests that Zuluness is not a vanishing relic, but a malleable construct, adapting to postcolonial currents. Indeed, in 2006 followers of deposed ANC Deputy-President Jacob Zuma rallied behind their fallen leader by conducting traditional Zulu strengthening rituals outside the magistrate's court where he was being tried for rape. A decade before the demise of apartheid, some scholars anticipated the postcolonial turn when they started to abandon orthodox Marxism, which emphasised how white settler capitalism, to the exclusion of other local, national and global processes, prefigured the arc of modern South Africa.[6] In particular, social historians' critiques of structural materialism pointed to ways in which culture operates not simply as an auxiliary mode of political economy but as a crucial dimension of power itself, reflecting contested racial, gender, ethnic, religious and linguistic dynamics, as well as class struggles.[7]

Informed by such postcolonial ideas, *Zulu Identities* explores the cultural alchemy of *ubuZulu bethu*, an idiom, according to Jabulani Sithole, that captures the shared narratives, hybrid expressions and contradictory meanings of 'our Zuluness', which different actors espouse or discard over time. *UbuZulu bethu* also provides the spatial metaphor to situate studies of Zuluness in a research commons, an area of inquiry defined more by its intersecting paths than by high boundaries; some routes vary from the worn to fresh; others vanish or rematerialise. This network can be navigated with multiple tools such as fluency in isiZulu, *mfecane* debates, Biblical exegeses, public health policy, cosmologies of traditional medicine, and so forth. Moreover, in contrast to the late-apartheid period, contributors to *Zulu Identities* now enter the commons without the overriding fear of reprisal. Not long ago, a stark choice confronted academics in the terrain of Zuluness: join an Inkatha guide or his ANC rival and risk fratricidal violence. But the predicted conflagration on election eve of 1994 never came to pass – a fact that profoundly frames this book. Thus from the opening chapters, hoary assumptions of 'Zulucentrism', which reified Shaka kaSenzangakhona and his legacies, present a problem to interrogate rather than a challenge to avoid. New contingencies, from ANC-government-sponsored land redistribution and heritage tourism to truth and reconciliation and sexual socialisation in the age of AIDS, not only guide the compass of analysis, they inspire an unprecedented number of isiZulu-speaking scholars in this book to probe how today's changing rituals and social transformations link past with present.

In the new South Africa there is much that still evokes the old – fossilised ethnic classifications, for one thing, which John Wright remarks in Chapter 3 continue to hold sway. It is striking how many accounts of Zulu history accept as their point of departure Shaka's boundless aggression. Even more conspicuous, themes of atavistic Zulu terror persist, despite research over the last twenty years that debunks conceptions of an all-determining *mfecane*, the upheavals attributed to an embryonic Zulu empire, which supposedly depopulated southeast Africa in the early nineteenth century.[8] Most scholars agree that harrowing images of the *mfecane* have to be retraced to their nineteenth-century sources, many of them white authors hoping to cloak their own predations or professing to save European civilisation from African chaos, or both. In Chapter 7 Dan Wylie elaborates on this line of inquiry in his dissection of the lies published by colonial critics of Shaka's 'wars of extermination', which reputedly victimised millions and instilled hatred of Zulu belligerence in neighbouring Xhosa chiefdoms. In the early 1990s journalists seized on this 'mother's milk' stereotype when reporting on what they said were casualties of an age-old animosity between Zulu IFP and Xhosa ANC members. Philip Bonner and Vusi Ndima uncover the fallacy of this supposition in Chapter 31. They identify far more relevant trigger factors such as rifts within unions, alienating labour migrants caught between their commitments to syndicalism and supporting rural kin in KwaZulu.

In the aptly titled Chapter 6, 'Revisiting the Stereotype of Shaka's "Devastations"', John Wright looks back to the objectives of white supremacists, who attempted to splinter mass resistance by classifying people into discrete races and tribes, each with its own destiny. Primary evidence from the colonial era, he indicates, invariably reveals the opposite – polyglot exchanges between actors across a range of classes, generations, genders and religions.[9] Wright applies this critical understanding of heterogeneous sources to his clarifying portrait of the Zulu kingdom, which he places within a 400-to-500-mile (640-to-800-kilometre) radius, hardly the colossal empire bestriding southern Africa. This 'conquest state' was far from monolithic, for it contained a changeable amalgam of chiefdoms. Many of the people labelled Zulu by the twentieth century, he contends, had been subjects of a paramount ruler who stood third on a list of fealty, below the homestead head and, at another remove, lineage chief. In Chapter 8, John Laband similarly punctures the idea of enduring Zulu supremacy. He points to Isandlwana, a battle that saw King Cetshwayo's uSuthu regiments annihilate Queen Victoria's redcoats in January 1879, as the pyrrhic victory crystallising myths of the preternaturally dominant Zulu nation. The detail regularly overshadowed in popular versions of the Anglo-Zulu War, Ian Knight asserts in Chapter 15, is that the outcome at Isandlwana drove British troops to destroy a royal house that reigned no longer than a single lifespan.

In his archaeological survey in Chapter 4 Gavin Whitelaw analyses the recent formation of Zulu identity in relation to Bantu migrations. He charts how 1 500 years of Nguni settlement patterns in KwaZulu-Natal gradually produced the 'cultural package' of patrilineal kinship mistakenly attributed to Shaka's genius. Whitelaw's findings are complemented in Chapter 5 – W.D. Hammond-Tooke's study of livestock husbandry, which comprised a set of agricultural practices that Nguni farmers conveyed from central and eastern Africa two millennia ago. They established the conventions of bovine exchange that later underpinned the extensive patron-client ties of Zulu royalty. Thomas McClendon's Chapter 23 links this discussion of evolving late Iron Age customs to twentieth-century politics. He traces how African peasants in segregation-era Natal embraced pre-Shakan lineage dynamics as white sugar barons sought to embed their version of retribalised Zulu tradition in the legal foundation of settler rule.

The postcolonial implications of tribalism prompt Mbongiseni Buthelezi to ask in Chapter 2 why so many isiZulu-speaking Africans regard Shaka as their illustrious father. Deconstructing the first king's praises, *izibongo*, Buthelezi parses the verses that herald a regal 'attacker, who has long been attacking them'. This tribute, Buthelezi argues, explains why elders of his own lineage strain to recite their distant ancestors' experiences, but in bardic style can reel off Zulu feats. When Shaka subjugated autonomous chiefs such as Phungashe Buthelezi, their *izibongo* and oral traditions were proscribed. To repair wounds of this precolonial past and salvage the lore of clans Shaka vanquished, Mbongiseni Buthelezi recommends another truth and reconciliation process that could investigate how an autonomous Zulu regime consolidated its sovereignty. In Chapter 9 Sifiso Ndlovu rearticulates Buthelezi's question: why should so many isiZulu-speaking Africans regard Shaka as their great patriarch when other figures have equal significance? Ndlovu trains the spotlight on Dingane kaSenzangakhona, who relied on guidance from a matriarch, namely Queen Mnkabayi, before deciding to remove his brother, Shaka, who was weakening the kingdom with untenable campaigns. King Dingane again acted on Mnkabayi's advice, Ndlovu illustrates, when mobilising against Piet Retief's armed voortrekkers, a major incursion that Shaka never had to face.

Other whites, of course, moulded how the kingdom would develop and be perceived. Though blinkered by prejudice, their accounts of indigenous social obligations illuminate aspects of nascent Zulu rule. In the 1820s a few European men transformed Port Natal into their hub of commerce and patriarchy, taking on the prerogatives of polygamous homestead heads. They, their Zulu wives and biracial children, as well as African clients, not only manipulated Shaka's power but recorded vivid evidence of one form of hybrid Zuluness. Yet by the mid-nineteenth century, so-called 'white Zulus' had slipped from the colonist's view, as Natal authorities adopted polemics against Dark Continent barbarism, relegating anyone brushed by Zuluness to the lowest rung of humanity. Hierarchical ('stadial') theories of civilisation, as Jeremy Martens explains in Chapter 11, convinced prominent settlers that kinship groups in KwaZulu were broken up by Shaka and uniformly reconfigured as 'Zulu (savage)'. Ironically, this effort to homogenise Zulu identity enabled Dingane's successor, Mpande kaSenzangakhona, to control chiefs on the margins of his heartland, whose pleas to British officialdom that they never recognised 'Zulu Law' fell on deaf ears.[10] Still, notions of Zuluness appealed to early missionaries such as Bishop Colenso who attracted converts by likening God to the Zulu creator, *Nkulunkulu*. Yet even as

Colenso and his counterparts integrated indigenous cosmology, they assumed the 'civilising mission' of the Victorian vanguard.

By the late nineteenth century certain impressions of Zuluness increasingly shaped British imperial discourses. As Jeff Guy describes in Chapter 16, Zulu symbols became vital markers of Anglo-Saxon manhood in the United Kingdom and elsewhere. Boy Scouts founder Robert Baden-Powell appropriated one such badge while serving as an English soldier, literally snatching it from the corpse of a Zulu woman during an 1888 civil war ravaging the former kingdom. Baden-Powell later emblazoned his outsized memories of combat against uSuthu foes on the 'wood cross'. He patterned the top Scoutmaster award on a trophy of masculine bravery, the *iziqu*, worn by Baden-Powell's Zulu 'noble savage', a splendid figure that obsessed Orientalists, according to John Laband. In Chapter 40 Jonny Steinberg exposes a modern paradox of the 'noble savage' trope in Alan Paton's classic book, adored by readers in the former empire. Steinberg compares the tribal Arcadia in *Cry, the Beloved Country* with today's Zulu 'marginals', whose poverty begets anomie and a common casualty, the slain white farmer.

British cultural imperialism, in turn, helped establish the calculus of 'Zulu cosmopolitanism'. In Chapter 22 Peter Alegi underlines how early twentieth-century mine clerks, *mabhalane*, spread their passion for English soccer to the urban masses. Inspired by the legendary intensity of Zulu fighters, township football teams huddled for pre-game drills that mimicked the fortifying rituals of Shaka's army. On weekends Zulu soccer fans came from their migrant workers' hostels to join in these spectacles, arriving at matches wearing their waistcoat, *intolibhantshi*, adorned with exquisitely beaded panels. Such finery, as Fiona Rankin-Smith writes in Chapter 34, represented a synthesis of city style and home colours, and signalled their desire to create beautiful art in an industrial world dulled by concrete and soot (see illustration on p. 11).

In Chapter 39, in a literary illustration of cross-cultural borrowing, David Attwell decodes the dramas of eminent Zulu nationalist authors such as H.I.E. Dhlomo, who revelled in the 'immortal Elizabethan' aesthetics imbibed by Oxford students. In Chapter 29 Timothy Parsons detects the spectre of Baden-Powell in one of Mangosuthu Buthelezi's commands to shore up Zulu patriarchy. As revolutionary youths fought the Pretoria regime in the 1980s, Buthelezi merged the duty-bound spirit of the wood badge with *ubunto botho*, a traditionalist ideology inculcating obedience in Zulu Boy Scouts.

In the latter half of the twentieth century ANC architects of public history, engaging the ideas of more militant nationalists such as Anton Lembede, cited both the sacrifices of Zulu heroes and the 'defeatist mentality' of Zulu traitors when coming to terms with ineffectual opposition against 'weapons of Western Culture and Civilisation'.[11] In Chapter 32 Nsizwa Dlamini chronicles how Dingane's 1838 defeat at the battle of Ncome (also known as the battle of Blood River), and subsequent murder by *abafokazana*, commoners, in northern KwaZulu were interpreted in a 1999 battlefield memorial sanctioned by Inkatha intellectuals. Until the 1980s, the chances of any Zulu nationalist approving such a plan were remote, for Mangosuthu Buthelezi disparaged Dingane as a worthless usurper. But, as Dlamini shows, when in 1982 Pretoria planned to cede an upper swathe of KwaZulu to the Swazi monarchy, this decision spurred the Inkatha leader to rehabilitate Dingane through *ukukhumelana umlotha*, a purification ceremony that converted the second king's grave into hallowed ground and deterred the land seizure. During the same period, Jabulani Sithole states in Chapter 27, ANC strategists in exile celebrated Dingane's anti-colonial resistance to bolster the morale of Umkhonto weSizwe (MK) guerillas, suffering setbacks in their operations against Boer counter-insurgents.

Similar contradictions swirl around post-apartheid 'Legacy Projects' and exhibitions that present diverse faces of Zuluness. One monument to freedom-fighting just north of Durban ran aground when scholars told the Department of Arts, Culture, Science and Technology that its honoured recipient, the late Albert Luthuli – Nobel laureate, ANC president and non-violent activist – had rebuffed Zulu royalty for peddling 'separate development'. In Chapter 28 Jabulani Sithole highlights Luthuli's objections to the ethnic politics of KwaZulu homeland and National Party rule. 'To us', Luthuli remarked, the 'bantustan means the home of disease and miserable poverty, the place where we shall be swept into heaps in order to rot . . .'. When heritage institutions take steps to overturn entrenched perceptions of chauvinistic Zuluness their audiences seem reluctant to appreciate this alternative approach. In Chapter 41 Nsizwa Dlamini details a case in point, a sprawling Natal Museum 2000 installation titled *Sisonke* ('We Are Together'). Rather than narrow the presentation to a familiar arsenal, curators arranged beadwork, ceramics, headrests – artefacts conveying what Juliet Armstrong and Yvonne Winters call customary scripts of sociability in Chapters 35 and 36 – in a broader perspective that included ANC and IFP T-shirts as well as other decorated items of street clothing. Visitors registered confusion in the museum comment book, admitting 'they [were] not sure what story is being told'.

Other arbiters of national opinion also strive to recast markers of Zuluness. In confronting some of the ills that beset post-apartheid society, proponents of the African Renaissance[12] exalt remedies such as *muthi*, 'medicine' in isiZulu. As a consequence, *muthi* practitioners are becoming community guardians in crime-plagued KwaZulu-Natal. With cases of murder and robbery overwhelming the police, township residents resort to *muthi* treatments in order to divert criminal harm and recover stolen property.[13] Long a fixture of the traditional-modern continuum, the *muthi* trade, as Karen Flint and Julie Parle relate in Chapter 26, received a boost a hundred years earlier from Natal government authorities, who licensed traditional healers to bring them into the colonial economy.

If the African Renaissance proposes one ambitious goal, it is to foster homegrown black entrepreneurs – warrior 'bulls in the boardroom', to employ Malcolm Draper's phrase from Chapter 51. They are extolled for their ethics 'learned from such great leaders as Shaka', who financier Cyril Ramaphosa believes is a model deal-maker for 'the digital millennium, as some people label it'.[14] Ramaphosa epitomises a small but growing class of activists-turned-capitalists seeking a controlling stake in major companies, some with tourism ventures promoting archetypal Zuluness. Over the past decade hotel and casino owners in KwaZulu-Natal, with partners in black economic empowerment sectors, have bankrolled theme parks trumpeting 'the Great Kraal of King Shaka' as 'more than just a tourist attraction – it is an enriching experience affording you a better understanding of the Zulu nation, its people and their intriguing customs'.[15] In the near future, Thembisa Waetjen and Gerhard Maré predict in Chapter 30, visitors flying to South Africa will touch down at King Shaka International Airport. Cruise ships, too, might glide by an immense statue of the Zulu founder in Durban harbour. Berthed passengers already travel to Kosi Bay, touted as the tropical jewel of Zululand, or the Umfolozi Game Reserve – 'Shaka's Royal Hunting Grounds', as it was christened by white rangers romanticising the Zulu wilderness, according to Shirley Brooks in Chapter 24. These excursions ensure profit for a hospitality industry that knows a good brand. They also confirm that the adventure package in Zululand is a select commodity for affluent consumers in a country with one of the world's steepest disparities between the haves and have-nots. Waetjen and Maré speculate: who benefits from tourism in KwaZulu-Natal? Not too many residents near Zulu heritage sites: they eke out a living, as Dingani Mthethwa and Cherryl Walker attest in Chapters 43 and 44. Holidaymakers pay a provincial park authority to enter Kosi Bay, and in their sport utility vehicles purr through a sanctuary denuded of chiefdoms. Mthethwa shows that their presence in camping areas has reawakened painful grievances that one-time reparations to 'the dispossessed' do not relieve. Walker notes that in nearby Greater St Lucia Wetland Park, apartheid forced removals have created unusually thorny problems of legitimacy. There, government officials try hard to balance environmental conservation with land restitution claims involving rival clans that refuse to be cajoled into a manageable Zulu front. Such community discord reflects a longer history of local wrangling over scarce resources.

From the late nineteenth century onwards, as John Lambert points out in Chapter 17, an intrusive Natal colonial government transferred the most productive African territory to settlers, boasting that their mechanised enterprises yielded more in a few seasons than subsistence-based homesteads harvested in a lifetime. It is no wonder that state interventions intending to improve land-poor communities have the capacity to rekindle bitter memories of past modernising schemes. Older isiZulu-speaking people remember the 'betterment' policies of the Natal Native Affairs Department that culled 'scrub' (Nguni) cattle, Aran MacKinnon writes in Chapter 20, to advance progressive farming and pasture preservation, thus winnowing one of the last stores of wealth held by rural people.

Today, neo-liberal modernisers promise to facilitate South Africa's leap into a borderless age of economic growth, controversially dubbed globalisation.[16] Whether globalisation represents a unique phenomenon or another phase of capitalist expansion is a matter of dispute. Nonetheless, debates over globalisation have influenced scholars of Zuluness to think beyond 'national or continental containers'.[17] In Chapter 52 Bill Freund contends that globalisation and its real-time technologies only bolster superficial aspects of Zulu identity. Christina Steyn's study in Chapter 25 of the famous *sangoma* Credo Mutwa implicitly tests this hypothesis. Mutwa now vends his special gifts on a website publicising virtual cosmological expeditions to Zululand. Some of his worldwide clients are New Agers enthralled by his tale of being chosen in a vision by Shaka as 'Vusamazulu, awakener of the Zulus'. The Internet conduit to the New Age Zulu awaits further investigation, as does a related concern: how have components of Zuluness changed as they reached far-flung audiences? The hemispheric dimensions of civilising imperialism and martial typecasting are particularly relevant to this question. Researchers might consult 1890s Singer Company postcards (see illustration on p. 11) to see how its formal portraits of Zulus around a sewing machine, yearning 'to be as forward in civilization as . . . in war', buttressed an idea that even fearsome tribes could be domesticated by an appliance exemplifying American know-how.[18]

One might also consider how accounts of white English-speaking troops in the First World War, bringing Zulu 'knobkerrie' clubs and traditional combat rituals to the European trenches,[19] dovetailed with early cinematic portrayals of Cetshwayo's 'man-slaying' army.[20]

The 1918 silent screen epic *Symbol of Sacrifice*, a tale of passion and bellicosity during the 1879 Anglo-Zulu War, offers an evocative example. The consultant for *Symbol*'s script was the isiZulu-speaking Natal settler Johan Colenbrander, who avenged British losses at Isandlwana, traded cattle with Zulus loyal to Queen Victoria, and advised Theodore Roosevelt on safari etiquette in the African interior. The film concluded with a few 'redeemable' blacks abandoning their 'savage ways' and rescuing besieged whites, a climax that both countered the plot of D.W. Griffith's *Birth of a Nation* (1915) and fulfilled a liberal paternalist wish for the Union of South Africa.[21]

In the decade following armistice, with Roosevelt's cry to embrace the 'strenuous life' and male fantasies of 'kill or be killed' echoing in America, the Zulu Toy Company in Battle Creek, Michigan, mass-produced a 'Zulu blow-gun'. Instructions for the plaything promoted 'health-giving' exercises such as a mock lion-hunt, which the brawny boy designated 'Chief Zulu' could instigate after a tribal dance.[22] By the 1920s, the Zulu Toy Company was stocking a 'line of . . . board, shooting, bowling and card games' and exhibiting them at national novelty fairs.

Corporations continue to manufacture fantasies of Zulu physical prowess, but now they attempt to cross the gender divide. In 2005 Champion sports apparel unveiled the 'White Zulu' cross-trainer for career women desiring 'to get back into something fun and ferocious'.[23]

*Waistcoat (intolibhantshi), adorned with beaded panels.*

*Postcard of Singer Manufacturing Co. 1892.*

'"Come on Over—It's Fine!" . . . Kaffir War Dance by men of the S.A. Scottish on the Western Front [France] . . . to welcome a newly arrived draft from South Africa', 1918; note knobkerrie on left and induna, 'war captain', on right directing the dance.*

'Kaffir War Dance', led by induna, Robinson Deep Mine, Transvaal, inter-war period. Photograph c. mid-1930; Derwin World Tour Album.*

*An 'irredeemable' in* Symbol of Sacrifice.

WHITE AND BLACK.
Melissa, the sweetheart of Tambookie, King's Messenger to Cetywayo, sees a white woman—Marie Moxter (Miss Mabel May)—for the first time, and compares the colour of their skins. This is during the time, after the Battle of Rorke's Drift, that Marie is a prisoner in the hands of the Zulus, where, however, she is befriended by Tambookie and Melissa.

*Photos by African Film Productions, Ltd.*

*Imagined future?* Symbol of Sacrifice.

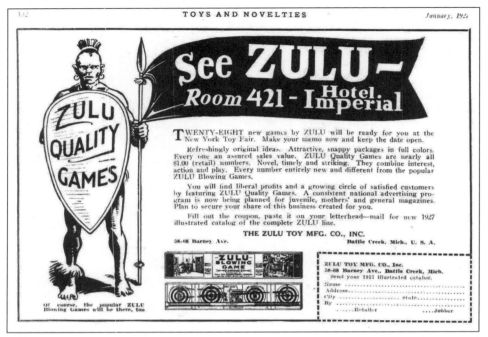

TOYS AND NOVELTIES                    *January, 192*

*Novelty Fair Advertisement, Zulu Toy Company, New York, January 1926,* Toys and Novelties *(trade magazine).*

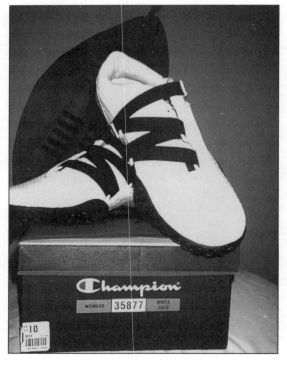

*Champion White Zulu cross-trainers, 2005.*

Nike running shoes also appear on South African televisions, with pitches in the planetary lingua franca, English, reinforcing isiZulu-speaking youths' 'growing disregard', Bill Freund argues, 'for African customs that seem out of step with the global-modern regime'. Yet as Liz Gunner and Imogen Gunner observe in Chapter 37 the global 'war on terror' has made some youths yearn for the solace of home. In *isicathamiya* (choir) groups they mourn the tragedies of 9/11 and voice scepticism about President George W. Bush's Christian-inflected crusade against the new evil.

Enfolded within these millennial developments are remnants of transnational forces that inspired past isiZulu-speaking Africans in seemingly opposite ways. By the turn of the twentieth century, bands of Protestant Zulu youths dubbed the *amaVoluntiya* (the Volunteers) were actively enlisting in an evangelical American cause to fight modern sin, a cause stoked by the charismatic Iowa preacher George Weavers, who came to South Africa in 1896. He brought the spirit of a 'Great Awakening', as Robert Houle explains in Chapter 18, kindling a Pentecostal faith that radiates in today's isiZulu-speaking churches. At the same time, elite mainstream Christians known as the *amakholwa* were emulating 'Negro' contributions to industrial progress, as Paul la Hausse de Lalouvière demonstrates in Chapter 21, in an effort to reconceive 'the Zulu nation in a globalising age'. For example, John Dube, editor of the Zulu newspaper *Ilanga lase Natal*, preached the 'Up from Slavery' gospel of Booker T. Washington, while urging labour migrants to glory in Shaka's feats.

Dube graduated from Union Missionary Training Institute in Brooklyn, New York. In the late 1890s he wanted to erect a Tuskegee-style vocational school in the Durban vicinity to cultivate African trades and self-sufficiency. His dream bound together influential Zulus and Americans, who crisscrossed the Atlantic in pursuit of initiatives that fostered Pan-African camaraderie. African-American men, in particular, saw Zuluness as a fount of 'archetypal black manhood and resistance to European domination', as Robert Vinson and Robert Edgar emphasise in Chapter 19.[24] Elements of the resistance ideal captivated audiences in the United States after reports of King Cetshwayo's triumph at Isandlwana shot through the telegraph wires. By the 1880s circuses were barnstorming through the Plains states with combat skits starring Zulu men recruited from Natal. African Americans, too, masqueraded as Cetshwayo's warriors in New York's dime museum acts. Their bravado incited some spectators, visiting from states in the Midwest which were notorious for lynching (along a line of 'southern' towns, i.e., Cincinnati, that stretched eastward from Illinois, Indiana and Ohio to Kentucky), to lash out at the performers.[25]

Such entertainment and the public backlash against it dates back at least to the ante-bellum heyday of minstrel and freak shows, when P.T. Barnum billed a prancing Zulu warrior as the latest humbug; and when morality plays, spawned by Harriet Beecher Stowe's *Uncle Tom's Cabin,* fired up the abolitionist cause by drawing parallels between tyrannical Zulu patriarchy and cruel plantation slavery.

Echoes of these diasporic currents are especially audible now in urban KwaZulu-Natal, where many young, upwardly mobile Zulus live. They listen to the black pride lyrics of hip-hop[26] and increasingly answer to their *igama lasekhaya* such as *uFunani*, a 'home' name, according to Adrian Koopman in Chapter 38, which evokes obligations to customary respect. Perhaps it is no coincidence that hip-hop's pioneers in the Bronx-based Universal Zulu Nation, who rhymed 'Say it Loud (I'm Black, I'm Proud),' might have motivated such a back-to-roots trend. Irony abounds here, for hip-hop borrows metre and parody from the plantation song, a vaudeville staple of African-American impresario Bert Williams and other blackface crooners such as the Grants whose 1900 sensation was *My Little Zulu Babe*.[27] This genre's sheet music like *Zulu Wail, His Zulu Gal Done Him Wrong* is replete with sketches of lascivious, grinning Africans lolling in a benighted Eden (see illustration on p. 17).

Even one of the great doyens of literature, who lampooned at every opportunity white supremacists in the United States, dabbled in motifs of minstrelised Zulus. While sailing 'the equator' in the mid-1890s, Mark Twain anchored in Durban, where he marvelled at the sight of 'splendidly built black' Zulu men. He said they were given to guffawing and flashing their teeth. During a trip into the coastal interior, Twain met 'sweet and musical' African women, 'just like those of the slave women of my early days'. His globetrotting diary, *Journey Around the World*, published in 1897, illustrated the 'good-natured' Zulu with a racial satire – an ink profile topped by the caption, 'Barnum's Claim' – and a photographic portrait that catered to consumers of the 'Zulu Gal' trope. Yet what was truly unique about Natal, as opposed to the United States, Twain acknowledged with a tone of anxiety, was that real Zulus outnumbered real Europeans ten to one.[28]

Burnt cork caricatures also circulated in colonial South Africa, which doubtless emboldened white supremacists to condemn what they saw as Shaka's corrupted progeny, the so-called teeming detribalised labour migrants who became foils of colonists fearing rampant promiscuity and disease in cities. Other isiZulu-speaking Africans were similarly rebuked, but not for their supposedly dangerous urban transformation; rather, they faced ridicule for enacting rural rites of passage believed to whet primitive appetites. At the same time, homestead patriarchs ostracised assertive youths such as unmarried couples that abandoned their vows of chastity.[29] As AIDS takes a terrible toll, these legacies of racist ridicule and taboo sexuality steer national debates over public health.

In KwaZulu-Natal medical bulletins warning individuals to avoid hazardous intercourse have collided with a movement claiming to safeguard female innocence through *ukuhlolwa kwezintombi*, virginity testing. A controversy has also ensued, Tessa Marcus contends in Chapter 45, about whether the safe-sex messages embedded in *ukuhlolwa kwezintombi* appeal to young people at risk of HIV infection. She interviewed isiZulu-speaking university students, probing why they suspected virginity testing was neither an ancient custom nor accurate physical inspection. Michael

'*A Thompson Street Zulu. A Cincinnati Citizen Declares War Against A Dime Museum Freak ...*', 1889.

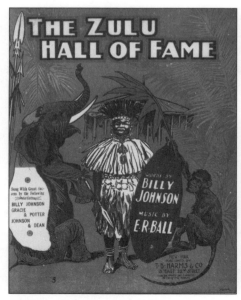

'*Zulu Hall of Fame*', c.1900.

'Zulu Wail', c.1920s.

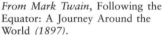
*From Mark Twain*, Following the Equator: A Journey Around the World *(1897)*.

Lambert broadens this critical approach in Chapter 46 by tracing the revival of *ukuhlolwa kwezintombi* to a recent university thesis by a female Zulu healer fascinated by the role of the 'Black Athena' in Afrocentric literature. In 1996, at one of the first virginity festivals, she took centre stage and hailed the return of Nomkhubulwane, a Zulu Demeter with powers to create utopian purity and fecundity. Such chastity celebrations tend to obscure other observances of female fertility that mediate the vital importance of youthful abstention. Indeed, Thenjiwe Magwaza illuminates a less heralded but more ubiquitous coming-out ceremony for older girls known as *umemulo*. With industrialisation, *umemulo* migrated from homestead to township, she notes in Chapter 42, a movement that altered norms of propriety for unmarried isiZulu-speaking young women in both rural and urban areas. While older girls were expected to refrain from premarital intercourse, in case they did not they could still be eligible for *umemulo*, particularly if it was known that they had been intimate with only one partner.

Reversing the gender perspective, in Chapter 48 Mark Hunter examines courtship patterns of isiZulu-speaking African men who seek higher patriarchal status by pursuing multiple lovers. He pinpoints periods of increasing poverty and un-employment, which depressed marriage rates. When bridewealth (*ilobolo*) cattle became all but unaffordable and jobs impossible to find – that is, during the past decade of neo-liberal structural adjustment – some single men adjusted their amorous pursuits, transacting numerous intimate relationships with a cell phone or another valuable gift. The consequences are tragically evident in the funeral tents that dot townships every weekend. In Chapter 49, Mxolisi Mchunu highlights additional modifications in male socialisation following the late nineteenth-century colonial dismantling of *amabutho*, the regiment system, and imposition of onerous taxes, which propelled older boys from rural chiefdom to wage work. Over the next century, coming-of-age idioms resonated with expressions that rejoiced in the completion of a young man's first job, usually as a suburban household's gardener dressed in a so-called 'kitchen suit' resembling an English child's tunic: '*Ngibheke nje, namuhla ngiyindoda ngoba ngangisebenza ezingadini*' (Just look at me, today I am a man because I was once a gardener). One of the hardships endured by gardeners could be their white madam who, folk wisdom holds, transmogrifies from mother figure to evil temptress, ready to seduce and contaminate them. This Zulu cosmological outlook, Suzanne Leclerc-Madlala maintains in Chapter 47, not only represents men as blameless recipients of illness, but also casts sexually active females and their bodily 'dirt' as fatal forces of pollution. In contemporary KwaZulu-Natal, if isiZulu-speaking women openly celebrate their romantic interests, they can be singled out for spreading untimely death.

The stigmas associated with HIV/AIDS, as Philippe Denis elaborates in Chapter 50, stifle communication between elders and youths in isiZulu-speaking African communities. Moreover, due to traditional social avoidance practices, young sons and daughters typically do not hear from their surviving guardian about 'why their mother or father, or both, suddenly wasted away', and thus find it difficult to release bottled-up grief. But this scenario is slowly changing, as initiatives such as Denis's Sinomlando ('We Have History') Project at the University of KwaZulu-Natal, Pietermaritzburg, assist intergenerational dialogue in families being affected by the pandemic.

Sinomlando deploys isiZulu-speaking 'memory facilitators', who use innovative oral history methodologies to create a space for the bereaved, especially mourning children, to consider emotional loss in open discussions. Invariably, uncomfortable disclosures and fond recollections get aired, starting a larger conversation that may be sustained after the memory facilitators are gone. Like the families involved in the Sinomlando Project, contributors to this volume face up to unspoken narratives. It is hoped, too, that their probing studies encourage searching questions and answers about Zuluness in postcolonial South Africa.

## Notes

1. See, for example, *Natal Witness*, 13 June 2005 and *New York Post*, 15 June 2005. For more recent critical views of Oprah Winfrey as the 'ultimate arbiter' of culture, see *New York Times*, 22 January 2006 and 27 January 2006.
2. *New York Post*, 15 June 2005.
3. *Mail & Guardian*, 23 January 2005.
4. Some important answers to this question are discussed by Shula Marks in ' "The Dog That Did Not Bark, Or Why Natal Did Not Take Off": Ethnicity and Democratization in South Africa – The Case of KwaZulu-Natal', in *Ethnicity & Democracy in Africa*, eds. Bruce Berman, Will Kymlicka and Dickson Eyoh (Oxford: James Currey, 2004), pp. 183–99.
5. On the complex phenomena of nation-building efforts and rising black elites, see Patrick Bond, *Elite Transition: From Apartheid to Neoliberalism in South Africa* (Pietermaritzburg: University of Natal Press, 2000) and Alan Hirsch, *Season of Hope: Economic Reform under Mandela and Mbeki* (Pietermaritzburg: University of KwaZulu-Natal Press, 2005). Another answer to the question of Buthelezi's plaintive message and Oprah's lineage-hunting could explore a dialectical relationship clarified by Lawrence Levine: how a crisis of belonging changes cultural actors and how cultural actors, in turn, alter perceptions of a crisis of belonging; see Ann Lage, 'An Interview with Lawrence W. Levine', *Journal of American History* 93:3 (2006): 800; and Lawrence Levine, *Black Culture and Black Consciousness: Afro-American Folk Thought from Slavery to Freedom* (New York: Oxford University Press, 1977).
6. Materialist scholars anticipated the postcolonial thinkers. See Shula Marks, *Ambiguities of Dependence in South Africa: Class, Nationalism and the State in Twentieth-Century Natal* (Johannesburg: Ravan Press, 1986). Such timely revisions informed *Political Economy and Identities in KwaZulu-Natal*, which sought to tackle the ambiguous forms of Zulu identity 'from a political economy position [while] trying to take an understanding forward, beyond inadequate . . . Marxist formulations'. See Robert Morrell's introduction to *Political Economy and Identities in KwaZulu-Natal: Historical and Social Perspectives* (Durban: Indicator Press, 1996), p. 5.
7. See Alan Lester, *Imperial Networks: Creating Identities in Nineteenth-century South Africa and Britain* (London: Routledge, 2001), pp. 2–3; and Tim Nuttall and John Wright, 'Exploring History with a Capital "H" ', *Current Writing* 10:2 (1998): 38–69.
8. This debate is encapsulated in Carolyn Hamilton, ed. *The Mfecane Aftermath: Reconstructive Debates in Southern African History* (Johannesburg: Witwatersrand University Press, 1995).
9. Wright's opinion is echoed by Carolyn Hamilton in *Terrific Majesty: The Powers of Shaka Zulu and the Limits of Historical Invention* (Cambridge, MA: Harvard University Press, 1998), pp. 28–29.
10. Natal Governor Pine to Government House (GH), 19 August 1852, No. 33, 376, p. 401, Vol. 1209A, 1/GH; see also Secretary for Native Affairs (SNA) T. Shepstone Reports, Statement and Messages, September 1853–April 1859, 1/7/3, 1/SNA, Pietermaritzburg Archives Repository (PAR); 'Message, delivered by Fokomifiya Andmunqulwana [*sic*], from Panda King of the Zulu Nation to the Lieutenant Governor', 6 March 1857 (witnessed and signed by SNA Shepstone), Vol. 1, 24, File 4, Fynn Papers, Killie Campbell Library (KCM), KCM 98/69/3, Durban.
11. Quotations are from Lembede's review of Benedict W. Vilakazi's *Nje-Nempela*, a book on 'Bambatha's bloody rebellion' of 1906, *Teachers' Quarterly Review* I:2 (1946): 8–10, reprinted in *Freedom in Our Lifetime: The Collected Writings of Anton Muziwakhe Lembede*, eds. Robert Edgar and Lyuanda kaMsumza (Athens, OH: Ohio University Press, 1996), pp. 141–46. For parallels between Lembede and ANC trailblazer Pixley Seme, see Paul la Hausse de Lalouvière, *Restless Identities: Signatures of Nationalism, Zulu Ethnicity and History in the Lives of Petros Lamula (c.1881–1948) and Lymon Maling (1889–c.1936)* (Pietermaritzburg: University of Natal Press, 2000), pp. 14–16. For debates over public history in South Africa, see Annie Coombes, *History after Apartheid: Visual Culture and Public Memory in a Democratic South Africa* (Durham, NC: Duke University Press, 2003), p. 5 and Leslie Witz, *Apartheid's Festival: Contesting South Africa's National Past* (Bloomington: Indiana University Press, 2003).
12. In the 1940s ANC leader Anton Lembede sought to repair black people's 'loss of self-confidence' by renewing pride in African achievements. See Anton Lembede, 'Policy of the Congress Youth League', *Inkundla yaBantu*, May 1946, reprinted in *From Protest to Challenge: A Documentary History of African Politics in South Africa*, eds. Thomas Karis and Gwendolen Carter (Stanford:

Hoover Institution, 1972), Vol. 2, pp. 317–18. See also Chris Dunton, 'Pixley kaIsaka Seme and the African Renaissance Debate', *African Affairs* 102 (2003): 555–73.

13. Thokozani Xaba, 'Witchcraft, Sorcery or Medical Practice? The Demand, Supply and Regulation of Indigenous Medicines in Durban, South Africa (1844–2002)' (Ph.D. diss., University of California, Berkeley, 2004), pp. 166–71, 176–81, 203–09.

14. From the back cover of Phinda Madi, *Leadership Lessons from Emperor Shaka Zulu the Great* (Randburg: Knowledge Resources, 2000).

15. Benedict Carton, 'Remaking Zulu Identity in the Era of Globalization', *Global Studies Bulletin* 5 (2005): 12.

16. On neo-liberalism and globalisation, see Gillian Hart, *Disabling Globalization: Places of Power in Post-Apartheid South Africa* (Pietermaritzburg: University of Natal Press, 2002).

17. Frederick Cooper, 'What is the Concept of Globalization Good For? An African Historian's Perspective', *African Affairs* 100 (2001): 190.

18. For more on African-theme advertising postcards, see Neal Sobania, 'But Where are the Cattle? Popular Images of Maasai and Zulu Across the Twentieth Century', *Visual Anthropology*, 15 (2002): 313–24. On 'Anglo-Saxon' technological advancement, see Gail Bederman, *Manliness and Civilization: A Cultural History of Gender and Race in the United States, 1880–1917* (Chicago: University of Chicago Press, 1995), p. 31 and Robert Rydell, *All the World's a Fair: Visions of Empire at American International Expositions, 1876–1916* (Chicago: University of Chicago Press, 1984), pp. 40–69.

19. For more on 'knobkerries' see *Washington Post*, 28 May 1916; see also an article on the use of 'Zulu clubs' to solve the 'eugenics problem' in the United States in *Newark Advocate*, 16 September 1916. A small number of isiZulu-speaking African men supported the South African-British imperial war effort during the First World War, but they were barred from enlisting as combat soldiers. Rather, they served in auxiliary units such as the South African Native Labour Contingent. See Norman Clothier, *Black Valour: The South African Native Labour Contingent, 1916–1918 and the Sinking of the Mendi* (Pietermaritzburg: University of Natal Press, 1987).

20. For more on Zulu ('noble savage') themes animating silent films in the United States, which include minstrelised cinema, see 'movie picture' listings for 'Among the Savage Zulus' (*Elyria Chronicle*, 31 January 1908). For more on (blackface) silent film, see 'The Zulu's Heart' by D.W. Griffith (Washington, DC: Library of Congress, 1908) and Peter Davis, *In Darkest Hollywood: Exploring the Jungle of Cinema's South Africa* (Athens, OH: Ohio University Press, 1996), pp. 8–9. On leisure and film-viewing (indicators of popular American culture), see Roy Rosenzweig, *Eight Hours for What We Will: Workers and Leisure in an Industrial City, 1870–1920* (New York: Cambridge University Press, 1982).

21. Johan Colenbrander played Lord Chelmsford in the film and drowned while crossing a swollen river in a scene for *Symbol*. See *Natal Witness*, 15 February 1918 and Death Notice, 27 March 1918, 34807, Master's Office, Transvaal Provincial Archives, Pretoria. On Colenbrander as cattle-dealer to Zulus, see Supreme Court (RSC) Illiquid Case, 8/1885, 1/5/116, 1/RSC, PAR. On Colenbrander as Roosevelt's safari adviser, see *New York Times*, 22 December 1908. On early cinema in South Africa, see Thelma Gutsche, *The History and Social Significance of Motion Pictures in South Africa, 1895–1940* (Cape Town: Howard Timmins, 1972), pp. 1–59; and Keyan Tomaselli, 'Ideology and Cultural Production in South African Cinema' (Ph.D. diss., University of the Witwatersrand, 1983), pp. 40–51. *Symbol of Sacrifice* was a popular film, but *De Voortrekkers* (1916), which also showed in American theatres as *Winning a Continent*, was a huge hit. See *De Voortrekkers*, South African Police (SAP), *De Voortrekkers* at Elsburg, 2/262/ 16, Correspondence, Vol. 87, 1/SAP, National Archives (SAB), Pretoria. See also Isabel Hofmeyr, 'Popularizing History: The Case of Gustav Preller', *Journal of African History* 29:3 (1988): 521–35. I thank M-Net for granting me rights to a version of *Symbol* restored by Dr Mark Coughlan who also generously shared his research. On the film script see Records of Chief Native Commissioner (CNC), CNC 111/1916, Correspondence 100–49, 1916, Vol. 228, 1/ CNC PAR.

22. 'Instructions for the Zulu Blowing Game' (1924), Zulu Toy Manufacturing, 1927, Edgar-Carton Collection, Washington, DC. On Roosevelt's macho cry, see Bederman, *Manliness and Civilization*, pp. 208–10 and Donna Haraway, *Primate Visions: Gender, Race, and Nature in the World of Modern Science* (London: Routledge, 1989), pp. 27–57. On early twentieth-century toy manufacturing and gender stereotyping, see Gary Cross, *Kids' Stuff: Toys and the Changing World of American Childhood* (Cambridge, MA: Harvard University Press, 1997).

23. Personal communication with Champion sportswear marketing representative, 3 October 2005.
24. For other scholarship on Pan-African camaraderie, see James Campbell, *Songs of Zion: The African Methodist Episcopal Church in the United States and South Africa* (New York: Oxford University Press, 1995); and Robert Vinson, 'Sea Kaffirs: "American Negroes" and the Gospel of Garveyism in Segregationist South Africa', *Journal of African History* 47:2 (2006): 281–303.
25. *The National Police Gazette*, 24 August 1889, Vol. LIV, No. 624, p. 5, Library of Congress, Washington, DC. On late nineteenth-century lynching in America and the Midwestern lynch belt, see Walter White, *Rope and Faggot: A Biography of Judge Lynch* (1929), Appendix, Table VI.
26. Musicians playing 'Zulu hip-hop' include H20, Zuluboy and Busi Mhlongo. On hip-hop and emerging youth ideologies in South Africa, see Lee Watkins, 'Rappin' the Cape: Style and Memory, Power in Community', in *Music, Space, and Place: Popular Music and Cultural Identity*, eds. Sheila Whiteley, Andy Bennett and Stan Hawkins (Burlington, VT: Aldershot, 2004).
27. On links between hip-hop and black vaudeville, see *New York Times*, 13 October 2004. On Afrodiasporic narratives in hip-hop see Tricia Rose, *Black Noise: Rap Music and Black Culture in Contemporary America* (Middletown, CT: Wesleyan University Press, 1994), p. 25. On Bert Williams's Zulu/African-inflected performances, see *New York Times*, 12 August 1900. W.S. Estren and Jas T. Brymn, *My Little Zulu Babe*, sung by Grant and Grant (Chicago, IL: Windsor Music, 1900), Performing Art/Music Division, New York Public Library (main branch). On Bert Williams's performance style and early films, some with blackface actors and Zulu plots, see Thomas Cripps, *Slow Fade to Black: The Negro in American Film, 1900–1942* (New York: Oxford University Press, 1993), pp. 11–25. On 'Negro comedians' Avery and Hart, (rivals of Williams and his partner Walker), who also dressed up Zulu for the New Jersey stage, see *Trenton Times*, 26 January 1904. On vaudeville and plantation song genre, see J. Dorman, 'Shaping the Popular Image of Post-Reconstruction American Blacks: The "Coon Song" Phenomenon of the Gilded Age', *American Quarterly* 40:4 (1988): 450–71 and Brainard's Ragtime Collection ('The Zulu patrol') c.1899, ZB 3479, Performing Arts/Music Division, Schomburg Center for Research in Black Culture, New York. Universal Zulu Nation, Music Division (EMI Records), Madison Building, Library of Congress, Washington, DC; *New York Observer*, 21 October 2001.
28. Mark Twain, *Following the Equator: A Journey Around the World* (Hartford, CT: American Publishing Co, 1897), pp. 643–46, 693. I thank Tad Suiter for this reference.
29. Peter Delius and Clive Glaser, 'Sexual Socialisation in South Africa: A Historical Perspective', *African Studies* 61:1 (2002): 27–54.

*Chapter 2*

# The Empire Talks Back
### Re-examining the Legacies of Shaka and Zulu Power in Post-apartheid South Africa[1]

MBONGISENI BUTHELEZI

POST-APARTHEID SOUTH AFRICA is now being reconceived as a coherent entity. Print and broadcast media, political speeches and church sermons constantly promote the image of a rainbow nation. But in the province of KwaZulu-Natal (KZN) the politics of cultural nationalism complicate this ideal of unity. One half of KZN, stretching north from the Thukela River, is still influenced by an almost exclusive ethnic/tribal identity. Much of this territory was once a Zulu homeland, governed during the late-apartheid era by Inkatha Yenkululeko Yesizwe/Inkatha National Cultural Liberation Movement, which in 1990 simplified its political title to the Inkatha Freedom Party (Inkatha or the IFP). In a speech at Nsingweni near Eshowe in January 2005, a seat of royal Zulu authority, the Inkatha president, Mangosuthu Buthelezi, implored his audience 'to preserve . . . Zuluness . . . to make our voice ring out across the hills and valleys of KwaZulu; to let the rest of South Africa know that we are Zulus'.[2]

Over the past three decades, Inkatha has been tied to the ideology of Mangosuthu Buthelezi, whose legitimacy rests on a reinvention of Zulu greatness. His vision has influenced the way that many South Africans – and people across the globe – continue to view *Inkosi*[3] (in colonial parlance, 'King') Shaka kaSenzangakhona, Inkatha's touchstone leader. Indeed, Buthelezi, who is known as *uNdunankulu wesizwe*, the 'traditional prime minister' of KwaZulu, invokes what he boasts of as the illustrious legacy of the Zulu kingdom to emphasise his time-honoured connection to Shaka's family. In so doing, Buthelezi avoids explaining how his claim to lead Zulu people – in the customary sense – comes from his own clan, *isizwe sakwaButhelezi*.[4] Why does Buthelezi maintain a public silence about his ancestors' relationship with Shaka? Were his forebears as ardent in their support of Zulu power?

This chapter seeks to explore such questions by probing what it means to be Zulu in South Africa. The first decade of democracy has seen intense nation-building, underpinned by aspirations that more open dialogue between South Africans might reduce the corrosive effects of colonial injustice. It could be argued that the human rights abuses aired by the Truth and Reconciliation Commission in the 1990s helped to improve racial understanding. Yet there has been no comparable effort to repair inequalities within African communities where the subjugator and the subjugated were both indigenous black people. The current political context, it can be argued, is an appropriate time for isiZulu-speaking Africans and others who accept the language of unadulterated tribalism to interrogate their long-held views of pure Zuluness.

I wish to propel this process. I, a Buthelezi, come from Zululand. Until the 1820s, my ancestors lived in an autonomous chiefdom headed by *inkosi* Phungashe Buthelezi. They lived in Mcakwini, nestled in the Babanango hills, a region that bordered on the territory of the Zulu clan. The Buthelezi people controlled their own affairs until *Inkosi* Shaka kaSenzangakhona started to forge a kingdom and forcibly incorporated scores of *amakhosi* (plural of *inkosi*), among them, Phungashe and his followers. This process of conquest prompts a question: Does the Buthelezi clan's subjugation by KwaZulu-Natal's famous empire-builder make them (and me) Zulu today? A partial answer might be found in the revisionist scholarship generated over the last two decades, which traces the complex historical trajectories that created Shaka's nation and tribal classifications in modern South Africa.[5]

As historians John Wright and Carolyn Hamilton convincingly demonstrate, the fate of *amakhosi* such as Phungashe and Shaka hinged on growing commercial activity in the late-eighteenth century Delagoa Bay-Thukela River region, an area buffeted by struggles between paramount chieftaincies from the Mabhudu and Ndwandwe to Mthethwa and Qwabe. At this time, the Zulu clan was but a minor entity and less prominent in stature than the Buthelezi clan. Paramount chieftaincies competed for vital exchange goods (ivory and cattle), natural resources (pasture and hunting land) and access to trade routes. Resultant rivalries stirred waves of instability that until fairly recently were attributed solely to a Napoleon-like genius named Shaka. By the turn of the nineteenth century, mounting conflicts between certain strengthening paramount chieftaincies set in motion a scramble for power, led by *inkosi* Zwide of the Ndwandwe and *inkosi* Dingiswayo of the Mthethwa. Whereas the Mthethwa clan sought a tributary system that subordinated smaller clans without resorting to wholesale violence, the Ndwandwe clan tended to subdue chiefdoms by military means.[6]

Historians have been unable to reconstruct Phungashe's extensive manoeuvres during the Ndwandwe and Mthethwa ascendancy in the Delagoa Bay-Thukela River region.[7] There was probably a military encounter between Phungashe's Buthelezi regiments and Mthethwa forces, while Shaka was ensconced in Dingiswayo's court and carrying out the assassination of Mahelana, a son of Senzangakhona with a military following.[8] Oral traditions further suggest that Phungashe did not fare well in battle against the Mthethwa, but managed to retain his political sovereignty, particularly after sealing an alliance with Zwide. Phungashe grew to depend on this paramount chief's protection after Shaka's soldiers attacked the Buthelezi clan and propelled Phungashe to seek haven in the court of the Ndwandwe.[9]

In the second decade of the nineteenth century, Shaka's Zulu clan became a client of Mthethwa power. After the Mthethwa were defeated by Ndwandwe regiments, the latter were to be vanquished by a Zulu-led army. During this phase of attack and counter-attack in the 1810s, Shaka became one of the most formidable leaders in the region that makes up present-day KwaZulu-Natal, eclipsing Zwide and moving to incorporate, at times through killing and intimidation, the region's chiefdoms, particularly those raided by his soldiers. This is how Phungashe's clan came to be absorbed by Shaka and his kingdom, which, among other things, institutionalised service in *amakhanda* (military headquarters and barracks) for all young to middle-aged men conscripted by the royal house, a recruitment system that brought Buthelezi generations into Zulu ranks.[10] Conscription served as an ideological instrument, fostering allegiance to Shaka's royal house, on the one hand, while eroding loyalties to *amakhosi*, such as Phungashe, on the other hand.[11]

Today, one of the consequences of this dramatic transformation is that very few Buthelezi people have a coherent sense of their own lineage history. To be sure, they know the canonical figures of certain *izithakazelo*, orally declaimed clan praises, in this case of Mangosuthu Buthelezi's line of patriarchs: Shenge, Sokalisa, Mnyamana kaNqengelele.[12] Nqengelele, in particular, was Buthelezi's great-great-grandfather, who, with his brother Khoboyela, contested Phungashe's rule by seeking to *khonza* (request refuge from) Shaka. In fact, Nqengelele became a favourite of the Zulu house and took command of some of its regiments to support Shaka's successful military campaign against Ndwandwe forces. A grateful Shaka granted Nqengelele control of a vast territory stretching from Mahlabathini through Louwsburg, Phongolo and Piet Retief.[13] With apartheid-era Zulu nationalism vanishing, Mangosuthu Buthelezi's uncritical embrace of Shaka's hegemony should raise issues about historical mythologising that extend beyond the ideas of a small circle of men who championed Inkatha's platform in different periods of white supremacy.

The earliest accounts of Zulu conquest were documented after the fact by English-speaking Europeans in colonial South Africa and imperial Great Britain. They brought to the literate world the first vivid details of Shaka, the so-called insatiable despot, hungry for blood and booty. Although they exaggerated events with the intent to demonise their protagonist, their writings were treated as reliable fact in many studies of Zulu history.[14] Such works have been assailed by twentieth-century Zulu nationalist intellectuals, among others, who claim that far more accurate insider accounts memorialised in *izibongo*, praises called out by special performance poets or *izimbongi*, highlight Shaka's true achievements. To date, *izibongo* have not received the same scrutiny as colonial versions of Shakan history.[15] Indeed, early Zulu nationalist discourses await more critical study, beginning with Shaka's *izibongo*. These verses revel in the Zulu founder's forcefulness, hailing him as '*uDlungwana*'

(Ferocious one) or '*uNomashovushovu*' (Voracious one), and extolling his ability to be the '*uSiphepho-shunguza*' (Rushing wind), '*Indlovu*' (Powerful elephant), '*Inyon' edl' ezinye*' (Bird that eats others), and '*Ingonyama*' (Mighty lion). But Shaka's *izibongo* also gloss over what loss meant to those that he defeated.[16]

Phungashe is one such vanquished character in Shaka's *izibongo*. A mere footnote and object of derision, Phungashe can be found in praises that roll on and on about the Zulu king's prowess; some of these lines appear in *Izibongo: Zulu Praises*, edited by Trevor Cope, a white scholar and isiZulu-speaking linguist of British descent:[17]

> [*UShaka*] *Obesixhokolo singamatsh' aseNkandla,*
> *Abephephel' izindlovu uba liphendule,*
> *Aphephel' uPhungashe wakwaButhelezi.*

> [Shaka] was a pile of rocks at Nkandla,
> Which was a shelter for the elephants in bad weather,
> Which sheltered Phungashe of the Buthelezi clan.[18]

> *UGasane kade lubagasela:*
> *Lwagasel'Phungashe wakwaButhelezi.*

> The attacker who has long been attacking them:
> He attacked Phungashe of the Buthelezi clan.[19]

> *Uhelele engimbon' ukwehla kwezikaMangcengeza;*
> *Kwathi kwezikaPhungashe wanyamalala.*

> Hawk that I saw descending from the hills of Mangcengeza,
> And from those of Phungashe he disappeared.[20]

Phungashe is again evoked in another version of Shaka's *izibongo* interpreted by the Zulu cultural scholar C.T. Msimang:

> *Uthi lwempundu oluhlal' izikhova,*
> *Ngoba luhlale uPhungashe wakwaButhelezi.*

> Gatepost on which owls sit,
> Because Phungashe of the Buthelezi sat on it.[21]

The quoted verses demonstrate that Phungashe's defeat was of little significance to the first Zulu king. They mention in passing Shaka regiments' attack on the Buthelezi people in the hills of Babanango; one line tells of Phungashe's flight to the rugged

Nkandla region; another line indicates that the Zulu state's founder became a gatepost on which the Buthelezi chief sat, an idiom that ratifies the fact that Shaka was far superior in stature than the vanquished Phungashe. The nine lines above comprise the only references to Phungashe in Shaka's seemingly endless *izibongo*. By contrast, *inkosi* Zwide is given a full portrayal, including a eulogy, where Shaka is hailed for his successful ('thundering') subjugation of this Ndwandwe paramount. A brief section is presented and translated below:

> *UMaswezisela wakithi kwaBulawayo,*
> *Oswezisel' uZwide ngamagqanqula.*
> *Izulu elimagwagwaba likaMageba,*
> *Elidume phezulu kuNomangci,*
> *Laduma' emva kwomuzi eKuqhobokeni laqanda,*
> *Lazithath' izihlangu zaMaphela naMankayiya,*
> *Amabheqan' ezimpaka asal' ezihlahleni . . .*

> Our own bringer of poverty at Bulawayo,
> Who made Zwide destitute by great strides.
> The sky that rumbled, the sky of Mageba,
> That thundered above Nomangci Mountain,
> It thundered behind the kraal at Kuqhobokeni and struck,
> It took the shields of the Maphela and the Mankayiya,
> And the little melons of the Zimpaka were left on the vines . . .[22]

Fortunately, since the early 2000s we have been able to recuperate more and more fragments of Phungashe's *izibongo*, which convey (contestable) accounts of Buthelezi history immediately before and during Shaka's rise. Several stanzas below might be interesting to admirers of the Zulu house:

> *Isiphungaphunga esiphungwe ngabasekhaya*
> *Saphungwa ngabasekwendeni.*
> *Ibamba elibambe uJama lamyekelela*
> *Wahlengwa ngezimagodla*
> *Labamba uMenzi lamyekelela*
> *Wahlengwa ngezimagodla*
> *Labamba uMalambule eNgonyameni.*

> *Inyathi yakithi emhlophe*
> *Ebisembethe izikhumba zezingwe neziNgonyama.*
> *Inhlabathi yoNdi noThukela*
> *Engifice beyihlela ngaze ngajubalala.*

*Imvukazi yakithi eMcakweni*
*Imaxhukazi mabili.*
*Inyathi yakithi emhlophe*
*Ibisembethe izikhumba zezingwe neziNgonyama.*
*Odle uQwangubane waseMaphiseni*
*Amakhubalo adliwa nguMabhedla.*

The driven one who is driven off by those of the family
And is driven off by those who have married.
The captor who seized Jama and then let him go
He was freed with oxen having long, winding horns.
He seized Menzi [Senzangakhona] and let him go
When he was ransomed with oxen with long, bending horns.
He seized Malambule of Ngonyameni.

The white buffalo of our home
Which wore the skins of leopards and lions
The soil of uNdi and uThukela
Which I found them arranging until I went away for a long time.
The ewe of our home at Mcakweni

It has two lambs.
The white buffalo of our home
Which was covered in the skins of leopards and lions
Who ate up Qwangubane of Maphiseni
And the medicines were eaten by Mabhedla.[23]

Simply put, Phungashe's *izibongo* provide a fulsome image of a Buthelezi commander with the military power to capture Jama, Menzi (Senzangakhona), Shaka's grandfather and father respectively, as well as other powerful leaders in KwaZulu-Natal – quite the counter-narrative to Shaka's *izibongo*, which render Phungashe as a non-figure obliterated by the son of Menzi's might.[24]

One major reason why the *izibongo* of Shaka and Phungashe offer competing views of history is that an *inkosi*'s praisers employed obscure phrasing for different ends, and not simply because they, as court performers, were compelled to rejoice in their subject's exploits. *Izimbongi* typically shifted the meanings of their declamations according to sundry dramatic contexts. For example, the same line that revelled in Shaka's prowess could be uttered differently, with satirical ends in mind. In other words, praises were and are, to this day, subject to constant recomposition. Thus, the Zulu *izibongo* appearing in books represent amalgamations of *izimbongi* performances. With this understanding in mind, scholars interested in Zulu and non-Zulu African pasts would do well to focus on *izibongo*, while being aware that this rich primary source contains multiple narratives and connotations. C.T. Msimang presents one effective way to approach *izibongo* research: '[I]zinkondlo ziqukethe *umlando. Zisichazela ngobunjalo bamaqhawe abongwayo. Zisifundisa amasu okuhlaba nokugxeka ube ubonga.* ([Praise] poems carry history. They explain to us the nature of the heroes being praised. They teach us ways to criticise while praising.)' Liz Gunner and Mafika Gwala echo Msimang's observation, remarking that *izibongo* allow 'wildly disparate elements to come together both in performance of the praises, and how they are remembered'. These elements comprise 'discourse[s] of the self' – of Shaka, Phungashe, or some other prominent figure – which 'may be partly dissident or subversive'.[25]

At the same time, it must be noted that English translations of *izibongo* have altered isiZulu poetics. I face this issue as a mother tongue isiZulu-speaker when I render *izibongo* into the language that I write in as a postcolonial critic. My immersion in the postcolonial debates shaping literary criticism further complicates matters. Postcolonial theories do not have a strong connection to Zulu oral culture, and thus must be carefully integrated into studies of *izibongo*. In particular, the problem of 'voice' – whether the voice is recorded in the vernacular and translated, and how these voices are then slotted into literary theory – is addressed by Gayatri Chakravorty Spivak, who asks, 'Can the Subaltern Speak?' Her answer is negative. '[I]n the context of colonial production,' she argues, 'the subaltern [invariably a Third World subject who experienced the legacies of white rule] has no history and cannot speak'.[26] If we accept Spivak's rejoinder, does the postcolonial theorist or critic automatically fall into an epistemological trap? Can a postcolonial theorist or critic with deep knowledge of a subaltern's language and customs ever attempt to represent the subaltern's complex pasts?[27]

The problem with Spivak's methodology is that it limits the possibilities of locating hidden testimony by insisting that the scholarly critic only understands her or his own subject position. It is more preferable to heed Duncan Brown's admonition that if 'the colonised has been unable to speak' it is largely because 'the coloniser (and too often the postcolonial critic) has been unable to hear'.[28] In this sense the postcolonial critic should not simply point to silences, but rather augment and analyse subjugated peoples' narratives, thus bringing to the fore once-lost cultural expressions and historical accounts.

Any critical assessment of a Zulu-centred past should consider as at least one useful point of departure the predictable pattern of silencing in Shaka's *izibongo*. The founding king's praises, heralding his might, heroism and generosity, smothered the spoken histories of the Africans that he sought to control. Indeed, Zulu rulers almost erased Buthelezi praises and guaranteed their replacement by the *izibongo* of Shaka's house. Thereafter, the nation for the Buthelezi people became *isizwe sikaPhunga noMageba* (the nation of Phunga and Mageba), that of Shaka's great-

great-grandfathers (who were twins). In contemporary South Africa many Zulu people whose ancestors were in Phungashe's precarious position are still called '*Mabandla kaMjokwana kaNdaba*', '*nina bakaMalandela*' and '*nina bakaMthaniya*', confirming that Shaka's ancestors Ndaba and Malandela as well as Shaka's grandmother, Mthaniya, have been made into the ancestors of every clan in KwaZulu-Natal.[29] Of course, this assertion of unbroken tribalism is not uniformly accepted.[30] The Zulu origin idiom, *isizwe sikaPhunga noMageba*, has greater resonance in rural and some peri-urban communities of KwaZulu-Natal (especially north of the Thukela River), where there exists a stronger continuity with precolonial social and political structures upheld by the Zulu kingdom. On the other hand, people in the traditional KwaZulu countryside are sometimes labelled disdainfully *uZulu wangempela* ('real Zulu') by urban Zulu people, who regard their identities as more fluid and open to various ethnic, racial and linguistic influences associated with modernity.[31]

The imposition of colonial rule also reinforced prevailing narratives of Zulu *izibongo*. From the mid-nineteenth century onwards, the many isiZulu-speaking Africans who might have directed protests or rebellions against Shaka's royal house opted, instead, to oppose European processes of dispossession and exploitation.[32] In this context, anti-colonial resistance in KwaZulu-Natal as well as elsewhere in South Africa and the continent was buoyed by Shakan symbols of autonomy and strength. Indeed, leaders of Negritude and black consciousness movements hailed the archetypal Zulu king's military brilliance and cultural pride, which kept whites at bay.[33]

As we attempt to move beyond the divisive nationalist narratives of exclusion, which served, paradoxically, to foment liberation in South Africa, there is a serious need now to recognise another side of restorative justice championed by the Truth and Reconciliation Commission. In the post-apartheid period, insufficient attention has been paid to the suffering endured by individuals, families and clans subjugated by Shaka and subsequent Zulu elites. The next wave of reconciliation in South Africa might then entail a reckoning of these dislocating and oppressive processes. St Kitts-British novelist Caryl Phillips offers one way that this might be done. He suggests a straightforward, non-violent strategy of subverting the past in a distinctly postcolonial era. He elaborates plainly: '[Y]ou take something which people presume they know about . . . and you make them look again from the point of view of people who have been written out [of that history].'[34]

Thus nineteenth- and twentieth-century Zulu history might be reconsidered from the perspectives of people such as *inkosi* Phungashe and his Buthelezi followers, who have been nearly expunged from the large repositories of oral history in KwaZulu-Natal, namely Zulu *izibongo*. Using critical techniques of literary and historical analysis that probe the ways in which *izibongo* glorify a celebrated subject, the postcolonial critic, in particular, could open new lines of inquiry into the lives of those who made up the lion's share of empire – the muted masses – allowing them to talk back, to reassert their speech into the lopsided tales of Zulu achievement. For example, when we next examine Shaka's praises and follow references to Phungashe, who postcolonial scholars would typically call a subaltern figure, we might note how the Buthelezi leader's escape to Nkandla and other events tied to Zulu conquest of Buthelezi people are represented. Can these representations be traced, contradicted, verified, and, most importantly, expanded on in other contexts? The answer is yes, when we juxtapose them with Phungashe's *izibongo*.

To the question of whether the subaltern can speak, the reply should be that he or she can, if their faint or fragmented voices (though probably not entire narratives) could be retrieved. Yet, as Duncan Brown asserts, this recovery procedure is not enough. Brown's contention is that the coloniser and the postcolonial critic have been unable to hear subaltern discourses because of an inability to know subaltern languages.[35] A scholar armed with good proficiency in isiZulu and knowledge of precolonial histories in KwaZulu-Natal – of which Phungashe's manoeuvres in relation to Shaka are a good example – could further challenge Mangosuthu Buthelezi's appeal to his audiences 'to let the rest of South Africa know that we are Zulus'. Such challenges might show Buthelezi people, in particular, that South African citizenship, rather than an ethnic classification, might be a more accurate personal and collective designation.

Still, the belief in being Zulu will probably not be discarded. It constitutes a part of post-apartheid society, which is why calls for greater national belonging should not simply dismiss Zulu cultural chauvinism as a tired relic of colonialism. Rather, they should encourage a wide-ranging investigation into what it means to be Zulu. For Mangosuthu Buthelezi's ancestor, *inkosi* Phungashe, being Zulu meant the elision of his ancestral pasts. As a consequence, today Buthelezi people and other clans continue to serve the harsh sentence imposed by Shaka, an indeterminate term of history-less-ness.

## Notes

1. The title of my chapter draws inspiration from B. Ashcroft, G. Griffiths and H. Tiffin's important postcolonial study, *The Empire Writes Back: Theory and Practice in Post-colonial Literatures* (London: Routledge, 1989).
2. 'Zulu nation must take a stand, says Buthelezi', *Mail & Guardian*, 23 January 2005.
3. In this chapter, I use *inkosi* instead of the colonial term 'chief' for two reasons. Firstly, I seek to point out how white rulers (beginning with British authority in the 1840s) undermined the institution of kingship in KwaZulu-Natal, particularly in relation to clans that made up the Zulu kingdom. The leaders of these clans were referred to as *amakhosi* (kings) by their respective followers, as are traditional leaders today. It must be noted that the term *inkosi* is used to refer to leaders of varying levels of importance, ranging from those whose polities comprise a few villages to the king of the Zulu ethnic group. I draw a distinction between the line of Zulu kings since Shaka's reign and more minor political figures in positions of traditional leadership by capitalising or not capitalising the 'i'

of *inkosi* respectively; i.e., a minor chief is *inkosi*, while a Zulu king is *Inkosi*. Secondly, I find the term 'chief' only appropriate to the co-opted and reformed institution of leadership during the colonial era, especially after the British partitioned the Zulu kingdom into thirteen chiefdoms (or kinglets) in the immediate wake of the Anglo-Zulu War of 1879. For a brief analysis of this historical transformation, see Carolyn Hamilton, *Terrific Majesty: The Powers of Shaka and the Limits of Historical Invention* (Cape Town: David Philip, 1998). Colonial conceptions of chieftaincy, of course, were central to the despotic rule of so-called traditional authority in apartheid 'bantustans', a system that Mangosuthu Buthelezi tapped into when ascending to new heights as leader of the Zulu nation. In the present, however, there is an important debate unfolding about whether the term 'chief' is a proper synonym for traditional leadership of a clan or nation.

4. For recent evidence of Mangosuthu Buthelezi evoking his title as 'traditional prime minister' of the Zulu nation, see *Mail & Guardian*, 23 January 2005. The term *isizwe* (plural, *izizwe*) is used here to mean clan, but it can also mean nation or race. I use the term 'clan' deliberately (following the ethnographer A.T. Bryant's definition of Zulu clan) to refer to lineage groups such as the Buthelezi or Zulu. For examples of the use of clan in Zulu history, see A.T. Bryant, *Olden Times in Zululand and Natal* (London: Longmans, 1929). For autobiographical commentary on Mangosuthu Buthelezi's lineage, see M.G. Buthelezi, 'The Early History of the Buthelezi Clan', in *Social Systems and Tradition in Southern Africa: Essays in Honour of Eileen Krige*, eds. J. Argyle and E. Preston-Whyte (Cape Town: Oxford University Press, 1978), p. 29 and M.G. Buthelezi, '*Izibongo zikaPhungashe kaNgwane Inkosi YakwaButhelezi*', (unpublished manuscript, 2003).

5. Over the past decade a few historians such as John Wright and Carolyn Hamilton have begun to analyse the complex regional struggles that contributed to Shaka's ascension, as well as to the wider recognition (and certainly fear) of Zulu identity in the nineteenth century. Among other things, they show that many of these struggles did not initially depend on Zulu agency, but rather were shaped by the actions of non-Zulu chiefdoms, which sought to enhance or uphold their political autonomy during increasingly turbulent times. See John Wright and Carolyn Hamilton, 'Traditions and Transformations in the Phongolo-Mzimkhulu Region in the Late and Early Nineteenth Centuries', in *Natal and Zululand from Earliest Times to 1910: A New History*, eds. A. Duminy and B. Guest (Pietermaritzburg: University of Natal Press and Shuter & Shooter, 1989), pp. 49–82. For other studies that examine the continued invention and maintenance of Zulu identity in the twentieth century, see John Wright, 'Political Mythology and the Making of Natal's *Mfecane*,' *Canadian Journal of African Studies* 22:2 (1989): 272–91; Shula Marks, 'Patriotism, Patriarchy and Purity: Natal and Politics of Zulu Ethnic Consciousness', in *The Creation of Tribalism in Southern Africa*, ed. Leroy Vail (London: James Currey, 1989), pp. 215–34 and Georgina Hamilton and Gerhard Maré, *An Appetite for Power: Buthelezi's Inkatha and South Africa* (Johannesburg: Ravan Press, 1987). See also Thembisa Waetjen's *Workers and Warriors: Masculinity and the Struggle for Nation in South Africa* (Urbana and Chicago: University of Illinois Press, 2004).

6. See Wright and Hamilton, 'Traditions and Transformations'. Julian Cobbing's controversial findings that slave traders, not Shaka's regiments, caused the violent disruptions associated with the *mfecane* were a crucial catalyst for the shift towards more ambivalent assessments of the figure of Shaka. See Julian Cobbing, 'The *Mfecane* as Alibi: Thoughts on Dithakong and Mbolompo', *Journal of African History* 29 (1988): 487–519.

7. Though the Ndwandwe and Mthethwa used armies to extend their authority, they also depended on consolidating ties through administrative structures that redistributed resources to allies in their fold, mainly *amakhosi* who pledged loyalty to Zwide or Dingiswayo. See Wright and Hamilton, 'Traditions and Transformations', p. 58.

8. Interview between Mbongiseni Buthelezi and Reggie Khumalo, a Zulu oral historian, 6 August 2003.

9. Ibid. See also interviews between Mbongiseni Buthelezi and Dede Buthelezi, 7 September 2003; Bonginkosi Buthelezi, 7 September 2003; Jethro Buthelezi, 7 September 2003; Musa Buthelezi, 3 October 2003 and Mzomusha Ndwandwe, 29 August 2003; these informants are oral historians of the Buthelezi clan.

10. The Buthelezi people are believed to have been one of Shaka's earliest conquests. According to one of James Stuart's interviewees, Baleka kaMpit[h]ikazi, '[Shaka] began with Macingwane, chief of the C[h]unu . . . After this he went to attack Phungashe, chief of the But[h]elezi, and also attacked other chiefs.' See C. de B. Webb and J.B. Wright, eds. *The James Stuart Archive of Recorded Oral Evidence Relating to the History of the Zulu and Neighbouring Peoples*, Vol. 1 (Pietermaritzburg:

University of Natal Press and Durban: Killie Campbell Collection, 1976), p. 5. Bryant makes a similar claim in *Olden Times*, p. 131, as does Buthelezi in 'The Early History', p. 29.

11. Even early Natal colonists (in this case the isiZulu-speaking British colonial administrator of native affairs, Theophilus Shepstone) deliberately propagating the stereotype of Shaka as a cruel monster, admitted that the Zulu founder preferred to 'intermingle [the people] as much as possible, and so rule them as to destroy their old associations . . .'. See Shepstone's quote in Hamilton, *Terrific Majesty*, p. 93; see also N.G. Biyela, 'The Figure of King Shaka in Past and Contemporary Oral Sources' (Masters thesis, University of Natal, 1998).

12. See Buthelezi, 'The Early History'.

13. Ibid., p. 32.

14. Dan Wylie offers a critique of white discourses on Shaka in *Savage Delight: White Myths of Shaka* (Pietermaritzburg: University of Natal Press, 2000).

15. Ibid. Whereas Wylie only focuses on colonial historical and literary representations of Shaka and beyond, works that have paid some critical attention to *izibongo* include Duncan Brown's *Voicing the Text: South African Oral Poetry Performance* (Cape Town: Oxford University Press, 1998), pp. 75–118; Liz Gunner and Mafika Gwala, *Musho! Zulu Popular Praises* (Johannesburg: Witwatersrand University Press, 1991) and Hamilton, *Terrific Majesty*. See also M.Z. Malaba, 'Shaka as Literary Theme' (Ph.D. diss., York University, 1986).

16. Trevor Cope, ed. *Izibongo: Zulu Praise Poetry* (London: Oxford Clarendon Press, 1968), pp. 88–117. See also C.T. Msimang, *Kusadliwa Ngoludala* (Pietermaritzburg: Shuter & Shooter, 1975), pp. 380–84.

17. For relevant scholarly views of *izibongo*, see Gunner and Gwala, *Musho!* and A.C. Nkabinde, *Zulu Prose and Praises* (KwaDlangezwa: University of Zululand, 1976). Generations later when proclaimed *izibongo* appeared frozen in written texts such as Trevor Cope's volume and then translated into English, the literate intermediary emerged as an essential figure – he or she became yet another gatekeeper of a once-oral tradition, further diluting the original scope and intent of *izibongo*. The version of the *izibongo*, entitled 'Shaka', that was eventually published by Cope bears a lengthy history of mediation: James Stuart, a nineteenth-century Natal native affairs official, collected and amalgamated his isiZulu version of the *izibongo* from 33 different performances that were conducted at his request (Brown, *Voicing the Text*, pp. 81–82). This was followed by Daniel McK. Malcolm of the Natal Native Affairs Department's translation of Stuart's version, which was later polished and published by Cope, who also made his own editorial interventions.

18. Cope, *Izibongo*, pp. 94–95.

19. Ibid., pp. 96–97.

20. Ibid., pp. 98–99.

21. C.T. Msimang, *Inkosi Yinkosi Ngabantu* (Cape Town: Kagiso Education: 1991), pp. 81–82.

22. Cope, *Izibongo*, pp. 100–01.

23. Most of the two blocks of verse can be found in '*Izibongo zikaPhungashe kaNgwane Inkosi YakwaButhelezi*', a document handwritten by Mangosuthu Buthelezi and given by him to the author of this chapter. The provenance of this important text remains uncertain, as no other version exists for the purpose of comparison. However some lines have been added after I recorded missing verses from interviews with Buthelezi *izimbongi* (Reggie Khumalo, 6 August 2003; Bonginkosi Buthelezi, 7 September 2003; Jethro Buthelezi, 7 September 2003 and Musa Buthelezi, 3 October 2003). I have provided the translation in this chapter. See also Buthelezi, 'The Early History'.

24. Interview between Mbongiseni Buthelezi and Reggie Khumalo, 6 August 2003; Bonginkosi Buthelezi, 7 September 2003; Jethro Buthelezi, 7 September 2003 and Musa Buthelezi, 3 October 2003.

25. Msimang, *Inkosi*, p. 3 and Gunner and Gwala, *Musho!*, p. 44. It is important to note here that *izibongo* are discourses of the public self as apprehended and appraised by the *izimbongi*, as well as the general public.

26. G.C. Spivak, 'Can the Subaltern Speak' in *Marxism and the Interpretation of Cultures*, eds. C. Nelson and L. Grossberg (Urbana and Chicago: University of Illinois Press, 1988), p. 287.

27. As a scholar who researched the legacies of the British Raj in India, Spivak's argument hinges on what is found in colonial historiography:

    'the peasant' is marked only as a pointer to an irretrievable consciousness. There is no subaltern voice that can be retrieved or made to speak, only the designations of texts that construct the peasant resisters as 'criminals' or 'mutineers' . . . [Hence] critics should resist the desire to retrieve the voices silenced by imperialism, first because they are irretrievable

and secondly because such a move would subscribe once more to the humanist notion of the voice as the free expression of an 'authentic' individuality.
(P. Childs and P. Williams, *An Introduction to Postcolonial Theory* [Harlow: Longman, 1997], p. 163.)

28. 'Introduction' in *Oral Literature and Performance in Southern Africa*, ed. Duncan Brown (Oxford: James Currey, Cape Town: David Philip and Athens: Ohio University Press, 1999), p. 10.

29. The Ndwandwe kingdom, because of its size and power, met a similar but intensified fate. See M. Buthelezi, '"Kof' Abantu, Kosal' Izibongo?": Contested Histories of Shaka, Phungashe and Zwide in Izibongo and Izithakazelo' (Masters thesis, University of KwaZulu-Natal, Durban, 2004), pp. 96–97.

30. There is a vigorous project of revising Buthelezi history currently in progress in northern KwaZulu-Natal. It entails recuperating the history of the clan through Phungashe and thus claiming back the land of which the Buthelezis were dispossessed by the Zulu kingdom and later during British colonial and apartheid rule. See Buthelezi, ' "Kof' Abantu" ', pp. 66–68.

31. Ibid., p. 4.

32. Not all resistance in this period was directed at the encroaching British and Boers. A confluence of succession disputes within the Zulu kingdom, as well as the presence of the British in Port Natal and that of the voortrekkers within the territories of the kingdom led to civil wars in 1839–40 and in 1856. In 1839–40, Mpande ousted Dingane from the royal throne with the assistance of the voortrekkers led by Andries Pretorius, under whose command the trekkers had routed Dingane's forces at Ncome in 1838. Mpande's victory led to his later estrangement from the Boers when they laid claim to and seized large tracts of land, both those from which Dingane had been withdrawing after the 1838 defeat and those that the Boers claimed for having aided Mpande's forces. Mpande's power and authority were in decline as he made manoeuvres between the British and the Boers in order to maintain his authority in the face of the threat posed by each of these new powers. By 1856, the succession dispute that had been developing between Mpande's sons, Princes Cetshwayo and Mbuyazi, led to a full-scale civil war. At the battle of Ndondakusuka, Mbuyazi's forces were defeated and the prince killed. Thereafter, Prince Cetshwayo ascended to the Zulu throne. See P. Colenbrander, 'The Zulu Kingdom, 1828–79', in *Natal and Zululand from Earliest Times to 1910: A New History*, eds. A. Duminy and B. Guest (Pietermaritzburg: University of Natal Press and Shuter & Shooter, 1989), pp. 83–115. See also Hamilton, *Terrific Majesty*, pp. 55–59.

33. See 'Chaka' in L.S. Senghor, *éthiopiques*, ed. P.G. N'diaye (Dakar and Abidjan: Les Nouvelles Editions Africaines, 1974), pp. 51–77. See also S. Biko, *I Write What I Like*, ed. Aelred Stubbs (Johannesburg: Ravan Press, 1996), pp. 95 and 128.

34. M. Jaggi. 'Crossing the River: Caryl Phillips talks to Maya Jaggi', *Wasafiri* 20: 26.

35. Brown, *Oral Literature*, p. 10.

*Chapter 3*

# Reflections on the Politics of Being 'Zulu'

JOHN WRIGHT

THE POPULAR VIEW of Zulu ethnicity today is that it is a fixed group identity that dates directly back to the emergence of the Zulu kingdom under Shaka kaSenzangakhona in the 1820s.[1] It is seen as a product of the establishment by the Zulu people of firm domination over the other peoples of what is now KwaZulu-Natal. The assumption is that from the time of Shaka's conquests onwards, his subjects unproblematically aligned themselves with the Zulu royal house and took on an overall identity as Zulu. This identity was strong enough to survive defeat at the hands of the British in 1879, devastating civil wars in the 1880s and the long ensuing period of white colonial rule. In the era of struggles against apartheid, Zulu identity was increasingly reasserted as a natural expression of a powerful and long-established group consciousness.

This view takes no notice of the argument, made by academic commentators for the last several decades, that ethnicity is never a fixed, primordial form of identity, but one which is always a product of historical processes. Nor does it take any notice of a well-established body of literature that indicates that the consolidation of a broad Zulu ethnic consciousness is primarily a phenomenon of the twentieth century, not the nineteenth.[2] It also overlooks a body of writings on modern Zulu nationalism that reveals how, in the period from the 1970s to the 1990s, competing Zulu identities were shaped and reshaped, taken up and abandoned, in a bitterly contested process involving black people and white people, isiZulu-speakers and non-isiZulu-speakers alike, in response to the pressures of contemporary politics.[3]

This chapter aims to underscore the argument that a generic Zulu ethnic identity did not take root before the twentieth century. It indicates that until the later nineteenth century not only was the need for such an identity not widely felt, but strong political and social forces at work in the Zulu kingdom and among black people in colonial Natal militated against its emergence. After the military defeat of the Zulu kingdom by British forces in 1879, the tightening of colonial rule over black people in Zululand and Natal from the 1890s onwards, the erosion of the old homestead-based rural order and the expansion of migrant labour in the same period, the conditions for the making of a broad Zulu identity began to fall into place. But it was not until after the First World War that claims to being Zulu began to be widely made.

## Zulu identity inside and outside the Zulu kingdom, 1820–80

The Zulu kingdom that emerged under Shaka in the 1820s, with its heartland in the territories between the Mkhuze and Thukela Rivers, was a conquest state.[4] Like other new conquest states, it was not, to begin with, a cohesive and united polity. It was an amalgamation of discrete, previously independent chiefdoms, each with its own established ruling house, its own identity, its own body of memories and traditions about the times before the Zulu conquest. Acceptance of Zulu overlordship by these chiefdoms did not add up to their acceptance of an identity as Zulu. Some notables, particularly those who had been placed in power by Shaka, had a basis for identifying to some extent with the political projects of the Zulu ruling house. Men of the new state's *amabutho*, or age regiments, who received, or hoped for, a share of the largesse in cattle distributed by their new ruler after successful raids, might also have had a reason for doing so. But for the majority of the people in the far-flung homesteads that yielded to the new paramount power tribute in the form of cattle, young women and the labour of young men, there was little, if anything, to draw them into identifying with the dominant Zulu group. Their identifications were with their own homestead-based communities and, at another remove, with their chiefs.

If the structures of the polity that Shaka dominated militated against the emergence of a common Zulu identity, so too did the policies that its ruling house was constrained to pursue, of deliberately fostering within it what in effect were ethnic lines of division. Like the rulers of the Mthethwa and Ndwandwe states before them and like the rulers of the contemporary Dlamini state in what is now Swaziland,[5] the Zulu leadership sought to maintain a clear distinction between a cluster of 'insider' chiefdoms in the state's heartland and various clusters of 'outsider' chiefdoms in its geographical peripheries north of the Mkhuze and south of the Thukela Rivers. The former collectively came to be known as *amantungwa*; the latter were designated by names, most of them opprobrious, such as *abambo, amalala, amanhlwenga, amazosha, iziyendane, izingadanqunu, amankengane* and others. The term 'Zulu' remained the designation exclusively of members of the royal house that dominated the new state. Members of other descent groups would have been actively prevented from claiming an identity as Zulu.

The Zulu body politic remained deeply divided against itself throughout the reign of Dingane (1828–40) and the first two decades of his successor Mpande (1840–72). On two occasions – in 1839–40 and in 1856 – tensions within the kingdom burst out into civil war. After 1838 the territories that the Zulu had dominated south of the Thukela passed under the control first of the Boer Republic of Natalia and then, in 1843, of the British colony of Natal. Henceforth, Zulu rule was confined to the territories north of the Thukela, occupied mainly by *amantungwa* chiefdoms. But, in the absence of a history of political unity, the greater ethnic homogeneity of the kingdom did not itself make for the development of a broader Zulu identity.[6]

It was probably not until the 1860s and 1870s that the kingdom started to achieve a greater degree of political unity, when its leading chiefs slowly drew together under Zulu leadership in common opposition to the external threats posed by the expansionism of the British in the south and the Boers in the west. It is possible that in these years a number of people in the kingdom, particularly the men who served in the king's *amabutho*, began to experience the first stirrings of a desire to identify themselves more specifically as Zulu, rather than more generally as *amantungwa*. By this time, memories of the pre-conquest period would have been growing dimmer, and people could acknowledge half a century of Zulu rule in attempting to broaden the meaning of what it was to be Zulu.

But local and regional identifications remained of major importance. In the reign of Cetshwayo kaMpande, (1872–79), the kingdom that he ruled remained an amalgamation of chiefdoms whose heads in many cases sought to retain some degree of autonomy from their Zulu overlords.[7] In the face of the British imperial invasion of 1879, the kingdom was able to hold together and to inflict a crushing defeat on the aggressors at the battle of Isandlwana. But once the British had resumed their march into the kingdom's heartland, important allegiances to the Zulu king crumbled. Numbers of chiefs were constrained to negotiate a separate peace with the British, even before the final defeat of the main Zulu army at Ulundi.[8] The settlement which followed the war saw the Zulu king exiled, his armies disbanded and the territories over which he had reigned partitioned among thirteen chiefs set up by the British as independent rulers. This was followed by a decade of destructive wars between supporters of the Zulu royal house and its antagonists. Playing an active role in fomenting them were British officials from Natal and Boers from the South African Republic: their motives were variously to seize land, to gain control over new sources of labour and to put an end to what remained of the influence of the Zulu royal house. By the end of the 1880s the basis for the existence of any broad Zulu identity north of the Thukela had largely crumbled away.

For most of the history of the Zulu kingdom, then, few of its members would have regarded themselves as Zulu. Until perhaps the time of Cetshwayo, people inside the kingdom applied the term solely to members of the ruling Zulu descent-group. Outside the kingdom, though, the term came to be used quite differently, particularly by white people. From the time of their earliest contacts with Shaka, Europeans in the neighbouring colonial world generically categorised all the people over whom he ruled as Zulu, both north and south of the Thukela. By the mid-1830s the word was well established in a growing English-language literary discourse. Many of the people so designated, particularly those living south of the Thukela, would emphatically not have called themselves Zulu.[9] As late as 1879, black people in Natal were prepared to take up arms for the British against the Zulu royal house.[10]

By the 1840s, if not earlier, some of the missionaries operating in the region were referring to the group of related dialects spoken by black people north and south of the Thukela as the Zulu language[11] and by the 1850s some early ethnographers were beginning to identify a cultural region which embraced both the Zulu kingdom and the colony of Natal.[12] Others revealed that the meaning of Zulu was still to some extent a contested one among white people by insisting on maintaining a distinction between the 'Zulus' of the Zulu kingdom and 'Kaffirs' of Natal colony.[13] Both these words were used by Natal colonists by the 1850s to refer to the colony's black population.[14] All these usages of the term 'Zulu' were rooted in the long-established European conception of people in Africa as living in distinct, bounded tribes, each with its own generic name; they did not at this stage reflect the usages of the people to whom they were applied. Whether Africans in the colony of Natal had any generic designation for themselves in this period is not clear; it may be that some of them were beginning to use the once-opprobrious term *amalala* to distinguish themselves from the Zulus north of the Thukela.[15]

## New contexts for Zulu identity, 1880–1920

In the last years of the nineteenth century and the early years of the twentieth, the very forces of imperialism and colonialism that had broken up the old Zulu order were establishing the conditions in which, for numbers of black people, the making of new kinds of alignments with the remnants of the Zulu royal house was becoming an attractive political proposition. These alignments provided the basis for the emergence of new claims to a Zulu identity.

A core of supporters of the Zulu royalist cause had survived the upheavals of the 1880s. By the 1890s they were beginning to receive support from a new quarter – the ranks of the mission-educated black people, or *kholwa*, who by then formed a distinct social category in the colony of Natal south of the Thukela. Increasingly frustrated as they were by the obstacles that white officials and settlers were placing in the way of their economic, social and political aspirations, members of this group were casting around for political allies.[16] In one direction lay the possibility of a nationalist alliance with similar groups in other regions of South Africa. In another, lay the possibility of an ethnic alliance with Zulu royalists north of the Thukela. From the 1890s onward, *amakholwa* leaders in Natal tended to veer between these positions as they sought to establish a political power base. In the process they developed a political discourse that combined elements of African nationalist ideology with elements of what can be called 'Zuluism', the self-conscious notion that the black people of the Natal-Zululand region were all Zulus by virtue of the fact that their forebears had once been ruled by the Zulu kings.[17]

This discourse converged in important respects with that of Natal colonial ideologues, who, in the pursuit of more effective administration of Africans in Natal and Zululand, promoted the idea that they constituted a single tribe called the Zulu. The annexation of much of the old Zulu kingdom as a British colony in 1887, followed by its incorporation into Natal colony in 1897, had largely erased the former sharp political distinction between the territories north and south of the Thukela. The notion that the isiZulu-speaking people of the two regions were all Zulus featured clearly in the detailed histories that colonial writers were beginning to produce at this time.[18] In contrast to earlier histories, which had depicted the Zulus as forming merely a branch of the 'Kaffir race',[19] these works were based on the premise that they constituted a discrete people with their own particular characteristics.

In the early years of the twentieth century the spread of Zuluist notions received support from yet another source. For the first time, some of the chiefs in Natal south of the Thukela were beginning to look to the Zulu royal house for leadership. Since the 1880s, common oppression at the hands of colonial governments had had the effect of gradually blurring many of the differences of interest that had previously existed between African communities north and south of the Thukela. This development was illustrated in the course of the Natal rebellion of 1906, when some of the handful of chiefs from south of the Thukela who went into open rebellion turned to Dinuzulu kaCetshwayo for support.[20] Dinuzulu, who had been allowed to return from exile in 1898, had no official status except as chief of a group of royalist supporters known as the uSuthu.

It is difficult to gauge the extent to which ordinary black people in Natal and Zululand were identifying with the Zulu royal house at this time. Some saw Dinuzulu as paramount among the chiefs of the region by virtue of his descent from the line of Zulu kings.[21] Others were ambivalent or hostile in their attitudes.[22] It is not possible to say how far people were actively identifying themselves as Zulu. But if analogies from other regions are anything to go by, the rapid growth in migrant labour from the rural areas of Natal and Zululand to towns such as Johannesburg from the 1890s onward would have served to foster the development, particularly among the younger men who constituted the bulk of the migrants, of an overarching generic identity. It is likely that in the towns where they came into competition with men from other regions for jobs, accommodation and access to women, they were starting to develop the beginnings of a regional solidarity and to take on the identity that white settlers, and probably Africans from other areas, had long conferred indiscriminately on black people from Natal and Zululand, that of Zulu.[23] This would not have been inconsistent with their continuing to identify strongly with their home communities in the rural areas.

But the extent to which a Zulu ethnic consciousness was emerging in the first two decades of the twentieth century should not be exaggerated. In part, its development would have been inhibited by the strong opposition shown since the

1880s by successive Natal administrations to the revival of the power and influence of the royal house. In Zululand, the hostility of many chiefs to the royal house was still strong. Numbers of influential chiefs pointedly did not attend Dinuzulu's funeral in 1913. For their part, even *kholwa* leaders who were sympathetic to the cause of the Zulu royal house, like John Dube, editor of the newspaper *Ilanga lase Natal*, were averse at this stage to being too closely associated with what they called 'tribalism'.[24] Among black people in Natal and Zululand there was as yet no firmly established political force to foster the development of a generic identity as Zulu.

The conditions necessary for the consolidation of a Zulu ethnic identity became more firmly established from the second decade of the twentieth century, when governments of the newly formed Union of South Africa began implementing segregationist policies in earnest. The 1913 Natives' Land Act, which put an end to the purchase of land by black people outside their scheduled reserves, struck a heavy blow to the aspirations of the small group of *kholwa* landowners. The Native Administration Bill of 1917, followed by the Native Administration Act of 1920, made clear to members of this class that their ability to pursue their economic and political aspirations outside the reserves was likely to be made more and more difficult. In 1917 more militant members ousted the conservative John Dube from the presidency of the South African Native National Congress to which he had been elected at its foundation meeting in 1912. In effect, he and his supporters were pushed back onto their regional political base in Natal. In seeking to strengthen this base, they were impelled by the growing radicalisation of black workers in the towns and in the countryside to look more seriously than before for a political alliance with more conservative leaders of rural communities in the reserves of Natal and Zululand.

For their part, many rural chiefs were becoming alarmed by the threats posed to their authority by the continuing growth of migrant labour and by the growth of working-class mobilisation in the towns. In looking for an alliance to help prop up the old rural order, many of them were beginning to align themselves with the cause of the figure whom they were now prepared to recognise as the most senior of their number, Solomon, son of Dinuzulu, of the Zulu royal house. In 1924 an alliance between *kholwa* landowners, chiefs north of the Thukela, and the Zulu royal house came together in an organisation named Inkatha ka Zulu. From this time on, isiZulu-speaking intellectuals, both *amakholwa* and traditionalists, were increasingly active in propagating an ideology that projected the head of the Zulu royal house as the leader by historical right of black people in Natal and Zululand.[25]

The complex history of the spread of this ideology among isiZulu-speaking people, and of resistance to it, belongs mainly to the period after the 1920s. But it is clear that from the 1910s onwards, the experiences of black people in Natal and Zululand made them more receptive to calls for ethnic solidarity. Overcrowding and loss of land in the reserves were propelling ever-increasing numbers of men into migrant labour, while for black people on white-owned farms conditions of labour tenancy were becoming more onerous.[26] Many isiZulu-speaking people, both in the rural areas and in the towns, faced lives of increasing hardship and uncertainty. Under these conditions, many of them, particularly in Zululand, were becoming increasingly receptive to calls to unite as a people and to give their allegiance to Zulu leaders whose forebears had fought against white domination. That these calls were beginning to strike a deep emotional chord among ordinary isiZulu-speaking people was graphically demonstrated at a public occasion in Eshowe when a crowd of 60 000 acclaimed Solomon kaDinuzulu as their king in 1925.[27]

## Notes

1.  This chapter is based on my unpublished paper entitled 'Notes on the Politics of Being "Zulu", 1820–1920', (University of Natal, 1992). It draws on another unpublished paper, jointly written with Carolyn Hamilton, entitled 'Ethnicity, History and the Limits of Imagination: Zulu Identity and the Metaphor of Shaka, 1820–1920', (University of the Witwatersrand and University of Natal, 1993) and on Carolyn Hamilton and John Wright, 'The Beginnings of Zulu Identity: The Image of Shaka', *Indicator South Africa* 10:3 (1993): 43–46.

2.  Shula Marks, *The Ambiguities of Dependence in South Africa: Class, Nationalism, and the State in Twentieth-Century Natal* (Johannesburg: Ravan Press, 1986); Shula Marks, 'Patriotism, Patriarchy and Purity: Natal and the Politics of Zulu Ethnic Consciousness', in *The Creation of Tribalism in Southern Africa*, ed. Leroy Vail (London: James Currey and Berkeley and Los Angeles: University of California Press, 1989), pp. 215–40; Nicholas Cope, 'The Zulu *Petit Bourgeoisie* and Zulu Nationalism in the 1920s: Origins of Inkatha', *Journal of Southern African Studies* 16:3 (1990): 431–51; Nicholas Cope, *To Bind the Nation: Solomon kaDinuzulu and Zulu Nationalism 1913–1933* (Pietermaritzburg: University of Natal Press, 1993); John Lambert and Robert Morrell, 'Domination and Subordination in Natal, 1890–1920', in *Political Economy and Identities in KwaZulu-Natal: Historical and Social Perspectives*, ed. Robert Morrell (Durban: Indicator Press, 1996), pp. 63–95; Paul Maylam, 'The Changing Political Economy of the Region 1920–1950', in Morrell, ed., *Political Economy*, pp. 97–118; Paul la Hausse de Lalouvière, *Restless Identities: Signatures of Nationalism, Zulu Ethnicity and History in the Lives of Petros Lamula (c.1881–1948) and Lymon Maling (1889–c.1936)* (Pietermaritzburg: University of Natal Press, 2000) and Bhekizizwe Peterson, *Monarchs, Missionaries and African Intellectuals: African Theatre and the Unmaking of Colonial Marginality* (Johannesburg: Witwatersrand University Press, 2000).

3.  Gerhard Maré and Georgina Hamilton, *An Appetite for Power: Buthelezi's Inkatha and the Politics of Loyal Resistance* (Johannesburg: Ravan Press, 1987); Paul Forsyth, 'The Past in the Service of the Present: The Political Use of History by Chief A.N.M.G. Buthelezi 1951–1991', *South African Historical Journal* 26 (1992): 74–92; Patrick Harries, 'Imagery, Symbolism and Tradition in a South African Bantustan: Mangosuthu Buthelezi, Inkatha, and Zulu History', *History and Theory* 32 (1993): 105–25; Daphna Golan, *Inventing Shaka: Using History in the Construction of Zulu Nationalism* (Boulder and London: Lynne Rienner, 1994); Carolyn Hamilton, *Terrific Majesty: The Powers of Shaka Zulu and the Limits of Historical Invention* (Cape Town: David Philip, 1998); Gerhard Maré, 'Versions of Resistance History in South Africa: The ANC Strand in Inkatha in the 1970s and 1980s', *Review of African Political Economy* 83 (2000): 63–79 and Laurence Piper, 'Nationalism Without a Nation: The Rise and Fall of Zulu Nationalism in South Africa's Transition to Democracy, 1975–99', *Nations and Nationalism* 8:1 (2002): 73–94.

4.  The first part of this section draws on John Wright and Carolyn Hamilton, 'Ethnicity and Political Change before 1840', in Morrell, ed., *Political Economy*, pp. 15–32.

5.  Philip Bonner, *Kings, Commoners and Concessionaires: The Evolution and Dissolution of the Nineteenth-Century Swazi State* (Cambridge: Cambridge University Press, 1983), pp. 33–37.

6.  For a similar conclusion, see M. de Haas and P.M. Zulu, 'Ethnicity and Nationalism in Post-apartheid South Africa: The Case of Natal and the "Zulus"', paper presented at conference of American Anthropological Association, Chicago, 1991, p. 7.

7.  Richard Cope, 'Political Power within the Zulu Kingdom and the "Coronation Laws" of 1873', *Journal of Natal and Zulu History* 8 (1985): 33–62 and Richard Cope, *Ploughshare of War: The Origins of the Anglo-Zulu War of 1879* (Pietermaritzburg: University of Natal Press, 1999).

8.  John Laband, 'The Cohesion of the Zulu Polity under the Impact of the Anglo-Zulu War', in *Kingdom and Colony at War: Sixteen Studies on the Anglo-Zulu War of 1879*, eds. John Laband and Paul Thompson (Pietermaritzburg: University of Natal Press and Cape Town: N & S Press, 1990), pp. 1–33.

9.  See many of the Cape colonial documents reprinted in B.J.T. Leverton, ed. *Records of Natal*, 4 vols., (Pretoria: Government Printer, 1984–92); George Champion, *Journal of the Reverend George Champion: American Missionary in Zululand 1835–9*, ed. Alan Booth (Cape Town: Struik, 1967) and Nathaniel Isaacs, *Travels and Adventures in Eastern Africa* (Cape Town: Struik, 1970; first published London, 1836).

10. See several of Paul Thompson's chapters in Laband and Thompson, *Kingdom and Colony*.

11. S.J.R. Martin, 'British Images of the Zulu, *c.*1820–1879' (Ph.D. diss., University of Cambridge, 1984), pp. 80–82.

12. J. Shooter, *The Kafirs of Natal and the Zulu Country* (London: E. Stanford, 1857) and Henry Callaway, *The Religious System of the Amazulu* (Springvale, Natal: J.A. Blair, 1870).

13. William Holden, *The Past and Future of the Kaffir Races* (Cape Town: Struik, 1963; first published London: William Holden, 1866), pp. 137–38.

14. G.H. Mason, *Life with the Zulus of Natal* (London: Longman, 1855). See also Martin, 'British Images of the Zulu', pp. 82–87.

15. Carolyn Hamilton and John Wright, 'The Making of the *Amalala*: Ethnicity, Ideology and Relations of Subordination in a Precolonial Context', *South African Historical Journal* 22 (1990): 21–22.

16. On the politics of this group, see Shula Marks, *Reluctant Rebellion: The 1906–1908 Disturbances in Natal* (Oxford: Clarendon Press, 1970), pp. 59–76, 114–15; Hamilton, *Terrific Majesty*; Andre Odendaal, *Vukani Bantu! The Beginnings of Black Protest Politics in South Africa to 1912* (Cape Town: David Philip, 1984), pp. 16–19, 59–62 and La Hausse de Lalouvière, *Restless Identities*, pp. 1–25.

17. For an example of the kind of history articulated by *kholwa* intellectuals at this time, see Magema Fuze's book, *Abantu Abamnyama Lapa Bavela Ngakona*. Although it was only published in 1922, it was apparently written in the early years of the century. An English translation by H.C. Lugg, edited by A.T. Cope, was published by University of Natal Press in 1978 under the title *The Black People and Whence They Came*.

18. J.Y. Gibson, *The Story of the Zulus* (Pietermaritzburg: P. Davis & Sons, 1903); Robert Plant, *The Zulu in Three Tenses* (Pietermaritzburg: P. Davis & Sons, 1905); A.T. Bryant, 'A Sketch of the Origin and Early History of the Zulu People', in his *A Zulu-English Dictionary* (Mariannhill: Mariannhill Press, 1905), pp. 12–66 and James Stuart, *A History of the Zulu Rebellion 1906* (London: Macmillan, 1913). In some of his other works, Stuart focused on the differences between the various peoples that made up the Zulu; his emphasis depended on the context in which he was writing.

19. Shooter, *The Kafirs* and Holden, *The Past*.

20. Marks, *Reluctant Rebellion*, pp. 114–16, 206, 253, 302–03.

21. Michael Mahoney, 'Between the Zulu King and the Great White Chief: Political Culture in a Natal Chiefdom, 1879–1906' (Ph.D. diss., University of California, 1998), pp. 227–37.

22. Benedict Carton, *Blood from Your Children: The Colonial Origins of Generational Conflict in South Africa* (Charlottesville and London: University Press of Virginia, 2000), pp. 114–15, 124–26, 139.

23. Mahoney, 'Between the Zulu King', pp. 148–64. On ethnic consciousness among black workers on the gold mines in the early years of the twentieth century, see Sean Moroney, 'Mine Worker Protest on the Witwatersrand: 1901–1912', in *Essays in Southern African Labour History*, ed. Eddie Webster (Johannesburg: Ravan Press, 1978), pp. 40–42. See also the reference in Odendaal, *Vukani Bantu!*, p. 62, to the existence in 1906 of a Cape Town and District Zulu Association.

24. Cope, 'The Zulu *Petit Bourgeoisie*', p. 433. See also La Hausse de Lalouvière, *Restless Identities*, pp. 9–25.

25. Marks, *Ambiguities of Dependence*, Chapter 2; Cope, *To Bind the Nation*, Chapter 4 and La Hausse de Lalouvière, *Restless Identities*, pp. 74–90.
26. Helen Bradford, *A Taste of Freedom: The ICU in Rural South Africa, 1924–1930* (Johannesburg: Ravan Press, 1988), Chapters 1, 2, and 6 and Thomas McClendon, *Genders and Generations Apart: Labor Tenants and Customary Law in Segregation-Era South Africa, 1920s to 1940s* (Portsmouth: Heinemann, Oxford: James Currey and Cape Town: David Philip, 2002), Chapter 2.
27. Cope, 'The Zulu *Petit Bourgeoisie*', p. 433.

# Foundations of Zuluness

## Iron Age to Late 1800s

*Chapter 4*

# A Brief Archaeology of Precolonial Farming in KwaZulu-Natal

GAVIN WHITELAW

TODAY, ZULU IDENTITY IS inextricably bound to KwaZulu-Natal. The province is marketed as the 'Kingdom of the Zulu', while its name could be translated as 'home and birthplace of the Zulu'.[1] One might ask if it was ever any other way. Archaeological and historical research provide an answer, showing that African farmers who were neither Zulu nor even Nguni-speakers also left their mark on the landscape during 1 600 years of a rich and relatively complex history. In this chapter I trace the outlines of this history.[2]

Archaeologists construct past identities from material culture, that is, the physical remains that people have left behind. Different kinds of identity are constructed from different kinds of remains. In KwaZulu-Natal, for instance, particular styles of homestead layout coincide with the distribution of eighteenth-century chiefdoms.[3]

Ceramics provide an example at a different scale. Pots, or their remains, occur on most farm sites and are stylistically variable in terms of shape and decoration. In southern Africa where the makers and users of pots were the same people, ceramic style zones represent groups of people who spoke the same language. The identification of such ceramic zones, or facies, allows archaeologists to detect the origin and subsequent history of linguistic groups. For example, the origin of Venda from interactions between Shona and Sotho speakers is represented in the archaeological record by a merger of Shona and Sotho ceramic styles.[4] Like homestead style, ceramic style is a material expression of identity, although on a larger scale.[5]

On an even larger scale, many cultural and linguistic entities in South Africa shared (and in many respects still share) a worldview, a particular way of organising the world. This is evident from a model of homestead organisation derived from nineteenth- and twentieth-century Nguni and Sotho-Tswana ethnography. The model, called the Central Cattle Pattern (CCP), depicts the layout of a homestead in terms of life forces, kinship and status.[6] It provides a unitary standard in which the essence of settlement layout is distilled and against which the extent and meaning of diversity can be assessed.

Briefly, wives live in houses arranged in ranked order around a central area containing cattle pens and a men's court or assembly area. Ceremonies such as weddings take place in the central area and important people are buried there, but women are normally excluded. Each wife stores grain from her fields in granaries in the courtyard of her house, but grain controlled by the homestead head is stored in the central area.

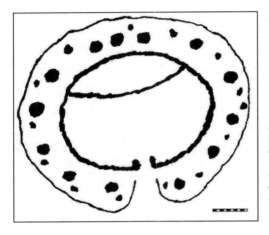

*Engraved depiction of a homestead, showing the cattle pen with an internal calf pen, the houses and their associated grain stores. These are surrounded by an outer fence. The engraving was probably made by children as a game board, possibly in the nineteenth century (Muden area).*

CCP homesteads are restricted to Eastern Bantu speakers who are patrilineal, maintain male hereditary leadership, have a preference for bridewealth in cattle and hold particular beliefs about the role of ancestors in daily life. The homestead is in fact a material expression of this cultural package. The archaeological presence of the CCP is therefore an indication of the past existence of this package. Other identities of this scale exist elsewhere in sub-Saharan Africa, represented materially by distinctive settlements. These include the Forest Pattern, associated with matrilineal Western Bantu speakers in Central Africa, and the Zimbabwe Pattern of Eastern Bantu speakers, associated with sacred leadership and class distinction.[7]

I construct the narrative that follows in terms of these three kinds of identity. It is important to recognise that they are *archaeological* identities derived from material remains and they do not have equivalent political consequences. Except possibly in the case of complex states such as Great Zimbabwe, ceramic style zones do not represent political entities. Activation of linguistic identity for political purposes would not have involved all members of a linguistic group. Local homestead style, on the other hand, could have been significant in establishing a distinctive political identity.

## The first millennium: Mzonjani and the Kalundu sequence

Two to three thousand years ago in the vicinity of modern Nigeria and Cameroon, African farmers speaking Bantu languages developed a new way of life and spread gradually around the fringes of the equatorial forests into eastern and southern Africa. This expansion is recognisable from distinctive settlement remains and pottery of the Chifumbaze Complex, divided on the basis of style into the Urewe and Kalundu traditions.[8]

The earliest date for settlement in South Africa, the fourth century AD, comes from the site of Silver Leaves in Limpopo province. Silver Leaves pottery belongs to the Urewe tradition, which shows that the ancestors of these pioneer farmers lived in East Africa. By 450 the Silver Leaves style had given rise to Mzonjani. The distribution of Mzonjani pottery indicates that by this time farmers had expanded into the coastal belt of what is now KwaZulu-Natal, reaching some 100 kilometres (62 miles) south of Durban. On current evidence there is a strong correlation in KwaZulu-Natal between site location and iron ore outcrops, suggesting that the discovery of ore reserves was an important motivating factor in the early expansion of farming settlements. Most Mzonjani sites lie within 6 kilometres (3.7 miles) of the shoreline, so this does not apply to the far more significant ore reserves further inland.[9] It seems possible that arid climatic conditions made the relatively dry interior unattractive; on the coast, annual rainfall is higher than further inland, whatever the prevailing conditions.[10] Farming as a way of life placed limits on where people settled.

It was, then, possibly the onset of wetter conditions in the seventh century that allowed farmers to settle in bushveld environments further inland and to push towards the southernmost limits of the summer rainfall region, near modern East London. The origin of this second phase of settlement differs from that of the Mzonjani phase. Second-phase pottery, called Msuluzi, is a Kalundu tradition style, indicating that the ancestors of these farmers came primarily from what is now Angola, which they had reached probably by moving south through the western margins of the equatorial forest. Both Msuluzi and Mzonjani people spoke Eastern Bantu languages, though the two groups were linguistically distinct. Evidence of interaction in the course of the expansion southwards is preserved in the richly decorated style of Msuluzi ceramics. As a result of stylistic drift, Msuluzi gave rise to a style we call Ndondondwane by 780, which in turn became Ntshekane by 940. Similar though gradually diverging changes are evident in the Kalundu ceramic sequence in the Eastern Cape.

Kalundu sites commonly cover 7–10 hectares, although it is unlikely that site size always reflects settlement size. Some sites were occupied for long periods, while others were abandoned and reoccupied through the centuries. Consequently, the various temporal layers must be teased apart to discern settlement size at any particular time. Nevertheless, at least some settlements were large: KwaGandaganda in the Mngeni valley near Durban was a little over 6 hectares in area during the ninth and tenth centuries.[11]

As a rule, sites are situated on deep arable soil close to rivers or lakes, indicating that fields and gardens were established close to the settlements. Crops included grain plants such as sorghum and bulrush and finger millet, as well as pulses (groundnuts and cowpeas) and cucurbits (African melons and gourds). Faunal remains show that farmers kept cattle, as well as flocks of sheep and goats, while chicken remains dating back to the seventh century show that this Asian fowl was an early introduction to Africa. Cattle typically provided the bulk of meat, although more sheep were eaten. Like small-scale farmers throughout history, it is likely that people made extensive use of wild resources. Plants were possibly especially important, although this is difficult to demonstrate with archaeological remains. Faunal remains show that people (probably with their dogs) hunted animals such as primates, carnivores, various ungulates, elephant and hippopotami, and smaller mammals such as the pangolin, water mongoose and hare. The dietary contribution of these animals was limited; instead hunting possibly served important social purposes, such as recreation, ritual, and to obtain items of value such as ivory.

The surrounding bushveld offered year-round sweet grazing and wood for industrial and domestic use. Looking further afield, it is reasonable to assume that some farmers exploited the summer grazing potential of grasslands on the higher ground above the valleys, as people have done in more recent times.[12] Resources of the seashore were clearly important for people living within easy reach of the coast. KwaGandaganda, some 25 kilometres (15.6 miles) inland, contained marine fish and shellfish remains. Harvesting trips to the shoreline may have been timed to coincide with spring low tides. On the beaches, the opposite end of the harvesting cycle is preserved in middens (refuse heaps) containing shellfish remains, ceramics, hearths and firestones.[13] KwaGandaganda also contains the remains of marine fish, including species that are easily trapped in estuaries, and black and white mussel crackers – landed today with some difficulty using lines off rocky promontories. By contrast, riverine foods were apparently considered less interesting – freshwater fish and mollusc remains are limited on sites both close to the coast and inland.

Food production would have absorbed most of the iron produced.[14] Indeed, metallurgy was a key component of farmer technology. Yet in contrast to the earlier Mzonjani phase, proximity to ore outcrops seems not to have been especially important for Kalundu tradition communities. Possibly iron production was organised differently by the two groups. Certainly the early association of ore bodies and settlements implies that Mzonjani ore-procurement strategies were small in scale. Later, ore collection in some areas required trips by work parties to outcrops some distance from settlements, especially in ore-deficient southern KwaZulu-Natal.

Iron ore smelting in the colonial period throughout much of sub-Saharan Africa was homologous to procreation and shrouded with the same supernatural danger that surrounds pregnancy and birth. Since it threatened the fertility of men and cattle, furnaces in southern Africa were generally situated outside settlements.

However, almost all Kalundu tradition sites contain residues of iron production, which some archaeologists interpret as evidence of a different belief structure.[15] A key issue is the nature of deposits, because forging in colonial times did not carry the same symbolic weight as smelting and in some societies was practised within settlements. KwaGandaganda, for instance, had forge remains in the men's court from the ninth century, but both smelting and forging debris in the seventh-century court midden. Since debris and structural remains are not equivalent data, the discovery of furnaces is important for resolving this problem. A furnace preserved at Ndondondwane in the Thukela valley was situated in a central activity area, while forging residues occurred in what was possibly the men's court near the cattle pen.[16] The organisation of iron production was clearly complex and recent research at Ndondondwane should generate new interpretations.[17] However, I suspect that these will be rooted in the general belief structure surrounding iron production that is so widespread in Africa.

From the seventh century onwards there was considerable movement of people and materials across the landscape. Sites contain exotic items such as ostrich eggshells, animal species not endemic to the region, copper beads and, late in the first-millennium sequence, glass beads and a fragment of a glazed ceramic vessel from the Sawad, the agricultural region of southern Iraq.[18] These artefacts point to the existence of a network of interactions that extended for great distances across South Africa and beyond.

*Settlement patterns and rites of passage*
Large-scale excavations have shown that the layout of Mzonjani phase and Kalundu tradition sites is consistent with the CCP.[19] The ninth- and tenth-century levels on KwaGandaganda had cattle pens closely associated with deep middens, which contained the waste generated from activities in the nearby men's court. These activities included ironworking, as the area also contained forge bases and broken slag. Surrounding this set of features was a residential area with huts, granaries and small midden deposits, probably associated with individual households. This layout is similar to that of the contemporary site of Ndondondwane. Data for the seventh- and eighth-century levels on KwaGandaganda are not as clean, but there is sufficient similarity in the association of particular features to suggest strongly that the same mental model was the basis for homestead organisation.[20]

The CCP provides compelling evidence that early farming communities were ranked societies with hereditary leaders. Political centres can be identified by the presence of ivory and exotic items, the size of court middens, the number of cattle pens, and longevity of occupation. Capitals may also contain residues of centralised rites of passage.[21] Such residues almost certainly include the remains of four hollow ceramic 'heads' with crocodilian 'beaks' or snouts and bulging eyes, recovered from Ndondondwane. Though somewhat different in appearance, they surely served the same purpose as the extraordinary ninth-century heads from Lydenburg, Mpumalanga,[22] which 'with fresh white slip, or paint and glittering specularite, . . . must have been dramatic objects to behold'.[23] These remarkable artefacts were most likely part of the paraphernalia used in premarital schools held in the central part of the settlement.[24]

Details of the sculpted mouths on four of the seven Lydenburg heads link them strongly to rites of passage. These contain evenly spaced peg-like teeth, separated into two groups by a gap in front, which most probably represents dental mutilation. In KwaZulu-Natal and elsewhere the lower four and upper two central incisors were extracted and the labial edges of the upper lateral incisors and neighbouring canines chipped to create rough points. Skeletal evidence shows this invasive procedure occurred in the teen years.[25] The operation marked a person indelibly as an adult.

Court middens especially contain other remnants of premarital education, including ceramic figurines of human females with featureless heads and stubby limbs, prominent navels and protruding buttocks, or a combination of these features. Some have rows of impressions and incised lines possibly representing scarification, other marks seem to represent genitalia. KwaGandaganda also yielded a penis-shaped object, underlining a focus on fertility. The figurines were commonly broken, apparently deliberately, prior to deposition. Since deliberate destruction is typically associated with an irreversible change in a person's status, these objects were probably didactic tools employed to teach young people proper behaviour.

Ceramic cooking and storage vessels also had a symbolic role. Deep pits on first-millennium sites from Tanzania to the southernmost reaches of farmer settlement in the Eastern Cape contain one or more pots with broken bases. The breakage was clearly intentional: although in some cases the hole has a ragged edge, in others the break was rubbed smooth. Similarly altered and complete pots occur in graves of children and infants.[26] Appropriate interpretations for these deposits should invoke the widespread metaphorical link in Africa between women and pots.[27] Pots, for instance, can represent the womb to which the dead infant is returned,[28] while a hypothesis for pit deposits invokes puberty rites for girls.[29]

Once they had reached adulthood, people could marry. The CCP shows that cattle were the preferred form of bridewealth. Some scholars have argued that first-millennium sites contain too few cattle remains for a cattle-based bridewealth system, but this view rests on shaky ground. Ethnographic information shows that the system can function even when cattle numbers are severely limited. Further, the presence of a single cow in the archaeological record implies the existence of a breeding population of at least 100 beasts. Certainly, there were sufficient numbers to produce the deep dung deposits common in first-millennium cattle pens.[30]

This defence of the model is critical because in more recent precolonial times, for which the existence of the CCP is uncontested, marriage was the primary mechanism men used to accumulate labour power – that is, human productive and reproductive capacity. Marriage, therefore, was central to men's exploitation of women and children, as well as male competition for labour power.[31] If the validity of the model holds on this point, it indicates that power relationships were structured and activated in the same way in the first millennium as in the more recent past.

### The second millennium: The Blackburn sequence

The final Kalundu tradition phase, Ntshekane, ends around 1030. This way of life was replaced by something markedly different. A deteriorating, drying climate possibly played a role in the change, although the effect appears to have been most marked south of what is now KwaZulu-Natal.[32] Of greater significance was the appearance on the landscape of new farmers from the north. The key evidence supporting this movement is the sharp stylistic disjunction in the pottery sequence.[33] The structured bands of incision, elaborate arcades and other motifs that characterised the Kalundu tradition are replaced by notches on vessel lips, stamping and incised slashes on pot shoulders, clusters of punctate impressions plus occasional elliptical or rounded bosses. Whereas almost all Kalundu pots are decorated, this is not the case with the new style, called Blackburn.

The Blackburn phase dates from about 1030 to 1300 and represents ancestral Nguni-speaking farmers – the third language group to settle in what is now KwaZulu-Natal. Ceramic data and kinship terms show that they originated in East Africa, probably in the Great Lakes region.[34] Blackburn may overlap with the end of the Kalundu sequence, but the limited evidence available does not enable us to examine this issue.

The next phase in the Blackburn sequence, Moor Park, dates from 1300 to 1700. Some Moor Park people were the first in South Africa to establish homesteads on the higher-altitude grasslands. Expansion into this new ecological zone opened the way to greater economic specialisation and interdependence. The debris of iron production is absent from grassland sites, for example, although two sites yielded fragments of iron blades, which must have been brought in from elsewhere.[35]

Moor Park settlements were the first in the region built of stone, a consequence of the absence of woody vegetation in the grasslands. Those excavated are situated on steep-sided hilltops or spurs, locations that provide rocky, uncomfortable places to live, often a good distance from water and arable lands.[36] Poorly preserved faunal remains include cattle and sheep or goats (or both), while dogs are identified from characteristic gnaw-marks on bones.[37] Grindstones and stone-paved platforms, probably for granaries, provide indirect evidence of crop cultivation and storage.[38]

Portuguese shipwreck survivors of the 1500s reported a range of foodstuffs: sorghum and millet, ground to produce porridge, beer and a kind of bread or cake, African melons, groundnuts, and beans (probably cowpeas). Domestic animals included chickens, sheep in grassland areas and goats in the coastal belt, while cattle provided milk, 'butter' (*amasi*)[39] and meat. As in the first millennium, farmers hunted and collected wild resources. Of interest are Manuel de Mesquita Perestrello's accounts of purchasing fish at the Mhlathuze lagoon and fishing in Delagoa Bay (in the 1550s).[40] Although he makes no mention of the activity further south, oral and written data describe fishing in Natal Bay in the 1700s and early 1800s. Here fish were highly regarded: they made a person 'fat and sleek', according to Maziyana kaMahlabeni, and were exchanged for iron tools.[41]

The Portuguese also noted the uneven distribution of resources. Survivors of the *Santo Alberto* wreck travelled through 'deserts' (probably sourveld grasslands) not occupied by farmers[42] and near the Thukela River found that 'for the same amount of copper, – of which they wear bracelets, – for which [people further south] gave three cows they would only give one, it not being so valuable among them, and they also value calico, which the others would not accept'.[43] This indicates either a higher value for cattle in the Thukela valley or reduced value for copper. Since neither copper nor brass were produced in KwaZulu-Natal, it is possible these communities already had access to imported copper and brass in the 1590s, especially as they had developed an interest in imported cloth. This could not have come from shipwrecked sailors passing through occasionally. It is worth noting that combined ceramic and radiocarbon data suggest reworking of imported brass at Mhlopeni in the Thukela basin between 1530 and 1700.[44] Thus, less than 100 years after Vasco da Gama reached the east coast of Africa in 1497, European trade was making an impact on life in the interior some 400 kilometres (250 miles) southwest of Delagoa Bay.

A significant consequence of Portugal's global reach was the introduction of American crops, especially maize. Maize is easier to cultivate than African grains and with sufficient rain provides higher yields per unit of land and labour. By the mid-eighteenth century maize was probably the staple crop in high rainfall areas. The archaeological record shows a marked increase in the number of sites in the interior grasslands at this time, suggesting a population increase built on the more productive cereal.[45] This period belongs to the Nqabeni phase, which lasts from around 1700 to the period of intensifying social and political disruptions around the beginning of the nineteenth century.

Several Nqabeni phase sites have been excavated, including Nqabeni itself on the Babanango plateau and Mgoduyanuka in the upper Thukela basin. Both are situated in the grasslands.[46] Nqabeni represents Type B sites, which consist of several roughly circular stone-walled enclosures connected by walling to form a large central enclosure. Huts would have been distributed around this central feature. Type B homesteads seem to have been restricted to an eighteenth-century Khumalo chiefdom.[47] By contrast, Zizi communities lived in Mgoduyanuka-style homesteads. The basic settlement unit here is a circular cattle pen surrounded by huts. Of special archaeological interest is that many of the cattle pens are constructed of stone-faced earth walls, a technique unknown elsewhere in South Africa. Middens on both types of sites contained maize and faunal assemblages dominated by cattle and caprines (probably sheep).

Mgoduyanuka sites occur over a large area and vary considerably in terms of their aggregation and dispersal – clusters of sites exist in some areas, in others sites are widely separated. They are not much differentiated, an exception being one site with nine cattle pens, and there is little to suggest that they represent a chiefdom like that represented by Type B sites. Rather, people living in them were organised in lower-level 'polities' – agnatic clusters or perhaps under a district headman.

Mgoduyanuka and Nqabeni contained iron items, but no trace of metalworking. Iron tools must have come from bush or thornveld areas because ironworking requires hardwood charcoal. At Mabhija in the Thukela valley, excavation revealed several smelting furnaces once fired by men of a Dlamini community. The area is agriculturally poor and, not surprisingly, oral traditions include stories of the exchange of hoes and spear blades for sorghum, sheep and cattle. Zizi people on the grasslands were an obvious market, while Sotho traditions indicate exchange across the Drakensberg Mountains.[48]

### Settlement patterns, conflict and expansion

There is limited evidence for the layout of Blackburn phase settlements. Excavation on Blackburn hill near Durban exposed the floors of two beehive huts 5.5 metres (5 yards) in diameter. There is sufficient space on the hilltop for up to fifteen similar structures, plus a cattle pen.[49] Patches of midden occurred on the slopes below the hilltop; these were most likely associated with different households. Although not yet demonstrated by excavation, it is most likely that Blackburn settlements had a CCP arrangement. The model is constructed primarily from Nguni and Sotho-Tswana ethnography. Nqabeni phase sites are organised in this way, as are the earliest Sotho-Tswana settlements in South Africa, dating from 1300 (like Nguni, Sotho-Tswana has East African origins).[50] Moor Park sites for the most part conform to the CCP, though its expression is frequently distorted by their location.[51] Blackburn is unlikely to have been different.

Written reports add colour to archaeological images of settlement and social organisation. Survivors of the 1593 *Santo Alberto* wreck 'came to a village consisting of a few houses around a kraal [livestock pen], in which there were about a hundred cows and a hundred and twenty very large sheep . . . Here lived an old man with his sons and grandsons'.[52] Groups of two or more such homesteads observed earlier in this century probably made up agnatic clusters, homesteads of men of common descent. These in turn could belong to larger socio-political units. Between the 1500s and 1800, chiefdoms in some parts of the region had territories of 15 to 20 kilometres (9 to 12.5 miles) across,[53] though the degree of centralisation varied. The account of the 1589 *São Thomé* survivors lists several 'kingdoms' in the coastal belt from Delagoa Bay southwards. Beyond the southernmost kingdom named, 'there are no other kings, but all is in the possession of chiefs called Inkosis [correctly, *amakhosi*], who are the heads and governors of three, four, or five villages'.[54] Possibly trade in ivory was already stimulating growth in the chiefdoms most affected.

Moor Park hilltop sites are of special interest. The location is defensive, an indication of a society in conflict – people had restricted freedom in establishing their homesteads.[55] The causes are unknown. However, annual growth rings of a yellowwood tree felled in 1916 indicate extremely slow growth for a long period in the fourteenth century, which Martin Hall has suggested was a result of limited availability of water (and, therefore, lower rainfall). An alternative possibility is that the slow growth was a consequence of the colder conditions brought by the onset of the Little Ice Age. Either way, the adverse conditions would have placed communities under severe stress, which at times resulted in enough conflict to force people to build in defendable locations. The violence must have been of some duration and there may have been episodes of aggression, given the spread of the Moor Park dates.

Since ethnographic data show that moving to new areas was a principle way of resolving tension, the conflict may have had another impact – prompting people to cross the Drakensberg Mountains to the highveld west of the mountains, which climatic changes had apparently made suitable for agriculture in the fifteenth century.[56] Alfred Bryant, for instance, maintained that the Fokeng who settled on the highveld in the 1400s were originally Nguni. Although his claim should not be accepted without reservation (David Ellenberger provides a different origin), new archaeological research suggests this was indeed the case.[57] Others took this route: archaeological and oral data suggests that Nguni speakers moved west-, north- and northwestwards out of the KwaZulu-Natal region from around 1500 onwards. According to Ellenberger and Bryant, offshoots of the Zizi spread west across the mountains from the early seventeenth century onwards, in one instance at least, says Bryant, to resolve tension. Nguni-like settlement layouts in the Caledon valley and near Winburg in the Free State may be a consequence of these movements. North of the Vaal River, Nguni-speakers intruded into areas occupied by Sotho communities, possibly from as early as the 1500s, but certainly from the early 1600s onwards.[58]

Increasing social and political fluidity occurred over a large area from mid-1750 onwards. This is popularly attributed to devastation wrought by the transformation of the minor eighteenth-century Zulu chiefdom into a major regional power. More nuanced interpretations see its origins in the interaction between African chiefdoms and European traders plying the east coast of Africa.[59]

Prior to the eighteenth century, most European trade on the east coast of Africa was with Shona states in the interior. Mozambique Island was an especially important port. Further south, the Venda traded through Sofala and Inhambane. Delagoa Bay became increasingly important from the early 1700s, and Natal Bay in the 1800s. Ivory was the principal export from Delagoa Bay, while slaving may have been a factor in the early nineteenth century. Key imports were copper, brass, glass beads and cloth.

In the hinterland of the bay, the 1700s witnessed a gradual acceleration of a process that had begun nearly two centuries earlier, as chiefs competing for trade wealth sought to consolidate and extend their spheres of influence. Competition became increasingly aggressive after 1750. Control and maintenance of chiefdoms required the distribution of largesse, which was obtained more and more by raiding communities outside the chiefdom. In response, some of those affected formed loose defensive aggregations. Other leaders abandoned their home territories to carve out chiefdoms elsewhere. Still other chiefs were killed, their followers incorporated into greater powers. Raiding for cattle escalated towards the end of the 1700s, to supply a growing demand from American and British traders. By consuming this key commodity, the trade threatened the reproduction of society outside the major chiefdoms. To make matters worse, a severe drought around 1800 ushered in the *Madlathule* ('let him eat and remain silent') famine. This must have led in turn to increasingly desperate and violent acquisition of resources, for sustenance, trade and redistribution.[60] Rock shelters throughout the region preserve evidence of occupation by refugees from political and economic turmoil.

Political and economic competition north of the Thukela River became dominated in the 1810s by a rivalry between the Ndwandwe and the Mthethwa, led respectively by Zwide kaLanga and Dingiswayo kaJobe. The Mthethwa polity collapsed after Dingiswayo's defeat and death in the late 1810s, though its Zulu ally under Shaka kaSenzangakhona evaded destruction. Shaka survived two Ndwandwe attacks, all the while employing a mixture of diplomacy and military action to draw neighbouring chiefdoms into a Zulu-dominated alliance. Bolstered by these resources, the Zulu repulsed a third attack. The Zulu success exposed dissent within the Ndwandwe chiefdom and hastened the end of Zwide's control of his larger polity. By 1820 the Zulu were the dominant power between the Phongolo and Thukela rivers.

### Conclusion

Even at the relatively coarse resolution of archaeological residues, farming history in KwaZulu-Natal recognisably relates to one of at least three distinct linguistic entities, represented by Mzonjani, Kalundu and Blackburn sequence ceramics. Smaller, chiefdom-level identities are evident in the archaeological record from the sixteenth century. This is a consequence of the construction of long-lasting stone-walled settlements in the grasslands and the availability of oral traditions and historical documents. Future research will hopefully seek to increase archaeological resolution in both millennia.

All these various linguistic and socio-political entities were rooted in a common worldview, represented by CCP settlements. The pattern endured for 1 600 years because it represents the mechanism that theoretically gave *all* men access to power. This allowed it to survive even the great upheavals of the early stages of colonisation. Indeed, one has to wonder if its persistence in the modern era is not partly a consequence of colonisation and apartheid, of the denial to Africans of an alternative route to power.

## Notes

1. 'Kwa-' is the locative prefix in Zulu, meaning 'place of', though it is usually used in the sense of 'home of' (Adrian Koopman, *Zulu Names* [Pietermaritzburg: University of Natal, 2000]). KwaZulu was the name of the self-governing homeland created for isiZulu-speakers under apartheid legislation. Natal is derived from the name 'Terre do Natal', meaning 'Land of the Birth' (of Christ), which Vasco da Gama gave on Christmas Day 1497. The current name of the province is a product of politically correct expediency in the run-up to South Africa's first democratic election in 1994. It binds an apartheid construction to a colonial one.

2. I exclude mention of hunter-gatherers who were present on the landscape before and during the last 1 600 years. This is not to suggest that they were unimportant or had little impact on farmers. Archaeological, historical, cultural, linguistic and genetic data show that this is not the case. They are excluded here simply due to space constraints.

3. M. Hall and K. Mack, 'The Outline of an Eighteenth-century Economic System in South-east Africa', *Annals of the South African Museum* 91:2 (1983): 163–94. Compare with T. Maggs, D. Oswald, M. Hall and H. Rüther, 'Spatial Parameters of Late Iron Age Settlements in the Upper Thukela Valley', *Annals of the Natal Museum* 27:2 (1986): 455–79.

4. Venda grammar and phonology are similar to Shona, Kalanga especially, while its vocabulary is closest to Sotho. See p. 150 of J.H.N. Loubser, 'The Ethnoarchaeology of Venda-speakers in Southern Africa', *Navorsinge van die Nasionale Museum, Bloemfontein* 7:8 (1991): 146–464.

5. T.M. Evers, 'The Recognition of Groups in the Iron Age of Southern Africa' (Ph.D. diss, University of the Witwatersrand, Johannesburg, 1988); T.N. Huffman, 'Ceramics, Classification and Iron Age Entities', *African Studies* 39:2 (1980): 123–73 and T.N. Huffman, 'Regionality in the Iron Age: The Case of the Sotho-Tswana', *Southern African Humanities* 14 (2002): 1–22.

6. T.N. Huffman, 'Archaeology and Ethnohistory of the African Iron Age', *Annual Review of Anthropology* 11 (1982): 133–50 and T.N. Huffman, 'The Central Cattle Pattern and Interpreting the Past', *Southern African Humanities* 13 (2001): 19–35.

7. T.N. Huffman, *Iron Age Migrations* (Johannesburg: Witwatersrand University Press, 1989) and T.N. Huffman, *Snakes and Crocodiles: Power and Symbolism in Ancient Zimbabwe* (Johannesburg: Witwatersrand University Press, 1996).

8. By convention pottery styles are given the name of the site at which they were first recorded. This name is also used to refer to the people who made the pottery. Pottery styles have both spatial and temporal limits. Broadly, contemporary sites with the same style make up a facies. Related facies make up branches and two or more related branches form a tradition. Temporally, stylistic sequences are divided into phases.

9. Mzonjani sites north of KwaZulu-Natal have a wider distribution. See M. Klapwijk and T.N. Huffman, 'Excavations at Silver Leaves: A Final Report', *South African Archaeological Bulletin* 51 (1996): 84–93.

10. G. Whitelaw and M. Moon, 'The Ceramics and Distribution of Pioneer Agriculturists in KwaZulu-Natal', *Natal Museum Journal of Humanities* 8 (1996): 53–79.

11. G. Whitelaw, 'KwaGandaganda: Settlement Patterns in the Natal Early Iron Age', *Natal Museum Journal of Humanities* 6 (1994): 1–64.

12. T. Maggs and V. Ward, 'Early Iron Age Sites in the Muden Area of Natal', *Annals of the Natal Museum* 26:2 (1984): 105–40.

13. L. Horwitz, T. Maggs and V. Ward, 'Two Shell Middens as Indicators of Shellfish Exploitation Patterns during the First Millennium AD on the Natal North Coast', *Natal Museum Journal of Humanities* 3 (1991): 1–28.

14. T. Maggs, 'Metalwork from Iron Age Hoards as a Record of Metal Production in the Natal Region', *South African Archaeological Bulletin* 46 (1991): 131–36. Although this paper deals with Zulu material, hoes probably accounted for most of the iron produced throughout southern Africa.

15. T. Maggs, 'The Early Iron Age in the Extreme South: Some Patterns and Problems', *Azania* 29–30 (1994–95): 171–78.

16. J.H.N. Loubser, 'Ndondondwane: The Significance of Features and Finds from a Ninth-century Site on the Lower Thukela River, Natal', *Natal Museum Journal of Humanities* 5 (1993): 109–51; L.O. van Schalkwyk, H. Greenfield and T. Jongsma, 'The Early Iron Age Site of Ndondondwane, KwaZulu-Natal, South Africa: Preliminary Report on the 1995 Excavations', *Southern African Field Archaeology* 6:2 (1997): 61–77. A furnace base was also preserved at Magogo; see Maggs and Ward, 'Early Iron Age Sites'.

17. Personal communication with Haskel Greenfield, University of Manitoba, Canada. See also G. Whitelaw, 'Comment on Greenfield and Van Schalkwyk's Ndondondwane, Azania, 2003', *Azania* 40 (2005): 122–27 and a response by H. Greenfield, 'On the Nature of Daga Houses, Kraals, Metallurgy and Intra-settlement Spatial Organisation of EIA Settlements in Southern Africa: A Response to Whitelaw', *Azania* 41 (2006): 165–178.

18. R.B. Mason, 'In Sindbad's Steps: A Sherd in Every Port', *Royal Ontario Museum Archaeological Newsletter* Series II:53 (1994): 1–4 and personal communication with the author.

19. T.N. Huffman, 'Broederstroom and the Origins of Cattle-keeping in Southern Africa', *African Studies* 49:2 (1990): 1–12; Loubser, 'Ndondondwane'; R.J. Mason, 'Early Iron Age Settlement at Broederstroom 24/73, Transvaal, South Africa', *South African Journal of Science* 77 (1981): 401–16; Van Schalkwyk, Greenfield and Jongsma, 'The Early Iron Age Site' and Whitelaw, 'KwaGandaganda'.

20. In particular, dung deposits are associated with deep middens containing ironworking debris and ceramic figurines throughout the sequence; see Van Schalkwyk, Greenfield and Jongsma, 'The Early Iron Age Site' and Whitelaw, 'KwaGandaganda'.

21. T.M. Evers and W.D. Hammond-Tooke, 'The Emergence of South African Chiefdoms: An Archaeological Perspective', *African Studies* 45:1 (1986): 37–41; and G. Whitelaw, 'Towards an Early Iron Age Worldview: Some Ideas from KwaZulu-Natal', *Azania* 29–30 (1994–95): 37–50.

22. For context, see T.M. Evers, 'Excavations at the Lydenburg Heads Site, Eastern Transvaal, South Africa,' *South African Archaeological Bulletin* 37 (1982): 16–33. For dating, see G. Whitelaw, 'Lydenburg Revisited: Another Look at the Mpumalanga Early Iron Age Sequence', *South African Archaeological Bulletin* 51 (1996): 75–83.

23. See p. 135 of R.R. Inskeep and T. Maggs, 'Unique Art Objects in the Iron Age of the Transvaal, South Africa', *South African Archaeological Bulletin* 30 (1975): 114–38.

24. Loubser, 'Ndondondwane'; see Van Schalkwyk, Greenfield and Jongsma, 'The Early Iron Age Site' for additional settlement pattern information.

25. A. Morris, 'Human Remains from the Early Iron Age Sites of Nanda and KwaGandaganda, Mngeni Valley, Natal, South Africa', *Natal Museum Journal of Humanities* 5 (1993): 83–98 and personal communication with the author.

26. L. van Schalkwyk, 'Wosi: An Early Iron Age Village in the Lower Thukela Basin, Natal', *Natal Museum Journal of Humanities* 6 (1994): 65–117; G. Whitelaw, 'Customs and Settlement Patterns in the First Millennium AD: Evidence from Natal, an Early Iron Age Site in the Mngeni Valley, Natal', *Natal Museum Journal of Humanities* 5 (1993): 47–81.

27. For instance, N. David, J. Sterner and K. Gavua, 'Why Pots are Decorated', *Current Anthropology* 29:3 (1988): 365–89.

28. S. Hattingh and S. Hall, 'The K2 Burials: Identifying Structure and Thinking about Meaning', paper read at the sixteenth conference of the Society for Africanist Archaeologists, Tuscon, USA, 18–22 May 2002; T.N. Huffman and M. Murimbika, 'Shona Ethnography and Iron Age Burials', *Journal of African Archaeology* 1:2 (2003): 237–46.

29. Whitelaw, 'Customs and Settlement Patterns' and Whitelaw, 'Towards an Early Iron Age Worldview'.

30. Huffman, 'Broederstroom' and Huffman, 'The Central Cattle Pattern'.

31. J. Guy, 'Analysing Pre-capitalist Societies in Southern Africa', *Journal of Southern African Studies* 14:1 (1987): 18–37.

32. F.E. Prins, 'Climate, Vegetation and Early Agriculturist Communities in Transkei and KwaZulu-Natal', *Azania* 29–30 (1994–95): 179–86.

33. T.N. Huffman, 'Ceramics, Settlements and Late Iron Age Migrations', *African Archaeological Review* 7 (1989): 155–82.

34. W.D. Hammond-Tooke, 'Southern Bantu Origins: Light from Kinship Terminology', *Southern African Humanities* 16 (2004): 71–78 and T.N. Huffman and R.K. Herbert, 'New Perspectives on Eastern Bantu', *Azania* 29–30 (1994–95): 27–36.

35. O. Davies, 'Excavations at the Walled Early Iron-Age Site in Moor Park near Estcourt, Natal', *Annals of the Natal Museum* 22:1 (1974): 289–323 and G. Whitelaw, 'Iron Age Hilltop Sites of the Early to Mid-second Millennium AD in KwaZulu-Natal, South Africa', in *Proceedings of the 11th Congress of the Pan-African Association for Prehistory and Related Studies*, Bamako, February 2001, eds. K. Sanogo, T. Togola, D. Keïta and M. N'Daou (Bamako: Soro Print Colour, 2004), pp. 38–51.

36. Davies, 'Excavations' and Whitelaw, 'Iron Age Hilltop Sites'.

37. Unpublished analyses of faunal material from iGujwana (by C.F. Beukes, Transvaal Museum) and Ntomdadlana and Sewula Gorge (by S. Badenhorst, Transvaal Museum).

38. In more recent times, stone-paved platforms, or 'stands', provided a hardened, relatively dry surface on which large grain baskets (*izilulu*) were placed. Impressions of woven articles on Moor Park hut floors confirm that they practised this craft. The impressions, however, are of more finely woven articles than the grain baskets in the Natal Museum collection.

39. Butter probably refers to *amasi*, although Ludwig Alberti reported a kind of butter used in leather-making by the amaXhosa. According to Alberti this butter was not eaten; see W. Fehr, *Ludwig Alberti's Account of the Tribal Life & Customs of the Xhosa, 1807*, translated from the original manuscript of 'The Kaffirs of the South Coast of Africa' (Cape Town: Balkema, 1968). Other ethnographies indicate the use of *amasi* in leather-making. I thank Shaw Badenhorst of the Transvaal Museum for this information.

40. G.M. Theal, *Records of South-eastern Africa*, Volume I, facsimile reprint (Cape Town: C. Struik, [1898] 1964). Perestrello was a survivor and chronicler of the wreck of the *São Bento* and the subsequent journey on foot of the shipwrecked party to Delagoa Bay. In 1575–76 he conducted a voyage from the Cape of Good Hope to Cape Correntes in order to produce a description of this part of the southern African coastline. The *São Thomé* survivors (1589) observed people fishing from small crafts in Delagoa Bay.

41. Maziyana was interviewed in 1905 by Natal public servant, Zulu linguist and ethnologist James Stuart (1868–1942). See *The James Stuart Archive of Recorded Oral Evidence Relating to the History of the Zulu and Neighbouring Peoples*, Vol. 2, eds. C. de B. Webb and J.B. Wright (Pietermaritzburg: University of Natal Press and Durban: Killie Campbell Collection, 1976), p. 276. Francis Farewell reported fishing in Natal Bay in 1824 and Ferdinand Krauss saw fish traps there in 1839 (F. Krauss, *Travel Journal, Cape to Zululand: Observations by a Collector and Naturalist 1838–40*, ed. O.H. Spohr [Cape Town: Balkema, 1973]).

42. Sourveld grasslands were quite possibly periodically occupied by hunter-gatherers.

43. G.M. Theal, *Records of South-eastern Africa*, Volume II, facsimile reprint (Cape Town: C. Struik, [1898] 1964), p. 326.

44. T. Maggs and D. Miller, 'Sandstone Crucibles from Mhlopeni, KwaZulu-Natal: Evidence of Precolonial Brassworking', *Natal Museum Journal of Humanities* 7 (1995): 1–16. The radiocarbon date calibrates from 1530–1800 but the pottery decoration includes lip-notching, a feature absent from assemblages postdating 1680.

45. T. Maggs, 'The Iron Age Farming Communities' in *Natal and Zululand from Earliest Times to 1910*, eds. A. Duminy and B. Guest (Pietermaritzburg: University of Natal Press and Shuter & Shooter, 1989), pp. 28–48.

46. M. Hall and T. Maggs, 'Nqabeni, a Later Iron Age Site in Zululand,' *South African Archaeological Society Goodwin Series* 3 (1979): 159–76 and T. Maggs, 'Mgoduyanuka: Terminal Iron Age Settlement in the Natal Grasslands', *Annals of the Natal Museum* 25:1 (1982): 83–113.

47. Hall and Mack, 'The Outline of an Eighteenth-century Economic System', see Figures 2 and 11. The authors suggest men of the neighbouring Mabaso chiefdom also built Type B homesteads, but Mabaso's capital and hence its boundaries are not precisely known. While the western boundaries of the Khumalo chiefdom are unknown, the distribution of Type B sites does nearly coincide with an approximation of Khumalo's eastern boundaries, derived from Thiessen Polygons. Type B sites cover an area approximately equivalent to the Buthelezi chiefdom east of Khumalo and may reasonably be assumed to provide an indication of Khumalo's area. The Type B style does not occur in the areas of the Buthelezi, Zulu and Mpungose chiefdoms east and southeast of Khumalo, at least not in stone-built form. The Buthelezi capital eLangeni was constructed of organic material, as were other settlements in these chiefdoms. Their homestead styles are not yet determined (and may for preservation reasons prove difficult to detect archaeologically), but it would be worth investigating the relationship between the eighteenth-century Zulu style and the style that came to dominate the region in the nineteenth century.

48. T. Maggs, 'Mabhija: Pre-colonial Industrial Development in the Tugela Basin', *Annals of the Natal Museum* 25:1 (1982): 123–41.

49. O. Davies, 'Excavations at Blackburn', *South African Archaeological Bulletin* 26:103–104 (1971): 164–78. See also T. Robey, 'Mpambanyoni: A Late Iron Age Site on the Natal South Coast,' *Annals of the Natal Museum* 24:1 (1980): 147–64.

50. Huffman, 'The Central Cattle Pattern'; see also E.O.M. Hanisch, 'Excavations at Icon, Northern

Transvaal', *South African Archaeological Society Goodwin Series* 3 (1979): 72–79. Hammond-Tooke, 'Southern Bantu Origins' and Huffman and Herbert, 'New Perspectives' place the origins of Sotho-Tswana in the East African interior.

51. Whitelaw, 'Iron Age Hilltop Sites'.
52. Theal, *Records*, Vol. II, p. 300.
53. Hall and Mack, 'The Outline of an Eighteenth-century Economic System' and Maggs, 'The Iron Age Farming Communities'.
54. Theal, *Records*, Vol. II, p. 199. The *São Thomé* account gives impossibly vast territories to each of the listed kingdoms. The territory of a king called Viragune extends 30 leagues (nearly 178 kilometres) inland from the coast. Mokalapapa extends from the St Lucia estuary to just south of Natal Bay. Nevertheless, the account provides names and hints that this awareness is a result of the ivory trade.
55. Whitelaw, 'Iron Age Hilltop Sites'.
56. A warm episode from 1420–1680 was evidently sufficient to make the highveld grasslands habitable (Huffman, *Snakes and Crocodiles*); see also M. Hall, 'Dendroclimatology, Rainfall and Human Adaptation in the Later Iron Age of Natal and Zululand', *Annals of the Natal Museum* 22 (1976): 693–703.
57. T.N. Huffman, *Handbook to the Iron Age: The Archaeology of Precolonial Farming Societies in Southern Africa* (Pietermaritzburg: University of KwaZulu-Natal Press, 2007). Apart from a different origin site from other Sotho speakers on the highveld, at Ntsuanatsatsi hill, the distinctiveness of the Fokeng is suggested by Ellenberger's claim that their dialect, customs and dress were adopted by later arrivals, especially the Kwena (T. Maggs, *Iron Age Communities of the Southern Highveld*, occasional publications of the Natal Museum, No. 2 [Pietermaritzburg: Natal Museum, 1976]; see also Huffman, 'Regionality in the Iron Age'). Alfred Thomas Bryant (1865–1953) was a Catholic priest and Zulu linguist and ethnologist who was appointed as a lecturer in Bantu Studies at the University of the Witwatersrand in 1920. David Frédéric Ellenberger (1835–1920) was a missionary and Sotho linguist and ethnologist.
58. T.N. Huffman, 'Obituary: The Waterberg Research of Jan Aukema', *South African Archaeological Bulletin* 45 (1990): 117–19 and J.H.N. Loubser, 'Ndebele Archaeology of the Pietersburg Area', *Navorsinge van die Nasionale Museum, Bloemfontein* 10:2 (1994): 61–147. Nguni communities north of the Vaal River are referred to as Ndebele, an anglicised form of *amaNdebele*, itself an Nguni form of the Sotho *Matabele*. Sotho and Nguni communities referred to intruding 'strangers from the east' as Ndebele or Matabele, irrespective of the language the strangers spoke (Loubser, 'Ndebele Archaeology': 63).
59. See, for example, *The Mfecane Aftermath: Reconstructive Debates in Southern African History*, ed. C. Hamilton (Johannesburg: Witwatersrand University Press and Pietermaritzburg: University of Natal Press, 1995).
60. J. Wright, 'The Dynamics of Power and Conflict in the Thukela–Mzimkhulu Region in the Late 18th and Early 19th centuries: A Critical Reconstruction' (Ph.D. diss., University of the Witwatersrand, 1995) and 'Political Transformations in the Thukela–Mzimkhulu Region in the Late Eighteenth and Early Nineteenth Centuries', in *The Mfecane Aftermath*, ed. Hamilton, pp. 162–81. See also J. Wright and C. Hamilton, 'Traditions and Transformations: The Phongolo-Mzimkhulu Region in the Late Eighteenth and Early Nineteenth Centuries', in *Natal and Zululand*, eds. Duminy and Guest, pp. 48–82.

*Chapter 5*

# Cattle Symbolism in Zulu Culture

W.D. HAMMOND-TOOKE

FOR AT LEAST a thousand years, cattle have been the most prized possession in Zulu culture, one of the few goods of real value owned outright by individuals and the only form of capital. They have been used in marriage exchanges that link families and underpin the legitimacy of children and they have been crucial in the operation of ancestor religion and chiefs' power. Finally, cattle products have always been vital to Zulu everyday life; they have been eaten, made into clothing and burned as fuel.

Cattle symbolism encompasses both the use of bovine-related images to capture important aspects of Zulu cultural life and also the unequivocal identification of this valuable commodity. In the latter case, the practical merged with the aesthetic. Many of the cattle terms are strikingly beautiful and, indeed, resemble poetic verse. In fact, they form an important part of the stock of knowledge that allowed for effective coping with the harsh realities of precolonial southern Africa. These very different types of symbolism will be treated separately in this chapter.

The period up to the end of the eighteenth century saw a steady increase in Zulu cattle holdings, although there were periods of extensive stock losses, notably during the great drought of 1803–04 and the devastating rinderpest pandemic of 1896–97. In general, however, herds flourished. Each beast was valued for itself and no culling was practised. The great prestige of cattle ownership was reflected by animal husbandry being solely in the hands of males, including milking. This was symbolically stressed by the belief that women of childbearing age possessed a ritual impurity (*umlaza*) that was a threat to both man and beast.

This opposition between women and cattle was strengthened by the wider symbolic association between sour milk (*amasi*) and kinship. Cattle were killed for food only with great reluctance, essentially as sacrifices to family ancestors: milk was, in fact, the daily dietary product of the family herd. Perhaps one of the most rigid rules in (even present-day) Zulu society was that sour milk could only be shared with kin members of the patriclan. To do so was to make a statement that one was related to the host. In a society preoccupied by fears of incest (see below), sharing *amasi* had vital implications for social bonds, especially sexual relations. To drink sour milk with a woman was to acknowledge her as a relative and thus not a potential sexual partner. This distinction obviously posed difficulty for a bride who was a stranger in her husband's family. The problem was overcome by allocating a special cow to a new wife, so that she could have access to milk during the first years of her marriage. There is some evidence that this identification of *amasi* with kinship is a prominent theme in Zulu folktales.[1] Significantly, violation of milk taboos is believed to bring weakness and disaster to cattle.

Zulu social life revolved around the homestead, a cluster of beehive-shaped huts built around a central cattle byre (enclosure). Each homestead was a self-contained economic and legal unit, with its own cattle and crops. In the nineteenth century the homestead, on the one hand, and the Zulu kingdom, on the other hand, were the two pillars on which Zulu society was built. At the local level the homestead head, *umnumzana*, was a little king in his domestic domain, with powers of life and death over those who lived in it. The impression one gets is one of self-sustaining social dynamics and, indeed, introversion.

This introversion perhaps had other functions. Of all South Africa's indigenous peoples, isiZulu-speaking Africans (and the isiXhosa speakers) are perhaps the most patriarchal, deriving from their extreme emphasis on patrilineal principle. Unlike other South African Bantu speakers, who maintain a greater balance between the father's and mother's side of the family, senior Zulu men belong to clans that rigidly prohibit marriage with any woman of the clans' four sets of grandparents. As we have seen, brides are strangers. It is thus tempting to see the scattered homestead pattern (so different from village life of Sotho and Venda peoples, for example) as a mechanism for monitoring the behaviour of wives.[2]

Indeed, the Zulu homestead resembled the Englishman's castle, but the South African variant required more complex organisation. The custom of polygyny and the practice of newly married sons setting up households within their father's homestead created an extended family. In Zulu polygynous households each wife had her own dwelling in which she lived with her children. The general term for a Zulu hut is *indlu*, yet the word has a wider significance. It also refers to the structuring of the homestead into distinct sections (for example, great house, right-hand house and left-hand house), each sheltering a wife and her children, as well as, initially, one or two cows to provide milk, property allocated to her by the husband. From time to time more cattle become part of the house property owned by a wife, and cannot be used by her husband without her permission, even when cattle are corralled in the byre with the family herd. On the death of the homestead head, the social structure of the deceased's homestead disintegrates; the component sections typically move off to establish their own domestic arrangements, with each male heir being accompanied by his mother.

What connects these changing portraits of family life is the economic and spiritual centrality of the central cattle byre. Not only does the byre protect much-prized cattle; it also harbours the ancestors themselves who brood over their descendants with a benevolent and critical eye. It is in the byre that animal sacrifices are made to elicit ancestral blessings, using the ritual spear that rests on the altar-like ledge (*umsamo*) at the back of the great hut, where other family heirlooms are also kept. There is, in fact, a line of spiritual force that ties the sacred *umsamo* to the world of men, and the byre, the home of the family herd. This symbolic link expresses a profound reality, for there is a fundamental identity between the members of the homestead and their cattle. Household and herd are one, constituting a single community. In fact this analogy was explicitly stated to an ethnographer by a Zulu man himself:

> [He] drew with his finger an incomplete oval in the sand, which stood for the trunk of a cow. Above, at the neck, he indicated the place of the homestead head . . . At shoulder height, on the right-hand side, he placed the heir, on the right flank the junior right-hand son. The left and junior left-hand sons were indicated on the left shoulder. According to them the homestead represents itself, structurally, like a cow.[3]

It seems that amaZulu also compared the homestead head and his wives with the bull and his cows. Johnny Clegg, the internationally known musician and anthropologically trained expert on Zulu customs, has recorded that the family head takes great care to rise and pass water each morning before his bull does. If he does not, it is believed that his authority over both human group and herd will be undermined.

But the place of the bull in Zulu society is ambiguous. While bulls are necessary for fertilising the cows, they are also essentially anti-social and difficult to control. Intractable and often dangerous, they are left to graze with other cattle, corralled in the byre at night, and treated with circumspection. Perhaps one of the best-known vernacular sayings is, 'You cannot have two bulls in one kraal'; that is why most bull calves are castrated within the first year. A bull's aggressive masculinity exudes virility and potential violence and yet there is an obvious association between a bull and the homestead head. How should this be understood? How far can the metaphorical relationship between *umnumzana* and his bull (and between the human family and its herd) be pushed?

An important difference between homestead members and their herd is that all males in the herd (except the bull) are castrated, thus eliminating disruptive competition for females. In a fundamental sense this is true, also, of human domestic life. We have become increasingly aware of the potentially devastating intra-family conflicts that can create social turmoil, if societies permit uncontrolled sexuality among kin members. It can be argued that this human danger is handled by the incest taboo, which acts as a selective psychological castration of young males. Is there an analogy here? The castration of bull calves is designed to maintain the authority of the bull: the incest taboo can be seen, from one point of view at least, as doing the same for the family head.

This correlation raises the question as to why amaZulu appear to prize oxen more than they do bulls. Informants almost always speak more fondly of their favourite ox, which is given a personal name and trained to come when called. They also comment on the sagacity and almost human attributes of their favourite ox, on how they use this beast to train other young oxen to plough and pull a wagon. Oxen are reliable, tractable and responsible. Within their limits they act as reasonable people – and the reasonable person is one who can be depended on to act in a responsible manner. There does seem to be ambivalence towards bulls. They behave on occasion like reckless youths, heedless of the consequence to others. This is emphatically not the image that Zulu society generally has of an adult male, who is expected to act with *gravitas*. In some Bantu-speaking societies in South Africa a common metaphor for circumcision is to 'castrate the young bulls', referring to the maturation that coming-of-age rituals bring about. The amaZulu do not have circumcision (it was said to be abolished at the time of Shaka's reign), but it may be significant that the galvanic, stamping dance of Zulu young men, in which the pawing, posturing and aggression of the bull is splendidly choreographed, is not considered appropriate for married men.

The metaphorical association between a Zulu homestead head and his herd is thus intricate. In terms of authority and sexuality an *umnumzana* is likened to a bull: in terms of social responsibility and value to the community he is seen as an ox. The two images reflect different sides of the complex role of maleness and masculinity in this (and every?) society.

Just as the male-dominated homestead is divided into component houses, so are the cattle in the byre, who themselves belong to those houses. When a homestead breaks up on the death of the *umnumzana*, house cattle will accompany their owners to newly established homesteads, where they will constitute a new family herd, the nucleus of which will come from the cattle descended from the original paternal herd. In a sense, then, cattle and their owners can be looked on as kinsmen, the original cattle being the shades of the present-day ones. The social group of the Zulu homestead can also be seen as analogous to, and identified with, its herd in its homestead (byre). The health of one depends on the other in symbiotic relationship.

Yet the symbolism of cattle extends beyond the homestead. Zulu domestic arrangements are part of a wider community, reflecting obligations of kinship and economic ties. Most importantly, such bonds are sealed by the exchange of cattle for wives. This is perhaps the primary role of the family herd. The movement of a bride from her father's group to that of her husband demands the offering of compensation for her family's loss. And what more appropriate way than to compensate for her loss through cattle used by her brothers to marry in their turn?

In nuptial negotiations bridewealth cattle represent the principal aim of marriage: to transfer two sets of rights, those over the bride herself and those over her children. Both sets express cattle imagery. Rights over the woman are those over her sexual access and to her domestic and field labour – matched, of course, by the duties of a husband to provide his wife with a house and lifelong security. There is also a close connection between a woman's children and her marriage cattle in that both cannot be together in the same homestead. A common Zulu saying goes: 'The children are where the cattle are not.' If a husband obtains a divorce from his wife, he is entitled to receive back the bridewealth, but the number of beasts returned depends on how many children were born from the union. In this sense, cattle equalled both a wife (they were exchanged for her in marriage) and her children (they balanced the equation between the family of the bride and the family of the groom).

The domestic community formed by homestead and herd (and strengthened and expanded through bridewealth exchanges) is ineluctably identified with its past; in turn, the relationship between the living and the dead is mediated through cattle. Ancestors can be moved to anger by the failure of their descendants to 'build up the homestead' (in other words, to produce children following marriage), or by allowing its reputation to be diminished, typically by omitting to provide generous hospitality to the wider community through beer and meat feasts. Particularly galling to ancestors is any expression of disrespect towards lineage seniors or the neglect of rituals due to them. In all such cases they may visit misfortune on the culprit and rituals have to be performed to appease them. Typically this takes the form of a blood sacrifice involving cattle (although goats are also used) – for the wrath of the ancestors is thought of in terms of their hunger for meat, and, especially, gall. The sacrificial beast comes from the family herd and the ritual officiator is the senior male member of the family. At each ritual an invocation is made to the august dead clan members, who are expected, as a collectivity, to be present. The beast symbolises both a propitiatory gift of food and a total subjection to patrilineal authority.

Ritual slaughters of animals are carried out in the upper section of the byre nearest the great house: the officiator calls on the ancestors to be present; a cow might first be consecrated by having beer poured over its back; then it is stabbed with the ritual spear to the invocation, 'Cry, beast of the ancestors!' The cow's bellowing informs the spirits of the event. If the ritual is directed at healing, gall is sprinkled on the sick person for the ancestors to lick. A possible explanation for the choice of gall is that this liquid defines the sacred as the opposite to the profane. Gall, because of its extreme bitterness, is the opposite of the food of men and thus an appropriate form of ambrosia for the shades.

The other aspect of cattle symbolism, as noted above, is rather different. It operates within the essential economic sphere of cattle ownership, but it is elaborated far beyond the utilitarian aim of merely identifying beasts. Each Sanga-Nguni beast, the name given to the hardy, indigenous cattle of the Zulu stock raisers, is not merely a commodity, but an individual animal with a distinct colour pattern, horn shape, gender, status and history. In a deep sense, amaZulu also regard each member of their herd as having a personality. This has resulted in a complex system of naming that uses metaphorical and appropriate analogies to express identity. For example, a cream beast, spotted lightly with rust, is known as (and *is*) 'the egg of the lark'; a dun and white-mottled beast *is* the 'castor oil bean'; a black beast with a white head *is* 'the Fish Eagle' and so forth. Thus, a beast and some other phenomenon – whether bird, animal, plant or domestic object – are brought into metaphorical relationship with one another, the latter becoming a cattle term that exists in its own right. For example, the phrase *inkomo engamatsh'oNgoye* translates into 'the beast, which is the stones of Ngoye Forest', describing an animal with coloured patches outlined by a dense white rim. This analogy reflects a feature of Ngoye in KwaZulu-Natal, where distinctive rocks dot glades, in which vegetation delineates a perimeter ring. The large rounded spots in the cowhide are named for this striking natural phenomenon.[4]

Clearly, knowledge of the environmental context is crucial to an understanding of the metaphors. Taken out of context, terms such as *ifukumuntu phakathi* ('that which is in the person in the middle'), *imatshehlathi* ('the stones of the forest') or *insingisuka* ('the Ground Hornbill takes to flight') are certainly obscure, if not incomprehensible, without further explication. Yet for knowledgeable isiZulu-speakers, a lucid image of the beast is immediately triggered.

It is not only by colour pattern that a beast may be identified. There are other descriptive terms that use criteria such as gender, status (age, fertility, virility, position in the ox-span, for example) and horn shape. Cattle may also be given individual names which describe some attribute or episode in their personal history or which may be honorific. Also, if a beast is being used for some specific purpose, such as bridewealth, a term may be applied to designate its role in transactions, for example, *imvulamlomo* ('what opens the mouth'), the animal given to pave the way for marriage negotiations. Neither of these latter two examples, however, forms part of the system of cattle-colour pattern terminology.

Colour pattern terminology should not be confused with the superficially similar scientific classification of plants, animals or birds. It arises, rather, from aesthetic constructs in the imagination of isiZulu-speaking people. At its simplest, a range of broadly similar colour and pattern conformations (for example, black and white markings) may be classified or interpreted by the same term. More creatively, the rich and varied number of terms handed down from previous generations may be combined in different ways to accommodate the subtly complex variety of individual configurations found among Nguni cattle. Such refinements are very much the province of pastoralists all over Africa, who may debate at length the classification of an animal bearing an ambiguous hide pattern. The colour pattern terminology is in some way fixed, but it is also open-ended with new configurations arising in different isiZulu-speaking regions. For example, a beast with a coloured body and a white face is traditionally known as *impemvu* ('White Helmet Shrike'), but one herder called it *ibullybeef*, after a brand of canned meat showing a Hereford-type beast with a red body and white face on the label.

One pattern that deserves attention is the *inkone*, particularly characteristic of Nguni cattle displaying a white stripe along the spine and a white underbelly, with the pattern on the left side mirroring the pattern on the right. While *inkone* are greatly favoured, the most distinctive cattle are the white *inyonikayiphumuli* of the Zulu monarch, with their milky hide and dark points at ears, muzzle, horns, hooves and eyes. Their name, meaning 'birds that have no rest', possibly refers to the white egrets (tick birds) that follow them everywhere. In colour terms, any white calf born in the byre of a commoner was automatically given to the king (the massive herds of the Zulu regent Cetshwayo were legendary). Among the amaZulu the colour white has spiritual and ritual importance, being associated with purity, harmony, coolness and the absence of pollution. White is the colour of the ancestors, diviners and protection against lightning. Black cattle, on the other hand, are associated with the herds of the Swazi monarchy.

If white and black are perceived to have symbolic associations, it is undoubtedly the variety of other colours – their great diversity of tones and range of combinations – which give a herd of Nguni cattle at pasture the resemblance of a flock of multi-coloured birds. Particularly rich are the shades of red, brown, dun and yellow that make the cattle appear enamelled in the light. The African writer and scholar Isidore Okpewhu speaks of an 'ecology of art' in Africa, and an African sense of belonging to the landscape of the continent: '[I]t would appear that much of the aesthetic nourishment of traditional African art derives from the nature of the surrounding landscape . . . In the words of an old griot: "Hunter, your words are obscure. Make your speech comprehensible to us, speak in the language of your savanna." '[5]

Cattle terms spoken by amaZulu, too, provide equally compelling insights into a worldview of nature, constituting the 'language of their savanna' in KwaZulu-Natal.

## Notes

1. W.D. Hammond-Tooke, 'Levi-Strauss in a Garden of Millet: The Structural Analysis of a Zulu Myth', *Man* 12 (1977): 76–86 and 'Twins, Incest and Mediators: The Structure of Four Zulu Folktales', *Africa* 62:2 (1992): 203–19.
2. For this connection, see M.C. O'Connell, 'Some Social and Cultural Repercussions of the Betterment Scheme in a Transkei Community', *Proceedings of the Sixth Biennial Meeting of the Transkei and Ciskei Research Society*, Umtata (1980): pp. 59–64. He writes: 'Because kinsmen cannot supervise [under village-like closer settlement], a woman can see a lover any time during the night', leading, according to his informants, to an increase in the incidence of adultery.
3. J.F. Holleman, '*Die Twee-eenheidsbeginsel in die Sosiale en Politieke Samelewing van die Zulu*', *Bantu Studies* 14 (1940): 31–75.
4. A full discussion of Zulu cattle terminology, including an exhaustive glossary of terms, with accompanying water colour illustrations, may be found in Marguerite Poland and David Hammond-Tooke, *The Abundant Herds: A Celebration of the Nguni Cattle of the Zulu People* (Cape Town: Fernwood Press, 2003).
5. Isidore Okpewhu, *The Epic in Africa: Towards a Poetics of the Oral Performance* (New York: Columbia University Press, 1979), p. 19.

# Chapter 6

# Revisiting the Stereotype of Shaka's 'Devastations'

JOHN WRIGHT

THIS CHAPTER CRYSTALLISED in the late 1980s.[1] It constituted the first extended attempt to develop an explanation of how the notion that Shaka Zulu's armies had 'devastated' Natal south of the Thukela River in the 1810s and 1820s – a period known as the *mfecane* – had become entrenched in the literature with little supporting evidence. At this time, the historian Julian Cobbing was honing a critique of the *mfecane*, which was beginning to attract wide scholarly attention; his ideas strongly influenced this chapter, although I seek to move beyond them.

In the new millennium the argument put forward here can be seen to require updating. Most obviously, the often fierce academic debates sparked by Cobbing's critique need to be recognised. Secondly, any critical investigation of the devastation stereotype ought to examine more deeply the thinking and writing of Cape colonial commentators, who from the 1820s to the 1830s showed keen interest in discovering the causes of upheavals, not only in Natal, but in the interior of the subcontinent. Thirdly, a carefully constructed, subtle portrait of the range of attitudes to Shaka held by European traders in Port Natal demands further research. Finally, much more should be made of the interplay between black and white observers of Zulu culture and history in creating images of Shaka from the 1820s to the present. To see these representations as having separate, racially defined origins gives a misleading picture of historical processes. This chapter, then, aims to focus on key early moments in the making of the stereotype of Shaka and his Zulu warriors as destroyers of southern Africa.

During a period that is difficult to define precisely, but that probably extended over the later 1810s and 1820s, the territories south of the Thukela River experienced a series of political and social upheavals that completely transformed the political map of the region. These upheavals are unproblematically regarded in the literature as having been caused by invasions of Zulu armies from across the Thukela. They are seen as part of a series of wars and migrations, allegedly set in motion by the explosive expansion of the Zulu kingdom, which disrupted life over a much wider area of southeast Africa. Since the late 1960s, these wars and migrations have almost universally come to be labelled as the '*mfecane*' or '*difaqane*'. The notion of the *mfecane* is now deeply entrenched as an organising concept around which much of the history of southern Africa in the first half of the nineteenth century is written.

In a series of papers and articles written since 1983, Cobbing has formulated a radical and sweeping critique of the whole concept of the *mfecane*.[2] While not denying that the history of African societies in the early nineteenth century was marked by a rising level of violence, Cobbing rejects the particular significance that white writers since at least the mid-nineteenth century have ascribed to this phenomenon. He argues that it was a continuation of conflicts that had begun long before the 1810s, conflicts whose primary causes are to be sought not in the expansion of the Zulu kingdom but in the intersection of forces emanating from two other epicentres of upheaval. These were the Eastern Cape, where first Dutch then British settlers and imperialists were engaged in persistent attempts to seize land and labour power from neighbouring African societies from at least the 1760s onwards and the Delagoa Bay region, where an export trade in ivory, cattle and slaves was developing at around much the same time.

In Cobbing's view the role attributed in the literature to the amaZulu is not based on historical evidence: rather it is a product of the search made by imperialist and settler ideologues for a plausible alibi for the colonial- and imperial-based interests whose aggressions were ultimately responsible for the violence and social disruptions of the period. For their own various ideological reasons, subsequent generations of historians, including that of the present, have either been concerned to maintain the alibi, or, at the very least, have done nothing to demonstrate its falsity. From this perspective, the notion of the *mfecane* is nothing but an interest-serving myth. Historians, Cobbing argues, urgently need to abandon not only the term itself, but the whole set of interlinked assumptions, distortions and falsehoods that it embodies and to address the business of developing an entirely new analysis of southern African history in the late eighteenth and early nineteenth centuries.

For historians currently doing research into this period, Cobbing's critique of *mfecane* theory raises a host of fundamental issues. Whether one agrees with him or not, it is impossible to sidestep the import of his arguments. Instead of being taken completely for granted, *mfecane* theory now has to be directly confronted, examined in depth on a region-by-region basis, and reasserted, modified, or rejected. Against the background of the debates that are beginning to emerge in response to Cobbing's critique, this chapter undertakes a survey of the historiography of the upheavals that took place south of the Thukela in the 1810s and 1820s. Its purpose is to investigate the basis of the established notion that these upheavals were the consequence of Zulu invasions.

Soon after the arrival of British hunters and traders at Port Natal in 1824, some of them were beginning to report that the neighbourhood of the bay was largely empty of population,[3] and to develop and publicise an explanation for this phenomenon. This explanation, to the effect that the previous inhabitants had either been killed or driven out by the amaZulu under Shaka a few years before, was beginning to appear in Cape Town newspapers in 1825 and 1826, and in printed books by 1827.[4] At the same time, specific literary images of the amaZulu and Shaka were beginning to take shape, with the amaZulu being described by writers such as King and Thompson as the warlike and bloodthirsty agents of Natal's devastation, and Shaka as the ferocious and savage leader who directed them.[5] Over the next decade these ideas were consolidated by a number of other writers – Owen, Pringle, Kay, Boteler, Steedman and, in particular, Isaacs – into literary forms, which in their essence, have survived to the present day.[6]

Few of these writers had actually set foot at Port Natal, and none of them had been eyewitnesses of the processes of destruction that they adumbrated. The evidence on which they based their descriptions was derived directly or indirectly from African informants, but nowhere in their works is there any mention of the identity of these people, or of the circumstances in which their testimony was obtained and recorded. Most of the historical information that found its way into published accounts was probably collected from members of the groups that the small community of white traders found living around Port Natal and in the neighbouring coastal regions. It is germane to make the point here that Port Natal was situated precisely in the one region of Natal that had in fact been overrun by Zulu forces, and it is likely that the generalised depictions of the destruction of Natal that were noised abroad by the traders were a reflection of the particular experiences of informants from this region.

As a Zulu-centric version of Natal's recent history took root among the traders, so the groups of Africans that were drawn to the bay to seek their protection came to shape their accounts of their own experiences accordingly. The process of reworking their recent history would in many cases have entailed only minor amendments, often involving simply the substitution of the amaZulu for other agents of destruction. Another factor in the making of the image of the amaZulu as the general destroyers of the region was very probably filtering of information on the part of the coloured interpreters whom the traders had brought with them, and whom they had to use in communicating with the local inhabitants until they learned the language. As servants and dependants, the interpreters very probably had their own particular interest in communicating a version of history palatable to their masters. It is likely, then, that a history that attributed the devastation of Natal to the amaZulu under Shaka gelled comparatively quickly, both among the traders and among the various categories of their clients and adherents. In the discourse of the amaZulu themselves with the traders there would have been nothing, one imagines, to dispel the notion of Shaka and his armies as conquerors and overlords of the regions south of the Thukela.

For their own part, the traders would have had no incentive to be critical of this notion, and every interest in formulating and propagating the idea that Natal was largely empty of inhabitants, and that Shaka and the amaZulu had been the agents of their dispersal or destruction. From the very first, the leading traders at Port Natal were concerned not only to open up commerce with the amaZulu but also to try to establish rights to large tracts of territory round Port Natal.[7] In the face of the express reluctance of the Cape government to sanction the acquisition of territorial possessions,[8] they attempted to minimise possible objections to their proceedings by asserting the claim that the land in question was virtually uninhabited.

If the Port Natal traders had a direct material interest in propagating the myth of the empty land, so too did the Cape merchants who in large part financed their early trading ventures.[9] In the late 1820s and early 1830s the rising commercial class and its associates in both the eastern and the western Cape were beginning to exert pressure on the British authorities in Cape Town and London to annex Natal and establish it as a colony of British settlement. This class's spokesmen used the notion of a depopulated Natal to underpin their arguments for the desirability of annexation.[10]

Propagation of the myth of the empty land thus served a clear material purpose. So too did the fostering of the image of Shaka as the cruel and despotic leader of a warlike Zulu nation. Although portraying Shaka and the Zulu in lurid detail, writers such as King and Isaacs clearly had an eye on their reading public; they and others also wrote to publicise and propagate the pro-annexationist cause. By depicting the amaZulu and their king as a potential threat to the security of the Cape's eastern frontier region, or alternatively as the potential allies of rival powers, they hoped to influence the British authorities into annexing Natal, thereby paving the way for the extension of British trade and settlement.[11] Some scepticism was voiced in the Cape Town press about the reality of the image of Shaka put about by the Natal traders,[12] but the idea that the 'numerous and warlike' Zulu were a potential 'threat' to the colony rapidly entered its public discourse.[13]

By the mid-1830s the notion that the territories south of the Thukela had been devastated by the amaZulu shortly before 1824 was becoming firmly fixed into a literary stereotype. This notion was essentially the product of Cape merchant interests and their associates. Of the writers so far cited as mainly responsible for fixing it in print, Farewell, King and Isaacs had all traded at Natal, while Farewell and Isaacs had close personal connections with Cape Town's business community.[14] Thompson and Steedman were Cape Town merchants; Bannister, although motivated in his writings partly by humanitarian concerns, was an associate of Farewell's and possibly one of his financial backers, and was later an active member of the South African Land and Emigration Association; Godlonton was 'a man of substance' in the rising eastern Cape business community.[15] Owen had played an important role in stimulating interest among the merchants of Cape Town in the commercial potential of Natal in 1822, and in 1823 seems to have provided Farewell with a chart of the Natal coast, a product of his survey of the previous year.[16]

All these authors directly or indirectly propounded the virtues of the regions beyond the borders of the Cape colony as fields for the expansion of Cape and British commerce. This intention was most explicitly stated by Isaacs in his *Travels and Adventures*, the last few pages of which formed an encomium to the commercial prospects of Natal. He wrote the book, he stated, partly to meet his readers' interest in 'novelty', but also so that 'the merchant, the speculator, and the capitalist will perceive new sources in which commercial enterprise may be successfully attempted; and new vents for the consumption of the manufactures of the United Kingdom, of which it is desirable to have some clear and unquestionable information'.[17]

From the later 1830s what will from now on be referred to as 'the devastation stereotype' began to be taken up and disseminated by members of another influential body of opinion-moulders and image-builders, the missionaries who were active in southern Africa. Although there might be wide differences of opinion between them as to the benefits or otherwise of the extension of European settlement, they were united in wanting to promote 'civilised' European government. Many aligned themselves with the merchants' call for the 'opening up' of the interior, and at the same time used much the same kind of historical rationale to justify it.[18]

The first author to go beyond the sketchy descriptions of the devastation stereotype in the settler literature was Father A.T. Bryant. The historical works that he published from 1905 onwards on the pre-European history of the Natal-Zululand region were far more detailed than any previous work on the subject and established him as the leading authority in the field. After its publication in 1929, his *Olden Times in Zululand and Natal* rapidly became, as it still largely remains, a standard source of reference.

Like Bryant's other works, *Olden Times* is universally regarded as being based on the oral traditions, which, the author indicates in its preface, he collected over a period of some 40 years. In fact, as far as his account of the upheavals of the 1810s and 1820s is concerned, detailed analysis of his sources reveals that it was almost entirely derived from other published sources.[19] Although it gave a much more elaborate account of the upheavals than any previous work had done, there was virtually nothing original in it by way of information or insights. This was not, however, apparent at the time and the overall impact of *Olden Times* was to cement the stereotype ever more firmly into the literature.

Although Bryant was well aware that several non-Zulu groups had in fact been responsible for much of the disruption that took place in Natal in the 1810s and 1820s, and that Zulu incursions south of the Thukela had been confined to a comparatively small area, he all but submerged the role played by these other groups in favour of an emphasis on the doings of the amaZulu. His dramatised and often hyperbolical description of Shaka's wars and conquests, one inherited directly from the settler stereotype, underscored the idea that Shaka and his 'Zulu murderers' were the main destroyers of Natal.[20] In addition, Bryant's method of presenting the region's history through a recital of the individual histories of the numerous chiefdoms of Natal had the effect of repeatedly bringing Shaka and the amaZulu into the narrative in the role of conquerors, exterminators and tribute-takers. In short, by adding a considerable amount of new, if repetitive, detail to the stereotype, Bryant's apparently authoritative account served to give it an empirical respectability that helped it to lodge firmly in the works of later writers.

It was not until the 1960s that there was a revival of interest in the writing of the history of African societies of southern Africa, including that of Zulu people under Shaka's leadership. The main stimulus in this development was the revolution in African historiography that accompanied the political decolonisation of most of the continent north of the Zambezi in the late 1950s and early 1960s.[21] The emergence of African nationalist movements and the ending of colonial rule outside the white-dominated states and colonies of the south generated an eager demand among African political activists and students, and among sympathisers in Europe and North America, for a decolonised African history, one that would rescue Africans from the virtual oblivion to which they had been consigned by colonial historiography, and one that emphasised African achievements. In the 1960s, an alliance of African nationalist and metropolitan liberal historians made the writing of this kind of history something of a growth industry at universities in Europe, North America and in black-dominated Africa.

The tendency in much of this history was to romanticise traditional African culture, and to emphasise the continuities in African history between the precolonial past and the postcolonial present, with the period of European colonial rule being seen as a period of corruption and disruption of African culture and development. Favourite themes were the emergence of great states in precolonial Africa, the mounting of resistance to European conquest and colonial subjugation, the growth of African nationalism, and the role of leaders, past and present.

Within this context the first work since Theal's to attempt a broad synthesis of the history of the upheavals that had taken place in southeast Africa in the 1820s and 1830s was published in 1966. This was J.D. Omer-Cooper's full-length study, *The Zulu Aftermath: A Nineteenth-Century Revolution in Bantu Africa.* In important respects Omer-Cooper's account was similar to Theal's. It saw the violence of the period as having emanated from a single epicentre, the Zulu kingdom, and as having radiated outward across much of southern and central Africa. Drawing on ideas previously put forward by writers such as Max Gluckman,[22] Omer-Cooper attributed the ultimate causes of the upheavals to a build-up of population pressure in southeast Africa in the later eighteenth century, rather than to the personality of Shaka, as Theal had done. He also went beyond Theal in seeing the effects of the violence as having extended over wide areas of Central Africa, and as having persisted into the latter half of the nineteenth century. But, as the title of his book indicates, like Theal, Omer-Cooper was looking for a compendium explanation to cover what he saw as a single historical phenomenon.[23]

In two respects, though, Omer-Cooper introduced major innovations into the treatment of the subject. Firstly, in sharp contract to Theal, who had emphasised the violence and bloodshed that had accompanied the upheavals in order to portray them as an indication of African barbarism and savagery, Omer-Cooper depicted them in positive terms as marking 'one of the great formative events of African history', as an episode of 'nation building' on the part of 'a galaxy of great leaders'.[24] Secondly, he gave the upheavals a single label, one which has stuck both in academic and in popular usage ever since. This was the term '*mfecane*', which he gave as meaning 'the wars and disturbances which accompanied the rise of the Zulu'.[25] The word had been used sporadically in the literature since the 1920s, although without a clearly defined meaning.[26] Omer-Cooper both standardised its meaning and projected it into general usage. In *The Zulu Aftermath* the compendium concept that had emerged in Theal's works in the late nineteenth century, and which in attenuated and sanitised form had been incorporated into liberal historiography from the 1920s onwards, was greatly amplified, given a positive gloss, and labelled for convenient usage.

In his treatment of the region south of the Thukela, to which he devoted a chapter, Omer-Cooper drew heavily on Bryant's *Olden Times in Zululand and Natal* to produce a much more detailed account than Theal had been able to do.[27] His was the first academic history to indicate clearly that Shaka's armies had been preceded into Natal by 'waves' of non-Zulu invaders (Bulpin, also drawing on Bryant, had previously done the same thing in a popular account),[28] but the paradigm within which he was working prevented him from using the evidence at his disposal to break with the devastation stereotype. With his main focus on the building of great states by great leaders, he was little concerned to look at the separate histories of the societies that became subject to them. By his own account, Omer-Cooper was not interested in trying to unravel the history of Natal before the period of upheavals.[29] The result was that he ended up, as Bryant had done, by making the amaZulu his main actors, and leaving the societies of Natal, together with their non-Zulu assailants, as all alike the victims of the mighty, all-conquering Zulu state. *The Zulu Aftermath* served to give the devastation stereotype further academic respectability, and, by presenting it as an integral part of the long-established and now revamped notion freshly packaged as the '*mfecane*', to publicise it more widely than ever. From this time on, the history of the stereotype was closely intertwined with that of *mfecane* theory.

Few works on southern African history have had so immediate and widespread an effect as *The Zulu Aftermath*. As Cobbing has pointed out, within a few years of the book's publication both the term *mfecane* (or *difaqane*) and the notion that the *mfecane* was one of the central events of southern African history had become embedded in African discourse outside South Africa.[30] It was widely established in general histories of Africa,[31] in academic articles and monographs,[32] in the *Encyclopaedia Britannica*,[33] and in university and school textbooks.[34]

In South Africa, the emergence of an academic Africanist historiography lagged some years behind its development elsewhere. In the 1960s liberal and Afrikaner nationalist historians alike remained primarily concerned with white political and, to a lesser extent, social history. The devastation stereotype lived on in their works in much the same forms as it had been cast by academic historians in the 1920s. Thus the first general history of Natal to be published since Russell's work early in the century, Brookes and Webb's *History of Natal*, which appeared in 1965, drew uncritically on Bryant for its interpretation of the regime's precolonial history.[35] So too did the popularisers, such as Bulpin, Ritter, Binns, Becker and Morris who in those years were helping to revive interest in the history of Natal and Zululand, and who, in advance of local academics, were tackling topics in the history of African societies.[36]

In the late 1960s and early 1970s South African academics began to catch on to the notion of the *mfecane*. The first to do so were Afrikaner nationalist historians, who were quick to spot the support which *mfecane* theory lent to the ideologically important notion that the first white settlers in the interior of southern Africa had moved into a land largely depopulated by inter-African warfare.[37] A little later, under the influence of overseas Africanists, liberal writers began to incorporate the *mfecane* into their work as the *fons et origo* of the processes of African state-formation (another term for 'nation building') around which they wrote the history of African societies in southeastern Africa in the first half of the nineteenth century.[38] They were followed by some African nationalist writers, particularly those sympathetic to Zulu ethnic nationalism, for whom the 'nation building' aspects of the *mfecane* were an obvious attraction.[39]

By the late 1970s the *mfecane* was accepted as an established fact of southern African history. Although by then a reaction against the more uncritical assumptions and assertions of Africanist history was manifesting itself among liberal and radical-revisionist historians alike,[40] the *mfecane* lived on in South Africa and abroad virtually unchallenged.[41] In 1983 *mfecane* theory was reproduced in standardised form in the first academic dictionary of South African history to be published.[42] In 1986 it achieved coffee-table status,[43] and in 1987, some twenty years on from *The Zulu Aftermath*, it was reinvigorated by Omer-Cooper himself in a new textbook on South African history.[44] In the late 1980s liberals, radicals, African nationalists and Afrikaner nationalists continued in an unlikely, if unwitting, alliance, some propounding, some merely accepting, but virtually none challenging the validity of the notion of the *mfecane*.

*Mfecane* theory emerged at a time when historians outside southern Africa were seeking to break away from racist and patronising colonial clichés about African culture and African history. It is easy to understand why the notion of the *mfecane* as a period of African nation-building caught on so rapidly among them, and why it survives today in the uncritically Africanist histories that continue to be produced. It is easy, too, to understand the continuing attraction of *mfecane* theory's depopulation thesis for the ideologues of apartheid.

More problematic is the failure of contemporary critical liberal and radical-revisionist scholarship to challenge *mfecane* theory. At a superficial level this failure can be explained in terms of the general decline of interest among scholars abroad in African history since about the mid-1970s.[45] Researchers are thinner on the ground than they used to be in the days of the Africanist boom and they have had little incentive to tamper with what appears to be a coherent and firmly grounded set of notions that puts the precolonial African states of southern Africa firmly on the historical map. In South Africa itself, after a brief flowering in the 1970s, interest in the region's precolonial history has waned as liberal and radical historians have increasingly focused their research and debates on the effects of capitalist penetration in southern Africa from the late nineteenth century onwards. Partly, then, *mfecane* theory survives today by default.

But, at a deeper level of explanation, it survives, as Cobbing has argued, largely because it functions to obscure the processes by which whites came to be politically dominant and in possession of most of the land south of the Limpopo River.[46] By omitting the role of white agency in the upheavals of the 1820s and 1830s, and by attributing them ultimately to the rise of the Zulu kingdom, *mfecane* theory is able to portray them as a consequence of internecine African conflict. African agency thus becomes responsible for opening the way for the penetration of white settlers into a largely empty interior, and the land-grabbing of whites later in the century can be downplayed. Cobbing's argument perhaps over-stresses the strength and cohesion of white settler societies in the nineteenth century, but its central point seems essentially correct. For liberal defenders of the capitalist order in South Africa, as well as for the ideologues of the country's Bantustan policies, *mfecane* theory helps to provide a convenient explanation of the historical basis of South Africa's present-day pattern of land distribution.

Among radical historians too, *mfecane* theory survives today partly for ideological reasons. The structuralist theories that were dominant among radical writers in South Africa in the 1970s did not encourage detailed scrutiny of historical evidence. While the reaction on the part of many contemporary radical historians against the often-reductionist analyses that were generated by their predecessors has made for the production of a far more textured and nuanced kind of history, it has also meant a loss of much of the political punch that radical history carried a decade ago. With their focus often on microstudies and with their tendency to be suspicious of schematising and generalisation, present-day radical historians are often less overtly concerned than the previous generation was to identify and hammer away at the ideological props, such as *mfecane* theory, which help sustain the current racial and social order in South Africa.

A hundred and sixty years after it first surfaced, the devastation stereotype lives on, embedded now in *mfecane* theory. Cape merchant interests created it in the 1820s and 1830s on the basis of hearsay evidence. Natal settlers from the 1840s onwards, the first South Africanists in the late nineteenth and early twentieth centuries, and Afrikaner nationalist historians from the early twentieth century onwards all had a common vested interest in keeping it alive. Early liberal historians in South Africa, with their attention elsewhere, incorporated it as an element in what they saw as the not very important history of the country's African underclasses. Later, liberal historians, first outside and then inside South Africa, helped to resuscitate and reconstruct it in a way that made it acceptable to emerging African nationalist elites. After a brief period of concern with developing new approaches both to pre-industrial history and to the macrohistory of southern Africa, the majority of radical historians turned away towards the more recent past and towards less deliberately politicised social history, leaving the stereotype intact. Present-day writers of all shades of opinion continue to pick it up from the previous literature and to incorporate it into their own work without attempting to seek empirical verification for it. Natal's *mfecane* exists today by virtue not of historical argumentation but of uncritical repetition of a colonial-made myth.

The primary evidence on which the stereotype is based is minimal in extent: a few sentences in tendentious accounts written by traders at Port Natal in the 1820s; the brief notes on 'Shaka's wars' recorded by colonial ideologues – Aldin Grout, Henry Francis Fynn and Theophilus Shepstone – in the 1850s and 1860s. Traditions on the subject published in isiZulu by Fuze and Stuart in the 1920s were fed into the version of the stereotype produced by Bryant in his *Olden Times in Zululand*, but the original texts remained quite outside either the ken or the field of interest of the academics who dominated the production of South African history from this time onwards.

The writings of materialist historians since the mid-1970s on the emergence of the Zulu state, together with the evidence available in the James Stuart Collection, provide the basis for an entirely new rendering of the history of the Thukela-Mzimkhulu region in the 1820s and 1830s. But before this can be put forward, the process of exorcising the devastation stereotype has to be taken a step further. So long as Bryant's magisterial and apparently authoritative account of the 'Zulu devastations' of Natal is allowed to stand unchallenged, the stereotype will be able to survive alongside any new interpretation put forward. Bryant is far too deeply entrenched as an authority simply to be brushed aside; his account has to be confronted in detail.[47]

## Notes

1. This work of scholarship reprints excerpts of Chapter 2 of my Ph.D. dissertation in History entitled, 'The Dynamics of Power and Conflict in the Thukela-Mzimkhulu Region in the Late 18th and Early 19th Centuries: A Critical Reconstruction', which I submitted to the University of the Witwatersrand in 1989. A slightly revised version of this chapter was published as 'Political Mythology and the Making of Natal's *Mfecane*', *Canadian Journal of African Studies* 23:2 (1989): 272–91. My thanks go to a number of colleagues, particularly Julian Cobbing, for their critical comments.

2. J. Cobbing, 'The Case against the *Mfecane*', unpublished paper, University of Cape Town, 1983; 'The Case against the *Mfecane*', unpublished paper, University of the Witwatersrand, 1984 (a slightly modified version of the UCT paper); 'The Myth of the *Mfecane*', unpublished paper, University of Durban-Westville, 1987; 'Jettisoning the *Mfecane* (with Perestroika)', unpublished paper, University of the Witwatersrand, 1988 and 'The *Mfecane* as Alibi: Thoughts on Dithakong and Mbolompo', *Journal of African History* 29 (1988): 487–519.

3. See the letter from Farewell to Somerset, 6 September 1824, in *Records of Natal*, Vol. 1, 1823–August 1828, ed. B.J.T. Leverton (South African Archival Records, Important Cape Documents, Vol. IV, Pretoria, 1984), p. 37. This letter also appears in *The Natal Papers*, ed. J. Chase (Cape Town: Struik, 1968 [1st ed. Grahamstown: Godlonton, 1843]), Part I, p. 18; and in *The Annals of Natal, 1495–1845*, Vol. 1, ed. J. Bird (Cape Town: Struik, 1965 [Pietermaritzburg: P. Davis and Sons, 1888]), p. 192.

4. See the extract from the *Cape Town Gazette and African Advertiser* of 4 June 1825 published in *Records of Natal*, Vol. 1, ed. Leverton, p. 51 and the passage from the article by James King, entitled 'Some Account of Mr Farewell's Settlement at Port Natal', originally published in *South African Commercial Advertiser* of 18 July 1826, and reprinted in G. Thompson, *Travels and Adventures in Southern Africa*, ed. V.S. Forbes (Cape Town: Van Riebeeck Society, 1968 [1st ed. London: Henry Colburn, 1827]), Vol. 2, p. 249. The relevant extract also appears in *Natal Papers*, Part I, ed. Chase, p. 21 and in *Annals*, Vol. 1, ed. Bird, p. 93. Both Chase and Bird erroneously give the author as Francis Farewell.

5. Thompson, *Travels and Adventures*, Vol. 1, pp. 172, 174–75; Vol. 2, pp. 248, 249.

6. H.B. Robinson, ed., *Narrative of Voyages . . . under the Direction of Captain W.F.W. Owen*, Vol. 1 (London: Richard Bentley, 1833), p. 71; T. Pringle, *African Sketches* (London: Edward Moxon, 1834), p. 362; S. Kay, *Travels and Researches in Caffraria* (London: John Mason, 1833), pp. 281, 341, 343, 344; T. Boteler, *Narrative of a Voyage of Discovery to Africa and Arabia*, Vol. 2 (London: Bentley, 1835), p. 303; A. Steedman, *Wanderings and Adventures in the Interior of South Africa*, Vol. 2 (Cape Town: Struik, 1966 [1st ed. London: Longman, 1835]), pp. 200–01; N. Isaacs, *Travels and Adventures in Eastern Africa* (Cape Town: Van Riebeeck Society, 1936 [1st ed. London: Edward Churton, 1836]), especially Chapter 18. See also the discussion in S.J.R. Martin, 'British Images of the Zulu, c.1820–1879' (Ph.D. diss., University of Cambridge, 1982), pp. 22–37.

7. H.F. Fynn, *The Diary of Henry Francis Fynn*, eds. J. Stuart and D.McK. Malcolm (Pietermaritzburg: Shuter & Shooter, 1950), pp. 86–88; Isaacs, *Travels and Adventures*, pp. 142, 180–81; *Records of Natal*, Vol. 1, ed. Leverton, letter from Farewell to Somerset, 6 September 1824, pp. 37–40 and notarial deed signed by J.A. Chabaud, 29 July 1828, pp. 247–48.

8. *Records of Natal*, Vol. 1, ed. Leverton, letter from Brink to Farewell, 5 May 1824, p. 36.

9. On the financing of these expeditions see Fynn, *Diary*, Chapter 3 and B. Roberts, *The Zulu Kings* (London: Hamish Hamilton, 1974), pp. 8–19, 75–76, 78–81.

10. S. Bannister, *Humane Policy; or, Justice to the Aborigines of New Settlements* (London: Thomas & George Underwood, 1830), Appendices 1, 6 and 7; *Natal Papers*, Part 1, ed. Chase, pp. 23–30, citing a letter from Bannister to the Secretary of State for the Colonies, 12 May 1829; *Natal Papers*, Part 1, ed. Chase, pp. 30–31, citing the *Graham's Town Journal* of 3 August 1832; P.R. Kirby, ed. *Andrew Smith and Natal* (Cape Town: Van Riebeeck Society, 1955), pp. 5–7, 145–46 and Roberts, *The Zulu Kings*, pp. 222–25.

11. King, 'Some Account' in Thompson, *Travels and Adventures*, Vol. 2, ed. Forbes, p. 249 and Isaacs, *Travels and Adventures*, p. 339.

12. Roberts, *The Zulu Kings*, pp. 154, 177, quoting the *South African Commercial Advertiser* of 15 November 1828 and 27 December 1828. This 'negrophilist' newspaper was frequently critical of European settler attitudes to, and treatment of, people of colour: see B.A. le Cordeur, *The Politics*

*of Eastern Cape Separatism 1820–1854* (Cape Town: Oxford University Press, 1981), pp. 43, 66.

13. *Natal Papers*, Part 1, ed. Chase, p. 27, citing a letter from S. Bannister to the Secretary of State for the Colonies, 12 May 1829; R. Godlonton, *Introductory Remarks to a Narrative of the Irruption of the Kafir Hordes* (Cape Town: Struik, 1965 [1st ed. Grahamstown: Meurant & Godlonton, 1836]), pp. 162–68, 172 and Kirby, ed. *Andrew Smith in Natal*, pp. 149–51, 153–54, 166–68, 171–72.

14. Roberts, *The Zulu Kings*, p. 18 and L. Herman and P. Kirby, 'Nathaniel Isaacs: A Biographical Sketch', in their edition of Isaacs, *Travels and Adventures*, p. xi.

15. V.S. Forbes, 'Biographical Sketch of George Thompson', in Thompson, *Travels and Adventures*, Vol. 1, pp. viii–xiii; *Dictionary of South African Biography*, Vol. 2, eds. W.J. de Klerk and D.W. Kruger (Cape Town: Tafelberg Publishers for Human Sciences Research Council, 1972), entry for Andrew Steedman, p. 706; Bannister, *Humane Policy*; *Natal Papers*, Part 1, ed. Chase, p. 23; A.F. Hattersley, 'Francis George Farewell, and the Earliest Natal Settlers', *Africana Notes and News* 14 (1960–61): 317–18; *Dictionary of South African Biography*, Vol. 1, eds. De Klerk and Kruger, entry for Saxe Bannister, p. 50 and Le Cordeur, *The Politics of Eastern Cape Separatism*, pp. 64–65.

16. *Dictionary of South African Biography*, Vol. 1, eds. De Klerk and Kruger, entry on Francis Farewell, p. 286; *Dictionary of South African Biography*, Vol. 2, eds. De Klerk and Kruger, entry on William Owen, p. 529; Roberts, *The Zulu Kings*, pp. 7–8, 10, 12.

17. Isaacs, *Travels and Adventures*, p. 339. For a comprehensive analysis of Isaacs's literary style and an assessment of his book's public impact, see Martin, 'British Images of the Zulu', pp. 37–58.

18. Kay, *Travels and Researches*, pp. 281, 341, 343, 344; D. Kotze, ed., *Letters of the American Missionaries 1835–1838* (Cape Town: Van Riebeeck Society, 1950), p. 97; G. Champion, *Journal of the Reverend George Champion 1835–1839*, ed. A. Booth (Cape Town: Struik, 1967), pp. 15, 62; W. Boyce, *Notes on South African Affairs* (Cape Town: Struik, 1971 [1st ed., Grahamstown: J. Mason, 1838]), pp. x, 171, 173–74; B. Shaw, *Memorials of South Africa* (Cape Town: Struik, 1970 [1st ed. London: Adams, 1840]), pp. 44–45; T. Arbousset and F. Daumas, *Narrative of an Exploratory Tour to the North-East of the Colony of the Cape of Good Hope* (Cape Town: Struik, 1968 [1st ed. Cape Town: Saul Solomon, 1846]), Chapter 17, especially p. 148.

19. The analysis is presented in Chapter 3 of my thesis. See also J. Wright, 'A.T. Bryant and "the Wars of Shaka"', *History in Africa* 18 (1991): 409–25.

20. The phrase occurs in his 'Sketch', *Dictionary of South African Biography*, eds. De Klerk and Kruger, p. 49.

21. On the development of Africanist historiography see P.D. Curtin, *African History* (London: Longman, 1978); American Historical Association publication No. 56 (New York: Macmillan, 1964), pp. 1–8; T. Hodgkin, 'Where the Paths Began', in *African Studies since 1945: A Tribute to Basil Davidson*, ed. C. Fyfe (London: Longman, 1976), pp. 6–16; I. Wallerstein, 'The Evolving Role of the Africa Scholar in African Studies', *Canadian Journal of African Studies* 17 (1983): 9–16 and C. Neale, *Writing 'Independent' History: African Historiography, 1960–1980* (Westport, Conn.: Greenwood, 1985), Chapter 1.

22. M. Gluckman, 'The Kingdom of the Zulu', in *African Political Systems*, eds. M. Fortes and E.E. Evans-Pritchard (London: Oxford University Press for International Africa Institute, 1940), p. 25.

23. J.D. Omer-Cooper, *The Zulu Aftermath: A Nineteenth-Century Revolution in Bantu Africa* (London: Longmans, 1966), Introduction and pp. 19–27.

24. Ibid., pp. 4–7.

25. Ibid., p. 5 n.

26. Cobbing, 'The Case against the *Mfecane*', p. 5.

27. Omer-Cooper, *Zulu Aftermath*, Chapter 10.

28. T.V. Bulpin, *To the Shores of Natal* (Cape Town: Timmins, 1953), pp. 40–47.

29. Omer-Cooper, *Zulu Aftermath*, p. 33 n.

30. Cobbing, 'The Case against the *Mfecane*', pp. 5–7; 'The Myth of the *Mfecane*', pp. 8–9.

31. For example, R. Hallett, *Africa to 1875: A Modern History* (Ann Arbor: University of Michigan Press, 1970), pp. 239–40; R.W. July, *A History of the African People* (London: Faber & Faber, 1970), pp. 232–37 and H.A. Gailey, *History of Africa from 1800 to Present* (New York: Holt, Rinehart & Winston, 1972), pp. 72–78.

32. For example W.F. Lye, 'The *Difaqane*: The *Mfecane* in the Southern Sotho Area, 1822–24', *Journal of African History* 8 (1967): 107–31; several of the articles in L. Thompson, ed. *African Societies* (London: Heinemann, 1969); L. Thompson, 'Co-operation and Conflict: The High Veld', in *Oxford History of S.A.*, Vol. 1, eds. L. Thompson and M. Wilson (Oxford: Oxford University Press, 1969), Chapter 9 and R.K. Rasmussen, *Migrant Kingdom: Mzilikazi's Ndebele in South Africa* (London: Collings, 1978), pp. 3, 7, 9.

33. See Shula Marks's article on history of southern Africa in *Encyclopaedia Britannica*, Vol. 17 (Chicago: Encyclopaedia Britannica Publishing, 1974), p. 281.

34. For example, R. Oliver and A. Atmore, *Africa since 1800*, 2nd ed. (Cambridge: Cambridge University Press, 1972), p. 55; J.D. Omer-Cooper, E.A. Ayendele, A.E. Afigbo and R.J. Gavin, *The Making of Modern Africa* (London: Longmans, Green, 1974), Chapter 5; G. Parker and P. Pfukani, *History of Southern Africa* (London: Bell & Hyman, 1975), Chapter 5.

35. E.H. Brookes and C. de B. Webb, *A History of Natal* (Pietermaritzburg: University of Natal Press, 1965), pp. 7–14.

36. T.V. Bulpin, *Shaka's Country* (Cape Town: Timmins, 1952) and *To the Shores of Natal*; E.A. Ritter, *Shaka Zulu: The Rise of the Zulu Empire* (London: Longmans, Green, 1955); C.T. Binns, *The Last Zulu King: The Life and Death of Cetshwayo* (London: Longmans, 1963) and *Dinuzulu: The Death of the House of Shaka* (London: Longmans, Green, 1968); P. Becker, *Rule of Fear* (London: Hamilton, 1966) and D.R. Morris, *The Washing of the Spears* (London: Jonathan Cape, 1966).

37. C.F.J. Muller, 'The Period of the Great Trek, 1834–1854', in *Five Hundred Years: A History of South Africa*, ed. C.F.J. Muller (Pretoria and Cape Town: Academica, 1969), p. 125; D. Ziervogel, 'The Natives of South Africa', in *Five Hundred Years*, ed. Muller, pp. 445–48; F.A. van Jaarsveld, *Van Van Riebeeck tot Verwoerd 1652–1966* (Johannesburg: Voortrekkerpers, 1971), Chapter 7; J.P. van S. Bruwer, article on Shaka in *Standard Encyclopaedia of Southern Africa*, Vol. 9 (Cape Town: Nasou, 1973), p. 598 and C.F.J. Muller, *Die Oorsprong van die Groot Trek* (Cape Town: Tafelberg, 1974), especially pp. 74–83.

38. For example, the present author's *Bushmen Raiders of the Drakensberg 1840–1870* (Pietermaritzburg: University of Natal Press, 1971), pp. 15–17; several of the articles in C. Saunders and R. Derricourt, eds. *Beyond the Cape Frontier* (London: Longman, 1974); C. de B. Webb, 'Of Orthodoxy, Heresy and the *Difaqane*', unpublished paper, University of the Witwatersrand, 1974 and 'The *Mfecane*' in *Perspectives on the Southern African Past* (Cape Town: Centre for African Studies, University of Cape Town, 1979), Chapter 9 and T.R.H. Davenport, *South Africa: A Modern History* (Johannesburg: Macmillan, 1977), pp. 10–17.

39. J.K. Ngubane, 'Shaka's Social, Political and Military Ideas', in *Shaka King of the Zulus in African Literature*, ed. D. Burness (Washington, DC: Three Continents Press, 1976), pp. 140, 147.

40. T.O. Ranger, 'Towards a Usable African Past', in *African Studies since 1945*, ed. Fyfe, pp. 17–30; A. Triulzi, 'Decolonising African History', in *People's History and Socialist History*, ed. R. Samuel (London: Routledge & Kegan Paul, 1981), pp. 286–97; A. Temu and B. Swai, *Historians and Africanist History: A Critique* (London: Zed Books, 1981); Neale, *Writing 'Independent' History*; D. Newbury, 'Africanist Historical Studies in the United States: Metamorphosis or Metastasis?' in *African Historiographies: What History for Which Africa?*, eds. B. Jewsiewicki and D. Newbury (Beverly Hills, CA: Sage, 1986), Chapter 12.

41. Besides Cobbing's work, the only critique so far to have been published is an article by V.E. Satir entitled 'The Difaqane: Fact vs. Fiction', *Educational Journal* 55:2 (1983): 6–10.

42. C. Saunders, *Historical Dictionary of South Africa* (Metuchen, N.J. and London: Scarecrow Press, 1983), pp. 107–08.

43. R. Edgecombe, 'The Mfecane or Difaqane', in *An Illustrated History of South Africa*, eds. T. Cameron and S.B. Spies (Johannesburg: Jonathan Ball, 1986), Chapter 9.

44. J.D. Omer-Cooper, *History of Southern Africa* (London: James Currey, 1987), Chapter 4.

45. Ranger, 'Towards a Usable African past', p. 17; P.D. Curtin, 'African History' in *The Past Before Us: Contemporary Historical Writing in the United States*, ed. M. Kammen (Ithaca and London: Cornell University Press, 1980), p. 115.

46. Cobbing, 'The Case against the *Mfecane*', pp. 1, 7–8, 16 and 'The Myth of the Mfecane', pp. 1, 9–10, 30.

47. The next chapter of my thesis therefore moves onto a critical analysis of Bryant's treatment of the upheavals that took place south of the Thukela in the 1810s and 1820s. See Note 19 above.

*Chapter 7*

# White Myths of Shaka

DAN WYLIE

WE KNOW ALMOST NOTHING for certain about Shaka. We do not know when he was born, or what he looked like, or exactly when he died. What has come down to us through the literature is an extraordinary palimpsest of half-understood rumours, speculations and plain old lies. This collage of inventions is more than mere fiction: it is a myth. A myth in this sense is more than just an untrue tale. It is a narrative imbued with the core values of a culture: it embodies and expresses widely held mental patterns of time and space, colour and creed – the aesthetics of judgement and power by which a culture identifies itself in contradistinction to other cultures. Shaka – the figure, largely propagated by white writers, familiar through novels, history textbooks and films – is a myth that has historically expressed and served the social, psychological and political needs of the white community in southern Africa. Shaka, in other words, has become, over the last 170-odd years, an icon against which white writers have habitually measured their own cultural norms. This is true whether Shaka is being vilified or praised.

Of course there have been many non-white writers on Shaka, from Mazisi Kunene in KwaZulu itself to Leopold Senghor of Senegal. This is a quite distinct stream of thought; however, here I survey the extraordinarily cohesive, even incestuous genealogy of white writing on Shaka. From the first eyewitness accounts of Nathaniel Isaacs and Henry Francis Fynn, through the voluminous studies of A.T. Bryant, to the television series *Shaka Zulu*, these writers have compulsively repeated one another's anecdotes and inventions, refurbishing them to suit their times and readerships, seldom bothering to question the veracity of their stories. Shaka has until now remained virtually impervious to rigorous scholarship or the inconvenience of facts.

Facts, to be sure, are hard to come by. It has been insufficiently recognised that all we have as historians is *text*, writing, a crafted literature, subject to all the limitations and wiles of language. Language conceals as much as it reveals. It is also crucial to realise that a culture identifies itself through commonalities and stabilities and such stabilities are recognised primarily through the communicative medium of language. Any examination that ignores the textual production and effect of the language itself is likely to miss the central purposes of texts such as those written about Shaka.

The eyewitness accounts are cases in point. Isaacs, Fynn and their few comrades depicted themselves – and were depicted by subsequent writers – as morally upright citizens carrying the light of European civilisation into the heart of darkness. They were, actually, frontier ruffians grubbing for a quick buck. They squabbled, sold slaves, fought as mercenaries and acquired harems of black wives and children whom they subsequently abandoned. Isaacs became a full-time slave trader in Sierra Leone; Fynn became a magistrate who laboured under persistent accusations of gun-running, cattle-rustling and cold-blooded murder – none of this comes out in their own accounts, of course. The primary purpose of their writing was not to reveal the Zulu reality; it was to conceal their own. Instead, Shaka was painted as the villain, the murderer – a clear case of psychological projection. And because it suited an invasive, often guilty, often beleaguered white colonial community to believe these lies, the projection became a whole society's and functioned as part of that society's very identity. Identity *is* style.

Isaacs's account (1836), and Fynn's so-called diary, published only in 1950, do retain *elements* of empirical factuality and of the writers' individuality. But they cannot be read as merely representational, or simplistically trawled for nuggets of fact. Even facts are deployed in a narrative structure serving other purposes. This is partly because Isaacs and Fynn scarcely wrote their accounts in the first place. Isaacs was then a semi-literate teenager: his *Travels and Adventures in Eastern Africa* was certainly rewritten by an unknown ghost-writer back in London – and it shows in the style. In part, colonial identity was invented 5 000 miles (8 000 kilometres) away by writers who had never left home. Many so-called facts about Shaka merely embody what *London* society thought Zulu society *ought* to look like, an image derived not from real contact, but from other literature, much of it legendary.

Similarly, Fynn's *Diary* is nothing of the sort: it is a collage of papers, mostly written for a variety of self-interested agendas decades after the event. Fynn's rough style has been extensively smoothed out and upgraded, its content censored and amplified by his editor, James Stuart. As a source of facts, it's extremely dubious.

Stuart is a particularly paradoxical nexus in this business. Although as a Natal administrator he collected enormous amounts of Zulu oral history – now our primary alternative source material – in his public appearances and editing he did everything possible to whitewash Fynn, in an obvious attempt to bolster white South African society's image of itself. He helped his brother Philip to write an egregiously racist novel on Shaka, and encouraged A.T. Bryant to rely on Isaacs's account of Shaka rather than his own collected traditions. And his nephew Huntly Stuart wrote a stage play, *Shaka* (1981), starring football hero Henry Cele. Cele went on to play Shaka in Bill Faure's appallingly inaccurate and violent television series, first screened in 1986 and rerun as recently as 2001. In this way Isaacs's improbable, Gothic vilification of Shaka lives on in cinemas worldwide.

*From Nathaniel Isaacs,* Travels and Adventures in Eastern Africa *(1836).*

*From D.C.F. Moodie,* A History of the Battles and Adventures of the British, the Boers and the Zulus *(1888).*

*From* Zwanna, Son of Zulu *comic book (1993).*

Amateur anthropologist/priest Bryant, too, demonstrates the inseparability of history, style and myth. Bryant's monumental *Olden Times in Zululand and Natal* (1929), a cornerstone of Zulu studies, is governed by another great myth: the destruction of Paradise, with Shaka starring as Satan. Obviously, this Christian mythology has nothing whatsoever to do with Zulu self-conceptions or sense of history. Everything in *Olden Times*, from its detailed stylistic flourishes to the grand narrative arrangements of evidence, serves this condemnatory, self-congratulatory, and ultimately, racist end.

Although profoundly indebted to Bryant, one work on Shaka – the most famous – belatedly injected a strand of glorification into the portrayal of the Zulu leader: E.A. Ritter's novel, *Shaka Zulu* (1955). This, too, was rewritten by a liberal London ghost-writer: a clumsily executed romance was refashioned into a lively history. Because it suited the prevailing preconceptions and societal desires – the mythology – it was read *as* history, as fact. This had everything to do with the style, nothing to do with factuality. Ritter inadvertently helped to launch a swathe of admiring histories of the Zulu, including Donald Morris's famous *Washing of the Spears* (1965) and John Omer-Cooper's *The Zulu Aftermath* (1966). Desperate, in the onset of postcolonial African independence, to show that Africans could be military geniuses and independent state builders, they swallowed Ritter whole. Nobody noticed that substantial chunks of the book were plagiarised.

There are no facts in *Shaka Zulu*. One example must suffice here: the battle of Qokli Hill. Ritter supplied a persuasively detailed account of the fight, which subsequently found its way into every textbook, encyclopedia and museum display. It features in the latest bizarre craze: adducing business principles from Shaka's mythical strategies. Everyone fell in love with Qokli Hill. But there is no evidence whatsoever that such a battle happened. There is no real evidence anywhere of Shaka's tactical acumen. Ritter made it up.

## Note

For examples of recent scholarship on Shaka, see especially Julian Cobbing (1988) and Carolyn Hamilton (1995, 1998), the unpublished theses by Hamilton (1986) and by John Wright (1989); and my own book, *Savage Delight*, of which this article is essentially a summary.

## References

Bryant, A.T. 1929. *Olden Times in Zululand and Natal*. London: Longmans.

Cobbing, Julian. 1988. 'The Mfecane as Alibi: Some Thoughts on Dithakong and Mbolompo', *Journal of African History* 29: 487–519.

Hamilton, Carolyn. 1986. 'Ideology, Oral Traditions and the Struggle for Power in the Early Zulu Kingdom' (Masters thesis, University of the Witwatersrand).

————. 1995. *The 'Mfecane' Aftermath: Reconstructive Debates in Southern African History.* Johannesburg: Witwatersrand University Press and Pietermaritzburg: University of Natal Press.

————. 1998. *Terrific Majesty: The Powers of Shaka Zulu and the Limits of Historical Invention.* Cape Town: David Philip.

Isaacs, Nathaniel. [1836] 1936. *Travels and Adventures in Eastern Africa.* 2 vols. Cape Town: Van Riebeeck Society.

Morris, Donald. 1965. *The Washing of the Spears.* London: Jonathan Cape.

Omer-Cooper, John. 1966. *The Zulu Aftermath: A Nineteenth-century Revolution in Southern Africa.* London: Longmans.

Ritter, E.A. 1955. *Shaka Zulu.* London: Longmans.

Stuart, James and D. McK. Malcolm, ed. 1950. *The Diary of Henry Francis Fynn.* Pietermaritzburg: Shuter & Shooter.

Stuart, P.A. 1927. *An African Attila.* London: Unwin.

Wright, John. 1989. 'The Dynamics of Power and Conflict in the Thukela-Mzimkhulu Region in the Late Eighteenth and Early Nineteenth Centuries' (Ph.D. diss., University of the Witwatersrand).

Wylie, Dan. 2000. *Savage Delight: White Myths of Shaka.* Pietermaritzburg: University of Natal Press.

# Chapter 8

# The Rise and Fall of the Zulu Kingdom

JOHN LABAND

THE ZULU KINGDOM THRUST itself into the world's attention when, in 1879, its armies inflicted a series of stinging reverses on the invading British forces before going down in final, but glorious defeat. Such was its consequent military renown that it is difficult to accept that the Zulu kingdom was a short-lived if spectacular phenomenon, enduring in its heyday no longer than a single lifespan. Nor is it possible to define the kingdom's boundaries definitively, for they fluctuated constantly, expanding in the second decade of the nineteenth century under King Shaka, and contracting and stabilising under his successors.

Until the late eighteenth century, there were no large chiefdoms in what was later to be the heartland of the Zulu kingdom, those lands between the Drakensberg Mountains and the Indian Ocean, bounded by the Phongolo River in the north and the Thukela River in the south. It was then that a process of political centralisation and expansion began, the myriad reasons for which are much debated by historians. Some have pointed to sharpening competition in time of recurring drought for limited resources, especially for suitable winter and summer pastures for cattle, which were central to the people's lives in terms of both ritual and wealth. More recently, other historians have emphasised the effects of the expanding international trade in ivory – and, more controversially, slaves – carried on by Europeans from Delagoa Bay and across the Orange River from the Cape Colony. Either way, the little chiefdoms of what was to become the Zulu kingdom were compelled to strengthen themselves in order to compete and survive.

The more successful competitors among them underwent necessary social and political adjustments. The most important of these involved the transformation of circumcision schools of young men of the same age into age-grade regiments, or *amabutho*, under the tighter authority of their chiefs. Chiefs increasingly employed these *amabutho* as instruments of internal control, and also as armies against external enemies. To keep them fed and rewarded necessitated raids against neighbouring chiefdoms, which in itself added to the growing cycle of violence. By the end of the eighteenth century three major chiefdoms had begun to emerge in the region: the

Mabhudu-Tsonga in what is now southern Mozambique; the Ndwandwe to the southwest of them between the Mkhuze and Black Mfolozi rivers; and the Mthethwa to the south of the Ndwandwe, between the lower Mfolozi and Mhlathuze rivers. In the late 1810s, intensifying warfare between these three rival chiefdoms caused their weaker neighbours to migrate out of harm's way and to set in train destructive conflicts in the South African interior still commonly – but not unproblematically – known as the *mfecane*, or 'the crushing'.

The Mthethwa chiefdom was seemingly less centrally controlled than the neighbouring Ndwandwe, and some of its subordinate chiefdoms were encouraged to expand their own military might to help obstruct Ndwandwe ambitions. One of these Mthethwa vassals was the obscure Zulu chiefdom in the valley of the middle White Mfolozi River, ruled over by Senzangakhona kaJama.

In about 1817 the Ndwandwe under Zwide kaLanga crushed the Mthethwa in battle and shattered their political hegemony in the central and southern parts of Zululand. All that was left standing between the Ndwandwe and final victory was the little Zulu chiefdom. Yet the amaZulu were powerful beyond their numbers and able to hold off the Ndwandwe successfully. The reason they were able to do so was because by then they were ruled by Shaka, Senzangakhona's son, a chief of extraordinary abilities who was transforming his *amabutho* into the most effective fighters in the region.

In 1816 (so far as the date can be known), Senzangakhona died and Shaka ruthlessly eliminated his rival half-brother, Sigujana, to secure the Zulu succession with the support of his patron and overlord, Dingiswayo kaJobe, the Mthethwa chief. Following Dingiswayo's death at the hands of the Ndwandwe, Shaka had to assert his position within his chiefdom, where many still considered him a usurper, while at the same time fighting off the Ndwandwe and other external enemies. Under Dingiswayo he had already become a renowned general, and he accordingly applied his experience to increase the size of his army, improve its military capability through rigorous training, and school it in effective strategic and tactical manoeuvres. These Shaka would most likely have first learned among the Mthethwa, although he certainly subsequently improved upon them. Shaka married his growing military weight with the exercise of ruthless but extremely skilful diplomacy to consolidate his position over the entire region between the White Mfolozi and the Thukela to the south. Smaller chiefdoms that prudently submitted to him provided additional manpower for the Zulu *amabutho* in return for his protection.

Shaka (whom we might now justifiably refer to as a king) brought the *amabutho* system to its mature development and, through marriage regulations, extended it to include the women of his growing kingdom. Indeed, this *amabutho* system was the basis of the Zulu king's power and authority, and continued to be so for Shaka and his successors until the fall of the kingdom in the late nineteenth century. Through this system, the Zulu monarch exercised social, economic, political and reproductive control over all his subjects, both men and women, and diverted their military and labour service away from their own homesteads and local chiefs into the service of the king.

Larger neighbouring chiefdoms, when confronted with waxing Zulu might, were faced with the unpalatable options of resistance, flight or submission. In 1819 Shaka took the fight to the Ndwandwe, pushed them north over the Phongolo and established Zulu control over their former territory. Shaka then broke up the chiefdoms to the west and south of him, and by the mid-1820s had extended his sway into the foothills of the Drakensberg Mountains and as far south as the Mzimkhulu River. Yet distance and difficult terrain were imposing a natural limit on the extent of territory that Shaka could effectively control. The amaZulu soon found they were not capable of establishing a permanent presence in the far-flung regions they had subdued to the west and south, and had consequently to confine themselves to frequent raids and the extraction of tribute from subordinate chiefdoms along the margins of their central domain.

In 1824 the establishment at Port Natal (later Durban) of a small settlement of British hunters and traders introduced a novel and deceptively benign element into the Zulu world. Their presence complemented the far-off Portuguese traders already at Delagoa Bay, and connected Zululand inexorably to the colonial world with all its apparent material advantages and many insidious dangers of foreign interference. Perhaps short-sightedly, Shaka welcomed the Port Natal adventurers because they were far more accessible suppliers of exotic goods than the Portuguese, and he saw how he could use them as intermediaries with the British authorities at the Cape who were growing suspicious and fearful of his armies operating near their borders. He also prized them as mercenaries with battle-winning firearms and struck a deal with them. In return for permitting them to live undisturbed at Port Natal, where he treated them like any other client chiefs under his suzerainty, they came to his aid in war. With their assistance, in 1826 Shaka finally crushed and dispersed the Ndwandwe who had been attempting a comeback.

All was not well, however, in Shaka's new kingdom. Disaffected groups among the recently conquered chiefdoms were persistently plotting his overthrow, his brothers and leading nobles had their inevitable ambitions, and there was discontent among many of the subjects of his high-handed and increasingly cruel and arbitrary rule. Most dangerous for him was growing resistance from the *amabutho*, the mainstay of his regime, to interminable and ever less-rewarding campaigns.

On 24 September 1828 disaffection coalesced, and at KwaDukuza Shaka fell to assassins in a well-laid coup. His half-brother Dingane seized the throne and moved swiftly to eliminate his co-conspirators and almost all his rivals in the royal house, to replace Shaka's high officials with his own, and to make concessions pleasing to the *amabutho*. He then proceeded to move vigorously against chiefdoms within the Zulu orbit whose loyalty he suspected, and his *amabutho* raided far and wide. Nevertheless,

Dingane realised that it was unrealistic to attempt to continue to exercise control over as extensive an area as Shaka had tried to maintain, and returned the centre of gravity of the Zulu kingdom to the White Mfolozi valley, largely relinquishing direct rule over the territory south of the Thukela. There the settlement at Port Natal was growing in size and independence and local influence, although the settlers remained in an uneasy tributary relationship with Dingane. Relations between the two almost broke down on several occasions during the 1830s, but self-interest on both sides averted a final rupture.

Then, in October 1837, emigrant farmers (or Boers) from the Cape, migrating with all their livestock and chattels in search of new lands to settle, streamed over the Drakensberg passes and laagered along the headwaters of the Thukela. As Dingane understood only too well, they came with firearms, horses and wagons, which they had deployed in the highveld in a series of crushing victories over the Ndebele, an old enemy whom the amaZulu had never succeeded in defeating. The mortal threat that the Boers posed to the Zulu kingdom was thus immediately apparent, especially since they rapidly proceeded to establish friendly contacts with the Port Natal settlers. In November Boer emissaries made known to Dingane their desire to settle in his loosely controlled territory south of the Thukela. Faced with this formidable threat to the integrity of his kingdom and to his own position as king, Dingane and his councillors tried to gain the advantage through guile over an adversary they despaired of overcoming in a direct military confrontation. Consequently, when a well-armed Boer deputation appeared at his capital, uMgungundlovu, to discuss terms with him, Dingane struck. On 6 February 1838 he ordered their execution and dispatched his armies to obliterate the rest of the Boers in their encampments in the foothills of the Drakensberg. Despite being taken completely by surprise, the Boers succeeded in beating off the amaZulu. An indecisive campaign then ensued during which, although the Boers suffered some defeats and their Port Natal allies were routed and forced temporarily to abandon their settlement, their military superiority was steadily asserted. Finally, on 16 December 1838, the Boers convincingly routed the Zulu army at the battle of Ncome (Blood River).

Worsted, but not destroyed, Dingane retired north across the Black Mfolozi and opened negotiations with the Boers. On 25 March 1839 he undertook to allow them to settle south of the Thukela. There the Boers established the Republiek Natalia with its capital at the recently founded village of Pietermaritzburg, and commenced dividing the land up into farms.

Dingane's first intention was to put space between himself and the Boers by relocating the focus of his kingdom further to the north. To that end he invaded the Swazi kingdom. But a stinging defeat at Lubuye in the winter of 1839 thwarted that possibility and further weakened Dingane's position. He was finally brought down as a consequence of a rebellion among his own subjects. In September 1839 his half-brother, Mpande, fearing that he was to be killed by the increasingly paranoid king who viewed him as a rival, fled with a considerable following to take refuge among the Boers. The canny Boers saw the advantage of an alliance with Mpande, and on 27 October 1839 agreed to make him king in return for his leaving them in control of the lands south of the Thukela, and ceding them St Lucia Bay and its possible harbour.

On 29 January 1840 Mpande's forces routed Dingane's at the Maqongqo Hills, and the defeated king fled across the Phongolo to die miserably as a fugitive. With their ally now the Zulu king, the Boers' ambitions waxed, and on 14 February 1840 they hubristically induced Mpande to cede to them – in addition to the territorial concessions he had already made – all the lands between the Thukela and the Black Mfolozi to the north. Yet the tiny Boer population had not the numbers to occupy and administer this additional territory, let alone the rest of the sprawling Republiek Natalia. To prevent the whole of southeastern Africa from being disrupted by the feeble yet unrealistically aggressive Boer republic, the British intervened in a long drawn-out process between 1842 and 1845 to annex Natalia as a British possession. As part of the general settlement of the region, on 5 October 1843 the British and King Mpande acknowledged their respective sovereignties. The Thukela, from its mouth to its confluence with the Mzinyathi (Buffalo), and then up that river to the Drakensberg Mountains, was recognised as the boundary between the Zulu kingdom and what eventually, on 15 July 1856, became the British Colony of Natal.

The Zulu kingdom now found itself wedged between British Natal to the south and the fledgling Boer republics on the highveld. The South African Republic

*Illustration from G.E. Angas,* The Kafirs Illustrated, *of Mpande reviewing his* amabutho *in 1847.*

(Transvaal) was to prove a perpetual menace, since the land-hungry Boer pastoralists were always trying to thrust into the good grazing lands of northwestern Zululand. The only land still open for raids by the *amabutho*, eager to prove their military prowess and to win the booty on which the military system depended, lay to the north, in the Swazi kingdom. Mpande's armies repeatedly campaigned there in the 1840s and early 1850s, but the British deprecated these disturbances to the regional balance and Mpande gradually desisted, for he was an astute ruler, and had early understood that it was necessary to cultivate the British, particularly in order to counteract his aggressive Boer neighbours. He thus did his best to foster good relations with the Natal authorities, permitting traders and hunters into his kingdom and, after 1850, missionaries.

The crucial matter of the royal succession remained unresolved, however. In polygamous Zulu society custom made it clear enough who a ruler's heir ought to be, although the brute fact was that Shaka and his two successors were all usurpers who gained the throne through assassination or civil war. Shaka and Dingane had vainly sought to postpone the issue of the succession by siring no legitimate offspring, but Mpande had many sons. He attempted to secure his position by playing one off against another, but only fostered a ferocious struggle for the succession between his favourite son, Mbuyazi, and Cetshwayo, whose claim was stronger. The two princes clashed on 2 December 1856 at the ferocious battle of Ndondakusuka, and Cetshwayo emerged the victor. Thereafter Mpande had no alternative but to share his authority with his over-mighty and undisputed heir. The old king died in September 1872, having succeeded, despite all perils, in maintaining the integrity of his kingdom.

Cetshwayo, no less than his father, was confronted, on the one hand, by white neighbours greedy to carve out farms in Zululand, and on the other hand, by ambitious great chiefs who were using their contacts with the colonial world to aggrandise their local power. Cetshwayo responded by strengthening royal authority, primarily through strictly enforcing its mainstay, the *amabutho* system, which had grown lax during the latter part of Mpande's reign. On the diplomatic front he continued his father's successful policy of fostering good relations with the British to counteract the more overt menace presented by the Boers.

Through no fault of Cetshwayo's the situation changed drastically when, in the later 1870s, the British began pursuing a policy of confederation in southern Africa. In the interests of imperial strategy, financial saving and economic opportunity they planned to bring all the white-ruled states in the region under their single authority. One of the major building blocks in the new structure was the Boer South African Republic, which the British annexed in April 1877 as the Transvaal Colony. To help placate their reluctant new subjects, it was necessary for the Transvaal authorities to support Boer land claims in Zululand and jettison their previous support for Cetshwayo. In any case, independent and militarily powerful black states such as the Zulu kingdom were perceived as a potential threat to the confederation process that ought to be neutralised. Finding to his dismay that his old ally had changed sides, Cetshwayo was compelled to negotiate fruitlessly while the British moved inexorably towards a military confrontation aimed at conclusively knitting together the threads of confederation.

On 11 January 1879 British and colonial forces invaded Zululand following Cetshwayo's failure to respond to an ultimatum that required him to abolish the *amabutho* system and make other concessions, thereby entirely disrupting the political, social and economic structure of his kingdom and placing it under British supervision. The ensuing Anglo-Zulu War, which cost the British several unanticipated defeats at the hands of the ably led and courageous Zulu army – notably at Isandlwana on 22 January and Hlobane on 28 March – and which took the invaders many months longer than envisioned to bring to a successful conclusion, came to an effective end at the battle of Ulundi on 4 July. Cetshwayo was captured several weeks later and sent to Cape Town as a prisoner.

While it was the British intention to break the military potential of the Zulu kingdom and destroy the unifying power of the monarch, it was not part of their plan to burden themselves with the future administration of the territory. It was sufficient to ensure that the Zulu would never again pose a military threat to their colonial neighbours, and this objective was pursued in the settlement General Sir Garnet Wolseley imposed on the Zulu chiefs on 1 September 1879. The institution of the Zulu monarchy was terminated; its main prop, the centralised *amabutho* system, was abolished and the former kingdom was divided up into thirteen independent chiefdoms under appointed chiefs, most of whom could be relied upon out of self-interest to ensure that there would be no resurgence of the centralised Zulu monarchy.

Wolseley's settlement soon broke down. Growing strife between the thirteen chiefdoms and the deliberate victimisation of the royalist party, known as the uSuthu, threatened to spill over into Natal and caused the British to rethink their Zululand policy. In August 1882 the exiled Cetshwayo was permitted to travel to London to plead his cause. On 11 December he agreed that he should be restored to the central part of his former kingdom. To be excluded from his authority was the chiefdom of Zibhebhu kaMaphitha in northeastern Zululand. Zibhebhu and his Mandlakazi people had emerged as the main oppressors of the uSuthu and, as the most reliable collaborators with the British, would help keep Cetshwayo in check. The territory between the Mhlathuze and Thukela rivers was not to be returned to Cetshwayo either, for it was to form a buffer between his reduced kingdom and Natal. It was placed under British protection and, as the Reserved Territory, was to be administered by officials recruited from Natal.

The restored Cetshwayo and Zibhebhu were immediately at war with each other. Zibhebhu was the best general in Zululand and, with his staunch ally, Hamu kaNzibe of the Ngenetsheni people, assisted by some white freebooters, soon gained the upper hand. On 21 July 1883, at the battle of oNdini, they were victorious, scattering the

*Illustration from the* Graphic, *10 March 1883, of Cetshwayo at his installation in January 1883.*

uSuthu and killing most of Cetshwayo's senior councillors and generals. Cetshwayo took refuge in the Nkandla forest in the Reserve Territory. Threatened by Zibhebhu's advance, he fled to British protection at Eshowe, where he died on 8 February 1884, poisoned, the uSuthu believed, by Zibhebhu.

Dinuzulu, Cetshwayo's teenaged heir, continued the struggle. But the British in the Reserve subdued uSuthu resistance there and Zibhebhu retained the upper hand in central Zululand. Repeatedly worsted, the desperate Dinuzulu forged an agreement with Boers from the South African Republic, which had regained its independence from Britain in 1881 at the conclusion of the First Anglo-Boer War. The Boers recognised Dinuzulu as the new Zulu king on 21 May 1884, and with their military assistance he crushed Zibhebhu at the battle of Tshaneni on 5 June 1884 and drove him in his turn into the Reserve. The Boers exacted an enormous reward for their help. On 16 August 1884 Dinuzulu ceded to them the northwestern two-thirds of that part of Zululand still outside the Reserve. The Boers proclaimed this territory the New Republic with its capital at the tiny village of Vryheid. The Zulu living in the New Republic – and they included some of the royal house's staunchest supporters, like the abaQulusi – found themselves instantaneously reduced to labour tenants on the farms that the Boers allocated to themselves.

The situation in Zululand continued to be unstable and turbulent. Britain was at last persuaded to intervene, not primarily out of concern for the plight of the Zulu people, but because its imperial position was threatened by German interest in the

Zululand coast and by the landlocked Boers' evident intention of pushing through Zululand to the sea. On 19 May 1887 the Reserve Territory and eastern Zululand (the rump of Zululand outside the New Republic under Dinuzulu's shaky control) were annexed as the British Colony of Zululand. Officials recruited from Natal were appointed to administer the new colony, which was to be run like one large African reserve, modelled on the locations set up in Natal after 1846 to control the African population and form reservoirs of labour. Chiefs, including Dinuzulu, were reduced to subordinate paid officials, and the whole administration was financed by a hut tax imposed on the people. However, to the discontent of Natal colonists, Zululand was not opened to white settlement.

Dinuzulu and his uncles found it difficult to accept their greatly reduced status in British Zululand, and querulously withheld their co-operation from the new administration. In order to bring them into line, but as an alternative to calling in the British troops of the Natal garrison, the Zululand officials adopted the short-sighted and disastrous expedient of restoring the uSuthus' arch-enemy, Zibhebhu, to his chiefdom to act as a counter-weight. His return in late 1887 inevitably sparked off renewed unrest. By April 1888 the uSuthu were in open rebellion, taking on both the British troops that were rushed in, and Zibhebhu's Mandlakazi and other collaborators like the Buthelezi people. By the end of September, after several sharp engagements, including an initial and ignominious repulse for the British at Ceza Mountain on 2 June, the British had dispersed the uSuthu from their strongholds and subdued the country with the passage of several punitive columns. Although defeated, Dinuzulu and the uSuthu had achieved at least one satisfaction, for at Nongoma on 23 June they had once again routed the hated Mandlakazi.

The ringleaders of the uSuthu rebellion were tried for high treason at Eshowe and found guilty in April 1889. Dinuzulu and two of his uncles were removed to St Helena to serve their sentences. A chastened Zululand administration then set about pacifying the colony and disentangling the land claims of the rival factions that remained a potent cause of unrest. It was believed that the return of Dinuzulu would help restore stability, but his restoration was strenuously opposed by the Natal colonists who insisted that it be coupled with the throwing open of Zululand to white settlement. Eventually, a deal was struck with the British government. On 30 December 1897 the Colony of Zululand (including British-ruled Ingwavuma and Tongaland) were annexed to Natal as the Province of Zululand. As a result of the findings of the Zululand Lands Delimitation Commission of 1902–04, two-fifths of the best land in Zululand was set aside, from 31 January 1906, for white occupation. The Zulu occupiers of the land at the time either became labour tenants on the white farms, or were removed to the remaining three-fifths of Zululand that had been declared African reserves. Thus the young men of Zululand, who in their *amabutho* had once served their king, became migrant labourers on farms and mines and in the towns of a white-ruled, industrialising South Africa.

When Dinuzulu returned to Zululand in January 1898 as part of the general settlement, it was no longer as a king, but merely as a 'government induna' and chief over the uSuthu locations Numbers 1 and 2. Nevertheless, many amaZulu persisted in recognising him as their legitimate king, and during the Union and apartheid years his heirs continued to provide a living link with the precolonial Zulu kingdom, and to act as a focus for a renewed sense of Zulu national consciousness, pride and unity.

## References

Brookes, E.H. and Webb, C. de B. 1965. *A History of Natal*. Pietermaritzburg: University of Natal Press.

Bryant, A.T. 1929. *Olden Times in Zululand and Natal*. London: Longmans, Green.

———. 1964. *A History of the Zulu and Neighbouring Tribes*. Cape Town: Struik.

Duminy, A. and Guest, B., eds. 1989. *Natal and Zululand from Earliest Times to 1910: A New History*. Pietermaritzburg: University of Natal Press and Shuter & Shooter.

Fuze, M.M. (translated by H.C. Lugg and edited by A.T. Cope). 1979. *The Black People and Whence They Came: A Zulu View*. Pietermaritzburg: University of Natal Press and Durban: Killie Campbell Africana Library.

Fynn, H.F. (edited by J. Stuart and D. McK. Malcolm). 1969. *The Diary of Henry Francis Fynn*. Pietermaritzburg: Shuter & Shooter.

Gibson, J.Y. 1911. *The Story of the Zulus*. London: Longmans.

Guy, J. 1998. *The Destruction of the Zulu Kingdom: The Civil War in Zululand, 1879–1884*. Pietermaritzburg: University of Natal Press.

———. 2001. *View Across the River: Harriet Colenso and the Zulu Struggle against Imperialism*. Oxford: James Currey.

Isaacs, N. (edited by L. Herman and P. Kirby). 1970. *Travels and Adventures in Eastern Africa*. Cape Town: Struik.

Laband, J. 1995. *Rope of Sand: The Rise and Fall of the Zulu Kingdom in the Nineteenth Century*. Johannesburg: Jonathan Ball.

———. 2001. *The Atlas of the Later Zulu Wars 1883–1888*. Pietermaritzburg: University of Natal Press.

Laband, J. and Thompson, P. 2000. *The Illustrated Guide to the Anglo-Zulu War*. Pietermaritzburg: University of Natal Press.

Leverton, B.J.T., ed. 1984, 1989, 1990, 1992. *Records of Natal, 1823–1839, South African Archival Records: Important Cape Documents, Vols. IV–VII*. Pretoria: Government Printer.

Lugg, H.C. 1949. *Historic Natal and Zululand*. Pietermaritzburg: Shuter & Shooter.

Samuelson, R.C.A. 1929. *Long, Long Ago*. Durban: Knox.

Shamase, M.Z. 1996. *Zulu Potentates from the Earliest to Zwelithini KaBhekuzulu*. Durban: S.M. Publications.

Taylor, S. 1994. *Shaka's Children: A History of the Zulu People*. London: HarperCollins.

Webb, C. de B. and Wright, J.B., eds. 1976, 1979, 1982, 1986, 2001. *The James Stuart Archive of Recorded Oral Evidence Relating to the History of the Zulu and Neighbouring Peoples*. Pietermaritzburg: University of Natal Press and Durban: Killie Campbell Collection.

# Chapter 9

# Zulu Nationalist Literary Representations of King Dingane

SIFISO NDLOVU

IN THE EARLY and middle years of the twentieth century King Dingane became a touchstone for isiZulu-speaking academics such as Bhambatha W. Vilakazi and Sibusiso Nyembezi. They were engaged in constructing a view of the Zulu past that overturned disparaging historical stereotypes presented by segregationist-minded people. The stringent restrictions on free speech imposed by national governments led Vilakazi and Nyembezi to write historical novels, many of them in isiZulu. Through such fictional accounts, which were based on actual primary evidence, they explored the legacies of Zulu kings and managed to bypass censors who looked for militant contemporary political pronouncements.[1] Employing Zulu oral sources, Vilakazi and Nyembezi grappled in particular with the ambiguous reputation of King Dingane to show that his reign was indeed full of machinations, but not for reasons cited by white authorities promoting the view that the 'civilised' voortrekker founders conquered their 'savage' Zulu rivals.

In keeping with other erudite African intellectuals such as Herbert and Rolfes Dhlomo, Bhambatha Vilakazi attributed his interest in intellectual endeavours to reading newspapers infused with the spirit of African and Zulu nationalism.[2] He remarked:

> It is very interesting to study the trend of thought espoused by Native papers and sometimes to discover how editors (Dhlomo brothers, Thema etc.) hold together the minds of the writers of their papers . . . I have always studied the style of thought of this wonderful journal [*Ilanga lase Natal*] (I call it wonderful because it is an unsurpassed effort of a single-headed Native, edited and supported by the Natives and thus proving native capacity and genius when given a chance) . . . Then comes R.R.R. [Rolfes] Dhlomo who has long patronised the paper and whose writings up to this day still hold good. One thing I like with this writer is that he is . . . a novelist with an open eye to everything that happens round him. He is good in political reports and criticisms.[3]

Vilakazi also turned to oral traditions to expand his knowledge of literary arts, especially when advancing his project to explore King Dingane.[4] Thus, one might say that Vilakazi was destined for cross-cultural successes – successes that elevated Zulu writers into academic settings buffeted by apartheid race politics – for he learned to straddle the formal education of colonial societies and traditional knowledge of Zulu communities.[5]

Bhambatha Wallet Vilakazi was born on 6 January 1906 to Christian parents in the coastal (American Board) Groutville Missionary Station north of Durban. He attended St Francis College at Mariannhill outside Pietermaritzburg, where he obtained a teacher's certificate in 1923 and then began his career as an instructor in the classroom at the Ixopo Catholic Seminary at the age of seventeen.[6] These early schooling and professional experiences propelled Vilakazi in 1936 to the position of teaching assistant in the University of the Witwatersrand's (Wits) Department of African Studies. While he was the first African person to lecture at a predominantly white university, his selection stirred controversy in academic and government circles.[7] It was still unheard of to offer a qualified black person the duties of a junior faculty position, which could entail teaching white students.[8] During the hullabaloo that trailed his appointment and tenure at Wits in the 1940s, no white authority complained that Vilakazi's job title, 'teaching assistantship', would have been an insult to white university lecturers with his accomplishments.[9]

Vilakazi was among the first black intellectuals to undertake research in Zulu storytelling, oral traditions and poetry. His 1945 doctoral dissertation, 'Oral and Written Literature in Nguni', challenged many stereotypes, among them that Zulu *izibongo* (praises) were inferior sources and could not be used in scholarly analysis. He hoped that his thesis would highlight the importance of the Zulu past in a racially divided country. In so doing he wanted to diversify the production of (historical) knowledge in a period of mounting political repression, when white academics also jealously safeguarded liberal, settler and Afrikaner nationalist historiographies. Vilakazi signalled such intentions in the 1930s after finishing an article on 'Bantu Views of the Great Trek', which he submitted for publication in an Institute of Race Relations journal examining the centenary of the expansionary Boer exodus from the Cape. His piece espoused radical views on South African citizenship and King Dingane's defensive reactions that culminated in the battle of 'Blood River',[10] but it was not included in the September 1938 special edition of the Race Relations Journal.

Vilakazi's unpublished article characterised whites as invaders and described the movement of the voortrekkers into Zulu territory as driven by racist imperialism:

> [T]here is no place for a black man in the Voortrekkers' scheme save when the black man prefers to lose his self. The same spirit has coloured the whole political situation of South Africa so that any measures at suppressing the

black man we ascribe them to the Voortrekker spirit. Perhaps today the word Voortrekker has changed into 'Afrikaner' and sometimes we say 'Dutch', for everything adverse to Bantu progress and interest.[11]

Vilakazi contended that the 'Voortrekker spirit' violated the sovereignty of King Dingane, the ruler of an African state recognised throughout Natal and across the Drakensburg.[12] When the voortrekkers descended into present-day Colenso and Weenen and began hunting in forbidden areas, the isiZulu-speaking people of the invaded region – namely Mchunu followers, the abasemaMbedwini, and scattered remnants of Qwabe chiefs – complained to King Dingane.[13]

If the voortrekkers sought to be honorary citizens of King Dingane's state, as custom allowed south of the Thukela River, they would be prohibited from owning or selling territory or independently granting settlement rights to any alien tribe or foreigners, whether black, white or brown. Moreover, Vilakazi argued, voortrekker chiefs like Gert Maritz could only exercise jurisdiction over land after accepting the obligation to offer tribute (*ukukhonza*) to their ruler, King Dingane. It was a privilege, therefore, for the voortrekkers to dwell on soil belonging to the Zulu nation.[14] Here Vilakazi evoked precolonial laws of land holding spelled out by Socwatsha kaPhaphu in an interview with the Natal colonial ethnographer James Stuart:

> In old days it was customary for very large kraals to be constructed. This was done for mutual protection against sudden attacks. These kraals were called amanxuluma. Hence they were really villages. Thus people lived together in large numbers, and although the district was a small one it supported a large population . . . A feature of that Zulu government is that the abamnumzane living under a given chief all exercised property rights over the land they occupied so much that if a newcomer applies to live under the chief and gave him his alliance, the chief is obliged to make special arrangement with the particular headman . . . The headman in question will object to accommodate the newcomer unless he submits and konza[s] [offers loyalty and tribute] to the headman himself . . . The land, as a matter of fact, all belongs to the king, but the headman of each tribe has rights which in practice [are] respected . . . as the king put it *ulahl'isihlangu sami na? Ati ikon'indoda ati 'ifika kumuntu itelwúmtwalo, ihlomísihlango sayo, iti, 'Ngetuleni'besekutiwa 'Dhlula na?' Kungatiwa 'etula' na 'yakalapha' na. Kanti wena ungambula ingubo ngiyembatileyo na? Ngoba izwi lakwaZulu ukuthi 'amadoda ingubo yokwembatha'. Abese uyaka njalo, ukuba sekupendula inkosi.*[15]

An English translation of the isiZulu passage above shows close parallels with Socwatsha kaPhaphu's oral testimony on the history of land use in the period immediately before Europeans arrived in KwaZulu-Natal. The regent or chief,

Socwatsha contended, parcelled out territory on behalf of the ancestors, the living, and those yet to be born in a recognised political region.

Vilakazi asserted that the Zulu royal house was haunted by the prophecy of King Shaka, who was said to have predicted the white conquest of his land. Whether the Zulu founder's dramatic forecast could be fabricated did not give pause to exponents of the prophecy story such as the Natal colonial ethnographer James Stuart, who elevated Shaka's prediction into fact; it could be argued that versions of this prophecy supported British imperial officials seeking a preordained justification for their invasion of late-nineteenth-century Zululand in the name of protecting 'civilisation' from 'savagery'. Whatever the case, it is remarkable that Shaka's so-called prophecy appealed to writers across the racial divide from Afrikaner nationalists and James Stuart to Rolfes Dhlomo and Vilakazi.[16]

In Vilakazi's account, King Dingane was obsessed by Shaka's prophecy, viewing 'the approach of white people in such numbers . . . [as] his death-warrant'.[17] What exacerbated King Dingane's fears, Vilakazi believed, was Piet Retief's disregard of traditions governing the Zulu royal house. When Retief's party arrived at King Dingane's, it was initially treated with hospitality, but as soon as the voortrekkers entered the king's palace with their guns and horses, Zulu suspicion intensified. Other breaches of royal etiquette doomed Retief and his party. After the voortrekkers had got drunk on beer at that night's festivities, they forgot to exit through the main entrance of the royal enclosure. Their massive horses were also alarmingly unfamiliar, having no horns and cloven hoofs like Zulu cattle and thus possibly resembling witchcraft familiars. At night the voortrekker horses roamed about, although it was strictly prohibited for any stock to wander after the sun went down. In these circumstances, the king's bodyguards became increasingly restive and protested that the uncontrolled, insolent behaviour of the strangers suggested that they were in fact agents of sorcerers.[18]

In *Body and Mind in Zulu Medicine*, the anthropologist Harriet Ngubane elaborates on the historical and cultural implications of sorcery in past Zulu society:

> (Ama)Zulu believe that a sorcerer was 'created or moulded with an evil heart' (*Wabunjwa ngenhliziyo embi*) . . . He harms people for no apparent reasons. He keeps baboons as familiars. When he visits homesteads at night to perform his evil acts, he rides naked on these baboons, facing backwards. Because he is thoroughly evil-hearted, on such nocturnal visits he also scatters medicines along pathways to harm anyone who may pass by. He is a danger to the community at large and is feared . . .[19]

Indeed, the earliest Zulu story of voortrekkers manoeuvring as witches emerges from an old tradition discussed in *Izindatyana Zabantu*, a signal collection of Zulu oral traditions that anticipated James Stuart's ethnographic pursuits by four decades.

William Ngidi and Bishop Colenso authored *Izindatyana Zabantu* in 1859, barely twenty years after King Dingane's death. A section titled '*Indaba yokubulawa kuka Piti*' highlights the deeply troubled relationship between King Dingane and Piet Retief:

> *Bafika abalungu . . . Wati (uDingane) bayolala lapaya kwaNkosinkulu ngaphandle esangweni . . . Kwati ebusuku abalungu bathi abawuhaqe uMgungundlovu. Babeyate abawuhaqe, bawuhaqe, wasala isinkeke, basebabuyela kona kwaNkosinkulu lapa belele kona.*[20]

> The whites arrived . . . Dingane ordered them to sleep outside the gate near to kwaNkosinkulu . . . During the evening the whites circled uMgungundlovu on a reconnaissance mission, and returned to kwaNkosinkulu as soon as they completed their mission.

In an unprecedented fashion, Vilakazi interpreted Retief's 'undisciplined activity [as] . . . mainly responsible for the massacre of . . . his followers'.[21]

**Vilakazi's handling of King Dingane's deadly retribution**
In his unpublished 1938 journal article, Vilakazi asserted that South African blacks had long paid the penalty for King Dingane's handling of Piet Retief, especially after the battle of Blood River on 16 December: the Zulu royal house lost hundreds of thousands of acres and a large measure of its cherished sovereignty.[22] The Zulu military defeat at Blood River also propelled another wave of white subjugations of black people, not simply in Zululand but throughout the African continent. Vilakazi lamented:

> [E]very year on Dec.16th Dingaan's Day there are demonstrations in South Africa, showing the prowess of the white man over the black man. We are told that this is a holiday, a day of worship . . . We know that the Voortrekkers have done very little or nothing for the Bantu in South Africa. They cannot take up a stand and pride themselves over our country as the purveyors of civilisation in Africa. We know that other bodies came along with altruistic and philanthropic motives at the background for African penetration. We know too that there have come other bodies with the dominant motives of predatory profits. Germany occupied East and West African areas for their minerals, diamonds and stock raising potentialities. France took North Africa with her eyes upon zinc, iron, and agricultural lands. Belgium seized the Congo for its rubber and ivory. And Britain seized upon Egypt and the Sudan for their cotton and minerals, and occasion for the seizure of the Orange Free State and the Transvaal was furnished by diamond fields and the gold. The interpretation of the word 'Voortrekkers' to-day has finally changed in a Bantu-man's mind.

> It means all those who prey upon and exploit us because of our ignorance and
> lack of opportunities to advance.[23]

Vaulting from Dingane's reign to the middle of the twentieth century, Vilakazi's article acknowledged that the voortrekkers' great-grandchildren had capable leaders in Jan Smuts and Jan Hofmeyr, among others, who might be able to promote some racial understanding. The author also considered that a strong African leader was needed to advance the cause of African nationalism beyond Zulu borders, as General Hertzog had done for Afrikaner nationalism after the Pact government gained power in South Africa following the 1924 all-white national election.[24] By the time Vilakazi wrote his 1945 doctorate, he had changed his pro-Dingane stance and, by implication, sharpened his view that the remaking of Zulu nationalism would require a more critical and comprehensive understanding of the past. One can attribute this shift to Vilakazi's more rigorous gathering of historical evidence. He interrogated a broader array of Zulu oral traditions and *izibongo*, which he ranged far and wide to collect. He elaborated on his fieldwork methodology:

> The investigation of *izibongo* and myth lore was not done in districts where the Nguni live under primitive conditions only, but the detribalised man in town was also studied . . . I owe much to Mr C.J. Mpanza, secretary of the Zulu Society, who placed the library of the Society at my disposal for use, and also introduced me to many chiefs of Natal and Zululand, to the Headman Daniel Vilakazi of Zululand and accompanied me to Chief Bokwe of the Mandlakazi, Amos kaMaseni Gumede who took me to uMthandeni, the Qwabe royal kraal, Mr A.B.C. Xaba who was the Headmaster of the Paulpietersburg Government School, rendered me very valuable service among the abaQulusi of Mnkabayi. Mr Xaba is responsible for all records made, of the poetry of womenfolk. [25]

The traditions he transcribed during this phase of primary research included oral accounts of King Dingane, which dismissed Shaka's usurper as an irresponsible coward who could not prevent the deaths of Piet Retief and his party. Many of these traditions portrayed the king as a weak regent easily manipulated by female royals. As a result, Vilakazi increasingly investigated the puppet masters controlling King Dingane, particularly Zulu Queen Regent Mnkabayi. As Jantshi kaNongila noted, 'Dingane was made king by Mnkabayi'.[26] Queen Mnkabayi was seen as the power behind King Dingane's throne for she was said to have orchestrated the massacre of the voortrekkers,[27] urging Ndlela, then prime minister, to give the order to 'Bulalani abathakathi, kill the wizards (Boers)'.[28]

    Yet contrary to histories written by some white historians of the time, Vilakazi exonerated King Dingane in Retief's final hour. Vilakazi asserted that the king was powerless to make decisions because he was confined to his sacred room undergoing the *ukweshwama* ceremony, a process of spiritual and bodily rejuvenation. Vilakazi based his argument on the lyrics of a period war song:

> *Zwan' isidumo sempi*
> *Inkos' inqab' ukuphum' ekhaya*
> *Ndaba yempi,*
> *Mababoboz' igazi*
> *Hlab'abezizwe, Ho yaye!*[29]

> Hear thou the battle cry
> The king won't come out of his hut
> O for the glory of war
> Let them spill blood,
> Stab thou the aliens, Ho yaye!

He further postulated another motive for the execution of the voortrekker party, claiming that the most prominent women in the royal palace, who thought that Retief's followers represented evil, commanded Zulu regiments to attack the visitors. This assertion was supported by Vilakazi's deconstruction of praises that chronicle how after the killing of Retief and his party the regiments responsible for this deed were seen as 'unclean, and soiled with bad blood' and sent away to abaQulusi lands, Queen Regent Mnkabayi's area that includes present-day Ladysmith, Newcastle and Vryheid.[30]

Many of the oral traditions Vilakazi collected for his unpublished doctoral thesis provided an anti-King Dingane perspective, especially the verses from Qwabe and Mandlakazi voices, as they were enemies of the Zulu royal house. While Vilakazi also read the Zulu primers published by James Stuart and the Catholic missionary and ethnographer A.T. Bryant, two important sources in the anti-Dingane camp, he also consulted rarely cited Zulu oral testimonies that rationalised the killing of Retief as an act of defending the Zulu nation: these latter testimonies were presented to Vilakazi by ranking members of the Zulu Society, an elite group of black isiZulu-speaking intellectuals promoting the concept of 'Zuluness'.[31] The Zulu Society sources lent considerable scholarly weight to Vilakazi's conclusions that Queen Regent Mnkabayi and other 'masculinised' royal women were responsible for manipulating King Dingane during the first wave of voortrekker encroachments. A fascinating comment follows on how Zulu women wielding power in a royal patriarchal setting embraced the cultural uniform of prominent men. Socwatsha kaPhaphu explained, detailing the Queen's penchant for things male and martial: 'The question of (Dingane's) succession was referred to Mnkabayi . . . She dressed as a man, [so] her identity could not be detected . . . She had a white shield with a black spot, assegais, . . . [and] she *dondoloza* [walked with a stick like an old man].'[32]

The revolutionary nature of Vilakazi's investigation into King Dingane and his female handlers provided inspiration to other emerging Zulu intellectuals, among them his own protégé, the late Sibusiso Nyembezi, who would continue his mentor's path-breaking research into oral traditions and *izibongo* until his death at the end of the twentieth century.

### Sibusiso Nyembezi: Scholar of oral traditions and King Dingane's history

Born on 5 December 1919 in Babanango, Zululand, Sibusiso Nyembezi trained as a teacher at the American Board Mission Adams College in Amanzimtoti. He obtained an honours degree from Wits in 1946, with a dissertation on 'The Historical Background of the *Izibongo* of the Zulu Military Age'. A version of this undergraduate thesis was published in a 1948 edition of the Wits journal, *African Studies*, doubtless helping Nyembezi to gain a post vacated by Dr B.W. Vilakazi, who died in 1948. Nyembezi went on to complete his masters degree in 1950 at Wits and lectured there until 1954, when he accepted the chair of Bantu languages at Fort Hare University in the Eastern Cape.

Like Vilakazi before him, Nyembezi undertook research trips in Zululand to collect oral traditions and *izibongo*. He contacted all sections of traditional society, from commoners to members of the Zulu royal family. He chronicled his odyssey:

> *Kuthe sengiphumile esikoleni, sengifundisa, ngaba nesifiso sokuba ngiphenye indaba yezibongo. Kodwa akukho lutho engalwenza kwaze kwaba ngunyaka ka 1945. Ngalowomnyaka ngangiseGoli, eWitwatersrand University. Kwathi sixoxa noMufi uDr B. W. Vilakazi, ngafumanisa ukuthi naye wudaba olwalusenhliziyweni yakhe lolu . . . Kuthe ngonyaka ka-1946, ngahambela ezindaweni ezithize kwaZulu, ngifunda ngoZulu . . . Ukufika kwami kwaNongoma ngafica umfundisi uShange . . . Ngasuka kwaNongoma ngaya kwaSokesimbone kuMufi uMshiyeni kaDinuzulu.*[33]

> After I had finished my formal schooling, during the time when I was employed as a professional teacher I had a wish to pursue research on *izibongo*. Nothing transpired until 1945 when I was at the Witwatersrand University in Johannesburg. It was during a conversation I had with the late Dr B.W. Vilakazi that I discovered that the latter had a keen interest and was committed to this issue . . . In 1946 I visited certain areas in kwaZulu, researching on amaZulu . . . When I arrived in kwaNongoma I met the Rev. Shange . . . From kwaNongoma I proceeded to kwaSokesimbone to meet the late (Prince) Mshiyeni kaDinuzulu . . .

Nyembezi's early fieldwork focused on three major episodes of King Dingane's biography: the king's rise to the throne, the arrival of voortrekkers in Zulu territory, and the king's fall. Nyembezi identified characteristics that he believed contributed to the king's enigmatic personality, among them Dingane's range of creative, introverted, indecisive, and unpredictable behaviour, as well as his brutal, cautious and cunning manoeuvres.[34] Following the analytical line established by Vilakazi, Nyembezi argued that King Dingane needed the support of Queen Regent Mnkabayi to seize the throne and purge rivals within the royal family, including many of his own siblings.[35]

Nyembezi was among the first isiZulu-speaking scholars to deconstruct *izibongo* consistently in order to tease out the biographical details of Zulu paramounts. For example, he identified key words in King Dingane's praises, *'uVezi, uNonyanda, uMgabadeli, owagabadela inkundla yakwaBulawayo'* (Vezi the huge one, the daring one who dared the courtyard of Bulawayo), to show that the king's accession followed the audacious assassination of Shaka at kwaBulawayo, which is still a source of controversy.[36] Most importantly, Nyembezi argued for King Dingane the 'producer' (uVezi, a procreator) because he killed the 'vicious' King Shaka and so 'produced' the people. His analysis also made it clear that King Dingane was by no means a better monarch than his predecessor; they both killed the very people they 'produced'.[37] Nyembezi demonstrates this line of reasoning with the verse, *'Umvuso omnyama wawo Sikhakha, Ovusela abantu ukuhlatswa'* (the black awakener of the kraal of Sikhakha, Who awakened people for slaughtering).

Furthermore, Nyembezi regarded King Dingane and King Shaka in a similar light; both regents decided to perpetuate bloodletting rather than impose a period of tranquillity.[38] But on this point Nyembezi distinguished King Shaka as more responsible for his own terrible fate. The Zulu founder's long-suffering siblings were not murderous by nature, but were made into murderers by their fear of King Shaka's 'narrow-minded' cruelty, which did not spare family members:

> To him the (male) children represented trouble. Whenever a child was born to one of his 'sisters' it was killed. Sometimes the woman was killed even before she gave birth. Thus it does seem strange that a man so careful of what may prove his own undoing should have spared some of his brothers. He little knew that his final exit would be engineered by these selfsame brothers.[39]

Nyembezi wanted to place King Dingane's action in the historical context of 'dictatorial' King Shaka, who ventured into overly ambitious murderous campaigns on the eve of his assassination in 1828. Immediately after the Zulu *amabutho* returned from fighting an amaMpondo army in the eastern Cape, King Shaka ordered these physically drained soldiers to march inland and battle King Soshangane's military.[40] King Shaka's brothers, who were part of the beleaguered Zulu forces, decided to disobey, suspecting that the king planned to eliminate them by sending them into the jaws of Soshangane's formidable soldiers. The Zulu princes then deserted and, back in the royal homestead kwaBulawayo, plotted to eliminate King Shaka. Nyembezi positioned Prince Dingane as a military general reluctant to take on Soshangane in what appeared to him to be a suicidal battle, and therefore chose to be '*uMashiya impi yakhe*', literally a deserter of his army. Nyembezi suggests that King Dingane behaved in a prudently cautious manner and was honoured for his action with the following *izibongo*, '*uMalunguza izindonga kade ukuwela*' (he who peers into gullies before crossing).[41] Other writers and historians present an entirely different event to explain the meaning of '*uMashiya impi yakhe*'. The Zulu nationalist author Petros Lamula, for one, interprets '*uMashiya impi yakhe*' to mean that King Dingane was a coward who left his regiments in dire straits after being defeated by his brother Prince Mpande in 1840.[42]

The view of King Dingane 'peering' before acting, Nyembezi countered, elevated Dingane to the highest position in the Zulu nation, especially after he and his brother Mhlangana arranged to have Shaka stabbed to death in 1828 – only to confront the reality that the throne accommodated just one of them. Mhlangana enjoyed a large following, and for King Dingane to eliminate his brother straight away might have sparked serious civil bloodshed. Therefore, a more cunning plan was devised, which received the approval of Queen Regent Mnkabayi.[43] According to Nyembezi's interpretation of Zulu oral traditions, the Zulu princes Dingane and Mhlangana walked to a nearby river and washed before one of them was appointed to be King Shaka's successor. Only Regent Mnkabayi's men joined the two royal bathers, and, carrying out the plan, her loyalists drowned Mhlangana. A story was then quickly circulated that whilst swimming Mhlangana had been seized by a severe cramp and failed to make it back to shore. The scenario behind King Dingane's ascension is memorialised thus: '*Isiziba esisemavivane Dingane, Isiziba esinzonzo sinzonzobele, Siminzise umuntu ethi uyageza, Waze washona ngesicoco*' (The pool at Mavivane Dingane, the deep pool is still, it drowned a person when he attempts to wash, and sunk even with his headring).[44]

Nyembezi also portrayed the king as a mysterious introvert who eventually succumbed to his worst weaknesses. In this regard Dingane was the opposite of King Shaka: '*Singqungqu kakhulumi, kanamlomo, kanjengaShaka, yena owaqeda umuzi ngokunkenkeza*' (The reserved one he does not speak, he has no mouth, he is not like Shaka, who used to finish a kraal speaking). Combing through other royal praises, Nyembezi found that King Dingane's reserve was also likened to that of a goat's silent, skittish disposition: '*Imbuzi kaDambuza, Ayibambe ngendlebe yabekezela, Ayinjengaka Mklaka ngase Ntshobozeni, yena ayimbambengendlebe, Yadabula yaqeda amadoda*'[45] (the goat of Dambuza that he held by the ears and was patient, unlike Mklaka's from nearby Ntshobozeni which though it was held by its ears it escaped and finished off men). The jerky movement of the goat alluded to the unpredictable nature of King Dingane who sometimes gave a false impression of himself: '*uVezi bathi umoya mnandi ngokunuka inyama*' (Vezi they say is sweet breathed by smelling meat). Nyembezi suggested that these praise words highlighted

King Dingane's deceptive qualities, which like the smell of meat only temporarily suppressed bad breath.

In Nyembezi's book *Izibongo Zamakhosi*, published in 1958, King Dingane emerges as the chosen hereditary Zulu leader, exercising rights to the throne as the proper heir to Shaka's father, Senzangakhona. Nyembezi based his argument on the fact that Queen Mpikase, Prince Dingane's mother, was King Senzangakhona's eldest wife. Nyembezi questioned whether Senzangakhona could have favoured his eldest son, Prince Sigujana whose mother was Queen Bhibi, over Mpikase's eldest son, Dingane. This patriarchal manoeuvring in the formative years of Prince Dingane's upbringing, Nyembezi speculated, must have influenced the later anxieties of the second Zulu king and his appetite for revenge, as the following verses begin to illustrate:

> *Ngazo zombili izindlela*
> *Niyobikela uNsimbini noMahlekeza*
> *Ukuthi abazi yini ukuthi*
> *uVezi yisizwa kubi?*
> *Angahl' athath'isihlang' asihlom' umgobo*
> *Ame ngas' emnyango kwaMpikase*
> *NakwaBhibhi, kuze kus'evevezela*
> *Engasalalanga nabuthongo?* [46]

> By using the two pathways
> go and notify Nsimbini and Mahlekeza
> that Vezi has heard the bad news
> He can therefore arm himself with a
> shield and assegai and post himself
> at Mpikase's and Bhibhi doorsteps, until sunrise
> he would be shaking
> because he would not have had a nap.

Nyembezi, like Vilakazi before him, envisioned Dingane driven by both the dread of being usurped and the determination to seek retribution for any real or perceived slight. In *Izibongo Zamakhosi*, Nyembezi attempted to show that when the voortrekkers came to the outskirts of the Zulu heartland to seize territory they triggered King Dingane's lifelong fear of being insulted in the most fundamental way through the loss of acquired power.[47] Thus did the white newcomers provoke King Dingane to act swiftly to safeguard his people's respect for a Zulu regent who could defend his nation's most cherished asset, land.

A unifying symbolic thread ran throughout Nyembezi's writings in *Izibongo Zamakhosi*, a project that also aimed to bolster black struggles against racism and apartheid. As Eliot Zondi, author of the influential Zulu nationalist exposé on King

Shaka's death, *Ukufa kukaShaka*, indicated, by the 1950s Nyembezi was a member of the African National Congress (ANC), working with Zulu nationalists like Professor Z.K. Matthews.[48] Nyembezi's representations of Dingane's decisive reaction to the invasion of the voortrekkers would, the author hoped, demonstrate to all South Africans that blacks were more than capable of defending their way of life. In this respect, the studies by Vilakazi and Nyembezi of King Dingane's complex reign aimed to provide a major signpost in the busy roadmap to liberation.

## Notes

1.  S.M. Ndlovu, 'The Changing Perceptions of King Dingane in Historical Literature: A Case Study in the Construction of Historical Knowledge in 19th and 20th Century South African History' (Ph.D. diss., University of the Witwatersrand, 2001), Chapter 5. Censors surveyed education boards, publishing houses and missionary schools. Examples of other historical novels on King Dingane include the xiTsonga booklet by T.M. Rikhotso, *Dingane: King of the Zulu* (Braamfontein: Sasavona, 1982).
2.  See for example, T. Couzens and N. Visser, eds. *H.I.E. Dhlomo: Collected Works* (Johannesburg: Ravan Press, 1985); *The New African: A Study of the Life and Work of H.I.E. Dhlomo* (Johannesburg: Ravan Press, 1985); B. Peterson, 'Monarchs, Missionaries and Intellectuals: Redemption and Revolution in South African Theatre' (Ph.D. diss., University of the Witwatersrand, 1997), p. 106 and N. Masilela, 'New African Intellectuals: Theorising a Structure of Intellectual and Literary History: The Cultural Role of African Newspapers in South Africa' (unpublished paper, n.d.).
3.  B.W. Vilakazi, *Ilanga lase Natal*, 17 March 1933.
4.  B.W. Vilakazi, 'Oral and Written Literature in Nguni' (Ph.D. diss., University of the Witwatersrand, 1945).
5.  See Peterson on Vilakazi in 'Monarchs, Missionaries'.
6.  For an eloquent description of Vilakazi's life influences and contributions, see his obituary in *Inkundla yaBantu*, 2 September 1946, written by the notable Jordan Ngubane. I excerpt a portion here:
    [A]t the time of the Bambata upheaval a boy was born at Groutville Station. Later he was known as Benedict Wallet Vilakazi. But his 'home name' as the Zulu saying is, was Bambata. Now, according to Zulu tradition, one's name shapes one character and destiny. However that may be, the boy Bambata was told not only the glorious saga of his namesake, but many other stirring historical and mythological stories of his people. Young Vilakazi, like most Missionary station children attended school as a matter of course. In those days education meant almost inevitably a teacher's course, a segregated inferior course improved by 'experts' on Education and African Affairs. Vilakazi followed tradition and became a teacher. At this time he was not aware of the divine smouldering fire in him that was to burn his soul out and give him fame and fortune. Like other young men of his day he delighted in acquiring a good physique, dressed well, played football, and coming from a musical family . . . he conducted choirs and played organ music. The changes came late when he was called to decide on two teaching posts offered . . . He decided on the rural post. It was the turning point – it was Ixopo – he was reborn. He began to take interest in private studies and oral traditions and his specialisation in African studies at University. Some people thought this foolish as the fashion then was to major in traditional subjects such as English, History, Ethics . . .
    See also J. Ngubane, 'Three Famous Authors I Knew: B.W. Vilakazi *imbongi yesizwe jikelele*, Dr Benedict Vilakazi', *Inkundla yaBantu*, April, First Fortnight, 1946.
7.  University of the Witwatersrand, B.W. Vilakazi File Misce. C/17/35 on 'Appointment of Native Language Assistant – Department of Bantu Studies'.
8.  Vilakazi's conditions of employment:

'(a) in regard to status: that this post of Language Assistant, decided upon by way of experiment, is not equivalent to the position of a Lecturer, either in status and privileges or in emolument; (b) in regard to authority and discipline: that all formal instruction in regular classes in which the Language Assistant is called upon to demonstrate, will be conducted by the Head of the department. Whilst the Language Assistant will also be available for giving informal assistance to students in the use of Zulu and Xhosa, no student will be compelled to avail himself for such assistance; nor will the Language Assistant have any disciplinary authority in virtue of his position over students who make use of this informal help.'
See University of the Witwatersrand, B.W. Vilakazi File Misce. S/48/35.

9. Peterson, 'Monarchs, Missionaries' and B. Murray, *Wits, the Early Years: A History of the University of the Witwatersrand, Johannesburg and its Precursors 1896–1938* (Johannesburg: Witwatersrand University Press, 1982).

10. Africans refer to this event, which took place on 16 December 1838, as *Impi yaseNcome*, see Ndlovu, 'The Changing Perceptions'.

11. B.W. Vilakazi, 'Bantu Views of the Great Trek', p. 4. This article is available at the University of the Witwatersrand Historical and Literary Papers Collection Library.

12. Ibid.

13. Ibid. See also J.B. Wright, 'The Dynamics of Power and Conflict in the Thukela-Mzimkulu Region in the Late 18th and 19th Centuries: A Critical Reconstruction' (Ph.D. diss., University of the Witwatersrand, 1989) and 'Political Transformations in the Thukela-Mzimkulu Regions in the Late 18th and 19th Centuries', in *The Mfecane Aftermath: Reconstructive Debates in Southern African History*, ed. Carolyn Hamilton (Johannesburg: Witwatersrand University Press and Pietermaritzburg: University of Natal Press, 1995), Chapter 6.

14. Wright, 'Political Transformations', p. 6.

15. Evidence of Socwatsha kaPhaphu, from the James Stuart Archives, KCM 24220/1, File 58, Killie Campbell Library, Durban. The last four lines capture the accommodative nature of African societies to foreigners and strangers seeking land and *ukukhonza*. The same principles applied when the voortrekkers moved into part of the southern Zulu kingdom.

16. Ndlovu, 'The Changing Perceptions', p. 39.

17. Vilakazi, 'Bantu Views', p. 5.

18. Ibid.

19. H. Ngubane, *Body and Mind in Zulu Medicine: An Ethnography of Health and Disease in Nyuswa-Zulu Thought* (London: Academic Press, 1977), pp. 31–32.

20. Church of England Missions, *Izindatyana zabantu: kanye nezindaba zase Natal* (Bishopstowe: Ekukhanyeni Mission Press, 1858), p. cxvi and Ndlovu, 'The Changing Perceptions', Chapter 1. This story was also repeated in the James Stuart Archives in the early twentieth century by Meshack Ngidi, among others, KCM 24324, 29/11/1921, Killie Campbell Library, Durban.

21. Vilakazi, 'Bantu Views', p. 4; see also p. 7. Peterson quotes in full Vilakazi's citation of Emerson's 'Essay on History': 'We sympathise in the great moments of history, in the great discoveries, the great resistance, the great posterities of men, because the law was found, or that blow was struck for us, as we ourselves in that place would have done or applauded.' See Peterson, 'Monarchs, Missionaries', p. 123.

22. Vilakazi, 'Bantu Views', p. 7.

23. Ibid.

24. Ibid., p. 8.

25. Vilakazi, 'Oral and Written Literature', pp. vii–viii.

26. Evidence of Jantshi kaNongila in C. de B. Webb and J. Wright, eds. *The James Stuart Archives of Recorded Oral Evidence Relating to the History of the Zulu and Neighbouring Peoples* (Pietermaritzburg: University of Natal Press and Durban: Killie Campbell Collection), Vol. 1, p. 196. Stuart interviewed him in 1903.

27. Queen Mnkabayi had power to enforce traditional, cultural practices and customs derived from her status as a high-placed elder within the Zulu royal family. King Dingane respected her authority as part of the political arrangement within his kingdom. Bhibi kaSompisi, Ndlela's sister, was also one of the most important women at uMgungundlovu. Another example is that of Queen Mother Ntombazi of the Ndwandwe. For further analysis of Regent Mnkabayi see Ndlovu, 'The Changing Perceptions', Chapters 1 and 6.

28. Vilakazi, 'Oral and Written Literature', p. 21.

29. Ibid., p. 22.
30. Ibid., p. 21.
31. Ibid., p. 424; A.T. Bryant, *Olden Times in Zululand* (London: Longmans, Green, 1929); J. Stuart, *uBaxolele* (London: Longmans, Green, 1924) and *uKulumetule* (London: Longmans, Green, 1925).
32. Evidence of Socwatsha kaPhaphu, KCM 24220, File 58, Killie Campbell Library, Durban.
33. S. Nyembezi, *Izibongo zamakhosi* (Pietermaritzburg: Shuter & Shooter, 1958).
34. S. Nyembezi, 'The Historical Background to the *Izibongo* of the Zulu Military Age' (Honours paper, University of the Witwatersrand, 1946), pp. 160 and 161. I use his path-breaking analysis of *izibongo zikaDingane* in Chapter 1 of my doctoral thesis; see Ndlovu, 'The Changing Perceptions'. This might be because *izibongo zamakhosi* were part of our vernacular curriculum during my primary education in Soweto. I still have vivid memories of talented praise-singers within our class. They were highly regarded by introverts who struggled to harness the performance skills of *izimbongi*. I used to dread those parades as our teachers had the right to ask any student to display his or her skills in front of the class; probably guys like the poet Mzwakhe Mbuli were brilliant during such occasions. I used to admire my talented colleagues.
35. Nyembezi, 'The Historical Background', p. 123.
36. Ibid. All the translations were done by Nyembezi. Other isiZulu oral traditions argue that King Shaka was assassinated at his kwaDukuza residence, where his grave is said to be located.
37. Ibid. See Ndlovu, 'The Changing Perceptions', Chapter 1 for a slightly different viewpoint.
38. Nyembezi, 'The Historical Background', p. 121.
39. Ibid., p. 122.
40. Evidence of Dinya kaZokozwayo, in *The James Stuart Archives*, eds. Webb and Wright, Vol. 1, p. 95. Stuart interviewed him in 1905.
41. Nyembezi, 'The Historical Background'; see also *Izibongo zikaDingane*, which are available under the title of 'Stuart Book of Eulogies' in the James Stuart Archives housed at the Killie Campbell Library in Durban, KCM 23478, File 28; KCM 23486, File 29a and A.B. Ngcobo and D.K. Rycroft, *The Praises of Dingane: Izibongo zikaDingane* (Pietermaritzburg: University of Natal Press, 1988).
42. P. Lamula, *uZulu kaMalandela: A Most Practical and Concise Compendium of African History Combined with Genealogy, Chronology, Geography and Biography* (Durban: Star Printing Works, 1924).
43. Nyembezi, 'The Historical Background', including the section on the Regent Mnkabayi.
44. Ndlovu, 'The Changing Perceptions', Chapter 1.
45. Nyembezi, 'The Historical Background'; see Ndlovu, 'The Changing Perceptions' for a different interpretation of this praise word.
46. S. Nyembezi, *Izibongo Zamakhosi*, (Pietermaritzburg: Shuter & Shooter, 1958), p. 61.
47. Ibid., p. 56; see also Ndlovu, 'The Changing Perceptions', Chapter 1.
48. Ndlovu, 'The Changing Perceptions', Chapter 5; see also E. Zondi, *Ukufa kukaShaka* (Johannesburg: Witwatersrand University Press, 1960).

*Chapter 10*

# A Reassessment of Women's Power in the Zulu Kingdom

SIFISO NDLOVU

THIS CHAPTER RE-EXAMINES the formative roles of women in the Zulu kingdom in the early and mid-nineteenth century.[1] It concentrates on Regent Queen Mnkabayi kaJama[2] and the portrayals of her legacy by recent Zulu intellectuals such as Eliot Zondi and Mazisi Kunene, who examined the recorded isiZulu-language (oral) accounts that documented how Zulu women actively participated in traditional networks of authority. To date, much of the scholarship reconstructing the lives of Zulu women 200 years ago falls within a gender studies paradigm. This academic field tends to rely on late-twentieth-century feminist analyses, which are informed by women's struggles in the industrialised West to win individual rights, rather than the historical realities of everyday collaboration between the sexes in precolonial Africa – a form of gender co-operation, as opposed to gender contestation, which both Zulu men and women acknowledged as essential to maintaining a collective (hierarchical) society.

What is interesting to note is that neither gender studies nor feminist analyses translate into an isiZulu phrase. They are essentially academic constructs formulated by mother-tongue English-speakers, whose opinions reflect modern ideas of human rights. That women in post-apartheid South Africa should share the same freedoms as men is an important aim, but this present goal does not help us understand fully the dynamics of precolonial southeast Africa, the area now referred to as KwaZulu-Natal. Thus, the most well-meaning scholar-activists who use feminist ideas to highlight women's oppression in the Zulu kingdom sometimes obscure, more than explain, the ways in which traditional gender relationships offered both males and females similar channels to customary influence and power.

In the decades leading up to the white conquest of King Cetshwayo's army in 1879, women in the Zulu kingdom were recognised, even revered, for their important contributions to one of the strongest polities in all of southern Africa. They were workers and decision-makers exercising agency in the agricultural economy (which included their involvement in crop cultivation and cattle husbandry); they were also leaders in the family homestead and key national institutions that oversaw expansionist phases of the Zulu state. Too often, however, these expressions of female power have been neglected by contemporary scholars such as professors Jeff Guy and Cherryl Walker, founders of the gender oppression school of historical analysis, which assails the rigid control that Zulu men exercised over women's reproduction and production.[3] The model of causality employed by Guy and Walker draws on Marxist theory, which, in turn, concentrates on the all-powerful mechanisms of class subjugation. It is this perspective of historical materialism that downplays the ways in which Zulu women in the 'exploited' ranks of 'reproducers of labour' could wield authority.[4]

An organising theme of the gender oppression school posits that the precolonial Zulu kingdom was rife with subjugated girls and women, toiling in single-sex units that followed a strict gender division of labour. Zulu girls and women were said to be responsible for tilling the fields and performing domestic duties such as cooking, serving food, fetching water, child-rearing and manufacturing household items such as pottery and thatching huts. Males, on the other hand, were said to dominate livestock husbandry totally; they also cleared the land for planting; built and repaired huts as well as homestead fences; made wooden and iron tools; and, most importantly, conducted warfare. While many of these activities generally capture elements of everyday Zulu life, they also present static portraits that conceal a range of cross-gender obligations. Existing oral traditions and *izibongo* are useful in questioning stereotypes perpetuated by contemporary scholars such as Guy and Walker.[5]

For example, during some important communal ceremonies Zulu girls – not their male counterparts – 'alusa[ed]' or 'look[ed] after cattle'.[6] Many of the cooking duties in the royal house were not carried out by women but by male members of the *izinceku* (singular, *inceku*) or attendants. In 1918 Baleni kaSilwana, a man appointed as King Mpande's *inceku*, recounted how he was responsible for serving the regent drink (milk and water) and roasting his meat. Baleni also brought water for the royals from a nearby river 'early in the morning and a long way off'.[7] Significantly, in commoner homesteads boys and girls performed interchangeable tasks, as the Zulu patriarch Ndukwana kaMbengwana explained in 1897. He catalogued a world of children serving the Zulu kingdom busy mingling at work:

> *Udibi*-carrier boys going to the great place (king's palace), to the *amakanda* [military barracks] . . . carried mats, stool, kaross and gourd for water, spoon, pot, basket, maize and *amabele* and other things. Girls accompany with a bag (*inqalati*, woven from rushes, like a mat) of mealies or *amabele* and other provisions. They carry for their elder brothers too . . . [T]he boys taken on a journey of this kind must be able to do the various domestic duties (and perform duties that were reserved for small girls). As soon as they get to headquarters, they must start by sweeping the hut (which perhaps might not have been occupied for a long time), then they smear it over with cow dung, go with a

gourd to fetch water, put the pot (*imbiza*) on, cook and also collect firewood. Food would always be fetched by girls from home . . . Girls might be placed in charge of the calves if the father is going to the royal kraal (thus performing duties reserved for small boys).[8]

As the above passage makes clear in its references to the presence of girls in military zones (*amakhanda* or barracks), females actively participated in the most masculine of male domains – warfare. Ngidi kaMcikaziswa, a former attendant of King Dingane, testified in 1904 that King Shaka launched campaigns with married women, *amakosikazi*, as well as girls in his army. Girls were, like boys, ritually enlisted in single-sex regiments; female conscripts cut their own shields (*sika'd izihlangu*) and hurled spears in skirmishes. They fought, for example, in the 1827 Zulu incursion into amaMpondo territory in what is today southern KwaZulu-Natal. In that engagement, Zulu women of the Ntshuku, Mcekeceke and Mvutwamini regiments rushed into battle under the command of their military leaders Magaya kaDibandhlela and Zihlando.[9] Finally, during times of peace, women with combat experience also wore their *iziqu*, a necklace of valour showing that they had killed enemy fighters in battle.[10] Such a diverse range of military functions defies any easy categorisation of female *amabutho* as largely ceremonial bodies with one major purpose: to provide a source of wives for male *amabutho* and agricultural labour for the Zulu state.[11]

Beyond investigating a greater range of female participation in war, one of the more incisive ways to determine the conceptual limits of the gender oppression school is to explore women's involvement in vital political spheres. Here, the stereotype of the beaten-down Zulu female is most problematic.[12] Such a materialist interpretation of female subordination functions on economic and ideological levels. One of the hallmarks of the gender oppression school is its preoccupation with victimising kinship relationships, which are described in terms of female labour and marital duties that supposedly enabled the Zulu elites to ruthlessly sustain the kingdom. These kinship relationships are seen as fundamental to a Zulu patriarchal system that taught girls early on to accept their lifelong material exploitation. On an ideological plane, three main forms of male domination are said to operate. Firstly, daily taboos and avoidances determined female social movement, expression and mobility within and outside the precolonial Zulu homestead; this general point will not be contested. Secondly, women were barred from exercising real political authority in the Zulu kingdom. In light of Regent Queen Mnkabayi's biography this statement needs to be reconsidered. And thirdly, the exclusion of females from power in Zulu society more widely was reinforced in grand ritual ceremonies tied to the royal house. There is compelling historical evidence in century-old Zulu testimonies about Queen Mnkabayi and some of her cohorts that challenge this final assertion.[13]

Indeed, a critical reassessment of recorded Zulu oral traditions, which memorialise the authority of Zulu women, provides a different portrait of material and ideological realities that contradicts key ideas of the gender oppression school. The establishment of Zulu state apparatuses saw the ascension of two institutions, *amakhanda* (singular, *ikhanda*), the military barracks system for regiments, and *izigodhlo* (singular, *isigodhlo*), roughly translated as 'seraglios' that served the king.[14] Both *amakhanda* and *izigodhlo* occupied central positions in the king's own colossal homestead enclosures. Heading the *amakhanda* were either old female relatives of the king or senior women appointed from within the ranks of *izigodhlo*. Childless, *amakhanda* leaders had no heirs. Since they were beyond the age of conceiving, they could not push their own sons into deadly succession rivalries, and thus were perceived as minor threats in royal intrigues. Moreover, such post-menopausal women were no longer considered 'unclean', with movements restricted by cattle taboos and other avoidance rituals (known more broadly as *ukuhlonipha*) observed by menstruating women.[15] This meant that they could function as a distinct kind of woman in Zulu society – possessing the customary authority to cross into both male and female domains.[16]

Leaders of *amakhanda* also wielded considerable power in the *isigodhlo*. Contrary to the scholarly views of the gender oppression school, *izigodhlo* were far more than harems of the king; they were focal points and sources of regal patronage.[17] However, the king exercised less personal authority within the *isigodhlo* than within his royal enclosures. Instead, the powerful women in charge of *isigodhlo* monopolised decision-making. Ngidi kaMcikaziswa, one of King Dingane's *izinceku*, elaborates:

> [I] used to take food out of the white *isigodhlo*; I would receive it from the *amakosikazi* of Senzangakhona. We would give it to *amahlengwa* who had arrived. We would give to *umpakati* who had come to *konza* . . . [Queen] Bibi [kaNkobe], sister of Ndhlela ka Sompisi, was the great *inkosikazi* of the white *isigodhlo*. She was wife of (King) Senzangakhona. [Queen] Langazana ka Gubetshe was at first in charge of the black *isigodhlo*. She was also [King] Senzangakhona's wife. When Langazana was removed and brought back to kwa Khangela [to be in charge there], [Queen] Mjanisi became in charge of the 'black' *isigodhlo* . . . [She] was [also] King Senzangakhona's wife .[18]

Yet prominent Zulu women did more than direct royal domestic labour and production. They managed ritual arenas. One such female leader was Queen Mnkabayi, the paternal aunt of three Zulu kings – Shaka, Dingane and Mpande – and leading authority in a royal *ikhanda* singled out for accolades in praises (*izibongo*) by the most creative bards (*izimbongi*) such as Magolwane and Mshongweni.[19] Mnkabayi's *izibongo* reveal that she exercised considerable jurisdiction over crucial customary matters in Zulu territory. Although it is generally argued that men controlled agricultural production through the *umkhosi*, an annual first fruits ceremony performed in every homestead following the king's great *umkhosi*, during the reign of Chief Senzangakhona, Queen Mnkabayi officiated over this grand ceremony, for she was recognised as the guardian of the royal Zulu mantle.[20]

During the 1820s and 1830s Queen Mnkabayi also ruled over the vast ebaQulusini area situated in the present-day Ladysmith-Newcastle-Vryheid region. Other female rulers within Zulu royal networks exercised power by ancestral writ. Queen Mmama, the twin sister of Queen Mnkabayi, for example, controlled enTonteleni, the original *ikhanda* of her brother Chief Senzangakhona. During Mmama's period of influence, Zulu commanders sought her out before launching a military campaign. In 1904 Ngidi kaMcikaziswa remembered that 'war has in the past had its seat in Mnkabayi's Mahlabaneni kraal. When the men of that place take the field, it is generally known that war has broken out in the land in earnest and will be universal in character.'[21]

Lines from Izibongo zikaMnkabayi, probably composed by Magolwane kaMkhathini Jiyane, which commences with the dramatic 'Father of guile!' provide us with a complex, multi-dimensional perspective of her life history:

> *uSoqili!*
> *Iqili lakwaHoshoza*
> *Elidl' umuntu limyenga ngendaba;*
> *Lidl' uBhedu ngasezinyangeni,*
> *Ladl' uMkhongoyiyiyana ngaseMangadini,*
> *Ladl' uBheje ngasezanusini.*
> *Ubhuku lukaMenzi,*
> *Olubamb' abantu lwabanela;*
> *Ngibone ngoNohela kaMlilo, umlil' ovuth' inaba zonke,*
> *Ngoba lumbambe wanyamalala.*
> *Inkomo ekhal'eSangoyana,*
> *Yakhal' umlomo wayo wabhoboz' izulu,*
> *Iye yezwiwa nguGwabalanda,*
> *Ezalwa nguMndaba kwaKhumalo.*
> *Intomb' ethombe yom' umlomo,*
> *Zase ziyihlab' imithanti ezawonina.*
> *Umthobela-bantu izinyoni,*
> *Bayazibamba usezibuka ngamehlo.*
> *Zibo bangene ngawo onk' amasango,*
> *Abanikazimuzi bangene ngezintuba.*
> *Umncindela kaNobiya,*
> *Umhlathuz' uzawugcwal' emini.*
> *Imbibizan' eyaqamba imigqa kwaMalandela,*
> *Yathi ngabakwaMalandela,*
> *Ithi yokhona bezoqanana ngazo zonk' izindlela.*[22]

Father of guile!
Cunning one of the Hoshoza people,
Who devours a person tempting him with a story;
She killed Bhedu amongst medicine men,
And destroyed Mkhongoyiyiyana amongst the Ngadini,
And killed Bheje among the diviners.
Morass of Menzi,
That caught people and finished them off;
I saw by Nohela son of Mlilo, the fire that burns on every hill,
For it caught him and he disappeared.
Beast that lows on Sangonyana,
It lowed and its voice pierced the sky,
It went and was heard by Gwabalanda
Son of Mndaba of the Khumalo clan.
She who allays for people their anxiety,
They catch it and she looks at it with her eyes.
The opener of all gates so that people may enter,
The owners of the homes enter by the narrow side-gates.
Sipper for others of venom of the cobra.
The Mhlathuzi River will flood at midday.
Little mouse that started runs at Malandela's,
And thought it was the people of Malandela
Who would thereby walk along all the paths.

These verses celebrate Queen Mnkabayi's capacity to solve her people's problems, including those of commoners, as the phrase 'bangene ngawo wonke amasango' (she who allays for people their anxiety) testifies. She also emerges in *izibongo* as a fighter against corrupt diviners such as Bhedu and Bheje, among others, indicating that she was not afraid to confront evil forces that might undermine Zulu power. What is most intriguing in this oral literature is that Queen Mnkabayi is sometimes depicted as a male figure; her praise name 'uSoqili' means the sly one, with the prefix (so) depicting a male instead of (no) which refers to a female.[23] One should not necessarily assume that a male *imbongi* called Queen Mnkabayi a 'man' in order to revel publicly in her notable accomplishments without upsetting a Zulu patriarchal order, though there is compelling testimony from one Zulu oral historian, Socwatsha kaPhapu, which suggests that she enjoyed breaching certain gender boundaries when called before the Zulu court to discuss matters of state. Socwatsha's account of how she 'dressed as a man' is quoted in the previous chapter.[24]

Ngidi kaMcikaziswa confirmed this tendency of Queen Mnkabayi's and its wider implications in terms of her participation in performing the war or '*impi*' ceremonies within the Zulu kingdom.[25] Finally, Prince Mgidlana kaMpande, son of king Mpande, recalled in 1921 another reason for Queen Mnkabayi's taking the attributes of a man: 'Her praises are like that of a man . . . *Imbibakazana ka Malandela, Eqamb'umugqa kwa Malandela'*. This may refer to two things; that she was a senior twin, who led Queen Mmama, her sister twin. Or the phrase may mean that Queen Mnkabayi was the first woman to become a Zulu Regent or Sovereign.[26] This possibility is ratified by the fact that she took power on behalf of her brother Senzangakhona when he was still a minor, and therefore unable to rule.

Queen Mnkabayi exercised her greatest ideological and political initiatives at two elite Zulu homesteads, kwaNobamba and esiKlebeni. The latter site was probably built by either Ndaba or Jama, two prominent Zulu ancestors of King Shaka.[27] Furthermore, esiKlebeni gained prominence because it housed the sacred *inkatha*, a large ring woven with the strands of materials that symbolically represented the unified clans of the Zulu nation.[28]

Regent Queen Mnkabayi's eminence in the Zulu state, which is memorialised in *izibongo* that chart her rise to national fame, has captured the imaginations of renowned twentieth-century Zulu intellectuals such as Elliot Zondi and Mazisi Kunene. These authors, writing (and thinking) in both isiZulu and English, used the voluminous (Zulu) oral sources on Queen Mnkabayi to reconstruct narratives of how she made and unmade Zulu kings. Such modern Zulu accounts of past royal intrigue have rarely been integrated into the recent scholarly works produced by the gender oppression school.[29]

For his part, Eliot Zondi elevated Queen Mnkabayi as the main protagonist in his historical drama published in 1960, titled *Ukufa kukaShaka* (The Death of Shaka).[30] This book became a standard work in the curriculum of apartheid-era (Bantu secondary) schools and universities. It is still prescribed in South African universities that offer courses in Zulu literature. The narrative begins with Prince Dingane at Queen Mnkabayi's court, where he is behaving like a timid, sly schemer whose ambitions depend on his powerful aunt, Queen Mnkabayi. To describe this opening scene, Eliot Zondi relied on his critical reading of the relevant *izibongo* to assert that Queen Mnkabayi already instilled a measure of fear in the hearts of cut-throat male Zulu rulers, for she was a voice of discretion and even-handedness. She stands in Zondi's narrative as a respected national leader, deeply disapproving of the autocratic and destructive policies of King Shaka, particularly his draconian restrictions on premarital courtship, which entailed delaying the reproduction of families for long service in the Zulu state's *amabutho* (regiments). In Zondi's tale, Queen Mnkabayi confides to Prince Dingane that she has misgivings about King Shaka's excesses, suggesting that she might have given the usurper the 'moral' grounds to overthrow his brother:

*Uyayibona Dingane imizi yezifunda ngezifunda iphenduka amanxiwa;*
*uyasibona isizwe sakithi siphela; izintombi zijendeviswa, izinsizwa zithenwa,*

*amakhehla nezalukazi kuthiwa akuganane kuzale . . . Nithule nithini Dingane? Ningamadoda ngoba nilengise amalengisi? Angiphenduke indoda yini? . . . Sukujama Dingane; isilonda sikaZulu siyabhibha, uZulu uselindele ihawu elisha. Zifudumela izandla oyakwamukelwa ngazo, libanzi iphiko engiyokwefumakela.*[31]

Dingane do you notice that households of the various regions are becoming old sites, do you notice the destruction of our kingdom, females being turned to old, childless, unmarried women, males being castrated, courtship being promoted among grandfathers and grandmothers so as to bear children . . . ? Why are you all silent Dingane? Are you men because of your private parts? Do you want me to change into a man? Do not stare at me Dingane; the open wound of the Zulu nation is festering, the Zulu nation is awaiting a new shield. You will be welcomed with warm hands, I will protect under my broad wings.

*Ukufa kukaShaka* positions Queen Mnkabayi as the consistent and manipulative voice in Prince Dingane's ear during what seemed like endless Zulu military campaigns, which stretched both national resources and resolve. This perpetual state of war made King Shaka's siblings regard his martial operations as a ploy to get rid of them, for they were required to fight in battle after battle far from their homesteads in distant, hostile locales, which increased their chances of being killed.[32] Sensitive to this outcome, Queen Mnkabayi warned her royal allies: '*[N]iyakubona ebengikusho? Niyazi kwaSoshangane? Kwamamangalahlwa? Aniyikubulawa indlala, niqedelwe isitha eniyosihlasela sizihlalele endlini yaso?*'[33] (Do you notice what I have alluded to? Are you aware how far is kwaSoshangane? Kwamamangalahlwa? Are you not going to die of hunger and finished off by a formidable enemy whom you have set out to attack in his own backyard?). Prince Dingane and his brother Prince Mahlagana seemed to heed the implication of her questions. In Zondi's book, both princes outmanoeuvred their king, deserted his weary army, returned to the royal palace at kwaBulawayo, and assassinated the founder of the Zulu kingdom.

Following in Zondi's literary footsteps, the late Zulu intellectual Mazisi Kunene published his now famous work, *Emperor Shaka the Great*, in 1979, the centennial year of Isandlwana. Kunene, like Zondi, drew key information from Zulu oral traditions.[34] While the central character in the 1979 classic is King Shaka, Queen Mnkabayi plays a commanding role. But unlike Zondi's story, Kunene's tale of royal power revolves around Prince Dingane, the usurper who poisoned the reputation of King Shaka and manipulated Queen Mnkabayi to adopt a negative view of the Zulu founder.[35] Portrayed as an empathetic ally of King Shaka, Queen Mnkabayi tells the impulsive and treacherous Prince Dingane to respect the Zulu throne, despite the extreme actions committed in its name. In this context, Kunene's Queen Mnkabayi is a circumspect and direct power broker, unafraid to dismiss Prince Dingane's 'jealous fits'. She councils King Shaka's fraternal rival:

> I, too, am beginning to see strange things in your brother's life . . . Despite all this I still have faith in him. Perhaps this dark cloud shall pass, and we may yet see a new and powerful king, Yes, I still have great faith in him. He is a king most needed in our times. Such sharpness of mind only comes as a gift from the Creator . . . You, too, must help your brother and consolidate his power.[36]

The voluminous oral evidence documenting the lives of prominent Zulu women and especially Regent Queen Mnkabayi – a body of knowledge consulted by Zulu scholars speaking and (in some cases) writing in isiZulu over the last 100 years – awaits closer examination by the gender oppression school. If the accounts provided by Baleni kaSilwana, Ngidi kaMcikaziswa, Socwatsha kaPhapu, Bhambatha Wallet Vilakazi, Eliot Zondi and Mazisi Kunene reveal anything, it is that precolonial Zulu women were neither automatically subordinate to Zulu men, nor barred by tyrannical patriarchs from the inner circles of Zulu power and monarchy. Indeed, the Zulu intellectuals cited in this chapter challenge what Guy and Walker characterise as the rigid (exploitable) class and gender division between Zulu men and women, which benefited the former at the expense of the latter. If Zulu women, functioning as important actors in the *amakhanda*, *izigodhlo* and Zulu royal family, were accorded a more important and central place in scholarly investigations, the prevailing view in today's gender currents of South African historiography could be subject to a long-awaited reconsideration.

## Notes

1. The author would like to dedicate this chapter to Carolyn Hamilton and Philip Bonner.
2. There are two variations of the Regent's spelling, namely, Mkabayi and Mnkabayi. This study adopts the latter (older) version. This spelling is used in many archival documents. According to existing oral traditions, Queen Mnkabayi held the Zulu throne on behalf of her brother, Prince Senzangakhona, when he was still a minor. She was briefly in charge of the monarchy during the transition periods following the deaths of both King Senzangakhona and King Shaka. She was also a skilful matchmaker, who arranged the relationship between Prince Senzangakhona and Princess Nandi, King Shaka's mother. Finally, it is also alleged Mnkabayi played a similar role regarding her father's marital affairs. Much of the analysis and interpretation in this chapter has been adapted from S.M. Ndlovu, 'The Changing Perceptions of King Dingane in Historical Literature: A Case Study in the Construction of Historical Knowledge in 19th and 20th Century South African History' (Ph.D. diss., University of the Witwatersrand, 2001).
3. J. Guy, 'Analysing Pre-capitalist Societies in Southern Africa', *Journal of Southern African Studies* 14:1 (1987): 18–37; J. Guy, 'Gender Oppression in Southern Africa's Precapitalist Societies', in *Women and Gender in Southern Africa to 1945*, ed. C. Walker (Cape Town: David Philip), pp. 33–47; and Cherryl Walker, 'Gender and the Development of the Migrant Labour System

c.1850–1930: An Overview', in *Women and Gender in Southern Africa to 1945*, ed. C. Walker (Cape Town: David Philip, 1990), pp. 168–96. For another example of recent historical scholarship on the status of marginal Zulu women in the kingdom, which grapples with but ultimately accepts the terminology of the gender oppression school, see Sean Hanretta, 'Women, Marginality and the Zulu State: Women's Institutions and Power in the Early Nineteenth Century', *Journal of African History* 39 (1998): 389–415.

4.  See C.A. Hamilton's path-breaking unpublished honours thesis in History: 'A Fragment of the Jigsaw: Authority and Labour Control Amongst the Early 19th-century Northern Nguni' (University of the Witswatersrand, 1980). Much of the analysis in the first part of this chapter draws on her excellent research. Hamilton's honours thesis contains a list of the most powerful women within the Zulu kingdom.

5.  For oral traditions and oral history regarding the Zulu Kingdom, see C.A. Hamilton, 'Ideology, Oral Traditions and the Struggle for Power in the Early Zulu Kingdom' (Masters thesis, University of the Witwatersrand, 1986). See also the original notebooks (nbk) that comprise the James Stuart Archives (JSA) housed in the Killie Campbell Africana Collection (KCM) at the University of KwaZulu-Natal, Durban.

6.  JSA, KCM 2423. Evidence of Ndukwana, 1/10/1900, File 59, nbk 34. See also Hamilton, 'A Fragment'.

7.  See evidence of Baleni kaSilwana, 28/6/1918 in C. de B. Webb and J.B. Wright, eds. *The James Stuart Archive of Recorded Oral Evidence Relating to the History of the Zulu and Neighbouring Peoples*, Vol. 1 (Pietermaritzburg: University of Natal Press and Durban: Killie Campbell Collection, 1976), pp. 35–36.

8.  See evidence of Ndukwana kaMbengwana, 11/9/03 in C. de B. Webb and J.B. Wright, eds. *The James Stuart Archive of Recorded Oral Evidence Relating to the History of the Zulu and Neighbouring Peoples*, Vol. 4 (Pietermaritzburg: University of Natal Press and Durban: Killie Campbell Collection, 1986), pp. 378–79. Ndukwana also remarked that young boys herded goats and tended poultry.

9.  JSA, KCM, 24283. Evidence of Ngidi kaMagumbukazi, 5/11/1904, File 61, nbk 47 and Hamilton, 'A Fragment'.

10. JSA, KCM, 24283. Evidence of Ngidi kaMagumbukazi, 5/11/1904, File 61, nbk 47. It should be noted that when King Shaka accompanied his army to Pondoland, an operation known as 'ihlambo lempi ka Nandi', he took with him Queen Mnkabi (King Senzangakhona's great *inkosikazi*). She fell ill after crossing the Mzimkulu River and died. Her corpse was then carried back to the Zulu kingdom and buried with honours. See evidence of Ngidi kaMcikaziswa, 11/8/1904 in C. de B. Webb and J.B. Wright, eds. *The James Stuart Archive of Recorded Oral Evidence Relating to the History of the Zulu and Neighbouring Peoples*, Vol. 5 (Pietermaritzburg: University of Natal Press and Durban: Killie Campbell Collection, 2001), p. 45.

11. Hamilton, 'A Fragment'.

12. See, for example, Guy, 'Analysing Pre-capitalist Societies' and 'Gender Oppression'.

13. Hamilton, 'A Fragment'.

14. One needs to take cognisance of the nationalist politics and linguistic problems when translating these isiZulu terms into equivalent English words.

15. Hamilton, 'A Fragment'.

16. JSA, KCM, 24283. Evidence of Ngidi kaMagambukazi, 5/11/1904, File 61, nbk. 47.

17. Ibid.

18. Evidence of Ngidi kaMcikaziswa, 24/6/1899 in *The James Stuart Archive*, eds. Webb and Wright, Vol. 5, p. 76.

19. Regent Queen Mnkabayi merits an in-depth study on her own. The role of royal women within royalty politics in southern Africa is now beginning to attract serious scholarly attention. See M. Genge, 'Power and Gender in Southern African History: Power Relations in the era of Queen Labotsibeni Gwamile Mdluli of Swaziland, ca.1875–1921' (Ph.D. diss., Michigan State University, 1999). In general, African women in positions of power have been studied elsewhere in Africa – and far more extensively. Genge cites an example: L.M. Aurbach, 'Women's Domestic Power: A Study of Women's Role in Tunisian Town' (Ph.D. diss., University of Illinois-Urbana-Champaign, 1980).

20. Hamilton, 'A Fragment' and Ndlovu, 'The Changing Perceptions'.

21. Evidence of Ngidi kaMcikaziswa, 11/8/1904 in *The James Stuart Archive*, eds. Webb and Wright,

Vol. 5, p. 67; Hamilton, 'A Fragment' and Ndlovu, 'The Changing Perceptions'. See also evidence of Madikane kaMlomowetole, 8/7/1903 in C. de B. Webb and J.B. Wright, eds., *The James Stuart Archive of Recorded Oral Evidence Relating to the History of the Zulu and Neighbouring Peoples*, Vol. 2 (Pietermaritzburg: University of Natal Press and Durban: Killie Campbell Collection, 1979), p. 47; P. Lamula, *uZulu kaMalandela: A Most Practical and Concise Compendium of African History Combined with Genealogy, Chronology, Geography and Biography* (Durban: Star Printing Works, 1924), p. 110 and B.W. Vilakazi, 'Oral and Written Literature in Nguni' (Ph.D. diss., University of the Witwatersrand, 1945), p. 46.

22. JSA, KCM 23478, 'Izibongo zikaMnkabayi'; the translations are from T. Cope, ed. *Izibongo: Zulu Praise Poems* (London: Oxford University Press, 1968). See also Vilakazi, 'Oral and Written Literature', Chapter 2 on 'Poetry Concerning Women', regarding his version of izibongo zikaMnkabayi; Sibusiso Nyembezi, 'The Historical Background to the Izibongo of the Zulu Military Age,' *African Studies* December (1948): 110–25, 157–74; M. Kunene, 'An Analytical Survey of Zulu Poetry Both Traditional and Modern' (Masters thesis, University of Natal, 1957); 'Portrait of Magolwane – The Great Zulu Poet', *Cultural Events in Africa* 32 (1976): 1–14 and Ndlovu, 'The Changing Perceptions'.

23. JSA, KCM 23478, File 28, 'Izibongo zikaMnkabayi'. For example, the names Nobantu and Sobantu mean 'of the people', but the former refers to a female and the latter to a male.

24. JSA, KCM 24220, File 58. Evidence of Socwatsha kaPhaphu.

25. See Ngidi's testimony: 'uMnkabayi inkosi yakwaZulu ete[a] impi. Amakosi akwaZulu abekwa uye' in JSA, KCM 24317.

26. JSA, KCL, File 57, nbk 7. Evidence of Mgidhlana kaMpande, 5/6/1921.

27. Evidence of Mayinga kaMbekuzana, 8/7/1905 in *The James Stuart Archive*, eds. Webb and Wright, Vol. 2, p. 252.

28. Ibid. and Hamilton, 'A Fragment'.

29. See Ndlovu, 'The Changing Perceptions'.

30. E. Zondi, *Ukufa kukaShaka* (Johannesburg: Witwatersrand University Press, 1960).

31. Ibid., p. 6.

32. Ibid.

33. Ibid., p. 40.

34. M. Kunene, *Emperor Shaka the Great: A Zulu Epic* (London: Heinemann, 1979).

35. Ibid., p. 303.

36. Ibid., p. 300.

*Chapter 11*

# Enlightenment Theories of Civilisation and Savagery in British Natal
## The Colonial Origins of the (Zulu) African Barbarism Myth

JEREMY MARTENS

A YEAR BEFORE HIS DEATH, Sir Theophilus Shepstone engaged in a debate with Orange Free State President F.W. Reitz over native policy in southern Africa. Reitz had proposed that indirect rule in Natal, with its recognition of native law and chieftainship, should be abolished. Natal's first Secretary for Native Affairs responded with a pithy defence of the system of government he had implemented and which bore his name:

> I hold that so long as the social condition of the natives is what it is chieftainship and tribalism are necessary. They are necessary to give us proper control of them, and proper control they must have. I do not believe in the efficacy of violent measures to destroy prejudices; to efface barbarism, or to commend civilised ideas and habits to a barbarous race . . . Their ancient institutions may be faulty, but they are efficient, and can be made so for the purposes of enlightened government . . . Civilisation will undermine them by the gradual but sure process of enforcing the fitness of things.[1]

Shepstone was not alone in asserting that societies should be understood through the lens of civilisation and barbarism, for similar views shaped settler perceptions of Africans, rationalised white supremacy, guided policy decisions and informed legislation throughout colonial South Africa.[2] The impact of theories of civilisation and barbarism also extended beyond southern Africa's borders into other territories under British imperial control. While nineteenth-century settlers did not think in terms of 'Zuluness', their assertion that all Africans in KwaZulu-Natal shared a homogeneous barbaric culture blinded them to the complex kinship identities that existed in southeast Africa. This monolithic characterisation profoundly influenced later constructions of Zuluness, which remain with us today.

For much of the nineteenth century, British attitudes towards colonisation were informed by a stadial theory of societal development.[3] Principally derived from the writings of influential Scottish Enlightenment thinkers, this theory posited that humankind was comprised of a diverse variety of peoples at different developmental stages. All societies occupied a place on the scale between savagery and civilisation; at the bottom of the scale were the 'rude' savage tribes of America and Australia, at the top the civilised 'polished nations' of Europe. This formulation rested on an assumption of European supremacy quite distinct from biologically racist theories of the late nineteenth and early twentieth centuries. Enlightenment philosophers rejected the idea that there were innate differences between the savage and civilised; for them, all people, regardless of origin, belonged to a single human family and inherited a universal human nature. Human differentiation resulted from environmental conditions, especially the state of societies in which people lived.

According to Enlightenment theory, all societies naturally passed through four economic stages, each phase corresponding to a different mode of subsistence. Hunting communities gradually evolved into pastoral societies, which, over time, developed agriculture. Eventually, agricultural communities made the final progression to commercial society, the apogee of human organisation. Moreover, it was argued that as the mode of subsistence varied in societies, so too did customs, manners and morals, as well as ideas and institutions relating to law, property and government.[4] The four-stage theory ignored differences between communities regarded as uncivilised. Thus pastoral societies in different parts of the world were often assumed to share similar laws, morals and customs. When translated to the colonial context, this assumption encouraged educated administrators to approach the governance of colonised peoples in certain prescribed ways.

This investigation will concentrate on those Enlightenment ideas relating to chieftainship, governance and the position of women in savage societies, and the extent to which they influenced native policy in colonial Natal.

### Chieftainship in early colonial Natal

When explaining the development of indirect rule in colonial Natal, historians emphasise a number of factors: the strength of Nguni institutions, the unwillingness of the British to spend large sums of money on African administration, the pragmatic genius of Theophilus Shepstone and the practical necessity of cultivating indigenous allies to safeguard colonial security. The validity of these factors is beyond dispute; nevertheless, it is possible that ideas about civilisation and savagery played a more significant role in shaping the Shepstone system than has hitherto been acknowledged.

From the early 1840s British colonial officials frequently contrasted the civilisation and security of British-administered Natal with the barbarism and tyranny of the Zulu kingdom on the colony's northern border.[5] Shepstone himself described the Zulu government as 'despotic and arbitrary' and characterised Mpande as a capricious tyrant who presided over an unhappy land rife with murder and bloodshed. 'Such a government as this upon our immediate border', he warned in 1846, 'must greatly influence the amount of native population, and the means of providing for it within the colony.' The short-sighted and cruel policies of the amaZulu had forced thousands of refugees, 'wearied by turmoil and war', to flee to Natal for British protection. It was therefore the responsibility of the colonial government to provide a counterpoint to Zulu despotism and to 'proceed at once with the worthy project of christianising and civilising 100 000 degraded human beings'. Shepstone argued that the key to effective administration of this large population was to govern through their chiefs, who themselves had been in 'a state of vassalage and abject servitude under the Zulu yoke'.[6]

Carolyn Hamilton has recently argued that Shepstone found in the Zulu monarchy a model for his system of indirect rule. While he cast Mpande as a capricious despot, Shepstone nevertheless believed that Natal's African community could only be effectively controlled through patriarchal command and a strong centralised government. He therefore sought to take on the 'mantle of Shaka' and rule over Natal Africans as Somtsewu, the Great White Father.[7] Shepstone maintained that the 'constant and exterminating wars' set in motion by Zulu depredations had led to anarchy and wanton violence. It was therefore necessary to provide 'a supreme restraining power, such as the Government now established, to which all look for protection, and from which all must expect punishment who contravene its regulations and break its laws'. He urged the British government to replace Zulu tyranny with an administration that, while benevolent, nonetheless recognised that Africans required a firm hand for

> [t]he whole of the native population has been born and brought up with the notions of the most implicit obedience to their rulers . . . they pretend to no individual opinion of their own, and are guided in every respect by the will of their legally-constituted superiors; and it is this feeling I so anxiously recommend the Government to take advantage of, before it gives way (as I already see indications of its doing) to more dangerous views, from continued relaxation from control.[8]

British preconceptions about the Zulu government and the effective administration of the indigenous inhabitants of Natal were in no small measure influenced by Enlightenment theories about appropriate forms of government for savage societies.[9] Adam Ferguson, John Millar and others had argued in the late eighteenth century that 'the uniform history of mankind in a barbarous state' demonstrated that when 'rude nations' made the transition from hunters to herders and farmers, their mode of government changed to reflect evolving distinctions between 'the leader and follower, the prince and the subject'. Chiefs emerged to lead large communities, but resorted to 'the bridle of despotism and military force' to control their followers' 'warlike and turbulent spirit'. Consequently '[r]apacity and terror' became the 'predominant motives of conduct', forming 'the character of the only parties into which mankind are divided, that of the oppressor, and that of the oppressed'. In this state, the power of superstition led to the creation of an 'order of men' who used magic and who sometimes gave communities 'an early taste of despotism and absolute slavery'. Over time chiefs asserted control over land and assumed legislative power. And, once members of the tribe were dependent on a chief with regard to their property, they were 'in no condition to dispute his commands, or to refuse obedience to those ordinances which he issues at pleasure'.[10]

The 1847 Natal Locations Commission report was one of the first documents to outline the principles of Shepstone's native administration and his assertion that prosperity depended on 'management and efficient control of the large native population' guided colonial policy into the twentieth century. The recommendation that locations be set aside for African habitation, that administration of law involve 'chiefs and councillors' and that legal decisions be adapted as much as possible 'to the usages and customs of the native law' were predicated on an understanding of society very similar to that of Ferguson and Millar. Africans' 'universal character' was 'superstitious and warlike', they had a low regard for human life, and their passions were 'easily enflamed'. These characteristics were not innate, however, but were formed by 'education, habits and associations'. Africans had 'grown up in habits of such servile compliance to the wills of their despotic rulers, that they still show ready obedience to constituted authority'.[11]

Earl Grey, Secretary of State for the Colonies, endorsed the Commission's assessment of African society. 'It is obvious', he asserted, 'that those who have hitherto been under a rule of despotic severity cannot without extreme danger be emancipated from all control.' It was therefore essential that the Natal government abstain 'from any sudden or violent interference with the authority exercised over these people by their own chiefs'. Africans should continue to 'administer justice towards each other as they had been used to do in former times', although chiefs should be restrained from 'those acts of cruelty and tyranny which are so common among savages'. However, this restraint should be sparingly exercised so that chiefly power was not diminished and the chiefs were not 'lowered in the eyes of their tribes', for their

> maintaining a strong authority affords the only means by which in the actual state of things absolute anarchy and confusion can be averted, and it would therefore be advisable to abstain from examining too minutely into the manner in which the chiefs may rule over their tribes, even though this should unfortunately allow of the existence of much oppression, and the commission of many acts highly repugnant to our notions of justice and humanity.[12]

These principles of government were embodied in the Royal Instructions of 1848, which recognised the validity of customary law and the powers that 'the laws, customs, and usages of the inhabitants' had vested in the chiefs. These principles also underpinned the enactment of Ordinance 3 of 1849, which gave to the Lieutenant-Governor 'all the power and authority which, according to the laws, customs and usages of the natives, are held and enjoyed by any supreme or paramount native chief'.[13] Indirect rule in Natal therefore fitted neatly within the theory that savage societies were suited to despotic rule and that any tampering with this rule would result in anarchy. An enlightened, 'decentralised despotism'[14] was the best that civilised government could provide.

The Natal administration thus characterised indirect rule as an enlightened alternative to the barbarous Zulu kingdom on its border. As in the Zulu kingdom, Natal native administration would be based on patriarchal control and a strong centralised government. However, Shepstone would assume Shaka's mantle and replace unbridled despotism with firm and benevolent government that would make use of chieftainship and tribalism, the institutions best suited to the barbarous social condition in which Natal's Africans found themselves. That Shepstone held these ideas for the whole of his career is evidenced by the quotation at the beginning of this chapter.

### Taxation in early colonial Natal

If the transition from barbarism to civilisation was a gradual process, enlightened government could at least facilitate the process through the encouragement of 'industry and the formation of a taste for the comforts and luxuries of civilised life'.[15] Ferguson had argued that in between 'the prospects of ruin and conquest' the barbarian spent 'every moment of relaxation in the indulgence of sloth. He cannot descend to the pursuits of industry or mechanical labour.'[16] Earl Grey applied a similar formula to the 'Zoolahs located in Natal'.[17] He agreed with Harry Smith's assessment that Africans in the colony had inherited 'that apathetic idea of comfort comprised in having a sufficiency to eat and time to sleep', arguing that this disposition was one 'which almost universally distinguishes uncivilised men'.[18]

The imposition of a system of taxation would not only increase the revenue of the colony, and provide funds for schools and other institutions, but would also encourage Africans to 'acquire habits of industry' and raise them in the scale of civilisation.[19] The form of taxation eventually adopted was a 'rate upon their huts', fixed at 7s per annum. Shepstone argued that a hut tax created 'every advantage of both a property and an income tax, and has the further recommendation of directly discouraging poligamy [*sic*], that great incentive to the exclusive acquirement of cattle, as the most desirable description of property'.[20] The adoption of the hut tax was a landmark in Natal's development of indirect rule, and the connections Shepstone drew between taxation, polygamy and civilisation continued to shape revenue collection in the colony throughout the nineteenth century.

Furthermore, future British efforts to raise isiZulu-speaking Africans in the scale of civilisation would not be confined to Natal. In 1879 Sir Bartle Frere rationalised the invasion of Zululand partly on the grounds that the Zulu 'belong to the same race which furnishes the good humoured volatile labourers and servants who abound in Natal, men capable of being moulded in the ways of civilisation, and when not actually trained to manslaughter not naturally blood-thirsty nor incurably barbarous'.[21] By the time the hut-tax system was introduced in Zululand in 1888, the transformation of young Zulu men into the 'volatile labourers and servants', which the southern African economy depended upon, was well advanced.

## Colonial debates over African marriage

The issue of African marriage as contracted in Natal and Zululand was central to settler discussions about civilisation and barbarism. Settler discussions of the Zulu kingdom frequently emphasised the king's tyrannical control over his soldiers' nuptials. As early as 1847, the Locations Commission had insisted that any 'improvement of the natives' in Natal depended on 'raising their women in the scale of native society', for 'polygamy and bartering for women prevail universally in their worst form in the district'.[22] No official action was taken in Natal until 1869, when regulations proclaimed under a new law imposed a tax on every marriage contracted by Africans, restricted the practice of *ukulobola* (the giving of bridewealth cattle) and required that brides publicly express their assent before an official witness for marriages to be valid. The implementation of these measures unleashed a storm of protest from white settlers and missionaries, and the controversy over polygamy further emphasises how colonial myths about the barbarism of isiZulu-speaking Africans shaped colonial policies.[23]

While economic considerations informed both the government's decision to pass the 1869 legislation and settlers' opposition to the law, both sides drew from ideas of civilisation and savagery to defend their positions. In Enlightenment theory, the condition of women was regarded as an index of the level of civilisation of any society. It was argued that among savages 'the women of a family are usually treated as the servants or slaves of the men' and that nothing could exceed the 'dependence and subjection in which they are kept, or the toil and drudgery which they are obliged to undergo'.[24] Wives in these societies were 'bought and sold, like any other species of property' by their husbands from their fathers and 'the conclusion of a bargain of this nature, together with the payment of the price, has therefore become the most usual form of solemnity in the celebration of their marriages'.[25] This theory helps to explain why settlers frequently compared African polygamous marriages in Natal and Zululand to slavery transactions. African men supposedly purchased large numbers of African women and regarded them as property, to be bought and sold like cattle. It was lamented that this savagery resulted in downtrodden women and unmanly, promiscuous, lazy men.

While all white Natalians agreed that female oppression was a sign of African barbarism, they could not agree on the best way to ameliorate the position of women and thereby raise African society in the scale of civilisation. Settlers and missionaries argued that moral legislation abolishing traditional African marriage practices would allow civilised domestic relations to emerge, and consequently black women and men would be rescued from barbarism. Conveniently, the enforcement of civilised monogamous marriages would also encourage black men to work for whites. Officials in contrast insisted that the only judicious way to facilitate civilisation was to employ indirect methods to regulate African marriage practices, rather than abolish them outright. Furthermore, officials insisted that the marriage tax would encourage Africans to enter the employ of settlers and augment the treasury.

In 1869 Shepstone recommended the new marriage regulations on the grounds that their implementation could 'only favour the operation of natural causes to achieve the extinction of polygamy'.[26] And, when called upon to defend the law, he reported that its provisions had the effect of 'protecting the young suitor from the mere property competition of the rich old polygamist: – in short, it makes the union a marriage, instead of practically a mere sale'. He went on to state that the application of the law since 1869 had greatly improved '[i]n every respect . . . the condition of both the young men and women . . . and native marriage has been placed on a better footing'.[27] It is possible also that Shepstone viewed these regulations as a further means by which he could appropriate the Zulu monarch's traditional control over marriage and thereby consolidate his position as the Great White Father.[28]

Lieutenant-Governor Keate endorsed Shepstone's appraisal of the measure.[29] In African society, Keate wrote, 'at present it is the wives and children who support by their labour the heads of families' and until 'surrounding circumstances so change as to throw upon the husband and the father the work and the duty of supporting wife and children polygamy will prevail'.[30] Any attempt to tackle polygamy directly would be imprudent because 'all that can be done by Legislative interference is to help on and remove obstructions [to] the natural causes which are leading however slowly to that result'.[31] The means by which the marriage registration measure would help on and remove these 'obstructions' would be by giving 'to the woman, what has hitherto been entirely denied to her, a voice in her own disposal, and by so doing tend to raise her in her own estimation and in the social scale, and thus give her an influence in the control and management of her own family and eventually beyond its limits'.[32] Furthermore, the marriage tax would serve to increase the supply of African labour to settlers by encouraging 'labour habits among the male portion of the native community upon which more than anything else the extinction of polygamy depends'.[33]

The leading settler opponent of the legislation was *Natal Witness* editor R.E. Ridley, who detailed how the legal recognition of 'a vicious and brutal polygamy' and 'woman slavery' condemned Africans to barbarism. If settlers wanted Africans to continue 'to be shrouded in the thick mantle of superstition and vice' and to remain impervious to Christianity and 'the gentle teaching of civilisation', they should strengthen and foster isiZulu-speaking Africans in their 'present depravity'. If, however, white Natalians had 'any faith that this tractable savage can be raised, can be weaned from his brutalising customs, can learn the practices of civilisation, and can appreciate the high truths and discharge the holy duties of our common Christianity, then let us cancel this foolish law'.[34] Legalising polygamy, Ridley maintained, had the effect of 'making the savage habits of the Kafir perpetual'.[35]

Ridley also maintained that polygamy presented a danger to settlers, in particular women and children. The controversy over the marriage law coincided with a 'rape scare' in the colony, which greatly alarmed white Natalians.[36] Ridley warned that when

> one man is allowed to have five wives, it is clear that four must go unmarried
> and wifeless, as nature is pretty uniform in the supply of the two sexes. If in
> England they point with sorrow to the fact that there are no less than 500,000
> unmarried women, in Natal we reverse the picture, and present to the world
> of philanthropists a formidable phalanx of savage unmarried men, greater by
> far in proportion to the respective populations.[37]

The view that polygamy ensured that only older richer men could marry, leaving 'hot-blooded youths frustrated'[38] anticipated colonial perceptions of the amaZulu ten years later. In justifying the invasion of Zululand in 1879 Sir Bartle Frere denounced 'regulations' in the kingdom that were 'directed to forming every young man in Zululand into a celibate man-destroying gladiator'.[39]

In the minds of other prominent colonists, the barbaric slavery of polygamy hindered the establishment of a civilised commercial society in Natal. Well-known settler Thomas Phipson argued that if it were not for the savage state of African society, the white settler 'would be able to sell his labour or produce in a fair market' and would be able to afford 'the food and clothing appertaining to civilised life'. Good prices would be obtained for agricultural products, on the one hand, and 'consumers, employed in arts, trades and commerce', would be found on the other hand. However, as things stood, none of these things could happen because

> [t]he black man either sets to work the girls and women whom he breeds or
> buys, or he '*sebenzas*' (for work it cannot properly be called) a few months for
> the white man, and spends his money in cattle and women; or lastly, he ploughs
> himself (or makes his boys do it more likely), and thus comes into the market
> as a competitor with his civilised neighbour.[40]

Although Phipson claimed that Africans had a right to live 'barbarously, to wear rags, or skins, or nothing, when at home, to eschew groceries and squat in a beehive hut', by doing so they tended 'to drag down to the same level' all who competed with them in agriculture. The settler farmer could not afford to live a civilised life 'so long as his savage competitor continues to be a savage, and so to undersell him'.[41]

Combined opposition from settlers and isiZulu-speaking patriarchs forced the government to abolish the marriage tax in 1875. Even so, Natal officials and settlers continued to employ Enlightenment theories about civilisation and savagery to defend their respective positions on polygamy after the controversy had receded.

### Conclusion

From the vantage point of the twenty-first century, it is easy to dismiss debates over Zulu or African barbarism and European civilisation as settler racism. However, the importance of Enlightenment theories of societal development should not be underestimated, for they helped to shape Natal's system of indirect rule and later informed both colonial and imperial policies toward the Zulu kingdom. With a near-obsessive focus on 'rapacious' habits of 'savage' life – polygamous customs in particular – Natal whites and their imperial overlords felt justified in typecasting isiZulu-speaking people as the progeny of pent-up, celibate warriors of Shaka's 'frightfully efficient man-slaying machine'. Such a view helped to justify colonial repression of African peoples in KwaZulu-Natal from the Anglo-Zulu War of 1879 to the 1906 Poll Tax Uprising and beyond.

### Notes

1. 'Sir Theophilus Shepstone Disagrees with the Orange Free State President, 1892', in *From the South African Past: Narratives, Documents and Debates*, ed. J.A. Williams (New York: Houghton Mifflin, 1997), p. 160.
2. For Enlightenment theories in the Cape colonial context see A. Bank, 'The Great Debate and the Origins of South African Historiography', *Journal of African History* 38 (1997): 261–81; 'Liberals and Their Enemies: Racial Ideology at the Cape of Good Hope, 1820 to 1850' (Ph.D. diss., University of Cambridge, 1995); E. Elbourne, 'Domesticity and Dispossession: The Ideology of "Home" and the British Construction of the "Primitive" from the Eighteenth to the Early Nineteenth Centuries' (unpublished paper, Princeton, 1999).
3. P. Maloney, 'Savagery and Civilisation: Early Victorian Notions', *New Zealand Journal of History* 35:2 (2001): 153–54.
4. See for example R. Meek, *Social Science and the Ignoble Savage* (Cambridge: Cambridge University Press, 1976), p. 2.
5. See for example H. Cloete's 1843 despatch to J. Montagu in J. Bird, *The Annals of Natal 1495 to 1845* Vol. 2 (Cape Town: Maskew Miller, 1965), pp. 290–99.
6. Shepstone Memorandum, 26 April 1846 in British Parliamentary Papers (BPP), *Correspondence Relating to the Settlement of Natal*. Presented August 1850 (London: Her Majesty's Stationery Office [HMSO], 1850), pp. 44–47.

7. C. Hamilton, *Terrific Majesty: The Powers of Shaka Zulu and the Limits of Historical Invention* (Cambridge, MA: Harvard University Press, 1998), pp. 72–129.

8. Shepstone Memorandum, 26 April 1846 in BPP, *Correspondence*, pp. 45–46. Shepstone's contention that the rise of the Zulu state caused widespread anarchy and violence in southeast Africa has long been debated by historians. For an introduction to the so-called *mfecane* debate, see C. Hamilton, ed. *The Mfecane Aftermath: Reconstructive Debates in Southern African History* (Johannesburg: Witwatersrand University Press and Pietermaritzburg: University of Natal Press, 1995).

9. For an introduction to Enlightenment theories of civilisation and savagery and the philosophers who espoused them, see Meek, *Social Science*.

10. A. Ferguson, *An Essay on the History of Civil Society 1767* (Edinburgh: Edinburgh University Press, 1966, reprint), pp. 100–05 and J. Millar, *The Origin of the Distinction of Ranks; or An Inquiry into the Circumstances which Give Rise to Influence and Authority in the Different Members of Society* (London: Longmans, 1779, 3rd edition), pp. 171–97.

11. Locations Commission Report in BPP, *Correspondence Relative to the Establishment of the Settlement of Natal.* Presented July 1848 (London: HMSO, 1848), p. 132

12. Grey to Smith, 10 December 1847 in BPP, *Correspondence*, 1848, pp. 138–39.

13. Cited in D. Welsh, *The Roots of Segregation: Native Policy in Colonial Natal, 1845–1910* (Cape Town: Oxford University Press, 1971), pp. 14, 17.

14. The term 'decentralised despotism' is Mahmood Mamdani's. See M. Mamdani, *Citizen and Subject: Contemporary Africa and the Legacy of Late Colonialism* (Princeton: Princeton University Press, 1996).

15. Grey to Smith, 19 June 1848 in BPP, *Correspondence*, 1848, p. 223.

16. Ferguson, *An Essay*, p. 101. See also Millar, *The Origin*, p. 43.

17. Grey to Smith, 19 June 1848 in BPP, *Correspondence*, 1848, p. 222.

18. Smith to Grey, 4 March 1848; Grey to Smith, 19 June 1848 in BPP, *Correspondence*, 1848, pp. 218, 222.

19. Grey to Smith, 19 June 1848 in BPP, *Correspondence*, 1848, p. 222.

20. Shepstone Memorandum on Hut Tax, 18 June 1849 in BPP, *Correspondence*, 1850, p. 65.

21. Cited in R. Cope, *Ploughshare of War: The Origins of the Anglo-Zulu War of 1879* (Pietermaritzburg: University of Natal Press, 1999), p. 202.

22. Locations Commission Report in BPP, *Correspondence*, 1848, p. 133.

23. For detailed analyses of the marriage law controversy see Welsh, *Roots of Segregation*, pp. 67–96 and J. Martens, ' "So Destructive of Domestic Security and Comfort": Settler Domesticity, Race and the Regulation of African Behaviour in the Colony of Natal, 1843–1893' (Ph.D. diss., Queen's University, Kingston, 2001), pp. 78–134.

24. Millar, *The Origin*, pp. 42–43.

25. Ibid., p. 49.

26. Pietermaritzburg Archives Repository (PAR), Secretary for Native Affairs Files (SNA) 1/7/8 (pp. 18–23), T. Shepstone, 'Memorandum: Registration of Native Marriages', 22 March 1869, p. 23.

27. PAR, SNA 1/7/7 (pp. 122–29), T. Shepstone, 'Memorandum . . . on the Law No. 1, 1869', 5 January 1875, p. 125.

28. For a discussion of the impact of the 1869 legislation on African communities in Natal, see B. Carton, ' "The New Generation . . . Jeer at Me, Saying We Are All Equal Now": Impotent African Patriarchs, Unruly African Sons in Colonial South Africa' in *The Politics of Age and Gerontocracy in Africa: Ethnographies of the Past & Memories of the Present*, ed. M. Aguilar (Trenton: Africa World Press, 1998), pp. 31–64.

29. PAR, Government House Files (GH) 1216 (pp. 313–29), Keate to Buckingham and Chandos, 24 October 1868, p. 321.

30. Ibid.

31. Ibid.

32. Ibid.

33. Ibid., pp. 322–23.

34. *Natal Witness*, 11 May 1869.

35. Ibid.

36. For an analysis of the rape scare, see N. Etherington, 'Natal's Black Rape Scare of the 1870s', *Journal of Southern African Studies* 15:1 (1988), pp. 36–53. For an analysis of legislation passed in response to the scare, see J. Martens, 'Polygamy, Sexual Danger, and the Creation of Vagrancy

Legislation in Colonial Natal', *Journal of Imperial and Commonwealth History* 31:3 (2003): 24–45.

37.  *Natal Witness*, 21 May 1869.
38.  Etherington, 'Natal's Black Rape Scare': 45.
39.  Frere to Hicks Beach, 24 January 1879 in BPP, *Further Correspondence Respecting the Affairs of South Africa*, presented March 1879 (London: HMSO, 1879), p. 46.
40.  R. Currey, ed. *Letters & Other Writings of a Natal Sheriff: Thomas Phipson 1815–76* (Cape Town: Oxford University Press, 1968), pp. 131–32.
41.  Currey, *Letters & Other Writings*, pp. 131–32.

# Chapter 12

# Awaken *Nkulunkulu,* Zulu God of the Old Testament

Pioneering Missionaries During
the Early Age of Racial Spectacle

BENEDICT CARTON

FEW HISTORIANS WOULD DISPUTE that nineteenth-century Natal was 'one of the most heavily-evangelised regions of the globe'.[1] Such a contention suggests that Christianity swept into this region of South Africa like an overpowering wave. After leaving their ships, the first proselytisers of the British Church Missionary Society (CMS) and American Board Mission (ABM)[2] were certainly convinced of their future success.[3] When ABM missionary Reverend George Champion made landfall in December 1835, he stood amid 'naked Kaffirs' (as the people of Port Natal are called, Zulus properly). Shortly thereafter he described in his journal the effect of this incident. 'Happily disappointed', he and his small group of American Congregationalists would move quickly to bring 'the gladness of salvation',[4] alongside their friends, Anglican CMS missionary Allen Gardiner and his successor Reverend Francis Owen.[5] They envisaged a Protestant promised land that even spanned the Zulu kingdom, then seen by Europeans, who heard stories of the 'monstrous' Shaka, as a repository of 'darkness & . . . death'.[6] This forecast soon required revision, as Champion's lament in 1836 attests: 'When speaking of God to any of these people, they have usually either stared about the heavens in wonder, or listened to our words as an unmeaning story'.[7]

The local experts that Champion tapped for insights offered misleading information.[8] When recruiting ABM preachers to South Africa in 1833, London Missionary Society superintendent in the Cape, Reverend John Philip, wrote to the American *Missionary Herald*, portraying what they might encounter east of his colony.[9] To establish an identifiable point of reference for his depiction[10] of 'Zoolah warriors', Philip compared them to 'Mohammedans'. Ingeniously, he went on to suggest that the latter had borrowed their concept of 'paradise' from the 'ancestors of the Zoolahs'. Next, he proposed a 'scale of civilisation' that located 'barbarous'

*Reverend George Champion.*

Zulus on the bottom rung, Muslims above them, and Christians at the top.[11] Philip's hierarchy evoked a tenet of the Great Chain of Being according to which God made various peoples but only enlightened some of them,[12] leaving much of humanity either totally ignorant or only faintly aware of 'true religion'.[13] This paradigm imbued proselytisers with confidence that if they could discern whether the 'Zoolah warrior' had glimpsed his ancestral paradise, they could also determine that he was ready to accept the gospel.

Evangelical estimates aside, from the 1830s to the 1850s (and in fact throughout the nineteenth century) the quest to redeem Natal and Zululand would produce few neophytes. Norman Etherington's *Preachers, Peasants and Politics in Southeast Africa* was one of the first books to consider why conversion proceeded at a glacial pace.[14] More specifically, he asked which Africans 'opposed . . . the missionaries in Natal'. His conclusion was 'nearly everyone: rich and poor; leaders and followers; old people and newly-weds; mothers and maidens; polygynists and single men'.[15] Many factors contributed to the rejection of the Bible, not least the British authorities' disregard for proselytisation. When in 1847 the Diplomatic Agent to the Native Tribes Theophilus Shepstone boasted of 'Christian government', he referred to practical, if not apostolic goals, among them winning the 'obedience' of one 'hundred thousand natives'. As an official charged with consolidating imperial power after the British annexation of Natal in 1842, he never forced Africans to attend churches; nor did he press the few *amakholwa*, or converted 'believers', to enlarge their communities.

Rather, Shepstone negotiated the imposition of indirect rule by recognising rights of isiZulu-speaking chiefs and homestead heads to preserve their customary realm, including ancestral worship.[16]

European travellers, hunters and traders also hindered the civilising mission by casting doubt on its motives.[17] For example, the French naturalist Adulphe Delegorgue, who lived with Africans from 1838 to 1844, denounced the judgmental 'machinations' of ABM clergymen. After one bush excursion, he stopped to rest at an isiZulu-speaking chief's homestead in the vicinity of an American '*omphindiss*' (missionary).[18] The chief was anything but welcoming: 'You are a white man; it is strange that you do not ask [the nearby evangelist] for hospitality and a place to spend the night'. Delegorgue answered:

> I prefer a black man to . . . white men who dress in white, and who live in white houses, but whose hearts are black; while there are black men living in smoky black houses whose hearts are white [good]. I believe you are one of those black men, and I would like to ask you for a hut where I may spend the night, some maize to satisfy my hunger, and some *tchoula* [*utshwala*, beer] to quench my thirst.

The chief allegedly replied: 'How can a white man dare to ask for *tchoula*, the black man's beer, which the *omphondiss* . . . forbids us to drink?' Delegorgue explained that the '*omphondiss* lies; *tchoula* . . . strengthens a man when he is weak, and takes away fatigue; much more than this, it gives rise to a gentle gaiety and, for that alone, I swear by [the Zulu king] Dingaan, it makes one a better man'. 'Yes,' the chief agreed, 'it nourishes and fortifies, but the *omphondiss* told us that it makes the heart black and wicked . . .'[19] This dialogue alludes to rituals of social belonging embedded in Zulu cosmology, such as drinking beer (*utshwala*) at gatherings, which typically began with a patriarch setting aside a pot of brew for the ancestors to express thanks for their sacred protection of clan and chiefdom. Champion and his cohorts, most notably Delegorgue's figure of scorn, the ABM Reverend Aldin Grout, often expressed disappointment that the individual message of salvation could not penetrate this strong collective ethos of kinship.[20]

More recently, scholars have reconsidered these missionary frustrations as part of ambiguous and evolving – rather than futile and sterile – interactions with intended converts. Indeed, the inability of nineteenth-century missionaries to appeal to isiZulu-speaking people raised pivotal questions for Jean and John Comaroff in their path-breaking 1991 exploration of the 'long conversation', or conversion, in colonial South Africa. Spreading the gospel, they argued, was never a one-sided affair, but rather a two-way religious drama. While Europeans may have directed the opening scene, Africans dominated subsequent acts using their script of Christianity, which missionaries had to learn.[21] In this context early proselytisers in Natal launched their 'long conversation' by probing 'heathen' knowledge of the Creator. The ensuing exchanges obliged them to comprehend 'a peculiar dialect', a necessity that provoked more humour than revelation.[22] One ABM minister recalled what happened to a colleague who 'preach[ed] too early [and] confounded the word *lalelani*, signifying "give attention" . . . [with] "*Lalani, nonke* (Go to sleep, all of you)"'. In another instance, the 'wife of a missionary, wishing to have a young man kill two ducks, had not noticed that the word for men differed from that for ducks in one letter: *Amadoda* (men), *amadada* (ducks). She said to him, "*Hamba bulala amadoda amabili* (Go and kill two men)." The young man looking up with a smile asked, "Which men shall I kill?"'[23]

Such linguistic confusions highlighted a pitfall awaiting evangelists in nineteenth-century Natal – their incapacity to communicate the gospel. Some coped with this impotence by turning to 'racial science', which helped them to justify their failures in terms of preordained biology. At first this 'natural determinism' had swayed few preachers who rejoiced instead in the universal right to divine 'civilisation'. By the 1840s, however, virulent racism had infected most of colonial South Africa, including Reverend Philip's church[24] and other mission societies that bemoaned the 'opprobrium' of Ham plaguing the 'Dark Continent'.[25] Many of these preachers shared fundamental views of land-hungry settlers in the eastern Cape who fought wars to eradicate what they termed Xhosa 'savagery'.[26] Proselytisers caught up in these frontier conflicts began to contemplate a polygenist ladder of separate races, arranged arbitrarily from Anglo-Saxon downward to lesser types, among them 'Zoolah', 'Kaffir' and 'Hottentot'. These rankings animated exhibitions objectifying Africans in Europe, America and South Africa[27] and reinforced the prominence of leading 'race scientists' such as the ethnographer James Prichard, anatomist Georges Cuvier, and craniometrist Samuel Morton.[28]

Of all race scientists, the Englishman Prichard and his studies of 'primitive religion' most influenced the incipient 'civilising mission' in Natal, according to Russell Martin. Prichard championed an Evangelical movement whose maxim was the natural unity of Man.[29] At the same time, he 'posited that the first people had been black . . . [and] identified the cause of subsequent whiteness as civilisation itself', thus making skin colour 'both a marker of civilisation and a product of it'.[30] This interpretation of monogenesis enabled clergymen in early nineteenth-century South Africa to account for the *visible* differences between 'heathen' Africans and 'civilised' Europeans.[31] Prichard opposed the social evolutionary argument of polygenists who claimed that 'the races of man were primordially distinct species'.[32] Though at odds with the Bible, polygenists influenced Natal missionaries who embraced the comparative anatomy associated with popular ethnographic spectacles.

Perhaps more than any 'freak show', the display of a Cape Khoi woman named Sara Baartman 'who suffered from steatopygia, enlargement of the behind', established a 'modern' taxonomy that classified Africans in a lower order of species. In London alone, tens of thousands ogled this 'Hottentot Venus'. From 1811 until her death in 1815, she would stand solemnly – barely cloaked and utterly denigrated – on podiums across Europe. In addition, her presence lifted the profile of comparative anatomists such as Georges Cuvier. He was renowned for examining Sara Baartman and insisting she was no *belle sauvage* but a species one notch above orang-utans, or troglodytes.[33] The Hottentot Venus similarly intrigued and repulsed apologists of slavery like William Harper, a member of the South Carolina slave-owning class that clashed with abolitionists in American Board circles.[34] His 1838 *Memoir on Slavery*[35] declared that eradicating the South's 'peculiar institution' would be as unnatural as comparing the Hottentot Venus to 'Medicean' women.[36] Harper seized on a trope in *Discovery and Adventure in Africa*, an 1832 travel guide consulted by American missionaries in Natal that described Baartman's 'unfortunate tribe' as one of 'the inferior orders of creation'.[37]

In the urban north, playwrights incorporated Venus-like stereotypes into 'African vogue' dramas in which black actors starred as Ethiopian belles. This theatre of racial worth would fuel Jump Jim Crow minstrelsy and the dissemination of inspirational pamphlets such as *The Zulu Blind Boy's Story* published by the American Tract Society (a booster of ABM work in Natal).[38] No doubt, the genre of African vogue stirred interest in the mid-nineteenth-century Manhattan monologue, 'Zooloo Kaffir Entertainment', a partial adaptation of Gardiner's monogenist account of Zulu religion[39] and P.T. Barnum's Broadway polygenist humbug, 'What Is It? Man-Monkey', with its accompanying skit of the 'Zulu War Dancer', staged decades before news of Isandlwana reached broadsheets in 1879.[40] More than leisure, these performances instructed Victorian masses to ask what divided monogenists from polygenists: did the Hottentot Venus or Man-Monkey confound the natural unity of Man? 'Black Atlantic cultural traffic'[41] carried critiques on this question to Natal[42] and back to English-speaking centres, where they stoked British anxieties over industrial 'barbarism' and American debates over Irish newcomers. Indeed, while Natal preachers failed to convert the 'primitive' Zulu, their fellow Evangelists at home struggled in vain to rescue the 'savage' poor. To social reformer Henry Mayhew the 'wandering tribes' of London's godless warrens presented as much of an insurmountable challenge to Victorian progress as the irredeemable South African 'native'.[43] The pool of racial stereotypes during Mayhew's slum investigations included caricatures of the 'simian' Irish who fled hunger in the countryside for cities on both sides of the Atlantic.[44] In New York 'nativist' American Board churches pondered whether these 'potato famine' immigrants, which newspapers disparaged as 'simian' Celts, could be saved from their 'backward' Catholicism and assimilated into a Protestant ('white') republic.[45] ABM missionaries probably joined in this 'long conversation' after reading a section in *Discovery and Adventure in Africa* explaining how *simia* species resembled 'the human race', but their low brain capacity negated their 'fancied alliance to mankind'.[46] By the early 1850s, Charles Dickens had summarised these commentaries in a far-reaching, stinging review of the London version of 'Zooloo Kaffir Entertainment' (titled 'Native Zulu Kafirs'), featuring isiZulu-speaking Africans from Natal playing tribesmen at St George's Gallery. The novelist's panned the production in his weekly journal *Household Words* and New York's *Spirit of the Times*. Dickens recapped the Zulu effort on stage by appraising a 'war song' and proffering an analogy:

> [E]very gentleman who finds himself excited by the subject, instead of crying 'Hear, hear!' as is the custom with us, darts from the rank and tramples out the life, . . . or performs a whirlwind of atrocities on the body of the imaginary enemy. Several gentlemen becoming thus excited at once, and pounding away without the least regard to the orator, that illustrious person is rather in the position of an orator in an Irish House of Commons. But, several of these scenes of savage life bear a strong generic resemblance to an Irish election, and I think would be extremely well received and understood at Cork.

Dickens decided the fate of this 'clucking, stamping, jumping, tearing' figure: 'I call a savage something highly desirable to be civilized off the face of the earth'.[47] A recent literary scholar has explained that the great defender of Victorian underdogs was almost certainly advocating 'improvement' over annihilation.[48] Yet Dickens should not receive such an easy pass. His tone echoed a conclusion in William Harris's 1839 *The Wild Sports of Southern Africa*, a book sold widely in London. Harris urged the 'necessity, dictated alike by reason, justice, and humanity, of exterminating from off the face of the earth, a race of monsters'. He referred to blacks in the Cape Colony.[49] Whatever the case, it should come as no surprise that Irish and Zulu people would soon appear together in cartoons that scorned the very notion that 'ape-like terrors' deserved a place in the British Empire.[50]

Needless to say, these controversies over 'citizenship and whiteness'[51] elevated the profile of race scientists such as Samuel Morton, whose specialty was to grade what he assumed a priori were superior Caucasian or inferior Negro mental faculties.[52] In the early nineteenth century Morton, the son of an Irish immigrant, left the United States to train in medicine at Edinburgh, Prichard's Alma Mater. Morton's education prepared him for one intellectual feat, to shift the ethnographic gaze from Venus's steatopygia to the 'savage's' head. His 1839 book *Crania Americana*, described how he developed American anthropology 'by patiently sifting birdseed or shot into human skulls'.[53] Among phrenologists, this experiment purportedly verified the presence of distinct races with wholly different levels of intelligence, which either lifted them into white societies or sunk them into black tribes. Given Morton's influence it is not surprising that some ABM missionaries who focused on African physiognomy – for example, the 'dark and greasy bodies'[54] of their Zulu flock – were attracted to popular phrenological ideas that assumed that the conformation of the skull fixed the 'national

TIME'S WAXWORKS.

*Victoria's 'chamber of horrors': Father Time introduces Zulu and Irish 'ape-like terrors'.*

character' of the 'predacious' Malay, 'indolent' Ethiopian, and so forth.[55] One American evangelist practically borrowed prose from George Combe's 'Phrenological Remarks' appended to *Crania Americana*,[56] when suggesting that an examination of converts' brains would illustrate that though 'Zulus have black skins and woolly hair . . . they have much to distinguish them from the negro of Western Africa . . . [And while] some of them have thick, protruding lips, and flat noses . . . it is not unusual to meet with the aquiline nose, straight lip, and . . . much intelligence'.[57] Such pronouncements demonstrated how the phrenologist's bible helped some ABM evangelists judge 'fitness for church fellowship in professed converts'.[58]

Despite this pat assessment, missionaries could rely on no scientific or aesthetic standard of appraising Zulu people. For example, the Cape-based missionary Stephen Kay, whose 1833 book *Travels and Researches in Caffraria* was sold in England, Natal and America, admired *abafazi*, a derogatory isiZulu term used to describe unmarried women: 'They are in many instances beautiful (laying aside the prejudice of colour).' But once *abafazi* married, he lamented domesticity ruined their allure, for 'the hard labour which they commence as soon as they enter the married state . . . [destroys what] nature may have gifted them, and they become, at an early age, even disgustingly ugly'.[59] Preacher Josiah Tyler, who left America for a Zulu mission in the late 1840s, liked the 'bodily strength [of] Zulus'. They surpass the 'average European', he contended, and with their 'good health, the result of simple food and moderate exercise, the natives are proof against a multitude of ills incident to a state of civilisation'. Tyler then dabbled in comparative anatomy: 'In contrasting Zulus with American negroes I perceive a marked difference. The former, as a race, are taller and more muscular, with loftier foreheads, higher cheekbones, and pleasanter expression of countenance. Their lips are not so thick, nor are their noses so flat . . . [S]ome of them bear a striking resemblance . . . [to] Arabic features . . .'[60]

Another European author who resided in Natal during the late 1830s and early 1840s was more explicit. 'Let me not be told', he intoned, 'that the Caucasian race is the most beautiful of all, and that it is universally pleasing . . .' If isiZulu-speaking Africans were 'to see the naked white body, [they] . . . would realise that they themselves were infinitely more beautiful, with their well-fleshed muscles and their firm rounded curves . . . At the moment, our bodies are so misshapen by our clothing, that our health is in danger and our sculptors in despair'.[61] He particularly revelled in the 'bearing of the Amazoulou girl [which] is so natural, or perhaps cultivated with such art, that I would defy the most rigid moralist, the severest of men, to find in their nudity anything to offend. This was my independent observation, but I do not claim to be unique in making it as it is apparent to every European upon his arrival in Natal'.[62] These portrayals – admiring, ambivalent or appalled – tended to reduce Zulu people to one-dimensional objects of nature and the modern European gaze.

Different notions of bodily fitness and function resonated with isiZulu-speaking Africans, especially in the assessments of the civilising mission they shared with religious colonisers. For example, in 1899 an 80-year-old man from a *kholwa* community just north of Durban, Sijewana kaMjanyelwa, told a Natal official conversant in the Bible that the 'first converts to Christianity as well as the missionaries were spoken of as those who *dunuza'd*, so that their anuses pointed upward'. The verb, *ukudunuza*, could describe the way people knelt, leaned forward, and prayed. *Ukudunuza* could also suggest a sexual union involving two males, or, more simply, an act of 'sodomy'.[63] Africans who attended services where food was served allegedly pointed to other parts of their bodies to express their feelings for the gospel. One Natal missionary noted:

> Not infrequently, they begin to talk in a comforting way about how they have now left their old, evil ways, how they are now going to heaven, how they now have white, perfect hearts and are now doing the will of the Lord, how they now love and serve God, and – to get to the main point – that they hope to get a lot of food so that they can become fat. (At this point they stretch out their arms to indicate the size of the stomach they want to have.) Unfortunately, one must say that the belly is their God, indeed their only God.[64]

*Josiah Tyler's sculpted ideal (c. mid-nineteenth century).*

*A Medicean Zulu painted by George Angas (1840s).*

By contrast, it is striking that the few Anglican missionaries, like Allen Gardiner, whose writings betray no obsession with the measurements of physiognomy or phrenology, appeared more able than his American counterparts to advance the 'long conversation'. Rather than dwelling on 'heathen' nakedness or brains, he persistently *asked* isiZulu-speakers questions about their cosmological outlook. For example, when Gardiner visited the Zulu court in the mid-1830s, he probed royals about whether they believed in God. They offered vague replies, but Gardiner pressed on until he said he learned of the existence of 'an overruling spirit', *uMvelingqangi*, and another, more diminutive Supreme Being called 'Koolukoolwani' or *uNkulunkulu*.[65] He also reconstructed the story of an epic journey involving a lizard and chameleon, which he interpreted as a crude parable of creation. A fuller version of this tale would be transcribed by a British army captain during a trip along the Natal coast with one of Gardiner's white translators, Henry Francis Fynn, who lived for a decade with his African wives and bi-racial children in traditional Zulu homesteads. Beginning in the mid-1820s the isiZulu-speaking Fynn, along with a few other British traders such as Francis Farewell and Henry Ogle, became 'clients' of the Zulu kingdom. They made Port Natal their base for selling cattle, skins and ivory to colonial and African commercial partners.[66] The army captain wrote the following account in his journal:

> Once upon a time The Great Spirit made a Man and a Woman. After their location it became a matter of consideration whether this couple should be endowed with Eternal or only Temporal Life [so] He forthwith dispatched a Cameleon [sic] and a Lizard each with a Message: and whichever Animal reached its destination first the Message of which it should be the Bearers [sic] was to be the future fate of the two Created Beings.

The opening lines bear some resemblance to Genesis, but the rest of the account reflects Zulu symbolism: 'The Message given the Cameleon was Makapile or Let him Live! That to the Lizard was Makafile or Let him Die! Both started together – but [the chameleon] went up into a tree to feed – and the Lizard . . . arrived first at the Man's abode and forthwith delivered the Message Dooming Man's [illegible word] to Death'.[67] This tale convinced Gardiner that his future converts recalled a dim memory of an afterlife with the 'Great Spirit' and a 'confused idea' of Jesus's resurrection.[68]

But rather than disentangle other possible biblical strands, Gardiner tied the thread that bound Zulu spirituality to patriarchal conventions that some of his counterparts associated with Hebrew kings Solomon, David and Herod. Here, again he probably counted on the observations of his isiZulu-speaking adviser Fynn,[69] who would later divulge:

[U]p to the period of their ['Kafirs'] becoming acquainted with white men they had but a very confused idea of a Deity. The opinion held by the most intelligent natives, during the reign of Chaka, was, that at death they would enter a world of spirits . . . [though] few Kafirs . . . state their belief that Umkulunkulu (the great great) shook the reeds with a strong wind, and there came from them the first man and woman.[70]

This remark was followed by a fuller account that compared Zulu spirituality to Hebrew worship. 'When I consider the perfection of their language, the remarkable suitability of their laws to their circumstances, and the nature of their offerings to their ancestral spirits, to say nothing of the resemblance of many of their customs to those of the ancient Jews, as prescribed in the ceremonial law, under the Levitical priesthood,' Fynn marvelled, 'I am led to form the opinion that the Kafir tribes have been very superior to what they are at the present time . . . I was surprised to find a considerable resemblance between many of the Kafir customs and those of the Jews.' He listed them: 'War offerings. Sin offerings. Propitiatory offerings. Festival of first fruits. The Proportion of the sacrifice given to the Isanusi (or witch doctor, as he is termed by Europeans). Periods of uncleanliness, on the decease of relatives and touching of the dead . . . Rejection of swine's flesh.' Fynn's comparison led 'him to form the opinion that the Kafir tribes have been very superior to what they are at the present time'.[71]

Gardiner's successor Reverend Owen – arguably, more driven than any pioneering evangelist to discover the vernacular definition of God – also acknowledged Fynn's expertise as a vital interlocutor.[72] In fact, Owen might have been better placed than any other missionary before the British annexation of Natal to comprehend indigenous spirituality. After all he was a special resident of the Zulu king from 1837 to 1838. But Owen had no converts to call on and felt isolated in his hut on the fringe of the royal Mgungundlovu residence.[73] Thus, he devoted more and more of his energies to discovering the local word for the creator, a quest that he urged other evangelists to join. In December 1837 he corresponded with Champion about the eventual need to invent an isiZulu term for God. Champion and his American cohorts opposed the praise name *uNkulunkulu*, which they said meant 'the great, great' and an 'ancient chief'. So, in keeping with Gardiner's findings on the matter, Owen and Champion agreed on one recommendation; they would use the Hebrew name 'Elohim' when speaking of the Zulu Supreme Being's 'action on the world'.[74]

Rooting Zulu ancestors in Palestine did not elevate their descendants to a privileged race. That Elohim's lost tribe could have been in South Africa might have confirmed assumptions of early nineteenth-century comparative philologists who reputedly traced 'physiological classification of racial difference' through 'historical linguistics'. In Britain and the United States, Champion, Gardiner and Owen enjoyed status as 'Caucasians' who spoke a vital Indo-European language, as opposed to Semitic people who spoke moribund Hebrew. While both Jew and Aryan supposedly had 'pure bloodlines' that flowed back to one 'Adamic' source, Semites were supposed to have degenerated into 'darkness' for they no longer saw the light of Christian truth.[75]

Furthermore, not every pioneering missionary considered the possibility that isiZulu-speaking Africans were related to Levi and Moses, but in the absence of an approved 'Christian' identity for *Nkulunkulu* they were sometimes regarded, in the words of Fynn, as the Jews of 'the Kafir tribes'.[76] Before Anglican Bishop John Colenso's decisive theological intervention in the 1850s ostensibly converted *Nkulunkulu* into the all-knowing and powerful being of the New Testament, the Zulu God in the minds of some of the first evangelists was not only the Great Spirit, with some worrisome pagan qualities, but also the deity of the ancient Mosaic faith.[77] As Jonathan Draper points out, by the early 1860s Colenso would relate to the Zulu as people of Semitic origin estranged from 'their ancestry as sons/grandsons of Abraham through Esau or Ishmael'.[78]

It is difficult to determine who fostered this Jew-Zulu contrivance. Were they neophytes embedding ancestral (*amadlozi*) worship in a newfound faith? Were they one of the more sympathetic, avowedly monogenist proselytisers like Gardiner who queried why the gospel was not meaningful to isiZulu-speaking Africans? Perhaps it was both. A comprehensive inquiry into this matter will require a deeper analysis of the Elohim analogy in evidence generated by *amakholwa* in the latter half of the nineteenth century. They revealed that some Zulu Christians reacted to colonial encroachment – the settlers who appropriated African land, employers who exploited labour, and officials who eroded customary authority – by seizing greater control of the discourse of righteousness. One of the more forceful voices in this chapter of the 'long conversation' came from Lazarus Mxaba, a Zulu patriarch who knew Colenso and many of the interpreters of missionaries, including the isiZulu-speaking Henry Francis Fynn. In 1901 Mxaba and two old Zulu men offered their testimony in an interview conducted by a fluent isiZulu linguist, the native affairs representative James Stuart. A question posed to the trio dealt with the tangle of ancestral tradition and *kholwa* theology. Mxaba weighed in by listing a

> number of Zulu customs . . . [and] identifying [them] with the Jews' such as
> 'slitting the ear, and the driving [of] a nail through a servant's ear who wished
> to live and die his master's servant'; to the *impepo* ceremony [a sweet-smelling
> plant burned as an offering]; to not destroying or throwing away of bones of
> a beast slaughtered, but burning same; to casting *umswani* [partly digested
> food in the slaughtered beast's small intestine] over the grave; to the manner
> of disposing of parts of a beast . . .

Stuart transcribed and interpreted some of what he heard:

> Mxaba, who is thoroughly well up in the whole subject, in native custom as
> well as biblical narrative etc., reminded me that one of the tribes, very soon
> after arriving in Palestine, took to worshipping the golden image of a calf. If
> *they* [emphasis in original], in a few years, could forget their God, is it not easy
> to believe that, after the lapse of many centuries, the two lost tribes might have
> fallen away from their original belief?

Stuart hazarded a guess as to why: '[H]ere are all these men [the Zulu trio, with
Mxaba in the middle] identifying themselves with the Jews and defending their
*amadhlozi*; they are in reality more Jews than Christians . . .! Fancy the Zulu can
claim to be related only to the Jews; they are in great distress; how can they expect
the Jews, themselves in misery, to help and deliver them?'[79] Stuart seemed amazed
that these three Zulu men embraced Judaism rather than have it claimed for them, as
it had been by prominent monogenists like Colenso, who saw in Zulu 'heathen' a
strayed brother capable of enlightened civilisation.[80] In addition, Stuart may have
been surprised to learn of the extent to which Mxaba, like other *amakholwa* at the
turn of the twentieth century, identified with biblical narratives that spoke to their
suffering under colonialism. It was during this period that revivalist 'Ethiopianism'
swept through isiZulu-speaking congregations, challenging missionary dominance
and condemning white rule. Ethiopian preachers were African men of God who
fostered modern 'black nationalism', a point that contemporary historians
demonstrate by quoting, 'let Ethiopia extend its hands to God', a line from Psalm 68
that 'Ethiopian' adherents deemed their clarion call.[81] Yet this invocation has its
rudiment in the biblical soil from which it springs, and needs to be explicated from
the scriptures that doubtless moved Mxaba. Crucially, the liberatory path of Jews is
identified as a universal signifier for the struggles of all oppressed peoples who yearn
for vindication of their claim on the 'ancient heavens'. The concluding verse of Psalm
68 should be quoted in full. It makes any providential design for Africa contingent
on a spiritual connection to 'the God of Israel' and his chosen people:

> Let nobles come from Egypt; let Ethiopia extend its hands to God. You
> kingdoms of the earth, sing to God, chant praise to the Lord who rides on the
> heights of ancient heavens. Behold as his voice resounds, the voice of power:
> 'Confess the power of God!' Over Israel is his majesty; his power is in the
> skies. Awesome in the sanctuary is God, the God of Israel; he gives power and
> strength to his people. Blessed be God!

## Notes

1. Norman Etherington, 'Christianity and African Society in Nineteenth-century Natal', in *Natal and Zululand from Earliest Times to 1910: A New History*, eds. Andrew Duminy and Bill Guest (Pietermaritzburg: University of Natal Press and Shuter & Shooter, 1989), p. 275.

2. The full title of the acronym ABM is the American Board of Commissioners for Foreign Missions.

3. This study does not focus on the first evangelists from France, Scandinavia, Prussia and Germany, who began to proselytise in colonial Natal in the 1840s and 1850s.

4. Alan Booth, ed. *Journal of Rev. George Champion: American Missionary in Zululand, 1835–1839* (Cape Town: Struik, 1967), pp. 1, 67. The Connecticut-born Champion (1810–41) graduated from Yale in 1831; three years later he sailed from Boston to South Africa accompanied by his new wife, Susanna Larner, and five ABM missionaries, among them Daniel Lindley and Aldin Grout and their families. See Booth, 'Introduction', *Journal*, p. viii. On ABM conversion strategies in Natal and Zululand, see *Missionary Herald*, January 1834, pp. 30–33.

5. George Cory, ed., *The Diary of the Rev. Francis Owen*, Vol. 7 (Cape Town: Van Riebeeck Society, 1926), pp. 7, 35, 85, 87, 89, 109, 122, 127. Letters from G. Champion to Collis, Cape Town, 2 April 1835, p. 55; and Venable to Anderson, Umhlatusi, 5 December 1837 in *Letters of the American Missionaries*, ed. D. Kotze (Cape Town: Van Riebeeck Society, 1950), pp. 55, 219.

6. Booth, *Journal*, p. 19; H. Robinson, ed. *Narrative of Voyages to Explore the Shores of Africa (Arabia and Madagascar) Performed in H.M. Ships Leven and Barracouta, Under the Direction of Capt. W.F.W. Owen R.N. by Command of the Lords Commanders of the Admiralty*, Vol. 1 (London: Richard Bentley, Publisher in Ordinary to His Majesty, 1833), p. 71; John Wright, 'The Dynamics of Power and Conflict in the Thukela-Mzimkhulu Region in the Late Eighteenth and Early Nineteenth Centuries: A Critical Reconstruction' (Ph.D. diss., University of the Witwatersrand, 1989), pp. 65–67.

7. Philippe Denis, *The Dominican Friars in Southern Africa: A Social History (1577–1990)*, (Leiden: Brill, 1998), pp. 39, 48. Champion's cohort, the British missionary and retired naval captain, Allen Gardiner (1794–1851), expressed similar sentiments: Allen Gardiner, *Narrative of a Journey to the Zoolu Country in South Africa* (Cape Town: Struik, [1936] 1966).

8. When ABM missionaries came to Natal, some complained that well-known travellers' accounts conveyed 'nonsense': Letter from Rev. Champion to Rev. Anderson, 10 Aug. 1837, in *Letters*, ed. Kotze, p. 199; see also *Boston Recorder*, 26 June 1835.

9. Reverend Philip (1775–1851) serenaded newly arrived ABM preachers with stories of David Livingstone and other icons of the Victorian gospel: Josiah Tyler, *Forty Years Among the Zulus* (Boston: Congregational Sunday School and Publishing Society, 1891), p. 22.

10. Reverend Philip's point of reference revealed a fascination with Orientalism. On early-nineteenth-century Orientalism in Great Britain and Europe, see Robert Young, *Colonial Desire: Hybridity in Theory, Culture and Race* (London: Routledge, 1995), pp. 100, 159–62; *White Mythologies: Writing History and the West* (London: Routledge, 1990); and, of course, Edward Said's classic *Orientalism: Western Representations of the Orient* (London: Routledge, 1978).

11. See 'Natural Capacity of the Human Race' in *Missionary Herald*, May 1833; for a Natal ABM endorsement of Philip's view of 'Mohammedans', see *New York Evangelist*, 20 June 1835 and *African Repository and Colonial Journal*, August 1835; on American Colonization Society interest in Philip's ranking of 'Zoolahs', see *African Repository and Colonial Journal*, December 1833. On Philip's influence on first missionaries in Natal, see 'Instructions of the Prudential Committee', Boston, 22 November 1834, Letters Received from the Board, 1834–59, II/1/1, 1/ABM, ABM Records, Pietermaritzburg Archives Repository (PAR). On Philip's trend-setting evangelism in the Cape, see Andrew Bank, 'The Great Debate and the Origins of South African Historiography', *Journal of African History* 38 (1997): 263.

12. Arthur Lovejoy, *The Great Chain of Being: A Study of the History of an Idea* (New York: Harper & Row, [1936] 1960), pp. 294, 204, 232–34.

13. On the Enlightenment-era Great Chain of Being, see Emmanuel Eze, 'Introduction', in *Race and the Enlightenment: A Reader*, ed., E. Eze (Cambridge, MA: Blackwell, 1997), pp. 1–7; see also Robert Gordon, 'The Venal Hottentot Venus and the Great Chain of Being', *African Studies* 51:2 (1992): 185–201. On missionary typologies of the heathen and converted, inflected by the vocabulary of racial science, see Paul Landau, 'Language' and Patrick Harries, 'Anthropology', in *Missions and Empire*, ed. Norman Etherington (Oxford: Oxford University Press, 2005), pp. 194–95 and

239–41. Natal missionaries such as Champion and Cambridge-trained Reverend Owen (1802–54) could thank their educational institutions for exposing them to monogenist-polygenist debates.

14. Norman Etherington, *Preachers, Peasants and Politics in Southeast Africa, 1835–1880: African Christian Communities in Natal, Pondoland and Zululand* (London: Royal Historical Society, 1978). On low conversion rates in Natal and Zululand, and neophyte responses to missionaries, see Norman Etherington, 'Kingdoms of This World and the Next: Christian Beginnings among Zulu and Swazi', in *Christianity in South Africa: A Political, Social and Cultural History*, eds. Richard Elphick and Rodney Davenport (Cape Town: David Philip, 1997).

15. Etherington, *Preachers, Peasants*, p. 59. Sheila Meintjies has also examined other processes impeding Christianity in Natal such as the legal restrictions on African converts' rights to own land. See Sheila Meintjies, 'Edendale 1850–1906: A Case Study of Rural Transformation and Class Formation in an African Mission in Natal' (Ph.D. diss., University of London, 1988).

16. Letter from Theophilus Shepstone, Pietermaritzburg to Superior Council of the African Institute, Paris, 10 November 1847, Despatched Letters 1847, November 10 – 1863 July 10, Vol. 70, (T.) Shepstone Papers, A96, PAR. On Shepstone's recognition of African patriarchs' rights in exchange for their loyalty to a white 'Supreme Chief', the Natal government, see David Welsh, *The Roots of Segregation: Native Policy in Colonial Natal, 1845–1910* (Cape Town: Oxford University Press, 1971), pp. 202–13.

17. British traders, too, resisted religious control of the civilising mission from the mid-to-late 1830s. See 'Protest of the Inhabitants of Natal against the Appointment of Capt. A. Gardiner, RN, as a Magistrate over Them for the Following Reasons', June/July 1837; and letters from Allen Gardiner, 'Ambanati, on the Umtongala', to Colonel Bell, Cape Town, 13 June 1837; and Colonel Bell, Cape Town, to Allen Gardiner, Port Natal, 24 July 1837 in *Records of Natal, Volume Three, August 1835–June 1838*, ed. B. Leverton (Pretoria: The Government Printer, 1990), pp. 178–81.

18. Adulphe Delegorgue, *Travels in Southern Africa*, Vol. 2 (Pietermaritzburg: University of Natal Press, 1997), p. 111. Delegorgue was referring to the Reverend Aldin Grout (1803–94), an American Board missionary. On Grout's legacy in colonial Natal, see Etherington, *Preachers, Peasants*, pp. 74–75.

19. Delegorgue, *Travels*, Vol. 2, pp. 109–10. Delegorgue's view of Zulu culture and Christianity was informed by the French thinkers he admired, namely the philosopher Jean Jacques Rousseau and the anatomist Georges Cuvier.

20. Booth, *Journal*, pp. 47, 64–65. Champion's cohorts recorded how the gospel went unheeded after only one prayer feast, where after serving food the assemby ate and refused religious instruction. Some missionaries admitted they did not save a single soul, though, as they maintained, refugees were ripe for conversion after being purportedly scattered by marauding Zulu regiments. See *Missionary Herald*, March 1837.

21. Jean Comaroff and John Comaroff, *Of Revelation and Revolution: Christianity, Colonialism, and Consciousness in South Africa*, Vol. 1 (Chicago: University of Chicago Press, 1991), pp. 17–18. See also Elizabeth Elbourne, 'Word Made Flesh: Christianity, Modernity and Cultural Colonialism in the Work of Jean and John Comaroff', *American Historical Review* 108 (2003): 435–59.

22. Missionaries such as Champion blamed his interpreter for draining scriptures of 'feeling' and 'unction'. See Booth, *Journal*, p. 12. One of Champion's principal interpreters was the Englishman Joseph Kirkman. See Cory, *The Diary*, p. 157. By 1838, Champion tried to conduct services before 'a few native women . . . in their own tongue', but there is no evidence that he converted Africans; see Cory, *The Diary*, pp. 127–28. It took several decades for ABM missionaries to find good isiZulu-speaking translators; see testimony of Rangu kaNotshiya, 12 November 1899, in *The James Stuart Archive of Recorded Oral Evidence Relating to the History of the Zulu and Neighbouring Peoples*, Vol. 5, eds. C. de B. Webb and J.B. Wright (Pietermaritzburg: University of Natal Press and Durban: Killie Campbell Collection, 2001), p. 256. Gardiner at one time had as his interpreter George Cyrus: Allen Gardiner, 'Treaty Concluded between Dingaan, King of the Zulus and the British Residents at Port Natal', 6 May 1835, p. 15 and 'Memorial of George Cyrus, Fort Peddie', 9 January 1838, p. 256, in *Records of Natal*, ed. Leverton.

23. Tyler, *Forty Years*, p. 34. See also Norman Etherington, 'Introduction', in *Missions and Empire*, ed. Etherington, pp. 1, 9–11.

24. Timothy J. Keegan, *Colonial South Africa and the Origins of the Racial Order* (Charlottesville, VA: University Press of Virginia, 1996), pp. 91, 127.

25. *Missionary Herald*, February 1841.

26. Keegan, *Colonial South Africa*, pp. 91, 127. The territorial wars between British troops and Xhosa fighters, which intensified in the 1820s and 1830s, increasingly spurred white farmers to justify, as God-given, their right to seize 'savage' land and labour. Malignant 'settler racism became more vituperative' in the eastern Cape frontier as colonial authorities envisaged armed conflicts with the amaXhosa as part of a battle between 'civilisation and barbarism'; see Paul Maylam, *South Africa's Racial Past: The History and Historiography of Racism, Segregation, and Apartheid* (Aldershot: Ashgate, 2001), p. 82. See also Clifton Crais, *The Making of the Colonial Order: White Supremacy and Black Resistance in the Eastern Cape, 1770–1865* (Cambridge: Cambridge University Press, 1992), pp. 117–28; Andrew Bank, 'Liberals and their Enemies: Racial Ideologies at the Cape of Good Hope, 1820 to 1850' (Ph.D. diss., University of Cambridge, 1995), pp. 194–205 and Alan Lester, 'The Margins of Order: Strategies of Segregation on the Eastern Cape Frontier, 1806–c.1850', *Journal of Southern African Studies* 23:4 (1997): 637–50.

27. *Illustrated London News*, 6 September 1845 and 12 June 1847; Richard Altick, *The Shows of London* (Cambridge, MA: Harvard University Press, 1978), pp. 269–72; Bernth Lindfors, 'Charles Dickens and the Zulus', in *Africans on Stage: Studies in Ethnological Show Business*, ed. Bernth Lindfors (Cape Town: David Philip, 1999), pp. 62–80. For the United States, see Robert Bogdan, *Freak Show: Presenting Human Oddities for Amusement and Profit* (Chicago: University of Chicago Press, 1988).

28. For scientific attitudes towards race in the first half of the nineteenth century in the United States, see William Stanton, *The Leopard's Spots: Scientific Attitudes Toward Race in America 1815–59* (Chicago: University of Chicago Press, 1960). I thank Michael Bottoms for the Stanton reference.

29. The composite name 'race scientist' is borrowed from Nancy Stepan, *The Idea of Race: Great Britain 1800–1960* (London: Macmillan, 1982). On James Prichard's intellectual milieu and influence on early missionaries in Natal and Zululand, see Russell Martin, 'British Images of the Zulu, c.1820–1879' (Ph.D. diss., University of Cambridge, 1982), pp. 177–79, and see Chapter 4 more generally.

30. Young, *Colonial Desire*, p. 35; Stepan, *The Idea of Race*, p. 38. Monogenists employed Prichard's ethnological outline to study the 'feelings, appetites, [and] aversions' of the 'ruder tribes'; see Matthew Jacobson, *Whiteness of a Different Color: European Immigrants and the Alchemy of Race* (Cambridge, MA: Harvard University Press, 1998), pp. 35–36.

31. Martin, 'British Images', pp. 177–79. For an ABM Natal evangelist's assurance to brethren in the United States that the 'people all consider white men as a superior race', see letter from Mr Grout, 12 February 1836 in *Missionary Herald*, September 1836. See Bishop Colenso's critical commentary on this issue: 'A Letter to An American Missionary from the Bishop of Natal', pp. 51, 61–2, Vol. 132, Colenso Collection, A204, PAR, 1856.

32. George Stocking, *Delimiting Anthropology: Occasional Essays and Reflections* (Madison, WI: University of Wisconsin Press, 2001), p. 15.

33. Cuvier insisted that 'only the most depraved and ludicrous could take [her] seriously as a woman and as a sex partner'; see Zoë Strother, 'Display of the Body Hottentot', in *Africans on Stage*, ed. Lindfors, p. 40 and Sander L. Gilman, 'Black Bodies, White Bodies: Toward an Ethnography of Female Sexuality in Late-nineteenth-century Medicine and Literature', *Critical Inquiry* 21:1 (1984): 204–42. On Cuvier's link to natural historians Linnaeus and Buffon, see Stocking, *Delimiting Anthropology*, p. 213.

34. For discourses involving racist biological determinists in the American Colonization Society, 'slave owners in South Carolina', American Board preachers, CMS Rev. Philip, and evangelising among the 'Zoolahs', see *African Repository and Colonial Journal*, December 1833.

35. Harper's *Memoir on Slavery* was published in Charleston, a port town that exhibited the orang-utan; see James Cook, *The Arts of Deception: Playing with Fraud in the Age of Barnum* (Cambridge, MA: Harvard University Press, 2001), pp. 108–18. On *simia troglodytes*, see Professor Jameson, James Wilson and Hugh Murray, *Discovery and Adventure in Africa* (New York: J&J Harper, 1832), pp. 293, 295; D/1/77, 1/ABM A608, PAR; this travel guide was carried by ABM missionaries to Natal. For historical connections between the Charleston port and southern African slave harbours in the Indian ocean, see Mabel Haight, *European Powers and South-East Africa: A Study of International Relations on the South-East Coast of Africa, 1796–1856* (London: Routledge, 1967), p. 89. On nineteenth-century southern Indian ocean trade, involving slavery and American ships, see journals of Richard Waters, Zanzibar, 1836–44, 1 January 1837, 22 February 1837 in *New England Merchants in Africa: A History Through Documents, 1802 to 1865*, eds. Norman Bennett

and George Brooks (Boston: Boston University Press, 1965), pp. 189–92. On American trade in the Port Natal area in the 1830s, see 'Statement of Andrew Smith', in *Records of Natal, Volume Two, September 1828–July 1835*, ed. B. Leverton (Pretoria: The Government Printer, 1989), p. 262.

36. William Harper, *Memoir on Slavery* (Charleston, SC: James S. Burges, 1838), p. 57. Harper studied medicine, which might have introduced him to Cuvier's view of Baartman. My thanks to Randolph Scully for this reference.

37. Jameson, Wilson and Murray, *Discovery and Adventure*.

38. Marvin McAllister, *White People Do Not Know How to Behave at Entertainments Designed for Ladies and Gentlemen of Colour: William Brown's African and American Theater* (Chapel Hill, NC: University of North Carolina Press, 2003), pp. 99, 100–112, 130–181. See also Eric Lott, *Love and Theft: Blackface Minstrelsy and the American Working Class* (New York: Oxford University Press, 1993); Shane White and Graham White, *Stylin': African-American Expressive Culture from its Beginnings to the Zoot Suit* (Ithaca, NY: Cornell University Press, 1998) and *A Zulu Blind Boy's Story* (New York: Tract Society, *c.* 1850s), Manuscripts and Rare Books, New York City Schomburg Library. On American Tract Society funding ABM work in Natal, see 'Minutes of the American Board Mission, 1846–1853', Vol. II, 102, A/1/1, 1/ABM, PAR.

39. 'Zooloo Kaffir Entertainment' was staged for a time at Drayton's Parlour in lower Manhattan: New York *Independent*, 29 Dec. 1859. In early 1860 the show and its producer, A.T. Caldecott, moved to a performance hall in a nearby church and made subsequent appearances in ethnological societies devoted to the study of philology and physiology, and 'tribes of Africans', see *Historical Magazine*, April 1861, New York. A.T. Caldecott was likely Charles Caldecott, the son of Natal businessman and promoter, A.T. Caldecott, who brought a troupe of isiZulu-speaking Africans to perform rituals on stage in 'Native Zulu Kafirs' at Hyde Park, London, in 1853; this acclaimed exhibition was seen by British royals and thousands more, including Charles Dickens. See 'Final Close of the St. George's Gallery, Hyde Park Corner, Piccadilly: Zulu Kafirs: Last few days in London', BL 10096.a.40, British Library, London. 'Native Zulu Kafirs' borrowed from the British missionary Allen Gardiner's book, *Narrative*; see Lindfors, 'Charles Dickens', pp. 73–74. The ABM probably did the most to introduce a particular image of warrior Zulu culture in the early-and-mid-nineteenth-century United States. See reports from ABM missionaries about Zulu king Dingane's killing of Piet Retief and his trekker party: *The Adams Sentinel*, 25 June 1838 (Gettysburg, Pennsylvania); *Alton Observer*, 8 February 1838 (Illinois) and *Ohio Repository*, 28 June 1838.

40. *Independent*, 27 December 1860, New York. On Barnum's 'What Is It?' and his Broadway Museum oddities, see Cook, *The Arts of Deception*, pp. 119–62 and Bogdan, *Freak Show*, pp. 101–11, 32–33. On Barnum's early fascination with the 'Great Chain Being', see Lovejoy, *The Great Chain*, p. 236. For headlines of the Zulu annihilation of British forces at Isandlwana in the Anglo-Zulu War of 1879, see *Brooklyn Eagle*, 11 February 1879 and *Harper's Weekly*, 12 April 1879. The buzz swirling around the 'War Dancer' presaged coverage of the Anglo-Zulu War in New York newspapers, which extolled the bravery and strength of the Zulu 'noble savage'; see *Brooklyn Eagle*, 11 May 1879. Sympathetic press coverage of Zulu struggles against British invaders was common in America in the 1880s; see 'Farini's N. American Circus and Show Activities, 1880–1889', 996.9.36, Subject 0028, File 0004, Box 0003, Peacock Papers, Ganaraska Regional Archives, Port Hope, Ontario, Canada.

41. Jennifer Brody, *Impossible Purities: Blackness, Femininity, and Victorian Culture* (Durham, NC: Duke University Press, 1998), p. 7. On (multi-)racial identities, whiteness, and blackness in the early-and-mid-nineteenth-century Atlantic cultural currents in America, see James Cook, 'Dancing across the Color Line', *Common-Place* 4:1 (2003), www.common-place.org, Parts I–V, accessed 6 May 2005. See also Paul Gilroy, *The Black Atlantic: Modernity and Double Consciousness* (Cambridge, MA: Harvard University Press, 1993).

42. Circulating periodicals containing commentaries on the African 'exhibition complex', see *Natal Witness* 16 December 1852; 17 June; 24 June; 1 July; 8 July; 22 July and 5 August 1853. See also 'ethnological lectures of interest' in 'Natal Society Records, 1851–1871', Vol. 1, Natal Society Library (NSL), Pietermaritzburg; Zine Magubane, *Bringing the Empire Home: Race, Class, and Gender in Britain and Colonial South Africa* (Chicago: University of Chicago Press, 2004), pp. 42–45; and *Independent*, 1 November 1860 and 13 May 1858, New York.

43. Mayhew quotations are taken from Gertrude Himmelfarb, *The Idea of Poverty: England in the Industrial Age* (New York: Alfred A. Knopf, 1985), pp. 325–30.

44. Magubane, *Bringing the Empire*, p. 50; L. Perry Curtis, *Apes and Angels: The Irishman in Victorian Caricature*, Revised Edition (Washington, DC: Smithsonian University Press, 1997), pp. ix–xxix, 24, 29–31; and Sean Wilentz, *Chants Democratic: New York City & the Rise of the American Working Class, 1788–1850* (Oxford: Oxford University Press, 1984), pp. 86, 119, 146, 266–67, 352–53.

45. *Missionary Herald*, July 1848; December 1850; June 1851. On ABM interests in converting Roman Catholic Irish that 'never heard so much of Jesus Christ', see *Missionary Herald*, May 1823. For scholarly analysis of New York 'nativist' churches and groups grappling with heavy Irish immigration, see Wilentz, *Chants Democratic*, pp. 86, 119, 146, 266–67, 352–53.

46. Jameson, Wilson and Murray, *Discovery and Adventure*, p. 293.

47. *Household Words*, 11 June 1853; *Spirit of the Times*, 22 October 1853. For earlier interest in the 'Kafir' of Natal, see *Spirit of the Times*, 19 March 1853.

48. Lindfors, 'Charles Dickens', pp. 76–77.

49. William Harris, *The Wild Sports of Southern Africa* (London: John Murray, 1839), p. 346.

50. Curtis, *Apes and Angels*, pp. 16–67, 89–129.

51. Jacobson, *Whiteness*, p. 29.

52. Stanton, *The Leopard's Spots*, pp. 26–35.

53. Michael O'Malley, 'Specie and Species: Race and the Money Question in Nineteenth-century America', *American Historical Review* 99:2 (1994): 369. On polygenesis, comparative anatomy, and cranium size, see Stocking, *Delimiting Anthropology*, p. 108.

54. Journal of Rev. William Ireland, 23 April 1849, Letters from the AZM (post) 1838 (15.4), 264, Vol. 4, American Board of Commissioner for Foreign Missions Collection (ABC), Houghton Library, Harvard University, Cambridge. On his first major tour of Natal missionary stations in 1854, Bishop Colenso noted that some ABM evangelists segregated their children from potential African playmates: W. Colenso, *Ten Weeks in Natal* (Cambridge: Macmillan, 1855), p. 23. On ABM Reverend Daniel Lindley (1801–80) and cotton plantation, see *Prospectus of the Protestant Co-Operative Emigrations and Colonization Society* (London: John Nichols Milton Press, 1849), p. 23; Natal Society Library Special Collection (NSLSC), Alan Paton Centre (APC), University of KwaZulu-Natal (UKZN) and Tyler, *Forty Years*, p. 36.

55. Stanton, *The Leopard's Spots*, p. 35; Rev. William Ireland, *Historical Sketch of the Zulu Mission in South Africa* (Boston: c.1860), p. 5, NSLSC, Vol. 266, APC, UKZN. On prevailing racial ideologies in the United States in the 1830s, see Reginald Horsman, *Race and Manifest Destiny: The Origins of American Anglo-Saxonism* (Cambridge, MA: Harvard University Press, 1981), pp. 120–24, 133–35. Although phrenology no longer commanded the attention of leading American intellectuals by the middle of the nineteenth century, this pseudo-science was still popular, with the *Phrenological Journal* publishing pictorials of 'kaffir' heads and 'the Kaffir race – physically and mentally considered with engravings from life, of young and old natives': *Harper's Weekly*, 10 June 1865.

56. Stanton, *The Leopard's Spots*, p. 35. Stanton questions whether Morton was a phrenologist, though *Crania Americana* included phrenological measurements and Combe's short manifesto on phrenology.

57. Ireland, *Historical Sketch*, p. 5. Champion also referred to 'jet black' skin; see Booth, *Journal of Rev. George Champion*, p. 19.

58. Rufus Anderson, *Foreign Missions: Their Relations and Their Claims* (New York: Charles Scribner, 1869). On Calvinist and Puritan influences on Anderson's ideas of race, see Winthrop Jordan, *White Over Black: American Attitudes Toward the Negro, 1550–1812* (Chapel Hill, NC: University of North Carolina Press, 1968), pp. 203–05.

59. Stephen Kay, *Travels and Researches in Caffraria: Describing the Character, Customs, and Moral Condition of the Tribes Inhabiting that Portion of Southern Africa* (New York: Harper & Brothers, 1834), p. 141. See also *Historical Magazine*, April 1861; Magubane, *Bringing the Empire*, p. 21; 'Account of Stephen Kay, Annexure 1, 17 March 1834', in *Records of Natal, Volume Three, August 1835–June 1838*, ed. B. Leverton (Pretoria: The Government Printer, 1990), p. 59. For similar British praise of Xhosa bodily form, see John Barrow, *Travels in the Interior of Southern Africa, in the Years 1797 and 1978*, Vol. 2 (London: T. Cadell Jun. and W. Davies, 1804), p. 99.

60. Tyler, *Forty Years*, pp. 188–89.

61. Delegorgue, *Travels*, Vol. 1, p. 169.

62. Delegorgue, *Travels*, Vol. 1, pp. 205–06. The Frenchman Delegorgue was a Rousseauist acolyte whose views of female Zulu beauty and 'fine' Zulu masculinity were shared by other British travellers

and hunters; see, for example William Humphreys, *The Journal of William Clayton Humphreys: Being a Personal Narrative of the Adventures and Experiences of a Trader and Hunter in the Zulu Country During the Months July–October 1851* (Pietermaritzburg: University of Natal Press, 1993), p. 9.

63. 'Testimony of Sijewana kaMjanyelwa, 17 November 1899' in *The James Stuart Archive*, eds. Webb and Wright, Vol. 5, p. 332. On '*dunuza'd*' and sodomy, see 'Testimony of Qalizwe, 13 August 1900', p. 243 and '11 December 1900', p. 247 in *The James Stuart Archive*, eds. Webb and Wright, Vol. 5. See also 'Testimony of Ndukwana, 10 December 1900', in *The James Stuart Archive*, eds. Webb and Wright, Vol. 4, p. 341.

64. 'Report of Pastor Hans Schreuder, 1 May 1846, Norwegian (Lutheran) Mission, Umhluti' in *Norwegian Missionaries in Natal and Zululand: Selected Correspondence, 1844–1900*, ed. Frederick Hale (Cape Town: Van Riebeeck Society, 1997), p. 28.

65. Gardiner, *Narrative*, pp. 178–79, 314 and Etherington, 'Christianity,' p. 277.

66. For Fynn's and the other white traders' plans to lure British authority to Port Natal, see Julie Pridmore, 'Henry Francis Fynn: An Assessment of His Career and an Analysis of the Written and Visual Portrayals of His Role in the History of the Natal Region' (Ph.D. diss., University of Natal, 1996), pp. 1–42; Carolyn Hamilton, *Terrific Majesty: The Powers of Shaka Zulu and the Limits of Historical Intervention* (Cambridge, MA: Harvard University Press, 1998), pp. 37–44; Dan Wylie, *Savage Delight: White Myths of Shaka* (Pietermaritzburg: University of Natal Press), pp. 105–27.

67. The author of these words, Captain Garden of Pietermaritzburg's 45th British regiment, recorded the lizard and chameleon story in his journal entry, 22 April 1852, 'Rambling Along the Sea Coast between Port Natal and the Umzimvooboo', p. 400, Vol. 2, Garden Papers, A1157, PAR.

68. Gardiner, *Narrative*, p. 314, see also pp. 178–79.

69. On Fynn's considerable influence on Gardiner, see Gardiner, *Narrative*, pp. 41, 95–96, 239; Cory, ed. *Diary*, p. 11; 'Letter from Gardiner, Port Natal, to Government House, Cape Town, 4 June 1835', in *Records of Natal*, ed. B. Leverton, p. 12. On Fynn as translator for Gardiner, see 'Letter from Gardiner to Fynn, 21 September 1835', File 4, Vol. 1, Fynn Papers, KCM 98/69/3, Killie Campbell Library (KCL), UKZN, Durban.

70. Mr Fynn's Evidence (Harding 'Kafir' Commission, 1852–3), 14 April 1853.

71. Mr Fynn's Evidence (Harding 'Kafir' Commission, 1852–3), 21 April 1853; *Natal Mercury*; File 8, 98/69/7, Fynn Papers, KCL, UKZN, Durban. On the 1852–3 'Kafir Commission', see Edgar Brookes and Colin Webb, *A History of Natal* (Pietermaritzburg: University of Natal Press, 1965), pp. 69–70. Fynn's evidence to the Commission is in the *Natal Government Gazette*, February and March 1853, p. 221, PAR. IsiZulu-speaking Africans who knew of Henry Fynn also spoke of a putative theological link between Jews and Zulus; see 'Testimony of Dinya kaZokowayo, 28 February 1905', in *The James Stuart Archives*, eds. Webb and Wright, Vol. 1, p. 98.

72. Fynn was an interpreter for Reverend Owen, who stayed in the Natal and Zululand region from 1837 to 1841; see Cory, ed., *The Diary*, pp. 1, 11.

73. 'Testimony of Baleni kaSilwane, 10 May 1914', in *The James Stuart Archive*, eds. Webb and Wright, Vol. 1, p. 20.

74. Cory, ed., *The Diary*, pp. 89–90; Martin, 'British Images', pp. 180–82. Elohim was/is the ordinary Hebrew name for God in his action on the world in contrast to Yahweh, which was/is used to describe the God of the covenant: Exodus 3.

75. On comparative philology and racial difference, see Young, *Colonial Desire*, pp. 65–71. On 'Adamic family', see Martin, 'British Images', p. 178.

76. For other period references to Zulus as an Old Testament tribe, see Thomas Jenkinson, *Amazulu: The Zulus, their Past History, Manners, Customs, and Language*, (London: W.H. Allen & Co., 1882), pp. 24–33; Lewis Grout, *Zulu-land: Or, Life Among the Zulu-Kafirs of Natal and Zululand, South Africa, with Map, and Illustrations* (Philadelphia: Presbyterian Publication Committee, 1864), Chapter 6; William Holden, *History of the Colony of Natal* (Cape Town: Struik, [1855] 1963), p. 182. See also David Chidester, *Savage Systems: Colonialism and Comparative Religion in Southern Africa* (Charlottesville, VA: University Press of Virginia, 1996), pp. 116–18, 124–26 and Jonathan Draper, 'The Bishop and the Bricoleur,' in *The Bible in Africa: Transactions, Trajectories, and Trends*, eds. Gerald West and Musa Dube (Leiden: Brill, 2001), pp. 424–28. Natal colonial official and fluent isiZulu-speaking ethnographer James Stuart was instrumental in promoting the Jew-Zulu comparison; see James Stuart, 'Are the Zulus Jews?' 17 April 1903, File 30, Stuart Papers, KCM 23521, KCL, UKZN, Durban.

77. J.W. Colenso to W.H.I. Bleek, 5 July 1861, Fol. A147, Colenso Papers, KCL, UKZN, Durban. In 1861, Colenso confidently stated full confidence that *uNkulunkulu* meant God. See Martin, 'British Images', p. 188.

78. Draper, 'The Bishop', p. 427 and Martin, 'British Images', p. 187.

79. 'Testimony of Lazarus Mxaba [with John Kumalo and Ndukwana kaMbengwana], 1 January 1901', in *The James Stuart Archive*, eds. Webb and Wright, Vol. 1, pp. 262–63.

80. Moreover, Stuart interviewed Mxaba at the height of the Second South African War, when Boers were more likely than Zulus to be called the Old Testament people of South Africa. In Delegorgue's accounts of Zulu life during the Great Trek, we find some of the first published references to the putative Boer-Jew parallel; see Leonard Thompson, *The Political Mythology of Apartheid* (New Haven, CT: Yale University Press, 1985), pp. 161–64, 178–79 and Andre du Toit, 'No Chosen People: The Myth of the Calvinist Origins of Afrikaner Nationalism and Racial Ideology', *American Historical Review* 88 (1983): 920–52. Stuart's surprise was probably compounded by the fact that English literature, which he read avidly, sometimes speculated on the 'genius' parallels between modern Britons and ancient Semites, both of whom were said to share an epochal destiny to build a 'New Jerusalem'. See Young, *Colonial Desire*, p. 84; also Brian Cheyette, *Constructions of 'the Jew' in English Literature and Society: Racial Representations, 1875–1945* (Cambridge: Cambridge University Press, 1993).

81. George Shepperson, 'Ethiopianism and African Nationalism', *Phylon* 14 (1953): 9–18 and Shula Marks, *Reluctant Rebellion: The 1906–1908 Disturbances in Natal* (Oxford: Oxford University Press, 1970), pp. 76–79.

*Chapter 13*

# Faithful Anthropologists
## Christianity, Ethnography and the Making of 'Zulu Religion' in Early Colonial Natal

BENEDICT CARTON[1]

[T]here is a faith in the Living Word, which speaks within [Zulu people]; there is a living obedience to the law of truth and love, which they find written upon their hearts by the finger of God, which is akin to the true living faith of a Christian.[2]

[Even] with the most careful effort to elevate the heathen people to a higher grade, . . . [they] will be prone to learn the vices more rapidly than the virtues of civilization; and in a few generations immorality and dissipation will not only decimate the unhappy race, it will gradually vanish from the face of the earth.[3]

DURING THE MID-TO-LATE nineteenth century, a version of the Victorian 'crisis of faith' buffeted the British colony of Natal in South Africa. There, officials such as magistrate John Bird and his colleague, Secretary for Native Affairs, Theophilus Shepstone, entrenched a stereotypical view of Zulu history, which posed a grave challenge to the mission enterprise.[4] Before the advent of white rule, they claimed, Shaka's 'savage wars' exterminated millions in southern Africa, leaving a razed landscape sparsely populated by '[t]ribes once powerful broken and scattered'.[5] Such devastation doomed any effort to save the 'heathen people' or to discover what made them unhappy, Bird wrote,[6] not least because they could never overcome the trauma inflicted by Shaka, the 'Scourge of God'.[7]

In contrast, a clutch of Anglican clergymen – led by Bishop John Colenso, his acolyte Reverend Henry Callaway, and to a lesser extent Reverend Joseph Shooter – expressed a strong desire to explore the living faith of their flock in Natal and Zululand. To this end, they conducted far-reaching fieldwork that examined local cosmological beliefs within the context of scriptural exegeses. Shaped by the contradictory forces of evangelical devotion and incipient cultural relativism, their inquiries represented the first comprehensive attempts to construct anthropological conceptions of 'Zulu religion' in published writings.[8]

Born in 1814, John Colenso came of age as a religious thinker in industrial Britain. He was exposed to London social reformers such as Henry Mayhew, who called the urban poor 'barbarous heathens', and evangelical texts authored by missionaries such as Robert Moffat, who sourced the ethnological rankings of black 'savages'.[9] In 1854, shortly after arriving in Natal as a new Anglican bishop, Colenso described a 'primitive' population ensnared by the 'Power of Darkness'.[10] Undeterred, he vowed to redeem them all with the 'gospel of love'. Colenso rejected everlasting punishment and exalted, instead, the fatherhood of God and brotherhood of men.[11] Here, he drew inspiration from F.D. Maurice's ethos of 'responsibility for the realisation of the Kingdom of God in earth', which Colenso interpreted to mean solidarity with all converts regardless of their race, creed or, most controversially, cultural outlook.[12] The last category encompassed the Zulu patriarch and his wives, a domestic group damned by virtually every white-controlled Christian body in the British Empire, Europe, and the Americas, except for Mormons in the United States.[13] Colenso defended his position on polygamy in widely disseminated printed statements. He wrote that what appeared to be repugnant about Zulu practices was not inevitably so in the eyes of God.[14] As a proselytiser, Colenso promised to meet 'the heathen, half way'.[15]

Colenso's 'heathen, half way' argument rolled across Atlantic waters and crashed into Great Britain and the United States; then, his argument rolled back to Natal.[16] By 1858, Colenso had angered England's Archbishop of Canterbury, President Woolsey of Yale College, and other elite theologians. They assailed the bishop in periodicals such as the New York *Independent* and *New Englander*, where editorials lampooned the new Zulu man of the gospel;[17] he was depicted as the only convert with a 'harem' of slave-wives.[18] As it happened, Colenso's writings fuelled ongoing debates in the United States over 'ethnological fallacies' and plantation slavery. Barbed exchanges from this national dialogue spilled into articles probing the origins of the 'Caucasian',[19] inhuman bondage and 'Hottentots',[20] whom Harriet Beecher Stowe, author of the great morality play, *Uncle Tom's Cabin,* portrayed as 'abysses of barbarianism'.[21] Her brief commentary on Khoe people of the Cape colony punctuated a December 1858 letter to the *Independent* in which she condemned slavery and the feeble protests against it by the American Board of Commissioners for Foreign Missions (ABM) in Boston. A few months earlier the *Independent* featured a dispatch from an ABM evangelist in Natal who signed off as Umhambi, 'the one who ventures'. This missionary lamented the 'dense mass of barbarism' bearing 'the Zulu name', and Colenso's 'admission of polygamists living in the practice of the crime, into the Church of Christ'. Such sacrilege sanctioned the 'purchase [of] women for wives, or for *slaves* rather', Umhambi said. He warned that the 'Bishop of the Episcopal Church

*Bishop John W. Colenso, c. late 1850s.*

in Natal' conspired to carry on the 'domestic slave trade . . . in Her Majesty's colony of Natal'.[22]

Colenso's 'gospel of love' also stirred the ire of whites in his own society. They decried his 'insane' influence over the colonial government, which considered granting isiZulu-speaking Africans redress in the case of employers' abuse.[23] White farmers similarly assailed Colenso's support for 'tribal titles' to territory.[24] After British annexation of Natal in 1842 made the imperial possession Crown property, new internal boundaries were mapped, which English settlers saw as a threat to their privileges as private landowners and speculators. By the 1850s, a controversy was brewing over the government's establishment of locations or reserves for the estimated 120 000 'heathens' in Natal, a population twenty times the size of colonial society. Such reserves protected communal rights to the land for indigenous family homesteads, which engaged in subsistence agriculture and livestock husbandry; and buttressed the rule of chiefs loyal to the head of 'native affairs', Theophilus Shepstone.[25] With this structure in place, Natal officials collected a hut tax imposed on each African homestead and enforced *isibhalo*, a policy compelling chiefs to organise government public works brigades. That colonial power could extract local resources hardly impressed white farmers who irritably complained that the African reserve system bolstered tribal self-sufficiency and encouraged a huge pool of labour to ignore their demands for workers. Such grievances – aired, for example, in the *Natal Mercury* and *Natal Witness* – were read weekly by Natal governors, their deputies, and Shepstone. But these officials would not acquiesce to angry settlers, fearing in part that deeper official incursions into homestead life would alienate 'the Kafirs' and drive them into an alliance with the Zulu kingdom to the north.[26]

With colonial dissatisfaction rife, Colenso was only one of several prominent British figures facing internal criticisms in the 1850s. It was not until the subsequent decade that his stand on polygamy provoked a full frontal attack on his reputation. In 1863 South Africa's 'High Church' charged Colenso with heresy and won conviction in a Cape Town ecclesiastical court. While the London-based Privy Council quickly overturned this judgment, Colenso had absorbed a major blow. One might think, then, that the bishop would become ever more dispirited. Yet, as serious as the temporary excommunication was, it did not permanently squelch Colenso's enthusiasm for pastoral work, a passion that he nurtured from the start of his Natal sojourn.[27] Indeed, as a missionary, Colenso showed a remarkably resilient, even euphoric, capacity to continue proselytising. A foretaste of this dedication can be found in an autobiographical account of a tour of his diocese in the mid-1850s in which he eagerly celebrated the charity of 'heathens', with little regard for the colonial ridicule that such ardour would doubtless invite. IsiZulu-speaking Africans longed to cosset their kin, Colenso reported, and greet newcomers with compassion. He pointed to these sentiments as 'a sign of hope – a token that they have human feelings like ours, and are therefore accessible to the tidings of great joy' and the rewards of piety.[28]

The Bishop gained insights into Zulu worship during a visit to Edendale Methodist mission, where he realised that the evangelists' vernacular word for God, *uThixo*, which they borrowed from isiXhosa-speaking missionaries from the Cape colony, barely resonated in Natal.[29] By contrast, he noted how *amakholwa*, Christian 'believers,' revelled in *iThongo*, the name for a 'Power of Universal Influence – a Being under whom all around were placed'.[30] Still, Colenso continued to canvas opinion, recording other praise names such as '*umKulunkulu*', which he translated as 'The Great-Great One', and '*umVelinqange*', the 'The First Comer-Out'.[31] These inquiries spurred Colenso to extend his etymological investigations. He subsequently considered *iNkosi yezulu* (Lord-of-the-Sky) and the neologism '*uDio*', a version of *uDiyo*, denoting both finality and, more problematically, a drinking pot.[32] In 1856 Colenso decided to introduce *uNkulunkulu* in his translation of the *Book of Common Prayer*.[33]

After Colenso established his Ekukhanyeni mission school in Bishopstowe outside the capital of Pietermaritzburg, he arranged discussions with isiZulu-speakers, many of them sceptics of the gospel. Their exchanges occasionally revolved around *ugovana* (evil disposition) and *unembeza* (good conscience), concepts that Colenso connected to Saint Paul's account of the conflict of the flesh and spirit. Furthermore, Colenso noted that Zulu descriptions of the 'shade' – a deceased man's shadow living on in an ancestral spirit – revealed beliefs in an afterlife 'already planted by the Divine Hand in the minds of these natives'. Even the first fruits ceremony (*umkhosi*), an annual festival honouring the Zulu king and the national protection afforded by his ancestors, had 'a right meaning', despite being 'purely heathen'. It seemed essential for Colenso to locate Zulu spirituality in a single framework 'grounded on truth', that is, an observable ceremony and its customary underpinnings.[34] Yet it is not entirely clear what Colenso had in mind by the 'right meaning'. Was the 'right meaning' embedded in 'heathen' ritual or was it a redeeming quality planted 'by the Divine Hand' in all of Adam's flock? Perhaps Colenso himself was undecided because he had not spent enough time in the field with his potential converts. Whatever the case, he seemed to be wrestling with contradictory questions: Were Zulu people already on their way to grasping salvation within a single framework 'grounded on truth'? Or, were they imminently redeemable because God thoughtfully and transcendentally inserted elements within their total belief structure that made it easier for a perceptive, ethnographically minded missionary such as Colenso to bring them into conformity with divine revelation?

Colenso's searching, analytical view of Zulu cosmology presaged an approach to the study of culture proposed by Franz Boas, whose groundbreaking scholarship in the late 1800s and early 1900s sought to reconstruct the whole life of non-European societies.[35] Boas's fieldwork, similar to Colenso's evangelism, saw potential in the 'mind of primitive man'. Boas urged 'greater tolerance of forms of civilization . . . [and] foreign races', who merited approbation 'so they will be capable of advancing the interests of mankind, if we are willing to give them a fair opportunity'.[36] He instilled this standard in students he trained, among them Melville Herskovits, 'America's first Africanist', who along with A.R. Radcliffe-Brown, Bronislaw Malinowski, Monica Hunter, and their cohorts charted the 'classical period' of anthropology (1920–60).[37] In analogous ways Colenso was also seen to be a path-breaking advocate of 'greater tolerance'. Indeed, at the turn of the twentieth century, *kholwa* thinkers such as Lazarus Mxaba and Johannes Kumalo commended the Bishop's 'energetic example'. They recounted how Colenso openly integrated Zulu cosmology and Christian principles into one evolving, long conversation about faith: 'His deeds on behalf of the natives, his questionings, discussions, the briefs he held, . . . tended to glow . . . The circumstances in which he laboured may pass and vanish from view, but . . . out of the very effort of discussion and questioning some light is derived.'[38]

Unlike Colenso, the English Reverend Joseph Shooter was not a missionary with many *kholwa* admirers. Shooter preached to British immigrants in Natal from 1850 to 1854.[39] One might suspect, then, that his resulting 1857 study, *The Kafirs of Natal and the Zulu Country*, published after his return to a curacy in England, would be tainted by the attitudes of settler churchgoers who endorsed Bird's prediction for the 'unhappy race'.[40] Yet Shooter was willing to recognise the vital presence of 'the heathen' for academic purposes. Despite the impression created by the chapter titled 'Superstition', *The Kafirs of Natal and the Zulu Country* embodied a determined effort to classify indigenous spiritual experiences of a society that, contrary to Bird, evinced no sign of disappearing from Natal.[41]

Shooter privileged first-hand accounts in his book. One of the most cited sources of *The Kafirs of Natal and the Zulu Country* was Henry Francis Fynn, a fluent isiZulu-speaking colonial magistrate and prominent witness in 1853 at the 'Commission Appointed to Inquire into the Past and Present State of the Kafirs in the District of Natal'. Fynn testified to an 'early inquiry . . . among these tribes regarding . . . the existence of a Supreme Being' and their understandings of the evil forces that morally and physically corroded their society.[42] Shooter paraphrased Fynn's extensive evidence before the Commission that focused on 'prophets', or diviners, and the manner in which they monitored malevolence through spirit messengers.[43]

Fynn's ethnographic expertise was widely recognised by Natal settlers who knew of his close relationships with Africans in the Port Natal region between the mid-1820s and mid-1830s.[44] With wealth he generated from trading ivory, animal skins and possibly firearms as well as gifts of livestock from King Shaka, Fynn pursued the patriarchal ambitions of isiZulu-speaking African men, including the accumulation of bridewealth cattle, *ilobolo*, which sealed multiple marriage arrangements. By the late 1820s, Fynn had embraced polygamy and established various homesteads containing his African wives and their bi-racial children. In addition he attracted political allies, namely *izinduna*, councillors, who helped manage his large households and govern the isiZulu-speaking Africans who acknowledged Fynn as their leader by giving him tribute and customary respect, *ukukhonza*.[45] Fynn's traditional obligations probably entailed the ceremonial propitiation of *amadlozi* (ancestors), where sacred praises were proclaimed to protect his followers and dependents.[46]

Like Shooter, Colenso relied on Fynn to elucidate the expectations of Zulu bridewealth, marriage and ancestral sanctions against '*umtagati*', evil. In fact, Colenso's 1856 peroration on polygamy, 'A Letter to an American Missionary' (a reply to an evangelist and critic, probably Umhambi from the *Independent*) lauded the knowledge Fynn derived from his 'intimate' connection with 'the Kafirs'. The letter elaborated:

> For those not acquainted with Natal, into whose hands this tract may fall, it may be necessary to say that Mr Fynn is one of the Resident Kafir Magistrates, who has been intimately connected with the Kafirs of this and the neighbouring districts, for more than thirty-one years, having been the first European who ever travelled through Natal, and who must be allowed by every one, cognizant, like yourself, of the facts of his personal history, to be one of the very best authorities upon the manners and habits of the Kafirs, that can be found in the whole of South Africa.[47]

*An aging Henry Francis Fynn in colonial Natal.*

Valuable as Fynn was, Colenso recognised the necessity of branching beyond one white isiZulu-speaking perspective. Shooter followed a similar strategy. *The Kafirs of Natal and the Zulu Country* draws extensively on oral traditions that the author claimed to have gathered from 'heathens' near Tongaat and Compensation (settlements just north of Durban), among them his own servant, Mopho, who assisted in recruiting key informants.[48] Such spoken testimony corroborated the existence of a heavenly creator with the praise name *uHlanga*, meaning a reed that the Lord-of-the-Sky used to bring forth man and beast. Shooter also learned of 'the Great-Great' or *uNkulunkulu*, which he said his informants once revered but no longer recalled after centuries of '[w]ar, change, . . . gradually darkened their minds, and obscured their remembrance of the true God'.[49] Significantly, Shooter called *amadlozi* 'false deities', a judgement confirming what scriptural orthodoxy upheld about the worship of (inferior) substitutes for the creator.

Here, Shooter overlooked crucial cosmological relationships clarified a century later by Zulu anthropologists and Christian intellectuals such as Absolom Vilakazi, who focused on how 'non-Christian people . . . meet the Christian assertions about God'. Vilakazi conducted research in the Nyuswa Reserve just west of Durban, an area not far from the informants that Shooter consulted. Vilakazi delved into the 'religious aspects of the social order', particularly the roles of ancestors (*amadlozi*, *isithunzi zakithi* or *onkulukulu bethu*) and *uMvenlinqangi*, the maker of the world.[50] He stressed that 'people worship the ancestral spirits because they were told to do so by *uMvelinqangi*', a deity that delegated spiritual authority to *amadlozi*.[51] 'It is as if,' Vilakazi said, 'after creating the world, *uMvelinqangi* retired far away, where he was out of the reach of the cries of human beings . . . [Therefore] it always is to the ancestral spirits that prayers are made', especially when 'seasons are out of joint, and [when] everything seems to be going wrong in nature'.[52] When compared to Vilakazi's analysis, the portrayal of 'false deities' in *The Kafirs of Natal* is more than a misinterpretation. Shooter held out hope that 'heathens' could be reminded of their biblical creator, if only they could realise their idolatry and accept the true 'Great-Great' God.

While Shooter distorted the meaning of *amadlozi*, his investigations into Zulu divination demonstrated a closer understanding of supernatural phenomena, specifically the functions of Zulu healers, whom he dubbed 'seers or prophets' (singular, *inyanga*; plural *izinyanga*). Eschewing condemnatory theories of witchcraft, Shooter called *izinyanga* 'clever practitioner[s]' capable of deducing prophetic signs and modifying their diagnoses to suit changing conditions.[53] He admitted, however, that *izinyanga* could spawn turmoil and tragedy when they ordered the killing of innocents accused of sorcery.[54] Yet even Shooter's most hyperbolic critiques of these executions never included lengthy tirades against the devil's work, a favourite trope of missionaries.[55] In fact the figure of Satan is largely absent from *The Kafirs of Natal*. Notions of preternatural evil do emerge in Shooter's sections on the fledgling healer's submission to the ancestors' call to combat malevolence, which could be received during a dream, a bout of sickness, and/or an hallucination. Although Shooter characterised some of these imaginings as states of derangement, he was reluctant to speculate on whether they indicated deep-seated mental pathologies.

*The Kafirs of Natal* tried to demystify the revelations of *izinyanga* by cataloguing how they disclosed their forecasts, wrestled with uncertainties and devised treatments. Shooter seemed bent on convincing the reader of his book that diviners exhibit rational behaviour. They rely not on haphazard guesswork, he asserted, but on visual surveillance, commonsense opinion and intuitive emotions.[56] In this regard Shooter anticipated the aim of 'psychological anthropology', a sub-discipline founded by Franz Boas in the late nineteenth century. Boas 'privileged subjective psychological grounding' and, like Shooter, saw the human psyche as ruled by 'the aesthetic/logical and the . . . affective impulse'.[57] Yet despite their congruencies, Shooter ultimately belonged to a much older tradition of anthropology, promoted in the first decades of the nineteenth century by James Cowles Prichard, a leading ethnographer in the English Evangelical movement and expert on 'primitive religion'. Prichard used the monogenesis model of analysis, which reasoned that the 'dispersion from the Tower of Babel after the Flood' connected the world's languages, customs, and physical types to the same 'human trunk'.[58] That 'all tribes were of one family' hardly bestirred most Britons to ask whether the 'primitive' was their equal. They, along with Prichard and Shooter, preferred to pose another question: was Anglo-Saxon hegemony to be benign or not? Thus, the tenor of white supremacy, not the fact of it, would have been a matter for debate.[59]

As *The Kafirs of Natal* garnered reviews in 1858, Charles Darwin announced the basis of biological evolution. In the ensuing year he published *The Origin of Species*, which ignited an epochal controversy and shook the ground on which monogenists stood (not to mention the ground of their rival polygenists).[60] Darwin's storm would leave something in its wake, a theoretical apparatus named 'natural selection'. When his sequel, *The Descent of Man*, reached booksellers in 1871, the term 'races' encompassed 'missing links' and their common ancestor, the ape. Suddenly, the roots of anthropology, which fed on biblical scripture, were uprooted and abandoned. Their desertion heralded the next 'necessary stage in the growth of modern relativism'.[61]

Edward Tylor, a British founder of evolutionary social anthropology, would become a parent of modern relativism.[62] In the mid-to-late nineteenth century, he pursued a line of inquiry that challenged racist assumptions about the purportedly immutable 'genetic inferiority' of 'colored peoples'. At the same time, Tylor expounded on a 'comparative method', which assumed 'coloured peoples' were on par with primitive Europeans, an analogy 'associated with the cultural relativism of Franz Boas'.[63] Tylor's paradigm contained 'what has since been called . . . the 'doctrine of survivals", an account of 'how humans, from being once culturally close to the ape, had risen to the status of civilised gentlemen'.[64] Period racism of a more paternalistic kind infused this teleological formulation.

Tylor's ideas appealed to Henry Callaway, a devoutly religious British medical doctor who took holy orders to assist Bishop Colenso in Natal.[65] Callaway expressed reservations about evolution, but he also welcomed secular challenges to faith.[66] In fact he placed science and revelation on the same plane by explaining 'one truth proceeds from God speaking by nature and by grace'. Reverend Callaway sailed to South Africa in the mid-1850s, settled in Pietermaritzburg, and started to collect testimonies from isiZulu-speaking Africans, both to master their language and record their folklore. Adhering to Tylor's 'doctrine of survivals', Callaway planned to use these sources, on the one hand, to compare (universal) modes of thought that might have existed in ancient Europe and, on the other hand, to discover if Zulu religion was truly devoid of any belief in God. Here, Callaway's approach corresponded with Prichard and Shooter. Callaway's letters and journals repeatedly mention a Genesis-like creation that isiZulu-speaking Africans were said to experience in the mists of time but too quickly forgot. Submerged within their testimonies, he sensed, was a 'substratum of truth – that their own ancients knew more than they, and that it is clear that traditions orally received have lost much in transmission and had much added to them'.[67]

After a serious disagreement in 1858 with Bishop Colenso over the significance of the word *uNkulunkulu*, Callaway removed from the Pietermaritzburg area to Springvale, where he built a mission.[68] There, he pursued his own research and wrote the life story of the neophyte Usetemba Dhladhla designed to show that 'Kafirs are not so devoid of moral and religious sentiments'. Callaway subsequently outlined Zulu worship, describing it much as Shooter had as 'the debris of some old theosophy'.[69] By the close of the 1860s, Callaway's fieldwork culminated in a wide-ranging investigation titled *The Religious System of the Amazulu* (1868–70), which appeared serially as a compilation of oral traditions in isiZulu text with English translation and discursive footnotes. This book was an intellectual feat in colonial Natal and a major contribution to nineteenth-century British anthropology, valued by none other than Edward Tylor.[70]

From the opening pages, it is clear that *The Religious System of the Amazulu* relied on 'the comparative method'. Callaway constructed parallels between the myths of 'heathens' – from isiZulu-speaking Africans to their 'contemporary primitive' neighbours on the fringe of the colony – and legends of primordial Europeans (the Greeks, for example). He tested Tylor's model to see if current 'savagery' and past 'civilisation' were on one continuum marking stages of social evolution.[71] Callaway was driven by an ambition to contribute 'a faithful record of man . . . and the varying states through which he has passed to the present'.[72]

For all the novel insights in *The Religious System*, the book reflects the author's uncritical acceptance of previous missionary opinions about the Zulu divinity. For example, Callaway approvingly details how Natal evangelists rejected the neologism uDio, explaining further that it smacked of Arianism, a body of religious thought centred on the trinity, which contended the Son, not the Father, was the agent of creation. *iNkosi yezulu* (Lord-of-the-Sky) was also shown to be lacking in biblical integrity because this deity was said to have the pagan powers of Zeus.[73] In other words Zulu religion embodied no theological idea of God, according to Callaway. However, this did not mean that they had no consideration for faith. Far from it, Callaway claimed that in the oral traditions he noted down Zulu people hinted at faint manifestations of God's 'truth' buried beneath their 'heathen' accretions.[74] Hence, he, like Tylor, envisaged 'primitive beliefs' as belonging to an embryonic stage of humankind.[75] What is striking about the argument that Zulu people possessed a vestigial spirituality found in 'the body of humanity' is that Callaway expressed very different opinions about their current cultural endowments in comparison to mid-to-late-nineteenth-century European society.[76] Profoundly shaped by the ethno-centrism of his day, Callaway's sermons dwelled on hoary assumptions that contradict the gist of *The Religious System*. When preaching to English congregations, for example, he presented indigenous inhabitants of Natal as the pathetic inheritors of age-old 'ignorance, darkness, degradation, [and] sin'.[77]

Yet Callaway's conviction that isiZulu-speaking Africans 'in every respect, possessed ... the same intellectual, ... and religious potentiality as ourselves' represented an extraordinary point of view.[78] In this respect he, along with Colenso and Shooter, could be seen to have pioneered a modern form of cultural relativism in the hopes of demonstrating that the 'heathen' were neither devoid of spiritually nor a sad 'race' doomed by the vices of modernity. Indeed, the three clergymen were among the first English-speaking writers to portray Zulu people, more broadly, as an open book made up of religious characters that could be read by those who knew the Word and anthropology.

## Notes

1. I owe a special debt to the scholarship and guidance of Russell Martin, with whom I worked on this chapter before completing it as the sole author.
2. John Colenso, *St Paul's Epistle to the Romans: Newly Translated, and Explained from a Missionary Point of View* (Pietermaritzburg: Ekukhanyeni Mission Press, 1861), p. 86. Colenso was an Anglican missionary and Bishop of Natal.
3. John Bird, 'The Form of Constitutional Government Existing in the Colony of Natal', 1869, Vol. 340–42, Natal Society Library Special Collection (NSLSC), Alan Paton Centre (APC), University of KwaZulu-Natal (UKZN), Pietermaritzburg. Bird was a Natal colonial magistrate and editor of *The Annals of Natal, 1495–1845* (Cape Town: Struik, [1888] 1965).
4. On the crisis of faith, see Richard Altick, *Victorian People and Ideas* (New York: W.W. Norton & Co, 1973), pp. 226–37.
5. Letter from Theophilus Shepstone, Pietermaritzburg, to Superior Council of the African Institute, Paris, 10 November 1847, Despatched Letters 1847 November 10 – 1863 July 10, Vol. 70, (T.) Shepstone Papers, A96, Pietermaritzburg Archives Repository (PAR), Pietermaritzburg, South Africa. Bird's *Annals of Natal* contain colonial writings on Shaka, for example, Shepstone's 'Early History of the Zulu-Kafir Race' (*Annals of Natal*, Vol. 1, pp. 203–06, 280–88). See John Wright, 'The Dynamics of Power and Conflict in the Thukela-Mzimkhulu Region in the Late 18th and Early 19th Centuries: A Critical Reconstruction' (Ph.D. diss., University of the Witwatersrand, 1989), pp. 2–3, 4, 6–8, 71, 76–101 and Carolyn Hamilton, *Terrific Majesty: The Powers of Shaka Zulu and the Limits of Historical Invention* (Cambridge, MA: Harvard University Press, 1998), pp. 90–93. On the ties between Bird and Shepstone, see 'Natal Society Records, 1851–1871, Vol. 1', pp. 32–58, Natal Society Library (NSL), Pietermaritzburg.
6. Bird, 'The Form of Constitutional Government'.
7. William Holden, *History of the Colony of Natal* (Cape Town: Struik, [1855] 1963), p. 48. On Holden's intellectual legacy, see Dan Wylie, *Savage Delight: White Myths of Shaka* (Pietermaritzburg: University of Natal Press, 2000), pp. 138–41. See also Alan Booth, ed. *Journal of the Rev. George Champion* (Cape Town: Struik, 1967), p. 62.
8. Russell Martin, 'British Images of the Zulu, *c.*1820–1879' (Ph.D. diss., University of Cambridge, 1982), Chapter 4 and Patrick Harries, 'Anthropology', in *Missions and Empire: Oxford History of the British Empire*, ed. Norman Etherington, (Oxford: Oxford University Press, 2005), p. 40. See also David Chidester, *Savage Systems: Colonialism and Comparative Religion in Southern Africa* (Charlottesville, VA: University Press of Virginia, 1996), Chapter 4. For a scholarly overview of methodological similarities between missionaries and early anthropologists, see Sjaak van der Geest, 'Anthropologists and Missionaries: Brothers under the Same Skin', *Man* 25 (1990): 588–601.
9. For Colenso's biblical view of a (racial) 'civilisation' gulf, see J.W. Colenso, *Minutes of Proceedings of the Conference of the Clergy and Laity of the Church of England in the Diocese of Natal Convened April 20 1858 by the Lord Bishop of the Diocese* (Pietermaritzburg, 1858), p. 35. On

London reformers and ethnological/racial rankings, see Zine Magubane, *Bringing the Empire Home: Race, Class, and Gender in Britain and Colonial South Africa* (Chicago: University of Chicago Press, 2004), pp. 40–54, 65–66 and Douglas Lorimer, *Colour, Class, and the Victorians: English Attitudes to the Negro in the Mid-Nineteenth Century* (Leicester: Leicester University Press, 1978).

10. *Natal Mercury*, 8 February 1854; J.W. Colenso, *Ten Weeks in Natal: A Journal of a First Tour of Visitation among the Colonists and Zulu Kafirs of Natal* (Cambridge: Macmillan, 1955), pp. 24, 121.

11. Peter Hinchliff, *John William Colenso, Bishop of Natal* (London: Nelson, 1964), p. 65 and Jeff Guy, *The Heretic: A Study of the Life of John William Colenso, 1814–1883* (Pietermaritzburg: University of Natal Press, 1983), pp. 24–29.

12. F.D. Maurice, *The Kingdom of Christ* (London: Darton and Clark, Holborn Hill, 1838); Jonathan Draper, 'The Bishop and the Bricoleur', in *The Bible in Africa: Transactions, Trajectories, and Trends*, eds. Gerald West and Musa Dube (Leiden: Brill, 2001), p. 422; Guy, *The Heretic*, pp. 24–29; Norman Etherington, 'Christianity and African Society in Nineteenth-century Natal', in *Natal and Zululand from earliest Times to 1910: A New History*, eds. Andrew Duminy and Bill Guest (Pietermaritzburg: University of Natal Press and Shuter & Shooter, 1989), p. 291.

13. Hinchliff, *John William Colenso*, pp. 33–37. A full statement of Colenso's views can be found in his *St Paul's Epistle*. This controversial work, 'a deliberate attempt . . . to expound a missionary gospel', was published at Colenso's residence, Bishopstowe (Ekukhanyeni). On Colenso's redemption of all peoples and the polygamy furore, see Guy, *The Heretic*, pp. 24–29, 73–74.

14. Colenso, *St Paul's Epistle*, pp. 48, 52–56, 79 and *A Letter to His Grace the Archbishop upon the Question of the Proper Treatment of Cases of Polygamy*, March 1861, (with margin notes), C 1269/2 Vol. 137, Colenso Collection, A204, PAR.

15. John Colenso, 'On the Efforts of Missionaries among Savages', *Journal of the Anthropological Society* 3 (1865): cclxxi–cclxxii.

16. The polygamy controversy crisscrossed the Atlantic between the mid-1850s and the 1860s.

17. Colenso, 'A Letter to His Grace'; New York *Independent*, 29 April 1858; New York *Independent*, 13 May 1858, Newspaper Collections, Library of Congress, Washington, DC; 'Bishop Colenso and Rev. Lewis Grout on Polygamy', *New Englander*, May 1856, The New York Historical Society, New York. The *New Englander* article contains marginalia, possibly from the pen of the editor William Kingsley, a New Haven resident and acquaintance of Yale President Woolsey.

18. See, for example New York *Independent*, 29 April 1858 and *New Englander*, May 1858.

19. New York *Independent*, 13 December 1860.

20. New York *Independent*, 1 November 1860; Matthew Jacobson, *Whiteness of a Different Color: European Immigrants and the Alchemy of Race* (Cambridge, MA: Harvard University Press, 1998), pp. 36–37.

21. On Stowe's *Uncle Tom's Cabin*, see Jennifer Brody, *Impossible Purities: Blackness, Femininity, and Victorian Culture* (Durham, NC: Duke University Press, 1998), pp. 74–78 and Hazel Waters, 'Putting on "Uncle Tom" on the Victorian Stage', *Race & Class* 42:3 (2001): 29–43.

22. New York *Independent*, 13 May 1858.

23. *Natal Mercury*, 6 November 1855 and 15 January 1857. See also *Natal Witness*, 22 May 1857. Like Colenso, Theophilus Shepstone was subject to settler backbiting, perhaps because in the mid-to-late 1850s Colenso and Shepstone were friends; see Guy, *The Heretic*, pp. 45–46.

24. *Natal Witness*, 22 May 1857.

25. Shepstone negotiated this settlement scheme with local chiefs. By 1850, his government had demarcated 'divisions' (encompassing reserves), over which white 'Kafir Magistrates' assumed considerable legal control. Yet Shepstone also relied on chiefs to adjudicate civil cases and some minor criminal cases. See Thomas McClendon, 'Coercion and Conversation: African Voices in the Making of Customary Law in Natal', in *The Culture of Power in Southern Africa: Essays on State Formation and the Political Imagination*, ed. Clifton Crais (Portsmouth, NH: Heinemann, 2003), pp. 56–57.

26. Contrary to colonial worries, in the 1850s the Zulu king Mpande did not invade Natal. Rather, he shored up control of the kingdom's heartland; see Benedict Carton, *Blood from Your Children: The Colonial Origins of Generational Conflict in South Africa* (Pietermaritzburg: University of Natal Press, 2000), p. 32.

27. After the reversal of the excommunication judgment, Colenso was reinstated as bishop of Natal; see Etherington, 'Christianity and African Society', p. 291 and Guy, *The Heretic*, p. 55.

28. Colenso, *Ten Weeks*, pp. 25, 44, 259–61. His feeling of 'common brotherhood' was to be reaffirmed in an 1859 visit to the Zulu court to secure a royal grant of land on which to establish a mission. There, Colenso saw Mpande convey 'family affection, human sorrow, [and] respect for the memory of the dead', principally his slain son, Mbuyazi, the brother of Cetshwayo. Mbuyazi and thousands of his followers had died in a civil war against rival Cetshwayo's regiments. See J.W. Colenso, 'On Missions to the Zulus in Natal and Zululand', *Social Science Review* 3 (1865): 490, 492–96, Guy, *The Heretic*, p. 88 and Peter Colenbrander, 'The Zulu Kingdom 1828–79', in *Natal and Zululand*, eds. Duminy and Guest, p. 104.

29. Colenso, *Ten Weeks*, p. 100. Colenso's sceptical view of *uThixo* received support from Theophilus Shepstone, who viewed evangelism through the lens of a Secretary for Native Affairs endeavouring to shield 'the African chiefly world' from colonial meddling (except his own, of course); see McClendon, 'Coercion and Conversation', p. 56 and Hamilton, *Terrific Majesty*, pp. 72–104. Still, as Jonathan Draper observes, Shepstone was not against conversion as long as it encompassed young men of Zulu royalty, the distant authority he hoped to monitor and influence. See Draper, 'The Bishop', p. 441 and Norman Etherington, *Preachers, Peasants and Politics in Southeast Africa, 1835–1880: African Christian Communities in Natal, Pondoland and Zululand* (London: Royal Historical Society, 1978), pp. 133–45.

30. Colenso, 'On Missions to the Zulus': 490. On *uThixo* and *iThongo*, see Colenso, *Ten Weeks*, pp. 56–58, 240 and Axel-Ivar Berglund, *Zulu Thought-patterns and Symbolism* (Bloomington, IN: Indiana University Press, 1976), p. 43. Colenso later concluded that *iThongo* referred to the spirits of the dead. On missionary vernacular terms for God, see William Worger, 'Parsing God: Conversations about the Meanings of Words in Nineteenth-century South Africa', *Journal of African History* 42 (2001): 417–47.

31. Colenso asserted that the vague symbolism of '*umKulunkulu*' and '*umVelinqange*' revealed the confusion of 'fathers of all the Kafir tribes' about 'God Himself'. '[U]mkulunkulu . . . Comer-Out': Colenso, *Ten Weeks*, p. 59; 'the fathers . . . religion': Colenso, *St Paul's Epistle*, p. 58; 'confused': Colenso, *Ten Weeks*, pp. 33, 238–99; 'God Himself': Colenso, *St Paul's Epistle*, p. 216.

32. William Shaw, *The Story of My Mission among British Settlers in South Eastern Africa*, (London: Wesleyan Mission House, [1860] 1872), p. 452.

33. Marion Benham, *Henry Callaway, M.D., D.D., First Bishop for Kaffraria: His Life-history and Work: A Memoir* (London: Macmillan and Co., 1896), p. 55 and letter from J.W. Colenso to W.H.I. Bleek, 5 July 1861, Fol. A147, Colenso Papers, Killie Campbell Library (KCL), UKZN, Durban. In 1861, Colenso expressed confidence that *uNkulunkulu* was the term for God.

34. Colenso, *Ten Weeks*, p. 100 and Colenso, *St Paul's Epistle*, p. 176.

35. Robert Young, *Colonial Desire: Hybridity in Theory, Culture and Race* (London: Routledge, 1995), pp. 50, 51. Boas is best known for his studies of Native Americans in the Pacific Northwest.

36. George Stocking, *Delimiting Anthropology: Occasional Inquiries and Reflections* (Madison, WI: University of Wisconsin Press, 2001), pp. 271–72.

37. Sally Falk Moore, *Anthropology and Africa: Changing Perspectives on a Changing Scene* (Charlottesville, VA: University Press of Virginia, 1994) pp. 10–11, 24–25, 28, 166. On the 'classical period', see George Stocking, *Victorian Anthropology* (New York: Free Press, 1987), p. 289. On British (African) anthropology, see Adam Kuper, *Anthropologists and Anthropology: The British School, 1922–1972* (London: Allan Lane, 1983), pp. 89–91.

38. 'Testimony of Lazarus Mxaba and Johannes Kumalo', in *The James Stuart Archive of Recorded Oral Evidence Relating to the History of the Zulu and Neighbouring Peoples*, Vol. 1, eds. Colin Webb and John Wright (Pietermaritzburg: University of Natal Press, 1976), pp. 260–61. On theological ties between Mxaba and Colenso, see Chidester, *Savage Systems*, pp. 116–18. On the anthropological content of the missionaries' 'long conversation', see Jean Comaroff and John Comaroff, *Of Revelation and Revolution: Christianity, Colonialism, and Consciousness in South Africa*, Vol. 1 (Chicago: University of Chicago Press, 1991), pp. 17–18. For critical views of the Comaroffs' approach to the 'long conversation', see Elizabeth Elbourne, 'Word Made Flesh: Christianity, Modernity and Cultural Colonialism in the Work of Jean and John Comaroff', *American Historical Review* CVIII (2003): 435–59.

39. Biographical information about Joseph Shooter can be found in the anonymous articles written by his wife, Mrs Shooter, entitled, 'Off to Natal, By a Clergyman's Wife', *Golden Hours: A Weekly Journal of Good Literature for Young Folks*, Jan.–Nov. 1868: 11–15, 302–08, 532–36, 606–10.

40. Bird, 'The Form of Constitutional Government'. On white clergymen's 'settler racism' in colonial South Africa in the early and middle nineteenth century, see Philippe Denis, *The Dominican Friars in Southern Africa: A Social History (1577–1990)* (Leiden: Brill, 1998), pp. 92, 95.

41. Joseph Shooter, *The Kafirs of Natal and The Zulu Country* (New York: Negro Universities Press, 1969 [London, 1857]), p. 159.

42. Fynn Testimony (Harding 'Kafir' Commission, 1852–53), 14 April 1853; 'When . . . flesh': Fynn Testimony (Harding 'Kafir' Commission, 1852–53), 21 April 1853; *Natal Mercury*; File 8, KCM 98/69/7, Fynn Papers, KCL, UKZN; Minutes '1852–53 Kafir Commission', II/1/1, Secretary for Native Affairs (SNA), 1/SNA, PAR.

43. Shooter, *The Kafirs of Natal*, pp. 172–74, 180–83.

44. Fynn, along with a few other British traders such as Francis Farewell, Henry Ogle and John Cane made Port Natal their base for selling cattle, animal skins, and possibly guns; securing tusks from elephant hunters and peddling ivory to Cape and Zulu commercial partners; and moving other lucrative commodities into colonial markets to the south and west. See Julie Pridmore, 'Henry Francis Fynn: An Assessment of His Career and An Analysis of the Written and Visual Portrayals of His Role in the History of the Natal Region' (Ph.D. diss., University of Natal, 1996), pp. 1–42; Wright, 'The Dynamics of Power', pp. 338–53; and Hamilton, *Terrific Majesty*, pp. 37–44.

45. 'Testimony of Ndukwana', in *The James Stuart Archive of Recorded Oral Evidence Relating to the History of the Zulu and Neighbouring Peoples*, Vol. 4, eds. Colin Webb and John Wright (Pietermaritzburg: University of Natal Press, 1986), pp. 291–92; 'Testimony of Mbovu', 'Testimony of Melapi' and 'Testimony of Mmemi', in *The James Stuart Archive of Recorded Oral Evidence Relating to the History of the Zulu and Neighbouring Peoples*, Vol. 3, eds. Colin Webb and John Wright (Pietermaritzburg: University of Natal Press, 1982), pp. 27, 73, 263. On white traders like Fynn and their polygamy, see 'Testimony of Jantshi' and 'Testimony of Dinya', in *The James Stuart Archive*, Vol. 1, eds. Webb and Wright, pp. 200, 111. On *ukukhonza*, see 'Testimony of Mcotoyi' and 'Testimony of Dinya', in *The James Stuart Archive*, Vol. 3, eds. Webb and Wright, p. 57. On the hierarchy of *izinduna*, see 'Testimony of Dinya', in *The James Stuart Archive*, Vol. 1, eds. Webb and Wright, p. 99.

46. Fynn's involvement in rituals of guardianship were memorialised in his *izibongo* (praises, which should be critically analysed). Zulu folksongs (composed before 1861) note Fynn's role as a homestead head with the power to commune with the ancestral realm; they also allude to Fynn's traditional leadership. See Trevor Cope, ed. *Izibongo: Zulu Praise-Poems* (Oxford: Oxford University Press, 1968), pp. 192–95 and 'Statement of Duka Fynn, Maguntsha, 16 Jan. 1907', p. 28, 'Notes on the Life of Henry Francis Fynn', File 10, Fynn Papers, KCL, UKZN. A Zulu folksong about Fynn can be found in 'Journal entry (10 March 1852)', pp. 66–70, 75, 'Rambling Along the Sea Coast between Port Natal and the Umzimvooboo', Vol. 2, Garden Papers, A1157, PAR.

47. Colenso, 'A Letter to an American Missionary', p. 59.

48. Shooter, *The Kafirs of Natal*, pp. v–vi.

49. Ibid., pp. 159–60. Mrs Shooter suggested that her husband believed that somewhere in the 'darkened heathen' mind there was 'an indistinct notion of the creation, fall, and the introduction of death; also a tradition of a universal deluge'; see 'Off to Natal', p. 608.

50. *uMvelingqangi*, 'the First Appearer or Exister', is derived from *vela* (to appear) and *ngqangi* (the origin); see Berglund, *Zulu Thought-patterns*, pp. 34–36.

51. A. Vilakazi, *Zulu Transformations* (Pietermaritzburg: University of Natal Press, 1965), p. 89. Vilakazi admitted that by the early 1900s Christian teachings started to influence more Zulu conceptions of the deity. Yet Vilakazi still attempted to outline Zulu cosmology by drawing on his interviews and linguistic studies. See also 'Testimony of Mkando' and 'Testimony of Ndukwana, Mkando, and Dlozi', in *The James Stuart Archive*, Vol. 3, eds. Webb and Wright, pp. 168–69, 171–72, 174; 'Testimony of Mqaikana' and 'Testimony of Mqaikana', in *The James Stuart Archive*, Vol. 4, eds. Webb and Wright, pp. 15–16, 301–05.

52. Vilakazi, *Zulu Transformations*, p. 89. For a similar perspective, see Harriet Ngubane, *Body and Mind in Zulu Medicine: An Ethnography of Health and Disease in Nyuswa-Zulu Thought and Practice* (New York: Academic Press, 1977), p. 50.

53. Shooter, *The Kafirs of Natal*, pp. 168–69 (also p. 167). In using the terms 'seers or prophets' Shooter acknowledged the information provided by Henry Francis Fynn, who noted that *ubuthakathi* (sorcery) referred to a wider field of malevolence than the English concept of 'witchcraft'; see 'Mr

Fynn's Evidence', (*Natal Mercury*, 21 April 1853, pp. 9–10, 13), File 8, KCM 98/69/7, Fynn Papers, KCL, UKZN, Durban.

54. Shooter, *The Kafirs of Natal*, pp. 191, 399 n. 8.
55. On macabre *izinyanga* behaviour, see Shooter, *The Kafirs of Natal*, pp. 184–91.
56. Shooter, *The Kafirs of Natal*, pp. 169–72.
57. Stocking, *Delimiting Anthropology*, pp. 49–52, 53–54, 55–62.
58. Ibid., p. 108.
59. See Jacobson, *Whiteness of A Different Color*, pp. 35–36.
60. Philip Appleman, ed. *Darwin* (New York: W.W. Norton, 2001), pp. 26–27.
61. Stocking, *Delimiting Anthropology*, p. 108. Just as momentous were new data from archaeologists and palaeontologists demonstrating that the antiquity of humankind extended to 'pre-historic' time.
62. On Tylor's evolutionary scheme, see Young, *Colonial Desire*, pp. 46–48.
63. Wilson Moses, *Afrotopia: The Roots of African American Popular History* (Cambridge: Cambridge University Press, 1998), p. 202. Tylor got field data from the young Boas, who offered a trenchant critique of 'the comparative method'; see Stocking, *Delimiting Anthropology*, p. 114.
64. Stocking, *Delimiting Anthropology*, p. 110.
65. Like Colenso, Callaway's evangelical awakening was stirred by F.D. Maurice. Callaway worked with Colenso from 1853 to 1858; see Etherington, 'Christianity and African Society', p. 293. Callaway's medical training would influence his subsequent ethnographic research; see Norman Etherington, 'Education and Medicine', in *Missions and Empire*, ed. Etherington, pp. 282–83.
66. Benham, *Henry Callaway*, pp. 200–06.
67. Ibid., p. 102.
68. Benham, *Henry Callaway*, pp. 56–59. Callaway and Colenso agreed on the existence of shades and 'knowledge of good and evil' (*unembeza* and *ugovana*), but their relationship deteriorated after a disagreement over the use of *uNkulunkulu*. Colenso maintained that Callaway's catechist, Mpengula Mbande, confused *uNkulunkulu* with the Lord-of-the-Sky and the shades; see Martin, 'British Images', pp. 196–202.
69. Henry Callaway, 'Usetemba's Tale', Preface, 'Callaway's Journal', Vol. 7, p. 852; letter from Dr Bleek to Callaway, 20 May 1862, Vol. 12, pp. 355–58, Fol. E, United Society for the Propagation of the Gospel Archives (SPG), London.
70. Benham, *Henry Callaway*, pp. 215, 239, 341.
71. Martin, 'British Images', pp. 196–202.
72. Henry Callaway, 'Preface', *Nursery Tales, Traditions, and Histories of the Zulus* (Pietermaritzburg: Davis and Sons, 1868), Vol. 1.
73. Henry Callaway, *The Religious System of the Amazulu: Izinyanga Zokubula; Or, Divination, As Existing Among the Amazulu* (Pietermaritzburg: Davis and Sons, 1870), pp. 101–25. Callaway's translation of the *Book of Common Prayer* used uDio as well as *uSimakade*, the Eternal, to represent God; see H. Callaway (transl.), *Incwadi Yokukuleka: yabantu abakristu* (London: Society for Promoting Christian Knowledge, 1882).
74. 'Callaway's Journal', Vol. 7, p. 825, Fol. E, SPG Archives, London.
75. Henry Callaway, *A Fragment on Comparative Religion*, (London: privately published, 1874) pp. 7–8 (reprinted in Irving Hexham, ed., *Texts on Zulu Religion: Traditional Zulu Ideas About God* [Lewiston: Edwin Mellen Press, 1987], pp. 400–49).
76. Henry Callaway, *Missionary Sermons* (London: George Bell & Sons, 1875), p. 135.
77. Callaway, *Missionary Sermons*, p. 18 and Benham, *Henry Callaway*, p. 83.
78. Callaway, *Missionary Sermons*, pp. 72, 135.

# Chapter 14

# 'Bloodstained Grandeur'
## Colonial and Imperial Stereotypes of Zulu Warriors and Zulu Warfare

JOHN LABAND

THE WESTERN IMAGINATION STILL entertains a counter-image of the noble, courageous tribal warrior, paradoxically admirable in his very savagery. Of all such warriors across the breadth of Africa it is the amaZulu of southeastern Africa who have captured and held the Western imagination as the epitome of the African fighting man. And, as Robert Edgerton has complained in his book about the Asante Empire, they have done so to the effective exclusion of all the other warrior peoples of Africa.[1]

This pervasive image of the amaZulu in the West has a long pedigree. Samuel Martin, basing his work on Edward Said's *Orientalism*, has shown how nineteenth-century British images of the amaZulu had a history and dynamic of their own and were in a constant state of transformation. The initial impression of forbidding savages was disseminated during the 1820s by the hunter-traders at Port Natal. In succeeding decades, Natal settlers and missionaries elaborated and crystallised the image of the amaZulu as a nation in arms, imbued with a fierce military ethos. The officials justifying the British invasion of Zululand in 1879 confirmed this tradition, which was sustained and elaborated by the sensational coverage of the campaign in the popular press. After the Anglo-Zulu War, the image of the terrible Zulu warrior was gradually transformed into one of a noble, heroic and worthy foe, not least through the novels of Sir Henry Rider Haggard.[2] Two recent books, one by Carolyn Hamilton, and the other by Dan Wylie – although dealing specifically with historical invention and literary mythology surrounding King Shaka, the founder of the Zulu kingdom – have both engaged more generally with the subsequent and continuing confirmation of the Zulu warrior stereotype, particularly in popular literature, film and the media.[3]

Perhaps the reason for the amaZulu continuing to hold pride of place over the last 40 years in the mind of the English-speaking world as Africa's quintessential warriors is, as Bruce Vandervort has suggested, the result of certain films and books that have persistently reinforced the stereotype.[4] Consider the cult nature attained by a war adventure film such as *Zulu*, which deals with the saga of the battle of

Rorke's Drift, or take the undiminished success of Donald Morris's much-reprinted *Washing of the Spears*, which tells the story of the Zulu kingdom from the rise of Shaka to the Anglo-Zulu War of 1879. No matter that the film is largely fiction and was not even filmed in Zululand, or that Morris's book has been comprehensively overtaken by subsequent academic research. Both have kept the amaZulu in the public eye and have attracted an audience that had not previously existed.

Fascination with the 'Zulu wars', verging almost on the morbid, can perhaps best be understood in terms of concepts of heroic masculinity and the residue of the pervasive military ethos that permeated late imperial Britain. In this milieu, it was not necessarily victory in Queen Victoria's 'little wars' that established a soldier's worth, but rather the qualities he showed in confronting defeat or certain death. The more dangerous and savage the foe, and the more overwhelming the odds, the greater the glory.[5] If this foe can also be projected as a worthy and courageous adversary – a noble savage, in fact – then a modern audience will respond even more positively to the drama.

A corollary of such romanticising of the Zulu warrior is the desire to turn him into an exploitable tourist resource, to transform him from icon into commodity. The heritage industry is economically increasingly important in KwaZulu-Natal and it requires for its marketing packages only carefully edited and uncritical 'history bytes'.[6] We already have phoney resorts such as Shakaland, where Western visitors can enjoy daily shows of dancing, spear-throwing and other apparently authentic traditional manifestations by warriors. However, these warriors have, in reality, become victims, wage-slaves in a modern, capitalist economy far removed from the precapitalist utopia being celebrated for its entertainment value.[7]

Moreover, a fundamental problem with this continued peddling of the warrior stereotype, no matter how domesticated, is that it can only reinforce the already pervasive Western expectation of the ferocious Zulu delight in things violent and military. Significantly, in an age that genuflects to the power of the mass media, Western photojournalists have accepted these assumptions and have been socialised into seeking out and confirming in their reporting the anticipated Zulu capacity for bloodshed. In 1994, amid the violence in the run-up to the first democratic elections in South Africa, the local media assisted in confirming the stereotypical image of the Zulu warrior by sensationally dwelling on Zulu men in traditional dress at political rallies or in the course of vigilante activities; the men carry shields and provocatively wield cultural weapons such as knobkerries and spears.

Yet we must not attribute the survival of the Zulu warrior stereotype solely to Western writers, films and the media. What seems to guarantee the unsinkability of this Western image is its reinforcement among many Zulu people today. Avoiding vexed debates about the creation of Zulu identity and ethnic consciousness,[8] it is perhaps enough to say that the Zulu past, especially its military tradition, has been exploited by contemporary Zulu intellectuals and politicians to legitimate modern

Zulu nationalism. Thembisa Waetjen and Gerhard Maré argue that the invocation of the blood brotherhood and worthy heritage of the proud and valorous Zulu warrior offered a dignified identity that could ease the anonymity and alienation of migrant working life in the apartheid era. This message has continued to resonate because it accords with popular Zulu attitudes concerning their masculinity and perceived ethnic characteristics as a warrior nation.[9] As a male Zulu migrant worker succinctly put it: 'The Zulu Nation is born out of Shaka's spear. When you say "Go and fight," it just happens.'[10] In a more general sense, Ali Mazrui has suggested that the affirmation of the warrior tradition in modern African culture is an attempt by males to heal the deep psychological wounds caused by the demilitarisation and dependency of the colonial experience by reasserting precolonial masculine virtues like martial valour.[11]

Dr Mangosuthu Buthelezi, the long-term leader of the Inkatha Freedom Party (IFP), which has always represented itself as the sole legitimate political representative of the Zulu nation, has paradoxically invoked the Zulu warrior heritage as the basis for the order that once supposedly existed in Zulu society, for discipline and, indeed, for civilisation. As Carolyn Hamilton has persuasively argued,[12] King Shaka's violent creation of the Zulu kingdom in the early nineteenth century at a time of major and general upheaval in southeastern Africa (a period still problematically known as the *mfecane*, or 'crushing')[13] is portrayed in this discourse as the price that people were prepared to pay for order and security. Those living in chaos on the peripheries of the centralised, disciplined and militaristic Zulu kingdom became the savage 'other'. The Zulu described them as 'cannibals', which was code for those living outside the recognised social order. And, by association, in the twentieth century Zulu nationalists have invoked the Shakan legacy and the warrior ethos as a bulwark, first against the chaos and upheaval inflicted on the Zulu people living under apartheid and then against the socialist policies of the urban-based African National Congress (ANC), which were portrayed by the IFP as threatening the traditional Zulu order and the powers of the chiefs in the rural areas.

These notions and images of the Zulu warrior are important for what they say about the ways in which cultural self-conceptions are propagated and enforced, cherished values proclaimed and those of outsiders thereby 'othered'. Yet it is also possible to demythologise the Zulu warrior and describe what he actually was, for nineteenth-century Zulu society can be normalised and understood like any other, as can the Zulu military system itself.[14]

The Zulu military system should be placed within its temporal limits. It only came into its full development in the 1820s during the reign of King Shaka and, as an institution, it was abruptly abolished in September 1879 in terms of the settlement the victorious British imposed on the defeated amaZulu at the end of the Anglo-Zulu War. It persisted in increasingly attenuated form during the civil wars and anti-colonial struggles of 1883–88 and 1906, but has lingered on only as a glorious memory to inspire present-day Zulus.[15]

*The striking representation in the* Illustrated London News
*of 6 September 1879 of Captain Lord William Beresford's
'encounter with a Zulu' during the reconnaissance of 3 July.*

When in 1879 Sir Bartle Frere, the British High Commissioner for South Africa, engineered his fatal war against the Zulu kingdom, with the object of ensuring the stable conditions necessary for the confederation of the subcontinent, he justified his actions to his apprehensive superiors in London by harping on the persistent military danger he asserted the Zulu kingdom posed to its British-ruled neighbours. He characterised the Zulu warriors as members of a 'frightfully efficient man-slaying machine',[16] and saw it as incumbent upon him as a Christian proconsul of empire to bring them the benefits of British civilisation. This meant releasing them from military servitude to their bloody tyrant of a king and putting them instead to productive labour for wages.[17] Frere's demonisation of the Zulu military system might have rung true to his white contemporaries and, as we have seen, still holds good in the popular mind. Yet the actuality was rather different from the myth.

From the outset, it must be understood that the Zulu army was never a professional standing army. Rather, it was a part-time militia that was integrated into the whole social and economic fabric of the kingdom, and was part of the labour system through which the king exercised power and authority over all his subjects, both male and female, in the interests of the state. The basis of the Zulu military system was the longstanding institution among the various chiefdoms of what was later to become the Zulu kingdom of the age-set regiment, or *ibutho* (plural, *amabutho*). Youths of the same age group were banded together to perform various forms of economic and military service for their chiefs in order to make for more effective management of resources. In the 1820s King Shaka brought this evolving *amabutho* system to its fully developed form as an instrument for integrating the members of the chiefdoms he had conquered into the new Zulu state, and for weaning them from their original loyalty to their old chiefs, now subordinated to the Zulu king. The *amabutho* were barracked in military homesteads, or *amakhanda* (singular, *ikhanda*), presided over by members of the royal family or trusted royal officers. These *amakhanda* provided the nodes of royal authority in the far-flung districts of the kingdom, and also the training and mobilisation points for the local elements of the *amabutho*.

Women were also part of the military system in that, as the major agricultural labour force in society, they fed the men when they were away from home serving the king. Girls were also formed into *amabutho* for the purpose of regulating marriage. At intervals the king gave a male *ibutho* leave to marry a designated female *ibutho*. By generally withholding permission until the men were in middle age, the king was prolonging the period in which they would be regarded as youths in Zulu society, and thus remain more firmly under the authority of their elders and, by extension, the king.

Newly formed *amabutho* spent seven to eight months continuously serving at the central *amakhanda* clustered in the heart of the kingdom. All *amabutho* would muster there annually for the national first fruits ceremonies presided over by the king. Otherwise, elements of the *amabutho* would take turns to serve at the regional *amakhanda* for a few months a year. While serving at an *ikhanda*, members of an *ibutho* would keep it in repair, herd and milk the royal cattle attached to it and cultivate the king's land. Their womenfolk would bring them additional food from home. When not serving the king in this way, the *amabutho* would stay at home and contribute their labour to their own homesteads.

The king would often call up a few *amabutho* for additional services, such as levying tribute from outlying subordinated people, or for collecting cattle fines and otherwise 'eating up' offenders against the king. Cattle and other commodities, which the *amabutho* collected on these forays, provided a vital source of royal power, for in redistributing a portion as largesse to the *amabutho* and great men of the kingdom, the king exercised an essential form of patronage that ensured their loyalty. Naturally, booty would be accumulated most spectacularly during full-scale military operations. It was thus in the interests of king, great chiefs and *amabutho* alike to go to war regularly. This occurred with the greatest frequency and covered the widest geographical area in the early days of the kingdom when Shaka was conquering and incorporating his neighbours, and creating a zone around the kingdom's core subject to incessant raiding and tribute gathering.[18] It is from this period, primarily in the 1820s, that the great legends and images of Zulu military prowess have arisen.

As early as 1824, however, British traders and hunters were established at Port Natal and were fighting as mercenaries in Shaka's campaigns. They were also acting as intermediaries with the government of the Cape Colony, which deprecated the unrest on its borders caused by Zulu raiding. From its earliest days, therefore, the Zulu kingdom became involved with the affairs of an encroaching colonial world.

This involvement accelerated rapidly in the late 1830s when many disgruntled Dutch-speaking settlers of the Cape Colony, the voortrekkers, moved away into the interior to establish republics free from British interference. Their advance denied the highveld of the interior to King Dingane's armies, and in 1837 they spilled over the mountains into the Zulu kingdom itself. In full-scale fighting during much of 1838 the voortrekkers eventually defeated Dingane's armies and seized the southern half of his kingdom.

The British then intervened and annexed the Boer republic as the Colony of Natal, fixing the southern boundary of the Zulu kingdom in 1843 along the Thukela River. Consequently, the Zulu armies could no longer raid south as had been their wont, while the consolidation of the fledgling Boer republics of the interior meant they could no longer raid west either. The people of the coastal lands to the northeast between Zululand and the Portuguese at Delagoa Bay were already Zulu tributaries. This left only the nascent Swazi kingdom to the north as a source of booty and military glory. King Mpande's armies raided Swaziland regularly throughout the 1840s, but by the early 1850s improved Swazi resistance in their mountainous terrain, as well as Boer and British interference, spelled the end of these military forays. Henceforth, the feared *amabutho* went to war only within Zululand itself in the civil conflicts that were a symptom of the strains being placed on the kingdom as it was steadily squeezed by its encroaching colonial neighbours.

What this meant in terms of Zulu military expertise was that when in 1879 Britain went to war against the warriors of Frere's so-called 'manslaying war-machine', these self-same, fearsome warriors had last pitted themselves against white fighters in December 1838, or 41 years before – a gap as large as that between the Crimean War and the Boer War. The last time the Zulu army had fought a major engagement was at Ndondakusuka in December 1856, when Cetshwayo destroyed his brother and rival, Mbuyazi, and secured the royal succession. That was 23 years before, a longer gap than that between the end of the First World War and the beginning of the Second World War.

In other words, when in January 1879 the Zulu army launched itself in several frontal mass attacks, intending to outflank and envelop the British in its famous bull's horn manoeuvre and finish them off in hand-to-hand fighting with stabbing-spears, in accordance with the close-order tactics required in fighting with edged weapons, the Zulu warriors involved had precious little battle experience, and none had previously faced the effects of concentrated fire from modern firearms. What remarkable military successes the amaZulu did achieve in 1879 were a testament to their great courage and determination (as well as to British military incompetence), and not to their atrophied fighting methods. For if these had made them the terror of the subcontinent in the 1820s, they had become completely outmoded by the 1870s.

As John Keegan has pointed out, it is 'a besetting fault of triumphant warrior systems . . . that they become fossilised in their moment of glory . . . [and] continue to concentrate all their energies in an exclusive military form'.[19] With the amaZulu, as so often elsewhere, the form was that which had determined their rise as a power, and the Shakan military system, although it efficiently served and protected a particular way of life, denied itself the chance to evolve and adapt to the changing world around it. The amaZulu did eventually acquire a considerable numbers of firearms by the 1870s, but they failed to adapt their tactics to the new weapon. They persisted in mass, frontal attacks with the stabbing-spear as their means to battlefield supremacy, and relegated the function of firearms to providing covering fire.

In this regard, Bruce Vandervort gives us the timely reminder that while it is certainly true that Africans who took the path of armed resistance to European invasion in the later nineteenth century faced daunting technological disadvantages and an enormous disparity in armaments, it would be to fall into the trap of technological determinism to attribute European success entirely to superior firepower. Equally significant was the unwillingness exhibited by people such as the amaZulu to rethink strategies and tactics that had proved ineffective against European methods of warfare so as to neutralise technological disparities.[20]

By stark contrast with the largely unmodified traditional Zulu military system, those of many other African peoples of the interior of southern Africa adapted more or less seriously to European weaponry and styles of fighting in order to resist colonial penetration. The Sotho people, for example, early embraced both horses and firearms, operating like mounted infantry. The Pedi, like the Sotho, put a premium on firearms and made effective use of natural features. These they turned into strongholds with the construction of stone sangars and rifle pits, and successfully resisted both Boer and Briton from 1876 until final defeat in late 1879. The Sotho fought a series of wars against their rapacious colonial neighbours between 1858 and 1881, eventually (unlike the amaZulu) securing their future independence as a nation.[21]

Indeed, if we were to identify an image epitomising the successful African fighting man in southern Africa during the later nineteenth century, it would not be that of the long-famed Zulu warrior with his tossing feather and leopard-skin headdress, beating his great cowhide shield with his stabbing-spear as he utters his terrible war cry. Rather, it would be that of a Sotho mounted on his sturdy pony, a high-crowned straw hat on his head and wearing a woven European-manufactured blanket over his Western-style jacket and trousers, taking careful aim with his rifled carbine. But that is not the stuff of legend.

## Notes

1. Robert Edgerton, *The Fall of the Asante Empire: The Hundred-Year War for Africa's Gold Coast* (New York: Free Press, 1995), p. 24.
2. S.J.R. Martin, 'British Images of the Zulu *c.*1820–1879' (Ph.D. diss., University of Cambridge, 1982), pp. 17–19, 166, 332–34.
3. Carolyn Hamilton, *Terrific Majesty: The Powers of Shaka Zulu and the Limits of Historical Invention* (Cape Town and Johannesburg: David Philip, 1998) and Dan Wylie, *Savage Delight: White Myths of Shaka* (Pietermaritzburg: University of Natal Press, 2000).
4. Bruce Vandervort, *Wars of Imperial Conquest in Africa, 1830–1914* (London: UCL Press, 1998), p. 102.
5. See Stephen Leech, ' "Aggressive by Nature, Depraved and Like Nazis": Images of Zulu Violence', *Kleio* XXX (1998): 94–95.
6. See John Wright, 'Making and Remaking Zuluist and Settlerist Histories in Shaka's Once-upon-a-time Kingdom', paper delivered at the conference on Memory and History: Remembering, Forgetting and Forgiving in the Life of the Nation and the Community, University of Cape Town, August 2000, pp. 10–12.
7. See D. Cloete, 'From Warriors to Wage-slaves: The Fate of the Zulu People since 1879', *Reality* 11:1 (1979).
8. See Robert Morrell, ed., *Political Economy and Identities in KwaZulu-Natal: Historical and Social Perspectives* (Durban: Indicator Press, 1996) for a collection of essays grappling with Zulu identity and ethnicity.
9. Thembisa Waetjen and Gerhard Maré, ' "Men amongst Men": Masculinity and Zulu Nationalism in the 1980s', in *Changing Men in Southern Africa*, ed. Robert Morrell (Pietermaritzburg: University of Natal Press and London: Zed Books, 2001), pp. 200–01, 205.
10. *Weekly Mail*, 30 August–5 September 1991.
11. Ali A. Mazrui, 'The Resurrection of the Warrior Tradition in African Political Culture', *The Journal of Modern African Studies* 13:1 (1975): 68, 71, 80, 83–84.
12. The following discussion is based on Hamilton, *Terrific Majesty*, pp. 208–14.
13. See Carolyn Hamilton, ed., *The Mfecane Debate: Reconstructive Debates in Southern African History* (Johannesburg: Witwatersrand University Press and Pietermaritzburg: University of Natal Press, 1995) for a collection of essays grappling with this contested concept.
14. For recent analyses of the Zulu army and military system, see John Laband and Paul Thompson, *The Illustrated Guide to the Anglo-Zulu War* (Pietermaritzburg: University of Natal Press, 2000), pp. 9–19 and Ian Knight, *The Anatomy of the Zulu Army from Shaka to Cetshwayo 1818–1879* (London: Greenhill Books, 1995).
15. For Zulu military organisation, fighting techniques and strategy during the 1880s, see John Laband, *The Atlas of the Later Zulu Wars 1883–1888* (Pietermaritzburg: University of Natal Press, 2001), pp. 4–8, 20–22. See also Benedict Carton, *Blood from your Children: The Colonial Origins of Generational Conflict in South Africa* (Pietermaritzburg, University of Natal Press, 2000), pp. 19–21, 36–41.
16. National Archives, Kew: Colonial Office 879/14: *African Confidential Print 166*, p. 5: notes by Frere, 3 February 1879.
17. See John Laband, *Kingdom in Crisis: The Zulu Response to the British Invasion of 1879* (Manchester: Manchester University Press, 1992), pp. 5–8. See also Richard Cope, *Ploughshare of War: The Origins of the Anglo-Zulu War of 1879* (Pietermaritzburg: University of Natal Press, 1999), pp. 257–64.

18. Detailed information on the wars in which the Zulu were involved from the 1810s to the 1870s can be found in John Laband, *The Rise and Fall of the Zulu Nation* (London: Arms and Armour Press, 1997), pp. 11–286.
19. John Keegan, *A History of Warfare* (London: Hutchinson, 1993), p. 31.
20. Vandervort, *Wars of Imperial Conquest*, pp. 48–51, 54, 113, 209.
21. See John Laband, 'War and Peace in South Africa to 1914' and Ian Knight, 'Military Opponents of the British Empire in South Africa, 1795–1914', both in *'Ashes and Blood': The British Army in South Africa 1795–1914*, eds. Peter Boyden, Alan Guy and Marion Harding (London: National Army Museum, 1999), pp. 14–16, 26–27.

*Chapter 15*

# 'What Do You Red-Jackets Want in Our Country?'

## The Zulu Response to the British Invasion of 1879

IAN KNIGHT

ON 11 JANUARY 1879, the British Empire went to war with a friendly power. British troops, massed at various points along the borders of their southern African colonies of Natal and the Transvaal, crossed into the sovereign territory of the independent Zulu kingdom, bringing to an end more than half a century of a largely amicable relationship.[1]

That a political crisis had been looming had, of course, been equally apparent to the powerful elite who administered the country and to ordinary Zulu people alike. If King Cetshwayo and his *ibandla*, the inner circle of trusted confidants who advised him, had been obliged to meet regularly to discuss the British threats, Zulu men from across the kingdom had experienced the rising tension through their obligation to serve the king in the frequent call-ups of the *amabutho* age-regiments. The gathering of the nation's young men at the *amakhanda*, the royal homesteads that served as centres of state administration, to meet earlier crises, and their subsequent dismissal in the event of a false alarm, had had an unsettling effect at all levels of Zulu society, spreading rumours and fuelling both fear and resentment of British intentions. These fears had become more prevalent throughout December 1878 and January 1879, as British troops could clearly be seen massing in the green hills opposite the principal points of entry into the kingdom. A Dutch trader, Cornelius Vijn, who had the misfortune to be in Zululand as the crisis unfolded, experienced the mixed feelings within the country:

> The Zulus were very friendly towards me, and trade was unusually good. Chief men came to me continually, both to buy and to talk over the now-impending war. The main part of the talk of the persons of most importance and of the people was that the Whites 'were very bad people. Since they had only just before set the King upon his throne, why had they now come to fight

177

with him, in order to kill him and take his country from him?'[2] In fact, the Zulus had the idea that the Whites had come to capture all the males, to be sent to England and there kept to work, while the girls would all be married off to (white) soldiers, and their cattle would, of course, all belong to the English government. Hence, when it came to fighting, they fought not for the King only, but for themselves, since they would rather die than live under the Whites.[3]

Others Europeans discovered that the ominous mood prevailing in the country found expression in the truculent behaviour of the young men when assembled in their *amabutho*. John Dunn, the white hunter and trader whom Cetshwayo had adopted as an adviser and raised up to a position of great influence, was in a particularly invidious position. At once a member of the inner circle and an outsider, he found himself the butt of the frustrations of those amaZulu who felt that Cetshwayo had been betrayed by his former white allies. In late 1878, Dunn was present at the muster of an *ibutho* when

> ... the gathering ... broke up in an unusual manner, as the soldiers shouted in an excited way, and a great number left their usual course and came in the direction of my camp ... [They] came swarming past, and several went right through my tents. On my speaking to them, they shouted out, 'That is past (meaning my authority); a white man is nothing now in this country; we will stab him with an assegai and disembowel him.'[4]

The British threat had initially come as something of a surprise to the Zulu kingdom, and was the result of a forward policy adopted in southern Africa in the mid-1870s. From 1877, the newly arrived British High Commissioner, Sir Henry Edward Bartle Frere, had come to see the existence of an independent Zulu state as a danger to British interests and had prepared the way for military intervention. On 11 December 1878 Frere's representatives had delivered an ultimatum to King Cetshwayo's envoys demanding, among other things, that the king surrender the family of the border *inkosi*, Sihayo kaXongo – whom the British accused of territorial violations – and disband the *amabutho* system.

That the British threat had produced such an apparent unanimity of feeling within Zululand was particularly ironic, since from the first they had hoped to minimise the need for force by dividing Zululand against itself. Colonial officials were well aware of the centrifugal forces at the heart of Zulu politics, of the sometimes very different aspirations of the state, represented by the king, and of the regional *izikhulu* and *amakhosi* who administered power at a local level. The British tried to alternately encourage and cajole regional *amakhosi* to abandon their loyalty to the king and to defect, thereby weakening the bonds that held the kingdom together. As early as

30 October 1878, the senior British Commander in southern Africa, Lieutenant-General Lord Chelmsford, wrote: 'I would also recommend that immediately war is proclaimed against Cetewayo, those now living under his rule should be informed that any desiring to escape from his tyranny will be allowed to take refuge in British territory.'[5]

By 11 December – the day of the ultimatum – he had expanded this idea, urging his Commanders that 'any other Chief who professes himself as anxious not to fight against us, that if they come out of Zululand and sit quiet in such locality as we may appoint, they will be reinstated in their own lands when the Zulu question has been finally settled, and that they will be recognised as independent owing allegiance only to Her Majesty through her representative'.[6]

It is certainly true that the *izikhulu* who sat on the *ibandla* were divided in the face of the British threat. Some, like the northern barons Prince Hamu kaNzibe – Cetshwayo's brother,[7] who was widely held to harbour ambitions to the throne – and the young and ambitious *inkosi* Zibhebhu kaMaphitha of the Mandlakazi section, had extensive commercial ties with the settler world that would be at risk from an open conflict. Others, like the king's immensely powerful senior *induna*, *inkosi* Mnyamana kaNgqengelele of the Buthelezi, were deeply uneasy at the cost to the country of armed conflict. Feelings against *inkosi* Sihayo ran high, blaming him for provoking the British, and some councillors went so far as to spit on him in council. Cetshwayo himself shared the prevailing unease but could not abandon his favourite and, indeed, the *ibandla* as a whole was united in its rejection of the central British demand: to disband the *amabutho* system quite clearly meant the end of Zulu political and economic independence. Even those in doubt accepted that, in the face of such a threat, there was no real alternative to fighting. In the first week of January 1879, as the British deadline loomed, King Cetshwayo once more assembled his *amabutho*.

British intelligence reports had suggested that the forces at Cetshwayo's disposal had a nominal strength of 40 000 men; this was perhaps true, but since the army represented the manpower of the nation concentrated – temporarily – in its defence, it was improbable that the turn-out would be universal. Many of the most senior *amabutho* were too elderly to fight, and in any case the king instructed *amakhosi* living in the border districts to hold back some of their men to watch for enemy movements. Others remained at home to guard homes, cattle and crops. Nevertheless, the army, which assembled at the royal homesteads of oNdini and kwaNodwengu in the third week of January, numbered some 29 000 men and included the leaders of all the great chiefdoms and lineages in the country. It was, in effect, an army of national unity, and it reflected the widespread indignation felt by the amaZulu at large to the attitude adopted by the British.

Once British troops actually crossed into Zululand at three points on 11 January they posed, of course, an immediate threat to those amaZulu living along their line of advance. Initially, the amaZulu were not at all overawed by the British presence, by the sight of the columns of redcoats and their impressive European weapons, as the British had hoped. On the coast, a patrol of Natal Volunteer troops encountered a party of Zulu scouts who asked them pointedly, 'What do you red-jackets want here in our country?'[8] One individual refused to be intimidated, even when taken as a prisoner into a British camp: '. . . this fellow put on such "side" when brought before the officers, that [the reporter] felt inclined to knock him down. "You have taken me," said this bumptious Zulu, and then added, as he drew himself up to erect form and twirled the end of his moustache, "but there are plenty more awaiting you over there".'[9]

It soon became apparent, however, that the local concentrations of warriors could not be expected to oppose the full weight of a British attack unaided. On 12 January Lord Chelmsford attacked the followers of *inkosi* Sihayo in the Batshe valley. As the British advanced, they heard the amaZulu begin 'to taunt us, making their voices sound through the still morning air in the curious way natives can: "What were we doing riding along there?" "We had better try and come up" "Were we looking for a place to build our kraals?" etc.'[10]

Yet in the military encounter that followed, the British easily dispersed the Zulu opposition, killing more than 60 men and scattering the rest, destroying Sihayo's homestead and carrying away some of his cattle. According to Muziwento, a Zulu boy who lived close to Isandlwana hill, news of the attack on Sihayo had a demoralising effect on fighting men locally, although most were determined to continue the resistance: 'Some said, "It is good that homage be paid to the white men." Said our father, "Whosoever desires to do homage, it is good that he be off, and go and do homage." . . . Our father went away with his men. Others deserted him and did homage.'[11]

The aggressive actions of Lord Chelmsford's column undoubtedly shaped King Cetshwayo's strategic response, for it was reported to him that 'the troops are laying waste to the country'.[12] Equally unsettling, the British on this front deliberately appeared to be targeting Cetshwayo's principal supporters on the central border; having defeated Sihayo's followers, they then seemed to be making forays into the territory of another favourite, *inkosi* Matshana kaMondisa. Moreover, British auxiliary forces attached to the column included not only representatives of powerful African elements in Natal, opposed to the influence of the Zulu kings, but also a renegade member of the Zulu royal house.[13] Lord Chelmsford's column, it seemed, was intent on mounting a direct challenge to King Cetshwayo's administration. Accordingly, the king and his council decided to direct their main strategic response against Chelmsford's column.[14] For three days in the middle of January the army was ritually prepared for war.[15] Then, on 17 January, after parading past the graves of King Cetshwayo's ancestors to secure the blessings of the spirits, it set out on its march to the front. Feeling within the army was high; there was a deep indignation against the British invasion, and the army was confident it could defeat the invaders.

King Cetshwayo himself did not fight, though he had decided the strategy with his military advisers, headed by Mnyamana kaNqgelelele, the army's commander-in-chief. Determined to maintain that he was the injured party, Cetshwayo ordered his field commanders not to fire the first shot if possible, but otherwise gave them the freedom to act as they saw fit. On the first day of the march, the army divided and a small portion under Godide kaNdlela moved southeast, to reinforce local troops defending the lower Thukela line, with instructions to oppose the British right-flank column, which was commanded by Colonel Charles Pearson. The main portion marched due west, towards Lord Chelmsford's column, under the command of Cetshwayo's most trusted General, Ntshingwayo kaMahole, and his associate Mavumengwana kaNdlela.[16] Elements from the abaQulusi section, who lived in the northern marches, were ordered to harass the British left-flank column, which was commanded by Colonel Henry Evelyn Wood. The Zulu intention was therefore to check the movements of the two British flanking columns, while directing the main army against the British centre.

It took three days for Ntshingwayo to march within striking distance of the invaders, and as it did so, the army was reinforced by men who had hitherto remained at home to serve their *amakhosi*. By the time it reached the front it was in excess of 25 000 strong. On 20 January it arrived at iSiphezi Mountain to find that the British were now only about 15 miles (24 kilometres) away. Lord Chelmsford had advanced from Rorke's Drift to Isandlwana hill, and that same day his patrols began to scout the territory of *inkosi* Matshana kaMondise along the Mangeni River. Rather than unnecessarily expose the army to the risk of discovery, Ntshingwayo and Mavumengwana shifted their advance away from Mangeni and occupied the sheltered Ngwebeni valley, which lay within Sihayo's territory, just 5 miles (8 kilometres) from Isandlwana.

Curiously, the Zulu response struck the British on all three fronts on the same day – 22 January, a day that was otherwise considered one of ill omen, because of an imminent new moon. Circumstances, however, contrived to overcome religious objections to fighting. On the coast, Godide manoeuvred his men with the intention of attacking Pearson's column on 21 January, but, finding that he had missed the British advance, retired to the hills above the Nyezane River. Here, early on 22 January, Pearson's scouts blundered into the Zulu vanguard, and the encounter provoked Godide's men to attack. Despite catching Pearson's column on the march, however, they were unable to deploy properly and lacked, in any case, the necessary numerical superiority. Faced with an extended firing line that inflicted heavy casualties upon his men, Godide was forced to call off the attack. Coincidentally, at the other end of the country, the abaQulusi were dispersed in a running fight with Wood around the Zungwini and Hlobane Mountains.

The main army, meanwhile, had accomplished its move across the British front, from iSiphezi to the Ngwebeni, on 21 January. British scouts had failed to intercept it, and the movement would prove to be arguably the Zulu army's greatest strategic masterstroke of the war. Late that evening, as the *amabutho* rested unseen on the British flank, British patrols intercepted *inkosi* Matshana's followers moving up the Mangeni to join it. This encounter profoundly shaped the reactions of the British Commander, Lord Chelmsford. Convinced that he had in fact encountered the main army approaching Mangeni, he divided his force at Isandlwana, and before dawn on 22 January personally led a strong detachment out to attack it. He left some 1 700 men behind him to defend the camp.[17]

At the Ngwebeni, Ntshingwayo hoped to let 22 January – the inauspicious day – pass by, and late that morning held a conference of the senior *izinduna* of the *amabutho* to discuss the king's instructions and to make contingency plans for an assault. Their deliberations were interrupted, however, by British scouts from Isandlwana who, pursuing Zulu foragers, suddenly stumbled across the bivouac at Ngwebeni. According to Cetshwayo himself, 'the chiefs, knowing that the work of death was being executed, broke up the meeting and went to their several regiments'.[18] This chance encounter provoked the uKhandempemvu *ibutho* to attack the British scouts, drawing the whole army behind them. There was considerable confusion among the *amabutho* until the *izinduna*, fresh from their interrupted command meeting, were able to establish some order. The army then deployed in the traditional 'chest and horns' formation and advanced to encircle the British camp. As it spilled off the heights and descended towards Isandlwana, Ntshingwayo himself came forward to command the battle. The British garrison made its initial deployments without any very clear impression of the strength or disposition of the Zulu *amabutho* and extended far out from the tents. As the Zulu centre advanced to contact, it came under heavy rifle fire and its advance was halted, but the wide encircling movement of the Zulu 'horns' effectively outflanked the British, making their positions untenable. When the British began to retire from their exposed forward positions, the centre renewed its attack, driving the British back through the camp. Although the British infantry tried to rally on the slopes below Isandlwana hill, and put up stubborn resistance, their line of retreat was cut by the 'horns' and their formations were eventually broken up. The last phase of the battle, fought out at close quarters, was extremely brutal and destructive.

The battle was a devastating defeat for the British. Over 1 300 men were killed, including almost all of the front-line white troops. The senior British Commanders were among the dead, as too was the heir to the amaChunu chieftainship in Natal, Gabangaye kaPakhade. Yet the battle had proved a costly victory for the amaZulu. As many as 1 000 warriors were killed outright, hundreds more mortally wounded and yet more disfigured by painful injuries that would scar them for life. Among the dead were Mkhosana kaMvundlana, the *inkosi* of the powerful Biyela chiefdom, who had been shot dead as he stood up to encourage his men, and Sigodi kaMasiphula, *inkosi* of the eMgazini. So too was Mtumengana, a son of Mnyamana Buthelezi, while two sons of Ntshingwayo were severely wounded. After looting the British camp, rather than returning to report to the king, the exhausted army had simply dispersed.

In the aftermath of Isandlwana, elements from the Zulu reserve, commanded by Prince Dabulamanzi kaMpande, crossed the Mzinyathi River onto Natal soil and assaulted the British supply depot at Rorke's Drift. The defenders improvised fortifications from sacks and boxes of supplies and, fighting for their lives, withstood the attacks for nearly ten hours. Although the battle was little more than a botched mopping-up operation from the Zulu perspective, the courage of the defenders allowed the British a propaganda victory and, more significantly, proffered tactical lessons which were to have ominous implications for the future Zulu conduct of the war.

The concerted Zulu response had been largely successful, in the short term at least, in halting the British invasion. Lord Chelmsford, returning from Mangeni to Isandlwana on the evening of 22 January, had little option to retire to the border. His flanking columns, left unsupported, were unable to advance. Yet if the British plan was in disarray, the cost to the Zulu nation of their defiance was appalling. No accurate figures exists, but the total number of dead on all fronts in those first few days of the war numbered between 2 000 and 4 000, and British border patrols reported the sound of mourning songs along the length of the border. The trader, Cornelius Vijn, encountered one party of mourners who 'kept on wailing in front of the kraals, rolling themselves on the ground and never quieting down; nay, in the night they wailed so as to cut through the heart of anyone. And this wailing went on, day and night, for a fortnight . . .'[19]

The effect of these losses left the nation as a whole emotionally drained. In the immediate aftermath of Isandlwana, there was a strategic possibility that King Cetshwayo might have mounted a successful foray into Natal, which lay largely undefended in the wake of the British defeat. In fact, he was determined to wage a solely defensive war for political reasons, but even had he wished to do so, the amabutho were not yet ready to obey his orders to reassemble. It would be the middle of March before they mustered again; by that time the tide of war had swung inexorably against the amaZulu.

News of Isandlwana had profoundly shocked both the British government and popular opinion. While this would lead, in due course, to a searching re-examination of British policies in southern Africa, the immediate response was to re-establish British military supremacy in the field. Large numbers of troops were shipped to Natal; granted a breathing space by Cetshwayo's enforced inactivity, Lord Chelmsford was able to plan the resurrection of British fortunes.

Throughout February and March, a low-intensity war spluttered across the northern and coastal fronts. On the coast, Pearson's column had dug in at the old Norwegian mission-station at Eshowe, much to the king's irritation. Zulu forces living in the area were directed to isolate the fort, to cut its line of communication with the British bases on the Thukela River and to harass patrols and foraging parties, in an attempt to lure the garrison into the open. Learning the lesson of Isandlwana, however, Pearson refused to be drawn from his earthworks and, learning the lesson of Rorke's Drift, the Zulus refused to attack him.[20] Two months of stalemate ensued. Only in the north was there a more fluid war of raids and counter-raids, in which the abaQulusi, assisted by a Swazi prince, Mbilini waMswati, who had given his allegiance to Cetshwayo – and who emerged as the most talented guerrilla leader in the Zulu cause of the entire war – sought to exert pressure on Wood's men.

By late March it was clear to the royal council that the British were again massing, and that the war was about to enter a new phase. The *amabutho* were assembled once more at oNdini, and again ritually prepared for combat. Cetshwayo's strategists urged him to strike at the existing British columns before fresh troops entered the country, and the choice of target was dictated by a heightening of the war on the northern front. On 12 March Prince Mbilini had led an attack that over-ran a company of the 80th Regiment, which had been stranded by bad weather on the flooded Ntombe River. The action had incensed the British, who had promptly raided Zulu settlements across the north in reprisal. The king therefore directed the main army to attack British bases in the north, instructing them to catch their opponents in the open if they could. Referring to the dangers of attacking an entrenched position, he is said to have told the assembled *amabutho* 'not to put their faces into the lair of the wild beasts, or else they would get clawed'.[21] To ensure that his instructions were obeyed, *inkosi* Mnyamana accompanied the army in person, a measure of the importance that the campaign had assumed in the council's eyes.

Despite rumours of its advance, the arrival of the Zulu army in the northern theatre seems to have caught the British largely by surprise. On 28 March Colonel Wood had accompanied a mounted foray against the abaQulusi stronghold at Hlobane Mountain. British troops had carried the summit and had captured large herds of Qulusi cattle but the Qulusi then rallied and began to cut the British lines of retreat. The action was still in progress when part of the main Zulu army crossed the iNyathi ridge and arrived within sight of Hlobane. Three *amabutho* – the uKhandempemvu, iNgobamakhosi and uVe – broke away from the army and hurried to assist the abaQulusi. The British forces were scattered and fled the mountain in something approaching a rout. The exultant victors rejoined the main army, which spent the night bivouacking near Hlobane.

The victory at Hlobane was to have unexpected consequences, however. If the approach of the main army had caught the British foray by surprise, it had at least warned Wood of their presence. His base at Khambula lay only a few miles beyond Hlobane, and before dawn the following morning he made sure it was on a defensive footing. Moreover, when the Zulu army broke up their bivouac at first light on 29 March, the young *amabutho*, elated by their role at Hlobane, were straining for battle. As the amaZulu drew close to Khambula, their commanders halted the advance and formed them into a circle for last-minute ritual preparation and *inkosi* Mnyamana took the opportunity to address the assembled *amabutho*, laying stress on the importance of the coming fight and increasing the general excitement in the ranks.

Despite the king's admonition to avoid defensive works, the amaZulu deployed to attack Khambula, apparently because popular feeling within the army still ran high against the British, and even senior commanders felt it their duty to attack the invaders wherever they found them. The sight, as the *amabutho* deployed in a great arc that stretched 10 miles (16 kilometres) from end to end, was certainly an intimidating one to the British, and the sense of menace was accentuated when Zulu speakers within the British camp heard warriors calling out from the distance, 'We are the boys from Isandlwana!'[22]

In fact, however, although the battle at Khambula was to prove the hardest fought of the war, it was a disaster for the amaZulu. The difficult ground meant that the Zulu right was in position before the rest of the army, a fact that Wood was determined to exploit. A mounted foray stung the over-eager young men of the iNgobamakhosi and uVe into an unsupported attack, which, met by a storm of concentrated British fire, failed to penetrate the British defences. Thereafter the amaZulu were condemned to launch a series of uncoordinated attacks, which allowed the British to meet each one in turn. Although some amaZulu fell dead at the very foot of the British defences, they could not over-run them. After four hours of hard fighting, the warriors were exhausted and the British noted signs that they were preparing to retreat. Wood's response was to attack them with his mounted troops, men who had survived the debacle at Hlobane the day before, and were now burning for revenge. At first the Zulu retreat was orderly, despite the British pressure, but the tired warriors were unable to resist effectively and all order gradually collapsed. The mounted men herded them away from Khambula, slaughtering them without mercy. The pursuit was only called off when darkness fell.

The British dragged 785 bodies away from their defences – noting that many of them were men in the prime of life, and that in the close-range fighting many had suffered ghastly wounds – and buried them in pits nearby. Hundreds more lay concealed in the long grass further off, and many more on the lines of retreat. Altogether British claims that they had killed 2 000 amaZulu were not implausible, and numbers of senior men were killed as they tried to encourage their men. Among the dead was a cousin of the king, Madlangampisi kaThondolozi, while many of the great men of the nation, including Mnyamana Buthelezi, Godide Ntuli and Mangqondo Maqwaza lost sons. In the aftermath of the rout, Mnyamana attempted to keep the army together to return in some order to the king, but for the most part the men were too shocked and tired to obey him.

Khambula was a particular calamity for the Zulu kingdom because the very *amabutho* that had triumphed at Isandlwana had been so undeniably defeated, but there was more bad news to come. At the end of March, at the other end of the country, Lord Chelmsford crossed the lower Thukela River to advance to the relief of Eshowe. Zulu forces concentrated in the coastal district gathered to stop him at kwaGingindlovu on 2 April but Chelmsford, drawing on the experience of Rorke's

Drift, formed his command into a square. As at Khambula, the Zulus were unable to break through the cordon of British fire that met them on all sides. Chelmsford relieved the Eshowe garrison the following day.

At the end of this second wave of fighting, Lord Chelmsford retired to the border to regroup. Any impression that the Zulus had once again succeeded in driving the British out of their country was, however, essentially misleading. In fact, the two defeats, at either end of the country, had seriously undermined the nation's capacity to resist. Lord Chelmsford, on the other hand, now had the time to martial his resources, await further reinforcements, and plan a renewed invasion at his leisure.

The new British invasion began on 1 June. Chelmsford was now advancing in two thrusts, from the lower Thukela River and from the Ncome River, north of Rorke's Drift, and both columns were significantly stronger than his January deployments. In the coastal sector, in particular, the amaZulu were able to offer no effective opposition, a fact that encouraged the British to open negotiations with local *amakhosi* in the hope of persuading them to surrender. It is noteworthy, however, that most refused to do so until the war in the field had been irrevocably decided. By contrast, King Cetshwayo's own attempts at peace negotiations were steadfastly rebuffed by the British. With the tide of war flowing firmly in his favour, Chelmsford had made the humiliation of the king an objective of victory.

Undoubtedly, the heavy casualties suffered by the Zulu people had had a sobering effect on popular support for the war. Nevertheless, if the easy truculence of January had evaporated, a determined feeling of defiance remained. With the British advancing deeply into Zulu territory, many *amakhosi* were more willing to hold men back from the general muster of the *amabutho* to defend their own homesteads. On 5 June the followers of *inkosi* Sihayo skirmished with British troops in an attempt to defend homesteads in the valley of the uPhoko River, while on 25 June members of the Magwaza, Ntuli and Cube chiefdoms mounted a raid across the Thukela into Natal territory, destroying African homesteads and carrying away cattle.

By that time, however, it was clear the war was drawing to a climax. Lord Chelmsford's own command had penetrated as far as the White Mfolozi valley, and Cetshwayo had assembled the *amabutho* for one last attempt to halt the invaders in the traditional heart of Zululand itself. At the last minute, the king attempted to send a herd of white cattle to the British as a peace offering; members of his own uKhandempemvu *ibutho* – in a gesture that indicates the strength of feeling still prevalent within the army – refused to allow it to pass through their lines.

The final battle of the war took place in the shadow of the great royal homesteads, which constituted the Zulu capital on the Ulundi plain on 4 July. The British had learned the tactical lessons of the war well; Lord Chelmsford formed his men into a square, the infantry lined four deep and the sides bristling with artillery. Zulu veterans admitted that, after the discouraging experience of Khambula and kwaGingindlovu, they did not 'fight with the same spirit'.[23] Even so, in some places individual amaZulu managed to reach to within nine paces of the British line before being shot down. For the most part, however, they could not penetrate the devastating curtain of British fire, and after only 45 minutes they began to withdraw. As Wood had done at Khambula, Chelmsford then sent out his cavalry to drive the amaZulu from the field. In triumph, the British cavalry then paraded around the plain, setting fire to each of the great royal homesteads in turn. By evening, Chelmsford had already retired, leaving only smoke, ashes, and a great circle of amaZulu dead in the long grass to mark the passing of Zulu unity and independence.

With the *amabutho* dispersed, the British noted a marked increase in the number of *amakhosi* who were prepared to negotiate for surrender. Nevertheless, although the population as a whole was undeniably exhausted by the war, support for the person of the king continued to the end, and it was not until 28 August that he was captured in the Ngome forest by a British patrol. He was taken to the coast and put on board a steamer, heading for Cape Town and captivity, and his exile marks the true end of the Anglo-Zulu War.

British perceptions of the Zulu people had changed dramatically across the course of the war, and their reactions continue to shape popular attitudes throughout the world to the Zulu today. At the beginning, the British regarded the Zulu army with disdain; they underestimated both the Zulu attachment to their independent political institutions and traditions, and their capacity to resist. Isandlwana changed all that, recasting the amaZulu into terrifying image of blood-stained bogeymen who, in the words of one young officer, haunted an African landscape grown suddenly alien and threatening: 'No one knows where the Zulu armies are; one day they are seen in one place, another at another; one meal lasts them for three days; and the bush they can creep through like snakes . . . they know everything that goes on. They are awfully wily . . .'[24]

This dread had been largely responsible for the climate of hatred and vengeance that had prevailed after Khambula and kwaGingindlovu and had been vented in the ferocious pursuits. Within days of the victory at Ulundi, however, the British lost their fear of the amaZulu, and began to reinvent them in the image of a proud and noble enemy, whose defeat had been a worthy achievement of British arms. British patrols operating in Zululand after Ulundi noted the apparent readiness with which individual amaZulu accepted the reality of defeat, finding solace in a mutual respect for each other's fighting capabilities. 'During this time,' recalled one officer,

> one of Somkele's warriors came up and asked if any of us had been at Isandhlwana, and on telling him that I was out with the Contingent at Isipezi at the time of the fight, he caught hold of both my hands and shook them firmly in a great state of delight, saying it was a splendid fight. 'You fought well, and we fought well,' he exclaimed, then showed me eleven wounds that he had received, bounding off in the greatest ecstasy to show how it had all

happened . . . Could anything more clearly show the splendid spirit in which the Zulus fought us? No animosity, or revengeful feeling, but just the sheer love of a good fight in which the courage of both sides could be tested, and it was evident that the courage of our soldiers was as much appreciated as their own.[25]

In finding a common ground with their enemies as soldiers, British participants in the war were given an opportunity to put aside any lingering feelings of disquiet about the righteousness of the cause and conduct of the invasion. From this has grown the popular impression that six months of unprovoked and brutal conflict was no more than a sporting match, fought out among equals to mutual laurels and without consequence, which continues to colour accounts of the war, and which is regularly offered up to reassure the British tourists who now stream steadily to the battlefields of 1879, or to sugar an uncomfortable pill in the presentation of British museum displays.

Yet whatever mutual sympathy the opposing warriors were able to achieve when the smoke at last cleared, it was not on the basis of equality, but of that of the victorious and the utterly defeated. British political interests triumphed at the expense of the interests of the Zulu people as a whole, and the concept that the war was essentially a noble struggle, where the cost can comfortably be accommodated within notions of gained acceptance and respect, is of course fallacious. Zulu losses in defence of their homeland numbered a minimum of 6 000 men, and may have run as high as 10 000. Thousands more were maimed by British bullets, shell and rocket fire. Hundreds of ordinary civilian homesteads were burned, and the invaders carried thousands of head of cattle away. The great royal homesteads, the material infrastructure of the state administration, were burned, and the king himself exiled. Furthermore, the British deliberately divided the surviving *amakhosi* against themselves in an attempt to neutralise any remaining popular resistance to European penetration, paving the way for a decade of bloody civil war.

For the Zulu people, the cost of their defiance in 1879 was ultimately paid in decades of dispossession, of political repression in their own country, and of the progressive subjugation of their economic needs to those of the victors.

## Notes

1. Only once, since King Shaka kaSenzangakhona had first extended his protection over the fledgling British settlement at Port Natal in 1824, had there been open conflict between British settlers and the Zulu kings. In 1838 the Port Natal settlers had allied themselves with the voortrekkers, who were then engaged in a protracted struggle with King Dingane kaSenzangakhona, and had raided Zulu territory. They were met on Zulu soil by a Zulu army on the banks of the lower Thukela River on 17 April 1838 and defeated. King Dingane then ordered Port Natal to be sacked in reprisal.

2. In September 1873 a deputation from Natal, headed by Natal's Secretary for Native Affairs, Theophilus Shepstone, had attended the ceremonies to install Cetshwayo as king. This was widely interpreted in Zululand as an expression of British support for Cetshwayo, an assumption, indeed, which Shepstone was later to exploit to bolster a British claim to intervene in Zulu affairs.

3. Cornelius Vijn, *Cetshwayo's Dutchman; Being the Private Journal of a White Trader in Zululand During the British Invasion*, trans. and ed. Bishop J.W. Colenso (London: Longmans Green, 1880), p. 15.

4. D.C.F. Moodie, ed. *John Dunn, Cetywayo and the Three Generals* (Pietermaritzburg: Natal Printing & Publishing, 1886), p. 73.

5. Lord Chelmsford, memorandum dated Pietermaritzburg, 30 October 1878, reproduced in *Lord Chelmsford's Zululand Campaign 1879*, ed. John Laband (Stroud: Alan Sutton Publishing 1994).

6. Lord Chelmsford to Colonel Evelyn Wood, Pietermaritzburg 11 December 1878, reproduced in *Lord Chelmsford's Zululand*, ed. Laband, p. 25.

7. Prince Hamu was the biological son of King Mpande kaSenzangakhona (Cetshwayo's father). However, Hamu had been raised on behalf of Mpande's dead brother, Nzibe kaSenzangakhona, and was considered heir to the House of Nzibe. This distinction barred him from any legitimate claim as Mpande's heir. Prince Hamu enjoyed considerable power in his own right, however, and was said to resent Cetshwayo's succession.

8. *Natal Mercury*, 16 January 1879.

9. *Natal Mercury*, 17 January 1879.

10. Henry Hallam Parr, *A Sketch of the Kafir and Zulu Wars* (London: Kegan Paul, 1880), p. 183.

11. George H. Swinney, *A Zulu Boy's Recollections of the Zulu War* (London: George Bell and Sons, 1883). Reprinted with a note by C. de B. Webb in *Natalia* 8, December 1978: 10.

12. King Cetshwayo's letter to Sir Hercules Robinson, Governor of the Cape, dated 29 March 1881, reproduced in *A Zulu King Speaks*, eds. C. de B. Webb and John Wright (Pietermaritzburg: University of Natal Press, 1978), p. 56.

13. The 3rd Regiment, Natal Native Contingent, included a substantial element from the amaChunu of Natal, led by Gabangaye kaPhakade, a son of the Chunu *inkosi*. The amaChunu had broken away from the Zulu kingdom *c*.1840. A number of iziGqoza, supporters of rival candidates for the Zulu throne, were also enrolled in the regiment; they were led by Cetshwayo's brother, Prince Sikhotha kaMpande.

14. For a discussion of Zulu strategic options, see John Laband, *Kingdom in Crisis: The Zulu Response to the British Invasion of 1879* (Manchester: Manchester University Press, 1992), pp. 54–60.

15. For a detailed description of these rituals, see Ian Knight, *The Anatomy of the Zulu Army* (London: Greenhill Books, 1999), pp. 157–67.

16. Mavumengwana was the younger brother of Godide. Their father, Ndlela kaSompisi, had been a senior *induna* under King Dingane kaSenzangakhona in the 1830s.

17. For a detailed account of the Isandlwana campaign see Ian Knight, *Zulu: The Battles of Isandlwana and Rorke's Drift* (London: Windrow and Greene, 1992) and Laband, *Kingdom in Crisis*, pp. 72–95.

18. King Cetshwayo, letter to Sir Hercules Robinson in *A Zulu King Speaks*, eds. Webb and Wright, p. 57.

19. Vijn, *Cetshwayo's Dutchman*, p. 28.

20. For a detailed account of the Eshowe campaign, see Ian Castle and Ian Knight, *Fearful Hard Times: The Siege and Relief of Eshowe* (London: Greenhill Books, 1994).

21. Statement of Mgelija Ngema, Bowden Papers, KwaZulu-Natal Museum, Pietermaritzburg, reproduced in Ian Knight, 'Kill Me In The Shadows', *Soldiers of the Queen* 74, September 1993: p. 12.

22. Quoted in John Laband, *Rope of Sand: The Rise and Fall of the Zulu Kingdom in the Nineteenth Century* (Johannesburg: Jonathan Ball, 1995), p. 270.

23. Evidence of Mehlokazulu kaSihayo, reported in the war supplement to the *Natal Mercury*, 1879.

24. Arthur Mynors, *Letters and Diary of the late Arthur C. B. Mynors* (Margate: privately published, 1879), p. 25.

25. Daphne Child, ed., *The Zulu War Journal of Col. Henry Harford, C.B.* (Pietermaritzburg: Shuter & Shooter, 1978), pp. 72–73.

# The Roots of Gathering Struggles
Late Nineteenth Century to Middle Twentieth Century

*Chapter 16*

# Imperial Appropriations
## Baden-Powell, the Wood Badge and the Zulu *Iziqu*[1]

JEFF GUY

THIS CHAPTER DEALS with the history of *iziqu*: carved, strung, interlocking wooden beads, which a standard Zulu-English dictionary says are badges 'of bravery (consisting of shaped wood or horn) worn round the neck by those who have killed an enemy in battle'.[2] Of course, dictionary definitions have a role to play, but this definition is a limited one and in the following pages I consider the dynamic range of interpretations attached to these wooden beads, together with the extraordinary variety of meanings invested in them in different historical contexts and across cultural boundaries. I do this by examining the progress of *iziqu* through the history of KwaZulu-Natal and the British Empire to a point where they can still be found lodged in the corners of neo-imperial thinking and practice. The story is far from complete, but there is sufficient information to suggest its main lines and nodal points and to do something to expose the mystifying process whereby the meanings of cultural artefacts are simultaneously fixed and radically changed in the course of history.

There are references to *iziqu* in the earliest historical documents on the Zulu kingdom. In Henry Francis Fynn's reconstruction of the Zulu army under Shaka kaSenzangakhona he writes that 'round the neck' of Zulu soldiers 'is hung a necklace of pieces of wood which are worn as medals of bravery. One is added for every one they kill in battle till there is no room left'.[3]

In the 1850s Charles MacLean (who was himself resurrected and recreated as the boy hero John Ross by a settler society in need of founding mythologies) wrote that in the 1820s in the Zulu kingdom he had seen soldiers at Bulawayo 'ornamenting and decorating their persons with beads and brass ornaments':

> The most curious part of these decorations consisted of several rows of small pieces of wood, about the size and shape of those used in playing drafts, strung together and made into necklaces and bracelets. Some of these warriors had their necks and arms ornamented with several rows of this description, and

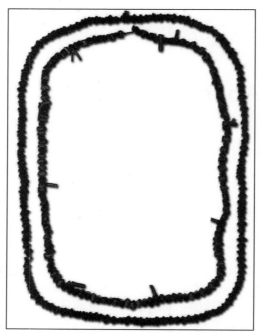

*Strings of* iziqu *housed in the Natal Museum.*

those particularly about the neck seemed to be very inconvenient to the wearer, and certainly were not very ornamental. But on inquiry we found that the Zulu warriors set great value on these apparently useless trifles, and that they were orders of merit conferred by Shaka on those who had distinguished themselves by daring deeds of bravery on the field of battle. Each row, whether round the neck or arm, was the distinguishing mark of some heroic deed, and which the wearer had received from Shaka's own hand. These were principally gained in the last amaMpondo war, from which Shaka had returned with a large booty. These of course were all the first class of warriors, high in favour with the Zulu monarch, and were now displaying their finery and decorations preparatory to presenting themselves before him.[4]

Strings of threaded items worn around different parts of the upper body are a feature of Zulu material culture and are made up, individually or in combination, of items such as seeds, pieces of wood such as *iziqu*, bone, beads, animal horns, teeth or claws. John Wright describes them as 'one part of a whole complex of "charms", medicines and practices that were used by men who had killed in battle to ward of misfortune. In this context, they seem to have been made and worn on the individual's own initiative.'[5]

*Maphelu kaMkhosana Zungu by Barbara Tyrell.*

*Laduma Madela, 1970, Ceza.*

My 1970 photograph of the sage and diviner, Laduma Madela, shows him wearing three such necklaces, one of berries, one of bones with a horn pendant, and the other consisting of snakes' vertebrae. Although none contain *iziqu*, the close interlocking of the various portions are reminiscent of them. Barbara Tyrrell's painting in the Killie Campbell Collection in Durban of Maphelu kaMkhosana of the Zungu, who led a life of great risk and adventure as a devoted soldier and servant of Dinuzulu kaCetshwayo, depicts him wearing *iziqu* interspersed with twigs. The *iziqu* are made of wood from the willow or *umnyezane*, which Axel-Ivar Berglund informs me is a tree associated with the shades and consequently treated with reverence and respect.

After the conquest of the Zulu kingdom, at the time of the tragic attempt by the royalist uSuthu to promote the son of the last independent Zulu king, Dinuzulu, as heir to the kingdom, he was photographed wearing a necklace of *iziqu* and twigs. In November 1888, when Dinuzulu made a highly dangerous visit to Pietermaritzburg, the colonial capital, photographs show that he was protected by long strings of *iziqu* around his neck and across his chest. He was then sent to Eshowe, the administrative capital of British Zululand, where he was gaoled before standing trial for public violence, high treason, and murder. Here he was visited by a Zulu chief who reported

*The son of the last independent Zulu king, Dinuzulu
kaCetshwayo, wearing* iziqu *while gaoled in Eshowe,
1889.*

to his superiors that 'Dinuzulu had round his neck several necklaces (Igiqu [*sic*]) such as are worn by natives, after they have killed an enemy or enemies in battle'.[6]

Another person who visited Dinuzulu during his detention was Harriette Colenso, daughter of the late bishop of Natal. It is therefore perhaps significant that while the early editions of Colenso's *Zulu-English Dictionary* refer to *iziqu* which are 'worn as charms upon the neck of a man',[7] editions subsequent to this visit, and revised by Harriette, bear the addition 'after he has killed or *hlomula*-ed a man in battle'.[8] Harriette Colenso may well have obtained this information directly from the Zulu royalists at Eshowe.

But the applications and the meanings of *iziqu* can be extended further, and, in their multiplicity of meanings, Axel-Ivar Berglund believes we have 'an important Zulu idiom to which not sufficient attention has been given by cultural anthropologists'.[9] Thus A.T. Bryant in his dictionary described the pieces of wood as 'prophylactic medicines' keeping harm at bay until the effective medicine arrives,[10] and by extension, as Berglund suggests, as charms to protect a man who has killed in battle, especially in the period of his greatest vulnerability before the purification ceremonies have been carried out. Literally *isiqu* is a root, the taproot, and by extension it refers to the origin of a matter, an issue or an event. Thus the fourth edition of Colenso's *Dictionary* refers to *iziqu* being used to refer to 'the main arguments, or the foundation facts'.[11] This meaning is in use to this day. Thus Berglund writes of 'traditional court cases' when

> a judge may call for *isiqu sendaba*, i.e. the origin of accusation or rumour. He thereby shifts the emphasis of the case from the dialogue between the accused and accuser, calling on witnesses to speak . . . [on] the origin/source of the issue at stake . . . *[I]siqu* carried considerable weight [with the judge when] passing judgement . . . as the source, origin and hence beginnings of the case discussed . . .

During the twentieth century more meanings were imposed as the word was mined at yet deeper levels. The grammatical root of *iziqu* is '*qu*', and the word came to be used in isiZulu to refer to the very concept of a grammatical root: a root of roots, as it were. Today the word is most widely translated and most frequently used to refer to a university degree or a diploma. Exactly when and how this extension happened I still have to discover, but the Doke and Vilikazi Zulu-English dictionary does not have this meaning, while the English-Zulu dictionary published in 1958 does.[12] Whether further research will reveal a conscious decision to find a suitable isiZulu word (as I suspect, by the self-appointed modernisers of the language) or whether it was an unconscious cultural adaptation, either discovery will be fascinating. It will indicate something of the way in which the meaning of the word *iziqu* has been transferred from an award given by the Zulu kings recognising victory in the field of war (as the epitome of courageous and committed service), to one given by the chancellor of a university, recognising victory in the field of learning (as the epitome of an often lonely and dogged pursuit of 'foundation facts').

### The imperial context

These are all examples of the changing meanings of *iziqu* in South Africa itself. But of course South Africa was made in its interaction with the imperial world and *iziqu* have made an extraordinary progress through imperial history as well. To demonstrate this I need to provide some of the background to the Zulu resistance to British annexation in 1888, and in particular to the immediately minor, but ultimately significant, role played by one Robert Baden-Powell.

After the failure to conquer the Zulu kingdom in 1879 by direct military means, the British divided the territory amongst a number of local leaders, thereby excluding the Zulu royal house from authority. Rallying around the exiled king's brothers and his son, Dinuzulu, the royalists (or uSuthu as they were called) attempted to regain something of their political autonomy. But they were actively opposed by some of the newly appointed chiefs who were backed by the authorities in the neighbouring colony of Natal. Civil war broke out and by 1883 the old political order had been effectively destroyed. Taking advantage of this, Zululand's colonial neighbours moved in to seize land and resources. The northwestern districts were incorporated into the Transvaal and in 1887 the territory between the Transvaal and the coast was annexed as British Zululand. Attempts by the colonial representatives of the new imperial authority to eradicate the last vestiges of royal power only provoked further resistance and British troops were authorised to support the civil authority in putting down what was characterised as a rebellion. At the end of June 1888 the Commander of British forces in South Africa, Lieutenant-General Henry Smyth, took direct control of military operations in Zululand.[13]

On his arrival Smyth came into conflict with the governor of Zululand, Sir Arthur Havelock, who was determined that overall direction of military operations should remain with the civil powers. As far as Havelock was concerned, the violence in Zululand was the work of a handful of unrepresentative royalists whose pretensions had to be checked by the civil authorities protected by the military. Military action outside of civil control might well provoke general Zulu resistance and Havelock was determined to do what he could to mount a policing operation in Zululand, rather than a military one. He was only too aware that the prospect of promoting a local conflict into one of Queen Victoria's little wars was far too attractive to younger military officers for whom bloodletting was a necessary prerequisite for military reputation and advancement. And one such officer was Smyth's aide-de-camp and nephew, 'Stephe', the 30-year-old Captain Robert Stephen Baden-Powell.[14]

Smyth and his staff arrived at Eshowe on 20 June 1888. Earlier in the month the Zululand Police had had to be rescued by the military from the consequences of their bungled attempt to arrest Dinuzulu in the defensive position he had constructed near the summit of Ceza Mountain. On 23 June Dinuzulu's uSuthu force left Ceza to attack its greatest enemy, Zibhebhu's Mandlakazi, which it defeated under the guns of the Zululand police in the fort at Nongoma.

In the aftermath the military and police authorities fell back on defended positions, while they attempted to raise 'loyal' forces from among the amaZulu to be used to bring the uSuthu under control. In the tense and occasionally violent situation that followed communication was broken between the chief magistrate at Eshowe and the resident magistrate in the Lower Mfolozi district. A flying column of 200 British regulars, supported by 2 000 men supplied by John Dunn and 200 mounted levies supplied by the baSotho chief Hlubi, was put together to relieve the Lower Mfolozi magistracy. It was under the command of Major A.C. McKean and Captain Baden-Powell accompanied him as staff officer. The column left Eshowe on 7 July 1888, reached the magistracy two days later and returned on 13 July, leaving a trail of burnt and looted homesteads.[15] It also left an angry governor, who earned the contempt of the military for his opinion that 'burning kraals' was not 'a judicious means of inflicting punishment for offences committed by British subjects living within British territory'.[16] The Colonial Office was to agree with the governor's attempts to keep the military under some control, but for different reasons: 'We have to look on these Usutus as potential tax payers, and it was of importance from that point of view, if from no other, to shoot as few of them as possible.'[17]

But Havelock's hold on the military was tenuous and there was still shooting to be done. General Smyth arrived at Nkonjeni on 1 August, sent a flying column to Ivuna on 4 August, and on 9 August established a military post under Lieutenant-Colonel Thompson in the upper reaches of the Black Mfolozi River. Baden-Powell was placed in command of the mounted infantry, dragoons, and a troop of African levies and ordered to prepare the ground for an attack on Dinuzulu's defended position at Ceza. But it was already too late: the British force was never able to have its military confrontation with the Zulu rebels that its officers so desired. On the evening of 7 August the members of the last active Zulu military mobilisation under the command of members of the royal house burnt their shelters at Ceza and moved northwards out of British Zululand before dispersing to their homes.

Deprived of a conclusive military action Baden-Powell's detachment began mopping up the enemy in the upper valley of the Black Mfolozi in preparation for a reconnaissance of the now-deserted uSuthu stronghold. On 10 August, it was reported that during the night some of Baden-Powell's African sentries had been threatened by uSuthu. They were said to be operating from a number of caves near Fig Tree Store on the border of the Transvaal. On the morning of 11 August the levies, supported by the British regulars, all under Baden-Powell's command, left at daybreak to clear the caves. Inhabitants in nearby homesteads fled, driving their cattle before them as the force approached. The African levies began to move towards the caves in horn formation, supported by volleys fired by the mounted infantry. After some skirmishing and an exchange of shots, the people in the caves were forced out, leaving behind at least three bodies, including that of a mentally deficient woman. More than 100 head of cattle were looted and 30 women and children captured, before the military discovered that they had terrorised and attacked their own allies, loyal Buthelezi, and that the caves in which they had taken refuge lay outside British Zululand and well within the Transvaal.[18] Baden-Powell pushed on that night to Ceza, which he was able to show his uncle, General Smyth, when he arrived on 16 August.

### Creating a heroic war in Zululand

The National Library of South Africa, Cape Town campus, contains drafts of Baden-Powell's reports on the Fig Tree raid in which he blamed the fiasco on the inaccurate 'Government map' and misleading information given by his guide and the African levies under his command.[19] With their many emendations, they are only the first of a series of attempts to obscure the multiple failures associated with the Fig Tree raid and in the process to recreate Baden-Powell's experiences in Zululand. For in time, of course, Baden-Powell was to become one of the most famous figures in the history of the British Empire.

After experience in two 'little wars' against the Asante and the Ndebele in the 1890s, he gained a world reputation as the defender of Mafeking in the South African War. Attracted towards the youth movements of the time, deeply concerned about the threats to the hegemony of the British Empire and the capacity of the nation's youth to confront them, fascinated by the subterfuge, guile and physical prowess required by military scouting and intelligence, between 1905 and 1907 he wrote *Scouting for Boys*. Suitably advanced by entrepreneurial interests in the publishing industry, it became, in the words of his most recent biographer, 'not only one of the world's greatest best sellers but the Boy Scouts' Bible: on one level a "how to do it" manual, but on another an almost theological statement of purposes and principles'.[20]

The Boy Scouts became a vast national, and later an international, movement in which millions of young people were to participate, and in which outdoor activities were organised so as to promote physical well-being, an individual moral code and sense of social responsibility. And, although Baden-Powell was only in Zululand for three months in 1888, his experiences there were to form a resource that inspired him for many years to come and which he was to incorporate into the mythologies and rituals of the Boy Scout movement.

For the first time in his military career, Baden-Powell had been responsible for deploying men and columns and had occasion to work with native levies and native spies. He had become thoroughly familiar with the skills involved in primitive warfare by actual practice in the bush and on the veld. He had learned the Zulu ways of living and of fighting. Throughout it all he had kept an exhaustive diary,[21] jotting down experiences and tips for future reference. He had added materially to his store of information for the booklet on 'scouting' he might some day write.[22]

It was this experience that he was to pass on to the youth of Britain, and then the world, warning them of the physical and moral challenges that they faced in a softer, degenerate, urbanised – and therefore equally dangerous environment – and giving advice on how to counter them. In an affidavit on the writing of *Scouting for Boys* he wrote that he had studied 'the principles adopted by the Zulus and other African tribes, which reflected the ideas of Epictetus, and the methods of the Spartans, ancient British and Irish for training their boys'.[23]

Baden-Powell presented the Zululand campaign as a glorious adventure. He was at the Cape, having to perform the social duties of a Military Secretary, which 'was great fun, a regular beano, when . . . bang came a bombshell': 'An alarming telegram came through from Zululand to say that the Usutus were up. They had defied the police; some troops from Natal had been sent to back up the civil force and had been driven back with loss. Generally the fat was in the fire.'[24]

*Baden-Powell: 'John Dunn and his* impis'.

Of course, for most of those caught up in the conflict in Zululand in 1888 it was a tragic affair, the crushing of the last desperate bid for autonomy by the surviving rulers of an African kingdom that the authorities had attempted to destroy by setting one faction against the other. The major clashes took place not between the military and the uSuthu but among the amaZulu themselves. There was no enemy uprising in the Lower Mfolozi district. Although officials tried to assert that the magistracy had been attacked, this was not so: the violence in the area was a symptom of the official manipulation of divisions among the amaZulu there. The African columns with the British troops were largely out of control and most of them were men provided by John Dunn, whose role in the calamities that had overtaken the amaZulu had been decidedly ignoble. Even now Dunn resisted giving military support until he was assured of a sufficient reward and the line of march was marked by burning kraals, looted cattle, and abducted women and children.

Baden-Powell saw none of this. As far as he was concerned he had been privileged to observe the noble Zulu warrior in all his glory. Forty years later, he could still remember the arrival of Dunn's force and depicted it as one of the most stirring of his memories:

When we topped the rise, we saw moving up towards us from the valley below three long lines of men marching in single file and singing a wonderful anthem as they marched. Both the sight and sound were intensely impressive. Every now and then one man would sing a few notes of a solo which were then responded to by an immense roar of sound from the whole impi of deep bass voices and higher tones singing in harmony. Then in the midst of their song there would be a sudden break and a shrill whistle would go up or a crash as they struck simultaneously their great hide shields with their assegais. The timekeeping and rhythm of these warriors in their singing was marvellous, accompanied as it was with stamping of the feet and booming and rattling at given periods . . . a glorious sound. The men themselves looked so splendid . . . very smartly decked out with feathers and furs and cows' tails. They wore little in the way of clothing and their brown bodies were polished with oil and looked like bronze statues.[25]

He sketched the scene, made notes on the singing and took down Dunn's translation.[26] In 1907, at the camp which Baden-Powell set up on Brownsea Island off the Dorset coast, where some of the activities which were to become intrinsic to Boy Scouts ritual were first practised, a journalist was to write how Baden-Powell

> . . . told true-life 'yarns' about being hunted by Zulus in the Matopo Hills . . . With experiences culled from all over the world and three small wars, not to mention a big one, [Baden-Powell] was in an unrivalled position to entertain his youthful audience. [A journalist] watched Baden-Powell at the camp fire leading the boys singing a Zulu war chant. This was the Eeengonyama chorus soon to be famous among all Boy Scouts. 'Eeengonyama – gonyama', sang Baden-Powell loudly, to be answered by the boys singing heartily: 'Invooboo. Yah bo! Invooboo.' This was supposed to mean, 'He is a lion!' Yes! He is better than that; he is a hippopotamus!' Everett was mesmerized. 'I can see him still,' he wrote twenty years later, 'as he stands in the flickering light of the fire – an alert figure, full of the joy of life, now grave, now gay, answering all manner of questions, imitating the call of birds, showing how to stalk an animal, fleshing out a little story, dancing and singing round the fire.[27]

Baden-Powell also remembered the magistrate's 'fine shooting', which killed two men under a euphorbia tree at a paced distance of 900 yards (822 metres). There was also the young Zulu woman with a bullet through the stomach: 'She was very plucky and knelt up when we told her to so that we could plug the holes and bind her up. Her only clothing was a bead girdle and a necklace of black and white beads.' But she died in the night. 'Before burying her I took the liberty of annexing her necklace as a memento, and it stood me in good stead later on.'[28]

Nothing that Baden-Powell wrote about his early military experiences in Zululand can be relied upon, but it would seem that he acquired his first *iziqu* from the corpse

*Baden-Powell: 'Surrendering one of Dinizulu's strongholds'.*

of a girl killed by a British raiding party. The Fig Tree raid and the reconnaissance of the deserted uSuthu camp on Ceza underwent transformation as well. Originally Baden-Powell held bad maps and faulty intelligence responsible for his attack on allies sheltering in foreign territory. But this was the report of an obscure officer seeking reputation and promotion and somewhat concerned about the effects of a scouting blunder on his career prospects. Forty years later Lord Baden-Powell of Gilwell wrote that uSuthu were trying to reach the safety of the Transvaal and 'we disregarded the border and followed them up, attacked, and got them'.[29]

The reconnaissance to the deserted uSuthu camp at Ceza was similarly recast. On the way Baden-Powell just escaped an attack by 'a splendid figure of a Zulu warrior, in all the glory of glistening brown skin and the white plumed head-dress from which the Usutu had their nickname of "Tyokobais"',[30] before being able to reach a crevice in the rocks 'packed with the brown faces, with rolling eyes and white teeth, of hundreds of women and children, refugees hiding from us' whom he was then able to reassure and lead to safety. And whereas the uSuthu had left Ceza a week previously, leaving Baden-Powell plenty of time to sketch the stronghold from different perspectives, pull down defensive walls and clear the paths, this was to be represented as the 'final dash' on Ceza, from which Dinuzulu 'decamped' before coming 'a few days later' to surrender, or 'I had been sent forward on a scouting expedition into his stronghold. He nipped out as we got in'.

Again it seems likely that he not only got into the Ceza stronghold, but also got out what loot he could – including *iziqu*. Baden-Powell never saw Dinuzulu. The Zulu prince only surrendered three months later – not to the military, but to the governor of Natal in Pietermaritzburg. And he did so after taking refuge in the house of the daughters of Bishop Colenso, his supporters, which he reached moving surreptitiously across country with an expertise that might have caught the attention of a man for whom subterfuge and scouting skills were so important.

But it is not only the conflicting and inaccurate accounts that Baden-Powell wrote of his Zululand experiences over the years – after all, in the 1920s the Chief Scout of the Empire could hardly admit to being misled by his spies and basic errors in map-reading. More interesting is the deep ambivalence in the way that he depicts his early African experiences. They can be as vile as anything that the history of British imperialism has to offer, as he flaunts his racism and cruelty. Throughout the Zululand campaign, it was his desire for violent confrontation that blocked any capacity he had to understand the obvious – that the people around him were not 'the enemy' – and which led him to attack his own non-combatant allies as they sought safety, and then shrug off the political, military and moral consequences of his actions. But at the same time there was in Baden-Powell the deep desire to romanticise this imperial violence, to sentimentalise both attacker and attacked, to idealise its objectives, and indeed to invest it with a moral quality.

When Baden-Powell was in Zululand the idea of the noble Zulu warrior was only just beginning to replace that of the barbarian who had slaughtered the British at Isandlwana. But by the time he wrote *Scouting for Boys*, the romanticisation of the Zulu was widespread, under the influence of the works of Rider Haggard especially. And by now there were independent sources promoting a romantic recreation of the primitive acting upon Baden-Powell as well. Ernest Thompson Seton was a naturalist living in North America who had just founded the Woodcraft movement and whose idealised recreation of Native American life was to give shape to a revolt against the experience of modernising industrial society. In 1905, as he was writing *Scouting for Boys*, Baden-Powell received from Seton a copy of his *The Birch-bark Roll of the Woodcraft Indians* with its call for a return to a more simple life, the enjoyment of outdoor adventure, close observation of nature and the materials it provided, and drawing on the wisdom and the lore of the tribe. The book gave substance to many of Baden-Powell's ideas and he adopted and adapted many of Seton's: the games, for example; the tribe and the totem, which provided the organisational principles, and the system of awards for achievement based on the natural world and its wild creatures amongst whom the young adventurers lived and played.[31] In the end Seton was to accuse Baden-Powell of appropriating his ideas. But as Jeal has written:

Baden-Powell learned from Seton and the Woodcraft Indians that romantic schemes conceived in a spirit of open opposition to industrial society had no future. Neither the industrialists of Progressive Era America nor Britain's beleaguered ruling class could be expected to see any merit in anything openly subversive. His Boy Scouts scheme would therefore have to promise to make boys not 'noble savages' but the patriotic and morally upright youngsters whom their 'betters' believed the country needed.[32]

Nonetheless, the call of the wild and the primitive remained a feature of the appeal of the Boy Scout movement's rituals and mythologies, and it drew for its inspiration on both Ernest Thompson Seton's recreation of Native American and Baden-Powell's imagined African experience.

### *Iziqu* in resistance

The *iziqu* that Baden-Powell looted from the amaZulu in 1888 were to play an important part in the promotion of the Boy Scout movement and thus the history of imperial iconography. But before giving an account of this, I want to relate briefly a counter-narrative – *iziqu*'s role in an attempt to frustrate the course of imperial power in Zululand. In the same year that Baden-Powell took possession of his *iziqu*, another white person gained hers – not by violence, however, but as a gift, in recognition of the bravery she had shown in the cause of Zulu independence. This was Harriette Colenso, who had been in contact with the uSuthu during the 1888 disturbances and was convinced that, far from being rebellious, the uSuthu leaders had been forced to defend their people against the violence initiated by the authorities and carried out by their Zulu appointees. Only when absolutely necessary, she believed, had Dinuzulu and his supporters acted violently against those acting against them.

It was Harriette Colenso who organised, and largely paid for, the defence of Dinuzulu and his uncles before the Court of Special Commissioners in Eshowe in 1888–89. She visited them in gaol, looked after their needs and interests as best she could, and made sure that Dinuzulu received an education in the long months he waited for confirmation of sentence. In so doing she was discharging a responsibility laid upon her by her father John William Colenso, the bishop of Natal, and his friend, Dinuzulu's father Cetshwayo kaMpande. In January 1890 Dinuzulu and his uncles were sent into exile on the island of St Helena. By then Harriette Colenso was already on her way to England, determined to bring his case before the British politicians and public. She planned to persuade the government to return the Zulu princes to Zululand where Dinuzulu, as heir to the Zulu throne, should be allowed the opportunity to lead his people in rebuilding the nation that Britain had treated so cruelly for the past decade.

She travelled to England on the same vessel as Baden-Powell and his uncle General Smyth, newly decorated for his role in ' "suppressing the Zulu rebellion" – and here he will find it on board the same steamer, as irrepressible as ever! Poor man,' she wrote.[33] The Colenso and Baden-Powell families knew one another. In the mid-century controversies on the nature of science and religion Professor Baden-Powell and Bishop Colenso had been allies. But on this voyage their children, now opponents on the Zulu question, did not speak to one another. And yet they had something in common. Baden-Powell had amongst his trophies the *iziqu* he was to claim belonged to Dinuzulu. Harriette Colenso carried *iziqu* with her as well – not as the trophy of the conqueror but as insignia identifying the emissary of the uSuthu, charged with bringing their case to the people of England so that justice might be done.

While in Britain she had to report back to her allies in Zululand and their leaders on St Helena. The effectiveness of her letters to them was necessarily limited not only by the effects of official surveillance but more significantly by the fact that most of the men and women she wanted to reach could not read. But the Colensos had always set great store in the photograph as a means of communication and Harriette Colenso paid particular attention to having photographs taken while she was in England campaigning for the uSuthu in the 1890s. When these photographs arrived in Natal, Zululand and St Helena the fact that she held the *tshokobezi*, the white cow's tail worn by the uSuthu, confirmed her continued commitment to their cause, while the *iziqu* indicated that the 'main arguments', 'foundation facts', *iziqu sendaba*, were before the parliament and the people of Great Britain.

*Harriette Colenso holding the* tshokobezi, *the white cow's tail worn by the uSuthu.*

The uSuthu cause failed. There was never enough support in this era of 'new imperialism' for 'new women' fighting for African autonomy. British Zululand was incorporated into Natal in 1897 and Dinuzulu was returned but stripped of authority. He and Harriette Colenso were soon to be caught up in that horror of colonial violence which history knows as the Bhambatha Rebellion. With the defeat of the uSuthu, its symbols declined, to be preserved in museum cabinets as records of extinct practices and dead beliefs. As for the other side, Baden-Powell went on to more African victories and, as one of the British Empire's great figures, he was able to revive and incorporate his memories of conquest and trophies of war into the rituals and iconography of the Boy Scout movement.

**The Wood Badge – 'the hope of the world'**
Over the years Baden-Powell was to write and rewrite his autobiography, drawing on his campaigns and adventures, changing and re-representing them as attitudes and demands of the times and movement changed. The effect of Baden-Powell's continual recreation and distortion of his past in his writings makes it extraordinarily difficult to construct even the simplest narrative of events. We do know that during his service in Zululand Baden-Powell acquired not only experiences that were to lead to the Boy Scout movement, but also the inspirations for the songs, chants and awards that were to become part of its ritual and iconography. And of these none are more significant than what became the Wood Badge, a small, wedge-shaped wooden bead, burnt on both ends, threaded on a leather lace.

The Wood Badge, given to Scoutmasters on completion of the Wood Badge Course, was the most prestigious symbol of scouting achievement and awarded only after a rigorous series of theoretical and practical training had been completed. Although it appears to have been phased out by the Scout movement in the United Kingdom over the last 30 years, it remains a feature of other scouting organisations. A visit to Wood Badge sites on the Internet shows that Wood Badge training is still a feature of scouting life in the United States and provides a number of versions of its history. As originally conceived, the Wood Badge was associated with Gilwell Park, the 54-acre estate that was acquired for the Boy Scouts in 1919. It was here that Baden-Powell first presented the Wood Badge to Scoutmasters and told them of its history:

> On the morning of September 8, 1919, a 61-year-old retired general of the British Army stepped out into the center of a clearing at Gilwell Park, in Epping Forest, outside London, England. He raised to his lips the horn of a Greater Kudu, one of the largest of African antelopes. He blew a long sharp blast. Nineteen men dressed in short pants and knee socks, their shirt-sleeves rolled up, assembled by patrols for the first Scoutmasters' training camp held at

Gilwell. The camp was designed and guided by Sir Robert Baden-Powell, the founder of the World Scouting Movement.

When they had finished their training together, Baden-Powell gave each man a simple wooden bead from a necklace he had found in a Zulu chieftain's deserted hut when on campaign in South Africa in 1888. The Scoutmasters' training course was a great success and continued to be held year-after-year. At the end of each course the wooden beads were used to recognize the completion of training. When the original beads ran out, new ones were whittled to maintain the tradition established by Baden-Powell. Because of these beads, the course came to be known as the Wood Badge Course. It continues to this day in England and around the world as the advanced training course for leaders in Scouting.[34]

Here is another version from what might be called the official biography:

B-P. did not care for certificates. He rummaged among his trophies and souvenirs for a suggestion and pulled out a long string of wooden beads he had found in Dinizulu's deserted hut in the Ceza bush during the Zulu War in 1888. He presented each man who had taken part in the camp with one of the beads.

These simple wooden beads signifying the completion of the training course became one of the most highly prized possessions a Scoutmaster could want. The beads gave the training its name of the Wood Badge Course. When Dinizulu's original beads ran out, the Gilwell training staff whittled others to keep up the tradition established by B-P.[35]

This latter account, published in 1964, has Baden-Powell finding the beads in the abandoned stronghold.[36] Jeal, however, has examined the original diaries and can find no account of this. The only references to beads are those worn by the injured girl whose necklace Baden-Powell annexed before burying her, and indeed some historians of the Boy Scout movement have taken these beads to be the original of the Wood Badge, no doubt under the influence of Baden-Powell's own statement that the necklace 'stood me in good stead later on'. But there are many other versions of the origin of the beads. There is a tradition that the beads were captured from Dinuzulu despite the fact that he had left Ceza over a week before Baden-Powell arrived there. In some cases the account becomes more confused: for example, the story that they were 'hand-carved beads he had taken from Zulu Chief Dinuzulu during the Ashanti campaign in 1888'.[37] The beads themselves gained their own character: they were part of a vast necklace some 12 feet (3.5 metres) in length and consisting of more than 1 000 South African yellowwood beads, which the giant 6.5-feet-tall (2 metre) famous Dinuzulu had worn.[38] Or they were given added significance as a sacred talisman, the guardian of the strength of nation:

*The Wood Badge.*

On state occasions, Dinizulu wore a necklace some 10 to 12 feet in length consisting of over a thousand beads, ranging in size from tiny emblems to others four inches in length. It was considered sacred by the warriors, and there was a belief that if it was ever captured all resistance by the natives would cease. The necklace was kept in a cave, high on a mountain and guarded night and day.

B-P. heard of this, and hoped that he would capture Dinizulu and acquire the necklace. It did come to pass, and his wish was fulfilled and B-P. took the necklace home to England where it was kept with his other military souvenirs. It was over 30 years before he made further use of it.[39]

None of these stories, however, sat particularly well with the Scouts movement as it was envisaged after Baden-Powell's death in 1941 and in the post-war era of decolonisation: 'To have stolen a Zulu ruler's property was thought underhand and unpleasant, as was the idea of the founder of worldwide multiracial brotherhood fighting against Africans. So it became policy within the Movement to claim that Baden-Powell had been given the necklace by Dinuzulu.'[40]

But annexed, purloined, captured, found or presented, the importance of the Wood Badge to the movement was indisputable and the symbolic weight attached to these beads was huge and continues in parts of the world to this day. We only have to consider the following:

Two tiny wooden beads on a leather thong. Doesn't sound like an outstanding badge or mark of distinction, but it is known and respected as such around the globe. It is symbolic of the efforts and interest of one man on behalf of others that created and launched the greatest movement for boys the world has ever known . . .

> It is the mark of men who have demonstrated that they are men of character and who are devoted to a cause . . . Striving for perfection in themselves that they might train others better. To this end exists Wood Badge . . .
>
> Who knows but that this effort, this crusade, may flourish to the end that two tiny wooden beads on a leather thong may yet become the symbol of a succeeding effort to bring about a World Brotherhood of Man under a Fatherhood of God. To that end may Wood Badge serve and her men never falter or fail. Two tiny wooden beads on a leather thong. They could symbolize the hope of the world. It's up to you.[41]

The religious overtones in this quotation are obvious and when reading of the beads' significance to the Boy Scout movement and its history, one is frequently reminded of other religious founding narratives, which suggests the mystical role that the Wood Craft Badge filled in the movement. But we can take the significance of the beads to another level as well. Consider the elements of the story. The founder of the movement, now realising that his active days are numbered, emerges from his place of retreat, holding an object made of commonplace material but which he has transformed and filled with spiritual significance. He breaks it up, takes the pieces, and gives them to his followers, as recognition of their achievements, and with the charge that they take what they have learnt and pass it on to others. The parallels with the Christian narrative and its associated rituals – the breaking of the bread, and the injunction that the disciples do likewise and spread the message through the world – seem to me to be significant. But what is unique and interesting about the Wood Badge myth – for it is not history – is the beads' primitive provenance and the spiritual power that they derive through association with a conquered savage people. In 1919, 40 years after the formal conquest of the Zulu kingdom, 30 years after he had been in Zululand and participated in its final subjugation, Baden-Powell stood before his successors, broke up his war trophy, and distributed its constituent parts with the charge that his successor do likewise. In so doing he created an 'Imperial Myth' as part of an 'Imperial Religion'. Decolonisation, contemporary anti-racial convention and liberal internationalism have buried it very deep in the Western unconscious. Nonetheless, the story of the Wood Badge is a ritual enactment of the appropriation and incorporation by the imperial conqueror of African power. By the same token it is a demonstration of the Africanisation of the imperial conqueror.

### Post-colonial *iziqu*

In South Africa, even while the idea of *iziqu* came to be applied to the highest achievements in formal education, its original meaning as 'exceptional courage in the field of battle'[42] has been retained and can be found occurring sporadically in the literature. In 1963 Mangosuthu Buthelezi was reported as having sent *iziqu* to a

Scout leader in Canada. Four 'replicas of Dinizulu's Necklace' were made by 'European Rover Crews in Natal and Zulu Scouts' and taken to the twelfth World Jamboree in Idaho in 1967. And in 1987, 'Chief Minister Mangosuthu Buthelezi of KwaZulu was the guest of honour at a huge Scout rally [where] the Chief Scout of South Africa, Garnet de la Hunt, took from around his neck a thong on which four Wood Badge beads were hung, and handed it to Chief Buthelezi, in a symbolic act of returning the beads to their rightful heir'.[43]

In 1996 an exhibition of 'the material culture of the Zulu People' included two *iziqu* under the title 'Valour-Award Necklace', with the incorrect information that they were 'last awarded in the Anglo-Zulu War of 1879' and this is now being repeated in tourist-oriented coffee-table books on Zulu culture.[44]

There are signs that *iziqu* are in the process of undergoing a major revival and substantial transformation. It would seem as if an important factor is the newly unveiled Isandlwana monument. It has been created by the sculptor Gert Swart and is in the form of a huge necklace cast in bronze that includes *iziqu*. Already this monument is reworking traditions, moving them away from the recognition of valour against the enemy in times of military conquest towards a yearning for tolerance and reconciliation in a rainbow nation. Staff at KwaZulu-Natal museums are being asked increasingly about *iziqu* and the monument. And in a letter in the press on the Isandlwana monument, the process by which traditions are recreated is almost tangible:

> My initial reaction to the *iziqu* was bewilderment. While I recognised the famous chest and horns formation in which it is laid, I drew a blank on the necklace itself. What a refreshing experience then to learn of the story behind the *iziqu*. Unlike most other military traditions whose medals of valour are bestowed upon the recipient, the *iziqu* is created by the warrior himself after being identified by the king as having distinguished himself in battle.
>
> I found the image of a warrior carefully crafting his own *iziqu* after confronting the violence and brutality of war moving and sympathetic. It seems to me that apart from its military aspects this ritual embodies remedial and healing qualities as well – serving as a kind of occupational therapy. This, together with its inherent themes of creativity and reconstruction for me make it a wonderful dedication, not only to the Zulu fallen, but to the English who died as well (not to mention the obvious symbolic reference to our present situation). [45]

Recently *iziqu* have appeared at the curio shop at the Rorke's Drift Museum. For R25, one can buy six pieces of dowelling, 'Hand made' and 'Crafted by Paddy', on a thong to which is attached a tag: 'Iziqu. A Zulu symbol of Courage . . . Painstakingly crafted from willow wood, the Zulu symbol of courage in battle'.

Observers of the politics and the history of KwaZulu-Natal would do well to monitor the contemporary and future progress of these small pieces of wood – in their new manifestations they should continue to gather new meanings in new contexts, even as their fixed, timeless, traditional powers are asserted.

## Notes

1. The original article on which this version is based can be found in the *Natal Museum Journal of Humanities* 11 (1999).
2. C.M. Doke and B.W. Vilikazi, *Zulu-English Dictionary* (Johannesburg: Witwatersrand University Press, [1948] 1972).
3. J. Stuart and D. McK. Malcom, eds., *The Diary of Henry Francis Fynn* (Pietermaritzburg: Shuter & Shooter, 1950), pp. 284–85.
4. Stephen Gray, ed., *Charles Rawden Maclean: The Natal Papers of 'John Ross'* (Durban: Killie Campbell African Library and Pietermaritzburg: University of Natal Press, 1992), pp. 113–14.
5. John Wright, personal communication.
6. British Parliamentary Papers (BPP). C.5892. No. 126, Havelock to Knutsford, 8 February 1889.
7. J.W. Colenso, *Zulu-English Dictionary* (Pietermaritzburg: P. Davis & Sons, [1864] 1884).
8. J.W. Colenso, *Zulu-English Dictionary* (Pietermaritzburg: Vause, Slatter & Co., 1905. Fourth authorised edition. Revised and enlarged).
9. I acknowledge and thank Axel-Ivar Berglund for his detailed communications with me on this subject.
10. A.T. Bryant, *A Zulu-English Dictionary* (Pinetown: Marianhill Mission Press, 1905).
11. See Note 8 above.
12. C.M. Doke, D. McK. Malcolm and J.M.A. Sikakana, *English-Zulu Dictionary* (Johannesburg: Witwatersrand University Press, 1958).
13. For details of these events, see Jeff Guy, *The View Across the River: Harriette Colenso and the Zulu Struggle against Imperialism* (Cape Town: David Philip, 2001).
14. Born 22 February 1857, Robert Stephenson Smyth Powell, Baden-Powell from 1869. Charterhouse, commissioned to the 13th Hussars in India, where he wrote *Reconnaissance and Scouting* (1885), and then to Natal where he wrote *Cavalry Instruction* (1885). Aide-de-camp to his uncle Lieutenant-General Henry Smyth in 1887 and accompanied him to Zululand in 1888 as military secretary.
15. For the official account, see BPP. C.5892. No. 4, Havelock to Knutsford, 7 August 1888, enc. 1 Smyth to Havelock 17 July 1888, which forwards Major A.C. McKean's report, dated 14 July 1888.
16. BPP. C.5892. No. 4, Havelock to Knutsford, 7 August 1888, enc. Havelock to Resident Commissioner, 7 August 1888.
17. Public Record Office. CO 427/2, 21012, Minute.
18. See documents in Pietermaritzburg Archives Repository (PAR). ZGH713. Z558, 565.
19. National Library of South Africa, Cape Town campus, Baden-Powell, R.S.B. Sir, MSB 66 Scrap Album: Zululand Campaign 1888. Items 24 and 34.1.
20. Tim Jeal, *Baden-Powell* (London: Hutchinson, 1989), p. 376.
21. I have not had the opportunity to consult this diary.
22. William Hillcourt (with Olave, Lady Baden-Powell), *Baden-Powell: The Two Lives of a Hero* (London: Heinemann, 1964), p. 84.
23. Jeal, *Baden-Powell*, pp. 582–83.
24. Lord Baden-Powell of Gilwell, *Lessons from the Varsity of Life* (London: C. Arthur Pearson, 1933), p. 147.
25. Baden-Powell, *Lessons*, p. 153.
26. Hillcourt, *Baden-Powell*, p. 82.
27. Jeal, *Baden-Powell*, p. 386.

28. Baden-Powell, *Lessons*, p. 152. See also Jeal, *Baden-Powell*, p. 134, quoting Wade, *Piper of Pax*.
29. Jeal, *Baden-Powell*, p. 136.
30. Correctly, '*tshokobezi*'.
31. This brief account of Seton draws on the interesting chapter 'Fortifying the Wall of Empire' in Michael Rosenthal's book, *The Character Factory: Baden-Powell and the Origins of the Boy Scout Movement* (London: Collins, 1986). Much of the depth in Jeal's *Baden-Powell* is the consequence of his ongoing argument with Rosenthal's important, but rather tendentious, interpretation of Baden-Powell's life.
32. Jeal, *Baden-Powell*, p. 381.
33. PAR. Colenso Collection. Box 73, H[arriette] E C[olenso] to Kate Giles, January 1890.
34. http://www.pinetreeweb.com/woodbadg.htm (accessed on 30 July 2004).
35. Hillcourt, *Baden-Powell*, p. 358. There are many other versions; of course, most of them are derivative. See for example, http://www.pinetreeweb.com/woodbadg.htm (accessed on 30 July 2004).
36. This is the version presented by D.J. Landsberg, Leader Trainer in his four-page typescript entitled 'Wood Badge Training'. I would like here to acknowledge Mr Landsberg's kind assistance in providing me with this material.
37. http://www.woodbadge.org/founding.htm (accessed on 30 July 2004). Nelson R. Block, 'The Founding of Wood Badge', *The Journal of Scouting History* 1994.
38. Photocopy of 'The Woodbadge Story' manuscript, provided by Mr Landsberg. See also 'Dinizulu's Necklace. Origin of the Wood Badge – Worldwide Symbol of a Trained Scoutmaster'. Printed with the badge of the World Jamboree 1967, Idaho, United States.
39. Photocopy of 'The First Gilwell Park Group' provided by Mr Landsberg.
40. Jeal, *Baden-Powell*, p. 134
41. http://www.woodbadge.org/BoyScout/wbtinybeads.htm (accessed on 30 July 2004).
42. For example, see J.L. Smail, *With Shield and Assegai* (Cape Town: Howard Timmins, 1969), p. 32.
43. I first came across this reference on a webpage called 'African Seeds of Scouting' at http://www.scouting.org.za/scouts/seeds/ (1 August 2004) but the original source is in an article by Elwyn Jenkins, 'Tradition Borrowed and Returned: The Wood Badge Beads', *Lantern* 44:3, Spring 1995: 78–79.
43. *Zulu Treasures: Amagugu kaZulu* (KwaZulu Cultural Museum and the Durban Local History Museums: 1996). The catalogue notes that *iziqu* were normally buried with the owner – an interesting observation if it could be validated.
44. *Zulu Treasures*.
45. 'The Story behind the Monument'. Letter by Patrick Makkink, *Natal Witness*, 6 February 1999.

*Chapter 17*

# 'Happy Are Those Who Are Dead'
## Crises in African Life in Late-nineteenth-century and Early-twentieth-century Colonial Natal

JOHN LAMBERT

UNTIL THE 1870s, many isiZulu-speaking Africans in Natal used the settler presence to their own advantage. Although much of the colony's land was in white possession, most settlers cultivated a small percentage of their farmlands, while about 400 000 hectares were owned by absentee landowners who made a profit by renting their lands to Zulu tenants. With the colonial farmers unable to meet the colony's food needs, the Natal administration bought staples from amaZulu in *imizi* (homesteads), with access to reserve, Crown, and settler lands. These productive farmers were able to move between the three designated territories with relative ease, establishing new gardens and seasonally driving their cattle between pastures. Until the early 1880s, over half their fields were devoted to maize (corn) and many *imizi* met the financial demands of the government and settlers by expanding their agricultural output for the market, rather than by labouring for wages.[1]

But as Zulu homesteads expanded production to meet the demand for grain, so individual *imizi* needed more land and between the late 1870s and early 1900s this need became difficult to meet. These years saw the colonial African population double to reach more than 600 000 by 1904.[2] Access to Crown and settler-owned land became restricted as the white population grew through natural increase and immigration from the Cape and Europe. Colonial farmers were making more use of their properties and reducing the available acreage for their tenants' gardens and grazing. At the same time, to satisfy the growing settler demand for arable soil, Crown and absentee-owned lands were being sold to private white owners, who either evicted their Zulu occupants or marginalised them to poor patches of the property.[3] By the early twentieth century, few lands remained in Crown or absentee hands other than those unsuitable for planting and grazing.[4] Both *kholwa* (Christian) and traditionalist amaZulu tried to ease their land shortage through purchases, but by 1901 they owned only 154 801 hectares, too little to make an appreciable difference.[5] Most amaZulu faced a grim future as either labour tenants or as poor peasants squeezed into reserves.[6]

Although many amaZulu in Natal were reluctant to move to the already crowded reserves, they had little choice.[7] Overpopulation became the norm in virtually all the reserves. Many chiefs made great effort to allocate fresh land to *abanumzana* (homestead heads); grazing was also restricted, and as early as the 1880s, many reserve inhabitants complained of reaching 'the end of their tether as far as cultivation goes'.[8] Methods of shifting cultivation, suited to conditions of abundant land, declined precipitously; *imizi* inhabitants tilling marginal gardens experienced a fall in the quality and quantity of their crops.[9] Some form of environmental degradation extended into every rural Zulu community, with attendant destruction of forest and bush cover on the fringes of homesteads further hastening erosion of rugged reserves of the coastal interior and Thukela valley.[10]

Thus, overpopulation, soil exhaustion, and environmental collapse contributed to a dramatic fall in overall *imizi* food production. By the early twentieth century, the amaZulu's share of Natal's maize crop dropped from 80 per cent in the early 1880s to 38 per cent.[11] Homestead farmers could not fill their stomachs, let alone supply a market.[12] Many were relying on hardy sorghum to survive, but as it contained little protein and diseases stemming from protein deficiencies such as kwashiorkor, which primarily affected children, spread unabated.[13]

Until the late 1890s, ecological pressures on the reserves were compounded by a sharp rise in cattle numbers. Many chiefs, *abanumzana* and commoners used money from produce sales to build up their herds. By 1896, African-owned cattle increased to just fewer than 500 000, compared with an estimated 330 000 in 1869.[14] Such swelling herds ate and walked their way across depleted veld, and eventually suffered from the kind of hunger that led to deteriorating milk production and poor health. Grazing practices were also curtailed in the early 1890s when the colony's farmers aggressively began to fence their properties and bar amaZulu from moving stock between different seasonal pastures.[15] A drought cycle between 1888 and 1893 also spawned crop failures that drove amaZulu into destitution and even starvation.[16] Many survived by selling livestock and horses, often at ridiculously low prices. In Ixopo in 1892, for example, in order to buy four bags of maize, a Zulu man had to barter a mare and foal.[17] To meet their needs, more and more Zulu men in Natal and Zululand turned to migrant labour, particularly as wage workers in towns and on the mines, leading to repercussions at all levels of Zulu society.

Migrant labour spurred social dislocation and unrest. With men away, women in homesteads had to take over male work, upsetting the sexual division of labour and causing considerable resentment, particularly among younger women. Then, having tasted freedom from homestead restrictions, returning migrant men were reluctant to conform to patriarchal codes within the *umuzi* (a single homestead), such as those dictating the proper drinking conduct around the beer pot. By ignoring such conventions, they effectively challenged the authority embodied in the homestead head. Moreover, their assertive attitudes emboldened women and youth in *imizi*, and instigated the formation of new social groupings of young men and women, which homestead authorities struggled to control.[18] Complaints from Zulu elders about deteriorating familial relations and the growing squalor of the *imizi* became commonplace, while their attempts to reinforce their domestic influence caused widening generational conflicts.[19]

The droughts that spanned the years 1888–93 continued intermittently into the twentieth century, and were accompanied by locust plagues between 1894 and 1896 and the rinderpest epizootic that destroyed about 85 per cent of African-owned cattle in Natal and Zululand between 1897 and 1899.[20] With the prosperity of local kinship so intimately bound up in cattle-keeping, rinderpest dealt a severe blow to the homestead economy. The magistrate of Weenen elaborated:

> Old headmen and fathers would cry like children, as I saw them, at the sight of their cattle and calves, their sole asset upon earth which they had watched for years grow and increase before their eyes, drop down and die by scores before them, cleaning out the coveted collection of a lifetime in fewer hours than it had taken them years to acquire them, the food for their children, and the wives for their young men taken from them without power of rescue ... To say that the consequences of this scourge have been the disorganization of their social system and the disaster of their domestic [world] is only to briefly compass the evils which its advent has entailed.[21]

The consequences of rinderpest made many Zulu fathers reluctant to allow their daughters to marry without the traditional bridewealth offering of cattle (*ilobolo*). This resulted both in the rise of so-called illegitimate births and a decline in the number of married men supporting more than one wife.[22]

Despite the natural crises, the Natal government gave little assistance to Africans, refusing even to postpone annual payment of hut tax.[23] Left to their own resources, *imizi* dwellers found it difficult to rebuild their herds. Although some used the boom conditions accompanying the South African War (1899–1902) to buy cattle, the process was interrupted in the early 1900s by a milder recurrence of rinderpest, and then by a devastating outbreak of deadly East Coast fever. Africans were never again to have the large herds of pre-rinderpest days.[24]

Inevitably, many *imizi* were no longer able to function properly. By the early twentieth century, human congestion and malnutrition had affected countless households. General reserve overpopulation reduced access to fresh water, creating the unsanitary settings that enabled typhus and dysentery to ran rampant; cramped conditions in homestead huts offered a breeding ground for tuberculosis. Intestinal complaints and enteritis were also everyday occurrences.[25] Children suffered the most, with endemic kwashiorkor undermining their immune systems.[26] In 1905 the district surgeon of Estcourt reported a high number of infant deaths caused by milk deficiencies, and estimated that Zulu mothers lost two out of three babies through abdominal complaints.[27] In this deteriorating world, many amaZulu had no choice but to depend on the narrow opportunities touted by exploitative commercial farmers, colonial traders and labour recruiters. Some impoverished Africans borrowed money and entered a cycle of crippling debt, which was only resolved after they handed over their valuable possessions to moneylenders (often traders) or white farmers who converted labour into serfs.[28]

Indebtedness reduced the ability of the *imizi* to function independently of migrant labour, in the process accelerating the proletarianisation of Zulu society. Without kinship networks to fall back on, a small but growing number of young men and women saw no point in sending money home. Breaking free of their homestead obligations, they deserted their *imizi*, moving to towns and mining centres – even youths as young as ten years of age followed this exodus. In 1904 the numbers of permanent African urban residents were still small, comprising only an estimated 4 per cent of Natal towns.[29]

Generally speaking, Africans experienced appalling urban conditions. Municipal authorities made little provision for housing; men and youths filled unsanitary outbuildings or burgeoning slums and many women lived in brothels.[30] Town police enforced laws and rules tightly regulating and restricting their lives. As popular African resentment over repressive treatment intensified, so too did incidents of criminal activity and armed resistance, often carried out by youth gangs who were dubbed *amalaita* and adopted traditional Zulu weapons and martial regimental identities.[31]

The milieu of urban violence seeped back into the countryside. Rural crime was growing by the beginning of the twentieth century, as were clashes between rival gangs and between bands of young men and African police.[32] Attacks on law enforcement reflected a widespread disregard for all forms of authority, which had repercussions on chiefs and *abanumzana*. The latter were particularly aware of the fragility of their position and bitterly complained to white officials of their inability to exercise authority over inhabitants of their *imizi*. In 1898 the *kholwa* landowner John Gama lamented, 'The behaviour of today is beyond me. Your own child can abuse you even as he helps himself to your food.'[33] In previous years, an *umnumzana* had been able to call on the support of his chief to discipline unruly members; now few chiefs were in a position to offer support.[34]

Although chiefly powers were undermined by the inability of chiefs to provide their followers with land, their disempowerment owed much to an alteration in government attitudes towards the amaZulu. At the most general level, this change reflected growing official indifference to the well-being of Africans. From the late 1880s, as the Natal colony relied more on white and Indian farmers to produce foodstuffs, 'native administrators' abandoned policies of protecting the homestead economy. Once Natal attained responsible government in 1893, settler farmers' ambitions dictated that competition from African cultivators be drastically reduced.

Thus, few official attempts were made to deal with the mounting homestead crises; in fact, government assistance was usually extended to white farmers who coveted land held communally by Zulu chiefs and African homesteads north and west of the Thukela River.[35]

By the early twentieth century, Africans throughout the Natal colony (greatly enlarged in 1897 by its annexation of Zululand as a province) faced official hostility, increased taxation (including the notorious 1905 £1 poll tax on unmarried men which precipitated the 1906 rebellion) and a barrage of legislation designed to undermine their independence. Attempts to restrict the amount of land available to Africans also continued to cause particular hardship. In 1903, they were prohibited from buying Crown land and steps were taken to discourage individual African land purchases.[36] The following year, the Zululand Lands Delimitation Commission alienated 1 057 467 hectares, or 40 per cent of this new province for settler farming.[37]

Government perceptions of Zulu *amakholwa* (Christian converts) also changed. There was mounting official acceptance of Social Darwinism – and its concepts positing that Africans were racially inferior and incapable of assimilation in white society – which militated against black Christian aspirations of equality with colonists. After 1893, legislation steadily reduced *kholwa* privileges. In the process, exemption from native customary laws, the foundation of white magistrates' rule of Zulu reserves, became almost meaningless. The prohibition against Africans buying Crown land was specifically aimed at *amakholwa*; mission schools were also closed or received smaller grants; the Natal government introduced regulations that prevented *amakholwa* from participating freely in town commerce. In the countryside, old established *kholwa* settlements such as Edendale and Groutville, once prosperous beacons to some African Christians, slipped into poverty.[38]

Zulu elders were no less affected by repressive government policies. In 1891 a new Natal Native Code was promulgated, and with each passing year more despotic amendments were added which further subordinated Africans to white control. Theoretically, the Code entrenched hierarchical patriarchal authorities in Zulu chiefdoms and homesteads. When put into practice, it transformed chiefs and *abanumzana* into puppets of the colonial administration.[39] In Natal, and later in Zululand, magistrates increasingly usurped powers of chiefs, thus depriving these traditional rulers of leverage to maintain patronage ties. Few Zulu chiefs were able to muster the labour of followers, while the government demanded with impunity that young men perform *isibhalo* (compulsory) service on colonial public works.

As chiefs attempted to meet their onerous obligations, their feelings of resentment and powerlessness grew. At the same time, their relationships with followers weakened and, as their authority waned, violent conflicts within and between chiefdoms multiplied. Succession disputes and local jostling over scarce land fuelled so-called faction fights.[40] To many elders, the government deliberately stoked the unrest. In 1905 Madikane kaMlomowelole pointed out: 'There is a restlessness in the hearts of all the people. What is now clear is that we shall be done harm, we shall die, we shall be done harm by the government.'[41] John Mpetwana was more explicit when he told the 1906–07 Native Affairs Commission that colonial ministers 'did not like to see people eating, because, when they saw them chewing anything, they seem to put their fingers into their very mouths and scoop the food out to eat themselves'.[42]

By 1906, the crisis in Zulu society in Natal and Zululand was reaching breaking point. Although many Africans retained some access to land, few lived in *imizi*, which were not, to a greater or lesser extent, dependent on cash earnings from migrant labour. During previous decades, many homestead dwellers had been forced to relocate to other plots where, although they were able to recreate some semblance of subsistence, they suffered trauma associated with the loss of ancestral burial sites. In many of the newly constructed *imizi*, the orderly pattern created by an interior cattle kraal ringed by huts was no longer widely evident, showing that a way of life had indeed begun to crumble.[43] Homestead gardens, with their stunted crops and choking weeds, and eroding pastures robbed of nutritious grasses, also bore eloquent witness to an ever-deepening crisis. Many in the homesteads would have empathised with the isiZulu-speaking Jobongo, who lamented to the 1906–07 Native Affairs Commission, 'Happy are those who are dead'.[44]

## Notes

1. J. Lambert, *Betrayed Trust: Africans and the State in Colonial Natal* (Pietermaritzburg: University of Natal Press, 1995), Chapters 1 and 3.
2. *Natal Blue Books (NBB)*, 1882, p. T5 and Natal, 'Report on the Condition of the Native Population', 1904, pp. 117–18. This figure does not include the province of Zululand nor the recently annexed Vryheid and Utrecht districts. Including these territories, the African population was more than 900 000.
3. Legislative Council (LC) *Hansard*, VII, 19 August 1884, Robinson and Hulett, p. 485 and Natal Land and Colonisation Company (NL&C), 183, No. 142, Haynes to General Manager, Durban, 13 January 1887. By the 1880s many of the sales were to Indian purchasers while absentee landowners now preferred Indian rent tenants who could afford to pay higher rents.
4. *NBB*, 1883, p. GG54; 'NBB Departmental Reports', 1884, pp. B16–17; Pietermaritzburg Archives Repository (PAR), Upper Umkomanzi Magistracy, 3/2/2, 109/92, Magistrate to Secretary for Native Affairs (SNA), 26 March 1892.
5. PAR, Legislative Assembly Sessional Papers, No. 3, 1901, p. 25.
6. Conditions varied from district to district. In northern Natal and the Vryheid and Utrecht districts, settler farming generally remained backward and the farmers continued to make less use of their land. Because of this, the level of African overcrowding was never as severe as in the rest of Natal; see J. Lambert and R. Morrell, 'Domination and Subordination in Natal 1890–1920', in *Political Economy and Identities in KwaZulu-Natal: Historical and Social Perspectives*, ed. R. Morrell (Durban: Indicator Press, 1996), p. 75.
7. *NBB*, 1881, p. GG8; PAR, SNA, 1/1/94, 945/86, SNA to Colonial Secretary, 13 January 1887.
8. *Evidence Taken before the Natal Native Commission, 1881* (Pietermaritzburg, 1882), Maweli, p. 203; Kukelela, p. 232; Madude, p. 240 and Umsutu, p. 367.
9. This was evident even in the early 1880s; see *Evidence Taken*, Mahoba, p. 376 and Ncapie, p. 384.

10. Lambert, *Betrayed Trust*, p. 109.
11. *NBB*, 1882, p. X7 and *Natal Statistical Year Book, 1902–1904*. The extent of the decline in Zululand cannot be estimated.
12. See *South African Native Affairs Commission (SANAC), 1903–1905* (Cape Town, 1905), 3, Mahashi, p. 896.
13. *NBB*, 1888–1893; 'NBB Departmental Reports, 1888–1893'; PAR, SNA (Natal Archives Depot), 1/1/137, 94/91, Fayle diary, 11 January 1891. See also A. Booth, 'Homestead, State and Migrant Labour in Colonial Swaziland', *African Economic History* 14 (1985): 107–45.
14. *NBB*, 1869, p. X12 and Natal, 'Report on the Condition of the Native Population', 1896. There are no figures for the increase in cattle numbers in either Zululand or the Vryheid and Utrecht divisions. It is unlikely, however, that the increase would have been as great as in Natal.
15. *Natal Mercury*, 19 April 1893.
16. PAR, SNA, 1/1/124, 472/90, Magistrate, Weenen to SNA, 13 April 1890.
17. PAR, SNA, 1/1/163, 1209/92, SNA to Governor, 2 December 1892.
18. See PAR, Natal Parliamentary Papers, 146, no. 111, 1886, Report of SNA, 16 July 1884 and SNA, 1/1/169, 441/93, Fayle diary, 8 April 1893.
19. See B. Carton, *Blood from Your Children: The Colonial Origins of Generational Conflict in South Africa* (Charlottesville: University of Virginia Press, 2000).
20. Lambert and Morrell, 'Domination and Subordination', p. 76.
21. PAR, 'Report on the Condition of the Native Population', 1897, pp. 104–05.
22. Lambert and Morrell, 'Domination and Subordination', p. 78.
23. PAR, SNA, 1/1/254, 1830/97, Precis of memorandums, 2 September 1897; 1/1/282, 1990/98, Notes of meeting, 8 September 1898.
24. By 1905 African-owned cattle numbered 276 997, far short of the 494 382 of 1896 (PAR, Department of Native Affairs, *Annual Report*, 1905, p. 129); population numbers had increased to 607 229 in 1904 compared to 455 983 in 1891 (PAR, *Census of 1891: Report with Tables and Appendices*, Pietermaritzburg, 1891 and PAR, *Census of the Colony of Natal, 17th April 1904*, Pietermaritzburg, 1904). All figures exclude Zululand and the northern districts of Vryheid and Utrecht annexed after the South African War.
25. PAR, 'Report on the Condition of the Native Population', 1901, p. B35; 1902, pp. A6, 27; 1903, pp. A11, 21, 25; and *SANAC*, 3, R.C. Samuelson, p. 505.
26. *NBB*, 1888–1893; 'NBB Departmental Reports', 1888–1893; PAR, SNA, 1/1/137, 94/91, Fayle diary, 11 January 1891.
27. PAR, Department of Native Affairs, *Annual Report*, 1905, p. 10.
28. Lambert, *Betrayed Trust*, pp. 171–73.
29. PAR, 'Report on the Condition of the Native Population', 1904.
30. *Natal Witness*, 16 August 1895; see also M.W. Swanson, ' "The Durban System": Roots of Urban Apartheid in Colonial Natal', *African Studies* 35:3–4 (1976): 159–76.
31. P. la Hausse de Lalouvière, 'The Struggle for the City: Alcohol, the Ematsheni and Popular Culture in Durban, 1902–1936' (Masters thesis, University of Cape Town, 1984), p. 35.
32. Lambert, *Betrayed Trust*, p. 185.
33. C. de B. Webb and J.B. Wright, eds. *The James Stuart Archive of Recorded Oral Evidence Relating to the History of the Zulu and Neighbouring Peoples*, Vol. 1 (Pietermaritzburg: University of Natal Press, 1976), p. 137.
34. The four volumes of the *James Stuart Archive* (1976–86) and the Natal, *Native Affairs Commission, 1906–07, Evidence* (1907) include numerous complaints by chiefs and *abanumzana* of their inability to exercise authority.
35. Lambert, *Betrayed Trust*, p. 166. For example, the annexation to the colony, first of Zululand in 1897 and then of the Vryheid and Utrecht districts in 1903, adversely impacted on Africans in these areas similarly subjected to the control of the Natal administration.
36. Ibid., p. 164.
37. J. Laband, *Rope of Sand: The Rise and Fall of the Zulu Kingdom in the Nineteenth Century* (Johannesburg: Jonathan Ball, 1995), p. 439.
38. Lambert and Morrell, 'Domination and Subordination', pp. 68, 71, 75.
39. Lambert, *Betrayed Trust*, p. 124.
40. Ibid., pp. 181–82.
41. C. de B. Webb and J.B. Wright, eds. *The James Stuart Archive of Recorded Oral Evidence Relating*

to the *History of the Zulu and Neighbouring Peoples*, Vol. 2 (Pietermaritzburg: University of Natal Press, 1979), p. 54.

42. PAR, *Native Affairs Commission, 1906–07, Evidence*, p. 716.
43. PAR, Department of Native Affairs, *Annual Report*, 1905, p. 48.
44. PAR, *Native Affairs Commission, 1906–07, Evidence*, p. 712.

*Chapter 18*

# The American Mission Revivals and the Birth of Modern Zulu Evangelism

ROBERT J. HOULE

SHORTLY BEFORE SUNRISE on the morning of 22 September 1896, the Holy Spirit descended upon Mbiya Kuzwayo, a young Zulu Christian living on the American Zulu Mission (AZM) station in Mapumulo division, northern Natal.[1] Although he had been born and raised a Christian, the spiritual intensity of this moment was unlike anything he had previously experienced in the congregational services of the AZM. That he did so now was due in part to his work translating the words of George Weavers, an itinerant Holiness preacher and a pioneer of the Pentecostal form of worship in Natal.[2] In the weeks preceding his own brush with the Holy Spirit, it had fallen upon Kuzwayo to put into isiZulu the central tenets of Holiness, particularly its belief that all could be perfected by first undergoing a process of consecration in which participants rid themselves of past sins through public confession, and then sanctification, in which it was thought the Holy Spirit descended into the purified soul to reside there and permit the believer to live a life free from future sin. Kuzwayo had spent the previous days praying for just such an occurrence and his 'heart leapt for joy' when he heard the Spirit command him: 'Go and tell Brother Weavers that this is a blessed day. No man or woman shall work. We shall have a whole day's service!' What followed turned first into a multi-day affair at Mapumulo, and then, in the coming months, spread from one mission station to the next before becoming an almost annual event in the century that followed. These revivals altered the nature of Christian worship in Natal, the relationship of the congregations to their white missionaries, and the *kholwa* (isiZulu-speaking African Christians) community's own sense of responsibility for spreading the Word, as small bands of Zulu revivalists suddenly took up evangelism with an enthusiasm never before witnessed. Although most of the community participated, the revivals were most thoroughly embraced by the youth, who had struggled in the decade before revival to reconcile their Christianity with the morally dangerous nature of their newly urban lives. Holiness theology represented an important tool in recasting what it meant to be an *ikholwa*, and revivals offered the necessary revolutionary space to accomplish this transformation.

Only the most optimistic missionary could have envisioned the dramatic growth of Christianity among the amaZulu that followed throughout the twentieth century. Today, a significant majority consider themselves Christian, and the faith they practise is among the most dynamic found anywhere in the world.[3] Some of these believers belong to one of the hundreds of African Independent Churches (AICs) that in the last century have blossomed not only in KwaZulu-Natal, but also across the entire continent.[4] The rest, however, attend one of the mainline churches established by missionaries in the nineteenth century and, although it is the potential tension between these two broad groups of evangelical churches that has most occupied the imagination of scholars, they share much in common.[5] Indeed, anyone attending services in a broad swathe of both AIC and mainline churches will notice Pentecostal influences traceable back to the 1896–97 revivals, particularly a penchant for charismatic revivals that emphasise the power of the Holy Spirit and demand the active participation of their audiences. This chapter examines how this came to pass.

*Zulu woman and three small children in Western dress, c.1900.*

## Pastoral Christianity and the problem of the urban

The birth pangs of the 1896–97 revival were mingled with the death throes of an earlier expression of Christianity. Working under the direction of its home organisation, the American Board Mission (ABM), the AZM was one of the first mission bodies in Natal and parlayed this advantage into more and larger grants of land than any other denomination that followed.[6] The first missionaries of the AZM believed in the moral efficacy of the church-centred farming community. The Christianity they preached was a muscular, agrarian faith in which work and education played equally important roles alongside worship. To promote this ideal, they developed the 'village plan' under which *amakholwa* lived in small settlements on mission reserves and leased plots of land from the mission to farm and graze cattle.[7]

Founded in 1844, the Groutville settlement became the AZM's most fully realised pastoral village. By 1867, its 433 residents owned nearly 50 wagons, many more ploughs and carts, and hundreds of trained oxen to pull them.[8] Transport-riding was a particularly popular and lucrative career for Groutville's *kholwa* community, allowing them to tend their farms while using their unique position as Zulu Christians to do business in both the traditional and Western worlds of Natal, buying grain from Zulu neighbours and reselling it to the white community. The residents of Groutville poured these profits back into the markers of their Christian identity – their 64 Western-style homes (including four made of brick), Victorian wardrobe, farming implements and small libraries.[9]

But during the last decades of the nineteenth century, the community began to crumble. Following the Anglo-Zulu War, in which some *amakholwa* from Groutville and elsewhere had made substantial sums of money in the transport trade, transport-riding became increasingly competitive as white settlers, traditionalists, and eventually the railroad all took business away. A second generation of missionaries also called into question the purity of their congregations, demanding that members abandon traditional customs such as brewing and drinking *utshwala* (beer), offering *ilobolo* (bridewealth, usually in cattle), and polygamy.[10] When *amakholwa* refused to don the AZM's blue ribbons symbolising abstinence, and warned that withholding *ilobolo* would scandalise their daughters as unworthy of marriage, the younger white missionaries became censorious, faulting their African congregations for not fulfilling the plan of God's chosen people. In the years following the Anglo-Zulu War in 1879, many Zulu believers were excluded from AZM churches for practices that earlier missionaries had frowned upon, but rarely punished.[11] Their Christian respectability challenged, they faced difficult decisions between new church laws and a desire to maintain a communal lifestyle suddenly deemed immoral.

Layered on the fight over purity was another, looming conflict within *kholwa* society, which reflected growing tensions between Zulu generations. As other scholars have demonstrated, the roots of this rift, in part, date back to the precolonial Zulu state, whose power depended on the ability of homestead patriarchs to mobilise young men (and to a lesser degree young women) into regiments. The collapse of this system in Natal following colonisation put greater pressure on African chiefs and fathers to control their youths.[12] For *amakholwa*, like their traditionalist neighbours, the fuel that fed this fire was the increasingly crowded land on which they lived; the demand of both cities and mines for migrant labour and the wages that allowed young men to bypass patriarchal authority by purchasing their own *ilobolo*. Although the increasing independence of juniors was translated differently in *kholwa* society, the implication for Zulu elders in the church was much the same as for traditionalists. By the 1890s, a generation of Zulu youth threatened to up-end accepted norms of generational respect.

Young Zulu converts were profoundly influenced by the wave of social changes spawned by industrialisation in South Africa, which intensified following the discovery of gold on the Witwatersrand in 1886. To be sure, *amakholwa* and the amaZulu in general experienced large-scale mining before it developed in the Transvaal. Yet prior 'mineral revolutions' such as the advent of diamond diggings in Kimberly in the late 1860s did not hold the same allure for Africans in Natal and Zululand as the gold strikes. Significantly, too, the two major mining booms would take time to affect Natal's overall economy, which remained stalwartly agricultural well into the early twentieth century.[13] In other words *kholwa* farmers did not initially need bustling cities or humming machines to prod them into embracing European modernity. From the mid-nineteenth century onwards, they adopted most things Western – from rocking chairs and feather beds, to suits and dresses and *amakholwa* also long served as a conduit through which many new fashions and behaviours flowed into Zulu society. This proved equally true for agricultural implements such as ploughs. Armed with this new technology, they sought to enter the South African and world economies as commercial producers of tea, coffee, cotton and arrowroot.[14]

Of all the cash crops, sugar promised quick riches, as Sydney Mintz has noted for other settler economies. In the eighteenth-century New World, the processing of sugarcane led to the building of mills, a factory-like institution that arguably industrialised British colonies well before either the cotton-mills of Manchester or James Watt's steam engine in the English metropole.[15] By the middle of the nineteenth century, the mills built in Natal were seen as industrial wonders by settlers and amaZulu alike; steam engines powered mechanical rollers, which crushed the cane; centrifuges in turn churned out molasses juice and vacuum-sealed kettles refined the remaining sugar into its preferred white state.

First grown in 1851, sugar did well on Natal's subtropical coast, where colonial authorities sought to encourage Zulu farmers, many of them recent Christian converts in AZM stations, to plant the crop and transport their harvest to a newly established mill at Groutville just north of Durban. Situated on prime arable land, the mill's first crushing of 70 tons earned $9 000 in 1857, bringing a significant influx of cash into the small *kholwa* community and prompting a short-lived sugar boom.[16] However, the Natal government-owned mill never turned a profit and was sold after twenty years to three *kholwa* farmers who struggled unsuccessfully over the next decade to compete against bigger, more efficient mills owned by prominent whites such as the Hulett family, which employed indentured Indian labour transported on ships by British labour recruiters from the 'jewel' of Victoria's empire to Durban.[17]

Sugar production spurred other developments, such as the construction of Natal railways. One major railroad line, which opened between Durban and Pieter-maritzburg in 1880 would serve another growing sector of the colonial economy, the small collieries that commenced operation in and around Newcastle and Dundee later. The coal-fed locomotive nudged the Natal colony into its own phase of proto-industrialisation just as news of an incredible gold strike on a small Witwatersrand farm was cabled round the world. This dramatic discovery attracted Zulu Christians and traditionalists alike; they travelled hundreds of kilometres, usually on foot, to the 'New Babylon, New Nineveh' of the Boer Transvaal.[18] The most potentially lucrative deposits were lodged in thin veins that extended deep in the ground and extracting such riches necessitated both a great deal of cheap labour and heavy machinery that could sink shafts. Almost overnight Johannesburg rose from the veld to become a modern hub of industry, particularly as newcomers from the British Isles, United States, Australia, Russia, and Lithuania, as well as Africans from southern sub-Saharan territories flocked to the gold mines.

Only a decade after the first haul of precious metal was refined, some 90 000 Africans worked in Johannesburg. However, as Charles van Onselen, David Coplan and other contemporary scholars have shown, most amaZulu experienced urbanisation, not as miners, but as service workers.[19] In the early years of Transvaal urban development, before steam laundries and racist regulations, Zulu washermen, *amawasha*, carved out a successful niche by cleaning the city's sheets and garments.[20] Other Zulu labourers entered Johannesburg to fill positions as artisans, preachers, clerks, musicians, shebeen (tavern) owners, beer brewers and petty thieves.

The Natal colony benefited in a variety of ways from the transportation links that stretched from the Witwatersrand to ports on the Indian Ocean coast. Like Johannesburg, the big towns of Durban and Pietermaritzburg sought to be incorporated into global networks and markets through Natal's railroad branches, which passed through main colonial centres and regions of the countryside, where farmers brought their harvested food and raw materials such as coal and wood to sidings. Trains also picked up thousands of migrant labourers in Natal and took them to the Transvaal. By the last decade of the nineteenth century, Durban had expanded considerably, becoming increasingly important as one of the closest ports through which goldfields cargo could exit South Africa. Needless to say, it was at this time that Zulu *togt* (day) labourers first crowded into the city to do the heavy lifting at the docks as stevedores.[21]

In 1896 few Zulu communities remained untouched in some way by industrialisation. Indeed, facing the imminent destruction of their cattle herds in the
rinderpest epizootic, a group of Zulu leaders took advantage of a scheduled meeting
with Natal's undersecretary for Native Affairs in October to vent their fears that
Johannesburg, more than the bovine disease wiping out their herds, was the real
harbinger of bad tidings to come, from the horrors of unrestrained alcohol
consumption to the indifferent leadership of their white 'handlers' (like J.S. Marwick,
the Natal representative for Native Affairs on the Witwatersrand) who seemed
unmoved by the social evils of a faraway gold city.[22] Johannesburg had forced its
way into the everyday consciousness of the amaZulu, not least into the modernising
communities of African Christians, with their wider knowledge of things Western,
namely the *amakholwa* of the American Zulu Mission.

Because AZM missionaries envisioned *kholwa* communities as self-contained and
agriculturally based, they frequently warned against the moral dangers of urban life.
Cities and towns were 'universities of vice', the Americans cautioned; their *kholwa*
charges needed to be wary of imitating degraded European habits or risk being
'smeared with the worst' that civilisation offered.[23] *Amakholwa* were rural farmers,
not rickshaw pullers and dockworkers in Durban, or miners in Johannesburg, AZM
authorities insisted. But agriculture could not support everyone on the mission stations,
and the material goods of 'civilisation' were expensive to acquire.[24] Thus, by the
mid-1890s many young *kholwa* men and women were seeking their fortunes in the
rapidly expanding urban centres of southern Africa.[25] Literate and bilingual, they
filled certain skilled niches and were paid comparatively well, often as clerks,
interpreters and overseers.[26]

While it helped to have some education, *kholwa* youth soon realised that in the
increasingly racialised environment of late-nineteenth-century South Africa, there
were limits to the usefulness of a higher degree. *Kholwa* elders, who promoted
education nearly as fervently as communion, were horrified when their children
deserted schools. Indeed, so few students graduated through the mission school system
at this time that in 1897 one of the leading secondary institutions open to Africans in
Natal, Amanzimtoti Seminary, nearly shut down. As teachers, the most probable
career path for *amakholwa* with high school educations, they would be fortunate to
earn £40 a year. As clerks, shop assistants, court interpreters and minor governmental
functionaries, they could earn as much as £13 a month in Durban.[27]

Undereducated, flush with cash, and steeped in the general lawlessness that
marked the southern African urban experience, *kholwa* youths returned home from
the city and found trouble. Where their parents put on Western clothes as a sign of
their newfound faith, their children were accused of vain 'overdress' in attempts to
seduce the opposite sex. Where older fathers had carefully husbanded their resources
to build their Christian standing, their sons used earnings to buy horses to race
against each other and gamble on the outcomes.[28] Drinking and illicit sex were not

only practised, but seemed to be flaunted, much to the consternation of *kholwa* elders and American missionaries.

Despite this assertive behaviour, it was clear from their demands upon the AZM to open churches in Durban and Johannesburg that young Zulu Christians did not want to discard their faith, but only to come to a meaningful understanding of what it now meant to be *amakholwa*. Given missionary patriarchy, the collapse of the village plan, and the attraction of urban life to *kholwa* youth, carving out a new identity addressing these issues was to be a critical step in the amaZulu making Christianity their own. The AZM, focused on their pastoral ideal, missed this important shift and only reluctantly and belatedly opened a church in Durban in 1890.[29] Ensconced on the mission reserves, the American missionaries declined to lead the effort and it fell to John Mdiwa, a *kholwa* teacher and preacher, to minister to a scattered but devoted and rapidly growing congregation. Prayer services were held every Wednesday and Friday but so many worshippers came on the Sabbath that Mdiwa held two separate services throughout the first year, and it soon became clear that a larger church was needed to meet the demand.[30]

As in Durban, young Congregationalist *amakholwa* in Johannesburg wanted to have their spiritual needs met. Many initially joined the Presbyterian Church, but its white congregation proved unwelcoming and in 1892 they wrote to the AZM, asking that the mission send them a pastor.[31] Reluctant to commit itself, the AZM asked the Congregational Union (an assembly of white Congregationalists in South Africa) to take up the work. Unhappy with the Congregational Union's proposal of sending a Xhosa preacher, Zulu *amakholwa* flooded the AZM with 'complaints and pleadings' to force the mission's hand – but they succeeded only after the AZM had garnered a promise from the young Zulu Christians in the city that they would match the funds spent by the mission in buying land and building a church.[32] The Johannesburg *amakholwa* then expected one of their own, Fokoti Makanya, to be appointed pastor – and when the AZM sent the American, H.D. Goodenough, to run the church, the congregation rebelled.

In early May 1896, the AZM received a letter from the *kholwa* congregation of Johannesburg, detailing their complaints against H.D. Goodenough.[33] While the letter briefly expressed disappointment that Makanya had not being appointed pastor, it more fully detailed the failings of Goodenough. He was faulted for looking after his business interests rather than the needs of the congregation, and constructing next to the church a boarding house 'swarming with Dutch Bastards and half-cast peoples' who engaged in 'adultery and licenciousness [*sic*]'. An investigative committee sent to Johannesburg by the AZM learned that Goodenough had compounded this mistake by hiring a female teacher to work with the coloured children. When Makanya sent his daughter to attend this school, the coloured children had 'put their fingers to their noses when going by her'.[34] Makanya refused to let her return, and the event further angered the *kholwa* community. It could hardly have come as a surprise when the *kholwa* wing of the church broke away in February 1897, and, along with another congregation outside Pietermaritzburg, formed the Zulu Congregational Church (ZCC).[35]

Was this in part a political struggle? Certainly, but it was also an issue of religion and identity. The pastoral Christianity of their parents did not suffice in the cities, and Zulu Christians needed to reimagine what it meant to be *amakholwa* in a project another author has seen as a 'mission community struggling to reproduce its class position in an urban setting'.[36] Goodenough's actions had highlighted the Americans' fallibility and allowed young *amakholwa* to cast about for other religious options. The members of the ZCC chose one path in reinterpreting what it meant to be *amakholwa*. As the year progressed most of the rest of the community would follow another path, with similar results: a Christian faith whose practice better fitted their needs and through which they would lay claim to spiritual autonomy from the mission overlords without abandoning the churches they and their parents had helped build.

### Revival and the altered nature of *kholwa* faith

In September 1896, young Zulu Christians ignited a series of revivals, which started in Mapumulo, Natal, and spread throughout southern Africa. By definition, revivals serve to reconnect the already converted to their faith and were thus not surprisingly seen as a useful tool by white church leaders. But revivals could also be revolutionary, creating spaces within which societal norms are up-ended and participants reorder the nature of their personal relationships with God, the church leadership and their brethren in general.[37]

The Zulu revival mirrored religious currents that animated Kentucky and Tennessee during the 'Second Great Awakening' in the early nineteenth century. Stressing individual faith, preachers from Presbyterian, Baptist and Methodist congregations in the Appalachian hills competed to save souls by delivering highly emotional sermons, which in turn swayed audiences to express ecstatic feelings for the Holy Spirit.[38] Revivalism evolved as it went west with the expanding American frontier. By the time the religious movement arrived in South Africa, it had absorbed the new theology of Holiness. Having imbibed John Wesley's Methodist ideas of being 'reborn' in God's love, advocates of Holiness argued that believers could undergo a dual process of consecration and sanctification that would empty the individual of sin and allow the Holy Spirit to enter a person's soul. Once sanctified, an individual could live free from sin and achieve a state of perfection before death: here Holiness departed most decisively from earlier Methodist doctrine. Given the promise of Holiness to wipe away past sins, it is not surprising that the fledgling theology's popularity soared following the horrors of the American Civil War. From 1867 on, tens of thousands participated in revivals across the United States; many then agreed to live 'in the world but not of it', and created distinct communities with other sanctified individuals.[39]

Under the direction of George Weavers, a Civil War veteran who had barely survived an ugly battle injury, a prominent Holiness community, the Hephzibah Faith Missionary Association, blossomed in Tabor, Iowa.[40] Like John Dowie's Zion City outside Chicago, the members of Hephzibah attempted to carve a Christian utopia out of the Midwestern soil. While members of Hephzibah sought to disconnect from the surrounding world, they also felt a duty to spread the Holiness message across the globe. As Hephzibah stalwarts embarked for Japan, India, China and Haiti, George Weavers boarded a ship to South Africa.

Weavers first docked in Cape Town in August of 1896 and then travelled to Natal where he was introduced to William Wilcox, the AZM missionary responsible for Mapumulo, who had recently come to believe in the possibility of achieving perfection before death. One month after landing in Cape Town, Weavers arrived at Mapumulo and began to hold meetings in the mission house.[41] Mbiya Kuzwayo, son of the *kholwa* headman and one of the many young *kholwa* men who had left Amanzimtoti Seminary before graduation to pursue opportunities in the cities, was one of the early participants and volunteered to interpret for the Iowan. Shortly thereafter he claimed to have been visited by the Holy Spirit and let Weavers know that the days of revival had arrived.

Word of divine intervention raced through the narrow social confines of the mission reserve; curious *amakholwa* swelled Weavers' congregation and broke out into spontaneous singing and prayer, which stretched from one day into another. Late in the second day of the revival, a young woman believed she was struck down by the Holy Spirit. She quickly initiated a process of consecration by publicly and loudly confessing her sins, then leapt to her feet and rushed through the church, clapping her hands and proclaiming the power of God. Her exaltations electrified the assembly, with those in attendance swearing later that the Holy Spirit had descended upon them in a moment that reminded Kuzwayo 'of my Saviour's words in Luke 24:19: "Tarry ye in the city of Jerusalem, until ye be endowed from power from on high"'. Some 50 *amakholwa* rose to their feet and, in a cacophony of religious ecstasy, began weeping, jumping and rollicking. The guest missionary in charge of Mapumulo reported: 'In all my experiences I have never seen such a meeting.'

Spent, the assembled returned home well after midnight. But even in their exhaustion they could not contain their spiritual enthusiasm and as they made their way along the darkened paths of the mission reserve they clapped and sang, making the air ring with their 'melodious voices'. Awakened by the commotion, those in the surrounding hills and valleys who had remained home could only wonder: 'Are these people mad, crazy, or possessed with evil spirits?'

The revival spread as Weavers, Mbiya and a band of young Zulu revivalists who came to call themselves *amaVoluntiya* (the Volunteers) moved between missions in Mapumulu, Groutville, Impapala, Inanda, Esidumbini and Noodsberg. Over six months the fervour portrayed by Kuzwayo affected nearly every station and outstation of the AZM, reaching other African congregations in Natal, Zululand and even Johannesburg. For the participants, including the veteran missionaries, the overall effect was unlike anything they had experienced. One American preacher observed: 'I have never before seen such a powerful work of the spirit among our people or indeed anywhere.'[42] Another echoed these sentiments: 'In the entire history of the mission there has been no such awakening among the people.'[43] Weavers, a solid Midwesterner with decades of revival experience and little given to hyperbole, recalled his months of preaching in Natal as 'some of the grandest meetings' he had ever witnessed.[44] Before returning to Iowa in February of 1897, Weavers publicly passed the torch of leadership for the revivals to the man he now called 'Elder' Kuzwayo (a Holiness honorific indicating the young Zulu man's sanctified state). After attending a revival meeting led by Kuzwayo, the Iowan wrote in his diary: 'He a lone [sic] has paid me by been [sic] filled with the Spirit for coming over to Africa.' Led by Kuzwayo and a growing number of young *amakholwa* formed into dedicated bands of Volunteers, the revival continued to pick up momentum as it was carried to previously unvisited sites.[45]

### 'Flames of fire to preach the Gospel . . .'[46]

Why did the revivals resonate so profoundly with young *amakholwa*? One reason lay in the immediate purification of the sinful individual offered by Holiness. Without the unburdening of sins in the act of consecration, sanctification was not possible. Young Zulu Christians willingly took part in consecration and what they had to tell shocked the American missionaries. Adultery, fornication, theft, drunkenness, witchcraft and even murders all came to light. When the revival reached nearby Groutville, one young man confessed to a murder and laid on the altar a suit of clothes he had stolen from the deceased.[47] The act underscored the brutal and dehumanising experience of life in the cities, where the exploitative nature of urban colonial capitalism stripped young Zulu migrants, Christian and traditionalist alike, of their humanity.[48] In this context, the revivalists' Holiness message gave the newly saved an opportunity to free themselves of guilt and reassert their claim to heaven. Critically, it did so almost instantaneously. Under normal conditions confessions of grave sin would have meant exclusion from communion, if not outright expulsion, followed by an extended period of reconciliation.[49] Sanctification moved at the Holy Spirit's speed, not the resident missionary's, a necessary reality for fast-paced youth in urban settings.

Another attraction of the revivals for young Zulu Christians was its revolutionary potential, allowing youth to challenge the leadership of both their elders and white missionaries as they remade what it meant to be *amakholwa*. This wasn't always easy; one young woman reported that her heart almost failed her when she prepared to address a congregation, but did so successfully after she prayed: 'Jesus you know I have no power to speak before my elders. You must help me and speak through me.'[50] Believing themselves filled with such spiritual authority, young Zulu men and women challenged their elders to publicly confess sins and urged them towards sanctification as they spread revival from one station to the next. Arriving at Groutville before Weavers, Mbiya Kuzwayo and eleven other youths from Mapumulo spent several days praying and fasting in the church and then moved out into the community, exhorting residents towards their own moment of *uvuswa*, or Christian rebirth.[51] Some, put off by these young firebrands, left the station, but the majority stayed, intrigued by the 'light and joy' in the faces of the young Zulu revivalists. Given the deep customary deference to elders, this youthful act of exhortation represented a considerable break from traditional generational norms.[52]

Gendered hierarchies were also up-ended during the revivals. Young women, more than their male counterparts, were expected to be subordinate, holding their tongues and serving the needs of the male-dominated household. But young women were also acutely aware of the personal and moral dangers that were found in the cities. During the revivals there are numerous examples of groups of young women spreading the message of sanctification not only to other women, but also to the men in their lives. One of the most astonishing moments in the 1896–97 revivals was what occurred at Umzumbe, a station located in the far southeastern corner of Natal and one not visited by Weavers in the nascent period of evangelical fervour. Demonstrating the virus-like nature of the revival message, young women from the girls' school located there returned for the start of the school year having clearly heard of what was happening in stations to the north and expressing a profound interest in the workings of the Holy Spirit. One of their teachers turned their attention to the New Testament book of Acts, and it was while reading this book, whose narrative focuses on the apostles' early missions following their endowment with the charismata, that on Friday 19 March the girls turned a morning Bible study held under the shade of banana trees into a day of consecration. As elsewhere, the girls confessed to a litany of sins before embracing the power of the Holy Spirit. Trapped inside by heavy rains in the following days, the girls passed the time in prayer, during which one of the girls claimed to have been spoken to by God, who bid her and her classmates to take their revival to *amakholwa* of the surrounding community.

When the rains abated, the small band of girls walked to the nearby Umzumbe church and led an impromptu service. Several men joined and were put 'under conviction' for their souls, crying out to Jesus for mercy. One of the men, a preacher, confessed that his life had become a lie; he had been living in sin and was a lost soul. He confessed all and expressed his elation at the willingness of God to 'abundantly pardon' and take him back into the Christian fold. The school principal at the AZM Umzumbe station commented on these matters: 'It seemed like a great search light – thrown upon the hearts of the church members – that marvellous power of the Holy Ghost bringing out inequities and sins hidden for long years.' Emboldened by their success, the girls then made their way from Umzumbe into the surrounding hills, preaching in kraals, outstations and other churches. Listening to the girls' testimonies, some homestead heads dropped to the floor and cried out, 'What must I do to be saved?' Others, in turn, entered states of semi-consciousness as they sensed a spiritual transformation. To the American missionaries, the sight of young Zulu women inducing old men into fits of tearful confession offered evocative evidence of the miraculous work of the Holy Spirit.

The revivals also profoundly altered a range of obligations between missionaries and *amakholwa*. For the latter, a central attraction of the Holiness message lay in the Christian purification of the self, following sanctification. So blessed, the *amakholwa* who adopted Weavers' message believed that, with careful vigilance, they could pursue sinless lives and achieve a state of grace that made all who underwent perfection 'brothers' and 'sisters' before God. Practically, what this meant was that Zulu Christians could claim spiritual equality with the Americans, shaking off the patriarchal relationship of children to a missionary father. Indeed, in most cases, the evangelical adherents could claim to be more fully people of faith than the white settlers around them who had not undergone revival. Missionaries who at first enthusiastically welcomed the revivals soon became concerned that the pastoral Christianity they had taught was being replaced by something too 'emotional'. One American noted that it would be their responsibility following the revivals to guide young *amakholwa* back to a more sober, well-trodden path by leading them, 'step-by-step to give precept upon precept, to boost this one up a hill of difficulty, to prop up that one against a chilling blast, to show by lesson upon lesson that serving Christ is being faithful in hoeing and grinding and studying, by telling the truth, by observing the rule of love, not by feeling feelings'.[53]

But any effort to draw *amakholwa* back into an older Christianity was doomed, for just as consecration allowed sinners the freedom to reveal their sins, so too did sanctification provide *amakholwa* with the authority and legitimacy to patrol the moral borders of their own churches, conduct their own services, and, in particular, to lead their own evangelisation efforts. At Mapumulo, the initial group of twelve revivalists quickly grew several times over, ranging far and wide through Natal and KwaZulu as they spread the Gospel. Following the initial revival, the Groutville congregation evidenced a 'missionary spirit from the pulpit to the pew and consecrated workers are continually going out to other parts'.[54] At Esidumbini, a group gathered at sunrise every Thursday for prayer and Bible study before breaking up into small groups to visit local homesteads.[55] When they met again the following week, leaders from each group reported successes and failures, recommended follow-up visits and suggested additional sites for evangelisation. At Inanda, 30 young lay ministers spread out across the neighbouring land, conducting weekly circuits so as to maximise their impact. After some of the *amaVoluntiya* visited the church at Umsumduzi, Nyuswa, its Zulu pastor, reported to the AZM: 'The work here is going with power indeed . . . The good news is that there is consecration of sins, throwing away of alcohol, smoking, and snuff tobacco. The young people have been greatly revived and are preaching in many places.' But demonstrating confidence in the power of his own sanctification, Nyuswa concluded his letter with a series of pointed questions: 'Am I Mr Harris's worker? [Harris being the missionary overseeing Umtwalumi] Am I not God's servant? Why am I under Mr Harris?'[56] At this critical moment *kholwa* youth had led Zulu Christians to high moral ground, an unassailable position from which they claimed sovereignty over their own institutions. While the era of the white missionary had not fully passed, *amaVoluntiya* represented the future of evangelisation in South Africa.[57]

Much of this future lay in urban areas. Almost inevitably the young *amakholwa* who had driven the revivals on the mission stations found that they needed to return to the cities. Speaking of the Esidumbini group a missionary noted that the young amaZulu involved 'would gladly remain at home to engage in the work for small salaries, forgoing the large wages of Johannesburg' but funds simply weren't available from the AZM to support them and many had migrated back. Once in the cities they reconstituted themselves into roaming evangelical bands. William Ngidi, one of the original band of twelve from Mapumulo, enthusiastically reported from Johannesburg: 'I preach out in the mines, and the Lord's work is going on rapidly and the people confess their sins and are converted and give themselves to the Lord.'[58] Within a few years in Durban, dozens of volunteers gathered every Sunday morning before dawn, held an hour of preparation through prayer, counsel and testimony, and then spread out into the city to hold services in barracks and other living quarters. They returned to the church before the 21h00 curfew to discuss their successes and failures and hand in tithes. An American missionary noted with awe that in one exhausting Sunday the *amaVoluntiya* he accompanied had preached to more than 2 000 people. 'Remember,' he urged his readers, 'they do not receive a penny. These men have been at their daily tasks right through the week. It means something for them to be up just as early Sunday as on other days.'[59]

Slowly, American missionaries recognised the new reality created by the revivals. No longer would they act as lords over their churches. By 1899 even those missionaries who had previously opposed giving daily control of the churches to a Zulu pastorate now admitted that their roles were irrevocably altered; the day of the American missionary ruling over an individual station as his personal fiefdom had passed.[60] In the years following the revival most of the AZM churches called *kholwa* pastors. For some twenty years, the AZM missionaries had prayed long and loud for their congregations to find '*moral earnestness*'.[61] When their prayers were seemingly answered by the revivals, they had little choice but to support 'God's Work', even as it shifted authority to a younger generation of Zulu Christians.

For *kholwa* youths, however, the revivals represented much more than their attainment of political control. The staid Congregationalism of their parents was replaced by a fervent Christianity that loudly promised the active and daily protection of the Holy Spirit, and rapid forgiveness should the need arise.[62] In this respect, Mbiya Kuzwayo's observations on his own life in the faith are enlightening: 'He was a good Christian before, all ready to receive those truths, but now says that he sees those things of God in such new light that it seems *as if he had never known them before*.'[63] Previously, Kuzwayo and other *kholwa* youths had freed themselves from the pastoral Christianity of their own parents and the missionaries, who tied their faith to its material potential to provide clothing, ploughs and brick homes. In unshackling Christianity, Holiness liberated urbanised Christian Zulu youth from expectations that they needed to follow their parents' footsteps in order to truly become worthy *amakholwa*. Given the growing exploitative nature of the colonial state and the brutality of city life, the revivals heralded a modern, more personal social transformation, which opened Christian worship to many more isiZulu-speaking Africans. They would increasingly embrace evangelical faith in the coming century to navigate between the worlds of traditional kinship and urban atomisation.

## Notes

1. *The Sent of God*, 3 December 1896, letter from Mbiya Kuzwayo. *The Sent of God* was the bi-monthly newspaper of the Hephzibah Faith Missionary Association, Weavers' mission, of which more will be said later.
2. Holiness and Pentecostalism are almost identical in theological thought. The one innovation that sets Pentecostals apart is their belief in glossolalia (speaking in tongues) as evidence of sanctification. After 1901, when a Holiness preacher in Kansas began advocating glossolalia, Holiness essentially became absorbed into the Pentecostal movement. Pentecostals are the second largest body of Christians (behind Roman Catholics) in the world today.
3. In the 2001 South African census, 69 per cent of some eight million African respondents in KwaZulu-Natal declared membership in a Christian church. See Statistics South Africa, *Census 2001: Primary Tables KwaZulu-Natal* (Pretoria: Statistics South Africa, 2004), pp. 24–28. The census is available online at: http://www.statssa.gov.za/.
4. Of the nearly 5.5 million Christians, some 2.5 million of them maintain membership in a mainline church, the largest of which is the Roman Catholic Church, with just over 800 000 members.
5. Most scholars have followed the work of Bengt Sundkler in his two groundbreaking studies of the AIC movement in South Africa: *Bantu Prophets in South Africa* (London: Oxford University Press, 1961) and *Zulu Zion* (London: Oxford University Press, 1976).
6. Although not without a protracted struggle, during which one of the missionaries presciently warned:
   I began to be afraid that the Crown may interfere with the rights of the natives. Reserve so little land that they will not be able to subsist on it, and the thing will be accomplished; for they will then have to ask permission to live on the lands of others, which will be granted on condition that they labor for their landlords. Here in their own country they will be made servants and beggars . . .
   See American Board of Commissioners for Foreign Missions Collection, Houghton Library Microfilm (henceforth ABM) Reel 175, Lindley to Anderson, 12 December 1845, p. 87.
7. The unrealised expectation was that *amakholwa* would eventually own these plots. In December 1893, Mfanefile Kuzwayo, the headman at Mapumulo wrote to the AZM:
   Some of us who are on the Glebe request to buy our land. This is because all of the areas around the Glebe are full and small now. And those who are already on the Glebe have spent a lot of money trying to beautify the area and have planted trees and built beautiful houses at their own expense. So we are making this request because we are tired of living

like birds who always wander the sky without a fixed place to stay. We want to make it clear that we are not happy to stay in these places because we know quite well that they do not belong to us. May the grace of our Lord Jesus Christ be with you if you approve our request.

Given how difficult it was for the mission to remove residents from mission lands, Kuzwayo and others were owners in all but name, but in the early 1890s *amakholwa* feared this was soon to change as Natal prepared to receive 'Responsible Government' from Britain, allowing the colony to manage its own affairs. Not surprisingly, many *amakholwa* felt betrayed in 1894 when the AZM agreed to hand legal control of the reserves to Natal. Left to the 'mercy of an intensely hostile colonial sentiment' *amakholwa* were, by December of 1895, 'already counting on the early sale of the reserve lands' to settlers. This did not happen, but the bitter taste over the experience coloured Zulu/missionary relationships for long after. See American Zulu Mission records, Natal Archives Repository, Pietermaritzburg (henceforth AZM) A/2/10, Mfanefile Kuzwayo to AZM, 27 December 1893; Bunker to Friends, 3 December 1895; AZM A/3/49, Goodenough to SNA, 25 June 1894; AZM A/3/49, AZM to members of the Ministry, 12 October 1895 and AZM A/3/46, Conclusions from studying the trust deed of AZM reserves, 1895.

8. ABM 180/42, AZM Annual Report for 1867–68.
9. Books became increasingly popular, and for many years the printing press owned by the AZM could not meet the demands of their newly literate, and apparently voracious, *kholwa* reading public.
10. Polygamy was never accepted by the Americans, but the debate had always revolved around the question of what polygamous men and women needed to do before entering the church. Following the financial windfalls of the Anglo-Zulu War, nearly a dozen *kholwa* men were disciplined for polygamy at Groutville alone. Among them were Umakabeni and Umyokana, two men who had moved from Aldin Grout's home school to become some of the earliest converts. They had translated their profits in a traditional manner, by buying cattle and exchanging them for second wives, who they clandestinely established off the stations at *inhlonhlo*, secondary cattle posts. When their actions came to light, the congregation at Groutville expelled the polygamous men. See ABM 212/216, Hance to Means, 15 May 1879.
11. Bridewealth was a particularly rancorous topic. Most of the older missionaries expressed sympathy for the plight of converts should it be forbidden. Younger missionaries, born and raised in the abolitionist milieu, saw the bridewealth custom as little less than a form of slavery and railed against it from the earliest moments of their arrivals in the 1870s. Not until the next decade, however, were they able to muster a majority to officially outlaw its practice by *amakholwa*. The battle between the two sides eventually led the director of the American Board to warn the younger missionaries: 'Your work is not to make American but Zulu Christians.' This was an admonishment the American evangelists rarely bothered to heed. See ABM 177/467–71, N. Clark to Zulu Mission, 2 June 1868.
12. Here I am following the lead of Benedict Carton's *Blood From Your Children: The Colonial Origins of Generational Conflict in South Africa* (Charlottesville, VA: University Press of Virginia, 2000).
13. The diamond mines did not lure Zulu migrant workers in the same volume as it did their Sotho neighbours. For an informative examination of Natal's colonial economy, both pre- and early industrial, see Bill Guest, 'The New Economy', in *Natal and Zululand From Earliest Times to 1910: A New History*, eds. Andrew Duminy and Bill Guest (Pietermaritzburg: University of Natal Press and Shuter & Shooter, 1990), pp. 302–23.
14. At Umtwalumi the government offered ploughs at cost in the early 1860s to any *amakholwa* willing to grow cotton for three years. Several young men took up the offer but abandoned cotton in frustration after the seedling would not take hold. See ABM 177/172, Umtwalumi station report, 1860–61.
15. Sydney Mintz, *Sweetness and Power: The Place of Sugar in Modern History* (New York: Viking, 1986). For Natal see, William Beinart, 'Transkeian Migrant Workers and Youth Labour on the Natal Sugar Estates 1918–1948', *Journal of African History* 32:1 (1991) and Patrick Harries, 'Plantations, Passes and Proletarians: Labour and the Colonial State in Nineteenth Century Natal', *Journal of Southern African Studies* 13:3 (1987).
16. ABM 175/987, A. Grout to Anderson, 3 June 1857; ABM 177/68, AZM annual letter, 1862–63.
17. ABM 188/88, Groutville station report, 1890–91; ABM 190/386–87, Bunker to Friends, 4 January 1897.

18. Charles van Onselen, *Studies in the Social and Economic History of the Witwatersrand, 1886–1914, New Babylon, New Nineveh* Vols. 1–2 (London: Longman, 1982).
19. David Coplan, 'The African Musician and the Development of the Johannesburg Entertainment Industry, 1900–1960', *Journal of Southern African Studies* 5:2 (1979) and Van Onselen, *Studies in the Social and Economic History*.
20. In a fascinating study, Keletso Atkins traces *amawasha* history back, not to Indian labourers as Van Onselen does, but to Durban of the early 1850s and the nearby Umgeni River where Zulu washermen, in the words of one source, dashed 'the brains out' of laundry for 'about a shilling a dozen'. For more references to and analysis of this 1850s period, see Keletso Atkins, 'Origins of the Amawasha: The Zulu Washermen's Guild in Natal, 1850–1910', *Journal of African History* 27:1 (1986).
21. Paul la Hausse de Lalouvière, '"The Cows of Nongoloza": Youth, Crime and Amalaita Gangs in Durban, 1900–1936', *Journal of Southern African Studies* 16:1 (1990).
22. *Natal Government Gazette*, 15 October 1896.
23. ABM 183, 582–83, Report of the Natal Missionary Conference 1890; AZM A/4/59, 'Point of Contact', paper presented by J.D. Taylor at Natal Missionary Conference, 1902. Taylor noted that white men frequently visited the African barracks with rum and cards, and that boys from the countryside learned, in this way, to drink and gamble. He also connected the rise of 'layita' gangs (*amalaita*), the organisations blamed for much of the crime in colonial Durban, on the influence of white men who used rickshaw pullers to tour the city's barrooms and brothels. For more on Durban's *amalaita* see La Hausse de Lalouvière, '"The Cows of Nongoloza"'.
24. Missionaries occasionally acknowledged the difficulties of being a poor Christian and the necessity of finding employment in the cities. The missionary at Inanda wrote: 'To wear the garb of civilisation they must have money to buy clothing and to meet the wants of their new life.' A/3/41, Lindley [Inanda] station report, 1890–91.
25. In 1895 the AZM built the 'Women's Durban Lodging House' for *kholwa* women visiting the city. It operated successfully until missionaries placed the project in the hands of the Durban businessmen who had originally contributed to its opening. Its closure didn't reflect lack of need, however, for even when fully funded the mission estimated the house only took in one per cent of those in town. Several prominent *amakholwa*, including Dr J. Nembula, urged the mission to permanently locate a female missionary at the house. AZM A/1/2, minutes volume VII, semi-annual meeting, 2–7 February 1895; AZM A/3/46, annual letter, 1895–96; AZM A/1/8, report of the Durban work, 1896.
26. AZM A/3/41, Amanzimtoti annual report, 1891–92. H. Marwick, Natal's SNA representative in Johannesburg, noted in 1896 that the bulk of *amakholwa* in the city worked as traders, transport riders and servants. He also noted that they were, with few exceptions, an upstanding and respectable group, including Fokoti Makanya, an AZM preacher discussed in more detail below. SNA 131/1896, Letter from H. Marwick, 14 May 1896. By 1895, the labour market had absorbed *amakholwa* seeking employment off the mission stations: AZM A/1/7, self-support committee, July 1895. See also Guest, 'The New Economy', pp. 302–14.
27. AZM A/3/41, Amanzimtoti Seminary report, 1896–97.
28. AZM A/3/41, Esidumbini station report, 1894–95; AZM A/3/41, Umzumbe station report, 1891–92.
29. *Amakholwa* repeatedly asked the AZM to establish a church in Durban and for a time the mission attempted to meet this request through an association with the local white Congregational Church. This deal fell through, however, when the Durban church failed to meet its pledge of support for the work. The AZM also criticised whites who sought to keep black churches out of their neighbourhoods. AZM A/1/2, AZM semi-annual meeting, 29–30 January 1885.
30. AZM A/3/46, Amanzimtoti station report, 1889–90. Two year later the AZM, forced to acknowledge the demand, opened the much larger Beatrice Street church.
31. AZM A/1/7, committee on mission work among the Zulu of Johannesburg, 1892.
32. AZM A/1/7, committee on Johannesburg work, 1893.
33. ABM 192/186, Curzon to Chairman or Secretary of the AZM, 1 May 1896.
34. AZM A/1/7, Committee report on meeting with Johannesburg church, 9 June 1896.
35. Like many other African independent churches, the ZCC was sensitive to the question of religious legitimacy. Following long-held missionary norms, the disaffected congregations passed a resolution inviting two *kholwa* preachers to be their pastors. Later, the ZCC took pains to explain its deeds, noting that its actions, including a consecration ceremony, had been in accordance with Congregational principles. AZM A/4/53, appointment of Shibe as minister, 20 February 1897.

36. James Campbell, *Songs of Zion: The African Methodist Episcopal Church in the United States and South Africa* (New York: Oxford University Press, 1995), p. 115.

37. For a discussion of the transformative properties of revivalism, see William McLoughlin, *Revivals, Awakenings, and Reform: An Essay on Religion and Social Change in America, 1607–1977* (Chicago: University of Chicago Press, 1978) and Jay Dolan, *Catholic Revivalism: The American Experience, 1830–1900* (Notre Dame: University of Notre Dame Press, 1978).

38. These included weeping, shaking, laughing uncontrollably, comas, writhing on the ground, and even barking. See Christopher Waldrep, 'The Making of a Border Society: James McGready, the Great Revival, and the Prosecution of Profanity in Kentucky', *The American Historical Review* 99:3 (1994): 767–84. For a perceptive work on these revivals, see Ellen Eslinger, *Citizens of Zion: The Social Origins of Camp Meeting Revivalism* (Knoxville: University of Tennessee Press, 1999). Eslinger challenges the view that the revivals represented a wild frontier religion for a people suffering through hardship and austerity. Instead, she argues, camp meetings offered participants an opportunity to reintegrate themselves into an American society that had changed dramatically following the end of the Revolutionary War and, echoing what the *amakholwa* were to accomplish through revival, to establish a common identity.

39. Gregory Schneider, 'A Conflict of Associations: The National Camp-Meeting Association for the Promotion of Holiness versus the Methodist Episcopal Church', *Church History* 66:2 (1997): 272.

40. 'The Close of a Notable Life: Obituary for Reverend George Weavers', *Tabor Beacon*, 30 April 1914; 'Obituary for Reverend George Weavers', *Mills County Tribune*, 30 April 1914 and Paul Worcester, *The Master Key* (Kansas City: Nazarene Publishing House, 1966).

41. The following account of the first days of the revival at Mapumulo is pieced together from the following sources: *The Sent of God*, 3 December 1896, letter from Mbiya Kuzwayo dated 30 September 1896, and letter from Frank Weiss dated 7 October 1896; AZM A/3/41, Mapumulo and Groutville Annual Report, 1896–97 and ABM 192/424–30, Price to Smith, 11 February 1897.

42. ABM 192/424–30, Price to Smith, 11 February 1897.

43. 'The Wonderful Revival', *The Missionary Herald*, August 1897, pp. 320–23.

44. *The Sent of God*, notice on Weavers' return to Iowa, 6 May 1897.

45. Weavers returned again in 1899 and during this second tour his fame had spread well beyond the AZM; he received numerous invitations from other mission bodies and even white congregations. He stayed until 1900, visiting several AZM stations he hadn't initially toured; he also spent considerable time in Johannesburg. Weavers returned a third time, in 1901, to set up Hephzibah's own mission, though he did not serve as a revivalist for the AZM. It is important to note that despite Weavers' great influence he drew few *amakholwa* away from the AZM – they had, by that time, successfully transformed the churches of the AZM into their own religious institutions.

46. In his annual report the missionary at Inanda wrote:

    Hundreds are now every Sabbath and during the week going forth to talk, hold meetings and preach to the people in the kraals. There has suddenly sprung into existence a mighty preaching force which is telling day and night the story of Jesus and of his salvation. Some of these men and women baptised by the Holy Ghost have become flames of fire to preach the Gospel and proving that they have indeed imbibed the spirit of the early Christians and showing as we think that they are working in the spirit of the Holy Master.

    See AZM A/3/41, Lindley Station Report, 1896–97.

47. *The Sent of God*, 11 February 1897, letter from M.E. Price and AZM A/3/41, Mapumulo and Groutville Annual Report, 1896–97.

48. Keith Breckenridge, 'The Allure of Violence: Men, Race and Masculinity on the South African Goldmines, 1900–1950', *Journal of Southern African Studies* 24:4 (1998); T. Dunbar Moodie, Vivienne Ndatshe and British Sibuyi, 'Migrancy and Male Sexuality on the South African Gold Mines', *Journal of Southern African Studies* 14:2 (1988) and Robert Morrell, 'Of Boys and Men: Masculinity and Gender in Southern African Studies', *Journal of Southern African Studies* 24:4 (1998).

49. After a week of revival, the AZM missionary Wilcox believed that all but four members of the congregation at Mapumulo had confessed to expulsion-worthy sins. But in the context of sanctification he was unwilling to follow these up with any disciplinary measures. AZM A/3/41, Mapumulo and Groutville Annual Report, 1896–97.

50. AZM A/3/47, Inanda Girls Seminary Report, 1896–97.

51. *The Sent of God*, 11 February 1897, letter from M.E. Price.

52. Nor did the revival's power to challenge norms end at the mission gate. At Mapumulo, a young male revivalist sent to pick up mail in a nearby town arrived at the post office and began preaching to several native policemen about their need for redemption. The policemen initially listened with amusement, but as the young man became 'drunk with the spirit', they became alarmed and threw him into jail. Undeterred, the young revivalist continued to preach, pray and praise God, rattling his cell with shouts of 'Hallelujah!' Unnerved, the police released him with the warning that he should never again return to fetch the mail and urged him to see a doctor for his illness. When he encountered another Christian on the road back to the mission, the two knelt down together to give thanks at the power of God in affecting his freedom. *The Sent of God*, 3 December 1896, letter from Frank Weiss.

53. AZM A/3/41, Amanzimtoti Seminary Report, 1896–97.

54. *The Sent of God*, 16 December 1897, letter from William Worcester, dated 5 November 1897.

55. AZM A/3/41, Esidumbini Station Report, 1896–97, AZM A/3/42, Esidumbini and Noodsberg Station Report, 1897–98.

56. AZM A/4/53, letter from Nyuswa to Bunker, 26 May 1897. In another episode, a group of boys from Amanzimtoti High School took an outbreak of dysentery at the school as a sign from the Holy Ghost that it was time to leave and preach to neighbouring traditionalists. The American principal disagreed. Fearing that a mass exodus might ensue, he forbade the boys' departure and threatened them with expulsion should they proceed. But the youths left anyway, filled with such 'spiritual pride'. The principal observed that 'they were sure they knew the Lord's will better than any or all of their teachers'. True to his word, the principal expelled many of the boys when they returned later in the school year. AZM A/4/59, Amanzimtoti Seminary Report, 1897–98.

57. AZM A/3/42, Inanda Station Report, 1898–99. Indeed, as the power of the group steadily increased over the years, they came to wield a disproportionate influence in the Congregational churches. In their zeal to ensure the purity of the churches, it became not uncommon for *amaVoluntiya* to clash with both missionaries and Zulu pastors. After over half a decade of revivals, an American missionary noted: 'To many Volunteers, membership means a higher order of purity and dedication than church membership. This can mean that a member will pride himself on being "better" than an ordinary church member.' Arthur Christofersen, edited by Richard Sales, *Adventuring With God: The Story of the American Board Mission in South Africa* (Durban: Robinson, 1967), pp. 129–30.

58. *The Sent of God*, 4 November 1897, undated letter of W.N. Ngidi would later play a key role in accomplishing the remarkable feat of bringing the Johannesburg wing of the ZCC back into the AZM fold.

59. *The Missionary Herald*, August 1902, pp. 348–52.

60. According to one missionary: 'It is an open question whether the time has not arrived for the people to assume control of their own evangelistic and pastoral work, looking to the missionaries for advice only. My personal feeling is that it has come or is near.' A reduced force of Americans would only act in the future as supervisors, advising, but not running the churches. ABM 190/450–51, Bunker to Smith, 9 March 1899.

61. ABM 183/417–48, AZM Annual Letter. Original emphasis.

62. I have gone into the theological underpinnings of this transformation in more detail elsewhere. See Robert J. Houle, ' "Today I am Delivered": Revival, Holiness, and the Naturalisation of Christianity in Turn of the Century Colonial Natal' (Ph.D. diss., University of Wisconsin, 2003).

63. ABM 190/424–30, Price to Smith, 11 February 1897; emphasis added.

*Chapter 19*

# Zulus, African Americans and the African Diaspora

ROBERT VINSON and ROBERT EDGAR

SINCE THE LATE nineteenth century, the amaZulu have captured the imaginations of African Americans. The popularity of film epics such as *Shaka Zulu*, histories of Zulu warfare, such as American Donald Morris's *Washing of the Spears*, the Zulu Social Aid and Pleasure Club (a pre-eminent New Orleans Carnival 'krewe'), pioneering hip-hop figures such as Afrika Bambaataa and his internationally known black nationalist group, the Universal Zulu Nation, and black nationalist leaders such as Malik Zulu Shabazz of the New Black Panther Party all attest to the salience of Zuluness in the African-American mind. This fact is even more remarkable because few African Americans claim blood ties with Zulu lineages.[1] This article demonstrates that these contemporary linkages have longstanding antecedents that can be traced to the influences of Zulu performers in American circuses and public exhibitions, Zulu students at American colleges and African-American travellers in colonial Zululand and Natal.

**'First American born in captivity': Zulu imagery in American culture**
The image of amaZulu became ingrained in the American mind around the time of the Anglo-Zulu War of 1879, when the American press featured the exploits of King Cetshwayo's regiments in their victory over the British at the battle of Isandlwana. During the European scramble for Africa, between 1885 and 1900, the amaZulu became a prominent symbol of both negative and positive African attributes. To many white Americans, the amaZulu represented an innate savagery, while to others – especially African Americans – they symbolised archetypal black manhood and resistance to European domination. As will be shown, Zulu visitors to the United States consciously reinforced these divergent perceptions.

The amaZulu appealed to the sensationalist instincts of Canadian-born promoter William Hunt, who saw enormous potential for displaying amaZulu to the so-called civilised world in exhibitions in Britain and North America. Shortly after the Anglo-Zulu War commenced, Hunt, who dubbed himself 'The Great Farini', dispatched an associate to South Africa to take several Zulu women to an exhibition in London.[2] In June 1879, six more amaZulu, whose authenticity was attested to by a Durban police sergeant, joined them. Billed as 'Farini's Friendly Zulus' and dressed in combat garb, they performed martial dances and hurled assegais.

After Farini merged his show with P.T. Barnum, the Canadian impresario presented four of the amaZulu – named Dingando, Possoman, Maguibi, and Ousan – as an opening act in Barnum's 'Greatest Show on Earth' at New York's Madison Square Garden. They toured with the Barnum show through northern and Midwestern American states. When a Zulu child was born in upstate New York, the show's route book recorded the event: 'Arrival into the world of the first American Zulu born into captivity, to use a Jumbonian expression . . . [T]here is a chance now of one of his many apprentices becoming President of this great republic.'[3] In Topeka Kansas, the *Daily Capital* of 13 August 1880 commented on one of their performances: 'The Zulus are a novelty to all visitors. They appear in native costume with their national weapons. They attract great attention, and seek to excite varied emotions in the minds of visitors.'[4]

Farini's Zulus also caught people's attention for other reasons. The *New York Times* reported the marriage of one of the troupe known as 'Zulu Charley' to an eighteen-year-old Italian music teacher, Anita Corsini, despite the strong objections of her father. After the ceremony, the couple went to the Brooklyn museum where 'Zulu Charley' had been performing a cultural skit, and 'the bridegroom took part in the usual Zulu war dances'.[5]

Some African Americans took advantage of the recognition of the amaZulu for personal gain or for reinventing their identities. Farini's Zulus, in particular, spawned many imitators. The entertainment magazine *New York Clipper* recorded instances in the 1880s of 'Zulu' performers – some of whom were whites in blackface – who performed at circuses and exhibitions. The figure of Zulu royalty inspired persons claiming to be sons of King Cetshwayo or other Zulu chiefs to seize the limelight and to lighten the wallets and purses of the unsuspecting. Borneo Moskego, for example, masquerading as a Zulu regent, collected offerings in 1893 at African-American churches in New Haven, Connecticut, for his 'benighted' brethren in Africa. He was finally arrested for taking money under false pretences after a person who had seen him posing in Milwaukee as Tippu Tip, an East African personage, reported him to the police.[6] In 1899 Private Thomas Taylor, an African-American soldier serving at Fort Alcatraz in San Francisco Bay, wove a story that he was the son of Zulu king 'Jerger' from the House of 'Okukudek' and that he and his ten sisters had been educated at Cambridge University.[7]

By the turn of the twentieth century, Mardi Gras performers in New Orleans were refashioning their acts to dramatise mythic Zulu history. In 1909, a group of African-American labourers belonging to a club called the Tramps attended a musical comedy, 'There Never Was and Never Will Be a King Like Me', which featured a send-up of Zulu politics. Shortly after that the Tramps began marching in the Mardi Gras parade as the Zulu Krewe. In 1916 they established the Zulu Social Aid and Pleasure Club.[8] Although the Zulu krewe's dress and accoutrements – raggedy pants, grass skirts, a king carrying a banana-stalk sceptre – bore no similarity to Zulu regalia, some have observed that the krewe's formation was in reality a biting social commentary on white domination and stereotypes of Africans and people of African descent.[9]

This use of Zulu narratives of the past served popularisers of black history in the United States. For example, in the 1920s journalist J.A. Rogers lionised African rulers who led resistance against European colonisers. He extolled King Cetshwayo and his soldiers as 'the pick of the pick of the human race' for inflicting 'on the British the most crushing defeat [at Isandlwana] that White men have experienced at the hands of any portion of a dark race in modern times'. Moreover, Rogers hailed Zulu chief Bhambatha, a leader of a rebellion in Natal in 1906, as a noble black nationalist 'who led the greatest revolt against white supremacy in modern times'. Rogers thought Bhambatha deserved to be revered in the same fashion as George Washington and other 'white patriots'.[10]

### 'Providential designs' of Zulu students in the United States and African Americans in Natal and Zululand, 1885–1930

The matriculation of Zulu students at American universities and colleges was a phenomenon quite distinct from the 'savage' Zulu exhibitionists who were in the United States for no discernible reason beyond entertaining gawking spectators and turning a profit for their bosses. By contrast, dignified Zulu students self-consciously tied their advancement – the continued acquisition of education, Christianity and cultural refinement – to that of their 'benighted' brethren in Africa. For a small portion of the estimated 200 to 400 black South African students who attended North American and English universities between 1880 and 1940, their educational mission was part of an implicit political project: to transfer knowledge learned in the United States in order to 'civilise' their fellow Africans and eventually end their subordinate status in South Africa.[11]

These students shared several basic characteristics. They hailed from *kholwa* (Christian) families, with most being affiliated to the Congregationalist American Board of Commissioners for Foreign Missions (ABM), an American organisation that established its first mission stations in Natal in the 1830s. The Zulu scholars tended to view the Hampton/Tuskegee model of industrial/agricultural training – which combined an ethos of self-help, morality and thrift with the learning of trades, agricultural production and domestic science – as an ideal vehicle for black advancement and helped transfer these educational standards to South Africa. Most importantly, their close ties with African Americans, including friendships with Booker T. Washington, the most famous proponent of the Hampton/Tuskegee model, links with Pan-Africanist organisations, and marriages to African-American women enhanced the Zulu students' privileged place within a small community of African elites who would nurture a democratic vision for South Africa.

The ABM/Zulu student pipeline to America opened with the passage of John Nembula to the Midwestern United States. In 1881 he accompanied ABM missionary S.C. Pixley to the United States to assist in the creation of a Bible in isiZulu. Nembula subsequently studied at Ohio's Oberlin College, the University of Michigan and the Chicago Medical College before returning to Natal in 1889 to become a district surgeon there. In 1893, he also helped to establish a hospital (later named McCord) at Adams mission. In 1895 he joined Joseph Booth's short-lived African Christian Union (ACU), which attempted to utilise co-operative agricultural and industrial training to create self-sufficient African communities. Pan-Africanist in orientation and with African-American and African officers, the ACU's objectives included the repatriation of Western-hemisphere blacks to an independent Christianised Africa. Nembula showed that Christianity and education would provide opportunities to prove African racial fitness as civilised citizens of modern society. Unfortunately, Nembula died prematurely in 1896, creating an open position of leadership, which was ably filled by his associate, John Langalibalele Dube.[12]

John Dube used Nembula's example to connect most Zulu students in the United States during the early twentieth century. In 1871, Dube was born into a *kholwa* community in Inanda district, Natal. His family had converted to Christianity shortly after a Zulu regiment killed his grandfather, a minor chief, in 1837. Dube's father, James, was one of the earliest ordained African ABM ministers and a prominent landowner and trader. Young John attended ABM secondary schools at Inanda and Amanzimtoti Theological School (later Adams College) and attended Oberlin during his first American sojourn (1887–92).[13] During his years abroad, he lectured widely on Christianity and industrial education, calling them the primary avenues to 'civilised' status. Accompanied by his wife Nokutela, he returned to the United States in 1896 and earned a theological degree from Brooklyn's Union Missionary Training Institute, along with his ordination, in 1899.

Dube had also come to the United States to raise funds for a Tuskegee-style industrial school in Natal that would train Africans to be Christianised, self-sufficient tradesmen instead of unskilled, exploited workers in a white-controlled colonial economy. To this end, he made a visit in May 1897 to observe the Tuskegee model, to meet with Washington and to speak at the school's commencement services. Affirming Tuskegee's methods, Dube's rousing address made him the 'hero of the commencement'.[14] In 1900, Dube also made an impassioned plea to African Americans, entitled 'A Zulu's Message to Afro-Americans'. This remarkable document argued that African Americans had a divinely ordained mission to help Christianise the African continent. The crucible of slavery and the coming light of Christianity had 'civilised' African slaves in the Western hemisphere and thus equipped them with a pious work ethic and modern technical skills that were to be transmitted to their racial cousins in Africa. Indeed, R.L. Scott, a West Indian-born Tuskegee graduate, heeded the call as he accompanied Dube back to South Africa to help establish Ohlange, where he became a popular teacher, mason, baker and merchant until his death in 1944.[15]

A handful of African-American missionaries also made their way to Natal. When Baptist missionary Charles Morris, a Howard University graduate, visited Natal in 1900, he echoed Dube's theology of redemption by arguing that the suffering African Americans endured in bondage gave them a special responsibility to return to Africa to civilise and uplift the continent. '[T]he American Negro,' Morris maintained, 'had been marvelously preserved and Christianised for a purpose, and that he was destined to play a star part in the great drama of the world's development.'[16] He extolled the amaZulu as 'the finest built people on the face of the earth', who benefited from a 'cracked corn' diet and vigorous physical activity in the hills. Morris called on African-American professionals to settle in Natal and bring their technical skills and entrepreneurial abilities to guide the amaZulu on the correct path to progress and civilisation. One of the few African-American missionaries who settled in Natal was Simon Crutcher of Shenandoah, Iowa, representing the Gospel Workers of America. Billing himself as the 'Black Moody' (after Dwight Moody, a white American evangelist), Crutcher arrived in Natal after the Anglo-Boer War and established a close relationship with John Dube in the few years he stayed there.

This African-American presence alarmed British colonial officials who regarded African Americans – especially African Methodist Episcopal Church (AME) clergy – as subversives who fuelled a seditious Ethiopian movement sweeping through Natal in the early twentieth century. 'Ethiopianism' was a name given to African independent churches that broke away from European mission denominations.

African police detectives kept a close watch on Dube, Crutcher and R.L. Scott, reporting Dube for boasting that 'when they [African Americans] come, then we will talk a lot about our country. It will be well if at sometime, the "first shall be last & the last shall be first." '[17] Comments like this fed the paranoia of white officials who were reluctant to allow African Americans to stop over or settle in Natal. Responding to Charles Dube's inquiry in 1910 about whether African Americans would be allowed to enter Natal, immigration officials politely informed Charles that any 'Negro arriving here from America' would be dealt with under existing immigration law. However, in private, the officials strongly opposed an 'invasion of American Negroes', basing their view on their experience in the 1890s with Joseph Booth who had been deported for his 'pernicious teachings'.[18]

Dube mentored successive Zulu students, including his younger brother Charles Dube and Isaac (Pixley) Seme, his cousin and future co-founder (in 1912) of the South African Native National Congress (SANNC), the forerunner of the African National Congress (ANC). Dube took Charles to the United States in 1897 and placed him at Wilberforce University in Ohio, an institution affiliated with the AME, which had just inaugurated its South African mission programme. Charles graduated from Wilberforce in 1904 and became Ohlange headmaster the following year. Isaac Seme resided with John Dube in Brooklyn before enrolling at Mount Hermon Preparatory School in Massachusetts. Dube paid half of Seme's $100 school costs, a considerable sum in 1898; Reverend S.C. Pixley paid the other half and convinced associates to pay Seme's fees for the duration of his time in the United States. The young Seme demonstrated his gratitude by changing his first name from Isaac to Pixley. He graduated from Mount Hermon in 1902 and visited Tuskegee the following year, telling Washington that 'we need your spirit in Africa'. Seme then enrolled at Columbia, earning a BA in 1906. He also won Columbia's top prize for oratory with his essay, 'The Regeneration of Africa', an affirmation of Africa's present and future contribution to world civilisation. Seme went on to earn a law degree at Oxford in 1910 before he returned to South Africa, where he and Dube joined forces again to launch what would become the SANNC.[19]

American audiences were quite curious about these Zulu students, who in their numerous public lectures demonstrated that Africans could debate successfully with or against Westerners. Yet students like John Dube also asserted that their non-Christian past contributed to their 'backwardness' relative to whites, a condition that necessitated financial support and public sympathy from African Americans willing to embark on mission work that would 'civilise' Africans. Madikane Cele, a Zulu graduate of Hampton Institute in 1912, exemplified this tendency. Cele was also within the Ohlange orbit as his father taught at the school. In 1907, Dube sent Cele to North Carolina's Slater Industrial School, then to Hampton, where Cele specialised in blacksmithing and wheelwrighting. Cele proved to be a sensation in America, performing in theatre productions that narrated colourful tales of Zulu life. Cele's embellished depictions, including hunting tigers in Africa, gave him the kind of notoriety that propelled him onto the political stage with Booker T. Washington during a New York conference. Upon graduation, Cele and Julia Smith, his African-American wife and Hampton classmate, returned to Zululand as Hampton-sponsored missionaries who also taught at Ohlange.[20]

By the 1920s, some Zulu students, like other Africans, began to reject the industrial education model as an auxiliary arm of white philanthropic paternalism. Sibusisiwe Makanya is a striking example of this phenomenon. Born in 1894, she studied at Inanda and Amanzimtoti. She left a secure position as teacher at Inanda in 1923 to operate a night school from her Umbumbulu home and to found the Bantu Purity League, an organisation particularly dedicated to the maintenance of virginity and high moral standards amongst unmarried African girls. By 1927, she had caught the attention of Charles T. Loram, whose Columbia University dissertation had been published in 1917 as *The Education of the South African Native*. His prominent posts in South Africa's Department of Education, connections to American philanthropic organisations like the Phelps-Stokes Fund and the Carnegie Corporation, and his position as Professor of Education at Yale University stamped Loram as one of the world's leading authorities on African education during the inter-war years.[21]

Loram was also a leading segregationist who looked to the rural-based Hampton/ Tuskegee industrial education model to produce African workers who would accept a subordinated role in the country's industrialising economy without challenging South Africa's white-over-black racial caste system. In 1927 Loram convinced Thomas Jesse Jones, the leading Phelps-Stokes official and an enthusiastic proponent of industrial education, to sponsor Makanya and her colleague Amelia Njongwana, both experienced teachers, to join the staff at South Carolina's Penn School. The Penn School was an industrial education centre designed to train teachers to establish rural-based community training centres in their home societies – a philosophy in keeping with South African segregationist conceptions of rural areas as the natural homes of Africans. Both women, coming from a rapidly urbanising society, became dismayed at a curriculum that studiously ignored urban social work conditions, and a 1928 transfer to Tuskegee did little to alleviate their grievances. Njongwana accepted Phelps-Stokes's offer to be transferred to the Atlanta School of Social Work, where she graduated and returned to South Africa. Makanya, however, severed her ties with the organisation, knowing that she now had no immediate means of funding her education or her passage back to South Africa.

Makanya paid for her education at the Congregationalist-affiliated Schauffler Training School in Cleveland, Ohio, and at Teachers College, Columbia University, by lecturing frequently on Zulu life and customs and by doing menial labor. At Columbia, Makanya was under the tutelage of Mabel Carney, a renowned liberal arts educator who had visited Natal in 1926.[22] While John Dube grumbled to his Phelps-Stokes allies that Makanya was 'ungrateful' to her initial patrons, he himself seemed to recognise the limits of industrial education. In 1927, he sent his own nephew Frederick to liberal arts-oriented Morehouse College, then on to Columbia University where he graduated with an MA degree in 1932. Frederick subsequently returned to South Africa with Marie, his African-American wife, who taught music at Adams College.[23]

These students were now amongst the most educated black people in South Africa. Dube, in addition to his ANC work, his attendance at the 1921 Pan-African conference in London and his continued leadership of the cash-strapped Ohlange, also became a leading proponent of an ethnic Zulu nationalism. He was also a co-founder of numerous Zulu cultural nationalist organisations, including the Zulu National Council (Inkatha) in 1922 and the Zulu Society in 1935, and became the first African to receive an honorary degree from the University of South Africa.[24] Pixley Seme, for his part, served as ANC president during much of the 1930s and as editor of the ANC newspaper *Abantu Batho*, and founded the African Farmer's Association while operating a thriving law practice. Makanya, in addition to the

Bantu Purity League, helped to establish, with Dube as chair, the Bantu Youth League to preserve Zulu cultural traditions and champion the Christian wholesomeness of Zulu youth. The Bantu Youth League and its 25 branches in Natal included several secondary and night schools, as well as a popular community centre in Umbumbulu. Her work must have been quite impressive; Dr A.P. Stokes, upon visiting her in Natal in 1932, recommended to his Phelps-Stokes Fund – the same entity that Makanya had spurned in America – that they support her work with a grant of at least $100.[25] Charles and Frederick Dube devoted their lives to teaching, a profession long nurtured by the African elite.

Several Zulu students never returned to South Africa. One was Arthur Bidewell Langa, who followed Seme from Amanzimtoti to Massachusetts and Mount Hermon in 1910. Unlike Seme, Langa's persistent financial difficulties and an unwillingness to accept the dictates of his white patrons caused Mount Hermon officials to expel him after two years. Langa's attempts to attend Oberlin Academy, Benedict College and Clark College failed, presumably from a lack of funds. He soon disappeared from the historical record. A 1936 inquiry into his whereabouts, conducted from South Africa where it was precipitated by the need to settle his deceased father's estate, failed to uncover clues to Langa's fate. Another Zulu expatriate was Isaac Msomi, who was a 46-year-old skilled welder when he met South African Prime Minister Jan Smuts and members of his delegation attending the landmark United Nations deliberations in San Francisco in 1945.[26] Born in Natal's Stanger district, Msomi received his education at Mariannhill Catholic mission before leaving South Africa in 1921 and entering the Carnegie Institute in Pittsburgh to commence a three-year course in mechanics. After Carnegie, he found skilled welding jobs in Detroit (where he worked for the Ford Motor company), Chicago and San Francisco. Msomi's long sojourn in the United States allowed him to tell Smuts about the differences between *de jure* segregation in the American South and *de facto* segregation in the rest of the country. Despite noting the pernicious effects of restrictive covenants in housing and racially exclusive trade unionism, Msomi believed that South African racism was far more corrosive than its American cousin. And he seized opportunities in the United States that dwarfed those available to his fellow Zulu students, who returned to a South Africa inexorably marching toward apartheid.[27]

Between 1879 and 1945, Zulu students and visitors in the United States gave dimension and depth to prevailing caricatures of the Zulu in lurid military accounts, theatrical exhibitions and shameless impersonations. Enamoured with the Zulu students, African Americans embraced the contradictory representations of their visitors. Some African Americans, like Simon Crutcher and Charles Morris, strengthened these linkages by travelling to South Africa, conducting religious and educational work among the amaZulu and contributing to American press reports that portrayed the amaZulu as icons of black masculinity and nationalism.

## Notes

1.  An exception is Col. W. Mallory, who claimed that his Zulu father was captured by Boers and taken to Mozambique, where he was sold to a Spanish slaver and taken to South Carolina. Born on a North Carolina plantation around 1825, Mallory escaped to freedom in 1860 and eventually settled in Canada. For his account, see Col. W. Mallory, *Old Plantation Days* (3rd edition, n.d.). A copy was found in the Academic Affairs Library of the University of North Carolina and has been placed on a website, North American Slave Narratives (http://docsouth.unc.edu/mallory/menu.html).
2.  See Shane Peacock's biography, *The Great Farini: The High-Wire Life of William Hunt* (Toronto: Viking, 1995).
3.  This child could have become a president because American citizenship is automatically conferred on any person born in the United States. Shane Peacock, 'Africa Meets the Great Farini', in *Africans on Stage: Studies in Ethnological Show Business*, ed. Bernth Lindfors (Bloomington: Indiana University Press, 1999), p. 93.
4.  The continuing popularity of the amaZulu as 'the pick of the human race' motivated Robert Ripley of 'Ripley's Believe It or Not' for other reasons. He hoped to display amaZulu at the Chicago's World Fair in 1933 and 1934. They had impressed him when he spent two months in South Africa on a round-the-world trip in 1933. Thus, he approached the South African government for permission to bring over a Zulu 'rickshaw man with the largest and highest headdress, a medicine man with the most complete outfit and a warrior with the most colorful regalia' for exhibition at his 'Odditorium' at the Chicago grounds. By then, however, the South African government had come to the conclusion that it was not in the interests of either itself or Africans for black people to be taken overseas for exhibitions and turned Ripley down. South African Government to International Oddities, Telegram, 10 July 1933; O.L. Simpson to Ralph Close, Ripley's Believe It or Not, 31 January 1934 (BWA 81/157/2, Vol. 3) Embassy of South Africa, Washington, DC (National Archives, Pretoria).
5.  *New York Times*, 27 August 1881.
6.  *New York Times*, 25 September 1893.
7.  *San Francisco Call*, 2 July 1899.
8.  See Joseph Roach, *Cities of the Dead: Circum-Atlantic Performance* (New York: Columbia University Press, 1996), pp. 18–25. See the website of the Zulu Krewe at www.mardigrasneworleans.com/zulu/.
9.  Roach, *Cities of the Dead*.
10. *Norfolk Journal and Guide*, 6 April and 1 June 1929.
11. R. Hunt Davis, Jnr. estimates that there were between 100 and 400 African students being educated overseas between 1890 and 1914 and it is a fair assumption that the minimum number of Africans would have been 200 between 1885 and 1930. See Davis, 'The Black American Education Component in African Responses to Colonialism in South Africa', *Journal of Southern African Affairs* III (1978): 65–83.
12. See, for example, *Imvo Zabantsundu*, 7 May 1889 and 9 February 1888.
13. Oberlin students renamed its main administration building after Dube during the mid-1980s to symbolise their successful efforts to force the college to divest from apartheid South Africa. See www.oberlin.edu/newserv/01mar/african_national_congress.html (accessed July 2004).
14. *Montgomery Advertiser*, 28 May 1897; *Birmingham News*, 1897, cited in W. Manning Marable, 'Booker T. Washington and African Nationalism', *Phylon* 35:4 (1974): 401. Dube also made a commencement address at Hampton's graduation ceremony in 1897.
15. *Ilanga Lase Natal*, 20 October 1905. Other diasporic black people who served at Ohlange included the West Indian-born preacher Simon Crutcher and the African-American Young Women's Christian Association (YWCA) worker Katherine Blackburn.
16. *Cleveland Gazette*, 31 March 1900.
17. Report re 'John Dube' of Inanda Mission Station, Chief Commissioner of Police, 13 December 1902 (Secretary of Native Affairs, File 1/4/12 C6/1903, Pietermaritzburg Archives Repository [PAR]). We thank Michael Mahoney for this reference. See also Shula Marks, *Reluctant Rebellion: The 1906–1908 Disturbances in Natal* (Oxford: Oxford University Press, 1970).
18. P.I.R. Officer to Charles Dube, 26 July 1910; A.U. Secretary Interior to Secretary of Interior, 27 July 1910; P.I.R. Officer to Charles Dube, 2 August 1910 (IRD [84 2350/1910], PAR).
19. Richard Rive and Tim Couzens, *Seme: The Founder of the ANC* (Johannesburg: Skotaville Publishers, 1991). One of Seme's close friends at Oxford was Alain Locke, the first African-American Rhodes scholar.

20. Cele, Dube's nephew, broke with Hampton in 1920 to affiliate with the Lott Carey African-American Baptist organisation.

21. For more on Loram and his close ties to American philanthropy, see R. Hunt Davis, 'Charles T. Loram and an American Model for African Education in South Africa', *African Studies Review* 19:2 (September 1976): 87–99 and his 'Producing the "Good African": South Carolina's Penn School as a Guide for African Education in South Africa', in *Independence Without Freedom: The Political Economy of Colonial Education in Southern Africa*, eds. Agrippah T. Mugomba and Muogo Nyaggah (Santa Barbara: University of California, 1977), pp. 83–112.

22. For more on Makanya and Carney, see Richard Glotzer, 'The Career of Mabel Carney: The Study of Race and Rural Development in the United States and South Africa', *International Journal of African Historical Studies* 29:2 (1996): 309–36. Carney's close relationship with Makanya influenced her decision to mentor several other amaZulu, including Reuben Caluza and Don Mtimkulu, during the 1930s.

23. Frederick Dube made national headlines in the black press by threatening a Morehouse cafeteria worker with a gun after a series of disagreements. See 'African Prince With Empty Gun Cleans Out', *Philadelphia Tribune*, 24 December 1931 and 'Lose Dignity When African Pulls Gun', *Amsterdam News*, 23 December 1931. It is important to note that Phelps-Stokes co-ordinated Frederick Dube's placement at Morehouse and also arranged for a financial sponsor for his fees. Phelps-Stokes also sponsored John Dube's 1926 Ohlange fundraising trip.

24. Shula Marks, *The Ambiguities of Dependence in South Africa* (Baltimore: Johns Hopkins Press, 1986), pp. 69, 71.

25. Shula Marks, *Not Either An Experimental Doll* (Bloomington: Indiana University Press and Pietermaritzburg: University of Natal Press, 1987), p. 35.

26. D. Smit, 'Note of Interview with Isaac Msomi, A Zulu Who Called upon Me at My Room at the Fairmont Hotel, San Francisco on 1.6.1945 (June 1)' (D.L. Smit Papers, Cory Library, Rhodes University).

27. Msomi remained in the United States and died in Wayne, Michigan in 1981.

*Chapter 20*

# Chiefs, Cattle and 'Betterment'
## Contesting Zuluness and Segregation in the Reserves

ARAN S. MACKINNON

IN THE EARLY twentieth century economic and ecological stresses deepened rural hardship, particularly in Zululand, a territory segregated from white South Africa. To contend with rapidly declining indigenous agricultural output during years of worldwide depression and periodic drought, government segregationists remoulded two pillars of the precolonial past. The central features of this reorganisation were tighter regulation of chiefs and 'betterment' schemes designed to shore up crumbling 'tribal' reserve land. But in Zululand segregationist discourse was not a one-way conversation. It also hinged on the actions of Zulu chiefs who struggled to maintain their customary authority and control over the material base of Zuluness.

During the 1920s and 1930s, the imposition of greater governmental restrictions on traditional power created tensions between local and national white officials. The central state in Pretoria attempted to bind Zulu chiefs to colonial administrators, who in turn needed to use traditional authorities to drum up labour for white-owned commercial interests. By contrast, the Natal Native Affairs headquarters in Pietermaritzburg, which oversaw magistrates in Zululand, feared a resurgence of any legacy of the formidable Zulu kingdom and aimed, instead, to curtail the sway of chiefs. Betterment schemes were less controversial among native affairs personnel, who embraced these programmes to offer a way of combating what they perceived to be 'deleterious methods' of cultivation and 'overgrazing' of Zulu 'scrub' animals.[1] In order to 'improve' reserve agriculture, state officials introduced the Livestock Improvement Proclamation No. 31 of 1939, a law that sought to reduce Zulu herds drastically and replace 'scrub' livestock with commercial breeds.

Agricultural improvement and betterment had a profound impact in Zululand, particularly in Chief Isaac Molefe's ward in the southern district of Nquthu. Such policies in large measure challenged Molefe's followers' understanding of the relationship between pastoral practice and cultural identity, not only by culling the base of Zulu survival, but also fraying ties between stock-keepers and their chiefs. For many Zulu farmers in the reserves, agro-pastoralism still comprised the foundation of both the homestead economy and Zulu ethnicity.

Chief Isaac Molefe always maintained an ambiguous relationship with people in Nquthu. Beginning in the 1920s, large numbers of African tenants evicted from neighbouring white farms streamed into Nquthu, putting greater pressures on the land. Rather than try to alleviate the overcrowding and ecological burdens, Molefe, the son of a government-appointed chief, enhanced his own position through corruption and strong-arming. He dispatched his *izinduna* (chief's deputies) to fleece the recent arrivals and intimidate newcomers preaching the radical politics of reclaiming African land rights. Moreover, Molefe continued to ride roughshod over well-established commoners, imposing indiscriminate fines and reserving the arable plots for his loyal followers. His favourite target was the so-called progressive, or modernising *amakholwa* (Christian Africans). They tended to challenge traditional chiefly authority. While many *amakholwa* embraced a scientific ('progressive') approach to commercial livestock 'improvement', especially sheep husbandry, Molefe sought to prevent them from developing an independent economic footing through their sales of wool.[2] In this context, increasing interventions by the Native Affairs Department (NAD) in Nquthu to reclaim land, halt soil erosion and regulate stock movement precipitated even wider disaffection, but this time oppositional currents were primarily directed at the South African state.

Chief Molefe responded to the meddling and unrest by agitating against betterment. Many of Molefe's followers then rallied around him and other Nquthu chiefs in the hope that these leaders could defend their interests. Despite tightening segregationist rule, Zulu commoners still saw their chiefs as bulwarks against unwanted intrusions. Clearly, many rural amaZulu on the fringes of industrialised South Africa also envisioned their cultural identity as intrinsically linked to land and cattle in the reserves. Broadly, the Molefe case highlights the paradoxical consequences of government intervention in rural South Africa. More specifically, this story demonstrates the limits of white supremacy when confronted by stalwarts of Zuluness.

### The material basis of Zuluness: Land, agriculture and cattle

In the early twentieth century the male Zulu domain of cattle-keeping managed to survive far better than the predominantly female domain of agriculture. While amaZulu produced fewer staples, they managed to increase their herds. Cattle remained an essential part of the customary Zulu economy. They had productive value in milk, hides and meat and they had reproductive value through the natural increase of the herds. Cattle were also used to cement social contracts such as marriage through the exchange of bridewealth or *ilobolo*. In 1895, prior to extensive colonial encroachment and the virulent rinderpest epizootic, there were an estimated 200 000 African-owned cattle in Zululand. Over the next 25 years, with effective herding practices and state veterinary measures, the herds recovered and reached their pre-rinderpest level by 1921. Thereafter, Zulu stock-keepers concentrated on amassing wealth and prestige through cattle.[3]

However, by the early decades of the twentieth century, state land expropriations and impinging white settlement had greatly restricted arable soil available to Zulu cultivators. As a result, the production of principal crops such as maize fluctuated perilously. In 1923 the total maize yield in the reserves was approximately 241 000 two-hundred-pound bags, but in 1946, a drought year, maize production had plummeted to 167 000 bags.[4] While Zulu families grew much of their own food in the 1920s, thereafter they increasingly relied on income secured from migrant labour and breeding and selling cattle to meet subsistence needs. It was in this context of rapidly declining reserve agriculture and growing reliance on the cattle economy that the state launched its plan to improve agrarian practices in the reserves, provoking Zulu resistance in Chief Isaac Molefe's ward. Molefe perceived this intervention as threatening his authority over local productive forces and started to mobilise opposition to state efforts to improve the reserves.

### 'Betterment' for the 'progressives', resistance from the 'scrub herders'

After 1920 Chief Molefe balanced the needs of his ward against unremitting pressure from the NAD to manage the demands of industrialising South Africa for Zulu labour and taxes. Despite staunch support from key Pretoria administrators, Molefe was constantly at odds with white Natal officials and had, on more than one occasion, drawn censure for his recalcitrance. For example, the Native Commissioner (NC) overseeing Nquthu, F.W. Ahrens, charged Molefe with being 'rude and impudent' after the chief launched a campaign against betterment.[5]

In fact, Molefe had long suffered harassment from Ahrens's office. In one correspondence, Ahrens disparaged the chief as 'weak, simple, secretive, suspicious and stubborn', adding that 'these qualities may be inherited: his father died in the Mental Hospital here'.[6] Many government-supporting Zulu authorities, such as the neighbouring Nquthu chief Mdhlalose, seemed to agree with official views that resistance to betterment was tantamount to 'lunacy'. Such opposition was likely to provoke state repression and curb progress for those who desired to implement modern farming and stock-keeping techniques.[7] For Mdhlalose and other 'progressives', longstanding Zulu agricultural practices threatened their ability to engage in market-oriented agro-pastoralism with a view to selling their goods to white buyers from the neighbouring farming districts and in Durban. By contrast, for Molefe and his traditionalist followers, reclamation represented the loss of Zulu customary autonomy: to choose how they, as the majority in Nquthu, would seek to survive.

An adept manipulator of state bureaucracy, Chief Molefe did not shrink easily from external challenges or backbiting internal politics. He knew how to pit officials against one another to get his way. He had already successfully disseminated a rumour that he had precipitated the replacement of NC Ahrens with a new NC, E. Lowe, in 1937. Molefe even claimed that his ally, the Secretary for Native Affairs (SNA),

D.L. Smit, had become disillusioned with Ahrens after Smit learned of a gathering radical protest movement, comprised of Zulu workers and peasants seeking more land, better living conditions, and political rights – the ICU *yase* Natal (Industrial and Commercial Workers' Union of Natal) operated openly in Zululand. Perhaps to show Zulu chiefs that they ought to rebuff ICU advances and back the state, Smit singled out the Natal administration and Ahrens for their bungling persecution of Molefe 'at a particularly sensitive time'. Shortly thereafter, Ahrens saw the writing on the wall and moved on to an otherwise distinguished career as a circuit court magistrate.[8]

By November 1938, however, the endless political manoeuvrings required of Molefe began to take a serious toll on his health. Insisting that he could 'no longer serve [his] people', Molefe requested leave from his position, this time to seek treatment for bronchitis in Durban, but the government refused permission.[9] Nevertheless, in December 1938 Molefe abandoned Nquthu, returning only intermittently over the next few years. Although he never proved it, the new NC Lowe suspected that Molefe went to Durban to meet members of the African National Congress (ANC) organising opposition to betterment in Nquthu and elsewhere in Zululand. Perhaps Lowe's assessment had some kernel of truth. While evidence to link Molefe and the ANC is suggestive, other traditionalist Zulu chiefs were looking to establish bonds with regional ANC leaders. The ANC, for its part, recognised the advantages to be gained from mobilising rural masses around the defence of Zulu practices that had long safeguarded domestic security. One of these vital practices was the keeping of 'scrub' cattle, which underpinned the ruling houses of Zulu elites, who allocated herds of Nguni (Zulu) cattle to feed regiments and maintain alliances.[10] By 1944, whether Molefe was in Durban or Nquthu, he remained stalwartly against betterment, and for this 'insubordination' he was officially suspended for three years.[11] His suspension, however, was far from a foregone conclusion in the protracted struggle with the local agents of the white state.

When Molefe came back to Nquthu in late 1947, the Livestock Improvement Proclamation No. 31 was already sparking widespread successful resistance.[12] In response to the promulgated NAD guidelines that restricted sheep herding, Chief Molefe obstructed reclamation of grazing land in his traditional jurisdiction. The South African state, nevertheless, erected additional shearing huts and sorting pens for the wool-producing merinos of isiZulu-speaking mission-educated 'progressives'. Molefe promptly wrote a stinging letter to the SNA protesting that he had never been apprised of these government plans.[13] He also condemned the 'anti-Zulu' actions of Zulu Christians in his ward for their support of the eradication of indigenous 'black' sheep. Although the breeds of cattle and smaller stock had great symbolic value in the making of Zulu ethnic identity, the SNA was not interested in these cultural subtleties; his angry reply to Molefe stated that the improvements were for the good of Nquthu, and that the matter was no longer open for discussion.[14] The good of

Nquthu did not extend to Molefe's followers, who witnessed firsthand what betterment signified: the culling of their valued animals. To bolster the quality of 'superior' sheep and cattle, the NAD set out to execute large numbers of 'scrub' stock, which officials considered to be inferior and destructive.[15]

Officials continued to impose distinctions between 'progressive' pastoralists who sought to improve their herds and 'Zulu scrub owners' who let their cattle graze in fragile grasslands cordoned off by white government.[16] Thus, the majority of amaZulu whose life strategies revolved around subsistence and opposition to betterment were pitted against the few amaZulu who could profit from agricultural trade in national markets and benefit from reclamation schemes.[17] The battle lines over idealised Zuluness, either for or against, were now drawn in the realm of livestock husbandry.

### Notes

1. Chief Native Commissioner's (CNC) files and correspondence, Natal, CNC Vol. 42A N2/8/2 (X), 39/1, Smit to CNC, 14 November 1936.
2. See Resident Magistrate and Native Commissioner Files for Nquthu (NQU) district, 1/NQU 3/4/1/1, 2/7/2, Reports of the NC to the CNC, 26 August 1929, 24 September 1929 and 6 January 1930.
3. Rinderpest was a devastating cattle disease that struck South Africa in 1896–97. It was the collapse of rural agriculture, in part however, which led to the veritable 'explosion' of the Zulu cattle herds. See A. MacKinnon, 'The Persistence of the Cattle Economy in Zululand, South Africa, 1900–50', *Canadian Journal of African Studies* 33:1 (1999): 98–136.
4. The population of Zululand increased by 34 per cent from 1921 to 1946, from 257 000 to 391 000. Statistics compiled by the author from Union of South Africa, *Report on Agricultural and Pastoral Production for 1923, Agricultural Census No. 6*, 1923, U.G. 25–'25, Chief Native Commissioner's Series, Vol. 97A, 112/110, District Reports for Zululand, 1930–1948, Union of South Africa, Social and Economic Planning Council, *Report No. 9, The Native Reserves and their Place in the Union of South Africa*, U.G. 32–'46 (hereafter, SEPC) and Union of South Africa, *Agricultural and Pastoral Census of the Union*, 1950, U.G. 34–'50.
5. Ahrens was reflecting upon his earlier experiences with the chief dating back to the 1930s. See his commentary on Molefe's career in Resident Magistrate and Native Commissioner Files for Nquthu district, 1/NQU 3/4/2/1, 2/1/2/1, Acting NC Martin to CNC, 20 September 1944.
6. See 1/NQU, 3/4/1/1, 2/7/2, NC to CNC, 10 July 1929. In fact Molefe's father, Hlubi, passed away peacefully at his home after a brief stay at the Charles Johnson Memorial Hospital for treatment of complications probably from malaria.
7. Ibid., annual reports for 1936. Molefe later brought a civil suit against Chief Mdhlalose for defamation. Mdhlalose used such 'defamatory' terms when he claimed that Molefe's opposition to the 'progress' of betterment was 'lunacy'.
8. 1/NQU, 3/4/1/4, 2/38/2/4, SNA to CNC, 19 June 1936. For F.W. Ahrens's life and career, see his autobiography, *From Bench to Bench* (Pietermaritzburg: Shuter & Shooter, 1948).
9. 1/NQU, 3/4/1/4, 2/38/2/4, NC to CNC, 8 December 1938.
10. For an elaboration of this political development see N. Cope, *To Bind A Nation: The Zulu Royal Family under the South African Government, 1910–1933* (Pietermaritzburg: University of Natal Press, 1994) and P. la Hausse de Lalouvière, 'History and Ethnicity in the Careers of Two Zulu Nationalists: Petro Lamula (*c.*1881–1948) and Lymon Maling (1889–*c.*1936)' (Ph.D. diss., University of the Witwatersrand, 1991).
11. For the details of Molefe's chequered career, see 1/NQU 3/4//1/1, 2/7/2.

12. This was provided for by the Natives Trust and Land Act of 1936. For a further discussion of the Proclamation, see B. Hirson, 'Rural Revolt in South Africa: 1937–1951', (paper presented at the Institute of Commonwealth Studies Postgraduate Seminar, No. 2, 1978); T. Lodge, *Black Politics* (London: Longman, 1983), pp. 3, 82; L. Platzky and C. Walker, *The Surplus People: Forced Removals in South Africa* (Johannesburg: Ravan Press, 1985), pp. 45–46, 93–94; T.R.H. Davenport and K.S. Hunt, *The Right to the Land* (Cape Town: David Philip, 1974), pp. 10, 44–46; J. Yawitch, *Betterment: The Myth of Homeland Agriculture* (Johannesburg: South African Institute of Race Relations, 1982), and for the official policy formulation see the Report of the NEC, pp. 10–13.
13. 1/NQU, 1/1/5/30, 3/4/2/4, copy of Molefe's letter to the SNA, 21 December 1937.
14. Ibid., SNA to CNC, 16 January 1938. For Smit's alleged 'liberal' stance, see A. MacKinnon, 'Land, Labour and Cattle: The Political Economy of Zululand, *c.*1930–1950' (Ph.D. diss., University of London, 1996) Chapter 1.
15. MacKinnon, 'Persistence of the Cattle Economy'.
16. For a further discussion of this difference, see for example, J. Ferguson, 'Bovine Mystique', *Man* 20 (1985): 647–74.
17. A similar point is made by P. Delius with regard to 'betterment' and Bantu Authorities in Sekhukuneland. See his *A Lion Amongst The Cattle* (Portsmouth: Heinemann, 1996).

*Chapter 21*

# 'Death is not the End'
## Zulu Cosmopolitanism and the Politics of the Zulu Cultural Revival

PAUL LA HAUSSE DE LALOUVIÈRE

IN 1917 A.B.H. NTULI, a mine hospital attendant, labour recruiter and dealer in animal hides, recorded the formation in Johannesburg of the Zulu Institute. His report, which appeared in *Ilanga lase Natal*, the mouthpiece of the Natal Native Congress,[1] captures something of the nationalist self-assertion that the Institute sought to galvanise in response to fears of racial extinction:

> [N]o success can come to any people except through co-operation and organisation, by means of . . . our own institutions, industries and businesses . . . [T]his Society is only the first step in our future hope of being one day able to supply all our needs strictly from within our own ranks . . . [to] rescue [us] from a life of misery and degradation for want of proper avenues of livelihood . . . [I]t is deplorable to think what the future of the children might be unless we of this generation leave something in life for them to live for . . .[2]

The Zulu Institute was a patriotic association, one of whose central purposes was to address a basic existential anxiety of Zulu migrants in temporary exile on the Rand: that in the event of their death far from home they would be accorded proper burial or their bodies returned to their kin. While the Zulu Institute has long since slipped from the historical record, it was probably one of the earliest burial societies on the Witwatersrand and the first self-consciously urban Zulu ethnic association in South Africa.

While the recent history of such ethnic organisations has attracted some scholarly attention,[3] our understanding of the creation of African ethnicities in early industrial South Africa remains very patchy.[4] Even more opaque is the history of ethnic identity and migrant association amongst the educated Christian (or *kholwa*) members of the large isiZulu-speaking population working in South Africa's industrial heartland, despite the fact that in the first two decades of the twentieth century graduates of Natal mission schools regarded employment on the Rand as a virtual rite of passage.[5]

The following narrative seeks to open a window on the history of the *amakholwa* on the Rand within the broader context of African nationalist politics in Natal and Zululand between 1900 and the early 1920s. Despite the fact that they ranged from down-at-heel harness-makers to mine compound managers, members of this elite were a clearly identifiable stratum within Rand society. As skilled and educated migrants, they moved between the goldfields and their homes in Natal and Zululand disseminating a new consciousness of the dangers of urban industrial society and of the ways in which modernity had, as one Zulu writer evocatively put it, 'reduced the dimensions of the earth'.[6] This chapter argues that intellectuals within this elite, spurred on by their experience of cosmopolitan life, played a vital role both in supporting a broader process of reimagining the Zulu nation in a globalising age and in shaping a form of nationalist politics in the isiZulu-speaking heartland that reflected this new identity.

As in the case of those black South Africans who travelled abroad to study or fight in the First World War, life in the distant mining towns of the Reef provided a space for skilled isiZulu-speakers to develop a cultural and political self-awareness – a cosmopolitanism – largely unimaginable before they left home.[7] And while the Witwatersrand was much closer to their ancestors' graves than the spires of American and Oxford colleges, or the mud of Flanders, it was sufficiently distant and dislocating to serve as a powerful stimulus to ethnic solidarity and patriotism. Zulu cosmopolitanism on the Rand, therefore, was a complex, ambiguous response to this anxiety of belonging amongst educated amaZulu. As much a cultural identity as a set of political ideas, Zulu cosmopolitanism had its roots in the Victorian liberalism and belief in Christian progress associated with the Natal mission stations. Its most important features, however, derived from two sources. The first of these was a desire to reform Zulu identity so as to make it speak to the concerns of a society undergoing disorientating and traumatic social change. The second was the result of an attempt to negotiate and domesticate radical ideas such as socialism and, more particularly, transatlantic notions of racial liberation and black economic self-sufficiency in the later 1910s.[8] Both were to produce the ethnic patriotism and racial nationalism characteristic of Zulu cosmopolitanism – an ideology that also provides a basis for a fresh understanding of the radicalisation of black politics on the Rand during and immediately after the First World War.

One dramatic index of the extent to which South Africa's industrial revolution altered isiZulu-speaking communities in Natal and Zululand was the vast number of gold coins offered in payment for hut tax by Zulu migrants returning from the Witwatersrand mines in the late nineteenth century. Indeed, the 'Kruger pound' entered Zulu folklore as a sign of both wealth and dislocation.[9] By the 1890s, the resilience of African homestead production had given way to intense struggles to retain land, pay taxes and control agricultural production, particularly in the Natal midlands and southern Zululand. In the process the crowded Natal reserves were transformed into major labour-exporting areas for white employers.[10] Then, in 1896, rinderpest carried off up to 90 per cent of cattle in some districts. At the time of the Bhambatha Rebellion (1906–08), over a third of the African male population of Natal and Zululand was engaged in some form of wage employment. After a half-century of migrancy, Zulu wage labourers were an enduring feature of colonial urban labour markets, particularly in Durban and Johannesburg. Indeed, in 1910 an estimated 80 per cent of adult males in Zululand entered migrancy to support their rural families. During that year, 34 679 Africans in Natal sought work in the Witwatersrand, nearly half of whom found jobs as mineworkers.[11]

The impact of industrialisation on the 20 000-strong isiZulu-speaking Christian African population (*amakholwa*) was no less dramatic.[12] In Natal, which had seen some of the most intensive evangelising in the world, thousands of mission-educated isiZulu-speakers had established themselves as successful peasant farmers by the 1880s. The improving *kholwa* farmer, expert in the use of the plough and Bible, combined cultivation with artisanal and entrepreneurial activities such as shoemaking, stone masonry and wagon-driving. Education and land conferred respectability on a social class whose members professed, like the prominent landowner Johannes Kumalo in 1863, to have 'left the race of [their] forefathers'. And even in Zululand proper, where chiefly authority, a homestead economy and the prevalence of polygyny inhibited mission enterprise, the rise of 'progressive' *kholwa* communities could be noted in the late nineteenth century. Yet the fervour of converts' faith in commercial farming, education and literacy brought them no closer to their dream of becoming British subjects.

Industrialisation further differentiated *kholwa* society, whose members ranged from magnates such as William Africa of Ladysmith, an owner of 1 600 acres of land, to humble, landless harness-makers and semi-skilled labourers.[13] After the granting of responsible government to Natal in 1893, the future of the *amakholwa* looked increasingly bleak. Subject to racially discriminatory laws and without an effective political voice, they found themselves locked in unequal competition with white farmers. Compounding this vulnerability within the changing regional political economy, the series of natural disasters after 1896 dealt progressive farmers, including over 1 500 African landowners, a blow from which many never recovered.[14] By the turn of the century, indebtedness, the ever-smaller yields of marginal agriculture and declining opportunities in trades such as transport-riding, had driven hundreds of struggling landowners and their educated sons to join thousands of Zulu migrants in search of work in the industrial centres of the Transvaal.

In the inhospitable environments of mine and compound, migrants took refuge in social solidarities rooted in language, age and kinship. In many respects this was hardly surprising; if anything, the migrant experience forged stronger ethnic identities

– in the historian John Lonsdale's words, 'Modern tribes were often born on the way to work.'[15] The corporate sense of belonging amongst Zulu migrants, which in turn nourished white stereotypes of, and vicarious attachment to, 'the proud Zulu', emerged full-blown at the outbreak of South African War in 1899, when an informal army of more than 7 000 Zulu workers, released from industrial employment across the Rand, gathered together and marched back to their homesteads in Natal and Zululand.[16] During the same period the Rand labour market manifested an increasing degree of ethnic job specialisation, of which the Zulu 'houseboy' and self-employed Zulu *amawasha* (washermen) were striking examples.[17]

While we possess an outline of a narrative of the history of Zulu migrants on the Rand, it is striking that the history and consciousness of the urbanised *amakholwa*, particularly those who made temporary homes for themselves on the goldfields, still eludes scholars. One could argue that this is precisely because in the sprawling, smoke-filled wood-and-iron landscape of the Witwatersrand, isiZulu-speaking mission-school graduates blended into a capacious culture encompassing numerous languages, creolised musical styles and syncretic religious movements.[18] In some respects this was certainly true. Yet there is evidence that, like manual labourers, educated isiZulu-speaking migrants not only created niches of informal control in the skilled job market, but also came to place a new emphasis on their shared identities and regional origins.[19]

The experience of Lymon Malinga, the Ohlange-educated son of a prominent African landowner and founding member of the Natal Native Congress (NNC), could stand for many others of his generation.[20] In 1910 he made his way from Newcastle in northern Natal to the Rand, probably in the company of an age-mate, Joel Maduna, with whom he had grown up on the same *kholwa*-owned syndicate farm. Much like Malinga, Maduna turned his back on the unpredictable future offered by his 29 acres of land and handful of cattle and, equipped with a Standard Five education, seized the opportunity to work on the Rand.[21]

Both young men were recruited as clerks (*umabhalana*) at Simmer Deep mine and over subsequent years these comrades-in-time-keeping separated and moved from one industrial employer to the next until, in 1918, they reunited at the Consolidated Main Reef West mine. During the intervening period Lymon Malinga's father, Petros, (now reduced to penury by disastrous land speculation) and his uncle Charles left for the Rand and found jobs as clerks: Petros at C.M. Hadley, the labour recruiters, and Charles at the New Comet mine. The vocation of clerk, which paid up to ten times the monthly wage of a mineworker, attracted scores of individuals with Malinga's social background, men whom white employers sometimes described as 'very respectful' and 'reliable'. They included the Inanda landowner Elka Cele, one of the first 'white collar' Zulus on the Rand mines; Stephen Molife, the son of one of the only African voters in Natal, who worked at Jumpers Deep; Robinson Deep's Peter Sioka, the (Lovedale) mission-educated son of Chief Dirk Sioka of

Pietermaritzburg; and future South African Native National Congress (SANNC) leader Saul Msane, an ambitious man who rose to the position of compound manager at the Jubilee and Salisbury mine after the South African War and emerged as one of the most influential Zulu leaders on the Rand during this period. 'The Zulus', as one white mine manager put it, 'have always played the game.'[22]

The Zulu clerk was only the most visible member of this elite community, which, particularly in the wake of the 1908 depression, incorporated legions of overseers, interpreters, teachers, clergymen, traders, typists, shoemakers, harness-makers, printers, labour touts and general brokers. Amongst this first wave of landless, unfulfilled younger sons of *kholwa* notables (many of whom were also Natal Congress members)[23] was a knot of professionals that included the Oxford-educated lawyer Pixley Seme and his Lincoln's Inn colleague, Alfred Mangena. Along with Saul Msane and Selby Msimang – a clerk and interpreter for a Johannesburg labour recruiter and then Seme's legal clerk – they were key isiZulu-speaking founders of the SANNC.

Whether in a transatlantic context or the polyglot environment of the Rand, displacement and social antagonisms generated by class formation led many members of the Zulu elite to reimagine their self-identity and social relations. As was the case in multi-ethnic industrial settings the world over, these reflections were a stimulus to a defensive enlargement of concepts of kin.[24] When the *kholwa* notable M.S. Radebe confidently declared, 'I am a Zulu [of Sesutu extraction]',[25] he anticipated the cultivation and spread of an ethnic identity that suited a global age where the stereotypical valorous Zulu was a well-established trope. Charles Dube, the American-educated brother of John Dube, described this phenomenon in 1907, evoking the terms of pure black manhood largely inconceivable a decade or so earlier: 'Among all the black races found in South Africa none surpasses the Zulus in physique and intellect . . . I am delighted to know that Cetywayo [*sic*], our former king, had the honour of representing us in the Royal House. Nearly everywhere you go the Zulu is looked upon as a man . . .'

Dube's expressed solidarity for the Zulu king and his racial origins revealed an acute sense of the dangers of social extinction in a class-ridden industrial civilisation. Here, for all to read, was an incipient politics of difference laced with racial tension. 'The Indians and Chinese', Dube added, 'have taken our positions in the canefields and [on the] Rand. Soon the avenues of Manual Labour will be closed to us, and we shall become servants to Indians and Chinese.'[26] John Dube himself pointed to the evisceration of indigenous peoples in Australia and North America as evidence of 'the utter impossibility of resisting the forces of the wonderful thing which the white man calls civilisation'. He continued:

> The question is how is the Zulu to join in this grand march of civilisation?
> Our advice to him is to commence at once to build up industries of his own, to
> leave off being entirely dependent upon the white man and to help

himself . . . Don't lose time; work while it is called day, for the night cometh when no man can work.[27]

John Dube's lament echoed the increasingly ubiquitous cultural idiom among literate amaZulu in Natal and on the Rand, particularly after the Bhambatha Rebellion. The ruthless repression of this uprising in 1906 provided the Zulu elite with a terrifying metaphor of racial eradication, fuelling their growing fear that the 'traditional' past would be severed from the unstable, modern present.[28] This Zulu-inflected Edwardian pessimism gave birth to new forms of *kholwa* identification with ordinary amaZulu, along with a growing appetite for Zulu history and an increasingly politicised sense of the Zulu past.[29] 'That we are indebted to foreigners for the dawning of Zulu literature', Dube thus bitingly commented to one of his colleagues at this time, 'is a dream invented by [you]. Long before the Europeans ever thought of the Zulu nation,' he continued, 'Zulu literature existed not in printed books, but in [the] mind of Zulu poets and orators who transmitted it from generation to generation.'[30]

This new sensibility also fostered that most enduring feature of twentieth-century African nationalism in South Africa – the co-operative organisation, which sought to defend the nation through the collective mobilisation of its resources. Amongst the first such bodies was Saul Msane's 1907 Native Centralisation Scheme (or *Isivivane*). Popularly known as 'Mayi-Mayi' (from whence the Johannesburg 'Mai Mai' market takes its name), Msane was a Natal landowner who combined his duties as a mine compound manager with land speculation and labour recruiting.[31] Borrowing vocabulary from Charles Dube's lexicon, Msane explained that the central aim of *Isivivane* was to promote co-operative land purchase and transfer of trade 'carried on by Indians' into African hands 'by establishing businesses from the central organisation under native management'.[32] By the early 1900s an undertow of anti-Indianism had emerged as a feature of collective self-assertion amongst Zulu intellectuals.

Saul Msane was perhaps the most prominent member of the small but influential Westernised Zulu diaspora on the Rand that played an important role in what I have elsewhere described as the first major Zulu cultural revival of the twentieth century[33] – a programme of ethnic and racial regeneration spearheaded by *kholwa* intellectuals seeking to integrate their vision of a morally unified community with a repackaged Zulu past. The experience of Zulu migrants informed this imaginative nation-building exercise, which in turn drew inspiration from debates conducted in print and in political, church and social meetings across the gold fields and throughout Natal and Zululand. At stake here was not only the creation of a new sense of Zulu communal identity but also the very definition of the meaning and objects of the Zulu nation itself – a process that would transform the prosaic time kept by the mine clerk and the providential time of the burial society into the transcendent temporality of the nationalist intellectual. This desire for moral regeneration is evocatively captured in the patriotic thought of the Zulu writer Magema Fuze, who early in 1918 entitled his series of essays linking Zulu and religious history 'Umuntu Kafi Apele' (A person does not die, he becomes complete).[34]

Early twentieth-century Zulu nation-building was a fraught process because *kholwa* identity hinged on converts distancing themselves, at least rhetorically, from their 'tribal' roots. Indeed, for these individuals without social recognition from traditional Zulu chiefs and their followers – who variously derided *amakholwa* as *amambuka* (traitors), *amaRespectables*, *izemtiti*, (the exempted), and Black Englishmen – resurrecting Zulu identity did not require an unconditional return to precolonial political and customary arrangements. Far from being a rejection of modernity, the *kholwa* rediscovery of their Zulu roots was a cultural nationalist initiative for its control. For this reason there was no necessary contradiction between the growing elite interest in Zulu folklore, language and history and those transatlantic and pan-ethnic ideas, which after 1912, animated the isiZulu-speaking, Rand-based architects of the SANNC such as Seme, Msane and Mangena. In seeking to mobilise a wider constituency in the years after Union, isiZulu-speaking intellectuals moved with ease in ambiguous terrain, simultaneously promoting the slogans '*Vukani Bantu!*' (Awake Africans!) and '*Pambili MaZulu!*' (Forward Zulus!).[35]

For Zulu intellectuals at home and on the Rand, the early African nationalist rallying cry '*Vukani Bantu*' thus evoked a complex set of nationalist longings, amongst them a surging Zulu ethnic consciousness more sharply defined and eagerly promoted by Natal's white segregationists in the decade after Union. Barely a year after the formation of the SANNC, prominent white Natal Congressmen began calling for territorial separation along racial lines and the restoration of the Zulu royal house. Then, in 1914, the NNC passed a resolution calling for the division of the 'White House [Natal] from the Black House [Zululand]',[36] a startling mobilisation of ethnic nationalism linked to the passage of the Natives Land Act and the death of Dinuzulu in exile in 1913.

The momentous Land Act undermined African rural independence in general but also struck a particular blow against *kholwa* farmers by restricting the amount of land available for African land purchase to specific 'scheduled' areas. It was a provision that created a fresh basis for elite identification with the plight of dispossessed Zulu. The new legislation drove isiZulu-speaking Congress leaders, notably John Dube and his colleagues in the Johannesburg area, Saul Msane and Pixley Seme, to launch their first political campaign in rural Natal and Zululand. Crucially, however, they never expressed outright rejection of the principle of territorial and racial separation. On the contrary, they and other influential figures such as Chief Martin Luthuli embraced the idea of radical segregation, but made this stance conditional upon a more equitable division of land. Between 1912 and 1914 the NNC briefly split into two factions, with Dube opposing Luthuli, not through any principled opposition to segregation, but rather because the former regarded the latter's separatism as impracticable. As Dube argued in a letter to Prime Minister Louis Botha in early 1914: 'We make no protest against the principle of segregation so far as it can be fairly and practically carried out. But we do not see how it is possible for this law to effect any greater separation between the races than obtains now.'[37]

If anything the popular Zulu response to the death of King Dinuzulu who, like many of his subjects, had been exiled to the Transvaal after the Bhambatha rebellion, added ballast to the idea that Zulu nationalist demands for land and political rights might be realised through segregationist policies. Dinuzulu's passing awakened powerful Zulu restorationist sentiment, which emboldened Natal Congress leaders John Dube and Pixley Seme to capitalise on these passions by – according to confidential official reports – 'labouring quietly and diplomatically amongst the Zulu speaking people' in order to secure 'a complete reunion of the Zulu Nation and thereby a resuscitation and revival of the Zulu Royal House and power'.[38] The reality, of course, was somewhat more complex. Rivalries and personality clashes involving isiZulu-speaking Congress stalwarts were an endemic feature of their 'big man' patronage politics. Dube, for one, was at loggerheads with Msane in Johannesburg over the conduct of the *Isivivane*; tensions also ran high between Mangena and Seme in their Johannesburg law practice. Moreover, both shared an uneasy relationship with Dube.[39] And while Zulu traditionalists in the heart of the old Zulu kingdom might have hailed John Dube as the 'New Moses', they could equally scorn Saul Msane as *ikhafula*, a derogatory term for an isiZulu-speaker from Natal whose ancestors were 'spat out' from Zululand.[40] Chiefs and headmen also greeted NNC plans for land purchase in Zululand with suspicion. Taking little notice of bickering Congress leaders, the Zulu royal family was too preoccupied – at least around 1914 – with renegotiating its position in relation to both traditionalist politics and the segregationist state.

While the political courtship between Congress leaders and the Zulu monarchy remained fraught, it did support the growing ethnic frame of reference of isiZulu-speaking nationalists in Natal and on the Rand. This was perhaps best registered in the co-operative movement, which enjoyed an astonishing renaissance after 1910 and canvassed popular support on the basis of appeals to both ethnic identity and racial solidarity. Pixley Seme, for example, established the Native Farmers' Association of South Africa in 1912 with a view to purchasing land – an organisation that bore a striking resemblance to the Zulu Industrial Improvement Company established by John Dube in 1908 'to ameliorate the condition of the Zulus and to improve their prospects for time and eternity'.[41] Then, in 1913, John Dube and Pixley Seme opportunistically mooted the establishment of a Dinuzulu Memorial Fund shortly before Saul Msane resurrected *Isivivane* in Johannesburg and renamed it the Native National Land Settlement and General Corporation of South Africa Limited. Msane's ambitions received a boost from Seme and another prominent Zulu Congress leader,

J.T. Gumede, both of whom threw their considerable reputations behind the organisation.

In 1916 these elite efforts to link the Zulu royal house to co-operative initiatives and NNC politics received significant new momentum from the Union government's limited recognition of Dinuzulu's heir, Solomon, along with a promise of his possible future confirmation as Zulu king. If anything, this attempt by the state to harness the popularity of the Zulu monarchy to serve government 'native policy' (and, in the short term, aid the recruitment of Zulu men for labour service on the Western Front) further embedded segregationist ideas in the political imagination of Zulu intellectuals.[42] But, as subsequent events demonstrated, there was a price to be paid for this flirtation with state ideology. Barely six months after Solomon's recognition as paramount of the uSuthu, in a dramatic coup, John Dube was forced to resign as president of the SANNC ostensibly because of his support for the principle of segregation. The SANNC, some of whose Transvaal leaders had unfairly come to view Dube as a remote leader based in Natal,[43] had sidelined not only a major intellectual, but also a leader originally elected as a unifying figure.

It would be misleading to view Dube's departure as part of a purge of isiZulu-speakers in the SANNC. In fact his Zulu colleague and rival, Saul Msane, was promptly elected its secretary-general in 1917. Nonetheless Dube's fall from grace was a defining moment in the history of African nationalism in South Africa. Indeed, his plight, which arguably had been prefigured in the Zulu cultural revival and the ethnic turn in nationalist politics in Natal, also breathed new life into nationalist mobilisation on the basis of appeals to Zulu history, language and ethnic identity. [44] Evidence of this can be found in the isiZulu press, where a range of subjects were increasingly subject to intense coverage and debate – including, for example, questions of language purity, the preservation of Zulu music and the social significance of Zulu customs. Articles dealing with the passing of the old Zulu military aristocracy, the future of isiZulu publishing and the purpose of writing works on Zulu history were also covered with novel urgency.[45] Although Zulu intellectuals in Natal drove much of this cultural debate, the Zulu intelligentsia on the Rand evidently followed these developments closely and it was to the goldfields that calls for the 'conservancy of IsiZulu' and reflections on the efficacy of establishing a monument to Shaka, for example, could be traced.[46]

This febrile literary output was an index of political turmoil and uncertainty, but it was on the Rand, paradoxically, that the most startling consequences of the coup that toppled Dube were to be found. Within weeks of S.M. Makgatho replacing Dube as Congress president, A.B.H. Ntuli, entrepreneur-extraordinaire and proprietor of the AmaZulu Trading Company, announced the formation of the Zulu Institute in language that managed to combine a sense of the terror of extinction ('misery and degradation') with a feature so vital to cultural nationalisms the world over: the idea of temporal regeneration and collective immortality.[47] An association that was at heart a burial society thus became a means of mobilising isiZulu-speakers around the fate of the nation. While it might be tempting to dismiss the Zulu Institute as the product of an obscure inspiration, the evidence suggests that Ntuli's political and cultural imagination was not uniquely his own, but was also shared by other isiZulu-speakers. The Institute reflected key elements of Zulu cosmopolitanism – a new ethnic patriotism framed by a racialised economic nationalism – and prefigured one significant reaction of the Zulu elite to the changing political climate on the Rand.

Ntuli founded his organisation as rampant inflation destabilised the economy of the Witwatersrand. Between 1918 and 1920 the soaring cost of living, combined with falling wages, led to the immiseration of workers and sparked strikes and popular protest (including anti-pass agitation) spearheaded by the Transvaal Native Congress (TNC). During this tumultuous period the African elite in the leadership ranks of the TNC, according to Philip Bonner, were radicalised and then fragmented along ideological lines.[48] Although Bonner is silent on the extent to which cultural identity and ethnic consciousness might have shaped the black politics of this period, it is evident that the Zulu nationalists on the Rand were drawn headlong into the radical ferment. The case of Reverend Gardiner Mvuyana, a charismatic isiZulu-speaking Natal preacher attached to the American Board Mission (ABM) in Johannesburg, is especially revealing in this respect.

In 1917, just after the leadership of the SANNC shifted decisively to the Rand, Mvuyana and his black colleagues broke from the ABM, complaining that their views were stifled and that they were excluded from the management of church property. Mvuyana's mostly isiZulu-speaking congregation apparently shared his belief, for they joined his breakaway African Congregational Church (ACC), led by a *kholwa* network that included a graduate of the Hampton Institute in America, the Reverend Q.M. Cele. A year later Mvuyana invited Solomon kaDinuzulu to lay the foundation stone of his flourishing church, an invitation that the government refused on the king's behalf, fearing his involvement with a controversial churchman, variously described as 'virulently anti-white', an 'excellent specimen of the better class Zulu' and sponsor of 'hero-worship of the Zulu kings from Tshaka down'.[49] These sentiments were a rough-hewn recognition of the combustible mixture of ethnicity and a racialised identity that came to characterise the outlook of many Zulu notables more generally on the Rand.

As worker discontent intensified and a section of the TNC, supported by the International Socialist League, planned a general strike, key members of the isiZulu-speaking nationalist intelligentsia began convening meetings of the 'Zulu Nation on the Rand' on the premises of the ACC. It would seem that many members of a brittle middle-class social grouping that constituted the Rand's Zulu elite recoiled in fear from the militancy of black workers, whose number included thousands of Zulu migrants. Certainly this was the case with the Congress 'big man' Saul Msane, who became a casualty of growing worker radicalism. By mid-1918, he stood condemned in the Transvaal's black press for being 'thick with the whiteman' because of his opposition to strike action. According to *Abantu-Batho*, the fiery mouthpiece of the Congress on the Rand founded by Pixley Seme in 1912, this was a betrayal symbolised by his European attire: a frock coat and silver hat.[50] Another Zulu public figure and TNC notable, Reverend M. Caluza, who divided his time between preaching and publishing isiZulu religious tracts in Johannesburg, appears to have succumbed to a similar fate.[51] That left C.S. Mabaso, editor of *Abantu-Batho*, an assimilated member of Johannesburg's multi-ethnic African middle class, as probably the only prominent Zulu active in the ranks of the TNC leadership during the industrial unrest between 1918 and 1920.

But if Msane was pilloried as *Isita ka Bantu*, the 'Enemy of the People',[52] this begged the question 'which people?'. Certainly not those in the Zulu Institute, which by early 1919 appears to have transformed itself into the Zulu National Association (ZNA) – an organisation which, despite being open to all Africans, was led by *kholwa* notables from Groutville in Natal and betrayed its fear of foreigners by writing into its constitution a provision 'excluding East Coast Natives' from membership. In addition to being a burial society, the Association intended to raise loans, purchase property, employ servants and establish clubs, stores, hotels and eating-houses.[53] Its president was Chief Martin Luthuli (uncle of future ANC president Albert Luthuli) and its secretary was A.D. Mxakaza, a clerk at Simmer Deep mine. Together they assembled a committee that included Saul Msane and J.H. Langeni, a veteran clerk at the Colonial Bank and Trust Company, entrepreneurs such as A.W.G. Champion (future provincial secretary of the Industrial and Commercial Workers' Union [ICU] in Natal), A.B.H. Ntuli himself and Ephraim kaTshumi, a tailor and general factotum of Natal's Qwabe people on the Rand.[54]

It is unlikely that the fate of what the isiZulu press referred to as the 'Zulu Nation on the Rand' lay in the hands of the ZNA – far from it. In August 1919 Zulu mineworkers placed their grievances before Solomon kaDinuzulu during his tour of the mines several months prior to joining strike action in 1920.[55] The reach of the organisation was sufficiently impressive, however, for it to create a branch of the NNC on the Rand.[56] Many in the ambit of the ZNA rose to prominence as nationalist leaders in Natal during the 1920s – among them future ICU organisers J.M. Ngcobo, D.L. Bopela, R.L. Ndima, Colley Mkize and Herbert Msane, all of whom were part of the Zulu salariat on the Rand in 1919. For some, then, including Saul Msane, the mobilisation of regional and ethnic identities was partly a response to a crisis of commitment generated by strikes, street violence and boycotts. But for others, such as the struggling butcher A.W.G. Champion, the indebted and periodically bankrupt A.B.H. Ntuli, and E.P. Mart Zulu, a trader in Alexandra township displaced by Indian and Chinese rivals, it was a desperate effort to arrest their descent into the ranks of the working class.

When in 1918 *Ilanga lase Natal* claimed that Africans were 'dying like dogs in their thousands',[57] organisations such as the ZNA promised a way out, especially to undercapitalised entrepreneurs who had lost access to rural incomes and sought opportunities for urban accumulation. A possible model of economic salvation was to be found in the co-operative Limited Liability Company, in which an older, progressive model of inter-racial mutual aid was reconfigured in terms of Zulu ethnic identity, indigenised transatlantic ideas of black liberation, and autarky. This approach resonated not only with the politics of Zulu elite struggles on the Rand, but also with broader political developments in Natal and Zululand, where the Zulu royal family had become a focal point of nationalism. Thus in 1918 Pixley Seme's Native Landowners' Association of Africa, in its fourth incarnation since 1912, elected Solomon kaDinuzulu as its patron.[58] After having discussions with Saul Msane, John Dube and Elka Cele, Seme hoped to enlarge the Association's money-raising efforts by launching a Zulu National Fund (an offshoot of the 1913 'Dinuzulu Memorial Fund'), which in turn underwrote the Zulu nationalist Inkatha organisation in 1923 – a Zululand-based movement that disappeared in 1930, only to be resuscitated in the apartheid era. Significantly, perhaps, in the early 1920s the first Secretary of Inkatha, the Reverend S.D. Simelane, abandoned Johannesburg's freehold Sophiatown township for rural Zululand, where twentieth-century Zulu nationalism would have its most powerful popular roots.

While migrancy fostered awareness amongst educated amaZulu of the politics of ethnicity, organisations such as the ZNA and the African Congregational Church underscored a new cosmopolitan Zulu identity, facilitating the self-conscious Zulu patriotism that would exercise a determining influence on African politics in Natal and Zululand during the 1920s and beyond. Far from being anachronistic in an industrial landscape of creolised cultures, the Zulu elite's attachment to the language of ethnic national belonging was, in its own way, as innovative – and perhaps even more globally conscious[59] – than those hybrid emerging urban subcultures such as *marabi* against which, in some respects, it sought to define itself.

It was thus from within the ranks of the ZNA on the Witwatersrand that Saul Msane began writing his *Miners' Companion in Zulu* shortly before his death in 1919; that A.D. Mxakaza emerged as a tireless advocate of isiZulu language purity; and that N.J.N. Masuku, a mine clerk and marginal Natal land owner, spearheaded the campaign to publish Magema Fuze's manuscript on Zulu history, which finally appeared as *Abantu Abamnyama Lapa Bavela Ngakona* in 1922.[60] It was around this time, and shortly before the influential Zulu intellectual R.R.R. Dhlomo portrayed a National Congress riven with factionalism, leadership conflicts and ethnic rivalries,[61] that *Abantu-Batho* critically questioned whether Natal 'was playing its part towards Africanism'.[62] Although the chief target of the newspaper was John Dube, *Abantu-Batho*'s invective could just as easily have been directed (and conceivably was) at Johannesburg-based Zulu cultural nationalists such as Masuku and Mxakaza. Both undoubtedly would have supported the Natal Congress in its attempts to cement an alliance with Zulu traditional leaders and Solomon kaDinuzulu in order to take advantage of the segregationist provisions of the 1920 Native Affairs Act.[63]

Criticisms of this 'Natal tendency' in Congress politics, however, took insufficient account of the complex and contradictory relationship between ethnic identity and racial nationalism (or 'Africanism') amongst isiZulu-speaking intellectuals. At the level of social biography one could find this portrayed especially vividly, for example, in the career of Saul Msane's son, Herbert Nuttall Vuma Msane. A pioneer of the East Rand Zulu football team, the 'Brave Natalians', Herbert Msane joined the International Socialist League around 1918 and thereafter assisted Seme in organising the Native Landowners' Association. A member of the Zulu National Association, Msane sought audiences with Solomon kaDinuzulu at Nongoma in 1919 before reappearing as a radical ICU organiser in the Natal after 1924.[64]

One also finds evidence of the tensions within Zulu cosmopolitanism in the remarkable career of the former policeman and butcher-turned-clerk, A.W.G. (George) Champion – one of the most important black South African nationalists of the 1920s who rose to become second-in-command of the ICU and then, in 1928, the Zulu populist boss of its secessionist Natal branch. Champion combined his membership of the ZNA with his duties as Patron of the United Native National Association of Commerce and Industry (UNNACI) – a Johannesburg organisation whose membership comprised mostly mine clerks drawn from a wide range of ethnic backgrounds. The slogan of the UNNACI – 'How long have we placed ourselves under slavery, working for other nations, which come from across the seas'[65] – betrays its origins in the ideology of liberation espoused by the radical racial nationalist Marcus Garvey, whose ideas took root in South Africa in 1919. A short time later, however, Champion can be found at the head of another more obscure organisation called the Exempted Natives' Association of South Africa, which represented a largely isiZulu-speaking Rand constituency that had been exempted from the Provisions of Native Law. Its motto was, 'Birds of the same feather flock together'. One suspects that the plumage of its members was coloured as much by their ethnic origins as it was by their shared legal status.[66]

But the early careers of George Champion and Saul Msane are instructive in another respect. They suggest the extent to which Zulu cosmopolitanism as a form of politics underwritten by a particular identity was being pulled apart by the radical post-war climate. During the course of the 1920s, when many members of the *kholwa* elite on the Rand appear to have returned permanently to Natal, this tension resolved itself into two recognisably distinct political tendencies. The first of these was the Zulu nationalism born of the uneasy alliance between moderate, mostly propertied Zulu Christian leaders and the Zulu royal house. This attempt to forge a politics based on a constitutional monarchy and shaped by the values of *kholwa* respectability and liberalism found organisational expression in John Dube's NNC and particularly in Inkatha – a movement linked to the Zulu cultural revival in which Natal intellectuals and the Zulu diaspora on the Rand had played so vital a part. In contrast to these *hamba kahle* (go carefully) politics was the Zulu populism and racial nationalism espoused by déclassé members of the *kholwa* elite such as George Champion. Responsive to the grievances of Zulu tenant labourers, migrants and urban workers, this populism found its home in the ICU and the radicalised section of the NNC, renamed the Natal African Congress – the Natal Branch of the ANC – in 1926.

It is to these tensions within African nationalist politics in Natal that the origins of competing regional political traditions over the following decades can be traced. At times probably more accurately described as a set of ideological entanglements than political fault lines, their common roots lay in the contested politics of Zulu identity in the early twentieth century – politics that were partly shaped by now largely forgotten members of the educated Zulu diaspora on the Witwatersrand.

## Notes

1. The Natal Native Congress (NNC) was one of a number of regional political organisations including the Transvaal Native Congress (TNC) that combined in 1912 to form the South African Native National Congress (SANNC, later African National Congress [ANC]). Despite the formation of the SANNC (which I often refer to here as the National Congress), these older regional Congress organisations continued to maintain local branches after 1912. While it was common for SANNC leaders to also simultaneously hold office in, say, the NNC or the TNC, these regional Congresses tended to reflect relatively distinct regional identities and political cultures.
2. *Ilanga lase Natal*, 6 July 1917.
3. See, for example, J. Guy and M. Thabane, 'The MaRashea: A Participant's Perspective', in *Class, Community and Conflict: South African Perspectives*, ed. B. Bozzoli (Johannesburg: Ravan Press, 1987); P. Delius, 'Sebatakgomo: Migrant Organisation, the ANC and the Sekhukhuneland Revolt', *Journal of Southern African Studies* 15:4 (1989) and P. Bonner, ' "Desirable or Undesirable Basotho women?" Liquor, Prostitution and the Migration of Basotho Women to the Rand, 1920–1945', in *Women and Gender in Southern Africa to 1945*, ed. C. Walker (Cape Town: David Philip, 1990).
4. The main exception here is C. van Onselen, *Studies in the Social and Economic History of the Witwatersrand 1886–1914, Vol. 1, New Babylon; Vol. 2, New Nineveh* (London: Longmans, 1982).
5. This relates to the more general failure of South African historians to explore the making of the African middle classes, despite the fact that the sources for such a project exist and that a generation has now passed since the first attempts were made to rescue 'the African petty bourgeoisie' from an historiographical no man's land. See B. Willan, 'Sol Plaatje, De Beers and an Old Tram Shed: Class Relations and Social Control in a South African Town, 1918–1919', *Journal of Southern African Studies* 4:2 (1978). Notable exceptions include H. Bradford, 'Mass Movements and the Petty Bourgeoisie: The Social Origins of ICU Leadership, 1924–1929', *Journal of African History* 25:3, 1984 and A.G. Cobley, *Class and Consciousness: The Black petty bourgeoisie in South Africa, 1924 to 1950* (New York: Greenwood, 1990).
6. *Ilanga lase Natal*, 12 December 1919; original in isiZulu (hereafter [Z]).
7. For the more general argument, see E. Gellner, *Nations and Nationalism* (Oxford: Blackwell, 1983), especially pp. 58–62.
8. The lineage of pan-African ideas, particularly in Natal, extended back at least to 1896 when the maverick missionary Joseph Booth announced the formation of the Christian African Union with the slogan 'Africa for the Africans' and an appeal to '[l]et the African be his own employer; develop

his own country; establish his own manufactures; run his own ships; work his own mines, and conserve the wealth from his labour'. See Natal Archives (hereafter NA), Secretary for Native Affairs (hereafter SNA), 391, 423/08, enclosed copy of *The Christian Express*, 1 October 1903, pp. 151–52.

9. The thousands of Zulu youths and men who entered employment on the Rand alongside many others of diverse ethnic origins were refugees of dislocated rural societies. P. la Hausse de Lalouvière, *Restless Identities: Signatures of Nationalism, Zulu Ethnicity and History in the Lives of Petros Lamula (c.1881–1948) and Lymon Maling (1889–c.1936)* (Pietermaritzburg: University of Natal Press, 2000), p. i.

10. See *Natal Census Report* (Pietermaritzburg: P. Davis, 1904); John Lambert, *Betrayed Trust: Africans and the State in Colonial Natal* (Pietermaritzburg: University of Natal Press, 1995), Chapters 6 and 7; Shula Marks, *Reluctant Rebellion: The 1906–08 Disturbances in Natal* (Oxford: Oxford University Press, 1970), Chapter 5 and B. Carton, *Blood from your Children: The Colonial Origins of Generational Conflict in South Africa* (Charlottesville: University Press of Virginia, 2000), Chapter 5. For hardship in southern Zululand see *Blue Book on Native Affairs, 1910.* U.G. 17–1911 (Cape Town: Cape Times, 1911).

11. See correspondence in NA, SNA, 392, 475/08 and NA, SNA, 477, 3566/1910, Act. Under SNA to Sec. Native Affairs Committee, Salisbury, 28 November 1911.

12. This figure is an estimate. In 1880 the African Christian population of Natal was around 10 000. Over the following decades mission enterprise amongst Africans expanded dramatically. See N. Etherington, 'African Economic Experiments in Colonial Natal, 1845–1880', in *Enterprise and Exploitation in a Victorian Colony*, eds. B. Guest and J.M. Sellers (Pietermaritzburg: University of Natal Press, 1985), p. 266.

13. See Etherington, 'African Economic Experiments', p. 267 for examples of large landowners and NA, SNA, 431, 1620/09, and exemption application of Fred Kuzwayo, 31 March 1909, for a typical profile of the landless *kholwa* artisan.

14. The number of African landowners in Natal was conservatively estimated at 1 548 in 1906. See *Native Affairs Commission 1906–07, Evidence* (Pietermaritzburg: P. Davis, 1907), p. 1005.

15. See J. Lonsdale 'The European Scramble and Conquest in African History', in *The Cambridge History of Africa*, Vol. 6, eds. R. Oliver and G.N. Sanderson (Cambridge: Cambridge University Press, 1985), p. 758.

16. See Killie Campbell Africana Library, Durban (KCAL) Marwick Papers, Ms Mar 2.08.5, KCM 2745. J.S. Marwick, the Natal Native Agent in Johannesburg, organised this march.

17. See Van Onselen, *New Nineveh*, Chapters 1 and 2 and Lambert, *Betrayed Trust*, p. 95 for Rand employers' stereotypes of Natal Africans.

18. See J. Campbell's illuminating discussion in *Songs of Zion: The African Methodist Episcopal Church in the United States and South Africa* (Oxford: Oxford University Press, 1995), p. 145. Also see D. Coplan, *In Township Tonight!* (Johannesburg: Ravan Press, 1985) and E. Koch, '"Without Visible Means of Subsistence": Slumyard Culture in Johannesburg 1918–1940' in *Town and Countryside in the Transvaal*, ed. B. Bozzoli (Johannesburg: Ravan Press, 1983).

19. For the predominance of amaZulu at particular mines, see A.E. le Roy, 'Does it Pay to Educate the Native?' *South African Journal of Science* 15 (1918–19): 348 and for later evidence see T.D.M. Skota, *The African Yearly Register* (Johannesburg: Esson, 1930), pp. 443–44.

20. John Dube's Zulu Christian Industrial School was established in 1900 on the lands of the American Board Mission in Inanda. Ohlange, as it became known, was based on the American model of Booker T. Washington's Tuskegee Institute. In its early years the school was starved of finances and crowded with pupils whose ages ranged from 12 to 30. A hostile white community viewed it as a crucible of 'Ethiopianism'. See La Hausse de Lalouvière, *Restless Identities*, pp. 168–69.

21. NA, SNA, 475, 3452/1910, J.M. Maduna to SNA, 9 Oct. 1910 and NA, Chief Native Commissioner (hereafter CNC), 129, 1129/1913, examination of Joel Moses Maduna, 9 September 1913.

22. A.E. le Roy, 'Does it Pay': 348. In 1911, 30 mine clerks on the Rand were graduates of the Amanzimtoti Institute alone.

23. For example, Stephen Molife (clerk at Jumpers Deep), Edwin Lutayi (compound clerk at Randfontein Central), Isaiah Mbonambi (hospital clerk at York gold mine) and Russell Mcanyana (clerk at Simmer East) were all sons of Natal Congressmen.

24. See J. Lonsdale's discussion 'Globalisation, Ethnicity and Democracy: A View from the "Hopeless Continent"', in *Globalisation in World History*, ed. A.G. Hopkins (London: Pimlico, 2002).

25. *South African Native Affairs Commission 1903–5, Volume III, Minutes of Evidence*, (Cape Town: Cape Times, 1904), p. 521. Radebe, a Pietermaritzburg founder of the NNC, was a journalist, clerk and eating-house keeper.

26. *Ilanga lase Natal*, 1 February 1907.

27. *Ilanga lase Natal*, 18 January 1907.

28. For a study that builds on my earlier discussion in *Restless Identities* of the *kholwa* experience of time and fears of extinction but with a particular reference to writing, see David Attwell, *Rewriting Modernity: Studies in Black South African Literary History* (Pietermaritzburg: University of KwaZulu-Natal Press, 2005), Chapter 2.

29. As A.D. Smith has argued: 'ethnic nationalism becomes a "surrogate" religion which aims to overcome the sense of futility engendered by the removal of any vision of an existence after death, by linking individuals to persisting communities whose generations form indissoluble links in a chain of memories and identities'. See *The Ethnic Origins of Nations* (Oxford: Blackwell, 1986), p. 176.

30. See La Hausse de Lalouvière, *Restless Identities*, pp. 12–14.

31. *Ilanga lase Natal*, 21 June 1907 and 17 October 1919 [Z].

32. Quoted in Marks, *Reluctant Rebellion*, p. 359.

33. See La Hausse de Lalouvière, *Restless Identities*, Introduction.

34. *Ilanga lase Natal*, February–March 1918 [Z].

35. See *Ilanga lase Natal*, 4 May 1906 [Z] and 1 November 1907 [Z], which translate as 'People Awake' and 'Forward Zulus' respectively.

36. NA, CNC, 62, 338/1912, report on NNC meeting, Pietermaritzburg, 13 February 1914.

37. See P. Walshe, *The Rise of African Nationalism in South Africa*, (Berkeley: University of California Press, 1971), p. 47.

38. NA, CNC, 144, 1818/1913, NC, Piet Retief to SNA, 9 January 1914.

39. See *Ilanga lase Natal*, 15 June 1917 (editorial) and B. Willan, *Sol Plaatje: A Biography* (Johannesburg: Ravan Press, 1984), p. 211, for a sense of these fierce rivalries.

40. NA, CNC, 62, 338/1912, report on a meeting held by S. Msane, Eshowe, 14 July 1913.

41. See *Ilanga lase Natal*, 12 June 1908. The Company aimed to raise £50 000 through shares in order to support a programme for land purchase and agricultural and industrial training.

42. For the significance and political background to this decision, see N. Cope, *To Bind the Nation: Solomon kaDinuzulu and Zulu Nationalism 1913–1933* (Pietermaritzburg: University of Natal Press, 1993), Chapter 3.

43. In fact Dube had spent 1916 in Johannesburg working as managing director of the Native Farmers' Association. See *Ilanga lase Natal*, 30 August 1918 (editorial).

44. Shula Marks has argued that after 1917 Dube was forced to retreat to his political base in Natal where he turned increasingly to ethnic mobilisation. See *The Ambiguities of Dependence*, p. 67. What should be added, however, is that Dube's fate had already been prefigured not only by the politics of the new Natal Congress movement and in the Zulu cultural revival, but also by his own desire to resuscitate the Zulu royal house. For Dube's support of the Zulu monarchy, see *Ilanga lase Natal*, 24 October 1913. It was probably not coincidental that Dube's loss of office followed the first reading of the Native Administration Bill in 1917, which embodied an ambitious, idealised form of segregation.

45. See La Hausse de Lalouvière, *Restless Identities*, Introduction and Chapter 3.

46. See *Ilanga lase Natal*, 24 April 1919, 7 November 1919 and 9 April 1920.

47. See B. Kapferer, *Legends of People, Myths of State: Violence, Intolerance, and Political Culture in Sri Lanka and Australia* (Washington: Smithsonian Institution Press, 1988), Chapter 1 for an analysis of nationalism as a religious form. Also see B. Anderson, *Imagined Communities: Reflections on the Origins and Spread of Nationalism* (London: Verso, 1983), p. 19.

48. See P. Bonner, 'The Transvaal Native Congress 1917–1920: The Radicalisation of the Black Petty Bourgeoisie on the Rand', in *Industrialisation and Social Change in South Africa: African Class Formation, Culture and Consciousness 1870–1930*, eds. S. Marks and R. Rathbone (London: Longman, 1982).

49. See correspondence in Central Archives Depot, Pretoria, (hereafter CAD), Native Affairs Department (hereafter NTS), 1444, 54/214.

50. See CAD, Government Native Labour Bureau (hereafter GNLB), 90, 144/13/D205(1), enclosed translation of *Abantu-Batho*, 4 July 1918.

51. See correspondence in CAD, GNLB, 60/26/30 and NA, CNC, 239, 783/1916.

52. This was according to Sol Plaatje. See Willan, 'Sol Plaatje, De Beers and an Old Tram Shed': 207.

53. See correspondence in CAD, GNLB, 313, 134/19/110.

54. In further evidence of the Rand's ethnicised labour market, at least three of the committee worked for Randles Bros. and Hudson – merchants who discriminated in favour of Zulu employees. See correspondence in CAD, GNLB, 324, 95/20/399; CAD, GNLB, 327, 219/20/53 and CAD, NTS, 9472, 6/400.

55. See Cope, *To Bind the Nation*, pp. 88–89.

56. See *Ilanga lase Natal*, 23 May 1919 [Z] and CAD, GNLB, 187, 1217/14/D110, cutting from *Abantu-Batho*, 15 May 1919 [Z].

57. *Ilanga lase Natal*, 1 November 1918.

58. CAD, GNLB, 380, 4/326, prospectus of the Native Farmers' Union of South Africa, 21 August 1918.

59. For further evidence of Zulu intellectuals' keen sense of comparative global history, see La Hausse de Lalouvière, *Restless Identities*, pp. 12–14, 58–59.

60. Masuku supported Fuze with money collected at public meetings and through financial subscriptions. See *Ilanga lase Natal*, 24 April 1919 and CAD, Master of the Supreme Court, 42409, Estate of S. Msane. For Masuku's intiatives on behalf of Fuze, see *Ilanga lase Natal*, 16 November 1917 [Z]; 9 July 1920 [Z] and M.M. Fuze, *Abantu Abamnyama. Lapa Bavela Ngakona* (Pietermaritzburg: City Printing Works, 1922).

61. See R.R.R. Dhlomo's article in *Ilanga lase Natal*, 4 August 1922.

62. See CAD, GNLB, 90, 144/13/D205(1), translation of article in *Abantu-Batho*, 6 April 1920.

63. See La Hausse de Lalouvière, *Restless Identities*, pp. 67–74.

64. See *Ilanga lase Natal*, 16 April 1909 [Z]; 1 August 1919; CAD, GNLB, 380, 4/326, SNA to CNC, 20 January 1922.

65. *Ilanga lase Natal*, 14 February 1919 and correspondence in CAD, NTS, 9472, 13/400.

66. See *Ilanga lase Natal*, 24 March 1922, for a discussion of the objects of the Association. Champion was also the founder of the Transvaal Native Mine Clerks' Association – another strongly Zulu association. Revealingly, too, the Witwatersrand District Native Football Association boasted discrete ethnic sections with mission-educated isiZulu-speakers accounting for over half of its office-bearers.

*Chapter 22*

# The Sport of Zuluness
## Masculinity, Class and Cultural Identity in Twentieth-century Black Soccer

PETER ALEGI

SPORT HAS LONG been a social space for playing out Zulu masculinities and cultural identities. In precolonial times, for example, boys and young men enjoyed stick fighting, hunting, dancing competitions, running events and cattle-racing. Indeed, these public displays of physicality offered compelling insights into how agrarian societies in southern Africa embraced *sportgeist* – the spirit of sport.[1] With the onset of industrialisation and tighter white rule in the late nineteenth century, this *sportgeist* would be transformed. The players in this transformation, both the literate isiZulu-speaking *kholwa* (Christian) elites and young rural commoners who migrated to the port city of Durban and distant Witwatersrand gold mines, adopted colonial leisure activities such as football (soccer) to cope with the dislocations of urbanisation and to build vital alternative networks.

From 1910 to 1945 educated, Westernising Zulu men shaped ethnic and class solidarities in burgeoning cities by organising football clubs. Inexpensive and relatively easy to play, soccer represented a sphere of action where expressions of Zulu modernity could be forged, tested and negotiated. A British colonial export, football drew on the experience of wage work in the city, as well as on longstanding customs and rituals of the precolonial past. Certain continuities linked traditional and modern sport. For example, generational dimensions influenced the formation of African athletic masculinities.[2] Additionally, Zulu migrants carried the tradition of praising and praise names from their homesteads to cities and towns, where the practice was then incorporated into African rituals of spectatorship. Finally, the transfer of propitiatory rituals associated with Zulu military campaigns further contributed to the making of a locally distinctive subaltern football culture.

Indeed, the symbolic regeneration of Zulu military prowess in the name of football displayed virtuous cultural identities while fostering team spirit. Match preparations often commenced with team officials consulting a diviner who threw bones to predict the outcome of a game. Before a key contest, clubs went on a retreat to re-enact purification ceremonies similar to those performed by nineteenth-century Zulu *amabutho* (age-regiments) before major battles.[3] The players drank a potent emetic and vomited, emulating the *ukuhlanza* (vomiting and cleansing) practice of Zulu soldiers on the eve of war. The sprinkling of *umuthi* on the football and on cleat-boots also recalled the doctoring of warriors' weapons, as did the burning of special roots. When fans exclaimed the special names (*izibongo*) of their favourite players another powerful element of Zuluness emerged on the pitches far from the homestead settings in Natal and Zululand.[4]

### Mine football and Zulu *umabhalana*

African football around the gold diggings of greater Johannesburg received an early boost from white mine managers who saw organised competitions in the compounds as a subtle means of social control. The 1920 African mineworkers' strike motivated firms to build leisure facilities for African clerks, policemen and other employees. Captains of mining also viewed sport as a production booster – for worker morale seemed to rise after soccer matches – and a safety valve for restive labourers perceived as faction fighters, alcoholics, dagga (cannabis) smokers and sexual predators.[5]

However, African football's founders on the Rand were mission-educated, isiZulu-speaking clerks from Natal. In 1917 the *umabhalana*, as these white-collar employees were commonly known, established the Witwatersrand and District Native Football Association, comprising the leadership of the mine league structured along ethnic lines.[6] Dressed in jackets and trousers, these secretarial workers occupied a key role between management and underground miners, leading 'mine companies to develop special recreational activities for them which not only occupied their leisure time and emphasised their élite status but also promoted an ethos of loyalty to the mine'.[7] As early as 1923 the Chamber of Mines newspaper *Umteteli waBantu* reported that 'all kinds of sports are organised and in various other ways provision is made to keep the Natives wholesomely amused'.[8]

Clerks with a Zulu background and privileged status held sway over black leisure outlets on the Rand. Sport suited this particular male elite, engaged in a hesitant struggle to be heard and seen in a hierarchical segregationist society. *Umabhalana* expressed a 'profound cultural ambivalence' about their identity, which straddled traditionalist and modern experiences, as well as the lower echelons of white supremacist society and the upper reaches of the black oppressed.[9] Having excelled in sport and physical education in mission schools, many clerks embraced aspects of colonial culture that gave voice to their aspiration – to be set apart from the mass of ordinary workers.[10] Through sport and attendant activities in politics, the *umabhalana* pursued a cosmopolitan Zulu identity 'shaped by common ties of blood, language and geography'.[11] At first, the clerks' vision accepted a major segregationist aim: that football should be separated by race and ethnicity.

Established in 1906 by *umabhalana* from northern Natal, the Old Natalians Football Club of Simmer and Jack Mine (Goldfields Group) became one of the most successful football teams on the Rand. Old Natalians dominated African football in greater Johannesburg for the next two decades, winning titles at club and district levels. A midfield player of note in this era, Enoch 'Joko Tea' Samaniso, named after a brand of tea popular among Africans, came from the *umabhalana* ranks at the Simmer and Jack mine. With his silky, irreverent dribbling skills and legendary toughness, Samaniso earned a reputation as a superstar among black footballers and their fans in the Transvaal. Off the pitch, Samaniso's team functioned as a mutual aid society-cum-social club, organising weekend concerts and dances that heightened members' social prestige. When Samaniso died in 1941, his teammates and other African soccer officials made financial contributions to his widow, while clerks from Old Natalians served as pallbearers at his funeral in Benoni.[12] The near cult status of 'Joko Tea', the midfield general, revealed a longing among blacks on the Rand to create a world of excitement beyond the doldrums of work.

In the 1930s and the 1940s the urban Zulu cosmopolitanism embodied by the Old Natalians and other clubs was shifting away from maintaining exclusive ethnic boundaries to using inclusive Zuluness as part of an increasingly pan-ethnic nationalist identity. After the mine league collapsed for unknown reasons in 1929, Zulu clerks resurrected it in 1931 without ethnic sections. Exploiting their intermediary role in mine labour relations, the *umabhalana* persuaded the Chamber of Mines and several small private companies to sponsor knockout and round-robin competitions such as the Native Recruiting Corporation Cup and the Hadley's Cup. Co-operation with management developed alongside a vigorous thrust to defend autonomous African leisure. Most notably, the new league dropped the appellative 'Native' from its title and renamed itself the Witwatersrand and District *African* Football Association (WDAFA). This name change alone suggests a more assertive opposition to white stewardship. A new propensity developed among some mine clerks to think of themselves as African, as well as Zulu. By the end of the Second World War, soccer's potential to foster an inclusive African nationalist identity was well established, not only on the gold mines of the Rand, but also in the city of Durban.

### Durban's 'fertile ground' for the 'loftiest to the most disreputable'
A focal aspect of everyday existence, football strengthened the connections between *amakholwa* and the African working poor in inter-war Durban. Zulu manual labourers joined the tiny *kholwa* elite as the game's major constituency, a trend reflected in the vertiginous increase in the number of African clubs: from 7 in 1917 to 26, with more than 1 000 players in 1931, and then 47 with 1 500 registered players in 1935.[13] Local conditions tended to facilitate solidarity in sport. For example, the presence of an overwhelmingly isiZulu-speaking African population reduced pressures to form ethnically defined sport networks. Another important consideration

was that in Durban the *kholwa* elite and other Africans endured similar racial discrimination, such as pass raids, curfews and the job colour bar.[14] The city's geography also affected the populist character of African leisure: '[D]ock workers in Durban's harbour area, the Point, lived within walking distance of the city-centre where dance halls, churches and soccer fields provided a fertile ground for the fusion of élite culture and working-class dance and music.'[15]

Soccer's capacity to bring together mission-educated groups and both migrant and non-migrant African workers in the city had a special appeal for Zulu leaders like Chief Albert Luthuli, future African National Congress (ANC) president and Nobel Peace Prize recipient. A teacher and prominent member of the *kholwa* community, Luthuli became vice-president of the Durban and District Native Football Association (DDNFA) in 1929, after serving for many years as secretary of the Adams College Shooting Stars Football Club, one of Durban's most respected sides. 'What has attracted me as much as the game,' he explained in his autobiography, 'has been the opportunity to meet all sorts of people, from the loftiest to the most disreputable.'[16] Such interactions were fraught with complications. Gideon Sivetye, a member of Shooting Stars and a teacher at Adams College, recounted the difficulties of bringing student athletes into regular contact with proletarian players and fans. 'As teachers we were criticised for going to Durban to play with the wild boys who were working in Durban,' Sivetye said. 'We had to answer questions of ministers, etc. I am glad to say our principals joined us; they thought it was a way of attracting them, to cooperate with us . . . It did a lot of good, this playing with those people in town. We got to know each other.'[17]

Football's growing appeal among urban Africans set the stage for a grand performance of Zulu patriarchal ambitions. In many ways, soccer competitions enabled military customs, undermined by colonial rule, to be reconstructed and unleashed in football combat. Indigenous traditions that valued physical force, toughness, skill, courage and territorial identities dictated soccer techniques and sensibilities. Images from the natural world dominated the names of urban football clubs, epitomising masculine elements in rural Zulu culture. But stereotypical colonial perceptions of warlike amaZulu also captured the essence of team purpose. Established teams such as Bush Bucks, Shooting Stars, Wild Zebras, Cannons, Wanderers, Ocean Swallows and Vultures were joined in the early 1920s by the Wild Savages, Rebellions, Assegais, Lions, Springboks, Antelopes, Railway Tigers and Fight for Evers.[18] The abundance of animal metaphors evoking 'viciousness, fury and savagery' can be linked to Zulu *izibongo* (praise poems), a resilient oral literature emphasising natural imagery and male virility.[19] For young men and adolescent boys, football's competitive rituals encouraged the pursuit of manly grace. Like stick-fighting in the countryside, engaging in soccer matches was the realm of vigorous unmarried youth, while the administration of football laws and discipline was seen as the customary domain of senior men.[20]

*Swallows boys' football team.*

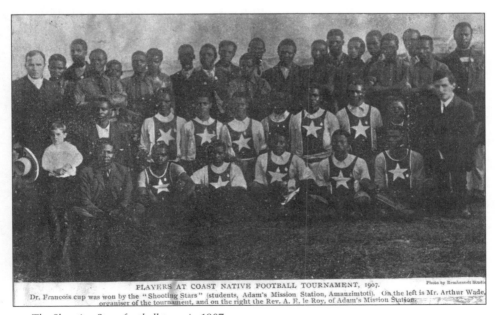

PLAYERS AT COAST NATIVE FOOTBALL TOURNAMENT, 1907.   Photo by Rembrandt Studio
Dr. Francois cup was won by the "Shooting Stars" (students, Adam's Mission Station, Amanzimtoti). On the left is Mr. Arthur Wade, organiser of the tournament, and on the right the Rev. A. E. le Roy, of Adam's Mission Station.

*The Shooting Stars football team in 1907.*

Generational divisions profoundly influenced male authority in soccer. Football players frequently called league officials 'elders'. Like homestead heads, football's patriarchs oversaw the everyday business of the Durban and District African Football Association (DDAFA) 'family', organised sport festivals, settled disputes and assigned playing fields. Referees represented another form of patriarchal authority; they oversaw competitions in the manner of headmen who umpired stick fights. In Durban, however, poorly trained soccer referees struggled to earn the respect of competitors. Because clubs provided game-day referees, a practice that carried on at least until the late 1940s, charges of favouritism were common, with the result that assaults on officials occurred with disconcerting regularity. Despite the elders' efforts to enforce obedience, crowd hooliganism persisted throughout the 1920s. The minutes of the Durban Association discuss incidents of mayhem on the fields; accompanying these accounts are the formal protests of referees and players who claimed to have been attacked by opponents and fans.[21] Such violence shows the limits of the control exercised by football's patriarchal elite over younger, independent men eager to assert their manhood during competitive spectacles.

### 'If Zulu were to be used other nationalities would suffer'

That urban football drew on Zulu conceptions of manhood reveals adaptation, rather than capitulation, to economic hardship and racial oppression. Alive to this development, Albert Luthuli used the popularity of football and the familiar authority structures it reproduced to resolve internal tensions within Durban's African community. He championed a vision of inclusive pan-ethnic African nationalism based, selectively, on respect for Zulu history and patriarchal order. His appreciation of customary tradition led him to teach isiZulu (as well as other subjects) at Adams College, and then in 1935 to establish a Zulu Language and Cultural Society, an arm of the Natal African Teachers' Association. Even so, as a member of the DDNFA executive committee, he helped to pass a constitutional amendment that made English the official language of the Durban Football Association. IsiZulu continued to be spoken at meetings, but the minutes were recorded in English. This practice stemmed partly from Pan-Africanist arguments that 'if Zulu were to be used other nationalities would suffer'.[22] Still, Luthuli's endorsement of isiZulu also exemplified the contradictions dividing *kholwa* people, torn between promoting a progressive, urbanised worldview and revelling in precolonial glories.

It was Albert Luthuli who tirelessly sought to change the name of the Durban and District Native Football Association in 1932 to Durban and District *African* Football Association. The deeper intrusion of Durban's white authorities into black sport in part accounted for Luthuli's pan-ethnic appeals to mobilise a more radical movement to combat colonialism. More generally, however, African sporting organisations, as seen in the case of the mine football league, were espousing an increasingly assertive, if polite, legal opposition to white paternalism.[23] This trend extended to Cape Town, where the Cape Peninsula Bantu Football Association, formed in 1927 in Langa, transformed itself into the Western Province African Football Association in 1936–37. Overall, the new titles highlighted how developments in football were tied to simultaneous changes in national politics and society, where 'race-conscious populism provided the African élite with a viable ideological approach to the problem of class division in the black community'.[24]

In twentieth-century South Africa colonialism and capitalist development created 'conditions that inspired new ideas about leisure, and in the process realigned relations of power and . . . boundaries of difference'.[25] During the early decades, Africans transformed the British sport of football into a leading form of popular culture. The vernacularisation of the colonial game was a product of a range of countervailing influences, emerging from foreign and indigenous, rural and urban, mission and traditional, and middle- and working-class sources. While Luthuli and members of the *amakholwa* were undeniably central to South African football's incipient years, the presence of traditional martial practices, praise names and ritual preparations before games points to enduring Zulu customary elements shaping soccer. Ultimately, isiZulu-speaking Africans on the Rand and in Durban moulded football into a crucible of pleasure and autonomy, and in so doing reformulated the boundaries of a more porous Zuluness in a modern urban world.

## Notes

1. S. Hardy, 'Entrepreneurs, Structures, and the *Sportgeist*: Old Tensions in a Modern Industry', in *Essays on Sport History and Sport Mythology*, eds. D.G. Kyle and G.D. Stark (College Station, TX: Texas A&M University Press, 1990), pp. 45–82.
2. J. Clegg, '*Ukubuyisa Isidumbu* – "Bringing Back the Body": An Examination into the Ideology of Vengeance in the Msinga and Mpofana Rural Locations, 1882–1944', in *Working Papers in Southern African Studies*, Vol. 2, ed. P. Bonner (Johannesburg: Witwatersrand University Press, 1981), pp. 164–98. For a discussion of a similar process in colonial Ghana, see E. Akyeampong, 'Bukom and the Social History of Boxing in Accra', *International Journal of African Historical Studies* 35:1 (2002): 39–60. Definition of patriarchal masculinity adapted from D. Moodie, *Going For Gold: Men, Mines, and Migration* (Johannesburg: Witwatersrand University Press, 1994), pp. 193–94 and B. Carton, *Blood from Your Children: The Colonial Origins of Generational Conflict in South Africa* (Pietermaritzburg: University of Natal Press, 2000). For recent South African studies on this topic, see R. Morrell, ed., *Changing Men in Southern Africa* (Pietermaritzburg: University of Natal Press, 2001) and 'Of Boys and Men: Masculinity and Gender in Southern African Studies', *Journal of Southern African Studies* 24:4 (1998): 605–30.
3. N.A. Scotch, 'Magic, Sorcery, and Football among Urban Zulus', *Journal of Conflict Resolution* 5 (1961): 72–73; 'Interview with Peter Sitsila', *Langa*, 27 July 1995 and 'Muti and Sport', *Drum*, March 1959. On the role of magic in Zulu war preparations, see J. Laband, *The Rise and Fall of the Zulu Nation* (London: Arms and Armor, 1997), pp. 26–27, 34–35.
4. For further details, see P. Alegi, 'Playing to the Gallery: Sport, Cultural Performance, and Social Identity in South Africa, 1920s–1945', *International Journal of African Historical Studies* 35:1 (2002): 17–38.

5.  C. Badenhorst and C. Mather, 'Tribal Recreation and Recreating Tribalism: Culture, Leisure and Social Control on South Africa's Gold Mines, 1940–1950', *Journal of Southern African Studies* 23:3 (1997): 473–89; P. Alegi, 'Katanga v. Johannesburg: A History of the First Sub-Saharan African Football Championship, 1949–50', *Kleio* 31(1999): 55–74 and Moodie, *Going for Gold*.
6.  'WDAFA Forges Ahead Despite Difficulties', *Bantu World*, 1 September 1934.
7.  A.G. Cobley, 'A Political History of Playing Fields: The Provision of Sporting Facilities for Africans in the Johannesburg Area to 1948', *International Journal of the History of Sport* 11:2 (1994): 224.
8.  'Life in Mine Compounds', *Umteteli waBantu*, 13 October 1923.
9.  P. la Hausse de Lalouvière, *Restless Identities: Signatures of Nationalism, Zulu Ethnicity and History in the Lives of Petros Lamula (c.1881–1948) and Lymon Maling (1889–c.1936)* (Pietermaritzburg: University of Natal Press, 2000), p. 14.
10.  Cobley, 'A Political History': 213; A. Odendaal, 'South Africa's Black Victorians: Sport and Society in South Africa in the Nineteenth Century', in *Pleasure, Profit, and Proselytism: British Culture and Sport at Home and Abroad*, ed. J.A. Mangan (London: Cass, 1988), p. 207 and J. Nauright, *Sport, Cultures and Identities in South Africa* (Cape Town: David Philip, 1997), pp. 47–75.
11.  La Hausse de Lalouvière, *Restless Identities*, p. 21.
12.  'Passing Away of Enoch "Joko Tea" Samaniso', *Bantu World*, 14 June 1941 and 'Transvaal African Football Association, Annual Report for 1941', *Bantu World*, 4 April 1942.
13.  Data on clubs and registered players in Durban collected from these sources: Collaborative Africana Microfilm Project (CAMP), Center for Research Libraries (Chicago), Leo Kuper Papers: Minutes of Meetings of the Durban & District Native Football Association (1924–35); 3/DBN, 4/1/2/1165, 11/352: Report of the Native Welfare Officer, 25 April 1931; 3/DBN, 4/1/3/1606, 352 v. I: Letter from Douglas Evans, Bantu Recreational Grounds Association, to Councilor J.L. Farrell, Chairman, Native Administration Committee, 31 January 1935 and B. Magubane, 'Sport and Politics in an Urban African Community: A Case Study of African Voluntary Organisations' (Masters thesis, University of Natal, 1963), 12.
14.  S. Marks, *Ambiguities of Dependence in South Africa* (Johannesburg: Ravan Press, 1986), p. 106.
15.  V. Erlmann, 'But Hope Does Not Kill: Black Popular Music in Durban, 1913–1939', in *The People's City*, eds. P. Maylam and I. Edwards (Pietermaritzburg: University of Natal Press, 1996), p. 68. For more insight on the politics of leisure, see G. Vahed, 'Control of African Leisure Time in Durban in the 1930s', *Journal of Natal and Zulu History* 18 (1998): 67–123.
16.  Albert Luthuli, *Let My People Go* (London: Collins, 1962), p. 38. The impact of pass raids, price increases, and declining real wages further encouraged many of the small-scale traders, artisans, policemen, and shopkeepers to identify closely with poorer, illiterate Africans, thereby encouraging the development of a socio-economically diverse subaltern football culture.
17.  T. Couzens, 'An Introduction to the History of Football in South Africa', in *Town and Countryside in the Transvaal*, ed. B. Bozzoli (Johannesburg: Ravan Press, 1983), pp. 202–03.
18.  Magubane, 'Sport and Politics', p. 12 and DDNFA minutes.
19.  Quote is from Magubane, 'Sport and Politics', p. 12.
20.  Moodie, *Going for Gold*, p. 192.
21.  Leo Kuper Papers: DDNFA Minutes, 1924–1931.
22.  Magubane, 'Sport and Politics', p. 15.
23.  Radical and progressive Africans increasingly used the term 'African' in the inter-war years, a pattern observed as early as 1923, when the South African Native National Congress became the African National Congress. For further discussion of the name change issue, see P. Limb, 'SANNC to ANC: Reply', in H-SAFRICA, http://www.h-net.org/~safrica/, 30 October 2001.
24.  C.R.D. Halisi, *Black Political Thought in the Making of South African Democracy* (Bloomington and Indianapolis: Indiana University Press, 1999), p. 57.
25.  E. Akyeampong and C. Ambler. 'Leisure in African History', *International Journal of African Historical Studies* 35:1 (2002): 5.

*Chapter 23*

# Generating Change, Engendering Tradition
## Rural Dynamics and the Limits of Zuluness in Colonial Natal

THOMAS McCLENDON

BETWEEN THE DEVASTATION of the bride-killing Great Flu in 1918 and the Ngongolo 'war' between the Chunu and Thembu chiefdoms in 1944 in the Weenen district, speakers of isiZulu in the heartlands of Natal experienced widening fissures along fault lines of gender and generation.[1] These tensions grew out of precolonial structures in southeastern Africa, including the Zulu kingdom and its neighbours, which shaped relations among genders and generations over matters of marriage, land, inheritance and seniority. Tensions were deeply exacerbated, however, by changes introduced through colonial rule and wage labour economies from the mid-nineteenth century. By the early twentieth century, rural Africans in Natal and Zululand were deeply immersed in colonial economies, while still recreating social structures that derived from precolonial times. They were encouraged to do so by a conservative white-supremacist state that sought to deflect radical tendencies among rural and urban Africans through a strategy of retribalisation. This strategy emphasised the stabilising force of patriarchal tradition, as enshrined in the codified version of customary law in force in Natal from the 1870s. While in urban areas, especially among men, there seems to have been a convergence of this strategy with new expressions of Zulu identity, in rural areas it was an appeal to hierarchical custom, described as emanating from 'time immemorial', that undergirded the state's strategy. Instead, restive sons and wives challenged static versions of custom through migration, disobedience and occasional litigation or testimony over matters of marriage, divorce and inheritance. This chapter argues that these matters of gender and generation, along with localised identities of lineage and chiefdom, were more central to rural dynamics than issues of Zuluness.

In the 1920s and 1930s, industrialising urban economies and the spread of commercial farming led to increased rural-urban migrancy, both temporary and permanent, as young rural Africans were pushed by declining conditions of accumulation on farms and reserves and simultaneously pulled by expanding urban opportunities. Not least of these was the opportunity for juniors to escape the control of seniors over wages, mobility and sexuality. The departure of young men and disparate disobedience of young women were sources of anxiety to labour-seeking white farmers and black patriarchs alike, while the latter also grew unnerved by youthful displays of disrespect. The branches of the state responsible for ensuring that African subjects remained compliant yet productive responded to these anxieties with an ideological and legislative commitment to the enforcement of traditional hierarchies, drawing on the system established in colonial Natal by its long-term Secretary for Native Affairs, Theophilus Shepstone. The virtues of traditional hierarchies in rural Africa became especially important to the state from the late 1920s onwards, in the wake of 'untraditional' challenges exemplified by the spectacular rise of the Industrial and Commercial Workers' Union (ICU) across wide areas of the South African countryside.

The Native Affairs Department (NAD) and other branches of the state were charged with ensuring that growing migrant labour, essential to the expansion of urban industries, did not unsettle the racial stratification that underlay the Union of South Africa. To do so, they sought to reinforce weakening structures of tradition in the countryside, both as a mask for authoritarian rule and in an attempt to prevent what they perceived as social disintegration. The state's endorsement of timeless tradition, encouraged by white farmers and African elders in Natal, was a response to a variety of social movements and currents that implicitly questioned a monolithic understanding of tradition. In urban areas, this effort encompassed encouraging politically neutralised identities such as a post-Bhambatha Zuluness. This, it was hoped, would deflect African workers from broader forms of identity along lines of class and race, which the supporters of the white supremacist and capitalist order saw as inherently threatening. African men and women in the countryside, however, belied the notion of static tradition by increasingly seeking new opportunities in urban life and occasionally offering open defiance to fathers and husbands. They also used the courts established to enforce tradition (through the vehicle of customary law) in order to challenge the official version of traditional arrangements, in effect subverting the state's aims. By the 1940s, rural dynamics were at best an uneasy stalemate and the flood of migration unleashed by the Second World War helped to create the call for the more draconian state controls eventually created by the white state under the banner of apartheid.

### Nineteenth-century preludes

Neither hierarchies of gender and generation nor changes in their dynamics appeared suddenly in the early twentieth century. Divisions along lines of gender and generation, and interplay between these categories, were fundamental to social arrangements in southeast Africa (as indeed they were and are elsewhere). The quickening economies, political centralisations and martial upheavals in the region from the late eighteenth century reshaped these fundamental categories, sharpening patriarchal hierarchies. Colonial rule and Christian missions brought ambiguous economic, political and ideological changes; these in turn made their mark on understandings of gender and generation, although without completely displacing earlier understandings or practices. To a large extent, the system created by Shepstone and his African allies was an attempt to manage the tensions of gender and generation that were inflamed by the colonial presence.

As a matter of practicality, the colonial government turned at a very early stage to a dual legal system that provided for Africans to be ruled by 'their own' laws, administered both by government-sanctioned chiefs and by white 'Administrators of Native Law'. Shepstone, as Secretary for Native Affairs, administered this system, in effect becoming the supreme authority on 'native law' as well as the political pointsman for relations between Africans and the state. 'Native' law remained unwritten through the first two-and-a-half decades of colonial rule, but in 1869 Shepstone began the process of codifying customary law by deliberately making significant changes through the marriage regulations of that year.[2] The changes were aimed at the multiple goals of raising revenue, enabling younger men to marry, reducing polygyny and ensuring brides' consent to marriage. Thus, from this stage at least, the colonial state recognised the centrality of relations of gender and generation in the social structures of isiZulu-speaking societies and sought to shape those relations to its own ends.

Colonists finally ended Shepstone's monopoly of control, after the disastrous Langalibalele affair of 1873–74, with the decision to produce a written code. The first version finally appeared in 1878, one year after Shepstone's departure for the Transvaal and one year before the related outbreak of the Anglo-Zulu War. The Natal Code of Native Law, both in its first iteration and in the 1891 revision, made no bones about putting hierarchies of gender and generation at its centre, listing as central principles the 'subjugation of the female sex' and primogeniture. It was this foundation that state authorities drew on in the struggle to 'retribalise' Africans in the 1920s and 1930s, with the severe and rigid hierarchies of the Code being used as a bulwark against contemporary social changes and their political undercurrents.

Labour tenancy, with its origins in the nineteenth century, lay at the heart of the changing economic and social structures of rural Natal in the early twentieth century and hierarchies of gender and generation lay at the heart of labour tenancy. Although the colonial authorities had established African reserves in the mid-nineteenth century, it was clear from the outset that the reserves were not large enough to provide for the land needs of Natal's large and growing African population.[3] Moreover, the settler population of Natal continually opposed expansion of the reserves, seeing correctly that reserve land provided households with a partial alternative to sending members to labour in the colonial wage economy. This was especially true for reserve lands located near colonial urban centres, since African homesteads there could profitably grow surpluses for urban consumers. It was essential to industrial concerns, to white-owned farms, and to urban whites' desires for household servants that large numbers of Africans live outside of or migrate regularly from the reserves. Africans also found advantages in living outside the reserves. White-owned farms afforded young men the opportunity to establish their own homesteads, independent of their seniors and free of the *isibhalo* (forced labour) demands of the state, conveyed through chiefs.

The type of labour tenancy that developed in Natal came to be known as the 'six-month system' or *isithupa* (six, hence a shorthand designation for working six months). A homestead head obtained access to farmland for grazing cattle, growing food crops and erecting dwellings by promising some of his homestead's labour for six months of the year. In practice, the goal of a labour tenant head of household was to secure his position on the farm through the labour of his sons and/or daughters, while his wife or wives anchored the homestead's own production. A married man who did not yet have children, or whose children were too young to perform *isithupa*, would labour during the required six months. Once he had dependants who were old enough to work full-time, however, he would send them in his place. This labour custom was recognised by the 1932 Native Service Contract Act (NSCA), which ensured the right of 'kraal heads' to contract on behalf of their minor children.

### Dynamics of the segregation era

One of the key goals of the Union of South Africa, founded in 1910, was to manage what white intellectuals and officials had come to call the 'native problem' in order to facilitate industrialisation. As in the contemporary United States, segregation was offered as the solution to this alleged problem. In South Africa's case, this meant building on the institutional arrangements that were a legacy of colonial rule, especially in the British colonies of the Cape and Natal. The combination of segregation, industrial expansion and commercialisation of farming in the 1920s and 1930s led to an exacerbation of tensions of gender and generation in the Natal countryside. This was apparent in the conflict over an alleged labour shortage on white farms in the 1930s, and the conflict found expression in a variety of ways in the courts designed to enforce traditional hierarchies.

Legislation that brought this ideology into full and unified practice in the four provinces of the Union encompassed territorial as well as political segregation. One of the key components, of course, was the 1913 Natives Land Act. This act infamously eliminated the right of Africans to purchase land, but it also outlawed new rent tenancies. As a result, in the expanding economy of the 1920s, white farmers increasingly evicted rent tenants or converted their status to that of labour tenants. At the same time, expansion of land use by commercial farmers in Natal's Midlands under the stimulus of rising prices for sheep and wool led to diminishing access to land – particularly grazing land – for tenants. Even with the crash in farm prices that came with the Depression of the 1930s, a new regime of farm subsidies and price stabilisation encouraged farmers to continue to expand production, and a growing ideology of rational, progressive farming led white farmers to continue to restrict tenants' access to land.

These changes, combined with the environmental disasters of the 1930s in the form of recurrent drought, disease and famine, were especially difficult for young men, both on farms and in the reserves. Since the late nineteenth century, the culture of labour migration had encouraged young men to travel to urban jobs for a period of time. There, they earned wages that enabled them to buy useful items such as guns and coats, and luxury goods such as musical instruments, as well as to pay taxes. But migrant labour also introduced a new tension into relations between juniors and seniors. Fathers demanded that wages be turned over to them for redistribution, but young men relished the independence of urban jobs, including the potential independence of earning and paying bridewealth without reference to the wishes or labour demands of seniors. The expanding urban economy of the inter-war years provided growing opportunities for urban employment at a time when the opportunities for rural accumulation were diminishing. As a result, young men were more likely to migrate to urban jobs, and more likely to overstay, failing to return on time to perform *isithupa*. This problem raised howls of protest from white farmers, who sounded the alarm of labour shortage in the mid-1930s. Even more disturbing, both to African patriarchs and to white officials, was the growing tendency for women to leave rural areas to seek urban opportunities or escape oppressive marriages.

From the late 1920s until the Second World War, the segregationist state and its allies – both white and African – attempted to control these trends through further elaboration of segregation ideologies and structures. In Natal, as Nicholas Cope and Shula Marks have argued, converging interests of native affairs authorities and theorists, white sugar barons and the *kholwa* elite led to the creation of Inkatha as an organisation designed to protect and advance the interests of the Zulu royal family.[4] Supporters hoped that identification with the *past* glories of the Zulu kingdom, now toothless but increasingly recognised as a unifying symbol, particularly by male migrants, might deflect dangerous forms of organisation by peasants, workers and migrants. As Paul la Hausse de Lalouvière has shown, Zulu intellectuals and elites had founded a series of organisations designed to promote Zulu unity and foster a nationalist history, beginning in the mid-1910s.[5] By supporting the creation of Inkatha and later creating the Native Administration Act (discussed below) state functionaries and white segregationists tried to tap into this cultural ferment in a way that was consistent with their own interests. This was to amount to supporting traditionalism (in this case Zulu traditionalism) in order to further the modernist goals of a white settler state.

The decade of the twenties was a time of considerable social ferment and political upheaval in South Africa, as urban workers and rural peasants flocked to organisations that offered new ways of engaging with economic change. They did so through rituals that inscribed positive meaning, as well as through protests that aimed to improve conditions.[6] The most dramatic instance of this was the spread of the ICU from the Cape Town docks in 1919 throughout the countryside in the mid-to-late 1920s.[7] In the process, the ICU grew from a workers' union to a millenarian social movement that promised restoration of African land. As such, it held great attraction for African labour tenants in Natal. The rise and rapid spread of such a movement in a decade that also saw the rapid spread of African independent churches caused considerable alarm in a government that had come to power on the heels of a white workers' revolt.

The Pact government's commitment to segregation was given added impetus by the rise of the ICU and parallel movements, which also provided both the incentive and the excuse to introduce further structures of repression. Most notable in this regard was the Native Administration Act (NAA), passed in 1927. Drawing on Shepstonian ideals of native administration, the Act gave the NAD unbridled powers to rule Africans by proclamation, acting through the administration of white Native Commissioners (NCs) and appointed African chiefs. It authorised what had long been normal practice in Natal, the use of customary law in civil cases among Africans. In the climate of retribalisation that prevailed in the late twenties and through the thirties, the NAD was committed to a conservative and rigid interpretation of customary law, as was apparent in the decisions of the NC courts (successors, under the act, to the former courts of the Administrators of Native Law) and bi-provincial Native Appeals courts.

This updating of the customary law regime in the context of segregation and industrialisation meant that when social tensions, exacerbated by a changing political economy, made their way to court, they were framed by the state's conservative neo-traditionalist discourse. The irony here is that according to the vision propounded by the Natal Code (now reinvigorated by the NAA), the cases of divorce, inheritance, disputes over bridewealth and the like that came before the NC courts should never have arisen (because custom should have dictated the outcome in a manner clear to all participants) or should have been matters of mere factual dispute. In real cases that arose in Natal's NC courts, however, litigants and witnesses had decidedly different views about the content of tradition and the proper workings of gender and generational hierarchies.

Three examples, each of which I have discussed elsewhere, will suffice to make this clear. In 1927, two brothers whose *isibongo* was Mazibuko brought an inheritance dispute to the Estcourt NC court.[8] The younger brother was the survivor of his recently deceased twin, whose property he claimed. The eldest brother claimed that under the rule of primogeniture all the homestead's property survived to him. Chief Peni, to whom the younger brother first brought his case, agreed with the younger brother on the theory that custom provided that twins were 'one person', so that on the death of one all his possessions should pass to the other. The NC court and the Native Appeals Court (NAC), however, decided that primogeniture superseded what they took to be an aberrant local practice that did not accord with the Code's vision of 'native custom'. Thus, the neo-traditionalist courts of the segregation era held to a vision enshrined in the Code, even when it contradicted the views presented by nearly every witness (and the relevant chief) in a particular case.

In another case a few years later, litigants disputed over whether an *ukungena* marriage had taken place, and thus whether the father was entitled to customary compensation, or whether it was 'simply an adultery'.[9] Testimony made clear that determination was difficult partly because some members of the community, though not all, were Christian, and thus eschewed the customary practice of slaughtering a goat to celebrate such a union. (At the same time, my interviews show that some Christians were nevertheless polygynous, despite the teachings of the European church on this matter. And *amakholwa*, of course, regularly participated in the giving and receiving of bridewealth, despite the counsel of early missionaries.) Finally, in a case arising in the 1940s, a witness asked to define the traditional practice of *ukusisa*, that is loaning of cattle to clients, defined it as 'hiding cattle on the white man's farm', that is evading restrictions on cattle movements and avoiding demands of bridewealth creditors by placing cattle with labour tenants on white-owned farms.[10]

Added to these definitional disputes are the divorce cases in which wives – and their fathers or brothers – implicitly challenged patriarchal views concerning women's proper behaviour, movements and exercise of sexuality. Although in the 1930s and 1940s many wives in divorce cases lost (either by failing to secure a divorce or by being found responsible, thus making their fathers or brothers liable for return of bridewealth), I conclude that the cases are evidence of women (and other juniors) refusing to accept the subordinate role assigned them by the Code. Review of a variety of cases in the NC courts in this period shows that rural Africans did not accept a unitary view of custom and tradition, despite the efforts of the NAD, white farmers and black fathers to impose a stable view. The very instability and change that the retribalisers sought to counteract instead tended to appear over and over again in the records of litigation.

The dynamics of gender and generation in rural life in this period were revealed in another context when authorities convened the Native Farm Labour Committee to try to understand why farms were experiencing (or at least perceiving) a shortage of labour in the mid-to-late thirties. Although the testimony made clear that young men left the farms due to low wages and senior monopolisation of meagre benefits, officials did not attempt any radical reforms. Indeed, attempts to regulate farm tenant mobility and labour, such as the NSCA and Chapter IV of the Native Trust and Land Act of 1936, had come mostly to naught in the face of the unwillingness of the NAD to risk the large-scale evictions, and consequent further overcrowding of depleted African reserves, that enforcement of these acts would require.

By the end of the Second World War, therefore, labour tenancy persisted as one of the most common forms of African land tenure, and as the most common method of obtaining farm labour (except for coastal sugar plantations, which relied mainly on migrant labour) in Natal. For commercial but cash-strapped white farmers, labour tenancy offered the advantage of securing a ready labour supply that needed only to be paid while 'in service', and then only minimally. Farmers who owned 'labour farms' could secure much of this benefit at little cost to the productivity of their commercial farms. For rural Africans, labour tenancy continued to offer access to land outside the crowded reserves. On the farms, homesteads had access to sufficient land for their own gardens, as well as some – albeit ever-diminishing – land for grazing the cattle that were such an important means of social exchange among rural Africans. There remained the inherent tension, however, that most of the benefits of labour tenancy accrued to senior men, while most of the burden fell on young men and women. That tension was the driving force in rural dynamics between the world wars.

In the late 1940s, the desire of some white ideologues and voters to solve 'the native problem' led to the election of the government that would institute a series of bureaucratic-segregationist measures known by the neologism 'apartheid'. The new spin on segregation included much tighter controls on the movements of rural and urban Africans, leading to a temporary solution to the draining of farm labour. By the 1950s and 1960s, however, the spreading of mechanisation combined with a drive under the second phase of apartheid to further segregate rural areas led to expelling 'surplus' people from the farms and dumping them in urbanised corners of rural reserves.

## Conclusion

Observant readers will have noted that this chapter has only rarely used the word 'Zulu' (except in reference to language or to the pre-conquest Zulu kingdom). While it is clear that changing Zulu identity was an important undercurrent – especially for men – in urban life, and among isiZulu-speaking intellectuals, this was not the case among non-literate peasants in rural Natal, at least southwest of the Thukela River within the bounds of the former colony.[11] Instead, divisions of gender and generation were the driving factors in rural dynamics in this period. Expansion of industry and declining conditions in rural areas (both in terms of conditions of labour tenancy and in terms of environmental difficulties that caused as much or more damage in reserves) led increasing numbers of young men and women to depart from rural areas, temporarily or permanently. This implicit challenge to established hierarchies was countered by the segregationist state, with some support from white farmers and African elders.

The South African state was more broadly concerned with challenges appearing in the form of organised social movements such as the ICU and African independent churches, but it channelled its structures of countervailing control through the neo-traditionalist ideologies of customary law and patriarchal chiefly control. Ironically, the courts established under the NAA proved to be venues for at least the voicing of resistance to a unitary and static vision of custom, indicating a broader resistance beyond the courthouse boundaries. These rural upheavals, with their spillover effects in urban environments, in turn led to a further state reaction, in the form of apartheid, from the 1950s onwards.

## Notes

1. This chapter is based on my book, *Genders and Generations Apart: Labour Tenants and Customary Law in Segregation Era South Africa, 1920s to 1940s* (Portsmouth, NH: Heinemann, 2002). The initial research was conducted with the support of a Fulbright-Hays dissertation fellowship and a Social Science Research Council Africa Program dissertation fellowship. As the project developed, it also received support from Foreign Language Area Studies fellowships, a summer fellowship from the National Endowment for the Humanities, and Southwestern University's Brown fellowship and Cullen faculty development grants.

2. See Thomas McClendon, 'Coercion and Conversation: African Voices in the Making of Customary Law in Natal', in *The Culture of Power in Southern Africa: Essays on State Formation and the Political Imagination*, ed. Clifton Crais (Portsmouth, NH: Heinemann, 2003), pp. 49–63.

3. The following discussion of land and labour in nineteenth-century Natal is drawn from John Lambert's work, particularly *Betrayed Trust: Africans and the State in Colonial Natal* (Pietermaritzburg: University of Natal Press, 1995).

4. Nicholas Cope, 'The Zulu Petit Bourgeoisie and Zulu Nationalism in the 1920s: Origins of Inkatha', *Journal of Southern African Studies* 16:3 (1990): 431–51; Shula Marks, 'Patriotism, Patriarchy and Purity: Natal and the Politics of Zulu Ethnic Consciousness', in *The Creation of Tribalism in Southern Africa*, ed. Leroy Vail (London: James Currey, 1989), pp. 215–40.

5. Paul la Hausse de Lalouvière, *Restless Identities: Signatures of Nationalism, Zulu Ethnicity and History in the Lives of Petros Lamula (c.1881–1948) and Lymon Maling (1889–c.1936)* (Pietermaritzburg: University of Natal Press, 2000), pp. 16–25.

6. See William Beinart and Colin Bundy, *Hidden Struggles in Rural South Africa: Politics and Popular Movements in the Transkei and Eastern Cape 1890–1930* (Johannesburg: Ravan Press, 1987).

7. For fuller discussion of the ICU in Natal, see Helen Bradford, *A Taste of Freedom: The ICU in Rural South Africa 1924–30* (New Haven: Yale University Press, 1987).

8. For a full explication of this case, see Thomas McClendon, ' "A Dangerous Doctrine": Twins, Ethnography, and Inheritance in Colonial Africa', *Journal of Legal Pluralism* 39 (1997): 121–40.

9. An *ukungena* marriage refers to the custom that a man has a right to 'enter' his dead brother's wife, if he has died without any children. This particular case is discussed more fully in McClendon, *Genders and Generations Apart*.

10. See Thomas McClendon, ' "Hiding Cattle on the White Man's Farm": Cattle Loans and Commercial Farms in Natal, 1930–1950', *African Economic History* 25 (1997): 43–58.

11. In 1992, an elderly male peasant I interviewed in the Weenen area made a point of impressing me with his literacy (gained while serving a sentence for a 'faction' killing), reading from one of the school readers created by James Stuart early in the century. The reader, created as part of the fashioning of the Zulu past by officials and missionaries just before Zulu intellectuals such as Magema Fuze took on that project, recounts the glorious past of the Zulu nation. However, identification with Zulu glories displayed by a conservative patriarch in the midst of KwaZulu-Natal's civil war should not be anachronistically cast backward to the time of that man's childhood. On the issue of school readers fashioning aspects of the Zulu past, see La Hausse de Lalouvière, *Restless Identities*, p. 12.

# Hybridities

Customary Traditions, Healing and Spirituality,
and Contentious Politics

*Chapter 24*

# Royal Precedents and Landscape Midwives
## Claiming the Zululand Wilderness

SHIRLEY BROOKS

IN CONTEMPORARY KWAZULU-NATAL (KZN), the provincial conservation authorities (formerly the Natal Parks Board, now Ezemvelo KZN Wildlife) have legitimised their preservationist aims by embracing Zuluness. This is particularly evident in the Umfolozi Game Reserve, founded in 1895, and currently part of the combined Hluhluwe-Umfolozi Park.[1] The park, a key tourist attraction for the province of KZN, spans approximately 964 square kilometres. Visitors can see the 'big five', including elephant, a species reintroduced in the 1990s. In the Umfolozi Reserve, white rangers have attempted to adopt elements of Zulu history and culture since the 1960s, while developing complex relationships with black isiZulu-speaking game guards. Umfolozi has long been called 'Shaka's royal hunting grounds' by conservationists who see their custodial role as rooted in martial Zulu tradition: to patrol its boundaries and keep trespassers from the warrior-king's sacred preserve.

The now famous relationship between conservation visionary Ian Player, who began his career as a young game ranger in the Umfolozi Reserve, and his partner in the wild, the Zulu game guard Magqubu Ntombela, was formed in Shaka's royal hunting grounds. In an interview promoting his 1997 book *Zululand Wilderness: Shadow and Soul*, Player described Umfolozi as a very 'ancient part of myself'.[2] Yet, he explained, for many years he was unable to understand the reserve's physical and psychological landscape because he remained imprisoned within a white colonial identity. Player boldly admitted that he required an aboriginal 'midwife' – Ntombela – to bring him to life as a conservationist.

Recently scholars Bill Adams and Martin Mulligan have suggested that in moving towards a post-colonial conservation practice, it is necessary for nature conservationists to enter into 'deep dialogue' with indigenous people. They argue that significant change has taken place in the world of conservation and that 'non-indigenous conservationists in many parts of the world have been forced to recognise that their

293

desire to preserve people-free wilderness areas has, in part, reflected the colonising imperative to rupture the link between the indigenous peoples and their lands'.[3] Together with several of their colleagues, Adams and Mulligan suggest that a more serious investigation of 'indigeneity', indigenous ways of knowing the land and its wildlife, may be crucial in 'decolonising' conservation practices.[4] This view signals a new direction in critical studies of nature conservation, which tend to regard with suspicion easy links between back-to-the-land environmentalism and indigeneity. In the Australian context, for example, scholars have rightly problematised ecotourist ventures that in highlighting the 'simplicity' of Aboriginal life, betray a 'general and variably expressed *modern* desire to (re)turn to Nature by way of indigenous cultures, to see indigenous peoples as the First Conservationists'.[5]

Adams and Mulligan are perhaps making a more pragmatic point. In the context of Umfolozi, it is significant that appeals to indigeneity have long been a central part of white (and black) ranger training, which depends on its recruits responding favourably to heroic invocations to protect the unsullied heritage of the Zulu nation. Umfolozi symbolises essentialist Zuluness for a number of constituencies, including tourists and white rangers, who have been 'touched' by the landscape, often through the agency of an indigenous person. Ian Player's *Zululand Wilderness* elaborates on a wider context:

> The friendship that existed between white game rangers and black game scouts in the former [white-ruled] Rhodesia overcame racial differences and antagonisms. This was the case throughout Africa with most of the men who served in the field. They shared food from the same pot, slept on the ground together, faced charging elephants and armed poachers together, believing in a cause that few could ever fully describe. The colour of one's skin, one's race or creed was irrelevant *once the Africa we carry within us was touched*.[6]

### Royal precedents

The story of Africa 'within us' follows the arc of the myth of Shaka's royal hunting grounds, which tourists have come to know as the Umfolozi experience. One documentary film made in 1997 focuses on this myth by showing visitors walking in the reserve's 'wilderness area' and observing old game pits used by Zulu hunters to capture their prey. The hikers listen to their guide: '[I]n Shaka's days, this area was set aside as a royal hunting ground and no one was allowed to live there.'[7] The theme of Zuluness, as well as the link between conservation practices and Zulu royalty, is repeated in the images and text of many of the display boards in the Centenary Centre Display Hall, located at the Nyalazi gate. The imposing display hall is intended as a centenary celebration of the park's heroic history, with particular emphasis on the thrill of game capture. Tourists are told:

[t]he Umfolozi area was the site of King Shaka's hunting pits and has great cultural importance to the Zulu nation . . . During the reign of King Shaka in the 1820s, game was abundant throughout Zululand. The Zulus were avid hunters but observed strict taboos and rules, with species such as lion, leopard, buffalo and rhino considered royal game. Hunts could only be initiated by chiefs or the King himself . . . The influence of the Zulu culture on conservation in the province continued due to the support of Dr Mangosutho Gatsha Buthelezi, a descendant of King Shaka.[8]

In addition to the appeal to the prestige of a conservation-minded Zulu royal house, the mythologising of Shaka's royal hunting grounds at Umfolozi is also closely linked to an appeal to a broader indigeneity. Several display boards make an explicit link between game capture or hunting techniques practised by the amaZulu, and those used historically by native people in the New World to trap wild animals. Native hunting and trapping expertise have long been admired by the promoters of the American wilderness ideal. In the case of Umfolozi, it is not coincidental that it was the southern part of the reserve – the place linked most closely in the popular imagination to hunting activities from the Shakan era – that was proposed by Ian Player in the 1950s as appropriate for a 'wilderness area', where access would only be on foot. Player is increasingly viewed by scholars as a key articulator of the wilderness model in South Africa, and clearly many of his ideas have been derived from the American conservation movement.[9] It comes as little surprise that a key sponsor of the Umfolozi-Hluhluwe Centenary Centre Display Hall is the United States Fish and Wildlife Service.[10]

The repeated assertions with respect to Shaka's royal hunting grounds are controversial, to say the least, yet it would be wrong to dismiss them as simply an entertaining fabrication. The idea that Shaka protected game in the territory between the White and Black Mfolozi rivers carries great significance for conservation workers, white and black, as well as for local Zulu men not directly involved in the park. During interviews I conducted in 1997 in 'tribal' authority areas outside the reserve, it was clear that for many ordinary Zulu men, the official narrative of the Umfolozi hunting grounds appropriately invokes the might of Shaka and the lost glory of the Zulu kingdom.[11] They spoke within an oral history tradition, seeing details of past hunts (and battles) as significant reminders of a now unattainable past, as well as a celebration of Zulu masculine prowess. Their testimony does not constitute an entirely invented tradition created for the benefit of tourists, although what is presented as historical fact is no doubt embroidered and suffused with local legend.

For local people, the space of the Umfolozi Game Reserve has, simultaneously, two meanings; the use of the appropriate language depends on context. In English, the Umfolozi Reserve is often referred to as 'Shaka's game reserve', a term used interchangeably with 'Shaka's royal hunting grounds'.[12] However, local amaZulu recounted some important linguistic distinctions between key terms, *isiqiwu* and *indawo yenkosi yokuzingela*. The word for 'game reserve', *isiqiwu*, means 'beacon' or 'boundary marker'.[13] This word reveals the link to colonial delimitation of wilderness with survey beacons and later fences, which barred people from access to conservation areas. The second phrase, *indawo yenkosi yokuzingela*, means, in essence, the royal hunting grounds. In an interview with Mr Gumede, an *induna* ('headman') from whose homestead it was possible to see the junction of the White and Black Mfolozi rivers, the reference is obviously to the second meaning. When asked about the area and Shaka's possible connection to it, Mr Gumede immediately spoke of hunting practices that invoked the days of Zulu independence:

> Yes, we know that place. It is between the two Mfolozi rivers. It is between Mfolozi Emhlope and Mfolozi Mnyama. If you remember, last time I showed you the place where the two rivers meet. Individual hunting was not allowed in that area. They only allowed group hunting. During group hunting, the [Zulu king's] regiments used to prepare themselves a day before the hunting day. Everything that happened during hunting was under the instruction of *nkosi* [the king].[14]

The *induna*'s brother, who had served as a game guard in the reserve since the 1950s, then joined the conversation, adding his view that the white authorities of Umfolozi simply reinvented and preserved the old *indawo yenkosi yokuzingela*:

> King Shaka had his own hunting ground. He gave his people a chance to hunt certain animals for him . . . That ground is still there and there is evidence that Zulu people were staying there because you can see grinding stones. There is also an area where Shaka used to rest. As far as we understand, he used to rest for almost a week. So I think people in the past had their own way of preserving animals. Although those ways were controlled by *amakhosi*. They had their own ways of guarding the animals. *This thing of preserving animals is not a new thing, but it was happening even in the past.*[15]

Local Zulu men such as these brothers have played a significant role in shaping the tourist narrative of Zululand game reserves and their contributions appear to celebrate a preservationist strand of the precolonial past.

For white rangers, such representations also have deep resonance. Men such as Ian Player, who spent formative adult years as young game rangers in Zululand, were fascinated by the oral history conveyed by game guards, who disseminated the compelling idea that the Umfolozi Game Reserve was Shaka's royal hunting ground. In his novel *Embrace*, the South African writer Mark Behr touches on the importance of this idea – well established in Natal Parks Board lore by the 1970s – in the life of a boy character growing up in the Umfolozi Reserve (his father is an officer in the Park).[16] The boy's knowledge that all around him is the old hunting ground of Shaka's *amabutho* (regiments), shapes his childhood understanding of this romantic and possibly dangerous landscape:

> From the house you could see the White Umfolozi snaking its dull water and white sand towards Chaka Zulu's hunting pits . . . [Reluctantly he] abandoned [his] idea of walking with the dogs all the way down to the White Umfolozi to look for the cave where Dr Ian Player said he had found a young boy's skeleton. Maybe killed in the times of Chaka, when Umfolozi was the hunting ground of the Zulus . . .[17]

In the 1970s archaeologist Martin Hall excavated the Umfolozi game pits and published his findings in an article that is often cited as scientific confirmation of the veracity of Shaka's royal hunting grounds.[18] Hall's research showed that the pits probably trapped wild animals in the early nineteenth century, but he issued a caveat:

> There is the disadvantage that it is now more than 150 years since Shaka's time. Consequently, informants with detailed knowledge are difficult to find, and their evidence is less substantial than that recovered by Bryant and Ritter. Furthermore, it is difficult to assess the originality of some of the information. The story of the game pits has now been known for some years, and there has probably been a degree of 'feedback' from the popularised written accounts, for instance in the face of demands for information from tourists.[19]

The historian John Wright, who accompanied Hall to Umfolozi to assist in the integration of archaeological evidence and oral sources, was also sceptical. Wright conducted interviews with two Zulu game guards. He wondered at the time 'how much of [the guard's] information was traditional, and how much was derived from outside sources'.[20] In 1998 Wright recalled this fieldwork and questioned whether the history of the royal hunting grounds is better described as an 'inverted pyramid', a partly invented history resting on a narrow base of fact – in effect, a myth.[21] The Umfolozi bush filled with game and tsetse flies may well have been used primarily for hunting, sometimes on the instructions of Shaka. However, to use the words 'game reserve' is perhaps to formalise this system of animal control in a way that is misleading. Writing about the formation of Kruger National Park in colonial South Africa, historian Jane Carruthers notes that for a myth to gain credence it must 'contain elements which conflate truth, semi-truth, distortion and fabrication'.[22] The successful myth is given coherence by a 'simple anecdotal story'; it might include an 'appeal to patriotism or nationalism' and provide 'evidence of a direct unchanging link between the past and the present'.[23] All these conditions are met in the case of Shaka's royal hunting grounds at Umfolozi.

## Landscape midwives

The pull of indigeneity – and white rangers' memories of romantic tales of regal landscape narrated in isiZulu – emerges most powerfully in the 1950s and 1960s, when young white men in the Natal Parks Board needed stories of ancient hunting and battles to justify their conservation work in a hallowed Zulu territory. Listening to the older Zulu game guards recollect the campaigns of brave regiments and Shaka's exploits, the white rangers responded by seeking to imbibe the spirit of the Zulu warrior as a way to prove their masculine worth in this manly wilderness.[24] The rangers who later wrote memoirs and other books about the reserves, all express admiration for the prowess of Zulu men who saw their destiny intertwined with nature.[25]

Nowhere is this more evident than in Ian Player's memoir, *Zululand Wilderness*, which charts his partnership with the game guard Magqubu Ntombela, an older man with whom Player was assigned to work in Umfolozi Game Reserve. Player initially accepted Ntombela because he came across as an authentic Zulu man:

> Maklwana Ntombela was Magqubu's father. He was son of Nkovana, son of Bidankomo, son of Ngogo, who was an *induna* of King Senzangakhona, an early Zulu king. Then he served Shaka and could imitate the way Shaka spoke. He passed this on to Magqubu. Magqubu would spend hours telling me his lineage and that of Zulu kings, his *induna*s and their praise names. Shaka was a hero of Magqubu's, and we were to walk for over thirty years together in Shaka's footsteps across the Zululand hills.[26]

Over the course of Player's lifetime as a conservationist, he moved beyond an early narrow identification with Zulu male prowess and admiration of the game guards' tracking skills, and sought to enter a realm of primordial power, which, he believed, special Zulu men such as Ntombela could show him.[27] Achievement of a personal oneness with and deep understanding of the African landscape, facilitated by the instruction of an authentically indigenous person, became a paramount goal in his life. As he developed his thinking about Umfolozi, Player began to identify strongly with an ancient human occupation of the reserve going back to the late Stone Age and hunter-gatherers. He felt that the depth of his connection to this lost world was facilitated by the gift of Ntombela's 'insider' ability to interpret and share treasures of the landscape with his white colleague.[28]

Forty years into their relationship, Player remembered a revelatory day in Umfolozi in the late 1950s:

> The three of us [Player, Ntombela and Player's dog] were alone in a small remnant of the once vast wildness of Zululand. There were no other extraneous

sounds or sights of so-called civilisation. We had all this to ourselves, and the warmth of the land, its shapes and contours, seemed to well up enough to dwarf and overwhelm us. *Magqubu for me was a link with the ancient spirit of this place. He knew and understood it from a Zulu perspective.* I thought and felt it too, but more from Stone Age man's existence and that of the Bushmen. Stone artefacts were everywhere. Our early ancestors had loved this place for its abundance of game, wild fruits, and tubers.[29]

At first, it was easier for Player to identify with the prehistory of Umfolozi than with the more recent past of Zulu occupation. Magqubu Ntombela provided a conduit back, through Zuluness, to the 'Bushmen', and before them, perhaps, to a common human ancestor.[30] In a 1998 radio interview promoting *Zululand Wilderness*, the interviewer John Richards asked Player about this primal link, made clear in the book: 'You have a very special feeling for that part of the earth. It must be some sort of – some sort of archetypal home for you.'[31] Player agreed. He elevated Umfolozi to a spiritual space, imbued with the presence of human forebears, and believed that the ancients could be coaxed from the womb of time by men such as Magqubu Ntombela, who had not suffered the loss of his union with the earth:

> Well, I think it was an archetypal home for *mankind*. I mean, early man had been there, and the Bushmen had been there. There are still remnants of Bushman paintings. And one – when you walk on that landscape, you know that you are walking inside a very ancient part of yourself. *But you need midwives – you need midwives to enable you to understand it.* And that's where old Magqubu was so wonderful.[32]

To access the 'ancient part of himself', Player underwent a test in the Zululand bush, which taught him to respect indigenous ritual and the Umfolozi landscape. In the process, Player shed his colonial skin and submitted to the authority of his 'midwife', Ntombela. This test was neither easy nor pleasant. Ntombela virtually bullied Player into being reborn as a man of the Zululand wilderness, one with deep reservoirs of self-knowledge (not all of it flattering). Player said this event was 'without doubt the most critical in my life as a white English-speaking South African'.[33]

The story revolves around Ntombela's insistence that his white partner honour a Zulu ritual by spitting on a stone and adding it to a cairn or *isivivane* (a mound of stones) they had just passed. Ntombela followed the ritual; Player did not, and, in fact, hardly noticed the cairn. The day was very hot, and Player was carrying a heavy gun in a canvas bag. 'The only thing that registered in my mind,' he recalled, 'was that it seemed strange to have a pile of stones in so isolated a part of the game reserve . . .'[34] Magqubu Ntombela explained the presence of the heaped stones: 'The cairns were put here for a purpose. They mark the place where something happened.

Perhaps a man died here . . . and the stones were started to honour the *amadhlozi* . . . No Zulu would pass by without paying respects.'[35] Ntombela challenged the young game ranger, telling him: 'It is the law, it is Zululand, and did you not say you wanted to learn about Zulu beliefs?'[36] Player wanted to learn, but not that day. The heat oppressed him and kept him from walking back to the cairn. 'Your beliefs have nothing to do with me,' he replied angrily.

In *Zululand Wilderness* Player reflects on his state of mind in the standoff with Ntombela. He saw himself as 'arrogant and unrepentant', arguing, 'was I not the senior ranger in charge of this reserve? I was the one who gave orders, and Magqubu could not dictate to me.'[37] More tellingly, he fell back on his racial standing: '[I]n any case I was white. Yes, a white man, and a senior one in this game reserve.'[38] An older, wiser Player recognised that 'I tried to rationalise my prejudices away, [but] deep down they were there and had now come to the surface under the duress of my fatigue, thirst and the unbearable heat.'[39]

Ntombela didn't flinch, commanding Player in Zulu, '*Uthi qi*,' which the author of *Zululand Wilderness* translated more glibly as 'You come here and you do so immediately.' Player describes his physical shock at this overturning of the hierarchical order in the Natal Parks Board: 'Everything around me ceased to exist. I grew cold in the heat of the sun and felt goose bumps burst out on my skin. It took a few moments before I breathed properly again.'[40] Yet he obeyed Ntombela, returning to the cairn, spitting on a stone, and adding it to the *isivivane*. On later reflection, Player thought he 'had been confronted with an aspect of myself that was decidedly unpleasant . . . I was not the superior person, and my white skin meant nothing. Like the trees that partially hid the white rhino in the pan, my skin was a screen stopping me from seeing the real person within, someone I did not really know or like.'[41]

The event might not have made a great impression on Player, but for the fact that shortly after the confrontation he and Ntombela unexpectedly confronted a black mamba rearing up to strike. The men remained motionless while the snake slithered away. Player associated the mamba with the incident at the *isivivane*, and expressed how his relationship with Ntombela had abruptly shifted:

> He was now very much the leader. I had spurned his requests to put a stone on the *isivivane* and pay my respects in the proper fashion, in a way that generations of passing travellers had done. In my white arrogance I had dismissed the beliefs of Magqubu until he had to command me to return, pick up a small stone, spit on it, and throw it onto the *isivivane*. I now knew how wrong I had been and linked the appearance of the mamba with my recalcitrance. My inner voice had already said, You are very lucky only to get a warning.[42]

In the 1998 radio interview, Player again touched on the mamba incident, telling listeners: '[Ntombela] said, "If you had not have [*sic*] listened to me, if you had not obeyed what is the right thing to do in this part of the world, then that snake would have bitten you and me, and both of us would have died".' When asked whether he knew at the time that the incident was central to his life, Player responded:

> Er – no. Well, I mean. Let's put it this way, that I knew – I did not – I had an inkling consciously. But I mean unconsciously it made an enormous impact on me . . . the situation changed. I mean from that moment onwards, I was not the boss anymore. I was not the great white *baas*. I was not. And Magqubu then became the teacher. Now it was a slow, gradual process. But the situation had changed. And that did it. And I think – thanks be to God that it happened. And that it happened that way. Because what he made me realise was that, what all of us should realise, is that we have to pay attention to the traditions and the cultures of other people. And in doing so, we are not lowering ourselves. In fact, we are lifting ourselves.[43]

Reflecting on the *isivivane* and mamba episodes, Player remembered that Ntombela devoted time to teaching his white partner to abide by deeply deferential Zulu ways of knowing and behaving, *ukuhlonipa*: 'With respect came understanding. It was an understanding that was not only an exterior understanding but an interior understanding too. We were reflected in the landscape, and the landscape was reflected inside us.'[44]

## Conclusion

Player's openness to indigeneity is a matter of pride that he sees as validated by Ntombela on the day of the mamba:

> He had seen something in me. My prejudice, my rejection, my lack of understanding and appreciation of everything that had been going on around me during the time that we had worked together – he understood this, but he knew somehow that I wanted to learn, and even though I did not speak his language with any degree of fluency, there was the other language of intuition and of unconscious understanding that could take place between two people.[45]

With Ntombela as his inspirational guide, Player went on from his snake encounter to start the Wilderness Leadership School, and almost single-handedly imported a 'cult of wilderness' from the United States into South Africa. Still, over the years, the overwhelmingly white participants in leadership activities in Umfolozi Game Reserve have continued to walk through an unpeopled landscape, or rather one peopled only by the ghosts of the Shakan past. Ultimately, the social practices that maintained the peopleless integrity of this game reserve proved stronger than the transformative energy of Player's spiritual journey – and were perhaps even strengthened by this white ranger's pilgrimage into his own Africanness, which brought him closer to Nature and to one Zulu man. As for the rest of black humanity in Zululand, they remained (and largely remain today) outside Shaka's royal hunting grounds, with the Gumedes, looking in.

## Notes

1. Government Notice, Zululand Proclamation No. 12, *The Natal Government Gazette*, 1895, p. 406. For official correspondence on the creation of game preserves in Zululand, see Pietermaritzburg Archives Repository, the Zululand Government House (ZGH) Collection, in particular ZGH 762, Minute Paper Z130/1895.
2. Interview with Ian Player, 'Total Exposure,' SAFM Radio, broadcast January 1998.
3. William M. Adams and Martin Mulligan, 'Conclusions', in *Decolonizing Nature: Strategies for Conservation in a Post-Colonial Era*, eds. William M. Adams and Martin Mulligan (London: Earthscan, 2003), p. 292.
4. For example, John Cameron, 'Responding to Place in a Post-colonial Era: An Australian Perspective', in *Decolonizing Nature*, eds. Adams and Mulligan. See in particular, 'Place, Indigeneity and Environmentalism', pp. 185–93.
5. Jane Jacobs, *Edge of Empire: Postcolonialism and the City* (London: Routledge, 1996), p. 136. The anthropologist Nicholas Thomas has also remarked on the new ecological imagination, its construction of aboriginality and Aboriginal associations with the land. See Nicholas Thomas, *Colonialism's Culture: Anthropology, Travel and Government* (Cambridge: Polity Press, 1994), pp. 174–77.
6. Ian Player, *Zululand Wilderness: Shadow and Soul* (Cape Town: David Philip, 1997), p. 256; emphasis added.
7. Shown on 'Life and Death', episode 1, 'Double Exposure: Game Park', a four-part documentary series on the Hluhluwe-Umfolozi Park, produced by the BBC and screened on SABC 2 in July 1998.
8. Display board, Centenary Centre Display Hall at Nyalazi gate, Hluhluwe-Umfolozi Park, 2003.
9. Malcolm Draper, 'Zen and the Art of Garden Province Maintenance: The Soft Intimacy of Hard Men in the Wilderness of KwaZulu-Natal, South Africa, 1952–1997', *Journal of Southern African Studies* 24:4 (1998) and Malcolm Draper and Gerhard Maré, 'Going In: The Garden of England's Gaming Zookeeper and Zululand', *Journal of Southern African Studies* 29:2 (2003). See also William Beinart and Peter Coates, *Environment and History: The Taming of Nature in the USA and South Africa* (London and New York: Routledge, 1995).
10. The other sponsors are WWF Netherlands and Richards Bay Minerals, a South African mining company.
11. These interviews were conducted with the assistance of Bheki Nxumalo. Note that an earlier version of this work was presented in Shirley Brooks, 'Re-reading the Hluhluwe-Umfolozi Game Reserve: Constructions of a "Natural" Space', *Transformation* 44 (2000).
12. This usage has not been sufficiently interrogated. For example, Jane Carruthers says in her history of the Kruger National Park that in the precolonial period in southern Africa, 'there were even royal hunting preserves, out of bounds to commoners, the best known of which was Shaka's game reserve in the Umfolozi district of Zululand, set aside in the 1820s'. See Jane Carruthers, *The Kruger National Park: A Social and Political History* (Pietermaritzburg: University of Natal Press, 1995), p. 7. My work aims to problematise this mythology.
13. R.C. Samuelson, *The King Cetywayo Zulu Dictionary* (Durban: Commercial Printing Co., 1923); C.M. Doke and B.W. Vilakazi, *Zulu-English Dictionary* (Johannesburg: Witwatersrand University Press, [1948] 1972). The meaning 'game reserve' is given in G.R. Dent and C.L.S. Nyembezi, *Scholar's Zulu Dictionary* (Pietermaritzburg: Shuter & Shooter, 1969).
14. Interview at Gumede homestead, Mpukonyoni tribal authority, 15 February 1997.

15. Ibid.; emphasis added.
16. Mark Behr, *Embrace* (London: Little, Brown and Co., 2000).
17. Ibid., p. 22. For the skeleton story, see Player, *Zululand Wilderness*, pp. 159–60.
18. Martin Hall, 'Shakan Pitfall Traps: Hunting Technique in the Zulu Kingdom', *Annals of the Natal Museum*, 23:1 (1977).
19. Ibid.: 7.
20. Ibid.: 11.
21. John Wright, personal communication, 5 June 1998.
22. Carruthers, *The Kruger National Park*, p. 81.
23. Ibid.
24. It must be emphasised that this was certainly an unusual relationship in the context of colonial Africa, especially apartheid South Africa.
25. See, in addition to Ian Player's books, Nick Steele, *Game Ranger on Horseback* (Cape Town: Books of Africa, 1968); *Poachers in the Hills: Norman Dean's Life in Hluhluwe Game Reserve* (Eshowe: Zululand Times, 1992) and Tony Pooley, *Mashesha: The Making of a Game Ranger* (Johannesburg: Southern Book Publishers, 1992).
26. Player, *Zululand Wilderness*, p. 128.
27. Interview with Ian Player, 'Total Exposure', SAFM Radio, broadcast January 1998.
28. It should be noted, however, that much of what Ntombela was saying, especially aspects related to ritual observance, was initially dismissed by Player when he was a young ranger.
29. Player, *Zululand Wilderness*, p. 162; emphasis added.
30. Some of this is no doubt a later construction by Player – in the 1950s sub-Saharan African had not yet been established as the 'cradle of humankind'. But this complex linkage of indigeneities fascinated Player.
31. Interview with Ian Player, 'Total Exposure', SAFM Radio, broadcast January 1998.
32. Ibid.; emphasis added.
33. Player, *Zululand Wilderness*, p. 180. The choice of the word 'midwife' is interesting, equating indigeneity with femaleness in a way that Player may not have intended.
34. Player, *Zululand Wilderness*, p. 180.
35. Ibid., p. 176. *Amadhlozi* are ancestral shades.
36. Player, *Zululand Wilderness*, p. 176.
37. Ibid., p. 177.
38. Ibid., p. 179.
39. Ibid.
40. Ibid.
41. Ibid., pp. 180–81.
42. Ibid., p. 183.
43. Interview with Ian Player, 'Total Exposure', SAFM Radio, broadcast January 1998.
44. Player, *Zululand Wilderness*, p. 184.
45. Ibid.

*Chapter 25*

# Credo Mutwa
New Age Zulu

H. CHRISTINA STEYN

CREDO VUSAMAZULU MUTWA is a controversial figure in South Africa.[1] Hailed as an authority on Zulu culture and healing, he is revered by some and disliked by others, particularly for his endorsement of ethnic chauvinism during apartheid. Whatever the case, he is now known locally and internationally as an author, prophet, painter, sculptor and custodian of traditional wisdom. Today, Mutwa's reputation as a great visionary appears to be reaching larger audiences, especially in the United States where he is celebrated as 'the Homer of Africa',[2] 'the most famous African traditional healer of the century',[3] and even 'His Holiness'.[4] Indeed, over the past two decades Mutwa's books have helped to globalise 'African beliefs and myths', particularly among New Age adherents abroad and the millions of Internet users who visit New Age websites.[5]

Telling the story of Credo Mutwa's extraordinary life is not without difficulties since he has presented conflicting autobiographical accounts. Allowing for lapses in his memory, as well as embellishments, we know that Mutwa was born in Natal on 21 July 1921 to a Roman Catholic father and a traditionalist mother. Through his mother, Mutwa claims to have descended from an unbroken line of 'Zulu High Witchdoctors'[6] stretching back to the 'High Witchdoctor' of the Zulu King Dingane.[7] Mutwa was raised a Christian and received eight years of mission education at different schools before seeking employment as a wage labourer.

When one considers Mutwa's minimal schooling, on the one hand, and the breadth of knowledge displayed in his books, on the other hand, one must consider how he mastered writing with such force and eloquence. An event portrayed in *Vusamazulu Credo Mutwa: Zulu High Sanusi* reveals that as a young man Mutwa worked for an Irishman in the town of Ladysmith, Natal, around 1940. While cleaning the Irishman's attic, Mutwa recalled finding a treasure trove of books that his employer no longer wanted, depicting this discovery as an episode that 'changed my life forever'.[8] Mutwa carried away many texts: dictionaries, histories, philosophical treatises, works on architecture, and entire sets of encyclopedias. In this massive body of written materials,

Mutwa came across a book that convinced him Christianity was 'a giant with feet of wet clay . . . a forgery . . . a false religion'.[9] He subsequently underwent a religious and emotional catharsis, rejecting the gospel and reassessing the cause of a strange illness that had afflicted him since his teenage years. He later identified this ailment as *utwasa*, the call to be a sangoma.[10]

### 'Historical fact and legendary fantasy . . . truth and nonsense'

In 1958, while Mutwa was employed at a curio shop in Johannesburg, he claimed to receive a vision in which a Zulu warrior appeared – a warrior later identified by Mutwa's grandfather as Shaka – and announced: 'You are named Vusamazulu, awakener of the Zulus, and you must help my people to awaken.' Mutwa said that he immediately accepted Shaka's appeal and began preparing with his grandfather to become a sangoma.[11] During Mutwa's clandestine training, his health recovered, and after 'more than two years' of apprenticing with his grandfather, he was initiated as a sangoma.[12] In 1963 Mutwa succeeded his ailing grandfather as High Sanusi of the Zulu people,[13] an elite position that Mutwa has described more ornately as the 'High Sanusi and also Guardian of Tribal History and Tribal Relics'.[14] Exactly how he was 'elevated to the rank of High Sanusi' is not clear, since there were, and are, no formal procedures for conferring such a title.

The next year Mutwa published his first book *Indaba: My Children*, detailing his initiation experiences, although he had sworn never to divulge these sacred secrets. Mutwa anticipated criticism from traditional healers and diviners, arguing that his special knowledge had to be shared with the world. His disclosures had grave consequences. While many sangomas and ordinary black people ostracised him, Mutwa defended his actions, insisting that he was promoting respect for African people by enhancing mutual understanding between the races of South Africa.[15] The deliberate breaking of the vow of secrecy was not done, he contended, 'to expose the Bantu to the scorn and ridicule of the so-called "civilized" world'.[16] Rather, Mutwa wanted 'the culture of my people' to live, adding that '[i]f it is threatened with destruction I must record it on paper. Then future generations will at least know that once Africa had a fascinating culture of its own.'[17]

Ironically, *Indaba* is hardly a tell-all book. It contains 'stories that old men and women tell to boys and girls' around the hearth, which bear little resemblance to any legends collected among the amaZulu previously or since. The fantastic plotlines in *Indaba* and in Mutwa's second book, *Africa is My Witness*, kindled even more debate, incredulity and bewilderment. Those who opened these books to seek the lost facts of Africa found mysterious riddles instead; for their part, isiZulu-speaking readers barely recognised their own folktales in Mutwa's narrative. Perhaps the author's diverse audience failed to take into account that Mutwa himself promised to deliver 'a strange mixture of historical fact and legendary fantasy . . . of truth and nonsense'.[18]

### 'Apartheid is what all the Bantu want'

The reasons for Mutwa's limited popularity at home were also political. His positive view of apartheid, which he qualified when protesting how Pretoria authorities callously enforced their laws, and his support for the white-minority government during the oppressive decades of the 1960s, 1970s and 1980s brought Mutwa many enemies. In 1966, for example, he wrote that the word 'apartheid' meant simply 'to tell different things apart', despite the fact that 'the whole world' had decided to translate its meaning into discrimination.[19] He elaborated that the 'laws of the present Government were not promulgated principally in the interest of the White community of this country; contrary to what most outsiders believe, these laws have been passed primarily in the interest of the Bantu tribes of this country. Apartheid is what all the Bantu want'.[20] These sentiments emerged again during the volatile year of 1976, when he voluntarily gave evidence before a commission of inquiry into the Soweto uprising and recommended that the mostly white army be sent into the townships to quell unrest.[21] He also publicly praised apartheid Prime Ministers Hendrik Verwoerd and B.J. Vorster. It is small wonder that after testifying at the commission, his house was gutted by youth activists.[22] Following this incident he fled Soweto for a short period, but then returned and moved into the security compound of the Department of Parks and Recreation for seven years.

It was during this period of surging popular protest in the early and middle 1970s that Mutwa embarked on a career path to build model African villages/museums in which to display his version of traditional culture. The first of these exhibition centres was erected in Soweto in 1975. Mutwa's employer at the time, the West Rand Administration Board, responsible for the administration of Soweto, sponsored this project as an attraction for tourists on guided bus visits though the township. The first model village/museum was unpopular with Soweto residents, and during the 1976 uprising, militant students destroyed it. Mutwa quickly reconstructed the centre, but it was again assaulted; it is now a crumbling structure containing faded sculptures, huts devoid of thatched roofs, signs linked to world religions (Judaism and Islam) and crude statues (of the Mother Goddess, a tiger, a few dinosaurs, an extraterrestrial and an enormous upright penis), stretching the imagination as to how these eclectic symbols illuminate aspects of African culture and religion. Mutwa persevered after his Soweto experiences and established two more villages/museums in Bophuthatswana and the Eastern Cape. But he eventually abandoned both projects; the land on which he built in Bophuthatswana was claimed by the National Parks Board in 1994,[23] while the Eastern Cape site was purportedly taken over by born-again Christians.[24]

The obstacles that Mutwa encountered never seemed to discourage the promotion of his worldview. In 1986 he published yet another defence of his right 'to tell different things apart' in *Let Not My Country Die*. This book passionately implored the outside world not to disinvest from South Africa and expressed his bitter opposition to the

African National Congress (ANC), which he saw as the most serious danger to the country.[25] As late as 1989, Mutwa persistently backed the white-minority government and wrote a foreword to a book that not only suggested the United States should incorporate South Africa as its 51st state, but also implored Americans not to impose sanctions on the apartheid regime.[26]

### 'Not to be missed!'

Despite many setbacks, Credo Mutwa emerged from the 1980s with a growing following, which paid him to speak on the global conference circuit. In the 1990s he was invited to address international gatherings devoted to the prophecies of the Andes (Peru, 1996); whales and dolphins (Queensland, Australia, 1997); traditional healing (Kampala, Uganda, 1997); nature conservation (Mono Lakes, California, 1999); AIDS (Durban, South Africa, 2000) and extraterrestrial intelligence (Australia, 2001). At home, Mutwa has been somewhat rehabilitated, perhaps due to the rise of the 'African Renaissance', an old clarion call of Mutwa's, which President Thabo Mbeki had seized on, as he urged South Africans to resurrect and reassert distinctly African cultural outlooks in their society. In 1996 a major national bank subsidised a visit by Mutwa to the British Museum of Mankind in London, where he retrieved African artefacts that had been stored there for years.[27] These objects were returned to South Africa and placed on display in a travelling exhibition for which Mutwa wrote a brochure. He has also joined forces with the Department of Welfare to devise programmes for the therapeutic use of traditional African folklore in counselling young criminal offenders. In 1999 Mutwa established the Vulindaba Trust to 'preserve ancient knowledge and to use this knowledge for the betterment of (the) people in Africa'. The trust claims responsibility for the distribution of traditional remedies produced from the indigenous plant *Sutherlandia*, which is employed as a treatment for AIDS and other illnesses.[28]

Today Credo Mutwa is in ailing health, stricken by diabetes and a stroke suffered in 2002. Yet even in 2003, his admirers could still reach him on the Internet for a 'shamanic expedition'.[29] One announcement aimed at New Age enthusiasts offers an occasion

> [n]ot to be missed! This unprecedented rare opportunity will not be available for very long, as this great Zulu Sanusi, high holy man, prophet and protector of the Zulu peoples and the Keeper of Zulu knowledge has invited us to be with him as he imparts knowledge from the stars, previously only divulged to initiates after many years of strenuous testing, now to be shared with the few who are called to him before he departs this life on Earth.[30]

The invitation extends to people who can pay $2 450, excluding airfare to South Africa, to join Mutwa in his own environs.

### The last reincarnation? New Age Zulu

It should come as no surprise that Credo Mutwa's teachings complement the doctrines of certain alternative religions. Indeed, his holistic ideas about African tradition mirror New Age views of God, humans and nature. Early on, Mutwa has preached that 'each tree, each blade of grass and each stone that you see out there, and each one of the things that live, be they men or beasts, are all parts of God . . . The sun is part of God; the moon is part of God and each one of the stars is but an infinitesimal part of Him'.[31] Whereas Christianity teaches that God created the soul, Mutwa says: 'Our belief in Africa is a little different from this. We believe that the soul is in fact an integral part of God and that our souls came into being when God created Himself. We exist because God exists, and our souls are fragments of this Universal Self.'[32]

Mutwa maintains that a comparison of folklore, cultural practices, and religious and philosophical sayings from all over the globe will confirm the presence of a 'tremendous unifying force . . . [that shows] we all are brothers and sisters, not only in our dreams, but in our mythologies and our very origins'.[33] Furthermore, he claims to find evidence for this statement in 'all languages spoken by the different races of Man [which] originated in one ancestral language just as all Bantu languages originated in one mother language'.[34] To support this point, he offers a personal example, telling of the time his wife had no difficulty communicating with her Japanese hosts, since she simply spoke isiZulu to them and they understood.[35]

Perhaps Mutwa's most imaginative effort has been to illuminate an entire 'Bantu symbol-language which is not taught to the common people but reserved for recording secret things'.[36] He contends that 30 per cent of Africans are able to use this type of writing. The Bantu symbol-language is also said to be the same for peoples throughout Africa. Although they cannot understand one another's spoken language, Mutwa believes that they can communicate through their Bantu ciphers.[37] Many of Mutwa's symbols are now being used as decorations on various items such as ostrich eggs for the export market and on buildings, such as the government-sponsored Coega Cultural Centre in the Eastern Cape.[38]

Needless to say, Mutwa's latest projects have stirred the interests of many in New Age circles, especially those aware of his recorded encounters with extraterrestrial life. Not only does Mutwa claim to have sighted space vehicles and their inhabitants, but he has also disposed of their waste; experienced the personal ordeal of being abducted and physically examined by them; studied one creature close up; been forced to have sex with another and even eaten some.[39] 'Oh yes,' he writes, 'Africa has had her own share of UFOs . . . Long before they were even heard of in other parts of the world, we, the people of Africa, had contact with these things and the creatures inside them. We call them fire visitors.'[40]

Unlike Mutwa's prior disclosures about the initiation processes of *isangoma*, he is quiet about the more elaborate details of his extraterrestrial contacts: ' I can only speak within certain constraints because we are not allowed to talk in any detail about these sacred things.'[41] He cautions people not to approach the fire visitors from outer space, but to summon sangomas who 'have been taught how to communicate with them and how to show them that this is a friendly world and that they need have no fear'.[42] To the delight of one international audience in Japan in 1985, Mutwa explained that the copper and bronze ornamental chain he wore around his neck indicated to extraterrestrials that they should rather talk to him.[43]

Many New Agers eagerly embrace Mutwa's philosophy about healing the mind and spirit. Their concern for learning more about traditional cultures and religion reflects a deep desire to be mystically attuned to the forces of nature through an expansive exploration of the mysterious depositories of knowledge on earth and in the entire cosmos. Mutwa often describes how he harnessed his visions and used them as guiding templates which 'greatly strengthened and broadened' his perception – of this world and of the entire cosmos. He also portrays how he was taught to tap 'the Hidden Lake' of the spirit realm, where all the knowledge of the universe is to be found.[44] Such pronouncements draw a rapt following in some New Age sectors.

Mutwa's more recent work is consciously directed at New Age listeners.[45] This trend might be understood from several angles. It has been Mutwa's self-proclaimed lifelong aim to gain respect for African traditions, culture and religion: New Age audiences are receptive to this aim, and they offer Mutwa his first truly globally connected audience. Mutwa has also employed whatever avenues open to him to champion his ideas: such pursuits during the apartheid period appeared to win him more angry enemies than welcoming friends. It is no coincidence, therefore, that towards the end of Mutwa's life, the 'new' is ever-present in his mind, whether the reference is to the opportunities of the new South Africa (distancing himself from his apartheid-tainted reputation) or fledgling alternative religious thought. New Age Zulu, indeed!

## Notes

1. The name 'Credo' (from Latin, meaning 'I believe') was given to him by his Roman Catholic father. 'Mutwa' is an isiZulu word for 'little Bushman'. Over the years, Mutwa has given different explanations as to why he became known as Vusamazulu, which means 'Awakener of the Zulu'. One explanation is that the name was given to him during a vision involving King Shaka who beckoned Mutwa to 'help my people to awaken'; see Vusamazulu Credo Mutwa, *Song of the Stars: The Lore of a Zulu Shaman* (New York: Station Hill Openings, 1996), p. 11. Other sources say that Mutwa was called Vusamazulu because he was a colicky baby and kept everyone in his family awake with his crying; see Bradford Keeney, ed. *Vusamazulu Credo Mutwa: Zulu High Sanusi* (Philadelphia: Ringing Rocks Press/Leete's Island Books, 2001), p. 20.
2. Mutwa, *Song of the Stars*, p. 228.
3. See the website of Leete's Island, a New York-based organisation that offers advice and counsel to start-up and mid-size not-for-profit organisations dedicated to art, education, and social betterment: http://www.leetesisland.com/imagination.profiles.html (accessed June 2003).

4. Before deteriorating health in 2002 curtailed his activities, Mutwa was often invited to speak at international conferences and was highly sought after as a diviner and healer in South Africa and beyond. See http://www.TheAfrican.Com (accessed May 2003).

5. An organisation called the Ringing Rocks Foundation whose aim it is to 'explore, document and preserve indigenous cultures and their healing practices' has facilitated a lifetime stipend in order that Mutwa may 'have the time, space and peace he needs to be inspired in his creative work'. See http://www.ringingrocks.org (accessed May 2003).

6. In the past Mutwa himself used the term 'witchdoctor' for what is today referred to as a sangoma, healer or diviner.

7. Vusamazulu Credo Mutwa, *Let Not My Country Die* (South Africa: United Publishers International, 1986), p. 227.

8. Keeney, *Vusamazulu Credo Mutwa*, p. 61.

9. Ibid., p. 62.

10. The term 'sangoma' is from the isiZulu word, *isangoma*, which refers to a traditional healer/diviner. The term 'shaman' is usually not applied to ecstatic healers from Africa, although Thorpe observes that 'there is no reason to exclude African traditional healers from being called shamans'. See S.A. Thorpe, *Shamans, Medicine Men and Traditional Healers* (Pretoria: Unisa Press, 1993), p. 7.

11. Mutwa, *Song of the Stars*, p. 11.

12. Ibid., p. 17.

13. A sanusi is superior to both a diviner and a herbalist. Mutwa himself describes a sanusi as an unmarried High Witchdoctor (see Vusamazulu Credo Mutwa, *Indaba: My Children* [Johannesburg: Blue Crane Books, 1964], p. 439), although he married Cecilia Ncobo in 1957. See Keeney, *Vusamazulu Credo Mutwa*, p. 99.

14. Mutwa, *Let Not My Country Die*, p. 227.

15. Mutwa, *Indaba*, pp. xv–xix.

16. Vusamazulu Credo Mutwa, *Africa is My Witness* (Johannesburg: Blue Crane Books, 1966), p. 558.

17. Ibid.

18. Mutwa, *Indaba*, p. 429.

19. Mutwa, *Africa is My Witness*, p. 318.

20. Ibid., p. 319.

21. *Rand Daily Mail*, 24 September 1976.

22. *Rand Daily Mail*, 27 September 1976.

23. Mutwa called his project Lotlamoreng Cultural Village, but when Bophuthatswana was reincorporated into South Africa in 1994, the National Parks Board claimed the land on which it stood and expelled him.

24. In the 1990s Mutwa designed and developed another site (with an emphasis on healing) named 'Kaya Lendaba' (Place of Enlightening Talk) in the Shamwari Game Reserve in the Eastern Cape. He dedicated this village to 'the preservation and restoration of ancient African culture and traditions'. But here, too, he was forced to leave, reportedly by born-again Christians. See Keeney, *Vusamazulu Credo Mutwa*, p. 168. The centre continues to function and attracts many foreign tourists interested in traditional culture.

25. Mutwa, *Let Not My Country Die*, p. 162.

26. Credo Mutwa, 'Foreword', in *South Africa: The 51st State*, eds. Stefano Ghersi and Peter Major (Randburg: Fastdraft, 1989).

27. This museum has recently been incorporated into the Ethnographic Department of the British Museum.

28. See the Vulindlela Trust website, containing information on the products derived from the *Sutherlandia* herb for the treatment of AIDS: http://www.credomutwa.co.za/PAGES/news/advertorialnaturalhealer.htm (accessed June 2003).

29. See also http://www.in-spirit.co.za, which provides information on tours to southern Africa using the promotional title, 'In Spirit – Soul Journeys to Sacred Africa' (accessed July 2003).

30. See http://www.dreamchange.org/programs/baba.html (accessed July 2003), a website promoting service to the 'earth through self-awareness' and offering trips and expeditions for experimental journeys involving indigenous peoples from diverse cultures.

31. Mutwa, *Indaba*, p. 455.

32. Mutwa, *Song of the Stars*, p. 18.

33.  Ibid., pp. 155–56.
34.  Mutwa, *Indaba*, p. 438.
35.  Mutwa, *Song of the Stars*, p. 163.
36.  Mutwa, *Indaba*, p. 537.
37.  Ibid.
38.  See http://www.theherald.co.za/herald/2002/12/20/news/n27_20122002.htm (accessed June 2003).
39.  See http://www.metatech.org/credo_mutwa.html (accessed July 2004), a website with a rare and astonishing conversation between Credo Mutwa and Rick Martin, 30 September 1999, which was a front-page story in *The Spectrum*. This newspaper gave permission for the conversation to be posted on the Internet.
40.  Mutwa, *Song of the Stars*, p. 122.
41.  Ibid.
42.  Ibid., p. 150.
43.  Ibid., p. xvi.
44.  Ibid., p. 14.
45.  This is clearly illustrated when he describes how he prays. The prayer process includes praising the ancestors, burning sweet-smelling herbs, holding a sacred crystal or rose quartz in order to create spiritual energy, bathing, visualisation exercises, smelling aromatic oils such as lavender, eating light and pure food, and getting rid of negative thoughts. See Keeney, *Vusamazulu Credo Mutwa*, p. 169.

# References

Chidester, David. 2002. 'Credo Mutwa, Zulu Shaman: The Invention and Appropriation of Indigenous Authenticity in African Folk Religion', *Journal for the Study of Religion in Southern Africa* 15:2: 65–86.

Mutwa, Credo. 1997. *African Signs of the Zodiac*. Cape Town: Struik.

Steyn, Christina H. 1996. 'Spiritual Healing: A Comparison between New Age Groups and African Initiated Churches in South Africa', *Religion & Theology* 3:2: 109–34.

———. 2003. 'Where New Age and African Religion Meet: The Case of Credo Mutwa', *Culture and Religion* 4:1: 67–92.

Thorpe, S.A. 1991. *African Traditional Religions*. Pretoria: Unisa Press.

*Chapter 26*

# Healing and Harming
## Medicine, Madness, Witchcraft and Tradition

KAREN FLINT and JULIE PARLE

IN OCTOBER 2003, Dr Zweli Mkhize, MB, Ch.B., Health Member of the Executive Council for KwaZulu-Natal (KZN) was present at the signing of a memorandum of understanding between the KZN Traditional Healers' Council and scientists, medical doctors and other biomedical health practitioners at the Nelson R. Mandela School of Medicine at the University of Natal.[1] In his speech, Mkhize pointed to the long history of animosity between African therapeutics and Western medicine and argued that recognition of African medicines must be a 'part of our emancipation as Africans [as] . . . we are now living in a new order where everyone is equal and everyone's right is protected'.[2] The following year, through the Traditional Health Practitioners' Act No. 35 of 2004, the South African state established a framework for the legal recognition of the hundreds of thousands of healers whose services had been criminalised since the passing of colonial laws in the nineteenth century.[3] The task of the Interim Traditional Health Practitioners' Council set up by this Act is to provide for a regulatory framework to ensure the efficacy, safety and quality of traditional healthcare services; to provide for the management and control over the registration, training and conduct of practitioners, students and specified categories in the traditional health practitioners profession; and to provide for matters connected therewith.

The Act thus legalises the practice of most traditional health practitioners and stipulates that such practice be based on 'traditional philosophy', defined as 'indigenous African techniques, principles, theories, ideologies, beliefs, opinions and customs and uses of traditional medicine'. While such a definition might seem straightforward and obvious, it masks both a complicated history and – more problematically – poses the assumption of an 'indigenous' African traditional medicine. Indeed, indigenous, or for the purposes of this chapter, 'Zulu', medicine is highly adaptive and cannot be entirely understood unless it is contextualised within the history of colonialism and white rule.

As in much of Africa, most healers in Natal and Zululand were outlawed through the nineteenth and twentieth centuries, and white missionaries and settlers commonly misunderstood the nature of many local therapeutic practices and idioms, mistakenly believing for example that diviners (*izangoma* in isiZulu) practised the evils of witchcraft (*ubuthakathi*) rather than the healing arts. However, the Natal colonial government did allow for the registration of *izinyanga* (herbalists), making the history of Zulu medicine unique in South Africa.[4] In this chapter, we look at two issues in the history of therapeutic beliefs and practices in this region in the nineteenth and early twentieth centuries. First, we examine the relationship between witchcraft, lawmakers and healers and second, we recount the story of the *amandiki*, women from Zululand who were tried under witchcraft suppression laws in 1910, but who declared themselves to be possessed by spirits that made them ill. Both illuminate instances of the historically complex relationship between different cultural conceptions of health and healing, and presage some of the legal difficulties that may lie in the future. Indeed, how society defines who is a healer, what causes illness, what medicine is, what remedies and practices could be harmful rather than helpful, and even what is traditional or indigenous, may prove to be just as fraught in the twenty-first century as it was in the past.

In colonial Natal and Zululand, *ubuthakathi* was a bane to both Africans and whites alike. African communities who suffered its consequences sought to discover and expose those who practised witchcraft, while whites aimed to protect the accused and persecute accusers. Each saw their intervention as necessary, just, and preventing imminent death. Consequently, each viewed the other with suspicion. Whites often cited African belief in, and fear of, witchcraft as proof of the irrational and superstitious nature of Africans and the need for white rule. Africans, however, argued that the white government had aligned itself with witches, giving them free reign. In 1852, Chief Phakade complained before the Natal Native Commission: 'The Government does not believe in the efficacy of witchcraft to kill people, and the Abatakati [*sic*] rejoice at this, because they see they can perpetrate their designs without molestation, and under its protection . . .'[5] Such variant views on witchcraft ensured that it would become an axis around which much cultural and political controversy would emerge.

In the nineteenth century, however, colonial officials who denied the existence of witches and witchcraft spent much time trying to resolve such cases, sometimes persecuting alleged witches and defending them at other times. For instance, colonists sought to differentiate between illness and death caused by poisons that could sometimes be verified in colonial laboratories versus witchcraft that could not. At issue was not only the idea of saving the life of the accused, but maintaining a sense of social and political order. Real or not, the existence of witchcraft threatened in subtle and not so subtle ways to undermine British colonial rule.

Within isiZulu-speaking communities, maintaining social and political order fell squarely on the shoulders of chiefs and *izangoma*. In the nineteenth and early twentieth centuries, Africans suffering from ill health or misfortune generally consulted with *izangoma* who ascertained whether such occurrences resulted from natural causes, displeased *amadlozi* (ancestors), or the work of *abathakathi* (loosely translated as evil-doers or witches). During the period of the Zulu kingdom, suspected witchcraft cases were tried by the king or his chief's *izangoma* at a national or chiefdom *umhlahlo* (judicial type hearing). An *umhlahlo*, attended by numerous representatives of a community, invited distinguished *izangoma* who then 'sniffed out' alleged *abathakathi*. Such persons, marked as dangerous and irredeemable, usually met immediate justice either through strangulation or anal impalement, although later kings instituted banishment from the community. The anti-witchcraft function of African healers made them particularly powerful individuals and rather unpopular with missionaries and government officials. Even after isiZulu-speaking communities and the Zulu kingdom were forcefully brought under British colonial rule and law, *izangoma*, at the urging of community members, continued to 'sniff out' alleged witches, who often then met banishment or death. As arbitrators of justice, healers represented the existence of a judicial and political system that threatened to interfere with the implementation of white rule. The further the British extended their political power within this region, the more they realised the need to limit the influence of African healers.

By the mid-1860s, British attention to witchcraft cases switched from one of concern for the alleged witches and punishing those who killed them to a focus on healers and a decision to outlaw them. Making a direct connection between the 'supernatural' power of African healers to unveil *abathakathi* and the powers of the chiefs, particularly hereditary chiefs, Theophilus Shepstone stated in 1881: 'With independent native tribes the witchdoctor becomes a political engine in the hands of the chief. For instance, if the chief fears a strong member of his tribe, it is only necessary for him to induce the witchdoctor to point him out publicly as guilty of witchcraft to accomplish his ruin.'[6] In 1892, he stated his objectives more bluntly: 'Take away the engine and nothing will be left to lean upon but the power of the government.'[7] Shepstone and other Natal administrators thus targeted *izangoma*, not only for their judicial functions, but also for their support of indigenous political structures.

This political support had a long history. According to Zulu oral traditions, both African healers and *umuthi* (a very general term meaning medicine) played a crucial role in the consolidation of powerful local chieftaincies and the emergence of the Zulu kingdom in the late eighteenth and early nineteenth centuries. *Umuthi* referred to medicine that healed or destroyed the physical body, and also that which helped kings and chiefs to usurp political power from rivals and kin. Furthermore, the king depended on the strength of healers and their *umuthi* to guard and maintain his own physical and political health as well as that of the nation. This included forging a sense of Zulu national identity through their participation in public and national ceremonies. One such ritual that helped foster new bonds of Zulu nationalism involved the *inkatha*, a ceremonial coil or stool (about 15 to 18 inches or 37 to 45 cm) created by the king's *izinduna* and doctored by the king's healers. Into the coil, national *izangoma* wove the ritual vomit of Zulu regiments, as well as the *insila* (body dirt containing one's essence) collected yearly from every corner of the Zulu nation. A respondent of James Stuart described it as follows: 'The inkata's [*sic*] purpose is to keep our nation standing firm. The binding round and round symbolizes the binding together of the people so that they should not be scattered.'[8] The *izangoma* not only helped to create a new sense of national identity in the Zulu kingdom, but also enabled Zulu communities to maintain a degree of social, cultural and political integrity once under British colonial law. Their political role, in legitimating indigenous political power and the judicial system, would inevitably lead to conflict between healers and the white colonists, who aimed to contest the political power of the Zulu kingdom and chiefdoms.

In addition to these more subtle threats, colonial officials soon learned that African healers could also directly challenge colonial rule. A number of early to mid-nineteenth century Xhosa uprisings in Natal's neighbouring colony of the Cape (Nxele, 1819; Mlanjeni, 1850–53; five prophets, 1855 and Nongqawuse, 1856) vividly demonstrated to British colonists the ability of healers to mobilise public opinion and action for anti-colonial purposes. While healers in the Eastern Cape had operated largely in-dependently of the Xhosa king and chiefdom, Zulu healers acted at the behest of the Zulu kingdom and Zulu chiefdoms. *Abasutu* war doctors functioned by treating and mobilising the Zulu army and partaking in strategic military planning. These healers participated in the Anglo-Zulu War of 1879 and continued to function militarily in local uprisings such as the 1906 Bhambatha Rebellion.

By the late 1880s, colonial officials decided that anti-witchcraft laws that aimed to reduce the power of healers had been unsuccessful. Following many discussions in which colonial officials weighed the merits of introducing biomedicine as a means of weaning Africans from witchcraft, it was decided to license those African healers who posed the least threat to the colonial state and most closely resembled biomedical practitioners. The 1891 Code of Native Law allowed for the licensing of a limited number of *izinyanga*. By limiting the type and number, colonial officials aimed to more successfully control the social and political power of African healers, while maintaining a minimal degree of healthcare. After all, the medicinal practices of healers isolated from their political and social functions seemed to pose little threat to the colonial state. The licensing of healers was unique to the colony of Natal and Zululand, which remained the only areas in South Africa where African healers were licensed and allowed to practice. As customary law sanctioned the political power of those chiefs most disposed to the colonial state, licensing sanctioned those healers who were least threatening. Licensing and urbanisation began to change local medicines in terms of how illness was diagnosed, the types of medicines included, and how and to whom they were sold. The resulting commercial and professional development of African *izinyanga* in this province soon brought them directly into commercial competition with white biomedical doctors and chemists in the urban areas of Natal in the early part of the twentieth century. Such competition invited further legal interference, narrowing how and to whom 'native medical practitioners' could attend within the province.

### An 'epidemic of hysterical mania': The *amandiki*

While the early twentieth century saw the professionalisation of some African healers, it was also a time when escalating illness and many epidemics – both of bodily disease and of fear – swept Natal and Zululand. In their wake it was not uncommon for new kinds of healing to emerge, some of which challenged both African and colonial notions of social and legal order. For instance, in Zululand between 1894 and 1914, an 'epidemic of hysterical mania' was said to be 'raging' through the region. In its attempts to quash this epidemic, the colonial state was vexed by its inability to distinguish between what was real and what was fake. It was forced to confront the question of whether the victims had willfully capitulated to a superstitious belief in witchcraft, or, alternatively, whether they were delusional, experiencing a genuine form of hysterical madness which, if the case, would absolve the sufferers from criminal responsibility. This debate, never satisfactorily resolved, had very real consequences for a number of women, known as the *amandiki*.

During the two decades that bracketed the turn of the century, disapproving missionaries and annoyed African men in Zululand complained repeatedly to colonial officials about the *amandiki*: numbers of ordinary African women who were banding together and travelling without permission through the countryside. Making a nuisance of themselves, the women danced and sang, held healing ceremonies, and then aggressively demanded gifts and sacrifices. The authorities' immediate response was to condemn the women for dabbling in the occult and for practising witchcraft. The women themselves, however, denied that they were in any way involved in witchcraft. Instead, they explained that they were the victims of a new form of spirit possession, called *indiki*, which had been introduced from the north. This, they said, caused them much physical suffering and mental anguish.

Considerable confusion ensued amongst officialdom as to whether the *amandiki* were indeed mentally ill – victims of a form of hysteria – or were merely fraudsters, the perpetrators of a criminal hoax. Was *indiki* an 'evil', an 'art', or a form of 'necromancy spread by false pretences by mountebank artifices and charlatans'? Or was it an affliction, a form of 'mania' with its roots in the power of suggestion, superstition and ignorance, especially amongst gullible women? After many months of deliberations between resident magistrates, district surgeons, the Secretary for Native Affairs, and the Attorney General's office, in June 1910, the District Native Commissioner of Zululand, R. Addison, instructed the Native Police to seek out and arrest any *amandiki* they could find. Five months later, eleven *amandiki*, their ages ranging from fourteen to thirty, were brought before A. Boast, the resident magistrate of Eshowe, on the charge that they 'did wrongfully and unlawfully pretend to practise witchcraft, or do acts criminally regarded as such, viz: pretending to be possessed by spirits'.[9]

In this trial of 'Nomlenze and Ten Others', the colonial government could not, however, reach a verdict, for while the women freely admitted to being *amandiki*, they were insistent that they were ill, the victims of a disease over which they had no control. Moreover, although witchcraft had been criminalised, its actual practices had not been defined. And, whereas many Europeans believed that Africans – especially African women – were particularly prone to hysterical feelings, late-nineteenth-century medical and psychiatric claims that the insane could not be held legally responsible for their actions compounded the existing ambiguity surrounding the consciousness and culpability of the *amandiki*. Eventually, after a further round of legal opinion had been sought – this time from the Attorney General himself – Magistrate Boast was forced to allow the *amandiki* to go free. Clearly, the threat of hysterical women was perplexing, but did not threaten to undermine colonial rule. But *indiki* possession continued to flourish, and over the next few years, several more women were tried on the same charges. Some were sentenced to terms of hard labour. In 1914 the resident magistrate of Mtunzini complained that 'ubundiki'[10] was rife in his district, and that he was quite unable to see 'how it can be stopped'. Intriguingly, this hapless official's plea for help is the last archival source we have about the *amandiki* of Zululand.

This epidemic was not the first, nor the last, of *indiki* possession in Zululand. Some early reports show the spirits as originating from beyond the territory's borders. Motivated by the need for revenge by those killed in battle, they affected both men and women. The possessed ate dog's flesh, and were driven to acts of violence against themselves and against others. Unlike for the later *amandiki*, relief was obtained through ceremonies where *izangoma* beat drums, performed particular rituals and songs, and received payment for providing a cure. Occasionally, the spirits drove the sufferer to suicide. *Indiki* spirits could also come from the mines, being brought back to Zululand by migrant workers. New forms of spirits with different manifestations and aetiologies often appeared in the wake of severe social dislocations, such as wars, political conquest, land loss, and devastating disease epidemics like the rinderpest in the 1890s and the Great Influenza pandemic of 1918. An extremely unpleasant possession by 'hordes of Indians and whites', called *ufufunyane* and believed to be caused by sorcery, appeared in the 1920s.

New illnesses called for innovative treatments within broader patterns of longstanding therapeutics. Some of these were specifically directed towards the alleviation of what might be described as 'mental' or psychological afflictions today. It was commonly understood, for example, that a particular form of madness, known as *iqunga*, was the result of failing to carry out the necessary purification rituals after killing another person. Being surrounded by a smouldering ring of burning faggots and herbs such as *iSimamlilo* (*Pentanisia prunelloides*, or wild verbena) would swiftly cure cases of paralysis that had no obvious cause. It was claimed that *isiphonso* medicines, 'combinations of all kinds of animal fats, flesh or excrements, plant-roots, and European chemicals and minerals, from loadstone to washing soda',[11] could cause others to become insane, and were especially effective in love magic and for inducing *umhayizo*, 'fits of hysteria' in young women. Urbanised *izinyanga*, privy to a wide variety of *umuthi* introduced by healers from other areas of southern Africa, as well as by Indians, who had come to Natal from the 1860s as indentured workers and traders, introduced many of these new remedies.

For the *amandiki* of Zululand from 1894 to 1914, however, no established cure or ceremony proved sufficient to contain the epidemic. *Izangoma* or *izinyanga* were not consulted: instead, the women took matters into their own hands. Only someone who had been affected by *indiki* could help another *amandiki*, and ultimately, the spirit could only be appeased by sacrifices made by the woman's family. In other ways, too, this epidemic was unusual in that its victims insisted that the cause of their suffering came not from outside Zululand, but from within. All the accused insisted that the possessing spirit was that of a recently deceased male relative. At her trial, along with Nomlenze and the others, Ungiqondile, for instance, stated that the *indiki* was 'in the form of [her] late father, Mzwakali'. For Tukutela, aged 25, the *indiki* was her 'grandfather, Mjoji', and that of Mankonai her 'late uncle'. Mankonai told the court that her *indiki* had caused her 'to die'. For all these women possession was by the spirit of a close male ancestor, suggesting a different cause for this new manifestation of *indiki*, one whose roots lay in more local dynamics and conflicts. In the context of a territory torn apart and experiencing profoundly traumatic social, ecological and spiritual upheaval, ruptures in Zulu familial bonds and mores would erupt in many guises, perhaps too in *indiki*.

Official sources concerning the *amandiki* fade after 1914, but *indiki* did not disappear. The phenomenon reappeared in 1918, and again in the wake of an outbreak of malaria in 1933. In the 1950s the psychologist S.G. Lee investigated *indiki*, in addition to other forms of emotional distress experienced by Zulu women in Nqutu. By this time, however, the spirits were no longer the troubling presence of a deceased grandfather, father, or uncle, but had once more become random and rootless. By the late twentieth century, *indiki* was once again a complaint of isiZulu-speaking men as well as women. Today, *indiki* remains a recognisable, if varied, force across much of southeastern Africa. Its origins are often unknown, and its symptoms may or may not be benign.

### 'Zulu' medicine

Asked what makes Zulu medicine uniquely Zulu, most healers today argue that there is nothing particularly remarkable about Zulu *umuthi*, and that regional similarities outstrip differences. Although medical practices and *materia medica* vary among South Africa's different cultural groups, historically they have shared medical cultures with many comparable key attributes. These included similar surgical and non-invasive therapeutic techniques, an occupational division between healers who used only herbs and those who healed through clairvoyant means, and the maxim of 'no cure, no pay'. Several medical word cognates such as *ti* (medicine), *inyanga* (doctor) and *ngoma* (diviner), also evince a long history of wider regional interaction and a possible ancient common origin.[12] Anthropologist John Janzen goes so far as to argue that cultures throughout central and southern Africa share the unique historical healing institution of *ngoma* (those ceremonies and rituals associated with a particular form of divination). Janzen demonstrates this through linguistic, behavioural and structural similarities. No doubt ancient trading routes, as well as more recent migrant labour patterns and increased urbanisation introduced many new herbal remedies, healing techniques and tools, along with new apparitions, diseases and psychological afflictions amongst peoples of southern Africa.

Some afflictions – such as *indiki* – transgressed national and cultural boundaries, afflicting people in Mozambique, Swaziland and across South Africa throughout the twentieth century. What remains uniquely Zulu, however, are the terms for ailments, apparitions and cures, and also some of the plants themselves, which can only be found in certain pockets of KwaZulu-Natal. *Isibhaha* (*warburgia slutaris*), popular for curing colds, malaria, toothache and other ailments, for instance, only grows in the most northern part of the province. Only two herbs in particular appear in the records of the James Stuart archives as emerging from the Zulu clan. The early predecessors of the amaZulu, the Ntungwa, were known in the region for providing *indungula* (*siphonochilus aethiopicus*), 'a medicine for chewing or giving to children when having a fever',[13] whereas the Zulu clan reputedly introduced *ikhathazo* (*alepideo amatymbica*) used for colds, a remedy now common in the current pharmacopoeia of southeastern Africa.[14] More recently, botanist Ann Hutchings, together with isiZulu-speaking healers, catalogued some 1 000 medicinal plants, demonstrating the large botanical variety of KwaZulu-Natal, as well as the absorption of exotic species into the local ecology and pharmacopoeia. Unfortunately much of this diversity is threatened by over-cultivation by itinerant traders seeking to furnish the large *umuthi* markets of Durban, Johannesburg and the smaller ones of Umlazi, Mthubathuba and Mona.[15] At a time when the search for cures for HIV/AIDS and associated infections has intensified the need for safe medicines – indigenous and otherwise – the cost of this loss could be great indeed.

Recently, there has been renewed interest in the research of local medicinal plants by universities and government laboratories as a means of resolving these ecological and health issues. For economic, ideological and political reasons there are many compelling arguments for the recognition of indigenous medicines and healers, especially at a time when biomedicine appears to offer little in the way of hope for the sufferers of new and old plagues and when belief in witchcraft as one of the underlying causes of illness and misfortune shows little signs of waning. Today, however, many healers of KwaZulu-Natal use herbs, substances and techniques of Indian and European extraction, which have been incorporated into the local pharmacopoeia for more than a century, raising questions for both healers and lawmakers about what exactly constitutes Zulu or indigenous medicine. Indeed, in twenty-first century KwaZulu-Natal contesting claims about the nature and causes of illness, about the authority and legal recognition of appropriate healers, and about how their cures can be verified, means that issues of safety, efficacy, management, control and criminalisation remain unlikely to be easily resolved.

## Notes

1. The term biomedicine, also referred to as 'Western medicine', 'cosmopolitan medicine', or 'orthodox medicine', is used to differentiate it from indigenous medical practices. On 1 January 2004, the University of Natal merged with the University of Durban-Westville to form the University of KwaZulu-Natal.
2. The speech can be found at http://www.doh.gov.za/docs/sp/2003/sp1022.html (accessed 24 April 2007).
3. The Act was promulgated in February 2005. In August 2006, some sections of the law were suspended for an eighteen-month period to allow for further consultation. However, the substance of the Act has not been altered.
4. While these terms reflect today's popular usage, the historical record shows wide regional variation. *Izangoma*, also known as *izanuse*, *abangoma* and *izinyanga zokubula* all refer to persons who derive knowledge and power from ancestors. Such persons are able to divine medical diagnosis, negotiate with ancestral powers and unveil witches and criminals. The word *izinyanga* translates as 'doctors' or 'specialists', but today is used to refer to healers who predominantly cure ailments using herbs. Thus *izinyanga zokwelapha* (*elapha* – to treat medicinally) or 'medical specialists', has been shortened to *izinyanga*.
5. *Natal Native Commission 1852*, 89, evidence of Umfulatela. Proceedings and report of the Commission appointed to inquire into the past and present state of the Kafirs in the district of Natal, and to report upon their future government and to suggest such arrangements as will tend to secure the peace and welfare of the district: for the information of His Honour Lieutenant-Governor Pine: 1852–3.
6. *Government Commission on Native Law and Custom* (Cape Town: Government Printer, 1883), G.4-'83.
7. T. Shepstone, 'Letter to the Editor', *Natal Mercury*, 19 January 1892.
8. C. de B. Webb and J.B. Wright, eds. *The James Stuart Archive of Recorded Oral Evidence Relating to the History of the Zulu and Neighbouring Peoples*, Vol. 1 (Pietermaritzburg: University of Natal Press, 1976), pp. 40–41, evidence of Baleni.
9. The colonial correspondence concerning the '*amandiki* nuisance' and court transcripts of the trial of Nomlenze and her co-accused can be found in the Pietermaritzburg Archives Repository (PAR), Secretary for Native Affairs (SNA), I/1/452 4045/1909, Enclosure No. 11, 'Copy of Notes of Evidence taken by the Magistrate, Eshowe in Criminal Case Rex vs Nomlenze and Ten Others (Rex 471/1910), Eshowe, 24 November 1910. Including Particulars of Charge Sheet in Summary Case Rex vs Nomlenze and Ten Others'.
10. PAR, Chief Native Commissioner (CNC), 157 1914/139, Native Affairs Department. 'From CNC, Natal, to Magistrate, Mtunzini Division, 14 February 1914'. *Indiki* possession was also sometimes referred to as 'ndiki' or 'ubundiki'.

11. Reverend W. Wanger, ed. *The Collector* (printed as MSS at Mariannhill, No. 1 [June 1911]), p. 41. Campbell Collection, Durban.

12. G. Waite, *History of Traditional Medicine and Health Care in Pre-colonial East Central Africa* (New York: Edward Mellen, 1992) and J. Jansen, *Ngoma: Discourses in Healing* (Berkeley: University of California Press, 1992).

13. C. de B. Webb and J.B. Wright, eds. *The James Stuart Archive of Recorded Oral Evidence Relating to the History of the Zulu and Neighbouring Peoples*, Vol. 2 (Pietermaritzburg: University of Natal Press, 1979), p. 263, evidence of Mmemi and C. de B. Webb and J.B. Wright, eds. *The James Stuart Archive of Recorded Oral Evidence Relating to the History of the Zulu and Neighbouring Peoples*, Vol. 4 (Pietermaritzburg: University of Natal Press, 1986), p. 37, evidence of Mruyi.

14. C. de B. Webb and J.B. Wright, eds. *The James Stuart Archive of Recorded Oral Evidence Relating to the History of the Zulu and Neighbouring Peoples*, Vol. 3 (Pietermaritzburg: University of Natal Press, 1982), p. 25, evidence of Mbovu and Webb and Wright, eds. *The James Stuart Archive*, Vol. 2, p. 84, evidence of Magidigidi.

15. M. Mander, *Marketing of Indigenous Medicinal Plants in South Africa: A Case Study in KwaZulu-Natal* (Rome: Food and Agricultural Organisation of the United Nations, 1998).

## References

Bryant, A.T. 1966. *Zulu Medicine and Medicine-Men*. Cape Town: C. Struik.

Edgar, R. and H. Sapire. 2000. *African Apocalypse: The Story of Nontetha Nkwenkwe, a Twentieth-century South African Prophet*. Johannesburg: Witwatersrand University Press.

Flint, K. Forthcoming. *Negotiating Tradition: African Healers, Medical Competition, and Cultural Exchange in South Africa*. Athens, Ohio: Ohio University Press.

Harries, P. 1944. *Work, Culture and Identity: Migrant Labourers in Mozambique and South Africa, c.1860–1910*. Johannesburg: Witwatersrand University Press.

Hutchings, A. 1996. *Zulu Medicinal Plants: An Inventory*. Pietermaritzburg: University of Natal Press.

Lee, S.G. 1969. 'Spirit Mediumship Among the Zulu', in *Spirit Mediumship and Society in Africa*, eds. J. Beattie and J. Middleton. London: Routledge and Kegan Paul.

Ngubane, H. 1977. *Body and Mind in Zulu Medicine: An Ethnography of Health and Disease in Nyuswa-Zulu Thought and Practice*. London: Academic Press.

Parle, J. 2003. 'Witchcraft or Madness?: The *Amandiki* of Zululand, 1894–1914', *Journal of Southern African Studies* 29:1: 105–32.

Parle, J. 2007. *States of Mind: Searching for Mental Health in Natal and Zululand, 1868–1918*. Pietermaritzburg: University of KwaZulu-Natal Press.

*Chapter 27*

# Changing Meanings of the Battle of Ncome and Images of King Dingane in Twentieth-century South Africa[1]

JABULANI SITHOLE

DURING THE REIGN of King Dingane kaSenzangakhona, the Zulu army under the command of Ndlela kaSompisi fought a fierce battle against invading Boers near Ncome River in the northeast of Natal. This clash, also known as the battle of Blood River, took place on 16 December 1838. The Boers prevailed and henceforth their victory became one of the most commemorated events in modern South African history, beginning with annual celebrations in the late-nineteenth-century Boer republics of the Transvaal and the Orange Free State. One year after the formation of the Union in 1910 an official annual holiday, named 'Dingaan's Day', was established on 16 December. Four years following the Nationalist Party victory in the 1948 election, Dingaan's Day became 'Day of the Vow', a religious phrase which encapsulated several meanings.[2]

Afrikaner nationalists in the Nationalist Party assumed that the frontier Boers, who dealt the first major blow against Zulu 'barbarism', benefited from divine intervention in the battle of Blood River. The victory, in other words, supposedly safeguarded Christian civilisation in a 'savage land'; to this end, they built a church to their Old Testament beliefs within sight of Ncome River. Most importantly, Afrikaner nationalists regarded 16 December 1838 as the beginning of a new era of God-sanctioned agrarian prosperity beyond the grasp of secular British authorities in the Cape colony.[3]

Although the National Party managed to impose this perspective of Blood River on a good part of South Africa, Africans were never passive spectators during Day of the Vow festivities in the latter half of the twentieth century. Instead, they held defiant remembrances, at which they rallied the oppressed majority to oppose racial segregation, which they located in Boer frontier aggression. In particular, they challenged the stereotypical views of inherent Zulu cruelty, which punctuated white writers' written accounts of the battle of Blood River. The counter-commemorations of Ncome gained momentum before the banning of the main liberation movements in 1960, and then accelerated as the African National Congress (ANC) and Pan-Africanist Congress (PAC) sustained the armed struggle between 1961 and 1990. Similarly, other movements such as Inkatha (and later its successor, the Inkatha Freedom Party) developed memorials to Ncome and its legacies, but for different purposes, namely to promote Zulu ethnic chauvinism.

### ANC views of the battle of Ncome and King Dingane

African intellectuals in the ANC and its allied organisations, the South African Communist Party (SACP) and progressive trade unions, played a leading role in promoting an alternative vision of King Dingane. But they differed over the implications of his martial strategies. Some ANC members, who could be regarded as socially conservative, argued that King Dingane lacked judgement and sowed the seeds of racial conflict when he ordered the killing of Piet Retief and his entourage at the Mgungundlovu royal palace in 1837.[4] By contrast, more radical ANC thinkers with links to the SACP and worker activism elevated Dingane as a freedom fighter who defended the sovereign Zulu state in the face of a relentless colonial assault. They promoted 16 December as an historic moment on their calendar of liberation milestones, especially when calling protests against white domination. The Ncome episode thus symbolised a turning point in which a new generation of militant cadres picked up their spears and died fighting Boer colonialism.[4] For his part, the ANC Secretary-General, Selope Thema, provided a third position, issuing a call in 1932 for 16 December to be recognised as the 'Day of Reconciliation'.[5]

When the ANC launched its armed wing, Umkhonto weSizwe (MK) on 16 December 1961 – subsequently to be named 'Heroes' Day' – legacies of the battle of Ncome finally took centre stage in struggle politics.[6] In fact, the first MK combatants to launch operations testified in interviews in the late 1990s that they saw themselves as seizing the spears (*imikhonto*) of their fallen Zulu comrades to free modern South Africa. Writing in the *African Communist*, an organ of the SACP, a famous commentator and supporter of the armed struggle, Mzala, commented: 'MK combatants, wherever they are, whether deployed or not, bow their heads on this day in memory of our martyred dead and rededicate themselves to spare neither courage nor life until South Africa is free. The dead of Income [sic] have risen with the banner of the Umkhonto we Sizwe [sic].'[7]

Soon Heroes' Day celebrations served as events to show the world that the ANC was pursuing a 'just war', given the refusal of the apartheid regime to listen to the non-violent grievances of black people.[8] This morality tale – rooted in Ncome metaphors – permeated the MK soldiers' manifesto, which happened to be issued on 16 December 1961. One illustrative extract reads:

> The People's patience is not endless. The time comes in the life of any nation when there remain only two choices: submit or fight. That time has now come to South Africa. We shall not submit and we have no choice but to hit back by all means within our power in defence of our people, our future and our freedom . . . We of uMkhonto we Sizwe [*sic*] have always sought – as the liberation movement has sought – *to achieve liberation without bloodshed and civil clash* [emphasis added].[9]

In the light of the Sharpeville Massacre in 1960, such justifications of 'hitting back' were needed, for the international community was uneasy about MK's mission; some Western powers also eyed the ANC as a potential terrorist organisation, or at the very least, a reckless group willing to expose unarmed black people to slaughter by the police.[10]

During the 1970s, the ANC and SACP referred to Ncome when rousing militant support at Heroes' Day ceremonies. These annual public pronouncements matched the persistent vigour and consistency of frequent official publications, which linked MK sabotage operations to the courage of Dingane's regiments to start a process of emancipationist nation building.[11] One telling example emerges in the statement of the National Executive Committee of the ANC (ANC NEC) released on 16 December 1986 to honour the 25th anniversary of MK:

> It was not by accident that we launched MK on December 16th. White South Africa observes that day as the triumph of its military might over our people. The violence that they celebrate is the violence of a minority aimed at subjugating the majority of the people of our country. It is a celebration of injustice and inhumanity of man against man. We chose that day to show how different we were. *We celebrate December 16, our Heroes Day, to underlie our commitment that we are waging a just pursuit of freedom, democracy and peace* [emphasis added].[12]

In his autobiography, *A Long Walk to Freedom*, Nelson Mandela reiterates another version of this view:

> On that day white South Africans celebrate the defeat of the great Zulu leader Dingane at the Battle of Blood River in 1838 . . . [the] day, the bullets of the Boers were too much for the assegais of the Zulu *impis*. We chose December 16 to show that the African had not only begun to fight, and that we had righteousness – and dynamite – on our side.[13]

Perhaps the 1980s, more than any other decade, entrenched the symbolic importance of Ncome among ANC activists. In September 1984, the month when a new tricameral constitution came into effect, there was an outbreak of fierce protests in African, Coloured and Indian communities, signalling the most serious anti-apartheid eruptions since the Soweto revolts of 1976 and 1977. The state and police enlisted the services of homeland-based vigilantes to quell the uprisings, and for the first time since 1960, deployed soldiers from the South African army in the townships.[14] This development created an opening for the ANC to reassert itself as the primary force commanding the struggle for liberation *inside* South Africa. In January 1985 the ANC called for the country to be made ungovernable. By this time MK had also stepped up its operations. In the late 1970s these armed actions had numbered no more than about twenty a year. By 1983 and 1984 this figure had risen to about 40 a year, and from 1986 onwards it rose to about 200 a year.[15] The 230 attacks in 1986 alone represented a 300 per cent increase of the number of guerrilla incursions mounted in 1983, a year before the outbreak of the township revolts.[16] The reaction of the South African government and its international allies, President Reagan in the United States and Prime Minister Thatcher in Britain, was to brand the ANC a terrorist organisation.[17] During this period, the battle of Ncome was again cited by media sources sympathetic to the anti-apartheid struggle, such as in the documentary films *The Anvil and the Hammer* in 1985 and *The Spear of the Nation* in 1986, to demonstrate the legitimacy of African military resistance and the need for black people to soldier on.[18]

Although the countrywide State of Emergency declared by the white-minority government in 1986 again extended a measure of draconian control, the crackdown ultimately failed to quiet the national rage, which received a boost from international sanctions that started to crimp the finances of the apartheid regime.[19] In the context of the deepening crisis in South Africa, an influential section within the leadership of the ANC considered very seriously a negotiated settlement, while a more militant coterie called for the intensification of revolutionary fervour and the forcible seizure of power.[20] Reflecting on this time, Mzala evoked the founding fathers of MK who selected 16 December to launch modern armed struggle in 1961 to indicate that the current heroic freedom fighters 'master the art of victory' and not risk another defeat against their conquerors.[21] ANC president Oliver Tambo's late-1980s Heroes' Day addresses carried this line forward when he hailed MK for carrying forward the work of the kings Dingane, Cetshwayo, Makana, Sekhukhune, Moshoeshoe and others who were committed to thwarting colonial aggression.[22]

Throughout this period, it is striking how little attention was paid to the complex image of King Dingane. The sketch of his life seemed to belong to a different set of biographers, who focused on Natal province and KwaZulu homeland during the 1970s and 1980s, namely Mangosuthu Buthelezi's Inkatha cultural nationalist organisation.

**Dingane: Traitor or hero?**

In the 1970s, Mangosuthu Buthelezi and other Zulu nationalist leaders resurrected Inkatha by promoting the worship of certain royal Zulu figures.[23] Following the precedents of conservative isiZulu-speaking politicians of the 1920s and 1930s, such as John Dube and Zulu regent Mshiyeni, Buthelezi's organisation elevated Shaka, and to a lesser extent Mpande, as symbols of ascendant Zulu ethnic politics. For example, Inkatha campaigned successfully for a public holiday known as 'Shaka Day' on 24 September.[24] This gave rise to a situation in South Africa where two kings, Shaka and Dingane, were commemorated annually by opposing camps. From the early 1970s onwards, the death of King Shaka was commemorated on 24 September, while the defeat of King Dingane's army at Ncome was celebrated on 16 December. When the uneasy alliance between Inkatha and the ANC dissolved into bitter rivalry in 1979,[25] Shaka's Day became an exclusive Inkatha affair, while 16 December remained Heroes' Day for the ANC, especially in the mid-to-late 1980s, when the latter's in-country partners, the United Democratic Front (UDF) and Congress of South African Trade Unions (COSATU), mobilised wide anti-apartheid protests.[26] At this time, supporters of Inkatha openly began to denounce King Dingane as a traitor who collaborated with his brother, Mhlangana, and others to assassinate the great King Shaka, thereby associating their modern-day political opponents with Dingane. Such a decision seemed at odds with Mangosuthu Buthelezi's rehabilitation of King Dingane in the wake of the 1982 Ingwavuma land deal.[27] Meanwhile, many supporters of the UDF and COSATU hailed King Dingane as a freedom fighter.

In 1987, when I was a teacher in a township school in Elandskop outside Pietermaritzburg, I was forced to deal with a group of armed youths who burst into my classroom shortly after COSATU and the UDF declared a stayaway for 5 and 6 May. Workers who refused to strike blamed drivers of the KwaZulu buses, many of them members of a COSATU affiliate known as the Transport and General Workers' Union, for joining the stayaway instead of ferrying them to their jobs. When buses resumed their normal runs on the morning of 7 May local residents blocked the roads. One pupil was run over and fatally injured when he and others stepped in front of a moving bus. After this tragedy, students whose political allegiance was unknown were called upon to announce publicly whether they were supporters of Inkatha or the UDF. Those known to be sympathisers of the UDF were immediately attacked. The morning these students crashed into my classroom, I asked them why they were so upset. A leader in the group replied in isiZulu: '*Asibafuni oDingane noMhlangana phakathi kwethu! Kufuneka kucace ukuthi umuntu uyiliphi. Amakula namaXhosa kufuneka ayodla upaku namanye amakula*' (We do not want Dinganes and Mhlanganas in our midst! People should come out into the open and make it known where they stand. Indians and Xhosas should go and share *upaku* with other Indians).[28]

A few days later, I took the opportunity to discuss the student outburst in one of my history lessons. Some of my pupils confidently told me that King Dingane was a deceitful leader because he and his half brother, Mhlangana, organised the assassination of King Shaka. Although these students never directly addressed what happened at the battle of Ncome, their views of Dingane eerily echoed the opinions expressed by John Dube and regent Mshiyeni, who initially championed Shaka's so-called empire-building record. Indeed, the anti-Dingane attitude that prevailed in Elandskop in the late 1980s intensified after Shaka Day rallies at eShowe (Elandskop) and Wadley stadium – facilities close to my township.[29]

The Inkatha perspectives of Dingane co-existed with another, less critical observation of the second Zulu king, which can be found in a 1988 article published in the journal *Injula*. The author of this article, Mandla (a pseudonym), provided evidence that youths from townships in the Pietermaritzburg area were in fact parroting what homeland school history books said about King Dingane, the useless ruler: 'Ngisho *nezithombe esidwetshelwa zona ezincwadini zemilando kaZulu* ... *kuthi kwimifanekiso kaDingane siboniswe isidlekeza nje sendoda esho ngomkhabakazi nomlomo olengayo kuhle kwesilimakazi*' (Even the pictures that are drawn for us in the textbooks and art books of Zulu history [with] pictures of Dingane . . . [show] an obese man who has a big belly and a drooping mouth like that of an imbecile).[30] Mandla questioned this colonial stereotype of the king by rejecting any suggestion that Dingane was a fool. And, like activists of the ANC and SACP, he proposed an alternative narrative: that the second Zulu king was actually an unheralded brave hero who confronted white invaders in the 1830s. Although the Zulu army lost at Ncome in 1838 and, later, at Maqongqo in 1840, Mandla claimed that Dingane made the supreme sacrifice when he chose to die in exile, rather than submit his people to colonial subjugation.[31]

In my interviews in the late 1990s with former MK operatives, Dumezweni Zimu and Nkosinathi Nhleko, Dingane was not vilified, but rather hailed as a crucial figure in the story of Zulu independence. Citing little difference between Shaka and his successor, Zimu and Nhleko regarded both Zulu kings as heroic nation-builders.[32] Zimu even stated that Dingane's role in the assassination of Shaka did not warrant any special mention.[33] Dingane, Zimu explained, instituted a coup d'état, a common form of political succession in the nineteenth-century Zulu state.[34] Coups, he further remarked, also determined the course of monarchies throughout the world. Then both MK fighters weighed in on the significance of whether the death of Shaka led to wholesale changes in the lives of ordinary Zulu subjects. Only a few big land barons (chiefs and *izinduna*) who were the top beneficiaries of Shaka's patronage, were affected by the shift in power to Dingane's allies. In other words, the ANC soldiers said, peasants within the Zulu state largely remained in their territories tilling soil and herding cattle after the coup in 1828. Zulu commoners would experience far greater shocks in the years following the armed Boer intervention in 1840 that uprooted King Dingane from the Zulu monarchy and paved the way for various British colonial incursions from Natal.

From this it is clear that Africans seeking to promote their freedom and Afrikaner advocates of apartheid did not share the same understanding of Ncome. This obvious point tends to obscure a far more complex dynamic of Blood River commemoration. From the early twentieth century to the end of the 1930s, radicalised members of the ANC increasingly viewed Dingane as a freedom fighter, in contrast to conservative leaders of the ANC such as John Dube, who criticised the second Zulu king for unleashing racial animosity in South Africa. On the eve of the armed struggle and well into the 1960s, the ANC and its allies jettisoned Dube's position and exalted in Dingane the hero. Negative images of King Dingane resurfaced again in the 1970s and 1980s, however, as the revivified Inkatha organisation in the KwaZulu homeland began to promote King Shaka as its icon of nationalist ideology. In particular, Mangosuthu Buthelezi's embrace of the Zulu founder swayed school-going youths in Inkatha's ranks to denigrate Dingane as a treacherous assassin; at the same time their political opponents in the UDF, COSATU, and later the ANC celebrated the second king as a great patriot of the nineteenth century.

What do we make of these contradictory currents? For one, they direct our attention to a central idea about how Zuluness, or perceptions of what made and continues to make Zuluness, are constructed, redistilled, and changed over time by various ideologues and activists competing in a political arena. Two words which carried great importance among the former MK informants I spoke to in the 1990s and among my students in the tumultuous 1980s were *ubuZulu bethu*, a phrase roughly translated as 'our Zuluness'. They expressed fierce opinions about the lessons that could be gleaned from key leaders and events that shaped the independent Zulu state (the fount of their Zuluness); they also acknowledged that rival Zulu royals fiercely sought to exercise exclusive rights to rituals of power that ultimately led to resistance against white invaders. Thus, Dingane's reign effectively provides a compelling example of how *ubuZulu bethu* is not a sealed vernacular idea, but a phrase that encompasses competing views held by different actors for different reasons.

### Notes

1. This chapter was initially presented at a one-day workshop that was organised by the Department of Arts and Culture at the University of Zululand at kwaDlangezwa in 1998.
2. S. Ndlovu, ' "He Did What Any Other Person in His Position Would Have Done to Fight the Forces of Invasion and Disruption": Africans, the Land and Contending Images of King Dingane (the Patriot) in the Twentieth Century, 1916–1950s', *South African Historical Journal* 38 (1998): 99–143.

3. C. Muller, 'The Period of the Great Trek, 1835–1854', in *Five Hundred Years: A History of South Africa*, ed. C. Muller (Pretoria: Academica, 1969), pp. 141–42. Such views of the battle of Blood River had remained dominant for more than century until, surprisingly, some Afrikaner scholars in the 1980s and onwards began to critically assess the legacies of the battle of Blood River. See for example, B.J. Liebenberg, 'Mites Rondom Bloedrivier en die Gelofte', in *South African Historical Journal* 20 (1988).

4. A.T. Nzula, 'Smash the Passes', and A.T. Nzula, 'Comrade Joe Nkosie: First African Revolutionary', in *South African Communists Speak, 1915 to 1980* (London: Inkululeko Publications, 1981), pp. 109, 111.

5. Ibid. S.M. Ndlovu, 'Johannes Nkosi and the Communist Party of South Africa: Images of Blood River and King Dingane in the Late 1920s–1930', *History and Theory* 39:4 (2000): 111–32.

6. See 'The Manifesto of uMkhonto weSizwe – issued on December 16, 1961', in *South African Communists Speak, 1915 to 1980*, pp. 274–76; F. Meli, *South Africa Belongs to Us: A History of the ANC* (Harare: Zimbabwe Publishing House, 1989), pp. 145–46 and M.A. van der Merwe, '"Private Armies" with Specific Reference to South Africa', *Strategic Review for Southern Africa* XIII:2 (November 1991): 59–60. On Heroes' Day, see SACP, 'In Honour of J.B. Marks on Heroes' Day – Moscow on 16 December 1974', *African Communist*, Second Quarter, No. 61 (1975): 90–94.

7. Mzala, 'The Battle of Income – Symbol of Our Armed Struggle', *African Communist* 116 (1989): 95.

8. See 'Opening Address by the President of the African National Congress, Oliver R. Tambo to the ANC Consultative Conference' in *Advance to National Democracy: Report on the ANC National Consultative Conference, 14–16 December 1990* (Johannesburg: African National Congress, 1991), p. 4; Joe Slovo, 'Interview in an ANC Documentary, Cassette No. 3, 1958–1969', in *Ulibambe Lingashoni Ilanga: Hold Up the Sun*, ed. S. Wells (Braamfontein: Thebe and ANC, 1993) and ANC, 'Second Submission to the Truth and Reconciliation Commission' (Johannesburg: ANC Department of Information and Publicity, May 1997).

9. 'The Manifesto of uMkhonto weSizwe', p. 275 and Meli, *South Africa Belongs to Us*, pp. 145–46.

10. N. Mandela, *Long Walk to Freedom: An Autobiography of Nelson Mandela* (New York: Little, Brown and Co., 1994), pp. 234–39.

11. See Sol Dubula, 'Ten Years of Umkhonto weSizwe: A Survey of the Achievements of South Africa's Freedom Fighters, and the Discussion of the Role of Armed Struggle in National Liberation', *African Communist* Fourth Quarter, 47 (1971): 22–38 and Yusuf Dadoo's address to a memorial to the former chairperson of the South African Communist Party, J.B. Marks, on Heroes' Day 16 December 1974 in Moscow entitled: 'In Honour of J.B. Marks', *African Communist*, Second Quarter, 61 (1975): 90. Mgobi Tshonyane's article commemorating the 25th anniversary of MK explains that 16 December was selected to recognise the 'length and breadth' of brutal white repression of the masses irrespective of their ethnic and regional background to fight for freedom: M. Tshonyane, 'The Pride of All the Oppressed', *African Communist* 108 (1987): 25–26.

12. See ANC, 'Umkhonto we Sizwe – Born of the People: Statement of the National Executive Committee Issued on 16 December 1986', *Sechaba* (March 1987): 18.

13. Mandela, *Long Walk*, pp. 248–49.

14. See W. Beinart, *Twentieth-Century South Africa* (Cape Town: Oxford University Press, 1994), pp. 244–51.

15. See ANC, 'Second Submission', Appendix Four, pp. 72–101; *Weekly Mail*, 18–22 December 1986 and 18–23 December 1987; R.M. Price, *The Apartheid State in Crisis: Political Transformation in South Africa, 1975–1990* (New York: Oxford University Press, 1991), pp. 192–97.

16. R.M. Price, *The Apartheid State in Crisis*, p. 193 and *Weekly Mail*, 18–22 December 1986.

17. L. Thompson, *A History of South Africa* (Rev. ed. New Haven: Yale, 1995), p. 232.

18. J. Hamburg and P. Tate, *The Anvil and the Hammer*, audio-visual tape (International Defence and Aid Fund for Southern Africa, 1985) and I. Stuttard and D. Tereshchuck, *The Spear of the Nation*, audio-visual tape (London, Thames Television, 1986).

19. R.M. Price, *The Apartheid State in Crisis*, Chapter 7.

20. See SACP, *Path to Power* (London: Inkululeko Publications, 1990), pp. 48–60 and *Sechaba*, 1986, 1987, 1988 and 1989 editions.

21. Mzala, 'The Battle of Income': 95.

22. O.R. Tambo, Heroes' Day addresses on Radio Freedom on 16 December 1986, 1987 and 1988, (audio cassettes in possession of the author). In keeping with this tradition, the ANC held its first consultative conference as an unbanned organisation from 14–16 December 1990. See 'Speeches by Oliver R. Tambo and Nelson Mandela to Soccer City Rally, 16th December 1990', in ANC, *Advance to National Democracy: Report on the ANC National Consultative Conference, 14–16 December 1990*, pp. 27–34; *Work In Progress* 70–71 (November to December 1990); *Mayibuye* 1:3 (1990) and *Mayibuye* 1 February 1991.

23. G. Maré and G. Hamilton, *An Appetite for Power: Buthelezi's Inkatha and Politics of 'Loyal Resistance'* (Johannesburg: Ravan, 1987), pp. 54–60.

24. C. Hamilton, *Terrific Majesty: The Powers of Shaka Zulu and the Limits of Historical Invention* (Cape Town: David Philip, 1998), p. 1. *Inkosi* Mangosuthu Buthelezi subsequently informed the author that it was his mother, Princess Magogo kaDinuzulu, who urged him to carry forward King Solomon's national project which he had died without completing in 1933. Author's informal conversation with *Inkosi* Mangosuthu Buthelezi at the Chief Albert Luthuli Memorial lecture, University of KwaZulu-Natal, Westville Campus, on 27 October 2007.

25. Mzala, *Gatsha Buthelezi: Chief with a Double Agenda* (London: Zed Books, 1988), pp. 126–28.

26. The United Democratic Front (UDF), which supported ANC ideals but maintained a separate identity, launched its 1986 'Christmas against the Emergency' campaign on 16 December. See *Weekly Mail*, 5–11 December 1986.

27. For more information on the 1982 Igwavuma land deal and the rehabilitation of King Dingane, see Nsizwa Dlamini's chapter 'Monuments of Division' in this volume.

28. The word *upaku* refers to a particular Indian food. In could have derogatory connotations and *amakula* is a derogatory term used against Indians in Natal. This talk was a reference to the UDF and COSATU, which had visible Indian membership and leadership at the time.

29. See for example, *Weekly Mail* 30 September to 6 October 1988.

30. Mandla, *'Inkulumo-mpikiswano ngoShaka kaSenzangakhona: Ngabe wayengumholi onjani?'* in *Injula* 1 (November 1988): 17.

31. Ibid.

32. Dumezweni Zimu and Nkosinathi Nhleko, conversation in Bergville, 18 October 1997.

33. Dumezweni Zimu, interview at Esinadini, 3 August 2003, SADET Oral History Project.

34. Dumezweni Zimu and Nkosinathi Nhleko, conversation in Bergville, 18 October 1997.

*Chapter 28*

# Chief Albert Luthuli and Bantustan Politics

JABULANI SITHOLE

CHIEF ALBERT LUTHULI remains one of the major icons of liberation politics in the apartheid era.[1] From his heyday in the 1950s to his death in 1967, he served as the president-general of the African National Congress (ANC). Luthuli enjoyed popularity and respect from the masses in South Africa for his talents as 'a profound thinker, a man of powerful logic with a keen sense of justice; a man of lofty principles, a bold and courageous fighter and statesman'.[2] He was also the first African recipient of the Nobel Peace Prize in 1960, accepting the award in Oslo a year later adorned with the regalia of a Zulu chief.[3] Today, Luthuli is widely accepted as the father of unitary national politics and non-violent resistance in modern South Africa.

Although Luthuli's reputation was of both national and international stature, he received little attention from scholars at home after his passing. Indeed, the complex nature of Luthuli's ideals – his mix of democratic principles, African nationalist goals, and Christian mores – made him a figure who did not readily serve arguments on either side of the Marxist-liberal debate conducted during the final two decades of apartheid.[4] In the 1970s, Mangosuthu Gatsha Buthelezi, chief minister of the KwaZulu bantustan[5] and president of Inkatha Yenkululeko yeSizwe (renamed the Inkatha Freedom Party in 1993), noted this discomfort and stepped forward to express public appreciation of Luthuli's political significance.[6] As Buthelezi's clandestine support from the exiled leadership of the ANC crumbled at the end of the 1970s, he sought to shore up his credentials as a freedom fighter by appropriating the mantle of his so-called mentor, the 'patriotic' leader Albert Luthuli, who was said to guide Inkatha's actions.[7] In response to rapidly shifting political exigencies within liberation politics and the intensifying anti-apartheid protests that gripped South Africa in the 1970s and 1980s, Inkatha confronted strong challenges to its reformist platform of cultural chauvinism, incremental negotiations with Pretoria, and free enterprise economics. Thus, the embattled KwaZulu bantustan leadership increasingly drew on Luthuli's legacies of 'non-violent' protest and purported 'mentorship' of Buthelezi as the Zulu nationalist model for social change in all of South Africa.

### Mentor and protégé: Buthelezi and Luthuli in the 1950s

Prior to Buthelezi's rise to power, he was a chief in Mahlabathini, Zululand, a position in the KwaZulu bantustan to which he was appointed by the apartheid government in the 1950s.[8] His confirmation in this position was clouded by controversy as his half-brother, Mceleli Buthelezi, objected to the succession proceedings. The matter was brought to a close when Pretoria ruled in favour of Mangosuthu Buthelezi and temporarily banished Mceleli Buthelezi to Sibasa in the Transvaal. This brush with ruthless, state-sponsored traditional politics would profoundly influence the way Mangosuthu Buthelezi considered his relationship to Luthuli.

Ben Temkin, Buthelezi's first major biographer, has established that his subject of study first met Luthuli and other prominent ANC leaders in 1949, when Buthelezi was in Durban after his expulsion from Fort Hare.[9] Temkin describes how 'Luthuli was . . . by comparison with Buthelezi, a minor chief of an exceptionally poor area and also not a member of the royal house'.[10] Luthuli contradicts the main part of this assertion in his 1961 autobiography, *Let My People Go*. According to this source, his grandmother and mother spent part of their childhood in the household of King Cetshwayo, in keeping with the Zulu custom through which esteemed members of the Zulu state showed respect to regal power by having their daughters raised in the royal court.[11] One may conclude that Buthelezi probably saw Luthuli as an important figure with royal Zulu legitimacy.

Temkin presents other assertions that are difficult to substantiate, given the political repression in apartheid South Africa. For example, he portrays a close mentor-protégé relationship between the elder Luthuli and younger Buthelezi. In fact, Temkin describes ANC leaders such as Luthuli, Masabalala Bonnie Yengwa and Dr Zamindlela Conco coming to talk about ideas and current affairs in Buthelezi's Mahlabathini home in the late 1950s. If these interactions did occur, Luthuli for one would have been openly flouting his strict banning orders. Temkin adds that despite the political risks involved, these visits continued for years, with Buthelezi learning the art of practical politics from his senior ANC teachers. An image conjured here is that of a young Zulu politician benefiting from the wisdom of Luthuli and other Zulu figures of note.

However, Temkin is careful to state that Luthuli never encouraged Buthelezi to participate in the bantustan system. Instead, Bishop Alpheus Zulu and Jordan Ngubane supposedly coaxed a reluctant Buthelezi to play a key role in KwaZulu governance and thereby draw attention to apartheid inequalities.[12] To refuse this mission, Temkin writes, would have meant that Buthelezi was spurning an opportunity to reunify the great Zulu nation and bring it into modern resistance politics.[13] This kind of proto-nationalist sentiment apparently struck a deep chord in Buthelezi, but not in Luthuli, who openly opposed any 'black version' of 'separate development'. A passage in *Let My People Go* elaborates:

There is no hope in the Bantustan Act for any African. There is not intended to be any. It is the white man's solution, at ruthless cost to the African, of the white man's problems. Its only disadvantage from the white man's point of view is that it will not work. Considered as an economic proposition, it is insanity and murder . . . It will create nothing but chaos, and it will, because of the frustration and unrest which will follow from it, be the direct cause of numerous police shootings.[14]

For Luthuli, the ultimate reason he repudiated the 'white man's solution' pivoted on a longer, blatant system of colonial exploitation that laid the groundwork for apartheid. He explains:

In the end bantustans become destitute reservoirs of cheap labour, to be kept in order to discipline city workers who might dare demand higher wages. There will be work enough for good doctors. To us bantustan means the home of disease and miserable poverty, the place where we shall be swept into heaps in order to rot, the dumping ground of 'undesirable' elements, delinquents, criminals created especially in towns and cities by the system. And the place where old people and sick people are sent when the cities have taken what they had to give by way of strength, youth and labour. [15]

Before 1967, Buthelezi wavered over whether to participate actively in the KwaZulu bantustan or not. This was in part a desire not to go against Luthuli; such a move would have cost Buthelezi dearly in terms of his credibility. His standing within the ANC was still good; he was welcomed in the Luthuli family, and had befriended one of Luthuli's sons when they studied together at the American Board Mission's Amanzimtoti School in southern Natal.[16] Buthelezi also arranged to speak with Albert Luthuli about Bantu Authorities, ensuring his elder that he hoped to be like the anti-apartheid paramount chief Dalindyebo Sabata.[17]

### Luthuli in the hands of Buthelezi

Following Luthuli's death, a new version of the relationship between Buthelezi and the late ANC president-general emerged, gaining coherence by the 1970s. Buthelezi's Inkatha began to use Luthuli's name to bolster its claim to be the vocal voice of anti-colonial resistance from the time of the independent Zulu kings to the formation of the ANC (as the SANNC in 1912) and beyond. In 1975 Buthelezi boldly stated that Inkatha was a reincarnation of the ANC.[18] With tacit approval of ANC exiles, he adopted ANC symbols and issued public pronouncements calling for the resurrection of a broad liberation movement.[19] In this way, he refashioned Inkatha as the 'ANC mission in South Africa', but with the primary aim of mobilising a Zulu ethnic following in the KwaZulu bantustan.[20] Then, in a bid to expand his support base,

Buthelezi began to portray himself as the heir of Albert Luthuli and other ANC luminaries such as Professor Z.K. Matthews. When members of black consciousness (BC) organisations promptly dismissed Buthelezi as a puppet of apartheid, he asked rhetorically whether Luthuli was a puppet of Jan Smuts's white-minority United Party government before the apartheid election in 1948, for Luthuli had participated in the Native Representative Council, established by the Union government.[21]

Buthelezi was in the process of establishing Inkatha as a political force as the exiled leadership of the ANC sought to urge homeland leaders such as Buthelezi to use 'the opportunities provided by the bantustan programme to participate in the mass mobilisation of the oppressed people' against apartheid.[22] The ANC president, Oliver Tambo, reasoned that emerging mass-based organisations such as Inkatha could assist the ANC's armed wing, Umkhonto weSizwe (MK) in its operations.[23] However, the alliance between the ANC and Buthelezi did not last long; rifts between the partners developed after the Soweto student uprisings. Inkatha's strength increased at this time, following Pretoria's crackdown on BC organisations in October 1977, which effectively curtailed Buthelezi's main political rivals within South Africa's borders. By 1979, tensions were mounting around the planning of an ANC-Inkatha meeting in London.[24] As Buthelezi's own internal support grew between 1975 and 1979, a conviction intensified within Inkatha that 'the true heir to the ANC' was Buthelezi himself.[25]

Reformists within the reigning National Party were simultaneously pressing for new policies to control large numbers of urban Africans in South Africa, with P.W. Botha's government creating additional political space for conservative black leaders to build multiracial alliances through a tricameral system that barely altered the apartheid order. These developments marked a shift toward class politics as the state moved to protect the existing investment base, seeking ways to sustain profits on the basis of a tested colonial formula: cheap black labour and white private ownership. By the late 1970s Buthelezi had decided to promote Pretoria's class politics and to oppose foreign sanctions against doing business in South Africa; this stance kept him on a collision course with the ANC, which had launched the armed wing, amongst other pillars of its struggles, precisely to undermine apartheid economics.

In October 1979 Buthelezi and his top Inkatha deputies finally met an ANC delegation in London. Buthelezi's comments immediately after the conference showed that there had been significant disagreement and antagonism.[26] At the start of the 1980s, the ANC was publicly denouncing Buthelezi and Inkatha as enemies of oppressed peoples in South Africa.[27] Such proclamations invariably dented Buthelezi's reputation as an anti-apartheid leader and forced him to rely almost exclusively on his KwaZulu bantustan constituency. More than ever before, he worked hard to link himself with Luthuli's putative support of Zulu nationalist ideals. First, Buthelezi tried to monopolise annual commemoration services for 'Chief' Luthuli. Second, he reformulated his public representation of the freedom struggle, keeping Luthuli as a defining figure while denying the ANC any substantial role in African opposition to apartheid.

### Contesting Luthuli's heritage: Inkatha versus the ANC and its allies

In mid-1982, Buthelezi persuaded the widowed Mrs Luthuli to allow him to organise Albert Luthuli's memorial service as an Inkatha rally in Groutville.[28] At this large gathering, Buthelezi condemned the radical confrontational politics of the ANC.[29] The commemorated icon's eldest daughter, Dr Albertinah Luthuli, did not take kindly to Buthelezi's attack, and subsequently issued a press statement that took Buthelezi to task for using her father's name to further his divisive objectives. She also accused the Inkatha leader of manipulating her aging mother to give him permission to hold the rally in Albert Luthuli's name.[30] Buthelezi responded, saying he did not need Mrs Luthuli as a 'political prop'.[31]

Buthelezi's split with the ANC forced him to reappraise, again, how he chose to characterise black freedom struggles in South Africa. Soon after the failed London meeting, he started to deride the overseas ANC leadership as a 'mission in exile' with no connection to the heroism of precolonial Zulu kings who embodied the true resistance to white invaders. Only Inkatha, he now asserted, could realise the principles of ANC founders such as John Dube and other Zulu intellectuals.[32] In 1983 Inkatha circulated a statement calling attention to an historic 'symbolic meeting between Chief Luthuli and the Honourable Chief M.G. Buthelezi' in the 1960s, where the heritage of the leadership of the struggle was said to have been passed on to the Honourable Chief Buthelezi. The document concluded that Inkatha was 'as much a descendant of the old ANC as the present external mission'.[33]

By the second half of 1983, anti-apartheid resistance had assumed a popular character. In August 1983, the formation of the United Democratic Front (UDF), an alliance of more than 600 ANC-leaning grassroots organisations, posed a fresh challenge to Buthelezi's government in KwaZulu. Inkatha's first major test came with extensive rent boycotts and open defiance of local councils – then dominated by Buthelezi's hand-picked members and sympathisers – in Hambanathi near Verulam and in the communities of Lamontville and Chesterville outside Durban. This resistance soon spread to other townships throughout Natal and KwaZulu; many of the UDF youths at the vanguard of these protests condemned the KwaZulu bantustan as an apartheid creation and Buthelezi as a puppet of Pretoria, especially when he attempted to incorporate Hambanathi, Lamontville and Chesterville into his homeland rule.

In the face of this increasingly violent opposition, Inkatha held fast to its post-1979 version of the roots of the anti-colonial struggle. The party continued to stress the Zulu role in battling settler invasions and the putative unbroken line of Zulu

*Albert Luthuli (left) and John Dube.*

resisters from King Cetshwayo and 'Chief' Luthuli to KwaZulu Chief Minister Buthelezi. During a July 1984 interview, Oscar Dhlomo, the Secretary-General of Inkatha, again made the distinction between ANC 'founding fathers' and the so-called dubious 'mission in exile'.[34] The former had operated legally in South Africa between 1912 and 1960, he insisted, organising valiant non-violent demonstrations. After 1960, however, Dhlomo claimed that the ANC's mission-in-exile fled the country to wage guerrilla war from the outside and thereby abdicated control over liberation strategies within South Africa. Writing for *Leadership South Africa* in 1984, he further clarified his opinion, referring to the 'so-called ANC . . . [being] sent overseas by the last constitutionally elected President . . . the late Chief Albert Luthuli . . . [who] never [had] any intention that the external mission would eventually develop into a completely autonomous movement that would be free to decide on any liberatory strategies . . .'. Or, in the words of Buthelezi, Inkatha considered the exiled ANC 'the proverbial tail that wags the dog'.[35] Buthelezi elaborated on this view in an interview published in *Leadership South Africa*, where he claimed that the 'external mission' had deviated from the principles of Luthuli by 'opt[ing] for violence', implying as well that the decision to embark on the armed struggle was taken outside South Africa.[36] Shortly thereafter, Buthelezi suggested that he had heard from Luthuli, who allegedly voiced misgivings about the possibility that the ANC 'were to resort to violence'; for this reason, Buthelezi implied that the 'external mission' intended to isolate the president-general after the award of his Nobel Peace Prize.[37]

Buthelezi's insistence that Luthuli entrusted the Inkatha leader with the 'non-violent' torch was crucial to KwaZulu government rejoinders to critics who labelled it as a protected stooge of the apartheid rulers. To bolster his legitimacy in homeland politics, Buthelezi reiterated the claim he made in the 1970s: that Luthuli, Mandela, Sisulu and others had advised Inkatha to participate in homeland politics.[38] Buthelezi would repeat this assertion during Inkatha's annual general meeting at Ulundi in June 1985.[39] It seems likely that Buthelezi emphasised Mandela's role in the alleged incident out of expediency, for by the mid-1980s, as a consequence of UDF protests featuring T-shirts and placards with the jailed ANC leader's face, Mandela was becoming much more popular than Luthuli both nationally and internationally. This trend certainly gained momentum as the memory of Luthuli faded in the minds of the younger generation of liberation fighters leading the anti-apartheid struggle into its final phase.

What should we make of Buthelezi's representations of Luthuli in the service of Inkatha's cause? We might reconsider the ways in which Buthelezi evoked Luthuli's name when advocating non-violent change in South Africa, in contrast to the ANC's pursuit of armed struggle. Fairly recent evidence presented by Luthuli's family casts serious doubts on Buthelezi's assertion. In the widowed Mrs Luthuli's 1993 biography of her husband, she writes that Chief Luthuli used the money from his Nobel Peace Prize to buy two farms in Swaziland for South African refugees fleeing Pretoria's brutality, suggesting strongly that he too endorsed the plans of exiled ANC leaders to support anti-apartheid advocates from outside South Africa.[40]

We might also review whether Buthelezi actually depended on the alleged advice of his mentor Luthuli to justify Inkatha's participation in the homeland system. Significantly, there is no reference to a relationship (sustained camaraderie or lasting association) between Luthuli and Buthelezi in *Let My People Go*. To be sure, many prominent African national and Natal-based leaders are mentioned, including Oliver Tambo, national deputy-president of the ANC until 1967; M.B. Yengwa, Luthuli's dear colleague and ANC Natal secretary; as well as countless others. The complete omission of Buthelezi's name from Luthuli's autobiography could mean several things. Buthelezi was either politically so insignificant during the 1950s and early 1960s that he did not warrant any mention. Or, the friendship between Buthelezi and the Luthuli family developed through the protégé's initiative. A crucial question should be raised, which future scholars might want to answer. Did Luthuli's purported acquaintance with Buthelezi necessarily imply that the ANC's president-general endorsed the man who would become the most prominent homeland leader of the apartheid era? A partial answer unfolds in Chapter 19 of *Let My People Go*. Here, Luthuli is unmistakably straightforward about what he believes. He labels the bantustan system a cruel 'deceit', which seeks to remove black people from the South African political landscape.[41]

## Notes

1. In this chapter, I refrain from using the title 'chief' to preface Mangosuthu Buthelezi since he and the other *amkhosi* from the KwaZulu-Natal province have objected to its usage because of its colonial baggage. Unless otherwise stated, Mangosuthu Buthelezi refers to 'Chief' Ashpenaz Nathan Mangosuthu G. Buthelezi, formerly the chairman of Mahlathini Tribal Authority and chairman of Mashonangashoni Regional Authority; previous chief minister of KwaZulu, minister of police in KwaZulu, president of Inkatha, chairman of the South African Black Alliance, minister of Home Affairs (1994–2004), and chairman of the House of Traditional Leaders; as well as current *iNkosi*YaKwaButhelezi eMahlabathini, KwaZulu-Natal.

2. V. Gorodnov, 'Outstanding People's Leaders: Part One', *Sechaba: Official Organ of the ANC of South Africa* (November 1982): 23.

3. In recognition of Luthuli's contribution to the struggle against apartheid, the Organisation of African Unity also bestowed on him a posthumous merit award in 1974; see B. Temkin, *Gatsha Buthelezi: A Zulu Statesman* (Cape Town: Purnell, 1976), pp. 83–84.

4. Radical revisionist historians, for example, felt uneasy about Luthuli's African nationalist ideology, for Marxists, in particular, denounced all forms of nationalism as narrowly framed, reactionary politics.

5. In June 1970, the Zululand Territorial Authority (ZTA) was formally constituted and later became KwaZulu bantustan, with Mangosuthu Gatsha Buthelezi as its chief executive officer: Republic of South Africa (hereafter RSA), *Government Gazette No. 2 713*, Proclamation No. 139 of 22 May 1922, pp. 1–14; M. Horrell, *A Survey of Race Relations in South Africa, 1970* (Johannesburg: South African Institute of Race Relations [SAIRR], 1971), p. 141; B. Temkin, *Buthelezi: A Biography* (London: Frank Cass, 2003), p. 117; T.G. Karis and G.M. Gerhart, eds. *From Protest to Challenge: A Documentary History of African Politics in South Africa, 1882–1990*, Vol. 5 (Pretoria: Unisa Press, 1997), pp. 254 and 669–73. In April 1972 the ZTA was granted its own legislative assembly in terms of the 1971 Bantu Homelands Constitution Act; Buthelezi then became the chief minister of the new institution. His control of the bantustan administration provided him with a powerful platform from which to launch himself into politics in Natal. Mangosuthu Buthelezi became so influential in South Africa that over time he came to personify the KwaZulu bantustan: RSA, *Government Gazette*, Proclamation No. R69 of 30 March 1972; M. Horrell, *The African Homelands of South Africa* (Johannesburg: SAIRR, 1973) and D. Bonnin, G. Hamilton, R. Morrell and A. Sitas, 'The Struggle for Natal and KwaZulu: Workers, Township Dwellers and Inkatha, 1972–1985', in *Political Economy and Identities in KwaZulu-Natal*, ed. R. Morrell (Durban: Indicator Press, 1996), p. 147.

6. Buthelezi formed Inkatha in March 1975 as a KwaZulu-based mass movement. Its primary aims were to serve as the ruling party in the KwaZulu legislative assembly, and to counter the emergence of political parties claiming to serve the interests of the Zulu monarch. Between 1975 and 1990, Inkatha grew into a powerful regional political movement that occupied an ambivalent relationship with both the apartheid state and South African liberation movements such as the African National Congress (ANC) and Pan-Africanist Congress (PAC). During Inkatha's first five years of existence, it enjoyed clandestine support from the exiled leadership of the ANC. For a full account of the origins of modern Inkatha and its political development, including alliances and enemies, see G. Maré and G. Hamilton, *An Appetite for Power: Buthelezi's Inkatha and Politics of Loyal Resistance* (Johannesburg: Ravan Press, 1988).

7. The use of the past (especially the Zulu past) by Buthelezi and Inkatha to serve Zulu nationalist ends has been closely studied by scholars: see Maré and Hamilton, *An Appetite for Power*, Chapter 2; D. Golan, 'Inkatha and its Use of the Zulu Past', *History in Africa* 18 (1991): 113–36 and P. Forsyth, 'The Past in the Service of the Present: The Political Use of History by Chief M.G. Buthelezi, 1951–1991', *South African Historical Journal* 16 (1992): 74–92. In Forsyth's article, he identifies five main phases into which Buthelezi's political career can be divided during the period 1951 to 1991; each one of these phases corresponds to Buthelezi's appeal to and reliance upon different reconstructed historical traditions, see Forsyth, 'The Past': 75.

8. Temkin, *Gatsha Buthelezi*, p. 61.

9. Ibid., p. 54.

10. Ibid.

11. See A.J. Luthuli, *Let My People Go: An Autobiography* (Glasgow: Harper Collins, 1962), p. 22. Luthuli says that his maternal grandfather, Chief Mnqiwu Gumede, had had his mother, Mthonya Gumede, placed in the house of King Cetshwayo.

12. Luthuli, *Let My People Go*, pp. 122–23.

13. Ibid.

14. Ibid., p. 184.

15. Ibid., p. 181.

16. Buthelezi's high standing within the Luthuli family was particularly evident when he was one of the speakers at Albert Luthuli's funeral in 1967. Interview with Tryfina Jokweni conducted by Jabulani Sithole at Umlazi Township on 19 September 2001, SADET Oral History Project and author's discussion with Dr Albertinah Luthuli at La Montagne Hotel on 10 June 2005.

17. In the Cape, Tembu paramount Chief Dalindyebo Sabata was putting up feisty opposition against Bantu authorities. Interview with Johannes 'Passfour' Phungula conducted by the author, 25 October 2001, Durban, SADET Oral History Project.

18. Maré and Hamilton, *An Appetite for Power*, p. 137.

19. On appropriation of ANC symbols, see Forsyth, 'The Past': 84. On Buthelezi's pronouncements calling for the resurrection of a broad liberation movement, see Karis and Gerhart, eds. *From Protest to Challenge*, Vol. 5, p. 257 and Jack Shepherd Smith, *Buthelezi: The Biography* (Johannesburg: Hans Strydom, 1988) pp. 121 and 126.

20. Forsyth, 'The Past': 84.

21. Mzala, *Gatsha Buthelezi: Chief with a Double Agenda* (London: Zed Books, 1988), pp. 81 and 86–87.

22. O.R. Tambo, 'Buthelezi and Inkatha', in *Preparing for Power: Tambo Speaks*, ed. A. Tambo (London: Heinemann, 1987), p. 146.

23. Karis and Gerhart, *From Protest to Challenge*, Vol. 5, p. 271.

24. There is a wider context – a dispute that needed to be ironed out – to this London meeting. Karis and Gerhart argue that 'throughout the decade of the 1970s, Buthelezi embraced the ANC and the ideals of its "founding fathers" while seeking ways to marginalise its leadership in exile': Karis and Gerhart, *From Protest to Challenge*, Vol. 5, p. 251.

25. Karis and Gerhart, *From Protest to Challenge*, Vol. 5, p. 258.

26. *Sunday Tribune*, 4 November 1979 and *Natal Mercury*, 5 November 1979.

27. Alfred Nzo, 'Statement to the June 6th Freedom Day Meeting', *Sechaba* (September 1980): 6 and Karis and Gerhart, *From Protest to Challenge*, Vol. 5, p. 274.

28. *Ilanga lase Natal*, 2–4 September 1982.

29. Ibid. and M.G. Buthelezi, 'Address at a Prayer Meeting', Groutville, 29 August 1982.

30. *The Star*, 16 September 1982 and Maré and Hamilton, *An Appetite for Power*, p. 41.

31. Maré and Hamilton, *An Appetite for Power*, p. 41 and Smith, *Buthelezi*, p. 258.

32. Forsyth, 'The Past': 87 and Maré and Hamilton, *An Appetite for Power*, pp. 137–38.

33. Maré and Hamilton, *An Appetite for Power*, p. 138.

34. Ibid., p. 137

35. O. Dhlomo, 'Inkatha and the ANC', *Leadership South Africa* 3:1 (1984): 47.

36. M.G. Buthelezi, 'Interview with Murray', *Leadership South Africa* 4:4 (1985): 26.

37. Wessel de Kock, *Usuthu! Cry Peace!: The Black Liberation Movement Inkatha and the Fight for a Just South Africa* (Cape Town: Open Hand Press, 1986), p. 72.

38. Maré and Hamilton, *An Appetite for Power*, p. 41.

39. Ibid., p. 220. This claim was relayed during an interview with his second biographer, Wessel de Kock in his book *Usuthu!*, p. 41. Buthelezi told the same thing to his third biographer, Jack Smith; see Smith, *Buthelezi*, p. 47. See also Buthelezi, 'Interview with Murray': 26.

40. Peter Rule, Marilyn Aitken and Jenny van Dyk, *Nokukhanya: Mother of Light* (Johannesburg: Grail, 1993), pp. 131–33.

41. Luthuli, *Let My People Go*, Chapter 19.

*Chapter 29*

# Undivided Loyalties
## Inkatha and the Boy Scout Movement

TIMOTHY PARSONS

ON 5 OCTOBER 2002, Mangosuthu Buthelezi, South Africa's minister of Home Affairs and the leader of the Inkatha Freedom Party, addressed the South Africa Scout Association's (SASA) Mack Omega Shange Scout Competition Rally at King Cetshwayo Stadium in Ulundi, KwaZulu-Natal. Buthelezi spoke of his longstanding connection with South African Scouting and, more importantly, claimed the Boy Scout movement for the Zulus. Noting that Robert, Lord Baden-Powell had a 'deep and lasting respect for African traditions', he argued that the movement's true roots were in Africa:

> Today, much of what has become international practice in training Scouts has been taken directly from my own Zulu culture, and from the cultures of other African peoples . . . Being a naturally observant, keen discoverer, Sir Baden-Powell took note of the characteristics of African people, from our social structures to our children's upbringing. He was inspired by what he saw and was moved to ensure that his own experiences of the African way of life were not lost to anyone who could benefit from them.[1]

He also recalled that Garnet de la Hunt, a former Chief Scout of South Africa, had given him four Wood Badge beads taken from King Dinuzulu's necklace, which the Scouts used to mark the completion of a rigorous Scoutmaster training course, at a 1987 Scout rally. Reminding his audience that Dinuzulu was his grandfather, Buthelezi used Scouting to strengthen his claim to the leadership of the entire Zulu community by asserting that De la Hunt had symbolically restored the beads to their 'rightful home'.

More significantly, Buthelezi claimed Scouting for Inkatha by linking Scout ideology with his party's doctrine of *uBunto Botho*, which he defined as the Zulu tradition 'whereby we each are responsible for one another'. In Buthelezi's view, Scouting and Inkatha worked together during the apartheid era to teach discipline to young people who were in danger of being led astray by radicals who told them that education could wait for liberation. By teaching 'education for liberation' both Scouting and Inkatha dissuaded boys and young men from 'blindly following the call to arms and violence'. Finally, Buthelezi reminded the Scouts that he had worked closely with Mack Omega Shange, the pioneering Zulu Scouter honoured by the rally, in the government of the KwaZulu bantustan.

Buthelezi's emphasis on the central role that Zulu people and culture played in the development of the Scout movement in general and in South African Scouting in particular was essentially correct. Yet SASA's relations with Inkatha were far more complex than Buthelezi's address would suggest. Prior to 1994, the Zulu leader envisioned a post-apartheid South African state based on ethnic federalism, rather than the pluralist democracy favoured by his rivals in the African National Congress (ANC). Claiming that Inkatha represented all amaZulu, Buthelezi turned Zulu history and tradition into a potent political weapon. Inkatha's version of *Ubunto Botho* was by no means as benign as he suggested in his address to the Scouts. Far from being an expression of African humanism, it became a rallying cry for aggressive Zulu cultural nationalism that Buthelezi and Inkatha used to mobilise an informal Zulu militia armed with 'traditional' Zulu weapons. These '*impis*' battled the young 'comrades' allied with the United Democratic Front (UDF) and the ANC for control of Natal during the last years of the apartheid era.[2]

Yet class and generational tensions undermined Buthelezi's claim that Inkatha spoke for all isiZulu-speakers. Many young amaZulu, particularly students, were impatient with his gradualist strategy in dealing with the apartheid regime. In 1976, Buthelezi created the Inkatha Youth Brigade to ensure that Zulu youth did not become radicalised or transfer their allegiance to rival political movements.[3] This step alarmed the white Scout authorities who worried that a rival youth organisation would draw off the Zulu boys who constituted 45 per cent of their roughly 25 000 African members in the mid-1970s.[4]

In time, the SASA leadership found that they did not need to worry. Although the Youth Brigade and the Inkatha Youth Service Corps had some success in attracting and controlling non-schoolboys and young labour migrants, many Zulu students, particularly those with a more radical agenda, distrusted Buthelezi's willingness to work within the apartheid system. Scouting, which shared Inkatha's message of respect for authority and social conformity, was far more appealing to schoolboys. In theory, the movement offered Buthelezi an alternative means of disciplining Zulu youth because its avowed apolitical philosophy would make it slightly more tolerable to activist students in KwaZulu. To be sure, Scouting did indeed provide young Africans with a means to challenge apartheid. The Fourth Scout Law, which declared that all Scouts were brothers, implicitly blurred racial boundaries in South Africa. Furthermore, the movement conferred a measure of legitimacy and self-respect on African boys who faced a marginal existence during the apartheid era. As a result,

Buthelezi found that Scouting offered a more effective means of reaching, if not controlling, Zulu students.

The Scout authorities were happy to work with Buthelezi in steering young Africans away from violent confrontation with the state. Yet the contested nature of the movement in South Africa meant that Scouting itself had the potential to be politically subversive.[5] These contradictions stemmed from South African Scouting's own problematic history. Buthelezi was correct in locating the origins of the Boy Scout movement in southern Africa. Baden-Powell's popularity as a hero of the South African War (1899–1902) meant that the first informal Scout groups emerged in Johannesburg in 1901, some seven years before he formally launched Scouting in Britain. These were all-European troops, and the white leadership of the Transvaal Scout Association rejected all requests from Africans, Coloureds and Indians to join the movement. Citing the need to unify South Africa's two 'white races', the Scouts asserted that Afrikaner youth would shun Scouting if they admitted non-Europeans. Baden-Powell himself supported their position, and claimed that neither he nor the British Scout Association's imperial headquarters could interfere in local South African affairs.

Although the Scout authorities refusal to adhere to their own Fourth Scout Law was blatantly hypocritical, African boys and community leaders still sought to become Scouts. Baden-Powell had originally conceived of Scouting as an instrument of social discipline to smooth over class tensions inflamed by industrialisation in Edwardian Britain. He originally intended that his admonition that 'a Scout is a brother to every other Scout' should only be applied to Britons and later to other 'civilised' peoples. In South Africa this conformist doctrine had the potential to undermine racial segregation by suggesting that Africans and Europeans could be equal members of the same movement. This was a primary reason that Africans, Coloureds and Indians demanded access to Scouting.

Missionaries and liberal social welfare experts favoured allowing Africans to become Scouts in segregated troops in the hope that Scouting would become a modernising force that would teach them to accept their place in South African society. The South African Scout authorities remained steadfastly committed to strict racial segregation, but in the early 1920s they reached a compromise with their liberal critics whereby Africans, Coloureds and Indians could join a Scout-type movement known as the Pathfinders. The Pathfinders were under the indirect control of the SASA and followed a slightly modified Scout curriculum. However, they could not call themselves Scouts and had to wear a distinct uniform that underlined this fact. This failure to uphold the core values of the movement made the original Pathfinder model unworkable, and in 1936 the white Scout leadership created four parallel Scout institutions for Europeans, Africans, Coloureds and Indians under the central leadership of the SASA. African boys won the right to call themselves Pathfinder-Scouts, but they still had to wear distinct uniforms and never mixed with their white brother Scouts, apart from a few carefully staged rallies.

SASA justified these restrictions on the grounds that the Second Scout Law, 'A Scout is loyal', prevented them from challenging or undermining government policies on strict racial segregation. Throughout the era of white rule in South Africa, Scout officials sacrificed their obligations to African, Coloured and Indian boys in an effort to maintain favoured relations with the state. They also continually sought to entice Afrikaner boys into the movement, but this hope proved chimerical: Afrikaners never forgot Baden-Powell's role in the South African War and distrusted Scouting as an imperial institution.

When the National Party came to power in 1948, it looked as though SASA was certain to lose its semi-official ties to the Union government. Yet while Afrikaner nationalists clearly disliked the Scouts, they had to admit that the movement had its uses. Scouting's emphasis on respect for authority and self-discipline discouraged African resistance to apartheid, and its celebration of African tribal culture strengthened the Nationalists' bantustan polices. Scouting survived by respecting apartheid's racial boundaries and claiming to be resolutely apolitical. The parallel association model lasted until 1976 when the end of petty apartheid finally allowed the Scout authorities to create a unified national South African Scout association.

In practice, very few African Scouts accepted or acknowledged SASA's official policies on race and apartheid. African boys and their parents embraced the movement because it brought a measure of status, respectability and some relief from pass laws and harassment by the police and security forces. It also allowed African students to prove their worth in comparison with European boys. Moreover, the movement proved particularly useful to cultural brokers such as Buthelezi who sought to mobilise an ethnic constituency for political purposes.

The amaZulu unquestionably constituted the backbone of African Scouting in South Africa. As Buthelezi correctly pointed out, the enormous popularity of Scouting in the Zulu community was due in part to Baden-Powell's celebration of Zulu culture. As a military man, Baden-Powell considered the amaZulu to be the prototypical ideal of the selfless, resourceful, well-disciplined 'tribal' warrior, a common view in late Victorian England that stemmed in part from Cetshwayo's defeat of the British Army at Isandlwana in 1879.[6] Although he freely used the word 'nigger' in referring to Africans, Baden-Powell had a cultural rather than a biological view of race and considered the amaZulu to be 'white men' at heart.[7] He therefore had no reservations about incorporating his interpretation of Zulu culture into the Scout movement. Age-grades were an inspiration for the Scout ranks, and Baden-Powell cited the Zulu practice of testing young warriors through 'ordeals' as a model for his Scout tests.[8] Similarly, he backed up his opposition to formulaic military-style drill by noting: 'The Zulu warrior, splendid specimen though he is, never went through Swedish drill.'[9] Finally, he based the 'Scouts' War Dance' on what he called the Zulu 'Een-Gonyama Song' and, as previously noted, used beads from a Zulu *iziqu*, or necklace of valour, as the centrepiece of the Wood Badge.

Yet Baden-Powell made no effort to draw Zulu boys into the Scout movement, and it fell to missionaries to bring Scouting to Zululand. Official Scout records offer no explanation of exactly how or why so many Zulu youths became Pathfinders during the inter-war era. Similarly, published works on Zulu history and politics make no mention of Scouting. It seems certain, however, that government education authorities in Natal played a key role in the expansion of Zulu Scouting. Daniel McK. Malcolm, the chief inspector of Native Education, was a member of the Pathfinder Council and played an instrumental role in brokering the 1936 compromise that granted Africans formal Scout status. Like many white liberals of the period, he saw the movement as a 'civilising' supplement to the destabilising formal literary education that promoted Westernisation without 'detribalisation'. In 1933, he reminded a gathering of Zulu Pathfinder masters that Scouting stressed 'traditional' Zulu respect for generational authority:

> You Zulus understand the power of tradition. You know what it means when a person says this is not done (*akwenziwa lokhu*). There is no law or written rule so strong as this simple phrase and you are going to build this up . . . 'A Pathfinder is loyal.' This is a quality that comes easily to the Zulu. It is bred in his bone to be loyal to those in authority and you will not find it difficult to get boys to appreciate this virtue.[10]

Buthelezi's 2002 address to SASA's Mack Omega Shange Rally echoed these sentiments very distinctly, and it is highly likely that the founders of the original Inkatha movement of the 1920s would have endorsed and aided Malcolm's efforts to spread Pathfinding/Scouting amongst the Zulu community.

Natal education authorities continued to back the movement during the apartheid era. The National Party's open hostility to the movement did not dissuade them from using the state bureaucracy to promote African Scouting. By the late 1950s, Zulu Scouting was almost entirely in the hands of Oscar Emanualson, a senior circuit inspector of Bantu Education and later, the deputy-director of Bantu Education, who ran the movement out of the provincial Bantu Education office. He often used his own money to keep the operation running when the Natal (African) Scout Division ran short of funds. Although SASA's leadership complained that Scouting in Natal was linked too closely to formal education, Emanualson's African teachers kept Zulu Scouting alive when the rest of the movement suffered during the turbulent period of the Sharpeville massacre and South Africa's withdrawal from the British Commonwealth in the early 1960s.[11]

Mack Omega Shange was one of these teachers. Born in Pietermaritzburg to Methodist parents in 1932, he joined the Scout troop at the Sobantu Secondary School at the age of fifteen. After graduating in the early 1950s, he trained as a woodworking instructor and most likely came to Emanualson's attention when he

*Mack Omega Shange invests
King Cyprian Bhekuzulu Nyangayezizwe
as a Scout, 1965.*

taught at the Howick Primary and Secondary School from 1956 to 1961. During this period, he earned the Wood Badge that signified his expertise as a Scoutmaster and became the secretary of the Natal (African) Scout Division.[12] Emanualson therefore nominated him to be the African field commissioner for Natal, a paid position that the South African Scout authorities created to supervise rural African troops.

SASA originally hired approximately eight professional African and Coloured Scouters, but only Shange and a Xhosa commissioner named Micksey N'thaba proved up to the job. Shange's salary was half of what he had earned as a teacher, but he worked tirelessly to promote the movement in Natal in the face of harassment by government officials and hostile African community leaders who suspected he was a government agent.[13] In explaining his reasons for shutting down an African troupe in Port Elizabeth that he considered substandard, Shange declared:

> Scouters fail to realise just how much of a boy's time it takes to be a good
> Scout. We have [a] twofold duty, first of repaying the loyalty of the boy who

gives up so much time, by making his sacrifice worthwhile and in the second place, of ensuring that this sacrifice does not deprive him of the interesting and exciting things he would have been able to do outside Scouting.[14]

Shange was unquestionably sincere in his commitment to the movement, but it is also likely that he sought to undercut racist white assumptions that Africans were inherently inferior by demonstrating that African Scouts were the equal of their European peers.

Although South African Scouting maintained that it was inherently apolitical, this was an implicitly political stance under apartheid. Shange himself worked to ally the movement with the Zulu royal family. In 1966, he invested paramount Chief Cyprian Bhekuzulu Nyangayezizwe as the patron of Natal African Scouting at an elaborate ceremony in the Zulu 'Royal Kraal' before an audience of 5 000 spectators, 1 500 Zulu Scouts, and representatives of the Department of Bantu Affairs. He also used the occasion to present several Zulu Scoutmasters with their Wood Badges, declaring it was the first time the beads had been bestowed in the Kraal since the 'days of Dinuzulu'. Four years after Cyprian died in 1968, Shange also invested his heir, Prince Goodwill Zwelithini, as a Scout.[15] The South African Scout leadership supported these measures as a step towards promoting the movement in Zululand, but it is almost certain that Shange had the dual agenda of placing the power and influence of Zulu Scouting in the hands of cultural brokers seeking to harness Zulu history and culture for political purposes.

By the mid-1970s, Zulu boys dominated SASA's African sub-association. From 1969 to 1974, the numbers of enrolled Zulu Scouts increased from 4 910 to 13 343.[16] There were also most certainly several thousand additional members of unofficial and unregistered Zulu troops. Scouting therefore had the potential to become a potent instrument of political mobilisation, but SASA was largely unaware of the full extent of the political activities of its Zulu Scouters. White Scout officials knew that Professor Otty Nxumalo, their figurehead Chief Scout Commissioner for the African sub-association, was 'Buthelezi's right-hand man' and a member of the Ubhoko committee that drew up the constitution for the modern-day movement. They also knew that Shange himself was working with Nxumalo.[17] Yet the Scout authorities assumed that the Zulu Scouters' primary loyalty was to the Boy Scouts.

For the most part, SASA did not object to the creation of Inkatha because Buthelezi's movement was largely compatible with the government's bantustan policies. SASA authorities were shocked, however, to learn that Buthelezi, Nxumalo, and even Shange were planning a compulsory 'junior arm' that would operate in the KwaZulu bantustan schools. Finally realising the extent of the Zulu leaders' divided loyalties, SASA feared that Inkatha would follow the example of Kamuzu Hastings Banda in Malawi, who disbanded the Scouts to ensure they did not compete with his Young Pioneers. F.W. Drysdale, the Natal field commissioner for the European Scout association, sounded the alarm in mid-1975 when he warned that Buthelezi had already ordered 200 000 scarves for the uniforms of the new Zulu movement. An organisation this size would dwarf the Scouts and place most of the young people in KwaZulu under the direct influence of Inkatha. Seemingly oblivious to the political implications of Buthelezi's plans, Drysdale blamed Oscar Emanualson for provoking the Zulu into creating their own youth movement through his 'racialist' patronising arrogance:

> Undoubtedly there is a feeling of frustration amongst the Zulus with regard to Scouting. They do not feel that Scouting is doing all it can to eliminate barriers within the movement and if they have to be held at arms length, then why not go the whole hog? Instead of being a 'poor relation' in the Scout Movement they keep their pride by having their own which is essentially Zulu in character.[18]

In making these observations, Drysdale seems to have believed, naively, that Buthelezi would have given up his plans if SASA lived up to the Fourth Scout Law by unifying the four racially based parallel Scout associations.

The white Scout authorities therefore offered to integrate the Scout movement in South Africa fully, while granting Zulu Scouting 'full autonomy' within the KwaZulu bantustan as a separate and independent Scout association under the nominal supervision of SASA.[19] In practice, this proposal was a non-starter. Buthelezi steadfastly resisted the South African government's pressure to accept apartheid's version of political independence for KwaZulu, and the international Scout movement made it clear that it would not sanction South African racism by recognising Scout institutions in the bantustans as national Scout associations.

Sure enough, Zulu Scouters showed little interest in SASA's plans to unify South African Scouting. Nxumalo and Shange failed to turn up for the 'Quo Vadis' committee meetings that dismantled the separate African, Coloured and Asian sub-associations. When Charles Martin, the Chief Scout of the European association, asked Nxumalo and Shange about Inkatha's youth plans, the Zulu Scouters avoided the issue and seemed surprised that he even knew about them. Nevertheless, they promised Martin that the Inkatha Youth Brigade would be a cultural movement that would not resemble or compete with Scouting. These reassurances put SASA's leadership at ease and they chose not to openly oppose Buthelezi's plans.[20]

It soon became clear that Nxumalo and his allies had led the Scouts astray. Founded in 1976, the Inkatha Youth Brigade (IYB) borrowed a great deal from Scouting in its uniform, organisation and demands for loyalty and obedience. Although the IYB did not openly oppose Scouting, the KwaZulu education department's decision to incorporate Inkatha's *uBunto Botho* philosophy into the official school syllabus and its warning that teachers who did not join the Youth Brigade might lose their jobs threatened to cut Zulu Scouting off from its vital educational roots.[21]

Yet Buthelezi soon found that he still had a use for Scouting in KwaZulu. Although Inkatha succeeded in keeping Natal relatively quiet during the 1976 Soweto uprising, it could not prevent Zulu students from joining the 1980 national school boycott. Preferring confrontational activism to Buthelezi's 'education for liberation', Zulu students resisted Inkatha's attempt to force them back into the classrooms. Less educated non-school-going boys may have found the IYB's celebration of Zulu ethnic nationalism appealing, but many Zulu students preferred to confront the South African government directly. In 1980, Buthelezi tried to gain a greater measure of control over young Zulus by creating the more strictly regimented Inkatha Youth Service Corps, but this too proved relatively ineffective in reaching the most politicised elements of Zulu youth.[22]

African Scouting, on the other hand, was almost entirely a school-based movement in South Africa. The most radical Zulu students had no more use for the Boy Scouts than they did for the IYB, but it appears that, ironically, Scouting gained some appeal as SASA dismantled the racial association model in keeping with the government's retreat from the most odious segregationalist aspects of petty apartheid. Through its emphasis on citizenship and respect for authority, Scouting at least still had the potential to reach Zulu students who stood aloof from the IYB.

Certainly Shange seems to have recognised this reality. Although he listed himself as an IYB leader in his 1978 *Who's Who in South Africa* bibliographical entry, he continued to serve as a professional Scouter.[23] He may have been influenced by financial considerations in that SASA provided him with a rent-free house on Scout land, but his overall salary was still much less than what he would have earned as a school inspector in the KwaZulu Education Department. Moreover, Shange never gave up his gruelling schedule of inspecting rural Scout troops, in spite of a heart attack and stroke that slowed him up considerably in the mid-1970s. In 1980, Colin Inglis, the Chief Scout of the unified SASA, considered him the cornerstone of Zulu Scouting and 'shuddered to think what would happen if Shange's health broke'. It finally did break in the early 1980s, and honour guards of Scouts and Inkatha members attended his funeral.[24]

Shange's dual status as a devoted Scout and a committed Inkatha member exposes the deeper implications of Buthelezi's address to SASA at the 2002 Mack Omega Shange Scout Rally. Buthelezi did not follow Banda's lead in creating a totalitarian youth movement to replace the Boy Scouts. Instead he sought to tease the Zuluness out of Scouting to enlist the movement in his larger goal of mobilising Zulu people under his leadership. Moreover, the Scout movement offered a potential solution to the generational tensions that troubled Inkatha. As Steven Biko noted, 'Gatsha [Buthelezi] is supported by oldies.'[25] Representing an older traditionalist ideal of Zulu nationalism that valourised Zulu royalty, Inkatha had difficulty capturing younger better-educated amaZulu who saw little reason to defer to Buthelezi and his more conservative constituency. Scouting's 'retribalising' focus on obedience, social conformity, and respect for authority offered a possible solution to Buthelezi's youth problem. It also allowed Mack Shange to serve faithfully both the Boy Scout movement and Inkatha without dividing his loyalties.

## Notes

1. The full text of Buthelezi's address is available on the Inkatha Freedom Party website: http://www.ifp.org.za/Archive/Speeches/051002sp.htm (accessed June 2002). All quotations from the speech in this chapter are from this source.
2. Gerhard Maré and Georgina Hamilton, *An Appetite for Power: Buthelezi's Inkatha and South Africa* (Johannesburg: Ravan Press, 1987), pp. 6 and 57 and Patrick Harries, 'Imagery, Symbolism and Tradition in a South African Bantustan: Mangosuthu Buthelezi, Inkatha, and Zulu History', *History and Theory* 32:4 (1993): 114, 122.
3. Maré and Hamilton, *An Appetite for Power*, p. 183.
4. South African Scout Association (SASA), BC 956/F/Census Returns and 'Zulus Flock to Join Scouts', *Natal Witness*, 24 May 1974.
5. For a detailed account of the development of South African Scouting, see Timothy Parsons, *Race, Resistance, and the Boy Scout Movement in British Colonial Africa* (Athens, OH: Ohio University Press, 2004).
6. Carolyn Hamilton, *Terrific Majesty: The Powers of Shaka Zulu and the Limits of Historical Invention* (Cambridge: Harvard University Press, 1998), p. 112.
7. In discussing the brutal treatment of Ndebele rebels, he wrote: 'Don't think me a nigger-hater for I am not. I have met lots of good friends among them – especially among the Zulus. But, however good they may be, they must, as a people, be ruled with a hand of iron in a velvet glove.' Lord Robert Baden-Powell, *The Matabele Campaign, 1896* (Westport, CT: Negro Universities Press, 1970), p. 63. See also Sir Robert Baden-Powell, 'White Men in Black Skins', *Elders Review of West African Affairs* 8:30 (July 1929): 6.
8. R.S.S. Baden-Powell, *Scouting and Youth Movements* (New York: Jonathan Cape & Harrison Smith, 1931), p. 27.
9. R.S.S. Baden-Powell, *Scoutmastership: A Handbook for Scoutmasters on the Theory of Scout Training* (London: G.P. Putnam's Sons, 1920), p. 77.
10. Report on the Second Natal Gilwell Pathfinder Masters' Training Course by G.W. Meister, Honorary Secretary Natal Division Pathfinder Movement, 20 July 1933, University of the Witwatersrand, South African Institution of Race Relations, Papers of J.D. Rheinallt Jones (UW SAIRR), AD 843/B 25.1 (1).
11. Natal Division (A) AR 1957, SASA, BC 956/A/Africa Scouts, 1936–60; Report on Natal Division by SAHQ Development Commissioner, 1961; Divisional Commissioner Natal (A) to SAHQ Development Commissioner, 2 July 1962 and SASA, BC 956/D/African Field Commissioner.
12. 'Obituary of Mack Omega Shange', SASA, BC 956/D/Condolences.
13. SAHQ, Field Commissioners and Association Secretaries, 1960, SASA, BC 956/A/CSIC, 1960; J.D. Fraser to CSSA, 14 November 1961, SASA, BC 956/D/General Correspondence 1960s and Natal African Field Commissioner to SAHQ Development Commissioner, 21 April 1964, SASA, BC 956/D/African Field Commissioner.
14. M.O. Shange to Camp Chief SABSA, 24 July 1966, SASA, BC 956/D/African Field Commissioner.
15. Report by SAHQ Commissioner for Development, 17 January 1966, SASA, BC 956/A/Council Circulars, 1964–65 and Natal Division (A), AR 1968, SASA, BC 956/A/African, 1968–70s.
16. 'Zulus Flock to Join Scouts', *Natal Witness*, 24 May 1974.
17. Maré and Hamilton, *An Appetite for Power*, p. 55 and 'Proposal for New KwaZulu Youth Movement', by F. W. Drysdale, Field Commissioner Natal (E), *c.*1975, SASA, BC 956/F/Quo Vadis Committee.

18. 'Proposal for New KwaZulu Youth Movement', and Doug Drysdale to P. Knightly, 27 October 1975, SASA, BC 956/F/Quo Vadis.
19. C.A. Martin, CSSA to O. Nxumalo, CSC (A), 22 December 1975, SASA, BC 956/F/Quo Vadis.
20. Conference notes, Lexton Maritzburg, 15–16 March 1975, SASA, BC 956/F/Quo Vadis; C.A. Martin, CSSA, to P. Knightly, *c.* October 1975, SASA, BC 956/F/Quo Vadis and Doug Drysdale to P. Knightly, 27 October 1975.
21. Maré and Hamilton, *An Appetite for Power*, pp. 183–84.
22. Ibid., pp. 69, 187.
23. Dee Shirley Deane, *South Africans: A Who's Who* (Cape Town: Oxford University Press, 1978), p. 171.
24. Otty Nxumalo, CSC (A), to CSSA, 23 January 1974, SASA, BC 956/B/African Field Commissioners; African Association, *c.*1976, SASA, BC 956/B/People and Personalities; Inglis to A.C. Cape Midlands, January 1980, SASA, BC 956/D/Urban Development and 'Obituary of Mack Omega Shange'.

Pd Hamilton, *An Appetite for Power*, p. 186.

*Chapter 30*

# Shaka's Aeroplane
## The Take-off and Landing of Inkatha, Modern Zulu Nationalism and Royal Politics

THEMBISA WAETJEN and GERARD MARÉ

ON 18 JANUARY 1992 boosters of the Isandlwana Historic Reserve in KwaZulu inaugurated a new visitor's centre at the site where, 113 years earlier, a Zulu army defeated a British military column invading the Zulu kingdom. The ribbon-cutting ceremony occasioned stirring speeches that boasted of an illustrious Zulu past. Yet it was the future that was most clearly at stake. Indeed, the political significance of this event during the violent years of South Africa's democratic transition could hardly have been more transparent. Communities surrounding the celebrated battlefield were in the throes of internecine fighting that pitted supporters of the Zulu nationalist movement, Inkatha, against the African National Congress (ANC). With the ANC poised to take power in a post-apartheid era, this political conflict had escalated into a civil war.[1] In recounting Zulu martial triumphs of the previous century, Inkatha representatives at Isandlwana delivered a message that the 'Zulu Nation' was again intent on resisting what it perceived as the intrusion of another government. This time, they warned, the fight would not be against agents of British colonialism, but against a rival political movement.

The reigning Zulu monarch, King Goodwill Zwelithini, was present for the festivities, demonstrating his support for Inkatha's orchestration of Zulu politics. Other guests included government officials, traditional leaders and representatives of corporate sugar companies. To this collusion of interests and hundreds of local residents, Inkatha's leader and primary spokesperson, Mangosuthu Buthelezi, delivered a speech. Employing the rhetorical style he mastered during decades of political campaigning, Buthelezi meditated on the heroic qualities of legendary nation-founder King Shaka kaSenzangakhona, who forged a regional Zulu empire in the first quarter of the nineteenth century.[2] On this occasion, however, invocations of King Shaka's bravery and military discipline were eclipsed by a much more extraordinary claim. 'King Shaka,' declared Buthelezi, 'that magnificent founding forefather of the Zulu nation, already saw the new South Africa as inevitable even as he was busy finally putting the Zulu Kingdom together. *Before he died he had visions of aeroplanes flying in the air carrying people . . .'³*

The notion of an early-nineteenth-century monarch prophesying the future in the form of a democratic capitalist state – and, even more extraordinarily, in the form of passenger planes – may seem an absurd, certainly outlandish, claim even when put forth by a zealous politician with so much at stake. Yet embellished veneration of founding fathers is common enough in nationalist rhetoric; the point here is not to single out Buthelezi as an especially audacious orator. In nationalist discourses, founding patriarchs supply all manner of mystical traits to confirm the political fate of their progeny. Attributing visions of the modern to a figure who embodies all that is incontrovertibly traditional exemplifies the enigmatic posturing of nationalism's relationship to historical time.⁴ Similar to other nationalist movements, Inkatha presented itself as the preordained bearer of a collective political vision and destiny. In this sense, the image of 'Shaka's aeroplane' offers an apt metaphor for Inkatha's Zulu nationalism: a modern reality accredited retrospectively to the brain of a long-dead warrior-king.

## A brief overview of Buthelezi's Inkatha

In the last quarter of the twentieth century, Mangosuthu Buthelezi's Inkatha movement was the most powerful agent to affect public meanings of Zuluness. Although Inkatha was certainly not the only voice of Zulu political resolve, nor the sole advocate of Zulu cultural pride, it cultivated its reputation during this time to become the most widely known and well-publicised representative of ethnic Zulu people.

The Inkatha National Cultural Liberation Movement was formed in 1975. It was not the first campaign to give organisational form to Zulu ethnic nationalism during the twentieth century, nor even the first that was mobilised under the name Inkatha. In the 1920s, prominent isiZulu-speaking intellectuals, businessmen and local leaders established an organisation called Inkatha under the patronage of King Solomon kaDinuzulu.⁵ This earlier Inkatha sought to advance a range of political concerns and economic ambitions that were suffering under the assaults of legislated racial segregation and exclusions, beginning with the Act of Union in 1910.⁶ The politicisation of Zulu cultural unity simmered for a number of years, one expression among other initiatives of black resistance to white political domination.

With the victory of the Afrikaner-led National Party in 1948, racial segregation was progressively entrenched and broadened through a new official doctrine known as apartheid. In this programme of social engineering, African ethnicity became the target of intensive political manoeuvring by the state. Partly as a response to apartheid's divide-and-rule policies, Zulu nationalism gradually was eclipsed by mobilisations around black solidarity. The ANC took a strong stand against the government's plan for ethnic balkanisation. Over the years, Pretoria became increasingly intolerant of a radicalising opposition and, in 1960, banned the ANC, forcing many leaders of this liberation organisation into exile. State repression mounted in the 1970s, and, when Buthelezi and others launched a *new* Inkatha to fight apartheid, this initiative was welcomed by exiled members of the ANC. Inkatha was viewed, at that stage, as a partner-in-struggle within a broad activist coalition.

Indeed, from its beginnings, while Inkatha called itself the custodian and advocate of Zulu tradition, its aims were embroiled in the struggle for a new liberal South Africa. Yet, Inkatha's relationship with other anti-apartheid organisations quickly became contentious. The issue of ethnicity became the pivotal source of discord. Because ethnic distinctiveness and segregation were foundations of apartheid's separate development policies, Inkatha's growing advocacy of Zulu nationalism came to be regarded with deep suspicion by those who were attempting to break down ethnic allegiances. In turn, as its support from the ANC waned, Inkatha promoted themes of ethnic pride to recruit popular support, especially from isiZulu-speaking men.[7]

While the deadly trajectory of clashes between the ANC and Inkatha could not have been predicted, from the outset Inkatha's career was rife with ambiguities. Perhaps most significant was its position in relation to Pretoria's Bantu affairs policies, particularly to the apartheid-created homeland parliament of KwaZulu, the KwaZulu Legislative Assembly (KLA). The Inkatha leadership was comprised of many of the same people, and had access to many of the same resources as the KLA. Buthelezi himself was not only the president of Inkatha but also presided over the KLA as its chief minister. In its defence, Inkatha represented its relationship to the homeland government as a practical necessity, a means of dismantling apartheid from within. But Buthelezi never found it easy to resolve the contradictions between sustaining anti-apartheid opposition and accumulating benefits from Pretoria's institutional bodies, including a vast police force, which buttressed notoriously fragile tribal homeland governments.

Even so, Zulu identity constituted a powerful appeal, mobilising large numbers of mainly rural people. Additionally, Inkatha's neo-liberal economic platform secured the support of local and international business interests since it promised an anti-communist alternative to the left-leaning ANC and trade unions. Among Buthelezi's conservative admirers were Ronald Reagan, Helmut Kohl and Margaret Thatcher.[8] Inkatha's adversarial relationship with the ANC heated up in the 1980s and, amidst a conflict that killed thousands of people, Inkatha faced well-founded accusations of collusion with the apartheid state and its military arm, the South African Defence Force (SADF).[9] Inkatha (and Buthelezi personally) adopted a more defensive and injured posture in relation to these criticisms, which, they claimed, represented attacks on Zuluness itself.[10]

Inkatha addressed a wider audience than had been possible for the earlier movement of the same name. A more literate public with access to radio and television, better transportation, and infrastructural backing for grand festivities of Zuluness (such as Shaka Day) contributed to Buthelezi's massive mobilisation campaigns throughout the region. From the 1970s to the 1990s, Inkatha intensified its nationalist project by linking Zulu cultural and linguistic identities to a collective vision of an apartheid-free South Africa. In effect, this process constituted a bold bid by the Zulu elite to marshal the poorest of the poor along with chiefs and *izinduna*, headmen, and other customary authorities whose mother tongue was isiZulu.[11]

Their efforts were more successful than many political observers and scholars are willing to acknowledge. In the post-apartheid period, support for Inkatha still runs deep among isiZulu-speakers in the consolidated province of KwaZulu-Natal, not only in rural areas, but also in urban communities where migrant labourers live. That Inkatha continues to reap the benefits of its ethnic appeal in some ways demonstrates the failure of the ANC, trade unions and other groups to adequately address the concerns of South Africa's most marginalised citizens. But Inkatha also confronts obstacles in the new South Africa. It is plagued by tensions between national and civic bodies, between regional identities and clan loyalties, and between neo-liberal capitalism and communal practices that prevent resources from being privatised. In fact, it was these intensifying contradictions in the 1990s that propelled Inkatha, the 'cultural liberation movement', to transform itself into the more encompassing (and less narrowly *ethnic*) Inkatha Freedom Party (IFP), a self-declared political stakeholder in the South African government of national unity after the first inclusive national ballot in 1994.

Despite the opening up of the IFP to incorporate non-Zulu people, the ethnic core of Inkatha still continues as a force in South African politics. Buthelezi persists in his role as a controversial player in South African politics. Since 1994, he has held a high position in cabinet as both a deputy vice-president and minister of Homeland Affairs, performing the duties of acting president in the absence of both the president and vice-president from the country. Indeed, in 1998, he narrowly lost the position of vice-president to another Zulu politician, Jacob Zuma. In contrast to ANC leaders, Buthelezi persistently advocated greater influence for traditional leaders, especially in KwaZulu-Natal, and the transfer of the provincial capital from Pietermaritzburg to Ulundi, an Inkatha stronghold. For many, he remains the voice of contemporary Zuluness.

### Buthelezi: Modernising the Zulu kingdom

Mangosuthu Buthelezi's personal history reflects complex manoeuvring around regional and national pressures long buffeting black intellectuals and leaders of resistance movements in the middle of the twentieth century. Born in 1928, he spent his formative years in an isiZulu-speaking community where clan origins and proper customary behaviour were held as paramount values. He claims royal lineage through his mother, Princess Constance Magogo (a daughter of King Dinuzulu), and was officially installed as chief of the Buthelezi clan in 1957.[12] Ethnic identity in this context reflected concerns that were primarily *local*.

However, as noted earlier, policy-makers of the white supremacist National Party had their own definition of cultural belonging in South Africa. From the 1948 election onwards, the cardinal project of the National Party was to elevate its version of primordial ethnic identity in order to implement a system of homelands, or bantustans, that recognised Africans in positions of clan, regional and territorial authority as black custodians of apartheid. The Zulu kingdom of old was earmarked to be a bantustan under Pretoria's command. As with other politically aware young people of his generation, Buthelezi responded favourably to calls for black liberation as apartheid ideologues alienated more and more South Africans. In the late 1940s he attended Fort Hare University, where African nationalism flowered, and in the years beyond sought out Zulu leaders such as Nobel Peace Prize winner Albert Luthuli, who became ANC president in 1952. Still, the politics of the local – his loyalty to clan and the 'Zulu Nation' – motivated the young Mangosuthu to pursue a different path in the 1950s. In 1955, at a meeting of 300 traditional Zulu leaders with the notorious apartheid stalwart, Minister of Native Affairs, Hendrik Verwoerd, Buthelezi vented concerns that remained consistent over the next 35 years: safeguarding the status of the Zulu king, land for rural amaZulu, and rights of local traders, among them members of the Zulu petit bourgeoisie who would eventually provide support for Inkatha. At the same time, Zulu parochial issues were linked to the broader struggle against apartheid. Buthelezi himself, and those close to him, protested against encroaching state repression. His wife, Irene, and his mother, Princess Magogo, participated in the marches organised by black women against the extension of passes to women in the 1950s.[13]

In 1970, the state established the Zulu Territorial Authority. At its launch, which was attended by the white minister of Bantu Administration and Development, Mangosuthu Buthelezi called for a transition to 'self-determination and self-realisation' for 'the Zulu nation'.[14] At the same time, in contrast to the acquiescence of other bantustan elites, Buthelezi rejected the puppet role he would have to assume as the independent leader of Zulu statehood under the banner of 'separate development'. His appeal to Pretoria for additional territory was central to an agenda that would seek first to protect the sovereignty of the historic Zulu Kingdom and the integrity of Zulu ethnic politics.

To implement this agenda, Buthelezi worked tirelessly to revive a particular royal brand of Zulu ethnic pride, as well as nationalist sentiment. From 1954, when he organised a cultural festival in September celebrating Shaka Day (later an annual event), Buthelezi turned public gatherings into recruitment drives for Inkatha. Of central importance in this effort was the figure of the contemporary Zulu monarch, King Cyprian. Zulu kingship gave meaning to the idea of Zulu politics; Zulu subjects in the Territorial Authority were to be distinguished for their Zuluness, in this case defined by their loyalty to the hereditary father of the 'Zulu Nation', as well as their residence in an area encompassed by the old borders of King Cetshwayo's Zulu

*King Goodwill Zwelithini (left), Mangosuthu Buthelezi (centre), Jacob Zuma (right).*

kingdom. Yet, in this grand scheme, the support of King Cyprian was a never a foregone conclusion. Moreover, King Cyprian died in 1968, before his young heir Goodwill Zwelithini reached an age to assume control of the monarchy. Buthelezi's relationship with the interim regent, Cyprian's half-brother Prince Israel Mcswayizeni, was frosty. Possibly because Mcwayizeni was pursuing a co-operative relationship with Pretoria,[15] Buthelezi was excluded from Zulu affairs. Well into the reign of King Goodwill Zwelithini, Buthelezi and his supporters in the KLA found the royal house difficult to manipulate. The king and his royalists ambitiously eyed an apartheid proposal to reinstate the executive powers of the Zulu monarchy in preparation for independent rule in the Zulu Territorial Authority. Thus, King Goodwill Zwelithini's compliance with Inkatha's political goals was uncertain as Buthelezi advocated shunning bantustan independence. After much acrimonious debate, the KLA constitution in 1972 stripped King Goodwill Zwelithini of executive power and converted his throne into a grand, if symbolic, office.

By the early 1980s, King Goodwill Zwelithini had emerged a bullied man, and an essential figure in the Inkatha mobilisation of isiZulu-speakers.[16] The king became Buthelezi's most important living cultural icon, representing the continuity of Zulu lineage from Shaka into the new South Africa. Inkatha leaders and their representatives in the KLA assumed the executive reins over Zulu politics and its royal figurehead in the context of the nation state. For his part, the Zulu king presented himself as the father of Zuluness, declaring that 'history has put me where I am and all Zulu history demands that I make the unity of my people my first priority'.[17] Although he vehemently denied being a political pawn, King Goodwill Zwelithini was absorbed into the Inkatha fold, following a course Buthelezi would steer for the royal house. At political rallies, the king arrayed himself sometimes in the smart, military uniform of European monarchs, sometimes in a suit and tie, and sometimes in the majestic traditional leopard hide of his forefathers. As Buthelezi confidently interpreted King Shaka's futuristic visions for a modern South Africa, King Zwelithini was there to concur.

### Securing a kingdom: Heritage, territory and changing political conditions
What signalled King Goodwill Zwelithini's willingness to embrace Inkatha was his ardent rejection of the apartheid government's manoeuvre in 1982 to offer the independent kingdom of Swaziland two expanses of bantustan territory. The area to be ceded was in the northern Ingwavuma district of KwaZulu, which included access to the Indian Ocean. The Swazi king would gain control of these strips of land in exchange for allowing the Pretoria government to crush ANC guerrillas crossing the border from Mozambique.[18] Inkatha vehemently protested seizure of this territory by invoking Zulu history and its royal lineage to keep hold of Ingwavuma. Buthelezi's speeches throughout 1983 saluted a historical figure, King Dingane (1828–37), for whom he had previously shown only disdain. Dingane held a dubious position in Inkatha's historiography, for he was the assassin of his brother, King Shaka. Yet King Dingane's readmittance into the ranks of great Zulu patriarchs was indicated in June 1983 when a memorial service was held in the Ingwavuma region where he had died. Buthelezi and King Goodwill Zwelithini presided over the ceremonial unveiling of a stone on Dingane's burial site and used this event to publicly oppose the Ingwavuma land deal. In his speech, Buthelezi announced: 'Part of the history which was enacted during [King Dingane's] reign represents our history and our cultural roots. That we cannot change in 1983. His bones are precious to us, just like the bones of any other Zulu king, and the ground in which lie his mortal remains is hallowed ground to each and every Zulu.' He continued: 'These memorials have been placed by us as evidence before all Africa, and the entire world, that if the Ingwavuma land deal is pursued, that there may be many Zulus who will consider it a noble cause to lose their blood in defence of what we regard as our heritage.'[19]

The endeavour to identify physical territory as belonging to a Zulu heritage was pursued in other ways and not simply as a project for securing contested land. In the early 1980s, Buthelezi enlisted social scientists from local universities on a special project called the Buthelezi Commission, which sought to investigate the political, cultural, demographic and economic features of Natal and KwaZulu. The commission asserted that, despite divisive apartheid, the province of Natal and the tribal homeland of KwaZulu were best understood *not* as discrete entities, but rather as a single, integrated territory. The heritage of the Zulu kingdom was also seen as an unassailable feature of the region. The commission's findings encouraged leading politicians and business people, white as well as black, in KwaZulu and Natal, to produce a constitution that could serve as a model for national change. This 1986 initiative known as the 'Indaba' urged a level of regional political unification in order to promote one major goal: economic development through capital investment. The Indaba broadcast the need for a special deal in a newly joined KwaZulu-Natal and advocated a high measure of regional autonomy within a *federal* model of government in post-apartheid South Africa.

Yet, as the *unitary* model of rule favoured by the ANC became a likelihood, Inkatha proponents of the Indaba, pressing for protection of their proclaimed ethnic homeland, announced that King Goodwill Zwelithini's people would secede from the rest of South Africa and declare independence for the Zulu kingdom. This threat of secession was abated rapidly, though Inkatha's commitment to participate in the 1994 elections remained tenuous right into the eleventh hour. During the historic April ballot, Inkatha pursued its agenda in a new guise as the IFP, lobbying for a national constituency. The subsequent landslide victory of the ANC was indeed a blow to the IFP. Buthelezi's loss was compounded when King Goodwill Zwelithini, who was courted by the ANC and sought to be among the ranks of the newly powerful, defected to the side of the victors.

**From identity politics to spectacle? Questions about the public future of Zuluness**

Up to 1994, Inkatha's complex achievement was in reinstating Zuluness as a core element of national politics in South Africa. But now in the post-apartheid period, what do we make of this legacy? Will Zuluness in the era of globalisation remain a potent instrument of mobilisation? What do we make of the cynical way in which the ANC also entered the fray of ethnic contestation, and of the even more cynical manner in which the apartheid state played its two-faced role – on the one hand, protecting Inkatha's version of Zuluness and, on the other hand, undermining the dignity of thousands of isiZulu-speakers through racially discriminatory laws? What is certain is that, despite the efforts of nationalists to capture and manipulate cultural allegiance for prescribed political outcomes, the complexities of ethnic identity are still here. And the big questions apply as ever before: how do isiZulu-speaking people define themselves? What other interpretations of so-called indigenous heritage in KwaZulu-Natal exist outside of modern political and economic pursuits? How will multiple interpretations of Zuluness be accommodated in the future South Africa?

As political conflict has subsided in KwaZulu-Natal, there are indications that Zuluness is now subject as much to the forces of global entertainment as to local political wrangling. While the conundrum of Zulu identity politics and uncertainties regarding the status of Zulu traditional authorities and customary laws remain unresolved issues, regional development strategists recognise that Zulu heritage as an ideal represents a wellspring of opportunity to draw tourists and foreign capital.[20] KwaZulu-Natal is now advertised as 'The Kingdom of the Zulu'; travel brochures and posters depict Zulu people in traditional dress alongside African wildlife; buses and billboards are splashed with the injunction, 'Wozani! Our Kingdom Calls'.

While Buthelezi and members of the Zulu royal house still speak eloquently about their warrior valour and noble resistance to colonialism – as they did at Isandlwana in 1992 – the purpose of such claims has changed. After King Goodwill Zwelithini's dramatic move to establish closer links with the ANC, he almost single-handedly shifted what it meant to be a politicised Zulu on the eve of the new millennium. In January 1997, he gave a speech that signalled the royal stamp of approval on the insurgent tourism industry in the rainbow nation, announcing his goal to 'educate KwaZulu-Natal youth and promote Zulu culture to tourists'. The king also planned to reinstate his control over the annual traditional reed dance, the first fruits ceremony – a great feast to honour kingship – and Shaka Day celebrations, where ANC, other public dignitaries and foreign visitors would be welcomed to attend. Reports also filtered from the monarchy that King Goodwill Zwelithini was 'backing moves to build a royal theme park "on the scale of Disneyland"' in KwaZulu-Natal. In 2002 a new 'Kingdom cultural venue' was launched to provide the foundation for a 'Zulu cultural route' that would end in Nongoma, Zululand, the site of the royal residence.[21] These moves by the king were part of a deliberate attempt, more directed than ever before, to open traditional Zuluness to a global market and public spectacle.

Since the transition to a democratic South Africa, international currents have uniquely transformed Zulu identity. It is ironic that, with Zulu political militancy now declining and with rural Zulu people confronting desperate poverty and HIV/AIDS, Zulu heritage is in unprecedented global demand. No longer do *National Geographic*, the film industry, or the political views championed by Buthelezi channel the dominant images of Zuluness in the twenty-first century. To be sure, in the province of KwaZulu-Natal local interests still commercialise Zuluness, but the primary vehicles of such promotions are now the developers of tourist sites – for example, the PheZulu Safari park, Izintaba Cultural Zulu Village at the Rob Roy Hotel (advertised to 'capture your imagination during a one-hour educational show') and other theme parks claim to offer international audiences an experience of the Shakan exotic.

The depth of feelings surrounding Zulu identity is difficult to reconcile with the economically motivated, shallow performances of Zulu culture geared to holiday-makers. Considering the blood spilt among the poorest of the poor in ten years of recent fratricidal political violence, it is remarkable that South Africa's renowned political transition has left virtually unaddressed the most vital questions of ethnic meaning, political selfhood and social inequality. In the forward march to new opportunities for new beneficiaries, the destitute and dead cannot tell their story of Zuluness. This history is concealed as Inkatha's elites take their places in government, reconcile with old enemies and reap the benefits of South Africa's neo-liberal capitalist vision.

As the imaginative uses of Zulu identity pass into new hands, the Zulu founder became the topic in Durban planning meetings about the development of a waterfront marine theme park, 'uShaka Island', and the positioning of a colossal statue of his regal figure at the harbour entrance. Periodically, the press raises the prospect of a new airport north of Durban that would be named 'King Shaka International'. If this latter possibility materialises, Shaka may get his fleet of aeroplanes after all – testimony to the malleability of his image to suit new political conditions and the aspirations of a twenty-first century tourism boom.

## Notes

1. The civic strife, which claimed more than 15 000 lives, is recounted in detail elsewhere. See, for example, Anthea Jeffrey, *The Natal Story: 16 Years of Conflict* (Johannesburg: South African Institute of Race Relations, 1997).

2. The iconic power of Shaka was also used in opposition to Buthelezi, for example by a political party founded by Zulu royalists in 1973, called Umkhonto kaShaka (Shaka's Spear).

3. Speech by Buthelezi, Isandlwana 18 January 1992; emphasis added.

4. See Anne McClintock, 'Family Feuds: Gender, Nationalism, and the Family', *Feminist Review* (Summer 1993); Benedict Anderson, *Imagined Communities: Reflections on the Origin and Spread of Nationalism* (London: Verso, 1991); Ernest Gellner, *Nations and Nationalism* (Oxford: Basil Blackwell, 1983) and Anthony Smith, *Theories of Nationalism* (New York: Torchbook Library Edition, 1971).

5. See Shula Marks, *The Ambiguities of Dependence in South Africa: Class, Nationalism, and the State in Twentieth-century Natal* (Johannesburg: Ravan Press, 1986) and Nicholas Cope, *To Bind the Nation* (Pietermaritzburg: University of Natal Press, 1993), Chapter 4.

6. This act, which unified territories in South Africa, effectively excluded black people from the full rights of citizenship.

7. See Thembisa Waetjen, *Workers and Warriors: Masculinity and the Struggle for Nation in South Africa* (Urbana-Champaign: University of Illinois Press, 2004), Chapter 3.

8. Several issues of the official Inkatha publication, *Clarion Call*, showcase such relationships, with Buthelezi shaking hands with Thatcher, Bush, Reagan, Kohl, and other figures.

9. Buthelezi has vehemently continued to deny Inkatha's relationship to the SADF, despite findings by the Truth and Reconciliation Commission (TRC) to the contrary. In 2003 he lost the suit he had brought against the TRC, which documents evidence of Inkatha units trained by the SADF in Namibia.

10. For example, King Goodwill Zwelithini, speaking in Johannesburg, in May 1991, told the ANC to 'stop this ugly vendetta against the Zulu people and their Zuluness'.

11. The theoretical perspective we assert here (but do not aim to develop in this chapter) links nationalism to class formation, and is similar to that outlined by John Saul in the chapter entitled 'The Dialectic of Class and Tribe', in *The State and Revolution in Eastern Africa: Essays by John Saul* (New York and London: Monthly Review Press, 1979). For a more substantial discussion, see Gerhard Maré and Georgina Hamilton, *An Appetite for Power: Buthelezi's Inkatha and South Africa* (Bloomington: Indiana University Press, 1987) and Marks, *The Ambiguities of Dependence*.

12. Buthelezi had presided in the role of acting chief for four years prior to his official instalment. After 1957, his claim to chieftaincy was challenged by his older brother in a battle that lasted for several years and was ended only with state intervention. For this reason, Buthelezi's political rivals sometimes questioned the legitimacy of his position as a chief.

13. See Ben Temkin, *Buthelezi: A Biography* (London and Portland, OR: Frank Cass, 2003), p. 57.

14. Muriel Horrell, ed. *A Survey of Race Relations in South Africa 1970* (Johannesburg: South African Institute of Race Relations, 1971), p. 143.

15. See Temkin, *Buthelezi*, p. 110.

16. See, for example, Gerhard Maré, *Ethnicity and Politics in South Africa* (London: Zed Books, 1993).

17. Speech by King Goodwill Zwelithini, 9 September 1989.

18. The matter was settled in the Supreme Court in Pietermaritzburg, with KwaZulu retaining control of Ingwavuma. Yet *The Mercury* reports that recently Swaziland restated their claim over Ingwavuma and 'are understood to be briefing lawyers to fight the case on their behalf'; see *The Mercury*, 13 May 2003.

19. Speech by Buthelezi, 18 June 1983, Gwaliweni, Ingwavuma entitled: 'King Dingane kaSenzangakhona: Unveiling of a Memorial near the Spot Where He Was Assassinated and of a Stone on His Grave by King Zwelithini Goodwill kaBhekuzulu – the Eighth King of the Zulus'.

20. Senior Zulu royal prince and IFP politician Gideon Zulu has taken Mbeki to task for failing to clearly define the status of the Zulu kingdom. The uncertainty clearly breeds sentiments of anger among traditionalists. At the book launch of his autobiography, Prince Gideon Zulu questioned why 'the great Zulu Kingdom was undermined and enjoyed a lesser status than the smaller Swazi and Lesotho Kingdoms' and 'urged the warriors to rise up and fight for the rights of the King and the kingdom', *The Mercury*, 13 May 2003.

21. *The Mercury*, 16 January 1997; *The Sunday Tribune*, 23 February 1997 and *The Mercury*, 16 July 2002.

*Chapter 31*

# The Roots of Violence and Martial Zuluness on the East Rand

PHILIP BONNER and VUSI NDIMA

BETWEEN JULY 1990 and the elections of April 1994, the Witwatersrand experienced the most sustained bloodletting of its 100-year existence. From July 1990 to April 1992, 1 207 people died and 3 697 suffered injuries in a sequence of conflicts between hostel dwellers and residents of townships. The East Rand was the epicentre of this violence, accounting for 36.3 per cent of the total deaths and 67.6 per cent of all injuries. The preponderance of these casualties occurred in Katorus, a region set aside for black settlement encompassing Katlehong, Thokoza and Vosloorus in the eastern Witwatersrand.[1] Much of the media coverage focused on two driving forces stoking the bloodshed: Zulu aggressors and a putative age-old animosity between Xhosa and Zulu people whose final outcome was competition between a Zulu-dominated Inkatha Freedom Party (IFP) and the Xhosa-dominated African National Congress (ANC).

While some journalists manipulated ideas of tribalism for political purposes, most failed to question ethnic stereotypes that located 'Zulus in a lineage of violence extending back to Shaka's supposed wars of extermination', a legacy which was said to have particularly victimised Mpondo people in the isiXhosa-speaking Cape in the late 1820s.[2] Accounts offered by left-leaning media were also misleading. In these reports police and so-called 'third force' operatives were blamed for manipulating the IFP and inciting Zulu hostel dwellers into murderous assaults on African residents of townships; the roots of these attacks were in turn traced to the launching of the IFP as a countrywide political organisation in July 1990 and its subsequent forced recruitment of members in isiZulu-speaking migrant workers' hostels.[3]

While journalists covering violence on the Witwatersrand and people enveloped in the combat sought to identify instigators, academics analysed the conflict in a sociological context. Morris and Hindson, for example, focused on the breakdown in the 1980s of apartheid laws restricting freedom of movement and the resultant rivalries between marginalised groups over dwindling resources; they argued that these dynamics contributed to civil bloodshed.[4] Similarly, Ruiters and Taylor presented the protagonists as those 'most severely exploited and disadvantaged by the apartheid system', particularly hostel dwellers who were competing for the few crumbs falling from apartheid's rickety table.[5] Minnaar and Chipkin broadened and sharpened their sociological focus in interesting ways. Minnaar placed special emphasis on the increasing ostracisation and isolation of hostel dwellers from township communities and located the trigger of violence in the conflict between isiXhosa-speaking residents of Phola Park squatter camp in Thokoza township and isiZulu-speaking hostel dwellers in neighbouring Khalanyoni hostel.[6] Chipkin saw the fighting as a product of five overlapping factors, including tension between Khalanyoni hostel and Phola Park. Most importantly, he highlighted an overlooked determinant – the Katlehong township taxi war of 1990.[7]

Ultimately the most illuminating studies make use of oral testimonies of hostel dwellers. Here, both Segal and Ndima catalogued a sequence of incendiary provocations fuelling the conflict, among them the slackening of municipal controls over hostel life in the 1980s and the consequent overcrowding and degradation of hostel units; the estrangement of Zulu migrants from militant trade unions; escalating political competition after the 1990 unbanning of the ANC; ethnic stereotyping and vengeful rumour; frictions between migrants in mushrooming squatter camps; and dirty tricks sponsored by the police and security forces.[8]

Yet this substantial research paints a picture that still remains unfinished. To date, the most pertinent studies neglect chronological descriptions. The few narrative analyses rarely foreground sociological considerations. Our aim is to integrate the two explanatory frameworks into one canvas by revisiting the violence through interviews conducted with combatants, refugees, hostel dwellers, labour migrants, township residents and squatter camp activists in the Katorus region. Ndima's interviews with Zulu migrants and ex-migrants from KwaZulu-Natal, a region falling into desperate poverty in the 1970s and 1980s under pressure from apartheid resettlement and mounting cattle theft, form the bedrock of this chapter. Carried out in 1996 in hostels in Katlehong, Thokoza and Vosloorus, as well as in the KwaZulu 'home' district of Nqutu, the interviews number 34 in total (including seven repeats). Such testimonies permit us to plot how migrants attempted to sustain their rural families by sending back their earnings; some statements allude to social dimensions of hostel life such as the customary discipline – rules about saving wages and respecting patriarchal control – that older workers imposed on younger colleagues. The interviews also speak to how isiZulu-speaking African men in the Witwatersrand job market felt squeezed between the needs of their relations in KwaZulu and radical aims of the Federation of South African Trade Unions (FOSATU) and its successor, the Congress of South African Trade Unions (COSATU), which launched stayaways in the 1980s as jobs became scarce in an era of retrenchment. Migrants did not idly watch these economic shocks; they actively sought channels to generate income by redeploying some of their earnings into black taxi businesses, then engaging in violent competition over routes and passengers. These bloody taxi rivalries would be reported erroneously as Zulu-Xhosa wars. Finally, the Nqutu interviews are complemented by interviews with trade unionists and Phola Park township residents, as well as a broad range of archival documentation that hitherto has not seen the light of day. This mix of oral and written sources offers deeper insights into the complex dynamics that erupted into internecine struggles on the Witwatersrand between 1990 and 1994.

### Cultural geography, social rules and conjugal visits: The hostel milieu

Between the early 1960s and late 1970s hostels were laid out across the eastern Witwatersrand, endowing the area with the second-largest concentration of contracted labour migrants in South Africa. By 1980, Katlehong hostels accommodated 15 800 people, Thokoza hostels 13 000, and those in Vosloorus 17 481.[9] Within their confines, a set of isiZulu-speaking migrant cultures thrived, governed by a gerontocratic patriarchal order that required younger newcomers to give 'complete submission' to hostel elders.[10]

These hostels were also situated in the heart of apartheid's new townships. Thokoza's dormitory complex on Khumalo Street, for example, sat on the main access road in and out of the township. Some hostel residents were not content to isolate themselves from this urban world. Migrant elders often entered the adjacent township to attend church or pursue trysts. Young migrants joined bands playing *isicathamiya* or *maskanda* music, staging shows for township audiences.[11] Although popular, these performances threatened older custodians of migrant values who feared youth assertiveness and outside influences. As one Zulu elder in Mazibuko hostel, Johannes Sithole, claimed, 'People who sang it [*isicathamiya* and *maskanda*] were known to be absconders because they were exposed to township women in halls and were easy targets. They also spent a lot of money on clothes, which made them attractive.'[12]

Before the age of minibus taxis, or 'Kombis', most migrant workers were only able to return home once or twice a year.[13] Many migrants broke the long periods of familial separation by inviting wives to town during fallow periods. Kwesine hostel resident, Wilson Magubane, sent for his wife (in Nqutu) 'in winter because there were no fields to plough and no harvests to reap. She stayed two to three months, and returned home at the first rains'. A singular intent of such visits was to conceive a child, or 'going to fetch the baby'.[14] To this end, migrant husbands rented lodgings in township houses for their wives, irrespective of different ethnic neighbourhoods. The couple would often sleep in the kitchen to ensure some privacy and rise early each morning, so that the wife could clean the toilets and the yard to offset some of the rent payments. Arrangements of this kind are remembered fondly; in fact, township residents waged campaigns against police harassment of migrant wives, who came to stay with their husbands without obtaining a permit.[15]

Indeed, in the 1960s and 1970s relationships between township residents and hostel dwellers were generally described as 'cordial', even 'family-like'.[16] Other hostel dwellers remember more ambivalence from township youths. Gabriel Ngcobo, a Zulu migrant who rented a room in Vosloorus in the 1970s, recalls being ridiculed by children as the man 'from the *plaas* [farm]'. Epithets hurled at Zulu migrants also mocked their pierced ears, '*omadlebe*'.[17] In response, some hostel dwellers sutured their dangling lobes because 'those with them were victims of violence on the trains and faced social exclusion in the township'.[18] The contempt of gangster, or *tsotsi*, youth became the most serious problem for Zulu migrants, who saw these toughs as their 'thorn'.[19] Still, a basically harmonious atmosphere prevailed between hostel dwellers and township residents, and, by the early-to-middle 1980s, both communities were being drawn into a surging trade union movement that urged all black workers to join ranks.

New forces were even then beginning to pick away at the threads of Zulu migrant culture, rendering it less intact and more vulnerable to collision with other sectors of the townships' population. The first aspect of migrant culture exposed to these corrosive forces was the urban space in which it was housed, the hostel itself. The second was the migrants' rural base: the rural homestead for which they sacrificed all else.

### The siege begins: The unravelling of hostel life

In March 1985 a civil engineering company named Con Roux wrote to the Vosloorus town council to complain that Con Roux employees in Vosloorus hostels lived in appalling conditions. 'For some years now,' the company protested, 'security at the gate had been almost . . . non-existent.' As a result, 'a large number of shop and shebeen owners' plied their trade in hostel rooms which led to 'theft [and] personal danger'. Amenities in the hostel were also decaying; hot water and lavatories were 'very seldom in working order'; broken windows were 'left for months'; and grass outside the dormitories 'grew window high'. Residents had 'a roof over their head' but 'very little else'. 'The attitude of the authorities', Con Roux concluded, 'seems to have been that they have given up.'[20]

Vosloorus's hostels shared the same plight with similar complexes throughout Katorus. The Soweto revolts in 1976 and 1977, as well as the resulting politicisation of the Witwatersrand's townships, compelled the apartheid regime's Bantu affairs department and their local arms, the East and West Rand administration boards, to implement urban programmes to upgrade the services of permanent black residents. By contrast, living conditions of Zulu migrants were largely ignored. The inauguration of self-financing black local authorities in Vosloorus's town council in 1983 merely exacerbated the problem. What few resources they had available, they directed towards their more politically vociferous, settled urban constituents. The deterioration of hostel infrastructure accelerated after the abolition of influx control in 1986.

Now the reservoir of unemployed, which had lain dammed up in rural towns and African reserves, flooded into industrial centres such as the Witwatersrand in search of jobs. To compound the situation, industries in Katorus and elsewhere in South Africa had languished in deep recession since 1984. Large numbers of Zulu migrants had already been laid off; they combed the surrounding urban areas looking for any paid work, often surviving by trading goods in the informal economy, stealing and offering illegal accommodation in their hostels. Municipal authorities were no longer responsible for enforcing influx control; consequently, they had little incentive to raid hostels in search of illegal residents. Hostel regulations were loosened so that people without employment could obtain a permit and a bed, provided they paid rent.[21]

Maviyo Sithole, a Zulu migrant from Nqutu, recalls his good fortune to move into Buyafuthi hostel when 'rules governing residence in hostels were relaxed due to high unemployed [*sic*]'.[22] By the late 1980s, the city council of Vosloorus had reported that paying residents of its hostels had declined to 50 per cent of the beds available; the other 50 per cent were occupied illegally. The number of women and children staying permanently in hostels, an unheard of scenario a decade ago, climbed precipitously.[23] In May 1989 the manager of community services spelled out the consequences of domestic life in Vosloorus hostels: 'Radios and electrical equipment such as fridges and deep freezers illegally connected to the electrical system originally installed for lights only . . . result [in] . . . numerous power failures.'[24]

## 'The kraal is at the centre of the homestead . . . and without it the homestead is a joke': Stock criminals and migrant hardship

Zulu migrants were also experiencing greater hardships far from their hostels. From the 1960s to the 1970s, African labour tenants on white farms and residents of apartheid 'black spots' were expelled in increasing numbers from their homes and relocated in overcrowded reserves. In Natal alone, two million black residents of 'white South Africa' were dumped into communally held plots in the KwaZulu bantustan.[25] To cope with the land shortage, the Bantu affairs department instituted a programme of resettlement, grouping scattered homesteads into 'closer settlements' and reducing strictly demarcated individual holdings reduced to only a few acres.[26] This policy in rural KwaZulu districts such as Nqutu, the traditional home of many Katorus migrants, was to remove grazing grounds far from their homesteads, placing cattle many miles from the watchful eye of their owner and herders. Stock theft suddenly proliferated. Previously, a thief whose usual aim was to alleviate hunger would seize a single cow. But by the late 1970s, 'a new kind of theft [had begun] to be practised', a trend which gathered momentum over the next decade.[27] Thieves formed criminal syndicates to raid cattle and sell their booty. Such cattle were instantly butchered and sold on the local market, for sometimes as little as half the normal price. Now, in one devastating swoop 'whole kraals were emptied'.[28] The terror associated with this organised crime rose dramatically, prompting Buyafuthi hostel resident Maviyo Sithole to observe:

> [B]oth the community and the thieves solicit the help of hired killers . . . There are areas like Hlazekazi and Qudeni where the stolen cattle and goats are kept. These areas have roads that are near to being impassable. The thieves in these areas are armed to the teeth when the conscientious police try to penetrate these areas they are attacked . . . The problem is made worse by the fact that other police are involved in this side-line business . . . The most common method is that of coming in the middle of the night. They knock at the door and tell the woman (where the father is at work) not to wake up if she still wants to live . . . Another method is that of going to the grazing camps where they just drive the cattle to their desired destination.[29]

The impact of stock theft was devastating to patriarchal Zulu migrants away at work, for they were largely powerless to protect their homes, families and belongings. As one Nqutu migrant and Buyafuthi hostel resident, Nqaba Ndima, explained, cattle raids destroyed 'the social fabric of the rural communities whose major building block is livestock possession'. A homestead without livestock 'is a non-existent homestead . . . There should be livestock in every homestead, and the absence of livestock is liable to alienate a man from his ancestors. The kraal is at the centre of the homestead, and without it the homestead is just a joke.'[30] The migrant lifestyle was thus being eroded at both rural and urban ends: Zulu hostel dwellers, in particular, were being subjected to mounting impoverishment, violence and stress. An incendiary situation began to develop in the hostels, with Zulu residents seeking ways out of this impasse that led them into conflicts with other sections of the Witwatersrand black urban population.

### Minibus taxis: '[A] mushroom industry' of commerce and war

Stock thieves in Hlazekazi and elsewhere in KwaZulu used their booty to buy taxis.[31] Migrant workers fleeced of their herds often gave up hope of returning home to become productive cattle farmers; instead, they started to invest in the eventual purchase of a minibus. Taxis were in some ways the logical substitute or supplementary investment, since the Zulu hostel dwellers' distance from home ensured a constant demand for transport. In the 1960s and 1970s the granting of licences to Africans to run taxis was tightly restricted by the white government, but with the easing of apartheid laws, especially in the aftermath of the 1976 Soweto uprising, taxi permits became easier to secure. The appearance on the vehicle market of the Kombi or minibus, which could carry eight passengers, spurred the growth of the taxi industry. Aspiring migrant entrepreneurs moved quickly to set up taxi services between homeland and town, charging considerably lower rates to travel than drivers of four-seat vehicles. Now hostel dwellers could be ferried back and forth to their homes many times a year for short periods, without consuming too much income or jeopardising their jobs by long absenteeism. The taxi industry truly took off in 1986 and 1987, when restrictive transport regulations along with pass laws were effectively abandoned. Kombi licences shot up from 7 093 to 34 378.[32] Overnight, too, minibus taxis became a principal avenue of capital accumulation for black South Africans. Almost as quickly, Kombi routes extended like a spider's web, with more and more operators spinning new circuits.

Before deregulation in the mid-1980s, local taxi associations had mobilised to guard their routes from interlopers and competitors. An estimated 38–60 per cent of taxi drivers and owners were 'pirates' without official authorisation.[33] In Germiston taxi operators from KwaZulu, who initially plied long distance routes to Zululand, established the Germiston and District Taxi Association (GDTA) to curb pirate encroachment. Elsewhere on the Witwatersrand competition between legal and illegal taxis, and between different taxi associations, stoked conflict and revenge attacks that ended in murders. In Katorus armed rivalries assumed a distinctive character, with isiZulu-speaking migrant taxi-operators and taxi-operators permanently resident in Katlehong township at the centre of the violence. Congress of South African Students (COSAS) president, Moses Maseko, who knew Katlehong well at this time, placed this development within an economic context: 'You remember around this time, at that stage, a lot of people were retrenched, out of work . . . Some, I would say ordinary citizens of Germiston, or Katlehong, some had to buy taxis because they see it as a mushroom industry.'[34]

Throughout Katlehong and Thokoza townships, tensions rose. A letter sent to *The Sowetan* newspaper in January 1988, signed by a 'Worried Resident', complained about 'taxi operators' who have hired hostel dwellers to attack 'pirate taxis', but who, to his 'surprise . . . cannot transport passengers to and from work on time'. 'These drivers', he added, 'think they own the roads.' And he concluded with an ominous warning, 'They must stop this or the residents will act.'[35]

At some point over the ensuing months, a rival Katlehong Taxi Association (KATO) emerged, comprising township taxi operators as opposed to hostel-based taxi owners and drivers. KATO exploited its familiarity with the township community. Maseko recalled that 'those guys opened new roads . . . which the old taxi association didn't want to operate through . . . and people started to behave like, look, there are taxis that can move close to us because they know Katlehong'. KATO also courted the students and ex-students. Maseko elaborated:

> You know that a number of young people who were not able to go to university, and all those things, there was no other option but to look at possible jobs around and they were employed within the taxi industry to be drivers and all those things. Because COSAS was a strong organisation, they met us, said, no

we will reduce fees for students, give us one rand . . . They are marketing themselves and obviously, once there are economic issues, there will be politics coming in at the end of the day. If I remember well, there was a situation where the Student Congress . . . hosted a number of events and KATO supported us.[36]

The scene was set for two black taxi associations to settle their differences through violence. Khosa locates the beginning of open conflict in November 1989 when a dispute flared over the allocation of routes.[37] One isiZulu-speaking hostel dweller, Sam Manyathi, describes the antagonists 'fight[ing] for routes. These were KATO and the G and D [Germiston and District]; KATO was supported by township people because it was a local organisation. G and D was supported by people from KwaZulu-Natal . . . KATO was able to manipulate the township youth to burn taxis that belonged to G and D.'[38] COSAS leader, George Nkosi, offers a slightly different, but complementary, account:

What happened was that they were fighting over routes, and also the other thing that worsened conflict was students refusing to catch the taxis of the G and D because they claimed that they were dirty and the taxi drivers are basically full of shit, and most of these taxi drivers are from the hostels from G and D, and that they wouldn't catch G and D taxis, they'd rather wait until the KATO taxi comes. KATO taxis were nice, they were clean and most of them were new ZolaBudds [a vehicle description referring to the famous long-distance South African female runner], so the G and D had these old Toyotas, which were called in the township *inkomosophosa* and people really didn't like those kinds. The students ended up saying we'll stick on the KATO taxis, and they also had different hooters.[39]

## Stayaways, taxis and union competition

Zulu hostel dwellers interviewed identified the taxi wars as a prelude to the civil war that raged through Katorus between 1990 and 1994. For the most part, they situate this first stage of violence in 1989 and 1990, a period of nascent killing precipitated by the torching of a taxi with passengers bound for Nqutu during a stayaway called by COSATU and its political allies in June 1989. The intensity of emotion unleashed by this event propelled a taxi-centred political war. Khosa, as we have seen, dates the first taxi conflict to November 1987, interpreting this battle as having roots in market competition. Economic rivalries were, however, already being amplified by and intertwined with political conflicts. In November 1985 the giant new trade union federation, COSATU, was formed. It aligned itself with the ANC, the United Democratic Front (UDF) and the latter's powerful youth constituency, noted for its participation in national and provincial stayaways.[40] Hostel-dwelling Zulu migrants, whose prime purpose for being on the Rand was 'to work for home', were rarely consulted about these stayaways and were generally reluctant to take part in what seemed to be initiatives driven by youngsters. In this context taxis became sources of simultaneous economic and political conflict. Khophakwakhe Ngobese still remembers with barely restrained emotion 'when their ears were cut and when they were stoned . . . on their way to work' by youths who taunted them with the chant of '*Sishaya Impohlo*' [we are beating the bachelors].[41] These attacks increasingly placed the two rival taxi associations in different political as well as economic camps.

While township-aligned KATO taxis generally observed the stayaway prohibition, G and D taxi operators carried Zulu migrants to work (or back home) and paid for their temerity by being stoned or worse. As COSAS and South African Students Congress (SASCO) stalwart Moses Maseko explained:

> If there was a stayaway, we call a stayaway; it was easy for us to inform the other taxi association, no operation . . . KATO were people who we were able to say too, look, this is our situation, some of them will understand, but the other guys did not understand and they were calling us children of Atcha [perhaps referring to a hot relish or Archie Gumede, the national president of the UDF] . . . You know at those times some of the actions that we took was to make sure that people like this come to our cause.[42]

The period 1986 to 1989 was peppered with stayaways. Ruiters identifies nine, spread over thirteen days in total between 1976 and 1988. Another three-day stayaway was mounted by COSATU in September 1989 to protest the Labour Relations Amendment Act of 1988.[43] Elias Monage, COSAS activist and later National Union of Metalworkers of South Africa (NUMSA) and COSATU organiser, recalls a significant moment in the escalation of the taxi feud during this three-day stayaway:

> Youth have to monitor and discipline those who do not keep unity. Workers call for a stayaway but they drink beer and sleep and see it as a holiday . . . While the youth played a role on the first day, this receded on the second day. Taxis did not operate after the first day of the stayaway making it difficult for those who wanted to go to work. Youth wanted to burn the taxis for operating on the first day but only two taxis were attacked . . . at Kwesine station a coach was burnt. There was no marching in the townships as that would be provocative.[44]

If Monage's recollection is accurate, a longer history of taxi politicisation preceded the outbreak of full-fledged war, which Zulu migrants on the East Rand interviewed for this chapter appear not to remember. All they recollect is one traumatising moment, which seems to have blotted out earlier occurrences. This inflaming event took place in the course of another stayaway the following year, according to hostel dweller Simon Ndima: 'Violence began in June 1989 when children were on stayaway. Taxis were not operating that day. A taxi left from Kwesine (hostel) on its way to Nquthu. The children burnt it.'[45] Other hostel dwellers gave the same date, and in so doing provide further indication of the elision of the different phases of the taxi conflict in their testimony. The 1989 stayaway occurred in September not June 1989. It was the 1988 stayaway that took place in June. Both, however, were in protest against the Labour Relations Bill/Act, which may account for the confusion.[46]

Wilson Magubane situates the major outbreak of fighting at the same time as Ndima, and in a similar context:

> [W]hen trade unions such as COSATU called for the 'Stick-away' stayaway . . .
> [h]ostel dwellers were still going to work because they did not know what was
> going on. There was a taxi that was full of people who were on their way to
> Nqutu. The owner of this taxi was Mr Ngobese. The driver of this taxi was
> afraid of getting out of the township alone because of fear of the township
> youth who had barricaded the roads. Another driver who was driving a taxi
> that was empty offered to accompany him to Boksburg . . . The taxis left, driving
> along Khumalo Street. When they were about to reach Mnisi Section they
> were stopped . . . petrol was poured on those minibuses and they were burnt
> to ashes . . . The most painful thing about the burning . . . is that one minibus
> carried a pregnant women who was also travelling with a small child.

Both drivers and all but one passenger were burned to death. Magubane claimed that police in a helicopter equipped with loudspeakers spurred the attackers to light the fire.[47] Khiphakwakhe Ngobese, who was on leave on that day and walking across a soccer field on his way back from his in-laws, recalls 'smelling a kind of smell which he had never smelt before . . . He found that the hostels had been barricaded and people had been burnt to death'.[48]

Episodes such as these exacerbated the estrangement between the COSATU-led union movement and Zulu migrants, who had been staunch COSATU supporters since its formation in November 1985. At a mass rally marking the foundation of COSATU at Kings Park Stadium in Durban, Elijah Barayi, the newly elected president at the time of its inauguration, launched an unauthorised attack on Chief Mangosuthu Gatsha Buthelezi, the president of Inkatha and homeland leader of KwaZulu. After dubbing Chief Buthelezi a bantustan 'puppet', Barayi urged the crowd to 'bury Botha and Gatsha' and to secure the release of the 'real leader', Nelson Mandela.[49] Ex-FOSATU leaders gaped. They had spent years trying to prevent a total breach with Chief Buthelezi and Inkatha. Now, in one gesture, Barayi had issued a declaration of war.

Almost immediately, Inkatha formed a rival federation, christened the United Workers' Union of South Africa (UWUSA) on May Day 1986, with Simon Conco as president.[50] UWUSA pledged to support foreign investment and contended that high profits for business and economic growth would lead to the dismantling of apartheid.[51] This by itself would have pointed it on a collision course with COSATU. Conco made doubly sure by promising his charges that 'the battle with COSATU would be won on the Witwatersrand'. UWUSA's main recruits were Zulu migrants employed in the metal works of eastern Witwatersrand and residing in Katorus hostels. In 1987, 6 000 members of the Metal and Allied Workers' Union's (MAWU) stronghold in the firm Scaw Metals defected to UWUSA.[52]

Until 1987 and the offensive by UWUSA, Zulu migrants working in metal industries remained loyal to MAWU and UWUSA. Douglas Manyathi, for example, said he joined MAWU in 1986 because 'without the unions it was easier for employers to expel the employees without any valid reason . . . The arrival of the trade unions ensured that the workers were protected. The shop-stewards . . . fought for the rights of the workers because they were workers themselves.'[53] Johannes Sithole signed up with MAWU in 1987 'because they [metal workers] were underpaid [and] the foremen used favouritism in the way they paid wages . . . [T]he unions [also] ensured there would be no unfair dismissals.'[54]

From 1986 onwards, migrant workers also became alienated from COSATU by repeated stayaways and strikes. Johannes Sithole stated that

> lazy and irresponsible people began to misuse the trade unions. A person expelled for late coming and absenteeism had to be protected by the union which would order other workers to stay away from work or to go slow. It happened sometimes that the worker is caught red-handed . . . stealing the property of the employer . . . and the other workers go on strike for that. Some employers decided to expel all those workers and employ scab labour . . . [which] in turn would inspire those who had been expelled to attack the 'rats' as scab labourers were called. The employers would elect to close down their firms, which created divisions in the ranks of the workers. We as Zulu do not believe in stayaways because we have come to the Rand for the sole purpose of working for our children.[55]

Nqaba Ndima echoed this view:

> In the mid-1980s [COSATU] began to fight for people who had been expelled for valid reasons such as absenteeism and the use of intoxicating liquor. People took advantage of this and started demanding more money, which in turn forced some firms to close down . . . It was the general view among migrants, Zulu in particular, that the firms were closing down due to trade union activity.[56]

Many migrant union or ex-union members repeated this same point, often citing individual firms that closed or moved out of the Katorus areas such as Lash, Kros Brothers, and so on.

Another major source of alienation for migrant workers were the repeated stayaways called by COSATU between 1986 and 1990. As one Katlehong migrant put it: 'The Zulu said they came to the Rand for the sole purpose of working [which meant they] left their families behind them. They [now] had to down tools and stay in the hostel, while the township people downed tools to stay with their families.'[57] There was also a perception of something more sinister unfolding. NUMSA member, Herbert Sibisi, left NUMSA when he realised that 'it was NUMSA that was fuelling violence by organising stayaways that led to the death of many Zulu workers who were on their way to work'.[58] Sam Manyathi quit COSATU when 'it became clear that [the union] was being manipulated by the UDF which was the arch-rival of the IFP'.[59] Johannes Sithole, 'began to detest stayaways because the unions were beginning to say they hated Buthelezi'.[60]

Many Zulu migrants associated the shift in union practice with the formation of a more militant COSATU. In Zibuke Manyathi's eyes a change occurred 'when the umbrella body became COSATU. Then the workers were now divided along political tendencies. The Zulu had been in leadership positions in FOSATU. This . . . led to UWUSA. This . . . profoundly hardened ethnic relationships.'[61] His fellow hostel dweller, Joseph Buthelezi, presented a more vocal perspective. Most people from Nqutu left the union and joined UWUSA because COSATU preached against investment.[62] And of course, as Inkatha endlessly reiterated, divestment cost jobs. Gabriel Ngcobo likewise observes: 'In the course of time COSATU became more politically than economically oriented. Our problems were not given first as it was the case before.'[63]

The two final stayaways that precipitated an open split between Zulu hostel dwellers and township residents were the 'stickaway' stayaway, which led to the incineration of Ngobese's taxi and its passengers in September 1989 and a further stayaway called for 2 July 1990 to protest the 'reign of terror' being conducted by Inkatha in Natal and to press the demand that Chief Mangosuthu Buthelezi, then KwaZulu's minister of police, be removed from office. Following the first outrage, Wilson Magubane, along with other hostel and township elders, attempted to broker a truce between the two sides.[64] This failed, following a further altercation over the allocation of taxi routes (the one Khosa singles out as the main escalator of conflict) in November 1989. Nearly three weeks of violence erupted, extending from February to March 1990. In one particularly savage episode on 27 February six pupils and teachers were murdered in a Katlehong school. Hostel vigilantes hunted from house to house for township suspects and even raided a local hospital to finish off wounded 'Komblese' (comrades). Ultimately 50 people would lose their lives in this conflict and 350 would be left wounded. On 7 March Katlehong residents organised a boycott of all taxis in an effort to curb the violence, an initiative which eventually led to a momentary cessation of armed hostilities and the establishment of a new combined taxi association.[65] It should be noted that in the early months of 1990, individual hostels were still multi-ethnic. Wilson Magubane described 'the hostel dwellers as speaking with one voice. There was no discrimination along ethnic lines. Zulu, Mpondo, Xhosa, Basotho as hostel residents gathered together [and] armed.'[66]

The final moment of rupture came with the 'reign of terror' stayaway called for 2 July 1990. This was one that Zulu migrant workers could not possibly join. It was at least partly in response to this call that the IFP announced its intention to relaunch itself as a countrywide political party, and initiated recruitment rallies at various townships across the greater Witwatersrand. At one of these gatherings in Sebokeng stadium on 22 July 1990, violence erupted leading to substantial loss of life.[67] This wave of killing spread and engulfed the Rand, pitting Zulu hostel dwellers against township residents in a remorseless cycle of violence in which thousands would die over four years.

### 'Holed up and starved': A war of attrition and the conclusion of violence

It was during these vicious contestations between township residents and hostel dwellers, according to several accounts, that the ethnic factor was truly invoked. Ethnic battles had racked the Witwatersrand a half-century before, pitting South Sotho men against either Mpondo or Zulu men.[68] Prior to this period, 120 years had elapsed since the sole recorded armed conflicts between Zulu and Mpondo, which occurred during Shaka's reign.[69] Thus, available historical evidence truly indicates that Zulu-Xhosa animosity developed in the late 1980s, shortly after the lifting of the pass laws, as self-identified Zulu and Xhosa factions battled for scarce resources and power. At this time, more Xhosa migrants from the Cape reserves were streaming into the Witwatersrand. Petrus Mlambo, an isiZulu-speaking hostel dweller from Kwesine hostel in Katlehong, recalled businesses in areas around Johannesburg being 'packed with Xhosa', adding that 'if you are a Zulu you won't get a job'.[70] Fellow Nqutu migrant, Sam Manyathi, describes Xhosa newcomers jamming into shack settlements and seeking beds in Katorus hostels.[71]

Ethnic stereotypes were now deployed far more frequently in the name of defending group integrity. IsiZulu-speakers increasingly disparaged isiXhosa-speakers as 'treacherous' thieves who 'live by the saying "a person's property is also mine"'. IsiXhosa-speakers identified Zulus as 'stupid war-mongers' and boss-boys.[72] Epithets stoked feelings of unrest that other interventions kindled into full-scale war. These interventions were in the first instance political: the unbanning of the ANC in 1990 and Buthelezi's launching of the IFP as a national party. Pickup Mtshali, a Zulu labour migrant from Nqutu district living in Kwesine hostel in Katlehong, recalls 'the jubilations that shook the whole country on the day that Nelson Mandela was released' in February 1990. Mtshali said: 'We of the Zulu migrants of Katorus hostels were also happy because we heard that the president had spent 27 years in detention for the sake of the oppressed people of this country.' Within days Zulu hostel dwellers expressed second thoughts. They feared 'elimination' by ANC comrades who saw

Zulu migrants as going against the black 'political mainstream'.[73] IFP organisers, in turn, demanded that amaZulu reject the ANC. Douglas Manyathi, a Zulu migrant, remembers an 'inflammatory' meeting at Kwesine hostel, Katlehong, where 'the speakers . . . insist[ed] that they were not going to be ruled by a Xhosa. A few days later . . . the Xhosa in the hostels were attacked by the Zulu', which led to a series of retaliatory strikes.[74] A Buyafuthi hostel dweller, Simon Ndima, elaborated on a pivotal incident in Lindela hostel, Katlehong township:

> Early in 1990, the Bhaca [an ethnic group from the far eastern Cape] and Xhosa attacked the Zulu at Lindela hostel. Most Zulu were stabbed to death because they were caught off-guard, even though there was a rumour that the Bhaca were sharpening their spears. Most Zulu then fled to Kwesine and other hostels that were predominantly Zulu . . . This very same day we took the train to Crossroads (squatter camp) to attack the shack township which was predominantly Xhosa-Bhaca. We arrived there at 4.00 a.m. We stayed till 1.00 p.m. Many Xhosa died.[75]

The Lindela slaughter features as the reason Zulu hostel dwellers invaded so-called Bhaca and Xhosa communities, even though this point is not mentioned in most published accounts of these events. Still, this conflagration could not have escalated without state provocateurs. In one long bloody incident between 10 and 13 September 1990, Zulu hostel dwellers from Khalanyoni hostel in Thokoza retaliated en masse against nearby Xhosa residents of Phola Park. They mounted two big assaults, burning 600 shacks and killing 80 people, with the assistance of government forces.[76] Armed with rifles and grenade launchers, white policemen dressed in balaclavas, with their faces smeared in black boot polish, fired into shacks, shouting, '*Kom Zulu, kom* [come Zulu, come].' Armoured police vehicles escorted the attackers. At least one white infiltrator was killed, his body later removed with other fatally wounded Zulu combatants by the police.[77] On 25 September, a curfew was finally imposed; by the next day widespread killing had ceased. But the war resumed in November when Zulu migrants from Nqutu and elsewhere ordered Xhosa to leave all hostels to join 'their brothers in the townships'.[78] Once again the police and third force incited these killings, spreading misinformation in forged pamphlets bearing antiquated ANC crests, which read: 'We want to destroy the Zulus . . . We have to end their Zuluness of which they are proud . . . There will be no peace as long as the Zulus are still powerful. Let us destroy them all in South African townships, hostels, and in the working places. Let us burn down their houses in townships and drive them out. Down with Zulus.'[79]

After an attack by Zulu migrants on Vosloorus hostels, one of their number, J.B., recalls that 'police allowed us to invade the township. We killed 38 that day.' Massacres soon moved to the trains, probably through the agency of Inkatha marauders and third force insurgents although to many outside observers these assaults appeared motiveless or simply blind acts of counter-terror.[80]

In 1993, as the political stakes were raised in anticipation of national elections the following year, internecine killing exploded with greater ferocity: in July and August, hundreds on the Witwatersrand were driven from their properties and lost their lives.[81] Many isiZulu-speaking people seeking the shrinking margin of a non-aligned political status, but suspected by both sides, hunkered down in the only place they could find refuge, the hostels. Douglas Manyathi, a neutral émigré from Nqutu who had bought a house in Sunrise View, Katlehong, faced accusations from fellow Zulu workers of being a 'sell-out'. They ordered him to pay a donation for firearms 'to show that he had not forsaken them'. Enoch Shoba, who likewise purchased a house in Hlongwane Section, Katlehong, survived 'by attending ANC meetings', despite the fact that he was not a member. To display any outward signs of Zuluness, such as wearing bracelets of animal skin (*iziphandla*), Vusi Lange reported, was to court death. Zwenke Mthembu 'survived by changing masks: when he was with the Zulu he behaved like Inkatha, when with the township people he became a comrade'.[82]

Among the refugees who flooded into hostels were vast numbers of Zulu women. Zulu hostel dwellers offered sanctuary 'because we would not forsake our own people'. The massive influx of women further upset the Zulu bachelor existence in the hostels. Competition over girlfriends was rife, and in this courting milieu the authority of elders over youth drastically eroded.[83] Generational conflicts brewed. 'Youth were no longer so submissive,' Joseph Buthelezi said. 'They dictated to elders, especially over war issues.'[84]

Many older migrants moved out of their hostels, either returning home or securing accommodation elsewhere in squatter camps and white suburbs. Their beds were taken by young unemployed rural migrants, many coming with the objective of fighting and looting. Rumours abounded, with some titbits of truth, that the IFP bussed in Zulu fighters from regions of KwaZulu and Natal terrorised by stock-theft syndicates. These new combatants knew the battlefield. 'People from Qudeni, Msinga and Hlazekazi played a leading role in the violent episodes because gunfighting was their daily bread,' one Zulu migrant said.[85] *Izinduna* organised regiments, *amabutho*, and collected financial levies to buy guns, displacing the command structure of elders and *isibonda* in the hostels.[86] Burial societies emerged to cover hostel residents with a guaranteed payment of R4 000 upon death.[87]

Youthful self-defence units also sprang up in township neighbourhoods around the hostels; they did everything in their power to extinguish the presence of Zulu migrants. Hostel dwellers were regularly attacked on their way to jobs; a key railway line between Natalspruit and the industrial areas was also torn up and made impassable. Zulu migrants had to travel circuitous, expensive routes to work, and sometimes lost their jobs as a result.[88] A profound sense of isolation and embattlement descended on hostel dwellers. On one nightmarish occasion, when hostel residents were 'holed up and starved', a group of them dissected a dead body in search of a liver to eat.[89]

## Conclusion

In their homesteads, adult Zulu men celebrate their 'bullness' and their power. When they moved to the Rand to take up contracts as migrant labourers, a remarkable and hitherto unrecognised transformation occurred. As they entered the domain of arbitrary white authority in the factories and streets of the Rand, they experienced a sense of being comprehensively disempowered. This shift is registered in the ethnic stereotypes that Zulu migrants hold of themselves, where they characterise their behaviour on the Rand with such terms as patient, obedient, strong in the face of adversity and heavy labour. Among the words that recur most frequently in migrant vocabularies and testimonies are 'perseverance' and 'to persevere'. The hard school of youthful herding, stick fighting and faction fighting is pictured as inuring and hardening Zulu youth so that as adult workers they can endure and persevere. A favourite metaphor employed by Zulu migrants to reflect their way of handling the disempowering urban milieu is *aziyon inkabi* – an ox perseveres.[90] This image is striking, for the virtues that are being extolled are the tractable, patient, obedient, long-suffering and ultimately emasculated characteristics of the ox. Occasionally the alter ego of bullness would surface during weekend dancing competitions, and in demands for being given precedence in hostel rooms, but for the most part it remained submerged.

Under intense pressures in both urban and rural environments in the 1980s, and in response to what its protagonists saw as the provocations of township youth, Zulu migrant culture underwent radical changes. Patience snapped, and the pliable ox was transformed into a raging, rampaging bull. Egged on by the IFP and the third force, Zulu migrants then embarked on a course of unprecedented bloodletting and destruction across much of the Rand.

In retrospect, however, it seems as if the alter ego aspect of oxness was not entirely expunged from migrant cultures. What remains truly astonishing today and constitutes a central part of the South African miracle is that the brutal civil war that raged on the Rand for nearly four years, came to an abrupt and near-complete end with the general elections of April 1994. The critical precondition for this outcome was the last-minute decision by Chief Mangosuthu Buthelezi and the IFP to take part in the 1994 election. This permitted Zulu migrants to register their votes and, again with hindsight, constituted the first and massively significant act in a ritual of reconciliation. As thousands of migrants along with many other South Africans queued patiently under scorching skies to cast their ballots, they metamorphosed imperceptibly back into the oxen they once were, yoked together once again by the common need and design to persevere.

# Notes

1. Independent Board of Enquiry into Informal Repression (hereafter IBI), *Fortress of Fear* (Johannesburg, 1992), pp. 11–15.
2. R. Taylor, 'The Myth of Ethnic Division: Township Conflict on the Reef', *Race and Class* 22:2 (October–December 1991) and an article by R.W. Johnston in *Sunday Star*, 21 October 1991.
3. IBI monthly reports, August 1990–March 1991; A. Mapheta, 'The Violence: A View from the Ground', *Work in Progress* (hereafter WIP) 69 (1990): 508; Lawyers for Human Rights, *Phola Park: 10–13 September 1990, as Witnessed by the Residents* (Johannesburg, 1990); IBI monthly reports August 1991; D. Everett, *Who is Murdering the Peace?* (Johannesburg: Johannesburg Community Agency for Social Enquiry, 1991).
4. M. Morris and D. Hindson, 'Political Violence and Urban Reconstruction in South Africa', unpublished paper, July 1991.
5. G. Ruiters and R. Taylor, 'Hostel War: Organise or Die', *WIP* 70/71 (1991): 20–23.
6. A. Minnaar, 'Hostels and Violent Conflict on the Reef', in *Communities in Isolation: Perspectives on Hostels in South Africa*, ed. A. Minnaar (Pretoria: Human Science Research Council [HSRC], 1993), pp. 10–47.
7. I. Chipkin, 'Democracy, Cities and Space' (Masters thesis, University of the Witwatersrand, Johannesburg, 1997), pp. 94–123.
8. I. Segal, 'The Human Face of Violence: Hostel Dwellers Speak', *Journal of Southern African Studies* 18:1 (1992): 191–231 and G.V. Ndima, '*Ayizon inkabi* (An ox perseveres): The Changing Lives of Migrants from the Nqutu District of KwaZulu-Natal to Germiston, 1950–1980s' (Masters research report, University of the Witwatersrand, 1997), pp. 1–201.
9. H. Mashabela, *Townships of the PWV* (Johannesburg: South African Institute of Race Relations [SAIRR], 1988), pp. 94, 158, 170.
10. Ndima '*Ayizon inkabi*', p. 95. 'Complete submission required that young labour migrants give their earnings to hostel elders for safekeeping, abide by prohibitions forbidding contact with township women, and single-mindedly support their rural homestead' – an injunction captured by the widely used axiom, 'A Zulu works for home'. Jacob Mncube, interview conducted by Vusi Ndima, Nqutu, December 1996, speaks of 'unconditional respect'.
11. Interview conducted by Vusi Ndima with Mbongeni Ngobese, Nqutu, July 1996.
12. Second interview conducted by Vusi Ndima with Johannes Sithole, Mazibuko hostel, September 1996. According to Zibuke Manyathi, 'Most people visited the township, a practice given its own name, "siyawela" (we are going across)'. Township residents reciprocated, visiting hostels to buy meat and liquor, as well as getting water and taking hot baths. Hundreds also attended weekend *ingoma* and other traditional dances on hostel grounds. Interviews conducted by Vusi Ndima with Zibuke Manyathi, Andreas Ngokwe, Augustine Mandlenkosi, Ngcobo, Nqutu, July and December 1996.
13. Interviews conducted by Vusi Ndima with Z. Manyathi and with Elliot Cebekhulu, Nqutu, December 1996.
14. Second interview conducted by Vusi Ndima with Wilson Magubane, Kwesine hostel, September 1996. For the phrase, see the second interview with Z. Manyathi, Nqutu, December 1996.
15. Because of their conspicuous traditional dress styles, migrant wives who had previously courted arrest when they went out on the streets were then routinely granted permits for three-month visits. Interviews conducted by Vusi Ndima; second interview with Petrus Mlambo, Kwesine hostel, September 1996; second interview with Maviyo Sithole, Buyafuthi hostel, September 1996; second interview with Johannes Sithole, Mazibuko hostel, September 1996; interview with Sam Manyathi, Zonkesizwe, September 1996 and interview with Jacob Mncube.
16. First interview with Zibuke Manyathi, Nqutu, July 1996.
17. Interview conducted by Vusi Ndima with Gabriel Nqcobo, Nqutu, December 1996. First and second interviews conducted by Vusi Ndima with Johannes Sithole, Mazibuko hostel, August and September 1996.
18. Muzikhawukhete Mkhize's family failed to recognise him when he returned home after an absence of several years with his ears stitched up. Interview conducted by Vusi Ndima with Muzikhawukhete Mkhize, Buyafuthi hostel, 4 August 1996.
19. Interviews conducted by Vusi Ndima with Philip Nene and Joseph Buthelezi, Nqutu, December 1996.

20. Vosloorus Archive (hereafter VA) T1/13 'Klaagtes'.
21. Segal, 'The Human Face': 211. One hostel resident described the overall climate at this time: 'There was less security, less municipal police . . . It was much less strict . . . Maybe this police were not well disciplined . . . there was no more security. . . so it's not safe.'
22. Interview with Maviyo Sithole.
23. VA Agenda, 20 November 1988.
24. VA T1/13 'Klaagtes'. Report of Town Engineer.
25. A. Sitas, 'African Worker Responses on the East Rand to Changes in the Metal Industry, 1960–1980' (Ph.D. diss., University of the Witwatersrand, 1983), pp. 261–65. For more specific data regarding Nqutu, see G. Maré, *African Population Relocation in South Africa* (Johannesburg: SAIRR, 1980), pp. 12–15.
26. Maré, *African Population Relocation*. Interview with Joseph Buthelezi; interview conducted by Vusi Ndima with Khophakwakhe Ngobene, Kwesine hostel, 3 August 1996 and Gerhard Maré and Georgina Hamilton, *An Appetite for Power: Buthelezi's Inkatha and South Africa* (Johannesburg: Ravan Press, 1987).
27. Second interview Petrus Mlambo and second interview conducted by Vusi Ndima with Nqaba Ndima, Buyafuthi hostel, September 1996.
28. Second interview with Johannes Sithole and second interview with Sam Manyathi.
29. Second interview with Maviyo Sithole. Not all areas were as acutely vulnerable to the depredations of stock thieves as Nquthu. Nevertheless, the same broad trend was evident elsewhere in South Africa. In other parts of Natal and in the homeland of Lebowa, the withdrawal of labour services supplied by young boys who were now going to school, left livestock unsupervised and exposed to roaming thieves. See P. Delius, *A Lion Among the Cattle* (Johannesburg: Ravan Press, 1996), p. 146 and an unpublished paper by N. Breslin and P. Delius for Operation Hunger. So, too, in Lesotho and the Transkei, cattle theft soared at this time, see J.B. Peires, 'Traditional Leaders in Purgatory in Local Government in Tsolo, Qunu and Port St. Johns, 1900–2000', *African Studies* 59:1 (July 2000): 98–104.
30. Second interview with Nqaba Ndima.
31. Second interview with Petrus Mlambo.
32. M.M. Khosa, 'Routes, Ranks and Rebels: Feuding in the Taxi Revolution', *Journal of Southern African Studies* 18:1 (March 1992): 235. Sam Manyathi records the dramatic change of being able to return home every month.
33. C. McCaul, *No Easy Ride: The Rise and Future of the Black Taxi Industry* (Johannesburg: SAIRR, 1990), pp. 58–63.
34. Interview conducted by Sello Mathabatha with Moses Maseko, 13 March 1999. Meftagodren with Moses Maseko.
35. *The Sowetan*, 8 January 1988.
36. Interview with Moses Maseko.
37. Khosa, 'Routes, Ranks': 245.
38. Interview with Sam Manyathi.
39. Interview conducted by Noor Niefthgodren with George Ndlozi, April 1999.
40. Interview conducted by Vusi Ndima with Simon Silwayiphi Ndima, Buyafuthi hostel, 4 August 1996.
41. Interview with Khophakwakhe Ngobese.
42. Interview with Moses Maseko.
43. G. Ruiters, 'South African Liberation Politics: A Case Study of Collective Bargaining and Leadership in Kathorus 1980–1989' (Masters thesis, University of the Witwatersrand, 1995), p. 171. See also J. Baskin, *Striking Back: A History of COSATU* (Johannesburg: Ravan Press, 1991), pp. 122–27, 140–31, 188–91, 223–89, and especially 389–91 for the 1989 stayaway.
44. Ruiters, 'South African Liberation Politics', p. 153.
45. Interview conducted by Vusi Ndima with Simon Silwayiphi Ndima, Buyafuthi hostel, 4 August 1996.
46. Here, the authors are persuaded that it is the 1989 event to which reference is being made. See Baskin, *Striking Back*, pp. 189–90, 283–89, 339–41.
47. Interview conducted by Vusi Ndima with Khiphakwakhe Ngobese with Wilson Magubane interjecting, Kwesine hostel, 3 August 1996.
48. Ibid.

49. Baskin, *Striking Back*, pp. 66–67.
50. Maré and Hamilton, *An Appetite for Power*, pp. 130–33.
51. Baskin, *Striking Back*, pp. 66–67.
52. Ibid., pp. 139–40 and Ruiters, 'South African Liberation Politics', p. 169.
53. Interview conducted by Vusi Ndima with Douglas Manyathi, Sunrise View, Vosloorus, September 1996.
54. Interview conducted by Vusi Ndima with Johannes Sithole, Mazibuko hostel, 4 August 1996. For similar endorsements, see, for example, interviews with Nqaba Ndima who joined MAWU 'when it started operating because it fought against ill treatment of workers and unnecessary expulsions. The union also fought against low wages paid to workers.' Petrus Mlambo who 'joined MAWU in 1979 . . . due to the fact that [he] wanted to see wages increased as well as to fight unfair dismissal' (second interview). Muzikawuthetki Mkhize joined MAWU in the late 1970s when he was working at Kros Brothers in Cleveland in order 'to protect himself against unfair treatment and expulsions which were common in those days' (interview conducted by Vusi Ndima, Buyafuthi hostel, 4 August 1996).
55. Second interview with Johannes Sithole.
56. Second interview with Nqaba Ndima.
57. Interview conducted by Vusi Ndima with Vusi Langa, Sunrise View, Katlehong, September 1996. See also second interview, Johannes Sithole.
58. Interview conducted by Vusi Ndima with Herbert Sibisi, Katorus, September 1992.
59. Interview with Sam Manyathi.
60. Interview with Johannes Sithole.
61. Interview with Zibuke Manyathi.
62. Interview conducted by Vusi Ndima with Joseph Buthelezi, Nqutu, December 1996.
63. Interview with Gabriel Ngcobo.
64. Interview with Khophakwakhe Ngobese, Wilson Magubane.
65. Khosa, 'Routes, Ranks': 245–47.
66. Interview with Khophakwakhe Ngobese, Wilson Magubane.
67. Baskin, *Striking Back*, pp. 426–27; UW, HLP, BIRR, submission to the TRC on the Reef Violence, 12 December 1996, pp. 6–7.
68. P.L. Bonner, 'The Russians on the Reef, 1947–1957: Urbanisation, Gang Warfare and Ethnic Mobilisation', in *Apartheid's Genesis, 1935–1962*, eds. Philip Bonner, Peter Delius and Deborah Posel (Johannesburg: Ravan Press and Witwatersrand University Press, 1993), pp. 160–174.
69. William Beinart, *The Political Economy of Pondoland 1860–1930* (Cambridge: Cambridge University Press, 1982), pp. 10–11.
70. Interview conducted by Vusi Ndima with Petrus Mlambo, Kwesine hostel, Katlehong, 4 August and September 1996.
71. Interview conducted by Vusi Ndima with Sam Manyathi, Zonkesiswe squatter camp, Vosloorus, September 1996.
72. Segal, 'The Human Face': 223.
73. Interview conducted by Vusi Ndima with Pickup Mtshali, Kwesine hostel, Katlehong, 3 August 1996.
74. Interview conducted by Vusi Ndima with Douglas Manyathi, Sunrise View, Vosloorus, September 1996.
75. Interview conducted by Vusi Ndima with Simon Silwayiphi Ndima, Buyafuthi hostel, Katlehong, 4 August 1996.
76. University of the Witwatersrand Library, Historical Library Papers, Planact Papers AL 2566 17.98, 'Development and Resistance: The Lessons for Planning of Phola Park', unauthored, no date.
77. Lawyers for Human Rights, *Phola Park*, p. 3.
78. Petrus Mlambo, first interview.
79. Segal, 'The Human Face': 223.
80. See IBI reports for the entire period, University of the Witwatersrand, Johannesburg. Independent Board of Enquiry Collection, monthly reports.
81. Peace Action, *When We Were Friends*, pp. 1–45.
82. Interview with Douglas Manyathi; first interview conducted by Vusi Ndima with Enoch Shoba, Nqutu, December 1996; interview with Vusi Langa; interview conducted by Vusi Ndima with Zwelonke Mthembu, Nqutu, December 1996.

83. Second interview with Nqaba Ndima.
84. Interview conducted by Vusi Ndima with Joseph Buthelezi, Nqutu, December 1996.
85. Interview with Joseph Buthelezi.
86. Second interview with Nqaba Ndima and second interview with Petrus Mlamba.
87. First interview with Nqaba Ndima, Buyafuthi hostel, 4 August 1991 and first interview with Petrus Mlambo.
88. Interview with Jabulani Ndima and comment by Falithenjwa Mncube during interview with Maviyo Sithole.
89. Interview, August 1996 and Ndima '*Ayizon inkabi*'.
90. Ibid.

*Chapter 32*

# Monuments of Division
## Apartheid and Post-apartheid Struggles over Zulu Nationalist Heritage Sites

NSIZWA DLAMINI

IN THE APARTHEID-ERA KwaZulu homeland, the early 1970s marked the beginning of annual ceremonies celebrating King Shaka as the founder of the great Zulu nation. Over the next two decades, the legacies of other famous Zulu rulers were also commemorated with the unveiling of monuments in their honour. Such memorials incorporated a version of heroic Zulu history championed by Mangosuthu Buthelezi, leader of Inkatha Yenkululeko Yesizwe (Inkatha), a political movement that ruled KwaZulu. Yet perhaps more than any other heritage tribute to epic symbols of Zuluness, the public rehabilitation of the notoriously 'useless' King Dingane revealed how an ambiguous past could be manipulated to support a nationalist present.

**Mangosuthu Buthelezi's reconstruction of King Dingane and the Zulu nation**
In the 1970s Buthelezi asserted himself as a major political figure in South Africa. To win a local following of isiZulu-speaking people, he campaigned for the Zulu Territorial Authority in 1970 within a wider Republic governed by the white supremacist National Party. Crucial to his rise to power was a steadfast insistence on the 'Zulu nation's self-determination'.[1] In 1972 the KwaZulu Legislative Assembly (KLA) was formed, which, according to Chief Minister Buthelezi, signalled the 'rebirth of KwaZulu'.[2] It was through the KLA that Buthelezi was able to petition apartheid officials for recognition of Shaka's Day on 24 September.[3] Throughout the 1970s, his frequent references to the great Zulu nation during Shaka Day celebrations, which originated without state sanction in the mid-1950s, aimed to raise awareness of the ethnic nationalism supposedly unifying the power of his growing Inkatha movement and fledgling KwaZulu homeland. Buthelezi would also reinforce his adaptation of the Zulu past through other institutional appendages, such as the KwaZulu Monuments Council (KMC), an organisation tasked with preserving Zulu heritage.

Buthelezi's idea of Zulu history focused on his favourite kings, Shaka kaSenzangakhona and Shaka's nephew, Cetshwayo kaMpande, during whose reign

British invaders suffered a devastating loss at Isandlwana on 22 January 1879. In fact, Buthelezi could and did claim that he was one of the few Zulu torchbearers whose 'quest for black unity' had familial links to kings Shaka and Cetshwayo, as well as to Chief Mnyamana, Cetshwayo's trusted prime minister.[4] By honouring the first and last independent rulers of nineteenth-century Zululand, Buthelezi deliberately excluded King Dingane kaSenzangakhona and his legacy of defeat at Ncome on 16 December 1838 (also known as the battle of Blood River). But in 1982 King Dingane suddenly entered Buthelezi's pantheon of Zulu heroes, only to be summarily dropped from this select group the following year. A decade-and-a-half later, King Dingane again vaulted back into the Inkatha-sanctioned tradition of Zulu history. This time the rehabilitating event was the 1998 unveiling of the Ncome Museum and Monument overlooking the 'Blood River' battlefield in the Nqutu region. It was here that armed voortrekkers, shooting from behind a wagon laager, prevailed over Zulu regiments. Later Afrikaner leaders hailed this victory as the Day of the Covenant, a divine sign that South Africa was destined to be their promised land.

During the decade before the first rehabilitation of King Dingane in 1982, the most significant events on the calendar of Zulu nationalists commemorated the clashes at Isandlwana and Ulundi during the Anglo-Zulu War. If the former battle was a Zulu triumph, the latter's significance for contemporary Zulu royalists was that it destroyed the 'mightiest kingdom in Southern Africa'.[5] The importance of these mini-wars of resistance was evident in 1979 when the centennials of Isandlwana and Ulundi were observed.[6] Missing in the period between the formation of the Zulu Territorial Authority and the early 1980s was any public recognition of King Dingane and the battle of Ncome. From the point of view of leading members of the KwaZulu homeland elite, Dingane's reign and the ignoble outcome (for Zulus) on 16 December 1838 undermined Inkatha's vision of a laudable Zulu nation. When Dingane was mentioned in government pronouncements, Mangosuthu Buthelezi reduced him to a 'useless' king who eliminated a gloriously useful Shaka.[7] Indeed, Buthelezi emphasised that King Shaka's political acumen 'overshadow[ed those who wanted] . . . to get rid of him'.[8] On another level, Mangosuthu Buthelezi compared his perilous situation as a homeland leader during a period of growing anti-apartheid protests to that of King Shaka, who had to be aware of plots to eliminate him. Both he and Shaka, Buthelezi contended, faced the threat of usurpers trying to murder them – an allusion to alleged hit squads of the African National Congress (ANC) targeting him for assassination.[9] Buthelezi went so far as to describe the spiritual cost of these looming dangers in an address to a crowd of thousands during the King Shaka memorial celebrations in 1981: '[T]hese are tragedies of life when God allows even foolish people to change the whole cause of history.'[10] A year later one of the 'foolish people' in this ring of Shaka's assassins, Dingane kaSenzangakhona, was brought back to the position of 'respected' ruler at a time when the KwaZulu homeland feared the consequences of an apartheid plan to seize Zulu territory containing King Dingane's bones.

**The black Boers, Ingwavuma land deal, and rediscovery of King Dingane's grave**

After ruling the Zulu nation for twelve years (1828–40), King Dingane was defeated by his brother King Mpande, who allied himself with Boer commandos of the neighbouring Republic of Natalia, following the Zulu defeat at the battle of Ncome. King Dingane fled north across the Phongolo River and hid in the dense Gwadileni forest in the Lubombo Mountains, where in 1840 he was ambushed, killed and interred by members of the Nyawo ethnic group, then clients of the Swazi monarchy. According to the 1904 testimony of an isiZulu-speaking oral historian, Ngidi kaMcikaziswa, King Dingane was stabbed to death by *abafokazana*, 'common people'.[11] The manner in which King Dingane died, Ngidi pointed out, led to 'humiliation and remorse' in the Zulu state. By the late twentieth century, the slain king's burial site had not only been lost in the thicket, but also incorporated within the northern KwaZulu district of Ingwavuma, which apartheid officials in 1982 hoped to give to independent Swaziland.

The Ingwavuma region is bounded by the Lubombo Mountains and Swaziland in the west, and by the Indian Ocean in the east. In the north is the Phongolo River and Mozambique. Over the past two centuries, Africans of diverse ethnic origins occupied Ingwavuma (otherwise known as Thongaland), among them groups of Swazi, Zulu and Thonga (also known as Tsonga) people who endured different foreign regimes in the late nineteenth century, from Portuguese colonialism and British imperialism to white settler government based in Natal.[12] In 1970, at the time of the establishment of the Zulu Territorial Authority, Ingwavuma was an expendable tract as far as white South Africa was concerned, and easily ceded to KwaZulu. Seven years later, when KwaZulu was granted self-government status, Ingwavuma was placed under the control of Buthelezi's homeland.

In June 1982 the apartheid state unilaterally announced that Ingwavuma and the nearby KaNgwane homeland would be given to Swaziland. This controversial plan became known as the Ingwavuma land deal.[13] Military and economic considerations were part of the apartheid government's decision. In 'exchange for allowing the Pretoria government to crush ANC guerillas crossing the border [to and] from Mozambique', National Party leaders boasted, Swaziland would gain better access to the trade routes of the Indian Ocean and other fertile strips of agricultural land.[14]

KwaZulu authorities at once opposed the land deal. Firstly, they voiced misgivings in the KLA that the Swazi monarchy was hatching yet another conspiracy to dilute Zulu power. Buthelezi, for one, protested that the land deal exposed the unholy link between the white South African Boers and the 'Black Boers' of Swaziland.[15] In the epithet 'Black Boers' he disparaged Swazi military collaboration with Boer commandos in battles against sovereign black polities such as the Pedi kingdom in the eastern Transvaal during the late 1870s.[16] Swazi forces also assisted the British imperial army late in the Anglo-Zulu War of 1879 by looting Zulu homesteads (*imizi*) in the northern reaches of Cetshwayo's kingdom, thus effectively preventing him from fleeing into Swaziland.[17] Finally, Buthelezi barred chiefs in the KwaZulu homeland from supporting the land deal;[18] he followed up this prohibition with a forceful campaign to recruit new Inkatha members and thus show that his was the political authority commoners needed to heed, before listening to their own local leaders.[19]

Other KwaZulu government officials went on the offensive, commissioning a researcher named Nicholas Wellington to conduct a study of the history of Ingwavuma. He drew on a range of evidence to conclude that people in this disputed area were predominantly isiZulu-speakers. He relied on ethnographic accounts constructed by Walter Felgate, an adviser to Buthelezi. Felgate contended that, despite the different ethnic influences in Ingwavuma, isiZulu was the main language of 'men', while Thonga was the preferred language of 'women'.[20] He claimed, too, that 'when asked why they did not speak Thonga, men in Thongaland invariably claimed that they were Zulus living in Zululand under the Zulu paramount chief, and that they were described as Zulu in their reference books'.[21]

The final and perhaps most noteworthy reaction to the 1982 land deal was the KLA's determination to transform Dingane's gravesite in Ingwavuma into a rallying point for homeland sovereignty and Inkatha control of KwaZulu. For the first time, Buthelezi and other Zulu nationalists broadcast that they 'respected' Shaka's successor 'as a King just like any of his predecessors and/or successors'.[22] In May 1982 KLA members accompanied Buthelezi to King Dingane's putative burial place in Ingwavuma.[23] The visit was supposed to salvage Dingane's reputation in the official historical narrative articulated by Zulu nationalists. On 18 June 1983 homeland authorities and figures in the Zulu royal house again travelled to Ingwavuma to conduct a cleansing ceremony, *ukukhumelana umlotha*, to honour the fallen King Dingane.[24] All the while there was uncertainty among local residents near the Mozambique border as to the exact location of Dingane's grave.[25] Buthelezi summarised the propitiations of *ukukhumelana umlotha* as an 'act of political and national rehabilitation'.[26] He also used this sacred occasion to level more accusations against 'Swazi' adversaries, namely Silevana Nyawo and Nondowana Mdluli, the men of the Nyawo ethnic group, who were said to have treacherously murdered King Dingane and, in a dramatic flourish, he reminded his audience that the Swazi monarchy and the white Boers had long worked together to undermine the Zulu nation. To balance this display of wrath, he reassured those Zulu nationalists who accused Dingane of 'usurp[ing] the Zulu throne after King Shaka's assassination . . . [that Dingane] was accepted by the Zulu nation as the king of the Zulus. Part of the history which was enacted during his twelve-year reign represents our history and our cultural roots.'[27] Buthelezi's fierce ceremonial protests, coupled with the KLA's strong opposition to the apartheid government's seizure of Ingwavuma, scuttled the 1982 land deal.

The planned reclamation of King Dingane's burial place spawned other initiatives by homeland elites to refurbish the tarnished image of Shaka's successor in the battle of Ncome. While Inkatha leaders did not shy away from the fact that a Zulu force succumbed to a Boer army on 16 December 1838, they minimised the impact of the military loss. Buthelezi, for example, asserted that King Dingane's regiments were 'split in 1838 and only a section of them was annihilated by the Boers'.[28] He also imbued the clash with renewed significance in terms of the Zulu struggle against foreign incursion. Indeed, in 1983 on 'Dingaan's Day' (16 December), a holiday normally celebrated by white South Africans as the start of the Christmas festive season, Buthelezi specially recognised the heroic resistance of Shaka's successor. The next year, after KwaZulu had secured Ingwavuma, King Dingane disappeared altogether from the public celebrations of 'Zuluness' (a term coined by Buthelezi as early as 1984) in the KwaZulu homeland.[29] Instead, Shaka and Cetshwayo would monopolise the mantle of the forebears of Zulu greatness.[30] The second tier of favoured monarchs included King Mpande, the brother of Shaka and Dingane, as well as Dinuzulu, the son of Cetshwayo. There was no longer a place for King Dingane.[31] Those who sought to add or subtract from the hierarchy of rulers revered by Inkatha, the contemporary Zulu royal house, and the KLA – Buthelezi warned – were merely academic (white) historians housed in 'English Universities'.[32] Until the 1990s, the sites of 'historical heritage', where the sacred list of kings would be heralded, came under the increasing scrutiny of Buthelezi, as did the major repositories and exhibition halls of Zulu culture in KwaZulu and Natal.

### Zulu heritage sites and the KwaZulu Monuments Council

Between 1983 and 1991, Buthelezi imposed his version of the Zulu past on public institutions such as the KwaZulu Monuments Council and its network of museums, which exhibited Zulu material culture and presented booklets on Zulu history that received KLA approval.[33] From its inception, the KMC was tasked by the 'KwaZulu political leadership' to identify 'flagship projects' of Zulu heritage.[34] Several pivotal endeavours were singled out: the reconstruction of King Cetshwayo's royal residence at oNdini, as well as the preservation of the Isandlwana battlefield and Shaka's homestead ruins in the Stanger-Dukuza area.

oNdini, the capital of the Zulu kingdom from 1872 to 1879, was targeted for immediate development. This project required the building of both a model of King Cetshwayo's enclosure and a modern 'Interpretive Cultural Centre', featuring diagrams that told the story of the last independent Zulu monarch as sanctioned by the KLA and Zulu royal house. With the first phase of construction completed in August 1983, the centre opened its doors to the public. Two years later the second phase of the project was finished with the launching of the KwaZulu Cultural Museum on the anniversary of King Cetshwayo's death (8 February 1884).[35]

The Isandlwana project began with the removal of all existing structures from the battlefield, namely some Zulu homesteads, a shop and a school.[36] In 1987 the KMC demarcated the boundaries of the Isandlwana Historical Reserve, on which they planned to erect an interpretive centre.[37] Five years later the Isandlwana Historic Reserve invited its first public visitors on 22 January, 113 years to the day after the shock defeat of the British invaders by Zulu soldiers.

Finally, the dual Stanger-Dukuza project commenced when in 1987 the KwaZulu homeland government purchased a residential property in Stanger municipality opposite the longstanding King Shaka monument.[38] This location once served 'as a much-needed formal rest facility for the Zulu Royal Family and Minister Buthelezi during King Shaka Day ceremonies'.[39] In September 1995 a new interpretive centre was opened there, elevating the Stanger-Dukuza project to the status of a formal heritage site.

However, the fields of Nqutu district where King Dingane's regiments experienced heavy casualties in the battle of Ncome, merited neither recognition nor investment. It was not until the late 1990s, when the first episode in the rehabilitation of Dingane was a mere memory, that politicians would honour this Zulu king's involvement in the events of 16 December 1838.

### The Ncome project: The ghost of King Dingane at Nqutu, 1998–99

In 1998 the ANC-led government promoted several 'Legacy Projects' to redress public representations of South Africa's past in the interests of nation-building. As part of this reconciliation process, two initiatives were to be inaugurated in the KwaZulu-Natal province on the site of the battle of Ncome and at the Groutville home of the first African Nobel Peace Prize laureate and ANC leader, Albert Luthuli, north of Durban. The *Inkosi*/Chief Albert Luthuli Memorial was started and suspended because – as Musa Xulu, then deputy director-general of the ANC-led national government's Department of Arts, Culture, Science and Technology (DACST) recalled – 'there were problems, you know KwaZulu-Natal'. He was alluding to the still-smouldering tensions between isiZulu-speaking ANC and Inkatha representatives in provincial politics.[40] The battle of Ncome monument, therefore, became the flagship legacy project in KwaZulu-Natal. The monument was unveiled on 16 December 1998, with the Ncome Museum, in turn, officially opening on 26 November 1999.

The Ncome memorial was to achieve two central goals. Firstly, it would commemorate the Zulu fighters who died fighting the voortrekkers. Secondly, it sought to 'correct' longstanding versions of this episode. To this end, the DACST appointed 'diverse' academic historians to devise a new official line for the battle of Ncome; it is significant that this revisionist process dwelled on the name Ncome as opposed to Blood River. The mixed group of scholars comprised Professor J.E.H. Grobler, an 'Afrikaner' historian, 'English' historians Professors J. Laband and C.A. Hamilton from the University of Natal and University of the Witwatersrand respectively, as well as Zulu 'nationalist historians' Professors J.S. Maphalala and L. Mathenjwa from the University of Zululand; also included in the assembly was Professor Mazisi Kunene, a doyen of Zulu literature and poetry. In amending perspectives of the Ncome war, general 'Zulu interpretations' of the battle were given greater weight.[41] Yet the group's final report focused more on specific Zulu nationalist reinterpretations of 16 December 1838. For example, it highlighted the glories of the Zulu kingdom before the treachery of the voortrekkers, who were described as land grabbers.[42] The report also recommended that 'any attempt to redress the current imbalance in the events at Blood River/Ncome needs to take into account the context in which King Dingane acted' in relation to aggressive white interlopers, particularly the iconic figure, Piet Retief.[43]

The ANC national government, for its part, sought to promote a presentation of Ncome that challenged monolithic views of 'ethnic' history. Furthermore, it hoped to fund the construction of a heritage site that would be inclusive, not only of Afrikaner and Zulu participants, but also of many other players.[44] Some of the prominent isiZulu-speaking members of the panel of historians seemed to foreground the role of voortrekker and Zulu actors in incidents that instigated the battle on 16 December 1838, ignoring the significance of Sekonyela, for one, a chief of the Tlokoa (Basotho) whose actions in antecedent events fuelled an irreparable rift between voortrekker and Zulu leaders.

Late in 1837, Piet Retief and his party of voortrekkers arrived at Mgungundlovu, King Dingane's homestead. Their intention was to negotiate a claim to a vast territory south of the Thukela River. Dingane apparently agreed to talk to them and even considered ceding land, providing that Retief rescued cattle taken from the kingdom by Chief Sekonyela. In December 1838, Retief and his commando crossed the Drakensberg Mountains to recover the stolen herds from Chief Sekonyela, who lived among the Basotho people. Retief apprehended and handcuffed Chief Sekonyela, retrieving many of the cattle Dingane wanted back. On 3 February 1838, Retief arrived in Mgungundlovu, driving the herds with Sekonyela in tow. It was three days after this incident, according to historian P. Colenbrander, that Retief and his party were put to death. The 'simple trick of handcuffing the unsuspecting Sekonyela', coupled with the news filtering into Zululand of voortrekker military successes against the formidable army of Chief Mzilikazi, argues Colenbrander, particularly unsettled Dingane and prompted him to kill the newcomers.[45]

In further contrast to the final report of the panel, one of the government-appointed historians, Professor Maphalala, dwelt on the role of Sekonyela in events preceding Ncome, challenging the very fact that Sekonyela ever pilfered the king's cattle. The cattle Sekonyela possessed, and which other historians claimed were stolen, Professor Maphalala asserted, 'were obtained as compensation after he had been invited by [another Basotho leader] Mini Hlubi to help him in an *ubukhosi* (traditional leadership) dispute with [Hlubi (Basotho) chief] Langalibalele long before the arrival of Boers in the Kingdom of kwaZulu'.[46] To back this assertion, Professor Maphalala cited the oral historical testimony of Mabonsa kaSidhlayi, transcribed in 1909 by the Natal colonial ethnographer and white government official, James Stuart: 'Mini now made a proposal to Sigonyela. Sigonyela had mounted men with him. They came as an *impi* to our district on horseback. They attacked the people living in the bush country, the Ngwekazi people of Langalibalele's tribe, on the north side of the Mzinyathi. They had guns. They killed everyone in the bush. They drove off the cattle.'[47]

Professor Maphalala suggested that Retief, rather than Sekonyela, robbed Dingane of cattle. Thus Sekonyela's innocence was enough to write him out of Ncome history and place full blame on a deceitful Boer leader for the 16 December 1838 conflict. This finding of Professor Maphalala, which made its way into the panel's conclusions, had a profound impact on the exhibits in the newly built heritage structures on the Blood River/Ncome site. The 'radical reinterpretation' promoted by the Ncome Museum, for example, asserted that the 'War of Ncome' was triggered by voortrekker belligerence, which justified Dingane's swift reaction to defend his territory.[48] This statement bore the imprint of Professor Maphalala's version of the short history of 16 December 1838, for there was no mention of Sekonyela's encounter with Piet Retief.[49]

One reason for the exclusion of Sekonyela might be attributed to many decades of uneasy interaction between so-called Zulu and Tlokoa (Basotho) residents, the latter who migrated in 1867 into north-western Natal. To implement a scheme to balkanise Zululand into thirteen 'kinglets' immediately after the Anglo-Zulu War, the British exiled Sihayo, chief of the Ngobese chiefdom in Nqutu and close ally of the vanquished Cetshwayo in August 1879.[50] With Sihayo gone, the 'loyal' Tlokoa chief Hlubi Molefe and his followers were settled in the expelled leader's strategic territory, abutting Natal at the junction of the Thukela and Mzinyathi rivers, largely to return a favour. Hlubi Molefe had mustered levies to assist British forces in a number of battles, including an assault on Chief Sihayo's homestead on 12 January 1979. Descendants of both chiefs presently live in the Nqutu district.

A decade before the Ncome monument was planned, Inkatha politicians challenged the legitimacy of Molefe ruling families in Nqutu. In September 1989 the KwaZulu homeland government removed Chief Elphas Molefe, whose ancestor was Hlubi Molefe, from his position.[51] On 15 June 1992, a letter signed by Buthelezi certified Chief Elphas Molefe's exclusion from traditional office. This order was reinforced by acts of violence against the deposed Basotho chief, which were initiated in the context of the bloody struggle between the United Democratic Front (UDF)/ ANC and Inkatha in the 1980s and the early 1990s.[52] The Basotho chief and a number of his subjects were accused of supporting the UDF/ANC, Buthelezi's rival.[53] Their supposed political affiliation invited reprisals from stalwarts of the KwaZulu homeland leadership who were keen to win a civil war that almost derailed the 1994 all-race national ballot. In the post-apartheid era these tensions have not diminished. Four years into Nelson Mandela's presidency, Chief Molefe's followers would be further marginalised, not by a defunct KwaZulu state, but by a group of individuals once linked to the former homeland. After the 1994 liberation elections, a coalition national government led by the ANC formed partnerships with several political parties, among them Buthelezi's Inkatha Freedom Party, which was 'given' control of the DACST as a gesture of reconciliation.

The minister heading the DACST was Lionel Mtshali, an IFP stalwart who, after his appointment in September 1996, expressed 'the need to have senior officials in the department [DACST] whom he could trust'.[54] As Buthelezi held a national post, he was largely occupied with other matters, and for the first time in decades, his grip on the heritage sphere seemed to loosen considerably. It was in this context that Professor Musa Xulu, a Zulu nationalist and IFP member, joined DACST as head of the arts and culture branch. Professor Xulu took charge of the implementation of the Ncome Museum and monument, but in 1998 he and Lionel Mtshali faced some opposition, particularly from detractors who said the duo were using the Ncome project to advance their party interests, which included 'Zulu ethnicism'.[55] This was a reference to a longstanding campaign to reinforce 'Zulu' rights over those of the Molefe chief and Basotho residents, who were blamed by Inkatha for illegally settling on ground in much the same way as the voortrekkers who laagered in Nqutu and defeated Dingane's regiments on 16 December 1838. This perhaps explains why the DACST has been seen to be speaking through Professor Maphalala and his colleague Professor Mathenjwa in directing the panel of historians to arrive at a narrow view of 16 December 1838. The Ncome monument effectively demonises the voortrekkers, celebrates the Zulu defence of royal territory, and all but ignores other 'non-Boer' and 'non-Zulu' participants. Could it be that one legend – Blood River – has been replaced by another legend, Ncome?

## Conclusion

It is fitting to propose that the newly constructed monuments to Zulu history in post-apartheid KwaZulu-Natal reveal the broader input of Zulu nationalists who have their own vision of the public reification of what Buthelezi has called 'Zuluness'. By contrast, memorials constructed for King Shaka and King Cetshwayo during the official period of white supremacy sought to champion the need to unify the 'Zulu state' as both an ethnic homeland and the personal domain of Buthelezi, who could boast that 'I trace my own ancestry back to the very founders of KwaZulu. From my mother's knee onwards I grew up being seeped in what it meant to be a Zulu and what Zuluness meant to a man and a woman.'[56] The most recent effort to commemorate King Dingane in Nqutu suggests that another brand of Zuluness had emerged on the eve of the new millennium. The Ncome Museum and monument honour a king that IFP ideologues have long ignored because of his link to a shameful setback in a war with white invaders that split a kingdom that Shaka worked so hard to forge. It is strange to gain access to the conversations of the panel of historians and not find evidence of lengthy accusations by Zulu nationalists – similar to the kind of accusations that once filled the KLA assembly – claiming that Dingane assassinated (literally in one case, metaphorically in the other) the great 'founders' (Shaka and Cetshwayo) to whom Buthelezi can trace his 'own ancestry'. In other words, there was a palpable change occurring in the sphere of monumental Zulu heritage, where struggles over Zulu nationalism and Zuluness are played out in DACST conference rooms far from the ears and eyes of Buthelezi; and where professed aims to 'redress' unequal historical representation offered opportunities to create new myths that echoed a period of myth-making in which black people, regardless of their Zuluness, were silenced in the name of white supremacy.

## Notes

1. P. Forsyth, 'The Past in the Service of the Present: The Political Use of History by A.N.M.G. Buthelezi 1951–1991', *South African Historical Journal* 26 (1992): 79. For a book-length analysis of the Zulu Territorial Authority and rise of modern Inkatha and its leader M.G. Buthelezi, see G. Maré and G. Hamilton, *An Appetite for Power: Buthelezi's Inkatha and South Africa* (Johannesburg: Ravan Press, 1987).
2. Mangosuthu G. Buthelezi, Chief Minister of KwaZulu, 'A Luncheon Address to Members of the Rotary Club of Durban South', 20 November 1972, Alan Paton Centre (APC), PC126/2 Natal Room Collection, BS (section of Gerhard Maré Collection [hereafter GMC]), University of KwaZulu-Natal (UKZN).
3. *Daily News*, 15 January 1971.
4. Mangosuthu G. Buthelezi, Chief Minister of KwaZulu, 'Unveiling of King Cetshwayo's Tombstone', Nkandla District, 27 September 1980, APC, PC 126/2, BS (GMC).
5. Mangosuthu G. Buthelezi, Chief Minister of KwaZulu and President of Inkatha Yenkululeko Yesizwe, 'Function to Commemorate the Battle of Ulundi – the Final Battle of the Anglo-Zulu War of 1879', Ulundi, 26 May 1979, APC, PC 126/2, BS (GMC).
6. Ibid. Buthelezi nominated the organising committee in charge of the commemoration of these battles.
7. Mangosuthu G. Buthelezi, Chief Minister of KwaZulu, 'King Shaka Memorial Celebrations', Stanger, 24 September 1981, APC, PC 126/2, BS (GMC).
8. Ibid.
9. Mangosuthu G. Buthelezi, Chief Minister of KwaZulu, 'Tenth Anniversary Celebrations of the Enthronement of His Majesty King Zwelithini Goodwill kaSolomon, kaDinuzulu, kaCetshwayo, kaMpande', Nongoma, 5 December 1981, APC, PC 126/2, BS (GMC).
10. Mangosuthu G. Buthelezi, President of Inkatha Yenkululeko Yesizwe and Chief Minister of KwaZulu, 'King Shaka Memorial Celebrations', 24 September 1981, APC, PC 126/2, BS (GMC).
11. C. de B. Webb and J.B. Wright, eds., *The James Stuart Archive of Recorded Oral Evidence Relating to the History of the Zulu and Neighbouring Peoples*, Vol. 5 (Pietermaritzburg, University of Natal Press, 2001), p. 53.
12. The Ingwavuma area has a complex political history; the British annexed it in 1895 and turned Ingwavuma into a magisterial division; see terms of Zululand Proclamation No. 9 of 1895 in *The Natal Government Gazette (Extraordinary)* Vol. XLVII, No. 2745, 16 July 1895. Then in 1897 the part of Thongaland closely linked (ethnically) to African communities in southern Mozambique

was incorporated into the British Colony of Zululand and the Ingwavuma district; see Zululand Proclamation No. 14 of 1897 in *The Natal Government Gazette (Extraordinary)* Vol. XLIX, No. 2923, 24 December 1897. Late the same year, Ingwavuma became part of Natal with the annexation of British Zululand by Natal on 29 December in terms of Act No. 37 of 1897; see Pietermaritzburg Archives Repository, *Acts of the Parliament of the Colony of Natal 1897–8.*

13. N. Wellington, *A Historical Study of the Ingwavuma Region* (Durban: KwaZulu Development Commission, 1983), p. 149.

14. T. Waetjen and G. Maré, 'Shaka's Aeroplane: The Take-off and Landing of Inkatha, Modern Zulu Nationalism and Royal Politics' in this volume. On views by contemporaries on why South Africa engaged in the land deal, see *Work in Progress* 4 (April 1978): 1–5; *Work in Progress* 5 (June 1978): 10–13 and *Work in Progress* 27 (June 1983): 14–22. Also see pro-Inkatha views in *Clarion Call* (October/November 1984): 16–17.

15. 'Verbatim Report of the Special Sessions of the Fifth and the Third KwaZulu Legislative Assembly' (hereafter 'KLA Debates'), Vol. 25, 21 April – 11 May 1982, p. 761, APC, PC 126, Natal Room Collection.

16. On these battles, see P. Delius, *The Land Belongs to Us: The Pedi Polity, the Boers and the British in the Nineteenth Century Transvaal* (Johannesburg: Ravan Press, 1983). Also see P. Bonner, *Kings, Commoners and Concessionaires* (Cambridge: Cambridge University Press, 1983).

17. See J. Laband, *Kingdom in Crisis: The Zulu Response to British Invasion of 1879* (Pietermaritzburg: University of Natal Press, 1992), pp. 239–42.

18. *Natal Witness*, 6 November 1984.

19. D. Webster, '*Abafazi bathonga bafihlakala*: Ethnicity and Gender in a KwaZulu Border Community', *African Studies* 50:1 and 2 (1991): 248.

20. W. Felgate, 'The Thembe Thonga of Natal and Mozambique: An Ecological Approach', cited in N.M. Wellington, *A Historical Study of the Ingwavuma Region* (Durban: KwaZulu Development Corporation, 1983), p. 146. For a detailed history and 'ethnic' composition of the area, see P. Harries, 'History, Ethnicity and the Ingwavuma Land Deal: The Zulu Northern Frontier in the Nineteenth Century', *Journal of Natal and Zulu History* VI (1983): 1–27.

21. Felgate, 'The Thembe Thonga', p. 146.

22. 'KLA Debates', p. 965; see also p. 861.

23. 'KLA Debates', Vol. 27, 4–28 June 1982, p. 861.

24. This phrase best describes the 'cleansing' act as King Dingane was reinstated into the royal house, despite the fact that he was held responsible for the killing of King Shaka. The occasion was therefore an act of forgiving and reconciliation within royalty. I thank Professor N. Ntshangase of the University of Natal, Durban, for clarifying key issues that pertain to a 'cleansing ceremony': personal communication with Professor Ntshangase, 18 July 2003.

25. It has been pointed out that 'the exact location of Dingane's grave was a matter which local people would not discuss'; see M.N. Burton, M. Smith and R.H. Taylor, 'A Brief History of Human Involvement in Maputaland', in *Studies on the Ecology of Maputaland*, eds. M.N. Burton and K.H. Cooper (Grahamstown: Rhodes University, 1980), p. 436.

26. Mangosuthu G. Buthelezi, Chief Minister of KwaZulu, 'Unveiling of a Memorial Near the Spot Where King Dingane was Assassinated and of a Stone on his Grave by King Zwelithini Goodwill kaBhekuzulu – the Eighth King of the Zulu', Ingwavuma, 18 June 1983, APC, PC 126/2, BS (GMC).

27. Ibid.

28. 'KLA Debates', Vol. 25, 21 April to 11 May 1982, p. 965.

29. 'Zuluness' was a concept that Buthelezi started using more extensively in 1984: see Mangosuthu G. Buthelezi, President of Inkatha Yenkululeko Yesizwe and Chief Minister of KwaZulu, 'King Shaka Day', Ongoye, 4 November 1984, APC, PC 126/2, BS (GMC).

30. Mangosuthu G. Buthelezi, President of Inkatha Yenkululeko Yesizwe, 'King Shaka Day', KwaMashu, 26 September 1987, APC, PC 126/2, BS (GMC).

31. Mangosuthu G. Buthelezi, Chief Minister of KwaZulu, 'Launching of the "House of Shaka", written by Charles Ballard', Hulett Country Club, 9 December 1988, APC, PC 126/2, BS (GMC).

32. Mangosuthu G. Buthelezi, Chief Minister of KwaZulu and President of Inkatha Yenkululeko Yesizwe, 'King Shaka Day', Stanger, 24 September 1991, APC, PC 126/2, BS (GMC).

33. G. Whitelaw, 'Archaeological Monuments in KwaZulu-Natal: A Procedure for the Identification of Value', *Natal Museum Journal of Humanities* 9 (1997): 99. See also Forsyth, 'The Past': 89.

34. N. Dlamini's interview with L. Van Schalkwyk, Pietermaritzburg, 16 August 1999 and N. Dlamini's interview with T. Maggs, 5 October 2000. Also see M.G. Buthelezi, 'The KwaZulu Government, Museums and Cultural Heritage', *SAMAB* 17:4 (1986): 175–76.

35. *'Amafa AkwaZulu Natali'*, draft document by J. van Vuuren to L. van Schalkwyk, 'The KwaZulu Monuments Council – its Development and History 1980–1998' (undated).

36. The KMC negotiated with the local Mangwebuthanani Tribal Authority to claim the entire Isandlwana area. N. Dlamini's interview with Barry Marshall, director, *Amafa AkwaZulu Natali*, Ulundi, 27 February 2001.

37. Van Vuuren to Van Schalkwyk, 'The KwaZulu Monuments Council'.

38. *Annual Report of the KwaZulu Monuments Council for the year ended 31 March 1988* (Ulundi: KMC, 1988), p. 2. The King Shaka Monument was officially recognised in 1939 by the Historical Monuments Council.

39. *Annual Report of the KwaZulu Monuments Council.*

40. N. Dlamini's interview with M. Xulu, former deputy director-general, Department of Arts, Culture Science and Technology (DACST), Pretoria, 8 August 2000.

41. Pietermaritzburg Archives Repository (hereafter PAR), John Laband Ncome Project (hereafter JLNP) file, M. Xulu, Convenor, Panel of Academic Historians, 'Legacy Project: Blood River Memorial; Towards a Reinterpretation of History' (undated), p. 1.

42. PAR, JLNP file, 'Report of the Panel of Historians Appointed by the South African Department of Arts, Culture, Science and Technology' by J.S. Maphalala, M. Kunene, J. Laband, C.A. Hamilton and J.E.H. Grobler, 1 September 1998, p. 4.

43. Ibid.

44. PAR, JLNP file, 'Legacy Project: Blood River Memorial: Towards a Reinterpretation of History', undated.

45. See P. Colenbrander, 'The Zulu Kingdom, 1828–79', in *Natal and Zululand from Earliest Times to 1910: A New History*, eds. A. Duminy and B. Guest (Pietermaritzburg: University of Natal Press and Shuter & Shooter, 1989), p. 93.

46. J.S. Maphalala, 'The Re-interpretation of the War of Ncome (Renamed Bloed Rivier and Blood River by Voortrekkers and the British Respectively), 16 December 1838', paper presented to a seminar held at the University of Zululand, 31 October 1998, p. 9.

47. Ibid. Cited from C. de B. Webb, and J.B. Wright, eds. *The James Stuart Archive of Recorded Oral Evidence Relating to the History of the Zulu and Neighbouring Peoples*, Vol. 2 (Pietermaritzburg: University of Natal Press, 1979), p. 32.

48. N. Dlamini's interview with B. Ndhlovu, Curator, Ncome Museum, Dundee, Pietermaritzburg, 14 July 2000.

49. See for example, Maphalala, 'The Re-interpretation of the War of Ncome', pp. 10–13.

50. For details of the history of Nqutu district, see E. Unterhalter, 'Confronting Imperialism: The People of Nquthu and the Invasion of Zululand', in *The Anglo-Zulu War: New Perspectives*, eds. A. Duminy and C. Ballard (Pietermaritzburg: University of Natal Press, 1981), pp. 98–119.

51. See testimony by Chief Elphas Molefe, Truth and Reconciliation Commission Proceedings held at Vryheid, 17 April 1997, http://www.truth.org.za/hrvtrans/Vryheid.vryheid2.htm (accessed June 1998).

52. Testimony by Chief Elphas Molefe. It should be noted that the legitimacy of Molefe chiefs is still being challenged in the post-apartheid era.

53. Testimony by Chief Elphas Molefe.

54. *Cape Argus*, 4 December 1998.

55. *Sunday Independent*, 27 January 1999. Indeed, a DACST source told other newspapers that the Ncome project was exploited to serve IFP objectives: *Mail & Guardian*, 20 November 1999. Also see *The Cape Times*, 28 December 1998.

56. Mangosuthu G. Buthelezi, Chief Minister of KwaZulu and President of Inkatha Freedom Party, 'Official Opening of Visitor Centre and Isandlwana Historic Reserve: Introduction of His Majesty King Goodwill kaBhekuzulu, King of the Zulu', Isandlwana, 18 January 1992, APC, PC 129/1/7/ 331–88, BS Gosney Collection.

*Chapter 33*

# Divisions and Realignments in Post-apartheid Zulu Local and National Politics

LAURENCE PIPER

AS A POPULAR political movement, Zulu nationalism is dead. Contrary to the pretensions of certain political elites and contrary to the mythology that continues to envelop their name, ordinary Zulu people are almost indistinguishable from other black South Africans in their political behaviour and beliefs. Most amaZulu support the African National Congress (ANC), most endorse a democratic and unitary state, and most identify themselves as South Africans first and foremost. In no small measure, Zulu nationalism has waned because ordinary Zulu people do not support it.

This conclusion would have seemed ridiculous in the build-up to South Africa's first democratic election in April 1994 when the 'warrior Zulu nation marched again'.[1] Rallying behind King Goodwill Zwelithini's calls for 'Zulu self-determination',[2] the Inkatha Freedom Party (IFP) organised militaristic resistance to the impending election in much of KwaZulu-Natal. Ignoring this brinkmanship, the ANC and the National Party (NP) pushed ahead with the ballot, forcing the IFP to choose between participation and civil war. After a terrifying moment of hesitation, the IFP decided to participate.[3]

Despite the avoidance of conflict, many observers expected Zulu nationalism to continue in a new guise after the 1994 election.[4] Remarkably, it did not. By the time of the local government elections of 1996, the IFP's militant Zulu nationalist rhetoric and mobilisation was replaced by a conservative-liberal and more co-operative politics.[5] Furthermore, for ten years until the 2004 election the IFP and ANC were voluntary partners in both the national and KwaZulu-Natal governments. Although it once threatened to explode with a bang, Zulu nationalism has withered away to a whimper.

This chapter interrogates the primordialist assumptions about 'being Zulu' expressed in the IFP's transition rhetoric and held by many observers – usually white and Western – for whom an essential Zuluness is a pet myth. What is missed in these accounts is that the Zulu nationalism of the transition was not so much rooted in a shared popular consciousness, as driven by a particular political elite who, through the IFP, expediently embraced and then jettisoned Zulu nationalism. Indeed, it is the very disjuncture between the elite and the people that allowed for the easy abandonment of Zulu nationalist politics after 1994. Had a truly popular Zulu nationalism been unleashed, it is inconceivable that it would have dissipated so quickly without realising its objectives.

### Zulus divided: The rural/urban nature of IFP/ANC support

In making this argument I begin by examining the distribution of political party support in KwaZulu-Natal from 1994 to 2000, as reflected in the results of local and national elections. These figures clearly demonstrate that the divide between the IFP and ANC was not an ethnic one, but rather a rural/urban one. Indeed, until 1999 this correlation was so strong that in the region of 90 per cent of urban amaZulu backed the ANC and 90 per cent of rural amaZulu endorsed the IFP. These figures are surprising, especially given the high degree of migrancy between urban and rural areas in KwaZulu-Natal. Notably, though, this urban-rural correspondence began to break down after 1999 – to the extent that, as I show in the epilogue, the IFP-ANC cleavage today divides the north of KwaZulu-Natal from the south.

In examining voting party support in post-apartheid KwaZulu-Natal, I shall consider returns from the 1994 and 1999 national elections, and from the 1996 and 2000 local government elections. While one might expect some significant differences in voter behaviour between national and local elections in most democracies, this is not the case with KwaZulu-Natal voters. Indeed, perhaps the most striking feature of the election returns is the consistency in voting trends. Thus I shall begin by outlining the 1994 results and then compare them briefly with the 1996, 1999 and 2000 results.

### 1994 national election

The results of the 1994 election were much as expected, with the exception of a stronger than expected third-place national showing by the IFP, with 10.5 per cent of the vote. Significantly, the overwhelming majority of the IFP's votes (86 per cent) came from KwaZulu-Natal, where it won by 50.3 per cent to the ANC's 32.2 per cent. Much controversy surrounded the results of the 1994 election for KwaZulu-Natal, and for good reason,[6] but the nature of the problems and the results from subsequent elections suggest that they were broadly accurate.[7]

Three main trends are evident from these results. Firstly, the massive returns of the ANC and IFP reflect that they are parties that enjoy the support of black people who constitute over 80 per cent of KwaZulu-Natal's population. Indeed, a rough calculation of the numbers suggests that the ratio of black support for the IFP and ANC can be split roughly 60:40, as the support from other race groups was relatively small.[8] Secondly, it is evident from Figure 33.1, which shows the distribution of

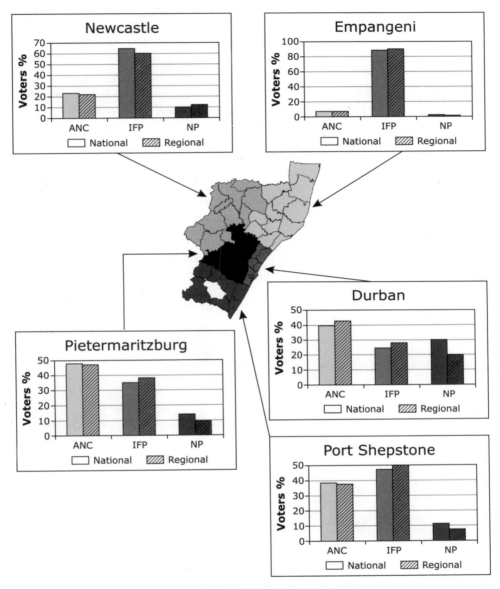

Figure 33.1    *1994 party support in KwaZulu-Natal by IEC sub-region.*

votes according to the five Independent Electoral Commission (IEC) sub-regions, that party support was spread unevenly across the province. The ANC was the largest party in only two of the five sub-regions, Pietermaritzburg and Durban, which are also the most urbanised. This fact, coupled with results for many townships where the ANC scored upwards of 90 per cent[9] and pre-election polling as to the typical profiles of IFP and ANC voters,[10] revealed that the line dividing IFP and ANC supporters was not racial or ethnic, but rural versus urban. Given that the 1996 census notes that 79.8 per cent of black people in KwaZulu-Natal are isiZulu-speaking, it seems safe to conclude that both the IFP and ANC enjoyed significant Zulu support. Lastly, there was some limited evidence that ethnicity was important *within* rural areas. Where the ANC did manage to win rural votes on any scale it was in historically black areas where the mother tongue is not isiZulu. This observation is suggested by a comparison of the election results with Figure 33.2, the distribution of language speakers in KwaZulu-Natal.

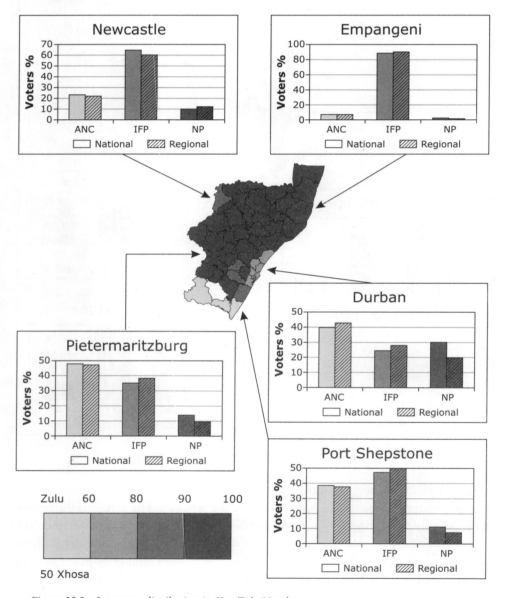

Figure 33.2  *Language distribution in KwaZulu-Natal.*

**The 1996 local government elections**

These general trends are confirmed by the 1996, 1999 and 2000 election results. Importantly the 1996 local government elections offered more trustworthy and accurate insights into the spatial distribution of party support. These elections were more trustworthy because the integrity of the election process was properly maintained, and they were more accurate because the results could be traced down to the local level, at least in urban areas. Although the 1996 local government elections did not include a ballot for the province, one can effectively manufacture a comparison by adding together the proportional returns for each local council. As illustrated by Table 33.1, the IFP remained the largest party in 1996 with 44.5 per cent, with the ANC in second place with 33.2 per cent. Thus while the ANC's returns remained almost constant, the IFP's were down by nearly 6 per cent.

Table 33.1   Party percentages in elections in KwaZulu-Natal 1994–2000.

| Party | 1994 | 1996 | 1999 | 2000 |
|-------|------|------|------|------|
| IFP | 50.3 | 44.5 | 41.9 | 48.83 |
| ANC | 32.2 | 33.2 | 39.4 | 3.79 |
| NP/NNP | 11.2 | 12.7 | 3.3 | |
| DP | 2.2 | 3.3 | 8.2 | 13.3 |
| MF | 1.3 | 2.3 | 2.9 | 1.26 |

The 1996 results confirmed the 1994 trends, with the IFP and ANC between them winning nearly 80 per cent of the vote, and winning it in historically black areas. Moreover, support for the two parties followed rural-urban lines. The IFP secured 77.35 per cent of the rural vote and, as reflected in Figure 33.3, was especially strong in Regional Councils One and Two, where it was closer to 90 per cent. Overall, 83 per cent of the IFP's support came from rural areas, with roughly 90 per cent of its votes from 'tribal' areas.[11] Conversely, the ANC dominated urban areas, winning most of the towns including Pietermaritzburg, Ladysmith and Mooi River, and was the largest party in the Durban Metropolitan, the grand prize of local councils, winning 48 per cent of the proportional vote and 36 of 70 seats. Overall, the ANC relied on urban areas for 70 per cent of its support, suggesting that upwards of 85 per cent of township voters endorsed the party. Furthermore, 60 per cent of its total support was from the Durban-Pietermaritzburg region.

The only qualification of this general trend was a slight decrease in IFP dominance from north to south, roughly proportional to the decreasing majority of Zulu people in rural areas (see Figure 33.3). Again, as in 1994, this suggests that non-Zulu rural people tend to vote ANC, as they did in the rest of the country in both 1994 and 1996. Hence ethnicity *might* be a third-degree predictor of party support in the black population of KwaZulu-Natal.

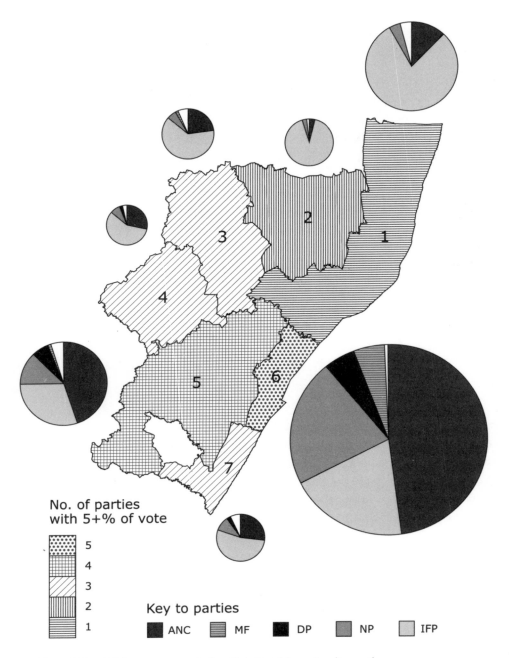

No. of parties
with 5+% of vote

5
4
3
2
1

Key to parties

ANC    MF    DP    NP    IFP

Figure 33.3    *1996 party support in KwaZulu-Natal by regional council.*

### The 1999 national election

Contrary to the negative predictions of the opinion polls, in the 1999 national election the IFP retained third place nationally, with 8.58 per cent, 87 per cent of which came from KwaZulu-Natal, slightly more than in 1994 (see Table 33.1). This showing also saw the IFP narrowly remain the largest party in the province, with 41.9 per cent to the ANC's 39.38 per cent. While the ANC and IFP may have struggled vigorously against each other, they kept the same percentage of the overall vote as in 1994, monopolising black support between them.

These results not only confirmed that the IFP's support was overwhelmingly concentrated in one province, but also showed that the party was rooted among *rural* Zulu people. Some 65.98 per cent of rural voters supported it, constituting 76.45 per cent of its total support in KwaZulu-Natal. Interestingly, this was less than in the 1996 local government elections, where the IFP secured 77.35 per cent of the rural vote, constituting 83 per cent of its total vote. Given that neither registration nor turnout significantly affected the result, the IFP's loss of nearly 10 per cent from 1994 and the ANC's corresponding gain of 7 per cent represented a direct gain by the ANC at the IFP's expense. Indeed, this time the ANC won 27.54 per cent of the rural vote compared to just 17 per cent in 1996, and the rural component of the total ANC vote correspondingly rose from 24.66 per cent in 1996 to 33.4 per cent in 1999. ANC gains were most remarkable in the south of the province, where it secured some 43.7 per cent of the vote, less than 5 per cent adrift of the IFP. However, most of the ANC's votes (72.46 per cent) came from urban areas where it secured over 50 per cent support, again, overwhelmingly from township voters.[12]

### The 2000 local government elections

Superficially the 2000 elections buck the trend of the preceding three. Thus, as illustrated in Table 33.1, the IFP appeared to win back much of its lost support. However, on closer inspection this shift was not due to more people voting for the IFP, but rather many urban ANC supporters not turning out to vote. Thus, in rural areas there was little change from 1999. The IFP did marginally better in areas such as Ugu and Ilembe, but, with the exception of Durban, its real gains were in the towns, especially Newcastle (+ 10 per cent), Ladysmith (+ 31 per cent) and Mooi River (+ 9 per cent). Critically however, this difference was not so much due to an increased number of votes for the IFP compared with 1996, but as in the rest of South Africa, a poor turnout by many ANC voters. Speculation was that this poor turnout reflected the growing discontent of the ANC rank-and-file.[13] Whatever the reason, the 2000 elections introduced a new variable into KwaZulu-Natal politics: the unreliability of the ANC core vote in local government elections.

In short, the four elections confirm the following three trends among party support in post-apartheid KwaZulu-Natal. Firstly, race is a good predictor of party support, with black voters supporting the IFP and ANC almost exclusively, and other races supporting opposition parties. As illustrated in 1999 and 2000, this 'black versus other' pattern remains, despite the changing identities and fortunes of specific opposition parties. Secondly, amongst black voters, the vast majority of whom are amaZulu, the rural-urban divide was the best indicator of IFP/ANC allegiance, although this began to change, especially in the south of the province. Thirdly, within the rural black vote, ethnicity roughly correlated with party preference, although to a lesser extent of late. In sum, in KwaZulu-Natal most rural amaZulu supported the IFP and all other black voters supported the ANC.

### Interpreting election results: Behaviour and attitudes of Zulu voters

What do the election results tell us about 'being Zulu'? Firstly, the distribution of party support along rural-urban lines rather than ethnic lines clearly explodes the myth that 'being Zulu' implies being a Zulu nationalist or even supporting the IFP. The reality is that most isiZulu-speaking people in South Africa support the ANC, with its emphasis on race and nation rather than ethnicity. Furthermore, as the election trends reveal, the IFP's majority support amongst the Zulu people of KwaZulu-Natal is dwindling fast. I would go as far as to argue that the election results demonstrate that the Zulu nation does not exist, given that nationhood requires a degree of common political self-awareness.[14]

Secondly, the rural-urban split and its more recent erosion suggest that factors other than ethnicity influenced voter behaviour. I would argue that this pattern of voter behaviour is only explicable through a history of IFP-ANC political competition set against the backdrop of a bifurcated state with divergent elites and constituencies.[15] It may be countered that a sense of nationhood *was* nevertheless important in influencing the popular vote in that while not all amaZulu voted for the IFP, those who felt strongly about their Zuluness. Was not some sense of nationhood or ethnic identity central to the way ordinary people voted? Why else would the IFP have embraced Zulu nationalism, and why else would so many commentators describe these elections as a racial or ethnic census?

However, the available empirical evidence does not support these claims to any substantial degree. Research into the self-understanding of Zulu people has found that while most embrace 'being Zulu' in some way, the constructions of Zuluness vary widely and only some are overtly Zulu nationalist. Most seem to intertwine Zuluness with being black or African, or even subsume it to the latter.[16] Indeed, for some time, social histories of KwaZulu-Natal have pointed to the complex and hybrid ways in which identities of 'Zulu' and 'black' have been intertwined,[17] thus confounding the basis for a simple Zulu nationalism. Moreover, research into the reasons given by voters for party choice notes that racial or ethnic identities are almost never cited. The only significant exception here were IFP voters of 1994, of whom 44 per cent supported the IFP because they were Zulu.[18] Thus while a significant minority of IFP supporters were ethnic voters, this was still a minority of their support, and only some 26 per cent of Zulu voters in total. This statistic is all the more remarkable given that 1994 was when militant Zulu nationalism was at its zenith.

## Conclusion

Being Zulu does not mean being Zulu nationalist. Both the election results and empirical research into the self-understanding of voters make this abundantly clear. Even during the 1994 election, the apogee of Zulu nationalism, Zulu people in KwaZulu-Natal were split down the middle, half for the Zulu nationalist IFP and half for its rival, the ANC. This division is nowhere better demonstrated than in the political violence between the two parties, which pitted Zulu against Zulu. Tellingly, the social basis of political division in KwaZulu-Natal was not ethnic, but rural versus urban. This, as I argue more fully elsewhere reflects the legacy of IFP/ANC competition for popular hegemony.[19] Set against the backdrop of a state bifurcated between rural and urban with distinct elites and constituencies,[20] Zulu nationalism was strategically embraced by the IFP in an attempt to capitalise on a popular ethnic identity, and then jettisoned when it no longer suited their purposes. The ease with which this was achieved reflects the limited popular resonance of Zulu nationalist discourse. To put it in Terence Ranger's terms, Zulu nationalism was 'invented from above' rather than 'imagined from below',[21] and thus constituted 'political tribalism'[22] rather than 'moral ethnicity'.[23] Indeed, all the evidence suggests that Zulu people see themselves as South Africans in pretty much the same way as their fellow black citizens. What is unique about KwaZulu-Natal politics is not the Zulu nation – it does not exist – but rather the dwindling IFP-ANC rivalry.

## Epilogue: The 2004 election

From the perspective of patterns of voter support, the 2004 election was remarkable in two respects. Firstly, the IFP lost the province of KwaZulu-Natal, winning just 36.82 per cent of the vote to the ANC's 46.98 per cent. For the first time in its history, the IFP is not leading the government of the province. Secondly, the IFP-ANC divide is no longer a rural-urban one, but a north-south one, as shown in Figure 33.4, confirming a change in a trend first noted in the 2000 local government elections. Despite these two changes, the fundamental racial pattern of voter support remains, with black voters supporting the IFP and ANC almost exclusively, while most voters of other races support opposition parties. The other consistent trend is that IFP losses were ANC gains, with a reasonably consistent rate of attrition from the IFP to the ANC between the national and provincial elections of 1994 and 1999, and of 1999 and 2004. With the ANC now in power in KwaZulu-Natal, this is bad news for the future of the IFP.

Notably, these new trends in the patterns of voter support offer no evidence contrary to my argument; indeed they reinforce it. The 2004 election confirms that ordinary Zulu people do not vote like Zulu nationalists, nor do the overwhelming

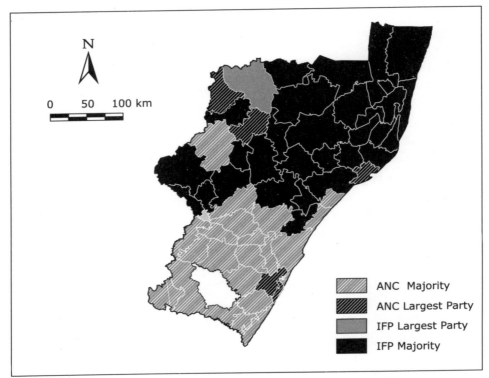

Figure 33.4    *KwaZulu-Natal municipalities by leading party in the 2004 election.*

majority favour a Zulu-based party. Indeed, isiZulu-speaking South Africans are today more similar than ever before to other black South Africans in their voting behaviour, and there is good reason to believe that this trend towards homogeneity will continue as the IFP-ANC rivalry works itself out to the disadvantage of the IFP.

## Notes

1. *Natal Witness*, 29 March 1994.
2. G. Zwelithini, 'Representation by His Majesty the King of the Zulus to the State President of South Africa, Mr F.W. de Klerk DMS on the Inalienable Rights of a Zulu King to Rule over his Father's People Within the Context of the Incorporation of KwaZulu/Natal in the Federal Republic of South Africa', Pretoria, 17 January 1994.
3. L. Piper, 'The Politics of Zuluness in the Transition to a Democratic South Africa' (Ph.D. diss., University of Cambridge, 2000), pp. 116–22.
4. S. Taylor, *Shaka's Children: A History of the Zulu People* (London: Harper Collins, 1994).
5. L. Piper and K. Hamilton, 'The Decline of "Militant Zulu Nationalism": The Sea-change in IFP Politics After 1994', *Politikon* 25:1 (1998).

6.  L. Piper and S. Piper, 'Hit & Myth: Zulu Ethnicity and the 1994 Elections in KwaZulu-Natal', South African Political Studies Association Conference, 27–29 September 1995.

7.  Piper, 'The Politics of Zuluness', pp. 132–33.

8.  Ibid., pp. 135–37.

9.  R. Haswell, 'Election Results in the "New Pietermaritzburg"', ANC pamphlet, 1994.

10. R.W. Johnson, 'How Free? How Fair?', in *Launching Democracy in South Africa: The First Open Election, April 1994*, eds. R.W. Johnson and L. Schlemmer (New Haven and London: Yale University Press, 1996).

11. D. Randall, 'The 1995/1996 South African Local Elections: HSRC/Wits Political Studies Department Monitoring Project – Case Study of KwaZulu-Natal', unpublished paper, 1996, p. 13.

12. L. Piper, 'Democracy for a Bargain: The 1999 Election in KwaZulu-Natal', *Politikon* 26:2 (1999).

13. *Mail & Guardian*, 8 December 2000.

14. L. Piper, 'Nationalism Without a Nation: The Rise and Fall of Zulu Nationalism in South Africa's Transition to Democracy, 1975–1999', *Nations and Nationalism* 8:1 (2002): 73–94.

15. Piper, 'The Politics of Zuluness' and 'Nationalism Without a Nation'.

16. A. Sitas, 'Inanda, August 1985: "Where Wealth and Power and Blood Reign Worshipped Gods"', *South African Labour Bulletin* 11:4 (1986) and C. Campbell, G. Maré and C. Walker, 'Evidence for an Ethnic Identity in the Life Histories of Zulu Speaking Township Residents', *Journal of Southern African Studies* 21:2 (1995).

17. B. Sundkler, *Bantu Prophets in South Africa* (London: Oxford University Press, 1961); A. Vilakazi, B. Mthethwa and M. Mpanza, *Shembe: The Revitalisation of African Society* (Johannesburg: Skotaville, 1986) and P. la Hausse de Lalouvière, 'Ethnicity and History in the Careers of Two Zulu Nationalists: Petros Lamula (*c.*1881–1948) and Lymon Maling (1889–*c.*1936)' (Ph.D. diss., University of the Witwatersrand, 1992).

18. R. Mattes, *The Election Book: Judgement and Choice in South Africa's 1994 Election* (Cape Town: Idasa, 1995), pp. 85–86.

19. Piper, 'The Politics of Zuluness' and 'Nationalism Without a Nation'.

20. M. Mamdani, *Citizen and Subject: Contemporary Africa and the Legacy of Late Colonialism* (Cape Town: David Philip, 1996).

21. T. Ranger, 'The Invention of Tradition Revisited: The Case of Colonial Africa', in *Inventions and Boundaries: Historical and Anthropological Approaches to the Study of Ethnicity and Nationalism*, eds. P. Kaarsholm and J. Hultin (Roskilde, Denmark: International Development Studies, 1994).

22. J. Lonsdale, 'Moral Ethnicity and Political Tribalism', in *Inventions and Boundaries*, eds. Kaarsholm and Hultin.

23. B. Berman, 'Ethnicity, Patronage and the African State: The Politics of Uncivil Nationalism', *African Affairs* 97 (1998): 305–41.

## References

Hutchinson. J. 1994. *Modern Nationalism*. London: Fontana.

Lodge, T. 1995. 'The South African General Elections, April 1994: Results, Analysis and Implications', *African Affairs* 94: 471–500.

SAIRR (South African Institute of Race Relations). 1994. *Watchdog on the South Africa Election, Five*. Johannesburg, 28 February.

Reynolds, A. ed. 1994. *Election '94: The Campaigns, Results and Future Prospects*. Cape Town: David Philip.

# Symbolisms of Culture

*Chapter 34*

# Beauty in the Hard Journey
## Defining Trends in Twentieth-century Zulu Art

FIONA RANKIN-SMITH

IN THE LAST third half of the nineteenth century, as isiZulu-speaking African migrants increasingly departed from their homesteads to toil in diamond and gold diggings, they took with them treasured objects such as sleeping mats, fighting sticks and headrests. Since their industrial residences – the mining compounds that confined them to work sites – provided only a concrete bed and bare walls, they quickly developed a deep nostalgia for their domestic artefacts, garments, rituals and songs. Indeed, to this day, many traditional Zulu migrant workers either make or purchase pieces of clothing such as migrant waistcoats (*intolibhantshi*) (Plate 1), reaffirming connections to their rural homes. However, over the past century and a half, their everyday art has incorporated techniques and materials that reflect the hybrid cultural influences of the metropolis and the mine.[1] This chapter begins to trace these artistic continuities and transformations.

**Migrant labour: 1930s to 1970s**
Into the early twentieth century, the migrant labour system primarily fed mining industries, but by the 1930s and during the next four decades, an expanding manufacturing sector afforded itinerant Zulu workers new opportunities for employment as messengers and factory hands. At the same time, with stricter pass laws, these migrants found it difficult to settle permanently in urban centres.[2] Despite intensifying influx control, Zulu men continued to secure work as domestic workers in the white households of Pretoria and Johannesburg, while more and more Zulu women trickled into cities in search of jobs, usually against the wishes of their elders, husbands, brothers and chiefs. With strong patriarchal constraints restricting female movement in the traditional countryside, however, the majority of Zulu women remained in their rural homesteads, looking after the very young and the old, and continuing to craft beautiful apparel and adornments. Beaded necklaces, *umgexo*, often incorporate objects obtained from city trading stores, such as locks and keys that are included to connect to a tradition, but also to acknowledge a world of modern technology (Plate 2).

## Zulu migrants in urban areas: Multiple identities

With the easing of influx control in the mid-1980s, unprecedented numbers of rural amaZulu flooded into informal settlements on the outskirts of cities in the Witwatersrand region. They swelled a century-old movement of Zulu migrants, who experienced life as a struggle to sustain both an urban existence and a rural abode, where the prospect of one day retiring to their ancestors held a powerful allure. In post-apartheid South Africa, isiZulu-speaking rural Africans still view urban centres as paradoxical destinations, holding possibilities, as well as hardships. Most importantly, they see the city as a necessary modern evil, offering a real prospect for steady employment and income.[3]

The idea of a 'home' refuge is a crucial organising principle of the worldview of the average Zulu migrant worker, who struggles to uphold the desire to support his distant family, while navigating in the often-hostile industrial metropolis.[4] Faced with such contradictory demands, Zulu migrants have long sought to mould and maintain multiple identities. For example, they formed urban associations that accommodated their hybrid cultural expressions, such as the *amalaita*,[5] which marched with traditional weapons such as *amawisa* (knobkerries) on Sundays to venues where they held boxing contests.[6] The South African writer Ezekiel Mphahlele, in particular, remembers how isiZulu-speaking *amalaita* men arrived at these gatherings 'dressed in shorts, tennis shoes and caps and handkerchiefs dangl[ing] from their pockets. They crouched, shook their fists in the air so that the bangles round their waists clanged.'[7] Here, Mphahlele refers to the *amadavathi*, beaded wrist- and leg-bands, which reflected patterns and colours associated with specific districts in KwaZulu-Natal.

The attire of Zulu migrants displays this amalgam of influences, spanning various past and contemporary styles, which African itinerant labourers across the continent have incorporated to create walking pieces of art that cover their bodies. Such aesthetic combinations are evident in studio photographs of Zulu migrants wearing tailored jackets replete with quixotic garments, accoutrements and beadwork panels. By the middle of the twentieth century, professional photographers in the Witwatersrand had set up studios that catered for migrant workers who wanted to sit for their black-and-white portraits. Plates 3, 4 and 5 in this volume, taken in the mid-1950s, are from one such studio in the Pretoria area. They show a mix of dress modes, attesting both to the inventive ways in which migrants negotiated their daily experiences and the critical value they attached to their evolving notions of beauty. For example, the beaded waistcoats (*intolibhantshi*) integrate longstanding indigenous art forms with the sartorial splendour commonly aspired to by black middle-class men. Often, a fedora would be worn to cap this style. In addition, the photographs reveal how some Zulu migrants decorate their prized *izinduku* (walking sticks), which were made in rural areas from hard woods and sometimes embellished in the city with plastic wires and rings.

## Everyday objects as art

Initially, Zulu migrants working in mining industries used their limited leisure time to make many of their own garments, which they wore on special occasions. Old photographs of early-twentieth-century compounds catalogue the presence of part-time tailors who sewed the uniforms that Zulu workers donned for soccer tournaments, boxing spectacles and dancing competitions. Other ceremonial clothes were obtained from second-hand shops, while the wives, mothers and girlfriends of Zulu migrants sewed in the beadwork sections. Later, garments of this kind were bought from urban traders at the Mai Mai hostel and adjacent market in Johannesburg, a commercial centre largely run by isiZulu-speaking artisans and entrepreneurs.[8]

Established in the 1940s by the Johannesburg city council, the Mai Mai hostel sheltered Zulu migrant workers employed in a variety of industries. Over time, this and other complexes became flourishing bazaars for traditional Zulu consumers seeking meat plates (*ugqoko*), headrests (*izigqiki*) and beadwork, many of which were obtained from rural artisans in Natal and Zululand. Traditional headrests were also modified into more idiosyncratic forms and carvers incorporated materials reflecting aspects of modernity, such as the use of brightly coloured letters in perspex, creating words like 'snuff' embossed on them (Plate 6).

Although the unknown male artist of the work in Plate 6 experimented widely, his work unmistakably mirrors the style of headrests from Thukela Ferry in Msinga, KwaZulu-Natal, perhaps his home region. Moreover, the function and use of his creations did not deviate radically from traditional expectations; many of his headrests were commissioned as valued objects that Zulu brides, living just south and north of the Thukela River, brought with them to their husband's household.[9]

## Traditional objects from modern materials

In recent years Mai Mai has spawned a wider popular interest in the creative objects of Zulu migrants. Taking advantage of this trend, female entrepreneurs, such as Zodwa Duma, who comes from the Ladysmith area of KwaZulu-Natal, travel regularly to Johannesburg, where they set up artistic wares on the street, selling 'traditional' telephone wire baskets for a collective of crafters in her home district (Plate 7).[10]

Until the early 1900s, all baskets were woven from grass. The increasingly common practice of using telephone wire to make items of this kind – and to embellish dancing and fighting sticks – appears to have originated in the first half of the twentieth century with isiZulu-speaking men, who after dusk guarded factories and other industrial properties (Plate 8). Unlike the Zulu migrants who faced arrest and legal penalties for bringing knobkerries and sticks into towns, Zulu night watchmen were exempt from laws making it an offence to carry what colonial authorities called traditional weaponry.[11] To wile away the hours of darkness, they plaited multi-coloured telephone wire into circular patterns on the shafts and heads of their sticks. Their artistic decisions reflected both aesthetic and economic concerns. They no longer relied on uncertain supplies of the copper and brass wire that they had used to emboss sticks in the nineteenth century. Night watchmen also began to construct telephone wire lids (*izimbenge*) for beer pots, establishing a lucrative style of art that to this day satisfies the tastes of local and international tourists.

Other imaginative *objets d'art* produced by Zulu migrants have long been popular in the marketplace: among these are *iziqhaza*, earplugs made from colourful pieces of plastic cut into geometric shapes before being nailed with fine metal shafts (apparently modified gramophone record needles) onto circular discs of wood. Inserted into stretched earlobes, *iziqhaza* remain fashionable items among older male migrants. Sold regularly at Mai Mai, the most contemporary (curio) earplugs are attached to the lobe with elasticised loops. The extraordinary freedom of artistic expression manifest in the making of *iziqhaza* literally extends from head to toe. Indeed, in producing mundane functional items such as sandals, artisans have created a new range of footwear, featuring the cross-strap, open-faced snake-tread of *izimbadada*, constructed out of car tyres and *odabuluzwane*, the hard rubber dancing sandals with diagonal thongs secured between the big and second toes of the foot.

Although the migrant labour system undoubtedly dislocated and burdened isiZulu-speaking Africans, they nevertheless managed to carve out spaces for their artistic innovations. While their creations often break traditional moulds – by using industrial materials and urban ideas to make something excitingly new – their artefacts simultaneously strengthen continuities between past and present and between rural homesteads and urban life. Indeed, Zulu migrants embrace a range of aesthetic expressions, demonstrating that they are less concerned with authenticity than with finding appropriate ways to articulate their complex identities.

## Notes

1. A. Nettleton, J. Charlton and F. Rankin-Smith, *Engaging Modernities: Transforming the Commonplace* (Johannesburg: University of Witwatersrand Art Galleries, 2003).
2. D. Hindson, *Pass Controls and the Urban African Proletariat* (Johannesburg: Ravan Press, 1987), pp. 43–48. For other scholarship on this subject, see B. Bozzoli, ed. *Town and Countryside in the Transvaal* (Johannesburg: Ravan Press, 1983); J. Lewis, *Industrialisation and Trade Union Organisation in South Africa, 1924–55: The Rise and Fall of the South African Trades and Labour Council* (Cambridge: Cambridge University Press, 1984) and P. Bonner, 'African Urbanisation on the Rand Between the 1930s and 1960s: Its Social Character and Political Consequences', *Journal of Southern African Studies* 21:1 (1995): 115–29.
3. P. Delius, *A Lion Amongst the Cattle: Reconstruction and Resistance in the Northern Transvaal* (Johannesburg: Ravan Press, 1996), p. 23.
4. On this broad migrant phenomenon, see D.B. Coplan, *In the Time of Cannibals: The Word Music of South Africa's Basotho Migrants* (Johannesburg: Witwatersrand University Press, 1994), p. 119.

5.  On *amalaita* culture in South African cities, see P. la Hausse de Lalouvière, ' "The Cows of Nongoloza": Youth, Crime and *Amalaita* Gangs in Durban, 1900–1936', *Journal of Southern African Studies* 16:1 (1990): 79–111 and C. van Onselen, *Studies in the Social and Economic History of the Witwatersrand, 1886–1914, Vol. 1: New Babylon* and *Vol. 2: New Nineveh* (London: Longman, 1982), pp. 54–60.

6.  For scholarship on migrant Zulu masculinity and sporting contests in urban spaces, with reference to *amalaita*, see P. Alegi, *Laduma! Soccer, Politics and Society in South Africa* (Pietermaritzburg: University of Natal Press, 2004), p. 35 and R. Morrell, 'Of Boys and Men: Masculinity and Gender in Southern African Studies', *Journal of Southern African Studies* 24:4 (1998): 623.

7.  E. Mphahlele, *Down Second Avenue* (London: Faber and Faber, 1959), pp. 100–01, cited in Delius, *A Lion Amongst the Cattle*, p. 41.

8.  F. Rankin-Smith and S. Klopper, 'Creating Beauty in, and between, Two Worlds: Contexualising the Art of South Africa's Migrant Labourers', in *Democracy X: Marking the Present, Representing the Past*, eds. A. Oliphant, P. Delius and L. Meltzer (Pretoria: University of South Africa Press, 2004), p. 64.

9.  Women from the impoverished Msinga region have also set up food shops at Mai Mai. Working from stalls, they cook hot meals such as braai (barbequed) meat and *pap* (boiled maize porridge) for a regular clientele. The ethnographic detail in this note comes from the author's numerous visits to Mai Mai market between 1990 and 2005.

10. When in Johannesburg, Zodwa Duma stays at a former used car workshop named KwaWondle in Jules Street, Jeppestown. KwaWondle resembles a 'compound', with partitioned dry walls dividing many small units from one another. This shelter is run by a young isiZulu-speaking man from the same rural region in KwaZulu-Natal; he allows only people from Ladysmith to rent space and conducts spot checks on the tenants to ensure an ordered establishment: Interview between Fiona Rankin-Smith and Zodwa Duma, 2 December 2002, KwaWondle, Johannesburg.

11. For scholarship on traditional weaponry as art, see Rayda Becker, 'Tsonga Headrests: The Making of a South African Art History Category' (Ph.D. diss., University of the Witwatersrand, 2001).

# Chapter 35

# Ceremonial Beer Pots and their Uses

JULIET ARMSTRONG

ISIZULU-SPEAKING AFRICANS use many types of pottery to prepare, transport, store and serve Zulu sorghum beer or *utshwala*. *Utshwala* is both a nutritious drink and an alcoholic beverage, consumed daily and at joyous occasions honouring ancestral spirits, or *amadlozi*. Beer is taken for granted when there is a ceremonial slaughter for a feast. However, when an animal is ritually killed in connection with sadness, there is no beer. Whatever the cause for the ceremony, the senior man of the homestead gives the final word to women of his domestic circle to brew beer. Women who are menstruating, breastfeeding or pregnant typically cannot prepare *utshwala*.[1]

The pottery commonly associated with the drinking of *utshwala* is made by women who have learned their craft from other women specialising in ceramics and firing. Women collect clay from alluvial sources with the help of children and perhaps a donkey that can carry heavy loads. Potters prefer storing the clay near the central byre (cattle enclosure) of a homestead. They mix different kinds of clay according to the type of vessel that is to be constructed. Small drinking pots such as *izinkamba* (singular: *ukhamba*) require finer clay than large containers, *imbiza*, in which beer is fermented and brewed (Plate 9). The basic foundation of a vessel is made from coils of clay. After this initial construction, the potter begins smoothing and tapering the walls. In the case of drinking and serving vessels, designs are always added onto the wet clay surface. There are several methods used to decorate a vessel, based on either removing clay from the pot surface by incising into the leather hard clay (Plate 10), or by adding further clay to raise the surface in relief.[2] The placement of these motifs is intrinsic to the grip of the vessel by the consumer when it is full of beer. Furthermore, the motifs should be read from the top as the vessel is usually stored upright on the floor, or is customarily seen from the top as it is passed around to the other celebrants.

Different tools are used to make various patterns for incised designs. Relief motifs are made by raising the surface of the pot with pellets or strips of clay. The pellets are grouped closely together to create a markedly tactile geometric pattern. This type of design is usually called *amasumpa* (Plates 11 and 12).[3]

There are many different ways of making *amasumpa* and there are historical associations between the use of this motif and the monarch.[4] The drying vessel is

Plate 1  *Waistcoat or* intolibhantshi.

Plate 2  *Necklaces with locks and keys.*

Plates 3–5   *Zulu migrant workers displaying their attire.*

Plate 6   *Zulu headrest*, isigqiki.

Plate 7   *Zodwa Duma with* izimbenge, *baskets with plastic coated telephone wire.*

Plate 8   *Contemporary telephone wire baskets.*

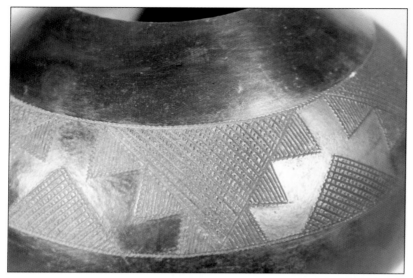

Plate 9   Ukhamba, *drinking pot, made by Nesta Nala.*

Plate 10   Ukhamba *made by Khulumaleni Magwaza, showing incised design.*

Plate 11   *Large* uphiso *claimed to be from Cetshwayo's homestead in oNdini showing* amasumpa *added onto the surface of the vessel.*

Plate 12   *Dinuzulu's drinking vessels, as further evidence of the use of* amasumpa *in the nineteenth-century courts of the Zulu kingdom.*

Plate 13   *Shoshlina Motlaung (Nqutu) burnishing a dried vessel with a smooth stone.*

Plate 14   *Children from the Magwaza homestead (mPabalane) blackening a vessel in the second carbonised firing or* ukufusa.

Plate 15   *Mancane Magwaza standing in her* umsamo *wearing the appropriate respectful attire.*

Plate 16   *A member of the Magwaza family drinking beer in the* isibaya *at an* umemulo *ceremony.*

Plate 17  *Mr Magwaza taking a refreshing drink in his home during an* umemulo *celebration.*

Plate 18  *Blackened, decorated and burnished* ukhamba *made by Shongaziphi Magwaza. It has been filled with beer, stirred and is ready for communal consumption.*

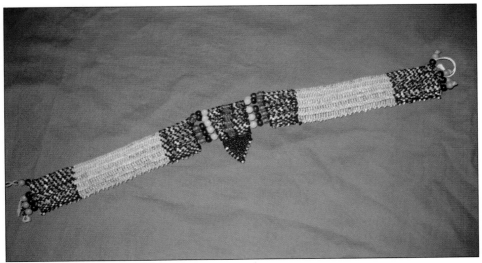

Plate 19  *Engagement necklace from Ndwedwe district.*

Plate 20  *A wooden headrest,* isigqiki.

Plate 21   *Marriage cape of MaNxele Mzolo.*

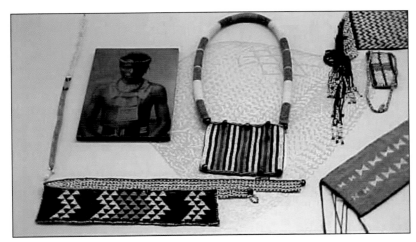

Plate 22   *Beadwork display items from the* Sisonke *exhibition.*

Plate 23   *Beadwork from Nongoma.*

Plate 24   *Beadwork from Msinga.*

Plate 25   *Beadwork displayed at the* Sisonke *exhibition.*

smoothed and then when dry, it is rubbed on the undecorated surface with a smooth stone lubricated with a little water, compacting the surface clay particles to create a burnished sheen, *ukugudla* (Plate 13).

The clay vessels are left in the sun to dry completely before being fired; the arid winter months are considered the ideal conditions for the incendiary process because the ground is dry. Flammable materials such as cow dung, grass, wood and dried aloe leaves fuel the first 'biscuit firing' in a shallow pit situated below the potter's homestead. Each vessel to be fired has a burning ember placed inside it to complete the drying process. The pots are then positioned in various layers and covered with the fuel before ignition. The firing temperature reaches approximately 900 °C. The intense heat changes the composition of the clay, making the fired vessel water resistant.[5]

Only the drinking and serving vessels are given a second carbonised firing to make them black (Plate 14). This process does not strengthen the vessels; the second firing is a customary ritual to honour the ancestors (*amadlozi*). Zulu traditionalists say that the *amadlozi* are enticed to beer ceremonies by the presence of black vessels. The *amadlozi* prefer dark cool places; the shiny black *ukhamba* with incised designs, for example, can serve as a welcoming beacon for the ancestors called to protect the living.

Beer is typically brewed in the drum-like *imbiza* vessel, an undecorated massive pot smeared after firing with desiccated cow dung to show respect (*ukuhlonipha*) to paternal ancestors. Cattle products typically mediate relations between the spiritual world and living members of a homestead. This smearing of dung, known as the *ubulongwe* covering, is also said to shield the homestead from lightning. An *imbiza* is stored in a sacred place called the *umsamo*, an area at the back of the main hut (*indl'enkulu*), marked out by a small raised wall in a semicircular configuration (Plate 15). The *umsamo* is where the ancestors commune with the *abaphilayo*, or living relatives. Should beer be brewed, an offering of this beverage in a small *ukhamba*-shaped vessel (*umancishana*) will be left overnight in the *umsamo* for the ancestors to bless. When a member of the household dies, a candle is lit and placed in the *umsamo* to inform the ancestors of the event.[6]

The large serving vessel (*iphangela*) is used to transport beer from the big *imbiza* to the drinking assembly.[7] The beer is strained through a woven sieve made of strips from Ilala palm fronds. It is sieved from the *imbiza* into the *iphangela* and then into sundry *ukhamba* with the use of a dried gourd. This is the biggest of the serving vessels and its capacity makes it useful for serving a large gathering of people. It is enormously heavy when full, so in order that the beverage may be delivered to the celebrants, it is carried outside slung between two pieces of cloth, the ends of which are firmly held by two strong women, thus evenly supporting the vessel and its contents. The beer is then scooped from this vessel into a drinking vessel with the use of a dried gourd and presented to the first drinker by a woman on her bended knees.

She will taste the beer, thus assuring the head of the household that she has brewed properly, and then hand him the *ukhamba* to drink and pass on to others at the gathering. Men and women usually drink in separate groups. If men are being offered beer, the *ukhamba* is usually covered by an *imbenge*, a woven fibre or grass plate that protects the brew from dust and insects. It is considered disrespectful for a man to stand or wear a hat when drinking beer. He should customarily sit on his haunches, or if he is older, he should sit on a stool or a chair (Plates 16 and 17). Custom dictates that the drinking and serving vessels are always kept on the floor or at ground level and never stored on tables. This is to ensure that the *amadlozi* (also known as the *abaphansi*) have constant access to the vessels.[8]

Finally, beer in black clay pots is consumed when communing with the *amadlozi* (Plate 18). The communal drinking of beer encourages *amadlozi* to engage in commensalisms and good neighbourliness. A reveller cradling a blackened decorated *ukhamba* will feel solace knowing that the beverage he sips and the vessel he touches are imbued with spiritual respect for the ancestors. A 'hot' or unblackened vessel would never be used for ceremonial occasions, as it is devoid of the protective symbolism that customary beer drinking and pottery embody.

### Notes

1. The guest honoured by the ritual beer drink is the first to be offered the beverage, regardless of age and status in the homestead.
2. None of these motifs, and this was said emphatically by my informants, would signify that the vessel is reserved for the exclusive use of the status or age group with which the person identifies (Interview, S. Magwaza, 2004).
3. The word '*amasumpa*' means nodules or dimples. It can be a laborious method of decoration and the potter usually charges a higher fee for work made in this way, or only makes it for commissions.
4. It has been noted in the field that none of the people interviewed south of the Tugela River have any notion of the uses and meaning of *amasumpa*. It is a convention specifically associated with the Zulu kingdom in northern KwaZulu-Natal.
5. Any firing lower than 850 °C will render the vessels too fragile for use.
6. When a child is born, the umbilical cord is buried near the *umsamo*, immediately to the left if it is a girl, and to the right if it is a boy. Senior members of the family, particularly diviners, will burn a dried plant called *imphepho* (*Helicrysum odoratissimum/cymosum* or *rugulosum*) in the *umsamo* to invoke the ancestors. As this is a sacred area, women can only enter when wearing certain clothing, usually placing a towel over their shoulders or a scarf tied over the left shoulder and under the right arm. In so doing they are practicing *ukuhlonipha*, a convention of deep deference.
7. If beer is transported between homesteads, it will be carried in an *uphiso*, a vessel with a small neck at the aperture to prevent the brew from spilling. This *uphiso* is also used to fill the *izinkamba* at a large gathering as it pours neatly. Beer would never be drunk from this vessel.
8. In 2002 Shongaziphi Magwaza from mPabalane told me that the *amadlozi* are unfamiliar with tables and so they would not be able to find the vessel should it be placed above ground level.

## References

Armstrong, J. 1995. 'The Relationship between Body Ornamentation and Pottery Decoration among the Zulu People', in *Women, the Arts and South Africa*, eds. A. Zaverdinos and E. Liebenberg, Conference Proceedings: Vol. 1. Pietermaritzburg: Gender Studies Program, University of Natal.

Berglund, A-I. 1976. *Zulu Thought-patterns and Symbolism*. London: Hurst.

Bryant, A.T. 1949. *The Zulu People as They Were before the White Man Came*. Pietermaritzburg: Shuter & Shooter.

De Haas, M.E. 1986. *Sorghum Beer in Southern Africa: Continuity and Change*. Durban: unpublished report prepared for Tetra Pak.

Doke, C.M., D.M. Malcolm, J.M.A. Sikakana and B.W. Vilakazi. *English-Zulu: Zulu-English Dictionary*. Johannesburg: Witwatersrand University Press, 1990.

Hamer, F. 1975. *The Potter's Dictionary of Materials and Techniques*. Cambridge: University Printing House.

Kennedy, C. 1967–68. 'Art, Architecture and Material Culture of the Zulu Kingdom' (Ph.D. diss., University of California, Los Angeles).

Lawton, A.C. 1967–68. 'Bantu Pottery of Southern Africa', *Annals of the South African Museum* 49.

McAllister, P.A. 1993. 'Indigenous Beer in Southern Africa', *African Studies* 52:1.

Reusch, D. 1998. '*Imbiza kayibil: Ingenambheki': The Social Life of Pots*. Ubumba Catalogue, Pietermaritzburg.

Schofield, J.F. 1948. *Primitive Pottery: An Introduction to South African Ceramics Prehistoric and Protohistoric*. Cape Town: South African Archaeological Society.

Stuart, J. ed. 1969. *The Diary of Henry Francis Fynn*. Pietermaritzburg: Shuter & Shooter.

# Chapter 36

# The Secret of Zulu Bead Language and Proportion and Balance of the Zulu Headrest (*Isigqiki*)

YVONNE WINTERS

BEADWORK AND HEADRESTS (*izigqiki*) represent major forms of Zulu artwork. While they are visually captivating, they also communicate deep emotions. In particular, the 'Zulu love letter',[1] *incwadi yothando*, a beaded necklace or pin, carries messages of love, which may explain why it is one of the popular curios bought by tourists in South Africa.[2] Commercially savvy beadwork sellers append a note to their wares, explaining in English what their designs say, thereby entrenching the idea that the love letter encodes special feelings. But contemporary scholars of Zulu material culture have scrutinised this assertion. Eleanor Preston-Whyte and Jo Thorpe, for example, critically note

> with beadmakers that there is no overall agreement about the meaning of the
> different colours. This has not prevented producers and middle-people trading
> on the romance of the love letter, to great effect . . . They combine the appeal
> of the 'ethnic' and 'different' with the romance of courtship and love – an
> unbeatable combination – in terms of money making potential they prove
> themselves time and again.[3]

Nevertheless, Preston-Whyte and Thorpe do not wholly debunk the belief that the Zulu love letter conveys passionate thoughts. Indeed, beadwork has long spoken to people who understand its intensely metaphorical meanings. Throughout the nineteenth and early twentieth centuries, when illiteracy remained the norm in traditional Zulu communities, oral poetry and articles of aesthetic value conveyed special intimate expressions of yearning and disappointment.[4] James Stuart, an early-twentieth-century, Natal colonial ethnographer and recorder of Zulu oral testimonies, elaborated on the significance of one such object, the beaded necklace:

[It is] a common ornament, well known to various Zulu tribes and full of significance, [arising] . . . out of the colours of the beads used and the way they are arranged. [Girls] . . . are always making bead-work . . . and forwarding the same by some trusted messenger to the lover . . . for purposes of correspondence . . . Hence the reason why a romantic and poetic charm attaches itself to these seemingly meaningless trivialities.[5]

Stuart preferred to study matters of Zulu politics and history; that he remarked on poetic charms is striking, not least because he – who recorded myriad small details of Zulu royal successions – took the time to consider seriously the implications of how love is articulated. Integral to modes of Zulu courting during Stuart's time was the use of bantering and florid language by the male suitor, followed by the mock rejection of his female love interest. She typically opened communication with her suitor after receiving permission from senior girls, *amaqhikiza*, in her age group, who strictly regulated sexual propriety. With consent from the *amaqhikiza*, she could signal her willingness to be wooed through a gift of beadwork that she created especially for her suitor.[6]

### Modernisation of beadwork tradition

Today, more and more rural women have basic literacy; they can pen a love letter if they so desire, and some do. Even so, beadwork continues to communicate their amorous sentiments, perhaps because it is still made by traditional Zulu girls and women who safeguard a material culture rich in symbolic motifs.[7] Moreover, unlike pencils and paper, beads have been exchanged in KwaZulu-Natal for centuries. During much of the nineteenth and twentieth centuries, beads were glass and somewhat costly. Factories in Italy and Czechoslovakia manufactured some of these beads to meet different consumer demands, including the tastes of Africans who sought to buy certain sizes and colours. Over the past few decades, beads were peddled by wholesalers such as W.G. Brown in Durban, exclusive jewellers such as Randals Brothers and Hudson (also of Durban), as well as urban store chains, among them J.W. Jagger & Co. More recently, Muslim and Gujarati families have taken over the wholesale bead trade, with Hoosen and Patel on Grey Street, Durban, leading the way.

By the end of the twentieth century, several major shifts in the production, distribution and use of beads were gathering momentum. In the 1970s, the Natal firm Fouché and Coke, based in Pinetown and Port Shepstone, started to manufacture plastic beads that resembled the glass prototypes. Plastic beads were cheaper to produce and are more affordable. Soon artwork in rural isiZulu-speaking communities (for example, in Ndwedwe and the Richmond area) revealed local preferences for plastic beads.[8] At roughly the same time, an evolving genre of beadwork, incorporating words and letters of the alphabet, also emerged, lending credence to the notion that a 'bead language' actually exists.

Yet while all can appreciate the beauty of the Zulu love letter, its messages remain somewhat enigmatic. Beadwork tends to be most accurately 'read' by people who understand its ceremonial and idiosyncratic purposes. For example, it can document relationships of power such as marriages that depend on the sanction of homestead and clan, which herald their agreement with specific colour arrangements in beadwork known only to these parties.[9] Beaded patterns also convey complex emotions associated with nuptial negotiations. This is illustrated by one necklace made in the 1970s by a common law wife for her 'husband' in Emkhambathini, Ndwedwe district, who had not fulfilled his cattle bridewealth (*ilobolo*) obligations (Plate 19).[10]

This necklace has three tiered bands, *izithokothela*, suggesting that the husband seeks to 'layer his wives'. The blue band, *ubumpangele*, evokes a guinea fowl and an idiom: '*Angazi ukuthi ngisahlalele bani ngoba ngisuka ngindize njeke pangele?*' (Why are you layering or taking wives when I am still waiting to be married? Do you want me to fly away [like a guinea fowl]?). Guinea fowl are not known to gain flight easily; they flap their wings and run quickly. It may be that the beadmaker experienced difficulty in articulating her disappointment and chose to indicate indirectly that her husband's polygynous aims, without first settling her *ilobolo* debt, will drive her away in a manner not typically associated with a 'wife' in her position.[11] The central black tab has a metaphorical meaning: '*indlela yenhliziyo yami imnyama*' (the way of my heart is black [discouraged]). The common law wife testified that her husband knew what she intended to say with the necklace.[12] Whatever the case, mixed metaphors and arcane similes shape this form of communication. Such linguistic permutations support the contention that beadwork, like words, expresses complicated emotions.[13]

Other examples of 'bead language' are embedded in large ceremonial garments such as the wedding cape (see Plate 21), which was worn by a bride named MaNxele Mzolo in Ndwedwe in the mid-1970s.[14]

MaNxele's decorated cloth is made from three joined panels, to which are pinned six beaded anklets, *amadavathi*, distributed in two diagonal rows. Typical of the style in this region and time, the small beads are plastic. The first of the three anklets depicts a series of triangles resembling *izindlu*, or huts, that demonstrate the bride's promise to 'to make a home'. The second anklet reflects H-shapes that close a homestead's central livestock enclosure and prevent a rival wife's *ilobolo* (in this case, cattle) from entering the pen.[15] The final anklet has three crosses, whose meaning is explained by the following idiom: '*Ngishayela iziphambano kathathu*' (I am driving [hammering] the cross three times).

The cross is a Zulu symbol for a valid wedding, or, in the case of isiZulu-speaking Christians (*amakholwa*), a solemnised marriage. The central blue cross stands for the husband, while the flanking mauve and red crosses, known singly as *ubheja* (to bet or win), signify that the bride draped in the cape intends to become the first wife. More generally, the cross (*isiphambano*) evokes the swearing of an oath, with two hooked fingers or the marking of the ground.[16] The image conjured by the three crosses is that of MaNxele, hammer in hand, hitting home the three crosses that epitomise her sacrament, and simultaneously venting her jubilant anticipation that she will 'win' over her rivals.[17]

### The wooden headrest, *isigqiki*

Such strong attitudes about competing for love and loyalty shape another work of (communicative) Zulu art, the wooden headrest, *isigqiki*.[18] When it came to nuptial arrangements, the male *umkhongi* or marriage negotiator for the bride, insisted that the groom provide two headrests, one for his wife-to-be and one for himself. Moreover, the bride usually dictated how the carver, who cut the wood, traced similar motifs that she designed for her engagement beadwork. In particular, the wife-to-be wished to show the groom that the incised lines on his headrest's legs acknowledged their converging paths: '*Imihlobisa ikhombisa ukuthi izindlela sezize zahlangana ekugcineni, useze waphumelela ezifisweni zakhe. Izindlela abezihamba efuna uthando zonke izinsuku sezizoncipha*' (The husband's wooing trips came together and led to the woman he vowed to look after). Indeed, the headrest in Plate 20 reveals a series of chevron lines scored through the centre by a vertical line. This pattern showed that the courting process had not only ended but that the groom had 'sawed' out his rival suitors to make his fiancée a happy woman.

Headrests have elegance, proportion and balance. They are individually owned and serve as pillows for married couples, and as stools for men. When headrests belong to a homestead head, they are subject to strict rules. He will appoint his senior wife to care for his headrest, along with his sleeping mat, spoon and clothes, making it taboo for his junior wives, children, or outsiders to handle this personal property. It is believed that intimate items absorb something of the man's spiritual essence, *isithunzi*, and thus their ordinary or disrespectful handling indicates ill intent, *umthakathi*, towards the owner.[19]

During the nineteenth century, Zulu kings insisted on exercising control over carvers who used iron tools. Consequently wooden items were broadly considered the property of the Zulu royal house and its ranking allies.[20] This combination of regal respect and high political status accorded to headrests meant that they could not be readily discarded. A headrest could be buried in the grave of its owner, a homestead head, or passed on to his heir as a vital family heirloom never to be used again.[21]

The prevailing design on Zulu headrests, the elliptical bosses, *amasumpa* or warts, are found on other crafts such as meat dishes and pottery in districts 'dominated by the courts of Shaka's nineteenth century successors'.[22] The warts tell of the large herd of cattle owned by a prominent homestead head, whose ritual and economic power was measured in livestock, and who commissioned all wooden artefacts for domestic functions.[23] The second distinctive type of Zulu headrest incorporated rounded supports, *amasondo*, rising into a neck-rest.[24] Resembling a cow's legs, *amasondo* in their more recent renditions are decorated with diagonally placed triangles called *indlela yegoli*, 'the road to Johannesburg'.[25] This pattern is emulated in beadwork made by a girl for her male lover who leaves his rural home as a migrant worker for urban centres, where young men have their best chance to earn the money to purchase *ilobolo* cattle.

## Conclusion

It is possible to conclude that 'language' emanates from beadwork and headrests. Nevertheless, one should be careful about reading too much into these forms of art. Beadwork and headrests might simply serve functional needs or enhance household decoration. Yet regardless of how they are interpreted, beadwork and headrests reveal the beauty of local creativity and emotional complexities of a changing Zulu past and present.

## Notes

1. I take phrases such as 'Zulu love letter' and 'Zulu bead language' from earlier popular writings on the subject. See, for example, Regina Twala, 'Beads, Fascinating Secrets of Zulu Letters: Stories behind Patterns and Colours of the Language of Beads', *Sunday Times*, 14 February 1954.
2. A large number of curio dealers in KwaZulu-Natal, for example, contract Zulu beadmakers to produce necklaces and pins for tourists. Personal communication with Danny Ramsuroop, S.A. Shewell cc, Durban, November 2006.
3. E. Preston-Whyte and J. Thorpe, 'Zulu Beadwork: A Romantic Past – A Vibrant Future', *The Condenser*, June 1989.
4. Written isiZulu was only familiar to a very small number of mission-educated Christian converts, *amakholwa*.
5. James Stuart, 'Manuscript Beadwork', 1908, KCM/30929, Killie Campbell Africana Library, Durban.
6. I owe thanks to my colleague Siyabonga Mkhize for this explanation of the links between courting rituals and the creation and presentation of beadwork. He deepened his own understanding of such links in interviews with traditional Zulu women in the 1990s at Kranskop, KwaZulu-Natal, when he worked for the private community radio station, Ikhwezi.
7. My understanding of the role of symbolic motifs in beadwork is informed by J. Beattie, *Other Cultures: Aims, Methods and Achievements in Social Anthropology* (London: Routledge and Kegan Paul, 1970), especially pp. 70–71.
8. Bead Trade Cards, MM2311, 2107, 2253–54, 2445, Campbell Collections of the University of KwaZulu-Natal.
9. Collectors have often reported cases in which they cannot persuade a person to part with an item of beadwork. Indeed, beadwork can be submitted in a court, adjudicating African customary law, as evidence of a declaration of intent (certainly in matters of marriage). Personal communication with Barbara Tyrrell, Scottburgh, November 2004.
10. Beadwork can help us interpret cultural ideals related to the negotiation of *ilobolo* (bridewealth), which not only seals a marriage, but also legitimises the future children born in this ritualised union. Because Zulu men sometimes support more than one wife, a polygynous husband often

appoints the woman he first marries as his head wife, a status that accords her more privileges than the other wives. However, in Ndwedwe, chronic unemployment and rural poverty prevent men from affording *ilobolo*; thus, some men engage in the 'abduction' or *ukuthwala*, of their intended bride. A poor man's friends will take away the chosen girl, who often has consented to this action, and bring her to his home. Thereafter marriage negotiations are begun. In such cases the payment of *ilobolo* is deferred, sometimes for decades. The 'abducted' woman can bear children while her 'husband' may fall in love with another girl and abduct her similarly, making her a second wife of sorts. Intense jealousy can result, with accusations of witchcraft poisoning co-operation between the wives. Personal communication with MaDube Sibisi, Wilfred Ncube and Dingani Mthethwa, Durban, July 1998.

11. Personal communication with Mxolisi Mchunu, January 2007.

12. Such personal information remains in a restricted file in museum records: Necklace, MM 4914, Campbell Collections of the University of KwaZulu-Natal.

13. Personal communications with among others MaDube Sibisi and Sandile Mkhize, Durban, 1980s–2000s and field-collector interview with MaMchunu Sibisi, Emqeku, Ekhambathini, November 1995.

14. It is noteworthy that no single piece of beadwork, whether a necklace, love letter, or cape, is created outside of the context of the entire regalia worn for the relevant occasion.

15. MaNxele's circumstances were of the same nature as those described in Note 10, except that she has had the good fortune of having her marriage legitimised.

16. Personal communication with Ndaba Dube, Durban, March 2001 and personal communication with Mxolisi Mchunu and Siyabonga Mkhize, Durban, January 2007.

17. This we understand by MaNxele's use of the verb 'shayela' which means to 'drive home' (oxen, nail, etc.), adding that she will do so 'three times'. Personal communication with Dingani Mthethwa, Durban, November 1999. Finally, MaNxele's garment also epitomises a Zulu social milieu of shared architectural conventions. Her triangles, for example, mirror the shape of rondavel (thatched and mud hut) roofs, which in turn highlight the home she aims to build for the children she will bear.

18. Collection of courting regalia and dowry objects of Mr S. Simelani, MM5345–55, Campbell Collections of the University of KwaZulu-Natal. MaDube Sibisi interview with Mr and Mrs Simelane, Vryheid, July 2004.

19. O.F. Raum, *The Social Functions of Avoidances and Taboos among the Zulu* (Berlin: Walter de Gruyter, 1973), pp. 99, 433.

20. C. Newman, *Zulu Headrests of the Msinga District in KwaZulu-Natal* (Port Elizabeth: King George VI Gallery, 1999).

21. It is for this reason that some rare pieces are still to be found in the field: 'AmaGugu III' exhibition catalogue, African Art Centre, March 2001, Durban.

22. Sandra Klopper, *Catalogue: Ten Years of Collecting (1979–1989)* (Johannesburg: The Standard Bank Collection of African Art and University of Witwatersrand Art Galleries, 1989), p. 36.

23. Sandra Klopper, *Art and Ambiguity: Perspectives on the Brenthurst Collection of Southern African Art* (Johannesburg: Johannesburg Art Gallery, 1991), pp. 84–85; see also Reverend W. Holden, *The Past and Future of the Kaffir Races* (London: Richards, Glanville and Co., 1862) and George Angas, *The Kafirs Illustrated: A Facsimile Reprint of the Original 1849 Edition of Hand-coloured Lithographs* (Cape Town: A.A. Balkema, [1849] 1974), Plate II, p. 55.

24. H.P.N. Muller and J.F. Snelleman, *Industrie des Cafres du Sud-est de L'afrique* (Leyden: E.J. Brill, 1893), p. xiv.

25. Headrest of Mr M. Ngcobo, MM4747, Campbell Collections of the University of KwaZulu-Natal.

# Chapter 37

# 'Where's it Gone, Freedom?'

## Composing *Isicathamiya* in Post-apartheid South Africa in the Age of 9/11

LIZ GUNNER and IMOGEN GUNNER

*A myth still haunts much writing about African music: the myth that Africa has no composers.*[1]

THIS CHAPTER IS a collaboration across the generations of mother and daughter and it attempts to put to use our joint skills and areas of expertise. While one of us has worked for many years on orality and performance and has studied forms of popular culture, the other has recently completed a graduate degree in ethnomusicology and is a practising musician. With our combined abilities, which in some ways complement each other, but could also tug us in different directions, we have tried to explore questions relating to how performers of the genre *isicathamiya*[2] approach the question of composition in the post-apartheid era. What wider issues relating to questions of identity in the new state emerge from our explorations? How does the genre fit into a wider pattern of social process and creativity, and how does it carve out its own rules and profile in the communities in which it operates as a social activity deeply connected to the making of culture and the making of meaning? We ask if the quite radical reconfiguration of cultural energies and political rights in the democratic era has affected the composers and singers in the genre of *isicathamiya*. Is there, we wonder, a kind of post-1994 'self-writing' taking place, in this hybrid and adventurous genre, itself a part of a wider presence of expressive forms in South Africa constantly in conversation as they make, modify and change culture?[3] What altered autobiographical acts have marked the songs and performances in the genre as the country has made the political transition to freedom?[4]

We focus on two *isicathamiya* groups with whom we worked early in 2003, Mkhamabathi Try Singers, led by Nkosinathi Ndlovu, and Mbheka Lion Singers, with the Dlamuka brothers, Mzi and Nkone, as their leaders and composers. Both teams practised in Number 3 Section of Mkhambathini, in the Valley of a Thousand

Hills, and took part in *isicathamiya* competitions in community halls close by. This was their base, rather than the dusty halls of Durban, or of downtown Johannesburg and its hostels.[5] We argue that our encounters in Mkhambathini with the two groups, Try Singers and Lion Singers, provide a few pointers that suggest both a search for the new and a careful building on old strengths. We suggest, too, that even within a wide configuration of genres, there are very clear profiles for each and that within a genre there is a great range of possibility for difference.[6]

### Friday, 31 January 2003, 15h30, KwaZulu-Natal, South Africa

We drive a sky-blue Toyota in the summer heat down the winding tar roads of the Valley of a Thousand Hills, a region between Pietermaritzburg and Durban. Mother and daughter, together with Wiseman Masango, Khule Ngubane and Dolly Simelane, who are all part of the research team, head for the far side of Mkhambathi, the great flat-topped mountain with high, basalt ridges that dominates the valley and gives the district its name.[7] We climb left up a winding dirt road, and pass Mcoseli's Store, leaving the fast-flowing uMngeni River behind us. Taking the track as far as it will go, we park and unpack our recording equipment. We walk single file in waist-high grass, passing homesteads, children, chickens and goats until we approach the Ndlovu home where the Try Singers practise. We hear singing and catch the words of a cryptic, melancholic and quite enigmatic lyric, a distinctly post-1994 one, we learn later: '*Yashonaphi Inkululeko yashonaphi na?*' (Where's it gone? Freedom, where's it disappeared to?). Later, in the large rondavel where the practice session is taking place, we hear the opening riffs of a second lyric, which suddenly connects us to the Twin Towers event that shook the world: '*Yaze yankulu le ndaba/ Lalelani sinixoxele*' (A terrible event took place/Listen and we'll tell you about it).[8] These two songs, coming almost a decade after the 1994 elections in South Africa and a little over a year after the 11 September 2001 attacks in the United States, are a reminder of the ways in which Zulu performance genres, ranging from *izibongo*, (praise-poetry) to *maskanda* music, have always engaged with the topical and the political.

### Composition and context in African music

A century ago, the *imbongi* or praise-poet still had the authority and the command of high rhetoric that enabled him to both make praise-poetry from the intricate life of the person he praised and produce it in the public sphere through his performance. Or he could work with an existing set of praises, reshape them and in so doing, give them his unique stamp in performance. Such artists still work within the genre, although they are far fewer now. In some cases, such as that of the *imbongi* of former President Mandela, Zolani Nkiva, the praising is accompanied by backing instruments and marketed as part of contemporary performance poetry. For the genre of *izibongo* there has always been a complex creativity that allowed for the talent of the individual through the addition of new poetic and metaphoric praise-names to the existing stock names and set devices to which the genre has access. Thus great composers such as Magolwana, the *imbongi* of King Dingane, successor to Shaka, and the contemporary praise-poet of King Goodwill, Ntuliwenkosi Dlamini, are recognised as *composers* as well as performers.[9] But, as Ruth Finnegan pointed out as early as 1961, and again in 1970, oral African forms do not spring from some mysterious communal source; they are *composed*. She confirmed this point in her discussion of global oral forms in *Oral Poetry*, showing how in instances as different as Yugoslavian oral poetry and Texan prison work songs, the poet composes and works within the parameters of a particular art form. Thus the idea of composition – and this would apply, too, to composers working within the *isicathamiya* creative context – needs to be understood as modulated by a framework of skills, and the sometimes shifting expectations of a specific culture and genre.[10]

Today guitar-strumming *maskanda* singers, often backed by support vocalists and drum and bass guitar, have a far higher public profile than praise-poets. These former troubadours of the streets, now with considerable access to electronic media, and marketed by companies such as Gallo, frequently insert their personal auto-biographies and *izibongo* into their songs that comment on the flux of contemporary events. Their recordings and the airtime they receive reach a wide and eager audience who listen for style and melody, but also for the message of the song. Indeed, the 2003 song, 'Amakhansela' (political councillors), by the *maskanda* artist Phuz'ekhemisi, which assailed self-seeking politicians and urged people not to vote for them, ignited controversy when it sold widely on CD and audio-cassettes in music shops and from makeshift pavement kiosks, and was played on uKhozi FM, the SABC isiZulu radio station. With its caustic comments on the abuse of power and its confident address to its public, it so enraged the premier of KwaZulu-Natal, Lionel Mtshali, that he publicly rebuked Phuz'ekhemisi and the song was banned from all SABC stations. A similar ban has been placed on the controversial song, 'Msholozi', recorded by the popular *maskanda* group of two women and one man, Izingane zoMa (Mother's Little Ones).[11] Referring to the former deputy-president, Jacob Zuma, by his clan praise-name, *Msholozi*, (and recorded in November 2005, just in time for Christmas) the song deals with the case of fraud brought against Zuma. Produced before the second charge of rape, the song calls for all charges to be withdrawn and for his reinstatement so that he can prepare to be the next president, which was what 'Mandela had wanted'.[12] These are two examples of the way in which singers in popular genres can enter a highly contested space in the public domain, capture an aspect of popular opinion and mediate it for a mass audience.

The songs of *isicathamiya*, similarly, have the choice to engage with difficult and controversial topics, although they do not command a mass market in the way the *maskanda* singers do. Some singers and composers see it as their duty to engage with controversy, rather than work with the well-worn themes of loneliness, love and courtship and the pain of the city that have marked the genre.[13] The freedom of voice of the new era has propelled some groups into making the deliberate choice to become 'messengers' for their community and thus heightened the didactic emphasis within the genre. Certainly that has seemed so with both Try Singers and their neighbours and fellow artists, Lion Singers. Yet this sense of speaking out has led to very different productions, as we will show, and points to the flexibility in the genre and the possibility of very different kinds of autobiographical acts.

Like Phuz'ekemisi and his fellow *maskanda* singers, the performers of *isicathamiya* are engaged in catching the consciousness of the times, particularly the conflicting views of gender power, patriarchal privilege, cultural loyalties, national interest, and so on. They listen intently in the marketplace, the taxis, busy streets, taverns and homesteads; they tune in to the radio, watch television and turn what they hear into their newest songs. They dive into controversy, compose, and put their goods on display in their performances. They exploit the latest turns of phrase, and if need be, they ransack other genres for the eloquence they need – linguistic, gestural, melodic or harmonic. They too are creators, bricoleurs, interpreters. They not only generate knowledge and debate through their performances, but also actively produce culture and an emergent consciousness.[14]

### Transcultural and transnational elements in post-1994 *isicathamiya*

Our experience with the members of Try Singers and Lion Singers in the Valley of a Thousand Hills in the early months of 2003 suggested that through performance and new (and old) lyrics, each group was re-examining its place in the world; that belonging and home were always important, even if they meant different things. To the Lion Singers, both belonging and home meant searching for a place in the present that included a rich and still-accessible past. This often meant creating a quite tactile sense of place in their songs through images of a peopled landscape, a landscape of stories and words with which people interacted and to which they ascribed their place in the world. Home for the Dlamuka brothers, Mzi and Nkone, the composers for Lion Singers, had to connect with a social ethic. As Njabulo Ndebele has expressed it, 'public intimacies do need private intimacies'.[15] Thus the songs of the Dlamuka brothers set out often from the private nexus of home, searching for corresponding 'public intimacies', for a consonance of value across the two domains. Their compositions (see the discussion of their song, '*Uthando*', later in this chapter) frequently highlight the tensions and contradictions between past and present home values and set these within a wider sphere of public well-being. There was a sense of their wanting to keep hold of symbolic capital, a certain 'strategic essentialism' when it came to the shaping of an identity which they wished to mark. There was an emphasis on keeping in the forefront of their compositions what Dipesh Chakrabarty calls 'a societally structured subjectivity'.[16]

For other groups, such as Try Singers, the place in the world, opened up by the fall of apartheid and the national citizenship that it brought, appeared to signal the chance for a more global reach, which resituated their local identities. It brought them, to use James Ferguson's phrase, a new 'worldliness at home'.[17] Yet Try Singers, too, wanted to keep a hold on home. Thus, their song we mention later, '*Sasesashaya lengoma ukuze sikhumbuz' ekhaya*' (We remember home), scripts the complex bundle of what home stands for in their new package of global awareness. The home strand is further complicated by their 'Where's it gone, freedom?' song, which gestures to the imagined pleasures of a past secure world now forever gone. But nostalgia is not their trademark, simply one among many tropes of their artistic message. For the genre as a whole, the post-1994 era has produced a new edge of confidence and certainty, both in lyrics and general style.

In this milieu, Try Singers embrace their role as 'messengers' with authority to speak to their community and to the public domain. Their song involving the events of 9/11 cries out sympathy for Americans, but advises the US president and world leaders *not* to take revenge. These lyrics recognise the huge influence of contemporary American popular culture on South African youth – particularly black youth. Yet Try Singers' song on 9/11 was foremost, for them, a part of their place in the world, and evidence of the easy stretch of their composing into global matters that influence their post-1994 home.

The transcultural and transnational elements, on which Try Singers draw, is not something new to the genre of *isicathamiya*. Veit Erlmann has stressed the profound influence on black South African popular culture of the African-American vaudeville groups that toured the country in the late nineteenth century.[18] In other words, black South Africans have long shared with other colonised black subjects transnational appropriations of the culture of the Black Atlantic. Thus, the 'active, performative process of consumption and the imagining of new communities through their bodies', which marked Akan performers of the early concert party genre in the 1930s, in colonial Ghana – then the Gold Coast – is true also of *isicathamiya* appropriation. They too, 'imagined new communities through their bodies' as they brought the new genre into being, drawing not only on early African-American popular culture, but also on Christian hymnody and Welsh and English choral traditions.[19]

Mkhambathini itself is no stranger to *isicathamiya*. A few of the present groups originated in the mid-1950s, according to Benedict Mlambo, leader of the Ocean Singers.[20] It is likely that the Ocean Singers, founded in 1956, are part of an even longer stretch of *isicathamiya* groups going back several decades earlier, as the first known singers in the area, The Crocodiles, led by landowner Enoch Mzobe, came from Botha's Hill in the southeastern section of the Valley of a Thousand Hills.[21] The Mkhambathini-based Try Singers and Lion Singers take their names from the actual location of members, rather than from a rural home to which they return, even nostalgically in their lyrics. Members of Lion Singers, in particular, travel from their base in Number Three Section, Mkhambathini, some to work in Durban and some further afield, but they return to the valley, practise there and live there. It is this rural locatedness that both groups accept as a part of their overall style. Yet home is a hugely multivalent signifier, calling up different associations of cultural memory and ties to history. While Try Singers loop their songs in an ever-widening circle which catches international events, the national and home, Lion Singers focus more intently on a multi-layered home, in which place, language and the echoes of older voices all carry heavy weight. They search, too, for ways of linking the 'intimacies' of the private and public domains.

### Try Singers and the creative process: Individual vision, collective realisation

On a number of occasions in early 2003, the two leaders of Try Singers, Nkosinathi Ndlovu and Sikhulu Ndlovu, discussed with us *how* they work from the seed of an idea to the realisation of a song in a group situation. In this section we focus on this key aspect of their craft and ask: How do Sikhulu and Nkosinathi negotiate and recreate their sonic environments?

The musical creativity of Sikhulu and Nkosinathi began in childhood. As is the nature of regeneration within oral traditions, the brothers learnt to sing and dance by watching and listening to those around them in the context of *isicathamiya* – principally their performing fathers and uncles. As we saw on our fieldwork trips, children, the next generation of performers, were present at both practices and performances, where they sat spellbound and formed an integral part of the audience. It is important to point out that initial steps of creativity involved learning the melodic and rhythmic content of other people's songs, a recurring theme in the process of composition. After learning a template of song, structure and melodies from their elders, what follows is a stage of decisive creativity, involving conscious decision-making as regards the creation of new music. It is on this stage that we wish to focus – after learning the vernacular, the framework, the structures, then what happens? How did Sikhulu and Nkosinathi take the genre and shape their own personal vernacular within the fluid parameters of *isicathamiya*?

Sikhulu started to write and compose his own songs at the age of eleven. At first he was one of a group of older singers; gradually as the older members drifted away, only the young remained. It was then that his role as composer began in earnest. The new, young group were still repeating the old songs and although he loved the music, it was time for a change, time for Sikhulu to make his own mark. With many musical groups, the end performance is the product of an individual vision, realised collectively. To what extent did Sikhulu craft each song and exactly how much input did the other members have? Sikhulu explained that initially a song topic would be discussed amongst group members. When this was agreed on, he would take off by himself so as not to be distracted, composing first the melody and then the lyrics, a process that would normally take one to two days: 'It's very easy once I have the title from others in the group. When I'm composing, it's very distracting to be around other people; I end up thinking about other things, so I prefer to be alone. I think very deeply at that time, and the tune just comes. The words follow. I can do half today and half tomorrow.'[22]

Articulating the exact process of composition, Sikhulu referred to three separate stages. First, he thought of an old song, which would serve as a melodic template for the new; then he took the fladgling version and did the same until he had a totally new song. He elaborated: 'I take an old song and play around with it until it's a new song. When I like the sound of it, I take that new song and play around with it, changing the key and trying out lots of different notes until I find the actual tune which is going to be perfect for the new song and then we stick to it.'

**Sources of original songs**
It is interesting to compare Sikhulu's mode of composing with that of Joseph Shabalala, the master of the tradition, whose influence on other singers and composers over the last 40 years has been profound. In his conversations with Christopher Ballantine, Shabalala mentioned the importance of dreaming, particularly in his early days as a composer, and subsequently working with the group.[23] We asked Sikhulu about the source of his original older songs. Did he get them from other groups, or the radio? 'No,' he answered. 'The original song that I sing, it's usually an old song from the group. At the beginning, I used to take some from other groups, but now I'm used to it. I'm experienced enough, so everything just comes, just like that. If you give me a topic then I can start the song. It's easy now.'

An important indication of individuality in Sikhulu's music is actually the regeneration of melodic ideas between songs. Indeed, many of Sikhulu's songs have a melodic hook, something that immediately gives them a trademark Try Singers sound. Within the songs we heard, one particular passage reappeared at the beginning of two of the most popular pieces in the Try Singers' repertoire – the song about 9/11 and the song about home – '*Sasesashaya lengoma ukuze sikhumbuz' ekhaya*'. The extract from '*Yaze Yankulu Lendaba*' that follows features exactly the same melody that appears in the song about home. It only differs slightly in rhythmic pattern to accommodate the different lyrics of each song. As is common in many African performance traditions, the leader begins the song in a free, flowing style, followed by the whole group bringing rhythmic emphasis.

This particular phrase not only enhanced the group's sound; it also acted as a bridge, a conduit between the two separate locations, distant New York and home, in South Africa. It is through this melody that Try Singers move swiftly between the global and the local. By embracing and expressing these two topics in the same distinctive melody, Try Singers use their own musical vocabulary to express what matters to them, right here and right now. The topic of 'home', which carries great historical significance, still remains crucial in the composing of *isicathamiya*, an ever-evolving genre that allows expression of current global concerns such as 9/11.[24]

Having explored individual creativity, we ask: at what point did the new melody and lyrics leave the hands of their creator and assume the collective sound of the

*Introduction to 9/11 song – 'Yaze Yankulu Lendaba' (This is a terrible story) (words by Sikhulu Ndlovu, music by Sikhulu Ndlovu and S'thembiso Ngidi). The arrow in bar 3 indicates a slide between notes. All four parts sing the lyrics written under the leader line.*

group? One evening at our home in Pietermaritzburg, Sikhulu explained further how the composing grew. The next stage of the process involved collaborating with just one other person, his brother Nkosinathi, co-arranger and leader of the group: 'There is a friend, a brother of mine, and we sit down and discuss the new song first. I sing it with him first to check that it's easy to sing; if it's easy, we then teach the choir. We start by teaching bass first because there are many of them and they are a bit older than the others, so they learn very quickly.'

The majority of the choir sing bass parts, but in a single song one might hear varying combinations of solo, duo, trio and whole choir. In our interview Sikhulu began singing the different parts of a song, first the melody and then the bass part that had been decided upon in collaboration with his brother. The song was '*Yaze Yankhulu Lendaba*' (This is a terrible story), written about America's 9/11.

Altogether there are four parts: the leader sings mostly by himself. The alto and tenor (to use Sikhulu's terminology) sometimes sing in thirds with the leader and are used to add, colour, depth and variation to each song. The bass pins down the harmonic structure of the songs and adds another spectrum of pitch.

Later in the conversation we asked Nkosinathi about the specific role of the middle layers of voice: 'Alto and tenor are very important to all *isicathamiya* groups, they add to the song, they make it nicer, they give it more harmony and they allow for the flexibility to throw in certain things.'

In crafting the overall sound, and designating roles to different singers, Sikhulu and Nkosinathi's talent for arrangement came to the fore. Working closely together, they would mould the collective voices of the choir to attain a desired sound. In performance, in the particular song about 9/11, two singers seemed to have a more supportive role to the lead voice than the other singers. They faced each other, sang in harmony and danced different steps to the rest of the group. Was this their role for most songs? Sikhulu's answer revealed a deep knowledge and insight of his creative medium:

> It depends on the song, and the person that is teaching them the song. For instance, if I were to dream of a song and then I were to teach those people a song, I know their voices very well, so I can say X you can do that, and X you sing that and X and B do that and following, so I designate roles as they are learning the song, according to their voices for that particular song, but it's not the same people all the time, just depending on the voice.

Nkosinathi added: 'If you put me in a new group of seven people, once I identify their voices, I'd be able to know what I want them to sing.' Sikhulu: 'Yes, we'd be able to arrange them according to their voices. It is better to record with five good voices than more that don't work as well. The emphasis is on quality.'

This description of their interaction with the vocal medium revealed the extent of their artistic vision. It showed them to be skilful artists with a palette of voices, using their full awareness of the colour and shape of every voice to craft a complex, layered song. Sikhulu and Nkosinathi's closeness was evident in every interaction. In our discussions they would sing parts of songs, and when they sang together, they sang in harmony, but with the contours of one voice, shaping phrases, louder, softer, swelling and clipping words in perfect unison. Their roles within the choir were also inextricably intertwined, one relying on the other to help the realisation of an individual idea, using the choir and the creation of new songs as a vehicle of expression.

## Lion Singers and the search for a new home

*Each generation has its own strengths.*[25]

Our discussion of creativity in relation to Lion Singers focuses less on the musical act of composition and more on the position from which they work as makers of culture and producers of new songs with messages – somatic, musical and semantic – for their audiences and devoted followers: how they re-imagine home both for themselves and for their searching audience who experience the dilemmas they encapsulate in their compositions.

It was only at the Lion Singers' practice on 31 January 2003, a week after our first meeting at the uMngeni Hall concert, that we realised how strong their focus is on the problematics of the contemporary moment, in which the conflicting demands and values of the generations have to be unravelled. Nkone Dlamuka, Mzi's brother, led the singing and the group saw him as their principal leader – who often 'dreamed a new song' and then brought it to the group. If he did not dream, he took his topic from what he saw around him in the community and set it in the narrative and dialogic structure that was a hallmark of the group's style.[26]

Attending a long evening practice at the Dlamuka homestead meant that we were able to listen to and watch the rehearsal of a larger number of songs than we could ever hear from a single group in a concert or competition. We were also able to learn at least the basic melodic outlines of some of the songs, so that we could recognise them on later occasions. Lion Singers did perform some short songs, but these compositions were in the main their entry or exit songs. In this repertoire 'Maliphathwe ngobungcwele igama lakho' (May your name be seen as holy), with its resonances of Western hymnody, was a favourite line. In general, many of their songs were long with a strong narrative quality. Many favoured a built-in dialogue that brought out tensions between two different positions expressed in the song and emphasised the dramatic and mimetic possibilities the genre contained, but on which performers did not always draw. The tensions expressed in song were a part of Lion Singers' trademark, as they wrestled with past and present, and asked their audiences to do the same.

Unlike Try Singers, whose two young leaders had taken on the task of remaking the group when the older members left, Nkone and Mzi of Lion Singers had been there from the group's beginning in 1977 (when they were both at Mbheka Primary School in neighbouring Swayimane).[27] Perhaps it was this prolonged period together that enabled their compositions to focus on what seemed for them a major issue: the difference between *intsha* (the young) and the generation that had already been young but were no longer so.[28] What was striking about their songs was the depth of this exploration of the changes in life perceptions as a result of shifts of biological and social age. For Lion Singers, change was not simply a brushing aside of an older generation. Rather it was an attempt to embrace them, but not to compromise, and to search for possible points of continuity. The group's sense of precisely what they were focusing upon was expressed by one of their members, Sino Dlamuka, in an interview with Wiseman Masango a few days before we watched the practice at the Dlamuka home:

> We show a picture of how it was when people were living in the old days and how it was that they reached their peak, and now the youth are here. They have a way of life that is quite different from that of the old days, that earlier time. Many of our songs point that out. They show that people did things in a way that the community approved of in those days. But now it's the new generation; we do things differently from the old days when they were young like us. For instance, the song called '*Uthando*' (Love). We try not to compose songs that discriminate, for instance, not to sing only to the young and leave out the older people. We want to reach out to every living person in this place. Like our song, '*Sinombiko*' (We have a message).[29] That song touches every kind of person who's here, it doesn't leave out a soul!

Their songs, on the theme of love particularly, tied into the wider concern of differences between this and earlier generations. Sino Dlamuka described how the song '*Uthando*' (Love) traced the shift in generational attitudes to marriage and finding a partner. To the older generation, it has to be the ritual exchange of cattle ('on foot' or as money), which formalises a relationship. Yet to the younger generation, often with little access to either cattle or money, this insistence is at worst, cruel, and at best, misguided. Two songs on the theme of love were part of their long practice on the night of 31 January 2003, and later, in performances in early February – both songs on love were listened to intently, and with deep satisfaction, by the mainly young audience. One in particular dwelt on generational swings and in its compressed narrative structure dealt obliquely with issues of patriarchal authority, of the right of parents to choose for their daughter, and the song set that against *her* desire, and that of her chosen lover. The 'Phansi' (Soft) style of Lion Singers, which Mzi referred to in conversations with us as 'the Mbube style', was in marked contrast to the 'swooping' and more strident 'Isikhwela Jo' style of Try Singers. It provided a fine medium for this lyrical meditation on youthful love chafing against the demands of an older generation who were calling for customary marriage practices, including the giving of bridewealth by a man who could afford it – an increasingly difficult option for young men who were often not earning regular wages and for whom farming the land was not an option. In the dramatic exchange in the song, the three proverbs are put into the mouth of the older generation as they try to make their point that marriage to a man who possesses nothing, is 'nothing'; their daughter must choose the 'old' man (with the cattle). What follows are the words without the repetitions – in most verses. Nkone as leader would sing the opening line solo, sometimes twice, and then the group in their part harmonies would enter; their mimetic movements were sinuous and expressive yet muted, drawing more on the light cat-like movements for which the genre is most known, than the flamboyant dance style with its shades of kwaito steps which was used by Try Singers, especially in their groundbreaking 'America' song:

| | |
|---|---|
| *Uma ukhuluma ngothando* (×2), *ucabange* | **If you think about love, just think** |
| *Ucabangisise ngobuthando akusiyo into yokudlala* | If you have to think about it, know it's not for fooling with |
| *Akusiyo into yokwenziwa* | You can't invent it |
| *Kodwa luyazifikela.* | It just appears. |
| | |
| *Ngeke kulunge, ingane uma uyikhombela* | It'll never do to choose for your child |
| *Ungamkhethela kanjani omunye umuntu?* | How can you choose for another person? |
| *Ngoba nawe wazikhethela* | Because you chose for yourself |
| *Iyeke, iyeke izikhombele* | Leave her; just leave her to point to someone |
| *Iyeke, izikhethele.* | Leave her to choose for herself. |
| | |
| *Ngaba iyamthanda-nje* (×2) | Just because she loves him |
| *Uma uyibheka* | If he looks at her |
| *Uyazibona izihlathi zigcwele uthando* | You can see her face shines with love |
| *Uma ibona abakubo* | If she looks at his family |
| *Iyashalaza* | She's shy |
| *Ibheke phansi njengesambane* | She glances down like the anteater |
| *Uma ibona yena* | If she sees him |
| *Ivusa amehlo kancane* | Her eyes widen a little |
| *Ibisiyamamatheka.* | And then she smiles. |
| | |
| *Kodwa ngoba akanalutho-nje* | But because he's got nothing it doesn't mean a thing |

| | |
|---|---|
| *Ngithi ngoba akanalutho-nje* | I say because he's got nothing |
| *Ukuthi akanalutho, akusho lutho* | Because he's got nothing it means nothing |
| *Ngoba iyona ezikhombela, iyona ezikhethele* | Yet she's pointed to him, she has chosen him herself |
| *Umendo awuthunyelwa 'gundane* | You can't tell how marriage will turn out |
| *Kuyokhanya, nakwaMakhanya kwazikhanyela.* | Things will just happen the way they're going to happen |
| *Alikho isoka elingenasici.* | There is no perfect lover. |
| | |
| *Khetha mntanami* | Choose my child |
| *Alikh' isoka elingenasici* | There is no perfect lover |
| *Kodwa yena usemdala* | 'But that one is so old! |
| *Ngizomenzenjani ngoba usemdala!* | What'll I do with him 'cos he's so old! |
| *Ngoba usemdala-nje!* (words repeated for the dance steps) | He's so old!' |

The song '*Uthando*' sets out the symbolic capital of earlier generation – its linkage of marriage and cattle – within a wider social system that saw this transaction as an essential element of generational stability and social reproduction, in which women played their own meek part. And against this, it sets love and asks the audience to weigh up the two positions. In a way, the song does not choose sides; it simply enunciates, eloquently, the dilemma for the young men and women for whom the group sings.

Thus Lion Singers search for a new modernity, within the frame of the post-1994 era. Their search causes them to look back, as well as at the contemporary moment; Try Singers look far more at the 'nowness' of things, which includes Twin Towers and the planes that destroyed them, as well as '*ekhaya*' (home). Each group shows us a particular view of modernity, which the genre mediates for its audiences and with which its composers wrestle. Where, then, is home? It is a fluid signifier with multiple and shifting meanings: is it the place from where you set out as a young migrant worker and to which you come back only to die? Is it the place from where you build your present and your future? Is it the most precious site of language where, as Mikhail Bakhtin would have it, all the past meanings and conversations of words impact on and refract onto your own use of it?[30] And is it also the somatic memory of the gestures of the encultured body through time, the sonic memory of the voice constantly reworked and shifted? The echoes through time, like the praises that stay '*emanxiweni*' in the old homesteads long after their owner has passed on? Is all this part of the sung home of Mkhambathini and the groups who sing *isicathamiya* and engage with the world from there?

# Notes

1.  Christopher Ballantine, 'Joseph Shabalala: African Composer', in *Senses of Culture: South African Music Studies*, eds. Sarah Nuttall and Cheryl-Ann Michaels (Oxford: Oxford University Press, 2000).

2.  *Isicathamiya* refers to an a cappella singing style (traditionally groups of Zulu men), usually accompanied by choreographed dance moves.

3.  For an overview of recent work on music and politics in Africa, see Lara Allen, 'Music and Politics in Africa', *Social Dynamics* 30:2 (2004): 1–19. See also Kelly Askew, *Performing the Nation: Swahili Music and Cultural Politics in Tanzania* (Chicago: University of Chicago Press, 2002).

4.  See Sarah Nuttall and Cheryl-Ann Michaels, 'Autobiographical Acts', in *Senses of Culture: South African Music Studies*, eds. Sarah Nuttall and Cheryl-Ann Michaels (Oxford: Oxford University Press, 2000), p. 316.

5.  Veit Erlmann's two classic studies of *isicathamiya* focus primarily on the urban expression of the genre. See *African Stars: Studies in Black South African Performance* (Chicago: University of Chicago Press, 1991) and *Nightsong: Performance, Power and Practice in South Africa* (Chicago: University of Chicago Press, 1996).

6.  For an insight into the range within Hausa expressive culture in Nigeria and the profiling of individual artists, see Graham Furniss, *Poetry, Prose and Popular Culture in Hausa* (Edinburgh: Edinburgh University Press, 1996), especially p. 10.

7.  The National Research Foundation, Indigenous Knowledge Systems category funded a small project on Youth, Identity and Performance, which enabled us to do this research. Liz Gunner is extremely grateful to them.

8.  Mkhambathi Try Singers, 'America' song, 25 January 2003.

9.  See the reference to Magolwana and precise praises attributed to him in Mike Chapman, *Art Talk, Politics Talk* (Pietermaritzburg: University of KwaZulu-Natal Press, 2006), p. 35. See also Liz Gunner, '*Ukubonga Nezibongo*: Zulu Praising and Praises' (Ph.D. diss., School of Oriental and African Studies, University of London, 1984), Chapter 8.

10. Ruth Finnegan, *Limba Stories and Storytelling* (Oxford: Oxford University Press, 1967); *Oral Literature in Africa* (Oxford: Oxford University Press, 1970) and *Oral Poetry: Its Nature, Significance and Social Context* (Cambridge: Cambridge University Press, 1976).

11. The CD and cassette came out on their own imprint, Izingane ZoMa Record Company, MCING 125 (DD), 2006 and is distributed by Gallo. For two recent accounts of the knotty relationship of music and politics in other African countries, see Maina Mutonya, 'Praise and Protest: Music and Contesting Patriotisms in Postcolonial Kenya', *Social Dynamics* 30:2 (2004): 20–35 and Silindiwe Sibanda, ' "You Don't Get to Sing a Song When You Have Nothing to Say": Oliver Mutukudzi's Music as a Vehicle for Socio-Political Commentary', *Social Dynamics* 30:2 (2004): 36–63.

12. Personal communication with Mpume Zondi, 15 March 2006 and Dudu Ngubane, 17 March 2006.

13. See Erlmann, *African Stars* and *Nightsong*.

14. Karin Barber, 'Views of the Field: Introduction', in *Readings in African Popular Culture*, ed. Karin Barber (Oxford: James Currey and Bloomington: Indiana University Press, 1997), pp. 1–12. See also Johannes Fabian, 'Popular Culture in Africa: Findings and Conjectures', *Africa* 48:4 (1978): 315–34, reprinted in *Readings in African Popular Culture*, ed. Karin Barber (Oxford: James Currey and Bloomington: Indiana University Press, 1997), pp. 18–28 and Johannes Fabian, *Moments of Freedom: Anthropology and Popular Culture* (Charlottesville: University of Virginia Press, 1998).

15. M.J. Daymond, 'From a Shadow City: Lilian Ngoyi's letters, 1971–1980, Orlando, Soweto', in *Moving Worlds* 5:1 (2005) (Special Issue on Postcolonial Cities in Africa): 49–68. Daymond quotes from Njabulo S. Ndebele, 'A Home for Intimacy', *Mail & Guardian*, 26 April–2 May 1996, pp. 28–29.

16. Gayatri Spivak uses the term 'strategic essentialism' somewhat differently, but it seems useful here. See Gayatri Spivak, *Outside in the Teaching Machine* (New York: Routledge, 1993). See also Dipesh Chakrabarty, *Provincialising Europe: Postcolonial Thought and Historical Difference* (Princeton: Princeton University Press, 2000).

17. James Ferguson, *Expectations of Modernity: Myths and Meanings of Urban Life on the Zambian Copperbelt* (Berkeley: University of California Press, 1999).

18. Erlmann, *African Stars*.

19. See Catherine Cole, *Ghana's Concert Party Theatre* (Bloomington: Indiana University Press, 2001), pp. 8, 14 and Chapter 5.

20. Benedict Mlambo interview with Liz Gunner and Wiseman Masango, 24 March 2003, Pietermaritzburg.

21. Erlmann, *African Stars*, pp. 207–08.

22. Quoted from an interview that took place on 25 January 2003 at the Number Three Community Hall, Valley of a Thousand Hills, between Imogen Gunner and Sikhulu Ndlovu. Wiseman Masango translated Sikhulu's responses.

23. Ballantine, 'Joseph Shabalala', pp. 235–44.

24. Ethnomusicologist Louise Meintjes outlines the polysemous nature of music, imbued with a significance that is never cast in stone; meaning is ascribed depending on a listener's particular associations with that sound: 'Paul Simon's Graceland: South Africa and the Mediation of Musical Meaning', *Ethnomusicology* 34:1 (Winter 1990): 37–73. To the audience of Try Singers, the hook, namely the movable musical phrase, became a trademark. It was the main composers' (Sikhulu and Nkosinathi) personal stamp on the music, which came to identify the whole group. Their arrangements exhibited a solemnity that differed from other riffs, appearing later in each song and containing a resonance of Western hymnody. This is also apparent in the arrangement and in the terminology applied to the voices of leader, alto, tenor and bass. The phrase could also have been based on a generic pattern, used by other *isicathamiya* groups. A not dissimilar phrase occurs in the Ladysmith Black Mambazo song '*Yinhle Ntombenhle*' (Beautiful girl), which they performed at a concert at the University of Limerick, Ireland, in April 2003. However, in the context of Try Singers' repertoire, *their* hook became autobiographical, a musical expression of self.

25. Mzi Dlamuka and Nkone Dlamuka to Wiseman Masango, 25 January 2003, uMngeni Hall, Mkhambathini.

26. Interview: Lion Singers with Wiseman Masango, 25 January 2003, uMngeni Hall, Mkhambathini.

27. Interview: Mzi Dlamuka with Liz Gunner and Wiseman Masango, 7 August 2003, KwaDlamuka, Mkhambathini.

28. Sino Dlamuka of Lion Singers to Wiseman Masango, 25 January 2003.

29. Ibid.

30. Mikhail Bakhtin, *Marxism and the Philosophy of Language*, trans. Ladislaw Matjeka and I.R. Titunik (Cambridge, Mass.: Harvard University Press, 1986 [1929 Russian edition published under the name of V.N. Voloshinov]).

*Chapter 38*

# Zulu Names

ADRIAN KOOPMAN

ZULU NAMES, WHETHER names of places (toponyms) or of people (anthroponyms), have long held a fascination for students of isiZulu and Zulu culture. This chapter looks specifically at the system of anthroponyms used in Zulu society.

An anthroponymic system refers to the different sets and types of names given by members of a particular society to themselves and to other members of society, and to the way in which these names interact with each other and with certain social aspects, such as the status, age and sex of the name bearer. Any anthroponymic system is strongly connected with perceptions of identity in society, and in this chapter the major theme is the relationship between concepts of identity and the different types of names in Zulu society.[1]

The first major subdivision is between 'official' and 'unofficial' identities. The official identity is contained in the documents of any bureaucratic system or administration: birth certificates, identity books (including the infamous *dompas* of the apartheid era), marriage certificates, bank or pension books, educational certificates, driver's licences and the like. Under this heading, three different types of names emerge: (1) the *igama lasekhaya* (the 'home' name, the 'real' name), (2) the *igama lesilungu* (the 'European' or 'Euro-Western' name, the 'colonial' name), and (3) the *isibongo* (the 'clan name'). Four other types of names seldom, if ever, find their way onto official documents, but may be no less an identity of the person concerned. Indeed, in many cases a person may be known entirely by one or more of the unofficial name types that follow, and not at all by any of the names that occur on his or her papers. These four name types are: (4) the *isithakazelo* ('clan praise'), (5) the *igama lomntwana* (the 'teknonym'), (6) the *igama likayise* ('patronym'), and (7) the nickname, for which there is no single, generally accepted, isiZulu term.

### Official identities: Personal and social dynamics of naming

The *igama lasekhaya*, literally the 'home name', is given to a child within a few days of birth, by either or both parents, occasionally by a grandparent or other close family member. This may be considered the 'real' personal name. It relates to the identity of the name in two very specific ways: firstly by linking a name with the person as a physical human being and secondly, by linking a name with the person as a unit within a variety of social dynamics.

Euro-Western anthroponymical systems generally regard an individual's name as a label that can be assumed or discarded at will. "Romeo, doff thy name,' says Shakespeare's Juliet, when she realises that the name Montague will spoil her chances of a satisfactory relationship with Romeo, she being a Capulet. 'Doff', from 'do off' or 'take off', equates the name with a piece of clothing such as a hat or glove, something that can be removed from the person and put aside. In African anthroponymic systems, as with similar systems in many other parts of the world, the personal name (the 'home' name, the 'real' name) is as much a part of the person as his or her limbs, ears and eyes. A person may be physically harmed through the name in the same way as injury may be done to the human body, and previously it was a standard belief in most African societies, Zulu society included, that possession of someone's name meant power over that person through witchcraft (*ubuthakathi*). For this reason the personal name was normally only used in the family circle, and the name was kept from outsiders as much as possible. Many scholars have cited different types of bans on the speaking aloud, not only of personal names of various members of society, but even of other 'non-name' words (common nouns, verbs, adjectives, etc.) in the language. This type of name avoidance has been well documented in Zulu society, under the general heading *ukuhlonipha*, although strictly speaking *ukuhlonipha* means 'respect' and includes a number of tabooed behaviours – ways of sitting, looking, eating, prescribed foodstuffs, and so on. Increasing Westernisation has lessened the belief that knowing a person's name gives one power over that person, although belief in witchcraft persists in Zulu society, and not only among rural or uneducated communities.

The *igama lasekhaya* may fix a person within the society through various relationships, which carry important social messages.[2] For example, if a newly married mother is continually being criticised by her mother-in-law, rules of *ukuhlonipha* prevent her from responding to the older woman. But it would be perfectly acceptable for the young mother to name a child *uFunani* ('What do you want?'), a question that everyone in the homestead would understand as being directed at the mother-in-law. A similarly functioning name is *uThulani* ('Be quiet'), again understood by the immediate family as being directed towards those who may be criticising the young mother. The names of dogs and oxen are frequently used in this way, particularly when a neighbour is suspected of witchcraft and social norms prevent outright accusations. In such situations a man may be heard calling out loudly to his ox *uBayangizonda* ('They hate me') or to his dog *uBayangihleba* ('They are whispering against me').

Names may also be used to convey the hopes and gratitude of parents. Zulu mothers and fathers may encode their wishes for the child's future proper behaviour in names such as *uBhekabafowabo* ('Look after your brothers'), *uBhekuyise* ('Look up to your father/Father') and *uThembinkosi* ('Trust God'), which act as a reminder to the child of the conduct expected in later life. A large percentage of Zulu personal names reflect the religious belief that God has had a hand in the successful birth of a child and must be thanked for this. Examples are: *uNkosinathi* ('The Lord is with us'), *uMandlenkosi* ('Strength of the Lord'), *uBonginkosi* ('Praise the Lord'), *uBusisiwe* ('She who is blessed'), and *uNomthandazo* ('Daughter of prayer').

Identity (and birth order) within the family structure is also important. Thus, many names have meanings equated with 'first boy', 'one of many girls', and so on, for example: *uNtombizodwa* ('Only girls'), *uMfanafuthi* ('Another boy'), *uNtombifikile* ('A girl has arrived [at last!]'), and *uNtombizine* ('The girls are [now] four'). The well-known practice of offering *ilobolo*, financial compensation for future children by the groom's family to that of the bride, is often referred to in names. A family with many sons may well be assured of a strong lineage, but the father will soon become short of cattle as he helps each son to marry. A daughter born after many sons is seen as the potential return of these cattle, and often gets a name based on the verb root – *buy* – ('return') as in *uZibuyile* ('They [cattle] have returned'), *uMabuyi* ('Miss Returner') and the like. The name *uNkomokazikho* ('The cattle are no longer here') has been recorded for the fifth son in a family with no daughters. In a patriarchal Zulu society, an adequate supply of sons is necessary to keep the family line going, and to ensure that the names of the living do not die forever. This importance is reflected in names such as *uVusumuzi* (literally, 'Wake up the family line' – a name given to a first-born son who 'kicks off' the next generation) and *uMuzikawupheli* ('The family line will never end' – a name given to a third or fourth son).

From names indicating identity within the family, we move to names that emphasise identity within the wider clan. Identity as a clan member reaches its height in clan praises, but is occasionally recorded in personal names such as *uMuntuwasembo* (literally 'A person from Embo-land', i.e. a member of the Mkhize clan) and *uZamantungwa* ('An Mntungwa girl', using the formative -*za*).

With the spread of Christianity, mission education and urbanisation, came the use of a new category of name – *igama lesilungu* (the *igama lesikole* or *igama lasedolobheni*) – that drew heavily on the European onomasticon. The *igama lesikole* ('school name') and *igama lasedolobheni* ('town name') can be regarded as a false or imposed identity, invariably related to European intrusion. Since the scramble for Africa (and in some cases starting centuries earlier during the height of Atlantic and Indian Ocean slave commerce), most African societies incorporated English, Arabic, French and Portuguese names. In South Africa, over the last fifteen years or so, probably because of intensifying anti-apartheid struggle, there has been a strong reaction against the use of a colonial name. Indeed, more and more younger, educated urban people are rejecting their *igama lesilungu* for their *igama lasekhaya*. Examples of *igama lesilungu* in Zulu society range from John, Mary and Sally, to Michael, Edward and Phyllis, and sometimes rather old-fashioned names such as Wilberforce, Cuthbert, Prudence, Constance and Charity. Other names come from the Bible, including Aaron, Cleopas, Abednigo, Ruth and Sarah; still others have American and European historical roots, such as Lincoln, Washington, Wordsworth, Churchill and Napoleon, while a range of *igama lesilungu* are drawn from random elements of modern Western culture, such as Sixpence, Lucky, Happygirl, Insurance, Beauty and Dolly.

From looking at names of the individual, we move on to look at names shared by members of a family or a clan, starting with the *isibongo*, a word often translated as 'surname'. Although the *isibongo* functions as a surname in the Euro-Western context of administrative documents, it is, strictly speaking, a clan name and not a surname. There are fundamental differences between the two. The possession of a clan name indicates membership of a clan, a sense of kinship among all those bearing the same name, as well as common descent from the clan founder. Relationships of descent can be reinforced through allegiance to a clan chief, common use of clan praises, identification with a specific geographical area, and the sharing of physical characteristics, such as scarification, beadwork styles, hairstyles, modes of speech and dancing and various other manifestations of clan identity. Having a particular surname presupposes none of these characteristics.[3] Some common Zulu clan names are Dlamini, Bhengu, Cele, Dlomo, Mkhize, Khumalo, Ntuli, Ntshangase, Ngcobo, Mthethwa, Gumede, Mhlongo, Zondi, Sibisi, Zulu, Mthembu and Maphumulo.

A typical way to address a married woman is by using her maiden *isibongo*, prefixed with *ma-*. Thus, friends, neighbours, family and even her husband may address Mrs Dlamini, born Miss Ngcobo, as MaNgcobo. The *izithakazelo* (see below) of the maiden surname may be substituted, so a woman born into the Khumalo clan, when she later marries, may be addressed as MaMntungwa or MaMabaso, Mntungwa and Mabaso being praise names for the Khumalo clan. An interesting onomastic phenomenon that arose in the mid-1990s in South Africa among married women of high public profile (primarily politicians, with a handful of television, stage and screen personalities) has been the use of double-barrelled surnames, with the maiden clan name prefixed to the clan name of the husband. Winnie Mandela, second wife of Nelson Mandela, was the first to be recorded, when the press began referring to her as Winnie Madikizela-Mandela. Other well-known public identities are Nkosazana Dlamini-Zuma, Manto Shabalala-Msimang and Khanyi Dlomo-Mkhize.

### Unofficial identities: Names off the record

Every clan name (*isibongo*) has its own clan praises, ranging from the brief two or three single names of illustrious ancestors to the lengthy 50- or 60-line praise poems.[4] When clan names are related, as frequently happens when a clan splits into two, or when clan breakaways take place, then their *izithakazelo* will overlap, and the longer these related clans have been part of a single clan, the more their clan praises will overlap.

Clan praises consist, for the most part, of the names of chiefs, heroes and other notables from the history of the clan, interspersed with descriptive or narrative phrases linked to these individuals. A clan name and its primary clan praise name (one that usually occurs first in a list of clan praises) may be so connected in terms of identity that they are interchangeable, such as the following pairs: Khumalo/Mntungwa, Xulu/Makhathini, Hadebe/Mthimkhulu, Ngema/Mngadi and Mthembu/Mvelase. Let us take the pair Ngema/Mngadi. A person known by the clan name Mngadi may be also known by other people as Ngema. Half of his/her documents may reflect Mngadi as the 'surname', the other half, Ngema. If the person identifies himself as Mngadi, then he can be praised as 'Ngema! Madlokovu!'. If the person identifies herself as Ngema, she may be praised with 'Mngadi! Madlokovu!'. In other words, the names Mngadi and Ngema serve as clan praise for each other, each with the secondary clan praise Madlokovu. This 'system', or better, 'possibility' of interchangeable surnames is incomprehensible to many Euro-Western minds.

Clan praises constitute the fullest possible identity of an individual. As they consist mainly of illustrious names from the history of the clan, going back usually to the name of the clan founder, they link the living individual with his or her ancestors (often known as *abaphansi*, 'those below'), who are, in turn, linked to the soil and earth. Thus, *izithakazelo* not only distinguish individuals as clan members, but as people with roots in Africa. To identify a person by one or more clan praises also flatters the person. *Izithakazelo* as single names are commonly used as forms of address, but when strung together in sequence they may be used to complement, thank and cajole. To call a person from the Mkhize clan 'Khabazela!' is but to use one name as an address form. To exclaim to him or her, '*Khabazela! Wena kaMavovo! Wena kaZihlandlo kaGcwabe! Sibiside! Siyingela! Wena owakhula thina silibele!*' ('Khabazela! Son of Mavovo! Son of Zihlandlo, born of Gcwabe! Sibiside! Siyingela! You who grew, while others remained behind!') is to reach deep into the heart of that person.

The single clan praise name implies the unstated potential of all the others that lie behind it. A person with the clan name Mhlongo may be addressed with the single praise 'Njomane!' but this is an abbreviated form of the full '*Njomane! Wena kaMgabhi! Wena owaduka iminyakanyaka ngowesine watholakala! Khuyamine! Yangeni! Dlomo!*' ('Njomane! You the son of Mgabhi! You who went astray for many years and returned in the fourth year! Khuyamine! Yangeni! Dlomo!'). In their fullest forms, clan praises are recited solemnly by the *umnumzane* (family head) at *imisebenzi* (ceremonies when a goat or a beast is slaughtered to honour the ancestors) such as weddings, funerals and the *ukubuyisa* ceremony, held one year after the death of a family head to call back his spirit.

More commonly in rural areas where traditional practices have endured longer than in urban areas, men and women may be referred to or addressed by a 'patronym', the *igama likayise* or name of their father, prefixed with a possessive indicating 'born of'. Catholic priest and ethnographer of the amaZulu, A.T. Bryant, stated in 1949 that a married woman's father's name could be used to refer to her with or without the prefix *oka-* ('she of').[5] Men commonly add their father's name to their own personal name, along with the possessive *ka-*, as does the central character in Kenneth Ngubane's novel *Uvalo Lwezinhlonzi* (*The Fear of the Eyebrows*), who invariably introduces himself, at various points in the novel, as '*NginguZulumacansi kaBhekokwakhe waseButhunqe bukaMagayi*' ('I am Zulumacansi, son of Bhekokwakhe from Buthunqe under chief Magayi'). Thereafter, most of the other characters in the book address him as '*wena kaBhekokwakhe*' ('you, son of Bhekokwakhe').[6] Although the second half of the twentieth century saw a general decrease in the use of the patronym, since the beginning of the new millennium, there has been a noticeable trend for high-profile members of the print media in South Africa to adopt as part of their public identity either patronyms, or what appear to be patronyms, with the placing of the Nguni possessive *ka-* in front of the surname. It was the secretary of the Pan-Africanist Congress, Thami kaPlaatjie, who seems to have started the trend. He has since been followed by, among others, *City Press* reporter, Themba kaMathe and journalists for the *Natal Witness*, Bhungani kaMzolo and Bheki kaNcube. Using a different possessive prefix are *Sunday Times* columnist, Mzilikazi waAfrika; *Sowetan Sunday World* writer, Moyahabo waMabeba and *City Press* reporters, Edward waMahlamela and Gabanapuo waSelomo.

This onomastic phenomenon is too new to be analysed fully here. Yet it seems clear that those who have adopted this style are trying to move away from a Euro-Western identity and to aim for more of an African personality. A theory recently put forward is that use of the patronymic or an implied patronymic joins the so-named person through time and space to the continent of Africa, a theme resonating in popular discourse associated with President Thabo Mbeki's African Renaissance at the start of the twenty-first century.[7]

From 'naming through the father' we move to 'naming through the child'. A form of identity common throughout Africa, but which appears to be non-existent in Euro-Western anthroponymic systems, is the use of the *igama lomntwana* ('name of the child'), the teknonym. Teknonymic usage refers to the addressing of either of a child's parents by prefixing the name of the child with 'mother of . . .' or 'father of . . .'. Zulu kinship terms include first-person, second-person and third-person terms for both father and mother, but the second-person term *uyihlo* ('your father') is mildly offensive, while the second-person term *unyoko* ('your mother') is extremely insulting. In polite social speech only the first- and third-person terms are used interchangeably, so in addressing a second person either the first-person *(u)baba* ('my father') and *(u)mama* ('my mother'), or the third-person *(u)yise* ('his/her/their father') and *(u)nina* ('his/her/their mother') may be used.[8] As a result, parents of the boy Dumisani may be referred to by outsiders and by each other as *unina kaDumisani* and *uyise kaDumisani* and addressed as *baba kaDumisani* and *mama kaDumisani*. While only the first child is living, parents will use both versions of this name, regardless of the sex of the child. However, once children of both sexes have been born, the general custom is for the mother to be addressed by the name of the eldest daughter, and the father to be addressed by the name of the eldest son. This is by no means an invariable rule, however, and in many families, the name of the eldest child, of whatever sex, is used for both father and mother. The teknonymous mode is extremely common in Zulu society. A study of urban families in the Pietermaritzburg area of KwaZulu-Natal in the early 1980s showed that well over half of the married women addressing their husbands using teknonyms, while well over a third of husbands regularly did so when addressing their wives.[9]

Nicknames in Zulu society, as elsewhere, share the curious irony that they are invariably *unofficial* names (rarely found in administrative documents),[10] but may be the most common way in which an individual is known; and they may be chosen to reflect some aspect of a person's character or circumstances specifically related to that individual. In other words, nicknames are generally coined for a person once that person's nature can be identified, whereas official names are either unrelated to the individual (as in surnames), or chosen for the individual (like personal names) at birth before the character or nature of the individual has been realised. In isiZulu-speaking communities, nicknames may be conferred at any age and by anyone, including oneself. They may be single words, short phrases of two or three words, or they may develop into fuller sentences. A person may have more than one nickname, and when these are extended into phrases and sentences, there is an overlap between names and oral poetry, which is widespread in Zulu society.[11]

For example, nicknames coined for behavioural patterns include *uMpangele ekhala igijima* ('guinea-fowl that sings as it runs': a man who habitually sang as he went about his business);[12] *uFishonamasondo* ('fish with wheels': a man who can do anything);[13] *uKhombanathingi* ('pointing at nothing': a manager concerned with trivial details) and *uLwembu* ('Miss Spider': from her habit of wrapping her arms around everyone).[14] While the following nicknames are descriptive of physical features: *uNomvukuzane* ('Mr Mole': a person with tiny slit eyes); *uMadevaphulinkomishi* ('moustaches that break a cup': very large moustache);[15] *uMbamboziyabalwa* ('ribs are counted': extremely thin person);[16] *Yinde lenyoni ayiboni kaZulu* ('it is tall, this bird, and does not see the sky': very tall person); *uMthunzi wokuphumula amatshitshi* ('shade where young maidens rest': tall person who rather fancies himself with the girls); *uShort Division isibalo sabantwana* ('Short division is the arithmetical problem of young children': a very short person.[17] Nicknames provide an endurable fascination for onomasticians, and nicknames in Zulu and other South African languages have been no exception.[18]

Evans-Pritchard, writing more than 60 years ago about the anthroponymic system of the Nilotic Nuer people, stated: 'Names of all kinds are social documents, which fix a person's position in the social structure and define his relations to other members of society.'[19] This statement is equally true of Zulu society. Whether it is an ox name that announces the discovery of witchcraft, a clan praise that links a man to his ancestry, or the name of a girl that tells how many older sisters she has, Zulu names undoubtedly 'fix positions' and 'define relationships' in society. Although their primary function, as with most names the world over, is to *identify*, at the same time, they set and extend Zulu cultural parameters through the everyday communicative acts of speech and social discourse.

**Appendix: The morphology of Zulu personal names (*amagama asekhaya*)[20]**
All Zulu anthroponyms belong to Zulu noun class 1(a), with the noun class prefix *u-*, and have a plural in class 2(a), with prefix *o-*. The exact meaning of the plural depends on the context. Thus, *oBonginkosi* could mean 'all people named Bonginkosi', 'a group of people named Bonginkosi' (*mabaphume eklasini oBonginkosi* – 'all the Bonginkosis should leave the class'), or 'Bonginkosi and friends', 'Bonginkosi and Co.'). Although every Zulu name is a noun, they may be derived from all parts of speech: nouns, verbs, possessives, adjectives, adverbs, etc. The two most common sources, which account for the vast majority of Zulu names, are other nouns and verbs.

In their simplest form, names are derived from nouns by replacing the initial vowel of a noun with the class 1(a) prefix: *inhlanhla* ('luck') becomes uNhlanhla; *amadoda* ('men') becomes uMadoda; *amantombazane* ('girls') becomes uMantombazane and *igugu* ('treasure') becomes uGugu. Rarely, the male marker -*so*- is prefixed to the base noun before prefixing class 1(a) *u-*: uSomfana from *umfana* ('boy') and uSobantu from *abantu* ('people'). Very commonly (in approximately 30 per cent of female names), the female marker -*no*- is likewise prefixed to a base noun: uNonhlanhla from *inhlanhla* ('luck'); uNomvula from *imvula* ('rain'); uNokukhanya from *ukukhanya* ('shining') and uNomazulu from *amaZulu* ('Zulu people').

In the case of names derived from verbs, the class 1(a) prefix *u-* is directly prefixed to the root of the verb suffixed with -*a*, the form in which the verb is regularly entered into dictionaries: uThemba from *themba* ('hope') and uBonga from *bonga* ('thank'). However, a wide variety of grammatical forms of the verb, covering the full range of possible subject and object concords, tense, mood, implications, and positivity as well as negativity, can be used as the base for personal names. The list below encompasses possibilities derived from the verb root *bong-* ('thank'):

| | | |
|---|---|---|
| uBongani | 'be grateful' | plural imperative |
| uBongekile | 'having felt grateful' | neuter extension with perfect |

| | | |
|---|---|---|
| uBongeka | 'feeling grateful' | neuter extension |
| uSiyabonga | 'we are grateful' | present tense positive |
| uSibongile | 'we are grateful' | perfect tense |
| uAsibonge | 'let us be grateful' | subjunctive (hortative) |
| uSiyambonga | 'we thank Him' | present tense positive with object concord |
| uBonginkosi | 'thank the Lord' | present tense with object |

A sample of the many compounds possible in the formation of Zulu names include:[21]

| | | |
|---|---|---|
| uThembinkosi | 'trust the Lord' | verb + object noun |
| uVumakonke | 'agree to everything' | verb + inclusive pronoun |
| uPhumasilwe | 'let us go out and fight' | verb + subjunctive verb |
| uMfanufikile | 'a boy has arrived' | subject noun + verb |
| uMuntukayithenjwa | 'a person is not trusted' | subject noun + negative verb |
| uMuzikawupheli | 'the family line will not end' | subject noun + negative verb |
| uMuzikawukho | 'there is no family line' | subject noun + negative copulative |
| uMandlenkosi | 'the strength of the Lord' | noun + possessive + noun |
| uNtombikayise | 'girl of her father' | noun + possessive + noun |
| uNtombenkulu | 'big girl' | noun + adjective |
| uMakhosonke | 'all chiefs' | noun + inclusive pronoun |
| uNtombizintathu | 'the girls are now three' | noun + adjective |

## Notes

1. Much of what follows here comes from research that culminated in my book *Zulu Names* (Pietermaritzburg: University of Natal Press, 2002).
2. For further reading on names as social messages, see N.S. Turner, 'Zulu Names and Indirect Expression', *Names* 48:2 (2000) and A. Koopman, 'Zulu Names as Social Messages', unpublished paper read at the 21st Congress of the International Council of Onomastic Sciences, Uppsala, Sweden, 2002.
3. See Koopman, 'Zulu Names as Social Messages', pp. 76–81 for a detailed comparison of Zulu clan names and Scottish clan names.
4. For further reading on clan praises, see D.M. Mzolo, 'Zulu Clan Praises', in *Social Systems and Tradition in Southern Africa*, eds. J. Argyle and E. Preston-Whyte (Cape Town: Oxford University Press, 1978), A. Koopman, '*Bongesihle sabaNguni*', in *Tinanatelo: Swazi Family Praises*, ed. W. Kamera (Durban: Centre for Oral Studies, University of Natal, 1999) and Koopman, 'Zulu Names as Social Messages', pp. 76–85.
5. A.T. Bryant, *The Zulu People as They Were before the White Man Came* (Pietermaritzburg: Shuter & Shooter, 1949), p. 209.

6.  K. Ngubane, *Uvalo Lwezinhlonzi* (Johannesburg: Educum, 1972).

7.  See A. Koopman, 'Possessives and Patronymics: Towards a New Identity for Zulu Males', unpublished paper read at the 12th Conference of the African Languages Association of Southern Africa, University of Stellenbosch, July 2003.

8.  The noun prefix (u)- is in brackets here because it is used in third person reference, but falls away in second person address.

9.  See A. Koopman, 'The Social and Literary Aspects of Zulu Personal Names' (Masters thesis, Pietermaritzburg, University of Natal, 1986) and *Zulu Names*, p. 28.

10.  There is no regularly accepted isiZulu term for nickname, although various writers have used terms such as *isithopho* (Bryant's 'fancy name'), *isangelo* ('kissing name', 'hugging name'), *isidlaliso* ('playing name'), *isifengqo, isifeketiso, isitheketiso* ('playful names'). Most of these terms refer to the 'pet' names which mothers give to their children in early infancy, usually used only by the mother, and then only in the child's early years, making these terms generally unsuitable for the kind of nickname which is given in, or endures until, the bearer's adult years.

11.  See Koopman, 'The Onomastic–Oral Literature Continuum', in *Zulu Names*, pp. 305–09 and A. Koopman, 'The Power of Names in Zulu Oral Poetry', *Nomina Africana* 14:2 (2000).

12.  See Koopman, *Zulu Names*, p. 58 and A. Koopman, 'The Praises of Young Zulu Men', *Theoria* 70 (1987): 41–54.

13.  See L. Molefe, 'Onomastic Aspects of Zulu Nicknames with Special Reference to Source and Functionality' (Ph.D. diss., Pretoria, University of South Africa, 2000).

14.  See N.S. Turner, 'Onomastic Caricatures: Names Given to Employers and Coworkers by Black Employees', *Nomina Africana* 11:1 (1997).

15.  Ibid.

16.  Molefe, 'Onomastic Aspects of Zulu Nicknames'.

17.  See Koopman, *Zulu Names* and 'The Praises of Young Zulu Men'.

18.  See, for example, V. de Klerk, 'Nicknaming Across Cultures: Borrowing and Other Linguistic Tricks', *Nomina Africana* 12:1 (1998); Koopman, 'The Praises of Young Zulu Men', *Zulu Names* and 'Zulu Names as Social Messages'; Molefe, 'Onomastic Aspects of Zulu Nicknames'; S.J. Neethling, '*Iziteketiso* in Xhosa', *Nomina Africana* 4:1 (1990); V. Prabhakaram, 'Nicknames: The Hardest Stone the Devil can Throw: Indian Caricature in South Africa', *Nomina Africana* 13:1 and 2 (1999) and Turner, 'Onomastic Caricatures'.

19.  E.E. Evans-Pritchard, 'Customs and Beliefs Relating to Twins Among the Nilotic Nuer', *Uganda Journal* 3 (1939): 237.

20.  For details of the grammatical structure of Zulu personal names, see A. Koopman, 'The Linguistic Difference between Nouns and Names in Zulu', *African Studies* 38:1 (1979); 'Male and Female Names in Zulu', *African Studies* 38:2 (1979) and *Zulu Names*, pp. 267–96. For details of the morphology of Zulu clan names, see A. Koopman, 'Some Notes on the Morphology of Zulu Clan Names', *South African Journal of African Languages* 10:4 (1991).

21.  For an extensive analysis of the structure of Zulu personal names, and the difference between male and female names, see Koopman, 'The Linguistic Difference'; 'Male and Female Names' and *Zulu Names*, pp. 267–96.

# Chapter 39

# Poetic Masters of Zuluness
## The Dhlomo-Vilakazi Literary Debate

DAVID ATTWELL

BETWEEN JUNE 1938 and July 1939, a dispute took place in the pages of *Bantu Studies* and *The South African Outlook* between H.I.E. Dhlomo and B. Wallet Vilakazi, eminent figures in Zulu literature.[1] Their vituperative disagreement might have seemed disproportionate to the subject at hand: the place of rhyme in Zulu poetry. That their argument became overheated reflected the fact that the two figures were rivals, as interpreters of Zulu tradition and pathfinders in the development of modern Zulu literature.[2] The conflict had its origins in the 1938 masters thesis Vilakazi submitted to the University of the Witwatersrand on 'The Conception and Development of Poetry in Zulu', a portion of which was published in the same university's recently founded journal *Bantu Studies*. By this time, Vilakazi's poetry was well known, since it had been published in *Ilanga lase Natal* and the *Native Teacher's Journal*, followed by the collection, *Inkondlo kaZulu* ('Zulu Songs'). In *Inkondlo*, Vilakazi experimented with rhyme, following a range of English models of versification – the couplet, rhyming quatrains, and others. For these efforts he earned sceptical notice, as he acknowledges later: 'By trying to adopt this rhyming I have found that there is a feeling among European critics that Zulu can achieve only a limited success with rhyming, since most of the words in Zulu end in [unstressed] vowels, and thus do not permit variety of sound that makes successful rhyming possible.'[3] Chastened, Vilakazi answered defensively, justifying the use of rhyme with reference to many alliterative derivatives in isiZulu that took similar forms. Vilakazi drew on examples of existing successful rhymed compositions, notably hymns; he also clarified his position by saying that it is not only the final syllable which should rhyme, but the penultimate one with its preceding consonant, *iphaba* with *ubaba* and *ukubaba*, *vela* with *fela*, *amatata* with *amathatha* and *amadada*, etc. In laying out this theory, he meticulously distinguished between successful and unsuccessful rhymes, paying attention to such elements as nasalisation, fricatives and clicks.[4]

Herbert Dhlomo found Vilakazi's elaboration to be overwrought. Dhlomo published two responses, 'Nature and Variety of Tribal Drama' in *Bantu Studies* and

449

'African Drama and Poetry' in *The South African Outlook*. In *Bantu Studies* he said that oral poetry, with the exception of certain *izibongo*, consists of incomplete records of communal performances. His scorn for his rival's efforts emerges in the second piece, in which he calls rhyme a 'cold tyrant' and Vilakazi's scheme 'rigid', 'inflexible' and 'crippling'. Particularly humiliating for Vilakazi, who was eager to preserve his academic reputation (let us not forget the pressures of being the first black appointment to the University of the Witwatersrand), is Dhlomo's citing of Sir Arthur Quiller-Couch to launch a retort:

> Those elders of you who have followed certain earlier lectures 'On the Art of Writing' may remember that they set very little store upon metre as a dividing line between poetry and prose, and no store at all upon rhyme. I am tempted today to go further, and to maintain that, the larger, the sublimer, your subject is, the more impertinent rhyme becomes to it: and that this impertinence increases in a sort of geometrical progression as you advance from monosyllabic to disyllabic and on to trisyllabic rhyme . . .[5]

Dhlomo himself was attempting to develop what he called 'literary drama' that dealt with 'actions, passions, and furies that burst through the stagnant, dam-like banks of rhyme' to the 'wider, less defined sea-basin of blank and parallel verse'.[6] His view sought validation in biblical Hebrew and in Shakespeare, and he emphasised rhythm rather than rhyme: 'In fact, one may almost say that the greatest gift of Africa to the artistic world will be – and has been – Rhythm.'[7]

Vilakazi was stung by Dhlomo's attack, and his riposte was vigorous. He dismissed Dhlomo's understanding of literary drama as superficial and unscholarly, saying Dhlomo had no grounding in isiZulu linguistics, let alone in classical languages or Shakespeare. But more tellingly, in a personal assault on Dhlomo's efforts in drama, he said, 'I do not know of any Bantu dramatists and their works; but I know there are poets with published works of reputable hallmark in all our South African Bantu languages which are worthy of study.'[8] Bearing in mind that Dhlomo was writing historical dramas on the Zulu kings in English, the full implications of Vilakazi's criticism (which resonate down to later generations) emerge in the final paragraph:

> By Bantu drama, I mean a drama written by a Bantu, for the Bantu, in a Bantu language. I do not class English or Afrikaans dramas on Bantu themes, whether these are written by Black people, I do not call them contributions to Bantu Literature . . . I have an unshaken belief in the possibilities of Bantu languages and their literature, provided the Bantu writers *themselves* can learn to love their languages and use them as vehicles for thought, feeling and will. After all, the belief, resulting in literature, is a demonstration of people's 'self' where they cry: '*Ego sum quod sum*'. That is our pride in being black, and we cannot change creation.[9]

It was an argument, then, about where one's deepest loyalties lay in the struggle for racial and national self-affirmation, and it was about the aesthetic consequences of these choices.

### Zulu tradition and British romanticism

Exactly how seriously Vilakazi would take J. Dexter Taylor's review of *Inkondlo* in subsequent years emerges from his doctoral thesis, 'The Oral and Written Literature in Nguni'. In 1938 Taylor had hailed Vilakazi for showing the spirit of the *imbongi* (praiser), but classified the Zulu intellectual as a follower of J.E.K. Aggrey (who had recently visited South Africa) rather than Shaka, meaning that he saw Vilakazi as a man thinking outside the primordial space purportedly created by Shaka. Taylor dubbed Vilakazi 'the human poet rather than the Zulu poet . . . in the attention he pays to his own emotions and those he observes in others. It is the *imbongi* come to consciousness of the abstract and of the inner self, through contact with the work of other poets and through the unconscious influence of education and European culture.'[10] Of course, Taylor was diluting Vilakazi's essential Zuluness by defining Vilakazi as a hybrid artist who sources European forms.

In a direct response in his thesis, Vilakazi contrasts the generation of S.E.K. Mqhayi with that of the slightly later J.J.R. Jolobe in Xhosa literature, and argues that the greatness of the earlier generation lay in their 'combining and using the knowledge and craft of the dead *izimbongi*, while the greatness of Jolobe and his confreres lies in experimentation and innovation, backed by their knowledge of past history, and in the delicate culture of mind drilled in the study of European literature which generates true poetic poise'. Vilakazi then cites Taylor's comments about himself (Vilakazi), making them represent his entire generation: 'A young African poet [who] composes in the truly African flavour of his imagery and in the exuberant extravagance of some of his descriptions is a true descendant of the *imbongi*. But the background of his thought is not that of the *imbongi*. He is not much concerned with warlike prowess.'[11]

In Vilakazi's critical prose it is clear that varieties of romanticism, which had become institutionalised in English literary-critical writing by the 1930s, hold sway. A poet's 'happiness', he wrote, comes from a special ability to interpret life 'in emotive words';[12] this ability stands in opposition to the sterility of mass culture;[13] the imagination of the poet is in touch with the ineffable, things 'which none of us can touch or handle'. Romanticism for Vilakazi separated traditional from modern aesthetics: the contemporary poet's imagination, his special ability to use words as 'elusive agents seeking answers to the final problems of life and even immortality' is what distinguishes him from 'the old world of primitive life, where savages wondered at the appearance of a train or at a minister of the Gospel'.[14] Such apparent self-alienation is puzzling because Vilakazi's life's work actually entailed the justification of traditional Zulu expression – even if this tradition necessitated reinvention through the terms of European culture.

Part of the explanation for Vilakazi's line between traditional and modern aesthetics lies in prevailing constructions of traditional expression. Journals such as *Bantu Studies* and *The Critic* (both read by Vilakazi and Dhlomo) were overwhelmingly ethnographic in their treatment of black expression, with the attendant 'fixing' of African ethnic identity in condescending and ahistorical terms. It is not surprising that Zulu intellectuals would have wished to put as much distance as possible between themselves and such static representations.

In the 1930s there was a good deal of public discussion about the social role of literature amongst black South Africans, a discussion which assumed a connection between race, ethnicity and literature as a marker of 'progress'. The debate was joined by liberal intellectuals such as C.M. Doke (Bantu Studies at the University of the Witwatersrand) and R.H.W. Shepherd (director of the Lovedale mission press), as well as black intellectuals such as Peter Abrahams (who recalls these years in *Tell Freedom*), D.D.T. Jabavu (author of two brief but pioneering monographs on black literary history), B.W. Vilakazi, Herbert Dhlomo and others associated with the Bantu Men's Social Centre (BMSC) in Johannesburg.[15]

The public discussion led in 1932 to the BMSC becoming a book distribution centre for the American philanthropic Carnegie Corporation, thus bringing into being the Carnegie Non-European Library, which by 1937 was run by Herbert Dhlomo. The intervention of the Carnegie Corporation in 1932 also spurred the founding of *The Critic*, which carried articles on black expression, including an essay by G.P. Lestrade, the government ethnographer, on praise-poetry to which both Dhlomo and Vilakazi would respond. In June and October 1936, two conferences of 'Bantu authors' were held, one in Bloemfontein and the other in Florida, near Johannesburg, in Shepherd's words, 'to emphasise the value of the use of literature'.[16] With white and black referring to the example of African-American literary achievement, the participants in these conferences had different emphases: white philanthropists emphasised progress towards non-racialism and civility; black authors complained about the poor level of support from the presses.[17] Although the proposal was never implemented, Clement Doke's idea of starting a 'Bantu Academy' was widely supported.[18]

By 1936, South Africa would see the refinement of segregationist ideology in the Herzog Bills, which entrenched the racial franchise and exacerbated existing laws governing access to landed property. In the absence of strong leadership from the African National Congress (ANC), the All-African Convention brought the elite together to protest. Dhlomo's signal play of this period, *Cetshwayo*, provides a critique of segregationist thinking by tracing its genealogy back to the 'native administration' policies provoking the Anglo-Zulu War in 1879.[19]

As these circumstances developed, Dhlomo and Vilakazi's generation would experience nothing but injury to its social and political aspirations, and the literate culture of the mission school would steadily become an anachronism. Except, perhaps, in one respect: in the experience of this group, romanticism was not merely around as dead convention. It spoke powerfully to young, ambitious people adrift in a world scarcely imagined by their forebears; then, as they faced exclusion, frustration and disappointment, the 'wounded self' of Shelley and Keats could provide a relevant idiom. In Dhlomo's case, even when in his later, more militant phase of the 1940s he was writing about the disappointments he personally suffered at the hands of white liberals (in poems such as 'Frustration' and 'Fired!') or the general disappointment felt by Africans to whom it was clear that the victory celebrations at the end of the War excluded them ('Our Country Dear', 'Not for Me', 'Royal Visit, 1947'), the pull of Shelley's 'thorns of life' is all too evident: 'this betrayal wounds and sears my soul. I bleed'.[20]

One may say that Dhlomo and Vilakazi encountered the culture of literary modernity through the institutionalisation of literature and criticism – 'Literature' – first in the mission school, then later, in the press, philanthropic organisations and universities. It seems safe to assert that the linkage of literary culture – coloured by the legacy of romanticism – and modernity was a significant feature of this generation's intellectual life. Repeating in a few compressed decades, perhaps, a history familiar in Europe, these institutions began taking over an Enlightenment tradition that had been the sole preserve of the church (as-mission). But this is to speak of only half of the encounter; equally important is to consider what African intellectuals brought to it, the prevailing constructions of African culture they inhabited, whether by circumstance or explicit affiliation. Their 'recognition' – to borrow the term used by John and Jean Comaroff to cover the range of apprehensions whereby colonised people engage with the culture of modernity – of the power of 'Literature' would have been governed by their particular circumstances, which were decisive in determining the forms of 'experimental practice' they could improvise in response.[21] The decisive aspect of these circumstances and the practices to which they gave rise was that they were profoundly split.

Intellectuals such as Dhlomo and Vilakazi moved from the poles of the urban and rural, literate and non-literate, traditional and modern, shuttling between them constantly, so much so that it would be no exaggeration to say that negotiation comprised their life's work. It is true that these oppositions constituted an historical reality; the question is how were they negotiated?[22] Far from being a choice between being authentic or being colonised, it was a choice between modes of synthesis, for the question was not whether to choose tradition or modernity, but how to put the two spheres together in a performance that best served one's interests. Dhlomo and Vilakazi, as intellectuals with roughly similar backgrounds, were united in confronting this dilemma; what divided them, as we shall see, was that they chose differently in the only choice that was really available: either to modernise tradition, or to traditionalise modernity, or at least, certain forms of modern literary culture. When in a poem such as '*Imfundo Ephakeme*' ('Higher Education'), Vilakazi contemplates the co-presence of the 'white man's books' and the praises of the 'black poets', then *'Namhla zixaben'ekhanda lami'* ('Today they quarrel in my mind') – the tension demands resolution. In Vilakazi's case, this takes the form of an injunction to write his books for the children of Zululand, but at the *behest* of the *amadlozi* (the spirits or shades), who irritate and badger him into action.[23]

### Vilakazi's poetics

'Poetry today', wrote Vilakazi, in a passage which reveals much about his poetics,

> is still but a trumpet call to those who cherish, in the midst of disillusion and despair, the ideal of intellectual and spiritual liberty, for it enables man to cultivate the philosophic mind. In other words, poetry means knowledge of the human heart in its depths, and it interprets to the world by creating a new feeling in the full of imagery and a pleasant recognition. There must be some witchery of word arrangement and selection together with the incantation of the rhythm. The writer can never forget the thrill of joy with which he recalls to mind the old man dressed in his Zulu war attire, adorned with a shining headring, reciting to the family the exploits of Zulu heroes in Shakan times, and in the midst of his narration, suddenly picking one Mvundlane kaMenziwa of the Biyela tribe and praising him. In the long praises he was always struck by one line: *uNdonga zeLungwe, ngiba ngiyazibize ziyesabela* (the echoing of the precipitous battle fields of Langwe [*sic*]). The line always brought home to my mind the echoing of the precipitous battlefields and the reverberation of the voices of herd boys I used to hear at sunset in the Valley of a Thousand Hills. The situation became real to me with the words: *Ziyesabela*.

He further recalled:

> as a college boy I was attracted by a very big church bell called 'Angelus' which rang with its mellow tone wafted over forests and mountains. I do not know why it became a habit that at 9 every Sunday we would listen to its voice with unsatisfied delight, for we could not express our feelings, until one day in a Latin class our lecturer who gloried in Classics, noticed the ringing of this bell. The sound threw him into ecstasy and he said it brought back to him his home in Germany, where, in the city cathedral, there hung a bell with this inscription: 'Vivos Voco, mortuos plango, fulgura frango.' My understanding of these lines brought me perpetual content, ever afterwards whenever I heard the toll of this Angelus. The quotation was at once connected in my mind with the old *Ngibengiyazibize, ziyasabela* [*sic*]. To my mind both these lines are great poetry. When I read them my mind is filled with pleasant recognition. I can hear the echoing broken cliffs, visualise thick forests and winding rivers.

While on the other hand on hearing the tolling of the 'Angelus' for a funeral, or, on the approaching of the storm with heavy dark clouds, a feeling of safety and relief from fear is immediately engendered by the remembrance of the 'Angelus' tolling on a Sunday morning and the people streaming to church along different winding footpaths, up and down the echoing mountains. The swinging of the bell is felt in the rhythm of the Latin composition, while the Zulu line presents a queer scanning, imitating the wafted waves of a re-echoing voice: *Ndonga zeLangwe, Ngibengiyazibize, ziyesabela*.[24]

Ndonga's praise-name merges in Vilakazi's mind with the memory of the bell Angelus, calling across the hills around the Mariannhill mission. Rhythm and place – the geography of the Drakensberg foothills – are reconstituted in such a way that the two lines reinforce one another in a collective set of associations. Vilakazi's Catholic teacher – in all probability, Mariannhill's principal, Father Bernard Huss – offered his students an impassioned aperçu, which (almost literally) resonates with an idea drawn from oral poetry, and in that (profoundly hybrid) resonance, the associations acquire form and memorability. 'Aesthetic distance' – a term Vilakazi uses – is achieved through transculturation and recollection, a combination, roughly, of oral culture, a particular cross-cultural encounter in the mission classroom, and Wordsworth's preface to the *Lyrical Ballads*.[25]

'Aesthetic pleasure', Vilakazi goes on to say, 'derived from content and rememberance, is a *psychic form*. I do not believe in *physical form*; I rely more on the *psychic* – the spirit of a poem.' Against his critics, Vilakazi asserts that he does not reduce everything to 'mechanical standards'; nevertheless, 'it is only when the genius who knows his work, plays with the *physical form* in interpreting the visions of his plastic soul, that we can have the *psychic form* revealed unspoilt in the art of poetry.'[26] The important aspect here is the *reworking*, which makes a statement oracular, beautiful and memorable, thus answerable to the 'plasticity' of the mind creating it. We can now see that Vilakazi's fondness for rhyme, together with his interest in prosody, were essentially means to an end, which was to enable Zulu writing to acquire abstraction, distance, monumentality and perfection, the qualities of modern, post-romantic aesthetics. Vilakazi hoped to modernise tradition, passing Zulu expressive forms through what he called a 'tempering' process and giving them a 'psychic form' recognisable to modern world literature.[27]

Using the mechanics of Western poetry was therefore not mere imitation. 'If we use Western stanza-forms and metrical system,' Vilakazi asserted, 'we employ them only as vehicles or receptacles for our poetic images, depicted as we see and conceive.'[28] Thus, the accession of modernity's aesthetics was not inimical to the expression of Zulu nationalist aspirations; on the contrary, it was instrumental. Comparing the famous line of the spiritual, 'Nobody knows the trouble I see' to a line from a Zulu burial song lamenting a dying warrior culture, Vilakazi says,

There is a dream in the song reflecting the Zulu mind's devastating experience, and the vanishing of his shadowy faith in war. The poet does not surrender his dream for he knows it has its counterpart when he lives by its enchantment. He has to make himself of a certain quality, to fashion himself to a certain temper . . . His dream works upon his soul and never diminishes. Even though his military faiths are wrecked. There remains one thing in which he believes without fear of disillusion, and that is the beauty of his dream.[29]

## Zulu gestalt versus tribal drama

Vilakazi drew on gestalt psychology and his ideas on psychic form to establish that a certain mental set or dreamscape is required to grasp Zulu oral poetry. Using a love poem, '*Umcayi kaVuma*' ('Vuma's daughter') as an example, he emphasised the technical elaboration of breath-units, stresses and prosody. Such a demonstration irritated Dhlomo, who used the same poem for his demonstration of the coherence of oral poetry. Dhlomo claimed that 'the tribal literary forms whose nature and construction have baffled many investigators, are in reality mutilated and distorted remains of primitive, tribal dramatic pieces'. The oral poet was 'handicapped and fettered' by traditional methods of composition and was forced to present what was, in fact, dramatic dialogue, in quasi-linear, unsuccessful monologue. Dhlomo transcribed '*Umcayi*', in English translation, into a piece of drama, with the lines being assigned to four contending characters, with movements on and offstage.[30] As was his wont, Vilakazi quickly countered in print. '*Umcayi*', he insisted, was a simple love poem, not an 'anthropologist's fallacy'.[31]

Dhlomo's ideological interest in traditional society was reinforced by his reading of the mythopoeic anthropology so favoured by literary critics of the period. His personal copy of Sir James Frazer's *The Golden Bough* was carefully annotated, from which he borrowed the idea of 'tribal drama'.[32] The 'tribal dramatist', Dhlomo remarked, was able to create great 'literary drama', modelled on the Greek and Elizabethan stages, partly because

> we live under conditions in many ways similar to those that produced great Greek dramatic literature and the immortal Elizabethan drama . . . It is a time when an old indigenous culture clashes with a newer civilisation, when tradition faces powerful exotic influences. It is a time when men suddenly become conscious of the wealth of their threatened old culture, the glories of their forefathers, the richness of their tradition, the beauty of their art and song.[33]

Dhlomo's writings on traditional drama reflected the Janus-faced orientation of all cultural nationalism: the desire for participation in a global modernity, but on the basis of an intrinsic, distinctive character.[34] The dramatist had to practise 'literary necromancy', raiding Zulu traditions to 'gather sticks to fight our literary and cultural battles, timber to build our dramatic genius, wood to make our poetic fires, leaves to decorate our achievements. *Izibongelo* [traditional poems] are the essence of our being, the meaning of our name . . . Above all they reveal the common origin, the spiritual unity, the essential Oneness, the single destiny of all Bantu tribes.'[35] Dhlomo's position reversed Vilakazi's line: to traditionalise modernity, the former argued, traditional forms needed a stamp of modern literary self-consciousness.

But Dhlomo's approach obliged him to work in a lingua franca, which could only be English, rather than isiZulu or another African language.[36] By the 1940s, he committed to publishing in 'English . . . the universal language of the future by force of commanding factors'.[37] It is possible that Dhlomo and Vilakazi held divergent positions on the language question due to differences in their mission education, with the Congregationalists of the American Board in Dhlomo's childhood more laissez-faire about the use of English than Vilakazi's Catholics teachers at Mariannhill. Mariannhill was bilingual, but the language question was foregrounded there by several disputes over the translation into isiZulu of the catechism.[38] As language assistant to Father Huss, the prolific priest at Mariannhill, Vilakazi was particularly invested in this debate, an experience that would later contribute to his being appointed as language adviser in Bantu Studies at the University of the Witwatersrand.[39] Dhlomo's drift towards English, by contrast, appears to have been confirmed for ideological reasons. In this respect, it is interesting that his brother, Rolfes, wrote mainly in isiZulu, and remained on the other side of the language debate.

Now the respective language positions of Vilakazi and Dhlomo become clear. In the *South African Outlook* essay that pricked Vilakazi, Dhlomo proposed that the repetition and parallelism of oral poetry could be maintained in English as the basis of literary poetry. Dhlomo also claimed that he had already achieved this in his own drama.[40] Vilakazi reacted by saying that it was one thing to apply 'such a purely primitive Bantu form of poetry as a criterion of a new English poetry by Bantu authors', but another to advocate 'the possibility of new Bantu forms being generated from the primitive material which is itself good poetry'.[41] This distinction crisply defines the dilemma dividing the two literary masters. The first position – deriving a theoretical criterion from oral poetry by which to develop and judge poetry in English – was Dhlomo's. Vilakazi followed by developing 'new [written] Bantu forms based on the oral material'.[42]

It is not enough to point to – much less to celebrate – a rather vaguely defined cultural 'synthesis' or 'hybridity' to characterise the choices writers of this generation were required to make. Vilakazi himself was to wrestle with suitable metaphors in describing the historic project that lay before his and subsequent generations: the new literature would be a creolised creation, 'something that has the elements of both, but which has its own Bantu life, and is yet new, harmonious, developing and integrally African'.[43]

Both strategies were neo-traditionalist, but while Vilakazi sought to build from a sense of continuity within isiZulu – since it is in the forms of this language that one hears the original speech community and imagines its survival – Dhlomo's relationship with Zulu tradition meant 'gather[ing] sticks to fight our literary and cultural battles, timber to build our dramatic genius, wood to make our poetic fires, leaves to decorate our achievements'. This statement reveals Dhlomo as assuming the position of the nation's genius, the pathfinder whose speech is uttered in conditions of relative isolation, to be understood by the people who are able to follow his call.[44] It was Dhlomo's strategy, rather than Vilakazi's, which best exemplifies Benedict Anderson's thesis that nationhood comes to fill a dizzying emptiness with heroic ideas.[45] The difficulty for these two writers was that the Zulu nation could only be imagined in conflicted terms.

Was Dhlomo's position revolutionary, Vilakazi's evolutionary? Perhaps, to some degree, but both positions carried a price. In fact, as with most rivalries, each writer needed most what the other possessed. Lewis Nkosi observes the failure of both poets 'to adapt lessons learned from English verse to their own native tradition', arguing that 'Vilakazi at least enjoyed the advantage of having written mostly in his mother tongue, with the result that however derivative his poetics it could not include the use of an exact European imagery and terminology as Dhlomo was sometimes compelled to do. Regrettably . . . lyrical "purity" is precisely what Dhlomo's poem ["Valley of a Thousand Hills"] fails to achieve.'[46]

Dhlomo's ideas of Zulu and African nationalism were thus somewhat tainted by lofty isolation. A close reading of the poem for which he is best known, 'Valley of a Thousand Hills', illustrates this point. There are good internal and contextual reasons for the poem to have acquired the reputation of being 'one of the early major poetic epics in South African literature'.[47] It is a poem of epic aspiration, from the opening section, which arranges the Zulu pantheon of gods and royal ancestors in an elaborate 'machinery' and constructs the land as fertile seedbed of a heroic history, to the final sections contrasting an idyllic past of independent communalism, a degraded present of disarray under oppression, and a resurgent future in which the glories inherent in a revered landscape will once again find political expression. The mythopoeic additions in the second edition, which were written into Dhlomo's copy of the first edition, came largely from the white anthropologist Eileen Krige, whose 1936 book, *The Social System of the Zulus*, was becoming a classic.[48] That Dhlomo's relation to his material should have been enhanced by Krige's findings is not altogether surprising, given his overall stance on Zulu cultural knowledge: 'If I could know more about Zulu custom then I could write very well but I don't know it very much. If I get the chance, I'll go around Zululand and see these old people. I think it's wrong because I haven't been to Zululand. I've been brought up in Johannesburg. Even if I've got inspiration to write sometimes I feel I cannot.'[49]

To this revelation, we might add the caveat that it is not simply a question of Vilakazi's (or anyone else's) having written more authentically in the mother tongue or with deep knowledge of natal customary idioms, since the production of literary aesthetics – in whatever language, or from whatever cultural outlook – entails an act of synthesis. Rather, it is a question of whether such a synthesis echoes a recognisable voice of the community whose interests it seeks to represent.

## Conclusion

While Vilakazi was equivocal to the end about Dhlomo's poetry, Dhlomo was more forgiving. By 1946, Dhlomo had decided to bury the hatchet, for in his review of Vilakazi's *Amal'ezulu*, he observed that the new volume 'reveals a revolutionary change or development in the poet's soul'. Previously, Vilakazi proved himself to be 'obsessed with the idea of classicism, an artist worshipping devoutly in the shrine of art for art's sake, a poet so enamoured of the beauty and music and meaning of Nature that he was oblivious of the grim tragedy, the struggle, the pathetic conditions and the call of his people'. The 'new Vilakazi' was a 'cultural Bambatha' who identified with 'the struggles of his people', and by so doing, he has 'gained in breadth, strength and stature'.[50] To argue this way, of course, is to ignore the poems in *Amal'ezulu* that are not especially militant, such as the final piece on the poet's father's death. There is also 'NgoMbuyazi eNdondakusuka', which opens up the ticklish question of Cetshwayo's assassinated brother, implying a lingering anxiety about the effects of succession disputes. In the light of the range of Vilakazi's concerns in his second collection, Dhlomo's review is somewhat overstated.

On Vilakazi's untimely death from meningitis in 1947, Dhlomo wrote an elegy ('Ichabod') recognising what previously he had denounced: 'How beautiful our native speech resounded/In the mellowed tones you weaved in Race-pride grounded.'[51] Dhlomo survived Vilakazi by ten years, dying during heart surgery in 1957. In this decade, his literary efforts were limited largely to journalism, working on *Ilanga lase Natal* with his brother, Rolfes. Both Vilakazi and Dhlomo died relatively young, and their dispute has about it a youthful assurance on both sides. But their debate was definitive, signalling the crucial ideological and aesthetic challenges which subsequent generations of African literary intellectuals would be required to face.

## Notes

1. As C.L.S. Nyembezi notes, R.R.R. (Rolfes) Dhlomo, the brother of H.I.E. (Herbert) was prominent, but he did not have the expansive vision of his brother, expressed in cultural criticism. See 'Benedict Wallet Vilakazi: A Biographical Note', in *Zulu Horizons*, B.W. Vilakazi (Johannesburg: Witwatersrand University Press, 1973), pp. xvii–xx. Born Bambatha, Vilakazi was rechristened Benedict at the Catholic Mission at Mariannhill in Pinetown. I am grateful to Adrian Koopman, Phiwe Mkhize, and Stephen Gray for their comments on an earlier version of this chapter. I am particularly grateful to Adrian Koopman for sharing with me his astute scholarship on Vilakazi.
2. Several critics mention the dispute, although not discussed in these terms. See Albert S. Gérard, *Four African Literatures: Xhosa, Sotho, Zulu, Amharic* (Berkeley and London: University of

California Press, 1971), pp. 235–36; David Johnson, *Shakespeare and South Africa* (Oxford: The Clarendon Press, 1996), pp. 133–35; Michael Chapman, *Southern African Literatures* (London and New York: Longman, 1996), pp. 213–14 and Bhekizizwe Peterson, 'Monarchs, Missionaries and African Intellectuals: Redemption and Revolution in South African Theatre, 1900–1940' (Ph.D. diss., University of the Witwatersrand, 1997), pp. 103–30. Maria K. Mootry, 'Literature and Resistance in South Africa: Two Zulu Poets', in *African Literature Today No. 7: Poetry in Africa*, ed. Eldred Jones (London: Heinemann, 1973), pp. 112–29 and Lewis Nkosi, *Tasks and Masks: Themes and Styles of African Literature* (Harlow: Longman, 1981) usefully compare the two poets.

3.  B.W. Vilakazi, *Inkondlo kaZulu*, Bantu Treasury Series No. 1 (Johannesburg: Witwatersrand University Press, [1935] 1982), p. 78. 'European critics' meant J. Dexter Taylor, whose review of *Inkondlo* mentioned this minor disagreeable note: ' "Inkondlo kaZulu" – An Appreciation', *Bantu Studies* 9 (1935): 163–65. See also Lewis Nkosi, 'Postmodernism and Black Writing in South Africa', in *Writing South Africa: Literature, Apartheid, and Democracy, 1970–1995*, eds. Derek Attridge and Rosemary Jolly (Cambridge: Cambridge University Press, 1998), p. 87.

4.  Vilakazi, *Inkondlo kaZulu*, pp. 77–81. It is not the case, as several writers assert, that after this criticism Vilakazi abandoned his efforts in rhyme in his second collection, *Amal'ezulu*. Adrian Koopman has pointed out to me the complex rhymes, *inter alia*, of the final poem, *'Sengiyakholwa'*. Also, Vilakazi was not alone in experimenting with rhyme; J.J.R. Jolobe uses rhyming couplets in his Xhosa poetry in *Umyezo*, as Vilakazi himself shrewdly notices in his Ph.D. dissertation, 'The Oral and Written Literature in Nguni' (University of the Witwatersrand, 1946), p. 29n.

5.  H.I.E. Dhlomo, 'African Drama and Poetry', *The South African Outlook*, 1 April 1939: 88.

6.  Ibid.: 89.

7.  Ibid.: 90. Gérard rightly remarks on the congruence between Dhlomo and the early Negritude scholars, at much the same time; see *Four African Literatures*, p. 239.

8.  B.W. Vilakazi, 'African Drama and Poetry', *The South African Outlook*, 1 July 1939: 166.

9.  Ibid.: 167. What we witness in the dispute – in these polemics, but also in the more sober essays and statements that surround them – is an acting out of the dilemmas facing the nationalist writer-intellectual of the day; an enactment of the ideological and aesthetic difficulties confronting writers in what Bhekizizwe Peterson calls 'the poetics of the crossroads' (see 'Monarchs, Missionaries and African Intellectuals', p. 103).

10. Taylor, ' "Inkondlo kaZulu" ': 164. Aggrey's visit to South Africa under the auspices of the Phelps-Stokes Trust in 1921 had, according to Tim Couzens, 'caused a sensation'; Aggrey's message of inter-racial co-operation was warmly appreciated by the liberal intelligentsia of the day, both black and white. See Tim Couzens, *The New African: A Study of the Life and Work of H.I.E. Dhlomo* (Johannesburg: Ravan Press, 1985), pp. 82–85.

11. Vilakazi, 'Oral and Written Literature', p. 348.

12. Ibid., p. 25.

13. Ibid., p. 26.

14. Ibid., p. 321.

15. Couzens, *The New African*, pp. 102–06. Tim Couzens, David Johnson, Leon de Kock and Bhekizizwe Peterson all document different aspects of this debate. Kwame Anthony Appiah traces the genealogy of the linkage of race and literature: see *In My Father's House: Africa in the Philosophy of Culture* (London: Methuen, 1992), pp. 74–78.

16. The Carnegie intervention and the founding of *The Critic* was motivated by a commissioned report that found 'there is no English critical periodical in the Union and no belletristic periodical of any value': see H.A. Reyburn, 'Prologue', *The Critic* 1:1 (September 1932): 1. Couzens describes the public discussion that led to the BMSC as the 'moralising leisure time'; see *The New African*, pp. 105, 110. At the second of the 'Bantu authors' conferences, Vilakazi was appointed to a committee to explore the feasibility of a literature 'Bureau' under the auspices of the Inter-University Committee for African Studies and the Christian Council.

17. See Couzens, *The New African*, p. 105.

18. Vilakazi, 'Oral and Written Literature', p. 364. In so far as Dhlomo and Vilakazi regarded orality as falling within the purview of literary history and criticism, they sought to extend the reach of what constituted literature in a sense not current at the time. Overwhelmingly, studies of oral tradition were ethnographic rather than treated as art in the post-romantic sense. Declining the ethnographic emphasis was therefore part of their achievement: see B.W. Vilakazi, 'Some Aspects of Zulu Literature', *African Studies* (cont. of *Bantu Studies*) 1 (1942): 270.

19. Couzens, *The New African*, pp. 125–34.

20. H.I.E. Dhlomo, *Collected Works*, eds. Nick Visser and Tim Couzens (Johannesburg: Ravan Press, 1985), p. 377.

21. Jean and John Comaroff, *Of Revelation and Revolution: Christianity, Colonialism, and Consciousness in South Africa* (Chicago and London: University of Chicago Press, 1991), pp. 29–31.

22. By the 1930s, rural (traditional) or indigenous life – the source of what we like to call Africanity – did not exist in a space free of the history of colonial rule; it had been subject, not only to encroachment, but also to administrative control – certainly in the case of Natal and Zululand – for nearly half a century. The general character of this control has again inspired lively debate, following Mahmood Mamdani's study of late-colonial modernity, *Citizen and Subject: Contemporary Africa and the Legacy of Late Colonialism* (Kampala: Fountain Publishers, Cape Town: David Philip and London: James Currey, 1996). Mamdani's thesis is that the British colonial authorities and after 1910, the South African state (Union government), consistently constructed and maintained a bifurcated world, with the rights of citizens within the framework of civil society being distinguished from the rights of communities living under customary law and traditional authority. Mamdani does not position these modes of power in a linear, developmental relationship: both were part of the armory of late-colonial modernity, which instituted racially exclusive democracy at the centre (largely for whites, settlers, or 'colons') and decentralised despotism at the periphery, largely for the black peasantry. Between these groups fell 'urban-based natives, mainly middle- and working-class persons, who were exempt from the lash of customary law but not from modern, racially discriminatory civil legislation. Neither subject to customs nor exalted as rights-bearing citizens, they languished in a juridical limbo.' (*Citizen and Subject*, p. 19). There is a pressing question whether 'limbo' was only juridical. The potential confusion here is whether individuals of the middle zone – by definition, where the intellectuals would belong – reside entirely within a sphere, or whether they inhabit both, as 'citizens' and 'subjects'. Presumably, Mamdani is implying the latter, but if so, do the poles of their experience remain permanently sealed off from one another, 'barricaded', in Mamdani's terms?

23. B.W. Vilakazi, *Amal'ezulu*, Bantu Treasury Series No. 8 (Johannesburg: Witwatersrand University Press, [1945] 1980), pp. 7–8.

24. Vilakazi, 'Oral and Written Literature', pp. 28–29.

25. Ibid., p. 30. In his poem, '*Izinsimbi Zesonto*', Vilakazi would ascribe a related meaning to the mission bells of his youth, in which, having once signalled conquest, they come to herald a 'bright new world' led by men such as Albert Luthuli, A.W.G. Champion, and John Dube.

26. Vilakazi, 'Oral and Written Literature', p. 29.

27. B.W. Vilakazi, 'The Conception and Development of Poetry in Zulu', reprinted from *Bantu Studies* 12: 105–34 in *Foundations of Southern African Oral Literature*, ed. Russell H. Kaschula (Johannesburg: Witwatersrand University Press, 1993), p. 83.

28. Ibid., p. 77.

29. Ibid., pp. 83–84.

30. H.I.E. Dhlomo, 'Nature and Variety of Tribal Drama', reprinted from *Bantu Studies* 13: 33–48 in *Foundations of Southern African Oral Literature*, p. 187.

31. Vilakazi, 'Oral and Written Literature', p. 94.

32. Couzens, *The New African*, pp. 161, 190n.

33. H.I.E. Dhlomo, 'Why Study Tribal Dramatic Forms?' reprinted from *Transvaal Native Education Quarterly* March 1939: 20–24 in *English in Africa* 4:2 (September 1977): 41.

34. In his late, unpublished essay, 'Reflections on the Circle in Zulu Life and Thought' (planned as part of a monograph entitled *Zulu Life and Thought*, unpublished manuscript, Campbell Collections, University of Natal, Durban, KCM 8266), Dhlomo was wrestling with the same tension. The circle represents Africanity, the square, the European mind, but the emphasis is not on permanent difference, since each figure captures aspects of a complex and dynamic reality.

35. Dhlomo, 'Why Study Tribal Dramatic Forms?': 37. A parallel dilemma was being played out by liberal segregationists who debated the relative merits of 'adaptionist' and 'assimilationist' policies. With cultural relativism coming into prominence over earlier Victorian notions of spreading universal civilisation, segregationism could present itself as concerned with the survival of authentic identities. Beneath such sentiments lay anxieties about the aspirations of upwardly mobile middle-class Africans, and class-based mobilisation amongst proletarianised Africans, fears articulated by white Natal

segregationist Heaton Nicholls: 'The adaptionist policy . . . assumes what is in effect the growth of a national consciousness amongst the Abantu themselves . . . the opposite policy of assimilation substitutes class for race, and if continued on its present basis must lead to the evolution of a native proletariat, inspired by the usual antagonisms of class war': Peterson, 'Monarchs, Missionaries and African Intellectuals', p. 112.

36. It is true that in the late 1930s Dhlomo supported the idea of the development of 'Union' languages – Nguni, Sotho, Venda, Thonga – each of which would represent a cluster of related languages, an idea widely discussed by linguists, anthropologists, missionaries and administrators. For Dhlomo's own purposes, the advantages of such a scheme seemed clear: 'First, there would be the blend of the genius of each racial group resulting in the greater genius of the nation. Second, there would be a richer field of tradition, folklore and ideas. Third, African literature would enjoy a wider circle of readers. Fourth, it would lead to the establishment of a national school of African Drama': H.I.E. Dhlomo, 'Language and National Drama', reprinted from *The New Outlook*, March 1939: 8–11 in *English in Africa* 4:2 (September 1977): 9. But since the Union languages scheme had little practical chance of success, and since English would accomplish most of these goals more effectively than Union languages anyway, Dhlomo was to fall back on the use of English.

37. Peterson, 'Monarchs, Missionaries and African Intellectuals', pp. 84, 225.

38. Ibid., pp. 85–94.

39. Nyembezi, 'Benedict Wallet Vilakazi', p. xviii.

40. Dhlomo, 'African Drama and Poetry': 89. In the *English in Africa* collection of Dhlomo's essays, this point is omitted from the original. I am quoting the original version from *South African Outlook*.

41. Vilakazi, 'Oral and Written Literature', pp. 276–77.

42. Ibid., p. 372.

43. Ibid. Vilakazi would assert further: 'What future literature needs is not a compromise between the old and the new ideas, but a fusion, as it were; not a mixture but an amalgam. The virile elements of both African and Western cultures must fuse and give birth to a new life, expressed in a new literature.'

44. Dhlomo, 'Why Study Tribal Dramatic Forms?': 40.

45. Benedict Anderson, *Imagined Communities: Reflections on the Origin and Spread of Nationalism* (London and New York: Verso, [1983] 1991), p. 24.

46. Nkosi, *Tasks and Masks*, p. 115.

47. Couzens, *The New African*, p. 220.

48. Ibid., p. 243.

49. Ibid., p. 352.

50. Ibid., pp. 220–21. Bambatha was Vilakazi's given name, which he shared with a celebrated chief who rebelled against the Natal colony in 1906. See also H.I.E. Dhlomo, 'Three Famous Authors I Knew – B.W. Vilakazi', *Inkundla YaBantu* 9:122 (August 1946). Dhlomo maintains this reading in his 'Masterpiece in Bronze' essay on Vilakazi in *Drum* 2:7 (July 1952).

51. Dhlomo, *Collected Works*, p. 352.

## Further reading

Cary, Joyce. 1947. *Mister Johnson*. London: Joseph.

De Kock, Leon. 1996. *Civilising Barbarians: Missionary Narrative and African Textual Response in Nineteenth Century South Africa*. Johannesburg: Witwatersrand University Press and Alice: Lovedale Press.

Koopman, Adrian. 1980. 'Aspects of the *Isangoma* in the Poetry of B.W. Vilakazi', *Theoria* 55 (October): 1–19.

Lestrade, G.P. 1935. 'Bantu Praise-Poems', *The Critic* 4:1 (October): 1–10.

Ndebele, Njabulo. 1983. *Fools and Other Stories*. Johannesburg: Ravan Press.

Ngwenya, Thengani. 1998. 'B.W. Vilakazi: The Poet as Inspired Prophet', *Alternation* 5:2: 127–46.

Ntuli, D.B.Z. 1984. *The Poetry of B.W. Vilakazi*. Pretoria: Van Schaik.

Ntuli, D.B. and C.F. Swanepoel. 1993. *Southern African Literature in African Languages: A Concise Historical Perspective*. Pretoria: Acacia Books.

Richards, I.A. [1924] 1994. *Principles of Literary Criticism*. London: Kegan Paul, Trench, Trubner & Co.

Vail, Leroy and Landeg White. 1991. *Power and the Praise Poem*. Charlottesville: University of Virginia Press.

Vilakazi, B.W. 1973. *Zulu Horizons*. Translations of *Inkondlo kaZulu* and *Amal'ezulu* by D. McK. Malcolm, J. Mandlenkosi Sikakana and Florence Louie Friedman. Johannesburg: Witwatersrand University Press.

Williams, Raymond. [1958] 1963. *Culture and Society: 1780–1950*. Harmondsworth: Penguin.

*Chapter 40*

# Cry, The Beloved Country
## A Murder in Alan Paton's Country, 1999[1]

JONNY STEINBERG

IN THE EARLY summer of 1999, I travelled to the southern Midlands of KwaZulu-Natal to investigate a story – the murder of a white farmer's son. The research ended up taking more than a year to complete.[2] While I was in the Midlands, it was difficult not to think of Alan Paton's novel *Cry, The Beloved Country*, for there were a number of striking parallels between the murder that I was investigating and the murder that is the subject of Paton's book. In both narratives, the victim was the son of a white southern Midlands farmer, the alleged perpetrator a son of Zulu peasant stock. In both, a young Zulu man was to die in retribution, at the hands of whites. And, in both stories, the unfolding relationship between the two surviving fathers was to prove significant. Paton published his book in 1948.

I read *Cry, The Beloved Country* twice during the course of my research, and the reading of it was a haunting experience. I sensed that Paton would have been unsurprised by the murder that I was investigating; that he had, in fact, almost foretold it. For, despite the evangelical moment of reconciliation with which *Cry, The Beloved Country* concludes, it is, ultimately, about the unthreading of a fabric of civility and order, about the dawn of an age in which scores are settled by the gun as a matter of course.

And yet at another level, I must confess that I found Paton's book irritatingly flawed. *Cry, The Beloved Country* is a eulogy to a dying Zulu tradition. The murder at the heart of his book is a symptom of this other murder, this other dying, of a traditional culture. Paton cannot see that anything good will come of this destruction. The post-traditional world he forecasts is bleak and murderous.

During the year I spent in the Midlands, I searched in vain for any vestige of Paton's romantic Zulu tribalism. I could not find it in archives or scholarly works, nor in the oral histories presented by the people of the southern Midlands. Instead, I found evidence of a long history of destruction and alienation. Paton's traditional idyll is little more than a fantasy. To truly understand the 1999 murder, there is a sense in which one must put his work aside.

**The murder of Peter Mitchell**

The man to whom I have given the name 'Peter Mitchell' was shot to death in the middle of an afternoon in October 1999 on the dirt track that runs from his father's farmhouse to his irrigation fields. He was 28 years old. It was clear at once that the killing was a premeditated execution. While the killers took the dead man's gun, they left everything else, including a wallet full of cash. They had clearly scoured the bush on either side of the dirt track; they picked a spot where the bush grows tall, right up against the roadside, where a man can stand at full height, unseen, with a clear view of his victim. On the morning of the killing, the murderers had walked a good 4 kilometres (2.5 miles) through a dense labyrinth of footpaths in order to get to the scene of the ambush. They had waited there, probably for more than two hours.

The father of the dead man, whom I have called 'Arthur Mitchell', knew immediately what the killing of his son was about. The morning after the murder, he went down to a derelict and informal shop called the Tea Room, patronised by the male tenants on his newly acquired farm Normandale. He wanted to tell the men he knew the murderers were among them. But he found the Tea Room deserted. For the first time in months, it was closed; the men were nowhere to be seen.

To understand what was going through Arthur Mitchell's mind as he went down to the Tea Room on the morning after his son's death, it is necessary to backtrack eight months, to February 1999. At that time, Mitchell owned two farms in the district: Eleanor, on which he lived and farmed beef, and Derbytin, where he grew tomatoes and cabbages. Wedged between Eleanor and Derbytin was a farm called Normandale, owned by a man that I have called 'Laurie Steyn'. Steyn, who had farmed Normandale for three decades, put the farm on the market some time in 1998. He had said he was leaving because 'crime in the area was becoming too extreme'.

While it is true that there was a great deal of crime in the district, Steyn's explanation was something of a euphemism. At the bottom of his farm, Normandale, was a settlement of nine homesteads called Langeni, where the farm tenants lived. The truth of the matter is that by the end of 1998, members of Langeni had pushed Steyn off his land. First, a fence came down. It was not stolen, just left on the side of the road. Then portions of his fields were burnt at night. A year before he left, his foreman, who lived in a caravan in the darkness of the farm, was shot in the ribs while watching television. A little later, Steyn's son was shot at one night outside his front door.

When Steyn first put his farm on the market, Mitchell was not interested in buying. However, when it became clear that Steyn was going to leave anyway, and that Normandale would lie empty, he bought. And for one reason: he did not want a piece of unmanaged land on his border. He wanted a buffer zone between his farming operation and the lives of Steyn's erstwhile tenants. So he bought Steyn's land in

February 1999 and he called a meeting with his new tenants to lay down his rules of tenancy.

He spoke through a Zulu translator. The tenants listened sullenly until Mitchell got to the rule that stated that he needed a list of names of everybody who lived in Langeni. At that point, a tenant, whom I shall call 'Mashabana', whose family had been living in Langeni since before Laurie Steyn's time, stood up and advised his co-tenants not to give *umlungu*, the white man, their names. He said that the white man would use the information against them. Mitchell called off the meeting.

In the months following the February encounter, Mitchell was subjected to the same treatment dished out to Steyn before him. Fences were torn down. A field was torched. A cottage on one of his farms burnt to the ground. On two occasions, Mitchell was threatened and provoked as he drove past his property on the district road. Once, the tenant who had stood up against him at the meeting, Mashabana, pulled a section of Mitchell's fence out of the ground as he drove past and invited Mitchell to have him arrested. On another occasion, three of Mitchell's tenants, the Cube brothers, stopped him on the road and demanded threateningly that he build a dirt track linking their home with the regional artery.

In August, Mitchell called a second meeting with his tenants. Once again, when he got to the part about taking names, Mashabana stood up and railed against him. This time, Mitchell responded by reading Mashabana an eviction notice. The meeting ended in acrimony.

Six weeks after the August meeting, Peter Mitchell was killed. His father had little doubt that the murder was a final, lethal tactic to remove him from his land.

### The missing motive

I arrived on the scene about three months after the murder. Getting to talk to some of the tenants who had attended the two meetings with Mitchell was slow and painstaking. The killing was, and has remained, to this day, unsolved.[3] There was a great deal of tension in the air, a great deal of suspicion about the motives of strangers. When people did finally agree to speak, they did so on condition of anonymity, and they spoke with extreme caution.

What they said was puzzling. I was told that Mitchell was killed because of his father's rules. Two, in particular, were mentioned. Firstly, when a Langeni tenant wants to build an extension to his property, he must seek Mr Mitchell's permission. Mr Mitchell will personally come down to Langeni to see whether the extension is necessary. If it is because a child has been born, or a son has married, that is fine. If it is for a stranger, it is not fine. 'Why is that offensive?' I asked. My question was greeted with amazement. 'The man is saying you cannot give birth without him examining the size of your wife's stomach,' I was told. 'You cannot bring a man or a woman into your household without the white *baas* coming down to examine the marriage papers. If the white man says no, where must the newborn baby sleep – on the roof? Where must the newly-weds conceive their first child – in their parents' bed? The white man decides these things.'

The second offensive rule was that each tenant family could keep a maximum of five head of cattle. 'Why is this rule offensive?' I asked. 'There are two ways of dying from poverty,' I was told. 'The first is when you have no food. The second is when you have no cattle and your sons cannot marry. They will have children, but the little ones will not be your grandchildren. They are vagrants, human beings with no ancestry. And then you have died because your family has died. You have disgraced everyone who came before you.'

I can see how these rules might have been offensive, but the fact of their offensiveness does not begin to explain the murder. They were, in fact, entirely orthodox rules and Mitchell was an orthodox farmer. The stipulation limiting each family to five head of cattle had been standard in the district for at least three generations, possibly longer. And the building extension rule was a stipulation typical of the old paternalist ethos that had developed in the southern Midlands in the late nineteenth century. For generations, farmers of the southern Midlands had used the labour of black people who lived on their farms. Much of the workers' wages was paid in kind. Farmers would build crèches and sports facilities and underwrite the maintenance of a local farm school. They would offer interest-free credit for hospital bills, pay for coffins and funerals. They would allow their tenants to plough small patches of land and keep limited quantities of livestock. But, in exchange, they exerted absolute control over the social life that took place on their properties. They told their tenants where they could build, where they could bury their dead, collect their firewood and draw their water. They regulated movement in and out of the tenant homesteads, decreeing who could sleep there and who ought to be removed. Above all, they could evict a tenant at a moment's notice, denying him, not only his job, but also his land, his children's education and his expectation of a comfortable old age.

Generations of labour tenants, denied the right to land ownership under successive white minority governments and, for one reason or another, expelled from communal and tribal land, abided by this quid pro quo. They did so in a complicated manner. They never thought the situation just, but they believed it would last forever. They resisted it passively, defying the territorial markers set down by whites in insouciant ways. For instance, tenants would make a point of hunting game on white-owned farmland. Tenant-owned cows would be let onto white-owned grazing land. Boundary fences would be moved overnight. These were subtle registers of resistance: they were a million miles from frontal rebellion. What had changed in the 1990s? Why had the laying down of a set of rules, over which nobody had died during the course of several generations, culminated in the murder of a white farmer's son?

The answer has a great deal to do with the things that worried Alan Paton. It has to do with the life experiences of the last two generations of Midlands labour tenants, experiences utterly foreign to their forebears, but which Paton may well have predicted.

The great bogeyman of *Cry, The Beloved Country* is the city. The mid-century Natal Midlands that Paton describes is hollowing out. The reserves into which his fictional amaZulu have been shepherded are too small to contain and feed their populations. Young adults are moving in droves to Johannesburg, and they do not return. Those who remain on the land struggle to eke out a living.

The protagonist of *Cry, The Beloved Country*, a Midlands pastor by the name of Stephen Kumalo, travels to Johannesburg in search of his scattered family. His brother, John, his sister, Gertrude, and his son, Absolom, have been swallowed up by the big city. Kumalo's first few days in Johannesburg constitute the most powerful moment of *Cry, the Beloved Country*. It is not so much the vastness of the city that captures our attention, but the sense that things are awry. The Johannesburg Paton describes is deluged by waves of first-generation rural migrants. They cluster together in the newly formed 'Shanty Town', in what would soon become Soweto and in the backyards of the freehold houses of Alexandra. Freeholders are forced, by economic circumstance, to let rooms in their houses to strangers – young men who ogle at their daughters, single women who eye their husbands. Everyone inhabits everybody else's space, but there are no settled rules of engagement; there is a mass of humanity on the one hand, and a sense of mutual estrangement, on the other hand.

Outside Park station, Kumalo is confronted by a beguiling man who offers him help and then cons him out of money. In Shanty Town, he meets his long-lost brother, John, a successful businessman steeped in slippery urban politics. John, who disregards isiZulu and prefers to speak English, has cheated on his wife, lost touch with his son and failed to rescue his own sister, Gertrude, who lost her moral compass and has become a prostitute. Most harrowing of all, Kumalo's son, Absolom, has killed a prominent white man in his own home and is to stand trial for murder. Kumalo feels 'deep down the fear of a man who lives in a world not made for him, whose own world is slipping away, dying, being destroyed, beyond any recall'.[4]

### Paton as commentator on the Mitchell killing

What has happened to both the city and the countryside in the half-century since Paton wrote his book was not precisely prefigured in *Cry, The Beloved Country*, but it certainly would not have surprised Paton. Practically every member of the last two generations of homestead cultivators and farm workers has migrated to the cities in early adulthood, swearing they would never return. They have quickly discovered that urban South Africa treats newcomers from the hinterland like dirt. They have settled on the periphery of the metropolis, making homes in tin shacks alongside acquisitive, untrustworthy neighbours, fruitlessly seeking work. Many have ended up returning to their rural homes again and again during the course of their failed lives; they are drifters, not urban, no longer rural, scavenging what they can from both the cities and the rural villages.

This is the social context of Peter Mitchell's murder. The Cubes and the Mashabanas, the two families most vocal in their opposition to Arthur Mitchell's proprietorship of Normandale, were both led by men in their late thirties and early forties. The three Cube brothers and Mashabana were born in the local district in the early and mid-1960s. They grew up as the sons of labour tenants, attended local farm schools, and worked for men like Mitchell on weekends and during school holidays. In their late teens, they all migrated to Durban and Pietermaritzburg. All four found employment at a single butchery. They experienced the city at its roughest and most acquisitive. Mashabana and one of the Cubes found themselves behind the urban barricades during the uprisings of the mid-1980s. Living on the margins of urban life, they also came into contact with the fast-growing contraband economy through which many of the urban periphery moved and earned livelihoods. In Alan Paton's imagination, such men abandon their ancestral homes and are never seen again in the villages where they were once boys. But this is not how things turned out. The city does not ingest migrants; it hurls them back into the countryside, where they impart urban ways.

No wonder that the rules Arthur Mitchell laid down at the side of the district road next to Langeni were greeted with such hostility. The puzzle of why a set of stipulations that had been accepted in generations past were now rejected, is not difficult to explain. The tragedy is that Mitchell was entirely unaware that he was laying down rules for the ears of a generation that was long dead. The men who heard his rules were light years from their parents and grandparents, who had been archetypal stoics. They had listened to the white man impassively, then retreated into their shells and negotiated the world from there. But their children, the Cubes and Mashabanas of 1999, were anything but stoics. They brought back to their ancestral homes both the political aggressiveness and the personal stubbornness of the city. They were not going to abide by the old quid pro quo of Midlands paternalism. They were going to grab what they could.

It is tempting to read poetic justice into the story. Smug white farmers lay down their paternalist rules as if they are still living in the heyday of apartheid, and they think they can get away with it. But they can't. Unlike them, their tenants have smelt the fragrance of post-apartheid South Africa. They sweep away the old paternalism for the distasteful relic it is. But things are not that simple, nor that agreeable. The end of apartheid has failed men such as the Cubes and the Mashabanas, and has, in all probability, made them more brutal. Few of the promises of the late 1980s have been fulfilled. In the countryside, they are still the sons of labour tenants and still asked to abide by the rules of white paternalists. In the city, they are still marginals, getting by through their own resourcefulness and ingenuity. I would imagine that the things they have seen since the end of apartheid have extinguished many of their hopes. I believe that the manner in which they live their lives has become more atomistic, more acquisitive. They are members of a swelling generation who believe that if they do not fend for themselves, nobody will; a generation who take what they can, any way they can.

Therein lies the lasting message of Alan Paton. He observed the growing anomie of twentieth-century South Africa. He understood that the great demographic movements of the mid-century were deeply inhospitable to human community. He knew that a political settlement, no matter how successful, no matter how carefully crafted, would never entirely erase the ugly legacies of his time.

### Paton the nostalgist

Yet there is also a less impressive aspect of *Cry, The Beloved Country*, which bothered me while I was researching the events around the murder of Peter Mitchell. It begins with Paton's depiction of Kumalo's home village, Ndotsheni, and widens into his entire prognosis for twentieth-century South Africa. Although it is written in English, Paton has us understand that when the isiZulu-speaking characters in the book converse with one another, they are speaking in isiZulu. What we are reading is an imagined translation. Paton pays close attention to the diction of his characters, marking their English with its isiZulu origin. For instance, when Kumalo is on his Johannesburg-bound train, and a fellow traveller describes to him the process of mining gold, his description runs thus: 'We go down and dig it out, umfundisi. And when it is hard to dig, we go away, and the white men blow it out with the fire-sticks. Then . . . we load it on to the trucks and it goes up in a cage, up a long chimney so long that I cannot say it for you.'[5]

Commenting on this passage in an essay on Paton, J.M. Coetzee points to the words 'fire-sticks', 'chimney' and 'go away'. 'The reader cannot be blamed for concluding', Coetzee writes, 'that Zulu lacks words for the concepts dynamite, shaft, take cover, that the speaker is using the best approximations his language provides, and that Paton has given literal translations of these approximations. In fact, this conclusion is quite false,' Coetzee continues. 'The Zulu for mine shaft is *umgodi*, a word quite distinct from *ushimula* (chimney in Zulu), whose English origin is clear. The word for dynamite, again in English origin, is *udalimede*, which has nothing to do with fire-sticks. *Banda*, take cover, is clearly distinguished from *suka*, go away.'[6] What is this faux-isiZulu diction about? 'The archaism of the English', Coetzee remarks a little later, 'implies an archaic quality to the Zulu behind it', as if the Zulu language, culture, and frame of mind, belonged to a bygone era.

> In its . . . preference for parable over abstraction, Paton's Zulu appears to belong to an earlier and more innocent era in human culture. From the fact that Kumalo's politician brother prefers to use English, the reader may further surmise that Zulu is as inhospitable to lies and deception as it is to complexity

and abstraction . . . [Paton's Zulu tells us that his characters] belong in an old-fashioned context of direct personal relations based on respect, obedience and fidelity.[7]

*Cry, The Beloved Country* is littered with linguistic oddities that give the impression of quaintness and innocence. An electrically powered train is described as a vehicle 'taking power from the metal ropes stretched overhead'.[8] Johannesburg itself is 'a great city with so many streets they say a man can spend his days going up one and down another, and never the same one twice'.[9] In describing a journey Kumalo takes through Ndotsheni, Paton writes, 'but at the first fork you go to the side of the hand that you eat with'.[10]

What is the purpose of Paton's faux-setting? When Kumalo returns from his trip to Johannesburg, and walks through Ndotsheni at sunset,

> . . . there is a calling here, and in the dusk one voice calls to another in some far distant place. If you are a Zulu you can hear what they say, but if you are not, even if you know the language, you would find it hard to know what is being called. Some white men call it magic, but it is no magic, only an art perfected. It is Africa, the beloved country.[11]

Paton is attempting to conjure something beautifully antiquarian. It is a world in which people communicate directly, by the unmediated sound of their own voices, and the things they have to say are gentle and nourishing. He seems to suggest that we, the readers, irretrievably tainted as we are by our submersion in the modern, would not understand these voices, even if we understood isiZulu. He suggests that the idyll he invokes is already lost, that it exists beyond the phenomenological registers of the modern world.

Like many pastoral fantasies, Paton's conjured place has no particular moral content. It contains women who mother with love and pastors who minister with care. It is a world best summed up in the homespun dictums of Mrs Lethebe, Kumalo's landlady for the duration of his stay in Johannesburg. When Kumalo asks Mrs Lethebe whether she will give shelter to the young girl pregnant with his grandchild, and when Mrs Lethebe assents, Kumalo thanks her. 'Mother, I am grateful. You are indeed a mother to me.' 'Why else do we live?' she replies.[12]

Against this background, one has less sympathy for Paton's pessimism. For one wonders whether he despairs of the debris of white domination, or bemoans the coming of the twentieth century. *Cry, the Beloved Country* sits firmly in a literary tradition of romantic conservatism. It finds its counterpart in an old and now quite antiquated strand of Tory thinking in England, which harks back longingly to feudal times. Nothing good can come of the modern era; the reservoirs of value all lie in the past.

**Life on the margins**

It is particularly unfortunate that Paton chose the southern Midlands as the receptacle of his fantasy. A sober reading of the region's history over the last 180 years reveals a portrait of fitful violence and dislocation. Indeed, in 1999, it seemed prudent to place the murder of Peter Mitchell in this long and unhappy history.

According to many of the white farmers I met near the Mitchell home, the district's past isn't even 180 years old. They claim that when the voortrekkers abandoned the eastern Cape frontier and arrived in the southern Midlands in 1837, they found it empty. The amaZulu only began to move up from the coast in the mid-to-late nineteenth century, white farmers told me, once the voortrekkers had left for the Transvaal, and British expatriates began to farm and offer wage labour opportunities.

In all myths of origin, there is a small grain of truth. The voortrekkers did leave the eastern Cape frontier in large streams during the 1830s. But when they arrived in the southern Midlands in 1837, they found thousands of people between the Umkomaas and Mzimkhulu Rivers. They were living strange and disturbed lives. The valleys and the grasslands, where you would expect to find pastoral settlements, had been evacuated. There were skeletons of former villages; their one-time occupants had scattered into small groups and dwelled in broken or forested country, living off edible roots and tiny patches of crops. They dared not rebuild permanent infrastructures or keep cattle in any numbers; the area was violent, and any permanent infrastructure would have to be defended.

The voortrekkers had stumbled into the aftermath of a period of great flux in southern African history: the upheaval that historians once referred to as the *mfecane*. More than 200 kilometres (125 miles) north of the ground on which Peter Mitchell was killed, dozens of chiefdoms had been displaced by warfare and were moving south. The Thembu, the Chunu, the Macaba chiefs, along with other rulers, had fled with their followers and crossed the Thukela River, making their way south. These people on the run had nothing – they had left the infrastructure of social life behind them – and they rebuilt by devastating the settlements they met on the way. They brought with them the violence and plunder from which they had escaped, and by the late 1820s, the southern Midlands was in turmoil.

The surnames of Normandale's tenants bear testimony to the fact that their forebears were in the thick of those ugly times. The Mashabanas, for instance, came from an amaWushe chiefdom that claimed the area around present-day Howick 200 years ago. They were pushed south in the 1820s, as Thembu and Chunu claimed Wushe land. The Mabhidas, another old tenant family at Normandale, fled from the Zulu kingdom to Natal in a 1830s exodus, after the Zulu regent Dingane killed their chief. The mid-nineteenth century forebears of the Normandale tenants were the sons and daughters of refugees. They found themselves wedged between an expansionist Zulu kingdom and intruding colonial powers – comprised first of voortrekker parties, then British settlers.[13]

By the 1840s, black communities in the southern Midlands were living on land recently annexed by the queen of England and English officials based in the Cape Colony. In Peter Mitchell's district, isiZulu-speaking cultivators and pastoralists resided on territory bought by London speculators investing in the Natal Land and Colonisation Company. Until late in the nineteenth century, this foreign ownership was merely nominal. Black communities worked the properties while whites held the title deeds. But in the early 1880s, the Natal Land and Colonisation Company started to sell large plots to aspirant settler farmers. In places like the hamlet I have called Sarahdale, where the Mitchells farm today, black people were evicted shortly after the turn of the century. Those that remained were to become the first generation of black labour tenants engaged in that precarious and complicated quid pro quo with white farmers. This was the fate of the great-grandparents of Normandale's current tenants.

There is a danger in reading a single action in the present – in this case, the murder of Peter Mitchell – against the backdrop of a tortuous past. The danger is one of reading motives and feelings in the here and now as if they were merely the sediments left by generations of previous experience. Nonetheless, I was struck by the nineteenth-century history of the southern Midlands and pondered the 180 years of creeping marginalisation endured by Normandale tenants.

When I spoke to white farmers about labour tenancy, most had the same response. They said that the tenants of white farmers in the southern Midlands were the lucky ones, that they were something of an aristocracy. Those stuck in 'tribal' homeland areas inhabited overcrowded land. Unemployment in some places reached the 80 per cent mark. Crime was rife. Tenants on white-owned farms, in contrast, had secure jobs. They could graze some cattle and plant crops. Their children could attend farm schools, and their hospital bills would be paid. Once they retired, they had a place to grow old.

Yet when I began to talk to people in the surrounding black communities and mission reserves, they told a different story. They did not regard tenants with envy, but instead, with something bordering on pity and scorn. An old man I interviewed who lived in Izita, the mission across the road from Normandale, laughed when I told him that the whites regarded their tenants as an aristocracy. 'We people who lived on tribal land were always free to move to the city and run our homes as we wished,' he told me. 'The tenants, those poor people were always forced to work on the land in order to keep their homes. And the white landlord controlled every corner of their lives. An aristocracy,' he laughed. 'No, those people are serfs.'

The Normandale tenants seemed to be the marginals among marginals, a pitied underclass among the descendants of refugees. They don't know why their forebears found themselves on white-owned rather than tribal land. The inherited memories of the Normandale tenants I spoke to only went back three generations; most of their families had been tenants for as long as they could remember.

The case of the Cubes is particularly telling. They fought the Mitchells more tenaciously than any of the other Normandale tenants. One of them, Mduduzi Cube, was arrested for Peter Mitchell's murder and then released. The detectives handling the Mitchell case shot dead his twenty-year-old son, Bheki, in suspicious circumstances.

Tracing the Cube's ancestry, I discovered something odd. In the case of other Normandale tenants, like the Mashabanas and the Mabhidas, it was quite easy to discover why they had found themselves living in the southern Midlands; their forebears had been displaced from north of the Thukela River during early-nineteenth-century Zulu expansionism. But the story of the Cubes is more mysterious. The amaCubeni clan had never migrated south of the Thukela. Their forebears were ironworkers, an invaluable skill exploited by warring chiefs in the 1820s. The forested division of Nkandla on the north side of the Thukela is where Cube artisans made battle weapons. Powerful Zulu elites courted and shielded them. Why, then, had some Cube people given up this privileged position to migrate south?

I visited the Nkandla stronghold of the amaCubeni to find out. I met with a group of old men and women and asked them questions about their history. They, too, were perplexed about why a Cube family had ventured so far south. They said they recalled a time in the 1920s when a fairly large group of Cubes was expelled and settled near Pietermaritzburg, but these refugees could not have been the Cubes of Normandale, for they had been in the south at the very least since the late nineteenth century. The Cube elders concluded that there must have been a scandal way back in the past; perhaps a man or a family was forced to move after offending somebody powerful. He, or they, must have drifted south and lost touch with the amaCubeni core.

When I told the gathering that the last three generations of the Cubes of Normandale had been tenants on white-owned farms, some of the old people shook their heads sagely, displaying a sense of pity. I then told them about the murder; that one Cube had been arrested for it and another killed for it, and the gathering fell silent. Like a group of aristocrats who shake their heads at the news that someone of their kin has slipped through the cracks and ended up a commoner, they meditated on the fate of these forlorn Cubes. And then I left and the old people probably forgot about their kinfolk in the southern Midlands.

It is tempting to place the murder of Peter Mitchell in the rubric of a history that Alan Paton did not tell. Perhaps the genesis of the murder is to be situated long before apartheid, perhaps before the Union of South Africa in 1910. In 1994, in the corner of the Midlands where Mitchell was killed, political power had just changed hands for the umpteenth time and, like all the times before, the tenants of Normandale found themselves on the periphery of the new order. Perhaps, in killing Mitchell, they were doing what many of their forebears did in times past, indeed, what many marginals across the world have done for generations: scavenged and fought dirty, in the knowledge that they have always been on the wrong side of history and always will be.

## Notes

1. In regard to the 1999 murder, the names of all people and places have been changed. You will see later that the particular clan histories of the Normandale tenants will come to play an important part in the story. In choosing pseudonyms for the Normandale tenants, I have endeavoured to keep their names consistent with their real clan histories.
2. This research culminated in my book, *Midlands* (Johannesburg: Jonathan Ball, 2002).
3. In late 2006, almost seven years after the murder, the state began proceedings to bring a 26-year-old man to trial for the killing. He, together with two others, had been charged with the murder in early 2000. The charges were subsequently dropped.
4. Alan Paton, *Cry, the Beloved Country* (London: Penguin, 1987), p. 15. First published by Jonathan Cape in 1948.
5. Paton, *Cry, the Beloved Country* p. 17.
6. J.M. Coetzee *White Writing: On the Culture of Letters in South Africa* (New Haven: Yale University Press, 1988), p. 127.
7. Ibid.
8. Paton, *Cry, the Beloved Country*, p. 186.
9. Ibid., p. 13.
10. Ibid., p. 230.
11. Ibid., p. 189.
12. Ibid., p. 105.
13. Zulu elites from in the kingdom north of the Thukela River called the dialect spoken in the south by the derogatory name '*lala*' – which meant 'menial'; they also extracted heavy tributes from the so-called menials on the periphery of their kingdom. See, for example, C. Hamilton, 'Ideology, Oral Traditions and the Struggle for Power in the Early Zulu Kingdom' (Masters thesis, University of the Witwatersrand, 1986).

# Chapter 41

# Failed Experiment? Challenging Homogenous 'Zululisation' in South Africa's Museums
## The Case of *Sisonke* in Natal

NSIZWA DLAMINI

THE POST-APARTHEID PERIOD has seen considerable shifts in the politics of South Africa's heritage institutions. In KwaZulu-Natal, for example, museums that formerly preserved relics of the colonial past are now hurrying to feature 'tribal' objects, especially the ever-popular curios of Zulu material culture. However, the Natal Museum in the provincial capital of Pietermaritzburg recently adopted a different, more incremental approach to heritage diversification that sought to challenge widespread views of idealised ethnicity. Through an exhibition titled *Sisonke* ('We Are Together'), the museum attempted to refocus public attention on the ways in which the Zulu past and present have been stereotyped at home and abroad. Indeed, in KwaZulu-Natal and elsewhere, the trope of the noble, if fearsome Shakan warrior represented one of the most enduring symbols of Zulu culture. To a great extent, then, the *Sisonke* display attempted to alter this trend and perception, but the display's reception confirmed that the new 'rainbow' nation inaugurated by Nelson Mandela would need many more museum critiques of monolithic Zulu identity.

With the establishment of the KwaZulu homeland more than two decades ago, a certain expression of glorious Zulu heritage was harnessed to support the ethnic chauvinism of the Inkatha Freedom Party (IFP), the region's dominant political movement that exercised influence over public exhibits of indigenous culture. Inkatha and its homeland auxiliaries believed that the best way to safeguard local indigenous history was to build museums into showcases, or perhaps shrines, for the narrated feats of Zulu royals in their sovereign kingdom. To this end, the Nodwengu Museum was opened at Ulundi in 1983 to honour the legacy of King Mpande. Two years later, the KwaZulu Cultural Museum at oNdini, the site of King Cetshwayo's former homestead in Ulundi, invited its first visitors to revel in preconquest uSuthu greatness. Both institutions functioned as repositories for a select view of the Zulu past, untainted by internal division and foreign control.

By contrast, during this period, Zulu artefacts occupied a marginal position in Natal museums, confined to static ethnographic 'spaces'. Where aspects of Zulu culture were highlighted, they bore the imprint of melodramatic tales of encounters between intrepid Europeans and bloodthirsty amaZulu. Pivotal frontier wars of conquest and defence – the battle of Blood River in 1838, for example – became touchstones of historical 'reality' that were sure to lure white audiences. Colonial leaders, their artillery and tactics, as well as faithful troops featured in the placard plots. The enemy multitudes were also important characters in this all-too-familiar story of civilisation versus barbarism, but the most developed vignettes hardly touched on the sacrifice of the ordinary Zulu soldier. Rather, Zulu royalty and their material symbols of martial authority were positioned most prominently so as to draw maximum attention.

In both KwaZulu and Natal museums, therefore, the presentation of 'Zuluness' followed a well-worn script that concluded with a summary of what makes ethnic identity homogeneous and naturally unified. For KwaZulu bantustan authorities, in particular, political imperatives dictated this script. A new homeland government, increasingly challenged by anti-apartheid liberation movements, needed institutional reminders – museum exhibits – to help legitimise its ideological platform of Zulu nationalism.[1] This singular way of displaying Zulu history and culture would begin to change, if only slowly, after the 1994 democratic election. By the late 1990s, the KwaZulu Cultural Museum at Ondini had moved away from presenting only Zulu ethnographic items. The curators seemed to acknowledge the idea of a multi-ethnic, post-apartheid nation and included, for the first time, cultural art of Xhosa, Ndebele, and Batlokoa peoples. Yet despite these attempts to inject heterogeneous perspectives, the standard practice of presenting monolithic Zulu identity continued as strongly as ever. It was only when the Natal Museum launched its *Sisonke* display in 1997 that the heritage world in KwaZulu-Natal took note of a new approach.

### Origins and layout of *Sisonke*
After the historic election in 1994 that brought the African National Congress (ANC) to power in a newly democratic South Africa, cultural diversity became the dominant discourse amongst policy-makers in the new national Department of Arts, Culture, Science and Technology (DACST). The ANC-led government urged the heritage institutions it funded countrywide to meet the needs of an embryonic rainbow nation. To this end, DACST appointed an assessment committee to visit all state-supported museums to evaluate their commitment to promoting a post-apartheid vision of the past.

In mid-November 1997, a DACST assessment committee visited the Natal Museum, interviewing heads of departments and evaluating exhibited materials.[2] The DACST final report noted that the museum had an extensive collection of artefacts from precolonial societies in the southeastern region of Africa. However, it also stressed that there were no displays of African culture relevant to contemporary KwaZulu-Natal.[3] DACST representatives were unclear about whether they wanted a show of recent Zulu culture, or of local liberation struggles that had dominated the region in the two previous decades. The museum was told to devise a strategy to present history most relevant to museum visitors. The History and Anthropology departments met and jointly combed through existing collections to see what could be utilised for this purpose, hoping to construct an exhibition that integrated objects that DACST would consider 'historical' and 'anthropological'. They concentrated on choosing and arranging items from the *Amandla* collection (a body of artefacts relating to the struggle against apartheid collected in the early 1990s) and the beadwork collection. What emerged from this effort was *Sisonke*.

The original name for the exhibition was to be 'Symbols and Identity', but museum curators thought that such a title sounded too 'dry and academic'. They settled on a more 'catchy Zulu word', *Sisonke*.[4] The scope of *Sisonke* was broad; it encompassed various themes that were not always compatible, but which nonetheless offered a complex perspective of a single concept, 'Zuluness', and its many strands and manifestations. The artefacts placed in cases and tacked to boards possessed symbolic significance to isiZulu-speaking people. The first section of the display included an array of items typically associated with Zulu culture: colourful beadwork (see Plates 22–25), spears and other 'traditional weapons'.

Some artefacts were made by amaBhaca people and isiZulu-speaking amaLala who were never truly incorporated into the Zulu kingdom; other items were constructed by Zulu communities in Nongoma, the seat of royal uSuthu power, or by artists in the Msinga district, a 'traditional' area where labour migrancy has long been part of a young man's rite of passage in a working world that embodies both rural and urban lifestyles.

The second part of *Sisonke* featured objects associated with local resistance struggles during the late-apartheid period, including bloody civil conflicts between supporters of the Zulu cultural nationalist IFP and proponents of the United Democratic Front (UDF)/ANC alliance. Political posters, banners, and T-shirts of the UDF, ANC, and IFP adorned a large section of the display. The central thread that linked these examples of material culture was that Zulu ethnic identity shifted according to the social, economic and political interests of a black isiZulu-speaking population.

### The deconstruction of Zulu stereotypes in *Sisonke*

The *Sisonke* display used material culture to make three conceptual points. Firstly, it scrutinised the issue of Zulu tradition, suggesting ways to conceive of Zulu customs as rooted in fluid expressions of ritual life. Secondly, the exhibit deliberately lifted the nostalgic cloud hovering over Zulu culture. And finally, *Sisonke* aimed to demonstrate the idea that there was no rigid tie between Zulu ethnic identity and membership of the IFP, UDF or ANC.

The museum curators were most troubled by the view that 'tradition is something static and old fashioned'.[5] Thus, they showed how beadwork conformed to no single repetitive pattern. The beadwork of Msinga, for example, revealed stylistic variations that evolved over the last 100 years. The curators were equally worried about the idyllic portrayal of Nguni people of KwaZulu-Natal 'as a homogeneous ethnic group known as the Zulu', sharing one lineage and uniform culture.[6] Here, the idea of KwaZulu-Natal as a province dominated exclusively by the 'Zulu tribe' was deconstructed through beadwork arrangements highlighting the different aesthetic preferences of craft artists living in Msinga and Nongoma.[7] Finally, *Sisonke* featured a diorama that suggested ways in which political identities were not wholly determined by ethnic loyalties. The first figure to greet visitors was the image of a Zulu warrior in combat regalia, a man supposedly epitomising true Zuluness in the global imagination. Next to him was a rendition of a Zulu man clad in an IFP T-shirt and traditional attire. Alongside him was a Zulu woman in an ANC T-shirt with an *isidwaba* (skin apron) typically worn by older girls and wives in Msinga. This representation of 'politicised' material culture was designed to spur museum guests to consider whether the IFP only served black people who, by their outward appearance, fit the category of member of the Zulu nation. As it turned out, *Sisonke*'s focus on the three conceptual points made this exhibit unpopular with both the Natal Museum's education department and the wider public.

The Natal Museum education officer observed that *Sisonke* was 'very abstract and . . . difficult for learners' to understand.[8] This officer oversaw the staff conducting tours for school children on field trips to the museum. The display also drew sharp criticism from visitors. One remarked: 'I did not understand some of the connections [between the materials on display].'[9] In the period between February 2000 and April 2001, out of 239 visitors who took the time to record their observations in the Natal Museum guest book, only two endorsed *Sisonke* as an impressive exhibit.[10]

There might be several interlocking explanations for the failure of *Sisonke* to evoke positive popular feedback. *Sisonke* offered no linear narrative of Zulu life and its contemporary characteristics; in fact, the exhibit did just the opposite. This, in part, explains why visitors said 'they [were] not sure what story is being told'.[11] Perhaps more significantly, since the museum is located in KwaZulu-Natal, a province promoted in tourist guides and highway billboards as 'the land and kingdom of the Zulus', the public coming to *Sisonke* probably anticipated some kind of ratification of this slogan.

## Conclusion

The curators of *Sisonke* hoped that offering multiple, often contradictory, perspectives of Zulu culture and history would intrigue, rather than alienate, the public. From the mid-1990s onwards, some former colonial museums in KwaZulu-Natal increasingly moved towards different representations of indigenous people to debunk static concepts of tribe beloved by apartheid lawmakers who wanted South Africans and the rest of the world to see ethnicity and race as fixed entities. It is striking that in the post-apartheid period many museums have given priority to representations of all things 'Zulu', doubtless hoping to attract visitors who know what they will be getting, the image of 'Zuluness' exploited in films such as *Zulu* and *Zulu Dawn*, and of course the television mini-series *Shaka Zulu*. The problem with many of these newer Zulu displays, however, is that they provide visitors with no broader context (in terms of written analysis), and thus tend to reinforce stereotypes rather than complicate them.[12] In the end, *Sisonke* stood alone as an experiment, perhaps doomed to failure in the near term.

Yet *Sisonke* might still prove to be a path-breaking exhibit. Under the pressure of DACST assessors, the easy way out for the Natal Museum would have been to create an exhibit that unified renditions of 'Zuluness'. That this did not happen, despite broad-based criticism, signals hope for the future. The display's failure to satisfy popular notions of what representations of 'Zuluness' should be was its strength.[13] In order to make the phrase 'rainbow nation' mean something, heritage institutions must break down what have been destructive stereotypes and, instead, highlight the cultural and historical diversity *within* ethnic groups, revealing the social transformations buffeting 'traditional' and 'modernising' Zulu lifestyles. Deconstructing the world-renowned Zulu warrior might be the best way to advance this crucial process.

## Notes

1. For a nuanced discussion of the relationship between museums and ideology in Natal and KwaZulu, see J. Wright and A. Mazel, 'Controlling the Past in the Museums of Natal and KwaZulu', *Critical Arts* 5:3 (1991): 59–78.
2. Natal Museum, 'Itinerary for Assessment Team', Natal Museum Assessment, 17–19 November 1997.
3. Author interview with Sibongiseni Mkhize, former curator of the *Sisonke* display, Department of Historical Anthropology, Natal Museum, 14 March 2000.
4. Author interview with Frans Prins, former curator of the *Sisonke* display, Department of Historical Anthropology, Natal Museum, 30 April 2001.
5. Frans Prins, revised *Sisonke* display text for the exhibition department (undated).
6. Prins, revised *Sisonke* display text. For academic research on this point, see J.B. Wright and C. Hamilton, 'Ethnicity and Political Change before 1840', in *Political Economy and Identities in KwaZulu-Natal: Historical and Social Perspectives*, ed. R. Morrell (Durban: Indicator Press, 1996), pp. 15–33.
7. Ibid.
8. Author interview with Iris Bornman, former head of the Natal Museum's education department, 8 May 2001.
9. Natal Museum, visitor comments, May 2000.
10. Natal Museum, visitor comments, February 2000 – April 2001.

11. Author interview with Peter Croeser, education officer, Natal Museum, 4 May 2001.
12. An example is the Voortrekker Museum's exhibition on 'Zulu' culture, which opened in November 2000. In this display, the warrior image of Zulu males predominated. Moreover, the exhibition reinforced distinct gender roles, which were hallmarks of stereotypical Zulu culture.
13. For a similar view of Museum Africa in Johannesburg, see C. Hamilton, 'Against the Museum as Chameleon', *South African Historical Journal* 31 (1994): 184–99.

# Chapter 42

# 'So that I will be a Marriageable Girl'
## *Umemulo* in Contemporary Zulu Society

THENJIWE MAGWAZA

BEFORE THE 1990s in KwaZulu-Natal, white authorities sought to control crucial indigenous rituals marking the passage of isiZulu-speaking youths to greater social standing. For example, from the mid-nineteenth century onwards, Natal colonists imposed 'native customary laws' that regulated bridewealth (*ilobolo*),[1] limiting the number of cattle that could be offered by a 'tribal' isiZulu-speaking man to his wife's family. White magistrates interfered with nuptial negotiations by insisting that an African 'official witness' employed by government verify whether a Zulu bride wished to marry her prospective husband, regardless of any agreement between elders of the betrothed. And, most notoriously, following the British conquest of Zululand in 1879 the enrolment of male and female youths into Zulu regiments was severely restricted. Yet *umemulo*, the 'coming-of-age' ceremony held for a girl reaching marriageable age, eluded disruptive external shocks and manipulation. Perhaps this is because a custom recognising the potential of adolescent girls was perceived as no threat to white minority power.[2]

Today, many Zulu people still enact *umemulo*.[3] Indeed, it is common for the isiZulu-language newspaper, *Ilanga lase Natal*, to highlight various *umemulo* celebrations as part of its topical coverage.[4] Why then, we might ask, is *umemulo* such a prominent feature of contemporary Zulu society in South Africa?

If Zulu parents do not elect to perform this coming-of-age ceremony, they can imperil their unmarried daughters, who may encounter serious problems in the future. For one, the ancestors, the *amadlozi*,[5] will not have been told of a girl's rise to nubile status, and will be unable to support her aspirations to become a wife and mother or, simply, a full woman. Indeed, *umemulo* is also known as *ukuthomba*, a 'blossoming forth' of a girl into womanhood, which requires ritual notification of and permission from the *amadlozi*. The ancestors in turn bless the girl, known as the *intombi emulayo* during her *umemulo*, with the capacity to bear children.[6] This link between spiritual sanction and female fertility hinges on the *intombi emulayo* learning from elders and peers the obligations of deference expected of a married woman. In this sense a girl's maturation involves much more than her capacity to reproduce.

*The combined meaning of political freedom and 'coming out'. The young woman,* intombi
emulayo, *being celebrated at the centre of the* umemulo *assembly is bestowed with monetary
donations and other presents. Her affirmation of traditional Zulu culture is made clear by the
grass mat,* ucansi, *upon which she sits (instead of a chair or modern carpet). She accepts a
blanket, which incorporates the colours of the new national flag, and reflects the transformation
to freedom in South Africa. The giver of the blanket also chants praises to and for the* intombi
emulayo. *A woman on the left gestures with a grass broom,* umshanelo, *reinforcing invocations
that celebrate multiple liberations of the Zulu people who were released from oppressive
apartheid and the* intombi emulayo *who will be free to marry.*

This chapter, based on fieldwork conducted between November 1987 and August
1999, examines the central features of *umemulo* in several locations in KwaZulu-
Natal, from Durban (eThekwini) and communities surrounding this city, to more
remote sites near the rural towns of Vryheid, Mahlabathini and Eshowe. I collected
relevant ethnographic data in interviews with 22 informants, many of them ceremonial
participants, and while attending (or viewing on video) thirteen *umemulo* rituals –
one of which was my own.[7] In unique ways the videos provided more useful evidence
than personal observations written on paper. For one, the taped images displayed a
broader range of audience reactions, while presenting the researcher, seeking to note
different angles of performance, with another advantage – being able to replay a
pivotal moment at slower speed.[8] I also created audio recordings of songs, speeches
and chants, which enabled me to transcribe the complex isiZulu verse associated
with various kinds of oral praising. Finally, my pool of evidence revealed remarkable
continuities in cultural outlooks that ranged across diverse settings, showing that

despite the social disruptions caused by colonisation, urbanisation and industrial-isation, *umemulo* retains much of its longstanding traditional character. Of course, changes in ritual protocol, objects and garments were also critically examined.[9]

Since at least the nineteenth century *umemulo* was connected to the onset of a girl's menarche, but nowadays this is not strictly the case. Some parents perform the ceremony for their daughter when she has finished higher education (completing either high school or university study); in this case *umemulo* represents a graduation party. Occasionally, an *umemulo* celebration is held on the same day as the *intombi emulayo*'s 21st birthday; or just before she marries, when her lover's elders have indicated their wish to proffer bridewealth. It used to be that youths were expected widely to maintain certain virtuous practices such as abstaining from premarital sex, which precluded the possibility of having a child out of wedlock. But now breaking vows of chastity is not a cause to halt a planned *umemulo*.

*Symbolism of the gifts. In keeping with* umemulo *custom (certainly within the last century, as more amaZulu entered the wage labour market), gifts in the form of money are conferred on the* intombi emulayo. *During this 1997 event, R10 notes (about $2.00 at the time) were fastened to her headgear. Since unemployment is rife in rural Zululand (also in urban areas in KwaZulu-Natal, where Zulu people live in large numbers) and few migrant workers earn sufficient wages to support their families, it comes as no surprise that the cash donations did not exceed R10 notes, the smallest paper currency in South Africa. Izinyongo, gall bladders from slaughtered animals, also adorn the head of the* intombi emulayo.

For a patriarchal father, initiating his daughter's coming of age is as much a milestone in his life as it is in hers. A father leading an *umemulo* ceremony publicly confirms that he is willing to uphold relationships of gendered authority. One major purpose of *umemulo* is for the father of the *intombi emulayo* to offer thanks to his daughter for embracing ideals of respecting one's elders, *ukuhlonipha*, a set of behaviours including stringent rules of avoidance that a wife follows when interacting with her husband and ranking members of his family. Just prior to the coming-of-age festivities, the father of the *intombi emulayo* expresses his joyous approval of her passage to womanhood by presenting a prized ox for slaughter; parts of this beast will be symbolically allocated to the *amadlozi*, while other parcels of meat and organs will support a feast to congratulate the *intombi emulayo* on reaching the age of maturity.[10] As a successful *umemulo* always needs spiritual blessing, the *intombi emulayo* is secluded the week before in a special room or hut called the *umgonqo*, where the ancestors can easily recognise and reach her.

### Seclusion in the *umgonqo*

The *intombi emulayo* stays in the *umgonqo* with other female age-mates, adhering to an austere regimen in the days before the *umemulo* celebration, which usually takes place on a Saturday.[11] She is not allowed to leave the *umgonqo* except at night, when few people might see her. Social isolation ensures that she is not affected by sorcery, for her intention to go through *umemulo* means that she will be acquainted with the targets of sorcerers, and that the revered *amadlozi* will consecrate her. Whoever wants to greet the *intombi emulayo* or give her a gift must walk into her room and not remain outside. Whenever she leaves the *umgonqo*, even for a short time, she adopts an extremely shy attitude, exhibiting deference common to *ukuhlonipha*. In *Social Functions of Avoidances and Taboos Amongst the Zulu*, the social anthropologist Otto Friedrich Raum writes that neither the parents nor brothers of the *intombi emulayo* may ordinarily enter the seclusion hut.[12] They can, however, come to the *umgonqo* if they have brought a present, but any conversations that occur must be kept at a whisper. Raum also describes other requirements and prohibitions placed on the *intombi emulayo*: she must not talk too much, speak loudly or laugh heartily, showing that she is becoming a suitable wife capable of *ukuhlonipha*; she must drink water medicated with a pinch of ash to make her a good cook for her future husband; to boost her fertility, she eats bitter roots of the *impindisa* shrub[13] and she avoids sour milk like a traditional married woman.[14]

There are clear reasons why so many *umgonqo* prescriptions pertain to marriage and motherhood. The *umemulo* ritual is designed to form part of a single woman's training to be an ideal wife in the eyes of her spouse and in-laws. Yet it must be noted that the typical *intombi emulayo* does not usually seek formal cultural/religious instruction of the coming-of-age ceremony itself, of the kind imparted to a Christian girl preparing for her confirmation or a Jewish boy learning to recite the Torah on the eve of his bar mitzvah. Indeed, an *intombi emulayo* is not explicitly taught how to participate in her *umemulo*, and she herself does not generally seek any formal lessons because she has likely seen and participated in many prior coming-of-age ceremonies.

Finally, special body adornment is also important in preparing the *intombi emulayo* for passage to womanhood. She puts red ochre on her face, arms and legs, but her age-mates keeping her company only put ochre on their faces. According to *Kusadliwa Ngoludala*, a study by the linguist and ethnographer Themba Msimang, this practice signals her state of seclusion and entices the ancestors to have greater contact with her than with the rest of the *umgonqo* girls.[15] He adds that if males see *umgonqo* girls wearing red ochre, they typically run away, an evasive action that demonstrates abiding respect and healthy fear of ancestral visits to the seclusion hut.[16]

*Women, bearers of tradition. This photograph captures the rhythms of young women dancing the* ukusina, *with men in the background keeping time by clapping their hands and chanting. The women are attired in traditional garments and artefacts, highlighting how* umemulo *ensures the continuation of Zulu material culture. The* intombi emulayo *is draped with the special caul (cape),* umhlwehlwe. *She also wears the married woman's customary* isidwaba, *skirt, to show that she is ready to become a wife. The* intombi emulayo's *head cloth,* umnqwazi, *which is donned by women in the front row and on the left, displays an intention to enjoy the affections of a boyfriend. Unlike the married women pictured at the back, the young women cover only a quarter of their heads, suggesting that they are in a liminal stage between youth and adulthood.*

The weeklong residence in the *umgonqo* can be exacting, as one of my informants, Mrs Nokuthula Dlamini of KwaMashu township north of Durban, reported. She performed *umemulo* ceremonies for her two daughters in 1990 and 1992, respectively, and made the *umgonqo* period a key part of their coming of age. Mrs Dlamini wanted to instil in her daughters an appreciation of adult hardships, particularly the prescriptions they would encounter in married life, such as not being able to consume sour milk, having to exhibit great deference every day, and generally being separated from natal kin – three realities that define a new wife's experience.

To end the *umgonqo* phase and initiate *umemulo* festivities, a goat is slaughtered or a significant amount of money is presented to the *intombi emulayo*. Thereafter, the father or recognised senior guardian of the *intombi emulayo* ritually kills a beast, calling attention to the fact that people are now invited to a big feast with dancing and singing.

### Umemulo day: Song and spear

With seclusion over, the *intombi emulayo* is also released to engage in the revelry of the *umemulo* day.[17] As her relatives, friends and scores of acquaintances of her family stream in, the *intombi emulayo* and her age-mates from the *umgonqo* wash off their red ochre and don married women's leather kilts, *izidwaba*, and other artefacts, which they can borrow from older women.[18] Today, much of this attire can be hired from shops such as Kwayikhulu in the Ndwedwe rural area and Emakhehleni in KwaMashu township, both of which specialise in traditional ceremonial wear. The girls then go to a place far from home, where they gather under a tree, next to a friend or relative's house, or just in an open space not visible to the *intombi emulayo's* family. There they wait until the father or guardian of the *intombi emulayo* sends a message calling them back. On their return they sing songs in call-and-response mode commemorating the special occasion. Some verses appear below:

A  Leader: *Ubaba uthe angimule*
   Father said I must celebrate the coming of age
   Girls: *Awe yehheni ngiyakwesaba*
   Oh no, I am afraid of it (i.e. *ukwemula*)
   Leader: *Khona ngizoba intombi*
   So that I will be a marriageable girl
   Girls: *Awu yehheni ngiyakwesaba*
   Oh no, I am afraid of it (i.e. *ukwemula*)
   Leader: *Khona ngizokweshelwa*
   So that I may be courted
   Girls: *Awu yehheni ngiyakwesaba*
   Oh no, I am afraid of it (i.e. *ukwemula*).[19]

B     Leader: *Mina ngeke ngibalekele ikhaya labazali*
      I won't run away from my parent's house
      Girls: *Ngeke ngilibalekele noma sengikhulile*
      I won't run away from it even when I have grown up.[20]

These songs describe the *intombi emulayo*'s predicaments: how to balance her fears
and aspirations. Song A, for example, expresses the continuum of hope and anxiety.
The *intombi emulayo*'s newly recognised fertility frightens her, as she does not know
what really to expect in the naked world of adulthood. Will she be courted right
away by a man who eventually becomes her husband? When she weds and stays
with her in-laws, will she be happy? Song B memorialises the *intombi emulayo*'s love
for her family home and promises to be forever loyal to her natal kin after she
marries and moves away.

'*You are victorious.*' *A spear is given to the* intombi emulayo. *Sometimes a father
may opt to conduct one* umemulo *ceremony for several maturing daughters close
in age; if this occurs, he may elect to present more than one spear on the day of
festivities, as is the case in this image. Another mark of achievement and elite
power is the* intombi emulayo's *donning of leopard skins (rare for commoners,
much less women), which in this photograph likely indicates that the family
sponsoring this coming-of-age ritual is of a chiefly or royal lineage.*

While members of the *umgonqo* group serenade one another, there is another indication that the *umemulo* celebration is about to commence. The *intombi emulayo* displays a spear in her hand, which she would have received from her father, his brother or her maternal uncle, if her father has passed away. In rare cases the *intombi emulayo*'s lover, a suitor accepted by her family, might be asked to buy the spear for her. I have observed that some people put paper, cloth or a potato at the tip of the blade indicating that the weapon is intended for goodwill.

One of my informants, Mr Mahlanaza Makhoba of Dlebe in Mahlabathini, elaborates on the implication of this practice:[21]

> Although the girl's spear is not for fighting, it however symbolises her victory, having fought and won childhood and teenage battles, which to some are difficult to conquer. And because she conquered childhood illnesses that killed some, her father amongst other things sees it necessary to perform the ceremony for her. She also conquered teenage immoral acts that led many to have illegitimate children. The spear symbolises the fact therefore that she is indeed a conquering hero, as no coward or loser can be made to carry a spear in public.[22]

## Ceremonial ritual and revelry

With the arrival of the *umgonqo* girls before the assembled guests, the *intombi emulayo*'s father performs a pivotal rite, preferably in a central cattle enclosure.[23] Away from the view of onlookers, he smears the thumbs and big toes of the *intombi emulayo* with gall from a beast slaughtered the day before the *umemulo* ceremony, tying the *inyongo*, the gall bladder, around her wrist. The presence of gall invites the ancestors to continue to protect the *intombi emulayo*.[24]

Before the bladder contents are used, they are stored in a safe place, with the precious gall hidden in the sacred *umsamo* section of a hut (the back part of the hut or chosen urban room used to communicate with the ancestors), shielded from evildoers like witches who may turn an ancestor against the whole living family.[25] Next, the father of the *intombi emulayo* puts the slaughtered beast's caul, *umhlwehlwe*, a layer of fat covering the viscera of a slaughtered beast that hangs like a cape over the girl's shoulders and breasts, which Themba Msimang says is also meant to invite the ancestors to ensure the girl's good fortune.[26] Whilst performing this rite, her father calls to the ancestors, *ukuthetha*, thanking them and requesting their blessing.[27] The father and his *intombi emulayo* then go to a chosen area, *isigcawu*, cleared for a large assembly, where the rest of the *umemulo* performance occurs and the guests are already waiting. In the *isigcawu* the father commences with a speech, telling the gathering and his familial ancestors about the significance of the 'coming-out' occasion.

*The dance of girls. During an* umemulo *ceremony, girls without boyfriends such as those pictured here gather to perform. This image depicts 'innocent' dancers, whose 'virginal' condition is corroborated by the white purity beads around their waists and necks. Such exhibitions of chastity boast to visitors that the ceremony is being held in a district that contains a good number of 'proper' girls. Clearly accustomed to each other, the dancers follow choreographed movements. It is likely that this routine called for rehearsals that probably took place when the girls previously came together on an errand to fetch water or collect wood, or perhaps when they accompanied one another home from school.*

### *Umemulo* speeches: Patriarchal and matriarchal influences in 'coming-out' prayers

This address was recorded in 1993 at Umbumbulu, a rural area 30 kilometres (18.5 miles) south of Durban. It was the *umemulo* speech for Sibungu Sekhwani Mshengu.[28]

1. *Uma umuntu elimile ensimini, uyavuna.*
   When a person has sown in the field, s/he reaps.
2. *Uma evuna, uyazidla izithelo.*
   When s/he reaps, s/he eats the fruit.
3. *Induku le ikhombisa ubuqhawe bakhe,*
   This stick (referring to a presented spear) shows bravery,
4. *Akekho umuntu olwa ngaphandle kwesikhali.*
   Nobody fights without a weapon.
5. *Induku le ikhombisa ubuqhawe bakhe,*
   This stick shows her bravery,
6. *Ngoba ngempela akekho umuntu ongalwa ngaphandle kwesikhali sakhe.*
   Because indeed nobody can fight without her/his weapon.
7. *Le nto le nguphawu lokukhombisa ukuthi usekhulile.*
   This thing is a symbol that shows that she is now grown up.

8. *Useyimbambile impi wayilwa, wayilwa, akaqhubeke nokuyilwa.*
   She has fought the battle, and fought, let her continue fighting.

9. *Lona kuyoze kube ngumkhonto wakho wokulwa njalo njalo ndodakazi yami.*
   This will be your fighting spear always, always my daughter.

10. *Ungihloniphe gugu lami, ngalokho-ke ngithi ngiyabonga Mshengu.*
    You have shown me respect my precious thing, because of that I am saying thank you Mshengu.

11. *Sihlangene lapha bantabenkosi ngalo mntwana uGugu.*
    We have met here today children of the king because of this child, Gugu.

12. *UGugu lo ungiphathe kahle ngaphenduka ingane kuyena,*
    Gugu has treated me well and I was like a child to her,

13. *Ekubeni mina ngimdala.*
    Whereas I am the elder.

14. *Ungiphathe ngenhlonipho, nami-ke kanjalo,*
    She respected me, therefore in turn,

15. *Ngamhlonipha njengengane ngoba engihloniphile.*
    Like a child I respected her because she acted respectfully first.

16. *Ngiyabonga, ngiyabonga kule ngane. Ngiyabonga Gugu.*
    Thank you, thanks to this child. Thank you Gugu.

17. *Futhi ngiyabonga kinina futhi abaphansi bakaMajola,*
    Again I thank you the ancestors of the Majola,

18. *BakaMacingwane, bakaMshengu.*
    Of the Macingwane, of the Mshengu.

19. *Gugu bathi angibonge kuwe abakaMshengu.*
    Gugu, the Mshengu say that I must thank you.

20. *Bathi angibonge, nomkhulu uStefani, uStefani ozala uMcondo,*
    They say I must thank you, and my grandfather Stephan, Stephan who begets Mcondo,

21. *UMcondo ozala mina, uSibungu sekhwani, uSibungu-ke ozala uGugu lo.*
    Mcondo who begets me, Sibungu Sekhwani who then begets Gugu.

In the opening lines (1 to 4) Sibungu evokes imaginative comparisons to inform his audience of the joy brought by his daughter's *umemulo*. One of these verses drawing on a biblical allusion particularly captures his happiness: 'A sower reaping that which he has sown, rejoicing as he is now eating the fruits of his labour.' In lines 3 to 7, Sibungu uses the stick metaphor to explain the power of bravery, explaining further that the implement is important to a person who has to fight to survive. Line 8 culminates with a description of the stick, which is now a symbol that the *intombi emulayo* has grown into a victor, a theme frequently celebrated in praise poetry about great personal feats.

Sibungu devotes lines 9 to 15 to rhetorical questions, which he poses to his daughter. Will she maintain her respect for proper customary behaviour? Revering parents and elders is a valued traditional act; an example of this obligation would be her daily use of the deferential terms *ubaba* and *umama*, which mean father and mother, respectively.[29] Line 10 especially focuses on the *igugu*, a precious object that personifies his daughter. It is worth noting that Zulu people do not randomly name their children; parents' wishes and life circumstances around the time of a child's birth influence her/his given name. It is also believed that one's name can determine personal behaviour, successes and failures. Lines 12 to 15 emphasise honouring and respect, themes repeated frequently by Sibungu.

At the end of his oration, Sibungu thanks the ancestors again for upholding the moral and social order that enabled his daughter to live a proper life. In keeping with a custom underpinning *umemulo*, the ancestors tend to be honoured at the start and conclusion of a ceremony. In a final statement (lines 17 and 18) Sibungu briefly extols them using lineage praises, which are held in highest esteem. I observed genealogical recitations in all the *umemulo* ceremonies I studied, which showed that if ranking family members of a girl coming out had a respectable, authentic lineage they sought to proclaim that they had traceable ancestors.

In a 1933 study on marriage customs in southern Natal, the ethnographer Marie Kohler demonstrated that presenting the order of lineage descent is a form of praying

*Synchronising old and new. At many* umemulo *ceremonies artistic individuals seize the opportunities to showcase their talents. The young woman in explosive stride seems to have carefully prepared for her star moment. Her leglets, izigqizo, made of tin, wire and fragments of beverage cans not only decorate her body but also augment the sounds arising from her stamping feet. Most significantly, Western materials and indigenous artefacts comprise her costume. She thus reflects a hybrid style prevalent even in remote Zulu communities affected by urban influences.*

among traditional Zulu people. During the recitation of genealogy, ancestors are enumerated in the putative order of their succession.[30] However, in the speech above, Sibungu starts with the most recent ancestors and goes only three generations back.

In *Orality and Literacy: The Technologizing of the World*, the linguistic theorist Walter Ong points out that a primary characteristic of oral thought and speech is the reliance on repetition, which keeps both speaker and listener on the same track.[31] Overall, this 1993 speech is profoundly shaped by spoken metaphors and repetitive words and phrases. But this tells us only part of the narrative. Marcel Jousse has explored how voiced language powerfully expresses ideas, but he also reminds us that manual gesticulations perhaps contribute even more to an audience's awareness of what is being communicated.[32] We tend better to understand a person when we see his bodily gestures. It should be noted that Sibungu's strong body movements punctuated his oration, for he sought to exhibit how the sower disseminates and the warrior fights.

Often a performance of clan praises and/or personal praises accompanies such speeches. These dramatic recitations might be exclaimed by a senior family member older than the *intombi emulayo*'s father, if there is one at the ceremony, or a talented

*Older women's endorsement of* umemulo. *Senior women are critical to the moral sanctity of the* umemulo *ceremony. During dances, for example, older married women excitedly cut the air with grass brooms. Such slicing movements symbolise the* intombi emulayo's *dramatic severance from childhood, express their joy that she has risen to adulthood and serve to ward off the evil that may disrupt her progress to marriage. It is crucial to note that neither male attendants nor unmarried women partake in this activity.*

family orator who can *ukuthetha* (call the ancestors) with expressive force. The missionary-ethnographer and fluent isiZulu linguist, Axel-Ivar Berglund, notes that eloquent addressing of the *amadlozi* is profoundly important, for it is a formal act of seeking spiritual favour.

## Conclusion

*Umemulo* is widely believed to be a traditional ceremony that should be performed for every girl or woman at some stage of her childbearing years. If for any reason a girl's father or any elder acting on behalf of her father is unable to perform a 'coming-out' ceremony, traditional Zulu people typically say that she will experience serious problems in her life. She might not get a husband, or she might marry and suffer infertility; in either case, she would probably endure considerable anguish. Such misfortune would be attributed to the ancestors who had no *umemulo* ritual through which to contact and protect the now-tormented woman.[33] Simply put, spiritual communication secured through the slaughter of livestock, seclusion in *umgonqo*, oral praising, dances and songs, speeches of thanks, and prayers not only make *umemulo* a momentous 'coming out,' but also turn this ritual into a celebration of kinship and its very life forces.

## Notes

1. *(I)-lobolo*: bridewealth. The term refers to livestock, household equipment, money, etc. paid by the bridegroom to his parents-in-law.
2. Robert Morrell, John Wright and Sheila Mentjies, 'Colonialism and the Establishment of White Domination 1840–1890', and John Lambert and Robert Morrell, 'Domination and Subordination in Natal 1890–1920', in *Political Economies and Identities in KwaZulu-Natal: Historical and Social Perspectives*, ed. Robert Morrell (Durban: Indicator Press, 1996). See also Norman Etherington, 'The "Shepstone System" in the Colony of Natal and Beyond the Borders', and John Laband and Paul Thompson, 'The Reduction of Zululand, 1878–1904', in *Natal and Zululand From Earliest Time to 1910: A New History*, eds. Andrew Duminy and Bill Guest (Pietermaritzburg: University of Natal Press and Shuter & Shooter, 1989).
3. In some families an *umemulo* ceremony for the first daughter is sufficient to symbolise all future 'coming-out' ceremonies of the rest of the daughters. Much of the context and interpretation in this chapter come from Thenjiwe Magwaza, 'Orality and Literacy in Some Zulu Ceremonies' (Masters thesis, University of Natal, Durban, Oral Studies Department, 1993).
4. See for example: '*Ukuziphatha Kahle Kuyabuyisela*', *Ilanga lase Natal*, 5 August 1991 and '*Bekukuhle Kanje Emcimbini Wokwemulisa Amadodakazi KaZikode*', *Ilanga lase Natal*, 14 September 1992.
5. *Idlozi* (plural: *amadlozi*) usually means a human spirit or soul; in this chapter the term is used to mean an ancestor.
6. The *umemulo* ceremony is also called *ukukhulisa intombazane*, literally meaning, 'causing the girl to grow', a passage of life facilitated by her father who performs *umemulo* for his daughter. A synonym is *(ukw)-emulisa*, meaning to initiate a daughter into a new life through public ritual acknowledgment that she has reached a marriageable age. See C. Doke, D.M. Malcom, J. Sikakana and B. Vilikazi, *English-Zulu Dictionary* (Johannesburg: Witwatersrand University Press, [1958] 1990). It is significant to mention that unlike other African groups such as the amaXhosa, Zulu

people do not have a corresponding ceremony for a boy child. In other words strict expressions of customary respect and chastity are 'ritualised' attributes expected of a girl or unmarried woman.

7. Informants were selected on the basis of their social and biological age (i.e., generation, and here I sought a range of old, middle-aged, and young people); knowledge of 'coming-out' ceremonies and participatory experiences in several *omemulo*, either in a rural or urban area, or in both settings. Before writing up my findings, I went back to some informants and re-interviewed them. Their responses were essential to my analysis, as they further clarified meanings of rituals and traditional expressions. Other primary evidence was collected during everyday conversation with isiZulu-speaking African people in their homes and while I listened to Radio Zulu (now Ukhozi FM) programmes that discussed Zulu culture. Unpublished university dissertations from the anthropology and isiZulu language and literature departments of the University of Natal, Durban (now University of KwaZulu-Natal), as well as articles in *Ilanga lase Natal*, an isiZulu-language newspaper, similarly offered topical information on the significance of *umemulo* ceremonies in Zulu communities.

8. It is interesting to note that there is a growing trend among prosperous Zulu people to videotape their *umemulo* ceremonies.

9. For further reading on garments worn by women over time and changes that have impacted on them, see Thenjiwe Magwaza, 'Function and Meaning of Zulu Female Dress: A Descriptive Study of Visual Communication' (Ph.D. diss., University of Natal, Durban, 2000); 'Private Transgression: The Visual Voice of Zulu Women', *Agenda* 49 (2001): 27–34 and 'The Conceptualisation of Zulu Traditional Female Dress in the Post-apartheid Era', *Kunapipi: Journal of Post-Colonial Writing* 1 (2002): 192–204.

10. At most of the ceremonies I attended, informants noted that *umemulo* mirrored a Western coming-of-age celebration.

11. The period of seclusion could vary in duration depending on whether the *intombi emulayo* attends school, works, secures holiday leave, or lives at home.

12. Otto Friedrich Raum, *The Social Functions of Avoidances and Taboos amongst the Zulu* (Berlin: De Gruyter, 1973).

13. This flowering climbing plant – a species of the coffee family – can effectively combat impotence, according to Doke et al., *English-Zulu Dictionary*.

14. During this phase, elderly women also enter the *umgonqo* to teach the *intombi emulayo* how to conduct herself as a woman.

15. Themba Msimang, *Kusadliwa Ngoludala* (Pietermartizburg: Shuter & Shooter, 1975).

16. In urban areas, a room within a house or outside building is often used for this purpose.

17. Her right to participate in *umemulo* revelry is a form of public recognition that she has passed into a marriageable state. Otto Raum also refers to the 'coming out' day of celebration as a release rite; see *The Social Functions*, p. 282.

18. Magwaza, 'Function and Meaning', pp. 141–72.

19. This song was recorded in 1991 at Umbumbulu during Sidudla Hlomuka's *umemulo*: see Magwaza, 'Orality and Literacy', p. 35.

20. The song was recorded in 1993 at Camperdown during Gugu Majola's *umemulo*: see Magwaza, 'Orality and Literacy', p. 35.

21. A male informant interviewed at a 1992 *umemulo* ceremony I attended in Dlebe, Mahlabathini in northern Zululand: see Magwaza, 'Orality and Literacy', pp. 37–39.

22. Another reason we can assume that the *umemulo* spear is not for fighting is that it may be encircled with white beads, which signal that the weapon symbolises the presence of who support the *intombi emulayo*. The girls secluded in the *umgonqo* assemble the white beads and put them around the spear. Axel-Ivar Berglund suggests that white in puberty ceremonies initiates ancestor brooding: *Zulu Thought-patterns and Symbolism* (Cape Town: David Philip, 1976), p. 98. A female informant, named Nokuthula Dlamini of KwaMashu township in the Durban area, clarified in an interview conducted in 1991 that 'white is symbolic of peace and love': see Magwaza, 'Orality and Literacy', pp. 39–43.

23. Due to urbanisation and unavailability of cattle kraals in townships, this important rite is more often enacted in the household yard or in a chosen area immediately beyond the household.

24. The majority of the respondents were convinced that the ancestors lick the gall (whenever it is poured) without the people concerned noticing it.

25. For more on gall, the *umsamo*, and witches destroying a family, see Eileen Krige, *The Social System of the Zulu* (Pietermaritzburg: Shuter & Shooter, 1936).

26. Msimang, *Kusadliwa*, p. 248.
27. *(Uku)-thetha*: literally 'to scold'. *Ukuthetha idlozi* gives the initial impression of an aggressive relationship between *amadlozi*, the ancestors, and their *abaphilayo*, living descendants, but the literal English translation is misleading. *Ukuthetha idlozi* means to address the ancestors.
28. At the time, the father of the girl celebrating the *umemulo* was a 59-year-old factory worker.
29. *Ubaba* and *umama* are used without possessives, but are understood to mean my father and my mother, respectively, reflecting Zulu cultural reverence for senior people.
30. Marie Kohler, *Marriage Customs in Southern Natal* (Pietermaritzburg: Government Printer, 1933), p. 123.
31. Walter Ong, *Orality and Literacy: The Technologizing of the World* (London: Methuen, 1982), p. 40.
32. Marcel Jousse, *The Oral Style* (New York: Garland Publishers, 1988), p. 39.
33. Ancestors must be formally alerted to what their descendants do or are about to do. On this general point, see for example: Barbara Tyrell and Peter Jurgens, *Beads and Beadwork: African Heritage* (Johannesburg: Macmillan, 1983). If the ancestors are not contacted, disaster or misfortune will befall the living. This explains why an *umemulo* might be performed for a married woman who has never been an *intombi emulayo*. This married woman may have encountered problems, ranging from a mysterious illness and infertility, to a troublesome husband and friction with in-laws. Such was the case for several of my informants, and their *omemulo* led to their greater fulfilment. For example, Sizo Ntshangase, a childless wife living in Umlazi township south of Durban, told me she had a 'coming-of-age' ceremony in 1989, ten years into married life. After consulting a diviner in 1987, her in-laws decided to send her back to her home so that her family could celebrate her *umemulo*. Three months after the ceremony she conceived, and today she has two children. Another informant, 36-year-old Zodwa Bhengu of Oyaya Sonani in Eshowe, was to have got married, but she remained single, bearing the stigma of the *umjendevu* epithet, meaning old unmarried woman. Zodwa's father, a staunch Christian, felt it necessary in 1990 to perform *umemulo* for her, so as to invite good fortune in her life. Three years later Zodwa Bhengu became a bride. Once again Zodwa's happiness was attributed to the success of her deferred 'coming-of-age' ceremony. The data for these two cases came from interviews held at the homes of the Nsthangase and Bhengu families: see Magwaza, 'Orality and Literacy', pp. 29–51.

# Futures of Zuluness

# Chapter 43

# Two Bulls in One Kraal
## Local Politics, 'Zulu History' and Heritage Tourism in Kosi Bay

DINGANI MTHETHWA

TOURISTS THE WORLD over have discovered KwaZulu-Natal (KZN), a province in post-apartheid South Africa with the slogan, '*Wozani KwaZulu!*' (Come to the Zulu Kingdom!). For the typical tourist, whether foreign or local, a vacation in KZN means fun, relaxation, natural wonders, and even the possibility that the money spent on leisure might generate wealth for an impoverished isiZulu-speaking community, usually in a rural area. There is no doubt that revenues from tourism are trickling down to local areas, but such benefits do not signify a fresh start for destitute people. The surge in tourist interest in KZN has laid bare the wounds of the rural poor living near leisure developments, especially communities that lost land and sovereignty to a range of invaders. In this sense tourism has created a different 'African Renaissance',[1] prompting a rebirth of local memory of suppressed identity that implicates the legacies of African leaders who complied with, rather than resisted, colonial rule.

Maputaland in northern KZN is one site of this revival. There, the clan of Makhuza Tembe, which dwells in the Kosi Bay region of Maputaland, one of the premier tourist destinations in South Africa, is reasserting its rights over what is now a World Heritage Site. This conflict has persisted from the late precolonial era to the present, and encompasses claims to ancestral territory and political authority.[2] Located on the border with Mozambique along the Indian Ocean coastline, Kosi Bay is a favourite place for beachcombers and campers. The remote bush and estuaries are renowned for their beauty; visitors can pitch a tent in grasslands inhabited only by birds; and lie on the sand, seeing only a few passers-by the whole day. Indeed, many tourists choose to visit Kosi Bay after reading brochures that describe the area as one of the last tropical preserves in the once mighty Zulu kingdom.

It is not surprising that tourist advertisements gloss over Kosi Bay's more complicated past. Operators of leisure businesses tend not to market complexity or conflict, preferring instead to offer tranquility and a unique Zulu setting. But local feuds over both resources and political allegiances have been part of the Kosi Bay landscape for at least a century. Contrary to the brochures, these disputes are affecting an area where residents have not welcomed Zulu royalty and apartheid-era KwaZulu homeland rule with particular warmth.

Many so-called isiZulu-speaking inhabitants of Kosi Bay still regard themselves as Thonga people living in Maputaland, who owe their allegiance to area clans rather than to the Zulu king. Some older people, many of them women, prefer to converse in isiGonde, a dialect of Maputaland related to isiThonga, which has deeper (and different) linguistic roots in the region than isiZulu.[3] Throughout the 1980s and 1990s, a significant number of Kosi Bay residents basically accepted the tourist brochures that called their area a tropical Zulu outpost because this claim generated some revenue from vacationers seeking a getaway among the once mighty tribe of South Africa.

Before the 1994 democratic national elections, profits made from tourism in Kosi Bay mostly went to a white-controlled Natal Parks Board (NPB), which had ties with the KwaZulu homeland government and oversaw the administrative control of the wetlands and beaches of Kosi Bay. A few clan elites who granted NPB access to traditional areas also received a small amount of revenue from gate receipts.[4] After the African National Congress (ANC) achieved its first landslide victory and the main KwaZulu political party, the Inkatha Freedom Party (IFP), started to lose its grip on KZN, tolerance for the old way of marketing Kosi Bay began to fade among the region's rural communities. More Thonga people, in particular, said they wanted to receive the benefits of tourism, which also meant claiming a voice in their 'heritage narrative'. Who gets to tell this 'heritage narrative' and who in turn controls the right to earn from tourist ventures, are major questions to resolve for local owners, stakeholders and promoters of recreational resources in the new South Africa.

The promise of more equitable opportunities for black people, a goal of the post-apartheid era, is a vital dimension in struggles over tourism in Maputaland. In the absence of a strongly mobilised Zulu ethnic nationalism, which IFP supporters tried to entrench in northern KwaZulu in the 1980s and early 1990s, Thonga people in Kosi Bay are expressing their loyalty to clan over the Zulu nation. In other words, they are seeking to be represented by traditional leaders of Maputaland. Two contending groups dominate this arena of political competition. Leaders of the Makhuza Tembe clan, a powerful Thonga lineage, are pitted against another Thonga lineage, the rulers of the Ngwanase Tembe family, which in the twentieth century allied itself with authorities in colonial Natal and apartheid governments, including KwaZulu homeland officials. The origins of this Tembe (Thonga) rivalry extend back roughly 100 years.[5]

### Three stories of the Makhuza-Ngwanase struggle

I first learned of the Makhuza-Ngwanase conflict as a boy growing up in sight of Kosi Bay. My childhood in Maputaland spanned the 1960s, 1970s and part of the

1980s (after which I left the area to find employment elsewhere). I returned to the smouldering rivalry in the late 1990s, as a History Masters candidate and researcher in the Killie Campbell (Collection) Library at the University of Natal, Durban. My course of study required that I conduct oral history interviews in Kosi Bay for a thesis, which in part critically examined Tembe and Zulu ethnicity in northern KwaZulu-Natal. Over twenty years (from the late 1960s to the early 1980s, and again in the mid-to-late 1990s), I pieced together three stories that pertained to the Makhuza-Ngwanase struggle.

An elderly woman named Bukiwe Tembe relayed the first tale. When I was a little boy, Bukiwe Tembe stayed in my homestead. She loved to impart lore, especially the feats of her lineage and her father.[6] While we occasionally talked in isiZulu, Bukiwe Tembe preferred to speak in isiGonde, a language that I still understand. The following narrative about her father, Makhuza, chief of Kosi Bay in the late 1890s, is a paraphrased account, which I have translated into English:

> Makhuza's relatives were in Portuguese territory where his half-brother, Ngwanase, was also a chief. One day Ngwanase invited my father (Makhuza) as a guest of honour to a family gathering in Portuguese territory. At the gathering a fat black bull was slaughtered. Before the ceremony ended, one old lady who knew about a conspiracy to assassinate the guest of honour warned Makhuza that his dead body would be wrapped in the skin of the slaughtered bull that evening. Makhuza immediately fled to Nhlangwini, one of his royal enclosures in Kosi Bay (in British colonial territory on the northern fringe of Zululand). Fearing that Ngwanase's army would follow him to Nhlangwini, Makhuza fled further south to hide in dense forests at Lake Sibaya.[7]

Although Makhuza hid safely for months in Kosi Bay, rumours found him. He did not know what to make of the whispers that said he was a marked man. Apparently, in 1895 Ngwanase Tembe, a paramount chief whose homestead was within a few days' walk of Kosi Bay, wanted to leave the (northern half of) Maputaland, then situated in the south of the colony of Portuguese East Africa (also known as Mozambique). Ngwanase Tembe let it be known that he planned to avoid his Portuguese colonial overlords who imposed heavy taxes and meddled in his affairs. He planned to settle in a country where another Tembe lineage reigned, and where he believed he would assume the position of regent. In this country called British Southern Maputaland (now part of northern KwaZulu-Natal), Makhuza Tembe was a chief with jurisdiction over about a dozen clans, some of which had either migrated from Portuguese territory or moved farther away from the Zulu kingdom to escape raiding *amabutho* (regiments). Makhuza Tembe's followers generally did not view Ngwanase Tembe as a legitimate leader of their chiefdom.[8]

As a teenager in 1981, I heard a second important story about contested royal politics in Maputaland. On most weekends, I helped my mother sell *isishimeyana*, beer she made from boiled sugar cane. Peddling *isishimeyana* required that I sit with customers so that if they wanted a drink, I could fetch it and help my mother earn more money. It was around the drinking assembly that I heard the history of the Ngubane lineage. Contemporary leaders of this clan claimed to have lived in Kosi Bay before both Makhuza and Ngwanase Tembe. The Ngubane people had recently formed an alliance with members of Makhuza Tembe's family against the Ngwanase house. On one Saturday, the regular crowd of older men and women gathered under a mahogany tree. Some men smoked tobacco, while women snorted snuff and carried on in isiGonde. As I took a rand note for my mother's beer from a grey-headed elder, I heard him say to some of his friends: 'The Ngubane were the original "landowners" of coastal Maputaland.'

This old man got the drinking assembly's attention. He said his clan lost power in Maputaland to the ruling Tembe through trickery. 'One day a group of Ngubane men killed a buck while hunting,' he recounted.

> They skinned the carcass with mussel shells. Soon a group of Tembe men arrived with a sharp metal instrument, which they gave as a tool for skinning the animal. They helped the Ngubane men to prepare the game. To show gratitude, the Ngubane men gave the left front leg of the buck to the Tembe men. The Ngubane presented this meat without knowing that Tembe customs recognised the offering of this specific portion as a gesture that Ngubane people were accepting Tembe superiority over them.

At the conclusion of the man's story, few people were paying attention, but I was listening. Another old man turned to the grey-haired one and retorted: 'The Ngubane men are cowards to have given up a chieftainship like that. I would fight to the death.' Many drinkers laughed uneasily. I then walked away to get my mother's customer his drink.

Sixteen years later this narrative resurfaced. In 1997 I was enjoying a big feast at an Ngubane homestead in Nkathwini, a district of southern Maputaland. A tall man stood up and spoke on behalf of the Ngubane clan. According to the etiquette of such festivities, this orator thanked guests for coming to celebrate with his family. He started to proclaim praises of the Ngubane clan: '*Nina abakaMzwaza, abakaPhangani, abakaMfulwa kawuwelwa, uwelwa zinkonjane,*' meaning, 'You the people of Mzwazwa, of Phangani, you are a river that no one can cross but the swallows'. This first verse referred specifically to the indomitable Ngubane. While singing the next verses, his voice got louder. 'The Tembe people know,' he roared, 'that we, the Ngubane clan, are the rulers of this area. Yet we are nothing in the land of our ancestors!' When he finished, the gathering rumbled in agreement, while the women ululated. Suddenly, a small group of old men leapt up and waved their hands as if they were carrying sticks and performing combat manoeuvres.[9]

## The Ngubane clan: An oral and documentay history

This event profoundly influenced my thesis research. In 1998 I started to conduct oral interviews with elders of the local Ngubane clan, so that I could re-construct their lineage genealogy in the Kosi Bay area. In the testimony I collected, there was no firm agreement as to when or where Ngubane people first arrived in Maputaland. Some informants indicated that Ngubane pioneers might have come from Zululand or from present-day Mozambique.[10] The fragmentary written evidence (in various KwaZulu-Natal archival repositories) that traced Ngubane migratory and settlement patterns offered few additional clues. With the collected oral testimony and some primary documentation, I started to piece together a narrative that revealed how and when Ngubane people arrived in Kosi Bay – in all likelihood during Shaka's youthful days when the houses of Makhuza and Ngwanase emerged as powerful entities. This latter point of history then helped me discover more about two centuries of Tembe history in Maputaland.[11]

About 200 years ago, Makhuza Tembe and Ngwanase Tembe were chiefs in the Mabhudu kingdom, one of the most powerful polities in southern Africa in the late 1700s to early 1800s.[12] Mabhudu Tembe, from whom the kingdom took its name, governed Tembe chiefdoms (including the chiefdoms of Makhuza and Ngwanase), in a sovereign territory stretching from Delagoa Bay south to the Mkhuze River, which became a northern boundary of Zululand.[13] Upon Mabhudu Tembe's death (*c.*1798), his son, Mwali Tembe, took his place. At some time in the first decade of the nineteenth century, one of Mwali Tembe's sons, Madingi Tembe (the grandfather of Makhuza Tembe) branched out with his followers and set up his own chiefdom in present-day (southern) Maputaland.[14] It seems as if this migration of Madingi Tembe went largely unnoticed by Zulu kings who commanded tribute from Madingi Tembe, but did not interfere in his affairs. Another son of Mwali Tembe, Makasana Tembe, paid tribute to the Zulu royal house while living in Portuguese territory.[15] Even with the late nineteenth-century extension of Natal colonial rule, along with English imperial intrusion, into African territories on the northern margins of a conquered Zululand (following the British victory over King Cetshwayo's army in 1879), Madingi Tembe's chieftaincy remained beyond the reach of aggressive white rule.[16] Such independence would be lost with Natal's incorporation of the British Crown Colony of Zululand in 1897.[17]

This colonial annexation of Cetshwayo's former kingdom, which now included southern Maputaland, made the white governor of Natal the final arbiter of disputes in Madingi Tembe's chiefdom. Now the governor could exercise great powers in the Kosi Bay region, including the application 'to the Province of Zululand any of the laws of Natal relative to: Police, Gaols, Customs and Excise, Audit, Post and Telegraph

Service, Registry of Deeds, and to repeal any existing law of Zululand relative thereto'.[18] But perhaps more importantly for the immediate fate of Madingi Tembe's sovereignty, Chief Ngwanase Tembe, who ruled Maputaland on the Mozambique side, had been declared an outlaw by Portuguese officials in 1896 due to his refusal to pay taxes and supply conscripted labour for colonial public works. This encounter between Ngwanase Tembe and the East African Portuguese government had been brewing for two years, and ultimately forced him to flee south across the colonial border in order to seek protection from the British authorities. On the British Maputaland side, Ngwanase Tembe established a homestead in the Kosi Bay area, then controlled by Makhuza Tembe, a grandson of Madingi Tembe. Ngwanase Tembe's sudden arrival meant that two sons of Tembe royalty were to live side by side.

Any possibility of collaborative rule, however, was quickly undermined by political rivalry. According to Tembe succession custom, the heir of the main house of the ruling family born to the designated senior wife was the ruler-in-waiting of a Tembe chieftaincy. Ngwanase Tembe fitted this position, for his mother was the senior wife in the main Tembe branch; that she happened to be a daughter of the Swazi king, Sobhuza II, strengthened Ngwanase Tembe's royal standing.[19] However, Makhuza Tembe also came from a reigning family. Approximately 30 years prior to Ngwanase Tembe's birth, Madingi Tembe ruled an autonomous chiefdom in (southern) Maputaland, breaking quietly from the control of Ngwanase Tembe's ancestors.[20] Notwithstanding these complex arrangements of sovereignty, Ngwanase Tembe's claim to govern British Maputaland was deemed legitimate by white authorities, and a compromise had to be reached. Makhuza Tembe reluctantly gave up the leadership of southern Maputaland to Ngwanase Tembe, but retained jurisdiction over a strip of coast from Kosi Bay mouth south to Lake Sibaya.[21]

Contemporary historians of English-speaking colonial administration in Africa point out that British indirect rule policies depended on co-operative African chiefs.[22] In southern Maputaland, Ngwanase Tembe represented one such compliant leader, who gave loyalty to white authorities in exchange for official recognition of his paramount status.[23] The colonial records indicate that Ngwanase was aware of the collaborative role he was playing in this era of white rule. He was supposed to be the eyes and ears of a stretched colonial bureaucracy, safeguarding, for example, the process of handing over traditional wealth (livestock) and migrant wages during colonial tax collection. In the early twentieth century, correspondence between the white magistrate in Ingwavuma district (situated within Ngwanase Tembe's territory) and the Chief Native Commissioner shows that Ngwanase Tembe was not only demanding higher annual salaries from the Natal government, but also 'tribute' in the form of food, clothes and blankets to support his polygamous homestead.[24] During this time and immediately before (at the close of the nineteenth century), white native affairs administrators in the capital, Pietermaritzburg, regarded southern Maputaland as a Thonga region separate from Zululand. It must be noted that this official perspective would undergo a change in 1897 when Zululand and Maputaland were annexed by the Natal colony.[25]

With government backing, Chief Ngwanase Tembe then sought to extend his authority over clans living in southern Maputaland, but with little success. The other Tembe rulers who derived their traditional powers from ancestral ties to the Mabhudu kingdom enjoyed a large degree of autonomy, and in the case of Makhuza Tembe even gave provisions to Ngwanase Tembe to help the latter, who suffered occasionally from want.[26] The oral testimony I collected in the late 1990s revealed that before Ngwanase Tembe departed Portuguese territory in 1896, he was an unknown entity, and perhaps a non-entity, among Thonga clans in southern Maputaland.[27]

It is interesting that today some of Makhuza Tembe's followers do not focus blame solely on white oppressors. They remember the nationalist government that implemented apartheid after 1948 as their enemy, along with African leaders who Afrikaner rulers were able to manipulate to carry out separate development. The entire system of colonial rule, many informants told me, undermined Makhuza Tembe's authority, especially after Ngwanase Tembe was granted official paramount status in the 1960s, just as bantustan tribal structures were being introduced in South Africa's rural areas. A 1997 account of Kosi Bay's twentieth-century history, authored by descendants of Makhuza Tembe, chronicles how the nationalist government was aware of the two royal families, but chose to adopt divide-and-rule tactics in order to destabilise the royal Mabhudu lineage represented by Makhuza Tembe.[28] Such documentation also made clear that the Tembe family and its rival, Ngwanase Tembe, were not in dispute over Zulu spoils; their disagreement was a Thonga affair about two 'bulls in one kraal'.[29] The account further asserted that the Makhuza Tembe family controlled coastal communities during Ngwanase Tembe's supposed reign, and fulfilled administrative responsibilities, including the collection of taxes, without sanction from Chief Ngwanase. In other words the Makhuza Tembe family also acted as rulers in their own domain, a fact that is confirmed by state records that show frequent meetings between Makhuza Tembe and Ngwanase Tembe, in which they jointly addressed political concerns in Maputaland. However, this trend would be reversed as the ambitious Walter Mlingo Tembe, the nominated successor of Makhuza Tembe, took over the latter's mantle in 1956. One of Walter Tembe's first initiatives was to say that the Makhuza Tembe lineage would secede from the Ngwanase royal family. He wanted to elevate his position above that of the apartheid regime's designation, according to which he was an *induna* (headman), performing the duties of a subordinate councillor to a chief.[30]

When Walter Tembe started to pursue his breakaway strategy, he recounted in 2000, it was because the apartheid government had already made chieftainship the avenue to greater wealth and influence in coastal Maputaland. 'Why would the Makhuza family compromise for a position that has no benefits?' Walter Tembe asked in an interview with me. 'The government does not recognise a headman and therefore allots no salary for that position,' was his answer.[31] Indeed, historians of African traditional leadership have shown how African chiefs were usually the richest men in their territories in precolonial times and during white rule.[32]

Walter Tembe understood what was at stake if he failed to secure an officially recognised chieftaincy. Under Bantu administration, coastal communities paid their fines to a government 'tribal' office controlled by the Ngwanase Tembe line. By the late 1950s, even the Tembe Tribal Court was now a local arm of the apartheid regime. Perhaps the biggest disappointment for Walter Tembe came in 1962 when the house of Ngwanase Tembe selected Hlabezimhlophe Tembe, a loyalist in the eyes of the nationalist government and Ngwanase Tembe's family, to be headman of an area originally controlled by the Makhuza Tembe family. Such an appointment not only gave further powers to Ngwanase Tembe's family, it also bolstered the authority of Chief Mzimba George Tembe, the youngest son and the second successor in the house of Ngwanase Tembe, who supported the promotion of Hlabezimhlophe Tembe. It was then that Walter Tembe seized what he regarded as his last opportunity to become a chief.

After years of preparation, Walter Tembe launched a legal challenge against the Ngwanase royal house and the apartheid state. The Johannesburg firm of Heinman, Dorp and Barker Associates represented Walter Tembe, filing the necessary court papers in March 1967.[33] Tembe's attorneys argued that their client was entitled to a position as chief, as he was a descendant of Makhuza Tembe, regent of Kosi Bay. The thrust of the case was that Walter Tembe deserved a government stipend, as well as the right to accumulate traditional wealth in the form of cattle, which his followers kept in coastal Maputaland. Walter Tembe apparently told his legal advisers: 'Without political rank my followers would neither listen to me nor offer tribute.'[34]

The court case lasted four years. In 1971 the judgment went against Walter Tembe. The nationalist government followed its own agenda, refusing to side with the plaintiff because of the historical precedent set by the South African Native Affairs Commission of 1903–05, which prohibited the involvement of attorneys in matters of native administration.[35] Injured but still resilient, Walter waited again to advance the standing of the Makhuza Tembe family.

Walter Tembe's next opportunity came in the late 1980s, as the apartheid regime faced pressure from liberation movements and the KwaZulu government under Chief Minister M.G. Buthelezi was ceded more responsibilities for nature conservation in his homeland territories. Although Maputaland had been considered a part of KwaZulu since its annexation by the Natal colony in 1897, Buthelezi's homeland officials did not closely manage the Kosi Bay region. At the same time, the growth of tourism in South Africa also created hope for new economic development, a prospect that spurred Buthelezi to attempt to wrest additional authority from the Natal Parks Board.[36] He formed the KwaZulu Bureau of Natural Resources (KBNR) in an effort to establish firm control over nature conservation in his homeland.[37] KBNR launched wide-ranging wilderness protection projects such as the Tembe Elephant Park and the Kosi Bay Lake preserve, both of which attracted tourists from all over the world. In this boom period, the coastal communities, comprised mainly of Walter Tembe's followers, received few real benefits. As visitors drove into Kosi Bay and paid entrance fees to the KwaZulu homeland government, the conservation schemes were extended deeper into local communities; some of the schemes required forced relocations of coastal homesteads, mainly containing followers of the house of Makhuza Tembe. While the KwaZulu homeland government liaised with the Tembe Tribal Authority (controlled by descendants of paramount chief Ngwanase) before ejecting members of Makhuza Tembe's ward, this process of negotiated displacement stirred discontent. Tensions escalated when it was learned that money generated by tourism in areas like Kosi Bay was going straight to the Tembe Tribal Authority. During one of my interviews with Walter Tembe, he asked rhetorically: 'Why was the KwaZulu government taking the food of the children of Makhuza and giving it to the house of Ngwanase?'[38]

### Challenges of the democratic era

With the dramatic end of apartheid in 1994, the controversy over tourism in Kosi Bay intensified. Shortly after the first democratic election, the Great St Lucia Wetland Park in coastal Maputaland was granted status as a World Heritage Site.[39] The Lubombo Spatial Development Initiative (LSDI), a project launched by the governments of Mozambique, Swaziland and South Africa, encouraged joint tourist endeavours with local entrepreneurs and communities. Visitors continued to pour into coastal Maputaland, which raised the value of land.[40] Chiefs and would-be chiefs saw a bright future. It was during this time that the house of Makhuza Tembe under Walter Tembe's direction again petitioned to control its own destiny, but this time his claim revolved around the restitution of land; public gatherings were called to mobilise a broad-based coalition that protested the prior removals conducted by KBNR with the Ngwanase Tembe royal house's compliance.

The post-apartheid rights-culture influencing heritage tourism steers the course of this latest challenge. With the Restitution of Land Rights Act 22 of 1994, the South African government of national unity inaugurated a major land reform programme that allowed dispossessed rural communities to seek back territory they could prove was theirs.[41] Yet Act 22 became only a secondary catalyst for the Makhuza Tembe claim. A memorandum written by Walter Tembe's followers spelled out the main strategy of their 'restoration' case, which evoked newly instituted democratic liberties: 'We now say that in terms of the given freedom of choice . . . it is erroneous and unacceptable to force individuals and communities to belong where they do not belong nor is it acceptable to force a tribe to pay tribute to the *inkosi* (chief) which is not theirs by right of origin . . .'[42]

How this predicament will be resolved is still not clear. Statutes of the post-apartheid Constitution, which enshrines individual human rights, complicate any chief's claim to redress an historical injury; his claim is invariably rooted in the ambiguous role of tribal authorities and traditional customs of communal ownership, which served as a cornerstone of the apartheid plan to extend Pretoria's control over distant rural areas.[43] The likely so-called winners in this struggle for control of commercial leisure and recreational ventures in coastal Maputaland will be the local families who come together and mobilise their past for present rewards. In this sense the profitable future promised by heritage tourism is fundamentally changing the way history is being told in Kosi Bay. Community-based projects to collect oral history of the region have already commenced. Ngubane elders, for example, have actively sought to discuss the feats of their lineage at ceremonies, funerals and feasts. Walter Tembe has done the same on behalf of the cause of Makhuza. These public discussions rarely, if ever, mention the name of a Zulu king. Rather, they focus on rival Thonga rulers in the competing houses of Tembe.[44]

There is so much more to Bukiwe Tembe's account of Makhuza's plight that does not appear in this chapter, not least the techniques I used to verify and weave together her narrative.[45] If anything, the next comprehensive investigation of Makhuza's escape from treachery at the feast should extend beyond the oral realm and into Mozambican colonial archives. Whatever methods future researchers employ, their fieldwork and write-up will take time to complete. By contrast, one of Bukiwe Tembe's storytelling legacies may be realised any day now, but not in ways she probably intended. Her tale of a ruling ancestor's fate, like the beer boast of the grey-haired man who described the ill-fated Ngubane hunt, reminds local audiences in Maputaland of the benefits that indigenous people can receive if they retrieve and present an accessible precolonial past. Walter Tembe certainly understands what is at stake. His contribution to oral history, his telling of Makhuza's lost sovereignty and Ngwanase's cunning intrusion, are motivated by what he believes can be gained with time, real resources and legitimacy for his community through ecotourism.

## Notes

1. The 'African Renaissance' is a notion that revolves around the restoration of pride in being African and rooting out of the shame in having a black skin and other associated Western perceptions. The African Renaissance in post-apartheid South Africa is generally associated with President Thabo Mbeki's administration, but the current state leader might be inclined to recognise that he follows in the footsteps of other proponents of an African Renaissance, which include African National Congress leaders, Pixley Seme and Anton Lembede. See Thabo Mbeki, *Africa: The Time Has Come* (Cape Town: Tafelberg, 1998). For a recent analysis of the historical roots of modern South Africa's African Renaissance in the politics of isiZulu-speaking intellectuals, see Benedict Carton, 'Fount of Deep Culture: Legacies of the *James Stuart Archive* in South African Historiography', *History in Africa* 30 (2003): 97–98.

2. A summary of this conflict appeared in a story published in the *Maputaland Mirror: The Pride of Thongaland*, 28 April 2000. Sam Masinga, the journalist who wrote this story, described growing tensions between two ruling Tembe families, the house of Ngwanase and the house of Makhuza. The roots of this dynastic struggle became the subject of my Masters thesis. Masinga sets the scene: 'There is now a clash ... [over] issues of development in the Tembe area ... a conflict that is becoming clearer even to those who were not aware about the antagonisms between these two houses.' Masinga then alludes to a Tembe leadership in disarray: 'No one can ever know who is from and not from Royal Family in KwaTembe. Whenever one is commissioned to serve this Community he ought to bow for every one s/he meets as the opposite may be to his/her disadvantage.' For more on Kosi Bay, Maputaland and World Heritage Sites, see Chris van der Merwe, 'World Heritage – A Win-win Situation', *South African Country Life*, March 2000 and Tammy Lloyd, 'Conservation and Tourism', *Financial Mail*, 10 November 2000.

3. See David Webster, '*Abafazi Bathonga Bafihlakala*: Ethnicity and Gender, KwaZulu Border Community', *African Studies* 50:1 and 2 (1991); Walter Felgate, *The Tembe-Thonga of Natal and Mozambique: An Ecological Approach* (Durban: Department of African Studies, University of Natal, 1982) and Sihawukele Ngubane, 'A Survey of the Northern Zululand Dialects in the Ingwavuma District' (Masters thesis, University of Natal, Durban, 1991).

4. Some researchers working in Maputaland have also noted that the conflict between the two Tembe families complicated fieldwork; see Raul Davion, 'A Contribution to Understanding Contemporary People-Environment Dynamics: South African Approaches in Context' (Masters thesis, University of Natal, Pietermaritzburg, 1996).

5. What is happening in Kosi Bay is not an isolated case in KwaZulu-Natal or other parts of South Africa. In the remarkably peaceful decade that followed the civil violence leading up to the 1994 elections, rural communities elsewhere have been plagued by tensions rooted in clan-level claims to recover and manage lost resources. See, for example, the Bhangazi claim: Yonah Seleti, 'Expropriation, Exploitation and Exhibitionism: The Quest for the Bhangazi Heritage Site in the Greater St Lucia Wetland Park' (unpublished paper, Killie Campbell Collections, University of Natal, Durban, 2001).

6. Isabel Hofmeyr analyses gendered oral narratives, especially the ways in which women tend to focus on different issues from men. See Isabel Hofmeyr, '*We Spend Our Years as a Tale that is Told': Oral Historical Narratives in a South African Chiefdom* (Portsmouth: Heinemann, 1993).

7. Bukiwe Tembe told this story to me in 1978, when we were living in Thandizwe, KwaNgwanase, Maputaland. The same story was later repeated by other people in the Kosi Bay region when I conducted my Masters thesis research: interviews with Albert Mabole Tembe, Star of the Sea, KwaNgwanase, 7 November 1997; Nkaphani Ngubane, Lake Shengeza, KwaNgwanase, 12 July 1999 and Walter Mlingo Tembe, Thengani, KwaNgwanase, 10 July 1999.

8. Interview with Nkaphani Ngubane, Lake Shengeza, KwaNgwanase, 12 July 1999. Nkaphani narrated stories of how a group of Ngubane people, after learning that King Shaka wanted to kill them, fled Zululand for Maputaland. Alfred Ngubane told a different version of this Ngubane story to me; he said that Shaka dispatched groups of Ngubane people to guard the northern frontier of the Zulu kingdom against Portuguese intruders. Yet other evidence suggests that the Ngubane may have come from present-day Mozambique. It is clear that Makhuza may have been a ruler in the Kosi Bay region, although English-speaking white officials during this time did not know this: interview with Albert Twayi Ngubane, Thengani, KwaNgwanase, 13 July 1999. See also an important study of Zulu relations with Maputaland rulers during Shaka's reign: Elizabeth Eldredge, 'Delagoa Bay and the Hinterland in the Early Nineteenth Century: Politics, Trade, Slaves and Slave Raiding', in *Slavery in South Africa: Captive Labor on the Dutch Frontier*, eds. Elizabeth Eldredge and Fred Morton (Pietermaritzburg: University of Natal Press, 1994), pp. 144–47.

9. Many scholars inside and outside South Africa have observed different oral constructions of history in various social arenas; the work of some of these scholars has shaped the way that I understand the collection and use of oral evidence. See, for example: Elizabeth Tonkin, *Narrating Our Past: The Social Construction of Oral History* (Cambridge: Cambridge University Press, 1992); Hofmeyr, *We Spend Our Years*; Leroy Vail and Landeg White, *Power and the Praise Poem: Southern African Voices in History* (Charlottesville: University of Virginia Press, 1991) and Richard Rathbone, *Murder and Politics in Colonial Ghana* (New Haven, CT: Yale University Press, 1993).

10. For a study of Thonga people adopting Zulu clan names in Maputaland, see David Webster, 'Tembe-Thonga Kinship: The Marriage of Anthropology and History', *Cahiers d'études africains* 104:XXVI-4 (1986): 615, 628–29 and '*Abafazi Bathonga Bafihlakala*'. See also Philip Warhurst, 'What's in a

Name? Ethnicity and the Kingdom of Maputo', *Journal of Natal and Zulu History* 6 (1983): 5–6. Some researchers working in Maputaland who observed the influence of Zulu customs on Thonga people include: Dennis Claude, 'The Hidden Architecture in Maputaland', *South African Journal of Art and Architectural History* 4 (1994): 453; 'Precis of Information Concerning Swaziland, Tongaland and North Zululand: H.M.S.O.', unpublished confidential report prepared for general staff, War Office, 1905, Killie Campbell Library (KCL), Durban and G.G. Campbell, 'Presidential Address: A Review of Scientific Investigations in the Tongaland area of Northern Natal', 1969, KCM 31860, KCL. I interviewed the anthropologist Walter Felgate about the immigration of the Ngubane clan from Mozambique to Maputaland. Felgate claimed that evidence from the Ingwavuma magistrate's records detailed the flow of migrant labourers in and out of Maputaland in the 1940s. Felgate noted that the Gubande clan name declined in the magistracy records from the 1940s to the 1960s, while the Ngubane clan name (which did not appear before the 1940s) was increasing. Using this documentation as irrefutable proof, Felgate concluded that the people with the clan name Gubande might have 'Zulu-ised' their identities by adopting the Zulu clan name 'Ngubane', thus aligning themselves with a supposedly chauvinistic ethnic group favoured by segregationist and apartheid government officials: interview with Walter Felgate, Killie Campbell Library, Durban, November 1997. In my investigations of the Ingwavuma magistrate's records in Pietermaritzburg and Ulundi archives, I could find none of the records discussed by Felgate. More significantly, contrary to Felgate's claim, the oral evidence I collected from elders of the Ngubane clan suggests that their ancestors were sent to Maputaland by King Shaka to guard the northern border of Zululand: interviews with Nkaphani Ngubane, Lake Shengeza, KwaNgwanase, 12 July 1999 and Albert Twayi Ngubane, Thengani, KwaNgwanase, 13 July 1999. For a detailed history of labour migrancy in southern Mozambique, see Patrick Harries, 'Migrants and Marriage: The Role of Chiefs and Elders in Labour Movements from Pre-colonial Southern Mozambique to South Africa', seminar paper, University of Cape Town, 1979 and *Work, Culture and Identity: Migrant Laborers in Mozambique and South Africa, c.1860–1910* (Portsmouth: Heinemann, 1994).

11. The history of Maputaland over the last 200 years has yet to be written. Few details about Maputaland appear in imperial and colonial records, despite the fact that Kosi Bay had been the subject of intense disputes between encroaching white powers, mainly Great Britain, Germany, Portugal and the South African Republic. Records of these disputes can be found in the British Parliamentary Papers (BPP), *Colonies Africa* (Shannon: Irish University Press, 1968–1971), Vols. 35 and 48; Colonial Secretary's Office (CSO), Minute Papers, 1887 to 1918, Pietermaritzburg Archives Repository (PAR); Secretary for Native Affairs (SNA), Minute Papers, 1887–1910, PAR; Zululand Government House (ZGH), Vols. for 1889–1899, PAR; Ingwavuma Magistrate Records, Minute Papers 1898–1954, PAR; Chief Native Commissioner (CNC), Minute Papers 1924–1972, Ulundi Archives Repository (UAR); CNC, Minute Papers, 1897–1928, PAR. See also: manuscript notes of Von Wissel (a trader in Maputaland at the turn of the nineteenth and into the twentieth centuries who owned stores with several partners at Ndumu, Manaba and Mangusi near the time Chief Ngwanase moved to British Maputaland) in the Miller Papers, 'Von Wissel Louis Charles: Reminiscences of Trading Days in Northern Zululand 1895–1919', KCM 2309, KCL. For other relevant perspectives, particularly missionary records, see E.H. Hurcombe, *A Walk Round Kosi Lake, Undertaken by Miss Prozesky, Nkosazane YaseMaputa* (Blysthswood: Blysthswood Press, 1925); E. and H. Wigram, *Soldiers of the Cross in Zululand* (London: Bemrose & Sons, 1906), pp. 155–75, Joseph Ballam Manuscripts, File 27, KCL; W.J. Leyds, *The Transvaal Surrounded: A Continuation of the First Annexation of Transvaal* (London: T. Fisher Unwin, 1919), pp. 376–80 and H.P. Braatveldt, *Roaming Zululand with Native Commissioner* (Pietermaritzburg: Shuter & Shooter, 1949), pp. 96–120.

12. David Hedges, 'Trade and Politics in Southern Mozambique and Zululand in Early Eighteenth and Nineteenth Centuries' (Ph.D. diss., University of London, 1978), pp. 229–32.

13. 'Testimony of Mahungane and Nkomuza, 9 November 1897', in *The James Stuart Archive of Recorded Oral Evidence Relating to the History of the Zulu and Neighbouring Peoples*, eds. C. de B. Webb and J. Wright, Vol. 2 (Pietermaritzburg: University of Natal Press, 1979), pp. 150–53. See also Warhurst, 'What's in a Name?' and Hedges, 'Trade and Politics', pp. 138–39.

14. Webster, 'Tembe-Thonga Kinship': 5 and Hedges, 'Trade and Politics', pp. 138–40.

15. In particular, Ndukwana kaMbengwana told the Natal colonial official and isiZulu-speaking ethnographer, James Stuart, that Makasana paid tribute to King Shaka. Makasana ruled the old Tembe chiefdom while Madingi Tembe left to establish his rule in the south. In this same period

Zulu power was said to be at its peak in southeastern Africa. Madingi Tembe's move to the south did not draw the attention of the Zulu royal house: 'Testimony of Ndukwana, 19 September 1900', *The James Stuart Archive of Recorded Oral Evidence Relating to the History of the Zulu and Neighbouring Peoples*, eds. C. de B. Webb and J. Wright, Vol. 4 (Pietermaritzburg: University of Natal Press, 1986), p. 285. For a broader analysis of the Zulu state's impact on Maputaland, see 'Testimony of Mahungane and Nkomuza, 20 November 1900', in *The James Stuart Archive*, eds. Webb and Wright, Vol. 2, p. 143 and 'Testimony of Ndaba, 24 October 1897', in *The James Stuart Archive*, eds. Webb and Wright, Vol. 4, p. 172.

16. The period of the 1870s, which saw the demise of the Zulu kingdom, was also momentous for the Mabhudu polity. In 1875 the Portuguese East African and British imperial governments divided the Mabhudu kingdom. The southern part fell under British influence, while a Portuguese East African government controlled the northern part. In the final two decades of the nineteenth century, the Natal Colonial government sought to expand the boundaries of northern Zululand to incorporate Tembe chiefs in the southern part of Maputaland. This included chiefdoms of Fokothi, Manaba, and Sibonda. The process of expanding the northern boundary of Zululand was started in July 1887 by Charles Saunders, who was commissioned by Sir Arthur Havelock, the governor of Natal. As a result of these negotiations, a British protectorate was proclaimed over Maputaland in May 1895. BPP, *Colonies Africa*, C6200, (Shannon: Irish University Press, 1968–1971), pp. 39–40, 54, 166–67, 174. For a record of correspondence between the Tembe royal family and British colonial offices, see Leyds, *The Transvaal Surrounded*, pp. 376–80. For a historical analysis of this period, see Philip Warhurst, 'Britain and the Partition of Maputo 1875–1897', unpublished paper presented to Natal and Zulu History Workshop, University of Natal, Durban, 1985. See also Dingani Mthethwa, 'The Mobilisation of History and the Tembe Chieftaincy in Maputaland: 1896–1997' (Masters thesis, University of Natal, Durban 2002), 55–71.

17. It should be noted that the Thonga were never conquered by the Zulu and remained autonomous until their incorporation into the Natal colony in the late nineteenth century and ultimately into the KwaZulu bantustan in the twentieth century. For more details regarding annexation of Maputaland, see Warhurst, 'Britain and the Partition of Maputo', which describes struggles of the Tembe dynasty involving Portuguese and British imperial governments.

18. For this and other terms of Zululand's incorporation into the Natal colony, see: PAR, Natal Colonial Publications (NCP), 8/3/65, The Zululand Annexation Act 1897, Zululand Land Delimitation Commission.

19. 'Testimony of Dhlozi, Ndukwana and Ndaba, 9 February 1902', in *The James Stuart Archive*, eds. Webb and Wright, Vol. 2, p. 158; interview conducted by Dingani Mthethwa and Ian Edwards with MaMkhwanazi Tembe (wife to Chief George Mzimba Tembe), Thandizwe Tembe Royal Palace, KwaNgwanase (Maputaland), 5 November 1997; interview with Themba Habile Tembe, Enkathwini, KwaNgwanase (Maputaland), 6 November 1997 and A.T. Bryant, *Olden Times in Zululand and Natal* (London: Longmans, 1929), p. 307.

20. This was a consistent theme in the oral evidence I collected from members of the Makhuza lineage, who repeatedly highlighted how Madingi left the Tembe main branch: interview with Walter Tembe, Thengani, KwaNgwanase, 10 July 1999 and 5 February 2000; interviews with Albert Mabole Tembe, Star of the Sea, KwaNgawanse, 7 November 1997 and Chithumuzi Mdlesthe, KwaChithumuzi, KwaNgwanase, 14 July 1997. The evidence that many researchers use is 'Testimony of Mahungane and Nkomuza, 9 September 1897', in *The James Stuart Archive*, eds. Webb and Wright, Vol. 2, p. 150–55.

21. It is interesting to note that in early 1905 the Natal colonial government recognised a coastal strip in the Kosi Bay area as 'Reserve XIV', containing 'Mabudu & Tengbi'. The Mabhudu reference seems to grant both Ngwanase and Makhuza Tembe the right to co-exist as branches of the Mabhudu kingdom; the 'Tengbi' reference might be a typo, but it seems more likely that it refers to [Makhuza] Tembe, thus confirming oral testimony that this leader had been recognised as traditional authority over a coastal strip of territory in the Kosi Bay region: *Natal Witness*, 25 January 1905 in PAR, SNA 1/1/316, Minutes Papers SNA, 1905. See corroborating documents in this file on the Zululand Delimitation Commission, which mapped out the political territory of Maputaland for the Natal colonial government.

22. For the tactics and repercussions of British indirect rule in colonial southern Africa and a summary of recent historical scholarship on this subject, see Mahmood Mamdani, *Citizen and Subject: Contemporary Africa and the Legacy of Late Colonialism* (Princeton: Princeton University Press, 1996).

23. Philip Warhurst, 'Britain and the Partition of Maputo 1875–1897', *Journal of Natal and Zulu History* 3 (1985): 26; with slight modifications, this journal article covers much of the same ground as Warhurst's 1985 paper presented to the Natal and Zulu History Workshop.

24. In the first decade of the twentieth century, the typical chief in Natal and Zululand was paid between 6 and 40 pounds sterling per year. By contrast, Ngwanase earned an average of 100 pounds sterling per annum. On top of this pay, he often demanded a 100 per cent salary increase. For more details about Ngwanase Tembe's demands and his role in the colonial order, see PAR, CNC 79/1021/1912, interview between Mr Shepstone, Acting Native Commissioner and Chief Ngwanase Tembe, Ingwavuma, 13 May 1912; UAR, Tembe Tribal Authority: Ingwavuma, CNC, 3226/1922, Boast to Wheelwright, 3 September 1925; UAR, Tembe Tribal Authority: Ingwavuma, CNC, 3102/1921, Notes of Proceedings, Manguzi Police Camp, 31 July 1922. See also Mthethwa, 'The Mobilisation of History', pp. 89–93. For an insightful historical analysis of government salaries paid to chiefs in Natal and Zululand at the turn of the twentieth century, see John Lambert, 'From Independence to Rebellion: African Society in Crisis, *c.*1880–1910', in *Natal and Zululand from Earliest Times to 1910*, eds. Andrew Duminy and Bill Guest (Pietermaritzburg: University of Natal Press and Shuter & Shooter, 1989), p. 379.

25. Philip Warhurst details how Maputaland was finally incorporated into Natal-controlled Zululand. See his 'Britain and the Partition of Maputo 1875–1897' in *Journal of Natal and Zulu History*.

26. PAR, CNC, Vol. 28/1911, CNC Minute Papers. The evidence from these volumes suggests a conflict between Ngwanase and other Tembe chiefs, namely Mzila, Manaba and Godi. My interview with Walter Tembe, Thengani, Maputaland, 5 February 2000, confirmed the written evidence. In addition, Walter Tembe said that Ngwanase would have starved to death if Makhuza Tembe had not helped him build a homestead and fed him. This point was corroborated in an interview with MaMpinga Ngubane (MaGumede), Mahlambani River, KwaNgwanase, 6 November 1997. MaGumede passed away a month later. MaMpinga and her husband lived in Kosi Bay when Ngwanase arrived in Maputaland. She recalled Chief Makhuza Tembe sending men from Kosi Bay (including her husband) to Emfihlweni, Ngwanase's new homestead, to help in construction of the palace. MaMpinga and other women travelled from Kosi Bay to Emfihlweni bringing food to their husbands.

27. This is one of the major reasons, a Ngwanase family rival testified, that members of Makhuza Tembe's clan felt growing resentment of the colonial-supported imposition of authority of Ngwanase Tembe's family in southern Maputaland: interview with Walter Tembe, Thengani, Maputaland, 5 February 2000.

28. 'Chieftainship, Re-definition of the Well Boundaries and Recognition of 11 Community Authorities Situated within the Late Traditional Inkosi Makhuza Tembe's Territory', 10 November 1996; 'Application for the Re-establishment of the Late Inkosi Makhuza's Chieftainship', 11 November 1996; 'The Establishment of Mading Chieftainship', 8 March 1997. These documents were sent to the post-apartheid Department of Traditional Affairs, KwaZulu-Natal, in order to lodge a claim that leading members of Makhuza Tembe's family need to recognise a future traditional structure of area governance called the Makhuza Tribal Authority.

29. 'Two bulls in one kraal' (*Akukho sibaya sinenkunzi ezimbili*) is an isiZulu idiom that suggests a nasty fight will arise when two bulls are confined in one place, especially when one bull desires to be the only mate of fertile heifers in his area.

30. The oral evidence collected during my Masters research generally confirms the genealogy of power succession in the house of Makhuza, which opened the opportunity for Walter Mlingo Tembe to rise to a leadership position in the house of Makhuza. In 1956, Mvutshana Tembe, the head the house of Makhuza Tembe, became ill and could no longer perform his chiefly duties. His son and heir, Ncelaphi Tembe, was too young at the time to succeed his father. As a result, Walter Tembe, a cousin of Mvutshana Tembe became the successor: interviews with Albert Mabole Tembe, Star of the Sea, KwaNgwanase, 7 November 1997; Chithumuzi Mdletshe, KwaChithumuzi, KwaNgwanase, 14 July 1997; Magwevu Tembe, KwaZibi, KwaNgwanase, 21 December 1997; Walter Mlingo Tembe, Thengani, KwaNgwanase, 10 July 1999; Solomon Hlomehlome Tembe, Manguzi, KwaNgwanase, 11 July 1999; Jalimane Nhlonzi, Thengani, KwaNgwanase, 13 July 1999; Bidi Ngubane, KwamaNdende, KwaNgwanase, 14 July 1999; Reverend J. Masinga, Thandizwe, KwaNgwanase, 22 June 2000; Jameson Makokozane Ngubane, Nkathwini, KwaNgwanase, 3 September 2000; Teka Tembe, Manguzi, Kwangwanase, 6 November 2000 and see also Indlu KaMadingi, '*Umlando Ngendlu KaMqingabhodo*', 20 January 1993 (paper prepared by the members of the Makhuza family as proof that the house of Ngwanase intruded on the land of Makhuza).

31. Interview with Walter Tembe, Thengani, Maputaland, 5 February 2000.
32. Wealth was measured in the form of cattle, which chiefs accumulated from raids and followers' tribute. Outsiders who wanted to be incorporated within a chief's territory usually provided him with a few head of cattle from their herd. Chiefs' access to wealth was limited under late nineteenth-century colonial rule. White governments paid chiefs meagre stipends and the collecting of traditional tribute was forbidden. Yet colonial power also provided new means to accumulate wealth by giving chiefs responsibilities to gather taxes for government coffers. As chiefs were also requested to aid in the running of labour recruitment, directing men to wage employment in mines and white-owned farms, for example, traditional leaders could take a portion of the salaries paid to migrants. From the early to middle twentieth century, when there was minimal colonial presence in Maputaland, Ngwanase Tembe combined traditional and official ways of extracting wealth from his followers to achieve financial security. Chief Mhlupheki Tembe, who succeeded Ngwanase Tembe, was considered wealthy enough (through inheritance) to approach white officials to buy a vehicle for him, a lifelong investment for any African leader. On chiefs' wealth and avenues of accumulation in precolonial and colonial south-eastern Africa, see Jeff Guy, 'Analysing Pre-Capitalist Societies in Southern Africa', *Journal of Southern African Studies* 14:1 (1987): 18–37; *The Destruction of the Zulu Kingdom: The Civil War in Zululand, 1879–1884* (London: Longman, 1979); Patrick Harries, 'Slavery, Social Incorporation and Surplus Extraction: The Nature of Free and Unfree Labour in South-east Africa', *Journal of African History* 22 (1981): 309–30 and *Work, Culture and Identity*.
33. UAR, N1/1/3/18/4, H. Heinman, M.A.S. Dorp & Barker, Johannesburg, to Bantu Commissioner, Ingwavuma, 26 January 1967 and UAR, N. 1/1/3/11, Zylstra to Mr Maarsdorp, 21 March 1967.
34. UAR, N1/1/3/11, Letter, Mr Zylstra to Mr Maarsdorp, regarding a private discussion between Mr Zylstra and Walter Tembe, 21 March 1967.
35. UAR, N1/15/1 (X), Memorandum: Intervention of Attorney in Administrative Matters of Bantu Affairs, 16 April 1963. The nationalist government conducted local research in Maputaland through Mr Woener, a government anthropologist. In 1967, he was commissioned to collect oral evidence on the history of the two Tembe houses (following Walter Tembe's claim). The 1971 judgment against Walter Tembe was based on Woener's report. According to Walter Tembe, Woener's report supported the house of Ngwanase because the government anthropologist only interviewed members of the Ngwanase family. See the original Woener report: UAR, N1/1/3/18/4, Mr Woener's Report on the History of the Tembe people, April 1967. Solomon Tembe confirmed that in the 1971 court judgment Walter was fined twenty head of cattle by the Tembe Tribal Authority: interview with Solomon Tembe, Manguzi, KwaNgwanase, 5 February 2000.
36. For an insightful history of nature conservation in greater Zululand, see: Beverly Ellis, 'Game Conservation in Zululand 1824–1947' (Honours thesis, University of Natal, Pietermaritzburg, 1975). See also Mthethwa, 'The Mobilisation of History', pp. 146–50 and interview with Jerry Mngomezulu, Dukuduku, Mtubatuba, 4 November 2000. Jerry Mngomezulu worked with the KwaZulu Bureau of Natural Resources in Kosi Bay. The KBNR was later changed to KwaZulu Nature Conservation Services.
37. When Chief Minister Buthelezi announced that he planned to take over nature conservation in KwaZulu homeland, he blamed the NPB for mishandling his people's resources, for example, by allowing white fishermen at Kosi Bay to take food from the water and therefore the mouths of his constituency. Buthelezi was hailed as a 'hero' by some local residents, for he was claiming to fight for the rights of inhabitants of Maputaland.
38. Interview with Walter Tembe, Thengani, KwaNgwanase, 5 February 2000. In the year before I interviewed Walter Tembe for the second time, a member of the Ngubane clan, Albert Twayi, posed the same question, directing to me: 'Is it right that the tribal authority (house of Ngwanase) take the money generated from Kosi Bay? Leave those people (inhabitants of Kosi Bay) with nothing, but the trash left by tourists?' Answering himself: 'I do not think so. Something must be done,' pointing to the direction of Kosi Bay. Albert Twayi felt that the Ngubane people were the legitimate owners of the coastal area (Kosi Bay), not the house of Makhuza.
39. Van der Merwe, 'World Heritage'; Lloyd, 'Conservation and Tourism' and 'People and Parks, Parks and People', conference summary proceedings in *Peoples & Parks*, eds. Jane Carruthers and Andrew Zaloumis, Occasional Paper No. 1 (1995).
40. For example, a survey conducted by the researcher Japhet Ngubane showed that an average of 17 000 tourists visited Kosi Bay area between 1997 to 1999: Japhet Ngubane, notes prepared for Ph.D. dissertation on environmental studies in Maputaland, University of Natal, 2000.

41. For an illuminating discussion of the provisions of this act, see Bertus de Villiers, *Land Claims and National Parks* (Pretoria: Human Sciences Research Council, 1999). See also Section 1 of the Restitution of Land Rights Act 22 of 1994. For examples of land resettlement and tourist ventures, see Leslie Witz, Ciraj Rassool and Gary Minkley, 'Repackaging the Past for South Africa Tourism', *Daedalus: Journal of the American Academy of Arts and Sciences* 1:130 (2001); the authors focus on land settlement schemes in the Northern Cape and Northern Province.

42. 'Application for the Re-establishment of the Late Traditional Leader, Inkosi Makhuza's Chieftainship, Re-definition of the Well Boundaries and Recognition of 11 Community Authorities Situated within the Late Traditional Inkosi Makhuza Tembe's Territory', 10 November 1996. This document was signed by residents of Makhuza Tembe's ward, 11 October 1997. During my interviews, Inkosi Nyanga Ngubane of the Department of Traditional Affairs confirmed that his department had received a complaint from the Maputaland coastal communities (i.e., members of the Makhuza family). Interview with Inkosi Nyanga Ngubane, Pietermaritzburg, 11 July 2000.

43. 'Discussion Document: Towards a White Paper on Traditional Leadership and Institutions', Department of Provincial and Local Government, 26 April 2000. A researcher for Programme for Land and Agrarian Studies (PLAAS), Lungisile Ntsebenza, argues that traditional authorities cannot perform decisive roles in a South African democratic government: Lungisile Ntsebenza, 'Land Tenure Reform, Traditional Authorities and Rural Local Government in Post-apartheid South Africa: Case Studies from the Eastern Cape', School of Government, University of the Western Cape, Research Report 3, 1999.

44. Interview with Albert Twayi Ngubane, Thengani Maputaland, 13 July 1999. Albert Ngubane was angry with members of his own family because they could not trace their own lineage history. He also expressed disappointment that the Ngubane clan was divided, and some of its members submitted themselves either to the house of Makhuza Tembe or Ngwanase Tembe.

45. For these methods, see Mthethwa, 'The Mobilisation of History'.

*Chapter 44*

# Claiming Community
## Restitution on the Eastern Shores of Lake St Lucia

CHERRYL WALKER

FROM THE 1950s to the early 1980s, some 1 200 isiZulu-speaking households were removed from what is now the Greater St Lucia Wetland Park (GSLWP), a World Heritage Site stretching along the northern reaches of the KwaZulu-Natal coastline. Some lost their land in the name of nature conservation, while others were dispossessed to make way for commercial forestry and the establishment of a South African Defence Force (SADF) missile base on the Ndlozi Peninsula in 1968.[1] The claims to this land of the dispossessed first began to receive serious recognition from national and regional policy-makers in the early 1990s, during the hard-fought battle between conservationists and mining interests over an application by Richards Bay Minerals (RBM), a multinational company, seeking to mine the valuable titanium deposits in the dunes on the eastern shores of Lake St Lucia.[2] After a protracted Environmental Impact Assessment (EIA) – the largest of its kind in South Africa to date – conservationists won a qualified victory in 1996, when the new, post-apartheid government decided in favour of conservation linked to ecotourism as the development strategy for the region.

Today the legacy of forced population removals remains one of the biggest challenges facing the GSLWP authorities. In coming to terms with the past and looking to the future, the park authorities and other conservation officials accept that they must respect local communities' claims to the area, thus distancing themselves from previous conservation policies that accorded little intrinsic value to African land rights and citizenship. However, turning this acceptance into practice in support of the mandate of conservation with development remains difficult. It also raises complex questions about how 'community' is to be understood in relation to the park. There are tensions between those people whom the post-apartheid state has recognised as legitimate land claimants and other, neighbouring groups who do not have direct ancestral ties to conservation land, yet still look to the park and the uncertain promises of ecotourism for improved livelihood opportunities. There have also been bitter

515

struggles among restitution claimants themselves over whose claims are legitimate and why, as well as who should represent them and why. Furthermore, external interest groups – government officials, local politicians, mining company representatives, environmental non-governmental organisations (NGOs), development consultants, researchers – continue to advocate their own understandings of community, land ownership and the public interest. They are driven by competing visions of how the public interest is constituted, what the landscape represents, and where responsibility for decisions about its future should lie. Of interest in the context of this publication is that in this turbulent history 'Zuluness' has not been pre-eminent as an axis of identity.

This chapter explores these knotty issues as they weave themselves through one of the pivotal land claims in this region – that of the Bhangazi (Mbuyazi) people – to the eastern shores of Lake St Lucia (see map).[3] This claim was formally settled in September 1999 in terms of the Restitution of Land Rights Act of 1994, thereby clearing the way for the declaration of the GSLWP as a World Heritage Site in 2000. For most local participants in this struggle, Zuluness was not so much non-existent as irrelevant, compared to the salience of deeply localised, patriarchal, clan-based histories and identifications with the land. Even where Zuluness might have been expected to play a stronger role, in the counterclaim of the Mpukonyoni *inkosi* (chief) and tribal authority to the eastern shores, Zulu identity was not invoked overtly, although a particular, nationalist version of it was implicit in the functioning of the tribal authority as an institution of the KwaZulu bantustan government and in the reading of chiefly relationships and hierarchies that informed the tribal authority claim.

### Human settlement on the eastern shores before 1956

It is tempting to think of the eastern shores as pristine wilderness,[4] but the imprint of human activity on this peninsula stretches back nearly two millennia. Indeed, the earliest Iron Age sites yet uncovered in South Africa, dating to AD 300 and 400, are located on this strip of land. Its marshlands, dune forests and coastline with 'rich shellfish beds' combined to provide 'ideal locations' for these pioneering farming settlements,[5] which long pre-date the ethnic histories inscribed in current restitution claims and proclaim the historical significance of the eastern shores for a much wider, southern African community.

However, within this broader historical continuum, the Mbuyazi clan occupies a substantial slice of the more recent past. Their residence on the eastern shores appears to span over 200 years, to the pre-Shakan era. Their name for this territory is Nkokhweni, according to the spoken traditions of Phineas Mbuyazi, the leader who spearheaded the Bhangazi claim for this land in the 1980s and 1990s.[6] In his telling, the sea is a significant marker of Mbuyazi identity. They are coastal people, 'people of the sea', who should not be separated from their land – 'It's like taking the fish

*Map showing the eastern shores of Lake St Lucia.*

from the ocean and thinking that the fish will survive.'[7] He describes his forebears as an offshoot of a chiefdom located in Kwambonambi to the south, near present-day Richards Bay, who first settled on the eastern shores in the early nineteenth century under their *inkosi*, Sokana. Documentation supporting the Bhangazi claim gives Sokana's dates as *inkosi* as 1812 to 1821 and recounts a genealogy of six *amakhosi* (chiefs), ending with Lokothwayo Njojela Mbuyazi, an *isangoma* (diviner) of considerable repute who headed the clan between 1913 and 1971.[8] In broad outlines, the oral traditions recounted by Mbuyazi corroborate those recorded by the isiZulu-speaking missionary-ethnographer, A.T. Bryant. In his *Olden Times in Zululand and Natal* he recounts how 'Mbonambi spear-smiths' vanquished the abaNtlozi (a group of 'artless arcadians' already living on 'that out-of-the-way peninsula') and 'subsequently develop[ed] into a separate and independent clanlet calling itself aba-kwa-Sokana (They of Sokana)'.[9]

From the late nineteenth century, Lake St Lucia began to feature on British maps drawn without cognisance of or interest in the local people whose land it was. In 1879, at the end of the Anglo-Zulu War, the English Crown divided the defeated Zulu kingdom into thirteen supposedly independent chiefdoms, and allocated (temporarily) the southern portion of Lake St Lucia and the eastern shores to the once powerful Somkhele (Mpukonyoni) chiefdom of the defeated Zulu kingdom, whose heartland lay inland, to the west of the lake.[10] The following year imperial authorities annexed Lake St Lucia to block the Transvaal Boers' ambitions for a sea harbour on the Indian Ocean.[11] In 1887 Britain annexed historic Zululand, excluding the substantial western tracts taken by Boer farmers. A decade later Zululand was incorporated into the Natal colony; henceforth the former kingdom's development was to be subordinated to the political and economic interests of white settlers to the south and west.

In the early twentieth century the people living on the eastern shores became, unbeknown to themselves and along with thousands of their compatriots, squatters on their own land. In 1904 Zululand was delimited by a commission of British and Natal colonial officials, which set aside 60 per cent of the territory for African occupation in 21 reserves. The remaining 40 per cent, which included the western and eastern shores of Lake St Lucia, was declared crown land.[12] A decade later the Natives Land Act of 1913 confirmed this devastating division between official native reserves and crown land. Yet while the Zululand Delimitation Commission had recommended that 'natives' be allowed to buy plots outside their reserves 'if they wish to do so', the 1913 Land Act prohibited African people from acquiring land beyond the 7 per cent of land on its national schedule.[13] With this foundational act of twentieth-century white rule, the Bhangazi people were reduced to rightless occupants, their continued existence on their land dependent on an inaccessible and unaccountable bureaucracy.

Missionary, leisure-holiday and conservationist concerns precipitated other encroachments on Bhangazi land. During the 1890s Norwegian Lutherans moved into the St Lucia area, establishing a mission at Mount Tabor.[14] From the 1920s to the 1930s the first lots of an all-white holiday town named St Lucia were laid out at the estuary mouth.[15] This meant that homesteads in the south had to shift northwards, while the Bhangazi community as a whole lost access to communal lands and the estuary mouth. A series of official conservation interventions between the 1890s and 1940s further reduced land use options.[16] Then, in 1956, some 25 000 hectares on the eastern shores were demarcated as the Cape Vidal Forest Reserve, opening the way for the Department of Forestry to plant exotic pine plantations in the southern section.[17] Ownership of this land remained vested in the Republic of South Africa, but the management of the eastern shores was split between several national and provincial arms of government, with the Natal Parks Board (NPB) responsible for conservation.[18]

By the mid-twentieth century, the Bhangazi people's way of life was being squeezed from all sides. The 1951 census recorded 2 075 'natives' resident in the Cape Vidal Forest Reserve, of whom 58 per cent were female.[19] The gender imbalance points to the prevalence of polygynous marriages, as well as the degree to which homesteads had come to rely on male migrant labour to supplement household income. Born in the 1940s, Phineas Mbuyazi, for example, worked as a young man on a sugar farm in Empangeni.[20] Yet the Bhangazi people continued to sustain many elements of their traditional way of life. Cattle constituted a major social and economic resource.[21] Homesteads practised shifting cultivation in the shallow soils, supplementing agricultural yields with hunting, fishing and the gathering of natural resources such as shellfish, despite pressure from conservation authorities who classified these activities as poaching.[22] The Bhangazi people also maintained cultural and spiritual rituals in which the sea and lake system featured prominently. Infants were baptised in the sea and Mbuyazi *amakhosi* enjoyed a totemic relationship with the hippo living in the lake system, never eating their meat and calling upon them in intercessionary ways in times of community conflict.[23] Social organisation was largely bound by and bound up with the local environment. Thus, speaking to field workers from the Commission on Restitution of Land Rights (CRLR) in the mid-1990s, Mbuyazi described the reasons why he wanted to return to the eastern shores as *isiko* (local clan-based custom), *ulwandle* (the sea) and the lake with its hippo.[24]

The political relationship between this isolated group and the Mpukonyoni Tribal Authority in the mid-twentieth century was ambiguous. The suzerainty accorded the Mpukonyoni chiefdom by the British in the late nineteenth century had formally lapsed with the subsequent annexation of the Zulu kingdom and the declaration of the eastern shores as crown land. In 1951 the Bantu Authorities Act reconstituted tribal chiefs and councils across South Africa as petty functionaries of the state, thereby radically compromising any claims by apartheid-era tribal authorities for direct political continuity between themselves and their nineteenth-century antecedents. At this time immediate authority over the African residents of the eastern shores lay with the local, white native commissioner and magistrate (first at Hlabisa, later Mtubatuba), who appears to have given the Mbuyazi a degree of recognition as a distinct entity, while also 'working closely with what [he] considered the relevant tribal authorities'.[25] In the 1990s the Mpukonyoni Tribal Authority, under *Inkosi* Mkhwanazi, argued that the Mbuyazi leaders were *izinduna* not *amakhosi*, and that the Mpukonyoni *inkosi* used to graze cattle on the eastern shores, which was evidence of his rights over it. This claim was disputed at the time by the NPB conservator on the eastern shores (Gordon Forrest), who could not recall a noticeable Mpukonyoni presence on the eastern shores when he started working for the NPB in 1964, but did remember strong links between the Bhangazi people and other coastal communities to the north.[26]

Phineas Mbuyazi insists that the Mbuyazi lived independently of the Mpukonyoni *inkosi* before they were removed, although he concedes that at one point the local magistrate demoted Lokothwayo and temporarily designated, but then never instituted, the Mpukonyoni *inkosi* as regent on behalf of Lokothwayo's son.[27] Regardless of others' interpretations of the Mpukonyoni/Bhangazi relationship, in his relationship to the eastern shores, it is Phineas Mbuyazi's identity as Mbuyazi that is core: 'My *isibongi* (clan name) is Mbuyazi, Mbonambi is my *isithakazelo* (praise name). I know who I am.'[28] Interestingly, when questioned specifically about the relationship between Mbuyazi and Zulu identity, he states that Lokothwayo was the first Mbuyazi *inkosi* to declare himself a Zulu – before that 'they were independent, they were not being regarded as Zulu, just Mbuyazi'.[29] He dates this shift to Zulu King Cyprian's reign (1948–64), and explains it in terms of 'a change in the system', an apparent reference to the political developments associated with the Bantu Authorities Act, which had begun the process of identifying all black South Africans with one of ten ethnic homelands, including KwaZulu. Since then, notes Mbuyazi, 'if you are a black person born in this province, then you are a Zulu'.[30]

### Apartheid-era forced removals, 1956–74

In the 1950s and 1960s, a series of decisions by various state agencies finally destroyed the Bhangazi people's precarious hold on their land. The first move came from the Department of Forestry, which in October 1956, after the proclamation of the Cape Vidal Forest Reserve, announced that henceforth only people who were prepared to work for it would be allowed to live in the areas under its control, and then on its terms. Addressing a meeting called with 'Induna Lokotwayo Mbuyaze and about 75 followers' at Lake Bhangazi, the Chief Native Commissioner, A.J. Turton, listed stringent terms of residence:

> Any family wishing to stay must have one member . . . in service. The family will be able to graze 5 head of cattle in [the] area. The family will have a kraal site and 1 acre of land for crops. You will ask – How do I feed myself? My answer is – from wages earned from the Forestry Department . . . [You] are given three months to make up [your] minds . . . If [families] go they must be gone by May. Some can find their own places in the Reserve.[31]

Having sounded the death knell for the Bhangazi, Turton limited discussion since, he said, he did not have 'all day . . . questions must be to the point'. In conclusion Turton's assistant described the stark choice facing the Bhangazi people as 'more generous than anything you could have expected'. He claimed that those people who had already been moved from the western shores, who previously had 'cried', 'have now told me that we should have moved them a long time ago because they have been living like baboons among the bushes but now have good land'.[32]

The second intervention was precipitated by a small conservation lobby, which began marshalling white public opposition to various commercial forestry, agricultural and irrigation projects in the region that had been identified as undermining the environmental health of Lake St Lucia and its environs. In response the government appointed the Kriel Commission, which released a report in 1966 extolling the 'unique environment' of the lake and recommending the enlargement of the existing conservation zone under a single management; this preserve, it argued, would 'represent a vignette of the original wild life of Zululand'.[33] The Kriel Commission ignored the interests of the Bhangazi people, recommending instead that they be removed and 'absorbed' into the adjacent African reserves.[34] In 1986 environmentalists achieved a significant victory when St Lucia was proclaimed a wetland of international importance in terms of the Ramsar Convention.[35]

At the same time, as the political isolation of South Africa and decolonisation on the rest of the African continent gathered pace, apartheid military forces entered the scene, emphasising the strategic importance of this remote coastal area. In 1968 the SADF established a missile-testing range extending from the tip of the Ndlozi Peninsula, over the northern reaches of Lake St Lucia and a coastal strip, to Sodwana Bay. This military installation led to the forcible and ill-planned relocation of some 3 400 Mbila people, the northern neighbours of the Bhangazi people, between 1972 and 1979.[36] The missile range also affected Bhangazi homesteads living north of Lake Bhangazi, who were forced to shift southwards before being moved from the area altogether.[37] Also at this time, and notwithstanding the growing conservation interest in Lake St Lucia, between 1969 and 1976 several mining companies applied for and received prospecting rights in three lease zones on the eastern shores from the Department of Minerals and Energy Affairs.[38]

By 1964, according to Gordon Forrest, there were no longer any African homesteads located south of Lake Bhangazi. Forrest describes the living conditions of those who remained on the eastern shores through the 1960s and early 1970s as 'rough'. A severe drought, followed by floods, decimated subsistence production; grazing was poor; hippos a problem, and money in short supply – in his view, this 'was not Eden'.[39] Throughout this time the charismatic Lokothwayo provided a focal point of Bhangazi solidarity, but in 1971 he died. In the laconic phrase of one unidentified white official, this old man, likely in his eighties at the time of his death, had always been 'somewhat adamant' against moving.[40] With his death the last flickers of Bhangazi resistance went out,[41] and in 1974 the Department of Forestry trucked the remaining 79 families out of the eastern shores.[42] For Phineas Mbuyazi, who was moved at this time, relocation meant that the Bhangazi people were severed not simply from livelihood opportunities but from the place that defined who they were:

> We left our food in the fields. Our mealies, our bananas, our *madumbe*, we left them like that. Some of our goats were left behind in the forest. When we returned to fetch them, they said, no, no one is allowed to enter here. We were the last. Those who were removed, their houses were burned. If you had money inside, it did not matter. Our removal was a great heaviness . . . We were separated from our environment. I am referring to the graves of our revered ancestors.[43]

Because the Bhangazi people were classified as squatters, they were not eligible for compensation, but were told to *ukukhonza* (declare allegiance to) neighbouring *amakhosi* to obtain homestead sites. Many ended up in the Mpukonyoni Tribal Authority; some moved illegally into the adjacent Dukuduku state forest, while others drifted north to Mbazwana. While the ecological health of the Lake St Lucia system was beginning to draw public attention, the Bhangazi removal passed unnoticed in the mainstream press; the Mpukonyoni Tribal Authority raised no protests, either.[44] Although the apartheid government's notorious forced removals policies were beginning to receive critical attention in some opposition quarters, the Bhangazi people were too small and isolated a community to be noticed.[45] They were merged into the seemingly routine impoverishment of the surrounding districts over a period of nearly twenty years, powerless in the face of official insistence and the lurking threat of state repression.

## Struggles for the eastern shores, 1974–95

The history of the land claim can be divided into three stages. The first phase covered the period 1974–89, when a small group of male elders toiled in obscurity to press their plea to return to their land, first to the newly established self-governing territory of KwaZulu[46] and, when that failed to garner any results, to the Natal Provincial Administration (NPA). At first the proponents of the claim were individual men, contemporaries of Lokothwayo (Geva, Alos, Makhuzakhuza, Mhlanga and Mpesheya), all of whom died within a few years of the final removal.[47] Phineas Mbuyazi dates his emergence as leader to '[P.W.] Botha's time', in the mid-1980s, when Lokothwayo appeared to him in a dream and instructed him to launch a struggle to restore his people's land.[48] The dream, Mbuyazi recalls, left him feeling sick and disturbed but, with the blessing of Lokothwayo's son Daniel (who was reluctant to take the lead himself), he submitted to its authority. 'When Lokothwayo came to me through the dream, I called the people of Bhangazi together. Then I explained to them about this representation. They gave me their support. Thereafter I pursued this matter.'[49]

To mark this momentous step, Mbuyazi's own father slaughtered a goat and 'told [Lokothwayo] that the child has received the burden and will carry it'. Lokothwayo has continued to haunt Mbuyazi's dreams ever since: 'There were times when I would get fed up and want to stop, but Lokothwayo would come to me and say, "Who said you could stop?"'[50]

Backing him was his wife, Thokozisiwe Mbuyazi, who, unlike her husband, was literate and played a key role in writing the letters Mbuyazi dictated to the sequence of officials to whom bureaucrats, well versed in the art of referral, directed him. A small group of older Bhangazi men constituted a support committee; one of them, V.J. Mlambo, owned a taxi in which the committee travelled 'up and down to Ulundi', the capital of the KwaZulu homeland.[51] The decision to approach officials in the

KwaZulu government was occasioned less by loyalty to the institution than by pragmatic considerations; in the 1980s it would have been hard for Mbuyazi to imagine options outside the homeland structures. However, he soon reached the limits of this route – 'At Ulundi they said they could not take the matter forward; I needed to reach up to the big government'[52] – and thereafter turned to the NPA and the NPB. Gordon Forrest remembers first meeting Mbuyazi about the land claim in 1987, when he was working for the NPB on the western shores.[53] Around this time Mbuyazi was briefly arrested at the gates to the eastern shores, when he arrived to announce his wish to return home.[54]

By 1989 South Africa was on the brink of a tumultuous period of transition. In August 1989 the more flexible F.W. de Klerk replaced the bellicose P.W. Botha as state president, clearing the way for formal negotiations between the ruling National Party and the leadership of the exiled African National Congress (ANC). In February 1990, De Klerk released Nelson Mandela from prison. The following year the National Party formally abandoned its apartheid policy and abolished the 1913 and 1936 Land Acts. Under mounting pressure to address the legacy of forced removals, it also established the Advisory Committee on Land Allocation (ACLA) to make recommendations on the disposal of state land, including to formerly dispossessed people.[55] Also during these momentous years, conservationists launched a nation-wide campaign to block RBM's plans to mine the eastern shores. The Campaign for St Lucia grew rapidly into one of the largest environmental campaigns yet mounted in South Africa, conducting an effective media campaign, collecting thousands of signatures for a national petition, and lobbying parliament. A prominent theme for the campaign was the need to protect what conservationists defined as the unique 'sense of place' that visitors to the eastern shores experienced; in summarising this position, the EIA report noted how 'the St Lucia subregion, which is perceived as wilderness, has gained a special symbolic value in the minds of many South Africans, and people overseas'.[56] A major partner in the campaign, the Zululand Environmental Alliance (ZEAL), argued that the St Lucia region 'constitutes a treasure of untold environmental richness which belongs to all the people of South Africa, indeed of the world'.[57] The De Klerk cabinet responded to the unprecedented pressure by commissioning a full EIA of the mining option, and in 1991 appointed a review panel under Judge Leon to make recommendations based on the EIA, once that was finalised.[58]

The seismic shifts in the South African political order marked the start of the second phase of the Bhangazi land claim, which profoundly influenced the future course of developments at Lake St Lucia. Initially the former residents of the eastern shores were largely invisible in the public debate that erupted around the EIA between the proponents of mining and of conservation. Both lobbies regarded the landscape over which they battled as essentially unattached to local social geographies – their conception of the 'public interest' did not include local black people as citizens but, rather, as abstract and undifferentiated beneficiaries of their preferred EIA outcomes. The managers of the EIA process themselves identified only one black organisation among fourteen 'interested and affected parties', and that was the National Union of Mineworkers, which was chosen to represent RBM workers and did not participate actively in the EIA.[59] However, as the process unfolded through the early 1990s, the previously submerged rights and interests of land claimants began to assume an unfamiliar legitimacy. In 1992 the expert commissioned to report on historically and culturally significant structures that might be affected by mining referred briefly to the history of removals and the possibility that 'in the present situation . . . the previous inhabitants of the area may feel that they have a rightful claim to the land';[60] the author of this chapter of the EIA (who located the history of the eastern shores unambiguously within a political history of the Zulu kingdom) recommended that some symbolic acknowledgment of their 'contribution to the history of the area' would be appropriate.[61]

The recognition of the history of dispossession introduced new uncertainties into the EIA, but also opened up strategic opportunities for some. For the Bhangazi people, their hitherto very locally framed objectives were now subsumed within national, even global, concerns, which were embedded in very different worldviews and struggles over resources from their own. Phineas Mbuyazi tried to use the changing dynamics to press his claim 'to go back to our land to Bhangazi if possible because we have . . . developed a special relationship [to the] shores'.[62] In late 1992 he submitted a claim to the NPB, again approached the KwaZulu government, and contacted a member of the Natal provincial executive, who referred him to ACLA. In March 1993 he wrote to ACLA. The following month he arrived unexpectedly at an unrelated ACLA hearing in Richards Bay, from where he was directed to the EIA review panel. The panel heard his story in November 1993 and referred him back to ACLA, which decided that it did not have clear authority and requested the deputy-minister of Land Affairs to determine whether it could consider Mbuyazi's claim.[63] By this time, however, Mbuyazi was no longer the only spokesperson for the claim. In September 1992, the Mpukonyoni Tribal Authority entered the fray, with active support from RBM, who hired lawyers to undertake research in support of the Mpukonyoni claim, as a precursor to negotiations with the *inkosi* about future land-use options. Taking the lead in the tribal authority claim were several youthful advisers of the *inkosi*, who had never lived on the eastern shores themselves, but were alive to the economic potential of its mineral wealth.[64] RBM also embarked upon a major public relations exercise that appealed to 'at least 100 *indunas* and *inkosi* from as far away as Eshowe' to back the Mpukonyoni claim.[65]

Compared to RBM, the conservation lobby's response to the land claims was less coherent. The Campaign for St Lucia was comprised of many organisations, overwhelmingly white, who had a common enemy in mining, but did not necessarily agree on the optimal relationship between conservation and human development.

Most organisations within the coalition downplayed the legitimacy of the claims, fearing that recognition of either claimant group as equal partners would play into the hands of RBM.[66] By 1992, however, a smaller grouping had emerged which was working to 'democratise the battle for St Lucia by consulting and involving local residents'.[67] They were receptive to new ideas about including local communities in the management of protected areas under the slogan: 'People and Parks'.[68] Their sympathies lay with the Mbuyazi grouping, which was seen as independent of RBM, although not necessarily fully supportive of the conservation option for their former land.

In November 1992 the EIA review panel requested that the public participation programme be extended to include a 'Rural Liaison Programme' to facilitate the involvement of 'rural communities', whom they defined as 'those communities living within or adjacent to the subregion who are largely illiterate, whose first language is Zulu, who are not communicable by post, and who are . . . affected by any of the two land-use options'.[69] In practice, however, the liaison programme was weighted towards black employees of RBM and the NPB, on the one hand, and KwaZulu structures on the other, with the Mpukonyoni Tribal Authority assumed to enjoy '*de facto* authority'.[70] However, during this programme, some 'union members' alleged that 'Chief Mkhwanazi knows full well that he is not the legitimate representative of the people of the Eastern Shores' and referred the facilitators to 'a certain old man [who] claims to have some documents that prove the ownership of the land by the Mbuyazi people'.[71] When interviewed by the programme facilitators, Mbuyazi emphasised the autonomy of the Bhangazi people and expressed concern 'that chief Mzondeni Mkhwanazi has entered into an understanding on the issue of mining on the Eastern Shores with RBM' because 'Chief Mkhwanazi . . . is not and his ancestors never were the traditional rulers of the territory across the St Lucia estuary'.[72]

The draft EIA report was released in 1993. It tentatively outlined a potential land-use compromise: mining in a reduced area, subject to mitigation, and the development of 'nature conservation and ecotourism activities' in the remaining area, within the framework of an enlarged wetland park.[73] The report stated that the resettlement of the previous inhabitants of the area was not an option it could consider 'on the grounds that present government policy determined that the area would revert to nature conservation', but suggested that this might have to be revisited 'in view of the developments with respect to this issue in South Africa today'.[74] The subsequent EIA review panel also identified the plight of the original inhabitants as in need of serious attention, but recommended in favour of the ecotourism option, because 'mining the Eastern Shores would cause unacceptable damage to a place which is special because of its rich history, ecological and biological diversity and the significance it has in the eyes of its many visitors. This unique combination makes the Greater St Lucia Area a very special asset for the nation.'[75]

In the meantime, however, senior officials in the Department of Regional and Land Affairs (DRLA) had advised the deputy-minister against referring the Mbuyazi claim to ACLA, arguing that the claim had no legal merits and forced removals had never taken place. These officials were anxious to prevent the claim from derailing their favoured land-use option – 'balanced development' encompassing both ecotourism and mining – and did not regard community structures operating outside the tribal authority as legitimate. Their plan was to establish a single claimant committee under *Inkosi* Mkhwanazi, and then bring selected parties together in a negotiations forum under the DRLA, to reach an agreement on the land claim as a preliminary step towards settling the land-use debate.[76]

In April 1994, in its dying days, the apartheid cabinet decided to delay the final decision on the EIA until the uncertainties around land ownership in the eastern shores had been resolved. At the time, this decision was seen to reward mining interests. While the first democratic elections ushered in a new dispensation, including an ANC minister of Land Affairs and a restyled Department of Land Affairs (DLA), they did not signal a rapid shift in the state bureaucracy. The same officials who had managed the eastern shores claim on behalf of the DRLA before the elections continued to do so for another year. In early 1995 they motivated successfully to the minister of Land Affairs (Derek Hanekom) to appoint a mediator, Professor de Clerq of the University of Zululand, to resolve the dispute about the leadership of the land claim.[77] This mediator, who had worked closely with the KwaZulu government on regional development initiatives in Zululand in the past, had no doubts about the right of the Mpukonyoni *inkosi* to represent the Bhangazi people in terms of Zulu customary law. At this point local tensions escalated sharply. In April 1995 Gordon Forrest had to escort Mbuyazi to safety after a threatening mob had surrounded the Mtubatuba hall where a mediation meeting was underway.[78] In this intimidating environment, the men who remained behind after Mbuyazi had left, including three members of Mbuyazi's own committee, signed an agreement as 'members of the Bhangazi sub-committee of the Mkhwanazi tribe' agreeing to submit 'one claim for the return of the land . . . to the Mkhwanazi tribe'.[79] Shortly thereafter, following the murder of a member of the Bhangazi group, Mbuyazi felt compelled to flee the Mpukonyoni district with his wife and moved north to a shack on the sandy flats west of Mbazwana.

## Negotiating the land claim, 1995–99

The third phase of the Bhangazi claim was initiated by the appointment of the national Commission on Restitution Land Rights (CRLR) by the ANC government in March 1995. A few months later, alerted by a lawyer acting for Mbuyazi at the DLA's in-house negotiations process,[80] the newly appointed Regional Land Claims Commissioner (RLCC) for KwaZulu Natal (the present author) intervened to take over responsibility for the claim. The RLCC tried to minimise the significance of the leadership dispute by arguing that the rights to the eastern shores belonged to the actual people who had formerly lived there, and that they could be represented by more than one set of leaders – a position that did not sit comfortably with either leader, both of whom operated within a traditionalist, chiefly mode. Now the balance began to swing towards locating those people who had been removed from the eastern shores, whose identities and views were blurred in the presence of their leaders and at large public community meetings called on their behalf within the Mpukonyoni district. Then, as now, the people with ancestral ties to the eastern shores were mostly poor, without records that documented their homestead histories, and scattered over large distances. They had to rely primarily on the radio, tribal authority meetings, neighbourhood and family networks, and rumour for information, and were extremely vulnerable to intimidation – several times the author had the disconcerting experience of being publicly condemned by members of Mbuyazi's committee, who on other occasions were friendly, when they appeared at certain meetings as members of the tribal authority delegation.[81] In a patriarchal society, women were particularly reluctant to make their voices heard.

In the meantime, Minister Hanekom had instituted his own review of the EIA, which was criticised as 'essentially an academic study' that was 'biased in favour of "concerned parties" with technical capacity, rather than the neighbouring communities who would be materially affected by the decision'.[82] For the ANC-aligned Land and Agricultural Policy Centre (LAPC), the consultants appointed to assist the minister with this task, the understanding of local community needed to extend beyond those involved in the land claim: 'Given the high levels of poverty in the Hlabisa district, it is arguable that the conceptualisation of the problem should be redefined to answer the question: how can the natural resources of the region be utilised in a manner that brings tangible and sustainable development to the sub-region?'[83]

Within this framework this ministerial review ultimately endorsed the ecotourism route, while urging that land claims be resolved as quickly as possible 'not through reoccupation of land, but through equity-sharing in ecotourism ventures and/or through the provision of alternative land'.[84] In March 1996 the national ANC cabinet finally rejected the mining option and adopted a development strategy that tied the conservation status of the future GSLWP to the promotion of ecotourism as a spur to economic growth for the entire sub-region. In the same month the RLCC formally accepted that the people who had been removed from the eastern shores had a valid claim, while also recognising that at that stage they had two sets of representatives.

Two major challenges facing the next round of negotiations were, first, to identify, enumerate and verify the actual claimants and, second, to establish the negotiating positions of the principal parties: the claimants, the NPB and the state (which was by then represented by a new echelon of DLA officials). Over several weeks in 1997 a team made up of community elders, a lawyer, a surveyor equipped with Global Positioning Satellite (GPS) technology, an anthropologist, and CRLR, DLA and NPB staff walked the eastern shores to locate old homestead sites that the surveyor had already identified from historical aerial photographs, and then record the names and whereabouts of the families who once had lived there. This mapping exercise also proved extremely significant in bridging the political divisions among the elders from the two leadership camps.[85] To make the wilderness area north of Lake Bhangazi accessible, the NPB provided a helicopter – for the old men who flew for the first time, it was a memorable experience to view their former land from the air. Andrew Spiegel, the anthropologist on the team, was struck by the ease with which the men walked – remembered with their feet – old pathways that were invisible to him; he also remarked on the contrast between their confident resurrection of place in the indigenous forests and grasslands and their acute disorientation in the pine plantations.[86]

During this time the DLA developed its negotiating position, based on the state's commitment to preserving the eastern shores as a protected area. At the same time, the NPB – always fiercely protective of the conservation integrity of the eastern shores – began to acknowledge the need to incorporate claimants more actively in the benefits and management of park resources. By early 1998 a settlement finally appeared within reach. The Mpukonyoni Tribal Authority, weakened by the loss of external support, effectively withdrew from the negotiations and in March 1998 a single committee, with one legal representative, was finally chosen at a claimant meeting in the NPB auditorium at St Lucia town. (After intense discussion among the men about the nature of South Africa's new democratic dispensation, the committee included a number of women as well.)[87] Thereafter the CRLR undertook two polls to gauge claimant settlement preferences, in which the overwhelming majority of respondents opted for financial compensation above land restoration. Mbuyazi was one of only seven who opted for the land. For many beneficiaries, especially younger descendants of the original inhabitants, whose links to the eastern shores were by then tenuous, cash was an attractive proposition. However, committee members also maintain that the outcome of the poll reflected claimants' belief that at the end of the day money was all the state was prepared to offer.[88]

The Bhangazi land claim was finally settled by means of two separate but interlocking agreements, which were signed by the parties at a major ceremony next to Lake Bhangazi on 24 September 1999 (Heritage Day) – a 'hot, hectic day' infused with last-minute tensions and logistical dramas.[89] In recognition of the importance of the settlement, Deputy-President Zuma, the premier of KwaZulu-Natal, the new minister of Land Affairs, the chief land claims commissioner, and members of the KwaZulu-Natal Conservation Authority (successor to the NPB) were present, as well as hundreds of local people who were bussed in to witness the event.[90] The first agreement, between the claimants and the minister of Land Affairs, formally settled the land claim by means of a financial settlement to the tune of R16 680 000.[91] The second agreement, between the claimants and the KwaZulu-Natal Nature Conservation Board, anticipated the establishment of the Bhangazi Community Trust, which would be the major beneficiary of a community levy on tourists visiting the eastern shores, and also committed the park management to the establishment of a 4.6 hectare Heritage Site for the Bhangazi people to develop at Lake Bhangazi, as well as a number of other benefits.[92] To operate for a period of 75 years, the community levy required hard negotiations, as the state was anxious not to exclude the Mpukonyoni Tribal Authority altogether from the benefits of the settlement, while the claimant committee wanted all proceeds to go to its Trust.[93] For Phineas Mbuyazi, putting his thumbprint to the settlement documents signalled an ambivalent conclusion to his dreams. While he could finally rest, for which he professed himself grateful, he also had to come to terms with the knowledge that his promise to Lokothwayo would not be fulfilled.[94]

## Conclusion

It is still premature to pass final judgement on the outcome of the eastern shores claim. The main provisions of the two agreements have been implemented, but the longer-term success of the settlement remains in the balance as the state's developmental vision for the sub-region struggles to take off in an extremely difficult socio-economic environment.[95] The payout process roused expectations of compensation beyond those homesteads identified as claimants by the settlement and also stirred tensions within extended beneficiary families as to who would receive the money and how it should be spent. The Bhangazi Community Trust now has a younger generation of leaders from those who fought the claim in key positions; the transition has been a bumpy one, with Mbuyazi particularly unhappy about the new dispensation, from which he feels excluded.[96] The development of the Heritage Site has not moved much beyond the concept stage, nor have trustees come up with a policy on what development projects the Community Trust should fund. To this group now falls the major responsibility for defining the relationship of the Bhangazi people to the new park management, the GSLWP Authority. While trustees are regularly called upon as representatives of the Bhangazi people in 'People and Parks' events,[97] engaging the dispersed members of the larger community of claimants in development initiatives remains a major challenge. Managing substantial community funds well, in the midst of poverty, is another.[98]

Given the history of the claim and the impoverished rural context in which the settlement must work, these problems are not surprising. Yet what may surprise those interested in the dynamics of land reform is just how contested the boundaries of community and attitudes to land have been in the Bhangazi claim. The struggle for restoration of the eastern shores was driven by leaders organised around a patrilineal clan-based identity, with a very specific relationship to place, that successfully challenged attempts to subordinate them to a larger tribal identity that was itself located within a particular, nationalist version of Zulu history. However, in the process the restitution claim came up against other struggles for the eastern shores, which drew on very different and ultimately more powerful constructions of place, development and the public interest, and guided the claim in a direction that has finally kept Phineas Mbuyazi's vision in the land of dreams. Today his confident articulation of Mbuyazi identity has given way to the still inchoate aspirations of a younger generation of Bhangazi leaders, who are struggling to find their own place in a post-apartheid, post-bantustan and, I would suggest, post-peasant world.

## Notes

I am grateful to the John D. and Catherine T. MacArthur Foundation for their generous support of my research. I also wish to thank Mzamo Mathe for his assistance with several interviews; Jeff Guy for discussion on the precolonial and colonial history of the eastern shores; Ben Carton for useful editorial comment, and all those who gave generously of their time and expertise in interviews. An earlier version of this chapter, called 'Land of Dreams: A History of the Land Claim on the Eastern Shores' was presented at the conference on 'Environment of the St Lucia Wetland: Processes of Change,' Cape Vidal, 4–7 September 2003.

1. This total is calculated from figures in the Surplus People Project, *Forced Removals in South Africa: The SPP Reports*, Vol. 4, Natal (Cape Town: Surplus People Project, 1983). The author co-ordinated the Natal region of the Surplus People Project and also dealt directly with the Bhangazi land claim as regional land claims commissioner for KwaZulu-Natal from 1995 to 2000; this experience afforded key information on the content and dynamics of this case, which is drawn on in this account.
2. Richards Bay Minerals was formed in 1976. In 1993 major shareholders were the RTZ Corporation (50 per cent), Gencor (25 per cent), the South African Industrial Development Corporation (16.8 per cent) and Old Mutual (8.2 per cent). RTZ had a wholly owned Canadian subsidiary company, QIT Fer et Titane Inc. See Council for Scientific and Industrial Research (CSIR) Environmental Services, *Environmental Impact Assessment: Eastern Shores of Lake St Lucia (Kingsa/Tojan Lease Area)*, Vol. 3, Environmental Impact Report (Pretoria: CSIR Environmental Services, 1993), p. 64. The CSIR Environmental Impact Assessment (EIA) resulted in the publication of four volumes, namely: Volume 1, Part 1, Specialist Reports; Volume 1, Part 2, Comments on the Specialist Reports; Volume 2, Reports on the Key Issues; Volume 3, Environmental Impact Report; Volume 4, Part 1, Final Report (Response to the Comments Received) and Volume 4, Part 2, Comments on the Environmental Impact Assessment.
3. 'Mbuyazi' is a clan name, while 'Bhangazi' is the name of the small lake on the eastern shores, near Cape Vidal, that lies at the heart of the claimants' former land. Terminology for the group of people associated with this claim has fluctuated over the years. While 'Mbuyazi' was more common in the land claim phase, 'Bhangazi' has become the dominant appellation since then and is the one I have preferred in this text.
4. There was an interesting debate on the applicability of the term 'pristine' and its implications for mining, conservation and land ownership during the eastern shores EIA in 1991–93; see Ruth Edgecombe, 'Comments' in CSIR Environmental Services, *Environmental Impact Assessment*, Vol. 4, Part 2, p. 307.
5. M. Hall, *The Changing Past: Farmers, Kings and Traders in Southern Africa, 200–1860* (Cape Town: David Philip, 1987), p. 36. There is also a string of Late Iron Age sites from the second millennium on the eastern shores. This archaeological evidence reveals dynamic patterns of human settlement around Lake St Lucia and challenges static notions of 'time immemorial', a term used in 1995 by the lawyer acting for the Bhangazi claimants, in support of his clients' rights.
6. Cherryl Walker, interview with Phineas Mbuyazi (the interview was assisted by Mzamo Mathe), Mbazwana, 26 February 2003.
7. Interview with Phineas Mbuyazi, 26 February 2003.

8. The claim form submitted by Phineas Mbuyazi records the following: Sokana Mbuyazi, 1812–1821; Makhungu Mbuyazi, 1821–1829; Dobo Mbuyazi, 1829–1840; Hlawukane Mbuyazi 1840–1910; Siyakatha Mbuyazi (regent), 1910–1913; Lokothwayo (Njojela) Mbuyazi, 1913–1971: Mbuyazi land claim form, Commission on Restitution of Land Rights (CRLR), File KRN6/2/2/E/8/0/0/1473 (Pietermaritzburg). When interviewed in 2003, Mbuyazi described a similar genealogy, but referred in addition to Mabhodla, a Moses-like figure with magical powers (reported to have parted waters with his stick), who appears in this account to have pre-dated Sokana; Mbuyazi also described Dobo as the son of Sokana, while omitting any reference to Makhungu: interview with Phineas Mbuyazi, 26 February 2003. The claim form supplied by *inkosi* Mkhwanazi on behalf of the Mpukonyoni Tribal Authority largely confirms the genealogy on the Mbuyazi claim form, but places Makhungu after Dobo and describes all the Mbuyazi leaders as *izinduna* (headmen) of the Mpukonyoni *amakhosi* (chiefs): Mkhwanazi land claim form, CRLR, File KRN6/2/2/E/8/0/0/1473 (Pietermaritzburg).

9. A.T. Bryant, *Olden Times in Zululand and Natal* (London: Longmans, Green & Co., 1929), pp. 105, 117–18. Bryant also mentions Mabhodla and speculates that Sokana could have been another name for Mabhodla, 'or that of his grandfather, or that perchance of his son': Bryant, *Olden Times*, p. 105.

10. Jeff Guy, *The Destruction of the Zulu Kingdom: The Civil War in Zululand 1879–1884* (Pietermaritzburg: University of Natal Press, 1994), pp. 72–74.

11. CSIR Environmental Services, *Environmental Impact Assessment*, Vol. 3, p. 20.

12. Surplus People Project, *Forced Removals in South Africa*, Vol. 4, Natal, p. 23.

13. E.H. Brookes and C. Webb, *A History of Natal* (Pietermaritzburg: University of Natal Press, 1965), p. 186. The 1936 Native Trust and Land Act, which brought the amount of territory allocated for African occupation to 13 per cent of South Africa, consolidated this position by excluding the eastern shores from the additional land it 'released' for addition to the reserves.

14. G. Dominy, 'History of Lake St Lucia Eastern Shores', in CSIR Environmental Services, *Environmental Impact Assessment*, Vol. 2, p. 430.

15. Regional Land Claims Commissioner (RLCC), 'Settlement of the Restitution Claim, Eastern Shores, Lake St. Lucia', 24 September 1999, media briefing pack (CRLR, KwaZulu-Natal, Pietermaritzburg).

16. In 1895 a game reserve was declared over Lake St Lucia and the eastern shores. Although the 1895 decree was withdrawn in 1928 (amidst settler pressure on the government to eradicate game in order to control tsetse fly), a bird sanctuary was proclaimed for the eastern shores in 1927 and a nature reserve reproclaimed over the lake and a reduced section of the eastern shores in 1938. See Shirley Brooks, Ruth Edgecombe, Bev Ellis, Steven Kotze and Milner Snell, 'Comments on Chapter 13, History of Lake St Lucia Eastern Shores' in CSIR Environmental Services, *Environmental Impact Assessment*, Vol. 4, Part 2, pp. 310–13.

17. This also resulted in the immediate closure of the mission station: Dominy, 'History', p. 430.

18. This synopsis of a very complex regulatory terrain is drawn from CRLR, 'Negotiations Report, Claim for Restitution of Land Rights, Eastern Shores Lake St Lucia', draft 26 February 1998 (Pietermaritzburg).

19. Letter, District Forest Officer, Eshowe to The Conservator of Forests, Pietermaritzburg, 24-1-56 (Annexure 26, CRLR, 'Negotiations Report, Eastern Shores Lake St Lucia' [1998]). This population total accords with the tally of 381 former homestead sites that the CRLR mapped as part of its claimant verification exercise in the mid-1990s: see CRLR, 'Negotiations Report', p. 8.

20. Interview with Phineas Mbuyazi, 26 February 2003.

21. The 1954/55 Agricultural Census recorded a total of 2 373 head of cattle at the Bhangazi and Mbelela Dips: Letter, District Forest Officer, Eshowe, 24-1-56.

22. Cherryl Walker, interview with Gordon Forrest (NPB conservator, eastern shores, 1993–97, and working in the area from 1964), Bergville, 25 August 2003. Through the course of the twentieth century several animal species, already severely depleted as a result of colonial hunting in the nineteenth century, disappeared or were reduced in numbers; Phineas Mbuyazi recalls that both elephant and leopard were found on the eastern shores during his youth: interview with Phineas Mbuyazi, 26 February 2003.

23. Interview with Phineas Mbuyazi, 26 February 2003. According to Mbuyazi, members of his clan can communicate directly with the hippo; he also recounts a story of how two hippo followed Lokothwayo to Lake Bhangazi from KwaNgwanase (next to Kosi Bay), after Lokothwayo had married two 'daughters' from that area.

24. Handwritten notes on a meeting with Phineas Mbuyazi, Mbazwana, 7 March 1997, copy in possession of Cherryl Walker.

25. G.W. Forrest, conservator E. Shores (NPB), 'Background – E Shores Land Claim', undated typescript, *c.*1995, copy in possession of Cherryl Walker. Jeff Guy, who was commissioned by the author when regional land claims commissioner to undertake archival research on the history of the Mbuyazi clan, reported, 'It is clear that this [Bhangazi] occupancy of the land was recognised by the magistrate and native commissioner, at least in the 1940s and 1950s when representatives of the Mbuyazi were sometimes present at the Quarterly Meetings of Chiefs, Headmen and People': Jeff Guy, 'Political Power and Land Distribution in the St Lucia Area from the Nineteenth Century', typescript, 17 July 1995 (Jeff Guy, History Department, University of Natal, 1995), p. 2. Official correspondence of the 1950s refers to Lokothwayo as an *induna*, rather than an *inkosi*, but this is not necessarily indicative of how his followers regarded him at the time.

26. Forrest, 'Background'.

27. Interview with Phineas Mbuyazi, 26 February 2003. At the time Lokothwayo was facing a charge of arson; the details of this case are not known.

28. Interview with Phineas Mbuyazi, 26 February 2003.

29. Ibid.

30. Ibid.

31. The account of this meeting comes from an apparently verbatim record headed 'Record of Meeting Held at Lake Bangazi, Hlabisa District, in Connection with Afforestation of Land East of St Lucia Lake and Conditions under Which Natives Will be Permitted to Remain in Area. 30/10/56', Annexure 31, CRLR, 'Negotiations Report'.

32. Ibid.

33. Dominy, 'History', p. 430.

34. Ibid.

35. The Ramsar Convention was established in 1971 when various 'contracting parties', i.e. national states, agreed to designate a list of wetlands of international importance and to formulate and implement plans for their conservation. South Africa became a signatory to the convention in 1975: Ramsar Bureau, 'Ramsar Convention Monitoring Procedure, Report No. 28, St Lucia System, South Africa', in CSIR Environmental Services, *Environmental Impact Assessment*, Vol. 4, Part 2, p. 643.

36. Surplus People Project, *Forced Removals in South Africa*, Vol. 4, Natal, pp. 261–67. The Surplus People Project also notes the co-operation of the KwaZulu bantustan government with the SADF in bringing about this removal.

37. Interview with Gordon Forrest, 25 August 2003.

38. CSIR Environmental Services, *Environmental Impact Assessment*, Vol. 3, pp. 21–24.

39. Interview with Gordon Forrest, 25 August 2003.

40. The quote comes from an undated and unsigned memorandum, 'Squatters in Crown Ground between the Sea and the St Lucia Lake System North of Mtubatuba', a document possibly generated by the NPB; copy in possession of Cherryl Walker.

41. Interview with Phineas Mbuyazi, 26 February 2003.

42. Memorandum, Regional Director, Zululand Forest Region, to Chief Bantu Affairs Commissioner, Durban, 13 May 1974 (Annexure 34, CRLR, 'Negotiations Report').

43. Interview with Phineas Mbuyazi, 26 February 2003.

44. Interview with Gordon Forrest, 25 August 2003.

45. For example, the dire conditions prevailing at the resettlement camps of Limehill in Natal and Dimbaza in the Eastern Cape drew some national as well as international condemnation in the late 1960s and early 1970s. For an account of population removals at this time, see C. Desmond, *The Discarded People* (Braamfontein: The Christian Institute, n.d.). For a more general history of apartheid removals, see L. Platzky and C. Walker, *The Surplus People: Forced Removals in South Africa* (Johannesburg: Ravan Press, 1985).

46. KwaZulu was established as an ethnic, isiZulu-speaking self-governing territory in 1977.

47. Interview with Phineas Mbuyazi, 26 February 2003.

48. Ibid. The exact nature of the relationship between Lokothwayo and Phineas Mbuyazi was a matter of considerable dispute during the land claim process. In different testimonies Phineas Mbuyazi describes Lokothwayo as his father, as well as the brother of his father, while other sources maintain that Phineas Mbuyazi's father and Lokothwayo were, in Western terms, cousins not brothers.

However, Phineas Mbuyazi recognised Lokothwayo's biological sons; for him Lokothwayo was a close, senior clansman who figured as a social, rather than strictly biological, father.

49. Interview with Phineas Mbuyazi, 26 February 2003.
50. Ibid.
51. Cherryl Walker, assisted by Mzamo Mathe, interview with Ephraim Mfeka, chairperson of the Bhangazi Community Trust, as part of a group interview with the Bhangazi Community Trust, Mtubatuba, 25 February 2003.
52. Interview with Phineas Mbuyazi, 26 February 2003.
53. Interview with Gordon Forrest, 25 August 2003. Gordon Forrest knew Phineas Mbuyazi before 1987.
54. Interview with Phineas Mbuyazi, 26 February 2003.
55. Republic of South Africa, *White Paper on Land Reform* (Pretoria: Government Printer, 1991).
56. CSIR Environmental Services, *Environmental Impact Assessment*, Vol. 3, p. 122.
57. Zululand Environmental Alliance (ZEAL), 'Submission by the Zululand Environmental Alliance (ZEAL) to the Review Panel of the Environmental Impact Assessment (EIA) of the Eastern Shores of Lake St Lucia (Kingsa/Tojan Lease Area)', in CSIR Environmental Services, *Environmental Impact Assessment*, Vol. 4, Part 2, p. 136.
58. CSIR Environmental Services, *Environmental Impact Assessment*, Vol. 3.
59. The fourteen 'interested and affected parties' were: the Chamber of Mines, Department of Environment Affairs, Department of Minerals and Energy Affairs, Natal Parks Board, Natal Provincial Administration, Regional Development Advisory committee (Region E), Richards Bay Minerals, KwaZulu Bureau of Natural Resources, Wildlife Society, Zululand Environmental Alliance, Department of Water Affairs and Forestry, Pinechem (Pty) Limited, St Lucia Town Board, and the National Union of Mineworkers (NUM): CSIR Environmental Services, *Environmental Impact Assessment*, Vol. 4, Part 1, pp. 1–21. NUM did not submit comments on the EIA report, although some members were interviewed as part of the Rural Liaison Programme initiated by the review panel in late 1992. Interestingly, this programme reported that NUM was anti-mining, because of scepticism about the nature of the job opportunities promised by RBM: CSIR Environmental Services, *Environmental Impact Assessment*, Vol. 4, Part 1, pp. 2–5.
60. Dominy, 'History', p. 437.
61. Ibid. This chapter also placed the history of removals within a catalogue of cultural resources, including buildings and shipwrecks.
62. The quote is extracted from a photocopied document headed 'Translation of a letter written in Zulu to the Advisory Land Commission dated 24-3-93, written by Mr Pheneas Mbuyazi', copy in possession of Cherryl Walker.
63. CRLR, 'Negotiations Report', p. 13.
64. This account is based on the author's involvement in the negotiation of the claim after 1995.
65. H. Marais, 'When Green Turns to White', *Work in Progress* 89 (1993): 35.
66. These comments are based on submissions made to the author and her own observations when she was RLCC.
67. Marais, 'When Green Turns to White': 35.
68. New Ground, *People and Parks* (A New Ground supplement recording the GEM [Group for Environmental Monitoring] Broederstroom conference, 21 to 23 May 1993).
69. CSIR Environmental Services, *Environmental Impact Assessment*, Vol. 4, Part 1, p. 2.
70. The criteria used to identify who to interview on the ground were given as proximity to the mining site; historical connection to the area; employment with either RBM or the NPB, and '*de facto* authority . . . in this case the Mpukonyoni Tribal Authority'. The parties interviewed were 'Kwa-Mpukonyoni-Dukuduku communities under chief Mkhwanazi within the MTA, black RBM personnel living in the sub-region, NUM in Richards Bay, black NPB staff in the sub-region, the local Inkatha Freedom Party representative, and the Hlabisa Regional Authority': Bonga Mlambo and Themba Mzimela, 'St. Lucia Rural Communications Programme: Comments from Rural Communities on the Environmental Impact Report', 1 June 1993, Appendix 1, CSIR Environmental Services, *Environmental Impact Assessment*, Vol. 4, Part 1, pp. 1–2.
71. Mlambo and Mzimela, 'St Lucia Rural Communications Programme', CSIR Environmental Services, *Environmental Impact Assessment*, Vol. 4, Part 1, p. 17.
72 . Ibid. The report goes on to state that Mbuyazi warned of a pending 'bloodbath' and claimed that RBM was manipulating the situation in its favour by 'giving chief Mkhwanazi the center stage'.

73. CSIR Environmental Services, *Environmental Impact Assessment*, Vol. 3.
74. Ibid., p. 39.
75. J. Baskin, *A Report Outlining the Key Choices that Decisions Makers Need to Consider with Regard to the Future of St Lucia*, (Johannesburg: Land and Agricultural Policy Centre, 1995), p. 4.
76. CRLR, 'Negotiations Report', p. 14.
77. This account draws on the author's observations of events as RLCC at the time, as well as the reports prepared by the mediator and reproduced in CRLR, 'Negotiations Report'.
78. Interviews with Phineas Mbuyazi, 26 February 2003 and Gordon Forrest, 25 August 2003.
79. CRLR, 'Negotiations Report', Annexure 63.
80. Mbuyazi had been referred to this lawyer, based in Empangeni, by some conservationists who were concerned about their own exclusion from the negotiations process and were also in touch with the RLCC.
81. These comments are based on the author's observations as RLCC at the time.
82. Baskin, *A Report Outlining the Key Choices*, p. 5.
83. Ibid., p. 6.
84. Ibid., p. 22.
85. A. Spiegel, 'Walking Memories and Growing Amnesia in the Land Claims Process: Lake St Lucia, South Africa', paper presented at the annual conference of the Association for Anthropology in Southern Africa, University of Zimbabwe, Harare and The Trauma and Topography Colloquium, University of the Western Cape, 1999. Revisiting the land separated those who had lived there from those who had not – already in earlier demonstrations at the park entrance to the eastern shores, former Bhangazi residents had observed that the *inkosi* did not know where to march to assert his claim: 'He could not take anyone, he could not show anything, he was weak. But Phineas went and said, "You see that bush, you see that there? That's where we were."': interview with Bhangazi Community Trust, 25 February 2003.
86. Spiegel, 'Walking Memories'.
87. CRLR, 'Minutes of Meeting, St Lucia/Eastern Shores Land Claim, NPB Auditorium, 28 March 1998', 2, Annexure B to Deed of Settlement, 'Agreement Entered into between the Republic of South Africa and the Community of Former St Lucia Eastern Shores/Bhangazi Beneficial Occupants and Their Direct Descendants', 24 September 1999 (CRLR, KwaZulu Natal, Pietermaritzburg).
88. Interview with Bhangazi Community Trust, 25 February 2003.
89. Cherryl Walker, 'The Land Claim Process', unpublished presentation, Greater St Lucia Wetland Park NGO Information Weekend, 10–11 May 2003.
90. In addition to the signing ceremony, there were speeches, a school drama performance, and a feast, for which the NPB and the St Lucia Town Board (relieved by the outcome of the settlement) donated beasts for slaughter.
91. In arriving at the amount, the state treated the land rights of the Bhangazi people as de facto equivalent to those of ownership, and then determined a total value for the land under claim, based on a determination of its presumed agricultural value in 1999. Through the process of negotiations the parties eventually settled on an amount of R16 680 000. They also agreed to fix the size of the dispossessed community at a maximum of 556 families; the financial settlement thus meant a cash payment of R30 000 per beneficiary family. Although the list of families was based on field evidence, its finalisation was, inevitably, a political process. The actual number of households on the list was set at 548, made up as follows: 342 identified in the field by the CRLR, with a living, verified beneficiary; 39 identified in the field, without a living, verified beneficiary; 167 identified by the claimant committee as valid community members and accepted as such by the RLCC through the negotiations.
92. The agreement stipulates that trust funds are to be used for the education and benefit of the community of beneficiaries as a whole. It also identifies the trust as the mechanism for representing the Bhangazi people in their future dealings with the GSLWP. The agreement also stipulates protection for important Mbuyazi grave sites and grants a number of additional benefits such as free access for Bhangazi people to the eastern shores during normal gate hours and eligibility for seeds, cuttings and culled animals 'in accordance with Board policy', although the conservation authorities retain their managerial prerogatives over how these are to be allocated. The claimant community also won the right to nominate candidates for employment consideration by the conservation authorities.
93. Eventually the parties agreed that 70 per cent of the gate levy would go to the Trust, 20 per cent to the tribal authority, and 10 per cent to the central community fund of the Conservation Board.

94. Interview with Phineas Mbuyazi, 26 February 2003. The ceremony encompassed a range of emotions. For conservationists it was a moment to savour. For myself as RLCC it was a bitter-sweet moment – there was 'the element of sadness . . . in this moment of congratulation' for those who 'had always hoped that one day they would be able to return to their former homes': see RLCC, 'Settlement of the Restitution Claim'.

95. One unfortunate lapse involves a DLA undertaking of assistance to the handful of claimants who had indicated that they were interested in buying alternative land with their payout, on which to settle. That undertaking was never actively pursued once the agreements were signed and with time became increasingly unrealisable as DLA staff involved in the negotiations moved on and beneficiaries spent their money.

96. Interview with Phineas Mbuyazi, 26 February 2003.

97. An example is the 'People and Parks' consultation held at Cape Vidal on the eastern shores as a precursor to the World Parks Congress that was held in Durban in September 2003.

98. In February 2003 trustees stated that the fund stood at over R750 000: interview with Bhangazi Community Trust, 25 February 2003.

*Chapter 45*

# Virginity Testing
## A Backward-looking Response to Sexual Regulation in the HIV/AIDS Crisis

TESSA MARCUS

IN CONTEMPORARY KWAZULU-NATAL the recent revival of virginity testing, *ukuhlolwa kwezintombi*, emerges within a social framework shaped by a confluence of factors: the deadly toll in isiZulu-speaking households plagued by HIV/AIDS, disassociation of marriage from family life and the allure of Zulu traditions that allegedly protected the past innocence of youth. Despite its nostalgic appeal, virginity testing is also fraught with contradictions that grip contemporary South Africa, reflecting divisions between traditional and modern practices, as well as the gender and generational tensions that such practices foster. Derived from an earlier period where sexual regulation was crucial to community stability, virginity testing has now been reinvented by older isiZulu-speaking women who bear a disproportionate share of the burden of AIDS, caring for gravely ill adult children and coping with the economic crises that sudden mortality creates. In this context, *ukuhlolwa kwezintombi* expresses a deep-rooted concern of female elders to strengthen controls over assertive youthful behaviour and reverse some of the devastating causes of domestic break-down.[1]

Undeniably, the idea of testing for virginity sparks considerable curiosity in South Africa and elsewhere, where the media features *ukuhlolwa kwezintombi* ceremonies. After hearing of or reading such reports, it is hard not to wonder: what is being tested, by whom, and for what purpose? Or to query: how do people conceptualise the value of virginity today? Or to ask: what conditions or circumstances would give rise to such a practice among isiZulu-speaking people without property or other wealth of note?

**Crises in sexual regulation: HIV/AIDS in South Africa and KwaZulu-Natal**
Perhaps it is best to start with the last question first. The context of HIV/AIDS translates into a public health calamity of unprecedented dimensions. Indeed, the pandemic foregrounds 'the social organisation of sexual experience and the social imagination

of the sexual subject' in a way that is exceptional in medical science and policy formulation.[2] Certain accepted assumptions of atomised behaviour have informed research and intervention efforts as AIDS has proliferated over the past decade. Yet the connection between sexual regulation, individual lifestyles and personal psychology is problematic. Such a link incorrectly assumes that once given adequate information about risky behaviour, a human being is able to make decisions in the sexual realm, as if she or he only operated in a world of rational choice. Extensive recent fieldwork in communities gutted by AIDS has revealed the fallacy of this universalising approach, particularly in explaining why a variety of intervention programmes fail and why reactive customary responses such as virginity testing appear, on the surface, to have gained momentum in contemporary KwaZulu-Natal.[3]

Sexual relations are embedded in relationships of power, which are in turn shaped by economic, political and cultural factors produced by historical change. Sexual dynamics reflect heterogeneous and contradictory social trajectories that depend on a shared set of norms mediated by choice. With the intrusion of HIV/AIDS, the regulation of sex in South Africa is in acute crisis, not least because of the pandemic's deleterious impact on individuals, their families and neighbourhoods in which they live. African communities of South Africa have positively acknowledged adolescent sexuality, partly because it was an area that was socially recognised as requiring proactive regulation. There were common practices that aimed to manage and monitor sexual socialisation, so as to reduce the possibility of premarital pregnancy and ensure the ritual reconstitution of family and community through marriage. At the same time, norms of sexual regulation reinforced a gendered hierarchy of power and authority. Typically, a male patriarch occupied the pinnacle of the domestic hierarchy. Below him in standing were his senior wives and other senior men of his homestead; they, in turn, were positioned above junior wives and women, while youth and children constituted the base of this idealised social pyramid.[4]

As the historians Peter Delius and Clive Glaser point out, African peer groups played an instrumental role in sexual regulation, particularly in societies that performed male and female rites of initiation.[5] Such peer organisation gave boys and girls periodic freedom from adult discipline and imbued them with a measure of autonomy. Despite generational struggles between old and young, this arrangement was only possible because mutual agreements bound youth and adult to a 'common inheritance' that was intimately tied to rules about sexual relations.[6] In other words, youth were assured of more property and a higher social standing as long as they behaved properly and honoured their elders through rituals of customary respect (*ukuhlonipha*), which included abiding by mores not to engage in full intercourse before marriage.

The transformations wrought by colonialism and industrialisation over the past century and a half profoundly affected indigenous practices regulating intimacy, making it increasingly difficult to link sexual activity to customary understandings of familial, economic and political inheritance. The processes of modernisation trailing white conquests also relegated African sexual relations to the realm of private domestic reproduction. At the same time, Christian injunctions imparted by white missionaries entrenched a variety of moral messages that a belief in Jesus Christ entailed suppression of human urges and the protection of virginity as the sacred state of unmarried people.[7] The complex legacies of these historical developments underpin the resurrection of traditions such as *ukuhlolwa kwezintombi*. This is clearly reflected in a case study conducted during the new millennium involving isiZulu-speaking students at the then University of Natal who replied to questions that probed why virginity testing has re-emerged today.

### 'You can't be like uMariya (Mother Mary)': Virginity testing in a time of AIDS

Confronted by the ravages of HIV/AIDS, the University of Natal launched initiatives to assess the impact of the pandemic on its own community, organising discussions with a cross-section of first-year students in April 2000 in a series of focus groups that were named Khwela, Rangana, Sipika, Moabi, and so forth. Ranging from 18 to 26 years old, the young adults interviewed were asked to debate issues of sexual regulation such as virginity testing.[8] The testimonies of students in these focus groups revealed gendered ideas of chastity; a range of definitions for virginity were also given, among them 'never being touched by a man's penis', 'being pure' and 'innocent', or resembling 'a Ricoffee tin which has not been opened'. Most associated virginity with not being sexually active. However, the students puzzled over whether non-penetrative sexual interactions, or even anal or oral sex violated virginity. Some classified virginity strictly in terms of penal/vaginal penetrative sex. For them, a girl remained 'pure' even if she may have been penetrated anally, orally, or manually (with fingers). Others thought that virginity could be breached with intense sexual activity that did not involve penetration.[9]

The definition of virginity is critically important to determining the social veracity of testing. Given the students' difficulty in demarcating virginity, they were even more challenged to define how the test assesses a pure condition. Fiona Scorgie elaborates on the *ukuhlolwa kwezintombi* procedure: '[T]he girls line up, then lie in a row on their backs on grass mats spread out on the ground. They part their legs while the *umhloli* (inspector) peers briefly at each girl's exposed genitals before making her judgement (occasionally, the *umhloli* will use her hands to part a girl's labia).'[10] In addition an *igosa lezintombi* – the female elder who leads, directs and inspects – noted the muscle tone of the assembled girls, as well as gauging the girls' general demeanour, which she took into account when determining their virginity status.

In the focus group discussions, where the students seemed to be aware of these subjective dimensions of *ukuhlolwa kwezintombi*, debates arose about traditional knowledge versus scientific verification. Numerous participants expressed unease that a life-affirming ritual depended on a female elder's visual inspection of girls' thighs, the back of their knees, breasts, genitalia, as well as how they presented themselves in public. The students' discomfort centred on doubts that personal judgement of a respected older woman constituted proof of virginity. They did not wholly believe that what was confirmed amounted to scientific evidence. This scepticism was even more apparent in their responses to procedures to ascertain male virginity, which essentially considered the intensity of impact of a boy's urine on the ground, or whether he could accurately direct his urine stream across a wire. There was considerably more confidence in the possibilities of physiological examination of girls because it could possibly determine a young female's virginity. However, as women in the focus groups were quick to point out, there was also scepticism that such an inspection could conclusively show virginal status, since many knew that sport, insertion of tampons, or visits to the gynaecologist tampered with the 'evidence'. For these university students to question the value of virginity in terms of whether it was scientifically assessable suggests that the meaning of testing chastity to an isiZulu-speaking young person is not simply framed by ahistoricised cultural values. Some students remarked that customs change over time and according to place. Moreover, their worldviews were infused with precepts of science, a body of critical thought that sat uneasily with their understanding of traditional practice.

The issue of virginity testing does not end with the problem of definitions or with the more evident difficulties surrounding proof of the condition. To be sure, a ritual can be entirely acceptable to people if it has some social value beyond its systematic corroboration. So what, if any, is the perceived social value of *ukuhlolwa kwezintombi* to the wider public? Not surprisingly, the response of students in the focus group discussions is a gendered one. Some women in the Rangana focus group stressed that virginity testing gave them a sense of pride. One participant explained: 'It's good to boost your self-esteem. Whenever you walk, you walk with your shoulders high, you know. Like "I've never been interfered with".' Their male counterparts, by contrast, considered their own virginity as having little intrinsic worth. More generally, several participants indicated that female virginity boosts male pride and authority, ensuring a young man that the girls or young women he courts are trustworthy and not 'damaged' (or, in the words, of one participant, 'the guy knows he [alone] broke the girl's virginity').[11]

The broad-ranging discussions brought to light other problems related to female virginity and intimate interactions. While one or two young women claimed that offering their virginity to a man was a way of showing their romantic and social commitment, a few men regarded female virginity as perilously entrapping. 'She can be stuck to me,' declared one male student in the Rangana focus group. He added: 'At least somebody should go first and then I'll come afterwards.' However, several men expressed a different disconcerting view. For them, a girl's virginity was an enticement, an opportunity to test a potential lover's will and prowess, and a way of establishing themselves amongst their peers. Their count of deflowered virgins helped establish their *isoka* (lover) status, as their conquests and the recounting of sexual successes made them real men, for they had the numbers to prove it.[12] Still other female and male students saw virginity as a hollow concept because the condition, in their estimation, countermanded individual desire, curiosity and sense of adventure. As one young woman put it: 'You can't be like UMariya (Mother Mary).'[13]

### The limits of virginity testing

If the social value of virginity is largely one-sided in the contemporary world of some isiZulu-speaking young adults, what merit might testing for virginity have in the South African population at large? Very little, as far as the focus group participants were concerned. The best defence of virginity testing that they could present was to contend that it promoted the preservation of the self, especially for women, and thereby raised awareness of the dangers of sexually transmitted diseases, especially HIV/AIDS. The *ukuhlolwa kwezintombi* could also be used to help a mother, they said, to encourage her children to remain virgins until they came of age or got married. A female student in the Sipika focus group explained: '[A] person could be a mother of four children, but with her certificate she can still tell her children "I was a virgin up to 21", maybe.' This sentiment resonates with Scorgie's argument, which stresses that the resuscitation of *ukuhlolwa kwezintombi* is driven by a reactive effort to ward off the further erosion of adult women's authority and the disintegration of family life.[14]

But equally important, it was also clear from discussions in the focus groups that testing could not safeguard virginity, even if that was the desired intention. Some remarked disparagingly that *ukuhlolwa kwezintombi* had no meaning beyond the event itself. 'Virginity testing is useless,' one student said. 'She can lose her virginity anytime after that certificate (given to show she took the test).'[15] In the words of another student, who questioned whether the ritual did anything to engage with issues of HIV/AIDS: 'You get a (ornamental) hood for your behaviour' and little else.[16] Several participants expressed fear that the test invited sexual aggression: 'In some areas, it is like you are advertising yourself,' said one young woman. Her counterpart admitted, 'Boys will follow you and come and get you.'[17]

Many students in the focus groups described how virginity testing collided with what they termed modern values such as human and individual rights, which they, as young adults, embraced. 'The question is all about privacy,' one student said.[18] Several commented that their parents, who were anxious about the spread of HIV/AIDS, forced them to be tested. In this context, students voiced concerns about the manipulated relationship between virginity testing and the pandemic. Other focus group participants worried that in an environment where the myth circulates that sex with a virgin is a cure for AIDS, public testing endangered girls because it made them visible targets of assault. These worries may not be misplaced, given the increase in reported rape and indecent assault of children, as well as the seeming increased attendance of men at virginity testing ceremonies.[19]

Perhaps more tellingly, given the heated public debates over virginity testing, only one of the isiZulu-speaking participants in the focus groups cited in this chapter was willing to undergo *ukuhlolwa kwezintombi*, or the alleged male equivalent. The other students remained largely sceptical of the ritual. One male student even admitted, 'If I was a girl, I don't think I would have gone for a virginity test.'[20] *Ukuhlolwa kwezintombi* clearly had no appeal to these young isiZulu-speaking women and men at the University of Natal. This begs the question: who is targeted for this purity test?

In theory *ukuhlolwa kwezintombi* is aimed at all women because it is designed to uphold female chastity. As 'a gendered response to a disease experience that is fundamentally "gendered"', Suzanne Leclerc-Madlala contends, virginity testing is 'another thread in the web of meaning that places women and women's sexuality at the epicentre of blame for the current AIDS epidemic'.[21] Her argument draws on public perceptions that women upset sexual social relations. Young single women are particularly accused of no longer conforming to cultural ideals of demure female obedience. This complaint often emanates from men and elders, who seem to echo similar protests of Zulu patriarchs a century before, as they lost customary powers over women and youths during a period of tightening white rule and expanding capitalist exploitation.[22] Rather than behaving responsibly and curbing aggressive male sexual advances (which are held to be naturally uncontrollable and socially acceptable), women and girls are now said to be initiating sexual relations and seeking numerous liaisons – a prerogative regarded as belonging to those who court them. As Mark Hunter observes, young 'women typically see multiple boyfriends as a means to gaining control over their lives, rather than as simply acts of desperation – although the two of course are linked. The very vocabulary of sex – centred for women around the verb *qoma* (to choose a man) – is suggestive of women's agency.'[23] In a world of need and desire where economic inequalities are profoundly gendered, proponents hail virginity testing as a way to bring female waywardness under stricter patriarchal authority.

Apart from the restorative allure of *ukuhlolwa kwezintombi*, especially for elders, the ritual also holds some importance for prepubescent girls and young teenagers. However, whether these youths are part of the educated elite or marginal masses in townships and informal settlements, few girls and boys appear to view virginity testing as a crucial step toward the fulfilment of basic human needs, such as the procurement of food, construction of shelter and pursuit of schooling. Whatever the positive association of *ukuhlolwa kwezintombi* with a bygone, if idealised, social order, there is perhaps a more powerful healing force in today's South African democracy: the validation of individual rights of all girls and women regardless of race and ethnicity and sexual orientation.[24]

## Virginity testing and family crises in AIDS-buffeted KwaZulu-Natal

Virginity testing will not alter the course of HIV infections, nor is it likely to safeguard idealised norms of chastity. In fact virginity testing seems to have little impact on young isiZulu-speaking people and other segments of contemporary South Africa at risk in the current pandemic. The concept of virginity itself has limited social worth because its preservation is no longer linked to a vital institution of sexual regulation: marriage. Marriage symbolises many social ideals: accomplishment, maturity, stability and good standing in communities, as well as personal commitment, fidelity and happiness. In KwaZulu-Natal and elsewhere in South Africa, irrespective of class or colour, marriage is still prized, if difficult to attain, for fewer and fewer African people can afford to negotiate nuptials.

Many isiZulu-speaking people either postpone marriage until later in life, or do not wed at all, particularly because marital arrangements entail prohibitively expensive customary obligations such as *ilobolo* (bridewealth), which can cost the prospective husband and his family up to R20 000 in gifts to the bride's family. The guaranteed virginity of a bride often requires her would-be spouse to secure as much as R5 000 over the set *ilobolo*; if he chooses to dispute her chaste status, he may stir interfamilial friction.[25] Most importantly, the grim evidence of AIDS-induced deaths shows starkly that marriage is no bulwark against the lethal pandemic.[26] In an environment where marriage is largely unrealisable, many unwed isiZulu-speaking women are likely to find that virginity does not enhance their prospect for becoming wives, especially when fidelity in marriage is merely a spoken ideal for some husbands.[27]

In KwaZulu-Natal and South Africa more broadly, female virginity is hardly going to serve as a barrier to keep girls from penetrative sex, an experience defined as much by 'coerced consent' as mutual agreement,[28] especially where coercion is seen as an intrinsic, even straightforward, part of intimate relations with the opposite sex.[29] Intimacy, not virginity, is the bargaining chip that isiZulu-speaking girls and women use to get things they need or desire from men. If anything, common sense suggests that the public identification of girls deemed pure makes them more vulnerable to potential male predation in a world of transactional sex.

Virginity testing is unlikely to make a positive contribution towards alleviating the burdens shouldered by older women in the HIV/AIDS epidemic. It may even aggravate domestic and community tensions since *ukuhlolwa kwezintombi* can fuel recriminations. Women are at the epicentre of this angry and confused thinking. IsiZulu-speaking men, for their part, add to the chorus of blame, accusing women of spreading disease, despite the fact that male *isoka* pursuits entail having multiple sexual partners. Rather than ensuring codes of sexual regulation and steering youths through danger, *ukuhlolwa kwezintombi* leads a litany of externalising responses to HIV/AIDS that underpin sexism, social intolerance and violence against women in a democratic society.

# Notes

1. F. Scorgie, 'Virginity Testing and the Politics of Sexual Responsibility: Implications for AIDS Interventions', *African Studies* 61:1 (2002).
2. R. Parker, R.M. Barbosa and P. Aggleton, eds. *Framing the Sexual Subject: The Politics of Gender, Sexuality and Power* (Berkeley: University of California Press, 2000).
3. Evaluative research conducted by Rachel King points to this inherent weakness; see 'Sexual Behavioural Change for HIV: Where Have the Theories Taken Us?' (UNAIDS Best Practice Collection, Key Material UNAIDS, 1999).
4. B. Carton, *Blood from Your Children: The Colonial Origins of Generational Conflict in South Africa* (Charlottesville: University Press of Virginia, 2000).
5. P. Delius and C. Glaser, 'Sexual Socialisation in South Africa: A Historical Perspective', *African Studies* 61:1 (2002).
6. Meyer and Meyer 1970, cited in Delius and Glaser, 'Sexual Socialisation'.
7. It should be noted that challenges to established patterns of sexual regulation were rarely acknowledged publicly or elevated to the level of a wider crisis that required grave moral appeals.
8. The primary data in this chapter is based on some of the testimonies drawn from 33 isiZulu-speaking students in a small range of focus groups. A broader project gauging sexual attitudes in many more focus groups than the four cited here involved students of all races. However, these early research findings are indicative.
9. 'Student Perspectives on Male Adult, Female Child Sex: Research Report, Khwela Focus Group', (University of Natal, 2000).
10. Scorgie, 'Virginity Testing'. She uses the term *umhloli*, which means inspector. However, the women who do virginity testing are also referred to as *igosa lezintombi*, which means inspector and guide to girls; the term *igosa lezintombi* means to lead and direct as much as check: personal communication, Dalifa Ngobese, Ncome Museum, 2003.
11. 'Virginity Testing: Research Report, Moabi, Rangana and Sipika Focus Groups', (University of Natal, 2000). Along the same lines, some students believed that female virginity reduced the risks of contracting AIDS.
12. M. Hunter, 'The Materiality of Everyday Sex: Thinking Beyond Prostitution', *African Studies* 61:1 (2002). This association of prowess with the conquest of virgins is not confined to isiZulu-speaking men. It is a widely spread expression of masculinity in many communities and cultures across South Africa (personal communication, M. Masoga, 24 June 2003) and is inseparable from the contradictions of sexual regulation that demands chastity and fidelity of women and sexual experience and multiple partnering of men.
13. Khwela Focus Group (University of Natal, 2000).
14. Scorgie, 'Virginity Testing' and Sipika Focus Group (University of Natal, 2000).
15. Sipika Focus Group (University of Natal, 2000).
16. Rangana Focus Group (University of Natal, 2000).
17. Moabi Focus Group (University of Natal, 2000).
18. Ibid.
19. Scorgie, 'Virginity Testing'.
20. Moabi Focus Group (University of Natal, 2000).
21. S. Leclerc-Madlala, 'Virginity Testing for AIDS Prevention: Consolidating the Gendered Epidemic', XIII International Conference on AIDS, Post Workshop on Social Inequality, Community Mobilisation and HIV-AIDS Vulnerability, 15 July 2001, University of Natal, Durban.
22. Carton, *Blood from Your Children*.
23. Hunter, 'The Materiality of Everyday Sex'.
24. For a broader analysis of the gender politics and struggles leading to the assertion of women's rights in South Africa, see C. Walker, *Women and Resistance in South Africa* (London: Onyx Press, 1982).
25. Personal communication, M. Masoga, 24 June 2003.
26. P. Badcock-Walters, C. Desmond, D. Wilson and W. Heard, 'Educator Mortality In-Service in KwaZulu Natal', (HEARD, University of Natal, 2003). Using as their case study teachers in South African schools, they conclude: 'In-service mortality rates for teachers in KwaZulu-Natal in the period 1998–2001 were three times higher than the normal ("without AIDS") mortality rate for South Africa in equivalent age bands'. In this period 90 per cent or more of the educators who died

were 49 years old or younger; 80 per cent had died of illness or natural causes. The fact that most of these deaths include women and men between the ages of 30 and 50 years old is suggestive that HIV infection and AIDS fatalities are to be found inside, as well as beyond, formalised relationships.

27. Hunter, 'The Materiality of Everyday Sex'.
28. R. Jewkes, J. Levin, N. Mbananga and D. Bradshaw, 'Rape of Girls in South Africa', *Lancet* 359 (2002): 9303.
29. A. Harrison, 'The Social Dynamics of Adolescent Risk for HIV: Using Research Findings to Design a School Based Intervention', *Agenda* 53 (2002) and Scorgie, 'Virginity Testing'.

*Chapter 46*

# Nomkhubulwane
## Reinventing a Zulu Goddess

MICHAEL LAMBERT

FROM 27 TO 29 SEPTEMBER 1996, an isiZulu-speaking African community in Bulwer, KwaZulu-Natal, conducted a three-day ritual in honour of Nomkhubulwane, the Zulu fertility goddess.[1] The first day of the ceremony began with a 'past' and apologies to the goddess for years of neglect; chanting and a relentless drumbeat set in motion male and female *izangoma* (diviners, plural of *isangoma*), who walked in a procession headed by the chief officiator, who was leading a tethered goat. They wound along a narrow dirt road to a clearing in a field above the Turn Table Trust where an animal sacrifice was to be held.[2] Here, a large fire was kindled and prayers exclaimed, telling both the ancestors and goddess that the ritual would result in peace, as well as the preservation of 'our culture' and 'children'. The goat's throat was slit and the animal carried around the fire, leaving a trail of blood. After the chief officiator and the goat bearers had marked their lips with the spilled blood, they presented the animal to the rest of the *izangoma*, who did likewise. After the limp goat was tossed into the fire and burnt, together with eleven chickens, similarly sacrificed, a large group of bare-breasted young women surged forward and launched into a frenzied traditional dance.[3]

During the second day of celebration, girls and young women gathered to have their virginity examined (*ukuhlolwa*) by older women, who marked with white clay the foreheads of those who passed the test. The graduates then proceeded down to the nearest river to bathe naked and beat the waters to call the goddess. Afterwards, they danced before the chanting older women. As night fell, a cow was slaughtered, cooked and eaten. One of the highlights of the evening was spirited storytelling around a bonfire, led by well-known South African author and playwright Gcina Mhlope.

The third and final day focused on 'the future'. The virgins sang the goddess's song 'Mabele, mabele oMama' ('Sorghum, sorghum o mothers') and marched to a field specially prepared for them. Moving in a group across open ground, the young women, clad in Zulu apron skirts (*imitsha*) and repeating the refrains of '*Mabele*', scattered seed onto the goddess's sacred soil while older women and a clutch of men and boys observed. Rain fell heavily two days later, thus apparently confirming both the goddess's forgiveness for years of neglect and her role in presiding over fertility.[4]

The Nomkhubulwane festival is now an annual event in rural isiZulu-speaking areas. It was apparently the brainchild of a prominent Zulu *isangoma* and teacher, Nomagugu Ngobese, who claimed to be inspired by a dream in 1994. Thereafter she committed to writing a university dissertation (for a BA honours degree in isiZulu) on Nomkhubulwane. Her studies were supervised by an American academic Dr Kathryn Limakatso Kendall, a white professor of Drama Studies at the University of Natal (Pietermaritzburg) from 1995 to 1998. In a recorded interview in 1996 for a documentary video of the Nomkhubulwane revival made by Kendall, Ngobese explains why she 'reinvented' the festival: to give the so-called lost generation a sense of Zulu identity. Her subsequent dissertation, titled 'Nomkhubulwane "Goddess of Rain" ', develops this idea more fully, arguing that the return of the goddess promises to aid the recovery and inculcation of traditional moral values and sexual practices, long eroded by Christianity, 'Urbanisation and Industrialisation', forces 'instrumental in bringing about gender discrimination'.[5] Ngobese predicted that resurrecting Nomkhubulwane (and, presumably, virginity testing) would help to fight the spread of AIDS and 'unnecessary' pregnancies, as well as foster reconciliation among the 'Black peoples of Africa'.[6] In a 2000 interview with a German television company, Ngobese added that her cultural projects seek to influence sex education from 'an African perspective' and thus are 'part of the African Renaissance the president (Thabo Mbeki) talks about'.[7]

Like Ngobese, Kendall uses the sweeping terms of an activist to describe her involvement in the Nomkhubulwane festival, although she accentuates different motives. With disarming honesty, Kendall portrays herself as 'a postmodern-deconstructionist-lesbian-feminist' with a 'materialist theoretical bias', who believes that the revived ritual can offer marginalised women 'visibility, public validation, and agency from the very public nature of the rituals'.[8] This theoretical position clearly influences Ngobese's dissertation, as well as the shape and content of the documentary video on Nomkhubulwane.[9] To be sure, Kendall emphasises that the ritual revival was her student's idea. Yet the teacher admits that she urged Ngobese to make the Nomkhubulwane festival the subject of her dissertation. Moreover, the Drama professor took the instrumental step of advancing her student's fieldwork by visiting Ngobese's rural home 'to help her begin the research on how to (re)create the rituals . . .'[10] Kendall's account of this early inquiry exposes how invested she was in the rebirth of a 'nonce ritual',[11] which promised 'empowerment' and 'enhanced self-esteem' to rural Zulu women in general, and female *izangoma* in particular.[12] Finally, she says that she embraced Nomkhubulwane in the context of healing a festering communal wound suffered during South Africa's recent colonial past. Thus, her focus on strengthening identity formation among *izintombi* (older girls, plural of *intombi*) is intended to counteract 'internalised racism absorbed from the views of Zulu history and culture taught in the infamous Bantu schools'.[13]

Interestingly, Kendall believes that the reinvigoration of spiritual beliefs is 'particularly likely to lead to increased female self-esteem'.[14] The rituals that morally fortify Zulu women and *izangoma*, she opines, would have been sustained more widely had they not been hijacked by certain sexual, patriarchal and organisational politics – a reference to the practice of virginity testing which is linked (although not restricted) to the Inkatha Freedom Party and its Zulu cultural nationalism. In this respect, Kendall clearly parts company with her erstwhile student, carefully stating her disapproval of Ngobese's alliance with the now well-known Andile Gumede, queen regnant of the virginity testers.[15]

Many of the isiZulu-speaking officiators, dignitaries and spectators attending the 1996 festival, who were interviewed by Kendall's students in the University of Natal Community Theatre class,[16] expressed a belief that the revival of Nom-khubulwane rituals would both unite communities fractured by violence and restore a 'lost' culture.[17] Bringing back the rituals of Nomkhubulwane was said to reinforce respect for ancestors, parents, members of the community and oneself.[18] Furthermore, interviewees declared the strict regulation of *izintombi*'s virginity essential to the giving of bridewealth (*ilobolo*) and the socio-economic survival of rural communities.[19] That a girl's virginity, checked and verified, entitled her family to ask for more *ilobolo* (usually an extra cow to be given to the bride's mother) is a practice that endures in many parts of rural KwaZulu-Natal today, where cattle, wealth and one's reputation in the community are still inextricably linked.[20] Most male respondents asserted that women were responsible for the moral well-being of the community. To support this view, one chief testified in an interview that 'when you have females . . . who are virgins you automatically get boys that are virgins'. Similarly, the minister of Environmental and Traditional Affairs in the KwaZulu-Natal legislature, Nyanga Ngubane, singled out 'young women [who] should first be vigilant'. A young male spectator remarked more glibly that 'male virginity depends on one's interest but female virginity is a *must*, because all men want to marry virgins, otherwise divorce will occur'. A male *isangoma* affirmed this view, proudly exclaiming 'a nation is a nation because of faithful women'.[21] Some female respondents reinforced these attitudes by claiming that 'the discipline is with the girls, not the boys'.[22]

There are remarkable similarities between Ngobese, Kendall and the interviewees, particularly in their expressed purpose for recreating the Nomkhubulwane festival. They all agreed that the three-day ritual enhanced essential qualities of *ubuntu* (respect for oneself and others, which entails reconciliation of perceived wrongs). Moreover, their reasons for elevating *ubuntu* as a goal depended on 'identity' discourse. However, whereas Ngobese and the interviewees spoke of recovering a 'lost identity' by incorporating general (ahistorical) notions of precolonial mores and sexual practices, Kendall employed the language of 'empowerment', drawing more explicitly on feminist and post-structuralist ideas that underpin the concept of identity-in-process and 'identity as the site of resistance' (in this case against internalised racism). Ngobese and the interviewees underscored the importance of virginity testing in the struggle against HIV/AIDS. Yet Kendall voiced misgivings about the possible link between ritual practices and biomedical outcomes, foregrounding instead the beneficial impact of a vague concept called 'African Spirituality', which she implied could be isolated from cultural politics. Finally, both Ngobese and Kendall ignored the question of *ilobolo* in relation to reviving the rituals, while the interviewees were strikingly attuned to the socio-economic benefits of sustaining customary exchanges of this kind.[23]

Differences aside, the reconstruction of the ritual itself was tackled rigorously. For her part, Ngobese used both oral and written sources. She formulated and disseminated a questionnaire about ritual structure, poems and songs, which aimed to collect information from observers and participants at the Nomkhubulwane festival. Over a period of eleven months, Ngobese consulted Bulwer *izangoma* and isiZulu-speaking traditionalists in nearby Impendle district, and also travelled with Kendall to Nongoma in northern Zululand to interview two elderly Zulu women, a member of the Zulu royal family, Princess Ntombini kaNdabuko and a local *isangoma*, Velenine Ndebele, who remembered the Nomkhubulwane song ('*Mabele oMama*') from her grandmother.[24] In addition, Ngobese gleaned evidence from classic ethnographic texts on Zulu culture and history, written by whites resident in Natal for long periods of their lives, such as A.T. Bryant's *The Zulu People as They Were before the White Man Came*, Eileen Krige's *The Social System of the Zulus* and Axel-Ivar Berglund's *Zulu Thought-patterns and Symbolism*.[25] She also referred to a study comparing the Greek goddess Demeter to Nomkhubulwane, which critically assessed how both Bryant and Krige patronisingly described the Zulu goddess as a 'child of the Mediterranean' or a 'Zulu Ceres'.[26] The listing of Erich Neumann's *The Great Mother: An Analysis of the Archetype* and Martin Bernal's *Black Athena: The Afroasiatic Roots of Classical Civilisation* in the bibliography of Ngobese's Honours dissertation suggests that Nomkhubulwane was destined to emerge as the primal Mother, an icon in both feminist spiritual and black nationalist quests to locate human origins in Africa.

Despite Ngobese's conscientious attempts to retrieve what she believed was a lost cultural event, there is much in her efforts that depended on elastic invention. There is no historical record (either oral or written) of mass three-day festivals for Nomkhubulwane requiring animal sacrifice and virginity testing. The burnt offering that occurred at the 1996 revival was not traditional Zulu sacrificial practice and was replaced by the sacrifice of a cow and two sheep at the festival in 1997.[27] Furthermore, the three-day festival, following a ritual rhythm reconstructed by Ngobese (for example, apologies for past neglect, *ukuhlolwa*, and 'sowing' seed for the future), eerily resembled female fertility rituals in the ancient Greek tradition and Easter *triduum* of the Christian liturgical calendar.[28] To be sure, Ngobese acknowledged that the new customary rituals did not come from some deep current of Zulu heritage; she sought to modernise the 'celebration so that the youth will participate'.[29] Kendall similarly noted that some *izintombi* interviewed recognised that the pivotal features of the Nomkhubulwane festival were more fiction than custom.[30]

Most importantly, one of the dramatic moments of the Nomkhubulwane ritual, the virginity testing of thousands of young women and their recognition with daubs of approbation – which in the 1997 festival ranged from green for virgins, yellow for semi-virgins, and red for mothers[31] – is not a delineated precolonial practice, although *ukuhlolwa* probably occurred in private Zulu households.[32] Neither Ngobese nor Kendall confronts the realities of public virginity testing. The videotape recording of the 1996 revival skims over the process entirely and only shows a parade of joyous virgins smeared with white clay frolicking after the procedure. Recent anthropological studies by Suzanne Leclerc-Madlala and Fiona Scorgie provide graphic accounts of just how invasive virginity testing can be. Young girls have to lie in a row on grass mats, often in football stadia before crowds, whilst the tester (*umhloli*, plural *abahloli*) parts their legs and examines their genitalia, frequently using her hands to part the girls' labia or pull their buttocks to see the *ihlo* (the 'eye', presumably hymen) more clearly.[33] The above-mentioned analyses also focus on the potential divisiveness caused by *ukuhlolwa*, which subverts the spirit of *ubuntu*.[34] For example, at Ngobese's first Nomkhubulwane festival (1996), one of the thirteen-year-old participants remarked that she was shocked by the 'checking' procedure and would not participate again. It should be noted, however, that a group of girls at the same ritual reported that since they practised *ukusoma* (non-penetrative sex) with their boyfriend they were happy to be checked.[35]

The contradictory nature of these responses reflects the ambiguities of virginity itself. In some ancient Greek and Roman all-female fertility rituals, married women became virgins again for important socio-cultural purposes: virgins were associated with the wildness of Nature, which was tamed by the acculturation of marriage, but which had to be collectively unleashed if the community were to survive.[36] Conversely, Rome's well-known Vestal Virgins enjoyed privileges accorded to married women and men.[37] As these examples illustrate, virginity has been for centuries a highly prized cultural category of infinitely malleable resilience, reconstituted and manipulated by patriarchal societies from the classical Greeks to modern amaZulu, particularly in relation to what men and many women perceived as the intimate (and mysterious) link between women, their natures and Nature itself.

In the video recording *Calling the Zulu Goddess Home*, made by Kendall in 1996, an *isangoma* revealed her perception of the amorphous status of virginity when she remarked that participation in the Nomkhubulwane rituals could cleanse girls who have been raped (presumably turning them into virgins again). The policing of virginity by cohorts of testers and the paradoxical association of *ukuhlolwa* with the revival of fertility rituals – for the Nomkhubulwane festival climaxes in the sowing of seed – reveals a transparent attempt to resurrect a set of cultural attitudes that have long shaped patriarchal perceptions of Zulu femininity.[38] Indeed, male *izinduna*, headmen, and *izangoma* gave Nomkhubulwane rituals their blessing and actively participated as well.[39] Young men attended the festivals, some for an afternoon of virgin spotting.[40] In this case Leclerc-Madlala writes that female initiates face a grave threat: they risk rape and contracting HIV/AIDS after their virginity is publicly proclaimed in the presence of a few predatory young men.[41]

The roles of women in the festival are indicative neither of the empowerment of women nor of the affirmation of Zulu female identity; instead they reflect the deep pervasiveness of certain patriarchal gender stereotypes. That women should bear the responsibility for a nation's moral and sexual well-being – for in the discourse surrounding the festival, the two are synonymous – seems to be endorsed by older women, who know intimately about the dire cost of unsafe sexual practices and illegitimate births of HIV-infected children.[42] No one would surely deny that any traditional Zulu effort to tackle the horror of HIV/AIDS in KwaZulu-Natal is laudable, but the revival of practices that appear to exonerate men from sexual accountability is especially dangerous.[43] Many Zulu men may well want virgin brides and many mothers may well get their *ilobolo* cows, but if a husband believes that 'the discipline is with the girls, not the boys', the virgin bride's right to life may well be cruelly flouted.[44]

Reinventing a long-dormant Zulu goddess and her rituals in contemporary KwaZulu-Natal is clearly not simply about recovering lost Zulu identities and cultural practices. Ngobese conceives of precolonial history as a golden age, a Utopia unblemished by colonial rapacity and 'gender discrimination'.[45] Kendall shares Ngobese's romanticised view of Zulu cultural history in her quest for the recovery of what she terms 'African Spirituality'. However, where Ngobese suggests that the recovery of this women-only ritual will usher in an age without 'gender discrimination', Kendall writes explicitly of the 'empowerment' of Zulu women and female *izangoma* in particular. What Kendall means by 'empowerment' is never adequately explained. It cannot simply mean 'increased visibility, public validation, and agency from the very public nature of the rituals'. This, of course, may be a hopelessly masculinist viewpoint, 'from the outside'. Kendall records of female *izangoma* that they *felt* empowered during the 1997 festival;[46] Leclerc-Madlala comments on the empowerment of older women through virginity testing 'in a society where women's voices have historically been muted'.[47] However, it is debatable whether 'feeling' empowered as the result of participation in a ritual or practice such as virginity testing can translate into a meaningful challenge to patriarchal power. Furthermore the role of senior Zulu women – Ngobese's chief sources of information – in reinforcing patriarchal gender stereotypes is well known.

As the above discussion demonstrates, the reinvention of the Nomkhubulwane rituals by Ngobese and Kendall reveals the interesting (but forced, and ultimately unhappy) marriage of Africanist romanticism, supported by current political rhetoric about the African Renaissance, indigenous knowledge systems and Western feminism. Where Ngobese clearly does not distinguish between sex and gender, and conceives of the recovery of an essential Zulu womanhood, Kendall, as an American feminist, not only makes such a distinction, but believes that participation in these rituals can change perceptions of gender, and thus contribute to altering patriarchal power relations in Zulu communities. Kendall is not alone in this: the human rights and feminist discourse of the South African Constitution makes the distinction between sex and gender too.[48] As Scorgie and other scholars have shown, the clash between the universal, humanist ideals of the Constitution and the beliefs and claims of local communities to reclaim 'our cultural traditions' stirs controversy in the identity politics of contemporary South Africa.[49] The tension between the Gender Commission and the isiZulu-speaking virginity testers (and between Kendall and Ngobese over precisely this issue) is yet another instance of this clash.

## Notes

1. As she is deemed in all the relevant ethnographies (see Michael Lambert, 'Nomkhubulwana: The Zulu Demeter', *Akroterion* 35:2 [1990]: 46–59): and in the opinions of nearly all the interviewed officials, guests and participants at the 1996 festival. These opinions may well have been formed by the research conducted by the initiator (Ngobese), who used Radio Zulu to broadcast information about the goddess and her rituals (98 *APD* 2:8; 98 *APD* 5:13). At least one of the participating *izangoma* refused to limit the functions of Nomkhubulwane to fertility and the bringing of rain and considered her as 'the female part of god' (see K. Kendall, 'The Role of *Izangoma* in Bringing the Zulu Goddess Back to Her People', *The Drama Review* 43:2 [1999]: 97). One interviewee (female) at the 1996 revival regarded her as a 'living princess' who died 'being a virgin' (98 *APD* 2:12), another (male) as one of 'our ancestors and heroes' (98 *APD* 5:14), yet another (male) as the first female goddess who 'created human beings on earth' (98 *APD* 7:6). The abbreviation *APD* refers to the unpublished Nomkhubulwane documents housed in the Alan Paton Centre at the University of KwaZulu-Natal, Pietermaritzburg; *APV* refers to the documents relating to the making of the videotape *Nomkhubulwane – Calling the Zulu Goddess Home*.
2. A trial run of the festival was first held in Impendle in 1995, attracting 'about 150 teenagers plus a few *izangoma* and interested parents' (see Kendall, 'The Role of *Izangoma*', 95 and P.N. Ngobese, 'Nomkhubulwane "Goddess of Rain"' (Honours dissertation, University of Natal, Pietermaritzburg, 1997), p. 25.
3. Two hundred *izintombi* at first (Kendall, 'The Role of *Izangoma*', 103), this group grew to approximately 4 000 on the second day (Kendall e-mail: 3 October 1996: 97 *APV* 37) and dwindled to 1 000 on the third day (ibid.); the total crowd in 1996 was estimated at 7 000, and at 11 000 in 1997 (Kendall, 'The Role of *Izangoma*': 107).
4. This account of the 1996 recreation of the rituals is based on Kendall's videotape of the ritual entitled *Nomkhubulwane – Calling the Zulu Goddess Home*, housed in the Alan Paton Centre (Pietermaritzburg, 97 *APV* 36), and on Kendall's personal accounts (97 *APV* 37; 1999: 103–105).
5. Ngobese, 'Nomkhubulwane', pp. 44–54, 52.
6. Ibid., pp. 45, 50. In the videotape, Ngobese stipulates that Nomkhubulwane could be adapted to 'all the peoples of South Africa, not only the blacks'.
7. Interview for a German television company, *Natal Witness*, 19 October 2000, p. 3.
8. Kendall, 'The Role of *Izangoma*': 113.
9. Kendall painstakingly attempts to appear to be as 'engaged' and as self-reflexive as possible ('The Role of *Izangoma*': 99–101).

10. Kendall, 'The Role of *Izangoma*': 95, 98, 99.

11. Ibid.: 105.

12. Ibid.: 94, 114.

13. Ibid.: 106.

14. Ibid. Elsewhere, Kendall states that the Nomkhubulwane rituals constitute 'an annual celebration of Ubuntu, the Goddess, sexual self-mastery, and African Spirituality' (e-mail, 3 October 1996: 97 APV 37).

15. Kendall, 'The Role of *Izangoma*': 112–15. For the controversy around virginity testing, which has been condemned by the Gender Commission as an abuse of human rights, see especially Suzanne Leclerc-Madlala, 'Virginity Testing: Managing Sexuality in a Maturing HIV/AIDS Epidemic', *Medical Anthropology Quarterly* 15:4 (2001): 533–52; 'Protecting Girlhood? Virginity Revivals in the Era of AIDS', *Agenda* 56 (2003): 16–25 and Fiona Scorgie, 'Virginity Testing and the Politics of Sexual Responsibility: Implications for AIDS Intervention', *African Studies* 61:1 (2002): 55–75. The local press has given the debate considerable attention: see, for instance, Nalini Naidoo's report on the conference on virginity testing organised by the Commission on Gender Equality (*Natal Witness*, 16 June 2000, p. 13) and various articles reporting on protest marches – using 'young virgins' – mounted by the testers against the Commission (*Natal Witness* (*Echo*), 27 July 2000, p. 12 and *Natal Witness*, 13 December 2000). Popular magazines such as *Bona* have also featured the controversy ('The Price of Virginity', November 2000, pp. 40–42). See also the admirable attempt to educate an isiZulu-speaking public about the debate in 'Old Traditions in Modern Times', *Learn with Echo*, no. 404, 28 September 2000. For Gumede's reputation, see Leclerc-Madlala, 'Virginity Testing': 539; 'Protecting Girlhood?': 19 and Scorgie 'Virginity Testing': 57.

16. Tape recordings of these interviews, transcripts, translations and commentaries by the interviewers form the bulk of the Nomkhubulwane documents in the Alan Paton Centre. Clearly the student interviewers are not professional anthropologists and wisely restrict themselves to a set of questions shaped in the classroom situation; furthermore the intellectual quality of the comment varies widely. In addition, a number of the students had no knowledge of isiZulu and used interpreters, often with questionable results. However, there is much of interest in this collection, which awaits comprehensive analysis.

17. 98 APD 1:2; 98 APD 1:7; 98 APD 3:11 and 98 APD 5:6–7.

18. 98 APD 6:5 (ancestors); 98 APD 5:15 (parents); 98 APD 8:3 (respect for ourselves) and 98 APD 2:11 (respect for one's body).

19. 98 APD 2:4–5 (the mother of the virgin will get a special cow); 98 APD 2:6 (a mother of three virgin daughters participating in the festival is confident she 'will get her three cows from her three daughters when they marry'); 98 APD 2:10 (*ilobolo* sustains community relationships); 98 APD 2:13 (if one's bride is not a virgin, the parents have to repay the *ilobolo* and a fine; the girl becomes an outcast in the community). One of the respondents in the 1997 festival claims that the parents of the girl who is no longer a virgin have to pay three cows: one for Nomkhubulwane, one for the boys from her area, and one for the chief (98 APD 12:6).

20. Scorgie 'Virginity Testing': 61 and Leclerc-Madlala 'Virginity Testing': 544 and 'Protecting Girlhood?': 18.

21. 98 APD 1:2 (chief); 98 APD 1:4 (minister); 98 APD 5:7 (young male) and 98 APD 7:2 (male *isangoma*).

22. 98 APD 2:5 and 98 APD 13:2, 4 (1997 festival). Interestingly, the 1997 female interviewees held fast to the opinion that the 'guys should be checked as well'. Virginity testing of young men involves the examination of their knees and analysis 'of the way they answer questions when asked' (98 APD 2:10). Attempts to clarify this resulted in my legs directly below the kneecaps being prodded by an obliging Zulu colleague: I was not issued with a certificate.

23. One of the student interviewers during the 1997 festival records that only one *isangoma* mentioned that she was there to celebrate Nomkhubulwane; the other *izangoma* that she interviewed emphasised that they were there to check young girls because 'virginity is an important factor when a young girl's *lobola* is being paid' (98 APD 25:5).

24. Ngobese, 'Nomkhubulwane', pp. 15–20 and Kendall, 'The Role of *Izangoma*': 96, 98.

25. A.T. Bryant, *The Zulu People as They Were before the White Man Came* (Pietermaritzburg: Shuter & Shooter, 1949); Eileen Krige, *The Social System of the Zulus* (Pietermaritzburg: Shuter & Shooter, 1950) and Axel-Ivar Berglund, *Zulu Thought-patterns and Symbolism* (Cape Town: David Philip, 1976).

26. See Ngobese's bibliography ('Nomkhubulwane', pp. 57–59).

27. For traditional Zulu sacrificial practice, see M. Lambert, 'Ancient Greek and Zulu Sacrificial Ritual: A Comparative Analysis', *Numen* 40 (1993): 293–317. For the nature of the sacrifice at the 1997 festival, see 98 *APD* 9:10 and Kendall, 'The Role of *Izangoma*': 113.

28. Both known to Ngobese. She comments on problems with her sources at Impendle precisely 'because of their strong affiliation to the Christian faith and their denomination is Roman Catholic' ('Nomkhubulwane', p. 16). Centocow, near Bulwer, is the site of a prominent Roman Catholic mission, established in the late nineteenth century and named after the Madonna of Czestochowa, patron saint of Poland: behind the modern Nomkhubulwane may well lurk the Virgin Mary.

29. Kendall 'The Role of *Izangoma*': 99.

30. Ibid.: 105.

31. 98 *APD* 13:2.

32. Scorgie, 'Virginity Testing': 57, 61.

33. Leclerc-Madlala, 'Virginity Testing': 537–38 and Scorgie, 'Virginity Testing': 58–59.

34. See Leclerc-Madlala, 'Virginity Testing': 540 for 'A', 'B' and 'C' grades given by the virginity testers: 'to be given a "C" grade . . . is to be marked with shame and disgrace. Depending on the particular tester and the host of the event, the girl's family may be asked to pay a fine.'

35. 98 *APD* 2:6–7 and 98 *APD* 2:16. Compare with Leclerc-Madlala, 'Protecting Girlhood?': 20.

36. H.S. Versnel, 'The Festival for Bona Dea and the Thesmophoria', *Greece and Rome* 39:1 (1992): 48–49.

37. M. Beard, 'The Sexual Status of Vestal Virgins', *Journal of Roman Studies* 70 (1980): 12–27.

38. Zulu masculinities have received considerable attention (see, for example, C. Hemson, '*Ukubekezela* or *Ukuzithemba* African Lifesavers in Durban', in *Changing Men in Southern Africa*, ed. Robert Morrell (Pietermaritzburg: University of Natal Press, 2001), pp. 57–73; Thokozani Xaba, 'Masculinity and its Malcontents', in *Changing Men*, ed. Morrell, pp. 105–24; Benedict Carton, 'Locusts Fall from the Sky: Manhood and Migrancy in KwaZulu', in *Changing Men*, ed. Morrell, pp. 129–40 and C.S. Rankotha, 'The Construction of Egalitarian Masculinities in the Midlands of KwaZulu-Natal' (Ph.D. diss., University of Natal, Pietermaritzburg, 2002] but, perhaps predictably, little attention has been paid to patriarchal constructions of Zulu femininity.

39. See Leclerc-Madlala's incisive comments on the role of men in powerful positions, who associate the recovery of 'lost' traditions, such as virginity testing, with the African Renaissance and the rediscovery of 'indigenous knowledge systems' ('Virginity Testing': 536).

40. One of the female *izangoma* at the 1996 virginity testing catches a 'boy peeping' (98 *APD* 2:14).

41. Leclerc-Madlala, 'Protecting Girlhood?': 22–23.

42. See Leclerc-Madlala, 'Virginity Testing': 535 for the role of older women, supporting households of younger children whose parents have died of HIV and AIDS, in advocating a return to the virginity testing tradition.

43. Compare with Leclerc-Madlala, 'Virginity Testing': 547: 'I would suggest that promoting virginity testing of girls helps to obscure the role of men and their abuse of sexual power and privilege, which are driving the rapid growth of HIV and AIDS.'

44. Underpinned by the cultural belief that the body of the sexually active woman is a dangerous pollutant, capable of generating and harbouring disease (Leclerc-Madlala, 'Virginity Testing': 541–42, 545–46). Compare with Gumede's views: 'the girls are the ones spreading the virus . . .' (*Natal Witness*, 21 September 2000).

45. Compare with Leclerc-Madlala's comments on the effect of rapid social changes on the 'rekindling of people's interest in the past' ('Protecting Girlhood?': 16).

46. Kendall 'The Role of *Izangoma*': 113–14.

47. Leclerc-Madlala, 'Virginity Testing': 546–47.

48. Constitution of the Republic of South Africa, Bill of Rights, Act 108 of 1996, Chapter 2, 9 (3).

49. Scorgie, 'Virginity Testing': 55, 62 and Leclerc-Madlala, 'Virginity Testing': 536.

# Chapter 47

# AIDS in Zulu Idiom
## Etiological Configurations of Women, Pollution and Modernity

SUZANNE LECLERC-MADLALA

BY MOST MEASURES, the results of campaigns to curb the growth of the African AIDS pandemic have not been encouraging. A 2002 United Nations evaluation report on 'first generation' HIV prevention programmes in 39 developing countries, 22 of which were in Africa, found no significant behavioural change in spite of high levels of HIV/AIDS awareness.[1] These findings coincide with renewed questioning of the relevance of commonly used models that guide communication programmes and policies in Africa, as well as in Asia and Latin America.[2]

In South Africa, as throughout the continent of Africa, models used for designing and developing strategies for communicating HIV/AIDS were, and still are, largely the same as those used in the West. These are models commonly based on the theories and principles of social psychology, and are couched almost exclusively in biomedical terms. Derived from a corpus of studies of people in Western middle-class cultures, social psychological models emphasise self-directed behavioural change applied at the level of the individual.[3] In accordance with these dominant models, efforts to halt the global spread of HIV/AIDS have been largely conceived as challenges in behavioural modification. Thus, fostering safer sex, the primary objective of most AIDS education interventions, has proceeded through an agenda to promote individual decision-making, increased self-esteem and empowerment, particularly of women.

Assessing the prospects for HIV prevention in Africa, Triandis was among the first to suggest that widely accepted social psychological models might have severe limitations when applied in contexts for which they were not designed.[4] At that time Triandis called for closer attention to be paid to the shaping force of the cultural context when trying to understand differences in health behaviours. By failing to recognise the centrality of culture as an organising theme in people's lives, Triandis posited that HIV/AIDS prevention in Africa could only be expected to have limited success.

This chapter explores local interpretations of HIV/AIDS in KwaZulu-Natal and draws upon ethnographic research spanning over a decade of study on the sociocultural constructions and meanings of AIDS among isiZulu-speaking people.[5] Primarily on the basis of fieldwork in the peri-urban region of Mariannhill, some 30 kilometres (18.5 miles) west of Durban, an attempt is made to illuminate the critical role played by cultural schemas in shaping people's ongoing experiences of and responses to HIV/AIDS. In our quest to develop more effective HIV/AIDS interventions, perhaps it is time to reconsider Triandis's views and to design ways to address the pandemic that relate more closely to people's own local truths about the disease.

**Exploring local meaning**

Early in the epidemic and recognising the importance of the cultural frame for understanding knowledge and behaviour related to illness and its management, several anthropologists set out to study HIV/AIDS and the nature of local idioms used to understand the new disease.[6] Although undertaken at a time when the epidemic was still largely one of rising HIV infection and barely visible in terms of increased illness and death, later studies from Kenya, Uganda, South Africa, Tanzania, Botswana and Zambia attested to broad similarities in the ways in which HIV/AIDS had been worked into local disease categories and prevailing discourses of contemporary life.[7]

While these ethnographic studies of HIV/AIDS in Africa drew upon pre-AIDS-era literature on medical cosmology, they went far beyond previous works in their depth of analysis and concern for actual behaviour in relation to illness. Most previous researchers who studied medically related phenomena were mainly concerned with identifying and analysing discreet 'systems of belief' amongst specific groups of people. Much of this literature demonstrates a preoccupation with developing various etiological categories of disease as part of a biomedically inspired exercise to discern local systems of medical classification. South African ethnographies were no exception.[8] When writing about people's notions of pollution and dirt in relation to illness, for example, these concepts were assigned to the causal category of 'ritual pollution', and then analysed almost exclusively in relation to the spiritual realm. The emphasis was on classifying disease, with little or no attention paid to illness experience and its local management. How these systems of belief, or medical worldviews, translated into therapeutic responses or health-seeking behaviours was rarely described or explained. Ngubane tells us about *umnyama*, a state of 'ritual pollution' meaning darkness that is contagious, capable of causing illness, and most especially associated with women.[9] What meaning this state held in relation to how 'infected' women behaved and managed the condition was left largely unexplained. Thus, while previous ethnographic accounts may provide valuable information on local causal categories of disease, they shed little light on how people engage with illness and how disease is embodied through common understandings of ethnopathological processes.

Knowledge of local disease categories is central to any understanding of medical cosmology. Yet, this knowledge alone is of limited use when trying to understand the process by which new diseases such as HIV/AIDS have been worked into local ways of thinking and have come to acquire meaning. As Pelto and Pelto point out, a cognitive explanation, what we label as belief and knowledge, are elements to which economic, social and political factors are joined, weighted and negotiated in the course of understanding and managing illness.[10] The process by which Zulu people have attempted to make sense of the current AIDS pandemic requires an analysis of common 'folk models' of the human body, particularly women's bodies, and close attention to discourses on morality, particularly women's morality, as linked to prevailing critiques of modern life. All of these are key strands in a common 'web of signification' that has provided a culturally coherent and meaningful way of understanding a disease currently having a tumultuous impact on the lives of isiZulu-speaking people.

**Pollution as presentation and representation**

Unlike Western biomedicine, Zulu medical cosmology is not standardised in theory or practice. Therefore it can be expected to vary, not only by researcher interpretation, but also by the region from which individual Zulu clans originated, and the contexts in which people find themselves today. Thus, what might describe typical medical epistemology in one locale at a particular historical moment may not have wide currency beyond that specific place and time. The lived experience of a particular disease in a Durban township, for example, may be considerably different from that found in a northern KwaZulu rural area. Among isiZulu-speaking people living in Mariannhill, it is widely believed that people living in the more northern reaches of the province have stronger medicines and secret knowledge about disease and therapeutic plants. Such a conception is no doubt linked to another prevalent idea; that amaZulu living in the northern parts of the province are in all facets of life more traditional. Nonetheless, there are some aspects of contemporary ethnomedicine that have fairly wide currency amongst people who identify themselves as Zulu. Notions of pollution and bodily dirt in relation to illness are significant in this regard.

Ideas about internal dirt and the state of being dirty, expressed in terms of a 'dirty stomach' for example, or a 'dirty chest' or a 'dirty womb', represent an important category of disease as well as an idiom for expressing ill-health. The state of being dirty is a broad ethnopathological explanatory model for disease that is encoded in common practices of bodily cleansing as therapeutic response. Beyond being conceived in terms of 'ritual pollution', or being in some sense spiritually unclean, notions of contamination and dirtiness have real meaning, in the sense that they represent pathogenic metaphors of ill-health. As a form of non-ritual pollution, the state of being dirty is a central concept of disease among the Zulu, through which *other* causal factors (such as witchcraft/sorcery, ancestral wrath or nature) work.[11] Rather than being a distinct causal typology, the state of being dirty can be understood as an explanatory model for illness. According to Jewkes and Wood, the amaXhosa of

Eastern Cape province hold similar views on dirt and disease. To say that one has 'dirty kidneys' or a 'dirty stomach', is to say that one is experiencing illness symptoms in relation to those organs.[12] As part of a therapeutic process to cure the specific illness, steps are taken to cleanse the body of dirt. Various preparations, some obtainable through modern pharmacies and others through traditional medical practitioners, are used to purge the body of harmful dirt as part of a cleansing therapy. Commercial laxatives and enema preparations are commonly used for cleansing dirt associated with the abdominal region. Diuretics are used in the case of urinary complaints. Emetics are believed to be effective against ailments in the upper chest or throat. Managing illness by taking steps to eliminate dirt associated with disease is often the first line of defence against illness and a routine part of most traditional approaches to therapy.[13]

An understanding of the concept of bodily dirt and its significance as an ethnopathological explanatory model for disease is central to the metaphoric construction of disease, including HIV/AIDS. According to local folk models of human anatomy and physiology, any dirt believed responsible for illness symptoms in a particular body part, whether dirt associated with 'dirty stomach' or dirt associated with a 'dirty chest', or dirt causing 'dirty kidneys', has the ability to 'mix with the blood' if not treated soon after symptoms occur. With common folk models maintaining that all organs in the body are interconnected, dirt producing illness symptoms in one part of the body may be conveyed to other parts of the body, via the blood, and thus cause symptoms of illness elsewhere. When this happens, one can expect symptoms of more generalised and severe sickness, with fatigue and debility as indicative of 'dirty blood'.

### 'Polluted' bodies

Research conducted among the Tswana of Botswana, the Giriama of Kenya and the Meru of Tanzania reveal similarities in the depiction of adult women's bodies as uniquely suitable for harbouring and hiding disease.[14] Ingstadt records how the Tswana people often compared women's bodies to suitcases that conceal and transport disease to others. Such imagery resonates in the way people from Mariannhill talk about women and HIV/AIDS, and ultimately blame women for the pandemic. Both men and women hold views that reflect a symbiotic relationship between women's bodies and disease in general. As a place where disease-causing 'dirt' is especially likely to be 'hiding', the vagina is widely thought to be an open-ended passage that leads up into the womb. This belief underlies a widespread fear that condoms might 'go up' and 'get lost'. Many women express anxiety that should a condom break or slip off during intercourse, it may 'float around inside' and eventually find its way up into the body cavity to cause grave illness. One informant asked: 'What if it (the condom) goes up to the heart or even the throat? It can choke you and then you can die.' Another suggested that a lost condom could become 'twisted', thus obstructing the blood flow and causing high blood pressure, a very common condition amongst urban Zulu women.

Along with notions that the vagina opens into the rest of the body and that it provides a suitable hiding place for dirt and disease, ideas about vaginal fluids are significant to the conceptualisation of women as disease-bearing vessels. The theme of a 'wet' vagina associated with sexually transmitted diseases and an ability to cause all manner of 'dirt' to stick to its walls, are features in both men's and women's discourses of HIV transmission. One young nursing student referred to the higher incidence of HIV infection amongst women as being due to the fact that 'women are wet down there, therefore when they are exposed to infections the germs just stick inside'. One young man expressed similar anxieties: 'Inside a woman it is dark, wet, not nice. AIDS can live there, waiting, and you wouldn't know. Even the woman herself wouldn't know because it just sticks inside. She really needs a blood test to know for sure.'

### Flaccid muscles, infectious fluids

The presence of vaginal fluids, together with the width and muscle tone of the vagina is believed to be useful as indices of a woman's moral character and sexual experience. Young women acknowledge the importance of being 'dry and tight' for pleasing men who are said to enjoy women who feel 'like a girl' as opposed to 'someone with many boyfriends', and therefore someone possibly harbouring disease. The ability to give the illusion of virginity by having a 'dry and tight' vagina was considered part of a Zulu woman's secret knowledge and sexual repertoire. Women report a variety of methods and substances used to 'tighten' and 'clean' the vagina and hence make sex more attractive and acceptable to men. The metaphor of dry-clean-virgin has significance as part of the ethnomedical logic that underlies a pervasive belief that sexual intercourse with a virgin can 'cleanse the blood' of a man with HIV/AIDS. In accordance with the cultural logic that governs the sympathetic-magic system described by Berglund and is still a relevant part of Zulu ethnomedicine today, AIDS is construed as a disease acquired through sex with a 'dirty' woman and therefore believed curable through sex with a 'clean' woman.[15]

In her study of Zulu medical cosmology, Ngubane makes the point that, compared to other bodily emissions, female sexual fluids are a class apart.[16] Ngubane attributes the unique status of these fluids to the fact that they represent a woman's power in the form of reproduction. It is within this context of a patriarchally structured and dominated Zulu society that the dank-and-disease model of female sexuality must be considered. Douglas argued that polluting substances (read 'vaginal fluids') symbolise threatening forces that pose a danger to the very symbolic order that produces them.[17] The vagina, simultaneously a site of male pleasure, as well as a site of birth, is a potent symbol of a woman's sexual and reproductive power, both acknowledged as necessary ingredients for life. Patriarchal fears of women's power coalesce in the symbolism of the vagina; the dark, wet, mysterious passage fraught with hazards in the form of 'dirt' and disease, yet associated with life's greatest pleasures in the form of sex and the issuing forth of babies, society's hopes for the future. Such strong negative symbolism could be understood as a reflection of culturally defined fears and insecurities vis-à-vis a woman's inherent power, a power at variance with her social inequality and general lack of power in society.

The dry-clean-virgin theme also holds great symbolic value for virginity testers who have revived virginity testing in recent years and hailed it as a culturally appropriate way to fight HIV/AIDS and high rates of teenage pregnancy. Virginity testers diagnose virginity with reference to a set of physical characteristics that include the 'dry and tight' vagina as a foremost indicator of chastity. The morally loose woman, whose behaviour is believed responsible for the current scourge of HIV/AIDS, is metaphorically represented in the loose vagina. Following the cultural logic that confers a deeply gendered meaning to the HIV/AIDS pandemic, the appropriate way to address the disease would be to reassert control over the bodies held responsible for the problem. The current revival of virginity testing amongst the amaZulu echoes what Gaitskell has described as the 'wailing for purity' that occurred in the 1920s and 1930s when women were increasingly leaving rural homes to seek job opportunities in town.[18] Publicly portrayed as concern for women's growing immorality, such anxiety may have had more to do with a desire to reassert control over women's agricultural labour at that time.[19] Similarly, virginity testing can be read as a contemporary iteration of attempts to reinstate control over women. In this case it is control over women's bodies at a time when those bodies are perceived to be out of control and supposedly wreaking havoc in the form of increased disease, death and orphaned children.[20]

### 'Polluted' behaviour

The HIV/AIDS pandemic has given renewed sustenance to long-established women-danger-disease ideologies. Pollution linked to women and bodies that represent reservoirs of hidden and threatening dirt and disease are ideologies that help to supply the rationale for gender discrimination. The infectious bodily fluids talked about in modern AIDS awareness campaigns may be new ideas, but they have been distilled and filtered through not-so-unfamiliar old ideas of women's pollution and the peril it represents to men and to society in general.

Shared perceptions of a modern femininity that transgresses moral boundaries defined by patriarchy not only supply the logic for reviving virginity testing, but also inform the process by which pollution ideology has been updated and reworked in the context of AIDS. Common views that women today are more sexually active than in the past, and that they often take the initiative to attract men and commence a sexual relationship, contribute to the perception of modern women as out of control. The traditional masculine ideal of the *isoka*, a man popular amongst women, is often recalled to describe a new femininity whereby women are said to compete for and pursue men (to *shela*, to propose love), as opposed to waiting and choosing a man (to *qoma*, to choose a lover).[21] Such active pursuit of men on the part of women is the antithesis of what is considered to be proper feminine behaviour. In attitude and behaviour, cultural ideals of quiet respect and obedience still apply. The image of a demure, soft-spoken girl who serves her family, and then grows up to serve her husband, her children, and her in-laws represents an ideal type of femininity. One of the highest compliments and forms of praise that can be directed at a woman in Mariannhill is to describe her as someone who can 'hardly speak'. Mutedness serves to condense a complexity of meanings related to how a proper Zulu woman should behave. A young unmarried woman should be preparing for a future of muted wifehood, where she is expected not to 'backchat' a husband or any member of his family, where control of the sexual encounter is firmly in the husband's hands, and where it is her duty as a wife to show love and respect by meeting his needs and not questioning his behaviour.

The popular perception of modern young women as being assertive and active in pursuing their sexual interests in a manner traditionally associated with men is a perception of transgression; an overstepping of accepted morality. Seen as challenging the culturally conceived codes of conduct that prescribe how women should behave, women are portrayed as out of control, a notion that reverberates through local discourses on contemporary women, their sexual behaviour, and the HIV/AIDS pandemic. As one 55-year-old grandmother stated: 'You see our girls today, poking around like chickens up and down? Any man who looks at them, they go for. This is why we have AIDS and all those things. What can we expect? Girls never did this before.'

Supporting pervasive views of a modern femininity gone wrong are general beliefs that women are increasingly using love potions to gain an unfair advantage over men. While the use of these substances, generally called *imithi*, has traditionally been associated with men, the view that women are increasingly buying and using them has wide currency. Such medicines are used in various ways for various effects. They may be used to attract a particular love interest, to secure unfailing love and fidelity, to harm an illicit sexual partner of one's lover, or to cause a couple to quarrel, divorce, or otherwise end their relationship. While there is no general agreement regarding the morality of Zulu men's supposed traditional use of these substances, there is a degree of social acceptance of such use. However, there is no comparable acceptance of women's use of love medicines. Dabbling in what is construed as the customary preserve of men, women who use love potions are widely condemned as immoral and such behaviour gives further indication that women are out of control.

## 'Polluted' context

Substantiated through the common occurrence of teenage pregnancy and the growing numbers of people sick and dying from AIDS, there is wide acknowledgement that traditional checks which were once successful in regulating the sexual activities of Zulu youth no longer operate.[22] Foreign media influences and the rigours of modernisation, with the subsequent erosion of traditional values, are viewed as having conspired to corrupt young people, and most especially the erstwhile quiet and complacent Zulu girl. General perceptions of sexual permissiveness among the youth and perceptions of young women today having multiple sexual partners as the norm rather than the exception, have some basis in day-to-day reality. The practice of gift giving is a pivotal feature of young people's sexual relations in Mariannhill and elsewhere in KwaZulu-Natal,[23] as well as in other provinces.[24] These studies reveal that for many women, especially those from urban areas, having relationships with a number of men is increasingly seen as an ideal premarital situation. Young women are aware of the economic benefits that can be derived from soliciting and maintaining numerous sexual liaisons. Where parents or guardians largely meet basic needs in the form of food and shelter, some women view relationships with men as a means of acquiring luxury goods. Reference to the high cost of living, growing difficulties in finding jobs, and great uncertainty about the future, all combine in the discourses of young women who say they 'need' several boyfriends to assist them materially in maintaining a modern lifestyle.[25]

The AIDS pandemic itself, attested to through constant media reports of high HIV infection rates and visible through increased sickness and death of family members and friends, also provides women with justification for living life in the present moment and enjoying the social and material benefits that come with having several concurrent partners. For many women, multiple sexual partnering is associated with newfound human rights and contemporary notions of gender equality. Both are seized upon in defence of behaviours that the women themselves often acknowledge as increasing their risk of HIV/AIDS.

Post-apartheid structural adjustments – with liberalisation of markets, growing privatisation of services, increased urban unemployment and the simultaneous strong promotion of consumer values – have conspired to propel women's engagements in multiple sexual relationships. Through liaisons that imply an exchange of sexual favours for material gain, a woman can acquire goods that symbolise modernity and confer upon her a certain prestige and public image. South Africa's democratisation (and all the changes that it has ushered in), has not only accentuated many underlying social pathologies, but may have given rise to new forms of social pathology that may have longer-term negative consequences and may ultimately be more difficult to address.

## Conclusion

Complex cultural and psychological meanings intervene in the contemporary representations of HIV/AIDS among isiZulu-speaking people from Mariannhill in KwaZulu-Natal. The process of casting AIDS into a local idiom has entailed a cultural reflection and an internal debate about morality and the consequences of social change and the loss of an older moral order. Longstanding ethnopathological explanatory models and constructions of women and their sexuality as dangerous and diseased have been brought into the AIDS meaning-making project. At the same time, these models have been updated and transformed by the pandemic and other broader historical processes. While new experiences and perceptions of modern life are framed by pre-existing ways of knowing, so the prevailing ways of knowing are being informed by new experiences and perceptions. The process is at once transforming and transformative. The daily realities of contemporary life, with its encroachment of globalisation and foreign values, changing roles and expectations of women, deteriorating economic circumstances, and young lives being ravished, children orphaned, and the elderly burdened by this new disease, all contribute to the crafting of a local understanding of HIV/AIDS. The cluster of metaphors that signify HIV/AIDS among the amaZulu call forth an image of diseased bodies behaving in a diseased manner, within a diseased environment. These metaphors reflect a bio-moral model of disease that has been invoked to make sense of the experience of greatly increased illness and death in this society at this particular point in time.

While many might recognise the need to develop more culturally relevant behavioural models and health communication strategies, there is little evidence of serious attempts to do this. With the scale of the AIDS pandemic representing nothing less than a global emergency, one could argue that giving consideration to local understandings of the disease (often viewed as products of superstition and lack of education) is an academic luxury. Yet, local understandings of HIV/AIDS should be considered important for properly contextualising the disease and imagining more effective ways to halt the infection and manage the pandemic. Perhaps their neglect has much to with what Schoepf refers to as 'the defining power of the international biomedical fraternity' and 'the choice of epistemology being political rather than disciplinary'.[26] In South Africa, the common ways in which Zulu people and others conceptualise and experience HIV/AIDS have been muted against the strong thrust of a well-resourced biomedical machinery that supports a wide variety of interventions and produces a vast array of HIV/AIDS media and educational materials. We need to acknowledge that the terms of reference used in the global AIDS effort – not only in South Africa, but throughout the world – are set in boardrooms far removed from the suffering of ordinary people, most especially those in the developing world.

Mann reminds us that voices contesting dominant paradigms and their implications should expect to be ignored. He argues that biomedical dominance legitimates a desire by public health workers to own the problem of AIDS, and helps to avoid inevitable accusations of 'meddling' in societal issues. The public health profession is sensitive to not being seen as 'going beyond its scope' and potentially putting its researchers at odds with government and other sources of power in society. Against such a backdrop, marginalisation of the 'views from below' as well as those of critical social scientists, is likely to be maintained. Local voices in the 'struggle for AIDS signification' will continue to be subdued by the overwhelming hegemony of a biomedical model of disease long at the vanguard of a Western-inspired colonisation (now turned globalisation) process. It remains to be seen whether 'second generation' HIV prevention programmes, in South Africa or elsewhere, will be substantively different from those of the first generation.[27]

## Notes

1. UNAIDS, 'HIV/AIDS Awareness and Behaviour in 39 Developing Countries', paper presented at a Special UN General Assembly on HIV/AIDS, Department of Social and Economic Affairs, Population Division, UNDP, 2002.

2. C. Airhihenbuwa and R. Obregon, 'A Critical Assessment of Theories/Models Used in Health Communication for HIV/AIDS', *Journal of Health Communication* 5 (2000): 5–16; S. Heald, 'It's Never as Easy as ABC: Understandings of AIDS in Botswana', *African Journal of AIDS Research* 1 (2002): 1–10 and E. Green, *Rethinking AIDS Prevention: Learning From Successes in Developing Countries* (New York: Praeger, 2003).

3. C. Airhihenbuwa, *Health and Culture: Beyond the Western Paradigm* (Thousand Oaks: Sage Press, 1995).

4. H. Triandis, 'AIDS in Sub-Saharan Africa: The Epidemiology of Heterosexual Transmission and the Prospects for Prevention', *Epidemiology* 41:1 (1993): 63–72.

5. This chapter draws from research on the ethnography of AIDS that was undertaken for Ph.D. purposes and took place mainly in the community of St Wendolin's, one of the six communities that comprise Mariannhill. Trappist monks from Europe, who reconstituted to form the Religious Missionary Order of Mariannhill, bought this peri-urban tract of land from the Land Colonisation Company of Natal. Settlement by Africans was reserved for newly converted Catholics who were allowed to purchase plots from the missionaries. A fuller description of the history and background of Mariannhill is provided in S. Leclerc-Madlala, 'An Analysis of the Sociocultural Construction and Gendering of HIV/AIDS in KwaZulu-Natal' (Ph.D. diss., University of Natal, Durban, South Africa, 2000). Although formal ethnographic study began in 1995, my academic interest in understanding local medical cosmology and people's engagements with HIV and AIDS stem from the time that I lived with my in-laws in St Wendolin's in 1985. Having come from the United States to marry an isiZulu-speaking man, I was conferred an 'honorary black' classification according to population registration laws of the time. This placed restrictions on where we could live, and until the demise of the Group Areas Act in 1991, I lived in St Wendolin's as a *mokoti* (an 'in-marrying wife') of the Madlala family. This afforded me much opportunity to collect information on the intricate ways in which people were experiencing the 'new' disease of HIV and AIDS as it began to present itself in their lives.

6. Most notable of these studies by Africanists were those in Botswana by B. Ingstadt, 'The Cultural Construction of AIDS and its Consequences for Prevention in Botswana', *Medical Anthropology Quarterly* 4 (1990): 28–40; in Rwanda by C. Taylor, 'Condoms and Cosmology: The "Fractal" Person and Sexual Risk in Rwanda', *Social Science and Medicine* 31:9 (1990): 1023–28; in what was Zaïre and now is the Democratic Republic of Congo by B. Schoeph, 'Women at Risk: Case Studies from Zaire', in *In the Time of AIDS: Social Analysis, Theory and Method*, eds. G. Heardt and S. Lindenbaum (London: Sage Press, 1992) and in Uganda by J. McGrath, C. Rwabukwali, D. Schumann, J. Pearson-Marks, S. Nakayiwa, B. Namande, L. Nakyobe and R. Mukasa, 'Anthropology and AIDS: The Cultural Context of Sexual Risk Behaviour Among Urban Buganda Women in Kampala, Uganda', *Social Science and Medicine* 36:4 (1993): 429–39.

7. For Kenya, see H. Mogensen, *AIDS is a Kind of Kahungo that Kills* (Oslo: Scandanavian Press, 1995) and M. Udvardy, 'The Lifecourse of Property and Personhood: Provisional Women and Enduring Men Among the Giriama of Kenya', *Research in Economic Anthropology* 16 (1995):

325–48. For Uganda, see C. Obbo, 'Gender, Age and Class: Discourses on HIV Transmission and Control in Uganda', in *Culture and Sexual Risk: Anthropological Perspectives on AIDS*, eds. H. Brummelhuise and G. Herdt (Chicago: Gordon and Breach, 1995). For South Africa, see Leclerc-Madlala, 'An Analysis of the Sociocultural Construction'. For Tanzania, see L. Haram, 'In Sexual Life Women are Hunters: AIDS and Women who Drain Men's Bodies – The Case of the Meru of Tanzania', *Society in Transition* 32:1 (2001): 47–55. For Botswana, see Heald, 'It's Never as Easy as ABC'. For Zambia, see C. Yamba, 'Cosmologies in Turmoil: Witch-hunting and AIDS in Chiawa, Zambia', *Africa* 67:2 (1997): 200–30 and M. Naur, *Indigenous Knowledge and HIV/AIDS: Ghana and Zambia* (Washington, DC: World Bank, IK Notes, 30 March 2001).

8. The following works reveal strong interest in disease categorisation and understanding the criteria used for consigning illness to one causal category as opposed to another: M. Hunter, *Reactions to Conquest: Effects of Contact with Europeans on the Pondo of South Africa* (London: Oxford University Press, 1936); E. Krige, 'The Magical Thought-Pattern of the Bantu in Relation to Health Services', *Africa* 6 (1944): 59–89; *The Social System of the Zulus* (Pietermaritzburg: Shuter & Shooter, [1936] 1974); A.T. Bryant, *The Zulu People* (Pietermaritzburg: Shuter & Shooter, 1949); *Zulu Medicine and Medicine Men* (Cape Town: C. Struik, 1970); A.-I. Berglund, *Zulu Thought-patterns and Symbolism* (London: Hurst, 1976); H. Ngubane, *Body and Mind in Zulu Medicine* (London: Academic Press, 1977); A. Ashforth, 'AIDS, Witchcraft, and the Problem of Power in Post-Apartheid South Africa', Occasional Paper No. 10, presented to the Institute of Advanced Study, School of Social Science, Princeton University, 2001; 'An Epidemic of Witchcraft? The Implications of AIDS for the Post-Apartheid State', *African Studies* 61:1 (2002): 121–42 and W.D. Hammond-Tooke, 'Urbanisation and the Interpretation of Misfortune: A Qualitative Analysis', *Africa* 40 (1970): 25–38; *Boundaries and Beliefs: The Structure of a Sotho World View* (Johannesburg: Witwatersrand University Press, 1981).

9. Ngubane, *Body and Mind*, p. 76.

10. P. Pelto and G. Pelto, 'Studying Knowledge, Culture and Behaviour in Applied Medical Anthropology', *Medical Anthropology Quarterly* 11:2 (1997): 147–63.

11. Ashforth, 'AIDS, Witchcraft', and 'An Epidemic of Witchcraft?', and B. Carton, 'The Forgotten Compass of Death: Apocalypse Then and Now in the Social History of South Africa', *Journal of Social History* 37:1 (2003): 199–218.

12. R. Jewkes and K. Wood, 'Problematizing Pollution: Dirty Wombs, Ritual Pollution and Pathological Processes', *Medical Anthropology* 18 (1999): 163–86.

13. S. Leclerc-Madlala, 'Zulu Health, Cultural Meanings and the Reinterpretation of Western Pharmaceuticals', paper presented at the annual conference of the Anthropological Association of Southern Africa, Durban, University of Natal, 1994.

14. On the Tswana of Botswana, see Ingstadt, 'The Cultural Construction of AIDS'; on the Giriama of Kenya, see Udvardy, 'The Lifecourse of Property'; on the Meru of Tanzania, see Haram, 'In Sexual Life'.

15. See Berglund, *Zulu Thought-patterns* and S. Leclerc-Madlala, 'On the Virgin Cleansing Myth: Gendered Bodies, AIDS and Ethnomedicine', *African Journal of AIDS Research* 1 (2002): 87–95.

16. Ngubane, *Body and Mind*.

17. M. Douglas, *Purity and Danger* (London: Routledge and Kegan Paul, 1966).

18. D. Gaitskell, ' "Wailing for Purity": Prayer Unions, African Mothers and Adolescent Daughters, 1912–1940', in *Industrialisation and Social Change in South Africa*, eds. S. Marks and R. Rathbone (Essex: Longman, 1989). Much of Gaitskell's study on social preoccupations with purity and the rise of African women's prayer unions during the early part of the last century resonate with the revival of virginity testing today. The same laments over women's growing immorality and lack of purity/loss of virginity are heard in the rallying cries of virginity testers and the older generation of African women. These practices point to ongoing intergenerational conflicts and struggles over the control of women. See B. Carton, *Blood from Your Children: The Colonial Origins of Generational Conflict in South Africa* (Pietermaritzburg: University of Natal Press, 2000) for a historical analysis of these trends in South Africa.

19. As S. Marks suggested in 'Patriotism, Patriarchy and Purity: Natal and the Politics of Zulu Ethnic Consciousness', in *The Creation of Tribalism in Southern Africa*, ed. L. Vail (Berkeley: University of California Press, 1989).

20. See S. Leclerc-Madlala, 'Virginity Testing: Managing Sexuality in a Maturing HIV/AIDS Epidemic', *Medical Anthropology Quarterly* 15:4 (2001): 533–52.

21. M. Hunter provides an excellent historiography of the shifting expressions of masculinity amongst the Zulu of KwaZulu-Natal. He suggests that in the current context of HIV and AIDS there may be an emerging counter-discourse and challenge to the traditional *isoka* ideal of multiple partnering; see 'Masculinities and Multiple-sexual-partners in KwaZulu-Natal: The Making and Un-making of *Isoka*', paper presented at the Historical Studies Seminar Series, University of Natal, Durban, March 2003. This is significant in relation to my own work with young women and changing expressions of femininity. I would suggest that some emerging femininities may have a stake in maintaining '*isoka*-dom' amongst men, as gaining material advantages through sexual liaisons depends on men subscribing to the ideals of multi-partnered sexual practices. The continued vigorous promotion of consumerism is likely to stimulate material desires amongst women, and thus may provide a counter-challenge to growing social objections to *isoka* masculinity.

22. See P. Delius and C. Glaser, 'Sexual Socialisation in South Africa: A Historical Perspective', *African Studies* 61:1 (2002): 27–54 for a recent and comprehensive account of changes in the sexual socialisation of African children from a historical perspective. They argue that where social structures and institutions once existed to allow for and monitor the limited sexual activities of youth, the combined forces of Christianity, urbanisation and migrant labour effectively undermined these practices and left little in the way of structures for socialising children into sex. Numerous conversations with people of the older generation in Mariannhill would support their views.

23. See, for example, M. Thorpe, 'Masculinity in an HIV Intervention', *Agenda* 53 (2002): 61–68; M. Hunter, 'The Materiality of Everyday Sex: Thinking Beyond Prostitution', *African Studies* 61 (2002): 99–119 and C. Kaufman and S. Stavrou, ' "Bus Fare Please": The Economics of Sex and Gifts among Adolescents in Urban South Africa', Working Paper 166, Population Council Policy Research Division, The Population Council, New York, 2002.

24. J. Wojcicki, 'She Drank His Money: Survival Sex and the Problem of Violence in Taverns in Gauteng Province, South Africa', *Medical Anthropology Quarterly* 16 (2002): 267–93 and T-A. Selikow, B. Zulu and E. Cedras, 'The Ingagara, the Regte and the Cherry: HIV/AIDS and Youth Culture in Contemporary Urban Townships', *Agenda* 53 (2002): 22–32.

25. See S. Leclerc-Madlala, ' "We do Sex to have Money": Modernity and Meaning in Contemporary Urban Youth Relationships', paper presented at the first annual Durban AIDS Conference, Durban, 3–6 August 2003.

26. B. Schoepf, 'International AIDS Research in Anthropology: Taking a Critical Perspective on the Crisis', *Annual Review of Anthropology* 30 (2001): 338.

27. J. Mann, 'Human Rights and AIDS: The Future of the Pandemic', in *AIDS Education: Interventions in Multicultural Societies*, ed. I. Schenker (New York: Plenum Press, 1996), p. 6.

# Chapter 48

# IsiZulu-speaking Men and Changing Households

## From Providers within Marriage to Providers outside Marriage

MARK HUNTER

PRIOR TO COLONIAL conquest in the nineteenth century, the life of isiZulu-speakers revolved around the self-sufficient African homestead, or *umuzi*. The centrality of the *umuzi* to production and reproduction is captured by the phrase *ukwakha umuzi*, roughly translated as 'to build a home', a patriarchal project established through marriage. Indeed, matrimony catapulted a man into the respected status of *umnumzana* (household head), a husband who might support several wives in his large *umuzi*.

Missionaries and ethnographers have long noted how white rule, expanding capitalism and forced labour migration undermined the independence of the *umuzi* and created turmoil in domestic relations. More recent scholarship has highlighted how gender and generational conflicts profoundly shaped these processes.[1] The disastrous effects of itinerant wage work on family relations is perhaps most apparent in the syphilis epidemic that peaked in the first half of the twentieth century. The disease, only partly thwarted by antibiotics available from the 1950s onwards, helped to permanently etch into historical records the association between family instability and debilitating illness.

Half a century later, when five million South Africans are said to be HIV-positive, scholars have understandably pointed to parallels between syphilis and AIDS, with the latter epidemic seen as an almost inevitable consequence of the collapsing homestead. This chapter draws on these comparisons, but suggests fundamental ways in which the household and sexuality shifted under the more recent weight of unemployment and rising social inequalities; significantly, these economic trends have extended into the new era of multiracial democracy.[2] In the contemporary period, marital rates have plummeted and material transactions – usually gifts from boyfriends to girlfriends – are common in sexual relationships. Consequently, many isiZulu-speaking men have shifted from acting as 'providers within marriage' to 'providers outside of marriage'.

### Coming of age in the 1940s and 1950s: Providers within marriage

By the 1940s virtually all isiZulu-speaking African men who wanted to marry entered labour migrancy, usually as paid workers for European settlers. The stretching of men's lives between rural and urban areas was symbolised by the shift in payment of *ilobolo* from bridewealth cattle secured through a man's father to cash earnings. The dangerous work, long journeys to and from towns, the self-discipline needed to resist abandoning one's home and tense dependence on employers shaped what it meant to be a Zulu man. Masculinities were multifaceted and in perpetual flux, but an enduring theme was the importance of marriage, a fact signalled by the powerful metaphor *ukwakha umuzi*. In urban factories, in mines and on white farms, apartheid workplace conditions demasculinised African men by positioning them as 'boys'. At the same time, wages allowed many single Zulu men to purchase *ilobolo* cattle independent of their fathers and become patriarchs sometimes more quickly through marriage.

The relationship between wage labour, migration and homestead reproduction influenced courting rituals and attendant meanings of love, amorous gifts and marriage. During interviews that I conducted with elderly isiZulu-speaking men in Mandeni, KwaZulu-Natal, from 2000 to 2004, informants remembered the *isoka* figure as a man who successfully wooed many women. The *isoka* was the opposite of the ignominious *isishimane*, a man too scared to talk with girls. Yet the *isoka* masculinity contained within it the seeds of its own constraints. While men had the right to court freely, without a job they found it difficult to secure girlfriends. Men with more than one lover, including husbands who pursued younger single women, were frequently asked to declare their intention (or financial ability) to marry. Unlike today, it was not men's gifts to women, such as cell phones and clothes, that attracted multiple partners, but a suitor's ability to support a wife. It is also evident that the *isoka* phase of a man's life occurred during his youth and had important restrictions. If a male suitor's ability to have multiple partners was enshrined in the word *isoka*, his courting limits can be discerned in the concept of *isoka lamanyala*. The word *amanyala* means 'dirt', or 'disgraceful act'. Thus, *isoka lamanyala* signifies a masculinity gone too far; its connotation is usually negative, although some men did celebrate their *amanyala* status.[3]

By the 1950s, increasing numbers of men and women were moving semi-permanently to urban areas. Apartheid hinged on separating races (whites, Africans, Coloureds, Indians) and on restricting the access of Africans to urban areas. One component of this project was the building of black townships that were set up to house African men and their families in four-roomed matchbox dwellings, often miles from the centre of towns. A housing boom spanned the 1950s and 1960s, a two-decade period in which apartheid rulers sought to create and exploit the African 'industrial man' by institutionalising nuclear, heterosexual families.[4]

This urbanisation not only involved great upheaval, but also continuity, as suggested by the linguistic endurance of the term *umnumzana*.[5] This personal title – conveying respect for patriarchal authority – once described the 'head of a homestead'. However, with the growth of factories and businesses, the *umnumzana* came to represent the 'urban gentleman', or simply 'Mr'. In this modern milieu, the *umnumzana* was basically a township provider, the father of a household in a matchbox unit whose members depended on white employers for work.[6]

### Contemporary masculinities: Providers outside of marriage

The years between the mid-twentieth century, when my elderly informants were young, and the early twenty-first century were tumultuous and bloody. In the aftermath of the 1976 Soweto uprising, thousands of African men left South Africa to engage in military training for the liberation struggle. In township uprisings, manliness was enacted in battles against white domination;[7] for this reason, the word *amandla* (power) became a potent rallying cry, answered with the call *ngawethu* (to the people). The violence that enveloped KwaZulu-Natal in the 1980s and 1990s exhibited an especially vicious internecine character with the supporters of the Zulu nationalist Inkatha Freedom Party (IFP) fighting a civil war against members of the African National Congress (ANC). The young urban comrades of the ANC repudiated KwaZulu homeland 'collaborators' and rebelled against the conservative, anti-activist politics of isiZulu-speaking migrant men who stayed in township hostels. To combat the insurgent, 'disrespectful' ANC youth, IFP leader Mangosuthu Buthelezi promoted an image of Zulu masculinity as embodying dignity, respect, wisdom and unity. A booster of big capital and industrial decentralisation, Buthelezi claimed that hardworking Zulu sons and fathers were the real men in South Africa, not the effeminate ANC exiles who shirked the everyday sacrifices necessary to support their families.[8]

Soon after the historic 1994 ballot heralded electoral power, *amandla*, for isiZulu-speaking men and a virtual end to political violence, Buthelezi's brand of personalised ethnic nationalism carried far less sway among his followers. Yet today grinding unemployment means that many isiZulu-speaking men remain disempowered in painfully familiar ways; especially since they are unable to accumulate *ilobolo* (bridewealth) and establish their own *umuzi*. To be sure, the advent of democracy has enabled a growing African middle class to relocate to formerly white suburbs and live a comfortable family life with their own children and an African maid – a domestic arrangement bearing all the markers of the middle-class prosperity previously preserved for whites. By contrast, in townships and rural areas, most isiZulu-speaking men are unable even to pay *ilobolo* and start their lives as husbands. Today, less than 30 per cent of adult Africans are married and unemployment rates are well over 40 per cent. Moreover, women are exerting rights in new ways. Particularly, they enter the labour force (even if often they struggle to find work) in much greater numbers than they did a generation ago when men were considered reliable providers.

These developments have destabilised dominant masculinities in my research site of Mandeni by remoulding the household and, consequently, the area's physical and social geography in major ways. Over the last twenty years the median household size in Mandeni's most urban community, Sundumbili Township, dropped from seven to just over two, as *ukwakha umuzi* receded as an achievable goal. When Sundumbili Township was constructed in the 1960s, virtually all men working in the area had access to a four-roomed matchbox dwelling, the infamous symbol of the social engineering mission of apartheid urban planners. In the last two decades, however, one-roomed *imijondolo* (shacks), usually attached to township houses or located on the outskirts of Sundumbili, have mushroomed. Indeed, since the construction of the neighbouring Isithebe Industrial Park, the former tribal area around Mandeni has become a sprawling informal settlement for jobseekers. Similar informal settlements have burgeoned elsewhere in South Africa, especially with the ending of influx controls (measures to restrict the presence of Africans in urban areas) in the 1980s.

Three of my most forthcoming informants, all single young men, described how they behaved as suitors amidst the matchbox houses and shacklands of the Mandeni area. They said they had girlfriends, with two of the young men, Khetha and Thanda, divulging that they had two girlfriends each, while the third informant, Joe, claiming he had only one. None of them had children. To some degree this interview, like many others, demonstrated that young men could celebrate having multiple girlfriends, over whom they could occasionally exercise violent control. At the same time, tensions and contradictions were apparent. Thanda said that they must 'look after their situation' before raising children. This included 'checking blood', or taking an HIV test, and being in a position to support their children. Khetha says that he doesn't yet have sex because he is scared of HIV. Even if informants tend to exaggerate the extent to which they practise safe sex, it is significant that both Thanda and Joe insisted that they were scared of AIDS and that they used condoms.

## Money and masculinities

Young men such as Khetha and Joe, in a similar way to my other informants, note the high value placed on *isoka* status. This figure is still contrasted to *isishimane*, a 'sissy' or male suitor with no ability to attract women. Indeed, the *isoka* masculinity continues to normalise heterosexual male power, being juxtaposed to the derisory term for a so-called loose woman, *isifebe*. But there are crucial contextual differences that alter the meaning of *isoka* today. In the mid-twentieth century successful courting meant that a man could secure many girlfriends, but there was a serious hitch: a respected man had to marry at least one of his lovers. Now with the possibility of marriage all but disappearing, money and gifts, from food to cell phone 'air time', typically given by men to women, facilitate intimate relationships.[9] Since many isiZulu-speaking men are unemployed, they frequently express dissatisfaction with their ability to woo women; men with jobs in formal or informal sectors of the economy are currently expected to provide for women, sometimes multiple women, in new ways. One consequence is that younger single women can have affairs with older men and when the age gap is very large the man is called a 'sugar daddy'. The HIV prevalence rates reflect this shift in intimate practices; they peak about ten years later for men than women.

Not all men, however, are considered winning suitors for supporting more than one girlfriend. My informant Khetha elaborates:

> [An] *isoka* is someone who comes to a girl and greets her and then the girl gets excited without him saying a thing about *shela* (proposing love) and then when he starts to *shela* he doesn't expect the girl to agree now but she is excited and if someone else comes to *shela* that same girl and she will only think of that *isoka* . . .

As Khetha suggests, it is men's assumed irresistibility to women that is celebrated in his ideal view of triumphant masculinity. If the link between money and securing a woman is too obvious or crass, the male suitor in question could be seen in a negative light, in the words of Joe, as a man who might 'give a woman his number and write it on a 100 rand note'. Even more significant, the *isoka lamanyala*, a man who 'wasted' nubile girls, is still used to denote an unacceptable masculinity. Yet today this concept has become partially delinked from marriage, according to Thanda; the *isoka lamanyala* is simply a man who goes too far by sleeping with so-called dirty women. Other informants explained *isoka lamanyala* as a male suitor who makes love to his woman's best friend.[10] Compared to the elderly informants, the young men I interviewed relayed how the once stringent restrictions on *isoka* behaviour appeared to have lessened; as long as a man is luring reasonably respectable women, he is seen as a positive *isoka*, they observe. It is not uncommon to hear men today talk of aspiring to have six or seven girlfriends, the limit determined by their disposable income, rather than their ability to marry women. Certainly, an expanding consumer culture has hamstrung jobless men who cannot afford flashy cell phones and designer clothes; they tend to be left behind in the pursuit of women.

The difficulties that poor unmarried men encounter in sustaining intimate relationships invariably raise issues about their perceptions of fatherhood. A prominent stereotype in the South African press is that black men impregnate black women and then brusquely deny paternity, thus rejecting the provider role. Many of my informants, however, offer a more complicated picture. Thanda, for example, told me that he did not want children until he could look after them, although he recognised their importance to his attainment of manhood. This response, quite typical in my interviews, points to a dilemma that unmarried men face as they struggle to integrate at least two different expressions of masculinity: one that elevates the responsibility of dependable father and household provider, and the other that revels in *isoka* virility.[11] Since isiZulu-speaking African masculinities are frequently depicted in national debates about gender inequality in negative (patriarchal) terms, what young men such as Thanda have to say about fatherhood is particularly important. They tend to grapple with more complex and contradictory portraits of manhood that encompass ambiguous dimensions such as the *isoka* figure, as well as the tensions inherent in men's role in acting as 'providers outside of marriage'.

Another powerful dynamic must be added to these currents – AIDS. The contradictions of *isoka* status are most tragically played out today in the many funerals punctuating life in townships and rural areas. If at the middle of the twentieth century, the end game of *isoka* behaviour was marriage, today the end game can be death. Consequently, isiZulu-speaking sexually active men are under great scrutiny, a fact boosted by radio and television programmes that talk of gender equality in the new democratic dispensation. In this environment some young men, such as Thanda and Joe, claim to use condoms and in some cases even go for a blood (HIV) test before starting sexual relationships. Of course, it is impossible to tell the extent to which they do actually practise safe sex. The fact that they do not yet have children suggests that they might, although a number of young men I know told me that they wear condoms, but later confided that at times they do not. Equally contradictory is how contemporary masculinities can manifest men's continued physical and social power in acts of sexual violence and risk-taking – despite men's economic disempowerment and the terrible reality of a 40 per cent HIV prevalence rate.

## Conclusion

The era of the male suitor who pursues several women and marries one of them is but a memory. Today, chronic unemployment confines poor isiZulu-speaking young men to a bleak economic existence, where their aspirations of achieving manliness, encapsulated by the phrase, 'building a home', are seldom realised. Indeed, young men are more likely to be 'providers outside of marriage', a route to contemporary manhood that pulls them into the vortex of a lethal pandemic.

## Notes

1. For more on homestead instability, see Colin Murray, *Families Divided: The Impact of Migrant Labour in Lesotho* (Cambridge: Cambridge University Press, 1981). For more on generational conflict, see Benedict Carton, *Blood from Your Children: The Colonial Origins of Generational Conflict in South Africa* (Charlottesville: University of Virginia Press, 2000).
2. This short chapter is largely based on 300 interviews that the author conducted in Mandeni,

KwaZulu-Natal, between 2000 and 2004; the oral data from these interviews became a major part of his Ph.D. dissertation. Over three extended stays in South Africa, the author, a white male originally from the United Kingdom, lived with a family in the Isithebe informal settlement and conducted interviews with informants ranging from the ages of 16 to 80. Many of the interviews were undertaken with the help of an isiZulu-speaking research assistant who lived in a nearby township, called Sundumbili. All of the names of informants in this paper (such as Thanda, etc.) are pseudonyms. For more details about the study and the author's methodology and positionality, see Mark Hunter, 'Building a Home: Unemployment, Intimacy and AIDS in South Africa' (Ph.D. diss., University of California, Berkeley, 2005).

3.  See Mark Hunter, 'Cultural Politics and Masculinities: Multiple-partners in Historical Perspective in KwaZulu-Natal', *Culture, Health, and Sexuality* 7:4 (2005): 389–403.

4.  For this policy in other parts of Africa, see Frederick Cooper, 'Industrial Man Goes to Africa', in *Men and Masculinities in Modern Africa*, eds. Lisa Lindsay and Stephan Miescher (Portsmouth: Heinemann, 2003).

5.  On upheaval, see, for example, ethnographic scholarship on this subject: Laura Longmore, *The Dispossessed: A Study of the Sex-life of Bantu Women in Urban Areas in and around Johannesburg* (London: Jonathan Cape, 1959).

6.  It should be noted that in the 1950s, although segregation and migrant labour fundamentally destabilised African families, marital rates in both rural and urban areas still remained high.

7.  See, for example, Thokozani Xaba, 'Masculinity and its Malcontents: The Confrontation between "Struggle Masculinity" and "Post-Struggle Masculinity" (1990–1997)', in *Changing Men in Southern Africa*, ed. Robert Morrell (Pietermaritzburg: University of Natal Press, 2001).

8.  Thembisa Waetjen, *Workers and Warriors: Masculinity and the Struggle for Nation in South Africa* (Urbana: University of Illinois Press, 2004).

9.  There is a lot of literature in African Studies on the inappropriate use of 'prostitution' to describe material relationships between men and women (for an excellent summary, see Hilary Standing, 'Conceptual and Methodological Issues in Researching Sexual Behaviour in Sub-Saharan Africa', *Social Science and Medicine* 34 [1992]: 475–83). Without going into this literature here, I argue that the period of chronic unemployment has heightened 'the materiality of everyday sex' in profound ways. On 'transactional sex' in modern South Africa, see Suzanne Leclerc-Madlala, 'Transactional Sex and the Pursuit of Modernity', *Social Dynamics* 29 (2003): 213–33; Mark Hunter, 'The Materiality of Everyday Sex: Thinking Beyond "Prostitution"', *African Studies* 61 (2002): 99–120 and Terry-Ann Selikow, Bheki Zulu and Eugene Cedras, 'The Ingagara, the Regte and the Cherry: HIV/AIDS and Youth Culture in Contemporary Urban Townships', *Agenda* 53 (2002): 22–32.

10. The term *amanyala* can also be used more generally to describe a disgraceful sexual act. It was used recently to describe the rape of a 50-year-old African woman by a 26-year-old white man on a sugar cane farm ('*Amanyala esimobeni*', *Umafrika*, 16–22 May 2003, p. 1) and the rape by a 71-year-old African man of a 5-year-old African child ('*Ixhegu lamanyala* (71) *linukubeze ingane eno* (5),' *Umafrika*, 31 January–6 February 2003).

11. The subject of fathering is discussed in Robert Morrell and Linda Richter, eds., *Ubaba? Men and Fatherhood in South Africa* (Pretoria: Human Science Research Council, 2005). This book marks an important development in the South African masculinities literature.

## Further reading

Breckenridge, Keith. 1998. 'The Allure of Violence: Men, Race and Masculinity on the South African Goldmines, 1900–1950', *Journal of Southern African Studies* 24.

Glaser, Clive. 2000. *Bo-tsotsi: The Youth Gangs of Soweto, 1935–1976*. Portsmouth: Heinemann.

Harries, Patrick. 1994. *Work, Culture, and Identity: Migrant Laborers in Mozambique and South Africa, c.1860–1910*. Portsmouth: Heinemann and London: James Currey.

Mager, Anne Kelk. 1999. *Gender and the Making of a South African Bantustan: A Social History of the Ciskei, 1945–1959*. Portsmouth: Heinemann and London: James Currey.

Morrell, Robert. 1998. 'Of Boys and Men: Masculinity and Gender in Southern African Studies', *Journal of Southern African Studies* 24.

Moodie, T. Dunbar. 1994. *Going for Gold: Men, Mines and Migration*. Berkeley: University of California Press.

Ouzgane, Lahoucine and Robert Morrell, eds. 2005. *African Masculinities*. New York: Palgrave.

# Chapter 49

# A Modern Coming of Age
## Zulu Manhood, Domestic Work and the 'Kitchen Suit'

MXOLISI MCHUNU

THE RITES OF Zulu male initiation have never been fixed. They have changed according to the conditions of the time, such as during the rule of the Zulu kings and, later, the imposition of colonialism. In the nineteenth century, older Zulu boys and young men enrolled in royal regiments, *amabutho*, which not only conducted physical training and military duties, but also fostered a group identity based on manly dignity, *indoda enesithunzi*. They were members of an armed body called *Ngobamakhosi*, for example, with an inspirational commander, special armbands, as well as songs (*amahubo*) celebrating their collective struggles and exploits.[1] By the end of the 1800s, the British conquest of Zululand in 1879 had all but crippled the *amabutho* system, and with each passing decade, colonial control of the most token Zulu warrior customs tightened.[2]

In the late nineteenth century and throughout the twentieth century, as Natal government taxes created heavier financial burdens on Zulu homesteads and white settlers appropriated more African land, young men barred from entering *amabutho* went into colonial domestic service to earn wages required to meet their families' needs. Coming-of-age idioms reflected this transformation. Whereas during Zulu political independence these idioms – captured in a regimental song, for example – revelled in the ideal pursuit of traditional manhood, under white rule they tended to express wage labourers' dirge-like resignation. Indeed, '*Angizisoli ngokuthi ngake ngasebenza ezingadini*' (I am not sorry that I was once a gardener) and '*Ngibheke nje, namuhla ngiyindoda ngoba ngangisebenza ezingadini*' (Just look at me, today I am a man because I was once a gardener) have become the standard phrases expressing how some isiZulu-speaking African young men envision the achievement of manhood. Needless to say, the wearing of martial garb also no longer announced that a young man was laying the foundation to assume greater patriarchal power. Such a quest was more likely indicated by his donning of a 'kitchen suit', a style of uniform that dates to the first days of servitude in the era of the mineral revolution.

As industrialisation transformed late nineteenth-century South Africa into a territory of burgeoning cities, black and white servants toiled side by side in urban colonial households. Most black servants tended to be males from rural areas, while many white servants were female immigrants from Europe. Archival sources reveal instances of close friendships between these domestic workers, which developed across colour lines and included sexual relations. These examples in part show that perceptions of racial difference did not stifle intimacy between servants. However, due to the enforcement of more rigid discriminatory laws, particularly after union of the two British colonies and two Afrikaner republics into a unitary South Africa in 1910, white women servants soon learnt to avoid contact with their black counterparts. The *Imperial Colonist*, a journal widely circulated among white madams in Johannesburg, Pietermaritzburg and Durban, urged employers to teach white housemaids how to act towards black servants. In one early twentieth-century article, the *Imperial Colonist* reminded readers to infantilise Africans and prescribe behaviour that segregated the home-workplace: 'They [white female servants] should be civil and kind,' the journal counselled, 'but they should never allow any familiarity . . . [such as] touch their [black male servants'] hands, or sit in a room where there are boys, or do anything whereby an insolent native may take liberties.'[3]

This advice and other factors, such as white housemaids' demands for higher wages and for rights to order around the Zulu 'house boy' created racial tensions between domestic workers. In the First World War era, this tension eased because white housemaids left their profession in droves (particularly on the Rand and in Natal); many sought better-paying employment elsewhere, married white husbands, and settled in Europeans-only neighbourhoods served by domestic workers drawn from a large pool of unskilled black men coming to the cities. In this milieu white women generally acted as managers exercising 'control over their workers, more so than other employers (except perhaps for . . . [those in] the mine compounds). The domestic workers lived and worked in the same place, under the watchful eye of the employer.' Indeed, '[o]ff-duty hours were almost as closely supervised as working hours', as '[e]mployers of all classes . . . inspect[ed] their servants' room and goods if they suspected them of theft or any other misdemeanour'.[4]

Originating in colonial Natal, the kitchen suit helped to reinforce this regime of labour surveillance.[5] The uniform was first sewn at the turn of the twentieth century by a Durban housewife for a twelve-year-old Zulu boy named P[h]endula, who had come to work for her dressed only in his *umutsha*, a loin cloth patch hung from the waist. Taken aback by his near nakedness, P[h]endula's madam promptly clothed him with a 'simplified version of her son's tunic and knickers . . . in navy with white braid trimming for everyday, and then in white with red braid for inside the house'. Word soon circulated in colonial society that there was a new outfit with which to identify Africans in service to white homeowners. Benjamin Greenacre, an apparel supplier visited the Durban housewife and asked if he might have P[h]endula's 'uniform copied for his store'. His business, known originally as Harvey, Greenacre & Co., was situated between West and Smith Street in Durban, and had branches in Natal and Johannesburg. Thereafter, use of the kitchen suit became widespread, not only in Natal but in other South African provinces as well.[6]

From the start, black servants – many of them rural migrants classified in traditional Zulu settings as *izinsizwa*, young unmarried men aged from their late teens to their twenties – regarded the tunic as offensive. They understood that they now reported to work in a white boy's outfit made from stiff, uncomfortable canvas material. However, they had little power to protest other than to vacate their position, a choice that would relinquish income to pay taxes, buy food and increase savings for *ilobolo* (bridewealth, usually in cattle). It is difficult to determine when precisely, but at some time in the early decades of the twentieth century the kitchen suit expanded into a line of clothing that distinguished domestic jobs, with the cook and inside staff wearing white, the outdoor crew wearing khaki, and the labourers who cleaned stoves and carried slop pails wearing blue. All three uniforms had red piping on the end of sleeves and trouser legs, which left uncovered skin from the foot to the upper calf, and sometimes up to the knee.[7]

### A personal lineage in the social history of the kitchen suit

Not long ago, I regularly wore a kitchen suit. I am from a family of 'gardeners', a broad designation encompassing indoor and outdoor domestic servants.[8] My father took up the profession until he found his first job at the University of Natal 35 years ago, working in the Department of Agriculture as a laboratories' assistant; later he was promoted to supervisor of departmental laboratories. All six of my brothers worked as gardeners; my late, eldest brother started as a gardener at the age of twelve before going to Madadeni Technical College, where he enrolled in a mechanical engineering course. My next two brothers worked as gardeners through high school. The brother before me quit as a gardener when he entered the University of Durban-Westville. I remained a gardener until my final undergraduate year at the University of Natal.

I began my days as a gardener in the twilight of apartheid, waking up early on Saturdays, leaving my rural Zulu home, and riding the minibus taxi or a bus to Pietermaritzburg, where my employer, 'Missus' Cronjé, lived.[9] My first morning of work commenced when I was thirteen years old in Standard Seven at Mtholangqondo Secondary School. I was not alone; my male cohorts, who two centuries ago might have been enrolled in *amabutho*, followed this path to wage labour. I remember we would meet on our way to Pietermaritzburg and joke about our vocation and daily negotiations with the boss or missus. The humourous stories we told were for our ears only; if outsiders heard us, we would be embarrassed. Being a Zulu gardener carried a mixed reputation in African communities where livelihoods depended on urban employment. Gardeners could be called the 'African Wanderers Players',

*A caricature of the colonial kitchen suit.*

*The cook and inside staff wore white, while the 'tiolet cleaners' wore blue.*

*Abaqulusi*, a reference both to a soccer club and a 'team of gardeners'. *Abaqulusi* also connotes a fraternity of young men 'who display their buttocks'. The Zulu term sounds derisive, but it is actually fitting. Soccer players, like gardeners, bend down on the grass when they engage in energetic manoeuvres that accidentally display their buttocks. While gardeners could show anger at an isiZulu-speaking African person who described them as *Abaqulusi*, they called each other this name in secret. This self-identification reflected a tacit understanding that their work shared a quality of strenuous physical exertion – and on-the-job humiliation. Without much inhibition, the boss or missus could call the gardener a 'boy' or 'piccanin', the latter slur meaning a small child in corrupted Portuguese (the word is probably of colonial Mozambican or Angolan origin).[10] An employer could also berate her domestic servants for real or imagined mistakes, labelling them '*dom*' (stupid) or diminishing them with remarks such as '*Ag nee, jou Kaffer*' (Oh no, you Kaffir). In my estimation gardeners rarely, if ever, objected candidly to these putdowns. Perhaps many felt that being 'temporarily' insulted was part of the rite of passage to a better job.

The gardeners that I knew in the Pietermaritzburg area secured jobs in white suburbs such as Hayfields, Scottsville and Prestbury; others took employment in the Indian township of Northdale or in a so-called poor-white community such as Oribi, near the airport. The gardeners in more affluent Scottsville and Hayfields boasted that they earned rather more than their counterparts in neighbourhoods with working-class residents. Gardeners often made these assertions while travelling on buses or minibus taxis to and from work. The commute provided a venue for conversing about sensitive matters such as degrading treatment by a boss, or a female employer's personal dealings with her young Zulu man in a kitchen suit, a subject that raised issues about sexuality in a remarkably open way. In public places, talk of intimacy is still considered taboo.[11]

Once I told a story of being ordered to mow under the washing line upon which hung the missus's stretch lace bloomers. While she was Afrikaans, I noted how her clothes were similar in style to the undergarments that I was told elderly Zulu women wore, an outfit jokingly termed '*MaMhlongo*', after the Zulu surname Mhlongo prefixed by 'Ma', meaning 'Mama' or 'Mrs'. It was a hot day and I was annoyed by Missus Cronjé's request to cut the grass in this spot. In traditional Zulu custom it is an affront for a male to be touched on the head and shoulders by a woman's underclothes; the place of the ancestors is considered to be in these body parts. Moreover, what Missus Cronjé asked me to do was said to bring bad luck in Zulu cosmology; being exposed to stretch bloomers was symbolically equivalent to seeing a naked woman. To view an African woman bathing in the river could evoke the following phrase in my traditional area: 'Oh, Oh . . . I don't want to see this!' The 'this' is understood as *ibhadi*, misfortune, a derivation of *umnyama*. Thus, I retaliated against the missus by loosening my hold on the garden hose and spraying her. I apologised and claimed that I doused her by accident.

I also remember telling my counterparts how I arrived each workday and went to the outside servant's toilet, where I changed into my khaki kitchen suit with its red binding on the sleeves and trousers legs. During my single meal break, I ate from my designated plastic plate; this dish was kept in an old, unused stove on the verandah. A fellow gardener relayed a tale about being jolted from his workday meal when his employer's dog started snarling. He ran away, leaving the food, whereupon the dog finished the rations. As it turned out, the gardener had been given his dinner on the dog's plate. Missus Cronjé, for her part, considered tea a privilege that could not be given to just any 'boy'. When the time came for a hot beverage, she called to me in Afrikaans, '*Kom* Russel (my Christian name) *kos is reg*', and then said in English, as if to reinforce her civilising mission, 'Here is your tea' (in my blue metal mug). What gardeners ate and drank seemed to be a topic of endless intrigue. One of the myths circulating among *Abaqulusi* alludes to the possibility that madams, white women but even more especially Indian women, feed their male servants their expressed breast milk. The explanation for this supposed phenomenon is that breast milk builds up a bond between the madam and servant, thus making it almost impossible for him to leave her employ. Some isiZulu-speaking Africans on the street sneer at gardeners saying, 'You go to work so that you may be fat!' The reference here is to the rich mother's milk that domestic servants are said to consume on the job.[12]

It is striking that gardeners could speak freely about private matters relating to work, but few appeared to dwell on the topic of the kitchen suit. I recall vividly that my elder brother, who worked for Missus Cronjé before I did, refused to tell me whether he put on the uniform. Still, certain rules about the kitchen suit were transmitted from older gardener to younger gardener. The uniform's ingrained racialised sanctions dealt with sexual taboos; these sanctions carried severe, if imaginary, penalties. For example, it was not uncommon for gardeners to believe that the red binding, which rimmed the short sleeves and trousers, indicated up to where a gardener could look on the body of the madam or daughter of the house – i.e., looking above or inside the red line were absolutely banned. Older gardeners insisted that a young apprentice not focus on the forbidden parts of the missus's body, for he would be punished, with his arm or leg amputated just below the red edging of his kitchen suit.[13]

Some gardeners who had house chores could not withstand the pressure of working in a 'personally degrading' kitchen suit. In an interview in 2004, one of my informants (Mr Joseph Gxabhashe of KwaVulindlela) described escaping to Johannesburg, as a young man in the late 1950s, to avoid the humiliation of being closely scrutinised by his missus in Howick, a wealthy white suburb of Pietermaritzburg.[14] But because he had no permit or pass to stay on the Rand he was sent back to his employer, and then demoted to outdoor work. Mr Gxabhashe recalled, 'By so doing I disgraced myself and my parents.' His reduction in status aside, he still found being a gardener too humiliating, so he quit. This time he went to Durban where he settled and got a job in the government railways as a 'fireboy'. His job was to make fire by boiling water and stoking a steam engine; he was also responsible for cleaning and polishing the trains, a skill he says he learned while engaged in gardening work. He considered his transition from gardener to railway employee to be a test of his mettle. In retrospect, Mr Gxabhashe said that he had to suffer through the 'disgrace' of the kitchen suit before moving on to becoming a 'fireboy', a position that allowed him to 'hold his head high' as a man in his community. His ability to withstand abuse from the missus made him a man. Without this experience, he would have been one of the 'masters of nothing', *bengelutho*, or, simply, a failed man. Mr Gxabhashe concluded that '*Isizathu esabangela ukuthi ngibekezelele ukusebenza njengo fireboy kwa Loliwe ukuthi ngasokwa*' (The reason why I could work as a fireboy was because of this *initiation* as a gardener).

Many Zulu gardeners such as Mr Gxabhashe told me that they underwent a similar rite of passage in the kitchen suit, which compared to enduring the trials of traditional African initiation schools, some of which, at least before Zulu King Shaka's reign, centred on adolescent male circumcision and humiliating tasks that taught the discipline and toughness required in manhood. Even the rite of enrolling in the *amabutho* shared parallels with the Zulu young man's first employment as a new member of a team of domestic servants with a collective identity and experience of hardship.[15] Most important, being a gardener has turned into a ritual of attaining manly dignity (*indoda enesithunzi*). It is, of course, ironic that madam-servant relations, imposed by colonial segregationists, provided the cultural ground for a longstanding practice, albeit in a different form. Certainly the most striking similarity between traditional male initiation and the trials of *Abaqulusi* is the emphasis on male separation (seclusion) from all things female, from the amputation warning of the red piping on the kitchen suit to the (breast) milk taboo, symbolising the (forced) severance of young men from their mothers – in this instance their figurative 'maternal' missus.[16]

There is another striking parallel with the social expectations of *amabutho* membership, in which a young warrior felt the need to establish himself as a battle-worthy man who could lead his age-mates as a headman of young men or *induna yezinsizwa*. Tales abound among gardeners of being elevated suddenly from their lowly position when they demonstrated dignity and strength. In my own experience, this attainment of manhood occurred one day at work when I refused to eat the food the missus prepared for me because it came very late in the day, violating the usual arrangement of a noontime meal. This act of defiance shocked my Afrikaans madam; ashamed, she 'graduated' me to the position of trusted employee who could sit on her verandah to eat with her, her family, and even her guests. Indeed, many older gardeners who stayed beyond their 'graduation' rose to become respected 'family retainers' or headmen (*izinduna*) of the madam's property.[17]

The madam's *induna* represents one of the 'positive' outcomes of the gardener's experience. There is, however, a darker side to *Abaqulusi* life rarely glimpsed publicly (except by the elite cultural set in KwaZulu-Natal), which also shows that not all patriarchal societies enable the abuse of women by men. Although the young male gardener could refer to his madam as a mother figure, certain circumstance could prompt him to envisage her as a potential temptress or, worse, a sexual sorcerer – a kind of lewd witch, *umthakathi*. The renowned, late Zulu artist Trevor Makhoba portrayed this phenomenon in a graphic canvas titled 'Great Temptation in the Garden'. The composition speaks for itself.[18]

'Great Temptation in the Garden' by Trevor Makhoba.

Enough eyewitness evidence can be marshalled from gardeners to confirm the scene in the 'Great Temptation'. But the fact that such testimony can be collected, cross-referenced, and verified might lead readers to think that working as a gardener primarily offered an avenue to forbidden fruits. This point obscures an important historical process underpinning the use and symbolism of the kitchen suit. Madams used their status as white employers of Zulu men dressed in a boy's tunic to indulge their proclivities, including a desire for racial dominance over Zulu males, often regarded by white settlers as larger-than-life fearsome figures. It goes without saying that the stereotypical Zulu man, mythically born in the mould of his creator, Shaka, represented the indomitable black warrior with a legendary prowess that defeated well-armed uniformed British men at Isandlwana in 1879. For members of the *Abaqulusi*, the 'Great Temptation', along with different humiliations and sanctions associated with their first job, paved the road to their initiation into modern manhood.

## Notes

1. A.T. Bryant highlights how at the time of the early Zulu kingdom 'the custom of circumcision became obsolete . . . [although] the practice of regularly banding together into "groups" (*amabutho*) all clan youths of a similar age continued as before. Until king Shaka turned them all into real soldiers and real "regiments" . . .'. See *The Zulu People as They Were before the White Man Came*

(Pietermaritzburg: Shuter & Shooter, 1949), pp. 494, 655. See also C. Wilkinson-Latham, *Uniforms and Weapons of the Zulu War* (London: B.T. Batsford, 1978), pp. 75–76.

2. A further blow to the vestiges of the *amabutho* system was dealt by the harsh colonial reprisals following *impi yamakhanda*, the Bhambatha Poll Tax Uprising of 1906. See B. Carton, *Blood from Your Children: The Colonial Origins of Generational Conflict in South Africa* (Pietermaritzburg: University of Natal Press, 2000), Chapters 3–5.

3. L. Callinicos, *Working Life in 1886–1940: Factories, Townships and Popular Culture on the Rand* (Johannesburg: Ravan Press, 1987), p. 56 and J. Cock, *Maids and Madams* (Johannesburg: Ravan Press, 1980). Important studies of African labouring conditions in Natal domestic service can be found in K. Atkins, *The Moon Is Dead! Give Us Our Money! The Cultural Origins of an African Work Ethic, Natal, South Africa, 1843–1900* (Portsmouth: Heinemann, 1993), Chapters 2–3 and 'Origins of the *AmaWasha*: The Zulu Washerman's Guild in Natal, 1850–1910', *Journal of African History* 27 (1986).

4. L. Callinicos, *Working Life*, p. 56.

5. Y. Winters and M. Mchunu, 'Great Temptation in the Garden: Trevor Makhoba as Taboo-breaker', *Trevor Makhoba Retrospective*, Memorial Catalogue, Durban Art Gallery, 2004.

6. J. Verbeek and A. Verbeek, *Victorian and Edwardian Natal* (Pietermaritzburg: Shuter & Shooter, 1982), p. 64.

7. The kitchen suit finally became outmoded garb by the end of the 1960s, although some die-hards continued the custom, with the uniform's obsolescence virtually guaranteed after the Natal provincial school hostel-staff discarded it (then still supplied by the original Harvey, Greenacre & Co. store in Durban). Ironically, the kitchen suit enjoyed a revival in the 1970s when white schoolboys wore it as a demonstration of their 'liberal' sympathies with the domestic staff living in hostels and working in Natal educational institutions: interview Y. Winters with J.S. Betram, head of Weston Agricultural College hostel staff and hotelier, c.1980s and M. Mchunu, personal communication with Y. Winters, 11 June 2004, Durban.

8. Many of these domestic servants worked for private employers, such as white and Indian families, as well as residential and licensed hotels in Natal. The period of contract typically spanned six months to a year, depending on whether the servant obtained an endorsed permit or pass (certainly up to the 1980s). Domestic servitude was often a stepping-stone to other jobs in urban areas: interview M. Mchunu with Y. Winters and M.G. Heera, Durban, 7 June 2004. See also M. Lacey's *Working for Boroko: The Origins of a Coercive Labour System in South Africa* (Johannesburg: Ravan Press, 1981) and J. Cock, *Maids and Madams*.

9. My former employer's surname had been changed for the sake of her privacy; she is a white lady of Afrikaans and French Huguenot extraction.

10. J. Branford, *A Dictionary of South African English* (Oxford: Oxford University Press: 1978). The use of the term *abaqulusi* is not intended to insult the Abaqulusi people of the Ladysmith area.

11. From interviews (i.e., 11 June 2004, KwaShange, Pietermaritzburg) that I conducted with my oral history informants, I heard a consensus opinion; that avoidance and respect (*ukuzila* and *ukuhlonipha*) almost always go together because they relate to the concept of avoiding the sacred, which is a highly valued cultural concept possessing taboo qualities. In traditional Zulu society, all that pertains to sexual activity is sacred taboo; thus mentioning the subject openly is seriously frowned upon. For examples of this phenomenon, see A-I. Berglund, *Zulu Thought-patterns and Symbolism* (London: Hurst, 1976). Berglund associates sex with extraordinary power, especially male power or *amandla*, and the wrathful realm of ancestral spirits. It is believed that a father imbues his son with spirit (from or via the ancestors) during the act of conception. In this sense, semen is considered to exemplify or convey a powerful spirit. Moreover, a man who is sexually active is considered to be 'hot', a status that might endanger society at large if it is not controlled. Hence, behaving with respect and avoidance, *ukuzila* and *ukuhlonipha*, can 'cool' down such dangerous forces and ensure that he has the proper *isithunzi* (dignity) or character befitting a man of rank. While it may seem obscure, this concept of 'cool' respect builds a man's dignity. Homestead heads or priests, for example, prepare to enter the domain of ancestral spirits during family prayers or sacrifices by abstaining from sexual intercourse, as well as behavior involving release such as eating meat and drinking alcohol.

12. Many ex-gardeners still insist on the truth of this story. The manner in which I came to know the truth – and thus the untruth – of the myth is that Missus Cronjé never expressed breast milk; she bought milk, which I unloaded with her groceries from the supermarket. Still out of respect for such traditional lore, I was reluctant to drink any milk in her home.

13. An interview with M. Kweyama and K. Madlala, 5 June 2004, KwaShange, Pietermaritzburg. The gardeners I knew considered this punishment and replied: 'Yes, they say that, but I know of no one whose arms were cut.' Some also said: 'Yes, I was told by my boss not to look beyond the red edge.'
14. I have changed the name of my informant to protect his privacy.
15. In southern Natal by the end of the 1800s, Bhaca people (isiZulu-speaking Africans who became gardeners and domestics in colonial homes) had done away with male initiation by circumcision, choosing to mark the passage to manhood as a journey of the young male migrant to wage work, sometimes to the mines or a white person's home: see W.D. Hammond-Tooke, 'The Bantu Tribes of South Africa', in *The Bantu Tribes of South Africa: Reproductions of Photographic Studies*, Vol. 3, ed. A.M. Duggan-Cronin (Cambridge: Deighton, 1935). Significantly, Bhaca young men also worked for the Pietermaritzburg and Durban Municipal Corporations as 'bucket boys', emptying the toilet (night soil) containers for pay. In mining cities such as Kimberley, other rural isiZulu-speaking migrants, many of them young men from the northern Natal district of Msinga who wore their hallmark ear-studs, performed bucket work, earning the derision of local Tswana people: Y. Winters interview with Nico Meyer, Head of Kimberley Bantu Administration in the 1960 and 1970s, June 2004, Durban. For migrant 'initiations' of Mpondo young men just south of Bhaca communities, see D. Moodie and V. Ndatshe, *Going for Gold* (Berkeley: University of California Press, 1993).
16. It seems, at least from some gardeners' work experience, that a relationship sometimes develops between a servant and the madam, where the former expects his female employer to sort out his personal crises, saying 'but you must, you are my mother': M. Mchunu interview with Mrs B. Eldridge, June 2004, Durban.
17. For example, strong family ties existed between the Gasa and Ndlovu families, on the one hand, and their bosses in the well-known old Natal family called the Campbells, particularly one of its matriarchs, the well-known Africana collector, Dr Killie Campbell. She is of course renowned for her collections of Zulu cultural items, which she donated to the University of KwaZulu-Natal.
18. It is generally known among a community of gardeners/domestics and their white employers, which madams tend to be sexually lascivious, M. Mchunu, personal communication; Y. Winters in discussion with ex-Pietermaritzburg resident J. Blackmore, January 2004, Rosetta. In Makhoba's painting the gardener in his 'kitchen-suit' is depicted as being 'trapped' by his seductress. Makhoba indicated that such happenings were common within the many circles of gardeners/domestics: see Winters and Mchunu, 'Great Temptation'.

*Chapter 50*

# Are Zulu Children Allowed to Ask Questions?

## Silence, Death and Memory in the Time of AIDS[1]

PHILIPPE DENIS

SINCE THE START of the new millennium, it is not exceptional in KwaZulu-Natal to find families who have lost two, three or more members in one year due to the epidemic of HIV/AIDS. A recent survey estimated that no less than 39.1 per cent of women seeking care in antenatal clinics – and probably, by extrapolation, one-third of the sexually active population in the province – is HIV-positive.[2] Without antiretroviral treatments, most people living with HIV/AIDS succumb to opportunistic infections. The consequences of HIV/AIDS among survivors, particularly children, are equally devastating. Some babies contract the deadly virus from their mothers and usually die at an early age. Other young sons and daughters experience trauma when parents with HIV/AIDS sicken and die. Currently, as a result of the epidemic, there are an estimated 1 200 000 orphans in South Africa.[3]

AIDS orphans endure a double loss. They lose their parents and also the more secure existence typically associated with a parent-headed household. Their quality of life deteriorates drastically, while they slip into greater isolation. For example, they do not go out to see relatives as they used to do. Sometimes they stop attending school because without their income-earning parent or parents to provide money, they cannot pay the fees; even if AIDS orphans can meet the financial obligations of education, the stigma of their tragedy is often so great that they do not want to face their peers and teachers in the classroom.[4]

HIV/AIDS not only tears the socio-economic fabric of families, but also upsets their emotional stability. The fact that a caregiver, usually an older female relative who has had to step into the parenting void, is unwilling to tell children why their mother or father, or both, suddenly wasted away worsens the plight of the youngest generation. As the children's situation deteriorates further, they are afflicted by anger, sadness or depression. They find it difficult to express their emotions because the cause of their problem has rarely been named. Tessa Marcus, a sociologist who has studied the impact of AIDS on children in the Natal Midlands points out that AIDS is surrounded by silence and secrecy. People generally do not refer to the disease by name.[5] They use euphemisms such as *amagama amathatu*, the 'three-letter word'. In the end, children victimised by AIDS are left alone in their grief. With time, their memories of deceased parents tend to fade, creating a state of confusion that prevents them from developing their full potential. The effect of bereavement on children is worse, as a recent study on childhood trauma shows, when they are not helped to understand and resolve their loss.[6]

But this bleak scenario might not be inevitable as patterns of communication between adults and children begin to change. Culture – and in this particular case, Zulu cultural values operating within and between families – shapes the way in which the dead are remembered. This supposition provokes crucial questions as the AIDS epidemic claims an ever-higher toll. In what circumstances do parents, or if they are absent, caregivers convey family history to young children? In the customary realm of *ukuhlonipha* (Zulu traditional respect for and avoidance of elders), can boys and girls children ask adults probing questions? How are family secrets aired?

Since 2000 the Sinomlando Centre for Oral History and Memory Work in Africa, a University of KwaZulu-Natal-based community organisation, has grappled with such open-ended concerns. It aims to facilitate an intergenerational dialogue around family accounts that deal with untimely illness and death. In Zulu, *sinomlando* means, 'we have a history'; this phrase captures the research aims of the project. Sinomlando devised a memory box programme that endeavours to use methodologies of oral history to develop resilience in children whose parents are living with, or have died from, AIDS. Resilience is a concept used by trauma specialists to designate 'the ability to resume personal growth in adverse circumstances'[7] – in this case the ability of children affected by HIV/AIDS to grow without the care and support of loving parents. With the assistance of the Sinomlando 'memory facilitators', family members in communities gutted by AIDS are encouraged to tell their life stories. Transcripts of conversations in isiZulu are edited and compiled in a booklet that accompanies an audiotape of all the voices. These materials are presented to the interviewed family and placed in a memory box created by the children with the help of memory facilitators.

### Oral history and the importation of life story work in Zulu communities
In 2001 the Sinomlando Centre and Sinosizo Home-based Care, a community organisation that provides AIDS patients and their children with vital support, launched a pilot study to assess the effects of the memory box in twenty mostly isiZulu-speaking families in the Durban area.[8] Currently, the memory box programme provides training and ongoing assistance to various community- and faith-based organisations in the KwaZulu-Natal, Eastern Cape and Gauteng provinces. The findings of the 2001 pilot study suggest that children who have a clearer recollection

of life with their parents are better able to cope with the hardships of AIDS-induced death. Such children know more about their family history and can deduce what happened to their parents.

The process of composing a memory box is designed to create the space for adults and children to discuss trauma in the family and recollections of domestic happiness. Indeed, these disparate personal accounts are known to aid healing. As the author of a recent study on memory and trauma demonstrates, 'by telling our story of the trauma(s) and working through the associated pain, i.e. by grieving it, we can slowly transfer and transform our traumatic memory into a healthier kind of ordinary memory – something that we were not allowed to do before'.[9]

The Memory Box Programme aims to collect multiple narratives. The texts and voices engendered by interviews allow children to put together the fragments of their family history. The Sinomlando Centre draws inspiration from the therapeutic value of oral history. Oral historians know how to encourage ordinary people to tell stories, particularly about life circumstances that have dealt a cruel blow to their basic family integrity.[10]

The reconstruction of family stories (to enhance resilience of children at risk) is not specific to South Africa. In countries such as Great Britain and France, counsellors encourage life story work, as this process is called, in children's homes, halfway houses and foster families.[11] Such state-supported children, many of them abandoned or given up for adoption, often question their origins. They have been placed – or rather displaced – once or several times in their lives without ever understanding why. Christine Abels-Eber, an expert on the life story method, explains: 'The child who is placed in an institution or a foster family is, in most situations, a child who suffers: he is buffeted from one place to another and his life is arranged as if he had no family. Yet, he is imbued with a family legacy to which he clings.'[12]

Are these techniques – oral history and life story work – applicable in contemporary Zulu society? This kind of question elicits a warning from Hugo Slim and Paul Thompson, two oral historians who discourage a culturally blind approach to research. In the West, they observe, conducting an interview has become a currency of inquiry. A job interview is generally a prerequisite for employment; the media features endless clips of people replying to questions in sound bites; few people escape having to participate in telephone polls and marketing surveys. In African societies, by contrast, these now standard interview techniques are largely foreign to indigenous systems of communication.[13]

Similar observations apply to the technique of life story work. In countries like France, where life story work has been developed, child abandonment – once a widespread phenomenon in medieval and industrial times – is now rare. The orphanage, for example, has altogether receded from the public sphere in most wealthy European societies. Instead, children's lives are disrupted by family abuse and neglect or, more commonly, by divorce. To be sure, Western parents have uncomfortable secrets that undermine the emotional stability of their children, but there are also numerous supporting mechanisms to help the very young take ownership of their family histories: a sprawling network of social services, affordable individual therapies, accessible computer databases, dependable transport systems and so on. Few if any of these resources are available on demand to the average family in South Africa.

### Disrupted family lives

Like other invasive historical processes such as conquest by the British Empire, AIDS in South Africa has profoundly altered socio-economic and generational dynamics, as well as patterns of communication between children and adults. There is a growing scholarly literature that explores the past trajectories of such complex forms of family disruption.[14] Long before the advent of the pandemic, nineteenth-century colonial forces buffeted Zulu households, particularly in rural areas, where families tended to be large. As a consequence, in this new millennium, the traditional capacious homestead – two or three generations on the same plot, with a patriarch, his one or two wives, their children, and grandchildren – is now an anachronism.

Over the course of the twentieth century, migrant labour, forced removals and unemployment so eroded the bonds of rural communities that widespread sexual violence, unwed motherhood and disintegration of conjugal ties are everyday realities in KwaZulu-Natal. Patriarchal order in homesteads, which on the one hand subordinated women to men and on the other hand, afforded women some domestic security, remains at best a fragmented certainty. No viable alternative structure to regulate marital or parental relations has emerged. In a climate of joblessness and landlessness, with patriarchal status declining as the cost of marriage extends beyond the reach of suitors, men have sought to reinforce their power over women in other ways. Continually in search of work and unable to pay the high price of *ilobolo* (bridewealth), more and more single men tend to pursue multiple short-lived relationships, leaving the children of these liaisons to be cared for by their lover or her mother. Procreation still gives social recognition both to unmarried mothers and fathers. But as far as many male suitors are concerned, having children does not mean taking responsibility for them. The maternal caretaker in these circumstances is often a single woman, either because she is a widow or because she has never married. Instead of enjoying the support of adult children, some of these grandmothers struggle again to bring up another generation of sons and daughters. Financially and emotionally this represents an enormous burden.

The pilot study conducted by Sinomlando memory facilitators documented these burdens in interviews with seventeen isiZulu-speaking families affected by HIV/AIDS in the Durban area.[15] Among the respondents, only three couples were or had been married; four lived together extramaritally, while in the remaining cases the primary caregiver was a single mother. Not surprisingly, Sinomlando researchers found that HIV/AIDS exacerbate the grim uncertainties of single parenthood and child abandonment. In many instances the principal caregiver does not know if the father of the children he has left behind is HIV-positive, or even if he is alive because he has been out of contact for years.[16]

### *Ukuhlonipha*, children and untimely death

Sinomlando fieldwork demonstrates that when children orphaned by AIDS are raised by a much older or traditionally minded guardian, or grow up in a household where Zulu customary respect, *ukuhlonipha*, is practised, they are silent participants in family matters. 'It is in our blood', a Sinomlando isiZulu-speaking memory facilitator asserted at a university seminar on bereavement, 'that children do not ask questions.' Under few circumstances, she continued, are they supposed to ask their caregivers to divulge information about an elder, especially a person who might have died from an illness regarded as shameful.[17]

A similar convention of deference prohibits women from approaching their husbands to discuss sensitive matters. 'Are you not allowed to talk to your husband in private and ask him if he noticed that there is a problem with chastity in the family?' one of Sinomlando's representatives recently asked the head of a local Christian African women's organisation in KwaZulu-Natal. This church leader suspected one of her daughters went out with boys. Given the high prevalence of HIV in her township some action needed to be taken. So she took this particular daughter for a virginity test but the mother did not know how to inform her husband of this action. 'Yes, we advise our husbands', the church leader explained, but 'our husbands have this attitude which makes them say: "I can never be told by a woman" . . . So you end up knowing that there is nothing you can say to your husband.'[18]

*Ukuhlonipha* requires that children, unmarried women, and junior wives show deference to their social 'superiors'. The Sinomlando memory facilitators have discovered that in isiZulu-speaking households they visit men who claim to be the social superior, even when they are not married. The same applies to older (widowed or single) mothers, especially when a son is, or was, the head of the family. The people seen as subordinates feel obliged to express themselves indirectly so that the superior does not have to acknowledge that he has something to learn from 'inferiors'. Unfortunately, this form of subtle communication does not always work, particularly when family tensions escalate and during bereavement. The head of the local Christian women's organisation voiced frustration: 'Yes, you try to use words that will be acceptable. But you end up not saying what you wanted to say. You burn inside because you do not get the result that you were expecting.'[19] Most importantly, the conventions of *ukuhlonipha* become a major hindrance to mourning children. How can they grieve if they cannot openly display their emotions and ask questions that are important to them? When considering these issues, one should bear in mind that in South Africa AIDS remains a taboo disease surrounded by stigma.[20]

*Ukuhlonipha* can also mislead caregivers when they try to understand children's hidden feelings. A grandmother might assume that if children do not pose questions they do not have concerns to voice, or their silence is attributed to their young age. Memory facilitators frequently record the following sentence, 'This child is too small to understand.' But in many cases children know more than they divulge about their parents' condition. Sometimes children overhear adult conversation, or, more simply, they discern the truth by discussing matters with peers. Some children, for example, know that their mother is HIV-positive, even though the issue was never discussed openly in their presence.

Sinomlando memory facilitators have found that for the grieving process to unfold in meaningful ways, children's perceptions need to be validated by a supporting adult. A conversation with caregivers might begin to resolve some of the children's general disorientation. Moreover, naming the cause of so much suffering doubtless accelerates mourning and, it is hoped, healing through dialogue.

One should not conclude that elements of traditional Zulu culture stifle intergenerational dialogue. In fact, storytelling is a well-known Zulu (and African) form of socialisation that bridges the perspectives of old and young. As literature scholar Isabel Hofmeyr writes: '[O]ne of the most enduring stereotypes in Southern African oral literary studies is that of woman-as-storyteller. Almost invariably a grandmother, preferably seated in the vicinity of a fire, this figure has dominated virtually all local research into oral narrative.' Hofmeyr notes, too, that older men also convey tales, although not to the same audiences.[21]

Hofmeyr's assessment is important to the fieldworkers of Sinomlando. In the context of ritual gatherings that honour the ancestors, grandparents proclaim lineage praises (*izibongo*) in the presence of children. Revered elders perform a similar act as caregivers of an AIDS orphan, when they recount family stories in the presence of memory facilitators. Thus, the concept of creating memory boxes is not wholly alien to broadly conceived Zulu cultural views.

## The culture of generational communication in Zulu families

*Ukuhlonipha* is neither static nor consistently hegemonic. It has undergone changes during this past century of urbanisation and minority white rule. Figures of authority, such as the Zulu father, teacher or priest seem to command less authority and young unmarried fathers earn no esteem for refusing to acknowledge their offspring. To be sure, patriarchal prestige was challenged long before the advent of AIDS.

A recent study of the social unrest in Zulu communities that preceded the 1906 Bhambatha rebellion in Natal shows that Zulu fathers struggled to maintain some semblance of their privileged standing as colonial officials imposed emasculating laws.[22] What this work of scholarship and the fieldwork of Sinomlando demonstrate is that some critical gender studies of patriarchal power tend to lose sight of the fact that erosion of *ukuhlonipha* can entail less respect for all in isiZulu-speaking communities. Women and children, for their part, lose a degree of patriarchal protection, as they are more exposed to abuse and neglect. But major cultural change also has positive aspects during this time of AIDS. After the memory facilitators' interventions, the children are less afraid to talk to their caregivers. Even if the behaviour of a boy or girl is seen as assertive, more and more adults accept such challenges and try to communicate with their children to build greater trust. At first caregivers appear hesitant to talk to their children for fear of possible fallout. Here, the memory facilitators act as a safety net. A caregiver can turn to them when the basic cohesion of the family is perceived to be at risk. But the memory facilitators only play a temporary role. In many instances, as the 2001 pilot study indicates, a family conversation initiated by Sinomlando representatives continues after their departure from a community.

The staff of the Memory Box Programme noticed that caregivers of AIDS orphans now admit that speaking to children about illness and death is beneficial. Moreover, the general outlook of children affected by AIDS tends to improve as they explore ways to express questions that haunt them. Nokhaya Makiwane, one of the memory facilitators, summed up this promising development at a Sinomlando seminar: 'The people we visit do not want to tell their family secrets. But to them this silence is a burden. They do not tell the family history because there is no space for a conversation on this subject in their lives. They find it appropriate if someone facilitates the process. When that happens, they are relieved to share their secrets with the children.'[23]

## Notes

1. I express my gratitude to Ben Carton, Sibongile Mafu, Nokhaya Makiwane, Thandeka Tshezi, Louise Vis and James Worthington who took part in a seminar of the Sinomlando Centre in January 2003, exploring Zulu cultural aspects of the methodology of the Memory Box Programme. Their input helped me write this chapter.
2. Statistics provided by the South African Department of Health (http://www.avert.org/safricastats.htm) (accessed September 2007). The survey was conducted in October and November 2006.
3. Statistics provided by UNICEF (http://www.avert.org/aidsorphans.htm) (accessed September 2007). See also J. Gow, C. Desmond and D. Ewing, 'Children and HIV/AIDS', in *Impacts and Interventions: The HIV/AIDS Epidemic and the Children of South Africa*, eds. J. Gow and C. Desmond (Pietermaritzburg: University of Natal Press, 2002), p. 6. An orphan is defined here as a person under the age of eighteen whose mother has died.
4. T. Marcus, 'Living and Dying with AIDS', prepared for the Children in Distress Network (CINDI), July 1999 and Gow, Desmond and Ewing, *Impacts and Interventions*.
5. Marcus, 'Living and Dying', p. 10.
6. S. Lewis, *Childhood Trauma: Understanding Traumatised Children in South Africa* (Cape Town: David Philip, 1999), p. 4.
7. E. Grotberg, *A Guide to Promoting Resilience in Children: Strengthening the Human Spirit* (The Hague: Bernard van Leer Foundation, 1995).
8. P. Denis, ed. *Never Too Small to Remember: Memory Work and Resilience in Times of AIDS* (Pietermaritzburg: Cluster Publications, 2005), pp. 19–26. For an overview of the Sinomlando Centre's activities see www.sinomlando.org.za.

9. C. Whitfield, *Memory and Abuse: Remembering and Healing the Effects of Trauma* (Florida: Health Communications, 1995), p. 44.

10. During the last decade of apartheid numerous attempts were made to document and record the voices of 'ordinary people' as an alternative to a history written 'from above'. Works such as Belinda Bozzoli, *Women of Phokeng: Consciousness, Life Strategy, and Migrancy in South Africa, 1900–1983* (Portsmouth: Heinemann and London: James Currey, 1991) and Isabel Hofmeyr, *'We Spend Our Years as a Tale That is Told': Oral Historical Narrative in a South African Chiefdom* (Johannesburg: Witwatersrand University Press, 1994) showed how marginalised and disenfranchised black people struggled to hold onto their oral histories during a repressive regime of white supremacy that sought to nullify black history. On oral history in South Africa, see P. la Hausse de Lalouvière, 'Oral History and South African Oral Historians', *Radical History Review* 46/7 (1990): 346–56 and P. Denis, 'Oral History in a Wounded Country', in *Orality, Literacy and Colonialism in Southern Africa*, ed. J. Draper (Atlanta: Society of Biblical Literature and Pietermaritzburg: Cluster Publications, 2003), pp. 205–16.

11. T. Ryan and R. Walker, *Life Story Work* (London: British Agencies for Adoption and Fostering, 1999); C. Abels-Eber, *Enfants placés et construction d'historicité* (Paris: L'Harmattan, 2000) and P. Denis, ed. *Never Too Small to Remember*, pp. 1–18.

12. Abels-Eber, *Enfants placés*, p. 23.

13. H. Slim and P. Thompson, *Listening for a Change: Oral Testimony and Development* (London: Panos Publications, 1993), p. 61.

14. See, for example, C. Walker, 'Gender and the Development of the Migrant Labour System *c.*1850–1930: An Overview', in *Women and Gender in Southern Africa to 1945*, ed. C. Walker (Cape Town: David Philip and London: James Currey, 1990); D. Webb, *HIV and AIDS in Africa* (London and Chicago: Pluto Press, 1997); Marcus, 'Living and Dying'; A. Whiteside and C. Sunter, *Aids: The Challenge for South Africa* (Cape Town: Tafelberg and Human Rousseau, 2000); B. Carton, *Blood from Your Children: The Colonial Origins of Generational Conflict in South Africa* (Charlottesville: University of Virginia Press, 2000); P. Delius and F. Glaser, 'Sexual Socialisation in South Africa in an Historical Perspective', *African Studies* 61:1 (July 2002): 5–54 and P. Denis, 'Sexuality and Aids in South Africa', *Journal of Theology for Southern Africa* 113 (March 2003): 63–77.

15. Three families of the original pool of twenty families were left out for various reasons.

16. P. Denis and R. Ntsimane, 'Absent Fathers: Why do Men not Feature in Stories of Families Affected by HIV/AIDS in KwaZulu-Natal', in *Baba: Men and Fatherhood in South Africa*, eds. L. Richter and R. Morrell (Cape Town: HSRC Press, 2006), pp. 237–49.

17. On the stigma of AIDS, see Marcus, 'Living and Dying', pp. 10–14. For a critical analysis of the *ukukhonipha* concept, see P. Mduli, 'Ubuntu-Mbotho: Inkatha's "People's Education"', *Transformation* 5 (1987): 67–69.

18. Interview conducted in Sobantu, Pietermaritzburg, 13 October 2001. See P. Denis, '"We also had to live with apartheid in our homes": Stories of women in Sobantu, South Africa', *Studia Historiae Ecclesiasticae* 30:1 (June 2004): 151–167.

19. Interview conducted in Sobantu, Pietermaritzburg, 13 October 2001.

20. Marcus, 'Living and Dying', p. 10.

21. Hofmeyr, *We Spend Our Years*, p. 25.

22. Carton, *Blood from Your Children*.

23. Memory Box Programme seminar, Pietermaritzburg, 18 January 2003.

# Chapter 51

# Bulls in the Boardroom
## The Zulu Warrior Ethic and the Spirit of South African Capitalism[1]

BENEDICT CARTON and MALCOLM DRAPER

IN CONTEMPORARY SOUTH Africa, new elites champion the African Renaissance, a philosophy of national rejuvenation integrating ideals of laissez-faire capitalism and black economic empowerment (BEE).[2] Before running foul of the law, Deputy-President Jacob Zuma was a vocal proponent of the African Renaissance. In the foreword to dealmaker Phinda Madi's book, *Leadership Lessons from Emperor Shaka Zulu the Great*, Zuma lauded his model strategist in the world of modern markets, Shaka, 'the visionary, the transformer, [and] the motivator'.[3] *Leadership Lessons* identifies the motives that purportedly spurred Shaka's 'sense of destiny', among them his drive to accumulate cattle, which he 'would sit and watch . . . sometimes the whole day'. The author of *Leadership Lessons*, a member of the 2001 Black Economic Empowerment Commission and public relations firm Madi, Sussens and HerdBuoys, recounts how the first Zulu king taught his regiments to 'sprout like the horns of bull' and overwhelm opponents.[4] This tactic not only made Shaka one of the 'globally revered' winners, according to Madi, it could also turn a 'fanatical team' of managers into unbeatable competitors. Thus, *Leadership Lessons* recommends that aspirant capitalists gain their edge by consulting the oral traditions that chronicle Shaka's relentless rise to power.[5]

Madi's pitch highlights certain BEE aims that President Thabo Mbeki promoted in 2006 to 'assist poverty alleviation'[6] through indigenous initiative. Mbeki announced: 'We have achieved steady progress towards the restructuring of our economy so that it gains the organic possibility to grow, expand and develop, producing greater volumes of wealth, demonstrating the possibility for a country of the South to stand its ground and advance, even in the context of a highly competitive and inequitable process of globalisation.'[7]

This discourse of ambition and reparation animates management guidebooks urging corporations in the post-apartheid era to embrace a 'Zulu competitive spirit';[8]

or the Johannesburg *Star*'s 'workplace' column, featuring tips to executives about harnessing their *ubukhosi*, regal presence, and exuding an 'inner Shaka' by 'dress[ing] to kill'.[9]

There is a reason why tales of the magnanimous and fearsome Shaka are grist for the motivational guru's mill, *Leadership Lessons* admits freely.[10] Madi acknowledges the imaginative power of his 'poetic licence' lies in his appeal to business people of 'all backgrounds' to shed their apartheid skin and slip into a suit of Zulu glory.[11] He ascribes a deeper understanding of the relationship between Shakan achievement and market success to the wisdom imparted by his academic mentor at the University of the Witwatersrand in Johannesburg, the anthropologist David Webster, an 'anti-apartheid campaigner and soldier of conscience . . . [who] was mowed down unmercifully by the bullet of an [apartheid hit squad] assassin' in May 1989. 'At just about that time', Madi writes, 'he had been doing tremendous work with a nobleman from our clan, uMntwana Bukhosibakhe Madi . . . [and] together [they had] unearthed a fascinating part of the Madi family history, from the times of Emperor Shaka to the present.'[12] In fact Webster conducted research in northern KwaZulu where, instead of a Zulu primordial identity, he found Thonga communities filled with 'consummate cultural entrepreneurs' drawing on 'a repertoire of ethnic features', including the stereotype of the strong Zulu warrior that appealed to European employers on the Witwatersrand.[13]

Webster provides crucial insights into the rationale behind management gurus' fixation on a great figure of the African Renaissance, Shaka Zulu, whose mythologised feats make up one model of social advancement and economic possibility. Here, it is important to note that the archetypal Zulu warrior was never monopolised by black business. Shaka long served as an idol in a range of companies, as Mike Boon's *African Way: The Power of Interactive Leadership* shows. His book emphasises that before the advent of democracy 'white Africans' (some of whom also studied with Webster) were turning to Zulu culture to navigate the 'complex and challenging marketplace'.[14] An English- and isiZulu-speaking South African, Boon grew up in rural KwaZulu-Natal and developed close ties with prominent 'white Zulus' such as world music star, the rock-*maskanda* mixer Johnny Clegg, a Webster protégé, as well as Barry Leitch and Kingsley Holgate, founders of Shakaland, an 'international tourist haunt' outside Eshowe.[15] Although Boon disclaims sexism, his guide to 'interactive leadership' borrows the language of martial patriarchy. Indeed, the ever-recurring Shaka seems to be the avatar of the *African Way*. However, Boon distances himself from the kind of Zulu ethnicity that 'fan[s] hatred of other groups'.[16] One of his partners in a company Boon formed, Group Africa of the Amavulandlela (the path-breakers), was Barry Leitch. Leitch is said to bring a 'Now African' attitude to work, a sentiment rooted in his own 'cross-cultural pollination', which he harnesses to develop free enterprise possibilities, especially in the tourist trade.[17]

In fact one could argue that either half of the name phrase 'Shaka Zulu' is the recognised brand of modern South Africa and perhaps the entire continent. Recently, *Africa Geographic* scrutinised this rarely verified assertion by canvassing surveys in the United States and across Europe. The magazine not only discovered that 'the word most often associated with Africa is "Zulu"', but also that 'there should be something exploitable in the combination of "Zulu" and international tourism'.[18] The negative side of this exploitation did not faze the African National Congress (ANC) minister for Environmental Affairs and Tourism Pallo Jordan when, in April 1997, he hailed the 'hospitality industry' as 'one of the key growth points in the [national] economy', singling out the conglomerate Tourvest and its white board for bringing African styles and people 'into the tourism industry'.[19] Indeed, Tourvest and its BEE partners have been at the forefront of the tourism boom, posting solid returns despite global recessions, threats of terrorism and the strengthening rand.[20] Tourvest's holdings include foreign currency exchange, retail merchandising, and package accommodations.[21] Tourvest's heritage lodges, according to Charl van Wyk (in 2003 the managing director of the premier Protea Hotel destination, Shakaland) particularly elevate the international reputation of the corporation. It is the Zulu warrior experience, Van Wyk says, that draws the tourists two hours' drive north of Durban where Shakaland stages martial dances and ethnographic skits of 'Zulu people at the Great Kraal'. The welcome brochure advertises a place that serves as 'an enriching experience affording you a better understanding of the Zulu nation, its people and their intriguing customs'.[22]

At a nearby Tourvest establishment, the Protea Simunye Zulu Lodge, another kind of 'primal and timeless . . . magic' is said to await visitors. They can ride an ox-cart to their accommodations and drink at the 'Cattle Station pub', where they learn from their printed guide that they stay under the 'protection of warriors of the Royal House'. The tourist is then offered a palette of 'fascinating cross-cultural' choices originally devised by Barry Leitch, who built and operated Simunye before Protea Hotels took it over. The idea for Simunye, Leitch recalled in 2004, was born in the 1980s, when he struggled to carve out 'space in white South Africa' for 'the Zulu cultural experience'. Leitch said he found his first clutch of white sympathisers as an undergraduate in the anthropology department of the University of Cape Town, but his true revelations as maverick entrepreneur had come much earlier, when he was barefoot in the bush and illiterate in the lingua franca of global commerce. The Zululand farm-boy Leitch spoke isiZulu before he learned English. As a schoolboy, he spent holidays with his surrogate AmaBiyela family in their homestead near the White Mfolozi River. Prince Gilenja, then the AmaBiyela patriarch, accepted Leitch as an honorary son whose name was not Barry, but Mkhomazi, after the Mkhomazi River that, like Leitch's creative energies, could flood without warning.[23] In this oral world, Leitch claimed to absorb more 'priceless' lessons than any formal education could afford, including masculine bonding with Zulu age-mates near the cattle dipping tank, where they acted like 'young bulls', squaring off in stick fights, and competing for the affections of girls. Years later, the AmaBiyela patriarch would endorse the establishment of Simunye, according to Leitch.[24]

After leaving university, Leitch started his career with the South African Broadcasting Company (SABC), where he designed documentary programmes, among them *Jikelele*, the first live television broadcast in isiZulu. He soon joined the film industry to help make *Zulu Dawn*, a movie about the battle of Isandlwana and a prequel to *Zulu*, which vaulted Michael Caine (as Lieutenant Gonville Bromhead) and Mangosuthu Buthelezi (as Zulu King Cetshwayo) to the big screen, and ended with Richard Burton, in a Shakespearean voiceover, reciting the names of British soldiers who won the Victoria Cross for their defence of Rorke's Drift. Leitch then accepted the position of first assistant director of the mini-series *Shaka Zulu*. In her critical study of Shaka called *Terrific Majesty*, Carolyn Hamilton shows how this made-for-television epic, idealising relationships between European traders and their patron, Shaka, exhibited a didactic agenda: to project a make-believe multiracial Zulu past that instilled hope in white South Africans that they could be friends with black people.[25] Emerging on screen as economic sanctions and cultural boycotts further ostracised South Africa, *Shaka Zulu* garnered praise and audiences – and has seldom been absent from TV screens since.[26]

In these heady days, Leitch joined forces with Kingsley Holgate, a businessman who owned a rural Mhlatuze store with two names, Kwabhekithunga and KwaPhobane. At the time, Holgate was already known as an isiZulu-speaking adventurer whose large feet earned him the name Nondwayiso, the lily-trotter. They pursued television contracts for which they were well positioned with Leitch's SABC connections. Although they worked on a follow-up to *Shaka Zulu* – the lack-lustre series *John Ross*, which traced the bush gambols of an English boy who supposedly struck up a friendship with the first Zulu king – film opportunities were receding fast. Holgate and Leitch hit hard times.[27] In 1987 the land bought by Holgate and Leitch, which served as a base-camp and movie set of Senzangakhona's royal homestead during the making of *Shaka Zulu*, was converted into a 'cross-cultural centre' named Shakaland. The same fiery orange-letter placard dividing each segment of the television mini-series now emblazoned the gate of a true 'hyper-reality'. Indeed, Shakaland was advertised as a film site, rather than a true-to-life depiction of Zulu heritage.[28] Tourists seemed to love the concept and almost immediately the Holgate-Leitch venture became one of the prized 'cultural villages' in South Africa. Holgate contributed marketing knowledge and personal charisma to the partnership, choosing not to take the lead on matters of staging Zulu culture. His business clothes consisted of an open-necked khaki shirt and frontiersman's veldskoens (simple leather shoes). Weather permitting, he walked naked from the waist up, priding himself on his considerable stomach. He recalled in 2003 that his pious and strict father, Reverend Arthur Holgate, introduced him to the 'real' Africa north of the Limpopo, which white travellers with pith helmets had romanticised: 'During school holidays he would cart us off from Natal on these missionary journeys to Southern and Northern Rhodesia. That, together with his interest in the early pioneers, is how I got my name Kingsley – after Kingsley Fairbridge, the missionary explorer . . .' [29]

Perhaps because he was the dutiful son of a minister, Holgate was reluctant to appear in Shakaland's dramatic acts alongside Leitch. Leitch preferred an array of clothes fusing Zulu and Swazi designs, as well as embroidered trousers, *imibondwe* (see picture below), favoured by Zulu male migrants who could not wear ceremonial skins in the city; one could argue that Leitch's attire manifested the way he liked to portray African culture as colourful, dynamic, porous and hybrid. He donned some of these outfits when mirroring the chesty movements of the '*inkunzi* (bull) warrior' dance, which he had mastered in childhood with AmaBiyela playmates around the dipping tank. These performances serenaded guests at twilight, as Leitch manoeuvred himself so that he was silhouetted against a blazing fire in the *isibaya*, the central pen where his Nguni cattle were kept at night.[30] Leitch told Carolyn Hamilton in an interview that he and Holgate behaved 'in the Zulu fashion. We don't conduct ourselves in a white fashion.'[31]

*Standing Gumede and Barry Leitch, cultural virtuosos of Shakaland, on stage, c.1987.*

*Kingsley Holgate, playing host*
*at Shakaland, c.1987.*

Yet Shakaland was never an unqualified success story. For one thing, it lacked a performance space to hold large paying crowds. Thus in 1987 Leitch and Holgate planned to erect an *indl'enkulu* (great hut) for large choreographed dances. Zulu King Goodwill Zwelithini and the top financial executive at First National Bank, who bankrolled the project, attended the inaugural ceremony. Back then, Shakaland offered a venue to broker the future for white capital – desperate, as Leitch explained in 2003, to position itself for the transition to majority rule.[32]

*King Goodwill Zwelithini at the First National*
*Bank Great Hut opening.*

With the fresh investment, Holgate and Leitch formed the Rural Television Network (RTV), which beamed *Shaka Zulu* and commercials on video machines at trading stores throughout KwaZulu. They wanted to take the mini-series to people who helped make it, funding this effort with revenues from advertisers of soap, food, Doom insecticide, tea and cosmetics, but they refused to plug skin lightener cream.

RTV put on live roadshows with movie actors, musicians and dancers from Shakaland, among them Mkhomazi, whose *inkunzi* warrior routine sparked enthusiasm among crowds.[33] Rural isiZulu-speaking markets, which had hitherto been ignored by many manufacturers, were now buffeted by the winds of modern demand-driven, leisure-oriented market forces. In this regard, Mkhomazi and Nondwayiso accelerated the pace of capitalist consumption in the heart of Chief Minister Mangosuthu Buthelezi's homeland, much as the early nineteenth-century British clients of Shaka had facilitated access to colonial goods in the Zulu kingdom. The analogy with earlier 'white Zulus' such as Henry Fynn is vital: the 'cross-cultural' commerce of the 1820s and 1830s presaged imperial conquest, which in turn paved the way for the free enterprise of Holgate and Leitch.[34]

*Barry Leitch and* Shaka Zulu *actor, selling Doom bug killer on RTV, 1987.*

The constant grind of roadshows took its toll on the white Zulu duo. Neither Holgate nor Leitch professed to enjoy the day-to-day tasks of running a small entertainment empire stretching across the challenging terrain (to commerce as to agriculture) of Zululand. Moreover, their 'cross-cultural centre' was drifting into insolvency, with subsidies from RTV earnings barely meeting creditors' demands. Just as bankruptcy seemed inevitable, Holgate and Leitch sealed a strategic alliance with Protea Hotels, which agreed to assume Shakaland's debts and boost their credit.

In next to no time the cross-cultural centre again became one of the most buoyant ventures of its kind in South Africa. While Protea executives controlled the hospitality side – handling the accounting, reservations, dining, etc. – Leitch managed the cultural capital, such as dance choreography, and Holgate oversaw labour relations with the isiZulu-speaking staff. Nowhere were the signs of Shakaland's future viability more evident than on top of the elevated *inqolobane*, which symbolised both a beehive storehouse that traditionally held grain for lean times and a vulnerable asset for enemies to target when attacking their rival's surplus.[35] At each corner of the *inqolobane* was a flag that gusty winds slowly shredded. One pennant showed the fiery letters of Shakaland, another the crest of Chief Minister Buthelezi's KwaZulu homeland, still another the national colours of apartheid South Africa, and the final cloth bore the insignia of private capital (Protea).[36]

*Flags on the* inqolobane, *clockwise from left: Shakaland, KwaZulu, South Africa, and Protea, 1989.*

Protea Hotels would convert Shakaland into a must-see global destination, with glossy advertisements in travel magazines promising 'the essence of Africa [and its] pulsating tribal rhythms, assegai-wielding warriors and the mysterious rituals of the Sangoma [diviner] interpreting messages from the spirits'. The cover of the main brochure, graced with the image of the head-ringed old AmaBiyela patriarch named Gilenja, 'spoke volumes about the authentic Zulu culture tourists could come and see'. A promotional CD with clips of performances at Shakaland also asked enticing questions: 'Have you ever been to a place where time stands still and wealth is measured in beautiful cattle?'[37] The resurrection of Shakaland as a well-financed corporate appendage enabled the two white Zulus to pursue other possibilities elsewhere, increasingly as individuals rather than as partners.[38]

As South Africa staggered toward the first democratic election in 1994, Holgate stepped away from the 'endless' board meetings to lead a band of land and water 'explorers' with backing from Captain Morgan Rum and Land Rover. Since the early 1990s, Holgate's swashbuckling treks through the frontline states, where ANC guerillas used to train, have captured the imagination of white South Africans, who spent *their* Mandela prison years as veritable pariahs on their continent and elsewhere in the world. When Holgate was pictured clutching his Captain Morgan and standing in front of his four-wheel-drive vehicle, he epitomised what was possible for the adult children of settler society in the post-apartheid era. Indeed, Holgate attributes the impetus behind his quests to the 'moment South Africa came of age' following Nelson Mandela's walk from confinement. '[H]it the road', Holgate thought, 'Madagascar, Uganda – and that led to the Cape to Cairo trip' that began with his party of travellers filling a Zulu calabash with water from Cape Point and ended a year later with that calabash being emptied into the Mediterranean at the mouth of the Nile. 'The trip had an amazing psychological effect on us,' says Holgate. 'We felt we were citizens of Africa, not just South Africa.'[39] After a Captain Morgan-sponsored 'African Odyssey' in 1993 that skirted the Tropic of Capricorn (a journey inaugurated by a 'Zulu send-off' from Shakaland), Holgate appeared to be tracing the fabled trajectory of a 'white-gone-native' in *Shaka Zulu*, the real-life character Henry Francis Fynn. T.V. Bulpin, the author of bestselling popular Natal colonial histories in the mid-to-late twentieth century, depicted Henry Francis Fynn as a 'kind and intelligent man' – more at heart 'an explorer and pioneer than a trader, and such achievements as were to be his were not to be counted in terms of cash or personal wealth'.[40]

*Kinglsey Holgate: Captain Morgan Explorer, 2002.*

In media interviews Holgate has delighted in downplaying the need to make and save money. Yet he, like Fynn, the one-time beneficiary of Shakan largesse, managed to earn enough to sustain his escapades. Holgate's pre-Shakaland entrepreneurial experiences as owner of the Kwabhekithunga curio shop in the Mhlatuze valley reveal a further connection with the Fynn legacy. When Protea stepped in to purchase Shakaland, the big hotel chain insisted that cross-cultural marketing activities remain their exclusive property, and to enforce this stipulation a restraint of trade agreement was slapped on the white Zulus to limit what they could peddle outside the resort. Protea may have worried about Holgate's ability to tap into the previously successful business practices that enabled him to run Kwabhekithunga, just across the road from Shakaland. When Holgate owned this store, it was also called Phobane, which was the Zulu name of Henry Francis Fynn's brother Frank Fynn, another one-time client of the Zulu royal house who supported multiple African wives.[41]

Recently, the aging if robust Holgate weighed up these hectic Zululand years: 'There is a trade-off between a life of earning bucks and a life of adventure. You can balance the two, but beware when you begin to get precious about your pension. I'd rather die poor with a wealth of experience than die wealthy with no stories to tell.'[42] His reflections were published in the online version of South Africa's *Men's Health*; this feel-good magazine's 'wealth section' typically features local and global entrepreneurs, among them 'white Zulu' Johnny Clegg who, in the edition extolling Holgate's 'trade-off' exploits, advised white men to stop whingeing and learn an African language. Holgate is more explicit about confronting (white) masculine fears:

> There will always be a thousand and one excuses for you to back out, but you have to push them out of your mind. You sh-t yourself, but when you're in the moment, your fear dissipates . . . Adventure doesn't have to be a place or an activity. It can happen in your mind . . . We all have in us an old warrior ethic that we have forgotten.[43]

For his part, Leitch's 'warrior ethic' continues to influence his pursuit of business ventures that he sees as a bulwark against the 'biggest tragedy being played out' in South Africa, 'the loss of the Zulu and other African cultures'. Since the mid-1990s, Leitch has focused his energies on this salvage mission because 'I love the people and the way they are'.[44] While he seems to overlook the ways in which history affects culture – for example, how coercive colonial policies such as compulsory public works and settler land appropriations disfigured rural Zulu life – Leitch's alarm over 'the biggest tragedy' actually masks an optimistic sentiment, one shared by the author of *Leadership Lessons*, Phinda Madi. Leitch and Madi see contemporary South Africans as uniquely placed entrepreneurs who can bolster their competitiveness by embracing indigenous ideals of success. Leitch elucidates: 'If you are seen to be giving something back to the community, you can earn tremendous consumer loyalty. As the Zulu expression goes, "the hands wash each other".'[45]

Leitch is applying this axiom to another cultural village, which he launched near the coastal town of Umdloti, north of Durban. His brainchild is called uMlilo KaZulu (Fire of the Zulu) after the praise name of the Biyela clan with whom it is a joint initiative, along with AfriSun KZN, a corporate player in the hospitality industry. The centre of this development is a giant statue of the Biyela warrior Prince Mkhosana who gave his life in the Zulu assault against the British at Isandlwana. Another focal point is the *indl'enkulu*, a 'big hut' where 'guests will experience the close-up thrill of the Zulu coming-of-age ceremony'. In 2004 the *Sunday Tribune* published a story on Leitch's uMlilo KaZulu, entitled 'Where Warriors Dare to Tread', picturing its chief executive officer and lead cultural impresario 'going at full tilt along a path he has set himself – and, by his own wry admission, scattering a fair amount of chaos along the way'.[46] Aside from this description, evoking a figure with palatable Shakan qualities, Leitch is said to be fast-tracking his Biyela workers into the African Renaissance by teaching them 'long-term earning capacity through computer literacy courses' that 'form the nucleus for a universal formula to bring to life President Thabo Mbeki's concept of bringing the third world into the first through empowerment'.[47]

Meanwhile Shakaland continues to overflow with foreign visitors and South African schoolchildren; the latter gain entrance with their teachers through low-cost, high-volume packages. Still run by white men, Protea Hotels is showing acute awareness of African Renaissance discourses that call for greater 'community participation' in heritage tourism, i.e., by extending inexpensive tours to historically marginalised groups and, of course, job opportunities that aim to enhance, as in the case of Simunye, black economic competitiveness through skills and management training programmes. This corporate embrace of how 'the hands wash each other' pleases Holgate and Leitch since they articulate a Zulu warrior ethic that merges self-help philanthropy with risk-taking accumulation. By contrast, the Protestant ethic in its seminal form envisaged the poor as victims of their own ungodly laziness. Thus, while the Zulu warrior ethic is touted by BEE advocates, it is still a beacon for white businessmen shedding their 'European' skin to conquer market share in the post-apartheid era. Eschewing the 'guns and steel' metaphor of Western imperialist hegemony, Holgate and Leitch derive their idea of success from symbolic modes of Zulu patriarchy. It appears that some corporate gurus who extol Shaka as the transcendental model of fearless achievement are doing the same, as democratic South Africa is laid bare to the ruthless competitors of the global economic system.[48]

## Notes

1. This chapter title is a play on Max Weber's *Protestant Ethic and the Spirit of Capitalism*, translated by Talcott Parson (London: Unwin University Books, 1930). Yet our aim is not to work within an explicitly Weberian framework. Rather, Weber's conceptual tandem, 'ethic and spirit', informs how we analyse emerging economic forces, which not only guide entrepreneurs, but also reduce precolonial political achievements, i.e., the rise of Shaka's Zulu kingdom, to a cultural package marketed in modern South African capitalism, although not always for profit. We thank Virgil Kihika Storr for his incisive comments on Weber and 'the warrior ethic' and for his scholarly interpretations of these themes in Bahamian economic development: see his 'Weber's Spirit of Capitalism and the Bahamas' Junkanoo Ethic', *The Review of Austrian Economics* 19:4 (2006): 289–309.

2. Alan Hirsch, *Season of Hope: Economic Reform under Mandela and Mbeki* (Pietermaritzburg: University of KwaZulu-Natal Press, 2005), pp. 210–11 and *Empowerment Guidelines for Investors 2003: Mapping State Requirements and Investor Experiences* (Johannesburg: BusinessMap Foundation, 2003).

3. Phinda Madi, *Leadership Lessons from Emperor Shaka Zulu the Great* (Randburg: Knowledge Resources, 2000), pp. xii–xiii. This book was a sequel to Phinda Madi's *Black Economic Empowerment in the New South Africa: The Rights and the Wrongs* (Randburg: Knowledge Resources, 1997).

4. Madi, *Leadership Lessons*, pp. 25, 42–43. See also Black Economic Empowerment Commission, *A National Integrated Black Economic Empowerment Strategy* (Johannesburg: Skotaville, 2001), p. 8.

5. Madi, *Leadership Lessons*, pp. x, 117, 24.

6. On BEE and dubious 'poverty alleviation', see Patrick Wadula, 'Does BEE Really Alleviate Poverty?', *Enterprise: Where Black Business Lives,* October 2005. A pro-business magazine editor, Wadulo expressed growing unease over BEE: 'Since the introduction of the Broad-Based Black Empowerment Act ... it has become quite clear that BEE seeks to give increased ownership to and control over businesses to blacks ... [but] the same few blacks [are] benefiting ... [T]he real challenge is to make BEE deals broad-based to the extent that they empower the masses.' For a trenchant critique of BEE, see Patrick Bond, *Elite Transition: From Apartheid to Neoliberalism in South Africa* (Pietermaritzburg: University of Natal Press, 2000), Chapter 1.

7. Letter from the President (Thabo Mbeki), 'The New South Africa – A Season of Hope!', Vol. 6.1, January 2006, http://www.anc.org.za/ancdocs/anctoday/2006/at01.htm (accessed March 2006).

8. Eddie Bond, 'The Zulu Competitive Spirit: Business Guide' (unpublished pamphlet, 2002) and 'Fifty Business Lessons Derived from Zulu Proverbs, History, Culture and Tradition' (unpublished manuscript, 2002). See also British merchant banker Jim Slater's get-rich-quick formula (now in its fifth impression): J. Slater, *The Zulu Principle: Making Extraordinary Profits from Ordinary Shares* (London: Texere Publishing, [1992] 2001).

9. *Star*, 14 December 2005.

10. Madi, *Leadership Lessons*, p. vii. Madi cites in his bibliography only nine published works, among them critical studies of Shakan myths such as Carolyn Hamilton's *Terrific Majesty: The Powers of Shaka Zulu and the Limits of Historical Invention* (Cambridge, MA: Harvard University Press, 1998).

11. Madi, *Leadership Lessons*, pp. vii, x–xi.

12. Ibid., p. vii. Before his death David Webster was conducting research in Kosi Bay on the Mozambique border, exploring how rural people constructed ethnic identity in an area designated part of the KwaZulu homeland. He focused on kinship relationships that drew on past Thongan politics and isiGonde-speaking elders, particularly matriarchs, rather than memories of clan loyalty to Zulu authority.

13. David Webster, '*Abafazi Bathonga Bafihlakala*: Ethnicity and Gender in a KwaZulu Border Community', *African Studies* 50:1 and 2 (1991): 249, 268. Webster's findings have been confirmed most recently by a historian (formerly of the University of Natal, Durban), born in the Kosi Bay region, who remembered as a child his presence in the area: interview, Benedict Carton with Dingani Mthethwa, 20 June 2000, Durban; 2 February 2002, Washington, DC and 25 November 2003, Washington, DC. Mthethwa fits Webster's profile of Kosi Bay residents, who grew up in matriarchal households, where female elders spoke isiGonde and celebrated their Thongan past.

14. Mike Boon, *The African Way: The Power of Interactive Leadership* (Johannesburg: Zebra Press, 1996), p. 11.

15. Hamilton, *Terrific Majesty*, pp. 187–204. On 'international tourist haunt' and associations between Boon, Leitch and Holgate, see *Natal Mercury*, 4 October 1993. Johnny Clegg developed his passion for Zulu culture and academic inquiry when he studied anthropology at the University of the Witwatersrand, with David Webster as one of his mentors. As Webster's colleague, Clegg also lectured in social anthropology at the university, but his love for *maskanda* music and Zulu dance, (including 'bull' ritual performance) propelled him to the global stage: see *Style*, January 2003; *Natal Witness*, 11 October 2002 and *Lethbridge Herald* (Canada), 22 October 1983. Clegg's anthropological training seemed to influence how he integrated his multiple identities in a society divided by colonialism. Clegg's ideas of racial justice and cross-ethnic belonging includes a Jewish-Zulu identity: see http://www.johnnyclegg.com/qanda.htm (accessed December 2003); Samuel Freedman, 'Johnny Clegg's War on Apartheid', *Rolling Stone*, 22 March 1990 and 'Cultural Weapons: Interview between Immanuel Suttner and Johnny Clegg, 11 and 12 July 1995, Johannesburg'. The authors thank Andy Friedland of Dartmouth College for these sources; personal communication between Benedict Carton/Malcolm Draper and Johnny Clegg, 6 and 7 January 2006, Makhabeleni, KwaZulu-Natal; interview, Benedict Carton/Malcolm Draper with Sipho Mchunu, 27 July 2001; interviews, Benedict Carton with Sipho Mchunu; 26 December 1996; 20 March 2000; 4 November 2002; Makhabeleni, KwaZulu-Natal; and Muff Anderson, *Music in the Mix: The Story of South African Popular Music* (Johannesburg: Ravan Press, 1981), pp. 160–62.

16. Boon *The African Way*, p. 63.

17. Ibid., p. 11.

18. *Africa Geographic*, February 2006.

19. 'Address by Minister Pallo Jordan to Tourvest, Sandton Sun Hotel, Johannesburg, 2 April 1997', South African Government Information, http://www.info.gov.za/speeches/1997/04070x85697.htm (accessed December 1999).

20. The release of a Human Sciences Research Council report on tourism growth in 2004 confirmed that the hospitality sector is slated to be 'the largest employer and GDP contributor to the economy over the next 10 years': see *Business Day*, 4 February 2004; see also *Sunday Times*, 12 May 2002; *Business Day*, 13 March and 15 March 2004 and *SABC News*, 9 March and 10 March 2004; http://www.sabcnews.co.za/economy/business/0,2172,7 (accessed June 2006). On Tourvest's role in burgeoning South African tourism, see *Business Day*, 20 August 2001; *Sunday Times*, 17 August 2003 and 'Tourvest Annual Report 2003'.

21. On Tourvest, BEE partners, and diverse holdings, see 'Tourvest Annual Report 2003' and 'Tourvest Annual Report 2004'.

22. Benedict Carton, 'Remaking Zulu Identity in the Era of Globalization', *Global Studies Review* 1:1 (2005): 8 and interview, Benedict Carton/Malcolm Draper with Charl van Wyk, managing director, Shakaland, 3 August 2003, Mhlatuze Valley, Eshowe. Tourvest's reliance on Zulu branding might have influenced the formation of Lesedi Cultural Village, a tourist destination outside Johannesburg. In 2000, Lesedi was staffed mostly by people hired in the Shakaland region; Zulu culture dominates while other ethnic/language groups (Pedi, Sotho and Tswana) whose histories are rooted in the Gauteng area are absent. According to Xolani Zungu, the deputy-manager: 'We want to showcase all cultures but the foreigners seem to be more interested in us Zulus because we beat the British at Isandlwana': *Sunday Times*, 9 April 2000. On Lesedi Cultural Village in the repertoire of heritage vacation products, see 'Tourvest Annual Report 2003', pp. 12–13 and 'Tourvest Annual Report 2004', p. 13.

23. Interview, Benedict Carton/Malcolm Draper with Barry Leitch, 3 August 2003, Simunye, Melmoth.

24. Interview, Benedict Carton/Malcolm Draper with Vincent Sikakhana, Simunye project partner and childhood friend of Barry Leitch in the AmaBiyela chiefdom, 3 August 2003, Simunye, Melmoth.

25. Hamilton, *Terrific Majesty*, pp. 30–31, 171–90 and Benedict Carton, personal communication with Henry Cele, Durban, May 2004.

26. For additional scholarly critiques of the historical inaccuracies and apartheid politics involved in the making of the film *Shaka Zulu*, see Keyan Tomaselli, 'The Semiotics of Anthropological Authenticity: The Film Apparatus and Cultural Accommodation', *Visual Anthropology* 14 (2001): 173–93; Dan Wylie, *Savage Delight: White Myths of Shaka* (Pietermaritzburg: University of Natal Press, 2000), pp. 23, 25, 239, 245 and Gary Mersham, 'Political Discourse and Historical Television Drama: A Case Study of *Shaka Zulu*' (Ph.D. diss., University of South Africa, Pretoria, 1989).

27. Gerhard Schutte, 'Tourists and Tribes in the "New" South Africa', *Ethnohistory* 50:3 (2003): 473–87, especially 479–80. The capital reserves of Holgate and Leitch were also drained by a national economic recession in South Africa that was worsened by mounting international sanctions.

28. Carolyn Hamilton critically examines the political and cultural niche that Shakaland filled in the 1980s: see *Terrific Majesty*, p. 193. See also Schutte, 'Tourists and Tribes': 479–80.

29. Stephen Coan, 'Crisscrossing Continents', *Natal Witness*, 13 March 2003; interview, Benedict Carton/ Malcolm Draper and Kingsley Holgate, 30 December 2005, Zinkwazi, KwaZulu-Natal and Benedict Carton and Malcolm Draper, 'Le Zoeloe Blanc: A Potent Pedigree', paper presented at The Burden of Race? 'Whiteness' and 'Blackness' in Modern South Africa Conference, University of the Witwatersrand, 2001.

30. On Holgate deferring to Leitch on matters of Zulu culture and history: personal communication between Kinglsey Holgate and Malcolm Draper, 31 July 2001. Leitch's sartorial choices demonstrated how he could envisage indigenous cultural expressions as more fluid, comprising dynamic elements of different ethnic identities. In the late 1980s Draper personally witnessed investor serenades in the cultural-business life of Leitch and Holgate. In August 2002 Carton and Draper attended dances with other tourists at Shakaland's *indl'enkulu*, the Great Hut; these performances were originally choreographed by Leitch and his local Zulu cultural consultants: interview, Benedict Carton/Malcolm Draper and Barry Leitch, 6 August 2003, Simunye, Melmoth; interview, Malcolm Draper and '45', former Zulu dancer at Shakaland, 2 August 2002, Mhlatuze, Eshowe and interview, Benedict Carton/ Malcolm Draper and Kingsley Holgate, 30 December 2005, Zinkwazi, KwaZulu-Natal.

31. Hamilton, *Terrific Majesty*, p. 201. Such commentary was in keeping with what Malcolm Draper heard and observed while working as an assistant for Holgate and Leitch in 1988. In her critique of Shakaland, Hamilton states that 'at one level it was a praiseworthy didactic and celebratory endeavour'. Although Holgate lived in a white area during the apartheid years, black friends and business associates would enjoy overnight hospitality in his house. Clearly, what is taken as a self-explanatory category – 'white Zulu patriarchy' – needs to be critically assessed if we are to have an understanding of how white isiZulu-speaking men maintain their supremacy in a changing social context.

32. Interview, Benedict Carton/Malcolm Draper and Barry Leitch, 6 August 2003, Simunye, Melmoth.

33. Often these acts spent time at Shakaland when on tour for RTV. They provided tourists with entertainment from far corners of the province and taught Shakaland dancers new routines. On Holgate co-ordinating the roadshow equipment and transportation needs, see Simon Burton, Tessa Marcus and Malcolm Draper, 'Bushwacking the Locals: A Preliminary Assessment of the Impact of the Rural Television Network in Natal', unpublished paper presented at the Making Media Work for South Africa's Development Conference, Grahamstown, 1993.

34. Carton and Draper, 'Le Zoeloe Blanc', pp. 18–19 and Hamilton, *Terrific Majesty*, pp. 46, 185.

35. Provincial depots containing archival documents in KwaZulu-Natal were also called *inqolobane* and during apartheid they were fortified with materials thought to withstand a 'terrorist'/freedom fighter bomb blast.

36. Interview, Benedict Carton/Malcolm Draper with Barry Leitch, 6 August 2003, Simunye, Melmoth; interview, Benedict Carton/Malcolm Draper with Charl van Wyk, 3 August 2002, Shakaland, Eshowe and Carton and Draper, 'Le Zoeloe Blanc'.

37. '[T]he essence . . . great nation': Protea Hotel Shakaland Brochure, 2002; 'Have you . . . cattle': Shakaland CD, 2002 and see also Carton, 'Remaking Zulu Identity in the Era of Globalization'.

38. Interview, Benedict Carton/Malcolm Draper with Charl van Wyk, 3 August 2002, Shakaland, Eshowe.

39. 'Kingsley Holgate: Adventurer and Explorer', *Men's Health*, http://www.menshealthsa.co.za/ (accessed June 2006) and interview, Benedict Carton/Malcolm Draper and Kingsley Holgate, 30 December 2005, Zinkwazi, KwaZulu-Natal.

40. 'Kingsley Holgate/White Man in Africa', *Carte Blanche*, SABC, 25 April 1999 and T.V. Bulpin, *Natal and the Zulu Country* (Cape Town: Books of Africa, 1966), pp. 51, 63.

41. Carton and Draper, 'Le Zoeloe Blanc', pp. 17–18, 24. On Henry Francis Fynn and his Fynn sibling legacies in early- and mid-nineteenth century Natal, see Julie Pridmore, 'Henry Francis Fynn: An Assessment of his Career and an Analysis of the Written and Visual Portrayals of his Role in the History of the Natal Region' (Ph.D. diss., University of Natal, 1996), pp. 1–42; John Wright, 'The Dynamics of Power and Conflict in the Thukela-Mzimkhulu Region in the Late 18th and Early 19th Centuries: A Critical Reconstruction' (Ph.D. diss., University of the Witwatersrand, 1995), pp. 338–53; Wylie, *Savage Delight*, pp. 105–27.

42. Interview, Benedict Carton/Malcolm Draper and Kingsley Holgate, 30 December 2005, Zinkwazi, KwaZulu-Natal.

43. 'Kingsley Holgate: Adventurer and Explorer', *Men's Health*.
44. *Natal Mercury*, 4 October 1993.
45. *Financial Mail*, 4 September 1993. See also Hamilton, *Terrific Majesty*, p. 201.
46. *Sunday Tribune*, 17 October 2004.
47. Ibid.
48. Malcolm Draper, 'African Wilderness® Pty Ltd: An Authentic Encounter with the Big Five, Death and the Meaning of Life', in *Taking Tourism to the Limits: Issues, Concepts and Managerial Perspectives*, eds. Chris Ryan, Stephen Page, and Michelle Aitken (Amsterdam: Elsevier, 2005), pp. 113–28 and interview, Benedict Carton/Malcolm Draper and Kingsley Holgate, 30 December 2005, Zinkwazi, KwaZulu-Natal.

# Chapter 52

# Zulu Identity in the International Context

BILL FREUND

IDENTITY IS A shifting, multifaceted concept that should be traced as it changes over time. While Zulu identity in the popular mind may be associated with an internally created, primordial structure, in fact it has been shaped more by external processes. If we wish to consider how Zulu identity today will weather new international currents, we should first review how it interacted with previous intrusive forces.

### Historic perceptions

The rapid nineteenth-century transformation in 'Zuluness' – from a local concept reflecting chiefly loyalty to a national identity associated with an expanding kingdom – occurred after intense contacts in the 1820s and 1830s between Zulu elites and encroaching white settlers just south of the Thukela River. With the establishment of the British Natal colony in the 1840s, the cultural/political dichotomy between colonial Natal and independent KwaZulu became more rigid. As with Lesotho, the menace posed by the growing white presence was a major factor in preserving the Zulu state through the middle of the nineteenth century, despite bloody factionalism in various royal houses. In 1879 British invaders conquered Cetshwayo's kingdom and attempted decisively to fragment Zulu power. Although this project created civil bloodshed and further subjugated Zulu elites, it largely failed. By the turn of the twentieth century, isiZulu-speaking African people in Natal and KwaZulu increasingly embraced positive memories of the extinguished Zulu state and a sense of being Zulu, a cultural identity that apparently spoke for itself in defining legitimate African actions, including anti-colonial resistance. Zulu markers became associated with continuity and reverence for the past, particularly as the Zulu cultural nationalist organisation – Inkatha – took off in the early twentieth century and influenced later African nationalist movements. The use of isiZulu, standardised through missionary use and a vehicle for books and periodical literature by the twentieth century, together with other cultural forms defined as Zulu, integrated the response of many people to the pressures of life under segregation and apartheid.

Scholarly studies by Shula Marks and Nicholas Cope have highlighted how the rise of Inkatha as a political movement in the 1920s was nurtured by state segregationists aiming to create a definable region for 'retribalised' Zulus, a scheme that looked particularly attractive to white Natal elites.[1] Where once the 'Zulus' were a collective menace, they now seemed transferable into a cordoned-off and controllable tribal community available for massive amounts of unskilled labour on a migrant basis. At the start of the apartheid era, the national government refined earlier segregationist aims by planning to shunt African people in the former Zulu kingdom and communities dotting the old colonial territory of Natal into a bantustan called KwaZulu, thus further encouraging the preservation of traditional ('tribal') Zulu behaviour, considered compatible with philosophies of separate development. White authorities recognised that their real long-term problem lay in the prospect of a unified black-run country. They provided Mahmood Mamdani with a classic example with which to defend his thesis of a bifurcated administration, a decentralised despotism, which was an important model for colonised Africa.[2]

Throughout the twentieth century, South Africa achieved greater integration into the wider world and, with attendant economic prosperity in the 1960s and 1970s bolstering white nation-building, the bantustan system became even more entrenched. At the same time, however, the accelerating rate of urbanisation and industrialisation undercut the position of white supremacists. The cities and towns of the Witwatersrand, for example, housed large heterogeneous populations, including a great many isiZulu-speaking labour migrants from KwaZulu and Natal. While derivations of isiZulu provided the foundation for a black lingua franca in and around the gold mines and some townships, other African languages became important in daily communication. As a result, isiZulu-speaking labour migrants and their children, many of whom grew up in urban centres, developed their own polyglot national identity: they belonged to a multi-ethnic, modernising South Africa, not simply to a Zulu homeland. Economic development, education with the diffusion of literacy and political and religious mobilisation – all happening to some degree in many townships – brought urban Zulu people together with other Africans in salient ways that shaped a hybrid cultural consciousness. These powerful impetuses paved the way for a black South African nationalism to emerge.

A set of identifiable (but far from immutable) cultural practices also enhanced a sense of Zuluness throughout the twentieth century. The patrimonial networks that governed life in townships still functioned, and in collusion with apartheid laws reifying traditional authority, Zulu patriarchal dynamics influenced family order in isiZulu-speaking urban households. However, it would be wrong to assume that this patriarchal Zuluness contradicted a parallel identification with being black and South African. Nor were more traditional expressions of Zuluness consistently, or even frequently, overtly clashing with other African identities in South Africa. In mining compounds, inter-ethnic male rivalries over resources and women occasionally sparked bloodshed, but in townships inter-ethnic rivalries did not have a widespread violent impact on social relationships. For example, in Durban, the major city in Natal province and the site of a dramatic urban expansion from the 1940s, Zulu culture predominated, while other African groups, notably Sotho-, Pondo- and Xhosa-speaking people, made up minority communities. Yet the omnipresent Zulu ethnic character rarely instigated inter-ethnic faction fighting. Indeed, Zulu identity, regional particularities and black nationalism were intermingled in the careers of Durban-based isiZulu-speaking notables such as John Dube, Selby Msimang, A.W. George Champion, Albert Luthuli, and Josiah and Archie Gumede, all of whom emerged as leaders in the early and middle decades of the twentieth century. Such defining factors can also be identified amongst communist militants Moses Mabhida and Harry Gwala, activists who channelled the protest politics of the late twentieth century.

The 1970s Inkatha movement under Mangosuthu Buthelezi exhibited ambivalence to the circumstances influencing Dube, Luthuli and Gwala. Established in 1972, Inkatha was successful as a movement that primarily defended chiefly patrimony in the countryside and, before 1990, fostered the interests of the isiZulu-speaking petit bourgeoisie in the KwaZulu homeland. Mangosuthu Buthelezi forcefully opposed the spread of socialism and the cult of armed resistance that marked the rise of the African National Congress (ANC); he manoeuvred Inkatha as a bulwark against such radical mobilisations. His strategy backfired in the 1980s when urban isiZulu-speaking people, many of them youths promoting the cause of the United Democratic Front (UDF) and ANC, turned against Inkatha. During resulting civil conflicts that intensified into the early 1990s, they ejected Inkatha members from many parts of the province. Young UDF and ANC comrades joined with trade union members to challenge the notion that Inkatha represented big pockets of isiZulu-speaking people in residential areas, except perhaps for workers' hostels outside Natal, which housed vast numbers of Inkatha-supporting Zulu migrants.

There was a serious prospect of a full-scale civil war erupting from such clashes over the salience of Zuluness, a prospect that seemed to parallel other recent historical patterns in the continent. Throughout much of British colonial Africa in the 1950s and 1960s, tribal and traditional authorities (like Inkatha leaders before the 1994 election) felt similarly threatened by Jacobin-minded black nationalists seeking to minimise the importance of ethnic identity and creating grave problems for the incremental onset of independence. Specialists in the history and politics of other parts of Africa will be able to draw obvious comparisons with the Kabaka crisis of 1953–55 that bedevilled the decolonisation of Uganda, where indirect rule was particularly entrenched under the British rulers.[3] This crisis ended when a governor with Jacobin sympathies, Sir Andrew Cohen, the official often considered the mastermind of British decolonisation in Africa, sent the Kabaka leader, Frederick

Mutesa, into exile. The Kabaka Yekka movement in Uganda culminated fatally for the royal party in Buganda, when Milton Obote turned to the army to assert his party's control in 1966, terminating the hope for democracy after only four years. Other parallel examples from Africa's recent past are also relevant:

- The secessionist movement in Barotseland, the so-called 'protectorate within a protectorate',[4] which threatened the nationalist movement's capacity to represent the whole territory in Northern Rhodesia, now Zambia. In this case Lozi voters rejected the claims of their paramount chief in the final colonial elections, pressurising him to agree to Zambian independence. Since then, however, Barotseland has often shown distinctive voting patterns.
- The tensions that marked the relationship between Kwame Nkrumah and the Asante elite in Ghana, the heart and soul of the opposition in the late colonial elections during the twilight of British colonialism. These tensions intensified as Nkrumah moved to create a one-party regime in 1961, albeit within a context of far more complex political rivalries.
- The split between ZANU and ZAPU in Southern Rhodesia (Zimbabwe) from 1963, which fuelled an Ndebele-Shona conflict, with the Ndebele again being identified as a tribal entity with strong Zulu historic links.
- The role of so-called traditional leaders in promoting the Northern Peoples' Congress as a vehicle for regional autonomy in northern Nigeria since the first colonial elections held in 1951.
- The formation in 1960 of KADU, an anti-Gikuyu political front in Kenya, which provided a base for national independence to proceed without regional violence. The early independence phase ended with the dissolution of KADU in 1964, with its leader, Daniel arap Moi, becoming Jomo Kenyatta's successor. However, ethnic politics have cast a very large shadow over Kenya ever since.

In the end, a full-scale civil war did not materialise in Natal, perhaps because the ANC-Inkatha rivalry was not a battle over the legitimacy of Zulu culture. During the period of negotiations that led up to the 1994 national ballot, the ANC, in particular, was careful to showcase high-ranking isiZulu-speaking members such as Jacob Zuma and Harry Gwala. In the post-apartheid era, South African presidents and ANC stalwarts Nelson Mandela and Thabo Mbeki have been conciliatory to Mangosuthu Buthelezi, and often requested ANC leaders in KwaZulu-Natal to tone down their anti-Inkatha rhetoric for the sake of national unity. Moreover, KwaZulu-Natal, which is poorer than the average South African province, has wisely not been excluded from central government patronage, or left out of ambitious state development initiatives.

Still, the new South Africa has not gone particularly far to promote a post-apartheid national identity. The initial tendency by the government to trumpet the existence of rainbow multiculturalism has been sidelined under the presidency of Thabo Mbeki, who advanced the African Renaissance through affirmative action and black empowerment legislation. In other words, he encouraged black South Africans to think of their society primarily in terms of race, not ethnicity.

It must be said that Buthelezi himself, long an opponent of apartheid-era independence for the KwaZulu homeland, only flirted with secession from 1990 to 1994. In the middle and late 1990s, he has championed the cause of chiefs and rural patronage as a loyal cabinet member of the ANC-dominated national government. While many doyens of African studies in the West have long assumed that primordial ethnic identity is the motor force of political life, the fate of Zulu identity, a political force of national mobilisation in South Africa, shows the limits of such conjecture.

## The contemporary picture

The future of Zulu identity in today's South Africa depends on an array of determining forces: domestic political and social factors condition the role of the international context, which invariably means globalisation. Globalisation entails the intensification of worldwide economic linkages through the use of technologies that facilitate real-time communications and financial integration. Globalisation goes together with the promotion of an international business culture and milieu that dominate corporate media and promote the interests of multinational corporations. Of course, foreign investment, mass media, and state-of-the-art technologies are not unknown in South Africa. Yet globalisation as an idea is posited on qualitatively new levels of economic penetration, spurring an unprecedented glorification of consumerism, on the one hand, and a denigration of marginalised local culture, on the other hand.

South Africa is being buffeted by globalisation. The inward-looking political and cultural development of the apartheid years, largely in conflict with the free rein that white supremacists offered to capitalists, has been thoroughly discredited since 1994. Zulu youths have many more opportunities to embrace variants of international (for which we should read 'American') consumerism, tailored for black people through the marketing of politically neutralised African-American icons. The pressure on isiZulu-speaking young people to communicate in English has also intensified, in response to the perceived prestige associated with the planetary lingua franca. So far, Zuluness seems unlikely to transmogrify into a sword to resist the forces of globalisation. While reinvented fundamentalism among groups threatened and demeaned by globalisation is ascendant in some parts of the world, thus far the new South Africa has seen no similar 'resistance' movements arise among its ethnic traditionalists. Current consumer trends demonstrate a growing disregard among black urban youths for African customs that seem out of step with the global-modern regime. Even so, local isiZulu idioms and fragmented elements of Zulu culture that young and old people can call theirs (virginity testing, for example) have not disappeared and could certainly stage comebacks in the future.

Since 1994 the ANC, the dominant force in a government of national unity, has been moderately successful in a politics of redistribution to the previously disadvantaged, largely black population through heavy taxation and delivery of social services. However, ANC leaders have not provided either much economic growth or new employment. If the judgement expressed in the previous paragraph needs to be qualified, it may be because of the relative failure of the ANC to deliver prosperity in the form of jobs and rapid social promotion for ordinary people. If this failure is not arrested, there is some potential for black people in KwaZulu-Natal once again to consider both Inkatha and Zulu patrimonial structures as alternative social benefactors.

In the late 1990s, political commentators tended to view Inkatha as a slowly dying phenomenon largely dependent on the presence of elder statesman Mangosuthu Buthelezi. But in the 2000 local election, Inkatha surprised observers by increasing its share of the vote in the province where it has a plurality. This probably reflects a decline in positive perceptions by black KwaZulu-Natal residents of ANC government delivery. By the 2004 provincial ballot, however, it was evident that Inkatha was in another decline. In overwhelming numbers Buthelezi's once loyal constituencies cast their ballots for ANC candidates. Now the current isiZulu-speaking ANC premier of KwaZulu-Natal, S'bu Ndebele, is using the Inkatha strategy of extolling Shaka's historical accomplishments (i.e., to build a mammoth statue to the founder-king), while promoting neo-liberal policies of President Mbeki. For the moment, the ANC has not only won the support of most isiZulu-speaking voters, but also the battle for political control of Buthelezi's brand of nationalism, an ideology that is losing salience as black nationalist and xenophobic sentiments surge to the fore.

Where modernity fails, people tend to turn to abandoned or semi-abandoned cultural bulwarks. Black South Africans have become notorious for their chauvinistic xenophobia towards immigrants from elsewhere on the Africa continent; the latter are frequently blamed for stealing the rightful post-apartheid gains of South Africa's massively expanded citizenry. In 1999 an Inkatha-leaning Durban newspaper *Ilanga lase Natal* published an editorial piece calling for the expulsion from South Africa of people of Asian origin, disparaging them as 'bloodsuckers who thrive on the blood of Africans'.[5] (The editor concerned was dismissed from the newspaper in short order.) This outburst reveals the possible evolution of new ethnic twists. As AIDS kills more and more Zulu men and women, some communities devastated by the pandemic are resurrecting virginity testing and other so-called Zulu rituals as traditional forms of healing and protection. But these are somewhat isolated occurrences. What is harder to imagine are self-conscious Zulu elites putting together a coherent traditional 'identity package' that would appeal to a mass audience in KwaZulu-Natal. Moreover, it would be rash to predict that serious Zulu cultural revivalism is likely to emerge to counter the effects of globalisation and reject the modern notion of state citizenship. So far, Zulu identity has shown no sign of becoming an engine of rivalry or competition with other equivalent identities in the new South Africa. Thus, assessing the impact of international and national forces on Zuluness remains a matter of speculation and material for future study.

## Notes

1. See Shula Marks, *The Ambiguities of Dependence in South Africa: Class, Nationalism and the State in Twentieth-century Natal* (Johannesburg: Ravan Press, 1986) and Nicholas Cope, *To Bind the Nation: Solomon kaDinuzulu and Zulu Nationalism 1913–33,* (Pietermaritzburg: University of Natal Press, 1993).
2. See Mahmood Mamdani, *Citizen and Subject: Contemporary Africa and the Legacy of Late Colonialism* (Princeton: Princeton University Press, 1996).
3. See Christopher Wrigley, 'Four Steps towards Disaster', in *Uganda Now Between Decay and Development,* eds. Holger Bernt Hansen and Michael Twaddle (London: James Currey, 1988), pp. 30–35.
4. Andrew Roberts, *A History of Zambia* (London: Heinemann, 1976), p. 221.
5. Thokozani Xaba, 'From Symbolic to Participatory Reconciliation: Race Relations in South Africa – The African-Indian Case', *Transformation* 45 (2001): 50.

## Further reading

Astrow, André. 1983. *Zimbabwe: A Revolution that Lost its Way?* London: Zed Press.

Dunn, John, ed. 1978. *West African States: Failure and Promise.* Cambridge: Cambridge University Press.

Freund, Bill. 1996. 'The Violence in Natal' in *Political Economy and Identities in KwaZulu-Natal,* ed. Robert Morrell. Pietermaritzburg: University of Natal Press, pp. 179–95.

S.R. Karugire, S.R. 1980. *A Political History of Uganda.* Nairobi: Heinemann.

Leys, Colin. 1975. *Underdevelopment in Kenya: The Political Economy of Neo-Colonialism.* London: Heinemann.

Maré, Gerhard. 1992. *Brothers Born of Warrior Blood: Politics and Ethnicity in South Africa.* Johannesburg: Ravan Press.

Whitaker, C.S. 1970. *The Politics of Tradition: Continuity and Change in Northern Nigeria.* Princeton: Princeton University Press.

# Credits for Illustrations

| | |
|---|---|
| 171 | *Illustrated London News*, 6 September 1879 |
| 194 | Natal Museum |
| 195 (top left) | Jeff Guy |
| 195 (top right) | Campbell Collections, University of KwaZulu-Natal |
| 196 | Campbell Collections, University of KwaZulu-Natal, Album A 42/009 |
| 201 | National Library of South Africa (Cape Town) |
| 203 | National Library of South Africa (Cape Town) |
| 206 | Pietermaritzburg Archives Repository, Photo Collection, C 776 |
| 223 | Pietermaritzburg Archives Repository, Photo Collection, C 744 |
| 277 (top) | Pietermaritzburg Archives Repository, 1/ABM, American Board Mission Records, 5576 |
| 277 (bottom) | Pietermaritzburg Archives Repository, 1/ABM, American Board Mission Records, American Board Photograph Book, p. 47 |
| 336 | Pietermaritzburg Archives Repository, 1/ABM, American Board Mission Records, 5549 |
| 346 | South African Scout Association, University of Cape Town, Special Collections, 956 |
| 357 | Gerry Freese and Ian Carbutt, *Natal Witness* |
| 483 | Zev Greenfield |
| 484 | Zev Greenfield |
| 486 | Zev Greenfield |
| 488 | Zev Greenfield |
| 490 | Zev Greenfield |
| 492 | Zev Greenfield |
| 493 | Zev Greenfield |
| 576 (top) | Pietermaritzburg Archives Repository, Photo Collection, C 86/4 |
| 576 (bottom left) | Mxolisi Mchunu Collection |
| 576 (bottom right) | Mxolisi Mchunu Collection |
| 580 | Campbell Collections, University of KwaZulu-Natal, William Campbell Picture Collection, WCP 3002 |
| 595 | Malcolm Draper |
| 596 (top) | Malcolm Draper |
| 596 (bottom) | Malcolm Draper |
| 597 | Malcolm Draper |
| 598 | Malcolm Draper |
| 599 | *Sunday Times*, 14 July 2002 |
| | |
| Plate 1 | Standard Bank Collection of African Art, Wits Art Galleries |
| Plate 2 | Standard Bank Collection of African Art, Wits Art Galleries |
| Plate 3 | Gibson and Rankin-Smith Private Collection, Johannesburg |
| Plate 4 | Gibson and Rankin-Smith Private Collection, Johannesburg |
| Plate 5 | Gibson and Rankin-Smith Private Collection, Johannesburg |
| Plate 6 | Standard Bank Collection of African Art, Wits Art Galleries |
| Plate 7 | Wits Art Galleries, University of the Witwatersrand |

| | |
|---|---|
| Plate 8 | Standard Bank Collection of African Art, Wits Art Galleries |
| Plate 9 | Juliet Armstrong |
| Plate 10 | Juliet Armstrong |
| Plate 11 | Local History Museum, Durban |
| Plate 12 | Pietermaritzburg Archives Repository, Photo Collection, C 611 |
| Plate 13 | Juliet Armstrong |
| Plate 14 | Juliet Armstrong |
| Plate 15 | Juliet Armstrong |
| Plate 16 | Juliet Armstrong |
| Plate 17 | Juliet Armstrong |
| Plate 18 | Juliet Armstrong |
| Plate 19 | Campbell Collections, University of KwaZulu-Natal |
| Plate 20 | Campbell Collections, University of KwaZulu-Natal |
| Plate 21 | Campbell Collections, University of KwaZulu-Natal |
| Plate 22 | Natal Museum |
| Plate 23 | Natal Museum |
| Plate 24 | Natal Museum |
| Plate 25 | Natal Museum |

# About the Contributors

PETER ALEGI is an Assistant Professor in the Department of History at Michigan State University, USA.

JULIET ARMSTRONG is a Professor in the Centre for Visual Art at the University of KwaZulu-Natal, South Africa.

DAVID ATTWELL is the Chair of Modern Literature at the University of York, United Kingdom.

PHILIP BONNER is a Professor in the Department of History at the University of the Witwatersrand, South Africa.

SHIRLEY BROOKS is a Senior Lecturer in the Geography Department at the University of KwaZulu-Natal, South Africa.

MBONGISENI BUTHELEZI is a Fulbright scholar in the Department of English and Comparative Literature at Columbia University, USA.

BENEDICT CARTON is an Associate Professor in the Department of History and Art History at George Mason University, USA.

PHILIPPE DENIS is a Professor in the School of Religion and Theology and Director of the Sinomlando Centre for Oral History and Memory Work at the University of KwaZulu-Natal, South Africa.

NSIZWA DLAMINI is a doctoral candidate at the Wits Institute for Social and Economic Research, University of the Witwatersrand, South Africa.

MALCOLM DRAPER is a Lecturer in the Department of Sociology at the University of KwaZulu-Natal, South Africa.

ROBERT EDGAR is a Professor in the Department of African Studies at Howard University, USA.

KAREN FLINT is an Associate Professor in the Department of History at the University of North Carolina, Charlotte, USA.

BILL FREUND is a Professor in the Department of Economic History and Development Studies Programme at the University of KwaZulu-Natal, South Africa.

IMOGEN GUNNER is a musician and ethnomusicologist based in Limerick, Ireland.

LIZ GUNNER is a Research Professorial Associate at the Wits Institute for Social and Economic Research, University of the Witwatersrand, South Africa.

JEFF GUY is a Research Fellow at the Campbell Collections of the University of KwaZulu-Natal, South Africa.

The late W.D. HAMMOND-TOOKE was a Professor of Anthropology at the University of the Witwatersrand, South Africa.

PAUL LA HAUSSE DE LALOUVIÈRE is a Research Associate in the Centre of African Studies at the University of Cambridge, United Kingdom.

ROBERT J. HOULE is an Assistant Professor in the Department of History at Fairleigh Dickinson University, USA.

MARK HUNTER is an Assistant Professor in the Department of Social Sciences/Geography, University of Toronto, Canada.

IAN KNIGHT is a writer and an authority on the Anglo-Zulu War of 1879 and is based in the United Kingdom.

ADRIAN KOOPMAN is a Professor in the School of isiZulu Studies at the University of KwaZulu-Natal, South Africa.

JOHN LABAND is a Professor in the Department of History at Wilfrid Laurier University, Canada.

JOHN LAMBERT is a Professor in the Department of History at the University of South Africa, South Africa.

MICHAEL LAMBERT is a Senior Lecturer in the Classics Department at the University of KwaZulu-Natal, South Africa.

SUZANNE LECLERC-MADLALA is a Professor in the Anthropology Department at the University of KwaZulu-Natal, South Africa.

ARAN S. MACKINNON is an Associate Professor in the Department of History at the University of West Georgia, USA.

THENJIWE MAGWAZA is a Professor in the Gender Studies Department at the University of KwaZulu-Natal, South Africa.

TESSA MARCUS is Professor Extraordinary in the Department of Family Medicine at the University of Pretoria, South Africa.

GERHARD MARÉ is a Professor in the Department of Sociology at the University of KwaZulu-Natal, South Africa.

JEREMY MARTENS is a Lecturer in the Department of History at the University of Western Australia, Australia.

THOMAS MCCLENDON is an Associate Professor in the Department of History at Southwestern University, USA.

MXOLISI MCHUNU is an Educational and Research Officer at the Campbell Collections of the University of KwaZulu-Natal, South Africa.

DINGANI MTHETHWA is an Instructor in the School of World Studies at Virginia Commonwealth University, USA.

VUSI NDIMA is the Chief Director of Heritage in the Department of Arts and Culture in the South African government.

SIFISO NDLOVU works at the South African Democracy Education Trust, Pretoria, South Africa.

JULIE PARLE is a Senior Lecturer in the History Department at the University of KwaZulu-Natal, South Africa.

TIMOTHY PARSONS is a Professor in the Department of History at Washington University, St Louis, USA.

LAURENCE PIPER is a Professor in the School of Politics at the University of KwaZulu-Natal, South Africa.

FIONA RANKIN-SMITH is Curator of Wits Art Galleries at the University of KwaZulu-Natal, South Africa.

JABULANI SITHOLE is a Lecturer in the History Department at the University of KwaZulu-Natal, South Africa.

JONNY STEINBERG is a writer and Senior Research Consultant at the Institute for Security Studies in Pretoria, South Africa.

H. CHRISTINA STEYN is a Professor in the Department of Religious Studies at the University of South Africa, South Africa.

ROBERT VINSON is an Assistant Professor in the Department of History at the College of William & Mary, USA.

THEMBISA WAETJEN is a Lecturer in the History Department at the University of KwaZulu-Natal, South Africa.

CHERRYL WALKER is a Professor in the Department of Sociology and Social Anthropology at the University of Stellenbosch, South Africa.

GAVIN WHITELAW is an archaeologist at the Natal Museum, and an Honorary Lecturer in the School of Anthropology at the University of KwaZulu-Natal, South Africa.

YVONNE WINTERS is Senior Museologist at the Campbell Collections of University of KwaZulu-Natal, South Africa.

JOHN WRIGHT is a Senior Research Associate in History at the University of KwaZulu-Natal, South Africa.

DAN WYLIE is a Senior Lecturer in the Department of English at Rhodes University, South Africa.

# Index

Zulu personal names are entered under their first names when followed by their *isibongo* (surname), prefixed with 'ka'. For example, Baleni kaSilwana will be indexed under 'B'. When personal names are not followed by their *isibongo*, they will be entered under their last names. For example, Joseph Buthelezi will be indexed under 'B'.

619

# FUN

NEW SERIES

VOL II

LONDON :

PUBLISHED (FOR THE PROPRIETORS) BY THOMAS BAKER,

80, FLEET STREET, E.C.

# The Dictionary of British Book

# ILLUSTRATORS and CARICATURISTS

# 1800~1914

*With introductory chapters on the Rise and Progress of the Art.*

# Simon Houfe

*Frontispiece:*
*EDMUND DULAC 1882-1953*
*'Beauty and the Beast'*
*Original drawing for* Fairy Tales
*by Sir Arthur Quiller-Couch, 1910*
*Pen, ink and watercolour*
*dated 1910*

Victoria and Albert Museum

British Library CIP data
Houfe, Simon
    Dictionary of British book illustrators, 1800-1914.
    1. Illustrators — Great Britain — Biography
    2. Illustration of books — Great Britain
    I.  Title II. Antique Collectors' Club
    741'.092'2        NC978

    ISBN 0-902028-73-1

Printed in England by Baron Publishing
Church Street, Woodbridge, Suffolk

# The Antique Collectors' Club

The Antique Collectors' Club, formed in 1966, pioneered the provision of information on prices for collectors. The Club's magazine *Antique Collecting* was the first to tackle the complex problems of describing to collectors the various features which can influence prices. In response to the enormous demand for this type of information the *Price Guide Series* was introduced in 1968 with **The Price Guide to Antique Furniture**, a book which broke new ground by illustrating the more common types of antique furniture, the sort that collectors could buy in shops and at auctions, rather than the rare museum pieces which had previously been used (and still to a large extent are used) to make up the limited amount of illustrations in books published by commercial publishers. Many other price guides have followed, all copiously illustrated, and greatly appreciated by collectors for the valuable information they contain, quite apart from prices.

Club membership, which is open to all collectors, costs £6.95 per annum. Members receive free of charge *Antique Collecting,* the Club's magazine (published every month except August), which contains well-illustrated articles dealing with the practical aspects of collecting not normally dealt with by magazines. Prices, features of value, investment potential, fakes and forgeries are all given prominence in the magazine.

In addition members buy and sell among themselves; the Club charges a nominal fee for introductions but takes no commission. Since the Club started many thousands of antiques have been offered for sale privately. No other publication contains anything to match the long list of items for sale privately which appears in each issue of the magazine.

The presentation of useful information and the facility to buy and sell privately would alone have assured the success of the Club, but perhaps the feature most valued by members is the ability to make contact with other collectors living nearby. Not only do members learn about the other branches of collecting but they make interesting friendships. The Club organises weekend seminars and other meetings.

As its motto implies, the Club is an amateur organisation designed to help collectors to get the most out of their hobby: it is informal and friendly and gives enormous enjoyment to all concerned.

*For Collectors — By Collectors — About Collecting*

**The Antique Collectors' Club, 5 Church Street, Woodbridge, Suffolk**

# Contents

# Acknowledgements

This opportunity is taken to thank the many people who have assisted in researches over the past three years. Among the families of the illustrators themselves must be included The Countess of Rosse, Miss O. Ault, L.F. Pape, Mrs. Eve Sheldon-Williams, Miss L. Wallis Mills and among collectors, C.R. Cone, Mrs. Christopher Day, Miss Julia Elton, Jeffrey Gordon, Dr. C. Lattimore, H. Newman and R.G. Searight, who gave enormous help from his unrivalled knowledge of Middle East illustrators.

The following trusts, foundations and art galleries have allowed works in their possession to be reproduced, The Trustees of the Bedford Settled Estates and The Most Hon. The Marquess of Tavistock, Birmingham City Art Gallery, The Garrick Club, The Paul Mellon Foundation and the Victoria and Albert Museum, Print Room and Library. Assistance has been received at various times from the staffs of the Print Rooms at the Ashmolean Museum, Oxford, the British Museum, The Fitzwilliam Museum, Cambridge, the Laing Art Gallery, Newcastle-upon-Tyne, as well as from the librarians at the British Library Manuscript Room, the London Library, the Westminster Public Library and the Witt Photo Library, Courtauld Institute, University of London.

Valuable help has been given by Eric Holder, Mr. and Mrs. Ronald Marshall, Christopher Mendez, Alister Mathews and Ben Weinreb in allowing access to original works in their possession.

Much information and advice has come from historians and collectors among whom should be mentioned, John Christian, Professor Robert Halsband, Professor Dudley Johnson, Lionel Lambourne, Lady Mander, Dr. Gerald Taylor and Lady (Micky) Reid.

A special note of thanks must go to Simon Richardson, who acted as research assistant during the summer of 1976 and did sterling service in many London libraries at various times in 1977 and 1978. Last but not least thanks are due to my publisher, John Steel, and to his able assistant, Mrs. Elizabeth Watson, who saw the book through its final stages.

Avenue House, Ampthill                                                    Simon Houfe
13th September, 1978

# Introduction

The task facing any historian or lexicographer of the nineteenth century is a daunting one. The industry and energy of that century seems to have been almost uncanny and its capacity to record and document every detail of its tirelessness absolutely unprecedented. Lytton Strachey, writing sixty years ago when nineteenth century studies had only just begun, put the historian's predicament in this way. 'He will row out over that great ocean of material, and lower down into it, here and there, a little bucket, which will bring up to the light of day some characteristic specimen, from those depths, to be examined with a careful curiosity.'

The work of the book illustrators in the years 1800 to 1914 is certainly characteristic of its age but even one of Strachey's buckets would produce an embarrassing haul! No book setting out to cover this immense subject could hope to be fully comprehensive, but by including popular artists as well as significant artists, minor figures as well as great ones, it could go some way towards seeing the period as the Victorians saw it themselves. Illustration has always been the Cinderella among the fine arts, even in the nineteenth century, but in some ways in those years it comes closest of all to the normal, the average, the everyday in national taste; its steel engravings, wood engravings and lithographs tell us as much about the people who were looking at them as they tell of the artists themselves. The growth of literacy during the early part of the century, which was sealed with official approval after 1870, meant that more and more people could benefit from books and cheaper periodicals. The designs in them were a help to the learner and an entertainment to the leisured, to the working class and also to many of the middle class, images were associated with letter-press and 'painting' *was* the black ink impression of a wood block on the printed page. The impact of the illustrated magazine on the Victorian household must have been tremendous; for the first time people in remote places and of all backgrounds had their own art galleries of portraits, landscapes, caricatures, battlepieces, still-lifes and miniatures delivered by the postman weekly. For some people their only contact with the visual arts was through magazine illustration and a proper appreciation of that fact helps us to understand much about them, the seriousness with which they regarded book illustration, their love of narrative painting and their enthusiasm for the long novel.

Victorian illustrated pages travelled great distances. Readers of Samuel Butler's symbolical story *Erehwon* will remember that the walls of the hero's hut in the distant outback were 'pasted over with extracts from the *Illustrated London News* and *Punch*...'. Nearer at home, but equally isolated, Flora Thomson describes in *Lark Rise,* the decoration of her 'privy' in deepest Buckinghamshire. 'On the wall of the "little house" at Laura's home pictures cut from the newspapers were pasted. These were changed when the walls were whitewashed and in succession they were "The Bombardment of Alexandria", all clouds of smoke, flying fragments and flashes of explosives; "Glasgow's Mournful Disaster: Plunges for Life from the Daphne", and "The Tay Bridge Disaster", with the end of the train dangling from the broken bridge over a boiling sea. It was before the day of Press photography and the artists were able to give their imagination full play.' It is these sort of comments that show most clearly what Victorian art was; sentimental, melodramatic, subjective perhaps, but also spontaneous and a medium in which everyone felt involved. The present writer therefore makes no apology for having been biased towards magazine work in both the introductory chapters and in the accounts of individual artists.

For the purposes of this book, a book illustration has been defined as any pictorial subject in topography, architecture, genre or literature which aids a text, however slender. This does not include engravings of literary subjects separately issued or technical books of architecture or science. The definition of British is wide enough to take in foreign artists who published their work in this country or artists who studied here but only published work abroad. Although the limits of this book are really from the Regency to the Edwardian period, some artists have been included whose major contributions were made in earlier or later years, but whose style or direction seems relevant to the case. This is true of a number of topographers working in the 1800s and in most of these examples a bibliographical reference to J.R. Abbey's stupendous volumes is appended, AL (Abbey *Life*) or AT (Abbey *Travel*). The introductory chapters should be seen as a guide line to the Dictionary rather than as a full scale survey of the period, the sections are simply subjects that have caught the writer's attention as a collector and, in the compilation of the artists' names, have interested him. Where a particular illustration in the Dictionary is discussed in detail in these chapters, a smaller version has been provided for the reader's convenience as close to the reference as possible.

No attempt has been made here to deal with technical matters, information on this can be found in Ruari Mclean's masterly work *Victorian Book Design and Colour Printing,* 1963, and in the much smaller but equally useful *Victorian Book Illustration* by Geoffrey Wakeman, 1973. Children's books are not considered separately, although many illustrators of them are listed, neither is any individual history of the private presses given, although many illustrators ran them or worked for them. Anyone working in this field must acknowledge the debt they owe to the pioneers of illustration history who worked at the turn of the century. Gleeson White's *English Illustration, The Sixties,* published in 1897, is a classic if somewhat unmanageable volume, Forrest Reid's *The Illustrators of the Sixties,* 1928, is still a very helpful book and far more compact. James Thorpe's *English Illustration of the Nineties* is very wide in its approach, the same author's biographies of illustrators are a mine of information.

Simon Houfe

# Chapter 1

# Regency Background

Although both the eighteenth and the twentieth centuries have produced outstanding illustrated books, it is perhaps generally recognised that it was in the nineteenth century that this art form reached its zenith. A wave of national self-awareness and cultural enthusiasm after the Napoleonic Wars became a basis for establishing a taste for books, which laid the foundations of solid mid-Victorian publishing. The early years of the century were brim-full of new ideas, which were waiting to burst out on a newly industrialised society, once the 'Corsican Monster' was safely locked up on St. Helena. They were ideas that were frequently at variance with each other, sometimes diametrically opposed, but usually having in common a thirst for experiment and a fresh vision of the future. The admixture of romanticism, hot-headed liberalism, evangelicalism, mass-production, popular education, self-help and scientific investigation, proved a very potent brew, and the richness of this society in transition is displayed to good effect in their illustrated books.

It was an age of expanding knowledge and therefore of expanding opportunities for the bookseller, the publisher, and through force of circumstances, for the illustrator as well. Books of travel, topography, architecture, science and natural history, archaeology and engineering, poured from the presses to satisfy the growing private library owners, while plain but serviceable magazines for mechanics, manuals of instruction, exemplars for the craftsman were in more ready supply than ever before. At the lower end of the market the literature of the streets, broadsheet and ballad was having a revival and the singly issued caricature print was in its heyday. Books were produced with fine mezzo-tint engravings, occasionally with stipple engravings, and firms in the years following 1800 were discovering the new techniques of aquatinting, one at least making its name with them. There were a wide variety of magazines being published, some on specialist subjects, but also political, religious, sporting and domestic, increasingly relying on illustration to appeal to an audience.

The inheritance from the eighteenth century in the illustrating of poetry and fiction was small in scale and theatrical in content, typified by the art of Robert Smirke, 1752-1845, and Richard Westall, 1765-1836. The decorative softness of the English rococo, which had re-interpreted the classics, and set figures against the background of an idyllic landscape, was disappearing. James Thomson's *The Seasons,* 1730, the perfect English idyll, but more naturalistic than anything preceding it, had passed from pastoral allegory to romantic tension between the illustrated editions of 1730 and 1830. The work of the late eighteenth century men tends to be divided between the sentimental and the neo-classical. In the first, conventional figures in a sylvan English setting languish or pine, in the second overtly classical figures in the style of Barry and Fuseli dominate the page. The strong decorative sense which is apparent in the French-inspired books, illustrated by Gravelot and others, recedes decade by decade, although powerful ornament was designed by some men outside the mainstream such as Richard Bentley, 1708-1782, for *Gray's Poems,* 1753.

The fashion was for small engravings in the sets of illustrated novels by Richardson, Fielding, Sterne, Smollett and Burney, to be used as tableaux rather than as explanations of the printed story. Charles Lamb, a Georgian by upbringing if not wholly by sentiment, enjoyed reading Shakespeare in the cheapest editions so that the poor plates could serve as 'maps' to the text without in any way emulating it! This was clearly the influence of Hogarth, who being more of an illustrator of life than of books, claimed that his engravings were 'dumb shows' and expected them to be 'read' quite independantly of a text. Hogarth's connection with the stage re-inforces this impression and the fact that contemporary British painting was most lively in its portrayal of actors underlines it yet again. To open an engraved page of an illustrated Smollett or Richardson is to look straight into a scene of theatrical portraiture. Joseph Wenman's edition of *Count Fathom,* published in 1780, for example, has several plates by a minor illustrator, Dodd; in each case the figures are taken in gesture and in placing from the contemporary stage or the portraits of it by Johann Zoffany. Later theatrical painters were also to be illustrators such as de Wilde and Clint.

Book illustration moved another step away from its primary object as a visual stimulus to the reader when various wealthy booksellers began projects for lavish publishing at the end of the century. Alderman Boydell's unsuccessful venture in creating a Shakespeare Gallery, where the greatest artists were asked to contribute paintings of the plays which would then be sumptuously published, emphasises this discrepancy. The art of the book illustrator and the historical painter are quite different and the policy, which reduced a large painting to a page size, ignored that difference. Boydell's artists were not only unacquainted for the most part with book illustration, they came from different sides of the classical tradition and were experiencing in 1786 the beginnings of a divergence between neo-classic and romantic ideals. Henry Fuseli, 1741-1825, started a similar venture, The Milton Gallery, between 1790 and 1800, and Thomas Macklin had established a Poets' Gallery in 1788. The latter was also responsible for an illustrated *Holy Bible* with seventy-one plates and one hundred and twenty-five vignettes by eminent artists including P.J. de Loutherbourg, 1740-1812, and Thomas Stothard, 1755-1834. The work came out in parts and was issued to subscribers, the whole edition being completed between 1789 and 1800.[1] Other illustrated classics included *Harrison's Novelists Magazine,* 1780-83, *Cooke's British Classics,* 1796, *Bell's British Poets* and *Theatre* and later on Rivington's pocket poets and *Sharpe's Classics,* 1822. The most illustrated volumes outside the series continued to be *Gil Blas, Don Quixote, The Spectator* and *The Adventurer* with, as the romantic 1800s progressed, increasing interest in *The Arabian Nights* and *The Waverley Novels.*

This group included many excellent artists. Richard Westall RA, became an academician in 1792 on the strength of his painting, but is best remembered as an illustrator. He was capable of handling subjects as various as Crabbe, Gray and Goldsmith but is probably strongest in working on the classical histories (Colour Plate I). A good pen and ink artist with a fine sense of colour, the majority of his illustrations, even the pretty vignettes to Thomson's *Seasons* of 1816-17, lack individual lustre. E.F. Burney, 1760-1848, is another artist who deserves mention, his vignettes, borders and trophies are beautifully executed, his sense of design imaginative, perhaps fired by that separate career of his as caricaturist in watercolours. Thomas Stothard was another prolific illustrator who became an academician and Librarian of the Royal Academy in 1812. According to his biographer, Stothard undertook over five thousand illustrations for books during his lifetime, probably only a slight exaggeration.[2] But implicit in all these works is the history painter who had painted the staircase at Burghley House and exhibited yearly at the Academy until 1834. The better examples are more like relief sculpture than illustration and some of the most delightful things are for trifles like pocket-books and almanacks, the bacchanals are strongly decorative, the rural pieces rather weak. So the combination of theatricality, sentimentality and small format gives the productions of these men little chance to breathe and the same can be said for R. Corbould, T. Uwins, T. Kirk and many others (Figure 1).

J.H. Mortimer, 1741-1779, an important neo-classical artist but also an illustrator, seems to have appreciated the opportunities and limitations of the book. In his contributions to the poems of Milton and Pope in *Bell's Poets of Great Britain,* 1776-82, the artist places the illustrations in roundels which are decorated with neo-classical features, festoons and medallions giving the effect of an architectural frontispiece to the works. It is only a small point that Belinda in *The Rape of The Lock* looks more like a Roman matron than a Georgian lady of fashion, but there is altogether more vitality about the drawing. This is true of most of the neo-classical illustrators who worked in that other fashionable style of the Regency, line engraving, the shadeless outline, the concentration on the two dimensional that had evolved from Roman friezes and Greek vases. The most famous artist to adopt this method was the sculptor John Flaxman, 1755-1826, whose first child-ish drawings had been illustrations to the poets. His ability in modelling attracted the eye of Josiah Wedgwood and he was employed by the firm from 1775, later being sent to Italy to supervise Wedgwood's Italian draughtsmen. While in Rome, Flaxman was commissioned by Mrs. Hare Naylor to illustrate *The Iliad* and *The Odyssey* and by Thomas

*Figure 1. 'Youth and Age' by Thomas Kirk. Ink and wash.*

Hope and the Countess Spencer to illustrate Dante and Aeschylus respectively. The set of four illustrated works were engraved by Thomas Prioli in Rome in 1793 and distributed throughout Europe, giving Flaxman a greater standing than any other British artist. *The Iliad* and *The Odyssey* were published in London by Longman, Hurst, Rees and Orme in 1805, and *The Theogony* in 1817. The drawings are sharp, almost stark in their linear purity, but beautifully placed on the page and accompanied by no other text than a few lines from *Pope's Homer.* These plates were very frequently re-issued and had a deep influence on certain artists of the 1830s and 1840s and in particular on Moritz Retsch and his Shakespearean illustrations. Flaxman, like Hogarth, was so big a figure that the reverberations of his art were still powerful fifty years after his death (Figure 2).

Line engraving appealed to Flaxman because he was a sculptor and it was ideal for showing the clear profiles of neo-classic architecture and ornament. An impressive example of its use is in the monumental three volumes of *Ancient Vases . . . in the Collection of Sir William Hamilton,* published by Tischbein in Naples, 1791-95. This fine set with English and French text was re-issued or reprinted four times between then and 1814 and certainly made line the medium for neo-classicism. The real doyen of line engraving however was a London artist, Henry Moses, 1782-1870. His list of books, all executed with great finesse, handsome lay-outs and border ornament, reads like a catalogue of Regency taste. He began by engraving *The Gallery of Benjamin West* in 1811, supplied the plates for Thomas Hope's *Modern Costume,* 1812, for three books on Greek vases between 1814 and 1820, and *Sculptures from the Museum of the Louvre,* 1828. Perhaps his most attractive work is the two volume *Works of Antonio Canova,* 1823-24, where Moses' status is given due recognition and the pages are packed with the artist's work, displayed with an almost French suavity. Thomas Hope's *Household Furniture,* with interiors of his own residence, was engraved in outline, so was *The Description of the House and Museum of Sir John Soane Architect,* 1835, and many guides to galleries and the fine arts in the intervening years. Some of the supplements to *The Repository of the Arts* were engraved in line, taking

*Figure 2. Illustration to* The Odyssey *by John Flaxman, RA. Line engraving.*

their style and designs from the plates of Percier and Fontaine; the moving spirit behind *The Repository* was a dynamic German publisher living in London, Rudolph Ackermann.

Rudolph Ackermann, 1764-1834, was one of those remarkable figures who rise up on the shoulders of one particular fashion and dominate it for a generation; his contribution was to architectural and topographical illustration and his method was the aquatint. Ackermann was born at Stolberg in Saxony in 1764, and trained as a designer of carriages, moving first to Paris and then to London, working for various firms making equipages. He settled in London with an English wife and, looking round for a more permanent occupation, opened print shops at 96 and then 101, The Strand, taking in up to eighty pupils at a separate house run as a drawing school. Ackermann's gift for giving the art loving public a whiff of Continental air in his establishment, proved to be a very successful and lucrative idea. By 1806 he had closed the school and was concentrating on selling books and prints, artists' materials and fancy goods made by the impoverished French emigrés whom he employed. A contemporary report states that there were 'seldom less than fifty nobles, priests, and ladies of distinction at work upon screens, card-wracks, flower stands and other ornamental fancy works of a similar nature.'[3] The print seller was naturalised in 1809, and from 1813 established the first Art Library in London, where the latest publications on the arts in every European language were available for consultation or purchase. Ackermann saw his role as that of instigator of new ideas and his shop as a meeting place for artists and writers. This was a more usual form of trading in the 1800s, a guide of the time says 'English booksellers shops which are frequented as lounging shops . . . are provided with all new publications, newspapers, etc.'[4] But Ackermann made his premises lavish, employed a well-known architect to design them and held receptions upstairs on Wednesdays, when drawings, lithographs and advances in book production were exhibited.

Ackermann's readers were the art conscious middle class who had been inspired by the cult of the picturesque and the cult of the Grecian. The picturesque had originated from

Edmund Burke's aesthetics of the 'Sublime' and the 'Beautiful'. The Rev. William Gilpin, while accepting the earlier idea that smooth landscapes and rugged mountains were the archetypal examples of sublimity and beauty, had further discovered the beauty of 'variety' which he termed 'the picturesque'. Landscape and buildings were picturesque if they had the qualities of composed paintings and perversely paintings were picturesque if they had the qualities of composed landscapes! The literature of this theory of design was stupendous; drawing-masters produced numerous books for the amateur student of the picturesque, writers of guide-books rewrote their texts to suit its teachings and topographical works and volumes on Gothic architecture abounded. Ackermann supplied a great deal of their wants both as artists' colourman and as publisher of sumptuous volumes on cathedrals and castles.

*Figure 3. Tomb of the Duke of Richmond in Westminster Abbey by Thomas Uwins. Engraving.*

The first of these great volumes was *The Microcosm of London or London in Miniature, the Architecture by A. Pugin, the Manners and Customs by Thomas Rowlandson,* 1808. This was a part work, issued in twenty-six instalments at 10s. 6d. each, finally being offered in three elephant quarto volumes at fifteen guineas in 1810. It was a new venture in that it treated the metropolis pictorially and ranged over new and ancient buildings and meeting places in an almost sociological way. Ackermann claimed in his introduction to have been disatisfied with the static quality of much architectural illustration and had therefore introduced Pugin for the buildings and Rowlandson for the crowds. The liveliness of the latter are certainly invigorating and the plates still bustle and jostle after a century and a half because of them. Rowlandson was given 'ample scope for the execution of his abilities', so the introduction runs, 'and it will be found that his powers are not confined to the ludicrous, but that he can vary with his subject, and wherever it is necessary descend "From grave to gay – from lively to severe".'

The next work to be issued was the famous *History of the Abbey Church of St. Peter's, Westminster,* published in sixteen monthly numbers and appearing in 1812 at £15 for two volumes. Here a variety of artists were used to bring out in page plates the glories of the stained glass windows and the 'dim religious light' of the chapels and the richness of the monuments in the national shrine. Thomas Uwins (Figure 3), Pugin, G. Shepherd, J. White, Frederick Mackenzie, Thomson and H. Villiers were extensively employed on a book that set out to 'give a history of this vast and beautiful fabric, this scene of human grandeur, this last repository of glory, in all its parts . . .' which would animate piety and awaken sensibilities.[5]

The next two books from 101, Strand were *The History of the University of Oxford,* 1814 and *The History of the University of Cambridge,* 1815. These are splendid works, real tributes to Ackermann's perfectionism, with glorious plates by Pugin, Nash, Mackenzie and Westall. They contained optional supplementary plates of the university costumes and the bound volumes were sold at £16. In 1816 he published *The History of the Colleges,* a survey of the major public schools, using some of the same artists.

In 1809, Ackermann began his own magazine the *Repository of Arts, Literature, Commerce, Manufactures, Fashions and Politics,* published at four shillings a number and designed as an illustrated imitation of *The Gentleman's Magazine* and *The European Magazine* which was not extensively illustrated. The *Repository* included book reviews, theatrical notices, art criticisms and stories, but was distinguished for the variety of its plates in woodcut, line, stipple and lithography after 1817, as well as for the profusion of coloured aquatints. It was edited by Frederick Shoberl, 1775-1853, and was full of drawings by Ackermann's established artists as well as by new recruits to his team; within the first year it had gained a total of three thousand subscribers.

Aquatint was favoured not only because it was a perfected process but because it imitated the brushwork obtainable with watercolour. Aquatinting is intaglio printing from a copper plate, the hollows being bitten out with the ink squeezed on to damp paper under pressure. Whole areas are evenly hollowed out to give a uniform tint and by this method a variety of tones are achieved throughout the print, some imitating the highlights of watercolour, working from light to dark tones. The places that were to appear dead white were stopped out during the plate's successive immersions in the acid, resulting in a more and more contrasted effect. The plate might be printed in brown, olive, green or red, sometimes in two or three colours, before being tinted by hand. It is known for example that in Ackermann's last major work *The History of the Royal Residences,* 1829, the interior views of the palaces were printed in one colour and the exterior views in two, blue and brown, for the sky and buildings. The process from original drawings by C. Wild, J. Stephanoff or W. Westall would have run thus: when the watercolour was handed to the engraver an aquatint would be made of it, and a proof returned to the artist for colouring; this would then be used as a model by Ackermann's large staff of experienced colourists (Colour Plate II).

The publisher's other great discoveries were Thomas Rowlandson, 1756-1827, already referred to and William Combe, 1741-1823, whose talents he brought together. Rowlandson was connected with Ackermann from 1799 when he illustrated the eighty-seven plates to the *Loyal Volunteers of London and Environs.* Combe, a jobbing writer who was in and out of debtors' prisons, was an old man before he met Ackermann and agreed to write verses to Rowlandson's drawings of a travelling schoolmaster. In this way *Dr. Syntax in Search of the Picturesque,* 1812, was born and became one of the classic illustrated books of its period (Colour Plate III). The black-clad doctor on his awkward horse became the hero of a whole generation and started a fashion for aquatint engravings opposite rhyming texts. There followed *The Second Tour of Dr. Syntax in Search of Consolation,* 1820, and *The Third Tour of Dr. Syntax in Search of a Wife,* 1821. Ackermann had the distinction of not only paving the way for picturesque illustrating in this country, but of seducing the wayward Rowlandson into the covers of a book and holding him there. The same sort of flow of drawings and incidents take place in *Poetical Sketches of Scarborough,* 1819 and *The History of Johnny Quae Genus,* 1822, 'The Foundling of the Late Dr. Syntax'. Pursuing this further one would arrive at the episodic literature of the late Regency, Pierce Egan's *Real Life in London,* 1827, with coloured plates by Heath, Dighton, Alken and Rowlandson and the serial parts of early Dickens drawn for by H.K. Browne. Another notable Rowlandson and Combe partnership was in *The Dance of Death,* 1815, and *The Dance of Life,* 1817, where the artist's satirical powers are more in evidence. Another example of Rowlandson's work is shown in Colour Plate IV.

Ackermann's contribution was not just a nice mix of artists and authors but the raising of topographical and literary illustration on to a more fashionable plane. The foremost artists gathered at his rooms and we find that lion of the Royal Academy, Joseph Farington, there on April 26, 1813. After noting in his diary that he saw 'Pyne and Heaphy in

*Right: Plate I*
*RICHARD WESTALL, RA*
*1765-1836*
*'Aeneas Triumphing over*
*Turnus.' Original drawing*
*for illustration to* The
Aeneid. *c.1800*
Victoria and Albert Museum

*Below: Plate II*
*CHARLES WILD 1781-1835*
*'The West Ante Room,*
*Carlton House.' Illustration for*
Pyne's Royal Residences, *1819*
*Hand-coloured engraving*

Ackermann's Museum Room' he adds acidly that 'the printseller has gradually risen & become a publisher of Books with prints & is supposed to be worth £20,000'.[6] His relations with the illustrators seem to have been very good and his preservation of their work was remarkable. Retaining the original drawings, the publisher's right, he had all those for the *History of Westminster Abbey* bound up with the letterpress printed on vellum. Papworth 'prepared a special design, with Gothic details, for the brass mountings and clasps for the two volumes, which cost £120. This copy Ackermann valued so highly that he used to provide a pair of white kid gloves for the use of the person to whom was granted the favour of inspecting it.'[7]

Costume was not a speciality of Ackermann's except where it touched on the fine fashion plates in his magazine or in the university plates. There was however one notable book produced by an Ackermann author, W.H. Pyne, for another publisher, *The Costume of Great Britain,* 1808. William Miller of Old Bond Street published a series of six books on costume between 1801 and 1807 with English and French texts and pretty if anaemic single figure illustrations. Interest in costumes was generated by romantic novels and exotic architecture, so the countries chosen tended to be remote and colourful; China, an obvious choice, was illustrated by a Cantonese artist, Pu-Qua, Turkey by a Frenchman, Dalvimart, Russia and Austria being unattributed. Pyne designed, engraved and wrote the whole of the seventh volume on *Great Britain* and it is certainly far the most interesting. Pyne had cut his teeth in a remarkable drawing-book called *Microcosm or a Picturesque Delineation of the Arts, Agriculture and Manufactures of Great Britain.* In a series of groups which he subtitles as an 'Encyclopaedia of Illustration' issued from 1805, he shows how picturesque figures can be used for embellishing landscape for the artist. Aquatinted by J. Hill, these charming studies of cottagers, brewers, gardeners, basket makers and millers are now valuable as scenes of everyday life. A further series *Rustic Figures* appeared in 1814. It is not surprising therefore that *The Costume of Great Britain* has fine compositions of figures, superbly grouped and more in the tradition of narrative painting than costume illustration. Among the best are 'The Halfpenny Showman', 'The Lamp Lighter', 'Dustman' and 'Brickmaker', street scenes and trades having a greater sense of reality through Pyne's eyes than the more formal 'Baron' or 'Speaker of the House of Commons'.

A contemporary, Jerdan, leaves a picture of the restless and enquiring life of W.H. Pyne, so typical of the early nineteenth century artist. Through this ceaseless activity Jerdan writes 'his facile pencil so ready and true in seizing every quaint and characteristic form or feature, as illustrated in his Microcosm of London, and other productions which gave celebrity to Ackermann's Repository, were still more captivating proofs of his genius in the arts. It was delightful to lounge out with him on a summer day, imbibe his conversation, and watch the execution of a dozen humorous and most fanciful sketches, of beggars, brewers, milkmaids, children at play, animals, odd-looking trees, or gates, or buildings — in short, of all curious or picturesque objects and everything else.'[8]

The Napoleonic Wars, which had hemmed in the British artists for more than a decade, seem to have acted like a *camera obscura,* throwing the image of the outside world into sharper relief and giving them a more concentrated vision. After 1814, the full effect of this was felt in topographical books where the services of the artist were required in depicting every aspect of foreign travel for a public hungry for information. The British watercolourists who had built up a great reputation in their engraved views for *The Copper Plate Magazine,* 1792-1803, *Angus's Seats* from 1784 and *Watts' Seats,* 1779-1786, came to the fore as painters of Continental and Eastern scenery. The subtleties of watercolour, the softness of the colour range and the gentleness of the rendering were aspects that it had taken a generation to appreciate, and just as the medium was emerging from the tinted drawing into its richer form, here was the aquatint process to capture it for a wider audience. A good example of this change from straightforward topography to a more powerful scenic style may be found in the *Selection of Twenty Views in Paris* published posthumously by Thomas Girtin in 1803, etched in outline and completed by F.C. Lewis in aquatint. The plates have no text, but this and other similar works showed the illustrator the way to a more picturesque rendering of buildings and a more poetically grand approach to landscape.

Just as Ackermann's contribution was chiefly in British topography, so the exploration of the Indian sub-continent was mostly the work of one publisher, Edward Orme. With his brothers, Daniel and W. Orme, all of them occasional illustrators, he succeeded in creating a library of Indian life that was second to none. The first book was *Twelve Views of Places in the Kingdom of Mysore* by R.H. Colebrook, 1794, which contained aquatints and was followed by *Picturesque Scenery in the Kingdom of Mysore,* 1805. But the most celebrated partnership began in 1808 with the publication of *Oriental Scenery* from the drawings of Thomas and William Daniell. Thomas Daniell RA, 1749-1840, was born at Kingston-on-Thames and studied at the RA Schools. In 1784 he left for India, taking with him his nephew William Daniell RA, 1769-1837, then aged fourteen, as his assistant. They spent ten years there, based in Calcutta, but travelling freely over the country and making a great number of oil and watercolour landscapes. Some of this material was published as *Views in Calcutta,* 1786-88, but most of it was issued by Orme of Bond Street, *Oriental Scenery* being followed in 1810 by *A Picturesque Voyage to India by the Way of China.* The success of the books enabled Thomas to retire, but William Daniell continued to issue fresh books, *Views in Bootan,* 1813, and the important *A Picturesque Voyage Round Great Britain,* 1814-25, many of the drawings for which are in the British Museum Print Room. He also shows his versatility in the uncoloured aquatint illustrations to *Memoir of Sicily,* 1824, by William Henry Smyth, including views and botanical drawings requiring a high degree of scientific accuracy. At a later date, 1836, he was providing the illustrations for *The Oriental Annual.*

Some other notable books contemporary with the Orme publications are Gold's *Oriental Drawings,* 1806, and Lord Munster's journal of a *Route across India,* 1819. Orme at first issued sporting subjects with his *Collection of British Field Sports* in 1807, a series of plates by Samuel Howitt, 1765-1822, later he augmented this with his Indian interests to produce *Oriental Field Sports* with illustrations by Howitt aquatinted by Havell and Merke. The introduction to this very beautiful work states categorically that the Englishman's domain is now much further extended than his own coasts. 'It is offered to the Public as depicting the Manners, Customs, Scenery and Costume of a territory, now intimately blended with the British Empire . . .' Howitt, a self-taught artist, never visited Bengal but worked up the watercolours from sketches made by the author, Captain Williamson, a tribute to the sort of co-operation that could exist between the amateur and the professional at this time (Figure 4).

Two artists who did travel abroad extensively however, were Sir John Carr, 1772-1832, whose *Stranger in France* was ridiculed by Byron in *English Bards and Scotch Reviewers,* and Sir Robert Ker Porter, 1777-1842. Carr, the typical amateur travelling for his health, went on to publish books on Holland, Spain and Scotland. Ker Porter was a much more substantial figure who was patronised by West as a battle painter and painter of panoramas and achieved success as Historical Painter to the Czar at St. Petersburg. His most representative work is found in two books *Travelling Sketches in Russia and Sweden,* 1809, and *Travels in Georgia, Persia, Armenia, Ancient Babylonia,* 1817-20. Greece was also a popular country for artists and travellers interested in archaeology and the Greek revival; Middleton's *Grecian Remains in Italy* appeared in 1812, Dodwell's *Views in Greece* in 1821 and P.F. Laurent's *Recollections of a Classical Tour* the same year. C.R. Cockerell,

*Figure 4.* 'Dooreahs of Dog Keepers Leading out dogs, Plate XXXVII'. *Illustration to* Oriental Field Sports *by Samuel Howitt, 1805-07.*

1788-1863, contributed illustrations to *Travels in Sicily, Greece and Albania* by the Rev. T.S. Hughes in 1820 and another architect, Professor T.L. Donaldson, published his *Pompei Illustrated* in 1829. Sir William Gell, 1774-1836, another topographer, sent out a continuous stream of books after settling in Italy. These included *Pompeiana*, 1817-19, *The Walls of Rome*, 1820, *Narrative of a Journey to the Morea*, 1823, and *Topography of Rome*, 1834. Gell also penetrated to Troy and Barbary but with the exception of draughtsmen like Luigi Mayer, who worked in Egypt, 1801-04, much of the landscape drawing was in Western Europe.

A lucrative side to the illustrated book market was the trade in elaborate folios of the recent campaigns from the Nile to Waterloo, and in some cases views of St. Helena where Napoleon was residing. The volumes had begun to appear during the war as the public demanded immediate representations of the sites and evidence of battles and sackings as they happened. One example of this was from the pencil of the artist-chaplain to Lord St. Vincent, the Rev. Cooper Willyams, 1762-1816, who gave his own account of the Battle of the Nile in *Voyage up the Mediterranean in the Swiftsure*, 1802. There were many others, St. Clair's *Views of the Principal Occurences in Spain and Portugal*, 1812, and Jacob's *Travels in the South of Spain*. The small village of Waterloo became the most drawn in Europe, from the grand volume of the *Martial Achievements of Great Britain and her Allies*, 1815, to the *Historical Account of the Campaigns in the Netherlands* with some plates by Cruikshank, and the *Victories of the Duke of Wellington*, 1819, with Westall illustrations. R. Bowyer of Marlborough Place, Pall Mall, were offering their *Campaign of Waterloo* within the year, complete with portraits and biographical notes of the allied generals, reprints of despatches and an account of St. Helena. This was in addition to maps, several coloured aquatints and a folding plate in aquatint of the battle from Mont St. Jean.

The great interest in British topography which resulted from the cult of the picturesque was not confined only to the house of Ackermann. Another publisher and promoter of equal stature was John Britton, 1771-1857, who was also a rather mediocre illustrator in his own right. Virtually untrained, but working as an architectural draughtsman from about 1787, Britton began to produce surveys of the architectural antiquities of the English counties in 1801 under the title of *The Beauties of England and Wales,* 1801-1821. Similar things had been attempted but Britton brought with him an expertise in business, a thoroughness in history and accuracy in draughtsmanship, that had not been seen before. Along with his more scholarly co-author, E.W. Brayley, 1773-1854, Britton actually walked over much of the countryside described in the early books and according to one report, traversed as much as fifty miles in a day! For the first five volumes in the series, the authors travelled 3,500 miles and between June and September 1800 had walked 1,350 miles on a route from London to Hereford and Ludlow, then to North Wales and finally back to London again. 'In the long run it was the seven hundred illustrations which made the greatest impact,' writes J.M. Crook, 'and for this Britton justifiably claimed the credit. It was only towards the end of the series that he handed over responsibility to the ubiquitous J.P. Neale.'[9] Britton trained up a whole team of young men as topographical illustrators whom he housed under one roof in London, providing them with books and materials for study such as the earlier prints of Buck and Hearne and the drawings of Cotman, Girtin and Turner. Among these pupils were Samuel Prout, 1783-1852, Frederick Mackenzie, 1788-1854, and W.H. Bartlett, 1809-1854. Engravers who learned their craft in the Britton atelier included John and Henry LeKeux, the watercolourist George Cattermole, 1800-1868, and the architect Edward Blore, 1787-1879. Britton gave evening parties which were well known for their conviviality and the affection in which he was regarded by his pupils is shown in part of a letter written to him many years later by Bartlett:

'I have a vivid . . . recollection of the awakening of the antiquarian spirit within me under your tuition; of drives and walks about the Wiltshire downs, and of the great gig-umbrella swaying to and fro, and the danger of all being capsized, of cromlechs, stone temples, old churches, and old gateways, and a host of other subjects.'[10]

Britton's generic name for his illustrators was 'scientific artists' suggesting the rigorous standards that he expected from them. At different times he employed Nash, Hearne, Wyatville, Buckler, Gandy, Wild, Westall, Dayes, Fielding, Turner, Shee and Repton. Even when he had ceased with *The Beauties,* he was busy producing other important series, *Cathedral Antiquities of Great Britain,* 1814-35, *The Dictionary of Architecture,* 1829 or individual guides to country houses, *Fonthill,* 1823, *Cassiobury,* 1837, and *Toddington,* 1841, which were still having a vogue. He completed his career by publishing a voluminous *Autobiography,* 1850, which shows how the seeds of the Gothic revival and of landscape illustration were sown in the Regency. Britton's importance lies not simply in this but in the fact that he understood the book as an art form and took pains with his design, his title pages, tail-pieces and headings. In many ways he was a forerunner of those industrious apprentices of the publishing trade who were to take the country by storm in the 1840s.

John Preston Neale, c.1780-1847, worked for both Ackermann and Britton at various times and published his own *Views of the Seats of Nobleman and Gentlemen,* 1818-24, and the second series from 1829, for which he executed over seven hundred drawings. He also drew for *Views of the Most Interesting Collegiate and Parochial Churches of Great Britain,* 1824-25, and *Jones's Views,* 1829-31. Original drawings for these works are seen on the market from time to time, beautifully finished, but often lacking the contrast or drama which one associates with the romantic movement. The urban counterparts to Neale were George Shepherd, fl.1800-1841, who drew for Wilkinson's *Londina Illustrata,* 1808, and *Architectura Ecclesiastica Londini* and his brother Thomas Hosmer Shepherd, fl.1817-1840.

The latter was a very prolific topographer, illustrating Bath and Bristol but most notably the new buildings of London in the 1820s. These were contained in *Metropolitan Improvements*, 1827-28, and *London and its Environs in the Nineteenth Century*, 1829, a show of confidence in the stuccoed terraces of Nash. These were published by Jones at his 'Temple of the Muses' in Finsbury Square and issued in parts at one shilling each. Each part contained a text by the architect James Elmes and four steel plates 'Engraved in The First Style of the Art' from Shepherd's drawings. The publisher offered subscribers special cheap rates during the progress of the work which would be doubled when the collected edition appeared. The artist depicted Regent Street, Regent's Park and the improved squares and crescents but also the smaller villas of Park Village and the Canal. Testimonials from famous architects were printed on the paper covers! A similar part work was issued for Scotland, *The Modern Athens! Or Views in Edinburgh: Exhibiting the Whole of the Splendid New Buildings and Modern Improvements*, 1830, priced at four shillings a section and containing sixteen steel engravings. A handsome two volume set by William Westall was *The Mansions of England*, 1830, a collaboration with Shepherd and Gendall of plates issued in *The Repository*. Another charming illustrated book is *Picturesque Rides and Walks with Excursions by Water, Thirty Miles Round the British Metropolis* by J. Hassell, 1817. With an eye for the remote and secluded, the artist shows the lesser-known country houses, churches and monuments of Hertfordshire, Kent and Surrey.

Among the growing number of topographers and view painters, many of whom were amateurs encouraged by Britton to draw their own localities, were one or two highly individual men whose work is on a different level. Georg Cuitt Junior, 1779-1854, was almost alone in using etchings for his antiquarian books on the North of England. A drawing-master at Chester, Cuitt used his vigorous and dramatic style, strongly influenced by Piranesi, to produce a remarkable series of plates including those to *Saxon and Other Buildings Remaining at Chester*, 1810-11, *Picturesque Buildings in Chester*, 1810-11, and *A History of Chester*, 1815. Cuitt used the deep contrasts possible in etching and the sketchy groups of figures among the old buildings of the city to lift topography out of the realm of mere hackwork (Figure 5).

*Figure 5. Chester by George Cuitt. 1815. Etching.*

*Right: Figure 6. Monument in Hingham Church by J.S. Cotman. Etching.*

24

Another artist to do this supremely well was John Sell Cotman, 1782-1842, a natural landscape painter whose hands were nevertheless tied by the publisher's demand for antiquarian views. Self-taught, but growing up in the fertile artistic ground of Norwich, Cotman had great advantages in being associated with watercolourists like John Varley and Thomas Girtin and having the encouragement of rich patrons. But recognition and worldly success did not come and he was thrown back on his own resources to become an illustrator of county histories and a teacher of drawing to young and not so young ladies. In 1804 Cotman came into contact with Dawson Turner, a scholarly amateur with a passion for medieval antiquities and particularly Gothic architecture and design. The artist was engaged almost at once on a long and tedious job of recording the historical monuments of Norfolk and Suffolk, the churches, castles, priories and brasses for which Turner felt such an enthusiasm. The sketches from which Cotman worked up his etchings are dated from 1805 to 1818 and were issued for circulation privately as *Specimens of the Architectural Antiquities of Norfolk*, 1812-18, in ten parts. The whole collection was published as *A Series of Etchings Illustrative of the Architectural Antiquities of Norfolk*, 1818, and *Specimens of Norman and Gothic Architecture in the County of Norfolk*, 1816-18. Besides these he produced ninety-seven plates and two ornamental title pages for *Excursions Through Norfolk*, 1818-19, which were badly engraved and lack any of the original brilliance as prints. It is rather depressing that such an individual genius as Cotman should have had to spend so much of his time on such unproductive book work, but his drawings and etchings show how personal his response was. As C.F. Bell wrote: 'It is paying him a very inadequate compliment to say that his touch transported the traditional "views of seats" so abundantly popular at that time, on to a plane which no other draughtsman dreamed of approaching.'[11] (Figure 6.)

Cotman was given greater scope when Turner sent him to Normandy in 1817, 1818 and 1820 to draw its Romanesque architecture as a comparative volume for the earlier work. The artist extended his range to the countryside and to its peasantry, although it was only the archaeological part of the tour that was published. This appeared as *The Architectural Antiquities of Normandy*, 1822 and 1832, a remarkable book in its scale and accuracy with a great deal of Cotman's unique vision. Some of the etchings are awe inspiring, the West Front of Rouen Cathedral for example which the artist called 'a work of more than twenty weeks hard labour'.[12] The most handsome set of the etchings is the one published by Bohn in 1838. But topographical illustration was not enough, disillusion produced in Cotman what has been described as 'self-tormenting melancholia'.[13] For long after his death in 1842, these drawings were still passing from collection to collection for only a few shillings, although a few discerning men, such as the Rev. Bulwer, had gathered them together, realising their merit.

Cotman eked out his living as a drawing-master and these years were notable for the great number of copy-books and exemplars produced by aspiring teachers for the amateur. The first books of this kind, as distinct from works on perspective, were really those by that herald of the Picturesque, the Rev. William Gilpin, 1724-1804, in the 1780s and 1790s. They included *Observations on the River Wye*, 1782, *Observations on . . . the Mountains and Lakes of Cumberland and Westmorland*, 1786, *Forest Scenery*, 1791, and *Picturesque Travel*, 1792, and several more. They were essays in aesthetics for the artist and the dilettante, but they were more than this for they were illustrated by Gilpin's own sketches in aquatint. These usually appear in ovals and have a yellowish tinge to the print, which the artist believed was preferable to the staring whiteness of paper; one of the books, *Forest Scenery*, had a series of 'picturesque animals' etched by Sawrey Gilpin on toned paper. This precedent brought a great flurry of similar books in the next twenty years, each claiming to show the most 'characteristic expression' of natural landscape. Among these might be mentioned *An Essay on Trees in Landscape* by Edward Kennion, 1815, with a fine group of tree studies by the author, J. Hassell's *Aqua Pictura,* which came out in monthly parts, 1811-13, showing progressive stages in landscape drawing and the same artist's short-lived and rare *Drawing Magazine,* 1809-11. There were few artists of stature who did not publish something illustrated by themselves; Pyne, as we have seen, produced his *Groups,* John Varley issued an eight part work *A treatise on the principles of landscape paintings* between 1816 and 1821, Robert Hills etched plates of cattle and horses for example in the years 1798 to 1817. David Cox's *An Essay on Landscape Painting & Effect,* 1814, and reprinted regularly until 1841, is among the best of these works containing coloured aquatints of such beauty as to be barely distinguishable from watercolours. Samuel Prout's earlier drawing books were illustrated by soft-ground etchings, Francis Nicholson's *The Practice of drawing and painting landscape from nature,* 1820, has a careful explanation on colouring and George Brookshaw tackled another side of the growing interest in watercolour with his three books on *Groups of flowers, Groups of fruit* and *Six Birds,* 1819.

Brookshaw's most accomplished piece of illustrating was his *Pomona Britannica,* 1805, with ninety-three coloured plates in stipple and aquatint and this as well as other books prove it to have been a heyday for botanical illustration. William Jackson Hooker illustrated *The Natural History of Fuci,* 1819, for that same Dawson Turner who had helped Cotman and it was the late 1820s that saw the publishing of the grandiose plates for *Birds of America* by John James Audubon. Other titles of note are *Conchology, or the Natural History of Shells* by George Perry, 1811, with their drawings by John Clarke and the magnificent run of Maund's *Botanic Garden,* 1825-35, with the exquisite hand-coloured plates of plants by the miniature painter, Edwin Datton Smith.

The most exceptional talent of these years in book illustration was not however to be found in London or even in metal engraving, but in one of the most distant provincial cities and in wood engraving. Thomas Bewick, 1753-1828, was a Northumbrian who was trained as a copper plate engraver at Newcastle-upon-Tyne under Ralph Beilby. Within a year of his apprenticeship, he was asked to engrave on wood for the illustrations of a scientific work and the tools and boxwood blocks were procured from London; this started him on a career which not only transformed the art of wood engraving but gave Bewick national recognition. Bewick brought to the wood block the same skill and finesse that he used for copper and, instead of cutting away the non printing areas as the early wood engravers had done, he used white line cutting. This meant that the surface was treated as solid black and each stroke of the graver was a white line giving a greater delicacy and creative expression in the design. Over a number of years, the engraver perfected his technique, lowered his blocks to obtain greater evenness in the presses, printed them lighter and papered over the dark areas to bring out the highlights. There were many advantages in the process, it was simpler to print wood engravings and text together for a book, the effect was often more pleasing on the eye and, if the artists were skilful enough, great richness could be obtained for a reduced cost.

Bewick, the Northumbrian and the country man, was highly skilled and highly perceptive as an artist. A constant observer of nature, both human and animal, his soft grey and silvery tones seem exactly fitted for the task of depicting natural history subjects and the fancies and foibles of ordinary simple people. This was his main work from about 1776 until his death, beginning with the engravings for *Select Fables* and continuing with *Gay's Fables* and *Trip's History of Beasts and Birds,* 1779, on to the great classic *A General History of Quadrupeds* which occupied him from 1785 to 1790. Bewick's viewpoint is a very personal one, the animals, drawn in pen and ink and then traced on to the block for engraving, are beautifully alive within their settings and more naturalistic than anything that had gone before. This is even more true of *A History of British Birds,* 1797 and 1804, where

*Figure 7. Vignette illustration of old country woman from Bewick's* British Birds. *1797-1804. Wood engraving.*

the attention to detail in plumage and habitat could only have been achieved by someone who had roamed the countryside for information. The human interest is provided by the delicate little vignettes and tail-pieces, minute slices of country life which follow chapter by chapter, often with a Rabelaisian wit. We are treated to glimpses of clumsy yokels, huntsmen, angry old crones and mischievous boys, as the backdrop to the teeming, restless and fascinating rural life of Bewick's countryside (Figure 7). The same spirit emerges in the delightful *Fables of Aesop,* 1818, on which he was engaged for seven years. Further books were projected on *British Fishes* and although they were never completed many drawings and engravings survive for them in the British Museum.

Even Bewick's proficiency and personal supervision of the printers could not entirely outbalance the variableness of the impressions, and the engraver's own clients were invited to choose their own wood engravings before having the books bound up.[14] It is also uncertain how much of a hand the more talented pupils had in some of the vignettes, according to Bewick very little, but according to Jackson rather more; this again might account for some discrepancies among the engravings in the same book. Bewick had numerous pupils and some left him for London and great success, but he appears to have carried a rather jaundiced view of some of them into old age. Despite this, the association with Bewick was of great importance and it was this continuity in wood engraving that was to prove invaluable when the revival of the art set in during the 1840s. Names such as John Jackson, William Harvey, John Thurston and Charles Thomson were to carry Bewick's influence forward if their work never reached his heights. The celebrated Dalziel Brothers were also in the line of succession from this master engraver.

The Regency was not only the age of the lavish colour plate book but the golden age of British caricature. The cream of London life, its politics, its fashions, its social misdemeanours were constantly placed before the public by the artists, and if it was often rather sour cream, it helped to vent the irritation with weak governments and a self-indulgent Court. Many years later Charles Knight recalled the excitement generated by each new production of this very urban art. 'A daily Caricature? Yes; and a wilderness of Caricatures, issuing in endless succession out of shops round which crowds gathered from Piccadilly to Cheapside.'[15] When J.P. Malcolm published his *Historical Sketch of The Art of Caricaturing* in 1813, the first survey of the subject, he excused himself by referring 'to the number of persons employed in this way, and the number of shops appropriated to the sale of Caricatures . . . a proof of the importance the Publick has attached to them.'[16] Malcolm felt bound to define caricature as an art form and to some extent today it still needs that definition. To some people it is any visual grotesque however far removed from portraiture, to others it is the world of diminutive figures with huge heads or the characters depicted on seaside postcards. Only an art as spontaneous and volatile as caricature could have slipped so easily into the language without explaining itself, so it is necessary to know a little of its background to appreciate the work of Gillray and Cruikshank, Dighton and Heath.

Caricature comes from the Italian word 'caricare' to overload and it was in the Italy of the early baroque that the art was born. Artists and sculptors had always interested themselves in the grotesque, Leonardo's heads are an example, and since the Renaissance had used emblems to make political or religious points in prints. But it was only with the painter, Annibale Carracci, 1560-1609, that it came to be realised that the pithy exaggerations of the most striking features of a man, were often more true to life than a portrait. Carracci made rapid sketches that 'overloaded' the characteristics of his friends and dubbed them 'caricature'. He claimed 'to grasp the perfect deformity and thus reveal the very essence of a personality'. Bernini and other artists were to develop this sideline to their more serious work.

By the early years of the eighteenth century, the Grand Tour was in full swing and the artistically-minded and the influential in British Society were making the journey to Italy. Not all of them were such serious connoisseurs and some no doubt agreed with Lord Chesterfield that it was not expected of a gentleman to do more than dabble in art. But caricature was different, it was witty and subtle and appeared to expend no energy; it exactly suited the dilettante who could show his flare for a likeness but remain an amateur, who could satisfy the urge to create something and yet know it would be ephemeral. So along with the opera, the ridotto and old master paintings, caricature entered this country in the baggage of returning *cicerones* and milords. One or two painters such as the Italians Zanetti and Pier-Leone Ghezzi became as celebrated for their thumbnail caricatures as for their history paintings, the English artist, Thomas Patch of Florence, specialised in caricature oil groups of his visiting fellow countrymen. The tourists and the artists saw these, were amused, and experimented for themselves, the Countess of Burlington, Lord Townshend and Sir Joshua Reynolds among them.

Alongside the growing interest in 'caricatura' was the much older tradition of portraying types. Leonardo had drawn contrasting faces much in the spirit of the medieval display of the different humours. Hogarth's prints are all of this kind, detections of passion, stupidity, grossness, cupidity and sloth in human countenances, but not caricatures. Hogarth has unfortunately been labelled 'the father of English caricature' but his work was quite alien to the light-hearted jottings of Court dandies. But Hogarth was far too powerful a figure in English draughtsmanship for his influence to escape the caricaturists. The 'caricatura' of types is a popular subject throughout the nineteenth century and this stems directly from him. A further boost to the character draughtsman was provided by the pseudo-scientific investigations of physiognomy and craniology. Johann Casper Lavater's writings were popular in England and in them he maintained that the virtues and vices of a man might be classified by his profile and salient features. The particular set of a nose or a mouth belonged inevitably to a certain type, craniology or the study of bumps led to similar conclusions about thirty years later.

So at the beginning of our period there were three branches of caricature, the amateur caricaturist who made lightning sketches for private circulation and occasionally had them published, the political and social caricaturist who drew portraits and mirrored current events and the draughtsman of types and characters. From the middle of the eighteenth century, caricature had come to occupy a more crucial place than as the mere doodlings of a dilettante, it became a sharp political weapon and crossed the threshold from the drawing-room to the club house. Malcolm believed that, 'Those Caricatures which apply to political events and characters are now considered as the necessary consequence of holding a place under the Government, or wishing to obtain one.'[17] George Townshend, Lord Townshend, 1724-1807, was the earliest amateur to use his talent for a cause. Identifying military setbacks on the Continent with the Duke of Cumberland, Townshend began savagely and mercilessly to caricature his former commander and published an anonymous print of 'A Brief Narrative of the Late Campaign in Germany' 1751. From 1756 he was associated with the printsellers Matthew and Mary Darley, thus setting a pattern for the caricaturist in the next seventy years, the amateur supplying the engraver with ideas and the printseller financing them. From the 1770s the amateurs were still in the lead and one in particular, Henry William Bunbury, 1750-1811, typifies the ill-drawn but spontaneous life of these prints. A country squire with a taste for humour, Bunbury poked gentle fun at life and was commended by Malcolm for never 'having wantonly injured the feelings of individuals, who were not accountable to him for the singularities of their features, persons or manners . . .'[18] The example shown (Figure 8) is called 'The Salutation Tavern' and was published in March 1773 by the Darleys. Its free drawing of the figures and its Italian setting show the connection still existing between caricature, high society and the Grand Tour. These uncoloured prints with two figures were called 'Macaronis', a word for fashionable people and the sub-title 'Macaroni & other Soups hot every day' referred to the daily publications of satires. However inadequate Bunbury might seem to be as an artist, it says something for the status of caricature at this time that Reynolds owned the caricaturist's original drawing for his popular 'A Barber's Shop', 1785.[19]

Another crude but competent hand was Francis Grose FRS, 1730-1791, the antiquary and author, who actually published a pamphlet on the subject. *Rules For Drawing Caricatures*, 1788, is a delightful booklet which gives much of the flavour of amateur

*Figure 8. 'The Salutation Tavern' by H.W. Bunbury. 1773. Engraving.*

draughtsmanship and must have accounted for many of the portfolios of scraps and albums of heads in country house libraries. Like Hogarth, Grose considers that caricature has a moral purpose and 'may be most efficaciously employed in the cause of virtue and decorum, by holding up to public notice many offenders against both, who are not amenable to any other tribunal.'[20] He instructs the reader to draw portraits from the antique or from plaster casts and then amuse himself by altering the proportions. But this is no substitute for observing the peculiarities of nature and with Georgian elegance he begins to rationalise the process, dividing the nose, the chin and the eyes into categories and giving each category names. A line should be drawn through a profile touching the extremities of the forehead, nose and chin, the general facial expression 'angular, concave, convex, right lined or mixed' being apparent from it. 'Mouths may be arranged under four different genera or kinds. Of each of these there are several species. The under-hung, the pouting or blubber, the shark's mouth and the bone box.'[21] Grose illustrates all these and goes on to point out that a caricature should be both spontaneous and a result of assimilation. 'Peculiarities of the eyes are best shown in a front face; those of the nose, forehead or chin [in profile]; for by these distinctions the different features of a face may be described as to convey a pretty accurate idea of it; wherefore, when a caricaturist wishes to delineate any face he may see in a place where it would be improper or impossible to draw it, he may commit it to his memory, by parsing it in his mind (as the school-boys term it) by naming the contour and different species of feature of which it is constructed, as school-boys point out the different parts of speech in a Latin sentence.'[22]

Grose concludes that his appended caricatures 'are not to be considered in any other light than as mathematical diagrams, illustrating the principles here laid down.'[23] The germ of caricature is almost accidental and Grose can hardly have believed that anything so febrile could be achieved by a nearly mechanical process. Nevertheless such manuals kept amateur work alive in the long evenings and provided a continuous flow of new recruits to book illustration and later to the magazines. In 1813 it could be said with some truth that 'the Caricatures of the Continent seem all forced and unnatural and entirely destitute of that fire and freedom and invention, conspicuous in our own.'[24]

The happy band of amateurs, Townshend, Bunbury, Grose, Henry Wigstead, G.M. Woodward and John Nixon, prepared the ground for the professional caricaturists who were to follow. Among the most important names from the 1780s were James Sayers, Isaac Cruikshank and James Gillray, 1757-1815. After conventional training at the Royal Academy and as a stipple-engraver, Gillray turned to caricature with the Bond Street print-shop of Miss Humphrey as his outlet. A far better craftsman and a more instinctive artist than the others, he very soon simplified the art and brought greater expression to the subjects and stronger imagery to their meaning. His work hit very hard and as the artist was something of a political maverick, the politicians wooed him continuously. So did the Prince of Wales, who could not forget the bloated image Gillray produced of him as 'A Voluptuary under the horrors of Digestion' 1792. At various times the Prince and the ministers paid pensions and bribes to him to keep their features out of the daily prints!

Much of the pungency of Gillray's work can be accounted for by his cynicism and pessimism. 'For Gillray, as for any perceptive humorist,' writes Draper Hill, 'comedy and tragedy were the opposite sides of the same coin. In his eyes, human experience seems to resolve itself into a grim sort of carnival roller-coaster on which trial is inevitably followed by error and aspiration necessarily results in disillusion.'[25] J.P. Malcolm, who was not a great sponsor of Gillray referred to his 'unbounded spirit and fire of genius' glowing 'in every line of his work' which distinguished him from the previous generation. In his single figures and small groups, he continued the amateur style of caricature, but his elaborate compositions benefited from his training as a history painter which Bunbury and the others had never had. A good pair of copper engravings of 1795 which show his talent in straight profile work are the 'Billingsgate Eloquence' and 'Pulpit Eloquence' (Figures 9 and 10). In 'Billingsgate Eloquence' he shows the scraggy features and bared arms of a Billingsgate fishwife, famed for their brutality and bad language. The gist of her argument is carried on the caption below, but the real humour lies in the fact that the caricature *is* a portrait of Lady Cecilia Johnston, well known for the bitterness of her tongue! In the other hand-coloured engraving 'Pulpit Eloquence', a fat and contented cleric preaches from a pulpit, but it is no ordinary cleric, but Archbishop John Moore, a frequent butt of Gillray's satire.

The sharp divisions along party lines which followed the French Revolution probably enabled Gillray to exercise his art with unprecedented asperity. Malcolm railed against faction and insisted 'that party spleen too often suggested a degree of severity which belongs only to crimes of the deepest dye.'[26] Charles James Fox's portrayal as a devil and Pitt's head rising out of excrement are rather overstating the case, even if the impact is powerful. It was in fact against the common enemy, the French, that some of Gillray's best work was done, in the same way as it was to be with that of Low one hundred and fifty years later. 'The Plum-Pudding in danger' of 1805 and 'Tiddy-Doll, the great French-Gingerbread-Baker' 1806, are unforgettable, as is 'The King of Brobdingnag and Gulliver, 1803 (Colour Plate V). The caricaturist has used an incident from Swift to show George III and Napoleon in a way that is practically visual alone. Gillray's original drawings are rare, but his surviving sketchbooks show that he worked 'in a lacy, delicate pencil to which ink (and occasionally colour) was later added'.[27] The wild maze of free penwork which typifies these studies is entirely different from that of Rowlandson, Dighton or any of his contemporary caricaturists.

Social caricature was at least as popular as political caricature under the Regency and the follies of society, connoisseurship, opera-going, military and sporting absurdities, medicine and the theatre, were ceaselessly ridiculed. The excesses of fashionable costume

*Figure 9. 'Billingsgate Eloquence' by James Gillray. 1795. Engraving.*

*Figure 10. 'Pulpit Eloquence' by James Gillray. 1795. Engraving.*

were an early favourite of the caricaturists. 'Nothing affords greater scope for ludicrous representations than the universal rage with which particular fashions of dress are followed by persons of all ranks, ages, sizes and makes,' wrote Grose in 1788, 'without the least attention to their figures or stations. Habilments also, not ridiculous in themselves, become so by being worn by improper persons, or at improper places.'[28] Gillray satirised superbly the elaborate coiffeurs, plumes, turbans and high-waisted dresses of his day and his followers relentlessly caricatured the sartorial coxcombery of the 1820s with its pantaloons, high collars and quizzing glasses for the men, enormous top-heavy hats, small waists and tiny feet for the women. The interaction between fashion plates and fashion comedies is touched on in a later chapter, but it was certainly this aspect of the art which was to find the most comfortable place in Victorian parlours. One of the earliest and most prolific of these artists concentrating on manners, was Robert Dighton, 1752-1814, an actor and caricaturist who took subjects from London life including those of

Figure 11. 'A Lesson Westward' by Robert Dighton. Pen and ink with watercolour. 1782.

parsons, barbers, ladies of the town and lamplighters. While not as bold in style or visual imagination as Gillray's, these engravings, usually charmingly coloured, give an interesting and detailed glimpse of late eighteenth century and early nineteenth century life.

In February 1978, Sotheby's sold the most important collection of original watercolours by Dighton that has so far come to light, a complete album of his work from the collection of the late Jeffrey Rose. The ninety-six drawings had belonged to the Carrington Bowles family, who were Dighton's publishers, and had been bound together in about 1830. The drawings were early, spirited, with both historical and literary content and in mint condition with their colours protected for a hundred and fifty years.[29] They covered the whole range of his work from the least caricatured of his groups 'Pheasant Shooting' and 'Snipe Shooting' to the macabre half skeletal watercolours of 'Life and Death Contrasted'. One which illustrated Dighton's delight in detail is 'A Lesson Westward' (Figure 11), poking fun at the fashion for ladies in high life to learn to drive phaetons. This one, expensively dressed and under instruction, has already killed a piglet and is terrifying the life out of an elderly gentleman! In the majority of cases, Dighton's pen line is harder than Rowlandson's and he is much less accomplished in the drawing; his figures stare rather stiffly out of the paper and their faces are usually grotesque.

The most important figure after Gillray was probably George Cruikshank, 1792-1879. He came from a caricaturing stable, the son of Isaac Cruikshank, and completed Gillray's last work for Miss Humphrey in 1811 and was the dying artist's natural successor. Satire became extraordinarily fierce again in the closing years of the Napoleonic campaign,

Figure 12. 'John Bull in the Council Chamber' by George Cruikshank. Engraving.

particularly in the turmoil surrounding the King's illness, Princess Caroline's misdemeanours and the Prince's extravagance; Cruikshank's eye was a match for all this. He inherited from Gillray the large scale of the latter's caricatures and to some extent his grotesqueness, devils, gremlins and exaggerated gestures are part of this. In other places, his imagery of a polluted countryside or a vision of future air travel, are more abstract. One of Cruikshank's typical productions is 'John Bull in The Council Chamber' drawn and issued by Jones of Newgate Street in 1813 (Figure 12). This engraving does demonstrate that Regency caricature was still something that had to be read as well as looked at, symbol and letter-press were still as important as recognisable portraiture. The central figure is that of Queen Charlotte, the German consort of George III, by 1813 the rather sad wife of the mentally disturbed King. Never a great beauty, she is shown by Cruikshank shrivelled and peevish, her elbow resting on a German sausage and her throne overflowing with sauer kraut. Various attendants offer up boxes of Royal Strasburgh to her, while Chinese figures holding money bags glare down at her from pillars, a reference to the royal extravagance at the Brighton Pavilion. A fat baby in a cradle, easily identified as the Prince of Wales, sleeps indulgently, while the Chancellor keeps a starving Irishman away. On the other side, the Liverpool administration refute the claims that the estranged Princess Caroline is worthy of censure. At the right-hand, John Bull, a fairly new recruit to the caricaturist's menagerie, looks on aghast and shouts out indignantly 'Is this the way I am bubbled?' That the artist should strike so many subtle nuances was a great test of his political awareness, Cruikshank scarcely left the drawing table when Parliament was in session. As Malcolm comments: 'He that would ensure success is aware that he is expected to draw with great correctness; which having attained, he flies to his pencil, and thence to etching; and thus he gives a spirit in every touch of the needle that could not be effected were he compelled to proceed with caution.'[30]

Neither Cruikshank nor his contemporaries Charles Williams, William Heath (Colour Plate VI), Newton or Rowlandson, spared their subjects and it is not surprising that Cruikshank was paid £100 on the new King's accession in 1820 'in consideration of a pledge not to caricature His Majesty in any immoral situation', the artist was indeed wielding power. The forerunners of the illustrated papers, they were sold at a penny plain and tuppence coloured but not yet in book form.

The art of caricaturing continued in the country houses where it had first flourished. Numerous sketchbooks are found with witty little drawings of house parties, shooting parties and amateur theatricals in broad caricature, but they are often difficult to identify. Two, who might be mentioned are Robert Browning Senior, 1782-1866, the father of the poet, who made crude political caricatures in ink and the Hon. Henry Graves, 1806-1892. Graves was a society figure who moved in aristocratic circles and drew his fellow guests with charm and humour in brown ink and wash. His vein of fantasy is sufficient to make the private jokes of the Paget and Wellesley families seem funny even today with their monstrous luggage, animals in hats and cigars flying through the air with wings!

A more substantial figure however and one with a humorous eye was the Rev. Walter Sneyd, 1809-1888, of Keele Hall, Staffordshire. Sneyd had the conventional background of the younger son, he was educated at Oxford and destined for the church and the occupation of a family living. Perhaps as an undergraduate he developed an aptitude for caricature, for as a young man he was prolific in both pencil and crayons. In 1829, he privately printed a delightful little book called *Portraits of the Spruggins Family,* an imitation of a family history with witty little drawings (Figure 13). Sneyd carried out all the work himself with the exception of one plate[31] and utilised the new invention of lithography, which enabled the amateur to come to grips with printing as well as sketching. As can be seen, Sneyd was still working in the manner of Gillray and in fact his uncle had supplied drawings for Gillray's prints. There is therefore some evidence that the art of caricature was handed down in families as a 'polite' accomplishment along with drawing and dancing. Other skilful draughtsmen were Alfred, Count D'Orsay, and W.M. Thackeray who will be discussed later, the link between the professional artist who played with the human countenance and the amateurs who dabbled with it, provided a useful middle ground in the years that lay ahead.

*Figure 13. Illustration to the* Spruggins Gallery *by the Rev. Walter Sneyd. Lithograph.*

## Footnotes

1. Mrs. Bray, *Life of Thomas Stothard R.A.,* 1851.
2. ibid.
3. S.T. Prideaux, *Aquatint Engraving,* 1909, p.113.
4. *Picture of London,* 1811, p.335.
5. *History of the Abbey Church of St. Peter's, Westminster,* 1812, p.xvi.
6. *The Farington Dairy,* Edited by James Greig, Vol. 7, p.168.
7. Wyatt Papworth, *The Life of J.B. Papworth,* 1879.
8. *Jerdan's Autobiography,* 1853, pp.78-79.
9. J. Mordaunt Crook in *Concerning Architecture,* 1968, p.108.
10. ibid. p.109.
11. C.F. Bell, *Walker's Quarterly,* Nos. 19-20, 1926, p.17.
12. Martin Hardie, *Watercolour Painting in Britain,* Vol. 2, 1967, p.87.
13. ibid. p.91.
14. *Thomas Bewick — Memoir,* Edited by Ian Bain, 1975.
15. Charles Knight, *Passages of a Working Life,* Vol.2, 1865, p.6.
16. J.P. Malcolm, *An Historical Sketch of the Art of Caricaturing with Graphic Illustrations,* 1813, p.iii.
17. ibid.
18. ibid. p.89.
19. ibid. p.92.
20. Francis Grose, *Rules For Drawing Caricatures,* 1788, p.4.
21. ibid. p.8.
22. ibid. p.10.
23. ibid. p.12.
24. Malcolm, op. cit. p.157.
25. Draper Hill, *Mr. Gillray The Caricaturist,* 1965, p.136.
26. Malcolm, op. cit. p.54.
27. Hill, op. cit. p.135.
28. Francis Grose, *Comic Painting,* 1788, p.2.
29. The sale on 23 February 1978 made a total of £50,960 and established caricatures as major works of art.
30. Malcolm, op. cit. p.157.
31. According to a note in the *Bodleian Library Record,* Vol. 8, No. 3, February 1969, states that all but the picture of the whole gallery were Sneyd's works, the exception being Lady Morley's.

# Chapter 2

# Albums, Annuals, Landscapes
# and Lithographs

The most dominant feature of the Regency book market had been topography, the most obscure countries, insignificant cities and curious journeys were dutifully recorded and engraved on the copper plate; abbeys, castles and country houses had their own guides and even the novels of Scott and the adventures of Dr. Syntax became the excuse for loosely delineated topography and travel illustrations. The appetite of the public for such descriptions was insatiable and there seems to have been little concern whether the texts were very accurate or very lengthy provided that the engravings were of a good standard. The limitations of this sort of book were really the limitations of the copper plate itself, for in 1800, a publisher would not normally expect to get more than four thousand good impressions from one plate, a lamentably small edition considering the potential readership. A more durable material was sought and this proved to be the steel plate, introduced here in about 1822 by Albert Warren. As the years went by these were improved to gain absolute consistency for the artist, no warping and any degree of hardness that was required. From 1820 to 1835, a whole generation of artists were bred up to this new invention, who completed their work with the burin (a type of chisel) and became specialists in the interpretation of tones and gradations. For the first time, a large number of British artists saw an opening for their drawings to reach the greatest possible audience, by the 1840s editions of between 20,000 and 30,000 prints were quite usual from the leading London printsellers. Some engravers reached a high degree of proficiency by the 1830s and had a European reputation, among them George Cooke, E. Goodall, R. Wallis, Edward Finder, W. Miller, J.C. Allen and W.B. Cooke. Both topographical and architectural illustrators learned to draw for the engraver, to adapt to his skill and recognise his limitations. Among the men who formed part of the new landscape school were James Duffield Harding, Thomas Allom, W.H. Bartlett, Alfred Gomershall Vickers, James Holland and William Callow; immense prestige was gained for this medium when J.M.W. Turner began to work for it in the 1820s. We are of course still in the province of the separately issued print. Walter Crane dismissed the whole group eighty years later as outside the range of pure illustration: 'Book illustrations of this type which largely prevailed during the second quarter of the century − are simply pictures without frames.'[1] But these 'pictures' did find their way into collections with covers between 1820 and 1840 and do carry the story of the illustrated book forward if somewhat hesitantly. The watercolourists and draughtsmen whose names became famous in early Victorian households through steel engravings, had reached those hallowed surroundings by one direction only, the illustrated annuals.

The craze for annuals, which lasted for about three decades from 1820 to 1850, was a hardly surprising reaction to the austerities and masculine emphasis placed on society by the Napoleonic Wars. Once free of the books on battles and sieges in aquatint, the decade of the 1820s developed a very soft and highly decorative standpoint in everything from its villas to its cuisine. It could be described as a very feminine and pretty period, frilly and fluffy in its dress, modulated in its satirical prints, gently edging forward to the Victorian concept of art and ornament being synonymous. It was a time when the small and the ephemeral were very fashionable just as the 'new' and the 'artistic' were to be in the 1890s and the pocket-sized annual, beautifully bound, exquisitely lettered 'full of sound and fury signifying nothing' became the touchstone of the moment. Pocket diaries and almanacks had been popular in the eighteenth century, often with an engraved frontispiece or a fashion plate. *The English Ladies Pocket Book For The Year 1795* for example has a folding plate of 'The most Fashionable Head Dresses of the Year'. *The London Almanack for the Year 1810* which is only thumb-size, has a diminutive engraving of 'the Naval Asylum Greenwich' as an introduction to a calendar and a table of lord mayors and current coins. Other illustrated almanacks included the *Ladies Polite Remembrancer* and the *Royal Repository,* and William Havell supplied many of the tiny illustrations for *Peacocks Polite Repository,* 1813-17. A number of these sheets have been seen on the market, usually done in sepia and wash with their locations written below, they are never more than one by two inches in size and must have proved some challenge to the engraver. Samuel Prout also supplied designs for these books and a large collection of proofs is in the British Museum.

It was the energetic Rudolph Ackermann who first spotted that this humble branch of book production could be a highly profitable enterprise. The firm of Rodwell and Martin of Old Bond Street were actually the first to lay plans for an annual and got as far as examining German models and deciding that they could surpass them in quality of engraving, before the financial outlay upset the project.[2] Ackermann was less diffident and knew well the German 'Taschenbucher' and the French 'Almanachs' which the others had no doubt consulted. Taking ideas from here and there, he produced this hybrid called *The Forget-Me-Not* in 1822, which was the first of the race 'the prototype of a new and splendid progeny'.[3]

It was an immediate success and was to last as a 'Christmas and New Year's Present' from then until 1847. The contents were always insubstantial, poems by minor bards and plates of minor thespians, all surrounded by borders and encased in covers that became more exotic every year. A few respectable literary figures began to grace the pages of the books after Alaric Watts started editing *The Literary Souvenir or cabinet of poetry and romance* in 1825-26, continuing in one form or another to 1842. Watts who had a circulation of six thousand copies for *The Souvenir* from its first years, prided himself on executing engravings from '*original* paintings and drawings by the first artists of the day'. Ackermann's and Watts' success led to a cascade of new titles, all rivals as Charles Knight recalled and with 'no lack of sentimental stories and verses, somewhat mawkish with their bowers and flowers'.[4] Over three hundred separate annuals are listed between 1823 and 1855,[5] many of them only reaching one edition, some like *Heath's Book of Beauty* having very long and popular runs, 1833 to 1849. Their names alone capture their trifling fascination and their perennial success, *Affections Keepsake,* 1836-46, *Apollo's Gift,* 1830, *The Bijou,* 1828-30, *The Christmas Box,* 1828-29, *Fisher's drawing-room scrap book,* 1832-38, *Gems of Loveliness,* 1843, *Juvenile Missionary Keepsake,* 1846, *Royal Repository and picturesque diary,* 1831. The flood had become a deluge after August 1834 when the stamp duty on almanacks was repealed. 'There were elegant bijou almanacks for the drawing-room table', Vizetelly records, 'Sunday almanacks for the prayer-book, miniature almanacks for the waistcoat pocket, circular almanacks for the crown of the hat and almanacks even printed upon pocket handkerchiefs.'[6] Where the almanacks led the annuals followed and there were annuals for children, young ladies, protestants, the military, naval and musical! 'Competition necessarily gave rise to prodigious efforts to obtain pre-eminence', wrote S.C. Hall, who was busy editing *The Amulet* from 1829 to 1836, 'In their earlier years, the Annuals were all bound up in tinted paper, and enclosed in a case. Paper yielded to silk, in which the majority of them soon made their appearance; then followed morocco — for the binding of which they had been accustomed to pay nearly as much as the cost of the whole work — illustrated by exquisitely engraved prints from

*Above: Plate III. THOMAS ROWLANDSON 1756-1827*
*'Dr. Syntax and The Gypsies.' Illustration to*
The Tour of Dr. Syntax in Search of the Picturesque
*Hand-coloured engraving. 1812*

*Below: Plate IV. THOMAS ROWLANDSON 1756-1827*
*'The Stocks at Tetbury.' Ink, watercolour and wash*
*8ins. x 13ins. (20.3cm x 33cm)*
Author's Collection

paintings by artists of the highest ability, any of which previously would have been valued at the charge demanded for the series, and containing prose and poetry, written for the several publications by leading popular writers of the age.'[7] A minor poet who wrote for *Friendship's Offering* was W.M. Praed who summed up the gossamer like pattern of these books in his verse 'Goodnight to the Season'.

> 'Good-night to the Season — the splendour
> That beam'd in the Spanish Bazaar;
> Where I purchased — my heart was so tender —
> A card case, — a pasteboard guitar —
> A bottle of perfume, a girdle
> A lithograph'd Riego full-grown
> Whom Bigotry drew on a hurdle
> That artists might draw him on stone
> A small panorama of Seville
> A trap for demolishing flies
> A caricature of the Devil
> And a look from Miss Sheridan's eyes.'

Miss Sheridan was Caroline Elizabeth Sheridan, afterwards the Hon. Mrs. Norton, 1808-1877, daughter of the playwright, who was editor of *The English Annual, Fisher's Drawing-room Scrapbook* and other journals. She was one of a number of society ladies who toyed with literature, the Countess of Blessington, Lady Emeline Stuart-Wortley and the Baroness de Calabrella were others, their portraits liberally spread through the pages among the pictures of J.R. Herbert, C.R. Leslie, G.S. Newton and H. Howard. Even if panoramas of Seville were included and full-grown Riegos, lithographs were never used for all the work was done in the medium of steel engravings. At the beginning of the period they were carefully engraved, but as time went on they were etched for speed and the later steel engravings in these books tend to have a rather mechanical appearance. 'There were Keepsakes', wrote Knight, 'and Gems and Bijous; but these delicate flowerlets of the literary hotbed had a brief existence. They did more for the arts than for letters.'[8] This statement is hardly corroborated by the books themselves. After looking at a great many their mild prettiness and embossed bindings do not seem to have anything very startling to say for book illustration at all. Beyond the title-pages, which were usually pleasantly designed (Figure 14) and gave the steel engraving an opportunity of cleverly showing medals by Wyon and sculpture by Flaxman, there was practically no use of the vignette and an

*Figure 14. Title-page for* The Keepsake, *1830.*

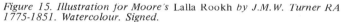

*Figure 15. Illustration for Moore's* Lalla Rookh *by J.M.W. Turner RA 1775-1851. Watercolour. Signed.*

*Figure 16. Title-page of* Heath's Picturesque Annual *for 1832, with illustration by Clarkson Stanfield, engraved by E. Goodall.*

unrelenting series of portraits and genre subjects. With titles like 'Lucy and Her Bird' or 'Do You Remember It', they were cabinet paintings encased in books. Obviously illustrations were commissioned directly for these books, small and highly finished grey and brown wash drawings that do appear by Fanny and Louisa Corbaux, F.P. Stephanoff, Alfred Chalon and the Corboulds were evidently destined for such plates, but the main commissions coming through the lady editors all seem to have gone to established oil painters. Absolutely no attempt was made by *them* to adapt their canvases for the small format. Thackeray ridicules this in *Pendennis,* 'it was the eminent poets who had to write to the plates and not the artists who illustrated the poem.'

J.M.W. Turner contributed regularly to *The Keepsake* from 1829 to 1837 and this influx of landscape engravings, though small in number in proportion to the book and always very small in scale, gave the annuals a more serious interest. Turner's involvement with book illustrations is almost a separate subject, his extraordinary powers and intellectual approach make them quite unlike anything else undertaken in the early nineteenth century. The artist had grown up very much in the topographical tradition but his first major attempt to codify his thoughts about the art and present 'a visual treatise on landscape' was his *Liber Studiorum* issued in fourteen parts between 1807 and 1819. This was inspired by Claude's *Liber Veritatis* and the project was carried out in mezzo-tint by Charles Turner, the engraver, although outlines of the designs were always etched on to the plate by Turner himself. Another large scale landscape work appeared between 1814 and 1826, *Picturesque View of the Southern Coast of England,* in which the master was joined by certain lesser stars like William Westall, Samuel Owen and William Havell, but had the lion's share of the

39

work. This series was a success, was issued as two volumes and was still being produced in large paper editions as late as 1849. Other illustrated books included a *History of Richmondshire,* 1823, *Picturesque Views of England and Wales,* 1832-38, and posthumous collections such as *Harbours of England,* 1856. Turner did venture into pure literary illustration with sketches after Tom Moore's lyrics (Figure 15). *Campbell's Poetical Works,* 1837, and *Rogers Italy,* 1830, and *Poems,* 1834. Probably greater attention to detail and finish of the engravings was applied to Turner's illustrations than to any comparable works by artists at the time; he personally supervised every stage and every work is an original in its own right. As sheer works of topography they are often of no interest at all but as the creations of a brilliant mind they repay careful study. As Percy Muir has written, 'The simple fact is that he was less interested in producing a faithful representation of a locality than in the creation of an original work of art, and if the natural ingredients of the landscape failed to conform with his requirements he changed them to suit his purpose.'[9]

Turner's example may have popularised the notion of having annuals that were solely filled with landscape engravings. *The Landscape Annual* began in 1830 and ran to 1837, and this was followed by *Heath's Picturesque Annual,* 1832-43, *The Continental Annual,* 1832, *The Landscape Album,* 1832, *Landscape Souvenir,* 1835-39 and *Landscape Wreath,* without date. In the case of the three best known ones, whole volumes were devoted to the work of one landscape artist, giving a pleasantly uniform appearance to the series, *The Continental Annual* was entirely illustrated by Prout, *The Landscape Annual* had J.D. Harding as its artist in 1832-34, David Roberts from 1835-38, and James Holland in 1839. Clarkson Stanfield's work was exclusively in *Heath's Picturesque Annual* from 1832-34 (Figure 16) and George Cattermole, A.G. Vickers, William Callow and J.D. Harding in succeeding years.

The only artist of the annuals to come anywhere near Turner's intensity of vision and grandeur of concept was John Martin, 1789-1854. Martin was born at Haydon Bridge, Northumberland, and after acting as heraldic painter and china decorator, finally established himself after 1812 as a painter of biblical and Miltonic subjects of enormous size and power. The more monumental and catastrophic the story, the greater the success Martin had with it, piling up huge and threatening edifices of rock and stone which topple and crush the struggling and wayward humanity below them. Among his favourite themes are 'The Fall of Nineveh', 'The Deluge', 'Belshazzar's Feast' and 'Pandemonium', all making use of the black ground and lowering aspect of the mezzotint. Martin therefore would seem the least likely candidate for the annuals, surely apocalyptic breezes blowing through *The Keepsake, The Amulet* and *The Forget-Me-Not* would overturn the tea-tray and bestir the drawing-room

*Figure 17. 'Opening of the Seventh Seal' by John Martin 1789-1854, issued in 1837.* Mellon Collection.

*Figure 18. 'The Flight Into Egypt' by John Martin 1789-1854.*

curtains? They do not seem to have done so, and his popularity and the high prices paid for his oil paintings are referred to by contemporaries. 'Sums of money that sound preposterous were lavished upon the several departments', writes S.C. Hall of *The Amulet,* 'five hundred pounds were given to Sir Walter Scott, and proportionable remuneration to other authors for articles contributed to a single volume of the Keepsake; amounts varying from twenty to one hundred and fifty guineas were paid to artists for the loan of pictures to be engraved; and it was by no means uncommon for the engraver to receive one hundred and fifty guineas for the production of a single plate. For one indeed, "The Crucifixion" after Martin, engraved by Le Keux, that gentleman received from me one hundred and eighty guineas (size 7 inches by 4), making the cost of the print, including the sum paid for the drawing, two hundred and ten guineas. The volume of The Amulet that contained this costly work had also two other engravings, which together cost two hundred and sixty guineas; the other nine prints amounted perhaps, to seven hundred guineas; so that for the embellishments alone the publishers had to pay nearly twelve hundred guineas. And yet, strange to say, that was the only volume of the whole series of The Amulet that yielded a profitable return upon the capital expended and the labour bestowed.'[10] As we notice, Martin was paid thirty guineas for his drawing, much less than the engraver, but one must remember that at exactly the same time Frank Stone was being paid five shillings each for his contributions to *Heath's Book of Beauty!*

Martin's cataclysmic visions appealed to the same audience that would today go to a horror film. The aspects of divine vengeance and natural disaster that were prevalent in all his paintings, lightning, raging seas, gigantic scale, seem to have touched a chord in the early Victorian breast which wanted to be a little discomforted and disconcerted in the face of growing prosperity. In some prints, such as 'Opening of the Seventh Seal', this disquiet and immense power are beautifully conceived, the tiny figure in the foreground silhouetted against the waves, being a typical Martin device (Figure 17). Some of his lighting and his structures have been convincingly linked to the influence of early industry, gas illumination and engineering in the 1820s and 1830s. A more gentle use of his prints is 'The Flight Into Egypt' (Figure 18) intended for *The Forget-Me-Not* of 1838.

The annuals and the albums are an intriguing sideline of book illustration, but not really a very important one. Their purpose obscure, their format constricted, they were pretty and ephemeral but had some lasting results in the gift-books of the 1850s and 1860s. While the fashion lasted however 'the returns were amply sufficient to requite writers liberally, to pay artists handsomely, and to satisfy publishers for their risks in advertising such heavy freights in such lightly built and showily painted vessels.'[11]

The public that had developed a taste for landscape illustrations from the engraved plates in the annuals and books of beauty were encouraged to take their scenery and architecture in a more personal way by the 1840s. The lithograph, which had been neglected since its first introduction to England by Senefelder in 1807, really came to the fore in the hands of C.J. Hullmandel, 1789-1850, who experimented with new processes and made it a commercial success. Hullmandel augmented the visual appeal of the lithograph by tinting it with one or as many as four lithographic tints, a method he called 'lithotint' and which he patented in 1840. The effects achieved were much richer than in pure lithography, the draughtsmanship of the chalk was now contrasted with toned areas and the use of white highlights. They were in essence tinted drawings and printed on toned paper with some colouring added by hand, they were very striking and convincing. With the graphic feel of the lithograph and gradations nearest to the watercolour, they were as close to autograph examples from the artist's sketch-book as the average art lover was likely to get outside aquatint.

This style was ideally suited to the more picturesque and romantic approach succeeding album art. Its subtle pencil technique softened the hard edges of topography and architecture and its pattern of colour gave all scenes a decorative uniformity as well as a sense of history and atmosphere. The medium exactly fitted the taste of the public which wanted a mood rather than a measured drawing, murky cavernous cathedrals and ivy-hung mansions rather than the trim squares and crescents of the metropolitan improvements. One associates with this time the impressive quartos and folios which show views of foreign cities on toned paper, the almost barren grandeur of Greece, India or Egypt, huge rugged monuments in stone, garrisoned by tiny ineffectual figures. Several artists travelled to the Near and Far East but others strayed no further than the Continent and its western coast. The volumes of lithotints that are most often seen in secondhand shops or framed singly on the walls of vicarages or hotels are views of Normandy, Brittany and Belgium.

The watercolour school was just beginning to discover French Gothic and Flemish Renaissance buildings, the dim religious light of Chartres, Beauvais and Amiens, the townhalls, market-places and burgher houses of Ghent, Bruges and Louvain. Although buildings, carvings, choir stalls and chimney-pieces were rendered with a feverish accuracy, the figures make these series a literary, almost narrative, form of illustration. Every market-place is thronged with people, every church with clerics, prelates and clouds of incense, cavaliers wander round the cloisters and here and there a hermit reads from a chained bible. It is a far remove from eighteenth century topography, but possibly because of their limited range of colour and their strongly graphic quality, the lithotinters are still among the most effective portrayers of old buildings.

Hullmandel was not slow to realise that this poetic treatment could be used for views of old manor houses and castles as successfully as Jones or Shepherd had used engraving for new buildings. He drew and published in 1833 a part work, *Ancient Castellated Mansions in Scotland* which captured the life and spirit of these great strongholds and may be said to have contributed to the Victorian idea of baronialism. But the most formidable work to appear was Joseph Nash's *The Mansions of England in the Olden Time,* 1839-49, subtitled as 'depicting the most characteristic features of the domestic architecture of the Tudor Age, and also illustrating the costumes, habits, and recreations of our ancestors.' Nash was trained under A.C. Pugin, the architectural draughtsman, but preferred a freer rendering of his subjects and a more secular choice of buildings. His chief interest was in Tudor domestic architecture and in *The Mansions* he illustrates nearly a hundred interiors and exteriors of the most famous sixteenth century houses. These include Hatfield, Burleigh, Haddon and Hardwick, the bedchambers and long galleries of Knole, the excesses of Wollaton and the glories of Hampton Court.[12]  Nash was also sensible enough to include small houses,

Waterstone in Dorset, Levens and Ightham as well as the black and white manors of Speke and Moreton. 'The artists object', runs the 1869 edition, 'was not to exhibit these as many of them now appear — gloomy, desolate and neglected; but glowing with the genial warmth of their fire-sides.' The artist achieved this by avoiding anything in furniture or decoration that was not in accord with the period of the house; the rooms were peopled by ladies in ruffles and gentlemen in doublet and hose taken straight from the portraits on the walls. Apart from the too frequent appearance of Henry VIII and Queen Elizabeth, the result is reasonably convincing though his figures do not have the presence or power of George Cattermole's.

The Low Countries and Germany were well served by Louis Haghe, 1806-1885, a Frenchman who came to London as a young man. He was a painter in the lithographic firm, Day and Haghe, but made his reputation as a watercolourist and as an illustrator in '*A Portfolio of Sketches in Belgium, Germany,* 1840-50. Haghe's range was greater than that of Nash, the scenes were usually more vigorously drawn, the figures larger in scale and their relationship to the architecture and surroundings more important. Such scenes as the 'High Altar, St Martin's Church, Hal' or 'Townhall, Louvain' contain an incredible breadth of expression with only the slightest chiaroscuro effects. This type of treatment was much more influential on ink draughtsmen than on topographers, the swashbuckling cavaliers of Haghe's market-places became the stock in trade of Sir John Gilbert and the ancestors of boys' adventure story heroes.

Samuel Prout, 1783-1852, was another watercolour painter who excelled in lithography. He was a talented architectural draughtsman and figure artist who transmitted to paper his great affinity with the crumbling stonework and sunlit piazzas of old Swiss and Italian towns. His groups of washerwomen, fishermen and stall holders stand picturesquely beneath the west doors of cathedrals or at the foot of battered medieval crosses. The peasant costumes, the rather undefined faces and the high coifs of the women which gleam in his highlights, are almost the hallmarks of his books. Prout considered that the arrangement of his figures was the most important key to success. 'There should always be one principal group and smaller groups, with here and there detached figures, to express distances, and render the composition and effect more picturesque.' Perhaps this concentration on figures as well as his short sight caused him to illustrate features rather than complete buildings. There was no composer of crowds to equal him and Ruskin, a neighbour of the artist's in London, loved 'the half sad half sublime' buildings and more especially that they were drawn from nature. Prout produced eighteen books, all those after 1820 were in lithography and included *Illustrations of the Rhine,* 1824, *Facsimiles of Sketches made in Flanders and Germany,* 1833, *Sketches in France, Switzerland and Italy,* 1839. Some of the artist's early publications had been manuals of examples for the amateur. The idea was repeated in lithography which proved itself ideal for copying and for expressing the freedom of the pencil to the pupil in easy stages. *Prout's Microcosm,* 1841, is a typical example, it concentrates on the figure in an architectural setting, stresses the homogeneity of a composition but, says Prout, the eye should never rest 'but wander through the picture unconscious of the rules and principles that have influenced the painter'.

J.D. Harding, 1798-1863, was a pupil of Samuel Prout and specialised in the countryside and trees where his master specialised in buildings and figures. His greatest output was as a drawing-master, issuing copybooks and exemplars. He contributed to *The Landscape Annual* as we have mentioned and produced through the delicacy of stone three charming books, *Sketches at Home and Abroad,* 1836, *Harding's Portfolio* and *The Park and the Forest,* 1841.

Just as Haghe is associated with the Low Countries and Prout with the south, Paris was the spiritual home of Thomas Shotter Boys, 1803-1874. Boys was a trained engraver but on going to Paris, came under the influence of the brilliant virtuoso watercolourist, R.P. Bonington. Boys' lucid renderings of ancient Paris, his marvellous light and rich colour are the nearest things to the actual work of that short-lived genius. Boys' greatest venture into lithography *Picturesque Architecture in Paris, Ghent, Antwerp, Rouen Etc Drawn From Nature on Stone,* is also the closest approach to watercolour art in the book. These twenty-six lithographs issued in 1839 were an opportunity for the public to have in their hands views treated with a personality and expression unparalleled in reproductive art. The introductory note did not let this unique character escape them. 'In developing the capabilities of Chromolithography, the artist has aimed at difference of style in his manner of treatment, as well as at variety in the aspects of nature. For example, the view of the Abbaye St Amand, Rouen, is intended to present the appearance of a crayon sketch heightened with colour; that of Ste Chapelle, Paris, a sepia drawing, with touches of colour; the Fish-Market, Antwerp, a slight sketch in watercolours; St Laurent, a finished watercolour drawing . . .' After this success, Boys produced in 1842 his *Original Views of London As It Is,* not in chromolithography but in monochrome lithography with a few copies coloured in by hand (Figure 19).

Two other artists ventured much further afield, David Roberts, 1796-1864, to Egypt and the Holy Land and Edward Lear to Greece and Syria. David Roberts, a Scottish artist who had made a reputation as a scene painter, began to travel abroad regularly in 1831 and published the fruits of a Spanish tour as *Picturesque Sketches in Spain during the years 1832 and 1833.* He contributed to *Jennings Landscape Annual,* 1835-38, but his greatest triumph was his visit to the Middle East in 1838. It was really the first time that an artist of Robert's calibre had visited Egypt and the Holy Land and with the new taste for archaeological accuracy, allied to mood, he came back with a portfolio of splendid results. Such hidden treasures as Aboo Simbel and Petra were suddenly within the grasp of ordinary people and the Holy Places of Jerusalem were drawn with a truth and directness that made these prints popular for a generation. Roberts' work was put on the stone by J.D. Harding and Louis Haghe and published in parts from 1842-1849 as *Views of the Holy Land, Syria Idumea, Arabia, Egypt and Nubia.* All the plates were finished in two tints but extra colour was added by hand from the originals, the whole project cost Moon, the publisher, £50,000, and the subscribers for the complete set of six volumes paid nearly £150 each.

Edward Lear, 1812-1888, is such a familiar figure on the Victorian scene, so appealing and yet so intangible that it is difficult to label him as a topographer. A brilliant ornithological artist, a wild humorist accompanying each zany verse of poetry with a more zany and surreal drawing, he nevertheless devoted much of his life to landscape watercolours. Published books of drawings played a large part in this and they were an important supplement to his income as

*Figure 19. St. James's Palace by Thomas Shotter Boys 1803-1874 from his* Original Views of London As It Is *1842. Lithograph.*

*Figure 20. Frascati by Edward Lear 1812-1888. Illustration in* Rome and Its Environs, *1841. Litho-tint.*

an artist. His three best-known landscape folios of drawings were *Excursions in Italy,* 1846, *Journals of a Landscape Painter in Greece and Albania,* 1851 and *Southern Calabria,* 1852. These are the ones most usually seen in bookshops, and sale-rooms frequently have sketches or studies that prove to be directly related to them. In Lear's very personal style of draughtsmanship, line predominated over watercolour and made his work ideal for lithography. In *Rome and Its Environs,* 1841, he is much more concerned for the overall balance of light and shade and is much less profligate with effects and highlights than some of his fellows. In his 'Frascati' view in this volume (Figure 20), Lear leans on no picturesque effects but just lets the weird shapes of the poplars outlined against the horizon of the campagna tell their own story. Figures are less important to him than the contour of the countryside, where they occur as in 'Cervara' or 'Collepardo' in the same volume, they stand to one side inviting the observer into the landscape where range upon range of mountains succeed each other into the distance.

The early Victorians were not so easily prepared to separate art and technology as we are and industry had its own sumptuous volumes in the new medium. Perhaps the most evocative of their period and the most interesting are the records of the building of railways by James Bourne, 1773-1854. Bourne brought from the world of architectural draughtsmanship a clear statement of what he saw, the complex world of the early engineers with their tunnels, embankments, earthworks and teams of navvies, all enlivened with his artist's eye but recorded with a scientific accuracy. The birth pangs of the railway age in the 1830s and 1840s, breathes again for us in his *London and Birmingham Railway,* 1839, and *The History and Description of the Great Western Railway,* 1846. His pencil transmits the excitement of machinery in such romantic plates as 'Engine and Tender emerging from Tunnel near Bristol' or 'Building retaining walls, etc. near Park St Camden Town'. From the original drawings for these in the Elton Collection it would appear that there were at least three stages before the completed compositions finally reached the stone. The first sketches of the people and objects were made in pencil, followed by inking over. At the same time broader watercolours were made of the whole scene and the view drawn on to the stone from this accumulated information. Bourne most resembles Prout and J.D. Harding and none of their delicacy is lost in these very different subjects; his accuracy in showing detail is amazing, especially as the larger sketches are all reduced on the stone and much of their finish is lost.

The major industrial event of the epoch, the Great Exhibition of 1851, is recorded in two lavish lithographic folios. The earlier *Recollections of the Great Exhibition* published in the same year contained selected views of the interior by various artists including John Absolom and W. Goodall. The twenty-five litho-plates were hand tinted and the volume was printed by Day & Sons. The second and more celebrated book was *Dickenson's comprehensive picture of the Great Exhibition of 1851* which has come to be associated with the names of its three artists, J. Nash, Louis Haghe and David Roberts. These illustrations, published in 1854 give a general survey of all the galleries and include fifty-five plates, all originally commissioned by the Prince Consort. The artists have given a pleasing spaciousness to the production, the plates are ample and crammed with detail, the blue and grey colours of the Crystal Palace's structure floats over the stands of rich red, the figures and groups animated and individual.

These are only a small fraction of the many decorative books produced during the zenith of litho-tint 1830 to 1856. It would be possible to mention two further well-designed works, *Eton College,* 1844 and *Memorials of Charterhouse,* 1844, drawn and lithographed by Charles W. Radclyffe. W.A. Delamotte, 1775-1863, published a similar series of studies in *Original Views of Oxford,* 1843 and George Barnard some plates of Germany at about the same time. Among the most charming of these is Douglas Morrison's *Views of Haddon Hall,* 1842, but almost every provincial town can claim one or two topographical books of this type, architectural, picturesque, but varying in quality from the masterly to the coarse. Many of them hardly qualify as illustrated books at all, and yet they form a substantial part of the nineteenth century story.

Although the impact of the lithograph was on landscape and architectural illustration, it had some slight success in the world of caricature. William Heath, 1795-1840, who was a prime caricaturist of social life as 'Paul Pry' 1827-29 (Colour Place VI) was the instigator of *The Glasgow,* later *The Northern Looking-Glass,* 1825-26, and *The Looking Glass,* 1830, which can claim to be the earliest caricature magazines, pre-dating even Charles Phillipon's French publications. They are rather flimsy things without much text but they have a rarity and curiosity value.

*Figure 21. 'A Scene of Confusion' 1836 by 'HB' John Doyle 1797-1868.*

John Doyle or 'HB' was in spirit if not in date the first political caricaturist of the nineteenth century. Trained as a portrait painter rather than in the strong satiric tradition of Gillray and Cruikshank, he brought to the art a need for likeness rather than for exaggeration, for reasoned argument rather than mud-slinging. Doyle was never a strong draughtsman and despite his Irish background no great wit either. His satire was in the line of Regency caricature, visual representations were adapted from the London stage and the rhetoric of politicians transferred to the print in gesture and stance, but the effect was weak (Figure 21). Perhaps it is not so much Doyle himself as the nature of lithography that is to blame; the soft pencilled effects that the process gives were a great contrast to the sharp, spiteful line of the copper-plate. The lithograph as a vehicle of satire needed strong draughtsmanship of the order of the French artists if it was to succeed and in England it never received this. Doyle's amateurishly composed pictures with their weightless figures are miles away from the stature of the Parisian artists. If one looks, for example, at a print of September 1831, a lead up to the Reform Bill controversy, one sees Doyle in his best and worst lights. Sketch No. 154 is entitled 'Another Sign of The Times or Symptoms of What Modern Architects, complacently term — Settling'. A pair of columns stand side by side supporting a collapsing cornice on which are chiselled the words 'The Bill The Whole Bill And Any-Thing But The Bill'. The column to the left is the Tuscan order of architecture, a Roman innovation and therefore a symbol of democracy and might, the right-hand one which is steady as a rock is a Greek Corinthian column in which the Crown features as the capital. The design like the title is not only a clever allusion to the two sides in the Reform debate but incidentally to the rivalry of Greek and Roman architecture at the time and the instability of late Regency building! Lord Brougham and others vainly try to steady the toppling mass with a pole inscribed 'The Times', needless to say the edifice is built on sand and the 'royal' column has emblazoned on it a pun on William IV, 'Reform Bill Alias The Kings Name'.

Although Doyle has achieved three or four strands of meaning in all this, the impact is not pungent and the drawing very thin. The figures are insubstantial and there is a lack of contrast, yet Doyle maintained a great following among the early Victorians who wished to be entertained not shocked or provoked as their forebears had been. 'You never hear any laughing at "HB" ', Thackeray wrote in 1840, 'his pictures are a great deal too genteel for that — polite points of wit, which strike one as exceedingly clever and pretty, and cause one to smile in a quiet gentlemanlike kind of way.'[13]

The postscript to this is that 'HB's' work never stirred any collectors after its period. Writing in 1893, Graham Everitt cites a projected sale of 'HB's' original drawings to have been held in about 1880. There were apparently no takers and only Disraeli was seen thumbing through the productions of a caricaturist who could never have done him any harm!

*Footnotes*

1. W. Crane, *Of The Decorative Illustration of Books,* 1901.
2. W. Jerdan, *An Autobiography,* Vol. IV, 1853, pp.241-242.
3. ibid.
4. Charles Knight, *Passages of a Working Life,* Vol. II, pp.53-54.
5. F.W. Faxon, *Literary Annuals and Gift Books,* Edited by Jamieson and Bain, P.L.A. 1973.
6. Henry Vizetelly, *Glances Back Over Seventy Years,* 1893, p.104.
7. S.C. Hall, *Retrospect of a Long Life,* Vol. 1, 1883, pp.306-311.
8. Knight op. cit.
9. Percy Muir, *Victorian Illustrated Books,* 1971, p.65.
10. Hall op. cit.
11. Jerdan op. cit.
12. Original watercolours for Speke, Knole and Hampton Court are in the Victoria and Albert Museum.
13. *Westminster Review,* June 1840.

# Chapter 3

# The Illustrated Magazine
## Early Periodicals 1820-1840

Until 1820 the idea of an illustrated periodical in Great Britain was an impractical dream or a very rare novelty. A crude woodblock of Nelson's funeral car had appeared in *The Times* of 1806, the earliest newspaper illustration in the country, but an expensive curiosity rather than the vanguard of new things. The story does not fully begin until the 1820s with the rise of mechanisation, a wider reading public and a politically explosive decade. In 1814, *The Times* installed at their London office, a Konig printing machine which was powered by steam, a great advance over hand printing methods, in the number of impressions and the speed of their production. But this alone would not have caused the spate of illustrated journals from 1820 to 1840 if it had not been for two further factors; a tremendous thirst for information and the change from print to book of an earlier visual tradition.

Although it is usual to think of the Victorians and popular educationalists in the same breath, many of the most active were well to the fore by the great reforming year of 1832. Carlyle was beginning to establish himself, Ruskin's first effort was published in 1834 and Gladstone was already an MP. But the most outstanding figure in illustrated journalism, who might well rank with these great names, and crops up time and time again in books, pamphlets and periodicals, is Charles Knight, 1791-1873, newspaper proprietor and publisher. Knight was one of those indefatigible promoters of multitudinous schemes for the public good, as dexterous a canvasser as William Cobbett and as prolific as Charles Kingsley or Tom Hood, both incidentally involved in illustration. Born in 1791, the son of a Berkshire printer who had published *The Windsor Guide*, Knight was evidently destined for greater things than a provincial newspaper office. He was apprenticed to the editor of *The Globe* in London, returned home to run his father's *Windsor and Eton Express* in 1812, but was already by 1814 formulating plans to become a popular educator. In his breezy and self-confident autobiography *Passages of a Working Life*, 1865, Knight wrote: 'I had acquired a little familiarity with the general ignorance of the working classes, knew something practical of their habits, saw in some few a desire for knowledge, and felt how ill their intellectual wants could be supplied.'[1] Knight looked with horror at the literature of the book hawker 'the worst sort of temptations in sixpenny Novels with a coloured frontispiece'[2] and 'the lesson books with blotches called pictures, that puzzled the school-boy mind half a century ago . . .'[3] Knight published a paper on 'Cheap Publications' in 1819 but was not able to become a real agitator until he was established as first the publisher of *The Plain Englishman*, 1820-22, and concurrently of *The Guardian*.

One of Knight's principal concerns was to strike a midway course between scurrilous pamphlets with coarse woodcuts and the more learned magazines; both existed in total isolation. The religious and political tracts and squibs were to Knight's mind too inflamatory and the established publications like *The Gentleman's Magazine* and the newly-founded *Blackwood's Magazine*, 1817, too specialised, and the latter unillustrated. Knight had a healthy respect for the aspirations of a working population, now urbanised and estimated to be two-thirds to three-quarters literate. He was alarmed by the revolutionary spirit abroad in the 1820s and particularly in its more radical forms in magazines like *Twopenny Register, The Black Dwarf, The Republican, The Medusa's Head* and *The Cap of Liberty*. Paradoxically, Knight picked up some of his most useful tips on a visit to anti-monarchist France from looking at a compendious publication of facts called *Le Bulletin Universal.*

Even so, Knight was not the first in the field, there were a few precursors though not on such a grand scale. *The Observer,* which can claim to be the earliest illustrated paper, ran a series of woodcuts in the mid-1820s, including one of Gurney's Steam Carriage, another of the Thames Tunnel accident and a third of the Ascot Races drawn by William Harvey. *The Observer* continued to illustrate events up to the time of Queen Victoria's Coronation in 1837 and her marriage in 1841, when it produced a complete supplement. Other newspapers to use illustrations included *The Weekly Chronicle, The Sunday Times, The Champion, Weekly Herald* and *The Magnet,* mostly in the 1830s. Rather earlier than these was a little magazine called *The Portfolio,* 1825, 'Comprising I. The Flowers of Literature. II. The Spirit of the Magazines. III. The Wonders of Nature and Art. IV. The Essence of Anecdote and Wit. V. The Domestic Guide. VI. The Mechanic's Oracle'. It had by 25 March 1825 already swallowed up a similar venture *The Hive* and contains on its title page a very crude woodcut of Eton College signed 'Blunt'. Another longer-lived magazine was *The Mirror of Literature, Amusement and Instruction,* edited by John Timbs, which according to Vizetelly was founded in 1822 and extensively illustrated by the late 1820s. It was priced twopence and published every Saturday until 1843 at the same price. Its cheapness would certainly have put it into the hands of the same artisans that Knight hoped to reach, his own comments on

it being that it was 'indifferently illustrated' and 'not crowned with success'.[4] Each issue had a page or half-page woodcut illustration under the heading, generally a view of a building, sometimes new sometimes old, but very seldom of an event or a news item. The only real departure from this was the coverage of George IV's death and funeral in 1830. *The Mirror* gave a full-page profile portrait of 'His Late Most Gracious Majesty' against a backdrop of a lake and Chinese temple, signed like others in the magazine, 'I Dodd' (Figure 22). Subsequent numbers showed interior views of Windsor Castle, the lying-in-state and the funeral at St. George's Chapel. Most of them are very hard and over hatched, crude representations of scenes, hardly conceivable only a decade after Bewick's triumphs.

It was this gap that Knight hoped to fill and from the late 1830s produced a whole series of journals of outstanding variety. He sowed some of his wild oats in the earliest and slightly scurrilous publication *Knight's Quarterly Magazine,* then followed *The London Magazine,* about 1828, *The Library of Entertaining Knowledge,* 1830, *The Quarterly Journal of Education,* 1831, *Gallery of Portraits,* 1832-34, *The Printing Machine — A Review For the Many,* 1834, and others. But he is best remembered for having established and run *The Penny Magazine,* the first number of which

Figure 22. *His Majesty King George IV from* The Mirror, *1830.*

appeared on 31 March 1832. Knight's contacts with authors, artists and men of science gave him a wider sweep of the academic spectrum than any popular journalist had had before. *The Penny Magazine* had the promotion of a very Victorian-sounding body *The Society For The Diffusion of Useful Knowledge,* its eminent governors including Lord Brougham, Sir H. Parnell and Dr. Arnold of Rugby. Not surprisingly it was nicknamed 'The Steam Intellect Society'. The aims of the magazine were to capture the imagination of the ordinary readership in 'Striking points of Natural History — Accounts of the Great Works of Art in Sculpture and Painting — Descriptions of such Antiquities as possess historical interest — Personal Narratives of Travellers — Biographies of Men who have had a permanent influence on the condition of the world ... '.[5] This formidable list which sounds pretty dry reading was liberally sprinkled with woodcuts. Fortunately Knight did not share the contemporary idea that something illustrated was something juvenile and his first year's figures thoroughly justified this piece of speculation. From March 1832 to the end of the year, the circulation of Knight's magazine rose to 200,000, an incredible figure for those days.

At the beginning *The Penny Magazine* relied on blocks from the other Knight publications, particularly *The Library of Entertaining Knowledge,* but as interest increased he was able to commission new work. Knight clearly saw the success as one of illustration and said as much in his printed preface to the first bound volume. 'It must not be forgotten that some of the unexpected success of this little work is to be ascribed to the liberal employment of illustrations, by means of Wood-cuts. At the commencement of the publication, before the large sale which it has reached could at all have been comtemplated, the cuts were few in number ... But as the public encouragement enabled the conductors to make greater exertions ... it became necessary to engage artists of eminence, both as draughtsmen and wood engravers to gratify a proper curiosity, and cultivate an increasing taste ...'[6] Knight had a high opinion of illustrators, considered their derisory treatment by painters as unjustified and was among the first to print the names of both illustrator and engraver, though not in *The Penny Magazine.*

The chief difficulties in this illustrated mass journalism were technical ones. First of all there was a complete dearth of competent wood engravers, those that existed concentrating on the production of expensive books, to the mind of the populist Knight, a complete betrayal of what wood engraving was about! Then there was the machinery, capable of printing sixteen thousand impressions daily, but not of giving a very satisfactory balance or clarity to the engravings. Knight's woodcuts and text were transferred to stereotype-plates and the impressions were rapidly printed from the plates by his new cylinder machinery. The early results from *The Penny Magazine* were not very successful and publisher and printer continued to experiment for some years, consulting the artists, obtaining a clarity in his lights and a uniform application of ink, difficult with the cylindrical pressure of the printing machine. Knight's part works continued to be issued regularly until the middle 1840s. 'Price 4s. 6d. in Nine Monthly Parts. 6s. bound in cloth'. *The Gallery of Portraits* also appeared in parts, monthly numbers at half a crown, widening the circulation by reducing the initial outlay. The publisher himself proceeded to travel all over England, visiting factories, concerning himself with pauper lunatics, mechanics' institutes and providing cheap suppers for poor scholars near the British Museum. He was foremost in pressing for the repeal of duty on almanacks, but strangely enough against the similar lifting of stamp duty on newspapers, the signal for a mammoth illustrated press. With the unexpected success of *The Penny Magazine,* Knight proudly laid before the public details of his distribution, the agents in the provinces, the booksellers collecting their profits direct from him, the ease of communication being a sign of civilization. Knight's exertions were not without their admirers from abroad. Frederick Von Raumer, visiting England in 1835, went to see the steam presses of *The Penny Magazine* at Lambeth and published an account of his guided tour. 'I learned many curious details,' he writes, 'for instance, how the single types are formed into stereotype plates: how plaster-casts are taken from the blocks of woodcuts, lead and antimony again cast into these matrices, and thus plates produced, which are used as substitutes for the blocks.'[7] Like Knight's, Von Raumer's view of illustrated books was clearly instruction rather than delight, but it was not coincidence that a German should be visiting the works for Knight claimed in 1836 to be supplying blocks to 'Germany, France, Holland, Livonia, Bohemia, Italy, the Ionian Islands, Sweden, Spanish America, the Brazils'.[8] Nevertheless something bigger was round the corner, the early 1830s were still after all, the era of the stage-coach.

The energetic Knight was not without his imitators; the Literature and Education Committee of the Society For Promoting Christian Knowledge were hard on his heels when in 1832 they published *The Saturday Magazine.* This was nearer to the earlier Knight schemes, except that it had a more distinctly religious nature, woodcuts of abbeys and churches and the history of saints. Other items included articles on plant growth, foreign lands, the manufacture of glass, Ancient Egypt, silk worms and the lives of famous painters, among them Rembrandt, Dürer and Richard Wilson. The woodcuts are often clearer than Knight's earlier work and those of buildings have a sort of obstinate chunky charm which excuses their shortcomings in accuracy. No reader confronted with a 'View of Jerusalem' in September 1833, would have any doubt what they were looking at! This could not have been said a decade earlier, but even *The Mirror* was now producing respectable views with passable figures. The run of *The Saturday Magazine,* which the writer has examined was from Woburn Abbey. It is hardly conceivable that the Duke of Bedford would have subscribed to it for himself and it seems likely that this cheap penny illustrated journal was reaching its right readership here in the library of the servants' hall.

Some of the earlier illustrated magazines had a similarity to the broadsheets, printed on poor paper and in small format, but idealists like Knight and the Chambers brothers made one mistake. Their uplifting penny papers contained no stories, nothing sensational and hardly any bones that the ordinary man could glamourise and romanticise with his lively imagination. The ballads with titles like 'The Taylor's Courtship', 'Death and The Lady' or 'The Fatherless Captain or Betray'd Virgin' were replaced with scenes of alpine villages and erudite articles on crabs! The restless and spontaneous world of the chapman, where every murder or public execution or scandal brought its fresh bundle of ballads, had not found a counterpart in the press. In the next ten years their vibrant, satirical and often bawdy outpourings were to be absorbed by a more official press, channelled by the restraints of Olympian editors into areas of more acceptable public taste. The cheaper end of the market persisted until it too was overtaken by the topical themes and songs of the music hall.

At the same time as the ballad sheet was in decline, the separately issued political caricature was ceasing to exist. Charles Knight, writing of the year 1810, gives a lively account of that trade as he remembered it which reminds one of Gillray's 'Very Slippery Weather' where idlers are seen gazing at the windows of Humphrey's print shop. 'I very often found myself staring into a window, if I could possibly get a look amidst the multitude which daily crowded about the shop of "T. McLean, 26 Haymarket, where Political and Other Caricatures are daily publishing" ', thus runs the imprint of one who was the chief patron of humourists for the age who were famous before *Punch.*[9] This teeming industry, which had lasted for nearly one hundred years, was the middle and upper class answer to the street ballad. Instant political and social comment came wet from the press daily, before the hue and cry had even died down. This amazing flurry of paper, caricature answering caricature, political party countering political party through rival engravers, the asperity and venom of faction bitten in to every line of print, acts like a daily diary of the reigns of George III and George IV. It bred several generations of rich artists, and in the

Cruikshanks, a whole dynasty of political caricaturists, Gillray at their head, but including Rowlandson, Newton, G.M. Woodward, William Heath and many others. The public were brought into direct touch with this work at such places as S.W. Fores Caricatura Exhibition Rooms, 3 Piccadilly 'the completest Collection in Kingdon, Admit 1s' where 'Folios of Caricatures' were 'lent out for the Evening'.[10] The approach of these artists was close to journalism and filled the gap left by the absence of any visual lampooning in the daily or weekly papers.

Book illustration was undoubtedly the respectable antidote to the virulent life of the caricature. By the end of the 1820s George Cruikshank had abandoned political satire for the art of the book and the same was true of Robert Seymour. The numerous draughtsmen and political caricaturists adapted their styles and were absorbed into the new world of illustrated papers. Something of their immediacy and personality was lost when an essentially ephemeral composition was the central point of a weekly or a monthly. Confined in the straight-jacket of covers, caricature took on much of the quality of book illustration proper, greatly invigorated the latter, but lost some of its separate identity and incidentally its colour.

Before the links with the old world were completely eclipsed, a number of minor illustrated weeklies and monthlies sprang up around the political excitement generated by the Reform Bill. The most important of them was *Figaro in London,* which had quite a long run from December 1831 to August 1839 and was less radical than some of its fellows. Its editors were Gilbert à Beckett and Henry Mayhew, both afterwards associated with the founding of *Punch. Figaro's* greatest claim to fame was that its centre focus was on a full-page drawing, an encapsulated caricature so to speak, drawn by Seymour and usually the subject of the leading article. This was to be a precedent and every great Victorian periodical was to follow its lead. A series of political woodcuts in serial form appeared in the years after the Reform Bill. *The Political Drama, John Bull's Picture Gallery* and the Chartist leaders, produced numerous unstamped penny newspapers with crude and anti-monarchial cuts by the artist C.J. Grant. Knight's self-improvement campaign was said to have killed off many of the more insubstantial squibs, but old habits die hard. When Mayhew made his survey of reading habits among Manchester operatives in 1849-50, he announced: 'That species of novel, adorned with woodcuts, and published in penny weekly numbers, claims the foremost place.'[11] This 'literary garbage' as Mayhew called it was selling six thousand copies weekly whereas *Chambers Journal,* a weekly, was only selling nine hundred copies. Knight himself blamed the eventual failure of *The Penny Magazine* on another publisher, as energetic as he but not so high principalled.

Edward Lloyd, 1815-1890, was a publisher whose aims were not very far removed from profit at any price, and who claimed to give the public what it wanted. The ballad printer and the caricaturist had made much coin out of sensational crime, Pitts and Catnach were famed for their circulation of 'dying speeches' and even Cruikshank had run a series like this entitled *Mornings At Bow Street,* 1824-25. Lloyd began in September 1841 a penny weekly called *The People's Police Gazette,* which exactly catered for this market. It was filled with lurid details of famous crimes accompanied by macabre illustrations as to how they were committed. Lloyd followed this with *The Weekly Penny Miscellany* and eventually *The Penny Atlas and Weekly Register of Novel Entertainment.* The high-flying titles were intentionally misleading and Lloyd claimed spuriously to be giving the public magazines that were 'elevated and impassioned'. Needless to say, Lloyd established the respectable-sounding *Lloyd's Weekly London Newspaper* in 1842 and died in 1890 as the proprietor of *The Daily Chronicle,* a sort of Victorian patriarch! It is curious however that the two great giants of the new illustrated era, discussed at length later, were to be founded on the basis of radical caricaturing and criminal reporting. Another magazine with less lofty ambitions to educate was *The Illuminated Magazine,* 1845, edited by Douglas Jerrold. Its contents and its illustrations were a mixture of the serious and the humourous; its illuminated frontispiece in two colours was an introduction to a diet of ballads, book reviews, instruction on the fine arts and a description of Birmingham. Kenny Meadows contributed spidery figure subjects and both Leech and H.G. Hine added their talent to its pages, but the fear of stamp duty prevented it from being anything like a newspaper, even in satirical drawings. A little later on we come to *The Illustrated Magazine of Art,* a Cassell publication, with numerous items on industry and art, that twin-headed Victorian goddess worshipped by the reformers. *The Illustrated London Magazine,* edited by R.B. Knowles had a strong visual side including the work of 'Phiz', John Gilbert, Cuthbert Bede, W. McConnell and A.S. Henning, but both of these magazines date from the early 1850s, a little ahead of our period. Others with Knight's missionary zeal were the Scottish Chambers brothers, Robert and William who founded *Chambers Journal* in that same *annus mirabilis,* 1832, and *The Miscellany,* 1848, and *Repository,* 1852. Chambers' moralizing gave way sometimes to woodcut illustrations, giving the magazine a more popular appeal.

The second reason for the great vitality in the illustrated press of the 1830s and 1840s was its rich inheritance from the eighteenth century. The educationalists and the engineers were providing the aims and the means, but the man in the street was neither so gullible nor so disloyal to his past as to abandon hard worn ways of amusement over night. The 'illustrated magazines' of ordinary folk in the 1820s were not Knight's books or even Lloyd's penny dreadfuls, but the chapbooks and broadsheets that they bought at street corners, printed by the chapmen of St. Giles. This very ancient tradition of hawking songs, ballads and news at a half-penny a sheet, was having a revival under the Regency in the hands of two celebrated rivals, John Pitts and James Catnach. The trade had received a boost from the Newspaper Stamp Act of December 1819, which Knight called a 'tax on knowledge'. Ballad sheets were not affected by this and flourished among the poor who could not afford seven pence for a newspaper. Both Pitts and Catnach produced sheets with crude but often expressive woodcuts on them and Leslie Shepard in *John Pitts Ballad Printer,* 1969, quotes an early source as saying that the woodcut was half of the attraction. By the time Knight and his friends came on the scene, the street ballad was beginning to decline and the reformers made a concerted attack on it. In 1836, a Mr. E. Cowper gave evidence before a House of Commons Committee and was questioned on this subject. Amongst the leading questions or observations by the committee was this: "In fact the mechanic and the peasant in the most remote districts of the country, have now an opportunity of seeing tolerably correct outlines of form which they never could behold before?" His answer was "Exactly; and literally at the price they used to give for a song."[12]

But the Victorian poor accepted the illustrated ballad as a natural part of their background more readily than an illustrated magazine. As Victor Neuburg has pointed out in *The Victorian City,* its elements and attraction were almost those of a tabloid newspaper, it dealt with topical themes, satirised popular events, but its illustrations were not specifically topical or satirical. Printers frequently introduced woodcuts that had no bearing on the text, a trick which Vizetelly tells us was to find its way into early magazines. Although the sheets dealt with religious, commercial, free-thinking, political and temperance topics, they were carefully generalised to appeal to the largest sale. 'The political tone of street literature, then, was muted "The great battle for freedom and reform" is clearly reformist, but by no stretch of the imagination extremist,' writes Mr. Neuburg.[13] The radical writer and caricaturist were to find a new home in the magazines after the 1830s, although their strident voice was to gradually become as tempered as those of their brother ballad mongers.

# Punch

*P*unch has become so much a national institution over the years, that its origins have always been hotly debated, leading almost to open controversy at the end of the Victorian era. When M.H. Spielmann sat down to write his monumental *The History of Punch* in 1895, the squabbling was at its height. 'It is not that his (Mr. Punch's) parentage has been lost to history in a discreet and charitable silence,' he wrote, 'on the contrary, it is rather that that honour has been claimed by over-many, covetous of the distinction.'[14] Spielmann is referring to the various families of the à Beckets, Jerrolds, Lasts and Landells who considered it to be their child and were saying so vociferously in the 1890s.

One of the clearest accounts of this complex business is given in R.G.G. Price's *A History of Punch,* 1957, and this summary is based on his conclusions. In late 1840 or early 1841, Joseph Last, the printer, and Ebenezer Landells, the engraver, proposed to start a periodical called *The Cosmorama.* Henry Mayhew, formerly of *Figaro in London* fame was introduced and he prepared a dummy, based on Phillipon's French paper and an abortive effort of his own called *Cupid.* Landells is believed to have had the first idea for the new paper, but Last claimed to have introduced Landells into the scheme and the Jerrolds maintained that the title and style of the magazine were based on Douglas Jerrold's *Punch in London.* Simultaneously, Mark Lemon, whose mother was licensee of the Shakespeare's Head in Wych Street, was attempting to start a weekly called *Pen and Palette.* The two projects came together and the name 'Punch', evolved from the beverage rather than the puppet, was finally agreed on when Douglas Jerrold relinquished his prior claim to the name. At this point a document was drawn up with a solicitor which described it as 'a new work of wit and whim, embellished with cuts and caricatures, to be called *Punch* or *The London Charivari*'. The printer and engraver were each to have a one third share and the three editors, Henry Mayhew, Mark Lemon and Stirling Coyne, the remaining share; Jerrold was to be the principal contributor.

*Below and at heading: Original drawing and wood engraving for* Punch's Almanack, *1849.*

The first months were not noticeably successful and three changes were made in the printers. The last printers, Bradbury and Evans were persuaded to buy the editors' share, Landells amid much bad blood sold his, and by the end of 1842, Bradbury and Evans were both printers and owners of *Punch*. It is significant that Bradbury's put their distribution into the hands of W.S. Orr and Co. from the beginning, the same firm that were agents for Chambers' magazines and presumably owners of lists of the better class of readership. Under the new regime Mark Lemon was sole Editor and Mayhew and Gilbert à Beckett wrote from time to time, the magazine settling down after its birth pangs to a period of unclouded success.

Those early numbers of *Punch,* witty and spontaneous though they are, leave an awful lot to be desired on the visual side. 'This Guffawgraph is intended to form a refuge for destitute wit,' reads the opening notice, 'an asylum for the thousands of orphan jokes — the superannuated Joe Millers — the millions of perishing puns, which are wandering about without so much as a shelf to rest upon!' Further facetious comments follow, but nowhere is there any reference to the illustrations and under 'Fine Arts' only to art criticism. The most striking features of the early pages are the bushels of tiny woodcuts, some of them in silhouette and known as 'blackies' which decorate the columns of the text. These were the work of William Newman who had worked for *Figaro in London,* 1841-49, and whose comic cuts were similar to the punning ones in Tom Hood's *Comic Annuals.* 'Returned by a Large Majority' showing a man kicked down the stairs by many boots or 'Real Irish Butter', a Pat with a shelalagh being attacked by a goat. All very simple stuff but at least providing continuity and better drawn than the main print of each issue by A.S. Henning. This artist took a social or political theme for his 'Pencillings' as they were called 'Candidates Under Different Phases' for example or 'Hercules Tearing Theseus From The Rock' or 'The Evening Party', all extremely weak in invention and drawing. Regrettably, *Pencilling* No. 4, 'Foreign Affairs', the first contribution of John Leech, is scarcely better. It was delivered so late that the artist was not asked again for a long time; Landells' hustle with the engraving may therefore account for its indifferent quality.

*Punch* is also responsible for having fathered the word 'cartoon' on satirical prints. In 1843, it published a series of mock entries for the mural decoration competition then taking place for the new Houses of Parliament. These replaced the usual 'Pencillings' and on 15 July 1843 appeared under the technical name for projected mural work 'cartoon'. This name gradually replaced 'Pencillings' and became the established term in Victorian England for the 'big cut' in a magazine.[15] Cartoon was never used in the nineteenth century as it popularly is now to describe almost any comic drawing.

The position of the artists on the paper was very anomalous to begin with. Lemon was out of his depth with artists, did not understand them and kept them quite separate from the writers who were his cronies. The illustrator worked with the text and there was no such thing as an individual joke illustration, there was indeed no artist strong enough had they been considered. Lemon eventually made some attempt to get acquainted with artists and enrolled Kenny Meadows, A.S. Henning's brother-in-law, for a series of cartoons up to 1844 and to illustrate 'Punch's Letters to His Son'. The young Birkett Foster began to contribute initial letters in 1841-3 and these little pieces of decoration, subtle and beautiful in execution, are as good a sign as any that *Punch's* draughtsmanship was speedily improving. Alfred Crowquill was recruited briefly, 'Phiz' joined the team but left when it was felt that *Punch* could not support two stars of the calibre of Leech and himself. W.M. Thackeray's influence on *Punch* was mostly literary, but scattered throughout the early numbers are his own contributions illustrated by himself in his inimitable untidy hand, signed by a pair of spectacles. One could mention 'Jeames's Diary' in 1845, 'The Snobs of England', 1846-47, 'Punch's Prize Novelists', 1847, as well as occasional cuts for Gilbert à Beckett or Percival

"My little friend Grildrig you have made a most admirable
panegyric upon yourself and Country but from what I can
gather from your own relation & the answers I have with
much pains wring'd & extorted from you, I cannot but conclude you to be one of the most pernicious little odious
reptiles that nature ever sufferd to crawl upon the surface
of the Earth —

The KING of BROBDINGNAG and GULLIVER

Vide Swift's Gulliver Voyage to Brobdingnag

Left: Plate V
JAMES GILLRAY
1757-1815
'The King of Brobdingnag
and Gulliver.' Political
caricature issued in
July 1803. Hand-coloured
engraving

Below: Plate VI
WILLIAM HEATH
'Paul Pry', 1795-1840
'Where Are You Going My
Pretty Maid?' Hand-
coloured engraving. c.1825

WHERE ARE YOU GOING MY PRETTY MAID

Leigh's writings, a grand total of three hundred and eighty.[16]

The constituents of early *Punch* were therefore a strange admixture of the old and the new as represented by the talented but very different men who ran it. Gathered together were the same strands discussed earlier in the chapter, that had come together in the crucible of the 1830s; a strong tradition of merciless caricaturing, an anti-monarchial vitality from the ballads and broadsheets, a Hogarthian chauvinism, a tremendous sympathy for the under-dog and a deep-seated but fair radicalism. Mark Lemon's connections with the stage, William Newman's coarseness and Albert Smith's racy writing numbered them among the old school of satirical journalism. Thackeray and Gilbert à Beckett in writing and Leech and Richard Doyle, when they joined, in drawing, represented a less savage and more light-hearted comment on the world around them. *Punch* was most modern, most sharply defined from the humours of the past when it took up the banner of middle-class life, depicted domestic scenes and involved 'the fair sex' increasingly in its pages. In the early issues the 'Pencillings' had been succeeded for a short time by 'Domestic Miseries', a clear inheritance from Heath and Alken but which R.G.G. Price suggests rightly are 'probably the ancestors of the independent joke drawing'.[17] The *Punch* men were most original where they worked as a team, bringing a precise and almost individual voice to its views, and probably thereby excluding artists like Cruikshank from its pages. This is most plainly seen in the *Punch* dinners on Wednesday nights, where members of the salaried staff met with the proprietor and printers round 'The Table' and decided on the big political cartoon for the ensuing week. These working meals, which Thackeray immortalised in his song of 'The Mahogany Tree', were lively, witty and punnish affairs, more boyish than business-like, but they worked because they brought authors and artists together and generated a feeling of mutual trust.

*Punch* had the great advantage over other magazines that it could appear to see things through the eyes of 'Mr Punch' himself. A point of view developed so personally that people could identify with *his* views and join *his* club, membership being the annual subscription to the magazine. Increasingly *Punch's* butts, pet aversions and recurring topics of satire became those people who were not members!

Thackeray was anxious from the start that the magazine should disassociate itself from tavern-shop wit and bumptiousness; Jerrold writing to Dickens in 1846 said: 'I am convinced that the world will get tired (at least I hope so) of this eternal guffaw at all things.'[18] If on the surface it appeared merely humorous, under-lying this was a strong vein of criticism. Both Henry Mayhew and Douglas Jerrold could be described as radical in some of their views but as Price says the generosity that accompanied Jerrold's radicalism was 'love of the ill-treated, not hatred of the powerful . . .'[19] It is all the same rather surprising to find in the early copies of the paper, articles and drawings attacking the Prince Consort, and the Crystal Palace, as well as more popular targets like Prince Louis Napoleon. The Queen came under some scrutiny, simply for being the wife of the Prince Consort and there were always references to the growing Royal Nursery! Spielmann writing in 1895 is at great pains to conceal this at a period when the Queen was at the height of her popularity. 'Towards the Queen herself,' he writes, '*Punch* has shown unswerving chivalry and reverence, even during the shouting days when democracy was more noisily republican than it is today.'[20] This is only half-true, for the disparity revealed in Disraeli's *Two Nations* was deeply felt by the first *Punch* men and was brought out in one of Richard Doyle's first cartoons for the paper in August 1844. 'Prince Albert's Bee Hives' provided a not very flattering cartoon of the Queen and an equally stony one of her consort. Doyle's composition takes as its theme the installations of new beehives at Windsor Castle by that ingenious and experimenting German Prince. The Royal Pair gaze down enchantedly on pretty, bell-shaped beehives, one of which is totally transparent for our benefit. Inside, tiny

*Figure 23. 'Prince Albert's Bee Hives' by Richard Doyle.*

busy figures, typically Doyleish, carry loads, scythe grass, hammer iron and, revealingly, work as artists. The caption, quoted from a newspaper report, reads 'These Hives are so constructed that the HONEY may be removed without DESTROYING THE BEES' (Figure 23).

*Punch's* outspoken views on foreign despotism resulted in it being banned in both France and Austria at various times and it was loud in its condemnation of sweat shops, the pollution of the Thames and the replanning of London that left many poor people homeless.

It had its rivalry during the first years from *The Squib, The Great Gun, Joe Miller The Younger* and later from *The Man in The Moon, The Comic Times, The Puppet Show* and *Diogenes. The Man in The Moon* was edited by Albert Smith, the writer who had been dropped from *Punch,* and was extremely hostile, although it only lasted for twenty-eight issues. In the 1860s and '70s it was to find competition in newer magazines built exactly like it, *Fun,* 1861, *Judy,* 1867, *Punch and Judy,* 1869, *Will o' The Wisp,* 1868, *Moonshine,* etc., but with the exception of a few brilliant cartoonists like Matt Morgan and John Proctor, their drawings never equalled those of the original.

The first great rise in circulation followed the publication of *Punch's Almanac,* when sales rose from 6,000 to 90,000 in the course of a week. There had been a great boom in the publication of almanacs since the repeal of Stamp Duty on them in 1834 and *Punch's* humorous one was a logical successor, though more packed with incident and anecdote than most. Highly decorative pages, calendaring the months, were contributed by H.G. Hine and Kenny Meadows and among the small print of the almanac's saints days, university terms and law sittings, sprang up puns and witticisms from the jolly dogs of the 'guffawgraph'. The drawings were much more full-blooded than in the main magazine, the head-pieces take on the substantiality of complete drawings and in the fourth and fifth almanacs in the hands of Leech and Doyle the metamorphosis of 'cut' to illustration is entire. *The Almanac* for 1848 was prepared in a luxurious coloured edition, price five shillings, an uncoloured version being half a crown, some indication that the artist was now on an equal footing with Grub Street.[21]

From 1843 to 1881, *Punch* published a *Pocket Book,* in many ways the counterpart to the almanac, but more useful in having twenty-five pages of diary in the centre, space for cash accounts, a pouch and a pencil. The whole book was neatly finished in red, blue or black leather and fastened with a tongue. This was supposed to reach a wider audience than the weekly *Punch* readership, part of its attraction being the folding coloured frontispieces by John Leech (Figure 24) and later by Charles Keene and Linley Sambourne as well as the vignettes by Tenniel and others. In some ways these books were an awkward compromise of fact and fancy but they remain, when they can be found, one of the most delightful pieces of *Punch* ephemera.

The career of John Leech, 1817-1864, is as much synonymous with early *Punch* as John Tenniel's and Richard Doyle's and this triumvirate must be considered individually. Leech's contributions to the magazine from 1841 to 1864 largely bridge the gap between

*Figure 24. Punch's Pocket Book For 1857, John Leech.*

Georgian and Victorian illustration and humour. One consciously avoids calling him a caricaturist, for though it would be unthinkable for a Regency artist to satirical papers to be anything else, Leech's work ushered in a more generous spirit of muted criticism. He can probably, as Ruskin wrote, be credited with having introduced this whole new genre of domestic satire which depended neither on verbal squibs or exaggerated drawing but on a greater naturalism of wit and draughtsmanship. Ruskin in *The Art of England* refers to that 'great softening of the English mind' which under Leech led to 'simplicity' and 'aerial space' in British humorous art.[22] This may not be so obvious to us today, but it was apparent to contemporaries.

John Leech was a Londoner and born in 1817, so that he came artistically of age in the 1830s, when illustration was uncertain in both aim and method. He had very little training, but did master etching, learnt drawing from the block from Orrin Smith and worked with lithography, one of the few English humorous artist to do so. His first published works, *Etchings and Sketchings* of 1835, were in lithography but he soon abandoned this for etching and the wood which were being used for books and magazines. All through his life he continued to contribute etched plates to more finished publications, but in many cases they lack the spontaneous touch which practice and speed had brought to his magazine work. It was above all the drawing on the wood that became Leech's natural medium of expression and it was perhaps that lack of academic training that left him with such a brilliantly sketchy effect. While his contemporaries produced harder and harder engravings, Leech danced rings round them with his rapidly drawn landscapes, seascapes and interiors, producing by a few lines of shadow or the skilful hatching of a hat or bonnet that wit and laughter which are free and immeasurable. Ruskin's admiration for the work was particularly directed to the flexibility and lightness of Leech's line, its condensation of elements, time, energy, thought and expression into a tiny area of paper and a few potent pencillings. Ruskin adds that the slightness of the sketches are their greatest strength because they have become slight, not through carelessness or cutting corners, but through studied realisation of the subject.[23] It is perhaps fortunate that most of the surviving drawings collected today have exactly that quality about them; they are preliminary jottings, rapid pencil sketches or a few more finished watercolours, the essence of Leech's talent. For the mid-Victorians they were unmechanical, individual and playful and if the subjects were undemanding, Ruskin could at least point out that this did not affect the purity of draughtsmanship which was like the silver points of the sixteenth century. The familiar 'JL' under a drawing or the sign manual of a leech in a bottle became almost the stamp of approval for bourgeois Victorian England.

Leech's art was like Leech himself. 'He was himself a typical middle-class British householder,' Spielmann writes, 'who liked to have everything nice and neat about him, including the pretty amiable, zealous h-less maidservant in nice white apron and clean print dress.'[24] So that his world was not one where vice or hypocrisy were viciously exposed but where the follies of the ordinary domestic round got a decent airing. We find the master and mistress of this perfect household in trouble with burst water pipes after a thaw or facing an invasion of cockroaches in their kitchen; they are found entertaining their friends in the crinoline and swallow-tail of the period or déshabillé whispering sweet nothings to their own looking-glasses. They interview their servants for us, have consultations with sweeps and dustmen, they are barricaded in their houses by builders, tried to death by casual labourers, bored to death by barbers and horrified by nursemaids. We find them on trains, shut into claustrophobic little compartments, on steamboats feeling sick, rowing on the river, hunting and shooting, negotiating the discomforts of the bathing machine or the glories of the exhibition and the aquarium. At their most tranquil they gather round the family dinner table, the children on their high chairs, the parents ranged at either end, family portraits, pier glasses and ornaments surrounding them, while the master complains of 'cold mutton again' and the mistress mumbles not for the first time of her little 'housekeeping'. Leech, the affable, lovable *pater familias* puts a great deal of friendly chiding into these scenes, they are drawn with absolute familiarity and sympathy for the situations and people. Some of his themes have become fragments of history, but others like the climate, the exaggeration of sportsmen, the hen-pecked husband, the effects of cheap furniture, the temperamental artist, are still with us. Unlike many later Victorian satirists, one does not have to know a great deal about social or political history to appreciate his humour and respond to his pencil; his sketches are effervescently funny. The spectrum of nineteenth century life, provided by these hundreds of drawings in the first twenty years of *Punch*, is truly amazing; in sheer diversity of subject from political cartooning to social cuts and characterisations, novel illustrations, tiny thumbnail sketches, there is nobody to equal Leech. His statesmen and aristocrats may not be as convincing as his butcher boys, army sergeants, huntsmen and middle class matrons, because he did not know them so well, but all are gathered into his stiuations by his quick eye and deft line. Unlike his colleague Keene, Leech's wit was usually his own.

Leech did not slavishly adhere to any method of work and oddly enough was regarded as unreliable and unpunctual in business. He never used models but made notes of landscape backgrounds, buildings and props that might be adapted to a particular event. The sands at Ramsgate were utilised on one occasion for a joke and his travels round the country gave him other vital details. The artist had taken up hunting and frequently went out with the Puckeridge Hunt so that his numerous subjects concerned with the pack, the huntsmen and the followers, all have Hertfordshire as the basis for their backgrounds. His friendship with John Everett Millais had led him to undertake shooting holidays in Scotland where he found the perfect scenery for the grouse-shooting, salmon-fishing and deer-stalking exploits of his comic hero Mr. Briggs. His power of observation was acute. Frith, his chatty biographer, cites the action of a young man putting on his coat in 'The Derby Epidemic', a movement lasting a fraction of a second and yet perfectly captured. All through his graphic work there are examples of this spontaneous memorising, the man-about-town with one foot on a chair, the baby with something stuck in its mouth, the inflections from the way a cigar is smoked. In the same way he has the genius to hide a figure behind a newspaper and tell everything about him from the set of his ankles! If Leech had relied less on this memory and more on strict accuracy, it is unlikely that so many fascinating stereotypes would have evolved in his work. This was not the derogatory stereotype of infinite repetition, but the inventive and essential signal of this or that type of behaviour. Leech expanded his originality by varying

Figure 25. The Gypsy's Prophecy by John Leech, 1860.

Figure 26. The Gypsy's Prophecy by John Leech, wood engraving.

his own schemes, Doyle by extending his into fantasy.

The most famous of Leech's creations was the Leech young lady, as famous in her own time as America's Gibson Girl. Modelled on his wife, whom he had romantically seen in the street, followed and married, she pouts and simpers through hundreds of *Punch* pictures, a ringleted, rather bird-like creature with sharp nose, dark hair and sparkling lustrefull eyes. Sometimes she is the daughter of the house, sometimes she is the maid-servant taken advantage of by a guest or caught trying on her mistress's bonnet. She is seen in droves at balls, at the flower show or riding in Rotten Row, embroidering by the fireside or warming her very small feet on the fender. She is often the foil to Leech's more exaggerated creations, the foppish army officer, the precocious juvenile, elderly curmudgeons and cockney hunting gentlemen and even appears in the Surtees novels as the fair enchantress of Mr. Jorrocks or the seeker of a fortune teller in *Plain or Ringlets,* 1860. Figures 25 and 26, a drawing and an engraving, give one an opportunity of seeing Leech at work. The sketch of the Gypsy has been prepared by the artist in pencil and ink with a light wash here and there, for the steel engraver. On this first draft, Leech has pencilled in his instructions to 'Bite up with this vigorously' and indicated the positions. He has also requested a 'hard paper proof' so that he can add the final colour as an example to the hand painters. The result as it appears, the portion on the left of the plate duely treated and the distance clarified, shows the close co-operation then existing between artist and engraver.

The artist's other popular creations which the public found amusing through familiarity rather than novelty were 'The Rising Generation' series and 'Flunkeiana'. In the first, Leech hit that chord in the Victorians that so admired the diminutive, miniature objects, General Tom Thumb, bright children dressed like tiny adults. The usual format of these is for the miniscule infant in studied adult pose to refer to 'a jeuced fine gurl' across the room or for a creature the size and appearance of Bubbles to call for 'a toast to the ladies!' It is not a type of humour that has survived and is much funnier in Leech's repertoire when it emerges as the pretension of the undergraduate who wishes to cut a dash or the ensign working up his moustachios.

Flunkeiana, the counterpart of Servantgalism, was a chronicle of the thoughts and aspirations of cockaded metropolitan 'James's' and 'Thomas's' who waited at a thousand London tables and polished silver in a thousand London pantries. Leech's pencil often flew round at the expense of these powdered exotics complaining of too much 'fizzical exercise' or enquiring from their employers whether they were engaged for 'use or ornament'. The

London flunkey at Brighton asked if he likes the seaside, replies to the French maid 'Par Bokhoo Mamzelle' and his friend visiting Suffolk says 'I don't like your champagne, its all Gewsberry!'

With Leech's illustrations collected in his own lifetime into volumes of *Life and Character*,[25] it is easy to assume that he had no more serious comments to make than these. But he was a cartoonist of considerable ability and some of the best political work of early *Punch* came from him. 'The Agricultural Question Settled', 1845, 'The Poor Man's Friend' of the same year and 'The Irish Cinderella and Her Haughty Sisters' 1846, spring to mind. Nor was he above satirising the throne in 1845, when the Railway mania and subsequent crash had the Queen asking Prince Albert 'Tell me, oh tell me, dearest Albert, have *you* any Railway Shares?' Leech's portraits were not the careful likenesses of the photographic age, where everyone knows the features of the great, but good token images explicable by uniform or situation. He successfully used the theme of the school-mistress and the naughty boy to project the Queen and her ministers — Disraeli and Palmerston and even Sir Joseph Paxton fell into this rôle. One of his most celebrated full-page subjects was 'General Février Turned Traitor' of 1855, the gaunt skeletal figure of a Russian winter placing his boney hand on the form of the dying Tsar Nicholas, chief protagonist of the Crimean War. He shared with Doyle and Tenniel a favourite ploy of putting the politicians into Dickensian rôles, Trotty Veck, Mrs. Gamp and Fagin, the last a brilliant substitution of the scraggy thief for the corpulent form of Louis-Phillippe. Leech's own ideals were simple and English, he tended to be chauvinist and anti-Papist, show sympathy but not understanding for the poor and most of the causes he took up lacked objectivity. He developed an obsession against street musicians, was rather anti-semitic and much angered by unpatriotic loafers during the Crimean War. His greatest achievement was probably in the war against sweated labour and the famous 'Cheap Clothing' cut of 1845, where skeletons darn away under the eye of a prosperous proprietor, was a powerful image for change. However the full page was a rather large area to cover for Leech's decidedly domestic talent and the cartoons lack the impact of the smaller drawings.

As can be seen, Leech owed a great deal to the Regency despite his new approach. His famous 'characters' of 'Tom Noddy' and 'Mr. Briggs', instantly recognisable by the tall hat and large cigar of the one and the puffy indignant face of the other, are the descendants of Seymour's comic sportsmen and Alken's albums. But however many times Noddy loses his horse or Briggs his hat, there is a delight in their indomitable spirit totally lacking in Georgian savagery. Leech openly used Cruikshank's subjects of an earlier generation for his political cartooning, for example 'Where Ignorance is Bliss', 1846, smartened, brought up to date and reissued.

He was probably closest to the earlier men in his caricaturing of fashion, which despite growing conformity still showed excesses of display in the 1850s. The crinoline vogue, the cravat and collar mania, bloomerism, the great bonnet question, Dundreary whiskers, all come under the magnifying glass of his friendly satire. As good an example as any and a gallery of Leech's female beauties into the bargain appears in *Punch's Pocket Book.* Entitled 'Dressing For the Ball in 1857' (Figure 24), it shows a harem of soft-cheeked, soft-eyed girls waiting patiently for a maid to pump up the monstrous form of a crinoline like a glorified inner tube, a delightful combination of delicate penwork and modern fantasy! His belles and his fops, their skirts billowing out to impossible size, their shirts astonishing all beholders, are only one step away from the fantasies of Heath and Cruikshank, but that step is all important.

It is sad to think that as *Punch* veered away under Thackeray from Bloomsbury to Belgravia, Leech became more conservative, more jingoistic and more determined to be a gentleman. Like so many illustrators, his profession had made his social position a rather ambiguous one and social standing was everything in Victorian England. Neither journalist nor artist, neither fish nor flesh, Leech adopted the life style of a country gentleman, hunting, fishing and attending parties, winning the sort of acceptance that his drawings alone could never gain him. As John Gilbert hid his insecurity behind piles of money, Leech and many others hid it behind respectability. It is rather tragic to find Leech at the end of his life in 1862, expending time and energy on pro-

Figure 27. The Knight and Jotun by Richard Doyle.

ducing oil paintings from his *Punch* drawings, hoping for the designation of 'painter'.[26] Tenniel, the mural painter of histories was to be remembered for *Alice,* Leech who fancied himself an oil painter, for the fat boys, flunkies and squires of *Punch.*

The second of the great triumvirate of early *Punch* was Richard Doyle. Doyle was the son of John Doyle 'HB' and came from a family of talented journalists and caricaturists, two of his brothers also having their drawings published. He was snapped up by Mark Lemon when hardly out of his teens, taught drawing on wood by Swain and was contributing his first border designs to Tom Hood's famous 'Song of the Shirt' on 16 December 1843. *Punch* was established in its drawings of political and social satire, Richard Doyle provided that other essential ingredient, fantasy. The legendary and fantastic were too integral a part of the Victorian scene in other literature to be excluded from a humorous magazine, and with Doyle's pen the allegories became whimsically funny, mythology impish and even the half sinister world of fairies and elves took on a wayward charm of its own (Figure 27). His most noteworthy successes in this line were the *Punch* covers, the first designed in January 1844, including a mock 'Triumph of Bacchus' and a border of tumbling figures, the second, a modification made in January 1849 and used for over a hundred years. Doyle really has two styles of drawing, the first used on the covers with such decorative effect was primarily ornamental, intricate and small of scale, superb groupings of tiny figures drawn with a sharp pen (Figure 28). The other method was

*Figure 28.* Punch *cover.*

developed later, a linear style of etched outlines, an obvious inheritance from Flaxman and the German classicists, where the same crowded figures were disposed like a frieze without shade or hatching. The artist used his more piquant decorator's style for the lovely initial letters, vignettes and head and tail pieces that are a feature of the 1840s. A recurring theme is the dream, either of Mr. Punch or some other character, who snoozes contentedly while the passions of past or present frolic above him in the air. The idea was well tried in the early Victorian period, 'Phiz' uses it in *Martin Chuzzlewhit* by Charles Dickens, 1844, and for the frontispiece to *Dombey and Son,* 1848. Doyle uses it again for Dickens in *The Chimes,* 1845, and *The Cricket On The Hearth,* 1846. Fairy illustration once established in *Punch,* remained a favourite until the turn of the century but usually in the Christmas issues. Doyle began this tradition in its pages which lasted until the beautiful drawings of Thomas Maybank in the 1900s and to Rackham and beyond in books.

Doyle's other great triumph was with his etched outlines. He used this medium for his long-running series of 'Manners and Customs of Ye Englyshe', later expanded in book form as *'Mr Pips Hys Diary',* 1849. Doyle took as his starting point contemporary society as viewed through a medieval drawing or tapestry, scenes showing among other things 'Ye Fashionable Worlde Takynge Its Exercyse In Hyde Parke' and 'Ye National Sporte!!! of Steeple Chasynge'. Doyle's drawings were a development from Gilbert à Beckett's comic histories which Leech had illustrated from the 1830s. The humour may seem a trifle laboured now, but it caught on and became the first in a long series of humours of history, leading down to the 'Prehistoric Peeps' of E.T. Reed and the early British lunacies of George Morrow.

It was perhaps ironic that one of Doyle's 'Manners and Customs' should have shown 'A Prospect of Exeter Hall Showynge A Christian Gentleman Denouncynge Ye Pope'. This is a much harsher picture than the others and refers to the anti-Catholic rumpus of 1849-50 when Rome established bishops in this country. The anti-papal stand taken by *Punch* was too much for the gently and deeply Catholic Doyle, who resigned his position in 1850. He devoted the rest of his life to book illustration and in particular to books for children to which his talent was ideally suited.

If Leech's drawings represented the domestic side of Victorian Britain, Tenniel's pointed to her political and imperial role in the grandly classical guises of John Bull, Mrs. Bull, The British Lion, Father Thames and Brittania, seen week by week from 1862 in the principal cartoon. Like so many *Punch* artists, Tenniel's work was sought out by Mark Lemon for its range rather than its purity Doyle had left the 'Table' at an awkward moment, the Almanac and *The Pocket Book* for 1851 were uncompleted and there was no decorative artist on the staff to tackle the ornaments, initial letters and frontispieces which were the entrée of *Punch* to the drawing-room. John Tenniel, 1820-1914, was a serious artist, whose training at the RA Schools had left him greatly influenced by Flaxman and greatly enamoured of German draughtsmanship in the works of Menzel and Rethel. Lemon had seen his illustrations for the Rev. Thomas James's *Aesop,* published by Murray in 1848 and evidently been impressed, but it was certainly a new departure to have a representative of high art on his team, Gilbert having been dropped years before.

Tenniel's first work was the frontispiece to the second half-yearly volume for 1850, but he very soon graduated from initials and frontispieces to 'socials' and cartoons, taking over from John Leech, that onerous weekly job to which the latter was somewhat unsuited. But Tenniel was one of the new breed of political cartoonists, as far removed from Gillray or Cruikshank as possible. 'As for political opinions,' he told Spielmann, 'I have none; at least, if I have my own little politics, I keep them to myself, and profess only those of my paper.'[27] As the one Conservative among a Liberal editorship, Tenniel shows remarkable restraint in this, but it emerges that above all *his art* mattered more to him than the subject picked for him by the *Punch* 'Table'. Tenniel felt that professionalism should rule over strong feelings, a stoically Victorian attitude, and his drawings are always finely executed, beautifully composed and fair in content. Mercifully he could be both stern and amusing on paper. This order and exactness in his dealings with *Punch*, the cartoon commissioned on Wednesday, sketched on Thursday, finished on the block on Friday, is in marked contrast to Leech! His perfectionism extended to working with a specially prepared six-H pencil, producing silvery grey strokes of a hair's breadth thickness on the paper, possibly the finest pencil work after Maclise of the Victorian era. He was also a fanatic for smooth blocks on which to draw and Swain, the engraver, had a hard job to keep him so supplied. Tenniel himself admitted that he traced the drawing on to the block and in his excellent study of this period, Percy Muir suggests 'that most of the old hands at drawing on wood habitually provided the engraver with no more than the bare essentials of a picture leaving him to supply the trimmings.'[28] This may be true, but does not quite account for the highly finished drawings on the wood that still exist in some collections, mostly by eminent artists of the 1860s. Despite the appearance of the half tone and improved reproductive processes, Tenniel continued to draw for or on the block for *Punch* until as late as 1892. After this it was his practice to draw on the chinese-whitened surface of cardboard, which was then photographed.[29]

His lightness of touch and feathery delicacy were not characteristics which the engraver could transpose at all. Swain had to interpret Tenniel's work into a thicker black line for the printed page without losing the areas of detail or the flat areas of white which gave the sketches their Germanic crispness. Spielmann mentions that Tenniel could never open the journal himself when the print was completed, it was handed to his sister who opened it to show him! This sort of squeamishness was very general among artists, who were less well-served by engravers than Tenniel was by Swain. But there is a tremendous contrast between the drawings and the printed page in the magazine, leaving a lot to be desired. The fact that so many finished drawings do survive to show Tenniel's mastery of the pencil line is left on record by the artist himself. 'The first sketch I may, and often do complete later on as a commission,' he told Spielmann, 'Indeed, at the present time I have a huge undertaking on hand, in which I take great delight — the finishing of scores of my sketches, of which I have many hundreds.'[30]

Another feature of Tenniel's method which links him more closely to John Leech is that he, like Leech, never drew from nature, only from observation. 'I never use models or Nature for the figure, drapery, or anything else,' he recorded, 'but I have a wonderful memory of observation, not for dates, but anything I see I remember.'[31] This was true of the whole generation of book illustrators raised before 1850. As with Leech this tended to lead to repetition in placing the figures in the cartoons and what was worse a slight air of unreality about the subjects. Under his pencil, politicians tended never to age at all and in the 1890s he was still depicting the bicycles and railway trains of his middle age!

Among the two thousand cartoons contributed to *Punch* by Tenniel, are some of the most famous of the century. In 1857 after the Indian Mutiny appeared his 'The British Lion's Vengeance on The Bengal Tiger', a dramatic but direct piece of political allegory showing the artist's fine handling of animal subjects. As late as 29 March 1890 came the celebrated 'Dropping The Pilot' a powerful interpretation of Bismark's dismissal by the German Emperor, suggested to Tenniel by G.A. à Beckett. The 1860s, such a great period for illustrations generally, were a golden era for Tenniel cartoons. We have 'The National Crinoline' in February 1863, where current fashion is used to satirise national extravagance, 'The American Juggernaut', where the American North is condemned for bloodshed in the Civil War, September 1863, and 'Where's The Irish Police?' with an inert Gladstone in volunteer's dress idly watching a bloody brawl. Like Leech, Tenniel resorts to themes from

Dickens, Shakespeare and the Classics for his armour (Figure 29) and on occasion goes back to earlier painters. It is amusing to find him using Henry Fuseli's 'Nightmare', paraphrased to such advantage by Gillray, as the basis of 'London's Nightmare' in March 1866. In this case the incubus is a parish beadle crouching on a contorted feminine figure of 'London', a cry against Vestry Government in the City. As the beadle is obviously Dickens' 'Mr. Bumble', the sources for the subject are deliciously mixed; even so one speculates as to who in 1866 would have recalled the original painting by Fuseli! He also uses a contemporary image, Frank Holl's celebrated oil painting of 'Newgate; Committed For Trial' and uses it with dramatic force to illustrate a bank failure of February 1869. The figures are always in large scale, almost muscular, well-handled and with a slight suggestion of fantasy. 'My drawings are sometimes grotesque,' Tenniel is recorded as saying, 'but that is from a sense of fun and humour. Some people declare that I am no humorist, that I have no sense of fun

*Figure 29. 'The Press as Scare Monger', 1892, by Sir John Tenniel.*

at all; they deny me everything but severity, 'classicality' and dignity. Now I believe that I have a very keen sense of humour, and that my drawings are sometimes really funny!'[32] Grotesque describes his drawings perfectly, because they are usually too hard on the page to be really comic. In some such as 'Before The Tournament', an election cartoon of November 1868, the weird stiff figures in armour have a lot of the innocent child's view that comes out so clearly in the 'White Knight' and other *Alice* characters.

Tenniel's association with Lewis Carrol on these books, *Alice in Wonderland*, 1865, and *Alice Through The Looking Glass*, 1871, form one of the most chronicled author-artist partnerships of our period, the wild imagination of Carroll stretching Tenniel's powers to the limit, but in the process creating some of the greatest comic characters of all time.

## The Illustrated London News

As the 1840s dawned, there was seen to be a place for a general illustrated journal of news, current events and comment that would appeal to a wide middle-class readership. *Punch* had had a slow gestation period, but was now reaping the benefit of the literary tradition of Hogarth, the satiric tradition of Gillray and the essay tradition of Junius and others; but *Punch* unquestionably needed a 'straight man' to compliment him. The founding of *The Illustrated London News* in 1842, made it very nearly Mr Punch's twin and the two magazines, still happily with us, became the bastions of Victorian Britishness and an essential part of the mid-nineteenth century household. If *Punch's* birth was protracted, that of *The Illustrated London News* was highly coincidental, not to say bizarre.

In about 1841, Herbert Ingram, a young businessman from Nottingham, who had been trained as a printer in Boston, Lincolnshire, approached the printer Henry Vizetelly for an engraved portrait of 'Old Parr' the legendary long-lived man. This engraving was to appear in a fictitious life of the old man and help to promote Morrison's Vegetable Pills, a somewhat dubious concoction, which Ingram was then selling in the Midlands. Ingram had an instinctive feel for business and realised that the 'Old Parr' story would be a most effective enterprise if linked to some sort of medical comfort. According to Vizetelly he had 'a harmless aperient bolus' made up and marketed it among the Nottingham lace-makers as 'Parr's Life Pills', later publishing *Old Moore* in almanac form to testify to the miraculous qualities of his first product! The little piece of job-work engraving brought Ingram and Vizetelly together and, as a result, Ingram made a suggestion which Vizetelly clearly jumped at with alacrity.

Ingram told him that after a sensational trial, the Greenacre murder of 1837, he had felt that there might be a place for a popular illustrated journal full of police cases and assize hearings, but aimed at a fairly literate market. Vizetelly was very impressed by the idea and in his own words gives Ingram the credit for it. 'The suggestion of a newspaper,' he writes, 'with every number of it more or less filled with engravings, came as a sort of revelation to me, and I at once realised the vast field it opened up.'[33] There was very little love lost between Vizetelly and Ingram in later years and it is difficult to know how much of his *Memories,* dealing with subsequent meetings is to be wholly trusted. Vizetelly drew up an elaborate prospectus which went far beyond the scope of Ingram's original and rather grubby little crime magazine and, if it was entirely his own scheme, was truly remarkable. Vizetelly recalled that the new paper would include 'scenes of state ceremonial, the important political gatherings [the agitation against the Corn Laws was then at its height] and the crowd of general public events, including every class of popular amusement, which were equally susceptible of illustration.'[34] He also emphasised the ease with which portraits could be drawn for the publication since the discovery of daguerrotypes and that the inclusion of drawings from war zones, such as the Chinese and Afghan conflicts then in progress, would arouse colossal public interest. This latter point was not taken up at once, but in other respects the structure of *The Illustrated London News* was forming. Mason Jackson, who was later in the employ of the Ingram family, took quite a different view of Herbert Ingram's intentions in *The Pictorial Press,* published in 1885. Jackson makes him out to be a high-minded and generous principalled philanthropist, in the style of Charles Knight. 'Though he had not himself received the advantages of literary or artistic culture, he was able to do much in diffusing a knowledge and love of art amongst the people,' he writes.[35] This was certainly to be the case, but taking into account what we know of the shrewd Nottingham businessman and quack medicine proprietor, it is likely to have been the promotion of the magazine rather than its scope for which *he* is to be congratulated. The perfect balance of text to pictures and the happy blending of current affairs with historical or natural interest must be laid at Vizetelly's door alone.

The title of the magazine, *The Illustrated London News,* was decided almost at once; F.W.N. 'Omnibus' Bailey was appointed the first Editor with Monahan as the sub-editor and John Gilbert as chief artist. The first issue appeared on 14 May, 1842 with sixteen pages, thirty-two woodcuts, the main one showing the destruction of Hamburg by fire. Ingram's innate business sense won, the magazine was an immediate success; by its seventh number it had reached a circulation of 20,000, and within a year 66,000, rising to 100,000 in 1851. Ingram performed feats of unprecedented promotion for Victorian England. He sent eight thousand free copies showing the Enthronement of the Archbishop of Canterbury to every beneficed clergyman in the land, boosting the circulation yet again, and assuring the respectability of the paper for the next fifty years! The main difficulties were the dearth of artists who were sure enough and quick enough for this sort of work, drawing rapidly on the block and returning the finished product in a matter of hours. Ingram adopted Knight's formula of having a number of staff engravers working under a chief engraver, in this case Landells, so that much of the work was undertaken on the premises. Landells' position was really that of Art Editor, although no acknowledgement was given to this position for many years. The other problem was that those artists who were competent, the book illustrators, felt themselves to be a profession apart, did not understand the magazine and according to Vizetelly 'looked with something like disdain upon the interloper'.[36]

If Knight had had a struggle to interest the mechanics in the printed word interspersed with drawings, Ingram did not at first capture the literary public although his page openings alternated text with cuts. The Victorian mind which 'read' pictures in other contexts, found it difficult to consider news and events seriously in illustrations, the Poet Laureate included. William Wordsworth saw in the illustrated press only the pictorial world of childhood and was prompted to write a sonnet on looking at *The Illustrated London News* in 1846.

'Discourse was deemed Man's noblest attribute,
And written words the glory of his hand;
Then followed Printing with enlarged command
For thought — dominion vast and absolute
For spreading truth, and making love expand.
Now prose and verse sunk into disrepute
Must lacquey a dumb Art that best can suit
The taste of this once — intellectual Land.
A backward movement surely have we here,

From manhood — back to childhood; for the age —
Back towards caverned life's first rude career.
Avaunt this vile abuse of pictured page!
Must eyes be all in all, the tongue and ear
Nothing? Heaven keep us from a lower stage!'

It is difficult today, on leafing through the magazine of the 1840s to see what had so affronted the septuagenarian poet. We find an undoubted paper of information and record, eight pages of wood engravings to eight pages of text, and that text divided into three columns and set for the most part in thickly inked Victorian 6 point type, a most daunting prospect! The unillustrated openings might be from any serious nineteenth century paper with their one and a half pages of Parliamentary Reports, the obituaries of 'Eminent Persons Recently Deceased', a column length of leading article, 'Court and Haut Ton' and 'Foreign Intelligence'. With records of Stock Market transactions, extracts from the *London Gazette,* reports on Tattersall's, national sports, chess problems and humorous verses, Ingram and Vizetelly had proved that an illustrated paper of popular appeal, could still be a paper for the whole family. The only quarrel possible with the infant *'Illustrated* would seem to be its diversity, the textual pages so unremittingly solid, its wood engravings so surprisingly big, perhaps it was the magnitude of this contrast that upset a word-based audience.

The intention was of course that text and pictures should be closely followed together, not in isolation as might be the case with modern glossies with their long captions. One has to imagine the Victorian reader, thumb in the text page, finger on the print, minutely following the details of the picture as they are described. For most of Ingram's readers, the serial novel in parts, or magazines like *Ainsworth's Magazine,* were the natural diet, and in them close study of the illustrations was the only way to provide a continuity week by week. The text running with some rural scenes by Birket Foster, published in an early number of *The Illustrated London News,* does show how integral was this relationship.

'Each bears the aspect of the month — a sort of pictured climatology, with the natural appearances of the season, and the monthly phases of the farmer's life. Thus, in January, the ground and roofs are thickly mantled with snow, the effect of which, against the black wintry sky, and the bare bough trees, is very telling; the scene is a farmyard, where the feeding of poultry, pigs and cattle, seems to break the sleep and silence of the season; the contrast of the still and busy life is excellent. The tail-piece is a shepherd carrying one of his flock in a snowstorm. The business of February is ploughing and sowing; the rooks are building, and all nature is just astir. In March we have felling timber; in April, angling, the ferry, and harrowing; with the landscape just freshened by a shower, and the bow in the sky. May is exquisitely redolent of whitethorn, and budding boys and girls in the roads and hedges. In leafy June, we have the mowers at their work, and the heavy load of hay.'

The narrator goes on to evoke the picturesque spirit of Foster's pictures with quotes from Robert Bloomfield and Alfred Tennyson. We are informed that the writer is 'Mr Thomas Miller', who has 'evidently luxuriated in such kindred subjects; his descriptions teem with eloquent poetry and truthful nature.'[37] The reader was confronted by a map with references, rather than by an independant work of art.

So entirely new and alien to the instincts of publishers was this venture, that even the industrious Charles Knight had his doubts. It was the reporting of events rather than facts that confused Knight and brought him nearly to disbelief.

'In 1842,' he writes, 'having occasion to be in attendance at the Central Criminal Court, my curiosity was excited by an unusual spectacle — that of an artist, seated amongst the city dignitaries on the bench, diligently employed in sketching two Lascars on their trial for a capital offence. What was there so remarkable in the case, in the persons, or even in the costume of the accused, that they should be made the subject of a picture? The mystery was soon explained to me. *The Illustrated London News* had been announced for publication on the Saturday of the week in which I saw the wretched foreigners standing at the bar. I knew something about hurrying on wood engravers for *The Penny Magazine,* but a Newspaper was an essentially different affair. How, I thought, could artists and journalists so work concurrently that the news and the appropriate illustrations should both be fresh? How could such things be managed with any approach to fidelity of representation, unless all the essential characteristics of a newspaper were sacrificed in the attempt to render it pictorial? I fancied that this rash experiment would be a failure. It proved to be such a success as could only be ensured by resolute and persevering struggles against natural difficulties.'[38]

Ingram was already employing a few artists for the paper but the roving 'Special Artist', dealt with in a later chapter was still a thing of the future. Vizetelly notes how primitive were the arrangements for collecting material: 'the system pursued with the majority of engravings of current events — foreign, provincial, and even metropolitan when these transpired unexpectedly — was to scan the morning papers carefully, cut out such paragraphs as furnished good subjects for illustration, and send them with the necessary boxwood blocks to the draughtsman employed.'[39]

The earlier volumes were certainly stronger in their decorative and allegorical pages, than in their news reporting. It was a considerable triumph for Ingram to have enlisted William Harvey, the foremost book illustrator of the period, for the magazine, and he was given full pages with titles such as 'Bringing in The New Year', 'Autumn' or 'To The Memory of O'Connell' where his talent for pathos or legend filled the space with weeping angels, dancing sprites or maidens with sheaves. John Gilbert was the other draughtsman in the classical mould who found a comfortable niche in these pages. He had begun life on *Punch*, designing the frontispiece to its second volume in 1842, which also served as its wrapper, but his statuesque men and beautiful women planting laurel leaves on their brows had not one ounce of humour in them. After Douglas Jerrold's famous witticism about him 'We don't want Rubens on *Punch!*', Gilbert migrated to the Ingram stable very readily.

Gilbert's popular appeal cannot be overestimated. After little formal training except some study with George Lance, he had emerged as a magisterial draughtsman, the doyen of the Christmas book market and the best-loved illustrator of the English poets. He was exactly what the Victorians respected, a history painter who happened to illustrate books rather than a book illustrator who struggled with historical subjects. His figure drawing was always faultless and his sense of majesty and grandeur on the printed page almost overwhelming. He was decidedly at his best in allegorical work where lofty sentiments and patriotism could be expressed through mythological deities, his work becoming a *sine qua non* of the Christmas issues. He was also a decorative artist of rare accomplishment and his page design for The Royal Agricultural Society of England's meeting at Northampton in July 1847 is one of many that must have delighted readers who did not want their pictures to be taken in at a glance. The opening motions of the meeting are contained within a tremendous ornamental frontispiece by Gilbert in which a richly foliated border, twined with crops and vines, includes the figures of a reaper and a scyther. Below is a delicate vignette of the town of Northampton and at the bottom of the composition a 'trophy' of agricultural implements, with sieves, sickles, a plough, hay fork, cider press and the inevitable symbol of Victorian endeavour — a beehive (Figure 30). Gilbert's heavy metaphor does pall, but his early works are among his best, and Ingram shrewdly realised that such visual symbols were good for business.

Although it was a novelty, *The Illustrated London News* had in it many seeds of earlier experiments with pictorial journalism. Its format was entirely that of the newspaper and yet its appearance in two cloth-bound volumes at the end of the year, blind stamped decoration

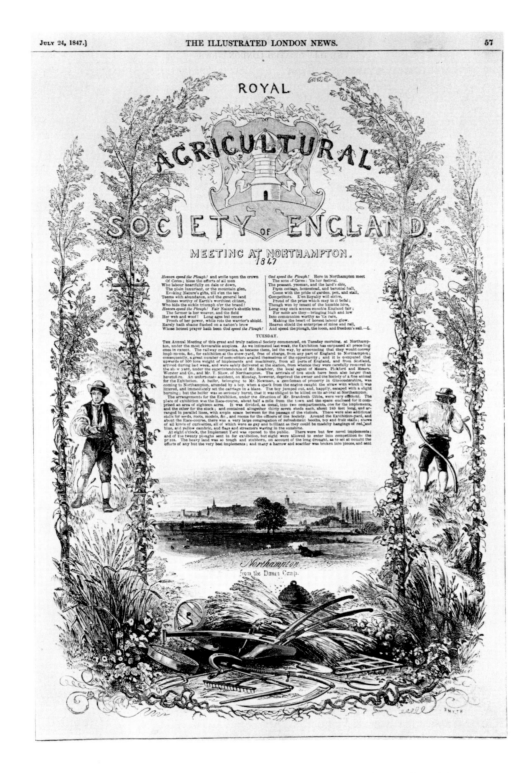

Figure 30. Northampton Agricultural Meeting by John Gilbert, July 1847.

at the corners, gilded cypher in the middle, gave it an air of permanence. This was not something to be discarded like a newspaper, but kept on the table in view of visitors, to be pored over like an album. There was much of the album in these volumes, with gilt edges, decorated spines, elaborate initial letters from the pen of John Gilbert and the lush treatment of the Fine Arts, usually a sentimental genre subject with a purple description below it. Even closer to the tradition of the albums, *The Gem* and *The Keepsake* was the inclusion of sheet music from time to time, seasonal lyrics such as 'Hymn For The Harvest' by 'A Lady' or patriotic songs by that arch-philanderer Sir Henry Bishop, all suitably embellished. Fashionable costumes were shown each month, most of them straight from French journals and by French artists but an equal coverage was given to the 'London Season' with graceful high life portrayed by Gilbert and evoked 'with a charming novelette'. Where fashion and current affairs joined forces, artists specialising in drawing objects were employed on page after page of Royal wedding presents, commemorative plate, race cups and in the case of the Marquess of Kildare, his wedding cake in every intricate detail!

From Charles Knight and the Penny Encyclopaedists there were borrowings of scientific investigation, astronomy and the charting of eclipses, home industry in 'A visit to Messrs Barclay and Perkins Brewery' or natural history, the 'Long-Eared Fox at the Gardens of the Zoological Society', each accompanied by an accurate drawing or diagram. These were often by technical or architectural artists, the earliest scientific draughtsman being one Thomas M. Hare. Ingram was also following Knight's lead in the way fiction was reduced to the barest minimum; in the 1850s there was practically none and in the 1840s only the occasional tale from the German translated by Miss Howitt with column measure blocks. It is also noticeable that sensational crime, which was supposed to have been the *raison d'être* for Ingram's first idea and was the mainstay of Reynolds' publications, appears here as a straight report of the police courts.

In its early numbers *The Illustrated* borrowed a style of satire which was very much that of *Punch* and continued to do so for many years, relying at the same time on a group of *Punch* artists. Comic drawings appeared about once every four or five weeks, usually in Kenny Meadows rather wooden but jolly hand, and Albert Smith ran an 'Everybody's Column' punctuated by tiny comic vignettes, quite anonymous. The targets were social or seasonal, dealing with railways or elections and the popular pastime of the Victorians in drawing grotesque 'Heads'. Richard Doyle supplied some of these, H.G. Hine was a frequent contributor and in the next few years, John Leech, Alfred Crowquill, 'Phiz', Cuthbert Bede, C.H. Bennett and Charles Keene were to play their part. After 1860 Du Maurier, Fred Barnard and William Ralston were to feature, the former two bringing with them a less boisterous humour and the latter by degrees the comic strip episode.

Another side of the magazine in the 1840s which became a consistent adjunct to the whole were the portraits, one would not dare say pictures, of prize bulls, cattle and poultry. For a paper that drew a lot of support from the shires and published a country edition, it was important that the agricultural scenes were life-like. Describing Edward Duncan's drawing of 'A Poultry Yard' on 20 March, 1847, the writer says: 'The busy group in the Illustration need not be individualized. Nor need we enquire how many of the pure Dorking breed there may be among them, or if the hand which scatters the food be that of a Dorking housewife . . . All these accessories combine in a very pleasing scene, not a painter's composition, but a picture of actual life.' Duncan's art could be implicitly relied upon and the reader clearly knew his hens!

Both J.F. Herring and Benjamin Robert Herring were active in these agricultural scenes, Harrison Weir drawing the Leicester, Hereford and South Down cattle. J.W. Archer assisted and later on J.W. Wood, Harry Hall and G.B. Goddard were to continue their work and Sam Carter drew cows for upwards of twenty years. These 'pictures of actual life' are of a continuing high quality and stand apart in the early days when figures are poor and printing indifferent.

A feature that developed out of the Victorian cult of Christmas as the main celebration, as opposed to the Georgians' New Year, was an enlarged Christmas issue with strong illustrative contributions. Until the end of the century, outside artists of high calibre were imported for this one occasion although the 'house' artists were used as well. In the 1850s we find in one supplement, Birket Foster, Abraham Solomon, John Tenniel, C.H. Bennett and Edmond Morin, in the 1860s James Godwin, George Thomas and John Everett Millais, with his only contribution to the magazine. As allegory and myth became less usual outside political cartooning, much of the fantasy and legendary illustration became concentrated in this section; it was also the first part of the magazine to have coloured pages from wood blocks in 1857.

This pattern of publication, once settled, was almost unchanging until the 1900s. The size of the journal nearly doubled from an average of 850 pages a year in the mid-forties to an average of 1,300 pages in the mid-fifties, the two comparatively slender yearly bound volumes becoming as bulky as family bibles. The proprietors supplied 'supplements gratis' at certain times of the year and at moments of national rejoicing or national crisis. There were several during the Crimean War, some issues had two supplements which had to be paid for, doubling the price of the magazine to one shilling. On 4 February 1854, there were sixteen extra pages on the Opening of Parliament, on 25 February another, mostly on the arts and one on the British Institution on 11 March. 'The Baltic Fleet' supplement appeared on 18 March with a marine frontispiece by E. Weedon, the chief marine artist of the magazine from 1848 to 1872, and nine wood engravings of engagements and uniforms as well as a map and a patriotic song. The coverage of naval and military activity was always extensive and became more so as artists themselves became more involved.

*The Illustrated London News* was not without rivals and imitators in its early days. The indefatigible Henry Lloyd tried to compete with its success for a few months in 1842, when he produced *Lloyd's Illustrated London Newspaper,* a short-lived speculation that fathered numerous other papers including *Lloyd's Penny Sunday Times and Peoples Police Gazette,* 1840-44, and *Lloyd's Weekly News.* Another inexpensive rival was *The London Journal,* 1845, which despite its sub-title as 'Weekly Record of Literature, Science and Art' depended for its popularity on sensational stories of barbarity and crude and lurid woodcuts. Selling at a penny a week, it had a circulation of 100,000. Mason Jackson mentions as other serious competitors, *Pen and Pencil* with woodcuts by Linton, *The Penny Illustrated Paper, The Pictorial World,* which specialised in large lithographic portraits and *The Ladies Pictorial.* [40] *The Field,* founded in 1853, began life with a strong team of artists including Leech, 'Phiz', Richard Ansdell, Harrison Weir and Harry Hall, but after its acquisition by E.W. Cox illustrations were dropped for a number of years. Cox gave as one of his reasons, the cost, and the fact that 'much better ones can be procured for a penny in John Cassell's illustrated sheet'. [41]

John Cassell, a reformed drunkard turned grocer, and a publisher from 1850, was making a name in inexpensive popular journalism. His papers were wholesome, homely, teetotal and illustrated, sufficient to make a formidable contender with *The Illustrated .* The one Cox refers to was *Cassell's Illustrated Family Paper* which had grown out of this earnest educator's other triumphs like *Cassell's Magazine of Art,* brought out after the Great Exhibition of 1851. The *'Family Paper,* which like *The Illustrated London News* had a folio format, lasted until 1865, when it became a quarto, changing its name to *Cassell's Family Magazine* in 1867. From 1854-57 it was priced at a penny, appeared like its rival on Saturday and contained eight pages of which four were illustrated. At this time it had designs by John Gilbert, including its headpiece, and illustrations by George Cruikshank (the teetotal lobby), T.H. Nicholson, Kenny Meadows and G Sargent. Generally speaking the artists were less impressive than Ingram's team as well as being restricted in space. Cassell's psychology of keeping in the penny market while employing *The Illustrated* artists was good business. Although *they* had twenty pages per issue in 1854 and fourteen were of illustrations, the *'Family Paper* was publishing stories in serial form running week to week. Nor were the authors inconsiderable. In 1854 appeared the following notice:

> 'John Cassell, being determined that this Periodical shall stand pre-eminent for popularity, has resolved to give it the increased attraction of a NEW, POWERFUL AND DEEPLY INTERESTING HISTORICAL TALE, which will be exclusively furnished under the Copyright Act, for Cassell's Illustrated Family Paper, by that celebrated Author ALEXANDER DUMAS.'

There followed serial instalments of the Dumas novel, completed each week by a busy and rather inky woodcut by T.H. Nicholson, who had taught Count d'Orsay. With the exception of Christmas numbers, it was only in the 1870s that *The Illustrated London News* finally succumbed to serial stories.

The greatest threat of all came from within, when in 1843, Henry Vizetelly, who was always willing to play maverick, left the magazine and founded his own *Pictorial Times.* This had a staff of brilliant men, Douglas Jerrold as leader writer, Thackeray as critic and reviewer, Mark Lemon as drama critic and Gilbert à Beckett as humorist. It foundered in 1847 and the tireless Vizetelly began again in 1855 with *The Illustrated Times* a far more ambitious paper. Its folio format was still modelled on *The Illustrated* , though slimmer, it had W. McConnell as the resident comic artist and employed that great designer H. Noel Humphreys to design borders and decorations. 'Phiz' worked for it, so did Doré, and between 1856 and 1866 it probably used more Continental artists than any other comparable magazine. A surprising contributor was the young Matt Morgan who was first employed to decorate and then to draw political demonstrations, showing his characteristic bite. *The Illustrated Times* was too successful for old Ingram, who at first took a third part share in it, then bought it and finally closed it down altogether.

No survey of these illustrated magazines would be complete without some mention of the part they played in perpetuating a strong tradition of black and white art, of providing a forcing house for young talent and constant employment for the less successful painter. Writing in 1885, Mason Jackson says 'Both *The Illustrated London News* and *The Graphic* may claim to have done good service to art and artists in this respect. Their pages have always been open to young artists, and while they have helped forward struggling genius they have opened up new sources of enjoyment to the general public.'[42] Jackson goes on to elaborate and say that 'the production of works in black and white, whether as engravings or drawings, is no doubt good artistic practice in the study of light and shade, and the young artist who draws on wood as a means of helping him to live while he is waiting for fame, is at the same time pursuing a useful branch of his art education.'[43] He cites Luke Fildes, Birket Foster, William Small, Caton Woodville and C. Gregory in this category and among the artists of our period, Samuel Read, Edward Duncan and F.W. Topham. He does not however mention the far wider scope of subjects or specialities available to the artist in the news magazines than in book illustration or their persistent use of the amateur. Both *Punch* and *The Illustrated London News* used much amateur drawing, some of it original or of high quality, but much of it merely perpetuating that link between professional and gifted gentleman that had made Georgian caricature and topography so varied.

1. Charles Knight, *Passages of a Working Life,* 1865, Vol. 1, P.226.
2. ibid., Vol. 2, p.227.
3. ibid., Vol. 2, p.116.
4. ibid., Vol. 1, p.244.
5. *Penny Magazine,* introduction to Vol. 1, 1832.
6. ibid.
7. F. Von Raumer, *England in 1835,* Vol. 1, p.193.
8. Charles Knight, *Passages of a Working Life,* 1865, Vol. 3, p.223.
9. ibid., Vol. 2, p.6.
10. Etched details on a caricature of S.W. Fores February 1803.
11. Quoted in John W. Dodd's *The Age of Paradox,* 1952, p.126.
12. Charles Knight, *Passages of a Working Life,* 1865, Vol. 2, p.223.
13. *The Victorian City* (V. Neuburg), Vol. 1, 1977, p.197.
14. M.H. Spielmann, *The History of Punch,* 1895, p.10.
15. R.G.G. Price, *A History of Punch,* 1957, p.43.
16. M.H. Spielmann, op. cit., p.314.
17. R.G.G. Price, op. cit., p.43.
18. ibid., p.49.
19. ibid., p.36.
20. Spielmann, op. cit., p.214.
21. George Cruikshank produced Comic Almanacs from 1835 to 1853 and *Punch* probably borrowed the idea from these.
22. John Ruskin, *The Art of England,* 1884, p.179.
23. John Ruskin, preface to *Children of the Nobility,* 1875.
24. Spielmann, op. cit., p.422.
25. Numerous editions, mostly undated were issued by Bradbury and Agnew between 1858 and 1886.
26. These were a considerable innovation in their time. An impression from an engraved wood block was made on india rubber and then enlarged by stretching. This 'blow-up' was then transferred to a lithographic stone and printed on canvas. Leech then painted in the whole composition with thin oil colour. Six examples were lent to an exhibition at Leicester Art Gallery in October 1967, the finest being 'The Fair Toxopholites' from the Croft-Murray Collection.
27. Spielman, op. cit., p.463.
28. Percy Muir, *Victorian Illustrated Books,* 1971, p.110.
29. Spielmann, op. cit., p.464.
30. ibid., p.464.
31. ibid., p.464.
32. ibid., p.463.
33. H. Vizetelly, *Memoirs,* 1893, p.223.
34. ibid.
35. Mason Jackson, *The Pictorial Press,* 1885. p.307.
36. Vizetelly, op. cit., p.238.
37. *Illustrated London News,* 30 October, 1847.
38. Knight, op. cit., Vol. 3, p.244.
39. Vizetelly, op. cit., p.232.
40. Jackson, op. cit., p.314.
41. *The Field.* In 1853, the magazine was running 16 pages weekly, 24 pages with supplements and had a circulation of 3,800.
42. Jackson, op. cit., pp.356-357.
43. ibid.

# Chapter 4

# The Continental Connection
# Cross Currents in Illustration 1840~1880

The assimilation of ideas from the Continent and particularly France, which had been something of a one way traffic in the eighteenth century, had become a more healthy cross-fertilisation by the second decade of the nineteenth. The rise of romanticism, particularly that of Byron, Goethe and Scott, made a deep impression on the French mind, so that illustration and caricature, the most literary sides of the visual arts, were bound to benefit. In passing one should mention the solid contacts already existing by the 1820s. R.P. Bonnington was established in France by 1818, shared a studio with Delacroix in 1825, and collaborated with Monnier on an illustrated book in 1828. Delacroix made his celebrated visit to London in 1825, the same year that Thomas Shotter Boys arrived in Paris. The latter had been the first Englishman to show his compatriots what the lithograph was capable of in his *Picturesque Architecture of Paris,* 1839, already dealt with elsewhere.

The revival of wood engraving in England which had stemmed from Bewick's work in the North East had caused considerable interest in France. The beautiful naturalism and earthy simplicity of Bewick's line, cut on the grain, struck a chord in the romantic spirit of the age. Charles Thompson, 1791-1843, a Londoner, who had studied under Bewick, established himself at Paris in 1816 and had won for himself considerable success by the 1830s. (Strangely enough it was his followers that cut the famous 'St. Paul's' headpiece for *The Illustrated London News* in 1841, see page 67, wood engravers being at a premium in England.) Vignette illustrations, a feature with Bewick, had been more common in France than in England in the eighteenth century and were ideally suited to the woodcut. They returned to this country in the 1840s with the popular landscape subjects of Birket Foster decorating poetry.

The most persistent influence from France in book illustration, was, and remained, the fashion plate. It was the only consistently well circulated medium for the British public to become acquainted with French draughtsmanship and figure studies, unsullied by English alteration or interpretation. The earlier frigid plates of the Empire that had appeared in *La Belle Assemblée* and other ladies' magazines were replaced in the 1820s by a more romantic approach, figures grouped gracefully together, scenes of the toilette or the promenade which included more props in the way of statuary, furniture and ornament. The people in these were no longer clothes pegs on which glorious apparel was hung, but stereotyped beings, moving with a sort of exaggerated realism. Even earlier, the French caricaturists of the Empire, had made play with the extremes and follies of fashion, in series like 'Le Supreme Bon Ton', and 'Mode du Jour'. In many like 'La Manie de la Danse' and 'Le Bon Genre', 1800-1827, Debucourt and other artists mimmick social manners, but provide a very accurate picture of dress scarcely distinguishable from fashion plates. By the late 1820s the two are very alike and become more so as the French caricaturists turn their attention to domestic and social satire. Even if French caricatures were not reaching English homes, French fashion plates *were* and it seems plausible that a public accustomed to them was more open to accept the work of Leech, Keene, F.M. Brown and Millais in the 1850s as a result. By the mid-century, the caricaturist could dispense with the grotesque in his art, that exaggeration which Baudelaire condemned from across the Channel, and substitute for it the comedy of manners.

*Punch* magazine was to be the chief vehicle for this new middle-class humour. As already mentioned, its founding in 1841 provided an important departure for English satirical journalism modelled on the French press. From the end of the Georgian phase, when prints ceased to be issued daily from the printsellers, the Continental style of ephemeral newspaper began to catch on. They were brief beauties that budded and flowered and disappeared within the year if not within the month, but they were spontaneous, topical, uninhibited and as slippery and elusive as the young men who ran them. *Punch* was in reality a successor to *Figaro in London* and had the sub-title of another great French publication, *Charivari.* As we have noticed, the first plans drawn up for the magazine had in fact included a separate lithographic cartoon by Leech with each issue, in the French manner.

But France could supply much more than a model for English journalists and artists, it could supply a different relationship between them and a new mode of expression. British comic artists had given full vent to their feelings in the penny plain and twopence coloured caricatures of the printsellers for fifty years. The foibles of monarchy, the scandals of society and the vagaries of every politician in the spectrum had been ruthlessly satirised from Gillray and Rowlandson to the last sketches of Cruikshank. But in France the situation was very different; a rigid censorship under the Empire and a controlled press under the restored Bourbons, gave the satirist no outlet for his brush. Without as strong a tradition of caricature and visual satire as in England, the French were far more open to new ideas when they came and far more inventive when the floodgates finally opened. The collapse of the Bourbons and the advent of Louis Philippe's July Monarchy was the watershed for French caricature. The pent up anger and frustration of the satirical artist was released on a public hungry for the blood of a corrupt government and a self-satisfied bourgeoisie; their medium was the lithograph.

Charles Philipon, 1806-1862, the editor, political agitator and artist, was the moving spirit behind this revitalisation of the humorous print and he founded the magazine *La Caricature,* a chief organ for freedom and later a factor in the birth of the Republic in 1848. In a very special way the drawing on stone spelled out an artistic freedom which the artists could identify with a political one. The work had the immediacy and the urgency of the sketch, the sense of the private message from the draughtsman to the public which copper or wood lacked, easy manoeuvrability and the advantage of being a break with the past. Psychologically it was ideal and the artists such as Grandville, Despret, Devéria, Monnier, Pigal and many more brought their searing wit to it, a wit which lay as much in the drawing as in the printed caption. The greatest of all Philipon's artists was Honoré Daumier, 1808-1879, who impressed himself on the national consciousness of French satire as strongly as Hogarth had on the British. Daumier's art is the new art of the nineteenth century as totally removed from the caricature of Cruikshank as anything could be. It is the lithe and elfin art of a sophisticated bohemian, who prefers the literary parry and thrust of the drawing room to the guffaw of the street corner; the former often being the more venomous.

The best commentator on the new age is Thackeray, himself an amateur illustrator and caricaturist and a keen follower of this branch of journalism. The vitality of the art that he found in France formed the subject of a whole chapter in *The Paris Sketchbook,* published in 1840. Thackeray, who considered that his own indefinite little drawings were ruined by the engravers, classified wood block and steel plate as mere 'art done by machinery'. In the direct drawing of the French lithographers he saw the only freedom. 'We get in these engravings the *loisirs* of men of genius, not the finikin performances of labored mediocrity, as with us; all these artists are good painters, as well as good designers; a design from them is worth a whole gross of Books of Beauty; and if we might raise a humble supplication to the artists in our own country of similar merit — to such men as Leslie, Maclise, Herbert, Cattermole and others — it would be, that they should, after the example of their French bretheren and of the English landscape painters, take chalk in hand, produce their own copies of their own sketches, and never more draw a single "Forsaken One" "Rejected One" "Dejected One" at the entreaty of any publisher or for the pages of any Book of Beauty, Royalty or Loveliness whatever.'[1]

Thackeray could see that where lithography had strengthened the arm of French humour, it had weakened the keen edge of English. The British treated the stone as a vehicle for soft and delicate portraits or the caricatures of 'HB' which were scarcely caricatures at all, the French gave full vent to their feelings day by day. *Charivari* became a daily Parisian paper which says much for the appetite of the French for visual satire; *Punch* started and remained a weekly. French artists came to London and drew its foibles, Thackeray went to Paris and *wrote* about theirs; the difference was one of spirit and temperament more than anything else. It is completely in accord with Thackeray's views therefore to find the cosmopolitan writer Mrs. Frances Trollope, 1780-1863, employing a French-trained artist for her books *Paris And The Parisians in 1835* and *Jonathan Jefferson Whitlaw,* 1835 and 1836. No British figure artist of this date would have been free of the distortions deplored by Thackeray and she chooses the draughtsman August Hervieu, fl.1819-1858, who contributes six 'Embellishments' to the first book and fifteen to the second, all in a straightforward literal style. They include in the Paris volume a superb engraving of a crowded room at the Louvre with its pushing throng of visitors drawn with great naturalness, and other similarly realistic groups of soldiers in 'Pro Patria (Figure 31), high society at the 'Soirée' and art lovers attending a 'Lecture à l'Abbaye-Aux-Bois'. Hervieu's sketches were criticised in the English press for having nothing to do with the text but one suspects it was their original format that rankled.

Philipon's celebrated 'poire' which metamorphosed into the jowell and visage of Louis Philippe, expressed in the simplest way the feelings of a generation who had been hoodwinked into a corrupt monarchy. It was a simple enough symbol to be scattered around Paris, scrawled on walls, to cause indignation at Court and result in an unsuccessful action against Philipon in November 1831. It was the kind of vitality that had been Gillray's at the height of his fame and in later years had lost its force as the plates became more and more smothered in words. Thackeray appreciated that the Frenchmen saw themselves first as artists and wished for a similar range of vision in his English friends.

'Now in looking, for instance, at HB's slim vapory figures, they have struck us as excellent *likenesses* of men and women, but no more: the bodies want spirit, action and individuality. George Cruikshank, as a humorist, has quite as much genius, but he does not know the art of "effect" so well as Monsieur Daumier; and if we might venture to give a word of advice to another humorous designer, whose works are extensively circulated — the illustrator of "Pickwick" and "Nicholas Nickleby" — it would be to study well these caricatures of Monsieur

*Figure 31. 'Pro Patria' by Auguste Hervieu. 1835.*

Daumier; who though he executes very carelessly, knows very well what he would express, indicates perfectly the attitude and identity of his figure, and is quite aware, beforehand, of the effect which he intends to produce.'[2]

Thackeray criticises Cruikshank for being 'a practised artist', taking his ease, and 'Phiz' a clever one who ought to think more and exaggerate less. In the whole gamut of Daumier's 'Macaire et Bertrand' series, there is nothing gross or absurdly exaggerated. Thackeray really finds that in England the intellectual approach is missing. 'Nothing merely intellectual will be popular among us; we do not love beauty for beauty's sake, as Germans; or wit, for wit's sake, as the French; for abstract art we have no appreciation.'[3]

Until the late 1840s none of these artists had appeared in British publications and they were never to be seen in the subtleties of lithograph. But from about 1835, Monsieur Michel P. Delaporte had a print and book emporium at 37 Burlington Arcade, where Thackeray and the public at large could see and purchase the genuine Parisian article. *The Illustrated London News* pressed Gavarni into its service in 1848 and Tony Johannot in 1851 but they, with Lami and Guys, remained aloof from *Punch* and other journals.

Tony Johannot, 1803-1852, was probably the best known French artist who worked for British authors. He had first appeared briefly as illustrator of the first three parts of *Windsor Castle* by Harrison Ainsworth, 1843, after the author had quarrelled with Cruikshank. He later illustrated further classics in English, *Don Quixote,* the *Vicar of Wakefield* and *A Sentimental Journey,* 1851, all containing his characteristically wiery figures. Another illustrator who would have been equally well-known was Jean-Ignace Isidore Gerard Grandville, 1803-1847, who specialised in humorous animals and metamorphosed objects which have an uncanny attraction and an almost surreal quality to them. Several of his books appeared in English editions, notably *Gulliver,* 1840, *La Fontaine,* 1843, *Comical People* and *The Flowers Personified,* 1855.

Daumier's art developed along a certain theme which was highly successful and certainly not unique to France. He took as his starting point a forgotten play called 'Auberge des Adrets' which had been transformed by the actor Lemaitre into a popular drama and taken Paris by storm. Lemaitre's clever interpretation of the main character Robert Macaire, an unscrupulous villain, became legendary, and his green coat, crimson pantaloons and enormous whiskers were written about, burlesqued and caricatured. When this bizarre figure had passed into popular mythology, Daumier transformed him and his seedy friend Bertrand and made them speak for the topical issue of the day, ridiculing the rogueries and corruptions of everything from the Parliament to the Bourse. If there was the whiff of scandal in high places, Macaire and Bertrand are there to dabble in it; if sharp practices exist in the law, the two villains will be hot on its heals, neither the institutions of monarchy or business are exempt from their crafty schemes. A similar running episode had been produced in England by the 'Paul Pry' caricatures of the 1820s and later Victorian artists were to benefit from a 'cast' of characters from Leech's 'Mr. Briggs' to Du Maurier's 'Sir Gorgias Midas'. In Daumier's case the effect was instantaneous; Louis Philippe took on M. Philipon's army of artists in the Gallerie Vero-Dodat, and it is posterity that is the richer. There were prosecutions, seizures, fines and even bribes instigated by the King of the French as prints of his family and himself continued to pour forth, each more ludicrous than the last.

At one point only, Daumier overstepped the mark, landed himself in prison for six months and immediately became the darling of radicalism. Daumier had drawn a plate entitled 'Gargantua' in which a pompous personage with a pear-shaped head, sits on a throne of state. A plank extends upwards towards his mouth and on it trip a hundred little mignons, to-ing and fro-ing in various robes of state and feeding him with gold pieces. On the extreme right artisans and the poor drop their meagre savings into his treasury. Strangely enough this suggests that Daumier was familiar with British caricature; the source for this seems to be Robert Seymour's 'The Great Joss and His Playthings', published in 1829, a milder version, satirising the Prince Regent's extravagance.

These attacks resulted in the 'law of September' which made it illegal to caricature the officers of state and changed the tenet of French humorous art. From the mid-1830s the artists had to confine themselves willy nilly to the *comédie humaine,* the fashionable dress shops, the café, the bar at the opera and the social indiscretions of the bourgeoisie behind their Brussels curtains. This had one dynamic result which never took place in England, it drove the illustrators and the caricaturists into the arms of the writers, who were just then exploring the same subjects in reaction to the academic and high-flown romantic. Hugo, the artist-writer held a salon for both his confreres: 'For a century and more, art had served the libretto, the novel, and the pamphlet; for almost as long, the writer had minded the artist's business, and had not been careful to hide his condescension. Now, when he began to show a new sympathy and respect, the yoke ceased to chafe and a pleasant partnership ensued.'[4]

The French artists were seeing what Thackeray hoped their counterparts across the Channel would see, the importance of social satire as an expression of the times. 'They form a very curious and instructive commentary upon the present state of society in Paris, and a hundred years hence, when the whole of this struggling, noisy, busy, merry race shall have exchanged their pleasures or occupations for a quiet coffin at Montmartre or Père la Chaise; when the follies here recorded shall have been superceded by new ones, and the fools now so active shall have given up the inheritance of the world to their children; the latter will at least have the advantage of knowing, intimately, exactly, the manners of life and being of their grandsires, and calling up, when they so choose it, our ghosts from the grave to live, love, quarrel, swindle, suffer and struggle on blindly as of yore.'[5]

It is curious to find Charles Baudelaire taking up this theme and developing it in an essay more than twenty years later. Baudelaire, the most compelling and lucid of French critics, was among the first to bother with the caricaturist and the illustrator and to rescue him from the relegation of a minor art. In his 'The Painter of Modern Life', which appeared in *Figaro* in November and December 1863, he outlined a philosophy for 'the painter of the passing moment' which was neither insignificant or ephemeral. He takes as his starting point the work of the mysterious and elusive artist, Constantin Guys, whose rapid pen sketches of Second Empire Paris have become classics of their type. 'Monsieur G', the artist's name is never spelled out, is referred to as a 'man of the world', one whose vision is not restricted but whose curiosity makes him want 'to know, understand and appreciate everything that happens on the surface of our globe.'[6] Guys' restless and ever changing vision of life, dashing horses, milling crowds, swaggering officers, are *felt* through his frenzied ink lines as the trembling vibrancy of a composite humanity. 'The crowd is his element,' Baudelaire writes, 'as the air is that of birds and water of fishes. His passion and his profession are to become one flesh with the crowd.'[7] Every age, Baudelaire argues, has its own 'gait and gesture' and the artist-recorders job is to set this down for posterity, at the same time loving the synthesis of modern life, which he distills, as heroic and exciting. Baudelaire like Guys, concentrates on subjects that are piquant and sensual, parades, battles, strollers, royalty, women of easy virtue, never on the humdrum and laborious middle class, whose object, one might say heroism, was money.

The connection here, which makes the Anglo-French flow of ideas important, is Baudelaire's identification of 'the painter of modern life' with dandyism. The contemptuous superiority of the artist, his disassociation from the vulgarity of money and gainful employment, were very much part of the romantic rebellion. In the mind of the French, dandyism was very much associated with the English, or at least with that part of the English character which was feudal and aristocratic. This must have had its roots in such publications as Pierce Egan's *Real Life In London*, the literature of sport, and the caricatures of George Cruikshank and his fellows. But if these and George Brummel were the inestimable models for the cult of French dandyism, they left a lot to be desired, none of them had an idea to their names and the new dandyism in France was 'an aristocratic superiority of mind'. Dress, that rich field of caricature, became the outlandish and defiant front of the artist against conventional patronage and academicism. The students of Paris paraded in the costume of the Middle Ages, colourful cloaks and waistcoats, doublet and hose, the literary garb of revived plays, novels or old legend. All this conspired to throw the artist and writer together too, a common enemy, the state, a common source of inspiration, ordinary life, and a common pride in Gautier's art for art's sake, which set artists as people apart. Contact with Gavarni and Monnier reconciled Balzac to the artists and recommended them to him as a study for his numerous novels. In England it was to be fifty years before artists played a prominent part in novels of the French-inspired writers like Wilde and Bennett. It was also more customary for serious artists to act as illustrators in France, not the case in England; Delacroix is one example and even Millet produced chalk drawings with popular journals in mind.

Constantin Guys was an apostle of this dandyism, in essence if not in appearance, Gavarni had it too. The latter's contacts in England are mentioned elsewhere, Guys long connection with *The Illustrated London News* and stay in London in the 1840s is sketchy in the extreme. It seems unlikely that he had any direct influence on English draughtsmen, his sketches were seen by few and such illustrations as were published lost their impressionistic sparkle. He has nevertheless left us the finest rapid notes of early Victorian England that can be found anywhere, whether they are the Brighton coach in quick motion or idlers in the Park (Figure 32).

One of the moving spirits behind this dandyism in England was also a Frenchman, Eugène Lami. It needed a Gallic illustrator to give a fashionable gloss to this worn out image that had died with that gross and unpopular dandy, George IV. Lami, a Parisian who trained

*Figure 32. 'The purple roans' by Constantin Guys.*

81

*Figure 33. 'Le Repos' by Eugène Lami.*

under Baron Gros, Horace Vernet and the École des Beaux-Arts, arrived in England in about 1828. For him it was an enchanted island and in many ways his spiritual home. Not only was it the country of Scott and the romantic novel but the country of the descendants of the Plantaganets and Tudors who re-gothicised their castles and dispensed boiling punch rather than boiling oil from the battlements. Lami's captivation first saw fruit in his *Voyage en Angleterre*, 1829-30. This was only a prelude to his obsession with English high life, and hundreds of ink and wash sketches of the most sensuous loveliness, which mirrored a generation or at least handed it a glass to see what it wanted to! Lami's evident enjoyment and uncritical view of the English, gave him influential friends. Unlike Gavarni, no doors were closed to him and he is there at the most intimate scenes of social life as well as at fêtes, balls, the hunt breakfasts, the farewell performance at the theatre or in a country house drawing-room. It is on record that Lami was very proud of his connections with old families and was well acquainted with their pedigrees; Baudelaire, who considered him minor, called him 'almost an Englishman in virtue of his love for aristocratic elegance'.[8] Lami gave English life that nonchalance and languid ease which it saw in the fashion plate. Spanking horses and sumptuous equipages collect frail girls, as light as fluff, from houses in Belgrave Square; doors open to reveal glittering staircases filled with unruffled fan-fluttering beauties; parties are set down in cool parkland to enjoy overflowing hampers, nothing disturbs the serenity of Lami's *beau monde*.

Lami was most successful with military processions and reviews, the officer being the archetypal dandy, but even intimate figure studies have a swagger and panache of their own. There is a splendid dandified figure, standing in half contemptuous gesture near the staircase in 'Queen Victoria at the Chateau d'Eu', 1843, now in the Royal Collection at Windsor Castle.

Another fine example is his 'Repos' which is typical both as to the treatment of the subject and the medium used (Figure 33). A pair of huntsman of studied elegance sprawl on the ground in a forest glade and chat to a cigar-smoking companion who perches in exaggerated jockey pose on his horse; in the background a groom waits respectfully with the two spare horses. Lami has done a fluid pen drawing on toned paper, washing in the landscape and foreground in brown or green shadow, concentrating the whole of his interest on the figures. The reds of the coats, the smudge of a blue cravat and a yellow waistcoat, the sunlight on patent boots, give life to the whole. Inspite of the English scene, it is not an English treatment, the watercolour is imprisoned in those wiry pen lines, however sensuous, which are the structure of the whole picture. This is not a party of countrymen, but Londoners or Parisians who wish to be seen hunting the fox, the landscape is a fashionable backdrop.

Lami's attitudinising about the English must have contributed to the image of military and social life in the 1840s and '50s, Lord Cardigan's obsession with uniform and the officerial lisping, satirised by many writers. By a strange quirk of fate, the caricature figure of the dandy returned to English pages from these foreign works in John Leech's 'Young Snobley' with his tiny feet, peg top trousers and enormous neckwear.

Apart from Thackeray, the only Englishmen to have regular and direct contact with the French illustrators and caricaturists were Blanchard Jerrold and the Mayhews. According to one writer they were frequent visitors in the 1840s at 'le Childebert' an infamous tenement in the Quartier-Latin, renowned for its avant-garde artists and caricaturists, one of whom was Tony Johannot. Henry Vizetelly, later Editor of *The Illustrated Times,* was another man with Gallic contact. He purchased blocks from Philipon's *Charivari* for his *Comic Nursery Tales* and illustrated 'Cham' alongside the home-grown Leech and Crowquill. He was also businessman enough to buy up old blocks from *L'Illustration* and sell his own clichés to Lillaud of *Le Journal Illustré*. Thackeray introduced 'Cham', Amédée, Comte de Noé, 1819-1879, to England in the 1840s, and though he dined with John Leech and Richard Doyle, was either ignored or missed by the Editor of *Punch.* There was still no salon for the illustrator and the author to meet on equal terms on this side of the Channel, although *Punch's* table and the 'boards' of the various magazines were to become their nearest equivalent. Thackeray's position as foremost novelist and creditable illustrator might have enabled him to play this part in England as Victor Hugo had done in France, both artists had progressed from clever caricatures in the 1830s to more serious ambitions, but Thackeray was less attuned to changes in the arts and his power as a draughtsman was more limited than the French writer's.

Baudelaire, in his essay on some foreign caricaturists, 1857, mentions besides Hogarth, both Cruikshank and Seymour, showing that English graphic satire was known there when the English School of painting was dismissed. It seems evident that Robert Seymour's sporting subjects were familiar to the French public as Baudelaire refers to them as 'excessive', 'simple' and 'ultra-brutal' without further attempt at explanation. A nice piece of cross-channel borrowing took place at about this time which shows the extent to which artists were relying on one another. H.K. Browne, whom Thackeray considered should 'study well these caricatures of Monsieur Daumier', did so for *Martin Chuzzlewhit,* 1844. Not only are the figures in this book drawn with greater characterisation and realism, but in the engraving of the nurse 'Mrs Sarah Gamp', Browne has translated one of Daumier's most witty female creations 'La Garde Malade' from a lithograph published in *Le Charivari* two years before in May 1842 (Figure 34).

Another strong link with the Continent was provided by the German artists, not only those who had influenced Pre-Raphaelitism but those who were illustrating fables, songs, children's stories and history in the 1840s and 1850s. Ludwig Richter was the most outstanding, producing a well-illustrated *Vicar of Wakefield* in German and English in 1841 and *The Black Aunt* and *The Book of German Songs* in 1848 and 1856 respectively. Some of the designs in the latter book are certainly by Charles Keene who was the most forthright exponent of German draughtsmanship in the decade; he had been fired by looking at the most celebrated German book of the time Kugler's *Frederick the Great* with its illustrations by Adolf von Menzel, 1815-1905. Two English editions of this mammoth work were published in 1844 and 1845 and the date, as well as the quality of their hundreds of black and white illustrations, can be seen as a turning point for the art in Britain. Several artists such as Holman Hunt were later to claim that they did not know the work of either Adolf Menzel or Alfred Rethel 1815-1859. Gleeson White's comments on the *Frederick the Great* are as near to the truth as we shall ever get. 'It is quite possible that any one of the men of the time might have seen it by chance, and turned over its pages ignorant of its artist's name.'[9] Charles Keene developed a correspondence with the German artist and they exchanged work. When an interviewer visited Menzel many years afterwards he was recorded as saying that 'He favoured the nocturnal cafés, where he hunted after the illustrated papers — amongst which he admired *Punch.*'[10] Keene's knowledge of Continental draughtsmanship was probably greater than most British illustrators and the admiration was mutual. On his death in 1891, he received long obituaries in both *Arte Moderne* and *La Chronique des Arts,* the last comparing his work to that of Menzel and Degas.

Figure 34. *'Sarah Gamp' by H.K. Browne from Dickens'* Martin Chuzzlewhit, *1844.*

German magazines were making important strides throughout this period, their artists evolving a free style of drawing, based partly on Menzel, partly on the wit of the amateur and developing new techniques and formats such as the strip cartoon. The best of these magazines was the *Fliegende Blätter* of Munich which had a formidable team of artists and issued small books of their work as it appeared in the magazine. The most important humorous illustrator associated with it was Wilhelm Busch, 1832-1908, whose books were finding their way to this country in the 1860s.

Busch was an original artist whose work consisted in vigorous nonsense, drawn with great sprightliness, a sort of German equivalent of Edward Lear. His shorthand is in some ways more similar to Caldecott than to Lear although his humour was more provincial and more coarse than either of them (Figure 35). His preposterous German peasants and country characters spill over the pages and demand attention. As Pennell says, 'Busch's work is a perpetual letter to the whole world, which one who runs may read.'[11] Busch seems to have been more influential on individual artists than on the reading public in this country, the development of the strip cartoon surely has his mark upon it. In 1868 the first strip joke is used in *The Illustrated London News* in the able hands of Fred Barnard and this genre was popularised in Caldecott's letter stories for *The Graphic*, ten years later. E. Morant Cox uses the same medium for his humour in *The Illustrated* in 1884-85 and is followed by similar sketches from S.T. Dadd; *The Graphic's* strip cartoonists were A.C. Corbould, a nephew of Charles Keene, and W. Ralston who both worked in the late 1880s, but none of these men had the lightness of touch and mobility of subject found in Busch. Interest in Busch's homeland was sufficient however in early 1882 for *The Graphic* to run to several pages on the art of caricature in Germany.

The only illustrator to capture the mischievous humour of Busch and to some extent his drawing line was J.F. Sullivan, 1853-1936, whose work was mainly done for the magazine *Fun* from 1878 to 1901. He invented and ran for years a series of story strips called 'The British Working Man' which included comic incidents of labourers, doctors, chemists, builders, gas-men and many others (Figure 36). Sullivan, whose cartoons were issued by *Fun* in book form, comes closest to his German counterpart in the unshaded drawings such as 'Time Work' and 'The British Bumpkin' both included in the 1878 volume and comparable to Busch's *Der Maulwurf*. He also illustrated books about comic insects, a derivation of Busch's most popular English book, *Buss-a-Buzz*, 1872, a tale of a bee-hive, and there is a refreshing modernity about Sullivan when he does not overwork his subjects.

After 1880 there was a considerable deterioration in printing and publishing in France and many illustrators began to appear in English and American editions. The most influential Parisian magazine remained, *L'Art et L'Idée* which was edited by Octave Uzanne, an interesting figure, who edited two gift books for the English market and published articles in both countries. *The Graphic* was the periodical with the strongest Continental links at this time, although both it and *The Illustrated London News* had relied on the foreign Special Artists for many years. W.L. Thomas of *The Graphic* had acquired the

*Figure 35. 'Der Maulwurf' by Wilhelm Busch.*

*Figure 36. A comic strip by J.F. Sullivan.*

virtuoso French cartoonist 'Mars' Maurice Bonvoisin, 1849-1912, for the paper in about 1880 and he contributed spasmodically from then until 1903, sharing his talents with *The Illustrated* from 1883 and including English subjects in his repertoire. Caran d'Ache otherwise Emmanuel Poirée, 1858-1909, appeared once in *The Graphic* in 1887 and once in *Punch* seven years later, it was perhaps difficult to wean such an international figure from his home ground of *Vie Parisienne* and *Chat Noir*. 'Caran d'Ache always spoke with enthusiasm of our black-and-white artists.' wrote A. Ludovici after his death, 'such as Charles Keene, Phil May, Dudley Hardy and Raven Hill, who were all then working for the comic papers.'[12] Poirée was given an exhibition at the Fine Art Society in 1898 and familiarity with his drawings and the circulation of his periodicals did much to loosen the English pen drawing from the straight-jacket of the *Punch* style. *The Graphic's* reputation abroad was enhanced in 1889 when it published two special numbers for the Continent. In June it announced 'L'Été' described as 'An Edition of the Graphic Summer No. Published in the French Language Price 1s 8d'. The following Christmas it published a similar number called 'Noël'. French artists like 'Mars', Caran d'Ache and A. Guillaume often appeared in colour in these supplements and provided a useful key of the subtle tones achievable in print compared to the stridencies in some English work.

Paris had given birth to a number of remarkable pen artists in the mid-1880s among whom might be named Jeanniot, Vogel, José, Loir and Robida. But the outstanding figure of this group was Daniel Vierge, 1851-1904. Vierge or Daniel Urrabieta Ortiz y Vierge to give him his full name, arrived in Paris from Spain in 1869 and began to publish his exquisite pen and ink drawings in *La Vie Moderne, Le Monde Illustré* and other Continental papers. His pen line was much purer than anything that had gone before it in book illustration, there was very little hatching, a delicate precision in every stroke and a strong *sense* of colouring without the use of any colour. There is a refinement in his buildings and figures that is quite breath-taking, somewhat aided by his habit of drawing large and having the sketch reduced for the page. Vierge had the sort of life of which legends are made. Struck down by a paralytic stroke in the middle of his most ambitious work, an illustrated volume of *Pablo de Ségovie*, he painstakingly learned to draw with his unaffected left hand in order to complete the book. Vierge undertook a lot of illustration for the American journal *Scribner's Monthly* and developed a large number of devotees in the United States as well as the admiration of American students working in Paris. The result was a school of pen draughtsmen who took Vierge as their exemplar and it was through the American connection that the refined pen technique of Vierge seeped into this country. E.A. Abbey, later to be discussed more fully, C.S. Reinhart and Howard Pyle who were typical illustrators in the new style, were featured in the pages of *The Graphic* by 1883 as well as illustrating classics for British publishers. This is not to discount the direct links that Vierge had with this country. 'He was so keen on exhibiting in England,' wrote Ludovici, 'that he not only sent us wash and pen and ink drawings framed, but a number of albums I had never asked for and did not know existed.'[13] When the completed English edition of *Pablo* was issued in 1892, Joseph Pennell was enthusiastic in his praise. 'There is really very little to be said about Vierge's drawings, except to advise the student to study them in the most thorough manner, and to remind him that their cleverness and apparent freedom are the result of years of the hardest study, and, in each drawing, of days and sometimes weeks of the most careful work.'[14] The magnificent illustrations by Bernard Partridge, W. Dewar, Christine Hammond, Fred Pegram and H.R. Millar which followed in the 1890s show that such advice was not wasted.

Paul Renouard, 1845-1924, began to work for *The Graphic* in about 1884 and was a continuing and powerful reminder of French practice until the 1900s. His stature as an illustrator of ordinary life is covered in a later chapter, but his introduction of chalk drawing to the English magazines was an important step towards more powerful graphics. F.L. Emanuel writing of the new school of illustrators in London and Paris in the 1890s makes mention of 'how much many of the most excellent of the younger artists — such as Steinlen, Léandre Malteste, Redon, Sabattier, Tilly and Huard in France, Lockhart Bogle, Hartrick, Almond and Gunning King in England, evidently owe to that giant among draughtsman — Paul Renouard.'[15] In France the rise of poster art and the influence of artists like Jules Chéret had greatly affected book illustration and turned the attention of younger illustrators from pen to chalk and charcoal. 'The perfection to which the photo-reproduction of drawings now attains,' wrote Emanuel, 'has been chiefly responsible for this, together with the praise-worthy attempt of the modern men to vie with the magnificent series of drawings on stone, done half a century ago by Gavarni, Daumier, De Beaumont, 'Cham' and other splendid draughtsmen.'[16] Chalk and crayon were used with greater frequency towards the turn of the century and there was a revival in lithography but the average illustrated book and periodical remained grey and unbending. The most original and most European blends still came from highly gifted individuals, Lucien Pissaro, 1863-1944, for example, who made a tentative visit to England in 1883 and settled here after 1890. Pissarro set up the Eragny Press in 1894 and the thirty or so titles issued by him are famous for their strong Normandy flavour in the illustrations and the use of colour wood engravings, unusual in England. Nevertheless these rare birds with their fresh impressionistic colours can only have been seen by the very few. Emanuel's comments on the cross-currents between the two countries might almost be read as an obituary of the whole subject. 'The fact that most of the papers in which these illustrations appear are unknown to, or unpalatable to the British public, renders it certain that, with but few exceptions, the accomplished work of these modern artists of black and white art will never be as widely appreciated in England as it deserves to be.'[17]

And what of the cross fertilisation in the field of caricature that Thackeray had spoken of so hopefully? The effects of French naturalism and the *comédie humaine* had done their work well in the 1850s and 1860s, allied to Victorian disapproval of anyting that was excessive or coarse. Frank Emanuel could look across to France at the end of the century and in the design of 'Ribot de Noël' by Charles Léandre, 1862-1930, see that 'in the largeness of the forms and the rollicking *abandon* of the whole scene we are reminded of our own Rowlandson, an artist whose work is thoroughly appreciated across the Channel.'[18] But ironically, for Augustin Filon, the French historian who published *La Caricature En Angleterre*, the essentially British exaggeration which he admires from Hogarth to Leech has evaporated. 'La caricature anglaise a cessé de vivre sa vie independante; elle a cessé d'être un genre.'

## Footnotes

1. W.M. Thackeray, *The Paris Sketch Book,* 'Caricatures and Lithography', pp.152-153.
2. ibid. p.172.
3. ibid. p.155.
4. Malcolm Easton, *Artists and Writers in Paris — The Bohemian Idea 1803-1867.*
5. Thackeray, op. cit. p.173.
6. Charles Baudelaire, *The Painter of Modern Life,* etc., edited by Jonathan Mayne, 1964, p.7.
7. ibid.
8. ibid. p.5.
9. Gleeson White, *English Illustration The Sixties,* 1906, p.150.
10. 'Conversations with Menzel', *The Studio,* Vol. 34, 1905, pp.257-261.
11. Joseph Pennell, *Pen Drawing and Pen Draughtsmen,* 1894, p.155.
12. A. Lucovici, *An Artist's Life in London and Paris,* 1926, pp.51-52.
13. ibid. p.126.
14. Pennell, op. cit. p.42.
15. Frank Emanuel, *The Illustrators of Montmartre,* 1904, p.76.
16. ibid. p.58.
17. ibid. p.84-85.
18. ibid. p.78.
19. A. Filon, *La Caricature En Angleterre,* 1902, p.269.

# Chapter 5

# The Pre-Raphaelite Illustrators

## (i) Lyric and Legend

he vigour and diversity which had characterised the illustration of books under the Regency was not sustained long after the 1820s. Blake and Rowlandson were dead by 1827 and Thomas Bewick, the bulk of whose work had been done in the previous decade, died the following year. The older tradition of caricatured illustrating was continued under George Cruikshank and to a lesser extent H.K. Browne, W.H. Brooke, Henry Alken, Robert Cruikshank, William Heath and a host of minor practitioners. As we have seen the romantic movement lived on in the apocalyptic visions of John Martin, engraved for albums like *The Gem, The Keepsake* and *The Literary Souvenir,* or in the more private world of Blake's follower, Edward Calvert. The best work being completed after 1830, as we have noticed, was by the topographers, in the generous folios of travel, architecture and engineering achievement which were bringing the new art of lithography to the fore under the names of T.S. Boys, Samuel Prout, J.S. Cotman, J. Bourne and Edward Lear.

A glance at the illustration of books during the 1840s gives an impression of dreary sameness, an increasing antiquarianism with artists like George Cattermole, or a cloying sentimentality as painters like John Gilbert, Myles Birket Foster and William Mulready reduced the miopic prettiness of their oils to the confines of the printed page.

Change was however in the wind. The young Alfred Tennyson had admired Bewick's woodcuts not only for their beauty but for their scientific accuracy. A new generation responded more readily to Flaxman's interpretation of *The Odyssey,* 1805, with its linear austerity than to the small scale work of Smirke, Corbould or Westall. A more critical approach to the arts was leading some painters back to the earliest printed sources of book illustrations, the German woodcuts of the early sixteenth century.[1] When William Bell Scott visited the exhibition of designs for the Westminster Hall Competition in 1843, he noticed a new style from the younger men, 'careful studies of form and design' not costume pieces or the elaborate effects of light and shade.[2] This trend was not long in appearing in the illustration and decoration of books, where epics, such as *The Pilgrim's Progress* and Kingsley's *Hereward The Wake,* 1844 and 1866, were depicted in outline by Henry Courtney Selous, 1803-1890. These were typical of the new school in which expression and gesture were investigated and the placing of the figures very carefully considered. They often have the appearance of toneless frescoes and these were frequently the source from German and French publications, no coloured versions being available.

Another brilliant exponent of the kind was Daniel Maclise, 1806-1870, whose debt to the German work of Retzsch and others can be seen in his decorative but rather harsh frontispieces to Dickens' Christmas books, *The Chimes,* 1845, and *The Cricket On The Hearth*, 1846. Predictably perhaps the artist used a German wood engraver. In 1845 he illustrated Moore's *Irish Melodies* (Figure 37), a particularly successful combination of text and designs which have worn better than his large scale canvases. This concentration on draughtsmanship, organisation of the picture space and detail, sowed the seeds of a great black and white tradition in this country.

A number of small illustrated books began to reflect this change, among them Bogue's edition of Longfellow's *Evangeline,* dated 1850 but presumably published in 1849. This little volume was produced uniformly with *The Minor Poems of H.W. Longfellow,* but is not mentioned by either Gleeson White or Forrest Reid in their comprehensive lists. It is very much a drawing-room gift copy of the period, a hard papier mâché cover in cream-colour with bevelled edges, is overlaid with a design of trailing leaves, the title in pseudo-medieval German script. In the centre of the design is an oval picture of a couple standing by the sea shore, the man in profile, the woman turned away, erect, stern and tense. The initials 'J.E.B.' below are for Jane E. Benham, a professional artist and illustrator, whose main reputation depends on two editions of Longfellow and some contributions to *Beattie and Collins Poems,* 1854. *Evangeline* has thirty-one pages or vignettes by Birket Foster, three half pages by John Gilbert and eleven by Jane Benham. Although the book was clearly to be sold on the strength of Birket Foster's reputation, it is interesting to note that Jane Benham's work is on the covers and reflects

*Figure 37. Page from* Moore's Irish Melodies *by Daniel Maclise, 1846.*

perfectly the current mood. She was one of a group of English artists who had studied under Wilhelm Kaulbach at Munich and brought back with her some of the intensity of approach and earnestness of method that had gained the Nazarene School a wide following and brought them under the patronage of the Prince Consort. It is not that she is a particularly strong draughtswoman, the engraving illustrated shows that she is not (Figure 38). For pure technique she is outdistanced by the suavity of Gilbert and the decorative sense of Foster. Where she triumphs is that her illustrations are very personal statements, unconventional in their simplicity of outline and lack of modelling, a great deal is left to the imagination of the reader, evoking a mystical rather than literal response to the words.

In the middle of 1847, that redoubtable trio of John Everett Millais, William Holman Hunt and Gabriel Rossetti, joined themselves together to form the Pre-Raphaelite Brotherhood, a bold attempt to recreate in their own work the naturalism of early Renaissance paint-

*Figure 38. Illustration to Longfellow's* Evangeline *by Jane E. Benham, 1850.*

ing. In Millais' Gower Street home, the three of them pored over engravings of frescoes by Benozzo Gozzoli, Orcagna and others from the Campo Santo at Pisa. The productions of the Brotherhood between then and 1851 slipped imperceptibly at first into the Royal Academy exhibitions. Millais had exhibited his masterpiece, 'Lorenzo and Isabella' and 'Christ in the House of His Parents', Hunt his 'Valentine' and Rossetti his 'Girlhood of Mary The Virgin' and 'Annunciation' separately. But then amid a growing storm of wrath, the British public became enraged by their fresh vision and new approach, until John Ruskin came to the rescue as 'a graduate of Oxford' in his celebrated supporting letter to *The Times* in 1851.

The Pre-Raphaelite assault on book illustration was not so dramatic as that on painting. The Brotherhood was already in disarray before their first illustrations had been commercially published. The four or five artists surrounding Rossetti had no revolutionary ideas to bring to the book itself, they had no crede of typography like Morris or ethic of decoration like Walter Crane, they simply wished to express the idea of the poetry of the day or of the day before yesterday as they saw it.

It was hardly surprising that they chose lyric, legend and mythology to do it. Not the mythology of the classical world which had lost its lustre for them, but the northern mythology of German romanticism, mysterious, cloudy and easy to paraphrase. Then there was contemporary poetry, the work of Tennyson and Longfellow, of Christina Rossetti and Jean Ingelow, much of it highly tuned and painterly, but not too tightly written. The Pre-Raphaelites proper seldom strayed very far outside *their* literature, either the writers whom they knew personally or the poets contemporary with the early painters they admired. Rossetti, the foreigner, turned his thoughts to early Italian themes and Dante, Madox Brown illustrated passages from Byron and Arthur Hughes tales from Macdonald. Biblical scenes were a source of inspiration and several of the group drew for *Sacred Poetry* much of it seventeenth century or for *Watts' Divine Songs.* Subjects from Scott or Shakespeare do not seem to have interested them as far as the book was concerned, not a single one of them illustrated an historical novel, and the works of Bunyan, Milton, Defoe, Swift, Goldsmith and Thomson as well as Cervantes and La Fontaine were left to their followers.

What they were beginning to bring to the illustration was a recognition that it had the status of a work of art. The endless preparatory studies, the research, the changes in direction, the demands on their engravers were quite new to men like the Dalziels. They had been used to the professionalism of John Gilbert, whose boast was that not one line had to be altered. That was the way of successful commercialism not of great art, Pre-Raphaelite pride owed nobody a living, the illustrator was now to be on a par with the poet. As their position improved, artists began to have their names on the contents pages of books, often from the 1840s with that of the engraver alongside.

It is only possible here to deal with representative books from the two main themes of Pre-Raphaelite illustration, the designs for contemporary poets and the biblical and sacred subjects. The most important book of the first group, and the first to appear, in 1855, was *The Music Master* by William Allingham, also known as *Day and Night Songs.* Allingham, 1824-1889, was an Irish poet and collector of ballads, who later became Editor of *Fraser's Magazine* and the husband of the well-known illustrator and watercolourist, Helen Allingham. The success of Allingham's *Poems,* 1850, and *Day and Night Thoughts,* 1854, must have encouraged him to think of an illustrated edition of the latter. In the eventual preface of the book, he thanks 'those excellent painters who on my behalf have submitted their genius to the risks of wood engraving. . . ,' making it plain that the idea had been his rather than Messrs. Routledge's. The amateur status of the project meant that each artist only received three guineas for each block. In April 1854, Rossetti and Ruskin were reading the first edition of the poems and the latter pronounced them 'heavenly'.[3] They held for the Rossetti circle exactly the right ingredients of romance, archaism and love of nature to make them irresistible. Practically the only one remembered today is 'Up the airy mountain, Down the rushy glen', a nursery song that seems to have become the perennial diet of every child's anthology. By May 1854, the scheme which had been nothing more than a vague idea was taking shape; Rossetti was already asking Allingham for two or three blocks to work on. The following month the artist again writes to him with customary vagueness about the commission in hand. 'I trust certainly to join Hughes in at any rate one of the illustrations of Day and Night Songs,' he writes, 'of which I hope his and mine will be worthy — else there is nothing so much spoils a good book as an attempt to embody its ideas, only going halfway.' The book was obviously taking on a coherent shape, Millais was enlisted and Arthur Hughes, closely associated with the Pre-Raphaelites was one of the best designers for the printed page.

Rossetti took the subject of 'The Maids of Elfen-Mere' for his wood engraving, a theme of unrequited love which he found congenial and gave him the opportunity of drawing three lovely but menacing women and a pining, dying figure from the world of mortal men (Figure 39). It was nevertheless January 1855 before the publishers had the completed block in their hands, following one unsuccessful attempt. Rossetti was unfamiliar with drawing on the wood and the first effort seems to have been untranslatable by the engravers. 'In this *second edition* of it,' Rossetti writes, 'I have tried to draw all the shadow in exact lines, to which, if the engraver will only adhere, I fancy it may have a chance, but hardly otherwise, as there is a good deal of strong shade — dangerous especially to the faces, but I could find no other way.' The cutting was given to the Dalziels, the most experienced of engravers but the resulting proofs horrified the sensitive Rossetti, he immediately requested Allingham to withdraw it from the book. The other side of the story was related to Arthur Hughes by the

*Figure 39. 'The Maids of Elfen-Mere' by D.G. Rossetti.*

Dalziels themselves. 'How', they asked him, 'is one to engrave a drawing that is partly in ink, partly in pencil, and partly in red chalk?' Allingham's wishes prevailed and after some doctoring, Rossetti was prepared to let it stand in March 1855. A cover design was also prepared by him for the book but never used.

Of the other two contributors. Arthur Hughes had the lion's share, designing the frontispiece 'Crossing the Stile', vignette and ornaments and six page illustrations. The ornament is small stark and naturalistic and in that sense Pre-Raphaelite, the illustrations less so. 'Lady Alice' except for gesture and drawing is on the same level as Selous or Benham, 'Milly' is a more carefully observed subject, three separate figures, all concealed from each other but all expressing inward emotion. The best of his in the book is 'Under the Abbey Wall', in which the figure of a young man lies head in hand on a grave, a derelict gothic transept, festooned with ivy behind him. This is the first appearance of the subject that was to fascinate Hughes and bring him to fame as the painter of 'Home From Sea', 1856-62. The more decorative side of Hughes' work is found in 'Fairies' (Figure 40), a delightful roundel of elfish figures dancing in front of the moon, their girations reflected in the calm waters of a lily pond. The gentle fantasy of this is somewhat akin to Richard Doyle's fairyland, but the design is much more organised and the flowers and lilies and reeds are preternaturally real. John Millais' single illustration 'The Fireside Story' is dealt with later.

*The Music Master,* with its nine illustrations and small duodecimo size, does not seem to compete with work like William Harvey's *Don Quixote* of 1839, with its three hundred wood engravings. But despite its size and lack of balance, it was an achievement for Victorian illustration and for Allingham in particular for introducing three great artists to the art of the book. Rossetti best expressed what he had done when he wrote later to Allingham that he preferred to illustrate those poems 'where one can allegorize on one's own hook on the subject of the poem, without killing for oneself and everyone a distinct idea of the poets.' His 'Maids of Elfen-Mere' had caught the idea of the poem, captured

*Figure 40. 'Fairies' by Arthur Hughes, 1855.*

the nervous rhythm, 'the pulsing cadence', but neither slavishly mirrors the verses or dominates them; the three spinning maidens and the doomed figure in the foreground exist quite independantly of the lines. In choosing to allegorize here, Rossetti was really liberating the most creative forces since Blake, forces that were to give the 1860s their most distinctive themes, symbols of passion, cruelty, hopelessness, that were to be used and abused and plagiarized for forty years. Even the small size of the block, which Rossetti disliked, worked for the best. It gives the print a more highly charged, crowded, sensual aspect, which was entirely new. Hughes' vignettes in the same book were the starting place of a whole generation of children's books where the child's senses and imagination were magically touched and developed.

If the *Music Master* proved to be too slight a production for convincing the public of the freshness, originality and poetry of the Pre-Raphaelite illustrators, *Moxon's Tennyson,* 1857 was too diluted to do so. The first was the personal idea of Allingham the poet in sympathy with his friends, the second the commercial undertaking of Moxon, the publisher and man of business! Rossetti still saw *this* book as he had the other as a declaration of Pre-Raphaelite principles with only the chosen few contributing. 'The right names would have been Millais, Hunt, Madox Brown, Hughes, a certain lady and myself', he wrote to Allingham, 'NO OTHERS. What do you think? Stansfield is to do *Break, break,* because there is the sea in it, and Ulysses, too, because there are ships. Landseer has Lady Godiva — and all in that way. Each artist, it seems, is to do about half-a-dozen, but I hardly expect to manage so many, as I find the work of drawing on wood particularly trying to the eyes.'[4] W.M. Rossetti mentions with what derision the older illustrators work was received by the young men when the book finally came out.

Over the years it has become Rossetti, Hunt and Millais' book, five illustrations by the former including some of his best work (see Colour Plates VII and VIII), seven by Hunt and eleven legendary subjects by Millais. This triumvirate certainly seized on those passages where it was possible to allegorize and extemporize in visual terms, 'The Palace of Art', 'A Dream of Fair Women' and the ballad stories like 'The Lord of Burleigh' and 'The Lady of Shalott'. William Holman Hunt emerges through these pages as a better composer than Rossetti, if without so fertile an imagination. His two designs for 'Recollections of The Arabian Nights' seem to have been tailor-made for him, the squatting figure of 'the Good Haroun Alraschid' no doubt sketched from a figure in the Holy Land. In the first drawing for 'The Ballad of Oriana', Hunt has brilliantly moved to medieval Europe, capturing in his drawings the inevitable, ruthless and doom-laden world of chivalry, the knight's lady struck down by the arrow as she looks out from the battlements. The 'Shalott' pictures are divided between Hunt and Rossetti because the latter complained that all the good subjects had been taken. Hunt's fine and stylised and stormy 'Lady', her hair flowing like a cascade fore and aft along the top of the engraving is the archetypal Pre-Raphaelite image. It is in fact more typical of Rossetti than of himself. This lank, slightly stooping titan was constantly repeated in book illustration and caricatured by such artists as George Du Maurier, 1834-1896, in his 'Legend of Camelot' based on the Moxon edition. In *Tennyson and His Pre-Raphaelite Illustrators* G.S. Layard refers to Tennyson's reaction to this drawing. 'My dear Hunt,' said Tennyson, when he first saw this illustration, 'I never said that the young woman's hair was flying all over the shop.' 'No,' said Hunt, 'but you never said it wasn't.'

In his other work, Hunt shows enormous subtlety, the 'Godiva' though highly finished throughout, concentrates attention on the beautiful figure of the woman, 'The Beggar Maid' is as lightly drawn as the other is deeply etched.

Rossetti's drawings are the result of the same brooding idiosyncratic vision which gave Allingham's 'Maids' such power and they brought much the same striving after perfection and outbursts of indignation from the painter poet. 'What ministers of wrath', Rossetti wrote of his engravers, 'Your drawing comes to them, like Agag, delicately, and is hewn in pieces before the Lord Harry. I took more pains with one block lately than I had with anything for a long while. It came back to me on paper, the other day, with Dalziel performing his cannibal jig in the corner, and I have really felt like an invalid ever since. As yet I fare best with W.J. Linton, he keeps stomache aches for you, but Dalziel deals in fevers and agues'. The most important of Rossetti's works here, the first illustration to 'The Palace of Art', was in fact engraved by the Dalziels with very creditable results, though Ruskin considered otherwise. It shows the artist at his most precocious; literary and mystical allusions abound, distant ramparts, greens, trees, harbours full of ships, a dove and a sundial. In the midst of this 'lordly pleasure house' sits the beautiful organist, St. Cecilia, swooning backwards at the heady sounds of her own melody, backwards to be kissed sensuously and on the cheek by an angel, the kiss of death (Figure 41 and Colour Plate VIII). Potent stuff this and whether it is suggested by Titian's organ player or the little masters of Germany, it remains indelibly Rossetti's in its glorious intensity and skilled eclecticism. Neither 'Mariana in the South' or 'Sir Galahad', two others of his contributions, quite sustain this pitch of poetic allegory. His illustration for 'The Lady of Shalott' is an admirable square composition with some of the confined feeling of a missal painting. The bending figure of Lancelot was modelled by the young Burne-Jones. 'The Palace of Art' remains the triumph, Madox Brown called it 'jolly quaint but very lovely' and Tennyson could not make it out at all. 'The illustration of St. Cecilia puzzled Tennyson not a little,' wrote W.M. Rossetti, 'and he had to give up the problem of what it had to do with his verses.'[5] Rossetti himself believed that Tennyson loathed his designs!

Even in the realm of legend and allegory, Millais was the most natural book illustrator of the three. Despite Rossetti's great powers of invention and Hunt's religious zeal, the pure, seemingly

*Figure 41. St. Cecilia by D.G. Rossetti from* Moxon's Tennyson, *1857.*

effortless line of the unbookish Millais surpassed them. The first drawing chronologically in the *Moxon,* is 'Mariana', illustrating Tennyson's haunting poem of a girl's forlorn love as she waits by a window (Figure 42). The very writing of this poem with its 'rusted nails', 'ancient thatch' and 'cluster'd marish mosses' has a sort of Pre-Raphaelite colouring to it. Millais' prostrate figure on the window seat lies like a great arc across the picture, the drapery of her dress catching the light of the window before falling into deeper shadow. The idea was frequently used by later artists and one suspects that the delightful window embrasure was the inspiration for many an aesthetic inglenook!

*Figure 42. 'Mariana' by John Everett Millais, 1857.*

Perhaps next in quality to this is the 'St. Agnes Eve', a drawing of great sensitivity and simplicity in which the young woman pauses on a turret stair and gazes out on a snow-covered moonlit landscape. The light on her gown, the stonework and even the warmth of her breath in the frosty air are given an almost ethereal delicacy. Two rather more severe subjects are his illustrations to 'The Sisters' and 'The Death of The Old Year', a step nearer than most to Dürer and his contemporaries. For 'The Sisters' he takes a dark and windswept castle tower directly from Tennyson's lines 'The wind is howling in turret and tree', a much more literal interpretation than Rossetti or Hunt. In the 'Death of The Old Year', we are in an empty bell turret based on that at Winterton church. The wheel and bell are still, but a quizzical owl perches in the shadows above the wooden frame. Forrest Reid considers that this may have been an illustration for Tennyson's unused poem 'The Owl'; it certainly bears no connection to the printed poem below.

Both the 'Sleeping Palace' illustrations are complex in composition and that of the king waking from his reverie, surrounded by the court, looks forward to the groups of *The Parables* a few years later. 'The Talking Oak' is disappointing, but with 'The Lord of Burleigh' at the end of the book, he returns to a tragic theme and produces a deathbed scene with astonishing control of the lights. Millais seems to have liked to minimise the whites and praised highly the cutting of this block.

*Moxon* was to remain a rich mine for Pre-Raphaelite followers. The 'Lady of Shalott' and other themes appear and reappear from Burne-Jones to Fortescue Brickdale. But closer in time and more relevant are the constant repetitions of the 1860s, linking the technical ability of that decade to the creative mastery of the Pre-Raphaelites. 'Mariana' for example turns up as a direct transcription, but reversed, in Arthur Hughes' 'Blessings in Disguise', published in *The Sunday Magazine* in 1869. The scene of leaded window and angle seat had already been utilised three years earlier by J.D. Watson in 'Too Late', an illustration for *London Society.* Frederick Sandys has raided Rossetti's 'Mariana in the South' for his own 'Rosamund Queen of the Lombards' in *Once a Week,* giving her a more slick and polished finish; the same artist's 'If' for *The Argosy* is a type of 'Lady of Shalott'. Turning to the work of M.J. Lawless, 1837-1864, we find that his 'Rung into Heaven', *Good Words,* 1862, is set in the same bell turret as 'The Death of The Old Year', the landscape glimpsed through the self-same opening, but he introduces figures of three orphans.

It would be possible to pursue this almost *ad infinitum,* but one further convention deserves to be looked at because it occurs so frequently, the deathbed. The only deathbed in the *Moxon Tennyson* is Millais' 'Lord of Burleigh'; the sombre tones of the bunched drapes and the dark areas of closely engraved line give it an extraordinary grandeur. The dying woman lies in a bed, the length of her body dividing the picture area laterally into two, a window is in the right corner and four figures lean gently over her. Whether Millais was thinking of some specific painting such as Hugo Van Der Goes' 'Death of the Virgin' or not it would be difficult to say, but his solution to making the picture read well and yet remain unsentimental, worked. The scene is a symbol rather than a representation. The same arrangement was used for his modern subject 'Last Words' in *The Cornhill,* 1860, in Holman Hunt's 'At Night' in *Once a Week,* (Figure 43), the same year, and repeated by that 'dealer in magics and spells', Frederick Sandys, for his 'Sleep', *Good Words,* 1863, and his 'Sailors Bride', *Once a Week,* 1861. M.J. Lawless uses it for his 'One Dead' in *The Churchman's Family Magazine,* 1862. The young George Du Maurier contributed 'On Her Deathbed' to *Once a Week* in 1860, the bed swung round at an angle, perhaps suggesting a familiarity with the 'Death of St. Anne' by Quentin Massys which he might have seen in Belgium. The same treatment of the bed at an angle appears in Lawless's 'The Bands of Love' for *Good Words,* 1862.

Although the Pre-Raphaelites had brought pictorial power and invention to the book, sharp observation of nature and increasing sympathy for the medium, the bulk of the work is scattered and not numerous. The most considerable series of drawings which can be judged together and represent the mystical side of the movement are *The Parables of Our Lord* published in 1863.

The Dalziels had suggested the idea to Millais in 1857 and in agreeing to it, he had said that he intended to make it 'a labour of love like yourselves'.[6] The plan was to have had thirty drawings but the number was reduced to twenty and even then it was six years before the artist completed them. In a letter to the Dalziels, Millais explained his attitude to the drawings and his method of work. 'They are separate pictures, and so I exert myself to the utmost to make them as complete as possible. I can do ordinary illustrations as quickly as most men, but these designs can scarcely be regarded in the same light — each Parable I illustrate perhaps a dozen times before I fix, and the "Hidden Treasure" I have altered at least six times. The manipulation of the drawings takes much less time than the arrangement, although you cannot but see how carefully they are executed.'

The Dalziels played their crucial part in the cutting, giving an exactitude in the facsimile which won high praise from Millais. Twelve of the subjects appeared in *Good Words* in 1862 by special arrangement with Strahan, the publisher. They included 'The

*Figure 43. 'At Night' by W. Holman Hunt from* Once a Week, *1860.*

Leaven', 'The Ten Virgins', 'The Prodigal Son', 'The Good Samaritan', 'The Unjust Judge', 'The Pharisee and The Publican', 'The Hidden Treasure', 'The Pearl of Great Price', 'The Lost Piece of Silver', 'The Sower', 'The Unmerciful Servant' and 'The Labourers of the Vineyard'. These were followed by eight others when the completed book was published, 'The Tares', 'The Wicked Husbandmen', 'The Foolish Virgins', 'The Importunate Friend', 'The Marriage Feast', 'The Lost Sheep', 'The Rich Man and Lazarus' and 'The Good Shepherd'.

One has to remain astonished at Millais' fecundity of invention. With twenty subjects, many of them representing similar passions, cruelty, remorse, retribution, compassion, reconciliation and wonder, the artist has left no room for overlap and has created a complete world in each. Millais lets the teaching or moral of each parable stand out clearly from personal sentiment. The cloying subjective character of much Victorian religious illustration is completely absent because of the strength and independance of the draughtsmanship. Had these illustrations been in colour, it is doubtful whether even Millais would have escaped the mediocre.

Perhaps the most distinguished of the group representing reconciliation and compassion respectively, 'The Prodigal Son' and 'The Good Samaritan', were both first published in *The Cornhill*. In 'The Prodigal', the returned wayward son is locked in the arms of his father as they meet on a grassy slope. Sheep sit unconcernedly nearby and above them is the conical shape of a granary where harnessed oxen wait for the normal day's work to be resumed (Figure 44). The dark shapes of the cedars contrast well with the pyramidal barn and the contrasting hair of father and son is splendidly rendered. Millais has realised that to show the faces at such a moment would be to betray the depth of the emotion. 'The Good Samaritan' is likewise balanced by a calm and unconcerned animal, this time a donkey and a carefully realised landscape. Again the faces of the two figures, the one bending over the other, are partially obscured.

The composition of these pictures is exceedingly diverse, 'The Sower' for example is shown silhouetted against the skyline, scattering the seed on a steeply sloping rocky hillside; in 'The Hidden Treasure' the dark haunches of the oxen are contrasted with the bright desert sky and the ploughman kneels in the shade to examine what he has found. In 'The Tares' an evil old man sows mischief among the crops with snakes and jackals around him, while the light in his unwitting neighbour's house burns brightly in the background. The most Jewish or Eastern in feeling of the series are 'The Pharisee and The Publican' and 'The Unjust Judge', not perhaps as accurate in Jewish detail as Simeon Solomon's work but with a powerful sense of ritual and the difference between inward and outward behaviour. In the first, the Pharisee stands in the full sunlight, his finely chiselled profile and beard gazing upwards; the Publican by contrast leans heavily on a pillar more twisted than himself in deepest shade. In the second, the more complex composition, an Eastern ruler, of incredible duplicity and cunning, turns aside from a pleading widow at his feet, while his various attendants try to restrain her (Figure 45). Millais has written here, in the indifference of the judge and the petulant movement of that tiny

*Figure 44. 'The Prodigal Son' by John Everett Millais.*

THE UNJUST JUDGE.

*Figure 45. 'The Unjust Judge' by John Everett Millais from* Good Words *1862.*

authoritative hand, reams about the abuse of power. The studies of the other heads are brilliant realisations of brutal ignorance in the man tugging at the woman, superiority and idle curiosity in the figures looking round the chair and subservient hostility in the scribe to the right. The heads in this and the earlier drawing suggest more than a passing debt to Bellini.

'The Lost Piece of Silver' is the most striking image of the set, Forrest Reid considers the line has 'the flowing elastic quality of a water weed streaming in a current'.[7] The background is in deep shade because it is night and the stooping figure of the girl is moulded out of this where the light from the candle catches her face, her arm or the edge of her broom, in her diligent search. In 'The Leaven', a woman works at the kitchen table while her daughter looks on. 'I send off by Post the Parable of "The Leaven which the woman hid in the three measures of meal",' Millais wrote to Dalziel, 'she is mixing the leaven in the last of the three. The girl at the back I have made near the oven with one of the loaves, and the other rests against the wall of the window.'[8] The clarity of this scene and Millais' description of it is reminiscent of the Flemish painters of the sixteenth century or even the work of his French contemporaries.

*The Parables of Our Lord* were no more a commercial success than *The Music Master* or *Moxon's Tennyson.* For Millais it was a triumph and for Victorian book illustration a break through to 'high art'. The impact that these designs made on artists if not on the public, led the way to a large number of illustrated biblical books of high quality during the 1860s, culminating in Dalziel's great *Bible Gallery* in 1881.

# (ii) Millais and Modern Episodes

The years after 1860 saw a great explosion of illustrations of contemporary life, both in the magazines and the novels, the one often proving to be the testing ground for the other. Authors such as Charles Dickens, W.M. Thackeray, Anthony Trollope, Wilkie Collins, George Eliot, and later Mrs. Henry Wood and Henry James, provided an absorbing account of middle class life in which the artist could not easily escape into medievalism or sentimentality. The illustrator had to face the nineteenth century on its own terms, revealing as he did so its morality, its dilemmas, its conscience or lack of it, much as the social realists were to do in the 1870s and 1880s. But the scenario for most of them was the gentler more claustrophobic world of those lives lived behind thick velvet curtains. The innuendoes of the croquet lawn and the Hunt Ball, the savagery of the moneyed, the gossip of the London dinner table, lingering illnesses, deathbeds and the private but terrible ruin facing the respectable family that erred. The tensions were as great as in the slop shop but more dramatic by being more concealed.

As Michael Sadleir put it: 'A tide of royal principle and popular disgust, by engulfing the *ancien regime,* had transformed the middle classes from unimportant sandhills into the bulwark between land and sea'.[9]

A great number of artists worked in the contemporary idiom and verged from the masterly to the banal, although the quality was consistently high during the 1860s. The mental leap one has to make between say Phiz's illustrations to *Little Dorrit* of 1857 and the same author's illustrated edition of *Our Mutual Friend,* 1865, requires some explanation; the first is exaggerated, caricatured, the figures crowded into the picture area with generalised expression, the latter by Marcus Stone, though not the best of their type, clearly presented, the figures larger in scale, the treatment naturalistic. There is a more subtle difference than one of medium, Phiz sticking to the steel plate and Stone preferring the wood engraving, the vision that society has of itself has shifted from synthesis to objectivity. Where did so much unbiased reporting and beauty of line spring from in the simple depicting of every day events? The answer must lie with the greatest illustrator of the mid-century, John Everett Millais.

Millais' career from infant prodigy to President of the Royal Academy is too well known to be given here, but his work as a book illustrator is less familiar. Millais' extraordinary aptitude for drawing led him to be entered at Henry Sass's School at the age of nine and gained him a Society of Arts silver medal the same year. He entered the Royal Academy Schools at the age of eleven and remained there for six years winning most of the major prizes. In the middle of 1847, when he was barely nineteen, he joined Holman Hunt and Gabriel Rossetti to form the Pre-Raphaelite Brotherhood, and make a return to the principals of early Christian painting.

Millais was a born draughtsman and therefore a born illustrator. Some of his earliest sketches are title pages for books in the confident line of Flaxman or the slightly more decorative manner of Stothard. It was he who had presented a portfolio to the group in which black and white drawings could be circulated and criticised and it was he who had contributed illustrations to that short-lived organ of their movement *The Germ,* 1849.

The work of Millais the illustrator happily falls into the years 1857 to 1867, although a few were done in the 1870s. The dates have a certain significance, for they form a bridge between the early career of the idealistic Pre-Raphaelite and the later career of the successful academician and man of the world. The reason that these illustrations were such powerful insights into the Victorian mind and such accurate realisations of the contemporary novel was despite rather than because of the artist's growing popularity. These drawings had their seeds in the early 1850s when Millais was still young and still outside the artistic establishment. If these ideas took some years to form themselves into a coherent pattern, they were well worth waiting for; from 1857 with the publication of *Moxon's Tennyson* to the conclusion of *Phineas Finn* a decade later, glorious images of what Hunt called 'modern episodes' spilled out from his pen.

The crucible for all this energy and draughtsmanship was the Pre-Raphaelite movement itself, its strongly felt but inexact aims, its mixture of poetry and painting and Millais' own turbulent life after his meeting with Mrs. Ruskin. At the back of the Pre-Raphaelite creed was a strong reforming zeal and a desire to be involved with great moral issues in contemporary life; in 1853 Holman Hunt's *The Awakening Conscience* and Rossetti's *Found* were on this theme and Millais' own contribution was a very remarkable series of highly finished drawings. In them Millais was working out for himself the strong emotions engendered by his love for another man's wife; 1853 was after all the *annus mirabilis* of his Associateship, but also of the famous visit to Scotland with the Ruskins.

The author of *Modern Painters,* his young wife and Millais, the most promising painter of the British School, spent a holiday together in the Highlands during the summer and autumn of 1853. Ruskin lionised Millais, but the young people were thrown together, Millais grew to resent the coldness and reserve of Ruskin to his wife, and Effie had confessed to him that her marriage to Ruskin was no marriage at all. The Ruskins remained in the North and Millais returned to London, his love for Effie a ferment, his sense of outrage and frustration almost unbearable. Christmas passed, Effie returned to London, but it was not until the end of April that she left Ruskin for her parents' home in Scotland. Millais had to wait till July of 1854 for the marriage to be annulled and a further year before his own marriage to Effie.

It was at this period of mental anguish and self-searching, between the winter of 1853 and the summer of 1854, that Millais drew his series of modern episodes, thirteen in all, excluding copies. They are crucial in the development of Millais' own work for contemporary literature and ultimately of the School of the 1860s. J.G. Millais in his *Life* [10] discusses them with his father's illustrations to Trollope, implying this link; their high finish, their strong moral interest, their frank criticism, make them illustrations in all but name, although only one was published. The theme in each case is dependance, the dependance of woman on man, the dependance of children on their parents, the dependance of the sick person on his nurses, the sense that no action is ever isolated from responsibility. The most domestic of the subjects is the group called 'Retribution' where the Victorian paterfamilias stands, head bowed, confronted by two wives and the family of one of them; the solid furniture and the watching domestic heightening for a moment the public success and the private failure.

'The Race Meeting' follows the same pattern; a pleasure carriage at the races is surrounded by touts and beggars, the spendthrift young owner is ruined but tries to put a brave face on it, only his kept woman, who sits behind him, buries her face in her hands knowing that he will no longer afford her. Millais' tight penwork, incisive detail and factual reporting were the best vehicles for expressing Victorian cruelty and injustice. 'Accepted', a more conventional lover's tryst shows the man on his knees to the girl on the lawn of a country house. A ball is in progress within, dancers can be seen through the arches of the terrace, the lawn is bathed in moonlight except for the pool of shadow cast by the lovers. Are they part of the dance or has he crept into the garden to meet her? Her anxious glance housewards suggest this is the case. The whole scene conjures up Tennyson's *Maud* but that was published two years later in 1855. 'Rejected' is less dramatic as a composition but no less tense, a woman in a riding habit turns away from her suitor, her riding crop trailing on the ground, while grooms hold their agitated horses behind. 'The Dying Man' shows a faded and

*Figure 46. 'Fireside Story' by John Everett Millais from Allingham's* Music Master, *1855.*

sick man gazing at the fire, while his young wife reads to him. In 'The Blind Man', a blind beggar is led across a busy street by a defiant but gentle young woman. It is easy to conjecture Millais as the blind man and Effie as the absent but ever compelling guide! This drawing, both in outline, washes and subject matter, suggests curious affinities with Richard Dadd, an obsessive and nearly pathological eye.

A significant step between the drawings of the early 1850s and the illustrations of the 1860s, is the delightful contemporary subject in Allingham's *Music Master* of 1855, the only one of its kind by Millais in the book. Entitled 'Fireside Story' (Figure 46), it shows a circular group of two adults and five children listening to a tale, the whole scene is concentrated on facial expression and gesture, particularly good in the small girl, buried in her mother's skirts, and the totally absorbed look of the nursemaid.

Millais may have taken up the idea of doing black and white work from his meeting with John Leech in 1851. Leech's position on *Punch* had become pre-eminent through his social cuts of sporting subjects. Ruskin credits him with bringing graceful subjects to the printed page.[11]  The two artists were to become fast friends and hunting and fishing companions. According to J.G. Millais, his father's attitude to illustrative work was not one of snobbery, he believed 'that the few men quite at the top of the tree, both in line and wash, were entitled to rank with the best exponents of oil and watercolour'.[12]  He admired Leech's drawings and through him was introduced to Bradbury and Evans in 1860; in August that year he was speculating that he might make £500 a year from black and white drawing. His son did not think it was a profitable exercise; Millais was painstaking and deliberate and made as many pencil studies as for an oil painting before drawing the composition out in pen. He would scrap the whole scheme, tearing the drawing to pieces if there was anything unsatisfactory. He was careful about locations too; the interiors for *Orley Farm* were copied from Trollope's boyhood home at Harrow[13] and he was in the habit of using models, actually borrowing a baby for the same book! All the work for the Trollope novels, the *Cornhill Magazine, Good Words* and *London Society*, excellently engraved as they were, can only be appreciated with reference to these earlier 'modern episodes'. As all his work was drawn on the block, the original was destroyed in the cutting and he alone among the artists of the 1860s has enough surviving finished work to point the way. The fact that most of them remained in the family surely shows what personal documents they were.

100

One of the series was actually published and is illustrated here (Figure 47). It is perhaps the best study of the artist's technique, those controlled pen lines and subtle washes that only the best engravers could translate. This is called 'Married For Money' or 'Woman in a Church watching her former Lover married',· and was engraved for *Moore's Irish Melodies* in 1856. Millais mentions in a letter, quoted in Mary Lutyens' *Millais and The Ruskins*[14] that he spent his time in early 1854, disconsolately looking at churches. Perhaps one of them gave him the idea for this ingenious composition; the dark shape of the woman cranes forward to look into the body of the church where the wedding party are congratulating each other. Her silhouette is marvellously thrown into relief by the bright light from the windows behind her, striking pillar and pew, nobody but Millais could be so brilliantly subjective and yet so devoid of sentiment.

This perfection of line owes something to the neo-classicists as well as to fresco painting and the flat effects of Dyce or the

Figure 47. 'Married For Money' by John Everett Millais.

Nazarene School. It is most obvious in 'The Ghost', another marriage subject where Millais' preoccupation with gesture is best seen. It is small wonder that Ruskin was later to refer to this School of illustration as closer to nature in the delineation of the faces than anything since Holbein.[15] 'They possess,' says Gleeson White, 'the immense individuality of a Velasquez portrait, which, as a human being, appeals to you no less surely, than its handling arouses your aesthetic appreciation. At this period it seems as if the artist was overflowing with power and mastery – everything he touched sprang to life . . .'[16]

The decision by Edward Moxon, the publisher, to use Millais and Rossetti as his illustrators for the 1857 edition of Tennyson was a daring step. His use of older and less controversial men like Creswick and Mulready as well, makes the book a specially queer melange and accentuates the new style of the Pre-Raphaelites. Rossetti's 'The Lady of Shalott' and 'The Palace of Art' were outstanding, as were Millais' historical subjects dealt with previously. But the *Moxon Tennyson* brought Millais to the fore as a portrayer of modern episode. There were seven of these out of his total of twenty-four. The Dalziels called it 'a landmark in the history of book illustration',[17] even after one hundred and thirty years these engravings have a freshness and clarity. It must have appeared startling to the mid-Victorians that any artist would dare to treat the poetry of the great Tennyson in such a direct manner, the almost Millet-like figures for *Edward Gray,* the engagingly plain couple kissing in *The Miller's Daughter* and the magnificently basic and unlyrical argument between Father Allan and William at the head of *Dora.* The novelty is only reinforced by the simpering drawings of J.C. Horsley for *Circumstance* and the repetitive landscapes of Myles Birket Foster. Ruskin would have supported him; in *The Art of England* he writes 'that literature has in all cases remained strongest in dealing with contemporary fact. The genius of Tennyson is at its highest in the poems of *Maud, In Memoriam* and *The Northern Farmer.'*[18] What was true of the poet was equally true of this illustrator.

A number of the illustrations relate to the earlier drawings. The family group of 'Retribution' is contracted into the circle of figures at the end of *Dora*, the baby drawn from the poet's son, Hallam.[19] 'Rejected' becomes the gentler parting of *Edward Gray* and 'Accepted' the deep embrace of *Locksley Hall;* the similarities are not striking but the spirit of them is there. Millais like the other artists, was paid twenty-five guineas, Rossetti to be different, thirty guineas. The book is quarto size sold at a guinea and a half and should have been a success, but it wasn't. Another edition from Routledge sold well, but its triumph was in its influence rather than the profit it put into the pocket of Edward Moxon.

Three years later in 1860, Millais was commissioned through George Smith to illustrate Anthony Trollope's *Framley Parsonage* for the *Cornhill Magazine.* Although Millais only entered at the third instalment, it was to be one of the most successful partnerships of author and illustrator, the artist once more drawing for his inspiration on the modern passions and completing eighty-seven designs for *Framley Parsonage, Orley Farm, The Small House at Allington, Rachel Ray* and *Phineas Finn.* Trollope, who took little interest in his illustrators was surprisingly enthusiastic. 'Should I live to see my story illustrated by Millais nobody would be able to hold me,' he wrote from Cambridge in February 1860.

Unaware of who his new illustrator might be, he had. written a month before to the publisher with a tedious list of instructions: 'I think the scene most suited to an illustration in Part 3 of Framley Parsonage would be a little interview between Lord Boanerges and Miss Dunstable.' He goes on to explain that the lord should be very old, the lady not very young and the artist would have to read his earlier novel *Dr. Thorne* to get a description of her. Although Trollope came to trust Millais' pen implicitly, this was to continue as their pattern of work; the novelist suggested the subject, the artist carried it out and the writer criticised the result. It was remarkable that Trollope could fault his collaborator on dress but never on character. 'There is a scene which would do well for an illustration', Trollope wrote to his publisher, 'It is a meeting between Lady Lufton and the Duke of Omnium at the top of Miss Dunstable's staircase. I cannot say the number or chapter, as you have all the proofs. But I think it would come in at the second volume. If Mr. Millais would look at it I think he would find that it would answer.' Mr. Millais did and it is one of the best groups in the book. Both artist and author were completely attuned to observing nature. 'The art practised by Millais and myself,' said Trollope, 'is the effective combination of details which observation has collected for us from every quarter.'[20]

Trollope wrote appreciatively of their work together in his autobiography, a rare honour for the working illustrator. 'An artist will frequently dislike to subordinate his ideas to those of an author, and will sometimes be too idle to find out what those ideas are. But this artist was neither proud nor idle. In every figure that he drew it was his object to promote the views of the writer whose work he had undertaken to illustrate, and he never spared himself any pains in studying that work, so as to enable him to do so. I have carried on some of these characters from book to book, and have had my own early ideas impressed indelibly on my memory by the excellence of his delineations.'[21] If Trollope's characters had very nearly become Millais' characters, it is arguable how much the inhabitants of Barsetshire owe to the artist in the popular imagination today. The Archdeacon and Mrs. Arabin, the Bishop and Mrs. Proudie, the Crawleys and Lady Lufton are Trollope's creations but we still remember them through Millais' exact and penetrating eye.

The most delightful of the illustrated books is *Framley Parsonage* the earliest and the freshest in concept. Outstanding in the second volume of the work is the group of the Crawley Family (Figure 48), one of the softest and most beautifully balanced domestic subjects to come out of Victorian fiction, it was particularly admired by the novelist himself. The placing of the figures on the page is always happy in Millais, as in the 'Miss Gresham and Miss Dunstable' or the later illustration of Mr. and Mrs. Robarts standing in front of their chimney-piece. It is noticeable that in 'The Crawley Family' Millais harks back to those earlier groups of 1853, in particular, 'Married For Love', the hard pressed cleric surrounded by his family and writing a sermon. Similarly, the Duke of Omnium appears as a younger version of the same nobleman in 'Married For Rank', led along on the arm of his much younger and ambitious bride.

*Rachel Ray,* 1863, was followed by *The Small House at Allington* in 1864. This has a splendid frontispiece to the second volume 'Mr. Palliser and Lady Dumbello', some good rural subjects in which Millais excelled, especially His Lordship discovering the sleeping Eames and another 'And Have I not Really Loved You' reminiscent of the 'Rejected' of 1853. Orley Farm, 1866, has the sensitive landscape frontispiece of the farm, based on Julian's Farm at Harrow, some delightful trios like 'Over Their Wine' and tête-à-têtes such as 'Never is a very long word'. For some reason Millais lost the commission of *The Last Chronicle of Barset.* 1867, to G.H. Thomas, a far inferior artist, who was instructed to work from Millais' originals. Millais again appears as the illustrator of *Phineas Finn* with some excellent work 'Lady Laura's Headache' and 'The Fact is mama, I love him' being among the best. But there is a distinct falling off in quality towards the end of this volume, which appeared as late as 1869.

Trollope did not however have a monopoly on modern subjects and there were a number of these by Millais, such as 'Last Words' (Figure 49), which appeared in *The Cornhill Magazine* in November 1860, and are equal to any of the Barchester series.

Many of the most significant artists of the time, followed Millais in tackling contemporary literature with a similar intensity and power. Among them were Whistler, a rare illustrator, Fred Walker, M.J. Lawless, Frederick Sandys, J.D. Watson, J. Mahoney, Luke Fildes, G.J. Pinwell, Ford Madox Brown and J.W. North. The pages of *The Cornhill Magazine, Once a Week, Good Words* and *The Quiver* are full of the exquisite drawings, not

THE CRAWLEY FAMILY.

*Figure 48. 'The Crawley Family' by John Everett Millais.*

LAST WORDS.

*Figure 49. 'Last Words' by John Everett Millais.*

103

only confounding Ruskin's strictures that the turban was superior to the hat, but giving a beauty and significance to the top hat, the crinoline, the frock coat and the parasol. The nearest approach to Millais was in the superb work of Fred Walker, who had originally acted as 'ghost' for Thackeray's feeble designs to his own *The Adventures of Philip,* 1861, eventually taking over the job fully and signing with his familiar 'FW'.

Another deft black and white artist was G.J. Pinwell whose forte was in rural life. His 'The Sailor's Valentine' published in *The Quiver* in 1867 shows a Jack Tar with a woman and a little girl in the back garden of a London house. It is certainly not a grand London house, the woman wears a crumpled dress, the little girl's frock is not of the newest and the backs of other houses run across the top of the picture like a frieze. Pinwell, like North and Fred Walker, has gone among the people with a contemporary eye, not with the eye of romantic hindsight.

Ford Madox Brown's rare illustration in *Dark Blue,* 'Down Stream', shows the same questing after modernity; the young man grasps his love coarsely and vulgarly as the oars drag idly from the boat, emphasising the power of the moment, the 'now' triumphing over the restraint of the 'later'. Boyd Houghton's domestic scenes such as 'My Treasure' engraved in *Good Words* in 1862 echo the same feeling, the ugliness of the Victorian furniture giving a strong sense of the contemporary to the timelessness of a mother's love for her children.

Some of the early editions of Wilkie Collins' novels had illustrations by G.H. Thomas, Sydney Hall and F.W. Lawson that were not up to standard, and those of his later books, illustrated by Arthur Hopkins, are flagrantly bad. Marcus Stone's adequate but unremarkable work for Dickens' *Our Mutual Friend* has already been mentioned, Luke Fildes marvellous darkened interiors for Dickens unfinished novel, *Edwin Drood,* 1870, are easily the best of the later illustrations. A catalogue like this could go on to include work by T. Morten, Harrison Weir, F.W. Slinger, G.A. Sala, M. Ellen Edwards, who drew for Trollope's *The Claverings* and many more. Among these secondary artists, none is more charming than Kate Edwards, whose sensitive draughtsmanship of 'The June Dream', *London Society,* 1866, reflects the influence that the assured penwork of George Du Maurier was already having on a younger generation of artists.

Millais illustrations are however part of a long-standing graphic tradition even if that tradition was observed with new eyes. William Allingham, writing to the artist while he was on the threshold of his black and white career, recognised this: 'I wish you would master the art of etching, and make public half a dozen designs now and again', he writes. 'Surely one picture in a year, shown in London and then shut up, is not result enough for such a mine of invention and miraculous power of reproduction as you possess. This is the age of printing and a countless public, and the pictorial artist may and ought to aim at exercising a wider immediate influence. Be our better Hogarth . . .' That Millais achieved this end with his Trollope designs was the climax of a ten year study of modern episode.

Three of Millais' important series of 'modern episodes' came up for sale at Christie's on 12 December 1972 and fetched prices in excess of £2,500, a recognition of their considerable rarity in the artist's oeuvres. 'Accepted', from the collection of the artist's family, also made a high price at auction. Considering the wide circulation of Trollope's novels in the 1860s and the stature of the artist illustrating them, it is extraordinary that this side of his work is not better known and the books themselves more collected.

*Right: Plate VII*
*DANTE GABRIEL*
*ROSSETTI 1828-1882*
*'King Arthur and the*
*Weeping Queens'*
*Design for* Moxon's
Tennyson, *1856-57*
*Pen and brown ink*
*3¼ins. x 3³/8ins.*
*(8.3cm x 8.6cm)*
Birmingham City
Art Gallery

*Left: Plate VIII*
*DANTE GABRIEL ROSSETTI*
*1828-1882*
*'St Cecilia'*
*Design for* Moxon's Tennyson,
*1856-57. Signed with mono-*
*gram. Pen and brown ink*
*3⁷/8ins. x 3¼ins.*
*(9.8cm x 8.3cm)*
Birmingham City Art Gallery

105

## Footnotes

1. John Christian, 'Early German Sources For Pre-Raphaelite Designs' *The Art Quarterly,* Vol. XXXVI, Nos. 1 and 2, 1978.
2. William Bell Scott *Autobiographical Notes,* 1892, p.171.
3. This and following quotations taken from *Letters of Dante Gabriel Rossetti to William Allingham 1854-1870.* Edited by G. Birkbeck Hill, 1897, p.97.
4. ibid.
5. ibid, p.104.
6. *The Brothers Dalziel A Record of Work 1840-1890,* 1901, p.94.
7. Forrest Reid, *Illustrators of the Sixties,* 1928, p.75.
8. *The Brothers Dalziel,* op. cit., p.102.
9. Michael Sadleir, *Anthony Trollope A Commentary,* 1927, p.24.
10. J.G. Millais, *The Life and Letters of Sir John Everett Millais,* 1899, Vol. 1, pp.357-362.
11. John Ruskin, *The Art of England,* 1884, pp.178-179.
12. J.G. Millais, op. cit., Vol. 1, p.358.
13. ibid.
14. Mary Lutyens, *Millais and the Ruskins,* 1967, p.126.
15. John Ruskin, op. cit., p.179.
16. Gleeson White, *English Illustration of The Sixties,* 1906, pp.22-23.
17. The Brothers Dalziel, op. cit., p.83.
18. John Ruskin, op. cit., p.6.
19. Charles Tennyson, *Alfred Tennyson,* 1968, p.278.
20. Michael Sadleir, op. cit., p.278.
21. ibid.

# Chapter 6
# The Eighteen Sixties
# Some Magazines and Some Artists

 obody can deny that with the 1860s one has arrived at the golden age of Victorian illustration, a decade and a half from 1855 to 1870, when drawing on wood came to its maturity, and the best artists in the country were engaged in it. A great deal has been written about this epoch and even before it closed, the works were legendary and the position of the artists almost sacrosanct. The tendency has always been to perpetuate the myth of this 'sudden' flowering as if it were entirely in the hands of a group of young artists, not in the hands of mid-Victorian society, its dictates, tastes and prejudices. The black and white art of the 1860s is principally remembered today through the pages of its magazines, endless publications with varying axes to grind, political, literary, religious, instructional, humorous and purely entertaining. The majority of these were run on strict business lines, earnestly improving perhaps, but unsentimentally meeting a demand from a vast reading public. The new magazines could follow the channels opened up by *The Illustrated London News* and benefit from the vast distributive organisation of W.H. Smith whose bookstalls were to be found at nearly every major railway station in England and Wales providing light reading for the journey.

Apart from Samuel Read of *The Illustrated London News,* there were no art editors on the magazines and therefore no pandering to the demands of the artists for their own sake. In fact the writer was still considered of greater value to the magazine than the illustrator, who was paid proportionately less by his editors, men totally unsympathetic to the visual arts. W. Tinsley, proprietor of the successful and fairly well-illustrated *Tinsley's Magazine,* grumbles in his memoirs that pictures 'cost from two to three pounds the square inch for drawing and engraving', a preposterous sum![1] Nevertheless by 1860, it would have been a foolhardy editor who did not liberally sprinkle his weekly or monthly with engraved illustrations. The public had become visually aware, printing and engraving were approaching a peak, literacy was spreading and punitive taxation was being repealed. The climate was ideal for magazines in this lull between the self-discovery of the Great Exhibition and the consolidation of the Queen as Empress after 1876. It was the heyday of family entertainment and the decorative covers of *Good Words* or *Once a Week* would be opened, read aloud and then passed from hand to hand for the designs to be examined. The editors were satiated with fiction and the middle class with leisure, the illustrators answered the call by improving the one without making too strenuous demands on the other.

The middle of the nineteenth century was a very art conscious period. Moral and social improvement joined with culture to form an Elysium of institutions. Institutions bred other institutions like rabbits, burgeoning government departments spread mutual benefit into the provinces, government schools of design were set up, literary and scientific societies established, architectural and archaeological institutes were born. The ground was well prepared for the book-conscious 1860s. The Art Union of London, which distributed engravings to its subscribers and bought and presented the works of modern artists by lottery, was flourishing. It had begun in 1836 with a capital of £489 and in 1857, at the beginning of our period, its assets stood at £13,218 -9s. with a largely middle class membership of twelve thousand. It became a patron of the book illustrator only spasmodically, issuing to subscribers albums of line engravings such as Thomson's *Castle of Indolence* with William Rimer's designs in 1845 and the following year Campbell's *Gertrude of Wyoming* illustrated by George Elger Hicks. Sir Noël Paton was another artist employed by the Union to draw subjects from Shakespeare. Significantly enough the chief agents for the Art Union in the United Kingdom were booksellers. Other cities had their own Art Unions and the uniformity of the public they created and the homogeneity of its taste, must have encouraged publishers and printers to bring out larger editions, more lavishly illustrated.

'It is sometimes urged as an objection to the Art-Union,' ran its Report for 1857, 'that its productions, being issued to large numbers of persons, become in consequence common and valueless. This is not the feeling in which works of art should be viewed. It is not so in literature; a book is prized for the instruction it contains, or the delight it affords, and the value of it as a work of mind is in no degree lessened because copies are multiplied in thousands, and the book is placed within the reach of everyone.'[2]

The illustrators of the 1860s were part of a much larger revolution which placed the artistic print in the hands of everyone. The same zest for improvement that had created a readership had also created the talent to satisfy it, many of the draughtsmen now emerging were the products of those self-same government institutions. Never before had the decorative and industrial arts stood so high in the estimation of most men, and book illustration, perhaps the most artisan of the fine arts, shared in this glory of utility and mechanisation.

From the early 1850s, the vestries were allowed to build Free Libraries although they built very few. Such records of these as exist show that the working man was ravenous for tales and romances that took him far away from the grimy present, *The Arabian Nights, Ivanhoe, Robinson Crusoe* and *Moll Flanders* being the favourites. There is no indication but probably some of these cheap editions were crudely illustrated.[3] Mechanics Institutes were to be found in most large towns and these included libraries, news-rooms and reading rooms where journals and magazines could be found, although they were often most used by the tradesmen.[4]

There was also a revolution in the way people read, the more dignified habit of the eighteenth century, became the more cursory familiarity with books of the nineteenth. The age of the three volume novel turned into the age of the instalment, the part novel and the serial. W.H. Smith's had recognised as early as 1848 that a new means of transport needed a new kind of book. They had provided for the bookstall *The Railway Anecdote Book*, 1849, a collection of stories and jokes. The key was to occupy the reader rather than absorb him, to catch his attention between the covers, and hold him there for the fascinating moving landscape around him. The new literature presupposed that there was something else going on, and the 'yellow-backs' of the bookstalls carried the message 'For the Fireside, Steamboat or the Rail'. The illustrated magazine or novel was the natural companion for rapid transit where plates might hold the wandering attention in a way that prose could not.

The reformers of the Stamp Duty had likewise seen to it that the late 1850s and early '60s were the first tax free periods for the newspaper. Alterations were made to the levy on newspapers in 1853 and in June 1855, the duty was totally abolished except where the paper passed through the postal service. The effect was immediate. In July and August 1854, 19,115,000 newspaper stamps were issued and in the same months in 1855 only 6,870,000. Although not all magazines were subject to the tax, there was a great sense of liberation and euphoria in the press after the repeals and a boom in new papers and new publications.

The struggles of the artists over the previous ten years to master the art of book illustrating was really symptomatic of the slow progress towards a desired goal. Rossetti's frantic consultations with J.R. Clayton, the engraver, and J.E. Millais' attempts to etch were only the birth pangs of a new movement. The desire to communicate with a wider public was there, but until that communication took the form of a happy partnership between illustrator and engraver, rather than a battleground, the vigour of creative ability and craft were not going to be united on the page. The engravers, Dalziel, Linton, Swain and their brethren continued to gain stature from the work fed to them by William Harvey, John Franklin, William Mulready, John Gilbert, Birket Foster and many more. The up-and-coming young men of the 1860s undeniably stood on the shoulders of such artists technically, even if they surpassed them in other ways; the younger group were to inherit the vision of the Pre-Raphaelites but to adopt a more craftsman-like approach to engraving. Until the middle of the 1850s the individuality of artists' work was virtually obliterated by the wood engravers. 'All that was to be recognised,' wrote Layard, 'was the composition and invention. There was not necessarily of the artist a line in the reproduction that corresponded to his pen and ink drawing. So we see in many illustrated books of the period the name of the engraver upon the title page, with no mention of the designer.'[5] It is important to note as one follows the course of the younger artists through the magazines and books of the time, how few of them were in any way architects of their destinies. Walter Crane, 1845-1915, the archetypal craftsman-illustrator had bought *Moxon's Tennyson* for 31/6d. while still an apprentice; Burne-Jones, the future apostle of poetic legend had raved at Oxford over Allingham's *Music Master;* du Maurier, the ascendant star of domestic manners, had given the same illustrated *Tennyson* to his bride! The 1860s were to flourish on their own account, but the seeds had been sown a long time before.

Gleeson White in his formidable book *English Illustration of The Sixties,* takes as his starting point the magazines of the period. He is correct to do so for not only were they pre-eminent, but from them stemmed the new role of the illustrator as a journalist. From then onwards until the demise of magazine draughtsmanship, the illustrator's staple diet was the weekly and the monthly, the periodical as opposed to the book. There were of course some magnificent books produced, but finance and caution among the publishers made the magazine the natural home for the pictorial journalist. 'For it must not be forgotten,' Gleeson White wrote, 'that every new books is, to a great extent a speculation; whereas the circulation of a periodical, once it is assured, varies but slightly. A book may be prepared for twenty thousand buyers, and not attract one thousand; but a periodical that sold twenty thousand of its current number is fairly certain to sell eighteen thousand to nineteen thousand of the next, and more probably will show a slight increase.'[6]

Just as the risk of a periodical was reduced over that of a book, so the problems of using one illustrator were reduced by employing many. The publisher who was unwilling to commit himself to an untried and inexperienced artist had the opportunity to give him minor work without any obligation to continue. From the point of view of the young illustrator, it was much easier to get his artistic foot in the door through magazine work than through the more prized book work. The first offered room for experiment and gradual improvement, the second greater discipline and an awesome sense of finality. Moreover the one led to continuous employment and the other to more patchy periods of activity punctuated by non-employment. The magazines therefore became the ateliers of students, amateurs and craftsmen who aspired to be painters. Just as the engraving establishments were the grammar schools, the editorial offices were the universities on the way to High Art. 'I shall always regard those early years in Mr Linton's office as of great value to me,' Walter Crane wrote at the end of his career, 'despite changes of method and new inventions, it gave me a thorough knowledge of the mechanical conditions of wood engraving at any rate, and has implanted a sense of necessary relationship between design, material and method of production, of art and craft in fact — which cannot be lost and has had its effects in many ways.'[7] Similarly, Mason Jackson writing in the 1880s could make a strong case for the unique value of the magazines. 'Both *The Illustrated London News* and *The Graphic* may claim to have done good service to art and artists in this respect. Their pages have always been open for young artists, and while they have helped forward struggling genius they have opened up new sources of enjoyment to the general public.'[8]

The hierachy of the new magazines was as rigid as any old order of chivalry. The same sort of 'trade' specialists that had existed at Day's Lithographic Office in the 1840s were perpetuated in the 1860s. At the apex of this pyramid were those artists on the staff of the magazine, the members of 'The Table' at *Punch,* the Special Artists and the permanent men of *The Illustrated London News* and the chief cartoonists of the smaller magazines. Most of them held special positions in their respective papers, were paid salaries or retainers, and had privileged places within the pages. John Tenniel's principal cartoon in *Punch* for example was always placed in the middle opening and was always unbacked by print, Linley Sambourne's second cartoon also had a customary place and had to contrast with Tenniel's. Of equal importance with these regulars were the artists who drew only for special numbers at Christmas time, in the Season, or for royal weddings and funerals. The most famous of these was Sir John Gilbert, who had made a reputation out of grandiose history and patriotic allegory, and acquired a fortune to go with it. Du Maurier reported that Gilbert was making £3,000 a year out of illustrating in 1860 which was probably accurate; a bachelor and proverbially mean, he was continually pursued by less fortunate artists to become godfather to their numerous progeny! His greatest claim to fame is that he brought some dignity and objectivity to news reporting in the early days and made illustration respectable.

Further down in the scale were the outside contributors who would be featured regularly while not forming part of the inner coterie, illustrators working on the second serial, artists illustrating a poem or the seasons of the year. Beneath these were the scavenging hordes of students, amateurs and hacks hoping that an initial letter might fall from the rich man's table. There was enormous pressure to get commissions from more prominent journals and the enterprising would take on almost anything, drawing out another man's work, improving for the engraver and preparing tedious decorations and headings. The graduation from the drudgery to a quarter page cut was a red-letter day! The benefit of the system was that every man went through it. The RAs of the 1880s were the initial designers of the 1860s. Du Maurier, fresh from the Continent, set to work on initials, Herkomer had to learn to drawn on the wood and Fred Walker's lovely drawings appeared anonymously because he was ghosting them for W.M. Thackeray. Tenniel himself, A.B. Houghton, J.W. North, William Small, Luke Fildes, M.J. Lawless and Charles Green all came into the profession by that same door.

The more elaborate the magazine, the more complex its structure, and *The Illustrated London News* had of course specialists in every field. Artists were employed solely on portraits or animals, shipping, scientific drawing, bird's-eye views, comic cuts or ornament. T.R. Macquoid, their decorative artist, was in quite a different category from the casual decorator, his ornamental details appearing over a score of years with regularity.

George du Maurier, 1834-1896, who arrived in this country at the very turning point for black and white art, 1860, recognised at once the enormous competition. Brimming over with confidence and a certain self-importance, he was nonetheless forced to strain his capacities to the utmost to be accepted. His letters to his mother are full of the colour of the period and the *sturm und drang* of youthful enthusiasm. 'It is utterly impossible for me to give you an account of this last week,' he writes in June 1860, 'all the troubles, fatigues and vexations I have wiped — Clambering up the staircases and knocking at the doors of editors who are always busy and always in a bad temper. Sometimes treated rudely, sometimes put off with much politeness and slight hopes of future employment.'[9] 'If I got as much work as I could do' he wrote more confidently in November 1860, 'I could make £800 or £1,000 a year.'[10] But the question was to get that work; there was no chance of the inexperienced man being taken on to the permanent staff although he sensibly realised that this should be his aim. 'My name hasn't yet sufficient weight to force on them drawings which they don't like, like Keene or Tenniel,' he remarks of *Punch* in April 1861, 'and I cannot illustrate all subjects with equal facility. This depending on one paper is certainly precarious . . .' Or again the following May he confides, 'Mark Lemon told me very kindly that as their artists, Leech, Tenniel and Keene received a yearly income, he could only take large sketches from me when they were very much better than theirs, which is sensible enough.'[11]

Du Maurier had set his sights on *Once a Week* and ultimately *The Cornhill Magazine,* but both were highly selective, *The Cornhill* had comparatively few illustrations and *Once a Week* cut down their number quite soon after he started contributing. 'There was no sketch of mine in this week's *Once a Week,'* he reported gloomily in October 1860, 'nor will there be in the next, as they are crammed full of drawings by Millais.' Late in 1862 he repeats much the same story – 'I went to see Smith about the Cornhill. No chance for a long time to come – Millais, Leighton and Sandys have the monopoly of that at present . . .' There were of course other tactics to be considered; the silly season was an ideal one for the aspiring illustrator. 'In August the Punch artists will be going out of town,' du Maurier wrote gleefully in the summer of 1861, 'and I shall be very necessary I fancy, and I will try and do my very best in the light comical line.'[12] Later he was using Keene's absences to get known 'such is everybody's advice'. In 1862 he was exercising his talents by dining with Miss Thackeray, the daughter of *The Cornhill's* editor. Du Maurier called her 'a tremendous jobber' and added, 'if I get on the right side of her I'm alright with the Cornhill.'

But the chief strength of book illustration in the 1860s was its emphasis on the syntax of draughtsmanship and its high degree of specialisation. The artists disciplined themselves to draw for a certain magazine or a certain public. Du Maurier recognised this at an early stage and made humorous social scenes, the comedy of high life, peculiarly his own. 'I do not see any others in the field against me,' he writes in June 1861, 'Little Walker who had the first start in *Once a Week* has cut me out there, his style is very much appreciated by the public and he has the knack of making his work easy to the engraver. But he is utterly without fun or humour of any kind, and so is Lawless, and therefore *Punch* is not for them.'

The prestige of magazine illustrating at this time can only be compared to the same status applied to the 'artistic' periodicals of the 1890s. As we have noticed the attraction of these publications was partly due to their growing technical excellence in reproduction, partly due to a more artistic readership and undoubtedly helped by the social position of editors like W.M. Thackeray, Mark Lemon, Edmund Yates and Dr. Norman Macleod. In the higher echelons of the arts they were also paying well; under no other circumstances would the great names have been persuaded to join this hitherto despised craft. 'Indeed the competition is becoming so pressing that it is only by unflagging industry that I can keep pace,' du Maurier wrote in 1862, 'There is Leighton drawing on wood now for *The Cornhill Magazine,* and other swells whom you have not heard of, who spare no expense in time, industry and models. There is little Walker who had greater talent than I and whom I can only hope to keep up with by straining every nerve so to speak . . .'[13]

A novel by George Eliot would have attracted Leighton no more than a novel by Trollope would have attracted Millais, if they had not embodied the ideals that swept the country in the 1850s. 'I am very anxious to be kept on O.A.W. as it is the swellest thing out,' du Maurier told his mother in 1861, 'and gets me known, and the more carefully I draw the better it will be for me in the end, as a day is coming when illustrating for the million à la Phiz and à la Gilbert will give place to real art, more expensive to print and engrave, and therefore only within the means of more educated classes, who will appreciate more . . .'[14]

It was particularly in their meticulous pen work and in their study of nature that the rising men most resembled the Pre-Raphaelite tradition. As soon as du Maurier came under the shadow of Frederick Sandys he came under that influence. He had been paying only £10 a year for a lay figure, even Leech had never used one, but with Sandys the study was nature or nothing. 'I never appreciated till now the full extent of Sandys' marvellous power of execution,' he wrote, 'but think it a thing to be acquired. Oh for the physical strength to work 10 or 12 hours a day like Sandys and not suffer.' Or again he admires the other artist's intensity of observation — 'If he has a path of grass to do in a cut, an inch square, he makes a large and highly finished study from nature for it first.' Something of this finesse and integrity comes over in du Maurier's drawings for *Once a Week* and *Good Words,* although more noticeably in the landscapes of Fred Walker, J. Mahoney, J.W. North and George Pinwell. If any further proof of the genesis of the new illustration was necessary it would be conclusively drawn from a remark by George Cruikshank. That irascible artist had burst out to the editor of *Once a Week* that du Maurier was 'a damned preraphaelite'. As du Maurier added delightedly, it was only likely to do him good and the other harm!

As the momentum of the new movement proceeded and three major magazines were founded, *Once a Week,* 1859, *The Cornhill Magazine,* and *Good Words,* 1860, it might have been expected that some support would come for the younger men from Rossetti and Ruskin. Rossetti's reactions were sweeping and perhaps ill-considered but not wholly unsympathetic. In a letter to William Allingham in November 1860 he says 'I quite agree with you in loathing *Once a Week* illustrations and all.' but he adds, that he would not mind opening a connection with the paper.[15] Ruskin's attitude, as might be expected, was much more mandarin in judgment.

Ruskin's antipathy was two-fold, a dislike of the cheapening effects of mass production and a mistrust of engravers that dated back to the time when he was writing *Modern Painters.* Of the first matter, Ruskin boiled over in the pages of *The Cornhill Magazine* in 1876, a splendid tirade of Victorian jargon and lofty sentiment.

'The cheap popular art cannot draw for you beauty, sense or honesty; but every species of distorted folly and vice — the idiot, the blackguard, the coxcomb, the paltry fool, the degraded woman — are pictured for your honourable pleasure in every page, with clumsy caricature, struggling to render its dulness tolerable by insisting on defect — if, perchance, a penny or two may be coined out of the cockneys itch for loathsomeness . . . These . . . are favourably representative of the entire art industry of the modern press — industry enslaved to the ghastly service of catching the last gleams in the glued eyes of the daily more bestial English mob — railroad born and bred, which drags itself about the black world it has withered under its breath.'[16]

The great critic's quarrel with the engravers was long-standing; there is scarcely a paragraph in *Modern Painters* that is not derisive of them and though much of this applied to steel rather than wood engraving, both came under much the same lash. The engravers of the earlier landscape books had altered his beloved Turner's landscapes on the plate, so his full fury was unleashed upon them. For Ruskin, facsimile engraving was too mechanical on the one hand and too subject to human error on the other. The engraving 'factories' and the dividing of blocks represented the hateful voice of the modern world and the interpretive rather than the craftsmanlike attitude of the engravers, a sort of tyranny. In his Oxford lectures he could speak with some reason — 'there is not one artist in ten thousand who can draw even simple objects rightly with a perfectly pure line; when such a line is drawn, only an extremely skilful engraver can reproduce it on wood; when reproduced it is liable to be broken at the second or third printing; and supposing it permanent, not one spectator in ten thousand would care for it.'[17]

Although this was probably over-stating the case, Ruskin's qualms about the result on the printed page were natural. He could point to Albrecht Dürer's woodcut of 'The Dragon in the Apocalypse', where the line of the landscape was coarsely cut but was perfect in expressing the facts.[18] It was, he maintained, the engraver's job to express character not complexion, to use the softness of the substance to reproduce the light and shade drawn by the human hand, not to produce colour by varied line. 'All attempt to record colour in engraving,' he writes in *Modern Painters,* 'is heraldry out of its place; the engraver has no power beyond that of expressing transparency or opacity by greater or lesser openess of line, for the same depth of tint is producable by lines with very different intervals.'[19]

Ruskin could have been thinking of some of the early blocks for *Once a Week*; two spring to mind as typical of the insensitive approach of which he complained. J.E. Millais' first block in the new magazine 'Magenta' is so finely hatched and scraped as to be almost black, after staring at it one realises that the woman, if it is a woman, sprawled upon the bed, is reading a *newspaper.* Even if we take into account bad printing, it is inconceivable that Millais' original drawing could have been so totally lacking in contrast. Similarly, in December 1860, Holman Hunt's drawing 'Temujin' is handled with such awful coarseness by Swain that it is difficult to believe that the superfine draughtsman of 'The Lady of Shalott' could have had anything to do with it. Other examples could be quoted from the cheaper periodicals, but generally speaking Ruskin's strictures are over critical; the competent or excellent work seems to far outstrip the bad or mediocre. Without the original drawing, block and print side by side, it is however difficult to judge. But there was nevertheless a continuing tension for all artists except those who engraved their own work. As Philip James wrote: 'there could never exist that unity which Bewick gave to his books in which he, as the originator of the designs himself, cut the blocks and supervised the press work.'[20]

But it is only too easy to quibble over the deficiencies of such work without recognising the range, the quantity and the quality covered by artists and engravers in these brief dozen years. Gleeson White records nearly sixty magazines in his book and mentions two hundred and fifty artists, Forrest Reid considerably added to this list as well as classifying them more elegantly. The ones already mentioned, *The Cornhill Magazine* and *Once a Week* were the *sine qua non* of having reached the zenith as an illustrator and much the same could be said of *Good Words.* But the host of smaller publications catering for every taste and viewpoint must not be forgotten: *The Sunday Magazine* published by Strahan from 1865, *Belgravia* started by Miss Braddon, Mrs. Henry Wood's *Argosy,* 1868, *The Quiver,* with contributors like Robert Barnes, Paul Gray, A.B. Houghton and George Pinwell, *Tinsley's Magazine* already referred to, *The Broadway* which ran for seven years, *Saint Pauls* and *Dark Blue,* 1871-73. A noticeable advance which may reflect a change in the readership is the employment of women as contributors, illustrators, and even as editors in the 1860s. Some journals following earlier patterns were published entirely for women, the most famous of the newer sort being *The Queen,* 1860-61, containing fashion plates and samplers but not illustrated stories. Many other magazines ran articles on servants, cuisine and society, which must have been directed towards a feminine readership. The illustrator Miss Georgina Bowers, fl.1866-1880, made her début in the pages of *Punch* in 1866 and drew many vignettes, initials and socials for it in succeeding years. The woman as humorist was almost unheard of however and remained very rare indeed. Both Charles Keene and Harry Furniss shied away from caricaturing them and they did not emerge as caricaturists in their own right. At the end of the century M.H. Spielmann stated rather pompously, 'No woman has ever yet been a caricaturist, in spite of the fact that her femininity befits her pre-eminently for the part. That she has desisted is a mercy for which man may be devoutly thankful.'[21]

A number of magazines with excellent engravings in them were started for children, *The Boy's Own Magazine,* 1863, *Every Boy's Magazine,* 1863, *Aunt Judy's Magazine,* 1866,

*Beeton's Annuals* and the best of them all *Good Words For The Young,* 1869. In some ways the adult magazines were so charming and so comprehensive that any child might reach for them with delight, but in all cases they lacked colour, a powerful argument for returning to the nursery bookshelf. It was also some credit to the influence of artists of the 1860s that so many were employed by temperance societies, evangelical bodies and philanthropic institutions on tracts that would normally have been badly designed and badly printed. *The Band of Hope Review* was supported by Harrison Weir, L. Huard and John Gilbert and *The Leisure Hour,* an organ of the Religious Tract Society, contained an immense amount of illustrative work, some by Gilbert, George du Maurier and Simeon Solomon.

The least satisfactory side of these volumes was their overall design, the illustrations appear to be inserted without much consideration to the page and the types used for the text are often too small and hideous. Some of the original publisher's cloth bindings are very pretty and these are preferable to the re-bindings, even contemporary re-bindings in dull calf. *The Cornhill's* lovely cover design by Godfrey Sykes loses something from the red cloth being blind stamped. *The Churchman's Family Magazine* has gold stamped cloth in a gothic pattern by Bone and *London Society,* a maroon cover of the same by Burn, *Good Words* in blue cloth is stamped with gold only on the title and the spine.

# The Cornhill Magazine

This publication was founded in 1860 with W.M. Thackeray as editor. Its aim was to maintain high standards in both literature and illustration and this it succeeded in doing during the forty-seven volumes of its first series. It was generally regarded to be at the zenith of magazine illustrating and du Maurier as we have seen was keen to enter its pages. The competition was increased by its policy of having fewer illustrations than its rivals and those mostly full page. The high standard of design runs through from the title-page and cover, commissioned from Godfrey Sykes, 1824-1866 (Figure 50). Sykes is best remembered today for his murals and decorations for the South Kensington complex of buildings, but here he has produced a vigorous Renaissance frontispiece, four vignetted figures in an architectural framework, owing something to the influence of Alfred Stevens. Sykes must also be credited with another unattributed classical design in illustration of 'Ariadne in Naxos' which appears in this first volume. It is surprising that although the artists employed were all in the first rank, neither this frontispiece nor any of the illustrations are given formal acknowledgement, though many are signed.

*Figure 50. Cover of* Cornhill Magazine *by Godfrey Sykes.*

114

Thackeray, the perennial illustrator of his own stories, is here, scratching through serial parts of *Lovel the Widower* and *The Four Georges,* but as his own editor, who could stop him! His figures seem weightless and scrappy, but he is too closely influenced by the Hogarthian tradition to adapt to the new drawing style. But in the same volume for July to December 1860 there were articles on William Hogarth, and the artists of the 1860s could feel that they were part of a school of British draughtsmanship.

*The Cornhill Magazine* did have a greater homogeneity about it than other publications such as *Once a Week,* all the illustrations were printed on higher grade plate paper and only initial letters on the text paper; initials and illustrations are usually by the same hand. The most remarkable feature of the magazine however was its power to attract the Victorian Olympians. Not only were Thackeray's novels appearing between its covers, but in successive volumes were the first appearances of works by Elizabeth Barrett Browning, Anthony Trollope, Matthew Arnold, George Eliot, Mrs. Gaskell and Wilkie Collins. It was clearly the attraction of such a team that persuaded Frederick Leighton, Frederick Sandys and John Everett Millais to contribute so regularly when so seldom illustrating elsewhere. But it was also in these pages that the young Fred Walker was first given his head as a black and white artist. Millais' formidable series of designs for the *Barchester* novels has been dealt with, Sandys and Walker will be considered separately, Leighton's illustrations for 1862-63 are exceptional, even in an oustanding decade.

Leighton's drawings for books are rare and it was a stroke of genius to combine his scholarly classicality with the texts of George Eliot's *Romola*. Without any doubt George Eliot's name gave the project an additional glamour to the thirty-two year old artist, only four years away from election to the Royal Academy. 'It is an Italian story,' wrote Leighton to his father in 1862, 'the scene and period are Florence and the fifteenth century, nothing could "ganter" me better. It is to continue through *twelve* numbers, in each of which are to be *two* illustrations.'[22] From the very first artist and author were on friendly terms and George Eliot consulted Leighton, an acknowledged Italian expert on the meaning of words and on costume. 'I never saw anything comparable to the scene in Nello's shop as an illustration,' she wrote to him in the early numbers, 'There could not be a better beginning.'[23] Later on she criticised the position of a head but added as an afterthought, 'You have given her attitude transcendently well, and the attitude is more important than the mere head-dress.'[24] George Eliot had the advantage of seeing all of Leighton's highly finished pen drawings before they were engraved, we only have the results after the cutting. Probably the ones that most impress us today are those least redolent of Victoriana. 'The Blind Scholar and His Daughter', 'Suppose You Let Me Look At Myself' or 'The Escaped Prisoner' have that curious sense of pantomime that nineteenth century history painting usually brings. But when Leighton looks at the fifteenth century through the mind of its own painters as in 'The First Kiss', 'The Dying Message' or 'Coming Home' (Figure 51) the effects are marvellously structural, great play being made with the folds of materials and the contrasts of light and

*Figure 51. 'Coming Home' by Frederick Leighton.*

shade. Leighton is one of the few artists of the period to use shadow sparingly but really effectively, and he does so with the central figure in 'Niccolo at Work', the best classical model to emerge during the whole period. The corpus of this work was so highly rated that it was issued in a special edition of the novel in 1880. Leighton's first work for the magazine had been 'The Great God Pan' in the summer of 1860 but he was not satisfied with the engraving. The latter was a Dalziel block and he seems to have demanded a change to Swain for *Romola,* the results of those being wholly admirable.

Other notable contributions are in du Maurier's drawings for Mrs. Gaskell's *Wives and Daughters* in Volume 9 and Sir Noël Paton's only appearance 'Ulysses' in the same volume. That stalwart artist, Miss M. Ellen Edwards, at the outset of a long career, supplied eleven illustrations for Trollope's *The Claverings* in 1867 and F.W. Lawson makes his début with four drawings in the same year. In the 1864 volume we find G.J. Pinwell, Charles Keene and G.H. Thomas, a nicely contrasted trio, Robert Barnes, that most regular artist in later issues, arrive for the first time and Luke Fildes comes on the scene in 1870.

Two artists persist from the earlier tradition, Richard Doyle and C.H. Bennett, 1829-1867, bringing with them a facetiousness and whimsicality which suits the Thackeray ethos rather better than that of the other authors. Doyle continues his 'physiognomies' which began with 'Manners and Costumes of Ye Englishe' in *Punch* in 1849. Here they have become 'Bird's-Eye Views of Society' even more densely packed with figures than their predecessors and more sharply drawn. In the opening pull-out plate 'At Home Small and Early' the artist shows a nightmare of a party; overblown guests in the voluminous and constricting costume of the day jostle for position and food while the gasoliers burn hot overhead. Every face is carefully realised and shadow is almost excluded; no wonder the Pre-Raphaelites liked Doyle; he even includes an intense Rossetti female in the right foreground of the composition! We are then shown a 'Juvenile Party' no less crowded than the adult one, 'A Morning Party', 'A State Party' and 'A Country Ball', everywhere a profusion of food, a vivid motley of clothes and character and a revealing study of temperament. We then move on to the more public world of 'The Picture Sale', 'At The Sea-side' and 'A Popular Entertainment' with the same painstaking detail, nearly photo-graphic sweep of vision and mass of isolated narrative incidents. Doyle looks at life with a strange fanciful innocence like that of a child, his lack of gradations in colour reflect his ingenuous observation of character, everything is either black or white. Doyle's richly imaginative side is seen here in the initial letters to the series, especially in that to 'A Charity Bazaar' where 'C' (Figure 52) becomes a turmoil of mischievous sprites reliev-ing an elderly man of his money, his watch and everything!

C.H. Bennett's poorly drawn but expressive illustrations of passengers on 'The Excursion Train' and at 'Covent Garden Market', make even stranger company with the dexterous work of Fred Walker, but like Doyle's, their vein of comedy is refreshingly

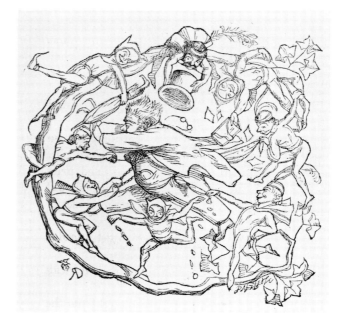

*Figure 52. Decorative initial by Doyle.*

116

pungent. It was to be a long time before such direct almost surreal creations as Bennett's reappeared in books with all their delightful crudities. The initial letter 'F' (Figure 53) of a train, half snake, half child's toy, blowing its preposterous way across the page, was lost for many years to come in the high-minded factualism of the later illustrators.

*The Cornhill Magazine* did not fall off in quality as dramatically as its rivals at the end of the 1860s. There are still some fine drawings and interesting literary contributions in the 1870s, Helen Allingham produces good work for Thomas Hardy's *Far From The Madding Crowd* in 1874 and the following year du Maurier tackles the same author's *The Hand of Ethelberta* and Henry James' *Washington Square* in 1880. Initial letters for this serial show what a deft designer du Maurier still was until the early 1880s. Well into the decade there are interesting names, Harry Furniss, R.C. Woodville, G.G. Kilburne, Frank Dadd and Towneley Green. Arthur Hopkins, 1842-1930, produces fussier and fussier social subjects and William Small develops a slick smooth technique without the beauty of his early work. Curiously enough the magazine lists the artists for the first time in 1883, two years later it dispensed with them altogether.

*Figure 53. Decorative initial by C.H. Bennett.*

# Good Words

This sixpenny religious publication edited by Dr. Norman Macleod, began in 1860 and had a meteoric rise to 1862, employing some of the best artists of the day. From 1863 with its change of venue from Edinburgh to London, there is a steady decline in its interest, drawings from photographs beginning to replace original work. Macleod, a chaplain to Queen Victoria and the son of a Moderator of the General Assembly, was more literary than visual but gave good scope to his evangelical leanings through the arts. During his early years, *Good Words* produced some outstanding things, in the *annus mirabilis* of 1862 came Millais' *Parables* already discussed but also fine work from lesser known artists. In that extraordinary year there is representative work by Millais, Sandys, Whistler, Keene, Holman Hunt, Burne-Jones and Boyd Houghton.

The greatest surprise of all are the two illustrations by the young Whistler, one showing the crouching figure of a girl by a fire and the other of a girl at a writing desk, both reflecting the vital line that was too powerful to contain this artist in book illustration. Edward Burne-Jones, who was to be one of the few artists to contribute to both the great periods of illustration, the 1890s as well as the 1860s, has two designs in 1862-63. The first is a rather grand composition to 'King Sigurd the Crusader', a poem by the Aberdeen poet, William Forsyth, and the second 'Summer Snow' a more typically lyrical subject of a girl bent over a letter, with the Pre-Raphaelite accessories of a full-flowing skirt, a brick wall and partly glimpsed tree branches. Burne-Jones seems to have disliked drawing on the wood and these are his only contributions to the magazines although he was later to draw for Dalziel's *Illustrated Bible*.

Both Sandys and Houghton are seen in 1862 in the height of their power and so are T. Morten and Holman Hunt. Morten is best represented by 'Pictures in the Fire' and 'The

Carrier Pigeon', Hunt by the distracted figure of 'Go and Come'. M.J. Lawless makes two splendid drawings 'Rung into Heaven' and 'The Bands of Love', rather softer than his usual mannered style. Works by H.H. Armstead, Fred Walker and J.D. Watson are scattered elsewhere and there is an infinite variety after 1863 in pictures by J. Wolf, R.P. Leitch, G. Pinwell, Florence Claxton and John Pettie. Two artists who sustain their early promise in the magazine from 1865 are Paul Gray and Robert Barnes, the first with some stirring costume subjects for Charles Kingsley's *Hereward the Last of the English* and the second in the protracted serial, *Alfred Hogart's Household,* by the now forgotten Alexander Smith. These are beautifully drawn and show in such plates as 'Come Along' and 'Puir Thing' a distinct debt to Millais' contemporary figures through the compositions of Fred Walker.

Until 1869 the quality of the magazine was maintained by the work of George Pinwell and Arthur Boyd Houghton, who will be dealt with separately. In April 1867, William Small illustrates Macleod's story, *The Starling,* with some very good country characters and Luke Fildes contributes an unusual scene 'In The Choir' for the following August. In 1868, Small is again very much to the fore with his domestic scenes for Mrs. Craik's story, *The Woman's Kingdom,* the initials for this

Figure 54. 'Macleod of Dare' by John Pettie.

being particularly charming, F.A. Fraser and J. Leighton also feature. Apart from the early work of Hubert von Herkomer, designs by J. Mahoney and Arthur Hughes, the later volumes tail off into the nondescript. There was an Indian Summer of the magazine's fortunes in 1878, when a group of 1860s men returned to draw for William Black's story, *Macleod of Dare.* The artists included G.H. Boughton, John Pettie (Figure 54), P. Graham, W.Q. Orchardson and J.E. Millais. Pettie in particular excelled himself in his portrayal of the Highlander.

# Once a Week

This was the first major magazine to be extensively illustrated by the new group of 1860s artists. It appeared for the first time on 2 July 1859, an attempt by the publishers Bradbury and Evans to rival Charles Dickens' popular but unillustrated magazine, *All The Year Round.* They chose as their editor Samuel Lucas, 1818-1868, a well-tried journalist with a strongly educational approach, accounting for the pictures of natural phenomena, archaeological specimens and topography in later numbers. His assistant and successor from 1867 was Edward Walford, a prolific journalist who was first an Anglican clergyman and then a convert to Rome. Both men benefited from sharing the same ownership as *Punch,* were frequent visitors to the *Punch* 'Table' and had the enormous advantage of being able to call on *Punch* artists. There is a very strong flavour of the other journal in early numbers,[25] especially in the contributions of John Leech, H.G. Hine and Hablot K. Browne, but it soon establishes its own identity with the younger men. Leech's socials are still marvellously vigorous and witty drawings but they do begin to date a little beside the subtlety of Fred Walker, M.J. Lawless and early Charles Keene.

It was probably Leech's influence that tempted Millais into *Once a Week,* with twenty illustrations in the first three volumes, July 1859 to December 1860. They vary a great deal in quality and in printing, the most enduring image being the engraving to Alfred Tennyson's poem 'The Grandmother's Apology', a sensitive study of the gentleness of age towards youth. But in 'A Wife', 'Practising', 'Musa', 'Violet' and 'A Head of Hair For Sale' we enter his most lyrical vein, lovely uncluttered outlines with superb light and shade. In 'La Fille Bien Gardée', a beautiful girl watched over by a dog, there is the gentlest hint that it is one of Leech's young ladies! There are several historical subjects too, less successful and less well interpreted by the Dalziels, although 'The Plague of Elliant' is very powerful.

Millais' contributions dwindle in 1861, the first half-year having like the second volume of 1860, only two works. In the last 1860 volume there is the warrior figure of 'Tannhauser' and 'Swing Song', a sentimental picture of childhood foreshadowing some of the later paintings. The illustrations for 'Thor's Hunt For His Hammer' and 'Iphis and Anaxarete' in

the first volume of 1861 are in his most poetic style, perhaps a reaction from the amount of modern genre subjects he was doing for Trollope at this time.

*Once a Week* gave a prominent place to Charles Keene at the start of his brilliant career, as an illustrator of serials. He begins with half pages for Charles Reade's *A Good Fight,* most unsuccessful work in a jocular medieval style imitating German woodcuts. Fortunately the proprietors gave him his head and he produced sketches of contemporary life where his penchant for humour and fine penwork were combined. 'The Foundation of My Picture Gallery' (Figure 55), the study of a connoisseur, shows the artist at his best, the central figure carefully finished, the background merely suggested. The following year, 1860, the commission to illustrate George Meredith's *Ewan Harrington* brought thirty-nine exquisite drawings into the pages. Keene's work on these is uneven but sometimes they are equal in handling to the figure studies of Millais and Walker, though with that heavy characterisation of the faces that Keene made his own.

Another of the magazine's early contributors was Sir John Tenniel, seen to advantage in both illustrations of Old Norse legend and Goethe and in

*Figure 55. 'The Foundation of My Picture Gallery' by Charles Keene.*

the domestic scenes for Shirley Brook's story *The Silver Cloud*. Tenniel emerges as a very much more versatile draughtsman than *Punch's* cartoons would lead one to suppose, but he is happiest in his drawing of 'Eckhart The Trusty', a vision of elfland to a poem by Goethe. Tenniel of course is just one of a number of Victorian illustrators whose childhood fears and delusions seem to smoulder under the surface, only to burst out in zaney worlds where children and hobgoblins have complete control. The owls, bats and puckish denizens of the woods seem far more alive than the bewildered youngsters they surround. The treillage of rustic woodwork and twisting ivy that frames this very decorative page, points to Tenniel as the artist of the magazine's frontispiece. C.H. Bennett, that very fertile artist already mentioned, whose comic invention usually outstripped his drawing ability, has one very weird drawing, 'The Song of the Survivor', conceived with the same disturbing impersonality as Tenniel at his most fantastic.

W. Holman Hunt supplies three illustrations, 'Temujin' which has been referred to, 'Witches and Witchcraft' and 'At Night', a contemporary deathbed scene, very even in tone and full of the artist's religious intensity. *Once a Week* was also unique in having secured no less than four illustrations by J. McNeil Whistler, very free in their execution and quite unlike any of the other work; his kneeling girl in 'The Relief Fund in Lancashire' must have appeared very novel to the readers, looking forward as it does to the mastery of the pen line in reproduction at the end of the century.

Charles Green, George du Maurier, Edward Poynter, F.J. Shields, J.D. Watson, F.W. Lawson and Paul Gray all contributed to the first thirteen volumes of *Once a Week*. A new series began in January 1866 and another in 1868, but the standard of creativity and execution, so notable in the early days, declined until there was little difference between it and the cheaper magazines. That great triumvirate of George Pinwell, Fred Walker and M.J. Lawless did much of their early work for the publication, and the two former illustrators and Frederick Sandys are dealt with below.

# The Churchman's Family Magazine

Although not as considerable as the 'big three' magazines, *The Churchman's Family Magazine*, founded by James Hogg in January 1863, is attractive and representative of the period. Its blue and gold cloth binding is very striking and like so many designs of the time is the work of John Leighton. The illustrative contents are surprisingly varied and exciting after that ominous sub-title that claims 'the Clergy and Distinguished Literary Men' as its contributors. J.E. Millais has two drawings of the 'Framley' type and similar domestic genre scenes are continued by J.D. Watson and A.W. Cooper, one of the best being the former's 'Sunday Evening' in Volume 1, page 191. Watson is equally at home in more dramatic company and two other works are 'The Christian Martyr', a free rendering of Sandys' 'Rosamund' in *Once a Week* a year or so before and 'The Hermit', a strong piece of figure drawing worthy of anything in Dalziel's biblical collection. E.J. Poynter makes an early appearance in two half pages that seem scratchy enough, but the poor paper probably accounts for it; his full page 'The Painter's Inspiration' is a fine thing (Figure 56), an artist with his back to the reader works on a Rossetti-ish canvas of a woman with a lute. F.R. Pickersgill is seen once again as the most interesting artist among the older generation; his 'Summer Evening Reverie' is boldly drawn, well composed and has a great sense of texture, expressed through the wood engraving. The trees are in a beautiful shadow and the stonework lit by the setting sun. Thomas Morten has a pair of seascapes, 'Black Peter's Little Passenger' and 'The Moment of Danger', in Volume 1. He is one of those artists to whom an incident of pathos comes easily and an incident of humour hardly at all; his one attempt here on page 432, is completely stylised and wooden. But his last illustration in Volume 2, 'The Bell-Ringer's Christmas Story', gains by the superb characterisation of the old man whatever it may lose by the feeble drawing of the girls. The location is suspiciously close to Millais' *Moxon* bell chamber! An artist who appears fairly consistently in both Volumes 1 and 2 is Charles Green, later to find fame as a Dickens illustrator, here confined to one or two small half-page genre subjects and a surprising 'Henry II and Beckett'. The earliest two volumes seem to have a good balance between the old and new illustrators, including in this the amateurism of Cuthbert Bede and the idiosyncracies of M.J. Lawless. Lawless's most celebrated illustration here, published by Gleeson White, is 'One Dead', a death-bed scene that is among his strongest and least mannered works. 'Harold Massey's Confession', Volume 3, page 64, is much more vintage

*Figure 56. 'The Painter's Inspiration' by E.J. Poynter.*

Lawless, figures in dark outline, crowded together in the lower part of the picture space, the background almost frieze like.

Louis Huard's genre scenes 'Decorating the Church', 'Hooray', and 'Bring Home the May' are pleasantly handled, and in Rebecca Solomon's work there is a fine flow, especially in 'An Ambiguous Direction', Volume 1, page 564, where the figures of the women and their full skirts form a great elipse in the centre of the page. But the canker was already present. Although the magazine continued its High Church articles and had work by J.D. Watson, M.E. Edwards and A.B. Houghton in the following two years, it was relying already on far inferior artists. Florence Claxton's dreadful social subjects predominate and it is possible without visual aids to guess the sort of meal she would make out of a title like 'Murmur, murmur, rippled the Happy Child's low toned Monologue'. Like many of its competitors, editorial discrimination soon could not distinguish between the first and second rate and cut-price; gradually hackwork succeeded real talent and imagination in its pages.

# London Society

Perhaps the most revealing way of looking at the problems of the magazines of the 1860s and of why such hopeful publications as *Once a Week* or *The Churchman's Family Magazine* declined in standard, is to examine their accounts. Few of these survive, but the papers and accounts of *London Society* from 1867 to 1873 do survive and provide valuable background information.[26] The magazine never had the prestige of *The Cornhill* or *Once a Week,* but it produced consistently good work in its pages and established artists as well as promising ones were eager to appear. Towards the end of its best period, in 1870 in fact, the magazine was acquired by the firm of Richard Bentley and continued by them for a further three years.

*London Society* had been started in February 1862 under the editorship of James Hogg, ubiquitous proprietor, to be run as a popular illustrated shilling magazine. Hogg, 1806-1888, was a canny Edinburgh publisher whose experiences had taken him through at least two earlier periodicals. Its appearance was heralded enthusiastically by du Maurier. 'I have done the cover for this Periodical,' he wrote in December 1861, 'which will appear every month from the 1st February under the name of London Society, and I shall probably have to bring out a series of these sketches for which I get 6 guineas a piece, but shall charge more if they are twigged.'[27] Du Maurier's ideas were not over optimistic, he illustrated for the magazine consistently, but this first drawing of London Bridge was considered a 'shocking failure' and had to be redrawn at the artist's expense!

Whatever Hogg's hopes for *London Society,* it maintained a good circulation among the public until he sold it to Bentley. In the autumn of 1870 the magazine had a print order of nearly 15,000 copies, only a fraction of a giant like *The Illustrated London News,* but a healthy number for mid-Victorian England. The following year it started a steep decline to just over 13,000 copies in March 1871, picked up once more during the summer issues and finally sank to 11,750 copies at the end of 1871 and the beginning of 1872. It would probably be too simple an explanation to relate this to Bentley's management and his lack of sympathy for an illustrated periodical. The boom in magazine publishing was dying down after the euphoria of repealed legislation, the editors who typified the quality of the early 1860s had moved on and the draughtsmen of the period had graduated to being painters. Paradoxically the black and white men of this decade were too good to prevent a lowering of standards. 'It must not be forgotten,' writes Gleeson White, of Millais, 'that high prices are often responsible for the desire, or rather the necessity, of using second-rate work. When an artist attains a position that monopolises all his working hours, it is obvious that he cannot afford to accept even the highest current rate of payment for magazine illustration; nor, on the other hand, can an editor, who conducts what is after all a commercial enterprise, afford to pay enormous sums for its illustrations. For later drawings this artist was paid at least five times as much as for his earlier efforts, and possibly in some cases ten or twelve times as much.'[28]

There is therefore a noticeable falling off of artistic quality in *London Society* between James Hogg's proprietorship and that of Richard Bentley; the former ran between ten and twenty illustrations to each monthly issue and although Bentley did much the same, the names that his predecessor was able to command are no longer there. The one exception, who was Bentley's discovery and Bentley's alone, was Randolph Caldecott who first came into prominence through its pages in late 1871.

*London Society* was far too small an organisation to have a permanent staff of artists, none of the monthlies did, although *The Cornhill Magazine* had a small number of illustrators tackling long series. The editorial policy seems to have been to employ the more important professional men in full page for stories and at certain seasons of the year, leaving the text illustrating to the secondary man and the amateurs. There were always a few of these, varying from vicars to society ladies and differing in competence between the professional and the downright awful! There were obvious disadvantages in employing them, much of their work would have to be redrawn and often they were unable to draw straight on the wood, meaning extra engraving work, time and money.

Payment depended on the illustrator's place in the hierarchy mentioned earlier, but also to some extent on the size of the work undertaken, initials and tail pieces running at a very reasonable rate, double page illustrations and work involving colour being exceedingly highly graded. The two special issues, the Christmas Number and the Holiday Number (June) carried higher honorariums, but for most illustrators there was no alteration to the standard rate and even this was often equal to some and more equal to others! The boasts of Millais and du Maurier, at the outset of the 1860s, about the sort of income they could make as illustrators were probably justified. £500 or £800 a year were the tokens of success and of great success when added to the prizes of fashionable landscape and portrait painting. The amateur artist was well pleased to make £100 out of his hobby. But for the majority of artists, unless it was a youthful stepping stone, the life of magazine illustrating must have been one of grind and frustration.

The usual fee for drawing a whole page illustration in *London Society,* usually a block of 7½ by 4½ inches, was five guineas. Between 1867 and 1870 the proprietorship seems to have erred on the side of generosity and increased it to six guineas. The rate for a half-page illustration was two guineas or three, depending on the quantity of work in it or the standing of the artist involved. For example George Pinwell received six guineas for drawing 'Beautiful Miss Johnson' in August 1867 and Charles Green seven guineas for 'All's Well That Ends Well' in September, slightly above the average price, presumably in recognition of their earlier work in illustrated books. Other artists to rate a higher price included William Small, eight guineas for an illustration to a poem in November 1867, J.D. Watson, ten pounds for a similar subject in March 1868 and Bouverie Goddard, six guineas for a full page animal subject in November 1867. Du Maurier who had drawn that first frontispiece in 1862 and hoped to get six guineas was getting ten guineas per drawing by January 1868 and his friend Charles Keene received twelve guineas for a full page in November 1868, both were by this time renowned *Punch* draughtsmen and to James Hogg the extra money would appear well spent. The most consistently highly paid illustrator in the magazine remained John Gilbert, who received ten guineas for every drawing quite irrespective of subject or issue. He was usually an indispensable part of the Christmas issue where his 'Spirit of Good Cheer' or 'The Old Year' gave him freedom to sentimentalise the feast, making it as much his own in line as Dickens had in print. The highest single price for a drawing on the block was fourteen guineas paid to H. Stacey Marks for a Christmas Number in 1870; Marks, who was elected an ARA the following year, had made a reputation out of rather conventional medieval subjects. In August 1868, when Hogg wanted a special cover for his Holiday Number, he commissioned it from John Leighton, the illustrator and book decorator, at a cost of seven guineas, a proportionately good figure when one considers it rated the same as a full page illustration and publishers thought of decorators as a minor branch of art.

It is amusing to find that a sensitive young draughtsman of twenty-four, who had trained as a Marine Engineer and had his first drawing published in *Punch* in 1867, was already on the books of *London Society* in 1868. His name was Linley Sambourne, 1844-1910, and he was earning three guineas for a full page illustration! Sambourne could have been described as an untried artist and his 'Sedan Chair' design of November 1869, for which he received the same sum, lacks assurance. Yet Sambourne was to gain a seat at the *Punch* 'Table' within a few years and live in considerable style at 18 Stafford Terrace, so for the successful artist there were attractive rewards. Sambourne would have thought of himself as a professional and yet T.S. Seccombe, an Indian army officer, and the Hon. Hugh Rowley were definitely amateurs. Seccombe drew for a hobby and Rowley, the son of Lord Langford, was a man of independant means with a house in Albert Gate, yet both received five guineas for their pages. Georgina Bowers, Florence Claxton, Louis Huard, J. Abbot Pasquier and Robert Dudley, professionals but not of the first rank, received from four to five guineas. M. Ellen Edwards, who was later to be the chief star in the Bentley galaxy as illustrator of all Mrs. Henry Wood's novels was not yet highly rewarded at five guineas per picture. Kate Edwards, that superb draughtsman of the single female figure, received four

*Left: Plate IX*
WALTER CRANE 1845-1915
*'I Saw Three Ships.' Illustration for a*
*book of Nursery Rhymes*

*Below left: Plate X*
ANONYMOUS ILLUSTRATOR
*Illustration to* Ten Little Soldier Boys
*One of a series of Warne's*
*Juvenile Drolleries, c.1870*

*Below right: Plate XI*
JOSEPH CRAWHALL Senior 1821-1896
*Illustration to* The Gloamin' buchte, *1883*
*Woodcuts coloured by hand*

Seven little Soldier Boys were playing funny tricks,
One, just in fun, let off his gun, and then there were but **6**.

**N**EVER a word ſpak' bonnie Jeanie
        Roole,
        But---" Shepherd let us gang : "
An' never mair, at a gloamin' buchte
Wad ſhe ſing another ſang.

pounds for her 'Autumn Reverie' in 1867 and though no records show it, probably the same sum for the brilliant 'June Dream' of a year earlier illustrated here (Figure 57).

*Figure 57. 'June Dream' by Kate Edwards.*

L. Straszynski received 15s. for a small initial letter and £2 5s. for a large one. Another contributor who was yet to make his name was W.S. Gilbert of Gilbert and Sullivan, who submitted an article illustrated by himself 'Thumbnail Sketches' in the middle of 1867 and a similar piece called 'Getting Up a Pantomime' at the end of the year. For the first he received £7 15s. and the second £10 4s., not princely for a man whose pen had two uses and was already known for the grotesque little sketches decorating the pages of *Fun*.

A certain disparity is accounted for by those artists who drew directly on the block and those whose work was drawn on it for them by the engravers. It is surprising to find the veteran illustrator James Mahoney having his drawing put on the block for him in September 1870 at a cost of £11 5s. 9d. One of Gilbert's subjects, for which he was paid ten guineas, cost a further six guineas to be engraved by J.W. Whymper. If Whymper had had to put it on wood as well, the cost would have been over twenty pounds; small wonder that the artist who only produced a sketch was paid less. Most of the artists and engravers were prepared to produce work at a discount as J.W. Whymper wrote to the editor in 1871, 'it will be obvious for you that it is only a regular supply of work that makes men keep their prices at the lower figure.'[29] Hogg occasionally employed foreign artists like Jules Pelcoq, Gustave Janet and Moullin, apparently with that Francophile, Henry Vizetelly, acting as agent. Their remuneration seems to have been very much below the British average. Pelcoq being paid eight pounds for '6 dessins sur bois' in the same half year that Marks received fourteen guineas for one!

The new company which took over the magazine in the autumn of 1870 did not greatly alter its payments although some earlier contributors benefited. Alfred Crowquill, who was distinctly old-fashioned and had been poorly recompensed under Hogg, received eight guineas for a Christmas page and George Cruikshank Junior, a very weak artist, got a three-quarter page subject to do for three guineas. H. Tuck did some socials at £2 10s. a time and Sambourne has a frontispiece of Valentine for which he was paid five guineas. Many of the older men and more distinguished names have disappeared, all the more surprising because Henry Blackburn, art critic and writer on illustration, was editor for the next two years!

Blackburn's great *coup de main* was the discovery and recognition of Randolph Caldecott, 1846-1886. A parcel of drawings addressed to him from Manchester arrived at his office in late 1870 and he at once realised that he was in possession of wildly original work. Drawings of matchless freedom spilled out, they were not conventionally well drawn, but pen and ink sketches full of humour, presenting a world as seen by a jovial overgrown schoolboy. They were in fact not of the 1860s at all, but looking forward to colour books for children and the establishment of Routledge and Warne's picture books. In his life of Caldecott, Blackburn refers to this period. 'The freshness of fancy, not to say recklessness of style, in many of the drawings which came by post at this time, the abundance of the flow from a stream, the course of which was not yet clearly marked — raised embarrassing thoughts in an editor's mind. What to do with all the material sent?'[30]

Blackburn bought it, or a lot of it and detailed accounts remain. Within the first year Caldecott was receiving £5 10s. for a full page drawing and a guinea for smaller subjects. His spirited work which really looked like pen work and not simply like an engraver's idea of it, depended a great deal on the minor items. Caldecott's spontaneous talent developed vignettes and jottings that were as important to the page as a full scale work. His accounts are therefore sprinkled with small items: '2 ball room sketches half page each £1-10-0', '1 small outline "Heigh ho the Holly" 15/-', 'Frieze — Irish landlord & tenants £2 : 2 : 0', '1 small outline Young Lochinvar 15/-'. During the first half of 1872, Caldecott earned £38 through the pages of London Society and by 1873 he was getting £10 14s. on every issue, thus giving him an income of £120 to £140 from this source alone. In addition of course he was working for the Manchester journals and was employed at his bank. As Blackburn rightly points out, it was *London Society* that gave him a London audience and the financial independance to migrate to the south and devote himself entirely to magazine and book illustration.

# G.J. Pinwell

George John Pinwell, 1842-1875, is best remembered today for his highly finished watercolours of rural scenes, the colour applied with a jewel-like brilliance, the whole spectrum giving a kind of radiant peace. It is often forgotten that he began life as a black and white artist and that many of his most successful paintings are based on illustrated work in anthologies and magazines.

Pinwell was a Buckinghamshire man, born at High Wycombe in 1842, the son of a builder. His father's death left him in very straitened circumstances and at a young age he was employed by a firm of embroiderers to make designs for them. This unusual training gave him a keen sense of design, pattern and colour which was a great strength in his later work. Pursuing his own fortune, despite difficulties, Pinwell entered himself at St. Martin's Lane School and in 1862 joined Heatherley's. That year he produced his first batch of illustrations for *Lilliput Levee,* 'The Happy Home' and 'Hacco The Dwarf', as well as sending a few drawings to *Fun.* He gained more practical experience when he was apprenticed to J.W. Whymper, 1813-1903, succeeding Fred Walker as chief figure draughtsman at the firm.

During 1863 Pinwell widened his scope to include work for *Once a Week, Good Words, London Society, The Cornhill Magazine* and others, as well as being befriended by W.J. Linton and becoming closely associated with the Dalziels. It was in fact these industrious brothers (dealt with below), who gave him his first great chance in 1864, the illustrations for their own edition of *Goldsmith's Works.* It was this volume, that Williamson called 'a model of what an illustrated book should be',[31] and its forty pages of drawings proved Pinwell's maturity to have arrived, the vision poetic enough but literal and accurate too. The artist worked methodically at this, producing the illustrations week by week for the parts, completing it in about six months. More work followed from Dalziels, *A Round of Days, Wayside Posies, Poems by Jean Ingelow, North Coast and Other Poems,* all with that distinctive arrangement and lyricism that Pinwell made his own.

Pinwell was much more of a landscape artist than his contemporary Fred Walker and, where he shows landscape, there is a great deal in it to occupy the attention. He accurately observes his backgrounds, they are never static like Walker's but filled with a continual flight of birds and movement of beasts. All the hedgerows are alive with activity and the figures are not intruders but merge naturally with the thickly growing grass and flowers. He returns frequently to Devon and Somerset for inspiration and the grey stone walls of a favourite manor house, Halsway Court, appear and re-appear in the drawings. They are the backdrop to the watercolour 'Away From Home' and also in 'The Unwilling Playmate' and 'The Dovecote' from *English Rustic Pictures,* 1865 (Figure 58). This variant, in the Victoria and Albert Museum, shows the same gables and chimneys framing the heads of the two rustic lovers, negligent of all around them, but so much a part of it, while inquisitive geese investigate the beautifully modelled basket. Every drawing is vibrant with this love of nature, some of the figures in *North Coast* are surrounded by a Noah's Ark, full of wild and domestic animals, decoratively placed, perfectly expressive of verse rather than prose. Even with his occasional sallies into urban life as with Dickens' *Uncommercial Traveller,* 1868, Pinwell searches out the passages that find people in relation to nature.

*Figure 58. 'The Dovecote' by G.J. Pinwell, 1865.*

The enduring memory of Pinwell is still as a watercolourist and not as an illustrator, so many of the former survive, so few of the latter. But they are really illustrations, these visionary fragments of the countryside, full of light, teeming with interest, Pre-Raphaelite in their hues but also looking forward to a more synthesised application of washes that would end with Wilson Steer. Walker, it is noted 'could not understand Pinwell's rough handling, or appreciate his touches of brilliant colour, and his experiments in the combined use of different colours and methods in the same picture.'[32] One leaves Pinwell with this impression of ethereal loveliness, hastily sketched women in the great bell-like dresses of the 1860s, parasols aloft, moving across meadows of yellow-green grass amidst a flurry of white birds. Even if Pinwell did not live long enough to develop his mature style, his influence on illustration was great. The *Goldsmith* series sowed the seeds of a simpler approach to historical illustrating and his bright colours found an echo in the sumptuous process books of the Edwardians.

# Fred Walker

Fred Walker, 1840-1875, was perhaps the most classically academic of all the illustrators of the 1860s. Far less adaptable than a Millais, and far less dramatically accomplished than a Sandys, his gifts were nevertheless of an extremely high order. In thinking of Walker one turns one's mind more to the inhabitants of the countryside than to the countryside itself, the reverse of Pinwell; women sitting by their fireplaces, sewing or stirring the embers, children at cottage doors, men trudging home from the fields. Walker would seem to be the perfect depictor of George Eliot or Thomas Hardy, in fact he missed the former and was too early for the latter, the long rural tales of which the Victorians were so fond seem to have eluded him. He served the Thackerays well, for W.M. Thackeray he illustrated *The Adventures of Philip in His Way Through The World* and for Miss Thackeray *The Story of Elizabeth* and *The Village on the Cliff.* But the first had a more or less metropolitan setting and the last consisted of only six designs, certainly Walker's short illustrating life, 1860-64, could have given him more opportunities.

Walker was born in Marylebone in 1840, the son of a designer of jewellery. The family were poor and the father's early death left them even poorer and gave little scope to the son in the choice of a career. But Walker was fortunate in being the first generation that had grown up with illustrated journalism and with his aptitude for drawing was able to copy engravings from Cassell's informative books and other plentiful and cheap periodicals. He was first of all placed with an architect, which lasted until 1857, and then entered Leigh's Newman Street Studio to learn drawing, studying the Elgin marbles in his spare time. This was followed by a spell as a student at the RA Schools from March 1858, but in all these places, Walker proved to be an original artist not a natural student. A more fruitful training opened up to him in November 1858, when he was apprenticed to the engraver J.W. Whymper, working in his establishment for three days a week for the next two years. Walker met J.W. North there and Charles Green, but more significantly he learnt the basic requirements that an artist needed to draw for the engraver, a knowledge that gave him pre-eminence as a technician.

Walker was small and slight and nervous, but had a disarming manner and generous nature that won him a wide circle of friends. Both the du Maurier and Millais circles referred to him affectionately as 'Little Walker' but this was not a disparagement, both recognised his great powers as an artist. Even before his name was established in 1859, he was clear about his intentions to use black and white work as a stepping stone only. 'I am busy now, and shall be; and for all the future shall look to making more by word drawing than painting, till I have advanced in practise to that extent, that I can *rely* on painting with safety.'[33]

His first important illustrations for *Once a Week,* beginning on 18 February 1860 with a characteristic subject 'Peasant Proprietorship', show no discernible strength in the drawing of country types. By April, Walker was contributing domestic genre subjects such as 'Apres' and 'Tenants At Number-Twenty-Seven' which are nicely balanced if unremarkable. With the second volume for 1860 we begin to recognise that gentle sympathy for the countryside by which he is most recognised. The first illustration for Eliza Cook's poem 'Once Upon a Time' has an elderly smocked rustic walking in front of a thatched barn with children in its shade and the more usual 'F.W.' signature superceding the full name. In October 1860 we find Walker promoted to the unusual position of illustrating a period story 'The Herberts of Elfdale', very strong figure drawing throughout, but what is more impressive, a real understanding of trees, grass and flowers. His tree trunks are especially convincing as not just examples of the genus but as individual trees; his gardens and old houses are not pasteboard but places he sees and interprets. It is on record that Walker would take his boxwood block into the countryside and finish backgrounds from nature, perhaps he was the first illustrator to do this.[34] Certainly Walker equated the study of nature with Greek art and this often gives his figures a sort of serenity. Those studies at the British Museum were deeply ingrained and Gleeson White rightly refers to his farm labourers as 'youths from the Parthenon in peasant costume'.[35]

The artist's best work was reserved for *The Cornhill Magazine,* every aspiring draughtsman's goal in the early 1860s. His entry into that august magazine is one of the legends of the illustrator. Swain, the engraver, who had the management of *Once a Week's* illustrations had considerable influence with Thackeray. It was Swain's job to find draughtsmen who could put the great novelist's own sketches on to the wood and generally tidy up their deficiences. Walker, anxious to get on to *The Cornhill,* called on Thackeray with Swain and showed the jealous·amateur artist some of his drawings. Thackeray promptly asked Walker to sketch his back while he was shaving in his dressing-room, and the result was so successful that Walker not only won the commission, but the block appeared in the journal in February 1861. But the object had been to get original work and the doctoring and 'ghosting' of Thackeray's designs would not satisfy him. After four ill-proportioned and wooden pages of Thackeray's own contributions to his *The Adventures of Philip,* Walker took over the compositions, though his presence was not acknowledged until June 1861. Thackeray's stepping down was unusual and the successful relationship was due to Walker's sensitive nature and great ability. The author gave his artist detailed verbal instructions, sometimes accompanied by a rough sketch, an indication of the expression of the passage rather than its exact rendering. In the last design of the 'Philip' series, 'Thanksgiving', Thackeray specified which church he wanted depicted — 'the Church is the one in Queen Square Bloomsbury, if you are curious to be exact',[36] he wrote.

The influence of Millais is stressed by Gleeson White but not overtly referred to in the biography. Walker is known to have consulted Millais about his *Cornhill* work[37] and can hardly have failed to be impressed by the Trollope designs by Millais appearing alongside his own (Figure 59). But Walker's originality is unquestioned, and his study of children alone would win him a high place, as would such natural groups as 'Out Among the Wild Flowers' which appeared in 1862 in *Good Words.* But he was also an innovator, among the earliest artists to use photographs for the details of his pictures, the first artist to introduce brushwork into his drawings on wood and the creator of the first Victorian poster for Wilkie Collins' *The Woman in White,* 1872. The latter is such a fluid image of a woman escaping through a door that it is difficult to believe it was done before the 1890s. Walker's four productive years of illustrating were the groundwork for a further ten years as water-colourist and oil painter, the field, the lane and the cottage door recurring frequently in these fresh mediums. His tragic death at the age of thirty-five in June 1875 was a sad loss for British art which expected great things from the new ARA. But by this time, book illustration had long since ceased to be a major factor in his life.

*Figure 59. 'In the November Night' by Fred Walker*

# A.Boyd Houghton

Arthur Boyd Houghton, 1836-1875, was a very different artist from those already mentioned. As fine a draughtsman, he was as well a painter, illustrator and Special Artist. His work for *The Graphic* is discussed later but his domestic and legendary work forms a major bulk in that working life that was so tragically short. Born into an Indian Army family in 1836, he returned with them to England and showing an aptitude for drawing was sent to the appropriate schools, Leigh's and the Royal Academy's. He benefited much more however from attending the Langham Art Society where he came under the influence of Charles Keene, a much older man and already well-established on *Punch*. Keene's bohemianism probably accorded with the unconventional in Houghton, that strain of compassion for the underdog which in the younger man's work became radical protest. A talented oil painter in small scale, Houghton turned in the later 1850s from historical subjects to those of everyday life, often the street and beach scenes that had attracted the Pre-Raphaelites and containing their bright palette. One of these, 'Holborn in 1861', has certain affinities with Madox Brown's 'Work', the sort of essay in realism that was to stand him in good stead as reporter-artist. A lack of success in selling paintings turned Houghton into an illustrator, as it did so many others. He was introduced to the Dalziel Brothers and began by doing domestic scenes for them on Wilkie Collins' novel *After Dark*. His domestic oil paintings owe rather more to Augustus Egg RA and the 1840s than to the Pre-Raphaelites, his illustrations based on his own happy family life, are more the descendants of Millais' 'Fireside Story' of 1855 and its aftermath. This connection is particularly noticeable in *Home Thoughts and Home Scenes,* 1865. The Brothers Dalziel continued to help the artist and in 1863-65 he illustrated for them with T.B.G. Dalziel, *The Arabian Nights,* contributing ninety-two designs. The Brothers record that he had an advantage for this work in having been born in the East and having access to 'articles of virtu, curios, costumes and every sort of thing invaluable for the illustrator's purposes . . .'[38] In his 'Three Blind Men', 'Aladdin in Despair' and other figure subjects, he produces some of the most powerful images of the whole decade. The masterly designs for the *Don Quixote* of 1866, another Dalziel commission, are better than the celebrated Doré ones, but neither book received proper recognition. The Dalziels talk of 'his fine sense of humour' being 'coupled with a pleasant tinge of satire, such as comes from a man who knows the world in its various phases of life, but always cultured and refined.'[39] It is this 'tinge of satire' that Paul Hogarth has suggested as the aspect of Houghton's work that middle class Victorians were not prepared to take.[40] Houghton was probably the right artist therefore to record the Paris Commune of 1870, which he did in a notable series in *The Graphic,* including those of the trial scenes after its collapse. Always a depressive man, Houghton became an increasingly persistent drinker and eventually died of his alcoholism in November 1875. He had been a meticulous worker, very professional, making several sketches before transferring the design to the wood block. Forrest Read found his most interesting style to be the early period, here he was closest to the idyllic artists, a more modern taste might prefer the dramatic and realistic quality of the later work.

# Frederick Sandys

Of all the illustrators of the 1860s, there is no artist who carried the spirit of the Pre-Raphaelites forward with greater conviction than Frederick Sandys, 1829-1904. His black and white drawings for the magazines and the art books of the time are not numerous, they number about thirty in all, but they retain the fire, the atmosphere and the intensity which was apparent in the *Moxon Tennyson* several years earlier. Sandys could sustain this dynamism from the first appearance in *Once a Week* in 1860 to the *Dalziel's Bible Gallery* of 1882, and Gleeson White wrote of him as 'the most potent factor' in giving the former magazine a distinctive place in the arts,[41] but what essentially did the Sandys mastery consist of? He was certainly the most accomplished draughtsman of the period, nobody but Millais could possibly equal his graceful and easy line, his virtuosity in composition and decorative treatment, his tender portraits and soft studies from nature. However it is difficult to look at any of Sandys' works from our standpoint and feel that the penetration of character or literary interpretation is anything more than gently sensuous, that the haughty figures and crowded symbols are anything more than the trappings of poetry and lyric. This brooding dissatisfaction with a drawing is often present when the artist is very young or an inveterate copyist and as we know, Frederick Sandys was a brilliant and witty copyist from the famous 'Nightmare' of 1857 which caricatured Millais' 'Sir Isumbras at the Ford'.

Turning to the pages of *Once a Week* one is alternately amazed and bewildered by the artist's contributions, amazed at his range, dazzled by his performance, bewildered by the impertinence of his borrowings. It would be impossible to expect an artist of Sandys' ability to develop in the 1860s, a period of flux, without some recourse to borrowings, but the reliance on Rossetti revealed in these pages goes a good deal beyond the purely inspirational. This is not to say that Sandys was a pure copyist, his study of nature was meticulous and there are numerous drawings to prove it.

Frederick Sandys was born in Norwich in 1829 and, though his family were in rather unpromising circumstances, he received a good education and was trained at the Norwich School of Design and patronised by a local amateur artist. On coming to London he obtained work in drawing for wood engravers and there learnt the syntax that was to stand him in good stead when he had to draw for the printed page. Sandys got to know Rossetti and his friends after the satirical print of 1857 and they recognised his genius as a draughtsman. This was the year of the *Moxon Tennyson* which must have left a deep impression on him, but he was also making himself acquainted with the sixteenth century German masters of the woodcut and particularly Dürer. The Pre-Raphaelites' absorption in early German art stemmed from the Nazarene influence on the Brotherhood and several artists of the Rossetti circle had collections of these prints. Rossetti himself had a few examples, Ruskin a considerable collection and William Bell Scott a connoisseur's collection, as befitted the author of a *Life of Dürer,* 1869. A hazy juggling of motifs, symbols and backgrounds took place among these painters, many of them garnered from sixteenth century originals through the eyes of the more penetrating and poetic Rossetti. This influence has recently been highlighted in a revealing article on the sources of Pre-Raphaelite design.[42] It is evident though that Sandys was not quarrying from the originals, or synthesising the work of Rossetti, but rather working in a Rossetti mannerism as a vehicle for his own precocious line. In the catalogue of the Sandys exhibition at Brighton in 1974, this duplicity in Sandys is referred to as a weakness. 'Mystery is of the essence of Sandys themes', says the writer, 'but the pictures are made with an explicitness that precludes it.'[43] Surely this is because the highly charged, brooding and very poetic subjects belong to a Rossetti and the slick presentation of them only to a Sandys.

Figure 61. 'The Waiting Time' by Frederick Sandys.
Left: Figure 60. 'Manoli' by Frederick Sandys.

The most glaring example of this is the 'Rosamond Queen of the Lombards' which came out in *Once a Week* for 30 November 1861, only the third contribution by the artist to the paper. As mentioned briefly before, it is a reversed figure of Rossetti's famous *Moxon* subject 'Mariana in the South', the background of which had been taken from a Dürer woodcut.[44] Although a more accomplished work technically than the Rossetti, the Rosamond is awkwardly crowded with symbols and more ambivalent in meaning than its famous predecessor. The first important work for *Once a Week* 'Yet Once More on the Organ Play' contributed in March 1861, has similar memories of 'St Cecilia' in the instrument and the reclining figure, though more obvious links with Titian's 'Venus and Cupid with an Organ Player'. Other designs that follow, 'The Sailor's Bride', 13 April 1861,[45] 'From My Window', 24 August 1861, and 'The Three Statues of Aegina', 26 October 1861, are not so closely inspired. 'The Old Chartist' of 8 February 1862 is markedly Düreresque in style and the finest work he did for *Once a Week*. Pennell wrote ecstatically of this print in 1896 — 'the Chartist is a figure that Sandys has seen for himself; but it is this evidence of things seen which gives such force to his drawings; his illustrations are as carefully studied as any one else's paintings . . .' [46] Sandys was earning extremely good money for his illustrations at this time, receiving forty guineas from *The Cornhill* for his 'Portent' in 1860, but he was conspicuously profligate in his business affairs.

Dating from the same period are the contributions to both *The Cornhill Magazine*, classical studies like 'Manoli' (Figure 60) and *Good Words*. The last contains only two Sandys illustrations 'Until her Death' strongly influenced by Rossetti and Dürer and 'Sleep' appearing successively in 1862 and 1863. Sandys continued to work for *Once a Week* until 1866 but the most significant design ever produced by him was first seen in *The Churchman's Family Magazine* in July 1863. 'The Waiting Time' (Figure 61), an illustration to a poem by Sarah Doudney on the Lancashire cotton distress, exactly captures the spirit

132

of Victorian labour through the deliberate archaism of line and hatching found in Dürer prints; the over-hanging frames of the silent loom, the sunlight on the wall and the carefully observed wood grain on stool and machine. There is something implicitly Pre-Raphaelite here which wishes to interpret a current moral dilemma in terms of the past. Sandys illustrated two books, 'Life's Journey' a design with all the delicacy of 'The Chartist' was included in Willmott's *Sacred Poetry* in 1862 and his 'Little Mourner' appeared in the same work; further illustrations were used in *Thornbury's Legendary Ballads,* 1876. The muscular Biblical illustration 'Jacob Hears The Voice of the Lord' was drawn in the 1860s but was not used until *Dalziel's Bible Gallery* first came out in 1881. Hindsight may have slightly dimmed our appreciation of Sandys, his magnificent portrait drawings certainly redress the imbalance, but so does the remark of Swinburne that he wanted nobody else to design for his verse![47]

# The Dalziel Brothers

The revival of wood engraving in the 1840s, its gradual perfecting in the 1850s and its flowering in the '60s greatly altered the status of the wood engraving workshops. In any less complicated time than the nineteenth century this trade might have remained a craft occupation as it had with Bewick, or the calling of a highly individual artist as it had in the late Renaissance, but the Victorians were at heart commercial and broadly based. By the middle of the century the facsimile wood engraver was sufficiently indispensable to command the respect of artist and publisher alike, his workshop was the meeting place of new talent with established names, his patronage was eagerly sought after and his advice taken. As we have already seen the Victorian artist diversified more than his predecessors; he was a designer as well as a painter, concerned himself with ornament, metalwork, stained-glass, as well as with history painting and landscape; he experimented with engraving and new methods of printing. The names of 'Landells', 'Swain' and 'Linton' printed prominently in the corners of otherwise unsigned wood engravings are often mistaken by the unwary for those of the artist. They were in fact the signatures of the leading engraving establishments, hives of industry from 1850 to 1880, the schools that made British black and white draughtsmanship pre-eminent for so long. The merchant princes of this trade were undoubtedly the Brothers Dalziel, whose name appears in almost every major book between 1840 and 1890.

The Dalziel Brothers have already been mentioned in connection with Rossetti for they were his dealers 'in fevers and agues' with their cutting! But less demanding artists than Rossetti fared better and their achievements are generally considered to be outstanding. The four brothers were born into that fertile ground for wood engraving, Northumberland, the three most prominent engravers being George Dalziel, 1815-1902, Edward Dalziel, 1817-1905, and John Dalziel, 1822-1869. Thomas Bolton Gilchrist Dalziel, 1823-1906, was the youngest brother and in many ways the most talented, combining like Edward, engraving with book illustrating, but also an active marine and landscape painter.[48] They were all the children of Alexander Dalziel, 1781-1832, a farmer who turned to painting late in life, but who nevertheless saw to it that his sons trained thoroughly and early. Both George and Edward Dalziel were apprenticed to Ebenezer Landells, a pupil of Bewick, and on their arrival in London in 1835 were befriended by William Harvey, 1796-1866, another Newcastle illustrator and pupil of Bewick, which accounts for the close connection with the

Bewick School that is mentioned in their memoir. John Dalziel joined the firm in 1852 and Thomas Dalziel arrived in London in 1857.

Although the firm was engaged on finely illustrated books from the 1850 Harvey edition of *Pilgrim's Progress* onwards, they only achieved real fame in the late 1850s, with their work on *The Music Master* by William Allingham, 1855 and the *Moxon Tennyson,* 1857. The convenience of wood engraving over its rivals, steel plates and lithography, was so obvious by the latter year that the Dalziels inaugurated a new side to their business. They established a printing works at 53 High Street, Camden Town, known as The Camden Press, which run together with the engraving shop, enabled them to commission their own books 'Dalziel's Fine Art Books' and superintend the production of them from start to finish. They were not their own distributors, but had agreements with publishing houses like Routledge, Longman and Warne, so that the titles could be retailed under their imprint. The 1860s were the Dalziels' heyday and they included among their employees and clients, the most astonishing list of Victorian giants, both artists and authors. The main part of their production was still in engraving blocks for the magazines, *Punch, The Cornhill Magazine* and *Good Words* among them, but since many of the serial stories were later reprinted in volume form, the book side to their business could expand simultaneously. Among the more attractive publications in which they had a hand are *Willmott's Poets of the Nineteenth Century,* 1857, Charles Mackay's *Home Affections,* 1858, *Montgomery's Poems,* 1860, *Wood's Natural History,* 1861-63, the *Barsetshire Novels,* 1861-64, *Alice in Wonderland,* with all its vicissitudes, 1865-66, and *Dalziel's Goldsmith,* already mentioned, 1865. Particular favourites of the present writer with which the Dalziels are associated are *A Round of Days* with its gentle rural illustrations, 1867, *Jean Ingelow's Fables,* 1867, and *Wayside Posies,* 1866-67, all contained in decorative art covers by John Leighton, Albert Warren, Owen Jones and others.

The Dalziel books are open to some criticism for being both melanges of various illustrators' work and insubstantial in text. The first problem was common to most of the books of the late 1850s and '60s, the second seems to have stemmed from a reluctance by the firm to commission from writers who were so much more expensive to use than artists. There was also a tendency to make anthologies pay their way in preference to new work and a not too scrupulous use of illustrative material when it was the firm's copyright. *Thornbury's Legendary Ballads* is a case in point, where eighty-two of the prime drawings for *Once a Week* are foisted on to the indifferent verses of G.W. Thornbury. Despite this, the advent of large illustrated volumes for the table, if not yet the 'coffee table', was a definite improvement on gift books and the Dalziels' record is an impressive one.

Gleeson White while emphasising their influence in engraving and in bringing forward the younger draughtsmen pays tribute to their own drawing. 'That these talented engravers were draughtsmen of no mean order might be proved in a hundred instances,' he writes, only a few of their own blocks 'establish their

*Figure 62. Illustration for* The Uncommercial Traveller, *Edward Dalziel.*

134

right to an honourable position as illustrators.'[49] These must include Thomas Dalziel's finely detailed illustrations to *The Arabian Nights,* 1864, and *The Arabian Nights Entertainments,* 1877, as well as his fourteen engravings in the Bible Gallery, 1881. After Thomas, the most competent artist in the family was Edward, his brother, a contributor to *Ballad Stories of The Affections,* 1866, and sole illustrator of *The Uncommercial Traveller* in Dickens' Household Edition, 1870 (Figure 62). E.G. Dalziel, 1849-1889, was Edward's eldest son and a strong figure draughtsman.

Had the Dalziel Brothers acquired or founded a magazine in the early 1860s it might well have been a great success. Their failure to do so, however, is probably explained by the fact that their real prosperity was after 1865 when the magazine market itself was starting to tail off. They did however acquire two magazines; *Fun* was bought by them somewhat later in 1870 and run by them until 1893 and *Ally Sloper's Half Holiday,* the paper that had been the brainchild of C.H. Ross, was run until 1903 by Gilbert Dalziel, 1853-1930, the journalist of the family and the most brilliant of Edward's sons.

## *Footnotes*

1. W. Tinsley, *Random Recollections,* 1900, pp.62-63.
2. *Art Union Annual Report,* 1857, p.4.
3. G.M. Young (Editor), *Early Victorian England,* 1934, Vol. 1, p.232.
4. ibid.
5. G.S. Layard, *Pre-Raphaelite Illustrators,* pp.23-24.
6. Gleeson White, *English Illustration 'The Sixties',* 1906, p.9.
7. Walter Crane, *Of The Decorative Illustration of Books,* 1901, p.148.
8. Mason Jackson, *The Pictorial Press,* 1885, pp.356-57.
9. Daphne du Maurier, *The Young du M: A Selection of His Letters 1860-67,* 1951.
10. ibid.
11. ibid.
12. ibid.
13. ibid.
14. ibid.
15. *Letters of D.G. Rossetti to W. Allingham,* 1897, p.248.
16. John Ruskin, *Ariadne Florentina,* 1877, p.235.
17. John Ruskin, *The Art of England,* 1884, pp.166-67.
18. John Ruskin, *Modern Painters,* 1904, Vol. 4, p.228.
19. ibid., Vol. 1, p.182.
20. Philip James, *English Book Illustration,* 1800-1900, p.37.
21. M.H. Spielmann, *The History of Punch,* 1895, p.392.
22. Mrs. Ward Barrington, *Lord Leighton,* 1906, Vol. 2, p.95.
23. ibid., p.96.
24. ibid., p.97.
25. Like *Punch, Once a Week* was prepared to publish drawings independant of a story or a text.
26. British Museum, Add, MSS 46560-46682, Bentley Papers.
27. Daphne du Maurier, op. cit.
28. Gleeson White, op.cit., p.25.
29. Bentley Papers.
30. Henry Blackburn, *Randolph Caldecott,* 1886. pp.21-22.
31. George C. Williamson, *G.J. Pinwell And His Works,* 1900, p.12.
32. ibid., p.71.
33. J.G. Marks, *Life and Letters of Fred Walker,* 1896, p.12.
34. ibid., p.27.
35. Gleeson White, op. cit., p.165.
36. J.G. Marks, op. cit.
37. ibid., p.40.
38. *The Brothers Dalziel, A Record of Work, 1840-1890,* 1901, p.222.
39. ibid.
40. Paul Hogarth, *Arthur Boyd Houghton,* Catalogue of Victoria and Albert Museum exhibition, 1975, p.10.
41. Gleeson White, op. cit. p.173.
42. John Christian, *The Art Quarterly,* 1973, Vol. 36, pp.56-83.
43. Frederick Sandys exhibition catalogue, Brighton 1974.
44. John Christian, op. cit.
45. The original uncut woodblock of an earlier version of this subject is in the Birmingham City Art Gallery.
46. Joseph Pennell, *The Quarto, 1896, pp.33-37.*
47. Frederick Sandys exhibition catalogue, op. cit.
48. Thomas Dalziel was also instrumental in teaching the student wood engravers. Information communicated to me by Miss Ailsa Dalziel, 1978.
49. Gleeson White, op. cit., p.178.

# Chapter 7
# The Special Artists

*Figure 63. 'The Trenches Before Sebastopol' by J.A. Crowe, Special Artist, 1855.*

The founding and development of *The Illustrated London News* and its rivals in the 1840s led to a much greater sophistication on the part of the reading public and a much greater awareness of the possibilities and shortcomings of the then pictorial press. A mercantile and predominantly middle-class clientele demanded something more precise and direct than a sedentary artist's idea of a besieged citadel or an attempted assassination, worked up from maps in his Bloomsbury lodgings. The steamboat and the rail were contracting the confines of Europe and even the distances to India and America had shrunk within a generation. To the proprietors of the illustrated periodicals it was obvious that businessmen in an expanding Empire would require greater and greater authenticity in their illustrations; the shipbuilders of Tyneside, the locomotive engineers of the Midlands and the captains of iron in South Wales, would not be fobbed off with one bolt out of place. If the ordinary reader was less scrupulous, he at least required the realism of news, the sense of immediacy transcribed through the pencil by an eye witness. Perhaps the rather static repertoire of *The Illustrated London News* and other journals would have continued with their royal processions, ship launches, house fires and trials, if events had not overtaken them.

On 28 March 1854, Great Britain and France jointly declared war on Russia and troops were despatched to the Crimea. It was the first major military campaign for more than a quarter of a century, the public were aroused to a fever of patriotism and an insatiable appetite for information of any kind. They wanted first-hand news of their troops operating in this remote corner of Asia Minor, details of their every-day life, pictures of the terrain, its inhabitants, and their customs (Figure 63). It was up to the illustrated magazines to provide this information, but for the most part they were unprepared. It was true that they had used

SKETCHING IN CHINA.

*Figure 64. Special Artists on location. R.P. Leitch and a colleague sketching for* The Illustrated London News *in China in early 1857.*

French artists during the French Revolution of 1848, but Paris was a centre of illustrated journalism and the Crimea was not. The artist William Simpson, later called 'Crimean Simpson', described the ludicrous situation facing the home-based illustrators. 'When the news of the Battle of the Alma came home,' he writes, 'I made a sketch, principally from the newspaper accounts, and put it on stone.'[1] Simpson found even greater difficulty in tracing prints of Sebastopol as the siege approached; there were few maps and the British Museum had only a silhouette of the city in the corner of one of them from which a complete drawing had to be made. Simpson was then employed as a lithographer at the printers Day and Sons, and it was proposed to him that he should go to the Crimea and collect material for Messrs. Colnaghi, who intended publishing a folio of the war.

William Simpson left in September 1854 and became the first of the 'special artists' although not accredited to a newspaper. Later writers suggest that 'while the signs of the coming storm were yet distant',[2] *The Illustrated London News* sent Samuel Read to the seat of war. Read was certainly in Constantinople for the magazine in 1853 but saw no action. Vizetelly also records that *The Illustrated London News* sales slumped because they had no artist on the spot on the Bosphorus, so Simpson's claim to be the first of a new breed seems substantiated.[3]

What an amazing breed they were to be, these special artists. They were the princes among illustrators − hardy, resourceful and flamboyant, engaging in every kind of subterfuge and intrigue to ensure that their masters in Fleet Street received both copy and sketches hot from the action. They were the eternal wanderers of the magazine world, following campaign after campaign, from one continent to another (Figure 64), sometimes fêted by governments, sometimes imprisoned, one minute enduring awful privations, the next commanding a retinue of servants. The Special 'provides himself with an abundant supply of tinned meats and champagne,' says Mason Jackson, 'plenty of clothing, the latest improvements in saddlery; and when he arrives at the scene of action he buys as many horses as he wants for himself and servants. Acting on the experience of previous campaigns, Mr. Prior was able in the Zulu War to travel much more comfortably than any member of the staff, not even excepting Lord Chelmsford himself.'[4] At various times other artists had their own covered carts, fitted up as 'studios' and sleeping quarters, but these luxuries were the exception in a very tough and rough life. Years after the Crimean campaign when the specials had developed a sort of rudimentary professionalism, the casualties were high. Melton Prior of *The Illustrated London News* caught sunstroke from which he never fully recovered, W.T. Maud of *The Graphic* died of syncope and, as late as 1906, C.E. Fripp collapsed and died from hardship. When the 'champagne' had run out and there were no more tins, Seppings Wright found himself eating bread that had gone into a hard brick in the Sudan campaign at a temperature of 130 degrees farenheit!

It is hardly surprising that René Bull, the war artist of *Black and White* at the end of the century, was also an illustrator of Anthony Hope's stories. Their lives were the pure stuff of Ruritania, of Rudolph Rasendel and 'Black' Michael, their feats of daring and disguise, ingenuity and escape would have made a splendid epic for the silent cinema. It is absolutely in character that G.A. Henty, the writer of more than seventy boys' stories, was a special for *The 'News* in the Abyssinian expedition of 1867. Such a life did not encourage the married man and many artists remained bachelors, adopting a sort of raffish bohemianism in dress and manner. Some like Melton Prior and Caton Woodville, despite illness, returned home to a distinguished old age of memoir writing, others like Frank Vizetelly vanished without trace.

William Simpson was not quite in this mould. A hard-working Scotsman from Glasgow, he had trained as a lithographer and risen from a salary of £2 a week in his native city to a commanding £8 a week in London. Simpson was an accomplished watercolourist, a talent he put down to the more painterly qualities of lithography as opposed to the more mechanical ones of wood or steel. He was, in fact, one of the few leading illustrators to spring out of the lithographic boom in the mid-century. As well as a competent hand and an eye for detail, Simpson possessed the unquenchable curiosity which make his drawings human documents that are fascinating to the historian. His intense interest in all the countries he visited led him to become an authority on eastern cultures and religions and publish several books.

On his arrival in the Crimea, Simpson was so much of a novice that he wandered about among the troops drawn up before Sebastopol like a kind of spectator and actually seated himself in front of the batteries and began to sketch! While working away with pencil and paper he records that he was dimly aware of objects falling around him from time to time, only to realise, when an officer shouted to him, that they were cannon balls. Simpson's work had value in showing the truth about the Crimea for he insisted in drawing actual situations under various conditions and including portraits, not the generalisations of later specials. In this way he spent long hours among the troops furnishing the publishers with a series of the trenches at different times of day, 'A Quiet Day in the Battery' or 'A Quiet Night in the Battery', etc.

The presence of an artist was as much of a novelty to the allied armies as their life was to Simpson. The only other correspondent in the field was the famous Dr. W.H. Russell, 'Russell of The Times', and the commanding officer, Lord Raglan, enjoyed showing off Simpson's work to his French opposite number because the great Parisian publications had no artists there. The fact that Lord Raglan approved of the work meant that the drawings could be sent home in his private letter bag with despatches. Every sketch that Simpson carried out had to be placed before the War Minister, shown to Queen Victoria and passed by both of them before going to the lithographers. This complicated procedure at least won Simpson and some later artists the Queen's patronage.

It was not always so easy to convince combatant officers of the accuracy of his drawings. An illustration of the Charge of the Light Brigade, composed from accounts given to Simpson was rejected time after time by the arrogant Lord Cardigan. It was only when

Simpson had the wit to place Cardigan in a gallant attitude in a prominent part of the drawing that the sketch was passed correct for the Foreign Office and Windsor!

The role of the special was being developed alongside that of the correspondent; sometimes the artist was called upon to write reports or letters, usually the functions were separate. Simpson considered perhaps rightly that the artist was rated lower than the correspondent by authority; less courted than the latter, he was also less hated in times of stress.

Simpson had no illusions about his function as a reporter. 'From the long peace that had existed before the Crimean War the technical terms belonging to seige operations had much the character of a foreign language to the British public,' he wrote. 'Gabions, fascines, sandbags, traverses, eparlements, etc., were words that conveyed no distinct meaning to the generality of readers and it was my function to make illustrations that would show what these things were.'⁵

It was unfortunately the great weakness of these draughtsmen that they had arrived on the scene at a time when British art had very little sense of direction. There was no tradition of news reporting; it was a new science. The strongest branches of local talent were landscape and topography, neither of which were suitable grafts for the febrile subjects of war painting. The nearest equivalent school was in history painting, almost non-existent since B.R. Haydon's tragic suicide in 1846, or in its near relation, battle painting, which had enjoyed some success in this country. It was this which was the starting point for much ensuing work. However much Simpson and his successors strove for a greater realism, a more objective and frank observance of the facts, the dead weight of historical battle painting was never far away. An illustrator such as T.H. Nicholson, who was special artist for *Cassell's Illustrated Family Paper* throughout the Crimean War, has a very heroic view indeed of the place and purpose of battles for the artist. His 'Battle of Alma' published on 11 November 1854, is an impressive and well-drawn full page woodcut, but the gesturing generals and serried ranks of soldiers do not leave a very striking impression of authenticity. The same artist's 'Death of Captain Vicars', 2 June 1855, where the officer staggers backwards on a pyramid of bodies, is hardly of its time and might almost be the work of Benjamin West or J.S. Copley. Caton Woodville, among the best of these men, developed a complete career as a battle painter and came to be known as 'the English Meissonier'. If these two identities became confused neither editors nor readers were dissatisfied; the same problem faced Frederick Remington in the 1890s when American publishers rejected his realism. In most cases the specials were not sufficiently strong as artists to develop their own individuality and resist the temptation to sentimentalise or dramatise their story. Nobody emerged of the calibre of Thomas Nast, whose American Civil War sketches affected a whole generation.

The results of Simpson's Crimean labours were eventually published in two folio volumes and were a great financial success. But by this time *The Illustrated London News* had a number of specials in the Crimea, *The Illustrated Times* one and, as mentioned, *Cassell's* one. By the middle of 1854, *The 'News* had W.O. Brierly stationed at the seat of war, supported by two naval officer artists, Lieut. Bredin and Lieut. Montagu O'Reilly of *The Retribution.* The concentration of the services on accurate draughtsmanship at this time was always a blessing to the harassed editor and officers were continually enlisted as illustrators in the course of these wars. At the beginning of 1855, Brierly had been recalled and replaced by E.A. Goodall, Samuel Read was at Scutari, and J.A. Crowe was officially designated 'Correspondent'. Local colour was provided by an army officer W.S.M. Wolfe and 'James Robertson of Constantinople', a resident with a useful pencil and also a photographer. The second half of this year saw the arrival of some first-rate illustrators, J.W. Carmichael, Constantin Guys, Gustave Doré and the return of Brierly. J.A. Crowe stayed on until 1856 perhaps as chief illustrator (Figure 63) and Landells arrived in the early part of that year as the war ended. Julian Portch had acted throughout for *The Illustrated Times.*

The Crimea was the last occasion on which the coverage was to be so haphazard; subsequently *The Illustrated London News,* later *The Graphic* and much later *Black and White, The Sphere* and their imitators, were to develop teams of artists, specialists in battles or naval engagements or simply explorers. *The 'News* relied on Marshall Claxton and W. Carpenter, both of whom happened to be in India during the Mutiny in 1857, but by 1870 it was relying more on its permanent staff. Nor was it easy to become a member of this august body. William Simpson noticing the change from lithograph to woodcut after 1865 determined to move with it; despite a life-time of experience he was not taken on to the permanent staff of *The 'News* until 1869, receiving a retaining fee with his services paid for in addition.

The circumstances of working were often hazardous in the extreme. Frank Vizetelly, who worked for his brother's *Illustrated Times* and was briefly editor of the Parisian *Monde Illustrée,* was sent by *The Illustrated London News* to Sicily in 1860. He landed with Garibaldi in Italy disguised as a sailor and managed to smuggle out some astonishing sketches of the thousand and their romantic leader. The following year he was sent to the United States to report on the Federal side of the American Civil War but not content with this decided to cross over the lines and draw the Confederates as well. After three days and nights on a river bank in the sights of a northern gunboat, he succeeded in his plan, once again bringing renown to *The 'News* which had failed before to get a correspondent into the blockaded southern ports.

Simpson encountered most difficulties in the France of the Second Empire, which, despite its glamorous reputation for Offenbach's music and café society was little more than a police state. The special, Vizetelly points out, was always at the mercy of the local populace and the local press ever ready to describe 'his pencils as stilettos, his india rubber as a pocket bomb, and his sketchbook as an infernal machine'.[6] He mentions in particular the artist Morin, whom he employed because he claimed relationship with the Emperor's chef. Later he discovered that this was a fabrication; Morin was actually one of the Emperor's agents. This double agent later redeemed himself in Vizetelly's eyes by sending a crucial sketch from the Battle of Sedan, drawn on the vellum of a drumhead! Simpson had an uncomfortable time during the same campaign in 1870, frequently under suspicion and once arrested, he nevertheless had to make sketches openly and then post them through the collapsing public service in the hopes that they would be in the Editor's hands for the Saturday after next! All the sketches for the build-up to the Battle of Forbach were drawn on cigarette papers which were then rolled and could be smoked in an emergency. The battlefield of Sedan was sketched on a strip of wallpaper removed from a deserted château, sealed up and sent to Mason Jackson in London.

The artists at the Franco-German front included not only Simpson but also G.H. Andrews, C.J. Staniland, Jules Pelcoq, G. Regamey and R.T. Landells, whose acquaintance with the Crown Prince gave him access to the German lines. After the fall of France, *The Illustrated London News* supported Pelcoq during the siege of Paris, paying for his hardship but none too generously. Pelcoq's and Regamey's sketches of the beleaguered capital were sent out to the world by balloon, first being photographed by Nadar and the prints sent out in another balloon to ensure that the precious work was not destroyed by one German gun. One of these is shown in Figure 65. During the five months not a single sketch was lost, making both the siege and the Commune among the most faithfully recorded nineteenth century events.

Later specials worked under even greater difficulties. The artist A.S. Hartrick records the sort of material he had to work from at *The Graphic* office, sent in by C.E. Fripp. 'I have handled volumes of sketches done by him during the Zulu War, which were ideal to work from. Some sketches made by him at the battle of Ulundi, drawn with a pen as he lay

*Figure 65. G. Regamey's impression of German shells bursting at the Porte d'Auteuil during the Siege of Paris, 1871. Regamey worked for* The Illustrated London News *throughout the sieges and his sketches were sent out by balloon.*

on the leather roof of a waggon, with Zulus charging close up armed with both assegais and rifles, were set out with full topographical details, as if executed in a chair at home.'[7]

Accuracy was often a criticism of the artist's work, even under these difficult circumstances, but a report in the *Morning Herald* of March 1855 gives a macabre insight into the draughtsman's truth to nature. 'I saw today the Sketching Correspondent of *The Illustrated London News,* who had been permitted to sketch amusing groups about the Camp. He has made a very clever and graphic sketch of the still unburied Russian bodies which have been lying in a putrid state, bordering the river Inkerman, ever since the 5th November. While engaged taking his sketch, the enemy fired a few shots upon him from the opposite side, but he succeeded in completing his work before he left the place.'

It was usual for these rapid sketches to be covered with notes and directions and to be sent back to competent home-based artists who could disentangle them and create a composition. But as one contemporary report of these artists put it, the special had to invest their drawings with something more than bare facts if they were to succeed. 'We are not moved by the accuracy with which a thousand and one details are realised; not by the material facts of masonry and cannon and armed men, though these in themselves are impressive; but by the intangible yet real idea they are made to express.'[8] The shorthand of the man in the field was a skeleton on which his colleagues could build a picture or a panorama, perhaps a 'two pager' double spread. As the century proceeded, the speed increased, but the mode of work remained the same, as Inglis Sheldon-Williams of *The Sphere* found in the Boer War; 'My Boer war drawings were, on occasion, the slightest sketches, but conveying the essentials to the artist at home. The drawings were always in outline, sketches sometimes from the top of my horse while the sergeant wasn't looking, the result could be slipped into an envelope and catch the first mail home to the office where, if considered advisable, it could be turned into a complete double page drawing in twenty-four hours by Wal Paget.'

Sometimes the drawing was divided into two for speed and two artists worked all night on the two halves, bringing them together in the morning. Gulich and Hatherell of *The Sphere* worked best on this kind of teamwork and it emphasises how vital the expertise of the supporting team was. The organisation behind the scenes was extensive; numbers of

141

artists were kept perpetually busy on the sketch notes of the specials, harmonising them for the page and drawing them on the boxwood blocks. Turkey boxwood was always used because of its close grain, hardness and lightness of colour, enabling the artist to use finer and sharper lines than on any other substance. These blocks were then transferred to the engravers, a handful of famous men — Orrin Smith, Landells, Whymper, Linton or Dalziel — whose services were retained by the better magazines over many years.

Ingram's hard business head had early appreciated the advantages of large blocks and quick engraving and he eagerly seized the idea of bolted blocks, developed at the time *The Illustrated London News* was founded. This process meant that the drawing covered an area of several blocks bolted together; the whole composition was sent to the engraver who set the lines across the joints of the block before dismembering it into individual pieces for the various engravers. The separated pieces therefore all had a small area of engraving prepared by the master engraver to act as a keynote in colour, texture and style for their particular fragment of the jigsaw. When this was followed, the woodcut came together again from various sources in perfect harmony and in a quarter of the time it would have taken one man to complete. A first proof would then be taken from the block and the supervising artist would add the retouching and corrections he thought necessary. After the block was finished it would be taken to the electrotyper, moulds made, overlays formed and the finished article would be ready to make 400,000 impressions from that first slight sketch of the artist on campaign.

Some of the magazines sent their work to outside artists and many younger men began careers in this way. George du Maurier notes in September 1861: 'The other day the *Illustrated Times* sent me a large block to do in a hurry, giving me 2 days. I did it in 6 hours; only three pounds, but that pays for it is coarse rapid work done anyhow.'[9] But most magazines had their own specialists, and Simpson's experience on coming to London in 1851 was typical. Day and Sons where he worked, had more than a dozen artists dealing with a variety of illustration. Edmund Walker concentrated on architectural subjects. T.G. Dutton on shipping, Lynch on elaborate portraits, Vintner on large figure subjects, Needham on trees, Haghe on interiors. All these artists worked in their homes, Simpson being considered unusual in working at the office. Vizetelly employed more than a score of artists during the nine years of his *Illustrated Times,* 1855-1864.

Speed was of the essence and later in the century some of the older men felt that it had lessened their control over their work. Simpson deputed to draw the Prince of Wales placing the last rivet in the new Forth Bridge, found it necessary to send Forrestier, a younger man, to fill in the background. The whole composition was more or less completed on the actual block before Simpson added a few touches and hurried it by rail to London.

'This was a Tuesday,' Simpson writes, 'and it was necessary to have the event in the paper on the Saturday following. This necessity indicates a great change in the history of *The Illustrated London News,* as well as in the history of illustrated journalism. When the paper was first started and for many years afterwards, what is called the "make up" was arranged on the Thursday week before the issue appeared. From improvements in the printing press, which produced greater speed in printing, events that took place on the Friday became possible. Later on events on a Saturday could be produced within the time. And at last, owing principally to greater speed in printing, important events taking place on the Monday were possible. Rivalry with *The Graphic* may have had something to do with these efforts at rapidity of production. One device which helped in such cases was to give the late event in a supplement, which being a smaller sheet than the body of the paper, could be run more quickly through the press. The floating of the *Daily Graphic* brought a new necessity for speed. It produced or intensified the feeling that if an event could not be given till the Saturday week after its occurrence, it had become "ancient history" which in these days of fast living would be all but forgotten.'[10]

The increase in mechanisation did not mean a fall in quality. Illustrated magazines burgeoned in the 1870s and those that had been founded in the 1840s like *The Illustrated London News* had doubled in size. The overseas readership had special colonial editions from 1880, printed on specially thin paper, but the proprietors did not recommend them for the best quality in the engravings.

On both *News* and *Graphic* there was a definite hierarchy with the 'Special War Artist' like R.T. Landells taking pride of place. But particular importance was attached to explorer artists designated 'Travelling Special Artist' such as J.M. Price, who was in Siberia in 1891. Maynard Brown that same year was called 'Special Artist at Public and State Ceremonies' — a very important recorder of the Victorian scene if less arduous than a war artist. He would be expected to 'fill up the intervals of waiting by

*Figure 66. Parisians selling their pets for meat during the Siege of Paris by Fred Barnard,* The Illustrated London News, *January 1871.*

making sketches of the various state costumes — perhaps "thumbnail" portraits of the functionaries who wore them — indicating little idiosyncracies of bearing and gesture and expression. He would make also, a variety of sketches of the broad general aspect of the scene, so as to get it thoroughly in his mind; thoroughly mastered and ready to hand as it were when the culmination of the ceremony should arrive.'[11] W.D. Almond, whose forte was in social realism, was also referred to as a 'Special Artist for Character Subjects' in 1887.

The great strength of these men was not in their specialisation but in their versatility; any of them could be called upon at a moment's notice to fill in a background, giving authenticity to fragmentary pencillings. Although it might seem now to be pure hackwork, it produced a surprising degree of accuracy if not great art and very little rancour in the profession. The work of the war artists did need specialist treatment and was given to Caton Woodville, a veteran campaigner, who could render on the block the sketches of Joseph Bell high in the mountains of Armenia in 1877, or to John Schonberg, who worked on Melton Prior's drawings of the Zulu War in 1879. Necessity can make strange bedfellows and it is a surprise to find Fred Barnard, the illustrator of Dickens, working up drawings from the Paris Commune in 1871 (Figure 66) and F.H. Townsend, later the first art editor of *Punch*, redrawing Seppings Wright's sketches of the Greek War of 1897! From the same war and the same artist we find a scene in Larissa interpreted by Cecil Aldin in an idiosyncratic and almost too individual style!

One change in the artist's status had definitely taken place since the early days, he was no longer an anonymous artisan. From about 1877, when Mason Jackson, a talented illustrator, took over the editorship of *The Illustrated London News,* the work of the specials is more frequently acknowledged and their travels explained. In June 1877 the magazine published a series of war leaves from artists' sketchbooks, not the more impersonal finished product, but the action drawings reproduced in line. To our modern tastes these are more exciting than the completed prints, their vigorous pen-line and dramatic excitement (Simpson even left the mud from a shell on his!) give us a blow by blow account of Queen Victoria's little wars from the Ashanti onwards. Furthermore they are likely to survive for the collector today when the full scale work would have been devoured by the engraver's tools. Simpson's drawings, the most commonly seen, are usually in pencil with light grey washes and squared up for division by the engraver. These facsimile sketches published by Mason Jackson were used from time to time, highlighting for the Victorian public 'the art' behind the special artist's rather mechanical prints. W. Luson Thomas, *The Graphic* editor came from a similar engraver background to Jackson and supported the artists by giving their work greater publicity.

Jackson kept his readers informed of the movements of his specials in the Turkish-Bulgarian campaigns of late 1877 with the pride of a general. Melton Prior, he tells us, was sent to Belgrade in 1875 to sketch preliminary skirmishing. When Servia declared war on Turkey, Chantrey Corbould joined the Servian forces and the *News* had Count Carriero as artist on the Turkish side. When Russia joined the war, John Schonberg was despatched to join them, but still there were not sufficient artists to supply the British public with news.

'In the meantime,' Mason Jackson writes, 'without delay or hesitation, we had despatched from London, solely and exclusively for the service of this journal, three more English artists: Mr. Bell, Mr. Irving Montague and Mr. E. Mathew Hale. The first named 'Special' proceeding to Constantinople, speedily found his way into Asia Minor, where he joined the army of Ahmed Moukhter Pasha, witnessed the battles of the road between Erzeroum and Kars, and was present at the raising of the Siege of Kars in the first week of July. Mr. Irving Montague who had likewise got a personal introduction to the Turkish naval and military authorities, sojourned for a time at Varna, which was the scene of great bustle in warlike preparations. He afterwards proceeded by sea to Armenia, where many of his sketches, with those of Mr. Bell, served to present a most complete set of pictures of travel and warfare in Asiatic Turkey . . . Mr. Hale, was enabled . . . to join the expedition of General Goucko across the Balakan . . . We have much satisfaction in announcing that a selection of original Sketches of the War by the Special Artists of the *Illustrated London News* will shortly be placed on view at the Royal Aquarium, Westminster, by an arrangement with the directors.'

Exhibitions of finished drawings became a standard way of supplementing the meagre salaries of the specials, but not at first. There was always strong feeling on the artists' side about the publishers' right to the sketches once they had been drawn out and engraved. Simpson was indignant about his Crimean sketches. 'The publishers afterwards sold my drawings and no doubt received as much as they gave me for them, so that they had the copyright for nothing.'[12] Sir Charles Eastlake, PRA, had in fact advised the Government to buy Simpson's work in 1856 as an historical record but they had refused, adjudging mere watercolours as of no value! Simpson was among the earliest artists to get a contract from *The Illustrated London News* for the return of his sketches which were then exhibited annually in 'Mr. Thompson's Gallery' in Piccadilly.

It was not only the artistic personality of the specials that was being recognised by the 1880s, but their social position. The importance of the specials was tremendously advanced when Melton Prior was asked to lecture on his work and illustrate it before the Prince of Wales at the Savage Club in February 1883. Prior had drawn the Prince's tour of India in 1875 and like Vizetelly with Garibaldi, had struck up as close a friendship with his subject as protocol allowed. Frederick Villiers of *The Graphic* had had his portrait exhibited at the Royal Academy 'in uniform hung about with revolvers, in his hand the flaming scarlet envelope in which despatches for *The Graphic* might be franked without waiting for tiresome delays at post offices or such-like formalities'.[13]

The profession of special artist must have been the only area of book illustration in Victorian England where there was fierce competition to be chosen. A writer in 1883 talks of journals 'constantly pestered by people whose artistic powers are indescribably slight' ready to 'sketch very badly, anything and everything'.[14] Aristocratic amateurs flocked to these offices, some with talent got jobs, the well-connected Richard Wake was sent out to Suakim in December 1888 and shot in battle after sending home his first drawing.

It is reasonable criticism of the specials to see them as a pack of adventurers and fame-hunters, at their best mundane reporters turning out hundreds of illustrations for a fact-hungry but philistine readership. This ignores the real stature of men like Simpson, Caton Woodville, Melton Prior, J.W. Carmichael, Seppings Wright, Sidney Hall and W.T. Maud who had separate careers as painters and watercolourists, exhibiting regularly at the Royal Academy and other exhibitions. It is true that book illustration and genre subjects attracted more of the big names than the ardours of special work, London salons being more attractive than the solitary life of a campaigner. But at least one great name enlisted with the artist correspondents and his work gives some measure of the beauty and strength of line possible in a popular periodical of the 1870s, this was Arthur Boyd Houghton of *The Graphic*.

The founding of *The Graphic* in December 1869 presented *The Illustrated London News* with its first serious challenge since it had swallowed up *The Illustrated Times.* In 1868-69, *The 'News* had sent the artist and alpinist Edward Whymper to the United States, furnishing the journal with a series of views and descriptions like a travelogue. Whether or not as a direct competition to this, *The Graphic* sent A.B. Houghton on a seven month tour of the United States from October 1869 to April 1870 to depict the brash and prosperous land of plenty five years after the Civil War. Houghton was not a topographer, but a brilliant book illustrator and figure draughtsman, schooled in the pages of *Good Words* and *Once a Week* where his biblical and family themes rivalled those of Walker, Pinwell, Fildes and du Maurier. The series was called 'Graphic America' and as well as being an important opening for the publication, released the artist from the drudgery of magazine work, enabling him to investigate a young and virile nation with the sort of scrutiny that only Dickens and Thackeray had before attempted. Boyd Houghton's pen, tinged with a gentle Pre-Raphaelite radicalism, opened up the East Coast and the frontiers of the West for middle class England as well as causing a considerable stir in the States itself. He was both amused and disenchanted by the oldest republic in the world, amused to follow in the steps of Fenimore Cooper and Longfellow and appalled by the corruption and the greed of the new American. He was nevertheless able to extract from it all with consummate skill, the tiny incidents of city life, the Boston News Room, the barber's saloon and the trotting races that epitomised the vital razamataz of American cities. Also in the East, he produced strikingly contrasted sketches of the austere Shaker Community at Mount Lebanon, the synthesis of American extremes.

In the West, Houghton was dealing with themes that were as much of interest to the Bostonians as to the Londoners, so remote and detached were they from pioneering life. Some of Houghton's best work was done there where he found a greater sympathy with the rugged character of the frontiersman pitting his strength against unrelenting nature, craggy mountains and vast forests. Houghton's art, which was an art of contrasting balance of black with white, found full scope in the camp fires and dark woods of the West. A master of composition, his effects of light and shade in prints such as 'Crossing a Canyon' borrow a good deal from Doré's tricks of verticality and silhouette. He drew Indians, visited the Mormons and struck up an acquaintance with 'Wild Bill' Cody, accompanying him on a three day buffalo hunt, and despatched his drawings with his own pithy text to London. Paul Hogarth is probably near the mark when he writes that 'No other artist had been given, or would be given again, the freedom to describe as well as to depict his impressions of such an important theme.'[15]

By the end of the century the role of the special was changing. He was far less independent, relied less on his own resourcefulness and was increasingly hampered by a panoply of red tape. 'The heyday of the war correspondent's adventurous life closed with the Boer War,' Sheldon-Williams wrote in an article during his old age.[16] At Ladysmith the relationship between military and artist was still informal. 'I do not care if you get a hole through your body as long as you don't go outside our lines,' Sheldon-Williams was told by Major Altham. On the same occasion, Bennet Burleigh of the *Daily Telegraph*, who was known for bluffing his way through anything, complained to the authorities half in jest, that Melton Prior's bald head was drawing the enemy's fire! Such camaraderie among the correspondents became less acceptable as the professionalism of scientific warfare increased. In the Russo-Japanese War of 1905, Melton Prior was forbidden to go to the front by the Japanese command as too old and too much of a liability. Sheldon-Williams says he wept, being unable to complete his work and therefore as good as finished. The First World War was like a new chapter for anyone like Sheldon-Williams who had worked under the old *ad hoc* methods of the specials. His position was officially recognised and he was provided with a chauffeur, a car and a batman, but was also expected to keep out of the way! The creation of official war artists in 1915 really swept aside the unique role of the artist correspondent and ended a profession that had lasted only a little more than sixty years.

Photography had much to do with the decline in the work of the artist reporter, but in this particular area the influence was very slow. In his introduction to *The Camera Goes to War, Photographs From the Crimean War 1854-6,* James Hannavy says that photographs exploded 'the lie that troops fought in dress uniforms — or for that matter any uniform at all — the war artist would rapidly become a dying breed'.[17] Although *The Illustrated London News* was using photographs as a basis for its engravings in the 1850s, there was no sense of rivalry at this early date and it was years before any process of printing photographs in acceptable form was developed. Mason Jackson used 'direct photo-engraving' in the magazine for 1886 and one illustration of a torpedo boat was photographed on to the block for an issue of 1889, but these were not yet substitutes for the action-packed drawings of Woodville or the spirited naval battles of J.R. Wells, the Fleet Special Artist. Many artists worked on photographs and had files of them for data. Apart from the technical problems, the photographer tended still to provide a static view of war, the artist on the other hand could give the sense and colour of action and continued to do so until well into the First War. The public craved for that 'instant when the scene resolves itself into a true picture, which remains for a minute perhaps, and then melts'.[18]

It was during the Russo-Japanese campaign of 1905 that artists like Sheldon-Williams felt the pressure of the camera really encroaching on their territory for the first time. It was a relentless progress from weekly to daily papers and then on to the early screens. Williams found himself in open competition with J. Hare, the official Japanese photographer, Bulla on the Russian side and R.S. Dunn of New York who had been sent out by *The Commercial Advertiser.*

But if the newspaper barons appreciated the use of photography it is clear from a strange story told by one of the specials that the public did not. Fred Villiers, who was always an experimenter, decided to take an early movie camera with him on the Graeco-Turkish campaign of 1897. Villiers had thought that if the artist's on-the-spot sketches were insufficient, here was the ideal substitute which was bound to be a commercial success. But it was a total failure. The flickering black and white impressions on the screen, in which it was difficult to make out either side, almost impossible to catch any dramatic moments and where there was practically no 'text', were useless to convey the story. The public which had been brought up on fiery penwork, the swirling smoke of naval engagements, the defence of Majuba Hill or the Relief of Khartoum, were not prepared to knuckle down to actuality. In fact news films had to be set up in the tradition of 'battle painting' for the early cinema to be able to use them! It was an extraordinary back-handed triumph for the artist that he had dominated the pages for so long and gripped the imagination of his audience so successfully that they preferred his view to that of the camera. It was H.V. Barnett's remark in 1883 that the special's job was to invest 'bare facts with charm'[19] that was the making and undoing of their work. It put history in aspic, delicious for the taste of the Victorians but less palatable for us. Caton Woodville's great oil paintings are less true to us than his vital sketches covered with notes though it was the former that made him famous. But the battle-painter tradition that persisted among these gallant gentlemen died hard and it was only the unsentimental still photographs of rotting corpses in the trenches of the First World War that finally made the public familiar, if sickened, with reality.

*Footnotes*

1. William Simpson, RI, *Autobiography,* 1903.
2. Mason Jackson, *The Pictorial Press, its Origins and Progress,* 1885.
3. Henry Vizetelly, *Glances Back Over Seventy Years,* 2 Vols., 1893.
4. Mason Jackson, *The Pictorial Press, its Origins and Progress,* 1885, p.342.
5. William Simpson, *The English Illustrated Magazine,* Vol. 14, 1895-6, p.230.
6. Vizetelly, op.cit., p.236.
7. A.S. Hartrick, *A Painter's Pilgrimage Through Fifty Years,* 1939, p.71.
8. Harry V. Barnett, 'The Special Artist', *Magazine of Art,* Vol. 6, 1883, p.166.
9. Daphne du Maurier, *The Young George du Maurier: A Selection of his Letters, 1860-1867,* 1951, p.82.
10. William Simpson, RI, *Autobiography,* 1903.
11. Harry V. Barnett, op.cit.
12. William Simpson, RI, op.cit.
13. A.S. Hartrick, op.cit.
14. Harry V. Barnett, op.cit.
15. Paul Hogarth, *Arthur Boyd Houghton,* Victoria and Albert Museum, 1975, p.13.
16. Inglis Sheldon-Williams, 'The War Correspondent: Then and Now', *The Sphere,* November 20, 1937.
17. James Hannavy, *The Camera Goes to War,* Scottish Arts Council, 1974, p.13.
18. Harry V. Barnett, op. cit.
19. ibid.

# Chapter 8

# Social Realism 1850-1890

here was no question of the strongly didactic and moralising Victorian conscience leaving illustration as a purely informing or entertaining medium. In 1865, Charles Knight, who had been at the centre of popular illustrating from its beginnings, was criticising news illustration for its lack of serious reporting. 'The staple materials,' he wrote, 'for the steady-going illustrator to work most attractively upon are, Court and Fashion; Civic Processions and Banquets; Political and Religious Demonstrations in crowded halls; Theatrical Novelties; Musical Meetings; Races; Reviews; Ship Launches — every scene in short, where a crowd of great people and respectable people can be got together, but never, if possible, any exhibition of vulgar poverty. This view of Society is one-sided. We must look further for its "many coloured life". We want to behold something more than the showy make-up of the characteristics of the age. We want to see the human form beneath the drapery.'[1]

Had Knight examined the serial parts or even the bound volumes of the foremost novelist of the period, Charles Dickens, he would have noticed a change in the style of illustrations from 1840 to 1860, a change towards that reality he so wished to see in the press. We have deliberately avoided here in these chapters, the tangled web of Dickens' illustration, but even a cursory glance at the engravings of H.K. Browne (Phiz) to *Pickwick* and then to *Martin Chuzzlewit*, 1844, and *Bleak House*, 1852-53, show a progression away from caricature and towards direct statement. As John Harvey has written, there is a 'new sharpness and energy'[2] in Browne's drawing which is partly derived from Daumier and partly from the way the novelist was changing in the new Victorian world. In *Bleak House,* Browne uses the so-called dark plates to express the feeling of the time; probably a sense that both novelist and illustrator felt together and decided to use, a brooding sense where the figures are dominated by their surroundings. As Harvey writes — 'On Browne's part, the development of this mode shows the depth of his response to Dickens' writing at this time, for it is ideally suited to conveying the oppressive gatherings of fog and darkness in human affairs so powerfully presented in the novel.'[3] This was a far remove from Phiz's illustrations for Grant's *Sketches in London* of 1838, where convicts and lunatics became burlesques much as they had been in the eighteenth century. There were only twenty-three years between that book and the 'literal description' of Henry Mayhew's *London Labour and The London Poor*, 1861, but what a world passes between them. The cold charity of Mr. Bumble was gradually replaced by a greater compassion and understanding from writers and their artists, this was reflected in the Pre-Raphaelite work of the 1850s but there had been earlier precursors.

Charles Knight himself had been an important force in showing life as it actually was away from romanticism and cottage door sentimentality. His two volumes on *London*, 1841, showed some events that were neither topographical, sentimental or caricatured about the ordinary life of citizens. The woodcuts were small and generalised but they gave facts, those on the sewerage of the growing city are among the most interesting. Knight had gathered round him minor delineators like Tiffin, Timbrill and Fairholt, who could not be expected to lift their work right out of the conventions of the time. In fact it was only after 1851 that the Victorian preoccupation with facts alone became dominant. Douglas Jerrold, writing in 1891, caught the spirit of the change from the earlier books, not simply the change in drawing techniques but the change in the way the new generation of 1851 looked at itself. 'Mr Knight's *London* of 1841,' he writes, 'is a book of the past. His streets and his Cockneys – even those of Dickens – are of another generation – the like of which we know no more. His picture of "a plug in a frost" is a part of London's history, it has ceased to be *our* plug in a frost – and the figures are less familiar to our sight than Chinaman.'[4]

Some earlier attempts had been made to depict the life of the metropolis in unvarnished form. A Regency book in which frankness vies with strangeness is John Thomas Smith's *Vagabondiana or Anecdotes of Mendicant Wanderers Through The Streets of London,* published in 1817. Smith, the morose Keeper of Prints at the British Museum, who brought out a barbed *Life of Nollekens,* filled his book with etchings after his own pen drawings. They present a dramatic survey of street folk, blind beggars, cripples, the indigent poor of all kinds, destitute sailors and hawkers of trifles, observed with objectivity

*Figure 67. Beggars by John Thomas Smith. Etching, 1817.*

(Figure 67). Smith has clearly taken Callot and Rembrandt as his models and some even mirror the prints of Goya. Although he was no great artist, Smith had the sense to perceive that it was more important to paint blindness, beggary and poverty than personifications of them. Smith worked for Knight at one time and in 1839 a posthumous book *The Cries of London* was published carrying much the same sort of illustrations but the threshold between curiosity and involvement between artist and subject had not really been crossed.

The suspicion of the truthfulness of the artist which was very much a part of the 'scientific' Victorian, stems from the strength of caricature and romanticism in the British School. It is certainly relevant that Mayhew, a founder of *Punch* and a friend of numerous illustrators, should choose daguerrotypes by Beard as the basis of the drawings in his three volume survey of *London Labour.* Nothing short of strict accuracy could be tolerated and no artistic humour or sentiment softens the confrontation of readers with these rejected individuals. *The Illustrated London News* had provided sketches of the Irish famine in 1847, which were not without social comment, and similar coverage was given to the Crimean veterans in 1856 and to the cotton distress in Lancashire in 1862 by a splendid series of illustrations of Manchester operatives' dwellings. Even George Cruikshank's temperance drawings such as the prints of *The Bottle,* 1847, have a stronger realism about them, but by and large the skill of artists was not equal to the situations shown. Irish sketches, Manchester sketches, only seem to tell half the truth and although from 1855 artists such as C.W. Sheeres, C.J. Durham, J. Palmer and R.C. Hulme were tackling industry, they were seldom getting behind the skin of the men who worked in it.

The political upheavals on the Continent between 1830 and 1848 produced a stream of disaffected artists who became temporary visitors to this country much as they did after 1870. Among the artists to come were Eugène Lami, already referred to, and H.G.S. Chevalier known as 'Gavarni', 1804-1866. Lami drew English high life with great panache, Gavarni, a more complicated figure, radical in outlook, bohemian in manner, left his impressions of the capital in a volume called *Gavarni In London, Sketches of Life and Character,* published in 1849. This was a postscript to the artist's English years, he actually remained here from 1847 to 1851, a period of not unqualified success.[5] Fashionable London had taken the handsome Frenchman to its heart, had fêted him, had invited him to its houses, filled his desk with the cards of artists and men of letters. It was hoped that Gavarni would immortalise the high society of the most prosperous capital in the world, its receptions, balls, garden parties, political functions and historical ceremonies in a volume of magnificent lithographs. This may have been in Gavarni's mind to begin with, but as the life of London became more familiar to him, it was with the humdrum aspects of ordinary life that he identified. At home in Paris, he had hardly been the quiescent well-behaved illustrator of the bourgeois monarchy of Louis-Philippe; in London the artist who had struggled from poverty and imprisonment for debt, drew with fascination and feeling the inhabitants of the grimy streets. Gavarni had been introduced to *Punch* but was disdainful; he had been given permission to paint the Queen but had failed to turn up for the sitting. The British public were not prepared to tolerate such cavalier behaviour and though some of his work appeared in *The Illustrated London News* in 1848 it was dismissed as 'too French'.

*Gavarni in London* of 1849 remains an interesting book. As was the case with Doré, more than twenty years later, it needed an outsider, a foreigner, to look frankly at the problems of London and provide a dispassionate portrait of its people. Nearly three-quarters of Gavarni's subjects are what Mayhew came to call 'street folk', pavement entertainers, door to door traders, stall holders, labourers or working people in their habitats of Covent Garden or Greenwich. We have a wonderful frontispiece of street acrobats, supple and muscular figures divesting themselves of cheap clothing to reveal an almost Greek nobility; Gavarni found a nobility in the slums and was not afraid to reveal it. He shows us the Potato-Can seller, crying his wares defiantly while shadowy bundles of rags in the background, greedily gobble them up. Next to him are a pair of dandies bound for a fancy ball and before that the demi-monde of Vauxhall and the vulnerable world of the barmaid, a pretty figure surrounded by leering approving faces (Figure 68). Elsewhere a car man and a coal heaver talk together in a gin palace watched by the same pretty barmaid, a crossing sweeper pleads a tip from a haughty citizen and two beautiful women in bonnets and shawls make their way to church followed by a cockaded footman carrying the books. It is as if a sharp knife has been cut into the cake of Victorian society and its varying layers laid bare for the first time.

It can be no accident that each sketch remains so compartmented on its own page, so seemingly isolated from the others and from the text, it was precisely as the London of 1849 appeared to Gavarni. The artist brings a fluidity of line and softness in the pencillings and shadings only achievable in lithography. Besides this an extra dimension is given by the tinting of the lithographs, rare in this type of book. These are French illustrations par excellence, at their most English in the heads of the thieves, but still the productions of the Gallic temperament. In nearly the last illustration in the book 'Foreign Gentleman in

*Figure 68. 'The bar-maid' by Gavarni.*

London' we see the be-whiskered features of Gavarni himself, a self-portrait, as he orders his menu in a chop house, defensive to the last of his right to be a foreigner and to have his own opinion of this strange paradoxical people.

A few attempts were made at an early date after this to draw the city as it actually was. George Godwin, Editor of *The Builder,* took graphic artists with him on his visits to investigate the slums in the early 1850s. This was to be 'a record of the curious — not to say frightful — condition of London and some of its denizens in the middle of the boasted nineteenth century.'[6] The choice of artists was strange, Alfred Concanen and William McConnell both being well-known humorous illustrators; the results were published as *London Shadows: A glance at the homes of the thousands,* 1854.

Perhaps the greatest piece of visual exploration in this sphere came not from the English illustrators but from another Frenchman, Gustave Doré, 1832-1883. Doré's background was that of many of the other visiting French draughtsmen, Gavarni included. A spell of working on Philippon's *Journal Pour Rire,* had been followed by a great success as the illustrator of classics by Rabelais and Cervantes. He had appeared briefly before the British public as the reporter of the Crimean War through the pages of *The Illustrated London News*, pages whose individuality and tortured humanity survived even the scalpels of the wood-engravers. The idea that this distinguished foreign artist should make a microcosm of London and follow more penetratingly in the steps of Rowlandson and Gavarni was not his own. It was suggested to him by Blanchard Jerrold, the playright and farceur, who offered to write an accompanying text. Neither was the idea brought to completion, but what was finished remains a masterpiece. Doré was a great enough artist to see that the way to understand a great city and to capture its spirit for the printed page was to synthesise. It was the distillation of the smokey, foggy, brutal and funny, hateful but engaging, poverty-stricken but luxury-laden city of four million people that he set out to capture.

Jerrold was later to write about his friend and the way *London A Pilgrimage* came to be written.

'We are pilgrims; not, I repeat, historians, nor antiquaries, nor topographers. Our plan is to present London in the quick to the reader — as completely as we may be able to grasp the prodigious giant, and dissect his Titan limbs, the floods of his veins, the iron beams of his muscles! We approach him by the main artery which feeds his unflinching vigour. We shall examine him at work and play; asleep and in his wakefullest moments. We shall pay court to him in his brightest and his happiest guises, when he stands solemn and erect in the dignity of his quaint and ancient state; when his steadfastness to the old is personified in the dress of a benefactor, or his passion for the new is shown in the hundred changes of every passing hour.'[7]

It is in fact 'the main artery' of the Thames which gives the book its symmetry, wherever our artist takes us we are conscious of the river producing the grime of the waterfront (Figure 69) as well as the luxuries of the drawing-room. In a large and generous piece of Victorian book production, Doré brings the contradictions and contrasts vividly into juxta-

*Figure 69. 'The Pool of London' by Gustave Doré.*

position, opening wide the London of Disraeli's two nations. Each nation is treated quite separately, The Docks, The Derby, The West End, Workaday London, divided territories, each totally ignorant of the other. And yet it is the similarities which make the irony for the artist; Jerrold perceptively remarks that only in London do the poor ape the rich in dress, becoming caricatures of the society that has rejected them. In both cases Doré's pictures are thick with humanity whether at the fashionable garden party at Holland House, or in the sleezy gaslight of a fourth rate music-hall; everywhere people are fighting for recognition in the anonymity of it all. The crowded full page illustrations are emphasised by the subtle inclusion of single figures in the opposite text; the chestnut woman or the blind beggar come struggling forward demanding our notice.

Doré's wit suffuses the book from the initial letter 'L' formed from oars pointing skywards and a boat jutting out from the bank, to the sinister rendering of the Lambeth Gasworks, an obvious allusion to Bosch or his followers with the *double entendre* of a Last Judgement! Throughout Doré has relied on foreign engravers which allied to his rather painterly flow of line gives the unique impression of figures on the streets and buildings being as much a part of the climate as the watery moon and the greyness. Doré is the prince of gaslight, both high and low are seen by its rays, the piled hair coils of society ladies come under its glow and so do the jigging bodies of wharfmen or children dancing to a barrel organ in a brick court.

With the founding of *The Graphic* in 1869, a more socially conscious epoch opened up to the illustrator. It was by no means solely *The Graphic* that reported the upheavals of the post industrial revolution cities or the drift from the land, although they fostered a group of artists who drew them with sensitivity, objectivity and great pictorial power. For the first time the illustrated journals became the vehicles of a passionate and persuasive point of view, whose purpose was to show the sufferings of the poor, the destitute and the ill, as they existed in the cold light of Victorian charity. In the hands of Luke Fildes, Hubert von Herkomer and Frank Holl, the homeless, the workhouse inmates and the flower girls, became actual voices demanding to be heard, to be understood, to be considered as part of that society. The unsentimental wood engraving was the ideal medium for this work, and the artist's skilful definition of a crowd as an individual, or a single person representing his whole group, could be seen with a detachment which excluded the morbid or banal.

These illustrators were partly influenced by the moralising of the Hogarth tradition, the novels of Dickens and George Eliot and the identification with work which was a feature of mid-Victorian radicalism. Such figures as John Cassell, the Ingrams and Walter Crane took a fairly vigorous line in social improvement and Crane like W.L. Thomas, 1830-1900, founder of *The Graphic,* had been apprenticed to the radical wood engraver W.J. Linton.

The catalyst in this whole development, from occasional realistic illustration to wholesale coverage of deprivation, seems to have been the Paris Commune in March to June 1871, very few pictures of strong social interest appearing before it. The Revolution exposed nerve ends which nobody recognised were there previously. French cartoonists displayed an amazing black humour in their illustrations of the siege and many French artists, with the tradition of Courbet behind them, flocked into England after the end of the Commune. There was already a great discipline in black and white art, a legacy from the 1860s and Regamey's sketches of Paris for *The Illustrated London News* and Boyd Houghton's powerful evocations of civic solidarity like the 'Women of Montmartre' in *The Graphic,* had a deep impact on the younger artists. Crane was not alone in reacting strongly to the executions of the communists that followed. 'The Commune, its ideals and its acts, were entirely misunderstood, or misrepresented in the English press, and it is only recently, after the lapse of years, that its true aims, with all its faults and almost superhuman difficulties, are beginning to be apprehended as an attempt to establish a true Civic

*Figure 70. Illustration to* Edwin Drood *by Luke Fildes, 1871.*

Commonwealth, on a basis of collective service and ownership.'[8] Fortunately the British artists preferred to extract the news of the moment from the heavy political theology of the time, making a visual comment outside faction and class rancour.

Fildes, Herkomer and Holl were not political animals. All were to be elected Royal Academicians and, though the third died comparatively young, the first two were to become influential figures in the artistic establishment. Luke Fildes, 1844-1927, a young painter who had already made his name as an illustrator in the mid-1860s, was showing some restlessness by 1869 at being confined to 'fancy' pictures. He was making it his habit to carry a notebook with him on his walks through London and when that year W.L. Thomas suggested he should illustrate a new publication that he was promoting, one of these sketches sprang to mind. It was a drawing that he had noted down of a group of homeless people waiting in the cold for admission to a Casual Ward. This was to be his first and most celebrated contribution to the new *Graphic.* It appeared on 4 December 1869 as 'Houseless and Hungry', a line of destitutes huddled against a bleak wall out of the wind, their heads bowed in subjection, their hands in their pockets and their meagre clothes wrapped inadequately round them. There is no trace of sentimentality anywhere, only a kind of stoical resolve in the adults, a weary inevitability in the figures of the children. The picture had immediate success, academicians praised it, the public were moved by it and Millais at once suggested Fildes' name as the illustrator of Dickens' new novel *The Mystery of Edwin Drood.* Fildes' work in social realism was to be limited; he translated this illustration into a canvas, 'Applicants for an Admission to a Casual Ward', 1874, and painted other subjects of a domestic rather than a social nature. But his enduring image of the queue as a symbol of social suffering was a powerful one and was used repeatedly by other realists, particularly William Small and E. Buckman for The Commune in *The Graphic,* 1870-71, and M. Fitzgerald in the *Illustrated* for the coal mining industry in 1875. Fildes' illustrations for the unfinished Dickens novel are fine and compelling (Figure 70) and provide a link between the novelist's frank expression and the artist's truth to nature which was a feature of the 1870s and 1880s, particularly in the designs for Hardy's novels by Helen Paterson (Allingham), M.E. Edwards, Fred Barnard, Robert Barnes and Charles Green.

Hubert von Herkomer, 1849-1914, some years Fildes' junior, came to illustrating rather late in the 1860s and his best work in black and white was done for *The Graphic,* 1871-79. His greatest strength was in his interiors with figures, observed with a Millet-like sense of form and compassion, melting into their surroundings. His illustrations of lodging houses, workhouses and hospitals are measured by a particular sympathy for the frailties of age, for instance 'Old Age' a study at the Westminster Union, 1877, 'Sunday at Chelsea Hospital', 1871, 'Low Lodging House, St Giles', 1872 and 'Christmas in a Workhouse', 1876. For some reason his contributions to *The Illustrated London News* from 1871-73 are purely social.

Frank Holl, 1845-1888, was a Londoner and most at home with the depiction of ordinary life in town and country. He entered the RA Schools in 1860 at the age of fifteen and eight years later won the travelling scholarship. He resigned this while on tour abroad, partly because it was not benefiting his art, and partly because he was an invalid. His talents really lay in figure drawing and specially the figures of the quayside and the pavement, fisherwomen waiting for their husbands, soldiers ordered off to service overseas. Holl became the painter of working class uncertainty, the uncompromising realities of those who had to fish, had to fight for their country or had to deliver their all to the pawnbroker. Frith had made the platform a place of drama in his 'Railway Station', Holl makes it one of personal tragedy in 'Gone – Euston Station', a *Graphic* illustration of 19 February 1876, and 'Ordered Off', *Illustrated London News,* 13 September 1884. Other facets of the artist are the intensely observed interiors of 'Shoe-making at The Philanthropic Society's Farm, Redhill' *The Graphic,* 18 May 1872, and the subtle street groups of 'Sketches in London' in the same magazine for 22 June 1872. Holl was widely acclaimed for his 'Newgate: Committed For Trial', 1878, and 'No Tidings From The Sea', specially commissioned by Queen Victoria, but his later work is almost entirely in portraiture. Holl was not primarily an illustrator, only occasionally developed his magazine illustrations from canvases, rather than the reverse, and did not usually think in terms of black and white.

E. Buckman was a fairly regular contributor of the social illustration in the early 1870s, working for both the *Graphic* and the *Illustrated.* For the latter he tackled subjects as various as 'A Statute Fair For a Farm Servant', 2 November 1872, and scenes in a 'London Dockyard', 1873. His 'Homeless' in the Christmas *Illustrated London News* of 1876 verges on the sentimental. Michael Fitzgerald, a shadowy figure, contributed some staggeringly simple drawings to the *Illustrated* in the early 1870s showing the hopelessness and monotony of prison life in Newgate and the Clerkenwell House of Correction. A series of character studies run by *The Graphic* entitled 'Heads of the People' gave artists such as Herkomer, Mathew White Ridley and William Small, the chance to show the passions expressed through a trade or a calling, diligence in the head of the miner, watchfulness in that of the coastguard and sober devotion in that of the labourer. Small's contribution, 'The British Rough', is a most astonishing image of brute force, unsurpassed in his later work, with all the strength of Goya.

Mathew White Ridley and C.J. Staniland provided vivid illustrations of the coal mining industry and other artists like A.E. Emslie, W.B. Murray and later W.D. Almond, came to grips with the 'dark satanic mills' of the big cities with their poorly paid female labour. H. Towneley Green formed one of this same group with his brother Charles Green, the Dickens illustrator, so too did R. Caton Woodville, the battle painter and J.D. Linton, the watercolourist. Robert Barnes contributed to *The Illustrated* from 1872 and Fred Barnard, A.D. McCormick and Matt Morgan all submitted illustrations of the Irish distress and British unemployment in 1886. J.C. Dollman's factual look at an opium den in *The Graphic* of 23 October 1880 is a great contrast to Doré's theatrical treatment of ten years earlier.

An interesting sidelight on this group of illustrators in the early 1880s is the development of a mannerism by themselves and their successors. From about 1884, A.E. Emslie, Edward R. King, William Rainey, Sidney Paget, Percy Tarrant, Gunning King and a few more, veer away from the traditional pen line and attempt broken effects as if they were anxious to give a texture like oil paint. This is best seen in Edward R. King's

'Workman's Train' published in *The Illustrated London News* of 14 April 1883. The new processes for photographing a drawing directly on to the block and the increased use of heavy bodycolour over the ink, must account for this thick 'impasto' style, much decried by illustrators of the old school.

W.L. Thomas's interest in showing social problems continues in *The Graphic* throughout the 1880s although the artists employed tend to be less interesting. The middle years of the decade have illustrations of vaccinations in poor districts, board schools, common lodging houses and hospitals, Barnes providing many of them and the drawings for Hardy's *Mayor of Casterbridge* serialised at the same time. The work of C.S. Reinhart, H. Johnson and J.R. Brown is competent in accuracy but does not have that insight which lifts a scene out of the pages of journalism and into the realm of great art. Very different however is the work of the Frenchman, Paul Renouard, 1845-1924, one of the great stars of *The Graphic*.

*Figure 71. 'Anarchist Oratory'. Front page of* The Graphic *by Paul Renouard.*

He first appears in 1884 and was still working for the paper well into the Edwardian period. He is arguably the greatest artist in chalk ever to work for a British publication and he provides another link in the chain that Thomas forged with the Continental journals. Although he excelled in Parliamentary portraits, Renouard's greatest triumphs were in sketches of the London Police Courts, 1887, and the London prisons in 1889, followed by equally beautiful but less testing subjects in France in the 1890s (Figure 71). His extraordinary mastery of this very soft and caressing medium without tint, gave *The Graphic* a visual lead over its famous rival which was to remain until the First World War. No artist could succeed to him, but chalk replaced wash in the work of the Specials, and when David Wilson became cartoonist in about 1910, his medium was also chalk.

The greatest barrier to accurate social reporting was the fact that both *The Graphic* and *The Illustrated London News* pursued a very general readership. The work of the artists was required to be fairly objective, untainted and untrammelled by prejudice or polemic, simply putting forward a statement of fact. *The Graphic* artists could maintain a certain independence as narrative and genre painting swept agricultural and industrial subjects into the illustrator's net,[9] but the pressures on the draughtsmen as journalists kept their comments muted and there was little text accompanying the blocks. As has been pointed out, the situation with the Victorian comic weeklies was rather different. 'Traditionally', wrote Wolff and Fox in *The Victorian City,* 'graphic humour has always been closely connected with comment, individual bias and prejudice. It is recognised as being a distortion of reality to point an effect or achieve a purpose ... In the small cartoons also, the contact between illustrator and audience did not involve the concept of impartiality, and in addition the artist rarely had to meet a topical deadline.'[10] The first cartoonist of *Punch* who had his subject chosen for him at a dinner on one day and had to produce a completed drawing three days later, would hardly endorse this, but *Punch* by the 1860s had become a paper of the *status quo* and Tenniel was not a political man. A more vital style of cartooning which must have had some social impact was that appearing in *The Tomahawk* between 1867 and 1870.

*The Tomahawk* was founded by A.W. à Beckett after he had been cold-shouldered by

Mark Lemon of *Punch*. A Beckett was twenty-one years old and determined to have a *Punch* of his own, which may account for the youthful verve of the paper and the great freedom of its one and only illustrator. It turned out to be very unlike *Punch*, 'a Saturday Journal of Satire' with a maximum of six pages of letter press and one 'big cut' for the price of twopence. With a staff of about six, mainly made up of young civil servants who were writers, it was more adaptable than its elder brother and more socially volatile. Its greatest strength was in having Alfred Thompson as writer and illustrator of its almanacs and Matt Morgan, 1836-1890, as cartoonist throughout its life.

Morgan is a rather shadowy figure but his work is amongst the most original of its time. He made rather conventional illustrations for *The Illustrated Times* and other periodicals before coming to *The Tomahawk* in 1867, and drawing for it with a fearlessness and conviction that had hardly been seen since Gillray. His draughtsmanship appears to have been very variable but the images that he produces are very modern, some deriving from French cartooning and some from the book illustrations of Doré. *The Tomahawk* made the innovation in political and social cartooning of printing from tinted wood blocks, the black outlines standing out from green, orange, yellow or blue tints, sometimes tremendously enhancing to a double page spread, sometimes creating 'an ultra-bilious effect to the jaundiced eye'.[11] The cartoons were decided by the staff much as those on *Punch* were chosen, but Morgan seems to have had great freedom and the editorial works very closely with his designs. *The Tomahawk* strongly criticised Disraeli, condemned the abuses of women by society, protested about the English attitude to Ireland and the misuse of money by city magnates. Morgan dared too on 14 November 1868 to criticise the Queen and her prolonged widowhood in 'Which Will It be?.' A throne is shown on one side of the cartoon occupied by a serene Queen Victoria and on the other side it is empty and draped with black; around it are symbols of the corresponding prosperity or poverty that the sovereign's influence brings. This cartoon was strongly criticised and Morgan had to atone for it by a more loyal one when the Queen finally emerged from her hibernation at Windsor.

Morgan's bête noire was Napoleon III and his small, lithe presence, with carefully waxed moustache, is seen frequently in *The Tomahawk* pages as the ravisher and destroyer of France. Amongst the most memorable of the series leading towards the defeat of 1870 are 'Alone With The Dead, Or Liberty And Her Murderer', 30 January 1869, showing Napoleon rowing a boat with the corpse of *La France* in its stern, a subject from Doré and 'The Modern Mazeppa' where the Emperor is lashed to a runaway horse, 5 June 1869. The cartoon of 24 July 1869 is ominously prophetic, a sombre panorama of Paris is titled 'The Doomed City' and the lurid green of the tints breaks in only one piece of sky to reveal the words 'Revolution'. His most remarkable engraving appeared on 30 July 1870 under the title 'Vive La Guerre', a menacing skeleton dressed as a French soldier gives out a cry from its gaping jaws and holds a torch and a sword high in its bony hands. Not only is this an indictment of the Franco-Prussian War but a statement about war as a whole. Morgan was especially outraged by the dependence of the urban population on such frivolities as the London Season and he voiced this in a cartoon of 21 August 1869 where a family face starvation in a garret because Society has left town for the summer. Another outrage depicted by his pen was that of baby farming, shown as 'The Devil's Trade' in July 1870 (Figure 72).

Morgan's position on *The Tomahawk* is credited with winning greater freedom for the cartoonist in other fringe papers for which he worked, *Fun, Judy* and *Will o' the Wisp*.[12] He made some further important contributions to *The Illustrated London News* in 1886, showing the London unemployed but later settled in the United States where he died in New York in 1890.

A further pair of artists working in this strongly social pictorial tradition were William

Strang and Jack B. Yeats. William Strang RA, 1859-1921, used the recently revived etching to show the rugged and arduous life of poor country people, rather in the style of Millet. They can show great contrasts in atmosphere and in character, very often they depict that sort of stoical determination which is seen in the group of his etching 'The Fair Ground', 1892 (Figure 73). Jack Yeats, 1871-1957, reveals another aspect of late Victorian society in his East End drawings of 'A Push Halfpenny Match', 1898, or 'Gaff in the East End' of the same date. They show a crowd of heads, usually craning forward over a game, an incident or a boxing match, and are among the most sturdily vivid works being done in the 1890s.

THE DEVIL'S TRADE!
(DEDICATED TO THE SUPPORTERS OF BABY-FARMERS)

Figure 73. 'The Fair Ground' by William Strang, 1892.

Left: Figure 72. 'The Devil's Trade' by Matt Morgan, July 1870.

### Footnotes

1. Charles Knight, *Passages of a Working Life*, 1865, Vol. 3, pp.246-47.
2. John Harvey, *Victorian Novelists and Their Illustrators*, 1970, p.134.
3. ibid., p.153.
4. Blanchard Jerrold, *Life of Gustave Doré*, 1891, p.175.
5. Gavarni must have been known to the British public by 1845 when W. Dugdale of Holywell Street, published sixteen woodcuts by the artist, price 2d.
6. Quoted by Dyos & Wolff in *The Victorian City*, 1973.
7. Blanchard Jerrold, op.cit., pp.175-76.
8. Walter Crane, *An Artist's Reminiscences*, 1907, p.102.
9. It was this aspect of the black and white artists that encouraged Vincent Van Gogh to collect their wood engravings from the magazines.
10. Dyos & Wolff, *The Victorian City*, 1973, p.567.
11. A.W. à Beckett, *The A Beckett's of Punch*, 1903, p.168.
12. Kemnitz, *Victorian Studies*, Sept. 1975, Vol. 19, No. 1.

# Chapter 9

# Fin de Siècle Magazines

*Head-piece for* The English Illustrated Magazine, *1883, by Heywood Sumner.*

The Victorian reading public was a magazine reading public and the originality and inventiveness of publishers and artists were kept in perpetual ferment by their demand to be entertained. After the rather dull days of the 1880s, the next decade produced a myriad of illustrated publications, some of them short-lived, some more hardy, but all of them self-consciously of the moment and determined to amaze, shock, delight and enthrall before the century ran out. Holbrook Jackson, writing in 1913 and almost within earshot of the 1890s, remarked that 'people felt they were living amid changes and struggles, intellectual, social and spiritual, and the interpreters of the hour — the publicists, journalists and popular purveyors of ideas of all kinds — did not fail to make a sort of traffic in the spirit of the times.'[1]

The words 'fin de siècle' were on everybody's lips as was the word 'new', there was the new art 'art nouveau', the new morals, the new socialism, the new drama and logically enough 'the new woman' who smoked, rode on a bicycle or had a career. Perhaps because of the entrenched academicism of the schools and galleries, perhaps because book work is the natural opening for a young artist, it was in the illustrations, in the decorations, in the posters and private presses, that the spirit of this new art flourished. 'In no other branch of pictorial art was there so much activity during the whole of the period,' wrote Holbrook Jackson, 'and, on the whole, so much undisputed excellence, as in the various pen and pencil drawings which blossomed from innumerable books and periodicals.'[2] It was after all the decade of Aubrey Beardsley and Phil May, of Walter Crane, William Morris, Charles Ricketts, Bernard Partridge, Linley Sambourne, Raven-Hill, S.H. Sime, J.F. and E.J. Sullivan to name only a few.

The decadent vision which has come to be associated with the period certainly stretches back to an earlier date than 1890, in fact to the aestheticism of the 1870s. The liberation of subject matter that had been won by the Pre-Raphaelites and continued by the artists of the 1860s had not penetrated the book as a whole. It was only in the pioneering work of Walter Crane and his followers that the artist left his allotted pages and flowed over into the text, establishing his right to be considered and consulted over type faces, frontispieces, covers, initial letters and all manner of decoration. Crane had come to realise the importance of the quality of space and black and white areas in a book opening, his inspiration being partly in the tradition of medieval illuminations, partly inspired by Dürer and to some extent by latent Pre-Raphaelitism. But although Crane's discovery of the 'mechanical relation' of decoration to the page, and the page to printing, resulted in many fine art books, a large proportion of this creativity went into children's books and the production of magazines. Crane's training under the socialist engraver W.J. Linton places him firmly in the craft tradition and his populist feelings about illustration are summed up in a book written at about this time. Graphic art he says 'is the most vital and popular form of art at the present day, and it, far more than painting, deals with the actual life of the people; it is too, thoroughly democratic in its appeal, and associated with the newspaper and magazine, goes everywhere — at least, as far as there are shillings and pence — and where often no other form of art is accessible.'[3] Crane with his eye on new ideas and a new public was not so dogged by the precious archaism which taints some of Morris's book design and was so prevalent among his imitators. He did not resist mechanisation or disallow the value of photography but saw possibilities in both and praised their fidelity in the best processes.

Concurrent with the Utopian dream of Morris and the radicalism of Crane, was the doctrine of 'art for art's sake' which had been nurtured by Walter Pater and been brought to a wider audience through the writings of Oscar Wilde. It was in many ways the antithesis of the craft approach, it held that art was responsible to nobody, that it had no moral or political message beyond itself and that it was the territory of a cultured elite among whom the artist himself was a sort of natural aristocrat. The art of such a doctrine was necessarily self-conscious, brittle and precious, and whereas in the hands of Whistler or Beardsley it could reach great heights, its presence in the schools produced work that was often imitative and mannered. Because it was a distinctly decorative style, its range was well suited to the book and some of the finest productions of these years were in art nouveau books and magazines. The concept of the 'artistic person' and the 'artistic house' was very fashionable at the turn of the century and it was undoubtedly a middle-class readership, fired by Morris and seduced by the new art, that enabled so many *fin de siècle* magazines to flourish.

These magazines were sometimes weeklies, sometimes monthlies but were distinctive for their decoration, hand-made paper, beautiful type forms and carefully chosen subject matter, the spiritual heirs of the books of beauty that were nice to feel and handle as well as to read. The other magazines of political, social or general interest continued to be issued, *The Strand Magazine, The Pall Mall Magazine, The Pall Mall Budget, The Sketch, Pick-Me-Up* and many more, each employing their own teams of good artists. But the drawings were for the most part purely pictorial, purely illustrative and little more than accomplished entertainment; the *fin de siècle* magazines on the other hand clearly demanded a critical response and an intellectual comparison of design with design from their readers.

The resulting mixture of aims and aspirations between the arts and crafts movement on the one side and art nouveau on the other give the 1890s that fragile doomed extravagance which we have come to admire. The tensions within the art of the time seem to have been more than usually creative and they are nowhere better seen than in the pained pierrots, glowering satyrs, grotesque masks, arabesques and lotus flowers that spread across the pages of the magazines.

Line blocks had been used from 1876 and the first half-tone was used commercially in 1884, bringing in an epoch where the artist was no longer drawing for the engraver but drawing for himself and gaining with it an independence of interpretation and a will to experiment. By the middle of the 1890s there were younger men on *The Graphic* who had never worked for the wood-engraver and whose vision was totally fresh. Another sign of the times was the rather tragic bankruptcy of the firm of Dalziel Brothers in the middle of 1893. The remarkable family of engravers and artists, who had been responsible for many of the finest art books of the mid-century, ceased trading with debts of £39,146. The Official Receiver commented of the famous brothers that they were 'over 70 years of age' and 'could not keep up with the times'.[4] But their own evidence was that their losses were due to 'the extinction of their wood-engraving business owing to the introduction of automatic processes; to loss by colour printing owing to foreign competition generally'. At the height of their fame in the 1860s, George, Edward and Thomas Dalziel had been the leading engravers and publishers of art books, their influence extending into magazines. For years they had supplied the engraved blocks for *Punch,* but in the 1890s even that magazine was changing, although it continued to be a forcing house for black and white art in the wood-engraved style until the 1920s.

For the more adaptable younger men like A.S. Hartrick, Charles Robinson, G.L. Stampa, Tom Browne, Jack B. Yeats and Reginald Cleaver, the half-tone was a spur to new things. As mass-production increased magazine coverage, and the process made illustration varied and cheap, the artist was more and more called upon to perfect his art and to extend his boundaries. The euphoria lasted out the decade. 'Gradually,' wrote James Thorpe, 'the development of the half-tone block facilitated the reproduction of photographs, and as the initial cost of these was far less, they began to take the place of drawings. Thus the new process, which had at first brought so much encouragement to the artist presently threatened to extinguish him.'[5] It was perhaps the constant presentiment of the camera breathing down their necks that drove so many of the best magazine artists of the day into areas where photography could not stray, pure decoration and pure humour.

## The English Illustrated Magazine

The *English Illustrated Magazine* which was begun by Macmillan's in 1883 was a half-way house between the finely illustrated periodicals of the 1860s with little page design and the very 'aesthetic' publications of the 1890s. As its name suggests it was profusely illustrated, but not too heavily to frighten away Henry James as an early contributor or F. Marion Craufurd, that steady favourite of Victorian fiction lovers. Travel articles were the mainstay with occasionally full-page, more usually half-page, illustrations or vignettes by T. Napier Hemy, W.J. Hennessy, R.W. Macbeth, A.D. McCormick, Lady Butler and J. Fulleylove. In almost all cases there was well-handled black and white or pen and wash, interspersed with chalk drawings, nothing very startling from the point of view of book production. But the aesthetic movement of the time was having its impact and there are some full-hearted contributions by Walter Crane, filling the page with his maidens, borders and cyphers, scarcely giving room for the scant verse it is intended to illustrate! This is at its best in 1884 and in 1887, Heywood Sumner takes up the clarion call with illustrations for Julia Cartwright's *Undine,* a double page spread of marvellously bold design, statuesque females, their long tresses mixing with a tightly meshed design of water-lilies and poppies. Sumner's inspiration is best seen in his headings and tail-pieces which are less

Burne-Jonesish in origin, more in the spirit of the woodcuts of Calvert and Palmer, small scale with an engaging lack of finish, one of a wagon veering across the page top is a small masterpiece (see the head-piece to this chapter, p.158).

An advance on the practice of many other journals was *The English Illustrated's* painstaking listing of all the artists appearing between its covers. Each illustrator is mentioned under the heading of 'artists' and again with the text he illustrates. Even the designers of the head-pieces, tail-pieces and initial letters come in for inclusion, a certain sign that the publishers were proud of their 'art for art's sake' approach. Some of this enterprise can be credited to the three Macmillan editors, J. Comyns Carr, Clement Kinloch-Cooke and Emery Walker, the first and the last in particular having close links with art and design. They managed to gather around them a very varied selection of talent. Sumner as has been mentioned contributed a great many wood engravings, but so did the Pre-Raphaelite artist Henry Ryland, the architect A.E. Sedding, the flower-painter Alfred Parsons and the lesser known S.R. Macquoid and A. Morrow. But even here there was no overall sense of design, not even that cohesion of 1860s magazines, head-pieces and borders come from different pens, illustrations from more than one artist per article, an *omnium gatherum* that does not sit easily together. One of Sedding's meticulous and delicate initials is placed immediately below a coarser, bolder design by R. Heighway. Elsewhere a mixture of original work and drawings based on photographs give an uncomfortable lack of direction to the whole venture.

The most homogeneous pages are those in which poetry is set into a free design and illustrations and text balance one another, as in Hugh Thomson's lyrical sketches to eighteenth century ballads. Hugh Thomson, 1860-1920, was principally a discovery of *The English Illustrated Magazine.* Arriving in London from Ireland, his work must have seemed like an answer to the editor's prayer after the tragic death of Randolph Caldecott in 1886. The two artists appear together in the same issue for 1885-86 making an interesting comparison. Thomson's art is in the straight tradition of Caldecott, superbly modulated pen and ink drawing, more meticulous perhaps, but not scratchy or unpleasantly hatched. His works for these numbers are as individual as Caldecott's, gentle humour pervading his huntsmen, dancers, dairy-maids and fishermen, as they did with the latter, but never becoming caricatures. Once Thomson was established as Caldecott's successor, and his frequent appearances after 1886 show this, the brilliantly versatile artist became the doyen of the eighteenth century pastiche. He had a collaborator of equal merit in Herbert Railton and during 1887-88, the two black and white artists gave readers a good piece of nostalgia, illustrating Outram Tristram's *Coaching Days and Coaching Ways,* dealt with later as a book. For their money, Macmillan's subscribers had Railton's tremulous drawings of old inns supported by Thomson's magnificent figures of grooms, coachmen and travellers.

If Thomson was very much the ascendant star, there were a number of exciting artists making their way through its pages. Louis Wain arrives in 1883 as a topographer and later as an illustrator of hunting scenes and dogs! W.D. Almond contributes superb figure studies, Harry Furniss comic scenes of low life, Holland Tringham and A.D. McCormick architectural studies. An amusing little pen artist is Harper Pennington who provides the thumbnail marginalia to Oscar Wilde's article on 'London Models' in 1889. Veteran illustrators like William Simpson RI and Harrison Weir worked for the magazine with sketches of campaigns and poultry respectively, but the editorship encouraged new blood such as the architectural drawings of Reginald Blomfield, the etchings of the young William Strang, and sketches to illustrate an article on 'Wolf Hunting' by a totally unknown student called Edmund J. Sullivan. From October 1888, there is a strong element of arts and crafts pervading the journal, this dates from the editorship of Emery Walker, lasting until about 1890. Younger artists are used for decorations, Annie Baker and Florence Ayling do Morrisy headings,

Matilda Stoker a very Celtic one, and A.C. Weatherstone a frieze in the style of Burne-Jones. The book itself is well covered by contributions on binding from Cobden Sanderson and on the *Punch* artists.

But after the first flush of interest, Macmillan's found the circulation dwindling and not even the talents of craft editors like Walker could do much about it. 'For a time the magazine prospered,' writes the official historian of Macmillans, 'but one cannot resist an impression that it never clearly made up its mind what its purpose was. The list of contributors is remarkable, but exceedingly mixed.'[6] The paper was sold to Ingram in 1893 and became for some years another arm of the great *Illustrated London News*. In succeeding years, particularly in 1893-96, the impetus was maintained and the new proprietors found Gilbert James as a good decorator for poetry and L. Bowley and C. May for headings and tail-pieces. E.J. Sullivan was employed again as an illustrator of stories, Phil May and Dudley Hardy appear infrequently, Laurence Housman designs for E. Nesbit's *Ballad of the White Lady*. It is pleasant to find Caran D'Ache making picaresque drawings in October 1895 and Cecil Aldin drawing animals in April 1896, but apart from

*Figure 74. Illustration to* The Century Guild Hobby Horse *by Selwyn Image, 1886.*

these it becomes 'run of the mill' work by *News* illustrators; W.H. Overend with his endless shipping, Caton Woodville's battling lancers and Montbard's stories. A delightful piece of light relief as always are the French influenced decorations by René Bull. The distinct character of *The English Illustrated Magazine* which made it the first of the 'artistic' magazines, has however completely vanished. Although it struggled on until 1909, its story is not that of a *fin de siècle* magazine.

Only three years after the birth of *The English Illustrated Magazine* in 1886, a publication of even greater artistic pretension had come on the scene. Herbert P. Horne and Selwyn Image produced *The Hobby Horse*, 1886-92, which was noted for its fine design and clear printing, a precursor of things to come (Figure 74). In 1888, the Arts and Crafts Exhibition was held which was to be an important step for the country. For the craftsman-printer and illustrator, the catalogue had a section on printing written by the ubiquitous Emery Walker. This influence bore immediate fruit in 1889 when Hacon and Ricketts founded their publication *The Dial*, and in 1891 William Morris opened his Kelmscott Press.

# The Butterfly

A refreshing feature of the 1890s is its openness to new talent and the readiness of publishers to accept young artists as illustrators of magazines, handing over both design and editorship to them to show the work of their contemporaries. The Lane enterprises were highly commercial ones, the Charles Ricketts and Gordon Craig publications highly personal, and between the two came periodicals like *The Butterfly.* Leonard Raven-Hill, 1867-1942, was only just twenty-six when he founded and edited this magazine in 1893. A Somerset man who had studied at the Lambeth School with Ricketts and Shannon, he had gone on to conventional atelier studies in France, concentrating on black and white drawing. Raven-Hill worked on *Judy,* and *Black and White* and was Art Editor of *Pick-Me-Up* before starting this new venture. His métier was the street scene and humours of society and both in style·and character he was the spiritual successor of Leech and Keene.

*The Butterfly's* sub-heading was 'A Humorous & Artistic Periodical Published on the 15th of each month', and its butterfly insignia on the front cover might easily have been mistaken for Whistler's signature, an association with aestheticism that cannot have been wholly unintentional! The informal note was struck by the 'Apology' in the first number which gave the impression that the readers were looking over a student's sketchbook, gleaned purely by chance. 'We propose to devote several pages of each monthly number to pictures of a really superior class,' it ran. 'These will be carefully done by some friends of ours who have learned drawing at school, and who have since devoted quite a lot of spare time to making sketches on odd pieces of paper and cardboard in order to acquire the pleasing facility in the use of the pencil which they now enjoy.'[7]

Chief among these friends were Maurice Greiffenhagen, 1862-1931, who illustrated stories and Edgar Wilson, an intriguing artist, who provided the decorations. The greatest strength of these little books is the pen drawing, but Greiffenhagen, a master of the lead pencil, reproduces superbly in the half-tone illustrations, making up about a quarter of the book. Raven-Hill fills these early numbers with sparkling cockney studies, some with the meticulousness of Keene, others more spare in line like Phil May or Tom Browne. E.J. Sullivan, 1869-1933, the greatest black and white artist of his day, appears briefly in the first volume as the illustrator of his own tale *The Story of Melloe's Play* in crisp inky lines. There are some reasonable genre scenes such as 'Bank Holiday at Brighton' by Oscar Eckhardt and other less known artists.

The contributor who most catches one's attention, presumably because so little is known about him, is Edgar Wilson, the principal decorator. It is his design on the cover and further penetration inside shows him to be a wildly enthusiastic follower of Whistler's and predictably of Japanese art. Wilson's eye for the page is excellent and his headings and tail-pieces lift the magazine out of the ordinary and place it in the forefront of design. In the early numbers there are some excellent Whistlerian drawings of jetties by Wilson, reproduced in silvery half-tones and in the final one of the first year an amusing piece of archaism in the decorations to the poem 'To My Garden'. Wilson shows here and in the drawings to 'A Wooden Waterloo' in 1894, his sensitivity to old woodcuts, anticipating the work of the Beggarstaff Brothers and Gordon Craig. In 1894 Wilson's work develops a slightly more grotesque dimension, and Greiffenhagen's story illustrations become more consciously French, Raven-Hill has a series of Jewish portraits, 'Ghetto Travesties', and there are some refined figure studies by a newcomer, Reginald Savage. Singularly enough, Raven-Hill's last series of drawings before the magazine closed down are illustrations to *Bab,* the story of a model, a neat piece of plagiarism from du Maurier's *Trilby.*[8]

*The Butterfly* began life again for a short spell in 1899-1900, altering its format and using not three or four artists as in its first flight but a large cast of black and white men, decorators and caricaturists. Half-tones are more widely used than in the first series to bring to life the animal drawings of G.D. Armour, the caricatures of G.R. Halkett and some mysterious lowering illustrations to *A Vision of Judgement* by S.H. Sime, 1867-1941. This artist is capable of straight pieces of impressionism, as in the 'Underground Railway Station' in one of these issues, but is best remembered for his disturbing black humour and insights into the uncanny. The best one in *The Butterfly* is probably 'The Edge of The Forest',

1900, which looks forward to the grimly menacing 'Wild Beast Wood' of a few years later and to his illustrations for Lord Dunsany's books. A bewildered group of figures cower around their diminutive cottages, dominated and crushed by the giant trees of the forest above them, Sime's personal vision of the inevitable power of nature. The timeless quality of these drawings and their power has seen to it that Sime is still remembered when other artists in these pages are forgotten. Gilbert James for example, another imaginative artist but a much weaker one, illustrates a Rackhamish medieval scene and decorative sentiment is found in a whole series of 'eighteenth century' portraits, 'The Virtuosos', 'The Sign-Painter', 'Violet', in the sensuous line of Dion Clayton Calthrop. The literary contributions to the pages are not particularly memorable but a *feuilleton* by Calthrop 'On The Prevalent Architecture of Hen Coops' typifies the satirical imitation of the essay style that little magazines seem to have attracted.

A more accomplished essayist is here as caricaturist, Max Beerbohm, 1872-1956, who took the germ of *portrait chargé* from *Vanity Fair* and invigorated it with brilliant feeling and wit, and is represented by two cartoons. The earlier one is an unkind but very funny portrait of Edward, Prince of Wales, entitled 'The Royal Box' from which the heir apparent leers through opera glasses, the second a sketch of M. de Sounal 'The Portugese Minister', the dandified sort of figure in whom Max delighted and who in many ways represented his own way of life. Raven-Hill continues to give the readers beautiful pen drawings and the Whistler influence of the early years persists in Joseph Pennell's etching of 'The Pool of London' and Frank Emanuel's charming drawing of Dieppe. Edgar Wilson's art has made great strides since 1894 and its decorative forms are much bolder, more symbolic and overtly Japanese than ever before. One superbly contrasted heading of a fish is so chunky and stylised that it could almost be taken for a piece of art deco rather than an explorative work by a young turn of the century artist. *The Butterfly,*[9] like most of its competitors, folded its wings for the last time in 1900. Raven-Hill had joined *Punch* and was filling its weekly pages with figure studies for which he was well suited and with political cartoons for which he was not; the student of 1893 had become the professional of 1900.

# The Studio

If the trends in the arts of the 1890s were diverse with styles and ideals pulling in opposite directions, they came nearest to speaking with one voice in a neat little monthly magazine which began appearing in 1893. *The Studio* would have had no success before the art-conscious 1890s and to some extent lived on borrowed time after the decade was over, but during those years it was as decidedly of its time as Beardsley or May. In its pages jostled the two major influences on the art of the period, the crafts movement of Morris and the aestheticism stemming from Whistler, Wilde and their followers. The first provided scope for articles on potteries, tapestries, wall-papers, iron and metalwork, cottage homes and extensive coverage of the Arts and Crafts exhibitions; the second gave the magazine its Continental outlook, its love of posters, book illustrations, Gallé glass and international art nouveau. The publishers had cleverly succeeded in appealing to an audience wide enough to be popular and yet exclusive enough to retain the image of the artist as a special person. The magazine was neither the realm of the professional alone nor of the amateur alone, it contained works of new painters and old, balancing out the smart with the established and giving the readership the aura of novelty and being in touch with experiments. It was the first attempt to tap the huge leisured middle-class which knew itself to be bored and suspected itself of being artistic, and the first attempt to involve that group principally with contemporary work.

*The Studio* was the brainchild of C. Lewis Hind, 1862-1927, who was its first promoter and who employed the very youthful Aubrey Beardsley to design the first wrapper, an outstanding design of tree stems and foliage with that signature of the new art, three open lilies in the left hand corner. Hind was succeeded almost at once by Gleeson White, 1851-1898, who was editor of the magazine for the first two years and stamped his personality and tastes on it in a quite remarkable way. White's background was more all-embracing than Hind's, he was not merely a critic, but a professional journalist and an amateur designer of talent. He had a more practical approach to the new art, having designed book covers for Elkin Mathews and the Bodley Head and was clearly most interested in the decorative side of designing, the side most in favour with his readership. The year he became Editor of *The Studio,* he published a book on *Practical Designing* and he brought with him to the post an immense amount of experience gained as Editor of the American journal *Art Amateur,* 1891-92. Perhaps most important of all he forged links with the art schools and the amateur sketching clubs, giving many column inches to their exhibitions and successes, publishing the work of unknown students and encouraging them through *The Studio* competitions, which were a great feature of the early volumes.

Besides this, White was an acknowledged authority on book illustration and particularly the artists of the 1860s. His book *English Illustration 'The Sixties' 1855-70,* was widely acclaimed on its first publication in 1897 and has been frequently quoted in this book. The fact that he should consider the artistic public of his own day as fertile ground for a book on illustration is borne out in its opening chapter 'The New Appreciation And The New Collector'. 'Today,' he writes, 'not a few people interested in the Arts find 'the sixties' a time as interesting as in the last century men found Praxiteles, or as still more recently, the Middle Ages appeared to the early Pre-Raphaelites.' White shows that the oil painters and the stained glass artists have been admired and the turn of the art of the book has come. 'Now, however, the humble illustrator, the man who fashions his dreams into designs for commercial reproduction by wood-engraving or 'process', has found an audience, and is acquiring rapidly a fame of his own.'[10] The re-appraisal of 1860s' work was undoubtedly coming from artists and critics like White and not from publishers and readers. Sir Seymour Haden and Joseph Pennell had both focussed attention on black and white work through etchings and drawings and Pennell had written about it in his formidable book of 1895.[11] The younger artists, particularly Laurence Housman and E.J. Sullivan, had looked over their shoulders at the earlier school and found kinship which greatly invigorated their work. Housman published an article on A.B. Houghton in *Bibliographica* for 1895 and then, such was his enthusiasm, produced a catalogue, *Forty Designs by A. Boyd Houghton* in 1896. Gleeson White understood how beneficial this cross-fertilisation could be. 'It is a healthy sign,' he wrote, 'to find that people today are interesting themselves in the books of the sixties; it should make them more eager for original contemporary work, and foster a dislike to the inevitable photograph from nature reproduced by half-tone, which one feared would have satisfied their love for black-and-white to the exclusion of all else.'[12]

It is hardly surprising therefore that *The Studio* began with a strong bias towards the art of the book generally and book illustration in particular. The first volume for April to September 1893 contained articles on 'Designing For Bookplates', 'The Collecting of Posters — A New Field For Connoisseurs' and a whole series on 'Drawing For Reproduction'. White's experience in the States is reflected in the contribution on 'The Art Magazines of America' and their strong emphasis on pen drawing, followed by an article on 'Pen Drawing

For Process'. But the article which set the seal of modernity on the whole venture was Joseph Pennell's celebrated essay on 'A New Illustrator, Aubrey Beardsley' which came out in the first month. Pennell like White wanted to see draughtsmanship that was working with, rather than fighting against, the new processes and in Beardsley he decided he had found it. 'The reproduction of the "Morte d'Arthur" drawing, printed in this number,' he wrote, 'is one of the most marvellous that I have ever seen, simply for this reason; it gives Mr Beardsley's actual handiwork, and not the interpretation of it by someone else. I know it is the correct thing to rave over the velvety, fatty quality of the wood-engraved line, a quality which can be obtained from any process-block by careful printing, and which is not due to the artist at all. But here I find the distinct quality of a pen line, and of Mr Beardsley's pen line, which has been used by the artist and reproduced by the process-man in a truly extraordinary manner.'[13] *The Studio* certainly became a continuing testimony to the Beardsley style although its pages also sheltered the woodcut style derived from Morris and Birmingham. White's catholic editing included the running of competitions for students, many of them devoted to illustration or other book craft.[14] The magazine organised prizes for 'all classes of decorative art', the designs being set by 'manufacturers, familiar with the purpose for which it is intended, who will also act as judges'. One of the earliest projects was to design a title-page for the new magazine and the variety of entries does show the eclectic influences from Crane to Kelmscott that prevailed in the art schools. In general the standard was high although frequent criticism came from the Editor about the inappropriateness of the lettering and the crowding of ornament. The competitions were continued long after White's death and must have had a marked effect on the art as a whole; for many aspiring illustrators it was the first time they saw their work in print. One finds the names of Evelyn Holden, Alfred Leete, Austin Osman Spere, Edmund Blampied and many others in this section.

*The Studio* gave an equal share of attention to photography, opened its columns to correspondence on such topics as 'Is the Camera the Friend or Foe of Art?' and published the work of Sutcliffe, Emerson and Henry Dixon. Artistic people were interviewed and artistic homes visited, pottery, sketching-grounds and Japanese art were discussed and the new movements spoken of with bated breath.

The second volume was less dramatic but continued White's themes with contributions on 'The Art of Book Binding', 'The Birmingham Municipal School of Art' with reproductions of the work of C.M. Gere, Winifred Smith, Sidney Heath, G.C. France and Florence Rudland, reviews of books and their decoration and fresh notices of the prodigy Aubrey Beardsley. The last were on the publication of *Morte d'Arthur* and *Salome*. In subsequent years it was *The Studio* which introduced that brilliant but soft-toned artist Charles Robinson to the public, and much the same was done for A. Garth Jones and Henry Ospovat in 1899 and the early work of Jessie M. King in the same year. In one number *The Studio* inserted a complete booklet printed by the Essex House Press entitled 'Beauty's Awakening' with decorations by C.R. Ashbee, Walter Crane, Harrison Townsend, C.W. Whall and H. Wilson, and bold penwork betraying its strong reliance on Morris. Phil May came to prominence here only after his death in 1903, but there were articles on animal illustrators such as Carton Moore Park and groups of illustrators such as The London Sketch Club. A tendency towards a more impressionistic genre is shown by an article on Constantin Guys in 1905 and to a more imaginative interpretation of children's books with A.L. Baldry's essay on Arthur Rackham later the same year.

Charles Holme's editorship from 1900 veered towards the crafts and architecture but the stamp of Gleeson White's concern for black and white art, the poster, the ex-libris, the book beautiful from the growing number of private presses, continued until after 1914. For the most informed criticism of E.H. New or Tony Sarg, George Sheringham or Hugh

Thomson, Kay Nielsen or Edmund Dulac, one still goes instinctively and confidently to the green and gold cloth volumes of *The Studio*. At the time of Gleeson White's premature death in 1898, the magazine published an appreciation stressing the wide scope of their first Editor's interests. 'The versatility and comprehensive knowledge which distinguished him have been exhibited here month by month in ways well fitted to appeal to the widest circle of art lovers; and to many readers of *The Studio* his death in the full tide of his ability will seem a personal loss.'[15] Magazines stand or fall by the quality of their editorship and White was unquestionably the right man for the job; but in the larger context of the *fin de siècle*, *The Studio* was the right magazine for the moment, it presented a more practical approach, a more pragmatic experience among the highly-polished and esoteric magazines of the 1890s.

# The Yellow Book and The Savoy

Ephemeral publications in which literary squibs, minute poems and stories of a Firbankian intensity and obscurity vied with the 'new' illustrations were irresistible to a public fed on Whistler's 'Ten O'Clock Lecture' and aestheticism. *The Yellow Book,* begun in April 1894, was one of those ventures which become famous overnight, and is nearly synonymous with the cult of the 1890s and the death-wish tragedies of Wilde and Beardsley.

It was started by John Lane who, together with Elkin Mathews, seems to have cornered the market in aesthetic books. Lane himself was considered a sound businessman, lucky in his illustrators and authors, but not a man of very developed tastes. 'That poor fly in the amber of modernity' was what Max Beerbohm called him. He appointed Henry Harland as Literary Editor and Aubrey Beardsley as Art Editor, an explosive combination which produced exactly the reaction from conservative London that would have been expected. Each quarter from April 1894 to April 1895, the stumpy yellow bound cloth volumes, with covers designed by Beardsley, slipped out from Lane's Bodley Head office in Vigo Street to astonish the world. Harland kept a literary salon, his wife sang French songs and the conspirators of *The Yellow Book* were encouraged to attend, adopt their Editors Continental bias and thoroughly represent the avant-garde. Habitués of the Café Royal, imbibers of absinthe, unimpressed, dandiacal, ostentatiously dishevelled or studiously immaculate, they could be the harbingers of ridicule, satire and ennui but also the provokers of outrage.

Both the literary and the artistic contributions were of a high standard, the first number contained work by Henry James, Lord Leighton, George Moore and Edmund Gosse, the younger generation being represented by Richard Le Gallienne, Arthur Symons and Max Beerbohm with illustrations by Joseph Pennell, Laurence Housman, Will Rothenstein, Walter Sickert and Charles Furse. The furore on its first appearance was divided between Beardsley's designs and Beerbohm's essay 'On Cosmetics', which was delivered with mock seriousness and swallowed whole by a disapproving press. It is interesting to note that *Punch,* an old arch-enemy of aestheticism rushed into the attack, perhaps seeing all too clearly that the satire in Beardsley's line was a confrontation with its own image as the arbiter of black and white.

Aubrey Beardsley, 1872-1898, had been born in Brighton and from an early age had shown a precocious talent for drawing as well as for literature and music, he was one of a number of 1890s' artists who were writers and illustrators, Laurence Housman and E.J.

Sullivan being others. After juvenile contributions to school magazines and a bit of menu card decorating, Beardsley became a clerk in the Guardian Life Assurance Company in 1889. There he might have remained if he had not been befriended by a Queen Street bookseller who showed a remarkable pen and ink drawing to Messrs. Dent, the publishers, in 1892. The drawing in question called 'Hail Mary' was strongly in the manner of Burne-Jones, one of a number of formative influences on the young artist and won him the immediate commission to illustrate Malory's *Morte d'Arthur* from Dents in 1893. A meeting with Joseph Pennell led to that important article in the first number of *The Studio,* already mentioned, where the critic talked of Beardsley's work as showing 'decisively the presence among us of an artist, of an artist whose work is quite as remarkable in its execution as in its invention; a very rare combination'.[16] Beardsley was a lover of literature and of books and therefore an instinctive illustrator; the designs for *Morte d'Arthur* were probably his most derivative work, echoing as they did the work of Morris and Burne-Jones but the restlessness in them that was the essential Beardsley, caught the spirit of the moment and made him the great figurehead of the *fin de siècle.*

His post on the new magazine made his position even more influential. But it was his drawings in its pages that were the principal target for the captious critics, particularly in the first issue, with 'L'Education Sentimentale' and 'Night Piece', both mildly suggestive and full of that ruthless power that the artist, obtained in his clinical separation of black and white. Even the portrait of 'Mrs. Patrick Campbell', the most marvellously controlled piece of line drawing, is hardly flattering and seems full of a sort of sensuous contempt. What was true of the first number remained true of its successors; the pages were lightly interspersed with the work of more academic artists, younger men were included but Beardsley remained very much the star. In the second volume, P.G. Hamerton was allowed to criticise the first volume, making some of the points raised by the critics but in gentler mood. 'There seems to be a peculiar tendency in Mr Beardsley's mind,' he writes, 'to the representation of types without intellect and without morals. Some of the most dreadful faces in all art are to be found in the illustrations to Mr Oscar Wilde's *Salome.* We have two unpleasant ones here in l'Education Sentimentale. There is distinctly a sort of corruption in Mr Beardsley's art so far as its human element is concerned, but not at all in its artistic qualities, which show the perfection of discipline, of self-control.' He criticises the elongation in Beardsley, the exaggerations of perspective and the absence of beauty in the faces. But Beardsley's vision and world, however vivid, was not beautiful, it was the doomed vision of an artist who knew he was dying of consumption and the sardonic world of youth, the youth whose innocence is looking evil in the face for the first time.

Subsequent illustrations included the 'Portrait of Himself', a tiny cynical head in a sea of rich and smothering curtain, the chiaroscuro studies of 'Lady Gold's Escort' and 'Wagnerites' and the rather Burne-Jones influenced 'Mysterious Rose Garden'. He also produces two drawings under the pseudonyms of Philip Broughton and Albert Foschter as well as the famous 'Garçons de Café', arguably the most compelling image to emerge in *fin de siècle* illustration on this side of the Channel.

In fact Beardsley was the only one of *The Yellow Book* artists who came to terms with the new processes and one of the very few who saw the possibilities and limitation of the page. In the first volume, only Pennell's fantastic architectural drawing, Laurence Housman's 'Reflected Faun' and J.T. Nettleship's startling 'Head of Minos' look as if they were designed for a book. In the other issues there are some splendid decorative pen and ink drawings by Patten Wilson, especially 'Rustan Firing The First Shot' in Volume 2, an intricate composition in the manner of a Dürer woodcut. A.S. Hartrick supplies a slightly sinister 'Lamplighter' to the same volume and a spirited sketch of a boxing match in Volume 5. From Volume 4 onwards, *The Yellow Book* ran a series of so called Bodley Heads, portraits of contributors, emphasising still further the close-knit circle of Harland's editorship. This gave a splendid opportunity for Will Rothenstein, fresh from the success of his *Oxford Characters,* to contribute a most lovely soft chalk drawing of John Davidson, others coming from the pencils and brushes of Walter Sickert, Sargent and E.A. Walton. Nothing could be a greater contrast to the tension of Beardsley's work than the refreshing and meticulous penmanship of Walter W. Russell's 'Westmorland Village' or William Hyde's open landscapes. Sickert's series of music-hall sketches give a delightfully raffish element to the volumes that might otherwise seem unnaturally precious in content. The cockney spirit of the 'Lion Comique' typifies the vitality of the halls, and 'Collins Music Hall' the French influence of Degas' stages, viewed across the orchestra. But as P.G. Hamerton points out Sickert's work, like that of C.W. Furse and Wilson Steer, is approached through the eyes of a painter not an illustrator.

In the October 1894 volume, Max Beerbohm had contributed only one drawing, a caricature of George IV, ringleted, double-chinned and gross and with an unaccountable look of Oscar Wilde. This presaged what was to come, because by the time the April 1895 volume was due to appear, Oscar Wilde was standing trial and the whole circle of decadents were under a cloud. Lane could not risk retaining an artist so strongly connected with Wilde in the public imagination as the illustrator of *Salome,* and though Beardsley was blameless he was immediately dismissed.

The mainspring of the exercise was gone, the elfin genius of the unpredictable Beardsley, but somehow the magazine managed to limp through eight further issues, not all lacking in interest. The design of the covers was now shared by various hands, J.D. Mackenzie, D.Y. Cameron, J. Illingworth Kay and Mabel Dearmer. Although the literary content remained high with Henry James and Arnold Bennett in July 1895, Baron Corvo, John Buchan and Richard Le Gallienne in April 1896, the graphic work did not equal it. The editor filled the first volume after the Wilde scandal with mediocrities like Fred Hyland, working in a sub-Beardsley manner, or wishy-washy amateurs like Sir William Eden, target

of one of Whistler's most searing attacks. Some fine pen drawings were obtained from Patten Wilson in these last three years, not only strongly reminiscent of German wood-cuts but like all Wilson's work, wild and Celtic, fighting to be released from the confines of the picture space (Figure 75). The October 1895 volume was devoted to the Newlyn School, that of January 1896 to the Glasgow School and the April 1896 issue to the Birmingham School. This was an interesting idea, giving added coherence to the magazine and focusing attention on the leading movements of the day. The first two volumes it must be confessed are very disappointing. The Newlyn School is not one that is strong on drawing and book illustration and the Glasgow School is treated entirely as a landscape group. By far the most valuable volume is that on the Birmingham School (culled from *The Quest*), which would have left no *Yellow Book* reader in any doubt as to where the strength in illustration really lay. The contributors include A.T. Gaskin, Sydney Meteyard, J.E. Southall and C.M. Gere

*Figure 75. 'So the wind drove us on . . . ' by Patten Wilson for* The Yellow Book, *1896.*

among the older men, and Mary J. Newill, Celia Levetus, Evelyn Holden (Figure 76), Bernard Sleigh and Florence M. Rutland among the younger students. E.H. New is represented by one of his fine architectural drawings and C.M. Gere shows a similar subject almost vying with it in its clarity of line. There are slight echoes of Burne-Jones in the allegorical subjects and E.G. Treglown's black and white work is Beardsleyesque, but otherwise the purity of draughtsmanship and the high quality of decoration is outstanding. The October 1896 volume contained the last Max caricature, an unusual coloured woodcut and the two succeeding issues were unremarkable except for the re-appearance of D.Y. Cameron and the emergence of Muirhead Bone.

Beardsley's highly indiviudal light was not easily extinguished and after *The Yellow Book* débâcle he flitted across from Lane to Leonard Smithers, the avant-garde publisher with whom he was to remain connected until his death. By

*Figure 76. 'Binnorie O Binnorie' by Evelyn Holden for* The Yellow Book, *1896.*

the end of 1895, both artist and publisher had decided to issue a new magazine of the arts, produced quarterly at 2/6d. and called *The Savoy*. It was in a slightly larger format than *The Yellow Book* but the paper was not so good and Beardsley returned to the medium of pure pen and ink. The move from Lane to Smithers coincided with a considerable shift in style, the curvilinear lines and black and white contrasts were replaced by rich decoration and stippling effects, mainly characterised by small dotted lines throughout the illustrations. The *Salome* of 1894, which predated even *The Yellow Book* was probably the most influential set of drawings that Beardsley ever created. The swirling lines, dramatic images and use of abstraction that runs through from the frontispiece to the 'Climax' plate at the end of the book were the most frequently copied by later illustrators and designers. His use of motifs from Whistler's Peacock Room, his tightly bunched borders of roses on the title page, but above all the very ascetic contrast of line to mass and black and white, recur again and again in the books of the 1900s and beyond.

The drawings of *The Savoy* period are finer compositions but give rise to the idea that Beardsley was principally a decorative illustrator. This was probably because of the artist's fascination with eighteenth century decoration, rococo detail, the hanging of lace and the forms of head-dresses which he used to such marvellous result in *The Rape of The Lock,* published by Smithers in May 1896. In an interview with Arthur H. Lawrence, Beardsley showed how much the current fashion for the eighteenth century had fired his imagination. Lawrence described how the artist always worked by candlelight with two old Empire ormolu candlesticks on the table, had Chippendale furniture and French Louis XV clocks as well as 'rare copies of last century *livres à vignettes . . .* and numerous pictures, engravings from Watteau, Lancret, Pater, Prud'hon and so on'.[17] It was these masterly plates for Pope's most elegant poem, 'The Dream', 'The Toilet', 'The Battle of the Beaux and The Belles' and 'The Cave of Spleen' which were to be a lasting memorial to the *fin de siècle* and an inspiration to the decorative artist for twenty years.

It is because *The Savoy* falls into Beardsley's richest period of illustrating that the eight volumes of the magazine have a special interest, demonstrating that the artist is a great draughtsman as well as a great illustrator. The atmosphere is still highly charged, but this time in the mannered rococo lines of 'The Coiffing' or the delicate bending figure of 'Mrs Pinchwife', reminiscent of another consumptive artist, the equally doomed and sardonic Watteau. Among the most striking of the works are those on the theme of Wagner and particularly 'The Fourth Tableau of Das Rheingold' (Figure 77) completed amid increasing illness, giving an extraordinary sweep of oriental mysticism and an unsurpassed glimpse of the beauty of his control of line. This series of drawings for a projected book the *Story of Venus and Tannhauser* was never finished; Beardsley left England for the last time in April 1897 and died at Menton on 16 March 1898 while still trying to work on his drawings for Ben Johnson's *Volpone,* published posthumously in 1898.

Holbrook Jackson, who did not much like Beardsley's art, wrote of his style as a sterile

*Figure 77. 'The Fourth Tableau of Das Rheingold' by Aubrey Beardsley.*

one. Too close to the period, he could not see the immense following the artist was to have, providing a rich inspiration to the gifted who could contain his manner without being overwhelmed by it, remaining a constant quarry to the hack and the amateur. In the following pages there are countless names who were grounded in the Beardsley discipline even if they failed to attain his literary vision or his finesse. Among them are Annie French, Harry Clarke, W.B. MacDougall, Austin O. Spare, H.H. Voight, A.E. Odle, W.H. Bradley, F.E. Jackson and George Plant.

# The Quest

This magazine which ran from 1894-96 was the shop window for the Birmingham School of Illustrators and as such was one of the most unified little productions of the entire decade. It first appeared in November 1894, priced at half-a-crown and printed at the press of the Birmingham Guild of Handicraft. From the beginning it was strongly reminiscent of the newly founded Kelmscott Press, the grey paper cover with the wood engraved design on it was very Morrisy indeed and showed how much *The Quest's* promoters Gere and Gaskin were involved with him. The first frontispiece by E.G. Treglown is closer to Burne-Jones than Morris in manner, very long figures set against a floriate background, and this strong decorative feeling is carried through to the ballad borders by H.A. Payne and the flame-like flowers in the initial letters designed by Treglown and Sydney Meteyard. E.H. New illustrates the old Grange at Broadway and C.M. Gere provides beautiful Celtic head-pieces to 'The Life of Saint Silvester', much lighter in tone than Treglown's heavy blacks in the page illustrations for the same legend. The editors are obviously at pains to include the work of student artists wherever possible and to give full credit to the engravers who have cut the blocks.

The second number of the magazine contains more interesting work by H.A. Payne and C.M. Gere and a very illuminating article on 'the Guild of Handicraft' with illustrations of the craftsmen, printers and engravers at work by E.H. New; Mary J. Newill supplies an initial letter. The pictures for the romance of 'Sir Generydes' by Payne, Meteyard and Tarling, show the two aspects of the Birmingham illustrative school at this time, Tarling's style being fluid with flowing draperies and curving lines, Meteyard's much more angular deriving from his craft background in ceramics and stained-glass. The third number is a little more varied, a bold frontispiece by A.J. Gaskin, an architectural description of Evesham (his home town) illustrated by E.H. New with characteristic wide foregrounds and labels, and Meteyard's drawings for Morris's ballad 'The Defence of Guenevere'. E.G. Treglown's illustrations to 'A Stranger in Love's Place' are even more in the style of early woodcuts than his earlier contributions and have sixteenth century originals very much in mind.

Morris's seal of approval was on *The Quest* from the beginning, in fact imitation was for him quite definitely the sincerest form of flattery. In November 1895 he lent a frontispiece of Kelmscott House by C.M. Gere for the magazine and actually contributed an article to its pages 'Gossip About An Old House On The Upper Thames' with illustrations by E.H. New. This essay and the whole issue gives a pleasant echo of William Morris in his last phase as printer after the fires of youth had somewhat subsided. The number is greatly strengthened by the use of full page drawings and one particularly fine example by Mary J. Newill shows a frieze of children's heads at the top and a trailing plant dominating the foreground, white skilfully cut into a black ground. The fifth issue in March 1896 has C.M. Gere's frontispiece 'Summer is Icomen In', a predictably Kelmscott style of design to fit in with the poem of Old England, and an article on vernacular buildings with brilliant sculptural sketches by E.H. New, accompanying A.S. Dixon's text. E.G. Treglown goes back to Rossetti for his 'A Ballad Upon A Wedding' and 'The Book of Tobit'. Designs by Treglown and Tarling run through this volume and into the next.

The last of these little books appeared in July 1896 with a frontispiece of 'Rapunzel' by Sydney Meteyard and an article on the guilds by W.R. Lethaby, the heading for it by Gere. Gere's full page drawing of a city steam roller entitled 'A Detail of Today' is really welcome after all the ballads and medievalising, showing just how far the Birmingham School were prepared to go with modernity! Other features of interest are an illustration to 'Childe Roland' by Inglis Sheldon-Williams, perhaps inspired by seventeenth century etchings and an architectural look at Warwick by E.H. New. Treglown's full-page drawing to the 'Life of St Kenelm' has interest in being inspired by Rossetti and returning in handling to the 1860s' school. Though short-lived, *The Quest* gives a very fair representation of arts and crafts illustrating at its best and has the merit of showing the work of masters and students alongside one another.

# The Quarto

*The Quest* was the magazine of the Birmingham School and the only other publication to exhibit mainly the work of one art school was *The Quarto*. This was begun in 1896 by J.S. Virtue & Co. and described itself as 'An Artistic Literary & Musical Quarterly'. It was formed from a mixture of modern talent, old masters and a rehabilitation of some of the great artists of the 1860s. Both Joseph Pennell and Gleeson White took a close interest

*Right: Plate XII*
*KATE GREENAWAY, RI*
*1846-1901*
*'The Gaudy Flower'*
*Illustration to* Little Ann,
A Book Illustrated By
Kate Greenaway, *1882.*

*Below: Plate XIII*
*GEORGE SAMUEL ELGOOD*
*1851-1943*
*'Bowls in a castle garden'*
*Original drawing for illustration*
*Watercolour*
*Signed and dated, 1887*
Lattimore Collection

in the venture and so the standard of draughtsmanship remained remarkably high. 'Our chief endeavour' runs the preface of the first number, 'is to bring before the world the work of young or unknown artists who have at some time or other received instruction at the Slade. This does not in the least preclude the work of others; our aims are broad and cosmopolitan, anything narrow or bigoted in Art, as in all else, being inimical to true progess, and therefore foreign to our intentions.'

From the beginning there was some very nice decorative work carried out by three talented artists, initial letters cut by Hugh Arnold, head- and tail-pieces by Alice B. Woodward and Cyril Goldie. One is struck at once by the tremendous sense of freedom and invention in these designs and by comparison some of the Birmingham designs seem stiff and contrived. Artists who were only just starting to emerge in 1896 are given some spectacular opportunities here, Robert Spence, the etcher, in a magnificent line drawing of 'The Legend of St Cuthbert' and Paul Woodroffe in his 'Nativity'. Something of a surprise is a ballad illustration by Ambrose McEvoy drawn completely in the style of the 1860s. In the second volume there is even stronger emphasis on the earlier illustrators with whom the new generation felt such obvious kinship. Millais' 'Foolish Virgins' is shown as well as Rossetti's 'Salutation of Beatrice', but the most astounding influence on a younger artist is Nellie Syrett's 'Time is short, life is short' which is based on A.B. Houghton's work. Other revealing drawings are 'The Brink' by Cyril Goldie, which shows him to have had nearly the imaginative temperament of a Rackham, and Alfred Jones' mixture of Celtic and Pre-Raphaelite symbolism in his illustration to Goethe's 'Der Erl König'.

In 1897 the pages are amplified by more Pre-Raphaelite work, Sir E.J. Poynter's 'Daniel's Prayer' and Burne-Jones' celebrated 'Parable of the Boiling Pot', both from the *Dalziel Bible* of sixteen years earlier. Robert Spence, who is still underrated, has a powerful work in his 'Legend of Fra Angelico And The Angels' and Paul Woodroffe a first class illustration to Bunyan's 'Holy War'. More of a curiosity than anything else is the oil painting by G.O. Onions 'Paolo and Francesca' showing the sort of thing Onions did as a student before going on to a career as a popular novelist. There is a single contribution by Rosie M.M. Pitman of 'Undine', a charming Pre-Raphaelite evocation by this delightful but minor Edwardian.

## The Page and the Broadsheet Style

One aspect of the new processes and the advances in mass-production was to make the sophisticated public of the 1890s hanker after a more personal type of book, a rough image on the page and a more tactile quality to type face and paper. The private presses and Kelmscott in particular were catering for the more exalted type of library with limited editions on hand-made paper in limp vellum covers, but several artists looked back to the chapbook and the broadsheet for inspiration, rather than to the illuminated books of the Middle Ages or rare incunabula. There had always been an attraction for the illustrator in being the master of his own destiny, and the ephemeral artists of the streets who were their own designers, engravers and printers, appeared to have a freedom denied to other men. The cheap ballad sheets of the late eighteenth and early nineteenth centuries with their crude woodcuts, have a directness and a spontaneity which is almost a visual assault and nearly impossible within a book. Bewick was the artist particularly admired by the Victorians for

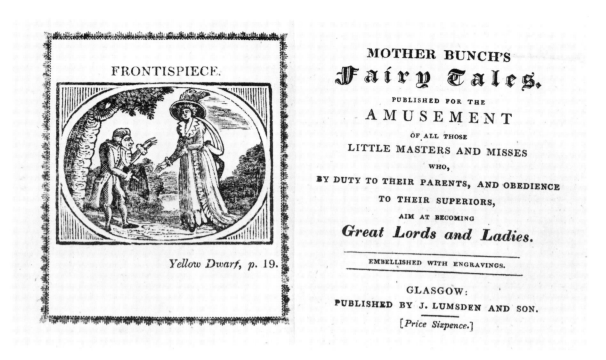

FRONTISPIECE.

*Yellow Dwarf, p. 19.*

MOTHER BUNCH'S
𝕱𝖆𝖎𝖗𝖞 𝕿𝖆𝖑𝖊𝖘.
PUBLISHED FOR THE
AMUSEMENT
OF ALL THOSE
LITTLE MASTERS AND MISSES
WHO,
BY DUTY TO THEIR PARENTS, AND OBEDIENCE
TO THEIR SUPERIORS,
AIM AT BECOMING
*Great Lords and Ladies.*

EMBELLISHED WITH ENGRAVINGS.

GLASGOW:
PUBLISHED BY J. LUMSDEN AND SON.
[*Price Sixpence.*]

*Figure 78. A chapbook by James Lumsden of Glasgow, c.1810.*

the sensitivity of his natural studies, studies that came directly from his pencil to his block and from his block to the printed sheet. But there were other cruder artists of the Northumbrian School whose cutting was heavier and coarser and whose work had a primitive tang in the wood which the younger men of the 1890s began to find very appealing. Partly derived from the arts and crafts movement, partly from that cult of the eighteenth century shortly to be mentioned, the naïve style of the broadsheet swept through the studios of the more individual artists for a decade or more. Some of the productions of the printer W. Davison of Alnwick have this attractive earthiness about them in the 1800s, as do the chapbooks of the Glasgow and Paisley booksellers and the sixpenny tales of James Lumsden and Sons of Glasgow (Figure 78), but there was also a more recent link with the craftsman-like past.

The earliest artist to involve himself with the broadsheet style was Joseph Crawhall, 1821-1896, a provincial and an eccentric whose genius for book making almost defies classification. The son of a prosperous ropemaker at Newcastle-upon-Tyne, Crawhall's interest in books grew out of his dual passions for antiquarianism and angling. The one made him familiar with the chapbooks and ballad sheets of earlier periods, the other fed him with subjects for his witty pen; in Newcastle it was impossible not to be attracted to wood-engraving in the early nineteenth century! In 1859, Crawhall designed and printed his first book, *The Compleatest Angling Booke,* a mixture of old and new fishing lore but very much reflecting the artist's love of old printed texts and archaic language. It was decorated with woodcuts, cut by him in a 'rich black expressionist style',[18] as well as work by his brothers Thomas and George, all making as unusual a mid-Victorian book as could be found anywhere. More were to follow: *Ye loving ballad of Lorde Bateman To itte's owne Tune herin sette fforth* in 1860, *A Collection of Right Merrie Garlands for North Country Anglers* in 1864 and *Chaplets from Coquet side,* 1873. Crawhall uses both decoration and figurative cuts to embellish his tales and songs, the former reflecting the work of the old artists but the latter taken with considerably more punch and wit. In his decoration, Crawhall often used a stipple effect for a background, a flower or symbol standing out from a black area covered with tiny white dots. In some of his more dramatic illustrations he cuts away the background to emphasise a bold black line, a technique which was to become popular with some of his imitators. Nineteen books were to come from this indefatigable angler and humorist, all printed from the original woodblocks and usually coloured by hand (Colour Plate XI p.124). From 1884 his work reached a wider public when it attracted the notice of Andrew Tuer, the printer, and the books were subsequently printed at the Leadenhall Press starting with *Old Aunt Elspa's ABC* and *Old Aunt Elspa's Spelling Bee,* 1884 and 1885. Tuer's commercialism and Crawhall's versatility extended the work to cards and posters, including some for Pears Soap and Brooke Bond Tea which have a refreshing sharpness for their date and actually bring humour to Victorian advertising The level of fun and lightness of touch makes these books peculiarly desirable and popular with the collector. 'Although Crawhall's humour had a satire edge to it,' writes C.S. Felver, 'it reflects none of the Swiftian *saeva indignatio* that Hogarth, whom he admired greatly, often shows. And there is a happy freedom in most of it from didactic moralism which frequently sinks Victorian humour under a weight of religious piety.'[19]

Crawhall's books with their rough paper, often discoloured with the years, blue covers, idiosyncratic initials and woodcuts, succeeded in rebuilding a bridge between the reader and the designer. It is only necessary to read his imprint at the back of one of the part works to feel the engraver's uncomplicated joy in his work — 'Gathyrd and newlie sett foorth with Titles, hede and tayle-peeces, ande various Sculptures (othyr than those signed) curiously engraven by Joseph Crawhall of Newcastle-upon-Tyne'. Crawhall died in London on 7 July 1896, his unique works still ignored by all except a small circle of admirers; within a few years the dramatic force of them and the expressionistic quality of the cuts were to become increasingly influential.

William Nicholson, 1872-1949, first noticed Crawhall's books in the early 1890s and they strongly appealed to his decorative sense where otherwise he was looking towards French graphic art. Nicholson and his brother-in-law James Pryde, 1866-1941, became partners in designing and printing woodcuts for posters, cards and book illustrations from about 1894. Working from a country cottage they produced results that were powerful, fresh and almost revolutionary in their simplicity. An early article on the 'Brothers'[20] stresses their admiration for the posters of Toulouse-Lautrec, their fascination for the line of Phil May and their obvious delight in being craftsman-artists. They took great trouble with the placing of their lines on the page and equal care in the choice of their lettering which is always bold and clear, the prints being characterised by the squared off black line round the edge which seems to give them body. This partnership produced some remarkable illustrated works in the broadsheet style between 1898 and 1900, they include *An Alphabet,* 1898, *An Almanac of Twelve Sports* with a text by Rudyard Kipling, 1898, *London Types* with a text by W.E. Henley, 1898, *The Square Book of Animals,* 1899, and *Characters of Romance,* 1900. In a sense these books are more like folios of beautifully designed pages than books in the conventional form, indeed the last one, *Characters of Romance* is actually a folder of loose plates with only a list of titles as a text. Nicholson and Pryde managed to break through the convention that an artistic book was a complicated piece of design or crammed with extraneous ornament; the enduring images of *An Alphabet* or *London Types* are fixed on the retina because they are so simple. In the London scenes, the coster-girl, the policeman and the life-guardsman rely almost entirely for their effect on thick black outline and an almost Japanese sense of two-dimensional rhythm. The range of scale is remarkable, the delightful coloured woodcut of 'The Fisher' which appeared in *The Dome* for 1897 measures four inches by four inches (Figure 79), the amazingly free but sinister rendering of 'Mr Vanslyperken' in the *Characters,* thirteen and a half inches by ten and a half inches (Figure 80). Only a limited number of these books were printed from the woodblocks and coloured by hand, the majority were reproduced in lithography.

Figure 79. 'The Fisher' by William Nicholson

Right: Figure 80. 'Mr. Vanslyperken' by William Nicholson.

The only artist to embark on the production of a magazine in this distinctive style of cutting was Edward Gordon Craig, 1872-1966, the actor, theatrical designer and writer. Craig's family background was as varied as his talents, his father was the Victorian architect E.W. Godwin and his mother the celebrated actress Dame Ellen Terry. Craig only developed as an important designer after youthful experiences as an actor. He trained himself to become a first-class wood-engraver and graphic artist and as the promoter of three magazines acted as his own editor, author, illustrator and publisher. One writer has called *The Page,* which

sprang to life in 1898 'a modest periodical'[21] but this is to miss the informality and camaraderie which Crawhall, the Beggarstaff Brothers and Craig were aiming at. The magazine which was brought out quarterly and only sold afterwards in yearly sets, had a high standard of design in type and illustrations and was an astonishing juggling act by Craig himself. He produced woodcuts (Figure 81) 'By the Editor' or 'By the Publisher' and even invented a fictitious artist called 'Oliver Bath' to spread the load more evenly; all of course were by himself! In the early volumes, however, there is some help from that beautiful but sombre artist J.J. Guthrie and from Charles Conder. Notable examples of Craig's work can be found in 'Waiting For The Marchioness' and 'The Horse' with its thick borders and dramatic darks, both in the first volume of 1899.

In the second volume of that year is the striking Puritan portrait subject 'Thoughts Apt, Hands Black' and the macabre and sardonically titled wood engraving of a hangman 'For what We are About to Receive'. The 'D'Artagnan in London 1649' is slightly looser than the others and the

Figure 81. 'Henry Irving', woodcut by E. Gordon Craig.

rather cloying effect of so much of the editor's work is relieved by a charming portrait drawing from Will Rothenstein. The third quarter for 1899 had fresh subjects by Craig on toned paper – 'Old Grimes, His Friend' and 'Mr Tom Peel', which was hand-coloured, as well as pen and ink drawings of Henry Irving and Sarah Bernhardt by J. Bastien Lepage.

*The Page* was also the advertising medium for Edward Gordon Craig's other designing projects, bookplates 'Designed, Engraved and Printed at the Sign of the Rose, Hackbridge, Surrey' and the famous *Gordon Craig's Book of Penny Toys – Twenty Original Colour Drawings of the most representative English, Dutch or German Wooden Toys and Twenty Verses. The Page Edition de Luxe* was sold to special subscribers and a pot pourri of contributions to the magazine, 1898-99, was issued in 1900. In the volume for 1901, Craig pays tribute to his predecessor in the broadsheet style by printing Haldane Macfall's article on 'Some Thoughts Suggested By The Art of Joseph Crawhall Illustrated With Woodcuts, The Presence of Which is Due To The Courtesy of The Leadenhall Press'. Some stage scenes in this number show the path Craig's art was going to take in the later magazines he edited, *The Masque* and *The Marionette.*

Craig's productions were too fresh and winsome to appeal to the heavy rhetoric of the Victorian critic and their very fragility came under attack. *The Dome* rather unfairly referred to the insubstantiality of the publication: 'To look at the cuts and read all the letter press took much less than ten minutes.' Some critics made comparisons with the Beggarstaff Brothers but not *The Weekly Sun,* which sums up the conventional disapproval with yet another side of *fin de siècle:* 'There is a charm in the work of an artist and also one in that of children but Mr. Craig is neither an artist nor a child, and why fair white paper should blush for his impertinences in line, or rather out of it, we do not see.' A great deal of *The Page's* influence however came much later in the 1900s and 1920s when Craig's shorthand began to be applied to scenery, books and posters. Pamela Colman Smith's illustrations such as that of 'The Wind' in 1901 certainly look towards the art deco designer and Claud Lovat Fraser's work is undeniably derived from Crawhall but through the deflecting glass of Edward Gordon Craig's *The Page.*

## The Beam, The Dome and The Acorn

*The Beam* was a short-lived and rare bird, published bi-monthly in 1896 and foundering after the January, March and May issues. Its format was much the same as the earlier issues of *The Butterfly* although it employed a different set of contributors. It was edited by Alfred Jones and was published according to the title page by 'Some Students of the National Art Training School'. The illustrations are patchy, some inspired by Morris and some by the attraction of Beardsley and art nouveau, many are full of student promise but do not quite make the grade as single drawings. Among the more interesting things to be found are early decorations by Leon Solon, figure subjects by J.W.T. Manuel and woodcutty and Pre-Raphelite subjects from W.R. Kean and W. Shackleton. The second number contained new art decorations by Arthur Orr and S. Stromquist, some tentative sketches by Oliver Onions and humorous sketches in the style of J.F. Sullivan from Alfred Jones. The May issue is perhaps the most coherent, the artists were obviously finding their feet and there are a number of new names. Edith Mason borrowing from Beardsley, Laurence Housman's refined illustrator's eye, more Oliver Onions' drawings of sturdy peasants in the manner of Fred Walker and excellent things by Alice B. Woodward and A. Hugh Fisher. Although the student tempo is very obtrusive, there are some interesting articles showing the influences on black and white artists of the time. One by A. Hugh Fisher is on 'Angelo Colarossi' under whom many of these men and women would study in Paris, another is on Whistler and there is a 'Counterblast' to the teaching at the South Kensington Schools. The circulation for this attractive little publication must have been very small and valuable mostly for the opportunities it gave the ardent contributors.

A similar publication but one which was more commanding in its field was *The Dome.* On its first title page in 1897, it calls itself 'a Quarterly containing Examples of All the Arts' and that of illustration was given a high place. *The Dome* at one shilling set itself apart by giving prominence to coloured wood engravings, the second volume containing the admirable engraving 'A Fisher' by William Nicholson, printed from four blocks and already referred to (Figure 79). Later volumes have similar work by Gordon Craig (Figure 81), more poster-like and rendered with less craft and more theatricality. The diet up to the last volume in February 1900 is none too rich but is refreshingly varied. There are some typically forbidding landscapes from the pen of J.J. Guthrie, a Housman that leans heavily on the Pre-Raphaelites, 'The Troubling of the Waters', some sombre works by W.T. Horton, a strange Celtic melange from the sinister to the poetic suitable to accompany W.B. Yeats' work, and excellent if bloodless topography by H.W. Brewer, R.J. Williams and F.L. Emanuel. Bernard Sleigh of the Birmingham School makes two appearances, Charles Pears three, and there are some fine things by A. Hugh Fisher, particularly 'Thatching', a Millet type subject treated with unsentimental thoroughness. All these volumes show a renewed fascination with wood engraving, prints by the German masters are reproduced, particularly Dürer and Cranach, interleaved with modern work in busy imitation. *The Dome* was the only illustrated art magazine of its time except *The Chord,* 1899-1900, to devote a regular section to printed music.

*The Acorn,* published by the Caradoc Press, never grew into an oak. It began life in October 1905 and was dead by February 1906, although it still had that *fin de siècle* preciosity about it. This again was a quarterly dealing with literature and art, but except for some etched frontispieces by Frank Brangwyn, an etching by Alfred East and rather ordinary decorations by H.G. Webb, it is of little account.

# Phil May's Illustrated Annuals

A hand-full of artists during our period were of sufficient popularity to have their own annuals, gift-books or journals,[22] easily the most famous of these was Phil May, 1864-1903. May was the obverse of the Beardsley coin, if the latter was the master of the refined line, the former was of the eliminated line. May was born in Leeds and on being left fatherless at the age of nine, took various jobs in offices and warehouses before joining the scene painters at Leeds' Grand Theatre. A natural artist with an instinctive sense of humour, he was quoted as saying in later life 'I can't remember a time when I didn't draw!'[23] May joined a touring theatrical company in 1879 and remained with them till 1882, gaining from this connection with the stage his delightful and unashamed bohemianism that became such a part of his life and his drawings. He made caricatures of his fellow actors and some of Irving, Toole and Bancroft, are in the manner of *portraits chargés,* perhaps based on the work of Carlo Pellegrini, 'Ape' of *Vanity Fair*. Arriving in London in 1883, he had months of severe hardship before finding illustrative work with *Society* and *The St Stephen's Review* where he deputised for the political cartoonist Matt Morgan. In 1885 he was offered a three year contract with the *Sydney Bulletin* and accepted it, sailing for Australia in November and completing during this spell abroad nearly nine hundred drawings, cartoons, caricatures and joke illustrations.

By this time the May style was emerging. The artist was beginning to reduce dramatically the number of pen lines that he worked with, and found it difficult to explain to editors that the seemingly effortless strokes on a board were nevertheless part of a rigid concentration. Within the established order of elaborate detail, feverish hatching and controlled tones for the wood-engraver, May's breath-taking virtuosity was nothing short of revolutionary. The enforced work on *The Bulletin*, its regular flow of drawings and the contact with other artists made May's stay in Australia a beneficial one. From being a talented but haphazard artist, he became a professional artist, broadening his outlook and probably acquiring that air of casualness in drawing and freedom in humour more typical of the exile than the home-based illustrator. May was the worthy successor of Cruikshank and Leech in English graphic satire but was even more indebted to Charles Keene whose cast of metropolitan characters were so close to his own. Like Keene he concentrated wholly on black and white work and like him relied entirely on the pen for his effects. 'By his genius for observation and selection,' wrote James Thorpe, 'and the extreme simplification of his method of presentation, he showed that a pen drawing can be a very eminent form of art.'[24] He had too the advantage over Keene that his wit was greater and his drawings and their captions are more intrinisically funny and punchy than the earlier artist's. Keene's beautifully toned drawings require a time fuse, usually the time fuse of a lengthy explanation, May's are instantaneous and explode on one like a fire cracker. The situation of the drawings is often the same, barrow boys and street vendors, waiters, overbearing shopkeepers, drunken gentlemen, fussy old ladies and gossips. Keene looks backwards to a harsher and more Hogarthian England, May forwards to a humour free of manners and prejudices and without letter-press. He claimed to have learnt a great deal about the placing of lines and parallel shading from Linley Sambourne, the *Punch* artist, and from Caran d'Ache, the Frenchman who relied on so few masterly pen strokes.

Although one might expect such an engagingly social artist as May to be working directly from nature in his sketchbooks, this was not always the case. The sketch was only the beginning of a process that whittled down the figure from complexity to bare essentials, some of his sketchbooks were on transparent paper enabling him to trace the study back from page to page knocking out all but the relevant lines, working from back to front of the book. It was only by dint of concentration and a perfect eye that he managed to retain the spontanaiety and freshness in the finished result, even when models were used the result is lively, boyish and enjoyable. As May absorbed the pure essence of a figure, the details of dress, surroundings and background were entirely sublimated to it.

May was a splendid portraitist from an early age and this certainly helped him to capture the expressions of pearly kings, 'Arries and 'Arriets, topers and urchins from his Battersea and East End sketchbooks. Corner sketches such as the bedraggled female ejected from a gin palace and saying '*Next* time I goes into a Publickhouse, I'll go somewhere where I'll be *respected*' are unforgettable as is the bibulous retort of another inebriate 'I'll do ellythik you like in reasol,Mria (hic) But I won't come 'home'. Many of the drawings rely on the ludicrous juxtapositions of the street scene almost as the camera has come to do, a good example is the crisp 'Fair Woman' in the Garrick Club collection (Figure 82). To look at these spirited sketches is to stare straight into the London of the music-hall, the hansom cab and the Gaiety Theatre, the London of the posters and Dan Leno and Marie Lloyd. May's humour like his drawings is clipped, quick and urban, a type recognisable to any cockney.

On his return from Australia and a period of study in London and Paris, May was engaged once more by *The St Stephen's Review* and began to make his famous series of drawings *The Parson and The Painter,* 1890. This featured a country clergyman the Rev. Joseph Slapkins and his nephew, visiting famous theatrical and sporting resorts and having picaresque adventures. When the drawings were published in book form in 1891, the edition of thirty thousand copies was sold out at once and Phil May became a household name. He was snapped up in November 1890 to work for the newly-founded *Daily Graphic* and was sent by them to cover the World Fair at Chicago. This proved to be less than successful, for May could not get to grips with the American character and preferred to be among his beloved Londoners. From this date onwards the artist could choose his own work and most of the leading magazines were anxious to have it. He published it in *The Sketch, Black and White, The*

Figure 82. 'Fair Women' by Phil May.

*Daily Chronicle* and many more. In 1892, he launched his first *Annual* which appeared regularly from then until 1905, thirteen Winter issues and three Summer numbers at one shilling each. They contained a wide selection of May's drawings but had literary contributions from writers as various as E.F. Benson, Conan Doyle, Kenneth Grahame and H.G. Wells. May was also appearing in *Fun, Frolic and Fancy,* a little periodical where his fine pencil studies are featured alongside the rather crude decorations of his brother Charles May. The *Annuals* were a personal triumph because he had greater freedom to draw what he liked and did not have to obey an editorial policy of captioned jokes.

In 1895, May received the accolade of black and white draughtsmanship and was elected to the staff of *Punch.* It was very much the appointment of an outsider, for though he had been contributing to its pages since 1893, his drawing and his way of life were totally different from the sedate illustrators of Bouverie Street. They were still living in the world of du Maurier and the highly pictured joke; May's presumptuous urchins with few lines and no backgrounds were a visual shock to them, not to say an unpalatable reminder of the outside world. *Punch's* radicalism and realism had long since departed and it remained a pocket of 1860s black and white drawings long after May's death and practically into the 1920s. On the other hand May's influence probably loosened the line of some of the younger men and is discernible in such later practitioners as Bert Thomas and Frank Reynolds. F.C. Burnand, the lordly editor of the magazine, remained wary of this amiable bohemian artist whose deadlines were rarely met and whose spendthrift nature was always causing embarrassment; but much of his best work appeared there.

May's other strength was in his keen observation of children and particularly the children of the streets; he was quoted as saying that he could understand them because he had been one of them. A few of these usually decorated the pages of the *Annuals* and many of them were gathered together as *Guttersnipes* and *ABC* published by the Leadenhall Press in 1896 and 1897. He is far less snobbish in these scenes than any of the other *Punch* men, he laughs with the boys round the gin palace door and not at them, and can see the pathos of poverty as well as its ludicrous side. For our own day his studies of lunatics in humorous situations are far less acceptable, reflecting the great change between the late Victorians and ourselves, and his ethnic jokes have likewise lost some of their appeal.

This brilliantly versatile artist died of cirrhosis of the liver on 5 August 1903 at the early age of thirty-nine. His reputation was assured and he had many imitators, all attracted by that deceptively easy line, few achieving any success with it. His monuments were the volumes of collected drawings and the *Annuals* which were continued for a year after his death. His spareness of line found its way most naturally into advertising and poster art in the early century, May himself had designed advertisements for Geradel's Pastilles and Player's Navy Cut. May qualifies as an artist of the *fin de siècle* not only because his work spanned that decade but because his approach to his art was so exclusive, so personal, so highly charged and nervous, filled with the self-conscious exuberance of those years. Like Beardsley, much of it was produced in the intervals between wracking illnesses, like Beardsley his last act was to be received into the Roman Catholic church.

# The Idler

Of all the magazines discussed here, *The Idler* is the most nearly an intruder and the least consciously 'artistic'. It began in 1892 and was called 'An Illustrated Monthly Magazine' in the joint editorship of Jerome K. Jerome and Robert Barr. Although extensively illustrated from the first volume onwards, its appearance is often not much above that of *The Strand Magazine,* one of the nastiest productions of the period! The first

THE ART GALLERY.

*Figure 83. The Strand Magazine Art Gallery, 1892.*

volume began well however with drawings from Bernard Partridge, smart wash illustrations to a story from Dudley Hardy and some nice decorations to a poem by J.F. Sullivan. Some of the best Hardy's to be seen also feature in 1892, his drawings for Jerome's article 'Variety Patter', a survey of the music hall stage. These include brilliant sketches of Albert Chevalier, Jenny Hill, Lottie Collins, and Charles Coborn, showing both artist and author in relaxed mood in the midst of a world they loved. In 1892-93 fresh illustrators arrive such as Fred Pegram, J. Gulich, Louis Gunnis and Louis Wain with cartoons by the rather crude artist 'Cynicus'. But the format of the magazine and the quality of the printing do not merit much attention and even the excellent pen drawings of A.S. Boyd in 1895-96 seem rather lost on the page.

After Volume 8 in 1895-96, there is a change in the design and appearance of the magazine and an increase in quality and quantity of black and white work. In the pages from this date are excellent illustrations by Max Cowper, H.R. Millar and S.H. Sime as well as delightfully Beardsleyish pastiches by Alan Wright and good figures in the style of May by Hounsom Byles. A. Jules Goodman contributes and there is a great advance in the use of headings and tail-pieces for decoration. But the real contribution of the magazines for the collector of illustration is the excellent series of articles on black and white artists running from Volume 8 to Volume 12. They include in their number Louis Wain, Raven-Hill, H.R. Millar, Dudley Hardy, E.T. Reed, Caton Woodville, Bernard Partridge, Aubrey Beardsley, Fred Pegram and S.H. Sime. These alone and their accompanying reproductions single out *The Idler* from its fellows as a magazine very much of its time.

Although *The Strand Magazine* does not qualify for inclusion here, it made its own contribution to fostering black and white art in a very original way. George Newnes, its proprietor, had two rooms at the magazine's offices laid out as an art gallery of illustrators' works. These were all original drawings by Paul Hardy, W.J. Boot, H.R. Millar and others that had previously appeared in the magazine. 'All these drawings are offered for sale,' runs an article in the magazine, 'but whether a possible purchaser or not, the passer-by will not waste the time occupied by a look round these two pleasant rooms.'[25] (Figure 83.) In 1901, the Victoria and Albert Museum held a big exhibition of black and white drawings and summed up on a national scale the extraordinary fecundity and originality of magazine and book illustrators from 1890.

*Footnotes*

1. Holbrook Jackson, *The Eighteen Nineties*, 1913, p.21.
2. ibid., p.339.
3. Walter Crane, *Of The Decorative Illustration of Books*, 1901, p.208.
4. Dalziel family documents sold at Sotheby's Belgravia as *The Dalziel Family*, 16 May 1978.
5. James Thorpe, *English Illustration The Nineties*, 1935, pp.12-13.
6. Charles Morgan, *The House of Macmillan*, 1943, p.125.
7. *The Butterfly*, 1893, No. 1, p.6.
8. First published in *Harper's*, January to July 1894.
9. Some yardstick of its success may be gauged by the fact that the Victoria and Albert Museum Library copy is from the collection of Gleeson White.
10. Gleeson White, *English Illustration 'The Sixties'*, 1897, p.3.
11. Joseph Pennell, *Pen Drawing and Pen Draughtsmen*, 1895.
12. White, op. cit., p.11.
13. *The Studio*, 1893, Vol. 1, No. 1, p.17.
14. *The Studio* devoted a Winter No. to book illustration in 1900-01 and a further Special Number in 1914.
15. *The Studio*, 1898.
16. ibid., April 1893, p.14.
17. *The Idler*, Vol. 11, pp.188-202.
18. C.S. Felver, *Joseph Crawhall*, 1972, p.15.
19. ibid., p.80.
20. *The Idler*, 1895, Vol. 8, pp.519-528.
21. G. Nash, *Edward Gordon Craig*, Victoria and Albert Museum, 1967, p.15.
22. Other artists to have annuals were Kate Greenaway, Louis Wain, John Hassall and Cecil Aldin.
23. James Thorpe, *Phil May*, 1932, p.20.
24. ibid.
25. *The Strand Magazine*, July to December 1892, Vol. 4, p.597.

# Chapter 10

# The Return of the Eighteenth Century

From the third quarter of the nineteenth century onwards till well beyond 1914, there were a group of illustrators who had one major element in common, whatever else may have divided them. They were landscape illustrators as well as illustrators of novels and included decorators and the avant-garde in their number. In brief they had all been fired by the literature, art, costume or atmosphere of England in the eighteenth century and became dealers in nostalgia on a very large scale. Some writers have referred to these artists as 'the Cranford School' in an attempt to give some coherence to the main contributors to period novels from 1890 to 1914. It is the intention here to broaden this group still further and take the sources of Georgian revivalism back into the middle of the century as well as to include two important illustrators of children's books Randolph Caldecott and Kate Greenaway. In a sense Aubrey Beardsley's decorative debt from the eighteenth century might almost warrant his inclusion too, but this aspect of him has been touched on in the previous chapter.

The romantic novelists of the generation of Sir Walter Scott had tended to set their stories in the remote past or the remote orient, accounting for wild inaccuracies in drawing and costume. The early Victorians such as Thackeray, Dickens and his imitators, though not to the same extent as Lytton or Ainsworth, favoured the recent past for their finest stories. Although one might quibble about the exact date of *Pickwick Papers,* its setting is surely before 1837, the year in which it appeared; Mr. Pickwick himself is totally Georgian as a type, so is Weller and the attraction of both of them for us and surely for the Victorians was that they belonged to a world before the railways, before industrialisation. No more precise date could be pin-pointed for *David Copperfield* or *Martin Chuzzlewhit; Barnaby Rudge* is early eighteenth century and *Tale of Two Cities* late eighteenth century in date. But in approaching the illustrators of these books, one is aware how much they are slowing down the process of time.

In book illustration the overriding influence in black and white work remained the prints of William Hogarth. For most early Victorians he was a figure outside time, the founder of the British School, the model of what every great painter should be, a great moraliser. Charles Lamb and William Hazlitt were both powerful advocates for the study of Hogarth's graphic works and most significant of all the two novelists already mentioned, Dickens and Thackeray, borrowed extensively from the artist in words and pictures. In his brilliant study of this relationship, *Victorian Novelists and Their Illustrators,* John Harvey argues convincingly that the elements of exaggeration, animism and the grotesque, find their way into the novels through the work of Hogarth. Dickens owned sets of some of the engravings and was clearly haunted by the artist's representation of 'Gin Lane', one of the most overtly allegorical of all Hogarth's prints. 'Dickens habitual mode of characterisation,' John Harvey writes, 'has the complexity we should expect to result from long immersion both in Hogarth's works and in the caricatures also. Although he brings a uniquely concentrated vision to bear on the physical details of his people, he does not submit these details to physical distortion; yet the reality is presented, none the less, through an elaborate play of far-fetched comparisons.'[1] This was a direct inheritance from the Georgian satirical print therefore, which outlawed by polite society had now taken refuge among the writers. An even stronger link is discernible in Thackeray, who as artist and writer clearly owed a lot to the great satirist. Thackeray was not only taught by George Cruikshank, the greatest exponent of the eighteenth century tradition, but Harvey traces one initial letter in his novel *The Virginians,* Chapter XXVII which is derived directly from Hogarth's 'Idle Apprentice' series.[2] A similar sort of connection can be seen in the delightful frontispiece which Thackeray drew for his own *Paris Sketchbook,* 1841 (Figure 84). A decorative frieze of heads which are satirical but not caricatured are grouped over the page, a succession of types that might have graced any eighteenth century work on physiognomy. But they are most akin to the compositions of heads which Hogarth liked to use as studies of character such as 'Arms of the Undertakers', 'The Chorus', 'The Laughing Audience' and 'Alma Mater' (Figure 85). For his highly successful book *The Four Georges,* serialised in *The Cornhill Magazine* in 1860, Thackeray made illustrations and initial letters from original eighteenth century material. In the published book, 1861, he acknowledges that the first initial letter 'is from an old Dutch print of Herenhausen', but he might also have added that

*Figure 85. 'Alma Mater' by William Hogarth.*

*Figure 84. Frontispiece of* The Paris Sketch Book *drawn by* W.M. Thackeray.

the initial in the fourth chapter is taken from Zoffany and the print of George IV and Queen Caroline comes from a popular stipple engraving. None of these have quite the Georgian feel of *The Paris Sketchbook* plate, but the initial of a drummer, at the head of the chapter on George II, is spirited and almost Hogarthian. With the money that he made on *The Four Georges*, Thackeray was able to build and furnish a new house in London where his enthusiasm for the 'Queen Anne' style could be given full rein.

It was perhaps significant that twenty years later it was Thackeray's works which gave a group of younger artists an opportunity of illustrating in the revived Georgian style. This was in the twenty-six volume Smith Elder Standard Edition of 1885 where Thackeray's original sketches were augmented by the works of Frank Dicksee, Linley Sambourne, Fred Barnard and G.A. Sala. The strongest period settings are by Fred Barnard who appears to go to original material for his inspiration and there is a splendid contribution by Fred Walker to 'Hogarth's Model' in *The English Humourists*. Linley Sambourne is weak as he often is with historical illustrating, but an added air of authenticity is introduced by the reproduction of eighteenth century engravings opposite each chapter in *The Four Georges*. For their 10/6d per volume, the readers of 1885 were receiving something that had not merely the sentiment of Georgian times about it, but a strong visual appeal as well.

By the middle of the 1860s there was a definite reaction against the sketchy, free and caricatured book illustrations that both Dickens and Thackeray had grown up with. H.K. Browne ended his partnership with Dickens after *Little Dorrit,* 1855-57, and the plates for *Tale of Two Cities,* 1859, and Fred Walker transformed Thackeray's pencillings for *The Adventures of Philip* into graceful and assured wood engravings for *The Cornhill*. It was a transition of style and temperament, a style which bade farewell to the copper-plate in a self-consciously progressive age and addressed itself to the greater subtleties of black and white art; a temperament which was as far removed from the volatile Regency as the pounding magazine presses were from the singly issued print of fifty years before. The French illustrators of the *comédie humaine,* the fashion plates, the middle-class novel and the softer characterisations of Leech, all had influenced the change. Ruskin, whose criticisms of book illustrations are curiously patchy saw fit to lampoon the illustrated edition of Dickens' *Barnaby Rudge,* 1841, in his *Ariadne Florentina,* natural perhaps that he should choose a period story with illustrators of the old school, H.K. Browne and George Cattermole. 'You have in that book,' writes Ruskin with marvellous over-statement, 'an entirely profitless and monstrous story, in which the principal characters are a coxcomb, an idiot, a madman, a savage blackguard, a foolish tavern-keeper, a mean old maid and a conceited apprentice — mixed up with a certain quantity of ordinary operatic pastoral stuff . . .'[3] This edition of *Barnaby Rudge* was published in conjunction with *The Old Curiosity Shop* as an omnibus edition, under the title 'Master Humphrey's Clock'. The engravings are mainly half-page figure subjects with an occasional landscape illustration and some lively initial letters linking section to section (Figure 86).

Ruskin's outburst was untimely. In 1872 Browne was already elderly and neglected, Cruikshank, obsessed with teetotalism, was more an historical figure than a practising artist and George Cattermole had ceased to illustrate at all. It was the impact of Pre-Raphaelite illustration on the younger men that had swept the carpet from under the Georgian satirists, the energies of the illustrator were now concentrated on naturalism and realism in interpreting the text of books. As we have already seen, the portrayal of modern episodes became an absorbing passion of the novel and the magazine illustrator while his more imaginative side was poured into the legendary and symbolic preoccupations of poetry and myth. It seemed for a few years as if the visual continuity that stretched in illustration from 1740 to 1840 had been broken.

There were some exceptions among the artists of the 1860s, however, one of whom has

*Figure 86. Illustration by George Cattermole for* The Old Curiosity Shop.

already been dealt with in some detail, George Pinwell. We have seen him as the brilliant draughtsman of country scenes which he touches with a magical sympathy and innocence, but his reputation as a major illustrator rests on his work in the Dalziels' *Illustrated Goldsmith,* 1865. In this book, Pinwell had the opportunity to produce a large and sustained amount of work from the stories and plays of a writer with whom he obviously felt a great kinship. It is true that all the one hundred illustrations are costume pieces and are therefore not the usual stock in trade of the artist, but the characters of Goldsmith are mostly culled from country life and by accepting this and fitting them into the settings and groups he knew so well, Pinwell breathes on them a naturalism which has not dated. *The Vicar of Wakefield* engravings and those for *She Stoops to Conquer* are probably the most successful, the group on page 155 of the former being marvellously composed and modelled and the figures by the harpsichord a characteristically well-defined piece of drawing. Forrest Reid hits the correct note when he points to the admirable figure of Goldsmith wandering the streets of London as showing 'a touch of Hogarth'.[4] It is the authenticity of the drawings which is still their strength, the Victorian idea of Georgian London may be there, but it is happily subdued and clothes, furniture and settings would seem to have been modelled from paintings and prints as well as from sensitivity to the writer. Although it would be difficult to establish it definitely, one suspects that the high praise given by Gleeson White and others to this book at the turn of the century, made it widely influential.

Matthew Lawless, the Irish-born illustrator who died in 1864 at the age of twenty-seven, was another powerfully individual artist who made some successful contributions to the eighteenth century idiom. He has already been touched upon as a Pre-Raphaelite follower but in *Good Words* for 1864 he illustrates a poem 'The Player and The Listeners' with an attractive musical subject in which both costume and instrument are eighteenth century, though a little indeterminate because of lack of knowledge. The year before he had drawn for *London Society,* a full page illustration 'A Box on the Ears and Its Consequences' which gave him the chance to show a crowded Georgian Assembly Room with outlined figures. Another subject managed with equal facility was 'Doctor Johnson's Penance' in *Once a Week* of the same year. A book of 1867 which reflects the same spirit is *The Story of a Feather,* illustrated by George du Maurier, again recapturing something of the atmosphere of scenes set in the previous century and even imitating in the penwork a little of the period's caricature.

In the same decade as Ruskin's portentous grumblings, a spate of books were issued to the public which were to have a considerable effect on the return of the eighteenth century to print. The publisher John Camden Hotten's list for 1871 included revived editions of *Hood's Whims and Oddities* of 1826, *Life in London* and *The Tours of Dr Syntax,* all Regency best-sellers. Cruikshank's *Comic Almanacks* were also on this list but by 1876 had migrated to Chatto and Windus, powerful supporters of caricature. Chatto's had been the publishers of the first major monograph on a Georgian figure with *The Works of James Gillray The Caricaturist* by Joseph Grego in 1873. Grego's thoughtful examination of the artist treats the caricatures in an historical and sociological fashion with passing references to 'HB', John Leech and Tenniel who he feels fulfill a similar function. This was followed by the yet more elaborate set of two volumes *Rowlandson The Caricaturist* by the same author in 1880. Thomas Wright had produced his *Caricature History of The Georges* in 1876 and a more general survey including chapters on the immediate past was available by 1893 in Graham Everitt's *English Caricaturists and Graphic Humourists.*

Such a wealth of illustrated material would have been of little use if it had not reached the notice of up and coming artists, but there is ample evidence that these books and the original drawings and prints were being re-discovered in studios and private collections. In 1883 a young girl visited the memorial exhibition of 'Phiz' (H.K. Browne) held in London. This was Beatrix Potter, the aspiring illustrator of flora and fauna, who found much in this unfashionable artist that was to her taste. She confided to her journal that she preferred his work to that of Leech and liked 'the wonderful difference in expression' of the original drawings in comparison with the published prints. Charles Keene, then at the height of his *Punch* fame, was the contributor who showed most clearly the free style of the magazine's early years. His figure work is incomparably the best of its kind in any illustrated journal but it was to Stothard that he claimed to look for inspiration and an obscure book illustrator of Polish extraction, Nicolas Chodowiecki, 1726-1801. This artist's scenes from Shakespeare, Lavater and others would seem to be the quintessence of good-mannered eighteenth century book illustration. Keene is on record as saying 'I consider him the most extraordinary demon of industry (and yet excellent art of its sort) I ever knew of.'[5] He also had a collection of Chodowiecki's originals. When Mr. John Jones left his outstanding collection of French eighteenth century furniture to the Victoria and Albert Museum in 1882, it contained a fine portfolio of hand-coloured caricatures of the same period, presumably collected in the 1850s and 1860s when interest in such things was supposed to be at its lowest.

*The Household Edition of Charles Dickens Works* that appeared between 1870 and 1879 reprinted all the major novels as well as fugitive pieces from *Household Words* and *All The Year Round* and a life of the author. The lion's share of this work went to Fred Barnard, the London born but French trained figure artist who had been working for *The Illustrated London News* since 1868. A good deal of Barnard's work had been in social realism, a good background for Dickens, but even with his considerable grasp of character and situation, the continuity of 'Phiz' and Cruikshank is not sustained through the volumes. A later edition of the illustrations only states that he took 'the types already created by his predecessors, preserved their characteristics, so that each was unmistakably himself and yet by the illuminating touch of genius transferred them every one from the realm of caricature to that of portraiture.'[6] This is only partially true for Barnard was a brilliant caricaturist and some of his creations in *Sketches By Boz* and *Martin Chuzzlewit* are closer to caricature. It is only necessary to look at the wood engravings in *Nicholas Nickleby* and then at the steel engravings in the 1839 volume to see how closely Barnard follows the dress and fittings and manners of the epoch and yet how totally he has missed the spirit of the age. The *Boz* illustrations are better, the characters live within the context of their writer and their period and in the 'Cold Thin Rain' engraving to Chapter II, Barnard has used as his source Gillray's 'Windy Day' and elsewhere, the half page sketch of the actor 'Jem Larkins' is a masterpiece but in reality a resurrected and re-moulded 'Jingle' from H.K. Browne.

Barnard's designs for *Tale of Two Cities* are very unconvincing, the costumes wildly inaccurate and the female revolutionaries looking more like the Parisians of 1870 than 1790. Charles Green, 1840-1898, was the other main contributor to this series, his best work being for *The Old Curiosity Shop* which gave him most scope for dramatic and atmospheric effects and strong characterisations. In drawings such as this, entitled 'A Consultation' one can see the strong influence of H.K. Browne's work (Figure 87). His surviving pen drawings show a freedom and a sprightliness one would not expect from the wood engravings, but the finished work for reproduction is often no longer linear but clouded with thick grey washes. The chief influence in this direction was William Small, 1843-1929, who also undertook period settings in some of his books. Artists like Barnard who remained loyal to line work, are not noticeably more accurate or close to the authors than those who experimented with washy effects on the wood engraving.

The most vigorous and spontaneous pastiches did not however come from established artists or amateurs but from an obscure bank clerk in Manchester, Randolph Caldecott. As mentioned in an earlier chapter, Caldecott was the discovery of James Hogg of *London Society*, 1871-72, and it was not long before he attracted the attention of W.L. Thomas of *The Graphic* and joined the recently founded magazine in October 1872. Caldecott's appeal was obviously in the freshness and vivacity of his drawing not in his accuracy. His tremendous capacity for humorous draughtsmanship and humorous story-telling was so effortless and attractive that it easily outbalanced the small blemishes natural in an untrained hand. An inveterate sportsman and lover of the country, Caldecott made the hunting party and the house party his school as Leech had before him. He also studied animals in the Zoological Gardens. There is still however some of the amateur's hesitancy and uncertainty in some of the earlier illustrations which in some ways give them their most enduring charm. Deriving some of his gentleness from Leech, Caldecott based his work directly on the spirit of the eighteenth century as it was found in the nostalgic Christmases and idylls of Dickens, Washington Irving and Thackeray, a pretty pastellish world, ideally suited for Victorians now living with industry, but dreaming of green countrysides and houses in blushing red brick (Figure 88).

Part of Caldecott's success was that he could convey the essence of a past age very easily but use his own texts. One of the ways he did this was to adopt the guise of a letter-writer or a diarist of the 'olden time' and illustrate with lively sketches his supposed

*Figure 87. 'A Consultation' by Charles Green.*

*Figure 88. 'Three Jovial Huntsmen' by Randolph Caldecott.*

adventures. *The Graphic* in those ten years between 1876 and 1886 contains numerous examples of this kind, 'Mr Carlyon's Christmas, Pictured by his Grandson', 'The Legend of the Laughing Oak', 'Diana Wood's Wedding', 'Christmas Visitors From My Grandfather's Sketches', 'The Cumudgeons Christmas' are some of them. A strangely fairy tale air of wonder fills the drawings to these stories, an unspoilt landscape stretches into the distance, great log fires seem to be perpetually burning and happy rustics are continually quaffing the health of the young squire in bright tankards. Yet these imaginary pieces were arranged in *The Graphic* for an adult readership who were enjoying to the full the greater use of colour printing in the magazines.

The artist happened to have arrived on the scene when what was needed was a humour of lightness, simplicity and verve, not too well drawn but adapted to colour work. Edmund Evans, the chief exponent of the new market, found ideal material for children's *Toybooks* in the designs of Walter Crane, Kate Greenaway and Randolph Caldecott, published by Routledges and Warnes from about 1865. Their simple black outlines and flat areas of subtle colours made them quite different from the crude and garish illustrations of other juvenile publications. (See Colour Plate X, p.124.) It was probably the whimsy of never-never land, combined with the sophisticated tonal range of the colours, that linked Caldecott and Kate Greenaway to the Aesthetic Movement. Their prettiness interested Ruskin and for him, Caldecott was 'dazzling' and most particularly for his landscapes, 'familiar landscapes, very English, interpreted with a bonhomie savante'.[7] Most of the artist's work has a remarkable economy of line which suggests comparisons with Phil May. The picture books had on average six coloured pages, the remaining openings being black and white or rather brown and white line drawings; only an artist of consummate skill could have linked the main plates with such slight and simple sketches so superbly. The artist certainly understood the world of childhood and the heroes and heroines of these *Toy Books* are always the children themselves.

In talking of the beauty of Caldecott's line, his biographer, Henry Blackburn, does say that the artist was not always well served by his engravers. This is certainly born out by the surviving pen drawings in letters and sketch-books and in the illustrations for *Old Christmas*, 1874, and *Bracebridge Hall*, 1877, both by Washington Irving. The drawing becomes much tighter in these illustrations, the compositions more considered and the figures more controlled, in some of them he would seem to have looked at Browne or Cruikshank with an affectionate eye. Drawings such as 'The Stage Coachman' and 'In The Stableyard' in the first book are marvellously evocative and in the second volume 'The Literary Antiquary' or 'Master Simon' only show a slight falling away. These two books were undoubtedly the most influential on the black and white artists of 1900, and from the amazing freedom of line and the imaginative use of vignettes, stems a great deal in Thomson, C.E. and H.M. Brock, Bernard Partridge and even E.J. Sullivan.

Caldecott's brief reign was not of course an entirely Georgian one. His French drawings were published as *Breton Folk* in 1878 and his *Graphic* contributions included light hearted views of contemporary life like 'The Strange Adventures of a Dog Cart' or 'Mr Chumley's Holidays'. But it is in the Georgian chronicles and the nursery books of Goldsmith's *Mad Dog* and Cowper's *John Gilpin* that the heart of Caldecott is to be found. There were numerous imitators but no single one could produce the magic of his parodies with the innocent child-like fun of his stories. In the year of his death, 1886, *The Graphic* published a pictured story by W. Ralston that was plainly an attempt to sustain the Caldecott manner, and another 'An Old Fashioned Christmas' followed in December 1889 with Arthur Hughes as the somewhat surprising Caldecott imitator. Others who caught this infectious style were W.B. Wollen, Cecil Aldin in his *Jorrocks* series and Percy Macquoid. Frank Dadd and the Brock Brothers carried the spirit of Caldecott Christmases up to 1914 and and Edwardian periodicals mercilessly aped the adventures of Regency bucks, even adopting the greens, browns and beiges of the coloured wood engraving for their own purposes. But it is some recognition of Caldecott's originality that while they have been forgotten, his evanescent picture books are still reprinted.

Kate Greenaway was a Londoner, born in Hoxton in 1846, a kinswoman of Richard Dadd and sister-in-law of the illustrator Frank Dadd. Like Caldecott, her urban background gave her a longing for the countryside and as he turned to the hunting field, she turned as readily to memories of childhood holidays in Nottinghamshire. Her aunt had a cottage at Rolleston near Newark and the young Kate spent summers there as well as much longer periods during a lengthy illness of her mother's. Rolleston with its haystacks and cornfields, country characters and farm animals, became mixed in her mind with the children's stories that were read to her, stories of the generation before last by the Misses Jane and Ann Taylor. An obvious aptitude for drawing led to her thinking of art as a career and she studied at both Heatherley's and the Slade School and shared a studio with Elizabeth Thompson, later Lady Butler. As early as 1868 she was specialising in legends and scenes from childhood and they began to bring her work from Marcus Ward for Christmas cards and valentines. In due course she was introduced to Edmund Evans and it was with his encouragement and expertise that she produced *Under the Window* in 1878, a book of her own verses, illustrated by herself. This was an immediate success in this country and also in Europe and America. Ruskin raved over her designs. 'The fairyland that she creates for you is not beyond the sky,' he told his Oxford audience, 'nor beneath the sea, but near you even at your doors.'

The 'fairyland' was 'olden time' in concept and Regency in dress as far as it could be. It corresponded to the Caldecott picturesque world perfectly. But the effect on the page was quite different; her garlanded children in bonnets and ribbons seem not only timeless but motionless as well, their waisted dresses and breached legs are as weightless and fleshless as feathers (Colour Plate XII, p.173). It is difficult to associate such robust tales as Red Riding Hood, Blue Beard and Puss in Boots with these solemn little girls, but she illustrated them all and the Victorian public loved them. The later nineteenth century was morbidly sentimental about children and here was an artist who not only treated them as serious little adults but gave them a period setting and an aesthetic costume! Kate Greenaway's sources were various, not only the children's books of the 1800s beautified, but the work of more considerable illustrators. Her friend Locker Lampson introduced her to the drawings of Thomas Stothard and she claimed elsewhere to have been influenced by Downman and certainly was by Reynolds in those finished watercolours of hers such as 'Winter', 1892, and 'Out For a Walk'. Her watercolours of country scenes are among her best work and are reminiscent in colouring of the art of Fred Walker and in their content, cottages and flower gardens, of her friend and contemporary Helen Allingham. She was unusual among the illustrators in attempting to create a genuinely historical representation. 'She did not merely pick up an old book of costumes and copy and adapt them second-hand to her own uses,' Spielmann records, 'She began from the very beginning, fashioning the dresses with her own hands and dressing up her models and lay figures in order to realise the effects anew.'[8] Whether copied or not, the garments have no genuine Regency counterparts, but the illustrations attracted the public who began to dress their children in Kate Greenaway costume. Du Maurier delightfully ridiculed the 'artistic couples' who decked their children out in flimsy dresses and monstrous bonnets apeing *The Kate Greenaway Almanack* which came out nearly every year between 1888 and 1897.

The fact that so much was done in the studio from the lay figure surely accounts for the static quality in Kate Greenaway's art and its impression of decoration rather than illustration. It was precisely this aspect that most worried Ruskin. 'There is no joy and very,

GULLIVER STANDS TO HIS FULL HEIGHT

*Left: Plate XIV*
*ALAN ELSDEN ODLE 1888-1948*
*'Gulliver stands to his full height'*
*Original drawing for a projected edition*
*of* Gulliver's Travels, *c. 1912*
*Pencil and watercolour*
*22½ins. x 15½ins. (57.2cm x 39.4cm)*
Author's Collection

*Below: Plate XV*
*ANNIE FRENCH fl. 1904-1925*
*'A Garlanded Wedding'*
*Pen and watercolour. Signed*
Private Collection

192

very little interest in any of these Flower book subjects,' he wrote to her in 1884, 'and they look as if you had nothing to paint them in but starch and camomile tea.'[9] Ruskin tried to persuade her to study from nature and considered her delicate colours were lost in the printing and should have been painted in by hand. 'What you Absolutely need,' he told her, 'is a quantity of practice from things as they are — and hitherto you have Absolutely refused to draw any of them so.'[10] But the books remained an overwhelming success. *Under the Window* was printed in an edition of 20,000 copies, at once sold out and reprinted, Evans eventually seeing it through to a total of 70,000 copies. The ones that followed, *The Birthday Book, Mother Goose, A Day in A Child's Life,* were equally popular and usually printed well over 10,000 copies. Her more conventional illustrating was not so individual, it harked back to the 1860s and in the case of *The Illustrated London News* included in Christmas 1874 'A Christmas Dream' which, with a sleeping child surrounded by elves and fairies, might have been a late work by Doyle. Her contributions to Charlotte M. Yonge's *The Heir of Redclyffe* in 1881 are very dry and reminiscent of M. Ellen Edwards at her least inspired.

But the essential Greenaway style of sugary sweetness, overlaid with Regency trappings, had it imitators well into the 1900s. It then became fused with the decorative motifs of 1890s work and died in the 1920s after a brief explosion of coy crinolined ladies. Among the better followers may be mentioned Mrs. Farmiloe, Winifred Graham, J.G. Sowerby, H.H. Emerson and R. André.

An illustrator who arrived from the United States in the late 1870s and who was to be widely influential here, was E.A. Abbey, 1852-1911, the American born and American trained draughtsman. Edwin Austin Abbey was born in Philadelphia and worked in a wood engraving office, studying art in the evening at the Pennsylvania Academy of Fine Arts, later moving to New York. His major American works were all for Harper Brothers' magazines, where the influence of German and French black and white art, already referred to, was transforming pen drawing. From the studio of Dietz in Munich, and Fortuny and others in France, a whole generation of American artists had returned to revitalise the art of illustration. The leading exponents were all Harper's or Scribner's men and it was therefore in American magazines and through American draughtsmen that the strongest Continental influences came. The essence of these drawings was a high standard of technique, a remarkable control of the pen line and a direct working from nature; perhaps most significant of all they did not treat illustrations as a minor but as a major means of artistic expression.

Abbey's contact with England was a tremendous spur to his historical work. His familiarity with the literature of the sixteenth to eighteenth centuries in this country was such that direct contact with the places and the landscape of the stories drove him on to fresh inventiveness. Settling first in London and then at Fairford in Gloucestershire, he became successively ARA and RA in 1901-02 and over the years captured the imagination of many younger artists with his renderings of Shakespearean subjects, *Herrick's Poems,* 1882, and *She Stoops to Conquer,* 1885 (Figure 89). In the latter book, he breaks completely away from the decorative convention of period illustrating and conjures

*Figure 89. Illustration by E.A. Abbey for* She Stoops to Conquer.

up people of flesh and blood living in imaginable surroundings. 'In England of the eighteenth century he is as much at home as Austin Dobson,' wrote his fellow American Joseph Pennell, 'He can reconstruct its old rooms and village streets and fill them anew with beauty and life.'[11] The artist's work also contains greater historical accuracy; Goldsmith's and Sheridan's characters sit on chairs of a discernible date, drink from vessels of a plausible appearance and wear clothes of a recognisable cut. Abbey had a considerable collection of old master paintings and antique furniture and these were presumably marshalled for use in his illustrations, probably the earliest attempt at such for a purely Georgian scene.[12] He also possessed an extensive library of the illustrated books of the 1860s, and a well-thumbed copy of A Round of Days with his bookplate is ample evidence that there was a strong link with the earlier artists.[13]

The drawings of Abbey had a very refined quality which made them difficult to reproduce in wood engravings. The etchings and original sketches, such as the one shown (Figure 89), often have a delicacy and sparkle that surpasses the book illustrations themselves. Old Songs, 1889, and She Stoops to Conquer, 1885 and 1901, are probably the high points of Abbey's art, but it is important to remember how versatile he was, humorous drawing was also in his line and he collaborated in delightful but uncharacteristic illustrations with Alfred Parsons in Quiet Life, 1890. In a note to the 1894 edition of Pen Drawing and Pen Draughtsmen, Pennell comments 'one can see that a new school is arising, and this is the school of Abbey, who has at the present moment followers in every illustrating country in the world, men who are seeking to carry out his method of brilliant drawing carefully and seriously executed.'[14] How true this was is proved by the list of artists working on eighteenth century literature in the 1890s, and 1900s and in fact right up until Abbey's death in 1911.

Chronologically after Abbey comes Hugh Thomson, 1860-1920, who was directly influenced by him. He was born at Coleraine near Londonderry and like Kate Greenaway began his career on the design of Christmas cards. His arrival in London and early work for The English Illustrated Magazine has been discussed in an earlier chapter, but his contributions as an illustrator of books are important for combining two strands of Georgian revivalism. He assimilated the humour and freedom of Caldecott with the fine line and careful expression of Abbey, bringing out between 1886 and 1900 a whole succession of small classics with crisp well-tuned pen sketches for Macmillans and Kegan Paul. That he recognised his debt to these artists is recorded in a reference quoted by Spielmann; of Caldecott he said 'It was a revalation to us all, when we saw what could be done with a simple unshaded outline, provided there was humour and fun in it. Hugh admired Abbey's work in Harper and the fine lines took his fancy.'[15] Again he recalls 'Hugh was immensely pleased with The Mad Dog, John Gilpin, The House That Jack Built'.

The first of his books is Days with Sir Roger De Coverley, 1886, a very neat little volume with beautiful figure drawings and some excellent pastoral decorations in the shape of headings, initials and vignettes. There are strong hints of Caldecott throughout, even down to the eclectic styles of dress, but also echoes of Fred Walker's unused illustrations for Henry Esmond. Other titles included The Vicar of Wakefield, 1891, the same work that Walker had made famous, The Ballad of Beau Brocade, 1892, a real feast of Augustan sentiment and Our Village, 1893, and Peg Woffington, 1899. His greatest success, Coaching Days and Coaching Ways, was published in 1888 and reprinted in 1903, as J.F. Sullivan said of him – 'He was the roundest of round pegs in the roundest of round holes, and his spirit and style seemed to me to fit the works he illustrated to a degree unattained by any other draughtsman that occurs to mind.'[16] His peppery squires and rubicund coachmen perfectly capture this aspect of Edwardian nostalgia (Figure 90).

Thomson's path through the forty years of his working life was predictable. He was to

"THEN HE, HANDING HER INTO HER COACH, STEPS IN AFTER."

*From a Drawing by HUGH THOMSON.*

The battle was over without any blows,

The heroes unharness and strip off their clothes;

The dame gives her captain a sip of rose-water,

Then he, handing her into her coach, steps in after.

John's orders are special to drive very slow,

For fevers oft follow fatigues, we all know;

*Figure 90. Illustration by Hugh Thomson to poem in* The English Illustrated Magazine.

illustrate, besides Goldsmith, Jane Austen, Fanny Burney, W.M. Thackeray, R.B. Sheridan, Hawthorne and Mrs. Gaskell. Any story in which costume illustration was appropriate was bound to persuade the publisher that Thomson should undertake it. The culmination was a series of handsome Edwardian volumes from Heinemann and Hodder in which Sheridan, Shakespeare and even J.M. Barrie were treated with a lush period sensuousness, fragile and beautiful interiors in pastel colours, lyrical decorations and vignettes, all between spacious margins. Although these caught the imagination of the public, they do not show Thomson at his best, because a black and white artist is usually diverted when he is engaged on colour work. The large plates are often flat and anaemic in tone and entirely lack the vigour of the pure pen drawings, neither do they make happy comparisons with the colour books of contemporaries like Rackham and Dulac. Thomson was also limited as an interpreter of legend and *The Illustrated Fairy Books*, 1898, lack the bite and the sinister element as well as the decorative appeal that made Rackham and Dulac so famous. Thomson's washy colours have most in common with the later watercolours of George Cruikshank and the surviving colour work of Leech and Doyle.

But Thomson had another side which is revealed in *The English Illustrated Magazine,* his love and sympathetic treatment of Londoners. In 1886-87 he illustrated an article 'In The Heart of London' filled with very lively cockney studies, gaiety as well as pathos. There is the germ here for a really great illustrator of the contemporary, a humourist of the streets like May, a forerunner of G.L. Stampa in his love of urchins. But it was not to be and Thomson always returned to the minuet, the pointed toe in the buckled shoe, the raised fan that his Edwardian admirers demanded.

A younger artist who must have been influenced by the Thomson manner was Sir J. Bernard Partridge, 1861-1945, better known as the cartoonist of *Punch.* Partridge, who in the 1880s was still making up his mind whether to be an actor or an artist was clearly struck by Thomson's work in *The English Illustrated Magazine.* He records this and elsewhere Thomson acknowledges a sort of friendly rivalry between them although they were little more than acquaintances. Partridge stressed Thomson's success in making the settings 'the compliment of his figures'[17] and he went on to achieve this in his own work. In 1893, he illustrated Austin Dobson's *Proverbs in Porcelain,* and made very accomplished pen drawings of the eighteenth century characters, somewhat dramatically gestured, but benefiting from his theatrical background in the knowledge of their costumes. Partridge's flirtation with the *dix-huitième* was brief and he was soon back in the weekly issues of *Punch* and illustrating the novels of F. Anstey.

The closest disciples of Thomson were definitely the Cambridge brothers, C.E. and H.M. Brock. These brothers (there were in fact three but the other was not a period illustrator) worked quietly in their Victorian house over a span of more than fifty years. Like a pair of latter-day Cheeryble Brothers, the Brocks worked away with tremendous industry and overflowed their benevolence into hundreds and hundreds of printed pages between 1891 and 1953. In some ways they were strangely isolated from other artists and unaffected by current trends, so that the pen drawings they were producing in the full flower of the 1890s were largely the same as those coming from their boards in the 1930s. Although they used the Cambridge college libraries for picture research and the City obviously gave them inspiration, they remained totally outside the priggish academic circles there and indeed the Fitzwilliam Museum still contains not a single work by either of them.

C.E. Brock, 1870-1938, began to draw for books in the early 1890s and found his feet completely after illustrating *Gulliver's Travels* in 1894 and *Annals of The Parish* and *Pride and Prejudice* in 1895. The eighteenth century proved to be his métier, but this was only after considerable experience with contemporary subjects in magazines like *The Quiver, The Strand* and *Pearsons.* In 1898 he made sixteen full page drawings for *The Vicar of Wakefield* in the *Illustrated English Library* series and the same year saw the appearance of Dent's Novels of Jane Austen, a collaboration between the brothers. Although they are usually bracketed together, the brothers can be very different artists. Usually C.E. Brock's line is more delicate than his brother's, more refined on the page surface and closer to Thomson or Abbey. His compositions are always excellent but his range was probably not so great, he did far less *Punch* work than H.M. and nothing after 1910. The older brother's drawings are much scarcer than H.M.'s, a strange fact considering they so often worked and published together. They followed their more famous predecessors step by step, not only *The Vicar of Wakefield* like Abbey and Thomson, but *Jackanapes,* 1913, which Caldecott had made a best-seller and *Sir Roger de Coverley* and *Old Christmas,* the chestnuts of the period book market. Between 1903 and 1911 they worked on various stories by Charles Dickens, mostly the minor works where their benign drawings would most accord with the words. In the 1930s C.E. was to illustrate several Dickens novels but with the reduced number of plates that followed publishing economies. When one has mentioned Whyte-Melville's novels, Lamb's belles-lettres, the adventure stories of R.D. Blackmore and Baroness Orczy, the school stories of Ian Hay and Desmond Coke, one has covered the whole range of Brock illustrating. It could not be described as very powerful work but it is full of the quiet charm of England before 1914, when the leisured reader wanted his book well pictured but in a rather decorative way.

The Brocks certainly score over some of their forerunners and contemporaries in matters of accuracy. The brothers had clothes specially made up to provide examples for their costume subjects and they used the model to some effect in the mobility and action of their figures. There are also references to their working collection including a great many costume prints and fashion plates of the Regency period.[18] They both collected antiques and the 'props' in their houses, Georgian bureau bookcases, mirrors, chairs and candlesticks, recur again and again in their illustrations. The more authoritative note creeping in came not only from the more favourable climate in the country towards Georgian England, but from the more knowledgable approach of antique dealers. The Brocks were very friendly with a number of these and in 1906 their interest saw them jointly employed as illustrators on Mallett's *History of Furniture,* making ink drawings of the originals in the dealer's Bath shop. Extensive files were kept of furniture and interiors, carefully clipped from *Country Life* and entered under the appropriate date.

Another pair of illustrators whom the Brocks would surely have heard of, were led by *their* historical appetites into a completely different field, that of writing. Percy Macquoid, 1852-1925, the artist son of *The Illustrated London News* decorative illustrator, T.R. Macquoid, gradually turned from pictures with period settings to the history of furniture. Trained at Heatherley's and in France, Macquoid moved from equestrian illustrations in *The Graphic* and costume pieces illustrating Scott to the three-dimensional theatre stage and finally to the museum. His critical illustrator's faculties were brought to bear on the cabinet-making of the early Stuarts, Queen Anne and the first three Georges and he produced in 1905 the earliest modern history of English furniture. It was in the form of four large volumes dealing with oak, walnut, mahogany and satinwood furniture.

Fred Roe, 1864-1947, began his career as a black and white figure artist on *Fun* and *Judy,* but developed a fascination for historical genre painting. Working with Stuart and Georgian settings he became absorbed by their detail and began to draw each object for its own sake. The result of this research was a number of books including *Ancient Coffers and Cupboards,* 1902, and *A History of Oak Furniture,* 1920, and many articles in *The Connoisseur* incorporating his own sketches. Both these illustrators cum writers were avid collectors of antiques and this brings out yet another strand of influence in the return to the eighteenth century. The reproduction of art objects by photograph in sale catalogues and books, which had begun in the 1880s in earnest, was paralleled by a school of French still-life illustrators who represented the art of the *ancien régime* with amazing virtuosity. The chief of these was Jules Jacquemart whose tightly drawn lines and careful rendering of light effects on polished surfaces, made the boulle, Sèvres plaques and gilded bronze of Louis Quinze live with an astonishing brightness. Other artists of this school include C. David and E. Prignot, Charles Goutzviller and Henri Toussaint, all capturing the spirit of the age in their drawings. These books were not only aids to interior decoration and material for the artists' shelves but slowly established a more critical response in the reader who opened up a new volume of Molière's *Femmes Savantes* or Fanny Burney's *Evelina,* fully illustrated.

This historical awareness was a tribute to the sophistication of the public too, and might have been a step closer to the text, but it did not always work for the illustrator's advantage. From the 1890s onwards there was a taste for having the original illustrations wherever possible, the frank and caricatured etchings of George Cruikshank, the lively work of 'Phiz', not reproduced in their original medium it is true, but having enough of the irreverent Regency in them to be authentic! As mentioned, Thackeray led the way in 1885 with the *Standard Edition* and the same became true of John Leech's plates to R.S. Surtees' novels and the whole early cycle of Dickens' novels. Chapman and Hall's *Household Edition,* which should have been a pace setter with its fine wood engravings from drawings by Fred Barnard, Charles Green, J. Mahoney, G.B. Frost and E.G. Dalziel, came too late in the 1860s tradition to become a classic. In fact it was not published in the 1860s at all but in the 1870s with some weak work by 'Phiz' being the only contributions of an original collaborator. Macmillan's reprint of the first editions in 1892 contained the original 'Phiz' plates as did the succeeding *Gadshill Edition* of 1897, with the illustrations printed from the original steel plates. The early years of the century saw *The Biographical Edition,* 1902-03, *The Fireside Dickens,* 1903-07, *The Authentic Edition,* 1901-05, and *The National Edition,* 1906-08, all with their inimitable characters seen through the 'Georgian' eyes of 'Phiz'. In some editions, the *London Edition,* 1901-02, and *The Authentic Edition,* colour was applied to the 'Phiz' and Cruikshank illustrations, giving them the same weak and washy look as contemporary illustrators' works. *The London Edition* has alternate plates in colour only, a weird compromise.

It was hardly surprising that such a bout of nostalgia and antiquarianism should have its counterpart in landscape. Following the Caldecott and Greenaway vistas of unspoilt and sylvan countryside, a group of artists emerged who recorded actual places, old inns, castles and towns with the same touch of romance as if they had been part of an Austen or Goldsmith story. It is really Caldecott, this time as the painter of manor houses and old farmsteads, that lies behind this lichen-encrusted phase of illustration, but sentimental watercolourists like Samuel Read and illustrators such as Nash with his *Mansions of the Olden Time,* must have helped. Hugh Thomson's co-artist in the successful *Coaching Days and Coaching Ways* had been Herbert Railton and it was he that stood at the head of this particular group.

Herbert Railton, 1857-1910, was an extremely prolific black and white artist whose sensitive pen strokes seem to caress and enliven the odd shapes and textures of ancient

*Figure 91. 'Old Tabard Inn' by Herbert Railton.*

decaying buildings. He was, moreover, an artist who did not attempt portraits of his streets and buildings but presented a pavement-eye view of life, searching out little nooks and crannies, hens scratching in inn yards, curious vistas through narrow alley-ways, pumps and pub signs, but always somewhere the tremulous line and dark presence of ivy or virginia creeper, choking and covering the walls (Figure 91). Sometimes the artist gives an effect of sparkling light by using broken lines, an idiosyncracy that can become just a mannerism. *Coaching Days* remains his masterpiece, the backs of these old hostelries from Bath to Guildford and from Smithfield to Chester, really do breathe out an infectious enthusiasm for the travels of Pickwick and Weller. And yet the stable yards are empty and one has to look across the page for Thomson's group of ostlers or the departure of a four-in-hand to be completely convinced. Railton contributed to the *Jubilee Edition* of *Pickwick* in 1887 and illustrated *The Select Essays of Dr Johnson,* 1889, *The Poems and Plays of Goldsmith* in the same year and editions of Peacock and Leigh Hunt in 1891. The latter part of his career was given over to the illustration of old buildings in travel books and his reliability and expression of regional characteristics must have paved the way for many city and cathedral series in the 1900s. Although influential, he had only one outstanding pupil, Holland Tringham, who died in 1909. He worked principally for *The Illustrated London News* and *The English Illustrated Magazine* and his penwork is often much sharper than that of his teacher.

The highly evocative world of Cecil Aldin, 1870-1935, fits neatly into this story, for he was not merely an equestrian illustrator of great talent but a humourist and a lover of the eighteenth century who could set his scenes against a highly convincing background. He has few equals in creating the atmosphere surrounding old buildings and peopling the thoroughfares and squares with recognisable but untheatrical bustle. His studies of old houses and timber-framed inns grow naturally out of the coloured paper and chalks that he generally used. His chalk drawings of the transport of the day, the flying stagecoach or the crawling heavy waggon are more believable than most of his contemporaries, because he knew his horse flesh from first hand and had studied the prints of James Pollard, Henry Alken and W.H. Pyne. His student days with the animal painter Frank Calderon were of tremendous advantage to him, although their result can be rather mixed. Some early contributions of comic animals to *The English Illustrated Magazine* are sickeningly sentimental and he can be very cloying in his portraiture of dogs and cats. But he is the true successor of Leech, even more than Caldecott was, and the full blooded hunting sketches and rapid line drawings balance perfectly with the knots of rustic figures to give a concentrated whiff of country air. Aldin's recognition after *Two-Well-Worn Shoes*, 1899, and a *Dog Day*, 1902, brought him a wider popularity than some of the other illustrators dealt with. He lent his strong outline work to advertising and produced a run of *Cecil Aldin Picture Books* from 1908; his *tour de force* in period genre is probably *The Romance of The Road*, a verbal and visual echo of Outram Tristram, which did not appear until as late as 1928. This has come to rely on contemporary engravings as much as on Aldin's own sketches of Georgian life. The present writer's favourites are four little books published by Heinemann in 1909, *Bachelors, Wives, The Widow* and *Jorrocks On 'Unting*. The texts are culled from various sources in Steele and Washington Irving as well as Surtees and the coloured plates show Aldin at his best, whimsical, mischievous and slight, some of the figures in pen-line and wash reminiscent of Hugh Thomson. The *Jorrocks* book has real affection in the sketches of this ebullient and over-weight sportsman, three years later Aldin illustrated *Handley Cross,* one of the most delightful of author-artist combinations before 1914. A similar rose-tinted view of the olden time came from the writer C.G. Harper, 1863-1943, who issued a number of coaching books between 1892 and 1900, the subjects usually well imagined and well drawn.

The most outstanding pencil artist in this group was probably Alfred Parsons, 1847-1920, a landscape painter with a great knowledge of flower and tree forms and with a strong sense of decoration. He was a natural partner with E.A. Abbey in *The Quiet Life* which has been mentioned and produced on his own the fine illustrations to *Old Songs*, 1889, and *The Sonnets of William Wordsworth*, 1891, his silver grey pencil drawings are quite unmistakable for softness and texture. Joseph Walter West, 1860-1933, is roughly comparable in the beauty of his draughtsmanship; he used his Quaker background for genre subjects and leaned heavily on the eighteenth century for both content and style in the book work that he undertook.

Probably the last and most important figure to come under this spell was Beatrix Potter, 1866-1943, whose enthusiasm for Georgian drawings was mentioned at the beginning of the chapter. Helen Beatrix Potter, the daughter of a wealthy Londoner, grew up from a rather lonely childhood to be a talented and painstaking amateur artist, mainly through her own exertions. She had the advantage of leisure, a book-filled house and at least some contacts with artists, provided by her father's wide circle of friends which included Millais. Beatrix's entry into illustration was through natural history; she soaked herself in the wood engravings of Bewick, pored over the illustrations of Mrs. Hugh Blackburn and kept tame dormice to make studies from. Visits to the Zoo resulted in accurate animal drawings and her preoccupation with making watercolours of fungi, gave her a colour discipline worthy of the Pre-Raphaelites. But there was another influence, as she confided to her biographer. 'I have always had the greatest admiration for Caldecott as an artist. At one time I tried in vain to copy him. We had all his picture books as they came out and my father bought many of his original drawings at a sale after Caldecott's death.'[19] In the secret journal that she kept from about 1882, the young artist shows an astonishing maturity in criticising the work of contemporary painters, she is rigorous in her search for good drawing and natural colouring, which she feels is lacking in all but the Pre-Raphaelites. Her solitary existence was relieved by letter writing and what was second nature to the Victorians, the illustrated letter, long, rambling histories of the household with amateur and not so amateur drawings in the margin. It is hardly surprising that when all these talents finally fused together, that uniquely fresh, translucent and charming art of Beatrix Potter came to be born. This innocent and inward world of childhood, only conceivable from a lover of nature and a secretive sketcher and writer, burst out onto the public in the series of books that have become household names. From a tentative offer of Christmas cards in the 1890s, came the private printing of *Peter Rabbit* in 1900 and its acceptance by Warne & Co. in 1902. The stream of books that followed from *Squirrel Nutkin,* 1903, to *Little Pig Robinson,* 1930, show a faraway world which is nevertheless realisable, inhabited by recognisable animals in period settings. Beatrix Potter's eye was relentless in pursuing a world that children and even adults might believe in, the waistcoat in *The Tailor of Gloucester,* 1903, was copied from an eighteenth century embroidered one in the Victoria and Albert Museum, the kitchen scenes with their friendly antique articles and furniture were copied from her own cottage and the landscapes were those of her beloved Lakes.

Edmund J. Sullivan, 1869-1933, one of the most brilliant illustrators to appear during the Edwardian years, turned his attention to eighteenth century literature on a number of occasions. Sullivan's amazing versatility and stature as a black and white draughtsman is only just being recognised and his prolific but in some ways unfulfilled career is beginning to be charted. His father was an artist and his brother was the talented cartoonist who created the character of 'The British Working Man'. Sullivan's training was on *The Graphic* and *The Pall Mall Budget,* but in some senses his work was too large scale for magazine illustrations, it was too big in concept and too grand and generous in line and colouring to accompany anything but the strongest texts. In 1896 he illustrated *The School For Scandal* and *The Rivals* for Macmillans in his own individual style and in 1898 Thomas Carlyle's *Sartor Resartus* with its witty studies of dress. In this, as in the Tennyson *Dream of Fair Women,* 1900, he stylises and synthesises his historic costume leaving an impression of both the period of the writing and his own period. The ink drawing (Figure 92) accompanying the juvenilia poem 'Airy Fairy Lilian' is based on the style of 1830 in waistline and shoulder width, but the fine accordion pleating and the appearance of chiffons are typical of 1899, the year in which the drawing was made! Sullivan is on record as disliking books that were simply sought out by illustrators for their costume appeal alone. His commission for illustrating Carlyle's *French Revolution* in 1908 was greeted by a friend with the comment 'a fine chance for costume' which angered him.[20] The result is anything but window dressing, a powerful combination of fact and symbol in which the period staging, though clear, does not distort the meaning. Sullivan's oeuvres also included *A Citizen of the World,*

1904, and the inevitable *Vicar of Wakefield,* 1914, comparatively straightforward tasks compared with many of the subjects he tackled. Sullivan's popular appeal seems to have wained after 1920, ironically enough at a time when his drawing skill was at its peak, and surviving sketches show this introspective man at his most interesting. He deserves to be better known and better understood for, as P.V. Bradshaw wrote of him, he was that rare thing among illustrators 'a literary Epicure and an Artist of distinction'.[21]

It would hardly be possible to think of a more different artist from Sullivan than Jack B. Yeats, 1871-1957, and yet he was engaged on illustrating similar subjects at about this time. The younger brother of W.B. Yeats, he started as a magazine illustrator in London before moving back to Ireland and becoming one of the country's most distinguished landscape painters. He was always involved with the illustration of character, both for comic journals like *Punch* and *Fun* and in the broadsheets issued under his own imprimatur. In 1895 he illustrated

*Figure 92. 'Airy Fairy Lilian' by E.J. Sullivan.*

200

for Messrs. Dent's *Pocket Series*, Defoe's *Life and Adventures of Captain Singleton* and five years later the same author's *Romance and Narratives*. Yeats' interpretation was sketchy, bold and rather hard, as unsentimental a view of the eighteenth century writer as one was ever likely to get in the 1890s.

A list of artists working in the eighteenth century idiom between 1880 and 1914 would be endless. It would include T. Blake Wirgman who imitated eighteenth century portraits, Lewis Baumer who revived the subtle effects of pastel in some of his books, Chris Hammond, the illustrator of Edgeworth, Frank Dadd, the gifted cousin of Kate Greenaway, F.D. Bedford, artist of Dickens and Barrie, W.J. Hodgson, producer of Regency children's books, Carl Scloesser, a follower of Thomson, H.M. Paget, A. Garth Jones, Margaret Jameson, Alan Odle (Colour Plate XIV) and George Belcher.

Such a brief glance over forty years of illustrating cannot hope to be all inclusive, especially as the period 1880 to 1914 proves to have been so rich. It has only been possible to pick up a few threads, which making themselves apparent in architecture, decorative art and fashion, are not always so obvious within the covers of a book. Changing attitudes to the eighteenth century not only reshaped the publisher's list of titles, but altered the artist's standpoint. What had been a highly expressive and individual period of history was softened and mellowed into pure decoration at its worst or into something quite new at its best. The least good artists compromised themselves for the sake of fashion or drew only with accuracy in view; the best, like Beardsley or Sullivan, took the germ of an idea but made the inspiration their own. The origins of the return to the eighteenth century stretched back a long way, but the Edwardians themselves tended to see no further back than the Caldecott and Greenaway *Picture Books*. These bright and charming productions were ideal for nursery ballads and songs, but by 1900 their direct descendants were expected to work alongside the prose of Fielding, Johnson and Scott. E.A. Abbey's drawings were serious and intellectual statements about the books that he was illustrating; E.J. Sullivan and Jack B. Yeats placed an individual interpretation on everything that they touched. In these men, that visual and verbal partnership that was so strong in the eighteenth century, lived on.

*Footnotes*

1. John Harvey, *Victorian Novelists and Their Illustrators*, 1970, p.63.
2. ibid., p.99, illus.
3. John Ruskin, *Adriadne Florentina*, 1872, p.235.
4. Forrest Reid, *Illustrators of The Sixties*, 1928, p.161.
5. G.S. Layard, *Charles Keene*, 1892, p.155.
6. *Scenes and Characters From Dickens*, 1908, p.x.
7. John Ruskin, *The Art of England*, pp.144-145.
8. M.H. Spielmann, *Kate Greenaway*, 1905, p.44.
9. ibid., p.128.
10. ibid., p.133.
11. Joseph Pennell, *Pen Drawing and Pen Draughtsmen*, 1894.
12. The Abbey Collection was sold at Sotheby's on 22 April and 13-14 June 1921.
13. In the possession of the author.
14. Pennell, op.cit., p.228, footnote.
15. M.H. Spielmann and Walter Jerrold, *Hugh Thomson*, 1931, p.15.
16. ibid., p.47.
17. ibid., p.230.
18. C.M. Kelly, *The Brocks: A Cambridge Family of Artists and Illustrators*, 1975, p.128.
19. Anne Carroll Moore, *The Art of Beatrix Potter With An Appreciation*, 1955, p.25.
20. Quoted by Gordon N. Ray, in *The Illustrator and The Book in England 1790 to 1914*, 1977, p.190.
21. Percy V. Bradshaw, *E.J. Sullivan The Art of The Illustrator*, c.1915, p.8.

# Chapter 11

# Collecting Original Illustrators' Drawings

The collecting of original book illustrations has always been a rather neglected subject in this country, a strange fact considering the tremendous diversity of talent in the last one hundred and fifty years and the reputation of the British as bibliophiles. With the exception of a few outstanding collectors such as Sir Harold Hartley, who have concentrated on one period, or scholars like Sir Geoffrey Keynes, who have concentrated on one artist, William Blake, there are no definitive collections of British book illustration. The Victoria and Albert Museum Print Room, which has the most comprehensive group of drawings, acquired them through two bequests, the Ingram Bequest in 1914 and the Harrod Bequest in 1948, rather than with a planned policy and other museums tend to hold isolated examples of home-grown talent or of artists working in a particular medium. These fortuitous acquisitions have netted some remarkable collections, the Dalziel Colection of proof engravings in the Print Room of the British Museum for example or the superb ink drawings for illustration by D.G. Rossetti in the Birmingham City Art Gallery illustrated in this book. But the omissions are even more extraordinary, very few examples of book illustration post 1900 at the British Museum, not a single cartoon by the well-known First World War artist, Captain Bruce Bairnsfather, at the Victoria and Albert.

In 1904, the illustrator and art critic Frank Emanuel summed up his feelings about illustrative work and its impact in Britain like this '. . . in London we are sadly in need of a National Watercolour and Black and White Gallery, for which the best obtainable examples of such work could be procured by gift or purchase, and thereafter exhibited. Stowed away in drawers and cupboards at the British Museum, at the National Gallery, and probably at South Kensington Museum and elsewhere, visible only in driblets after regulated application, is untold wealth of beautiful drawings which should rightly be *displayed* on the walls of such a gallery as is suggested. Beautiful examples of work by living illustrators, both British and foreign, could be obtained for a comparatively nominal sum, and would exemplify a powerful and fascinating development of modern art; which meets the requirements of the day, in its own line, as fully as did those early Italian masters in *their* time, which the nation's art buyers collect so assiduously and at so much cost.'[1] What was true of 1904 is still largely true of our own time, there is still no major comparative collection to help the amateur and foster interest in the subject, there are still no dealers who specialise exclusively in this field. Not for the collector of illustrations the carefully culled rows of watercolours lit by spotlights, rather the odd drawing in the darkest corner of a picture show or a portfolio brought in at the last moment! Given these factors, the enthusiast should not despair but develop his own innate sense of quality and discrimination and make the apathy and ignorance about the subject work to his own advantage. Contemporary illustration is well served by shows at the National Book League and other centres and local museums will sometimes devote a month or two to a particular artist.

The truth is that the book illustration, meaning the original drawing or watercolour by the artist, is neither fish nor flesh. Its apparent slightness eludes the hardened collector of English watercolours and its position outside the cover of a book bothers the librarian; collectors are notoriously conservative and if something does not fit into a category it can usually be ignored! Illustrations also have stiffer competition in their own sphere in Britain than in most other countries, the Frenchman or German who cannot own oil paintings turns instinctively to drawings whereas his equivalent in this country turns automatically to watercolours. For the average British collector a move from the applied arts of antique pottery, glass, metalwork to the fine arts, generally means a move to watercolours and landscape watercolours in particular. It would be ridiculous to ignore this rich tradition stretching from Cozens to Cox with all its ramifications in the art of portraiture, still-life and architecture, but its roots are in the climate and in the strange, atmospheric, changeable and vari-coloured countryside that we all know. Most illustrations on the other hand are figurative, linear and monochrome, they have to rely on their forms alone to appeal to our eye, there is texture in the work but not colour, there is mood rather than atmosphere. The drawings are also intended to be seen in consort or in contrast to a text, so that one is not working alone with the artist in studying them, as would be the case with a landscape watercolour, but the story or poem or description is continually demanding attention. There is also a school of thought which I believe sincerely to be wrong, that does not rate any art associated with commercial ventures very highly. For them the full flow of artistic inspiration is lost if the draughtsman is constricted by publishers, authors and deadlines, the mode seems mechanical and somehow the magic is lost. The problem then is to wean ourselves away from watercolour to ink or wash, to step back from our pervading love of landscape and begin to look at the figure and above all to rid ourselves of the notion of book art as mechanical.

Fortunately our set ideas are beginning to change about all this. The suspicion that black and white art is a pedestrian medium should have been exploded years ago with Aubrey Beardsley and Phil May, but it is really only recently that drawings have gained by being connected with books or magazines rather than the reverse. The Victorian illustrators, who, with a few exceptions have long been out in the cold, are beginning to gain recognition. The last ten years has seen a meteoric rise in the price of minor works by the great names such as Millais, Leighton and Sandys, and a gradual increase of interest in secondary figures such as John Gilbert, John Leech and Richard Doyle in the mid-century and Arthur Rackham, E.J. Sullivan, Byam Shaw and Fortescue Brickdale at the end of it. It is partly a shift of taste but partly a lack of availability of major works to the serious collector who is not simply a broker! This is an acceptance long overdue, for the professional illustrator in the period from 1830 to 1890, not only interpreted, but often created a literary character that became a legend. Our view of Victorian literature is still an illustrator's one. It was the reputation of Robert Seymour, the comic draughtsman, which persuaded a publisher to ask Charles Dickens to write a text to his drawings, launching *Pickwick* on to the world. Although Dickens' description of the fat clubman is detailed, it is really Seymour's and later Browne's corpulent figure in tight gaiters and swallow-tail coat that lives on to the present day and is even continued by current illustrators and contemporary film producers. Similarly the world of *Alice* either in *Wonderland* or *Through The Looking-Glass* remains indelibly that of Sir John Tenniel, the toothy illogicality of the Mad Hatter, the sinister medievalism of the Duchess and the tip-toeing innocence of Alice herself. The visual impression of Sherlock Holmes, deer stalker, Inverness cape and spats, was very much the creation of Conan Doyle's illustrator Sidney Paget, whose wash drawings, recently re-issued, appeared in *The Strand Magazine* in serial form in the 1890s.[2] The best illustrators naturally worked closely with the author's text but it is undoubtedly true that characters such as Fagin, Mr. Jorrocks, the Duke of Omnium and the Lady of Shalott, remain as much the property of their first artists as their authors.

Apart from considering the intrinsic worth of a drawing's literary interest, and most collectors of illustrations are ardent readers, there is the great variety of work obtainable within the subject and its access to the collector. Because of their lack of popularity in the past, illustrators' drawings are still grossly under-valued and have become the refuge of those with narrow purses. It is astonishing to think that a neat early nineteenth century design in pen and ink may be obtained for a tenth of the cost of a watercolour of the same period because it is an illustration and in monochrome. Sometimes a drawing can be obtained for a fraction of the amount of a watercolour by the very same hand and in this same perverse way a classical or religious theme may keep the price down for the modest collector. Book illustrations also have a built-in protection against pure investment collecting, they are rarely showy enough for this sort of buyer and their names are generally not eye-catching. Everybody has met name dropping collectors and it is essential in this as in other fields not to collect names; with illustrations one is in a jungle of minor figures and quality and individuality of style are all that matter.

There are three main periods of book illustration where it is still comparatively easy to collect, the first and last being much easier than that in between. The first one we might call the early Victorian phase although it actually stretches from the 1820s to the 1850s, the second is the great period of black and white art from the 1860s to the 1870s and the third is the heyday of ornament and book design from about 1895 to 1914.

One of the first questions an aspiring collector might ask himself is how do I identify a book illustration? Faced with a drawer of figure studies in a dimly-lit gallery it is not always easy to be certain, but a few general guide lines can be given period by period. All the illustrations of the early Victorian phase were for the copper-plate or the steel engraving and the illustrations to novels and annuals tended to be fairly restricted in size. Most of the designs for them by artists such as Smirke, Westall and Corbould are in pen and ink with grey or sepia washes, the finished drawing often squared up for the engraver (Figure 93). There are very clear indications of light and shade and very clear washed areas with hatching to indicate the latter to the engraver. Facial expressions and gestures are very exact and there is an overall balance in the finish of the drawing which makes it like the cartoon for an oil painting. Frequently you find pencil notes on the edge or on the verso of the drawing, indicating instructions to the engraver or making some comment to the printer about its place in the order of the book. The years 1820 to 1850 were plentiful ones for genre painting and even for genre paintings taken from literature. The distinction between a genuine drawing for illustration and a genre drawing is misleading, but the illustration tends to be more highly defined, more expressive in action and to contain details relative to the

*Figure 93. Original pen and wash illustration by H. Corbould.*

story which a more painterly approach would not have included. The riddle is usually resolved however by the small scale of the illustrations, 2 by 3 inches or 6 by 4½ inches; no genre painter would wish to work for those measurements if he was not engaged on a book.

Drawings from the first decade of the century which were intended for a book may have ornamental borders, swags, decorative cartouches, but this tended to die out before 1820. Illustrations in the following years were generally simple rectangles or landscape shapes but in the 1840s ornament returns in profusion and there is often a good deal of vignette illustration, that is small tightly drawn compositions for page decoration, often conceived in the round and often receding in definition towards the edges like a poorly exposed photograph. Myles Birket Foster was the greatest Victorian master of this in his numerous books of the countryside. Samuel Palmer, a rare enough illustrator, provides a charming example of decoration of this period for Charles Dickens' *Picture of Italy,* 1846 (Figure 94). Both these artists are prohibitively expensive today, but the joy about collecting the ephemeral output of the Victorian book designing world remains that these trifles, borders, initial letters, tiny vignettes by artists such as William Harvey, John Gilbert, H. Anelay, John Franklin and others can be found for reasonable sums, possibly a few pounds.

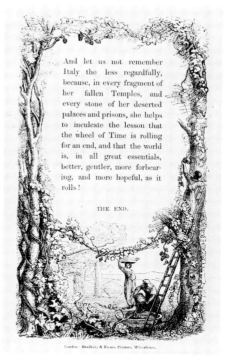

*Figure 94. Vignette illustration and ornament by Samuel Palmer for Charles Dickens'* Picture of Italy, *1846.*

The arrival of wood engraving as the most commercially viable form of illustration from the 1850s has advantages and disadvantages for the collector of drawings. Whereas the nature of copper and steel plate meant that the finished drawing was likely to survive its visit to the engraver, the advent of the woodblock meant that it was not. During the amazingly productive period from 1860 to 1870, many illustrators prepared their final version of a composition on the block and this was cut away when the engraving was made. By no means all the artists of the 1860s drew directly on the wood but as the facsimile wood engravers became more and more adept at their work, the artist was probably encouraged to indicate what he wanted by fewer and fewer directions. One author has argued convincingly on the basis of surviving drawings and versions for the Tenniel *Alice,* that the illustrators were able at this zenith of engraving to use a kind of shorthand when sending their sketches to Swain or the Dalziels, correcting discrepancies only at the first proof stage.[3] This would certainly be supported by the number of sketchy versions by Tenniel, Leech and others of otherwise important works and the occasional appearance of traced copies. The absence of finished drawings is obviously accounted for by the hungry graving tool on the block before the age of photographic reproduction.

In either case it means that completed designs for books and magazines in one of the greatest periods of black and white art are difficult to come by. There are exceptions of course where the artist made a finished sketch before transferring it to the block, where a version was finished but never used or where the block itself remained unused with the clear pen lines still standing out from a whitened ground. Some artists like Tenniel made carefully detailed duplicates of their celebrated cartoons for sale or for friends, men like Fred Walker and G.J. Pinwell often completed watercolours based on illustrative work, but if a collector is a purist, he will find this period a challenge to his time and his resources. Some of the finest drawings by the Victorian Olympians, Leighton, Burne-Jones, Ford Madox Brown,

Sandys, Poynter and Holman Hunt, are preserved because the Dalziel Brothers commissioned their Bible Gallery in the 1860s but did not prepare it until 1880 when drawings were already being photographed on the block. Some of these are illustrated here from the Victoria and Albert Museum, but it is noticeable that very few contemporary drawings exist now outside museums and are even absent from such recent collections as that formed by Gordon N. Ray.

The most important ink drawings which are forerunners of the 1860s group and which have been dealt with in Chapter 5, are Millais' modern episodes. At sales in December 1972, 'Married For Money' made 2,800 guineas, 'Married For Love' 2,200 guineas and 'Married For Rank' 1,100 guineas, the first was later offered for sale at 3,000 guineas. A work from exactly the same group, Millais' 'Accepted' signed and dated 1853, fetched £1,995 in 1967 so that in general terms their value has doubled as they have become scarcer and scarcer. A much earlier but less significant drawing of 'The Lempriere Family', 1845, made only £400 in late 1975, showing how much depends on the date of an artist's maturity even with the

greatest figures. Drawings by other hands during this key period are expensive if they are well-known, Rossetti's brilliant pencil and grey ink study of 'Dante in Meditation' made 2,100 guineas at Christie's in October 1975. At the recent sale of the Dalziel Family Collection at Sotheby's Belgravia on 16 May 1978, some works by a famous artist were undervalued. G.J. Pinwell's 'The Goose', the original pen drawing for Wayside Posies, 1866-67, made £280. Considering that this was a work for one of Pinwell's most important books, was very finished and such an opportunity is unlikely to recur again, it could not be thought of as expensive (Figure 95). The appearance of colour on a drawing greatly increases its price so that an excellent pencil sketch by Houghton, sold in 1976, made £120 because there were slight colour washes, pure pencil might have kept it below £100.

*Figure 95. 'The Goose', by George Pinwell for* Wayside Posies, *1866-67, 5¼ins. x 5½ins. (13.3cm x 14cm).*

The drawings most commonly seen from this date are therefore preparatory studies in pencil, details worked up in ink over pencil and the penultimate compositions where elements of both are combined. The last stage is invariably missing as we see in the complete series of Luke Fildes' designs for 'The Duet' published in *Once a Week* for 30 January 1869. The subject was a domestic one so the artist begins by making a study of a standing female from the life, barely indicating the fireplace and the presence of a pianist (Figure 96). Then the pianist figure takes greater shape and the lines and the lights of the piano are indicated in a spirited sketch (Figure 97). The folds of the standing figure's dress are worked upon in greater detail in a larger scale than is necessary (Figure 98) and at last the composition is brought together in the page size (Figure 99). There is then a jump from the penultimate sketch to the completed wood engraving in reverse, the finished drawing having been cut away to complete it (Figure 100).

These sort of drawings in preliminary pencil or ink are readily found at auction and in galleries and are very nice to own. It is usually not too difficult to discover in a reference book the main magazines for whom these artists worked and to locate the wood engraving for which the studies were made. (A fairly exhaustive list of works is included after each biographical paragraph in the second section of this volume.) It would be useful to acquire studies that stand up as works of art in their own right as these obviously do, there are quite

206

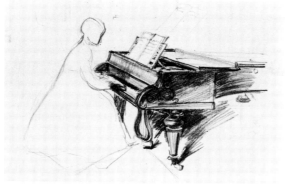

Figures 96-100. Preparatory drawings and finished illustration for 'The Duet' by Luke Fildes 1844-1927, published in Once a Week, 1869.

a number of very slight pencillings on gallery walls which are over-priced simply because of the names attached to them. Gleeson White, the first historian of this period who concentrated more on the wood engravings themselves than on the drawings, suggested that collections of the former should be made, removed from the books for comparative purposes! I have seen two such collections, presumably formed on this advice, Forrest Reid's files contained in boxes at the Ashmolean Museum, Oxford, and an anonymous collection on the London market with each print stamped with the artist's name. It would be a heinous crime to dismember these books and magazines today, but it is fascinating to form a library of reproduced works alongside ones own collection of originals and many of the books and specially the magazines are still easily obtainable.

The characteristic of this period is the very fine penwork and very exact statements of texture and 'colour' in black and white, prepared for engraving. Good examples of this are found in artists like Charles Keene and George du Maurier, both of whose drawings are still in good supply. Keene's sketchy designs have much charm but he is such a beautiful draughtsman that it is a pity to miss the more finished *Punch* jokes when they emerge; du Maurier's drawings fall short in composition after about 1880, his 'aesthetic' jokes of the 1870s are usually the most highly prized. John Leech has a looser pencil and his slight sketches are easy to find. More attractive than these are the finished watercolours from *Punch* subjects, large, airy and not too finished either, they seldom rise above £100 in price.

Between the 1870s and the 1880s great steps were taken in process printing which greatly alter the style and the abundance of the drawings. Although drawings were photographed on the woodblock earlier, the idea was in general use from only about 1868 and was followed by line blocks and eventually the half-tone in the 1880s. As greater and greater demands were made on the illustrator to provide bigger and bigger blocks for the magazines, a system of parallel ruling was introduced which as well as taking away some of the slavishness of drawing for the engraver, enabled the artist to enjoy a greatly extended tonal range. This was increased by the half-tone process by which the picture on the page was made up of a great quantity of dots, screened from the original negative and varying in concentration between light and dark areas of the subject. This method meant not only that finished drawings were no longer slaughtered but that they changed from the meticulous pen strokes of the 1860s to a broader and more oily style reminiscent of painting. Artists like Charles Green, Seymour Lucas, William Hatherell and William Small painted their illustrations on stiff card, filling out their effects in thick grey washes with overlaid chinese white, giving the whole surface a creamy texture almost like impasto.

Some artists drew their illustrations in oil on board and the writer has seen one sketch prepared for illustration in oil on canvas, but this is unusual. It can be said that all these media are universally recognisable as illustrations because of their monochrome effects and their ample size for the pages of *The Graphic, Black & White, The Sphere* and *The Illustrated London News.* Although this period does not have the panache of the 1860s or 1890s, it is a good one to collect, the designs are superbly executed and much material can still be found. Comparatively recently a pair of William Hatherell *Graphic* drawings were seen for about £20 and a fine figure piece by Edward Killingworth Johnson for £18, grossly undervalued considering the pure draughtsmanship in them.

The 1890s saw an explosion of new black and white talent which was led by those champions of the art, Aubrey Beardsley and Phil May. The illustrators of that decade were the first to grow up with the half-tone and the line block and make it work for them, so the surviving drawings are typified by a purity of line and a sense of breathing space and air. This is a field that should be limitless for the collector, the fact that it is not, is due to the fashion for art nouveau which has attached itself to nearly everything produced at the time, irrespective of its real origins. The art nouveau book has always attracted attention and, perhaps because of this, the *fin de siècle* is one of those rare periods where the original illustrations have rivalled or surpassed the books themselves in price. The drawings of Aubrey Beardsley are now of extreme rarity and even the slightest sketches from his hand, initial letters, page decorations and tiny vignettes, make hundreds of pounds. A small grotesque figure from *Bon Mots* made over three hundred pounds in 1976, a price that would probably be doubled today. Any illustrators who imitate the Beardsley manner or are self-consciously of the 1890s in their subject matter, have steadily risen in price together with the master. This is particularly true of men like Charles Robinson and his brothers William Heath and Thomas, whose earlier works are decorative and elaborate and can be expected to fetch well over a hundred pounds. W.T. Horton's rather black studies are also making about the same and S.H. Sime at his most sinister can achieve £500-£600, but very much less for his single figure subjects. The magnificent pen drawing 'The End of All Knowledge' by this artist, which was being offered in a provincial gallery in 1975 for £200, was priced at £650 when exhibited in London in 1977, a quite remarkable jump for an illustrator's drawing in a period of two years. This may well presage a return to higher prices for the macabre and mystical side of black and white art which Beardsley engendered. The Glasgow School, which took some of its inspiration from the Beardsley idiom and is flagrantly art nouveau throughout, has gained tremendous success with collectors in recent years. Sotheby's sale of Miss Jessie M. King's studio on 21 June 1977 was a considerable eye opener to the seriousness beginning to be given to illustrations. A special catalogue was produced, every lot was illustrated and some of the items deserved such cosseted attention;

*Figure 101. 'Percival and The Damsel', original drawing for the illustration in* The High History of the Holy Graal, *1906 by Jessie M. King.*

a marvellously stylised bookplate design in ink on vellum fetched £2,000 and a collection of the artist's views of Paris reached £3,000, but the average for drawings was between £100 and £300 with many charming works below this. The drawing of 'Percival and The Damsel' for a 1903 edition of *The High History of the Holy Graal,* made £700 (Figure 101).

The designs discussed might be considered the cream of the market but there are many other examples which are noteworthy but undervalued. Phil May's illustrations are very variable in quality but the best are very good indeed. His extraordinary industry and amazing output must account for the fact that they are still so plentiful and still obtainable by the most modest collector. The apprentice work of the Australian years can be rather rough, but in his mature period in the 1890s he is supreme and little studies by this great figure artist can still be found for £25 to £50, an absolute necessity in a really comprehensive collection. The other magazine artists and caricaturists should fall into the same pattern but I have noticed that there are many ordinary men such as Lucien Davis and Maurice Greiffenhagen whose work is more expensive when it captures the feeling of the period in a very tangible way.

After 1900, when the Edwardian publishing houses began to turn their attention to grand gift-books, glorious travel books and elaborate children's books, the scene shifts from strong drawing and black and white to luscious effects and bright colouring. The change to colour printing is not always a satisfactory one, type and black and white drawings marry well together, strident colour less so, and even subtle colours compete rather than blend with the text. Apart from this the collector finds himself once more in the multi-tinted jungle of watercolour collecting where the price is immediately increased by one hundred per cent, or more. The world of Arthur Rackham, a very tempting mythical world, has ceased to tempt all but the most daring purchasers. The parchmenty watercolours with their sinewy lines that have frightened and captured the hearts of children for seventy years, have always remained relatively expensive. Ten years ago £60 might have gained you a very nice example of moderate size, in the early 1970s they could still be found for £150. When Sotheby's sold their large watercolour of 'Two Girls' in April 1976, an optimistic estimate placed the probable price at £800: the drawing made £1,232. Most of this artist's watercolour work is still in the £600 to £800 range and rising steadily, the black and white drawings have made a comparable progress. One has to remember when thinking about this artist's original illustrations that first editions of his books are now sold for £250 and upwards. Rackham's pencil sketches and contemporary subjects remain very much cheaper, a clear instance of the nonsensical idea that a designer's 'characteristic' sketches are the only ones that matter! The collector should be able to enjoy and appreciate the unusual in any illustrator's oeuvres, the investor cannot be expected to!

Edmund Dulac (Frontispiece) follows hard on the heels of Rackham in popularity and his watercolours of Eastern romance are very much in demand. A splendid 1906 drawing of

'The Forty Thieves' was sold at Sotheby's in late 1976 for well over £1,000. His cheeky little caricatures and less finished studies are often seen between £50 and £150 however and usually contain that spark of imagination that makes any Dulac work so special. The highly detailed animal watercolours of E.J. and C. Detmold are also among the nicest things in watercolour illustrations, the works by the latter are rarer, although a delightful subject of a panther for one of Kipling's books made only £68 in 1975.

A good example of how the expected element in an artist or a period disturbs its true price might be found in a work by an almost unknown Edwardian, Mrs. Averil Burleigh. A highly elaborate watercolour of 'Motherhood' was exhibited in London in 1977 at the astonishing price of £650; it was an extremely competent piece of work, wonderfully coloured and detailed, but selling on its archetypal Edwardian-ness rather than on its merits as an important illustration. The same exhibition had a series of four watercolours by Byam Shaw of Biblical subjects in modern dress most sumptuously framed, a sort of Rake's Progress in the dress of the *Forsyte Saga*. Period atmosphere breathed out a high price in every line, but a delightful study for a Chiswick Press book by Byam Shaw was only £45.

Colour is not such a barrier to the collector if the artist's work is less known or the subject matter is difficult to assimilate. A case in point is the brilliant watercolour painter of the 1900s and 1920s, Warwick Goble. His filmy translucent watercolours, with their subtle tints and Japanese compositions, are unique in British illustration, but are not noticed by the collectors of Rackham and Dulac. A fine watercolour by him for *Stories of the Pentamerone* was offered for sale by a suburban dealer at £65 in 1978 and two illustrations for his best book, *The Green Willow*, were sold by a bookseller for £140 each in 1975. This does incidentally highlight the fact that it is always best to buy from specialists, drawings from drawings dealers and books from book dealers, rather than vice-versa; unfamiliarity with a subject tends to slightly over-price the items. Another artist working in colour before 1914 was Alan Odle, whose immensely powerful figure study of 'Gulliver Standing to His Full Height' is illustrated here (Colour Plate XIV p.192). This drawing appeared on the market for £80 in 1976 and fulfils most of the requirements for a memorable illustration; it is very dramatically conceived, the drawing is powerful and the concept of Gulliver as a grotesque, everyman figure rather than a sleek mariner is entirely original. Odle and Goble are artists who are just being discovered and their qualities will be properly appreciated in the next few years.

There was still a lot of supporting black and white illustration for all this colour work and it has tended to be almost entirely overlooked. Where are the collectors of H.R. Millar's beautiful virtuoso pen drawings or the figures of Paul Hardy or the wash and ink work of W. Rainey, Dudley Hardy and Jacomb-Hood? They are still unconsidered and obtainable at a very low price indeed. E.J. Sullivan, whose draughtsmanship is stronger and more individual than Rackham's, seems to have remained loyal to pen in an age of colour. Henry Ospovat's short working life probably did not allow him to experiment in this direction. Neither illustrator is appreciated as he should be and their ink works pass through the sale-rooms for between £50 and £100, a negligible sum considering their stature as draughtsmen. Both men developed a very personal style, so did Lawrence Housman whose career as an illustrator stopped short in about 1900. His refined and sensitive pen drawings, inspired by Pre-Raphaelite illustration have a fatal fascination for those who would like an original Rossetti but cannot afford it. His works are therefore rather expensive and the best examples which are like contributions to *Moxon's Tennyson* seen through half-closed eyes, sell on the London market for £300 to £400.

The early 1900s were years in which animal illustration made great leaps and bounds. It is quite striking that between 1890 and 1910, a whole generation of nature artists grew up who combined accuracy with great decorative sense. Foremost among them are the

Detmolds, already mentioned, H. Seton Thomson, Carton Moor Park and Warwick Reynolds; G.D. Armour and Cecil Aldin were also excellent in straight animal studies. These artists are rather overshadowed by Archibald Thorburn, who is really just a careful painter of 'stuffed' birds, and J.G. Millais who brings a greater touch of life to his subjects. A slightly earlier illustrator, J. Wolf, who is comparable to Thorburn in every respect, continues to be totally neglected. Any sketches by Seton Thomson and Park should be eagerly acquired by the collector for their sheer perception of an animal's form and habitat and their break from the tyranny of showing every feather. J.A. Shepherd was a humorous draughtsman who knew his animals well and whose comic animals are nearly credible, never distorted. Louis Wain's cat subjects appeal to a special sort of audience and are grossly inflated in price for that reason. At a recent Sotheby's sale on 21 March 1978, a series of elaborate and large grisaille drawings 'The Seven Ages of Man', all comic cat subjects, made a total of £3,300, one single picture in the series making £550. 'A Quiet Game at Nap', a card party of cats, signed and dated 1894, was sold for £320. Both Cecil Aldin and Harry B. Nielsen do the same sort of drawings even if with less manic intensity and it is difficult to see why their works are not so valued.

The area in which one might begin a collection is so wide that it is a matter of some thought to choose a subject. Specific subjects, stemming from the collector's interests, spring to mind, illustrations of a particular sport, of hunting, fishing or golf, legal or medical topics, royal events, early industry and shipping, house interiors, trades or occupations. A possible line of development would be to take a certain fictional person such as King Arthur, Tom Thumb or Falstaff and try to collect different aspects of them through various artists' eyes. Important collections of *Pilgrim's Progress, The Seasons* by James Thomson and *The Rape of The Lock* have already been made, but it would not be difficult to cull other subjects from literature; the resulting group of drawings would have great intrinsic value as a collection. One of the nicest small collections made recently in London, has taken politics as its theme and includes every sort of caricature and figure drawing from amateur work to the careful pencil of Tenniel. Another distinguished collector of Middle Eastern life has swept the illustrators into his net along with their more famous brothers, the watercolourists, to create an archive of national importance.

As has been mentioned earlier, the collector of illustrations is not primarily a house decorator or a fine art expert. His reasons for collecting at all are often twin-headed, a love of drawing, coupled with a love of literature, a curiosity about history joined with a wish to see it with the eyes of contemporaries, a fascination for a cause which has only been consistently chronicled by these humblest of all artists. It is obvious that such catholicity of taste will result in pictures that are not easy to display together or to display at all. Some drawings will be very small, designed to be seen on the closely-held printed page, others enormous as intended for double pages in Victorian weeklies. The one can hardly be seen against a wall-paper and the other is considerable enough to fight with oil paintings. The collector has to resign himself to having portfolios or presses of drawings that are not normally displayed, but there are plenty of good ink designs that will hold their own in any normal sized room.

A collector would be well-advised to know as much as possible about the method and technique of the drawings he is purchasing as well as the normal practice that illustrators worked by. This sort of information is found, not in their biographies, but in the manuals that they wrote for students. Two excellent books are *How To Draw In Pen and Ink* by Harry Furniss, 1905, which gives information on processes, papers, brushwork, scraping out and thumb shading, and a later publication *The Art of Illustration* by E.J. Sullivan, 1922; the same artist's book *Line An Art Study,* 1921, is also well worth looking at.

The main London auction rooms hold regular sales of drawings but the items in our category are usually included in watercolour sales at Sotheby's Belgravia, Christie's South Kensington and Bonham's. They are sometimes sold separately if they are considered important enough but more often are lotted together or even parcelled. Sotheby's Chancery Lane rooms are also an outlet for book illustrations and one should not assume that they only appear in the drawings catalogues. Chancery Lane holds twenty or more major book sales a year and at least two will generally include a good selection of original drawings. Several dealers run mailing lists and these are an invaluable guide to one's knowledge of the subject as well as a useful aid to collecting.

I have not touched on caricature specifically and this remains a very promising field for the enthusiast. It is if anything less fashionable than pure illustration, perhaps because people are squeamish about sharing their houses with grotesque heads! The successful sale of the large album of caricatures by Robert Dighton at Sotheby's, on 23 February 1978, certainly stimulated interest in this famous contemporary of the highly priced Rowlandson. Dighton, an infinitely less skilled draughtsman, scores on his pleasing colours and interior views, the sale totalled £50,000, indicating that caricatures must be considered a major part of British art. Victorian caricature drawings are still very virgin territory, the work of Tenniel, Sambourne, Partridge and Raven-Hill is to be found for well under £30, the slighter sketches even less. That serious people are starting to turn their attention to this area shows that recognition has been long overdue. One hopes that the breezes will not blow too hard through this backwater before a few collectors have been able to look long and carefully at these orphan children of the British School.

*Footnotes*

1. F.L. Emanuel, *The Illustrators of Montmartre*, 1904.
2. *The Sherlock Holmes Illustrated Omnibus*, 1978, Murray, pp.84-85.
3. Percy Muir, *Victorian Illustrated Books*, 1971, pp.110-111.

# The Dictionary

*SIR MAX BEERBOHM 1872-1956. 'Sir Henry Irving.' Signed. Ink and wash.*
The Garrick Club

# Abbreviations used in The Dictionary

| | |
|---|---|
| AJ | *Art Journal* |
| AL | *Life* by Major J.R. Abbey |
| ARWS | Associate of the RWS |
| Ashmolean | Ashmolean Museum, Oxford |
| AT | *Travel* by Major J.R. Abbey |
| B | Birmingham |
| Barber | Barber Institute, Birmingham |
| BI | British Institution, 1806-67 |
| Bibl: | Bibliography |
| BM | British Museum |
| CL | *Country Life* |
| Colls: | Examples of the artist's work can be found at the listed places |
| Colnaghi | Colnaghi's Gallery, London |
| Contrib: | Contributed illustrations to the listed publications |
| Dulwich | Dulwich College Picture Gallery |
| Exhib: | Exhibited paintings at the listed places |
| FAS | Fine Art Society, London |
| Free Society | Free Society of Artists |
| FRGS | Fellow of the Royal Geographical Society |
| FRS | Fellow of the Royal Society |
| G | Glasgow |
| GG | Grosvenor Gallery |
| Greenwich | National Maritime Museum |
| ICS | Indian Civil Service |
| Illus: | illustrated the listed books |
| ILN | Illustrated London News |
| L | Liverpool |
| Leicester Gall. | Leicester Galleries, London |
| Liverpool | Walker Art Gallery, Liverpool |
| London Salon | Allied Artists' Association. |
| M | Manchester |
| Manchester | City Art Gallery, Manchester |
| Mellon | Mellon Collection, Richmond, Virginia |
| Mercury Gall. | Mercury Gallery, London |
| NEA | New English Art Club |
| New Gall. | New Gallery |
| NG | National Gallery |
| NG, Ireland | National Gallery, Ireland |
| NG, Scotland | National Gallery, Scotland |
| NPG | National Portrait Gallery, London |
| NWS | New Watercolour Society |
| OWS | Old Watercolour Society |
| P | Royal Society of Portrait Painters |
| Paris | Paris Salon |
| Paris, 1900 | Universal Exhibition |
| PRA | President of the Royal Academy |
| PRWS | President of the RWS |
| Publ: | Published but did not illustrated the listed books |
| RA | Royal Academy |
| RBA | Royal Society of British Artists |
| RCA | Royal College of Art |
| RCam.A | Royal Cambrian Society |
| RE | Royal Society of Painters & Etchers |
| RHA | Royal Hibernian Society |
| RI | Royal Institute of Painters in Watercolours |
| RIBA | Royal Institute of British Architects |
| RMS | Royal Miniature Society |
| ROI | Royal Institute of Oil Painters |
| Royal Coll. | Royal Collection |
| RSW | Royal Scottish Society of Painters in Watercolours |
| RWA | Royal West of England Academy |
| RWS | Royal Society of Painters in Watercolours |
| Soc. of Antiq. | Society of Antiquaries |
| SWA | Society of Woman Artists |
| Tate | Tate Gallery, Millbank, London |
| Tooth | Tooth's Gallery, London |
| V & AM | Victoria and Albert Museum |
| Walker's | Walker's Gallery, London |
| Witt Photo | Witt Photographic Library, Courtauld Institute of Art, London |

The name of a town 'Chester', 'Lincoln' under Collections
denotes its Art Gallery unless otherwise specified.

## ABBEY, Edwin Austin   RA ARWS     1852-1911

Black and white artist and illustrator. Born in Philadelphia, 1 April 1852, and was educated at the Pennsylvania Academy of Fine Arts. After studying with a wood engraver, he began work with *Harper's* in New York in 1871 and was sent by them to England in 1878. With the exception of a brief visit to the United States, Abbey made his home in England from that date and became a very prolific draughtsman and illustrator. Specialising in costume and figure subjects, he established a reputation for fineness of execution and accuracy of detail; he was an important link with American drawing for British artists and was influential in introducing the taste for 18th century subjects and themes. He exhibited his first oil painting at the RA in 1890, was elected an Associate in 1901 and Academician in 1902. He worked in his later years at his home in Fairford, Gloucestershire, and died 2 August 1911.

Illus: *Herrick's Poems [1882]; The Rivals [1885]; Sketching Rambles in Holland [1885]; Old Songs [1889]; The Quiet Life [1890]; Comedies of Shakespeare [1896]; She Stoops to Conquer [1901].*
Contrib: *Scribner's Monthly, St. Nicholas [1875-1881]; The Graphic [1880,1883]; Longfellow's Portfolio [1887]; The Scarlet Runner [1899-1900].*
Exhib: RA; FAS, 1888, 1895.
Colls: Ashmolean; V&AM.
Bibl: The work of EAA, *The Artist,* Sept. 1900, pp.169-181 illus.; E.V. Lucas, *Life and Work of EAA,* 1921; R.E.D. Sketchley, *Eng. Bk. Illus.* 1903, pp.36, 64, 87, 144.

*EDWIN AUSTIN ABBEY RA 1852-1911. Study for illustration to Oliver Goldsmith's* She Stoops To Conquer, *1901. Pen and ink, signed and dated, 1885.*
Victoria and Albert Museum

## ABSOLON, John   RI     1815-1895

Painter and illustrator. Born in Lambeth, May 1815, and studied under an Italian, Ferrigi, earning his living as a portrait painter. He then acted as an assistant to Grieve, the theatrical scene-painter for about four years, before going to Paris in 1835. He remained there some years and returned there again for a year in 1839, practising as a miniaturist. In 1850 he assisted T. Grieve and Telbin with their diorama 'The Route of the Overland Mail to India'. He went to the Continent about 1858, visiting Italy and Switzerland. He became a member of the New Water Colour Society in 1835, resigning in 1858 and rejoining in 1861 to become Treasurer. He made drawings of the battlefields of Crécy and Agincourt which were published by Graves, 1860. He died 26 June 1895.

Absolon stands midway between the illustrators of the old tradition like Mulready and the new generation of the 1860s. He was most successful in figure drawing and particularly so in his contemporary genre subjects and his illustrations to children's books, outlined and with very little shadow.

Illus: *Aunt Carry's Ballads For Children [Mrs. Norton, 1847].*
Contrib: *L'Allegro and Il Penseroso [Art Union, 1848] and The Traveller [Art Union, 1851]; Recollections of The Great Exhibition [1851]; Beattie and Collins Poems [1854]; Goldsmith's Poetical Works; Lockhart's Spanish Ballads; Longfellow's Poems [1856]; Rhymes and Roundelayes [1858]; The Home Affections [C. Mackay, 1858]; Favourite English Poems [1859]; Churchman's Family Magazine [1864].*
Exhib: BI; NW; RA; RBA.
Colls: Ashmolean; BM; Leeds; V & AM.
Bibl: Chatto and Jackson, *Treatise on Wood Engraving,* 1861, p.576.

## ACKLAND, F.

Black and white artist contributing humorous figure subjects to *Fun,* 1901.

## ADAM, Emil     1843-

Sporting painter and caricaturist. Born at Munich 20 May 1843, he was principally a painter of horses and came to London in 1885, where he was an instant success among the sporting fraternity. He contributed one cartoon to *Vanity Fair,* 1909.

Colls: Jockey Club.

## ADAMS, H. Isabel

Decorative illustrator contributing to *The Yellow Book,* 1896.

## ADAMS, W. Dacres     1864-

Landscape painter and occasional illustrator. Born Oxford, 1864, and educated at Radley and Exeter College, Oxford. Studied at the Birmingham School and at the Herkomer School, Bushey, before working in Munich. His most important illustrated work is *A Book of Beggars,* published by Heinemann about 1912-13, strongly influenced by the Beggarstaff Brothers. Worked at Lechlade, 1889-91, and Dorchester, Oxon, 1902-3.

Exhib: FAS, 1924, 1925, 1927, G; L, Paris, 1937-9; RA, 1892.

## ADAMSON, Sydney     fl.1892-1914

Painter and illustrator. Born in Dundee and working in London for the principal magazines in the 1890s. He designed a book cover for *The Idler* in 1895 and exhibited at the RA in 1908 and at Liverpool in 1914, at which time he was residing in Paris.

Contrib: *Fun [1892]; The Sphere [1894]; The Yellow Book [1894]; The Pall Mall Magazine; Illustrated Bits; The Idler; The Minister.*
Colls: V & AM.

## ADCOCK, Frederick     fl.1913

Topographical artist and brother of Arthur St. John Adcock, essayist and novelist, for whom he illustrated *The Booklover's London,* c.1913.

## ADCOCK, George H.     fl.1827-1832

Engraver and illustrator working in London. Best known as an engraver of portraits but also engraved an edition of *The Compleat Angler* after G. Hassell and *The Works of Sir Walter Scott,* 1832.

Exhib: RBA, 1827.

215

**AIKMAN, George W. ARSA**         **1831-1905**

Painter and engraver. Born in 1831 and began work as an engraver on leaving Edinburgh Royal High School. For many years he was engaged on engraving portraits for *The Encyclopaedia Britannica,* but also executed portraits, landscapes and etchings. The Victoria and Albert Museum has a series of architectural studies of Edinburgh for an unidentified book. Died 8 January 1905.

Illus: *A Round of The Links [J. Smart, 1893]; The Midlothian Esks, [T. Chapman and J. Strathesk, 1895].*
Exhib: L; RA; RHA, from 1874; regularly at RSA.
Colls: V & AM.

**AIREY, F.W. RN**

Amateur artist contributing drawings of China to *The Graphic,* 1901.

**ALANDY, Sydney**

Figure artist contributing to *Punch,* 1901.

**ALBERT, Charles Augustus Emmanuel, HRH Prince**   **1819-1861**

Consort of Queen Victoria, amateur etcher and draughtsman. Born at Rosenau, 26 August 1819, and married at St. James's Palace 10 February 1840. Prince Albert was an important patron of the arts during the mid-Victorian era, was largely responsible for the idea of the Great Exhibition of 1851 and established at Court a taste for idealistic German art. He is included here as the illustrator of his home country, Gotha. Sketches by him were engraved for *The Illustrated London News* and published in 1845.

Colls: BM; Windsor.

**ALBERT, V.**         **fl.1890-1899**

Fashion Illustrator in watercolour, working for *The English Illustrated Magazine,* 1896-99 and *The Lady's Pictorial,* 1890.

Colls: V&AM.

**ALDER, W. Brooke**

Wash and pen and ink artists contributing to *The English Illustrated Magazine,* 1899.

Colls: V&AM.

**ALDIN, Cecil Charles Windsor**       **1870-1935**

Sporting artist and humerous illustrator. Born at Slough, 28 April, 1870, and educated at Eastbourne College before studying anatomy at South Kensington and animal painting under Frank W. Calderon. He published his first drawing in *The Graphic* in 1891, but continued to do much straight reporting work for the magazines before gaining a reputation for humerous hunting subjects. Aldin's activities as a countryman (he was MFH of the South Berkshire Foxhounds and a member of the Hunter's Improvement Society) enabled him to draw the funny side of horsemanship from inside that exclusive group. His brightly coloured books, the illustrations simply outlined, were the staple diet of country houses between the wars. His ability was in putting the spirit of an incident on to paper rather than the accuracy of it, in this he shared something with Leech and Caldecott who clearly influenced him. He was the ideal illustrator for *Pickwick* and *Handley Cross,* which were issued in 1910 and 1912 respectively. He died 6 January 1935.

Illus: *Everyday Characters [W.M. Praed, 1896]; Two Well-Worn Shoe Stories [1899]; The Fallowfield Hunt [1899-1900]; A Dog Day [1902]; Cecil Aldin's Picture Books [c.1908]; White-Ear and Peter [N. Heiberg, 1911]; 12 Hunting Countries [1912-13]; The Romance of the Road [1928].*
Contrib: *Sporting and Dramatic News [1892]; Good Words; The Ludgate Monthly; The Boys Own Paper [1892]; Pall Mall Budget — Kipling's Jungle Stories [1894-5]; The Sketch [1894]; ILN [1892-1911 (X)]; Pick-Me-Up [1897]; Black and White [1899]; English Illustrated Magazine [1893-7]; Lady's Pictorial; The Gentlewoman; The Queen; The Windsor Magazine; Pearson's Magazine; Punch.*
Exhib. FAS, 1899, 1935.
Colls: V & AM.
Bibl: *C4, Time I Was Dead,* 1934; *Mr. Punch With Horse and Hound,* New Punch Library, 1930.
See illustration (right).

**ALDRIDGE, Sydney**

Illustrator. Contributed to *The Royal Magazine* and *The Windmill,* 1899.

**ALEXANDER, Captain James Edward**

Amateur artist, illustrated his own *Travels to The Seat of War in the East,* 1830, AT 229.

**ALEXANDER, William**         **1766-1816**

Travelling draughtsman and illustrator. Born at Maidstone in 1766, he became a pupil of W. Pars and J.C. Ibbetson before entering the RA Schools. He went to China in 1792, with Lord Macartney's embassy and his drawings of this were published in G. Staunton's official account, 1797. The sketches for this are in the British Museum. He was Professor of Drawing at the Military College, Great Marlow, 1802-8, and Keeper of Prints and Drawings at the British Museum from 1808. He died at Maidstone 23 July 1816.

Illus: *View of the Headlands, Islands etc. of China [1798]; The Costumes of the Russian Empire [1803]; The Costumes of China [1805, AT 534]; Engravings From The Egyptian Antiquities in the BM [1805]; Picturesque Representations of the Dress and Manners of the Austrians [1813]; Picturesque Representations of the Dress and Manners of the Russians [1814]; Picturesque Representations of the Dress and Manners of the Chinese [1814]; Picturesque Representations of the Dress and Manners of the Turks [1814].*
Contrib: *Travels in China [Sir J. Barrow, 1804]; Voyage to Cochin China [Sir J. Barrow, 1806]; Architectural Antiquities [J. Britton, 1804-14].*
Colls: Ashmolean; BM; Fitzwilliam; Leeds; Maidstone; V & AM.

**ALFORD, W.**

Architectural draughtsman, employed on *The Illustrated London News,* 1888-89.

*CECIL ALDIN 1870-1935. A Street Scene in Larissa, ink and wash drawing fron sketches supplied by H.C. Seppings Wright for* The Illustrated London News *1897.*
        Victoria and Albert Museun

**ALKEN, Henry Thomas**                1785-1851

Sporting artists, engraver and illustrator. Born in London in 1784 into a family which became celebrated for its sporting artists and engravers. He is said to have worked as a trainer for the Duke of Beaufort, before studying under J.T. Barker Beaumont, the miniaturist, and he exhibited miniatures at the RA in 1801-2. He moved to Melton Mowbray in 1810 to train horses and eke out a livelihood in decorating trays with hunting scenes. His success really began when he issued prints under the name of 'Ben Tally Ho' in 1813 and he was at his most prolific in the 1820s and 1830s. His work was less interesting after that date and he died in poverty on 8 April, 1851. His son H.G. Alken copied his father's work extensively.

Alken's illustrations and separate prints are lively and very colourful and are closer to the 18th century caricature than to the 18th century sporting print. He enlarged Gillray's idea that the mishaps of hunting could be depicted in the same format as scenes of the chase and his publisher was significantly Thomas M'Lean of 'The Repository of Wit and Humour'. Shaw Sparrow considers that he was most influential in creating a medium in which Phiz, Leech and Caldecott could flourish. His *Sketchbook*, 1823 and *Scrapbook*, 1824, with their pages crammed with nearly related but separated incidents, may have influenced strip stories in the Victorian magazines. His drawings are most often seen in soft pencil with colour washes.

Illus: *The Beauties and Defects in the Figure of the Horse comparatively delineated [1816]; National Sports of Great Britain [1821]; Humorous Specimens of Riding [1821]; Symptoms [1822]; Sketchbook [1823]; Sporting Scrapbook [1824]; Shakespeare's Seven Ages [1824]; Flowers From Nature [1824]; A Touch of the Fine Arts [1824]; Humorous Illustrations of Popular Songs [1826]; Don Quixote [1831]; Life and Death of John Mytton [1837]; Jorrocks Jaunts and Jollities [1837]; The Sporting Review [1842-6]; The Art and Practice of Etching [1849].*

Colls: BM; Fitzwilliam; Leeds; Leicester; V & AM.
Bibl: W.S. Sparrow, *British Sporting Artists,* 1922, with full bibliography, p.209; W.S. Sparrow, *HA,* 1927; A. Noakes, *The World of HA,* 1952; Arts Council, *British Sporting Painting 1650-1850,* 1974.
See illustration (below).

**ALLEN, James**                fl.1881

Figure draughtsman probably working on children's books. A series of pen, ink and watercolour drawings, signed and dated 1881, are in the Victoria and Albert Museum.

**ALLEN, Olive**                fl.1900-1908

Illustrator of children's books. Student at the Liverpool School. 1900. Illustrated *Grandmother's Favourites: Holiday House,* C. Sinclair, 1908, in a pretty and whimsical Regency style.

Exhib: Walker AG, 1900.
Bibl: *Studio,* Vol.20, 1900, p.196; *Studio,* Winter No.1900-01, p.78 illus.

**ALLEN, Walter James**                fl.1859-1891

Genre painter and illustrator. He specialised in comic animals, humanised dogs and children. His work appears in *The Churchman's Family Magazine,* 1864 and in *The Illustrated London News,* 1888-91.

Exhib: RA and other exhibitions 1859-61.

**ALLEN, Rear-Admiral William**                1793-1864

Amateur artist. Lieutenant, 1815, commander, 1836, captain, 1842, rear-admiral, 1862. A highly decorated officer who took part in the Niger expeditions of 1832 and 1841-42.

Illus: *Fernando Po [1838, AT 283]; Picturesque Views of the River Niger [1840, AT 284]; The Dead Sea [1855, AT 365].*
Exhib: RA and RBA, landscapes, 1828-47.

*Go breeze that sweeps the orange grove*

*Happy's the love that meets return.*

*I wander'd once at break of day*

*He woo'd he won her simple heart.*

*How imperfect is expression.*

*HENRY ALKEN 1784-1851. Hand coloured engravings to* Illustrations to Popular Songs, *1826.*

217

**ALLINGHAM, Helen   RWS**                                1848-1926
Watercolourist and illustrator. Born on 26 September 1848, the
daughter of Dr. A.H. Paterson, M.D. She attended the Birmingham
School of Design and the Royal Academy Schools from 1867, where
she was influenced by the work of Fred Walker. She visited Italy in
1868 but between that time and 1874, drew extensively for the
magazines. In 1874 she married the Irish poet, William Allingham, one
of the earliest encouragers of the Pre-Raphaelites, and was elected
ARWS in 1875 and RWS in 1890. Her scope as an illustrator was in
cottage and rural life with some portraits. An early success was for the
serial *Far From the Madding Crowd* by ,Thomas Hardy in *The Cornhill
Magazine,* 1874. She died at Haslemere in 1926.

Illus: *A Flat Iron for a Farthing [Mrs. Ewing, 1872]; Jan of the Windmill [Mrs.
Ewing, 1876]; Gentle and Simple [M.A. Paul, 1897]; Happy England [M.B.
Huish, 1903]; The Homes of Tennyson [c.1905]; The Cottage Homes of
England [1909].*
Contrib: *Once A Week [1868]; London Society [1870]; Cassells Magazine
[1870]; The Graphic [1870-74]; ILN [1871-98].*
Exhib: FAS, 1886, 1887, 1889, 1891, 1894, 1898, 1901, 1904, 1908, 1913;
RA; RWS.
Colls: BM; Manchester; V & AM.
Bibl: H.B. Huish, *Happy England as Painted by H.A.,* 1903; J. Maas, *Victorian
Painters,* 1970, p.231; Arts Council, *English Influences on Van Gogh,* 1974-75,
p.53.

**ALLINGHAM, Wallace J.**                                fl.1898-1907
Illustrator of stories for *The Illustrated London News,* 1898.

Exhib: RA, 1902.

**ALLINSON, Adrian or Alfred Paul   ROI RBA**            1890-1959
Painter, sculptor and caricaturist. Born 9 January 1890. Educated at
Wrekin and studied at Slade School, becoming scenic designer to the
Beecham Opera Company. Taught painting and drawing at
Westminster School of Art and designed posters. He contributed
occasional caricatures to magazines, always in black and white with

great economy of line, a good example is that to *The Gypsy,* 1915,
of G.K. Chesterton

Exhib: FAS, 1919, 1939; London Salon, 1913; NEA, 1911-16; RA.
Colls: V & AM.

**ALLISON, R. Gordon**
Topographical illustrator, working for Ingram publications, 1898.

Colls: V & AM.

**ALLOM, Thomas**                                        1804-1872
Architect and topographical illustrator. Born in London, 13 March
1804, and articled to the architect, Francis Goodwin in 1819. He was
a founder member of the RIBA and was associated with Sir Charles
Barry on various buildings. He carried out some of his own designs for
buildings in the London area and died at Barnes on 21 October 1872.
Works are mostly meticulous and in sepia washes.

Illus: *Devonshire Illustrated [1829]; Cumberland and Westmoreland, Scotland
Illustrated, The Counties of Chester, Derby and Nottingham [c.1836]; France
Illustrated [G.N. Wright, 1840]; China in a Series of Views [Rev. G.N. Wright,
1843]; China, Its Scenery, Architecture, Social Habits, Illustrated [c.1843];
Constantinople and Its Environs [1843].*
Contrib: *ILN [1851].*
Colls: BM; Chester; Fitzwilliam; G; Newcastle AG; V & AM.

**ALLON, Arthur**
Architectural illustrator, working for *The Illustrated London News* for
which he supplied drawings of The Crystal Palace, 1851.

**ALMA TADEMA, Sir Laurence**                            1836-1912
Painter. Born at Dronryp, Netherlands, on 8 January 1836. He studied
at the Antwerp Academy and under Baron Leys, but settled in
London in 1870 and very soon became one of the Victorian
Olympians, living in a lavish house in St. Johns Wood and having a
wide circle of students and admirers. He became an ARA in 1873 and

*WILLIAM DOUGLAS ALMOND RI 1868-1916. The Gas Workers' Strike. Chalk drawing for* The Illustrated London News, *January 4, 1890.*
Victoria and Albert Museum

218

an RA in 1879 as well as Member of the OWS in 1875. Alma Tadema was knighted in 1899, received the OM in 1905 and many other honours. His reputation which suffered a decline after his death, has had a revival in recent years mainly due to the taste for slick and highly coloured classical subjects of which he was a master. He arrived too late in this country to benefit from the great period of illustration, but a few examples from the 1880s exist, most notably an India proof of Findusi's *Epic of Kings*, 1882 in the Victoria and Albert Museum.

Colls: BM; Manchester; V & AM.
Bibl: P.C. Standing, *Sir L. A-T.* 1905; J. Maas, *Victorian Painters*, 1970, pp.181-183.

**ALMA TADEMA, Laura Theresa, Lady**          **1852-1909**
Artist and occasional illustrator. Born in 1852, the daughter of G.N. Epps, she was a pupil of Sir Laurence before she married him in 1871. She specialised in scenes of childhood, dressed up in the same classical guise as those of her husband.

Contrib: *The English Illustrated Magazine [1889, Vol. VII, p.625]*.
Exhib: FAS, 1910.
Colls: V & AM.

**ALMOND, William Douglas   RI RBA**          **1868-1916**
Illustrator. Born in London, 28 April 1868, he was educated at King's College and became a Member of the Langham Sketching Club. He joined the staff of *The Illustrated London News* in 1887 and during the next decade did most of his best work for it while acting as an occasional contributor to other periodicals. He was designated 'Special Artist for Character Subjects' in 1891 and it is in social realism that his great strength lies. He was clearly influenced by the earlier generation of realists, Herkomer, Fildes and Holl, but his medium was

*G. AMATO. The Assasination of the King of Italy at Monza, wash drawing for* The Illustrated London News, *1900.*

chalk, adapted to new processes, and more lively than the old engravings. Almond's studies of the workhouses, sweat shops and hospitals of Victorian London have never been surpassed and it is strange that he has never received due recognition. He was also a topographical artist, but these works like his watercolours are much weaker in handling. RI, 1897.

Illus: *Sally Dows [Bret Harte, 1897]*.
Contrib: *ILN [1887-1894]; Good Words [1891-2]; The Sphere [1894]; Good Cheer [1894]; English Illustrated Magazine [1894-99]; Penny Illustrated Paper; Cassells Family Magazine; The Idler; The Pall Mall Magazine; The Windsor Magazine; The Strand Magazine.*
Exhib: Paris, 1900; RA; RBA; RI; ROI.
Colls: V & AM.
See illustration (p.218).

**ALTSON, Abbey   RBA**          **fl.1892-1925**
Painter and illustrator. Working at Swiss Cottage, London, 1902, and at Bedford Park, London, 1903-1925. Worked for *The Illustrated London News*, 1897; *The Pall Mall Magazine; The Windsor Magazine*. His drawings are very clear and photographic.

Exhib: G; Salon, 1892-93; RA.

**AMATO, G.**          **fl.1894-1901**
Special artist for *The Illustrated London News*, 1894-1901, for *The Graphic*, 1901 and for *L'Illustration*. Amato appears to have been a travelling artist for these papers, in Russia, 1894, in Crete, 1896 and in Rome, 1901. He specialised in royal events and did wash drawings in a mechanical, photographic and dull style.

Colls: V & AM.
See illustration (below left).

**ANASTASI, Auguste Paul Charles**          **1820-1889**
French landscape painter. He was a pupil of Delacroix, Corot and Delaroche and specialised in views of Normandy, Holland and Rome. He abandoned painting due to blindness. Vizetelly says that he worked for *The Illustrated London News* in its early years.

**ANDERSON, Martin   see 'CYNICUS'**

**ANDRÉ, R.**          **fl.1880-1907**
Illustrator of children's books. Worked at Bushey, Hertfordshire, 1890-1907. Designed covers for *Old Fashioned Fairy Tales*, Mrs. Ewing, c.1880 and the same author's *Grandmother's Spring* and *Master Fritz*, 1885.

**ANDREWES, Miss D.**
Illustrator of children's books. Working at Folkestone, 1902-1907. Drew illustrations for *The Little Maid Who Danced To Every Mood*, 1908, with Agnes Stringer.

**ANDREWS, Mrs. E.A.   see CUBITT, Miss Edith Alice**

**ANDREWS, George Henry   RWS FRGS**          **1816-1898**
Marine painter and illustrator. Born at Lambeth in 1816 and trained as an engineer. Principal naval artist to *The Illustrated London News*, *1856-1860* and to *The Illustrated Times*, 1859. Worked for *The Graphic*, 1870. OWS, 1878. Died 31 December 1898.

Illus: *Operations at the Pyramids of Gizeh [H. Vyse, 1840]; English Landscape and Views [J.C. Anderson, 1883]*.
Exhib: BI; OWS, 1840-50; RA, 1850-93; RBA.
Colls: Cardiff; Greenwich; V & AM.
Bibl: Chatto and Jackson, *Treatise on Wood Engraving*, 1861, p.598.

**ANELAY, Henry**          **1817-1883**
Landscape painter and illustrator. Born at Hull in 1817 and lived at Sydenham from 1848. He was first of all a portrait illustrator and provided numerous plates for *The Illustrated London News*, 1843-1855 and may have been sent to Constantinople for the paper in 1853. He exhibited in London from 1845 and at the RA, 1858-73.

Contrib: *London [edited by Charles Knight, 1840]; Illustrated London Magazine [1853-54]; The British Workman [1855]; The Band of Hope Review [1861]; Sandford and Merton; Merrie Days of England; Favourite English Poems; Uncle Tom's Cabin [1852]*.
Bibl: Chatto and Jackson, *Treatise on Wood Engraving*, 1861, p.575.

*ANTON VAN ANROOY RI fl.1897-1925. Illustration for 'The Observant Friar' by F.H. Melville, wash drawing published in* The English Illustrated Magazine, *1900.*

**ANGAS, George French** 1822-1886

Topographical illustrator. Born in Durham, 1822, the son of one of the founders of South Australia. He studied anatomical drawing and lithography in London and in 1841 travelled to Malta and Sicily, issuing the result of the journey in 1842. He went to Australia in 1843 and became director of the Sydney Museum in 1851. Returned to England, 1873, and published a book of poems, 1874.

Illus: *The New Zealanders Illustrated [1846-47, AT 588]; Savage Life and Scenes in Australia and New Zealand [1847]; Description of the Barossa Range [1849, AT 580]; The Kafirs Illustrated [1849, AT 339]; Gold Fields of Ophir [1851, AT 582]; Gold Regions of Australia [1851, AT 583]; South Australia Illustrated [1846-47].*
Exhib: RA; RBA, 1843-74.
Colls: BM; Sydney.

**ANGUS, Miss Christine** fl.1899-1900

Children's book illustrator. Student at City and Guilds, 1899, and at Liverpool, 1900. Her work shows a slight Greenaway influence. There is no record of published books.

Exhib: Walker AG, Liverpool, 1900.
Bibl: *The Studio,* Vol.17, 1899, p.188 and Vol.20, 1900, p.196.

**ANNISON, Edward S.**

Illustrator of stories for *The Graphic,* 1912.

**ANROOY, Anton van  RI** 1870-

Born in Holland, but came to England at an early age and spent all his working life here. Principally a painter. Signs V. Anrooy or V.A.

Contrib: *The Dome [1897]; The Parade [1897]; The English Illustrated Magazine [1899]; The ILN [1901].*
Exhib: Brighton; Liverpool; RA; RI.
Colls: V & AM.
See illustration (p.220).

**ANSDELL, Richard  RA** 1815-1885

Animal and sporting painter and illustrator. He was born at Liverpool in 1815 and was educated at the Blue Coat School and the Liverpool Academy. He practised in his native city but moved to London in 1847 and became one of the most successful Victorian sporting artists, collaborating on huge canvases with artists such as T. Creswick and W.P. Frith. ARA, 1861, and RA, 1870. He is a rare illustrator but contributed a few spirited designs to books.

Contrib: *The Illustrated Times [1855-56]; Once a Week [1867]; Rhymes and Roundelayes [1858].*
Exhib: RA from 1840; BI from 1846.
Bibl: Chatto & Jackson *Treatise on Wood Engraving,* 1861, p.598.

**ANSTED, H.**

Architectural illustrator. Worked during 1827 on *Britton's Cathedrals* 1832-36. He exhibited architectural subjects at the RA, 1826.

**ANSTED, William Alexander**

Landscape draughtsman, illustrator and etcher, working at Chiswick from 1888-99. He was one of a number of late Victorian artists who specialised in popular and inexpensive travel books.

Illus: *Rivers of Devon [1893]; The Riviera [1894]; The Coast of Devon [1895]; Episcopal Palaces of England [1895]; The Master of The Musicians [1896]; London Riverside Churches [1897]; English Cathedral Series [1897-98]; The Romance of our Ancient Churches [1899]; Life of Johnson [1899].*
Contrib: *Good Words [1894].*

**APE**  See PELLEGRINI, C.

**APE JUNIOR** fl.1910-1911

Pseudonym of caricaturist working for *Vanity Fair,* 1910-11.
Colls: V & AM.

*GEORGE DENHOLM ARMOUR 1864-1949. Illustration for* Punch, *pen and ink. The Point to Point Season. Yokel (to persevering sportsman who in spite of several falls is doggedly completing the Course) " 'Urry up mister or the next race'll be catchin' you up!"* Author's Collection

**ARCHER, John Wykeham  ARWS**                    **1808-1864**

Watercolourist and topographical illustrator. Born at Newcastle-upon-Tyne, 2 August 1808, coming to London in 1820 to serve his apprenticeship with John Scott, the animal engraver. He worked as an engraver in Newcastle in partnership with William Collard and then in Edinburgh. Finally in 1831 he returned to London to work for W. and E. Finden. He slowly abandoned engraving for watercolour, although he did a great number of wood engravings in the 1840s and carried out many drawings of old buildings for topographical works. He became an ARWS in 1842, and died in London, 25 May 1864.

Illus: *The Castles and Abbeys of England [W.Beattie, 1844]*.
Contrib: *Winkle's Illustrations of the Cathedral Churches [1836-37]; London [Charles Knight, 1841]; ILN [1847-49 (animals)]; Household Song [1861]; Vestiges of Old London; Douglas Jerrold's Magazine; William Twopenny's Magazine.*
Exhib: NWS, 1842-64.
Colls: BM; V & AM.
Bibl: Chatto and Jackson, *Treatise on Wood Engraving*, 1861, p.599.

**ARIS, Ernest Alfred**                    **1883-**

Watercolour artist and illustrator. Born 22 April 1883 and studied at the Bradford College of Art and the RCA; diploma at Bradford, 1900. Art master ICS School, 1909-12. His works were widely reproduced in America, Canada and Australia and he did much commercial work. Contributed children's illustrations to *The Graphic*, 1910.

Exhib: RA; RBA; RI; RWS.
Bibl: *Who's Who in Art 1964*.

**ARMFIELD, Maxwell  RBA**                    **1882-1972**

Painter, watercolourist and etcher. Born at Ringwood in 1882, studied at the Birmingham School and in Paris under Collin, Prinet, and Dauchez. Armfield wrote and lectured extensively. As well as painting, he published *The Hanging Garden*, 1914, and *White Horses* and some books on technique. His only illustrated book is *Sylvia's Tales* by C. Armfield, 1911, which has vignettes of animals and elaborate colour plates.

Exhib: B, from 1902; FAS, 1970, 1971, 1973; L; NAC, from 1907; RA; RHA; RWA; Salon from 1905.
Bibl: *Modern Book Illustrators, Studio*, 1914.

**ARMITAGE, Edward  RA**                    **1817-1896**

Historical and religious painter and illustrator. Born in London in 1817 and in 1835 went to the École des Beaux-Arts in Paris to study with Paul Delaroche. Entered the Houses of Parliament competition and in 1847 his prize-winning painting 'The Battle of Meeanee' was purchased by Queen Victoria. He visited Russia during the Crimean War and painted military subjects on his return. He became an ARA in 1867, RA in 1872, and was Lecturer on Painting at the RA, 1875.

Contrib: *Lyra Germanica [1861]; Pupils of St. John The Divine [1867-68]; Dalziel's Bible Gallery [1880]*.
Exhib: G; L; RA, from 1848-93; Salon, 1842.
Colls: BM; Royal Collection.
Bibl: J.P. Richter, *Pictures and Drawings of EA*, 1897.

**ARMOUR, George Denholm  OBE**                    **1864-1949**

Black and white artist and illustrator. Born in Lanarkshire, 30 January 1864, and was educated at St. Andrews University, Edinburgh School of Art and the RSA, from 1880 to 1888. He worked in London from about 1890 as a painter and illustrator but only achieved wide recognition after his appearance in *Punch*, 1894. During the First World War, Armour commanded the depot of the Army Remount Service and served in Salonica, 1917 to 1919, being awarded the OBE in that year.

His drawings are almost exclusively of sporting and country subjects and many of them derived their humour from the Leech tradition. Armour's penwork was impeccable and he could seldom be faulted on his drawing of the horse. An unusual subject, a bullfight in the Victoria and Albert Museum is reminiscent of J. Crawhall, of whose drawings Armour had a collection. Nevertheless, the artist was criticised by Seaman of *Punch* for being too repetitive and of not introducing enough motor cars into his subjects!

Illus: *Handley Cross [1908]; Foxiana [L. Bell, Country Life, 1929]; Humour in the Hunting Field [1928]; Sport and There's the Humour of It [1935]*.

Contrib: *The Graphic [1892]; The Pall Mall Budget [1893]; Pick-Me-Up [1896]; The New Budget [1895]; The Unicorn [1895]; The Pall Mall Magazine [1897]; The Longbow [1898]; The Butterfly [1899]; Sporting and Dramatic News; The Windsor Magazine; Judge [New York].*
Exhib: FAS, 1924; Leicester Gall.; RSA; RWA.
Colls: Glasgow; *Punch*; V & AM.
Bibl: R.G.G. Price, *A History of Punch*, 1955, pp.176, 205-206.
See illustration (p.221).

**ARMOUR, Jessie Lamont**

Student at Armstrong College, Newcastle, producing designs for illustration in Birmingham School style. No record of published books.

Bibl: *The Studio*, Vol.44, 1908, p.275 illus.

**ARMSTEAD, Henry Hugh  RA**                    **1828-1905**

Sculptor and occasional illustrator. Born in London, 18 June 1828, and studied at the RA Schools. ARA, 1875, and RA, 1879. He was a prolific sculptor as well as a wood engraver and chaser; he carved the south and east panels of the podium of the Albert Memorial and part of the frieze of the Albert Hall. He was a frequent exhibitor of busts and reliefs at the RA from 1851. His illustrations, especially his religious subjects, were rather hard and Germanic, his modern genre subjects could be delightful with a good sense of composition. He died 4 December 1905.

Contrib: *Eliza Cook's Poems [1856]; Good Works [1861]; Sacred Poetry [1862]; Churchman's Family Magazine [1863]; Touches of Nature [1866]; Dalziel's Bible Gallery [1880]; Art Pictures from the Old Testament [1897]*.

**ARMSTRONG, Francis Abel William Taylor  RBA, RWA**
                    **1849-1920**

Landscape painter. Armstrong was born at Malmesbury, 15 February 1849, and although trained for a business career eventually devoted himself entirely to art. He drew for *The Art Journal* and *Portfolio*. He practised in Bristol and died there on 1 December 1920.

Contrib: *Lorna Doone [De Luxe Edition, 1883]; an unrecorded edition of Mathew Arnold's Poems, n.d.*
Exhib: Berlin; Cologne; FAS, 1923; Paris; RBA; RWA.
Colls: V & AM.

**ARMYTAGE, J. Charles**                    **fl.1863-1874**

Figure artist and illustrator. He contributed to *The Cornhill Magazine* and did architectural subjects — perhaps for books.

Colls: V & AM.

**ARNALD, George  ARA**                    **1763-1841**

Landscape painter and topographer. He was born in Berkshire in 1763 and was a pupil of William Pether. Like his master he specialised in seascapes and moonlight scenes. He is best known as a watercolourist and travelled in North Wales with John Varley in 1798 or 1799. He won a prize for his painting 'The Battle of the Nile' and from 1825 did some commissions for the Duke of Gloucester. He died at Pentonville, 21 November 1841. ARA, 1810.

Illus: *The Border Antiquities of England and Scotland [Walter Scott, 1814-17]; Picturesque Scenery on the Meuse [1835, AT 95]; History and Topography of Essex [1836]*.
Exhib: RA, 1788.
Colls: BM; Greenwich Hospital; V & AM.

**ARUNDALE, Francis Vyvyan Jago**                    **1807-1853**

Architect and draughtsman. He was born in 1807 and became a pupil of A. Pugin (q.v.) and accompanied him to Normandy. He studied at the RA Schools in 1829 and in 1831 he went out to Egypt to assist Robert Hay in his archaeological works, later assisting Bonomi and Catherwood, 1831-40. Arundale made many fine architectural studies many of which were exhibited in London on his return, but his books were not a financial success. He married the daughter of H.W. Pickersgill, RA and died in 1854, probably as the result of a disease contracted in the Egyptian tombs.

Illus: *Illustrations of Jerusalem and Mt. Sinai [1837]; Operations Carried on at The Pyramids of Giza, 1837 [Howard Vyse, 1840]*.
Contrib: *Specimens of the Architectural Antiquities of Normandy [1826-28]; Britton's Union of Architecture [1827, AL 7]*.
Exhib: BI; RA.
Colls: Searight Coll.

**ASHLEY, Alfred** fl.1841-1853

Landscape artist and illustrator. Ashley was a draughtsman and etcher of figure subjects working in the style of 'Phiz' but less certain in his drawing and more scratchy in his line. He published *The Art of Engraving*, 1849.

Contrib: *Punch [1841]; Christmas Shadows [1850]; Old London Bridge [G.H. Rodwell, c.1850].*
Exhib: London, 1850-53.

**ASHTON, G. Rossi** fl.1875-1901

Australian artist and illustrator. He appears to have worked in Australia till about 1885 and was for some time a colleague of Phil May on *The Sydney Bulletin*. Came to England and did prolific humorous work for the magazines.

Contrib: *The Graphic [1875, 1885 (Australia)]; Daily Graphic [1890-95]; Lika Joko [1896]; Pearson's Magazine [1896]; St. James's Budget [1898]; Fun [1901]; Illustrated Bits; The Pall Mall Magazine; The Sketch.*

**ASTOR**

Pseudonym of unidentified caricaturist, *Vanity Fair*, 1913.

**ATKINSON, Captain George Franklin** 1822-1859

Son of the artist James Atkinson. Officer in the Bengal Engineers and amateur artist. He was present at the Indian Mutiny and supplied sketches for *The Illustrated London News*, 1857. Published *The Campaign in India*, 1859, AT 486; *Curry and Rice*, 1860, AT 487.

**ATKINSON, John Augustus OWS** c.1775-c.1833

Painter, etcher and illustrator. Born in London about 1775, he was taken to Russia by his uncle, James Walker, in 1784 and was patronised by the Empress Catherine and the Emperor Paul. He returned to London in 1801 and published books on costume and manners of Russia. Atkinson was an accomplished caricaturist and a battle painter, and he visited the site of the Battle of Waterloo in 1815 as a topographer. He was a Member of the OWS from 1808 to 1812. He remained in London until about 1818 but little is known of his subsequent life.

Illus: *Hudibras [1797 (Russian edition)]; Miseries of Human Life [1807]; A Picturesque Representation of the ... Costumes of Great Britain [1807]; A Picturesque Representation of ... the Russians [1812]; Voyage Round the World [1813, AT 1]; Foreign Field Sports [1814 AT 2].*
Exhib: BI; OWS; RA, 1803-33; RBA.
Colls: BM; Dublin; Greenwich; Leningrad; Manchester; V & AM.

**ATKINSON, John Priestman** fl.1864-1894

Humorous black and white artist. Official in General Railway Manager's office, Derby, 1864. Began to draw for *The Derby Ram* and later turned completely to art, studying in Paris and becoming a close friend of Harry Furniss. He was a regular contributor to *Punch* under the name 'Dumb Crambo Junior'. Specialised in comic genre subjects. Signs with monogram JPA.

Illus: *Thackeray's The Great Hoggarty Diamond, Paris Sketch Book, Ballads, [1894].*
Contrib: *ILN [1881, 1884]; The Cornhill Magazine [1883]; Moonshine [1892]; The St. James's Budget; The Backslider.*
Colls: V & AM.
Bibl: M.H. Spielmann, *The History of Punch*, 1895, pp.524-525.

**ATKINSON, Thomas Witlam** c.1799-1861

Architect, traveller and topographer. Born at Cawthorne, Yorkshire, of poor parents and began life as bricklayer and stone carver. In 1827 he settled in London and in 1834 moved to Manchester where he went into partnership with the architect, A.B. Clayton. He designed a number of churches and other buildings in the Manchester area and in 1844 he left England for Hamburg and St. Petersburg, where he abandoned architecture for the life of a painter and traveller. He visited Egypt and Greece and made an extensive tour through Russia, 1848 to 1853.

Illus: *Gothic Ornaments Selected from the different Cathedrals [1829]; Oriental and Western Siberia [1858, AT 530]; Travels in Upper and Lower Amoor [1860].*
Exhib: RA, 1830-42.
Bibl: *Art Journal*, October 1861; *Builder*, XIX, 1861, p.590; H.M. Colvin, *Biog. Dict. Eng. Architects*, 1954, p.47.

**ATTWELL, Emily A.**

Student competitor in *The Studio* book illustration competitions. Working from address in the Mile End Road, London E.

Bibl: *The Studio*, Vol.10, 1897, illus; and Vol.12, 1897, illus.

**ATTWELL, Mabel Lucie (Mrs. H.C. Earnshaw)** 1879-

Artist and illustrator, author of children's stories and verse. She was born in London 4 June 1879 and was educated at the Cooper's Company School. She studied art at the Regent Street Art School and at Heatherley's. In 1908 she married Harold Earnshaw (q.v.), the illustrator, and in 1925 she was elected SWA. She illustrated works by Charles Kingsley, Hans Andersen, Grimm, Lewis Carroll and J.M. Barrie.

Exhib: SWA, 1924.

**AULT, Norman** 1880-1950

Writer and illustrator. Born 17 December 1880 and attended West Bromwich Art School, 1895 to 1900. On leaving he obtained work with *The Strand* and other magazines and collaborated with his artist wife on children's books. He specialised in costume, architecture, furniture and landscape, giving great attention to period details. He worked for the children's annuals *Chatterbox* and *Sunday*. Did little for books after 1920. Close friend of H.R. Millar.

Illus: *Sammy and the Snarleywink [1904]; The Rhyme Book [1906]; The Podgy Book [1907] (all with his wife). The Mabinogion [Lady Guest, 1902]; The Story of an Old Fashioned Doll [J. Connolly, 1905]; Alice in Wonderland [1907]; England's Story for Children [M.B. Williams, 1908]; The Lays of Ancient Rome, [T.B. Macaulay, 1911]; Tennyson, The Children's Poets [1913]; The Seven Champions of Christendom [F.J.H. Darton, 1913]; Caravan Tales [W. Hauff, n.d.]; The Shepherd of the Ocean [G.I. Whitham, 1914]; New Tales of Old Times [W.E. Sparkes, 1914]; Chambers Dramatic History Readers [W.Hislop, 1914-15]; Life in Ancient Britain [1920]; Dreamland Shores [1920]; The Poet's Life of Christ [1922].*
Bibl: *The Artist*, c.1900.

**AUSTIN, Henry**

Topographical illustrator contributing to *The Pall Mall Budget*, c.1890.

**AUSTIN, Samuel OWS** 1796-1834

Watercolourist and topographer. He was born at Liverpool in 1796 and after working as a bank clerk, he took lessons from Peter de Wint. He was a founder member of the SBA and was elected AOWS in 1827 and OWS on his deathbed in 1834. He painted extensively in Lancashire and North Wales but also in Belgium, Holland and Normandy.

Illus: *Views in the East [Elliott, 1833].*
Contrib: *Lancashire Illustrated [1829].*
Exhib: OWS; RA; RBA.
Colls: Ashmolean; Fitzwilliam; Liverpool; Manchester.

**AVRIL, Édouard Henri (called Paul)** 1849-1928

Painter and illustrator. Born in Algiers, 21 March 1849, and studied under Pils and P. Lehmann in Paris. He exhibited at the Salon 1878 to 1884. Avril is included here because he illustrated three lavish books by Octave Uzanne, which were published in England. They are *The Fan*, 1884; *The Sunshade*, 1883, and *The Mirror of the World*, 1890. All the drawings are more French than English and are extremely eclectic and ill-assorted; they make an interesting comparison with contemporary English black and white work.

**AYLING, Florence**

Book decorator in the William Morris style. She contributed headings to *The English Illustrated Magazine*, 1888.

## BACON, John Henry Frederick ARA 1865-1914

Portrait painter and illustrator. Painted the Coronation Portrait of King George V and Queen Mary, 1912. ARA, 1903. MVO, 1913. Died in London, 24 January 1914.

Illus: *Things Will Take a Turn [B. Harraden, 1894]; The Ravensworth Scholarship [H. Clarke, 1895]; The King's Empire [1906]; Celtic Myth and Legend [C. Squire, 1912].*
Contrib: *The Girl's Own Paper [1890-1900]; Black & White [1891-96]; The Quiver [1892]; The Ludgate Monthly [1895]; Cassell's Family Magazine [1896-97]; The Windsor Magazine.*
Colls: BM.

## BADEN-POWELL, Robert, 1st Baron OM 1857-1941

General, Founder of the Scout Movement, sculptor and illustrator. Born 22 February 1857 and after attending Charterhouse, joined the 13 Hussars, 1876; served in India, Afghanistan and South Africa, Assistant Military Secretary in South Africa, 1887-89 and Malta, 1890-93. At the Defence of Mafeking, 1899-1900. Major-General, 1900. Lieutenant-General, 1908. CB, 1900; KCB, 1909; KCVO, 1909; Baronet, 1922. Like many army officers of his generation, Baden-Powell was a talented artist and sculptor. He contributed sketches to *The Graphic* from South Africa in 1891 and from Ashanti to *The Daily Graphic*, 1895. A further sketch of scouting appeared in *The Graphic* in 1910. Died in Kenya, 1941.

Publ: *Pig-sticking or Hog-hunting [1889]; Reconnaisance and Scouting [1890]; Vedette [1890]; Cavalry Instruction [1895]; The Downfall of Prempeh [1896]; The Matabele Campaign [1896]; Aids to Scouting [1899]; Sport in War [1900]; Sketches in Mafeking and E. Africa [1907]; Scouting for Boys [1908]; Indian Memories [1915].*
Exhib: RA, 1907.

## BAINES, Thomas 1822-1875

Artist, explorer and illustrator. Travelled with the British Army during the Kafir war, 1848-51, and accompanied expeditions to North-West Australia, Victoria Falls, the Tati goldfields and the Zambesi under Livingstone. His drawings of African travel appeared in *The Illustrated London News*, 1869.

## BAIRNSFATHER, Bruce 1888-1959

Illustrator, cartoonist and journalist. Born at Murree, India, in July 1888, the son of an army officer. He attended the United Service College and served with the Warwickshire Militia from 1911 to 1914. At the outbreak of war that year he returned to the Royal Warwickshire Regiment and served in France until December 1916. Bairnsfather was already becoming known to the public by his humorous sketches of trench life in the pages of *The Tatler* and other magazines. An amateur artist who worked in the poster style developed by Hassall and others, his individual view of the Front, its cockney humour, its unheroic fortitude and chauvinism, was exactly right for the grim period after the Somme. His pipe-smoking tommy 'Old Bill' typified British determination with his 'If you know of a better 'ole go to it!' Bairnsfather was Official War Artist to the U.S. Army Europe in the Second World War, 1942-44.

Publ: *Fragments From France [6 Vols.]; The Better 'Ole; Bullets and Billets; From Mud to Mufti; Old Bill; Wide Canvas [1939]; Old Bill Stands By [1939]; Old Bill Does It Again [1940]; Jeeps and Jests [1943]; No Kiddin' [1944]; C'est Pour La France; Back to Blighty.*
Coll: Imperial War Mus.

## BAKER, Annie

Artist working at Egremont, Cheshire, and exhibiting at Liverpool, 1890. She contributed to *The English Illustrated Magazine*, 1688.

## BAKER, Colonel Bernard Granville fl.1911-1930

Military painter and illustrator. He worked in London and Beccles, Suffolk and illustrated his own *The Danube with Pen and Pencil*, 1911.

Exhib: L.

## BAKER, Sir Samuel White 1821-1893

Traveller and sportsman. Went to Ceylon in 1846 and remained until 1848. He established an English colony at Newera Eliya and travelled in Asia Minor, 1860-61, Abyssinia, 1861-62, Khartoum, 1862, and to the White Nile in 1864. He received the Gold Medal of the Royal Geographical Society and was knighted in 1866; FRS, 1869. He published in 1855 *Eight Years Wanderings in Ceylon*, AT 415, with his own sketches.

## BAKEWELL, Robert

Illustrated *Travels in the Tarentaise [1823 (coloured acquatints)*, AT 56].

## BALCOMB, J.T.

Illustrator specialising in scientific and biological drawings. He worked regularly for *The Illustrated London News*, 1876-83.

*RONALD E. BALFOUR 1896-1941. Drawing for illustration to Omar Khayyam, published by Messrs. Constable, 1920. Pen and ink.*
Victoria and Albert Museum

**BALFOUR, Maxwell**                                    fl.1896-1907

Painter and draughtsman. Working from an address in Cheyne Walk, Chelsea, 1901-2. He contributed to *The Quarto,* 1896, and exhibited at the NEAC, 1901-2.

**BALFOUR, Ronald E.**                                  1896-1941

Balfour appears to have been working as a book illustrator between about 1910 and 1925. In 1920 he illustrated an edition of *The Rubaiyat of Omar Khayyam* for Messrs. Constable. He frequently designs in pencil in an early art deco style and signs with monogram REB.

Colls: V & AM.
See illustration (p.224).

**BALKIN, Lance**

Portrait illustrator, working for *The Graphic,* 1887.

**BALL, Alec C.**

Illustrator of social realism for *The Graphic,* 1902-5 and 1906-10.

**BALL, Fred H.**                                       fl.1899-1925

Black and white and decorative artist for books. Working in Nottingham, 1899, and at Mapperley, Notts., 1914-25. His style is based on that of the French poster artists and much influenced by designers such as Alphonse Mucha.

Exhib: RA, 1913.
Bibl: *The Studio,* Vol.15, 1899, p.68 illus; pp.144, 295 illus; and Vol.63, 1914, pp.62-63; *Modern Book Illustrators and Their Work,* Studio, 1914, illus.

**BALL, Wilfred Williams**                              1853-1917

Illustrator, watercolourist and etcher. Born in London 4 January 1853. He was from a Lincolnshire family, settled in London, and was placed with a firm of accountants, devoting his spare time to painting and etching and studying at Heatherley's. In 1877 he gave up the City for professional painting, working from Putney, where he came into contact with Whistler undertaking his Thames views. He was a member of the Society of Painter Etchers from 1881 and a member of the Hogarth and Arts Clubs. His work was mainly topographical and landscape and it took him on tours abroad to Italy, 1877, Holland, 1889, Germany, 1890, Egypt, 1893. After 1895 he worked at Lymington and died at Khartoum on 14 February 1917 while working in a civil capacity for the army.

Illus: *Hampshire, Sussex [Varley, 1905].*
Contrib: *The Yellow Book [1895].*
Exhib: FAS, 1899, 1904, 1909, 1912, 1915, 1917; Leicester Gall.; New Gall.; RA, 1877-1903; RE.
Colls: V & AM.

**BANNISTER, F.**

Figure artist. He contributed to *The Strand Magazine,* 1892.

**BARBER, C. Burton**                                   1845-1894

Sporting and animal painter. Born in 1845 and worked latterly at Regents Park, London. He became a Member of the ROI, in 1883.

Contrib: *The Graphic [1882-86 (dogs)].*
Exhib: FAS, 1895; G; L; M; RA; ROI; Tooth.

**BARBER, T. or J.**

Engraver. He engraved views of Scotland and illustrated *Picturesque Illustrations of The Isle of Wight,* c.1830.

**BARCLAY, Edgar**                                      1842-1913

Landscape painter and illustrator. He studied in Dresden, 1861, and in Rome, 1874-75. He seems to have specialised in figure drawing and in illustrating stories of eastern life. Practised from Haverstock Hill, Hampstead, and died there in 1913.

Illus: *Orpheus and Eurydice [H.D. Barclay, 1877]; Mountain Life in Algeria [1882].*
Contrib: *English Illustrated Magazine [1888-91]; The Graphic [1899]; The Picturesque Mediterranean [1891].*
Exhib: G; L; M; New Gall.; OP; RA.

**BARNARD, Frederick**                                  1846-1896

Illustrator. Born in St. Martin's-le-Grand, London, 26 May 1846. He studied at Heatherley's in Newman Street in 1863 and at Paris under Bonnat. Barnard exhibited at the RA from 1866 to 1887, although he freely admitted that he never had the same confidence in oil as in black and white work. He began contributing the latter to *The Illustrated London News* in 1863 and remained until his death one of its most prolific artists. His *forte* was genre subjects and social realism which brought him the admiration of the young Vincent Van Gogh during his English years. He exhibited at the Paris Exhibition of 1878 and at home contributed to *Punch* and Furniss's *Lika Joko.* His Dickens illustrations are powerful, but his best work is perhaps the London sketches of *How The Poor Live* by George R. Sims, published in 1883, and also engraved for *The Pictorial Times.* His superb character drawing has only one fault, that it tends to be humorous when it is not required to be; the figures in the Paris Commune sketches of 1870, *Illustrated London News,* are a case in point.

Barnard was suffocated or burnt to death at Wimbledon on 28 September 1896. His work is usually in pen and ink, sometimes in chalk or wash, signed: F.B.

Illus: *Dickens Household Edition [1871-79], Barnaby Rudge, Bleak House, Sketches by Boz, etc.; Episodes of Fiction [1870]; All Sorts and Conditions of Men [Walter Besant]; The Four George's [Thackeray, 1894]; Armorel of Lyonesse [1890].*
Contrib: *ILN [1863-96]; Punch [1864, 1884]; The Broadway [1867-74]; Cassell's Illustrated Readings [1867-68]; London Society [1868]; Cassell's Family Magazine [1868]; Once A Week [1869]; Good Words [1869 and 1891-92]; Good Words For The Young [1869]; Fun [1869]; Judy [1887-90]; Boy's Own Paper [1890]; Black and White [1891]; Chums [1892]; Sporting and Dramatic News [1893]; Lika Joko [1894]; The Penny Illustrated Paper; Cassell's Saturday Journal.*
Exhib: Paris, 1878; RA from 1866.
Colls: V & AM.
See illustrations (below and p.143).

*FREDERICK BARNARD 1846-1896. One of a series of 'London Sketches' in pen and ink, for George R. Sims'* How The Poor Live, *1883.*

Victoria and Albert Museum

*ROBERT BARNES 1840-1895. A Welsh seller of lace, Llandudno, pen and ink for an unidentified magazine illustration.* Author's Collection

## BARNARD, George

Illustrator and drawing master. A pupil of J.D. Harding, he was a regular exhibitor at London galleries from 1832 to 1884 and became art master at Rugby in 1870. He published a number of books on technique, *Handbook of Foliage and Foreground Drawing*, 1853; *The Theory and Practice of Landscape Painting in Water Colours*, 1855; *Drawing From Nature*, 1856; *Barnard's Trees*, 1868.

Illus: *The Brunnens of Nassau and The River Lahn [1843, AT 61]; A Lady Tour Round Monte Rosa [Cole, 1859, AT 59]*.
Contrib: *ILN [1858]*.

## BARNES, G.E

Illustrator. Working for *The Broadway*, c.1867-74 and exhibiting at the RBA, 1866. Specialised in architecture.

## BARNES, Robert    ARWS                    1840-1895

Painter and illustrator. Worked first at Berkhampstead and later from Ormonde House, Cliveden Place, Brighton. Barnes was among the best of the second rank of illustrators of the 1860s; his drawing was always excellent if it lacks the originality of a Walker or a Pinwell. His range was very much theirs, because he was at his best in rural genre subjects and one of his most important commissions was to illustrate the first serialisation of 'The Mayor of Casterbridge' in *The Graphic*, January to June, 1886. He was elected ARWS in 1876.

Illus: *Sybil and Her Live Snowball [1866]; Gray's Elegy [1868]; A Prisoner of War [G. Norway, 1894]*.
Contrib: *London Society [1862]; Churchman's Family Magazine [1863]; Once A Week [1864]; Cornhill [1864, 1869-70, 1884]; The Leisure Hour [1864]; British Workman [1865]; The Band of Hope Review [1865-66]; The Sunday Magazine [1865-66, 1869]; The Sunday at Home [1866]; Touches of Nature by Eminent Artists [1866]; The Quiver [1867-69]; Idyllic Pictures [1867]; Golden Hours [1868]; Christian Lyrics [1868]; Taylor's Original Poems [1868]; Good Words [1869, 1891]; Cassell's Magazine [1870]; ILN [1872-77]; The Graphic [1880, 1885-89]; Cassell's Family Magazine [1890]; Our Life Illustrated by Pen and Pencil [1865]; The Months Illustrated With Pen and Pencil [1864]; Pictures of English Life [1865]; Foxe's Book of Martyrs [1865]*.
Colls: V & AM; Dorset County Museum.
Bibl: F. Reid, *Illustrators of The Sixties*, 1928, pp.256-258.
See illustration (above).

226

---

## BARNETT, R.C.                                 fl.1798-1831

Painter of landscape and draughtsman. Worked in London and exhibited there at the RA and BI, 1798 to 1821. Published at Manchester in 1831, *The Beauties of Antiquity*.

Colls: Ashmolean.

## BARRAUD, Frances                               -1924

Painter of portraits and genre subjects. Son of Henry Barraud, artist, and nephew of William Barraud, the sporting artist. He studied at the RA Schools, where he won the silver medal, and afterwards at Heatherley's, the Beaux-Arts, Antwerp. Barraud worked from the St. John's Wood area of London and was a frequent contributor to exhibitions. His most celebrated work is probably the original advertisement of 'His Master's Voice'. He died 29 August 1924.

Contrib: *The Graphic [Christmas, 1912]*.
Exhib: M; RA; RBA; RI; ROI; RWA.
Colls: Liverpool.
Bibl: *Who Was Who, 1916-28*.

## BARRETT, C.R.B.                               fl.1889-1930

Topographical illustrator.

Illus: *The Tower [1889]; Essex Highways, Byways and Waterways [1892-93]. The Trinity House of Deptford Strand [1893]; Barrett's Illustrated Guides [1892-93]; Somersetshire [1894]; Shelley's Visit to France [C.J. Elton, 1894]; Chaterhouse in Pen and Ink [1895]; Surrey [1895]; Battles and Battlefields of England [1896]*.
Bibl: R.E.D. Sketchley, *English Book Illustration*, 1903, pp.47, 48, 132.

## BARRIAS, Felix J.                             1822-1907

Distinguished French academic painter who won the *grand prix de Rome* in 1844. He contributed sketches of Italy to *The Illustrated London News*, 1847.

## BARRIBAL, W.H.                                fl.1907-1925

Portrait illustrator. He worked through London agents from 1914 to 1925.

Contrib: *ILN, Christmas [1907]; The Graphic [1911]*.

## BARROW

Wood engraver and illustrator, working in a rather crude and old fashioned style in the second quarter of the 19th century. His chief interest lies in W.J. Linton's claim that he was Charles Dickens's uncle. Charles Knight says much the same: 'His uncle, Mr. Barrow, was the conductor of *The Mirror of Parliament* and sometimes meeting him at the printing-office of Mr. Clowes, he would tell me of his clever young relative . . .' *Passages of a Working Life*, 1865, Vol. 3, p.37.

Illus: *Gulliver's Travels [1864]*.
Contrib: *ILN [1843, Queen Victoria's visit to the Midland counties]*.

## BARROW, Sir John                             1764-1848

Amateur draughtsman. Traveller, secretary of the Admiralty and Founder of the Royal Geographical Society. He contributed to the Encyclopaedia Britannica and wrote his autobiography.

Illus: *A Voyage to Cochinchina [1806, AT 514]*.

## BARTLETT, William Henry                       1809-1854

Topographical illustrator. Born in Kentish Town in 1809 and was apprenticed to the topographer, J. Britton. He travelled on the Continent in about 1830 and made visits to Syria, Egypt, Palestine and America. He died on board ship on his last tour, 1854.

Illus: *Britton's Cathedral Antiquities [1832-36]; Picturesque Antiquities of English Cities, Scotland Illustrated [1838]; American Scenery [1839-40, AT 651]; Walks About Jerusalem [1845]; Forty Days in the Desert [1848]; The Nile-Boat or Glimpses of Egypt [1849]; The Overland Route [1850]; Footsteps of our Lord and his Apostles in Syria, Greece and Italy [1851]; Pictures From Sicily [1852]; The Pilgrim Fathers [1853]; Scripture Sites and Scenes [1854]*.
Exhib: NWS, 1831-33; RA.
Colls: BM; Fitzwilliam; Leeds; V & AM.
Bibl: W. Beattie, *Brief Memoir of WHB*, 1855; J. Britton, *A Brief Biography of WHB*, 1855.

**BARTLETT, William H. ROI**        1858-

Painter. Born in 1858 and studied at the École des Beaux-Arts under Gerome and then with Bouguereau and Fleury. Exhibited at Paris in 1889 and received a silver medal and the Legion of Honour. He published various photogravures and his work was reproduced in *The Art Journal,* 1894-97. His rare illustrations are strongly drawn with the use of thick black ink.

Contrib: *ILN [1887, Vol.XC p.595].*
Exhib: B; FAS, 1892; G; L; M; New Gall; RA; RI; ROI; RWA.
Colls: Auckland; Bradford; Brighton; Leeds; Liverpool; Reading Savage Club; V & AM.

**BARTON, Rose M. RWS**        1856-1929

Watercolourist. Worked in Dublin until about 1903 and then in London specialising in townscapes. She was elected ARWS in 1893 and RWS in 1911.

Illus: *Picturesque Dublin Old and New [1898]; Familiar London [1904].*
Exhib: GG; RA; RBA; RWS from 1889.

**BATEMAN, Henry Mayo**        1887-1970

Comic artist in black and white and caricaturist. Born at Sutton Forest, New South Wales, Australia, 15 February 1887. Returned to England as a child and was educated at Forest Hill House School and at the Westminster and New Cross Art Schools. At a very young age, Bateman was encouraged to go ahead with his career by Phil May and was in the studio of Charles Van Havenmaet for several years before starting to draw for reproduction in 1906. Bateman's inimitable style of humour and line only developed after 1911, when, as he put it, he 'went mad on paper' and drew people how they felt rather than how they looked. His vigorous wholly visual approach was closer to the German work of *Simplicissimus* and Caran D'Ache than to anything in England. His infuriated colonels, gauche little men and haughty dames, spring out of the page with an extraordinary freshness. His art was an infusion to the stuffy pages of *Punch* which had been laughing at social indiscretions rather than with them. Bateman was a master at giving inanimate objects, palpable personality, the complete disintegration of a street in 'Love at First Sight' or the ricocheting chandeliers and twisting columns of 'The Man Who Asked for a Double Whisky in the Grand Pump Room at Bath'. Bateman revolutionised humorous art in Great Britain, making it spontaneous, hilarious and economical. Despite this his success and his failure is in stereotypes, he seldom moved away from Mr. Doolittle's 'middle-class morality' and the sequence of the faux pas. He contributed to almost all the leading weekly and monthly journals and designed several theatrical posters. In later life he was obsessed by Inland Revenue officials, an eccentricity in which he is not alone, and caricatured them mercilessly. Died in Gozo.

Illus: *Scraps [1903]; The Royal Magazine; The Tatler [1904]; London Opinion [1913]; Punch [1915]; The Graphic [1915]; Burlesques [1916]; After Dinner Stories [George Robey, 1920]; A Book of Drawings [1921]; Suburbia [1922]; More Drawings [1922]; Life [1923]; Adventures at Golf [1923]; Reed's The Complete Limerick Book [1924]; A Mixture [1924]; Our Modern Youth [Desmond Coke, 1924]; Colonels [1925]; Reed's Nonsense Verses [1925]; Bateman and I in Filmland [Dudley Clark, 1926]; Further Nonsense Verses and Prose [1926]; The Art of Drawing [1926]; Rebound [1927]; Brought Forward [1931]; Bateman's Booklets [1931]; Fly-Fishing For Duffers [1934]; Considered Trifles [1934]; The Art of Caricature [1936]; H.M. Bateman By Himself [1937]; Spinning for Duffers [1939]; On The Move in England [1940]; Art Ain't All Paint [1944]; Walton's Delight [1953]; The Evening Rise [1960].*
Exhib: FAS, 1962; Leicester Galleries, 1919, 1921, 1936, 1974.
Colls: Annabels; Author; Guards Club; V & AM.
Bibl: Michael Bateman, *The Man Who Drew The Twentieth Century:* The drawings and cartoons of HMB., 1969; John Jensen, *The Man Who and Other Drawings, HMB.,* Eyre Methuen, 1975.
See illustration (right).

**BATEMAN, James**        1814-1849

Sporting artist and illustrator. Born in London in 1814 and exhibited at the RA, BI, RBA, 1840-50. Contributed to *The Sporting Review,* 1842-46. Died at Holloway, 24 March 1849.

**BATEMAN, Robert**

Painter of figures. Exhibited at the RA and Grosvenor Gallery, 1866-89 and illustrated *Art in the House,* 1876.

**BATES, Dewey**        1851-1899

Landscape painter and illustrator. He was born in Philadelphia, USA, in 1851, but settled in England by 1880 and died at Rye, Sussex in 1899.

Contrib: *The English Illustrated Magazine [1887 (figs.), 1888-91 (land.)].*
Exhib: L; M; P; RA; RBA; RI; ROI.

**BATES, Frederick D.**

Illustrator for *The Sketch,* 1895. Worked from Grosvenor Chambers, Deansgate, Manchester, and specialised in chalk drawings of northern subjects. He signs his work F.D. Bates.

Colls: V & AM.

**BATTEN, John Dixon**        1860-1932

Painter and illustrator. Born at Plymouth, 8 October 1860. He studied at the Slade School under Alphonse Legros and began exhibiting pictures at the RA, New Gallery and Grosvenor Gallery in 1886. Batten was probably the best of that group of illustrators who took mythology as the keynote for their work and assisted such popularisers of it as Andrew Lang. His drawings derive partly from the German woodcuts that were admired by Pre-Raphaelites and partly from the arts and crafts book decoration of Morris and his followers. Batten was closely associated with the later Pre-Raphaelites and in particular with the amateur, George Howard, later Earl of Carlisle. Pennell considered that 'he has a keen appreciation of humour, and is

*HENRY MAYO BATEMAN 1887-1970. 'The C.O. – A Man's Man', pen and ink illustration for* Punch, *signed and dated 1917.*     Author's Collection

very intelligent in his handling.' Batten took his inspiration from Celtic, Norse and even Indian legend and fairy tales, his penmanship has close affinities with the Birmingham School.

Illus: *English Fairy Tales [1890]; Celtic Fairy Tales [1892]; Fairy Tales From The Arabian Nights [1893]; Indian Fairy Tales [1893]; More Celtic Fairy Tales [1894]; More English Fairy Tales [1894]; More Fairy Tales from The Arabian Nights [1894]; A Masque of Dead Florentines [1895]; The Book of Wonder Voyages [1896]; The Saga of the Sea Swallow [1896]; Dante's Inferno [1933].*
Colls: Author; V & AM.
Bibl: J. Pennell, *Pen Drawing and Pen Draughtsmen,* 1894, p.316; *Studio,* Winter No. 1900-01, p.58 illus.; R.E.D. Sketchley, *English Book Illus.,* 1903, pp.109, 110, 158; *Modern Book Illustrators and Their Work,* Studio, 1914; B. Peppin *Fantasy Book Illus.,* 1975, p.185 illus.
See illustration (below).

*JOHN D. BATTEN 1860-1932. Illustration of 'The Hunter Finds His Wife' for The Swan Maiden, pen and ink, c.1895.* Author's Collection

## BATTY, Lieutenant-Colonel Robert  FRS  1789-1848
Topographer and illustrator. He was the son of a surgeon who was also a landscape painter and was educated at Caius College, Cambridge. He entered the Grenadier Guards in 1813 and served in the Peninsular War and at Waterloo, where he was wounded. He spent the remainder of his life in travel and published numerous books illustrated from his own drawings.

At the Mentmore sale in May 1977, the unprecedented price of £40,000 was paid for more than sixty original drawings for Batty's *Hanoverian and Saxon Scenery,* 1829.

Illus: *A Sketch of the Late Campaign in the Netherlands [1815]; An Historical Sketch of the Campaign of 1815 [1820]; French Scenery [1822]; Campaign of the Left Wing of the Allied Army . . . [1823]; Welsh Scenery [1823]; German Scenery [1823]; Scenery of the Rhine, Belgium and Holland· [1826]; Hanoverian and Saxon Scenery [1829]; Six Views of Brussels [1830]; A Family Tour Through South Holland [1831]; Select Views of the Principal Cities of Europe [1832]; The Mutiny and Piratical Seizure of H.M.S. Bounty [1876].*
Exhib: RA, 1813-48.
Colls: Gibraltar Mus.; Nat. Mus., Wales; Wolverhampton.

## BAUERLÉ, Miss Amelia  R.E.
Illustrator of children's books and decorator. Working from Willesden, 1894-1907.

Illus: *Happy-go-lucky [1894]; A Mere Pug [1897]; Allegories [1898]; Sir Constant [1899]; Glimpses from Wonderland [1900]; Tennyson's The Day Dream [1901].*
Contrib: *The English Illustrated Magazine [1895-97]; The Yellow Book [1897].*
Exhib: L; RE; RI.
Bibl: R.E.D. Sketchley *English Book Illus.,* 1903, p.14.

## BAUGNIET, Charles  1814-1886
Painter, lithographer, engraver and illustrator. Born at Brussels, 27 February 1814, and after studying at the Brussels Academy he became a very succesful portrait painter and illustrator. He settled in London for some time after 1841 and had wide popularity, publishing a portrait of the Prince Consort. He contributed to *The Illustrated London News,* 1851. Died at Sèvres, 5 July 1886.

Exhib: BI, 1847-70; RA.
Colls: BM; Brussels.

## BAUMER, Lewis C.E.  1870-1963
Pastellist and illustrator. Born 8 August 1870, educated at University College School and studied at St. John's Wood Art School and Royal Academy School. Baumer is chiefly remembered for his black and white work during the 1920s and 1930s and he was a prolific contributor to *Punch* and other weekly magazines. He also painted portraits and flower pieces in oils, pastel and watercolour, was a member of the Pastel Society, the Royal Institute of Painters in Watercolours and regularly exhibited with them. All Baumer's drawings are beautifully executed in pen, even if they lack contrast and are in natural succession to Du Maurier, the humour lying in the letter-press rather than in the line; he is the classic suburban artist. Earlier Baumer drawings are often tinted and in softer line than his later work, all reveal an affinity with 18th century French drawings which he admired. He illustrated a number of children's books between the Wars.

Illus: *Jumbles [1897]; Hoodie [Mrs. Molesworth, 1897]; Elsie's Magician [1897]; The Baby Philosopher [1898]; The Story of The Treasure Seekers [E. Nesbit, 1899]; Henny and others [Mrs. Molesworth, 1898-1900].*
Contrib: *The Queen [1892]; The Pall Mall Magazine [1893]; Pall Mall Budget [1894]; The New Budget [1895]; The Unicorn [1895]; Pick-Me-Up [1895]; The English Illustrated Magazine [1896-97]; The Sketch [1896-1901]; St. James's Budget [1898]; Illustrated Bits; The Idler; The Minister; The Royal Magazine; The Graphic [1910-11]; Punch [1912].*
Exhib: FAS, 1913, 1924; Liverpool; RA; RBA, 1892-93; RI.
Colls: Author; V & AM.
Bibl: *Studio,* Vol.30, 1902, pp.233-239; R.E.D. Sketchley *English Book Illus.,* 1903, pp.99, 159; R.G.G. Price *A History of Punch,* 1955, pp.206-207.

## BAXTER, William Giles  1856-1888
Caricaturist. He was born of English parents in the south of Ireland, where his father had a small business. The venture was not successful and the family moved to America but later returned to England where the father died leaving the widow in difficult circumstances. The young Baxter was apprenticed to a Manchester architect, but at the end of his indentures decided to give it up in favour of black and white work. His first attempt was produced at the age of twenty-one, a series of lithographed pictures entitled *Buxton Sketches.* Early in 1879, he established a satirical weekly in Manchester called *Comus* later changed to *Momus,* which featured among other things a remarkable series of life-size heads, 'Studies From Dickens'. This weekly was not long-lived and Baxter moved to London and with an artist friend concentrated on designing humorous and political Christmas cards. At this point, he met Charles H. Ross, newspaper proprietor and amateur cartoonist, who had started a journal *Ally Sloper's Half Holiday,* loosely written round an imaginary character 'Ally Sloper'. Baxter was able to take Ross's rather feeble drawings and turn them into the lovable but monstrous 'Sloper' who soon became a Victorian legend. He had added to Ross's spindly and bottle-nosed 'Sloper', the props of battered hat, enormous brolly and shaggy dog which were to go with him for a generation and make him instantly recognisable.

Baxter's penwork and detailing, the inheritance from the architectural days, were meticulous, his studies of politicians, frequently introduced, brilliant. His great importance was that he foreshadowed 20th century cartoons, sustaining his public issue after issue with, in Pennell's words, 'a mystic and symbolic meaning . . . only to be comprehended by his constant followers'. Pennell adds that he was the most original caricaturist of his period and it was a sad day for British illustration when, after the first few numbers of a new publication, *Choodle,* Baxter died of consumption on 2 June 1888. He signs his work W.G. Baxter or WB (monogram).

Illus: *Comus* or *Momus [1879]; Ally Sloper's Half Holiday.*
Contrib: *Judy [1886]; The Graphic [1887-88]; Choodle [1888]; C.H. Ross's Variety Paper [1887-88].*
Colls: V & AM.
Bibl: *The Star,* July 1888; *The Graphic,* 4 August 1888, p.114 illus.; J. Pennell *Modern Illus.,* 1903; J. Pennell, *Pen Drawing,* 1895; J. Thorpe, 'A Great Comic Draughtsman', *Print Colls Quart.,* 1938.

### BAYARD, Émile Antoine                 1837-1891
Painter and draughtsman. Born at La Ferté-sous-Jouarre on 2 November 1837. He was a pupil of Cogniet and worked for most of the major French magazines including *Journal pour rire, L'illustration, Journal des Voyages, Bibliothèque rose.* In England he worked for *The Illustrated London News,* 1889 and *Cassell's Magazine,* 1887.

Exhib: Paris, 1853-61.
Colls: Pontoise; Rouen; Saintes; Saint-Étienne; V & AM.

### BAYES, Alfred Walter    RE RWS          1832-1909
Painter and draughtsman. Born at La Ferté-sous-Jouarre on 2 most of his life in London. Bayes was a second generation Pre-Raphaelite follower and specialised in illustrating fairy stories and children's books. He was killed by a motor cab in 1909.

Illus: *What the Moon Saw [1866-67]; Original Poems [Taylor, 1868]; Old Fashioned Fairy Tales [Mrs. Ewing, c.1880].*
Contrib: *Golden Light [1864]; London Society [1865]; The Sunday Magazine [1866]; A Round of Days [1866]; The Boys' Own Magazine; Aunt Judy's Magazine.*
Exhib: B; BI, 1859-67; G; L; M; RA; RBA, 1861-; RE; RHA; RI, 1890-1902; ROI; RWS.

### BAYLE, Gertrude E.
Artist working in Margate, contributor to *The Studio* title page competition.

Bibl: *The Studio,* Vol.8, 1896, p.253 illus.

### BAYNES, Philip
Humorous illustrator, specialising in comic strips. *The Graphic,* 1910.

### BEACH, Ernest George                    1865-
Portrait and landscape painter and lithographer. He lectured on art and worked in Holland, Belgium and France.

Contrib: *The English Illustrated Magazine [1890-91, 1897 (topography)].*
Exhib: G; L; NEA; RA; RI; ROI.

### BEALE, Evelyn                    fl.1906-1925
Illustrator of children's books, watercolourist, working in Edinburgh in 1907 and at Glasgow, 1925.

Illus: *The Apple Pie [Jack, 1908].*
Exhib: G; RSA, 1906-24.

### BEARD, Dan-Carter                    1850-
American illustrator, who succeeded C. Dana Gibson as President of the Society of Illustrators, U.S. He studied under Sartrain and Carroll Beckwith at the Art Students' League, New York, and is included here as the illustrator of English editions of Mark Twain's works, notably *A Connecticut Yankee At the Court of King Arthur,* 1889, and *Tom Sawyer Abroad,* 1894.

### BEARD, Frank-Thomas or Francis       1842-1905
American illustrator. He was born in Cincinnatti on 6 February 1842 and became one of the most celebrated illustrators of the American Civil War and a Director of *Illustration* and a frequent contributor to *Harper's Weekly;* he is included here as an occasional artist for *The Illustrated London News.*

### BEARDSLEY, Aubrey Vincent          1872-1898
Book illustrator, caricaturist, poster-designer and novelist. Born at Brighton on 21 August 1872 and was educated at Brighton Grammar School. A close-knit family group consisting of a weak father, a dominant mother and a much-loved sister, gave Beardsley that strange love-hate relationship with women which tinges his pictures and gives his sexual allegiances a weird character. He was ailing at school, unable to play games, but developed his own aloof arrogance as a witty and spirited caricaturist. Beardsley's circumstances allowed for no formal training and on leaving school he became a clerk to the Guardian Life Insurance Company in London. He began to admire the prints of the Italian Renaissance and among contemporaries the work of Burne-Jones (q.v.). This led to a meeting with the painter and some encouragement resulting in his attending evening classes at the Westminster School of Art. A visit to Paris in 1892 brought him into contact with the mainstream of French art and the posters of Lautrec. Later the same year, he received a windfall commission from Messrs. Dent to illustrate their new edition of Malory's *Le Morte d'Arthur,* the job that gave him independance to work wholly as an artist. Lewis Hind, the architect of *The Studio* was so impressed by the artist's work that he asked Pennell to write about him ir the first number of it, 1894, publicity that immediately placed him in the front rank.

From 1894 to 1896, Beardsley was in his hey-day, these were the years of *The Yellow Book, The Rape of the Lock* and *The Lysistrata of Aristophanes,* and Wilde's *Salome.* Beardsley's identification with Wilde in the public mind was such that he was damaged by the Wilde scandal of 1895 and lost his art-editorship with *The Yellow Book.* But it was temporary, and in the following year he began on *The Savoy* a successor publication run by Arthur Symons and was engaged on Illustrations to *Mademoiselle de Maupin* and *Volpone.* From 1895, Beardsley's early diagnosed tuberculosis worsened, bringing discomfort and lassitude. After advice from London specialists, he was moved to Mentone where he died on 16 March 1898 at the age of twenty-five.

Beardsley's influence stretches a long way beyond his short life, its linear effects were to recur in architecture, textiles, in the applied arts right up to the 1920s and in a host of major and minor book illustrators' work. He received inspiration from various sources, Japanese prints, the Italian masters, the Pre-Raphaelites, 18th century books, but he remained quintessentially just Beardsley. He was the high priest of aesthetic black and white art, arriving at the moment when half-tone and photogravure were perfected, stretching them to the limit. It was part of the tension in the designs that made them at once astounding and repellant, the menacing presences of androgonous figures, the sickly appearance of over ripe rococo decoration and the melancholy of Harlequin, give his work its disturbing eroticism. In an interview he said, 'If I am not grotesque I am nothing', *The Idler,* Vol.11, p.198.

His various styles can be divided into three groups; an entirely linear style like that of a bas-relief with black and white contrast, a dotted effect as in *The Rape of the Lock* and the later mannerism of *Mademoiselle de Maupin* where line and wash are used with intermediate tones. Apart from his international reputation, Beardsley united book decoration and illustration in this country and gave it credibility with serious artists of the *avant-garde.*

Illus: *Past and Present [Brighton School magazine, 1887-89]; The Bee [1891]; Evelina [cov.]; Malory's Le Morte d'Arthur [1893-94]; Bon Mots [1893-94]; Pastor Sang [1893 (frontis.)]; The Wonderful History of Virgilius the Sorcerer of Rome [1893]; Keynotes series [1893-96 (frontis., cov. & tail)]; Young Ofeg's Ditties [Hansson, 1895 (tail)]; Lucian's True History [1894]; Pagan Papers [Kenneth Grahame, 1894]; Salome [Oscar Wilde, 1894]; The Barbarous Britishers [1895 (frontis. & tail)]; Plays [John Davidson, 1894, (frontis.)]; The Cambridge ABC [1894 (frontis.)]; Baron Verdegris [J. Quilp, 1894]; Today [1894]; The Works of EA Poe [1894-95]; Earl Lavender [John Davidson, 1895]; Sappho [1895]; The Thread and The Path [1895 (frontis.)]; A London Garland [1896]; The Rape of the Lock [1896]; The Life and Times of Madame Du Barry [1896]; Verses [Ernest Dowson, 1896]; The Parade [1897]; A Book of Bargains [Vincent O'Sullivan, 1896]; The Pierrot of the Minute [1897]; Scenes of Parisian Life [1897]; The Souvenirs of Leonard [1897]; Mademoiselle de Maupin [1898]; A History of Dancing [1898]; Volpone [Ben Jonson 1898 (illus., cov. & frontis.)]; The London Yearbook [1898].*
Contrib: *Pall Mall Budget [1893]; The Studio [1893-95]; Pall Mall Magazine [1893]; The Idler [1894].*
Posthumous books: *The Early Work of Aubrey Beardsley [1899]; The Second*

Book of Fifty Drawings by Aubrey Beardsley [1899]; Five Drawings Illustrative of Lucian and Juvenal [1906]; A Portfolio of Aubrey Beardsley's Drawings [1907]; The Later Work of Aubrey Beardsley [1901]; The Uncollected Work of Aubrey Beardsley [1925].
Colls: Ashmolean; Barber Institute; Birmingham; Brighton; BM; Cecil Higgins Art Gallery, Bedford; Fitzwilliam; NPG; Reading Lib.; Sheffield; Tate; V & AM.
Bibl: *The Studio,* Vol.1, No.1, 1893; Vol.13, 1898, pp.252-263; Robert Ross *AB,* 1909; A.E. Gallantin, *AB Catalogue of Drawings and Bibliography,* 1945; Brian Reade, *B Studio Vista,* 1967; B. Reade and F. Dickinson, *AB, Exhibition at the V & AM,* 1966.
See illustrations (below and right).

*AUBREY VINCENT BEARDSLEY 1872-1898. Frontispiece to Walt Rudding's* An Evil Motherhood, *1896.*

*AUBREY VINCENT BEARDSLEY 1872-1898. The fourth tableau of* Das Rheingold, *1896, pen and ink.*                    Victoria and Albert Museum

**BEATRICE, H.R.H. The Princess**                    **1857-1944**
Youngest child of Queen Victoria, born 14 April 1857, and married 1885 H.R.H. Prince Henry of Battenberg. She was an amateur artist and produced *A Birthday Book Designed by Her Royal Highness The Princess Beatrice* London, 1881. This has borders of flowers, insects and berries in colour lithography from her designs. She died 26 October 1944.

**BEAUCÉ, Jean-Adophe**                    **1818-1875**
Military painter. He was born at Paris on 2 August 1818 and went on many military expeditions to Algeria, Syria and Mexico and was present at the siege of Metz. He contributed to *The Illustrated London News,* 1859-60 and 1862, including sketches of Garibaldi. Died at Boulogne, 13 July 1875.

**BEAUMONT, J. Herbert**
Amateur bookplate designer, working at Hessle, East Yorkshire.
Bibl: *The Studio,* Vol.10, 1897, p.274, illus.

**BECKEN, A.L.**
Contributor to *The Ladies Pictorial,* 1895.

**BEDE**
Pseudonym of caricaturist contributing two cartoons to *Vanity Fair,* 1905-6.

**BEDE, Cuthbert (The Rev. Edward Bradley)**                    **1827-1889**
Author and illustrator. Born at Kidderminster in 1827 and was educated at University College, Durham, 1848, taking a licenciate in theology, 1849, ordained 1850. He held various Midland curacies before becoming Vicar of Denton, Peterborough, from 1859-71. He was subsequently in the livings of Stretton, Oakham, 1871-83, and Lenton with Harby, 1883-89. He learnt wood engraving from George Cruikshank but remained very much the amateur, illustrating his own books, *Mr. Verdant Green* and others in a jolly and careless style. He was one of the first humorous illustrators to satirise photography. He died at Lavington in 1889.

Illus: *The Adventures of Mr. Verdant Green, an Oxford Freshman [1853-56]; Little Mr. Bouncer [c.1877 (child's book)].*
Contrib: *Bentley's Miscellany [1846]; Punch [1847-56]; ILN [1851 and 1856]; The Month [1852]; The Illustrated London Magazine [1855]; Churchman's Family Magazine [1863].*
Colls: BM.
Bibl: M.H. Spielmann, *The History of Punch,* 1895, pp.191-195.

**BEDFORD, Francis Donkin**                    **1864-**
Illustrator. He was born in London in 1864 and trained as an architect at South Kensington and the RA Schools. He was articled to the church architect, Sir Arthur Blomfield RA, but turned his attention to illustration in the 1880s and gained a wide popularity in the realm of children's books and as a landscape illustrator. He practised in the

Kensington area until 1914 and was working at Wimbledon in 1925.

Illus: *Old Country Life [1890]; The Deserts of Southern France [1894]; The Battle of the Frogs and Mice [1894]; Old English Fairy Tales [1895]; A Book of Nursery Rhymes [1897]; The Vicar of Wakefield [1898]; Henry Esmond [1898]; A Book of Verses For Children [E.V. Lucas, 1898]; The Book of Shops [E.V. Lucas, 1899]; Four and Twenty Tailors [E.V. Lucas, 1900]; The Original Poems of Taylor and O'Keefe [1903]; Two are Company [Louise Field, 1905]; Old Fashioned Tales [E.V. Lucas, 1905]; A Night of Wonder [1906]; Forgotten Tales of Long Ago [E.V. Lucas, 1906]; Runaways and Castaways [E.V. Lucas, 1908]; Maggie, A Day Dream [Lady Algernon Percy, 1908]; Anne's Terrible Good Nature [E.V. Lucas, 1908 (cover)]; Peter Pan and Wendy [J.M. Barrie, 1911]; The Magic Fishbone [C. Dickens, 1921]; Billie Barnicole [G. Macdonald, 1923]; At the Back of the North Wind [G. Macdonald, 1924]; The Princess and The Goblin [G. Macdonald, 1926]; A Cricket on the Hearth [C. Dickens, 1927]; Count Billy [G. Macdonald, 1928]; A Christmas Carol [C. Dickens, 1931].*
Exhib: RA, 1892.
Bibl: R.E.D. Sketchley, *English Book Illus.*, 1903, p.106, 159; B. Peppin, *Fantasy Book Illustration*, 1975, p.185 illus.

## BEDWELL, Frederick LeB.

Assistant Pay-Master on *H.M.S. Actaeon,* coast of China survey, 1862. Accompanied *H.M.S. Nassau* on Admiralty Survey of South America, 1869, contributed sketches to *The Illustrated London News.*

## BEECHEY, Henry W.   FSA                                          1870

Painter and explorer. He was the brother of Sir William Beechey and became Consul-General at Cairo, 1816. He explored the Nile with his brother, G.D. Beechey, and surveyed the coastline from Tripoli to Derna, 1821-22. He was elected FSA in 1825 and is believed to have died in New Zealand.

Illus: *Expedition to Explore The Northern Coast of Africa [1828, AT 305].*
Exhib: Sea pieces at RA and BI, 1829-38.

## BEER, John-Axel-Richard                                    1853-1906

Illustrator. He was born at Stockholm on 18 January 1853, but went to America as a young man in 1869 and stayed there for five years. He travelled to Russia and worked as an artist at the Imperial Court, eventually settling in London where he worked for the principal magazines. Beer was an excellent figure artist, at his best in free pen and wash sketches with effective atmospheric backgrounds.

Contrib: *Journal Illustré de Leipzig; The Graphic [1886 (horses)]; Black and White [1891]; The Sporting and Dramatic News [1894]; ILN [1900].*
Colls: V & AM.

## BEERBOHM, Sir Max                                          1872-1956

Caricaturist, novelist and broadcaster. Born in London on 24 August 1872, the youngest son of Julius E. Beerbohm and younger brother of Sir Beerbohm Tree, the actor. Educated at Charterhouse and Merton College, Oxford, the young Max was already cutting a figure in his undergraduate days as a wit, caricaturist and man-about-town. He referred to Oxford as 'the little city of learning and laughter' and this admirably sums up his attitude to life and to his art; he remained the perpetual impish undergraduate, cocking a snook at society and the philistines but never with very heavy artillery. From the circle of Oxford aesthetes, Max graduated to that of the Café Royal and Will Rothenstein, Oscar Wilde and Lord Alfred Douglas. But he remained on the edge of these groups like a good caricaturist, portraying his friends with an elfin touch and setting a seal on the 1890s as much as Beardsley or May. Max was a great admirer of the cartoons of Carlo Pellegrini (q.v.), for *Vanity Fair* and his own drawings are extensions of the type known as *portraits chargés.* He introduced his figures into situations, real or imagined, which gave an extra dimension to the cartoons as well as making them more literary than their proto-types. Max's range was wide but among his favourite targets were Edward, Prince of Wales, Rudyard Kipling, H.G. Wells, Edmund Gosse and the Rothschilds. They were usually drawn with pen, ink and wash, sometimes with a little colour added and always with a fastidious eye for detail. Max's talent was a small and brilliant one which he used with great care and the same miniature scale and perfection is found in his books, a stream of which appeared between 1896 and 1946. From 1910, the year in which he married, Max lived the life of an exile in Italy, his subjects and sources of inspiration remaining totally Edwardian to the end of his days. He died on 19 May 1956 at Rapallo.

Publ: *The Works of Max Beerbohm [1896]; Caricatures of Twenty-Five Gentlemen [1896]; More [1899]; Second Childhood of John Bull [1901]; Poets' Corner [1904]; Book of Caricatures [1907]; Yet Again [1909]; Zuleika Dobson [1910]; A Christmas Garland [1912]; Fifty Caricatures [1913]; Seven Men [1919]; And Even Now [1921]; A Survey [1921]; Rossetti and His Circle [1922]; Things New and Old [1923]; Observations [1925]; The Dreadful Dragon of Hay Hill [Lytton Strachey]; Mainly on the Air [1946].*
Contrib: *Pick-Me-Up [1894]; The Yellow Book [1894-96]; The Unicorn [1895]; The Savoy [1896]; Vanity Fair [1896 and 1905-06]; Eureka [1897]; The Parade [1897]; The Butterfly; The Idler; The Sketch; The Strand; The Pall Mall Budget; John Bull [1903].*
Exhib: Leicester Galleries, 1925.
Colls: Ashmolean; V & AM.
Bibl: S.N. Behrman, *Portrait of Max*, 1960; David Cecil, *Max a Biography*, 1964; Rupert Hart Davis, *A Catalogue.*
See illustration (p.213).

## BEEVER, W.A.

Topographer. He contributed to *Public Works of Great Britain*, 1838, AL 410.

## BEGG, Samuel                                          fl.1886-1916

Illustrator and sculptor working in Bedford Park. A prolific contributor to *The Illustrated London News* in the late Victorian and Edwardian periods. Begg seems to have preferred military subjects but also drew sport and the theatre. In many ways he represents the worst features of later illustration, technical perfection in representing almost photographic scenes with heavy use of body-colour but no imagination.

Contrib: *ILN [1887-1916]; Black and White [1892]; Cassell's Family Magazine [1895-96]; The Sporting and Dramatic News [1896].*
Exhib: RA, 1886-91, sculpture.
Colls: V & AM.
See illustration (below).

*SAMUEL BEGG fl. 1886-1916. The Gordon Highlanders embarking for South Africa, published in* The Illustrated London News, *1899. Grey wash heightened with white.*                                          Victoria and Albert Museum

231

**BEHNES, William**                                                    **1794-1864**

Sculptor. He was born in London in 1794 and studied in Dublin and at the RA Schools. He exhibited portraits at the RA from 1815-18 but then abandoned painting for sculpture, being commissioned to do many political and royal celebrities. In 1837 he became Sculptor in Ordinary to The Queen but this brought him little new work and he died in abject poverty in 1864. The Victoria and Albert Museum has a pencil drawing of *The Seven Ages of Man,* prepared for *The Saturday Magazine,* December 1832.

Bibl: R. Gunnis, *Dict. of British Sculptors, 1660-1851,* pp.45-48.

**BELCHER, George Frederick Arthur   RA**                              **1875-1947**

Black and white artist. Born in 1875, Belcher was educated at the Edward VI School, Berkhampstead, and at Gloucester School of Art. His *forte* was in charcoal drawing which he made very much his own in the *Punch* of the inter-war years. He was described by Kenneth Bird as 'Phil May in chalk' and R.G.G. Price says that he was 'A Regency buck in manner and a close observer of the appearance of low life by vocation'. Belcher's low life was different from May's in that it was more rural and less barbed, his favourite characters were the charladies, gossips and workmen whose speech he mimmicked so perfectly in his humorous touching figures. An early writer on Belcher in *The Studio* calls his humour 'intrinsic' adding that he had found charcoal the most sympathetic and responsive medium for rendering the subtleties of his models. His backgrounds are carefully observed but wholly atmospheric and a decided break with traditional *Punch* methods. His ability was recognised when he became an ARA in 1931 and an RA in 1945, a highly unusual distinction for an illustrator. He died in 1947.

Illus: *Portfolio of London Types and Characters [1922]; Members and Boxers of the National Sporting Club; Odd Fish [1923]; Potted Char; Taken From Life by George Belcher.*

*GEORGE BELCHER RA 1875-1947. Illustration for* The Tatler *c.1920, charcoal heightened with white. "Shall I open the other egg sir?" "Certainly not, open the window!"*                    Victoria and Albert Museum

*ROBERT ANNING BELL RA 1863-1933. 'Ophelia', illustration probably for* Lamb's Tales from Shakespeare, *1899, pen and watercolour.*
Victoria and Albert Museum

Contrib: *Punch; The Tatler, The Graphic.*
Exhib: FAS, 1924; Leicester Gall; RA from 1924.
Bibl: *The Studio,* Vol.52, 1911, pp.84-94 illus.; R.G.G. Price, *A History of Punch,* 1957, p.214.

**BELL, J.**                                                           **fl.1874-1894**

Special artist for *The Illustrated London News,* Russo-Turkish War and Constantinople, 1874-78, and Mombassa, 1890. He illustrated George Macdonald's *Phantastes,* Chatto, 1894.

**BELL, Robert Anning   RA**                                          **1863-1933.**

Sculptor, illustrator, designer of mosaics and stained glass artist. Born in London in 1863 and educated at University College School and then at Westminster School of Art under Fred Brown and at the RA Schools. He later studied under Aimé Morot and visited Italy where he took part in exhibitions. Bell was associated with the Arts and Crafts Society and was Master of the Art Workers' Guild. He taught at Glasgow, 1914, and was Professor of Design at the RCA, 1918-24. Outside his numerous illustrations, Bell's best work is probably his mosaic in the Houses of Parliament and his tympanum over the west door of Westminster Cathedral.

Bell's early work as an illustrator lies heavily on the Crane style, rather long and angular figures without shading contained in decorative borders. All his work is reminiscent of the woodcut and its two-dimensional quality perhaps results from the large amount of work undertaken in stained glass. He was elected ARA in 1914 and RA in 1922. Died 27 November 1933.

Illus: *Jack the Giant Killer, The Sleeping Beauty, Cinderella, Beauty and the Beast [1894]; After Sunset [G.R. Thomson 1894 (title and cov.)]; White Poppies [M. Kendall, 1894]; A Midsummer Night's Dream [1895]; The Riddle [1895]; Verspertilia [R.M. Watson, 1896]; An Altar Book [B. Updike, Boston, 1897]; Poems by John Keats [1897]; English Lyrics From Spenser to Milton [1898]; The Pilgrim's Progress [1898]; The Milan [1898]; The Christian Year [1898]; Lamb's Tales From Shakespeare [1899]; The Tempest [1901]; The Odes of John Keats [1901]; Grimm's Household Tales [1901]; Isabella and St. Agnes Eve [1902]; Poems by Shelley [1902]; Rubaiyat of Omar Khayyam [1902]; Shakespeare's Heroines [A.B. Jameson, 1905]; Palgrave's Golden Treasury [1907]; English Fairy Tales [E. Rhys, 1913].*
Contrib: *English Illustrated Magazine [1891-94]; The Yellow Book [1894-95]; Pall Mall Magazine.*
Exhib: B; FAS, 1907, 1934; G; L; NEA from 1888; RA from 1885; RHA; RSA; RWA; RWS.
Colls: V & AM
Bibl: *Studio*, Winter No.1900-01, p.21, illus.; *Modern Book Illustrators and Their Work*, Studio, 1914; R.E.D. Sketchley, *English Book Illus.*, 1903, pp.7, 121. *Who Was Who 1929-40*.
See illustration (p.232).

### BELLEW, Frank Henry Temple      1828-1888
Humorous illustrator specialising in outline drawings. Born at Cawnpore in 1828. He emigrated to the United States and from there contributed comic genre subjects to *Punch*, 1857-62. He also illustrated more serious subjects of American character and the Civil War for *The Illustrated Times*, 1861. He died at New York in 1888, his son became 'Chip', cartoonist of New York *Life*.

### BENDIXEN, Siegfried Detler      1786-1864
Painter, engraver and lithographer. He was born at Kiel on 25 November 1786 and studied under the Italian artist J.A. Pallivia at Enkendorf. He then travelled to Italy in 1808, to Dresden in 1810 and to Munich and Paris in 1811. Returning to Hamburg in 1813, he opened an art school there in 1815, finally settling in London in 1832. Bendixen produced *Preceptive Illustrations of the Bible*, in about 1840, a child's book of rather 'wooden' colour lithographs.

Exhib: BI; NWS, 1833-64; RA; RBA.

### BENHAM, Jane E. (Mrs. Hay)      fl.1850-1862
Painter and illustrator. She was a close friend of the artist daughter of William and Mary Howitt and of Miss Jessie Meriton White, a Garibaldi supporter. She studied for some years with the latter under Kaulbach at Munich, and then travelled in Italy. Vizetelly, who says that she married and lived in Paris, describes her as 'a grave and enthusiastic young lady'. There is little doubt that she was an interesting one, her few illustrations, notably those for *Longfellow's Evangeline*, 1850, show German influence, but also a familiarity with Blake, unusual for the date.

Illus: *Evangeline. A Tale of Arcady by Longfellow [1850 (with Birket Foster and John Gilbert)]; Longfellow's Golden Legend [1854]; Beattie and Collins' Poems [1854].* (Vizetelly records a further illustrated edition of Longfellow.)
Exhib: RA, 1848-49; other exhibitions 1859-62.
See illustration (right).

### BENNETT, Charles Henry      1829-1867
Illustrator and caricaturist. Apparently untrained but was already contributing to the illustrated press by 1855 with cuts in *Diogenes* and *The Comic Times*. He worked for *Comic News* between 1863 and 1865 and achieved wide popularity with his 'Shadows' and 'Studies in Darwinesque Development' for Vizetelly's *Illustrated Times*. He joined *Punch* in 1865 but only contributed for two years before his death. He was sponsored by Charles Kingsley in producing illustrations for Bunyan and commanded the respect of a wide group of literary men. But his caricature portraits with big heads and tiny bodies were in the style of an earlier humour. White criticised his Bunyan figures for over characterization.

Bennett was a poor business man and left his family in distress. *Punch* staged a benefit night at Manchester for them in 1867 under the superintendance of Sir Arthur Sullivan. His earliest work is signed with an owl and later an owl with a 'B' in its beak for a phonetic pun on Bennett.

Illus: *The Fables of Aesop [1857]; Proverbs with Pictures [1858-59]; Pilgrim's Progress [1859]; Fairy Tales of Science [1859]; Quarles Emblems [1860]; Nine*

*JANE E. BENHAM, MRS. HAY fl. 1850-1862. Vignette illustration for H.W. Longfellow's* Evangeline – A Tale of Arcadie, *1850.*

*Lives of a Cat [1860]; Stories little Breeches Told [1862]; London People [c.1864]; Mr. Wind and Madam Rain [c.1864]; Lemon's Fairy Tales; The Sorrowful Ending of Noodledo [1865].*
Contrib: *ILN [1857 & 1866]; The Illustrated Times [1856]; The Cornhill Magazine [1861]; The Welcome Guest [1860]; Good Words [1861]; London Society [1862-65]; Every Boys Magazine [1864-65]; Beeton's Annuals [1866].*
Bibl: Gleeson White, *English Illus.*, 1895; M.H. Spielmann, *The History of Punch*, 1895; Chatto & Jackson, *Treatise on Wood Engraving*, 1861.
See illustration (p.117).

### BENNETT, Fred
Contributor of vigorous and well drawn illustrations to *Chums*, first quarter of the twentieth century.

### BENNITT, Colonel Ward
Amateur illustrator; officer in the 6th Inniskilling Dragoons who contributed social cartoons and initial letters to *Punch*, 1875.

### BENSON
Working at Plymouth and contributing to *The Illustrated London News*, 1844.

### BENSON, Miss Mary K.      fl.1879-1907
Artist and decorator of books. Working in Hertford, 1879-90, at Dublin, 1890-1902 and in Bath in 1907. She drew a headpiece for *The Quarto*, 1896, and exhibited at the RA, RBA and RHA. She was the sister of Charlotte E. Benson, the artist, 1846-1893.

### BENSON, Robert
Traveller and topographer. Published *Sketches of Corsica*, 1825, AT 76.

**BENWELL, Joseph Austin**

Painter, watercolourist and illustrator working in Kensington. He specialised in Eastern subjects but sometimes illustrated modern genre subjects with less assurance. He travelled to India and China prior to 1856 and to Egypt and Palestine, 1865-66. Mrs. Benwell was also an artist.

Illus: *Our Indian Army [by Capper]*.
Contrib: *The Welcome Guest [1860]; The Cornhill Magazine [1860]; ILN [1863-64]*.
Exhib: NW, 1865-86; RA; RBA.

**BÉRARD, Evremond de**                    fl.1852-1863

French landscape painter, born at Guadeloupe and exhibited at the Salon in 1852. He contributed illustrations of Madagascar to *The Illustrated London News*, 1863.

**BERESFORD, Captain G.D.**

Illustrated *Scenes in Southern Albania*, 1855, AT 46.

**BERKELEY, Stanley**                      fl.1878-1907

Painter and illustrator of animals. Berkeley was a regular contributor to magazines in the 1880s and 1890s either in fancy pictures or for serials. His work shows a heavy use of bodycolour but, though sentimental in character, is seldom ill drawn. He worked at Esher, 1890-1902, and at Surbiton to 1907; his wife Edith Berkeley was also an artist.

Contrib: *ILN [1882-96]; The Graphic [1886]; Black and White [1891]; The Sporting and Dramatic News [1896]; The Sketch [1896]; The Boys' Own Paper; Chums.*
Exhib: B, 1889; L, 1889; NWS; RA, 1878-92; RBA.
Colls: V & AM

**BEWICK, Robert Elliot**                   1788-1849

Engraver and illustrator. Born at Newcastle in 1788, the only son of Thomas Bewick (q.v.), the reviver of English wood engraving. He went into partnership with his father in 1812 and assisted him with the illustrations for Aesop's Fables, 1818, and on the uncompleted *History of British Fishes*. Sketches by him for the latter book as well as some illustrations for *British Birds*, 1826, are in the BM. He died at Newcastle.

BRITISH BIRDS.                    57

**THE COMMON BUZZARD,**

OR PUTTOCK.

*( Falco Buteo, Lin.—La Buse, Buff.)*

*THOMAS BEWICK 1753-1828. The Common Buzzard or Puttock, wood engraving from* A History of British Birds, *1816.*
*Right: THOMAS BEWICK 1753-1828. The Domestic Cock, wood engraving from* A History of British Birds, *1816.*

234

**BEWICK, Thomas**                         1753-1828

Called the 'restorer of wood engraving in England'. Born at Cherryburn House, Ovingham, Northumberland, 10 August 1753 and was apprenticed to Ralph Beilby, the Newcastle-upon-Tyne copper plate engraver. The young Bewick found his work with Beilby unrewarding because it gave him little opportunity to develop as an artist, but he did find that wood engraving was more expressive. After working in London in 1776, he returned to Newcastle and in partnership with Beilby assembled material for a *History of Quadrupeds*, 1790, entirely illustrated by wood engravings. This was followed by a celebrated print of 'The Chillingham Bull' and his most famous work, *British Birds*, 1797 and 1804. Bewick died at 19 West Street, Gateshead, on 8 November 1828 and was buried at Ovingham..

Bewick's career runs parallel to the rise of the romantic school in painting and poetry. He was the first person to translate wood engraving from the crudities of the broadsheets to a fine art and the first person to recognise that naturalism was the vehicle rather than the enemy of book illustration. His first edition of *Quadrupeds* contained tailpieces borrowed from continental sources, but later editions and subsequent books had vignettes which in originality and observation are among his masterpieces. His miniature landscapes, his foliage, houses and animals are drawn with accuracy and his country folk with a humour and gentle truth. Chatto and Jackson, who were writing in 1838, only a decade after his death, express this well. 'Bewick was truly a *countryman*.....for though no person was capable of closer application to his art within doors, he loved to spend his hours of relaxation in the open air, studying the character of beasts and birds in their natural state; and diligently noting those little incidents and traits of country life which give so great an interest to many of his tailpieces.' *Treatise on Wood Engraving*, p.479. Bewick was a believer in a clean line and did not like cross-hatching, he liked to cut on the block from dark to light which was an innovation from old practice. His influence established Newcastle as the centre of wood engraving and he had a number of pupils; these include, John Bewick, Robert Johnson, Charlton Nesbit, Luke Clennel, and William Harvey (qq.v.).

Illus: *History of Quadrupeds [1790]; History of Birds [1797 and 1804]; Select Fables [1784]; Gay's Fables [1779]; Aesop's Fables [1818]; A Tour Through Sweden.*
Exhib: FAS, 1880.
Colls: BM (large collection); Newcastle; V & AM; Northumberland Nat. Hist. Soc.
Bibl: F.G. Stephens, *TB Notes on a Collection of Drawings and Woodcuts*, 1881; D.C. Thomson, *The Life and Works of TB*, 1882; D.C. Thomson, *The Watercolour Drawings of TB*, 1930.
See illustrations (below, left and p.235).

280                    BRITISH BIRDS.

**THE DOMESTIC COCK.**

*THOMAS BEWICK 1753-1828. Tailpiece wood engraving from* A History of British Birds, *1816*

**BEWLEY, Miss**
Landscape illustrator for *Good Words*, 1880.

**BIDDARD, C.**
Contributor of social subjects to *Punch*, 1902.

**BIDDULPH, Major-General Sir Michael Anthony Shrapnel GCB**
**1823-1904**
Soldier and artist. Born at Cleeve Court, Somerset, 1823. Major, 1854, and Colonel, 1874. Served throughout the Crimean War and was at the Siege of Sebastopol. Groom in Waiting to H.M. Queen Victoria and Keeper of the Regalia. Died 23 July 1904.
Illus: *Norway [Forester, 1849]*.
Contrib: ILN, 1880.
Exhib: RBA, 1889-90.

**BILLINGS, Robert William**                                    **1815-1874**
Landscape painter and architectural illustrator. Born in London in 1815. Worked at Bath, 1834-37. Died at Putney, 4 November 1874. H.M. Colvin suggests that he was a member of the Billing family, who were builders in Reading.
Illus: *Britton's Cathedrals [1832-36 (vignettes)]; Architectural Illustrations...of Carlisle Cathedral [1840]; Architectural Illustrations....of Durham Cathedral [1843]; Architectural Illustrations....of Kettering Church [1843]; Baronial Antiquities of Scotland [1848-52]*.
Exhib: RA, 1845-72.
Colls: Bath AG.

**BILLINGHURST, Percy J.**                                    **fl.1899-1900**
Illustrator, designer of bookplates. RA Schools, 1897. There is no biographical information about this talented animal draughtsman who did clever pen drawings in elaborate frames for children's books around 1900.
Illus: *A Hundred Fables of Aesop [1899]; A Hundred Fables of La Fontaine [1900]; A Hundred Anecdotes of Animals [Lane, 1901]*.
Bibl: 'P.J. Billinghurst Designer and Illustrator', *The Studio*, Vol.14, 1898, pp.181-186, illus; *The Studio*, Winter No. 1900-01, p.49, illus; R.E.D. Sketchley, *English Book Illus.*, 1903, pp.117, 160.

**BILSBIE, Charles**
Contributor of cockney figures to *Punch*, 1906. His style is broadly based on that of Phil May.

*THOMAS BEWICK 1753-1828. Vignette wood engraving from* A History of British Birds, *1816*.

**BINGHAM, The Hon. Albert Yelverton**                        **1840-1907**
Landscape painter. He was born on 11 February 1840, the third son of Denis, 3rd Baron Clanmorris and was D.L. for County Mayo. He died on 31 March 1907.
Illus: *The Voyage of The Sunbeam [Lady Brassey, 1891]*.
Exhib: RA, 1878.

**BINT**
Contributed one cartoon to *Vanity Fair*, 1893.

**BIRCH, Charles Bell    ARA**                                **1832-1893**
Sculptor and illustrator. Born in London September 1832 and studied at the RA Schools and in Berlin with Rauch, later becoming assistant to J.H. Foley, RA. His only illustrated work is *Lara, a Tale of Lord Byron*, Art Union of London Album, 1879. This is very hard and teutonic and quite out-moded for its date. Some further unidentified illustrations are at the Victoria and Albert Museum. ARA 1880.

**BIRCH, Reginald**
Illustrator of *Little Lord Fauntelroy* by Frances Hodgson Burnett, 1886, and *The One I Knew Best of All*, by the same author, 1894.

**BIRD, John Alexander H.**                                    **1846-**
Painter of animals and illustrator. He specialised in horse subjects and exhibited at the RA, RI and Canadian Academy. He contributed to *Dark Blue*, 1871-73.

**BIRD, W.**
Pseudonym in *Punch* of Jack B. Yeats (q.v.).

**BIRKENRUTH, Adolph**                                        **1861-1940**
Illustrator. Born at Grahamstown, South Africa, 28 November 1861. He was educated at University College School, at Frankfort and studied art in Paris. He settled in London by 1883 and from 1890 was a prolific contributor to the magazines, illustrating work by 'Q' and Walter Besant. Birkenruth handled plain chalk with greater mastery than he handled his washes and was more at home in social realism than in anecdotal subjects. He died on 15 September 1940. Signs with monogram AB.
Illus: *The Rebel Queen [Walter Besant, 1894]*.
Contrib: *Black & White [1892]; ILN [1892-99]; The Pall Mall Budget [1893]; The Butterfly [1893]; English Illustrated Magazine [1893-96]; The Sphere [1894]; Pick-Me-Up [1894]; The New Budget [1895]; The English Illustrated Magazine [1895]; The Idler*.
Exhib: Grafton Gall; L; RA from 1883; RBA; RI; ROI; RWS.
Colls: V & AM.
See illustration (p.236).

*ADOLPHE BIRKENRUTH 1861-1940. 'A Hopper's Wife', black chalk and wash drawing for a story in* The English Illustrated Magazine, *March 1895.*
Victoria and Albert Museum

## BLACKBURN, Mrs. J. (née Wedderburn)                1823-1909

An important animal and bird illustrator. The daughter of an influential Scottish family, she showed an early ability for drawing animals and birds. She was influenced by the naturalism of Bewick's woodcuts and on a visit to London in 1840 became acquainted with Mulready and Landseer, the latter telling her that he had nothing to teach her about drawing. She married Professor Hugh Blackburn, Professor of Mathematics in the University of Glasgow and continued to paint and illustrate until the 1890s. She died at Edinburgh in 1909.

Mrs. Blackburn was strongly influenced by the Pre-Raphaelites and admired by both Millais and Ruskin. In a letter of 1861, George du Maurier wrote '. . . look at Mrs. Blackburn, who has monopolised the large page of Good Words, and is decidedly well paid for it too and courted much more for her talent than she ever could be for the title she possesses in common with some 2 or 500 other ladies'. *The Young George Du Maurier*, p.84.

Publ: *Scenes From Animal Life and Character [1858]; Birds Drawn From Nature [1862]; A Few Words About Drawing For Beginners [1893]; Birds From Moidart [1895].*
Illus: *The Instructive Picture Book [A. White, 1859]; Songs and Fables [W.J.M. Rankins, 1874].*
Contrib: *Good Words [1861].*
Exhib: RA from 1863.
Colls: BM.

## BLACKWOOD, Lady Alicia

Lithographer and amateur illustrator. She published *Scutari, Bosphorus, Crimea*, 1857, at Bristol, AT 242, and exhibited landscapes at the RA from Box Wood, 1878-80.

## BLAIKIE, F.

Contributor of silhouette cartoons to *Punch*, 1904.

## BLAIKLEY, Alexander                                1816-1903

Portrait painter. Born in Glasgow in 1816 and exhibited at the BI, RA and RBA, 1842-67. He was a contributor to *The Illustrated London News*, 1856.

## BLAIKLEY, Ernest                                      1885-

Painter and etcher. He was born in London on 12 April 1885 and was educated at University College School, London, before studying art at the Slade School. He became Keeper of Pictures at the Imperial War Museum, 1919.

Illus: *The Artist's London [n.d.]*
Contrib: *Punch [1906].*
Exhib: RA; RBA; RI; RSA.

## BLAKE, William                                        1757-1827

Engraver, poet, painter and mystic. Born in London at 28 Broad Street, Golden Square, on 28 November 1757, the son of a hosier. He joined William Pars's Drawing School at the age of ten and was writing poetry at fourteen. He was apprenticed to the engraver James Basire and made drawings of London churches for engraving, entering the RA Schools as an engraving student in 1779, and exhibiting there from 1780. From that date onwards he was engaged in commercial engraving to supplement his meagre income. This included plates after other artists in numerous publications like *The Wits' Magazine*, 1784; *Harrison's Novelists Magazine, Wollstonecraft's Works*, 1791 and various work by the minor author, William Hayley, 1800-09. He illustrated Lavater's *Essays on Physiognomy*, 1789, Young's *Night Thoughts*, 1793-1800, *Leonora*, 1796, *Hayley's Ballads*, 1805, Malkin's *A Father's Memories of His Child*, 1806, Thornton's *Virgil*, 1821, and wood engravings for Phillips *Pastorals*, 1820-21.

Blake's most powerful and individual contribution to illustration was in his Prophetic Books. Blake used his own printing method of relief etching for these, though some are intaglio etched, and then he or Mrs. Blake coloured the figures in imitation of drawings. As Bland says, 'Blake's calligraphy embraces the whole page — borders, figures, and words without distinction. The verse flows into the borders and the figures encroach on the verse. In this Blake goes back to the very earliest manuscripts of the Middle Ages before there was a division between scribe and illuminator and before the attempt was made to add a third dimension to the page.' The dating and printing of these mystic books, text and design, is very complex and can best be understood by reference to *A Bibliography of William Blake* by Sir Geoffrey Keynes, 1921, and the subsequent Blake studies by this author. They are as follows — *Songs of Innocence*, 1789; *Visions of the Daughters of Albion*, 1793-95; *The Gates of Paradise*, 1793; *The Argument*, 1793; *The Book of Thel*, 1789-94; *Songs of Experience*, 1794; *The Book of Urizen*, 1794; *Europe: A Prophecy*, 1794; *America: A Prophecy*, 1793; *Milton*, 1804; *Jerusalem*, 1804-18; *The Marriage of Heaven and Hell*, 1815-21; *Paradise Lost*, 1806; *Paradise Regained; The Song of Los; The Book of Ahania; Dante's Inferno* (incomplete); *The Illustrations of The Book of Job* (incomplete), 1825.

Blake was very influential but not until late in life. From 1818, he gathered round him a group of disciples including John Linnell, Samuel Palmer, Edward Calvert, George Richmond and F.O. Finch. To the Victorians he was a more substantial poet than artist, Ruskin admired his figures but not his colour, though David and William Bell Scott owe much to him (qq.v.). It was only at the end of the century that the growth of the private presses singled him out for praise as the precursor of the book as a total work of art.

Exhib: London, 1809.
Colls: Bedford; BM; Fitzwilliam; Leeds; Manchester; Tate; V & AM.
Bibl: W.B. Scott, *WB Etchings From His Works*, 1878; R.L. Binyon, *The Art of WB*, 1906; G.K. Chesterton, *WB*, 1920; W. Gaunt, *Arrows of Desire*, 1956; D. Bland, *A History of Book Illus.*, 1958, pp.242-246. M. Butlin, *Catalogue Tate Gallery*, 1978.
See illustration (p.237).

WILLIAM BLAKE 1757-1827. 'The Whirlwind of Lovers' from Dante's Inferno, Canto V, 1824-27. Line engraving        Author's Collection

**BLAMPIED, Edmund   RE RBA**                          **1886-**
Artist and caricaturist. Born in Jersey of a Jersey family, 30 March
1886. As a schoolboy he worked on farms and studied their animals,
especially horses, eventually going on to study at the Lambeth School
of Art. He exhibited book illustrations in the National Competition,
1905-6 and won an L.C.C. scholarship. Blampied was a witty and fluid
pen artist but concentrated on painting as a career. He took up
etching in 1913, becoming an Associate of the RE in 1920, and RBA,
1938. He lived in Jersey throughout the Occupation and designed the
liberation stamps, 1945.

Illus: *Peter Pan [Hodder, 1939]*.
Contrib: *The Graphic [1915]*.
Exhib: Leicester Gall., 1923; Salon.
Colls: V & AM.

**BLANCHARD, F.L.**
Marine painter. Contributor to *The Graphic*, 1905.

**BLANCHARD, Ph.**                                **fl.1853-1860**
Figure illustrator. He was chiefly employed on French illustrated
papers according to Vizetelly. He contributed French subjects to *The
Illustrated London News*, 1853.

**BLATCHFORD, Montagu**
Amateur cartoonist. By profession a carpet designer, Blatchford lived
in Halifax and contributed cartoons to *Punch* in the style of Linley
Sambourne from 1876-81.

**BLAYLOCK, T. Todd**                             **fl.1897-1925**
Artist and illustrator. Studied at Poole School of Art and exhibited at
National Competition, 1897. Worked in London in 1907 and at Poole,
1914-25. Exhibited at RA, 1906-13.

Bibl: *The Studio*, Vol. 11, 1897, p.260, illus.

**BLOMFIELD, Sir Reginald   RA FSA**                  **1856-1942**
Architect, historian and draughtsman. Born in Kent on 20 December
1856 and was educated at Haileybury and Exeter College, Oxford.
Architect of many domestic and civil schemes and gardens. RIBA
Gold Medal. RA 1914, ARA 1905, PRIBA 1912-14. Knighted 1919.
Blomfield was an authority on French architecture and on
architectural draughtsmanship of which he was an accomplished
exponent.

Publ: *The Formal Garden in England [1892]; A History of Renaissance
Architecture in England [1897]; A Short History of Renaissance Architecture
in England [1900]; Studies in Architecture [1906]; The Mistress Art [1908];
History of French Architecture, 1494-1661 [1911]; Architectural Drawing and
Draughtsmen [1912]; History of French Architecture, 1661-1774 [1920]; The
Touchstone of Architecture [1925]*.
Contrib: *The English Illustrated Magazine [1888-90]*.
Colls: RIBA; V & AM.

**BLORE, Edward   FRS FSA**                          **1787-1879**
Architect and architectural draughtsman. Born in Rutland, 1787, the
son of Thomas Blore, FSA. He lived as a youth in Stamford and
developed a passion for Gothic architecture and a talent for drawing
it. An introduction to Sir Walter Scott resulted in the chance
commission to rebuild Abbotsford in the Gothic style. He had a very
large practice in the early Victorian period, was a 'special architect' to
William IV and Queen Victoria and as such completed Buckingham
Palace, 1831-37. Surveyor of Westminster Abbey, 1827-49.

Illus: *History of Rutland [T. Blore, 1811]; History of Durham [Surtees,
1816-40]; Northamptonshire [Baker, 1822-41]; Hertfordshire [Clutterbuck,
1815-27]; Britton's Cathedrals [1832-36]; The Provincial Antiquities and
Picturesque Scenery of Scotland; The Monumental Remains of Noble and
Eminent Persons [1824]; Essay on Gothic Architecture [Sir J. Hall, 1813]*.
Exhib: RA, 1813-36.
Colls: BM; RIBA; Soc. of Antiq.; V & AM.
Bibl: H.M. Colvin, *Biographical Dict. of English Architects, pp.78-82.*

**BLOW, Detmar FRIBA**                                    **1867-1939**

Artist and architect. He was born on 24 November 1867 and was educated at Hawtrey's. He was a major domestic architect in the first quarter of the century, and specialised in the restoration of old buildings. He died 7 February 1939.

Contrib: *The English Illustrated Magazine [with E.H. New, 1891-92]*.
Exhib: RA, 1924.

**BLUM, Robert Frederick**                               **1857-1903**

American illustrator who worked for *Scribner's Magazine*. Contributed pen, pencil and wash drawings to *Japonica*, Sir E. Arnold, 1892. Exhibited figures at the RA, 1888.

**BLYTH, S.R.**

Contributed figures in a posterish style with thick lines to *Fun*, 1900.

**BOGLE, W. Lockhart**                                         **-1900**

Portrait painter and illustrator. Born in the Highlands and studied at Glasgow University followed by seven years apprenticeship to a lawyer. Abandoned law for painting and studied in Düsseldorf, specialising on his return in Highland subjects and subjects associated with Scottish history. Bogle was also an accomplished archaeologist and a champion wrestler. Died 20 May 1900. He signed his work 'Lockhart Bogle' or 'LB'.

Contrib: *ILN [1886-89]; The Graphic [1882-89]; Good Words [1891-94]*.
Exhib: New Gall; RA, 1886-93.
Colls: V & AM.

**BOND, A.L.**

Illustrator. Nothing is known of this draughtsman who illustrated *The Miller's Daughter* by Alfred Tennyson in about 1855. This book contains fine vignette and page designs with large trees and flowers in juxtaposition with small landscape and in ornamental borders. It is possible that the artist was 'J.L.' Bond, a Welsh landscape painter.

**BOND, H.**

Draughtsman. He designed the frontispiece for *The Surrey Tourist or Excursions Through Surrey*, 1821, with H. Gastineau.

**BONE, Herbert**                                        **fl.1882-1907**

Craftsman designer and illustrator. Working in Dulwich, 1902-7. Exhibited at the RA, RBA, RI, 1874-92, and contributed to *The Quiver*, 1882.

**BONE, Sir Muirhead**                                    **1876-1953**

Etcher, draughtsman and painter. Born in Glasgow on 23 March 1876, the son of a journalist, he studied at the evening classes of the Glasgow School of Art. He moved to London in 1902 and in 1903 married Gertrude Dodd, the sister of Francis Dodd. Bone was a member of the New English Art Club from 1902, having exhibited there from 1898 and was a member of the Society of 12. He made extensive tours with his wife, she providing the text for a number of books illustrated by her husband. Bone did a great deal of his best work as Official Artist on the Western Front and with the Fleet, 1916-18; in the Second World War he was Official War Artist to the Admiralty, 1940-43. He was a Trustee of The National Gallery, 1941-48 and of The Tate Gallery.

Bone's early training as an architect's pupil led him to study buildings, and it is the structure and form of towns, cities and streets which appear most often in his work. But he was very far from being a mere topographer; his *Western Front*, best seen in the large paper edition of 1917, brings the contrasts and the anonymity of that First World War to life in chalk and pencil. Bone was particularly good at observing vast industrial activity and in showing myriad figures from above, a sort of Piranesi in reverse.

Illus: *Glasgow in 1901 [1901]; Children's Children [1908]; Glasgow, Fifty Drawings [1911]; The Front Line [1916]; Merchant Men-at-Arms [1919]; The London Perambulator [1925]; Days in Old Spain [1938]; London Echoing [1948]; Merchant Men Rearmed [1949]; The English and Their Country [1951]; Come to Oxford [1952]*.
Contrib: *The Yellow Book [1897]*.

Exhib: Colnaghi, 1930; FAS, 1953, 1974, 1975; G; L; Mercury Gall, 1974; NEA; RA; RSA.
Colls: V & AM.
Bibl: Campbell Dodgson, *Etchings and Dry Points of MB*.

**BOOT, William Henry James RBA RI**                      **1848-1918**

Landscape painter and illustrator. Born at Nottingham in 1848, he studied at the Derby School of Art. Moved to London and practised in Hampstead, devoting himself in his early years almost exclusively to illustration. He was Art Editor of *The Strand Magazine*, 1895-1915, and a contributor to the first numbers of *The Graphic*. He published two technical books, *Trees and How to Paint Them*, 1883, and *Tree Painting in Watercolours*, 1886. He became a member of the RBA in 1884 and was Vice-President, 1895-1915. He died on 8 September 1918.

Illus: *Picturesque Europe; British Battles; Our Village; Our Own Country; British Ballads; Royal River; Rivers of England; Greater London; Picturesque Mediterranean [1891]*.
Contrib: *The Graphic [1870-81]; ILN [1884-86]; Good Words [1890]; The Quiver. [1890]; Boys' Own Paper; The Art Journal; The Magazine of Art*.
Exhib: B; RA, 1874-84; RBA, 1889-1913; RHA; RI; RWA.
Colls: Derby.
Bibl: *Who Was Who 1916-28*.

**BOOTH, J.L.C.**

Black and white artist contributing to *Punch*, 1896-1906. He usually draws hunting subjects and sometimes signs 'JC Booth'.

**BOSSOLI, Carlo**                                        **1815-1884**

Painter and draughtsman. Born at Davesco, near Lugano, in 1815 and specialised in military and political subjects, many of which were undertaken in pen and ink. He travelled to Russia, Sweden, Spain and England where he was made a painter to Queen Victoria, finally settling at Turin.

Illus: *Views on the Railway Between Turin and Genoa [1853, AT 176]; The War in Italy [1859-60, AT 177]*.

**BOSTOCK, John**                                         **fl.1826-1859**

Portrait painter. He made a number of drawings for the Annuals, especially *The Chaplet*, c.1840. He exhibited at the RA, RBA, BI and Old Watercolour Society, 1826-69, at first from Regent's Park, later from Manchester and Kensington.

**BOTHAMS, Walter**                                       **fl.1882-1925**

Landscape painter and illustrator of rural life. Working in London, 1882, Salisbury, 1885-1902 and Malvern, 1903-25. He contributed to *The Illustrated London News*, 1883-84 and 1894, (fishing and architecture).

Exhib: RA; RBA, 1882-91.

**BOUCHER, William H.**                                        **-1906**

Illustrator. Cartoonist of *Judy*, 1868-87 in succession to J. Proctor (q.v.). Associate of the RWS. Died 5 March 1906.

Exhib: RA, 1888-91.
Bibl: Dalziel, *A Record of Work*, 1901 p.318.

**BOUGH, Samuel RSA**                                     **1822-1878**

Landscape painter and illustrator. Born at Carlisle on 8 January 1822 and learnt engraving under Thomas Allom, in London. He was for some years in the Civil Service although he continued to associate with artists and in 1845 went to Manchester as scene painter to the Theatre Royal. This was followed by periods at the Princess Theatre, Glasgow, 1848, and the Adelphi Theatre, Edinburgh, 1849. An argumentative and individualistic man who became a well-established Edinburgh character and a popular landscape painter. ARSA 1856, and RSA, 1875. He died in Edinburgh, 19 November 1878.

Illus: *Poems and Songs [Robert Burns, 1875]; Edinburgh, Picturesque Notes [R.L. Stevenson, 1879]*.
Exhib: RA, 1856-76; RSA.
Colls: Aberdeen; BM; Dundee; Fitzwilliam; Glasgow; Manchester; NG, Scotland; V & AM.
Bibl: S. Gilpin *SB*, 1905.

**BOUGHTON, George Henry   RA RI**                    **1833-1905**
Painter and illustrator. Born near Norwich on 4 December 1833, the
son of a farmer. The family emigrated to the United States in 1839
and Boughton was brought up at Albany where he taught himself to
paint. He returned to England in 1853, studying art in London and
then went back to the States to practise as a landscape painter. He
remained in New York, 1854-59, and then left for France to study
under Édouard Frère. He finally settled in London in 1862 and
became a regular exhibitor at the RA, being elected ARA, 1879 and
RA, 1896.

Boughton established himself as a popular Victorian illustrator who
specialised in strongly historical costume subjects with a decidedly
literary setting. Van Gogh admired these when they appeared in *The
Illustrated London News* and the artist's articles on Holland in
*Harper's Magazine*, 1883. Boughton's figures derive a great deal from
Fred Walker, but his historical revivalism is very much his own. He
died 10 January 1905.

Illus: *Rip Van Winkle; Legend of Sleepy Hollow [Washington Irving, 1893];
The Trial of Sir Jasper [1878].*
Contrib: *ILN [1870-82]; Good Words [1878]; The Pall Mall Magazine.*
Exhib: B; BI; FAS, 1894; G; GG; L; M; New York, 1857; NW; RA from 1862.
Colls: Ashmolean; V&AM.

**BOURNE, James**                                    **fl.1800-1810**
Topographer. He exhibited at the RA, 1800-9, and published
*Interesting Views of the Lakes of Cumberland, Westmorland and
Lancashire,* n.d.

**BOURNE, John Cooke**                               **1814-1896**
Topographer and illustrator. Although little is known of this artist, he
was solely responsible for one of the most heroic illustrating
achievements of the early Victorian period, the publication of two
volumes on railway construction. Bourne's *Drawings of the London
and Birmingham Railway,* 1839, with its 35 tinted lithographic plates
on 30 leaves, united art and industry with the lithograph. *The History
and Description of the Great Western Railway,* followed in 1846, with
43 tinted lithographs on 34 leaves with 3 maps. The series provide a
unique insight into Victorian engineering stage by stage but, more
than that, the artist's role is a new one. 'The revelation of the book is,
not surprisingly, of an artist relatively unknown ... with his action
pictures of the building of the London and Birmingham Railway ... He
apparently foresaw the up-and-down and roundabout viewpoint of the
cinema lense for he looks as up to date as Vertov and the most
advanced of his documentaries'. John Grierson, *Scotsman,* 18 May
1968. Bourne stood unsuccessfully for election to the New
Watercolour Society between 1866 and 1877 and exhibited there and
at the RA and RBA. He visited Russia in about 1864.

In general the drawings resemble the work of Prout and J.D.
Harding, his figures in particular being large, vigorous and very
detailed in the preparatory sketches. He drew on stone for Hay's
*Views in Kairo,* 1840, AT 270, and for *The Illustrated London News,*
1860.

Colls: BM; Elton Collection.

**BOW, Charles**
Contributor to *The Illustrated London News,* 1855.

**BOWERS, Miss Georgina (Mrs Bowers-Edwards)**        **fl.1866-1880**
*Punch's* second woman cartoonist. She supplied initials, vignettes and
social subjects for the magazine from 1866-76. A keen hunting
woman, she lived at Holywell House, St. Albans, and was first
encouraged to draw by John Leech. She exhibited in London,
1878-80.
Illus: *Canters in Crampshire [c.1880]; Mr. Crop's Harriers [c.1880].*
Contrib: *Once a Week [1866]; London Society [1867].*

**BOWLER, Thomas William**                            **-1869**
Landscape painter and illustrator. Born in the Vale of Aylesbury and
lived in Brighton from where he exhibited at the RA and the RBA,
1857-60. In about 1860 he left for South Africa where he became an
astronomer at the Cape of Good Hope. He drew many landscapes and

drawings of the Cape Town area and contributed some to *The
Illustrated London News* in 1860. He died in 1869.
Colls: Cape Town.

**BOWLEY, A.L.**
Book decorator. Contributing ornament to children's stories in *The
English Illustrated Magazine,* 1895-97.

**BOWRING, W. Arminger**                              **fl.1902-1922**
Portrait and figure painter. He worked in London and was elected
ROI in 1922.
Contrib: *Punch [1902-5 (children)].*
Exhib: L; P; RA; ROI.

**BOYD, Alexander Stuart**                            **1854-1930**
Illustrator. Born in Glasgow on 7 February 1854; practised in his
home city until about 1890, contributing humorous drawings to *Quiz*
and *The Bailie of Glasgow* under the pseudonym of 'Twym'. After
moving to London, Boyd worked at St. John's Wood and drew for
most of the leading magazines of the day. His parliamentary subjects
were always very accurate and Spielmann considered that the
drawings were 'executed with great care and with singular
appreciation of the value of his blacks'. His wife, Mary Stuart Boyd,
was a writer and they collaborated on a number of books. He
emigrated to New Zealand after 1914 and died near Auckland on 21
August 1930.

Illus: *Peter Stonnor [Blatherwick, 1884]; The Birthday Book of Solomon
Grundy [Roberts, 1884]; Novel Notes [J.K. Jerome, 1893]; At the Rising of
the Moon [Mathew, 1893]; Ghetto Tragedies [Zangwill, 1894]; A Protegée of
Jack Hamlin's [Bret Harte, 1894]; The Bell Ringer of Angels [Bret Harte,
1894]; John Inglefield [J.K. Jerome, 1894]; The Sketchbook of the North
[1896]; Rabbi Saunderson [1898]; Lowden Sabbath Morn [R.L. Stevenson,
1898]; Days of Auld Lang Syne [1898]; Gillian the Dreamer and Horace in
Homespun [1900]; Our Stolen Summer [1900]; A Versailles Christmas-Tide
[1901]; The Fortunate Isles [Mrs. Boyd]; Wee Macgregor and Jess and Co.
[Bell]; Cottars Saturday Night [Burns]; Hamewith [Murray].*
Contrib: *Good Words [1890]; The Idler [1892]; Sunday Magazine [1894];
Black and White [1897]; The Graphic [1901-4]; Daily Graphic [1911]; Punch
[1896-]; The Pall Mall Magazine; Pictures from Punch [Vol. VI, 1896].*
Exhib: G, 1889-1906; RA, 1884-87 and 1913; RSA, 1889-1913; RSW.
Colls: Author; Glasgow; V & AM.
Bibl: M.H. Spielmann, *The History of Punch,* 1895, p.567.
See illustration (p.240).

**BOYLE, The Hon. Mrs. Richard   'E.V.B.'**           **1825-1916**
Illustrator of poetry and children's books. Born Eleanor Vere Gordon,
youngest daughter of Alexander Gordon of Ellon Castle, Aberdeenshire, she married in 1845, the Hon. and Rev. Richard Boyle, MA,
Chaplain in Ordinary to Queen Victoria, Vicar of Marston Bigott,
Somerset. She received advice from Boxall and Eastlake and was
admired as an illustrator by some of the Pre-Raphaelites. Her
delightful little books appeared at intervals from 1853 to 1908 and
are full of wide-eyed love of nature and a quirky charm of their own.
Her inspiration is often in the work of Holman Hunt or Millais and her
decorations and mystical pictures come directly from Arthur Hughes
or are softened fantasies from Doyle. Her *May Queen* of 1861 is her
most successful book, her *Story Without An End,* 1868, perhaps her
most famous. At the close of her career, a writer to *The Bookman,*
October 1908, p.54, said 'E.V.B. is an aesthete of Ruskin's school, a
lover of beautiful things, of what is decent and quiet and old, of
gardens, of nature in selections, and of art'. She is indeed the only
woman illustrator of competence to emerge before the 1860s. She
lived at Maidenhead in middle life and died on 30 July 1916. Signs
with monogram.

Illus: *A Children's Summer [1853]; Child's Play [1858]; The May Queen
[1861]; Woodland Gossip [1864]; The Story Without An End [1868 (coloured
pls.)]; Andersen's Fairy Tales [1872]; Beauty and The Beast [1875]; The Magic
Valley [1877]; The New Child's Play [1880]; A Book of Heavenly Birthdays
[1894]; Seven Gardens and a Palace [1900]; The Peacock's Pleasaunce [1908].*
Contrib: *ILN [Christmas, 1863].*
Exhib: Dudley Gallery; Grosvenor Gallery, 1878-81.
Bibl: B. Peppin, *Fantasy Book Illus.,* 1975, pp.8, 11, 57, 60 illus.
See illustration (p.241).

## BOYS, Thomas Shotter                                   1803-1874

Painter and lithographer. He was born at Pentonville on 2 January
1803 and articled to G. Cooke, the engraver. In 1825 he went to Paris
where he worked for French publishers and met R.P. Bonington. This
was the most important influence of his life, for the precocious young
painter persuaded him to abandon engraving for watercolours and
lithography. Boys grasped the importance of tinted lithographs and
the fact that 'painting on stone' was the way to bring the effect of
watercolours to the widest public. His masterpiece in this medium was
*Picturesque Architecture in Paris, Ghent, Antwerp and Rouen*, 1839,
AT 23, which was published at eight guineas. This was followed by
*Original Views of London As It Is,* 1842, hand tinted this time and
only a small number coloured.

Boys was the most sensitive colourist of the mid-Victorian
topographers, his rendering of sunlight on massive building and his
patches of local rich colour put him almost on a level with Bonington.
But he was not successful and spent the latter part of his life on hack
work, illustrating Blackie's *History of England,* and etching plates for
Ruskin's *Modern Painters* or preparing lithographs for the *Stones of
Venice.* He died at St. John's Wood on October 10 1874.

Exhib: NWS, 1832-73; RA, 1847-48; RBA, 1824-58.
Colls: Ashmolean; Bedford; BM; Fitzwilliam; Liverpool; Mellon, Richmond,
Virginia; Newcastle; V & AM.
Bibl: E.B. Chancellor *Original Views of London,* 1926; E.B. Chancellor
*Picturesque Architecture in Paris,* 1928; J. Roundell *TSB,* 1974; *Walker's
Quarterly,* XVIII, 1926; M. Hardie *Watercolour Paint in Brit.,* 1967, Vol. III,
pp.183-185, illus.
See illustration (p.242).

## BRACEBRIDGE, Mrs Selina   née Mills                      -1874

Watercolourist and traveller. She was born at Bisterne, Hampshire and
became a pupil of Samuel Prout (q.v.). Her journeys included visits to
Italy in 1824, Italy and Germany in 1825 and the Near East in about
1833. She was in Sweden in 1840 and in the Pyrenees in 1842. She
was a friend and sponsor of Florence Nightingale at Scutari and may
have been an acquaintance of Edward Lear who owned a sketchbook
of hers, now in the Victoria and Albert Museum. Her style is like that
of both Lear and W. Page and although her work was usually
lithographed by others, she was apparently an amateur lithographer.
She died in 1874.

Publ: *Panoramic Sketch of Athens [1836].*
Contrib: *Finden's Landscape Illustrations of the Bible [1837-38].*
Colls: Searight Coll; V & AM.

## BRADDELL, Kyo

Contributor of two cartoons to *Vanity Fair,* 1891-92. The name is
given in Puttick & Simpson's sale catalogue, 17 March 1916.

## BRADDYLL, Lt.-Colonel Thomas Richard Gale        1776-1862

Amateur caricaturist. Presumably the owner of Conishead Priory near
Ulverston, Lancs. He was the originator of Gillray's famous caricature
of *Gulliver and the King of Brobdingnag,* 1803.

Bibl: M.D. George *English Political Caricature,* 1959, pp.69, 72, 83, 261.

## BRADFORD, Rev. W.

Church of England clergyman of St. John's College, Oxford. He
illustrated his own *Sketches of the Country, Character and Costume
in Portugal and Spain,* 1809-10, AT 135.

## BRADLEY, Basil RWS                                     1842-1904

Sporting painter and illustrator. He studied at the Manchester School
of Art and was a consistent exhibitor in London and provincial shows
He became chief equestrian artist to *The Graphic* in 1869 and his
spirited pen did much to enliven its earliest and best years. He became
an Associate of the RWS in 1867 and a full Member in 1881. He
travelled to New South Wales.

Contrib: *Once a Week [1866]; Cassell's Magazine [1867]; The Graphic
[1869-76].*
Exhib: B; M; RA; RBA; RWS.
Colls: BM; Manchester; Sydney.

*ALEXANDER STUART BOYD 1854-1930. A page of sketches in pen and ink
for* Immediate Parliament, *1898.*                    Author's Collection

## BRADLEY, Cuthbert                                     fl.1885-1907

Equestrian illustrator. Working at Folkingham, Lincolnshire, in about
1907. Contributed to *Moonshine,* 1885, *The Graphic,* 1904 and *The
Boy's Own Paper.*

## BRADLEY, C.H.

Illustrator and decorative artist. He contributed initials, and social
subjects to *Punch,* 1852-60, in a weak and watered-down Tenniel
style. His monogram is easily mistaken for that of C.H. Bennett (q.v.).

## BRADLEY, Miss Gertrude M.                            fl.1893-1902

Illustrator of children's books. She worked at Brocton, Staffordshire,
and produced colourful story-books and fairy tales.

Illus: *Songs For Somebody [1893]; The Red Hen and Other Fairy Tales
[1893]; New Pictures in Old Frames [1894]; Just Forty Winks [1897]; Tom
Unlimited [1897]; Nursery Rhymes [1897-98]; Puff-Puff [1899]; Pillow-
Stories [1901].*
Bibl: R.E.D. Sketchley *English Book Illus.* 1902, pp.106, 160.

*THE HON. MRS. RICHARD BOYLE 'E.V.B.' 1825-1916. Illustration for Alfred, Lord Tennyson's* The May Queen, *1861.*

**BRADLEY, William H.**      **1868-**

American illustrator, working at New York. He was Art Director of *Colliers Magazine, Metropolitan* and *The Century*. His work is one of the best examples of the Beardsley manner exported to the United States. Pennell writing in 1895 says, 'The decorative or decadent craze has also reached America and its most amusing representative so far, is W.H. Bradley.' *Modern Illustration*, p.124. He was a talented poster designer and is included here as an artist working for John Lane and exhibiting in this country.

Illus: *Fringilla [R.D. Blackmore, Cleveland, 1895]; The Romance of Zion Chapel [Le Gallienne, 1898]; War is Kind [Stephen Crane, New York, 1899]; Peter Poodle; Toy Maker to The King [1906]; The Wonderbox, Stories [1916]; Launcelot and The Ladies [1927].*

**BRADSHAW, Percy Venner**      **fl.1905-1949**

Illustrator, writer and art teacher. He was born in London and after being educated at Askes School, he studied art at Goldsmiths and Birkbeck Colleges. He was an illustrator for the magazines for many years before developing an art correspondence course and founding the Press Art School at Tudor Hall, Forest Hill, in 1905. He issued portfolios on *The Art of the Illustrator* from about 1914. He had a large private collection of this work.

Publ: *Art in Advertising [1925]; They Make Us Smile [1942]; I Wish I Could Paint [1945]; The Magic of Line [1949].*
Contrib: *The Boys' Own Paper [c.1890].*

**BRAGER, Jean Baptiste Henri Durand**      **1814-1879**

Marine painter and illustrator. Born at Dol, France, on 21 May 1814, and studied with Eugène Isabey. The artist was very adventurous and a keen traveller and ranged through most of Europe and Africa (including Algeria and Senegal), in search of subjects. He attended the expedition that brought back the Emperor Napoleon's body to France and published his drawings. Died at Paris in 1879.

Illus: *La Marine française; La Marine du commerce; Études de marine; Types et physionomie des armées d'Orient.*
Contrib: *The Illustrated Times [1859 (Piedmont campaign), 1860 (Palermo)].*

**BRANDARD, Robert**      **1805-1862**

Landscape painter and engraver. Born at Birmingham in 1805, and came to London for a year in 1824 to study with E. Goodall. He was really a professional engraver and in this capacity worked on Turner's *Picturesque Views in England and Wales,* 1838, and engraved work by Stanfield and Callcott. He drew some illustrations for Knight's *London*, 1841-42. Worked mostly in Islington.

Exhib: BI, 1835-58; OW; RA; RBA, 1831-47.
Colls: Leicester; Manchester; V & AM.

*THOMAS SHOTTER BOYS 1803-1874. The North Front of St. James's Palace from the set of twenty-six lithographs published as* London As It Is, *1842.*

### BRANDLING, Henry Charles                    fl.1847-1861

Watercolour painter and occasional illustrator. He was an Associate of the Old Watercolour Society from 1853-57, and exhibited at the RA from 1847-50. In 1848, he published *Views in the North of France,* tinted lithographs, AT 98, and in 1851, illustrated W. Wilkie Collins *Rambles beyond Railways;* sepia sketches for the latter were on the art market in London, 1976. Gleeson White records his illustrations to *The Merchant of Venice,* 1860.

Bibl: Chatto & Jackson *Treatise on Wood Engraving,* 1861, p.599.

### BRANGWYN, Sir Frank  RA                      1867-1956

Born at Bruges in 1867, the son of a Welsh architect. Brangwyn was an all round figure, being painter, designer, etcher, lithographer and book illustrator, but basically self-taught. He worked with William Morris at Merton Abbey before going to sea, then travelled extensively in Asia Minor, 1888, Algeria and Morocco, 1889, South Africa, 1891, and in the same year to Spain with Arthur Melville. This is reflected in the very colourful mural and stained glass work which he undertook for town-halls and public buildings, his choice of subjects is in the tradition of the Newlyn School, but some of his wilder schemes are reminiscent of the northern symbolism of Ensor. In illustration, Brangwyn's range was equally wide; he gave full play to the Edwardian love of colour plate books of travel or romance but could hold his own with the best black and white work, preferring chalk to pen, but sometimes powerfully using black and white contrasts. He became an ARA in 1904, and an RA in 1919. He was knighted in 1941 and died in 1956. There are two museums devoted entirely to his work, that at Bruges, opened in 1936, and another is at Orange in the South of France.

Illus: *The Life of Admiral Lord Collingwood [1890]; The Captured Cruiser [Hyne, 1892]; The Exemplary Novels of Cervantes; The Wreck of the Golden Fleece [1893]; The Cruise of the Midge [1894]; Tales of Our Coast [1896];*

*Arabian Nights [1896]; Don Quixote [1898]; Tom Cringle's Log [Scott, 1898]; Bread Upon the Waters [Kipling]; Devil and the Deep Blue Sea [Kipling]; Eothen [A.W. Kinglake]; The Book of Bridges [W. Shaw Sparrow, 1915]; Omar Khayyam [1920].*

Contrib: *The Graphic [1891-1904]; Pall Mall Budget [1891]; The Idler; The Pall Mall Magazine; The Acorn [1905-6].*

Exhib: FSA, 1908, 1910, 1912, 1915, 1916, 1924, 1948, 1952, 1958, 1967; G; New Gall; RA from 1885; RE; RWA.

Colls: BM; Fitzwilliam; Glasgow; V & AM; Witt Photo.

Bibl: W. Shaw Sparrow *FB and His Work,* 1910; H. Furst *The Decorative Art of FB,* 1924; *The Artist,* May 1897, pp.193-200, illus.

See illustration (below).

### BRANSON, Paul                                1885-

American painter and illustrator, born in Washington in 1885. He illustrated Methuen's 1913 edition of *The Wind in The Willows.* This came in for adverse criticism at the time. 'The author tells the story of some obviously "fairy tale" animals, but in depicting the various characters with so much fidelity to nature . . . the artist seems to us to have entirely missed the spirit of this delightful romance.' *The Studio,* Vol.60, p.249.

### BRANSTON, F.W.

Comic illustrator and watercolourist. Contributor to *Hoods Comic Annual,* 1830, exhibited at RBA, 1833, from address at the Old Mint, Tower of London.

### BREDIN, E.G.

Army officer and amateur artist. Lieutenant, Royal Regiment of Artillery, 1847; acting Major 1855; Crimean War Medal. Contributed sketches of the Crimea to *The Illustrated London News,* 1854-58.

*SIR FRANK BRANGWYN RA 1867-1956. Illustration for* The Arabian Nights, *Gibbings Edition, 1896.*                    Victoria and Albert Museum

**BRENNAN, Alfred**
Decorative illustrator to *The Artist,* August 1897.

**BRETON, William H.**
Naval officer and amateur artist. Lieutenant RN, 1827; Reserve, 1862.
He published *Excursions in New South Wales,* 1833, AT 575;
*Scandinavian Sketches,* 1835, AT 255.

**BREWER, Henry Charles   RI                1866-1943**
Landscape painter and architectural illustrator. He was the son of
H.W. Brewer (q.v.), and studied at the Westminster School of Art. He
specialised in views of Spain, Venice and Tangier, all of which he
visited. He practised in West London, 1902-25.
Contrib: *The Graphic [1887-1910].*
Exhib: FSA, 1908, 1911, 1932; L; RA; RI; RWA.

**BREWER, Henry William                        -1903**
Architectural illustrator specialising in panoramic views. He was born
and educated at Oxford, though living most of his working life in
North Kensington. He exhibited at the RA from 1858, and was in
1869 an unsuccessful candidate for the NWS. After his death in 1903,
H.C. Brewer (q.v.), moved into his house.
Illus: *Old London Illustrated [1921].*
Contrib: *The Graphic [1870-1901]; English Illustrated Magazine [1887]; The
Daily Graphic [1890]; The Pall Mall Magazine [1894-98]; The Girl's Own Paper
[1897-98]; The Dome [1897-99].*
Colls: V & AM.
Bibl: *Art Journal.*

**BREWER, J. Alphege**
Possibly another son of H.W. Brewer (q.v.), practising at Acton, about
1925. Contributor to *The Graphic,* 1910, architectural subjects, and
exhibited with the Royal Cambrian Academy, 1924.

**BREWER, W.H.**
Watercolourist. There are two drawings in the Victoria and Albert
Museum, one for *Master Humphreys Clock* by Charles Dickens, 1840,
and the other of fairies, the first signed 'W.H. Brewer delt'.

**BREWTNALL, Edward Frederick   RWS       1846-1902**
Landscape painter and illustrator. He was an early contributor to *The
Graphic* supplying narrative pictures to that magazine and *The
Illustrated London News.* He was a member of the RBA from
1882-86, having exhibited there from 1868, and a member of the
RWS from 1883. He died at Bedford Park on 15 November, 1902.
He signs his work 'EFB'.
Illus: *The Oceans Highway.*
Contrib: *Once a Week [1867]; Good Words For The Young[1869]; The
Graphic [1870-74 and 1889]; Punch [1870]; The Illustrated London News
[1873-74 and 1892]; Dalziel's Bible Gallery [1880]; Cassell's Family Magazine;
English Illustrated Magazine [1887]; The Quiver [1890]; Black and White
[1891]; Pall Mall Magazine [1892].*
Exhib: RA; RBA; RWS from 1875.
Colls: Sheffield; V & AM; Warrington.

**BRIAULT, Sydney Graham                    1887-1955**
Portrait painter and illustrator. He studied at the Regent Street
Polytechnic, London, 1900 and at the St. Martin's School of Art.
Contrib: *Punch [1914].*
Exhib: RA.

**BRICKDALE, Eleanor Fortescue   RWS       1871-1945**
Illustrator, painter and designer. She was born in 1871, the daughter
of a barrister and studied at the Crystal Palace School of Art, the RA
Schools and with Byam Shaw. She won a prize for the best decoration
of a public building in 1896 and began to exhibit at the RA the same
year. She represents the last phase of Pre-Raphaelitism, her highly
detailed and meaningful little pictures are crammed with medievalism
and moral sentiment. She was the ideal illustrator of legend and
particularly for those expensive coloured gift books of the 1900s
where her bright colours and haughty figures were set off to advantage

on the ample pages. She was also a talented stained glass artist and
designed windows for Bristol Cathedral. Her work was sometimes
criticised for its confusion of black to white making outlines difficult
to see and occasionally on scale 'piggies the size of white rats need a
good deal of ingenious defence'. *The Studio,* Vol.13, pp.103-108.
ARWS, 1902; RWS, 1919.
Illus: *A Cotswold Village [J.A. Gibbs, 1898]; Ivanhoe [1899]; Tennyson's
Poems [1905]; Child's Life of Christ [M. Dearmer, 1906]; Pippa Passes [R.
Browning 1908]; Dramatis Personae [R. Browning, 1909]; Beautiful Flowers
[Wright, 1909]; Tennyson's Idylls of the King [1911]; Story of Saint Elizabeth
of Hungary [W. Canton, 1912]; The Gathering of Brother Hilarius [M. Fairless,
1913]; The Book of Old English Songs and Ballads [1915]; The Golden Book
of Famous Women [1920]; Fleur and Blanchefleur [1922]; Palgrave's Golden
Treasury [1924]; Christmas Carols [1925]; A Diary of an Eighteenth-century
Garden [D.C. Calthrop, 1926]; The Gentle Art [D.C. Calthrop, 1927].*
Exhib: Leighton House, 1904; L; RA; RWS.
Colls: Birmingham; Leeds.
Bibl: *The Studio,* Winter No., 1900-1 p.71 illus.; *Modern Book Illustrators and
Their Work,* Studio, 1914, illus.; M. Hardie *Watercolour Paint in Brit.,* Vol. III,
1968 pp.130-131; G.L. Taylor *EFB Centenary Exhibition* Ashmolean, 1972-73.

**BRIDGENS, Richard                        fl.1818-1838**
Architect, practising in Liverpool, 1818, and later in London, in the
gothic style. He published and illustrated *Manners and Costumes of
France, Switzerland and Italy,* 1821, AT 21; *Sefton Church . . . ,*
1822; *West India Scenery,* 1836, AT 680; *Furniture with
Candelabra and Interior Decorations . . . ,* 1838.
Exhib: RA, 1813-26, architecture.
Bibl: H.M. Colvin *Biog. Dict. of Eng. Architects,* 1954 p.97.

**BRIERLY, Sir Oswald Walters   RWS       1817-1894**
Marine painter. He was born in Chester in 1817, the son of a doctor,
and studied at Sass's School and at Plymouth. In 1841, he made a
voyage round the world, but settled in New Zealand for a time and
then visited Australia and North and South America. He accompanied
the British Fleet to the Baltic on the outbreak of the Crimean War in
1854, and then proceeded to the Black Sea, making drawings that
were later published in two books. He travelled with various members
of the Royal Family on tours, notably to Norway, 1867-68, and to
the Crimea again in 1868. He was elected ARWS in 1872, and RWS in
1890. He became Marine Painter to the Queen in 1874 and was
knighted in 1885.
Illus: *Marine and Coast Sketches of the Black Sea [1856, AT 240]; The Englis
and French Fleets in the Baltic [1858].*
Contrib: *ILN [1851, 1854 (Crimea); 1855 (Finland)].*
Exhib: Pall Mall Gallery, 1887.

**BRIGHT, Henry of Thames Ditton**
Painter of figure compositions, cartoons and an occasional book
illustrator. A large gouache picture of humanised frogs was exhibited
at the NWS, 1876. It probably had political implications, the two
central frogs being identified as the German Emperor and Bismarck.
Bibl: *Country Life,* Nov. 29, 1956 illus.

**BRIGHTWELL, L.R.                         fl.1914-1938**
Animal painter and etcher. He studied at the Lambeth School of Art
and at the Zoological Gardens.
Contrib: *Punch [1914 (figs.)].*
Exhib: L.

**BRINE**
An early cartoonist for *Punch.* He studied in Paris and in London at
the same time as T. Woolner (q.v.), and A. Elmore (q.v.), and worked
closely with A.S. Henning (q.v.). He is believed to have taught Birket
Foster figure drawing.

**BRISCOE, Arthur John Trevor            1873-**
Painter and engraver. He was born at Birkenhead on 25 February
1873 but spent most of his life in East Anglia. Exhibited at the NEA
1896 and 1900 and at the RA. His one attempt at illustration is 'The
Mother', published in *The Quarto,* 1896, showing both the influence
of Japan and the Birmingham School illustrators.
Exhib: FAS, 1926, 1928, 1930, 1934, 1936, 1940, 1943.

**BRISCOE, Ernest Edward** 1882-
Watercolourist and illustrator. He was born on 5 March 1882 and exhibited at the RA and RI from Caterham. He illustrated *By Ways of London,* 1928, and specialised in drawings of old houses.

**BRITTAIN, I.G.**
Contributor of agricultural subjects to *The Strand Magazine,* 1891. This may be identified with Miss Isabel Brittain of Scarborough who exhibited at Dowdeswell Galleries that year.

**BRITTEN, William Edward Frank** fl.1873-1901
Genre painter and illustrator. Britten was working in London from about 1873, the year in which he began to exhibit at the RBA. He was not a prolific illustrator but an eclectic one, his designs ranging from Victorian classicism to smokey Pre-Raphaelite chalk drawings. He excelled as a decorative artist, placing his subjects in elaborate frames, the Shaftesbury Tribute in *The Graphic* of 1885 is a good example. He was still working in Pimlico in 1890.

*Illus: Carols of the Year, Algernon Swinburne; The Elf Errant [1895]; Undine, [Baron de la Motte Fouqué, 1896]; The Early Poems of Alfred Lord Tennyson [1901].*
Contrib: *The Graphic [1885-86].*
Colls: V & AM.

**BRITTON, John FSA** 1771-1857
Architectural draughtsman and antiquary. He was born at Kingston St. Michael, Wiltshire in 1771 and after being apprenticed to a publican, became a hop merchant and ballad writer. He joined forces with Edward Brayley in 1801 to produce their first book, *The*

*Beauties of Wiltshire,* the first of a giant series which was to set the seal on romantic topographical guides for a generation. Britton gave up his interest in the project after Volume VII but was supplying illustrations for his successor J.C. Smith in 1814. A poor draughtsman, Britton was a brilliant self-made and irrepressible editor. For his works he gathered illustrative artists together calling them 'scientific artists' and showed a definite feel for book-making, highlighted by his use of Whittingham as his printer. He died in 1857 having published his mammoth *Autobiography,* 1850.

Publ: *Architectural Antiquities of Great Britain [1805-14]; Cathedral Antiquities of England [1814-35]; Specimens of Gothic Architecture [1823-25]; The Architectural Antiquities of Normandy [1825]; Dictionary of Architecture and Archaeology of the Middle Ages [1829]; Public Buildings of London [1825-28]; History . . . of the . . . Palace . . . of Westminster [1834-36, with Brayley]; Architectural Description of Windsor [1842].*
Exhib: RA, 1799-1819.
Colls: Ashmolean; BM; Devizes.
Bibl: *RIBA Papers,* 1856-57; *AJ* February 1857; J. Mordaunt Crook 'John Britton and the Genesis of the Gothic Revival', *Concerning Architecture,* Penguin, 1968, pp.98-119.

**BROCK, Charles Edmund RI** 1870-1938
Book illustrator and portrait painter. Born at Cambridge in February 1870 and spent the whole of his working life there. Educated at the Cambridge School and in the studio of Henry Wiles, sculptor. Like his younger brother, H.M. Brock, (q.v.), his metier was in the illustration of period books, the worlds of Jane Austen, Charles Lamb, Oliver Goldsmith, and Daniel Defoe, but also of Scott's classics and the stories of Whyte-Melville. His career began in earnest in the middle 1890s and he continued to produce a regular output until his death in

Sang to him instead of the cruelty of Barbara Allen

*CHARLES EDMUND BROCK RI 1870-1938. Illustration for an 18th century story, pen and ink, signed and dated 1906.*

*HENRY MATTHEW BROCK RI 1875-1960. Illustration for 'Mrs. Bellamy's Diamonds', c.1905, pen and ink.*                    Author's Collection

1938. In general his pen drawings have a lighter touch than his brother's and are softer in their contrasts, the finished watercolours have an all over pastel hue which to the present writer is less successful than the black and white work.

The Brocks worked closely together in the same studio and gained stimulation from each other. One of their influences was undoubtedly the work of Hugh Thomson (q.v.), but their accuracy in period settings was greater than his, they collected Georgian furniture and clothing to study from. He became RI, 1908; and died at Cambridge 28 February 1938.

A full Bibliography of illustrated books is found in *The Brocks, A Family of Cambridge Artists and Illustrators,* by C.M. Kelly, 1975.

Contrib: *Good Cheer [1894]; Sunday Magazine [1894]; Good Words [1895-96]; Punch [1901-10]; Fun [1901]; The Graphic [1901-10]; ILN [1912] Tucks Annuals; Blackie's Annuals.*
Exhib: L; RA, from 1906; RI.
Bibl: *The Studio,* Winter No. 1900-01 p.37 illus.; *Modern Book Illustrators and Their Work,* Studio, 1914 illus.; C.M. Kelly, op. cit.
See illustration (p.244).

### BROCK, Henry Matthew  RI                    1875-1960
Book illustrator and landscape painter. Born at Cambridge 11 July 1875, the younger brother of C.E. Brock (q.v.). He was educated at Cambridge Higher Grade School and at the Cambridge School of Art before joining his brother's studio. He married in 1912 his cousin, Doris Joan Pegram, sister of Fred Pegram (q.v.). There is little difference in the careers of the two brothers, except that H.M.'s was longer and in many respects more varied, he painted landscapes and was more gifted as a humorous artist. Although meticulous in signing

their drawings, H.M.'s can usually be told apart by their thicker ink lines and bolder handling. He was elected RI in 1906 and died at Cambridge in 1960.

A full Bibliography of illustrated books is found in *The Brocks, A Family of Cambridge Artists and Illustrators,* by C.M. Kelly, 1975.

Contrib: *Cassell's Family Magazine [1896-97]; The Quiver [1897-98]; Good News [1898]; The Captain; C.B. Fry's Magazine; Chums Annual; Blackie's Annuals; The Strand Magazine; Fun [1901]; The Graphic [1901]; Punch [1905-40, 415 drawings]; The Sphere [c.1912].*
Exhib: B; L; RA, 1901-1906; RI.
Colls: V & AM; Witt Photo.
Bibl: *Modern Book Illustrators and Their Work,* Studio, 1914 illus., C.M. Kelly, op. cit.
See illustration (above).

### BROCK, Richard Henry                    fl.1902-1925
Landscape painter and illustrator. Brother of C.M. and H.M. Brock (qq.v.). He practised at Cambridge in the family studio but concentrated more on the illustrations of boys' annuals.

Contrib: *Punch [1916-17]; Chatterbox and Prize Annuals [1908-25]; Blackie's Boys' Annuals.*
Exhib: L; M; RA, 1901-13; RI.
Bibl: C.M. Kelly, op. cit.

### BROMLEY, Clough W.                    fl.1880-1904
Landscape and flower painter, engraver and illustrator. He worked in London and contributed pastorals, architecture and decoration to *The English Illustrated Magazine,* 1885-87, 1896.

Exhib: B; L; M; RA; RBA; RHA; RI; ROI.

**BROMLEY, Valentine Walter**                    **1848-1877**
Painter and illustrator. Born in London in 1848 and exhibited at
London exhibitions, 1865-77. He married Miss A.L.M. Atkinson, the
landscape painter and was assistant on *The Illustrated London News*,
1873. He travelled to the United States in 1875, illustrating Lord
Dunraven's *The Great Divide* and died at Fellows Green, near
Harpenden in 1877. Member of RBA, 1871.

Contrib: *The Graphic [1872-73]; ILN [1873-79]; Punch [1876]*.
Exhib: NWS; RA; RBA, 1867-74.
Colls: Shipley; Witt Photo.

**BROOK, Ricardo**
Illustrator of comic genre. He contributed to *Punch*, 1914.

**BROOKE, Sir Arthur De Capel, Bt.**                    **1791-1858**
Amateur artist, son of Sir R. De Capel Brooke, he travelled in Europe
and published several books illustrated by himself. These included *A
Winter in Lapland and Sweden*, 1827; *Winter Sketches in Lapland*,
1827; *Sketches in Spain and Morocco*, 1837.

**BROOKE, E. Adveno**
Topographer exhibiting at the RA, BI and RBA, 1844-64, from
addresses in Islington and Shepherd's Bush. He illustrated *The Book
of South Wales* by Mr. and Mrs. S.C. Hall, 1861.

**BROOKE, Leonard Leslie**                    **1863-1940**
Painter and illustrator. Born at Birkenhead and educated there before
being trained in the RA Schools, Armitage medal, 1888. Brooke's
talent lay in the illustration of children's books, his figure drawing is
strong, characterised by cross hatching and he is capable of
considerable humour. He is best remembered as the illustrator of Mrs.
Molesworth's works, 1891-97. He died at Hampstead, 1 May 1940.

Illus: *Miriam's Ambition [1889]; Thorndyke Manor [1890]; The Secret of the
Old House [1890]; The Light Princess [G. Macdonald 1890]; Brownies and
Rose Leaves [1892]; Bab [1892]; Marian [1892]; A Hit and a Miss [1893];
Moonbeams and Brownies [1894]; Penelope and The Others [1896]; School in
Fairyland [1896]; Mrs. Molesworth's Works [1891-97]; Pippa Passes [Robert
Browning, 1898]; A Spring Song [1898]; The Pelican Chorus [E. Lear, 1900];
The Jumblies [E. Lear, 1900]; Johnny Crow's Garden [1903]; The Book of Gilly
[Emily Lawless, 1908]; Johnny Crow's New Garden [1935]*.
Contrib: *English Illustrated Magazine [1896]; The Parade [1897]*.
Exhib: B; L; M; New Gall; NWS, 1887-1901; RA.
Colls: Manchester.
Bibl: *The Studio*, Winter No. 1900-01, p.74 illus.; R.E.D. Sketchley, *English
Book Illus*, 1902, pp.99, 160; *Who Was Who*, 1929-40.

**BROOKE, William Henry**                    **1772-1860**
Illustrator and caricaturist. Born in 1772, the nephew of Henry
Brooke, the historical painter. He exhibited portraits and figure
subjects at the RA, 1810-26, but is best known as an illustrator in the
style of Stothard. His comic cuts are in the manner of William Heath
(q.v.). He practised first in Soho, moving to the Adelphi and finally to
Bloomsbury. He died at Chichester in 1860.

Illus: *Moore's Irish Melodies [1822]; Hone's Every Day Book [1826-27]; The
Fairy Mythology [T. Keightley, 1828]; Greek and Roman Mythology [T.
Keightley, 1831]; Walton's Angler; The Humorist [W.H. Harrison, 1832];
Antiquarian Etching Club*.
Contrib: *Satirist [1812-14]; Britton's Cathedrals [1832-36, figures only]*.
Colls: BM; V & AM.

**BROOKES, Warwick**                    **1808-1882**
Designer and illustrator. Born at Salford in 1808 and was one of the
first pupils of the new School of Design established at Manchester in
1838. He then became a leading figure among the group of artists in
the North-West who wished to study from the life and came together
as The United Society of Manchester Artists. Brookes made a
considerable local reputation and after the Manchester Exhibition of
1857, received encouragement from the Prince Consort and made
yearly visits to London. He was head designer of the Rossendale
Printing Company from 1840-66.

Illus: *Marjorie Fleming [J. Brown, 1884]; WB's Pencil Pictures of Child Life
[T. Letherbrow, 1889]*.

Contrib: *A Round of Days [1866, heads]*.
Colls: BM.

**BROOKSHAW, George**                    **fl.1818-1819**
Flower painter and drawing-master. He illustrated his own *New
Treatise*, 1818, AL 96 and *Groups*, 1819, AL 97.

Exhib: RA, 1819.

**BROUGH, Robert    ARSA**                    **1872-1905**
Painter. Born at Invergordon, Ross, in 1872 and was educated in
Aberdeen and Glasgow. Studied art at Aberdeen Art School and at the
RSA, Edinburgh and later in Paris. In Edinburgh he gained the Watters
medal and Chalmers bursary. His first London success was with his
portrait of W.D. Ross of *Black & White* shown at the New Gallery. He
died 22 January 1905.

Contrib: *The Evergreen [1896]*.
Exhib: Dresden, 1901; G; L; Munich, 1897; N; Paris, 1900; RA, 1897; RSA.

**BROWN, A.**
Contributed architectural subjects to *Illustrated London News*, 1847.

**BROWN, Major Cecil    MA RBS**                    **1867-**
Equestrian artist and sculptor. Born at Ayr, 1867 and educated at
Harrow and Oxford. He designed the medal for the International
Medical Congress, London, 1913, and served in the First World War,
1914-18. Art master at Bedford School, 1925.

Illus: *The Horse in Art and Nature*.
Contrib: *ILN [1896]*.
Exhib: Paris Salon; RA from 1895.

**BROWN, Ford Madox**                    **1821-1893**
Painter and occasional illustrator. He was born in Calais in 1821 and
studied art in Belgium and Rome. He came into contact with the
newly formed Pre-Raphaelite Brotherhood in 1848, when he took
D.G. Rossetti (q.v.), as a pupil. Brown remained on the edge of the
group, but his contact with them was mutually beneficial; it is
particularly marked in his illustrative work where an earnestness and
attention to detail is predominant. In 1857, he spent three days in a
mortuary getting accurate information on the decomposition of the
body for a woodcut illustration measuring 3¾ins. x 5ins.! Perhaps his
finest works were the two illustrations for Rossetti's poem 'Down
Stream' which combine technical mastery and an objective view of
love and nature. Brown taught at the Camden Town Working Men's
College from 1854 and was a designer for Morris, Faulkner and Co.,
1861-74. He signs his name 'FMB' or 'FMB/89'.

Illus: *The Feather [1892]*.
Contrib: *Willmott's Poets of the Nineteenth Century [1857]; Lyra Germanica
[1868]; Once A Week [1869]; Dark Blue [1871]; Dalziel's Bible Gallery
[1880-81]; The Builder [1887]; Brown Owl [1891, title and illus.]; Dramas
in Miniature [Mathilde Blind, 1897]*.
Exhib: BI, 1841-67; RA.
Colls: Ashmolean; Bedford; BM; Manchester; V & AM.
Bibl: F.M. Hueffer, *Memoir of MB*, 1896; Gleeson White, *English Illustration,
The Sixties*, 1906; F. Reid, *Illustrators of The Sixties*, 1928, pp.48-50; J. Maas,
*Victorian Painters*, 1969, pp.131-132.

**BROWN, Isaac L.**
Draughtsman. Contributor to *London Society*, 1868.

**BROWN, James**
Illustrator for *Judy*, 1887.

**BROWN, John**
Architect and County Surveyor of Norfolk. Contributed a church
genre subject to *The Illustrated Times*, Christmas, 1856. He exhibited
at the RA, 1820-44.

**BROWN, J.D. or J.B.**
Contributor to *Good Words*, 1860. Exhibited at the RBA, 1862.

**BROWN, J.R.**                                    fl.1874-1890

Illustrator. Working at Sefton Park, Liverpool and contributing regularly to *The Graphic*, 1874-77 and 1885-88. The artist has a wide range, tackling comic and genre subjects as well as social realism. Among his best work here is 'Common Lodging House', 1888.

Exhib: L, 1889.

**BROWN, M.**

Landscape illustrator for *The Illustrated London News*, 1888. Presumably the same as artist practising in Edinburgh and exhibiting at the RSA, 1889.

**BROWN, Oliver Madox**

Painter. Son of Ford Madox Brown (q.v.). He illustrated with his father, Moxon's edition of the *Poetical Works of Lord Byron*, 1870.

**BROWN, T.R.J.**

Illustrator working exclusively for *Ally Sloper's Half Holiday*, c.1890.

**BROWN, Thomas**                                    fl.1842-1856

Painter, sculptor and illustrator. He worked at Pentonville and exhibited at the RA and BI from 1842-55. He illustrated *The Complete Poetical Works of William Cowper*, for Gall & Anglis, Edinburgh, n.d., c.1840.

Colls: Witt Photo.

**BROWN, Thomas Austen   ARSA**                     1857-1924

Painter of genre and landscape, illustrator. Born at Edinburgh, 18 September 1859 and was educated there. He was an RA exhibitor from 1885 and a Member of the RI, 1888-99 and a member of The National Portrait Society. He exhibited abroad at Munich, Dresden and Barcelona and won many medals. He died at Boulogne.

Brown has a very individual style both in his watercolours and in the coloured woodcuts he undertook. The figures are sketchy and undefined, the buildings wavy in soft tints. He signs his name with a monogrammed TAB.

Illus: *Bits of Old Chelsea [1922, lithographs]*.
Contrib: *ILN [1899]*.
Exhib: FAS, 1900, 1903; NWS; RA; RSA.
Colls: BM; V & AM.
Bibl: *Who Was Who, 1916-28*.

**BROWN, W.**

Illustrator of *The Comic Album*, and contributor to *Punch*, 1844. The same artist may be William Brown exhibiting at the RBA from 1825-33 with an address in Chelsea.

**BROWNE, Gordon Frederick   RI**                     1858-1932

Painter and illustrator. Born at Banstead, Surrey, the younger son of H.K. Browne, 'Phiz' (q.v.). He was educated privately and then studied art at Heatherley's, following his father into book illustration as a profession. From about 1880, Browne illustrated a truly amazing quantity of boys' stories, tales and novels, among them works by Defoe, Swift, Bunyan, Scott, R.L. Stevenson, Andrew Lang, and E.F. Benson. In many ways he was the superior of his father as a figure draughtsman, but although very prolific never reached the latter's stature, principally because he had no one writer to collaborate with. He was clearly an artist who pleased editors and in this way there is a sameness about his work which dulls it; characters look much alike whether they are Besant's or Henty's! He was elected RI in 1896 and died 27 May 1932. He signs his name 'GB'.

Illus: *Stevenson's Island Nights Entertainments [1893]; Grimm's Fairy Tales [1894]; National Rhymes of the Nursery [1894]; Sintram and His Companions Undine [1896]; Dr. Jolliboy's ABC [1898]; Stories from Froissart [1899]*; Mrs. Ewing's works including: *Man's Meadow, Melchior's Dream, The Peace Egg, Dandelion Clocks; F. Anstey's Stories For Boys and Girls [1898, covers and illus.]; A Book of Discoveries [J. Masefield, 1910]*.
Contrib: *ILN [1881-87, 1891-98]; The Quiver [1890]; Black & White [1891]; Good Words [1891-97]; Chums [1892]; The Captain; Lika Joko [1894]; The New Budget [1895]; The Sporting and Dramatic News [1899]; Cassell's Saturday Journal; Cassell's Family Magazine; The Boy's Own Paper; The Girl's Own Paper; The Pall Mall Magazine; The Sunday Strand [1906]*.
Exhib: L; RA, 1886; RBA; RI, 1890-1925; RWA.
Colls: Author; BM; Doncaster; Hove; V & AM.
Bibl: R.E.D. Sketchley, *English Book Illus.*, 1902, pp.161-5, (this contains a full bibliography to 1901); *The Studio*, Winter No. 1900-01, p.27, illus.

*HABLOT KNIGHT BROWNE 'PHIZ' 1815-1882. Illustration of a beach scene for unidentified book, pen and ink.*          Victoria and Albert Museum

*TOM BROWNE RI 1872-1910. 'A Dispute with a servant.' Illustration for unidentified periodical, pen and ink and crayon.* Author's Collection

**BROWNE, Hablot Knight 'Phiz'**                    **1815-1882**
Watercolourist, book illustrator and humorous artist. He was born at Kennington in 1815 and after being educated in Suffolk was apprenticed to Finden, the engraver, subsequently opening a studio of his own and attending the St. Martin's Lane School. He was the artist who most benefited from the untimely death of Robert Seymour (q.v.), when he succeeded him as Dickens' illustrator for *Pickwick Papers,* 1836. The same year he had produced the illustrations for another Dickens work *Sunday As It is,* and he was to continue to do so with the major novels, until unseated by more modern illustrators in the 1860s. Browne's draughtsmanship was in the tradition of the Regency, verging on caricature, scratchy in execution and not always very assured in the penwork. His work would not perhaps have remained so stereotyped and old fashioned if he had not stuck to plates when the whole world was enjoying the woodblock. By the time that *Little Dorrit* appeared in 1857 he was moving towards a greater naturalism. Dickens seems to have found the artist companionable and took him on two trips to collect material. He became paralysed in 1867 and moved to Brighton in 1880, where he died in 1882.

*Illus: Sunday under Three Heads [Dickens, 1836]; Posthumous Papers of the Pickwick Club [Dickens, 1836-37]; Sketches of Young Ladies by 'Quiz' [1837]; Sketches in London [Grant, 1838]; A Paper of Tobacco [1839]; Nicholas Nickleby [Dickens, 1839]; Harry Lorrequer [C. Lever, 1839]; Master Humphrey's Clock – Old Curiosity Shop and Barnaby Rudge [Dickens, 1840-41]; Legendary Tales of the Highlands [1841]; Charles O'Malley [C. Lever, 1841]; Peter Priggins [1841]; Rambling Recollections [Maxwell, 1842]; Jack Hinton [C. Lever, 1842-43]; Irish Peasantry [W. Carleton, 1843-44]; Martin Chuzzlewit [Dickens, 1844]; Tom Burke [C. Lever, 1844]; St. Patrick's Eve [C. Lever, 1845]; Tales of the Train [C. Lever, 1845]; Nuts and Nutcrackers [1845]; The O'Donoghue [C. Lever, 1845]; Fiddle-Faddle's Sentimental Tour [1845]; Fanny the Little Milliner [1846]; The Commissioner [1846]; Teetotalism [1846]; Dombey & Son [Dickens, 1846-48]; The Knight of Gwynne [C. Lever, 1847]; The Fortunes of Colonel Torlogh O'Brien [1847]; Irish Diamonds [1847]; Old St. Paul's [W.H. Ainsworth, 1847]; Pottleton Legacy [Albert Smith, 1849]; David Copperfield [Dickens, 1849-50]; Roland Cashel [C. Lever, 1849-50]; Sketches of Cantabs [Albert Smith, 1850]; The Illustrated Byron [1850]; The Daltons [C. Lever, 1850-52]; Ghost Stories [1851]; Lewis Arundel [Frank Smedley, 1852]; Bleak House [Dickens, 1852-53]; Letters Left at the Pastrycooks [Horace Mayhew, 1853]; Crichton [W.H. Ainsworth]; Christmas Day [1854]; The Water Lily [H. Myrtle, 1854]; The Dodd Family Abroad [C. Lever, 1854]; Harry Coverdale's Courtship [Frank Smedley, 1854]; Martins of Cro' Martin [C. Lever, 1856]; Home Pictures [1856]; Little Dorrit [Dickens, 1855-57]; Spendthrift, Mervyn Clitheroe [W.H. Ainsworth, 1857-58]; Davenpot Dunn [C. Lever, 1859]; The Minister's Wooing [H.B. Stowe, 1859]; Tale of Two Cities [Dickens, 1859]; Ovingdean Grange [W.H. Ainsworth, 1860]; Twigs for Nests [1860]; One of Them [C. Lever, 1861]; Puck on Pegasus [C. Pennell, 1861]; Barrington [1862-63]; Tom Moody's Tales [Mark Lemon, 1864]; Facey Romford's Hounds [1864]; Luttrell of Arran [C. Lever, 1865]; Ballads and Songs of Brittany [1865]; Can You Forgive Her? [A. Trollope, 1866]; Dame Perkin's and Her Mare [1866]; Phiz's Funny Alphabet [1883].*

Contrib: *New Sporting Magazine [1839]; London Magazine. [1840]; Punch [1842-44, 1861-69]; The Great Gun [1844]; ILN [1844-61]; Ainsworth's Magazine [1844]; The Illuminated Magazine [1845]; The Union Magazine [1846]; Life [1850]; Illustrated London Magazine [1853-55]; The Illustrated Times [1855-56]; New Monthly Magazine; Only a Week; Tinsley's Magazine; London Society; St. James's Magazine; Illustrated Gazette; Sporting Times; Judy; The Welcome Guest.*

Exhib: BI, 1843-67; FAS, 1883; RA; RBA, 1865-86.
Colls: BM; Manchester; V & AM.
Bibl: Chatto & Jackson, *Treatise on Wood Engraving,* 1861, p.599; F.G. Kitton, *Phiz a Memoir,* 1882; D.C. Thomson, *Life and Labour of HKB,* 1884; S.M. Ellis, *Mainly Victorian,* 1924.
See illustrations (pp.84 and 247).

**BROWNE, N. Robert**
Humorous illustrator for *Fun*, 1901.

**BROWNE, Tom   RI**                          **1872-1910**
Painter and black and white artist. Born at Nottingham in 1872 into a working class family and after attending the National School, left at the age of eleven to work in the city's Lace Market. Browne had a talent for sketching which led to his being apprenticed to a firm of lithographers in 1886 where he remained until 1893. He had been doing commercial illustration from 1889 and in 1895 settled in London, where he exhibited at the RA in 1897.

Browne was one of the artists among whom can be counted Beardsley and Phil May, who were young enough to be free of the constraints of wood engraving by hand. They appreciated at once the possibilities of photographic engraving and reproduction and developed their style accordingly. Browne's was a linear style with wide hatching and often a rather obvious contrast of areas of black and white. His stage-door Johnnies and bottle-nosed footmen sometimes have the feeling of May but rarely his subtlety. Browne's humour was more earthy than that of *Punch* and he used convicts and vicars and fat ladies with less discrimination than May and seems to make little social comment. He was, however, enormously popular in mid-Edwardian England and had his own *Tom Browne's Comic Annual.* He made a trip to Korea in 1909 and the drawings completed show a greater range than one would expect and an incredible facility with pure pencil line. He died 16 March 1910.

Illus: *Tom Browne's Comic Annual; Tom Browne's Cycle Sketch Book; The Khaki Alphabet Book; Night Side of London.*
Contrib: *The Graphic [1898-1911]; Pick-Me-Up [1898]; Eureka [1897]; Black and White [1899]; Moonshine [1900]; Chums; Fun [1901]; Pearson's Magazine; The Royal Magazine; The Sketch [1899].*
Exhib: FAS, 1899.
Colls: V & AM.
Bibl: *TB, RI Brush, Pen and Pencil,* c.1905.
See illustration (p.248).

**BROWNE, Walter**
Illustrator. Son of H.K. Browne and brother of G.F. Browne (qq.v.). He contributed to *Punch,* 1875, and then worked on *Fun,* finally devoting himself to news drawing and some book illustration.
Exhib: RBA, 1865.

**BROWNING, Robert, Snr.**                   **1782-1866**
Father of the poet, amateur caricaturist and draughtsman. For many years a clerk in the Bank of England, he left an album of 172 caricatures, heads figure and groups, now in the Victoria and Albert Museum Library.
See illustration (below).

**BROWNLIE, R.A.   'R.A.B.'**                  **-1897**
Illustrator and landscape painter. Born in England but worked for most of his life in Scotland, principally in Glasgow. He was a talented caricaturist, contributing spirited cartoons to many magazines. He was influenced by Phil May, excelled in cockney subjects which he treated either with broad grey washes or in a more linear posterish style. He died at Edinburgh in 1897.
Contrib: *The Sketch [1893-95]; St. Paul's; Judy [1893]; The Pall Mall Maga: in [1893]; The English Illustrated Magazine [1894-96].*
Exhib: G; L; NEA; RSA; RSW.
Colls: V & AM.

**BRUCKMAN, William L.**                      **1866-**
Landscape painter. Born at the Hague and worked in London and Essex, 1904 to 1917. He contributed illustrations to *The Dome,* 1898.
Exhib: FAS, 1913.

**BRUHL, Louis Burleigh   RBA**              **1862-1942**
Landscape painter. He was born at Baghdad on 2 July 1862, and was trained in Vienna; President of the British Watercolour Society.
Illus: *Essex [Hope Moncreiff, c.1905 (colour)].*
Exhib: RA, 1889-1924.

**BRUNDAGE, Francis**
Illustrated *Tales From Tennyson* by Nora Chesson, Tuck, c.1900. A rather sugary artist not improved by chromo-lithography.

**BRUNELLESCHI**
Pseudonym of contributor to *The Illustrated London News,* 1913, colour plates in the style of Poiret.

**BRUNTON, William S.**                       **fl.1859-1871**
Illustrator. He was of Irish extraction and was a founder member of the Savage Club. Dalziel refers to 'Billy Brunton' as 'a constant contributor of comic sketches dealing with passing events of everyday life'. He has an unusual sign-manual of arrow-pierced hearts, or monogram 'WB'.
Contrib: *Punch [1859]; The Illustrated Times [1861 (military), and 1866, (comic)]; London Society [1863, 1865, 1868]; Fun [1865]; Tinsley's Magazine*

*ROBERT BROWNING SENIOR 1782-1866. Amateur caricature in pen and ink.*

Gordon Collection

*[1867]; The Broadway [1867-74]; Moonshine, [1871].*
Colls: V & AM.
Bibl: Dalziel, *A Record of Work*, 1901, p.314.

**BRYAN, Alfred·**      1852-1899
Caricaturist and illustrator. Born in 1852 and worked chiefly for *The Sporting and Dramatic News* where he did weekly cartoons as 'our Captious Critic'. He worked also for *Entracte, The Hornet,* and *Judy,* 1890, but is best remembered as chief cartoonist of *Moonshine.*
Colls: Brighton Art Gallery.

**BRYANT, Joshua**
Landscape artist and topographer, exhibiting at the RA and BI, 1798-1810, from address in Oxford Street, London. He travelled widely in France and illustrated Thornton's *A Sporting Tour Through France,* 1806, AT 84.

**BRYDEN, Robert  RE**      1865-1939
Wood engraver, etcher and sculptor. He worked in Glasgow after studying at the RCA, RA Schools and in Belgium, France, Italy, Spain and Egypt. ARE, 1891; RE, 1899. Died 22 August 1939.

Publ: *Etchings of Ayrshire Castles [3 Vols, 1899, 1908, 1910]; Etchings in Italy [1894]; A Series of Burns Etchings [1896]; Etchings in Spain [1896]; Auld Ayr and Some Ayr Characters [1897]; Woodcuts of Men of Letters of the 19th century [1899]; Workers, or Wanting Crafts [1912]; Edinburgh Etchings [1913]; Glasgow Etchings [1914]; Ayrshire Monuments [1915]; Twenty Etched Portraits From Life [1916]; Ayr Etchings [1922]; Parables of Our Lord [1924].*
Contrib: *The Dome [1900].*
Exhib: G; L; RA; RE; RSA.

**BUCHANAN, Fred**
Humorous draughtsman, working for *Fun* 1900, *The Graphic,* 1906 and *The Strand.* He was a member of the Strand Club in 1906.

**BUCHEL, Charles A.**      1872-1950
Portrait painter who made some illustrations of theatrical events and some posters. He practised in Hampstead, 1902-14, and in St. John's Wood, 1925.
Exhib: G; L; RA; RBA; ROI; RWA.
Colls: Witt Photo.

**BUCK, Adam**      1759-1833
Portrait and miniature painter. He was born at Cork in 1759, the son of a silversmith and acquired a considerable reputation before coming to England in about 1795. Buck's drawings with watercolour finish over pencil, and the face usually given a miniature-like treatment, epitomise slick Regency neo-classicism. His engravings are often of family virtues 'Affection' etc., and frequently include Greek revival ornament and are very decorative. The drawings are much rarer and desirable.
Illus: *Sentimental Journey [Sterne, n.d.]; Paintings on Greek Vases [100 pls., 1812].*
Exhib: BI; RA; RBA.
Colls: Ashmolean; BM; Fitzwilliam.

**BUCKLAND, Arthur Herbert  RBA**      1870-
Painter and illustrator. He was born at Taunton on 22 January 1870, and studied at the RCA and at Julian's, Paris, 1894. He subsequently worked in London and Barnet, 1911-25. RBA, 1894.
Illus: *Anne's Terrible Good Nature [E.V. Lucas, 1908].*
Contrib: *The Pall Mall Magazine; The Windsor Magazine; ILN [1898 and 1907]; The Quiver [1900].*
Exhib: RA; RBA; RI; ROI.
Colls: Witt Photo.

**BUCKLER, John Chessel**      1793-1894
Architect and topographical draughtsman. Born in 1793, the eldest son of John Buckler, FSA, the architect. Buckler was an antiquary like his father and his architectural practice was of houses in the gothic style. His meticulous drawings belong more to the 18th than to the 19th century.
Illus: *Views of Cathedral Churches in England [1822]; Observations on the*

*Original Architecture of St. Mary Magdalen, Oxford ... [1823]; Sixty Views of Endowed Grammar Schools [1827]; An Historical and Descriptive Account of the Royal Palace of Eltham [1828]; Remarks Upon Wayside Chapels [1843]; History of the Architecture of the Abbey Church of St. Albans [1847]; Description of Lincoln Cathedral [1866].*
Contrib: *Oxford Almanac [1816, 1817, 1820].*
Exhib: OWS; RA; RBA.
Colls: Ashmolean; BM; Bristol; Manchester; Norwich.
Bibl: H.M. Colvin *Biog. Dict. of English Architects,* 1954, p.106.

**BUCKLEY, Walter**
Illustrator of Sir H.M. Stanley's *My Dark Companions,* 1893.

**BUCKMAN, Edwin**      1841-1930
Watercolourist and illustrator. Born on 25 January 1841 and, after being educated at King Edward's School, Birmingham, he acquired the rudiments of drawing at the Birmingham Art School. Buckman was one of the original staff of *The Graphic* and contributed to its reputation as a paper of social concern. His drawings of the poor and neglected in Victorian society and his illustrations of the Paris Commune are amongst the strongest works of their kind. Van Gogh admired his work in his London years and wrote of it as 'drawn especially broadly and boldly and in a whole-hearted manner'. He was later drawing master to Her Majesty Queen Alexandra. ARWS, 1877. He died 15 October 1930.
Contrib: *The Graphic [1869-71 and 1889]; ILN [1871-76].*
Exhib: RA to 1877; RWS.
Bibl: *English Influences on Van Gogh,* Arts Council, 1974-75 p.51.

**BUCKMAN, W.R.**
Illustrator contributing to *Good Words,* 1868, and *Cassell's Magazine,* 1870.

**BULCOCK, Percy**      1877-1914
Illustrator specialising in ink drawing. Working at Burnley, 1899, and Liverpool, 1907.
Illus: *Blessed Damozel [Rossetti (Lane), 1900].*
Contrib: *The Dome [1899].*
Bibl: R.E.D. Sketchley, *English Book Illus.,* 1903, p.14, 122.

**BULL, René**      -1942
Illustrator and special artist. He was born in Ireland and went to Paris to study engineering, but left this for art work in London, 1892. After working for various magazines, he was appointed 'special' for *Black and White,* 1896, attending the Armenian massacres and the Graeco-Turkish War as artist. He made trips for the paper to the North-West Frontier and to the Atbara and Omdurman campaigns. He served in the First World War in RNVR, 1916, and RAF, 1917.

Bull was one of the most versatile specials because his stature as an artist was above average. Not only an accurate reporter, he was a talented comic draughtsman and a brilliant illustrator of fairy stories. His most successful humorous sketches were in strip cartoon form and were the nearest things in England to the subtle line of Caran D'Ache.
Illus: *Fables [J. de la Fontaine, 1905 (with C. Moore Park, q.v.)]; Uncle Remus [J.C. Harris, 1906]; The Arabian Nights [1912]; The Russian Ballet [A.E. Johnson, 1913]; Rubaiyat of Omar Khayyam [1913]; Carmen [P. Merimée, 1916]; Gulliver's Travels [J. Swift, 1928].*
Contrib: *Black & White [1892]; Chums [1892]; Pall Mall Budget [1893]; ILN [1893]; St. Paul's [1894]; Lika Joko [1894]; English Illustrated Magazine [1894-96]; Pick-Me-Up; The New Budget [1895]; The Sketch [1895-1918]; The Ludgate Monthly [c.1896]; The Bystander [1904].*
Colls: V&AM; Witt Photo.
Bibl: *Modern Book Illustrators and Their Work,* Studio, 1914, illus; B. Peppin *Fantasy Book Illustration,* 1975, p.186 illus.

**BULTEEL, Lady Elizabeth**      1798-1880
Amateur illustrator. Daughter of the 2nd Earl Grey, and wife of John Crocker Bulteel of Flete and Lyneham, Devon. She produced several books for her grandchildren, illustrated by herself, one small volume being printed.

**BUNBURY, Sir Henry Edward**      1778-1860
Soldier, military historian and amateur caricaturist. He was the son of Henry William Bunbury, 1750-1811, the amateur caricaturist who

published numerous satires at the end of the 18th century. His work strongly reflects the influence of his father.

## BUNDY, Edgar   ARA   1862-1922
Historical painter and illustrator. He was born at Brighton in 1862 and was largely self-taught. RI, 1891; RBA, 1891; ROI, 1892; ARA, 1915. One of his paintings acquired for the Chantrey Bequest, 1905. He died 10 January 1922.

Contrib: *The Graphic [1899]*.
Exhib: B; G; L; RA, from 1881; RBA; RI; ROI.

## BURCHELL, William John   1782-1863
Explorer, naturalist and artist. Born in 1782, he worked as a botanist at St. Helena, 1805-10, and then moved to Cape Town to study Cape-Dutch and travel in South Africa, 1811-15. He later explored the interior of Brazil, 1825-29, collecting plants and specimens.

Illus: *Travels in the Interior of Southern Africa [1822-24, AT 327]*.
Exhib: RA, 1805-20.

## BURGES, William   ARA FRIBA   1827-1881
Architect. One of the most original Victorian designers, combining a brilliant understanding of structure with a wild imagination. He was the son of a wealthy engineer and in early middle age met Lord Bute who became his enthusiastic and faithful patron. For this eccentric peer he created Cardiff Castle and Castell Cock, both of which have such an air of gothic fantasy that they might easily be three dimensional extensions of *Moxon's Tennyson*! Burges is included here because of his powerful and exciting ink drawing in the Victoria and Albert Museum of 'St. Simeon Stylites'. This masterpiece inspired *by* rather than *for* literature, is signed and dated 1861, and is totally in the spirit of the grandest 1860s illustration with German woodcuts as its inspiration. ARA, 1881.

Exhib: RA, 1860-80.

## BURGESS, Arthur James Wetherall   RI   1879-1956
Marine artist and illustrator. Born at Bombola, New South Wales, 6 January 1879, and settled in England in 1901. He studied shipping in the Royal Dockyards and became Art Editor of *Brassey's Naval and Shipping Annual*, 1922-30. He contributed to many illustrated papers, particularly *The Graphic*, 1910. RI, 1916; ROI, 1913.

Exhib: B; G; L; RA, from 1904; RBA; RI; ROI.
Colls: New South Wales, Nat. Gall.

## BURGESS, Ella
Illustrated P. Hay Hunter's *My Ducats and My Daughter*, 1894.

## BURGESS, Ethel K.   fl.1896-1907
Figure painter, illustrator, designer of bookplates. She was resident in Camberwell in 1896 and was a student at the Lambeth School in 1900, winning a first prize in the Gilbert Sketching Club. She was a good pen artist, basing her style on the rugged contrasts of the Newlyn School and capable of interesting period designs for children's books.
Exhib: L, 1901-07; RA.
Bibl: *The Artist*, 1897, pp.7-9 illus.; *The Studio*, Vol.10, 1897, p.113, bk. pl; Vol.20, 1900, pp.191-195 illus.

## BURGESS, H.G.
American artist, working as an illustrator in Boston in about 1907. He contributed illustrations to *The Illustrated London News*, 1896-97; *English Illustrated Magazine*, 1897; *Cassell's Family Magazine*, 1898; *Pearson's Magazine*.

Colls: V & AM.

## BURGESS, Walter William   -1908
Etcher. He was elected RE in 1883 and, in 1894, published *Bits of Old Chelsea*, illustrated by himself.

Exhib: RA; RE.

## BURLEIGH, Averil Mary   -1949
Painter and illustrator. She studied at Brighton School of Art and

seems to have worked all her life in Sussex; she married the painter C.H.H. Burleigh. Her mannered medievalism is rather like that of E.F. Brickdale (q.v.), and she tackled the same sort of subjects, the works of Shakespeare and Keats. ARWS, 1939.

Exhib: FAS, 1925, 1934; GG, Arts & Crafts Exhib., 1913; RA; RI; RWS.
Bibl: *The Studio*, Vol.58, 1913.

*SIR EDWARD COLEY BURNE-JONES RA 1833-1898. Caricature of William Morris, the poet and designer in a wooden bath tub.*

## BURNE-JONES, Sir Edward Coley Bt.   RA   1833-1898
Artist, book illustrator, caricaturist and writer of illustrated letters. Born at Birmingham 28 August 1833 and after being educated at King Edward's School, Birmingham, went up to Oxford in 1833. There he met William Morris (q.v.), and in the succeeding year became influenced by the paintings of Rossetti and the writings of Ruskin, whom he met in 1856. Burne-Jone's position as a quasi-member of the Pre-Raphaelite group and his development as a major subject and decorative painter are not of primary importance here; his work as an illustrator falls into three categories. In 1857, he illustrated *The Fairy Family*, for his friend Maclaren, rather conventional designs and typical of the romantic school of the 1840s. In the 1860s he contributed a few illustrations to the magazines that were thriving on the revival in wood engraving. In the last years of his life, 1892 to 1898, he had a fruitful partnership with the Kelmscott Press in designing for books of high typographic quality. His influence in the latter venture lasted well into the 1900s in private press work. ARA, 1885; ARWS, 1886. Baronet, 1894.

Illus: *Good Words [1862-63]*; *Parables From Nature [1865]*; *Dalziel's Bible Gallery [1880-81]*; design for title to one of Ruskin's lectures, 1865 (not used); *King Poppy [Lytton (title and frontis.)]*; *The Queen Who Flew: A Fairy Tale [Hueffer, 1894 (title and frontis.)]*; *The High History of The Holy Grail [1898]*; *The Beginning of The World [1903]*; *Letters to Katie [1925]*.

Kelmscott Press Books: *A Dream of John Ball [frontis.]; A King's Lesson [1892 (frontis.)]; The Golden Legend [1892 (woodcuts)]; The Order of Chivalry [1893 (frontis.)]; The Wood Beyond the World [frontis.]; Sir Pereccyvelle of Gales [1895 (frontis.)]; The Life and Death of Jason, The Well at the World's End [1896]; The Works of Geoffrey Chaucer [1896]; Sire Degrevaunt [1897]; Syr Ysambrace [1897]; Love is Enough [1897]; The Story of Sigurd the Volsung [1898].*
Exhib: FAS, 1876; GG; New Gall; OW; RA.
Colls: Ashmolean; Bedford; Birmingham; Fitzwilliam; Manchester; V&AM.
Bibl: M. Bell, *Sir E B-J*, 1898; M. Harrison and B. Waters, *B-J*, 1973; *B-J*, Cat of Exhibition, Arts Council 1975 (J. Christian).
See illustrations (below, right and p.251).

## BURNE-JONES, Sir Philip Bt.     1862-1926
Portrait painter. He was born on 2 October 1861, the only son of Sir E.C. Burne-Jones Bt. (q.v.). He was educated at Marlborough College and University College, Oxford. He died 21 June 1926.

Illus: *The Little Iliad [Maurice Hewlett, 1915].*
Exhib: B; G; L; M; P; RA; ROI; RSA.

*SIR EDWARD COLEY BURNE-JONES RA 1833-1898. Pencil drawing for the frontispiece of* Syr Percyvelle of Gales, *published by William Morris at the Kelmscott Press, 1895.* Victoria and Albert Museum

## BURNEY, Edward Francis     1760-1848
Illustrator and caricaturist. Born at Worcester in 1760, the son of Dr. Burney, the composer, and brother of the novelist Fanny Burney. He studied at the RA Schools and exhibited there from 1780 both book illustrations and portraits. Among his earlier works were a set of illustrations for his sister's novel *Evelina*. But Burney's general run of illustrations give no indication of the inventive mind that lies behind his large caricature subjects 'An Elegant Establishment for Young

*SIR EDWARD COLEY BURNE-JONES RA 1833-1898. Frontispiece for* Syr Percyvelle of Gales, *published by William Morris at the Kelmscott Press, 1895. Wood engraving from the preceding drawing.* Victoria and Albert Museum

Ladies', 'The Waltz' etc. These superbly finished compositions of many figures are in direct succession to Hogarth and especially from their theatrical and literary standpoint. An album of drawings sold at Christie's on 5 March 1974 gave some indication of the artist's scope, including religious, classical, poetic and comic subjects. The smaller decorative subjects are not uncommon, he excelled in small groups, head and tail pieces.

Illus: *Buffon's Natural History [1791]; The Copper Plate Magazine [1792-1803]; Ireland's Avon [1795]; The Pleasures of Hope [Thomas Campbell, 1806]; Burney's Theatrical Portraits; Sporting Magazine [frontis.]; The New Doll [c.1825].*
Colls: BM; V & AM; Witt Photo.
Bibl: Iolo Williams, *Early English Watercolours*, 1952, pp.132-133; M. Hardie, *Watercolour Paint in Brit.*, Vol.I, 1966, pp.152-153.

## BURNS, Cecil Lawrence     c.1863-1929
Portrait and genre painter. He studied under Herkomer (q.v.), and at RA, becoming the Principal of Camberwell School of Arts and Crafts, 1897, and Principal of Bombay School of Art in 1899. He was curator of the Victoria and Albert Museum, Bombay, 1902-1918. He became a Member of the NEA, 1887 and RBA, 1899. He died 26 July 1929.

Illus: *Belle Dame Sans Merci [n.d.].*
Exhib: L; M; NEA; RA; RBA; ROI.
Bibl: *The Studio*, Vol.6, 1896, illus.

## BURNS, M.J.
Marine artist. Contributed illustrations to *The Graphic*, 1910.

**BURNS, Robert ARSA** 1869-1941

Figure and portrait painter. He was born at Edinburgh in 1869 and after studying at South Kensington and in Paris, 1890-92, worked for the whole of his life in the city. Burns was specially successful with crowded figure subjects built up densely as in a medieval tapestry; a sketch-book of such subjects of Border legend was sold at Sotheby's in April 1976. The artist was President of the Society of Scottish Artists, ARSA, 1902, resigned 1920, and Director of Painting at Edinburgh College of Art, 1914.

Illus: *The Evergreen [1895]*.
Exhib: B; G; L; M; RA; RHA; RSA; RSW.

**BURTON, E.J.**

Contributor to *Punch,* 1847-49.

**BURTON, Sir Frederick William RHA RWS FSA** 1816-1900

Painter. He was born at Corofin House, County Clare, on 8 April 1816, the son of an amateur landscape painter. In 1828 he went to Dublin and studied under the Brocas brothers, attracting the attention of George Petrie, the landscape painter and archaeologist. He studied in Munich from 1851-1858 although he continued to exhibit in London. He was elected ARHA in 1837 and RHA in 1839; ARWS, 1854 and RWS, 1855, Hon Member, 1886. Burton was immensely successful as a miniature painter and watercolourist and became Director of the National Gallery in 1874, receiving a knighthood on his retirement twenty years later. He died at Kensington, 16 March 1900.

Contrib: *ILN, [1896]*.
Exhib: G; RA from 1842; RHA.
Colls: Ashmolean; BM; Nat. Gall., Ireland; V & AM.

**BURTON, Sir Richard Francis** 1821-1890

Scholar, explorer, translator and artist. Born in 1821 and was educated at Trinity College, Oxford, 1840. He followed an army career from 1842, was an assistant on the Sind survey. but abandoned this for a wandering life studying Moslem beliefs and customs. He explored Somaliland in 1854, the Nile in 1856-59, and travelled in North America, 1860. Burton served in the Crimean War, but from 1861 was in the diplomatic service as British Consul in Fernando Po, Santos, Damascus and finally Trieste, 1872. He was made a KCMG in 1885, but his fame really rests on his knowledge of Asiatic languages and his translation of classics like *The Book of The Sword',* 1884 and *The Arabian Nights,* 1885-88.

Illus: *Falconry in the Valley of the Indus [1852, AT 479]; Personal Narrative of a Pilgrimage to El-Medinah and Meccah [1855-56, AT 368]*.

**BURTON, William Paton** 1828-1883

Landscape painter. Born in Madras in 1828, the son of an Indian army officer. He was educated in Edinburgh and proposing to take up architecture as a career, entered the office of David Bryce. He left Bryce for a life of landscape painting in oils and watercolours and travelled on the Continent and in Egypt in search of subjects. He died on 31 December 1883, near Aberdeen.

Contrib: *Willmott's Sacred Poetry of the 16th, 17th and 18th Centuries [1862]; Legends and Lyrics [1865]; Golden Thoughts From Golden Fountains [1867]*.
Bibl: Aberdeen; BM; Manchester; V & AM; Witt Photo.

**BURTON, William Shakespeare** 1830-1916

A minor Pre-Raphaelite who exhibited the 'Wounded Cavalier' at the RA in 1856. He studied at the RA Schools and won the gold medal there in 1851. His only known illustration is for *Once a Week,* 1865.

Exhib: RA; RI.

**BURY, Rev. Edward John MA** 1790-1832

Amateur artist. He was the son of Edward Bury of Walthamstow, Essex, and was educated at University College, Oxford, BA, 1811, MA, 1817. He was Rector of Lichfield, Hants from 1814 and married in 1818, the Lady Charlotte Campbell, daughter of the 5th Duke of Argyll, and died in May 1832. He illustrated his wife's *The Three Great Sanctuaries of Tuscany,* 1833.

Bibl: *Alumni Oxonienses 1715-1886*.

**BURY, Thomas Talbot** 1811-1877

Architect and artist. He was born in London and became a pupil of Pugin in 1824 although left him to set up his own practice in 1830. He was one of the draughtsmen of Pugin's *Paris,* 1831.

Publ: *Remains of Ecclesiastical Woodwork [1847]; Rudimentary Architecture [1849]*.
Colls: BM; Manchester.

**BURY, Viscount** **See KEPPEL, William Coutts**

**BUSBY, Thomas Lord**

Figure artist. He exhibited portraits at the RA from 1804-1837. He illustrated *Costumes of the Lower Orders in Paris,* c.1820, AT 107; *Costumes of the Lower Orders of The Metropolis,* 24 plates, 1818.

**BUSHBY, Lady Frances** 1838-1925

Amateur flower artist. She was born in 1838, the daughter of the 6th Earl of Guilford and wife of the Recorder of Colchester. In 1866 she illustrated *Early Rising by a Late Philosopher,* for private circulation.

**BUSHNELL, A.**

Contributed illustration to *Good Words,* 1861.

**BUSS, R.W.** 1804-1875

Painter and illustrator. He was born in London in 1804, the son of R.W. Buss, engraver and enameller. He studied drawing under George Clint, ARA, but began his career as an illustrator by working for Charles Knight. He was particularly closely associated with Knight in producing the *Penny Magazine* and an oil by him in the Victoria and Albert Museum shows the interior of the magazine office with a wood engraver at work. Buss's greatest test was to produce etched work of sufficient quality for use in *Pickwick,* 1836, but he failed in this and was succeeded by H.K. Browne (q.v.). He was Editor of *The Fine Art Almanack* and wrote a book *The Principles of Caricature,* 1874. He died at Camden Town, 1875.

Illus: *London [Knight, 1841]; Old England; Chaucer; Widow Barnaby [Frances Trollope, 1839]; Peter Simple [Marryat]; Jacob Faithful [Marryat, 1834]; The Court of King James II [Ainsworth]*.
Exhib: BI; RA; RBA, 1826-1859.
Colls: BM; Fitzwilliam; V & AM.
Bibl: Alfred G. Buss, *Notes and Queries,* April 24, 1875; G. Everitt, *English Caricaturists,* 1893, pp.363-366.

**BUTLER, Lady (Elizabeth) née Thompson RI** 1846-1933

Battle painter and illustrator. She was born in Lausanne in 1846 and studied at South Kensington, Florence and Rome. She was the sister of Alice Meynell, the poetess, and married in 1877 Lt-General Sir William F. Butler. Although she specialised in military and equestrian subjects, she did an extensive amount of black and white work and illustrated her sister's poems. She died 2 October 1933.

Illus: *Poems [Alice Meynell]; Ballads [Thackeray]; Campaigns of the Cataracts [W.F. Butler]; Letters From the Holy Land [1905]; From Sketch-Book and Diary [c.1905]*.
Contrib: *Merry England; The Graphic [1873 and 1889]*.
Exhib: B; FAS, 1877; G; L; M; RA from 1873.
Colls: BM.
Bibl: *An Autobiography,* 1923.

**BUXTON, Dudley**

Contributor of half tone comic sporting subjects to *Punch,* 1904.

**BYLES, W. Housman RBA** fl.1890-1925

Landscape and figure painter, practising in London, 1903, and at West Hamprett, Chichester, 1907-25. Byles contributed illustrations to *The Pall Mall Magazine* and *The Sketch* in the 1890s. RBA, 1901.

Exhib: B; L; New Gall; RA; RBA; ROI.

**BYRNE, Claude**

Painter working at Rathmines, Dublin. He contributed illustrations of Irish distress to *The Illustrated London News,* 1886, and exhibited at the RHA, 1884.

**BYRNE, E.R.**

Contributed marine subjects to *The Graphic,* 1873.

Christmas and *Bracebridge Hall [Washington Irving, 1876]*; *North Italian Folk [1878]*; *The House That Jack Built* and *John Gilpin [1878]*; *Elegy on a Mad Dog* and *The Babes in the Wood [1879]*; *Aunt Judy's Magazine [1879]*; *Jackanapes, Daddy Darwin's Dovecote [1879]*; *Three Jovial Huntsman, Sing a Song of Sixpence [1880]*; *Breton Folk [1880]*; *What The Blackbird Said [1880]*; *The Queen of Hearts, The Farmer's Boy [1881]*; *Hey Diddle Diddle, Baby Bunting [1882]*; *Greystoke Hall [1882]*; *The Fox Jumps Over The Parson's Gate, A Frog He Would [1883]*; *A Sketch Book, Some of Aesop's Fables [1883]*; *Come Lasses and Lads, Ride a Cock Horse [1884]*; *The English Illustrated Magazine [1884-86 (initials)]*; *Mrs. Mary Blaize, The Great Panjandrum [1885]*; *The Complete Collection of Pictures and Sons [1887]*; *The Complete . . . Contributions*; *The Boys' Own Paper*.
Exhib: RA, 1872-85.
Colls: Ashmolean; Bedford; BM; Fitzwilliam; V & AM; Walsall.
Bibl: Henry Blackburn, *RC A Personal Memoir*, 1886; *The Artist*, June 1898, pp.65-69 illus.; M.G. Davis, *RC*, 1946; R.K. Engen, *RC*, 1976.
See illustrations (below and p.255).

### CALDER, Scott
Amateur illustrator working at Chelsea. Winner of book illustration competition, *The Studio*, Vol.8, 1896, p.184, illus.

### CALDERON, William Frank    ROI                1865-1943
Figure, landscape and sporting painter. Born in 1865, son of P.H. Calderon. He studied at the Slade School and became founder and Principal of the School of Animal Painting, St. Mary Abbots Place, Kensington, 1894-1916. Calderon worked in London 1883-90 and then in Midhurst, 1889, and finally at Charmouth, Dorset. He was elected ROI in 1891 and married the daughter of H.H. Armstead RA (q.v.).
Contrib: *Black and White, 1891*.
Exhib: B; G; L; M; New Gall; RA; RBA; RHA; ROI.

### CALDWELL, Edmund                                 -1930
Animal painter. He worked in Swanley and Guildford, 1887-90 and in Haverstock Hill, London, 1902-25. He contributed to *The Sporting and Dramatic News*.
Exhib: L; M; RA, 1880; RBA, 1881-83; RHA; RI; ROI.

### CALKIN, Lance    ROI                          1859-1936
Portrait painter. Born 22 June 1859 and studied at South Kensington, Slade and RA Schools. He painted all the leading Edwardian figures including King Edward VII, Captain Scott and Joseph Chamberlain. He was elected RBA in 1884 and ROI in 1895. He died 10 October 1936.
Contrib: *The Graphic [1887-89 (portraits) and 1901-02 (genre)]*.
Exhib: B; G; L; M; New Gall; RA; RBA; ROI.
Bibl: *Who Was Who 1929-40*.

### CALLAWAY, Rev. William Frederick
Amateur cartoonist. He was a Baptist minister at York and contributed to *Punch*, 1855. He exhibited at the RA, BI, and at other exhibitions 1855-61.

# C

### CADENHEAD, James    ARSA RSW                 1858-1927
Landscape painter and illustrator. Born at Aberdeen in 1858 and studied at the RSA School and then in Paris under Duran. He was elected ARSA in 1902 and RSA in 1921 and was a founder member of the NEAC, 1889. Cadenhead was a talented printmaker and in his few book illustrations the influence of the Japanese print on his work is very striking. He signs his work ⓒ
Illus: *Pixie [Mrs. G. Ford, 1891]*; *Master Rex [Mrs. G. Ford, 1891]*; *Hell's Piper [ballad by Riccardo Stephens, n.d.]*.
Contrib: *The Evergreen [1894-96]*.
Exhib: G; L; M; NEA, 1899-1900; RSA from 1880.
Bibl: *The Studio*, Vol.10, 1897, p.67 illus.; Vol.55, 1912, pp.10-20 illus.

### CALDECOTT, Randolph    RI                     1846-1886
Watercolourist and illustrator. Born at Chester on 22 March 1846, the son of an accountant and was educated at the King's School. He became a bank clerk at Whitchurch and Manchester, but had greater success as a draughtsman for local periodicals, 1868-69. His wish to reach a wider public was only realised in 1871, when sketches by him were published in *London Society;* this was his real début and in the next decade he became the most popular illustrator of children's books of the period published by Edmund Evans, and second only to Kate Greenaway (q.v.). Caldecott shared with Kate Greenaway a love of the past and especially the last days of the 18th century before industrialization. A keen sportsman, Caldecott's world is always rural, pretty and untroubled, a landscape of manor houses, hunts and skating parties loosely hung round a story. His costume subjects for *The Graphic*, often in the form of letters, are better than his contemporary cartoons and he is an artist who comes across more vividly in colour than in black and white.

Caldecott was a very finished artist, but his illustrations lack the humour of Leech and indeed of the period he depicts. His flat colour and slick outlines were to have many successors, in particular Phil May (q.v.), and Cecil Aldin (q.v.), his spiritual follower being Hugh Thomson (q.v.). Caldecott's promising career was cut short by illness and he died at St. Augustine, Florida, where he was seeking a cure on 12 February 1886.
Illus. and Contrib: *Will o'the Wisp [1867]*; *The Sphinx [1867]*; *London Society [1871-72]*; *Punch [1872 and 1883]*; *The Harz Mountains [1872]*; *Frank Mildmay [1873]*; *The Graphic [1873-86]*; *Pictorial World [1874]*; *Old*

*RANDOLPH CALDECOTT RI 1846-1886. 'The Three Huntsmen.' An illustration to* The Complete Collection of Pictures and Songs, *1887.*

*RANDOLPH CALDECOTT RI 1846-1886. 'Cupid in Society.' Outline drawing in pen and ink.* Jeffrey Gordon Collection.

## CALLOW, William      1812-1908

Watercolourist. He was born at Greenwich in 1812 and his first art employment was in colouring prints for the Fielding brothers. He went to Paris in 1829 to help in engraving views of the city for a book, remaining there with a group of English artists until 1841. He was intimate with Turner and Bonington and shared a studio with T.S. Boys (q.v.) but his book illustrating is limited to the one work, Charles Heath's *Picturesque Annual: Versailles,* 1839, compiled in the years 1829-36. RWS, 1848. He died at Great Missenden, 20 February, 1908.

Bibl: *Autobiography,* Edited by H.M. Cundall, 1908; *Walker's Quarterly,* 1927 XXII; M. Hardie, *Watercolour Paint in Brit,* Vol.III, 1968, pp.35-42.

## CALOR, Tom

Figure artist. He contributed to *Punch,* 1914.

## CALTHROP, Dion Clayton      1878-1937

Artist, writer and stage designer. Born on 2 May 1878, son of John Clayton, the actor. Educated at St. Paul's School and studied art at St. Johns Wood, Paris, with Julian's and Colarossi's. In early life he did a good deal of commercial work for magazines but then concentrated entirely on illustrating his own books. He served with the RNVR during the First World War and died 7 March 1937.

Illus: *History of English Costume; King Peter; Guide to Fairyland; The Dance of Love; Everybody's Secret; Tinsel and Gold; The Charm of Gardens; Perpetua; St. Quin; A Trap to Catch A Dream; Bread and Butterflies; A Bit of a Time; Beginners Please; All For the Love of A Lady; English Dress.*
Contrib: *The Dome [1897]; The Quartier Latin [1898]; Pick-Me-Up [1899]; The Idler; The Butterfly [1899]; The Connoisseur [1910 (décor)].*
Exhib: RA; ROI, 1900-03.
Bibl: *Modern Book Illustrators and Their Work,* Studio, 1914 illus; *My Own Trumpet,* 1935 (autobiography); *Who Was Who 1929-40.*

## CALVERT, Edith L.      fl.1886-1907

Flower painter and illustrator. Working in London 1893-1907.

Illus: *Baby's Lays [Elkin Mathews, 1897]; More Baby's Lays [Elkin Mathews, 1898].*
Contrib: *The Quarto [1898].*
Exhib: RBA; SWA, 1886-93.
Bibl: R.E.D. Sketchley, *English Book Illus,* 1903, pp.102, 165.

## CAMERON, Sir David Young    RA      1865-1945

Painter and etcher. Born at Glasgow in 1865 and was educated at Glasgow Academy and studied at the Glasgow School of Art and at Edinburgh. Cameron was one of the outstanding group of print-makers who rose to fame before the First World War. He excelled in landscape but also did excellent illustrative work and even bookplates; his oils and watercolours are sensitive interpretations of his native Scotland, but the earlier work is purer. He served as War Artist for the Canadian Government, 1917, and in 1919 taugnt at the British School at Rome. He became ARA, 1911; RA, 1920 and RSA, 1918. He was knighted in 1924.

Illus: *Old Glasgow Exhibition [1894 (title)]; Charterhouse Old and New [1895]; Scholar Gipsies [John Buchan, 1896]; An Elegy and Other Poems [R.L. Stevenson, 1896 (title)]; Story of the Tweed [Sir Herbert Maxwell, 1905]; The Compleat Angler [1902].*
Portfolios: *The Clyde Set [1890]; North Holland [1892]; North Italy [1896]; The London Set [1900]; Paris Etchings [1904]; Etchings in Belgium [1907].*
Contrib: *Good Words [1891-92]; Black and White [1892]; The Ludgate Monthly [1895]; The Quarto [1896]; The Yellow Book [1896,(cover)].*
Exhib: Antwerp; Brussels, 1895; Chicago, 1893; Munich, 1905; NEA; Paris, 1900; RA; RE; ROI.
Colls: BM; V & AM.
Bibl: *The Studio,* Winter No, 1900-01, pp.34-5, illus.; R.E.D. Sketchley, *English Book Illus,* 1903, pp.41, 64, 133; F. Rinder, *An Illustrated Catalogue of . . . Etched Work,* 1912; *Modern Book Illustrators and Their Work,* Studio, 1914.

## CAMERON, Hugh    RSA RSW      1835-1918

Portrait and genre painter. He was born at Edinburgh in 1835 and studied at the Trustees Academy. He worked partly at Edinburgh and partly at Largs, travelling on the Continent. ARSA, 1859 and RSA, 1869; RSW, 1878.

Contrib: *Pen and Pencil Pictures From the Poets [Nimmo, 1866]; Idyllic Pictures [Cassell, 1867]; Good Words.*
Exhib: GG; RA; RBA.

## CAMERON, John

Etcher and dry-point artist. He was working at Inverness in 1917 and at Corstorphine, 1918-1925. A coloured illustration by this artist for *Treasure Island* is in Witt Photo Library.

Exhib: B; G; L; RHA; RSA.

255

**CAMERON, Katharine (Mrs. Kay) RSW ARE**      1874-1965

Painter and etcher. Born in Glasgow, daughter of the Rev. Robert Cameron and sister of Sir. D.Y. Cameron (q.v.). She was educated in Glasgow and studied at Glasgow School of Art and in Paris at Colarossi's. She was a prolific illustrator of children's books, giving full vent to her gift for flower studies and in 1928 she married Arthur Kay, HRSA. RSW, 1897 and ARE, 1920.

Illus: *In Fairyland; The Enchanted Land; Legends of Italy; A City Garden; Water Babies; Idylls of the King; Aucassin and Nicolette; Undine; Rhyme of the Duchess May; Flowers I Love; Haunting Edinburgh; Where The Bee Sucks; Iain the Happy Puppy; Stories From the Ballads [Macregor, 1908].*
Contrib: *The Yellow Book [1897].*
Exhib: Berlin; L; Leipzig; RA; RSA; Venice.

**CAMPBELL, John E.**

Illustrator of the boys' story *Wulnoth the Wanderer,* H. Escott Inman, 1908.

**CAMPBELL, John P. (Seaghan MacCathmhaoill)**      fl.1904-1912

Illustrator of Celtic legends. He illustrated *Celtic Romances; Irish Songs; The Tain, Four Irish Songs,* all c.1909-1912. His penwork is reminiscent of wood engraving and his figures usually have a strange bending posture as if floating. No biographical details are known.

Colls: Witt Photo.
Bibl: *An Illustrator of Celtic Romance,* The Studio, Vol.48, 1909, pp.37-43; *Modern Book Illustrators and their Work,* Studio 1914.

**CAMPION, George Bryant NWS**      1796-1870

Painter, topographical artist and lithographer. He specialised in military subjects and was for some time a drawing master at the Royal Military Academy, Woolwich. He emigrated to Munich where he died in April 1870. NWS, 1834. Wrote *The Adventures of a Chamois Hunter.*

Illus: *Virtue's View in Kent [1830].*
Exhib: NWS; RBA, 1829-31.
Colls: Ashmolean; BM; Witt Photo.

**CANZIANI, Estella Louisa Michaela RBA**      1887-1964

Portrait painter and illustrator. Daughter of the painter Louisa Starr, was born 12 January 1887 and studied with Sir Arthur Cope, at Watson Nichol's School and at the RA Schools. RBA, 1930.

Illus: *Round About Three Palace Green [1939]; Costumes Traditions and Songs of Savoy; Piedmont; Through The Appenines and the Lands of the Abruzzi; Songs of Childhood [Walter de la Mare]; Oxford in Brush and Pen; The Lord's Minstrel [C.M.D. Jones, 1927]; Good Adventure [E. Vipont, 1931].*
Exhib: L; New Gall, 1906; RBA; RI, 1913-; RSA; SWA.
Colls: V & AM.

**CAPON, William**      1757-1827

Topographical artist and architect. He was born at Norwich in 1757, the son of a painter. At a young age he began to paint portraits but, on moving to London, he showed an aptitude for architecture and was apprenticed to Novozielski as scene painter at Ranelagh Gardens and the Italian Opera. Capon acted as scene painter to Kemble at Drury Lane, 1794, and was generally associated with his productions. He was able to establish a small architectural practice and in 1804 was accredited architectural draughtsman to the Duke of York. He died at Westminster in 1827.

Contrib: *Britton's Beauties of England and Wales [1808, 1815].*
Exhib: BI; RA; RBA, 1788-1827.
Colls: Bath; BM; Witt Photo.
Bibl: H.M. Colvin, *Biog. Dict. of English Architects,* 1954, p.121; *Views of Westminster by William Capon,* London Topographical Society, 1923-24.

**CARAN D'ACHE (Emmanuel Poirié)**      1858-1909

French caricaturist. Born in Moscow in 1858 and studied there before settling in Paris. He first came to fame as cartoonist on *Chronique Parisienne,* but also with shadow pictures in *Chat Noir.* He was particularly popular for his silhouette caricatures and for his historical jokes; a vogue for both of these caught on in England, largely due to his influence. Caran D'Ache contributed in his fluid outline to *Figaro, L'Illustration, La Revue Illustrée* and drew for his own books,

*Comédie du Jour, Comédie de Notre Temps, Les Courses dans L'Antiquité, Carnet de Chèques, The Discovery of Russia.* He played a leading part in the Dreyfus affair and started the magazine *Ps'itt.* Died in Paris in 1909.

Contrib: *The Graphic [1887]; Punch [1894]; English Illustrated Magazine [1896].*
Exhib: FAS, 1898.
Bibl: J. Pennell, *Pen Drawing and Pen Draughtsmen,* 1894, p.112 illus.

**CARLILE, Lieutenant W.O. RA**

Contributor to *The Illustrated London News,* 1873.

**CARLISLE, The 9th Earl of**      See HOWARD, George

**CARMICHAEL, John Wilson**      1800-1868

Marine painter and illustrator. Born at Newcastle-upon-Tyne in 1800 and went to sea at an early age, later being apprenticed to a shipbuilder and employed in drawing and designing. He was really a watercolourist, but from 1825 experimented with oils and became a regular exhibitor in London. He moved to London in 1845 and was employed by *The Illustrated London News* to make drawings in the Baltic during the Crimean War, 1853-56. He left London in 1862, due to illness and settled at Scarborough where he died on 2 May 1868.

Publ: *The Art of Marine Painting in Watercolours [1859]; The Art of Marine Painting in Oil Colours [1864].*
Contrib: *Views on the Newcastle and Carlisle Railway [1839]; Howitt's Visits to Remarkable Places [1841].*
Colls: BM; Greenwich; Newcastle; V & AM.

**CARMICHAEL, Stewart of Dundee**      1867-

Portrait painter, decorator and architect. He studied at Dundee, Antwerp, Brussels and Paris, before practising in Dundee. He produced three design in 1899, 'The Unhappy Queen', 'The Players of the Jews Harp' and 'Disinherited', which show strong Beardsley influence and may have been intended for a book.

Exhib: G; L; RSA.
Colls: Witt Photo.

**CARNEGIE, Rook**

Artist for *The Graphic* in Roumania, 1910.

**CARPENTER, William**      1818-1899

Painter and etcher of oriental subjects. He was born in London in 1818, the son of Mrs. M.S. Carpenter, the portrait painter. He spent most of his life in India, sketching the country's manners and customs and an exhibition of these works was held at South Kensington in 1881. He contributed to *The Illustrated London News,* 1857-59, his Indian scenes being among the first reproduced in colour for the magazine.

Colls: Ashmolean; BM; V & AM.

**CARR, David**      1847-1920

Figure and bird painter. Born in London, 1847 and was educated at King's College, London. He was articled as a pupil engineer to W.H. Barlow, CE, Consulting Engineer to The Midland Railway, and worked there in civil engineering. He left this career and became an art student for three years at the Slade School under Alphonse Legros, finally going to Paris, 1881. Carr's interests were wide ranging and as well as practising as a painter in Campden Hill, Kensington, 1890-1902, and at Bedford Park, 1902-14, he designed several country houses in the West of England. He died 25 December 1920.

Contrib: *The Pall Mall Gazette; The England Illustrated Magazine [1884-87 (birds and landscapes)].*
Exhib: B; GG; L; M; New Gall; NWS; RA from 1875; RBA, from 1875; RI.
Colls: Witt Photo.
Bibl: *Who Was Who,* 1916-28.

**CARR, Ellis**

Illustrator of *Climbing in the British Isles,* Alan Wright, 1894. He exhibited at the ROI, 1884.

**CARR, Mrs. Geraldine**                                fl.1896-1916
Sculptor and painter on enamel. She worked in London and supplied a decorative headpiece to *The Quarto*, 1896.

Exhib: L, 1901-16; RA.

**CARR, Sir John**                                      1772-1832
Miscellaneous writer, minor poet and illustrator. Carr was a gentleman of private means, who travelled for his health and was knighted in 1806. He was pilloried by Lord Byron in a cancelled passage of *English Bards and Scotch Reviewers*, 1809.

Publ: *The Stranger in France; A Tour From Devonshire to Paris; A Northern Summer [1805]; A Tour Through Holland [1807, AT 216]; Caledonian Sketches [1808].*
Illus: *Descriptive Travels . . . in . . . Spain [1811, AT 144].*
Colls: BM.

**CARRICK, J. Mulcaster**                               fl.1854-1878
Painter and illustrator. An extremely interesting minor Pre-Raphaelite who specialised in landscape painting. He illustrated *The Home Affections*, Charles Mackay, 1858, contributing four drawings, and in 1865 designed some for *Legends and Lyrics* by A.A. Proctor. At least one illustration 'An Episode From Life' was turned into an oil painting. Carrick uses great contrasts of light and shade, dappling the backs and clothing of his figures in sunlight, minutely hatching in the shadow.

Exhib: BI, 1854; RBA, 1856; RI.
Colls: Witt Photo.

**CARROL, Lewis    see DODGSON, Charles**

**CARSE, Alexander    'Old Carse'**                     fl.1796-1838
Scottish genre painter. He was probably born in Edinburgh where he worked as a young man before going to London in 1812. There he exhibited at the RA and BI, 1812-20, before returning to Scotland for the last twenty years of his life. He designed title pages and vignettes for editions of Burns and Schiller, c.1830.

Colls: BM; Witt Photo.

**CARTER, David Broadfoot**                             fl.1905-1910
Illustrator and designer. He studied at Glasgow School of Art and afterwards in Paris, before settling in London as a professional lithographer. He undertook comic illustrations for books in strong pen line.

Exhib: G.
Colls: Witt Photo.

**CARTER, Frederick    ARE**                            1885-1967
Painter and etcher. He was born near Bradford in 1885 and studied in Paris and at the Académie Royale des Beaux-Arts, Antwerp. On his return to England he worked for poster printers, but went back to study at the Polytechnic, and won gold medals for book illustrations. He studied etching under Sir Frank Short (q.v.), ARE, 1910 and 1922.

Illus: *The Wandering Jew; The Dragon of the Alchemists; Eighteen Drawings; The Dragon of Revelation; D.H. Lawrence and The Body Mystical; Symbols of Revelation; Introduction and Drawings for Byron's Manfred; Florentine Nights [Heine]; decorations for Cyril Tourneur's works.*
Contrib: *various magazines about 1916.*
Exhib: L; NEA; RA; RE; ROI.
Colls: Witt Photo.

**CARTER, Owen Browne**                                 1806-1859
Topographical draughtsman and architect. He worked mainly at Winchester but travelled to Egypt in about 1829-30.

Publ: *Picturesque Memorials of Winchester [1830]; Some Account of the Church at Bishopstone [1845].*
Illus: *Illustrations of Cairo [Robert Hay, 1840].*
Exhib: RA, 1847-49.
Colls: BM.

**CARTER, Reginald Arthur Lay**                         1886-
Black and white artist contributing humorous illustrations to magazines, c.1910-13.

Colls: V & AM.

**CARTER, Rubens Charles**                              1877-1905
Painter and comic draughtsman. Born at Clifton in 1877 and studied at the Bristol School of Art. He worked for numerous magazines, his cartoons being in the style of Tom Browne (q.v.).

Illus: *Punch [1900]; Pick-Me-Up [1899].*
Colls: BM; Witt Photo.

**CARTER, Samuel John    ROI**                          1835-1892
Animal painter and illustrator. Born at Swaffham, Norfolk in 1835 and studied in Norwich. For many years he was the principal animal illustrator for *The Illustrated London News,* contributing many fine drawings of cattle, sheep and horse shows all over Britain. ROI, 1883.

Contrib: *ILN [1867-89]; The Graphic [1886].*
Exhib: BI, 1863-66; GG; RA; RBA, 1861-68; ROI.

**CARTER, Z.A.**
Contributor of 'Edwin and Angelina' social subjects to *Punch,* 1900.

**CASELLA, Miss Julia**
Sculptor. Contributing illustration to *The Graphic,* 1880, and exhibiting at Grosvenor Gallery, 1885.

**CASTAIGNE, A.**                                       fl.1902-1910
Illustrator of royal events and social subjects for *The Graphic,* 1902-03 and 1905-10.

**CATCHPOLE, Frederic T.**                              fl.1897-1940
Landscape and figure painter. Worked in Chelsea and was elected RBA in 1913. He was drawing for *Judy* in 1890.

Exhib: GG; L; NEA, 1904; RA; RBA, 1914-25; RI; ROI.

**CATHERWOOD, Frederick**                               1799-1854
Architect and topographer. He was born in London in 1799 and became a pupil of the architect, Michael Meredith. He travelled in Italy, Greece and Egypt from 1821-25 and again in 1831 up the Nile Valley to record its antiquities. He settled in New York after 1836 and made a celebrated voyage to South America with J.L. Stephens in 1839, the results appearing in *View of Ancient Monuments in Central America, Chiapas and Yucatan,* 1844. Lost on the steamer *Arctic,* 1854.

Exhib: RA, 1820-31.
Bibl: H.M. Colvin, *Biog. Dict. of English Architects,* 1954, p.129.

**CATTERMOLE, Charles**                                 1832-1900
Watercolourist. Born in 1832, nephew of George Cattermole (q.v.). He was elected RI, 1870; RBA, 1876 and ROI, 1883. He illustrated a number of books and died 21 August 1900.

Exhib: BI, 1858-93; RBA; RI.

**CATTERMOLE, George**                                  1800-1868
Watercolourist and illustrator of romance. He was born at Dickleburgh, Norfolk in 1800, the youngest brother of the Rev. R. Cattermole (q.v.). He worked first as an architectural draughtsman, contributing largely to Britton's *English Cathedrals,* 1832-36. By the 1830s his emphasis was changing from historic buildings to historic incidents in which figures played a more important part than their backgrounds. Cattermole established a vogue for the swash-buckling 17th century where duels and sieges took place in accurate surroundings and alluring watercolours. His drawings were probably due to a mammoth edition of Scott which he undertook, *Poetical and Prose Works of Sir W. Scott* and *Landscape Illustrations of the Works of Sir W. Scott,* 1833. He had a great sense of history, his costumes were accurate and the figures drawn in with vivid spontaneous pen

GEORGE CATTERMOLE 1800-1868. 'Little Nell's Grave at Tong church, Staffordshire.' Watercolour heightened with white. 14⅝ins. x 19⅜ins. (37.1cm x 49.2cm).
Victoria and Albert Museum

lines; sometimes individual illustrations were re-drawn as finished watercolours.

Cattermole enjoyed enormous success especially after illustrating *Barnaby Rudge* and *The Old Curiosity Shop* in Dickens's *Master Humphreys Clock,* 1841. Dickens was an intimate friend, called him 'Kittenmoles' and through him and others, the artist became part of the Kensington Gore set and a Member of the Garrick Club. Although he refused a knighthood in 1839 and was frequently patronised by Queen Victoria, his later life was clouded by unsuccessful attempts to establish himself as an oil painter. AOWS, 1822, and after a lapse, OWS, 1833. He died in London in 1868.

Illus: *Roscoe's North Wales [1836]; Cattermole's Historical Annual: The Great Civil War [R. Cattermole, 1841-45]; Cattermole's Portfolio [1845].*
Contrib: *Heaths Gallery [1836-38].*
Exhib: BI, 1827; OWS; RA, 1819-.
Colls: Ashmolean; BM; Glasgow; Leeds; Manchester; V & AM.
Bibl: OWS Club, IX, 1932; M. Hardie, *Watercol. Paint. in Brit.* Vol.III, 1968, pp.88-91.
See illustrations (above and p.259).

**CATTERMOLE, The Rev. Richard**                    c.1795-1858
Topographical artist. The eldest brother of George Cattermole (q.v.), studied under John Britton and drew nine illustrations for *Pyne's Royal Residences,* 1819, and *The Cathedral Antiquities of Great Britain,* 1814-35. He went up to Christ's College, Cambridge and took a BD in 1831, entering holy orders. He was minister of the South Lambeth Chapel from 1844 and Vicar of Little Marlow from 1849. He compiled the *Historical Annual,* illustrated by his brother and wrote *The Book of the Cartoons of Raphael,* 1837. He died at Boulogne-sur-mer, 1858.

Exhib: OWS, 1814-18.

**CATTERSON, Albert**                    fl.1895-1896
Illustrator. He specialised in coloured crayon drawings of sentimental subjects in a pretty posterish style. His work appears chiefly in *The*

*Sketch,* 1895-96. He signs his work Bert Catterson.
Colls: V & AM.

**CAWSE, John**                    1779-1862
Portrait painter and caricaturist. He published political caricatures with an anti-Foxite bias between 1799 and 1801. He was also a very talented personal caricaturist and the British Museum has a fine one by him of Joseph Witon, RA. Published *The Art of Oil Painting,* 1840.

Exhib: OWS; RA, 1801-45.
Bibl: M.D. George, *English Political Caricature,* 1959, Vol.II, p.261.
Colls: Witt Photo.

**CECIONI, Adriano**                    1838-1886
Italian sculptor and caricaturist. He contributed twenty six cartoons to *Vanity Fair,* 1872.

**CHALON, Alfred Edward    RA**                    1780-1860
Portrait and history painter, caricaturist. He was born in Geneva in 1780, the son of a Huguenot refugee and the younger brother of J.J. Chalon (q.v.). The family moved to Kensington and the two brothers lived and worked there for the rest of their lives. He studied at the RA Schools, 1797, and began exhibiting at the RA in 1801. After working in Ireland, Chalon established himself as a fashionable painter of beauties and actresses, many of the portraits appearing in the albums of the period. He became Painter in Watercolours to Queen Victoria and it is his portrait of the Queen that appeared on many early issues of Colonial stamps. Chalon was a Member of the Association of Artists in Watercolours, 1807-08, and founded The Sketching Society in 1808. His caricatures in brown wash were done for private circulation only. He was elected ARA in 1812 and RA, 1816. He died

258

at Campden Hill, Kensington, 3 October 1860 and was buried at Highgate.

Illus: *Gallery of Graces [1832-34]; Portraits of Children of the Nobility [L. Fairlie, 1838]; The Belle of a Season [M. Gardiner, 1840]; A Memoir of Thomas Uwins [S. Uwins, 1858].*
Contrib: *Heath's Gallery [1836, 1838]; The Chaplet [1840]; ILN [1843].*
Exhib: BI, 1807-38; RA, 1810-60.
Colls: Ashmolean; BM; Leeds; NPG; Nottingham; V & AM; Witt Photo.
Bibl: *Art Journal,* January, 1862; M. Hardie, *Watercol. Paint in Brit.,* Vol.II, 1967, p.149.

### CHALON, John James  RA OWS                1778-1854

Landscape painter, genre painter and caricaturist. He was born in Geneva in 1778, the son of a Huguenot refugee and came to England with his family and younger brother A.E. Chalon (q.v.). He studied at the RA Schools, 1796, after giving up a commercial career and exhibited there from 1800. He travelled widely in the south and west of England making sketches and, after a visit to Paris in 1819-20, published a set of lithographs of the city, 1822. Associate of the OWS, 1805, and Member, 1807. He was elected ARA in 1827 and RA, 1841. Like his brother he practised caricature and had more success with it in a spirited and free style of wash. The Laing Art Gallery, Newcastle has a more conventional series of classical book illustrations in sepia, showing the influence of The Sketching Society which he helped to found in 1808. He died at Campden Hill, Kensington, 14 November 1854, and was buried at Highgate.

Illus: *Scenes in Paris [1820-22, AT 108].*
Exhib: BI, 1808-43; OWS; RA, 1800-54.
Colls: BM; Maidstone; Newcastle; V & AM.
Bibl: *Art Journal,* January, 1855; M. Hardie, *Watercol. Paint. in Brit.,* Vol.II, 1967, pp.149-150.

### 'CHAM' Comte Amedée Charles Henri De Noé      1819-1879

French draughtsman and caricaturist. He was born in Paris on 26 January 1819, and was intended to study at the École Polytechnique.

After several failures, he turned his talent for drawing into a career and began work under the caricaturist Charlet and with Paul Delaroche. He quickly became one of the leading lithographic caricaturists and published his first series in 1839. A friend of W.M. Thackeray, Cham was persuaded to complete some blocks overnight for Mark Lemon and these appeared in *Punch* in 1859. He died in September 1879.

### CHAMBERLAIN, D.                             fl.1887-1914

Watercolourist and illustrator. Working in Glasgow from 1887 to 1914 and exhibiting there and at the RSW. This artist drew in the late *art nouveau* style of the Glasgow School and won the chapter heading competition in *The Studio,* Vol.12, 1898, illus.

### CHAPMAN, C.H.

Comic illustrator. He was the principal illustrator of the 'Billy Bunter' stories from 1912 when he first met their author, Frank Richards. He was the first artist to give all the Greyfriars boys a distinctive character in the pen drawings, working closely to Richards' texts, but choosing his own subjects. He lived near Reading and died at the age of ninety.

Bibl: W.O. Lofts and D.J. Adley, *The World of Frank Richards,* 1975.

### CHAPMAN, Captain E.F.

Amateur illustrator. He travelled to Asia on the Yakund Expedition, 1874, and his sketches appeared in *The Illustrated London News.*

### CHAPMAN, George R.                          fl.1863-1890

Portrait painter who did some illustrations. He exhibited at the RA, 1863-74, and illustrated his own *The Epic of Hades,* c.1890. He also published a book *Songs of Two Worlds.*

Colls: Witt Photo.

*GEORGE CATTERMOLE 1800-1868. 'Little Nell's Grave at Tong church, Staffordshire.' Original wood engraving from* The Old Curiosity Shop *by Charles Dickens, published in* Master Humphrey's Clock, *1841.*

**CHARLES, William**                                                    **-1820**
A caricaturist who worked in England, 1803-04, and drew anti-British satires during the Anglo-American War of 1812. He died in Philadelphia in 1820.
Bibl: M.D. George, *English Political Caricature*, Vol.11, 1959, p.261.

**CHARLTON, C. Hedley**
Illustrator. He contributed drawings of children in a poster style to *Punch*, 1908.

**CHARLTON, Edward William   RE**                                       **1859-1925**
Landscape painter. Working at Ringwood, Hants, 1890-99 and at Lymington, Hants, 1899-1925. ARE, 1892 and RE, 1907.
Exhib: L; RA; RE; ROI; RWA.
Bibl: *The Studio*, Winter No. 1900-1, pp.56-57 illus.

**CHARLTON, Miss Gertrude**
Portrait painter and illustrator of children's books. She worked in Chelsea, 1899-1902, and illustrated her own *Excellent Jane*, 1899. She exhibited at the NEA, 1901.

**CHARLTON, John**                                                      **1849-1917**
Animal and battle painter and illustrator. He was born at Bamburgh, Northumberland in 1849 and after working in a bookshop, studied at the Newcastle School of Art under W.B. Scott (q.v.). He then went to South Kensington and worked for some time under J.D. Watson (q.v.), thereby forming an important link between the 1860s illustrators and those of the 1890s. He was at his best when drawing scenes from high life, particularly hunting subjects and royal occasions. He settled permanently in London in 1874 and his connection with *The Graphic* dates from two years later. His work for the magazine on the Egyptian Campaign of 1882 turned his attention to battle scenes, and he became one of the leading exponents of military paintings. He died in London, 5 November 1917. RBA, 1882 and ROI, 1887.
Illus: *Twelve Packs of Hounds [1891]; Red Deer [H.A. Macpherson, 1896].*
Contrib: *The Graphic [1876-95].*
Exhib: B; G; L; M; New Gall; RA; RBA, 1871-   ; ROI; RSA.
Colls: Newcastle; V & AM; Witt Photo.

**CHARTRAN, Théobald**                                                  **1849-1907**
Portrait painter. He was born at Besançon in 1849 and had a distinguished career painting state portraits and elaborate mural schemes. He exhibited regularly in Paris from 1872 and at the RA from 1881. He contributed several cartoons to *Vanity Fair*, 1878-88.
Colls: V & AM.

**CHASEMORE, Archibald**                                                **fl.1868-1901**
A regular cartoonist for *Judy*, 1875-89. He was a contributor to *Punch* 1868-79, and supplied jokes for his friend Charles Keene (q.v.) to draw. His own work was in very finished pen and ink but tending to be rather stiff. His political subjects are amusing and collectable. Contributed to *Pick-Me-Up*, 1901; *Ally Sloper's Half Holiday; The Boys' Own Paper.*

**CHATTERTON, Henrietta Georgina Marcia, Lady**                        **1806-1876**
Writer and artist. She married in 1824 Sir William Abraham Chatterton of County Cork, but lived in England from 1852. On his death she married Edward Heneage Dering in 1859. She published poems and travels, 1837-76.
Illus: *The Pyrenees with Excursions into Spain [1843, AT 211].*

**CHEESEMAN, Thomas Gedge**                                             **fl.1890-1925**
Painter of domestic subjects. He worked at Highbury, 1890, and at Battersea, 1908-25. Exhibiting at the RA, 1890-91, and ROI. He contributed to *The Cornhill Magazine*, 1885.

**CHESTERTON, Gilbert Keith**                                           **1874-1936**
Author, novelist and critic. He was born at Campden Hill in 1874 and studied at the Slade School. Before he established himself as a

novelist, Chesterton reviewed art-books for *The Bookman*. He was a competent amateur artist and his chalks of humorous subject have considerable charm.
Colls: Witt Photo.

**CHESWORTH, Frank**
Prolific illustrator in the 1890s.
Contrib: *The Sketch [1894]; The New Budget [1895]; The Sporting and Dramatic News [1895]; Pick-Me-Up [1896]; Illustrated Bits; The Pall Mall Magazine.*

**CHINNER, J.A.**
Amateur illustrator. He contributed to *Punch*, 1908.

**CHRISTIAN, W.F.D.**
Illustrator contributing to *The Cambridge Portfolio*, 1840.

**CHRISTIE, James Elder**                                               **1847-1914**
Figure and portrait painter. He studied at Paisley School of Art and South Kensington. Visited Paris and worked in London, 1880-94, and at Glasgow, 1894-1914. He became a Member of the NEA in 1887.
Illus: *Susy [Bret Harte, 1897].*
Exhib: B; G; GG; L; M; NEA; New Gall; RA; RSA.

**CLARK, Christopher**                                                  **1875-**
Painter of military subjects and illustrator. He was born 1 March 1875 and was self-taught. He drew frequently for magazines from c.1900 and was also a poster artist. He served in the RNVR, 1917-19. RI, 1905.
Illus: *Lorna Doone [R.D. Blackmore, 1912]; Tales of the Great War [Sir H. Newbolt, 1916].*
Exhib: L; RA; RI.
Colls: Witt Photo.

**CLARK, John Heaviside   'Waterloo Clark'**                           **c.1771-1863**
Landscape painter and book illustrator. He worked in London between 1802 and 1832, but died in Edinburgh in 1863. He earned his nickname from the series of sketches that he undertook immediately after the Battle of Waterloo.
Illus: *Foreign Field Sports [1814, AT 2].*
Publ: *Practical Essay On The Art of Colouring and Painting Landscapes [1807]; Practical Illustrations of Gilpin's Day [1814].*
Exhib: RA, 1801-32.
Colls: Glasgow.

**CLARK, Joseph**                                                       **1834-1926**
Painter and illustrator. He was born at Cerne Abbas in Dorset in 1834 and was educated there by the Rev. William Barnes. He studied art at Leigh's School and was a student at the RA Schools. Two of his pictures were bought by the Chantrey Bequest and many were engraved. He died at Ramsgate 4 July 1926.
Contrib: *Passages From Modern English Poets [1862].*
Exhib: NWS; RA, 1857-1925; RBA; RI.
Colls: Tate.
Bibl: *Who Was Who*, 1916-28.

**CLARK, Joseph Benwell**                                               **1857-**
Painter, draughtsman and illustrator. He was the nephew of Joseph Clark (q.v.) and specialised in interiors and animal painting. He was a pupil of Alphonse Legros and although much of his output is unremarkable, he was responsible for a handfull of exceptional book illustrations in the 1890s. In 1895, he drew the pictures for a Lawrence & Bullen edition of *The Surprising Adventures of Baron Munchausen*, pen and ink work in a bold and woodcutty style, very advanced and imaginative. The publishers clearly thought highly of his work, for he is one of the supporting illustrators in *Lucian's True History*, 1894, where Beardsley was the star. He worked for most of his life in North London, sometimes in conjunction with V.M. Hamilton.
Illus: *Ali-Baba [1896] Sinbad the Sailor [1896].*
Contrib: *Judy [1889-90 (strip cartoons)]; ILN [1891].*
Exhib: GG; RA; RBA, 1876-91.
Colls: V & AM.
See illustration (p.261).

*JOSEPH BENWELL CLARK b.1857. Illustration to* The Surprising Adventures of Baron Munchausen, *1895. Ink and chinese white. Signed with initials and dated 1894. 6ins. x 5ins. (15.2cm x 12.7cm).* Victoria and Albert Museum

**CLARKE, Arthur**        -c.1912
One of the original illustrators of 'Billy Bunter'. He succeeded Hutton Mitchell (q.v.), as artist on *The Magnet* and died about 1912. He also worked for *The Gem*.
Bibl: W.O. Lofts and D.J. Adley, *The World of Frank Richards*, 1975.

**CLARKE, Edward Francis C.**        fl.1867-1887
Painter, architect and illustrator. He practised in London and exhibited there 1872-1887.
Contrib: *The Churchman's Shilling Magazine [1867]; Dark Blue [1871-73].*
Exhib: L; NWS; RBA, 1882-84; RI; RSA.

**CLARKE, Harry**        1890-1931
Illustrator and decorative artist. Born in Dublin in 1890 and was apprenticed to his father, head of a large firm of stained glass artists in 1906. Attended the Dublin Metropolitan School of Art, 1910-13, and was awarded three gold medals and one which took him to the Île-de-France. On his return he set up an independent stained glass workshop in Dublin and carried out a great deal of work in Ireland, England and abroad. As a book illustrator, he was one of the most successful followers of Beardsley, capturing a great deal of the latter's sinister atmosphere, although his finish was less polished. He died of tuberculosis in Switzerland in 1931. RHA, 1925.
Illus: *Fairy Tales [Hans Christian Andersen, 1916]; Tales of Mystery and Imagination [Edgar Alan Poe, 1919]; The Years at the Spring [Lettice D'O Walters, 1920]; The Fairy Tales of Charles Perrault [1922]; Faust [Goethe, 1925]; Selected Poems [A.C. Swinburne, 1928]; The Playboy of the Western World [J.M. Synge].*
Exhib: RHA; St. George's Gall.

Colls: V & AM; Witt Photo.
Bibl: *Modern Book Illustrators and their Work,* Studio, 1914; B. Peppin, *Fantasy Book Illustration,* 1975, pp.21-22, 186 illus.
See illustration (below).

**CLARKE, Joseph Clayton**   'Kyd'        fl.1883-1894
Illustrator and caricaturist. He drew illustrations for an edition of Dickens in 1883 and made a caricature of Aubrey Beardsley (q.v.), in 1894.
Colls: Witt Photo.

**CLARKE, Miss Maud V.**
Horse painter. Contributor to *English Illustrated Magazine,* 1887, *The Illustrated London News,* 1889, and *The Sporting and Dramatic News,* 1890.

**CLAUSEN, Sir George**   RA RWS        1852-1944
Landscape painter and painter of rural life. He was born in London in 1852, the son of a Danish sculptor and was much influenced by continental art and the French School in particular. Member of the NEA, 1888; he was elected ARA in 1895 and RA in 1908, having exhibited there since 1876. Clausen was Professor of Painting at the RA, 1903-06, and Director of the Schools. He was knighted in 1927. RWS, 1898. He provided a single illustration for *The Quarto,* 1897.
Exhib: L; M; RA; RWS.
Colls: Bedford; BM; Fitzwilliam; Manchester; V & AM.

**CLAXTON, Adelaide (Mrs. George Turner)**        fl.1858-c.1905
Illustrator. The younger daughter of Marshall C. Claxton (q.v.), who was the first artist to take an exhibition of pictures to Australia. She accompanied her father there and afterwards to Ceylon, and India, 1860. Vizetelly says she 'satirized the social follies' and her pictures had great popularity, but the drawing was often very stiff and the proportions of the figures poor.
Illus: *A Shillingsworth of Sugar Plums [1867]; Brainy Odds & Ends [1900].*
Contrib: *ILN [1858]; The Illustrated Times [1859-66]; London Society [1862-65, 1870]; Judy [1871-79]; Sidelights on English Society [Grenville Murray, 1881].*
Exhib: RA; RBA, 1865-76; SWA, 1880-89.
Colls: V & AM.

*HARRY CLARKE 1890-1931. Tail-piece for Goethe's* Faust, *G.G. Harrap, 1925, limited edition.*

**CLAXTON, Florence A. (Mrs. Farrington)** fl.1855-1879
Illustrator. She was the eldest daughter of Marshall C. Claxton (q.v.), and sister of Adelaide Claxton (q.v.). Accompanied her father to Australia, Ceylon and India and made sketches of the last two countries which were later published. She was a more serious artist than her sister and specialised in historical drawings and the illustration of romantic stories rather than purely humorous subjects. Her work is, however, often poor in composition and coarse in execution.

Contrib: *The Illustrated Times [1855-67]; ILN [1860]; London Society [1862]; The Churchman's Family Magazine [1863]; Good Words [1864].*
Exhib: RA; RBA, 1865-73; SWA, 1896.
Colls: V & AM.

**CLAXTON, Marshall C.** 1811-1881
Historical painter and illustrator. He was born at Bolton in 1811 and was a pupil of John Jackson RA. He entered the RA Schools in 1831, won a medal in the Painting School, 1832, and a Society of Arts Gold Medal in 1835. He travelled to Australia in the 1850s with the idea of starting an art school and exhibiting pictures, the first man to do so. He returned through Ceylon and India and made sketches of life and scenery there. He signs his work *CM*

Contrib: *ILN [1852-58]; The Illustrated Times [1859]; The Churchman's Family Magazine [1863].*
Exhib: BI, 1833-67; RA; RBA, 1832-75.
Colls: V & AM (Designs for an edition of Pilgrim's Progress).

**CLAYTON, Benjamin**
Illustrator of military scenes. Contributed to *The Illustrated Times,* 1856-60.

**CLAYTON, Eleanor 'Ellen' Creathorne** c.1846-
Novelist and illustrator. She was born in Dublin and after studying at the British Museum began to contribute humorous drawings to magazines. She undertook the designing of calendars, valentines, etc. in the 1870s.

Illus: *Miss Milly Moss [1862].*

**CLAYTON, John R.**
Wood engraver and draughtsman, specialising in figure subjects. He was a High Victorian artist whose greatest claim to fame is that he was consulted by D.G. Rossetti (q.v.) about the wood engravings for the *Moxon, Tennyson,* 1857.

Contrib: *George Herbert's Poetical Works [1856]; Pilgrim's Progress [1856]; Course of Time [1857]; Poets of the Nineteenth Century [1857]; Dramatic Scenes and Other Poems [1857]; Lays of the Holy Land [1858]; The Home Affections [1858]; Krummacher's Parables [1858]; Architectural Sketches From the Continent [R. Norman Shaw, 1858 (border of frontis.)]; English Poets, Illustrated by the Junior Etching Club [1862]; Barry Cornwall's Poems.*
Colls: V & AM; Witt Photo.
Bibl: Chatto & Jackson, *Treatise on Wood Engraving,* 1861, p.599; Forrest Reid, *Illustrators of the Sixties,* 1928, pp.32-36.

**CLEAVER, Dudley**
Contributor to *The Penny Illustrated Paper,* c.1890.

**CLEAVER, F.R.**
Illustrator of genre subjects for *The Illustrated London News,* 1889.

**CLEAVER, Ralph** fl.1893-1926
Black and white artist. He was employed on many illustrated papers in the 1890s but regularly on *The Graphic* and *Daily Graphic* from 1906. He served in the RNVR throughout the First World War. Cleaver specialised in naval and military subjects, but also drew theatrical performances and cartoons. He enlivened his straight magazine reportage by introducing comic elements, and his drawing is always clear.

Illus: *Mating of Clopinda [James Bank, 1909].*
Contrib: *Judy [1893]; ILN [1895-1901]; The St. James's Budget; The Gentlewoman; Penny Illustrated Paper; The Temple Magazine; The Royal Magazine; Punch [1900].*
Colls: V & AM.
Bibl: *The Studio,* Winter No, 1900-01, p.84 illus.

*REGINALD THOMAS CLEAVER c.1954. Study of a seated woman for an illustration in* Punch, *c.1900. Pencil and grey wash. 9½ins. x 6¾ins. (24.1cm x 17.1cm).*
Author's Collection

**CLEAVER, Reginald Thomas** -1954
Black and white artist. He was employed on *The Graphic* staff from about 1893 and worked for that paper and *The Daily Graphic* until 1910. Spielmann calls his drawing 'somewhat hard but of great beauty in its own line', but this hardness wore off to make Cleaver, according to Thorp, the most important *Graphic* artist of the Edwardian era. His studies for drawings, where washes are subtly added to sensitive pencil lines, are among the most beautiful of their type. Cleaver was a marvellous portrayer of women and of the social scene as numerous *Punch* cuts testify.

Contrib: *The Graphic [1893-1910]; Punch [1894-1930].*
Colls: Author; V & AM.
Bibl: Spielmann, *The History of 'Punch',* 1895, pp.92, 565; J. Pennell, *Pen Drawing and Pen Draughtsmen,* 1894, pp.330-331; J. Pennell, *Modern Illustration,* 1895, p.106; *The Studio,* Winter No, 1900-01, p.84 illus.; *Mr. Punch With Horse and Hound,* New Punch Library, c.1930, p.115.
See illustration (above).

**CLEGG, Ada**
Book decorator. Contributing to *The English Illustrated Magazine,* 1896-97.

**CLEGHORN, John** fl.1840-1880
Painter of landscapes, wood carver and sculptor. He exhibited in London from 1840-80.

Contrib: *Winkle's Illustrations to the Cathedral Churches [1836-37]; Knight's London [1842].*

**CLENNELL, Luke** 1781-1840
Wood engraver, illustrator and watercolourist. He was born at Ugham, near Morpeth, on 8 April 1781, the son of a farmer. Although started in trade, Clennell was apprenticed in 1797 to Thomas Bewick (q.v.),

262

*LUKE CLENNELL 1781-1840. Fashion illustration for* La Belle Assemblée, *c.1805-6. Watercolour.*

and became one of his best pupils. He left Newcastle in 1804 and on becoming a wood engraver in London, was awarded the golden palette of the Society of Arts in 1806 and 1809. Chatto records that, 'Clennell who drew beautifully in watercolours, made many of the drawings for the Border Antiquities; and the encouragement that he received as a designer and painter made him resolve to entirely abandon wood engraving.' He became an Associate of the OWS in 1812 and won the 150 guinea premium offered by the BI for the best sketch of 'The Decisive Charge of the Life Guards at Waterloo'; it was published in 1821. In April 1817, he became insane and although he continued to make small sketches and write poems, his professional career was at an end. Clennell died in Newcastle Lunatic Asylum, 9 February 1840.

Clennell brought to book illustration some of the freedom which was associated with the Bewick School and the naturalness of head and tail pieces which characterised it. He designed some bookplates and in surviving designs looks backwards to French illustration and forwards to the insouciant charm of Kate Greenaway.

Contrib: *La Belle Assemblée or Fashionable Companion [1805-06]; Ackermann's Religious Emblems [1809]; Britton's Beauties of England and Wales [1814]; Border Antiquities of England and Scotland [1814-17]; The Antiquarian Itinerary [1818].*
Exhib: OWS; RA.
Colls: BM; Greenwich; Newcastle; V & AM.
Bibl: Chatto & Jackson, *Treatise on Wood Engraving,* 1861 pp.521-527.
See illustration (above).

### CLIFFORD, Harry P. RBA — fl.1895-1938
Black and white artist, specialising in architectural subjects. He worked in Kensington, 1902-25, and exhibited at many exhibitions. RBA, 1898.

Exhib: B; L; RA; RBA; RI.
Bibl: *The Studio,* Winter No., 1900-01, p.68 illus.

### CLIFFORD, Maurice
Figure artist. Working in Bedford Park, London and winner of *The Studio* tailpiece competition, Vol.12, 1897-98, illus.

Exhib: L; M; RA; ROI, 1890-95.

### CLINT, George ARA — 1770-1854
Portrait painter and engraver. He was born in London in 1770 and after working as a decorator and a miniature painter, he began to paint personalities from the London stage. He was an ARA from 1821 to 1836.

Contrib: *The British Theatrical Gallery [1825, AL 418].*
Exhib: BI; OWS; RA; RBA.
Colls: BM.

### CLUTTON, Henry — 1819-1893
Architect. He was a pupil of Edward Blore and a friend of William Burges (q.v.). With Burges he won the first place in the Lille Cathedral Competition, and in the course of a long career designed many schools, houses and churches.

Illus: *Remarks ... On The Domestic Architecture of France [1853 (tinted liths.) AT 100].*

### COBB, Ruth
Figure artist. She contributed to *Punch,* 1914.

### COCK, Eianley
Perhaps E.C. Loveland Cock, recorded in *The Years Art,* 1909-30. He contributed a cartoon to *Vanity Fair,* 1913.

### COCKERELL, Charles Robert RA — 1788-1863
Architect, draughtsman and etcher. He was the son of Samuel Pepys Cockerell, the architect and was educated at Westminster. After studying with his father, he went on a prolonged tour of Greece, Asia Minor and Sicily, 1810-17, discovering the frieze of the Temple of Apollo at Phigaleia, 1812. He was the leading exponent of Victorian classical architecture, designing the Taylor Buildings at Oxford, 1841-52. RA, 1836; Professor of Architecture at RA, 1840-57.

Publ: *The Antiquities of Athens etc. [1830]; The Temple of Jupiter Olympus at Agrigentum [1830]; The Iconography of the West Front of Wells Cathedral [1851]; The Temples of Jupiter Panhellenus etc. [1860].*
Illus: *Ancient Marbles in the British Museum [1820-30 (frontis.)]; Travels in Sicily, Greece and Albania [Rev. T.S. Hughes, 1820, AT 203].*

Exhib: RA, 1818-58.
Colls: BM; RIBA; V & AM.
Bibl: A.E. Richardson, *Monumental Classic Architecture in Great Britain and Ireland*, 1914; David Watkin, *CRC, 1975*.

**COHEN, Ellen Gertrude**  fl.1884-1905

Figure painter and illustrator. She worked in London and contributed to *The English Illustrated Magazine*, 1890-94.

Exhib: B; L; M; P; RA; RBA; RI; ROI; SWA.

**COÏDE  See TISSOT, J.J.**

**COKE, Thomas William  Earl of Leicester**  1752-1842

'Mr. Coke of Holkam', created 1st Earl of Leicester, 1837. He was a talented caricaturist in the style of Ghezzi, but his drawings were only for private circulation.

Colls: Windsor.

**COLE, C.W.**  fl.1884-1905

Humorous artist. He contributed comic genre subjects to *The Graphic*, 1884-85, and collaborated with C.J. Staniland (q.v.) in views of Japan in the same magazine, 1887.

**COLE, Herbert**  1867-1930

Draughtsman, illustrator and engraver, designer of bookplates. There is little biographical material on this important artist. He appears to have worked for many magazines in the 1890s, either in a flamboyant art nouveau style or in comic illustrations in the manner of Charles Keene. By the 1900s, Cole was combining a fluid pen with the most sensuous colouring, his designs are always inventive if they lack the

*Such was the dirge the violet-crowned Muses sang over the son of Thetis*

*HERBERT COLE 1867-1930. 'Sunset of the Heroes.' An illustration for a book published by W.M.L. Hutchinson in 1911. Pen and ink with watercolour. 12¹/8ins. x 8³/8ins. (30.8cm x 21.3cm).*  Victoria and Albert Museum

dramatic force of a Rackham or a Harry Clarke, returning more perhaps to the book design of Crane.

Illus: *Gulliver's Travels [Lane, 1899]; The Rubaiyat* and *Flowers of Parnassus [1901]* and *A Ballade upon a Wedding [in the same series]; The Nut-Brown Maid [1901]; The Rime of the Ancient Mariner [1900]; The Poems and Songs of Shakespeare [1904]; Songs and Lyrics From the Dramatists, 1533-1797 [1905]; The Dragon Volant [Le Fanu, 1907]; The Sunset of the Heroes [W.M.L. Hutchinson, 1911]; Fairy Gold: A Book of English Fairy Tales [Ernest Rhys, 1926]; Rise of the Romantic School in France [C. Yriarte, n.d. (decor)]*.
Contrib: *Fun [1901]; The Pall Mall Magazine*.
Exhib: RA, 1898 and 1900.
Colls: V & AM; Witt Photo.
Bibl: R.E.D. Sketchley, *English Book Illustration*, 1903, pp.13-14, 122.
See illustration (below left).

**COLEMAN, Edmund Thomas**  fl.1839-1877

Landscape painter and topographer. He specialised in alpine scenery.

Illus: *Sketches on the Danube [1838, AT 79]; Scenes From The Snow Fields [1859, AT 68]*.
Exhib: BI, 1852-59; RA; RBA, 1850-1877.

**COLEMAN, William Stephen**  1829-1904

Landscape and figure painter and illustrator. He was born at Horsham, Sussex in 1829, the son of a physician. He was a keen naturalist and this led him to the arts and the illustration of books. He illustrated the Rev. J.G. Wood's natural history books and worked in oil, pastel and etching. His landscapes are idealised and romantic although his scientific work is accurate. In later life he became associated with Minton's Art Pottery Studio for which he designed. He was on the committee of the Dudley Gallery until 1881 and died on 22 March 1904 at St. John's Wood.

Illus: *Our Woodlands, Heaths and Hedges [1859]; British Butterflies [1860]*.
Contrib: *The Illustrated Times [1856]; ILN [1857]; The Book of The Thames [S.C. Hall, 1859]; The Book of South Wales [Mr. and Mrs. S.C. Hall, 1861]; Mary Howitt's Tales; The Field*.
Exhib: 1866-79; RBA, 175.
Colls: Blackpool; Glasgow; V & AM; Witt Photo.

**COLEMAN-SMITH, Pamela**  fl.1899-1917

Painter and illustrator of children's books. She was working at Knightsbridge, London, 1907 and exhibited at the SWA and the Baillie Gallery, 1905-17. She illustrated *Widdicombe Fair* in a limited edition, 1899, the drawings done in stumpy black outline in the style of the Beggarstaff Brothers.

**COLES, E.**

Contributor to *Fun*, 1900.

**COLLIER, The Hon. John**  1850-1934

Figure, portrait and landscape painter. He was born in London, 27 January 1850, son of 1st Baron Monkswell. He was educated at Eton and the Slade School and then under E.J. Poynter (q.v.), and J.P. Laurens, Paris. He married successively two of the daughters of T.H. Huxley.

Although a very popular artist in the grand manner, Collier was a rare illustrator and reveals himself to be a weak pen artist. He illustrated Thomas Hardy's 'The Trumpet Major' for *Good Words* in 1880, which was not successful and in 1894 tackled *Thackeray's Ballads* in the Cheap Illustrated Edition, *English Illustrated Magazine*, 1890-91. He published various manuals on oil painting. Died 11 April 1934.

Exhib: GG; RA; RBA.
Colls: Blackburn; Sydney; V & AM.
Bibl: E.C.F. Collier, *A Victorian Diarist, Monkswell, 1873-95*, 1944.

**COLLINGS, Arthur Henry**  -1947

Portrait and figure painter. He worked in North London, 1902-25, and won a gold medal at Paris Salon 1907. RBA, 1897; RI, 1913.

Contrib: *The Lady's Pictorial [1895]*.
Exhib: L; RA; RBA; RI; ROI.

**COLLINGS, J.P. or T.P.**

Illustrator, specialising in ornament and works of art, contributing to *The Graphic*, 1875-1889.

**COLLINGWOOD, Professor William Gershom  MA FSA  1854-1932**
Landscape painter and illustrator. He was born in 1854, the son of W. Collingwood, RWS, and was educated at Liverpool College and at University College, Oxford. He then attended the Slade School under Legros and followed a career in art teaching. He was Professor of Fine Art, University College, Reading and President of the Cumberland and Westmorland Antiquarian Society and President of the Lake Artists Society. He published a number of books but made a special study of Scandinavian art and lore. He illustrated *The Elder or Poetic Edda: The Mythological Poems,* by Olive Bray, in 1909. These are very beautiful Norse designs, based on the sculpture of Pre-Norman monuments in the north of England. He lived much of his life in the Lake District and died at Coniston on 1 October 1932.

Exhib: G; L; M; New Gall; RA; RBA; RI.
Bibl: Who Was Who 1929-1940.

**COLLINS, Charles Allston**                                    **1828-1873**
Pre-Raphaelite painter and brother of Wilkie Collins and son-in-law of Charles Dickens. He studied at the RA Schools and worked with Millais and was thus drawn into the Pre-Raphaelite circle. His output was small and imbued with tremendous religious sentiment as well as Pre-Raphaelite colouring and exactitude. He wrote articles for *Good Words* and *All The Year Round* and exhibited at the RA from 1847 to 1855, when he finally abandoned painting. He designed the wrapper of the first American edition of Dickens's *Edwin Drood,* 1870.

Colls: Ashmolean; BM.
Bibl: J. Maas, *Victorian Painters,* 1969, p.127.

**COLLINS, William Wiehe**                                    **1862-1951**
Painter of architecture and military subjects. He was the son of an army doctor and was educated at Epsom College, followed by study at Lambeth School of Art and at Julian's, Paris. He was in the RNVR, 1914-18, in the Dardanelles and in Egypt, which furnished him with material for pictures. He lived at Wareham, Dorset, 1903-25, and died at Bridgwater, Somerset, 1951. RI, 1898.

Publ: *The Cathedral Cities of England [1905]; Cathedral Cities of Spain [1909]; Cathedral Cities of Italy [1911]; The Green Roads of England.*
Contrib: *Black and White [1891].*
Exhib: FAS, 1901.

**COLOMB, Wellington**
Landscape painter who exhibited at the RA and RBA, 1865-70. He contributed an illustration to *Good Words,* 1864.

**COMPTON, Edward Theodore**                                    **1849-**
Painter and alpinist. Lived most of his life in Austria and Germany but exhibited regularly in London. He was interned during the First World War, but continued to work near the Italian frontier.

Illus: *A Mendip Valley [T. Compton, 1892]; Germany [J.F. Dickie, 1912]; Germany [G.W. Bullet, 1930].*
Contrib: *The Picturesque Mediterranean [Cassell, 1891].*

**CONCANEN, Alfred**                                    **1835-1886**
Music cover illustrator. He was born in London in 1835 of Irish descent and began designing covers for music in 1859. He was the most prolific of these artists and the best, giving his subjects great verve and clarity and specialising in what Ronald Pearsall has called 'London out-of-doors' subjects.

Illus: *Carols of Cockayne [H.S. Leigh, 1874]; Low Life Deeps [J. Greenwood, 1874]; The Queen of Hearts [Wilkie Collins, 1875]; The Wilds of London [J. Greenwood, 1876].*
Contrib: *Illustrated Sporting and Dramatic News.*
Bibl: Ronald Pearsall *Victorian Sheet Music Covers,* 1972.

**CONDER, Charles Edward**                                    **1868-1909**
Landscape painter and designer of fans. He was born in London in 1868 and spent much of his early life in India. He was educated at Eastbourne and then spent five years in Australia as a civil servant, 1885. While there he worked for the *Illustrated Sydney News* and attended Melbourne School of Art. In 1890 he went to Paris and studied at Julian's becoming an Associate of the Société Nationale

des Beaux Arts, 1893. He settled in London in 1897 and was elected to the NEAC in 1901. He died at Virginia Water in 1909.

Contrib: *The Yellow Book [1895]; The Savoy [1896]; The Page [1899].*
Des: *Impressionist Exhibition [1899 (cover)];* invitation card for Conder Exhibition, Paris, Dec. 1901.
Colls: Bedford; BM; Fitzwilliam; Leeds; Manchester; V & AM; Witt Photo.

**CONDY, Nicholas Matthew**                                    **1818-1851**
Marine painter. He was the son of Nicholas Condy, 1793-1857, the painter, and taught art at Plymouth.

Publ: *Cotehele . . . the seat of the Earl of Mount Edgecumbe [1850].*
Contrib: *ILN [1845-50 (naval subjects)].*

**CONNARD, Philip  RA CVO**                                    **1875-1958**
Painter and illustrator. He was born at Southport in 1875 and after being educated at the National Schools, he studied at Julian's in Paris. Settling in Fulham in 1901, he became Art Master at the Lambeth School of Art and concentrated on book illustration. These works, principally for John Lane, were in a late Pre-Raphaelite style in the manner of Laurence Houseman (q.v.). Elected to the NEAC in 1909; ARA, 1918, and RA, 1925. Keeper of the RA, 1945-49; ARWS, 1933.

Illus: *Flowers of Parnassus [Browning, Lane, 1900]; Narpessa [Stephen Phillips, 1900 (frontis.)].*
Contrib: *The Idler; The Dome [1899-1900]; The Quartier Latin [1898].*
Exhib: G; L; M; NEA, from 1901; RA; RHA; ROI; RSA; RSW; RWS.
Colls: Aberdeen; Bradford; Cardiff; Dublin; Manchester; Southport; Tate.
Bibl: R.E.D. Sketchley *English Book Illus.,* 1903, pp.13-14, 122.

**CONNELL, M. Christine**                                    **fl.1885-1907**
Painter of domestic subjects. She worked in Chelsea and Chiswick and contributed decorative subjects to *The English Illustrated Magazine,* 1896, and *The Sketch,* 1897.

Exhib: L; M; New Gall.; RA; RBA; ROI; SWA.
Colls: V & AM.

**CONNOR, Arthur Bentley**                                    **fl.1903-1925**
Portrait painter. He worked in London, 1903, in Penarth, 1915, and Weston-super-Mare from 1918-1925. He illustrated *Highways and Byways in Hampshire.*

Exhib: P; RA.

**COODE, Miss Helen Hoppner**                                    **fl.1859-1882**
Illustrator and watercolourist. She worked at Notting Hill, London, and Guildford, Surrey, and specialised in figure subjects. They are often brittle little drawings with large heads and rather weightless. She was the first woman cartoonist to work for *Punch,* 1859-61 and contributed small illustrations to *Once a Week,* 1859. She signs her work ⊬⊖⊢

Exhib: BI, 1859-66; M; RA; RBA, 1876-81.

**COOK, Richard  RA**                                    **1784-1857**
Painter and book illustrator. He was born in London in 1784 and entered the RA Schools in 1800. He specialised in historical scenes and illustrated numerous works from poetry and classical literature. His handling of the drawings typifies the beautiful ink and grey wash approach which was a legacy from the 18th century but which often lacked punch. The BM has a fine album of his studies for *The Lady of the Lake* by Sir Walter Scott, published in 1811. He became ARA in 1816 and RA in 1822 after which date he ceased to paint.

Illus: *Inchbald's British Theatre [1802]; Young's Night Thoughts [1804]; The Pastoral Care [1808]; The Idler [1810]; Park's British Poets; Miller's Shakespeare* etc.
Exhib: BI, 1807-26; RA, 1808-22.
Colls: BM; Swansea; V & AM; Witt Photo.

**COOKE, Arthur Claude**                                    **1867-**
Figure and animal painter. He was born at Luton, Bedfordshire, in 1867 and studied at the RA Schools. He worked in London, 1890-92, and again from 1903-14, finally settling in Radlett in 1925. He supplied illustrations of dogs to *The Lady's Pictorial* in the 1890s.

Exhib: B; L; RA; RBA; ROI.

**COOKE, Edward William    RA FRS**                 **1811-1880**

Marine watercolourist, topographer and illustrator. He was born at Pentonville on 27 March 1811, the son of George Cooke (q.v.), the engraver. He was making wood engravings of plants by the age of nine, some of which were used in J.C. Loudon's *Encyclopaedia of Plants,* 1829, and Loddidge's *Botanical Cabinet* 1817-33. He married the latter's daughter but after meeting Clarkson Stanfield (q.v.) in 1825, began to draw boats for him and to study shipping. Cooke travelled extensively in Europe, visiting Normandy in 1830 and Belgium and Holland between 1832 and 1844. He went further afield to Italy, 1845-46, and Spain and North Africa. His watercolours are rare but his fine pencil studies and leaves from his sketch-book, showing picturesque groups of fishermen, crowds and shore-lines, are quite common. He became ARA in 1851 and RA in 1864, dying at Groombridge, Kent, on 4 January 1880.

Illus: *Coast Sketches: British Coast [1826-30]; Fifty Plates of Shipping and Craft [1829]; Finden's Ports, Harbours and Watering Places [1840].*
Contrib: *Good Words [1863].*
Exhib: BI, 1835-67; RA; RBA, 1835-38, 1876.
Colls: BM; Glasgow; Greenwich; Leeds; Salford; Sheffield; V & AM.
Bibl: M. Hardie, *Watercol. Paint. in Brit.*, Vol. III, 1968, p.79.

**COOKE, George**                                    **1781-1834**

Topographical illustrator and engraver. Born in London in 1781 and engraved many works after Turner, Callcott and his son E.W. Cooke (q.v.). Died at Barnes in 1834.

Illus. or contrib: *Britton's Beauties [1803-13]; Pinkerton's Voyages and Travels; The Thames [1811]; The Southern Coast of England [1814-26]; History of Durham [Surtees, 1816-40]; Hertfordshire [R. Clutterbuck, 1815-27]; Italy [J. Hakewill, 1818-20]; D'Oyly and Mant's Bible; The Botanical Cabinet [1817-1833]; London and Its Vicinity [1826-28].*
Exhib: RBA.
Colls: BM.

**COOKE, William Bernard**                           **1778-1855**

Topographical illustrator and engraver. Elder brother of George Cooke (q.v.). He was a pupil of W. Angus, the topographer, and assisted his brother in publishing *The Thames*, 1811, and *The Southern Coast of England,* 1814-26.

Illus: *A New Picture of The Isle of Wight [1808]; Britton's Beauties [1808-16].*
Colls: Witt Photo.

**COOKE, William Cubitt**                            **1866-1951**

Watercolourist and book illustrator. He was born in London in 1866 and was educated at the Cowper Street Schools, City Road. At the age of sixteen he was apprenticed to a chromo-lithographer, but taught himself drawing and painting. He went later to Heatherley's and the Westminster School of Art. Cooke had his first black and white drawing published in 1892 and this was followed by a steady stream, some for short stories with an eastern flavour and some for period novels. He was a very competent figure artist indeed, although his compositions lack great individuality.

Illus: *Evelina* and *Cecilia [Fanny Burney, 1893]; The Man of Feeling [Mackenzie, 1893]; My Study Fire [1893]; The Vicar of Wakefield [1893]; Reveries of a Bachelor [1894]; The Master Beggars [1897]; The Singer of Marly [1897]; The Temple Dickens [1899]; Novels of Jane Austen [1894]; British Ballads [1894]; By Stroke of Sword [1897]; John Halifax [1898].*
Contrib: *The Quiver [c.1895]; The Idler; The Pall Mall Magazine; The English Illustrated Magazine [1896-98]; The Windsor Magazine.*
Exhib: RA, from 1893; RBA, from 1890; RI.
Colls: V & AM.
Bibl: R.E.D. Sketchley, *English Illus.*, 1903, pp.84, 149.
See illustration (right).

**COOPER, Abraham    RA**                            **1787-1868**

Sporting artist. He was largely self-taught although he had some drawing lessons from Ben Marshall. His inclusion here rests solely on some compositions that appeared in *The Sporting Magazine* and the frontispiece that he designed for *A Treatise on Greyhounds,* 1819. ARA; 1817, and RA, 1820.

Exhib: BI and RA, 1812-1869.
Colls: BM; With photo.

**COOPER, Alfred W.**                                **fl.1850-1901**

Illustrator of domestic subjects. One of the best of the second rank of 1860s artists about whom little is known. He was living in North London, 1853-54, and had moved to Twickenham by 1866, where he seems to have worked for the rest of his life. Cooper's earlier drawings are his best. Those in sepia ink or black ink in the Laing Art Gallery, Newcastle, come closest in feeling to Millais and are dated 1857-59. His published work begins with *Good Words*, 1861, and this and succeeding work such as 'On The Hills', *Churchman's Family Magazine*, 1863, retain the quality of line and show an affinity with Fred Walker's rustic illustrations. His later domestic and high life drawings are contrived and the use of gesture is overplayed and almost ludicrous. An early ink drawing by this artist would be very desirable and very rare. He signs his early drawings, which are very rare, and his later drawings *AWC*

Illus: *Une Culotte [Digby, 1894]; Walton's Compleat Angler [n.d.].*
Contrib: *Good Words [1861]; London Society [1862-68]; Churchman's Family Magazine [1863]; Tinsley's Magazine [1868]; Dark Blue [1871]; The British Workman; Aunt Judy's Magazine; The Graphic [1870].*
Exhib: B; BI, 1853-66; RA; RBA, 1852-1880; RI; ROI.
Colls: Newcastle; V & AM.
Bibl: Gleeson White, *English Illustration: The Sixties,* 1897.

**COOPER, Florence**                                 **fl.1886-1935**

Miniature painter. She illustrated with James Cadenhead (q.v.), two children's books, *Master Rex* and *Pixie* by Mrs. G. Ford, 1890-91.

Exhib: L; New Gall.; P; RA; RI; RMS; SWA.

*WILLIAM CUBITT COOKE 1866-1951. 'Mystery of the Balkans.' An illustration for* The English Illustrated Magazine, *Vol.16, 1896. Pen and grey wash. Signed and dated 1890. 7¾ins. x 5¼ins. (19.7cm x 13.3cm).*
Victoria and Albert Museum

**COOPER, Frederick Charles**
Landscape painter and archaeological illustrator. He went to Nineveh in 1849 to work for H.A. Layard, and drew for the latter's *Nineveh and Babylon*, 1853.

**COOPER, Will**
Contributor to *Fun*, 1900.

**COPE, Charles West   RA**                                    1811-1890
Historical painter, watercolourist and illustrator. He was born at Leeds, 28 July 1811, and was educated at Leeds Grammar School. He went to London in 1826 and studied at Sass's School in 1827 followed by some time at the RA Schools, 1828. He travelled to Paris, 1831, and to Italy, 1833-35, and again in 1845. He won a premium in the Houses of Parliament frescoes competition in 1843 and was an authority on Renaissance frescoes. He was a founder member of the Etching Club and was elected ARA in 1843 and RA in 1848. He represented the Academy at Philadelphia in 1876. Cope died at Bournemouth on 21 August 1890.

Contrib: *The Deserted Village [Goldsmith, Etching Club, 1841]; Songs of Shakespeare [Etching Club, 1843]; Poems and Pictures [1846]; Sacred Allegories [1856]; Favourite English Poems [1858-59]; A Book of Favourite Modern Ballads [1859]; The Churchman's Family Magazine [1863]; Cassell's Sacred Poems [1867]; Excelsior Ballads; Burns Poems; The Poetry of Thomas Moore.*
Exhib: BI and RA, 1833-82.
Colls: BM; Leicester; Liverpool; Melbourne; Preston.
Bibl: Chatto & Jackson *Treatise on Wood Engraving*, 1861, p.598; C.H. Cope, *Reminiscences of CWC*, Art Journal, 1869; J Maas, *Victorian Painters*, 1969, pp.28, 216, 238.

**COPPING, Harold**                                          1863-1932
Illustrator. He studied at the RA Schools and won the Landseer scholarship to Paris. He travelled to Palestine, Egypt and Canada, finally settling at Sevenoaks in 1902 and remaining there till his death, designing children's books and illustrating scriptural stories. He died 1 July 1932.

Illus: *Hard Lines [1894]; A Newnham Friendship; Toy Book; Mrs. Wiggs of the Cabbage Patch [A.H. Rice, 1908]; Canadian Pictures; The Gospel in the Old Testament; Scenes from the Life of St. Paul; Scripture Picture Books; The 'Copping' Bible.*
Contrib: *The Girls' Own Paper [1890-1900]; The Temple Magazine [1896]; English Illustrated Magazine [1897]; Black & White [1899]; The Windsor Magazine; The Royal Magazine.*

**CORBAUX, Louisa   NWS**                                        1808-
Painter and lithographer. She was the elder sister of Fanny Corbaux (q.v.) and specialised in pictures of animals and children. She collaborated with her sister in gift books and annuals. NWS, 1837.

Illus: *Pearls of the East, Beauties From Lalla Rookh [Tilt, 1837].*
Exhib: RBA, 1828-50.
Colls: BM.

**CORBAUX, Marie Françoise Catherine Doetter 'Fanny'   NWS**
                                                            1812-1883
Watercolourist and illustrator. Born in 1812, she was recognised as an infant prodigy, and won silver medals at the Society of Arts in 1827 and 1830. She was a writer on oriental subjects and a biblical scholar but is best known for her illustrations to gift books. She was granted a Civil List pension in recognition of her work and died at Brighton 1 February 1883. NWS, 1839.

Illus: *Pearls of the East, Beauties From Lalla Rookh [Tilt, 1837, 'drawn on stone by Louisa Corbaux']; Cousin Natalia's Tales [T. Moore, 1841].*
Contrib: *Heath's Gallery [1836]; Finden's Byron Beauties; Le Souvenir [1848].*
Exhib: NWS; RBA, 1828-40.
Colls: BM.
Bibl: R. Maclean, *Victorian Book Design*, 1972, pp.26, 28, 53 illus.

**CORBOULD, Aster Chantrey   RBA**                              -1920
Sporting artist and illustrator. He studied with his uncle Charles Keene (q.v.) who introduced him to *Punch*, in which magazine much of his work was afterwards published. Corbould was at his best in illustration when horses were involved, but his range did include social

and military drawings and cartoons. His sketches appear to lose a great deal in the printing. Sheets of sepia illustrations on the market in 1976, had the clarity of penwork and finesse of Keene, but on the magazine page they look coarse. Elected to RBA, 1893. He signs his work ⟨A⟩

Illus: *The Sword of Damocles [frontis.].*
Contrib: *Punch [1871-90]; The Graphic [1873-89]; ILN [1876 (acting Special Artist, Servia)]; Cornhill Magazine [1883]; Daily Graphic; Black & White [1891]; St. Paul's [1894]; Lika Joko [1894]; The New Budget [1895]; The St. James's Budget [1898].*
Exhib: B; L; RA; RBA; RHA; RI; ROI.
Colls: V & AM.
Bibl: R.G.G. Price, *A History of Punch*, 1957, p.120; *Mr. Punch With Horse and Hound*, New Punch Library, c.1930.

**CORBOULD, Edward Henry   RI**                                 1815-1905
Painter, sculptor and illustrator. He was born in London 5 December 1815 and became a pupil of his father, Henry Corbould (q.v.), also a very prolific illustrator. He studied at Sass's and at the RA Schools. In 1851 he was appointed drawing master to the children of Queen Victoria, retaining the post until 1872. His illustration drawings are all in the conventional monochrome washes of the period with fine ink detail, many of them bear the stamp of the artist's studio sale. RI, 1838.

Illus: *Lalla Rookh [1839]; Scott's Works, 1825.*
Contrib: *The Sporting Review [1842-46]; L'Allegro and Il Penseroso [Art Union, 1848]; The Traveller [Goldsmith, Art Union, 1851]; Tupper's Proverbial Philosophy [1854]; ILN [1856 (decor.), 1866]; Willmott's Poets of the Nineteenth Century [1857]; Merrie Days of England [1858-59]; London Society [1863]; The Churchman's Family Magazine [1863]; Cassell's Magazine [1870]; Favourite Modern Ballads; Burns Poems; Poetry of Thomas Moore; Barry Cornwall's Poems; Thornbury's Legendary Ballads [1876].*
Exhib: BI, 1846; GG; NWS; RA; RBA, 1835-42.
Colls: Ashmolean; BM; Soane; V & AM.
Bibl: Chatto & Jackson, *Treatise on Wood Engraving*, 1861, p.598.

**CORBOULD, Henry   FSA**                                       1787-1844
Illustrator, third son of Richard Corbould (q.v.), and father of E.H. Corbould (q.v.). Born at Robertsbridge in 1787, he studied with his father, later becoming a student at the RA Schools under H. Fuseli. He was a close friend of the leading neo-classical artists, Flaxman, Stothard, West and Chantrey, some of whose works he drew. J. Britton says that he was 'extensively employed by publishers to make drawings for engraving; and the number of his designs, which adorn many books, amount to several hundreds. He was one of the sufferers from an accident on the Eastern Counties Railway, when the train, falling off a lofty embankment, involved passengers in a smash . . . he was killed . . .' *Autobiography* Vol. 11, p.172. He spent thirty years on drawings for *Ancient Marbles*, published after his death. He illustrated the marbles at Woburn and Petworth.

Illus: *Paradise Lost [1796]; Rasselas [1810]; Swiss Family Robinson [1814]; Rosara's Chain [Lefanu, 1815]; Letters of Lady R. Russell [1826]; Cecilia [Burney, 1825].*
Contrib: *Heath's Gallery [1836-37].*
Colls: BM; Leeds; V & AM.
See illustration (p. 204).

**CORBOULD, Richard**                                          1757-1831
Painter of oils and watercolours, miniaturist, enamellist, portraitist. He was born in London in 1757 and most of his life was employed in the illustration of books, principally the series of miniature classics produced by Cooke, 1795-1800. His drawings were either in muted watercolours or monochrome washes, very gem-like and often within decorative frames or feigned ovals. Their quality is usually higher than those by the other members of the Corbould family. Much of his best work falls earlier than the scope of this book, but a selection of work is given below. He died at Highgate, 1831.

Illus: *The Adventurer; Tom Jones; Thoughts in Prison; Howlett's Views in the County of Lincoln [1800]; Broome's Works; Adventures of a Guinea.*
Contrib: *The Copper Plate Magazine [1792-94].*
Exhib: BI, 1806-17; Free Soc.; RA.
Colls: BM; V & AM.
See illustration (p. 268).

RICHARD CORBOULD 1757-1831. 'Pamela giving up her parcel of Papers to her Master.' An illustration for Richardson's Pamela, c.1805. Oval vignette in ink and watercolour with decoration. Victoria and Albert Museum

**CORDINER, Rev. James**         **1775-1836**
Traveller and topographer. Son of the Rev. Charles Cordiner of Banff. M.A., Aberdeen, 1793. Army chaplain at Madras, 1797, and at Colombo, 1798-1804. He was minister of St. Paul's Episcopal Church at Aberdeen, 1807-34.

Illus: *A Description of Ceylon [1807, AT 409]; A Voyage to India [1820]*.

**CORNILLIET, Jules**         **1830-1886**
History painter. He was born at Versailles in 1830 and studied with Ary Scheffer and H. Vernet. Exhibited at the Salon from 1857. He contributed drawings of the Franco-Italian campaign to *The Illustrated London News*, 1859.

**COTMAN, Frederick George    RI ROI**     **1850-1920**
Landscape and genre painter in watercolour and oil. He was born in Ipswich and was a nephew of J.S. Cotman (q.v.). After being educated at Ipswich, he went to the RA Schools in 1868, winning the gold medal for historical painting, 1873. He accompanied the Duke of Westminster on a Mediterranean tour and was employed to make watercolours of the places visited. His illustrative work is very rare but boldly handled in quite large scale, using a great deal of sepia and bodycolour. He became RI in 1882, ROI, 1883, and died at

Felixstowe on 16 July 1920.

Contrib: *ILN [1876 and 1880]; The Yellow Book [1895]*.
Exhib: B; FAS, 1893; G; L; M; Paris, 1889; RA; RBA; RI; ROI; RSA.
Colls: Norwich; V & AM.
Bibl: *The Studio*, Vol. 47, 1909, p.167.

**COTMAN, John Sell**         **1782-1842**
Painter and etcher, a principal figure of the Norwich School of painters, he is included here as an architectural illustrator. After spending his boyhood in Norwich, he went to London and learnt a good deal about the world of engraving and publishing, acting as a colourer of aquatints for Rudolph Ackermann of the Strand. He collected material for a volume of Norfolk antiquities and visited Normandy in 1817, 1818 and 1820 for a similar project. He produced one hundred etchings for the latter, often arduous work but showing his own individual view of the subject. The 1820s were clouded by mental anxiety and financial problems, but in 1834 Cotman was appointed drawing master at King's College, London, a post he held until his death in 1842.

Illus: *Miscellaneous Etchings of Architectural Antiquities in Yorkshire [1812]; Architectural Antiquities of Norfolk [1812-17]; Sepulchral Brasses in Norfolk [1813-16]; Architectural Antiquities of Normandy [1822]; Sepulchral Brasses of Norfolk & Suffolk; Liber Studiorum; Britton's Cathedrals [1832-36]; Eight Original Etchings [n.d.]*.
Exhib: BI, 1810-27; OWS; RA; RBA, 1838.
Colls: Ashmolean; BM; Glasgow; Manchester; Norwich; V & AM.
Bibl: S.D. Kitson, *Life of JSC*, 1937; M. Hardie, *Watercol. Paint. in Brit.* Vol. II, 1967, pp.72-96.
See illustration (below).

JOHN SELL COTMAN 1782-1842. The Morley Monument, Hingham church, Norfolk. An etching for Eight Original Etchings By The Late John Sell Cotman, Norwich, n.d. 15½ins. x 10ins. (39.4cm x 25.4cm). Author's Collection

**COTTON, Lieutenant J.S.**

Amateur caricaturist. He illustrated *The New Tale of a Tub* by F.W.N. Bayley, 1841, in lithography.

**COULDERY, Thomas W.**                    fl.1877-1898

Domestic painter and illustrator. He was working in London in 1882, at Pulborough and Chichester, Sussex, 1890-93, and at Brighton in 1897.

Illus: *A Woman Hater [Charles Reade, 1877].*
Contrib: *ILN [1888, 1894]; Cassell's Family Magazine; English Illustrated Magazine [1891-94].*
Exhib: B; L; M; RA; RBA; RI.
Colls: Sydney.

**COWELL, G.H. Sydney**                    fl.1884-1907

Domestic painter and illustrator of urban genre, sculptor. He worked in London and specialised in drawings for school stories and boys' and girls' novels. His work is competent but not exciting

Illus: *A Peep Behind the Scenes [Mrs. O.F. Walton]; Every Inch a Briton [1901].*
Contrib: *ILN [1889-92]; The Quiver [1890]; The English Illustrated Magazine [1891-92, 1896]; The Idler [1892]; The Sporting and Dramatic News [1893]; The New Budget [1895]; Pearson's Magazine [1896]; The Temple [1896]; The Minister [1895]; The Girls' Own Paper; The St. James's Budget; Cassell's Family Magazine; The Pall Mall Magazine; The Windsor Magazine.*
Exhib: B; M; RA; RBA; ROI.

**COWHAM, Hilda Gertrude (Mrs. Edgar Lander)**       1873-1964

Artist, author and book illustrator. She was born in 1873 and after being educated at Wimbledon College, attended the Lambeth School of Art. Miss Cowham had drawings published while she was still at school in *Pick-Me-Up* and *The Queen*. She later became a prolific contributor to magazines, designed posters and made dolls. Her claim to be the first woman to draw for *Punch* is quite incorrect, that honour going to Helen Coode (q.v.).

Her drawings in pencil and ink for children's books are very decorative and whimsy. She usually signs: H. Cowham.

Illus: *Fiddlesticks; Our Generals; Blacklegs; Curly Locks and Long Legs; Kitty in Fairyland.*
Contrib: *The Sketch [1894-95]; Moonshine [1896]; The Royal Magazine [1901]; The Graphic [1902-05, 1908, 1912, (Christmas supps.)]; The Sphere; The Tatler.*
Exhib: G; L; RA; RWS; SWA; Walker's.
Colls: V & AM.

**COWPER, Frank Cadogan   RA RWS**          1877-1958

Portrait and subject painter. He was born on 16 October 1877 at Wicken Rectory, Northamptonshire, and was educated at Cranleigh. He studied first at the St. John's Wood Art School, 1896, then at the RA Schools, 1897-1902, and worked for six months in the studio of E.A. Abbey, RA (q.v.). Cowper did numerous portraits but specialised in subject pictures of romantic type: 'French Aristocrat', 'Venetian Ladies' etc., etc. He was also responsible for painting panels and altar-pieces. He worked in London but died in Cirencester in 1958. ARA, 1907; RA, 1934; RP, 1921; RWS, 1911.

Contrib: *The Idler; The Graphic 1906.*
Exhib: B; G; GG; L; M; P; RA; ROI; RWS.

**COWPER, Max**                            fl.1892-1911

Figure painter and illustrator. He was working in Dundee in 1893, in Edinburgh in 1894 and in London from 1901. Cowper made illustrations for a large number of magazines, his ink drawing is very good and his grey wash drawings are delicate, but he sometimes swamps his fine line with wash.

Contrib: *Fun [1892-93]; St. Pauls [1894]; The Rambler [1897]; The Longbow [1898]; Pick-Me-Up; Illustrated Bits; The Quiver [1899]; The Idler; The Pall Mall Magazine; The Minister; The Strand Magazine.*
Exhib: G; L; RA; RSA.
Colls: V & AM; Witt Photo.

**COX, David   OWS**                        1783-1859

Landscape painter and watercolourist. He was born at Deritend, Birmingham in 1783 and began as a scene painter for the Birmingham Theatre. He moved to London in 1804 and in the next decade became highly influential as a drawing-master and practitioner. He travelled abroad between 1826 and 1832 and developed as a colourist and in his later years as a forerunner of impressionism. He is included here for his one recorded work of illustration *A Treatise on The Aeropleustic Art by means of Kites,* 1851, AL 395. He died at Harborne on 7 June 1859.

Publ: *Treatise on Landscape Painting and Effect in Watercolour [1814]; Progressive Lessons on Landscape for Young Beginners [1816]; A Series of Progressive Lessons [c.1816]; The Young Artist's Companion [1825].*
Exhib: BI; OWS; RA; RBA.
Colls: Ashmolean; BM; Birmingham; Nottingham; V & AM.
Bibl: Trenchard Cox, *DC,* 1947.

**COX, Everard Morant**                    fl.1878-1891

Black and white illustrator, working in London and producing comic genre and sporting subjects for the magazines.

Contrib: *ILN [1883-84, 1888, 1891]; Punch [1883].*
Exhib: RA, 1884-85.

**CRAFT, Percy Robert   RBA**              1856-1934

Landscape and coastal painter. He studied at Heatherley's and at the Slade School under Legros and Poynter, where he was a gold and silver medallist. He worked in London until 1910 with a brief spell at Penzance in 1890. He was elected RBA, 1898, and died in London 26 November 1934.

Contrib: *ILN [1883 (Cornwall)].*
Exhib: B; G; L; M; New Gall.; RA; RBA; RE; ROI; RSA.

*EDWARD GORDON CRAIG 1872-1966. Portrait of Henry Irving for* The Dome, *October to December 1898. Woodcut.*

**CRAFTY**

Pseudonym of cartoonist to *The Graphic*, 1871.

**CRAIG, Edward Gordon**                                         1872-1966

Designer, woodcut artist and propagandist for simplicity in the theatre. He was born 16 January 1872, the son of E.W. Godwin, 1833-1886, the Victorian architect, and Ellen Terry, 1847-1928, the actress. Although much of Craig's energy was concentrated on theatre design, he was a dynamic and original illustrator and typographer. After being educated at Heidelberg and Bradfield, he went on the stage for a short period. After moving to Uxbridge, he came under the influence of William Nicholson (q.v.) and James Pryde (q.v.), then living at Denham, and he was taught the rudiments of wood engraving by them. This contact proved a turning point and he immersed himself in Renaissance wood engravings and the study of architecture of the same period. The years 1893-98 saw the production of a number of splendid bold and chunky woodcuts, particularly character studies of Irving and Ellen Terry. Craig designed and produced *The Page* at The Sign of the Rose, Hackbridge, from 1898-1901. He was his own editor, illustrator and publisher for *The Mask* and *The Marionette*. In later years he produced numerous stage sets in Britain and Europe and wrote extensively.

Publ: *The Page [1898-1901]; The Art of The Theatre [1905]; The Mask [Florence, 1908-29]; On The Art of The Theatre [1911]; Towards a New Theatre [1913]; The Theatre Advancing [1921]; Scene [1923]; Woodcuts and Some Words [1924]; Books and Theatres [1925]; A Production [1926, 1930]; Fourteen Notes [1931]; Ellen Terry and Her Secret Self [1931].*
Contrib: *The Minister; The Dome [1898-99]; Book of Penny Toys [1899].*
Exhib: G; RHA.
Colls: BM; V & AM; Witt Photo.
Bibl: *EGC* Cat. of Exhibition. V & AM, 1967; *EGC* Bibliography (Ifan Kyrle Fletcher).
See illustration (p.269).

**CRAIG, Frank**                                         1874-1918

Black and white illustrator. He was born at Abbey, Kent, on 27 February 1874 and studied at the RA Schools. He began working on *The Graphic* in 1895, succeeding Gulich as collaborator with William Hatherell (q.v.). He was sent by *The Graphic* as Special Artist to the South African War, 1900. Craig was an accomplished illustrator of stories, using grey wash drawings to powerful effect and drawing in with the brush. He illustrated some of George Gissing's work, some of Rudyard Kipling's and a little of Arnold Bennett who disliked his style. One of his paintings was purchased for the Chantrey Bequest in 1906.

Contrib: *The English Illustrated Magazine [1894-95]; The Graphic [1895-1910]; The Quiver [1894-1900]; The Temple [1896]; Cassell's Family Magazine [1898]; The Pall Mall Magazine; The Sketch; The Strand Magazine.*
Exhib: G; L; M; RA; RBA, 1892-94; ROI; RSA.
Colls: Author; V & AM.
Bibl: *The Art Journal*, 1906, p.881; *The Studio*, Vol. 38, 1906, pp.4-11; *Arnold Bennett, Letters to J.B. Pinker*, Vol. 1, 1966, pp.168-169, (Edited by J. Hepburn).
See illustration (below).

**CRAIG, William Marshall**                                         c.1765-c.1834

Illustrator, drawing master, painter of portraits. He was living in Manchester in 1788 and practising as a drawing master, exhibiting miniatures and landscapes at various exhibitions. He was established in London from 1790 and there became Water-colour Painter to the Queen in 1812 and Court Painter to the Duke of York in 1820. He may have travelled to Russia in 1814 and he gave lectures at the BI.

Craig's output as an illustrator was considerable, all his work was done in the meticulous neo-classic style of drawing favoured for books, charming but not individual. His work is occasionally seen on

*FRANK CRAIG 1874-1918. 'A Group of Diners.' Illustration for unidentified story. Ink and grey wash. Signed and dated 1895. 7¼ins. x 8½ins. (18.4cm x 21.6cm)*
Author's Collection

the market.

Illus: *A Wreath For The Brow of Youth [1804]; Scripture Illustrated [1806]; An Essay on Transparent Prints [1807]; The Economy of Human Life [1808]; Cowper's Poems [1813]; Foxe's Book of Martyrs.*
Contrib: *Britton's Beauties [1803-12]; Inchbald's British Theatre; Bell's British Theatre; Britton's Gallery of Contemporary Portraits.*
Exhib: BI, 1806-20; RA, 1788-1827; RBA, 1826-28.
Colls: Nottingham; V & AM.
Bibl: I. Williams, *Early English Watercolours,* 1952, pp.134-135, illus.

## CRAMPTON, Sir John Twistleton Wickham Fiennes    1805-1886
Amateur artist and caricaturist. He was born in 1805, the son of Sir Philip Crampton and entered the Diplomatic service, acting as Secretary of the Legation at Berne, 1844 and Washington, 1845. He was recalled in 1856 after his attempts to recruit American citizens for the Crimea and became Minister at Hanover, 1857, and St. Petersburg, 1858. He finally retired in 1869 and died at Bushey Park, Co. Wicklow in 1886. His ink drawings of figures are very competent although they have a decidedly Georgian look to them.

Colls: BM.
Bibl: *Agnew... Exhib. of Watercolours,* Jan-Feb. 1975.

## CRANE, T.
Designer. He was the elder brother of Walter Crane (q.v.), and was art director of the firm of Marcus Ward and Co. He designed ornament for Christmas cards, calendars and children's books, the figure work being by Mrs. Houghton of Warrington. He decorated *At Home,* in the style of Kate Greenaway, 1881.

Bibl: W. Crane, *An Artist's Reminiscences,* 1907.

## CRANE, Walter   RWS       1845-1915
Painter, decorator, designer, book illustrator, writer and socialist. He was born in Liverpool on 15 August 1845 and was self-taught as an

*WALTER CRANE RWS 1845-1915. 'They saw a Knight in dangerous distresse.' An illustration for Spenser's Faerie Queen, Book V, 1896. Pen and ink. Signed with monogram. 9⅝ins. x 7⅝ins. (24.4cm x 19.4cm).*
Victoria and Albert Museum

artist before being apprenticed in London to W.J. Linton (q.v.) in 1857. From this technical background, Crane was able to develop a much greater craftsmanship in the art of the book than any other contemporary artist. He had the great strength of being principally an illustrator and not merely a painter who illustrated books. In the following years he studied early printed books, medieval illuminations, Japanese prints and the work of the Pre-Raphaelites in order to adapt them to his own linear patterns. His children's books are the most famous and are characterised by strong outlines, flat tints and solid blacks, all ideally suited to colour wood engraving and the *Picture Books* produced for Messrs. Routledge by Edmund Evans. From 1867, Crane was associated with the Dalziels and in the years following his marriage in 1871, he travelled widely in Italy, later to Greece, Bohemia and the United States. The Paris Commune had a powerful influence on him in 1871 and after it he became associated with William Morris (q.v.) and with the socialist cause.

Crane was associated as well with every project in art education, he was examiner in Design to the Board of Education, to London County Council and the Scottish Board of Education. He taught design at Manchester, 1893-96, was Art Director at Reading College, 1898, and Principal of the RCA, 1898-99. He was first President of the Arts and Crafts Exhibition Society, 1888, and a Master of the Art Workers' Guild. Although direct followers are hard to pin down, Crane was widely influential and the Crane style appears in the Art School work of the 1890s and 1900s. He died at Kensington 14 March 1915.

Publ: *The Basis of Design [1898]; Line and Form [1900]; Of The Decorative Illustration of Books [1901].*
Illus: *Children's Sayings [1862]; Stories of Old [1862]; The New Forest [1863]; Stories From Memel [1863]; True Pathetic History of Poor Match [1863]; Goody Platts and Her Two Cats [1864]; Toy Books [1865-76]; Broken in Harness [Lemon, 1865]; Wait For The End [1866]; Miss Mackenzie [Trollope, 1866]; Poetry of Nature [1868]; Legendary Ballads [Roberts, 1868]; King Gab's Story Nag [1869]; Magic of Kindness [1869]; Merrie Heart [1870]; Labour Stands on Golden Feet [1870];* Mrs. Molesworth's stories from 1875; *Songs of Many Seasons [1876]; Baby's Opera [1877]; The Baby's Bouquet [1879]; Grimm's Fairy Tales [1882]; Aesop's Fables [1886]; Flora's Feast [1889]; Queen Summer [1891]; The Old Garden [Margaret Deland, 1893]; Hawthorne's Wonder Book For Girls and Boys [1892]; Spenser's Mutabilitie [1896]; Spenser's Faerie Queene [1897]; Bluebeard's Picture Book [1899]; Don Quixote Retold [Judge Parry, 1900]; Last Essays of Elia [1901].*
Contrib: *Entertaining Things [1861]; London Society [1862]; Good Words [1863]; Once a Week [1863-65]; Every Boy's Magazine [1864-65]; Punch [1866]; The Argosy [1868-69]; Churchman's Shilling Magazine [1868]; English Illustrated Magazine [1883-88]; Black & White [1891]; The Quarto [1898]; The Art Journal [cover]; The Graphic [Christmas cover]; Pears Magazine.*
Exhib: Dudley; FAS, 1891; RI; RWS.
Colls: Ashmolean; Bedford; BM; Fitzwilliam; Glasgow; V & AM.
Bibl: Walter Crane, *An Artist's Reminiscences,* 1907; *The Studio,* Winter No., 1900-01, p.53, illus.
See illustrations (left, Colour Plate IX p.124, and p.272).

## CRAWHALL, Joseph       1821-1896
Illustrator of chapbooks and ballads. He was born at Newcastle in 1821 and ran a family ropery business. Living in a city which was famous for its wood engravers and still basking in the glory of Thomas Bewick (q.v.), Crawhall enjoyed the spirit of book making and began to assemble material from various sources, writing, illustrating and putting the book together himself. The result is a unique kind of production, part archaism, part bibliomania and part wit. The crude woodcuts, coloured by hand, are in sympathy with the rough paper and the earthy ballads printed below them. Crawhall attempted to bring back the personality to books, dead since industrialisation.

He was a friend of Charles Keene and supplied many of his *Punch* jokes for the artist to work up. He was secretary of the Newcastle Arts Club.

Illus: *The Compleatest Angling Booke that ever was writ [1859]; Ye loving ballad of Lorde Bateman... [1860]; A Collection of Right Merrie Garlands... [1864]; Chaplets from Coquetside [1873]; Northumbrian Small Pipe Tunes [1877]; Border Notes and Mixty-Maxty [1880]; Chap-Book Chaplets [1883]; Olde Tayles... [1883];* Etc.
Colls: BM; Glasgow.
Bibl: Charles S. Felver, *JC The Newcastle Wood Engraver 1821-96,* 1972 (complete bibliography).

See illustrations (Colour Plate XI p.124).

WALTER CRANE RWS 1845-1915. 'Simple Honesty.' An illustration to A Floral Fantasy Set Forth in Verses, 1899. Pen and watercolour. 10ins. x 14⅝ins. (25.4cm x 37.1cm).                    Victoria and Albert Museum

**CRAWHALL, Joseph E.   RSW**                    **1861-1913**
Animal painter. The son of Joseph Crawhall (q.v.) and one of the most distinguished artists connected with the Glasgow School. His sketches of animals in action are particularly fine. He was a contributor to *The Pall Mall Magazine*.
Colls: V & AM.
Bibl: A.J.C. Bury, *The Man and The Artist* 1958.

**CRAWSHAW, J.E.**
Amateur artist. He contributed drawings of comic machines to *Punch*, 1906.

**CREALOCK, Lieutenant-General Henry Hope**                    **1831-1891**
Amateur artist. He was educated at Rugby and joined the Army in 1848, serving in the Crimea and China, 1857-58, the Indian Mutiny, New Brunswick, 1865, and Zululand, 1879. He was promoted Lieutenant-Colonel in 1861 and Lieutenant-General in 1884.
Illus: *Wolf-Hunting and Wild Sport in Lower Brittany [1875]; Katerfelto [G.J.W. Melville, 1875]; Sport [W.D.B. Davenport, 1885].*
Contrib: *The Illustrated Times [1855].*
Colls: BM.

**CRESWICK, Thomas   RA**                    **1811-1869**
Landscape painter and illustrator. He was born at Sheffield in 1811 and studied at Birmingham with Joseph Vincent Barber before settling in London in 1828. His métier was the English landscape in high summer, his compositions are always good, many of them were done in collaboration with animal painters such as Ansdell and Goodall or figure painters like Phillip and Frith. He was an early member of the Etching Club and he was commended by Ruskin, rare distinction, for a book illustration to 'Nut Brown Maid' in the *Book of English*

*Ballads*. ARA, 1842 and RA, 1851. He died in 1869 and was buried at Kensal Green.
Illus: *Walton's Compleat Angler; Works of Goldsmith.*
Contrib: *Deserted Village [Goldsmith, Etching Club, 1841]; Gray's Elegy [Etching Club, 1847]; L'Allegro [Etching Club, 1849]; Songs and Ballads of Shakespeare [Etching Club, 1853]; Moxon's Tennyson [1857]; Favourite English Poems of the Last Two Centuries [1858-59]; Early English Poems [1863]; The Churchman's Family Magazine [1863].*
Exhib: BI, 1829-30; RA, 1828-
Colls: BM; Glasgow; Manchester.
Bibl: Chatto & Jackson *Treatise on Wood Engraving*, 1861, pp.588-589.

**CRISP, Frank E.F.**                    **-1915**
Artist working in St. John's Wood, who probably died on active service. He illustrated Edward Hutton's *The Cities of Romagna and The Marches*, 1913, with 12 colour plates.
Exhib: L; RA; RSA.

**CROMBIE, Benjamin William**                    **1803-1847**
Draughtsman, engraver and caricaturist. He was born in Edinburgh and published a set of caricatures for *Modern Athenians*, 1839, in a style akin to that of Dighton.
Colls: Edinburgh.
Bibl: Veth, *Comic Art in England*, 1930, p.41, illus.

**CROMBIE, Charles**                    **fl.1904-1912**
Cartoonist in black and white and watercolour. He worked for *The Bystander*, 1904, *The Graphic*, 1906, comic illustrations, and *The Illustrated London News* and *Graphic*, Christmas numbers, 1911 and 1912.
Colls: Witt Photo.

**CROPSEY, Jasper F.**                    **1823-1900**
American painter established in England. He worked in New York 1845-62 and then travelled to Turkey. He was a founder member of the Academy in New York, 1851, before settling in London in 1857.
Illus: *The Poetical Works of E.A. Poe [1857]; The Poetry of Thomas Moore [n.d.].*
Bibl: Chatto & Jackson, *Treatise on Wood Engraving*, 1861, p.598.

**CROSS, A. Campbell**                    **fl.1895-1898**
Illustrator, working in Chelsea for the magazines. His drawings are usually in black chalk with colour washes and are in a late Pre-Raphaelite style.
Contrib: *The Sketch [1895-98]; The Idler; The Quartier Latin [1896]; The Quarto [1896-97].*
Exhib: RA, 1897.
Colls: V & AM.

**CROSS, Stanley**
Black and white artist. He contributed to *Punch*, 1914 and specialised in drawings of hen-pecked husbands.

**CROW**
Comic illustrator to *Judy*, 1889.

**CROWE, Eyre   ARA**                    **1824-1910**
Painter and illustrator. He was born in London on 3 October 1824, the son of Eyre Evans-Crowe, the historian. He studied with William Darley and at the Atelier Delaroche in Paris as well as at the RA Schools, 1844. He was secretary to his cousin W.M. Thackeray and lived in the United States, 1852-57. He was elected ARA in 1875 and died in London, 12 December 1910. He was an occasional caricaturist.
Illus: *With Thackeray in America [1893]; Haunts and Homes of W.M. Thackeray.*
Contrib: *ILN [1856-61].*
Exhib: BI, 1850, 1861; RA; RBA, 1854, 1856.
Colls: V & AM.

**CROWE, J.A.**
Artist. Described by *The Illustrated London News* as their 'Correspondent' in the Crimea, 1855-56.
See illustration (p.136).

**CROWLEY, Nicholas J. RHA**            **1813-1857**

Portrait painter. He was born in 1813, probably in Ireland, and lived and worked for the whole of his life in Dublin, visiting England briefly in 1838. He was elected RHA, 1838, and died in 1857.

Contrib: *ILN [1853-54].*
Exhib: BI, 1839-57; RA, 1835- ; RBA, 1836.
Colls: NG, Ireland.

**CROWQUILL, Alfred**
**pseudonym of Alfred Henry Forrestier**     **1804-1872**

Writer and comic artist, caricaturist and illustrator. Born in London in 1804 and already contributing caricatures to the publishers by the age of eighteen. He worked for John Timbs on *The Hive* and *The Mirror*, before becoming associated with *Punch* from its earliest days, after its predecessor *Charivari* had foundered. Crowquill wrote extensively for *The New Monthly* and *Bentley's* magazines and was more widely regarded as a literary man than as an artist. Nevertheless his drawings are incisive and charming and have an element of fantasy at a time when grotesqueness was more usual. He left *Punch* in 1844 and found a highly successful career from the 1850s onwards as an illustrator of children's books. In his early career he sometimes drew social satires that were engraved by George Cruikshank (q.v.). His best work is found when he uses fine ink lines and pastel colours on toned paper. He signs his work

Illus: *Ups and Downs [1823]; Paternal Pride [1825]; Despondency and Jealousy [1825]; Der Freyschutz Travestied, Alfred Crowquill's Sketch Book, Absurdities in Prose and Verse [1827]; Goethe's Faust [1834]; Pickwickian Sketches, Bunn's Vauxhall Papers [1841]; Sea Pie [1842]; Dr. Syntax Tour in Search of the Picturesque [1844]; Comic Arithmetic [1844]; Woman's Love [1846]; Wanderings of a Pen and Pencil [1846]; A Good-natured Hint about California [1849]; The Excitement [1849]; Pictorial Grammar, Pictorial Arithmetic; Gold [1850]; A Bundle of Crowquills Dropped by Alfred Crowquill [1854]; Fun [1854]; Griffel Swillendrunken [1856]; Aunt Mavor's Nursery Tales [1855]; Little Pilgrim [1856]; Little Plays For Little Actors [1856]; Fairy Tales [1857]; Merry Pictures [1857]; Bon Gaultier Ballads [with Leech and Doyle, 1857]; A New Story Book [1858]; Fairy Tales [C. Bede, 1858]; Baron Munchausen [1858]; Twyll Owlglass [1859]; Honesty and Cunning [1859]; Kindness and Cruelty [1859]; The Red Cap [1859]; Paul Prendergast [1859]; Strange Surprising Adventures of the Venerable Gooros Simple [1861]; Fairy Footsteps [1861]; Chambers Book of Days; Pickwick Abroad [G.W. Reynolds]; The Boys and The Giant [1870]; The Cunning Fox [1870]; Dick Doolittle [1870]; Little Tiny's Picture Book [1871]; Guide to the Watering Places.*
Contrib: *Punch [1842-44]; ILN [1844-70]; The Illustrated Times [1859].*
Exhib: RA, 1845-46.
Colls: Author; V & AM.
Bibl: G. Everitt, *English Caricaturists*, 1893, pp.368-371; M.H. Spielmann, *The History of Punch*, 1895, pp.449-450.
See illustrations (right and p.274).

**CROWTHER, T.S.C.**           **fl.1891-1902**

Illustrator. His work is characterised by a very thin pen line.

Contrib: *The Daily Graphic; The Windsor Magazine; The Temple Magazine; The Idler; The English Illustrated Magazine [1891-92]; The Graphic [1902].*

**CRUIKSHANK, George, Snr.**         **1792-1878**

Artist, etcher and polemicist on temperance, caricaturist. Born at Duke Street, Bloomsbury, on 27 September 1792, the second son of the caricaturist, Isaac Cruikshank. He worked with his father from an early age, engraving lottery tickets and chapbooks, his first published design appearing in 1806. From his father's death in about 1810, he developed as the foremost political caricaturist of the Regency, both spiritually and physically taking over the place of the insane Gillray at Mrs. Humphrey's establishment. As early as 1820 when the caricature boom was still at its zenith, Cruikshank had begun contributing to ephemeral journals like *The Wits' Magazine* and was establishing himself as a book illustrator. His first major work in this medium was the Regency best-seller, *Life in London*, by Pierce Egan. This was followed by similar publications, including *Life in Paris*, and then a number of smaller books which became little more than vehicles for his own lively drawings. By the 1830s he was the leading illustrator and was engaged on works by Charles Dickens, Harrison Ainsworth and Sir Walter Scott. At the same time yearly almanacks were issued from 1835 to 1853 under the artist's name and these were succeeded by *George Cruikshank's Magazine*, 1853-54.

*ALFRED CROWQUILL (A.H. Forrestier) 1804-1872. Title page design for* Music On The Waves, A Set of Songs by The Honble Mrs Norton. *Ink and watercolour. Signed. 12¼ins. x 8¼ins. (13.1cm x 21cm).*
                             Victoria and Albert Museum

Cruikshank's conversion to the teetotal cause in the late 1840s gave him a fresh zest for life at exactly the moment when his fame was starting to diminish. The next thirty years witnessed an incredible activity from his pen, mostly for the Temperance League and including his mammoth 'The Worship of Bacchus', the vast unmanageable canvas which took him three years to complete and is now relegated to the cellars of The Tate Gallery. This frenzied picture, with its hundreds of tiny figure groups in various stages of dissipation says a great deal about the artist. Strongly inventive and with a keen eye for the absurd and the pathetic, he had delusions of grandeur which were unsuited to his small scale genius. Although Ruskin gave him fulsome praise for his children's books, the vigour of his line and the bombast of his humour belonged to the 18th century rather than the 19th.

Cruikshank died at Mornington Crescent on 1 February 1878 and was buried at Kensal Green; his body was later removed to St. Paul's at the instigation of the temperance lobby rather than for his acknowledged importance as an artist.

Finished drawings by Cruikshank are rare, the most common items met with are pencil studies in small scale on white paper, the major figures drawn over in ink in preparation for the completed work.

Illus: *Nelson's Funeral Car [1806, first illus.]; Life in London [1820]; Life in Paris [1822]; Peter Sclemihl [1824]; Greenwich Hospital [1826]; Phrenological Illustrations [1826]; Illustrations of Time [1827]; Punch and Judy, Scraps and Sketches [1828]; Three Courses and a Dessert [1830]; Hogarth Moralized, Roscoe's Moralists Library [1831]; Salis Populi Suprema Lex [1832]; Sundays in London [1833]; Cruikshankiana [1835]; My Sketchbook; Comic Almanack [1835-53]; Sketches by Boz [Dickens, 1836]; Waverley Novels [1836-38]; Oliver Twist [Dickens]; Jack Sheppard, Guy Fawkes [1838]; The Tower of London [Ainsworth, 1840]; George Cruikshank's Omnibus [1841]; The Bachelor's Own Book, Arthur O'Leary [1844]; George Cruikshank's Table*

*ALFRED CROWQUILL (A.H. Forrestier) 1804-1872. A page from the artist's Ramsgate sketchbook. Pen and ink. Signed and dated 1857. 6¾ins. x 9¼ins. (17.1cm x 25.5cm).*
Author's Collection

Book, *Maxwell's Irish Rebellion [1845]; Outline of Society [1846]; The Bottle [1847]; The Drunkard's Children [1848]; 1851 or The Adventures of Mr. and Mrs. Sandboys [1851]; Uncle Tom's Cabin [1852]; George Cruikshank's Fairy Library [1853-54]; The New Political House That Jack Built [1854]; Life of Falstaff [1857]; A Pop Gun Fired Off [1860]; The British Bee Hive [1867]; Our Gutter Children [1868]; The Brownies and Other Tales [Mrs. J.H. Ewing 1871]; The Trial of Sir Jasper [1873]; Peeps at Life [1875]; The Rose and The Lily [1877].*
Contrib: *Bentley's Miscellany [1837-43]; Ainsworth's Magazine [1842]; The Illustrated Times; ILN [1877].*
Exhib: BI, 1833-60; RA.
Colls: BM (large collection); Manchester; Tate; V & AM.
Bibl: Chatto & Jackson *Treatise on Wood Engraving,* 1861, pp.595-596; J. Grego *C's Watercolours,* 1904; R. McLean, *GC,* 1949; William Feaver, *GC,* Arts Council, 1974.
See illustration (p.275).

### CRUIKSHANK, George, Jnr.                    fl.1866-1894
Son of George Cruikshank (q.v.). His drawings are very weak imitations of his father, he contributed to magazines in the 1870s and 1880s and usually signs George Cruikshank Junior.

Contrib: *Beeton's Annuals [1866]; London Society [1866, 1874]; Aunt Judy's Magazine [1866-71]; ILN [1882]; The Sphere [1894].*
Colls: V & AM.

### CRUIKSHANK, (Isaac) Robert                    1786-1856
Caricaturist, illustrator and miniature painter. He was born in 1786, the eldest son of Isaac Cruikshank and brother of George Cruikshank, Snr. (q.v.). He served as midshipman with the East India Company until 1814, setting up as a miniature painter in London and changing to etching and caricatures in 1816. Between then and 1825 he attained almost as wide a popularity as his brother, issuing caricatures on the follies of fashion, the foibles of military life and those of the stage. He achieved great success with the illustrations for *Life in London,* the book adapted from the play which he had himself designed at the Adelphi Theatre, He also provided lively and well-executed illustrations for *The English Spy,* but after the 1820s he dropped out of favour and published slovenly uneven work. Everitt considers that the new forms of caricature adapted by HB and others

killed his not very original talent. He died in poverty, 13 March 1856.

Illus: *Age of Intellect [J. Moore, 1819]; Lessons of Thrift [1820]; Nightingale's Memoirs of Queen Caroline [1820]; Radical Chiefs [1821]; Life in London [1821]; The Commercial Tourist [1822]; Annals of Sporting and Fancy Gazette [1822-25]; Ramsey's New Dictionary of Anecdote [1822]; My Cousin in the Army [1822]; Westmacott's Points of Misery [1823]; Spirit of the Public Journals [1823-24]; Life and Exploits of Don Quixote [1824]; Bernard Blackmantle's English Spy [1825]; Westmacott's Punster's Pocket Book [1826]; London Characters [1827]; Grimm's Fairy Tales [1827]; Thompson's Life of Allen [1828]; Smeeton's Doings in London [1828]; British Dance of Death [1828, frontis.]; Spirit of the Age [1828]; Universal Songster [1828]; London Oddities [1828]; The Finish to the Adventures of Tom, Jerry and Logick [1828].* Etc.
Exhib: RA, 1811-17.
Colls: BM; V & AM.
Bibl: G. Everitt, *English Caricaturists,* 1893, pp.89-124; W. Bates, *GC the Artist, the Humorist and The Man, with some account of his brother Robert,* 1878.

### CRUIKSHANK, Percy                    fl.1853-1854
Probably the son of (Isaac) Robert Cruikshank (q.v.). Worked with his uncle and father and illustrated *Sunday Scenes in London and the Suburbs,* twelve illustrations on stone, May 1854.

Colls: BM.
See illustration (p.276).

### CUBITT, Miss Edith Alice (Mrs. Andrews)                    fl.1898-1940
Flower painter and illustrator. She studied at the New Cross Art School and won the prize for black and white illustrations at the National Competition, South Kensington, 1898. She attended Goldsmith's College in 1909. She was working in London in 1900 and at Kent in 1909 and 1931.

Illus: A Book of Nursery Rhymes, Ernest Nister, c.1900.
Exhib: B; L; RA; RI.

### CUCUEL, Edward                    1875-
American painter and illustrator. He was born in San Francisco in 1875, but worked in Switzerland and Germany, 1924.

Contrib: *ILN [1905].*
Exhib: L; Salon, Paris.

GEORGE CRUICKSHANK, Snr. 1792-1878. 'John Bull in The Council Chamber.' A satirical print coloured by hand and published by W.N. Jones, 1 July 1813.
Author's Collection
Engraving. 7¾ins. x 19½ins. (19.7cm x 49.5cm)

275

*PERCY CRUIKSHANK fl.1853-54. 'Sunday Evening at the Red Cross Gin Shop, Barbican.' Illustration for* Sunday Scenes in London and the Suburbs, *May 1854. Lithograph.*

## CUITT, George
1779-1854

Topographical illustrator and etcher. He was the son of George Cuitt 1743-1814, the landscape painter, and was born at Richmond, Yorks in 1779. He followed his father as a painter, but specialised in etchings of buildings, ruins and landscapes in a dramatic Italianate style. He taught drawing at Richmond, then at Chester from 1804 to 1820 and it is that city with which he is usually associated. Cuitt was the only artist of his generation to apply the romantic view of buildings to practical illustration as in guides and histories, his crowded streets and small figures are influenced by Piranesi. Cuitt's books, which are very desirable, cannot be obtained easily, but his separate plates from these can be found. He died at Masham, 1854.

Illus: *Six Etchings of Saxon and Other Buildings Remaining at Chester [1810-11]; Six Etchings of Old Buildings in Chester Six Etchings of Picturesque Buildings in Chester [1810-11]; A History of Chester [1815]; Yorkshire Abbeys [1822-25]; Twenty-four Etchings of Select Parts of Yorkshire [1834]; Wanderings and Pencillings Among Ruins of the Olden Times [1848].*
Colls: BM; Leeds; Newcastle; V & AM; Witt Photo.

See illustration (below).

## CULLIN, Isaac
fl.1881-1894

Figure and portrait painter. He exhibited at the RA and Liverpool, 1881-89, and drew sporting subjects for *The Illustrated London News*, 1893-94.

*GEORGE CUITT 1779-1854. Street scene, Chester. An illustration to* A History of Chester, *1815. Etching.*

*CYNICUS (Martin Anderson). Political cartoon possibly for* The Satires, *1890. Pen and ink.*

Jeffrey Gordon Collection

**CUNEO, Cyrus Cincinnato  ROI**                           **1879-1916**
Painter and illustrator. He was born in San Francisco of Italian parents and came to Paris to study under Girardo, Prenet and Whistler, 1900. Settled in London in 1902 and died there in 1916. He became ROI in 1908. His illustrative work is unusual in often being in oil on board.

Illus: *The Lost Column [C. Gilson, 1908 (boys' novel)]*.
Contrib: *The Pall Mall Magazine; The Strand Magazine [1906]; ILN [1908-12]*.
Exhib: G; L; RA; RHA; ROI.
Colls: V & AM.

**CURTIS, Dora**
Figure painter and illustrator. She designed bookplates, one of which appeared in *The Quarto*, 1896, and exhibited at the NEA, 1899-1901.

**CUTHBERT, E.S.**
Contributing illustrations of Arabia to *The English Illustrated Magazine*, 1887.

**'CYNICUS'   Pseudonym of Martin Anderson**
Political and social cartoonist, designer of postcards. Anderson seems to have originated from Dundee and produced satirical books, in limited editions from an address at 57 Drury Lane, London. The sketches are inventive if not very masterly in the drawing, according to Thorpe they were popular at the time.

Illus: *The Satires of Cynicus [1890]; The Humours of Cynicus [1891]; The Fatal Smile A Fairy Tale [1892]; Cartoons Social and Political [1893]*.
Colls: Gordon.
See illustration (above).

## D, H.P.
Unidentified illustrator for *Fun*, 1887.

## DA COSTA, John ROI         1867-1931
Portrait painter and illustrator. He was born in 1867 and after being educated in Southampton, studied art in Paris for three years. He did most of his illustrative work in the 1890s before becoming a fashionable portrait painter, elected ROI 1905 and RP 1912. He was living at Newlyn in 1880 and in London 1898-1931, except for a brief period at Clanfield, Oxon, 1908. He died 26 May 1931.

Contrib: *The Yellow Book; The Quarto [1896]; Eureka [1901]; The Graphic [1901].*
Exhib: G; GG; L; M; New Gall.; Paris, 1907; P; RA; RHA; ROI; RSA.

## DADD, Frank RI         1851-1929
Black and white artist and figure illustrator. He was born in London on 28 March 1851 and educated at South Kensington and the RA Schools before starting work as an illustrator in about 1872. Dadd did much work for the magazines, particularly drawing for boys' adventure stories; he joined the staff of *The Graphic* in 1884. His style is very photographic with heavy application of bodycolour and clever uses of grey wash, but it is technically excellent and very accurate in detail. He became RI, 1884 and ROI, 1888 and in 1908 one of his pictures was purchased by the Chantrey Bequest. Dadd was a cousin

of Kate Greenaway (q.v.), and his brother married her sister. He died at Teignmouth, Devon, 7 March 1929. Dadd's pictures and drawings are models of Edwardian eloquence, if not of high art.

Illus: *Lead Kindly Light [J.H. Newman, 1887]; Dick O' the Fens [G.M. Fenn, 1888].*
Contrib: *Cornhill Magazine [1870-79]; The Graphic [1876-1910]; ILN [1878-84]; The Quiver [1882]; Boys' Own Paper; The Windsor Magazine.*
Exhib: B; G; L; M; RA, 1905; RI; ROI.
Colls: Author; BM; Exeter.
Bibl: *Who Was Who 1924-40.*
See illustration (below).

## DADD, Philip, J.S.         -1916
Painter and illustrator, killed in action 1916. There are two pen and ink drawings by this artist of war subjects in the Victoria and Albert Museum, one dated 1899. He worked in Hornsey and exhibited at the RA, RI, ROI and Liverpool, 1905-14. He signs his work 'PD'.

## DADD, Richard,         1817-1886
Painter, draughtsman and illustrator. He was born at Chatham, the son of a tradesman and after being educated there, studied art at William Dadson's Academy. In 1834 his family moved to London and the young Dadd became friendly with notable artists, including David Roberts (q.v.) and Clarkson Stanfield (q.v.). He entered the RA Schools on their recommendation in 1837 and he specialised in the painting of fancy pictures in which fairies took a principle role. In 1840 he won the medal for life drawing at the RA and began to exhibit regularly in London.

Dadd was fortunate to be encouraged by Sir Thomas Phillips, the art connoisseur, and was taken on an extensive European tour by him in 1842, visiting, Italy, Greece and the Middle East. On this expedition he first showed unusual behaviour and delusions about the Pope and his patron, Sir Thomas, whom he was convinced were devils. Although he was clearly insane by his return, the symptoms were not recognised until, on August 28 1843, he brutally murdered his father

*FRANK DADD RI 1851-1929. 'A duel.' Illustration for unidentified serial story. Ink and wash with Chinese white. Signed. 5½ins. x 7ins. (14cm x 17.8cm).*
Author's Collection

in Cobham Park, Kent. He immediately fled to France, but was arrested and returned to this country in 1844 and confined in Bethlem Hospital. He was encouraged to continue painting in the asylum and Dr. W.C. Hood, who became physician at Bethlem in 1853, became a collector and admirer of his work. He was moved to Broadmoor in 1864 where he died in 1886. Dadd's work is interesting because of his isolation from the art world for so many years. His watercolours show a microscopic observation of detail and a fresh and rather disturbing use of colour. Some of his drawings might be compared to those of the Pre-Raphaelites, particularly the more intense visions of Millais and Rossetti in the early 1850s. Dadd's work as an illustrator was short-lived. He drew for *The Book of British Ballads*, 1842, contributing vignettes of 'Robin Goodfellow' and made a frontispiece for *The Kentish Coronal* 1840, which is remarkably bold for its date.

Exhib: BI, 1839; RA; RBA, 1837.
Colls: Bedford; BM; Fitzwilliam; Newcastle; V & AM.
Bibl: D. Greysmith, *RD* 1973. Tate Gallery RD Exhibition catalogue, 1974.

### DADD, Stephen T.                                   fl.1879-1914
Figure painter and illustrator. He worked at Brockley, South London, and contributed domestic and animal subjects to magazines.

Contrib: *The Graphic [1882-91, 1901]; ILN [1889]; Daily Graphic [1890]; The Quiver [1890]; Sporting and Dramatic News [1890]; Black and White [1891]; The Rambler [1897]; Chums; Cassell's Family Magazine.*
Exhib: L; M; NWS, 1879-92; RBA; RI.

### DALE, Lawrence
Amateur artist. He contributed to *Punch*, 1909.

### DALTON, F.T.
Perhaps 'Dallon' who contributed cartoons to *Vanity Fair*, 1895-1900.

### DALZIEL, Edward                                    1817-1905
Engraver on wood and illustrator. He was born at Wooler, Northumberland, on 5 December 1817, the fifth son of Alexander Dalziel and brother of E. and T.B. Dalziel (qq.v.). He was in business at first, but spent much of his spare time studying art, finally joining his brother George in London in 1839 as a wood engraver. He formed part of the firm of Dalziel for over fifty years. Edward was the brother who took on the role of illustrator more earnestly than the rest of his family; he studied at the Clipstone St. Academy alongside Charles Keene (q.v.), and Sir John Tenniel (q.v.) and exhibited from time to time at the RA. He collaborated with his brother on their book, *The Brothers Dalziel, A Record of Work, 1840-1890,* and died 25 March 1905.

Illus: *The Hermit [Thomas Parnell].*
Contrib: *Bryant's Poems [1857]; Dramatic Scenes [1857]; Poets of the Nineteenth Century [1857]; The Home Affections [Mackay, 1858]; Dalziel's Arabian Nights [1865]; A Round of Days [1866]; The Spirit of Praise [1866]; Ballad Stories of the Affections [1866]; Golden Thoughts from Golden Fountains [1867]; North Coast [1868]; National Nursery Rhymes [1870]; The Uncommercial Traveller [Dickens Household Edition, 1871]; The Graphic [1873-74]; Dalziel's Bible Gallery [1881].*
Bibl: The Brothers Dalziel, *A Record of Work, 1840-90,* 1901; Gleeson White, *English Illustration The Sixties,* 1897; F. Reid, *Illustrators of the Sixties,* 1928, pp.252-258, illus.; Simon Houfe, *The Dalziel Family,* Sotheby's Belgravia, 1978.
See illustration (right).

### DALZIEL, Edward Gurdon                              1849-1889
Illustrator. He was born in 1849 and was the eldest son of Edward Dalziel (q.v.). For some years he was a contributor to *Fun,* 1878-80 choosing subjects of country life and manners, with figures in the tradition of Pinwell and Walker. In *The Brothers Dalziel* he is described as 'a young artist full of promise and great ability. Had he given continued attention to his oil painting he must undoubtedly have taken a very high position. He exhibited many pictures at the Royal Academy, the Grosvenor and other galleries, but the allurement of black and white became too much for him, and he laid aside his brush for the pencil.' *A Record of Work,* 1901, p.10. His work in this medium was much admired by Sir John Gilbert, but he died at the comparatively early age of thirty-nine in 1889.

Exhib: NWS, 1865-87; RA; RBA.

### DALZIEL, Thomas Bolton Gilchrist Septimus          1823-1906
Illustrator and wood engraver. He was born at Wooler, Northumberland, in 1823, the son of Alexander Dalziel, painter. He joined his brothers George, Edward and John in the London engraving business in 1860. He was the only one of the brothers to be a noted draughtsman, he was a more accomplished figure artist than Edward, and he contributed to a number of books that were either augmented or financed by the firm. He was a fine landscape illustrator and some of his best work is in Dalziel's Arabian Nights.

Contrib: *Dramatic Scenes [1857]; Bryant's Poems [1857]; Poets of the Nineteenth Century [1857]; Gertrude of Wyoming [1857]; The Home Affections [Mackay, 1858]; Lays of the Holy Land [1858]; The Pilgrim's Progress [1863]; The Golden Harp [1864]; The Churchman's Family Magazine [1864]; The Sunday Magazine [1866-68]; Dalziel's Arabian Nights [1865]; The Arabian Nights [1866]; A Round of Days [1866]; Ballad Stories of the Affections [1866]; The Spirit of Praise [1866]; Jean Ingelow's Poems [1867]; Golden Thoughts From Golden Fountains [1867]; North Coast [1865]; National Nursery Rhymes [1870]; Christmas Carols [1871]; Dalziel's Bible Gallery [1881]; Art Pictures From The Old Testament [1891, etc.].*
Exhib: BI, 1858; RA; RBA, 1846, 1866.
Bibl: *The Brothers Dalziel – A Record of Work 1840-1890,* 1901; F. Reid, *Illustrators of the Sixties,* 1928, pp.251-252; Simon Houfe, *The Dalziel Family,* Sotheby's Belgravia, 1978.

### DANCE, Sir Nathaniel, Bt.   RA                     1734-1811
Caricaturist. He was the eldest son of George Dance, the architect, and was born in London in 1734. He showed a talent for painting from an early age and studied with Francis Hayman, followed by nearly nine years in Italy, where he met and fell in love with Angelica Kauffmann. On his return to England he married a wealthy widow and enjoyed a comfortable life in which he was able to devote his time to politics, eventually being given a baronetcy as M.P. for East Grinstead. Dance was known in his day as a history and portrait painter and as a founder member of the RA, but ironically is best remembered now for the brilliant caricatures done for his own amusement and for

EDWARD DALZIEL 1817-1905. 'The Son of His Filthy Old Father Thames.' Illustration for The Uncommercial Traveller, Dickens Household Edition, 1870.

279

private circulation.

His style of pen drawing is close to Rowlandson (q.v.) in outline and like Hogarth in subject manner. Although it is very much in the tradition of Lord Townshend, it is softer in touch.

Exhib: RA.
Colls: NPG; Witt Photo.

## DANIELL, Samuel                    c.1775-1811

Watercolourist and illustrator. He was born in 1775, the brother of William and the nephew of Thomas Daniell (qq.v.). He studied under Medland and travelled in Africa as secretary and draughtsman for the Bechuanaland mission, 1801. He returned to England in 1804 and travelled to Ceylon; in the following year he died of illness contracted there in the swamps.

Illus: *African Scenery and Animals [1804-05, AT 32]; Barrow's Travels Into The Interior of Southern Africa [1806, AT 322]; The Scenery Animals and Native Inhabitants of Ceylon [1808]; Scenery of Southern Africa [1820]*
Exhib: RA, 1792-1812.
Colls: V & AM.
Bibl: Iolo Williams, *Early English Watercolours*, 1952, p.58 illus.

## DANIELL, Thomas   RA               1749-1840

Landscape painter. He was born at Kingston-upon-Thames in 1749, the son of an innkeeper. After being apprenticed to a coach painter, he began to work for Thomas Catton RA, and entered the RA Schools in 1773. During this period he worked as a landscapist in the English Shires, but in 1785 he made the journey that was to alter the course of his career, by travelling to India with his nephew, William (q.v.). He worked in Calcutta, 1788-89, then toured North India, returning to Calcutta in 1791. In 1792 they undertook a tour of Southern India and Ceylon, returning to Bombay in 1793 and leaving for home later the same year.

Much of Daniell's subsequent career was taken up with completing and publishing his Indian work. His drawings and watercolours are careful topographer's work, the colours more like tints than full-blooded watercolours. He became ARA in 1796 and RA in 1797. He was a Fellow of the Royal Society and of the Asiatic Society. He died at Kensington on 19 March 1840.

Illus: (with W. Daniell) *Oriental Scenery [1795-1808]; A Picturesque Voyage to India by the Way of China [1810]*.
Illus: *Views in Calcutta [1786-88, AT 492]*.
Exhib: RA, 1772-84.
Colls: BM; Fitzwilliam; India Office Library; V & AM.
Bibl: T. Sutton, *The Daniells*, 1954; M. Shellim, *The Daniells in Indias*, 1970; *Walker's Quarterly*, Vol.35-36, 1932; M. Archer, *Cat. of Drawings in the India Office Library*.

## DANIELL, William   RA              1769-1837

Landscape painter and topographer. He was born in 1769 and was trained as his uncle, William Daniell's assistant and accompanied him to India, 1785-94 (q.v.). On his return, Daniell concentrated on making topographical drawings and watercolours, specialising at first in Indian scenery and later in English and Scottish views. He was a very fine aquatinter and engraver and engraved most of the prints for his uncle and family from 1808. His greatest success was probably his *Voyage Round Great Britain*, produced in the years 1813 to 1823 and published 1814-25. He produced some of his best watercolours for this work although many of the studies for the prints are in sepia wash. Daniell was an early follower of Turner in wiping out highlights in his watercolours but otherwise belonged to the older tradition of watercolours. He died at New Camden Town on 16 August 1837. ARA 1807, and RA 1822.

Illus: *Oriental Scenery [1795-1808, 1812-16, AT 432]; Interesting Selections From Animated Nature [1807-12]; A Picturesque Voyage to India by the way of China [1810]; A Familiar Treatise on Perspective [1810]; Views in Bootan [1813]; A Voyage Round Great Britain [1814-25]; Illustrations of the Island of Staffa [1818, after S. Daniell]; Sketches of the Native Tribes . . . of Southern Africa [1820]; Views of Windsor, Eton and Virginia Water [1827-30]; The Oriental Annual [1838]; A Brief History of Ancient and Modern India [Blagdon, 1802-5]*.
Exhib: BI 1807-36; RA from 1795.
Colls: Bedford; BM; Fitzwilliam; Greenwich; India Office; V & AM..
Bibl: T. Sutton, *The Daniells*, 1954; M. Shellim, *The Daniells in India, 1970*; M. Archer, *Catalogue of Drawings in the India Office Library*.

## DANIELS, George                    1854-c.1917

Landscape painter, miniaturist, stained glass artist. He probably undertook some illustrations and a period subject dated '28 February 1874' is in the Victoria and Albert Museum.

Exhib: RA, 1884-93.

## DARBYSHIRE, J.A.                    fl.1886-1893

Figure illustrator, working in the Manchester area at Flixton and Prestwick. His work is rather exaggerated and weak in drawing.

Exhib: M, 1886-93.
Colls: V & AM.

## DARLEY, J. Felix   RBA ACA          -1932

Landscape and figure painter and illustrator. He contributed many competent landscape subjects to books in the 1860s and was elected RBA in 1901. He worked in London from 1886 and at Addlestone, Surrey, from 1898, he died at Woking on 17 October 1932.

Contrib: *The Poetical Works of Edgar Allan Poe [1857]; Poets of the West; London Society [1863]*.
Exhib: B; L; RBA; ROI.
Bibl: Chatton & Jackson *Treatise On Wood Engraving, 1861*, p.599.

## DARRÉ, G.                           fl.1883-1889

French illustrator. He worked extensively for Parisian satirical publications including, *Charivari, Journal Amusant, Le Grelot, Le Carillon*. He illustrated a *Histoire de France* before coming to London in 1883. There he found work on *Punch*, 1888-89, and some work on *Judy*, 1889. After that date he abandoned illustration for commercial work in black and white.

## DAVENPORT, W.

Topographer. He illustrated a *Life of Ali Pasha*, 1823, AT 206.

## DAVEY, George

Illustrator and contributor to *Fun*, 1901, working in West Hampstead, London, 1901-2.

## DAVEY, H.F.

Topograher. Working in Newcastle-upon-Tyne and contributing drawings to *The Illustrated London News*, 1887.

## DAVID, S.

Illustrator of the 1822 edition of *Walton's Compleat Angler*.

## DAVIDSON, Alexander   RSW           1838-1887

Painter and illustrator who studied in Glasgow. He exhibited at the RA and at the RBA, 1873-92. He made drawings for an edition of Scott's *Waverley Novels*.

## DAVIDSON, Thomas                    fl.1880-1908

Painter of history and genre. He worked in Hampstead from 1880 and specialised in figure subjects. He contributed the latter to *Good Words*, 1880.

Exhib: B; G; L; M; RA; RBA; RHA; ROI.

## DAVIEL, Leon                        fl.1893-1930

Portrait painter, wood engraver and illustrator. In his earlier years he specialised in figure subjects for the magazines, 1897-1907; he worked in Chelsea, 1914-25.

Contrib: *Good Words [1897]; Black and White [1900]; Pearson's Magazine; The Temple Magazine; The Illustrated London News [1907, Christmas]*.
Exhib: NEA, 1912; New Gall; P; RA; ROI.

## DAVIES, Edgar W.                    fl.1893-1910

Historical, mythical and architectural draughtsman. He was working in Manchester in 1893 and subsequently in London. He designed book covers and made studies of foreign towns possibly with a view to illustration. An important group of his drawings in a late Pre-Raphaelite style were sold at Sotheby's Belgravia on 24 January 1978.

Exhib: B; L; M; New Gall; RA; RBA.

**DAVIES, Scrope**
Figure artist. Contributed to *The English Illustrated Magazine*, 1897; *The Dome*, 1899.

**DAVIS, A.L.** fl.1899-1925
Figure painter. Probably the same artist who lived at Hither Green, Kent, from 1914-25 and exhibited at the RA, 1914. He contributed to Newnes edition of *The Arabian Nights*, 1899.

**DAVIS, G.H.**
Marine illustrator, contributing naval subjects to *The Graphic*, 1910.

**DAVIS, Joseph Bernard** 1861-
Painter of landscapes, genre and portraits, and illustrator. He was born at Bowness, Windermere, in 1861, and worked in London, 1890-1911, and from then until 1925 at Gerrards Cross, Bucks. He was a fairly regular illustrator in the 1890s and excelled in robust genre scenes, such as 'Bank Holiday at the Welsh Harp' for *The Graphic*.

Contrib: *The Temple Magazine* [1896]; *The Quiver* [1900]; *The Graphic* [1903]; *The Ludgate Monthly*; *The Pall Mall Magazine*; *The Windsor Magazine*; *The Royal Magazine*.
Exhib: B; G; L; NWS; RA; RBA; RCA; RI; ROI; RSA.
Colls: Witt Photo.

**DAVIS, Louis RWS** 1861-1941
Book decorator and illustrator. He worked at Ewelme, Pinner, 1897-1925, and designed borders and bookplates in the style of Morris and Burne-Jones. From 1886-87 he was designing decoration in the form of stylised birds for *The English Illustrated Magazine*, and in 1891-92 contributed topographical work. His drawings are delightful period pieces. He was elected ARWS, 1898.

Exhib: L; New Gall; RWS.

**DAVIS, Lucien RI** 1860-
Artist and illustrator. He was born at Liverpool in 1860, the son of William Davis, the Liverpool artist. He was educated at St. Francis Xavier's College, Liverpool, and entered the RA Schools in 1877 where he won several prizes. He began his career as an illustrator with Cassell's publications in 1878, but had his first important drawings published in *The Graphic*, 1880-81. He joined the staff of *The Illustrated London News* in 1885 and remained for the next twenty years as one of its chief artists, specialising in social subjects and in work for the Christmas numbers. He was described in the magazine in 1892 as 'singularly successful in representing the sheen of a silk or satin dress'; certainly his figures are rarely seen out of the ballroom or the drawing room! Davis was elected RI in 1893. His two brothers, W.P. and Valentine Davis, were also artists.

Illus: *Willow the King* [1899 (child's book)]; *Cricket, Lawn Tennis* and *Billiards* in the Badminton Library editions.
Contrib: *The Graphic* [1880-81]; *ILN* [1885-1905]; *The English Illustrated Magazine* [1885]; *Fun* [1886-87]; *The Quiver* [1890]; *Cassell's Family Magazine*.
Exhib: G; L; M; Paris, 1900; P; RA.
Colls: V & AM; Witt Photo.

**DAVIS, Vaughan**
Animal artist. Illustrated Cassell's *The Book of the Dog*, c.1870.

**DAVY, C.** fl.1833-1846
Architectural draughtsman. He contributed to *Public Works of Great Britain*, 1838, AL 410.
Exhib: RA.

**DAWSON, Alfred** fl.1860-1889
Landscape painter. He worked at Chertsey as painter and etcher and exhibited at London exhibitions from 1860. He made illustrations for a history of Dorset and contributed to *The Portfolio*, 1884-92.
Exhib: B; RA; RBA; RE; ROI.
Colls: V & AM; Witt Photo.

**DAWSON, Charles Frederick** fl.1909-1933
Painter and designer. He studied at Shipley School of Art and then in Bradford, Manchester and Newlyn Cornwall. He was for some years headmaster of the Bingley, Nelson and Accrington Schools of Art.
Contrib: *The Page*, 1899.
Exhib: L; M; RA.

**DEAN, Christopher**
Draughtsman, illustrator and book decorator. He was born in Glasgow and worked there until 1895, settling in Marlow, Bucks., in 1898 and in Chelsea from 1925. He designed illustrations and book covers in a bold Celtic style, using distinctive interlaced borders to the page plates.
Designs for: *Hans Sachs His Life and Work* [c.1910]; *The Odes of Anacreon* [c.1910].
Exhib: G and RSA, 1895-99.
Bibl: *The Studio*, Vol.12, 1898, pp.183-187, illus. Winter No.1900-01, p.64, illus.

**DEAN, Frank RBA** 1865-
Painter of genre and illustrator. He was born near Leeds in 1865 and studied at the Slade School under Legros and then at Paris with Lefevbre and Boulanger, 1882-86. He was a close friend of A.S. Hartrick (q.v.) and joined the staff of *The Graphic* with him in 1890, he later shared a flat with E.J. Sullivan (q.v.). Dean travelled to the Middle East and India in search of subjects and worked at Headingley near Leeds from 1914. He was elected RBA, 1895.
Exhib: L; M; NEA; New Gall; RA, from 1887; RBA; RCA; RI; ROI; RSA.
Bibl: A.S. Hartrick, *Painters Pilgrimage Through Fifty Years*, 1939.

**DEANE, William Wood OWS** 1825-1873
Painter, watercolourist and draughtsman. He was born in Liverpool Road, Islington, on 22 March 1825, the son of J.W. Wood, amateur watercolourist. He began his career in architecture, but gradually abandoned this for painting. He attended the RA Schools in 1844, where he won a silver medal and travelled to Italy, 1850-52. He was an intimate friend of F.W. Topham (q.v.) and visited Spain with him in 1866; he married the sister of Professor George Aitchison, ARA, the architect. He was elected ARIBA, 1848, Associate of the NWS, 1862, and Member, 1867, resigning in 1870 to join the OWS. He was a prolific painter of views of France, Spain and Venice, very colourful and moody compositions. He died at Hampstead, 18 January 1873.

Contrib: *The Illustrated Times*, [Naples, 1856].
Exhib: BI, 1859-64; OWS; NWS; RA; RBA, 1857-66.
Colls: V & AM; Wakefield.
Bibl: M. Hardie, *Watercol. Paint in Britain*, Vol.3, 1968, p.21 illus.

**DEAR, Mary E.** fl.1848-1867
Portrait and genre painter and illustrator. She worked in London and exhibited at various exhibitions through Messrs. Colnaghi, Pall Mall East; by 1867 she was working from Rottingdean, Sussex. Her figure drawing is always of high quality.
Illus: *The Scarlet Letter* [Nathaniel Hawthorne, 1859].
Contrib: *The Illustrated Times* [1855, Christmas]; *The Art Journal* [c.1865 (a series of Seasons)].
Exhib: RA; RBA, 1848-67.

**DEARMER, Mrs. Percy (née Mabel White)** 1872-1915
Writer, dramatist and illustrator. She was born on 22 March 1872 and studied art at the Herkomer School, Bushey. In 1892 she married the Rev. Percy Dearmer, Editor of the *English Hymnal*, and became one of the most popular illustrators of children's books, many of them written by herself and printed in bright colours. She was also engaged in poster work before her death and died at Primrose Hill, London, 10 July 1915.

Illus: *Wymps and Other Fairy Tales* [Evelyn Sharp, 1897]; *Roundabout Rhymes* [1898]; *The Book of Penny Toys* [1899]; *The Noah's Ark Geography* [1900]; *The Seven Young Goslings* [Laurence Housman, 1900].
Contrib: *The Yellow Book* [1896 (cover), 1897]; *The Parade* [1897].

**DE GRIMM see GRIMM**

**DE HAENEN, F.**      fl.1896-1910
War artist and illustrator. He was a Frenchman, working for the magazine, *L'Illustration*, and contributing to *The Illustrated London News*, 1896. He went to South Africa as correspondent for *The Graphic*, in 1900 and continued to work for the journal until 1910.

**DE KATOW, Paul de**      1834-1897
Battle painter and illustrator. He was born in Strasbourg on 17 October 1834 and became a pupil of Delacroix; he exhibited regularly at the Salon, 1839-82, and was war correspondent of *Gaulois* in 1870. He drew illustrations of the Siege of Paris for *The Illustrated London News*, 1870, and contributed to *The Graphic*, 1872.

Exhib: RBA, 1872-73.

**DE LA BERE, Stephen Baghot   RI**      1877-1927
Figure and landscape painter and illustrator. He was educated at Ilkley, Yorks, and studied at Westminster School of Art. He worked in Kensington for most of his life, but at Bishop's Stortford, 1913-14. He was elected RI in 1908. De La Bere was an occasional illustrator, capable of very fine pen and ink work, he died in 1927.

Illus: *Lazarillo de Tomes [Hurtado de Mendoza, n.d.]*.
Contrib: *ILN [1911]*.
Exhib: FAS, 1912; L; RA; RI; RWA.

**DE LACEY, Charles John**      fl.1885-1925
Landscape and naval artist and illustrator. He worked for *The Illustrated London News*, 1895-1900, and was Special Artist with the Russian Fleet, 1897. He later worked for *The Graphic* and acted as Special for the Admiralty and the Port of London Authority.

Illus: *A Book About Ships [A.O. Cooke, 1914]; Our Wonderful Navy, [J.S. Margerison, 1919]*.
Contrib: *The Pall Mall Magazine*.
Exhib: L; M; RA; RBA, 1885-1918.

**DELAMOTTE, E.**
Contributed decorative initials to *The Illustrated London Magazine*, 1855.

**DELAMOTTE, William Alfred**      1775-1863
Watercolourist and draughtsman. He was born at Weymouth 2 August 1775 and, through the interest of George III, was placed under Benjamin West in 1794. He studied in the life classes of the RA Schools and eventually settled in the Oxford area as a drawing master and topographer. In 1803, he gained the official appointment of drawing master to the Royal Military Academy, Great Marlow, and two years later, became an early member of the OWS. Our view of Regency Oxford and the Thames valley is generally taken through his soft pencil drawings with colour washes, many of which were engraved for books. He died at St. Giles's Field, Oxford, 13 February 1863.

Illus: *Thirty etchings of rural subjects [1816]; Illustrations of Virginia Water [1828]; Memorials of Oxford [J. Ingram, 1837]; Original views of Oxford, 1843 (liths)]; Windsor Castle [W.H. Ainsworth, 1843]; An Historical Sketch ... Hospital of St. Bartholomew [1844]; Smokers and Smoking [G.T. Fisher, 1845]; Journey to India [Broughton, 1847, AT 522]*.
Contrib: *Britton's Beauties of England and Wales [1813]*.
Exhib: BI 1808-46; OWS, 1806-8; RA; RBA, 1829-31.
Colls: Ashmolean; BM; Fitzwilliam; Manchester; V & AM.
Bibl: Iolo Williams, *Early English Watercolours*, 1952, p.63, illus.

**DELFICO, Melchiorre**      1825-1895
Draughtsman, musician and caricaturist. He was born at Teramo in 1825 and became well known in Italy for his caricature albums of celebrated people. He died in Naples in 1895. In 1872-73, he contributed 8 cartoons to *Vanity Fair*.

**DELL, John H.**      1830-1888
Painter of rustic subjects and animals. He worked in the London area and had addresses at various times in Hammersmith, Chertsey and New Malden. He was noted for the accuracy of his work and his masterpiece in book illustration was *Nature Pictures*, published in 1878, consisting of thirty plates in which were shown, as Gleeson

White put it, 'years of patient painstaking labour on the part of artist and engraver'.

Exhib: B; BI, 1851-67; M; RBA, 1851-86.

**DE MARTINO, Commendatore Eduardo   MVO**      1834-1912
Marine artist and illustrator. Born at Meta, near Naples, in 1834 and trained at Naples Naval College for a career in the Italian Navy where he remained until 1867. He then travelled to Brazil and was engaged by the Emperor to make official sketches of the Paraguayan War. Settling in England in 1875, he was made Marine Painter in Ordinary to Queen Victoria and the Royal Yacht Squadron, MVO, 1898. He accompanied the Duke of York on his royal tour in 1901. He died at St. John's Wood, 21 May 1912.

Contrib: *The Graphic [1896-1905]*.
Exhib: GG; L.

**DE MONTMORENCY, Lily**      fl.1895-1904
Landscape and figure artist. She was working in Streatham in 1895, and at Bushey, 1898, where she may have attended the Herkomer School. She was elected ASWA in 1898.

Illus: *Little Tales of Long Ago [1903 (child's book)]*.
Contrib: *The Parade [1897 (initials)]*.
Exhib: L; RA; SWA.

**DE MORGAN, William**      1839-1917
Artist, author and potter. He was born in 1839, and educated at University College and at the RA Schools, 1859. He came under the influence of the Pre-Raphaelite circle and experimented with stained glass and tile processes, founding a pottery at Chelsea in 1871. He is best remembered today for his re-discovery of coloured lustre, a craft he put to good use in making large chargers and vases. He was associated with William Morris (q.v.) in the Merton Abbey venture, 1882-88, and then on his own at Fulham. He retired in 1905 to Florence and became well-known as a novelist. He died in 1917.

De Morgan was a witty draughtsman of comic sketches and illustrated a book for children, *On a Pincushion and Other Fairy Tales*, 1877. His humorous drawings occasionally come on the market.

**DE PARYS or DE PARIS, Alphonse G.**      fl.1902-1933
Figure painter and illustrator. He contributed to *The Graphic*, 1902-3, mostly crowded social subjects and in particular the Coronation of King Edward VII. He worked in Kensington.

Exhib: RA, 1933.

**D'EPINAY   see EPINAY**

**DEROY, Isidore Laurent**      1797-1886
Architectural illustrator. He was well-known in France as a painter and lithographer and exhibited at the Salon. He drew views of churches and castles for some English publications, notably *The Illustrated London News* (Vizetelly).

**DERRICK, Thomas C.**      1885-1954
Artist in stained glass, mural painter and cartoonist. He was born in Bristol in 1885, and was educated at Didcot and studied at the RCA. He was instructor in decorative painting at the RCA for five years, but was best known as a cartoonist contributing to *Punch* and *Time and Tide*. His slick chalk drawings, more like the medium of advertising than the stateliness of *Punch*, typify the 1930s, but probably seemed very untypical at the time. His work was never straight reporting, but a synthesis and abstraction of an event. R.G.G. Price says, 'Reality was patterned and a social point that would be dull presented in a unitary setting gained enormously by being presented rhythmically and decoratively ...' *A History of Punch*, 1955, p.283, illus. Derrick married the daughter of Sir George Clausen, RA, (q.v.).

Publ: *The Prodigal Son and Other Parables; The Nine Nines [Hilaire Belloc]; Everyman [(72 wood engravings) 1930]*.
Exhib: FAS, 1910; G; NEA; RA.

**DETMOLD, Charles Maurice ARE**                     **1883-1908**

Animal painter, illustrator and etcher. He was born on 21 November 1883, the twin brother of E.J. Detmold (q.v.), with whom he collaborated. He studied animals in the Zoological Gardens with his brother and exhibited watercolours from the age of fourteen. He was strongly influenced by Japanese art and produced with his brother, a portfolio of etchings of birds and animals of unusual technical ability in 1898. He committed suicide in 1908. Elected RE, 1905.

Illus: *Pictures From Birdland; The Jungle Book [Rudyard Kipling, 1908].*
Exhib: FAS, 1900; G; NEA, 1899; RE; RI, 1897-

**DETMOLD, Edward Julius**                          **1883-1957**

Animal painter, illustrator and etcher. The twin brother of C.M. Detmold (q.v.). He worked with his brother making sketches at the Zoological Gardens and exhibited with him from the age of fourteen. He was strongly influenced by Japanese art but also by the woodcuts of Dürer and became one of the best Edwardian animal illustrators. His sense of composition and the decorative placing of the animal in its natural habitat was much more subtle than the natural history painters or for example A. Thorburn (q.v.). E.J. Detmold's range was considerable and he published a number of books of fantasy drawing in the early 1920s which show a vivid imagination, fine drawing and warm colouring. Detmold settled at Montgomery in Wales and died there in 1957. He was elected RE in 1905.

*EDWARD JULIUS DETMOLD 1883-1957. 'Dormice among brambles.' Illustration for a publication of Messrs. Dent. 19⁷/₈ins. x 13³/₄ins. (50.5cm x 34.9cm).*
Victoria and Albert Museum

Illus: *Pictures From Birdland [1899 (with C.M.D.)]; Sixteen Illustrations of subjects from Kipling's 'Jungle Book' [1903 (with C.M.D.)]; The Jungle Book [R. Kipling, 1908]; The Fables of Aesop [1909]; The Life of the Bee [M. Maeterlinck, 1911]; Birds and Beasts [C. Lemmonier, 1911]; The Book of Baby Beasts [F.E. Dugdale, 1911]; The Book of Baby Birds [F.E. Dugdale, 1912]; Hours of Gladness [M. Maeterlinck, 1912]; The Book of Baby Pets [F.E. Dugdale, 1915]; The Book of Baby Dogs [Charles J. Kaberry, 1915]; Our Little Neighbours, Animals of the Farm and Woodland [1921]; Rainbow Houses [A.V. Hall, 1923]; Tales From the Thousand and One Nights [1924].*
Contrib: *ILN [1912, Christmas].*
Exhib: FAS, 1900; G; GG; L; M; NEA, 1899; RA; RBA; RHA; RI; ROI.
Colls: BM; Fitzwilliam; V & AM.
Bibl: 'A Note on Mr. Edward J. Detmold's Drawings and Etchings of Animal Life', *The Studio*, Vol.51, 1911, pp.289-296, illus; B. Peppin *Fantasy Book Illustration*, 1975, p.186, illus.
See illustration (below left).

**DEVAMBEZ, André Victor Édouard**                 **1867-1943**

French book illustrator. He was born in Paris in 1867, and studied with Constant and Lefevrbre, winning the *prix de Rome* in 1890. He illustrated many books by French authors, including *La Fête à Coqueville*, Émile Zola, and *Le Condamnes à mort*, Claude Farrere. He contributed to *The Illustrated London News*, 1912-13.

**DEWAR, William Jesmond**                          **fl.1890-1903**

Figure artist and illustrator. A competent black and white artist in pen who uses bold hatching and outline in the manner of C.D. Gibson (q.v.).

Contrib: *Moonshine [1885]; Illustrated Bits [1890]; Pick-Me-Up [1894]; Black & White [1896-99]; The Ludgate Monthly [1896]; The Rambler [1897]; The Temple Magazine; Pearson's Magazine.*
Exhib: RA, 1903.

**DE WILDE, Samuel 'Paul'**                         **1748-1832**

Dramatic portrait painter and illustrator. He was brought to England when a child by his widowed mother and apprenticed to a wood carver in Soho. His earliest works are a series of etchings and mezzotints after Steen, Van Loo, Reynolds, Vernet and Wright which were published under the pseudonym of 'Paul', 1770-77. From 1795, De Wilde was almost totally absorbed in theatrical portraiture, producing a long series of scenes with actors in character, mostly in oil but also in watercolour. He was also a political caricaturist and contributed anonymous plates to the Tory *Satirist*, 1807-8.

The Victoria and Albert Museum has a series of wash drawings of decorative designs for frontispieces, presumably dating from De Wilde's early years in illustration, c.1770; the Garrick Club has the finest collection of his theatrical portraits. He died 19 January 1832.

Exhib: BI, 1812; RA, 1782; SA, 1776.
Colls: Ashmolean; BM; Richmond, Virginia; V & AM.
Bibl: M.D. George, *English Political Caricature*, Vol. 2, 1959, p.106; Iolo Williams, *Early English Watercolours*, 1952, pp.148-149, illus.

**DIBDIN, Thomas Colman**                           **1810-1893**

Painter and illustrator. He was born at Betchworth, Surrey on 22 October 1810, the son of Thomas Dibdin, the dramatist and probably the grandson of Charles Dibdin, the actor-dramatist. He began work as a clerk in the GPO at the age of seventeen, but after eleven years left it to paint. Dibdin travelled in Northern France, Germany and Belgium drawing their old towns and picturesque buildings. In later life he claimed to be the inventor of chromo-lithography. He died at Sydenham on 26 December 1893.

Publ: *Progressive Lessons in Water Colour Painting [1848].*
Illus: *Heman's Works [1839]; Bacon's Oriental Annual; Rock Cut Temples of India [Ferguson, 1845, AT 467].*
Exhib: BI, 1832-50; NWS; RA; RBA, 1831-83.
Colls: Ashmolean; BM; Nottingham; Sydney; V & AM.

**DICKES, William**                                 **fl.1841-1883**

Illustrator, engraver and publisher. He was a prolific illustrator in the 1840s but turned his attention to publishing and was chief manager of the Abbotsford Edition of Sir Walter Scott's Works. Chatto records in 1861 that 'Mr. Dickes' attention is now turned to Colour-Printing'. He was living at Loughborough Park, London in 1881.

Illus: *Masterman Ready [Captain Marryat, 1841]; London [Charles Knight, 1841]; Glaucus or Wonders of the Shore [Charles Kingsley, 1855, (frontis.)].*

*SIR FRANCIS BERNARD DICKSEE, PRA RI HRSA, 1853-1928. 'An elderly couple.' Drawing for unidentified illustration, c.1873-80. Pencil.*

Contrib: *ILN [1843]*.
Exhib: RA, etc, 1843-81.
Bibl: Chatto & Jackson, *Treatise on Wood Engraving*, 1861, p.599; M.H. Spielmann, *'The History of Punch'*, 1895, p.248.

**DICKINSON, F.C.**                           **fl.1898-1906**
Black and white artist and watercolourist. He contributed to *The Quarto*, 1898, and *The Graphic*, 1899-1906. He does quite strong watercolours of figure subjects and may have illustrated an edition of Hans Andersen.

**DICKINSON, J. Reed**                        **fl.1867-1895**
Figure and portrait painter working in Regent's Park and Hammersmith.
Exhib: Dudley; L; M; RA, 1867-81; RBA, 1867-78.

**DICKSEE, Sir Francis Bernard   PRA RI HRSA     1853-1928**
Painter and illustrator. He was born in London in 1853, the son of T.F. Dicksee, the portrait painter. He was trained at the R.A. Schools, 1870-75, and was influenced by Leighton and Millais. He became a very competent book illustrator in the best black and white tradition of the 1870s, illustrated Longfellow's *Evangeline* in 1882 and *The Four Georges*, W.M. Thackeray, 1894. But his success as a society portrait painter enabled him to abandon this side of his art. He was elected ARA, 1881; RA, 1891, and PRA, 1924. He died in London 28 October 1928.
Exhib: G; GG; L; M; RA; RHA; RI; ROI; RSA.
Colls: BM; Manchester; V & AM.
Bibl: E.R. Dibdin, FD, 1905.
See illustration (above).

**DICKSEE, Margaret Isabel**                  **1858-1903**
Landscape and figure painter and illustrator. She was born in 1858, the daughter of T.F. Dicksee, the portrait painter and sister of Sir Frank Dicksee (q.v.). She drew ink illustrations for a number of magazines including *The Quiver*, 1890, and *The Girls' Own Paper*. She was also a good decorative artist and designed borders for some of Woolner's poems. She died in London 6 June 1903.
Exhib: L; RA; RBA; RWS.
Colls: V & AM; Witt Photo.

**DIGHTON, Denis**                            **1792-1827**
Military painter and draughtsman. He was born in London in 1792, the son of Robert Dighton (q.v.), and studied at the RA Schools. He was patronised by the Prince of Wales and became Military Draughtsman to him from 1815, sometimes travelling abroad. He died at St. Servan, Brittany in 1827.
Illus: *Sketches [1821, 15 liths., AL 121]*.
Exhib: BI; RA.

**DIGHTON, Joshua**                           **fl.1820-1840**
Caricaturist. A son of Robert Dighton and a brother of Richard Dighton (qq.v.). Like his brother he drew small full-length watercolour portraits in profile, concentrating on sporting celebrities.
Colls: Witt Photo.

**DIGHTON, Richard**                          **1795-1880**
Caricaturist. Son of Robert Dighton (q.v.) whose successor he was. He was born in London in 1795, and on his father's death in 1814, he continued the series of portrait etchings, 1815-28. These were all in the 'Dighton style' of small full-length portraits in profile, coloured by hand, usually of sporting celebrities but also of politicians. The whole series of originals by father and son were purchased by King George IV. Dighton also etched some Anti-Radical caricatures between 1819-21 and died on 13 April 1880. His portrait drawings are still occasionally seen on the market, they are often in pencil and watercolour and well-handled. Work by other members of the family is stiffer and less convincing.
Colls: NPG; V & AM.
See illustration (p. 285).

**DIGHTON, Robert**                           **1752-1814**
Painter, caricaturist and actor. He was the founder of the dynasty of Dightons that flourished in English caricature for a hundred years. Dighton began exhibiting as a watercolourist and etcher in 1769 at the Free Society of Artists and was an occasional exhibitor at the RA, 1775-1799. He worked for Carrington Bowles on humorous mezzotints or 'postures' between 1774 and 1794. In 1793, he brought out a *Collection of Portraits of Public Characters* which were an immediate public success and from this date he concentrated wholly on caricature. The series was something new in England as it was more natural than exaggerated and spelled the way for Regency and Early Victorian work. Dighton continued to do ordinary political caricaturing which Williams found coarse compared with the portraits. Dighton appears to have been a fairly reprobate personality and was discovered in 1806 to have removed prints out of the British Museum and replaced them with copies! He died in London in 1814.
Colls: Ashmolean; BM; Fitzwilliam; Manchester; V & AM.
Bibl: H.M. Hake, *Print Collectors Quarterly*, XIII, pp.136ff, 242ff.

RICHARD DIGHTON 1795-1880. 'The King and Noblemen before the stag is turn'd out.' Vignette illustration. Ink and watercolour. Signed: Dighton del.

**DINKEL, Joseph**                    fl.1833-1861
Architectural and botanical illustrator. He was born in Munich and travelled widely in Europe for The Linnaen Society, the Royal, Geological and Palaeontological Societies. Chatto records that he was 'a very accurate draughtsman of subjects of Natural History, especially of Fossil remains; but though he has most practice in this department, he also undertakes Architectural and Engineering drawings.'

Illus: *Poissons Fossiles [Agassiz, 1833-43]*.
Exhib: RA, 1840.
Colls: Neufchâtel.
Bibl: Chatto & Jackson, *Treatise on Wood Engraving*, 1861, p.593.

**DINSDALE, George**                    fl.1808-1829
Landscape painter and topographer. He was working in Chelsea, 1818, and Bloomsbury, 1828-9, and contributed illustrations to Griffith's *Cheltenham*, 1826.

Exhib: BI, 1808-29; RA.

**DINSDALE, John**
Figure artist working in Camden Town, 1884-90. He contributed humorous drawings to *Fun*, 1890. Exhibited at the RI.

**DISTON, A.**
Topographer. Illustrated *Costumes of the Canary Islands*, 1829, AT 75 (liths).

**DIXON, Charles Edward    RI**                    1872-1934
Marine painter and illustrator. He was born at Goring in 1872 and after exhibiting at the RA from the age of sixteen, he became a prolific iliustrator in *The Graphic*, 1900-10. He was a member of the Langham Sketching Club and was elected RI in 1900. His work is always very accurate, but he was able to create the atmosphere and mood of the great shipping lanes by skilful washes, careful uses of colour and sombre skies. He died at Itchenor, 12 September 1934.

Illus: *Britannia's Bulwarks [C.N. Robinson, 1901]*.
Exhib: FAS, 1916; G; L; M; RA; RI; ROI.
Colls: Greenwich; V & AM.

**DIXON, May**
Amateur illustrator. Hon Mention in *The Studio* book illustration competition, Vol. 8, 1896, p.184, illus.

**DIXON, O. Murray**
Contributed colour illustrations of animals to *The Illustrated London News*, 1909.

**DOBELL, Clarence M.**                    fl.1857-1866
Figure painter and illustrator. He contributed to *Good Words*, 1860, and *Once a Week*, 1865, and illustrated *One Year*, 1862, for Messrs. Macmillan. He was working in London, 1857-65, and then at Cheltenham.

Exhib: BI, 1858-66; RA; RBA, 1857-66.

**DOBSON, William Thomas Charles    RA RWS**                    1817-1898
Scriptural painter and illustrator. He was born at Hamburg in 1817 and entered the RA Schools in 1836, becoming a teacher in the Government School of Design in 1843. He left this work in 1845 and travelled abroad, mostly in Italy and Germany. He was elected an ARA in 1860 and RA in 1871 and RWS, 1875. Many of his pictures were engraved by Graves & Co. He died at Ventnor on 30 January 1898.

Illus: *Legends and Lyrics [A.A. Proctor, 1865]*.
Exhib: OWS; RA; RBA.
Colls: Sheffield; V & AM.

RICHARD DIGHTON 1795-1880. Mr. Hobhouse. 1819. Etching.

**DODD, A.W.**
Illustrator. Made illustrations of 'The Four Elements', *The Studio*, Vol. 34, 1905, p.350, illus.

**DODGSON, Charles Lutwidge 'Lewis Carroll'**     **1832-1898**
Writer and creator of 'Alice'. He was born at Daresbury, Cheshire, on the 17 January 1832 and after being educated at Rugby, gained a Fellowship at Christchurch, Oxford, where he remained for the rest of his life. Carroll, as he was known from 1856, produced his own small sketches to illustrate the first manuscript of *Alice in Wonderland*, January 1863, but because of their weakness he approached Sir John Tenniel (q.v.) in February 1864 to undertake the work. Carroll remained a scrupulous critic of his illustrators till his death.
Bibl: G. Ovenden, *The Illustrators of Alice*, 1972.

**DODGSON, George Haydock**     **1811-1880**
Topographer, landscape painter and illustrator. He was born at Liverpool on 16 August 1811 and was apprenticed to George Stephenson, the railway engineer, from 1827 to 1835. He left this employment due to the pressure of the work and began to paint, moving to London in 1836 and drawing its architecture. He did a great deal of illustration in the 1850s before turning his attention to landscapes. He then drew extensively on the Thames and made visits to Whitby and Wales. He was an ARWS from 1842-47 when he resigned and became OWS in 1848. He died on June 4 1880 at 28 Clifton Hill, St. John's Wood.
Illus: *Illustrations of the Scenery on the Line of the Whitby and Pickering Railway [1836]*.
Contrib: *The Illustrated London News [1853-6]; The Cambridge Almanack; Lays of the Holy Land [1858]; The Home Affections [C. Mackay, 1858]*.
Exhib: BI; OWS; RA; RBA, 1835-39; RWS.
Colls: BM; V & AM.
Bibl: Chatto & Jackson, *Treatise on Wood Engraving*, 1861, p.598.

**DODWELL, Edward FSA**     **1767-1832**
Topographer and draughtsman. He was born in Dublin in 1767 and after being educated at Trinity College, Cambridge, travelled in Greece, 1801 and 1805-6. He died at Rome in 1832.
Illus: *Alcuni Bassi rilievi della Grecia [1812]; A Classical and Topographical Tour of Greece [1819]; Views in Greece [1819-21, AT 130]; Views and Descriptions of Cyclonian or Pelasgic Remains . . . [1834]*.

**DOLBY, Edwin Thomas**     **fl.1849-1870**
Landscape and architectural illustrator. He specialised in views of churches and was a candidate for the NWS between 1850 and 1864.
Illus: *Great Britain as it is [E.H. Nolan, 1859]; A Series of Views . . . during the Russian War [1854]; D's Sketches in the Baltic [1854]*.
Contrib: *Recollections of the Great Exhibition of 1851 [1851]; ILN [1854, Denmark]; The Illustrated Times [1855, Crimea]; The Graphic [1870]*.
Exhib: RA, 1849-65.

**DOLBY, Joshua Edward Adolphus**     **fl.1837-1875**
Landscape painter. He specialised in picturesque buildings and drew for *Prague Illustrated*, 1845, AT 74 (liths.). He exhibited at RA and RBA, 1840-46.

**DOLLMAN, Francis Thomas**     **1812-1899**
Architectural draughtsman. Illustrated his own *Examples of Ancient Pulpits Existing in England*, 1849. Exhibited at the RA, 1840-78.
Colls: V & AM.

**DOLLMAN, John Charles RI**     **1851-1934**
Painter and illustrator of animals. He was born at Hove, 6 May 1851, the son of a bookseller and after being educated at Shoreham, studied art at South Kensington and the RA Schools, where he won prizes for drawing from the living model. He practised black and white drawing for the magazines until 1901 when he began to paint in watercolours, specialising in historical genre subjects. He was elected RI, 1886; ROI, 1887; ARWS, 1906, and RWS, 1913. He died at Bedford Park 11 December 1934.
Illus: *In the days when we went Hog-Hunting [J.M. Brown, 1891]; Curly [John Coleman, 1897]; Told by the Northmen [E.M. Wilmott Buxton, 1908]*.

Contrib: *The Graphic [1880-88 (stories and theat.)]*.
Exhib: B; FAS, 1906; G; L; M; Paris, 1900; RA; RHA; RI; ROI; RSA.
Colls: Glasgow; Manchester; Nottingham.
Bibl: *English Influences on Vincent Van Gogh*, Arts Council, 1974-75.

**DONNELLY, W.A.**
Contributed illustrations to *The Sporting and Dramatic News*, 1890 and *The Illustrated London News*, 1894.

**DONNISON, T.E.**
Illustrator, working at Rock Ferry, Cheshire, and contributing to the *The Boys' Own Paper* in the 1890s. Exhibited at Liverpool, 1882.

**DORÉ, Paul Gustave Louis Christophe**     **1832-1883**
Painter, illustrator and sculptor. He was born at Strasbourg on 6 January 1832 and took up lithography at the age of eleven while living at Bourg-en-Bresse. He then went to Paris and in 1848 attached himself to Philippon's *Journal Pour Rire*, where he contributed a weekly page. He showed pen and ink drawings at the Salon of 1848 and a painting in 1851 but really made his reputation in 1854 with his illustrated *Rabelais*, followed by a whole series of classic titles in English and French editions. He became known to the British public with his contributions to *The Illustrated London News* from 1853, and with Crimean sketches from 1855-56 and in 1858. Vizetelly employed him even more extensively on *The Illustrated Times*, 1855-60, and there is no mistaking his crowded and wildly dramatic battle scenes. His great projected work on London with a text by Douglas Jerrold was prepared in the late 1860s but only came out in a shortened version in 1872 as *London: A Pilgrimage*. A similar scheme for Paris never materialised. Doré's success in England enabled him to open his own gallery here for a number of years, but his obsessive ambition to be recognised as a great painter rather than a great illustrator clouded his later years.

Doré's earlier work tends to be linear and his later work tonal. By the end of his career he was treating the page like a canvas and his dominance of the illustrated book here and in France was not very beneficial. His greatest works like the *Inferno* and *Don Quixote*, 1863, are extremely dramatic; Doré plays on the horror of emptiness and height very cleverly, but sometimes loses his hold with a super-abundance of detail. His later books, where tone was all important, did not have the drawings carefully inked out for the wood engraver but were simply supplied as wash drawings. These are occasionally seen on the market.

A further side to Doré's genius is provided by his caricature sketches, many of these were published as *Two Hundred Sketches, Humorous and Grotesque* in 1867; they show him as a brisk satirist of society, the drawing is rather harsh and there is a tendency to adopt the old tradition of caricature in enormous heads and skeletal bodies.
Illus: *The Wandering Jew [Sue, 1856]; Jaufry the Knight and the Fair Brunissende [A. Elwes, 1856]; The Adventures of St. George [W.F. Peacock, 1858]; Boldheart the Warrior [G.F. Pardon, 1858]; the History of Don Quixote [Cervantes, 1863]; The Ancient Mariner [S.T. Coleridge, 1865]; Days of Chivalry [L'Epine, 1866]; The Adventures of Baron Munchausen [1866]; Fables of La Fontaine [1867]; Elaine, Guinevere, Vivien, Enid and Idylls of the King, [Tennyson, 1867-68]; The Bible [1867]; Popular Fairy Tales [1871]; Poems of Thomas Hood [1872]; London: A Pilgrimage [1872]*.
Colls: V & AM.
Bibl: Blanchard Jerrold, *Life of Gustave Doré*, 1891, (complete bibliography); David Bland, *A History of Book Illustration*, 1958, pp.289-295.

See illustration (p. 287).

**DORING, Adolph G.**
German landscape painter and etcher, working at Bernbourg and Ostsee, Germany. He contributed illustrations of animals to *The Strand Magazine*, 1894.
Exhib: RA, 1897.

*GUSTAVE DORÉ 1832-1883. 'Inside The Docks.' Illustration for* London, a pilgrimage *by Douglas Jerrold, 1872.* Victoria and Albert Museum

**DOUGLAS, Edwin**                                      **1848-1914**
Sporting and animal painter. He was born at Edinburgh in 1848 and studied at the RA Schools, and the RSA. He spent most of his life working in the south of England, in Surrey, 1880-90, and then in Sussex until his death. His paintings are in the style of Edwin Landseer.

Contrib: *Poems and Songs of Robert Burns [1875].*
Exhib: B; G; L; M; RA; ROI.

**DOWD, James H.**                                      **1884-1956**
Painter, etcher and black and white artist. He was a regular contributor to *Punch* from about 1906, specialising in the humours of childhood and later in the illustrations for film criticism; R.G.G. Price calls him 'the Baumer of the nursery'. He was working at Sheffield in 1912 and in London from 1918. He must not be confused with L. Dowd, another *Punch* artist.

Contrib: *The Graphic [1915].*
Exhib: G; L; P; RA; RMS; RSA.
Bibl: R.G.G. Price, *A History of Punch,* 1957, p.210.

**DOWNARD, Ebenezer Newman**                            **fl.1849-1892**
History painter, engraver and illustrator. He specialised in genre subjects and contributed work to *The Illustrated London News,* 1873-79.

Exhib: BI, 1861-66; G; RA; RBA; RHA; ROI.

**DOWNEY, Thomas**                                      **fl.1890-1935**
Figure painter and illustrator, caricaturist. He was a pupil of Alfred Bryan (q.v.) and worked for numerous magazines in the 1890s.

Illus: *Patsy [H. de V. Stacpoole, 1908 (frontis.)].*
Contrib: *Daily Graphic [1890]; Moonshine [1890]; The Sketch [1894-95]; Judy [1898]; The Idler; Chums; The Boys' Own Paper.*
Exhib: Arlington Gall., 1935.

**DOWNING, Henry Philip Burke   FRIBA**                 **1865-**
Architect, etcher and illustrator. He was born in 1865 and after studying at the RA Schools and at the Architectural Association, he was articled to Hessell Tiltman, FRIBA. He then became Chief Assistant to Joseph Clarke FSA, Canterbury Diocesan architect, and started in private practice in 1888. He served on the RIBA Council and was a member of the London Topographical Society. His pen and

ink drawings of buildings are in the style of Herbert Railton and Holland Tringham (qq.v.).

Illus: *Architectural Relics in Cornwall [1888]; Monumental Brasses.*
Contrib: *St. Paul's [1894]; Black & White; Lady's Pictorial.*
Exhib: RA; RSA, 1904-32.
Bibl: *Who's Who in Architecture,* 1914.

**DOYLE, Charles Altamont**                             **1832-1893**
Humorous and fairy illustrator. He was the fourth son of John Doyle (q.v.) and was born in London in 1832. He was a professional civil servant for most of his life but worked as an illustrator in an amateur capacity. His sketches of imaginary subjects often have a rather sinister quality somewhat akin to those of his brother Richard Doyle (q.v.). He was the father of Sir Arthur Conan Doyle and died at Dumfries in 1893.

Illus: *Our Trip to Blunderland [Jean Jambon, 1877 (60 illus.)].*
Contrib: *The Illustrated Times [1859-60]; Good Words [1860]; London Society [1863-64]; The Graphic [1877].*
Exhib: RSA.
Colls: Witt Photo.

**DOYLE, Henry Edward   RHA**                           **1827-1892**
Portrait and religious painter and caricaturist. He was born in Dublin in 1827, the third son of John Doyle (q.v.). He was trained in Dublin and on coming to London worked as a wood engraver and draughtsman for satirical journals. He made a number of small cuts for *Punch* in 1844, and was a contributor of caricatures to *The Great Gun,* 1845, and was cartoonist of *Fun,* 1867-69. His brother James Doyle (q.v.) rather dismisses this work as 'the merest child's play' but as Spielmann says, 'the spirit of humour was strong within him'. Doyle's public image was certainly very different (his illustrations to Telemachus were admired by Prince Albert) and in 1869 he became Director of the National Gallery of Ireland, formed an important collection there and carried out the decorations of a Roman Catholic chapel. He became ARHA in 1872 and RHA in 1874 and was awarded the CB in 1880. He died in Dublin, 17 February 1892.

Doyle's caricatures which are occasionally to be found, are usually diminutive full-length portraits in watercolour with large heads; he frequently signed with a hen or 'Fusbos'.

Bibl: M.H. Spielmann, *The History of Punch,* 1895, p.459.

**DOYLE, James William Edmund**                         **1822-1892**
Heraldic artist and illustrator. He was the eldest son of John Doyle (q.v.) and born in London in 1822. He studied under his father but soon turned all his attention to historical research, although he made a few designs in pen, ink and watercolour. He wrote and illustrated *A Chronicle of England,* 1864, which has colour plates printed by Edmund Evans; some authorities consider it finer work than Baxter's. He was the author of the *Historical Baronage of England,* 1886, and died in London in 1892.

Colls: V & AM.
Bibl: M. Hardie, *English Coloured Books,* 1906; Ruari McLean, *Victorian Book Design and Colour Printing,* 1972, p.184.

**DOYLE, John   'HB'**                                  **1797-1868**
Lithographer, portraitist and caricaturist. He was born at Dublin in 1797 and studied there under an Italian landscape painter, Gabrielli, and under the miniaturist, W. Comerford. He attended the Dublin Society's Drawing Academy and in about 1822 travelled to London to work as a portrait painter. This proving unsuccessful, he set himself up as a portrait lithographer, publishing portraits of well-known people such as Wellington, George IV at Ascot, and the Princess Victoria in her pony phaeton. All of these were signed 'JD'. Doyle took to political caricature in 1827, publishing anonymous lithographs in that year and the next, and beginning in 1829 his famous series of *Political Sketches* signed 'HB'. The monogram was made up of two conjoined 'JD's, intended to hide the identity of the artist and excite curiosity, which it did! The series with its characteristically weightless but well observed figures, ran from 1829 to 1849 with a further plate in 1851, an astonishing output of nearly one thousand prints.

Doyle was fortunate to work during a period of reform and change ideally suited to his talents. Although there was intense political

*JOHN DOYLE 'HB' 1797-1868. 'A Scene of Confusion.' No. 423 in* HB's Sketches, *published by McLean, 30th January 1836. Lithograph.*

activity, the public desired it to be treated with a gentler wit than the savage satire of the Gillray and Cruikshank era. Doyle therefore is less of a caricaturist than a political illustrator. The plates were issued by McLean in volume form, 1841 and 1844, with an *Illustrative Key.* Many of the pencil studies are in the British Museum. John Doyle died in London 2 January 1868.

Exhib: RA, 1825-35.
Colls: BM; Windsor.
Bibl: G. Everitt, *English Caricaturists*, pp.235-276; M.D. George, *English Political Caricature*, 1959; G.M. Trevelyan, *The Seven Years of William IV, a reign cartooned by John Doyle*, 1952.
See illustration (above).

**DOYLE, Richard    'Dick Kitcat'**                                1824-1883
Humorous artist, cartoonist and fairy illustrator. He was born in London, September 1824, the second son of John Doyle (q.v.). He was the most gifted artist in a very gifted family and began from an early age to illustrate juvenilia, *Home for the Holidays*, a book for family circulation in 1836 (first published 1887) and *Dick Doyle's Journal*, 1840 (first published 1885). His first published work was the comic medieval book *The Eglinton Tournament*, 1840, which was widely acclaimed and the same year he collaborated with John Leech (q.v.) on the novel *Hector O'Halloran* by W.H. Maxwell; other book illustrating commissions followed from Dickens and Thackeray, Doyle working in wood and steel and sometimes signing 'Dick Kitcat'.

In 1843, Doyle was introduced to *Punch* and soon became a very regular contributor of decorations and initial letters, but did not graduate to cartooning until March 1844, eventually sharing about a third of the work with Leech. In January of the same year, Doyle designed *Punch's* sixth cover which remained in use until 1954, a spirited procession of tiny figures based on Titian's 'Bacchus and Ariadne'. By the middle 1850s, Doyle was almost a household name through his popular series 'Manners and Customs of Ye Englishe' and the later 'Bird's Eye Views of Society', and he had become a very proficient wood engraver after taking lessons from Swain. The source for much of Doyle's comedy remained the books of his childhood, the legends and the chivalry which gave him ideas but also an open-hearted naïveté in the drawing. It was probably this romance and

freshness, the lack of shadow, that recommended his work to an artist like Holman Hunt and a critic like Ruskin, whose work he illustrated.

Doyle's break with *Punch* came in 1850, when its attacks on the Papacy were more than Doyle, a devout catholic, could tolerate. He devoted the rest of his life to the illustration of books and in particular children's stories and fairy tales where his delight in the grotesque is given full rein and he reveals himself as a vivid and magical colourist. Perhaps his masterpiece was *In Fairyland* by William Allingham, 1870, a folio with colour wood engravings by Edmund Evans. Doyle continued to paint landscapes and died after a visit to the Athenaeum on 11 December 1883. He signed his work with: ℞

Illus:. his own work: *Mr. Pip's Diary: Manners and Customs of Ye Englishe [1849]; An Overland Journey to The Great Exhibition [1851]; Bird's Eye Views of Society [1864]; The Foreign Tour of Brown, Jones and Robinson [1854]; The Doyle Fairy Book [1890]. Grimm's Fairy King [1846]; A Jar of Honey From Mount Hylba [Hunt, 1847]; Fairy Tales [Montalba, 1849]; The Enchanted Doll [M. Lemon, 1849]; Rebecca and Rowena [W.M. Thackeray, 1850]; The King of the Golden River [J. Ruskin, 1851]; The Story of Jack and The Giants [1851]; the Newcomes [W.M. Thackeray, 1845-55]; A Juvenile Calendar and Zodiac of Flowers [1855]; The Scouring of the White Horse [Hughes, 1859]; A Selection From the Works of Frederick Locker [1865]; An Old Fairy Tale [Planché, 1865]; Irish Biddy, The Visiting Judges, The Troublesome Priest [1868]; Lemon's Fairy Tales [1868]; In Fairy Land [W. Allingham, 1870]; Piccadilly [Oliphant, 1870]; The Enchanted Crow [1870]; The Feast of the Dwarfs [1871]; Fortune's Favourite [1871]; Snow White and Rose Red [1871]; Princess Nobody [A. Lang, 1884]; The Family Joe Miller.*
Contrib: *The Fortunes of Hector O'Halloran [W.H. Maxwell, 1842]; Punch [1843-51]; The Chimes [Charles Dickens, 1845]; The Battle of Life [Charles Dickens, 1846]; The Cricket on the Hearth [Charles Dickens, 1846]; ILN [1847]; L'Allegro and Il Penseroso [Milton, 1848]; Life of Oliver Goldsmith [J. Forster, 1848]; Gaultier Ballads [1849]; Merry Pictures By The Comic Hands of H.K. Browne and Richard Doyle [1857]; Puck on Pegasus [C. Pennell, 1862]; Disraeli in Cartoon,[1878]; Cornhill Magazine [1861-62]; Pall Mall Gazette [1885-87].*
Exhib: GG; L; RA, 1868-83.
Colls: Ashmolean; BM; Fitzwilliam; V & AM.
Bibl: G. Everitt, *English Caricaturists*, 1883, pp.381-394; Chatto & Jackson, *Treatise on Wood Engraving*, 1861, pp. 578-579; F.G. Kitton, *Dickens and His Illustrators*, 1899; Daria Hambourg, *RD English Masters of Black and White*, n.d.; B. Peppin, *Fantasy Book Illustration*, 1975. pp.9, 11, 20, illus.

See illustrations (pp. 63, 116 and 289).

*RICHARD DOYLE 1824-1883. 'The Knight and Jötun.' Illustration for a fairy story. Ink and watercolour. 4⅜ins. x 7ins. (11.1cm x 17.8cm)* Victoria and Albert Museum

### PRINCE ALBERT'S BEE-HIVES.

"These Hives are so constructed, that the HONEY may be removed without DESTROYING THE BEES."—*Morning Paper*

*RICHARD DOYLE 1824-1883. 'Prince Albert's Bees Hives.' Cartoon for* Punch, *1844.*

**D'OYLY, Sir Charles, 7th Bt.**                    **1781-1845**

Amateur artist and illustrator. He was born in Calcutta in 1781 and served for the whole of his life in India, first as assistant to the Registrar, Calcutta Court of Appeal, 1798, and then as Collector of Dacca and Resident at Patna, 1831. He studied drawings under George Chinnery in Dacca and made sketches of Anglo-Indian life and society. He returned to Europe in 1838 and died at Livorno in 1845.

Illus: *The European in India [1813]; Antiquities of Dacca [1814-15]; Behar Amateur Lithographic Scrap Book [1828; AT 446]; Indian Sports [1828, AT 447]; Tom Raw The Griffin [1828, AT 450]; The Feathered Game of Hindoostan [1828, AT 451]; Extra Behar Lithographic Scrap Book [1829, AT 452]; Oriental Ornithology [1829, AT 453]; Sketches of the New Road [1830, AT 455]; Views of Calcutta [1848, AT 497].*
Exhib: RA, 1815.
Bibl: *The Connoisseur*, Vol.CLXXV, 1970.

**DRAKE, William Henry**                    **1856-**

American illustrator. He was born in New York on 4 June 1856 and studied in Paris at the Académie Julian. He is included here as the illustrator of *Stories of Child Life*, and *The Jungle Book*, by Rudyard Kipling, 1894. He was a noted still-life illustrator, specialising in black and white drawings of gold and silver antiquities and old armour.

Bibl: J. Pennell, *Pen Drawing and Pen Draughtsmen*, 1894, pp.242-243 illus.

**DRAPER, Herbert James**                    **1864-1920**

Portrait, subject painter and illustrator. He was born in London in 1864, and studied at the St. John's Wood School, RA Schools and in Paris at Julian's, 1890 and Rome 1891. His painting 'The Lament for Icarus' was bought by the Chantrey Bequest in 1898. He died in Hampstead on 22 September 1920.

Illus: *St. Bartholomew's Eve [G.A. Henty, 1894]; A Young Traveller's Tales [Hope, 1894].*
Contrib: *The Yellow Book [1895].*
Exhib: G; L; M; New Gall.; Paris, 1900; RA; RBA; RHA.

**DRAW  see WARD, Leslie**

**DRUMMOND, James  RSA**                              **1816-1877**

History painter. He was born in Edinburgh in 1816 and worked as a
draughtsman for ornithological works. He then entered the Trustees
Academy, Edinburgh, and studied with Sir William Allan, exhibiting
at the RSA from 1835 and becoming ARSA in 1846 and Member in
1852. Drummond made a close study of archaeology and is noted for
his historical accuracy in his large canvases of Scottish history.

Illus: *Ancient Scottish Weapons [J. Andersen, 1881]*.
Contrib: *Good Words [1860]*.
Exhib: RBA; RI.
Colls: Blackburn; Edinburgh; V & AM.

**DUANE, William**

Principal cartoonist of *Fun*, 1900.

**DUDLEY, Ambrose**                                    **fl.1890-1919**

Portrait painter and illustrator. He worked in London and exhibited at
the RA, 1890-1919. A pleasant ink and wash drawing of a pedlar,
probably intended for illustration was in a London collection in
1976.

**DUDLEY, Robert**                                     **fl.1858-1893**

Painter, lithographer and illustrator. He specialised in English and
continental views and seascapes, but outside his landscape work was
an interesting minor figure in illustration. He first appears
contributing the topography of Birmingham to *The Illustrated
London News* in 1858 and seven years later in 1865, the same paper
sent him as correspondent on *The Great Eastern* when the
Trans-Atlantic Cable was laid. The result of this was a handsome book
of lithographs *The Atlantic Telegraph,* 1866, with text by W.H.
Russell of *The Times*. A watercolour worked up from one of these
subjects was shown by Dudley at the RBA in 1866. He was also
well-known as a book decorator and drew designs for brass cut
publishers' bindings, many of them signed. He worked in Kensington,
1865-75, and at Notting Hill from 1875 and died there about 1893.

Illus: *A Memorial of the Marriage of H.R.H. Albert Edward, Price of Wales and
H.R.H. Alexandra, Princess of Denmark [W.H. Russell, 1863]*.
Contrib: *ILN [1858-73]; The Illustrated Times [1861]; The Boys' Own
Magazine [1863]; London Society [1864-71]; The Graphic [1869]*.
Exhib: B; G; L; M; RA; RI.
Bibl: Ruari McLean *Victorian Book Design and Colour Printing*, 1973, pp.139,
220, 221.

**DUFF, Sir C.G.   'G C D' or 'Cloister'**

Contributing cartoons to *Vanity Fair*, 1899-1900 and 1903. Nobody
of this name can be traced.

**DUGDALE, Thomas Cantrell  RA**                       **1880-1952**

Painter and illustrator. He was born at Blackburn on 2 June 1880, and
was educated at Manchester Grammar School, studied art at
Manchester Art School and later in South Kensington and at Julian's,
Paris. He served throughout the First World War mostly in the Middle
East and the Balkans, being mentioned in despatches, 1915. In his
student days, Dugdale designed some book decorations in a woodcut
style and was an occasional illustrator in ink and watercolour. He later
abandoned this for oil painting. He was elected ROI, 1910; ARA,
1936, and RA, 1943. He held a one man show at the Leicester
Galleries in 1919.

Illus: *The Gateway to Shakespeare [Mrs. Andrew Lang, 1908]*.
Contrib: *The Graphic [1910]*.
Exhib: G; GG; L; M; NEA, 1910-13; P; Paris, 1921; RA; RHA; ROI; RSA.
Bibl: The *Studio*, Vol.12, 1897-98 p.137 illus.

**DULAC, Edmund**                                      **1882-1953**

Artist and illustrator. He was born at Toulouse on 22 October 1882
and after attending the university there, he studied law and took up
art, joining the drawing and painting classes of the Toulouse School of
Art. He then went to Paris and studied at the Académie Julian for
three weeks, concentrating from then onwards on work as a book
illustrator, portrait painter, designer of costumes and stage sets and
modeller. Dulac settled in London in 1906, and by the outbreak of
war had established himself as one of the leading artists in the field.
He became a naturalised British subject in 1912 and really cemented a

*EDMUND DULAC 1882-1953. Caricature of Arnold Bennett, novelist and man
of letters. An illustration for* The Evening Standard, *c.1922. Pen and ink. 5ins. x
5½ins. (12.7cm x 14cm)*                              Author's Collection

popularity with his adopted country which has remained to the
present day. Dulac was immensely versatile and had more sense of
colour and design than most of his English contemporaries, excepting
Rackham. He looked to the Middle and Far East for inspiration, his
watercolours of legendary subjects have a gemlike brilliance found
only in Mogul miniatures, their flat, stylised and sleepy beauty
sometimes comes from the Japanese print, sometimes from the
Pre-Raphaelites and even occasionally from the Renaissance. There are
clearly a few borrowings from Rackham mannerisms but when he is
depicting a tale like *Beauty and the Beast,* the repertoire is his own,
the paper parchmenty, the colour vivid and thick and the design
dominating the story. Dulac's early work is a precursor of Art Deco
and in fact his middle period fell right into the 1920s when such
highly-coloured and self-conscious work was in vogue. The artist
played his own part in this, designing a smoking room for one of the
great luxury liners, *The Empress of Britain*.

Dulac was also a remarkable caricaturist, a disciplined artist in
black and white who could capture a personality or situation in very
few lines, but remain sympathetic. He also brought to this country the
very French tradition of caricature sculpture, many examples of this
were in his studio at his death.

Illus: *The Arabian Nights [1907]; Lyrics Pathetic and Humours [1908]; The
Tempest [1908]; The Rubaiyat of Omar Khayyam [1909]; Fairies I have Met
[1910]; Studies from Hans Andersen [1911]; The Sleeping Beauty and Other
Tales [1912]; Princess Badoura [1913]; Sinbad the Sailor [1914]; Edmund
Dulac's Book For The French Red Cross [1915]; Edmund Dulac's Fairy Book
[1916]; Tanglewood Tales [1918]; The Kingdom of the Pearl [1920]; The
Green Lacquer Pavillion [1926]; Treasure Island [1927]; The Fairy Garland
[1928]; Gods and Mortals in Love [1936]; The Golden Cockerel [1950]*.
Contrib: *The Graphic [1906]; ILN [1911]; Princess Mary's Gift Book [1915];
The Outlook [1919]*.
Exhib: L; Leicester Gall., from 1907; Paris, 1904-5; RI.
Colls: Author; BM; Fitzwilliam; V & AM.
Bibl: F. Rutter, *The Drawings of ED; The Studio*, Vol.45, 1908-9, pp.103-113
illus; *Modern Book Illustrators and Their Work*, Studio, 1914; D. Larkin, *Dulac*,
Coronet Books, 1975; *Times Literary Supplement*, 29 October 1976.
See illustration (above, frontispiece and p. 291).

**DU MAURIER, George Louis Palmella Busson**          **1834-1896**

Black and white artist, illustrator and novelist. He was born in Paris
and came to London as a student to read chemistry at University
College, 1851. He returned to Paris as an art student in 1856-57 to
work under Gleyre and there made the acquaintance of J. McNeill
Whistler and E.J. Poynter (qq.v.), a period of his life which was
afterwards featured in his novel *Trilby*. Du Maurier moved on to

*EDMUND DULAC 1882-1953. 'The Entomologist's Dream.' Pen and ink, and watercolour. Signed and dated 1909. 10⅜ins. x 11⅜ins. (26.3cm x 28.9cm).*
Victoria and Albert Museum

Antwerp from 1857-60 to study under De Keyser and Van Lerius, but the loss of an eye precluded him from following the career of a painter, and he decided to concentrate on black and white work which was at a new peak at the beginning of the 1860s. A naturally lazy man, although a very talented one, du Maurier returned to London in 1860 and gradually broke into book and magazine illustrating, developing as a fine figure draughtsman and the greatest social satirist of the period. An occasional contributor to *Punch* from 1860, du Maurier became a regular part of the magazine from 1864 when he succeeded John Leech (q.v.) as the chief observer and caricaturist of fashion and high life. His accuracy in depicting the houses and habits of the rich bourgeoisie was astonishing and his ink drawings remain a very complete chronicle of Victorian life. It is the situations that are humorous in du Maurier's work rather than the drawings, he satirises certain traits of the Victorians admirably, their artiness and aestheticism in 'Mrs Cimabue Brown', a culture-loving hostess, and their snobbery in the social-climbing 'Mrs Ponsonby de Tompkyns'. It was only late in life that du Maurier emerged as an important novelist with his three books, *Peter Ibbetson*, 1891, *Trilby*, 1894; and *The Martian*, 1896, all illustrated by himself. He died in Hampstead, 8 October 1896.

Du Maurier's pen drawings for *Punch* in black or brown ink are among the most delightful of the Victorian era, they are usually very finished, carefully hatched with little shadow on the faces but a concentration of black in hair and clothes. They are more usually signed than dated. There is a definite falling off of quality after 1880 and his compositions are sometimes awkward after this date.

Illus: *The Story of a Feather [Douglas Jerrold, 1866]; Frozen Deep [Wilkie Collins, 1875]; Poor Miss Finch [Wilkie Collins, 1872]; The New Magdalen [Wilkie Collins, 1873]; Misunderstood [F. Montgomery, 1874]; Pegasus Re-saddled [H.C. Pennell, 1877].*
Contrib: *The Welcome Guest [1860]; ILN [1860 (decor.)]; Once a Week [1860-68]; Punch [1860-96]; Good Words [1861]; The Illustrated Times [1862]; London Society [1862-68]; The Sunday At Home [1863]; The Cornhill Magazine [1864, 1870, 1875-80]; English Sacred Poetry of The Olden Time [1864]; Our Life Illustrated in Pen and Pencil [1865]; Divine and Moral Songs [1866]; Legends and Lyrics [1866]; Foxe's Book of Martyrs [1866]; Touches of Nature by Eminent Artists [1867]; The Savage Club Papers [1867]; Lucile [1868]; Pictures From English Literature [1870]; The Graphic [1871, 1888]; Thornbury's Legendary Ballads [1876]; Sons of Many Seasons [1876]; Harper's Magazine [1889-94]; Black & White [1891].*
Exhib: FAS, 1884, 1887, 1895, 1897; OWS, 1870-93; RA.
Colls: Ashmolean; Bradford; BM; Fitzwilliam; Manchester; V & AM.

Bibl: T. Martin Wood, *G du M*, 1913; D.P. Whiteley, *G du M*, English Masters of Black and White, 1948; Leonee Ormond, *G du M*, 1969; M.H. Spielmann, *The History of Punch*, 1895, pp.503-516.
See illustration (p. 292).

**DU MOND, Frank Vincent**                                    1865-
Painter of genre subjects, landscapes and illustrator. He was born in Rochester, U.S.A., in 1865 and became a pupil of Boulanger and Constant in Paris. He illustrated the English edition of *Personal Recollections of Joan of Arc*, Mark Twain, 1897.

**DUNCAN, A.**
Figure painter. He was working at London from 1853 to 1862 and illustrated *The Ancient Mariner*, 1856.
Exhib: BI, 1855-62; RBA, 1853-62.

**DUNCAN, D.M.**
Figure painter. He contributed illustrations to *Good Words*, 1880, and exhibited in Glasgow, 1880-82.

**DUNCAN, Edward    RWS**                                    1803-1882
Marine and coastal painter and illustrator. He was born in London in 1803 and, showing artistic ability, was articled to Robert Havell and his son, the aquatint engravers. He then worked for Fores, the printsellers before giving up all engraving in favour of watercolours, becoming a member of the NWS in 1834. He became interested in marine subjects after making the acquaintance of William Huggins, the marine artist, and subsequently married his daughter; it was this side of his work that made him celebrated. He was a brilliantly clear colourist and showed life at the water-front and in the harbours of southern England with vividness and clarity. Duncan was specially good at representing old jetties, nets drying and baskets piled with fish and the general impediments of fisher life. These watercolour studies for the exhibited pictures survive in abundance as do leaves from his sketch-books showing boats, gear and busy figures, drawn in careful pencil line. The artist resigned from the NWS and joined the OWS in 1847 and throughout the next twenty years made long sketching tours in England, Scotland and Wales, once visiting Holland and once travelling to Italy. Duncan was an accomplished illustrator of marine subjects and his output was extensive. He died at his home in Haverstock Hill, Hampstead, on 11 April 1882.

Duncan's watercolours and drawings are usually signed 'E. Duncan', and many of the sketches have the red stamp of the artist's studio sale at Christie's, March 11, 1885.

Publ: *Advanced Studies in Marine Painting [1889]; British Landscape and Coast Scenery [1889].*
Illus: *Southey's Life of Nelson.*
Contrib: *Poems and Pictures [1846]; ILN [1847-58 and 1868]; Willmott's Poets of the Nineteenth Century [1857]; The Home Affections [Charles MacKay, 1858]; Lays of the Holy Land [1858]; Favourite English Poems [1859]; Book of Favourite Modern Ballads [1860]; Montgomery's Poems [1860]; Early English Poems: Chaucer to Pope [1863]; Once a Week [1866]; Book of Rhymes and Roundelayes; Moore's Poems; The Soldier's Dream.*
Exhib: BI, 1833-57; NWS; RA; RBA, 1830-82; RWS.
Bibl: Chatto & Jackson *Treatise on Wood Engraving*, 1861, p.583; M. Hardie, *Watercolour Paint. in Brit.*, Vol.III, 1968, pp.75-77 illus; F.L. Emanuel, *Walker's Quarterly*, xiii, 1923.
Colls: Bradford; BM; Glasgow; V & AM.

**DUNCAN, James Allen**                                    fl.1895-1910
Illustrator, decorator and type-face designer. He worked at Glasgow, 1895-97, and at Milngorie, 1902, and was a regular contributor to magazines, an illustrator of children's stories and the designer of two alphabets for the Chiswick Press, c.1899.

Contrib: *The Daily Graphic [1895]; The English Illustrated Magazine [1897]; Fun [1900]; The Graphic [1901-6]; The Connoisseur [1910 (decor.)].*
Illus: *Children's Rhymes [1899].*
Exhib: G and RSA, 1895-1901.
Bibl: *The Studio*, Vol.15, 1899, pp.184-189, illus.

*GEORGE DU MAURIER 1834-1896. 'Appreciative Sympathy: Herr Bogoluhoffski plays a lovely Nocturne. which he has just composed. To him, as he softly touches the final note, Fair Admirer, "Oh Thanks! I am so fond of that Dear Old Tune!"' Illustration for* Punch, *20 November 1880. Pen and ink. 5ins. x 8ins. (12.7cm x 20.3cm).*
Author's Collection

**DUNCAN, John RSA**        **1866-1945**
Painter of legend and history and illustrator. He was born at Dundee in 1866 and studied art there and in London and Düsseldorf before settling in Edinburgh and working in Edinburgh and Glasgow, where for a time he was on the staff of *The Glasgow Herald*. He drew for both magazines and books, his earlier work showing a strong influence from Japanese art and particularly Japanese prints. As a decorative artist, his main work was the scheme for the University Hall, Edinburgh, as a teacher, his main contribution was as Professor at Chicago University, 1902-4. He was elected ARSA in 1910 and RSA in 1923. RSW, 1930.

Contrib: *The Evergreen [1895]*.
Bibl: *The Artist*, 1898, pp.146-152 illus.

**DUNLOP, Marion Wallace**        **fl.1871-1905**
Portrait painter, figure artist and illustrator. She was working in London from 1871 and in Ealing 1897-1903. Her black and white work is extremely competent and heavily *art nouveau*.

Illus: *Fairies, Elves and Flower Babies [1899]; The Magic Fruit Garden [1899]*.
Exhib: G; NEA; RA; SWA.
Bibl: *The Studio*, Vol.10, 1897, illus. (competitions); Vol.12, 1897, illus. (competitions); R.E.D. Sketchley, *English Book Illus.*, 1902, pp.106, 165.

**DUNN, Edith (Mrs T.O. Hume)**        **fl.1862-1906**
Domestic painter and illustrator. She was working at Worcester, 1863, and in London, 1864, and exhibited at the RBA, 1862-67, and at the BI, 1864-67. She married the landscape painter Thomas O. Hume and lived after her marriage at South Harting, Petersfield, Hants.

Contrib: *The Quiver [1866]*.

**DURAND, Godefroy**        **1832-**
Illustrator. He was born in 1832 at Düsseldorf but was of French extraction. After studying with Leon Cogniet, he settled in London in 1870 probably as a result of the French defeat of that year. He exhibited pictures of the Siege of Paris at the RBA in 1873. Durand joined the permanent staff of *The Graphic* in 1870 and remained on it for many years supplying the paper with military and horse subjects and foreign views. He was still there in 1890, when Hartrick joined the staff and he described him as 'an elderly Frenchman . . . permanently

on the paper to do hackwork'.

Illus: *La Guerre au Maroc [Yriarte, n.d.]; The Life of Christ [Ernest Renan, n.d.]*.
Exhib: M, 1882; RA; RBA, 1873.

**DURDEN, James ROI**        **1878-1964**
Landscape and portrait painter. He was born in Manchester in 1878 and studied at Manchester School of Art and the Royal College of Art. He worked at Claygate, Surrey, 1909, London 1910 and 1927, finally settling at Keswick, Cumberland. He was elected ROI in 1927.

Illus: *The Five Macleods [C.G. Whyte, 1908]*.
Contrib: *The Quartier Latin [1898]; The Graphic [1911-12]*.
Exhib: G; L; M; P; Paris, 1927; RA; RI; ROI; RWA.

**DURHAM, C.J.**        **-1889**
Figure painter and illustrator. He was a teacher at the Slade School and contributed drawings of industry to *The Illustrated London News*, very regularly, 1861-74.

Exhib: RA, 1859; RBA, 1872-80.

**DUTTON, Thomas G.**
Marine watercolourist. He worked in London and contributed drawings of shipping to *The Illustrated London News*, 1877.

Exhib: RBA, 1858-79.

**DUVAL, Marie**        **see ROSS, C.H.**

**DYSON, William Henry**        **1883-1938**
Cartoonist. He was born at Ballarat, Australia, in 1883, was educated in Melbourne and came to England in 1909. He was chief cartoonist to the *Daily Herald*, 1913-25, and again in 1931-38, noted for his extreme radical outlook and as an ardent supporter of socialist change. Dyson was a talented etcher, but his drawings, scratchy penwork over pencil and dark shading, are more reminiscent of Daumier than of English caricature. Veth considered that Dyson in his 'wild extravagance' often overshot the mark. He died 21 January 1938.

Illus: *Collected Drawings*.
Exhib: Leicester Gall.; RHA; RSA.
Colls: V & AM.
Bibl: John Jensen, *WD: 20th Century Studies*, 1976.

## EARLE, Augustus 1793-1838

The son of Ralph Earle, the American painter. He studied at the RA, 1813, and began to travel, visiting the Mediterranean, Africa, Tristan da Cunha, the United States, New South Wales and New Zealand. He worked as a portrait painter in Madras before returning to England by way of France. His most famous voyage was made about 1833 when he acted as draughtsman to Charles Darwin on the expedition of H.M.S. Beagle. Earle was a skilled topographer but also drew caricatures and genre subjects.

Illus: *Journal of a Voyage to Brazil [M. Graham, 1824, AT 708]; Journal of a Residence in Chile [M. Graham, 1824, AT 714]; Sketches Illustrative of the Native Inhabitants and Islanders of New Zealand [1832, AT 587].*
Exhib: RA, 1806-38.
Colls: BM.

## EARLE, Percy

Contributed cartoons of horse subjects to *Vanity Fair*, 1909-10.

## EARNSHAW, Harold fl.1908-1926

Watercolour painter and illustrator. Husband of Mabel Lucie Atwell (q.v.). He specialised in the illustrating of boys' novels and exhibited at the RI.

Illus: *The Rebel Cadets Charles Gleig, 1908]; Princess Mary's Gift Book [1915].*
Contrib: *The Graphic [1912].*

## EAST, Sir Alfred    RA FRS 1849-1913

Landscape painter and watercolourist. He was born at Kettering, Northants, 15 December 1849, and began life in business at Glasgow before attending the Glasgow School of Art, studying under Robert Greenlees. He then went to Paris and was strongly influenced by the Barbizon School. East was an etcher as well as a painter and was an early member of the Royal Society of Etchers, Painters and Engravers, President of the RBA in 1906, ARA, 1899, and RA, 1913. He visited Japan in 1909 and was knighted in 1910. He died in London 28 September 1913 and was buried at Kettering.

East is included here by virtue of the fact that his etchings and paintings were sometimes used for books, for example in *Cassell's Picturesque Mediterranean*, 1891. His *Brush and Pencil Works in Landscape* was published posthumously, 1914.

Exhib: RA, 1883-1913.
Colls: Ashmolean; BM; Leeds; V & AM; Wakefield.
Bibl: F. Newbolt, 'The Etchings of Alfred East' *The Studio*, Vol. 34, 1905, pp.124-137; A. East, 'Art of the Painter Etcher' *The Studio*, Vol. 40, 1907, pp.278-282.

## EBBUTT, Phil

Figure and humorous illustrator. Working for magazines 1886-1903.

Contrib: *Fun [1886-87]; The Daily Graphic [1890]; The Quiver [1892]; Lady's Pictorial [1895]; The Graphic [1901-03].*

## ECKHARDT, Oscar    RBA fl.1893-1902

Painter and illustrator, working in Kensington. He worked for numerous magazines in thin pen and ink, 1893-1900. He was elected RBA, 1896. He signs his work Eckhardt.

Contrib: *The Butterfly [1893]; Black & White [1894]; St. Paul's [1894]; Daily Graphic [1895]; The Unicorn [1895]; The Windsor Magazine [1895]; The Sketch [1895]; Eureka [1897]; The St. James's Budget [1898]; Illustrated Bits [1900]; Pick-Me-Up; The Ludgate Monthly; The Idler; The Strand Magazine.*
Exhib: L; RBA; ROI.
Colls: V & AM.

## EDMONSTON, Samuel 1825-

Landscape and marine painter, occasional illustrator. He was a pupil of Sir William Allen and the RSA Schools and worked in Edinburgh, painting in watercolour and drawing in chalks.

Contrib: *Pen and Pencil Pictures from the Poets [Edinburgh, 1866]; Burns Poems [n.d.].*
Exhib: RA, 1856-57; RSA.
Colls: N.G. Scot; Witt Photo.
Bibl: Chatto & Jackson, *Treatise on Wood Engraving*, 1861, p.599.

## EDWARDS, Amelia B.

Illustrator and contributor to *The Girl's Own Paper*, c.1890.

*KATE EDWARDS fl.1865-1879. 'The June Dream.' Illustration to* London Society, *Vol. 9, No. 54, 1866. Wood engraving.*

**EDWARDS, D.**                                          fl.1850-1857

Illustrator of poetry in a rather weak and sentimental manner. He contributed two drawings to *Willmott's Poets of the Nineteenth Century*, 1857.

Colls: Witt Photo.

**EDWARDS, The Rev. E.**                                 1766-1849

Amateur topographer. He was a Norfolk vicar and antiquary and founded the Kings Lynn Museum in 1844. He was a competent pen and wash artist and contributed views to *Britton's Beauties of England & Wales*, 1810.

**EDWARDS, George Henry**

Figure and landscape painter and illustrator. He worked in London for juvenile magazines and novels and specialised in fairy and romantic subjects.

Illus: *The Temple of Death [E. Mitchell, 1894]; The Crimson Sign [Keightley, 1894]*.
Contrib: *ILN [1900]; The Boys' Own Paper; The Girls' Own Paper; The Royal Magazine*.
Exhib: L; RA; RBA, 1883-93; RI; ROI.

**EDWARDS, Henry Sutherland**                            1828-

Author and minor illustrator. He was for some time Editor of the comic paper *Pasquin* and was engaged as a writer for *Punch*, 1848. He published *The Russians at Home*, 1858, *A History of the Opera*, 1862, *Malvina*, 1871. In 1867 he contributed some illustrations to magazines.

Colls: Witt Photo.

**EDWARDS, Kate**                                        fl.1865-1879

Illustrator. Nothing is known of this outstanding figure artist who worked in the middle 1860s. Her drawings of women can only be compared to those by M. Ellen Edwards (q.v.) and George Pinwell (q.v.) by whom she was clearly influenced.

Contrib: *London Society [1865-66]; Once a Week [1867]*.
Exhib: RBA, 1879.
See illustration (p. 293).

**EDWARDS, Lionel Dalhousie Robertson    RI**          1878-1966

Painter, illustrator and writer on sporting subjects. He was born 9 November 1878, the son of Dr. James Edwards of Chester. He studied art under A. Cope and Frank Calderon (q.v.) at the School of Animal Painting, Kensington. Edwards worked extensively for the press, specialising in hunting subjects, first for *The Graphic* in about 1910 where he reported the Lisbon Revolution. He was the successor of Alken and Leech in his love of country pursuits, and eventually of G.D. Armour (q.v.), but his drawings lacked their humour. He worked for *Punch* before the First World War and regularly in the 1920s, but his black and white work is more scratchy than Armour's although his figures and landscapes are very authentic. Edwards was most at home in straight hunting sketches, ink and watercolour sometimes varied with colour chalk, or skilful smudges of bodycolour. The whole hunting field vividly realised, springing over fences or drawing a wood. In the inter-war years he made portraits of hunting celebrities, and there were few clubs or pubs at the time that did not possess a print of at least one of them. He was working in Wales, 1901-06, and Abingdon, 1909. He finally settled at Salisbury, Wiltshire, in 1923 and died there in 1966. He was elected RI in 1927.

Edward's work has always been popular with the hunting fraternity and both paintings and drawings have risen in demand.

Illus: *Hunting and Stalking Deer [1927]; Huntsmen Past and Present [1929]; My Hunting Sketch Book [1928 and 1930, 2 vols.]; Famous Fox Hunters [1932]; A Leicestershire Sketch Book [1935]; Seen From the Saddle [1936]; The Maltese Cat [Kipling, 1936]; My Irish Sketch Book [1938]; Horses and Ponies [1938]; Scarlet and Corduroy [1941]; Royal Newmarket [1944]; Getting to Know Your Pony [1947]*.
Contrib: *The Graphic [1910-16]; Punch*.
Exhib: L; RA; RCA; RI.
Bibl: *Mr. Punch with Horse and Hound*, New Punch Library, c.1930; Autobiog. *Reminiscences of a Sporting Artist*, 1948.

**EDWARDS, Louis**

Illustrator of military subjects. Contributed to *The Illustrated London News*, 1889.

**EDWARDS, Mary Ellen**                                  1839-c.1910
**(Mrs. Freer 1866-69; Mrs. Staples 1872).**

Book illustrator and figure artist. She was born 6 November 1839 at Kingston-upon-Thames and became one of the most prolific secondary illustrators of the third quarter of the 19th century. Her drawings of domestic life never advanced much beyond the competent and pretty, but she did illustrate Anthony Trollope's *The Claverings* and the novels of Mrs. Henry Wood in serial and book form. She was particularly good at child studies and in handling groups of children in a natural way. She was also associated with *The Argosy*, a magazine run by Mrs. Henry Wood's son. She used her maiden name until 1869, then Mrs. Freer until 1872 and finally her second husband's name, Mrs. Staples, from 1872. She lived at Chelsea, 1865-66, and at Hedingham, Essex, 1875-76, finally settling at Shere, Surrey, 1892. She died about 1910.

Illus: *The New House That Jack Built [Mrs. W. Luxton, 1883]; The Boys and I [Mrs. Molesworth, 1883]; A World of Girls [L.T. Meade, 1887]*.
Contrib: *Puck on Pegasus [1862]; Churchman's Family Magazine [1863-64]; Parables From Nature [1861 and 1867]; London Society [1864-69]; Family Fairy Tales [1864]; The Quiver [1864]; Once a Week [1865-68]; Watts Divine and Moral Songs [1865]; Legends and Lyrics [1865]; The Sunday Magazine [1865]; Good Words [1866]; Aunt Judy's Magazine [1867]; Cassell's Magazine [1867-70]; The Churchman's Shilling Magazine [1867]; The Broadway [1867-70]; Golden Hours; The Illustrated Times; Idyllic Pictures [1867]; The Illustrated Book of Sacred Poems [1867]; Argosy [1868]; Dark Blue [1871-73]; Graphic [1869-80]; Mother's Last Words; ILN [1880-  ]; The Quiver [1890]; The Girl's Own Paper*.
Bibl: F. Reid, *Illustrators of The Sixties*, 1928, pp.261-262; *English Influences On Van Gogh*, Arts Council, 1974-75, p.51.

**EGERTON, M.**                                          fl.1824-1827

Social caricaturist. He worked in London in the 1820s in the manner of George Cruikshank.

Illus: *Humorous Designs [1824, AL 288]; Sponge [1824, AL 289]; Airy Nothings [1825 AL 290]; Collinso Furioso [1825 AL 291]; Matrimonial Ladder [1825 AL 292]; Cross Readings [1826 AL 293]; Olla Padeida [1827 AL 294]*.

**EGLEY, William Maw**                                   1826-1916

History painter and miniaturist who undertook some illustrations. He was born in 1826, the son of William E. Egley, 1798-1870, the miniaturist. Egley worked as a book illustrator from 1843 to 1855, but thereafter concentrated on scenes of contemporary life and period subjects under the influence of W.P. Frith. A design for a frontispiece in the Victoria and Albert Museum, dated 1843, is in pencil, heightened with white, a charming mock Gothic drawing, the handling reminiscent of 'Phiz' or G. Cruikshank. The same museum has a manuscript catalogue of the artist's work in its library.

Exhib: B; L; M; RA; RBA; RI; ROI, 1843-98.
Colls: BM; Fitzwilliam; V & AM.

**EHNINGER, John W.**                                    1827-1889

American landscape painter and illustrator. He was born in New York in 1827 and travelled to Paris in 1847 where he became a pupil of Thomas Couture, 1815-1879. He visited many European countries and returning to the United States, became a member of the National Academy in 1860. He later published many engravings of his English drawings. He died in 1889.

Contrib: *Good Words [1864]*.
Exhib: RA and RI, 1864.

**ELCOCK, Howard K.**                                    fl.1910-1923

Figure artist and illustrator. He contributed sporting subjects to *Punch* and designed dust jackets, notably that for the 1923 edition of *The Prisoner of Zenda* by Anthony Hope.

**ELGOOD, George Samuel  RI**                    1851-1943
Painter and illustrator of gardens. He was born in Leicester, 26
February 1851, and was educated privately and at Bloxham. He
studied art at South Kensington and specialised in very finished
watercolours of formal gardens, parterres and country house views,
often peopled by figures in historic costume. Elgood became an
authority on Renaissance gardens in England, Italy and Spain and
generally spent five months of every year abroad, painting them. He
worked in London, 1872-77, and afterwards in his two houses at
Tenterden in Kent and at Markfield in Leicestershire. He was
brother-in-law of J. Fulleylove RI (q.v.). RI 1882, ROI 1883.

Illus: *Some English Gardens [Gertrude Jekyll, 1904]; The Garden That I Love
[Alfred Austin, 1905]; Larnia's Winter Quarters [Alfred Austin, 1905]; Italian
Gardens [1907]*
Exhib: FAS, 1891, 1893, 1895, 1898, 1900, 1904, 1906, 1908, 1910, 1912,
1914, 1918, 1923; L; M; RBA, 1871-78; RI; ROI.
Colls: Brighton; Wakefield.
Bibl: 'The Garden And Its Art with Special Reference to the Paintings of G.S.
Elgood'; *The Studio*, Vol.V, 1895, p.51, illus.; 'George S. Elgood's Watercolour
Drawings of Gardens', *The Studio*, Vol.31, 1904, pp.209-215, illus.
See illustration (Colour Plate XIII p. 173).

**ELLESMERE, Francis, 1st Earl of   see GOWER, F. Leveson**

**ELLETT**
Illustrator working c.1903. The Victoria and Albert Museum has one
example by this rather weak artist in watercolours and body colour.

**ELLIOTT, Alma**
Black and white artist, probably for illustration. She is recorded as
working in Leicester in 1926 and was a working member of the Design
and Industries Association. She made drawings of period subjects with
thin angular pen lines.

**ELLIOTT, E.G.**
Topographer. Draughtsman for *Travels in the Three Great Empires of
Austria, Russia and Turkey*, by Charles Boileau Elliott, 1838, AT 31.

**ELLIS, Edwin John**                              1841-1895
Landscape and marine painter and illustrator. He was born in
Nottingham in 1841 and worked in a lace factory before studying art
with Henry Dawson. He settled in London after completing his art
studies in France and became a popular landscape painter,
concentrating on the Welsh and Yorkshire coasts. He was a gifted poet
and a champion of the poetry of William Blake (q.v.) and a friend of
W.B. Yeats. RBA, 1875.

Publ: *The Real Blake, A Portrait Biography, 1907.*
Illus: *Fate in Arcadia [E.J. Ellis, 1868-69].*
Contrib: *Punch [1867]; London Society [1868-69]; Cassell's Magazine [1870].*
Exhib: RA; RBA, 1868-91.
Colls: Manchester; Nottingham.
Bibl: M.H. Spielmann, *The History of Punch*, 1895.

**ELLIS, Tristram James  ARPE**                   1844-1922
Artist. He was born at Great Malvern in 1844 and was educated at
Queenswood College and King's College, London. He was articled to
an engineer and worked on the District and Metropolitan Railways
until 1868. He then went to Paris to study painting under Bonnat,
1874, travelling to Cyprus, 1878, and to Syria, Asia Minor and
Mesopotamia, 1879-80, Egypt, 1881-82, Portugal, 1883-84 and
Greece and Turkey, 1885-86. He made later tours to Spitzbergen,
1894, and Russia, 1898. He became ARE in 1887 and at about this
time undertook some competent but not exciting book illustrations.
Phil May shared his studio in London for some months. He died 25
July 1922.

Publ: *On a Raft and through the Desert [1881].*
Illus: *Fairy Tales of a Parrot [A.C. Stephen, CB, CMG, 1873].*
Exhib: GG; New Gall.; RA; RBA; RG.

**ELLWOOD, George Montagu  SGA**                  1875-1955
Artist and writer. He was born at Eton in 1875 and studied at South
Kensington, Camden School of Art and in Paris, Vienna, Berlin and
Dresden. He was Designer of Applied Art at Holloway School of Art
and Design Master at Camden School of Art. He was also a member of
the Architectural Association, the Art Workers' Guild and the Society
of Graphic Art, and was Joint Editor of *Drawing and Design*, 1916-24.
Ellwood's interests were catholic and his work wide ranging from
interior schemes for houses and churches to posters, books and
pottery. He published handbooks for artists and died at Boscombe in
1955.

Publ: *English Furniture [1680-1800]; Some London Churches; Figure Studies
for Artists; The Human Form; Pen Drawing; Art in Advertising; English
Domestic Art; Human Sculpture.*
Contrib: *The Dome [1899].*
Bibl: *The Studio*, Vol. II, 1897, p.210, illus; Winter No.1900-01, p.69, illus.

**ELMORE, Alfred  RA**                            1815-1881
History and genre painter. He was born at Clonakelty, County Cork,
on 18 June 1815, the son of an army doctor, and moved to London
with his family while still young. Showing an aptitude for art, he
began drawing from the antique at the British Museum entering the
RA Schools in 1834 and exhibiting regularly there from the following
year. He made an extensive tour to Paris, Munich, Venice and
Florence, finally settling in Rome for two years and returning to
England in 1844. He was elected ARA in 1846, and RA in 1857, and
RHA 1878. He died in Kensington on 24 January 1881.

Elmore contributed one illustration, the frontispiece to *The Home
Affections* by Charles Mackay, 1858; it is well drawn and decorative
in the medieval idiom of the period and it is a pity the artist did not
produce more work of this type.

Contrib: *Midsummer Eve [Mrs. S.C. Hall, 1842].*
Exhib: BI, 1835-47; RA; RBA, 1836-79.
Colls: Ashmolean; BM; Edinburgh; V & AM.
Bibl: S.C. Hall, *Retrospect of a Long Life*, 1883, pp.219-220; J. Mass, *Victorian
Painters*, 1870, pp.239-240.

**ELTZE, Fritz**                                    -1870
The son of Mr. Eltze, private secretary to Sir Richard Mayne, Chief
Commissioner of Police. He spent his early life at Ramsgate but was
unable to live actively due to progressive consumption. He was
introduced to *Punch* in May 1864 when he submitted some sketches
to Mark Lemon. In the same year he took over the production of the
social illustrations that had been the responsibility of the recently
deceased John Leech (q.v.). Eltze was best when allowed to mirror the
follies of fashion, or the *bon mots* of childhood; his drawing was
slightly amateurish and very distinctive for its broad outline. In *Once
a Week*, 1869, Eltze perpetuates the vignette humour of the 1820s,
'Alteration in the Court Costume', 'A Siamese Twinge', etc.

Contrib: *Good Words [1864]; Punch [1864-70 (post: 1872 and 1875)];
Sunday Magazine [1865]; Once a Week [1866-67]; A New Table Book [Mark
Lemon, 1866]; ILN [1867]; Legendary Ballads [1876].*
Colls: Witt Photo.

**ELVERY, Beatrice Moss (Lady Glenavy)  RHA**      1883-1970
Painter, stained-glass artist and illustrator. She was born in 1883, the
elder daughter of William Elvery of Foxrock, Dublin, and married in
1912, 2nd Baron Glenavy. She studied at the Dublin School of Art
and the Slade School where she won the Taylor scholarship and then
became teacher at the Dublin Metropolitan School of Art. She was
elected ARHA, 1932, and RHA, 1934. She illustrated *Heroes of the
Dawn*, Violet Russell, c.1914, in a rather nationalistic Celtic style.

Exhib: RA; RCA; RHA; SWA.

**ELWES, Alfred Thomas**                          fl.1872-1884
Illustrator of animals and birds. He was working in London, 1872-77,
and was chief draughtsman of natural history subjects for *The
Illustrated London News* during those years.

Illus: *The Pleasant History of Reynard the Fox [Sampson Lowe, 1872].*
Contrib: *The Graphic [1875]; The Cornhill Magazine [1883-84].*

**ELWES, Robert**                                         **fl.1854-1871**

Landscape artist. He worked at Congham, near Lynn, 1861-71, and illustrated *A Sketcher's Tour Round The World*, 1854, AT 9 (liths.).

Exhib: BI, 1861; RBA, 1872.

**EMANUEL, Frank Lewis**                                  **1865-1948**

Topographer, etcher and illustrator. He was born in Bayswater in 1865 and was educated at University College School, University College and studied art at the Slade School. He worked in Paris at the Académie Julian and first exhibited at the Salon in 1886. After travelling to South Africa and Ceylon, he worked as a town planner and taught etching at the Central School of Arts and Crafts; he was also President of the Society of Graphic Art and a member of the Art Workers' Guild. He acted as special artist for *The Manchester Guardian* and was art critic of *The Architectural Review* for many years.

Emanuel was a copious writer, historian and polemicist for the arts; he wrote monographs on W.R. Beverley, Edward Duncan, William Callow and Charles Keene and his picture 'A Kensington Interior' was bought by the Chantrey Bequest in 1912. He was most at home with drawings of old buildings, principally those of London and the northern cities, which he drew very effectively in chalk or pencil, the contours of the houses built up with close hatching. He also reveals himself as a very good figure artist, capturing the spirit of cockney humour and the bustle of city life and produced one or two humorous sketches in the style of the Beggarstaff Brothers. He died at St. John's Wood, 1948. His work is signed 'Frank L. Emanuel' or 'F.L. Emanuel' or monogram

Illus: *Manchester Sketches; The Illustrators of Montmartre.*
Contrib: *The Graphic; The Dome [1899]; The Butterfly [1899]; The Studio [1899]; The Bystander [1904]; The Manchester Guardian [1906-].*
Exhib: G; L; M; NEA; P; RA; RE; RI; ROI; RSA.
Colls: Author; London Museum; V & AM.

See illustration (below).

*FRANK LEWIS EMANUEL 1865-1948. 'The Merry Month of May.' Unidentified illustration. Pen and ink. 7½ins. x 6⅜ins. (19.1cm x 16.2cm).*
Victoria and Albert Museum

**EMSLIE, Alfred Edward**                    1848-1918

Watercolourist, painter of genre and illustrator. He was born in 1848 and exhibited in London from 1867. He contributed many illustrations of social realism and industry to *The Illustrated London News* and *The Graphic*, 1880-85, and these were admired by Van Gogh during his London years. He was elected ARWS in 1888 and won a medal at the Paris Exhibition of 1887.

Exhib: B; G; GG; L; M; RA; RBA; RWS; FAS, 1896.
Colls: Manchester; V & AM.
Bibl: *English Influences On Vincent Van Gogh*, 1974-75, Arts Council, p.51.

**EPINAY, Prosper Comte d'**                    1836

French sculptor and caricaturist who exhibited at the Salon des Humoristes in 1909. He contributed one cartoon to *Vanity Fair*, 1873.

**ERICHSEN, Nelly**                    fl.1883-1901

Figure painter and illustrator. She specialised in figures in landscape and did some architectural illustration. Signs with monogram NE

Illus: *The Novels of Susan Edmonstone Ferrier [1894]; The Promised Land [1896]; Emanuel or Children of the Soil [1896]; Mediaeval Towns, Dent [1898-1901]*.
Contrib: *The English Illustrated Magazine [1886 (North of England), 1896-97(figs.)]*.
Exhib: L; RBA; RA ; ROI; SWA, 1883-97.

**EVANS, H.**

Black and white artist, contributing to *The Rambler*, 1897.

**EVANS, William**                    fl.1797-1822

Engraver and draughtsman. He worked from Newman Street, London, and illustrated Boydell's publications and drew for Cadell's *Gallery of Contemporary Portraits*, 1822, and engraved plates for the Dilettanti Society's *Specimens of Ancient Sculpture*, 1799-1807, published 1808.

Exhib: *BI and RA, 1797-1808*.

**EVANS, William, of Bristol    AOWS**                    1809-1858

Landscape painter. He was born in Bristol in 1809 and spent his earlier years living in a remote area of North Wales, studying mountain scenery. He was elected AOWS in 1845 and lived in Italy from 1852. He illustrated an edition of Scott's works in 1834.

Exhib: OWS; RBA, 1844-59.
Colls: BM; Bristol.

**EVERETT, Ethel Fanny**                    fl.1900-1939

Portrait painter and illustrator of children's books. She studied at the RA Schools and worked in Wimbledon, 1900, and Kensington 1915-25. She specialised in goblin drawings with vigorous compact pen lines and in a very decorative style. She signs her work E F E.

Exhib: L; RA; SWA.

**EVISON, G. Henry**                    fl.1890-1925

Illustrator. He was working at Bootle, 1890, and in London, 1896-1925. He is a particularly good figure artist and uses pen and ink with heavy bodycolour often in conjunction with a spray giving a speckled effect to the finished drawing. He signs 'G. Henry Evison', or 'G. Henry Evison/oo'.

Contrib: *Judy [1896]; The English Illustrated Magazine [1900]*.
Exhib: L; RA.
Colls: Author; V & AM.

See illustration (above right).

**EWAN, Frances**                    fl.1897-1929

Figure painter. She was working at Cricklewood, London, in 1907 and at St. Ives, Cornwall, in 1929. She contributed illustrations to *The English Illustrated Magazine* in 1897.

Exhib: RA, 1906; SWA.

*G. HENRY EVISON fl.1890-1925. Illustration for a story. Pen heightened with white. 8½ins. x 6ins. (21.6cm x 15.2cm).*                    Author's Collection

**EYRE, J.**

Topographer. He illustrated Mann's *Picture of New South Wales*, 1811, AT 566.

**EYRE, John    RI ARCA**                    -1927

Watercolourist and book illustrator. Born in Staffordshire and studied art at the South Kensington Schools. After designing for pottery he became a painter in watercolours and enamels and worked as a book illustrator. RBA, 1896, RI, 1917. He died at Cranleigh, 13 September 1927.

Illus: *English Poets*.
Exhib: G; L; M; RA; RBA; RHA; RI; RWS.

**EYRE, Colonel Vincent, CB**

Colonel in the Bengal Artillery, 1858. Contributed illustrations of India to *The Illustrated London News*, 1857.

**FABIAN, J.**          fl.c.1900
Illustrator, specialising in figure subjects, usually in pencil.
Colls: V & AM.

**FAHEY, Edward Henry   RI**      1844-1907
Oil and watercolour artist and illustrator. Born in London in 1844 and
studied at South Kensington Schools, RA Schools and in Italy,
1866-69. ARI 1870, RI 1876, ROI 1883. He held a one-man show
entitled 'English and Foreign Landscape', 1905. Died at Notting Hill,
13 March 1907.
Contrib: *The Graphic [1870 and 1877, (architecture)]*.
Exhib: GG; New Gall; NWS; RA; RBA; RHA; RI; ROI.

**FAIRBAIRN, Hilda**         fl.1893-1925
Figure painter and illustrator. She was born at Henley-on-Thames and
studied art at the Herkomer School, Bushey, and in Paris. She made a
specialty of portraits of children in watercolour or pastel. ASWA,
1902.
Illus: *The Saga of the Sea Swallow [1896, with J.D. Batten (q.v.)]*.
Exhib: L; New Gall; RA; ROI; SWA.

**FAIRFIELD, A.R.**
Amateur illustrator and clerk to the Board of Trade. He was born into
an artistic family and had only three months training at South
Kensington in 1857 before he began drawing on wood for *Fun*, 1861.
He started to draw for *Punch* and appeared regularly in 1864-65 and
again in 1887, contributing both drawings and initial letters. He was a
talented caricature portraitist, and a sketch of Austin Dobson dated
1874, is in the National Portrait Gallery. He signs his work with the
symbol ✗
Contrib: *The Leisure Hour; Once a Week [1860-65]; Thornbury's Legendary
Ballads [1876]*.
Colls: NPG; Witt Photo.
Bibl: M.H. Spielmann, *The History of Punch*, 1895, pp.522-523.

**FAIRHOLT, Frederick William   FSA**     1814-1866
Illustrator and engraver. He was born in London in 1814, the son of
German immigrants, and won a Society of Arts medal at an early age.
After working as a scene painter, he became assistant to S. Sly, the
wood engraver, in 1835. He soon established himself as an authority
on medieval heraldry and design and, as Chatto says, became
'distinguished for his knowledge of Costume and Medieval art, which
he has exemplified in a considerable number of shaded outlines,
mostly drawn and engraved by himself'. He was patronised by the Earl
of Londesborough and accompanied him or his son to Italy and Egypt
after 1856. Much of his work first appeared in *The Art Journal* of
which he was assistant editor. He died in London in 1866.

Illus: *Lord Mayor's Pageants [1841]; Robin Hood [Gutch, 1847]; The Home
of Shakespeare [1847]; Costume in England [1856]; Tobacco its History and
Association [1859]; Gog and Magog [1860]; Up the Nile [1862]; History of
Richborough [C.R. Smith]; Roman London [C.R. Smith]*.
Contrib: *London [Charles Knight, 1841]; Archaeological Album [1845]; The
Book of the Thames [S.C. Hall, 1859]; Book of British Ballads; Arts of the
Middle Ages [Labarte]*.
Colls: BM; V & AM.
Bibl: Chatto and Jackson, *Treatise on Wood Engraving*, 1861, p.592; S.C. Hall,
*Retrospect of a Long Life*, 1883, pp. 360-362.

**FAIRHURST, Enoch**          1874-
Portrait and miniature painter, etcher and illustrator. Elected ARMS,
1918. He was working in London until 1918 and then at Bolton,
1924. A talented delineator of architecture in pen and ink. Fairhurst
contributed a number of drawings to *The Ludgate Monthly* in the
1890s.
Exhib: L; M; RA; RCA; RMS; RSA; RWA.
Colls: V & AM.

**FANE, Brigadier-General Walter**     1828-1885
Amateur artist and illustrator. He was born 6 January 1828, the third
son of the Rev. E. Fane of Fulbeck, and served for most of his career
in India. His best works are of Indian landscape and architecture, with
brilliant colouring and creamy impasto. He contributed sketches of
Afghanistan to *The Illustrated London News*, 1880, which were
completed by Caton Woodville (q.v.) and he was a friend of W.
Simpson (q.v.). Died 17 June 1885.
Exhib: Dudley Gall.; OWS; RBA; RI.

**FARMILOE, Edith**
Children's book illustrator. She was the second daughter of Colonel
the Hon. Arthur Parnell and second cousin of C.S. Parnell, and
married the Rev. William D. Farmiloe, Vicar of St. Peter, Soho. Her
fanciful sketches of a make-believe world were partly influenced by
Caldecott and partly by Kate Greenaway. She was elected ASWA,
1905, and SWA, 1907.
Illus: *All the World Over [1898]; Rag, Tag and Bobtail [1899]*.
Contrib: *Little Folks [1895]; The Child's Pictorial [1896]*.
Exhib: SWA.
Bibl: *The Studio*, Vol.18, 1895 pp.172-179 illus.; Winter No. 1900-1 p.22.

**FARREN, Robert**
Etcher and illustrator. He was working in Cambridge in 1880 and at
Scarborough in 1889 and contributed 26 etched plates to *The Graphic*
and *The Cam*, Cambridge, 1880-1.
Exhib: L; M; RA; RE.

**FATIO, Morel**          fl.1843-1859
Italian illustrator, contributing topographical works of France to *The
Illustrated London News*, 1843, and of Italy to *The Illustrated Times*,
1859.

**FAU, Fernand**
French caricaturist. He contributed comic genre subjects to *Fun*,
1900.

**FAUCONNET, Guy Pierre**        1882-1920
Painter, etcher, designer for the theatre and book illustrator. Became a
pupil of J.P. Laurens and Benjamin Constant. He worked in London
as a miniaturist and book illustrator during the First World War, his
style being influenced by Beardsley; his friendship with Poiret is also
reflected in his work.
Illus: *Form and Substance [Charles Marriott, 1917]*.
Contrib: *La Gazette du bon ton [1914-20]*.

**FAULDS, James**
Painter and illustrator. He was working in Glasgow, 1896-1938, and
contributed to *The Graphic*, 1903.
Exhib: G; RSA; RSW.

**FAULKNER, A.M.**
Illustrator contributing to *The Lady's Pictorial*, 1895.

**FAUX, F.W.**
Illustrator contributing to *The Quest,* 1894-96.

**FAWKES, Francis Hawksworth**                    **1797-1871**
Amateur caricaturist. He was born in 1797, the eldest son of Walter Fawkes of Farnley Hall, Yorkshire, Turner's friend and patron. He was also a friend of Turner and did spirited caricatures in wash.

**FAWKES, L.G.**
Irish artist and contributor to *Punch,* 1875.

**FELL, Herbert Granville**                    **1872-1951**
Artist, illustrator, journalist and Editor of *The Connoisseur,* 1935-51. He was born in 1872 and married the daughter of Sir J.D. Linton, PRI (q.v.). Fell was educated at King's College, London and studied art at Heatherley's, in Paris, Brussels and in Germany before joining the firm of George Newnes Ltd. as editor of its Art Library. In 1907 he became Art Editor of *The Ladies Field,* holding the post until 1919, and in 1910-12 he was Art Editor of *The Strand Magazine.* He was Editor of *The Queen* from 1924-28 and Director of Drawing, Painting and Design at the Royal Albert Memorial College, Exeter. Fell was a well-known art journalist but his name as an artist deserves more recognition. He was a prolific book illustrator before 1910, drawing competent black and white figure studies for biblical and allegorical books, all strongly influenced by the late Burne-Jones; his pencil studies of *The Song of Solomon,* reproduced in half-tone, have more of the quality of Alphonse Mucha and international art nouveau.
Illus: *Our Lady's Tumbler [1894]; Wagner's Heroes [1895]; Cinderella [1895]; Ali-Baba [1895]; The Fairy Gifts [1895]; The Book of Job [1895]; Poems [W.B. Yeats, 1895]; The Song of Solomon [1897]; Wonder Stories from Herodotus [1900]; Tanglewood Tales [Nathaniel Hawthorne]; Stories of Siegfried [1908].*
Contrib: *The Ludgate Monthly [1892]; The Pall Mall Magazine; The Windmill [1899]; The Ladies Field.*
Exhib: New Gall.; RA.
Colls: Witt Photo.
Bibl: *The Artist,* 1897 pp.97-105 illus.; *The Studio,* Winter No. 1900-1 p.70 illus.; R.E.D. Sketchley *English Book Illus,* 1902 pp.27, 126.

**FELLER, F.**                    **1848-1908**
Painter and illustrator. He was born at Bumpliz, Switzerland, on 28 October 1848 and studied in Geneva under the enamellist Albert Feller and then at Munich, Paris and in London, where he settled. He specialised in book and magazine illustration and in comic genre subjects and depicting the humours of mountaineering. He died in London, 6 March 1908.
Contrib: *ILN [1880-84]; Black & White [1891]; St. Pauls [1894]; Good Cheer [1894]; Chums.*
Exhib: RA and RBA, 1878-95.

**FELLOWES, William Dorset**
Draughtsman and engineer. He illustrated *Antiquities of Westminster,* J.T. Smith, 1800 and *Historical Drawings,* 1828 by the same author and *A Visit to the Monastery of La Trappe,* 1818, AT 86.

**FELLOWS, Henry**
Amateur etcher who published privately *Etchings by H.E.,* 1866.

**FENNELL, John G.**                    **1807-1885**
Landscape watercolourist and caricaturist. He studied with Henry Sass in London and became an intimate friend of H.K. Browne, 'Phiz' (q.v.) and also of Dickens and Thackeray. His best works in art are landscape studies and caricatures. He was a noted angler.

**FENNING, Wilson**
Figure artist. He contributed an illustration to *Punch,* 1914.

**FERGUSON, James**                    **fl.1817-1866**
Landscape painter and illustrator. He worked in London, Edinburgh, Darlington and Keswick and was an unsuccessful candidate for the NWS in 1850. He made vignette illustrations for an edition of Scott's *Gertrude of Wyoming* and was probably the illustrator of *Army Equipment,* 1865-66.
Exhib: BI, 1821-57; RA; RBA, 1827, 1849 and 1856.
Colls: Witt Photo.

**FERGUSSON, James**                    **1808-1886**
Architectural writer. He was born in 1808 and started an indigo factory in India, at the same time devoting himself to the study of Indian art and architecture. He was elected a Fellow of the Royal Asiatic Society in 1840 and was awarded the Gold Medal of the RIBA in 1871. He published *An Historical Enquiry into the Five Principles of Beauty in Art,* 1844, *A History of Architecture in All Countries,* 1865-67, and *Fire and Serpent Worship,* 1868.
Illus: *Ancient Architecture in Hindoostan [1852, AT 480].*
Exhib: RA, 1850 and 1864.

**FFOULKES, Charles John   FSA**                    **1868-1947**
Curator and draughtsman. He was born on 26 June 1868, the son of the Rev. E.S. ffoulkes and great-grandson of Sir Robert Strange, the eighteenth century engraver. He was educated at Radley, Shrewsbury and St. John's College, Oxford, before becoming a student of Doucet and Duran in Paris. He was appointed lecturer on Armour and Medieval Subjects to Oxford University, became Master of the Armouries, Tower of London, 1912-38, the first curator of The Imperial War Museum, London, 1917-33. ffoulkes wrote numerous books on armour and a study of Sir Robert Strange. He was given the OBE in 1925.
Illus: *The Happy Wanderer [Percy Hemingway, 1895-96].*
Exhib: L; Paris, 1900; RA; RBA.

**FICHOT, Michel-Charles**                    **1817-1903**
Architectural draughtsman, painter and illustrator. Born at Troyes in 1817 and exhibited at the Salon regularly, 1841-75, being awarded the Chevalier of the Legion of Honour, he contributed to *The Illustrated London News,* 1867.
Colls: Troyes.

**FIDDIAN, Emmil**
Figure artist, contributing colour illustration to *The Graphic,* Christmas, 1889.

**FIDLER, Gideon M.**                    **fl.1883-1910**
Figure painter and illustrator. He worked at Telfont-Magna in Wiltshire and contributed drawings for a story to *The English Illustrated Magazine,* 1893-94.
Exhib: B; L; RA; RBA; RI; ROI.

**FIELD, G.C.**
A very fine pen and wash drawing by this artist for an illustration to *The Ancient Mariner* appears in *The Studio,* 1911.

**FILDES, Sir Samuel Luke   KCVO RA**                    **1844-1927**
Painter of genre and English and Venetian subjects, illustrator. He was born in Liverpool on 18 October 1843 and studied at the Liverpool Mechanics Institute, the Warrington School of Art, the South Kensington Schools and the RA Schools. At the outset of his London career in 1866, Fildes entered the world of black and white art and magazine illustration, remaining an outstanding figure in it until 1872. During these years he concentrated primarily on social realism, images of the poor and destitute that came across very powerfully on the printed page. Many of them especially those done for *The Graphic,*

*SIR LUKE FILDES RA 1844-1927. Study of a female figure for 'The Duet', an illustration in* Once a Week, *30 January 1869. Pencil.*

*SIR LUKE FILDES RA 1844-1927. Detail of a dress from studies for 'The Duet', an illustration in* Once a Week, *30 January 1869. Pencil.*

*SIR LUKE FILDES RA 1844-1927. Study of a piano for 'The Duet', an illustration in* Once a Week. *30 January 1869. Pencil.*

Victoria and Albert Museum

*SIR LUKE FILDES RA 1844-1927. Study of the whole group for 'The Duet', an illustration in* Once a Week, *30 January 1869. Pencil and wash.*

*SIR LUKE FILDES RA 1844-1927. Illustration for 'The Duet'.* Once a Week, *30 January 1869. Wood engraving.*

Victoria and Albert Museum

became famous and some like 'Applicants For Admission To a Casual Ward' were afterwards turned into large oil paintings. In spite of this, Fildes' genius as an observer of social need is much more satisfactory in black and white and his decision to concentrate on painting after 1872 was a loss to this side of book illustration. In 1869, he was chosen by Charles Dickens to illustrate his novel *Edwin Drood*, which was left uncompleted at the author's death in 1870. Fildes' reputation was increased by this work and by the drawing of Dicken's study at Gads Hill Place entitled 'The Empty Chair' done the day after the novelist's death. Published in *The Graphic* it was much admired by Van Gogh. Practically the whole of Fildes' archive of drawings, preparatory studies and proofs of wood engravings was presented to the Victoria and Albert Museum by his son, Sir Paul Fildes in 1971.

Fildes continued in his career as one of the foremost subject and portrait painters of the Edwardian era. He painted state portraits of King Edward VII, Queen Alexandra and King George V, was elected ARA in 1879 and RA in 1887. He was married in 1887 to the sister of H. Woods, RA (q.v.) and was knighted in 1906. He died 27 February 1927.

Illus: *Peg Woffington [Charles Reade, 1868]; Griffith Grant [Charles Reade, 1869]; Edwin Drood [Charles Dickens, 1870]; The Law and The Lady [Wilkie Collins, 1870]; Miss or Mrs. [Wilkie Collins, 1885]; Catherine [W.M. Thackeray, Cheap Illustrated Edition, 1894].*
Contrib: *Once a Week [1866-69]; Foxe's Book of Martyrs [1866]; Illustrated Readings [1867-68]; Good Words [1867-68]; The Sunday Magazine [1868]; Cassell's Magazine [1868-70]; The Quiver [1868-69]; The Sunday At Home [1868]; The Gentleman's Magazine [1869-70]; The Graphic [1869-74 and 1880]; The Cornhill Magazine [1870-73]; The Leisure Hour [1870]; Pictures From English Literature [1870]; ILN [1880]; Time [1880 (cover)].*
Exhib: B; G; L; M; RA, 1872-1927.

Colls: Glasgow; Holloway College; V & AM.
Bibl: L.V. Fildes, *LF, RA, A Victorian Painter*, 1868; *English Influences on Vincent Van Gogh*, Arts Council 1974-75 p.51.
See illustrations (below and pp.300 and 301).

**FINBERG, Alexander Joseph**                                          1866-1939
Art historian and illustrator. He was born in London in 1866 and after being educated at the City of London College and King's College, studied art at the Lambeth School and in Paris. In his early career Finberg alternated black and white illustration for the leading magazines with work as a journalist. For some years he was the art critic of the *Morning Leader, The Star, The Manchester Guardian* and *The Saturday Review*, and became a well known historian of the English romantic school. In 1905 he re-organised the Turner Collection at the National Gallery and made important discoveries among the paintings in the Turner Bequest, resulting in the building of the Turner Gallery. Finberg became the recognised Turner authority between the wars, and was Editor of the Walpole Society volumes, 1911-22 and lecturer in the history of painting at the London University. He died 15 March 1939.

Finberg's drawings in pen and ink or wash are quite common; he handles figure subjects well if not with great sparkle. Signs: AJF.

Publ: *English Watercolour Painters [1906]; The Drawings of David Cox; Ingres; The Watercolours of JMW Turner; Inventory of Turner's Drawings in the National Gallery [1909]; Turner's Sketches [1910]; The History of Turner's Liber Studiorum [1924].*
Contrib: *Fun [1890]; Lady's Pictorial [1890]; Puck and Ariel [1890]; The Ludgate Monthly [1892]; The Idler [1892]; The Sketch; Penny Illustrated Paper.*
Exhib: L; NEA; NWS; RA; RI.
Colls: V & AM.

*SIR LUKE FILDES RA 1844-1927. 'Sleeping It Off.' Illustration for* The Mystery of Edwin Drood, *by Charles Dickens, 1870. Wood engraving.*

**FINCHETT, T.**
Figure artist contributing to *The Illustrated London News,* 1896. Perhaps a relation of D.R. Finchett, artist working in Manchester, 1885.

**FINNEMORE, Joseph   RI RCA**                              **1860-1939**
Painter and illustrator. Born in Birmingham 1860 and studied at the Birmingham Art School and in Antwerp with Charles Verlat. He returned to England in 1881 and then went on an extended tour of Malta, Greece, Turkey, South Russia and Bessarabia. He settled in London in 1884 and specialised in book and magazine illustration and black and white work. Finnemore was later to concentrate on colour work for English and Continental colour printers in the 1900s. He was elected RBA, 1893; RI, 1898. He died 18 December 1939.
Illus: *When London Burned [G.A. Henty, 1894].*
Contrib: *The Graphic [1886-1910]; English Illustrated Magazine [1887-88]; Black and White [1891]; The Strand Magazine [1891]; Chums [1892]; The Wide World Magazine [1898]; Cassell's Saturday Journal; Cassell's Family Magazine; The Boys' Own Paper; The Girls' Own Paper; The Windsor Magazine.*
Exhib: B; G; L; RA; RBA; RCA; RHA; RI; ROI; RWA.

**FISH, Anne Harriet (Mrs Sefton)**                              **-1964**
Black and white artist and magazine illustrator. She was born at Bristol and after being educated at home, studied under C.M.Q. Orchardson and John Hassall (q.v.), and at the London School and at Paris. Her very individual style of drawing, which typifies the period of Art Deco, is partly influenced by poster design and partly by fashion drawing. Fish's art is the art of reduction, mouths, eyes or ears are omitted in the pursuit of a harsh satire and the whole of society becomes a symbol in a few black lines. Her greatest vogue was in the inter-war years when her work appeared regularly in all the principal magazines. She also designed textiles and worked in London from 1913 and then at East Grinstead, 1934, and latterly at St. Ives where she died in 1964. Her drawings are not uncommon.
Illus: *The Rubaiyat of Omar Khayyam [1922];*
Contrib: *Eve; Punch; Tatler; Vanity Fair; Vogue; Harper's Bazaar; Cosmopolitan.*
Exhib: FAS, 1916; RA.
Bibl: C. Veth, *Comic Art in England,* 1930 pp.196-197 illus.; *Caricature of Today,* Studio 1928 illus.

**FISHER, Alfred Hugh**                              **1867-1945**
Painter, etcher, illustrator and writer. He was born in London on 8 February 1867 and was educated at the City of London and University College Schools before going into business for nine years. He then turned to art and studied at Lambeth School and South Kensington before going to Paris to work under Laurens and Constant. He travelled widely in Europe and the Near East for the Visual Instruction Committee of the Colonial Office before settling at Amberley, Sussex. ARE, 1898.
Publ: *The Cathedral Church of Hereford [1898]; Poems [1913]; The Marriage of Ilario [1919]; The Ruined Barn and Other Poems [1921].*
Illus: *Through India and Burmah with Pen and Brush [1911].*
Contrib: *The Idler; The Dome [1899-1900]; The Windmill [1899].*
Exhib: L; NEA; New Gall.; RA; RBA; RE; RI; ROI; RWA.
Colls: Witt Photo
Bibl: F. Emanuel 'Exhib. of Works by Mr. A.H.F.', *The Artist,* Jan. 1901.

**FISHER, Harrison**                              **fl.1899-1906**
Figure artist and illustrator working until about 1906. He illustrated *The Market Place* by H. Frederics, 1899.

**FISHER, Henry Conway   'Bud'**                              **1884-**
Contributor of strip cartoons to various children's comics, c.1917.
Colls: V & AM.

**FISHER, Joshua Brewster**                              **1859-**
Landscape and figure painter and illustrator. He studied at Liverpool School of Art and spent the whole of his working life in the city.
Illus: *The Tyrants of Kool Sim [J. McLaren Cobban, 1896].*
Exhib: L; RCA, 1884-1933.

**FITCHEW, Dorothy**
Landscape and figure painter and illustrator. She worked at Bromley, Kent and made large and elaborate watercolours of Shakespearean and legendary subjects, particularly from 1911-15.
Exhib: L; RA; RI; SWA.

**FITCHEW, E.H.**
Portraitist and illustrator. Contributed studies of heads to *The English Illustrated Magazine,* 1886.

**FITTON, Hedley   RE**                              **1859-1929**
Editor and illustrator. He was born in Manchester in 1859 and worked for *The Daily Chronicle,* specialising in etchings of architectural subjects. Practising in Runcorn, Cheshire until 1890 he settled at Haslemere, Surrey in 1902 and remained there until his death, winning in 1907 the Gold Medal of the Société des Artistes Français. He was elected ARE in 1903 and RE in 1908. Besides his book illustrations Fitton produced a long series of etchings of London, Florence, Edinburgh and Paris. He died on 19 July 1929.
Illus: *English Cathedral Scenes [Isbister, 1899-1901]; Aeschylos [1901].*
Contrib: *The English Illustrated Magazine [1887]; The Quiver [1894]; Daily Chronicle [1895]; Good Words [1898].*
Bibl: R.E.D. Sketchley, *English Book Illus.,* 1902 pp.46, 133.

**FITZCLARENCE, George Augustus Frederick, 1st Earl of Munster**
                              **1794-1842**
Amateur artist. He was born on 29 January 1794, the natural son of King William IV by Mrs. Jordan. A professional soldier, he was the Lieutenant of the Tower of London and Governor of Windsor Castle, becoming a Major-General and ADC to Queen Victoria. He died 20 March 1842.
Illus: *Journal of a Route Across India [1819, AT 519].*

**FITZCOCK, Henry**                              **1824-**
History painter and illustrator. He was born at Pentonville in 1824 and studied at the RA Schools and with Benjamin Robert Haydon. Fitzcock was a regular exhibitor in London from 1853, taking his subjects from literature and chiefly from the works of Longfellow and Cowper. He may have travelled to Sweden to make studies in about 1856.
Illus: *The Holy War [John Bunyan, 1864]; All About Shakespeare.*
Contrib: *ILN [1856-60 (Sweden)]; The Churchmen's Family Magazine [1864].*
Exhib: BI, 1853-64; RA; RBA, 1853-72.

**FITZGERALD, Lord Gerald**                              **1821-1886**
Amateur draughtsman and watercolourist. He was born in 1821, the second son of the 3rd Duke of Leinster. A professional soldier who served in the Scots Fusilier Guards, Lord Gerald became a member of the Etching Club of Dublin, and engraved ten scenes to illustrate the poems of Tom Hood.
Contrib: *Passages From Modern English Poets [1862].*

**FITZGERALD, J. St M.**
Contributor to *The Idler,* c.1890.

**FITZGERALD, John Anster**                              **1832-1906**
Figure and fairy illustrator. He was born on 25 November 1832 and exhibited regularly at London exhibitions, 1845-1903 from Newington. He contributed fairy subjects to the Christmas numbers of *The Illustrated London News,* 1863, 1876-77.
Exhib: B; G; L; RA; RBA; RI; ROI.
Colls: Cardiff; Liverpool.
Bibl: J. Maas, *Victorian Painters,* 1969 pp.143-144 illus.

**FITZGERALD, Michael**                              **fl.1871-1891**
Figure painter and illustrator. He was working in London from 1875 and contributed Irish peasant subjects and middle class subjects to various magazines. Van Gogh admired the former and considered his prison illustrations as fine as Régamey (q.v.).
Illus: *The Irish Sketchbook; Ballads; The Roundabout Papers [W.M. Thackeray,*

*HANSLIP FLETCHER 1874-1955. Charing Cross Hospital. Illustration for unidentified book. Ink and sepia wash. Signed and dated June 1914. 8¾ins. x 12ins. (22.2cm x 30.5cm).*
Author's Collection

*Cheap Illustrated Edition, 1894].*
Contrib: *Dark Blue [1871-73]; ILN [1872-86, 1891]; The Pictorial World [1874-75]; The Cornhill Magazine [1885].*
Exhib: D; L; RA; RBA; RHA.
Colls: V & AM.
Bibl: *English Influences on Vincent Van Gogh,* Arts Council 1974-75.

**FITZMAURICE, Major The Hon. William Edward**     **1805-1889**
Amateur artist. He was born 21 March 1805, the second son of the Countess of Orkney and after serving as Major in the Life Guards he was MP for Buckingham, 1842-47. Died 18 June 1889.
Contrib: *ILN [1860 (Messina)].*

**FITZPATRICK, Edmond   ARHA**     **fl.1848-1872**
Figure artist and illustrator specialising in Irish genre subjects. He contributed a series of drawings of the Irish Famine to *The Illustrated London News* in 1848 and further genre subjects, 1853-59. He was drawing for *London Society* in 1872. ARHA 1856.
Exhib: BI, 1867; RBA, 1856-70.

**FITZPATRICK, Thomas**     **1860-1912**
Draughtsman and cartoonist. He was born at Cork in 1860 and after working as an apprentice to a printing and publishing firm there left for Dublin where he became a lithographer and cartoonist for the *Weekly Freeman* and the *Weekly National Press.* He started his own monthly *The Leprechaun* in 1905 and drew the cartoons for it.

**FLAGG, E.**
Contributor of cartoons to *Vanity Fair,* 1899 and 1902.

**FLEMING-WILLIAMS, C.R.**     **fl.1899-1925**
Black and white artist and watercolourist. He was cartoonist of *Judy,* 1899, his drawings showing strongly the American influence of C. Dana Gibson (q.v.). He was working at Letchworth, Herts, 1920-25.
Contrib: *Sketchy Bits; The Graphic [1905-6]; ILN [1908].*
Exhib: RA, 1920.

304

**FLÈRE, Herbert H.**     **fl.1893-1903**
Painter of genre. He was working in London in 1893. He contributed to *The Graphic,* 1902-3; *The Illustrated London News,*1903.

**FLETCHER, Hanslip**     **1874-1955**
Architectural draughtsman and etcher. He was born in London in 1874, the son of G. Rutter Fletcher, FSA, and was educated at the Merchant Taylors School and at the Birkbeck College, University of London. Fletcher concentrated his efforts on depicting vanishing corners of London and other old cities, drawing every detail of their architecture and street scenes with meticulous pen work. For many years he was artist for *The Sunday Times* and his weekly drawings were a feature of the paper, later being gathered together in book form as *Changing London,* 1925-28 and 1933. Fletcher was a close friend of many artists and writers including F.L. Emanuel (q.v.), James Bone, Sir Albert Richardson and Sir Muirhead Bone (q.v.). He was a member of the Art Workers Guild and served on the Committee for the Protection of Ancient Buildings. A large collection of his drawings of London was purchased by the Guildhall Library. He died at Northampton in 1955 after a long illness.
Contrib: *The Pall Mall Magazine; The Dome [1900]; The Architect and Builders Journal.*
Illus: *The Path to Paris [Frank Rutter, 1908]; London Passed and Passing [1908]; Oxford and Cambridge Delineated [1909]; Edinburgh Revisited [James Bone, 1911]; Bombed London [1947].*
Exhib: G; L; NEA; RA; RI; RSA.
Colls: Ashmolean; Author; Nat. Mus., Wales; V & AM.
Bibl: S.R. Houfe, *'Delineator of Change',* Country Life. Jan. 18, 1973.
See illustration (above).

**FLETCHER, S.P.**
Illustrator. He illustrated *Rowland Bradshaw, His Struggles and Adventures on The Way to Fame By The Author of The Raby Rattler* 1848. Fletcher's style is a clear derivative of the work of 'Phiz' (q.v.).

*SIR WILLIAM RUSSELL FLINT 1880-1969. 'Then he blew three deadly notes...' Illustration to* Morte d'Arthur, *Riccardi Press.*
*Watercolour, signed and dated 1910. 11⅛ins. x 8¾ins. (28.2cm x 22.2cm).*
Victoria and Albert Museum

**FLINT, Sir William Russell RA PRWS** 1880-1969

Draughtsman, watercolourist and illustrator. He was born at Edinburgh, 4 April 1880 and was educated at David Stewart's College and the Royal Institute of Art, Edinburgh. He settled in London in 1900 and after studying at Heatherley's, he was on the staff of *The Illustrated London News*, 1903-7. From this period onwards, Flint turned increasingly to watercolour, particularly for the illustration of colour books. He was influenced strongly by the illustrations of *Rip Van Winkle* by Arthur Rackham (q.v.) and between about 1905 and 1924 produced a whole series of brilliant luxury editions for the Riccardi Press of the Medici Society. His figures are finely modelled and contain elements of a Burne-Jones influence by way of Byam Shaw. From the 1920s Flint became the unquestioned master of the watercolour nude and these, and the prints from them, made his reputation, even if they were less original than his illustrative work.

Flint served in the First World War with the RNVR Airship section and made the first Atlantic crossing by airship in the R34, 1918-19. He was elected ARWS in 1914, RWS, 1917 and was President of the RWS from 1936. He became ARA, 1924 and RA, 1933 and was knighted in 1947. He died in London in 1969.

Illus: *The Duel [ Joseph Conrad]; King Solomon's Mines [Rider Haggard, 1905]; The Imitation of Christ [1908]; The Song of Solomon [1909]; Marcus Aurelius [1909]; The Savoy Operas [1909-10]; The Scholar Gypsy [1910, 2 vols.]; Morte d'Arthur [1910-11]; The Heroes [C. Kingsley, 1912]; The Canterbury Tales [1913]; Theocritus [1922]; Odyssey [1924]; Judith [1928]; Airmen or Noahs [1928]; The Book of Tobit [1929].*
Contrib: *The Studio [1899]; Opthalmological Society's Journal [1901]; The Pall Mall Magazine [1903]; Pearson's Magazine [1903]; Nash's Magazine [1903]; The Sketch [1903]; The Tatler [1903]; The Bystander [1903]; The Quiver [1903]; The English Illustrated Magazine [1903]; Black & White [1903]; The Idler [1903]; Illustrated Sporting and Dramatic News [1903]; Sunday at Home [1903]; The Sphere [1903]; The World and his Wife [1903]; The Graphic [1904].*
Exhib. FSA, 1909, 1911, 1914, 1919, 1922, 1923, 1925, 1932, 1937, 1950, 1975; G; L; M; RA; RE; RHA; RI; ROI; RSA; RSW.
Colls: BM; Glasgow; Leeds; V & AM.
Bibl: *Modern Illustrators and Their Work*, Studio, 1914; Arnold Palmer, *More Than Shadows - A Biography of WRF*, 1943; W.R. Flint, *Drawings*, 1950 (with prologue, descriptive notes and bibliography).
See illustration (p.305).

**FLORENCE, Mary Sargant** 1857-1954

Decorative mural painter in tempera. She was born in London on 21 July 1857, and studied art at the Slade School under Legros and in Paris at the Studio Merson. She carried out the mural decoration of Chelsea Old Town Hall. In 1896, she illustrated *The Crystal Ball*, designs which Walter Crane found full of 'power and decorative feeling'. She became a Member of the NEA in 1911. Two of her pictures were purchased for the Chantrey Bequest in 1932 and 1949. She worked latterly at Marlow, Bucks.

Exhib: L; NEA; RA; SWA.
Bibl: K. Spence, 'A Country Refuge From Bloomsbury', *Country Life* November 15, 1973.

**FLOWER, Clement** fl.1899-1908

Portrait and figure painter. He was working at Bushey, Herts., 1899-1908 and contributed illustrations of social realism to *The Graphic* in 1901.

Exhib: RA, 1899-1908.

**FOLKARD, Charles James** 1878-

Artist, illustrator and author of children's books. He was born in 1878 and after being educated at Lewisham, was apprenticed to a firm of designers but left them to become a professional conjuror. He later joined the *Daily Mail* staff as an artist, and invented the cartoon character 'Teddy Tail', but abandoned this career to follow that of book illustrator.

Illus: *Flint Heart [1910]; Swiss Family Robinson [1910]; Pinnochio [1911]; Grimms Fairy Tales [1911]; Aesop's Fables [1912]; Arabian Nights [1913]; Jackdaw of Rheims [1913]; Ottoman Wonder Tales [1915]; Mother Goose Nursery Rhymes [1919]; British Fairy and Folk Tales [1920]; Songs From Alice in Wonderland [1921]; Magic Egg [1922]; Granny's Wonderful Chair [1925]; The Troubles of a Gnome [1928]; Land of Nursery Rhyme [1932]; Tales of the Taunus Mountains [1937]; The Princess and the Goblin [1949]; The Princess and Curdie [1949].*

**FOLKARD, W.A.**

Artist, contributing comic illustrations to Tom Hood's *Comic Annual*, 1834.

**FORBES, Elizabeth Adela (née Armstrong, Mrs. Stanhope Forbes)** 1859-1912

Landscape painter, etcher and illustrator. She was born in Canada on 29 December, 1859 and studied at the Art Students' League, New York. She married in 1889, Stanhope Forbes, RA, and with him founded the Newlyn School of Art, 1899. As an illustrator Elizabeth Stanhope Forbes worked in pen· and ink, or in watercolour in a very broad and atmospheric way, reflecting her oil style. She became NEA in 1886 and RE, 1885-89, ARWS, 1899. She died at Newlyn, 22 March 1912. Signs early work: Elizabeth A. Armstrong, or with monogram: EA

Illus: *King Arthur's Wood [written and illus. by ESF, 1905]; Robert Herrick [Golden Poets, 1908].*
Contrib: *Black & White [1891]; The Yellow Book [1895].*
Exhib: B; FAS, 1900; G; L; M; NEA; RA; RBA; RI; ROI; SWA.
Colls: BM; V & AM.
Bibl: L. Birch, *SA Forbes and EF*, 1906; R. Pearsall, 'SF and the Newlyn School of Painting', *The Antique Collector*, Vol.44, August 1973 pp.213-216.

**FORBES, Professor James David** 1809-1868

Scientist and draughtsman. He was elected FRSE at the age of nineteen and was one of the joint founders of the British Association in 1831 and FRS 1832. In 1833 he became Professor of Natural Philosophy at Edinburgh and Principal of St. Andrews in 1859.

Illus: *Travels Through The Alps of Savoy [1843]; Norway And Its Glaciers [1853, AT 257].*

**FORBES, J.**

Topographical artist. Contributed to Griffith's *Cheltenham*, 1826.

**FORD, Henry Justice** 1860-1941

Artist and illustrator. He was born in London in February 1860 and was educated at Repton and Clare College, Cambridge; 1st Class Classical Tripos, 1882. He studied art under Alphonse Legros at the Slade and under Herkomer (q.v.) at Bushey. Ford was a friend of Edward Burne-Jones (q.v.) and was strongly influenced by the latter's iconography if not directly by his style of drawing. Ford concentrated on legend and folklore as subjects to illustrate and mixed carefully observed objects from the real world with fantasy creatures from an imagined world in a very convincing way. His penwork is assured and clear and placed on the page with great decorative effect; he often supplied borders and vignettes to his published work. A whole generation of Edwardians grew up on Ford's illustrations to Andrew Lang's fairy tales, the long series of little books appearing between 1889 and 1913. The black and white work owes something to Walter Crane and a great deal to *Moxon's Tennyson*, but it is really in the later colour picture books that Ford's debt to the Pre-Raphaelites emerges; their minute detail and brilliant colours show that they are his real source. He died in 1941. Ford's pen drawings are sometimes seen on the market.

Illus. for Andrew Lang: *The Blue Fairy Book [1889]; The Red Fairy Book [1890]; The Blue Poetry Book [1891]; The Green Fairy Book [1892]; The True Story Book [1893]; The Yellow Fairy Book [1894]; The Animal Story Book [1896]; The Blue True Story Book [1896]; The Red True Story Book [1897]; The Pink Fairy Book [1897]; The Arabian Nights Entertainment [1898]; The Red Book of Animal Stories [1899]; The Grey Fairy Book [1900]; The Violet Fairy Book [1901]; The Disentanglers [1902]; The Red Romance Book [1905]; Tales of King Arthur [1905]; Tales of Troy [1907]; The Marvellous Musicians [1909].*
Illus: *Aesop's Fables [1888]; When Mother Was Little [1890]; A Lost God [1891]; Early Italian Love Stories [Vera Taylor, 1899]; The Luck Flower [G. Walker, 1907]; The Book of Princes and Princesses [L.B. Lang, 1911]; The Book of Saints [L.B. Lang, 1912]; The Strange Story Book [L.B. Lang, 1913]; Old Testament Legends [M.R. James, 1913]; Pilot [H.P. Greene, 1916]; The Happy Warrior [H. Newbolt, 1917]; David Blaize and the Blue Door [E.F. Benson, 1918]; The Pilgrim's Progress [1921].*
Exhib: FAS, 1895; G; L; M; New Gall.; RA; ROI.
Colls: V & AM.
Bibl: R.E.D. Sketchley, *English Book Illus.*, 1902, pp.109, 110, 165; B. Peppin, *Fantasy Book Illus.*, 1975, p.187, illus.
See illustrations (p.307).

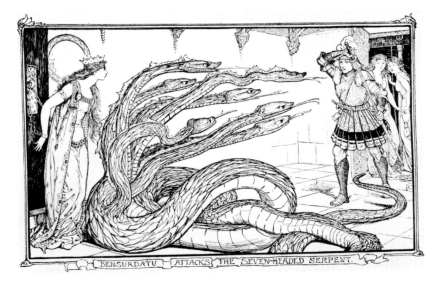

*HENRY JUSTICE FORD 1860-1941. 'Bensurdatu Attacks the Seven-Headed Serpent'. Illustration to* The Grey Fairy Book, *Andrew Lang, 1900.*

**FOREST, Eugène Hippolyte**                    1808-

French painter and lithographer. He was born at Strasbourg, 24 October 1808 and studied under Roqueplan and exhibited at the Salon from 1847. He contributed to *The Illustrated London News*, 1848.

**FORREST, Archibald Stevenson**                    1864-

Landscape painter and illustrator. He was born at Greenwich in 1869 and was educated at Roan School, Greenwich, and in Edinburgh. He studied art at the Westminster School, the City and Guilds College and Edinburgh School of Art. He worked in Blackheath, 1908, and at Lymington, Hants, 1926, specialising in black and white work in the 1890s, colour work in the 1900s, and pure landscape painting from about 1910. He designed a poster for *The Idler*.

*HENRY JUSTICE FORD 1860-1941. Fantastic bird. Pen and ink. Signed. 8ins. x 7⅜ins. (20.3cm x 18.7cm).*                    Victoria and Albert Museum

*HENRY JUSTICE FORD 1860-1941. 'Udea Found Lifeless.'*
*Illustration to* The Grey Fairy Book, *Andrew Lang, 1900.*

Illus: *South America [W.H. Koebel]; Morocco [S.L. Bensusan]; The West Indies [John Henderson, 1905].*
Contrib: *Judy [1894]; St. Paul [1895]; Black and White [1899]; Moonshine [1900]; Illustrated Bits; The Idler.*
Exhib: L; RBA, 1893-1909.
Colls: Witt Photo.

**FORREST, Isabelle**

Illustrator. Contributed a frontispiece to *Twelve Moons* by Frances A. Baidswell, 1912.

**FORRESTIER, Alfred Henry    see CROWQUILL, Alfred**

**FORRESTIER, Amedée**                    1854-1930

Special artist and illustrator. He was probably born in Belgium but came to England to work for *The Illustrated London News* in 1882. He acted as Special Artist for that paper regularly until 1899, attending mostly royal occasions and ceremonial functions at home and abroad. He visited Morocco, Russia, Germany, Belgium, Italy and Scandinavia, attended the coronation of Nicholas II in Russia, 1896, and the Quebec Tercentenary of 1908. Forrestier was a very good portraitist in chalk and drew several members of the Royal Family from life. In later life he devoted himself entirely to the study and illustration of archaeology. He died 14 November 1930.

Illus: *Blind Love [Wilkie Collins, 1890]; Barker's Luck [Bret Harte, 1896]; The World Went Well Then, For Faith and Freedom, In Deacon's Orders [Walter Besant, 1897]; Pablo The Priest [Baring Gould, 1899]; Belgium [G.W.T. Ormond]; Bruges and West Flanders, Brabant and East Flanders [1905]; Liège and the Ardennnes.*
Contrib: *ILN [1882-99]; The Girls' Own Paper [1890-1900]; The Strand Magazine [1891]; The English Illustrated Magazine [1895-96]; Pearson's Magazine [1896]; The Quartier Latin [1898]; The Sporting and Dramatic News [1899]; The Lady's Pictorial; The Windsor Magazine.*
Exhib: RBA, 1882-83.
Colls: V & AM.
Bibl: W. Simpson, *Autobiography*, 1903.

**FORSYTH, Adam**
Landscape painter working at Harlesden, London, 1889-92. He contributed a topographical illustration to *The Illustrated London News* in 1891 and exhibited at the RA and RI.

**FOSTER, Marcia Lane (Mrs. Jarrett)** 1897-
Wood engraver and illustrator. She was born at Bonn and studied at the St. John's Wood School of Art and at the Central School of Arts and Crafts. She specialised in figure painting and exhibited with the NEA in 1924.

Illus: *Canadian Fairy Tales [Cyrus Macmillan, 1922].*

**FOSTER, Myles Birkett** 1825-1899
Pastoral painter and illustrator. He was born into a Quaker family at North Shields on 4 February 1825. His grandfather was an acquaintance of Thomas Bewick, the wood engraver, and from a very early age he was set on being an artist himself. He went to Quaker Schools in Tottenham and Hitchin after the family had moved to London and at the age of sixteen he was apprenticed to an engraver named Stone, who unfortunately committed suicide on the day the indentures were completed. Foster was then moved to Ebenezer Landells, 1806-60, who had been a pupil of Bewick. He left Landells in 1846 at the age of twenty-one and began a career of his own in book illustration. This very productive period of his life lasted until 1859, when success enabled him to abandon this kind of work. He made his name with the public through the vignettes to Longfellow's *Evangeline*, 1850, and thereafter followed commissions for most of the classics and many books of modern poetry. Foster supplied initial letters to *Punch* in 1841-43, but his work for the magazines was very limited in comparison with his output on books. The latter were much more suitable vehicles for his gentle and subtle art, much of it in a small scale and low key, tiny detailed landscapes with pretty vegetation, herds of sheep and cows and cottagers at their doors. He was elected ARWS in 1860 and RWS in 1862. He died at Weybridge, 27 March 1899. He was brother-in-law of J.D. Watson (q.v.).

Foster designed book covers as well as illustrations and was one of the first artists to have his work reproduced by colour block in *The Illustrated London News* of 1857. He was on friendly terms with the Pre-Raphaelites and travelled abroad with Fred Walker (q.v.) whose figure work his own landscapes complement. His watercolours are very sentimental but have always attracted a large following among collectors.

Illus: *Burns Poems and Songs [1846]; Longfellow's Evangeline [1850]; Gray's Elegy [1853]; Longfellow's Poems [1854]; Proverbial Philosophy [1854]; Cowper's The Task [1855]; Adam's Sacred Allegories [1856]; Herbert's Poetical Works [1856]; Rhymes and Roundelays [1856]; Ministering Children [1856]; The Ancient Mariner [1856]; Bloomfield's Farmer's Boy [1857]; Course of Time [1857]; Poets of the Nineteenth Century [1857]; Kavanagh [1857]; Moore's Poetry [1857]; Gertrude of Wyoming [1857]; Choice Series [1857-64]; Poe's Poetical Works [1858]; Lays of the Holy Land [1858]; Home Affections [1858]; Favourite English Poems [1859]; Odes and Sonnets [1859]; The Seasons [1859]; Montgomery's Poems [1860]; The Book of South Wales [1861]; Household Song [1861]; Merrie Days of England [n.d.]; Early English Poems [1863]; Poetry of the Elizabethan Age [n.d.]; Christmas with the Poets [n.d.]; Legends and Lyrics [1866]; Moore's Irish Melodies [1867]; Beauties of Landscape [1873]; The Trail of Sir Jasper [n.d.]; Pictures of English Landscape [1881]; Picturesque Mediterranean [1891].*
Contrib: *Punch [1841-43]; ILN [1847-57]; The Illustrated London Almanac For 1853; The Illustrated Times [c.1855].*
Exhib: G; L; M; RA; RE; RWS.
Colls: Aberdeen; Ashmolean; BM; Blackburn; Greenwich; Hitchin; Newcastle; Sydney; V & AM.
Bibl: Chatto & Jackson, *Treatise on Wood Engraving*, 1861, p.558; H.M. Cundall, *BF*, 1906.

**FOSTER, William** 1853-1924
Landscape watercolourist and black and white and animal illustrator. He was born in 1853, the son of Myles Birkett Foster (q.v.). He lived near his father at Witley, Surrey, and later with him at Weybridge, 1899. He specialised in ink and wash illustrations to children's stories, including sketches of comic animals. He was a Fellow of the

Zoological Society.
Exhib: L; M; RA; RBA; RI; RSA.
Colls: V & AM.

**FOTHERGILL, George Algernon** 1868-
Watercolourst and illustrator. He was born in 1868 and although trained as a doctor, he gave up the profession in order to become an artist. He was Medical Officer in charge of 1st Cavalry Brigade, 1918-19 and lived and worked principally in the north of England or in Scotland.

Illus: *Notes From The Diary of a Doctor, Sketch, Artist and Sportsman . . . 220 Illustrations . . . [York, 1901].*
Exhib: L; RSA; Walker's Gall.

**'FOUGASSE' Cyril Kenneth Bird** 1887-
Black and white artist. He was born 17 December 1887 and was educated at Cheltenham College and King's College, London. He became Art Editor of *Punch* in 1937, succeeding George Morrow (q.v.), and had a great deal to do with modernising the paper's rather old fashioned image. He was Editor from 1949-52 and successfully steered the humour and drawing into the post-war world. Fougasse's own style was pithy and diagrammatic, due perhaps to the fact that he was trained as an engineer. His favourite form was the strip cartoon in which small outline figures, full of movement, but consisting of only the barest essentials for the story, raced along over the simplest of captions. He achieved great fame during the Second World War as a poster artist with his series 'Careless Talk Costs Lives'.

Illus: *A Gallery of Games [1920]; Drawn at a Venture [1922]; P.T.O. [1926]; E. and O.E. [1928]; Fun Fair [1934]; The Luck of the Draw [1930]; You Have Been Warned [1935]; Drawing the Line Somewhere [1937]; Stop or Go [1938]; Jotsam [1939]; The Changing Face of Britain [1940]; and the Gatepost [1940]; Running Commentary [1941]; Sorry No Rubber [1941]; Just a Few Lines [1943]; Family Group [1944]; Home Circle [1945]; A School of Purposes [1946]; You and Me [1948]; Us [1951]; The Neighbours [1954]; The Good-tempered Pencil [1956]; Between the Lines [1958].*
Exhib: FAS, 1966; RSA.
Bibl: R.G.G. Price, *A History of Punch*, 1957, pp.285-286, 300-301, illus.

**FOXLEY, C.**
Flower illustrator. Contributed decorative pages of the seasons to *The English Illustrated Magazine*, 1896-97.

**FOX-PITT, Douglas RBA** 1864-1922
Watercolourist and illustrator. He was born in London in 1864, the fifth son of General Pitt-Rivers, FRS. He studied art at the Slade and became a member of the London Group and a friend of Walter Sickert (q.v.). He made extensive tours abroad to Canada, Poland, Greece and the Ionian Isles and Ceylon. He visited Morocco in 1905-6 for Count Sternberg. He lived at Brighton from 1911 to 1918 and died at Chertsey, 19 September 1922. RBA, 1906.

Illus: *The Barbarians of Morocco [Count Sternberg, 1908].*
Exhib: GG; Leicester Gall.; M; NEA; RBA; RI.
Colls: Brighton; Fitzwilliam; Imperial War.
Bibl: *The Studio*, Vol.64, 1914, pp.56-57, illus.

**FRAMPTON, Edward Reginald ROI** 1870-1923
Painter and illustrator. He was born in 1870, the son of Edward Frampton, stained-glass artist. He was educated at Brighton and Westminster School and studied art in France and Italy. He was a member of the RBA, 1894, the Tempera Society, 1907, and the Art Workers Guild, 1910. Elected ROI, 1904. Frampton was for many years on the staff of the L.C.C. Higher Education Art Committee and published numerous papers on art. He is best known as a mural artist, he executed a number of designs for public buildings and most notably those in All Saints Church, Hastings, as well as designing stained glass and carrying out sculpture. His illustrated works were not extensive, they are in the black and white woodcutty manner which originates with Morris. Some of his drawings are very akin to those of Burne-Jones.

Illus: *The Poems of William Morris [n.d.].*
Exhib: B; FAS, 1924; G; L; M; New Gall.; P; Paris, 1910, 1920; RA; RBA; RI; ROI.
Colls: Bradford; V & AM.
Bibl: *The Studio*, Vol.58, 1913, p.21, illus.; *Who Was Who*, 1916-28.
See illustration (p.309).

*REGINALD EDWARD FRAMPTON ROI 1870-1923. St. Brandon. Illustration for unidentified book. Pencil on card. Signed. 7ins. x 8¾ins. (17.8cm x 22.2cm).*
Victoria and Albert Museum

**FRANKLIN, John**                                    **fl.1800-1861**

Landscape, historical and architectural painter and illustrator. He was
born in Ireland and studied at the RDS Schools before working in
Dublin. He exhibited at the RHA from its foundation in 1826 but
settled in London in 1828. S.C. Hall calls him 'an artist of prodigious
capability, who never gave himself fair play, frittering away his
marvellous talent in comparatively small things, and avoiding the great
works in which he would undoubtedly have excelled'. He was a fairly
regular book illustrator in the 1850s, and his work was much admired
by the young Walter Crane.

Illus: *The Psalms of David; Midsummer Eve [Mrs. S.C. Hall, 1842]; Seven
Champions of Christendom; Poets of the West; Ireland Its Scenes and Character
[S.C. Hall, 1841]; The Irish Peasantry [Carleton, 1852].*
Contrib: *The Book of British Ballads*
Exhib: BI, 1830-68; RA; RBA.
Bibl: Chatto & Jackson, *Treatise on Wood Engraving*, 1861, p.599; S.C. Hall,
*Retrospect of a Long Life*, 1883, Vol.1 p.332.

**FRASER, Claud Lovat**                                **1890-1921**

Artist, book illustrator and decorator, theatre designer. He was born
in London in May 1890 and was educated at Charterhouse, and
afterwards studied with Walter Sickert (q.v.) for six months. He did
some illustrating before the First World War but joined up in 1914
with the Durham Light Infantry and was severely shell-shocked and

gassed at Loos, subsequently being invalided out of the army. He
worked for two years in the Record Office but entered his most
productive period after 1918, when he made a name as a theatrical
designer, designing sets and costumes for *As You Like It* and *The
Beggars Opera*, 1920. He developed a style of drawing and of
illustration in the tradition of the chapbook with black outlines and
flat areas of bright colour. There are hints of Crawhall in his work but
also perversely, echoes of Nielsen. Fraser was an excellent decorator
of pamphlets and among his most striking works are the rhyme sheets
he drew for Harold Monro's Poetry Bookshop. Their self-conscious
simplicity and unaffected charm make them very much a part of art
deco mannerism. Fraser's active service had so damaged his health
that he died after this short-lived success at Sandgate on 18 June
1921.

Illus: *Eve and Other Poems [Ralph Hodgson, 1913]; Nursery Rhymes [1919];
The Chapbook; Poems from the Works of Charles Cotton Newly Decorated by
Claud Lovat Fraser [1922]; The Luck of the Bean-Rows [C. Nodier, 1921];
Peacock Pie [Walter de la Mare, 1924].*
Contrib: *Methuen's Annual, 1914, (cover).*
Exhib: International Soc., NEA, 1917; Memorial Exhibition, 1921.
Colls: Tate (Curwen Press Gift); V & AM.
Bibl: E. Craig and De La Mare, *Catalogue of the Lovat Fraser Memorial
Exhibition*, 1921; D. Bland, *A History of Book Illustration*, 1958, p.374; Joy
Grant, *Harold Monro and The Poetry Bookshop*, 1967, pp.113-114.

**FRASER, Eric George** 1902-
Painter and etcher. He worked in Westminster and exhibited at the RA in 1924.

**FRASER, Francis Arthur** fl.1865-1898
Figure painter and illustrator. He was working in London from 1867 and at Dorking and Shere, Surrey, from 1881-82. He was a very prolific artist, especially in the late 1860s and his work which is pleasantly ordinary, was considered decadent by Gleeson White. He was employed on *Fun* from 1878 and became cartoonist in 1898. His brother G.G. Fraser (q.v.) was also an illustrator.
Illus: *Great Expectations [Dickens Household Edition, 1871]; The Innocents at Home [Mark Twain, 1897].*
Contrib: *The Sunday Magazine [1865-69]; Once a Week [1867]; Cassells Magazine [1867-70]; St. Pauls [1868-69]; Good Words For The Young [1869-72]; Good Words [1870]; London Society [1870]; ILN [1874]; Fun [1878-98]; The Chandos Poets; Judy [1894].*
Exhib: RA; RBA.

**FRASER, G.G.** fl.1880-1895
Humorous illustrator. He was the brother of F.A. Fraser (q.v.) and specialised in comic figure subjects and strip cartoons. He was a regular contributor to *Judy* and died in 1895.
Contrib: *Fun [1890-92]; The Ludgate Monthly [1892]; The Strand [1894]; The Idler.*
Exhib: G; L; RA; RI.

**FRASER, James Baillie** 1783-1856
Traveller, writer and artist. With his brother W. Fraser, he explored Nepal and the sources of the Ganges and the Jumna in 1815. In 1821 he made the journey from Persia to Tabriz and rode through Asia Minor, 1833-34. He published a *Memoir of Lt-Colonel James Skinner,* 1851.
Illus: *Views of Calcutta [1824-26, AT 494]; Views in the Himala Mountains [AT 498].*
Exhib: BI and RBA, 1827-31.

**FRASER, P.**
Illustrator of genre. He contributed drawings of urchins to *Punch,* 1914.

**FREDERICS, A.** fl.1877-1889
Illustrator. He worked chiefly for *Harper's Magazine* in what Pennell considered the English tradition. He illustrated *Three Men in a Boat* by Jerome K. Jerome, 1889, and exhibited at the RBA in 1877.

**FREER, Mary Ellen    see EDWARDS, Mary Ellen**

**FRENCH, Annie (Mrs. G.W. Rhead)** fl.1900-1925
Painter, etcher and illustrator. She was probably trained at the Glasgow School and made many watercolours and pen drawings to illustrate children's books. Her style is influenced by the Pre-Raphaelites with its vivid colours, languid figures and garlands, but also present is a Beardsley influence, particularly in the use of massed dots giving the drawings a speckled appearance. In 1914 she married the etcher and stained-glass artist, George Wooliscroft Rhead (q.v.). Her work has had a great upsurge of popularity in recent years.
Contrib: *ILN [1913].*
Exhib: B; G; GG; L; M; RA; RHA; RI; RSA; RWA.
Colls: V & AM; Witt Photo.
See illustration (Colour Plate XV p.192).

**FRENCH, Henry** fl.1868-1875
Domestic painter and illustrator. He was working at Kentish Town in 1872-75, and exhibited at the RBA.
Contrib: *London Society [1868]; The Sunday Magazine [1869]; Good Words For The Young [1869]; Our Mutual Friend [Dickens Household Edition, 1871]; The Chandos Poets.*

**FRENZENY, Paul** fl.1887-1899
Illustrator. He appears to have acted as a Special Artist for *The Illustrated London News* in the Spanish American War of 1898 and had worked for the paper since 1887. He also specialised in theatrical studies, his work usually being in grey wash.
Illus: *Fifty Years on the Trail [H. O'Reilly, 1889]; The Jungle Book [Rudyard Kipling, 1894 (with others)].*
Exhib: RI, 1898.

**FRIEDENSON, Joseph T.** fl.1899-1909
Landscape painter and illustrator. He worked in London and contributed some ink drawings of rural life to the magazines. He signs his work J.T F.
Exhib: NEA; RA.
Colls: V & AM.

**FRIPP, Charles Edward    ARWS** 1854-1906
Watercolourist, Special Artist and illustrator. He was born in London in 1854 and was of G.A. Fripp, RWS, the landscape painter. Fripp was a war correspondent on *The Graphic* from 1878, and in that capacity covered a great number of Queen Victoria's 'little wars'. He was special artist in the Transvaal, 1881, Ceylon, 1881, South Africa, 1885 and China, 1895-1903. He visited Japan, but died at Montreal in 1906 as a result of the hardships endured during the Manchurian campaign of the Sino-Japanese War of 1905. Hartrick describes him as ' a little terrier of a man'. He was elected ARWS in 1891.
Illus: *Fairy Tales [B. Field, 1898].*
Contrib: *Black and White [1893]; The Pall Mall Magazine.*
Colls: V & AM.
Bibl: A.S. Hartrick, *Painter's Pilgrimage . . . .* 1939, p.71.
Exhib: L; M; RA; RHA; RWS.

**FRISTON, David Henry** fl.1853-1878
Figure painter and illustrator. He was working in Regent's Park in 1854 and in Kensington in 1863. Friston seems to have specialised in theatrical scenes and portraits in black and white.
Contrib: *The Churchman's Family Magazine [1863]; Tinsley's Magazine [1867]; ILN [1869-78 (theatrical)]; Dark Blue [1871-73].*
Exhib: BI, 1854-67; RA; RBA, 1863.

**FRITH, William Powell    RA CVO** 1819-1909
Domestic and genre painter. He was born on 9 January 1819 and was educated at Knaresborough and Dover, before studying art under Sass and at the RA Schools. He began to exhibit at the RA in 1840 and from that period became the doyen of English subject pictures, including 'Ramsgate Sands', 1853, 'Derby Day', 1858, and 'The Railway Station', 1862. Frith tried unsuccessfully to be a moral painter in the manner of Hogarth and although he illustrates Victorian society in a very finished and photographic way, he did not penetrate its skin and remained a prosperous popular painter. He made one excursion into book illustration by contributing to S.C. Hall's *Book of British Ballads* in 1842, and there is a wash drawing in the Victoria and Albert Museum which may be a study for illustration. He became ARA in 1845, and RA in 1853, and was created CVO in 1908 in recognition of his long connection with the Royal Family as a painter of ceremonial events. He died at St. John's Wood, 2 November 1909.
Bibl: W.P.F. *My Autobiography . . . Further Reminiscences, 1887-88; J. Laver* and J. Mayne, *Cat. of . . . Paintings by WPF, RA, at Harrogate Art Gallery,* 1951.

**FROHAWK, F.W.**
Ornithological draughtsman who contributed illustrations to *British Birds Their Nests and Eggs,* 1891.

**FRÖHLICH, Lorens**                                      **1820-1908**

Painter, engraver and illustrator. He was born in Copenhagen on 25 October 1820, and studied in Denmark and at Munich, Dresden and Rome. In 1877, he was appointed professor at the Academy of Fine Art in Copenhagen but established his reputation more as an illustrator than a painter. He illustrated numerous Danish books of legend and contributed to English children's stories. He died at Copenhagen on 25 October 1908.

Illus: *What Makes Me Grow? [1875].*
Contrib: *Mrs. Gatty's Parables From Nature [1861]; Legends and Lyrics [A.A. Proctor, 1865]; ILN [1872].*
Exhib: FAS, 1883.


**FROST, Arthur Burdett**                                 **1851-1928**

Painter and draughtsman. He was born at Philadelphia on 17 January 1851 and was associated from an early date with *Harper's* for which he did many drawings serious and humorous. Pennell considered him to be the finest comic artist in the United States, but was even more impressed by his accuracy as a domestic illustrator. 'Mr. Frost's drawings of the farmer in the Middle States will later be as valuable records as Menzel's uniforms of Frederick the Great.' Frost was an exhibitor at the Paris Exhibition of 1900 and died in 1928.

Illus: *American Notes [Dickens Household Edition, 1871]; Phantasmagoria [Lewis Carroll, 1911].*
Contrib: *The Quiver [1882].*
Bibl: J. Pennell, *Pen Drawing and Pen Draughtsmen*, 1894.


**FRY, Roger Elliott**                                    **1866-1934**

Art critic and artist. He was born in 1866, the son of the Rt.Hon. Sir Edward Fry, one of the distinguished Quaker family. After being educated at Clifton and King's College, Cambridge, where he read science, Fry devoted himself to art and studied under Francis Bate and in Paris. After visiting Italy, he turned his attention to connoisseurship and writing and became the director of the Metropolitan Museum of Art, New York, 1905-10. He sponsored the first French Post-Impressionist exhibitions at the Grafton Gallery, 1910 and 1912, and founded the Omega Workshop in 1913. He wrote many books and articles, championing modern art and became Slade Professor of Fine Art at Cambridge in 1933. He died on 9 September 1934. Member of NEA, 1893.

Illus: *In a Garden [Rev. H.C. Beeching, 1896 (title)].*
Exhib: G; L; M; NEA; RSA.


**FRY, Windsor**

Contributor of domestic illustrations to *The English Illustrated Magazine*, 1897.


**FULLEYLOVE, John   RI**                                 **1845-1908**

Landscape painter, watercolourist and illustrator. He was born at Leicester on 18 August 1845, and was at first apprenticed to an architect, Flint and Shenton of Leicester, before taking to painting as a profession. Fulleylove travelled abroad widely and painted architecture and gardens in Versailles, Florence, Rome and Athens and visited the Near East and the Holy Land. His work was published in a long series of late Victorian and Edwardian colour plate books and although attractive is often a too rich diet for today's taste. He was elected RI in 1879 and died in London on 22 May 1908. His brother-in-law was George S. Elgood RI (q.v.).

Illus: *Henry Irving [1883]; Oxford [Edward Thomas, 1889]; Pictures and Sketches of Greek Landscape [1897]; The Stones of Paris [1900]; The Holy Land [Rev. John Kelman MA, 1905]; Middlesex [Hope Moncrieff]; Edinburgh [Rosaline Masson]; In the Footsteps of Charles Lamb [c.1905].*
Contrib: *The English Illustrated Magazine [1886]; The Picturesque Mediterranean [1891]; Good Words [1891]; ILN [1894]; Pastorals of France [F. Wedmore, 1894 (title)].*
Exhib: B; FAS, 1886, 1888, 1890, 1894, 1896, 1899, 1902, 1906; G; Leicester Gall.; RA; RHA; RI; ROI.
Colls: Cardiff; Leicester; Liverpool; V & AM.
Bibl: 'Mr. Fulleylove's Drawings of Greek Architecture and Landscape', *The Studio*, Vol.7, 1896, pp.77-82, iillus.; R.E.D. Sketchley, *English Book Illus.*, 1902, pp.31, 39, 134.


**FURNISS, Harry**                                        **1854-1925**

Black and white artist, caricaturist and author. He was born at Wexford, Ireland, in 1854, the son of an English engineer. Furniss drew from an early age and first submitted work to A.M. Sullivan's Irish version of *Punch* and then to *Punch* itself, after he had settled in London in 1873. His sketches were rejected by *Punch's* editor, Tom Taylor, and only accepted after Burnand had taken over the editorship; he joined the staff in 1880, but was never on the salaried staff. Furniss was well-travelled, visited America, Canada and Australia, and was sent to the Chicago World Fair as Special Artist by *The Illustrated London News*. For the same paper he also tried his hand at social realism, but it is as a humorous illustrator that he is most widely remembered.

There is little doubt that Furniss was one of the most talented black and white artists of his time, certainly one of the quickest in executing work. His pen line, which looks effortlessly precise, was often worked up from pencil, but when he introduces washes, the effect is far less successful. A master of political caricature, of the silhouette caricature and of the inspired doodle, he lacked the consistency to become a great illustrator. He was notoriously argumentative and egotistical as is shown by obsessive use of self-portraits and his famous break with *Punch* in 1894 when he founded *Lika Joko* and *The New Budget*. He was at his most brilliant however in metamorphic caricatures such as 'Getting Mr. Gladstone's Collar Up' and subtly imitating the works of famous artists. His Parliamentary sketches are occasionally seen on the market. He died at Hastings, 14 January 1925 and signs his work ⌇%ₐ

Illus: *Happy Thoughts; Incompleat Angler; The Comic Blackstone; Sylvie and Bruno [Lewis Carroll, 1889]; Thackeray's Ballads [Cheap Illustrated Edition, 1894]; All in a Garden Fair [W. Besant, 1897]; The Wallypug of Why [G.E. Farrow, 1900]; The Works of Charles Dickens [1910]; The Works of W.M. Thackeray [1911].*
Publ: *Royal Academy Antics [1890]; America in a Hurry [1900]; Peace with Humour; P and O Sketches [1898]; Confessions of a Caricaturist [1901]; Harry Furniss At Home [1903]; How To Draw in Pen and*

HARRY FURNISS 1854-1925. *Caricature of Lord Brampton.* **Pen and ink.** *3½ins. x 2¾ins. (8.9cm x 7cm).*                    Author's Collection

*HARRY FURNISS 1854-1925. 'The Race for the Country. Waiting for the Signal by our Americanised Artist.' Illustration for* Punch, *18 June 1892. Pen and ink.*
Woburn Abbey Collection

*Ink [1905]; Friends without Faces [1905]; Our Lady Cinema [1914]; More about How to Draw in Pen and Ink [1915]; Peace in War [1917]; Deceit a reply to Defeat [1917]; My Bohemian Days; The Byways and Queer Ways of Boxing [1919]; Stiggins, Some Victorian Women [1923]; Some Victorian Men [1924].*
Contrib: *ILN [1876-86]; Punch [1880-94]; Vanity Fair [1881]; Cornhill Magazine [1883-85]; The English Illustrated Magazine [1883, 1890-91]; The Graphic [1889]; Good Words [1890]; Black & White [1891]; The Pall Mall Budget; The Sketch; The Windsor Magazine; Cassell's Family Magazine; Illustrated Sporting and Dramatic News.*
Exhib: FAS, 1894, 1898, 1925; RA; RHA.
Colls: V & AM.
Bibl: H.F. *Confessions of a Caricaturist*, 1901.
See illustrations (above and p.311).

### FURSE, Charles Wellington   ARA          1868-1904
Portrait painter. He was born in 1868, the son of the Ven. C.W. Furse, Archdeacon of Westminster. He was educated at Haileybury College and studied at the Slade School under Legros, winning a Slade Scholarship and then working in Paris. He was a member of the NEA in 1892 and was elected ARA in 1904. He died 17 October 1904.

Contrib: *The Yellow Book; The Autobiography of a Boy [G.S. Street, 1894 (title)].*

### FUSSELL, Joseph          fl.1821-1845
Landscape painter. He was probably the brother of A. and F.R. Fussell, and painted from addresses in Sadlers Wells and Bloomsbury, 1821-45. He contributed illustrations to Virtue's *Views of Kent*, 1829, and to Knight's *London*, 1841.

Exhib: BI, 1822-45; RBA, 1821-45.

### FYFE, William Baxter Collier          1836-1882
Figure painter and illustrator. He was born at Dundee in 1836 and studied art at the RSA in Edinburgh. He specialised in Scottish genre subjects, exhibited his first picture in 1861, and settled in London in 1863, working latterly at St. John's Wood.

Contrib: *Good Words [1861].*
Exhib: G; RA; RI; RBA.

**GAILDRAU, Jules**      **1816-1898**
Figure artist and illustrator. He was born in Paris 18 September 1816, and worked for numerous French papers, principally for *L'Illustration* and contributed to *The Illustrated London News* (Vizetelly). He exhibited at the Salon, 1848-57, and died in Paris in January 1898.

**GAILLIARD, François**      **1861-**
Painter of genre and illustrator. He was born at Brussels on 30 November 1861 and exhibited at Berlin in 1886. He worked for *L'Illustration* and contributed to *The Illustrated London News*, 1900.

**GALE, William**      **1823-1909**
Painter of history and religious themes. He was born in London in 1823 and studied at the RA Schools before travelling to the Continent, the Middle East and North Africa for study. He was a frequent exhibitor at London exhibitions, 1844-1892.
Contrib: *Passages From The Modern English Poets [1862].*
Exhib: B; BI, 1844-67; G; L; M; RA; RBA, 1844-92; RI; ROI; RSA.
Colls: Glasgow.

**GALLAGHER, F. O'Neill**      **fl.1901-1910**
Landscape painter and illustrator. Working at Corbeil, France, in 1910 and exhibiting at the NEA the same year.
Bibl: *The Studio*, Winter No.1900-01, p.62, illus.

**GALPIN, Will Dixon**      **fl.1882-1891**
Figure painter and illustrator. He was working at Roehampton, 1882-85, and at Bushey in 1884. In 1891 he contributed illustrations to Cassell's *The Picturesque Mediterranean.*
Exhib: B; G; L; RA; RBA.

**GAMMON, Reginald**      **1894-**
Watercolour artist, landscape painter and illustrator. He was born at Petersfield in 1894 and contributed black and white drawings to *Punch*, mostly of country subjects.
Exhib: NEA; RA; RBA; RI, 1938-40.
Bibl: *Mr. Punch With Horses and Hound*, New Punch Library, c.1930.

**GANDY, Herbert**      **fl.1881-1911**
Figure and domestic painter. He exhibited regularly from 1881-1911 and contributed fairy illustrations to *The Illustrated London News*, Christmas, 1903.
Exhib: B; G; L; M; RA; RHA; RI; ROI.

**GARDEN, G.M.**
Book decorator, contributing endpieces to *The English Illustrated Magazine*, 1896.

**GARDNER, W. Biscombe**      **c.1849-1919**
Landscape painter, wood engraver and etcher. He was born in about 1849 and painted in both watercolour and oil, but was best known as an engraver. He engraved work for *The Illustrated London News* and *The Graphic*, but specialised in work after such artists as Alma Tadema, Lord Leighton and G.F. Watts. He was working in London in 1880 and 1897, in Surrey, 1893 and 1883 and 1891, finally settling in Tunbridge Wells, 1906.
Contrib: *The Pall Mall Magazine; The English Illustrated Magazine [1887-88 and 1891-92].*
Exhib: G; L; New Gall.; RA; RI; ROI; RSW.
Colls: Margate; V & AM.

**GARLAND, Charles Trevor**      **fl.1874-1907**
Landscape, portrait and child painter and illustrator. He was working in London from 1874 and exhibiting regularly. He was living in Rome in 1880 and on his return to this country the following year, worked first in London and then in Penzance, 1892-1903. He was living in Colchester in 1907.
Contrib: *The Graphic [1874]; ILN [Christmas, 1882-86 (genre) and Christmas, 1892-93 (genre)].*
Exhib: B; G; L; M; RA; RBA; RI; ROI.

**GARLAND, Henry**      **fl.1854-1892**
Painter of landscape, genre and animals. He was born at Winchester and worked in North London from 1854 and in Leatherhead, Surrey from 1887, exhibiting regularly at the major exhibitions.
Contrib: *ILN [1868].*
Exhib: B; L; M; RA; RBA; ROI.
Colls: Leicester; Sunderland.

**GARLAND, Robert**      **c.1808-**
Draughtsman. He entered the RA Schools in December 1827 and drew views of London and its vicinity. He made the drawings for Winkle's *Cathedral Churches of England and Wales*, 1838.
Exhib: RA, 1826-31.

**GARRATT, Arthur Paine**      **1873-**
Portrait painter and illustrator. He was born in London on 17 July 1873 and was educated at the City of London School. He probably taught drawing at the Leys School, Cambridge and after some years portrait painting in America, returned to this country and settled in Chelsea. As a young man, Garratt was a prolific illustrator, and as a Londoner specialised in scenes of London life, crowded figure subjects such as the music hall and the riverside. A large pen and wash drawing of the Great Hall at Chelsea Hospital was recently on the market, the figures heavily built up in bodycolour.
Illus: *Lucian's Wonderland [St. J.B. Wynne Willson, 1899].*
Contrib: *The Graphic [1899-1910]; Black & White [1899-1900]; The Quiver [1900]; The Pall Mall Magazine [1900]; Pearson's Magazine; The Royal Magazine; Punch; The Sphere.*
Exhib: FAS, 1911; L; P; RA; Salon, 1903.
Bibl: *Who's Who in Art 1927.*

**GARRETT, Edmund Henry**      **1853-**
Painter, illustrator and engraver. Although an American artist, born in Albany on 19 October 1853 and working in Boston, after studying in Paris, he is included here as the illustrator of English editions of Ouida's novels.

**GASCOIGNE, John**
Figure artist. Contributed illustrations to *London Society*, 1865.

**GASKIN, Arthur Joseph**      **1862-1928**
Painter, illustrator, portraitist, designer. He was born at Birmingham in 1862 and married in 1894 Georgie Evelyn Cave France, (Mrs. Arthur Gaskin, q.v.). He was educated at Wolverhampton Grammar School and then studied at the Birmingham School of Art, eventually teaching there. Gaskin became increasingly interested in the crafts after contact with William Morris (q.v.) and the influence of the Kelmscott Press, for which he designed, is discernible in his own work and those of his students. He became the Director of the Jewellers and Silversmiths School at Victoria Street, Birmingham and was a member of the Royal Birmingham Society of Artists, he died on 4 June 1928.
Illus: *Stories and Fairy Tales [Hans Andersen, 1893]; Good King Wenceslas [Dr. Neale, 1895-96]; The Shepheardes Calender [Spenser, Kelmscott Press, 1896].*
Contrib: *The English Illustrated Magazines [1893-94]; A Book of Pictured Carols [Birmingham School, 1893]; A Book of Fairy Tales [Baring Gould, Birmingham School, 1894]; The Yellow Book [1896]; The Quarto [1897].*
Exhib: B; G; L; M; New Gall.; RA; RBA; RE.
Bibl: R.E.D. Sketchley, *English Book Illus.*, 1902, pp.10 and 126; Joseph E. Southall, *The Drawings of AG; The Studio*, Vol. 64, 1914.

**GASKIN, Mrs. Arthur (née Georgie Evelyn Cave France)**
Illustrator of children's books. She married Arthur J. Gaskin (q.v.), in 1894, helped him to design jewellery and exhibited 1896-1930.

Illus: *An ABC Book Pictured and Rhymed by . . . [1895-96]; Watts Divine and Moral Songs for Children [1896]; Horn-book Jingles [1896-97]; Little Girls and Little Boys [1898]; The Travellers and Other Stories [1898].*
Exhib: B; L; New Gall.; RMS.
Bibl: R.E.D. Sketchley, *English Book Illus.*, 1902, pp.101, 166.

**GASTINEAU, Henry G.   OWS                 1791-1876**
Landscape watercolourist and topographer. He was born in 1791 and studied at the RA Schools after being trained as an engraver. He travelled widely in Great Britain, painting picturesque scenery and was elected AOWS in 1821 and OWS in 1823. He worked as a drawing-master in Camberwell from 1827. He died there on 17 January 1876.

Publ: *Wales Illustrated [1829].*
Contrib: *The Surrey Tourist or Excursions Through Surrey [1821].*
Exhib: BI; OWS; RA.
Colls: BM; V & AM.

**GATCOMBE, George                       fl.1887-1897**
Black and white figure artist, specialising in theatrical illustrations.

Contrib: *Fun [1887-92]; Ally Sloper's Half Holiday [1890]; The Rambler [1897].*

**GAUGNIET**
French contributor to *The Illustrated London News*, 1848.

**GAVARNI   H.G.S. Chevalier             1804-1866**
Caricaturist and lithographer. He was born in Paris at 5 Rue des Vieilles-Haudriettes on 13 January 1804, his father having been an active revolutionary and his mother a member of a theatrical and painting family. In 1818 he went to study at the Pension Butet and then at the Conservatoire des Arts et Métiers, concentrating on machinery design. The artist had a few plates issued in Paris about 1825 signed 'HG' or 'H. Chevalier' but his main work was as an architectural etcher for Jean Adam and later surveying in the Haute Pyrénées. He settled in Paris again in June 1828.

From 1829, 'Gavarni' as Chevalier now called himself, began to develop as a designer; his early productions were costumes and fashion plates and in 1830, during the Revolution of that year, he produced two satirical prints of the departing Bourbons. Gavarni's interests were always the study of humanity, faces, figures, groups on the Paris streets. A series of lithographs was published in the *Artiste* on the 'Physionomies de la Population de Paris' and followed by 'Travestissements' in a similar vein, both attracting enormous attention. He joined the staff of *Charivari* and from this time onwards, his work appeared there and in *Le Musée des Familles, Le Caricature, Le Figaro, La Renaissance, Le Bulletin de L'Amis Des Arts* and *La Sylphide*. He also contributed to *La Revue et Gazette Musicale, L'Illustration, Le Bossu, the Puppet Show* and *Paris*.

On November 21 1847, Gavarni left for England and spent the next four years there, travelling widely, making a journey to Scotland and meeting English artists. This resulted in *Studies: Rustic Groups of Figures*, published by Rowney. In 1850 he published a series of tinted wood engravings, *Gavarni in London* and on his return to Paris in 1851, *Les Anglais peints par aux-mêmes*. Gavarni profited by his visit to England by developing a much wetter and broader technique in watercolours. His work fell out of favour in the late 1850s and he died of consumption on 24 November 1866. Gavarni admired the work of his great contemporary Daumier, but unlike him was more of a humorist than a caricaturist.

Illus: *The Wandering Jew [Sue, 1845]; Dames Aux Camélias; Petits bonheurs de la vie; Mille et Une Nuits; Symphonies de L'Hiver; Gil Blas [1863].*
Contrib: *ILN [1848-55].*
Colls: V & AM.
Bibl: Edmond and Jules de Goncourt, *Gavarni*, Paris, 1924; Franzt and Uzanne, *Daumier and Gavarni*, Studio, 1904.

See illustrations (right and p.315).

**GAVIN, Miss Jessie                      fl.1903-1914**
Illustrator. She was working at Oxton, Cheshire from 1903-14 and contributed frontispieces to some of Messrs. Jack's publications. She was a good portraitist in solid outline and was clearly influenced by the Beggarstaff Brothers. She signs G

Illus: *Stories of Hoffmann; Stories of Poe; Stories of Gautier [1908].*
Exhib: L, 1903-12.

**GEAR, J.W.                             fl.1851-1852**
Painter of portraits and engraver. He specialised in family groups in watercolours, in theatrical personalities and paintings on porcelain. Contributed to *The Illustrated London News*, 1848.

Exhib: RA; RBA, 1821-52.

**GELL, Sir William                      1774-1836**
Topographical draughtsman and traveller. He was born in 1774 and after studying at the RA Schools and practising as an architect, he settled in Italy in 1820 and became Chamberlain to the exiled Caroline, Princess of Wales. He is best remembered by his series of illustrated books and he died at Naples in 1836.

Illus: *The Topography of Troy [1804, AT 399]; Geography and Antiquities of Ithaca [1807]; The Itinerary of Greece [1810, AT 129]; Views in Barbary [1815, AT 297]; Attica [1817]; Itinerary of the Morea [1818]; Pompeiana [1817-19]; The Walls of Rome [1820]; Narrative of a Journey to the Morea [1823]; Topography of Rome [1834]; A Tour in the Lakes [1797 (edited by W. Rollinson, 1968)].*
Colls: Barrow-in-Furness; BM.

*GAVARNI (H.G.S. Chevalier) 1804-1866. 'The Bar-Maid.' An illustration for* Gavarni in London, *1850. Tinted lithograph.*

*GAVARNI (H.G.S. Chevalier) 1804-1866. 'The Queen's State Coachman.' An unpublished study for Gavarni in London, 1850. Pencil and chinese white.*
Victoria and Albert Museum

**GENDALL, John**　　　　　　　　　　　　**1790-1865**

Topographical artist. He was born in 1790 on Exe Island, Exeter and after showing early talent was noticed by Sir John Soane and introduced by him to Rudolph Ackermann. He worked with him for many years as draughtsman, lithographer and manager, travelling all over Britain and to Normandy to make drawings. He settled at Exeter again in 1830 and taught drawing at Cole's School, dying in the city in 1865.

Illus: *Picturesque Tour of the Seine [1821, AT 90 (with A. Pugin)]*; Westall's *Country Seats [1823-28]*.
Exhib: BI, 1818-63; RA.

**GÉNIOLE, Alfred André**　　　　　　　　**1813-1861**

Painter of genre and portraits. He was born at Nancy, France on 1 January 1813 and became a pupil of Baron Gros, exhibiting in the Salon from 1839. He contributed illustrations to *The Illustrated London News*, 1853. Died at Bicêtre on 12 January 1861.

**GERE, Charles March　RA ARWS**　　　　**1869-1957**

Portrait painter and watercolourist, illustrator, decorator and designer of stained glass. He was born at Gloucester in 1869 and was educated at Birmingham and in Italy, training as an artist with the Birmingham School of Art, remaining for many years as a teacher. He was associated, like his colleague Arthur Gaskin (q.v.), with William Morris at the Kelmscott Press and later with C.H. St. John Hornby at the Ashendene Press. He was an accomplished decorative artist and designed for embroidery, but after settling at Painswick, Gloucestershire in 1902, began to specialise in landscapes of the Cotswolds and North Italy. He became a member of the NEA in 1911, ARWS, 1921,

RWS, 1927 and was elected ARA in 1933 and RA in 1939.

Gere's illustrations in black and white have the rather mannered angularity of the Birmingham School and his topographical work is very close in feeling to that of E.H. New (q.v.).

Contrib: *News From Nowhere [William Morris, Kelmscott Press, 1893 (frontis.)]*; *Russian Fairy Tales [1893]*; *A Book of Pictured Carols [The Birmingham School [1893]*; *The Imitation of Christ [1894]*; *The Quest [1894-96]*; *The Yellow Book [1896]*.
Exhib: B; G; L; M; NEA, 1910-24; New Gall.; RA 1890-1956; RHA; RWS.
Bibl: R.E.D. Sketchley, *English Book Illus.*, 1902, pp.12, 50, 126.

**GERMAN, Dick**

Figure artist. He contributed to *Punch*, 1914.

**GIBBS, Percy W.**　　　　　　　　　　　　**fl.1894-1937**

Portrait and landscape painter and illustrator. He studied at the RA Schools and won the Creswick prize in 1895. Worked at East Molesey. Contributed to *The Graphic*, 1906.

Exhib: G; L; RA.

**GIBERNE, Edgar**　　　　　　　　　　　　**fl.1872-1890**

Sporting artist and illustrator. He worked from Epsom and drew Highland and Indian sporting subjects for magazines and illustrated children's books.

Illus: *Binko's Blue [H.C. Merivale, 1884]*.
Contrib: *ILN [1889-90]*.
Exhib: RA; RBA, 1872-88.

**GIBSON, Charles Dana**　　　　　　　　　**1867-1944**

Black and white artist and illustrator. He was born at Roxbury, Massachusetts, U.S.A. on 14 September 1867 and was educated at Flushing High School, followed by training at the Art Students' League, New York. Gibson studied with Augustus Saint Gaudens and attended Julian's in Paris. Within a year or so of his first drawing from life in 1888, Gibson had become an international figure and recognised on both sides of the Atlantic. He was the chronicler in visual terms of American high society, the world of luxury-laden and zestful New York and Boston where East Coast aristocrats hunted as a group and rigorously excluded all newcomers. Gibson did more than create a beautiful type of American girl 'the Gibson Girl', he created a fashion. As Pennell remarks, 'Not only has he countless artless imitators on both sides of the Atlantic, but Fifth Avenue today is like an endless procession of Gibsons.' Although his subjects were mostly American, he made visits to Europe and drew society in Paris and London. *The Studio*, in 1897, considered that they were unsuccessful, Gibson remaining a foreigner who could not capture a cockney or a society figure. His sister-in-law was Lady Astor.

His penwork was done on a very large scale which was greatly reduced, giving an incredible fineness and finish to the printed page. The execution is brilliant, but the compositions are often repetitive and a nauseating sentimentality creeps in from time to time. Gibson remains very much an American collecting field.

Illus: *Drawings by C.D. Gibson; Pictures of People [1897]; London As Seen By C. Dana Gibson [1897]; People of Dickens [1897]; Sketches and Cartoons; The Education of Mr. Pipp; Americans; A Widow and Her Friends; The Social Ladder; The Weaker Sex; Everyday People; Our Neighbours; Other People [1911]*.
Contrib: *Life*.
Exhib: FAS, 1896.
Bibl: Joseph Pennell, *Pen Drawing and Pen Draughtsmen*, 1894, pp.244-245.
See illustration (p.316).

**GILBERT, Frederick**　　　　　　　　　　**fl.1862-1877**

Painter, watercolourist and illustrator. He was the brother of Sir John Gilbert (q.v.), and lived with him at Blackheath. He specialised in genre and history subjects and illustrations from Tennyson's works.

Contrib: *Cassell's Magazine [1866]; Aunt Judy's Magazine [1866]; London Society [1870]*.
Exhib: RBA.

CHARLES DANA GIBSON 1867-1944. 'His Sister.' Illustration to Pictures of People, 1897.

## GILBERT, Sir John
**1817-1897**

Historical painter and illustrator. He was born at Blackheath in 1817 and after being apprenticed to an estate agent, he studied with George Lance and taught himself to draw on the block, engrave, etch and model. He was the first major figure to emerge alongside Harvey (q.v.) in the revival of wood engraving. Chatto & Jackson date his success from the publication of *Hall's English Ballads* in 1843, 'the first work of any consequence that presented a combination of the best artists of the time. Indeed it was the leader in what may be called the Illustrated Christmas Books of the present day. Since this period Mr. Gilbert has probably produced more drawings on wood than any other artist ...' Gilbert was the first serious artist to tackle news illustrating for *The Illustrated London News*, 1843 and remained as a major contributor until late in life. He made a reputation however, out of elaborate semi-allegorical pages, festive Christmas scenes and representations of the seasons for special issues of magazines, for which he was paid enormous sums of money. The acclaim with which Gilbert's work was met seems almost incredible, the Victorians considering his rather dull historical set-pieces as equal to the work of Doré! He became President of the Royal Society of Painters in Watercolours in 1871, was knighted in the following year and elected ARA in 1872 and RA in 1876. He died on 5 October 1897, having given a large collection of his works to various provincial art galleries in 1892.

Illus: *City Scenes [1845]; Children of the New Forest [Capt. Marryat, 1847]; The Pleasures of the Country, Stories For Young People [Mrs. Myrtle, 1851]; The Salamandrine [1853]; Hide and Seek [Wilkie Collins 1854]; Basil [Wilkie Collins, 1862]; Fairy Tales [Countess D'Aulnoy, 1881]; Shakespeare's Works [1856-58]; Adele [J. Kavanagh, 1862].*
Contrib: *Punch [1842(frontis.)-1882]; ILN [1843-79]; Sunday at Home [1852]; The Illustrated London Magazine [1853]; Proverbial Philosophy [M. Tupper, 1854]; Longfellow's Poems [1855]; Scott's Lady of The Lake [1856]; The Illustrated Times [1856]; Poets of the Nineteenth Century [Willmott, 1857]; The Book of Job [1857]; The Proverbs of Solomon [1858]; Lays of the Holy Land [1858]; The Home Affections [Charles Mackay, 1858];*
*Montgomery's Poems [1858]; Poetry of the Elizabethan Age [1860]; Songs and Sonnets of Shakespeare [1860]; The Welcome Guest [1860]; Eliza Cook's Poems [1861]; The Leisure Hour [1861-63]; The British Workman [1862]; The Band of Hope Review [1862]; English Sacred Poetry [Willmott, 1862]; Boys' Book of Ballads [1862]; Early English Poems [1863]; The Months Illustrated [1864]; Wordsworth's Poems [1865]; Legends and Lyrics [Proctor, 1866]; Foxe's Book of Martyrs [1866]; Once a Week [1866-67]; Cassell's History of England [1867]; London Society [1868-69]; Cassell's Family Paper [n.d.]; Choice Series [1857-64]; The Standard Poets and Standard Library; The Graphic [1877].*
Exhib: B; L; M; RA, 1838-51 and 1867-97; RBA, 1836-1892; RWS.
Colls: Ashmolean; BM; Manchester; Nat. Gall., Scotland; V & AM.
Bibl: F. Reid, *Illustrators of The Sixties,* 1928, pp.20-23; *Who Was Who 1897-1916;* M. Hardie, *Watercol. Paint. in Brit.,* Vol. III, 1968, pp.94-96, illus. See illustration (p.71).

## GILBERT, Sir William Schwenck 'BAB'
**1836-1911**

Journalist, playwright and amateur illustrator. He was born at Southampton Street, Strand on 18 November 1836 and was educated at Ealing and London University. He was called to the Bar in 1864 and served as Clerk to the Privy Council, 1857-1902. From his first introduction to Sir Arthur Sullivan in 1869 developed the fertile production of Savoy operas up to the year 1896. Gilbert's earlier career and reputation was made as 'Bab' the contributor of humorous verse to *Fun* illustrated by the author's own grotesque thumbnail sketches. There were really two sides to his artistic productions, the monstrous and savage creatures of the *Bab Ballads,* very much in the tradition of Lear, and rather pretty fairy sketches and drawings of young girls. Although the sketches were slight, they won the admiration of that fastidious critic Max Beerbohm. Gilbert died at Harrow Weald 29 May 1911. He was knighted, 1907.

Contrib: *Juvenile Verse Picture Book [1848]; Fun [1861]; Magic Mirror [1867-68]; London Society [1868]; Good Words For The Young [1869]; The Graphic [1876].*
Colls: BM.
Bibl: Leslie Baily, *The Gilbert and Sullivan Book,* 1952, p.44; Philip James, Introduction to *Selected Bab Ballads,* 1955.

## GILES, Alice B.  fl.1896-1924

Illustrator. She was a student at the New Cross Art School in 1896-97 and was working at Surbiton, Surrey in 1924 and was a member of the Design and Industries Association. She specialised in the illustration of child's stories where animals were included.

Exhib: RA, 1903.
Bibl: *The Studio*, Vol.8, 1896, p.229, illus.; 1897.

## GILES, Godfrey Douglas  1857-1923

Painter of horses and military scenes and illustrator. He was born in India in 1857 and served as a professional soldier there, and in Afghanistan and Egypt. He studied in Paris and was a regular exhibitor in London, 1882-1904. He was also a caricaturist.

Contrib: *The Graphic [1885, (horses)]; Black & White [1891, (sport)]; Vanity Fair [1899-1909, 1903]*.
Exhib: G; GG; L; M; RA; RBA; ROI; RSA.

## GILKS, Thomas  fl.1840-1876

Wood engraver, writer and illustrator. His bill head describes him as 'Draughtsman, Engraver, Ornamental Printer'. He was active from about 1840, engraved the plates for John Leech's *The Comic English Grammar*, and H. Fitzcock's *All About Shakespeare*. He illustrated his own *Study of the Art and Progress of Wood Engraving*.

Contrib: *ILN [1858, (Australia)]; London Society [1870]*.
Exhib: RBA, 1870.

## GILL, Arthur J.P.

Contributor to *Judy*, 1889.

*JAMES GILLRAY 1757-1815. 'Billingsgate Eloquence.' Published 6 January 1795. Engraving. 5ins. x 3¼ins. (12.7cm x 8.3cm).*

*JAMES GILLRAY 1757-1815. 'Pulpit Eloquence.' Published 6 January 1795. Engraving. 5ins. x 3¼ins. (12.7cm x 8.3cm).*

## GILLETT, (Edward) Frank  RI  1874-1927

Sporting artist and illustrator of equestrian subjects. He was born at Worlingham, Suffolk on 23 July 1874, son of the Rev. Jesse Gillett of Aldeby and was educated at Gresham's. He left school at sixteen and after six years as a Lloyds' clerk, joined the staff of the *Daily Graphic*, 1898, remaining on the paper until 1908. He was subsequently with *Black & White*, 1908-11 and with *The Illustrated Sporting and Dramatic News*, 1910-23. Gillett, who was elected RI in 1909, was working at St. Albans that year, in London 1911 and in Aldeby, Suffolk from 1918. His pen drawings of horses are always convincing but they can be stiff.

Contrib: *Fun [1895]; Judy [1898]; The Ludgate Monthly; The Idler*.
Exhib: G; L; RA; RI.

## GILLRAY, James  1757-1815

Caricaturist and engraver. He was born at Chelsea in 1757 and after being educated by the Moravians at Bedford was apprenticed to a letter engraver and worked under classical engravers such as Ryland and Bartolozzi in stipple. He trained at the R.A. Schools and did some book illustrations for Macklin's *Tom Jones* before turning to caricature in about 1780. His earlier works were published by the printseller Robert Wilkinson of Cornhill, forsaking him for Fores in about 1787. Gillray finally came to rest as chief caricaturist to Mrs. Humphrey at New and Old Bond Street, where he lodged till his death. Gillray was the first professional caricaturist in this country, he simplified the art of the amateurs by replacing archaic symbols with forceful design and his art training enabled him to work on a more heroic scale than his predecessors. His work hit very hard and as the artist was something of a poltical maverick, he was assiduously courted by all parties. His frequent satires on Royal extravagance such as 'A Voluptuary under the horrors of Digestion' 1792 and the caricatures of Napoleon and Charles James Fox, created in their realism and savagery a whole new field for the caricaturist. Although much of his work dates from before 1800, a group of marvellous caricatures appeared in the early 1800s including 'Tiddy-Doll, the great French-Gingerbread Baker', 1806, 'Uncorking Old Sherry', 1805, 'The Plum-pudding in danger', 1805 and most famous of all 'The King of Brobdingnag and Gulliver', 1803. Gillray's last work was engraved in 1811 shortly before he became insane; his position was taken by the young George Cruikshank (q.v.). Original drawings by this artist are very rare, they show a very free pen line and strong influence of the Old Masters. He died on 1 June 1815 and was buried at St. James's Church, Piccadilly.

Colls: Ashmolean; BM; New York Pub. Library; V & AM.
Bibl: T. Wright, *The Caricatures of JG*, 1851; Joseph Grego, *The Works of JG*, 1873; Draper Hill, *Mr. G The Caricaturist*, 1965; Draper Hill, *Fashionable Contrasts: Caricatures by JG*; 1966; *Country Life*, 12 January 1967.
See illustrations (Colour Plates V p.56 and p.317).

**GLAZIER, Louise M.**          fl.1900-1912
Wood engraver and illustrator. She was working at Mitcham in 1902 and at Bruges in 1906. Her domestic and village scenes recall the Newlyn School. She designed book plates and examples of her work occasionally come on the market.

Illus: *The Field Flowers Lore [1912]*.
Contrib: *The Dome [1900]*.
Exhib: Baillie Gall.; L.

**GLENNIE, J.D.**          1796-1874
Painter, etcher and amateur lithographer. He was born in 1796 and illustrated Maria Graham's *Letters On India* and *Views on the Continent* and contributed to *The Antiquarian and Topographical Cabinet*, 1811.

Exhib: RA, 1810-19.

**GLICK**
Contributor of cartoons to *Vanity Fair*, 1897. This has been identified as Count Gleichen, 1833-1891, who died in London or his daughter, Countess Feodora Gleichen who worked there as a sculptor.

**GLIDDON, Charles**          fl.1865-1870
Illustrator. He apparently drew for an edition of Walter Scott's novels, studies for *Red Gauntlet* and *The Fortunes of Nigel* in pencil, brown ink and brown wash are in the Ashmolean Museum, Oxford.

**GLOAG, Isobel Lilian   ROI**          1865-1917
Painter of romantic subjects, portraits and illustrator. She was born of Scottish parents in London in 1865 and studied at the St. John's Wood School, South Kensington and Paris and worked with M.W. Ridley (q.v.). She undertook poster design, flower paintings and stained glass work and was elected ROI in 1909. She died on 5 January 1917.

Illus: projected editions of: *William Tell* and *Loves Labour Lost*.
Contrib: *The Graphic [1910]*.
Exhib: B; G; L; RA; RBA; RI; ROI; SWA.

**GLOVER, G.C.**
Figure artist. He contributed illustrations to *Fun*, 1890-92, *Chums* and *Cassell's Saturday Journal*.

**GOBLE, Warwick**          fl.1893-1925
Watercolour painter and illustrator. After being educated at the City of London School, he joined the staff of *The Pall Mall Gazette* and later *The Westminster Gazette* as artist. Goble was strongly influenced by Japanese art and by Chinese paintings, his colour washes are extremely subtle and stroked on with the brush, his compositions consciously oriental. He worked almost entirely for publishers like Messrs. Black and Messrs. Macmillan who were specialising in colour plate books. He made a tour of the French battlefields in 1919.

Illus: *Constantinople [A. Van Milligen, 1905]; The Water Babies [C. Kingsley, 1909]; The Green Willow and Other Japanese Fairy Tales [Grace James, 1910]; Folk Tales of Bengal; The Fairy Book [Mrs. Craik, 1914]; The Modern Readers. Chaucer; Treasure Island; Kidnapped [1924]; The Alhambra; The Greater*

*Abbeys of England; The Book of Fairy Poetry.*
Contrib: *The Minister [1895]; ILN [1897-98, 1912]; The World Wide Magazine [1898]; The Pall Mall Budget; The Windsor Magazine.*
Exhib: FAS, 1910, 1911; L; RA.

**GODDARD, George Bouverie**          1832-1886
Animal painter and illustrator. He was born at Salisbury in 1832 and after recognition as an infant prodigy, travelled to London in 1849 and spent two years studying at the Zoological Gardens. After this he returned to Wiltshire for a period and finally settled in London in 1857. Goddard made drawings for many magazines and contributed some humorous and sporting subjects. He died at Brook Green, London in 1886.

Contrib: *ILN [1865-84]; Punch [1865]; Once a Week [1866]; London Society [1868]; The Graphic [1880-84]*.
Exhib: B; G; L; RA; RBA, 1864-72.
Colls: Liverpool.

**GODDARD, Louis Charles**          fl.1904-1921
Portrait painter. He worked at Stockport, Manchester and Wallasey, Cheshire. He contributed social subjects to *Punch*, 1904.

Exhib: B; L; N.

**GODEFROY**
French illustrator contributing comic genre strips to *Fun*, 1900, in the style of Caran D'Ache (q.v.).

Bibl: J. Pennell, *Pen Drawing and Pen Draughtsmen*, 1894, p.129, illus.

**GODWIN, James**          -1876
Painter of genre, draughtsman and illustrator. Working in Kensington from 1846, having studied at the RA Schools. Godwin's draughtsmanship was very influenced by the German School and although his pencil work is extremely exact and delicate, it lacks real power. He was a regular exhibitor at London exhibitions and died there in 1876.

Illus: *The Dream Chintz [1851 (child's book)]*.
Contrib: *ILN [1853-67 (Christmas and decor)]; The Poetical Works of E.A. Poe [1853]; Poets of the Nineteenth Century [Willmott, 1857]; The Home Affections [Charles Mackay, 1858]; London Society [1863]*.
Exhib: BI, 1846, 1850; RA; RBA, 1846-51.
Colls: V & AM.

**GOEDECKER, F.**
Contributor to *Vanity Fair*, 1884-85, signing 'GD' or 'FG' in monogram.

**GOLDIE, Cyril**          fl.1910-1925
Painter and illustrator, working in Liverpool. He contributed a headpiece and full page illustration to *The Quarto*, 1896, in a grotesque art nouveau style.

Exhib: L; NEA, 1910-22.

**GOLDSMITH, J.**
Amateur draughtsman. He contributed an illustration to Britton's *Beauties of England and Wales*, 1814.

**GOODALL, Edward Angelo   RWS**          1819-1908
Landscape painter and illustrator. He was born on 8 June 1819, the son of E. Goodall, the engraver, and brother of F. and W. Goodall (qq.v.). He was educated at University College School, London and at the age of seventeen, won a Society of Arts silver medal for watercolour, 1836-37. In 1841 he was appointed artist to the British Guiana Boundary Expedition and travelled there with Sir Robert Schomburgh, remaining in South America for three years. In 1854-55, Goodall was artist correspondent to *The Illustrated London News* in the Crimea, and in succeeding years made study trips to France, Italy, Spain, Egypt, Tangiers, Turkey and Greece. He was elected ARWS, 1858 and RWS, 1864. He died on 16 April 1908 and was buried at Highgate.

Illus: *Twelve Views in the Interior of Guiana [Bentley and Schomburgh, 1840-41, AT 720]*.
Contrib: *ILN [1855]; Poets of the Nineteenth Century [Willmott, 1857]; Rhymes and Roundelayes.*

Exhib: BI, 1841; L; M; RA; RBA, 1841-60; RWS.
Colls: Ashmolean; BM; Dublin; Liverpool; Manchester; Sydney; V & AM.
Bibl: Chatto & Jackson, *Treatise on Wood Engraving*, 1861, p.598; M. Hardie, *Watercolour Paint. in Brit.*, Vol.III, 1968, pp.163-164 illus.

## GOODALL, Frederick   RA HRI                    1822-1904

Landscape, genre and biblical painter and illustrator. He was born on 17 September 1822, the son of Edward Goodall, the engraver and brother of E.A. and W. Goodall (qq.v.). Studied engraving with his father and brother, encouraged by Ruskin and in 1837 won a Society of Arts silver medal. He travelled to Normandy in 1838, 1839 and 1840, to Brittany in 1841, 1842 and 1845 and to Ireland with F.W. Topham (q.v.) in 1843. He went to Egypt for eight months in 1858-59 and this to some extent changed his style; his earlier works followed the genre subjects of Wilkie, his later ones took the Nile and the Pyramids as their centre piece. He returned to Egypt again in 1870 with his brother E.A. Goodall. Goodall was elected RI, 1867, ARA, 1853 and RA, 1863 and became an Honorary Retired Academician in 1902. He died at Harrow, in the house designed for him by Norman Shaw, on 28 July 1904.

Contrib: *The Traveller [Goldsmith, Art Union, 1851]; Passages From The Poets [Junior Etching Club, 1862]; Rhymes and Roundelayes; Ministering Children.*

Exhib: B; FAS, 1894; G; GG; L; M; RA; RI; ROI.
Colls: BM; Leicester; Liverpool; Manchester; V & AM.
Bibl: *Reminiscences of FG*, 1902; Chatto & Jackson, *Treatise on Wood Engraving*, 1861, p.599; M. Hardie, *Watercol. Paint. In Brit.*, Vol.III, 1868, pp.163-164, illus.

## GOODALL, Walter   RWS                    1830-1889

Painter and watercolourist. He was born in London in 1830, the son of Edward Goodall, the engraver and brother of E.A. and F. Goodall (qq.v.). He studied art at the Clipstone St. Academy, the Government School of Design and at the RA Schools. He was elected RWS in 1853 and spent the winter of 1868 in Rome making Venetian studies. He died at Clapham, Bedfordshire in 1889.

Contrib: *Recollections of the Great Exhibition of 1851 [1851].*
Exhib: RA; RWS.
Bibl: M. Hardie, *Watercol. Paint. in Brit.*, Vol.III, 1968, p.164.

## GOODMAN, Arthur Jule                    fl.1890-1913

Illustrator and special artist. He was born at Hartford, Connecticut, U.S.A. and studied as an architect at the Institute of Technology, Boston. He worked as a lithographer with Matt Morgan (q.v.) and then left for Europe to study at Julian's in Paris and under Bouguereau. His

*SIR FRANCIS CARRUTHERS GOULD 1844-1925. 'Birds of a Feather.' Caricatures of Kruger and the Duke of Bedford. Pen and ink. Signed with initials.*
Woburn Abbey Collection

319

first published work was for *Harper's* in 1889 and on arrival in London, he became Special for *The Pall Mall Gazette* and contributed 'War Notes' making a considerable reputation as an illustrator of military subjects. He was working at Gedling, Nottinghamshire, from 1902 to 1913.

Illus: *Clarence [Bret Harte, 1897].*
Contrib: *The Girls' Own Paper [1890-1900]; The Pall Mall Magazine; The Pall Mall Budget [1893]; ILN [1893]; St. Pauls [1894]; Good Words [1894]; Good Cheer [1894]; The Minister [1895]; Pearson's Magazine [1896]; The English Illustrated Magazine [1895-97]; Madame; The Idler.*
Exhib: Nottingham; P.
Colls: V & AM.
Bibl: *The Idler,* Vol.9, pp.803-816, illus.

**GOODMAN, Walter**                                    1838-
Painter of portraits, genre and illustrator. He was born in London, 11 May 1838, the son of Julia Goodman, née Salaman, the domestic painter. He studied at Leigh's and travelled in Europe and in Cuba, 1864-69 and to North America. He exhibited regularly in London from 1859, including a portrait of Wilkie Collins. He was living at Brighton in 1889 and latterly at Henfield, Sussex in 1906.

Publ: *The Pearl of The Antilles or an Artist in Cuba.*
Contrib: *ILN [1877].*
Exhib: BI, 1859-61; RA; RBA, 1859-90; RSA.

**GOODWIN, Ernest 'GEE'**                    fl.1894-1903
Black and white artist in the style of Phil May. He was working at 20 St. Bride St., London E.C., 1902-03.

Contrib: *St. Pauls [1894]; Pick-Me-Up, [1895]; The Sketch; The Idler.*

**GORDON, G.A.**
Contributed illustration to *The Parade,* 1897.

**GORDON, Godfrey Jervis (Jan)**                    1882-1944
Painter, etcher, lithographer and illustrator. He was born at Finchampstead, 11 March 1882 and was educated at Marlborough College and Truro School of Mines. He was art critic of *The New Witness,* 1916-19, of *The Observer* and *Athenaeum,* 1919 and of *Land and Water,* 1920. He collaborated with his wife on illustrated travel books. RBA, 1935. He signs his work 'J.G.' or 'Gordon'.

Illus: *Poor Folk in Spain [1922]; Misadventures with a Donkey in Spain [1924]; Two Vagabonds in the Balkans [1925]; Two Vagabonds in Languedoc [1925]; Two Vagabonds in Sweden and Lapland [1926]; Two Vagabonds in Albania [1927].*
Exhib: L; NEA; RA; RBA; RI.

**GOSSE, Philip Henry**                    1810-1888
Zoologist and artist. He farmed in the United States and Canada before returning to England to devote himself to the study of insects in 1839. He illustrated many of his own books and was elected FRS in 1856; he was the father of Sir Edmund Gosse.

Publ: *The Canadian Naturalist [1840]; Introduction to Zoology [1843]; Birds of Jamaica [1847]; A Naturalist's Sojourn in Jamaica [1851, AT 688]; Rambles on the Devonshire Coast [1853]; The Aquarium [1854]; Manual of Marine Zoology [1855-56]; Actinologia Britannica [1858-60]; Romance of Natural History [1860].*
Bibl: E. Gosse, *Father and Son,* 1907.

**GOSSOP, Robert Percy**                    fl.1901-1925
Black and white artist, sometimes working in wash. He was a contributor to *Fun,* 1901, and was working at Henrietta St., Covent Garden, London in 1925.

Colls: V & AM.

**GOUGH, Arthur J.**                    fl.1897-1914
Landscape painter and illustrator. He was working at West Hampstead, 1903-14 and contributed black and white drawings to *The Rambler,* 1897.

Exhib: RA; RI.

**GOULD, Elizabeth (née Coxon)**                    1804-1841
Ornithological painter. She was born at Ramsgate, the daughter of a sea captain and in 1829 married John Gould FRS, 1804-81, the author and publisher of *Gould's Birds.* She worked with the young Edward Lear in producing watercolours as guides to the finished illustrated works. She helped with *The Birds of Europe,* and *A Century of Birds From The Himalayan Mountains* and accompanied her husband to Australia, for his *Birds of Australia,* 1838-40. Her husband frequently took the credit for her work.

Bibl: *Country Life,* June 25 1964.

**GOULD, Sir Francis Carruthers**                    1844-1925
Political cartoonist and caricaturist. He was born at Barnstaple on 2 December 1844, the son of an architect and after being educated in private schools, joined the London Stock Exchange. While working as a broker and jobber, he began to draw caricatures for his own amusement, eventually endowing them with his own brand of radicalism and publishing them. Gould illustrated for the Christmas numbers of *Truth,* became a member of the staff of *The Pall Mall Gazette* in 1890 and of *The Westminster Gazette,* 1893-1914, acting as assistant editor in 1896. He founded his own paper, *Picture Politics,* which ran from 1894-1914 and published numerous illustrated books. His reputation in the Edwardian period was considerable and Lord Rosebery was reported to have called him 'the greatest asset of the Liberal Party'. Gould was not a great artist, but he was a very political animal and had the talent to catch a likeness and develop a theme. His

*PAUL MARY GRAY 1842-1866. Woman and child. Illustration study for* The Quiver. *Pencil. 6⅜ins. x 4¾ins. (16.2cm x 12.1cm). Victoria and Albert Museum*

sketches of the sharp face of Joseph Chamberlain are amongst his best works and he introduced silhouette work into political satire. He was knighted in 1906 and died on 1 January 1925.

His cartoons are among the more attractive ephemera of the 1890s still obtainable.

Illus: *Michael's Crag [Grant Allen, 1893]; Who Killed Cock Robin? [1897]; Tales Told in the Zoo [1900]; Froissart's Modern Chronicles; The Struwwelpeter Alphabet [H. Begbie, 1900]; Political Caricature [1903]; Cartoons in Rhyme and Line [Sir W. Lawson, 1905].*
Contrib: *Vanity Fair [1879, 1890, 1897-99]; The Strand Magazine [1891]; Cassell's Family Magazine; Fun [1901].*
Exhib: Brook St. and Walker's Galleries, 1907-24.
Colls: BM; V & AM.
Bibl: *The Studio,* Winter No., 1900-01, p.40, illus.
See illustration (p.319)

## GOURSAT, George   See 'SEM'

## GOW, Mary L. (Mrs. Hall)   RI                    1851-1929
Figure artist and illustrator. She was born in London in 1851 and studied at the Queens Square School of Art and at Heatherley's. She married Sydney P. Hall, MVO, the painter and illustrator (q.v.) and was elected NWS in 1875 and RI in the same year.

Contrib: *The Quiver [1890]; The Graphic [1892]; Cassell's Family Magazine.*
Exhib: B; G; GG; M; New Gall.; RA; RI.

## GOWER, Charlotte
Botanical illustrator. She provided the illustrations in colour and tail-pieces for *The Wild Flowers of Great Britain,* by R. Hogg and George W. Johnson, 1863-64.

## GOWER, Francis LEVESON-, 1st Earl of Ellesmere   KG   1800-1857
Amateur artist. He was born 1 January 1800 and is only known to have illustrated one work, his wife's *Journal of a Tour in the Holy Land.* 1841, AT 384. He died 18 February 1857.

## GOWER, S.J.
Contributor to *The Illustrated London News,* 1860.

## GRAHAM, J.                                    fl.1810-1840
Contributor to *Bell's British Theatre* and *Cookes British Theatre.*

## GRAHAM, Peter   RA ARSA                        1836-1921
Landscape painter. He was born in Edinburgh and studied under R.S. Lauder at the Trustees Academy and with John Ballantyne. He settled in London in 1866, being elected ARA in 1877 and RA in 1881. He made a considerable reputation as a painter of Scottish scenery and was elected ARSA in 1860. He died at St. Andrews on 19 October 1921.

Contrib: *London Society [1878].*
Exhib: B; G; L; M; RA; RSA.
Colls: Worcester.

## GRAHAM, Thomas Alexander Ferguson             1840-1906
Figure and portrait painter. He was born at Kirkwall in 1840 and studied at the Trustees Academy, 1855 alongside Orchardson, J. Pettie, P. Graham and J. MacWhirter (qq.v.) under R.S. Lauder. On moving to London, he set up house with Pettie and Orchardson and exhibited there from 1863. He was elected HRSA in 1883 and received a commendation at the Paris Exhibition, 1900. He died in Hampstead, 24 December 1906.

Contrib: *Good Words [1861-63].*
Exhib: B; G; GG; L; M; New Gall; RA; RBA; RI; ROI; RSA.

*CHARLES GREEN RI 1848-1898. 'Quilp in a Wherry.' Illustration for* The Old Curiosity Shop, *by Charles Dickens 1871. Pen and wash with chinese white. 3⅞ins. x 5½ins. (9.9cm x 14cm).*
Victoria and Albert Museum

**GRAHAM, Winifred**
Illustrator of children's books. She was described in *The Studio,* Vol.18, 1899-1900, as an artist of 'poke-bonnetted and short waisted maidens . . . made familiar to us by Miss Greenaway'.
Illus: *Lamb's Poetry for Children [1898]; Mrs. Leicester's School [C. & M. Lamb, 1899].*
Bibl: R.E.D. Sketchley, *English Book Illustration,* 1902, pp.101, 166.

**GRANBY, The Marchioness of      See RUTLAND, Violet, Duchess of**

**GRANDVILLE, Jean-Ignace Isidore Gérard      1803-1847**
Draughtsman, watercolourist, caricaturist and lithographer. He was born at Nancy on 15 September 1803 and went to Paris in 1823, where he had considerable success as a lithographer and produced a series of cartoons on domestic and political matters. He made many drawings for *La Caricature,* specialising in metamorphosed objects and animals, wildly fantastic and offering a nineteenth century foretaste of surrealism. His books were widely bought in England and many English versions appeared. He died insane on 17 March 1847.
Illus: *The Flowers Personified [1855]; Comical People [c.1860]; Vie Privée et Publique des Animaux [1867].*
Colls: Nancy; Rochefort; Tours.
Bibl: C. Baudelaire, *The Painter of Modern Life,* edited by J. Mayne, 1964, pp.181-182.

**GRANT, Charles Jameson  'CJG'      fl.1831-1846**
Draughtsman, wood engraver and caricaturist. He was the leading artist of the penny Radical papers during the Chartist agitation, producing spirited if rather coarse work. He does not appear to be the same as Charles Grant, portrait painter, exhibiting at RA, 1825-39.
Colls: Witt Photo.
Bibl: M.D. George, *English Political Caricature,* Vol.II, 1959, pp.237-238, 245, 250, illus.

**GRANT, William James      1829-1866**
History painter, wood engraver and illustrator. He was born at Hackney in 1829 and attended the RA Schools in 1845. He concentrated on scriptural subjects, occasionally borrowing themes from modern poetry. He died at Hackney in 1866.
Illus: *Favourite Modern Ballads; Bloomfield's Farmers Boy.*
Exhib: BI, 1849-63; RA.
Bibl: Chatto and Jackson, *Treatise on Wood Engraving,* 1861, p.598.

**GRAVE, Charles      1886-**
Black and white artist, illustrator and watercolourist. He was born at Barrow-in-Furness in 1886 and was educated at Tottenham Grammar School. He began to draw for *Punch* in 1912 and was then successively on the staff of *Sporting Life, The Daily Chronicle,* and *The Daily Graphic,* serving in the First War with the Middlesex Regiment. Grave was at his best with low life characters, especially those of dockland and was a good draughtsman of shipping and boats although the situations are usually less funny than the sketches. For a time in the 1930s he was relief cartoonist of *Punch.* His work is not uncommon. He signs his work Chas Grave.
Contrib: *Lest We Forget, Illustrated Sporting and Dramatic News.*
Bibl: R.G.G. Price, *A History of Punch,* 1957, p.248.

**GRAVES, The Hon. Henry Richard      1818-1882**
Amateur caricaturist and portrait painter. He was the second son of the 2nd Baron Graves and was born on 9 October 1818. On marrying in October 1843 Henrietta Wellesley, Graves formed links with the Paget and Wellesley families whose members frequently feature in his sepia caricatures. They are very amateur works, but delightfully fanciful, the characters dramatised and cigars and other objects flying about with wings. An album of society portraits in pencil was sold at Sotheby's on 1 January 1976.
Exhib: RA, 1846-1881.

**GRAY, Alfred**
Contributor of comic strips and caricatures to *Judy,* 1887-89.

**GRAY, D.B.**
Black and white artist. He specialised in animal drawings, particularly horses and humanised dogs.
Contrib: *The English Illustrated Magazine [1895]; Punch [1902].*

**GRAY, George Kruger      fl.1915-1940**
Painter, poster artist and sculptor, working in London. The Victoria and Albert Museum has a series of process engravings by him for book illustration.
Exhib: RA, 1919-40

**GRAY, Millicent Ethelreda      1873-**
Figure and portrait painter and illustrator. She was born in London, 12 September 1873, and studied at the Cope and Nicols School of Art and at the RA Schools.
Illus: *A Book of Children's Verse; Little Women [Alcott].*
Contrib: *The Queen's Gift Book [c.1915]; Princess Mary's Gift Book [c.1915].*
Exhib: G; L; Leicester Gall; P; RA; ROI; SWA.

**GRAY, Paul Mary      1842-1866**
Illustrator. He was born in Dublin on 17 May 1842 and after attending a convent, worked in Dublin as an artist. He taught drawing at the Tullabeg School and worked for Dillon, the Dublin printseller, at the same time exhibiting at the RHA, 1861-63. He worked in London from 1863, getting his earliest commissions from *Punch* for whom he drew initials and socials which were thought very attractive. By the middle 1860s he was quite successful, but was struck down by consumption and died in London on 14 November 1866. Spielmann considered that Gray's drawings lacked 'backbone' and Reid considered them rather overrated, but they are among the most gentle pastoral studies of the great black and white period.
Illus: *Medwyns of Wykeham; Kenneth and Hugh.*
Contrib: *Punch ·[1863-65]; Once a Week; Good Words; London Society; Shilling Magazine; The Argosy; The Quiver; The Broadway; Jingles and Jokes for Little Folks [1865]; A Round of Days [1866]; Idyllic Pictures [1867]; Ghosts Wives [1867]; The Spirit of Praise [1867]; The Savage Club Papers [1867]; Longfellow [The Chandos].*
Exhib: RBA, 1867.
Colls: BM; V & AM.
Bibl: M.H. Spielmann, *The History of Punch,* 1895, p.517; Forrest Reid, *Illustrators of The Sixties,* 1928, p.262.
See illustration (p.320).

**GRAY, Mrs. Robert**
Amateur artist. She was the wife of Bishop R. Gray and is believed to have designed churches in her husband's South African diocese. She illustrated *Three Months Visitation,* 1856, AT 346.

**GRAY, Ronald  RWS      1868-1951**
Figure and landscape painter and illustrator. He was born in 1868 and studied at Westminster School of Art under Fred Brown and at Julian's. One of his oil paintings, 1908, was bought by the Chantrey Bequest in 1925. He was elected NEA, 1923, ARWS, 1934 and RWS, 1941.
Contrib: *Cassell's Family Magazine [1898-99]; The Pall Mall Budget; The Idler.*
Exhib: G; GG; L; M; NEA; P; RA; RHA; RI; RSA.
Colls: BM; Imperial War; Tate; V & AM.

**GRAY, Tom**
Subject painter, working from Howland Street, London in 1866. He exhibited at the BI that year and contributed illustrations to *London Society,* 1860, 1868; *The Graphic,* 1872 (rural).

**GREAVES, R.B. Brook**
Caricaturist in watercolours, working in art deco style, c.1920.

**GRECO, J.**
Wood engraver, who contributed illustrations to *The Book of the Sword,* Sir Richard Burton, 1884.

**GREEN, Charles   RI**                                    **1840-1898**

Painter and illustrator. He was born in 1840 and studied at Heatherley's and with J.W. Whymper (q.v.), thereby establishing himself as a master of figure and genre subjects and an accomplished draughtsman on the block. He was elected ARI in 1864 and RI in 1867, quickly establishing himself in the forefront of book illustrating, particularly in novels with a period setting. One of his major achievements was in illustrating *The Old Curiosity Shop* for Dickens *Household Edition,* in 1871, bringing a delicacy to the pen work and softness to the washes that made a great contrast with the earlier interpretations. Green was also involved in the early numbers of *The Graphic,* and his work was admired by Van Gogh there; this was yet another side of his character, the social realist, with sketches of street folk and factory workers. He exhibited oils at the RA from 1862-83. He died at Hampstead 4 May 1898.

The finest of Green's drawings date from the 1860s and 1870s and are rare. He signs his work CG.

Illus: *Playroom Stories [Craik, 1863]; Our Untitled Nobility [Tillotson, 1863]; Tinykins' Transformation [M. Lemon, 1869]; The Doom of St. Querec [Burnand, 1875]; The Old Curiosity Shop [1876]; Dorothy Forster [Walter Besant, 1897].*
Contrib: *Once A Week [1860]; Churchman's Family Magazine [1863-64]; ILN [1866]; Cassell's Magazine [1867]; The Graphic [1869-86]; London Society; Sunday Magazine; Good Words For The Young; Sunday at Home; English Sacred Poetry of the Olden Times [1864]; Life and Lessons of Our Lord [1864]; Choice Series [1864]; Watts Divine and Moral Songs [1865]; The Nobility of Life [L. Valentine, 1869]; Episodes of Fiction [1870]; Thornbury's Legendary Ballads [1876]*

Exhib: B; G; L; M; RA; RI; ROI.
Colls: BM; Cardiff; Leicester; V & AM.
Bibl: J. Pennell, *Pen Drawing and Pen Draughtsmen,* 1894, pp.279-300, 304, illus.; *English Influences on Vincent Van Gogh,* Arts Council, 1974-75.
See illustration (below and pp.321, 324).

**GREEN, Henry Towneley   RI**                             **1836-1899**

Illustrator. He was born in 1836 and was the brother of Charles Green (q.v.). After a career in banking, he took up art and followed his brother into illustrating and watercolour work, though never with the same success. He was elected ARI in 1875, RI in 1879 and ROI in 1883.

Contrib: *Once A Week [1867]; The Sunday Magazine [1869]; Cassell's Magazine [1870]; Golden Hours [1869]; Good Words For The Young [1870]; Thornbury's Legendary Ballads [1876]; ILN [1872 and 1887]; The Cornhill Magazine [1885].*
Exhib: B; L; M; RA; RBA, 1865-67; RI.
Colls: V & AM.
Bibl: *English Influences On Vincent Van Gogh,* Arts Council, 1974-75.

**GREEN, William Curtis   RA ARIBA**                       **1875-1960**

Architect. He was born on 16 July 1875 and was educated at Newton College, South Devon, and studied at the RA Schools. He is best remembered as the architect of the Dorchester Hotel, Park Lane, London. He was elected ARA in 1923 and RA in 1933. He won the RIBA Gold Medal in 1922.

Illus: *Old Cottages and Farmhouses in Surrey [1908].*
Exhib: G; RA; RSA.
Bibl: *The Drawings of W. Curtis Green,* foreword by A.E. Richardson, 1949.

*CHARLES GREEN RI 1848-1898. 'A Consultation.' Sketch for unidentified illustration. Pen and ink. 4³/₈ins. x 6ins. (11.1cm x 15.2cm).*          Victoria and Albert Museum

*CHARLES GREEN RI 1848-1898. 'The Caledonian Market.' Pen and ink with chinese white. 12ins. x 20ins. (30.5cm x 50.8cm).*     Victoria and Albert Museum

**GREENAWAY, Kate   RI**                                    **1846-1901**
Watercolourist and illustrator. She was born in London, the daughter of J. Greenaway, engraver to *The Illustrated London News* and was a cousin of Richard and Frank Dadd (qq.v.). She studied art at the Islington School, Heatherley's and at the Slade under Legros and began to exhibit at the RA in 1877. The same year, she began to work for Edmund Evans, the printer and publisher, who recognised her unusual talent for capturing an enchanted Regency world, and used it in the illustration of numerous children's books. Her style was loosely based on designs by artists such as Stothard, whom she admired, but endowed with a child-like innocence and charm which greatly appealed to the Victorians. Ruskin liked her work and encouraged her although he would have liked her to study directly from nature which she never did. Her popular books were being produced in editions of over ten thousand copies in the 1880s and beginning to sell widely in the United States. From 1883-1895 she produced a yearly almanack and at other times designed bookplates and painted portraits in oil. She was elected RI in 1889. She died in Hampstead in 1901.

Kate Greenaway's style had its effects on clothing and other accessories as well as on book illustration where it spawned a great number of copyists. Her meticulous pen drawings in outline, with no shadow, are charming if rather static studies; her watercolours are really the pen drawings lightly washed over with muted colours. Miss Greenaway's work was never very difficult to copy or imitate, and fakes abound.

Illus: *Aunt Louisa's London Toy Books: Diamonds and Toads [1871]; Madam D'Aulnoy's Fairy Tales [c.1871]; Fairy Gifts [Kathleen Knox, 1874]; The Quiver of Love [1876]; Poor Nelly [Mrs. Bonavia Hunt, 1878]; Topo [G.E. Brunefille (Lady C. Campbell), 1878]; Under The Window [K. Greenaway, 1878]; The Heir of Redclyffe [C.M. Yonge, 1879]; Amateur Theatricals [W.H. Pollock, 1879]; Heartsease [C.M. Yonge, 1879]; The Little Folks Painting Book [1879]; Kate Greenaway's Birthday Book [1880]; The Library [Andrew Lang, 1881]; A Day in a Child's Life [1881]; Mother Goose [1881]; Little Anne [1882]; Almanack [1883-95]; Fors Clavigera [John Ruskin, 1883-84]; A Painting Book [1884]; Language of Flowers [1884]; The English Spelling Book [W. Mavor, 1884]; Dame Wiggins of Lee [1885]; Marigold Garden [1885]; Kate Greenaway's Alphabet [1885]; An Apple Pie, The Queen of the Pirate Isle [Bret Harte, 1886]; Queen Victoria's Jubilee Garland [1887]; Rhymes For The Young Folk [William Allingham, 1887]; Orient Line Guide [1888]; The Pied Piper of Hamelin [R. Browning, 1888]; Kate Greenaway's Book of Games*

*[1889]; The Royal Progress of King Pepito [B.F. Creswell, 1889]; The April Baby's Book of Tunes [1900].*
Contrib: *The People's Magazine [1868]; Little Folks [1873-80]; Cassell's Magazines [1874-   ]; ILN [1874-82]; St. Nicholas; The Graphic; The American Queen; Every Girl's Annual [1882]; The Girls' Own Paper [1879-90].*
Exhib: FAS, 1894, 1898, 1902; RA; RBA, 1870-75; RI.
Colls: Ashmolean; BM; Manchester; V & AM.
Bibl: M.H. Spielmann, *KG*, 1905; H.M. Cundall, *KG Pictures From Originals Presented by Her to John Ruskin...*, 1921; A.C. Moore, *A Century of KG*, 1946; M. Hardie, *Watercol. Paint. in Brit.*, Vol.III, 1968, p.143, illus.
See illustration (Colour Plate XII p.173).

**GREGORY, Charles   RWS**                                  **1849-1920**
Historical and genre painter and illustrator. He was born at Milford, Surrey and was working in London, 1880 and at Godalming, 1894, finally settling at Marlow, Bucks, where he died on 21 October 1920. He was elected ARWS in 1882 and RWS in 1884.

Contrib: *ILN [1876, 1877, 1879].*
Exhib: B; G; L; M; RA; RBA; RWS.
Colls: Bristol; Liverpool.

**GREGORY, Edward John   RA PRI**                           **1850-1909**
Painter and illustrator. He was born at Southampton on 19 April 1850, grandson of John Gregory, engineer to Sir John Franklin's Expedition. He was educated in Southampton and worked for some time in the P & O Company's drawing office, 1865, and with Hubert Von Herkomer (q.v.). On the latter's advice he went to London in 1869 and studied at the South Kensington Schools and at the RA Schools, 1871-75. Gregory was employed on the decorations of the new Victoria and Albert Museum and was employed by *The Graphic* to draw on the wood, often finishing the work of S.P. Hall (q.v.). He was elected RI in 1876 and became PRI in 1898. He was elected ARA in 1879 and RA in 1898. He settled at Great Marlow, Buckinghamshire and died there on 22 June 1909.

Gregory specialised in scenes of life aboard ship and did some illustrations of the Battle of Hastings for an unidentified edition. The former genre subjects were admired by Vincent Van Gogh.

Contrib: *The Graphic [1870-83].*
Exhib: B; G; L; M; RA; RI; ROI; RSA.
Colls: Ashmolean; Tate.
Bibl: *The English Influences On Vincent Van Gogh*, Arts Council, 1974-75.

**GREGORY, Margaret**

Irish illustrator and daughter of Lady Gregory of Coole Park. She contributed woodcut illustrations to *The Kiltartan Wonder Book* by Lady Gregory, c.1918, and is associated with the Cuala Press, Churchtown, Dundrum, County Dublin. Her brother, Robert Gregory contributed two designs for the Press including one for this book, before being killed in action, January 1918. She signs her work [MG]

Bibl: Liam Miller, *The Dun Emer Press, Later The Cuala Press*, with a Preface by Michael B. Yeats. Dolmen Press, Dublin, 1973.

**GREIFFENHAGEN, Maurice   RA                    1862-1931**

Painter and illustrator. He was born in 1862 and studied at the RA Schools, where he won the Armitage Prize. He became Headmaster of the Life School, Glasgow School of Art, in 1906, was elected ARA in 1916 and RA in 1922. His painting 'Women By A Lake' was purchased by the Chantrey Bequest in 1914 and 'Dawn' in 1926. The earlier part of Greiffenhagen's career was devoted almost exclusively to illustrative work for books and magazines. Throughout the 1890s he was producing high quality black and white work, some of it in its economy of line and free handling, clearly influenced by Phil May. He is particularly associated with the illustrations to Sir Henry Rider Haggard's novels and somewhat oddly appears to have been D.H. Lawrence's favourite artist. He died at St. John's Wood, 26 December 1931.

Illus: *Vain Fortune [George Moore, 1894]*.
Contrib: *Judy [1889-90]; Black and White [1891-96]; Fun [1892]; ILN [1892-98]; The Butterfly [1893]; The Pall Mall Budget [1894]; Daily Chronicle [1895]; Pick-Me-Up [1895]; The Unicorn [1895]; Ally Sloper's Half*

*MAURICE GREIFFENHAGEN RA 1862-1931. 'The Holy Flower.' Illustration to a book of the same name, by Sir H. Rider Haggard, 1915. Watercolour and chinese white. 19ins. x 13ins. (48.3cm x 33cm).*          Author's Collection

*Holiday; The Sketch; The Lady's Pictorial; The Windsor Magazine.*
Exhib: B; G; L; M; NEA; RA; RBA; ROI; RSA.
Colls: Author; V & AM.
Bibl: J. Stanley Little, *Maurice Greiffenhagen and his Work*, The Studio, Vol.9, 1897, pp.235-245, illus.
See illustration (below left).

**GREIG, James   RBA                    1861-1941**

Painter and illustrator in black and white. He was born at Arbroath in 1861 and went to London to study art in 1891 and to Paris in 1895, settling in London in 1896. Greig became art critic of *The Morning Post* and a noted historian, publishing a monograph on Raeburn and editing *The Farrington Diaries*, 1922-28. RBA, 1898. His domestic and rustic figure drawings in Punch and elsewhere are attractive if a little weak.

Contrib: *Black & White [1892]; The English Illustrated Magazine [1893-96]; St. Pauls [1894]; The Sketch [1895-96]; The Temple [1896]; Good Words [1898-99]; Punch [1902-3]; Cassell's Family Magazine; The Ludgate Monthly; The Idler; The Pall Mall Magazine; The Windsor Magazine; The Quiver.*
Exhib: RBA, 1897-1907.
Colls: V & AM.

**GREIG, John                    fl.1807-1824**

Landscape painter. A draughtsman, engraver and lithographer, he was associated with J.S. Storer in publishing *The Antiquarian Cabinet*, and supplying many antiquarian drawings.

Illus: *Promenades Across London [D. Hughson, 1817]; Views of London [J. Hakewill]; Tours in Cornwall [F.W.L. Stockdale, 1824].*
Contrib: *Britton's Beauties of England & Wales; Border Antiquities of England and Wales [1817].*

**GRIFFITHS, Tom                    fl.1880-1904**

Landscape painter and illustrator. He was working for *The Graphic* from 1880-87, mostly military subjects. He may have acted as a Special in Africa in 1881, but it is more likely that he was an under-study to T.W. Wilson and worked up his sketches at home. He was living at Amberley from 1893 and at Bideford from 1901.

Exhib: B; G; L; M; RA; RBA; RHA; RI.

**GRIGGS, Frederick Landseer Maur   RA                    1876-1938**

Draughtsman, etcher and book illustrator. He was born at Hitchin, Hertfordshire in 1876 and was educated privately. Griggs was one of the younger group of artists, who, influenced by Morris, brought to their art a great exactitude and a reverence for the work of past craftsmen. He had established himself by the early 1900s as the most sensitive of architectural illustrators, chiefly through his drawings to Messrs. Macmillans 'Highways and Byways' series, which appeared between 1902 and 1906 and then at longer intervals till 1928. Griggs removed to Chipping Campden, Gloucestershire before the First World War, and remained there till his death, strongly identifying himself with its Guild. 'Though his sympathies extended to Georgian and later architecture' ran The Times obituary, 'it can be said of Griggs, who was a Roman Catholic, that his spiritual home was in the Middle Ages and his works were full of a nostalgia for that period.' His meticulous work shows a direct sympathy for stone buildings, carving and the clean structure of regional styles from which a craftsman would be able to work stone by stone; his landscapes are akin to those of Samuel Palmer (q.v.). Griggs' range included the designing of two sets of Roman letters, known as Littleworth and Leysbourne in 1933 and 1934. He bacame ARA in 1922 and RA in 1931. He was made Hon. ARIBA in 1926. He died on June 7 1938 after being taken ill on a visit to London. A centenary exhibition was held at the Ashmolean Museum, March-May, 1976.

Illus: *The Collected Works of William Morris; The Life of G.F. Watts; Seven Gardens and a Palace [EVB, 1900]; Stray Leaves From a Border Garden [1901]; The Chronicle of a Cornish Garden [1901]; Highways and Byways in Hertfordshire [1901]; Memorials of Edward Burne-Jones [1904]; Highways and Byways in London; Highways and Byways in Berkshire [1906]; A Book of Cottages and Little Houses [C.R. Ashbee, 1906]; Highways and Byways in Buckinghamshire [1908]; Old Colleges of Oxford [1912]; Highways and Byways in Lincolnshire [1912]; Highways and Byways in Northamptonshire [1914]; Highways and Byways in Leicestershire [1918]; Highways and Byways in Nottinghamshire [1928]; Highways and Byways in Sussex; Highways and Byways in Oxford and The Cotswolds; Highways and Byways in South Wales; Highways and Byways in Cambridge and Ely; Essex.*

Contrib: *The Oxford Almanack [1922-23]*.
Exhib: G; L; RA; RE; RSA.
Colls: Ashmolean; BM; V & AM.
Bibl: *The Studio*, Winter No., 1900-01, p.63, illus.; R.E.D. Sketchley, *English Book Illus.*, 1902, pp. 54, 134; H. Knight, *The Work of FLG*, Print Collectors Club, No. 20, 1941; F.A. Comstock, *A Gothic Vision: FLG*, Ashmolean, 1966.

**GRIMM, Constantine von   'Nemo' or 'C de Grimm'**
German painter and illustrator. He contributed six cartoons to *Vanity Fair*, 1884.

**GRIP   pseudonym of Alfred BRICE**                     c.1895-1896
Cartoonist for *The Sketch*, c.1895-96. Brice specialised in grey wash figures with large and detailed heads, highlighted with white on cheeks and hair. His range is usually political and literary, although the Victoria and Albert Museum has an admirable caricature of Aubrey Beardsley. He signs his work GRIP (with toucan), thus
Contrib: *The Ludgate Monthly [1893-94]*.
Colls: V & AM.

**GRISET, Ernest Henry**                                  1844-1907
Illustrator and comic draughtsman of animals. He was born at Boulogne-sur-Mer in 1844, and studied under Louis Gallait, presumably in Brussels. The latter had strong links with England and it may have been through him that Griset came to London in the mid-60s. Although intending to become a serious watercolourist, he was spiritually akin to Grandville (q.v.) in his delight in drawing animals and people and showing their basic similarities, not in caricature, but in behaviour. His mournful beasts and gangling half-savage hunters in pursuit of them, occupy a world of half legend, critical and comic. His work was exhibited first in a bookshop in Leicester Square and after attracting the notice of the Dalziel Brothers and Tom Hood, he was invited to join *Fun* and eventually *Punch*. Griset's style, delicate pen drawings, beautifully tinted with soft colours, are more French than English in their subtlety; one would not guess from the economic use of line and the precision of hand that the artist was a very rapid and hard worker, dashing off hundreds of such for *Griset's Grotesques*, 1867. Griset died on 22 March 1907, having outlived his popularity, but his sketches have a charm that has gained them a special place among collectors.

Illus: *The Hatchet Throwers [James Greenwood, 1867]*; *Legends of Savage Life [James Greenwood, 1867]*; *Among The Squirrels [Mrs. Deniston, 1867]*; *Vikram and The Vampire [1869]*; *Robinson Crusoe [1869]*; *The Rare Romance of Reynard The Fox [1869]*; *The Hunchback of Notre Dame [Hugo, 1879]*.
Contrib: *Fun; Punch [1867]*; *Once a Week [1867]*; *The Broadway [1867]*; *Good Words For The Young [1870-71]*; *The Graphic [1870-71]*; *Hood's Comic Annual [1878]*.
Exhib: RBA, 1871-72 (animals).
Colls: Author; BM; V & AM.
Bibl: Hesketh Hubbard, 'A Forgotten Illustrator'; *The Connoisseur*, 1945; L. Lambourne, *Country Life*, January, 1977.
See illustration (below).

**GROB, Conrad**                                         1828-1904
Painter of history and genre, lithographer, engraver and illustrator. He was born at Andelfingen, Switzerland on 3 September 1828 and did not begin his artistic career until he was thirty-eight, when he joined the Munich Academy and studied under Ramberg. He died at Munich 4 January 1904.

Contrib: *The Illustrated Times [1860. (Italian War)]*.
Exhib: Paris, 1900.
Colls: Basle; Berne.

*ERNEST HENRY GRISET 1844-1907. 'Two Ragamuffins.' Pen and washes. 4½ins. x 6ins. (11.4cm x 15.2cm).*        Author's Collection

**GROOME, William Henry Charles** RBA      fl.1881-1914

Landscape painter and illustrator. He was working at Ealing from 1881-1914 and became RBA in 1901.

Contrib: *ILN* [1889-92 (rustic)]; *Chums*.
Exhib: GG; RA; RBA; RI; ROI.

**GROSSMITH, Walter Weedon**      1854-1919

Painter and actor. He was born in 1854, the brother of George Grossmith and was educated at Simpson's School, Hampstead, before being trained at the Slade and RA Schools. He was the author of the Victorian classic, *Diary of a Nobody,* which first appeared in *Punch* in 1888. Grossmith was a talented black and white artist and landscape painter, but this increasingly gave way to his success as a comedy actor and later to his management of the Vaudeville Theatre, 1894-96 and the Avenue Theatre, 1901. He died 14 June 1919.

Exhib: B; GG; L; M; RA; RBA; RHA; ROI.
Colls: V & AM.
Bibl: WG *From Studio to Stage,* 1912.

**GROVES, S.J.**

Draughtsman. Contributed illustrations to *Pen and Pencil Pictures From The Poets,* Edinburgh, 1866.

**GUERARD, Eugène Charles François**      1821-1866

Painter and lithographer. He was born at Nancy 6 July 1821 and died there 6 July 1866. He studied with Paul Delaroche and exhibited at the Salon in 1842, 1848, and 1852. He contributed to *The Illustrated London News,* 1855.

**GUILLAUME, Albert**      1873-1942

Figure painter and humorous draughtsman. He was born in Paris on 14 February 1873 and studied in the Atelier Gérome and illustrated numerous French books. He died at Faux in the Dordogne in 1942.

Contrib: *The Graphic* [1901-03].
Exhib: L, 1910-24.

**GULICH, John Percival** RI      1865-1898

Illustrator, engraver and caricaturist. He was born at Wimbledon in 1864 and worked for many of the leading magazines in the 1890s, having begun with *The Graphic,* 1887 and *Harper's Magazine.* He was elected RI, 1897 and was a member of the Langham Sketch Club. He died of typhoid fever in 1898.

Illus: *Three Partners* [Bret Harte, 1897]; *John Ingerfield* [Jerome K. Jerome, 1897].
Contrib: *The Graphic* [1887-97]; *The Strand Magazine* [1891]; *Black & White* [1892]; *The Idler* [1892]; *Chums* [1892]; *The Quiver* [1895]; *Cassell's Family Magazine; The Pall Mall Magazine.*
Exhib: GG; L; Paris, 1900; RA; RBA; RI.
Colls: V & AM.

**GUNNIS, Louis J.**      fl.1887-1897

Painter and illustrator. He worked in London 1887-97 and specialised in domestic scenes.

Contrib: *ILN* [1889]; *Judy* [1889]; *The Sphere* [1894]; *The Sketch* [1895 (dramatic ports)]; *The English Illustrated Magazine* [1895-96]; *The Ludgate Monthly; Chums; The Idler; The Royal Magazine.*
Exhib: L; RA, 1887-97.
Colls: V & AM.

**GURNEY, Ernest T.**

Landscape painter. He was working at Ampthill Square, Hampstead Road in 1900-02. He contributed to *The Idler* and exhibited at the RA in 1900.

**GUTH, Jean Baptiste**      fl.1883-1921

French painter and caricaturist. He was a regular contributor to *Vanity Fair,* 1889-1908. He signs his work GUTH or JB GUTH.

**GUTHRIE, James Joshua**      1874-1952

Painter and illustrator and designer of bookplates. He was born in 1874 and although he had no formal training, studied as assistant to Reginald Hallward (q.v.). Guthrie was a talented hand printer and founded the Pear Tree Press at South Harting, Hampshire in May 1905. Guthrie was one of the leading wood engravers associated with the development of the private presses and the return to romanticism. His range extended from the illustrations to children's books to those of poets living and dead. His mood was a direct inheritance from the work of Blake, Palmer and Calvert (qq.v.) with his own idiosyncracies of curly trees, eddying water and wild sky, ideal for the brooding quality of Poe. The poet Gordon Bottomley has left an amusing description of his method of work. 'So far as I have seen he takes a piece of granulated cardboard and washes it over with a few brushfuls of a thin mixture of plaster of Paris. Then he digs into that with a pen and Indian ink. Then he puts on a film of Chinese White (Paris, India, China) what riches all at once.' This was in a letter to John Nash with whom some comparison might be found. Guthrie founded and illustrated a magazine called *The Elf* in 1895 and decorated rhymesheets for Harold Monro's Poetry Bookshop.

Illus: *Wedding Bells* [1895]; *The Elf* [1895-1904]; *The Little Man in Scarlet* [1896]; *An Album of Drawings* [1900]; *Virgil's Alexis* [1905]; *The Beatitudes* [1905]; *Midsummer Eve* [Gordon Bottomley, 1905]; *In Summer Time* [Dorothy Radford, 1906]; *A Second Book of Drawings* [1908]; *Echoes of Poetry* [1908]; *The Poems of E.A. Poe* [1908]; *The Riding of Lithend* [Gordon Bottomley, 1909]; *The Paradise of Tintoretto* [1910]; *The Blessed Damozel* [1911 (decor)]; *Six Poems* [Edward Eastaway]; *Trees* [Harold Monro, 1916]; *Root and Branch* [1916]; *Space and Man; The Castle of Indolence.*
Contrib: *The Yellow Book* [1896]; *The Quartier Latin* [1896]; *The Dome* [1897]; *The Windmill* [1899]; *The Page* [1899]; *The Idler.*
Colls: V & AM.
Bibl: *The Artist,* May-Aug., 1898, pp.238-241, illus; Sept., 1900, pp.197-202, illus.

See illustration (below).

DREAMLAND.

*JAMES JOSHUA GUTHRIE 1874-1952. 'Dreamland.' Wood engraving. 9ins. x 7⅝ins. (22.9cm x 19.4cm).*      Victoria and Albert Museum

*CONSTANTIN GUYS 1802-1892. 'The Strawberry Roans.' Ink and wash.*

**GUYS, Constantin Ernest Adolphe Hyacinthe**      **1802-1892**

Figure artist in pen and watercolour. The known facts about this great French draughtsman are scarce. He was born at Flushing, Holland of French parentage in 1802 and died in Paris in poverty at the advanced age of ninety in 1892. He is believed to have gone to Greece to fight in the War of Independence alongside Byron, action of any kind and particularly that of soldiers and horses always inspiring him. By the 1840s he was in England, acting as French tutor to the family of Dr. T.C. Girtin, son of Girtin the watercolourist. Guys gained employment with the newly-founded *Illustrated London News* in 1843 and appears to have worked for them until as late as 1860. He covered the Crimean War for the magazine in 1854-56, although his work is often unsigned though very recognisable, in the journal. He also went to Spain, Italy, Germany, Turkey and Egypt as their special correspondent. He seems to have been particularly associated with the English press, even by the French — the Goncourts mention him in their Journal in April 1858 as "the draughtsman of the ILLUSTRATED LONDON". Baudelaire brilliantly analysed Guys' style in his celebrated essay 'The Painter of Modern Life' (*Figaro*, 1863). Guys, characteristically mercurial and elusive, is referred to by his initials only. This and much else about his work, his casual attitude to completed drawings, his sketching from memory not life, his dismissal of the conventions, place him squarely in the literary bohemia associated with Balzac.

With little else to go on, the drawings speak for themselves about the originality and verve of Guys the artist. Baudelaire describes him as 'the painter of the passing moment' and links him to the vision of the moralist and the novelist. These rapid pen and ink sketches with light colour washes radiate their own period in a way that the finished illustrators could not attain. For Guys they are statements about society and leaves from the notebook of a reporter, in which the symbols of crowd or event matter more than their delineation. For Baudelaire they were living history, the documents on which the age

would be judged, for him, a very valid role for a minor master. The drawings have remained time-less with the sparkle of life so vividly apparent, the tawdry mock heroic demi-monde, the glitter of soldiery in the Park, the vibrant rapidity of the Brighton coach. In later years Guys used less colour and his sketches became more synthesised, but he had left actual illustrative work far behind. Although he was not widely known in his own time (Thackeray mentions him, Gavarni copied him) he had a growing following by the early twentieth century when many of his values, freedom of expression and immediacy came to be recognised. He is now a much sought-after artist and his drawings are among the highest priced of illustrators work.

Colls: BM; Paris (Petit Palais); V & AM.
Bibl: Charles Baudelaire, 'Un peintre de la vie moderne' *Figaro* 3 December 1863; Armand Dayot, *Catalogue de l'Exposition de l'oeuvre de Constantin Guys*, 1904; Henri Frantz, 'A Forgotten Artist', *The Studio*, Vol.34, 1905, pp.107-112; Gustave Geffroy, *CG, l'historien du Second Empire*, 1904-20; *CG, Collection Des Maîtres*, 1949; *The Painter of Modern Life and Other Essays By Charles Baudelaire*, edited by Jonathan Mayne, 1964. See illustration (above).

**GWENNETT, W. Gunn**      **fl.1903-1940**

Landscape painter and illustrator. He worked in Richmond, Surrey, 1903 and London.

Contrib: *Punch [1909]*.
Exhib: L; RA; RI; RSA.

**GYFFORD, Edward**      **1772-1834**

Architect, draughtsman and illustrator. He was born in 1772 and studied at the RA Schools, winning the Gold Medal in 1792. He published *Designs For Small Picturesque Cottages and Hunting-Boxes*, 1807 and contributed illustrations to *The Beauties of England and Wales*, 1810.

Exhib: RA, 1791-1801.
Bibl: H.M. Colvin, *Biog. Dict. of English Architects*, 1954, p.256.

## HAAG, Carl        1820-1915
Watercolourist and illustrator. He was born at Erlangen in Bavaria on 20 April 1820, the son of an amateur artist. He studied art at Nuremberg, 1834, and Munich, 1844-46 while working as a miniaturist and book illustrator. He worked in Brussels and then came to London in 1847 to study watercolour and attend the RA Schools. He visited Italy in 1847, travelled to Cairo with F. Goodall (q.v.) in 1858 and to Egypt in 1860, where he lived with the desert tribes. He ran studios in both London and Oberwesel, finally retiring to the latter in 1903 and dying there on 24 January 1915. He was elected AOWS in 1850 and OWS in 1853.

Contrib: *ILN [Christmas, 1869]*.
Exhib: FAS, 1882; L; M; RA; RBA; RWS.
Colls: BM; Leeds; V & AM.
Bibl: M. Hardie, *Watercol. Paint. in Brit.*, Vol.III, 1968, p.67.

## HACKER, Arthur   RA        1858-1919
Portrait and genre painter and occasional illustrator. He was born in London on 25 September 1858, the son of Edward Hacker, the line engraver. He was educated in London and Paris and studied art at the RA Schools, 1876, and under Bonnat in Paris, 1880-81. He became a popular portrait painter and travelled widely in Italy and North Africa collecting material for classical and religious subjects. He was elected ARA in 1894 and RA in 1910. He died in London 12 November 1919.

Contrib: *The Graphic [1903 (story illus.)]*.
Exhib: B; G; L; M; RA; RI; ROI.

## HADDON, Arthur Trevor        1864-1941
Portrait and genre painter. He was born in 1864 and studied at the Slade School under Legros from 1883-86, winning the painting medal in 1885. He worked in Spain, 1887 and at the Herkomer School, Bushey. 1888-90, becoming a Fellow of it in 1891. He then studied in Rome from 1896-97 and was elected RBA in 1896.

Publ: *The Old Venetian Palaces; Southern Spain.*
Illus: *The Snow Garden [Elizabeth Wordsworth, 1897]*.
Exhib: FAS; L; M; New Gall; P; RA; RBA; RHA; RI; ROI.

## HADGE
Contributor of a cartoon to *Vanity Fair*, 1899.

## HAGHE, Louis   RI        1806-1885
Painter and illustrator of architecture with figures. He was born at Tournai, Belgium, in 1806 and studied lithography under de la Barrière and J.P. de Jonghe, afterwards coming to London where he went into partnership with William Day, the publisher. From the 1830s onwards, Haghe issued collections of lithographs of his travels and frequently lithographed the works of other artists, particularly David Roberts's *Holy Land*. He was President of the RI from 1873-1884 having been a member since 1835. Haghe's work is extremely accurate if lacking in imagination. He died in London in 1885.

Illus: *Sketches in Belgium and Germany [1840-50, AT 35 and 37]; Portfolio of Sketches [1850, AT 41]*.
Contrib: *Bold's Travels Through Sicily [1827, AT 265]; Dickinson's Comprehensive Picture of the Great Exhibition of 1851.*
Exhib: NWS, 1835-
Colls: BM; Glasgow; Manchester; V & AM.
Bibl: M. Hardie, *Watercol. Paint. in Brit.*, Vol.III, 1968, p.93, illus.

## HAITÉ, George Charles   RI        1855-1924
Landscape painter and illustrator. He was born at Bexley in 1855, the son of a designer. After being educated at Mitcham College, he taught himself to draw and began work as a designer at the age of sixteen. He exhibited at the RA from 1883 and worked in black and white for a number of magazines, designing the covers of *The Strand Magazine* and *The Strand Musical Magazine*, 1891. He was the President of the Langham Sketching Club, 1883-87 and 1908. He was elected RI in 1901, and died at Bedford Park, 31 March 1924.

Illus: *Haité's Plant Studies.*
Colls: BM; Leeds; Manchester.
Bibl: *Who Was Who 1916-28.*

## HAKEWILL, James        1778-1843
Architect, draughtsman and illustrator. He was born in 1778, the son of John Hakewill, painter and decorator, and trained as an architect and exhibited designs at the RA from 1800. He was however more of an antiquary than a practical designer and turned increasingly to the publications of tours undertaken by him and his wife, also a talented artist. Hakewill had some association with J.M.W. Turner (q.v.) who made finished drawings from his Italian sketches. He died on 28 May 1843.

Illus: *The History of Windsor and Its Neighbourhood [1813]; A Picturesque Tour of Italy [1818-20, AT 683]; Picturesque Tour in the Island of Jamaica [1825]; Plans, Sections and Elevations of Abattoirs of Paris [1828]; An Attempt to Determine the Exact Character of Elizabethan Architecture [1835]; Antiquarian and Picturesque Tour [1849].*
Bibl: H.M. Colvin, *Biog. Dict. of English Architects*, 1954, p.259.

## HALCOMBE, Will        fl.1897-
Black and white artist specialising in comic history subjects. He contributed pen and watercolour drawings to *The Sketch*, 1897, mostly signed and dated.

Colls: V & AM.

## HALE, Edward Matthew   ROI        1852-1924
Painter and illustrator. He was born at Hastings in 1852 and studied art in Paris under Cabanel and Carolus Duran. He was Special Artist for *The Illustrated London News* in the Russo-Turkish War, 1877-78 and in Afghanistan. He was a Colonel in the Middlesex Rifle Volunteers. Elected ROI in 1898 and died at Godalming, 24 January 1924.

Exhib: B; G; L; M; RA; RBA; RI; ROI.
Colls: Leeds.

## HALKETT, George Roland        1855-1918
Artist, illustrator and writer on art. He was born at Edinburgh on 11 March 1855 and studied art in Paris. He later returned to Edinburgh and concentrated on making caricatures for the press and producing book illustrations. He was art critic of the *Edinburgh Evening News*, 1876, joined the *Pall Mall Gazette* as political cartoonist in 1892 and was successively art editor of *The Pall Mall Magazine*, 1897, and Editor, 1900-05. He was most celebrated for his caricatures of Mr. Gladstone which he issued in *New Gleanings From Gladstone* and a *Gladstone Almanack* and for *The Irish Green Book* produced during the Home Rule debates of 1887. His style is of the *portrait chargée* type adopted by 'Ape', but in the 1900s there is a definite Beggarstaff influence, chalky black lines on toned paper. He travelled extensively in the colonies and died in London, December 1918.

Contrib: *Edinburgh University Liberal Association [booklet, 1883 (frontis.)]; St. Stephen's Review [1885]; Pall Mall Budget [1893]; Pall Mall Magazine [1897]; Punch [1897-1903]; The Butterfly.*
Illus: *The Elves and The Shoemaker [child's book, n.d.].*
Exhib: G; RSA.
Colls: V & AM.

## HALL, Basil        fl.1886-1888
Black and white artist specialising in military subjects. He contributed story illustrations to *The Graphic* in 1886-87 and events in 1888.

## HALL, E.
Black and white artist contributing genre and social subjects to *The Illustrated Times*, 1856-59.

**HALL, Frederick**                                    1860-1948

Figure and landscape painter. He was born at Stillington, Yorks, in 1860 and studied at Lincoln Art School and under Verlat at Antwerp. He worked for fifteen years at Newlyn, Cornwall and drew for *The Graphic* in 1902, and caricatured for *Black & White,* 1891, *The Sketch,* 1894.

**HALL, Harry**                                    fl.1838-1886

Equestrian artist and illustrator. Hall worked first as a horse painter at Tattersall's in London, later moving to Newmarket where he became friendly with Mark Lemon, the Editor of *Punch.* He became chief artist on *The Field* and contributed only one drawing to *Punch.* He was the father of Sydney Hall (q.v.).

Contrib: *Tattersall's British Race Horses; Sporting Review [1842-46 (engs. and title)]; ILN [1857-58, 1866-67].*
Exhib: BI, 1847-66; RA, 1838-86; RBA, 1839-75.

**HALL, L. Bernard**                                    1859-1935

Portrait and figure painter. He was born in Liverpool, 28 December 1859 and was educated at Cheltenham College before studying art at South Kensington, Antwerp and Munich. He began his professional career in 1882, exhibiting at the RA from that year. In 1892, he was appointed Director of the National Gallery of Victoria at Melbourne, a post he held until his death on 14 February 1935.

Contrib: *The Graphic [1887]; Black & White.*
Exhib: L; M; NEA; RA; RBA; ROI.

**HALL, Sydney Prior   MVO**                                    1842-1922

Painter, draughtsman and illustrator. He was born at Newmarket in 1842 and studied with his father Harry Hall (q.v.), with Arthur Hughes (q.v.) and at the RA Schools. Hall was a popular painter of military subjects and illustrated many stories, his most famous collaboration being on *Tom Browne's School Days,* 1869, with his teacher, Arthur Hughes. He was a favourite painter of the Royal Family and accompanied Lord Lorne to Canada in 1881. He was a *Graphic* contributor from its first year, 1870, and a Special Artist in the Franco-Prussian War. See E.J. Gregory.

Illus: *The Law and The Lady [Wilkie Collins, 1876].*
Contrib: *The Quiver [1869]; The Graphic [1870-1906]; Dark Blue [1871-73]; The Sketch.*
Exhib: G; L; M; New Gall.; RA; RHA; RI.

**HALLIDAY, Michael Frederick**                                    1822-1869

Amateur artist and illustrator. He exhibited at the RA from 1853-56 and at the RBA in 1853. The National Portrait Gallery has his portrait of Joseph Priestley; he died at Thurlow Place, London in 1869.

Contrib: *Passages From the Poems of Tom Hood [Junior Etching Club, 1858].*

**HALLS, Robert**                                    fl.1892-1909

Miniature painter. He worked in London and Birkenhead and contributed to *The Yellow Book,* 1895.

Exhib: NEA; P; RA; RMS.

**HALLTHORPE**

Comic artist contributing to *Fun,* 1901.

**HALLWARD, Cyril R.**                                    fl.1886-1890

Comic artist in pen and ink specialising in figure subjects. His drawings are poor and the penline rather scratchy.

Contrib: *Judy [1886-89]; ILN [1889]; Lady's Pictorial [1890]; Puck and Ariel [1890].*

**HALLWARD, Ella F.G.**                                    fl.1896-98

Illustrator. Perhaps the daughter of Reginald and Adelaide Hallward, (qq.v.). She exhibited at the Arts and Crafts Exhibition Society in 1896 an illustration for an untraced book issued by Messrs. H.S. Nicholls. *The Studio* said: 'One can scarce recall any other attempt to work in white upon black which has mastered the problem so easily.'

Exhib: New Gall., 1898.
Bibl: *The Studio,* Vol. 9, 1897, p.283, illus.

**HALLWARD, Reginald**                                    1858-1948

Painter, stained glass artist, illustrator and designer. He was born 18 October 1858 and studied art at the Slade and at the Royal College of Art. He had J.J. Guthrie (q.v.) as an assistant for some time. Hallward ran The Woodlands Press at Shore near Gravesend from about 1895 to about 1913, printing various books of verse by Michael and Faith Hallward illustrated by his own chalk drawings. His wife, Adelaide (q.v.) was also an artist and illustrator.

Illus: *Vox Humana; Apotheosis; Wild Oats; Flowers of Paradise; The Babies Quest [1913, all Woodlands Press]; Rule Britannia; Quick March; The Religion of Art; The Next Step; Stories From The Bible [E.L. Farrar, 1897].*
Contrib: *Punch [1876]; Root and Branch [No. 4, 1916].*
Exhib: G; L; NEA; New Gall.; RA; RBA.

**HALLWARD, Mrs. Reginald (née Adelaide Bloxam)**       fl.1888-1922

Artist and illustrator. She was married to Reginald Hallward (q.v.) and helped him with his various ventures. She illustrated *The Child's Pictorial* for The S.P.C.K. and exhibited five works at the RA between 1888 and 1890. She was still painting though not exhibiting in 1922.

**HALSWELLE, Keeley   ARSA**                                    1832-1891

Landscape painter and illustrator. He was born at Richmond, Surrey, of Scottish parents on 23 April 1832. After studying at the British Museum and in Edinburgh, Halswelle started a career in book illustration from 1860 onwards, working for a number of leading magazines. Gleeson White comments that 'in these you find those water-lilies in blossom which in after years became a mannerism in his landscape foregrounds.' From 1869 he lived in Italy for some years painting peasant subjects, and he also worked in Paris. A new dimension to his art as an illustrator was revealed in November 1975, when Sotheby's Belgravia offered a remarkable ink drawing of 1858, entitled 'A Child's Dream of Christmas'. Centred on a sleeping child surrounded by many small fairy figures, it places him firmly in the tradition of Richard Doyle (q.v.). He was elected ARSA in 1865 and RI in 1882.

Illus: *The Princess Florella and the Knight of the Silver Shield [1860]; Six Years in a House-boat.*
Contrib: *ILN [1860]; Good Words [1860]; Pen and Pencil Pictures From the Poets [1866]; Scott's Poems [c.1866].*
Exhib: RA, 1862-91; RBA, 1875-79.
Colls: Dublin; Glasgow; Leeds; Tate.
Bibl: *The Art Journal,* 'The Works of KH', 1879, p.49.

**HAMERTON, Robert Jacob   RBA**

Illustrator and lithographer. Born in Ireland, he was teaching drawing in a school in County Longford by the age of fourteen and then travelled to London to study lithography under Charles Hullmandel. He contributed to *Punch,* 1843-48 a number of cartoons of an Irish flavour, signing himself first 'Shallaballa' and then with a 'Hammer on the side of a Tun'. He continued to work on stone as a book illustrator until 1891 'when the drawings on the huge stones became too much for my old back' (Spielmann, pp.452-453). He was a close friend of H.G. Hine (q.v.). RBA, 1843.

Illus: *Comic Blackstone [G. a'Beckett]; Life of Goldsmith [Forster].*
Exhib: BI, 1831-47; RA and RBA, 1831-58.

**HAMILTON, Lady Anne**                                    1766-1846

Amateur artist. She was born in 1766, daughter of the 9th Duke of Hamilton and died unmarried in 1846. She contributed a drawing of Ashton Hall to *The Beauties of England and Wales,* 1807.

**HAMILTON, James**                                    1819-1878

American illustrator. He was born in Ireland in 1819 but went to America when young. He returned to England during the years 1854-56 and later became an art master in Philadelphia, where he died in 1878. He was most celebrated for illustrating an edition of the *Arabian Nights.*

**HAMLEY, General Sir Edward Bruce**                                    1824-1893

Amateur illustrator. He was born in 1824 and after entering the Royal Horse Artillery in 1843, became Colonel in 1855 and served in the Crimean War. He contributed articles to *Blackwood's* and *Fraser's* magazines in 1858 and was Professor of Military History at Sandhurst, 1859-64. He was Commandant of the Staff College, 1870-77 and KCB, 1882, serving as MP for Birkenhead, 1885-92.

Illus: *The Campaign of Sebastopol [1855, AT 236].*

### HAMMERSLEY, James Astbury          1815-1869
Headmaster of the Manchester School of Design, 1849-1862. He illustrated *The Shipwreck of the Premier*, G.R. Dartnell, 1845.

### HAMMOND, Christine M. Demain "Chris"      fl.1886-1910
Painter and illustrator. Sister of Gertrude E. Demain Hammond (q.v.). She lived with her sister in London, 1886-90 and with her was the principal illustrator to *St. Paul's,* 1894. Her penwork is rather free and she excels in costume subjects in a style not unlike that of the Brocks eighteenth century pastiches.

Illus: *Goldsmith's Comedies [1894-96]; Sir Charles Grandison; Castle Rackrent* and *Popular Tales; The Absentee [Maria Edgeworth, 1895]; Belinda* and *Helen [Edgeworth, 1896]; The Parents Assistant [Edgeworth, 1897]; The Charm [W. Besant]; Henry Esmond [W.M. Thackeray, 1897]; Emma; Sense and Sensibility [Jane Austen]; John Halifax Gentleman [Mrs. Craik, 1898]; Stories From Shakespeare [T. Carter, 1910].*
Contrib: *The Pall Mall Budget [1891-92]; The Ludgate Monthly [1891 and 1895]; The Idler [1892]; The English Illustrated Magazine [1893-96]; St. Paul's [1894]; The Quiver [1894-95]; Madame [1895]; The Temple [1896]; Pearson's Magazine [1896]; Cassell's Family Magazine [1898]; Pick-Me-Up.*
Exhib: RA, 1886-93; RBA, 1886-90; RI; ROI.
Colls: V & AM.
See illustration (below).

*CHRISTINE HAMMOND fl.1886-1910. 'Lor! Ain't I glad!' Drawing for illustration in* The English Illustrated Magazine. *Pen and ink. Signed.*
Victoria and Albert Museum

### HAMMOND, Gertrude E. Demain    RI         1862-1953
Painter and illustrator. She was born in Brixton in 1862 and studied art at the Lambeth School, 1879 and at the RA Schools, 1885, gaining sketch and decorative design prizes there. From about 1892 she was engaged in illustrative work, becoming a very accomplished pen draughtsman particularly of female figures. She worked in oil and watercolour as well as in black and white and after her marriage in 1898, painted from West Kensington, 1902-14 and from Stow-on-the-Wold, 1925.

Illus: *The Clever Miss Foillett [J.K.H. Denny, 1894]; frontis. to novels by Robert Barr [1897]; The Virginians [W.M. Thackeray, 1902]; Martin Chuzzlewhit; Our Mutual Friend [Dickens, 1903]; George Eliot [American edition, 1907]; Arethusa [Marion Crawford, 1907]; The Beautiful-Birthday Book [c.1907]; Fairies of Sorts [Mrs. Molesworth, 1908].* Colour illus. to *Shakespeare [1902-03]; The Pilgrims Progress [1904]; Faerie Queen [1909]; Stories From Shakespeare [1910].*
Contrib: *The Quiver [1890]; The Ludgate Monthly [1891]; The Queen; The Idler [1892]; St. Paul's [1894]; Madame [1895]; The Yellow Book [1895]; The Minister [1895]; Lady's Pictorial; Pick-Me-Up.*
Exhib: L; M; RA; RBA, 1887-89; RHA; RI.
Colls: Gateshead; Shipley; V & AM.

### HAMNETT, Nina                        1890-1956
Portrait and landscape painter and illustrator. She was born in Tenby, South Wales in 1890 and studied at the London School of Art and became a member of the London Group, 1917. She contributed lively and linear figure sketches to *The Gypsy,* 1915.

Exhib: L; NEA, 1913-17.

### HANCOCK, Charles                 fl.1819-1868
Sporting artist, illustrator and drawing master. He was teaching at Marlborough in 1819, Reading, 1827-28, Wycombe, 1829, Aylesbury, 1830, Knightsbridge, 1831-49 and Highbury, 1849-67. He was a very prolific artist, illustrated an edition of *Nimrod* and contributed to *Tattersall's English Race Horses* and *The Sporting Review,* 1842-46.

Exhib: BI, 1827-67; NWS; RA, 1819-47.

### HANKEY, William Lee                1869-1952
Landscape painter in oil. He was born at Chester on 28 March 1869 and educated at King Edward's School, Chester; he served in the First World War, 1914-18 and was a member of the RI from 1898-1906 and 1918-1924. He died in 1952.

Illus: *The Deserted Village [Goldsmith]; The Compleat Angler [Walton].*
Publ: *An Old Garden; At the Well.*
Exhib: Paris; RA; RBA; RI.

### HANSCOM, Adelaide
Illustrator. She contributed drawings to an edition of *Omar Khayyam* published by Messrs. Harrap in 1908.

### HARDING, Emily J.                fl.1877-1902
Miniaturist and illustrator of children's books. She was married to the painter Edward William Andrews, worked closely with T.H. Robinson (q.v.) and was a translator as well as artist.

Illus: *An Affair of Honour [Alice Weber, 1892]; The Disagreeable Duke [E.D. Adams, 1894]; Fairy Tales of the Slav Peasants and Herdsmen; Hymn on the Morning of Christ's Nativity [1896].*
Exhib: RA, 1877, 1897-98; RMS.
Bibl: R.E.D. Sketchley, *English Bk. Illus.,* 1903, pp.112, 166.

### HARDING, James Duffield           1798-1863
Watercolourist, topographer, lithographer and teacher. He was born at Deptford in 1788 and studied with Samuel Prout and Charles Pye, the engraver. Preferring drawing to engraving, he worked from an early age as a landscape artist, exhibiting at the RA from 1810. He was an excellent lithographer and worked for Hullmandel producing folios from the works of Bonington, Roberts and Stanfield. He visited the Rhine, Italy and Normandy in the 1820s, 1830s and 1840s, producing books of his travels and at the same time issuing copy-books for amateur artists. He was highly regarded by John Ruskin, whose drawing-master he had been. Finished watercolours and studies are seen with some frequency on the market, those prepared for the

books, in pencil with slight high-lighting.

Publ: *Lithographic Drawing Book [1832]; Art, or the Use of the Lead Pencil [1834]; Principles and Practices of Art [1845]; Lessons on Trees [1852]*.
Illus: *Views in Spain [E.H. Locker, 1824, AT 147]; Britton's Cathedrals [1832-36 (figures)]; Sketches At Home and Abroad [1836. AT 29]; The Book of South Wales [S.C. Hall, 1861]*.
Exhib: BI; OWS; RA; RBA.
Colls: Ashmolean; BM; Fitzwilliam; Glasgow; Manchester; Nottingham; V & AM.
Bibl: M. Hardie, *Watercol. Paint. in Brit.*, Vol. III, 1968, pp.24-27.

### HARDWICKE, Elizabeth Yorke, Countess of         -1858
Amateur artist. She was the daughter of 5th Earl of Balcarres and married Philip, 3rd Earl of Hardwicke in 1782. She died on 26 May 1858.

Publ. and Illus: *The Court of Oberon or The Three Wishes [1831, AL 421 lith.]*.

### HARDY, Dorothy         fl.1908-1925
Illustrator of children's books. Contributed drawings to *In Nature's School* by Lillian Gask, 1908. Working at Long Eaton, Derby in 1925.

### HARDY, Dudley   RBA RI         1865-1922
Artist and illustrator. He was born at Sheffield, 15 January 1867, the son of T.B. Hardy, the marine painter. He was educated at Boulogne School and at University College School, London, and studied art at Düsseldorf, at Antwerp with Verlat, 1884-85 and in Paris. It was his period in Paris and his contact with French chalk drawings and poster art that had the most lasting influence on his style. On his return to England, he was able to give a panache to his illustrative work which was only surpassed by Phil May (q.v.), using his black lines economically and mastering the black and white spaces of the page. He is at his best when most dashing, the more careful sketches can sometimes verge on the pretty. A prolific magazine artist, he drew many theatrical posters, including most of the Gilbert and Sullivan operettas and other Savoy Theatre productions. His oil paintings, colourful and with strong impasto are often of oriental and biblical subjects. He became RBA, 1889 and RI, 1897.

Illus: *The Humour of Holland [Werner, 1894]; The Bell Ringer of Angels [Bret Harte, 1897]; Sensations of Paris [R. Strong, 1912]*.
Contrib: *ILN [1889-94]; Illustrated Bits; Puck and Ariel [1890]; The Idler [1892]; The English Illustrated Magazine [1893-97]; The Pall Mall Budget [1894]; The Ludgate Monthly [1895]; Eureka [1897]; The Longbow [1898]; The Gentlewoman; The Sketch; The Minister; Punch [1900-02]; The Graphic [1902, 1910]*.
Exhib: G; L; M; New Gall.; RA; RBA; RI; ROI.
Colls: Author; Leeds; Newport.
Bibl: E. Spence, 'Some Leaves From Mr. Dudley Hardy's Sketch Book', *The Studio*, Vol.8, 1896, pp.33-38; A.E. Johnson, edited by, *DH, RI, RMS Brush, Pen and Pencil Series*, c.1920; P.V. Bradshaw, *The Art of the Illustrator*, 1918.
See illustration (below).

### HARDY, Evelyn
Contributed small military drawing to *The Illustrated London News*, 1889.

### HARDY, F.C.
Brother of Dudley Hardy (q.v.). He contributed to *The Longbow*, 1898.

### HARDY, Heywood   RWA         1842-1933
Animal painter, etcher and illustrator, decorator. He came from Bristol but settled in London in about 1870 having exhibited landscapes and animal paintings from 1861. He was elected RE, 1880, ROI, 1883 and ARWS, 1885. He contributed illustrations to *The Illustrated London News,* 1876 (Christmas) and *The Graphic,* 1880 (Christmas colour). He worked in North London and latterly at Littlehampton.

*DUDLEY HARDY RBA RI 1866-1922. 'Their College Boys.' Illustration for* London Opinion, *1894. Pen and ink, and wash, 9½ins. x 15ins. (24.1cm x 38.1cm).*

Author's Collection

**HARDY, M.D.**
Animal illustrator. Contributed to *The Strand Magazine,* 1891.

**HARDY, Norman H.** fl.1864-1914
Illustrator, etcher. He worked for most of his life in London, but in 1896 was attached to the *Sydney Herald,* New South Wales. He specialised in archaeological drawings for *The Illustrated London News,* 1889-90.
Exhib: Dudley Gall.; RA, 1891.

**HARDY, Paul** fl.1886-1899
Historical painter and illustrator. Hardy worked at Bexley Heath, Kent and married the artist Ida Wilson Clarke. He is seen at his best in costume romances and adolescent series, like Jarrald's 'Books For Manly Boys', 1894. A prolific, competent but unexciting purveyor of adventure.
Illus: *Little Peter [L. Malet, 1888]; Children of the New Forest [1892]; A Jacobite Exile [G.A. Henty]; The Whispering Wilds [Debenham]; Afloat in a Gypsy Van [Thompson]; That Bother of a Boy [Stebbing]; Sayings and Doings in Fairyland; Lord Lynton's Ward [1892]; Barker's Luck [Bret Harte, 1897].*
Contrib: *The English Illustrated Magazine [1886]; Sporting and Dramatic News; The Quiver; The Boys' Own Paper [1890]; Black & White [1891]; Strand Magazine [1891]; Chums [1892]; St. Pauls [1894]; The Rambler [1897]; The St. James's Budget [1898]; Cassell's Family Magazine; Cassell's Saturday Journal; The Gentlewoman; The Ludgate Monthly; The Girls' Own Paper; The Wide World Magazine.*
Exhib: L; RA.

**HARDY, Ruth** fl.1895-1898
Portrait and figure painter. Contributed social illustrations to *The English Illustrated Magazine,* 1895.
Exhib: P.

**HARDY, T.D.**
An illustration by this untraced artist appears in Willmott's *Poets of the Nineteenth Century,* 1857. It seems unlikely to be an error for Thomas Bush Hardy 1842-1897.

**HARE, Augustus John Cuthbert** 1834-1903
Writer of guide-books, illustrator and topographer. He was born in Rome in 1834 and, left an orphan, was adopted by his aunt and uncle. After an unhappy childhood, he was educated at Harrow and University College, Oxford. He travelled abroad in the 1860s and began to publish guide-books of the places he had visited. on his own admission he had visited every town and almost every village in Italy and France. He settled in England at St. Leonards, and died there in 1903.
Publ: *Epitaphs From Country Churchyards;* Murray's Handbooks for *Berks, Bucks, Oxfordshire, Durham* and *Northumberland; Memorials of a Quiet Life [1872-76]; Walks in Rome [1871]; Days Near Rome; Cities of Northern Italy; Cities of Central Italy; Cities of Southern Italy; Venice; Wanderings in Spain; Sketches of Holland and Scandinavia; Walks in London.*
Exhib: Leicester Gall., 1902.
Colls: Dundee; Leeds.

**HARE, St. George RI** 1857-1933
Portrait and subject painter and illustrator. He was born in Limerick in 1857 and studied with N.A. Brophy and then at the South Kensington Schools, 1875. RI, 1892. Died 30 January 1933.
Illus: *The Dead Gallant [Tristram, 1894 (with Hugh Thomson)].*
Contrib: *The Graphic [1893, 1899 and 1912].*
Exhib: G; L; M; RA; RBA; RHA; RI; RWA.
Colls: V & AM.

**HARE, Thomas M.**
Scientific illustrator to *The Illustrated London News,* 1847-49.

**HARGRAVE, John Gordon** 1894-
Artist and writer. He was born in 1894, the son of Gordon Hargrave, landscape painter. Educated at the Wordsworth School, Hawkshead, Hargrave produced illustrations for *Gulliver's Travels* and *The Rose and The Ring,* 1909 and was chief cartoonist of the *London Evening*

*Times* in 1911 at the age of seventeen. He joined the staff of C. Arthur Pearson in 1914.
Bibl: *Modern Book Illustrators and their Work,* Studio, 1914.

**HARKER, E.**
Contributed illustration to *The Illustrated London News,* 1860.

**HARMSWORTH, Alfred Charles William** 1865-1922
**Viscount Northcliffe**
Millionaire newspaper proprietor and founder of *The Daily Mail,* 1896. Harmsworth apparently contributed sketches of the Arctic to *The English Illustrated Magazine,* 1895, perhaps in connection with exploration schemes that he was financing.

**HARPER, Charles G.** 1863-1943
Artist, illustrator and author. He was born in 1863 and from the late 1880s was producing a steady stream of books on the English countryside, illustrated by himself. He specialised in coaching scenes and represented another nostalgic look backwards at the 18th century, a favourite Edwardian pastime. He died in Surrey on 8 December 1943.
Illus: *Royal Winchester [1889]; The Brighton Road [1892]; From Paddington to Penzance [1893]; The Marches of Wales [1894]; The Dover Road [1895]; The Portsmouth Road [1895]; Some English Sketching Grounds [1897]; Stories of the Streets of London [1899]; The Exeter Road [1899]; The Bath Road [1899]; The Great North Road [1900].*
Contrib: *The Pall Mall Budget [1891-92].*
Exhib: L, 1886.
Bibl: R.E.D. Sketchley, *English Bok. Illus.,* 1903, pp.47, 134.

**HARPER, Henry Andrew** 1835-1900
Author and painter. He was born at Blunham, Bedfordshire in 1835 and specialised in landscapes of the Holy Land. He accompanied the Earl of Dudley to the Near East, but in 1874, failed to be elected to the NWS. He died at Westerham in 1900.
Contrib: *ILN [1872 (Christmas)].*
Exhib: L; RA; RBA; RI.

**HARPER, H.G. "G G"** 1851-
Sporting journalist and artist. He was born in Cheshire in 1851 and lived for most of his life at Epsom, where he trained and rode his own race-horses. He hunted with the Surrey foxhounds and wrote several sporting novels and books.
Illus: *Romance of the Brighton Road [c.1892].*

**HARPER, T.** fl.1817-1843
Portrait painter and miniaturist. He exhibited at the RA from 1817-1843 and contributed illustrations to *Heath's Gallery* 1836.

**HARRISON, Charles**
Black and white artist and cartoonist. A very prolific contributor to *Punch* in the period 1896-1914, Harrison brought a rather more modern and jokey style into the paper during its formal years. His drawings are not carefully hatched black and white work, but vigorous and imaginative cartooning with the flatness of the Japanese print and the outline of French caricaturists such as Mars (q.v.). He was one of a number of artists who used comic ancients for his jokes. He was later cartoonist on *The Daily Express* and contributed work to American magazines. He sometimes signs his work Harry's Son.
Contrib: *The Strand Magazine [1891]; Chums; The St. James's Budget; Funny Folks; Cassell's Saturday Journal; Punch [1896-1914].*

**HARRISON, Emma Florence** fl.1887-1914
Figure painter and illustrator. She was working in London from 1887 and specialised in illustrating poetry and children's books in a later Pre-Raphaelite style deriving something as well from William Morris.
Illus: *In The Fairy Ring [1908]; Poems of Christina Rossetti [1910]; Guinevere [Tennyson, 1912]; Early Poems of William Morris [1914].*
Exhib: RA, 1887-91.

**HARRISON, George L.**                          fl.1881-1904
Figure and domestic painter, working in West Kensington. He
contributed hunting subjects to *The Illustrated London News,*
1884-86.

Exhib: RA; RBA, 1881-1904.

**HARRISON, Thomas Erat**                          1853-1917
Sculptor, painter, illustrator and engraver. Although not a very
prolific illustrator, Harrison drew for books at various times and
designed bookplates. Two examples of the latter, dated 1887 and
1907 are in the Victoria and Albert Museum.

Exhib: GG; L; RA; RHA.

**HART, Dorothy**
Possibly a member of the Birmingham School, clearly influenced by
it. She was working at Heathdale, Harborne, Birmingham in 1897,
when she won a *Studio* competition.

Bibl: *The Studio,* Vol.II, 1897, p.71, illus.

**HART, Frank**                          1878-1959
Black and white figure artist. He was born at Brighton on 1 November
1878 and was drawing for magazines from the age of twenty. He was a
regular contributor to *Punch,* most frequently in the 1920s, where his
work is notable for fine penmanship and a carefully observed view of
country life and ways. Hart was a lecturer on black and white art and
gave many talks throughout the country, drawing directly on to the
blackboard. He died in 1959.

Publ: *Dolly's Society Book [1902]; How The Animals Did Their Bit [1914-18];
Andrew, Bogie and Jack; One Long Holiday.*
Illus: *Master Toby's Hunt; Little Lass; Peter and Co.*
Contrib: *The Temple Magazine [1896-97]; The Graphic; Punch [1914].*
Exhib: RA; RI.
Colls: Brighton; Eastbourne.

**HART, William**                          fl.1823-1894
Landscape painter. He was born at Paisley, 31 March 1823 and
emigrated to the United States. He worked first as a coach painter,
then as a portrait painter, finally setting up a studio in New York in
1853. He became a member of the National Academy in 1858 and
President of the Brooklyn Academy of Design. He made a number of
illustrations for the books of John Gould.

**HARTE, George C.**                          fl.1885-1893
Genre painter. He was working at Bedford Park, 1885-86 and
contributed boating subjects to *The Illustrated London News* in 1893.
Exhib: L.

**HARTRICK, Archibald Standish   RWS**                          1864-1950
Painter, black and white artist and illustrator. He was born at
Bangalore on 7 August 1864, the son of an army officer and was
educated at Fettes College and Edinburgh University. He studied art
at the Slade School under Alphonse Legros, 1884-85, in Paris under
Boulanger and Cormon, 1886-87 and joined the staff of *The Daily
Graphic* in 1890. Although Hartrick was very prolific as a magazine
artist and often worked as a special for *The Graphic,* his style
remained consistently high and he was almost unsurpassed in chalk by
any other British artists. It was perhaps typical of the man that he did
not think of himself as an illustrator and went on to become an
excellent watercolourist and a significant lithographer. He was at his
best when depicting rural characters and many of them have an
uncanny affinity with the rustic illustrators of the 60s. A whole set of
these drawings called Cotswold types was acquired for the British
Museum. He was a member of the NEA from 1893 and became ARWS
in 1910 and RWS in 1920. He died in 1950.

Illus: *Soldiers Tales [Rudyard Kipling, 1896]; The Body Snatcher [R.L.
Stevenson].*
Contrib: *The Graphic [1889-95]; Daily Graphic [1890]; The Pall Mall Budget
[1893]; Daily Chronicle; The Quiver; The New Budget [1895]; Black and White
[1899-1900]; The Butterfly [1899]; Cassell's Family Magazine [1899]; Fun
[1901]; The Yellow Book; The Ludgate Monthly; The Strand Magazine;
Pearson's Magazine; The Pall Mall Magazine.*

ARCHIBALD STANDISH HARTRICK RWS 1864-1950. 'Pulling Down The
Strand.' Drawing for illustration, unpublished. Pen and ink. 16¼ins. x 11⅜ins.
(41.3cm x 28.9).                                    Victoria and Albert Museum

Exhib: B; G; L; M; NEA; RA; RBA; RHA; RSA; RWS.
Colls: Aberdeen; BM; Liverpool; Manchester; Melbourne; Sydney; V & AM.
Bibl: *The Studio* Winter No., 1900-1, p.72, illus.; *Apollo,* XXIV, 1936; A.S.
Hartrick. *Painter's Pilgrimage Through Fifty Years,* 1939.
See illustration (above).

**HARVEY, Sydney**                          fl.1897-1907
Cartoonist for *Moonshine,* about 1901. He worked at Muswell Hill
and contributed drawings to *Punch,* 1897-1902.

**HARVEY, William**                          1796-1866
Wood engraver and illustrator. He was born at Newcastle-upon-Tyne
on 13 July 1796 and was apprenticed to Thomas Bewick (q.v.) who
employed him on the woodcuts for the famous edition of *Aesop's
Fables,* published in 1823. Harvey left Bewick in 1817, retained
contact with the engraver till his death, but became a pupil of B.R.
Haydon in London. He studied anatomy under Sir Charles Bell and
became associated with Charles Knight, the popular journalist and
educator for whom he undertook work. Harvey did little wood
engraving after his success in engraving Haydon's 'Dentatus' in the
manner of a copper plate. This heralded a new style and expertise in
wood engraving which was to result in elaborate Victorian
compositions. Harvey gradually became the most popular illustrator
of the 1840s, taking on work of such a scale, hundreds of vignettes in
*The Arabian Nights* and three thousand illustrations in the decade
1828 to 1838, that it almost revolutionised the market. Harvey was
one of the first to use numerous outside engravers on his work, thus
opening the way for a less personal approach but also for speed. His
shortcomings were his lack of success with modern subjects and his
total lack of humour in drawing. He designed the third cover of *Punch*
in July 1842 but it was considered too serious and his initial letters

were thought too graceful! By the 1860s his decorative pages, elegant figures and balanced foilage, was considered 'too mannered' but his influence on Gilbert and early Fred Walker was considerable. He died at Richmond on 13 January 1866.

Illus: *History of Wines [Henderson, 1824]; The Tower Menagerie [1828]; Northcote's Fables [1828]; The Garden and Menagerie of the Zoological Society [1831]; Children in the Wood [1831]; The Blind Beggar of Bethnal Green [1832]; Story Without An End; Pictorial Prayer Book; Thousand and One Nights [Lane, 1840]; London [Knight, 1841]; Metrical Tales [Samuel Lover, 1849]; The Pilgrim's Progress* and the *Holy War [1850]; Oriental Fairy Tales [1854]; The Fables of John Gray [1854]; Tales From Shakespeare [C. and M. Lamb, 1856]; The Queen of Hearts [Wilkie Collins, 1859]; Eugene Aram [T. Hood]; Natural History [J.G. Wood].*
Contrib: *The Observer [1828]; Bell's Life; Punch [1841-42]; ILN [1843-59 (decor and political)]; The Illustrated London Magazine [1854].*
Colls: BM; Fitzwilliam; V & AM.
Bibl: M.H. Spielmann, *The History of Punch,* 1895, pp.42-44; The Brothers Dalziel, *A Record of Work,* 1840-1890, 1901, pp.12-21; P. Muir, *Victorian Illustrated Books,* 1971, pp.28-33, illus.

## HARWOOD, John                                fl.1818-1829
Architectural and landscape painter. He worked in London and contributed to *Lancashire Illustrated,* 1829.

Exhib: BI; RA; RBA.

## HASELDEN, William Kerridge                          1872-1953
Cartoonist and caricaturist. He was born at Seville in 1872 and began drawing professionally in 1903. He joined the staff of the *Daily Mirror* in 1904 and began to contribute to *Punch* in 1906, concentrating on theatrical caricatures. In the 1920s and 1930s he was well-known for his 'art deco' caricatures of Edith Evans, Gertrude Lawrence, Shaw, Ivor Novello etc.

## HASSALL, John   RI                              1868-1948
Watercolourist, poster-designer and illustrator. He was born at Walmer in 1868 and educated at Newtown Abbot College, Devon and Neuenheim College, Heidelberg. He began life as a farmer in Manitoba, abandoning this for art and studying at Antwerp and Paris, 1891-94, in the former under P. Van Havermaet and in the latter with Bougereau. Hassall was an original and versatile designer of illustrations from 1895 onwards, contributing cartoons to many leading magazines, designing theatre posters, commercial posters for Messrs. David Allen and greetings cards, boys' books and nursery rhymes. His chief influence would seem to be the flat colours and two-dimensional decorative quality of Japanese prints, which he adapts to his own work with thick outline and careful patterning. He also executed fine watercolours for boys' adventure stories, the scene drawn in with the brush and the washes applied dryly and carefully. Hassall's work is synonymous with colour except for his First War booklets in line. He was elected RI in 1901, and RMS, the same year. A Centenary Exhibition was held at Leighton House 1-11 April 1968 He signs his work *Hassall* or *JH*

Illus: *Two Well Worn Shoes [1899]; The Princess and The Dragon; John Hassall's New Picture Book [1908]; Ye Berlyn Tapestrie Wilhelm's Invasion of Flanders [1916]; Keep Smiling [c.1916].*
Contrib: *The Daily Graphic [1890]; The Sketch [1894]; Judy; Moonshine; Pick-Me-Up; The New Budget [1895]; The West End Review [1898]; The Graphic [1899-1911]; Illustrated Bits; The Idler; Eureka; ILN [1900, 1908 (Christmas)]; The Sphere.*
Exhib: B; G; L; RA; RI; RMS; RSW.
Colls: Author; V & AM.
Bibl: 'The London Sketch Club' *The Magazine of Art,* March 1899, p.229; 'The Poster Paintings and Illustrations of John Hassall RI' *The Studio,* Vol. 36, 1906, illus.; *The Studio,* Winter No., 1900-1, pp.44-47, illus.; A.E. Johnson (editor) *JH, RI,* Pen and Pencil Series, c.1920.
See illustrations (below and p.336).

*JOHN HASSALL RI 1868-1948. 'Drunken Man and Teetotaler.' Pen and watercolour. 5ins. x 3½ins. (12.7cm x 8.9cm).*                Author's Collection

*JOHN HASSALL RI 1868-1948. 'Diner and Waiter.' Pen and watercolour. 5ins. x 3½ins. (12.7cm x.8.9cm).*                Author's Collection

*JOHN HASSALL RI 1868-1948. Gunfight. Illustration for a boys' magazine. Watercolour. 10ins. x 12ins. (25.4cm x 30.5cm).*     Author's Collection

**HASSELL, Edward**                                     **-1852**
Topographical artist and lithographer. He was the son of John Hassell 1767-1825, the engraver and drawing master, and was awarded premiums by the Society of Arts, 1828-29. He was a member of the RBA from 1841 and held the office of Secretary. He died at Lancaster in 1852.

Illus: *Historical Account of the Parish of St. Marylebone [Thomas Smith, 1833].*
Exhib: BI; RA; RBA.

**HASSELL, John**                                     **1767-1825**
An engraver and drawing master and close friend of George Morland. He produced numerous guide-books with aquatints after his own drawings.

Publ: *Tour of the Isle of Wight [1790]; Picturesque Guide to Bath [1793]; Life of George Morland [1806]; Speculum or the art of Drawing in Watercolours [1808]; Aqua Pictura [1813]; Picturesque Rides and Walks [1817]; The Tour of the Grand Junction Canal [1819]; Camera or the Art of Watercolour [1823]; Excursions of Pleasure and Sports on the Thames [1823].*
Contrib: *The Antiquarian Itinerary [1816].*
Exhib: RA, 1789.
Colls: BM; Guildford; Manchester.

**HASWELL**
Landscape artist and designer of initial letters in the style of Richard Doyle. He contributed to *The Illustrated London Magazine,* 1853-54.

**HATHERELL, William   RI RWA**                       **1855-1928**
Landscape and figure painter and illustrator. He was born at Westbury-on-Trym on 18 October 1855 and was educated at private schools before entering the RA Schools in 1877. He was a regular contributor to magazines from about 1889, having done his first illustrative work for Cassell's. Hatherell was at his best with stories, where his moody wash drawings and his care to reflect accurately a town, country or historical period could be shown to the full. Thorp says that his flowing wash style was influential on younger men, it is certainly typical of the 1890s. He was one of the few artists to produce illustrations in oil on board, grey monochrome studies which often have a rather French appearance. He was elected RI in 1888, ROI, 1898 and RWA in 1903. He died 7 December 1928.

Illus: *Annals of Westminster Abbey [E.J. Bradley, 1895]; Tantallon Castle [E.R. Pennell, 1895]; Sentimental Tommy [J.M. Barrie, 1897]; Romeo and Juliet [1912]; Island Night's Entertainments [R.L. Stevenson, 1913]; The Prince and the Pauper [S.L. Clemens, 1923].*

Contrib: *The Graphic [1889-1912]; The Quiver [1890]; Black and White [1891]; The Picturesque Mediterranean [1891]; The English Illustrated Magazine [1891-92]; The Pall Mall Budget [1892]; Cassell's Family Magazine; Chums; Cassell's Saturday Journal; Harper's Magazine; Scribner's Magazine.*
Exhib: B; G; L; M; NEA; RA; RBA; RI; ROI.
Colls: V & AM.

**HATTON, Brian**                                      1887-1916
A promising young black and white artist who was killed in the First World War. He gained a Bronze Medal from the Royal Drawing Society at the age of eight and later studied at Oxford, 1905-6 and at South Kensington and Julian's in Paris. An extremely strong draughtsman of the country and its people, in thick ink lines.
Contrib: *The Graphic [11 Dec. 1915].*
Exhib: P; RA; ROI.
Colls: Witt Photo.
Bibl: W. Shaw Sparrow, 'BH' *Walker's Quarterly*, Feb. 1926.

**HATTON, Helen Howard (Mrs. W.H. Margetson)**        1860-
Watercolourist and pastellist. She was born in Bristol in 1860 and studied art at the RA Schools and at Colarossi's in Paris. She married the painter W.H. Margetson 1861-1940 (q.v.), and worked mainly in Berkshire.
Contrib: *The English Illustrated Magazine [1886 (architecture)].*
Exhib: B; G; L; M; RA; RI; ROI.

**HAVELOCK, Helen**
Amateur topographer and daughter of W. Havelock of Ingress Park. She contributed an illustration to *Britton's Beauties of England and Wales,* 1808.

**HAVERS, Alice (Mrs. Frederick Morgan)**             1850-1890
Watercolourist and illustrator. She was born in Norfolk in 1850, the daughter of the manager of the Falkland Islands, where she was brought up. She returned to England in 1870 to study at South Kensington and in 1872, married the artist Frederick Morgan. She exhibited at the Salon, receiving a special mention in 1888 and was patronised by Queen Victoria.
Illus: *Cape Town Dicky; The White Swans [1890].*
Contrib: *Cassell's Family Magazine.*
Exhib: G; L; M; RA; RBA; RHA; SWA.
Colls: Cardiff; Liverpool; Norwich; Sheffield.

**HAWEIS, Mrs. H.R.**
Wrote and illustrated *Chaucer For Children, A Golden Key,* 1877.

**HAWKER, J.**                                         fl.1804-1812
Topographer and landscape painter. He exhibited at the RA 1804-09 and contributed to *Britton's Beauties of England and Wales* 1812.

**HAWKER, Peter**                                      1786-1853
Artist, soldier and author. He served in the Peninsular War with the 14th Light Dragoons and afterwards patented improvements to the pianoforte and wrote a sporting journal. He died in 1853.
Illus: *Instructions to Young Sportsmen [1824, AL 389].*

**HAWKSWORTH, John**
Topographer, working in London about 1820. He contributed to *The History and Antiquities of Islington,* 1823.

**'HAY'**
Pseudonym of caricaturist contributing to *Vanity Fair,* 1886, 1888-89 and 1893. His style is close to that of Pellegrini.

**HAY, George    RSA**                                1831-1913
History and subject painter and illustrator. He was born in Edinburgh in 1831 and studied in the RSA School and at the Trustees Gallery, entering the architectural profession at the age of seventeen. He later abandoned this for painting, specialising in pictures of Scottish life and history. He was elected ARSA in 1869, RSA in 1876 and

Secretary, 1881-1907. He died 31 August 1913.
Illus: *Pen and Pencil Pictures From the Poets [1866]; Poems and Songs by Robert Burns [1875]; Red Gauntlet [Walter Scott, 1894].*
Exhib: G; RSA.

**HAY, Helen**                                         fl.1895-1940
Black and white artist. She was probably associated with the Glasgow School and contributed to *The Evergreen,* 1895-96. She was working in Paisley in 1933 and at Egglesham, 1937.
Exhib: G; RSA.

**HAYDON, G.H.**                                       fl.1860-1892
Barrister, traveller and amateur artist. According to G.S. Layard, Haydon went to Australia as a youth to seek his fortune and made a number of sketches of the interior, later reproduced in the *Australian Illustrated* in about 1876. He was back in England by 1860 and became steward of Bridewell and Bethlem Hospitals. Haydon was a member of the Langham Sketch Club, became a friend of Charles Keene and John Leech, and was used by the latter as a model in some of his sporting drawings. He himself drew for *Punch,* 1860-62.
Bibl: G.S. Layard, *Charles Keene,* 1892, p.247.

**HAYES, Frederick William    ARCA FRGS**             1848-1918
Landscape painter, illustrator and author. He was born at New Ferry, Cheshire on 18 July 1848 and was educated at Liverpool College and privately. He trained as an architect with a firm in Ipswich, but turned to painting and studied with H. Dawson. Returning to the North-West, Hayes helped to found the Liverpool Watercolour Society; he remained in the city until about 1880 when he moved to London. A socialist and historian, Hayes specialised in the scenery of North Wales and illustrated his own books. He died 7 September 1918.
Illus: *The Story of the Phalanx [1894]; A Kent Squire [1900]; Gwynett of Thornhaugh [1900]; The Shadow of a Throne [1904]; A Prima Donna's Romance [1905]; Captain Kirk Webbe [1907]; The United Kingdom Limited [1910].*
Exhib: B; L; M; RA; RBA; RCA; RI; ROI.
Colls: BM; Glasgow; V & AM.

**HEAPS, Chris**
Black and white artist. Contributor to *The Graphic,* 1915.

**HEATH, Charles**                                     1785-1848
Engraver and illustrator. He executed plates for popular works and engraved the pictures of Benjamin West. He is best remembered as the publisher of illustrated 'Annuals' during the 1830s.
Exhib: RA and RBA, 1801-25.

**HEATH, Ernest Dudley**                               fl.1886-1927
Painter and illustrator. He was the son of Henry Charles Heath, Miniature Painter to Queen Victoria. He studied at the RA Schools and became lecturer on art, University of London Extension, 1903-08, Principal of the Hampstead Garden Suburbs School of Arts and Crafts, 1914-26, and lecturer on Principles of Art Teaching, Royal College of Art, 1927.
Contrib: *The English Illustrated Magazine [1893-94 (cockney figures)].*
Exhib: L; M; RA; RBA; RMS; ROI.

**HEATH, Henry**                                       fl.1824-1850
Probably the brother of William Heath (q.v.). He was a versatile and imitative artist, working in the loose and coarse Heath manner between the years 1824-30. He did imitation caricatures in the style of John Doyle 'HB' signed 'HH' for Messrs. Fores, 1831 and etched vignettes in the style of Cruikshank and lithographs in the style of Seymour from 1834. He was employed to make political caricatures by Spooner, the publisher and his work was collected and published by Charles Tilt. Heath undertook one cartoon for *Punch* in 1843 and his sets include *London Characters,* 12 pls., 1834 and *Domestic Miseries, Domestic Blisses,* 12 liths., 1850. He is believed to have emigrated to Australia.

**HEATH, Thomas Hastead of Cardiff**      fl.1879-1905

Portrait and figure painter. He specialised in seascapes but did fine figure studies in sepia ink, reminiscent of Wilkie. He also designed a fixture card for the 'Cardiff Harlequins'.

Exhib: L; RA; RBA.

**HEATH, William 'Paul Pry'**      1795-1840

Watercolourist and caricaturist who worked mostly under the pseudonym of Paul Pry. He called himself 'Portrait and Military painter' and was reputed to be an 'ex-captain of dragoons' but is not recorded in the Army List. Heath began life as a draughtsman and his main claim to fame rests on his having produced the first caricature magazine in Europe, *The Glasgow* later *Northern Looking-Glass,* 1825-26. Although this was a provincial work and without much text, it does pre-date Charles Philipon's similar publication. The height of his popularity fell between the years 1809-34, after which his humour was displaced by that of Robert Seymour and John Doyle (qq.v.). After this period he concentrated on topography and straight illustration.

Illus: *The Looking-Glass [1830]; The Life of a Soldier [1823]; Minor Morals [Bowring, 1834-39]; The Martial Achievements of Great Britain and Her Allies* and *Historical Military and Naval Anecdotes.*
Colls: V & AM.
See illustration (Colour Plate VI p.56).

**HEAVISIDE, John Smith**      1812-1864

Engraver. He was born at Stockton-on-Tees in 1812 and worked in London and Oxford. He illustrated Parker's archaeological books and died at Kentish Town on 3 October 1864.

**HEAVISIDE, T.**

Brother of John Smith Heaviside (q.v.). He engraved portraits of Thomas Bewick and John Owen and contributed to *The Illustrated London News,* 1849-51.

**HEBBLETHWAITE, H. Sydney**

Black and white artist. Thorpe describes him as an artist of promise and invention who died young. He contributed drawings to *Pick-Me-Up* in 1899 and another drawing, perhaps posthumous appeared in *The Graphic,* 1908.

**HEFFER, Edward A. of Liverpool**      fl.1860-1885

Decorative designer, architect and illustrator. He contributed work to *The Illustrated London News,* 1860-61.

Exhib: L; RA.

**HELLÉ. André**

French theatrical designer and illustrator. He was closely associated with the Opera Comique at Paris and did a great deal of work for children's books.

Contrib: *The Graphic [1910].*

**HELLEU, Paul César**      1859-1927

Painter and etcher. He was born at Vannes on 17 December 1859 and became a pupil of Gérome at the École Nationale des Beaux-Arts. Helleu was a talented painter of churches and of architecture but was best known in this country during the Edwardian period for his sensitive and charming etchings of society beauties. Among his subjects were Queen Alexandra, the Princess of Connaught and the Duchess of Marlborough. He became ARE, 1892, and RE, 1897. He died at Paris, 23 March 1927.

Contrib: *The Graphic [1901].*
Exhib: L; P; RE.

**HELMICK, Howard**      1845-1907

American figure painter and illustrator. He was born at Zanesville, Ohio, in 1845 and studied in Paris under Cabanel. He lived in London for some years and on returning to the United States became Professor of the History of Art at Georgetown University. He died on 18 April 1907. RBA, 1879, and RE, 1881.

Contrib: *The Graphic [1880].*
Exhib: B; G; L; M; RA; RBA; RE.

**HEMING, Matilda (Miss Lowry)**      fl.1808-1855

Portrait painter. She was the daughter of the engraver Willson Lowry and exhibited at the RA, 1808-09 and 1847-55. She contributed an illustration to Britton's *Beauties of England and Wales,* 1807.

**HEMY, Charles Napier**    RA RWS      1841-1917

Marine, landscape and still-life painter. He was born at Newcastle-upon-Tyne on 24 May 1841 and studied with William Bell Scott (q.v.). From 1850 to 1852, he sailed round the world developing a great knowledge of and interest in shipping, but on his return entered the Dominican order and studied for three years in monasteries at Newcastle and Lyons. He finally abandoned this life in 1862 and went to Antwerp to study art under Henri Leys, settling in London in 1870 and finally moving to Falmouth. Hemy's reputation is principally as a marine artist and he made many studies from his own yacht, the *Van der Meer,* which he kept at Falmouth. He was elected ARA in 1898 and RA in 1910, and RWS in 1897. He died on 30 September 1917.

Contrib: *The English Illustrated Magazine [1883-87].*
Exhib: B; G; L; M; New Gall.; RA; RI; RSA; RWS.
Colls: Birmingham; Bristol; Leeds; Newcastle.

**HENDERSON, Keith**    OBE RWS      1883-

Writer and illustrator. He was born in 1883 and after being educated at Marlborough, studied art at the Slade School and in Paris. He served in the First World War and was War Artist to the Royal Airforce in 1940.

Publ: *Letters to Helen; Palmgroves and Hummingbirds; Prehistoric Man; Burns by Himself; Romaunt of the Rose [1911]; No Second Spring; Christina Strang.*
Illus: *Conquest of Mexico [Prescott, 1922]; Green Mansions [W.H. Hudson, 1931]; Buckaroo [E. Cunningham, 1934].*
Exhib: B; FAS, 1914, 1917; G; L; NEA; RA; ROI; RSA; RWS.
Colls: V & AM.
Bibl: *Modern Book Illustrators and their Work,* Studio, 1914.

**HENDRY, Sydney**

Black and white artist specialising in children. He contributed to *Punch* in 1903.

**HENFREY, Charles**

Contributed illustrations to *Public Works of Great Britain,* 1838, AL 410.

**HENLEY, A.W.**      fl.1880-1908

Landscape artist working in West London. He contributed illustrations to R.L. Stevenson's *Fontainbleau.*

Exhib: GG; RHA; RSA.

**HENLEY, Lionel Charles**    RBA      1843-c.1893

Genre painter. He was born in London in 1843 and studied art at Düsseldorf, making his début at exhibitions in Magdebourg. He returned to England and exhibited regularly from 1862, becoming RBA in 1879.

Contrib: *London Society [1865]; Fun [1865]; Foxe's Book of Martyrs [1867]; The Graphic [1870].*
Exhib: B; L; RA; RBA; ROI.

**HENNESSY, William John**    ROI      1839-1917

Landscape and genre painter and illustrator. He was born at Thomastown, Ireland, in 1839 and emigrated with his family to America when very young, remaining there till 1870. He attended the National Academy in New York in 1856 and became a member in 1863, but in 1870 settled in England, alternating his residence from time to time between Normandy and Sussex. Hennessy was something of an expert on American art and his own drawing style, very finished and slick, owes a good deal to that school. Amongst his best work is probably the series of illustrations to Jean Ingelow's 'Sarah de Berenger' in *Good Words,* 1880. He became ROI in 1902.

Illus: *Broken Wings [Avery Macalpine, 1897]; Marriage [Susan Ferrier, 1895]; The Suicide Club; The Rajah's Diamond [R.L. Stevenson, 1913].*
Contrib: *ILN; Dark Blue [1871-73]; The Graphic [1872-76, 1880]; Punch [1873-75]; The English Illustrated Magazine [1884-92]; Black & White [1891]; The Girls' Own Paper.*
Exhib: B; G; GG; L; M; NEA; NG; RA; RHA; ROI.

**HENNING, Archibald Samuel** -1864
Comic illustrator. He was the third son of the sculptor John Henning and the brother-in-law of Kenny Meadows (q.v.). A rather slap-dash artist and bohemian character, he designed *Punch's* first wrapper and was rated 'a fair and prolific draughtsman on wood' by W.J. Linton. He may have undertaken medical and natural history illustrations in the 1850s.
Contrib: *Punch [1841-42]; The Squib; The Great Gun; Joe Miller The Younger; The Man in The Moon; The Comic Times; The Illustrated London Magazine [1854].*

**HENRY, Paul RHA** 1876-
Landscape painter. He worked in Liverpool, Belfast, Dublin and County Wicklow, and was elected ARHA in 1926 and RHA, 1929. He contributed illustrations of children to *The Graphic*, 1910.

**HENRY, Thomas** fl.1891-1914
Painter and illustrator. He contributed to *Punch*, 1914.
Exhib: Dowdeswell Gall.

**HENTY, George Alfred** 1832-1902
Author, journalist and amateur artist. He was born at Trumpington, Cambridge, on 8 December 1832 and educated at Westminster and at Caius College, Cambridge. Henty went out to the Crimea in the Purveyors' Department of the Army and after being invalided home, served with the Italian Legion. From 1866, he was special correspondent for *The Standard* in the Austro-Italian, Franco-Prussian and Turco-Serbian Wars and the Abyssinian and Ashanti Expeditions. His illustrated reports attracted considerable attention, but for their writing rather than their drawing! Henty went on to use these experiences in numerous adventure books for boys. He died 16 November 1902.
Contrib: *ILN [1868].*
Bibl: G.M. Fenn, *GAH The Story of an Active Life*, 1907, p.27.

**HERALD, James Watterson** 1859-1914
A landscape and coastal painter. He was born at Forfar in 1859 and studied under Herkomer (q.v.). His style is closely associated with the Glasgow School, he died at Arbroath in 1914. Some prints by this artist dating from about 1900, may have been intended as book illustrations.

**HERBERT, John Rogers RA RHI** 1810-1890
Portrait, romantic and religious painter. He was born at Maldon, Essex, in 1810 and studied at the RA Schools, 1826. He was an early teacher of art at the Government School of Design at Somerset House, Herbert was a regular book illustrator in the early part of his career, but after his conversion to Roman Catholicism, he gave this up to concentrate on large religious paintings. He was elected ARA in 1841 and RA in 1846, retiring in 1886.
Illus: *Legends of Venice [Edited by Roscoe, 1840].*
Contrib: *The Keepsake [1836]; Heath's Gallery [1838].*
Exhib: BI; NWS; RA; RBA.
Colls: BM; L; V & AM.

**HERDMAN, Robert RSA** 1829-1888
Portrait and history painter. He was born at Rattray on 17 September 1829 and after studying at St. Andrews University, became a pupil of R.S. Lauder at the Edinburgh Trustees Academy. He travelled to Italy, 1855-56 and established himself from 1861, when he became ARSA, as a leading portrait painter and painter of Scottish history. He left his large collection of artists' portraits to Aberdeen. He died at Edinburgh on 10 January 1888.
Contrib: *Poems and Songs by Robert Burns [1875].*
Exhib: RA; RSA.
Colls: Edinburgh; Glasgow.

**HERING, George Edwards** 1805-1879
Painter and illustrator. Born in London in 1805, the son of a bookbinder of German extraction. He studied art and worked in

Munich and then travelled in Italy and Turkey, Hungary and Transylvania, which were the most usual subjects for his pictures. He settled in London, but frequently travelled on painting expeditions.
Illus: *Sketches On The Danube, in Hungary and Transylvania, [1838]; The Mountains and Lakes of Switzerland, The Tyrol and Italy [1847, AT 63].*
Exhib: BI; RA, 1836; RBA, 1838-
Colls: V & AM.

**HERKOMER, Sir Hubert von RA** 1849-1914
Painter and illustrator. He was born at Waal, Bavaria, on 26 May 1849, the son of Lorenz Herkomer, who settled in England in 1857. He studied art at South Kensington from 1866, founded the Herkomer School of Art at Bushey in 1883 and was Slade Professor at Oxford, 1885-94. Herkomer was one of the grandees of Victorian painting in the 1880s and 1890s, receiving many honours both at home and abroad. He became ARA in 1879, RA in 1890 and was knighted in 1907.

Herkomer's greatest strength was as a composer of pictures and as a figure painter. His principal achievement in book illustration was the series of social realistic subjects that he drew for *The Graphic*, 1870-79. These included his famous 'Heads of the People', 1875, and such famous images of Victorian society as 'Christmas in a Workhouse'. Herkomer's talent for expressing the plight of the under-privileged was again used when he illustrated Hardy's *Tess of the D'Urbevilles* for the same magazine in 1891. Herkomer died at Budleigh Salterton on 31 March 1914.

Contrib: *The Quiver [1868]; The Sunday Magazine [1870]; Good Words For The Young [1870]; The Graphic [1870-79]; ILN [1871-73]; London Society [1872]; The Cornhill Magazine [1872]; Fun; Black & White [title]. & White [title].*
Exhib: B; G; GG; L; M; New Gall; P; RA; RBA; RE; RHA; ROI; RSA; RWS.
Colls: BM; Leeds; Manchester.
Bibl: *Autobiography*, 1890; *English Influences On Vincent Van Gogh*, Arts Council 1974-75, p.52.

**HÉROND, L.J.**
French artist, contributing illustrations of Paris to *Cassell's Illustrated Family Paper*, 1857.

**HERRING, Benjamin** -1871
Sporting artist. He was the son of J.F. Herring (q.v.) who looked upon him as his real successor in equestrian art. He was, however, a rather mediocre painter but contributed to *The Illustrated London News*, 1850-60 and 1864.
Exhib: BI; RBA, 1861-63.

**HERRING, John Frederick** 1795-1865
Sporting artist and illustrator. He was born in Surrey in 1795, the son of an American, and was inspired at an early age to draw horses. He worked as a coach painter and even for some time as a coach driver, later residing in Doncaster and setting up as a horse portraitist. He worked also at Newmarket, London and at Tunbridge Wells, where he died in 1865; he became a member of the SBA in 1841.
Contrib: *The Sporting Review [1842-46]; ILN [1844-45, 1864]; The Illustrated Times [1859]; Bell's Life in London.*
Exhib: BI; RA; RBA.
Bibl: W. Shaw Sparrow, *British Sporting Artists*, 1922, pp.215-227.

**HERRING, John Frederick, Jnr.** 1815-1907
Sporting artist. He was born in 1815, the eldest son of J.F. Herring (q.v.) and the brother of the B. Herring (q.v.). He made a speciality of farmyard scenes but was a less inspired painter than his father whom he mercilessly imitated. He died at Cambridge in 1907.
Contrib: *Old Sporting Magazine.*
Exhib: B; BI; RA; RBA.

**HESTER, R. Wallace** fl.1897-1913
Engraver and caricaturist. He worked at Tooting, 1897, and at Purley, 1901, and contributed to *Vanity Fair*, 1910-13.
Exhib: RA, 1897-1904.

**HEWERDINE, Matthew Bede**                    1871-1909
Cartoonist and book illustrator. He worked in Hull and Oxford and illustrated *Lest We Forget Them,* Lady Glover, 1900, and *Cloister and the Hearth,* C. Reade, 1904.

**HEWETSON, Edward**
Architectural draughtsman. He contributed illustrations to *Ackermann's Repository,* 1825.

**HEWITT, John**
Contributed illustrations to *Public Works of Great Britain,* 1838, AL 410.

**HICKLING, P.B.**                    fl.1895-1914
Illustrator. A very competent but unrecorded pen artist who worked for magazines. Contributed to *Fun,* 1895; *The Boys' Own Paper* and *The Graphic,* 1902-06; *Punch,* 1914. He also illustrated a novel *The Three Clerks,* John Long, c.1908.

**HICKS, George Elger**                    1824-1914
Genre and portrait painter and illustrator. He was born at Lymington in Hampshire in 1824 and trained as a doctor, abandoning this career for one of a painter and training at the Bloomsbury and RA Schools. Hicks was one of the most lush painters of Victorian life, such busy subjects as 'The General Post Office - One Minute to Six', 1860 and elaborate wedding pieces with every present shown in glittering oil, are his. He was also a very competent illustrator of figures and did a fair amount of this work in early life. He died in London in 1914. RBA, 1889.

Publ: *A Guide to Figure Painting,* 1853.
Contrib: *Campbell's Gertrude of Wyoming [Art Union of London, 1846]; Sacred Allegories [1856]; The Farmer's Boy [Robert Bloomfield, 1857]; Favourite Modern Ballads [1859].*
Exhib: B; GG; L; M; RA; RBA; RSA.
Colls: Ulster Museum.
Bibl: Chatto & Jackson, *Treatise on Wood Engraving,* 1861, p.598; J. Maas, *Victorian Painters,* 1969, p.117.

**HIGHAM, Bernard**                    fl.1895-1925
Landscape painter and illustrator. He was working at Wallington, Surrey, 1917-25. Contributed drawings to *The Idler,* c.1895; *The English Illustrated Magazine,* 1897.
Exhib: RA, 1917-19.

**HIGHAM, Sydney**                    fl.1890-1905
Comic artist in black and white. His drawings are amusing but rather coarse in execution, he worked for a number of magazines and may have emigrated to Canada in about 1905.
Contrib: *Daily Graphic [1890]; Penny Illustrated Paper; The Graphic [1901 and 1903-05].*
Colls: Author.

**HIGHAM, Thomas**                    1796-1844
Topographer and engraver. Contributed to *The Antiquarian Itinerary,* 1817. Exhibited at RA, 1824-30.

**HILL, David Octavius  RSA**                    1802-1870
Landscape painter, illustrator and photographer. He was born at Perth in 1802 and studied with Andrew Wilson at Edinburgh, making his début in exhibitions in 1823. Hill specialised in Scottish life and landscape pictures, but he was always an experimenter and worked also in lithography. He was the first Secretary of the Royal Scottish Academy, 1830-69, and ARSA in 1826 and RSA three years later. He was one of the first artists to appreciate the potential of photography when he used calotypes made by the Adamsons for his celebrated painting 'The Disruption', commemorating a religious furore of the 1840s. From about 1843, he concentrated on photography and died in Edinburgh 17 May 1870.

Illus: *Sketches of Scenery in Perthshire [liths.]; The Abbot, Red Gauntlet, The Fair Maid of Perth [Scott]; Poems and Songs by Robert Burns [1875]; The Land of Burns.*
Exhib: BI; RA; RBA; RSA.
Colls: Birkenhead; Edinburgh; Glasgow.
Bibl: D. Bruce, *Sun Pictures,* Studio Vista, 1973.

**HILL, Leonard RAVEN-    see RAVEN-HILL, Leonard**

**HILL, Rowland    see 'RIP'**

**HILL, Vernon**                    1887-
Illustrator, lithographer and sculptor. He was born in Halifax in 1887, apprenticed to a trade lithographer at thirteen and was a student teacher at seventeen. In 1908 he was working under John Hassall RI (q.v.) and published his first illustrations the year following. Hill is strongest as a figure draughtsman and his swirling bodies and large wave and plant shapes, make him a classical equivalent of the Beardsley eroticism. In November 1909, *The Bodleian,* referred to him as 'a youth only just past his teens, his inventions have the eternal quality of beauty, his imagination is so rich so astonishing in its originality, and he is beside so gifted with rare humour, that his work defies comparison with anything known to us . . .'

Illus: *The Arcadian Calendar for 1910 [1909]; The New Inferno [Stephen Phillips Jnr., 1911]; Ballads Weird and Wonderful [Richard Chope, 1912]; Tramping with a Poet in the Rockies [Stephen Graham, 1922].*
Exhib: Leicester Gall; NEA; RA; RSA; 1908-27.
Colls: V & AM.
Bibl: *The Studio,* Vol.57, 1912-13; *Modern Book Illustrators and Their Work,* Studio, 1914, illus.; B. Peppin, *Fantasy Book Illustration,* 1975, pp.155-163, illus.

**HILLS, Robert**                    1769-1844
Watercolourist. He was born in Islington on 26 June 1769 and received drawing lessons from John Gresse. He is principally remembered as a painter and etcher of animals and as a founder of the OWS in 1804 and its first Secretary and Treasurer. He died in London on 14 May 1844. Hills is included here for his book *Sketches in Flanders and Holland,* 1816, AT 186.
Exhib: OWS; RA.
Colls: Ashmolean; BM; Fitzwilliam; Leeds; V & AM.
Bibl: M. Hardie, *Watercol. Paint. In Brit.,* Vol.II, 1967, pp.139-141, illus.

**HILLS, W. Noel**                    fl.1889-1924
Landscape painter and illustrator. He was working at Leyton, London in 1920-24 and contributed comic genre subjects to *Judy,* 1889.
Exhib: RA.

**HILTON, Robert**                    fl.1886-1907
Architectural illustrator. He worked in Cricklewood in 1886 and in Chester, 1902-07.
Exhib: RA; RBA, 1886.

**HINDLEY, Godfrey C.**                    fl.1880-1910
Figure and flower painter and illustrator. He became a Member of the ROI in 1898. Specialised in boys' books.
Illus: *In The Heart of the Rockies [1894].*

**HINE, Henry George  VPRI**                    1811-1895
Watercolourist and illustrator. He was born in Brighton in 1811, the son of a coachman and was largely self-taught. He was apprenticed in London to Henry Meyer, the stipple engraver and after completing indentures, worked for two years in Rouen, France, before joining the Landell's firm as a wood engraver. During the 1840s and early 1850s, Hine was a considerable illustrator, working in particular for *Punch* and drawing for one of Wilkie Collins earliest stories in part works, 1843-44. Hone was like 'Phiz', a competent but not inspired humorous artist. In later life, Hine became a serious landscape watercolourist, concentrating on views of the Downs and coastal subjects showing the influence of Copley Fielding. He became RI in 1864 and Vice-President, 1888-95. He died in London on 16 March 1895.

Illus: *Change for a Shilling [H. Mayhew, 1848].*
Contrib: *Punch [1841-44]; The Illuminated Magazine [1843-45]; ILN [1847-55]; Illustrated London Magazine [1853-54]; The Welcome Guest [1860].*
Exhib: L; M; RA; RBA; RI.
Colls: BM; Fitzwilliam; Leeds; V & AM.

**HIPSLEY, John Henry**        fl.1882-1910

Flower painter. He was working at Liverpool, 1882, and Hemel Hempstead, 1891, and at Birmingham in 1899. He contributed to *The Strand Magazine,* 1891.

Exhib: B; L; RBA; RI.

**HITCHCOCK, Arthur**        fl.1884-1898

Watercolourist and illustrator. He illustrated *Hero and Heroine* by A.R. Hope, 1898 and exhibited at the RBA in 1884.

**HODGSON, Edward S.**        fl.1908-1925

Landscape painter. He worked at Bushey, Herts., and exhibited at RA in 1922. He illustrated *A Middy in Command,* Harry Collingwood, 1908.

**HODGSON, John Evan  RA**        1831-1895

Landscape and historical painter. He was born in London 1 March 1836 but spent the early part of his life in Russia, returning at the age of twenty-two to study at the RA Schools. He was a good military painter and specialised in oriental scenes after travelling in North Africa. He was elected ARA in 1873 and RA in 1880, becoming Librarian and Professor of Painting in 1882 until his death.

The Victoria and Albert Museum has a series of drawings by Hodgson for unidentified illustrations, one dated 1855. They are large figure drawings rather loosely handled in pencil, sepia, ink and watercolour.

Contrib: *The Graphic [1876]*.
Exhib: B; G; L; M; RA; RE; ROI.
Colls: Cardiff; V & AM.

*EVELYN B. HOLDEN fl.1894-1907 d.1920. 'Binnorie, O Binnorie.' Design for* The Yellow Book, *Vol. 9, April 1896.*

**HODGSON, William J.**        fl.1878-1903

Black and white sporting artist. He was working at Scarborough in 1878 and at Clovelly, Devon in 1891. His book illustrations for children are in the style of Caldecott and his *Punch* work, contributed most regularly from 1892-97 is in the best tradition of pen draughtsmanship.

Illus: *The Men of Ware [F.E. Weatherley, c.1884]; The Maids of Lee [F.E. Weatherley, c.1884]*.
Contrib: *Punch [1892-97, 1900, 1902-3]*.
Exhib: L; RA, 1891-93.

**HOFFLER**

Artist who supplied illustrations of Cuba to *The Illustrated London News,* 1869. Possibly the same as Adolph HOEFFLER of Frankfurt who travelled to North America in 1848.

**HOGG, H. Arthur**

Black and white artist, specialising in horses. Contributed to *Fun,* 1901, and *Punch,* 1906-7.

**HOGGARTH, Arthur Henry Graham**        1882-1964

Black and white artist and watercolourist. He was born at Kendal in 1882 and was educated at Kendal School and Keble, Oxford. He was Headmaster of Churcher's College, Petersfield, Hants., from 1911.

Contrib: *Punch [1904-06]*.
Exhib: L; RA; RI.

**HOLDEN, Evelyn B.**        fl.1894-1907 d.1920

Illustrator. She was closely associated with the Birmingham School and probably attended it in about 1894. She was strongly influenced by the work of Walter Crane (q.v.) and worked with her sister Violet M. Holden. She died by drowning in 1920.

Illus. with V.M. Holden: *The Real Princess [B. Atkinson, 1894]; The House That Jack Built [1895]*.
Contrib: *The Quest [1894-96]; The Yellow Book [1896]*.
Exhib: B; L; RA; SWA.
Bibl: *The Studio,* Vol.7, 1896; R.E.D. Sketchley, *English Book Illus.,* 1903, pp.102, 167; *The Diary of an Edwardian Lady,* 1977.
See illustration (left).

**HOLDING, Frederick**        1817-1874

Watercolourist. He was born in Manchester in 1817 and was the brother of H.J. Holding, landscape painter. There are two illustrations of Shakespearean subjects in the Victoria and Albert Museum collection.

**HOLE, William  ARSA**        1846-1917

Painter and illustrator. He was born at Salisbury on 7 November 1846 and after being educated at the Edinburgh Academy, served an apprenticeship as a civil engineer. He abandoned this career for art in 1870 and travelled in Italy, studied at the RSA and took up etching and mural painting. He is best known as an illustrator of Scottish subjects. He was elected ARSA in 1878, RSA, 1889, and died 22 October 1917.

Illus: *A Widow in Thrums [Barrie, 1892]; The Heart of Mid-Lothian [Scott, 1893]; The Little Minister [Barrie, 1893]; Auld Licht Idylls [Barrie, 1895]; Kidnapped [R.L. Stevenson, 1895]; Catriona [R.L. Stevenson, 1895]; Beside the Bonnie Brier Bush [1896]; Poetry of Robert Burns [1896]; The Master of Ballantrae [R.L. Stevenson [1897]*.
Contrib: *The Quiver [1882]*.
Exhib: B; G; L; M; RA; RE; RHA; RSA; RSW.
Bibl: R.E.D. Sketchley, *English Book Illus.,* 1903, pp.92, 151; *Who Was Who 1916-28*.

**HOLIDAY, Gilbert**        1879-1937

Black and white artist. He was born in 1879 and studied at the RA Schools and served in the First War with the RFA. He worked in London and at East Molesey, Surrey.

Contrib: *The Graphic [1900-02 (military)]; Punch*.
Exhib: M; RA; RI; ROI; RSA.

HENRY JAMES HOLIDAY 1839-1927. 'The Beaver.' Illustration for The Hunting of The Snark by Lewis Carroll, 1876. Wood engraving.

**HOLIDAY, Henry James**                **1839-1927**

Painter, sculptor, illustrator and stained glass artist. He was born in London on 17 June 1839 of an English father but French mother. He went to Leigh's Academy, 1854, and RA Schools the same year, becoming deeply interested in the work of the Pre-Raphaelites and forming friendships with Holman Hunt and Burne-Jones (qq.v.). While at the RA he formed his own sketching club with Albert Moore, Marcus Stone (q.v.) and Simeon Solomon (q.v.). Holiday's chief importance lies in his work as a glass designer, he started his own glass-works in 1890, and as a decorative artist in murals and mosaics. He wrote extensively on techniques and invented a new form of enamel on metal in relief. He died on 15 April 1927.

As an illustrator, Holiday's fame rests on the drawings for Lewis Carroll's *The Hunting of the Snark*, 1876, which show a weird intensity of detail which is among the most disturbing aspects of Victorian literature. The source of this drawing is Pre-Raphaelite and an even more astonishing example of the artist's work was on the London market in 1977, 'Beethoven at the First Performance of His Ninth Symphony', dating from about 1860.

Illus: *The Hunting of The Snark [L. Carroll, 1876]; The Mermaid [Hans Andersen, n.d.]*.
Exhib: GG; L; M; RA.
Colls: Liverpool.
Bibl: *Reminiscences*, 1914; A.L. Baldry, 'HH' *Walker's Quarterly*, 1930, No.32-32.

See illustration (above).

342

**HOLL, Francis Montague**
**'Frank' RA ARWS**               **1845-1888**

Portrait painter in oils, chalk draughtsman and illustrator. He was born in London, 4 July 1845, the son of Francis Holl, RA, the engraver. He studied at the RA Schools in 1861 and won a travelling scholarship which was not useful to him and which he never completed. He worked as an illustrator in the middle 1870s, chiefly on *The Graphic*, where he gained a great reputation for social realistic subjects, such as 'Sketches in London' which were admired by Van Gogh. Some of these compositions were taken from his oil paintings and others were developed into oil paintings, Queen Victoria bought 'Home From The Sea' in 1870 and Holloway 'Newgate — Committed For Trial', 1878. Holl worked almost entirely as a portrait painter from 1878, when he was elected ARA, becoming an academician in 1883. He died from heart disease on 31 July 1888.

Illus: *Phineas Redux [A. Trollope, 1874]*.
Contrib: *The Graphic [1872-83]; ILN [1881, 1884]*.
Exhib: B; GG; L; M; RA; RE; RHA; RI; RSA.
Colls: Birmingham; Bristol; Leeds; Royal Holloway College; Royal Collection.
Bibl: A.M. Reynolds, *Life and Work of FH*, 1912; A.L. Baldry, *FH; English Influences on Vincent Van Gogh*, Arts Council, 1974-75, p.52.

**HOLLAND, Frank**

Contributed strip cartoons to *Fun*, 1900-01.

**HOLLAND, Henry T.**             **fl.1879-1906**

Figure painter and illustrator. He contributed humorous figure subjects to *Judy*, 1879-87, and to *Punch*, 1906. He worked in Bloomsbury and exhibited at the RI in 1887-90.

**HOLLANDS, S.D.**

Still-life and fruit painter. He made drawings and a tailpiece for *The English Illustrated Magazine*, 1888.

**HOLLIDAY, F.**

Figure artist, contributing to *Punch*, 1907.

**HOLLOWAY, Herbert**

An unrecorded artist who illustrated *Fairy Tales From South Africa*, 1908.

**HOLME, C. Geoffrey**             **fl.1906-1914**

Artist and illustrator working at Fleet, Hants., 1911-14. He was elected RBA, 1912, and illustrated *The Old Man Book*, R.P. Stone, 1906.

Exhib: L; RBA.

**HOLMES, George**

Irish topographer and illustrator. He studied art in Dublin and worked as a landscape painter and engraver. He made a tour of Southern Ireland with J. Harden in 1797 and settled in London in 1799.

Illus: *Sketches of Some of the Southern Counties of Ireland . . . [1801]*.
Contrib: *Sentimental and Masonic Magazines; Copper Plate Magazine; Antiquities of Ireland [Ledwich]; Beauties of Ireland [Brewer, 1825-26]*.
Exhib: RA; RHA.
Bibl: D. Foskett, *John Harden of Brathay Hall 1772-1847*, 1974.

**HOLMES, George Augustus RBA**        **-1911**

Genre painter. He worked at Chelsea and was elected RBA in 1869.

Contrib: *ILN [1882]*.
Exhib: BI; RA; RBA.

**HOLT, W.G.**

Figure artist. Contributed to *Punch*, 1878.

**HOMERE, Stavros**

Engraver and illustrator. He studied at Paris with Jules Lefebvre and Robert Fleury. He was working at Bridgnorth, 1897, and at Étaples and Wallingford in 1907 and 1913.

Exhib: L; RA.
Bibl: *The Studio*, Vol.11, 1897, p.211, illus.

**HOMEWOOD, Florence M.**
Black and white artist.
Bibl: *The Studio*, Vol.8, 1896, p.227, illus.

**HOOD, George Percy JACOMB- MVO** 1857-1929
Painter, etcher and illustrator. He was born at Redhill, 6 July 1857,
the son of an engineer. He was educated at Tonbridge School and
studied art at the Slade School and under J.P. Laurens in Paris. For
most of his career Hood worked in Chelsea and followed the calling of
an illustrator while continuing to paint portraits. He was attached to
*The Graphic* for many years and was sent by them to Greece in 1896
and to India for the Prince of Wales's tour, 1905-06. He was a founder
member of the NEA, of the Society of Portrait Painters and a member
of the ROI. A very dependable and accurate artist for the story or the
event, his work lacks fire. He was created MVO in 1912 and died 11
December 1929. He signs his work ⊢H⊣

Illus: *Odatis, An Old Love Tale [Lewis Morris, 1888]; Lysbeth A Tale of The
Dutch [H. Rider Haggard, 1900]*.
Contrib: *ILN [1889-94]; Black & White [1891]; Daily Chronicle [1895]; The
Graphic [1896-1911]; The Quarto [1896]*.
Exhib. B; G; L; M; NEA; RA; RBA; RE; ROI.
Colls: V & AM.
Bibl: *With Brush and Pencil*, 1925.

See illustration (below).

**HOOD, Sybil Eleanor JACOMB-** 1870-
A sketchbook of designs for illustrations by the above artist is in the
Victoria and Albert Museum collection and dated 1897 'Slade
School'.

**HOOD, Thomas** 1799-1845
Poet and humorous draughtsman. He was born in London in 1799 and
while living at Dundee during his adolescence, contributed sketches to
local papers. Returning to London, he was apprenticed to an engraver
called Harris, then to his uncle Robert Sands and finally to the Le
Keux brothers. Hood worked on comic illustrations until his literary
efforts such as 'The Song of The Shirt' made that unnecessary. He
drew for *The Comic Annual*, 1830, 1834, 1837 and 1838, his humour
and line being that of the punster, his drawing reflecting the savage,
brutal and callous wit of the 18th century. Most biographies or
notices of him neglect his work as an illustrator and even the 1869
edition of *The Works* with notes by his family, does not refer to it.

Publ: *Whims and Oddities [1826-27]; Comic Annual [1830-38]; Hood's Own
[1838]; Up The Rhine [1839]; Hood's Magazine [1844]; Whimsicalities
[1844]; Collected Works [1882-84]*.
Colls: BM.
Bibl: Douglas Jerrold, *TH His Life and Times*, 1907; J.C. Reid *TH*, 1963.

*GEORGE PERCY JACOMB-HOOD 1857-1929. 'The Heir.' An illustration to* The Graphic, *6 January 1906. Chalk and wash. Signed with monogram.*
Victoria and Albert Museum

**HOOK, Bryan**                                                    fl.1880-1923
Landscape painter and etcher. He was the son of James Clarke Hook
RA (q.v.) and travelled widely in Africa. He was working at Churt,
Surrey, in 1880 and at Brixham in 1923.

Contrib: *The English Illustrated Magazine [1887 (animals)]*.
Exhib: L; M; RA; RI; ROI.

**HOOK, James Clarke   RA**                                        1819-1907
Landscape and portrait painter. He was born in London in 1819 and
after being educated at the North London Grammar School, studied
art at the RA Schools in 1836. He travelled in France and Italy
between 1845 and 1848 and worked in Cornwall and the Scilly Isles.
Hook specialised in his early career in history and poetic subjects and
his only illustrations date from this period. He was elected ARA in
1850 and RA in 1860, dying in Churt on 14 April 1907.

Contrib: *Songs and Ballads of Shakespeare Illustrated by The Etching Club
[1853]; A Selection of Etchings . . . Etching Club [1865, 1872, 1879]*.
Exhib: B; G; L; M; RA; RE; RSA.

**HOOKER, Sir Joseph Dalton   OM FRS**                             1817-1911
Botanist, artist and author. He was born at Halesworth, Suffolk, on
30 June 1817 and was educated at the High School and the
University, Glasgow. He was surgeon and naturalist on Ross's
Antarctic Expedition, 1839-43, travelled in the Himalayas, 1847-51,
Syria, 1860, Morocco, 1871, and the Rocky Mountains, 1877.
Director of the Royal Gardens, Kew, 1865-85 and President of the
Royal Society, 1872-77. He was made KCSI in 1877 and OM in 1907.
He died 10 December 1911.

Publ: *Flora of Tasmania [1860]; Genera Plantarum [1862-83]; Handbook of
the New Zealand Flora [1867]; Flora of British India [1883-97]*.
Illus: *The Rhododendrons of Sikkim – Himalaya [1849]*.

**HOOPER, William Harcourt**                                       1834-1912
Designer and engraver. He was born in London on 22 February 1834
and was a pupil of Bolton. He worked principally for magazines, but
towards the end of his life was associated with William Morris (q.v.) at
the Kelmscott Press and in particular with the production of *The
Golden Legend of Master William Caxton,* 1892, and the *Kelmscott
Chaucer,* 1896. Hooper was afterwards employed at the Essex House
Press, 1902, and was engraving from the designs of C.M. Gere (q.v.) at
the Ashendene Press in 1909 for *Tutte le opera di Dante Alighieri.* He
died at Hammersmith, 24 February 1912.

**HOPE, Mrs. Adrian C. (née Laura Trowbridge)**                    -1929
Portrait and figure painter, illustrator. She specialised in children's
books and worked in Chelsea 1893-1929.

Illus: *The Sparrow with One White Feather [Lady Ridley, 1908]*.
Contrib: *The English Illustrated Magazine [1891-92 (fairies)]*.
Exhib: L; New Gall; P; SWA.

**HOPKINS, Arthur   RWS**                                          1848-1930
Watercolourist and illustrator. He was born in London in 1848, the
brother of Gerard Manley Hopkins, poet and of Everard Hopkins
(q.v.). He was educated at Lancing College and spent some years in
the city before becoming an artist and entering the RA Schools in
1872. He painted in watercolour but was chiefly known by his social
subjects contributed to the leading magazines. Hopkins' figure
drawing is rather stiff and he has a very fussy pen line which works
against him when he appears in *Punch* alongside Du Maurier. He died
at Hampstead, 16 September 1930.

Illus: *Sketches and Skits [1900]; The Haunted Hotel [W. Collins]*.
Contrib: *ILN [1872-98]; The Cornhill Magazine [1875, 1884]; The Graphic
[1874-86]; The Quiver [1890]; Cassell's Family Magazine; Punch [1893-1902]*.
Exhib: B; G; L; M; RA; ROI; RSW; FAS, 1900.
Colls: Ashmolean; BM; Exeter; V & AM.

**HOPKINS, Everard**                                               1860-1928
Watercolourist and illustrator. He was born in London in 1860, the
brother of Gerard Manley Hopkins, the poet, and of Arthur Hopkins
(q.v.). He worked extensively for the magazines and was a much more
accomplished black and white artist than his more celebrated brother.
He studied at the Slade School and was a Slade scholar in 1878 and

344

Assistant Editor of *The Pilot.* He died on 17 October 1928. He signs
his work ЄН

Illus: *A Costly Freak [Maxwell Gray, 1894]; Sentimental Journey [1910]*.
Contrib: *The Graphic [1883-85]; ILN [1887-92]; The Quiver [1890]; Punch
[1891-1904]; Black & White [1891]; Cassell's Family Magazine*.
Exhib: G; M; RA; RI.
See illustration (below).

*EVERARD HOPKINS 1860-1928. 'Worth Knowing.' Pen and ink. Signed with
initials. 9⅜ins. x 5¾ins. (23.8cm x 14.6cm).*     Victoria and Albert Museum

**HOPKINS, Fritz**
Contributor to *Fun,* 1900.

**HORNE, Adam Edmund Maule**                                       1883-
Figure artist. He contributed to *The Graphic,* 1908 and to *Punch,*
1913.

Colls: V & AM.

**HORNE, Herbert P.**                                              1864-1916
Architect, writer, designer and connoisseur. He was born in London
on 18 February 1864. He designed a number of buildings including
the Church of the Redeemer, Bayswater Road, Brewhouse Court at
Éton College and part of St. Luke's, Camberwell. Horne retired to
Florence in 1892 and became a writer, producing a number of notable
books on the Rennaissance, among them, *Life of Leonardo da Vinci,*
1903 and of *Sandro Botticelli,* 1903. He devoted his time to collecting
fine paintings and sculptures in the Palazzo Alberti, Florence, which
he left to the Italian State as the Horne Museum on his death on 14
April 1916.

Publ: *Diversi Colores: Poems [1891]*.
Contrib: *The Hobby Horse [1886-93]*.
Exhib: RA, 1875.
Colls: BM.
Bibl: Carlo Gamba, *Il Museo Horne a Firenze,* 1961.

**HORNEL, Edward Atkinson**           **1864-1933**

Genre painter of the Scottish School. He was born in Australia in July 1864 and studied at Antwerp under Professor Verlat. He visited Japan, 1892-94, and Ceylon and Australia, 1907. He died July 1933.

Contrib: *The Evergreen [1895-96].*
Exhib: B; G; L; M; NEA; RA; ROI; RSA.

**HORWITZ, Herbert A.**           **fl.1892-1925**

Portrait painter. He studied at the RA Schools and was working in North London until 1925. He contributed to *The English Illustrated Magazine,* 1896 (decor).

Exhib: G; L; New Gall; RI; RBA.

**HORSLEY, John Callcott   RA**        **1817-1903**

Painter and etcher. He was born on 29 January 1817, the great-nephew of Sir Augustus Callcott RA. A prolific artist, he studied at the RA Schools and concentrated on book illustration in the earlier part of his career, favouring in both oil and black and white, subjects from history or from Shakespeare. He was elected RA in 1864, became Treasurer in 1882 and was Professor of Drawing. He died at Cranbrook, 19 October 1903.

Illus: *The Beauty and The Beast, The King was in the Counting House, Puck Reports to Oberon, The Home Treasury series [Felix Summerly, 1843]; The Little Princess [1843]; Poems and Pictures [1846].*
Contrib: *The Deserted Village [1841]; Etch'd Thoughts [1844]; Gray's Elegy [1847]; L'Allegro [1849]; Songs and Ballads of Shakespeare [1853]; Etching Club; Etchings for Art Union [1857, 1865, 1872, 1879]; Moxon's Tennyson [1857]; A Book of Favourite Modern Ballads [1859]; The Churchman's Family Magazine [1863]; Adam's Sacred Allegories; Burn's Poems; The Poetry of Thomas Moore.*
Exhib: B; BI; G; M; RA.
Colls: Sheffield; V & AM.

**HORSLEY, Walter Charles**         **1867-1934**

Figure and landscape painter. He was the son of J.C. Horsley RA (q.v.), and worked in London. He contributed to *The Graphic,* 1880.

Exhib: B; G; M; RA; RBA; RI; ROI.

**HORTON, Alice M.**           **fl.1897-1911**

Illustrator. Studied at Mount Street School of Art and contributed to *The Studio.* Working in Birkenhead, 1911.

Exhib: L.
Bibl: *The Studio,* Vol.13, 1897, pp.192-193, illus.

**HORTON, William Thomas**        **1864-1919**

Black and white artist and illustrator. Born in Brussels in 1864 and was educated there and at Brighton Grammar School where he was a schoolmate of Aubrey Beardsley (q.v.). Studied architecture at the RA Schools, 1887, but abandoned architecture in 1894 for novel writing, drawing and mysticism. He was a member of 'The Brotherhood of New Life'. It is on record that Beardsley considered Horton to have some 'kind of talent' and he was clearly influenced by the younger man. His drawings are mannered, sharp and with strong contrasts of black and white, but miss the subtle nuances of Beardsley. Some of his drawings and their sources are influenced by William Blake's work.

Illus: *A Book of Images [Introduced by W.B. Yeats, 1898].*
Contrib: *The Savoy [1896]; Pick-Me-Up [1897]; The Dome [1898-99].*
Exhib: RA, 1890.
Bibl: *The Studio,* Vol.35, 1905-06, p.335; *Modern Book Illustrators and their Work,* Studio, 1914; Roger Ingpen, *WTH,* London, 1929.

**HORWOOD, Arthur M.**

Contributed comic strip illustrations to *The Graphic,* 1904.

**HOSKINSON, E.**

Contributed genre and figure subjects to *Punch,* 1903.

**HOUGHTON, Arthur Boyd**        **1836-1875**

Painter and illustrator. He was born at Kotagiri, Madras, in 1836. He studied at Leigh's and entered the RA Schools in 1854 and through Charles Keene (q.v.) was probably introduced to J.W. Whymper (q.v.) and soon afterwards began work for the Dalziels. Financial

circumstances forced Houghton to concentrate on book illustrations rather than on oil paintings and ironically drove into the field of black and white one of the most original geniuses of mid-Victorian England. He was a very powerful draughtsman and as an illustrator of romance, the *Arabian Nights* for example, was the only artist on this side of the channel to rival Doré in visual effects. He brought many aspects into his drawing, the composition of the Japanese print, the domestic humour of Leech and the imagination and accuracy of Rossetti and Holman Hunt. The founding of *The Graphic* in December 1869, gave Houghton a unique opportunity. He was sent to the United States for several months to draw the Americans and their way of life. The results are among his best work and perhaps the finest piece of pictorial journalism carried out by a Special Artist in the whole period. Houghton was elected ARWS in 1871 and died of progressive alcholism on 25 November 1875.

Houghton's drawings and oil paintings are tinged with Pre-Raphaelitism and often follow similar themes. A comprehensive exhibition of the artist's work was held at the Victoria and Albert Museum in May 1975.

Illus: *Dalziel's Arabian Nights, Victorian History of England [1864]; A Round of Days, Home Thoughts and Home Scenes, Don Quixote [1865]; Ernie Elton, The Lazy Boy, Patient Henry, Stories Told to a Child, The Boy Pilgrims [1866-67]; Ballad Stories of the Affections, Foxe's Book of Martyrs, Touches of Nature [1866]; Jean Ingelow's Poems; Idyllic Pictures; Spirit of Praise, Longfellow's Poems, Golden Thoughts From Golden Fountains, Savage Club Papers [1867]; Christian Lyrics, North Coast [1868]; The Nobility of Life [1869]; Novellos National Nursery Rhymes [1871]; Thornbury's Legendary Ballads [1876]; Dalziel's Bible Gallery [1880].*
Contrib: *Good Words [1862-68]; Churchman's Family Magazine [1864]; ILN [1865-66]; The Sunday Magazine [1865-71]; The Argosy, The Quiver, Every Boy's Magazine [1866]; Fun [1866-67]; Tinsley's Magazine, The Broadway [1867]; Golden Hours [1868]; The Graphic [1869-75].*
Exhib: BI; OWS; RA; RBA.
Colls: Ashmolean; BM; Fitzwilliam; V & AM; Witt Photo.
Bibl: Laurence Housman, introduction to *ABH A Selection From His Work in Black and White,* 1896; P. Hogarth, *ABH,* V & AM, 1975.
See illustrations (below and pp.346, 347).

*ARTHUR BOYD HOUGHTON 1836-1875. 'The Meeting of the Prince and Badoura.' Illustration for* Dalziel's Arabian Nights, *1865. Pencil. 6⅞ins. x 5⅛ins. (17.4cm x 13cm).*     Victoria and Albert Museum

THE MEETING OF THE PRINCE AND BADOURA.

*ARTHUR BOYD HOUGHTON 1836-1875. 'The Meeting of The Prince and Badoura.' Completed illustration for* Dalziel's Arabian Nights, *1865. Wood engraving. 6⁷/8ins. x 5¹/8ins. (17.4cm x 13cm).* Victoria and Albert Museum

## HOUGHTON, Elizabeth Ellen                                    1853-1922
Illustrator. She worked at Warrington, Lancashire, between 1886 and 1910 specialising in children's books. Her style owed a great deal to the influence of Randolph Caldecott both in line and tinting. She signs her work E.E.H.

Illus: *The Adventures of Little Man-Chester [1887].*
Contrib: *The Dome [1899].*
Exhib: L; M.
Colls: V & AM.

## HOUGHTON, J.H.                                               fl.1886-1900
Cartoonist for *Judy*, 1897. He also contributed to *Fun*, 1886-92 and 1900.

## HOURY, J.J.
Amateur illustrator. Contributed to *The Studio* competitions, 1896, Vol.8, p.253, illus., from Bristol.

## HOUSMAN, Clemence                                            1861-1955
Woodcut artist. Sister of Laurence Housman (q.v.). Engraved many blocks after her brother's designs, including illustrations to *The Field of Clover, The Imitation of Christ*, 1898; *The Little Land with Songs from its Four Rivers*, 1899; *The Blue Moon*, 1904; *Maud*, 1905; *Prunella*, 1907, etc.

Exhib: Baillie Gall.

346

## HOUSMAN, Laurence                                            1865-1959
Painter, illustrator and author. He was born on 18 July 1865 and during the 1890s established himself as a leading book illustrator, basing his style on the traditional wood engraving of the 60s. He has been described as the last of the 'facsimile' engraver-illustrators and his wish to be in this line of succession, gives his work a marvellous purity of style and a freedom from *fin de siècle* mannerism. Housman was a great admirer of A.B. Houghton (q.v.) and published and edited his work in 1896. But it is not so much to this great black and white artist that Housman is in debt as to the Pre-Raphaelites and to artists such as Leighton. Housman paraphrases some of their best illustrative work, but with sufficient inventiveness and good manners to set himself well apart from the copyists. Like Rossetti, whose figures he imitated, Housman was a literary man as well as an artist and his books have a pleasant cohesion in design and text which was praised by contemporaries. He remained a rather isolated and nineteenth century figure and died at Street, Somerset, at a great age in 1959.

Signs: ⊢⊣

Illus: *Jump to Glory Jane [George Meredith, 1892]; Goblin Market [Rossetti, 1893]; Weird Tales From Nothern States [1893]; The End of Elfintown [J. Barlow]; A Random Itinerary [John Davidson]; A Farm in Fairyland; Poems [Francis Thompson]; Cuckoo Songs [Katharine Tynan, 1894]; The House of Joy [1895]; A Pomander of Verses [E. Nesbit]; Sister Songs [Francis Thompson]; Green Arras: Poems by Laurence Housman [1895]; The Were Wolf, All Fellows, The Viol of Love [C.N. Robinson, 1896]; The Sensitive Plant [P.B. Shelley]; The Little Flowers of St. Francis, Of The Imitation of Christ [1898]; The Little Land [1899]; At the Back of the North Wind [Macdonald, 1900]; The Princess and the Goblin [Macdonald, 1900]; The Blue Moon [1904]; Prunella or Love in a Dutch Garden [1907]; A Doorway in Fairyland [1923 etc.].*
Contrib: *The English Illustrated Magazine [1893-94]; The Pall Mall Magazine [1893]; The Yellow Book [1896]; The Pageant [1896]; The Parade [1897]; The Dome [1897-99]; The Quarto [1898].*
Exhib: Baillie Gall; FAS, 1901; NEA, 1894-1901.
Colls: V & AM.
Bibl: *The Studio,* Vol.19, 1897, p.220; *The Artist,* Feb. 1898, pp.99-103, illus; *The Studio,* Winter No., 1900-01, p.19 illus; R.E.D. Sketchley, *English Book Illus.,* 1903, pp.15, 127.
See illustration (p.349).

## HOUSTON, Mary G.
Painter and decorative artist. She contributed to *The Studio* competitions (Vol. 8, 1896, p.184, illus.). She was working at Chelsea, 1901-04 and exhibited at the R.A.

## HOWARD, Francis                                              1874-1954
Painter and writer. He was born 1 January 1884, great-great-grandson of Benjamin Franklin. He studied art in Paris and London and was for many years art critic of *The Sun,* and a contributor on the arts to many periodicals. He founded the International Society of Sculptors, Painters and Engravers in 1898, and the National Portrait Society, 1910. He was Managing Director of the Grafton and the Grosvenor Gallery and arranged many exhibitions at home and abroad. He contributed a series of portrait drawings entitled 'Bodley Heads' to *The Yellow Book,* 1896. He died in 1954.

Exhib: G; L; New Gall; P.

## HOWARD, George   9th Earl of Carlisle   HRWS        1843-1911
Watercolourist and illustrator. He was born on 12 August 1843, a grandson of the 6th Earl of Carlisle. He studied at South Kensington and was a patron of William Morris, Edward Burne-Jones, H.J. Ford and J.D. Batten (qq.v.). He was M.P. for East Cumberland, 1879-80 and 1881-85, but was more notable for the artists and radicals that he gathered round him at Naworth Castle, Cumberland. He travelled widely in Europe and Africa and was chairman of the Trustees of the National Gallery. He died 16 April 1911.

Illus: *A Picture Song Book by the Earl of Carlisle [1910].*
Contrib: *The English Illustrated Magazine [1895].*
Exhib: G; L; M; New Gall; RA; RHA; RWS.

FOR THE KING !

*ARTHUR BOYD HOUGHTON 1836-1875. 'For The King.' Illustration to a story in* Tinsley's Magazine, *1868. Wood engraving.*

**HOWARD, Captain Henry R.**                    **-1895**

Black and white artist. He was born at Watford, the son of a country gentleman and studied art under Ramburg in Hanover before being taught by John Leech (q.v.) to draw on the block. According to Spielmann he had the unusual practice of buying wood blocks from Messrs. Swain instead of having them supplied in his contract. He specialised in humanised beasts and birds and signed first with a manx emblem and then with a trident. He contributed to *Punch,* 1853-67 and died on 31 August 1895.

**HOWELL, Charles A.**

Amateur illustrator working in Upper Tooting. Contributed to *The Studio* competitions, Vol.15, 1899, p.144 illus.

**HOWITT, Samuel**                    **1756-1822**

Sporting artist and illustrator. He was born in 1756, the son of an old Nottinghamshire family who were squires at Chigwell in Essex. Howitt was an amateur artist who turned professional after experiencing financial troubles. He worked as a drawing-master at a private academy in Ealing and began to exhibit at the Incorporated Society of Artists in 1783. He acquired great skill as an animal draughtsman, his studies usually taken from life at the Tower of London Menagerie. He married the sister of Thomas Rowlandson, whose penwork Howitt's sometimes resembles. He died at Somers Town, London in 1822.

Illus: *Miscellaneous Etchings of Animals [1803]; Oriental Field Sports [1805-07 and 1808, AT 427]; Fables of Aesop, Gay and Phaedras [1809-11]; The British Sportsman [1812].*
Exhib: RA, 1784-
Colls: BM; Fitzwilliam; Mellon; V & AM.
Bibl: M. Hardie, *Watercolour Paint. in Brit.,* Vol.1, 1966, p.225, illus.
See illustration (p.22).

**HOYNCK, C. van Papendrecht**                    **1858-**

Dutch history and military painter and illustrator. He was born at Rotterdam on 18 September 1858 and exhibited in Munich and Berlin from 1888 and in Paris in 1900. He contributed to *The Graphic,* 1901-04.

Colls: V & AM (prints).

**HUARD, L.**                    **-1874**

Illustrator of genre. He was born at Aix-en-Provence and studied art at Antwerp. He worked in London for more than twenty years and contributed regularly to magazines. Gleeson White had a low opinion of this artist because he worked for the penny journals, his drawings are not inspired but he was thought good enough to succeed Sir John Gilbert on *The London Journal* in about 1859.

Contrib: *The British Workman [1855]; The London Journal [1859]; ILN [1861-63, 1875-76 and 1881]; London Society [1863]; Churchman's Family Magazine [1863]; Cassell's Magazine [1865]; The Band of Hope Review.*
Exhib: BI, 1857-72.

**HUDSON, Gwynedd M.**                    **fl.1912-1925**

Painter and illustrator of fairy tales. She studied at the Municipal School of Art, Brighton, and worked in Hove, Sussex.

Illus: *Peter Pan and Wendy [J.M. Barrie, c.1925].*
Exhib: RA, 1912.

**HUGHES, Arthur**                    **1832-1915**

Painter and illustrator of genre and history, decorator and illustrator of children's books. He was born in London on 27 January 1832 and was educated at Archbishop Tenison's Grammar School, showing such ability in drawing that he was allowed to attend the Government

School of Design at Somerset House at the age of fourteen and work under Alfred Stevens. Entering the RA Schools in 1847, he won the silver medal for antique drawing in 1849. Shortly afterwards he came into contact with the Pre-Raphaelite Brotherhood, who particularly admired his paintings exhibited at the RA in 1851, 1854 and 1856. He posed for Millais in 1853 as 'The Proscribed Royalist' and was much admired as an artist by John Ruskin. He worked on the Oxford Union murals and painted a number of famous pictures including 'Home From Sea' in the Ashmolean Museum and 'The Long Engagement' in the Birmingham City Art Gallery. Hughes lived a rather withdrawn life at Kew Green and died there on 22 December 1915.

Hughes was alone among the Pre-Raphaelites in recognising that book illustration was more than the illustration itself. All his designs are conceived as part of the text and the ornament of the book and perhaps his classical study under Stevens, gave him this greater discipline. He is fond of placing his figures in a circle or a semi-circle, often gives them the arched neck of the Pre-Raphaelites and in his fairy drawings, the delicacy of Doyle. Although he is best-known for his black and white work, Hughes was a most brilliant colourist. He signs his work with gothic monogram ⟨monogram⟩.

Illus: *The Music Master* [W. Allingham, 1855 (with others)]; *My Beautiful Lady* [T. Woolner, n.d.]; *Enoch Arden* [Tennyson, 1866]; *Dealings with the Fairies* [George Macdonald, 1867]; *Five Days Entertainment at Wentworth Grange* [F.T. Palgrave, 1868]; *Tom Brown's Schooldays* [T. Hughes, 1869]; *Mother Goose* [1870 (with others)]; *At the Back of the North Wind* [George Macdonald, 1871]; *Ranald Bannerman's Boyhood* [George Macdonald, 1871]; *The Princess and The Goblin* [George Macdonald 1872]; *Parables and Tales* [T. Gordon Hake, 1872]; *Story of Elizabeth* [Anne Thackeray, 1872]; *Sing Song* [Christina Rossetti, 1872]; *Gutta-Percha Willie* [George Macdonald 1873]; *Sinbad the Sailor* [1873]; *Speaking Likenesses* [Christina Rossetti, 1873]; *Old Kensington* [Anne Thackeray, 1874-76]; *Four Winds Farm* [1887]; *Babies Classic* [1904]; *The Magic Crook* [Greville Macdonald, 1911]; *Trystie's Quest* [Greville Macdonald, 1912]; *Jack and Jill* [Greville Macdonald, 1913].

Contrib: *Poets of the Nineteenth Century* [Willmott, 1857]; *The Queen* [1861]; *The Cornhill Magazine* [1863]; *Good Words* [1864-72]; *London Society* [1865-70]; *Good Cheer* [1868]; *Sunday Magazine* [1869-72]; *Good Words For The Young* [1870-73]; *Novello's National Nursery Rhymes* [1870]; *The Graphic* [1887, 1889]; *London Home Monthly* [1895]; *The Girls' Own Paper*.

Exhib: B; G; GG; L; M; New Gall; RA; RI; ROI.
Colls: Ashmolean; BM; Manchester; V & AM.
Bibl: Forrest Reid, *Illustrators of The Sixties*, 1928, pp.83-95.
See illustrations (pp.350, 351).

### HUGHES; Arthur Ford                                                1856-1914
Landscape painter and painter of windmills. He was born in 1856 and studied at Heatherley's and at the Slade and RA Schools. He was working at Wallington, Surrey in 1880 and in London in 1890. He contributed headpieces to *The English Illustrated Magazine*, 1886-87.

Exhib: G; L; RA; RBA; RI; ROI.

*ELIZABETH ELLEN HOUGHTON 1853-1922. Illustration to* The Adventures of Little-Man-Chester, *1887. Pen and ink, and watercolour. 8½ins. x 8⅞ins. (21.6cm x 22.5cm).*
Victoria and Albert Museum

*LAURENCE HOUSMAN 1865-1959. 'King Bugdemagus Daughter.' Pen and ink. Signed L.H. 7⅝ins. x 4⅛ins. (19.4cm x 10.5cm).*

Victoria and Albert Museum

**HUGHES, Edward**                                    **1832-1908**
Portrait and genre painter and illustrator. He worked in Kensington, Chelsea and Notting Hill and contributed literary and historical subjects to the magazines.

Illus: *Poor Miss Finch [Wilkie Collins, 1872 (with Du Maurier)].*
Contrib: *Once a Week [1864-66]; The Shilling Magazine [1865-66]; The Sunday Magazine [1866, 1869]; Cassell's Magazine [1870]; The Argosy [1866]; Hurst and Blackett's Standard Library, etc.; ILN [1870-75]; The Graphic [1871].*
Exhib: BI; GG; RA; RBA.

**HULL, Edward**                                    **fl.1827-1877**
Genre painter and illustrator, working in London. He contributed figure subjects to *The Illustrated Times*, 1859-61.

Exhib: RA; RBA.

**HULLMANDEL, Charles-Joseph**                        **1789-1850**
Artist and lithographer. He was born in London on 15 June 1789 and studied under Faraday. He travelled widely, experimented with lithography and perfected the litho-tint. He died on November 1850.

Illus: *Views of Italy [1818, AT 167]; The Art of Drawing on Stone [1824]; Ancient Castellated Mansions in Scotland [1833].*

**HULME, Frederick J. or E.**                        **fl.1880-1940**
Flower painter and illustrator. He illustrated his own book *Flower Painting in Watercolours*, 1886, and a children's book *The Little Flower Seekers*, c.1880.

Exhib: NEA; RA.

**HULME, Frederick William**                        **1816-1884**
Landscape painter and illustrator. He was born at Swinton on 22 October 1816 and studied under a Yorkshire artist before going to London in 1844 to work for engravers. He died in London 14 November 1884.

Contrib: *The Illustrated London Magazine [1853]; The Poetical Works of E.A. Poe [1853]; The Book of South Wales [Mr. and Mrs. S.C. Hall, 1861]; Rhymes and Roundelayes.*
Exhib: B; BI; L; RA; RBA; ROI.
Colls: Leicester; Liverpool; Montreal.

**HULME, Robert C.**                                **fl.1862-1876**
Still-life painter and illustrator. He contributed drawings of ceremonies to *The Illustrated London News*, 1864-69 and 1873.

Exhib: RA; RBA, 1862-76.

**HULSTROP, T.**
Illustrator. A very competent pen draughtsman, inclined to spoil his work with heavy washes. He illustrated *The Refugees, A Tale of Two Continents*, by Conan Doyle, on its first appearance in 1891 and when reissued in 1912.

Contrib: *The Graphic [1889]; ILN [1895].*

**HUMPHREY, Miss K. Maude**                        **fl.1883-1894**
Portrait and figure painter. She worked in London and illustrated *The Light Princess* by George Macdonald, 1894.

Exhib: B; M; RA; RBA; SWA.

**HUMPHREYS, H. Noel**                                **1810-1879**
Numismatist, naturalist and illustrator. He was born in Birmingham on 4 January 1810 and after working for some time in Italy, returned to England in 1843 to work as an illustrator. Humphreys was a very original designer in all the fields of art that he tackled, especially in that of illustration. A master of Chromo-lithography, he produced the finest illuminated gift-books of the Victorian age under the inspiration of Italian and Flemish illumination of the Middle Ages. He died intestate on 10 June 1879.

Illus: *The Illuminated Calendar [1845]; Parables of Our Lord, The Poets Pleasance, Insect Changes [1847]; The Coins of England [1846]; The Miracles of Our Lord, Maxims and Precepts of The Saviour [1848]; A Record of the Black Prince, The Art of Illumination and Missal Painting [1849]; The Book of Ruth [1850]; Sentiments and Similes of William Shakespeare [1851]; The History of Writing [1853]; Proverbial Philosophy [1854]; Coinage of the British Empire [1855]; Roman Anthology [1856]; River Gardens [1857]; Ocean Gardens [1857]; Rhymes and Roundelayes in Praise of Country Life [1857]; The Butterfly Vivarium [1858]; The Shipwreck [Falconer, 1858]; The Genera and Species of British Butterflies [1859]; Goldsmith's Poems [1859]; Thomson's Seasons [1859]; The White Doe of Rylstone [1858-59]; The Penitential Psalms [1861]; A Little Girl's Visit to a Flower Garden [Routledge Toy Books].*
Contrib: *The Illustrated Times [1855 (decor.)].*
Bibl: Chatto and Jackson, *Treatise on Wood Engraving*, 1861, p.599; R. McLean, *Victorian Book Design . . .* 1972, pp.99-113.

**HUMPHRIES, A.**
Illustrator. Contributing half tone work to *Punch*, 1905, in a poster style.

**HUMPHRIS, William H.**                            **fl.1881-1916**
Figure painter and illustrator of social realism. He worked in London, Wales and Cornwall and exhibited regularly.

Contrib: *The Graphic [1905-10].*
Exhib: B; L; RA; RI; ROI.

**HUNT, Alfred**                                    **fl.1860-1884**
Painter and illustrator. He was a student of the RA Schools and practised as a painter in Yorkshire until about 1860 when he returned to London and joined the staff of *The Illustrated London News*. He contributed large comic genre subjects to the paper, mainly for Christmas numbers at first and then more regularly. His double pagers present crowds of figures, usually rather wooden but interesting for their period details.

Illus: *Life and Lessons of Our Lord [Cummings, 1864].*

*ARTHUR HUGHES 1832-1915. Illustration for Tennyson's* Enoch Arden, *Moxon Edition, 1866. Pen and ink. Signed with monogram.*   Victoria and Albert Museum

**HUNT, William Holman   OM**                                           **1827-1910**
Painter and illustrator. He was born in Wood Street, Cheapside, London, on 2 April 1827, the son of a warehouse manager. He worked for some years as a clerk to an estate agent, but received lessons from the portrait painter, H. Rogers. He also studied at the British Museum, the National Gallery and after 1844 at the RA Schools. He began to exhibit at the Academy in 1846 and in 1848-49, he joined Millais and Rossetti in founding the Pre-Raphaelite Brotherhood. Thereafter followed a whole series of visits abroad, first to the Continent with Rossetti in 1849 and then as his ideas became more eastern and mystical, Egypt and Syria in 1854, a long stay in the Holy Land, 1869-71, and return visits to Palestine, 1875-78 and 1892. Hunt's greatest contribution was in portraying religious truth in terms of aesthetic truth as seen by the Pre-Raphaelites. His 'Light of The World' was to become a Victorian favourite and for his 'Finding of Christ in the Temple' he was paid the handsome sum of 5,500 guineas.

Hunt was not a prolific illustrator of books, but the work that he did was outstanding and highly inventive. His 'Lady of Shalott' in the *Moxon Tennyson,* 1857, set a seal on black and white drawing for a decade and his other contributions to magazines have a directness and mystery which makes them very compelling. He was awarded the OM in 1905 and died 7 September 1910.

Contrib: *Moxon's Tennyson [1857]; Once a Week [1860]; Parables From Nature [1861]; Willmott's Sacred Poetry [1862]; Good Words [1862]; Watt's Divine and Moral Songs [1865]; Macmillan's Golden Treasury Series; Studies From Life [Hurst and Blackett's Standard Library].*
Exhib: B; FAS, 1885-86; G; GG; L; M; NEA; New Gall; RBA; RHA; RSA; RWS.
Colls: Ashmolean; BM; Manchester; V & AM.
Bibl: W.H. Hunt, *Pre-Raphaelitsm and the Pre-Raphaelite Brotherhood,* 1905; F.W. Farrar, *WHH,* 1893; Diana Holman Hunt, *My Grandmothers and I.*

See illustration (p.351).

**HUNTER, John Young**                                                   **1874-1955**
Figure and portrait painter. He was born in Glasgow in 1874 and studied at the RA Schools. He married Mary Y. Hunter (q.v.), and became RBA in 1914.

Illus: *The Clyde [1908].*
Exhib: B; FAS, 1903, 1907; G; L; M; P; RA; RBA; RI; ROI; RWA.
Colls: Liverpool.

**HUNTER, (George) Leslie**                                             **1879-1931**
Landscape and portrait painter, illustrator. He was born at Rothesay in 1879 and studied art in San Francisco and Paris. He worked in Scotland from 1906 and contributed to *The Graphic,* 1910.

Exhib: G; L; RSA.

**HUNTER, Mary Young**                                                   **fl.1900-1925**
Landscape and figure painter and illustrator. The wife of John Y. Hunter (q.v.), elected ASWA, 1901. She was working in Kensington 1902-14 and at Helensburgh, 1925.

Illus: *The Clyde [1908 (with JYH)].*
Contrib: *The Graphic [1912].*
Exhib: FAS, 1903, 1907; G; L; New Gall; P; RA; ROI; SWA.

**HURST, Hal**                                                           **1865-c.1938**
Painter, watercolourist, miniaturist and illustrator. He was born in London on 26 August 1865, the son of Henry Hurst, the African traveller. He began as an artist by drawing scenes of the Irish evictions and had work published at the age of twenty-three. He then went to America and worked as a special artist on the *Philadelphia Press* and several New York newspapers, covering the Atlantic City flood and other major events. He studied in the Art League in the United States

*ARTHUR HUGHES 1832-1915. Illustration for* The Music Master *by William Allingham, 1855.*

before returning to Europe to train under Bouveret and Constant in Paris. His drawing line is strongly American and influenced by the studies of Dana Gibson (q.v.). He claimed to be the 'Artist of the man and woman about town'. RBA, 1896 and ROI, 1900.

Illus: *The Sikh War [G.A. Henty, 1894]; Sou'Wester and Sword [St. Leger, 1894]; The American Claimant [Mark Twain, 1897];* various novels by Robert Barr, 1897.

Contrib: *Fun [1890-1901]; The Idler [1892]; St. Paul's [1894]; Pick-Me-Up [1894]; The Minister [1895]; Vanity Fair [1896]; The Gentlewoman; Illustrated Bits; The Pall Mall Magazine; ILN [1912-13].*
Exhib: L; New Gall; RA; RBA; RHA; RI; RMS; RWS.
Bibl: *The Idler,* Vol.9, pp.657-670, illus.

### HUTCHINSON, George W.C.        fl.1881-1892

Figure and domestic painter. He worked in London, 1881, and in Bristol, 1889, and contributed the illustrations to Stevenson's 'Treasure Island' in *Chums,* 1892.

Contrib: *ILN [1889]; The Ludgate Monthly [1891]; Black & White [1892]; The Idler [1892]; Chums [1892]; The Pall Mall Budget; Puck and Ariel.*
Exhib: RA; RBA; RHA.

### HUTTULA, Richard C.        fl.1866-1888

Domestic painter. He contributed to *The Broadway,* c.1867-74.

Illus: *Hurricane Harry [W.H.G. Kingstone, 1874].*
Exhib: B; L; RBA; RI.

### HYDE, Edgar

Artist working in Limerick, Ireland. He contributed drawings to *The Illustrated Times,* 1859.

### HYDE, William Henry        1858-

Portrait painter and illustrator. He was born in New York on 29 January 1858 and studied under Boulanger in Paris and exhibited at the Paris Exhibition of 1900. Hyde was a mainstay of *Harper's Magazine,* producing fine ink studies in a gently humorous vein. He appears to have lived and worked in England for some considerable time and kept close contacts with British publishers.

Illus: *An Imaged World [E. Garnett, 1894]; Beyond the Dreams of Avarice [Walter Besant, 1897]; The Nature Poems of George Meredith [1897]; London Impressions [Alice Meynell, 1898 (cover and end papers)]; The Cinque Ports [Blackwood, 1901]; The Victoria County Histories: Hampshire and Norfolk [1901]; The Poetical Works of John Milton [Astolat Press, 1904].*
Contrib: *The Yellow Book [1894-95]; The Pall Mall Magazine.*
Bibl: *The Studio,* June, 1894; *The Artist,* January, 1898, pp.1-6; R.E.D. Sketchley, *English Book Illus,* 1903, pp.39, 135.

### HYLAND, Fred

Illustrator working in London, 1894. He contributed a drawing in the Beardsley idiom to *The Yellow Book,* 1895.

Exhib: RBA, 1894.

*WILLIAM HOLMAN HUNT 1827-1910. 'At Night.' Illustration to* Once a Week, *Vol. 3, 1860. Wood engraving.*

**ILLINGWORTH, F.W.**
Figure artist. He contributed to *Punch*, 1914.

**ILLINGWORTH, S.E.**
Illustrator, contributing to *London Society*, 1868.

**IMAGE, Selwyn**                              **1849-1930**
Watercolourist, illustrator and poet. Born at Bodiam, Sussex in 1849, the son of the Rev. J. Image. He was educated at Marlborough and New College, Oxford and then at the Slade School, Oxford under John Ruskin. He took Holy Orders in 1872, becoming curate at various London churches from 1875-80. He designed stained glass windows for the Paris Exhibition in 1900 and for St. Luke's, Camberwell and Morthoe Church, Devon. He was elected Master of the Art Workers' Guild in 1900 and was Professor of Fine Art at Oxford, 1910-16. He was an occasional illustrator, a designer of ex-libris, and died 21 August 1930.

Illus: *Lyric Poems [Laurence Binyon, 1894]; A London Rose and Other Rhymes [Ernest Rhys, 1894]; A Little Child's Wreath [E.R. Chapman, 1895-96]; Stephania [Michael Field, 1895-96]; Poems [Vincent O'Sullivan, 1895-96]; (in each case, title and cover).*
Contrib: *The Century Guild Hobby Horse [1884-91].*
Exhib: FAS.
Colls: BM; V & AM.
See illustration (right).

**IMARGIASSI, Mario**
Contributor to *The Illustrated London News*, 1889.

**INCE, Charles**                              **1875-**
Landscape painter and illustrator. He was educated at the Cowper School and at King's College, London, and studied art with Henry George Moon, the landscape painter. Ince was an accountant and a director of a family printing firm as well as an artist. He was for some years the auditor of the RBA, after being elected to it in 1912. He contributed to *Punch*, 1905-06, favouring chalk drawings reminiscent of Belcher's work.

Exhib: G; L; M; RA; RBA; RI; ROI; RWS.

**INCE, Joseph Murray**                         **1806-1859**
Watercolourist and topographer. He was born at Presteign, Radnorshire in 1806 and became a pupil of David Cox in 1823, remaining with him for three years. Ince then lived in London and later lived in Cambridge, returning finally to Presteign in about 1835 on inheriting property there. He died 24 September 1859.

Illus: *Views Illustrating the County of Radnor [1832]; The Cambridge Portfolio [Rev. J.J. Smith, 1838-40].*
Exhib: RA; RBA.
Colls: BM; Fitzwilliam; V & AM.
Bibl: M. Hardie, *Watercolour Paint in Brit.*, Vol.III, p.19, illus.

**INGLIS, Archie**
Figure artist. Contributed a 'portrait' of Mr. Punch to *Punch*, 1904.

**INGLIS, G.**
Illustrator and book decorator. He illustrated *Ditties of the Olden Time*, c.1840, the ornamental work of a high quality, the figures less successful.

*SELWYN IMAGE 1849-1930. Book illustration for* The Century Guild Hobby Horse, *1884.*

**INGLIS, Lionel**
Humorous figure artist. He illustrated with R.A. Sterndale *The Lays of Ind* by Aliph Cheem, Calcutta, 1883, a satire of the British Raj.

**INGRAM, Master H.**                              **-1860**
Amateur artist. He was the son of Herbert Ingram, founder of *The Illustrated London News* and contributed illustrations to the paper in 1859 and 1860. He perished with his father in a steamer accident on Lake Michigan in 1860.

# J

**JACK, Richard RA** **1866-1952**
Portrait, figure and landscape painter. He was born in Sunderland in 1866 and studied at the York School of Art, winning a National Scholarship to South Kensington in 1886. He studied at the Académie Julian in Paris, 1890-91 and won medals at the Academy Colarossi and exhibited a prize-winning portrait at the Paris Exhibition, 1900. Jack was elected an ARA in 1914 and an RA in 1920, having become RP in 1900 and RI, 1917. He was working in Montreal, Canada in 1932.

Contrib: *The Windsor Magazine; The Idler [1892].*
Exhib: G; GG; L; M; New Gall; P. RA; RI.

**JACKSON, Francis Ernest ARA** **1872-1945**
Portrait painter, lithographer. He studied in Paris and was for some time drawing instructor at the RA Schools. Jackson was very influential in bringing the art of lithography back into notice by serious artists and taught it at London County Council Schools in the 1900s. He ran his own lithography class in Camberwell and with Spenser Pryse (q.v.) he ran *The Neolith,* 1907-08, a magazine with both text and illustrations lithographed. His early work is clearly influenced by Beardsley and Mucha and with its candles and ironwork and 'coquettish' delicacy, looks forward to art deco. Jackson also carried out posters for the Underground Railway. ARA, 1944.

Exhib: G; L; M; NEA; P; RA; RHA; RSA.
Bibl: *The Studio,* competition, Vol.5, 1895, illus.; Vol.18, 1899-1900, pp.282-285.

**JACKSON, Frederick Hamilton** **1848-1923**
Painter, illustrator and designer. He was born in 1848 and entered his father's wholesale book business, but gave this up to follow art. He studied at the RA Schools, later becoming master in the Antique School of the Slade under Poynter and Legros (qq.v.). He founded with E.S. Burchett the Chiswick School of Art in 1880, was lecturer on perspective at South Kensington and a member of the Art Workers' Guild from 1887. He also worked on schemes for ecclesiastical decoration and designed for mosaics. He was elected RBA in 1889 and died 13 October 1923.

Illus: *The Stories of the Condottieri; A Little Guide to Sicily [1904]; The Shores of the Adriatic [1906]; The Italian Side and the Austrian Side; Rambles in the Pyrenees [1912].*
Exhib: B; G; GG; L; M; New Gall; RA; RBA; RHA; RI; ROI.

**JACKSON, J.**
Illustrator, contributing drawings of Spain to *The Illustrated London News,* 1875.

**JACKSON, James Grey**
Artist. He wrote and illustrated *An Account of the Empire of Morocco,* 1809, AT 296.

**JACKSON, Mason** **1819-1903**
Wood engraver and illustrator. He was the son of John Jackson, the wood engraver, who with W.A. Chatto published *A Treatise on Wood Engraving,* 1838. He was a pupil of his brother John Jackson 1801-1848 and became Art Editor of *The Illustrated London News* in 1860 and Editor in about 1875. He was the first historian of illustrated journalism. He died in West London in 1903.

Illus: *Walton's Compleat Angler [Bohn]; Ministering Children.*
Contrib: *Cassell's Illustrated Family Paper [1857]; ILN [1876-78].*
Exhib: RA.
Bibl: M. Jackson, *The Pictorial Press,* 1885.

**JACKSON, Sir Thomas Graham, Bt.** **1835-1924**
Architect and draughtsman. He was born at Hampstead 21 December 1835 and was educated at Brighton College and Wadham College, Oxford. He was a pupil with Sir Gilbert Scott, 1858-61 and in 1864 became a Fellow of Wadham College, remaining at Oxford until 1880. He was a notable architect of collegiate buildings, mostly in Oxford and carried out many restorations of Tudor and Jacobean houses. He was elected ARA in 1892 and RA in 1896. He was created a Baronet in 1913 and died on 7 November 1924.

Illus: *Wadham College: Its History and Buildings [1893].*
Exhib: RA.
Colls: Ashmolean (book-plates).
Bibl: *Recollections of TGJ,* 1950.

**JACOBS, Louise R.** **fl.1910-1938**
Landscape and flower painter and illustrator. She was working in London in 1910 and in Hull, 1923-25.

Contrib: *The Graphic [1915 (allegory)].*
Exhib: L; RA; RBA; RCA; RHA; RSA; SWA.

**JACOMB-HOOD, Percy** **See HOOD, Percy JACOMB-**

**JACQUE, G.H.**
French figure artist. He contributed drawings to *The Illustrated London News,* 1851.

**JALLAND, G.H.** **fl.1888-1908**
Black and white artist specialising in equestrian subjects. He was a regular contributor to *Punch* from 1888 and was considered by M.H. Spielmann to be a natural successor to Leech with his humours of the hunting field and of sport. He did small free pencil sketches which are very lively. He signs his work

Contrib: *Punch [1888-1905]; ILN [1891-98]; The Sporting and Dramatic News [1892]; The Pall Mall Magazine; The Graphic [1908].*
Exhib: FAS, 1901.
Bibl: *Mr. Punch with Horse and Hound* New Punch Library, c.1930.

**JAMES, Gilbert** **fl.1895-1926**
Figure and still-life painter and illustrator. He was born at Liverpool and after working in commerce, turned to art and on moving to London began to contribute black and white drawings to the leading magazines. James worked mostly in a heavy art nouveau style, strong contrasts and very mannered and symbolic subjects often with an Eastern setting. His work is very variable in quality.

Illus: *Contes de Grimm [1908]; Contes de Anderson [1908]; The Rubaiyat of Omar Khayyam [1910].*
Contrib: *The Ludgate Monthly [1891]; The English Illustrated Magazine [1895-97]; The Sketch [1897]; Pick-Me-Up [1897]; The Quartier Latin [1898]; The Butterfly [1899].*
Exhib: L; NEA.
Colls: V & AM.

**JAMES, The Rt. Rev. J.T. Bishop of Calcutta** **1786-1828**
Author and artist. He was born in 1786 and educated at Rugby, Charterhouse and Christ Church, Oxford. M.A., 1810. He lived at Barnet, 1810-16, was Vicar of Flitton-cum-Silsoe, Bedfordshire, 1816-27, and Bishop of Calcutta, 1827-28. He published some papers on painting, 1820-22.

Illus: *Journal of a Tour in Germany, Sweden and Russia, Poland [1816, AT 16]; The Semi-Sceptic [1825]; Views in Russia, Sweden, Poland and Germany [1826-27 (liths.) AT 23].*
Exhib: RA, 1810-16.

**JAMES, Lionel**
Special Artist for *The Graphic* in Russia, 1904, and during the Russian political outrages, 1905-10. This artist is not further recorded.

**JAMESON, Margaret** **fl.1909-1920**
Flower and portrait painter and illustrator. She worked in London and illustrated *The Vicar of Wakefield,* for Chapman and Hall in 1910 with lucid ink and watercolour drawings.

Exhib: L; RA; SWA.

**JANE, Fred T.**                                        1870-1916

Naval artist and author and originator of *Jane's The World's Warships,*
1915. He was born at Upottery, Devon, on 6 August 1870 and was
educated at Exeter School. Jane was the inventor of the Naval War
Game and a successful naval journalist, being correspondent for *The
Engineer, The Scientific American* and *The Standard.* He contested
Portsmouth as Navy Interest Candidate in the General Election of
1906. Lived at Havant, Hants and died 8 March 1916.

Publ: *The Imperial Russian Navy [1900]; The Imperial Japanese Navy [1904];
All The World's Aircraft [1910]; The British Battle Fleet [1912].*
Contrib: *ILN [1892-96]; The English Illustrated Magazine [1893-95]; The
Penny Illustrated Paper.*
Exhib: RA, 1894.

**JANET, Gustave**                                        1829-

Draughtsman, lithographer and illustrator. He was born in Paris in
1829 and was the brother of Janet Lange (q.v.). He worked for most
of the leading French magazines, particularly *Monde illustrée* and
*Revue de la Mode.* He did a certain amount of fashion illustration and
was employed by Henry Vizetelly on English publications. The latter
writes of him that he 'excelled in depicting such scenes as a ball or
reception at the Tuileries, his women always being very gracefully
drawn although they were remarkably alike in face — being in fact so
many portraits of the artist's handsome wife.'

Publ: *Caricatures Politiques [1849]; Souvenirs de L'Opera; La Mode artistique.*
Contrib: *Cassell's Illustrated Family Paper [1853]; The Illustrated Times
[1855-66]; ILN [1867-71].*

**JANOWSKI, C.**

Illustrator of genre. A series of designs of French markets by this
artist are in the Victoria and Albert Museum collection, signed and
dated 1904. The book for which they were intended has not been
identified.

**JEHNE, Linton**

Political cartoonist. He illustrated *Alice in Blunderland* by Louis
Carllew, 1910.

**JELLICOE, John**                                        fl.1865-1903

Figure painter and illustrator. He drew mainly domestic scenes for
novels and popular magazine stories.

Illus: *Queen of Beauty [Mrs. Henry, 1894]; Cherry and Violet [Miss Manning,
1897].*
Contrib: *ILN [1889]; The Sporting and Dramatic News [1890]; Good Words
[1891]; St Paul's [1894]; The Lady's Pictorial; The Windsor Magazine.*
Exhib: RBA, 1887-88.

**JENKINS, Joseph John  RSA**                            1811-1885

Genre painter, watercolourist and engraver. He was born in London in
1811, the son and pupil of the painter D. Jenkins. He became a
member of the NWS in 1842 and an Associate of the OWS in 1849
and Secretary, 1854-64. He was a considerable historian of the
progress of watercolour in this country, Roget basing his *History* on
Jenkins notes. He was also the first artist to introduce the idea of
private press views of exhibitions in this country. He died on 8 March
1885.

Contrib: *The Chaplet [c.1840].*
Exhib: BI; NWS; OWS; RA; RBA.
Colls: V & AM.

**JENKINS, Will**

Book decorator. He contributed borders and ornament to *The
Connoisseur,* 1914.

**JENNER, Stephen**                                      fl.1820-1830

Amateur caricaturist. He was a great-nephew of Dr. Jenner and drew
portrait figures in pencil, usually signed 'S. Jenner del'.

**JENNINGS, Edward**                                     fl.1865-1888

Landscape painter in watercolour and illustrator. He contributed to
*Good Words,* 1880.

Exhib: NWS; RA; RBA; RI.

**JENNINGS, Reginald George**                            1872-1930

Figure, portrait and landscape painter and illustrator. He studied at
the National Art Training School and at the Westminster School of
Art, becoming Instructor at King's College for Women and Instructor
in Painting and Design to Middlesex County Council.

Contrib: *Fun [1900].*
Exhib: L; New Gall; RA; RI.

**JENNIS, Gurnell Charles**                              1874-1943

Black and white artist and etcher. He specialised in country and horse
subjects in an individual scratchy style which he contributed to *Punch*
and other magazines. He worked in London and was elected ARE in
1914.

Contrib: *Pick-Me-Up [1896]; Punch [1913-22]; The Graphic [1916].*
Exhib: L; NEA; RA; RE.
Colls: V & AM.
Bibl: *Mr Punch with Horse and Hound,* New Punch Library, c.1930.

**JESSOP, Ernest Maurice**                               fl.1883-1907

Painter, etcher and illustrator. He worked in London and specialised
in domestic subjects and children's books.

Illus: *The Knight and The Dragon [Tom Hood, 1885].*
Contrib: *The Girl's Own Paper [1890-1900]; The Idler [1892].*

**'JEST'**

Cartoonist contributing one caricature to *Vanity Fair,* 1903.

**JEWITT, Thomas Orlando Sheldon**                       1799-1869

Architectural draughtsman and illustrator, engraver on wood. He was
born in 1799, the son of Arthur Jewitt and worked with his father on
the latter's newspaper *The Northern Star.* He established himself at
Oxford in 1838 and later moved to London where he became
well-known as an illustrator of Gothic architecture and ornament.
According to Chatto he was 'one of the very few who continue to
combine designing and drawing with engraving'. He died in London on
30 May 1869.

Illus: *Bloxham's Gothic Architecture [1829]; Bohn's Glossary of Ecclesiastical
Ornament [1846]; Glossary of Architecture [J.H. Parker, 1849]; Brick and
Marble Architecture of Italy [G.E. Street, 1855]; Murray's English Cathedrals
[1861-69, 7 vols]; Baptismal Fonts [Van Voorst]; Westminster Abbey [Scott].*
Bibl: Chatto & Jackson *Treatise on Wood Engraving,* 1861, pp.584-585.

**JOBLING, Robert**                                      1841-1923

River painter and illustrator of panoramic views. He was born in
Newcastle in 1841 and trained there as a glass-maker. He attended
evening classes in art and after acting as the foreman painter at a
shipyard, he became a full-time artist in 1899. He was married to a
painter, Isa Thompson and died at Whitley Bay in 1923.

Illus: *Tales of the Borders [Wilson].*
Contrib: *Illustrated London Magazine [1885]; The Graphic [1889].*
Exhib: B; L; RA; RBA.

**JOHANNOT, Tony**                                       1803-1852

French illustrator. He was born at Offenbach on 9 November 1803
and was the foremost illustrator of the 1840s in France, following
the romantic tradition and introducing vignette work into his books.
His popularity in England was not widespread although some English
editions of his illustrated volumes did appear. He died in Paris, 4
August 1852.

Illus: *Don Quixote [1836-37, English edition 1842]; The Works of Molière
[1835-36]; Sentimental Journey [Sterne, 1851]; Summer at Baden Baden
[Guinot, 1853].*
Contrib: *ILN [1851].*
Bibl: Percy Muir, *Victorian Illustrated Books,* 1971, pp.221-222.

**JOHNSON, Alfred J.** fl.1874-1894

Figure and domestic painter and illustrator. Worked in North London and was a very regular contributor to the magazines. He signs his work 〒

Illus: *Seven Little Australians [Ethel S. Turner, 1894].*
Contrib: *ILN [1874-93]; The Quiver [1890]; The Strand Magazine [1894]; The Wide World Magazine.*
Exhib: L; RA; RBA; RI.

**JOHNSON, C.K.**

Contributor of comic genre subjects to *The Graphic,* 1887.

**JOHNSON, Cyrus RI** 1848-1925

Genre painter and illustrator. He was born at Cambridge on 1 January 1848 and after studying at the Perse School, worked in London as a domestic and portrait painter. He was elected RI in 1887 and died at Baron's Court, 27 February 1925.

Contrib: *The Strand Magazine [1891].*
Exhib: RA; RBA; RWS.

**JOHNSON, Edward Killingworth RWS** 1825-1896

Rustic artist and illustrator. He was born at Stratford-le-Bow in 1825 and taught himself to paint, taking up the career of a painter in 1863. He attended some classes at the Langham Life School but preferred to study from nature in the countryside and moved to Essex in 1871, remaining there for the rest of his life. He was a popular contributor to *The Graphic* and in 1887, was described by that magazine as 'Our Country Artist'. In 1855, Johnson was employed to draw illustrations on the wood for the Cundall Edition of Goldsmith's *The Deserted Village.* He was elected AOWS in 1866 and a full member in 1876. He died at Halstead in 1896.

Contrib: *The Welcome Guest [1860]; London Society [1863]; The Churchman's Family Magazine; The Graphic [1874-89].*
Exhib: OWS; RA; RBA.

**JOHNSON, Ernest Borough RBA ROI RI** 1867-1949

Lead pencil artist and illustrator, painter, etcher, lithographer. He was born at Shifnal, Salop in 1867 and studied at the Slade School under Legros and at the Herkomer School, Bushey. Johnson was Professor of Fine Arts at Bedford College, University of London and Headmaster of the Art Department at Chelsea Polytechnic. He also taught at the London School of Art, the Byam Shaw School and the Vicat Cole School. He was a writer, a collector of antiques and porcelain and his drawings of 'Blitzed London' were acquired by the Guildhall Museum in 1945. He collaborated with Sir H. Von Herkomer (q.v.) in illustrating Thomas Hardy's *Tess* for *The Graphic* in 1891. He was elected RBA in 1896, RMS, 1897, ROI, 1903 and RI, 1906.

Publ: *The Drawings of Michaelangelo; The Woodcuts of Frederick Sandys; The Techniques of the Lead Pencil; Chalk and Charcoal; A Portfolio of Rapid Studies From the Nude; The Art of the Pencil.*
Contrib: *The Graphic [1889-91]; Black & White [1891].*
Exhib: B; G; L; M; New Gall; P; RA; RBA; RI; RSA; ROI.
Colls: V & AM.

**JOHNSON, Herbert** 1848-1906

Figure and landscape painter and illustrator. He worked mostly at Clapham, London, but was sent by *The Graphic* as Special Artist on the Royal Tour of India, 1875 and to Egypt in 1882. He specialised in military and ceremonial subjects.

Contrib: *The Graphic [1870-89]; The English Illustrated Magazine [1888]; The Daily Graphic [1890]; The Girls' Own Paper; The Windsor Magazine.*
Exhib: G; L; M; RA; RBA; ROI.
Colls: Witt Photo.

**JOHNSTON, Sir Harry Hamilton FRGS** 1858-1927

Painter and explorer. He was born at Kennington on 12 June 1858 and was educated at Stockwell Grammar School and King's College, London. He studied at the RA Schools, 1876-80 and was a medallist at South Kensington Schools, 1876. Johnston travelled in North

Africa, 1879-80, West Africa and the River Congo, 1882-83, and led the Royal Society's expedition to Kilimanjaro in 1884. He became British Vice-Consul in the Cameroons in 1885, Consul General of The British Central African Protectorate, 1891 and Consul General at Tunis, 1897-99. He was created KCB, 1896 and GCMG in 1901, and died in Sussex on 31 July 1927.

He was a very talented painter of African scenery and animals in watercolours, which he contributed to various publications and magazines.

Contrib: *The Graphic [1889-1906].*
Exhib: L; M; RA; RWS.
Bibl: *The Story of My Life,* 1923.

**JOHNSTONE, Alexander** 1815-1891

Genre painter and illustrator. He was born in Scotland in 1815 and studied at the Edinburgh Academy and at the RA Schools, principally painting history subjects. He died in March 1891.

Contrib: *The Home Affections [Charles Mackay, 1858].*
Exhib: BI; RA; RBA.

**JONES**

Various engravings to *The Illustrated London News,* 1843 are signed 'Jones del'.

**JONES, Adrian** 1845-1938

Sculptor. He was born on 9 February 1845, the son of James Brookholding Jones of Ludlow and was educated at Ludlow Grammar School. He served for twenty three years as a veterinary officer in the regular Army before devoting his time entirely to sculpture. He executed a large number of military statues and the Victoria and Albert Museum has a drawing by him for illustration. MVO, 1907. He died 24 January 1938.

Exhib: G; GG; L; RA; ROI.
Bibl: *Memoirs of a Soldier Artist,* 1933.

**JONES, Alfred Garth**

Landscape painter, illustrator and poster artist. He studied first in Manchester and then at the Westminster School of Art and the Slade, followed by working under Laurens and Constant in Paris, 1893 and a period at South Kensington. He was influenced by the works of Dürer and his pen drawings have a strong woodcut style that was sometimes criticised. A very versatile artist, he was as much at home in imaginative work as in political cartooning or pure decoration. He was better known in France in the early part of his career, working for *Revue Illustrée,* later establishing himself in this country as design master at the Lambeth and Manchester schools.

Illus: *The Tournament of Love [Brentano, 1894]; The Minor Poems of Milton, [1898]; Contes de Haute Lisse [Doucet, 1900]; Contes de la Fileuse [Doucet, 1900]; The Essays of Elia [Charles Lamb, 1902]; A Real Queen's Fairy Book; In Memoriam [Tennyson, 1903]; Goldsmith's Works; Poems and Dramatic Works of Coleridge; Journal to Stella [J. Swift]; Keat's Poems; The Voyage of Marco Polo.*
Contrib: *The Quartier Latin [1896]; The Quarto [1896-97]; The Parade [1897]; Fun [1901]; The Graphic [1910].*
Exhib: NEA; RA.
Bibl: *The Studio,* Winter No, 1900-01, p.82, illus; Vol.25, 1901-02, p.131; R.E.D. Sketchley, *Eng. Bk. Illus.,* 1903, pp.14-15, 128; *Modern Book Illustrators and their Work,* Studio, 1914.

**JONES, E.A.T.**

Illustrator. Four coloured ink drawings for a book, signed by this artist and dated 1871-85, were on the art market in 1976.

**JONES, F.**

Contributed drawings to *Small Arms,* published by the War Office in about 1900.

Colls: V & AM.

**JONES, G. Smetham** fl.1888-1894

Black and white artist, specialising in horses. Worked in North London and exhibited at the RA and RBA, 1888-1893.

Contrib: *Pick-Me-Up [c.1890]; Judy; St. Pauls [1894].*
Colls: Witt Photo.

**JONES, George Kingston** fl.1890-1925

Illustrator. He worked in London and according to A.S. Hartrick (q.v.) was on the staff of *The Graphic*, 'established as toucher-up of photographs and general utility man '.

Contrib: *The Daily Graphic [1890]; The Windsor Magazine; The Graphic [1890-1910].*
Exhib: RA, 1896-99.
Bibl: A.S. Hartrick, *A Painter's Pilgrimage*, 1939, p.67.

**JONES, Maud Raphael** fl.1889-1902

Landscape and rustic painter. She worked at Bradford and exhibited in London, 1889-93.

Colls: Witt Photo (illus.).

**JONES, Owen Carter** 1809-1874

Architect, designer and topographer. He was of Welsh descent and born in Thames Street, London on 15 February 1809. For six years he was a pupil of Lewis Vulliamy, the architect, and attended the RA Schools, 1830. Jones made extensive visits to France, Italy, Egypt and Spain in 1836, beginning a book on the Alhambra which was not completed for nine years and cost £24 a copy! He had also become interested by Sir Henry Cole's attempts to improve industrial design and contributed many illustrations to the latter's *Journal of Design and Manufactures,* 1849. He supervised the decoration of the Great Exhibition in 1851 and of the Crystal Palace at Sydenham, 1852. Jones was influential in opening up new possibilities for lithography and for applying new styles to wall-papers and textiles. He died on 19 April 1874.

Illus: *Ancient Spanish Ballads [J.G. Lockhart, 1841]; Alhambra [1836-42]; The Grammar of Ornament [1856]; The Victoria Psalter [1861].*
Exhib: RA, 1831-61.
Colls: BM.
Bibl: Chatto & Jackson, *Treatise on Wood Engraving*, 1861, p.599; Ruari McLean, *Victorian Book Design*, 1972, pp.73-98, illus.; P. Muir, *Victorian Illustrated Books*, 1971, pp.154-155.

**JONES, Sydney Robert** 1881-1966

Painter, etcher and illustrator. He was born on 27 February 1881 and studied art at the Birmingham School. A very accomplished pen artist, he made tours of England, France, Belgium and Holland and published the results in a series of travel books. He worked for *The Studio* in 1912-13, designing for their special numbers and was associated with Messrs. J. Connell, publishers. He died at Wallingford in 1966.

Illus: *Old English Country Cottages [1966]; The Charm of the English Village [P.H. Ditchfield; 1908]; The Manor Houses of England [1910]; Old Houses in Holland; Cottage Interiors and Decoration; On Designing Small Houses and Cottages; The Village Homes of England [1912]; England in France [C. Vince, 1919]; Posters and Their Designers; Art and Publicity; Touring England; Old English Household Life; London Triumphant; Thames Triumphant.*
Contrib: *The Sphere.*
Exhib: L; RA; RI.
Colls: V & AM.
Bibl: *Modern Book Illustrators and their Work*, Studio, 1914.

**JONES, T.W.**

Figure artist. Contributed drawings to *Punch*, 1904.

**JONES, Thomas** fl.1836-1848

Caricaturist. He was active in the early Victorian period, drawing very much in the style of Bunbury.

Colls: Witt Photo.

**JONES, V.**

Contributor to *The Illustrated London News*, 1858.

**JOPLING, Joseph Middleton** 1831-1884

Painter, portraitist and caricaturist. He was self-taught and was elected ARI, 1859. He married Louisa Goode, the first woman to be elected RBA, 1902. He contributed two cartoons to *Vanity Fair*, 1883.

**JOSEPH, George Francis ARA** 1764-1846

Portrait and miniature painter. He entered the RA Schools in 1784 and won the gold medal, 1792. He was elected ARA in 1813 and died in Cambridge in 1846. He designed some illustrations for historical books.

Colls: BM.

**JOUQMART, W.**

Contributor of social subjects to *Punch*, 1900.

**JOY, Thomas Musgrove** 1812-1866

Historical painter and book illustrator. He was born at Boughton Winchelsea, Kent, in 1812 and studied art with Samuel Drummond ARA. He moved to London and became the teacher of John Philip RA, and was patronised by Queen Victoria, 1841-43. His illustrative work makes use of vignettes and elaborate borders. He died in London, 7 April 1866.

Exhib: RA; RBA, 1832-
Colls: York.

**JUNGMANN, Nico W. RBA** 1873-1935

Dutch artist who became a British subject, painter and illustrator. He was born in Amsterdam in 1873 and was apprenticed at the age of twelve to a church decorator. He then attended the Academy of Plastic Art in Amsterdam and won a scholarship to London to study its life. He settled in London but continued to paint Dutch scenes, much of the illustrative work being in large chalk drawings with pastel colours and very sculptural in effect. He is much influenced by the Japanese colour print, but also by Millet and his sympathy for the peasant at work. He was a close friend of the artist Charles W. Bartlett with whom he worked.

Illus: *Holland [Beatrix Jungmann, c.1905]; Norway [Beatrix Jungmann, c.1905]; Normandy [G.E. Mitton, c.1905]; The People of Holland [c.1905].*
Contrib: *The Parade [1897].*
Exhib: B; L; M; RA; RBA; RHA.
Bibl: *Some Drawings by Mr. NJ*, Studio, Vol. 13, 1898, pp.25-32, illus.

**JUSTYNE, Percy William** 1812-1883

Landscape painter and book illustrator. He was born at Rochester, Kent in 1812 and was principally a contributor to the magazines. Justyne specialised in architectural illustration and particularly church architecture, gothic buildings and the monuments of the East and Spain, where he lived from 1841-48.

Illus: *History of Greece [Smith]; Biblical Dictionary [Fergusson]; Handbook of Architecture [C. Kingsley]; Christmas in the Tropics.*
Contrib: *Cassell's Illustrated Family Paper [1857]; Churchman's Family Magazine [1863]; The Graphic [1873]; ILN; Floral World.*
Exhib: RA; RBA.
Colls: Nottingham.

# K

## KAPP, Edmond Xavier                    1890-1978

Painter, draughtsman and caricaturist. He was born in London on 5 November 1890, and was educated at Owen's School and Christ's College, Cambridge before studying art in Paris and Rome. Although Kapp's training dates from before the First World War, in which he served with the BEF, his popularity as a caricaturist stemmed from his first one man show in London, 1919. He became one of the leading artists of the 1920s in this field, drawing most of the writers, musicians, artists and actors of the decade and publishing a number of books. He subsequently turned his attention to more serious painting and particularly abstract work. He died on 31 October 1978.

Illus: *Personalities, Twenty-Four Drawings* [1919]; *Reflections, Twenty-Four Drawings* [1922]; *Ten Great Lawyers* [1924]; *Minims, Twenty-Eight Drawings* [1925]; *Pastiche, A Music Room Book* [1926 (with his wife)]; publications of original lithographs from 1932; *The Nations at Geneva* [1934-35, twenty-five portraits on stone].
Contrib: *The Sketch; Trimblerigg* [L. Housman, 1924]; *The Law Journal* [1924-25].
Exhib: Leicester Gall; Wildenstein.
Colls: Ashmolean; Birmingham; BM; Manchester; V & AM.
Bibl: Charles Spencer, 'From Caricature to Abstraction', *Studio*, June 1961.

See illustration (below)

*EDMOND XAVIER KAPP 1890-1978. Caricature of Wyndham Lewis at the Café Royal, 1914. Ink and watercolours, chalk. 10¾ins. x 8ins. (27.4cm x 20.5cm).*                    Victoria and Albert Museum

## KAUFFER, Edward McKnight                    -1954

Artist, poster-designer and illustrator. He was born at Great Falls, Montana, U.S.A. and educated at American public schools. He began his career as a theatrical scene painter, attending evening classes at the Art Institute, Chicago and then studying at Munich. He spent two years in Paris before settling in London in 1914, making his name there with his poster work for the Underground Railways. He was the first poster-artist in Britain to design advertisements where the visual and the verbal were totally integrated. He worked extensively for the private presses but his book illustration is less well-known. He became a member of the London Group, 1916.

Illus: *Anatomy of Melancholy* [Robert Burton, Nonesuch, 1925]; *Benito Cereno* [Herman Melville, Nonesuch, 1926]; *Elsie And The Child* [Arnold Bennett, Curwen Press, 1929]; *Don Quixote* [Cervantes, Nonesuch, 1930]; *Marina* [T.S. Eliot, Ariel, 1930]; *The World in 2030 A.D.* [The Earl of Birkenhead, 1930].
Contrib: *The Broadside* [Harold Monro, Poetry Bookshop].
Exhib: NEA.
Colls: V & AM.
Bibl: EMcKK, *The Art of the Poster*, 1924.

## KAY, J. Illingworth                    fl.1894-1918

Designer of covers and title-pages. He worked for Lane's Bodley Head and exhibited at the RA, 1917-18.

Illus: *Orchard Songs* [Norman Gale, 1894]; *Poems* [Richard Garnett, 1894]; *Romantic Professions* [1894]; *The Lower Slopes* [Grant Allen, 1895].
Contrib: *The Yellow Book* [1896 (cover)].

## KAY, John                    1742-1826

Caricaturist and miniaturist. He was born in Dalkieth in 1742 and apprenticed to a barber and print-seller at Edinburgh. In 1782, a customer left him a legacy which enabled him to live independantly as an artist. From that time until his death he produced nine hundred portrait caricatures and some political squibs. His drawings are in profile and spindly, rather like the work of Robert Sayer, but they were considered good likenesses and cover the whole of Edinburgh Society. *Kay's Edinburgh Portraits* were issued in 1837-38 and a further *Series of Original Portraits by John Kay, Edinburgh,* followed in 1877.

Colls: Witt Photo.

## KEARNAN, Thomas                    fl.1821-1850

Watercolourist and draughtsman. He worked in London and contributed to *Public Works of Great Britain*, 1838, AL 410. NWS, 1837.

Exhib: NWS; RA; RBA.

## KEELING, William Knight   RI                    1807-1886

Portrait painter and watercolourist. He was born at Manchester in 1807 and was apprenticed to a wood-engraver there before moving to London to work under the portrait painter, W. Bradley. He returned to Manchester in 1835 and helped to found the Manchester Academy of Fine Arts of which he was President, 1864-77. He was elected AWS in 1840 and NWS the following year. Keeling made a voyage to Spain in middle life and died at Manchester 21 February 1886.

Contrib: *The Chaplet* [1840].
Exhib: BI; M; RA.
Colls: V & AM.

## KEENE, Charles Samuel                    1823-1891

Black and white artist, illustrator and etcher. He was born at Hornsea, London in 1823 and when a child moved with his family to Ipswich where he remained until his father's death in 1838. He was articled first to a solicitor and then to Pilkington, the architect, finally being articled to Charles Whymper, the wood-engraver. After leaving Whymper in 1852, he set up on his own in the Strand and worked for various publishers, especially for the nearby office of *The Illustrated London News*. Keene began to draw for *Punch* in 1852, a connection that was to last until the day of his death and bring him great celebrity. A rather withdrawn and slightly bohemian man, he relied principally on urban social life for his subjects, often taking his characters from the alley-way and the market where Du Maurier's folk

*CHARLES SAMUEL KEENE 1823-1891. 'The Struggle.' Pen and ink. Signed with initials. 5½ins. x 4½ins. (14cm x 11.4cm).* Author's Collection

would not be seen! He relied heavily on his friends for amusing situations and was supplied with many by his friend Joseph Crawhall (q.v.).

Keene's career as a draughtsman runs through several phases. His earlier works for Thomas Barrett's *Book of Beauty,* 1846, show an almost Georgian burlesque and caricature. By the 1850s he was under the influence of Menzel and develops a rather hard and Germanic drawing line, which gradually softens during the 1860s. In his last drawing, 'Arry on the Boulevard', published in *Punch* in 1891, his economy of line is such that he might almost be compared to the French draughtsmanship of a master like Lautrec. A memorial exhibition of the artist was held at the Fine Art Society in March 1891. He signs his early work: ⊂ʂκ̄  and his later work: ₭

Illus: *Robinson Crusoe [1847]; Green's Nursery Annual [1847]; The Wooden Walls of Old England [1847]; The De Cliffords [Mrs. Sherwood, 1847]; The White Slave [1852]; A Story with a Vengeance [1852]; Marie Louise [1853]; The Giants of Patagonia [1853]; The Book of German Songs [W.H. Dulcken, 1856]; A Narrative of the Indian Revolt [Sir Colin Campbell, 1858]; The Boy Tar [Mayne Reid, 1860]; The Voyage of the Constance [1860]; Jack Buntline [W.H. Kingston, 1861]; Sea Kings and Naval Heroes [1861]; The Cambridge Grisette [H. Vaughan, 1862]; Tracks for Tourists [F.C. Burnand, 1864]; Mrs. Caudle's Curtain Lectures [1866]; Roundabout Papers [W.M. Thackeray, 1879]; The Cloister and The Hearth [Reade, 1890].*
Contrib: *Willmott's Sacred Poetry [1862]; Ballads and Songs of Brittany [1865]; Legends and Lyrics [A.A. Proctor, 1866]; Touches of Nature [1866]; Thornbury's Legendary Ballads [1876]; Passages From Modern English Poets [1876]; ILN [1850-56]; Punch [1852-91]; Once a Week [1859-65 & 1867]; Good Words [1862]; The Cornhill Magazine [1864]; London Society [1866-70].*
Exhib: FAS.
Colls: Ashmolean; BM; Fitzwilliam; Newcastle; V & AM.
Bibl: G.S. Layard, *The Life and Letters of CSK,* 1892.; G.S. Layard, *The Work of CK,* 1897; F.L. Emanuel, *CK,* Print Collectors' Club, 1935; D. Hudson, *CK,* 1947.
See illustrations (above and pp.119, 359)

**KEENE, Thomas**
Relation or follower of Charles Keene (q.v.). There are some prints of his work in the Witt Photo Library.

**KELLER, Arthur L.**
Illustrator of Winston S. Churchill's only novel *Mr. Crewe's Career,* 1908.

**KELLY, Robert George Talbot    RBA RI**    **1861-1934**
Landscape painter and illustrator. He was born at Birkenhead on 18 January 1861, the son of R.G. Kelly, the landscape painter. He was educated at Birkenhead School before studying art with his father. He specialised in oriental scenery and from 1882 onwards travelled abroad in Morocco, Egypt and Burma, undertaking the illustrations of travel books for Messrs. Black in the 1900s. He became RI in 1907, RBA, 1893, and died on 30 December 1934.
Illus: *Fire and Sword in the Sudan [Sir R.C. Slatin, 1896]; Egypt Painted and Described [1902]; Burma [1905]; Peeps at Many Lands [1908].*
Exhib: B; FAS, 1902, 1904, 1916, 1924; G; L; M; RA; RBA; RHA; RI; RSA.

**KELLY, Tom**    **fl.1887-1901**
Landscape painter, topographer and flower illustrator. He was working in Newmarket, 1888, Bedford in 1892 and London in 1901. He travelled to South Africa in 1890-91 and exhibited at the New Gallery.
Contrib: *The English Illustrated Magazine [1887-91, 1896].*

**KEMBLE, Edward Windsor**    **1861-**
American magazine illustrator. He was born at Sacramento on 18 January 1861 and is associated with pen drawings of the Deep South, a similar sort of realism to that of F. Remington (q.v.). He is included here as the illustrator of *Mark Twain's Library of Humour, The Adventures of Huckleberry Finn,* etc., Chatto, 1897. Pennell considers him a fine but uneven draughtsman, tending to carlessness.
Bibl: J. Pennell, *Pen Drawing and Pen Draughtsmen,* 1894, pp.236-240.

**KEMP, Percy**    **fl.1890-1895**
Black and white artist showing the strong influence of Phil May.
Contrib: *Daily Chronicle [1895]; Pick-Me-Up.*

**KEMP-WELCH, Lucy Elizabeth    RI**    **1869-1958**
Horse and animal painter. She was born at Bournemouth in 1869 and studied at the Herkomer School, Bushey, Herts. She was Principal of the Kemp-Welch School of Painting at Bushey, was elected RBA, 1902 and RI, 1907. She was President of the Society of Animal Painters in 1914 and had paintings purchased by the Chantrey Bequest in 1897 and 1917. A one man exhibition of her work was held in London in 1938.
Illus: *The Making of Mathias [1897].*
Exhib: B; FAS, 1905; G; L; M; RA; RBA; RCA; RHA; RI; ROI; RSA; RWA; SWA.
Bibl: *The Studio,* Winter No., 1900-01, p.67, illus; *LK-W,* Antique Collectors' Club, 1976.
See illustration (p.362)

**KENNARD, Edward**
Illustrator. Contributed drawings of sport to *The Graphic,* 1888.

**KENNION, Edward    FSA**    **1744-1809**
Landscape painter and drawing-master. He was born in Liverpool in 1744 and travelled to Jamaica and Cuba as a young man from 1762 to 1769. He returned to England and worked in Bath, London and Malvern, making frequent visits to the North-West and the Lakes. He was a member of the Society of Artists and died in London in 1809.
Publ: *Elements of Landscape and Picturesque Beauty [1790]; An Essay on Trees in Landscape [1815, AL 147].*
Exhib: RA; SA.

*CHARLES SAMUEL KEENE 1823-1891. 'A Soft Answer.' Illustration for* Punch, *1879. Pen and ink. Signed with initials. 5ins. x 7½ins. (12.7cm x 19.1cm).*
Victoria and Albert Museum

**KEPPEL, William Coutts, Viscount Bury and 7th Earl of Albermarle**
**1832-1894**
Artist and politician. He was born on 15 April 1832, the only son of the 6th Earl of Albermarle whom he succeeded in 1876. He exhibited in London from 1878-83 while living in Nuremburg. He died 28 August 1894.

Contrib: *Passages From Modern English Poets [1862].*

**KERR, Charles Henry Malcolm   RBA**                      **1858-1907**
Portrait and landscape painter. He worked in London and was elected RBA in 1890. He died at Campden Hill, Kensington on 27 December 1907.

Illus: *The Curse of Carne's Hold [G.A. Henty, 1890].*
Exhib: L; M; NEA; RA; RBA; RHA; RI; ROI.

**KERR, Henry Wright   RSA RSW**                          **1857-1936**
Genre and landscape painter, and character painter. He was born at Edinburgh in 1857 and studied in Dundee and at the RSA Schools. He travelled in Ireland in 1888 and was elected ARSA in 1893 and RSA in 1909. He died on 17 February 1936.

Illus: *Reminiscences of Scottish Life and Character [Dean Ramsay]; Annals of the Parish [M.R. Mitford, 1911]; The Lighter Side of Irish Life [G.A. Birmingham, 1911]; The Last of the Lairds [J. Galt, 1926].*
Exhib: G; L; RA; RI; RSA; RSW.
Colls: Dundee.

**KERR-LAWSON, James**                                   **1864-1939**
Figure and landscape painter, mural painter and lithographer. He was born at Anstruther, 28 October 1865, and was taken to Canada in early childhood. He was educated in Rome and Paris and studied art with Lefevbre and Boulanger, before returning to live in Chelsea.

According to Hartrick he was one of the early experimenters in the revival of lithography in the 1900s. He contributed to F.E. Jackson's *The Neo-Lith,* 1907-08. He carried out the decorations to the Senate in Ottawa and in later life retired to Italy.

Exhib: B; G; L; M; RBA; ROI.

**KEYL, Frederich Wilhelm**                               **1823-1871**
Engraver and animal illustrator. He was born at Frankfurt on 17 August 1823, coming to London in 1845. He studied under Landseer and Verboeckhoven and began exhibiting in 1847. Several of his works were bought for the Royal Collection. He died 5 December 1871.

Illus: *Homes Without Hands [Rev. J.G. Wood]; Featherland: Or How The Birds Lived at Greenlawn [G.M. Fenn, 1877].*
Contrib: *ILN [1864-69]; Churchman's Family Magazine [1864]; Beaton's Annual [1866]; Gatty's Parables From Nature [1867].*
Exhib: BI; RA.

**KIDD, John Bartholomew**                               **fl.1807-1858**
Contributor to *The Antiquarian and Topographical Cabinet,* 1808.

**KIDD, Joseph Bartholomew   RSA**                       **1808-1889**
Genre and landscape painter. He was born in Edinburgh in 1808 and studied with Thomson of Duddingston. He was a founder member of RSA in 1829, resigning from the institution when he settled in London in 1836. He practised as a drawing master at Greenwich, and died in May 1889.

Illus: *The Miscellany of Natural History [Sir T.D. Lauder, 1833]; West Indian Scenery [1838-40, AT 686].*
Exhib: BI; RSA.

**KILBURNE, George Goodwin   RI ROI**                    1839-1924

Painter, watercolourist, engraver and illustrator. He was born in Norfolk on 24 July 1839 and was apprenticed to the Brothers Dalziel whose niece he married. He turned from engraving to painting and specialised in hunting scenes and genre subjects set in the 18th century. A very talented draughtsman, Dalziel records of his apprentice work that it was 'so perfect, that it was published with the set to which it belonged '. He died in London in September 1924. RI, 1868 and ROI, 1883.

Illus: *Thackeray's Ballads [Cheap Illus. Edit., 1894]*.
Contrib: *ILN [1873]; The Graphic [1873-77 (domestic & theatrical)]; The Cornhill Magazine [1884]*.
Exhib: B; G; L; M; RA; RBA; RI; ROI.

**KIMBALL, Katharine   ARE**                    fl.1906-1926

Painter and illustrator. She was born in New England and educated at Jersey Ladies' College and at the National Academy of Design, New York, 1897. She specialised in pen illustrations of towns and cities for travel books. She was elected ARE, 1909.

Illus: *Paris [Okey, 1904]; Brussels [Gilliatt Smith, 1906]; Canterbury [Sterling Taylor, 1912]; Rochester [1912]*.
Contrib: *The Century; The Studio; The Artist; Gazette des Beaux Arts; The Queen*.
Exhib: L; RA; RE.
Colls: BM; Congress Library; V & AM.

**KING, Edward R.**                    fl.1883-1924

Genre painter and illustrator. He was probably the brother of Gunning King (q.v.) and began contributing to *The Illustrated London News* in 1883. He was one of the group of artists who treated both rural and metropolitan subjects in a new and realistic way, giving through sensitive drawing and minute hatching, a sympathetic view of poor Londoners and country folk. He was one of the artists much admired by Van Gogh. He was still working at East Molesey, Surrey in 1924. He became NEA in 1888.

Contrib: *ILN [1883-87]; The Pall Mall Magazine; Punch [1905]*.
Exhib: B; G; L; M; NEA; RA; RBA; ROI.
Colls: Witt Photo.
Bibl: *English Influences on Vincent Van Gogh*, Arts Council, 1974-75.

**KING, Gunning**                    1859-1940

Painter, etcher and illustrator. He studied art at the South Kensington and the RA Schools and became a member of the NEA in 1887. King was one of the most vigorous illustrators of rural life to emerge during the eighties, combining great human interest with fine quality penwork. He was an early advocate of chalk drawings and in his figure subjects owes something to the freedom of Charles Keene (q.v.). He worked for most of his life at Petersfield, Hants.

Contrib: *ILN [1882-99]; The Graphic [1883]; The Windsor Magazine; Punch; The Sketch; The Sporting and Dramatic News [1896]; The English Illustrated Magazine [1896]; Pick-Me-Up [1897]; The Quiver [1897]*.
Exhib: B; G; GG; L; M; NEA; RA; RBA; RI; ROI.
Colls: V & AM; Witt Photo.
Bibl: R.G.G. Price, *A History of Punch*, 1955, p.158.

**KING, H.W.**

Illustrator. Contributed drawings of animals to *The Graphic*, 1871.

**KING, Henry John Yeend   RBA RI**                    1855-1924

Landscape painter and illustrator. He was born in London on 25 August 1855 and was apprenticed to Messrs. O'Connors, glass painters of Berners St. He left after three years and studied painting with William Bromley, RBA, later going to Paris and working with Bonnat and Cormon. He began to exhibit at the RA in 1876 and was elected RBA in 1879, RI in 1887 and VPRI in 1901. King's work for the magazines is usually rural or domestic in character. He died on 10 June 1924.

Contrib: *The Graphic [1880-82]; ILN [1887-94]*.
Exhib: B; G; GG; L; M; RA; RBA; RHA; RI.
Colls: Liverpool; Reading; Witt Photo.

**KING, Jessie Marion (Mrs E.A. Taylor)**                    1876-1949

Painter and illustrator. She was born in 1876 and studied at the Glasgow School of Art, where she won a travelling scholarship to France and Italy, in the latter coming under the influence of Botticelli's paintings. She was considered unsuccessful as a student because of her individuality, 'language of line' and imaginative sense, *The Studio*, Vol.26, p.177. Her style is inseparable from the angular *art nouveau* concepts of the Glasgow School and her decorative work in books is often the counterpart of C.R. Mackintosh's applied art. A great deal of her work was done on parchment, built up with carefully drawn thin pen lines and delicately coloured and tinted. Most of her designs have elaborate borders of stylised birds or foliage, suggesting metal-work rather than the printed page. It is not surprising to discover that she was in fact a jewellery designer and a painter of murals. Miss King lived in Paris from 1911 to 1913 and then at Kirkcudbright after her marriage to the artist E.A. Taylor. She died in 1949.

The drawings have become extremely popular in recent years and are among the more sought after illustrations. Sotheby's held an important sale of her work at the Charles Rennie Mackintosh Society in Glasgow on 21 June 1977, when the contents of her studio were auctioned by request of her daughter.

Illus: *The Light of Asia [Arnold, 1898]; Jeptha [G. Buchanan, 1902]; The High History of The Holy Graal [trans. by S. Evans, 1903]; The Defence of Guenevere [William Morris, 1904]; Comus [John Milton, 1906]; Poems of Spenser [intro. by W.B. Yeats, n.d.]; Budding Life [1906]; The Legend of Flowers [P. Mantegazza, 1908]; Dwellings of An Old World Town [1909]; The Grey City of the North [1910]; The City of the West [1911]; The Book of Bridges [E. Ancambeau, 1911]; Ponts de Paris [E. Ancambeau, 1912]; Songs of the Ettrick Shepherd [James Hogg, 1912]; Isabella and The Pot of Basil [John Keats, 1914]; A House of Pomegranates [Oscar Wilde, 1915]; The Little White Town of Never-Weary [1917]; Good King Wenceslas [1919]; L'Habitation Forcée [Rudyard Kipling, 1921]; How Cinderella Was Able To Go To The Ball [1924]; Mummy's Bedtime Story Book [1929]; Whose London [c.1930]; Our Lady's Garland [Arthur Corder, 1934]; Kirkcudbright [1934]; The Fringes of Paradise [Florence Drummond, 1935]; The Enchanted Capital of Scotland [I. Steele, 1945]; The Parish of New Kilpatrick [J. McCardel, 1949]*.
Contrib. (covers): International Library Editions, *The Marriage Ring [Jeremy Taylor, 1906]; Everyman [1906]*.
Exhib: G; L; RHA; RSA; RSW; SWA.
Colls: V & AM.
Bibl: *The Studio*, Vol. 26, 1901-02, p.177, illus; Vol. 36, 1906, pp.241-246, illus; Vol. 46, 1909, pp.148-150, illus. *The Studio Yearbook*, 1909, 1911, 1912, 1913, 1919; *Modern Book Illustrators and their Work*, Studio, 1914. *JMK.*, Scottish Arts Council Exhibition Cat., 1971.
See illustration (p.209).

**KING, W.H.**                    fl.1808-1836

Topographical illustrator. He worked at Edmonton and contributed to *Brittons Beauties of England and Wales*, 1808.

Exhib: RBA, 1836.

**KINGSFORD, Florence**                    fl.1899-1903

Figure and domestic painter. She worked in West London from 1899 and 1902 and designed initial letters for the Essex House Press.

Decor: *Tam O'Shanter [Essex House, 1902]; Rime of The Ancient Mariner [Essex House, 1903]*.
Exhib: RA.

**KINGSLEY, Charles**                    1819-1875

Author and amateur artist. After leaving Cambridge in 1842, young Kingsley worked on a life of St. Elizabeth of Hungary, illustrated by his own pen and ink drawings. This was not intended for publication but as a present for his wife. He continued to sketch on holidays after his marriage and, as a lecturer illustrated all his points with chalk on a blackboard. In 1855 he tried to establish drawing classes for artisans at Bideford and later on was consulted by C.H. Bennett and Frederick Shields (qq.v.) over their editions of Bunyan. He died in 1875.

Illus: *The Heroes [1856 (eight illus. by the author)]*.
Bibl: *CK His Letters and Memories*, Edited by His Wife, 1877.

**KIPLING, John Lockwood**               **1837-1911**

Architect, sculptor and illustrator. He was born at Pickering, Yorks, in 1837 and was educated at Woodhouse Grove and South Kensington. He taught at the Bombay School of Art and was Principal of the Mayo School of Art, Lahore, 1865-75, and became Curator of the Central Museum, Lahore from 1875-93. He was related by marriage to Sir E.J. Poynter and Sir E. Burne-Jones (qq.v.) and was the father of Rudyard Kipling (q.v.). He died 26 January 1911.

Illus: *Beast and Man in India [1891]*.
Contrib: *The Jungle Book; The Second Jungle Book [1894 (with R.K.)]*.
Colls: India Office Lib.

**KIPLING, Rudyard**                   **1865-1936**

Author and occasional illustrator. He was born in Bombay in 1865 and clearly influenced by the study of Indian art and culture made by his father, J. Lockwood Kipling (q.v.). He was educated in England, living in the vacations with the family of his uncle Sir E. Burne-Jones (q.v.). He returned to India as a journalist from 1882-89 and after early success, travelled to the United States and settled at Bateman's in Sussex. Kipling's black and white illustrations to *Just So Stories*, 1902 show a good decorative sense, if not a very developed manner of execution.

See illustrations (below and right).

*RUDYARD KIPLING 1865-1936. Initial letter for* The Just So Stories For Little Children, *1902.*

*RUDYARD KIPLING 1865-1936. 'The Elephant.' An illustration to* The Just So Stories For Little Children, *1902.*

**KITTON, Frederick George**             **1856-1903**

Author, artist and illustrator. He was born in Norwich on 5 May 1856 and was educated there before training as an engraver and draughtsman on wood with W.L. Thomas of *The Graphic*. From 1882, Kitton began to write on both illustration and English literature, eventually having a dozen works to his credit. He was a prolific if not very dazzling pen draughtsman and died at St. Albans on 10 September 1903.

Publ: *Phiz - A Memoir [1882]; John Leech, Artist and Humorist [1883]; Dickensiana [1886]; Charles Dickens by Pen and Pencil [1889-90]; The Novels of Charles Dickens [1897]; Dickens and His Illustrators [1898-99]; Zechariah Buck [1899]; The Minor Writings of Dickens [1900]; Charles Dickens, His Life, Writings and Personality [1902]; Autograph Edition of Dickens [Editor]*.
Illus: *Hertfordshire County Homes [1892]; St. Albans Historical and Picturesque [1893]; St. Albans Abbey [1897]; The Romany Rye [1900]*.
Contrib: *The Graphic [1874-85]; ILN [1889-90]; The English Illustrated Magazine [1891-92]; Black & White [1892]; The Sunday Magazine [1894]*.
Exhib: Norwich, 1886-87; RBA, 1880.
Bibl: R.E.D. Sketchley, *Eng. Bk. Illus.*, 1902, pp.48, 135.

**KITTON, R.**                       **fl.1832-1847**

Draughtsman at Norwich. He contributed illustrations to *Brittons Cathedrals*, 1832-36.

Exhib: RA, 1847.

**KLEMPNER, E.G.**

Contributor of military figure subjects to *Punch*, 1905.

**KNIGHT, Captain Charles Raleigh**

Amateur illustrator. He illustrated his own *Scenery on the Rhine*, 1850, AT 220.

**KNIGHT, Henry Gally**            **1786-1846**
Writer, traveller and amateur artist. He was born in 1786 and educated at Eton and Trinity College, Cambridge. He had independent means and an estate in Langold, Yorkshire, enabling him to travel throughout Europe and Palestine, writing about his journeys. He was a friend of J.M.W. Turner (q.v.) and illustrated his own books.

Illus: *An Architectural Tour of Normandy [1836]; The Normans in Sicily [1838]; Saracenic and Norman Remains to illustrate the 'Normans in Sicily' [1840]; The Ecclesiastical Architecture of Italy [1842-44].*

**KNIGHT, J. Louis**
Contributed scenes of Dockland to *The Illustrated London News*, 1889.

**KNIGHT, John William Buxton**          **1843-1908**
Landscape painter, watercolourist, occasional illustrator. He was born at Sevenoaks in 1843 and studied with J. Holland in Kent before attending the RA Schools, 1860. He was elected RBA in 1875 and RE in 1881.

Contrib: *The English Illustrated Magazine [1887 (figs. and lands)].*
Exhib: B; G; GG; L; M; RA; RBA; RE; RI.

**KNOWLES, Davidson**           **fl.1879-1902**
Landscape painter, figure painter and illustrator. He worked in London and was elected RBA in 1890, specialising in country genre subjects and animals.

Illus: *Songs and Lyrics For Little Lips [W.D. Cummings, n.d.].*
Contrib: *The Graphic [1880]; ILN [1883-96]; The English Illustrated Magazine [1893-94].*
Exhib: B; G; L; M; NEA; RA; RBA.

**KNOWLES, George Sheridan RI**       **1863-1931**
Genre painter and illustrator. He was born in Manchester on 25 November 1863, and studied at the Manchester School of Art and the RA Schools, 1884. He was elected RI in 1892 and became Treasurer. He died on 15 March 1931.

Contrib: *The Quiver [1890]; ILN [1894-99, (short stories)].*
Exhib: B; G; L; M; NEA; P; RA; RBA; ROI.

**KNOWLES, Horace J.**
Decorator of books. Worked with his brother Reginald L. Knowles (q.v.).

**KNOWLES, Reginald Lionel**        **fl.1905-1925**
Illustrator. A talented Edwardian artist of whom very little is known. He worked in the manner of Arthur Rackham, muted watercolours with highly decorative penwork and borders. He also designed book covers and book plates, and was responsible for Dent's *Everyman Library.*

Illus: *Legends From Fairyland [Holme Lee, 1908]; Norse Fairy Tales [P.C. Asborjornsen and J.I. Moe, 1910]; Marie de France - Old World Love Stories [1913].*
Bibl: *The Art of The Book,* Studio Year Book, 1914, illus; B. Peppin, *Fantasy Book Illustration,* 1975, pp.17, 188, illus.

**KOEKKOEK, H.W.**
Illustrator. Presumably one of the large family of Dutch painters of this name. He illustrated *Barclay of the Guides,* Herbert Strang, 1908.

**KRETSCHNER, Albert**          **1825-1891**
Genre painter and illustrator. He was born at Burghof, Germany on 27 February 1825, and studied at the Berlin Academy. He died in the same city on 11 July 1891.

Contrib: *The Illustrated Times [1859].*
Exhib: RA, 1852.

**KRIEGHOFF, Cornelius**          **1812-1872**
Painter of Canadian scenery and life. This very popular artist was active in the 1850s and 1860s. He illustrated *Construction of the Great Victoria Bridge,* 1860, AT 631.

**'KYD'    Joseph Clayton Clarke**      **fl.1882-1899**
Caricaturist and illustrator, who worked under the name 'Kyd'. His work is usually very delicate and in small scale with nice colour washes. He was employed on an 1889 edition of Dickens, and the drawings for this and a caricature of Whistler are in the V & A Museum.

Contrib: *ILN [1882]; Fun [1890-92].*

*LUCY KEMP-WELCH 1869-1958. Original drawing for an illustration.*                  Messum Studio Collection

**L, E.H.** late 19th century
A watercolour for illustration by this artist is in the Victoria and Albert Museum.

**L, R.**
Illustrator, contributing to *The Illustrated London News,* 1872.
Colls: V & AM.

**LABY, Alexander** fl. 1840-1879
History painter and illustrator. He was working in Paris and exhibiting there, 1840-44. He contributed drawings of Flemish industry to *The Illustrated London News,* 1879.
Exhib: RBA, 1864-66.

**LADER, A.S.**
Contributor to *The Illustrated London News,* 1889, topography.

**LAMB, Henry** fl. 1826-1861
Landscape painter. He worked at Malvern, Worcestershire, for most of his life and contributed illustrations to *Griffith's Cheltenham,* 1826.
Exhib: BI; NWS, 1834-61.

**LAMBERT, George ARA** 1873-1930
Portrait painter and illustrator. He was born in Russia in 1873 and came to England in 1878. He went to Australia in 1891 and studied at the Sydney School of Art, where he won a scholarship to Paris. He taught at the London School of Art in 1910 and returned to Australia

in 1928, having been elected A.R.A. in 1922. He died on 29 May 1930.
Contrib: *The Graphic [1887-88]; The Strand Magazine [1891]; The English Illustrated Magazine [1893-94].*

**LAMBERT, John** fl.1806-1814
Topographer and traveller. He visited N. America to study the cultivation of hemp in 1806 and travelled widely 1806-08. He illustrated *Travels Through Canada and the United States,* 1814, AT 613.

**LAMI, Eugène** 1800-1890
Genre painter, watercolourist, lithographer and illustrator. He was born in Paris on 12 January 1800 and studied under Baron Gros, H. Vernet and at the École des Beaux-Arts. Lami was an important lithographer and watercolourist during the reigns of Louis-Philippe and Napoleon III. His elegant ink drawings with watercolour washes of courtly interiors and scenes of high life were popular both in England and in France, typifying the artificial life of mid-19th century France. Lami produced a series of prints of *Uniforms of the French Army, 1791-1814,* in 1822 and *Uniformes français 1814-1824,* in 1825. His output was considerable, he produced 344 lithographs as well as numerous illustrations for books. He exhibited regularly at the Salon from 1824 to 1878 and as well as becoming a Chevalier de la Légion d'honneur in 1837, founded the French Society of Watercolourists. He died in Paris, 19 December 1890.
Illus: *Voyage en Angleterre [1829-30 (with Monnier)]; L'Hiver et L'Eté [Janin]; Les Ouevres de Alfred de Musset.*
Contrib: *ILN [1853].*
Exhib: RA, 1850.
Colls: Author; Louvres; Royal Coll.; V & AM; Versailles; Wallace Coll.
Bibl: P.A. Lemoisne, *L'Oeuvre de EL.*
See illustration (below).

**LAMONT or LA MONTE, Elish** 1800-1870
Miniature painter. She was born in Belfast in about 1800 and worked in Belfast and Dublin. She contributed portraits to *The Court Album* 1857 and did some illustrations for Swain in the 1860s.
Exhib: RA, 1856-69; RHA, 1842-57.

*EUGÈNE LAMI 1800-1890. 'Le repos.' Ink and watercolour on brown paper. 5¾ins. x 10½ins. (14.6cm x 26.7cm).*     Author's Collection, formerly Demidoff Collection

**LAMONT, Thomas Reynolds** ARWS 1826-1898
Landscape painter and illustrator. He was born in Scotland in 1826 and studied art in Paris with George Du Maurier (q.v.) who immortalised him as 'the Laird' in his novel *Trilby*. He was elected ARWS in 1866 but did little work after 1880.

Contrib: *London Society [1865]; The Shilling Magazine [1865-66]*.
Exhib: GG; OWS: RA.
Colls: V & AM.

**LANCELOT, Dieudonné Auguste** 1822-1894
Lithographer and illustrator. He was born at Sezanne in 1822 and became a pupil of J.F. Arnaud de Troyes. He exhibited at the Salon from 1853 to 1876 and illustrated landscapes and views in books. He died in Paris in 1894.

Illus: *Le Tour du Monde; Le Magasin pittoresque; Jardins [1887]*.
Contrib: *ILN [1857, Paris]*.

**LANCON, Auguste André** 1836-1887
Painter, engraver and sculptor. He was born at Saint-Claude in 1836 and studied art in Lyons and Paris, specialising in the painting and sculpting of animals. Lancon was implicated in the Commune of 1871 and imprisoned, but with the new regime he became a Special Artist for *L'Illustration* and went to the Balkans for them in 1877.

Contrib: *ILN [1870]*.

**LANDELLS, Ebenezer** 1808-1860
Engraver and illustrator. He was born at Newcastle-upon-Tyne in 1808 and worked as a pupil to Thomas Bewick (q.v.) and for a short time to Isaac Nicholson. He went to London in 1829 and became the right-hand man of John Jackson and William Harvey (q.v.) superintending the fine art department of the firm of Branston & Vizetelly. Landells was inventive and original as a projector of newspapers, but lacked business acumen. He was intimately concerned with the founding of *Punch*, but left it in 1842 to become Editor of the less successful *Illuminated Magazine*, 1843. He started *The Lady's Newspaper* in 1847, which was incorporated in *The Queen* and had M.B. Foster, the Dalziels and Edmund Evans (qq.v.) as his pupils. Landells was not a very strong artist, but acted as *The Illustrated London News* Special on Queen Victoria's first tour of Scotland. The Queen later bought the drawings, the first of their kind to be made for a newspaper on the spot. Landells died at Brompton on 1 September 1860.

Contrib: *The Sporting Review [1842-46]; ILN [1844-56]*.
Exhib: RBA, 1833 & 1837 (engravings).
Bibl: M.H. Spielmann, *The History of Punch*, 1895, pp.15-19; *The Brothers Dalziel, A Record of Work, 1840-1890*, 1901, pp.4-10.

**LANDELLS, Robert Thomas** 1833-1877
Illustrator and War artist. He was born 1 August 1833, the eldest son of Ebenezer Landells (q.v.). He was educated in France but studied drawing and painting in London, specialising in battles and military subjects. He was Special War Artist for *The Illustrated London News* from 1855 to 1871, covering the Crimea, Schleswig-Holstein, 1864, Austro-Prussia, 1866, and the Franco-Prussian compaign of 1870-71. He was awarded the Prussian Iron Cross on this occasion. Landells also acted for *The Illustrated London Magazine*, 1853-55. He died in London in 1877.

Exhib: RBA, 1863-76.

**LANDER, Edgar** 1883-
Black and white artist. He was born in 1883 and worked in North London. He regularly exhibited watercolours and etchings and married Hilda Cowham (q.v.).

Contrib: *Punch [1902, 1904-05 (social)]*.
Exhib: G: L: RA: RSA.

**LANDSEER, Charles** RA 1799-1878
History painter and illustrator. He was the second son of John Landseer, ARA, and brother of Sir E.H. and T. Landseer (qq.v.). He was a pupil of B.R. Haydon and studied at the RA Schools in 1816, afterwards travelling to South America. He became RA in 1845.

Illus: *Days of Deerstalking [W. Scrope, 1883]; Days and Nights of Salmon Fishing [1898]*.
Contrib: *Finden's Illustrations .... To the Life and Works of Lord Byron [1833-34]*.

**LANDSEER, Sir Edwin Henry** RA 1802-1873
Animal painter and caricaturist. He was born in 1802, the youngest son of John Landseer, ARA, and became the most popular painter of animals in Victorian England, his work widely engraved and admired from the Queen downwards. He is included here for his brown ink and wash caricatures which he often made while staying in country houses.

Colls: BM: Fitzwilliam; V & AM.

**LANDSEER, Thomas** ARA 1795-1880
Engraver and illustrator. He was the eldest son of John Landseer, ARA, and brother of Sir E.L. and C. Landseer (qq.v.). He was a pupil and assistant to his father and studied with B.R. Haydon, but became best known for his engravings from his famous brother's works. Early in his career, Thomas Landseer indulged in some humorous engraved caprices which are his most delightful works. They consisted of vigorous prints of animals, often in flight or fighting with men, mostly published by Moon, Boys & Graves in the 1820s or 1830s. Linton describes him as 'a short, broad-shouldered deaf man ... evincing more originality and vigour of drawing than is to be seen in the excellently painted pictures of the more famous Sir Edwin'. He was elected ARA in 1868.

Illus: *Monkeyana or Men in Miniatures [1827-28]; The Devil's Walk [S.T. Coleridge, 1831]; Characteristic Sketches of Animals [1832]; The Boy and The Birds [Emily Taylor, 1840]*.
Contrib: *The People's Journal [1846]; ILN [1844]*.
Exhib: BI, NWS: RA: RBA.
Colls: BM: Witt Photo.

**LANE, Richard James** ARA 1800-1872
Engraver. He was born in 1800 and was a great-nephew of Thomas Gainsborough. Lane's career was mainly in making engravings after the work of Landseer, Leslie, Lawrence and Gainsborough and in teaching at the engraving school at South Kensington. He became ARA in 1827 and was made lithographer to the Queen in 1837. The Victoria and Albert Museum has three drawings for illustration by this artist, two of them of Shakespearean subjects.

**LANE, Theodore** 1800-1828
Painter and caricaturist. He was born at Isleworth in 1800 and was apprenticed to J.C. Barrow at Battle Bridge. Shortly after completing his time, he produced *The Life of an Actor*, 1822, six pls., which had some popular success. After meeting Pierce Egan, he issued with him as author, *Life of an Actor Peregrine Proteus*, 1825 with 27 colour plates, and many woodcuts. During the Queen Caroline scandals, Lane worked for the printseller Humphrey, 1820-21, and did several satirical prints probably in collaboration with Theodore Hook. He died tragically on 21 February 1828 by falling through a skylight, being so badly mutilated that he was only recognisable by his card case. The RA ran a subscription for his widow.

Exhib: RA, 1819-20, 1826.
Colls: BM.
Bibl: G. Everitt, *English Caricaturists*, 1893, pp.84-88, illus; D. George, *English Political Caricature*, Vol.II, 1959, pp.197-198.

**LANGE, Janet** fl.1855-1860
French illustrator. He was the brother of Gustave Janet (q.v.) and according to Vizetelly an artist 'whose reputation stood high as a delineator of military episodes, Court pageants, and the like ...'

Contrib: *Cassell's Illustrated Family Paper [1855]; The Illustrated Times [1860]; ILN*.

**LANOS, Henri** fl.1886-1905
French genre painter and watercolourist. He contributed drawings of the Simplon Tunnel to *The Graphic*, 1902-03 and 1905. He was a member of the Artistes Français.

**LARSEN, Carl Christian**                    **1853-1910**
Painter and illustrator. He was born at Viborg, Denmark on 16 March 1853 and studied at the Copenhagen School of Art. He was Special Artist for *The Illustrated London News* in Siberia in 1882. He died at Vienna on 6 June 1910.

**LARUM, Oscar**
Contributed drawings of comic animals to *Punch,* 1909.

**LATHBURY, Mrs (née Miss M.A. Mills)**         **fl.1807-1815**
Amateur artist. She contributed topographical drawings of the West Country and Wales to *Britton's Beauties of England and Wales* 1812-15 and to *The Antiquarian and Topographical Cabinet,* 1807.

**LAUDER, Sir Thomas Dick, Bt.**               **1784-1848**
Amateur landscape artist. He was born in 1784 and succeeded his father as 7th Baronet of Fountainhall, County Haddington in 1820. He died 29 May 1848.
Illus: *A Voyage Round the Coasts of Scotland and the Isles [James Wilson, FRSE, 1842. Engraved by Charles H. Wilson].*

**LAUGHLIN, J.E.**
Illustrated *Three Boys in The Wild North Land* by E.R. Young, 1897.

**LAURENS, Jules Joseph Augustin**             **1825-1901**
Draughtsman and watercolourist. He was born at Carpentras, France, on 26 July 1825 and became a pupil of his brother J.J.B. Laurens. He exhibited regularly at the Salon and died at St. Didier 5 May 1901.
Contrib: *The Illustrated Times [1856 (Persia)].*
Colls: Angôuleme; Avignon; Bagnères; Carpentras; Metz; Montpellier; Narbonne, Orleans; Paris; Rouen.

**LAVEROCK, Florence**                         **fl.1900-1915**
Black and white artist working at Warrington. She did several pretty 'crinoline story-book' type illustrations in about 1900 which may have been published.
Exhib: L.

**LAWLESS, Matthew James**                     **1837-1864**
Illustrator and etcher. He was born in 1837, the son of Barry Lawless, a Dublin solicitor. As a catholic he was educated at the Prior Park School, Bath and then at the Langham, Cary's and Leigh's Art Schools in London. He was for some time a pupil of Henry O'Neill, RA and was influenced by the Pre-Raphaelites and by the Dutch masters of the 17th century. Although often unequal in his compositions and his handling of figures, sometimes very large and sometimes very small, Lawless at his best ranks very high among the artists on the wood. He worked briefly for *Punch* but made his name in the more serious or poetic areas of illustration, particularly in *Good Words* and *Once a Week*. He was one of a number of the 1860s' illustrators who had tragically short working lives. He was ill from 1860 onwards and died at Bayswater in 1864.
Contrib: *Once a Week [1859-64]; Punch [1860-61]; Lyra Germanica [1861]; Life of St. Patrick [1862]; Good Words [1862-64]; London Society [1862-70]; Passages from Modern English Poets [1862]; Churchman's Family Magazine [1863]; Pictures of Society [1866]; Touches of Nature [1867]; Thornbury's Legendary Ballads [1876].*
Exhib: RA; RBA, 1857-63.
Colls: BM.
Bibl: Chatto & Jackson, *Treatise on English Wood Engraving,* 1861, p.599; G. White, *English Illustration The Sixties,* 1895; F. Reid, *Illustrators of the Sixties,* 1928.

See illustration (below).

*MATTHEW JAMES LAWLESS 1837-1864. 'The Headmaster's Sister.' Illustration to* Once a Week, *28 April 1860. Wood engraving.*

**LAWSON, Cecil Gordon** 1851-1882

Landscape painter in oil and illustrator. He was born at Wellington, Salop, in 1851, the son of William Lawson, the Scottish portrait painter. He came to London with his father in 1861 and in 1870 began to draw on the wood for the engravers. In some ways Lawson was a proto-impressionist and his oils of the Thames and the countryside of Kent and Yorkshire are having a revival among collectors. Lawson suffered from acute ill health and after travelling to the South of France in 1881, returned to London and died on 10 June 1882. He was the younger brother of F.W. Lawson (q.v.).

Contrib: *The Quiver; Good Words; The Sunday Magazine; Dark Blue [1871-72]; Poems and Songs by Robert Burns [1875].*
Exhib: GG; RA; RBA.
Colls: Birmingham; BM; Edinburgh; V. & AM.
Bibl: F. Reid, *Illustrators of The Sixties,* 1928 pp.266.

**LAWSON, Francis Wilfrid** 1842-1935

Painter and illustrator. He was born in 1842, the elder brother of Cecil G. Lawson (q.v.) whom he taught. He was a very versatile artist, specialising not only in the figure but in landscape work as well. Reid considers his best work to be that for *The Cornhill Magazine* and Foxe's *Book of Martyrs.* Charles Keene (q.v.) had a studio in Lawson's house.

Illus: *The Law and The Lady [Wilkie Collins, 1876 (with Fildes and Hall)].*
Contrib: *Once a Week; London Society; The Cornhill Magazine [1867-69]; Book of Martyrs [Foxe, 1866]; Heber's Hymns [1867]; The Shilling Magazine; The Sunday Magazine; Cassell's Magazine; The Broadway; Dark Blue; Aunt Judy's Magazine; Fun; The Graphic [1869-76]; Punch [1876].*
Exhib: B; G; GG; L; M; NEA; RA; RBA; ROI; RI; RSA.A.
Colls: Liverpool; V & AM; Witt Photo.

**LAWSON, G.**

Illustrator. The British Museum has drawings by this artist of Reading Room personalities, published in *Atlanta,* 1888.

**LAWSON, John** fl.1865-1909

Landscape painter and illustrator, working mostly in Scotland, but at Sheffield, 1892-93. He is rated by Reid and White as a very competent draughtsman of the second rank, producing excellent figure work for the magazines of the 1860s.

Contrib: *Once a Week [1865-67]; The Sunday Magazine; Cassell's Magazine; The Quiver [1865]; The Children's Hour [1865]; The Shilling Magazine [1866]; The Argosy [1866]; British Workman [1866]; Pen and Pencil Pictures from the Poets [1866]; Ballad Stories [1866]; Golden Thoughts from Golden Fountains [1867]; Roses and Holly [1867]; Ballads, Scottish and English [1867]; Nursery Time [1867]; Early Start in Life [1867]; The Children of Blessing [1867]; The Golden Gift [1868]; Original Poems [1868]; Tales of the White Cockade [1870]; The Runaway [1872]; The Childrens Garland [1873]; The Fiery Cross [1875]; The World Well Lost [1877]; Clever Hans [1883]; There Was Once [1888]; Childhood Valley [1889].*
Exhib: G; L; M; RI; RSA.
Colls: Witt Photo.
Bibl: F. Reid, *Illustrators of the Sixties* 1928, pp.228-229, illus.

**LAYARD, Major Arthur** fl.1894-1911

Watercolourist and illustrator. He worked in Hammersmith and at Pangbourne, 1902-03. He was principally a figure artist.

Illus: *The People of The Mist [H.R. Haggard, 1894]; The Winged Wolf [Ha Sheen Kaf, 1894].*
Contrib: *The Pall Mall Magazine; Fun [1901].*
Exhib: Bruton Gall; NEA.

**LEAR, Edward** 1812-1888

Topographical artist, ornithological and comic illustrator. He was born at Holloway on 12 May 1812 and by the age of fifteen was already making his living by bird drawings. In 1831 he became a draughtsman at the Zoological Society's Gardens and in 1832 published his first book of coloured plates of parrots. From 1832 to 1836, Lear was employed as drawing-master to the children of the Earl of Derby at Knowsley, where he continued to paint and drew and wrote *The Book*

*EDWARD LEAR 1812-1888. 'Frascati.' Illustration to* Views in Rome, *1841. Tinted lithograph.*

*of Nonsense* for the Earl's children. The result of his Knowsley years was the privately printed book *Knowsley Menagerie*, 1856 and an introduction to Queen Victoria to whom he gave lessons in 1846.

From 1831 onwards, Lear made extensive tours abroad, publishing the resulting drawings in albums of lithographs. His chief excursions were to Rome in 1837, where he remained and taught until 1848, to Greece, Albaniá and Malta in 1848 and Egypt in 1849. At this point Lear returned to England and studied at the RA Schools, meeting W. Holman Hunt (q.v.) before commencing another period abroad from 1853 to 1857, visiting Greence, Egypt and the Holy Land. From about 1860, he was living entirely abroad, based at Cannes, Corfu and finally at San Remo. He visited India and Ceylon in 1872-74 and returned to England for the last time in 1880 before settling in San Remo where he died in January 1888. Lear's sketches are unusual among the art of the Victorians for being principally pen and ink works with wash, rather than drawn in watercolours. Many of them have lengthy inscriptions about their locations and the date and time of day that they were done.

Illus: *The Family of Psittacidae, or Parrots [1832]; The Naturalists Magazine [n.d.]; Views in Rome [1841, AT 183]; Excursions in Italy [1846, AT 172 (two parts)]; A Book of Nonsense [1846 and 1861]; The Knowsley Menagerie [1846]; Journal of a Landscape Painter in Albania and Illyria [1851]; Journal of a Landscape Painter in Southern Calabria [1852, AT 175]; Views of the Seven Ionian Islands [1863]; Journal of a Landscape Painter in Corsica [1870]; Nonsense Songs, Stories, Botany and Alphabets [1871]; More Nonsense, Pictures, Rhymes, Botany Etc. [1872]; Tortoises, Terrapins and Turtles [1872]; Indian Pheasants [n.d.]; Laughable Lyrics, A Fourth Book [1877]; Nonsense Songs and Stories [1895].*

*GILBERT LEDWARD RA 1888-1960. 'An aged enchanter.' Illustration to* The Story of Princess Carena. *Indian ink. Signed with monogram. 9¹/8ins. x 6ins. (23.2cm x 15.2cm).*  Victoria and Albert Museum

Exhib: FAS, 1938; RA; RBA.
Colls: Ashmolean; BM; Glasgow; Greenwich; Mellon; V & AM; Witt Photo.
Bibl: Vivien Noakes, *EL, The Life of a Wanderer*, 1968.
See illustration (p.366):

**LE BRETON, Miss Rosa**
Domestic painter, exhibiting in 1865. She contributed similar subjects to *Cassell's Illustrated Family Paper*, 1857.

**LEDWARD, Gilbert  RA**                                    **1888-1960**
Sculptor. He was born in 1888, the son of the sculptor R.A. Ledward. He studied at the RCA and the RA Schools and was awarded the first sculpture scholarship at the British School of Rome in 1913, and the RA travelling scholarship. He was Professor of Sculpture at the RCA, 1926-29 and was elected ARA in 1932 and RA in 1937. He died in 1960.
Illus: *The Story of Princess Carena [n.d.].*
Exhib: G; GG; L; RA; RSA.
Colls: V & AM.
See illustration (below left).

**LEE, Arthur**
Humorous artist, working in Coventry and exhibiting at Birmingham 1910. He may have worked for *The Pall Mall Magazine*.

**LEE, J.**
Perhaps John Ingle Lee, a figure artist who exhibited at the RA and RBA, 1868-91.
Contrib: *Book of Martyrs [Foxe, 1866].*

**LEE, Joseph Johnson**                                      **1876-**
Artist and author. He was born in Dundee in 1876 and studied at the Slade School and at Heatherley's. He served in the First World War 1914-18 in the Black Watch.
Publ: *Tales of Our Town [1910]; Fra Lippo Lippi [1914]; Ballads of Battle [1916]; Work-a-day Warriors [1917]; A Captive at Carlsruhe [1920].*
Contrib: *Punch.*
Colls: Witt Photo.

**LEE, William  NWS**                                         **1810-1865**
Watercolourist. He was born in 1810 and was a member and secretary of the Langham Sketch Club and elected NWS in 1848. He died in London on 22 January 1865.
Contrib: *London [Knight, 1841].*
Exhib: NWS; RA; RBA.
Colls: V & AM.

**LEECH, John**                                              **1817-1864**
Artist and illustrator. He was born in London on 23 August 1817, the son of a vintner and showed a remarkable aptitude for drawing from an early age. After being educated at Charterhouse and then entering St. Batholmew's Hospital to study medicine, Leech abandoned it for the career of an artist. At Charterhouse he had become a friend of W.M. Thackeray (q.v.) and at St. Bartholomew's he had made the acquaintance of Albert Smith and Percival Leigh, the writers, all of whom were to further him in his profession. He produced his first book *Etchings and Sketchings,* caricatures of Londoners, in 1835 and followed this with a series of satirical and political lithographs. Leech was taught to draw on the wood by Orrin Smith and it was in this field of black and white work that he was to make his name. His humour was like his talent, gentle, warm-hearted and positive, his world, the ups and downs of middle class life, the sports of the squirearchy, and the peccadilloes of army officers and undergraduates. He became really established in 1840 when he joined the staff of *Bentley's Miscellany,* contributing over one hundred and forty etchings to the magazine. In August 1841 he contributed his first block to the newly-established satirical journal *Punch*; Leech's art was ripe for this type of pictorial satire and within a few months he had made it his own, establishing a convention of social humour that was to last until the 1920s. From 1843, Leech shared the cartoons with Tenniel, completing no less than seven hundred and twenty before 1864. But his strength was in the drawings of the hunting field and London fashion, epitomised in the characters of Tom Noddy and Mr.

JOHN LEECH 1817-1864. Frontispiece and title-page to Punch's Pocket Book For 1857. Wood engravings coloured by hand.

Briggs. Extravagantly praised by Ruskin, Leech's often careless but never crude drawings have survived in charm and humour to give us a refreshing glimpse of mid-Victorian society. He died after a short illness in 1864.

Leech prepared sketches in oil of some of his illustrations and exhibited them in the Egyptian Hall, Piccadilly, in June 1862. The pencil sketches for the *Punch* cartoons are more generally available, though often slight.

Illus: *Etchings and Sketchings [A. Pen, 1835]; Droll Doings, Funny Characters [1835]; The Human Face Divine and De Vino [1835]; Bell's Life in London [1836]; Jack Brag [T. Hook, 1837]; American Broad Grins [1838]; Local Legends and Rambling Rhymes [John Dix, 1839]; Pencillings By The Way [N.P. Willis, 1839]; The Comic English Grammar [Paul Prendergast, 1840]; The Comic Latin Grammar [G. à Beckett, 1840]; The Fiddle-Faddle Fashion Book [Percival Leigh, 1840]; The Ingoldsby Legends [1840]; The Clockmaker [T.C. Haliburton, 1840]; The Bachelors Walk in a Fog [Peter Styles, 1840]; The Children of the Mobility [1841]; Written Caricatures [C.C. Pepper, 1841]; Stanley Thom [Henry Cockton, 1841]; The Porcelain Tower [1841]; Merrie England in the Olden Time [Daniel, 1842]; The Barnaby's in America [Mrs Trollope, 1843]; The Wassail Bowl [A.R. Smith, 1843]; Jack The Giant Killer [1843]; A Christmas Carol [Charles Dickens, 1843-44]; Jessie Phillips [Mrs Trollope, 1844]; Nursery Ditties [1844]; The Adventures of Mr Ledbury [Albert Smith, 1844]; The Comic Arithmetic [1844]; Sketches of Life and Character [George Hodder, 1845]; The Fortunes of the Scattergood Family [Albert Smith, 1845]; Hints on Life [1845]; The Quizzology of the British Drama [G. à Beckett, 1846]; The Battle of Life [Charles Dickens, 1846]; Mrs Caudle's Curtain Lectures [D. Jerrold, 1846]; The Comic History of England [G. à Beckett, 1847]; The Silver Swan [de Chatelain, 1847]; The Handbook of Joking [1847]; Hillside and Border Sketches [W.H. Maxwell, 1847]; The Haunted Man [Charles Dickens, 1847-48]; Life and Adventures of Oliver Goldsmith [Forester, 1848]; The Rising Generation [1848]; The Struggle and Adventures of Christopher Tadpole [Albert Smith, 1848]; Ballads of Bon Gaultier [1849]; A Man Made of Money [D. Jerrold, 1849]; The Natural History of Evening Parties [Albert Smith, 1849]; Toil and Trial [Mrs Crosland, 1849]; The Crock of Gold [M.F. Tupper, 1849]; Fun, Poetry and Pathos [W.Y. Browne, 1850]; Dashes of American Humour [Howard Paul, 1852]; The Comic History of Rome [G. à Beckett, 1852]; Picturesque Sketches of London [Thomas Miller, 1852]; Uncle Tom's Cabin [H.B. Stowe, 1852]; The Fortunes of Hector O'Halloran [W.H. Maxwell, 1853]; Mr. Sponge's Sporting Tour [R.S. Surtees, 1853]; The Great Highway [S.W. Fullom, 1854]; Handley Cross [R.S. Surtees, 1854]; Reminiscences of a Huntsman [The Hon. G. Berkeley, 1854]; The Paragreens [Ruffini, 1856]; The Militia Man At Home and Abroad [1857]; A Month in the Forests of France [The Hon. G. Berkeley, 1857]; The Encyclopaedia of Rural Sports [1858]; Ask Mama [R.S. Surtees, 1858]; The Cyclopaedia of Wit and Humour [1858]; The Path of Roses [F. Greenwood, 1858]; The Fliers of the Hunt [John Mills, 1859]; A Little Tour in Ireland [Reynolds Hole, 1859]; Newton Dogvane [J. Francis, 1859]; Soapey Sponge [1859]; Paul Prendergast [1859]; Mr Briggs and His Doings [1860]; Plain or Ringlets [R.S. Surtees, 1860]; Life of a Foxhound [John Mills, 1861]; The Follies of the Year [1864]; Mr Facey-Romford's Hounds [R.S. Surtees, 1864]; Carols of Cockayne [1869].*
Contrib: *The London Magazine [1840]; Bentley's Miscellany [1840-49]; Colin Clink [Hooton, 1841]; Punch [1841-64]; New Monthly Magazine [1842-43];*

*The Sporting Review [1842-46]; Hoods Comic Annual [1844-46]; The Illuminated Magazine [1843-45]; The Cricket on the Hearth [Charles Dickens, 1845-46]; Jerrold's Shilling Magazine [1845-48]; ILN [1845-57]; The Month [1851]; Illustrated London Magazine [1854]; Merry Pictures [1857]; Once A Week [1859-64]; Puck on Pegasus [Pennell, 1861]; The Gardener's Annual [1863].*
Colls: BM: Fitzwilliam; V & AM.
Bibl: John Brown, 'JL' *North British Review,* March 1865, pp.213-244; 'JL and Other Papers' *North British Review* Edinburgh, 1882; C.E. Chambers, *A List of Works containing Illustrations by JL,* 1892; 'JL and His Method', *The Strand,* March 1903, pp.158-164; Graham Everitt, *English Caricaturists . . .,* 1893; W.P. Frith, *JL, his Life and Works,* 2 vols, 1891; F.G. Kitton, *Charles Dickens by Pen and Pencil,* 1890; F.G. Kitton, *JL Artist and Humourist,* 1883; R.G.G. Price, *A History of Punch,* 1957, pp.62-65; H. Saint-Gaudens, *JL, The Critic,* Oct. 1905, pp.358-367; H. Silver, 'The Art of JL' *Magazine of Art,* Vol. XVI; Russell Sturgis, 'JL' *Scribners,* Feb. 1879, pp.553-565; Harry Thornber, 'JL' 1890; Rev. G. Tidy, *A Little About Leech,* 1931; J.N.P. Watson, 'JL in the Hunting Field' *Country Life,* 20 Jan. 1977; Stanley Kidder Wilson, *Cat. of . . . Exhibition of Works by JL,* Grolier Club, New York, 1914.
See illustrations (above and pp.369, 370).

**LEETE, Alfred Chew**                                    **1882-1933**
Black and white artist and cartoonist. He was born at Thorpe Achurch, Northamptonshire in 1882 and educated at Weston-super-Mare Grammar School before starting work in printing at the age of fifteen. From 1905 to 1933, Leete was a regular contributor to *Punch* specialising in figure drawings in ink and some political cartoons and caricatures. His surviving drawings tend to be on a rather large scale. He died on 17 June 1933.

Contrib: *The Pall Mall Gazette; London Opinion [1913].*
Bibl: *The Studio,* vol. 18, 1900, p.72.
See illustration (p.371).

**LE FANU, G. Brinsley**                                **fl.1878-1925**
Landscape painter and illustrator. He worked in London and exhibited regularly at the RA and RBA.

Illus: *Nursery Rhymes [1897-98 (with Gertrude Bradley)].*
Contrib: *The Ludgate Monthly [1891].*

**LEIGHTON, Edmund Blair   ROI**                     **1853-1922**
Painter of genre. He was born in London on 21 September 1853, the son of Charles Blair Leighton, the artist. He was educated at University College School and studied art at the RA, exhibiting there from 1887. He became ROI in 1887. Leighton amassed a large collection of historical musical instruments, arms and furniture at his house in Bedford Park, where he died on 1 September 1922.

Contrib: *The Quiver [1887].*
Exhib: B; G; L; M; RA; RBA; ROI.
Colls: V & AM.

**LEIGHTON, Frederic, Lord Leighton of Stretton PRA 1830-1896**

Painter. He was born at Scarborough in 1830, the son of a doctor, and received a very wide visual education, travelling with his father on the Continent. He learnt drawing from F. Meli at Rome and attended the Florence Academy and studied under J.E. Steinle at Frankfurt after 1849. He set up his own studio in 1852 and spent three years working in Rome, settling in London in 1859. Leighton had great success with his 'Cimabue's 'Madonna' exhibited at the RA in 1855 and very quickly became one of the grandees of the Victorian art world. He was elected ARA in 1864, RA in 1868 and became PRA, 1878; this was followed by his creation as a baronet in 1886 and a peer in 1896, the only artist to be so honoured. He died on 25 January 1896.

Leighton was a very strong black and white artist and made contributions to *The Cornhill Magazine* which rank among the best work of the 1860s. Forrest Reid refers to them as having 'a kind of cold, formal dignity' rather underrating the power of the draughtsmanship in George Elliot's medieval story of *Romola,* ideally suited to the artist. These plates were brought together in a special limited edition in 1880.

Contrib: *The Cornhill Magazine [1860-63]; Dalziel's Bible Gallery [1881]; Black and White [1891].*
Exhib: B; FAS, 1896-97; G; GG; L; M; RA; RHA; RSA.
Colls: Ashmolean; BM; V & AM.
Bibl: Mrs. Barrington-Ward, *The Life, Letters and Work of FL,* 1906; R. and L. Ormond, *Lord L,* 1975.

See illustrations (pp.372, 373).

**LEIGHTON, John FSA 'Luke Limner' 1822-1912**

Artist, illustrator, book decorator and designer of ex-libris. He was born in London on 22 September 1822 and studied under Henry Howard RA. Leighton was a lecturer and polemicist on behalf of the arts and in pushing forward technical innovations, an early friend of the camera, he joined with Roger Fenton to found the Photographic Society in 1853, now the Royal Photographic Society of Great Britain. Leighton was best known for his designs for frontispieces and decorative borders, what Gleeson White refers to as 'a pioneer of better things' in their simplicity. He was a founder proprietor of *The Graphic* in 1869 and designed their title page which remained in use until 1930! Leighton designed bookbindings from about 1845 and also turned his hands to Christmas cards. He wrote extensively under the name of 'Luke Limner' and died at Harrow on 15 September 1912.

Illus: *Contrasts and Conceits [c.1850, 20 liths]; London Out of Town [c.1850, 16 liths]; Life of Man Symbolised [1866]; The Poems of William Leighton [1894].*
Contrib: *Lyra Germanica [1861 and 1868]; Moral Emblems [1862]; Good Words [1864]; Once a Week [1866]; London Society [(cover), 1868]; The Graphic [1869 (title)]; The Sunday Magazine [1871]; Dalziel's Bible Pictures [1881]; Puck and Ariel [1890]; Fun [1890-92]; Punch [1900-02].*
Exhib: L, 1898.
Bibl: Chatto and Jackson, *Treatise on Wood Engraving,* 1861, p.582; R. McLean, *Victorian Book Design,* 1972, pp.218-219.

*JOHN LEECH 1817-1864. 'The Gypsey's Prophecy.' Original study for illustration to* Plain or Ringlets *by R.S. Surtees, 1860. Pencil, ink and wash.* The Garrick Club

*JOHN LEECH 1817-1864. 'The Gypsey's Prophecy.' Illustration to* Plain or Ringlets *by R.S. Surtees 1860. Engraving coloured by hand.*

**LEIST, Fred RBA**                                   fl.1901-1930
Portrait and figure painter and illustrator. He was elected RBA in 1913 and ROI in 1916. Working in Australia, 1901-02.

Illus: *The Gold-Marked Charm [B. Marchant, 1919].*
Contrib: *The Graphic [1901-10 (realism)].*
Exhib: L; P; RA; RBA; ROI.

**LEITCH, Richard Principal**                         fl.1840-1875
Drawing-master and illustrator. He was the brother of W. L. Leitch (q.v.) and painted landscapes and wrote instructional books. He was sent by *The Illustrated London News* to Italy in 1859 to cover the Franco-Italian War.

Contrib: *ILN [1847-61]; Poets of the Nineteenth Century [1857]; Good Words [1864]; The Sunday Magazine [1865]; Idyllic Pictures [1867]; The Quiver.*
Exhib: RA, 1844-60; RBA, till 1862.
Colls: BM; Maidstone; V & AM.
See illustration (p.137)

**LEITCH, William Leighton RI**                       1804-1883
Landscape painter. He was born in Glasgow on 22 November 1804, the son of a manufacturer, and brother of R.P. Leitch (q.v.). He was apprenticed to a lawyer after being educated at the Highland Society School and later studied art with D. Macnee. After working for a sign painter, he became scene painter at Glasgow's Theatre Royal in 1824, later moving to London to work at the Pavilion Theatre where he became a friend of D. Roberts and C. Stanfield (qq.v.). Leitch went to Italy in 1833 and did not return for five years, having used his time in extensive travel, teaching and sketching. He then set up in London as a fashionable watercolourist and teacher being patronised by Queen Victoria. He died 25 April 1883.

Contrib: *ILN [1859].*
Exhib: BI; NWS; RA; RBA.
Colls: BM; V & AM.
Bibl: A. MacGregor, *Memoir of WL*, 1884.

**LE JEUNE, Henry L. ARA**                            1819-1904
Painter of genre. He was born in London on 12 December 1819 and studied at the RA Schools, becoming Drawing-master there in 1845 and curator in 1848. He was elected ARA in 1863 and died at Hampstead 5 September 1904.

Contrib: *Ministering Children [1856]; Lays of the Holy Land [1858]; The Poetry of Thomas Moore.*
Exhib: BI; RA; RBA.
Colls: Witt Photo.

**LELONG, René**                                      fl.1895-1912
Painter. Born at Arrou, France, and exhibited at the Salon, 1895, becoming a medallist, 1898. Contributed to *The Graphic*, 1912.

**LE MAIR, H. Willebeek**                             1889-1966
**Baroness H. van Tuyll van Serooskerken**
Dutch designer and illustrator. She was born in Rotterdam on 23 April 1889, the daughter of a wealthy family who were artists and patrons of the arts. At an early age she was influenced by the French illustrator Maurice Boutet de Monvel whom she met at her father's and was advised by him to attend the Rotterdam Academy, 1909-11. From 1911 she had growing contacts with London publishers and was to remain very popular as an illustrator of children's books for the British public throughout the 1920s and 1930s. Her style is rather flat in the drawing with muted colours and decorative borders. A sideline of her artistic life was making designs for children's breakfast sets for the Gouda pottery, dating from about 1923. She lived the whole of her married life in the Hague and died there on 15 March 1966.

An exhibition of books and drawings by H. Willebeek Le Mair was held at the Bethnal Green Museum, London, in October 1975.

Illus: *Premières Rondes Enfantines [1904]; Our Old Nursery Rhymes [1911]; Little Songs of Long Ago [1912]; Schumann Album of Children's Pieces [1913]; Grannie's Little Rhyme Book; Mother's Little Rhyme Book; Auntie's*

Little Rhyme Book; Nursie's Little Rhyme Book; Daddy's Little Rhyme Book [c.1913]; The Children's Corner [1914]; What the Children Sing [1915]; Old Dutch Nursery Rhymes [1917]; A Gallery of Children [A.A. Milne, c.1925]; A Child's Garden of Verses [1926]; Twenty Jatka Tales [1939]; Christmas Carols; The Births of the Founders of Religion [1950-53].

**LEMANN, Miss E.A.**                    fl.1878-1889
Landscape painter and illustrator. She worked at Bath and specialised in children's books.

Illus: *The Gold of Farnilee [Andrew Lang]; King Diddle [H.C. Davidson]; Under the Water [Maurice Noel, c.1889].*
Exhib: RBA; SWA.

**LENFESTEY, Gifford Hocart    RBA**                    1872-1943
Landscape painter and illustrator of architectural subjects. He was born at Faversham on 6 September 1872 and studied art at the RCA and in Florence and Paris under Raphael Collin. He was elected RBA in 1898 and served on the Council. He died on 22 December 1943.

Exhib: M; RA; RBA; RI; ROI.
Bibl: *The Studio,* Vol.8, 1896, pp.142-148, illus.

**LE QUESNE, Rose**                    fl.1886-1895
Painter, sculptor and illustrator, working in London, but at Jersey in 1890. She contributed drawings of social realism, child workers etc. to *The Strand Magazine,* 1891.

Exhib: L; NEA; RA; RBA.

**LESLIE, Charles Robert    RA**                    1794-1859
Historical and portrait painter. He was born of American parents at Clerkenwell in 1794 and left with them for America in 1799 where he was brought up. He returned to England in 1811 to study art under Benjamin West and Washington Allston, becoming a student of the RA in 1813 and exhibiting for the first time in that year. He was elected ARA in 1821 and RA in 1826 and returned to the States in 1833 to become Drawing-Master at West Point. He settled in London finally the following year, becoming Professor of Painting at the RA, 1847-52 and as a painter specialised in very finished oil paintings of subjects from 17th and 18th century literature. He is included here for his series of illustrations for the novels of Washington Irving. Leslie, who became a notable art historian, died at St. John's Wood on 5 May 1859.

Pub: *Life of Constable [1845]; Life of Sir Joshua Reynolds.*
Exhib: BI; OWS; RA.
Colls: BM; V & AM.
Bibl: *Autobiographical Recollections,* Edited by Tom Taylor, 1865.

**LESLIE, George Dunlop    RA**                    1835-1921
Landscape and figure painter. He was born on 2 July 1835, younger son and pupil of C.R. Leslie, RA (q.v.). He was educated at the Mercer's School, before becoming a student at the RA in 1856. He was elected ARA in 1868 and RA in 1876. He specialised in views of the Home Counties and Thames Valley and White described his book illustrations as 'pretty half mediaeval, half modern . . .' He died at Lingfield, Sussex, on 21 February 1921.

Contrib: *Two Centuries of Song [1867]; ILN [1878].*
Pub: *Our River [1881]; Letters to Marco [1894]; Riverside Letters [1896]; The Inner Life of the Royal Academy.*

**L'ESTRANGE, Roland    'Armadillo'**                    1869-1919
Amateur caricaturist. A member of the family of L'Estrange of Hunstanton Hall, Norfolk. He contributed cartoons to *Vanity Fair,* 1903-04 and 1907. He signs his work Ao for Armadillo.

**LEVESON, Major A.H.**
Amateur draughtsman. He contributed drawings to *The Illustrated London News* during the Abyssinian Expedition of 1868.

**LEVETUS, Celia**                    fl.1896-1901
Illustrator. She was born in Birmingham, the sister of Edward, Lewis and Amelia Levetus, writers and critics. She studied at the Birmingham School and published black and white work in the Morris manner but as Sketchley comments 'in a more flexible style'.

ALFRED CHEW LEETE 1882-1933. Black and white illustration for humorous magazine, c.1914. Pen and ink.                    Jeffrey Gordon Collection

Illus: *Turkish Fairy Tales [1896]; Verse Fancies [1898]; Songs of Innocence [1899].*
Contrib: *The Yellow Book [1896]; English Illustrated Magazine [1896].*
Bibl: *The Artist,* May 1896; R.E.D. Sketchley, *English Book Illustrations,* 1903, pp.12, 128.

**LEVIS, Max**                    1863-
Portrait and figure painter. He was born in Hamburg, on 27 January 1863 and after studying at the Karlsruhe Academy and at Munich, worked in Vienna from 1888. He contributed an illustration to *The Illustrated London News,* 1892 (Christmas).

**LEWIN, Frederic George**                    fl.1902-1930
Humorous illustrator in black and white and colour. He worked throughout his life at Redland, Bristol, and specialised in rural figure subjects and children's books in the chap-book style.

Illus: *Rhymes of Ye Olde Sign Boards [c.1910].*
Contrib: *Punch [1902-08].*
Bibl: *Mr. Punch With Horse and Hound,* New Punch Library, c.1930

**LEWIS, Arthur James**                    1825-1901
Landscape and portrait painter, working in London. He contributed illustrations to *Passages From Modern English Poets,* 1862.

Exhib: BI; GG; New Gall; RA.

**LEWIS, F.**
Animal artist, contributing illustrations to *The Graphic,* 1886 from Dublin.

**LEWIS, Frederick Christian**                    1779-1856
Engraver and painter. He was born in London on 14 March 1779 and apprenticed to J.C. Stadler, the German engraver. He attended the RA Schools and was later appointed as engraver to Princess Charlotte of Wales, then successively to Leopold I, Geoge IV, William IV and Queen Victoria. He acquatinted Plate 43 of Turner's *Liber Studiorum.* He died at Enfield on 18 December 1856.

Illus: *Scenery of the River Dart [1821]; The Scenery of the Rivers Tamar and Tavy [1823].*
Exhib: BI; OWS; RBA.

*FREDERIC LORD LEIGHTON PRA 1830-1896. 'Coming Home.' Illustration for* Romola *by George Eliot, published in* The Cornhill Magazine, *Vol. 6, July to December 1862. Wood engraving.*

**LEWIS, George Robert**                                  **1782-1871**
Genre painter, landscape painter and illustrator. He was born in London in 1782, the younger brother of F.C. Lewis (q.v.). He was a pupil of Fuseli at the RA Schools and after working with his brother for Chamberlain and Ottley, made an extensive tour on the Continent in 1818. This journey made with the eccentric bibliophile Thomas Frognall Dibdin, was the start of a partnership which lasted some years, Dibdin writing reminiscences and Lewis illustrating them. He died at Hampstead in 1871.

Illus: *The Bibliographical Decameron [T.F. Dibdin, 1817]; Muscles of The Human Frame [1820]; The Bibliographical Tour [T.F. Dibdin, 1821 & 1829, 3 vols.]; Illustrations of Kilpeck Church [1842]; Banks of The Loire Illustrated; Early Fonts of England [1843]; British Forest Trees; Description of Shobdon Church [1856].*
Exhib: RA, 1820-59.
Colls: BM; Leeds.
Bibl: E.J. O'Dwyer, *Thomas Frognall Dibdin,* Private Libraries Association, 1967.

**LEWIS, John Frederick**                                  **1805-1876**
Painter of Figures and Eastern scenes. He was born in 1805, the eldest son of F.C. Lewis (q.v.) and began work as an animal painter in oils, exhibiting at the RA from the age of sixteen. His precocious talent attracted the notice of Sir Thomas Lawrence, who employed him as his assistant for a year. He published six mezzotints after his own work in 1825, which gained him a commission from George IV to paint sporting scenes at Windsor. His first visit to Spain in 1832 was of major significance to his work, his style became more assured, his

colours brighter and he developed an interest in the peninsular and the Middle East that soon became his hall-mark. Lewis lived abroad, first at Rome and then in the East from 1840 to 1851, basing himself at Cairo but visiting Greece and Albania. He was President of the OWS in 1855, having been elected in 1829, was elected ARA in 1859 and RA in 1865. Lewis's watercolours which are much sought after today are among the most brilliant Victorian achievements in the medium, brilliantly coloured and finely drawn. He died at Walton-on-Thames in 1876.

Illus: *Sketches and Drawings of the Alhambra [1835, AT 148]; Sketches of Spain and Spanish Character [1836, AT 149]; Sketches of Spain [1836, AT 150]; Illustrations of Constantinople [1838, AT 394].*
Exhib: BI; OWS; RA; RBA.
Colls: Birmingham; Blackburn; Fitzwilliam; V & AM.
Bibl: *Walker's Quarterly,* XXVIII, 1929; M. Hardie, *Watercol. Paint. in Brit.,* Vol.III, 1969, pp.48-55, illus.

**LIGHT, Kate**
Black and white artist. Contributed illustration and decor to a poem in *The Studio,* Vol.6, 1896.

**LILLIE, Charles T.**                                  **fl.1881-1882**
Comic draughtsman. He trained as an engineer and travelled widely to Africa and America before settling at Haverstock Hill, London, as an author and artist. He contributed to *Punch* in 1881 and exhibited flower paintings at the RBA in 1882.

**LINDSAY, G.**
Contributed drawings of comic fashions to *Punch,* 1906

**LINDSAY, Norman Alfred William**                      **1879-**
Black and white artist. He was born at Creswick, Victoria, Australia, on 23 February 1879 and joined the art staff of *The Sydney Bulletin* in 1901. He was chief cartoonist of the paper for many years, developing a pungent satirical style and a virtuosity of pen line that makes him the greatest black and white artist Australia has produced. He illustrated a number of books in addition to his cartooning, most of his work being left-wing, pacifist and anti-clerical in subject.

Illus: *Theocritus; Boccaccio; Casanova; Petronius; Satyrs and Sunlight [Hugh McCrae]; Songs of a Campaign [Colombine and Geelert]; Norman Lindsay's Book No.1 [1912]; No.2 [1915].*
Colls: V & AM.
Bibl: *Pen Drawings of NL,* Sydney, 1918.

**LINDSELL, Leonard**                                  **fl.1890-1907**
Illustrator. He was working in Bedford Park, London, during the 1890s and 1900s, contributing to the leading magazines.

Contrib: *The Girls' Own Paper [1890-1900]; The Lady's Pictorial [1895]; The Idler; The Royal Magazine.*
Colls: V & AM.

**LINNEY, W.**
Contributed a drawing to *Good Words,* 1861.

**LINSDALE, J.**
Contributed figure subjects to *Fun,* 1892.

**LINTON, Sir James Drogmole   PRI**                    **1840-1916**
Historical painter and illustrator. He was born in London on 26 December 1840 and educated at Clevedon House, Barnes, before studying art at Leigh's in Newman Street. He exhibited at the Dudley Gallery and the RI from 1863, was elected RI in 1870 and became the first President, 1883-97. He was knighted in 1885. Linton worked in black and white during the early part of his career, his best work being done for *The Graphic.* He died in London on 3 October 1916.

Illus: *The Pilgrim's Progress.*
Contrib: *Good Words [1870]; Cassell's Magazine [1870]; The Graphic [1871-74].*
Exhib: B; G; GG; L; M; New Gall; P; RA; RHA; RI; ROI.
Colls: Ashmolean; V & AM.
Bibl: *English Influences on Vincent Van Gogh,* Arts Council, 1974-75, p.52.

*FREDERIC LORD LEIGHTON PRA 1830-1896. 'Moses views the Promised Land.' Drawing for the illustration in* Dalziel's Bible Gallery, *1881. Indian ink and black chalk. 8¼ins. x 5ins. (21cm. x 12.7cm).* Victoria and Albert Museum

### LINTON, William                                         1791-1876

Landscape painter. He was born at Liverpool in 1791 and after being educated at Rochdale, entered a merchant's office in Liverpool. He spent much of his time in sketching the scenery of North Wales and studied the work of Claude and the Richard Wilson paintings at Ince Blundell Hall. He made extensive tours of Italy, Sicily and Greece in 1840 gathering information on classical antiquities which he incorporated in his pictures. Died in London in 1876.

Illus: *Ancient and Modern Colours [1852]; The Scenery of Greece [1856]; Colossall Vestiges of the Older Nations [1862].*
Exhib: BI; RA; RBA.
Colls: BM; Fitzwilliam; Woburn; V & AM.

### LINTON, William James                                   1812-1898

Engraver, poet and socialist. He was born in London on 7 December 1812 and was apprenticed to G.W. Bonner, the engraver, before entering partnership with Orrin Smith in 1842. He established *The National* in 1839, which reprinted pieces from other papers for the benefit of the working man; in 1845 he became editor of *The Illuminated Magazine* and founded *The English Republic,* 1850-55. In 1857 he was responsible for engraving the blocks to the historic *Moxon Tennyson* and was brought into contact with the Pre-Raephalites, in the 1860s he engraved for many books and was influential on a great many black and white artists who were his pupils, particularly Walter Crane (q.v.). He emigrated to the United States in 1866 and was elected a member of the Academy in 1882. He died at Newhaven, Conn., 1 January 1898.

Contrib: *Poems and Pictures [1846]; Good Words [1866]; The Lake Country [1864]; Wise's Shakespeare; Book of British Ballads [1842].*
Exhib: RA; RBA.
Bibl: *A History of Wood Engraving in America,* 1882; *Masters of Wood Engraving,* 1890; *Memories,* 1895.

### LINTOTT, Edward Barnard                                 1875-1951

Portrait and landscape painter. He was born in London in 1875 and studied at Julian's, the Sorbonne and the École des Beaux-Arts, Paris. He won a Carnegie Prize for work exhibited at the Salon and in the 1900s did a certain amount of illustrative work. He may have visited Russia in 1918 during the Revolution, was based in Chelsea after the First World War and died there in 1951.

Exhib: G; GG; L; M; NEA; P; RA.
Illus: *The Philharmonic-Symphony Orchestra of New York [W.G. King, 1940].*
Colls: V & AM.

### LINVECKER, J.B.

Animal illustrator, contributing to *The Graphic,* 1872.

### LIOTROWSKI

Russian artist, contributing drawings of the Revolution of 1905 to *The Graphic.*

### LIVETT, Berte

Comic black and white artist. He contributed illustrations to *Judy,* 1899 and *Fun,* 1900.

### LIVINGSTON-BULL, Charles

Illustrator of children's books. Drew for C. Lee Bryson's *Tan and Teckle,* 1908.

*FREDERIC LORD LEIGHTON PRA 1830-1896. 'Moses views the Promised Land.' Illustration in* Dalziel's Bible Gallery, *1881. Wood engraving.*
Victoria and Albert Museum

373

**LIX, Frédéric Théodore**                                    1830-1897
Genre painter. He was born in December 1830 and began to exhibit at the Paris Salon in 1859. He contributed equestrian subjects to *The Illustrated London News,* 1862-63 and died in Paris in 1897.

**LLOYD, Arthur Wynell**                                       1883-
Cartoonist and illustrator. He was born at Hartley Wintney in 1883 and after being educated at Rugby and Queen's College, Oxford, he served in the 25th Royal Fusiliers, 1916-17 and won the MC. He was chief cartoonist for the Essence of Parliament in *Punch* from 1914 and cartoonist of *The News of the World*. Signs: ⟨signature⟩.

Exhib: Cooling Gall., 1934.

**LLUELLYN, Mrs Y.A.D.**
Black and white artist, working for *The Longbow* and *The Ludgate Monthly* in the 1890s.

Exhib: ROI, 1889.

**LOCK, Agnes**                                               fl.1905-1925
Black and white artist working at Frencham, Surrey, from 1918 to 1925. She illustrated *Haunts of Ancient Peace* by Alfred Austin, c.1905.

Exhib: RI, 1918-19.

**LOCKE, William**
Genre painter and etcher. He was a pupil and friend of Henry Fuseli and worked in Paris and Rome. An undated drawing for Pope's *The Rape of the Lock,* possibly intended for illustration, is in an American private collection.

**LOCKWOOD, Sir Frank (Francis)**                             1847-1897
Amateur caricaturist. He was born in 1847 and was educated at Manchester Grammar School, St. Paul's, London and afterwards at Caius College, Cambridge. He was called to the Bar at Lincolns Inn and became Recorder of Sheffield in 1884, MP for York and Solicitor-General, 1894-95. He specialised in legal caricatures and contributed them to *Punch* for many years. R.G.G. Price says that they were 'worked up' by E.T. Reed (q.v.). He died 19 December 1897.

Contrib: *Punch; The Sketch; ILN [25 Dec., 1897].*
Bibl: A. Birrell, *Sir FL,* 1898; R.G.G. Price, *A History of Punch,* 1955, p.168.

**LODGE, George Edward**                                      fl.1881-1925
Figure and landscape painter. He specialised in natural history subjects and continental views, which he illustrated with great accuracy. He was working in London to 1917 and then at Camberley.

Contrib: *The English Illustrated Magazine [1886, 1893-94]; The Pall Mall Magazine.*
Exhib: B; L; M; RA; RBA; ROI.

**LOEB, Louis**                                               1866-1909
American illustrator. He was born at Cleveland in 1866 and became a member of the National Academy in 1906, dying at Canterbury, New Hampshire in 1909. He is included here as the illustrator of the English edition of *Pudd'nhead Wilson* by Mark Twain, 1897.

**LOEFFLER, Ludwig**                                          1819-1876
History painter and lithographer. He was born at Frankfurt-sur-Oder in 1819 and studied under Hensel and attended the Berlin Academy. He died at Berlin in 1876.

Contrib: *ILN [1868-74].*

**LOGSDAIL, William**                                         1859-1944
Portrait, architectural and landscape artist. He was born at Lincoln in 1859 and was educated at the Grammar School and School of Art at Lincoln. He won Gold Medals in the National Competition, 1875-76 and began to exhibit at the RA in 1877. He made further studies at the Académie des Beaux-Arts in Antwerp and worked as a painter in Venice, Cairo and Sicily. He was elected to the NEA in 1886.

Contrib: *The Graphic [1889 (topog.)].*
Exhib: G; GG; L; M; New Gall; RA; RBA; ROI.

**LONGMIRE, R.O.**                                            fl.1904-1923
Black and white artist working in Liverpool. He contributed illustrations to *Punch,* 1904.

Exhib: L.

**LORAINE, Nevison Arthur RBA**                               fl.1889-1908
Figure and landscape painter. He was elected RBA in 1893 and contributed to *The Illustrated London News,* 1895.

Exhib: L; RA; RBA; ROI.

**LORIOU, Felix**
French illustrator. Contributed colour plates to *The Illustrated London News,* Christmas 1916, in the style of Poiret.

**LORNE, The Marquess of**                                    1845-1914
**PC KG afterwards 9th Duke of Argyll.**
Amateur artist. Born 6 August 1845, eldest son of George, 8th Duke of Argyll. He was educated at Eton and Trinity College, Cambridge and was MP for Argyllshire in 1868. In 1871, he married HRH Princess Louise (q.v.), fourth daughter of Queen Victoria, becoming successively Governor-General of Canada, 1878-83 and MP for South Manchester, 1895. Lord Lorne published numerous books including *Canadian Pictures,* 1885 and died 2 May 1914.

Contrib: *The Graphic [1883].*

**LORON, G.A.**                                               fl.1895-1914
Illustrator. The Victoria and Albert Museum has illustrations by this artist for *The Heptameron* by Margaret of Navarre, in pen, ink, black chalk and wash on primed canvas.

**LORSAY or LORSA, Louis Alexandre Eustache**                1822-
Portrait painter and draughtsman. He was born at Paris on 23 June 1822 and studied with Paris and Monvoisin, exhibiting at the Salon in 1847 and 1859. He contributed figure subjects to *The Illustrated Times* in 1855.

**LOUDAN, William Mouat**                                     1868-1925
Genre and portrait painter. He was born in London of Scottish parents in 1868 and educated at Dulwich College before attending the RA Schools for four years, and winning the travelling scholarship. He then worked in Paris under Bouguereau and returned to England where he was elected NEA in 1886 and RP in 1891. He later devoted himself entirely to portraiture and died in London on 26 December 1925.

Contrib: *ILN [1889-94].*
Exhib: B; G; GG; L; M; NEA; New Gall; P; RA; RBA.
Colls: Leeds; Liverpool; V & AM.
Bibl: *The Artist,* 1899, pp.57-63, illus.

**LOUGHRIDGE, E.G.**
Amateur. Contributed some portrait into caricature subjects to *Punch* in 1903.

**LOUISE, HRH**                                               1848-1939
**The Princess Louise Caroline Alberta, Marchioness of Lorne.**
Artist, sculptress and writer. She was born at Windsor Castle on 8 March 1848, the sixth child and fourth daughter of HM Queen Victoria. She was married at Windsor on 21 March 1871 to the Marquess of Lorne, later 9th Duke of Argyll (q.v.). Princess Louise studied sculpture under Sir E. Boehm and was elected HRE, 1897, and RSW, 1884. She died at Kensington Palace in 1939.

Exhib: G; GG; L; M; RMS; RWS.

**LOUTHERBOURG, Philippe Jacques de RA**                      1740-1812
Landscape painter, illustrator and inventor. He was born, according to the inscription on his tomb, on 1 November 1740 at Strasbourg, the son of a painter of Polish extraction. He studied at Strasbourg University and under F.G. Casanova and Carlo Vanloo in Paris, becoming a member of the Académie Royale in 1767. He settled in England in 1771, painting battle pieces and scenery for David Garrick

at Drury Lane. An incurable romantic, Loutherbourg invented in 1781 the Eidophusicon for Spring Gardens, a machine that gave the illusion of changing light and movement on a stage set. He began to exhibit at the RA in 1782, was elected ARA in 1780 and RA in 1781. He died at Hammersmith Terrace, Chiswick on 11 March 1812.

Between 1775 and 1780, Loutherbourg developed an interest in caricature based on a study of P.L. Ghezzi and a knowledge of Hogarth. In 1775 he published *Caricatures of the English* from the shop of G.M. Torre. From this period many of the subsidiary groups in his landscapes develop a slightly caricatured form like those of Rowlandson. Loutherbourg gathered together his topographical paintings to form *The Picturesque Scenery of Great Britain*, 1801, and *The Picturesque and Romantic Scenery of England and Wales*, 1805. In 1789, Loutherbourg agreed to contribute plates to Thomas Macklin's edition of *The Holy Bible*. He provided twenty two out of the seventy one plates, plus one hundred and twenty five vignettes. The project lasted from 1789 to 1800 and was based on subscription, Macklin holding annual exhibitions in his Poets' Gallery.

Illus: *Hume's England [Bowyer's Edition]; Nelson's Victories [frontis]*.
Colls: BM; Derby; Dulwich; Glasgow; Louvre; Stockholm; V & AM.
Bibl: Rudiger Joppien, *PJ de L, RA, 1740-1812*, Catalogue of exhibition at Iveagh Bequest, GLC, 1973.

**LOW, Sir David**                                          **1891-196**
Cartoonist and caricaturist. He was born in Dunedin, New Zealand on 7 April 1891 and educated at the Boys' High School, Christchurch. He became Political Cartoonist of *The Spectator*, Christchurch, in 1902 and joined *The Sydney Bulletin* in 1911. He became cartoonist of *The Star*, London, 1919, and from 1927 worked for *The Evening Standard*, where much of his finest work appeared, and on *The Daily Herald* from 1930.

Publ: *Low's Annual [1908]; Caricatures [1915]; The Billy Book [1918]; Man [1921]; Lloyd George & Co. [1922]; Low & I [1923]; Low & I Holiday Book [1925]; Lions and Lambs [1928]; The Best of Low [1930]; Low's Russian Sketch Book [1932]; Portfolio of Caricatures [1933]; Low and Terry [1934]; The New Rake's Progress [1934]; Ye Madde Designer [1935]; Political Parade [1936]; Low Again [1938]; A Cartoon History of Our Time [1939]; Europe Since Versailles [1939]; Europe at War [1940]; Low's War Cartoons [1941]; Low on the War [1941]; British Cartoonists [1942]; The World at War [1942]; C'est La Guerre [1943]; Valka Zacala Mnichovem [1945]; Dreizehn Jahre Weltgeschehnen [1945]; Kleine Weltgeschichte [1949]; Years of Wrath [1949]*.
Bibl: *Low's Autobiography*, 1956.

**LOW, Harry (Henry Charles)**                              **fl.1914-1939**
Landscape painter and black and white artist. He was working at Wimborne, 1939-40 and contributed figure subjects to *Punch*, 1914.

**LOW, K.**
Illustrator and designer. He supplied illustrations and initials to an edition of Oscar Wilde's *A House of Pomegranates*, c.1900-10. He signs his work 'KL'.
Colls: V & AM.

**LOWELL, Orson**
Illustrator. Contributed drawings to *The Choir Invisible* by James Lane Allen, c.1908.

**LOWINSKY, Thomas Esmond**                                 **1892-1947**
Painter and illustrator. He was born in London on 2 March 1892 and was educated at Eton and Trinity College, Oxford. He studied art at the Slade School and enlisted in August 1914, serving throughout the War and on active service in France. Lowinsky was closely associated with the private presses in the 1920s and worked as illustrator for The Nonesuch Press, the Fleuron Press and The Shakespeare Head Press at various times. He specialised in coloured wood cuts, rather linear in style with strong art deco mannerism. He worked in Sunninghill, Berks., until 1914 and then at Kensington Square, London and Aldbourne, Wilts., where he died on 24 April 1947. He became a member of the NEA, 1926. He signs his work ⚒ ⚒

Illus: *Sidonia the Sorceress [William Meinhold, 1923]; Elegy on Dead Fashion [Edith Sitwell]; Paradise Regained [John Milton, 1924]; Dr Donne and Gargantua [Sacheverell Sitwell]; Exalt the Eglantine [Sacheverell Sitwell]; The*

*Princess of Babylon [1927]; Plutrach's Lives [1928]; The School For Scandal [1929]; Modern Nymphs [Raymond Mortimer, 1930]*.
Exhib: G; L; NEA; RA.
Colls: Fitzwilliam.

**LUARD, John Dalbiac**                                     **1830-1860**
Genre painter and illustrator. He was born in 1830 at Blyborough and followed a military career, serving in the Crimean War. Luard then joined the Langham Sketching Club and studied under John Philip RA. White had little regard for his work which he felt 'shows . . . a pre-Raphaelite manner and promise which later years did not fulfill'. He died at the early age of thirty, at Winterslow.

Contrib: *Once A Week*.
Exhib: RA, 1855-58.
Bibl: Stacy Marks, *Pen & Pencil Sketches*, p.59.

**LUCAS, Horatio Joseph**                                   **1839-1873**
Amateur etcher. He was born on 27 May 1839 and exhibited at the RA, 1870-73. Died 18 December 1873.

Contrib: *Good Words [1863]*.

**LUCAS, John Seymour   RA RI**                             **1849-1923**
Historical and portrait painter and illustrator. He was born in London on 21 December 1849, the nephew of John Lucas, the portrait painter. He studied at the St Martin's School of Art and at the RA Schools, specialising in sculpture but later turning to painting. He began to exhibit at the RA, in 1872, was elected NWS and RI in 1877 and ARA and RA in 1886 and 1898 respectively; visitor at the RA, 1886. Lucas did a considerable amount of illustrating in the 1890s, mostly of historical stories for magazines, the sketches for these are in grey washes with heavy bodycolour. He died at Blythborough, Suffolk on 8 May 1923.

Illus: *The Cruise of the River [1882]; The Grey Man [S.R. Crockett, 1896]*.
Contrib: *The Graphic [1893, 1901-06]*.
Exhib: B; G; L; M; RA; RBA; RCA; RHA; RI; ROI; RSA.
Colls: Birmingham; Leicester; Sydney; V & AM; Witt Photo.

**LUCAS, John Templeton**                                   **1836-1880**
Portrait painter and author. He was born in 1836, the son of John Lucas, the portrait painter and cousin of J. Seymour Lucas (q.v.). He wrote a farce and published some fairy tales in 1871, but is included here for the contributions he made to *The Illustrated London News*, in 1865 (genre subjects) and 1879 and in 1876 (Christmas subjects). He died at Whitby in 1880.

Exhib: BI, 1859-76; G; RA; RBA.

**LUCAS, Sydney Seymour**                                   **fl.1904-1940**
Portrait painter and illustrator. The son of J. Seymour Lucas, RA (q.v.) with whom he collaborated in illustrations. He worked in Bushey, Herts., in 1909 and at London and Blythborough, Suffolk in 1934 and 1936.

Contrib: *The Graphic [1904, 1905 (military)]*.
Exhib: P; RA; RSA.

**LUDLOW, Henry Stephen   'Hal'**                           **1861-**
Portrait and domestic painter and illustrator. He was born in 1861 and studied at Heatherley's and Highgate College and worked in London from 1880. Ludlow was a very competent all round magazine illustrator, his subjects ranging from theatrical sketches to Parliamentary reporting, stories and cattle shows. He was chief cartoonist to *Judy*, 1889-90. He worked at Hanwell, 1902-25.

Contrib: *Fun [1879-87]; ILN [1882-89]; Judy [1889-90]; The Queen [1892]; The Rambler [1897]; The Sketch; Ally Sloper's Half Holiday; Illustrated Bits; Cassell's Family Magazine; Chums; The Strand Magazine*.
Exhib: B; G; L; RA; RI.
Colls: V & AM.
See illustration (p.377).

**LUDLOW, S.**
Contributed illustrations of birds to *The Graphic*, 1870.

**LUDOVICO or LUDOVICI, Albert, Junior**     **1852-1932**

Figure and landscape painter and illustrator. He was born at Prague on 10 July 1852, the son of Albert Ludovici Senior, the artist. He painted genre subjects and worked in London and Paris after studying in Geneva. He was elected RBA in 1881 and NEA in 1891. His Parisian years brought him into contact with many famous artists and he was influenced by J.M. Whistler (q.v.). He died in London in 1932.

Contrib: *The Strand Magazine [1891 (legal)]*.
Exhib: BI; G; GG; L; M; NEA; RA; RBA; RHA; RI.
Colls: Sheffield.
Bibl: *An Artist's Life in London and Paris,* 1926.

**LUKER, William   RBA**     **1867-**

Animal and figure painter and illustrator. He was born in Kensington in 1867, the son of William Luker, the portrait, genre and animal painter. He was educated at private schools in London and Oxford before studying art at South Kensington and the RI Schools of Art. He worked for most of his life in London, but at Stanford-le-Hope, Essex, 1902-03 and at Amberley in Sussex after 1948. RBA, 1896.

Illus: *Kensington Picturesque and Historical; London City; London City Suburbs; Textile London; The Children's London [1902]*.
Contrib: *Souvenir of Indian Peace Contingent*.
Exhib: B; L; M; NEA; RA; RBA; RHA; RI; ROI.

**LUMLEY, Arthur**     **1837-1912**

American illustrator. He was born in Dublin in 1837 but emigrated to the United States where he worked as a painter in New York. He died there 27 September 1912.

Contrib: *ILN [1875-76, 1881]*.
Exhib: RA, 1876.

**LUMLEY, Augustus Savile**     **fl.1855-1899**

Genre and portrait painter. He exhibited at the RA, RBA and BI as well as at Liverpool, and contributed illustrations to *Sketchy Bits*.

**LUNT, Wilmot**

Illustrator. He was born at Warrington, Lancs. and was educated at the Boteler Grammar School and studied art at the Beaux Arts and Julian's in Paris. Lunt was principally a figure artist in black and white and contributed to many magazines. He worked at Elstree, Hertfordshire from 1914.

Contrib: *Punch [1908-09]; The Graphic [1915-16]; The Bystander; The Tatler*.
Exhib: L; RA; RI.
Bibl: *Who's Who in Art,* 1927.

*ILBERY LYNCH fl.1905-1925. 'Just Published.' An illustration in the style of Aubrey Beardsley. Pen and ink. Signed and dated 1909, and inscribed to Robert Ross 8¼ins. x 11¼ins. (21cm x 28.6cm).*
Victoria and Albert Museum

**LUTYENS, Sir Edwin Landseer PRA**     **1869-1944**
Architect and caricaturist. He was born in 1869 and studied at South Kensington under Sir Ernest George. He began to practise in 1888 and built country houses and later the brilliant New Delhi complex, 1913-30. Throughout his life, Lutyens was a talented and compulsive caricaturist and many of his letters and drawings are decorated in the margins with his humorous inspirations. He was elected PRA in 1938 and died in office in 1944; he had been knighted in 1918 and received the OM in 1942.

Colls: RIBA.
Bibl: A.S.G. Butler, *The Architecture of Sir EL*; C. Hussey, *The Life of Sir EL,* 1960.

**LYDON, A.F.**     **1836-1917**
Engraver and illustrator. He worked at Great Driffield, Yorkshire, and specialised in ornithological and natural history illustration.

Illus: *Houghton's British Fresh-water Fishes [1879].*
Contrib: *ILN [1890]; The English Illustrated Magazine [1891-92].*
Exhib: RA, 1861.
Colls: Witt Photo.

**LYNCH, F.**
Caricaturist, contributing portrait chargés to *Fun,* 1901.

**LYNCH, Ilbery**     **fl.1905-1925**
Black and white artist. Very little is known about this talented follower of Aubrey Beardsley. He illustrated *The Transmutation of Ling* by Ernest Bramah and designed a cover for *The Wallet of Kai Lung.* The Victoria and Albert Museum has an extremely fine pen

drawing in pastiche of Beardsley, signed and dated 1909.

Exhib: FAS, 1913.
Colls: V & AM.
Bibl: Grant Richards, *Author Hunting,* 1960.
See illustration (p.376).

**LYNCH, J.F.A.**
Topographical artist. He contributed to. *The Illustrated London News* and *The Illustrated Times* in 1860.

**LYNCH, J.G. Bohun**     **1884-**
Author and caricaturist. He was born in London on 21 May 1884 and was educated at Haileybury and University College, Oxford. Lynch was a popular caricaturist in the early 1920s, usually working in chalk and drawing large heads. He wrote a perceptive study of Max Beerbohm (q.v.).

Publ: *Glamour [1912]; Cake [1913]; Unofficial [1915]; The Complete Gentleman [1916]; The Tender Conscience [1919]; Forgotten Realms [1920]; A Perfect Day [1923]; Menace From The Moon; Max Beerbohm in Perspective [1921]; A Muster of Ghosts [1924]; Decorations and Absurdities.*
Bibl: *Caricature of Today.* Studio, 1928, pl.89.

**LYON, Captain George Francis**     **1795-1832**
Naval officer and traveller. He was born in 1795 and entered the Navy in 1808. He travelled to Africa in 1818-20 and published a narrative account of this in 1821. He formed part of Parry's Arctic Expedition in 1821-23 and after visiting Mexico and South America died at sea in 1832.

Illus: *The Private Journal of Captain GFL of HMS Hecla [1824].*

*HENRY STEPHEN LUDLOW*
*'HAL' 1861-*     *'Scenes at*
*Smithfield Cattle Show'.*
*Signed and dated.*

**MACBETH, Ann**                                    fl.1902-1925
Watercolour artist. She may have been trained at the Glasgow School and was working in the city, 1902-7 and again in 1925. Her style of drawing in pen and ink heightened with bodycolour and stippled, is close to that of Jessie M. King and Annie French (qq.v.) who offer an interesting comparison. Her drawing of 'Sleeping Beauty' sold by Sotheby's on 15 November 1977, may be for illustration.
Exhib: G; L.

**MACBETH, James**                                  1847-1891
Landscape painter and illustrator. He was born in Glasgow in 1847, the son of Norman Macbeth, RSA and brother of R.W. Macbeth, RA (q.v.). He worked in London and at Churt, Surrey and died in 1890.
Contrib: *ILN [1872-73]; The Graphic [1872-74].*
Exhib: G; GG; L; M; RA; RBA; RI; ROI; RSA.
Colls: Norwich.

**MACBETH, Robert Walker   RA**                     1848-1910
Painter and illustrator. He was born in Glasgow on 30 September 1848, the son of Norman Macbeth, RSA, and was educated at Edinburgh and at Friedrichsdorf, Germany. He studied art at the RSA Schools and on coming to London in 1870, began to work as an illustrator for *The Graphic,* then in its first year. Macbeth drew a wide variety of subjects for the paper, including sketches of the Commune, but became well-known for his rustic scenes and his etchings. As an etcher he was much influenced by Velazquez and Titian and was elected RE on the foundation of the Society. Macbeth, who gave his recreation in *Who's Who* as 'sleeping when too dark to work', became ARA in 1883 and RA in 1903. He died in London on 1 November 1910.
Illus: *A Thousand Days in the Arctic [F.G. Jackson, 1899].*
Contrib: *The Graphic [1870-71, 1901-03]; Once a Week [1870]; The Sunday Magazine [1871]; The English Illustrated Magazine [1883-85].*
Exhib: G; GG; L; M; New Gall; P; RA; RBA; RE; RI; ROI; RSA; RWS.
Colls: Aberdeen; V & AM; Witt Photo.

**MACBETH-RAEBURN, Henry Raeburn   ARA**            1860-1947
Artist and engraver. He was born in Glasgow on 24 September 1860, the son of Norman Macbeth, RSA and brother of R.W. and J. Macbeth (qq.v.). He was educated at the Edinburgh Academy and University and studied art at the RSA and at Julian's in Paris. He began his career as a portrait painter in London in 1884 and turned to engraving in 1890. In 1889, he made a visit to Spain and in 1896-97 etched a series of frontispieces for Osgood & Co.'s edition of *The Wessex Novels* by Thomas Hardy. Macbeth-Raeburn was best known in the 1920s for his engravings after the works of old masters, especially Raeburn. He was elected RE in 1899, ARA in 1921 and RA in 1933. He died in 1947.
Contrib: *ILN [1894-96].*
Exhib: G; L; M; P; RA; RBA; RE; RI; ROI; RSA.
Colls: V & AM.

**McCLURE, Griselda M.**
Illustrator, contributing drawings to *The Dawn at Shanty Bay,* a boy's story by R.E. Knowles, 1908.

**McCONNELL, William**                              fl.1850-1865
Cartoonist and comic artist. He was the son of a tailor of Irish extraction, learnt wood engraving from Swain and was a popular contributor to illustrated papers in the 1850s. He had two official appointments that of cartoonist to *Punch,* 1852 and cartoonist of *The*

*Illustrated Times,* 1855-56. His style is always exaggerated and grotesque with slight similarities to 'Phiz' or John Leech but never so well drawn. Spielmann says that he was a friend of G.A. Sala (q.v.) and was much commended by Mark Lemon for his *Punch* work which had included fierce attacks on Prince Louis Napoleon. According to Spielmann he 'revelled in beggars', 'swells' and 'backgrounds' and died of consumption soon after 1852. This must be incorrect information as he was still contributing to other periodicals in the 1860s.
Illus: *Twice Round The Clock [G.A. Sala, 1859]; The Adventures of Mr Wilderspin [1860].*
Contrib: *Punch [1850-52]; ILN [1851-58, 1860]; The Illustrated London Magazine [1855]; The Illustrated Times [1855-61]; The Welcome Guest [1860]; London Society [1864]; The Churchman's Family Magazine [1864]; The Sunday Magazine [1865].*
Bibl: M.H. Spielmann, *The History of Punch,* 1895, pp.460-461; Dalziel, *A Record of Work,* 1901, p.190.

**McCORMICK, Arthur David   RBA FRGS**              1860-1943
Artist and illustrator. He was born at Coleraine on 14 October 1860 and was educated at Coleraine and Belfast, studying art at South Kensington, 1883-86. He accompanied Sir Martin Conway's expedition to Karakoram, Himalayas, as artist in 1892-93 and Clinton Dent to the Caucasus in 1895. He was elected RBA in 1897 and ROI and RI in 1905 and 1906 respectively. He was FRGS from 1895 and died at St John's Wood in 1943. An exhibition of his work was held at the Alpine Gallery in 1904.
Illus: *Climbing and Exploring in the Karakoram Himalayas [W.M. Conway, 1894]; Silent Gods and Sun-Steeped Lands [R.W. Frazer, 1895]; Climbs in the New Zealand Alps [E.A. Fitzgerald, 1896]; The Kahirs of the Hindu-Kush [Sir G.S. Robertson, 1896]; New Climbs in Norway [E.C. Openheim, 1898]; Prince Patrick [A. Graves, 1898]; From the Cape to Cairo [E.S. Grogan, 1900]; Wanderings in Three Continents [Sir R. F. Burton, 1901]; The Alps [Sir W.M. Conway, 1904]; The Netherlands [M. Macgregory, 1907]; New Zealand [R. Horsley, 1908]; India [V. Surridge, 1909].*
Contrib: *The English Illustrated Magazine [1885-88]; ILN [1886-97]; Good Words [1898]; Arabian Nights [1899]; Strand Magazine [1906].*
Exhib: B; G; L; RA; RBA; RHA; RI; ROI; RWA.
Bibl: *An Artist in the Himalayas,* 1895.

**McCORMICK, Fred**
Artist. Contributed sketches of China to *The Graphic,* 1902-03.

**McCULLOCH, Horatio   RSA**                        1805-1867
Landscape painter. He was born in Glasgow on 9 November 1805, the son of a weaver and studied art with W.L. Leitch and Daniel Macnee. He first worked with the latter, painting snuff boxes and then moved to Edinburgh where he became an engraver. He began to exhibit at the RA in 1829 and was elected ARSA in 1834 and RSA in 1838. He specialised in Highland scenery and was influential on the younger generation of Scottish painters. He died at Edinburgh on 24 June 1867.
Contrib: *Scotland Illustrated [1838].*
Exhib: BI; RA; RSA.
Colls: Edinburgh; Glasgow.
Bibl: A. Frazer, *H. McC.,* 1872.

**MACDONALD, A.K.**                                 fl.1898-1925
Illustrator. Contributed to *The Longbow,* 1898 and was working in London, 1914-25.

**MACDONALD, Margaret**                             1865-1933
Designer. She set up a studio with her sister in Glasgow in 1894 and married the architect Charles Rennie Mackintosh in 1900. One of the Glasgow 'Four', she was a highly original designer in the fields of textiles, brassware, leather, illumination and posters. Her only contribution to illustration was a geometric design which appeared in *The Yellow Book,* July 1896.
Bibl: *Charles Rennie Mackintosh, 1868-1928, Architecture, Design and Painting,* Scottish Arts Council Catalogue, 1968.

**MACDOUGALL, William Brown** -1936

Painter, etcher, wood engraver and illustrator. He was born in Glasgow and educated at the Glasgow Academy. He studied art in Paris at Julian's and under Bouguereau, J.M. Laurens and R. Fleury. Macdougall was a regular exhibitor at the Salon and became a member of the NEA in 1890. His style changes distinctly after his appearance in *The Yellow Book* in 1894 and contact with Aubrey Beardsley (q.v.). From this point his illustrative work is symbolic and sombre with a great emphasis on black and white contrasts, but he lacks the wit of his great predecessor. He died at Loughton, Essex, 20 April 1936.

Illus: *Chronicles of Streatham [1896]; The Book of Ruth [1896]; The Fall of the Nibelungs [Margaret Armour, 1897]; Thames Sonnets and Semblances [1897]; Isabella . . . [1898]; The Shadow of Love and Other Poems [Margaret Armour, 1898]; The Eerie Book [Margaret Armour, 1898]; The Blessed Damozel [D.G. Rossetti, 1898]; Omar Khayyam [1898]; Fields of France; St Paul [F.W. Myers].*
Contrib: *The Yellow Book [1894]; The Evergreen [1894]; The Savoy.*
Exhib: G; L; M; NEA; RA; RSA.
Bibl: *The Studio,* Vol.10, 1897, p.141; Vol.15, 1898, p.210; R.E.D. Sketchley, *Eng. Bk. Illus.* 1902, pp.26, 128.
See illustration (below).

*WILLIAM BROWN MACDOUGALL -1936. 'The Mother and the Dead Child.' An illustration to* The Eerie Book *by Margaret Armour, 1898.*

**McEVOY, Arthur Ambrose  ARA ARWS** **1878-1927**

Landscape and portrait painter, born at Crudwell, Wiltshire in 1878 and studied at the Slade School. He was strongly influenced by J.

McNeil Whistler (q.v.) worked with Augustus John and Walter Sickert, and developed a free style of watercolour portraits for which he is best known. He was commissioned to paint portraits of the naval VC's in the First World War and was elected ARA in 1924 and ARWS in 1926, having been a member of the NEA, 1902. An exhibition of his watercolours was held at the Leicester Galleries in 1927 and memorial exhibitions at the RA and Manchester in 1928 and 1933. He died in London on 4 January 1927 of pneumonia.

Contrib: *The Quarto [1896].*
Exhib: G; GG; L; M; NEA; RA; RHA; RSA; RSW; RWS.
Colls: Bradford; Leeds; Manchester; Paris.
Bibl: C. Johnson, *The Works of AM,* 1919; R.M.Y. Gleadowe, *AM,* 1924; OWS Club, VII, 1931.

**McEWEN, D.H.**

Illustrator. Contributed to *The Book of South Wales* by Mr and Mrs S.C. Hall, 1861.

**MACFALL, C. Haldane** **1860-1928**

Figure, landscape and military painter. He was born on 24 July 1860 and was educated at Norwich Grammar School and Sandhurst before being gazetted into the West India Regiment in 1885. He retired in 1892 but served in the First World War. Macfall was a man of letters and a connoisseur and in the early part of the century published numerous books on literature, painting and collecting, he was an admirer of Whistler, Aubrey Beardsley and C. Lovat Fraser and wrote books on all three. He was awarded a Civil List Pension for his services to literature in 1914, and was increasingly known as an author rather than an artist, although he continued to design book covers. He died in London, 25 July 1928.

Contrib: *The Graphic [1891].*
Exhib: Int. Soc.; RA; RWA.

**MacFARLANE, T.D.** **fl.1894-1908**

Illustrator of children's books. He was working in Glasgow, 1894-97 and illustrated *Minstrelsy of the Scottish Border,* Noyes, 1908 and *Days That Speak,* 1908, both in colour.

Exhib: G.

**MACGILLIVRAY, James Pittendrigh  RSA** **1856-1938**

Sculptor. He was born at Inverurie, Aberdeenshire, in 1856 and studied art under William Brodie, RSA and John Mossman, HRSA. He became RSA in 1901, LLD, Aberdeen, 1909 and Kings Sculptor for Scotland, 1921. Macgillivray was a fine black and white draughtsman and some prints in the Witt Photo Library appear to be for book illustration. He died at Edinburgh, 29 April 1938.

Publ: *Verse Pro Patria [1915]; Bog Myrtle and Peat Reek [1922].*
Exhib: G; GG; L; M; NEA; RA; RSA.

**MACGREGOR, Archie G.**

Sculptor and illustrator. Working in London, 1884 to 1907 and exhibiting regularly.

Illus: *Katawampas [Judge Parry, 1895]; Butterscotia [Judge Parry, 1896]; The First Book of Klab [Judge Parry, 1897]; The World Wonderful [Charles Squire, 1898].*
Exhib: L; M; New Gall; NWS; RA; RHA; RI; ROI.
Bibl: R.E.D. Sketchley, *Eng. Bk. Illus.,* 1903, pp.107, 167.

**MACGREGOR, G.**

Probably G.S. Macgregor, working in Glasgow, 1891 and exhibiting at the RSA.

Contrib: *ILN [1887 (figures)].*

**MacGREGOR, Jessie** -1919

Portrait, genre and historical painter and illustrator. She was working in Liverpool from 1872 and in London from 1886 and was elected ASWA in 1886 and SWA in 1887.

Illus: *Christmas Eve at Romney Hall [1901].*
Exhib: B; G; L; M; RA; ROI; SWA.

**McHUTCHON, F.**

Humorous animal artist. Contributed illustrations to *Punch,* 1904-05.

Wreath the bowl
    With flowers of soul,
The brightest Wit can find us;
    We'll take a flight
    Tow'rds heaven to-night,
And leave dull earth behind us.
    Should Love amid
    The wreaths be hid,
That joy, th'enchanter, brings us,
    No danger fear,
    While wine is near,
We'll drown him if he stings us.

*DANIEL MACLISE RA 1806-1870. 'Wreath The Bowl.' Illustration to* Irish Melodies *by Tom Moore, London 1846.*

**McIAN, Robert Ronald ARSA** 1803-1856

Genre painter and illustrator. He was born in 1803 and worked as a professional actor as well as being a painter. He specialised in scenes of the Highlands and after 1840 abandoned the theatre for the life of a painter, having exhibited at the RA from 1836. He was elected ARSA and died at Hampstead in 1856.

Illus: *The Clans of the Scottish Highlands, Illustrated by Appropriate Figures [James Logan, 1845-47 (2 vols.)]; The London Art Union Prize Annual [1845].*
Exhib: BI; RA; RBA; RSA.

**MacINTOSH, John MacIntosh** 1847-1913

Landscape and view painter. He was born at Inverness in 1847 and studied at Heatherley's, the West London School of Art and in Versailles. He worked at Woolhampton near Reading, and died at Shanklin in 1913. He illustrated E.G. Hayden's *Islands of the Vale,* 1908.

Colls: Reading; V & AM.

**MACKAY, Wallis 'WV'** fl.1870-1893

Black and white artist and caricaturist. He was a social cartoonist for *Punch,* 1870-74 but offended Tom Taylor, the Editor and was dismissed, although work by him was still appearing in 1877. He became cartoonist of *Fun* in 1893.

Contrib: *Judy; ILN [1880].*
Bibl: M.H. Spielmann, *The History of Punch,* 1894, pp.540-541.

**MACKENZIE, Frederick OWS** 1787-1854

Topographical draughtsman. He was born in 1787 and became a pupil of John A. Repton and began a career as an architectural draughtsman for leading publishers such as Britton, Ackermann and Le Keux. He became an Associate of the OWS in 1822, and a Member in 1823 holding the post of Treasurer from 1831 till his death. Mackenzie was a very accurate delineator of gothic buildings at a time when clarity was all important. His drawings in grey washes are small and feathery and beautiful and have the definition that seems to be lost in the prints after his works. In later life his work was superceded by early photography. He died in London on 25 April 1854.

Illus: *Etchings of landscapes for the use of students [1812]; History of the Abbey Church of St. Peter, Westminster [1812]; Britton's Salisbury Cathedral [1813]; History of the University of Oxford [1814]; History of the University of Cambridge [1815]; Illustrations of the Principal Antiquities of Oxfordshire [1823]; Graphic Illustrations of Warwickshire [1829]; Memorials of Architectural Antiquities of St Stephen's Chapel, Westminster [n.d.].*
Contrib: *Britton's Beauties of England and Wales [1810-15]; The Oxford Almanack [1822, 1827, 1838, 1848, 1850, 1851, 1853].*
Exhib: OWS; RA; RBA.
Colls: Ashmolean; BM; Fitzwilliam; Lincoln; Manchester; V & AM; Witt Photo.
Bibl: M. Hardie, *Watercol. Paint. in Brit.,* Vol.3, 1968, pp.17-18 illus; Petter, *Oxford Almanacks,* 1974.

**MACKENZIE, John D.** fl.1886-1896

Painter, black and white artist and illustrator. He was working in London from 1886 and at Newlyn, Penzance from 1889. He supplied a cover and title page to *The Yellow Book* in October 1895, and exhibited at the RA and RBA.

Illus: *Sonnets and Songs [May Bateman, 1895-96 (title etc.)].*

**MACKEWAN, Arthur**

Amateur contributor to *Punch,* 1907.

**MACKIE, Charles Hodge RSA RSW** 1862-1920

Genre and landscape painter. He was born at Aldershot of Scottish parents in 1862 and was educated at Edinburgh University before studying at the RSA Schools. He travelled in Spain, Italy and France, where he met Gauguin and Vuillard and settled at Murrayfield. Mackie was a prolific and diverse artist and engaged in etching, mural decoration, sculpture and colour printing as well as painting. He was elected ARSA in 1902 and RSA in 1912, RSW, 1902. He died on 12 July 1920.

Contrib: *The Evergreen [1895].*
Exhib: G; L; M; NEA; RA; RHA; RSA; RSW.
Colls: BM; Edinburgh; Leeds; Liverpool; V & AM; Witt Photo.
Bibl: *The Studio,* Winter No., 1900-01, p.48 illus; Vol.58, 1913, pp.66, 137,

295; Vol.68, 1913, pp.61, 122, 125; Vol.70, 1913, p.107; *A.J.* 1900, p.287; *The Connoisseur,* Vol.37, 1912, p.53.

**McKIE, Helen Madeleine** fl.1915-1936

Illustrator. She studied at the Lambeth School of Art and was for a time on the staff of *The Bystander.* She contributed to *The Graphic,* Christmas number, 1915.

Exhib: RHA; SWA.

**MACKLIN, Thomas Eyre** 1867-1943

Painter and sculptor. He was born at Newcastle-upon-Tyne in 1867 the son of a journalist, and was educated privately before studying art at the RA Schools and in Paris. Macklin became Special Artist to *The Pall Mall Budget* from 1882 to 1892 and made many designs for books, magazines and posters. He travelled in Italy and lived for some time in France but also painted in his native Newcastle. He died in 1943. He was elected RBA, 1902.

Illus: *The Works of Nathaniel Hawthorne [1894].*
Exhib: L; RA; RBA; RSA.
Colls: Gateshead.

**McLEISH, Annie**

Illustrator. Pupil of the Mount Street School of Art and contributed illustration to *The Studio,* Vol. 13, 1897, pp.192-193.

**McLEOD, Lyons**

Artist. Illustrated *Travels in Eastern Africa and Mozambique,* 1860. AT 277.

**MACLISE, Daniel RA** 1806-1870

Historical and portrait painter. He was born at Cork in 1806, the son of a former Scottish soldier and while attending the Cork Art School was brought to public notice by a sketch he made of Sir Walter Scott, 1825. He travelled to London in July 1827 and attended the RA Schools, winning the silver and gold medals in 1828. He exhibited at the RA from 1829 and after a brief spell in Ireland that year, returned in 1830 to make a career in book illustration. Maclise contributed eighty caricatures to *Fraser's Magazine* between then and 1836. Most of them were drawn with a lithographic pen and suited his linear style and meticulous rendering. The caricatures were accompanied by biting literary sketches from the pen of William Maginn and relied more for their effect on their stylization than on their grotesqueness. Thomas Carlyle sitting for his caricature described Maclise as 'a quiet shy man with much brogue'. *Fraser's Illustrations,* the originals of which are now in the BM, made the artist's name and he illustrated many books of legend in the 1840s. Always concerned as an illustrator in fantasy rather than reality, Maclise found his sources in contemporary German illustration. He had been elected ARA in 1835 and RA in 1840 and became an immenseley popular painter, declining a knighthood and the Presidency of the RA in 1866. But by the time his illustrations for *Moxon's Tennyson* were appearing in 1857 and 1861, these and his *Norman Conquest* for The Art Union, 1866, were already in an outmoded style. He died at 4 Cheyne Walk, Chelsea on 25 April 1870.

Illus: *Fairy Legends [Crofton Croker, 1826]; Tour Round Ireland [John Barrow, 1826]; Ireland its Scenery and Character [1841]; The Chimes: A Goblin Story . . . [Charles Dickens, 1844]; The Cricket on The Hearth, A Fairy Tale . . . [Charles Dickens, 1845]; Thomas Moore's Irish Melodies [1845]; Leonora [Gottfried Burger 1847]; Moxon's Tennyson [1857, 1861]; The Princess [Tennyson, 1860]; Idylls of The King [Tennyson]; Story of the Norman Conquest [Art Union, 1866].*
Contrib: *Fraser's Magazine [1830-36]; The Keepsake [1835]; Heath's Gallery [1836, 1838]; The Old Curiosity Shop [Charles Dickens, (Chap.55) 1841].*
Exhib: BI; RA; RBA.
Colls: Ashmolean; BM; Ireland; Nat. Gall; NPG; V & AM; Witt Photo.
Bibl: Chatto & Jackson, *Treatise on Wood Engraving,* 1861, p.569; R. Ormond, *DM 1806-1870,* NPG, 1972.
See illustration (p.380).

**MACLURE, Andrew** fl.1857-1881

Landscape painter and lithographer. This artist illustrated *Queen Victoria in Scotland,* 1842 and *Highlands and Islands of The Adraitic,* 1849, AT 44.

Exhib: G; RA, 1857-81.
Colls: Witt Photo.

**MACMICHAEL, William** 1784-1839

Amateur artist, physician and writer. He was educated at Christ Church, Oxford, MA, 1807 and became Radcliffe Travelling Fellow in 1811, MD in 1816 and FRCP in 1818. He was appointed physician to William IV in 1831.

Pub: *The Gold-headed Cane [1827]*.
Illus: *Journey from Moscow to Constantinople [1819, AT 20]*.

**MACNAB, Peter  RBA** -1900

Genre painter and illustrator. Working in London and Woking, Surrey and exhibiting from 1864. He was elected RBA in 1879.

Contrib: *ILN [1882-83]; The Cornhill Magazine [1884]; The English Illustrated Magazine [1885]*.
Exhib: B; BI; FAS; G; L; M; RA; RBA; RI; ROI.

**MACNEIL, H.**

Illustrator. Contributed military subjects to *The English Illustrated Magazine*, 1896.

**MACPHERSON, Douglas** 1871-

Illustrator. He was born in Essex on 8 October 1871 the son of John Macpherson, artist. After being educated at a private school, he studied art at Westminster School of Art and became a member of the original staff of *The Daily Graphic*, 1890-1913. He served as Special Artist at home and abroad for *The Daily Graphic* and *The Graphic* until he joined *The Sphere* in 1913, attending among other events, The Spanish-American War, 1898, The St Petersburg Revolt, 1905 and the Assasination of Don Carlos in 1908. He served with the RNVR, 1914-18 and was present for *The Sphere* at Tutankhamun's Tomb, 1923-24. Drew the Coronation of King George VI for *The Daily Mail*, 1937 and sketches of the Second World War for *The Sphere, Daily Telegraph* and *Daily Mail*, 1939-45.

Contrib: *The Daily Graphic [1890-1913]; St Pauls [1894]; The Ludgate Monthly; The Graphic [1901-10]; Punch [1906-09]*.
Exhib: L; RA.

**MACQUOID, Percy T.  RI** 1852-1925

Artist, illustrator, designer and historian of English furniture. He was born in 1852, the son of T.R. Macquoid (q.v.) and was educated at Marlborough and studied art at Heatherley's, at the RA Schools and in France. He worked for *The Graphic* from 1871, at first concentrating on animal subjects but later painting historical and genre pictures. He was elected RI, 1882 and ROI, 1883. He was a designer of theatrical costumes but in his later years concentrated wholly on the study of English furniture, publishing his four volumes *History of English Furniture*, 1905. He died on 20 March 1925.

Illus: *The Bridal of Triermain [Walter Scott, Art Union, 1886]*.
Contrib: *ILN [1874-82]; The Graphic [1871-90]*.
Exhib: B; FAS; G; L; M; RA; RI; ROI.
Bibl: *English Influences on Vincent Van Gogh*, Arts Council, 1974-75, p.52.

**MACQUOID, Thomas Robert  RI** 1820-1912

Painter, illustrator and ornamental designer for books. He was born in Chelsea on 24 January 1820 and after being educated in Brompton, studied art at the RA Schools and specialised in book illustration. He is specifically mentioned by Chatto for his work on 'ornamental Letters and Borders' and supplied much decoration of this kind to the early volumes of *The Illustrated London News*, all showing great architectural accuracy and delicacy of execution. He collaborated with his wife, Mrs K.S. Macquoid on a number of travel books. RI, 1882 and ROI, 1883, he died on 6 April 1912. A memorial exhibition of his work was held at the New Dudley Gallery, London in 1912.

Illus: *Little Bird Red and Little Bird Blue [M.B. Edwards, 1861]; The Primrose Pilgrimage [M.B. Edwards, 1865]; Through Normandy [K.S. Macquoid, 1874]; Pictures and Legends of Normandy and Brittany [K.S. Macquoid, 1897]; Pictures in Umbria [K.S. Macquoid, 1905]; The Paris Sketchbook [W.M. Thackeray, 1894]*.
Contrib: *Examples of Architectural Art in Italy and Spain [1850]; ILN [1851-61, 1863-69]; Favourite English Poems [1857]; The Welcome Guest [1860]; The Churchman's Family Magazine [1863]; The Graphic [1873]; Rhymes and Roundelayes; Burns Poems; Thornbury's Legendary Ballads [1876]; Good Words [1880]; The English Illustrated Magazine [1886-87 (architecture)]; The Pall Mall Magazine.*

Exhib: G; L; M; RA; RBA; RI; ROI; RSW.
Bibl: Chatto & Jackson, *Treaties on Wood Engraving*, 1861, p.599.

**McTAGGART, William  RSA, RSW** 1835-1910

Painter and Scottish impressionist. He was born at Aros, near Campbeltown, and began by painting portraits of the inhabitants of this Scottish burgh in his spare time. He attended the Trustees Academy at Edinburgh for seven years from 1852, studying alongside Sir W.Q. Orchardson (q.v.) and J. MacWhirter (q.v.). He became ARSA in 1859 and RSA in 1870. He was Vice-President of the RSW in 1878 and died at Broomieknowe on 2 April 1910.

Contrib: *Good Words [1861]*.
Exhib: G; L; NEA; RA; RHA; RSA; RSW.
Colls: Aberdeen; Glasgow; Nat. Gall., Scotland.

**MacWHIRTER, John  RA** 1839-1911

Landscape painter and illustrator. He was born at Slateford near Edinburgh in 1839, the son of a papermaker and was educated at Peebles School, the Edinburgh School of Design and the Trustees Academy. He was elected ARSA in 1867 and moved to London in 1869, where he attracted the notice of Ruskin and became a popular painter of Highland and Continental landscapes. He made extensive tours in France, Switzerland, Italy, Austria, Turkey and Norway and visited the United States. He was a strong advocate of drawing direct from nature and published a book on technique. Most of his book illustrations date from his early career in Scotland. He was elected ARA in 1879 and RA in 1893 and died at St John's Wood on 28 January 1911.

Illus: *Landscape Painting in Watercolours [1901]; The MacWhirter Sketchbook [1906]; Sketches from Nature [1913]*.
Contrib: *Good Words [1861]; The Golden Thread [1861]; Wordsworth's Poems for the Young [1863]; The Sunday Magazine [1869]; Pen and Pencil Pictures from the Poets [1866]; Poems and Songs of Robert Burns [1875]; The Picturesque Mediterranean [1891]*.
Exhib: B; FAS; G; GG; L; M; New Gall; RA; RE; RHA; RI; RMS; ROI; RSA; RSW.
Colls: BM; Dundee; Glasgow; Manchester; Nat. Gall; Scotland; V & AM.
Bibl: M.H. Spielmann, *The Art of J McW*, 1904.

**MADOT, Adolphus M.** -1864

Figure artist and illustrator. He was a pupil of the RA Schools and studied at Julian's in Paris. He exhibited figure subjects in London, 1852-64, but died young.

Contrib: *The Home Affections [Charles MacKay, 1858]; The Poetical Works of E.A. Poe [1858]*.
Exhib: BI; RA; RBA.

**MAHONEY, J.** fl.1865-1876

Illustrator and engraver. He was practically uneducated and spent some years as errand boy for the firm of Vincent, Son and Brooks, lithographic printers. He was said to be a natural artist and his drawings came to the notice of J.W. Whymper, to whom he had to deliver proofs. Whymper took him into his employ and he made quick progress as a draughtsman, being given small illustrations to do after a comparatively short time. He was later with the Dalziel Brothers, but in both cases had to leave because of drunkenness and disorderly behaviour, finally dying in a latrine in London in the same unhappy condition. He undertook some important commissions such as *Oliver Twist*, *Little Dorrit* and *Our Mutual Friend*, 1871, for Dickens 'Household Edition' and did a great deal of magazine work. Reid is however critical of his uneven style — 'A curious tendency to dwarf his figures is carried, one might fancy, into the very shape of many of Mahoney's designs, and into the square squat monogram with which they are signed.'

Illus: *Scrambles on the Alps [Whymper, 1870]; Oliver Twist, Little Dorrit, Our Mutual Friend [Dickens 'Household Edition', 1871]; Three Clerks [A. Trollope (frontis.)]; Little Wonder-Horn [Jean Ingelow, 1872]; Frozen Deep [Wilkie Collins, 1875 (with Du Maurier)]*.
Contrib: *Leisure Hour [1865-66]; Sunday Magazine [1866-70]; The Argosy [1866]; Cassell's Magazine [1867]; Touches of Nature [1867]; Cassell's Illustrated Readings [1867]; The Peoples Magazine [1867]; The Quiver [1868];*

*The Nobility of Life [1869]; Good Words For The Young [1869]; National Nursery Rhymes [1870]; Little Folks [1870]; Judy; Fun; The Day of Rest.*
Colls: V & AM.
Bibl: Forrest Reid, *Illustrators of The Sixties*, 1928, pp.255-256, illus.

**MAHONEY, James**                    **1816-1879**
Watercolourist and engraver on wood. He was born at Cork in about 1816 and studied in Rome and other European centres, before returning to work in London, where he died on 29 May, 1879. He was a member of the NWS.
Contrib: *ILN [1847]*.
Exhib: RA, 1866-77.

**MALCOLM, James Peller**                    **1767-1815**
Draughtsman and engraver. He was born in Philadelphia in 1767 and came to England in 1788-89, attending the RA Schools for three years. He was acquainted with Benjamin West and J. Wright of Derby, who patronised him, but he never made a success of painting and turned to engraving for a living. Malcolm was also a writer, a Fellow of the Society of Antiquaries and one of the first artists to write a treatise on caricature. He died in London in 1815.
Illus: *Twenty Views Within Ten Miles of London [1800]; Excursions in the County of Kent [1802]; The History of Leicestershire [Nichols]; Biographical Dictionary of England [Granger]; Londinium Redivivum [1902-07]; Manners and Customs of London during the XVIII Century [1808, 50 views]; Excursions in the Counties of Kent, Gloucester, Hereford, Monmouth and Somerset [1813]; An Historical Sketch of The Art of Caricaturing with Graphic Illustrations [1813]*.
Contrib: *The Gentleman's Magazine; Lyson's Environs of London [1797-1800]; The Beauties of England and Wales [1801-05]*.
Exhib: RA, 1791.
Colls: V & AM; Witt Photo.

**MALLETT, R.W.**
Artist. Contributing illustrations of industry to *The Illustrated London News*, 1875.

**MANN, Harrington**                    **1864-1937**
Portrait painter and illustrator. He was born at Glasgow in 1864 and studied art at the Slade School and in Paris and Rome. He was a member of the Royal Society of Portrait Painters and of the International Society of Sculptors, Painters and Gravers. He was an important member of the Glasgow School of painters and an accomplished decorative artist, working as an illustrator for both *The Daily Graphic* and *The Scottish Art Review*. He is represented in most British galleries and died on a visit to New York, 28 February 1937.
Publ: *The Technique of Portrait Painting [1933]*.
Exhib: B; G; GG; L; M; NEA; New Gall; P; RA; RBA; RE; RI; ROI; RSA.
Bibl: *The Artist*, August 1897, pp.363-369, illus.

**MANSEL, Miss    afterwards Mrs Bull**
Amateur artist. She contributed one drawing to *Punch* in 1863, which was touched up by John Leech!

**MANTON, G. Grenville    RBA**                    **1855-1932**
Portrait painter and illustrator. He was born in London in 1855, the son of Gildon Manton, gunmaker. He was educated in London and Paris and was an RA medallist, but left England for America in 1890 and worked there for some years as a portrait painter, exhibiting at The National Academy. On returning to London, he became a staff artist on *Black and White*. He was working at Bushey, Hertfordshire from 1895 till his death on 13 May 1932. He was elected RBA in 1899.
Illus: *True to The Core [Jarrold's Books for Manly Boys, 1894]*.
Contrib: *Black & White [1892]; The Quiver [1892]; Pearson's Magazine [1896]; The Ludgate Monthly; The Pall Mall Magazine; The Sphere*.
Exhib: B; L; P; RA; RBA; ROI.

**MANUEL, J. Wright T.**                    **-1899**
Illustrator. He worked in London from about 1894 and specialised in comic sporting subjects in black and white but also in chalk and watercolour. He became RBA in 1896 and died in 1899.

Contrib: *Pick-Me-Up [1894]; The Unicorn [1895]; ILN [1896]; Eureka [1897]; The Butterfly [1899]; The Idler; The Minister*.
Exhib: RBA; ROI.
Colls: V & AM.

**MARGETSON, William Henry    RI**                    **1861-1940**
Landscape and genre painter in oil and watercolour, illustrator. He was born at Denmark Hill, London, in December 1861 and after being educated at Dulwich College, studied art at South Kensington and at the RA Schools. He lived and worked in Berkshire from 1914, first at Blewbury and then at Wallingford and was elected RI in 1909. Margetson has a pleasing eye for colour and was most popular as an illustrator of adventure stories. He died 2 January 1940.
Illus: *The King's Pardon [Overton, 1894]; The Village of Youth [B. Hatton, 1895]; With Cochrane The Dauntless [G.A. Henty, 1897]; A Missing Witness [Frank Barrett 1897]; Aglyaine and Selysette [Sutro, 1898]; The Wild Geese [S.J. Weyman, 1908]; Humphrey Bold [H. Strang, 1908]*.
Contrib: *The English Illustrated Magazine [1885, 1891-92]; The Quiver [1890]; Black & White [1891]; Cassell's Family Magazine; The Idler; The Pall Mall Magazine; The Graphic [1904-06]*.
Exhib: B; G; GG; L; M; RA; RBA; RI; ROI.

**MARIE, Adrien-Emmanuel**                    **1848-1891**
Painter and illustrator. He was born at Neuilly-sur-Seine on 20 October 1848, and was a pupil of Bayard, Camino and Pils. He was a regular exhibitor at the Salon from 1866 to 1881 and won a bronze medal at the 1889 Exhibition. His connection with England began in 1873, when he started to contribute French genre and social realistic subjects to *The Graphic*. A bold figure draughtsman, he was most prolific in the pages of the magazine from 1885-89, supplementing a rather weak period for English illustrators. He died at Cadiz in April 1891.
Exhib: FAS; M.
Colls: Calais; Tourcoing; Sydney.

**MARKLEN, H.**
Contributed illustrations to *Griffith's Cheltenham*, 1826.

**MARKS, A.J.**
Amateur caricaturist. Contributed cartoons to *Vanity Fair*, 1889. Signs his work AJM.

**MARKS, Henry Stacy    RA**                    **1829-1898**
Painter and illustrator. He was born in London on 13 September 1829 and studied art at Leigh's School, Newman Street and at the RA Schools, 1851. He spent some months in Paris with Calderon in 1852 and began exhibiting at the RA in 1853. Marks was very clearly influenced by the Pre-Raphaelites at this time and became a very brilliant pen and ink draughtsman and a masterly painter of animals. Marks seems to have been a very lazy artist and his drawings fall away dramatically after the 1860s into thick outline and clumsy handling. He was obsessed by the Middle Ages and painted many ludicrous subjects of them including 'Toothache in the Olden Time'. His best work is in his bird paintings and his stained glass design. He was elected ARA in 1871 and RA in 1878, and RSW in 1883.
Illus: *Sketching From Nature [T.J. Ellis, 1876]; The Good Old Days [E. Stuart, 1876]*.
Contrib: *Home Circle [1855]; Legends of the Cavaliers and the Roundheads [Thornbury, 1857]; Punch [1861 and 1882]; Willmott's Sacred Poetry [1862]; Passages From Modern English Poets [1862]; Once a Week [1863]; The Churchman's Family Magazine [1863]; Two Centuries of Song [1867]; Ridiculous Rhymes [1869]; London Society [1870]; National Nursery Rhymes [1871]; The Quiver [1873]; The Child's History of England [1873]; ILN [1876 and 1879]; The Graphic*.
Exhib: B; BI; FAS, 1889, 1890, 1895; G; L; M; RA; RCA; ROI; RWS.
Colls: Ashmolean; Exeter; Liverpool; V & AM.
Bibl: H.S. Marks, *Pen and Pencil Sketches*, 2 vols. 1894; Forrest Reid, *Illustrators of The Sixties*, 1928, pp.254-255; J. Maas, *Victorian Painters*, 1970, p.82, illus.
See illustration (p.384).

**MARKS, Lewis**                    **fl.1814-1815**
Amateur caricaturist, specialising in well-drawn figures of Napoleon and Paul Pry.
Colls: Witt Photo.

**The Sleepy Porter**

*Knock, knock: Never at quiet!* (*Marks.*)

*HENRY STACY MARKS RA 1829-1898. 'The Sleepy Porter.' An illustration for Shakespeare's* Macbeth. *Pen and ink, signed with monogram and dated 1859. 10½ins. x 7½ins. (26.7cm x 19.1cm).* Author's Collection

**MARRYAT, Captain Frederick  CB  FRS**  1792-1848
Novelist, draughtsman and caricaturist. He was born in Great George Street, Westminster on 10 July 1792, the son of an MP, and went to sea in 1806, serving throughout the Napoleonic Wars. He served in St Helena, 1820-21, and in North America, 1837-38. On his retirement he became celebrated as novelist and writer of books for children and died at Langham, Norfolk on 9 August 1848.

Publ: *The Children of the New Forest; The Naval Officer [1829]; Peter Simple [1834]; Midshipman Easy [1836]; The Metropolitan Magazine [Editor, 1832-35].*
Colls: V & AM.

**'MARS'  Maurice BONVOISIN**  1849-1912
Draughtsman, engraver and cartoonist of the Belgian School. He was born at Verviers on 26 May 1849 and became a regular illustrator in the French papers *Journal amusant* and *Charivari*. He was the only continental artist to be used consistently for cartoon work by British periodicals, his sketchy crayon style, based on the poster and anticipating May, being rather avant-garde here. He was a master of the purely visual joke without text and his books seem to have been popular in this country, some of his subjects being British ones. He died in 1912.

Illus: *Nos Cheris [Plon, Paris, 1886].*
Contrib: *The Graphic [1880-91]; ILN [1882-92]; The Daily Graphic [1890]; The Sketch [1894]; Illustrated Bits.*
Colls: V & AM.

**MARSHALL, Benjamin Marshall**  1768-1835
Sporting artist. He was born in Leicestershire on the 8 November 1768 and went to London in 1791 to follow the career of a painter. He exhibited at the RA from 1801 and between 1812 and 1825 had his studio near Newmarket. He died in London on 24 July 1835. He is included here for the illustrations of his work that appeared in *The Sporting Review*, after his death, 1842-46.

**MARSHALL, C.A.**  fl.1889-1890
Amateur artist and solicitor at Retford in Nottinghamshire. Contributed two drawings to *Punch*, 1889 and one to *Judy*, 1890.

**MARSHMAN, J.**
Artist working at Bangor, N. Wales. He contributed sporting subjects to *The Graphic*, 1876 and exhibited in the same year.

**MARTEN, John II**  fl.1808-1834
Topographical artist and son of John Marten of Canterbury, the landscape painter. He contributed drawings to Britton's *Beauties of England and Wales*, 1808 and exhibited at the RA and NWS, 1822-34.
Colls: V & AM.

**MARTENS, Henry**  fl.1828-1854
Battle painter in oil and watercolour. He worked in London and improved drawings by serving officers for engravings and published his own work.
Illus: *Yeomanry Costumes [1844-47, AT 369]; Costumes of the Indian Army [1846]; Costumes of the British Army in 1855 [1858, both for Ackerman].*
Exhib: BI; RBA.
Colls: Witt Photo.

**MARTIN, Charles**
Watercolourist and caricaturist. He was the son of John Martin, (q.v.) but according to Spielmann was too indolent to succeed as a painter. He contributed illustrations to *Punch*, in 1853.

**MARTIN, John**  1789-1854
Historical and biblical painter and illustrator. He was born at Eastlands End, Haydon Bridge, near Hexham on 19 July 1789 and was apprenticed to a coach painter in Newcastle before running away and studying with an Italian artist, Boniface Musso. He reached London in 1806 and began to exhibit regularly, winning a prize at the BI in 1816 and a premium of 200 guineas for his 'Belshazzar's Feast' in 1821. Martin achieved great popular acclaim from this period onwards for his huge canvases of classical or biblical subjects, most of them featuring dramatic effects of earthquake, destruction and flight. S.C. Hall, the sober editor of *The Art Journal* considered that Martin 'possessed the genius that to madness nearly is allied', two of the artist's brothers were deranged. Martin's imagery was drawn partly from the mystical and partly from the industrial, while being an incurable romantic he was also a child of the Industrial Revolution and his vast palaces, gorges and subterranean caverns have a quality of fact and experimental engineering about them. His work was exhibited abroad and he was made a member of the Belgian Academy and St Luke's Academy, Rome. Although much of his work was prepared in small scale brown and black ink and wash sketches for album books, a great deal was for straight mezzotint and not book form at all. Martin's most lasting achievements were probably the *Last Judgement* series, on which he was still working, when he died in the Isle of Man on 17 February 1854.

Illus: *Characters of Trees [1817]; Imposing Edifice in the Indian Style [1817]; Paradise Lost [1823-27]; Illustrations of The Bible [1831-35]; The Poetical Works of John Milton [1836]; The Wonders of Geology [1838]; The Wars of Jehovah [1844]; The Imperial Family Bible [1844]; The Holy Bible [1861-65]; Art and Song [1867].*
Contrib: *The Amulet; Forget-Me-Not; Friendship's Offering; The Gem; The Keepsake; The Literary Souvenir [1826-37]; The Wonders of Geology [G. Mantell, 1838, (frontis.)]; The Book of the Great Sea Dragons [Thomas Hawkins, 1840 (frontis.)]; The Traveller [1840, Art Union].*
Exhib: BI; RA; RBA.
Colls: Glasgow; Liverpool; Manchester; Newcastle; Nottingham; V & AM.
Bibl: W. Martin, *A Short Outline of the Philosopher's Life. . . . and an Account of Four Brothers and a Sister*, 1833; W. Feaver, *The Art of JM*, 1975.

See illustrations (pp.40, 41).

**MARTIN, Jonathan 'Mad'**                                1782-1838
Artist and fanatic. He was born at Hexham in 1782, the brother of
John Martin (q.v.). He was unbalanced and was responsible for setting
York Minster on fire in 1829, for which offence he was confined in St
Luke's Hospital, London as insane. He was responsible for producing
numerous strange caricature drawings.

**MASON, Abraham John**                                        1794-
Illustrator and wood engraver. He was born in London on 4 April
1794 and became a pupil of Robert Branston. He engraved the plates
for George Cruikshank's *Tales of Humour*, 1824, exhibited at the
RBA, in 1829 and emigrated to New York the same year. He became
a member of the National Academy in the United States.
Contrib: *ILN [1851]*.

**MASON, Ernold E.**                                    fl.1883-1902
Figure painter working in London. He contributed to *The Illustrated
London News* in 1889, a series of comic sketches. Exhibited at the
RA in 1883 and was living at Tilford, Surrey in 1902.

**MASON, Frank Henry**                                     1876-1965
Marine painter, etcher, illustrator and poster designer. He was born at
Seaton Carew, County Durham in 1876 and was educated at private
schools and on H.M.S. Conway. Worked at sea and later became an
engineer in Leeds and Hartlepool and was Lietenant RNVR, 1914-18.
He became RBA in 1904 and RI in 1929.
Illus: *The Book of British Ships*.
Contrib: *The Graphic [1910]*.
Exhib: B; G; L; M; RA; RBA; RHA; RI.

**MASON, Fred**                                         fl.1893-1897
Black and white artist and illustrator. He belonged to the Birmingham
School and illustrated a number of books in the 1890s, leaning heavily
on the Morris style.

*PHILIP WILLIAM MAY RI 1864-1903. 'Fair Women at the Grafton Galleries.
Pen and ink. Signed and dated 1894.*                    The Garrick Club

Illus: *The Story of Alexander, retold by Robert Steele [1894]; Huon of
Bordeaux, retold by Robert Steele [1895]; Renaud of Montaubon, retold by
Robert Steele [1897]*.
Contrib: *A Book of Pictured Carols [Birmingham School, 1893]*.
Bibl: R.E.D. Sketchley, *Eng, Bk. Illus.*, 1903, p.12, 128.

**MASON, George Finch**                                    1850-1915
Sporting painter and illustrator, caricaturist. He was the son of an
Eton master and attended the school from 1860-64, painting a set of
caricatures of Eton life, entitled 'Eton in The Sixties'. He died in July,
1915.
Publ: *The Run of the Season [1902]; Sporting Nonsense Rhymes [1906]*.
Contrib: *Punch [1881-83]*.
Exhib: London, 1874-76.
Colls: V & AM.

**MASON, W.G.**
Contributor to *The Illustrated London News*, 1850.

**MASTERS**
Illustrator, contributing to *London*, edited by Charles Knight, 1841.

**MASTERSON, H.I.**
Contributor of figure subjects to *Fun*, 1900.

**MATANIA, Professor Eduardo**                                1847-
Painter and illustrator. The father of F. Matania (q.v.), he was born in
Naples on 30 August 1847 and was an occasional contributor to *The
Sphere*.

**MATANIA, Fortunino RI**                                  1881-1963
Historical and battle painter. He was born in Naples in 1881, the son
of Professor Eduardo Matania (q.v.) and was trained in his father's
studio, illustrating his first book at fourteen. He worked in Milan as
Special Artist for *Illustrazione Italiana*, followed by work in Paris for
*L'Illustration Française* and in London for *The Graphic*. He returned
to Italy at the age of twenty-two in 1903 to do military service with
the Bersaglieri and then settled in London where he joined the staff of
*The Sphere*, becoming Special Artist in 1914 and seeing action on all
fronts. He was elected RI in 1917. Matania's style of drawing was
heroic rather than realist and his work has gone completely out of
fashion. The greatest attention paid to the shape of a bridle or the cut
of a uniform is useless when the picture itself is lifeless.
Contrib: *Illustrazione Italiana [1895-1902]; The Graphic [1902-05]; The
Sphere [1904-26]; Britannia and Eve [1929-30]*.
Exhib: L; RA; RI.
Bibl: Percy V. Bradshaw, *FM and His Work*, The Art of The Illustrator,
1916-17.

**MATANIA, Ugo 'M. Ugo'**                                      1888-
Figure painter. He was born at Naples 1 December 1888 and was the
nephew of Professor Eduardo Matania (q.v.) and cousin of F. Matania
(q.v.). He trained with his uncle and contributed drawings to *The
Sphere*.
Exhib: L; RA, 1909-18.

**MATHES, Louis**
Decorator of books. Contributing ornamental headpieces to *The
English Illustrated Magazine*, 1883.

**MATHEWS, Minnie**                                      fl.1886-1896
Flower and landscape painter. She drew the title and cover for *Pansies*
by May Probyn, 1895-96.
Exhib: RA, 1886-87.

**MATTHEWS, Winifred**                                         -1896
Painter and illustrator. She specialised in drawing children and some
of her work was published by Cassell & Co.
Exhib: NEA, 1894.
Bibl: Prof. Fred Brown, 'WM' *The Quarto*, 1896, pp.9-14, illus.

**MATTHISON, William**                                    fl.1885-1923

Landscape and coastal painter. He was living in Banbury, 1885 to 1902, and in Oxford, from 1905. He illustrated *Cambridge* by M.A.R. Tuker 1905.

Exhib: B; FAS; G; L; M; RA; RBA; RI.

**MAUD, W.T.**                                            1865-1903

Portrait painter and war artist for *The Graphic*. He was born in 1865 and became a pupil of the RA Schools, winning the Landseer Scholarship in 1893. He was appointed to *The Daily Graphic* the same year and succeeded A.S. Hartick on *The Graphic*, 1895. His campaigns as Special Artist for the magazine were considerable. He rode through Armenia from the Mediterranean to the Black Sea, 1895, was with the insurgents in Cuba, 1896, with the Greek Army in Thessaly, 1897; the Soudan, 1897, the North-West Frontier, 1897-98; he was at the Siege of Ladysmith and volunteered as A.D.C. to Sir Ian Hamilton, but was invalided home with enteric fever. He died during the Somali War on 12 May 1903. The Graphic obituary on 16 May 1903 referred to him as 'A Vigorous, capable artist, he had not only an eye for a good subject but the ability to transfer that sketch rapidly to his notebook.'

Illus: *Facey Romford's Hounds, Hawbuck Grange [R.S. Surtees]; Wagner's Heroines [Miss C. Maud, 1896].*
Contrib: *Punch.*
Exhib: RA; ROI.

**MAUND, Miss S.**                                        fl.1840-1873

Flower painter and illustrator. She illustrated *Flowering Plants*, 1873, and contributed to *The Botanist*, c.1840.

**MAXWELL, Donald**                                       1877-1936

Painter, illustrator and writer. He was born in London in 1877 and after being educated at Manor House School, Clapham, studied art at South Kensington, 1896, Slade School, 1897, and at Clapham Art School. From about 1910, Maxwell was Naval Artist to *The Graphic*, travelling widely and being appointed official artist by the Admiralty during the First World War, 1914-18. He accompanied the Prince of Wales on his Indian Tour and made numerous illustrations for travel books. He was working at Rochester, 1914-25, and afterwards at Harrietsham, Kent, where he died on 25 July 1936.

Illus: *The Enchanted Road; The Log of the Griffin [1905]; Adventures with a Sketchbook [1914]; The Prince of Wale's Eastern Book* etc.
Exhib: L; M; RA.
Bibl: *The Studio*, Vol.34, 1905, pp.113-117; *Modern Book Illustrators and their Work*, Studio, 1914.

**MAY, Charles**                                          1847-1932

Artist and decorator. He was the elder brother of Phil May (q.v.) and contributed to magazines as well as designing wall-papers.

Contrib: *Fun, Frolic and Fancy [1894]; Madame [1895]; The English Illustrated Magazine [1895-97]; Pearson's Magazine.*
Exhib: New Gall, 1896.

**MAY, E.M.**

Decorative designer for *The Connoisseur*, 1914.

**MAY, Philip William   'Phil' RI**                       1864-1903

Black and white artist, caricaturist and illustrator. He was born on 22 April 1864, the son of a Leeds engineer whose family had been landowners. He was educated at St George's School, Leeds, and became assistant scene painter at the Grand Theatre there, gaining a reputation for caricatures of members of the company. He left for London in about 1883 and joined *Society* and *St Stephen's Review* as artist, before leaving for Australia for the years 1885 to 1888. There he worked for *The Sydney Bulletin* and on returning to Europe studied art in Paris for a time. He made a major success of the highly popular *Parson and Painter*, series of drawings, published in 1891 and continued it by issuing *Annuals* from 1892 to 1904. He was on *The Graphic* staff until 1903 and joined *Punch* in 1895 making an instant mark with the readership that had enjoyed the drawings of the recently deceased, Charles Keene (q.v.). He lived a raffish bohemian life, squandered his money and died of cirrhosis of the liver and tuberculosis at the age of thirty-nine, on 5 August 1903.

May was the most important black and white artist to emerge in the 1890s in the British tradition. In many ways he was the reverse of the Beardsley coin, the discovery of line which was easy to print and which was used with great economy. His *dramatis personae* were the same as Keene's, urchins, costers, cabbies and drunks, but he reduced the fine pen of the latter to a simplified language of strokes. His drawings are always lively but vary a great deal in execution, some include self-portraits and some are tinted with watercolour. He was elected RI in 1897 and his remaining drawings were exhibited at a memorial show in the Leicester Galleries in 1903.

Illus: *The Parson and the Painter, their Wanderings and Excursions among Men and Women [Rev. Joseph Slapkins (Alfred Allison) and illus. by Charlie Summers (Phil May), 1891]; Phil Mays Winter and Summer Annuals [1892-1904]; The Comet Coach [H.H. Pearse, 1894]; Fun, Frolic and Fancy [1894]; Guttersnipes, Fifty Original Sketches [1896]; Zig-Zag Guide [F.C. Burnand, 1897]; Songs and Their Singers [1902]; East London [Walter Besant, 1902]; Littledom Castle [Mrs. H.M. Spielmann, 1903].*
Contrib: *The Yorkshire Gossip; The Busy Bee [Leeds, 1878]; St Stephen's Review [1883-85 and 1890-91]; The Penny Illustrated Paper [1883]; The Pictorial World [1883]; Society [1885]; The Sydney Bulletin [1886-94]; Puck and Ariel [1889]; The Daily Graphic [1890-96]; The Graphic [1891-92]; Black & White [1891]; Pick-Me-Up [1891-93]; ILN [1892-97, with advertisements]; The Sketch [1893-1903]; The Pall Mall Budget [1893-94]; The English Illustrated Magazine [1893-94]; Punch [1893-1903]; Daily Chronicle [1895]; The Unicorn [1895]; Eureka; The Savoy [1896]; The Mascot [1897]; The Century Magazine [1900]; The Tatler [1901]; The Jewish Chronicle [1903].*
Exhib: FAS; G; RA.
Colls: BM; Bradford; Glasgow; Leeds; V & AM.
Bibl: J. Thorpe, *PM*, 1932; *The Studio*, Vol.29, 1903, pp.280-286 'Life and Genius of Late PM'; *The Graphic*, Dec. 19, 1903, pp.840-841.

See illustrations (below and p.387).

*PHILIP WILLIAM MAY RI 1864-1903. The cover for the Christmas Number of The Graphic, 1893.*

**MAY, Captain Walter William** **RI** **1831-1896**

Marine artist and illustrator. He served in the Royal Navy from 1850 to 1870, retiring with the rank of Captain. He did rather accurate and traditional work in the style of Clarkson Stanfield (q.v.) and illustrated many books. He was elected ANWS in 1871 and NWS in 1874 and died in 1896.

Publ: *Marine Painting [1888]*.
Illus: *Fourteen Sketches Made During the Voyage Up Wellington Channel [1855, AT 646]; Quedah [Osborn, 1857, AT 526]; Will Weatherhelm [V..H.G. Kingston, 1879]; Sea Fishing [J. Bickerdyke, 1895]; In The Queen's Navee [C.N. Robinson and J. Leyland, 1902]*.
Contrib: *The Book of South Wales [Mr and Mrs S.C. Hall, 1861]; ILN [1875 Discovery expedition]; The Graphic [1869-75]*.
Exhib: BI; L; M; NWS; RA; RBA; RI; ROI.
Colls: Greenwich.

**MAYBANK, Thomas** **fl.1898-1925**

Fairy illustrator and genre painter. He practised in Beckenham, Croydon and Esher, contributing a number of startling fairy designs to *Punch* between 1902 and 1904. These include 'A Bank Holiday in Goblin Land', 'Coronation of Titania' and 'New Years Eve', all taking their inspiration from Doyle's work, pages of meticulous little figures drawn with pen and ink.

Contrib: *Punch [1902-09]; Pick-Me-Up [1899]*.
Exhib: RA; RBA; RHA; ROI.
Colls: V & AM.

**MAYE, H.**

Contributed illustrations to Wyatt's *Industrial Arts of the 19th Century*.

Colls: V & AM.

**MAYER, Henry** **1868-**

Caricaturist and illustrator. He was born at Worms in Germany in 1868 and worked in New York.

Contrib: *Illustrated Bits; Punch [1906]*.

**MAYER, Luigi** **fl.1776-1804**

Watercolourist and draughtsman. He was of Italian origin and worked as view painter to Sir Robert Ainslie, British ambassador at Constantinople, 1776 to 1792. He was later employed in making watercolours for aquatints, some of which were from sketches by the Countess of Harrington. Mayer was the most accurate delineator of the Near East before David Roberts (q.v.), most of the finished watercolours are identified by inscriptions in classical lettering running along the bottom; it is believed that he was assisted in some of them by his wife Clara.

Illus: *Lyric Airs [Edward Jones, 1804, AL 417 (etched by Rowlandson)]*.
Colls: Searight Coll.

**MAYSON, S.** **fl.1850-1856**

Illustrator. An oil over pencil on millboard, presumably for a book is in the Ashmolean Collection.

**MEADOWS, Joseph Kenny** **1790-1874**

Illustrator and caricaturist. He was born at Cardigan on 1 November 1790, the son of a retired naval officer. He was making a reputation in London by the 1830s and was one of the first illustrators to recommend wood engraving to publishers. In 1832, he collaborated with Isaac and Robert Cruikshank in *The Devil in London*, and in 1840 illustrated *Portraits of the English*, published by Robert Tyas, which achieved some success. In 1843, the same publisher issued his *Shakespeare*, which was specially well received in Germany; Meadows worked for *The Illustrated London News*, among his best work being designs for its Christmas numbers. He also appears in the first seven volumes of Punch, before being superceded by the stronger draughtsmanship of Leech and Doyle.

Meadows was an unoriginal but competent hand whose designs suffered most in mechanical figures with puffy faces and straight arms. He was a kindly but temperamental artist and this shows clearly in his uneven work. He was the brother-in-law of Archibald S.

Henning (q.v.). He died in London in August 1874.

Illus: *Costume of Shakespeare's Historical Tragedy of King John [1823]; Shakespeare's Works [1839-42]; Autobiography of Jack Ketch [1835]; Lalla Rookh [Moore, 1842]; Palfrey, A Love Story of Old Times [Leigh Hunt, 1842]; Whist, Its History and Practice; Backgammon, Its History and Practice; Leila; Calderon [E. Lytoon Bulwer, 1847]; The Family Joe Miller [1848]; Sketches From Life [Laman Blanchard, 1849]; Metrical Poems and Tales [Samuel Lover, 1849]; The Magic of Kindness [The Brothers Mayhew]; Midsummer Eve [Mrs S.C. Hall]*.
Contrib: *Bell's Life in London; London [Charles Knight, 1841]; Punch [1841]; Book of British Ballads [S.C. Hall, 1842-44]; The Illuminated Magazine [1843-45]; The Pictorial Times [1843-47]; The Illustrated Musical Annual [F.W.N. Bailey]; The Man in the Moon; Cassell's Illustrated Family Paper [1853]; The Book of Celebrated Poems; The Illustrated London Magazine [1854-55]; The Illustrated Times [1855-59]; The Welcome Guest [1860]*.
Exhib: RA; RBA, 1830-38.
Colls: V & AM; Witt Photo.
Bibl: G. Everitt, *English Caricaturists*, 1893, pp.355-363; M.H. Spielmann, *The History of Punch*, 1895, pp.446-449; The Dalziel Brothers, *A Record of Work, 1840-1890*, 1901, pp.38-41.

MARIANA.

"Mariana in the moated grange."—*Measure for Measure.*

*SIR JOHN EVERETT MILLAIS PRA 1829-1896. 'Mariana.' Illustration for Moxon's Tennyson, 1857. Wood engraving.*

**MEASOR, W.** **fl.1837-1870**

Painter of scriptural and marine subjects, working at Exeter. He exhibited at the BI, RA and RBA between 1837 and 1864 and contributed to *The Illustrated London News*, 1848, and *The Graphic*, 1870.

*SIR JOHN EVERETT MILLAIS PRA 1829-1896. 'A Fireside Story.' Illustration to* The Music Master *by William Allingham, 1855. Wood engraving.*

**MEIN, W. Gordon 'Will Mein'**                    fl.1886-1925

Figure painter and illustrator. He was working in Edinburgh, 1894, and afterwards in London. Specialised in boys' stories.

Illus: *Hidden Witchery [Nigel Tourneur, 1898]; My Two Edinburghs [S.R. Crockett, 1913].*
Contrib: *The Dome [1899-1900].*

**MELLOR, Sir John Paget, Bt. 'Quiz' KCB**         1862-1929

Amateur artist and caricaturist. He was called to the Bar at the Inner Temple, 1886, and served as a barrister and assistant solicitor to the Treasury, 1894-1909, and as solicitor, 1909-23. He was created CB in 1905 and KCB, 1911, and died on 4 February 1929. Mellor's cartoons are usually *portraits chargés* and signed 'Quiz'.

Contrib: *Punch [1886-88]; Vanity Fair [1890, 1893, 1898].*
Bibl: M.H. Spielmann, *The History of Punch*, 1895, pp.558-559.

**MELVILLE, Arthur ARWS, HRSA**                    1858-1904

Painter and watercolourist. He was born at the Loanhead of Guthrie, East Linton, Scotland on 10 April 1858 and was apprenticed to a grocer. He studied at the RSA and with J. Campbell Noble, before working his way round France and studying in Paris. He returned to Edinburgh, but left again in 1881 to tour in Egypt, Persia, Turkey and Asia, riding from Baghdad to the Black Sea. He made a special study of oriental subjects, became a friend of Frank Brangwyn (q.v.) and visited Spain with him in 1892. He died in London 29 August 1904.

Contrib: *The Graphic [1882].*
Exhib: B; BM; G; GG; L; M; New Gall; P; RA; RI; RSA; RWS.
Colls: Edinburgh; Glasgow; Liverpool; V & AM.

**MELVILLE, Harden Sidney**                        fl.1837-1882

Painter of landscapes, animals and sport. He worked in London for most of his life, but may have made tours abroad, possibly to Australia.

Illus: *Sketches in Australia [1849, AT 581]; The War Tiger [W. Dalton, 1859]; Wild Sports of the World [J. Greenwood, 1862]; Curiosities of Savage Life [J. Greenwood, 1864]; The Adventures of a Griffin [1867].*
Contrib: *London [Charles Knight, 1841]; ILN [1848 and 1865-66]; The Illustrated Times [1865]; The Welcome Guest [1860].*
Exhib: B; BI; RA; RBA.
Colls: BM.

*Opposite: SIR JOHN EVERETT MILLAIS PRA 1829-1896. 'Married For Money.' Pen and black and brown ink, brown wash. Signed. 8¼ins. x 6ins. (21cm x 15.2cm).*

**MENPES, Mortimer FRGS**                          1860-1938

Painter, etcher, raconteur and rifle shot. He was born in Australia in 1860 and educated at a grammar school in Port Adelaide, but came to England in the early 1880s and was working with J.M. Whistler as a studio assistant by 1884. He became one of those disciples of the American master who scouted out streets and corners and alleys for him to paint and working alongside him, absorbed much of his style in their etchings and oil paintings. Menpes travelled extensively and was particularly influenced by the arts of Japan, but also by those of India, Mexico, Spain, Morocco and Venice. He was instrumental in holding an exhibition of coloured etchings, an attempt to revive this art. He was Special Artist for *Black & White* in South Africa, 1900. He was elected RE, 1881, RBA, 1885, NEA, 1886 and RI, 1897, and died at Pangbourne, Berks, 1 April 1938.

Illus: *War Impressions [1901]; Japan [1901]; World Pictures [1902]; World's Children [1903]; The Durbar [1903]; Venice [1904]; Brittany [1905]; India [1905]; Thames [1906].*
Publ: *Whistler as I Knew Him [1904].*
Exhib: FAS, 1901, 1902, 1908, 1911; G; GG; L; M; New Gall; RA; RE; RI; ROI.
Colls: V & AM.
Bibl: *The Studio*, Winter No., 1900-01, p.61, illus.

**MERRITT, F.R.**

Contributor to *The Graphic*, 1884.

**MERRY, Tom**                                      1852-1902

Caricaturist and cartoonist. Merry was for many years the chief cartoonist of *St Stephen's Review*, being most prolific in the period 1885-90. He became cartoonist of *Puck and Ariel* in that year. His style is rather wooden, although he has a good eye for portraiture and making his political points on a large scale. All his work appeared as two-pager coloured lithographs, often wittily taken from famous paintings of the day by Seymour Lucas, Stanley Berkeley, or parodies of Hogarth. He died in 1902.

**METCALFE, Gerald Fenwick**                       fl.1894-1929

Portrait painter, miniaturist, illustrator and modeller. He was born at Landour, India and studied art at South Kensington, St John's Wood School and the RA Schools. He was working in Chelsea, 1902-03 and at Albury, Surrey, 1914-25.

Illus: *The Wrecker [R.L. Stevenson].*
Contrib: *Punch [1906].*
Bibl: *Modern Book Illustrators and Their Work*, Studio, 1914.

388

John Everett Millais

THE CRAWLEY FAMILY.

*SIR JOHN EVERETT MILLAIS PRA 1829-1896. 'The Crawley Family.'*
*Illustration to* Framley Parsonage *by Anthony Trollope,* The Cornhill Magazine,
*August 1860. Wood engraving.*

## METEYARD, Sidney Harold                1868-1947
Artist, stained-glass designer and illustrator. He was born in
Stourbridge in 1868 and is associated with the Birmingham School,
where he studied under E.R. Taylor. His paintings and drawings are
strongly influenced by Burne-Jones; he was elected a member of the
R.S.B.A., 1908.

Illus: *The Golden Legend [H.W. Longfellow, 1910].*
Contrib: *The Quest [1894-96]; The Yellow Book [1896].*
Exhib: B; L; New Gall; RA.

## METEYARD, Tom B.                1865-
Painter and illustrator. He was born at Rock Island, U.S.A. on 12
November 1865 and worked as an artist at Fernhurst, Sussex.

Illus: *Songs From Vagabondia [Bliss Carmen and Richard Hovey, 1895-96].*
Exhib: FAS, 1922.

## METTAIS, Charles-Joseph                fl.1846-1857
French portrait painter and illustrator. He exhibited at the Salon from
1846-48 and contributed to *Cassell's Illustrated Family Paper,* 1857.

## MICHAEL, A.C.                fl.1903-1916
Painter and etcher, working in Bedford Park, London. He was artist
for *The Morning Star* and illustrated books.

Illus: *The Ghost King [H. Rider Haggard, 1908]; King Solomon's Mines [H.
Rider Haggard, 1912].*

Contrib: *The Graphic [1903]; The Illustrated London News [1915-16].*
Exhib: RA; RI.
Bibl: M.A.C. *An Artist in Spain,* 1914.

## MICHAEL, J.B.
Architectural illustrator on *The Illustrated London News,* 1873.

## MICHAEL, L.H.                fl.1845-1874
Architectural illustrator. He contributed drawings to Wyatt's
*Industrial Arts of the Nineteenth Century, The Welcome Guest,* 1860
and *The Illustrated London News,* 1865-66.

Exhib: RA; RBA.
Colls: V & AM.

## MILES, Marie                fl.1897-1914
Black and white artist, specialising in children.

Contrib: *The Parade [1897]; Cassell's Family Magazine [1898]; The Royal
Magazine; Punch [1914].*

## MILLAIS, Sir John Everett, Bt.  PRA                1829-1896
Painter, illustrator and President of the Royal Academy. He was born
in Southampton in 1829 and was brought up in Jersey and Brittany,
coming to London in 1838 to study at Henry Sass's Academy and at
the RA Schools, 1840. With Holman Hunt (q.v.) and D.G. Rossetti
(q.v.) founded the Pre-Raphaelite Brotherhood, 1848. From the first,
Millais was a masterly draughtsman and excelled in line drawings,
preparing some for *The Germ,* the magazine of the Pre-Raphaelites in
1850. His most powerful black and white work was done in the period
1851-55 when he was concerned with modern moral subjects, but

LAST WORDS.

*SIR JOHN EVERETT MILLAIS PRA 1829-1896. 'Last Words.' Illustration to a
poem in* The Cornhill Magazine, *November 1860. Wood engraving.*

390

these remained unpublished. His most influential work was published in Moxon's edition of *Tennyson*, 1857, where he showed two styles of drawing developing, a highly finished manner for the romantic subjects and a more sketchy modern style for the contemporary illustration. The latter is best seen in his fine series of drawings prepared for the novels of Anthony Trollope, which appeared in *The Cornhill Magazine*, 1860. Millais' brilliant groups grasp perfectly the underlining tensions and complexities of Victorian society and are arguably the best of their kind done for a novelist in the entire 19th century.

Millais ceased to do illustration after the 1860s, although he undertook some for his son, and his falling away in expression dates from the same time. Marriage with Effie Ruskin in 1855 was followed by election as RA in 1863 and increasing popularity as a portrait painter of the great. He was created a baronet in 1885 and was elected PRA in 1896, serving only six months before dying of cancer of the throat on August 13 that year.

The drawings prepared by Millais for his famous book illustrations were mostly lost in the cutting, but his Pre-Raphaelite sketches and finished drawings sometimes emerge on the market. A group 'Married For Money', 'Married For Love' and 'Married For Rank' appeared in the London galleries in 1972.

Illus: *Framley Parsonage [Anthony Trollope, 1860-62]; Orley Farm [Anthony Trollope, 1861-62]; Small House at Allington [Anthony Trollope, 1862]; Phineas Finn [Anthony Trollope, 1869]; Kept in the Dark [Anthony Trollope, 1882].*
Contrib: *The Germ [No. 5, 1850 (not used)]; Mr. Wray's Cashbox . . . A Christmas Sketch [Wilkie Collins, 1852]; The Music Master [W. Allingham, 1855]; Poems [by Tom Hood, 1858]; Moxon's Tennyson [1857]; The Poets of the Nineteenth Century [Rev. R.A. Willmott, 1857]; Lays of the Holy Land [1858]; The Home Affections [Charles Mackay, 1858]; Once a Week [1859-63 and 1868]; The Cornhill Magazine [1860-63]; Good Words [1861-64, 1878, 1882]; London Society [1862-64]; The Illustrated London News [1862];*

SIR JOHN EVERETT MILLAIS PRA 1829-1896. 'The Prodigal Son. *Illustration for* The Parables of Our Lord, *1863. Wood engraving by the Brothers Dalziel.*

*Cornhill Gallery [1864]; The Churchman's Family Magazine [1863]; Papers For Thoughtful Girls [Sarah Tytler, 1862]; Puck on Pegasus [Pennell, 1862]; Parables of Our Lord [1863]; Punch [1863 and 1865]; Lilliput Levee [1864]; Little Songs For Me To Sing Touches of Nature By Eminent Artists [1866]; St. Pauls [1867]; Gems of Poetry [Mackay, 1867]; Leslie's Musical Annual [1870]; Passages From Modern English Poets [1876]; The Memoirs of Barry Lyndon Esq. [W.M. Thackeray (Complete Works, Vol. XIX) [1879]; Game Birds and Shooting Sketches [J.G. Millais, 1892 (frontis)].*
Colls: Ashmolean; BM; Bedford; Glasgow; Manchester; V & AM.
Exhib: BI; GG; G; L; M; New Gall; RA; RHA; RSA.
Bibl: J.G. Millais, *Life and Letters of JEM*, 1899. M. Lutyens, *M and the Ruskins*, 1967. M. Bennett, *M*, RA Exhibition Cat., Jan-April, 1967.
See illustrations (above, left and pp.387, 388, 389, 390).

## MILLAIS, John Guille FZS        1865-1931

Animal painter and illustrator. He was born on 24 March 1865, the fourth and youngest son of Sir John E. Millais (q.v.). He was educated at Marlborough and Trinity College, Cambridge and after serving with the Somerset Light Infantry, 1883-86, travelled in Africa, Canada, America and the Artic as a big game hunter. Millais published numerous books on these subjects, many illustrated from his own drawings. He became FZS and died on 24 March 1931.

Illus: *A Fauna of Sutherland [1887]; A Fauna of the Outer Hebrides [1888]; A Fauna of the Orkney Islands [1891]; Game Birds and Shooting Sketches [1892]; A Breath From the Veldt [1895]; British Deer and Their Horns [1897]; The Wild Fowler in Scotland [1901]; Surface-Feeding Ducks [1902]; The Mammals of Great Britain [1904-06]; Newfoundland [1907]; British Game Birds [1909]; British Diving Ducks [1913]; Deer and Deer Stalking [1913]; European Big Game [1914]; American Big Game [1915]; Rhododendrons and Their Hybrids [1917]; Wanderings and Memories [1919]; Far Away up the Nile [1924]; Magnolias [1927].*
Contrib: *The Graphic [1886]; Pearson's Magazine.*
Exhib: FAS, 1901, 1919, 1923.
Bibl: R.E.D. Sketchley, *Eng. Bk. Illus.* 1903, pp.54, 135.

SIR JOHN EVERETT MILLAIS PRA 1829-1896. 'The Unjust Judge.' *Illustration for* The Parables of Our Lord, *1863. Wood engraving by the Brothers Dalziel.*

**MILLAIS, William Henry**                                   **1828-1899**

Painter, watercolourist and illustrator. He was the elder brother of Sir John E. Millais (q.v.) and was born in 1828. He worked at Farnham and specialised in landscapes.

Publ: *The Princess of Parmesan [1897]*.
Contrib: *Parables From Nature [Mrs. Gatty, 1861, 1867]; Legends and Lyrics [A.A. Proctor, 1865]*.
Exhib: FAS; M; RA; RI.
Colls: Ashmolean; BM; V & AM.

**MILLAR, Harold R.**                                        **fl.1891-1935**

Painter and illustrator. He was born at Dumfries and intended to study engineering, but abandoned this for art and became a student of the Birmingham School. His earliest work was for Birmingham magazines such as *Scraps* and *Comus*, and he derived a very strong and free ink style based on the work of Vierge and Gigoux. A collector of ancient weapons and eastern works of art, Millar became known for his authenticity in illustrating eastern stories in the 1900s.

Illus: *The Golden Fairy Book [George Sand, 1894]; The Humour of Spain [1894]; Fairy Tales From Far and Near [1895]; The Adventures of Haji Baba [Morier, 1895]; The Silver Fairy Book [Bernhardt, 1895]; Headlong Hall, Nightmare Abbey [Peacock, 1896]; The Phantom Ship [Marryat, 1896]; The Diamond Fairy Book [Bellerby, 1897]; Untold Tales of the Past [B. Harraden, 1897]; Frank Mildmay [Marryat, 1897]; Snarleyow [1897]; Phroso [Anthony Hope [1897]; Eothen [A.W. Kinglake, 1898]; The Book of Dragons [E. Nesbitt, 1900]; Nine Unlikely Tales For Children [E. Nesbitt, 1901]; The Story of the Bold Pecopin [Hugo, 1902]; Queen Mab's Realm [1902]; The Phoenix and the Carpet [E. Nesbitt, 1904]; The New World Fairy Book [1904]; Oswald Bastable and Others [E. Nesbitt, 1905]; Kingdom Curious [Myra Hamilton, 1905]; Puck of Pook's Hill [Rudyard Kipling, 1906]; The Enchanted Castle [E. Nesbitt, 1917]; The Magic City [1910]; The Wonderful Garden [E. Nesbitt, 1911]; Wet Magic [E. Nesbitt, 1913]; The Dreamland Express [1927]; Hakluyt's Voyages [1929]*.
Contrib: *Judy [1890]; The Girl's Own Paper [1890-1900]; Fun [1891-92]; The Strand Magazine [1891, 1905]; The English Illustrated Magazine [1891-92]; Chums [1892]; Good Words [1893]; Good Cheer [1894]; The Sketch [1898]; Black & White [1899]; The Quiver [1900]; Punch [1906-09]; The Ludgate Monthly; Pick-Me-Up; Cassell's Family Magazine; The Idler; The Minister; Eureka*.
Exhib: RA.
Colls: V & AM.
Bibl: *The Idler,* Vol. 8, pp.228-236; R.E.D. Sketchley, *Eng. Bk. Illus.,* 1903, pp.109, 112, 167; Brigid Peppin, *Fantasy Book Illustration,* 1975, pp.188-189, illus.
See illustration (right).

**MILLER, F.**

Book decorator. Contributed tail-pieces to *The English Illustrated Magazine* 1895.

**MILLER, J.H.**                                             **fl.1803-1829**

Landscape painter and topographer. He contributed to Britton's *Beauties of England and Wales,* 1805 and exhibited at the RA, RBA and OWS from 1803 to 1829.

**MILLER, William Edwards**                                  **fl.1873-1929**

Portrait painter. Worked in London and contributed one cartoon to *Vanity Fair,* 1896.

Exhib: B; G; L; New Gall; RA; RSA.

**MILLER, William Frederick**                                **1834-1918**

Architectural draughtsman. He undertook some illustrative work for Messrs. T. Nelson & Sons, 1853-54.

Coll: V & AM.

**MILLS, A. Wallis**                                         **1878-1940**

Black and white artist. He was born in 1878, the son of the rector of Long Bennington, Lincolnshire, and trained at the South Kensington Schools, becoming a friend of F.H. Townsend, G.L. Stampa and G.K. Haseldon (qq.v.). He was working for illustrated magazines from about 1898, specialising in drawings of old country characters, many of them modelled on those he had known in Lincolnshire or who lived near him at Little Gransden, Hunts., in the 1920s. He served in the Royal Artillery in the First World War and made official war sketches, he died at his club in St. James's in April 1940.

Illus: *Novels of Jame Austen [n.d.]*

HAROLD R. MILLAR *fl.1891-1935.* 'The Amulet.' Drawing for illustration in The Strand Magazine, *Vol. 21, 1905. Pen. Signed and dated 1905. 7³⁄₄ins. x 6⁷⁄₈ins. (19.7cm x 17.4cm).*                Victoria and Albert Museum

Contrib: *Judy [1898]; The Strand Magazine [1906]; Punch [1907-14]; The Humourist; The Ludgate Monthly; The Royal Magazine; The Graphic [1915]*.
Exhib: Nottingham; RA.
Bibl: R.G.G. Price, *A History of Punch,* 1957, p.205.

**MILLS, Charles A.  ARHA**                                  **-1922**

Painter and illustrator. He worked in Dublin and contributed figure drawings to *Fun,* 1901 and to *The Graphic,* 1903-05. He was elected ARHA in 1913 and died in 1922.

Exhib: RHA.

**MILLS, Walter**                                            **fl.1880-1903**

Painter and illustrator working in Dublin. He acted as *The Graphic* Special in Ireland, 1903.

Exhib: RHA.

**MINNS, B.E.**                                              **fl.1895-1913**

Illustrator. He worked at Hendon, London and contributed to magazines in the 1890s.

Contrib: *The Idler; The Minister; Pearson's Magazine; Punch [1914]*.
Exhib: G; L; RA; RI.

**MITCHELL, Hutton**                                         **fl.1892-1925**

Illustrator and the original creator in line of Billy Bunter. He is recorded as being an able but dilatory artist who was replaced after thirty-nine issues of *The Magnet* by Arthur Clarke (q.v.). He was working at Paignton, S. Devon, 1920-25.

Contrib: *Fun [1892]; Daily Graphic [1893]; The Longbow [1898]; The Gem*.
Exhib: L.
Bibl: W.O. Lofts and D.J. Adley, *The World of Frank Richards,* 1975.

**MOIRA, Gerald Edward  RWS**                                **1867-1959**

Landscape, flower and decorative painter. He was born in London in 1867 as Giraldo de Moura, the son of a Portuguese miniaturist, and anglicized his name. He was elected ARWS in 1917 and RWS in 1932,

serving as Vice President from 1953. He died at Northwood in 1959.
Illus: *Shakespeare's True Life [J. Walter, 1890]*.
Colls: BM.
Bibl: J.H. Watkins, *The Art of GEM*, 1922.

**MONCRIEFF, Robert SCOTT-**
Amateur caricaturist. His drawings of Scottish lawyers of the years 1816-20 were published as *Scottish Bar*, 1871.
Colls: Witt Photo.

**MONNIER, G.**
French artist contributing to *The Illustrated London News*, 1870.

**MONRO, A.**
Illustrator of boys' stories. He contributed to *Chums*, c.1890 in a style like that of Gordon Browne (q.v.).

**MONSELL, J.R.**
Illustrator, who drew for *Grimms Fairy Tales*, 1908 and *The Buccaneers*, 1908, published by Cassells.

**MONSON, Frederick John  5th Baron Monson  1809-1841**
Amateur artist. He illustrated *Views in the Department of The Isère and The High Alps*, 1840. Lithographs by L. Haghe from Monson's drawings.

**MONTAGU, H. Irving  fl.1873-1893**
Figure painter, illustrator and war artist. He was Special Artist for *The Illustrated London News* from 1874, when he was present during the Carlist uprising in Spain and later served in Hungary, Turkey and Russia.
Contrib: *The Sunday Magazine [1881]*.
Exhib: B; RA; RBA.
Bibl: H.I.M., *Wanderings of a War Artist*, 1889; H.I.M., 'Anecdotes of the War Path' *The Strand Magazine*, Vol. I, 1891, pp.576-585.

**MONTBARD, G.  Charles Auguste Loyes  1841-1905**
Landscape painter, illustrator and caricaturist. He was born at Montbard on 2 August 1841 and took his professional name from the town. He worked first with O'Shea on *Chronique Illustrée* and had his introduction to the English public when he illustrated scenes at Compiègne for *The Illustrated London News* in 1868. Montbard was strongly political and after taking the side of the Commune in 1871, was proscribed from France and resided in England until his death. He very soon became a regular contributor to *The Illustrated*, making a series of drawings of country houses, usually devoid of figures at which he was very weak. He also undertook some flower paintings and died in London on 5 August 1905.
Illus: *The Land of the Sphinx [GM, 1894]*.
Contrib:*ILN [1868-99]; The Graphic [1871-73]; Judy [1871]; Vanity Fair [1872]; Good Words [1880-99]; The English Illustrated Magazine [1895]; St James's Budget; The Windsor Magazine; The Pall Mall Magazine.*
Exhib: L; M; RA; RBA; RI; ROI.
Colls: V & AM.

**MONTEFIORE, Edward Brice Stanley  fl.1872-1909**
Landscape and genre painter, working in London and Newnham, Glos., 1909.
Contrib: *Sporting & Dramatic News [1894]*.
Exhib: M; RA; ROI.

**MOODY, Fannie (Mrs. Gilbert King)  1861-**
Animal painter and illustrator. She was born in London on 10 May 1861, the daughter of T.W. Moody 1824-1886, master at the South Kensington Schools. She studied under J.T. Nettleship and became well known for her sentimental dog subjects, beloved of the Victorians. She drew for advertisements and was still working in Battersea 1920. SWA, 1887.
Contrib: *ILN [1892-99]*.
Exhib: B; L; M; RA; RBA; RMS ROI; SWA.
Bibl: 'The Animal Sketches of Miss Fannie Moody' *The Artist*, 1899, pp.121-130.

**MOODY, John  1884-**
Painter, etcher and black and white artist. He was born 21 June 1884 and studied at the Regent St Polytechnic and then in Paris and in Italy. He became a member of the Society of Graphic Art in 1920 and worked at Hampstead and Highgate from 1914 to 1925 and then at Burpham, Sussex. Principal of Hornsey School of Art, 1927. ARE, 1921; RE, 1946; RI, 1931.
Exhib: G; L; RA; RE; RI; ROI.
Bibl: *The Studio*, Vol. 38, 1906, p.317, illus.

**MOORE, Albert Joseph  1841-1893**
Figure painter and illustrator. He was born at York in 1841, the son of the portrait painter William Moore. On his mother's widowhood in 1855, he settled in London, travelling to Scotland and to France and visiting Rome in 1862. Moore was often employed by architects and worked as a mural painter. He was a frequent exhibitor at the RA from 1857 and developed a reputation for classical Greek studies which are the forerunners of Alma Tadema (q.v.). He died in London in 1893. RWS, 1884.
Contrib: *Specimens of Medieval Architecture [W. Eden Nesfield, 1862]*.
Exhib:B; FAS; G; L; M; NEA; New Gall; RA; RI; RWS.

**MOORE, Alexander Poole  1777-1806**
Topographer. He was born about 1777 and entered the RA Schools in 1792, winning the silver medal in 1794. He was a pupil of James Lewis, the architect, and was described as 'a young man of very eccentric habits but a clever Artist'.
Contrib: Britton's *Beauties of England & Wales*, 1802.
Exhib: RA, 1793-1806.
Colls: Witt Photo.
Bibl: H.M. Colvin, *Biog. Dict. of Eng. Architects*, 1954.

**MOORE, C. Aubrey**
Illustrator of the child's book *Adventures in Noah's Ark*, 1908.

**MOORE, Henry  1776-1848**
Topographer and drawing master at Derby. He was born in 1776 and won a Society of Arts medal for his process of etching on marble.
Illus: *Excursions from Derby to Matlock, Bath and its Vicinity [1818]*.
Contrib: *Beauties of England & Wales [Britton, 1802-13]; Antiquarian and Topographical Cabinet [Britton, 1806]*.
Colls: Derby; Witt Photo.

**MOORE, Henry  RA RWS  1831-1895**
Marine painter and engraver. He was born at York on 7 March 1831, the son and pupil of the portrait painter William Moore and brother of Albert Joseph Moore (q.v.). He studied at the York School of Design and at the RA Schools, 1853, and after settling in London made a series of tours abroad to France, Switzerland and Ireland. He was principally a marine painter but did landscapes, the earlier works being influenced by the Pre-Raphaelites. He was elected ARA in 1885 and RA in 1893, RWS, 1880. He died at Margate, 22 June 1895.
Contrib: *ILN [1856]; Poems [Tom Hood]; Passages From Modern English Poets [1862, Junior Etching Club]*.
Exhib: B; BI; FAS, 1887; GG; G; L; M: New Gall; RA; RBA; RHA; ROI; RSA; RWS.
Colls: Birmingham; Tate; V & AM.

**MOORE, R.H.  1875-1890**
Animal and bird illustrator. He was a sculptor and black and white artist and worked extensively for *The Illustrated London News*, 1875-90.
Contrib: *Lady's Pictorial; Sporting & Dramatic News [1890]*.
Exhib: NWS; RBA.

**MOORE, Thomas Sturge  1870-1944**
Illustrator, wood engraver and poet. He was born on 4 March 1870 and studied wood engraving at the Lambeth School of Art under Charles Roberts. Moore had strong connections with the private presses and particularly with the Essex House Press and was a member

of the Society of Twelve. Moore's designs were not so consciously archaic as Morris's and extremely well balanced in light and shade. He was also engaged in decorations for the rhyme sheets produced by Harold Monro's Poetry Bookshop.

Publ: *The Vine dressers and Other Poems [1899]; Aphrodite Against Artemis [1901]; Absalom [1903]; Danae [1903]; The Little School [1905]; Poems Marianne [1911]; The Sicilian Idyll and Judith [1911]; The Sea is Kind [1914]; The Little School Enlarged [1917]; The Powers of the Air [1920]; Tragic Mothers [1920]; Judas [1923].*
Illus: *The Centaur, The Bacchante [de Guerin, 1899]; Some Fruits of Solitude [William Penn, 1901].*
Contrib: *The Dial [1895].*
Exhib: RSA.
Colls: Witt Photo.
Bibl: R.E.D. Sketchley, *Eng. Bk. Illus.* 1903, pp.18, 24, 129; *The Studio*, Vol. 66, 1916, p.28 and Winter, 1923-24, pp.34 and 105; *The Connoisseur*, Vol. 55, 1919, p.187; *Print Coll Quarterly*, No. 18 1921, No. 3 p.276.

### MORCHEN, Horace          fl.1880-1890
Humorous illustrator and caricaturist. He studied under Alfred Bryan (q.v.) and specialised in theatrical subjects.

Contrib: *ILN [1880-83]; Moonshine [1890]; Sporting & Dramatic News; Cassell's Saturday Journal.*

### MOREL, Charles          1861-1908
French draughtsman and illustrator. He was born in 1861 and became a pupil of Detaille. He contributed to the Graphic, 1904, and died in Paris, 27 July, 1908.

### MORELAND A.
A cartoonist of *The Morning Leader,* c.1895. A book of 160 of these designs in colour was issued at the same date entitled *Humours of History.*

### MORGAN, Frederick  ROI          1856-1927
Painter of genre and children. He was born in 1856 and married the painter, Alice Mary Havers. He worked in Aylesbury in early life and later in London and at Broadstairs, 1914-25. He became ROI in 1883.

Contrib: *The Sunday Magazine [1894].*

Exhib: B; BI; FAS; G; L; M; RA; RBA; RI; ROI.
Colls: Leeds; Liverpool; Sheffield.

### MORGAN, Matt Somerville          1836-1890
Painter of social realism, lithographer and caricaturist. He was born in London in 1836 and from the late 1850s gained a high reputation as a figure artist and decorator in the magazines. He went to Italy in 1859-61 and covered the campaigns there for both *The Illustrated London News* and *The Illustrated Times* as a Special, later travelling in Algeria. From about 1866, he became interested in social questions and drew powerful studies of reform demonstrations and the poor in London. On becoming cartoonist to *The Tomahawk,* a radical paper, in 1867, his talents for figure drawing and brilliant political images were brought together on the page. His sharp satire established for him a greater freedom than any other Victorian cartoonist and his work was marked by its individuality in being printed from tinted wood blocks. Morgan emigrated to the United States and painted panoramas of the Civil War, he died in New York in 1890.

Illus: *Miles Standish.*
Contrib: *The Illustrated Times [1859-66]; The ILN [1859-86]; London Society [1863]; The Broadway [1867-74]; The Tomahawk [1867]; Judy; Britannia [1869]; Arrow; Will o' the Wisp.*
Bibl: Chatto & Jackson, *Treatise on Wood Engraving*, 1861, p.599; Clement & Hutton, *Art of the 19th Cent*, 1893; Fielding, *Dict of American Painters*, 1926; *Victorian Studies*, Vol. XIX, No. 1, Sept. 1975.
See illustrations (below and p.157)

### MORGAN, Walter Jenks  RBA          1847-1924
Genre painter and illustrator. He was born in 1847 and studied at the Birmingham School and at South Kensington. He worked for the magazines and Messrs. Cassell's, chiefly on domestic and children's subjects. He died at Birmingham on 31 October 1924. RBA, 1884.

Illus: *Spenser For Children [1897].*
Contrib: *The Graphic [1875-76]; ILN [1877-81].*
Exhib: B; L; RA; RBA; RI.

### MORIN, Edward          1824-1882
Watercolourist, lithographer and illustrator. He was born at Le Havre on 26 March 1824 and became a pupil of Gleyre, exhibiting at the Salon from 1857. He came to London to work for the illustrated magazines and was taught wood engraving by Sir John Gilbert (q.v.)

MATT SOMERVILLE MORGAN 1836-1890. 'The Unemployed at the East End of London.' Wood engraving in The Illustrated London News, 1886.

and was described by Vizetelly as 'a spirited French artist'. Although Benezet says that he returned to Paris in 1851, his work was still appearing in English journals until 1861. He died at Sceaux on 18 August 1882.

Contrib: *Cassell's Illustrated Family Paper [1853-55]; The Illustrated Times [1855-61]; ILN [1856-57]*.
Bibl: Vizetelly, *Memoirs,*1893.

**MORRELL, G.F.**
Draughtsman, contributed scientific drawings to *The Graphic*, 1910.

**MORRIS, William**                                    1834-1896
Poet, designer and polemicist. He was born at Walthamstow in 1834 and after studying at Oxford was converted to craft design and socialism, founding manufactures for the production of textiles and tapestries, stained-glass and furniture, having a profound influence on Victorian design. Morris developed an interest in the decoration of books over many years, culminating in his illumination of some works by hand in the early 1870s. He supervised the production of *The House of Wolfings* at the Chiswick Press, 1888, and founded the renowned Kelmscott Press in 1890. During the last six years of his life, Morris concentrated most of his energies on book production, upwards of fifty books being produced at Kelmscott for which he had designed borders and initial letters. He believed that 'ornament must form as much a part of the page as the type itself' and in many of the books, the decoration based on early printed motifs, seems rather to impinge on the text than otherwise. Morris employed Sir E. Burne-Jones, Walter Crane and C.M. Gere as illustrators, the most famous production being the former's Kelmscott *Chaucer*, May 8 1896. Morris died at Hammersmith in 1896.

Colls: BM; V & AM; Walthamstow; Wightwick, Nat. Trust.
Bibl: Aymer Vallance, *WM His Art His Writings & Public Life,* 1897.
See illustration (right).

**MORRISON, Douglas**                                fl.1842-1845
Lithographer. He illustrated his own *Views of Haddon Hall*, 1842 and *Views of Saxe-Coburg and Gotha*, 1846, AT 121.

**MORROW, Albert George**                          1863-1927
Black and white and poster artist. He was born in 1863 at Comber, County Down, Ireland, the son of a decorator. He studied in Belfast and at South Kensington and began illustrating for magazines in 1884. He was the brother of George and Edwin Morrow (q.v.). He died at West Heathly, Sussex in October 1927.

Contrib: *The English Illustrated Magazine [1884]; Illustrated Bits [1890]; Good Words [1890]; Punch.*
Exhib: RA; RBA.
Colls: V & AM.

**MORROW, Edwin A.**                                fl.1903-1914
Landscape painter and illustrator. Brother of George and Albert Morrow (qq.v.).

Contrib: *Punch [1914]*.
Exhib: RA.

**MORROW, George**                                  1869-1955
Comic artist and illustrator. He was born in Befast in 1869, the brother of Albert and Edwin Morrow (qq.v.), and studied in Paris in the 1890s being greatly influenced by the work of Caran d'Ache (q.v.). He began to contribute to *Punch* in 1906 and soon bcame known for his humourous historical episodes, in which history was treated in light-hearted manner in subject and in line. He joined the staff of *Punch* in 1924 and was Art Editor from 1932-37 and continued to draw for the paper until a month before his death on 18 January 1955. *The Times* wrote of him on that occasion as 'probably the most consistently comic artist of his day'.

Illus: *Country Stories [Mary Russell Mitford, 1896]*.
Contrib: *Pick-Me-Up [1896]; The Idler; The Windsor Magazine; Punch [1906-54]*.
Exhib: RA; RBA.

**MORROW, Norman**                                  fl.1911-1916
Irish illustrator. He contributed drawings to *The Graphic*, 1911-16.

*WILLIAM MORRIS 1834-1896. Initial letters and page decoration for* Maud! A Monodrama *by Alfred, Lord Tennyson, Kelmscott Press, 1894.*

**MORTEN, Thomas**                                  1836-1866
Illustrator and occasional painter. He was born at Uxbridge in 1836 and studied at Leigh's of Newman Street from an early age, specialising in drawing on wood. He worked for most of the leading magazines of the 1860s and his finest illustrations were for *Gulliver's Travels*, 1866, where he brought to the subject a new wit and vision. In other works, Reid considered him to be rather a plagiarist, borrowing ideas from Doré, Sandys and J.D. Watson (qq.v.) among others. He died in the autumn of 1866, probably by committing suicide due to pecuniary difficulties.

Illus: *Gulliver's Travels [1866]*.
Contrib: *Good Words [1861-63]; Once a Week [1861-66]; Entertaining Things [1861-62]; The Laird's Return [1861]; London Society [1862-69]; Every Boy's Magazine [186-63]; Churchman's Family Magazine [1863-64]; Dalziel's. Arabian Nights [1863]; A Round of Days [1865]; Watts Divine and Moral Songs [1865]; Legends and Lyrics [1865]; Jingles and Jokes For little Folks [1865]; The Quiver [1865-66]; Aunt Judy's Magazine [1866]; Beeton's Annuals [1866]; Cassell's Family Paper [1866]; Idyllic Pictures [1867]; Two Centuries of Song [1867]; Young Gentlemen's Magazine [1867]; Foxe's Book of Martyres [1867]; Belgravia [1871]; Thornbury's Legendary Ballads [1876]; Cassell's History of England.*
Exhib: BI; RA.
Colls: V & AM.
Bibl: Forrest Reid, *Illustrators of the Sixties,* 1928, pp.211-216.

**MOSER, Oswald   RI**                              1874-1953
Painter and illustrator. He studied at St. John's Wood Arf School and worked in London until 1925 and afterwards at Rye. He exhibited at the Salon in 1907 and was elected RI, 1909 and ROI, 1908. He died 31 March 1953.

Illus: *John Halifax, Gentleman [Mrs. Craik, Black, 1905]*.
Exhib: G; L; RA; RI; RSA.

**MOSES, Henry**                1782-1870

Draughtsman and engraver. He was born in London in 1782 and became the foremost outline engraver of his generation, specialising in antiquities and closely associated with the Greek Revival. He was engraver to the British Museum and died at Cowley, Middlesex on 28 February, 1870.

Illus: *The Gallery of Pictures Painted by Benjamin West [1811]; The Mausoleum at Castle Howard [1812]; A Collection of Vases [1814]; Picturesque Views of Ramsgate [1817]; Select Greek and Roman Antiquities from Vases ... Gems ... [1817]; Vases From the Collection of Sir Henry Englefield [1819-20]; Modern Costume [1823]; Sketches of Shipping [1824]; The Marine Sketchbook [1825-26]; The Works of Canova [1824-28]; Selection of Ornamental Sculptures From the Museum of the Louvre [1828]; Visit of William IV to Portsmouth [1840].*
Exhib: RBA.
Colls: Witt Photo.

**MOULIN**                fl.1859-1860

French figure artist and illustrator. Vizetelly records that Moulin had access to the palaces of the Second Empire because he was related to Napoleon III's chef but in fact he was an informer of the secret police!

Contrib: *The Illustrated Times [1859-60]; ILN [1860].*

**'MOUSE'**

Contributed one cartoon to *Vanity Fair*, 1913.

**MUCKLEY, Louis Fairfax**                fl.1889-1914

Painter, etcher and illustrator. He was born at Stourbridge and studied at Birmingham School of Art, contributing to various lavish books in a late Pre-Raphaelite style with Morris decoration. He was associated with the Birmingham School of Handicraft and designed for *The Quest*; he may have been a relation of W.J. Muckley, Art Director at Manchester and Wolverhampton.

Illus: *Fringilla [R.D. Blackmore, 1895-96]; Spenser's Faerie Queen [1897].*
Contrib: *Rivers of Great Britain [1889]; The Graphic [1889]; The Quiver [1890]; ILN [1893-96]; Cassell's Family Magazine.*
Exhib: B; New Gall; RA.
Bibl: R.E.D. Sketchley, *Eng. Bk. Illus.*, 1903, pp.12, 129.

**MULREADY, Augustus Edward**                -1886

Genre painter. He worked with F.D. Hardy, G.B. O'Neill and T. Webster as a member of the Cranbrook 'Colony'. He concentrated on domestic subjects and died in London in 1886.

Contrib: *ILN [1886].*
Exhib: RA; ROI.
Bibl: *Cat. of Works of Art, Corp. of London*, 1910.

**MULREADY, William    RA**                1786-1863

Genre painter and illustrator. He was born at Ennis, County Clare in 1786 and brought to London as a child where he early showed a talent for drawing. He received instruction from Thomas Banks, the sculptor, and entered the RA Schools in 1800. He formed a friendship with John Varley, whose sister he married in 1803, but the marriage ended after a few years. Mulready concentrated on oil paintings in the Wilkie style, but was also a very prolific illustrator, producing huge numbers of vignette designs in the period around 1810. He was elected ARA in 1815 and RA a few months later, but continued his illustrative work into late middle age, appearing under the same covers as the Pre-Raphaelites. Mulready is a charming but never a strong illustrator of fiction and his delicate drawings were best suited to the age before the wood engraving. He designed the first Penny Postage envelope for Sir Rowland Hill in 1840 and died at Bayswater on 7 July 1863.

Illus: *The Vicar of Wakefield [Goldsmith, 1843]; The Mother's Primer [1844]; Peveril of the Peak [Walter Scott 1846]; Frontispiece to Moore's Irish Melodies [1856]; Tennyson [Moxon, 1857].*
Exhib: BI; RA; RBA.
Colls: BM; Burnley; Glasgow; V & AM.
Bibl: F.G. Stephens, *Memorials of WM*, 1867; Chatto & Jackson, *Treatise on Wood Engraving*, 1861, p.598; Anne Rorimer, *Drawings of WM*, V & AM Cat., 1972.

**MUNN, George Frederick    RBA**                1852-1907

American genre and flower painter. He was born at Utica in 1852 and studied under Charles Calverley at the National Academy and at South Kensington. He was elected RBA in 1884 and died in New York on 10 February 1907.

Contrib: *ILN [1891].*
Exhib: RA; RBA; ROI.

**MUNNINGS, Sir Alfred    PRA**                1878-1959

Painter, sculptor and poet. He was born at Mendham, Suffolk on 8 October 1878 and studied at Framlingham School and Norwich School of Art. Munnings' great love of his native county and his knowledge of its life, made him one of the finest painters of the horse since George Stubbs. Although never strictly an illustrator, he began life in poster work at Norwich, designing wrappers for Caley's Chocolates and calendars for Bullard's Brewery. In later life he illustrated his own *An Artist's Life*, 1950. Elected RA in 1925, he was President of the RA from 1944 to 1949.

**MURCH, Arthur**                fl.1871-1881

Black and white artist. He was apparently working in Italy, 1871-73, and Walter Crane says that he was a meticulous man who produced little. His wife was a frequent exhibitor at the Grosvenor Gallery 1880-90.

Contrib: *Dalziel's Bible Gallery [1881].*

**MURDOCH, W.G. Burn**                fl.1882-1919

Painter, lithographer and etcher. He studied at the Antwerp Academy and under Carolus Duran in Paris, then in Madrid, Florence and Naples. He worked in Edinburgh and contributed to *The Evergreen*.

Exhib: G; L; New Gall; RA; RSA.

**MURRAY, Sir David    RA ARSA PRI**                1849-1933

Landscape painter. He was born at Glasgow in 1849 and after studying at the Art School, moved to London and became a very fashionable painter in the tradition of Constable. He was elected ARA in 1891 and RA in 1905 and was President of the RI, 1916-17. He is included here for the illustrations he drew for *The English Illustrated Magazine* in 1887.

Colls: Birkenhead; Glasgow.

**MURRAY, Charles Oliver    RPE**                1842-1924

Painter and etcher. He was born at Denholm in 1842 and was educated at Minto School and at the Edinburgh School of Design and the RSA. He gained medals there for his anatomical studies and drawings from the antique and the National Medallions Queens Prize. He worked as engraver and illustrator for the magazines but later devoted himself entirely to etching and worked on pictures after famous artists. He became RPE on its foundation in 1881 and was a member of the Art Workers Guild. He died 11 December 1924.

Illus: *Spindle Stories [Ascot R. Hope, 1880].*
Contrib: *Golden Hours [1869]; Good Words [1880]; The English Illustrated Magazine [1891-92].*
Exhib: FAS; L; M; RA; RE; RSA.
Colls: BM.

**MURRAY, George**                fl.1883-1922

Painter and decorative designer. He was working in Glasgow in 1883, in London 1899 and 1903 and in Blairgowrie, 1902. A title page design by this artist appears in *The Studio*, Vol.14, 1898, p.71.

Exhib: G; L; RA; RI; RSA.

**MURRAY, W. Bazett**                fl.1871-1890

Illustrator. This artist specialised in social realism and drawings of an industrial nature which are fine studies of the Victorian working class. His work was admired by Vincent Van Gogh during his English years.

Contrib: *The Graphic [1874-76]; ILN [1874-90].*
Exhib: RA, 1871-75.

**MURRELL, Claire**

Contributing decoration to *The Studio*, Vol.12, 1897, illus.

**NAFTEL, Maud    ARWS**                                1856-1890
Flower painter and illustrator. She was born in 1856, the daughter of
the artist Paul Naftel, a family of Guernsey origin. She studied at the
Slade School, then in Paris with Carolus Duran, and became a member
of the SWA in 1886 and was elected ARWS in 1887. She died in
London in 1890.
Publ: *Flowers and How to Paint Them [1886].*
Exhib: B; FAS; GG; G; L; M; New Gall; RA; RI; RWS; SWA.
Colls: Liverpool.

**NAIRN, Mr.**
Illustrator contributing drawings of the New Zealand Gold Rush to
*The Illustrated London News,* 1863. He may be identified as the
father of J.M. Nairn, the New Zealand artist who died at Wellington
on 2 February 1904.

**NANCE, Robert Morton**                               fl.1895-1909
Illustrator, painter and ship modeller. He probably studied at the
Herkomer School at Bushey in 1895 and then lived in South Wales,
1903 and at Penzance, 1909 where he was associated with the St. Ives
artists.
Exhib: L; New Gall; RA.
Bibl: *The Studio,* Bk. Illus. Competition, 1897; Vol.14, 1898 pp.257-262, illus.

**NANKIVELL, Frank Arthur**                            1869-
Painter, etcher and comic artist. He was born in Australia in 1869 and
studied in New York, London, Japan and China.
Contrib: *Punch [1903 (figures)].*
Exhib: FAS, 1930.

**NASCHEN, Doria**                                     fl.1910-1935
Figure artist and illustrator, working at Stamford Hill, London.
Exhib: RA; ROI.

**NASH, Frederick    OWS**                             1782-1856
Painter, watercolourist, lithographer and architectural illustrator. He
was born at Lambeth in 1782 and learned drawing with T. Malton,
Junior, and studied at the RA Schools. He exhibited at the RA from
1800 and began by working as an architectural draughtsman,
occasionally being employed by Sir R. Smirke RA. He contributed to
numerous publications and was one of a number of artists who gained
success by satisfying the early 19th century craving for extreme
accuracy. It was this which won him the post as artist to the Society
of Antiquaries in 1807, made Turner commend him and Ackermann
employ him. Nash was elected a member of the OWS in 1811 and five
years later began a series of foreign sketching tours to Switzerland,
France and Germany, some of the results of which were published. He
made tours in Great Britain, from 1827-41 and was accompanied on
some of them by Peter de Wint. His work becomes more moody in his
later years when he had almost ceased illustration and concentrated
on views of Windsor and Brighton, where he settled and died in 1856.
Illus: *The Collegiate Chapel of St. George at Windsor [1805]; Twelve views of
the Antiquities of London [1805-10]; Picturesque views of the City of Paris and
its Environs [1819-23].*
Contrib: *Howlett's Views in the County of Lincoln [1802]; Britton's Beauties
of England and Wales [1801-15]; Ackermann's Oxford [1814]; Antiquarian
and Topographical Cabinet [1809].*
Exhib: RA; RBA; BI; OWS.
Colls: Bradford; Nottingham; V & AM.
Bibl: Martin Hardie, *Watercol. Paint. in Brit.,* Vol.3, 1968 pp.16-17.

**NASH, John    RA**                                   1893-1977
Artist, flower painter and illustrator. He was born in Kensington in
1893, the brother of Paul Nash (q.v.). He was educated at Wellington
College and on the advice of his brother took no formal art training
and thus developed a very personal style in his interpretation of
nature, both innocent and observant. He served in the Artists Rifles
1916-18 and was appointed an official War Artist in 1918. During the
1920s both brothers were very successful artists, notably in
landscape, where they led a school that sought out a more abstract
direction, based on its colour, structure and massing. Nash's talent as a
comic artist and writer, led him to the field of book illustration which
was having a revival at the time with the Cresset, and Golden
Cockerell presses. Although most of his work post-dates our period,
he is included here as an artist active before 1914. He was elected
ARA in 1940 and RA in 1951; he was a member of the London
Group and was an assistant teacher of Design at the RCA, 1934. A
one man exhibition of his work was held at the RA in 1967.
Illus: *Dressing Gowns and Glue [1919]; Drawings in the Theatre [1919]; The
Nouveau Poor [1921]; Directions to Servants [1925]; Ovid's Elegies and
Epigrams [Sir John Davies, 1925]; Bats in the Belfry [1926]; Catalogue of
Alpine and Herbaceous Plants [1926]; Poisonous Plants [1927]; Celeste
[1930]; The Shepherds Calendar [1930]; Cobbett's Rural Rides [1930]; When
Thou Wast Naked [T.F. Powys, 1931]; The New Flora and Sylva [1931]; One
Hundred and One Ballades [1931]; The Curious Gardener [Jason Hill, 1931];
Flowers and Faces [1935]; Wild Flowers in Britain [1938]; Plants with
Personality [1938]; The Contemplative Gardener [1940]; The Almanack of
Hope [1946]; English Garden Flowers [1948]; The Natural History of Selborne
[1951]; Parnassian Molehill [1953]; The Tranquil Gardener [1958]; The
Guinness Year Book [1959]; Thorntree Meadows [1960]; The Native Garden
[1961]; B.B.C. Book of the Countryside [1963]; The Art of Angling [1965].*
Contrib: *The Broadside; Rhyme Sheets [Poetry Bookshop]; The Listener
[1933-34 (plant illus.)].*
Bibl: *JN,* RA Cat., 1967.

**NASH, Joseph**                                       1808-1878
Draughtsman and illustrator. He was born at Great Marlow on 17
December 1808 and worked as an assistant to Pugin, who took him to
Paris in 1829 to prepare topographical sketches for *Paris and its
Environs,* 1830. Nash is best remembered however for his large
lithographed books of picturesque architecture which appeared in the
1830s and 1840s and are still regarded as the most accurate views of
medieval houses and castles. Nash's figures in the style of Cattermole,
brought the buildings to life, without detracting from the serious
antiquarianism of the book. He was elected AOWS in 1834 and OWS
in 1842, but his work declined in later years possibly due to illness.
He died at Bayswater on 19 December 1878.
Illus: *Architecture of the Middle Ages [1838]; Mansions of England in the
Olden Time [1839-49]; Views of Windsor Castle [1848]; Scotia Delineata
[Lawson, 1847]; Merrie Days of England [E.A. MacDermott]; Dickenson's
Comprehensive Picture of the Great Exhibition of 1851; Old English Ballads
[1864].*
Exhib: BI; NWS; OWS; RA.
Colls: Fitzwilliam; Glasgow; Greenwich; Maidstone; V & AM; Witt Photo.

**NASH, Joseph, Jnr.    RI**                           -1922
Marine and landscape painter and illustrator. He was the son of Joseph
Nash (q.v.) and worked in London from 1859, latterly at Bedford
Park. He undertook some magazine work, mostly shipping subjects
and is the artist of the amusing plate in *The Graphic* 1874, showing
Ruskin's navvies mending the Oxford Road! He was elected RI in
1886 and died in 1922.
Illus: *The Dash For Khartoum [G.A. Henty, 1892].*
Contrib: *The Graphic [1872-1902].*
Exhib: B; G; L; M; RA; RHA; RI; ROI.
Bibl: *The Studio,* Winter No., 1923-24, p.27; *Apollo,* 1925, p.126; *The
Connoisseur,* Vol.71, 1925, p.112.

**NASH, Paul**                                         1889-1946
Painter, wood engraver, illustrator and theatrical designer. He was
born in London on 11 May 1889, the elder brother of John Nash
(q.v.). He was educated at St. Pauls and studied at Chelsea Polytechnic
and the Slade School, 1909-10. He held his first exhibition of
drawings at the Carfax Gallery in 1911 and followed this with an
exhibition of work jointly with his brother at the Dorien Leigh

Gallery, 1913. Nash enlisted with the Artists Rifles in 1914 and after being transferred to the Hampshire Regiment was wounded at Ypres, 1917 and the same year appointed official War Artist on the Western Front. The war drawings, grey wash studies of tortured landscapes and crabbed humanity were the most significant contribution that Nash made to twentieth century art. The shapes and symbols from this time recur again and again in his later landscape paintings and drawings. An exhibition of the war work was held at the Leicester Galleries in 1918 and another was held in 1924. Nash was a member of the London Group, the Modern English Watercolour Society and the Society of Wood Engravers and founded a group of imaginative painters called 'Unit One'. He was author of *Room and Book*, a series of essays on decoration, published in 1932 and he died in July 1946.

Illus: *Loyalties [John Drinkwater, 1918]; Images of War [Richard Aldington, 1919]; Places, Prose Poems and Wood-Engravings [1922]; Genesis [12 engravings on wood, 1924]; Urn Burial [Sir Thomas Browne]; Abd-er-Rahman [Jules Tellier, 1928]; The Seven Pillars of Wisdom [T.E. Lawrence].*
Contrib: *The Graphic [1918]; The Broadside; Rhymesheets [The Poetry Bookshop].*
Exhib: FAS; L; M; NEA; P; RSA; RSW.
Bibl: *Poet and Painter,* Oxford, 1955, edited by Abbott and Bertram.

**NASH, Thomas**
Illustrator working for *The Broadway,* 1867-74.

**NASMYTH, Alexander**                      **1758-1840**
Portrait and landscape painter. He was born at Edinburgh on 9 September 1758 and after becoming a pupil of Allan Ramsay, he worked in London and studied at Rome 1782-84. On his return to Edinburgh, he established a wide reputation for soft and sensitive oil landscapes in the manner of Claude. Nasmyth ran art classes in his house and five of his daughters and one son became distinguished artists. He died at Edinburgh on 10 April 1840.

Illus: *The Border Antiquities of England and Scotland [Walter Scott, 1817].*
Exhib: BI; RA; RBA.
Colls: Bristol; Edinburgh; Glasgow; Mellon; Nottingham.
Bibl: Peter Johnson, *The N Family of Painters.*

**NAST, J.**                      **1840-1902**
American caricaturist. He was born at Landau on 27 September 1840 of American parentage, but left with his parents for the United States and settled with them in New York. He began his career as an artist for various American magazines but came to England in 1860 for *The New York Illustrated Newspaper* to cover the boxers Heeman and Sayers. A man who clearly preferred action to the newspaper office, Nast enlisted with Garibaldi and became a Special Artist to English, French and American magazines during the Italian campaign. On his return to the United States in 1861, he fought in the American Civil War with distinction and became the leading cartoonist of his generation, noted for the power of his images and his draughtsmanship. He died at Guayaquil on 7 December 1902.

Contrib: *The Illustrated Times [1860]; The Illustrated London News [1860-61]; Vanity Fair [1872].*
Bibl: A.B. Paine, *N His Period and His Pictures,* 1905; *American Art Journal,* Vol.4, 1903 p.143; T. Nast St Hill, *N Cartoons and Illustrations,* Dover, 1974.

**NATTES, John Claude**                      **c.1765-1822**
Topographer and drawing master. He was born in England in about 1765 and studied under Hugh P. Dean and was a founder member of the OWS in 1804, but was expelled in 1807 for exhibiting other artists' works under his own name. He travelled to Italy and the South of France in 1820-22 and specialised in Italian landscapes and topographical views. He died in London in 1822.

Illus: *Scotia Depicta [1801-04]; Hibernia Depicta [1802]; Bath and its Environs Illustrated [1804-05]; Versailles, Paris and Saint Denis [1810, AT 103]; Select Views of Bath, Bristol [1805].*
Exhib: RA, 1782-1814.
Colls: Barnsley; BM; Leeds; Lincoln; V & AM.
Bibl: Hardie, *Watercol. Paint. in Brit.,* 1967 Vol.2, pp.133-134 illus.

**NEALE, Adam**
Amateur artist who illustrated his own *Travels Through Germany, Poland, Moldavia and Turkey,* 1818, AT 19.

**NEALE, Edward**                      **fl.1880-1899**
Animal and bird artist and illustrator. Worked in London and contributed to *The Illustrated London News,* 1899.
Exhib: B; L; RA.

**NEALE, John Preston**                      **1780-1847**
Architectural and topographical illustrator. He was born in 1780 and after working in the Post Office, turned to draughtsmanship and became one of the leading topographers of the gothic revival. His pen drawings which were exceptional for their accuracy, were often in monochrome washes and were used for numerous books as well as those published under his own name. He died at Tattingstone on 14 November 1847.

Illus: *The History and Antiquities of the Abbey Church of Westminster [1818]; The Seats of Noblemen and Gentlemen [1818-29]; Views of the Most Interesting Collegiate and Parochial Churches of Great Britain [1824-25].*
Contrib: *Britton's Beauties of England and Wales [1808-16]; London and Middlesex [Brayley]; Jones's Views [1829-31].*
Exhib: BI; OWS; RA; RBA.
Colls: Ashmolean; BM; Nottingham; V & AM.
Bibl: Iolo Williams, *Early English Watercols.,* 1952, p.225, illus.

**NEIL, H.          See O'NEILL, Hugh**

**NEILSON, Harry B.**                      **fl.1895-1901**
Illustrator of comic animal subjects. He worked at Claughton, Cheshire and published books for children which *The Studio* called 'wild and domesticated beasts disporting themselves in human garb', Vol.12.

Illus: *Micky Magee's Menagerie [1897]; Droll Days [1901].*
Contrib: *The Sketch; Cassell's Family Magazine.*
Exhib: L.

**NELSON, Harold Edward Hughes**                      **1871-**
Artist, illustrator and designer of bookplates. He was born at Dorchester on 22 May 1871 and studied at the Lambeth School of Art and the Central School of Arts and Crafts, London. Nelson made a speciality of medieval illustrations with elaborate borders and was particularly accomplished as a decorator of books. He was influenced by the books of Morris and by the Pre-Raphaelites, but made his mark as a designer of bookplates. He was also an early designer of Cadbury's advertisements.

Publ: *25 Designs by HN [Edinburgh, 1904].*
Illus: *Undine and Aslauga's Knight [F.H.C. de la Motte Fouqué, 1901]; Early English Prose Romances [W.J. Thomas, 1904].*
Contrib: *The Graphic [1915]; The Sphere; The Queen; Ladies Field; Royal Academy Pictures [cover, 1908]; Old Colleges of Oxford [Aymer Vallance, 1912 (frontis)].*
Exhib: L; RA; RI; RMS.
Bibl: H.W. Fincham, *Art of the Bookplate,* 1897; C.P. Horning, *Bookplates by HN,* New York, 1929; B. Peppin, *Fantasy Book Illustration 1860-1920,* 1975, p.189; *The Studio,* Vol.7, 1896, p.93; Vol.8 1896, p.226; Vol.24, 1902, p.63; Vol.63, 1915, p.148; Vol.73, 1918, p.67; Vol.81, 1921, p.19; Vol.83, 1922, p.96.

**NESBIT, Charlton**                      **1775-1838**
Illustrator and wood engraver. He was born at Swalewell in 1775 and became a pupil for four years of Beilby and Thomas Bewick (q.v.), working on his *British Birds.* He began painting in about 1795 and established himself in London in 1799, where he gained a reputation for book illustrations. He died there in 1838.

Illus: *Shakespeare's Works; The Works of Sir Egerton Bridges; Hudibras; Ackermann's Religious Emblems [1809]; Northcote's Fables [1828-33].*
Colls: BM; Witt Photo.

**NESBITT, Frances E.**                      **fl.1864-1934**
Landscape, figure and marine painter. She was elected ASWA in 1899 and illustrated her own *Algeria and Tunis* for Messrs. Black in about 1905.

Exhib: L; New Gall; RA; RBA; RHA; RI; ROI; SWA.

**NESFIELD, William Eden**          1835-1888

Architect and artist. He was the son of the artist William Andrews Nesfield and was closely associated with Richard Norman Shaw in the development of the romantic Victorian country house. He illustrated his own *Specimens of Medieval Architecture Chiefly Selected From Examples of the 12th and 13th Centuries in France and Italy*, 1862.

**NETTLESHIP, John Trivett**       1847-1902

Animal painter, illustrator and author. He was born at Kettering on 11 February 1841 and was educated at Durham School before joining the staff of his father's law firm. He abandoned this career for art and studied at Heatherley's and the Slade School, working as an illustrator in pen and ink and making drawings in the Zoological Gardens. He visited India in 1880-81, but made his reputation from expressive paintings of animals in the style of Delacroix. He died in London on 31 August 1902, having been elected ROI in 1894.

Publ: *Robert Browning Essays and Thoughts [1890]; George Morland [1898]*.
Illus: *An Epic of Women [A.W.E. O'Shaughnessy, 1870]; Emblems [Mrs. A. Cholomondeley, 1875]; Natural History Sketches Among the Carnivora [1885]; Ice-bound on Kolguev [A.R. Battye, 1895]*.
Contrib: *The Boys' Own Paper*.
Exhib: G; L; M; New Gall; RA; RHA; RI; ROI.
Colls: Ashmolean.
Bibl: *The Magazine of Art*, 1903 pp.75, 79; *The AJ*, 1907, p.251.

**NEW, Edmund Hort**          1871-1931

Landscape painter, architect and illustrator. He was born in Evesham in 1871, the son of a solicitor and was educated at Prince Henry's School, Evesham and at the Birmingham Municipal School of Art under E.R. Taylor and A.J. Gaskin (q.v.) 1886-95. New taught at a branch school of the School of Art and became well-known in the Midlands, spending much of his working life in Oxford. His black and white illustrations are characteristic of Birmingham, cleanly drawn in the woodcut style with large foregrounds and meticulous care in the delineation of each building and its materials. New was a member of the Art Workers Guild, was elected Hon. ARIBA, and died at Oxford on 3 February 1931.

Illus: *The Gypsy Road [Cole, 1894]; In the Garden of Peace [1896]; The Compleat Angler [1896]; The Vale of Arden [Alfred Hayes, 1896 (title and cover)]; White Wampum [Pauline Johnson, 1896 (title and cover)]; Oxford and Its Colleges [1897]; Cambridge and Its Colleges [1898]; Shakespeare's Country [1899]; Pickwick Papers [1899]; The Life of William Morris [1899]; The Natural History of Selborne [1900]; Westminster Abbey [1900]; Oliver Twist [1900]; Outside the Garden [1900]; Sussex [1900]; The Malvern Country [Windle, 1901]; The Wessex of Thomas Hardy; Some Impressions of Oxford [1901]; Haunts of Ancient Peace [1902]; Wren's Parentalia [1903]; Chester [1903]; Evesham [1904]; [Temple Topographies series, College Monographs series]; The Scholar Gypsy* and *Thyrsis [1906]; Poems of Wordsworth [1907]; Berkshire [1911]; Coleridge and Wordsworth in the West Country [Professor Knight, 1913]; Highways and Byways in Shakespeare's Country [1914]; Cranford [1914]; The New Loggan Guides to Oxford Colleges [1907-25, issued together 1932]; Prints issued of: The Towers of Oxford [1908]; High Street, Oxford [1912]; Firenze [1914]; The City and Port of London [1920]*.
Contrib: *The English Illustrated Magazine [1891-92]; The Quest [1894-96]; Daily Chronicle [1895]; The Yellow Book [1896]; The Pall Mall Magazine*.
Exhib: B; FAS; RA.
Colls: Birmingham; V & AM.
Bibl: R.E.D. Sketchley, *Eng. Bk. Illus.*, 1903, pp.10, 38, 50, 136; *Modern Book Illustrators and Their Work*, Studio, 1914.
See illustration (right).

**NEWCOMBE, Bertha**         fl.1880-1908

Landscape, figure and flower painter and illustrator. She worked in London and at Croydon and was elected NEA in 1888. She contributed illustrations of church and village life to *The English Illustrated Magazine*, 1895-97.

Exhib: FAS; L; M; NEA; RA; RBA; RI; ROI; SWA.

**NEWELL, Rev. Robert Hassell**      1778-1852

Amateur artist and illustrator. He was born in Essex in 1778 and after being educated at Colchester and St. John's College, Cambridge where he was admitted Fellow in 1800, he became Rector of Little Hormead, Hertfordshire in 1813. He studied with W.H. Payne (q.v.) and illustrated his own works.

**NEWHOUSE, C.B.**          fl.1834-1845

Artist and traveller. He illustrated his own *Scenes On The Road*, 1834-35. 18 aquatints, AL 406, and *Roadster's Album*, 1845, 17 aquatints, AL 407.

**NEWILL, Mary J.**          fl.1884-1925

Black and white artist, illustrator and embroider. She studied at the Birmingham School of Art and worked in Edgbaston, basing many of her designs on the Morris style. She was particularly imaginative in her renderings of wood and foilage and *The Studio* in 1897 referred to her trees having 'the strength of those by a little master of Germany'.

Illus: *A Book of Nursery Songs and Rhymes [1895]*.
Contrib: *The Quest [1894-96]; The Yellow Book [1896]*.
Exhib: B; FAS.
Bibl: *The Studio*, Vol.5, 1895, p.56, illus; Vol.10, 1897, p.232.

**NEWMAN, William**          fl.1842-1864

Comic artist. A friend of Ebenezer Landells (q.v.), he was much employed on *Punch* in the period, 1846-50. A talented humorist he was most versatile in small comic cuts in the manner of Tom Hood, but was rather despised for his coarse manners by the *Punch* Table and was poorly paid. He is believed to have emigrated to the United States in the early 60s.

Contrib: *The Squib [1842]; Puppet Show; Diogenes; Comic News [1864]*.
Bibl: M.H. Spielmann, *The History of Punch*, 1894, pp.413-414.

*EDMUND HORT NEW 1871-1931. 'Stanstead Abbots.' Illustration for* The Yellow Book, *1896*.

**NEWTON, Gilbert Stuart**    **RA**       1795-1835

Painter and illustrator. He was born at Halifax, Nova Scotia in 1795 and began studies with his maternal uncle Gilbert Stuart, the American portrait painter at an early age. He visited Italy in 1817, and after spending some time in Paris, settled in London and studied at the RA Schools, concentrating on painting in the style of Watteau. Newton had some success in painting genre and historical subjects and was patronised by the 6th Duke of Bedford. He was a friend of Washington Irving and died on 5 August 1835, having been insane since 1833. He was elected ARA in 1828 and RA in 1832.

Contrib: *The Literary Souvenir [1826]*.
Exhib: BI; RA.
Colls: V & AM.

## NEWTON, Richard                                              1777-1798
Caricaturist and miniaturist working in the manner of Gillray.

Illus: *Sentimental Journey [Sterne, 1795, AL 250]*.
Colls: BM.

## NIBBS, Richard Henry                                         1816-1893
Musician and painter. He was born in London in 1816 and worked principally in London with a studio in Brighton, settling permanently there after 1841. He travelled on the Continent and illustrated his own publications.

Publ: *Marine Sketch Book of Shipping Craft and Coast Scenes [1850]; The Churches of Sussex [1851]; Antiquities of Sussex [1874]*.
Exhib: BI; L; RA; RBA.
Colls: BM; Brighton; Greenwich; V & AM.

## NIBLETT, F.D.                                                fl.1882-1884
Illustrator working at Edinburgh. He illustrated *Dulcima's Doom and Other Tales* by Willis, c.1880.

Exhib: RSA.

## NICHOLL, Andrew    RHA                                       1804-1886
Landscape painter. He was born in Belfast in 1804 and trained with a printer on the newspaper *The Northern Whig*. He was self-taught as an artist and worked in London, Dublin and Belfast, being elected ARHA in 1832 and RHA in 1837; he taught art in Ceylon during 1846, having previously illustrated S.C. Hall's *Ireland its Scenery and Character*, 1841. He died in London in 1886.

Contrib: *The Illustrated London News [1851]*.
Colls: BM; V & AM.

## NICHOLSON, George                                            c.1795-c.1839
Topographer, working in Liverpool with his elder brother Samuel Nicholson. He published *Twenty-six Lithographic Drawings in the Vicinity of Liverpool*, 1821; *Plas Newydd and Vale Crucis Abbey*, 1824. He exhibited at Liverpool, 1827-38.

## NICHOLSON, J.B.R.                                            fl.c.1815
Illustrator. A series of watercolour drawings of soldiers and bandsmen one showing Edinburgh Castle, signed and dated by this artist 1815, were sold at Sotheby's in November 1976.

## NICHOLSON, Thomas Henry                                      -1870
Draughtsman, illustrator, engraver and sculptor. Nicholson worked in London and excelled in equestrian subjects, some of which he modelled in plaster, teaching the technique to Count Alfred d'Orsay. He was the principal artist for *Cassell's Illustrated Family Paper*, 1853-57 and worked for other magazines. Much of his work is busy and mannered in the style of H.K. Browne (q.v.). He died at Portland in 1870.

Illus: *Faces in the Fire [1850]; Works of Shakespeare [n.d.]*.
Contrib: *ILN [1848]; The Illustrated Times [1855-59]*.

## NICHOLSON, William    RSA                                    1781-1844
Portrait painter and etcher. He was born at Ovingham-on-Tyne in 1781 and after working in Newcastle, moved from there to Edinburgh in 1814. He was a Founder Member of the RSA and was its Secretary from 1826 to 1830. He published *Portraits of Distinguished Living Characters*, 1818.

Colls: Edinburgh; Newcastle.

## NICHOLSON, Sir William                                       1872-1949
Painter and illustrator. He was born at Newark-on-Trent in 1872, the son of W.N. Nicholson MP. He studied at Julian's, Paris, and from about 1894, collaborated with his brother-in-law James Pryde (q.v.), on a series of posters and illustrated books. Their style was based on the French poster which they admired in the hands of Toulouse Lautrec and others and the designs were most different from contemporary work in their careful lettering and effects gained by massing of the shadows and bold outlines. The artists became known as 'The Beggarstaff Brothers' and their work, which was mostly in woodcut coloured by hand and then lithographed, became widely influential. The books produced were designed as a whole and have very little text, the lay-out and the squared illustrations give them the freedom and charm of the early chapbooks which both 'Brothers' had come to admire. After 1900, Nicholson's contributions to illustrations were spasmodic although he carried out a certain amount of it in the 1920s. His later career was almost entirely devoted to portrait painting. Nicholson was elected RP in 1909 and was knighted in 1936. He died in 1949.

Illus: *Tony Drum [1898]; An Alphabet [1898]; An Almanac of Twelve Sports [R. Kipling, 1898]; London Types [W.E. Henley, 1898]; The Square Book of Animals [Arthur Waugh, 1899]; Characters of Romance [1900]; Moss and Feather [W.H. Davies, Ariel Poem, 1928]; Memoirs of a Fox-Hunting Man [Siegfried Sassoon, 1929]; The Pirate Twins [n.d.]; Time Remembered [Lady Horner, 1930 (end papers)]*.
Exhib: FAS; GG; G; L; M; NEA; P; RHA; ROI; RSA; RSW.
Colls: Fitzwilliam; Tate; V & AM.
Bibl: *The Idler*, Vol.8, pp.519-528, illus; *The Studio*, Vol.12, 1898, pp.177-183; Marguerite Steen, *WN*.

See illustrations (below and p.401).

Mr Vanslyperken.

SIR WILLIAM NICHOLSON 1872-1949. 'Mr. Vanslyperken.' *Illustration to* Characters of Romance, *Heinemann, 1900. Lithograph.*

## NICKSON, Fred J.                                             fl.1902-1903
Black and white figure artist contributing social subjects to *Punch* 1902-03.

*SIR WILLIAM NICHOLSON 1872-1949. 'A Fisher.' Illustration for* The Dome, *1897. Colour woodcut from four blocks.*

**NICOL, Erskine    ARA RSA**                           **1825-1904**
Painter of Irish genre subjects. He was born at Leith in 1825 and trained at the Trustees Academy at the age of twelve after being apprenticed to a house-painter. He worked as a drawing-master at Leith before moving to Dublin in 1846, where he began to gain a reputation for Irish peasant scenes. Although settling in London, he continued to make visits to Ireland; he was elected RSA in 1859 and ARA in 1868. He died at Feltham on 8 March 1904.

Illus: *Tales of Irish Life and Character [A.M. Hall, 1909]; Irish Life and Humour [W. Harvey, 1909].*
Contrib: *Good Words [1860].*
Exhib: G; RA; RSA.
Colls: BM; Edinburgh; Sheffield; Tate; V & AM.

**NICOL, John Watson    ROI**                           **1856-1926**
Genre painter and illustrator. He was born in 1856, the son of Erskine Nicol ARA (q.v.). He worked in Scotland and France as well as in London and was elected ROI in 1888.

Contrib: *Good Words [1890]; Black & White [1896].*
Exhib: B; G; L; M; RA; ROI; RSA.

**NIELSEN, Kay**                                        **1886-1957**
Illustrator and designer for the theatre. He was born at Copenhagen on 12 March 1886 and was a pupil of L. Find, before studying at Julian's in Paris and at Colarossi's, 1904-11. Nielsen worked in London from 1911 until 1916 which accounts for his inclusion here, it was an intensive period of work and he was strongly influenced by Aubrey Beardsley. In general Nielsen is a brilliant colourist and a highly decorative illustrator, his works formed into frieze-like patterns, are closest to Persian or Middle Eastern designs and therefore akin to Leon Bakst or Edmund Dulac (q.v.). He uses stippling effects and elaborate rococo motifs which are reminiscent of Beardsley, but also the swirling lines of Vernon Hill (q.v.) and the more sculptural lines of incipient art deco. Nielsen held a big exhibition in New York in 1917 and after acting as stage designer to the Theatre Royal, Copenhagen, 1918-22, he emigrated to the United States, living in California from 1939 and designing for the Hollywood companies. He died there in 1957.

Illus: *In Powder and Crinoline [A. Quiller Couch, 1912]; East of the Sun, West of the Moon [Asbjornsen and Moe, 1914]; Old Tales From The North [1919]; Fairy Tales by Hans Andersen [1924]; Hansel and Gretel [1925]; Red Magic [Romer Wilson, 1930].*
Contrib: *ILN [1912-13 (Christmas)].*
Exhib: Dowdeswell Gall., 1912; Leicester Gall., 1914.
Colls: V & AM.
Bibl: Marion Hepworth Dixon, 'The Drawings of KN', *The Studio*, Vol.60, 1914; B. Peppin, *Fantasy Book Illustration* 1860-1920, 1975, p.189 illus.; Keith Nicholson, *Introduction to KN*, Coronet Books, 1975.
See illustration (p.402)

**NINHAM, Henry**                                       **1793-1874**
Watercolourist and engraver. He was born at Norwich in 1793 the son of an heraldic artist and engraver. He was a topographical artist, specialising in street scenes and was a member of the Norwich School and friendly with J.S. Cotman. He died in the city in 1874.

Publ: *8 Original Etchings of Picturesque Antiquities of Norwich [1842]; Views of the Gates of Norwich made in 1792-93 by the late John Ninham [1861]; 23 Views of the Ancient City Gates of Norwich [1864]; Remnants of Antiquity in Norwich, Views of Norwich and Norfolk [1875]; Norwich Corporation Pageantry.*
Illus: *Castle Acre [Blome]; Eastern Arboretum [Grigor, 1841].*
Colls: BM; Norwich; V & AM.

**NISBET, Hume**                                        **1849-1923**
Painter and author, illustrator. He was born in Stirling on 8 August 1849 and studied art under Sam Bough RSA. At the age of sixteen he began to travel and spent seven years exploring Australia, being appointed on his return, Art Master at the Watt College and Old Schools of Art, Edinburgh. He resigned the post in 1885, when he was sent by Cassell & Co. to Australia and New Guinea, 1886; visited China and Japan, 1905-06. He concentrated on his work as novelist in the latter part of his life and died at Eastbourne in 1923.

Illus: *Her Loving Slave [1894]; A Sappho of Green Springs [Brett Harte, 1897]; The Fossicker [Ernest Glanville, 1897].*
Contrib: *The English Illustrated Magazine [1890-91 (ornament)].*
Exhib: G; RA; RBA; RHA; RSA.

**NIXON, J. Forbes**                                    **fl.1864-1867**
Still-life painter working at Tonbridge. He designed the cover for *The Young Gentleman's Magazine*, 1867.

Exhib: RBA.

**NIXON, James Henry**                                  **fl.1830-1847**
History painter and expert on heraldry. He was born in about 1808 and became a pupil of John Martin (q.v.).

Illus: *The Eglinton Tournament [Rev. J. Richardson, 1843, AL 388].*
Contrib: *Scott's Works [1834].*
Exhib: BI; RA; RBA.
Colls: Witt Photo.

**NIXON, John**                                         **c.1750-1818**
Landscape painter and amateur caricaturist. He was born about 1750 and carried on the business of merchant in Basinghall Street, befriending many artists and going on sketching tours with some of them. Nixon had business connections with Ireland and visited the island frequently in the 1780s and 1790s, once in 1791 in company with Captain Grose, the antiquary. Some of his drawings were used in *Watt's Seats*, 1779-1786 and he visited the Continent in 1783-84 and in 1802 and 1804, when he was at Paris. Nixon was at Bath with Thomas Rowlandson (q.v.) in 1792 and a drawing of the Abbey by him, sold at Christie's in March 1974, shows strong similarities to this artist in pen outlines. Although Nixon remained a coarse draughtsman compared with Rowlandson, he has something of his bravura and sense of the grotesque and his best works are datable from this contact to the period after 1800. Nixon was Secretary to The Beefsteak Club and a member of the Margravine of Anspach's circle at Brandenburg House in Hammersmith. He died in 1818.

Contrib *European Magazine; Journey from London to The Isle of Wight [Thomas Pennant, 1801]; Guide to The Watering Places [1803].*
Exhib: RA, 1781-1815.
Colls: BM; V & AM; Witt Photo.
Bibl: H. Angelo, *Reminiscences*, 1830.

*KAY NIELSEN 1886-1957. 'The Czarina's Violet.' Head piece for* In Powder and Crinoline *by Sir Arthur Quiller-Couch, 1913. Pen and ink. 2³⁄₄ins. x 6⁵⁄₈ins. (7cm x 16.8cm).*

Victoria and Albert Museum

**NOBLE, John Edwin   RBA FZS**                1876-
Animal painter and illustrator. He was born in 1876, the son of John Noble RBA 1848-96 and studied at the Slade, Lambeth and RA Schools. He worked in London and Surrey and at Milford on Sea, Hants from 1922; he was elected RBA in 1907 and FZS in 1908.

Bibl: *The Studio,* Vol.14, 1898, p.145, illus.

**NORBURY, Edwin Arthur   RCA**                1849-1918
Painter and illustrator. He was born in Liverpool in 1849, the son of Richard Norbury, RCA. He was educated at Dr. Wand's School, Liverpool and at the age of fifteen began sending contributions to *The Illustrated London News* and *Illustrated Times,* later joining *The Graphic* as artist correspondent. He lived in North Wales 1875-90 and went to Siam in 1892 to teach at the Royal School of Arts and while there acted as *Graphic* Special Artist during the Franco-Siamese War, 1893. He was a Founder Member of the Royal Cambrian Academy and ran his own Norbury Sketching School and St James' Life School in Chelsea. He was Principal of the Henry Blackburn Studio and died in London, 16 October 1918.

Illus: *The Kingdom of the Yellow Robe [Ernest Young, 1898]; The Arabian Nights Entertainments [1899]; Animal Arts and Crafts.*
Exhib: L; M; RA; RCA; RHA; RI; ROI.

**NORIE, Orlando**                1832-1901
Military artist and illustrator. He belonged to a celebrated family of Edinburgh artists but worked in London and Aldershot where he kept a studio. He is notable for his great accuracy in depicting uniforms and military customs, but is not a particularly imaginative painter.

Illus: *The Memoirs of the 10th Royal Hussars [R.S. Liddell, 1891].*
Exhib: NWS; RA.
Colls: India Office Lib.; Nat. Army Mus.; V & AM; Royal Collection.

**NORMAN, Philip   FSA**                c.1843-1931
Draughtsman and antiquary. He was born at Bromley Common in about 1843, the son of a Director of the Bank of England and was educated at Eton and studied at the Slade School. Norman devoted his life to the study of old London buildings and made many hundreds of pencil drawings of its old courts and alleys during the last quarter of the 19th century. They are reliable records of vanished architecture, but not strong drawings, he was a rather weak figure draughtsman. A collection of these was presented to the Victoria and Albert Museum by the artist and an *Annotated Catalogue of Drawings of Old London* by the artist, was issued by the museum in 1900. He died in London 17 May 1931.

Publ: *The Inns of Old Southwark [1888 (with W. Rendle)]; Cromwell House, Highgate [1917].*
Illus: *London Signs and Inscriptions [1893]; Modern History of The City of London [C. Welch, 1903].*
Contrib: *The English Illustrated Magazine [1890-92 (taverns)].*
Exhib: L; M; NEA; New Gall; RA; RBA; RI; ROI.
Colls: V & AM.

**NORMAND, B.**
Artist contributing illustrations of Italy to *The Illustrated London News,* 1847.

**NORRIS, Arthur**                1888-
Landscape painter and teacher. He was born in 1888, the son of William Foxley Norris, Dean of Westminster, and studied at the Slade School, 1907-10. He contributed figure subjects to *Punch* in 1909 and 1914.

Exhib: FAS; NEA; P; RA.

**NORRIS, Charles**                1779-1858
Architectural draughtsman and amateur engraver. He was born at Marylebone in 1779, and though from a wealthy family became an orphan at an early age. He was educated at Eton and Christ Church, Oxford, before serving in the Army. After his marriage, Norris concentrated on the arts and made ambitious plans to publish antiquarian and picturesque views, teaching himself engraving in the process. He settled at Tenby in 1810 and died there in 1858.

Illus: *The Architectural Antiquities of Wales [1810]; Saint David's in a Series of Engravings [1811]; Etchings of Tenby [1812]; An Historical Account of Tenby [1818].*
Bibl: A.L. Leach *CN,* 1949.

## NORTH, Lady Georgina
**1798-1835**

Amateur figure artist and illustrator. She was born in 1798, the third daughter of the 3rd Earl of Guilford and his second wife, Susannah Coutts. Since the appearance of some of this artists watercolours on the market in 1973, she has emerged as one of the most accomplished amateurs, working in the style of Fuseli. An illustration to *The Rape of The Lock*, dated 1831 was published and this together with a drawing of 'The Infancy of Wellington' are in an American private collection. She died unmarried on 25 August 1835.

## NORTH, John William    ARA RWS
**1842-1924**

Landscape painter, watercolourist and illustrator. He was born on the outskirts of London in 1842 and was apprenticed to J.W. Whymper's wood engraving workshop where he came into contact with Fred Walker and G.J. Pinwell (qq.v.). From 1862-66, North did a great deal of work for the Dalziel Brothers,and illustrated their *Wayside Poesies* 1867 and other books. North was a close friend of Fred Walker and they went on sketching tours together, Walker finding his subjects in the country folk and North in the landscapes. His work represents the best landscape work of the 1860s, a broad treatment of the countryside, superb detail showing up in the foreground, but as Reid has pointed out 'in his own day his work never attained popularity, and was underrated even by his fellow-artists'. North moved to Somerset in 1868 and the Halsway and Withycombe areas were to provide frequent subjects for his drawings. He was elected AOWS in 1871, RWS in 1883 and ARA in 1893. The later years of his life were spent in patenting and marketing a special watercolour paper which greatly impoverished him. He died at Washford on 20 December 1924.

Illus: *English Sacred Poetry of the Olden Time [1864]; Our Life Illustrated by Pen and Pencil [1864]; A Round of Days [1865]; The Sunday Magazine [1865-67]; Good Words [1866]; Once a Week [1866-67]; Touches of Nature by Eminent Artists [1866]; Longfellow's Poems [1866]; Poems by Jean Ingelow [1867]; Wayside Poesies [1867]; The Spirit of Praise [1867]; The Months Illustrated with Pen and Pencil [n.d.]; The Illustrated Book of Sacred Poems.*
Contrib: *The English Illustrated Magazine [1887].*
Exhib: B; FAS; GG; G; L; M; New Gall; RA; RHA; RSW; RWS.

Colls: Ashmolean; BM; Bristol; V & AM.
Bibl: Gleeson White, *English Illustration The Sixties,* 1906; Forrest Reid, *Illustrators of the Sixties,* 1928, pp.163-165; Martin Hardie, *Watercol. Paint. in Brit.,* Vol.3, 1968, pp.137-138; *Country Life,* 18 August 1977, 'A Somerset Draw For Painters' by R.M. Billingham.

## NORTHCOTE, James    RA
**1746-1831**

Painter and author. He was born in Plymouth in 1746, and was apprenticed to a watchmaker, before going to London in 1771 and being patronised by Sir Joshua Reynold's, whose assistant he became. He studied at the RA Schools and after a brief return to Plymouth, left for Italy in 1777 where he copied the old masters and particularly the works of Michaelangelo, Raphael and Titian. He returned to London in 1780 and became a successful portrait painter, contributing illustrations to various works. He was elected ARA in 1786 and RA in 1787. At the end of his career, Northcote devoted himself to animal painting and to writing, he published a standard life of Sir Joshua Reynolds in 1813 and his *Conversations* were published by William Hazlitt in 1830. In 1828, he produced an edition of *One Hundred Fables,* illustrated by himself, which includes 280 wood engravings of animal and landscape subjects which have almost the charm and romance of Bewick about them.

Contrib: *Boydell's Shakespeare [1792].*
Exhib: BI; RA; RBA.
Colls: Witt Photo; NPG; V & AM.
See illustration (below).

## NORTON, Eardley B.
**fl.1895-1902**

Caricaturist. He was working in London and contributed two cartoons to *Vanity Fair,* 1895 and 1902. Signs: E.B.N.

## NORTON, Val
**fl.1902-1905**

Contributor of figure subjects to *Punch,* 1902-05.

## NYE, Herbert
**fl.1885-1927**

Painter and sculptor. He was working at Walton on Thames, 1895-1902 and at Pulborough, 1923. He made nine etchings for Garnett's edition of *Vathek* by William Beckford, 1893.

Exhib: L; RA; RI; ROI.

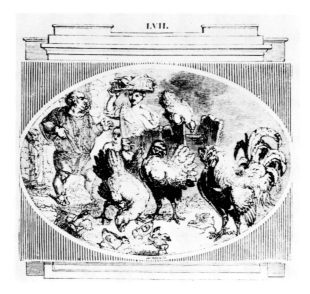

*JAMES NORTHCOTE RA 1746-1831. Vignette illustration for* One Hundred Fables, *1878. Wood engraving.*

**OAKES, John Wright  ARA HRSA**                     1820-1887

Landscape painter. He was born at Sproston House, Middlewich, Cheshire on 9 July 1820 and was educated at Liverpool College and at the Mechanics Institute under W.J. Bishop. Oakes concentrated on fruit paintings in the early part of his career but after 1843, worked with landscapes, especially the scenery of Wales, Scotland and Devon. He moved to London in 1859 and was elected ARA in 1876 and Hon. RSA in 1883. He was Secretary of the Liverpool Academy from 1839, and died in London on 8 July 1887.

Contrib: *Passages From The Modern English Poets [Junior Etching Club, 1862 and 1876].*
Exhib: BI; L; NWS; RA; RBA.
Colls: Birkenhead; V & AM.

**OAKLEY, William Harold**                     fl.1887-1925

Architect and illustrator. He practised in Maiden Lane, Strand, 1881-88 and was still active in 1925. He contributed architectural drawings to *The English Illustrated Magazine,* 1887-92 and to *The Strand Magazine,* 1891.

**ODLE, Alan Elsden**                     1888-1948

Illustrator, black and white artist and caricaturist. He was born in 1888 and studied at the Sidney Cooper School of Art, Canterbury and at the St John's Wood Art School. Odle specialised in Black Comedy subjects and in the grotesque, his drawings are often in chalk or black ink and show crowded and tortured scenes of revelry, with a strong sinister element derived from Beardsley. He apparently sold few of his drawings in his lifetime and illustrated few books for an artist with so powerful and individual a vision. Two sales of his work, much of it unused, at Sotheby's in April and November 1976 have helped to put his art into perspective. He was married to the novelist Dorothy Richardson, and died in 1948.

Illus: *Candide [Voltaire, 1925]; The Mimiambs of Herondas [trans by Jack Lindsay, Fanfrolico Press, 1926].*
Contrib: *The Gypsy [1915]; The Golden Hind.*
Exhib: RSA.
Colls: Author; V & AM.
Bibl: John Rosenberg, *The Genius They Forgot,* 1973; *Drawing and Design,* Vol.5, July 1925, p.40; *The Studio.* Vols.89, 95.
See illustration (Colour Plate XIV p.192).

**OFFORD, John James**                     fl.1860-1886

Figure painter and illustrator. He contributed drawings to *The Illustrated London News,* 1860.

Exhib: RA, 1886.

**OGDEN, H.A.**                     1856-

American illustrator. He was born at Philadelphia on 17 July 1856 and was a pupil of the Art Students League of New York. He specialised in military and historical subjects and contributed to *The Illustrated London News,* 1885.

**OLIPHANT, Laurence**                     1829-1888

Artist and war correspondent, traveller. He was born at Capetown in 1829 and travelled with his parents throughout Europe, 1846-48. He practised as a barrister in Ceylon and was secretary to Lord Elgin at Washington and in Canada, 1853-54. He represented *The Times* in Circassia, accompanied Lord Elgin to China, 1857-59 and worked with Garibaldi in Italy, 1860-61. He was *Times* correspondent again in the Franco-Prussian War of 1870 and was MP for Stirling, 1865-67. Oliphant was a contributor to *The Owl* and was associated with the spiritual teachings of T.L. Harris. He died in 1888.

Publ: *Journey to Khatmandhu [1852].*
Illus: *The Russian Shores of the Black Sea [1853, liths., AT 233].*
Contrib: *ILN [1855].*

**OLIVER, Lieutenant Samuel P.**

Amateur artist and Royal Artillery officer. He contributed to *The Illustrated London News,* 1867.

**O'NEILL, Harry**                     fl.1902-1915

Painter and illustrator. He contributed figure and social subjects to *Punch,* 1902-03.

Exhib. RHA.

**O'NEILL, Henry**                     1798-1880

Artist and antiquary. He was born at Clonmel in 1798 and in 1815 entered the RDS Schools and worked for a Dublin printseller. He worked as an illustrator before settling in London for some time, but making little success, he returned to Dublin where he became known for his publications. He was elected ARHA in 1837 but resigned in 1844. He died in Dublin in 1880.

Illus: *Picturesque Sketches of some of the Finest Landscapes and Coast Scenery of Ireland [1835 (with Nicholl and Petrie)]; Fourteen Views in the County of Wicklow [1835 (with Nicholl)]; Ireland its Scenery and Character [Hall, 1841]; Descriptive Catalogue of Illustrations of the Fine Arts of Ancient Ireland [1855]; Illustrations of the most interesting of the Sculptured Crosses of Ancient Ireland [1863]; The Round Towers of Ireland, Part 1 [1877].*
Colls: Belfast.

**O'NEILL, Hugh**                     1784-1824

Topographer and illustrator. He was born in Lascelles Place, Bloomsbury on 26 April 1784, the son of an architect and was patronised by Dr Thomas Monro. He won a Society of Arts silver palette in 1803 and in 1806 applied for the drawing-mastership at the RMC, Great Marlow. He eventually became a drawing-master in Oxford, Edinburgh, Bath and Bristol and died in the latter city on 7 April 1824.

Publ: *Bristol Antiquities [1826, etched by Skelton].*
Contrib: *Britton's Beauties of England and Wales {1801-13]; Antiquarian and Topographical Cabinet [1807]; The Oxford Almanac [1809, 1810, 1811, 1812, 1814].*
Exhib: RA, 1800-04.
Colls: Ashmolean; BM; Manchester; Reading; V & AM.
Bibl: Martin Hardie, *Watercol. Paint. in Brit.,* Vol.3, 1968, p.219.

**ONIONS, G. Oliver**                     1873-1961

Author and illustrator. He was born in Bradford in 1873 and after studying art, worked as a draughtsman for the Harmsworth Press. He married Bertha Ruck, the novelist and artist. Onions devoted himself entirely to novels from about 1910, winning the Tait Black Memorial Prize in 1947. He died on 9 April 1961.

Contrib: *Lady's Pictorial [1895]; The Quartier Latin [1896]; The Quarto [1897].*

**ONSLOW, A.G.**

Amateur artist contributing illustration to *Punch,* 1903.

**ONWHYN, Thomas**                     -1886

Illustrator. He was born in London, the youngest son of Joseph Onwhyn a bookseller and publisher of the magazine *The Owl,* 1864. Young Onwhyn produced 21 illegitimate drawings to an edition of *Pickwick Papers,* published by E. Grattan in 1837 and signed 'Sam Weller'. Further pirated examples followed, 40 for *Nicholas Nickleby* issued by Grattan in 1838 and another Pickwick set was begun but not published till 1893 by Albert Jackson. Onwhyn carried Dickens imitation to its logical conclusion by drawing in the manner of H.K. Browne and George Cruikshank (qq.v.). He never adapted to wood engraving and his best work is etched, but even that is rather wooden though he has an eye for the comic. He sometimes etched other people's work as in *Oakleigh* by W.H. Holmes, 1843 and drew for guidebooks and letter heads. He did no illustration for the last thirty years of his life and died on 5 January 1886.

Illus: *Memoirs of Davy Dreamy [1839]; Maxims and Specimens of William Muggins [Selby, 1841]; The Mysteries of Paris [Eugene Sue, 1844]; The Life and Adventures of Valentine Vox [Henry Cockton, 1849]; Etiquette Illustrated by an XMP [1849]; Marriage à la Mode, Mr and Mrs Brown's Visit to the Exhibition [1851]; Peter Palette's Tales and Pictures in Short Words For Young Folks [1856]; 300L a Year Or Single and Married Life [1859].*
Contrib: *Punch [1847-48].*

**OPPENHEIM, E. Phillips**                                    1866-1946
Illustrator. He began to work in 1887 and supplied ink drawings for *A Monk of Cruta*, c.1900.

**ORCHARDSON, Sir William Quiller**                          1836-1910
Painter of subject pictures and portraits. He was born in Edinburgh in 1836 and entered the Trustees Academy there in 1850 where he was a fellow student with John Pettie (q.v.). He moved to London in 1863 and exhibited Shakespearean subjects at the RA, but he became increasingly known for his High Life paintings in the 1880s, where great play is made of dramatic figures in a large pictorial space. As a young artist he had undertaken a small amount of illustration for magazines in a competent unremarkable style. He became ARA in 1868, RA in 1877, and was knighted in 1907. He died on 13 April 1910. An exhibition was held at the RA in 1911 and at FAS, 1972.

Contrib: *Good Words [1860-61, 1878]; Touches of Nature [1866]*.
Exhib: B; GG; G; L; New Gall; P; RA; RHA; RSA.
Bibl: J. Maas, *Victorian Painters*, 1970, p.244 illus.

**ORD, G.W.**
Illustrator of children's books, illustrated *Tommy Smith's Animals*, Edmund Selous, 1899.

**O'REILLY, Rear-Admiral Montague Frederick**               1822-1888
Amateur artist and illustrator. He was born in 1822 and as a professional naval officer, he served in North Australia and Hong-Kong and took part in the Chinese war of 1841. From 1845 he served on the West coast of Africa and in the Mediterranean and between 1851 and 1852 was on the South African station. He joined H.M.S. *Retribution* at Sebastopol and during this time made numerous sketches and diagrams of the Fleet in action in the Crimea. In 1856 he was appointed commander and from 1862 was commander of *Lapwing* in the Mediterranean and was promoted rear-admiral in 1878. O'Reilly sent many sketches to *The Illustrated London News*, in the years 1854-56 and in the issue of October 21, 1854 appears a self-portrait of him explaining his sketches.

Illus: *Twelve Views in the Black Sea and Bosphorus [1856, AT 241]*.
Contrib: *Cust's Naval Prints [1911]; Moore's Sailing Ships [1926]*.
Colls: Greenwich.
Bibl: *ILN*, June 7, 1888.

**ORFORD, H.W.**
Amateur illustrator contributing to *Fun*, 1900.

**ORME, Edward**                                              1774-
Publisher, engraver and architectural draughtsman. He was the brother of Ernest and William Orme (qq.v.) and studied at the RA Schools in 1793. He published numerous books on drawing from his address at 59 Bond Street and was still active in 1820.

Publ: *A Brief History of Ancient and Modern India [1805]; Orme's Graphic History of . . . Horatio Nelson [1806]; Essay on Transparent Prints [1807]; An Historical Momento [1814]; Bartolozzi Prints [1816 (a re-issue)]; Historic, Military and Naval Anecdotes [1819]*.
Colls: V & AM.

**ORME, Ernest**                                             fl.1801-1808
Architectural draughtsman and illustrator. He was a brother of Edward and William Orme and shared the latter's London address when he exhibited portraits at the RA, 1801-03. He published a drawing-book and illustrated a *Collection of British Field Sports*, 1807-08.

Colls: V & AM (sketchbook); Witt Photo.

**ORME, William**
Landscape artist and illustrator. He was born in Manchester, the brother of Ernest and Edward Orme (qq.v.) and worked there as a drawing-master from about 1794 to 1797. He had been awarded a silver palette by the Society of Arts in 1791-92. From 1797 when he moved to London he exhibited regularly at the RA and worked closely with his publisher brother.

Illus: *The Old Man, his Son and the Ass [c.1800]; Costume of Hindustan [1800]; Twenty-Four Views of Hindustan [1805]*.
Contrib: *The Copperplate Magazine*.
Colls: Greenwich; V & AM.

**ORMEROD, George**                                          fl.1801-1827
Amateur artist. Possibly George Ormerod of Charlton Hall, Cheshire, listed in *Patterson's Roads*, 1824.

Contrib: *Britton's Beauties of England and Wales [1801]*.

**ORPEN, Sir William    RA RI**                              1878-1931
Landscape painter and occasional caricaturist. He was born at Stillorgan in Ireland on 27 November 1878 and studied at the Dublin Metropolitan School of Art and at the Slade School, 1897-99. Although Orpen established his reputation in portrait painting and is remembered for very competent and slick studies of famous Edwardians in a lavish manner derived from Sargent, he made an impressive contribution as War Artist, 1917-18. These drawings which were exhibited as War Pictures in 1918 were later published as a book and many of them were presented to Government collections. Orpen was knighted in 1918, and elected RA in 1919 and was President of the International Society of Sculptors, Painters and Gravers from 1921. He was elected ARHA in 1904, RHA 1907 and RI in 1919, having been a member of the NEA since 1900. He died on 29 September 1931.

The Ashmolean collection has two caricatures by this artist, one of which is a self-portrait.

Illus: *An Onlooker in France [1921]; Stories of Old Ireland and Myself [1924]*.
Exhib: B; FAS; GG; G; L; M; NEA; P; RA.
Colls: Ashmolean; Imperial War Mus.

**ORR, Monro Scott**                                         1874-
Painter, etcher and illustrator. He was born at Irvine on 7 October 1874, the brother of Stewart Orr (q.v.) and studied at the Glasgow School of Art under Newbery. Orr's work is bold and rather posterish and is comparable in style to that of John Hassall (q.v.). He was also much influenced by William Nicholson as is clear from the thick border line to his drawings and his direct imitation of that artist in *Twelve Drawings of Familar Characters* . . . 1903. A contemporary criticism was that his drawings seemed to be cramped into a space too small for them.

Illus: *Twelve Drawings of Familar Characters in Fiction and Romance [1903]; Ye Twelve Months; The Old Ayrshire of Robert Burns; Poems of Robert Fergusson; The Arabian Nights; Grimms Fairy Tales; Mother Goose; Jane Eyre*; Book covers for: *The Unchanging East; Our Naval Heroes; Towards Pretoria; The Blessings of Esau; Kidnapped*.
Exhib: G; L; RSA; RSW.
Colls: Witt Photo.
Bibl: *Art Journal*, 1900, p.310; *The Studio*, Vol.29, 1903, p.215-217; *Modern Illustrators and Their Work*, Studio 1914.

**ORR, Stewart    RSW**                                      1872-1944
Watercolourist and book illustrator. He was born in Glasgow on 21 January 1872, the brother of Monro S. Orr (q.v.). He studied at the Glasgow School of Art and Glasgow University and after working in Essex in about 1902, lived chiefly in Glasgow or the Isle of Arran. He died in 1944, having been elected RSW in 1925.

Exhib: G; L; RA; RI; RSA; RSW.
Bibl: *Modern Book Illustrators and Their Work*, Studio 1914.

**ORROCK, James    RI**                                      1829-1913
Landscape painter, collector and lecturer. He was born in Edinburgh in 1829 and was educated at Irvine, Ayrshire and at Edinburgh University where he read surgery and dentistry. He then studied art with James Fergusson and J. Burgess in Leicester and with Stewart Smith at the Nottingham School of Design until 1866, when he moved to London. He took lessons from W.L. Leitch (q.v.) in London and was elected ANWS in 1871 and NWS in 1875.

Orrock was however best known for the books that he published on the arts and for his fine collections of Chippendale furniture and Nankin china which he had in his home at Bedford Square, Bloomsbury. He presented watercolours and drawings to both the

Victoria and Albert Museum and the Glasgow City Art Gallery, 1899.
He died on 10 May 1913, at Shepperton, Middlesex.

Illus: *In the Border Country [W.S. Crockett, 1906]; Mary Queen of Scots [W.S. Sparrow, 1906]; Old England [1908].*
Exhib: B; G; L; M; New Gall; RA; RI; ROI.
Colls: Bradford; Maidstone; Nottingham; V & AM.
Bibl: B. Webber, *JO*, 1903.

**OSBORNE, Walter Frederick   RHA**                    **1859-1903**
Portrait painter. He was born in Dublin in 1859 and studied at the
RDS Schools, 1876 and then at Antwerp, 1881 to 1883. He made
extensive painting tours in England, France and Spain, was elected
ARHA in 1883 and RHA in 1886. Osborne was an accomplished
painter of animals and of town and country life; he died in London in
1903.

Contrib: *Black & White [1891].*
Colls: BM; Nat. Gall; Ireland.
Bibl: T. Bodkin, *Four Irish Landscape Painters*, 1920.

**OSPOVAT, Henry**                    **1877-1909**
Painter, draughtsman and illustrator. He was born in Russia in 1877
and migrated with his family to Manchester where they settled.
Ospovat was trained at the Manchester School of Art in 1897 and was
perhaps encouraged by Walter Crane (q.v.) whose bookplate he
designed. He then attended the South Kensington School and received
some important commissions at a very early age and was much
influenced by the Pre-Raphaelites and the work of C.S. Ricketts
(q.v.). His drawing style might be compared to that of Laurence
Housman, another Rossetti devotee, but his line is much broader and
his effects altogether more powerful and sensuous. He was also a
brilliant caricaturist, particularly of the London music-hall and his
death in London on 2 January 1909 removed a significant figure from
English illustration. A memorial exhibition was held at the Baillie
Gallery in 1909.

Illus: *Shakespeare's Sonnets [1899]; The Poems of Matthew Arnold [1900]; Shakespeare's Songs [1901]; The Song of Songs [1906]; Browning's Poems [projected but not issued].*
Contrib: *The Idler.*
Exhib: NEA.
Colls: V & AM.
Bibl: *The Studio*, Vol.10, 1897, p.111, illus; Vol.43, 1908, p.235; Winter No., 1923-24, pp.37, 133; R.E.D. Sketchley, *Eng. Bk. Illus.*, 1903, pp.13-14, 129; Oliver Onions, *The Works of HO With An Appreciation By . . .*, 1911. Arnold Bennett, *Books and Persons*, 1917.
See illustration (right).

**OVEREND, William Heysman**                    **1851-1898**
Marine painter and illustrator. He was born at Coatham in Yorkshire
in 1851 and was educated at Charterhouse. He began principally as a
marine artist but increasingly from about 1872, undertook work for
*The Illustrated London News* and for book illustration. During the
next three decades his output was extensive and nearly every issue of
the magazine has pages of his coastal realism, fishermen and
trawlermen fighting the sea and anxious women waiting on shore. He
was elected ROI in 1886 and died in the U.S.A. 1898.

Illus: *The Fate of the Black Swan [F.F. Moore, 1865]; On board the Esmerelda [J.C. Hutcheson, 1885]; One of the 28th [G.A. Henty, 1889]; Benin the City of Blood [R.H.S. Bacon, 1897]; Devils Ford [Bret Harte, 1897].*
Contrib: *ILN [1872-96]; The English Illustrated Magazine [1891-94]; Good Words [1894]; The Rambler [1897]; The Boys' Own Paper; Chums; The Pall Mall Magazine.*
Exhib: G; L; RA; ROI
Colls: V & AM.
Bibl: Joseph Pennell, *Modern Illustration*, 1895 p.108.

**OVERNELL, T.J.**
Illustrator and designer and student of RCA working in an art
nouveau style and contributing programme covers and book plates to
the National Competition, South Kensington, 1897.

Bibl: *The Studio*, Vol.8, 1896, p.224, illus.

**OWEN, Rev. Edward Pryce**                    **1788-1863**
Amateur artist and topographer. He was born in 1788 and was
educated at St John's College, Cambridge before becoming Vicar of
Wellington and Rector of Eyton-upon-the-Wildmoors, Shropshire in

*HENRY OSPOVAT 1877-1909. 'Andrea del Sarto.' Illustration for Browning's Men and Women. Pen. 14ins. x 10ins. (35.6cm x 25.4cm).*
Victoria and Albert Museum

1823. He made extensive tours to the Continent, making sketches that
he used for watercolours and etchings. He died at Cheltenham in
1863.

Illus: *Etchings of Ancient Buildings in Shrewsbury [1820-21]; Etchings [1826]; The Book of Etchings [1842-55].*
Exhib: RBA, 1837-40.
Colls: Shrewsbury Lib.

**OWEN, Samuel**                    **1768-1857**
Marine painter. He was born in 1768 and is associated with
watercolour sketches of the south coast and the Thames estuary. He
published with W. Westall (q.v.) *Picturesque Tour of the River
Thames*, 1828 and illustrated W.B. Cooke's *The Thames*, 1811.

Exhib: RA, 1794-1807.

**OWEN, Will   RCA**                    **1869-1957**
Artist, caricaturist and lecturer. He was born in Malta in 1869 and
educated in Rochester and at the Lambeth School of Art. Owen
worked in a humorous poster style and did much commercial work,
his chief contribution to books was as illustrator of W.W. Jacobs
novels.

Publ: *Old London Town [n.d.].*
Contrib: *Pick-Me-Up [1895]; The Windsor Magazine; The Temple Magazine; Punch [1904-07]; The Strand Magazine [1906]; The Graphic [1912]; ILN [1915].*
Exhib: RCA;
Colls: V & AM.

**PADDAY, Charles Murray  RI**                                fl.1889-1937
Marine and landscape painter and illustrator. He was a leading illustrator of shipping for *The Illustrated London News* from 1896 until about 1916. He worked in London from 1889-93 and then at Bosham, 1902, Hayling Island, 1914 and Hythe, 1925, he also travelled on sketching tours to Brittany. He was elected ROI in 1906 and RI in 1929.

Illus: *Gun Boat and Gun Runner [T.T. Jeans, 1915].*
Contrib: *Black & White [1899].*
Exhib: L; RA; RBA; RI; ROI.
Bibl: *A.J.,* 1906 p.168.

**PADGETT, William**                                          1851-1904
Landscape painter. He worked in Twickenham, 1881 and Campden Hill, London from 1882. He contributed one illustration to *Punch* in 1882.

Exhib: GG; G; L; M; New Gall; RA; RBA; ROI.

**PAGE, P.N.**
Architectural draughtsman contributing to *The Illustrated London News,* 1858 (col. block).

**PAGE, William**                                             1794-1872
Landscape painter and topographer. He studied at the RA Schools, 1812-13 and travelled in Asia Minor and Greece in the period 1818 to 1824. He was an accurate depictor of buildings and a competent figure artist and contributed drawings to *Finden's Landscape and Portrait Illustrations To The Life and Works of Lord Byron,* 1833-34 and to *Finden's Landscape Illustrations of the Bible,* 1836.

Exhib: RA, 1816-60.
Colls: BM; Coventry; Searight Coll.
Bibl: *Country Life,* September 26, 1968.

**PAGET, Henry Marriott**                                     1856-1936
Artist and illustrator. He was born in London on 31 December 1856, brother of Sidney and Walter Stanley Paget (qq.v.). He was educated at Atherstone Grammar School, the City Foundation Schools and entered the RA Schools in 1874. He made a series of foreign tours beginning in 1879 to Italy, Greece and Crete and was in Western Canada, 1909. He was sent as Special Artist by *The Sphere* to Constantinople to cover the Balkan War, 1912-13 and served with the BEF in the First World War, 1916. He was elected RBA, 1889 and died in London, 27 March 1936.

Illus: *The Bravest of the Brave [G.A. Henty, 1887]; The Talisman, Kenilworth [Walter Scott, 1893]; Quentin Durward [Walter Scott, 1894]; Pictures From Dickens [1895]; Annals of Westminster Abbey [Bradley, 1895]; The Vicar of Wakefield [Goldsmith, 1898]; The Black Arrow [R.L. Stevenson, c.1913].*
Contrib: *The Graphic [1877-1906]; The Quiver [1890]; The Illustrated London News [1890]; The Windsor Magazine.*
Exhib: B; FAS; GG; G; L; M; RA; RBA; ROI.
Colls: Bodleian.

**PAGET, Sidney E.**                                          1860-1908
Artist and illustrator. He was born in London on 4 October 1860, the brother of Henry Marriott and Walter Stanley Paget (qq.v.). He was educated privately and studied art at the BM and at Heatherley's and the RA Schools, where he was a bronze and gold medallist, 1884. Paget was a very prolific illustrator and was the first artist to draw Sherlock Holmes for Conan Doyle's short stories in *The Strand Magazine,* 1892-94. He was on the staff of *The Illustrated London News* and *The Sphere,* and died in London on 28 January 1908.

Illus: *The Adventures of Sherlock Holmes [1892]; The Memoirs of Sherlock Holmes [1892-94]; Rodney Stone [1896]; The Tragedy of Korosko [1898];*

*Old Mortality [Walter Scott, 1898]; Terence [1898]; The Sanctuary Club [1900].*
Contrib: *ILN [1884]; The Quiver [1890]; The Strand Magazine [1891-94]; Cassell's Family Magazine; The Graphic.*
Exhib: L; M; New Gall; RA; RBA; RI.
Colls: Bristol.
Bibl: R.E.D. Sketchley, *Eng. Bk. Illus.,* 1903, pp.68, 152; *The Times,* 27 November 1976, Correspondence.

**PAGET, Walter Stanley  'Wal'**                              1863-1935
Artist and illustrator. He was born in 1863, the brother of Henry Marriott and Sidney E. Paget (qq.v.).

Illus: *The Black Dwarf, Castle Dangerous, The Talisman, A Legend of Montrose [Walter Scott, 1893-95]; Robinson Crusoe [1896]; At Agincourt [G.A. Henty, 1897]; Treasure Island [1899]; Lamb's Tales From Shakespeare [1901].*
Contrib: *The English Illustrated Magazine [1891-92]; ILN [1892-98]; The Queen [1894]; The Quiver; Cassell's Family Magazine.*
Exhib: G; L; M; New Gall; RA; RBA; ROI.
Bibl: R.E.D. Sketchley, *Eng. Bk. Illus.,* 1903 pp.92, 152.

**PAILLET, Fernand**                                          1850-1918
French portrait, watercolour and enamel painter. He exhibited at the Salon from 1873 and illustrated *Persian Lustre Ware* by Henry Wallis, 1899.

Colls: V & AM.

**PAILTHORPE, F.W.**                                          fl.c.1880-c.1899
Illustrator. A number of watercolours by this artist for an edition of Dickens are in the Victoria and Albert Museum. They are very Georgian in spirit and reminiscent of the work of H.K. Browne.

Illus: *Posthumous Papers of the Pickwick Club [1882]; Great Expectations [1885]; Oliver Twist [1886 (all issued by Robson & Kerslake)].*

**PAINE, Henry A.**
Black and white artist of the Birmingham School, contributed to *The Quest,* 1894-96.

**PALEOLOGU, Jean de  'PAL'**                                 1855-
Figure artist and caricaturist of Rumanian origin. He was a contributor to *Vanity Fair,* 1889-90 and to *The Strand Magazine,* 1892-94. Signs: PAL.

**PALMER, John**                                              fl.1856-1887
Genre painter and illustrator. He specialised in industrial and theatrical scenes as well as in domestic subjects and contributed to *The Illustrated Times,* 1856-61 and *The Illustrated London News,* 1864-66.

Exhib: RA; RBA.

**PALMER, Samuel  RWS**                                       1805-1881
Visionary landscape painter and watercolourist. He was born at Newington on 27 January 1805, the son of a bookseller and began painting at the age of thirteen. He started exhibiting at the RA in 1819 at the age of fourteen and soon after came under the influences of Varley, Stothard and Linnell, and that of William Blake (q.v.) whom he met first in 1824. Fired by Blake and forming one of his mystical circle of 'Ancients' at Shoreham, Palmer produced a series of watercolours of the area, outstanding for their poetic beauty and innocence. He married Linnell's daughter in 1837 and travelled in Italy for two years, returning to live near his father-in-law and to teach drawing. His later work is usually considered to have lost the intensity of his early vision of landscape. He was elected OWS in 1856 and died at Redhill in 1881.

Palmer's work as a book illustrator is very small. It was Blake's small wood engravings that first inspired him, but in his long life, only Charles Dickens' *Pictures from Italy,* 1846, has four tiny vignettes from his hand. Two important posthumous works were Virgil's *Eclogues,* 1883, and Milton's *Minor Poems,* 1888, issued by his son and filled with fine etchings. The Ashmolean has a print for an edition of *The Pilgrim's Progress,* 1848.

Exhib: BI; OWS; RA; RBA.
Colls: Birkenhead; Birmingham; Blackburn; BM; Manchester; V & AM.

Bibl: A.H. Palmer, *SP: A Memoir*, 1882; A.H. Palmer, *Life and Letters of SP*, 1892; R.L. Binyon, *The Followers of W. Blake*, 1926; G. Grigson, *The Visionary Years*, 1947; E. Malin's, *SP's Italian Honeymoon*, 1968; David Cecil, *Visionary and Dreamer*, 1969; R. Lister, *SP*, 1974.
See illustration (p.205).

**PALMER, Sutton**                                                    1854-1933

Landscape painter and illustrator. He was born at Plymouth in 1854 and was educated at Camden Town High School before studying at the South Kensington School. He changed from being primarily a still-life painter to a landscape painter and illustrated a number of colour plate books. He was elected RBA in 1892 and RI in 1920. He died on 8 May 1933.

Illus: *Rivers and Streams of England [A.G. Bradley]; Bonnie Scotland [Hope Moncreiff]; Surrey [Hope Moncreiff]; The Heart of Scotland [Hope Moncreiff, 1905]; The Wye; Berks and Bucks.*
Exhib: FAS; G; L; M; RA; RBA; RI.
Colls: V & AM.

**PANNET, R.**                                                       fl.1895-1925

Figure artist and illustrator working in London.

Contrib: *The Lady's Pictorial [1895]; St. Pauls [1899]; Illustrated Bits [1900]; The Temple Magazine; The Royal Magazine; The Graphic [1908].*

**PAPE, Frank Cheyne**

Black and white artist and illustrator.

Illus: *Children of the Dawn [E.F. Buckley, 1908]; The Book of Psalms [1912]; The Story Without An End [1912].*

**PAPWORTH, John Buonarotti**                                        1775-1847

Architect and topographical illustrator. He was born in London on 24 January 1775 and studied architecture on the advice of Sir William Chambers, learning drawing from John Deare and working under the architect John Plaw. He entered the RA Schools in 1798 and by that date had already exhibited drawings there and designed his first house, in Essex, for Sir James Wright, 1793-99. Papworth was well established as an architect by the age of twenty-five and had a large practice in country houses and villas and designed such Regency landmarks as the Cheltenham Pump Room, 1825-26. As a draughtsman, Papworth was much employed by R. Ackermann and on his own books, many of them issued by Ackermann. He had public appointments as Architect to the King of Württemberg, 1820 and was Secretary of the Associated Artists, 1808-10. He died at Little Paxton, Huntingdonshire on June 16 1847.

Illus: *The Social Day [Peter Coxe, 1823]; Select Views in London [1816]; Designs For Rural Residences, consisting of a series of Designs for Cottages, small villas, and other Buildings, [1818, 2nd Ed., 1832]; Hints on Ornamental Gardening [1823]; Forget-Me-Not Annual [1825-30 (covers)].*
Contrib: *Ackermann's Repository [1809-28].*
Exhib: RA.
Colls: RIBA; V & AM.
Bibl: W.A. Papworth, *JBP*, 1879; *Arch Review*, Vol.79, 1936; H.M. Colvin, *Biog. Dict. of Eng. Arch.*, 1954 pp.436-443.

**'PAQUE'    see PIKE, W.H.**

**PARK, Carton Moore**                                               1877-1956

Portrait, decorative and animal painter and illustrator. He was born in 1877 and studied at the Glasgow School of Art under Francis Newbery and his first efforts at illustration were published in *The Glasgow Weekly Citizen* and *St. Mungo*. Park was a talented book decorator and caricaturist, but concentrated on animal illustration which he was able to treat in a strong and unsentimental way derived from Japanese prints. In 1899 he was elected RBA, resigning in 1905, and he continued to exhibit in the UK before emigrating to America in about 1910. He was editor and illustrator for Messrs. George Allen's *Child's Library*. He died in New York on 23 January 1956.

Illus: *An Alphabet of Animals [1899]; A Book of Birds [1900]; A Book of Elfin Rhymes [1900]; A Book of Dogs; A Child's London [1900]; The Child's Pictorial Natural History [1901]; La Fontaine's Fables For Children; The King*

*of the Beasts; Mural panels – The Zoo; The Farmyard; Lithographs – Uncle Remus; Tales of the Old Plantation; Breer Rabbit; For Allen's Child's Library – A Countryside Chronicle [S.L. Bensusan]; The Bee; Biffel; The Story of a Trek-Ox.*
Contrib: *The Butterfly [1899]; The Idler.*
Exhib: G; L; NEA; RA; RBA.
Bibl: *The Studio*, Winter No., 1900-01 pp.16-17, illus.; R.E.D. Sketchley, *Eng. Bk. Illus.*, 1903 pp.118, 168; *Modern Book Illustrators and Their Work*, Studio 1914.
See illustration (below).

**PARKES, David**                                                    1763-1833

Amateur artist and schoolmaster. He was born at Cakemore, Salop in 1763 and ran a school at Shrewsbury. He died there on 8 May 1833.

Contrib: *Britton's Beauties of England & Wales [1813-14]; The Gentleman's Magazine.*

**PARKINSON, William**                                               fl.1883-1895

Figure artist and cartoonist of *Judy*, 1890. He worked in London and contributed to various magazines including, *Ally Sloper's Half Holiday*, 1890 and *Black and White*, 1891.

Exhib: RA.
Colls: V & AM.

**PARNELL, R.**

Illustrator of children's books. He was the brother of Mrs. E. Farmiloe (q.v.) and worked for *The New Budget, Lika Joko* and *Little Folks*. He made a speciality of comic animals.

Bibl: *The Studio*, Vol.21, 1900-01 pp.51-54.

**PARRIS, Edmund Thomas**                                            1793-1873

Portrait painter. He was born in London on 3 June 1793 and entered the RA Schools in 1816, exhibiting there from that year. He worked at Horner's Colosseum in Regents Park from 1824 to 1829 and became Historical Painter to Queen Adelaide in 1838. His restorations to the Thornhill paintings in the cupola of St. Paul's cathedral, 1853-56 were unsympathetic and his sentimental style and pretty washes were best suited to album illustration. He died in London on 17 November 1873.

Illus: *Flowers of Loveliness [Lady Blessington, 1836]; Confessions of an Elderly Gentleman [Lady Blessington, 1836]; Confessions of an Elderly Lady [Lady Blessington, 1838].*
Contrib: *The Keepsake;* 1833, 1836-37.
Exhib: BI; NWS; RA; RBA.
Colls: BM; Doncaster; V & AM.

*CARTON MOORE PARK 1877-1956. 'Panthers.' Illustration for* The Studio, *1900.*

**PARRISH, Maxfield**                                              1870-1966

Painter and illustrator. He was born in Philadelphia on 25 July 1870
and studied at the Boston Academy of Fine Arts under Howard Pyle
(q.v.). Although principally an American illustrator, he made the
designs for *Dream Days* by Kenneth Grahame, 1906. He died 30
March 1966.

Bibl: *The Studio*, Vol.38, 1906 pp.35-43 (Herkomer on his illus.).

**PARRY, James**                                                  c.1805-1871

Landscape and figure artist at Manchester. He drew and engraved
some illustrations of topography for Corry's *History of Lancashire*.
Exhib: M, 1827-56.

**PARRY, John**                                                   1812-c.1865

Caricaturist. He was probably an amateur and the Victoria and Albert
Museum has two sheets of his work, one inscribed 'Whims' and dated
'1850'. He seems to have specialised in silhouette caricatures of men,
women and animals, often done on visiting cards.

**PARSONS, Alfred    RA PRWS**                                    1847-1920

Landscape painter, watercolourist and illustrator. He was born at
Beckingham, Somerset on 2 December 1847 and started his life as a
Post Office clerk before studying at South Kensington. Parson's made
a speciality of garden and plant drawings and was a masterly book
decorator in designs for initial letters. He did a great deal of magazine
work before turning his attention to books and was elected ARA in
1897 and RA in 1911. He became RWS in 1905 and was President in
1913. His meticulous pen landscapes have a slight similarity to Joseph
Pennell (q.v.), but his pencil drawing is quite special in its toned
softness. He died at Broadway on 16 January 1920. Signs: [AP]

Illus: *God's Acre Beautiful [W. Robinson, 1880]; Poetry of Robert Herrick
[1882]; Springham [R.D. Blackmore, 1888]; Old Songs [1889]; Sonnets of
William Wordsworth [1891]; The Warwickshire Avon [Quiller Couch, 1892];
The Danube [F.D. Millet, 1892]; The Wild Garden [Robinson, 1895]; The
Bamboo Garden [Freeman-Mitford, 1896]; Notes in Japan [1896]; Wordsworth
[Andrew Lang, 1897].*
Contrib: *The English Illustrated Magazine [1883-86, 1891-92]; The Quiet Life
[1890 (with E.A. Abbey)]; Harper's Monthly Magazine [1891-92]; The Daily
Chronicle [1895].*
Exhib: B; FAS, 1885, 1891, 1893, 1894; GG; G; L; M; NEA; New Gall; RA;
RHA; RI; ROI; RSW; RWS.
Colls: V & AM.
Bibl: *The Studio*, Winter No., 1900-01 p.73, illus.; R.E.D. Sketchley, *Eng. Bk.
Illus.*, 1903 pp.31, 35, 137; Martin Hardie, *Watercol. Paint. in Brit.*, Vol.3, 1968
p.96, illus.

See illustration (right).

**PARTRIDGE, Sir J. Bernard    RI**                               1861-1945

Black and white artist and principal cartoonist of Punch. He was born
in London on 11 October 1861, the son of Professor Richard
Partridge, Professor of Anatomy to the RA and nephew of John
Partridge, Portrait Painter Extraordinary to Queen Victoria. Partridge
was educated at Stonyhurst College and then trained with a firm of
stained-glass artists, studying the design of drapery, 1880-84. He was
extremely interested in the theatre and acted for some time under the
name of 'Bernard Gould' appearing in the first production of Shaw's
*Arms and The Man*. Many of his early drawings are of theatrical
subjects or personalities and some of his finest caricatures in later life
were still drawn from the world of the stage. He was introduced to
*Punch* by F. Anstey and G. Du Maurier (q.v.) and joined the staff in
1891, becoming successively second cartoonist, 1901 and principal
cartoonist, 1909-45. An artist who was well suited to theatrical
sketches and book illustrations, he found himself having to do most of
the 'heavy' work of the magazine. Although he was trained with the
woodblock, he adapted his pen line to process quite easily, but some
of his cartoons are overworked and lack contrast. By the close of his
working life, the statuesque figures of symbol looked slightly out of
place on the magazines pages even when accompanied by excellent
portraits of Churchill, Hitler and Mussolini. Partridge also painted in
oil, watercolour and pastel, was elected a member of the NEA in 1893
and RI in 1896. He died in 1945.

*ALFRED PARSONS RA PRWS 1847-1920. The Old Mosque at Rustchuk,
Bulgaria. Illustration for* Harper's Monthly Magazine, *July 1892. Pencil. Signed
with monogram. 7⁷/₈ins. x 6¹/₄ins. (20cm x 15.9cm).*

Victoria and Albert Museum

Illus: *Stageland [Jerome K. Jerome, 1889]; Voces Populi [F. Anstey, 1890];
The Travelling Companions [F. Anstey, 1892]; My Flirtations [Margaret
Wynman, 1892]; The Man From Blankley's [F. Anstey, 1893]; Proverbs in
Porcelain [Austin Dobson, 1893]; Mr Punch's Pocket Ibsen [F. Anstey, 1893];
Under the Rose [F. Anstey, 1894]; Lyre and Lancet [F. Anstey, 1895];
Barrie's Works [1896]; Puppets at Large [1897]; Baboo Jabberjee B.A.,
[1897]; Lyceum Souvenirs; The Crusade of the Excelsior [Bret Harte, 1897];
The Tinted Venus [1898]; Wee Folk [1899]; A Bayard From Bengal [F.
Anstey, 1902].*
Contrib: *ILN [1885-89 (theat.)]; Judy [1886]; The Quiver [1890]; Punch
[1891-1945]; Black & White [1892]; The Idler [1892]; New Budget [1895];
Vanity Fair [1896]; Sporting and Dramatic News [1899]; Lady's Pictorial; The
Sketch; Lika Joko; Pick-Me-Up; Illustrated Bits.*
Exhib: FAS, 1902, 1946; G; L; NEA; RA; RI.
Colls: BM (Millar Bequest); V & AM; Mus. of London.
Bibl: Joseph Pennell, *Pen Drawing and Pen Draughtsmen*, 1894 pp.332-333;
M.H. Spielmann, *The History of Punch*, 1895 pp.564-565; *The Studio*, Winter
No., 1900-01 pp.11-13, illus.; R.E.D. Sketchley, *Eng. Bk. Illus.*, 1903 pp.58, 86,
153; R.G.G. Price, *A History of Punch*, 1957 pp.160-163, illus.; Martin Hardie,
*Watercol. Paint. in Brit.*, Vol.3, 1968 p.96.

See illustrations (pp.410, 411).

**PASQUIER, C.A.**

Decorative illustrator contributing to *The Graphic*, 1911 (Christmas).

409

*SIR BERNARD PARTRIDGE RI 1861-1945. 'The Wings of Victory.' A preliminary sketch for the cartoon that appeared in* Punch *on 14 May 1912, marking the inauguration of the Royal Flying Corps. Pencil, pen and ink. 14¹/8ins. x 11¹/2ins. (35.9cm x 29.2cm).*

Victoria and Albert Museum

*SIR BERNARD PARTRIDGE RI 1861-1945. 'The Comic Lovers.' A design for a music title cover, about 1895. Pen and ink. Signed. 9½ins. x 7¼ins. (21.4cm x 18.4cm).*
Author's Collection

## PASQUIER, J. Abbott                                    fl.1851-1872
Genre painter, watercolourist and illustrator. Although very little is known about him, Dalziel credits him with being 'a clever artist in black and white, and a skilful painter in watercolours'. His drawings for illustration have a very soft line with nice washes and slight caricature reminiscent of Leech. His favourite subjects were London ones, crossing sweepers, rainy days etc.

Contrib: *The Home Affections [Charles Mackay, 1858]; ILN [1856, 1866]; The Illustrated Times [1860]; London Society [1865-68]; Foxe's Book of Martyrs [1865]; Aunt Judy's Magazine [1866]; Beeton's Annuals [1866]; The Broadway [1867]; The Sunday Magazine [1868]; The Quiver [1868].*
Bibl: Dalziel, *A Record of Work, 1840-1890,* 1901 p.190.

## PATON, Frank                                           1856-1909
Figure painter and illustrator. He worked in London and Gravesend and contributed one cartoon of an equestrian subject to *Vanity Fair,* 1910.

Colls: BM.

## PATON, Sir Joseph Noël                                 1821-1901
Religious and fairy painter and illustrator. He was born at Dunfermline on 13 December 1821 and educated there before entering the RA Schools in 1843. He was awarded a premium in the Westminster Hall Competition, 1845 and again in 1847, becoming ARSA, in 1847 and RSA in 1850. He was a very versatile man working as poet and sculptor as well as painter; he had close connections with the Pre-Raphaelites in his early days and retained their colouring, he remained a lifelong friend of J.E. Millais (q.v.). His most famous illustrated book was Kingsley's *Water Babies,* 1863 and though he was approached by Dodgson to illustrate the second

volume of *Alice,* he declined. Paton was most at home in the realm of fairyland where Celtic romance and myth mixed together in his powerful imagination. Such paintings as the 'Reconciliation of Oberon and Titania' in the National Gallery of Scotland are among the best works in this field. Some of this spills over into his books for The Art Unions. An immensely successful public figure, Paton was made Her Majesty's Limner for Scotland in 1866 and knighted in 1867. He died at Edinburgh on 26 December 1901.

Illus: *Compositions from Shakespeare's Tempest [1845]; Compositions from Shelley's Prometheus Unbound [1845]; Silent Love [James Wilson, 1845]; Coleridge's Life of the Ancient Mariner [1863]; Lays of the Scottish Cavaliers [W.E. Aytoun, 1863]; The Water Babies [Charles Kingsley, 1863]; Gems of Literature [1866]; The Story of Wandering Willie [1870]; The Princess of Silverland and other Tales [E. Strivelyne, 1874]; Rab and his Friends [John Brown, 1878].*
Contrib: *A Book of British Ballads [1842]; Puck on Pegasus [Pennell, 1861]; The Cornhill Magazine [1864].*
Exhib: GG; G; L; RSA.
Colls: BM; Glasgow; Nat. Gall; Scotland.
Bibl: J. Maas, *Victorian Painters,* 1970 pp.152-153, illus.

## PATON, Walter Hugh   RSA                               1828-1895
Landscape painter and illustrator. He was born at Dunfermline on 27 July 1828 the brother of Sir J.N. Paton (q.v.). He began his career as an industrial designer in the textile industry until 1848 and then became a pupil of J.A. Houston. He was elected ARSA in 1866 and RSA in 1868. He died in Edinburgh on 8 March 1895.

Illus: *Lays of the Scottish Cavaliers [W.E. Aytoun, 1863 (with J.N. Paton)]; Poems and Songs by Robert Burns [1875].*
Exhib: G; L; M; New Gall; RA; RHA; RI; RSA; RSW.
Colls: Dundee; Glasgow.
Bibl: *Art Journal,* 1895.

## PATTEN, Leonard                                        fl.1889-1914
Painter. He contributed one humorous drawing in the style of Meryon to *Punch,* 1914.

Exhib: RA, 1889.

## PATTEN, William
Topographer. He contributed illustrations to *Westminster* by Walter Besant, 1897.

## PATTERSON, J. Malcolm                                  fl.1898-1925
Black and white artist, etcher and illustrator. He was born at Twickenham in 1873 and educated at Clifton. He worked at St. Andrews, Scotland where he was art master at St. Leonard's School, and specialised in rustic genre subjects with finely detailed cottage interiors.

Contrib: *Fun [1896]; The Dome [1898]; The Quiver [1900]; Punch [1900-07]; Illustrated Bits; Sketchy Bits; The Idler; The Windsor Magazine; The Royal Magazine.*
Exhib: L; RSA.

## PAUL, Evelyn                                           fl.1906-1911
Illustrator. She studied at South Kensington in about 1906 and exhibited in the National Competition that year.

Illus: *Cranford [Mrs. Gaskell, 1910]; Stories From Dante [Susan Cunnington, 1911].*
Bibl: *The Studio,* Vol.38, 1906 p.316.

## PAUL, Sir John Dean, Bt.                               1802-1868
Amateur illustrator. He was born on 27 October 1802 and was educated at Westminster and Eton before joining the family bank of Snow, Paul and Paul, from 1828. He succeeded his father as second baronet in 1852 and in 1855 the bank stopped payment and its partners were tried for fraud and sentenced to transportation. He died at St. Albans in 1868.

Publ: *A.B.C. of Foxhunting [1871].*
Illus: *The Country Doctor's Horse [Sir J.D. Paul, 1847].*

## PAUQUETTE, Hippolyte Louis Emile                       1797-
French illustrator. He was the brother-in-law of Gustave Janet (q.v.) and was an occasional ·contributor to *The Illustrated London News* in about 1869. He exhibited at the Salon, 1821-49.

**PAXTON, Robert B.M.** fl.1895-1925

Portrait painter and illustrator. In his early years he shared a studio with A.S. Hartrick (q.v.) and later worked in Fulham and Putney.

Contrib: *The Daily Graphic [1895]; The Windsor Magazine; The Graphic [1902-07]; The Strand Magazine [1906].*
Exhib: G; RA.

**PAYNE, C.N.**

Contributed motoring sketches to *Punch*, 1906.

**PAYNE, Charles J.**

Contributor to *The Graphic*, 1915.

**PAYNE, Dorothy M.** fl.1910-1914

Illustrator. She was a student of the Lambeth School and shows a strong influence of Walter Crane in her work. She exhibited at South Kensington, 1910-11.

Bibl: *The Studio*, Vol.53, 1911 p.299; *Pen, Pencil & Chalk*, Studio, 1911; *Modern Book Illustrators and Their Work*, Studio, 1914.

**PAYNE, Henry Albert RWS** 1868-1940

Portrait and landscape painter, stained-glass artist and illustrator. He was born at Kings Heath, Birmingham in 1868 and studied art under E.R. Taylor at the Birmingham School and taught at it for eighteen years. He learnt the craft of stained glass and made many windows and painted frescoes for the chapel of Lord Beauchamp and for the House of Lords. He married the flower painter Edith Gere in 1903 and was elected ARWS in 1912 and RWS in 1920. He lived at Amberley, Gloucestershire from about 1912 and died on 4 July 1940.

Contrib: *The Strand Magazine [1891]; A Book of Carols [1893]; The Dome [1898].*
Exhib: B; FAS; G; L; M; New Gall; P; RA; RSW; RWS.

**PEACOCK, Mildred A.**

Illustrator working at West Bromwich and possibly a student of the Birmingham School.

Bibl: *The Studio*, 1897, p.273, illus.

**PEACOCK, Ralph** 1868-1946

Portrait and landscape painter and illustrator. He was born in 1868 and studied at the Lambeth School of Art, 1882, the St. John's Wood School and the RA Schools, 1887, where he won the gold medal and Creswick prize. He was a teacher at the St. John's Wood School for many years and died on 17 January 1946.

Illus: *Wulf The Saxon [G.A. Henty, 1894]; Both Sides The Border [G.A. Henty, 1897].*
Contrib: *The English Illustrated Magazine [1896]; The Graphic [1899].*
Exhib: B; G; GG; L; M; New Gall; P; RA; RBA; RCA; ROI.
Colls: Birmingham; Liverpool; Tate.
Bibl: 'Ralph P and His Work', *The Studio*, Vol.21, 1900, pp.3-15, illus.

**PEAKE, Richard Brinsley** fl.1816-1819

Figure and domestic painter. He illustrated *The Characteristic Costume of France*, 1819, AT 87.

Exhib: RA.

**PEARS, Charles ROI** 1873-1958

Marine painter, illustrator, lithographer and poster artist. He was born at Pontefract 9 September 1873 and was educated at Hardwick College. He served in the RM in the First World War and was Official War Artist to the Admiralty, 1915-18 and again in 1940. He was a regular magazine illustrator in the 1890s and 1900s and was elected ROI in 1913. He wrote extensively on sailing and yachting and died in 1958.

Illus: *Two Years Before The Mast; Saltwater Ballads [John Masefield]; Dickens Works; The Pedlars Pack [Mrs. Alfred Baldwin, 1904-05].*
Contrib: *The Yellow Book [1896-97]; Judy [1896]; The Quartier Latin [1896]; The Dome [1897-99]; Punch [1897-1914]; The Longbow [1898]; The Windsor Magazine; The Ludgate Monthly; The Sketch; Fun [1901]; The Graphic [1910].*
Exhib: FAS; L; NEA; RA; RI; ROI; RWA.
Colls: V & AM.

**PEARSE, Alfred** c.1854-1933

Painter, black and white artist and illustrator of boys' books. He worked in London from about 1877 and died in 1933.

Illus: *By England's Aid [G.A. Henty, 1890]; Westward with Columbus [Gordon Stables, 1894].*
Contrib: *ILN [1882]; Boys' Own Paper [1890]; The Girls' Own Paper [1890-1900]; The Strand Magazine [1891-94, 1906]; The Wide World Magazine [1898]; Cassell's Family Magazine [1898]; Punch [1906].*
Exhib: RA; RBA.

**PEARSE, Susan B.** fl.1898-1937

Watercolour painter. She studied at the New Cross Art School and exhibited book illustrations at the National Competition, South Kensington in 1898.

Exhib: RA; RI; SWA.

**PEARSON, Mathew**

Black and white artist. He drew 189 drawings for *An Inventory of the Church Plate of Leicestershire*, by the Rev. Andrew Trollope, 1890.

Colls: V & AM.

**PEARSON, William** fl.1798-1813

Landscape painter and topographer. He was a friend of the watercolour artist F.L.T. Francia and probably illustrated *Select Views of the Antiquities of Shropshire*, 1807. Contributed to Britton's *Beauties of England and Wales*, 1812-14.

Exhib: RA.
Colls: BM; V & AM (sketchbook); Witt Photo.

**PEGRAM, Frederick RI** 1870-1937

Black and white artist and illustrator. He was born in London on 19 December 1870 and was first cousin of H., C.E., and R. Brock (qq.v.). He joined the staff of *The Queen* and then *The Pall Mall Gazette* in 1886, having studied under Fred Brown and spent some time in Paris. From then onwards he became one of the most prolific and consistent of magazine illustrators, his pen work is always of a high standard and his own preference was for drawing subjects with a Georgian setting. He was also an etcher and did occasional advertisements for the papers. Elected RI, 1925, he died in London on 23 August 1937.

Illus: *Macmillans Illustrated Standard Novels – Midshipman Easy [1896]; Masterman Ready [1897]; Poor Jack [1897]; The Last of the Barons [Bulwer Lytton, 1897]; The Arabian Nights Entertainments [1898]; The Bride of Lammermoor [1898]; The Orange Girl [Besant, 1899]; Ormond [Maria Edgeworth, 1900]; Concerning Isobel Carnaby [1900].*
Contrib: *Pall Mall Gazette [1886]; Pictorial World [1888]; ILN [1889-1916]; Judy [1889-90]; Lady's Pictorial [1893]; Punch [1894-1917]; The New Budget [1895]; The Quiver [1895]; Daily Chronicle [1895]; The Rambler [1897]; Black & White [1897]; Pall Mall Budget; The Gentlewoman; The Idler; The Pall Mall Magazine; The Minister; Cassell's Family Magazine.*
Exhib: FAS, 1938; G; L; P; RA; RI.
Colls: V & AM.
Bibl: *The Idler*, Vol.11, pp.673-683, illus.; J. Pennell, *Pen Drawing and Pen Draughtsmen*, 1894, p.370, illus.

**PELCOQ, Jules** fl.1866-1877

French artist and illustrator. He was born in Belgium of an old family and studied art at the Antwerp School and then went to Paris to work as a caricaturist. He worked for *Charivari* and *Journal Amusant* and illustrated some of Dumas novels and specialised in subjects from Parisian life. He was employed by *The Illustrated London News* in figure drawing and was their chief artist in Paris during the Siege of 1870, his work being despatched by balloon. He visited Vienna for the magazine in 1873 to cover the International Exhibition.

Bibl: H. Vizetelly, *Glances Back Over Seventy Years*, 1893, pp.340-342.

*CARLO PELLEGRINI 'APE' 1838-1889. Sir Charles John Forbes, Bt., of Newe. Original drawing for the illustration in* Vanity Fair, *14 August 1880. Watercolour and bodycolour on grey paper. Signed. 12ins. x 7ins. (30.5cm x 17.8cm).*

Author's Collection

## PELLEGRINI, Carlo 'APE' 1838-1889

Caricaturist, draughtsman and lithographer. He was born in Capua in 1838, the son of landed aristocrats, and made a considerable name in Neapolitan Society for his caricatures, which were directly inspired by the *portraits chargés* of Baron Melchiorre Delfico. The young Pellegrini was politically minded and before leaving Italy was associated with Garibaldi's liberation struggle to free Italy from foreign oppression. He moved to London in November 1864, where he soon became a central figure in the Prince of Wales' Marlborough House Set. He joined Thomas Gibson Bowles' *Vanity Fair* in 1865 and virtually made its name for the publisher, each issue having caricatures by the artist done in *portraits chargés* manner, quite new to an English public. He was later succeeded to some extent by James Tissot (q.v.) and then by his understudy Sir Leslie Ward (q.v.). Pellegrini had ambitions to be a serious portrait painter but his eccentricity and dilettante life style were against this; he exhibited some portraits at the RA and Grosvenor Gallery. He was very influential on Max Beerbohm (q.v.), who considered him his master and dedicated his first book to him in 1896. Pellegrini died in London on 22 January 1889.

Colls: NPG; Royal Coll., Windsor; V & AM.
Bibl: Eileen Harris, 'Ape or Man', *Apollo,* Jan. 1976, pp.53-57; *Vanity Fair,* NPG Exhibition Cat., July-August, 1976.

See illustration (above).

## PELLEGRINI, Professor Ricardo 1866-

Genre painter and illustrator. He was born at Milan in 1866 and illustrated an edition of *Gil Blas.* He acted as Special Artist for *The Graphic,* 1905.

## PENGUILLY L'HARIDON, Octave 1811-1870

French illustrator, watercolourist and engraver. He was born on 4 April 1811 and after serving as a professional soldier studied under Charlet. He was curator of the Artillery Museum in Paris and exhibited at the Salon, 1835-70.

Illus: *The Works of Scarron.*
Contrib: *ILN [1853].*

## PENNELL, Joseph 1860-1926

Artist, illustrator and author. He was born in Philadelphia in 1860 and educated at the School of Industrial Art there and at the Pennsylvania Academy of Fine Arts. He married Elizabeth Robins Pennell, the authoress, and they settled in England in the 1880s swiftly becoming members of the circle surrounding James McNeil Whistler (q.v.). Pennell was an extremely competent topographer in black and white and with his wife illustrated numerous travel books which she wrote. He is perhaps most significant however as the chronicler of late Victorian illustration in a number of books which not only brought new names to the fore, but were powerful advocates for the new processes of mechanisation. He was Art Editor of *The Daily Chronicle,* 1895, and was elected RE in 1882 and was a member of the American Academy of Arts. He returned to New York about 1914 and died there on 23 April 1926.

Publ: *Pen Drawing and Pen Draughtsmen [1889]; Modern Illustration [1895]; The Illustration of Books [1896]; The Work of Charles Keene [1897]; Lithography and Lithographers [1900]; The Life of James McNeil Whistler [1907]; Etchers and Etching [1919]; The Whistler Journal [1921]; The Graphic Arts [1922]; Adventures of an Illustrator [1925].*
Illus: *A Canterbury Pilgrimage [1885]; An Italian Pilgrimage [1886]; Two Pilgrims Progress [1887]; Our Sentimental Journey Through France and Italy [1888]; Our Journey to The Hebrides [1889]; The Stream of Pleasure [1891]; The Jew At Home [1892]; Play in Provence [1892]; To Gipsyland [1893]; A London Garland [W.E. Henley, 1895]; The Alhambra [1896]; Highways and Byways Series, Devon and Cornwall [1897]; N. Wales [1898]; Yorkshire [1899]; Normandy [1900]; A Little Tour in France [Henry James, 1900]; Gleanings From Venetian History [1908]; Pictures of The Panama Canal [1912]; Pictures of War Work in England [1917].*
Contrib: *The English Illustrated Magazine [1884]; The Graphic [1888]; ILN [1891]; The Pall Mall Budget [1893]; The Yellow Book; The Savoy [1896]; The Pall Mall Magazine; The Quarto [1896-97]; The Butterfly; The Neolith [1907-08].*
Exhib: FAS, 1896, 1912, 1917, 1922; G; GG; L; NEA; RSA.
Colls: V & AM.
Bibl: E.R. Pennell, *Journal of JP,* 1931.
See illustration (p.414).

## PENNINGTON, Harper 1854-

American illustrator. He was born at Newport in 1854 and while in Europe, 1874-86, was a pupil of Gérome, Carolus Duran and J.M. Whistler (q.v.). He contributed to *Punch* in 1886.

## PETERS, C.W.

Contributor of railway sketches to *The English Illustrated Magazine,* 1896.

## PETHERICK, Horace William 1839-1919

Painter and illustrator. He was working at Addiscombe in 1891 and at Croydon from 1919 and specialised in children's stories and particularly those with costume subjects. He did some work for the Kronheim 'Toy Book' series.

Illus: *Home For the Holidays [1880]; Among the Woblins [S. Hodges]; Among the Gibjigs [S. Hodges, 1883]; Cornet of Horse [G.A. Henty, 1892].*
Contrib: *ILN [1870-77, 1887, 1890].*
Exhib: L; RA; RBA.
Colls: V & AM.

## PETHERICK, Rosa C. fl.1896-1903

Illustrator. She was probably the daughter of Horace William Petherick (q.v.) and competed in book illustration competitions run by *The Studio,* Vol. 8, 1896, p.184. She later illustrated *Mother Hubbard's Cupboard of Nursery Rhymes,* 1903.

*JOSEPH PENNELL 1860-1926. 'Old Shops in Gray.' Original drawing for illustration in* The Saône *by P.G. Hamerton, 1887. Pen. 7¹/8ins. x 7¹/4ins. (18.1cm x 18.4cm).*
Victoria and Albert Museum

**PETHYBRIDGE, J. Ley**                     fl.1885-1897
Figure and landscape painter and occasional illustrator. He was working at Lyndhurst, 1885 and at Launceston, 1889 and was described by Thorpe as 'a too infrequent contributor to magazines'.
Contrib: *The Ludgate Monthly; The Temple Magazine [1896-97].*
Exhib: L; RA; RBA.

**PETIT, The Rev. John Louis**               1801-1868
Amateur topographer. He was born at Ashton-under-Lyne in 1801 and educated at Trinity College, Cambridge, and was for many years curate of Bradfield, Essex. He moved to Shropshire in 1846 and died at Lichfield in 1868.
Publ: *Remarks on Church Architecture [1841]; The Abbey Church of Tewkesbury [1848]; Architectural Studies in France [1854].*
Colls: Lichfield; V & AM.

**PETO, Gladys Emma**                        1891-1977
Black and white artist and illustrator. She was born in 1891 at Maidenhead and studied at the Maidenhead School of Art and the London School of Art. Her style was strongly influenced by the work of Aubrey Beardsley, and she worked for *The Sketch* from 1915-26. She married Col. C.L. Emmerson and died in Northern Ireland in 1977.
Illus: *The Works of Louisa M. Alcott [1914]; Malta, Egypt, Cyprus [1928].*

**PETRIE, George   PRHA**                    1789-1866
Landscape painter and topographer. He was born in Dublin in 1790 and studied at the RDS Schools and with his father, a miniature painter, before turning wholly to landscape. He made extensive tours in Ireland and Wales with fellow artists such as F. Danby and J.A. O'Connor in the years 1808-19. He was elected ARHA in 1826 and RHA in 1828, becoming Librarian in 1829 and President in 1856-59. He wrote antiquarian articles for the *Dublin Penny Journal*, 1832-33, and was Editor of the *Irish Penny Journal*, 1842. His ink drawings are reckoned to be more attractive than his watercolour drawings which are rather formal in composition. He died in Dublin on 17 January 1866.
Publ: *Ancient Music of Ireland [1855].*
Illus: *Excursions Through Ireland [Cromwell, 1819]; New Picture of Dublin [J.J. McGregor, 1821]; Historical Guide to Ancient and Modern Dublin [C.N. Wright, 1821]; Beauties of Ireland [Brewer, 1825-26].*
Contrib: *Guide to the County of Wicklow [C.N. Wright].*
Exhib: RHA.
Colls: BM; Nat. Gall., Ireland; V & AM.
Bibl: A. Stokes, *Life of G.P.,* 1868.

**PETRIE, Henry   FSA**                       1768-1842
Topographer and antiquary. He was born at Stockwell, Surrey in 1768 and was patronised by Thomas Frognall Dibdin and Earl Spencer. In 1818 Petrie began editing the *Monumenta Historica Britannica* of which one volume appeared by Sir T.D. Hardy, 1848. He was also involved in making a survey of Southern English Churches from about 1800 which was not completed and not published. His watercolours for this work are clear and accurate if somewhat dead through lack of figures and anything but architectural interest. He died at Stockwell in 1842, having been Keeper of the Records at The Tower since 1819.

**PETT, Norman**
Amateur illustrator, contributed one rustic subject to *Punch,* 1914.

414

**PETTIE, John  RA**                                    **1839-1893**
Painter and illustrator. He was born at East Linton, Scotland, on 17
March 1839 and showed early promise as a figure draughtsman. He
studied with his uncle Robert Frier in Edinburgh and then at the
Trustees Academy, 1856, under R.S. Lauder, where his fellow
students were Orchardson, MacWhirter and McTaggart (qq.v.). In
1862 he moved to London with Orchardson and shared a studio with
him, becoming an ARA in 1866 and an RA in 1873. He died at
Hastings on 23 February 1893. Although Pettie's output in
illustration is small it is among his most charming work; he excelled in
costume pieces and produced figures of incomparable strength with
subtle grey washes.

Illus: *The Postman's Bag [J. de Lefde, 1865]; The Boys of Axelford [L.G.
Seguin, 1869]; Rural England [1881].*
Contrib: *Good Words [1861-63]; Wordsworth's Poetry for the Young [1863];
Pen and Pencil Pictures from the Poets [1866]; Touches of Nature by Eminent
Artists [1866]; The Sunday Magazine [1868-69]; Good Words For the Young
[1869].*
Exhib: B; G; GG; L; M; P; RA; RHA; ROI; RSA.
Colls: Ashmolean; Glasgow; V & AM.
Bibl: M. Hardie, *JP,* 1908.
See illustration (right).

**PEYTON, A.**
Illustrator of comic strips of sporting subjects to *The Graphic,* 1904.

**PHILIPS, John**                                       **fl.1832-1838**
Illustrator. He worked in Soho and was an early contributor to *Punch*
and collaborated with Alfred Crowquill (q.v.) in the illustrations of
Reynolds' *Pickwick Abroad: or a Tour in France,* 1838.
Exhib: NWS; RBA.

**PHILIPS, Nathaniel George**                           **1795-1831**
Landscape painter and topographer. He was born in Manchester in
1795 and was educated at Manchester Grammar School and
Edinburgh University. He travelled in Ireland and the Lake District
and visited Italy in 1824-25, where he was elected to the Academy of
St. Luke in place of Henry Fuseli. He died at Liverpool in 1831,
having published etchings in 1822-24.
Illus: *Lancashire and Cheshire [1893].*

**PHILLIPS, John  FRS**                                 **1800-1874**
Lithographer and geologist. He was Keeper of the York Museum,
1825-40 and Professor of Geology at Trinity College, Dublin,
1844-53. He was Keeper of the Ashmolean Museum, Oxford,
1854-70, having been elected FRS in 1834. He published *The Geology
of Yorkshire* and illustrated *The Rivers, Mountains and Sea Coast of
Yorkshire,* 1853.

**PHILLIPS, Paul**
Fashion illustrator, contributing to *The Graphic,* 1871.

**PHILLIPS, T.W.**                                      **fl.1808-1826**
Landscape artist and topographer. He contributed drawings to
*Britton's Beauties of England and Wales,* 1808.
Exhib: BI; RA; RBA.

**PHILLIPS, W. Alison**
Illustrator of rustic genre subjects. Contributed to *Punch,* 1896-97.

**PHILLIPS, Watts**                                     **1825-1874**
Artist, illustrator and dramatist. He was born in 1825 and became the
only pupil of George Cruikshank (q.v.). He was an early contributor
to *Punch,* the founder of a short-lived periodical *Journal for Laughter*
and was on the fringe of the arts and the stage in Paris and then
in London where he settled in 1853-54. He brought out plays at the
Adelphi, 1857-59 and published novels in the *Family Herald.*

Illus: *M.P. Drawn and Etched by Watts Phillips [c.1840, AL 313].*
Contrib: *Punch [1844-46]; Puck; Diogenes; ILN [1852].*
Colls: Witt Photo.
Bibl: M.H. Spielmann, *The History of Punch,* 1895, pp.458-459.

*JOHN PETTIE RA 1839-1893. 'Macleod of Dare.' Original drawing for
illustration of a story by William Black,* Good Words, *1878. Wash. Signed.
14³/₈ins. x 8¹¹/₈ins. (36.5cm x 20.6cm).*          Victoria and Albert Museum

**'PHIZ'  see BROWNE, H.K.**

**PHOENIX, George**                                     **fl.1886-1935**
Figure and landscape painter. He worked at Wolverhampton, 1889 to
1925 and contributed spirited black and white drawings of rustic and
cockney genre subjects to *Punch,* 1902-03.
Exhib: B; L; New Gall; RA.

**PICKEN, Andrew**                                      **1815-1845**
Lithographer and illustrator. He was born in 1815, the son of the
author, Andrew Picken, and studied with Louis Haghe (q.v.). Due to
poor health, Picken settled in Madeira in 1837 and lived in London
again from 1840 until his death in 1845. He lithographed Dillon's
*Sketches in the Island of Madeira,* 1850, AT 193.
Illus: *Madeira Illustrated [1840, AT 191].*
Exhib. RA.

**PICKERING, George**                 **1794-1857**

Landscape painter and illustrator. He was born in Yorkshire in 1794 and became a pupil and close follower of John Glover. He began as a drawing-master at Chester, taking over the practice of George Cuitt (q.v.) and opening a studio at Liverpool in 1836. He taught drawing at Birkenhead, where he died in 1857, having been for many years a non-resident member of the Liverpool Academy.

Illus: *History of Cheshire [G. Ormerod, 1819]; History of the County Palatine of Lancaster [E. Baines]; Traditions of Lancashire [J. Roby, 1928].*
Contrib: *Fisher's Scrapbook [1834].*
Exhib: L; OWS; RBA.
Colls: V & AM; Witt Photo.

**PICKERSGILL, Frederick Richard RA**       **1820-1900**

Historical painter and illustrator. He was born in London in 1820, nephew of H.W. Pickersgill, RA, and W.F. Witherington under whom he studied. He entered the RA Schools and exhibited there from 1839, being elected ARA in 1847 and RA in 1857; he was Keeper from 1873-87. Pickersgill was a beautiful colourist and much influenced by William Etty, his illustrative work is full of fine figure drawing even if with a characteristic German hardness in places. The finest collection of his drawings of this sort of work is at the Barber Institute, Birmingham. He died on the Isle of Wight on 20 December 1900.

Illus: *Virgin Martyr [P. Massinger, 1844]; Illustrated Life of Christ [1850]; Comus [Milton, 1858]; Poetical Works of E.A. Poe [1858].*
Contrib: *Book of British Ballads [1842]; Tupper's Proverbial Philosophy [1854]; Poets of the Nineteenth Century [Willmott, 1857]; The Home Affections [Charles Mackay, 1858]; Lays of the Holy Land [1858]; The Seasons [James Thomson, 1859]; Montgomery's Poems [1860]; Sacred Poetry [1862]; The Lord's Prayer [1870]; Dalziel's Bible Gallery [1880]; Art Pictures From The Old Testament [1897].*
Exhib: BI; RA.
Colls: Barber; V & AM.
Bibl: Chatto & Jackson, *Treatise on Wood Eng.,* 1861, p.598.

**PIDGEON, Henry Clark**                **1807-1880**

Landscape watercolourist, etcher and illustrator. He was a teacher of drawing in London until 1847, when he moved to Liverpool to become Professor of Drawing at the Institute and successively a member and Secretary of the Liverpool Academy, 1850. He was a founder of the Historic Society of Lancashire and Cheshire and is notable for the antiquarian details in his drawings and prints. In London, where he taught again from 1851, he was a member of the Clipstone St. Academy. He died there in 1880.

Contrib: *Recollections of the Great Exhibition of 1851; Wyatt's Industrial Arts of the Nineteenth Century.*
Exhib: BI; RA; RBA.

**PIFFARD, Harold H.**               **fl.1895-1903**

Military painter and illustrator. He worked in Bedford Park, London, and was a prolific illustrator in the style of Caran d'Ache (q.v.).

Contrib: *Cassell's Family Magazine [1899]; The Quiver [1900]; The Windsor Magazine; Pearson's Magazine; Illustrated Bits.*
Exhib: B; L; RA.

**PIKE, W.H.**  **'Oliver Paque' RBA**          **1846-1908**

Landscape painter and illustrator. He was born at Plymouth in 1846 and painted in Devon and Cornwall until 1881 when he settled in London. He was elected RBA in 1889.

Contrib: *The Daily Graphic [1890]; The Sketch [1894]; The Graphic [1902].*
Exhib: L; RA; RBA; RHA; RI; ROI.

**PILKINGTON, Major-General Robert W.**      **1765-1834**

Landscape painter and soldier. He trained at the RMA, Woolwich and saw service in Canada and North America and was appointed Major-General in 1825 and Inspector-General of Fortifications in 1832. He painted in the manner of Richard Wilson and contributed a drawing to Britton's *Beauties of England and Wales,* 1814.

Exhib: RA, 1808-27.

**PILOTELLE, Georges**

Fashion illustrator to the *Lady's Pictorial,* c.1890.

**PIMLOTT, E. Philip**                **fl.1893-1940**

Painter and etcher. He worked at Aylesbury and London and was ARE, 1901-11. He supplied an ink drawing for *The Yellow Book,* 1897.

Exhib: NEA; RA; RE.

**PINWELL, George John**             **1842-1875**

Painter and illustrator of rural life. He was born at Wycombe on 26 December 1842, the son of a builder and had his first employment as a designer for embroiderers. He entered the St. Martin's Lane Academy and in 1862 studied at Heatherley's, earning money to support himself by supplying drawings to *Fun* and designs to Elkingtons, silversmiths. He began to work for the Dalziel Brothers in 1864 and there met J.W. North and Fred Walker (qq.v.), the three of them becoming the outstanding rustic and landscape illustrators of the 1860s. He was elected AOWS in 1869 and OWS in 1870 and received important commissions such as the *Illustrated Goldsmith,* 1864, for which he made one hundred drawings, completed in six months. Pinwell's health began to fail in 1873 and he went to Tangiers in 1875 to recover but died in London on his return, 8 September 1875.

Pinwell was closely allied in style to Fred Walker but he was more of a figure artist and less of a landscape artist than the other. He was a brilliant colourist and Reid considered him to have greater decorative sense than Walker and to be at his best in contemporary subjects.

Illus: *Dalziel's Illustrated Goldsmith [1864]; The Happy Home [H. Lushington, 1864]; Hacco the Dwarf [H. Lushington, 1864]; The Adventures of Gil Blas [1866]; Jean Ingelow's Poems [1867]; The Uncommercial Traveller [C. Dickens, 1868]; It Is Never Too Late To Mend [Reade, 1868].*
Contrib: *Punch [1863]; Once a Week [1863-69]; Good Words [1863-75]; The Churchman's Family Magazine [1863-64]; The Sunday at Home [1863-64]; London Society [1863-67]; Lilliput Levee [1864]; The Cornhill Magazine*

*GEORGE JOHN PINWELL 1842-1875. 'By The Dovecote.' Original drawing for illustration in* Wayside Posies *by R. Buchanan, 1867. Pen and pencil. Signed with monogram and dated 1865. 7¹/8ins. x 5¹/2ins. (18.1cm x 14cm).*
Victoria and Albert Museum

416

[1864, 1870]; The Sunday Magazine [1865-72]; The Leisure Hour [1865]; Our Life Illustrated by Pen and Pencil [1865]; Dalziel's Arabian Nights [1865]; The Quiver [1866-68]; The Argosy [1866]; The Spirit of Praise [1866]; Ballad Stories of the Affections [1866]; A Round of Days [1866]; Wayside Poesies [R.W. Buchanan, 1867]; Golden Thoughts From Golden Fountains [1867]; Cassells Magazine [1868]; Good Words For the Young [1869]; Leslie's Musical Annual [1870]; Novellos National Nursery Rhymes [1870]; The Graphic [1870-73]; Fun [1871]; Judy [1872]; Sunlight of Song [1875]; Dalziel's Bible Gallery [1894].
Exhib: Deschamps Gall., Bond St., Feb. 1876; FAS, 1895.
Colls: Aberdeen; Bedford; BM; Nottingham; V & AM; Witt Photo.
Bibl: G.C. Williamson, G.P. and His Work, 1900; F. Reid, Illustrators of the Sixties, 1928, pp.152-163; 'English Influences on Vincent Van Gogh', Arts Council, 1974.
See illustrations (pp.206, 416)

## PIOTROWSKI, Antoine                    1853-1924
Painter and illustrator. He was born at Kunow on 7 September 1853 and studied at Warsaw and Munich. In 1877 he became a pupil at the Mateiko School in Krakow and worked there until his death in Warsaw on 12 September 1924. He was The Graphic Special Artist in the Servo-Bulgarian War of 1885-86.

## PIRKIS
Figure artist contributing drawings in the manner of John Hassall to Punch, 1905.

## PISSARRO, Lucien                    1863-1944
Artist, landscape painter, wood engraver, designer and printer of books. He was born in Paris on 20 February 1863, the eldest son of the French painter Camille Pissarro. He was educated in France and studied with his father and the wood engraver Lepere, before coming to England to work in 1883. Here he met Charles Ricketts and C.H. Shannon (qq.v.) and came into contact with the revived interest in wood engravings and the new ideas in book design formulated by Kelmscott and other private presses. He contributed designs to The Dial and started the Eragny Press in 1894, producing a whole series of French classics in the next twenty years, most of them slightly illustrated but beautifully ornamented and designed. Pissarro stayed close to the Morris tradition in books, but his wood engravings do have a naturalism and flow that is not always present in Morris. Pissarro broke most new ground in his use of colour woodcuts and brought them to new heights in his Livre de Jade, 1911 and La Charrue d'Erable, 1912. Both his wife and Sturge Moore (q.v.) collaborated on these books. He designed the Brook type face for use in his books after 1902. As a landscape painter he provided an important bridge between English art and impressionism; he was also a talented caricaturist. He was a member of the NEA from 1906.
Illus: The Queen of the Fishes [1896]; Moralités légendaires [Laforgue, 1897]; Choix de sonnets [Ronsard, 1902]; Peau d'Ane [Perrault, 1902]; Areopagitica [1904]; Livre de Jade [Gautier, 1911]; La Charue d'Erable [1912].
Exhib: G; L; NEA; RA; RHA; RSA.
Colls: Ashmolean; Birmingham; Manchester.
Bibl: Colin Franklin, The Private Presses, 1969 (full bibliog.).

## PITMAN, Rosie M.M.                    fl.1883-1907
Illustrator of children's books. She worked in Manchester, 1883, London, 1894-1902 and at Ledbury, 1907.
Illus: Maurice or The Red Jar [Lady Jersey, 1894]; Undine [Fouqué, 1897]; The Magic Nuts [Mrs. Molesworth, 1898].
Contrib: The Quarto [1896].
Exhib: G; L; M; RA; RSA.
Bibl: R.E.D. Sketchley, Eng. Bk. Illus., 1903, pp.117, 168.

## PITTMAN, Oswald    ROI                    1874-1958
Landscape painter. He was born in London on 14 December 1874, the son of Robert Pittman, ACA, and was educated at Palace School, Enfield and at the RA Schools. He took part in a number of The Studio book illustration competitions. He was elected ROI, 1916, and died on 25 October 1958.
Exhib: G; L; RA; RI; ROI.
Bibl: The Studio, Vol.13, 1897, p.64 illus; Vol.14, 1898, p.71 illus.

## PIXELL, Maria                    fl.1793-1811
Landscape painter. She may have been a pupil of S. Gilpin and she exhibited at the RA and BI, 1793-1811. She contributed a drawing to Britton's Beauties of England and Wales, 1813.

## PLANK, George
Black and white artist who illustrated The Freaks of Mayfair by E.F. Benson, 1916, in the style of Aubrey Beardsley.

## POCOCK, E.
Architectural illustrator, contributing to The Illustrated London News, 1875.

## POGANY, William Andrew    'Willy'                    1882-
Painter, etcher and illustrator. He was born at Szeged in Hungary on 24 August 1882 and educated at the Budapest Technical University and at the Art Schools of Budapest, Munich and Paris. Pogany settled in the United States where he designed many stage-sets and illustrated more than one hundred books. His art was very strongly decorative in character and has begun to return to favour with the advent of the cult of Art Deco. He is included here for the many books that he illustrated for the English market during the Edwardian years.
Illus: A Treasury of Verses for Little Children [M.G. Edgar, 1908]; Tannhauser [1911]; Goethe's Faust [1912], etc.
Contrib: ILN [1913].

## POIRSON, V.A.
French artist and illustrator of comic genre subjects. He contributed to The Graphic, 1888-89.

## PONT, J.
Topographer. He contributed drawings to Britton's Beauties of England and Wales, 1813.

## POOLE, G.T.
Amateur artist. He acted as Special Artist for The Graphic in Russia in 1904.

## POOLE, William                    fl.1826-1840
Portrait painter. He worked in London, 1826 to 1838, and contributed to The Chaplet, c.1840.
Exhib: RBA.

## 'POPINI'
Name or pseudonym of artist contributing to Illustrated Bits, c.1890.

## PORTCH, Julian                    -1865
Illustrator and Special Artist. He came from a very poor background and was self-taught as an artist. He was a pupil of Henry Vizetelly (q.v.) who gave him a lot of work and sent him as Special Artist for The Illustrated Times to the Crimea in 1855. Portch caught rheumatic fever in the camps of the Crimea and was afterwards paralysed, although he continued to do theatrical illustrations, comic animals and decoration for the Punch Pocket Books. He died in September 1865.
Illus: The Illustrated Book of French Songs [John Oxenford, 1855].
Contrib: The Illustrated Times [1855-61]; Punch [1858-61, 1870]; The Welcome Guest [1860]; Puck on Pegasus [C. Pennell, 1861]; London Society [1862]; Poetry of the Elizabethan Age [1862]; Uncle Tom's Cabin; Boswell's Life of Johnson.

## PORTER, J.L.
This is likely to be John Porter, the historical and landscape painter who worked in London and Folkestone and exhibited at the BI, RA and RBA, 1826-70.
Contrib: Good Words [1861].

**PORTER, Sir Robert Ker**          **1777-1842**

Historical painter and illustrator. He was born at Durham in 1777, the son of an army officer and spent his boyhood at Edinburgh, becoming a student in the RA Schools in 1790 through the influence of Benjamin West. He won a Society of Arts silver palette in 1792 and joined the Sketching Club in 1799. In 1800, Porter was engaged in scene painting at the Lyceum Theatre and in producing panoramas and battle subjects. In 1804 he went to Russia and was appointed Historical Painter to the Czar and married the Princess Marie Schertakoff. He was knighted in 1813 and then went on extensive tours that took him to Sweden, Spain and Persia and he acted as British Consul in Venezuela from 1826 to 1841 before returning to St. Petersburgh where he died in 1842. His important collections were sold at Christie's on 30 March 1843.

Publ: *Narrative of the Campaign in Russia [1812, 1813]; Travels in Georgia, Persia, Armenia and Ancient Babylonia [1821-22, AT 359].*
Illus: *Travelling Sketches in Russia and Sweden, 1805-1808 [1809, AT 13]; Letters From Portugal and Spain [1809, AT 130].*
Exhib: RA; RBA.
Colls: BM; V & AM.

**POTT, Charles L.**          **fl.1886-1907**

Landscape painter and illustrator. He specialised in military and sporting subjects and worked at St. John's Wood, London. He was a regular contributor to many magazines but particularly to the pages of *Punch,* 1900-07.

Contrib: *Cassell's Saturday Journal [1890]; The Sporting and Dramatic News [1891]; Chums [1892]; Illustrated Bits [1900]; The Graphic [1902-03].*
Exhib: RBA; ROI.

**POTTER, Helen Beatrix**   **(Mrs. Heelis)**     **1866-1946**

Illustrator of children's books. She was born in London in 1866, the daughter of a wealthy family who had connections in the arts and knew contemporary artists, among them J.E. Millais (q.v.). Beatrix Potter had a repressed girlhood, however, and found her chief solace in sketching fungi, fossils and animals on her Scottish holidays and in keeping a secret journal. She wrote illustrated letters to children and it was this that led to the creation of *Peter Rabbit*, a masterpiece that was quietly and privately printed in 1900. It was accepted by Warne & Co. and published in 1902, gaining instant success for its brilliant watercolours and interplay of text and pictures. Many books followed, which gave her independence from her family and eventually the opportunity to buy her own farm in the Lake District and marry William Heelis, a solicitor. She claimed to have been influenced by the Pre-Raphaelites and by Randolph Caldecott (q.v.) and is known to have admired the drawings of Mrs. Blackburn (q.v.) and the woodcuts of Thomas Bewick (q.v.). But she was essentially an amateur artist who loved children and wished to enliven their books with animals that were still recognisably animalish. She died at Sawrey in 1946 and left her home and farm to the National Trust. An exhibition was held at the V & A Museum in December 1972.

Illus: *Peter Rabbit [1902]; Squirrel Nutkin [1903]; The Tailor of Gloucester [1903]; Benjamin Bunny [1904]; Two Bad Mice [1904]; Mrs. Tiggy-Winkle [1905]; The Pie and the Patty Pan [1905]; Mr. Jeremy Fisher [1906]; A Fierce Bad Rabbit [1906]; Miss Moppet [1906]; Tom Kitten [1907]; Jemima Puddleduck [1908]; The Roly-Poly Pudding [1908]; The Flopsy Bunnies [1909]; Ginger and Pickles [1909]; Mrs. Tittlemouse [1910]; Timmy Tiptoes Rhymes [1922]; Little Pig Robinson [1930]; A Happy Pair [F.E. Weatherly, n.d.]; and posthumously The Fairy Caravan [1952]; The Sly Old Cat [1971].*
Colls: BM; Nat. Bk. League; Tate.
Bibl: M. Lane, *The Tale of BP*, 1947; Anne Carroll Moore, *The Art of Beatrix Potter With An Appreciation*, 1955; *The Journal of BP*, 1966.

**POTTER, Raymond**          **fl.1893-1898**

Illustrator. He specialised in theatrical subjects, current events and may have visited India in 1898.

Contrib: *The Ludgate Monthly [1892]; The English Illustrated Magazine [1893-97]; ILN [1897]; The Sketch; The Penny Illustrated Paper; The Windsor Magazine; Pearson's Magazine; The Royal Magazine.*
Colls: V & AM.

**POWELL, Sir Francis**  **PRSW**         **1833-1914**

Marine and landscape artist. He was born at Pendleton, Manchester, in 1833 and studied at the Manchester School of Art, becoming OWS in 1876. He was first President of the RSW in 1878 and was knighted in 1893. He died at Dunoon on 27 October 1914.

Contrib: *Passages from Modern English Poets [1862].*
Colls: Dundee; Glasgow; V & AM.

**POWELL, Joseph**  **PNWS**         **1780-1834**

Landscape painter and topographer. He was a drawing-master and specialised in views of the South Coast, Wales and the Lakes. He was first President of the NWS in 1832 and made etchings and lithographs as well as drawings.

Contrib: *The Antiquarian and Topographical Cabinet [1809].*
Colls: BM; V & AM.

**POYNTER, Ambrose**          **1796-1886**

Architect, still-life and landscape painter and illustrator. He was born in London in 1796 and became a pupil of T.S. Boys (q.v.), and of John Nash. He travelled in Italy during the years 1819-21 and on his return set up as an architect designing government schools and London

THE PAINTER'S INSPIRATION.

Drawn by E. J. Poynter.         *See page* 131.

*SIR EDWARD JOHN POYNTER, Bt. PRA 1836-1919. 'The Painter's Inspiration.' Illustration to a story in* The Churchman's Family Magazine, *1862. Wood engraving.*

*SIR EDWARD JOHN POYNTER, Bt. PRA 1836-1919. 'Joseph distributing corn.' Original drawing for illustration to* Dalziel's Bible Gallery, *1881. Pen and ink. Signed with initials and dated 1864. 8¾ins. x 10¼ins. (22.2cm x 26cm).*
Victoria and Albert Museum

churches and becoming a founder member of the RIBA in 1834. He retired from practice in 1858 due to failing eye sight and died at Dover on 20 November 1886; he was the father of Sir E.J. Poynter (q.v.). Poynter did a considerable amount of illustrative work for Charles Knight who referred to 'the most beautiful architectural drawings, which imparted a character of truthfulness to many scenes' in his *Pictorial Shakespeare.*

Publ: *An Essay on the History and Antiquities of Windsor Castle [1841].*
Illus: *Genealogical History of England [Sandford].*
Contrib: *Knight's London [1841-42].*
Exhib: RA
Colls: BM; Fitzwilliam; V & AM.
Bibl: H.M. Poynter, *The Drawings of AP,* 1931.

### POYNTER, Sir Edward John, Bt. PRA      1836-1919
Painter and illustrator. He was born in Paris on 20 March 1836 the son of Ambrose Poynter (q.v.). He studied art in Paris under Gleyre, 1856-59 at the same time as Alma Tadema, Du Maurier and Whistler (qq.v.), having previously attended the RA Schools. He was elected ARA in 1868 and RA in 1877, having become the first Slade Professor of University College, 1871-75, and Principal of the South Kensington School, 1875-81. He was Director of the National Gallery, 1894-1904, and President of the Royal Academy from 1896 to 1918. He was knighted in 1896 and created a baronet in 1902. He died in London on 26 July 1919.

Poynter was very influential as a teacher in late Victorian Britain and especially through holding so many public appointments. His illustrations were all confined to the early part of his career but show a great aptitude for figure work and even a flare for handling modern subjects.

Contrib: *Once a Week [1862-67]; London Society [1862, 1864]; The Churchman's Family Magazine [1863]; Poems by Jean Ingelow [1867]; The Nobility of Life [1869]: ILN [1870]: Dalziel's Bible Gallery [1880].*
Exhib: B; FAS, 1903; G; GG; L; M; New Gall; RA; RE; RHA; RSA; RWS.
Colls: BM; Bradford; Manchester; V & AM.
Bibl: A. Margaux, *The Art of EJP.* 1905: M. Bell, *Drawings of EJP,* 1906; J. Maas, *Victorian Painters,* 1969, pp.183-184.
See illustrations (above and p.418).

### PRATER, Ernest      fl.1897-1914
Black and white artist and illustrator. He worked at London and Westcliffe-on-Sea and was on the staff of *Black & White, The Sphere* and *The Graphic,* acting as Special Artist for the first in the Sino-Japanese War of 1894.

Illus: *The Castle of the White Flag [E.E. Green, 1904].*
Contrib: *The St. James's Budget; The Boys' Own Paper; The Ludgate Monthly; The Idler; Chums; Pearson's Magazine; The Graphic [1905-10].*
Exhib: RA.

### PRATT, Edward      fl.1810-1812
Topographer. He contributed to Britton's *Beauties of England and Wales,* 1812.

### PREHN, William      fl.1862-1890
Sculptor. He was working in London in the last quarter of the nineteenth century and contributed to *Punch* in 1865.

Exhib: G; GG; L; RA.

419

**PRENTIS, Edward** 1797-1854

Genre painter and illustrator. He was born at Monmouth in 1797 and was an early member of the Society of British Artists. He specialised in domestic scenes of a humorous nature, many of which were engraved and he died in London in December 1854.

Contrib: *Layard's Monuments of Nineveh [1849, AL 29].*
Exhib: BI; RA; RBA.
Colls: Glasgow.

**PRESCOTT-DAVIES, Norman    RBA** 1862-1915

Portrait, flower and miniature painter and illustrator. He was born at Isleworth in 1862 and educated at the London International College and at South Kensington, City Guilds and Heatherley's Art Schools. He worked in London and at Radway, Warwickshire, and was elected RBA in 1893 and ARCA in 1891. He died on 15 June 1915.

Illus: *Gray's Elegy [De Luxe Edition].*
Contrib: *The Strand Magazine [1891].*
Exhib: B; G; L; M; New Gall; RA; RBA; RCA; RHA; RI; ROI.

**PRICE, Edward**

Topographer. The son of the Vicar of Needwood, he was a pupil of John Glover and accompanied him on tours of North Wales and Dovedale. He corresponded with John Constable, RA, and was patronised by the Duke of Sutherland. He helped organise some exhibitions of Glover's work in London, 1820-24, and was living in Nottinghamshire in 1856.

Illus: *Norway Views of Wild Scenery [1834]; Dovedale, 12 Views in Dovedale and Ilam [1845]; Views in Dovedale [1868].*
Exhib: BI; RA; RBA.
Bibl: *John Constable's Correspondence,* Vol.4, 1966, pp.312-313.

**PRICE, Julius Mendes** -1924

Illustrator and Special Artist. He was born in London, the son of a merchant and was educated at University College School and in Brussels, before studying at the École des Beaux-Arts in Paris. He joined the staff of *The Illustrated London News* in about 1884, and was described as 'Travelling Special Artist' although his chief function was as war correspondent. He took part in the Bechuanaland Campaign of 1884-85, enlisting as a trooper in Methuen's Horse, visited Siberia, Mongolia and the Gobi Desert, 1890-91, and the Western Australian Goldfields in 1895. He represented the magazine at the Graeco-Turkish War, 1897, Klondike, 1898, at the Russo-Japanese War, 1904-05, and on the French front throughout the First World War. He was appointed a lecturer in the British Army of Occupation in Germany in 1919. He died on 29 September 1924.

Publ: *From the Arctic Ocean to the Yellow Sea [1892]; The Land of Gold [1896]; From Euston to Klondike [1898]; Dame Fashion [1913]; My Bohemian Days in Paris [1913]; My Bohemian Days in London [1914]; Six Months on the Italian Front [1917]; On the Path of Adventure [1919].*
Contrib: *ILN [1884-1919]; The Sporting and Dramatic News [1890]; The English Illustrated Magazine [1893-94].*
Exhib: Paris; RA; RBA; RHA; ROI.

**PRIMROSE, Priscilla**

Amateur artist. She contributed drawings of Rome to *The Illustrated Times,* 1859.

**PRINCE, Val R.** fl.1890-1893

Painter and illustrator. He was working in Kensington in 1890 and contributed to *The Pall Mall Budget* in 1893.

**PRINSEP, James** 1799-1840

Architect, orientalist and draughtsman. He was born in 1799, brother of Charles Robert Prinsep, the economist. He acted as Assistant Assay-Master at the Calcutta mint, 1819, was appointed Assay-Master in 1832 and carried out some architectural works there including the completion of the Hooghly Canal.

Illus: *Benares Illustrated in a Series of Drawings [1831].*
Colls: Witt Photo.

**PRINSEP, Val C.    RA** 1838-1904

Painter and author. He was born at Calcutta on 14 February 1838 and educated at home. He studied art at the RA Schools and with Gleyre in Paris before spending some time in Rome. He was elected ARA in 1879 and RA in 1894, and was Professor of Painting from 1900 to 1903. He died on 11 November 1904.

Publ: *Imperial India, An Artist's Journal [1879].*
Contrib: *Once a Week [1869].*
Exhib: B; G; GG; L; M; New Gall; RA; RHA.
Colls: Hamburg; Sheffield; Tate.

**PRIOLO, Paolo** fl.1857-1890

Historical and biblical painter and illustrator. He worked in Stockwell, London, 1857-90, and contributed an illustration to *The Churchman's Family Magazine,* 1863.

Exhib: RA; RBA.

**PRIOR, Melton** 1845-1910

Special Artist and illustrator. He was born in London in 1845, the son of W.H. Prior (q.v.) and studied under his father in Camden Town. From about 1873 he was war correspondent of *The Illustrated London News,* and served in numerous campaigns. He followed the Ashanti War in 1873, the Carlist Rising, 1874, the Servian, Turkish, Kaffir, Zulu and first Boer Wars, the Egyptian Campaign, 1882, the Cretan Insurrection, the Siege of Ladysmith, 1900. He also went on a number of Royal Tours including the Prince of Wales's visit to Athens, 1875, the King of Denmark's visit to Iceland and the Marquess and Marchioness of Lorne's (qq.v.) visit to Canada. He was present at the Berlin Conference and drew for the magazine at the marriage of Tsar Nicholas II and later travelled with Prince George of Wales through Canada, 1901. He attended the Delhi Durbar of 1902, was on the Somaliland Expedition of 1903 and reported on the Russo-Japanese War of 1904. He died in London on 2 November 1910.

Contrib: *The Sketch; The English Illustrated Magazine [1893-94].*
Colls: V & AM.
Bibl: *The Idler,* Vol.8, pp.337-346; S.L. Bensusan (Editor), *Campaigns of a War Correspondent,* 1912.

**PRIOR, William Henry** 1812-1882

Landscape painter and illustrator. He was born in 1812 and worked in London and painted views in the South of England and on the Rhine. He was the father of Melton Prior (q.v.).

Illus: *Lyrics of a Life-Time [S. Smith, 1873].*
Contrib: *Knight's London [1841]; The Illuminated Magazine [1845]; ILN [1850]; Cassell's Illustrated Family Paper [1853]; The Illustrated London Magazine [1854]; The Illustrated Times [1866].*
Exhib: BI; RA; RBA.

**PRITCHETT, Robert Taylor    FSA** 1828-1907

Illustrator and gunsmith. He was born at Enfield in 1828, the son of a gun manufacturer and was educated at King's College School. He became a partner in the family business and was the originator of the Enfield rifle and invented with W.E. Metford the 'Pritchett bullet' in 1853, and the three grooved rifle in 1854. As an artist he specialised in black and white work and watercolours of the sea and ships, accompanying Lord and Lady Brassey on their tours of 1883 and 1885 on the *Sunbeam.* He was an intimate friend of John Leech, Charles Keene and Birket Foster (qq.v.). He died on 16 June 1907.

Illus: *Brush Notes in Holland [1871]; Gamle Norge [1878]; Smokiana [1890]; Pen and Pencil Sketches of Shipping [1899].*
Contrib: *Punch [1863-69]; Once a Week; Good Words [1864-80]; The Sunday Magazine [1865]; Cassell's Magazine [1867]; The Leisure Hour [1867]; The Graphic [1887].*
Exhib: RA; RBA.
Colls: Glasgow; V & AM.
Bibl: M.H. Spielmann, *The History of Punch,* 1894, pp.520-521.

**PROCTOR, J. James**

Black and white artist and illustrator. He illustrated *Yarns On The Beach,* by G.A. Henty, 1885, and contributed to *Illustrated Bits.*

WHERE IS JOHN BRIGHT NOW?

WELL, PEACE PROFESSIONS HAVING PLUNGED US INTO ALMOST UNIVERSAL WAR, JOHN BRIGHT IS—HIDING.

*JOHN PROCTOR fl.1866-1898. 'Where is John Bright Now?' A cartoon for* Moonshine, *25 August 1885.*

**PROCTOR, John**            **fl.1866-1898**

Cartoonist. Although little is known about his background or training, Proctor developed as one of the best political cartoonists of the end of the Victorian period, characterised by invention and strong drawing of animals. He was chief cartoonist for *Judy* 1867-68, following this with a period on *Will o' The Wisp* and *Moonshine,* 1868-85 and as chief cartoonist on *The Sketch,* 1893 and *Fun,* 1894-98. He was apparently employed by *The Illustrated London News* to act as Special Artist in St. Petersburg in 1874 and he also worked for *Cassell's Saturday Journal.*

Illus: *Dame Dingle's Fairy Tales [1866-67].*
Exhib: RBA.
Colls: Witt Photo.
See illustration (above).

**PROSPERI, Liberio**

Italian caricaturist. He contributed to *Vanity Fair,* 1886-94 and 1902-03.

**PROSSER, George Frederick**        **fl.1828-1868**

Artist and topographical illustrator. He worked at Winchester and Eton and published a number of books.

Illus: *Select Illustrations of the County of Surrey [1828]; Select Illustrations of Hampshire [1833]; Scenic and Antiquarian Features . . . of Guildford [1840]; The Antiquities of Hampshire [1842].*

**PROUT, John Skinner**   NWS        **1806-1876**

Architectural painter and illustrator. He was born at Plymouth in 1806, the nephew of Samuel Prout (q.v.) and was virtually self-taught but specialised in subjects similar to his uncle. As a young man he made a lengthy visit to Australia and lived in both Sydney and Hobart, forfeiting by his absence the membership of the NWS, which he had gained in 1838. He was re-elected on his return in 1849 and settled at Bristol where he became a close friend of the artist W.J. Muller. He died at Camden Town 29 August 1876.

Illus: *Sydney Illustrated [1842-44, AT 576]; Antiquities of Bristol [n.d.].*
Exhib: NWS; RI.
Bibl: M. Hardie, *Watercol. Paint. in Brit.,* Vol.3, 1968, pp.11-12.
Colls: BM; Fitzwilliam; V & AM.

**PROUT, Samuel**             **1783-1852**

Watercolourist, topographical illustrator and drawing-master. He was born at Diss, Norfolk on 17 September 1783 and was taught by J. Bidlake, master of the Plymouth Grammar School. He was friendly with B.R. Haydon, the historical painter and with him made sketching tours in Devonshire. In 1796, John Britton (q.v.) employed him to tour Cornwall for his *Beauties of England and Wales,* but his work proved unsatisfactory. By 1802 his work had improved and on sending fresh drawings to Britton, he was re-employed by him and lived with him at Clerkenwell for two years. Prout was continually dogged by ill health, but managed to finish work for Britton in Cambridgeshire, Essex and Wiltshire, 1804, and in Devon and Cornwall, 1805. From 1819 onwards, when he made his first visit to France, Prout became a frequent traveller on the Continent, visiting Belgium, the Rhine and Bavaria and Italy in 1824. He made his last tour to Normandy in 1846 by which time he was a sick man and unable to do much work between then and his death.

Prout's sympathy in rendering Gothic architecture with great accuracy and yet giving it mood and atmosphere was exactly suited to the romanticism of the 1820s and 1830s. His effects of light on crumbling masonry and flecks of colour on figures contrasting with the whites and greys of the buildings was widely copied for a generation. Perhaps this was partly due to the championship of John Ruskin who calls him in *Modern Painters* 'among our most sunny and substantial colourists'. He became a member of the OWS in 1819 and was Painter in Watercolours to George IV and Queen Victoria. He died at Denmark Hill on 10 February 1852.

Illus: *Rudiments of Landscape in Progressive Studies [1813, AL 170]; Rudiments [1814, AL 171]; New Drawing Book [1819, AL 172]; Series of Easy Lessons in Landscape Drawing [1819, AL 173]; Views of Cottages [1819, AL 174]; Illustrations of the Rhine [1824]; Facsimiles of Sketches made in Flanders and Germany [1833]; Hints [1834, AL 176]; Sketches in France, Switzerland and Italy [1839, AL 34].*
Contrib: *Beauties of England and Wales [1803-14]; Antiquarian and Topographical Cabinet [1809]; Jennings Landscape Annual [1831]; Microcosm [1841]; Sketches At Home and Abroad [1844]; Rhymes and Roundelayes; ILN [1850]; The Continental Annual [1832].*
Exhib: BI; OWS; RA.
Colls: Aberdeen; Ashmolean; BM; Birkenhead; Blackburn; Derby; Exeter; Fitzwilliam; Leeds; Manchester; V & AM.
Bibl: J. Ruskin, *Notes on SP and Hunt,* 1879; *The Studio,* Special No., 1914; J. Quigley, *Prout and Roberts,* 1926; A. Neumeyer, *Collection of Eng. Watercols. at Mills Coll.,* 1941; C.E. Hughes,' *O.W.S.* Vol.6; M. Hardie, *Watercol. Paint. in Brit.,* Vol.3, 1968, pp.4-11.

**PROUT, Victor**                                    fl.1888-1903
Watercolour painter. He contributed an angling subject to *The Graphic,* 1903.
Exhib: Goupil Gall., 1888.

**PROVOST, W.**
French illustrator. He contributed views of Paris to *Cassells Illustrated Family Paper,* 1857.

**PRY, Paul    see HEATH, William**

**PRYDE, James Ferrierr**                            1866-1941
Painter and illustrator. He was born at St. Andrews on 30 March 1869 and was educated at George Watson's College, the RSA Schools and in Paris at Julians under Bouguereau. He married Mabel Nicholson, sister of William Nicholson (q.v.) and with his brother-in-law began to design and produce posters and illustrations as the Beggarstaff Brothers. Pryde claimed to be part of the Glasgow School but his work is closer to the French poster art of Toulouse Lautrec and of Phil May. Both artists experimented with woodcuts and produced a periodical, *The Page,* 1898, based on archaic chap-book printing. Pryde was less of a book illustrator than a designer and his later career was devoted to stage design and dramatic paintings of shadowy interiors. Pryde was elected HROI, 1934 and died in 1941.
Illus: *The Little Glass Man [Wilhelm Hauff, 1893].*
Contrib: *Tony Drum [1898]; The Page [1898-99].*
Exhib: G; GG; L; NEA; RHA; RSA.
Colls: V & AM; Witt Photo.
Bibl: Derek Hudson, *JP, 1866-1941,* catalogue, 1949.

**PRYSE, Gerald Spencer**                            1882-1956
Painter and illustrator. He was born in 1882 at Ashton and was educated privately, studying art in London and Paris. He served in the First World War and won both the MC and the Croix de Guerre. Pryse was a member of the International Society and exhibited at Venice from 1907. He was working at Hammersmith from 1914 to 1925 but lived in Morocco after 1950. He died in 1956.
Publ: *Through the Lines to Abd el Karim's Stronghold in the Riffs; Four Days.*
Illus: *Salome and the Head; a Modern Melodrama [E. Nesbitt, 1909]; The Book of the Pageant [Wembley Exhibition, 1924].*
Contrib: *Punch [1903-04 (children), 1905]; The Neolith [1907-08]; The Strand Magazine [1910]; The Graphic [1910].*
Colls: V & AM.

**PUGIN, Augustus Charles**                          1762-1832
Architect, antiquary and architectural illustrator. He was born in France in 1762 into an old family, and fled to England in about 1798 where he was befriended by John Nash, the architect. Pugin was extensively employed by Nash as a Gothic draughtsman and his accuracy and knowledge of it was influential in establishing a purer appreciation of the style. He had lessons in aquatinting from Merigot in London and attended the RA Schools, at the same time carrying out a great deal of work for Ackermann, the publisher. At about the same time he set up a school of architectural drawing and published his own works, visiting Normandy in 1825 and Paris in 1830. His drawings reflect the current fashion in architectural work, meticulous tinted penwork, the figures frequently added by other artists such as Rowlandson and Stephanoff (qq.v.). His son was A.W.N. Pugin (q.v.). He died in Bloomsbury on 19 December 1832.
Illus: *Ackermann's Microcosm of London [1808]; Specimens of Gothic Architecture From Oxford; Specimens of Gothic Architecture [1821-23]; Views of Islington and Pentonville [1823]; Illustrations of Public Buildings in London [1825-28]; Specimens of Architectural Antiquities of Normandy [1826]; Examples of Gothic Architecture [1828-31]; Views of Paris and Environs [1828-31]; Gothic Ornaments from Ancient Buildings in England and France [1831]; Ornamental Gables [1831]; Cassiobury Park [Britton, 1838].*
Contrib: *Ackermann's Repository of the Arts [1810-27].*
Exhib: BI; OWS; RA.
Colls: BM; Lincoln; Nat. Gall., Scotland; RIBA; V & AM; Witt Photo.
Bibl: B. Ferrey, *Recollections of Welby and his Father ACP,* 1861.

**PUGIN, Augustus Northmore Welby**                  1812-1852
Architect, designer, draughtsman and polemicist. He was born in London in 1812 the son of A.C. Pugin (q.v.). He was educated at Christ's Hospital and studied architecture with his father, before being discovered by Rundell's the silversmiths and being employed by them and Jeffery Wyattville as a designer. He was received into the Roman Catholic church in 1835 and from then onwards had an extensive practice among wealthy co-religionists, notably the Earl of Shrewsbury and Ambrose March Phillips. He continued to design ecclesiastical buildings and ornaments until his death, his best work in illustration being the etchings for Ackermann which express in their fine lines an almost medieval mysticism. Pugin's large practice and obsessive pamphleteering caused him to lose his reason in 1851 and he died at Ramsgate in 1852.
Illus: *Gothic Furniture consisting of twenty-seven coloured engravings ... [1828]; Gothic Furniture in the style of the 15th century [1835]; Ornaments of the 15th and 16th centuries [1835-37]; Contrasts [1836]; Details of ancient timber houses of the 16th and 17th cent. ... [1836]; Designs for Gold and Silversmiths [1836]; Designs for Iron and Brass work in the style of the XV and XVI centuries [1836]; The True Principles of Pointed or Christian Architecture [1841]; An Apology For the Revival of Christian Architecture in England [1843]; Glossary of Ecclesiastical Ornament and Costume [1844]; Floriated Ornament, a series of thirty-one designs [1849]; Modèles d'orfèrerie, argenterie, etc. ... [1850]; A Treatise on Chancel Screens and Fonts [1851]; A series of Ornamental Timber Gables, from existing examples in England and France [1854].*
Exhib: RA.
Colls: BM; Maidstone; RIBA; V & AM.
Bibl: B. Ferrey, *Recollections of Welby and his Father A.C.P.,* 1861; *Victorian Church Art,* V & A Museum Cat., 1971-72.
See illustration (below).

*Right: AUGUSTUS NORTHMORE WELBY PUGIN 1812-1852. Title page to* Designs for Gold & Silversmiths, *1836. Etching.*

**PURSER, William**      c.1790-c.1852

Architect and topographical draughtsman. He was born about 1790, the son of an architect at Christ Church, Surrey. He entered the RA Schools in 1807 and travelled in Italy and Greece in 1817-20 with John Sanders, undertaking major archaeological work. He may have visited India.

Illus: *Syria [J. Carne, 1836].*
Contrib: *Finden's Landscape and Portrait Illustrations To The Life And Works of Lord Byron [1833-34]; Fisher's Scrapbook [1834].*
Exhib: RA; RBA.
Colls: BM; V & AM; Witt Photo.
Bibl: H.M. Colvin, *Biog. Dict. of Eng. Architects, 1660-1840*, 1954 p.481.

**PYLE, Howard**      1853-1911

Author and illustrator. He was born at Wilmington, Delaware, U.S.A. in 1853 and after being privately educated, studied at the Art Students League, New York. Pyle was among the most assured black and white draughtsmen of the American School excelling in 18th century subjects and in drawings in the manner of Durer whom he studied closely. Pennell considered that his early works suffer from having no direct contact with Europe, which he did not visit until his early middle age. He was a prolific illustrator of books for English as well as American publishers and died in Florence on 9 November 1911.

Illus: *The Merry Adventures of Robin Hood [1883]; Pepper and Salt [1885]; Rose of Paradise [1887]; The Wonder Clock [1887]; A Modern Aladdin [1891]; Poems [O.W. Holmes, 1892]; Twilight Land [1895]; The Garden Behind the Moon [1895]; Rejected of Men [1903]; The Story of King Arthur and His Knights [1902]; The Story of the Champions of the Round Table; The Story of Sir Launcelot and His Companions; The Ruby of Kishmoor [1908]; The Story of the Grail [1910].*
Contrib: *ILN [1880]; The Graphic [1883].*
Colls: V & AM.
Bibl: J. Pennell, *Pen Drawing and Pen Draughtsman*, 1894, pp.232-234; J. Pennell, *Modern Illustration*, 1895 pp.124-125.

**PYM, T.**

Illustrator of children's books. Contributed illustrations to *Victoria Bess; The Ups and Downs of a Doll's Life*, c.1880.

**PYNE, Charles Claude**      1802-1878

Landscape and genre painter. He was the second son of W.H. Pyne, (q.v.) and brother of G. Pyne (q.v.). He travelled on the Continent and practised as a drawing master at Guildford, where he died in 1878.

Contrib: *Lancashire Illustrated [W.H. Pyne, 1829].*
Exhib: BI; NWS; RA.
Colls: Nottingham; V & AM.

**PYNE, George**      1800-1884

Topographical watercolourist. He was born in 1800, the elder son of W.H. Pyne (q.v.) and brother of C.C. Pyne (q.v.). He was an excellent architectural artist and specialised in views of the Oxford and Cambridge Colleges and Eton, but was a less competent hand than his father. He was elected AOWS in 1827 and married the daughter of John Varley but later separated from her.

Publ: *A Rudimentary and Practical Treatise on Perspective for Beginners [1848]; Practical Rules on Drawing for the Operative Builder and Young Student in Architecture [1854].*
Contrib: *Lancashire Illustrated [W.H. Pyne, 1829].*
Colls: BM; Coventry; V & AM; York.

**PYNE, William Henry**      1769-1843

Landscape and genre painter in watercolours, illustrator, etcher, caricaturist and author. He was born in London in 1769 and studied with H. Pars, before beginning a career in book illustration. He was a founder member of the OWS in 1804 and remained a member until 1809 when he resigned. His greatest successes were in his collaborations with the publisher Rudolph Ackermann, when they were jointly engaged in issuing colour plate books from about 1803 to 1819. Pyne produced several drawing books for amateurs which are notable for their fine groups of figures and it is probably this aspect of his contribution to the romantic school that is most significant. He

was an assiduous art critic, catalogued Benjamin West's collection in 1829 and Watson Taylor's in 1832 and was editor of *The Somerset House Gazette* under the pseudonym of Ephraim Hardcastle and author of *Wine and Walnuts,* an anthology of the former, in 1823. *The Microcosm,* 1803-05 is his largest undertaking and many of the original drawings for the illustrations are in the Leeds City Art Gallery. He was a poor businessman and spent the last years of his life in the King's Bench Debtors' Prison, before dying at Pickering Place, Paddington on 29 May 1843.

Illus: *Microcosm or a Picturesque Delineation of the Arts, Agriculture and Manufactures of Gt. Britain [1803-08, AT 177]; Nattes Practical Geometry [1805 (title and vignettes)]; The Costume of Great Britain [1808]; Rudiments of Landscape Drawing [1812, AT 178]; Rustic Figures [1815, AT 179]; The History of the Royal Residences [1819]; Microcosm [1822-24, AT 80]; Lancashire Illustrated [1831].*
Contrib: *Knight's London [1841].*
Exhib: OWS; RA; Witt Photo.
Colls: BM; Leeds.
Bibl: M. Hardie, *Watercol. Paint. in Brit.*, 1968, Vol.3 pp.280-281; A Bury, *O.W.S.*, Vol.XXVIII, 1950.

**QUENNELL, Charles Henry Bourne**      1872-1935

Architect, author and illustrator. He was born on 5 June 1872 and was educated at South Kensington, beginning practice in Westminster in 1896. Quennell worked as a church architect as well as carrying out numerous houses in the arts and crafts style before 1914. In later life he devoted himself principally to books on social history, most of them illustrated by himself and his wife Marjorie Courtney whom he married in 1904. He held many posts at the RIBA and died on 5 December 1935.

Publ: *Norwich Cathedral [1900]; Modern Suburban Houses [1906]; A History of Everyday Things in England [1918-34]; Everyday Life in the Old Stone Age [1921]; New Stone, Bronze and Early Iron Age [1922]; Roman Britain [1924]; Anglo-Saxon, Viking and Norman Times [1926]; Everyday Things in Homeric Greece [1929]; Everyday Things in Archaic Greece [1931]; Everyday Things in Classical Greece [1932]; The Good New Days [1935].*

**QUESTED, George R.**      fl.1895-1901

Illustrator and book plate designer. He was working at St. John's Wood, 1895 and Edgbaston, 1897. He won prizes in *The Studio* book illustration competition, 1895.

Exhib: RA.
Bibl: *The Studio*, Winter No., 1900-01 p.59, illus.

**QUINTON, Alfred Robert**      1853-

Landscape and watercolour painter. He was born in 1853 and studied at Heatherley's and contributed to *The Illustrated London News*, 1884-86, 1894 and to *The Sporting & Dramatic News* 1890.

Illus: *Cycling in the Alps [C.L. Freeston, 1900]; The Historic Thames [J.H.P. Belloc, 1907]; The Avon and Shakespeare's Country [A.G. Bradley, 1910]; A Book of the Wye [E. Hutton, 1911]; The Cottages of Rural England [P.H. Ditchfield, 1912].*
Exhib: B; GG; G. L; M; RA; RBA; RHA; ROI.

**'QUIZ'**    **See MELLOR**

**R, N.**

Unidentified illustrator of landscape subjects, dating from about 1900.

Colls: V & AM.

**RACKHAM, Arthur   RWS**                                      **1867-1939**

Illustrator and watercolourist. He was born at Lewisham on 19 September 1867 and after being educated at the City of London School, studied art at Lambeth School where he was influenced by his fellow student Charles Ricketts (q.v.). Rackham joined the staff of *The Westminster Budget* in 1892 and from that time forward concentrated on the illustration of books and particularly those of a mystical, magic or legendary background. He very soon established himself as one of the foremost Edwardian illustrators and was triumphant in the early 1900s when colour printing first enabled him to use subtle tints and muted tones to represent age and timelessness. Rackham's imaginative eye saw all forms with the eyes of childhood and created a world that was half reassuring and half frightening. His sources were primarily Victorian and among them are evidently the works of Cruikshank, Doyle, Houghton and Beardsley (qq.v.) but also the prints of Dürer and Altdorfer. He was elected RWS in 1902 and after 1922 he undertook oil painting and some stage designing. He was a member of the Langham Sketch Club, exhibited widely at home and abroad and died on 6 September 1939.

Illus: *The Dolly Dialogues [1894]; Sketchbook, Tales of a Traveller [Washington Irving, 1895]; Bracebridge Hall [1896]; The Money Spinner [1896]; The Grey Lady [Seton Merriman, 1897]; Two Old Ladies etc. [M. Browne, 1897]; Evelina [Fanny Burney, 1898]; The Ingoldsby Legends [1898]; Gulliver's Travels [1899]; Tales From Shakespeare [Lamb, 1899]; Grimm's Fairy Tales [1900]; The Argonauts of the Amazon [C.R. Kenyon, 1901]; Rip Van Winkle [1905]; Peter Pan in Kensington Gardens [J.M. Barrie, 1906]; Alice's Adventures in Wonderland [Lewis Carroll, 1907]; A Midsummer Night's Dream [Shakespeare, 1908]; Undine [Fouqué, 1909]; The Book of Betty Barber [M. Browne, 1910]; The Rhinegold and The Valkyrie [Wagner, 1910]; Siegfried and the Twilight of the Gods [Wagner, 1911]; Aesop's Fables [1912]; The Old Nursery Rhymes [1913]; Arthur Rackham's Book of Pictures [1913]; A Christmas Carol [Charles Dickens, 1915]; The Allies Fairy Book [1916]; Little Brother and Little Sister [1917]; The Romance of King Arthur and his Knights of the Round Table [1917]; English Fairy Tales Retold [Flora Annie Steel, 1918]; The Springtide of Life [A.C. Swinburne, 1918]; Cinderella [1919]; Snickerty Nick, Rhymes by Whitter Bynner [J.E. Ford, 1919]; Some British Ballads [1919]; The Sleeping Beauty [1920]; Irish Fairy Tales [James Stephens, 1920]; A Dish of Apples [Eden Philpotts, 1921]; Comus [Milton, 1921]; A Wonder Book [Nathaniel Hawthorne, 1922]; Where the Blue Begins [Christopher Morley, 1925]; Poor Cecco [M.W. Bianco, 1925]; The Tempest [Shakespeare, 1926]; The Legend of Sleepy Hollow [Washington Irving, 1928]; The Vicar of Wakefield [Goldsmith, 1929]; The Compleat Angler [Izaak Walton, 1931]; The Night Before Christmas [C.C. Moore, 1931]; The King of the Golden River [J. Ruskin, 1932]; Fairy Tales [Anderson, 1932]; Goblin Market [Christina Rossetti, 1933]; The Pied Piper of Hamelin [Robert Browning, 1934]; Tales of Mystery and Imagination [E.A. Poe, 1935]; Peer Gynt [H. Ibsen, 1936]; A Midsummer Night's Dream [Shakespeare, 1939]; The Wind in the Willows [K. Grahame, 1940].*
Contrib: *Pall Mall Budget [1891-92]; Westminster Budget; The Graphic [1901]; Punch [1905-06]; The Sketch; Black & White; The Gentlewoman; Cassell's Magazine; Cassell's Family Magazine; Chums.*
Exhib: B; FAS, 1917; G; L; RA; RBA; RI; ROI; RSA; RSW; RWS.
Colls: Bradford; Fitzwilliam; Tate; V & AM.
Bibl: *The Studio*, Vol.34, 1906 pp.189-201, illus.; F. Coykendall, *A Bibliography*, 1922; O.W.S. Club, XVIII, 1940; D. Hudson, *AR, Life and Work*, 1960; F. Gettings, *AR*, 1975; B. Peppin, *Fantasy Book Illustration*, 1975; Gordon N. Ray, *The Illustrator and the Book in England*, 1976 pp.203-206.

See illustration (pp.425 and 507).

**RADCLYFFE, Charles Walter**                              **1817-1903**

Landscape painter, watercolourist, lithographer. He was born at Birmingham in 1817 and worked there throughout his life specialising

in views of old buildings in tinted lithographs and especially illustrations of the public schools. He came from a distinguished family of engravers and died at Birmingham in 1903.

Illus: *The Palace of Blenheim [1842]; Memorials of Shrewsbury School [1843]; Memorials of Charterhouse [1844]; Memorials of Eton College [1844]; Memorials of Westminster School [1845]; Memorials of Winchester College [1847].*
Exhib: B; RA; RI; ROI.
Colls: B; V & AM.

**RAEMAKERS, Louis**                                        **1869-1956**

Cartoonist. He was born at Roermond, Holland on 6 April 1869 and educated there and in Amsterdam and Brussels and received many diplomas for drawing. He was Director of a drawing school at Wageningen in Gelderland and about 1908 began to produce political cartoons and posters. Raemakers first attracted the attention of the British public during the First World War with his powerful chalk cartoons of the European situation, 1914-18. His bold and unsparing criticism of German atrocities was something new and his style has been compared to that of Steinlen. He later worked for French newspapers and died in 1956. Elected HRMS, 1916.

Illus: *The Great War in 1916; The Great War in 1917; Devant L'Histoire [1918]; Cartoon History of the War [1919].*
Exhib: FAS, 1915, 1916, 1917, 1918, 1920.
Colls: V & AM.

**RAFFET, Denis Auguste Marie**                            **1804-1860**

Battle painter, illustrator, engraver and lithographer. He was born in Paris on 2 March 1804 and after being apprenticed to a wood turner he went to Cabanel as a decorator of porcelain. In 1824 he worked for Charlet who taught him lithography and on leaving in 1829 he became a pupil of Gros. He failed to win the Prix de Rome in 1831 and from then concentrated entirely on lithography and illustration, publishing a number of albums. Raffet followed the French army to Italy in 1849 and attended the siege of Rome. He was patronised by Prince Demidoff and visited England and Scotland with him during his later years. He died at Gênes on 11 February 1860.

Illus: *Musée de la Revolution; Histoire de France; La Revolution; Le Consulat et L'Empire; History of Napoleon; Voyage en Crimée.*
Contrib: *The Illustrated Times [1855].*

**RAFTER, H.**

Illustrator and sporting artist. He was working in Coventry in 1856 and contributed to *Wyatt's Industrial Arts of the 19th Century.*

Colls: V & AM.

**RAILTON, Fanny (Mrs. Herbert Railton)**                   **fl.1894-1902**

Illustrator of children's books. Wife of the black and white artist Herbert Railton (q.v.).

Illus: *Lily and Lift [Seeley, 1894]; A Midsummer Night's Dream [1902].*

**RAILTON, Herbert**                                        **1857-1910**

Black and white artist and illustrator. He was born at Pleasington, Lancashire on 21 November 1857 and educated at Mechlin, Belgium and at Ampleforth. Railton's picturesque pen drawings of old buildings set a fashion in topographical draughtsmanship that lasted for many years, concentrating on the atmosphere and maturity of stone and brick. His drawings are characterised by an individual wriggly line and a strong decorative sense of the book page. Pennell considered him very influential, this is best seen in his follower Holland Tringham (q.v.). He died on 15 March 1911.

Illus: *Windsor Castle [1886]; Pickwick Papers [Charles Dickens Jubilee Edition, 1887]; Coaching Days and Coaching Ways [1888 (with Hugh Thomson)]; Westminster Abbey [1889]; Select Essays of Dr. Johnson [1889]; Poems and Plays of Goldsmith [1889]; Pericles and Aspasia [W.S. Landor, 1890]; Dreamland in History [1891]; The Citizen of the World [Goldsmith, 1891]; Beddoes Poetical Works [1891]; Collected Works of T.L. Peacock [1891]; Essays and Poems of Leigh Hunt [1891]; The Peak of Derbyshire [Leyland, 1891]; Ripon Millenary [1892]; The Inns of Court [Loftie, 1893]; Living English Poets [1894 (frontis)]; H. Kingsley's Novels [1894]; The Household of Sir Thomas More [1896]; The Haunted House [Hood, 1896]; Hampton Court [1897]; Cherry and Violet [Miss Manning, 1897]; English Cathedral Series [1897-99]; Travels in England [Le Gallienne, 1900]; Natural History of Selborne [White, 1900]; The Story of Bruges [1901]; Life of Johnson [1901].*

*ARTHUR RACKHAM RWS 1867-1939. 'The Death of Balder.' Original illustration in pen and ink. Signed and dated 1904. 15ins. x 11¹/₈ins. (38.1cm x 28.2cm).*

HERBERT RAILTON 1857-1910. 'The Old Tabard Inn.' Original drawing for illustration. Pen. 7⅞ins. x 10⅜ins. (20cm x 26.3cm).    Victoria and Albert Museum

Contrib: *The English Illustrated Magazine [1884-96]; The Graphic [1887]; ILN [1889-99]; The Sporting & Dramatic News [1890]; Good Words [1890-94]; The Pall Mall Budget [1891-92]; Daily Chronicle [1895]; The Sketch; The Idler; The Windsor Magazine; The Temple Magazine.*
Colls: Blackburn; V & AM.
Bibl: J. Pennell, *Pen Drawing and Pen Draughtsmen*, 1895 p.360, illus.; R.E.D. Sketchley, *Eng. Bk. Illus.*, 1903 pp.31, 38, 45, 74, 139.
See illustration (above).

**RAIMBACH, Abraham**                    **1776-1843**
Miniature painter and engraver. He was born in London in 1776 of Swiss extraction and after being educated at Archbishop Tenison's Library School, he attended the RA Schools. He was then employed by J. Hall, the engraver and worked on Smirke and Forster's edition of the *Arabian Nights, Macklin's Bible, Hume's History of England, Woodmason's Shakespeare* and *Bell's British Theatre* . . . He engraved a number of plates after Wilkie's works and died at Greenwich in 1843. Although not principally an illustrator, Raimbach's *Memoirs and Recollections*, 1843, remain an important source for the history of the art.
Colls: BM.

**RAINEY, William   RBA RI**              **1852-1936**
Artist and illustrator. He was born in London on 21 July 1852 and studied art at South Kensington and at the RA Schools before starting his career in book illustration. Rainey was much influenced by the 18th century revivalism of Thomson and others, was an assured pen artist and a fine wash artist. Much of his best work was done for the magazines but he illustrated a number of boys' stories. He was elected RI in 1891 and ROI, 1892, becoming HROI in 1930. He lived for the latter part of his life in Eastbourne and died on 24 January 1936.
Publ: *All the Fun of the Fair [1888]; Abdulla [1928]; The Last Voyage of the 'Jane Ann' [1929]; Admiral Rodney's Bantam Cock [1938]; Who's on My Side [1938].*

Illus: *Sweet Content [Mrs. Molesworth, 1891]; At Aboukir and Acre [G.A. Henty, 1898]; The Rebel of the School [L.T. Meade, 1902]; The Giant of the Treasure Caves [1908]; The Court Harman Girls [Meade, 1908].*
Contrib: *ILN [1884-94]; The Graphic [1884-1901]; The Quiver [1890]; Good Words [1891]; Black & White [1891-92]; The Strand Magazine [1891, 1906]; The Ludgate Monthly [1896]; The Temple Magazine [1896]; Cassell's Family Magazine; Chums.*
Exhib: G; L; M; RA; RBA; RI; ROI.
Colls: Leeds.
Bibl: J. Pennell, *Pen Drawing and Pen Draughtsmen*, 1894 p.352.
See illustration (p.427).

**RALSTON, John Mc L.**                   **fl.1872-1880**
Figure artist, illustrator and watercolourist. According to Dalziel this artist came from Scotland to work in London in about 1873. He worked for magazines and contributed to books.
Illus: *A Child's History of England [Charles Dickens, The Household Edition, 1873]; The Pilgrim's Progress [1880].*
Contrib: *ILN [1872-73, 1880-81].*
Exhib: Dowdeswell Galleries.
Bibl: The Brothers Dalziel, *A Record of Work, 1840-1890*, 1901.

**RALSTON, William**                      **1848-1911**
Comic artist. He was born in Dumbarton in 1848 and probably studied under his younger brother after abandoning a career as a photographer. He contributed a great many drawings to *Punch* from 1870 to 1886, specialising in genre and military subjects. He later became a master of the episodic illustration and strip cartoon, making up in humour for a certain deficiency in his drawings. He died at Glasgow in October 1911.
Illus: *Barry Lyndon [W.M. Thackeray, 1894].*
Contrib: *Punch [1870-86]; ILN [1870-73]; The Graphic [1870-1911]; The Cornhill Magazine [1883-84]; The Daily Graphic; The Sporting and Dramatic News [1895].*
Exhib: G.
Bibl: M.H. Spielmann, *The History of Punch*, 1895 p.543.

426

**RAMBERG, Johann Heinrich**                    **1763-1840**
Painter, engraver and caricaturist. He was born in Hanover in 1763 and came to England in 1781 to study at the RA Schools. He was a pupil of Sir Joshua Reynolds and Bartolozzi and after travelling to Italy and Dresden was appointed Court Painter at Hanover in 1792. His caricatures are mostly political ones dating from the later 1780s. He died at Hanover on July 6, 1840.

Exhib: RA.
Colls: BM; Hanover; Nottingham.
Bibl: M.D. George, *English Political Caricature*, Vol.1, 1959 p.194.

**RAMBLE, Fred**
Illustrator. Contributed to *Public Works of Great Britain*, 1838 AL 410.

**RANKIN, Andrew Scott**                         **1868-**
Animal painter. He was born at Aberfeldy in 1868 and studied at the Manufacturers School, Royal Institute and Life School, Edinburgh. He was on the staff of *Today* and was caricaturist of *The Idler*, c.1893. He worked at Strathtay, 1902-14 and at Pitlochrie, 1925.

Exhib: G; L; M; RA; RCA; RSA; RSW.

**RANKIN, Arabella Louisa**                      **1871-**
Painter and colour woodcut artist. She was born at Muthill, Perthshire in 1871 and worked at Edinburgh, 1903, Crieff, 1914 and in London 1922-35.

Bibl: *The Studio*, Vol.8, 1896 p.252, illus.

**RAVEN-HILL, Leonard    RWA**                   **1867-1942**
Black and white artist and cartoonist. He was born at Bath on 10 March 1867 and was educated at Bristol Grammar School and Devon County School before entering the Lambeth School of Art where he met Charles Rickettes and Charles H. Shannon (qq.v.). He then went to Paris and studied with Bouguereau and Aimé Morot and exhibited

at the Salon from 1887. Raven-Hill's connection with *Punch* began in 1896, but he had had a varied career on the magazines before this. He was appointed Art Editor of *Pick-Me-Up* in about 1890 and in 1895 founded his own illustrated publication *The Unicorn*, which had a short run. Other notable successes included his drawings for Rudyard Kipling's *Stalky & Co*. which first appeared in *The Windsor Magazine*.

Raven-Hill was one of the most versatile of the Edwardian *Punch* artists. He was strongly influenced by Ricketts, admired Japanese art and studied closely the work of Charles Keene (q.v.) with whose delicate pencil line and superb washes his own work has the closest affinities. He was second cartoonist and under-study to Partridge until 1935, but he was more at home in the domestic and genre subjects which he handled simply and brilliantly.

Illus: *The Promenaders [1894]; Stalky & Co., [Rudyard Kipling, 1899]; Raven-Hill's Indian Sketchbook [1903].*
Contrib: *Judy [1889]; Pick-Me-Up [1890]; Daily Graphic [1890]; Black & White [1891]; The Butterfly [1893-94, 1899-1900]; The Pall Mall Budget [1893]; ILN [1893]; The Unicorn [1895]; Punch [1896-1935]; The Minister [1895]; The Rambler [1897]; The Sketch [1897]; Fun [1901]; The Graphic [1906]; St. Paul's; Pearson's Magazine; The Pall Mall Magazine; The Nutshell.*
Exhib: FAS, 1899; GG; G; L; NEA; RA; RBA; RI; ROI; RSA.
Colls: Author; Birmingham; V & AM; Witt Photo.
Bibl: J. Pennell, *Pen Drawing and Pen Draughtsmen*, 1895 pp.340-341; *The Idler*, Vol.8 pp.124-132, illus; *The Studio*, Winter No., 1900-01 p.25, illus; R.G.G. Price, *A History of Punch*, 1957 pp.217-218.
See illustration (pp.428, 429).

**RAVERAT, Gwen**                                **1885-1957**
Wood engraver. She was born at Cambridge in 1885, the daughter of Sir George Darwin, Plumian Professor at Cambridge. She studied at the Slade School and worked mostly in Cambridgeshire but also in France, her style influenced by Eric Gill. ARE, 1920, RE, 1934. An exhibition of her work was held at the Fitzwilliam Museum in November 1977.

Illus: *The Bird Talisman, An Eastern Tale [H.A. Wedgwood].*
Exhib: G; L; NEA; RE; RHA; RSA.
Bibl: G. Raverat, *Period Piece*, 1952.

*W. RAINEY RBA RI 1852-1936. 'A Regency skating party.' Original drawing for illustration. Grey wash and bodycolour. Signed and dated 1891.*          Newman Collection

*LEONARD RAVEN-HILL 1867-1942. 'Edwin and Angelina find the only place they can meet in London!' Original drawing, probably intended as an illustration for* Punch. *Pen and ink. Signed and dated 1891. 8ins. x 9½ins. (20.3cm x 24.1cm).* Victoria and Albert Museum

**RAWLE, Samuel**       1771-1860

Landscape painter in oil and watercolours. He drew a number of illustrations for *The Gentleman's Magazine* and for J. Britton's publications. He illustrated *The Arabian Antiquities of Spain* by Murphy and died in London in 1860.

Colls: V & AM.

**RAWLINGS, Alfred**       1855-1939

Landscape and flower painter and illustrator. He was born in London in 1855 and became an art master at Leighton Park School, Reading and a member of the Berkshire Art Society where he exhibited.

Publ: *Anthology of Sea and Flowers [1910, 1913]; Book of Old Sundials [1915].*
Illus: *Our Village [M.R. Mitford, 1910].*
Exhib: B; RA.
Colls: Manchester; Northampton; Reading.

**RAWLINS, Thomas J.**       fl.1837-1860

Topographer and illustrator. Rawlins specialised in sporting subjects and was employed to illustrate works by Nimrod, Charles James Apperley, with H.T. Alken (q.v.). It seems that the artist visited India either in 1837 or in 1858-60.

Illus: *Gamonia or The Art of Preserving Game [L. Rawstorne, AL 392]; Elementary Drawing as Taught at St. Mark's College, Chelsea [1848].*
Contrib: *ILN [1858-60].*
Exhib: RA.

**RAYNER, Samuel A.**       -1874

Architectural and historical painter and illustrator. Rayner began exhibiting in London in 1821, most of his work being in the style of George Cattermole (q.v.). He was a successful artist and prints were made after his drawings and he was elected AOWS in 1845. He was however struck off in 1851 after being convicted of fraud. He had five daughters who painted architecture in his style and he died at Brighton in 1874.

Illus: *Sketches of Derbyshire Scenery [1830]; The History and Antiquities of Haddon Hall [1836]; The History . . . of Derby [1838].*
Contrib: *Britton's Cathedrals [1832-36].*
Exhib: BI; OWS; RA; RBA.
Colls: Birkenhead; Coventry; Derby; Ulster.

**READ, Edward Henry Handley**       1870-

Portrait and landscape painter and illustrator. He studied at South Kensington, at the Westminster School of Art and at the RA Schools where he won the Creswick prize. He was elected RBA in 1895 and was an Official War Artist for the Army, 1918.

Contrib: *The English Illustrated Magazine [1897]; The Graphic [1902].*
Exhib: FAS; G; L; M; RA; RBA; RI; ROI.
Colls: Bedford.

**READ, H. Hope**       fl.1906-1928

Figure painter. He was working in London from 1908 and contributed subjects to *Punch,* 1905-07.

Exhib: M; NEA; RA.

**READ, Samuel**   RWS       1815-1883

Landscape and architectural painter and illustrator. He was born at Needham Market, Suffolk in 1815 and was placed in a lawyer's office at Ipswich and then as an assistant to an architect. Neither professions suiting him, he went to London and learnt drawing on wood under J.W. Whymper (q.v.). He also studied with W.C. Smith and became an accomplished watercolour painter, sending many works to exhibitions. In 1844 he began to work as an illustrator for *The Illustrated London News,* a connection which lasted until his death. In 1853, just before the outbreak of the Crimean War, Read was despatched to Constantinople, the first occasion that the paper had sent an artist abroad on an assignment. He also travelled to Germany and North Italy and Spain as well as visiting and recording nearly every well-known ecclesiastical or manorial landmark in Great Britain. Over the years his pictures became an institution in *The 'News* and he was unofficially retained as Art Editor. His drawings of cathedrals, ruins and mysterious castles are delightfully dank and gloomy, always covered in thick undergrowth and with the appearance of having been painted in partly melted candle wax. He died at Sidmouth on 6 May 1883, having been elected OWS in 1880.

Illus: *Zoological Studies [S.P.C.K., 1844].*
Contrib: *The Home Affections by the Poets [Charles Mackay, 1858]; Willmott's Sacred Poetry of the 16th, 17th and 18th Centuries [1862]; Rhymes and Roundelayes.*
Exhib: OWS; RA; RBA.
Colls: Newcastle; Reading; V & AM.
Bibl: *Leaves From a Sketch-Book,* 1875.

**REASON, Florence**       fl.1896-1914

Genre and flower painter. She studied at the Queen's Square School of Art and won a National Silver Medal and Gilchrist Scholarship. She contributed figures to *The English Illustrated Magazine,* 1896.

Exhib: B; L; M; RA; RBA; RI; SWA.

**REDFARN, William Beales**       fl.1870-1916

Topographical artist. He made drawings of old buildings at Cambridge which were published as *Old Cambridge,* 1876 and he illustrated J.W. Clark's *Ancient Wood and Ironwork in Cambridge,* 1881.

Colls: Fitzwilliam.

**REDGRAVE, Richard**   RA       1804-1888

Genre painter and illustrator. He was born in Pimlico on 30 April 1804, the son of a wire fence manufacturer, and worked with his father before studying at the RA Schools. Redgrave became a drawing master in 1830 and was always heavily committed to art education and art history. He was associated with the Government School of Design from 1847, was on the Paris Exhibition Committee in 1855 and was Director of the Art Division, South Kensington, until 1875. He was Surveyor of the Queen's Pictures from 1857 to 1880 and was made CB in that year. Redgrave returned to the Bible and the English poets for much of his inspiration and this was also true of the small body of illustrative work he undertook. He was elected ARA in 1840, RA in 1851 and died in London on 14 December 1888.

Publ: *An Elementary Manual of Colour [1853]; A Century of Painters of the British School [1866].*
Contrib: *The Deserted Village [Etching Club, 1841]; Book of British Ballads [1842]; Songs of Shakespeare [Etching Club, 1843]; The Song of the Shirt [Etching Club]; Favourite English Poems [1859]; Early English Poems, Chaucer to Pope [1863].*
Exhib: BI; RA; RBA.
Colls: BM; V & AM; Witt Photo.
Bibl: F.M. Redgrave, *RR, a Memoir,* 1891.

*LEONARD RAVEN-HILL 1867-1942. Customer: 'Quite a Fancy Article. But what can it be used for?' Salesman: 'Well I really couldn't say, Madam, but I think its intended for a Christmas present.' Original drawing for illustration in* Humorists of the Pencil, *1903. Pen and ink. Signed and dated 1899. 7ins. x 11¼ins. (17.8cm x 28.6cm).*
Author's Collection

**REDON, Georges**                                    **1869-1943**
Painter, lithographer, humorous illustrator. He was born at Paris on 16 November 1869 and exhibited at the Salon. He died in 1943.

Contrib: *The Graphic [1901].*

**REED, C.W.**
Illustrator of *Jack the Fisherman,* E. Stuart Phelps, 1897.

**REED, Edward Tennyson**                              **1860-1933**
Cartoonist and illustrator. He was born on 27 March 1860, the son of Sir Edward James Reed, the naval architect and MP. He was educated at Harrow and then travelled to Egypt, China and Japan in 1880, before being appointed to the *Punch* staff in 1890 by Sir F. Burnand. He very soon became an established part of the paper, introducing his 'Prehistoric Peeps' series in 1893 and following Furness (q.v.) as parliamentary caricaturist in 1894, a post he held till 1912. He was also a talented lecturer and published a number of books.

Reed introduced the grotesque into *Punch* art once again after a long absence, he was also unusual in drawing principally in pencil with careful hatching and shading. A good portraitist and very inventive, his drawings are nevertheless rather angular and somewhat bizarre in quality. He died 12 July 1933.

Illus: *Mr Punch's Prehistoric Peeps [1896]; Tales With a Twist [1898]; Unrecorded History Mr Punch's Animal Land [1898]; Mr Punch's Book of Arms [1899]; The Tablets of Azit-Tigleth-Miphansi; The Scribe [1900]; The Unlucky Family [Mrs De La Pasture, 1908].*
Contrib: *Punch [1889-1933]; The Sketch [1894]; The Graphic; The Bystander.*
Exhib: FAS, 1899; G; New Gall; ROI.
Colls: V & AM.
Bibl: M.H. Spielmann, *The History of Punch,* 1895, pp.560-563; *The Idler,* Vol.9, pp.493-508; *The Studio,* Winter No., 1900-01, p.23 illus; Shane Leslie, *ETR,* 1957.

**REED, Ethel**                                        **1876-**
American illustrator. She was born at Newburyport in 1876 and specialised in babies and children's books which were published in the United Kingdom.

Illus: *Arabella and Araminta Stories; Verses [Mrs. L.C. Moulton].*
Contrib: *The Yellow Book [1897 (cover and illus.)].*
Bibl: 'The Work of Miss ER', *The Studio,* Vol.10, 1897, pp.230-236.

**REES, F.**
Amateur artist contributing to *Punch,* 1908.

**REEVE, A.**
Illustrator of comic genre subjects for *The Graphic,* 1886.

**RÉGAMEY, Félix Elie**                                **1844-1907**
Portrait and history painter, engraver and illustrator. He was born in Paris on 7 August 1844, the son and pupil of the artist L.P.G. Régamey. He started his career as a caricaturist on *Journal Amusant, la Vie Parisienne, au Monde Illustré, l'Illustration, l'Éclipse, La Lune, Paris Caprice, Monde Comique* and *La Guêpe.* He founded his own journal *Salut Public* in 1870. Régamey remained at Paris during the Siege and acted as reporter and Special Artist for *The Illustrated London News,* producing very strong and rugged work. He left France in 1873 and travelled to England and then to Japan and the United States where he made powerful sketches of American prisons. He became an inspector of drawings at the Paris Schools in 1881 and died there on 7 May 1907.

Exhib: London 1872.
Bibl: *English Influences on Vincent Van Gogh,* Arts Council, 1974-75.
See illustration (p.141).

**REGNAULT, Henri Alexandre Georges** 1843-1871
Genre and history painter. He was born in Paris on 30 October 1843 and entered the École des Beaux Arts in 1860, winning the Prix de Rome in 1866 and studying in Italy until 1868. He travelled in Spain and Morocco but was killed with the 19th Infantry Regiment after enlisting in 1870.

Contrib: *The Graphic [1871 (carnival)]*.
Colls: Boston; Chicago; Marseilles; Louvre.

**REID, Sir George   RSA HRHA** 1841-1913
Black and white artist and illustrator. He was born at Aberdeen on 31 October 1841 and was educated at Aberdeen Grammar School. He studied art in Edinburgh, Utrecht and Paris and returning to this country became the leading landscape pen draughtsman of his time. Pennell regarded his powers very highly — 'he can, in a pen drawing, give the whole character of northern landscape . . . while his portraits contain all the subtlety and refinement of a most elaborate etching by Rajon.' Reid exhibited his work very widely, received many honours, was knighted in 1891 and was President of the RSA, 1891 to 1902. He died in Somerset on 9 February 1913.

Illus: *The Selected Writings of John Ramsay [1871]; Life of a Scotch Naturalist [Smiles, 1876]; George Paul Chalmers [1879]; Johnny Gibb [W. Alexander, 1880]; Twelve Sketches of Scenery [1882]; Natural History and Sport in Norway [1882]; The River Tweed [1884]; The River Clyde [1886]; Salmon Fishing on the Ristigouche [1888]; Lacunar Basilicae [1888]; St. Giles' Edinburgh [1889]; Royal Edinburgh [Mrs Oliphant, 1890]; Familiar Letters of Sir Walter Scott [1894]*.
Contrib: *The English Illustrated Magazine [1890-91]*.
Exhib: B; G; L; M; New Gall; P; RA; RHA; ROI; RSA.
Bibl: J. Pennell, *Pen Drawing and Pen Draughtsmen*, 1904, pp.277-279 illus; R.E.D. Sketchley, *Eng. Bk. Illus.*, 1903, pp.31, 141.

**REID, John Robertson   RI** 1851-1926
Genre, history and landscape painter. He was born in Edinburgh on 6 August 1851 and studied at the RSA Schools under Chalmers and McTaggert. He specialised in marine and coastal paintings, many of them of Cornwall and distinguished for their clarity and colour. He was elected RI in 1897 and died at Hampstead on 10 February 1926.

Contrib: *The Graphic [1892 (birds)]; The Sketch [1894]*.
Exhib: B; FAS, 1899; G; GG; L; M; NEA; New Gall; RA; RBA; RHA; RI; ROI; RSA.
Colls: Leicester; Liverpool; V & AM.

**REID, Stephen** 1873-1948
Painter and illustrator. He was born at Aberdeen in 1873 and studied at the Grays School of Art, Aberdeen and at the RSA Schools. In his early years he was strongly influenced by the work of E.A. Abbey (q.v.) and favoured Georgian settings and costume pieces for his work, he was also a competent topographer in pen and ink. He was elected RBA in 1906 and died at Hampstead on 7 December 1948.

Illus: *The Magic Casement [Alfred Noyes, 1908]*.
Contrib: *The Windsor Magazine; The Temple Magazine [1896-97]; The Idler; The Strand Magazine [1906]; The Connoisseur [1910 (decor)]*.
Exhib: L; M; RA; RBA; RI; RSA.

**REID, W.E.**
Illustrator. Contributed drawings to *Embassy to the Court of Ava* by J. Crawford, 1829, AT 405.

**REINAGLE, George Philip** 1802-1835
Marine painter. He was born in 1802 and was the younger son of R.R Reinagle and began his career by copying Dutch masters. He was present with the Fleet at the Battle of Navarino in 1827, the last battle under sail, and with the Fleet off Portugal in 1833.

Illus: *Illustrations of the Battle of Navarino [1829]; Illustrations of the Occurences at the Entrance of the Bay of Patras . . . [1828]*.
Colls: BM.

**REINAGLE, Philip   RA** 1749-1833
Sporting artist and animal painter. He was born in Scotland in 1749 and entered the RA Schools in 1769 after which he studied with Allan Ramsay. He made botanical and anatomical drawings for book illustrations and was elected ARA in 1787 and RA in 1812. He died in London in 1833.

Illus: *Sportsman's Cabinet [Taplin, 1803]; Sexual System of Linnaeus [1799-1807]; Philosophy of Botany [1809-10]*.
Exhib: BI; RA; RBA.
Colls: BM; V & AM.
Bibl: *AJ*, 1898.

**REINHART, Charles Stanley** 1844-1896
American painter and illustrator. He was born at Pittsburg in 1844 and studied art at Paris and in Munich with Strahuber and Karl Otto. He worked principally in New York but contributed to British publications. These included the illustrations to Thomas Hardy's 'Romantic Adventures of a Milk-Maid' in *The Graphic*, 1883. He died in 1896.

Exhib: L; RI.

**REJCHAN, Stanislas**
Polish artist and illustrator. He worked in Paris and contributed Belgian scenes to *The Graphic*, 1902.

**RÉNAUD, G.**
Humorous artist. Contributed to *Judy*, 1886-89.

**RENÉ**
Decorative artist contributing to *The English Illustrated Magazine*, 1895.

*CHARLES PAUL RENOUARD 1845-1924. 'Anarchist Oratory in France.' An illustration to* The Graphic, *24 February 1894.*

*CHARLES PAUL RENOUARD 1845-1924. 'Recruiting the Sandwich Men.' Illustration for* The Graphic, *1894.*

**RENNELL, Joseph**

Draughtsman. He contributed illustrations to *Public Works of Great Britain*, 1838, AT 410.

**RENOUARD, Charles Paul**                                          **1845-1924**

Painter, engraver and illustrator. He was born at Cour Cheverny on 5 November 1845 and studied at the École des Beaux Arts after which he worked as a mural painter. Renouard worked for the Parisian papers *l'Illustration* and *Paris Illustré* before starting work for *The Graphic* in 1884. Renouard's forte was in pencil and chalk drawings which had a power and expressiveness quite new in the pages of English magazines. For a decade he was the giant among illustrators and his flamboyant full page sketches of social realism, London life and Parisian fashion burst on the British public. For some reason this masterly artist who must have been widely influential on such Paris trained Englishman as Dudley Hardy (q.v.) has been almost forgotten. He exhibited at the Salon from 1877 and died in Paris on 2 January 1924. Elected RE, 1881.

Contrib: *The Graphic [1884-1910]; ILN [1886-89]; The Butterfly [1893]; The English Illustrated Magazine [1893-94]; Daily Graphic.*
Exhib: L; NEA; P; RE.
See illustrations (above and p.430).

**RENTON, John**                                                     **1774-c.1841**

Figure and landscape painter. He lived in London and worked in the Thames Valley and Lake District. Contributed illustrations to *The Border Antiquities of England and Scotland*, Walter Scott, 1817.
Colls: BM.

**REPTON, Humphry**                                                 **1752-1818**

Landscape gardener and watercolourist. He was born at Bury St Edmunds in 1752 and educated at Bury, Norwich and on the Continent. He became interested in botany and landscape design and from the 1780s developed a large practise in the new 'picturesque' style of gardening. Repton developed a habit of presenting elaborate Red Books to his clients in which projected improvements were set out in 'before and after' scenes in brilliant watercolours. He was not strictly an illustrator at all, but drew for some of his own works. He died at Romford on 14 March 1818.

Publ: *Sketches and Hints on Landscape Gardening [1794]; Observations on the Theory and Practice of Landscape Gardening [1803]; Odd Whims and Miscellanies [1804]; Fragments on the Theory and Practice of Landscape Gardening [1816].*
Exhib: RA.
Colls: BM; V & AM.
Bibl: J.C. Loudon, *The Landscape Gardening . . . of HR*, 1840; D. Stroud, *HR*, 1962.

**REPTON, John Adey    FSA**                                       **1775-1860**

Architect. He was the eldest son of H. Repton (q.v.) and was born in Norwich on 29 March 1775. He became a pupil of the architect William Wilkins and made drawings of Norwich cathedral, but although he went into practice with his father, he was stone deaf and could only lead a retired life, but was the teacher of F. Mackenzie (q.v.). He was elected FSA in 1803 and died at Springfield, Essex on 26 November 1860.

Publ: *A Trewe . . . Hystorie of the . . . Prince Radapanthus [1820]; Some Account of the Beard and Moustachio [1839].*
Contrib: *Britton's Cathedrals [1832-36].*
Exhib: RA.
Colls: RIBA; Soc. of Antiquaries.
Bibl: H.M. Colvin, *Biog. Dict. of Eng. Architects*, 1954, p.491.

**REYNOLDS, Ernest G.**

Humorous artist. Contributed to *Judy*, 1886 and *Fun*, 1887.

**REYNOLDS, Frank    RI**                                          **1876-1953**

Black and white artist and illustrator. He was born in London on 13 February 1876 and studied at Heatherley's before working for *The Illustrated London News* and *The Sketch*. He joined the staff of *Punch* in 1919 and was Art Editor from 1920-32, having been a contributor from 1906. Reynolds was most successful in urban genre subjects, interiors, street corners and where groups of people were included. His characters, portly policemen, charladies and drunks were not as individual as Belcher's, but Fougasse later considered that his fluid pen line had done a lot to alter the image of *Punch*. He was elected RI in 1903 and died in April 1953.

Illus: *Pictures of Paris and Some Parisians [Raphael, 1908]; The F.R. Golf Book [1932]; Hamish McDuff [1937]; Off to the Pictures [1937]; Humorous Drawings [1947].*
Contrib: *Pick-Me-Up [1896]; The Longbow [1898]; Judy [1899]; Sketchy Bits; Punch [1906-53]; ILN [1909-11]; The Sketch.*
Exhib: L; RI; Walker's.
Colls: Author; Fitzwilliam.
Bibl: *FR, RI*, Ed. by A.E. Johnson, Brush, Pen, Pencil series, c.1910; *Modern Book Illustrators and Their Work*, Studio, 1914.
See illustration (p.432).

**REYNOLDS, H.**                                                    **fl.1882-1896**

Artist and illustrator. He worked at Birmingham and contributed decoration to *The English Illustrated Magazine*, 1896.
Exhib: B.

**REYNOLDS, J.H.**

Humorous artist. Contributed illustrations to *Hood's Comic Annual*, 1830.

**REYNOLDS, Percy T.**                                              **fl.1890-1914**

Humorous artist. He worked in London at Muswell Hill and contributed to *Fun*, 1890-92 and *Punch*, 1914.
Exhib: RA.

*FRANK REYNOLDS RI 1876-1953. 'Sir Henry Irving and companion.' Pen and ink. Signed with initials. 9½ins. x 5½ins. (24.1cm x 14cm).* Author's Collection

**REYNOLDS, Warwick**      fl.1871-1879

Black and white artist. He contributed comic heads to *Judy*, 1871-79. He was a member of the NWS from 1864-65.

**REYNOLDS, Warwick**      1880-1926

Black and white artist and illustrator. He was born in Islington in 1880, the son of Warwick Reynolds (q.v.). He was educated at Stroud Green and studied at the Grosvenor Studio, St. John's Wood Art School and at Julians in Paris, 1908. He made a particular study of animals in the collection of the Zoological Society, 1895-1901, and began to work for the magazines in 1895. He died in Glasgow on 15 December 1926.

Illus: *Babes of the Wild [1912].*
Contrib: *The Strand Magazine; Pearson's Magazine; Royal Windsor Magazine; The Quiver; The Idler; Ally Sloper's Half Holiday.*
Exhib: G; L; RA; RSA; RSW.
Colls: Glasgow; Witt Photo.

**RHEAD, F.A.**

Humorous figure artist. Contributed to *Punch*, 1914.

**RHEAD, George Wooliscroft   RE**      1855-1920

Painter, etcher and illustrator. He was born in 1855 and won a National Art Scholarship and silver medals before studying with Alphonse Legros and Ford Madox Brown. Rhead designed for stained glass, wrote on ecclesiastical art and was a member of the Art Workers

Guild and Hon. ARCA. He was elected RE in 1883 and in 1914 married the illustrator Annie French (q.v.). He died on 30 April 1920.

Publ. his own etchings: *The Foundation of Manchester by the Romans; The Dream of Sardanapalus.*
Illus: *Bunyan's Pilgrim's Progress; Life of Mr Badman; Idylls of the King [Tennyson].*
Exhib: G; L; New Gall; RA; RBA; RE; RI.
Bibl: *The Studio*, Vol.9, 1897, p.282 illus.

**RICE**

Illustrator contributing to *London Society*, 1868.

**RICH, Anthony**      fl.1854-1914

Landscape painter and illustrator working at Croydon and Hassocks. He contributed to *Thornbury's Legendary Ballads*, 1876.

**RICH, E.**

Topographer. He was a pupil of J. Hawksworth and illustrated *The History and Antiquities of Islington*, 1823.

**RICHARDS, Frank**      fl.1883-1925

Landscape and figure painter. He was probably born in Birmingham where he worked early in his career before settling in Dorset and the West Country from 1887. He was elected RBA in 1921.

Contrib: *Pick-Me-Up [1894]; The Graphic [1898]; The Queen; The Sketch; The Windsor Magazine.*
Exhib: B; L; M; RA; RBA.

**RICHARDS, G.E.**

Figure artist specialising in children. He contributed to *Punch* 1903 and may be the George Richards exhibiting at Liverpool in 1900.

**RICHARDSON, Charles**      1829-1908

Landscape and marine painter. He was born in 1829, the son of T.M. Richardson (q.v.) by his second marriage. He assisted his brother H.B. Richardson but moved to London in 1873, finally settling in Hampshire. He died in 1908.

Illus: *The Conquest of Camborne [Sir W. Lawson, 1903].*
Exhib: L; RA; RI.

**RICHARDSON, Charles**

Animal and bird illustrator. He contributed comic sketches to *Punch*, 1905.

**RICHARDSON, Charles James**      1806-1871

Architect and draughtsman. He was born in 1806 and became a pupil of Sir John Soane and a specialist on Tudor and Jacobean buildings and ornament. He was Master of the Architectural Class at Somerset House, 1848-52.

Illus: *Architectural Remains of the Reigns of Elizabeth and James I [1838-40]; Studies from Old Mansions, their Furniture, Gold and Silver Plate . . . [1841]; Studies of Ornamental Design [1848]; Picturesque Designs for Mansions, Villas, Lodges . . . [1870].*
Exhib: RA.
Colls: Soane Museum; V & AM (Lib.).

**RICHARDSON, Henry Burdon**      1811-1874

Landscape artist and topographer. He was born at Warkworth in about 1811, the son of T.M. Richardson (q.v.). He travelled widely before settling down as a drawing-master at Newcastle-upon-Tyne and undertaking the series of large views of the Roman Wall, illustrated in Sir Gainsford Bruce's *History of the Wall*. He died at Newcastle in 1874.

Exhib: RA; RBA.
Colls: Newcastle.

**RICHARDSON, Ralph J.**      fl.1896-1925

Painter and illustrator. He specialised in comic genre subjects in black and white mostly associated with horsemanship.

Contrib: *Punch [1896-1907]; The Graphic [1901].*
Exhib: RA, 1900.

**RICHARDSON, Thomas Miles**                    1784-1848
Landscape painter and watercolourist. He was born at
Newcastle-upon-Tyne on 15 May 1784 and after being apprenticed to
an engraver, became a drawing-master and devoted his time entirely to
painting from 1813. He travelled widely and his work is chiefly
associated with the more picturesque areas of Italy, Switzerland and
France. Richardson was a fine colourist and by far the most
distinguished watercolourist of the North East, founding the
Newcastle Watercolour Society in 1831. He was ANWS from 1840 for
three years and exhibited regularly. He began to publish a work on
Newcastle in 1816 and in 1833 began to issue *The Castles of The
English and Scottish Borders*. He died in Newcastle on 7 March 1848.

Contrib: *Howitt's Visits to Remarkable Places [1841]*.
Exhib: BI; NWS; OWS; RA, 1814-45; RBA.
Colls: BM; Bradford; Derby; Leeds; Manchester; Newcastle; V & AM.
Bibl: *Memorials of Old Newcastle on Tyne . . . with a sketch of the artist's life*,
1880.

**RICHARDSON, Thomas Miles, Jnr.    RWS**       1813-1890
Landscape painter and watercolourist. He was born at Newcastle-
upon-Tyne in 1813, the son of T.M. Richardson (q.v.). He worked
closely with his father, but moved to London in 1846 after being
elected AOWS in 1843; he became a full OWS in 1851. Richardson
made tours of the Continent and chose many of the same localities as
his father for his exhibition works. These are always brightly coloured
and highly finished, tending towards an over elaboration and a too
great size for the medium. His smaller studies are often charming with
an effective use of chinese white. He died at Newcastle on 5 January
1890.

Illus: *Sketches in Italy, Switzerland, France etc., [1837]; Sketches at Shotley
Bridge Spa and on The Derwent [1839]*.
Contrib: *Howitt's Visits to Remarkable Places [1841]*.
Exhib: BI; L; M; RA; RBA; RWS.
Colls: Blackburn; BM; Cardiff; Manchester; V & AM.

**RICHTER, Willibald**                          fl.1840-1856
Watercolourist and illustrator. He worked at Vienna and travelled to
England, Italy and Poland, exhibiting views of these countries at the
Vienna Academy 1840-50.

Contrib: *ILN [1855-56 (Turkey)]*.

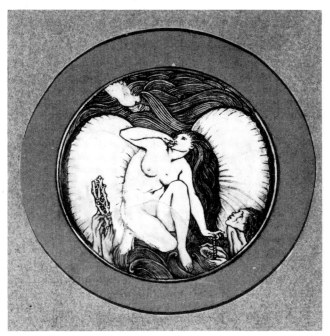

*CHARLES DE SOUSY RICKETTS RA 1866-1931. 'Venus Bird Messenger.'
Original drawing for wood engraving in* The Marriage of Cupid and Psyche, *Vale
Press, 1899. Circular pen and wash, touched with white. Diameter 3ins. (7.6cm)*
Victoria and Albert Museum

**RICKARDS, Edwin A.**                          1872-1920
Architect, draughtsman and caricaturist. He was born in Chelsea in
1872 and spent some time in the RA Schools and at the Architectural
Association but chiefly taught himself from study in the museums. He
entered the office of Richard J. Lovell in 1887 as an architectural
assistant and later joined the firms of Howard Ince and George
Sherrin. Toured Italy and made himself familiar with the baroque
before returning to England to do competition work and enter
partnership with H.V. Lanchester in 1897. He died as a result of war
disabilities in 1920.

Illus: *Parisian Nights and Other Impressions of Places and People [Arnold
Bennett, 1913]*.
Bibl: *The Art of EA with a Personal Sketch by Arnold Bennett, an Appreciation
by H.V. Lanchester and Technical Notes by Amor Fenn*, 1920.

**RICKETTS, Charles de Sousy    RA**            1866-1931
Painter, printer, stage designer, writer and collector. He was born in
Geneva in 1866, the son of the marine painter C.R. Ricketts (q.v.). He
was brought up in France and Italy and studied at the Lambeth
School of Art where he met his lifelong friend C.H. Shannon (q.v.).
With him he owned and edited *The Dial*, 1889-97 and ran the Vale
Press, 1896-1904, producing eighty-three volumes, many with type,
bindings or illustrations by him. Among them were *Daphne and
Chloe*, the first book of the new woodcut revival. Ricketts
concentrated in later life on stage designing and sculpture, was elected
ARA in 1922 and RA in 1928 and died in London on 7 October
1931.

Illus: *A House of Pomegranates [Wilde, 1891]; Poems Dramatic and Lyrical [de
Tabley, 1893]; Daphne and Chloe [1894]; Hero and Leander [1894]; In the
Key of Blue [J.A. Symonds; 1894 (cover)]; The Sphinx [Wilde, 1894]; The
Incomparable and Ingenious History of Mr W.H. [Wilde, 1894]; Dramatic Works
of Oscar Wilde [1894]; Nymphidia [1896]; Spiritual Poems [T. Gray]; The
Early Poems of John Milton [1896]; The Poems of Sir John Suckling; Fifty
Songs of Thomas Campion; Empedocles on Etna [Matthew Arnold]; Songs of
Innocence [Blake, 1897]; Sacred Poems of Henry Vaughan [1897]; Cupide and
Psyche [1897]; The Book of Thel [Blake, 1897]; Blake's Poetical Sketches
[1899]; The Rowley Poems of Thomas Chatterton [1898]; Julia Domna
[Michael Field, 1903]*.
Contrib: *Black and White [1891]*.
Exhib: FAS; G; GG; L; M; RA; RBA; RI; ROI; RSA.
Colls: Ashmolean; BM; Fitzwilliam; Leeds; Manchester; Reading; V & AM.
Bibl: T.S. Moore, *CR*, 1933; R.E.D. Sketchley, *Eng. Bk. Illus.*, 1903, pp.18,
129; C. Franklin, *The Private Presses*, 1969. For full bibliography of Vale
Press see Franklin, C.
See illustration (below left).

**RICKETTS, Charles Robert**                    fl.1868-1879
Marine painter. He worked in London and contributed to *The Graphic*
1871.

Exhib: RA; RBA.

**RIDCOCKS, E.F.**
Black and white artist in New Zealand. Contributed to *Punch*, 1902.

**RIDDELL, Robert Andrew**                      fl.1790-1807
Landscape, painter and topographer who illustrated *A History of
Mountains*, J. Wilson, 1807.

**RIDLEY, B.**
Black and white artist. He contributed to *London Society*, 1869.

**RIDLEY, Mathew White**                        1837-1888
Landscape painter, illustrator and engraver. He was born at
Newcastle-upon-Tyne in 1837 and studied at the RA Schools under
Smirke and Dobson. Ridley became the earliest pupil of James McNeil
Whistler (q.v.) and a friend of Fantin Latour. He developed a very
direct reportage in his illustrations of social realism in the 1870s and
these were admired by Van Gogh. He contributed to numerous
magazines and died on 2 June 1888.

Contrib: *Cassell's Family Magazine [1867]; The Quiver [1867]; Every Boy's
Magazine [1867]; The Graphic [1869-77]; ILN [1872-81]*.
Exhib: G; GG; RA; RI.
Bibl: *English Influences on Vincent Van Gogh*, Arts Council, 1974-75; 'Artists
Fruitful Friendship', V. Gatty, *Country Life*, 7 March 1974.

**RIMER, William**                                      fl.1845-1888

Historical and subject painter and illustrator. His drawings are usually in pencil, very meticulous in execution and showing strong German influence. He worked in Westminster and London and illustrated *Thomson's Castle of Indolence* for the Art Union of London, 1845.

Exhib: BI; RA; RBA.
Colls: Witt Photo; V & AM.

**RIMMER, Alfred**                                       1829-1893

Black and white artist, woodcut artist and antiquary. He was born at Liverpool on 9 August 1829 and worked for some years as an architect, spent a period of time in Canada, finally settling at Chester as an artist and writer. He died there on 27 October 1893.

Illus: *Ancient Streets and Homesteads of England; Pleasant Spots About Oxford; Rambles About Eton and Harrow; About England with Dickens.*
Contrib: *The English Illustrated Magazine [1885].*
Exhib: L; M.
Colls: BM.

**RIOU, Edouard**                                        1833-1900

Landscape painter, designer and illustrator. Born at Saint-Servan on 2 December 1833 and exhibited at the Salon from 1859. He specialised in book illustration including the works of Jules Verne and the poetry of A. Riou. He died in Paris on 27 January 1900.

Contrib: *The Illustrated Times [1859]; ILN [1894].*
Colls: Witt Photo.

**'RIP'   Rowland HILL**                                 1873-p.1925

Cartoonist. He was born at Halifax in 1873 and worked at Halifax before studying at Bradford School of Art and at the Herkomer School, Bushey. Travelled on the Continent and settled at Hinderwell, Yorks, 1908.

Contrib: *Black & White; Truth; The Sketch.*
Exhib: L; RA.
Colls: Leeds.

**RISCHGITZ, Edward**                                    1828-1909

Landscape painter. He was born at Geneva on 28 July 1828 and became a pupil of Diday and worked in Paris. He settled in London before 1878 and was elected RE in 1881. He died at the home of his daughter the artist Mary Rischgitz on 3 November 1909.

Contrib: *Good Words [1880].*
Exhib: GG; RE.

**RITCHIE, Alick P.F.**                                  fl.1892-1913

Caricaturist and illustrator.

Contrib: *The Ludgate Monthly [1892]; St Pauls [1894]; The Pall Mall Budget [1894]; Sketchy Bits [1895]; Eureka [1897]; Penny Illustrated Paper; Vanity Fair [1911-13].*

**RIVERS, A. Montague**                                  fl.1910-1915

Painter and illustrator. He worked in Hornsey, London and contributed to *The Illustrated London News*, 1915.

Exhib: M; RA; RI.

**RIVIERE, Briton   RA**                                 1840-1920

Genre, landscape and animal painter. He was born in London on 14 August 1840, the son of William Riviere, drawing-master at Cheltenham College. He was educated at Cheltenham and St Mary Hall, Oxford, where he began making humorous pen drawings. These came to the notice of Mark Lemon of *Punch*, who gave him work and he then undertook drawing for American magazines. Riviere maintained that one of his eyes was permanently damaged by the strain of this drawing and he only painted after 1870. He became very well-known for his animal subjects and was elected ARA in 1878 and RA in 1881. He died in London on 20 April 1920.

Contrib: *Punch [1868-69]; Good Words [1868]; Good Words For The Young [1869]; ILN [1870].*
Exhib: B; FAS; G; GG; L; M; RA; RCA; RHA; RSA.
Colls: BM; Blackburn; Manchester; V & AM.
Bibl: *AJ*, 1878, 1891.

**RIVIERE, Hugh Goldwin**                                1869-1956

Portrait painter. He was born at Bromley, Kent on 1 January 1869, the son of Briton Riviere (q.v.). He was educated at St Andrews and studied at the RA Schools, being elected RP in 1900 and ROI in 1907. He died in 1956.

Illus: *John Halifax Gentleman [Mrs Craik, 1897].*
Exhib: B; FAS; G; L; M; New Gall; P; RA; RHA; ROI; RSA.

**RIVINGTON, Reginald**                                  fl.1908

Illustrator of children's books. He illustrated *The Snow King* and *Buffs and Boys,* Amy Sims, 1908.

**ROBERTS, Charles J. Cramer**                           1834-1895

Landscape painter and illustrator. He was a professional soldier who joined the Army in 1853 and served in India and the Crimea retiring in 1887. He contributed portraits, social and military illustrations to *The Graphic,* 1872-77.

Colls: India Office Lib.

**ROBERTS, David   RA**                                  1796-1864

Landscape and architectural painter. He was born at Stockbridge, Edinburgh on 2 October 1796, the son of a shoemaker and was apprenticed for seven years to a house painter, before working as scene painter at theatres in Carlisle, Glasgow and Edinburgh. In 1822 he went to London and while scene painting at Drury Lane formed his lifelong friendship with Clarkson Stanfield (q.v.). Roberts was very successful in what he undertook, became Vice-President of the SBA on its foundation in 1823-24 and President in 1830. He began travelling on the Continent in the 1820s and on Wilkie's recommendation visited Spain and Tangier in 1832-33, following this with trips to Egypt and Palestine in 1838 and Italy in 1851 and 1853. Roberts' great accuracy as a draughtsman, his strong sense of country and place, combined with his love of architecture, made his Middle Eastern views the touchstone of a fashion among the early Victorians. The temples and monuments brought to life for the first time were drawn on the stone by J.D. Harding and Louis Haghe (qq.v.) and issued in amazingly lavish form to subscribers. Roberts was elected ARA in 1838 and RA in 1841 and acted as a Commissioner for the Great Exhibition. He died in London on 25 November 1864, still at work on a series of Thames views.

Illus: *Picturesque Sketches in Spain during the years 1832 and 1833 [AT 152]; Views in the Holy Land, Syria, Idumea, Egypt, Nubia [1842-49].*
Contrib: *Jennings Landscape Annual [1835-38]; The Chaplet [c.1840]; Scotland Delineated [Lawson, c.1845]; Lockhart's Spanish Ballads.*
Exhib: BI; RA; RBA.
Colls: Aberdeen; BM; Fitzwilliam; Glasgow; Leeds; Manchester; Nat. Gall. Scotland; V & AM.
Bibl: J. Ballantine, *The Life of DR,* 1866; J. Quigley, DR, *Walker's Quarterly,* X, 1922; M. Hardie, 'DR' *O.W.S.,* 1947; M. Hardie, *Watercol. Paint. In Brit.,* Vol.III, 1968, pp.179-183 illus.

**ROBERTS, Edwin**                                       fl.1862-1890

Genre and rustic painter. He worked in Chelsea and contributed figure illustrations to *Judy,* 1889.

Exhib: RA; RBA.

**ROBERTS, Henry Benjamin**                              1832-1915

Genre painter and watercolourist. He was born in Liverpool in 1831, the son of a landscape painter and studied with his father. He closely followed the work of W.H. Hunt, was elected a member of the Liverpool Academy in 1855, of the NWS in 1867 and the RBA in 1878. He was living in Leyton, Essex from 1883 except for a period in North Wales. He died in 1915.

Contrib: *ILN [1871-75].*
Exhib: B; L; RI.
Colls: Birkenhead; V & AM.

**ROBERTS, I.**

Contributed a social illustration to *The Graphic,* 1870.

*WALFORD GRAHAM ROBERTSON RBA ROI 1867-1948. 'The Man Whom The Trees Loved.' Illustration in* The Studio, *1914.*

### ROBERTS, J.H.
Black and white artist. He was an architect who had become a caricaturist, journalist and political versifier. He contributed to *Punch,* 1892-97; *Fun*, 1893; *Chums.*

### ROBERTSON, George Edward                    1864-
Portrait painter and illustrator. The son of a painter, he studied at St Martin's School of Art and worked in London.

Contrib: *The Graphic [1905].*
Exhib: G; L; M; RA; RBA; ROI.

### ROBERTSON, Henry Robert            1839-1921
Landscape, genre and figure painter and engraver. He was born at Windsor in 1839 and studied at the RA Schools. He worked in Hampstead and was elected RE, 1881 and RMS, 1896. He died on 6 June 1921.

Illus: *The Trial of Sir Jasper [S.C. Hall, 1870]; Life on the Upper Thames [1875]; The Art of Etching Explained and Illustrated [1883]; The Art of Painting on China [1884]; The Art of Pen and Ink Drawing [1886]; Plants we Play With [1915]; More Plants we Play With [1920].*
Contrib: *ILN [1874, 1881]; The English Illustrated Magazine [1886].*
Exhib: B; G; L; M; New Gall; RA; RBA; RE; RI; RMS; ROI.
Colls: Sheffield.

### ROBERTSON, James  of Constantinople
Amateur artist and photographer. He contributed an illustration of the Crimea to *The Illustrated London News* in 1855 and produced daguerrotype pictures of the War after Roger Fenton the photographer left the front. After the War he worked with Felice Beato and became an official British photographer. Drawings based on his photographs appeared in *The Illustrated Times*, 1856.

Bibl: *The Camera Goes to War,* Scottish Arts Council, 1974-75, p.58.

### ROBERTSON, Walford Graham   RBA ROI            1867-1948
Portrait and landscape painter, illustrator and designer. He was born in 1867 and educated at Slough and Eton. He studied art at South Kensington with Albert Moore and became a member of the NEA, 1891, the RBA in 1896 and the ROI in 1910. Robertson was part of the talented group of artists and illustrators who flourished in London in the 1890s, his portrait was painted by Sargent and he claimed to have been influenced by W. Crane and the Glasgow School and must have admired W. Nicholson (q.v.).

Illus: *Old English Songs and Dances [1903]; A Masque of May Morning [1904]; The Napoleon of Notting Hill [G.K. Chesterton, 1904]; Gold, Frankinsense and Myrhh and other Pageants for a Baby Girl [1906]; A Year of Songs; The Baby's Day Book; Wind in the Willows [Kenneth Grahame, 1908 (frontis)]; Old Fashioned Fairy Tales [n.d.].*
Contrib: *The English Illustrated Magazine [1896].*
Exhib: B; G. GG; L; M; NEA; New Gall; RA; RBA; ROI.
Bibl: 'The Illustrated Books and Paintings of WGR', by T.M. Wood, *The Studio,* Vol.36, pp.99-107 illus; *Modern Book Illustrators and Their Work,* Studio, 1914; *Time Was,* a book of Memories, WGR, n.d.
See illustration (left).

### ROBINSON, C.                    -1881
Illustrator and engraver. He was born in London the son of a wood engraver and book binder and was apprenticed to the firm of Maclure, Macdonald and Macgregor, lithographers before joining *The Illustrated London News* in about 1862. He had attended Finsbury School of Art in about 1857, winning a silver medal in the National Competition. He contributed regular and rather wooden work to *The 'News* until his death and also to *The Illustrated Times* in 1865. He was the uncle of Charles, T.H. and W. Heath Robinson (qq.v.).

Bibl: L de Fretas, *Charles Robinson,* Academy Edit, 1976.

### ROBINSON, Charles   RI            1870-1937
Painter in watercolours, illustrator and decorator. He was born in London on 22 October 1870, the son of Thomas Robinson, wood engraver, and nephew of C. Robinson (q.v.). He was educated at Islington High School and Highbury School of Art, but spells at the RA Schools were abandoned for lack of finance, 1892. He was then apprenticed to Waterlow & Sons as a lithographic artist but came to the fore in 1895 when his drawings were published in *The Studio* and he was asked to design for R.L. Stevenson's *A Child's Garden of Verses.* Robinson in company with his brothers T.H. and W. Heath Robinson (qq.v.) became one of the most popular Edwardian black and white artists. His style was very decorative, flowing and imaginative scenes were surrounded by elaborate borders and in the faces and forms of his children he recaptured something of the innocence of childhood. His drawings were partly inspired by the prints of Dürer, partly by the Pre-Raphaelites, their space often suggestive of Japanese prints. But he was no copyist and his colouring and fantasy are often highly original, perhaps based on his lack of formal training. He was elected President of the London Sketch Club, and was elected RI in 1932. He died in Buckinghamshire on 13 June 1937.

Illus: *Come Ye Apart [Sunday School Union, 1894]; Aesops Fables; A Child's Garden of Verses [R.L. Stevenson]; The Infant Reader; The First Primer; The*

Second Primer [1895]; Animals in the Wrong Places [E. Carrington]; The Child World [G. Setoun]; Christmas Dreams [Awfly Weirdly]; Make Believe [H.D. Lowry]; Minstrel Dick [C.R. Coleridge, 1896]; Dobbie's Little Master [Mrs. A. Bell]; Lullaby Land [E. Field]; Cranford [Mrs. Gaskell, 1897]; King Longbeard [B. MacGregor]; Lilliput Lyrics [W.D. Rands]; Richard Wagner and The Ring [1898]; Fairy Tales From Hans Christian Andersen [With T.H. and W.H.]; The New Noah's Ark [J.J. Bell]; Pierrette [H. de V. Stacpoole]; The Suitors of Aprille [N. Garstin, 1899]; The Adventures of Odysseus [Homer]; Child Voices [W.E. Cule]; Jack of All Trades [J.J. Bell]; The Little Lives of the Saints [P. Dearmer]; The Master Mosaic Workers [G. Sand]; Sintram and His Companions [de la Motte Fouqué]; Tales of Passed Times [C. Perrault]; The True Annals of Fairyland [Ed. W. Canton, 1900]; A Book of Days For Little Ones [C. Bridgman]; The Farm Book [W. Copeland]; The Mother's Book of Song [J.H. Burn]; Nonsense! Nonsense! [W. Jerrold]; The Shopping Day [C. Bridgman]; Stories For Children [Charles and Mary Lamb]; The True Annals of Fairyland; [J.M. Gibbon, 1901]; The Bairns Coronation Book [C. Bridgman]; The Book of the Zoo [W. Copeland]; The Coronation Autograph Book [1902]; The Big Book of Nursery Rhymes [W. Jerrold]; Fireside Saints [D. Jerrold]; The New Testament of Our Lord . . . [1903]; Siegfried [Baring Gould, 1904]; The Black Cat Book [W. Copeland]; A Bookful of Fun; The Book of Ducks and Dutchies [W. Copeland]; A Book of The Dutch Dolls [W. Copeland]; The Book of the Fan [W. Copeland]; The Book of the Little Dutch Dots [W. Copeland]; The Book of the Little J.Ds [W. Copeland]; The Book of the Mandarinfants [W. Copeland]; The Cloud Kingdom [I.H. Wallis]; The Ten Little Babies [1905]; Awful Airship [W. Copeland]; Baby Town Ballads [Netta]; The Books of Dolly's Doings [W. Copeland]; The Book of Dolly's House [W. Copeland]; The Book of Dollyland [W. Copeland]; Bouncing Babies [W. Copeland]; The Child's Christmas [E. Sharp]; Fanciful Fowls; A Little Book of Courtesies [K. Tynan]; Mad Motor [W. Copeland]; Peculiar Piggies; Road, Rail & Sea [C. Jerrold]; The Silly Submarine [W. Copeland, 1906]; Alice's Adventures in Wonderland [L. Carroll]; Black Bunnies; Black Doggies; Black Sambos; The Cake Shop [W. Copeland]; Prince Babillon [Netta]; Songs of Love and Praise [A. Matheson]; The Story of the Weathercock [E. Sharp]; The Sweet Shop [W. Copeland]; The Toy Shop [W. Copeland, 1907]; Babes and Blossoms [W. Copeland]; The Book of Other People [W. Copeland]; The Book of Sailors [W. Copeland]; The Book of Soldiers [W. Copeland]; A Child's Garden of Verses [R.L. Stevenson]; The Fairies Fountain [Countess Cesaresco]; Songs of Happy Childhood [I. Maunder, 1908]; Babes and Birds [J. Pope]; The Vanishing Princess [N. Syrett, 1909]; Brownikins and Other Fancies [R. Arkwright]; Grimm's Fairy Tales; In The Beginning [S.B. Macy, 1910]; The Baby Scouts [J. Pope]; The Big Book of Fairy Tales [W. Jerrold]; The Secret Garden [F. Hodgson Burnett]; The Sensitive Plant [P.B. Shelly, 1911]; Babes and Beasts [J. Pope]; Bee: The Princess of the Dwarfs [A. France]; The Big Book of Fables [W. Jerrold]; The Four Gardens [Handasyde]; Longfellow [M. MacLeod]; Old Time Tales [Ed. L. Marsh]; Songs of Innocence [W. Blake, 1912]; A Child's Book of Empire [A.T. Morris]; Fairy Tales [C. Perrault]; The Happy Prince [O. Wilde]; Margaret's Book [Fielding-Hall]; The Open Window [E.T. Thurston]; Rainbows [M. Dykes Spicer]; Topsy Turvy [W.J. Minnion, 1913]; Our Sentimental Garden [A. & E. Castle, 1914]; Arabian Nights; The Open Window [E.T. Thurston]; Rip Van Winkle [W. Irving]; Robert Herrick; The Songs and Sonnets of Shakespeare; What Happened At Christmas [E. Sharp, 1915]; Bridget's Fairies [Mrs. S. Stevenson, 1919]; Songs of Happy Childhood [I. Maunder]; Teddy's Year With the Fairies [M.E. Gullick, 1920]; The Children's Garland of Verses [G. Rhys]; Father Time Stories [J.G. Stevenson, 1921]; Doris and David All Alone [E. Marc]; The Goldfish Bowl [P. Austin, 1922]; Wee Men [B. Girvin & M. Cosens, 1923]; Once On A Time [A.A. Milne, 1925]; The Saint's Garden [W. Radcliffe, 1927]; Mother Goose Nursery Rhymes; The Rubaiyat of Omar Khayyam [1928]; Granny's Book of Fairy Stories [1930]; Young Hopeful [1932].
Contrib: Black & White [1895]; The Yellow Book [1896]; ILN [1912]; The Graphic [1915]; The Queen.
Exhib: G; L; RA; RI.
Colls: V & AM.
Bibl: The Studio, Vol.63, pp.150-151 illus; R.E.D. Sketchley, Eng. Bk. Illus., 1903, pp.102, 114, 169; Modern Book Illustrators and Their Work, Studio, 1914; L. de Freitas, CR, Academy Edit., 1976.

### ROBINSON, Frederick Cayley ARA 1862-1927

Painter, illustrator and poster artist. He was born at Brentford on Thames on 18 August 1862 and after being educated at the Lycée de Pau, studied art at the St Johns Wood and RA Schools. He lived on a yacht, 1888-90 and studied at Julian's 1890-92, later studying in Italy. He became Professor of figure composition and decoration at Glasgow, 1914-24 and was elected ARA in 1921. He had been RBA since 1890 and NEA since 1912. Robinson's style of work was based on Italian quattrocento sources and was not best adapted to the book. He did however, illustrate The Book of Genesis for the Riccardi Press in 1914. He died in London on 4 January 1927.

Exhib: G; L; M; NEA; New Gall; RA; RBA; ROI; RSA; RSW; RWS.
Colls: BM; Fitzwilliam; Manchester.
Bibl: FCR, FAS Cat., 1969, 1977; The Studio, Vol.31, 1904, pp.235-241 illus.

### ROBINSON, Gordon fl.1905-1913

Illustrator of children's books. He illustrated Puss in Boots in about 1905 and contributed to The Illustrated London News, 1908-13 in the style of J. Hassall (q.v.).

### ROBINSON, H.R.

Contributor of cartoon to Punch, 1864.

### ROBINSON, Joseph fl.1882-1885

Landscape painter working in London. He contributed a view of Thanet to The Illustrated London News, 1885.

Exhib: RI.

### ROBINSON, Ruth H.

Amateur illustrator. The Studio book illustration competition 1897 shows her work.

### ROBINSON, Miss S.A.H. fl.1890-1902

Illustrator. She contributed to the Daily Graphic, c.1890 and to The Graphic, 1902.

### ROBINSON, Thomas

Wood engraver and illustrator, probably the father of C., T.H. and W. Heath Robinson (qq.v.). Worked chiefly for The Penny Illustrated Paper, contributed to Dark Blue, 1871-73.

WILLIAM HEATH ROBINSON 1872-1944. 'Inspecting Stockings on Christmas Eve.' Original drawing for illustration in The Sketch. Pen and ink and wash. Signed in full. 15¾ins. x 11¼ins. (40cm x 28.6cm). Victoria and Albert Museum.

**ROBINSON, Thomas Heath**                    fl.1896-1902
Black and white artist and illustrator. He was the son of Thomas
Robinson (q.v.) and elder brother of C. and W. Heath Robinson
(qq.v.). He studied with his father and by 1896 had an extensive
output among the magazines and was developing as a designer of
bookplates.

Illus: *Legends From River and Mountain [1896]; Cranford [Mrs Gaskell,*
*1896]; Henry Esmond [W.M. Thackeray, 1896]; The Scarlet Letter*
*[Hawthorne, 1897]; A Sentimental Journey [Sterne, 1897]; Hymn on the*
*Morning of Christ's Nativity [1897]; A Child's Book of Saints [1898]; The*
*Heroes [Kingsley, 1899]; Fairy Tales From The Arabian Nights [1899]; Fairy*
*Tales from Hans Andersen [1899]; A Book of French Songs For The Young*
*[1899]; Lichtenstein [1900]; The Scottish Chiefs [1900].*
Contrib: *Cassell's Family Magazine [1898-99]; The Windmill [1899]; The*
*Quiver [1900]; The Idler; The Pall Mall Magazine.*
Bibl: R.E.D. Sketchley, *Eng. Bk. Illus.*, 1903, pp.114, 170.

**ROBINSON, Will B.**                          fl.1892-1902
Architectural draughtsman and illustrator. He was working in
Lincoln's Inn, London in 1902 and specialised in industrial subjects,
views of international exhibitions and decorations.

Contrib: *ILN [1892-1900]; The English Illustrated Magazine [1895-97].*

**ROBINSON, William Heath**                     1872-1944
Black and white artist and illustrator, the only British illustrator to
become a 'household name'. He was born in London on 31 May 1872,
the son of Thomas Robinson (q.v.) and younger brother of C. and
T.H. Robinson (qq.v.). He was educated in Islington and studied at
the RA Schools before beginning to draw for the publishers. His
earliest work was conventional book illustration very much in the
idiom of his brother Charles and it was only with the approach of the
First World War that the Robinson fantasy developed in him as a
passion for mad machinery. His pen and ink drawings of inventions
and contraptions were ideally suited to the industrial age and were in
some ways the visual counterparts to Lewis Carroll's prose, having as
their base, a kind of perverse logic. With his success, Robinson was
imitated and taken into the language as the arch-priest of
scatter-brained improvisation. He expanded into stage design and had a
large following abroad.

Illus: *The Pilgrim's Progress [1897]; Don Quixote [1897]; The Giant Crab*
*[1897]; Danish Fairy Tales [1897]; Arabian Nights [1899]; The Talking*
*Thrush [Rouse, 1899]; Tales For Toby [1900]; Rabelais; Twelfth Night; A Song*
*of the English [Rudyard Kipling]; Kipling's Collected Verse; a Midsummer*
*Night's Dream [1914]; The Water Babies; Perrault's Tales; Peacock Pie [Walter*
*de la Mare].*
Illus: *Uncle Lubin [1902]; Bill the Minder [1912].*
Contrib: *The Sketch; The Bystander; The Graphic [1910-]; The Illustrated*
*Sporting & Dramatic News; London Opinion; Puck; The Strand Magazine; The*
*Quiver; The Sportsman and Humorist [1931].*
Exhib: FAS, 1924; RA (Memorial Exhib, FAS 1945).
Colls: BM; V & AM.
Bibl: A.E. Johnson, *WHR*, Brush, Pen and Pencil series, 1913; *My Line of Life*
*by WHR*, 1938; Langton Day, *The Art and Life of WHR*, 1947.
See illustration (p.436).

**ROBLEY, Major-General Horatio Gordon**        1840-1930
Amateur black and white artist. He was born at Funchal, Madeira on
28 June 1840 the son of Capt. J.H. Robley and served as a
professional soldier in Burma, 1859-63, the Maori War, 1864-66, in
Zululand, 1884 and Ceylon, 1886-87. He was one of a number of
artists who sent suggestions to Charles Keene (q.v.) and some of his
drawings were improved by Keene for *Punch.* Robley was well-known
for his collection of preserved and tattooed Maori heads! He died on
29 October 1930.

Contrib: *Punch [1873-78]; The Graphic; ILN.*
Bibl: G.S. Layard, *Charles Keene,* 1892, p.179.

**ROE, Fred   RI**                             1864-1947
Genre painter and illustrator. He was born in 1864, the son of Robert
Henry Roe, landscape and miniature painter and studied at
Heatherley's and with J. Seymour Lucas (q.v.). He was elected RBA in
1895 and RI in 1909. Roe, who became a leading expert and collector
of antique furniture, wrote many articles for art magazines and died in
London in 1947.

Illus: *Ancient Coffers and Cupboards [1902]; Vanishing England [1910]; Old*
*Oak Furniture; A History of Oak Furniture [1920].*
Contrib: *Fun [1892]; Judy [1895].*
Exhib: B; L; M; RA; RBA; RI; ROI; RWA.
Colls: Greenwich; V & AM.

**ROE, John   of Warwick**
Landscape painter and topographer in watercolours. He worked
chiefly in the Midlands and drew ruins, exhibiting at the RA and the
Society of Artists. He was still active in 1812.

Illus: *Warwick Castle, a Poem [1812].*
Contrib: *Antiquarian and Topographical Cabinet [1811].*
Colls: BM; Coventry; V & AM.

**ROFFE, F.**
Illustrator. Contributed drawings of modern sculpture to *The Art*
*Journal,* 1862-71 and 1891.
Colls: V & AM.

**ROGERS, James Edward   RHA**               1838-1896
Architectural and marine painter. He was born in Dublin in 1838 and
practised as an architect before giving this up to become a
watercolourist. He was elected ARHA in 1871, RHA in 1872 and
moved to London in 1876. He died on 18 February 1896.

Illus: *More's Ridicula; Ridicula Rediviva; The Fairy Book [Miss Mulock,*
*c.1870].*
Contrib: *The English Illustrated Magazine [1893-94].*
Exhib: L; RA; RE; RHA; RI; ROI.
Colls: Nat. Gall., Dublin.

**ROGERS, W.A.**
Genre illustrator. Illustrated *City Legends* by Will Carleton, 1889 and
contributed to *The Graphic,* 1887.

**ROGERS, William Harry**                      1825-1873
Illustrator and designer. He was the son of W.G. Rogers and
specialised in ornament, emblems and designs based on German books
of the 16th century. He worked at Wimbledon and died there in 1873.

Illus: *Poems and Songs [Robert Burns, 1858]; Quarle's Emblems [c.1861];*
*Spiritual Conceits [c.1862]; Poe's Poetical Works [1858]; The Merchant of*
*Venice [1860].*
Bibl: Chatto & Jackson *Treatise on Wood Eng.*, 1861, p.600; Ruari McLean,
*Victorian Book Design*, 1972, pp.145-146, illus.

**ROLLER, George R.   RPE**                     1858-
Domestic and portrait painter and illustrator. He was born in 1858
and studied at Lambeth School of Art and in Paris under Bouguereau
and Fleury. He was the designer of advertisements for Burberry's for
thirty years and also picture restorer at the RA. He worked at
Basingstoke, 1889 to 1914 and in London from 1925. He was elected
RE, 1885.

Contrib: *Black & White [1894]; Pick-Me-Up; The Pall Mall Magazine; Fun*
*[1901].*
Exhib: FAS; L; RA; RBA; RE; ROI.

**ROLLESTON, D.**
Marine illustrator. Contributed to *The English Illustrated Magazine,*
1895.

**ROLLINSON, Sunderland**                       1872-
Painter, etcher and lithographer. He was born at Knaresborough in
1872 and studied at Scarborough School of Art and at the RCA. In
his student years he contributed a number of landscape illustrations
with enormous foregrounds to the National Competitions and *The*
*Studio* book illustration competitions. He was working at Fulham,
1902 and at Cottingham, Yorks, 1914 to 1925, he married the artist
Beatrice Malam.

Exhib: G; L; RA; RBA; RI; RSA.
Bibl: *The Studio,* Vol.11, 1897, p.261 illus.; Vol.14, 1898, p.144 illus.; Winter
No., 1900-1, p.60 illus.

*DANTE GABRIEL ROSSETTI 1828-1882. Design for frontispiece to* The Early Italian Poets, *1861, unused. Pen and ink over pencil. 6ins. x 4⁷/8ins. (15.2cm x 12.4cm).*
Marshall Collection

**ROLT, Charles** fl.1845-1867
Figure artist working at Merton and in Bloomsbury. He illustrated *The Sermon on The Mount*, 1861 (chromo-liths).

Exhib: BI; RA; RBA.

**ROOKE, Noel** 1881-1953
Painter, engraver and book illustrator and decorator. He was born in 1881, the son of T.M. Rooke, portrait painter. He studied at the Slade School and at the Central School of Arts and Crafts, becoming the Head of the School of Book Production there. He was elected ARE in 1920 and died in 1953.

Illus: *An Inland Voyage [R.L. Stevenson, 1913]; Travels with a Donkey [R.L. Stevenson, 1913]*.
Exhib: NEA; RA; RE.

**ROPE, George Thomas** 1845-1929
Landscape and animal painter. He was born at Blaxhall, Suffolk in 1849 and became a pupil of the landscape painter W.J. Webbe, visiting the Continent in 1882. He worked for most of his life at Wickham Market and excelled as a pencil artist. He died in 1929.

Illus: *Sketches of Farm Favourites [1881]; Country Sights and Sounds [1915]*.
Exhib: L; RA.

**ROSE, Robert Traill** 1863-
Painter, designer and lithographer. He was born at Newcastle-upon-Tyne in 1863 and studied at the Edinburgh School of Art. He worked chiefly in Edinburgh and Tweedsmuir and produced a series of fine

symbolic illustrations to *The Book of Job*, c.1912.

Exhib: G; L; RSA; RSW.
Bibl: *The Studio*, Vol.55, 1912, p.312 illus.; *Modern Book Illustrators and Their Work*, Studio, 1914.

**ROSS, Charles H.** fl.1867-1883
Dramatist, novelist and illustrator. He was employed in the Civil Service at Somerset House and began to write and draw in his free time. He was brought to the notice of William Tinsley, the publisher who gave him two Christmas annuals to edit describing him as a 'very clever, but very nervous young man'. Ross's facility with writing and drawing won him the Editorship of *Judy* where many of his quips and drawings were published in the years 1867-78. Dalziel mentions that they were 'generally signed "Marie Duval", his wife's maiden name and the subjects often savoured somewhat of a French origin'. His small lively figures were full of humour but not great satiric art although they had in them the makings of real satire. One such was a large-headed man who became Ally Sloper and was taken to great heights by the artist W.G. Baxter (q.v.). Ross was also the proprietor of *C.H. Ross's Variety Paper*.

Illus: *Queens and Kings and Other Things; The Boy Crusoe; Merry Conceits and Whimsical Rhymes written and drawn by CHR [1883]*.
Contrib: *Every Boy's Magazine*.
Bibl: W. Tinsley, *Random Recollections*, 1900, pp.267-268; The Brothers Dalziel, *A Record of Work, 1840-1890*, 1901, p.320.

**ROSS, Sir John** 1777-1856
Arctic explorer. He was born at Inch, Wigtonshire in 1777 and joined the East India Company in 1794 and the Royal Navy in 1805. He was commander in the Baltic and North Sea in 1812-17 and made his famous expeditions in search of the North-West Passage in 1818 and 1829-33. He was consul at Stockholm, 1839-46 and Rear-Admiral, 1834. He died in London in 1856.

Illus: *A Voyage of Discovery [1819, AT 634]; Narrative of a Second Voyage in Search of a North-West Passage [1835, AT 636]*.
Colls: BM; Greenwich.

**ROSSETTI, Dante Gabriel** 1828-1882
Painter, poet and occasional illustrator. He was born in London on 12 May 1828, the son of Gabriel Rossetti, an Italian refugee and Professor of Italian at King's College. He was educated at King's College, studied drawing under J.S. Cotman (q.v.) and in 1845 entered the RA Schools, going in 1848 into the studio of Ford Madox Brown (q.v.). It was this meeting and later those with Millais and Holman Hunt (qq.v.) that caused the foundation of the Pre-Raphaelite Brotherhood of which Rossetti was the mainstay. The movement which lasted from 1848 until 1853 was to have repercussions right through the Victorian age, although it was first met with hostility. From 1857-58, when Edward Burne-Jones helped him with the decoration of the Oxford Union, Rossetti was much involved with the younger Pre-Raphaelite followers and poets and craftsman like William Morris (q.v.). His model, Elizabeth Siddal, whom he married in 1860, was the source of much of his inspiration in both painting and poetry, most of his important illustration was done prior to her death in 1862.

Rossetti can be seen as a larger than life influence on the later illustrators although his own contribution was small. He provided much of the hot imagery and passion in the decade following which made the 1860s memorable in book art. Rossetti lived for some time at 16 Cheyne Walk, Chelsea with W.M. Rossetti, A.C. Swinburne and George Meredith. He died at Birchington, Sussex on 9 April 1882 and was buried there.

Illus: *The Music Master [William Allingham, 1855]; Tennyson's Poems [Moxon Edition, 1857]; The Goblin Market [Christina Rossetti, 1862]; The Prince's Progress and other Poems [Christina Rossetti, 1866]; Flower Pieces [1888]; Early Italian Poets [n.d. (unused frontis)]; The Risen Life [R.C. Jackson, 1884 (cov. & frontis)]*.
Exhib: London, 1849-50.
Colls: BM; Birmingham; V & AM.
Bibl: W.M. Rossetti, *DGR his Family Letters*, 1895; F.M. Hueffer, *R, A Critical Essay*, 1902; H.C. Marillier, *R*, 1904; Surtees, *DGR*, 1971; *DGR, Painter and Poet*, RA Cat., Jan.-March, 1973; Gordon N. Ray, *The Illustrator and The Book in England*, 1976, pp.101-103 illus.

See illustrations (above left, p.439 and Colour Plates VII and VIII p.105).

*DANTE GABRIEL ROSSETTI 1828-1882. 'The Maids of Elfen-Mere.'*
*Illustration to* The Music Master *by William Allingham, 1855. Wood engraving.*

**ROSSITER, Charles**                        1827-c.1890
Genre painter. He was born in 1827 and taught painting. He married
in 1860 Miss Frances Fripp Seares, the artist.

Contrib: *Passages From Modern English Poets [Junior Etching Club, 1862].*
Exhib: L; M; RA; RBA.

**ROTHENSTEIN, Sir William**                 1872-1945
Painter and portrait artist. He was born at Bradford, Yorks in 1872
and educated at Bradford Grammar School and studied at the Slade
School and at Julians, Paris, 1889-93. He made his debut as a
draughtsman at Oxford in 1893, when he drew its celebrities. His
portrait drawings are very French in treatment and some have a
decidedly Whistlerish feel to them. Rothenstein travelled to India in
1910 and was Official War Artist, 1917-18 and to the Canadian
Occupation, 1919. From 1917 to 1926 he was Professor of Civic Art
at Sheffield University and Principal of the RCA, 1920-35. He was
elected NEA, 1894, RP, 1897 and was knighted in 1931. He died in
1945.

Illus: *Oxford Characters, A Series of Lithographed Portraits by Will Rothenstein*
*[1894]; English Portraits [1898]; Manchester Portraits [1899]; Liber Juniorum*
*[1899]; The Fench Set and Portraits of Verlaine [1898]; Six Portraits of Sir*

*Rabindranath Tagore [1915]; Twenty-Four Portraits [1920]; Twenty-Four*
*Portraits, 2nd Series [1923].*
Contrib: *The Yellow Book; The Savoy ·[1896]; The Quarto [1898]; The Page*
*[1899]; The Dome [1899].*
Exhib: B; FAS; G; GG; L; M; NEA; P; RA; RHA; RSA; RSW.
Colls: Liverpool; Tate.
Bibl: Robert Speaight, *WR, The Portrait of an Artist in His Time,* 1962.

**ROUNTREE, Harry**                          1878-
Illustrator in black and white and colour. He was born in Auckland,
New Zealand in 1878 and was educated at Queen's College, Auckland.
He came to London in 1901 and studied with Percival Gaskell at the
Regent Street Polytechnic before getting commissions through the
Editor of *Little Folks.* Rountree's métier was always comic animals
and books for children although he undertook a certain amount of
poster work. His drawings are characterised by subtle colours and
fluid washes with a great accuracy of natural background.

Illus: *The Magic Wand [1908]; The Wonderful Isles [1908]; Peep in the World*
*[F.E. Crichton, 1908]; Alice's Adventures in Wonderland [1908].*
Contrib: *Little Folks; The Strand Magazine; Punch [1905-9, 1914]; The*
*Graphic [1906, 1911]; ILN [1911].*
Bibl: *Modern Book Illustrators and Their Work,* Studio, 1914; *HR and His*
*Work, The Art of the Illustrator,* P.V. Bradshaw, 1916.

**ROUS, Eva**
Illustrator contributing drawings to a story in *The Graphic,* 1910.

**ROUSE, Robert William Arthur    RBA**      fl.1883-1927
Landscape painter, etcher. He worked in Surrey, Buckinghamshire and
Oxfordshire and was elected RBA in 1889. He illustrated a series of
articles by W. Raymond in *The Idler* called 'The Idler out-of-doors'
and contributed to *The Windsor Magazine.*

Exhib: G; L; M; RA; RBA; RHA; RI; ROI; RSA.

**ROWLAND, Ralph**
Humorous illustrator. Contributed golf sketches to *Punch,* 1905.

**ROWLANDSON, George Derville**             1861-
Sporting illustrator. He was born in India in 1861 and studied art in
Gloucester, Westminster and Paris. He worked in Bedford Park and
the majority of his contributions are military or equestrian. He signs
his work GDR.
Contrib: *ILN [1897-1900]; The English Illustrated Magazine [1899-1900].*
Exhib: RI.

**ROWLANDSON, Thomas**                       1756-1827
Watercolour painter, illustrator and social caricaturist. He was born in
London in 1756, the son of a bankrupt merchant and was educated at
Dr Barrow's School and at the RA Schools, which he entered in 1772.
He made visits to Paris in 1774 and 1777 to visit relatives and the
rococo delicacy of his pen and wash drawings probably owes
something to this French connection. Rowlandson hereafter made
extensive journeys on the Continent to France, Italy, Germany and
Holland and in Great Britain, filling notebooks with a mixture of
grotesque humanity and sylvan ideal landscapes. He often travelled
with other caricaturists, notably, H. Wigstead and J. Nixon (q.v.). His
work is always tinted pen drawing rather than full-scale watercolour,
but he changed his humorous style to do drawings after the Old
Masters and figures reminiscent of Thomas Gainsborough. He was one
of the major caricaturists to become an extensive book illustrator,
particularly in his work for Ackermann from 1798 in *The Tours of*
*Dr. Syntax* and *The Microcosm of London,* 1808. In later life,
Rowlandson's quality of work tailed off, a not surprising feature of
someone who was a gambler, dissolute and naturally lazy. The later
drawings often show a sloppiness and lack of interest in the subject
and as countless versions of one subject exist this is not wholly
surprising. The artist was extensively faked, but these copies tend to
be wooden although the signature is often convincing. He died in
London in 1827.

Illus: *Poems of Peter Pindar [1786-92]; Tom Jones [Fielding, Edinburgh, 1791*
*and 1805]; Joseph Andrews [Fielding, 1793]; Siebald [Smollett, 1793];*
*Humphrey Clinker [Smollett, 1793]; The Beauties of Sterne [1800]; Remarks*

On a Tour to North and South Wales in the Year 1797 [1800]; Matrimonial Comforts [1800]; Country Characters [1800]; Jones's Bardic Museum [1802]; A Compendious Treatise On Modern Education [1802]; Pleasures of Human Life [1807]; The Microcosm of London [1808]; Smollett's Miscellaneous Works [1809]; Poetical Magazine [1808-11]; Beauties of Tom Brown [1809]; Gambado [1809]; Baron Munchausen's Surprising Adventures [1809]; Antidote to The Miseries of Human Life [Beresford, 1809]; Advice to Sportsmen [1809]; Rowlandson's Sketches From Nature [1809]; Views in Cornwall, Devon . . .; The Art of Ingeniously Tormenting [1809]; Annals of Sporting [1809]; The Trial of the Duke of York [1809]; Chesterfield Burlesqued [1811]; The Tour of Dr Syntax in Search of the Picturesque [1812]; Petitcoat Loose [1812]; Poetical Sketches of Scarborough [1813]; Letters From Italy [Engelbach, 1813]; The Military Adventures of Johnny Newcome [1815]; Naples and the Campagna [Engelbach, 1815]; The Dance of Death [1815]; The Grand Master [1816]; Figure Subjects For Landscapes [1816]; Relics of a Saint [1816]; Vicar of Wakefield [Goldsmith, 1817]; The Dance of Life [1817]; Grotesque Drawing Book; World in Miniature [1817]; The Second Tour of Dr Syntax [1820]; Rowlandson's Characteristic Sketches of the Lower Orders [1820]; Voyage du Docteur Syntaxe [1821]; Journal of Sentimental Travels in the Southern Provinces of France [1821]; The History of Johnny Quae Genus [1822]; The Third Tour of Dr Syntax: In Search of a Wife [1822]; Die Reise des Doktor Suntax [1822]; Crimes of the Clergy [1822]; The Spirit of the Public Journals [1823-25]; Bernard Blackmantle, English Spy [1825]; The Humorist [1831].
Exhib: RA; Soc. of Artists.
Colls: Aberdeen; Ashmolean; Bedford; Birmingham; BM; Fitzwilliam; Leeds; Manchester; Mellon Coll; Wakefield; V & AM.
Bibl: Joseph Grego, R, The Caricaturist, 1880; A.P. Oppé, TR, Drawings and Watercolours, 1923; O. Sitwell, TR, 1929; F.G. Roe, TR, 1947; A.W. Heintzelman, Watercolour Drawings of TR, 1947; A. Bury, R Drawings, 1949; B. Falk, TR, Life and Art, 1949; J. Hayes, R, 1972; R. Paulson, R, A New Interpretation, 1972.
See illustrations (Colour Plates III and IV p.37).

## ROWLEY, The Hon. Hugh                          1833-1908
Flower painter and amateur illustrator. He was born in 1833, the son of the 2nd Baron Langford. He was educated at Eton and Sandhurst, taking a commission in 10th Lancers, 1852 and retiring in 1854. He lived at Westfield House, Brighton and was the author of various humorous publications and Editor of a short-lived magazine, Puniana. He died on 12 May 1908.
Illus: Gamosagamnon or Hints on Hymen [1870].
Contrib: London Society [1867].
Exhib: RA, 1866.

## ROYLE, C.   RN
Amateur illustrator. He contributed a drawing to The Illustrated London News, 1859.

## RUDGE, Bradford                          1805-1885
Landscape painter and teacher. He was the son of Edward Rudge, a competent Midlands artist who taught at Rugby School. He settled at Bedford in 1837, having been an unsuccessful candidate for the NWS that year, and became the first drawing-master on the staff of the Harpur Schools. His early work is more in the tradition of the romantics, his later work very flowery. He painted mostly on the Ouse, in Surrey and in North Wales and retired in 1875, dying at Bedford in 1885.
Illus: A Short Account of Buckden Palace [1839].
Exhib: L; RBA; RSA.
Colls: Author; Bedford; Coventry.
Bibl: Bedfordshire Magazine, Vol.7, 1960-61, pp.247-250.

## RUSDEN, Athelstan
Cartoonist at Manchester. He worked for Moonshine and for Punch, 1879.

## RUSKIN, John                          1819-1900
Poet, painter and critic. He was born in London on 8 February 1819, the son of a Scottish wine importer with artistic inclinations. He studied at King's College, London and learned drawing under Copley Fielding and J.D. Harding (q.v.). He went up to Christ Church, Oxford in 1836 and won the Newdigate Prize three years later, then travelling in Europe, 1840-41. He had become acquainted with Turner in 1840 and paid his first visit to Venice in 1841, two events which were crucial to his writing career, his championship of Turner and his love of Venetian architecture. He published his first volume of Modern

Painters in 1843 and the series continued until 1860, by which time he was the leading art critic in the country and a stout defender of the Pre-Raphaelites. In 1869 he was elected Slade Professor of Art at Oxford, where he gave regular lectures until 1884. Ruskin's reforming zeal was demonstrated by his founding of the Guild of St George in 1871 for the 'workmen and labourers of Great Britain'. He went to live at Coniston in 1871 and became more and more a recluse from recurring attacks of brain fever. He died there of pneumonia in 1900.
Inspite of his vast literary output, Ruskin did not neglect his own considerable talents as a watercolourist. His pencil drawings of buildings are accurate and delicate, owing something to the work of Harding and Prout, his watercolours very much in the style of Turner, his still-life pictures having a Pre-Raphaelite detail. He was elected HRWS, 1873.
Illus: The Seven Lamps of Architecture [14 etched pls., 1849]; The Stones of Venice [1853]; The Poems of John Ruskin [Ed. W.G. Collingwood, 1891]; Poetry of Architecture [1893].
Exhib: FAS, 1878, 1907; RHA; RWS.
Colls: Ashmolean; Birkenhead; Birmingham; BM; Brantwood; Fitzwilliam; Glasgow; Sheffield; V & AM.
Bibl: T.J. Wise and J.P. Smart, Bibiography, 1893; W.G. Collingwood, The Art Teaching of JR, 1891; J.H. Whitehouse, The Painter and His Work at Bembridge, 1938; P. Quennell, JR, 1949; J. Evans, JR, 1954; M. Lutyens, Millais and the Ruskins, 1967; P.H. Walton, The Drawings of JR, 1972.

## RUSSELL, Sir Walter Westley   RA RWS                    1867-1949
Painter, teacher and illustrator. He was born at Epping in 1867 and studied at the Westminster School of Art under Fred Brown. He was Drawing Teacher at the Slade School from 1895 to 1927 and served with the Camouflage Corps in the First War, 1916-19. Russell was elected ARA in 1920 and RA in 1926. He was Keeper of the RA, 1927-42 and was influential in altering the teaching arrangements of the Schools and in bringing them up to date. He was an important link between the Academy and outsiders like P. Wilson Steer and Henry Tonks who were his friends. He was made CVO in 1931, knighted in 1935 and died on 16 April 1949.
Contrib: ILN [1892-94]; Daily Chronicle [1895]; The Graphic [1895]; The Yellow Book [1895]; The Quarto [1898]; Lady's Pictorial; The Pall Mall Magazine.
Exhib: G; GG; L; M; NEA; P; RA; RHA; RSW; RWS.
Colls: V & AM.
See illustration (p.441).

## RUTHERSTON, Albert Daniel                          1881-1953
Artist, stage designer and illustrator. He was born in Bradford on 5 December 1881, the son of M. Rothenstein and brother of Sir W. Rothenstein (q.v.). He was educated at Bradford Grammar School and studied at the Slade School, 1898-1902 and became Visiting Teacher at the Camberwell School of Arts and Crafts and Ruskin Master of Drawing at Oxford from 1929. He served in the First War with the Northants Regiment in Palestine, 1916-19. Rutherston did a considerable amount of designing for private presses in the 1920s and was responsible for some wrappers, all in the current craze for linear naïvety in startling colours. He was a member of the NEA, 1905 and RWS, 1941.
Publ: Decoration in the Art of the Theatre; A Memoir of Claude Lovat Fraser [with John Drinkwater]; Sixteen Designs For The Theatre.
Illus: The Children's Blue Bird [G. LeBlanc, 1913]; Cymbeline [1923]; The Cresset Herrick; The Soncino Haggadah; A Box of Paints [Geoffrey Scott, 1923]; Yuletide in a Younger World [Thomas Hardy, 1927].
Contrib: The Gypsy [1915]; The Broadside; The Chapbook [1921].
Exhib: Carfax Gall; FAS; G; L; M; NEA; RSA; RWS.
Colls: Ashmolean; V & AM.

## RUTLAND, Elizabeth   Duchess of                          -1825
Amateur artist. She was the daughter of the 5th Earl of Carlisle K.G. and married the 7th Duke of Rutland in 1799 and became a leader of taste and fashion, extensively altering her husband's home Belvoir Castle. She died on 29 November 1825.
Illus: Journal of a Short Trip to Paris, 1814, 1815 [AT 106, privately printed].

## RUTLAND, Florence M.
Illustrator. Student of the Birmingham School who contributed to The Yellow Book, April 1896.

*SIR WALTER WESTLEY RUSSELL RA RWS 1867-1949. Mr. and Mrs. Gladstone at Gorebridge, 4 July 1892. Original drawing for illustration in* The Illustrated London News, *Vol. 101, 1892. Black crayon. 8¼ins. x 7¼ins. (21cm x 18.4cm).*                                            Victoria and Albert Museum

**RUTLAND, Violet   Duchess of**                          **1856-1937**
Amateur artist. She was born at Wigan, Lancs in 1856, the daughter of Col. the Hon. C.H. Lindsay. She married the 8th Duke of Rutland. She concentrated on portrait drawings in pencil and chalks but also did sculpture. She died on 27 December 1937. Elected SWA, 1932.

Illus: *Portraits of Men and Women [1899].*
Exhib: FAS; G; GG; L; New Gall; P; RA; RMS; SWA.

**RYLAND, Henry   RI**                                    **1856-1924**
Painter and illustrator. He was born at Biggleswade, Bedfordshire in 1856 and became a pupil of Benjamin Constant, Boulanger, Lefebvre and Cormon in Paris. Ryland was a versatile artist and after being strongly influenced by Pre-Raphaelite art, turned his attention to stained glass, decorating and book illustrations as well as to the painting of subject and legend. He was elected RI in 1898 and died in Bedford Park, London on 23 November 1924.

Contrib: *The English Illustrated Magazine.*
Exhib: B; G; GG; L; M; New Gall; RA; RBA; RHA; RI; ROI; RSW.
Colls: Manchester.
Bibl: *Cassells Mag.,* CXCIV; *The Artist,* September 1898, pp.1-9.

## S., C.L.
Unidentified illustrator working about 1900.

Colls: V & AM.

## S., M.H.
Unidentified illustrator working in the second half of the 19th century. Contributed to *The Gentleman's Journal and Youth's Miscellany.*

Colls: V & AM.

## SABATTIER, Louis Rémy                    fl.1894-1910
French portrait painter. He was born at Annonay and studied with Gêrome and de Boulanger, exhibiting at the Salon from 1890.

Contrib: *The Graphic [1910].*

## SACHS, William J.
Topographical illustrator. He contributed to *The Illustrated Times,* 1866.

## ST CYR                                        fl.1912
Fashion illustrator working in pen and ink and watercolour for magazines, about 1912.

Colls: V & AM.

## SAINTON, Charles Prosper    RI           1861-1914
Portrait, figure and landscape painter and silver point artist. He was born in London on 23 June 1861 and educated at Hastings, before studying at the Slade School and in Florence and Paris. He held a one man show of silverpoints at the Burlington Gallery in 1892 and exhibited at the Salon from 1889. He was elected RI, 1897 and RMS, 1904. Died on 7 December 1914, possibly at New York.

Contrib: *The English Illustrated Magazine [1893-94, portraits].*
Exhib: B; FAS; G; GG; L; M; RA; RI; RMS; ROI.
Colls: V & AM.

## SALA, George Augustus Henry              1828-1896
Journalist, author and illustrator. He was born in 1828 and educated in Paris before studying drawing in London. He worked as a clerk and a scene painter at the Princess's and Lyceum Theatres before becoming a book illustrator and the Editor of *Chat.* Sala was sent by Dickens to cover the Crimean War on the Russian side in 1856 and contributed articles to *All The Year Round,* 1858. He founded and edited *Temple Bar,* 1860-66 and was a correspondent of *The Illustrated London News,* 1860-86 and of *The Daily Telegraph* in the American Civil War, 1863. In his early days he was a strong opponent of the youthful *Punch.*

Illus: *A Word With Punch [Bunn].*
Contrib: *The Cornhill Magazine [1860].*
Bibl: *The Life and Adventures of GS,* 2 vols., 1895; Ralph Straus, *GAS,* 1942.

## SALMON, J.M. Balliol                        1868-1953
Artist and illustrator. He was born on 1 June 1868, the son of a surgeon and barrister. He was educated privately and studied art under Fred Brown at the Westminster School and afterwards at Julian's in Paris. He was a teacher of drawing for a short time before becoming a full-time illustrator on *The Graphic* in about 1901. He was working in Glasgow in 1914 and at Bedford Park at the time of his death on

EDWARD LINLEY SAMBOURNE 1844-1910. 'Falstaff drinking from a tankard with Doll Tearsheet beside him.' Original drawing for illustration. Pen and ink. Signed and dated 1886. 5⅝ins. x 9¼ins. (14.3cm x 23.5cm).
Victoria and Albert Museum

LEAR. AND·COOL, CLEAR·AND·COOL,
BY·LAUGHING·SHALLOW,·AND·DREAMING·POOL
COOL·AND·CLEAR,·COOL·AND·CLEAR,
BY·SHINING·SHINGLE,·AND·FOAMING·WEIR;

"The Water Babies."
Charles Kingsley. Page 51.

*EDWARD LINLEY SAMBOURNE 1844-1910. Original drawing for illustration to* The Water Babies *by Charles Kingsley, 1886. Pen, ink and bodycolour. Signed and dated 1881. 6¾ins. x 4¾ins. (17.1cm x 12.1cm).*
Victoria and Albert Museum

443

3 January 1953. He was one of the best pencil and chalk artists to work for the press in the Edwardian period.

Contrib: *The Quiver [1890]; The Pall Mall Budget [1893]; The New Budget [1895]; The Graphic [1899-1930]; The Sporting and Dramatic News [1900]; Cassell's Family Magazine; The Ludgate Monthly; The Pall Mall Magazine.*

**SALT, Henry**            **1780-1827**
Topographer. He was born at Lichfield in 1780 and took lessons from J. Glover, J. Farrington and J. Hoppner. He accompanied Lord Mountnorris to India in 1802 as secretary and draughtsman and returned via Egypt and Ethiopia in 1806. He was sent on a diplomatic mission to Ethiopia in 1811 and became Consul-General in Egypt in 1815. He died at Alexandria in 1827.

Illus: *Voyages and Travels to India [Lord Valentia, 1809]; Twenty-Four Views in St Helena [1809]; A Voyage to Abyssinia [1814].*
Colls: BM; India Office Lib.
Bibl: J.J. Halls, *Life of S*, 1834.

**SAMBOURNE, Edward Linley**      **1844-1910**
Black and white artist, cartoonist and designer. He was born in London on 4 January 1845 and was educated at the City of London School and Chester College. In 1860 he was apprenticed to a firm of marine engineers and continued in that career until his drawings began to be received by *Punch* in 1867. He under-studied Sir John Tenniel as cartoonist and succeeded him as first cartoonist of the magazine when he retired in January 1901. Sambourne was well-known for the great accuracy of his drawings and the care he took over details of dress and construction. He was an inventive artist who appreciated page design and fantasy although his ink sketches can show a Germanic hardness of line. He was considered by Du Maurier to be the only artist in London who could draw a top hat correctly! He died in Kensington on 3 August 1910.

Illus: *The New Sandford and Merton [1872]; Our Autumn Holidays on French Rivers [1874]; The Royal Umbrella [1880]; The Water Babies [Charles Kingsley, 1885]; Buz or The Life and Adventures of a Honey Bee [Maurice Noel, 1889]; The Four Georges [W.M. Thackeray, 1894]; The Real Adventures of Robinson Crusoe [1893].*
Contrib: *London Society [1868]; ILN [1876]; Good Words [1890]; Black & White [1891]; The Sketch [1893]; The Pall Mall Magazine [1893]; Daily Chronicle [1895]; The Minister [1895].*
Exhib: FAS, 1893; G; L; RA.
Colls: V & AM.
Bibl: M.H. Spielmann, *The History of Punch*, 1895, pp.531-537; *The Studio*, Winter No., 1900-1, p.85 illus.
See illustrations (pp.442, 443).

**SAMBOURNE, Maud**          **fl.1892-1895**
Illustrator. She was the daughter of Linley Sambourne (q.v.) and contributed occasional drawings to *Punch*, 1892-94.

Contrib: *The Pall Mall Magazine; The Minister.*

**SANDERCOCK, Henry Ardmore**     **fl.1865-1907**
Marine and landscape painter in watercolour, illustrator. He worked at Bideford, Devon and illustrated for children's stories. He signs his work
Exhib: L; RA; RBA; RI; RWS.
Colls: Montreal.

**SANDERSON, H.**           **fl.1862-1865**
Figure artist. He illustrated *Legends from Fairyland*, Holmeden, 1862 and contributed to *London Society*, 1862-63, *The Churchman's Family Magazine*, 1863, *Fun*, 1865.

**SANDHEIM, May or Amy**       **fl.1908-1929**
Artist and illustrator. She illustrated *The Prince's Progress* by Christina Rossetti in 1908.

Exhib: L; SWA.

**SANDS, J.**             **fl.1862-1888**
Minor Scottish poet and amateur draughtsman. He was a close friend of Charles Keene (q.v.) whom he first met in 1862. He subsequently went on expeditions in Scotland with Keene in 1869, 1871 and later in the 1870s. Although trained as a solicitor Sands fancied himself as

an artist and at one time drew for a newspaper in Buenos Aires. He began to contribute to *Punch* in 1870 and continued to do so for a decade, also supplying Keene with material for his jokes. He finally broke with *Punch* because he considered that they were more interested in printing the work of Keene's nephew A. Corbould (q.v.) than his. He became a recluse at Walls, Shetland for the remainder of his life. Signs with an hour glass device.

Publ: *Out of this World or Life in St Kilda [1876].*
Colls: V & AM (album).
Bibl: G.S. Layard, *The Life and Letters of Charles Samuel Keene*, 1892, pp.123-128.

**SANDY, A.C.**           **fl.1897-1901**
Illustrator. Contributed to *The Rambler*, 1897, *Moonshine*, 1898, *Fun*, 1899-1901, *Illustrated Bits*, 1900 and *The Sketch* and *Sketchy Bits*.

MANOLI.

*FREDERICK AUGUSTUS SANDYS 1832-1904. 'Manoli.' Illustration to a poem in* The Cornhill Magazine, *1862. Wood engraving.*

THE WAITING TIME.

*Drawn by Frederick Sandys.*　　　　　*See "The Hardest Time of All."*

*FREDERICK AUGUSTUS SANDYS 1832-1904. 'The Waiting Time.'*
*Illustration in* The Churchman's Family Magazine, 1863. *Wood engraving.*

**SANDYS, Frederick Augustus**　　　　　**1832-1904**
Portrait-draughtsman and illustrator. He was born at Norwich in 1832, the son of a journeyman dyer who had set up as an artist. He showed promise at an early age and was noticed by the Rev. Bulwer and was enabled to attend Norwich Grammar School. He studied also in the newly established Government School of Design there and by the time that he arrived in London in about 1851, had already contributed illustrations to *The Birds of Norfolk* and *The Antiquities of Norwich*. He worked for wood engravers but showed his first picture, a portrait at the RA that year. After 1857, Sandys became part of Rossetti's circle at a time when the artists surrounding him were embarking on the production of illustrated books. Sandys was to join them in this and it is on these superbly finished designs that his reputation really rests. His influences were Rossetti himself, but also the prints of Dürer (he copied his own monogram freely from Dürer) and the work of Alfred Rethel, 1816-59. From the late 1860s, Sandys concentrated mostly on chalk drawings of women on toned paper, a surer medium for his exquisitely fine draughtsmanship than oils had ever given him. Despite some success, the artist remained largely unrecognised, partly due to his lack of business sense and pecuniary troubles. He died at 5 Hogarth Road, London on 25 June 1904.

Contrib: *Once a Week [1861-67]; The Cornhill Magazine [1860, 1866]; Good Words [1862-63]; Willmott's Sacred Poetry [1862]; The Churchmans Family Magazine [1863]; The Shilling Magazine [1865]; The Quiver [1866]; The Argosy [1866]; The Shaving of Shagpat [Meredith, 1865]; Christian's Mistake [Mrs Craik, 1866]; Touches of Nature by Eminent Artists [1866]; Idyllic Pictures [1867]; Thornbury's Legendary Ballads [1876]; The British Architect [1879]; Cassell's Family Magazine [1881]; Dalziel's Bible Gallery [1881]; Pan [1881]; The Century Guild Hobby Horse [1888]; The English Illustrated Magazine [1891]; The Quarto [1896]*.
Exhib: FAS; L; New Gall; P; RA.
Colls: Ashmolean; BM; Bradford; Fitzwilliam; Leeds; V & AM.
Bibl: *Woodcuts by FS*, Pub. by Hentchel, c.1904; *The Artist*, Dec. 1897, pp.7-63 illus.; Gleeson White, *English Illustration 'The Sixties'*, 1906, pp.172-175; Forrest Reid, *English Illustrators of the Sixties*, 1928, pp.59-64; *FS*, Cat. of Exhib. at Brighton, 1974; Gordon N. Ray, *The Illustrator and The Book in England*, 1976, pp.107-108 illus.

See illustrations (left and p.444).

**SANSOM, Nellie**　　　　　**fl.1894-1936**
Portrait painter and illustrator. She studied at the RCA and was elected RMS in 1896.

Contrib: *ILN [1903]*.
Exhib: B; G; L; M; RA; RBA; RCA; RI; RMS; SWA.

**SARG, Tony**　　　　　**1880-**
American painter, illustrator and caricaturist. He was born in Guatemala in 1880, worked for many magazines and executed mural paintings in New York hotels. He became a member of the London Sketch Club in 1914 and illustrated a number of English books.

Illus: *Children For Ever [J.F. Macpherson, 1908]; Molly's Book [1908]*.
Contrib: *Punch [1907-12]; The Graphic [1908-10]*.

**SARGENT, G.F.**　　　　　**fl.1840-1860**
Illustrator. Lived in London and was a prolific illustrator of topographical and antiquarian works. He was considered too poor an artist to be seconded for the NWS in 1854.

Illus: *Polite Repository [T.L. Peacock]*.
Contrib: *Knight's London [1841-42]; Shakespeare Illustrated [1842]; The Pilgrim's Progress and the Holy War Illuminated [c.1850]; Cassell's Illustrated Family Paper [1853]; The Illustrated London Magazine [1853-55]; The Seasons and The Castle of Indolence [1857]; The Welcome Guest [1860]; ILN [1860]*.
Colls: Nottingham.

**SARGENT, John Singer**　　　　　**1856-1925**
Portrait and landscape painter and watercolourist. He was born in Florence in 1856, the son of an American doctor and travelled widely in Europe and America, before studying in Rome, Florence and Paris, under Carolus Duran. Although principally known as a portrait painter of exceptional dexterity and sparkle in the Edwardian years, he was also a fluid watercolourist, making great effects with rapid washes and brilliant colours, particularly those undertaken during the First World War. He received many honours, the Légion d'Honneur, was elected ARA in 1894 and RA in 1897. He died in Chelsea on 15 April 1925 and his studio was sold at Christie's on July 24 and 27, 1925.

Illus: *Five Songs From a Book of Verses [W.E. Henley (title page)]*.
Exhib: B; FAS; G; GG; L; M; NEA; New Gall; RA; RHA; ROI; RSA; RSW; RWS.
Colls: Ashmolean; BM; Bradford; Fitzwilliam; Imperial War; Manchester; Tate.
Bibl: The Hon. E. Charteris, *JSS*, 1927; M. Hardie, *JSS*, 1930; R. Ormond, Cat. of Exhibition, Birmingham, *JSS*, Sept-Oct., 1964; R. Ormond, *JSS*, 1970.

**SARGENT, Waldo**
Illustrator, contributing to *London Society*, 1863.

**SARGISSON, Ralph M.**　　　　　**fl.1906-1937**
Artist and illustrator. He worked in Birmingham and contributed good ink drawings of interiors with figures to *Punch*, 1906. He was elected RBSA, 1935.
Exhib: B.

**SATCHWELL, R.W.**　　　　　**fl.1793-1818**
Miniaturist and portrait painter. He designed frames and border ornament for an edition of *The Rambler*, c.1795.
Colls: V & AM.

445

**SAUBER, Robert   RBA**                                   **1868-1936**
Painter and illustrator. He was born in London on 12 February 1868,
the grandson of Charles Hancock, the animal painter. He studied at
Julian's, Paris and in Munich and was an exhibitor in both places.
From about 1890, Sauber was living in London and working for most
of the leading weekly and monthly magazines. He claimed to be most
influenced by French 18th century art in his drawings, a particular
mannerism of his work being heavy washes with busy pen work on
top of them. He became RBA in 1891 and RMS in 1896, acting as
Vice-President of the RMS, 1896-98. He lived at Hartwell near
Northampton from about 1925 and died on 10 September 1936.

Illus: *Mrs Tregaskis [Mrs Praed, c.1894]*.
Contrib: *The English Illustrated Magazine [1893-96]; The Sketch [1894]; St
Pauls [1894]; The Sporting & Dramatic News [1895]; The Minister [1895];
Pearson's Magazine [1896]; ILN [1897-99 (theat.)]; The St James's Budget;
The Queen; The Windsor Magazine; The Idler; The Pall Mall Magazine; Fun
[1901]*.
Exhib: B; L; New Gall; RA; RBA; RMS; ROI.
Colls: V & AM.
Bibl: 'An Illustrator of Note' *The Artist*, June 1897, pp.241-248 illus.

**SAVAGE, Reginald**                                       **fl.1886-1904**
Portrait and figure painter and illustrator. He was a talented and
imaginative designer and woodcut artist, closely associated with the
Essex House Press. His subjects are usually from history and poetry
and he was commended by Walter Crane (q.v.) for his 'weird designs'.

Illus: *Pilgrim's Progress [1899]; The Poems of William Shakespeare [1899];
Venus and Adonis [1900-01]; The Eve of St Agnes [1900-1]; The Journal of
John Woolman [1900-1]; The Epithalmion of Spenser [1901]; Alexander's
Feast [John Dryden, 1904]; (All Essex House Press)*.
Contrib: *Black & White [1891]; The Dial [1892]; The Butterfly [1893]; St
Pauls [1894]; Madame [1895]; The Ludgate Monthly; The Pageant [1896];
Fun [1901]*.
Exhib: New Gall; RA; RBA; RI; ROI.
Colls: V & AM.
Bibl: *The Art of The Book*, Studio, 1914; R.E.D. Sketchley, *Eng. Bk. Illus.*,
1903, pp.18, 24, 130.

**SAWYER, Amy**                                            **1887-1909**
Figure and decorative artist. She worked at Bushey, 1887 where she
probably attended the Herkomer School. She later worked from
Ditchling, Sussex and was elected ASWA, 1901.

Contrib: *Black & White [1891]*.
Exhib: B; FAS; L; M; RA; ROI; SWA.

**SCANNELL, Edith S.**
Illustrator of children's books. She illustrated *The Child of the
Caravan*, E.M. Green, c.1888.

**SCHARF, George**                                         **1788-1860**
Miniature painter, drawing-master and illustrator. He was born at
Mainburg, Bavaria in 1788 and studied at Munich before travelling in
Flanders and France. During the Empire, he was in the Low Countries
and escaped from Antwerp during the siege of 1814. He studied in
Paris at the Musée Napoleon after 1815 and came to England in 1816,
where he learnt lithography and became an employee of Moser and
Hullmandel. He was employed for many years to draw on stone for
the illustrations of the Geological Society's *Transactions* and made
topographical drawings of London. He was a member of the NWS
from 1833 to 1836 and he died in London in 1860. He was the father
of Sir G. Scharf (q.v.).

Exhib: RA; RBA; NWS.
Colls: BM; V & AM.

**SCHARF, Sir George**                                     **1820-1895**
Draughtsman and illustrator. He was born in London in 1820, the son
of G. Scharf (q.v.) and was educated at University College School and
studied at the RA Schools, 1838. In 1840 he accompanied Sir Charles
Fellowes to Asia Minor as draughtsman, visiting Italy on the way and
returning to Asia Minor again in 1843. He assisted Charles Keene in
the scenery and costumes of his Shakespearean revivals, 1851-57 and
became celebrated for his work as an art historian and cataloguer. He
was made as a result of this the first Secretary and then Director of
the National Portrait Gallery, 1857 and 1882. He was knighted in
1895.

Publ: *Catalogue of the Collection of Pictures at Knowsley Hall [1875];
Descriptive and Historical Catalogue of the Collection of Pictures at Woburn
Abbey [1890]*.
Illus: *Recollection of Scenic Effects [1839]; Smiths Classical Dictionaries;
Keats Poems [1866-67]*.
Exhib: RA; BI.
Colls: BM; Witt Photo.

**SCHETKY, John Christian**                                **1778-1874**
Draughtsman and drawing-master. He was born in Edinburgh in 1778,
the son of a Hungarian musician and Maria Reinagle. He took lessons
from Alexander Nasmyth and from an early age taught drawing to
support his family. He worked as a scene painter and in 1801, walked
to Rome, returning through France. He was then drawing-master at
Oxford, at the Military College at Marlow and after 1810 was
appointed master at the Portsmouth Naval Academy where he
remained until 1836. Schetky's official appointments included being
Watercolour Painter to the Duke of Clarence and Marine Painter in
Ordinary to George IV and Queen Victoria. He died in London in
1874.

Illus: *Sketches and Notes of a Cruise in South Waters [Duke of Rutland, 1850];
Court Martial [Hon. H.S. Rous, AL 343]*.
Exhib: BI; OWS; RA; RBA.
Colls: BM; Greenwich.
Bibl: S.F.L. Schetky, *Life of JCS*, 1877.

**SCHLOESSER, Carl Bernhard**                              **1832-1914**
Portrait painter and etcher. He was born in Darmstadt in 1832 and
studied under Couture and at the École des Beaux Arts, exhibiting at
the Salon from 1861. He was living in London by 1890 and died there
in 1914.

Illus: *Ormond [Maria Edgeworth, c.1895]*.
Exhib: B; FAS; G; GG; L; M; RA; RHA.

**SCHNEBBLIE, Robert Blemmel**                                 **-1849**
Topographical draughtsman. He was the son of the celebrated
topographer J.C. Schnebblie, 1760-92. He worked in his father's style
and illustrated for *The Gentleman's Magazine* and Wilkinson's
*Londina Illustrata*, 1808. He died of starvation in 1849.

Exhib: RA.
Colls: BM; V & AM.

**SCHONBERG, Johann Nepomuk**                              **1844-**
Figure artist and illustrator. He was born in Austria in 1844, the son
of the lithographer Adolf Schonberg, 1813-68. He studied at the
Vienna Academy and then went to France where he worked for
*Monde Illustré* and *Journal Illustré*. He was appointed Special Artist
to *The Illustrated London News* in Roumania in 1877 and worked for
the magazine until 1895, often improving drawings sent in by other
artists. His style is characterised by heavy use of bodycolour with grey
washes.

Illus: *History of the Popes [Patuzzi]; Universal History [Alvensleben]; The
Young Buglers [G.A. Henty, 1880]; The Dash For Khartoum [G.A. Henty,
1892]*.
Exhib: RA, 1895.
See illustration (p.447).

**SCHWABE, Randolph   RWS**                                **1885-1948**
Watercolourist and illustrator. He was born in Manchester in 1885 and
after being educated privately, studied at the Slade School and then at
Julian's in Paris, 1906. Schwabe was a member of the NEA from 1917
and of the London Group from 1915, being elected ARWS in 1938
and RWS in 1942. In 1930 he was appointed Slade Professor of Fine
Arts in the University of London. Schwabe was a fluid draughtsman
with pen and ink and his views of cities in this medium are among his
best works. He carried out some book illustration in the 1920s and
died in 1948.

Illus: *Historic Costume, 1490-1790 [1929, with F.M. Kelly]; A Short History
of Costume and Armour, 1066-1800 [1931, with F.M. Kelly]; Summer's Fancy
[Edmund Blunden, Beaumont Press, 1930]; Costume in Ballet [Cyril W.
Beaumont]*.
Contrib: *Oxford Almanac [1940]*.
Exhib: FAS; G; GG; L; M; NEA; RSA; RWS.
Colls: Ashmolean; V & AM.

*JOHANN NEPOMUK SCHONBERG 1844- . 'Crossing the Citrol.' Original drawing for illustration, perhaps for* The Illustrated London News. *Pen, grey wash and bodycolour. 20½ins. x 14ins. (52.1cm x 35.6cm).* Author's Collection

**SCOTT, David RSA** 1806-1849

Painter and illustrator. He was born at Edinburgh in 1806, the son of the engraver Robert Scott and elder brother of W.B. Scott (q.v.). He worked as an engraver before turning to painting, studied at the Trustees Academy and was one of the founders of the Edinburgh Life Academy Association in 1827. He worked for a short time in Italy in 1832-34 where he made anatomical studies in the Hospital for Incurables. His paintings are heroic in concept and his illustrations have considerable interest, deriving as they do in both symbol and style from William Blake (q.v.). He died at Edinburgh in 1849.

Illus: *The Ancient Mariner [S.T. Coleridge, 1837]; Architecture of the Heavens [Prof. Nichol, 1851]; The Ancient Mariner; Pilgrim's Progress [1860].*
Exhib: RA; RSA.
Colls: BM.
Bibl: W.B. Scott, *Memoir of DS,* 1850; W.B. Scott, *Autobiographical Notes of the Life of,* Vol.2, 1892, pp.216-219 and 259-268.
See illustration (p.449)

**SCOTT, Georges** 1873-c.1948

French portrait painter. He was born in 1873 and worked in Paris, contributing illustrations of events to *The Graphic,* 1901-11. He painted a portrait of King George V now in the Bristol City Art Gallery.

Exhib: L; RA, 1909-12.

**SCOTT, J.**

Figure artist. Contributed comic illustrations to *Thomas Hood's Comic Annual,* 1837-38.

**SCOTT, Septimus Edwin** 1879-

Landscape painter and poster artist. He was born at Sunderland on 19 March 1879 and studied at the RCA. He was elected ARBA in 1919, RI in 1927 and ROI in 1920.

Contrib: *The Graphic [1910].*
Exhib: B; L; RA; RBA; RI; ROI.

**SCOTT, Stuart H.**

Topographer. Contributed to *The Illustrated London News,* 1896.

**SCOTT, Thomas D.** fl.1850-1893

Portrait illustrator and miniaturist. He worked at Peckham and was described by White as 'a well-known portrait engraver' and by Chatto as an 'able reducer and copyist of pictures on wood'.

Illus: *The Gold of Fairnilee [Andrew Lang, c.1889 (frontis)].*
Contrib: *The Book of British Ballads [S.C. Hall, 1842]; The Illustrated London News [1850]; Examples of Ornament [Bell & Daldy, 1855]; Heber's Hymns [1867]; Once a Week [1867].*
Exhib: RA.
Bibl: Chatto & Jackson, *Treatise on Wood Engraving,* 1861, p.600.

**SCOTT, William** fl.1880-1905

Painter and etcher. He was elected RE in 1881 and lived much of his life in Italy, at Rome, 1882, Venice, 1884 and Bodighera 1896.

Illus: *Lamia's Winter Quarters [Alfred Austin, c.1905 (head and tail pieces)].*
Exhib: B; G; M; RA; RBA; RE; ROI.

**SCOTT, William Bell** 1811-1890

Painter, illustrator, critic and poet. He was born at Edinburgh on 12 September 1811, the son of Robert Scott, the engraver and younger brother of David Scott (q.v.). He studied art with his father and then attended the Trustees Academy in Edinburgh in 1831. He assisted his father in the engraving business and then in 1837 left for London where he hoped to earn a livelihood as an illustrator. This proved not to be a success and he turned to painting, making friends with W.P. Frith and Augustus Egg. In 1842 he entered an unsuccessful design for the Houses of Parliament Cartoon Competition and the next year was appointed master of the School of Design at Newcastle-upon-Tyne, where he remained till 1863. Scott developed a considerable facility as a mural painter and did major works at Wallington Hall, Northumberland for the Trevelyan family and at Penkill Castle, Ayrshire for his patron Mr. Boyd. A friend of Rossetti and the Pre-Raphaelites, Scott was often inspired in his compositions and clumsy in his executions, giving a slightly provincial echo of the Brotherhood. His watercolours are generally conceived on too large a scale, their symbolism often borrowed from Dürer or Blake. He died at Penkill Castle in 1890.

Publ: *Antiquarian Gleanings in the North of England [1851]; Half-hour Lectures ... of the Fine and Ornamental Arts [1861]; Our British Landscape Painters [1872]; William Blake [1878].*
Illus: *The Ornamentist or Artisan's Manual [1845]; The Year of the World [1846]; Landon's Poetical Works; Pilgrim's Progress [1860, with D. Scott].*
Contrib: *Landscape Lyrics [c.1837]; The Observer [1842]; The Family Bible [1867].*
Exhib: BI; RA; RBA; RSA.
Colls: Author; Newcastle.
Bibl: *Autobiographical Notes on The Life of WBS,* 1892; M.D.E. Clayton-Stamm, 'Observer of the Industrial Revolution', *Apollo,* May 1969, pp.386-390; R. Trevelyan, *WBS, Apollo,* September 1977.
See illustration (p.448).

**SEARLE, A.A.**

Equestrian draughtsman. Contributed to *Punch,* 1907.

*WILLIAM BELL SCOTT 1811-1890. 'The Rending of the Veil in the Temple.' Original drawing for illustration in* The Family Bible, *1867. Ink. This version signed with initials and dated 1869. 10⅜ins. x 12¾ins. (26.3cm x 32.4cm).*

Author's Collection

**SECCOMBE, Colonel Thomas S.**                    fl.1865-1885

Military painter and illustrator. He joined the Royal Artillery in 1856 and retired with the rank of Colonel. He illustrated a considerable number of children's books and some period novels, his style of drawing being lively and humorous but often very wooden.

Ilus: *The Poetical Works of Thomas Moore; The Poetical Works of William Cowper; The Poetical Works of James Thomson [c.1870 (all Moxon's Popular Poets)]; Miss Kilmansegg [T. Hood, 1870 (2 edits.)]; Army and Navy Drolleries [c.1875]; The Rape of the Lock [1873]; The Story of Prince Hildebrand and the Princess Ida – Related in Rhyme [1880].*
Contrib: *Punch [1864-66, 1882]; London Society [1865]; Fun; The Illustrated Times.*
Exhib: RBA.
Colls: Witt Photo.

**SEDDING, A.E.**

Designer of ornaments. This must be an error for the architect J.D. Sedding, 1838-91, contributing two geometric initial letters to *The English Illustrated Magazine,* 1887. Sedding was a member of the RIBA from 1874 and attempted to start a school of carvers and gilders.

**SEELEY, Miss E.L.**                    fl.1873-1880

Figure painter and illustrator. She worked in Camden Town and illustrated a child's book *Eva's Mulberry Tree,* c.1880.

Exhib: RA; SWA.

**SELBY, Prideaux John**                    1788-1867

Botanical and ornithological illustrator. He was born at Alnwick, Northumberland in 1788 and after studying at University College, Oxford, he lived entirely in Northumberland and devoted himself to natural history. He became a member of the Royal Society of Edinburgh and of the Linnaean Society. He died at Twizell in 1867.

Illus: *Illustrations of British Ornithology [1821-34]; Illustrations of Ornithology [1825-43, with Sir W. Jardine]; British Forest Trees [1842].*

**SELOUS, Henry Courtney**                    1803-1890

Portrait and landscape painter and illustrator. He was born at Deptford in 1803, the son of George Selous, the miniature painter. He became a pupil of John Martin (q.v.) and was admitted a student at the RA Schools in about 1818. Selous entered the Westminster Hall Competition in 1843, having previously worked for a panorama painter and specialised in mural treatments. This background was to continue to influence his work, which though powerful, was always rather flatly conceived. He excelled in rather Germanic outline book illustrations and was an author of children's books under the names of 'Aunt Cae' and 'Kay Spen'. He died at Beaworthy in North Devon on 24 September 1890.

Illus: *The Pilgrim's Progress [Art Union, 1844]; The Life of Robert The Bruce; Hereward the Wake [1870].*
Contrib: *The Book of British Ballads [S.C. Hall, 1842]; Sintram and His Companions [Fouqué, c.1844]; Poems and Pictures [1846]; The Churchman's Family Magazine [1863]; Cassell's History of England; Our Life Illustrated by Pen and Pencil [1865]; Cassell's Shakespeare [1865]; Heber's Hymns [1867]; The Illustrated Book of Sacred Poems [1867]; The Man-Eaters of Tsaro [J.H. Patterson (1908 Edit.)].*
Exhib: BI; RA.
Colls: BM; Fitzwilliam; V & AM.
Bibl: Chatto & Jackson *Treatise on Wood Engraving,* 1861, p.599.

Christian enters the Valley of the Shadow of Death.

DAVID SCOTT RSA 1806-1849. 'Christian enters the Valley of the Shadow of Death.' Illustration engraved by W. Bell Scott for The Pilgrim's Progress, 1860. Wood engraving.

**'SEM' George GOURSAT**        1863-1934

French portrait painter and caricaturist. He was born at Perigueux, Dordogne on 23 November 1863 and from the first had a talent for rapid sketching, giving the feel of his subjects faces rather than direct portraits of them. He epitomised the Paris of the Entente Cordiale and drew fashionable scenes in the style of poster art. He was a frequent visitor to England in the years 1905-10 when he sketched the celebrities of Newmarket and Cowes and left indelible images of Edward VII. He had an exhibition at the Baillie Gallery in 1907, and died in Paris in 1934.

Illus: *Messieurs les Ronds-de-cuir [G. Courteline].*

**SETON, Ernest Thompson**        1860-

Animal illustrator in black and white. He was born at South Shields on 14 August 1860 and emigrated with his family to Canada. He studied in Paris under Gérome, Bouguereau, Ferrier and Mosler, 1878-81. He returned to America and worked as a writer and naturalist at Santa Fe. His drawings are notable for their accuracy but also for their strong decorative sense in the context of the book.

Illus: *Wild Animals I Have Known; Art Anatomy of Animals; Birds of Manitoba; Mammals of Manitoba; Trail of the Sandhill Stage; Biography of a Grizzly; Lives of the Hunted Containing a True Account of The Doings of Five Quadrupeds and Three Birds [1901]; Two Little Savages; Pictures of Wild Animals; Monarch, The Big Bear; Woodmyth and Fable; Animal Heroes; Birch Bark Roll of the Woodcraft Indians; Natural History of the Ten Commandments; Biography of a Silver-Fox [1909]; Life Histories of Northern Animals [1910];*

*Manual of Scouting [1910]; Rolf in the Woods [1911]; The Arctic Prairies [1911]; The Forester's Manual [1911]; The Book of Woodcraft and Indian Lore [1912]; Wild Animals At Home [1913]; Wild Animal Ways [1916]; The Sign Language [1918]; The Preacher of Cedar Mountain [1917]; Sign Talk Dictionary [1918]; Woodland Tales [1921]; Bannertail [1922]; Lives of Game Animals [1925].*

**SEVERN, Joseph Arthur Palliser RI**        1842-1931

Watercolourist. He was born in Rome in 1830, the son of Joseph Severn, artist and consul. He studied in Rome and Paris and in 1872 accompanied John Ruskin (q.v.) to Italy and nine years later married his niece Joan Ruskin. He was responsible for Ruskin during the latter's derangement and lived with him at Brantwood, painting Lake District views. In later middle age, Marie Corelli, the novelist developed an embarrassing passion for Severn and he illustrated her book *The Devil's Motor* in 1910. RI, 1882.

Exhib: FAS; G; L; M; RA; RI; ROI.
Colls: BM.

**SEVERN, Walter RCA**        1830-1904

Landscape and marine painter. He was born at Rome in 1830, the son of Joseph Severn, the artist and the brother of Arthur Severn. He was educated at Westminster and entered the Civil Service for a time before devoting himself to painting. He was interested in the applied arts, fostered needlework and embroidery designing and collaborated as a designer with Sir Charles Eastlake. He became President of the Dudley Art Society and RCA. He died in London on 22 September 1904.

Illus: *Good Night and Good Morning [Lord Houghton, 1859]; Golden Calendar; Deer and Forest Scenery; Morning and Evening Service.*
Contrib: *Passages From Modern English Poets [1862].*
Exhib: G; L; RBA; RCA.
Colls: V & AM.

**SEWELL, Ellen Mary**        1813-1905

Drawing and school mistress, amateur artist. She was born at Newport, Isle of Wight and lived most of her life in the island where she ran a school, from 1851 to 1891.

Publ: *Sailors' Hymns [1883].*
Illus: *Sacred Thoughts in Verse [W. Sewell, 1885].*

**SEYMOUR, George L.**        fl.1876-1916

Genre and animal painter and illustrator. He worked in London and illustrated architecture and topography for many of the magazines.

Illus: *Songs and Lyrics For Little Lips [W.D. Cummings, n.d.].*
Contrib: *Good Words [1880, 1890-95]; The Graphic [1886]; ILN [1887-92]; The English Illustrated Magazine [1888, 1897]; The Pall Mall Magazine.*
Exhib: FAS; L; M; RBA; RI; ROI.
Colls: Witt Photo.

**SEYMOUR, Robert**        1798-1836

Humorous illustrator and caricaturist. He was born in Somerset in 1798 and apprenticed to a London pattern designer, where he slowly developed an interest in history painting. He had little success with this and turned his hand to caricature and comic illustration, where his talent for the grotesque and the absurd could be given full range. Seymour was a somewhat inadequate draughtsman, but modelled himself on the far stronger repertoire of George Cruikshank (q.v.) and even aped the latter's signature by signing himself 'Short Shanks'. Seymour learnt the art of copper engraving in about 1827 and used lithography in the 1830s, much of his work was in the form of folios of prints with little or no text. His greatest contribution was in creating the routine of comic sportsmen from London having adventures in the country, a theme that established itself for a hundred years. It was his fame in this field that led the publishers, Chapman and Hall to commission the text of *Pickwick Papers* from young Charles Dickens as an accompaniment to Seymour's sketches. Only two issues were produced before the sensitive Seymour committed suicide in London on 20 April 1836.

Illus: *Vagaries in Quest of the Wild and Wonderful [1827]; The Heiress [1830, AL 319]; New Readings [1830-35, AL 320]; Journal of a Landsman From Portsmouth to Lisbon [1831, AL 346]; Humorous Sketches [1834, 1836]; Pickwick Papers [1836].*

Contrib: *Friendship's Offering [1824-36]; The Looking Glass [1830-32]; The Comic Offering [1831-35]; Figaro in London [1831-36]; The Comic Magazine; Hood's Comic Almanack [1836]; The Squib Annual [1836]; Sayings Worth Hearing; Terrific Penny Magazine; Book of Christmas [Hervey].*
Exhib: RA, 1822.
Colls: V & AM; Witt Photo.
Bibl: Graham Everitt, *English Caricaturists*, 1893, pp.208-234 illus.; M. Dorothy George, *English Political Caricature*, 1959, illus.

### SHACKLETON, William                    1872-1933

Landscape, figure and portrait painter. He was born at Bradford on 14 January 1872 and educated at Bradford Grammar School and Technical College before studying at the RCA, 1893. He won a travelling scholarship to Paris and Italy in 1896 and worked in London from 1905 undertaking sketching tours with W.E. Stott. He was a dramatic colourist in the Turner tradition and was successful enough to have one man shows in London in 1910 and 1922. He became NEA in 1909 and died on 9 January 1933.

Contrib: *The Quartier Latin [1896]; The Parade [1897].*
Exhib: B; G; GG; L; M; NEA; New Gall; RA; RBA; RHA; RI.
Colls: Bradford; Manchester.

### SHANNON, Charles Hazelwood  RA         1863-1937

Portrait and subject painter. He was born at Sleaford, Lincolnshire in 1863 and studied wood engraving at the Lambeth School of Art in 1882, where he met his lifelong friend Charles Ricketts (q.v.). They joined together with Sturge Moore (q.v.) to form *The Vale Press*, 1894-1904, which produced forty-eight books conspicious for their fine design and unassuming quality. Shannon was principally an artist and Ricketts was the guiding hand in design and production. He was a member of the Society of Twelve, was elected an ARA in 1911 and an RA in 1921. He died in London on 18 March 1937.

Illus: *House of Pomegranates [1891]; Daphnis and Chloe [1893]; Hero and Leander [1894];* etc.
Contrib: *Judy [1887]; Black & White [1891]; The Savoy [1896].*
Exhib: FAS; G; GG; L; M; NEA; New Gall; RA; RBA; RE; RHA; RI; ROI; RSA.
Colls: BM; V & AM; Witt Photo.
Bibl: *Catalogue of Mr S's Lithographs,* Vale Press, 1900; E.B. George, *CS,* Benn Contemp British Artists, 1924; Colin Franklin, *The Private Presses,* 1969.

### SHARPE, Charles Kirkpatrick            1781-1851

Portrait painter, caricaturist and antiquary. He was born at Hoddam Castle, Dumfriesshire on 15 May 1781 and was educated at Edinburgh University and Christ Church, Oxford. Although destined for the church, he became interested in painting and antiquarian research, spending most of his life in Edinburgh engaged in these pursuits. He also practised etching. He died in March 1851.

Contrib: *Witch of Fife [Hogg, 1820]; Fugitive Scottish Poetry [1823]; The Romances of Otuel, Roland and Vernagu [Abbotsford Club, 1836]; Flora's Fete.*
Colls: BM; Nat. Gall., Scot.
Bibl: A. Allardyce, *CKS's Letters,* 1868; *The Etchings of CKS,* 1869.

### SHAW, A.                               fl.1826-1839

Architectural draughtsman. He was a friend of R.P. Bonington and illustrated for *Pugin's Paris,* 1831.

Exhib: BI; RA; RBA.
Colls: Witt Photo.

### SHAW, Henry  FSA                       1800-1873

Architectural draughtsman, illuminator and antiquary. He was born in London on 4 July 1800 and concentrated on the research, decoration and production of a number of lavish Victorian heraldic books. Shaw was a perfectionist whose skills coincided with the beginning of the high Gothic revival culminating in the works of A.W. Pugin (q.v.). The books were usually published by William Pickering, printed by the Chiswick Press, and as McLean says 'are among the finest achievements of Victorian book design and illustration'. He was elected FSA in 1833 and died at Broxbourne, Herts on 12 June 1873.

Illus: *The History and Antiquities of the Chapel at Luton Park [1829]; Illuminated Ornaments [1833, AL 234]; Examples of Ornamental Metalwork [1836]; Specimens of Ancient Furniture [1836]; The Encyclopaedia of Ornament [1842]; Dresses and Decorations of the Middle Ages [1843]; Alphabets, Numerals and Devices of the Middle Ages [1845, AL 235]; The Arms of The Colleges of Oxford [1855]; The Art of Illumination [1866].*
Contrib: *Britton's Cathedrals [1832-36]; New Testament [Longman, 1864].*
Bibl: Ruari McLean, *Victorian Book Design,* 1972, pp.65-71 illus.

### SHAW, James                           fl.1883-1902

Illustrator. He worked in Edinburgh and contributed to *Punch*.

Exhib: G; L; RSA.
Colls: V & AM.

### SHAW, John Byam Liston  ARWS           1873-1919

Painter, designer and illustrator. He was born at Madras on 13 November 1872 and came to England in 1878 and to London in 1879. He was educated privately and studied at the St John's Wood Art School, entering the RA Schools in 1889. Shaw was strongly influenced by the work of the Pre-Raphaelite painters and by the illustrators of the 1860s. His black and white drawings are more successful than his colour, his organisation of the page is usually good but his imagination weaker. He went into partnership with Rex Vicat Cole to found a School of Art at Campden Hill, which still continues today. He was elected RI in 1898 and ARWS, 1913. He died in London on 26 January 1919.

Illus: *Browning's Poems [1897]; Tales From Boccaccio [1899]; Chiswick Shakespeare [1899]; Old King Cole's Book of Nursery Rhymes [1901]; Pilgrim's Progress [1904]; Coronation Book [1902]; Ballads and Lyrics of Love [1908]; The Cloister and The Hearth [1909]; Tales of Mystery and Imagination [E.A. Poe, 1909]; The Garden of Kama [Laurence Hope, 1914].*

*JOHN BYAM LISTON SHAW ARWS 1876-1919. Original drawing for an illustration in Reade's* The Cloister and The Hearth, *1909. Pen and ink. Signed. 7¾ins. x 5¾ins. (19.7cm x 14.6cm).* Author's Collection

Contrib: *The Dome [1898]; Cassell's Family Magazine [1898]; The Graphic [1899-1905]; The Connoisseur [1902, decor]; Punch [1905-7].*
Exhib: B; G; L; M; New Gall; RA; RI; ROI; RSA; RWS.
Colls: Ashmolean; V & AM.
Bibl: *The Studio*, Vol.12, pp.173-176; Vol.13, p.129; Winter No., 1900-1, p.75 illus.; R.E.D. Sketchley, *Eng. Bk. Illus.*, 1903, pp.13, 130; *Modern Book Illustrators and Their Work*, Studio, 1914.
See illustration (p.450).

**SHEERES, C.W.**　　　　　　　　　　　fl.1855-1859
Illustrator. He contributed views of industrial subjects to *The Illustrated London News*, 1855-59.

**SHEIL, Edward**　　　　　　　　　　　1834-1869
Figure painter. He was born at Coleraine in 1834 and worked in Cork where he died on 11 March 1869.

Contrib: *Once a Week [1867].*
Exhib: RA; RBA.

**SHELDON, Charles M.**　　　　　　　　fl.1891-1907
Figure artist and illustrator. He was, according to A.S. Hartrick, born in the United States and came to England to work as Special Artist for *Black & White*. He was sent by that magazine to the Sudan in 1897-98.

Illus: *Won By The Sword [G.A. Henty, 1900].*
Contrib: *The Pall Mall Budget [1891-92]; Black & White [1897-98]; The Ludgate Monthly [1895]; The Strand Magazine; Chums; The Wide World Magazine.*

**SHEPARD, Ernest Howard**　　　　　　1879-1976
Black and white artist and cartoonist. He was born in St John's Wood, London on 10 December 1879, the son of an architect. He was educated at St Paul's School and then studied art at Heatherley's and the RA Schools, 1897-1902. He worked in Glebe Place, Chelsea, from 1901-3 and in 1904 moved to Shamley Green, Guildford. Shepard began drawing for *Punch* in 1907 and was elected to the *Punch* table in 1921, becoming chief cartoonist in 1945. His delicate caressing pen and ink style was more suited to episodes of childhood than political cartooning, but he managed to produce some striking subjects connected with the Second World War. His great success and chief celebrity came when he undertook the splendidly imaginative drawings for A.A. Milne's *Pooh* series, 1926. He died in 1976, when his last picture was exhibited at the RA, his first having been shown there seventy-five years previously.

Illus: *When We Were Very Young [1924]; Playtime and Company [1925]; Holly Tree [1925]; Winnie-the-Pooh [1926]; Everybody's Pepys [1926]; Jeremy [1927]; Little Ones Log [1927]; Let's Pretend [1927]; Now We Are Six [1927]; Fun and Fantasy [1927]; The House at Pooh Corner [1928]; The Golden Age [1928]; Everybody's Boswell [1930]; Dreamy Days [1930]; Wind in the Willows [1931]; Christmas Poems [1931]; Bevis [1931]; Sycamore Square [1932]; Everybody's Lamb [1933]; The Cricket in the Cage [1933]; Victoria Regina [Housman, 1934]; Modern Strewelpeter [1936]; Golden Sovereign [Housman, 1937]; Cheddar Gorge [1937]; As The Bee Sucks [E.V. Lucas, 1937]; The Reluctant Dragon [1939]; Gracious Majesty [Housman, 1941]; Golden Age and Dream Days [1948-49]; Bertie's Escapade [Grahame, 1948-49].*
Contrib: *The Graphic [1906-7].*
Exhib: B; G; L; M; RA.
Colls: BM; V & AM; Witt Photo.
Bibl: R.G.G. Price, *A History of Punch*, 1957, pp.210-212.

**SHEPHEARD, George**　　　　　　　　1770-1842
Landscape painter and caricaturist. He was born in Herefordshire in 1770 and studied at the RA Schools before working chiefly in Surrey and Sussex. He visited France in 1816 and Wales in 1825, his caricature drawings are spirited and in the manner of Hogarth.

Illus: *Vignette Designs [1814-15].*
Colls: BM; Leeds; Witt Photo.

**SHEPHERD, E.**
Topographer. Contributed Herefordshire view to *Britton's Beauties of England and Wales*, 1808.

**SHEPHERD, F.H. Newton**　　　　　　fl.1898-1902
Figure artist and illustrator. He contributed to *The St. James's Budget*, 1898; *The Longbow*, 1898; *The Graphic*, 1902.

**SHEPHERD, G.E.**
Figure artist. He illustrated *Bubbles in Birdland* by H. Simpson, 1908.

**SHEPHERD, George**　　　　　　　　c.1782-c.1830
Architectural draughtsman and topographer. He had great success in the first decade of the 19th century and won the Society of Arts silver palettes in 1803-4 for draughtsmanship. He was principally an illustrator but did some landscape work.

Illus: *Londina Illustrata [Wilkinson, 1808]; The History of the Abbey Church of St Peter's, Westminster [1812]; History of the County of Kent [1829-30].*
Contrib: *Beauties of England and Wales; Knight's London [1841].*
Exhib: BI; RA.
Colls: BM; Chester; Greenwich; Manchester; Nottingham; V & AM.
Bibl: M. Hardie, *Watercol. Paint. in Brit.*, Vol.3, 1968, pp.14-15.

*CLAUDE ALLIN SHEPPERSON ARA ARWS 1867-1921. Original drawing for unidentified book illustration. Pen and ink. Signed. 10¾ins. x 6ins. (27.3cm x 15.2cm).*　　　　　　　　Author's Collection

451

**SHEPHERD, James Affleck** 1867-c.1931

Comic animal draughtsman. He was born in London on 29 November 1867 and was educated at various private schools. He had no formal training, but worked with Alfred Bryan (q.v.) the cartoonist of *Moonshine* for two years on that magazine. Shepherd was a master draughtsman of animals and birds in pen and ink and this enabled him to do humorous drawings in which the creatures wore human attire and had human personalities. This became his speciality and he invented a series of caricatures called 'Zig-Zags' for *The Strand Magazine,* of which this was the main attraction. He was invited to join *Punch* in 1893 and contributed many drawings over the years, living latterly at Charlwood, Surrey.

Illus: *Zig-Zag Fables [1897]; Illustrated Uncle Remus [1901]; Wonders in Monsterland [1901]; Nights With Uncle Remus [1903]; The Three Jovial Puppies [1907]; The Life of a Foxhound [1910]; The Story of Chanticleer [1913]; The Bodley Head Natural History [1913].*
Contrib: *Judy [1886-89]; Moonshine [1890-93]; The Sporting & Dramatic News [1892]; Chums [1892]; The Strand Magazine [1894]; Punch [1894]; Good Words [1894]; Black & White [1896]; Cassell's Family Magazine; The Boy's Own Paper.*
Exhib: G.
Colls: Witt Photo.
Bibl: M.H. Spielmann, *The History of Punch,* 1894, p.567; *The Studio,* Vol.12, 1898; Winter No., 1900-1, p.77 illus.

**SHEPHERD, Thomas Hosmer** c.1817-c.1842

Topographical illustrator. He was the son of George Shepherd (q.v.) and he was employed by Frederick Crace to make drawings of London which were outstanding for their skill and beauty.

Illus: *Metropolitan Improvements [1827]; London and Its Environs in the Nineteenth Century [1829]; Modern Athens Displayed or Edinburgh in the Nineteenth Century [1829]; Bath and Bristol [1829-30]; London Interiors [1841].*
Exhib: RBA.
Colls: BM; Newcastle.
Bibl: M. Hardie, *Watercol. Paint. in Brit.,* Vol.3, 1968, p.15.

**SHEPPARD, Raymond**

Illustrator of bird subjects in about 1890.

**SHEPPARD, W.** fl.1801-1814

Topographer. He contributed illustrations to *Britton's Beauties of England and Wales,* 1801-14.

**SHEPPERSON, Claude Allin ARA ARWS** 1867-1921

Painter and illustrator. He was born at Beckenham, Kent on 25 October 1867 and was intended for the law, which he studied. He studied art at Heatherley's in 1891 and then at Paris, taking up principally illustration and lithography but also some watercolour. He is a graceful artist whose work is at its best when children and pretty young women are involved, he was a regular contributor of this sort of drawing to *Punch* from about 1905. He was elected RI in 1900 and ARWS in 1920, but was exceptional among illustrators in being elected ARA in 1919. He died in Chelsea on 30 December 1921.

Illus: *Shrewsbury [Weyman, 1898]; Merchant of Venice [1899]; The Heart of Mid-Lothian [1900]; Lavengro [Borrow, 1900]; Coningsby [Disraeli, 1900]; As You Like It [1900]; Magic Dominions [Arthur F. Wallis, 1912]; The Open Road [E.V. Lucas, 1913].*
Contrib: *The English Illustrated Magazine [1893-96]; St Pauls [1894]; The Graphic [1895-1910]; The Idler; Pick-Me-Up; The Sketch; Illustrated Bits; Cassell's Family Magazine; The Queen; The Pall Mall Magazine; The Wide World Magazine [1898]; The Strand Magazine [1906]; The Windsor Magazine; ILN [1912-13].*
Exhib: FAS; G; GG; L; M; RA; RI; RMS; RSA; RWS.
Colls: Birmingham; Leeds; V & AM; Witt Photo.
Bibl: R.E.D. Sketchley, *Eng. Bk. Illus.,* 1903, pp.68, 74, 154; *Cat. of CS Memorial Exhibition,* Leicester Gall., March-April 1922.
See illustration (p.451).

**SHÉRIE, Ernest F.**

Military illustrator. He worked for *The Royal Magazine* and *The Illustrated London News,* 1899-1900, supplying South African War drawings.

**SHERINGHAM, George** 1884-1937

Decorative designer, theatrical designer and illustrator. He was born in London in 1884 and was educated at the King's School, Gloucester before studying at the Slade School and in Paris. Sheringham's work is decidedly art deco in form, he uses primary colours and a rather sculptural line that of Gill. He painted fans in the tradition of Conder (q.v.) and made studies for book covers and magazines and posters. A one man show of his work was held at the Brook Street Art Gallery in 1908. He died on 11 November 1937.

Illus: *The Happy Hypocrite [Max Beerbohm, 1918]; Canadian Wonder Tales [Cyrus Macmillan]; La Princesse Lointaine [Edmund Rostand]; The Duenna [R.B. Sheridan, 1925].*
Contrib: *The Sketch [1933].*
Exhib: FAS, 1937; L; M; RA; RMS; ROI; RSA.
Colls: BM; Fitzwilliam; Manchester; V & AM.
Bibl: *The Studio,* Vol.53, 1911, pp.136-139 illus; Special Spring No., 1922, 'Pen and Pencil Drawings'.

**SHERLOCK, William P.** c.1780-c.1820

Landscape painter and topographer. He was the son of William Sherlock, the portrait painter and worked in London producing Wilson-like ideal landscapes. He was also an etcher and made prints after his own work and that of Cox, Prout and Girtin.

Illus: *Dickinson's Antiquities of Nottinghamshire [1801-6].*
Contrib: *Howitt's Views in the County of Lincoln [1800]; Britton's Beauties of England and Wales [1808-14].*
Exhib: RA.
Colls: BM; Birkenhead; Leeds; V & AM; Witt Photo.

**SHERWILL, Captain George** fl.1848-1856

Amateur artist. He was an officer in the Royal Marines from 1848 and contributed views of India to *The Illustrated London News,* 1856.

**SHETKEY See SCHETKY, J.C.**

**SHIELDS, Frederick James ARWS** 1833-1911

Landscape artist, mural painter and illustrator. He was born of poor parents at Hartlepool in 1833 and was educated at a charity school before beginning work for a commercial lithographer at Manchester from the age of fourteen. Shields was influenced by the Pre-Raphaelites from an early date and carried out a considerable number of frescoes which show their marked effect on him, among them the Chapel of the Ascension, Hyde Park Place and Eaton Hall. He was a very strong illustrator, his powerful drawings and fine washes only losing a little of their crispness in wood engraving. He was elected ARWS in 1865 and died at Merton in Surrey on 26 March 1911.

Illus: *History of the Plague of London [Defoe, 1862]; The Pilgrim's Progress [1864].*
Contrib: *The Greyt Eggshibishun [Manchester, 1851]; Touches of Nature By Eminent Artists [1866]; The Sunday Magazine [1866]; Once a Week [1867]; Punch [1867-70].*
Exhib: L; M; New Gall; RWS.
Colls: BM; Fitzwilliam; Hartlepool; Manchester; V & AM.
Bibl: E. Mills, *Life and Letters of FJS,* 1912; *The Chapel of the Ascension,* 1912; Ball, *The Eng. Pre-Raphaelite Painters,* 1901; M. Hardie, *Watercol. Paint. in Brit.,* Vol.3, 1968, pp.128-129; J. Maas, *Victorian Painters,* 1970, p.146.
See illustrations (pp.453, 454).

**SHINDLER, H.** fl.1900-1908

Illustrator of children's books. Worked in London and contributed rather weak drawings to *Fun,* 1900.

Illus: *Hullabulloos at Hucksters [W.A. Clark, 1908].*

**SHIRLAW, Walter** 1838-1910

Landscape painter. He was born at Paisley and became the first President of the Society of American Artists. He died at Madrid in 1910. He designed initial letters for books.

Exhib: RA.

**SHOUBRIDGE, W.** fl.1831-1853

Topographical artist. He worked in Clapham, London and contributed to *The Cambridge Portfolio,* 1840.

Exhib: BI; NWS; RA; RBA.

*FREDERICK JAMES SHIELDS ARWS 1833-1911. Study for scrambling figure. Original drawing for illustration in* The Pilgrim's Progress, *1864. Pen and ink with chalk and bodycolour.*
Victoria and Albert Museum

## SHURY, J.

Topographer. He contributed drawings of Oxfordshire to *Britton's Beauties of England and Wales,* 1813.

## SHUTE, Mrs. E.L.                                    fl.1883-1907

Portrait painter. She worked in London and illustrated a child's book *The Kelpie's Fiddle-Bow,* in 1892.

Exhib: G; L; RHA; RI; SWA.

## SIBSON, Thomas                                      1817-1844

Painter, etcher and illustrator. He was born at Cross Canonby, Cumberland in 1817 and worked in Edinburgh before coming to London in 1838. According to W.J. Linton his first effort in illustration was a series of drawings to Dickens's *Old Curiosity Shop* and *Barnaby Rudge* which were not a success. He was then paid for by subscription to study under Kaulbach in Munich, 1842-44, but returned with consumption and lived with Linton. He died at Malta in 1844.

Illus: *Anatomy of Happiness [Ackermann, 1838]; The Old Curiosity Shop [Dickens, 1841 (frontis)]; Hall's British Ballads; The History of England.*
Colls: BM; V & AM (sketchbook).
Bibl: W.J. Linton, *Memoirs,* 1895, p.70.

## SICKERT, Bernard                                    1862-1932

Landscape painter, architectural painter and engraver. He was born at Munich in 1862, the brother of W.R. Sickert (q.v.). He became a member of the NEA in 1888 and died at Jordans on 2 August 1932.

Contrib: *The Yellow Book [1894 (portrait)].*
Exhib: G; GG; L; M; NEA; New Gall; RA; RBA; ROI.

## SICKERT, Walter Richard                             1860-1942

Street, interior and genre painter, etcher and illustrator. He was born in Munich in 1860, the brother of B. Sickert (q.v.). He studied at the Slade School in 1881 and then with Whistler from 1882, who took him on etching expeditions in London and taught him discipline in colouring. Sickert's best period was that following the death of his master, 1905 to 1920. During this time he made the drab areas of North London and particularly Camden Town his very own haunt, inspiring young painters with his French technique and contemptuous of fashion. He also painted in Dieppe and in Venice but never flattered these places or the sitters who came to his house for portraits. Sickert was a highly individual and bohemian figure who had the strength as artist and man to carry with him a circle of friends including critics like Roger Fry and artists such as Henry Tonks, Wilson Steer and Matthew Smith. He was a member of the London Group, 1916, was elected to the NEA in 1888, RE, 1887-92 and ARA, 1924 and RA, 1934. He resigned from the RA in 1935. He died in Bath in 1942.

Contrib: *The Idler; Cambridge Gazette; The Yellow Book; The Savoy; The Pall Mall Pudget; Whirlwind; Vanity Fair;* all 1887-97, mostly portraits.
Exhib: FAS, 1973; G; GG; L; M; NEA; RA; RBA; RE; RHA; RI; ROI; RSA.
Colls: BM; Manchester; Tate.
Bibl: Osbert Sitwell, *Noble Essences,* 1950, pp.163-206; Marjorie Lilly, *S The Painter and his Circle,* 1971; Wendy Barron, *S,* 1973. Denys Sutton *WS* 1976.

*FREDERICK JAMES SHIELDS ARWS 1833-1911. Initial letter C. Original drawing for decoration in* The Pilgrim's Progress, *1864. Pen and pencil.*
Victoria and Albert Museum

453

*FREDERICK JAMES SHIELDS ARWS 1833-1911. Initial letter C. Completed wood engraving for decoration in* The Pilgrim's Progress, *1864.*
Victoria and Albert Museum

## SIME, Sydney Herbert            1867-1941

Draughtsman and caricaturist. He was born in Manchester of a poor family and went down the mines as a boy to work as a scoop pusher. He then worked for a linen draper and a barber, before turning to sign-writing and entering the Liverpool School of Art. He moved to London and began to work for *Pick-Me-Up* and various halfpenny papers, his style being influenced by Aubrey Beardsley and Raven-Hill (qq.v.). He was Editor of a paper called *Eureka,* and became Joint Editor of *The Idler* from Volume 15.

Sime was a master of the macabre and the sinister finished with a beautiful cold pen line. Thorp saw in him the influence of Doré as well as Beardsley and considered that 'Pattern and colour were introduced not as a cover but as an aid to capable draughtsmanship . . .'. Sime claimed to be influenced by the Japanese print and many of his more startling compositions have a distinctly eastern composition and penmanship. The quality of brooding menace had its admirers and he was extensively employed for Lord Dunsany's stories and much patronised by Desmond Coke and Lord Howard de Walden. He held a one man show at the St George's Gallery in 1927 and died at Worplesdon, Surrey in 1941.

454

Illus: *The Sword of Welleran [Lord Dunsany, 1908; A Dreamer's Tale [Lord Dunsany, 1910]; Tales of Wonder [Lord Dunsany, 1917]; The Gods of Pegana [Lord Dunsany, 1919]; Time and the Gods [1923]; The King of Elfland's Daughter [Lord Dunsany, 1924]; Bogey Beasts [1930].*
Contrib: *The Ludgate Monthly [1891]; The Boy's Own Paper [1891-93]; The Sporting & Dramatic News [1893]; The Minister; The Windsor Magazine; The Pall Mall Magazine; The Idler; The Unicorn [1895]; Pick-Me-Up [1895]; Eureka [1897]; The Butterfly [1899]; Black & White [1899]; The Tatler [1901]; The Sketch [1904].*
Exhib: L; RBA.
Colls: V & AM. Worplesdon Hall.
Bibl: *'Apotheosis of the Grotesque',* The Idler, Vol.12, pp.755-766 illus; *The Studio,* Winter No., 1900-1, p.79 illus; Desmond Coke, *Confessions of an Incurable Collector,* 1928, pp.222-225; B. Peppin, *Fantasy Book Illustration,* 1975, pp.7, 18 illus.
See illustration (below).

## SIMKIN, Richard            1840-1926

Military painter and illustrator. He worked at Aldershot and specialised in watercolours of uniforms and in designing posters for military recruitment. He died at Herne Bay in 1926.

Illus: *The Boy's Book of British Battles [1889]; Our Armies [1891]; Where Glory Calls [1893].*
Contrib: *Army and Navy Gazette; Chums [1892].*
Colls: India Office Lib.

## SIMMONS, Graham C.            fl.1913-1919

Illustrator of comic genre subjects with bold hatching. He worked in London and contributed to *London Opinion,* 1913 and *Punch,* 1914.

Exhib: Inter Soc., 1916-19.

*SYDNEY HERBERT SIME 1867-1941. 'Midnight Oil.' Original drawing perhaps for illustration. Signed. 8¼ins. x 6¼ins. (32cm x 15.9cm).*
Victoria and Albert Museum

**SIMMONS, W. St Clair**          **fl.1878-1917**

Portrait, landscape and genre painter. He worked mostly in London, but at Hemel Hempstead, 1883.

Contrib: *The Pall Mall Budget [1893]; The English Illustrated Magazine [1893-95]; The Temple Magazine [1896]; The Windsor Magazine.*
Exhib: B; G; L; M; NEA; New Gall; P; RA; RBA; RI; ROI.

**SIMONSEN, Niels**          **1807-1885**

Painter, sculptor and lithographer. He was born in Copenhagen on 10 December 1807 and became a pupil of J.L. Lund, later visiting Italy and Algeria. He is described as 'Our Danish Artist' in *The Illustrated London News,* 1864.

**SIMPSON, Joseph W.    RBA**          **1879-1939**

Illustrator and caricaturist. He was born at Carlisle in 1879 and educated at Carlisle, studying art in Edinburgh. He became a close friend of D.Y. Cameron (q.v.) and was elected RBA in 1909. Simpson designed covers for Edinburgh publishers and was a prolific designer of bookplates, many of which were exhibited abroad. He died on 30 January 1939.

Publ: *Twelve Masters of Prose and Verse [1912]; God Save The King in La Grande Guerre [1915]; War Poems From The Times [1915].*
Illus: *Simpson His Book [1903]; The Book of Book Plates [1903]; Ibsen [1907];*

*Lions [1908]; Literary Lions [1910]; Edinburgh in 1911.*
Contrib: *The Student [Edinburgh]; London Opinion.*
Exhib: G; L; RBA; RSA; RSW.
Bibl: Haldane Macfall, '*JS Caricaturist',* The Studio, 1905-6, pp.21-25.

**SIMPSON, William    RI FRGS**          **1823-1899**

Artist, special artist and illustrator. He was born at Glasgow on 28 October 1823. He was educated in Perth and Glasgow and after starting in an architect's office, was apprenticed to Glasgow lithographers and moved to Day & Sons of London in 1851. His first major commission was to prepare drawings for a lithographic folio of the Crimean War published by Colnaghi's, and he was sent to the Baltic and the Crimea itself. He can claim to be the first Special Artist to be in action. This was the beginning of a long series of tours, many of them for *The Illustrated London News* whose permanent staff he joined in 1866. He was in India for three years, visited Kashmir and Tibet, was on the Abyssinian campaign of 1868, at the Franco-German War of 1870 and witnessed the Paris Commune, 1871. He accompanied the Prince of Wales to India in 1875-76 and illustrated Dr Schliemann's excavations in 1877 and the work of the Afghan Boundary Commission in 1884-85. Simpson was not a great artist, but an able recorder in pencil, wash and watercolours. Many of his sketches are in pencil only with detailed colour notes and instructions added and usually accurately dated. He died in London

*WILLIAM SIMPSON RI FRGS 1823-1899. 'The Mont Cenis Railway — Ascent from Lanslebourg.' Original drawing for* The Illustrated London News, *1869. Watercolour and wash. Signed and dated 1869. 8⅝ins. x 9⅛ins. (21.9cm x 23.2cm).*
Victoria and Albert Museum

on 17 April 1899. RI, 1879.

Illus: *Illustrations of the War in the East [1855-56]; Meeting the Sun, a Journey Round the World [1873]; Picturesque People or Groups from all Quarters of the Globe [1876]; Shikar and Tamasha [1876]; The Buddhist Praying Wheel [1896]; The Jonah Legend [1899]; Glasgow in the Forties [1899].*
Contrib: *The Quiver [1890]; The Picturesque Mediterranean [1891]; The English Illustrated Magazine [1893-96].*
Exhib: G; L; RI; ROI.
Colls: Glasgow; V & AM; Witt Photo.
Bibl: *WS, RI,* Autobiography, 1903.
See illustration (p.455).

**SIMSON, William   RSA**                    **1800-1847**
Portrait and marine painter. He was born at Dundee in 1800 and studied at the Trustees Academy and visited the Low Countries in 1827. He was elected RSA in 1830 and travelled to Italy to study in the 1830s. He died on 29 August 1847, in London.

Illus: *Sinbad the Sailor [n.d.].*
Exhib: BI; RA; RBA; RSA.
Colls: Birkenhead; V & AM.

**SINCLAIR, Helen Mok**                      **fl.1912-1917**
Miniature painter, black and white artist and illustrator. She illustrated children's books and worked in London.

Exhib: L; RA.
Colls: V & AM.
Bibl: *Modern Book Illustrators and Their Work,* Studio, 1914 illus.

**SINGLEHURST, Mary**
Student at Liverpool School of Art, 1906. A book illustration by her appears in *The Studio,* Vol. 38, 1906 p.77.

**SINGLETON, Henry**                         **1766-1839**
Historical painter. He was born in London in 1766 and after studying at the RA Schools, he became a very prolific and successful painter, but failed to be elected to the RA. He undertook a great many book illustrations, his later work verging on the sentimental. He died in London in 1839.

Exhib: BI; RA; RBA.
Colls: BM; V & AM.

**SKELTON, Joseph Ratcliffe   RWA**          **fl.1888-1927**
Figure painter and illustrator. He was born at Newcastle-upon-Tyne and was working in Bristol in 1893 and in London in 1925. Skelton's drawings are rather 1890s in style but the figures and drapery are North Country and solid. He was elected RWA.

Illus: *Our Empire Story [Jack, 1908].*
Contrib: *The Graphic [1885-1912]; The Sketch [1897]; The Bystander [1904]; ILN [1907].*
Exhib: M; P; RA; RI; ROI.
Colls: V & AM.

**SKELTON, Percival**                        **fl.1849-1887**
Landscape painter and illustrator. He was a relation of the 18th century engraver Joseph Skelton and a prolific illustrator of books. He was an unsuccessful candidate for the NWS from 1852 to 1861 and specialised in Scottish and coastal scenes in a detailed and sentimental mid-Victorian manner.

Illus: *The Tommiebeg Shootings [T. Jeans, 1860]; Harry's Big Boots [S.E. Gay, 1873].*
Contrib: *Metrical Tales [Samuel Lover, 1849]; The Poetical Works of Edgar Allan Poe [1858]; Childe Harold [1858-59]; ILN [1860]; The Illustrated Times [1860]; The Welcome Guest [1860]; The Churchman's Family Magazine [1863]; The Water Babies [Kingsley, 1863 (with Paton)]; Life and Lessons of Our Lord [1864]; Once a Week [1866]; Heber's Hymns [1867]; Episodes of Fiction [1870]; The Graphic [1870-76]; Thornbury's Legendary Ballads [1876].*
Exhib: RA; RBA.
Bibl: Chatto & Jackson, *Treatise on Wood Engraving,* 1861, p.569.

**SKILL, Frederick John   RI**               **1824-1881**
Landscape and portrait painter and illustrator. He was born in 1824 and trained as a steel engraver, working as a portrait artist on *The London Journal.* He lived in Venice for several years and acted as a Special Artist for *The Illustrated London News* during the Schleswig-Holstein affair. He may have been sent by the magazine to

China, but had little success with his work and committed suicide as a result of depression in London on 8 March 1881. He had been elected NWS in 1876.

Illus: *Holidays among the Mountains [M.B. Edwards, 1861].*
Contrib: *Metrical Tales [Samuel Lover, 1849]; ILN [1854-67]; The Illustrated Times [1860-65]; Cassell's Family Paper [1860-61]; The Welcome Guest [1860]; London Society [1862]; Foxe's Book of Martyrs [1866]; Beeton's Annual [1866]; The Graphic [1870-71].*
Exhib: NWS; RA; RBA.
Colls: BM; V & AM; Wallace; Witt Photo.
Bibl: *Art Journal,* 1881.

**SKINNER, Edward F.**                        **fl.1888-1925**
Portrait and landscape painter and illustrator. He worked in London, 1888, Lewes, 1891 and St Ives, Cornwall, 1925. He contributed to *The Royal Magazine* and *Black & White,* 1891.

Exhib: L; RA; RBA; RWA.

**SKINNER, Captain H.F.C.**                   **fl.1904-1915**
Figure artist. He worked in London and contributed to *Punch,* 1904 and 1914.

Exhib: RA; RI.

**SLADER, Alfred**                            **fl.1856-1866**
Landscape painter. He contributed to *The Illustrated Times,* 1856-66 and especially to its Christmas issues.

**SLEIGH, Bernard**                           **1872-**
Watercolourist, wood engraver, illustrator and decorator. He was born at Birmingham in 1872 and studied there, becoming associated with the Birmingham Guild of Handicraft. He was also connected with the Campden Guild of Handicraft and with the Essex House Press, for which he carried out work and cut blocks from the designs of William Strang (q.v.). His illustrations are characterised by a certain naïve charm combined with strength of design. He was elected RBSA in 1928.

Illus: *The Sea-King's Daughter [A. Mark, 1895]; The Faery Calendar [1920].*
Contrib: *A Book of Pictured Carols [Birmingham School, 1893]; The Yellow Book [1896]; The Dome [1899-1900].*
Exhib: B; FAS; G; L; New Gall; RA.
Colls: V & AM; Witt Photo.
Bibl: '*The Future of Wood Engraving*', The Studio, Vol.14, 1898, pp.10-16 illus; R.E.D. Sketchley, *Eng. Bk. Illus.,* 1903, pp.12, 130; C. Franklin, *The Private Presses,* 1969, pp.78, 153.

**SLEIGH, Henry**
Book decorator. He contributed ornament to *Odes and Sonnets,* 1859 illustrated by Birket Foster (q.v.).

**SLEIGH, John**                              **fl.1841-1872**
Landscape painter and illustrator. He worked in London and was a close friend of Charles Keene (q.v.) with whom he went on a sketching tour of Brittany. A record of this is preserved in twenty-four drawings by Keene, contributed to *Punch* on 6, 13 and 20 September 1856.

Contrib: *The Home Affections [Charles Mackay, 1858]; Passages From Modern English Poets [1862]; Sacred Poetry of the 16th, 17th and 18th Centuries [c.1862].*
Exhib: RA; RBA.
Bibl: G.S. Layard, *C.K.* 1892, p.59.

**SLINGER, F.J.**                             **fl.1858-1871**
Genre painter and illustrator. He worked in London and was assistant at the Slade School to Alphonse Legros.

Contrib: *Once A Week; The Graphic [1871].*
Exhib: BI; RA.
Bibl: W. Shaw Sparrow, *Memories of Life and Art,* 1925.

**SLOCOMBE, Alfred**                          **fl.1865-1886**
Flower painter, etcher and watercolourist. He was a member of the RCA and did decorations for *The Illustrated London News,* 1866.

Exhib: BI; OWS; RA; RBA.

*WILLIAM SMALL RI 1843-1929. Illustration to* Amelia. *Ink and wash with bodycolour. Signed and dated 1882. 4¼ins. x 7ins. (10.8cm x 17.8cm).* Author's Collection

**SLOCOMBE, Edward C.** -1915
Painter and etcher. He was the brother of Alfred Slocombe (q.v.) and worked at Watford, Hertfordshire from 1883. He contributed social and military subjects to *The Graphic,* 1873.

Exhib: FAS; L; New Gall; RA; RE; RHA.

**SLY, B.**
Topographer. He contributed drawings to *Knight's London,* 1841.

**SMALL, William   RI** 1843-1929
Artist and illustrator. He was born in Edinburgh on 27 May 1843 and studied at the RSA Schools before coming to London in 1865. He had worked at Edinburgh in the art department of Messrs. Nelson, the publishers, and was already a highly competent black and white artist when he began to work for the leading magazines. Small was a very quick worker, very powerful in conception and very prolific. His genre subjects are drawn with a brilliance of detail and truth to line which is among the best work of the 1860s, but it is this early period up to 1870 which contains his most attractive work. Afterwards, Small begins to innovate and lose his way. He experiments with wash effects and these gradually supercede the beautiful line work and because of his reputation are copied by a whole generation of artists. He has therefore been quite rightly condemned by both White and Reid. His power was still expressed in the double pages that he was given in *The Graphic* until about 1900, vast areas for which he was paid sixty guineas, making him the most highly paid illustrator of his time. Small's life span stretches amazingly from the early numbers of *Once a Week* right up to the avant-garde *Gypsy* of 1915. For the last few

years of his life he lived at Worcester, having been elected RI in 1883 and HRSA in 1917. He died on 23 December 1929.

Illus: *Words for the Wise; Miracles of Heavenly Love; Marion's Sundays [all 1864]; Washerwoman's Foundling [1867]; A Protegée of Jack Hamilton's [Bret Harte, 1894].*
Contrib: *Shilling Magazine [1865-66]; Once a Week [1866]; Good Words [1866-68]; The Sunday Magazine [1866-68, 1871]; Cassell's Family Paper [1866, 1870]; Sunday At Home [1866]; Pen and Pencil Pictures From the Poets [1866]; Touches of Nature by Eminent Artists [1866]; Ballad Stories of the Affections [1866]; London Society [1867-69]; The Argosy [1867]; The Quiver [1867]; Poems by Jean Ingelow [1867]; Idyllic Pictures [1867]; Two Centuries of Song [1867]; Foxe's Book of Martyrs [1867]; Heber's Hymns [1867]; The Spirit of Praise [1867]; Illustrated Book of Sacred Poems [1867]; Golden Thoughts From Golden Fountains [1867]; Ode on the Morning of Christ's Nativity [1867]; North Coast and Other Poems [1868]; The Graphic [1869-1900]; Pictures From English Literature [1870]; Good Words For The Young [1871]; Novellos National Nursery Rhymes [1871]; Judy's Almanac [1872]; Thornbury's Legendary Ballads [1876]; Dalziel's Bible Gallery [1880]; Chums [1892]; Fun; The Gypsy [1915].*
Exhib: B; FAS; G; L; M; RA; RHA: RI; ROI; RSA.
Colls: Birmingham (St George's Soc.); V & AM.
Bibl: Forrest Reid, *Illustrators of the Sixties,* 1928, pp.216-227 illus.
See illustration (above).

**SMALLFIELD, Frederick   ARWS** 1829-1915
Genre and portrait painter and illustrator. He was born at Homerton in 1829 and studied at the RA Schools and was elected ARWS in 1860. He was a prolific watercolourist, worked in London and died there on 10 September 1915.

Contrib: *Willmott's Sacred Poetry [1862]; Passages From Modern English Poets [1862].*
Exhib: B; BI; G; GG; L; M; RA; RI; ROI; RWS.

457

**SMALLWOOD, William Frome** 1806-1834
Architect and draughtsman. He was born in London on 24 June 1806 and became a pupil of the architect D.N. Cottingham. He travelled to the Continent to make drawings of churches for *The Penny Magazine* and exhibited landscapes. He died in London on 22 April 1834.

Contrib: *Knight's London [1842].*
Exhib: RA; RBA.
Bibl: *Architectural Magazine,* Vol.1, 1834, p.184.

**SMIRKE, Robert RA** 1752-1845
Artist and illustrator. He was born at Wigton near Carlisle in 1752 and came to London in 1766, studying at the RA Schools in 1771. Smirke was one of the most prolific book illustrators of the early 19th century, working for all the leading publishers and specialising in the 'conversation piece' drawing within decorative borders which augmented so many three volume novels. His drawings are usually very fine in execution, the pen line clear, the shadows and modelling in washes sometimes with a trace of blue. He was elected an ARA in 1791 and an RA in 1793. He died in London in 1845.

Illus: *Bowyer's History of England; The Adventure of Hunchback [1814, AT 366]; Don Quixote [1818].*
Exhib: BI; RA; RBA; Soc. of Artists.
Colls: BM; V & AM.

**SMITH, A.T.** fl.1899-1914
Humorous figure artist. He contributed wooden doll subjects to *Punch,* 1902-14 and to *Fun,* 1899.

Colls: Witt Photo.

**SMITH, Arthur Reginald RWS RSW** 1872-1934
Landscape and figure painter. He was born at Skipton-in-Craven in 1872 and studied and taught at the Keighley School of Art and then at South Kensington. He travelled in Italy and had a one man show at Leighton House in 1907-08. He was elected ARWS in 1917 and RWS in 1925 and RSW in 1925. He died at Bolton Abbey in 1934.

Illus: *The Lake Counties [W.G. Collingwood, 1932].*
Exhib: B; FAS; G; L; M; RA; RI; RSW; RWS.
Colls: Bradford; Bristol; V & AM.

**SMITH, Lieutenant-Colonel Charles Hamilton** 1776-1859
Topographical draughtsman and antiquary. He was born in East Flanders in 1776 and was educated at Richmond, Surrey before training as an officer in the Austrian military academy at Malines and Louvain. He joined the British Army in 1797 as a volunteer and served in the West Indies and Holland before becoming quartermaster on the Walcheren Expedition. After a visit to the United States he retired in 1820 and settled at Plymouth where he formed an artists' club. For most of his life, Smith made watercolours of costume and natural history which he used to illustrate his books. He died at Plymouth in 1859.

Publ: *Selections of Ancient Costume of Great Britain and Ireland, 7th to 16th Century [with S.R. Meyrick, 1814]; Costume of the Original Inhabitants of the British Isles to the 6th Century [1815]; Natural History of the Human Species [1848].*
Colls: BM; Greenwich.

**SMITH, Charles John** 1803-1838
Engraver and antiquary. He was born in Chelsea in 1803 and became a pupil of Charles Pye, the engraver. He painted views of London buildings, illustrated antiquarian works and was elected FSA in 1837. He died in London on 23 November 1838.

Colls: BM.

**SMITH, Edwin Dalton** 1800-
Miniaturist and painter of flowers. He was the son and pupil of Anker Smith and was born in London on 23 October 1800. He made drawings for *The Botanic Garden,* B. Maund, 1825-35.

Exhib: NWS; RA; RBA.

**SMITH, J.**
Contributor of genre subjects to *The Illustrated London News,* 1873.

**SMITH, J. Moyr** fl.1885-1920
Decorative designer and occasional illustrator. After starting as an architect, he began to produce illustrations for *Fun* and other magazines in the 1870s. He was Editor of *Decoration,* 1880-89 and drew in a flat Etruscan style derived from his study of ancient art. The drawings are very often as flat as the jokes; there was one example of this artist in the Handley-Read collection.

Illus: *Shakespeare For Children: Lamb's Tales [c.1897].*
Contrib: *Fun; Doré's Thomas Hood [1870, decor]; Punch [1872-78].*
Exhib: B; G; L; RA; RBA; RSA; RSW.
Colls: Witt Photo.

**SMITH, James Burrell** 1822-1897
Landscape painter. He was born in 1822 and between 1843 and 1854, lived at Alnwick and studied under T.M. Richardson (q.v.) during his first years. He set up as a drawing-master in London in 1854 and made sketches in the manner of Richardson, particularly of waterfalls. He died in London in 1897.

Contrib: *ILN [1883-87].*
Exhib: RBA.
Colls: Alnwick Castle; Fitzwilliam; Newcastle; V & AM.

**SMITH, Jessie Wilcox** -1935
Artist and illustrator. She was born in Philadelphia and worked in New York, many of her books being published in this country. She studied with Howard Pyle (q.v.) at the Philadelphia Fine Art Institute and specialised in children's books. She died in New York on 4 May 1935.

Illus: *A Child's Garden of Verses [R.L. Stevenson, 1905].*

**SMITH, John Thomas** 1766-1833
Draughtsman and antiquary. He was born in London in 1766, the son of Nathaniel Smith, the sculptor and printseller. He studied art with Joseph Nollekens and J.K. Sherwin and then set up for himself as a portrait and topographical engraver. He worked at Edmonton from 1788 and was made Keeper of Prints and Drawings at the British Museum from 1816. Smith is better remembered as a writer on the arts than as an artist, he produced a number of books of memoirs which form important links between the 18th and 19th century schools and are valuable sources of facts. His own work as an etcher is incisive and reminiscent of Callot and sometimes even of Rembrandt. He died in London in 1833.

Publ: *Nollekens and his Times [1828]; A Book for a Rainy Day [1845, re-issued 1905].*
Illus: *Remarks on Rural Scenery [1797]; Antiquities of London [1800]; Antiquities of Westminster [1807]; The Ancient Topography of London [1815]; Vagabondiana [1817]; The Cries of London [1839].*
Contrib: *Knight's London [1842].*
Exhib: RA.
Colls: BM; Fitzwilliam.

See illustration (p.459).

**SMITH, Joseph Clarendon** 1778-1810
Topographical draughtsman. He worked in the Thames Valley and the Home Counties, touring in Warwickshire in 1805 and Cornwall in 1806. He died after a visit to Madeira which he had visited as a cure for consumption, 1810.

Contrib: *The Beauties of England and Wales [1803, 1814-15]; Topographical Cabinet [1811]; The Antiquarian Itinerary [1817].*
Exhib: BI; RA.
Colls: BM; V & AM; Witt Photo.

*JOHN THOMAS SMITH 1766-1833. 'A Blind Man and his boy.' Plate in* Vagabondiana or Anecdotes of Mendicant Wanderers, *1817. Etching.*

**SMITH, Percy John Delf**         **1882-1948**

Painter, etcher and illustrator. He was born in London on 11 March 1882 and was mainly self-taught although he studied at the Camberwell School of Art. After service in the First War, he worked in the US, 1927, and in Palestine, 1932. Smith specialised in fine lettering and the illumination of books but also designed alphabets and worked for private presses. There is a bookplate by this artist in the Victoria and Albert Museum.

Illus: *Quality in Life [1919]; The Dance of Death [1914-18]; Twelve Drypoints of the War, 1914-18; The Bible in Spain [1925]; The Metamorphosis of Aiax [Sir J. Harrington, Fanfrolico, 1927].*
Exhib: L; RI.
Colls: V & AM; Witt Photo.

**SMITH, Robert Catterson**         **fl.1880-1892**

Landscape and figure painter. He worked in London and contributed figure subjects and architecture to *The English Illustrated Magazine,* 1890-92.

Exhib: L; M; RA; RBA; RHA; RI.

**SMITH, Thomas C.**

Figure artist. Contributed to *Punch,* 1903.

**SMITH, W.G.**         **fl.1866-1880**

Botanical illustrator. He contributed drawings to *The Wild Flowers of Great Britain,* R. Hogg and George W. Johnson, 1866-80 and drew an initial letter for *Punch* in 1878.

**SMITH, W. Thomas**         **1862-**

Portrait, figure and historical painter. He was working in London in 1890, but may have emigrated to Canada before 1925.

Illus: *The Wilds of the West Coast [Oxley, 1894].*
Contrib: *The Quiver [1890]; Good Cheer [1894]; The Boy's Own Paper.*
Exhib: L; M; P; RA; RBA; RI.

**SMITH, Winifred**         **fl.1890-1896**

Illustrator of children's books. She won commendations at the Nat. Competition, South Kensington in 1896 and was described by *The Bookman,* in August 1894 as an artist 'whose designs in black and white are witty, pretty and effective'.

Illus: *Childrens Singing Games [c.1890].*
Bibl: *The Studio,* Vol.8, 1896, p.228 illus.

**SMYTH, Dorothy Carleton**         **fl.1901-1925**

Painter and illustrator. She studied at the Glasgow School, c.1901 and worked in Glasgow, 1907 and at Cambuslang, 1925.

Exhib: G; L; RSA; RA.
Bibl: *The Studio,* Winter No., 1900-1, p.55 illus; Vol.25, 1901-2, pp.281-286.

**SMYTHE, Ernest**         **fl.1896-1899**

Illustrator and watercolourist. He specialised in hunting subjects and contributed to *The Sketch,* 1896 and *The Illustrated London News,* 1899.

Colls: V & AM.

**SMYTHE, Lionel Percy   RA**         **1839-1918**

Figure and landscape painter in watercolours. He was born in London on 4 September 1839 and was educated at Kings College School and studied art at Heatherley's. Smythe worked in the warm colours and genre subjects popularised by Fred Walker (q.v.) and worked chiefly at the Chateau de Honvault, Wimereux, Pas-de-Calais. He was elected ARA in 1898 and RA in 1911, having been RWS from 1894. He died on 10 July 1918.

Contrib: *ILN [1874, 1879, 1880].*
Exhib: B; FAS; G; L; M; RA; RBA; RI; ROI; RWS.
Colls: Greenwich; V & AM.
Bibl: R.M. Whitlaw and W.L. Wyllie, *LPS, RA,* 1923; M. Hardie, *Watercol. Paint. in Brit.,* Vol.3, 1968, p.140-141.

**SNEYD, Rev. John**         **1766-1835**

Amateur caricaturist. He was born in 1766, the son of Ralph Sneyd of Keele Hall, Staffs, (now Keele University) and was Rector of Elford for over forty years. He was a friend and patron of Gillray and died unmarried on 2 July 1835. His nephew was the Rev. W. Sneyd (q.v.).

Bibl: M.D. George, *English Political Caricature,* Vol.2, 1959, p.263.

**SNEYD, Rev. Walter   FSA**         **1809-1888**

Amateur caricaturist. He was born in 1809, the son of Walter Sneyd of Keele Hall and his wife the Hon. Louisa Bagot, and nephew of the Rev. John Sneyd (q.v.). He was educated at Westminster and Christ Church, Oxford, taking his BA in 1831. He succeeded his brother at Keele Hall in 1870 and died there on 2 July 1888.

Illus: *Portraits of the Spruggins Family [1829, privately printed].*
Bibl: *Walford's County Families; Alumni Oxoniensis.*
See illustration (p.34).

**SNOW, J.W.**         **fl.1832-1848**

Horse painter. He worked in London and contributed illustrations to *Tattersalls British Race Horses,* 1838 and *The Illustrated London News,* 1848.

Exhib: RBA, 1832.
Colls: BM.

**SNOWMAN, Isaac** 1874-

Genre and portrait painter. He was born in London in 1874 and studied at the RA Schools before becoming a pupil of Bouguereau and Constant in Paris. He painted state portraits of Edward VII and George V and eventually emigrated to Israel.

Contrib: *ILN [1897-98]*.
Exhib: B; L; RA; ROI.

**SOLOMON, Abraham** 1824-1862

Painter and illustrator. He was born in London in May 1824 and studied at Sass's Bloomsbury Art School in 1838, entering the RA Schools in 1839. Solomon painted a great number of subjects from literature but scored instant success with his railway carriage dramas of 1854, 'First Class — The Meeting' and 'Second Class — The Parting'. His work was well-known to the public through its popularisation in prints and he was a regular RA exhibitor. He died at Biarritz on 19 December 1862. He was the brother of Simeon and Rebecca Solomon (qq.v.).

Contrib: *ILN [1857]; Favourite Modern Ballads; Household Song [1861]*.
Exhib: BI; RA.
Bibl: Chatto & Jackson, *Treatise on Wood Engraving*, 1861, p.599; J. Maas, *Victorian Painters*, 1970, p.238.

**SOLOMON, Rebecca**

Portrait and history painter. She was the sister of Abraham and Simeon Solomon and exhibited regularly between 1852 and 1869. She contributed illustrations to *The Churchman's Family Magazine*, 1864 and *London Society*.

Exhib: RA.
Colls: Witt Photo.

**SOLOMON, Simeon** 1840-1905

Painter, draughtsman and illustrator. He was born in London in 1840, the brother of Abraham and Rebecca Solomon (qq.v.). He was a pupil of Cary's Academy in Bloomsbury and then entered the RA Schools, exhibiting at the exhibitions from 1858. Solomon became part of the Rossetti circle, was a friend of Burne-Jones (q.v.) and A.C. Swinburne and these contacts had a strong influence on his work. He travelled to Florence in 1866 and to Rome in 1869, but gradually sunk into a life of idleness and dissipation. His most vivid works are those featuring contemporary Jewish life such as the illustrations to *Jewish Customs* and they have an almost Rembrandtesque intensity. He was capable of evoking an air of eastern mystery in his drawings and fortunately his best work is his earliest and it was at this time that he was working for the book. He died in penury in 1905.

Publ: *A Vision of Love Revealed in Sleep [1871]*.
Contrib: *Once A Week [1862]; Good Words [1862]; The Leisure Hour [1866]; Dark Blue [1871-73]; Dalziel's Bible Gallery [1880]; Art Pictures From The Old Testament [1897]; Lives of the Minor Saints [Mrs. Jameson, c.1860]*.
Exhib: RA.
Colls: V & AM.
Bibl: A.C. Swinburne, *SS*, The Bibelot, XIV, 1908; B. Falk, *Five Years Dead*, 1937; Forrest Reid, *Illustrators of the Sixties*, 1928, pp.103-104; J.E. Ford, *SS*, 1964; J. Maas, *Victorian Painters*, 1970, p.146; L. Lambourne, *A SS Sketch-Book*, Apollo, Vol.85, 1967, pp.59-61.

See illustration (right).

**SOLOMON, Solomon Joseph** 1860-1927

Portrait and figure painter and illustrator. He was born in London on 16 September 1860 and studied at Heatherley's and the RA Schools before going to the Munich Academy and the École des Beaux Arts in Paris, 1879. He travelled and worked in Italy, Spain and Morocco and became Vice-President of the Maccabeans Society and President of the RBA, 1918. He had been elected ARA in 1896 and RA in 1906, having been a member of the NEA since 1886. He was the first artist to initiate camouflage for the British Army in the First World War. He died in London on 27 July 1927.

Illus: *For The Temple [G.A. Henty, 1887]*.
Contrib: *Black & White [1891]; The Graphic [1897-1904]*.
Exhib: B; G; GG; L; M; NEA; New Gall; P; RA; RBA; RHA; ROI.
Bibl: J. Maas, *Victorian Painters*, 1970, p.232.

**SOLON, Leon Victor** 1872-

Artist, sculptor and decorator. He was born at Stoke-on-Trent in 1872, the son of Louis M. Solon, artist and author. He was educated privately and then studied at the RCA where he was a scholar and medallist. Solon's connection with the Staffordshire potteries provides an interesting relationship between illustration and ceramics, many of his designs for Mintons for example, reflect the Symbolists and the work of Aubrey Beardsley (q.v.). Solon was the designer of one of the early posters for *The Studio*, but he emigrated to the United States early in the century and worked in Lakeland, Florida.

Contrib: *The Parade [1897]; Les Trophées [De Herdia, 1904]*.
Bibl: *The Studio*, Winter No., 1900-1, p.65 illus.

**SOMERVILLE, Edith Anna Œnone** 1858-1949

Author and illustrator. She was born at Drishane, Ireland in 1858, the daughter of Lt.-Colonel Somerville of a leading Anglo-Irish family. After being educated at home, she studied art in Paris under Colarossi and Delecluse and attended the Westminster School of Art. Edith Somerville returned to Ireland and set up house with her cousin Violet Martin, collaborating with her on a number of books on Irish life and character. Her knowledge of the country and particularly its sport gained from two spells as Master of the West Carbery Foxhounds, made her books both individual and popular. Most of them were illustrated by black and white sketches which typify the shabby genteel life of the Irish landowner before 1914. Edith Somerville

*SIMEON SOLOMON 1840-1905. 'Jepthah and his daughter.' Original drawing for illustration probably intended for Dalziel's Bible Gallery, 1881, not used. Pen and ink. Signed. 6¼ins. x 4¼ins. (15.9cm x 10.8cm).*
Victoria and Albert Museum

continued to write after the death of Violet Martin and became a vociferous and ardent feminist, dying at her old childhood. home of Drishane in 1949. She had one man shows at Goupil and Walker's Galleries in 1920 and 1923.

Illus: *The Real Charlotte [1894]; Clear As The Noon Day [E. Penrose, 1894]; The Silver Fox; Some Experiences of an Irish R.M. [1899]; Further Experiences of an Irish R.M. [1908]; Dan Russel the Fox [1911]; In Mr Knox's Country [1915].*
Contrib: *Black & White [1893].*
Exhib: FAS; L; RHA; SWA.

**SOMERVILLE, Howard**                              1873-c.1940
Figure painter, illustrator and etcher. He was born at Dundee in 1873 and after being privately educated, studied science and engineering at Dundee but abandoned this for art. He settled in London in 1899 and began to contribute to *Punch* and other magazines. Somerville, who also specialised in interiors and still-life, worked for some time in New York and Glasgow and was elected RPE in 1917. His ink drawings of women are rather highly finished and mannered.

Contrib: *Moonshine [1900]; Punch [1903-6]; ILN [1911].*
Exhib: B; G; GG; L; NEA; P; RA; RSA.
Colls: Liverpool; Witt Photo.

**SONNTAG, W. Louis**                               1870-
American illustrator. Born in New York in 1870. Contributor of railway drawings to *The English Illustrated Magazine,* 1896.

**SOPER, George   RE**                              1870-
Watercolourist, etcher, wood engraver and illustrator. He was born in London in 1870 and studied with the etcher Sir Frank Short. He worked at Harmer Green, Welwyn, Hertfordshire from about 1911 and was still exhibiting in 1930.

Illus: *The Water Babies [Charles Kingsley, 1908].*
Contrib: *ILN [1897 (S. Africa)]; Cassell's Magazine [1898]; The Boy's Own Paper; Chums; The Graphic [1901-4].*
Exhib: FAS; G; L; NEA; RA; RBA; RE; RHA; RI; RSA.

**SOUTHALL, Joseph Edward**                         1861-1944
Painter, designer and engraver. He was born at Nottingham in 1861 and educated at York and Scarborough before serving an apprenticeship to an architect, 1878-82. In 1883 he came to realize that all fine art was architectural and that the architect must study art and therefore he spent some time in Italy studying tempera painting. He was also much influenced by John Ruskin and studied drawing and carving and interested himself in furniture design and embroidery. He painted frescoes at the Birmingham Art Gallery and was examiner at the Birmingham School of Art. He was elected RBSA in 1902, NEA in 1926 and RWS in 1931. Southall's work is often anaemic in colouring and lifeless in content but it had some popularity at the time. He died in 1944.

Illus: *The Story of Bluebeard [1895].*
Contrib: *The Quest [1894-96]; The Yellow Book [1896];* political pamphlets during the First World War, n.d.
Exhib: B; FAS; G; GG; L; M; NEA; New Gall; RA; RWS.
Colls: Birmingham; Witt Photo.
Bibl: *Modern Book Illustrators and Their Work,* Studio, 1914.

**SOWERBY, James**                                  1757-1822
Botanical illustrator. He was born in London in 1757 and studied at the RA Schools. He set up in practice as a portrait and flower painter in London but finally abandoned this for the study of botany. He issued and illustrated *English Botany,* 1790-1814, *English Fungi,* 1797-1815, *English Botany or Coloured Figures of British Plants,* 1832-40. He died in London in 1822, leaving a large family many of whom became botanical artists.

Publ: *An Easy Introduction to Drawing Flowers [1778].*
Exhib: RA; Soc. of Artists.
Colls: BM; Nat. Hist.

**SOWERBY, John G.**                                fl.1876-1925
Landscape and flower painter. He worked in Newcastle-upon-Tyne, Gateshead and Ross-on-Wye and contributed a number of illustrations to children's books, all showing the marked influence of Kate

Greenaway (q.v.). Father of Millicent Sowerby (q.v.).

Illus: *Afternoon Tea – Rhymes for Children [c.1880]; At Home [1881].*
Exhib: B; G; L; M; RA; RI; RSA.

**SOWERBY, Millicent**                              fl.1900-1913
Watercolourist and illustrator. She was the daughter of John G. Sowerby (q.v.) and was working at Colchester, 1900 and Abingdon, 1904. She illustrated *A Child's Garden of Verses,* R.L. Stevenson, 1913.

**SPARE, Austin Osman**                             1888-1956
Painter, engraver, imaginary artist and illustrator. He was born at Snowhill on 31 December 1888 and studied at the Lambeth School and the RCA, exhibiting in the National Competition of 1903. Spare was a mystic and poetic draughtsman who was strongly influenced by Aubrey Beardsley's work in his early years. He was Editor of *Form,* 1916-17 and *The Golden Hind,* 1922-24 and illustrated in pen and ink as well as in chalk and watercolour and designed bookplates. He became unbalanced in later life and died in 1956.

Illus: *Earth Inferno [1905]; A Book of Satyrs [1907]; The Book of Pleasure; The Psychology of Ecstasy [1913]; Anathema of Zos; The Sermon of Hypocrites.*
Exhib: RA.
Colls: Ashmolean; Leeds; V & AM; Witt Photo.
Bibl: K. Grant, *Oracles of AOS,* 1975; *The Left Hand Path,* 1976.

**SPECHTER, Otto**
Illustrator. He contributed to *Parables From Nature* by Mrs Gatty, 1867.

**SPEED, Harold**                                   1872-1957
Landscape and portrait painter. He was born in London in 1872, the son of Edward Speed, the architect and was educated privately before studying at the RCA, 1887, at the RA Schools, 1890, and in Paris, Vienna and Rome, on a travelling scholarship, 1893. He was elected RP in 1897 and was Master of the Art Workers Guild in 1916.

Publ: *The Science and Practice of Drawing [1913]; The Science and Practice of Oil Painting [1924].*
Contrib: *The Graphic [1899-1902].*
Exhib: B; FAS, 1914, 1922, 1938; G; L; M; NEA; New Gall; P; RA; RBA; RCA; RHA; ROI; RSA.
Colls: Belfast; Birmingham; Bristol; Liverpool; Manchester.

**SPEED, Lancelot**                                 1860-1931
Coastal painter and black and white illustrator. He was born in London in 1860, the son of a barrister and was educated at Rugby and Clare College, Cambridge. Speed worked principally as a book illustrator from about 1890, concentrating on shipping subjects. He worked in Barnet and Southend-on-Sea and died there on 21 December 1931.

Illus: *The Red Fairy Book [c.1890]; The Limbersnigs [1896]; The Last Days of Pompei [Lytton, 1897]; Hypatia [C. Kingsley, 1897]; Novels of Robert Barr [1897]; The Romance of Early British Life [1908].*
Contrib: *ILN [1887-94]; The Sporting & Dramatic News [1892]; The English Illustrated Magazine [1895-97]; Good Words [1898]; The Sphere; Punch; The Windsor Magazine.*

**SPENCE, Percy F.S.**                              1868-1933
Painter and illustrator. He was born at Sydney, N.S.W., in 1868 and spent his early career in Australia and Fijii, exhibiting his work with the Art Society at New South Wales. He came to London in 1895 and resided there for the rest of his life, working from Kensington and contributing to many magazines. Spence was a fine figure draughtsman, his pen work frequently used with colour washes. He was acquainted with R.L. Stevenson in the South Seas and drew portraits of him. He died in London in September 1933.

Contrib: *The Graphic [1900-6]; Punch [1903]; ILN [1905]; The Ludgate Monthly; The Pall Mall Magazine; The Windsor Magazine.*
Exhib: B; L; New Gall; RA.
Colls: V & AM.

**SPENCE, Robert RE**                                   **1870-**
Painter, etcher and illustrator. He was born at Tynemouth on 6 October 1870 and studied at the Newcastle School of Art, at the Slade School, 1892-95 and in Paris with Cormon. Spence is an important and original figure because of his use of the etched plate for both illustrations and text in the book, thus continuing the visionary tradition of William Blake (q.v.). His most notable achievement in this medium is the *George Fox His Journal*. He also etched scenes from Wagner and illustrated for magazines. His work was particularly commended by Walter Crane for its romantic feeling and dramatic force. He was elected ARE in 1897 and RE in 1902.

Contrib: *The Quarto [1896]*.
Exhib: FAS; L; NEA; RA; RE; RWA.
Bibl: *British Book Illustrators Yesterday and Today*, Studio, 1923.

**SPILSBURY, Francis B.**                               **fl.1799-1805**
Amateur artist and draughtsman. He was a naval doctor and made drawings on his voyages, some of which were used in publications. Some of these were published by Daniel Orme as *Picturesque Scenes in the Holy Land and Syria*, 1803, AT 381.

Colls: Searight Coll; Witt Photo.

**SPOONER, Mrs. Minnie Dibdin (neé Davison)**          **fl.1893-1927**
Portrait painter and etcher. She drew for children's books and married the artist C.S. Spooner. She was elected RMS in 1901.

Illus: *The Gold Staircase [Wordsworth, 1906]*.
Exhib: L; New Gall; RA; RHA; RMS.

**SPOTTISWOODE, William**
Amateur artist. He published *Journey Through Eastern Russia*, 1857, AT 232, illustrated by lithos from his own drawings.

**SPREAT, William**                                     **fl.1841-1848**
Landscape painter working in the Exeter area. He published *Picturesque Sketches of the Churches of Devon*, 1842.

Colls: Exeter.

**SPURRIER, Steven   ARA RBA**                          **1878-1961**
Painter, black and white and poster artist. He was born in London in 1878 and studied art at Lambeth School and Heatherley's being elected ROI in 1912, RBA in 1934 and ARA in 1943 and RA in 1952. In his early days he specialised in genre and social realistic subjects for the magazines, later undertaking theatre illustration. He died in 1961.

Contrib: *The Graphic [1910]; Radio Times [1936]*.
Exhib: G; GG; L; M; RA; RBA; RHA; RI; ROI; RSA.
Colls: RA; V & AM; Witt Photo.

**SPURRIER, W.R.**                                      **fl.1896-1905**
Figure artist specialising in cockney children. He contributed to *Fun*, 1896-1900 and to *Punch*, 1902-5.

**STACEY, Walter S.**                                   **1846-1929**
Landscape and genre painter and illustrator. He was born in London in 1846 and studied at the RA Schools and was elected RBA in 1881 and ROI in 1883. He worked in Hampstead, 1890 to 1902 and then in the West Country at New Milton, Tiverton and Newton Abbot. His largest output of illustrations was for boys' books of adventure. He died at Newton Abbot in September 1929.

Illus: *Follow My Leader [T.B. Read, 1885]; Bible Pictures [1890]; In Greek Waters [G.A. Henty, 1893]; The White Conquerors of Mexico [Kirk Munroe, 1894]; In Press Gang Days [Pickering, 1894]; Bible Stories [L.L. Weedon, 1911]*.
Contrib: *The Cornhill Magazine [1883-84]; The Quiver [1891-95]; The Strand Magazine [1891-1906]; Good Words [1891]; Chums [1892]; The Temple Magazine [1896]; The Wide World Magazine [1898]; Cassell's Family Magazine; The Boy's Own Paper; The Girl's Own Paper; Black & White*.
Exhib: L; M; NEA; RA; RBA; RI; ROI.

**STAFFORD, John Phillips**                             **1851-1899**
Painter and humorous artist. He was born in 1851 and acted as cartoonist for *Funny Folks* for a number of years and was also a contributor to *Punch*, 1894. He made stage designs for the theatre and died in March 1899.

Exhib: RA, 1871-86.

**STAMP, Winifred L.**                                  **fl.1899-1925**
Figure and miniature painter. She worked in Stepney, London and was trained at the Regent Street Polytechnic. She exhibited some book illustrations in the National Competition, South Kensington in 1905-6.

Exhib: RA; RMS.

**STAMPA, George Loraine**                              **1875-**
Black and white artist. He was born in London on 29 November 1875, the son of an architect, and was educated at Bedford Modern School. He studied art at Heatherley's, c.1892 and at the RA Schools, 1895-1900. Stampa was a raffish bohemian who was the spiritual successor of Charles Keene and Phil May (qq.v.), preferring the London streets for his drawings to the salons of Mayfair. It was not surprising therefore to find him adopted as a *Punch* artist from 1895, contributing bushels of urchins, street arabs, cockney servant gals and drunken cabbies. He gave a touch of realism to *Punch* which was much needed, but his pen work was very traditional. He undertook some decorative work such as covers and initial letters and also made portraits.

Illus: *Easy French Exercises; Ragamuffins [1916]; Anthology – In Praise of Dogs*.
Contrib: *Punch [1895-1950]; Moonshine [1898]; The Graphic [1910]*.
Exhib: RA; Walker's Gall.
Bibl: R.G.G. Price, *A History of Punch*, p.249.

**STANDFUST, G.B.**
Draughtsman and illustrator. He illustrated *Shelley's Poetical Works*, 1844 and drew humorous subjects. There is a delightful study of Count D'Orsay by this artist in the Witt Photo Library.

Exhib: RA, 1844.

**STANFIELD, William Clarkson**                         **1793-1867**
Marine and landscape painter and illustrator. He was born at Sunderland in 1793, the son of J.F. Stanfield, an Irish actor and anti-slavery writer. He was apprenticed to an Edinburgh heraldic painter but went to sea in 1808 and was pressed into the Navy in 1812. He made voyages on an East Indian ship to China, but left the service in 1818 to devote all his time to theatrical scene painting. He met and became a close friend of David Roberts (q.v.) and went to London with him in 1820, where they were employed on the stage work at Drury Lane Theatre. Stanfield soon had great success, became part of the Charles Dickens's circle and an intimate with Douglas Jerrold and Captain Marryat whose books he illustrated. He was a founder member of the SBA in 1823 and was elected ARA in 1832 and RA in 1835. He made tours to Italy, France and Holland and visited Scotland on a number of occasions in later life, settling from 1847 in Hampstead. Stanfield's seascapes are remarkable for their accuracy and his Continental views were much used in the Annuals of the 1830s. He died at Hampstead on 18 May 1867.

Illus: *The Pirate and The Three Cutters [Capt. Marryat, 1835]; Poor Jack [Capt. Marryat, 1840 (20 engrs.)]; Coast Scenery [1847]; American Notes [C. Dickens, 1850 (frontis)]*.
Contrib: *Heath's Picturesque Album [1832-34]; Heath's Gallery [1836-38]; Finden's Life and Poems of the Rev. G. Crabbe [1834]; Sketches on the Moselle, The Rhine and the Meuse [1838, AT 32]; The Chimes, A Goblin Story [C. Dickens, 1845]; The Cricket on The Hearth [C. Dickens, 1846]; The Haunted Man and The Ghost's Bargain [C. Dickens, 1848]; Moxon's Tennyson [1857]*.
Exhib: BI; RA; RBA.
Colls: Aberdeen; BM; Fitzwilliam; Greenwich; Leeds; Manchester; V & AM; Garrick Club; Witt Photo.
Bibl: *Gentleman's Magazine*, IV, July 1867; J. Dafforne, *CS Short Biographical Sketch*, 1873; C. Dickens, *The Story of a Great Friendship*, 1918; M. Hardie, *Watercol. Paint. in Brit.*, Vol.3, 1968, pp.68-70 illus.

See illustration (pp.39, 463).

*WILLIAM CLARKSON STANFIELD 1793-1867. Charles Dickens in the character of 'Bobadil'. Watercolour and wash.*    The Garrick Club

**STANIFORTH, J.M.**                                    fl.1895-1906
Cartoonist and humorous artist. He was chief cartoonist of the
*Evening Express,* Cardiff and of *The Western Mail.* He contributed
comic animals and figures to *Punch,* 1906.

Illus: *The General Election 1895, Evening Express Political Cartoons; Cartoons
of the Welsh Coal Strike [1898].*

**STANILAND, Charles Joseph**                            1838-1916
Marine painter and illustrator. He was born at Kingston-upon-Hull on
19 June 1838 and studied at the Birmingham School of Art,
Heatherley's, South Kensington and the RA Schools, 1861. He was
elected ARI in 1875 and RI in 1879, becoming ROI in 1883.
Staniland's strength was in marine illustrations where the ships and
tackle were seen at close quarters and the working seaman was
observed in large scale. His many contributions to *The Illustrated
London News* and *The Graphic* were a mainstay of those periodicals
in the 1870s and 1880s, readers had practically to wipe the brine from
their faces as they turned the pages. He was also an excellent portrait
artist and painted still-life and bird subjects in watercolour. He was
among the most prolific artists of the period and was much admired
by Van Gogh during his English years. Staniland died in London in
1916.

Illus: *The Gentleman Cadet [A.W. Drayson, 1875]; The Dragon and the River
[G.A. Henty, 1886]; Traitor or Patriot [M.C. Rowsell]; Britannia's Bulwarks
[C.N. Robinson, 1901].*
Contrib: *The Leisure Hour [1866]; Cassell's Family Magazine [1867]; Idyllic
Pictures [1867]; The Quiver [1868]; Episodes of Ficton [1870]; ILN
[1870-87]; The Graphic [1880-90]; The English Illustrated Magazine
[1886-92]; The Boy's Own Paper [1892-93]; Chums [1892]; Cassell's Family
Magazine [1895-96]; The Pall Mall Magazine [1896-97]; The Wide World
Magazine [1898].*

Exhib: B; FAS; G; L; M; RA; RI.
Colls: Greenwich; Sunderland; V & AM; Witt Photo.
Bibl: *English Influences on Vincent Van Gogh,* Arts Council, 1974-75.

**STANLAWS, Penrhyn**
Figure artist. He contributed drawings to *Punch,* 1903-4 in a spirited
but scratchy style.

**STANLEY, Lady    See TENNANT, Dorothy**

**STANLEY, G.**                                        fl.1800-1817
Topographical artist. He may be the same artist who exhibited a
landscape at the RA in 1800.

Contrib: *The Antiquarian Itinerary [1817 (Yorkshire)].*
Colls: Witt Photo.

**STANLEY, Harold J.**                                   1817-1867
Painter and illustrator. He was born at Lincoln in 1817 and went to
Munich to work under Kaulbach. He travelled to Italy but returned to
Munich to work and died there in 1867.

Exhib: BI; RA; RBA.

**STANLEY, Sir Henry Morton**                            1841-1904
African explorer and amateur artist. He was born at Denbigh on 29
June 1841 with the name of John Rowlands, but being left an orphan
was brought up in the St Asaph workhouse, 1847-56. As a boy he
shipped to America and was adopted by Henry Stanley, a New
Orleans cottonbroker whose name he took. Stanley served in the

463

Confederate army, 1861-62 and in the United States navy, 1864-65, afterwards adopting the life of a roving journalist in Asia Minor, Abyssinia and Africa. In October 1869, he was ordered by the *New York Herald* to mount an expedition to find Dr Livingstone in central Africa. He found Dr Livingstone at Ujiji on 10 November 1871 and published his account of the journey in *How I Found Livingstone,* 1872. He was Governor of the Congo and knighted in 1899, he served as MP for Lambeth, 1895-1900 and married on 12 July 1890 Dorothy Tennant (q.v.) the artist and illustrator. He died on 10 May 1904.

Contrib: *ILN [1878].*

**STANLEY, L.**

Topographer. He contributed illustrations of Palermo to *The Illustrated Times,* 1860.

**STANNARD, Henry John**                                    **1844-1920**

Landscape and sporting artist and illustrator. He was born at Woburn, Bedfordshire in 1844, the son of John Stannard, 1795-1881. He studied at the South Kensington Schools and established his own Academy of Arts at Bedford in 1887, specialising in bird studies and publishing a number of country books illustrated by himself. He was elected RBA in 1894, was a member of the Dudley Art Society and died at Bedford on 15 November 1920.

Contrib: *ILN [1897-99 (decor and birds)]; Encyclopaedia of Sport; Bailey's Magazine; The Sporting & Dramatic News.*
Exhib: B; L; M; RA; RBA; RCA; RI.

**STANNARD, Lilian   (Mrs. Silas)**                         **1884-1944**

Flower painter. She was born at Woburn, Bedfordshire in 1884, the daughter of Henry John Stannard (q.v.). She lived at Blackheath and specialised in flower and garden pictures, having one man shows at the Mendoza Gallery, 1906, 1907 and 1927. She died in 1944.

Illus: *Popular Garden Flowers [W.P. Wright, 1912].*
Exhib: B; L; RA; RBA; RCA; RI; SWA.
Colls: Newport.

**STANNUS, Anthony Carey**                                  **fl.1862-1909**

Genre, landscape and marine painter. He drew views of Cornwall but also visited Ireland and Belgium for subjects and may have made a trip to Mexico in about 1867. He is probably the brother of the architect and writer H.H. Stannus, 1840-1908.

Illus: *The King of the Cats [1903].*
Contrib: *ILN [1867].*
Exhib: BI; L; RA; RBA; RHA.
Colls: V & AM.

**STANTON, G. Clark   RSA**                                 **1822-1894**

Sculptor, painter and illustrator. He was born at Birmingham in 1832 and studied as a designer for a commercial firm and attended the Birmingham School of Art. He visited Italy for some years and returned in 1855 to settle permanently in Edinburgh. He was a prolific painter of genre subjects with an 18th century tinge to them, popular in the third quarter of the century, but also designed stained glass windows and sculpted. He was elected ARSA in 1862 and RSA in 1883 and was also Curator of the RSA Life School. He died at Edinburgh on 8 January 1894.

Contrib: *Good Words [1860]; Poems and Songs by Robert Burns [1875].*
Exhib: B; G; L; M; RSA; RSW.
Colls: Dundee; Glasgow.

**STANTON, Horace Hughes**                                  **1843-1914**

Landscape painter. He was born in 1843 and worked in Chelsea and Kensington until 1913 when he went to America. He died in New York on September 13, 1914.

Contrib: *London Society [1869].*
Exhib: B; G; GG; L; M; RA; RHA.

**STAPLES, Sir Robert Ponsonby   12th Baronet**            **1853-1943**

Painter and illustrator. He was born on 30 June 1853, the third son of Sir Nathaniel A. Staples Bt. He was educated at home, and studied at the Louvain Academy of Fine Arts, 1865-70, with Portaels in

Brussels, 1872-74 and in Dresden, 1867. Staples visited Paris in 1869 and made tours to Australia, 1879-80 and was elected RBA in 1898. He was art master at the People's Palace, Mile End Road in 1897 and was a member of the International Union. He did a considerable amount of figurative work for magazines and died on 18 October 1943.

Contrib: *ILN [1893-96]; The Sketch [1894].*
Exhib: B; G; GG; L; M; NEA; P; RA; RBA; RHA; ROI.
Colls: Witt Photo.

**STARR, Sydney**                                           **1857-1925**

Landscape and decorative artist and illustrator. He was born at Kingston-upon-Hull in 1857 and worked in St John's Wood until 1890 when he emigrated to the United States. He was a friend of Walter Sickert (q.v.) and worked up paintings after the latter's drawings. His black and white work is characterised by very pronounced vertical hatching, and some of it appeared in *The Whirlwind.* He was elected NEA and RBA in 1886 and died in New York on 3 October 1925.

Exhib: G; GG; L; M; NEA; RA; RBA; RI; ROI.
Colls: V & AM; Witt Photo.

**STAYNES, Percy Angelo   ROI**                            **1875-**

Painter, designer and illustrator. He was born in 1875 and studied at the Manchester School of Art, at the Royal College of Art and at Julian's in Paris. He worked in Bedford Park, London, 1914-48 and was elected ROI in 1916 and RI in 1935.

Illus: *Roundabout Ways [Ffrida Wolfe, 1912]; Gulliver's Voyages [1912].*
Exhib: G; RI; ROI.

**STEAVENSON, C. Herbert**                                  **fl.1900-1917**

Landscape painter at Gateshead. He published *Colliery Workmen Sketched at Work,* 1912.

**STEELE, Gourlay   RSA**                                   **1819-1894**

Animal painter. He was born in 1819 and studied at the Trustees Academy in Edinburgh under R.S. Lauder. He was appointed painter to the Highland and Agricultural Society and Animal Painter for Scotland to Queen Victoria. He became Curator of the National Gallery of Scotland and was elected ARSA in 1846 and RSA in 1859. He died at Edinburgh in 1894.

Contrib: *Poems and Songs by Robert Burns [1875].*
Exhib: L; M; RA; RSA.
Colls: Edinburgh; Witt Photo.

**STEEPLE, John**                                           **-1887**

Landscape and coastal painter. He worked in Birmingham and London and specialised in subjects of Welsh, Midlands and Sussex scenery. He was an unsuccessful candidate for the NWS in 1868 and in subsequent years.

Illus: *Through Norway With a Knapsack [Williams, 1859, AT 258].*
Exhib: B; FAS; RA; RBA; RI; RSA.
Colls: Birmingham; Manchester; V & AM.

**STEER, Philip Wilson**                                    **1860-1942**

Landscape, portrait and genre painter in oil and watercolour. He was born at Birkenhead in 1860 and studied at Gloucester School of Art and at Julian's in Paris, 1882. He was teacher of painting at the Slade School from 1895 and a member of the NEA from 1886. Steer was very impressionistic in his treatment of landscape and although it was usually the English countryside that he was painting, the feeling remains French. Most of his illustrative work is landscape although he contributed chalk drawings to the *Pall Mall.*

Contrib: *The Whirlwind [1890]; The Pall Mall Budget [1893]; The Yellow Book [1894-95]; Albermarle; Prose Fancies [Le Gallienne].*
Exhib: FAS; G; GG; L; M; NEA; P; RA; RBA; RHA; ROI; RSA; RSW.
Colls: BM; Bedford; Bradford; Exeter; Fitzwilliam; Gloucester; Leeds; Manchester; Tate; V & AM.
Bibl: R. Ironsode, *PWS,* 1943; D.S. Macoll, *PWS,* 1945.

**STEPHANOFF, Francis Phillip**      **1788-1860**

Painter and illustrator. He was born in London in 1788, the younger brother of James Stephanoff (q.v.). He exhibited with the AA from 1809 and with the OWS from 1813. He remained less well known than his brother with whom he is often confused. He contributed designs to Heath's Gallery, 1836-38 and died after suffering from poor health at West Hanham, near Bristol in 1860.

Exhib: BI; OWS; RA; RBA.
Colls: BM; Exeter; Nottingham; V & AM; Witt Photo.

**STEPHANOFF, James**   **OWS**      **c.1786-1874**

Historical painter and topographer. He was born in Brompton, London in about 1786, the elder brother of F.P. Stephanoff (q.v.). He studied for a short time from 1801 at the RA Schools and was a frequent exhibitor in London from about 1810. He concentrated principally on scriptural, poetic and legendary subjects which he treated realistically and with attention to costume and detail. He was made Historical Painter in Watercolours to King William IV in 1831 and was elected OWS in 1819. He retired from the society due to ill health in 1861, having moved to Bristol in 1850; he died there at Frederick Place, Clifton, in 1874.

Contrib: *Pyne's Royal Residences [1819]; Finden's Tableaux [1841]*.
Exhib: AA; BI; RA.
Colls: BM; Bradford; Nat. Gall; Edinburgh; V & AM.

**STEPHENSON, James**      **1828-1886**

Engraver and lithographer. He was born in Manchester on 26 November 1828 and was described by Chatto as 'a skilful engraver on steel'. He engraved all the illustrations for *Manchester As It Is,* 1839 and contributed to *Clever Boys* and *Wide Wide World*. He died on 28 May 1886.

Bibl: Chatto & Jackson, *Treatise on Wood Engraving,* 1861, p.600.

**STERNER, Albert Edward**      **1863-1946**

Genre and portrait painter, etcher and illustrator. He was born in London on 8 March 1863, the son of American parents and worked chiefly in New York. He studied at Julian's in Paris with Boulanger, Lefèvre and Gêrome, returning to the United States in 1879 and founding his own atelier in 1885. Sterner's pen drawing which was mostly done for *Harper's Magazine* is very typical of the American school, bold lines with concentration on the figures and little background detail. Sterner exhibited at the Paris Exhibition of 1900 and won a bronze medal.

Illus: *L'ennui Madame [D. Meunier]*.
Contrib: *Harper's Magazine; The Quiver [1895]; Pick-Me-Up; The English Illustrated Magazine [1896]; The Savoy [1896]; Black & White [1896]*.
Exhib: FAS.
Colls: V & AM.
Bibl: Joseph Pennell, *Pen Drawing and Pen Draughtsmen,* 1894, p.259.
See illustration (right).

**STEVENSON, Robert Louis**      **1850-1894**

Author and amateur woodcut artist. He was born in Edinburgh in 1850 and studied engineering at the university there and was admitted an advocate in 1875. Stevenson's adolescent talent for writing rapidly developed in the 1870s and he published a series of best-sellers which rapidly became classics. They included *An Inland Voyage,* 1878, *Travels with a Donkey on the Cevennes,* 1879, *Treasure Island,* 1882, *Kidnapped* and *Dr Jekyll and Mr Hyde,* 1886. He travelled to America in 1887 to recover his health and after visiting Australia, settled at Samoa in 1890 where he died in 1894. None of his illustrations were ever published during his life time.

Bibl: J. Pennell, *RLS, Illustrator,* The Studio, Vol.9, 1897, pp.17-24 illus.

**STEWART, Allan**      **1865-1951**

Military and historical painter and illustrator. He was born in Edinburgh on 11 February 1865, and educated at the Edinburgh Institution, studying art at the RSA Schools. He worked for *The Illustrated London News* from about 1895 and acted as their Special Artist in South Africa. He later accompanied King Edward VII on his Mediterranean tours for the same magazine and contributed fairy illustrations to its Christmas numbers. He worked at Kenley, Surrey

*ALBERT EDWARD STERNER 1863-1946. 'My Unwilling Neighbour.' Original drawing for illustration in* The English Illustrated Magazine. *1896. Signed with initials and dated 1896.*      Victoria and Albert Museum.

till about 1925 and then at Castle Douglas, Kircudbright. He died on 29 January 1951.

Illus: *Red-Cap Adventures [S.R. Crockett, 1908]*.
Contrib: *ILN [c.1895-1908]*.
Exhib: FAS; G; L; M; RA; RSA; RSW.

**STEYERT, Auguste**      **1830-1904**

French draughtsman and designer of book plates. He was born at Lyons in 1830 and died there in 1904.

Contrib: *The Illustrated Times [1856]*.

**STOCK, Henry John**   **RI**      **1853-1930**

Portrait, genre and imaginary painter and illustrator. He was born in Greek St, Soho on 6 December 1853 and studied at the RA Schools. He worked in Fulham until 1910 and then at Felpham, Sussex, being elected RI in 1880. He died on 4 November 1930.

Illus: *West Indian Fairy Tales [Gertude Shaw, 1912]*.
Exhib: FAS; L; M; RA; RI; ROI.
Colls: Witt Photo.

**STOCKDALE, Frederick Wilton Litchfield**      **fl.1803-1848**

Topographer. He was assistant to the Military Secretary of the East India Company until forced to resign through ill-health. He was a prolific contributor to travel works.

Illus: *Etchings . . . of Antiquities in . . . Kent [1810]; A Concise . . . Sketch of Hastings, Winchelsea and Rye [1817]; Excursions in . . . Cornwall [1824]; The Cornish Tourist [1834]*.
Contrib: *The Beauties of England and Wales [1801-13]; Antiquarian Itinerary [1818]; Ackermann's Repository [1825-28]*.
Exhib: RA.
Colls: BM; Fitzwilliam; Nat. Mus., Wales; V & AM; Witt Photo.

**STOCKDALE, W. Colebrooke**                    fl.1852-1867

Draughtsman. He specialised in buildings and sporting subjects and contributed to *The Illustrated London News* in 1852.

Exhib: RA, 1860-67.

**STOCKS, Lumb RA**                              1812-1892

Portrait draughtsman, miniaturist, illustrator and engraver. He was born at Lightcliffe on 30 November 1812 and became a pupil of Charles Cope. He settled in London in 1827 and learnt the art of engraving with Rolls for six years, becoming one of the most competent of Victorian engravers. Chatto mentions that 'Mr Stocks has considerable reputation as an engraver on steel'. He was one of the few engravers to be elected on that art to the RA, becoming ARA in 1853 and RA in 1872. Many of his works are crayon portraits and he was an assiduous engraver after Stothard's works. He died in London on 28 April 1892. He was the father of the artists, Arthur, Bernard, Katharine and Walter Fryer Stocks.

Contrib: *Ministering Children; Ministry of Life; English Yeoman.*
Exhib: RA; RBA.
Bibl: Chatto & Jackson, *Treatise on Wood Engraving,* 1861, p.600.

**STOKER, Matilda**                              fl.1880-1886

Book decorator. She worked in Dublin and London and contributed Celtic ornament to *The English Illustrated Magazine,* 1886-88.

Exhib: RHA, 1880-84.

**STOKES, Adrian Scott RA ARWS**                1854-1935

Landscape painter in oil and watercolour and tempera, occasional illustrator. He was born at Southport in 1854 and was educated at the Liverpool Institute and studied at the RA Schools, 1872-75 and in Paris under Dagnan Bouveret, 1885-86. Stokes travelled widely in Europe and wrote extensively on Renaissance art, he exhibited work at the major exhibitions of Paris, 1889 and Chicago and two of his paintings were acquired by the Chantrey Bequest, 1888 and 1903. He was elected ROI, 1888, ARA, 1910 and RA, 1919, his talent as a watercolourist being recognised by his election as RWS in 1926 and VPRWS in 1933. He died in London on 30 November 1935.

His wife, Marianne Stokes (q.v.), née Preindlsberger, 1855-1927 was also an artist. A joint exhibition of their work was held at the FAS in 1900.

Publ: *Landscape Painting [1925]; Pansy's Flour-Bin [1880]; Hungary [1909].*
Illus: *The Three Brides [Charlotte M. Yonge]; The Clever Woman Of The Family [Charlotte M. Yonge]; Tyrol and its People [C. Holland, 1909].*
Exhib: B; FAS; G; GG; L; M; NEA; New Gall; RA; RBA; RHA; RI; ROI; RSA; RSW; RWS.
Colls: V & AM.
See illustration (below).

*ADRIAN SCOTT STOKES RA ARWS 1854-1935. 'Mackarel Lane.' Original drawing for illustration to* The Clever Woman of the Family *by Charlotte M. Yonge. Indian ink. 3¹/2ins. x 4⁷/8ins. (8.9cm x 12.4cm).*                    Victoria and Albert Museum

**STOKES, George Vernon**                    **1873-1954**
Landscape and animal painter and etcher. He was born in London on 1 January 1873 and after a private education specialised in black and white illustration and was elected ARBA in 1923 and RBA in 1929. He worked at Carlisle, 1911-14 and latterly at Deal, dying there in 1954.

Publ: *Colour Etchings in Two Printings; How to Draw and Paint Dogs.*
Contrib: *The Gentlewoman [c.1890]; Punch [1905 (dogs)]; ILN [1915]; The Graphic; The Sphere.*
Exhib: FAS; New Gall; RA; RBA; RI; RMS.
Colls: Carlisle.

**STOKES, Marianne   (née Preindlesberger)**    **1855-1927**
Portrait and biblical painter. She was born in Southern Austria in 1855 and studied under Lindenschmidt in Munich and worked at Graz. She married Adrian Stokes, RWS (q.v.) and died in London in 1927. She was elected NEA in 1887 and ASWA the same year, becoming ARWS in 1923.

Contrib: *The Graphic [1886].*
Exhib: B; FAS; G; GG; L; M; NEA; New Gall; RA; RBA; ROI; RWS; SWA.

**STONE, Frank   ARA**                    **1800-1859**
Figure painter and illustrator. He was born in Manchester in 1800 and began life as a cotton spinner before setting up for himself as a painter. He settled in London in 1831 and began to make illustrations for the albums and watercolours for the dealer Roberts. He was elected OWS in 1842 but resigned in 1846 in order to be elected an ARA in 1851. He was a close friend of Charles Dickens and his circle and acted with him. Stone's son Marcus (q.v.) was more successful than his father, who died in London in 1859.

Illus: *The Haunted Man [Charles Dickens, 1848].*
Contrib: *Heath's Gallery [1836].*
Exhib: BI; OWS; RA; RBA.
Colls: Manchester; NPG; V & AM; Witt Photo.
Bibl: *The Connoisseur*, Vol.62, 1922.

**STONE, Marcus   RA**                    **1840-1921**
Genre painter and illustrator. He was born in London on 4 July 1840, the second son of Frank Stone, ARA (q.v.). He studied art under his father and began exhibiting at the RA in 1858, specialising in figure subjects in interiors. He was elected ARA in 1877 and RA in 1887. He died in London on 24 March 1921.

Illus: *Great Expectations [Charles Dickens, 1860-61]; Our Mutual Friend [Charles Dickens, 1865].*
Contrib: *London Society [1863-64]; The Sunday Magazine [1865]; Touches of Nature by Eminent Artists [1866]; The Graphic [1872]; The Cornhill Magazine [1873]; ILN [1873].*
Exhib: B; FAS; G; L; M; RA.
Colls: BM; Manchester; V & AM; Witt Photo.
Bibl: *Art Annual*, 1896.

**STONEY, Thomas Butler**                    **fl.1899-1912**
Coastal painter and illustrator. He worked in London in 1899 and 1912 and at Portland, Co. Tipperary in 1910. With John Hassall (q.v.) he illustrated *The Princess and The Dragon*, 1908.

Exhib: B; L; NEA; P; RA; RHA.

**STONHOUSE, Charles**                    **fl.1833-1865**
Painter and engraver. He specialised in genre and literary subjects and worked in Bloomsbury from 1833 to 1865. He contributed to *The Deserted Village*, Etching Club, 1841.

Exhib: BI; RA.

**STOPFORD, Robert Lowe**                    **1813-1898**
Marine and view painter and lithographer. He was born at Dublin in 1813 and became a drawing-master in Cork where he worked as Special Artist for *The Illustrated London News*. His son was W.H. Stopford, 1842-90. He died at Cork on 2 February 1898.

Contrib: *The Illustrated Times [1859 (Ireland)].*

**STORER, Henry Sargant**                    **1797-1837**
Topographer, draughtsman and engraver. He was born in 1797, the son of James Sargant Storer (q.v.) with whom he collaborated on many books. He worked at Cambridge with his father but moved to London and died there on 8 January 1837.

Exhib: RA.

**STORER, James Sargant**                    **1771-1853**
Topographer, draughtsman and engraver. He was born in Cambridge in 1771 and practised there, his chief works being illustrative surveys of the medieval buildings and the cathedrals of England. 'The Messrs Storer had not the artistic skill of the artists employed by Ackermann, and moreover their drawings are on a very small scale. On the other hand, the general accuracy of their representations of existing buildings induces us to conclude that those which have been destroyed were delineated with equal accuracy.' (Willis & Clark, *Arch. Hist. of Univ. of Cambridge,* Vol.1, p.128.) The elder Storer died in London in 1853.

Illus: *Cathedrals of Great Britain [1823-24]; Illustrations of Cambridge [1827-32]; Britton's Cathedrals [1832-36]; The Cambridge Almanac [1832]; Cantabrigia Illustrata [1835]; Collegiorum portae apud Cantabrigium [1837]; Delineations of Fountains Abbey; Delineations of the Chapel of Kings College; Delineations of Trinity College.*

**STOREY, George Adolphus   RA**                    **1834-1919**
Genre and portrait painter and illustrator. He was born in London on 7 January 1834 and educated in Paris, where he studied paintings and mathematics under Professor M. Morand. He returned to London and spent some time with an architect before entering J.M. Leigh's Art School in Newman Street. He subsequently became a student at the RA Schools in 1854 and came strongly under the influence of the Pre-Raphaelites. He worked in Hampstead and St John's Wood where he was a founder-member of the Clique. He was elected ARA in 1876 and RA in 1914, having been Professor of Perspective from 1900 to 1919. He died on 29 July 1919.

Publ: *Sketches from Memory [1899]; Theory and Practice of Perspective [1910].*
Illus: *Homely Ballads and Old-Fashioned Poems [1880].*
Contrib: *Punch [1882]; The Ludgate Monthly [1892]; ILN [1893].*
Exhib: B; G; L; M; RA; RI; ROI; RSA.
Bibl: *AJ*, 1875; A.M. Eyre, *Saint Johns Wood*, 1913, pp.181-199; *Apollo*, June, 1964; J. Maas, *Victorian Painters*, 1970, p.13.

**STOTHARD, Charles Alfred**                    **1786-1821**
Painter and illustrator. He was born in London on 5 July 1786, the son of Thomas Stothard, RA (q.v.) and attended the RA Schools in 1807. He made a tour of Northern England in 1815, gathering material for illustrating Lyson's *Magna Britannia*. Having some skill as a classical draughtsman, he was made Draughtsman to the Society of Antiquaries and in 1816 visited Bayeux to draw the tapestry. He married the novelist Anna Eliza Bray who wrote biographies of both him and his father. He died at Beerferris, Devonshire on 27 May 1821 as the result of an accident in France.

Illus: *Monumental Effigies of Great Britain [1817]; Letters Written During a Tour Through Normandy, Brittany and Other Parts of France, 1820 [by Mrs CAS, AT 88]; Painted Chamber [J.G. Rokewode, 1842, AL 69].*
Contrib: *Lyson's Devonshire [1822].*
Exhib: RA.
Colls: BM.
Bibl: Mrs A.E. Bray, *Memoirs of CAS*, 1823; Mrs E.A. Bray, *Autobiography*, 1889.

**STOTHARD, Robert T.   FSA**                    **fl.1821-1857**
Miniature painter. He worked in London and there is an undated illustration in the V & A Museum for Scott's *Lady of the Lake* by this artist.

Exhib: BI.

**STOTHARD, Thomas   RA**                    **1755-1834**
Illustrator. He was born in London in 1755 but on being left an orphan he was brought up in Yorkshire and educated in Tadcaster. He began his career as a silk pattern designer, but went to London and entered the RA Schools in 1777, where he attracted the notice of

John Flaxman (q.v.). He had already begun to design book illustrations by 1779, doing work for *The Town and Country Magazine,* on Bell's *British Poets* and Harrison's *Novelists Magazines.* In the period 1780-83, Stothard was engaged on shop-cards, pocket-books and other ephemera at the same time studying Dürer prints and becoming a friend of William Blake (q.v.). He was elected ARA in 1785 and RA in 1794, following this with an important mural commission at Burghley House for Lord Exeter. Stothard was by far the most successful and distinguished illustrator of his day, his total contributions are estimated to be over five thousand, most of them figure subjects which the artist took from nature. His work is usually well finished, generally in monochrome wash but sometimes in full watercolours. He died on 27 April 1834.

Illus: *Peregrine Pickle [1781]; Clarissa [1784]; Robinson Crusoe [1790]; Pilgrims Progress [1789]; Young's Night Thoughts [1802]; Shakespeare's Works [1802]; The Spectator [1803]; Poems of Burns [1809]; Tales From Landlord [1820]; Cupid and Pysche [1820]; The Songs of Burns [1824]; Walton's Angler [1825]; Dramatic Works of Shakespeare [1826]; The Surprising Adventures of Baron Munchausen [1826];* etc.
Contrib: *The Novelists Magazine [1780-83]; The Poetical Magazine; Macklin's Bible [1791]; Boydell's Shakespeare; Bell's British Theatre; The Bijou [1828]; The Keepsake [1828-30];* etc.
Exhib: BI; RA; RBA.
Colls: Ashmolean; Birkenhead; BM; Fitzwilliam; Manchester; Nóttingham; Tate; V & AM; Witt Photo.
Bibl: Mrs A.E. Bray, *Life of TS,* 1851; *Memorial to TS,* 1867-68, V & AM MSS; A. Dobson, *Eighteenth Century Vignettes,* 1897; A.C. Coxhead, *TS,* 1906; I. Williams, *Early Eng. Watercolours,* 1952, pp.129-133; M. Hardie, *Watercol. Paint. in Brit.,* Vol.I, 1966, pp. 138-141 illus.

## STOTT, William R.S.        fl.1905-1934
Portrait and landscape painter and illustrator. He worked in Chelsea for most of his life, but worked at Aberdeen in 1909. He was employed by *The Graphic* from 1903 to 1923 to illustrate royal and public events.

Illus: *Kidnapped [R.L. Stevenson, c.1913].*
Exhib: G; L; RA; RHA.
Colls: Witt Photo.

## STOWERS, Thomas        fl.1778-1814
Illustrator. He may have been a friend of Rowlandson, but his figure work is more like that of J.H. Mortimer. He exhibited at the BI, RA and OWS.

## STOWERS, T. Gordon        fl.1880-1894
Portrait painter. He worked in London and contributed to *Punch,* 1880.

Exhib: B; RA; RBA.

## STRANG, Ian   RE        1886-1952
Painter and etcher. He was born in 1886, the eldest son of William Strang, RA (q.v.) and was educated at Merchant Taylors' School before studying art at the Slade School, 1902-6 and at Julian's, Paris, 1906-8. He travelled in France, Belgium, Sicily, Spain and Italy, where he became a member of the Faculty of the British School at Rome. He was elected ARE in 1926 and RE in 1930. He died at Wavendon, Bucks in 1952.

Publ: *The Students Book of Etching [1937]; Town and Country in Southern France [Frances Strang, 1937].*
Exhib: FAS; G; L; M; NEA; RA; RE; RHA; RSA.
Colls: V & AM.

## STRANG, William   RA        1859-1921
Painter and etcher. He was born at Dumbarton on 13 February 1859 and was educated at Dumbarton Academy and studied at the Slade School. He worked in London from 1875, carrying out some book illustrations but issuing a series of etchings notable for their imaginative power and insight and their concern with a wide range of subjects from poetry to social realism. He was elected RE in 1881 and ARA and RA in 1906 and 1921. He was President of the International Society of Sculptors, Painters and Gravers from 1918 to 1921, was LL.D. of Glasgow University, 1909 and a medallist of the Paris Exhibition of 1897. Strang's artistic debt is to the master engravers like Rembrandt, Forain and Daumier, but also to Alphonse Legros with whom he studied. He died on 12 April 1921.

Illus: *The Earth Friend [1892]; Death and the Ploughman's Wife [1894]; Nathan the Wise [1894]; The Ballad of Hadji [Ian Hamilton, 1894]; Baron Munchausen [1895]; Pilgrim's Progress [1895]; Christ Upon the Hill [1895]; Sinbad the Sailor and Ali Baba [1896, with J.B. Clark]; Milton's Paradise Lost [1896]; A Book of Ballads [Alice Sargant, 1898]; A Book of Giants [1898];*

*WILLIAM STRANG RA 1859-1921. 'The Fair Ground.' Etching. Signed and dated 1892. 7¾ins. x 9¾ins. (19.7cm x 24.8cm).*
Author's Collection

*Western Flanders [Laurence Binyon, 1899]; Etchings From Rudyard Kipling [1901]; The Praise of Folie [1901]; Walton's The Compleat Angler [1902]; Tam o'Shanter [Burns, 1902]; The Rime of the Ancient Mariner [Coleridge, 1902]; Thirty Etchings of Don Quixote [1903].*
Contrib: *The English Illustrated Magazine [1890-91]; The Yellow Book [1895]; The Dome [1898-1900].*
Exhib: FAS; G; GG; L; M; NEA; P; RA; RE; RHA; RSA.
Colls: Ashmolean; Leeds; V & AM; Witt Photo.
Bibl: F. Sedmore, *Frank Short & WS,* English Illustrated Magazine, Vol.8, 1890-91, pp.457-466; R.E.D. Sketchley, *Eng. Bk. Illus.,* 1903, pp.58, 154.
See illustrations (below and p.468).

*WILLIAM STRANG RA 1859-1921. Original drawing for illustration to* The Surprising Adventures of Baron Manchausen, *1895. Ink and bodycolour. Signed with intials.* 8⁵/8ins. x 6¹/8ins. (21.3cm x 15.5cm). Victoria and Albert Museum

**STRASYNSKI, Leonard Ludwik**　　　　**1828-1889**

Artist and lithographer. He was born on 11 January 1828 at Tokarowka, Poland and studied art at the St Petersburg Academy, 1847-55. He then travelled to Berlin, Paris, Brussels and Rome and was a member of the Academies of both Rome and St Petersburg. He appears to have been in London in 1867-68 when he designed initial letters for *London Society.* He died at Shitomir on 4 February 1889.

Contrib: *Punch [1867-68]; Once A Week [1867].*

**STRATTON, Helen**　　　　**fl.1892-1925**

Portrait and figure painter and illustrator. She worked in Kensington and Chelsea and specialised in children's stories and fairy tales.

Illus: *Songs For Little People [1896]; Tales From Hans Andersen [1896]; Beyond the Border [W.D. Campbell, 1898]; The Fairy Tales of Hans Christian Andersen [1899].*
Contrib: *Arabian Nights [1899].*
Exhib: L; RA; RBA; RHA; RI; SWA.
Colls: Witt Photo.
Bibl: R.E.D. Sketchley, *Eng. Bk. Illus.,* 1903, pp.116, 172.

**STREATFIELD, Rev. Thomas　FSA**　　**1777-1848**

Topographer and heraldic artist and illustrator. He was born in London in 1777 and educated at Oriel College, Oxford, becoming curate of Long Ditton and Tatsfield, Surrey and Chaplain to the Duke of Kent. He lived at Westerham from 1822 and collected material for a history of Kent, he died there in 1848.

Illus: *The Bridal of Armagnac [1823]; Excerpta Cantiana [1836]; Lympsfield and its Environs [1839]; Hasted's History of Kent, corrected and enlarged [1886].*
Contrib: *The Copper Plate Magazine [1792-1802]; Britton's Beauties of England and Wales [1813].*
Exhib: RA, 1800.
Colls: BM; Greenwich.

**STRETCH, Matt**　　　　**fl.1880-1896**

Figure and humorous artist. He worked for *The Gentlewoman* and for *Fun,* 1886-96 and *Moonshine,* 1891.

Exhib: RHA, 1880.

**STRINGER, Agnes**　　　　**fl.1900-1908**

Illustrator. She worked at Sunbury and Putney and illustrated with D. Andrewes (q.v.) *The Little Maid Who Danced To Every Mood,* 1908.

Exhib: RBA; SWA.

**STRONG, Joseph D.**　　　　**1852-1900**

American illustrator. He was born at Bridgeport, Connecticut in 1852 and studied in California and Munich under Piloty before travelling in the South Seas. He died in San Francisco on 5 April 1900.

Illus: *The Silverardo Squatters [R.L. Stevenson, 1897].*

**STRUBE, Sidney**　　　　**1891-1956**

Artist. There is a pencil and watercolour caricature by this artist in the V & A Museum, signed and dated 1916.

**STRUTT, Alfred William　RE FRGS**　　**1856-1924**

Animal, figure and landscape painter and illustrator. He was born at Tarahaki, New Zealand in 1856, the son of William Strutt, the genre painter, (q.v.) under whom he studied. He studied at South Kensington and exhibited in Paris and in Colonial exhibitions. He accompanied King Edward VII as official artist on a hunting trip to Scandinavia and was an occasional magazine illustrator. He was elected RBA in 1888 and ARE in 1889. He died at Wadhurst, Sussex on 2 March 1924.

Contrib: *ILN [1894 (rustic)].*
Exhib: FAS; L; M; RA; RBA; RCA; RE; RHA; RI; ROI; RSA; RWS.

**STRUTT, Jacob George**　　　　**1790-1864**

Painter of portraits and forests, etcher. He was born in 1790 and worked in London until 1831 when he moved to Lausanne and Rome. He died in Rome in 1864.

Illus: *Bury St Edmunds illustrated [1821]; Sylva Britannica [1822]; Deliciae Sylvarum [1828].*

## STRUTT, William                                    1827-1915

Animal and genre painter. He was born at Teignmouth, Devon in 1827, the grandson of Joseph Strutt, the antiquary and artist. He studied in Paris and went to Australia in 1850 where he founded the *Australian Journal* and *The Illustrated Australian Magazine.* He worked in New Zealand from 1856 and returned to England in 1862 and died at Wadhurst, Sussex in 1915. His son was A.E. Strutt (q.v.). He was elected RBA in 1891.

Exhib: L; M; RA; RBA; ROI.

## STUDDY, G.E.                                    1878-1925

Illustrator. He was born in Devonshire in 1878 and after studying at Heatherley's, specialised in drawings of children and contributed to *Punch,* in 1902 and to *The Graphic* in 1910 and 1912.

Colls: Witt Photo.

## 'STUFF'   See WRIGHT, H.C. Seppings.

## STURGESS, John                                    fl.1875-1903

Sporting painter and illustrator. He worked in London and was the principal hunting and racing artist for *The Illustrated London News* for about ten years from 1875. His drawings are accurate though somewhat wooden and he was among the first black and white artists to go wholeheartedly into advertising with his hunting sketches for Ellerman's Embrocation.

Illus: *The Magic Jacket [Nat Gould, 1896].*
Contrib: *ILN [1875-97]; The English Illustrated Magazine [1884]; The Sporting & Dramatic News [1890].*
Exhib: RBA; RHA.
Colls: V & AM; Witt Photo.

*EDMUND JOSEPH SULLIVAN RWS 1869-1933. 'Night and Morning.' Original drawing for unidentified magazine illustration. Chalk and wash. Indistinctly signed and dated 1 Jan 1903. 14ins. x 10ins. (35.6cm x 25.4cm).*
Author's Collection.

HERR DIOGENES

*EDMUND JOSEPH SULLIVAN RWS 1869-1933. 'Herr Diogenes.' Illustration for* Sartor Resartus *by Thomas Carlyle, 1898.*

## STYCHE, Frank                                    fl.1913-1925

Black and white figure artist. He worked at Hendon and Golders Green and contributed to *London Opinion,* 1913.

## SULLIVAN, Edmund Joseph   RWS                  1869-1933

Painter, watercolourist and illustrator. He was born in London in 1869, the son and pupil of M. Sullivan, an artist working at Hastings. He studied under his father and was in 1889, one of the new recruits along with Dean and Hartrick (qq.v.) for Thomas's new venture *The Daily Graphic.* From then onwards Sullivan established himself as one of the foremost illustrators of his time, although eclipsed by his contemporaries Rackham and Dulac. He was a superb figure draughtsman, especially in chalks and had a strong and inventive imagination. Hartrick later said of his colleague 'he could do anything with a pen and do it with distinction,' *Sullivan,* by Thorpe, p.14. Sullivan was a careful textual illustrator, his work on such books as *Sartor Resartus* are very accurately thought out, the decorative element in the design beautifully balanced. His preliminary sketches are very vivid and dramatic and sometimes they lose their greatest impact when completed as a finished drawing, but they never lack virtuosity. Sullivan had two main drawing styles, a very clear black and white one, used with most consistency about 1900 for books and a more atmospheric treatment with washes and swirling chalk lines, closer to the rough working notes. Less well known is his character study work, among the best of these being a series of Gloucestershire portraits which were purchased by the National Art Collections Fund for the BM.

Sullivan's lasting influence was probably not so strong in his books

*EDMUND JOSEPH SULLIVAN RWS 1869-1933. 'Airy Fairy Lilian.' Original drawing for illustration to* Dreams of Fair
Women *by Alfred Tennyson, 1900. Pen and ink. Signed and dated '99. 9ins. x 6ins. (22.9cm x 15.2cm).*

Author's Collection

as in his teaching. He was lecturer on Book Illustration and Lithography at the Goldsmith College for a number of years and was examiner in art for the Board of Education. He wrote two important text books on his subject. He was elected ARWS in 1903 and ARE in 1925. He died in London on 17 April 1933. His brother was J.F. Sullivan (q.v.).

Publ: *Line, an Art Study* [1921]; *The Art of Illustration* [1922].
Illus: *Lavengro* [Borrow, 1896]; *Tom Brown's School Days* [1896]; *The Compleat Angler* [1896]; *The Pirate and Three Cutters* [Marryat, 1897]; *Sartor Resartus* [Carlyle, 1898]; *Maud* [Tennyson, 1900]; *A Dream of Fair Women* [1900]; *The Pilgrim's Progress* [1901]; *Poems by R. Burns* [1901]; *A Citizen of the World* [1904]; *A Modern Utopia* [H.G. Wells, 1905]; *Sintram and His Companions* [1908]; *The French Revolution* [1910]; *The Rubaiyat of Omar Khayyam* [1913]; *The Vicar of Wakefield* [1914]; *The Kaiser's Garland* [1915]; *Legal and Other Lyrics* [G. Outram, 1916].

Contrib: *The Graphic* [1889]; *The Daily Graphic* [1890-]; *The English Illustrated Magazine* [1891-94]; *The Pall Mall Budget* [1893]; *The Yellow Book* [1894]; *The Daily Chronicle* [1895]; *The New Budget* [1895]; *A London Garland* [W.E. Henley, 1895]; *Good Words* [1896]; *The Lady's Pictorial* [1898]; *The Pall Mall Gazette* [1899]; *Black & White* [1900]; *Natural History of Selborne* [Gilbert White, 1900-1]; *The Old Court Suburbs* [Leigh Hunt, 1902]; *The Penny Illustrated Paper*; *The Pall Mall Magazine*; *The Gentlewoman*; *The Ludgate Monthly*; *The Windsor Magazine*; *Pearson's Magazine*; *Punch* [c.1920].
Exhib: FAS; G; L; NEA; RA; RE; RHA; RSA; RSW.
Colls: Ashmolean; BM; Bradford; V & AM; Witt Photo.
Bibl: *The Studio*, Winter No., 1900-1, pp.28-29 illus.; R.E.D. Sketchley, *Eng. Bk. Illus.*, 1903, pp.15, 74, 77, 155; *Modern Book Illustrators and Their Work*, Studio, 1914; J. Thorpe, *EJS*, 1948; B. Peppin, *Fantasy Book Illustration*, 1975, pp.98-99 illus.; Gordon N. Ray, *The Illustrator and The Book in England*, 1976, pp.186-193 allus.
See illustrations (pp.470, 471).

JAMES FRANK SULLIVAN 1853-1936. *'The Artist As He Should Be.'* Original drawings for illustration to *Fun*, 10 June 1885. Pen and ink. One signed with monogram. 4ins. x 10ins. (10.2cm x 25.4cm). Author's Collection

He had that sense of delicacy! His corn hurt him dreadfully, till he said "I will cut it". Then it flashed upon him that it would involve looking upon his toe in a state of nudity! He crimsoned to the roots of his hair (an asterisk shows position of corn).

For a while he contemplates cutting the corn from the outside.

With a strong effort against the innate delicacy inseparable from the pure-minded, he forced himself to remove the slipper.

Then — but with what mental torture! the sock. But the sense of impropriety was fearful.

But he steeled himself, Ah, how easy it is to lose all shame when once we have overstepped the bounds! And as he was about to operate HIS LANDLADY CAME IN!

**SULLIVAN, G.M.**
Contributor of humorous figure subjects to *Punch,* 1908.

**SULLIVAN, James Frank**       **1853-1936**
Draughtsman, illustrator and author. He was born in 1853, the son of M. Sullivan, an artist working at Hastings, and elder brother of E.J. Sullivan (q.v.). He went to the South Kensington Schools and began to work for the leading periodicals from about 1878. His greatest success was through the pages of *Fun,* where he was resident illustrator for about twenty-four years. Sullivan favoured the strip story cartoon and created a popular character 'The British Working Man' who features in issue after issue of his magazines. The main character is conceived in traditional cartoon idiom of small body and large head but is always very well drawn. Sullivan died in London on 5 May 1936.

Contrib: *Fun [1878-1901]; Black & White [1891]; The Strand Magazine [1891]; The Idler [1892]; The Butterfly [1893]; Lady's Pictorial [1893]; Punch [1893-94, 1905]; The Sketch [1893]; St Pauls [1894]; The Minister [1895]; The New Budget [1895]; Pearson's Magazine [1896]; Lika Joko; Pick-Me-Up; Cassell's Saturday Journal; Cassell's Family Magazine.*
Exhib: FAS; RBA.
Colls: Author; V & AM.
Bibl: *The Studio,* Winter No., 1900-1, p.76 illus.
See illustrations (pp.85, 472).

**SULMAN, T.**       **fl.1855-1890**
Architectural illustrator. This artist specialised in topographical views and panoramas and was architectural illustrator for *The Illustrated London News* from 1859 to 1888. His work was still appearing in 1890. He was described by Chatto as expert in 'Ornamental Borders and Vignettes'.

Illus: *Kalidasa-Sakoontala [Indian Drama, Monier Williams, 1855].*
Contrib: *Churchman's Family Magazine [1863]; The Illustrated Times [1860-65]; Once A Week [1867]; Good Words For The Young [1869]; The Boy's Own Paper [1882]; Lalla Rookh.*
Bibl: Chatto & Jackson, 1861, p.600.

**SUMMERS, W.**
Caricaturist. He published a series of illustrations entitled *Black Jokes,* 1834, AL 322.

**SUMNER, George Heywood Maunoir**       **1853-1940**
Etcher and archaeologist. He was born in 1853 and was a leading figure in the revival of wood engraving in the 1880s and 1890s. His work which is associated with the countryside, has a lyrical quality about it owing something to Blake and Palmer, his decorative illustration is somewhat akin to Morris. He died in 1940.

Illus: *The Itchen Valley [1881]; The Avon From Naxby to Tewkesbury [1882]; Epping Forest [1884]; Sintram and His Companions [1883]; Undine [1888]; The Besom Maker [1888]; Jacob and the Raven [1896].*
Contrib: *The English Illustrated Magazine [1883-86].*
Exhib: G; RA; RE.

Bibl: *The Studio,* Winter No., 1900-1, p.50 illus.; R.E.D. Sketchley, *Eng. Bk. Illus.,* 1903, pp.6, 130. Richard Bassett, *C.L.* 28 Sept. 1978.
See illustration (below).

**SUMNER, Margaret L.**       **fl.1882-1914**
Landscape painter and illustrator. She was working at Grasmere in 1898 and contributed to *The Yellow Book* in 1895.
Exhib: L.

**SUTCLIFFE, John E.**       **-1923**
Figure painter and illustrator. He worked in London, Bushey and Richmond and was married to the domestic painter E. Earnshaw. He contributed to *The Illustrated London News,* Christmas Number, 1916. He was elected ROI in 1920 and died in 1923.
Exhib: RA; RBA; RI; ROI.

**SUTHERLAND, Elizabeth Duchess of**       **1765-1839**
Amateur artist. She was born in 1765, the daughter and heir of the 18th Earl of Sutherland and married in 1785 the 1st Duke of Sutherland. Her claim to the title of Countess was allowed by the House of Lords. She was a pupil of Girtin and many of her watercolours of Continental scenes were engraved. Her *Etchings of the Orkney Isles* and *Views on the Northern and Western Coasts of Sutherland,* were privately printed in 1807.

**SWAINSON, William**       **1789-1855**
Zoological illustrator. He travelled widely in Europe and formed a natural history collection. He lived in Brazil from 1816 to 1818 and after returning to England in 1819, he finally emigrated to New Zealand in 1837, dying at Hutt Valley in 1855. He illustrated many of his own works.

Illus: *Zoological Illustrations [1820-23]; Ornithological Drawings, Birds of Brazil [1834-35]; Birds of Western Africa [Sir J. Richardson, 1837].*

**SWAN, Mary E.**       **1889-1898**
Fruit and flower painter. She worked in Bromley and London and drew the title page for *Poems by Emily H. Hickey,* 1895-96.
Exhib: B; FAS; L; New Gall; RA; ROI.

**SWETE, Rev. John**       **c.1752-1821**
Topographer. He was educated at University College, Oxford and became Prebendary of Exeter in 1781, the majority of his drawings being of Devonshire. He settled at Oxton House near Exeter, but made sketching tours to Scotland and Cumberland as well as to Switzerland and Italy, 1816. An important group of his drawings of country houses was sold at Christie's on 15 July 1976.

Contrib: *Antiquarian and Topographical Cabinet [1808]; Britton's Beauties of England and Wales [1813].*
Colls: Exeter.

*GEORGE HEYWOOD MAUNOIR SUMNER 1853-1940. Head piece for* The English Illustrated Magazine, *1883. Wood engraving.*

473

**SYDDALL, Joseph**                        fl.1898-1910
Portrait and genre painter. He was trained at the Herkomer School,
Bushey and worked from 1898 to 1910 at Chesterfield. He
contributed illustrations with Sir H. von Herkomer (q.v.) to *Tess of
the D'Urbevilles* when serialised in *The Graphic*, 1891.

**SYKES, Charles 'Rilette'**                1875-1950
Sculptor and illustrator. He was born in 1875 and worked in London
as a poster designer and magazine illustrator, contributing to *The
Sunday Dispatch* and *Woman* under the name of 'Rilette'. He also
designed De Reske cigarette advertisements, fashion plates and in
1911 the mascot for the Rolls Royce car that is still in use. He was
responsible for designing the Ascot race cups from 1926.

Exhib: G; L; RA; RI.
Colls: V & AM.

**SYKES, Godfrey**                          1824-1866
Landscape and interior painter and designer. He was born at Malton in
1824 and studied at the Government School of Design at Sheffield,
while serving his apprenticeship to an engraver. He subsequently
became a teacher in the School under Young Mitchell and painted
scenes of mills and forges. He worked with Alfred Stevens on coming
to London and then with Captain Fowke on the decoration of the
South Kensington Museum and the Horticultural Gardens. Linton
who much admired his work says that he 'was starved on a low salary'
and in consequence died of consumption in 1866. A memorial
exhibition was held at South Kensington in the summer of 1866.

Contrib: *Cornhill Magazine [1860 (first cover design)]*.
Exhib: RA.
Colls: Manchester; V & AM.
Bibl: W.J. Linton, *Memoirs*, 1895, p.182.
See illustration (right).

**SYMES, Ivor I. J.**                        fl.1899-1937
Genre painter and illustrator. He studied at the Herkomer School,
Bushey and married Mabel Gear, RI. He worked at Tadley, Hants.

Contrib: *The Graphic [1906]*.
Exhib: RA; ROI.

**SYMINGTON, J. Ayton**                      fl.1890-1908
Illustrator. He specialised in adventure stories and contributed to
numerous magazines.

Illus: *Tom Cringle's Log [Michael Scott, 1895]; Peter Simple [Captain Marryat,
1895]; The Wonderful Wapentake [J.S. Fletcher, 1896]; The Enchanting North
[J.S. Fletcher, 1908]*.
Contrib: *The Sporting & Dramatic News [1890]; Good Words [1893]; Chums;
The Windsor Magazine*.

**SYMONS, William Christian**                1845-1911
Portrait, genre, landscape and still-life painter and illustrator. He was
born in London in 1845 and studied at the Lambeth School of Art
and the RA Schools. He worked as a stained-glass designer and
produced the controversial mosaics for the new Westminster
Cathedral. He was elected RBA but resigned with Whistler in 1888
and later worked in Newlyn and Battle, dying in London in 1911. A
memorial exhibition was held by the Goupil Gallery in 1912.

Contrib: *The Graphic [1885]; The Strand Magazine [1891]; Good Words
[1898]; The Wide World Magazine [1898]*.
Exhib: B; G; L; M; NEA; RA; RBA; RHA; RI; ROI.
Colls: BM.

**SYNGE, Edward Millington**                 1860-1913
Painter and etcher. He was born at Great Malvern in 1860 and
educated at Norwich Grammar School and Trinity College,
Cambridge. He became a land agent and practised etching in his spare
time, being elected ARE in 1898. He devoted himself entirely to art
from 1901 and travelled in Italy and Spain. He died in 1913.

Illus: *Romantic Cities of Provence [A.M. Caird, 1906]*.
Exhib: G; L; RA; RE; RHA.

*GODFREY SYKES 1824-1866. Original drawing for the first cover of The
Cornhill Magazine, 1860. Pen. 7½ins. x 4⅝ins. (19.1cm x 11.7cm).*
                                    Victoria and Albert Museum

**SYRETT, Nellie or Netta**
Illustrator. Artist drawing in the black and white style of L. Housman
(q.v.). She contributed to *The Yellow Book* and *The Quarto*, 1896.
Exhib: SWA.

**TABER, I.W.**
Illustrator. He supplied the drawings for *Captains Courageous* by Rudyard Kipling, 1908.

**TADEMA**  See Sir L. ALMA- and Lady L.T. ALMA-

**TAFFS, Charles H.**　　　　　　　　　　　**fl.1894-1911**
Black and white artist. He worked in Clapham, London and illustrated for the leading magazines.

Contrib: *St Pauls [1894]; Lady's Pictorial [1895-98]; The Quiver [1895]; The New Budget [1895]; Pick-Me-Up [1897]; Sketchy Bits; The Royal Magazine; The English Illustrated Magazine [1897]; ILN [1899, 1908]; The Graphic [1910-11].*
Exhib: RA.

**TARLING, G.T.**　　　　　　　　　　　**fl.1894-1907**
Artist and illustrator. He was a member of the Birmingham Guild of Handicraft in 1907.

Contrib: *The Quest [1894-96].*

**TARLTON, J.**　　　　　　　　　　　**fl.1872-1875**
Wood engraver and illustrator. He worked in London and contributed to *The Illustrated London News*, 1874-75.

**TARRANT, Percy**　　　　　　　　　　　**fl.1881-1930**
Landscape, coastal and figure painter and illustrator. He worked in South London and then at Leatherhead and Gomshall, Surrey.

Illus: *Tom's Boy [Chambers, 1901].*
Contrib: *ILN [1884-89]; The Quiver [1890]; Black & White [1891]; Cassell's Family Magazine; The Girl's Own Paper; The Graphic [1911].*
Exhib: B; L; RA; RBA; RI; ROI.

**TATHAM, Helen S.**　　　　　　　　　　　**fl.1878-1891**
Landscape painter and illustrator. She worked at Shanklin, Isle of Wight and illustrated a children's book *Little Margaret's Ride*, 1878.

Exhib: B; L; M; RA; RBA; SWA.

**TATTERSALL, George**　　　　　　　　　　　**1817-1852**
Architectural and sporting illustrator. He contributed to *Tattersall's English Race Horses*, c.1841, under the name of 'Wildrake'.

Exhib: RA, 1840-48.
Colls: Witt Photo.

**TAVERNER, J.**
Illustrator. Contributed railway scenes to *The Graphic*, 1870.

**TAYLER, John Frederick  RWS**　　　　　　　　　　　**1802-1889**
Landscape and figure painter, etcher and illustrator. He was born at Boreham Wood, Hertfordshire in 1802, the son of an impoverished squire and was educated at Eton and Harrow. He was intended for the Church but instead attended art classes at Sass's and the RA Schools and studied in Paris under Horace Vernet, sharing rooms with R.P. Bonington. He worked with Samuel Prout (q.v.) and then lived in Rome before returning to London and achieving considerable fame as a watercolourist. He was elected AOWS in 1831 and OWS in 1834 becoming President from 1858 to 1871. Tayler was most fond of painting country scenes involving hunting and hawking and based on the landscapes of Scotland where he was a frequent visitor; these were also the most frequent subjects for his book illustrations. He died at West Hampstead in 1889.

Contrib: *The Deserted Village [Goldsmith, Etching Club, 1841]; The Traveller [Art Union, 1851].*

Exhib: BI; L; RA; RCA; RWS.
Bibl: M. Hardie, *Watercol. Paint. in Brit.*, Vol.III, 1968, pp.91-92.

**TAYLOR, Edwin**　　　　　　　　　　　**fl.1858-1884**
Landscape painter. He worked in Birmingham and published *Pictures of English Lakes and Mountains*, 1874.

**TAYLOR, Horace Christopher  RBA**　　　　　　　　　　　**1881-1934**
Painter, illustrator and poster artist. He was born in London on 10 January 1881 and was educated at Islington High School and studied at the Camden School of Art, 1898 and the RA Schools, 1902. He then worked in Munich, 1905 and was lecturer in commercial art at Chelsea School, 1931-34. Taylor worked as a caricaturist and cartoonist for *Pan* in about 1920 and also for *The Manchester Guardian*. He was one of the very few humorous artists to paint caricatures in oil. He died at Hampstead on 7 February 1934. He was elected ARBA in 1919 and RBA, 1921.

Illus: *Prehistoric Parables; The Second Show – Atta Troll.*
Exhib: RA; RBA; ROI.
Colls: Witt Photo.
Bibl: *The Studio*, Vol.48, 1909.

**TAYLOR, Leonard Campbell  RA**　　　　　　　　　　　**1874-1963**
Portrait painter and illustrator. He was born at Oxford on 12 December 1874, the son of Dr. J. Taylor, Organist to the University. He was educated at Cheltenham College and studied at the Ruskin School, Oxford, the St. Johns Wood School and the RA Schools. He was working at Hindhead, Surrey in 1905 and at Odiham, Basingstoke in 1921. He was elected ARA in 1928 and RA in 1931. He died in 1963.

Contrib: *The English Illustrated Magazine [1900-1].*
Exhib: B; L; M; New Gall; RA; RHA; RI; ROI; RSA; RWA.
Bibl: Herbert Furst, *LCT, RA His Place in Art*, 1945; G.E. Bunt, *LCT, RA*, 1949.

**TAYLOR, Thomas**　　　　　　　　　　　**c.1770-1826**
Topographer. He entered the RA Schools in 1791 and practised as an architect in the Leeds area, designing a number of churches. He illustrated Whitaker's *Loidis and Elmete* and his edition of Thoresby's *Ducatus Leodiensis*, both published in 1816. He died in March 1826.

Colls: BM.
Bibl: F. Beckwith, 'TT, Regency Architect', *Thoresby Society*, 1949.

**TAYLOR, Tom**　　　　　　　　　　　**fl.1883-1911**
Figure and domestic painter and illustrator. He worked in Camden, London from 1883 and contributed to *The Illustrated London News*, Christmas number, 1895-96.

Exhib: B; L; M; RA; RBA; RHA; RI; ROI.

**TAYLOR, Weld**
Amateur artist. He belonged to the family of Mitford and contributed illustrations to *Howitt's Visits to Remarkable Places*, 1841.

**TAYLOR, Zillah**
Amateur illustrator. She lived in Nottingham and won a *Studio* book illustration competition, 1895-96.

**TEALL, Gardner C.**
Ornamental artist. He designed the Contents page for *The Quartier Latin*, Vol.3, September 1897. An artist called Miss E. Teall was working and exhibiting at Birmingham, 1920-25.

**TEBBY, Arthur Kemp**　　　　　　　　　　　**fl.1883-1928**
Landscape, figure and flower painter and illustrator. He was working in Bloomsbury in 1883 and later moved to Heybridge, Essex; he acted as *The Graphic* naval artist for some time.

Contrib: *Daily Graphic [1890]; The Graphic [1903-5]; The Windsor Magazine; Pearson's Magazine.*
Exhib: RA; RBA; ROI.

SIR JOHN TENNIEL 1820-1914. 'The Press As Scare Monger'. A cartoon for
Punch, 1892. Pencil. Signed with monogram and dated.     Gordon Collection

**TEIGNMOUTH, Commander Henry Noel Shore   5th Baron**
                                                    **1847-1926**
Painter of oriental subjects. He was born in 1847 and joined the Navy
in 1868 becoming Lieutenant in 1872 and Commander in 1891. He
died on 25 February 1926 at Clevedon, Somerset.

Publ: *The Flight of the Lapwing [1881]; Smuggling Days and Smuggling Ways
[1892]; Three Pleasant Springs in Portugal [1899]; The Diary of a Girl in
France in 1821 [1905]; The Smugglers [1923 (with C.G. Harper)]*.
Exhib: RI.

**TEL, S.**
Contributed one cartoon to *Vanity Fair*, 1891.

**TENISON, Nell Marion   (Mrs. Cyrus Cuneo)**     **fl.1893-1940**
Figure painter and illustrator. She studied at the Cope and Nicholl
School, London, 1879 and afterwards in Paris. She married Cyrus
Cuneo (q.v.) and was elected SWA in 1918.

Contrib: *The Graphic [1904]*.
Exhib: L; RA; RBA; RHA; ROI; SWA.

**TENNANT, C. Dudley**     **fl.1898-1918**
Marine and sporting painter and illustrator. He worked in Liverpool,
1898 and Surrey, 1913 and contributed to *Punch*, 1907-8 and The

*Graphic*, 1910.
Exhib: L; RA.

**TENNANT, Dorothy   Lady Stanley**     **-1926**
Genre painter, illustrator and writer. She was the daughter of C.
Tennant of Cadoxton Lodge, Glamorgan and studied at the Slade
School and with Henner in Paris. She made a study of domestic
subjects and children and in 1890 she married Sir H.M. Stanley (q.v.)
the African explorer. She was RE from 1881 and died on 5 October
1926. Signs: △

Publ: *Autobiography of H.M. Stanley [1909]*.
Illus: *London Street Arabs [1890]*.
Contrib: *The English Illustrated Magazine [1885]*.
Exhib: FAS; G; L; M; New Gall; RA; RE; RHA; ROI.
Colls: Tate; Witt Photo.

**TENNANT, N.**
Topographer. He was producing illustrations of Scotland for books in
about 1849.

**TENNIEL, Sir John**     **1820-1914**
Cartoonist and illustrator. He was born in London in 1820 and
studied at the RA Schools and the Clipstone Street Life Academy,
rising to notice through his animal drawings in the 1840s. It was his
edition of *Aesop's Fables*, 1848 that brought him to the attention of
Mark Lemon of *Punch* and he joined the magazine as second
cartoonist in 1851, graduating to principal cartoonist in 1864. Tenniel
drew during his half century of association with the paper over 2,000
cartoons. They represented not only the essence of Victorian *Punch*,
but of Victorian society, imperial, dignified and Olympian. Tenniel's
superb draughtsmanship, meticulous silvery grey pencil strokes made
with a special 6H pencil produced some of the household images of
the period 'The British Lion Attacking The Bengal Tiger' and
'Dropping the Pilot'. Despite a serious vein in his work, Tenniel was a
fine illustrator of fantasy and his greatest opportunity for really
humorous drawing came with his work for Lewis Carroll's *Alice in
Wonderland*, 1865, a singular example of painstaking professionalism
for both artist and author. *Through The Looking Glass* followed in
1872. Tenniel was elected ANWS in 1874 and a full member the same
year. He was knighted in 1893 and died in London in early 1914.
*Punch* issued a special Tenniel Supplement on March 4, 1914 to mark
his death.

Contrib: *Undine [1845]; The Juvenile Verse and Picture Book [1848]; Aesop's
Fables [1848]; Pollok's Course of Time [1857]; Poets of the Nineteenth
Century [1858]; The Poetical Works of E.A. Poe [1857]; ILN [1857, 1868];
The Home Affections [Charles Mackay, 1858]; Blair's Grave [1858-59]; Once a
Week [1859-67]; Lalla Rookh [1861]; Parables From Nature [1861]; Good
Words [1862-64]; Puck on Pegasus [Pennell, 1862]; Passages From Modern
English Poets [1862]; Arabian Nights [1863]; The Ingoldsby Legends [1864];
English Sacred Poetry [1864]; Legends and Lyrics [1865]; The Mirage of Life
[1867-68]; A Noble Life [c.1870]. (For full bibl. see Sarzano, F.).*
Exhib: FAS, 1895, 1900; NWS; RA; RBA.
Colls: BM; V & AM; Witt Photo.
Bibl: M.H. Spielmann, *The History of Punch*, 1895, pp.461-474; Frances
Sarzano, *Sir JT*, English Masters of Black and White, 1948; R.G.G. Price, *A
History of Punch*, 1957, pp.70-74.
See illustration (left).

**TERRY, George W.**     **fl.1854-1858**
Ornamental artist. He contributed decorative work to *The Illustrated
London News* in 1854 and initial letters to *Punch*, 1856-58.

**TERRY, Herbert Stanley**     **1890-**
Illustrator of comic genre subjects. He was born in Birmingham on 13
March 1890 and was educated at Bede College, Northumberland and
at the Wolverhampton School of Art. He specialised in comic genre
subjects and contributed to the major magazines from about 1914.

Contrib: *Punch [1914]; The Bystander; The Tatler; The Sketch; Illustrated
Sporting and Dramatic News; London Opinion; Humorist; Passing Show;
Windsor Magazine*.

**THACKERAY, Lance RBA**                                    **-1916**

Painter, illustrator and writer. He worked in Notting Hill Gate,
London and specialised in sporting subjects, often with a humorous
side to them. He travelled extensively in the Middle East and had one
man exhibitions at the Leicester Galleries, 1908, the FAS, 1910 and
at Walker's Galleries, 1913. He was elected RBA in 1899 and died at
Brighton on 11 August 1916.

Illus: *The Light Side of Egypt [1908]; The People of Egypt [1910].*
Contrib: *The Sphere [1894]; Sketchy Bits [1895]; The Graphic [1904-11];
Punch [1905-8].*
Exhib: FAS; RA; RBA; RI.

**THACKERAY, William Makepeace**                            **1811-1863**

Novelist, illustrator and caricaturist. He was born in Calcutta in 1811
and after the family fortune was lost he turned to his aptitude for
drawing for a living before his aptitude for writing. His pen drawing
with light washes was always free and in the spirit of the amateur
caricaturists of the 18th century and with undoubted borrowings
from Hogarth. Despite a rather wooden appearance, Thackeray's
figures have great value as being the only illustrations by a major
writer for his own works. These began with the slight lithographs in
*Flore et Zephyr,* 1836, made at a time when he was studying art in
Paris and lead on to the more sustained work of *The Book of Snobs*
and *Vanity Fair,* 1847-48. Thackeray was an able critic of caricature
and humorous art both at home and on the Continent and his interest
in artists was continued by his connection with *Punch,* 1842-54. His
own attempts to illustrate his novel *Phillip* in the early numbers of
*The Cornhill Magazine,* which he was editing, resulted in the young
artist Fred Walker (q.v.) being employed. He died in London in 1863.

Illus: *Flore et Zephyr [1836]; The Paris Sketchbook [1840]; Comic Tales and
Sketches [1841]; The Irish Sketchbook [1843]; Christmas Books [1846-50];
Vanity Fair [1847-48]; The History of Pendennis [1849-50].*
Contrib: *Figaro in London [1836]; Punch [1842-54]; The Cornhill Magazine
[1860-61].*
Colls: BM; Fitzwilliam; V & AM; Witt Photo.
Bibl: Graham Everitt, *English Caricaturists,* 1893, pp.375-380; M.H. Spielmann,
*WMT,* 1899; Melville, *T. As Artist,* The Connoisseur, March 1904; Gleeson
White, *English Illustration,* 1906, p.18; *American Magazine,* Vol.28, 9
September 1935, p.555; Gordon N. Ray, *The Illustrator and the Book in
England,* Morgan Library, 1976.
See illustration (p.185).

**THIEDE, Edwin Adolf**                                     **fl.1882-1908**

Miniature portrait painter and illustrator. He worked in Lewisham and
London and worked for the leading magazines.

Contrib: *The Queen [1892]; ILN [1893, 1900]; The Ludgate Monthly; The
Windsor Magazine; The Temple Magazine.*
Exhib: RA; ROI.

**THIELE, Reinhold**

Illustrator. He illustrated *After School,* Robert Overton and *Lights
Out,* by the same author in Jarrold's series 'Books For Manly Boys',
1894.

**THIRTLE, John**                                          **fl.1896-1902**

Painter and illustrator. He worked at Ewell, Surrey and drew pen and
ink illustrations in the style of the Birmingham School for *The Studio*
competitions, 1896-97.

Exhib: RA; RI.
Bibl: *The Studio,* Vol.8, 1896, p.184 illus.; Vol.10, 1897; Vol.12, 1897.

**THOMAS, Bert**                                           **1883-1966**

Black and white artist and illustrator. He was born at Newport,
Montgomery in 1883, the son of the sculptor Job Thomas and was
educated at Swansea. He worked in London for many of the leading
magazines, taking as his subjects a raffish metropolitan world of
policeman, waitresses, soldiers and sailors, set down with a
spontaneous broken line. He drew a number of posters and died in
1966.

Contrib: *Fun [1901]; Punch [1905-35]; The Graphic [1910]; London Opinion
[1913-].*
Exhib: London Salon, 1909.
Colls: BM; V & AM.
Bibl: *Mr Punch with Horse and Hound,* New Punch Library, c.1930; R.G.G.
Price, *A History of Punch,* 1957, p.221 illus.

**THOMAS, George Housman**                                  **1824-1868**

Wood engraver and illustrator. He was born in London in 1824, the
brother of W.L. Thomas (q.v.). He worked from the age of fourteen
with the wood engraver Bonner, and won a Society of Arts silver
palette at the age of fifteen. He began his career as a book illustrator
in Paris where he worked with Henry Harrison and had a small
workshop with half a dozen assistants. During this period he was
employed by an American journal and to engrave U.S. bank notes and
went to New York in 1846, where he and his brother founded a
magazine which was unsuccessful. On his return in 1848, Thomas
went to Rome and was present at Garibaldi's defence of the city.
illustrations of it being accepted by *The Illustrated London News.* His
work for books and magazines was quite extensive after this date, but
his drawing lacks the fire to make him a great illustrator, although his
work was much admired by Queen Victoria. He died at Boulogne in
1868 after falling from his horse; a memorial exhibition was held at
the German Gallery the following year.

Illus: *Uncle Tom's Cabin [1852]; Hiawatha [1855-56]; Vicar of Wakefield
[1857]; Pilgrim's Progress [1857]; Robinson Crusoe [1865]; Armadale [Wilkie
Collins, 1866]; The Last Chronicle of Barset [Anthony Trollope [1867].*
Contrib: *ILN [1848-67]; Punch [1851-52]; Merrie Days of England [1858-59];
The Home Affections [Mackay, 1858]; Thomson's Seasons [1859]; Household
Songs [1861]; Early English Poems [1862]; London Society [1863]; The
Churchman's Family Magazine [1863]; The Cornhill Magazine [1864-65];
Legends and Lyrics [1865]; Aunt Sally's Life [1866-67]; Foxe's Book of
Martyrs [1866]; Cassell's Magazine [1867]; The Quiver [1867]; The Broadway
[1867]; Idyllic Pictures [1867].*
Exhib: BI; RA.
Colls: Fitzwilliam; V & AM.
Bibl: *In Memoriam GHT,* n.d., Cassell; Gleeson White, *English Illustration,*
1906, pp.155-156; Forrest Reid, *Illustrators of the sixties,* 1928, p.248.

**THOMAS, Inigo**                                          **fl.1891-1903**

Architectural illustrator. He contributed to *The English Illustrated
Magazine,* 1891-92 and illustrated Reginald Blomfield's *The Formal
Garden,* 1892.

Bibl: R.E.D. Sketchley, *Eng. Bk. Illus.,* 1903, pp.50, 142.

*WILLIAM F. THOMAS fl.1890-1907. 'Ally Sloper canvassing for votes.'
Original drawing for illustration in* Ally Sloper's Half Holiday, *1906. Pen and
ink. 10¾ins. x 9¾ins. (27.3cm x 24.8cm).*                Author's Collection

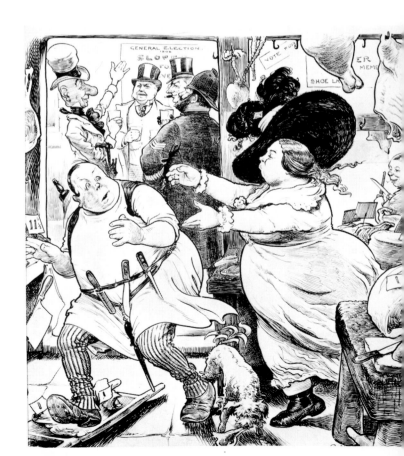

**THOMAS, Margaret**                                      -1929

Artist, illustrator, sculptor and author. She was born at Croydon and emigrated with her parents to Australia. There she studied with Charles Summers and returned to Europe to study in the RA Schools and in Paris and Rome. She lived in Melbourne and London and made extensive tours of the Mediterranean coasts, her researches being published in a number of books. She died on 24 December 1929.

Illus: *A Hero of the Workshop [1880]; A Scamper Through Spain and Tangier [1892]; Two Years in Palestine and Syria [1899]; Denmark Past and Present [1901]; From Damascus to Palmyra [1905].*
Exhib: RBA; RHA; ROI; SWA.
Bibl: *Who Was Who*, 1929-40.

**THOMAS, William F.**                              fl.1890-1907

Landscape painter and cartoonist. He followed W.G. Baxter (q.v.) as chief cartoonist on *Ally Sloper's Half Holiday* in 1890 and produced meticulous and detailed pen drawings of this character until at least 1906. He lived from about 1901 at Lydstepp House, Southwold, Suffolk.

Contrib: *Judy [1886-90]; Lika Joko [1894]; Punch [1895].*
Exhib: RA.
See illustration (p.477).

**THOMAS, William Luson    RI**                    1830-1900

Wood engraver and newspaper proprietor. He was born in 1830, the brother of G.H. Thomas (q.v.), and in 1846 left with him for the United States where they founded the unsuccessful journals, *The Republic* and *The Picture Gallery*. They returned to Europe in 1848 and lived in Paris and Rome and in 1855, W.L. Thomas married the daughter of the watercolourist and illustrator J.W. Carmichael (q.v.). Thomas's work for *The Illustrated London News* from about 1850, gave him the idea of another illustrated periodical and *The Graphic* was founded in December 1869. Mainly due to Thomas's dynamism and first hand knowledge of the work, the new paper flourished in the 1870s and attracted a remarkable group of young social realistic artists who published their best work in its pages. In 1890, he became the first promoter of a daily illustrated paper *The Daily Graphic*. Although principally a businessman, Thomas was an able water-colourist and was elected ANWS in 1864 and NWS in 1875. He died at Chertsey in 1900. His son, W. Carmichael Thomas, b.1856, was a wood engraver on *The Graphic* and managing director from 1900-17.

Exhib: L; M; RI; ROI.

**THOMPSON, Alfred**                                      -1895

Amateur painter, draughtsman and caricaturist. He was a cavalry officer, who took the advice of Mark Lemon of *Punch* to abandon the army and study art in Paris. He contributed to many periodicals, his caricatures reflecting the delicate portraits chargés of Tissot (q.v.). He finally became manager of the Theatre Royal at Manchester and designed costumes and scenery and edited the magazine *Mask*. He died in New York in September 1895.

Contrib: *Journal Amusant [Paris]; Diogenes [1854]; Punch [1856-58]; Comic News [1865]; The Arrow [1865]; Vanity Fair [1862-76]; The Broadway [1867-74]; ILN [1867]; Fun [1870].*

**THOMPSON, George**                              fl.1892-1894

Portrait painter. He worked in London and contributed to *The Yellow Book*, 1894.

Exhib: London, 1892.

**THOMPSON, Margaret**                            fl.1883-1923

Figure and flower painter and illustrator. She was a student at the New Cross School of Art and won a gold medal at South Kensington in 1898. She won a *Studio* competition in 1899 and worked in Hitchin and Hereford.

Exhib: B; RA; RBA; RI; RSA; SWA.
Bibl: *The Studio*, Vol.15, p.294 illus.

**THOMSON, Emily Gertrude    RMS**                   -1932

Portrait painter, miniaturist, sculptor and illustrator. She was born in Glasgow and studied at the Manchester School of Art and was elected ARMS in 1911 and RMS in 1912. She worked at Brook Green,

London from 1908 and died in 1932.

Illus: *A Soldier's Children [1897 (with E. Stuart Hardy)]; Three Sunsets and Other Poems with Twelve Fairy Fancies by EGT [1898].*
Exhib: G; L; M; RMS.
Colls: V & AM.

**THOMSON, George**                                1860-1939

Townscape painter and illustrator. He was born at Towie, Aberdeenshire in 1860 and studied at the RA Schools and was a lecturer at the Slade 1895 to 1914. He settled at Chateau Letoquoi at Samer in the Pas-de-Calais in 1914 and died at Boulogne on 22 March 1939. He was elected NEA in 1891.

Contrib: *The Pall Mall Budget [1891-92].*
Exhib: B; G; GG; L; M; NEA; RA; RBA; RHA; RI; ROI.

**THOMSON, Gordon**                               fl.1864-1886

Figure artist and illustrator. He was originally a civil servant and then cartoonist for *Fun*, 1870-78, having made his name with double page illustrations of the Franco-Prussian War for *The Graphic*. Dalziel refers to the 'large pictures for Christmas and other Holiday Numbers ... remarkable for the varied topical events he crowded into them, and those who remember his "Academy Skits" will know what quaint burlesques they were'. He signed his work

Illus: *Pictures From Italy [C. Dickens, 1870].*
Contrib: *Punch [1864]; London Society; The Graphic [1869-86]; Fun [1870-78, 1890-93].*
Exhib: RA, 1878.

"THEN HE, HANDING HER INTO HER COACH, STEPS IN AFTER."
*From a Drawing by* HUGH THOMSON.

The battle was over without any blows,

The heroes unharness and strip off their clothes;

The dame gives her captain a sip of rose-water,

Then he, handing her into her coach, steps in after.


John's orders are special to drive very slow,

For fevers oft follow fatigues, we all know;

*HUGH THOMSON 1860-1920. '... Handing Her into Her Coach ...' An illustration to a poem, published in* The English Illustrated Magazine, *1883.*

## THOMSON, Henry RA                                                                   1773-1843

Painter of history and allegory. He was born at Portsea on 31 July
1773 and studied in Paris before the Revolution, returning to this
country to become a pupil of John Opie. He travelled to Italy and
Germany, his main illustrative work being for Boydell's *Shakespeare*
and portraits for *The Theatrical Recorder*, 1805. He was elected ARA
in 1801 and RA in 1804, serving as Keeper from 1825-27. He died at
Portsea on 6 April 1843.

## THOMSON, Hugh                                                                        1860-1920

Watercolour artist and illustrator. He was born at Coleraine, Co.
Londonderry in 1860 and first came to prominence with his series of
drawings of 18th century ballads and stories in *The English Illustrated
Magazine*, 1883. Thomson was an instinctive artist with little formal
training. He had left Coleraine for Belfast in 1877 and started work in
the factory of Messrs Marcus Ward, engaged in Christmas card colour
printing. He attended a few classes at the Belfast School of Art, but
his real teacher was the artist and designer John Vinycomb (q.v.). His
contact with Carr of *The English Illustrated* gave him the opportunity
for figurative work and the partnership with W. Outram Tristram, the
author, provided him with an ideal text. His name was made with
*Coaching Days and Coaching Ways,* by the latter, 1888 and in such
delightful examples of nostalgia as *Days with Sir Roger de Coverley,*
1886. Influenced by Randolph Caldecott and the novels of Thackeray
(qq.v.), Thomson created an idyllic world of stage coaches, sedan
chairs, feasts and port wine, which was a little more convincing than
the earlier artists but very pretty. From the late 1880s he was
continuously in demand for the novels of Jane Austen, Fanny Burney,
Mrs. Gaskell, Charles Reade and others as well as for contemporaries
like J.M. Barrie and Austin Dobson. His studies of London life and the
cockney poor are a notable achievement and show the diversity of this
talented artist. Thomson was most prolific in the years 1900 to 1914
when his watercolour work was put to good use in the colour gift
books, page plates of period scenes, their colour washed into a gentle
ink drawing, usually pastellish and muted. He was elected RI in 1897
and retired in 1907. He died at Wandsworth on 7 May 1920. The
artist was influential on the following generation especially on the
work of C.E. and H.M. Brock (qq.v.).

Illus: *Days with Sir Roger de Coverley [1886]; Coaching Days and Coaching
Ways [Outram Tristram, 1888]; The Vicar of Wakefield [1891]; Cranford [Mrs.
Gaskell, 1891]; The Antiquary [1891]; The Bride of Lammermoor [1891];
The Ballad of Beau Brocade [1892]; Our Village [Miss Mitford, 1893]; The
Piper of Hamelin [1893]; Pride and Prejudice [Jane Austen, 1894]; Coridon's
Song [1894]; The Dead Gallant [Outram Tristram, 1894]; St. Ronan's Well
[1894]; The Story of Rosina [1895]; Sense and Sensibility [1896]; Emma
[1896]; The Chase [1896]; Highways and Byways in Devon and Cornwall
[1897]; Mansfield Park [1897]; Northanger Abbey [1897]; Persuasion [1897];
Riding Recollections [1898]; Highways and Byways in North Wales [1898];
Jack the Giant Killer [1898]; Peg Woffington [Reade, 1899]; Highways and By-
ways, Donegal and Antrim [1899]; Yorkshire [1899]; This and That [1899];
Ray Farley [1901]; The History of Samuel Titmarsh [1902]; Evelina [1903];
Scenes of Clerical Life [George Eliot, 1906]; Highways and Byways in Kent
[Jerrold, 1907]; As You Like It [1909]; The Merry Wives of Windsor [1910];
The School for Scandal [1911]; She Stoops to Conquer [1912]; Quality Street
[J.M. Barrie, 1913]; The Chimes [1913]; The Admirable Crichton [J.M. Barrie,
1914]; Tom Brown's School Days [1918]; The Scarlet Letter [Hawthorne,
1920].*
Contrib: *The English Illustrated Magazine [1883-92]; Pall Mall Budget [1890];
The Graphic [1890-1905]; Black & White [1891]; The New Budget [1895];
The Ludgate Monthly [1895].* (See Spielmann and Jerrold for complete bibl.)
Exhib: FAS, 1887, 1893; Leicester Galls; Walker's Galls.
Colls: BM; Ulster Mus; V & AM.
Bibl: *The Studio*, Winter No., 1900-1, p.30 illus.; R.E.D. Sketchley, *Eng. Bk.
Illus.*, 1903, pp.68, 79, 156; M.H. Spielmann and W. Jerrold, *HT*, 1931.
See illustrations (above right and p.478).

## THOMSON, James William                                                         c.1775-c.1825

Architectural draughtsman. He entered the RA Schools in 1798 and
contributed illustrations to *The History of the Abbey Church of St.
Peter's Westminster*, 1812 and *Ackermann's Repository*, 1825.

Exhib: RA, 1795.

HUGH THOMSON 1860-1920. 'The Gods – The Vaudeville Gallery.' *Original
drawing for* The Graphic. *Pen, pencil and watercolour. Signed and dated 1899.
11⁷⁄8ins. x 9³⁄4ins. (30.1cm x 24.8cm).*              Victoria and Albert Museum

## THORBURN, Archibald                                                            1860-1935

Painter of birds. He was born on 31 May 1860, the son of Robert
Thorburn, RA, the miniature painter. He was educated at Dalkeith
and Edinburgh and married the daughter of C.E. Mudie, the proprietor
of Mudie's Libraries. Thorburn was a very scientific painter whose
renderings of colour and texture in his ornithological books cannot be
faulted, at the same time the works can be dull. He had a wide
following among the sporting fraternity and lived latterly at
Godalming, Surrey. He died on 9 October 1935.

Illus: *British Birds [1915-18]; A Naturalists Sketchbook [1919]; British
Mammals [1920]; Game Birds and Wild Fowl of Great Britain and Ireland
[1923].*
Contrib: *The Sporting and Dramatic News [1896]; The Pall Mall Magazine; ILN
[1896-98]; The English Illustrated Magazine [1897]; British Diving Ducks
[1913].*
Exhib: FAS; L; RA; RBA.
Colls: BM; V & AM; Woburn.
Bibl: *The Studio*, Vol.91, 1926.
See illustration (p.480).

## THORIGNY, Felix                                                                    1824-1870

Landscape painter and draughtsman. He was born at Caen on 14
March 1824 and studied with Julian at Caen. He then went to Paris to
work for *Monde Illustré; Magazin Pittoresque; Musée des Familles* and
*Calvados Pittoresque*. He died in Paris on 27 March 1870.

Contrib: *ILN [1859-68]; Illustrated Times [1859].*

## THORNELY, H.

Equestrian illustrator. He contributed drawings to *The Penny
Illustrated Paper*.

*ARCHIBALD THORBURN 1860-1935. Original drawing for illustration to* British Divine Ducks, *1913. Watercolour. Signed.*

Woburn Abbey Collection

**THORNTON, Alfred Henry Robinson**                    **1863-1939**
Landscape painter. He was born in Delhi on 25 August 1863 and was educated at Harrow and Trinity College, Cambridge, then studying at the Slade and the Westminster School of Art. He was a member of the NEA from 1895 and Hon. Secretary from 1928 to 1939. He lived at Bath until 1914 and then at Painswick, Gloucestershire. He died on 20 February 1939.

Publ: *Fifty Years of the NEAC [1935]; The Diary of an Art Student of the Nineties [1938].*
Contrib: *The Yellow Book [1894-95].*
Exhib: FAS; L; M; NEA; RA; RBA; RSA.
Colls: BM; Cheltenham.

**THORPE, James H.**                    **1876-1949**
Painter and illustrator. He was born on 13 March 1876 and after being educated at Bancrofts School, studied at Heatherley's. He served in the First World War, 1915-19 and was the first designer of advertisements to the London Press Exchange, 1902-22. Thorpe's posterish style with heavy outline owes something to Hassall but is less competent in execution; his main contribution was as the historian of 1890s illustration and of monographs of two famous illustrators. He died in 1949.

Illus: *The Compleat Angler [Izaak Walton, 1911]; Over [de Selincourt, 1932].*
Contrib: *Punch [1909-38]; The Graphic [1908-15]; Windsor Magazine.*
Publ: *A Cricket Bag [1929]; Phil May [1932]; Jane Hollybrand [1932]; Happy Days [1933]; English Illustration The Nineties [1935]; Edmund J. Sullivan [1947].*
Exhib: RI.
Colls: Author; V & AM.

**THRUPP, Frederick**                    **1812-1895**
Sculptor. He was born at Paddington, London on 20 June 1812 and studied at Sass's Academy before working in Rome 1837-42. Thrupp won a Society of Arts silver medal in 1829 and designed statues for Westminster Hall. He died at Torquay on 21 May 1895.

Illus: *Paradise Lost [n.d.].*
Exhib: BI; RA; RBA.
Colls: BM; Winchester.
Bibl: R. Gunnis, *Dict. of Brit. Sculp.,* 1954, pp.394-395.

**THURSTON, John** 1774-1822

Watercolourist, illustrator and wood engraver. He was born at Scarborough in 1774 and specialised in copper plate and wood engraved book illustrations to stories. He was elected AOWS in 1805 and died in London in 1822.

Illus: *Rural Tales [R. Bloomfield, 1802]; Thomson's Seasons [1805]; Religious Emblems [1808]; Shakespeare's Works [1814]; Falconer's Shipwreck [1817]; Somerville's Rural Sports [1818].*
Contrib: *Hood's Comic Annual [1830].*
Exhib: OWS; RA.
Colls: BM; Greenwich; Nottingham.

**TIDMARSH, H.E.** fl.1880-1925

Landscape and figure painter. He worked in North London and at Barnet from 1914, specialising in architectural subjects.

Contrib: *The Graphic [1886-87]; ILN [1889-91].*
Exhib: B; M; RA; RBA; RI.

**TIFFIN, Henry** fl.1845-1874

Landscape painter. He worked in London and contributed to *Knight's London,* 1841.

Exhib: BI; RA; RBA.

**TIMBRELL, James Christopher** 1807-1850

Marine and genre painter. He was born at Dublin in 1807 and specialised in studies of sailors and shipping, contributing to *Knight's London,* 1841. He died at Portsmouth on 5 January 1850.

Exhib: BI; RA; RBA.

**TISSOT, Joseph James Jacques** 1836-1902

Painter of social genre, illustrator and caricaturist. He was born at Nantes on 15 October 1836 and studied art with Lamotte and Flandrin, exhibiting at the Salon from 1851. Tissot took an active part in the Franco-German War of 1870-71 and afterwards came to England and studied etching with Seymour Haden. In the 1870s he became the supreme genre painter of high life, the portrayer of balls and receptions, fashionable marriages and galas, transformed into luscious paint and correct in every detail. It was perhaps his observation that enabled him to be a good caricaturist for Vanity Fair, 1869-77, although Leslie Ward (q.v.) felt that the subjects in portrait chargé were too soft for caricature. In later life, Tissot became a convinced christian and devoted all his time to religious painting, some of this work is foreshadowed in his book illustrations of 1865. He died at Buillon on 8 August 1902. He was elected RE in 1880.

Illus: *Ballads and Songs of Brittany [1865]; The Life of Our Lord Jesus Christ [1897, 2 Vols.].*
Exhib: B; FAS; G; L; M; RA; RE.
Colls: V & AM.

**TITCOMB, William Holt Yates** RBA 1858-1930

Landscape, figure and flower painter. He was born at Cambridge in 1858 and studied at South Kensington and at Antwerp under Verlat and in Paris with Boulanger and Lefebvre. He also attended the Herkomer School at Bushey and was elected RBA in 1894. Titcomb worked at St. Ives, Cornwall and at Bristol and died in 1930.

Contrib: *The Graphic [1886 (story)].*
Exhib: FAS; G; L; M; NEA; New Gall; RA; RBA; RHA; RI; ROI.

**TOD, Colonel James** 1782-1835

Army officer and artist. He was sent to India in 1800 and carried out surveys, later acting as political agent at Rajput until 1822. He published and illustrated *Annals and Antiquities of Rajasthan,* 1829-32 and *Travels in Western India,* 1839. He died in London in 1835.

**TOFT, Albert** 1862-1949

Sculptor, modeller and designer. He was born in Birmingham in 1862 and studied at the Hanley and Newcastle-under-Lyme Schools of Art. He was at the RCA under Professor Lanteri for two years before being apprenticed to Messrs Wedgwood as a modeller. Toft undoubtedly designed Christmas cards and may have done some book illustration.

He died in 1949. FRBS, 1923.

Publ: *Modelling and Sculpture.*
Exhib: B; G; L; RA.
Colls: Birmingham; Glasgow; Liverpool.

**TOMKINS, Charles** c.1750-1810

Landscape painter and engraver. He was born about 1750, the son of William Tomkins, a landscape painter.

Contrib: *Britton's Beauties of England and Wales [1801-8].*
Exhib: RA.

**TOMKINS, Charles F.** 1798-1844

Landscape painter and caricaturist. He worked with David Roberts and Clarkson Stanfield (qq.v.) and was elected SBA in 1838. He contributed drawings for the early numbers of *Punch,* and died in 1844.

Exhib: RBA.
Colls: V & AM.

**TOMKINS, Peltro William** 1759-1840

Engraver and illustrator. He was born in London in 1759 and studied with F. Bartolozzi before working on *Sharpes's British Poets* and *The British Theatre.* He acted as a printseller in Bond Street and produced *The British Gallery of Art* by Tresham and Ottley and *The Gallery of the Marquess of Stafford.* He died in London in 1840.

Colls: BM; Manchester.

**TONKS, Henry** 1862-1936

Painter of interiors and caricaturist. He was born at Solihull in 1862 and educated at Clifton before training at the London Hospital and becoming Senior Medical Officer at the Royal Free Hospital and FRCS. He left medicine for art and studied under Fred Brown at the Westminster School, becoming his assistant at the Slade School, 1894. Tonks was Slade Professor of Fine Art at University College, London from 1917-30 and Emeritus Professor from 1930. He was elected NEA in 1895 and died in London on 8 January 1937.

Contrib: *The Quarto [1896].*
Exhib: G; L; M; NEA; RA; RHA; RSA.
Colls: Ashmolean; Manchester.

**TOPHAM, Edward** 1751-1820

Caricaturist. He was a Captain and Adjutant in the First Life Guards and was also a journalist and playwright. He made some Cambridge caricatures in 1771 and worked for W. Darly of the Strand in 1771-72, his most celebrated print 'The Macaroni Shop' appearing under his imprint on 14 July 1772. He was later caricatured by Rowlandson and Gillray. He died in 1820.

Colls: BM; Witt Photo.

**TOPHAM, Francis William** 1808-1877

Painter of genre subjects, illustrator and engraver. He was born in Leeds on 15 April 1808 and apprenticed to an uncle who was an engraver. He came to London in 1830 and became an heraldic engraver and then a line engraver, illustrating Moore's and Burns's works. He studied with the Clipstone Street Academy and gradually abandoned engraving for watercolour at which he was very proficient. He made a speciality of peasant scenes and figures and particularly those of Ireland, which he visited in 1844 and Spain where he travelled in 1852-53 and 1864. Topham was elected ANWS in 1842 and NWS in 1843, followed by OWS in 1848. He revisited Spain in 1876 and died there at Cordova on 31 March 1877.

Contrib: *Book of Gems; Fisher's Drawing Room Scrapbook; History of London [Fearnside and Harrall]; Midsummer Eve [Mrs. S.C. Hall]; Book of British Ballads [S.C. Hall, 1842]; The Sporting Review [1842-46]; ILN [1852]; Child's History of England [Dickens, 1852-54]; The Home Affections [Charles Mackay, 1858].*
Exhib: BI; NWS; OWS; RA; RBA.
Colls: BM; Reading; V & AM.
Bibl: Chatto & Jackson, *Treatise on Wood Engraving,* 1861, p.600; F.G. Kitton, *Dickens and His Illustrators,* 1899; J. Maas, *Victorian Painters,* 1970, p.240.

**TOPPI, W.**
Amateur figure artist. He contributed to *Punch,* 1902.

**TORRANCE, James**                    **1859-1916**
Painter and illustrator. He was born at Glasgow in 1859 and specialised in fairy books for children. He died in Helensburgh in 1916.
Illus: *Scottish Fairy Tales and Folk Tales [1893]; The Works of Nathaniel Hawthorne [1894].*
Exhib: G.
Colls: V & AM.

**TORRY, John T.**                    **fl.1886**
Landscape painter. He contributed social realism subjects to *The Illustrated London News,* 1886.
Exhib: RBA; RI.

**TOVEY, John**                    **fl.1826-1843**
Topographer. He contributed to *Griffith's Cheltenham,* 1826.
Exhib: BI, 1843.

**TOWNSEND, Frederick Henry Linton Jehne**                    **1868-1920**
Illustrator, black and white artist and etcher. He was born in London on 25 February 1868 and studied at the Lambeth School of Art. He was contributing figure drawings to *Punch* from 1903 and became the magazine's first Art Editor in 1905. Townsend's pen line is always assured and his compositions are good, but the subjects themselves lack humour and have little individuality in the *Punch* oeuvre. Before his connection with the magazine in the 1890s, Townsend was a prolific illustrator of books, having some claim to be influenced by Abbey (q.v.) and the draughtsmen of the 1860s. He died in London on 11 December 1920. His early work is sometimes signed 'Fin de ville'.
Illus: *A Social Departure [S.J. Duncan, 1890]; An American Girl in London [S.J. Duncan, 1891]; The Simple Adventures of a Memsahib [S.J. Duncan, 1893]; The Jones's and the Asterisks [Campbell, 1895]; Maid Marian and Crotchet Castle [T.L. Peacock, 1895]; Melincourt [1896]; Gryll Grange [1896]; Jane Eyre [1896]; The Misfortunes of Elfin; Rhodaphne [1897]; Shirley [1897]; Rob Roy [1897]; The Scarlet Letter [1897]; The House of the Seven Gables [1897]; Bladys of the Stewponey [1897]; The Blithedale Romance [1898]; The King's Own [Marryat, 1898]; For Peggy's Sake [1898]; The Cardinal's Snuff Box [1900].*
Contrib: *ILN [1889-99]; The Gentlewoman; Judy [1892]; The Pall Mall Budget [1893-94]; Good Words [1894]; The Unicorn [1895]; The New Budget [1895]; Daily Chronicle [1895]; The Quiver [1897]; Pick-Me-Up [1897]; Black & White [1897]; The Longbow [1898]; St. James's Budget [1898]; The Graphic [1899-1901]; Penny Illustrated Paper; The Lady's Pictorial; The Queen; The Idler; The Pall Mall Magazine; The Royal Magazine; Cassell's Family Magazine; The Windsor Magazine; Fun [1901]; The Sphere; The Tatler.*
Exhib: FAS, 1921; NEA; New Gall; RA; RBA; RE; RSA.
Colls: Author; BM; V & AM.
Bibl: *The Studio,* Winter No., 1900-1, p.52 illus.; R.E.D. Sketchley, *Eng. Bk. Illus.,* 1903, pp.68, 69, 72, 157; P.V. Bradshaw, *The Art of the Illustrator FHT,* 1918; R.G.G. Price, *A History of Punch,* 1957, pp.156-157.

**TOWNSEND, G.**
Ornamental artist. He supplied decoration for *The Illustrated London News* in 1860 and was then working in Exeter.

**TOWNSEND, Henry James**                    **1810-1890**
Surgeon, painter and etcher. He was born at Taunton in 1810 and between 1839 and 1866 taught art at the Government School of Design, Somerset House. He died in 1890.
Illus: *The Book of Ballads [Mrs. S.C. Hall, 1847].*
Contrib: *The Deserted Village [Etching Club, 1841]; Gray's Elegy [Etching Club, 1847]; Milton's Allegro [Etching Club]; The Illustrated Times [1855].*
Exhib: BI; RA; RBA.
Colls: V & AM.

**TOWNSHEND, George   1st Marquess**                    **1724-1807**
Soldier, politician and amateur caricaturist. He was born in 1724, the son of the 3rd Viscount Townshend and was educated at St. John's College, Cambridge, joining the 7th Dragoons in 1745, he fought at

the Battle of Culloden, 1746. He had a distinguished career in the Army, acting as aide-de-camp to George II and as general under Wolfe at Quebec. He succeeded his father in 1764 and was made Lord-Lieutenant of Ireland in 1767 and created a marquis in 1786. Concurrently with this career, Townshend developed a superb hand for caricature and was the first amateur artist to publish his work in the country and the first caricaturist to apply caricature to political satires. He worked closely with Darly, the printseller from 1756, and may have learnt the art from Darly's wife, Mary. His drawings created many enemies and irritated both William Hogarth and Horace Walpole. He died on 14 September 1807.
Bibl: Eileen Harris, *The Townshend Album,* National Portrait Gallery, 1974.

**TOY, W.H.**
Amateur figure artist. He contributed to *Punch,* 1909.

**TOZER, Henry E.**                    **fl.1873-1907**
Marine painter and illustrator. He worked at Penzance and was a very extensive contributor of shipping scenes to *The Illustrated London News,* 1873-80.
Exhib: B; RA.
Colls: Cape Town.

**TREGLOWN, Ernest G.**                    **-1922**
Artist and illustrator. He was a student of the Birmingham School and contributed black and white work to *The Yellow Book,* 1896 in a strong Beardsley idiom, and to *The Quest,* 1894-96.
Exhib: B; L, 1891-1916.

**TRESIDDER, Charles**
Illustrator. He drew for *The Old Miller and His Mill* by M.G. Pearse, a child's story of 1881.

**TRINGHAM, Holland   RBA**                    **-1909**
Painter and architectural illustrator. He was a pupil of Herbert Railton (q.v.) whose work his much resembles. He lived in Streatham and did a great deal of magazine work up to the time of his death, he was elected RBA in 1894.
Contrib: *The Quiver [1891]; Black & White [1891]; ILN [1892-1908]; The Gentlewoman; The Sketch; Cassell's Family Magazine; Chums; The English Illustrated Magazine [1894].*
Exhib: B; RA; RBA.
Colls: V & AM.

**TRUE, Will**
Poster designer and illustrator. He contributed to *Fun,* 1892.

**TUCK, Harry**                    **fl.1870-1907**
Landscape and genre painter and illustrator. He was on the permanent staff of *Fun,* 1878-1900 and worked at Haverstock Hill, London.
Contrib: *The Strand Magazine [1891].*
Exhib: B; G; L; M; RA; RBA; RI; ROI.

**TUCKER, Alfred Robert, Bishop of Uganda**                    **1860-1914**
Amateur artist. He was educated at Oxford and was curate at Bristol and Durham before entering the Colonial Episcopate as Bishop of Uganda from 1890 to 1911. He died after retiring to Durham in 1914.
Publ: *African Sketches [1892]; Toro [1899]; Eighteen Years in Uganda [1908].*
Bibl: J. Silvester, *ART,* 1926.

**TUCKET, Elizabeth Fox**
Black and white artist. She illustrated *Zigzagging Amongst the Dolomites* for Longmans in 1871.
Colls: V & AM.

**TURBAYNE, Albert Angus** 1866-1940

Designer and book decorator. He was born at Boston, United States in 1866 of Scottish parents and was educated there and at Coburg, Canada. From about 1900, Turbayne concentrated on the design of books, winning bronze medals in the Paris Exhibition of that year for his tool bindings for Oxford University Press. He was for many years Demonstrator in Design at the LCC School of Photoengraving and Lithography. He lived at Bedford Park, London and died on 29 April 1940.

Designed: *The Beautiful Birthday Book [Black, 1905 (borders)]; Prose Works of Rudyard Kipling [1908 (cover)].*
Publ: *Alphabet and Numerals; Monograms and Ciphers.*

**TURNER, Joseph Mallord William RA** 1775-1851

Landscape painter in oils and watercolours. He was born in London on 23 April 1775, the son of a barber and wig maker in Covent Garden. He entered the RA Schools in 1789, becoming a pupil of T. Malton and in 1791 and 1792 went on sketching tours in the Bristol and South Wales areas. He joined Dr. Monro's evening study classes in 1794 and in the following years visited the 'picturesque' landscapes of the Lake District and Wales and worked for William, Beckford at Fonthill Abbey. He was elected ARA in 1799 and RA in 1802, making his first Continental trip to France and Switzerland that year. Turner's tours increased after the Napoleonic Wars to include visits to Italy in 1819, Paris and Normandy in 1821, Holland, Belgium and the Rhine in 1825, the French rivers in 1826, France and Italy in 1828 and Northern France in 1829. These visits were interspersed with tours of England and stays with patrons like the Fawkes of Farnley Hall and Lord Egremont of Petworth. In the 1830s he was touring in the Baltic, Germany and Austria and paid his first visit to Venice in 1833 and made trips to the Rhine and Germany in 1840 and to Switzerland in 1841 and 1842 and again in 1844. He was in Normandy for the last time in 1845.

Turner's first move towards engraved work was in 1806 when W.F. Weils suggested that his paintings would reach a wider public if published. The result was the *Liber Studiorum,* a series of studies which were intended to classify his ideas about landscape. Turner etched the plates before they were mezzotinted and carefully superintended every stage under skilled engravers such as Lupton, Charles Turner and William Say. As Hardie has put it 'He trained a whole school of engravers and personally superintended their work'. In these inspired and harmonious productions the complete effect of a Turner drawing remains supreme. The fashion for the picturesque and for landscape annuals grew in the 1820s and the artist continued to work for these publications which were not so much books as plates between covers with a text. In many cases Turner, not principally a figure painter, had to crowd his foregrounds with interest to satisfy the public and his accuracy as a topographer was never a strong point. An extremely literary artist, Turner's pictures were full of allusions but he was too big an artist to sit comfortably in an ordinary volume and the *Liber* was never really surpassed. Turner acted as Professor of Perspective at the RA from 1807 to 1837 and died in London in 1851.

Contrib: *The Copper Plate Magazine; The Pocket Magazine [c.1798]; Cooke's Picturesque Views of the Southern Coast of England [1814-26]; Views in Sussex [1816-20]; The Rivers of Devon [1815-23]; Hakewill's Picturesque Tour of Italy [1818-20]; Whitaker's History of Richmondshire [1818-23]; Provincial Antiquities of Scotland [1819-26]; Picturesque Views in England and Wales [1827-38]; Roger's Poems [1834]; Byron's Life and Works [1832-34]; Rivers of France [1833-35]; Scott's Poetical and Prose Works [1834-37].*
Exhib: BI; RA; RBA.
Colls: Aberdeen; Ashmolean; Bedford; Birkenhead; BM; Derby; Exeter; Fitzwilliam; Glasgow; Leeds; Lincoln; Manchester; Nottingham; Tate; V & AM.
Bibl: W. Thornbury, *Life of JMWT,* 1862; A.J. Finberg, *T's Sketches and Drawings,* 1910; A.J. Finberg, *T's Watercolours at Farnley Hall,* 1912; A.P. Oppe, *Watercolours of T,* 1925; A. J. Finberg, *Life of JMWT,* 1939; J. Rothenstein, *T,* 1962; M. Butlin, *T. Watercolours,* 1962; L. Hermann, *JMWT,* 1963; J. Gage, *Colour in Turner,* 1969; Agnew *exhib. cat.,* Nov-Dec. 1967; RA *exhib. cat.,* Nov. 1974-March 1975.
See illustration (p.39).

**TURNER, William** 1792-1867

Diplomat and amateur topographer. He was attached to the embassy at Constantinople and was envoy to Columbia 1829-38. He illustrated his own *Journal of a Tour in the Levant,* 1820, AT 375.

**TWIDLE, Arthur** 1865-1936

Painter and illustrator. He worked at Sidcup, Kent from 1902-13 and then at Godstone, Surrey. He died in 1936.

Contrib: *The Quiver [1890]; The English Illustrated Magazine [1893-94]; The Temple Magazine [1896]; The Strand Magazine [1906 (Conan Doyle)].*
Exhib: RA.

**TWINING, Louisa** 1820-1900

Artist and writer. She was born on 16 November 1820 and published a number of books on art and social matters illustrated by herself. She was made a Lady of Grace of St. John of Jerusalem and died on 25 September 1911.

Publ: *Recollections of Life and Work [1893]; Workhouses and Pauperism [1898].*
Colls: BM.

**TYNDALE, Walter Frederick Roofe RI** 1856-1943

Architectural painter. He was born at Bruges in 1856 and came to England in 1871, later studying art at Antwerp and Paris. He began as an oil painter but after contact with Helen Allingham (q.v.) turned entirely to watercolour. He made tours of Morocco, Egypt, Lebanon, Syria and Japan and lived in Venice. During the First World War he acted as Head Censor for the Army at Boulogne. He died in 1943. He was elected RI in 1911, and one man shows were held at the FAS in 1920 and 1924.

Publ. or Illus: *The New Forest [1904]; Below the Cataracts [1907]; Japan and the Japanese [1910]; Japanese Gardens [1912]; An Artist in Egypt [1912]; An Artist in Italy [1913]; An Artist on the Riviera [1916]; The Dalmatian Coast [1925]; Somerset [1927].*
Exhib: B; FAS; G; GG; L; M; New Gall; RA; RBA; RHA; RI; ROI.
Colls: BM; Bradford; V & AM.

**TYRER, Mary S.**

Amateur illustrator. She was living at Cheltenham in 1896 and at Willesden in 1897 and won *The Studio* illustration competitions, Vol. 8 p.252 and Vol. 11 p.210 illus.

**UBSDELL, Richard Henry Clements**          fl.1828-1856
History painter, miniaturist, illustrator and photographer. He worked in Portsmouth and drew watercolours of churches. He contributed to *The Illustrated Times*, 1856 (marine).

Exhib: RA; RBA.
Colls: Portsmouth.

**UNDERWOOD, Edgar Sefton   FRIBA**          fl.1898-1914
Architect and humorous draughtsman. He was a Fellow of the RIBA and practised at Queen Street, Cheapside.

Contrib: *Fun [1901]*.
Exhib: RA.

**UPTON, Florence K.**          -1922
Portrait painter and illustrator. She was working in Paris from 1905-7 and produced a whole series of children's books called the 'Golliwog Books' in the years 1899-1905. Her drawings of figures and toys are imaginative if rather stiff. She died in 1922.

Illus: *The Adventures of Two Dutch Dolls [1895]; The Adventures of Borbee and The Wisp [1908]*.
Contrib: *The Strand Magazine [1894 (French ports)]; The Idler [1895]*.
Exhib: FAS; L; P; RA.

**URQUHART, Annie Mackenzie**          fl.1904-1928
Watercolour painter and illustrator. She studied at the Glasgow School of Art under F.H. Newbury and in Paris with M. Delville. She worked in Glasgow and specialised in drawings of children and foliage, often on vegetable parchment with the colour stippled on to an outline drawing.

Exhib: L; RA; RSA.
Bibl: *The Studio*, Vol.47, 1909, pp.60-63 illus.

**UWINS, Thomas   RA**          1782-1857
Painter and illustrator. He was born at Pentonville on 24 February 1782, the son of a Bank of England official and was apprenticed to the engraver Benjamin Smith in 1797. He left this employ after a year to study at a Finsbury drawing school and at the RA Schools, making his living by book frontispieces and vignette illustrations. He was elected AOWS in 1809 and OWS in 1810, acting as Secretary from 1813-14. He resigned from this due to poor health in 1818 but money difficulties caused him to undertake another intensive round of book illustrating, 1818-24. He was employed as a topographer and visited France in 1817, and lived in Italy from 1824 to 1831. A commission to illustrate *Scott's Works* resulted in him living in Edinburgh for a time, but it was the copying of miniature portraits that was supposed to have ruined his eyesight and cost him his career. He later turned to oil painting and was elected ARA in 1833, RA in 1838 and served as Librarian to the Academy 1844 and Surveyor to the Queen's Pictures from 1845. He died at Staines on 25 August 1857.

Illus: *Nourjahad [Mrs. Sheridan]; Histoire de Charles XII [Voltaire]; Don Quixote*.
Contrib: *Ackermann's Repository [fashion pls.]; The History of the Abbey Church of St. Peter's, Westminster [1812]; History of the University of Oxford [1813-14]; History of the University of Cambridge; Britton's Cathedrals [1832-36]*.
Exhib: BI; NWS; OWS; RA; RBA.
Colls: BM; Birkenhead; Fitzwilliam; V & AM.
Bibl: Mrs. T. Uwins, *Memoir*, 1858; M. Hardie, *Watercol. Paint. in Brit.*, Vol.1, 1966, p.157 illus.

See illustration (right).

*THOMAS UWINS RA 1782-1857. 'The Duke of Richmond's Tomb'. An illustration to* The History of the Abbey Church of St. Peter's Westminster, *1812. Engraving coloured by hand.*

**V**

**VALENTIN, Henry**                                    **1820-1855**
Painter and illustrator. He was born at Allarmoint in the Vosges in 1820 and worked for *l'Illustration*, drawing figures in the style of Gavarni (q.v.). He was French correspondent of a number of British papers and died in Paris in 1855.
Contrib: *ILN [1848-56]; Cassell's Illustrated Family Paper [1855]; The Illustrated Times [1859].*

**VALERIO, Theodore**                                  **1819-1879**
Painter, engraver, etcher and lithographer. He was born at Herserange on 18 February 1819 and became a pupil of Charlet, exhibiting at the Salon from 1838. He travelled widely and visited Italy, Switzerland, Hungary and England and made studies of the Crimea. He died at Vichy on 14 September 1879.
Contrib: *The Illustrated Times [1856, 1860 (Arabia and Austria)].*

**VALLANCE, Aymer**                                        **-1943**
Flower painter, illustrator and designer. He worked in London and designed initial letters, endpapers and ornament for his own books and made playing card designs. He died in 1943.
Publ: *William Morris His Art, Writings and Public Life [1897]; Old Colleges of Oxford [1912]; Old Crosses and Lychgates [1919].*
Contrib: *The Yellow Book [1894].*
Exhib: RBA.

**VALLENCE, William Fleming   RSA**                     **1827-1904**
Marine and landscape painter. He was born at Paisley on 13 February 1827 and apprenticed to a gilder in 1841 after which he studied at the Paisley School of Design and the Trustees Academy, Edinburgh. He was a full time artist from 1857 and was elected ARSA in 1875 and RSA in 1881. He died at Edinburgh on 31 August 1904.
Contrib: *Pen and Pencil Pictures From The Poets [1866].*
Exhib: RA; RSA.

**VAN ASSEN, Benedictus Antonio**                          **-1817**
Watercolour painter and engraver. He worked in England during the last decade of the 18th century and in the early 19th century. He engraved a portrait of Belzoni, 1804, J.H. Mortimer RA in 1810 and died in London in 1817.
Illus: *Emblematic Devices [1810].*
Exhib: RA, 1788-1804.
Colls: BM.

**VANDERLYN, Nathan**                                 **fl.1897-1937**
Watercolourist, etcher, engraver and illustrator. He studied at the Slade School and at the RCA. He was Painting Instructor at the LCC Central School of Arts and Crafts and was elected RI in 1916 although his name was removed in 1937.
Contrib: *The English Illustrated Magazine [1897].*
Exhib: L; RA; RBA; RI; RMS.

**VEAL, Oliver**
Illustrator. Contributed drawings to *Sketchy Bits*, 1895.

**VEDDER, Simon Harmon**                                   **1866-**
Painter, sculptor and illustrator. He was born in New York on 9 October 1866 and studied at the Metropolitan Museum School, N.Y. He studied in Paris at Julian's under Bouguereau and Robert Fleury and at the École des Beaux Arts. He settled in London by 1896 and married the painter Eva Roos.
Contrib: *Black & White [1900]; The Strand Magazine [1906]; Cassells Family*

*Magazine; The Idler; The Pall Mall Magazine.*
Exhib: B; FAS; L; RA; ROI.

**VENNER, Victor L.**                                 **fl.1904-1924**
Humorous illustrator. He contributed to *Punch*, 1904.
Exhib: L.

**VERHAEGE, L.**
Silhouette illustrator. He contributed scenes of Paris to *The English Illustrated Magazine*, 1896.
Colls: V & AM.

**VERHEYDEN, Francois**                                **1806-1890**
Genre painter and caricaturist. He was born at Louvain 18 March 1806 and studied in Paris before working at Antwerp. He contributed six cartoons to *Vanity Fair* in 1883 and died in Brussels about 1890.

**VERNER, Captain Willoughby**
Amateur artist. He was an officer in the Rifle Brigade, taking part in the Nile Expeditionary Force, 1884-85.
Illus: *Sketches in the Soudan [1885 (col. liths.)].*

**VERNON, R. Warren**                                 **fl.1882-1908**
Painter, etcher and illustrator. He worked mostly in the South of England but in Dresden in 1903. He contributed a drawing to *Punch* in 1903.
Exhib: B; G; L; RA: RBA; RCA; RHA; RI; ROI.

**VERPEILLEUX, Emile**                                 **1888-1964**
Portrait and landscape painter, engraver and illustrator. He was born of Belgian parents in London on 3 March 1888 and studied in London and at the Académie des Beaux Arts, Antwerp. He produced coloured wood engravings and views of London and was elected RBA 1914. He died in 1964.
Contrib: *The Graphic [1915].*
Exhib: L; NEA; RA; RBA; RSA.

**VICKERS, Alfred Gomersal**                           **1810-1837**
Landscape painter and illustrator. He was the son of the artist A. Vickers and was sent by Charles Heath to St. Petersburg to record the city for *The Picturesque Annual*, 1836 and *Heath's Gallery*, 1838. He died at Pentonville in 1837.
Exhib: BI; NWS; RA; RBA.
Colls: BM; V & AM; Witt Photo.

**VICKERS, Vincent Cartwright**                            **1879-**
Black and white artist. He was born in 1879 and was a member of the armament and shipbuilding family. He lived and worked at Royston.
Illus: *The Google Book [1913].*
Exhib: Arlington Gall; RA.
Bibl: *Strand Magazine*, Dec. 1926.

**VIERGE, M. Daniel   'Vierge Urrabieta Ortiz'**       **1851-1904**
Genre painter, draughtsman and illustrator. He was born at Madrid on 5 March 1851, the son of a leading Spanish illustrator and studied at the Madrid Academy. In 1867 he was working for the *Madrid la nuit* and in 1869 left for Paris to find an opening in illustrated journalism but his plans were prevented by the Franco-Prussian War. After returning to Madrid he was recognised by Yriarte, editor of *Monde Illustré* and worked for the paper from that time. Vierge illustrated an important edition of Victor Hugo's works, 1874 to 1882 and Quevedo's *Don Pablo*, 1882 and *Cervantes*, 1893. The artist was severely crippled by a stroke in 1881 but recovered sufficiently to do much good work subsequently.
   Pennell points out that Vierge's influence on illustration in France, Spain and the United States was very considerable. His pen line was very pure, there was little cross hatching and yet a great suggestion of colour without colour at all. Several of the Edwardian artists such as H.R. Millar (q.v.) owe a debt to him and Ludovici records that Vierge

485

was interested in his English public and wished to exhibit in London. Vierge won many honours including the Legion of Honour and died at Boulogne-surs-Seine on 4 May 1904.

Contrib: *ILN [1897]*.
Exhib: International, 1904.
Bibl: *The Century Magazine*, June 1893; J. Pennell, *Pen Drawing and Pen Draughtsmen*, 1889; A. Ludovici, *An Artist's Life In London and Paris*, 1926.

**VIGNE, Godfrey Thomas**                                    **1801-1863**
Amateur artist and illustrator. He worked at Woodford and specialised in figure subjects. He travelled overland to India, 1833-39.

Illus: *A Personal Narrative of a Visit to Ghuzni, Kabul and Afghanistan [1840 AT 505]*.
Contrib: *ILN [1849]*.
Exhib: RA.
Colls: Searight.

**VILLIERS, Fred**                                          **1851-1922**
Special Artist and illustrator of military subjects. He was born in London on 23 April 1851 and was educated at Guines in the Pas-de-Calais. He studied art at the BM and at South Kensington, 1869-70 and was a student at the RA Schools in 1871. He became Special Artist for *The Graphic* in 1876, being sent first to Servia and then to Turkey in 1877. He went on a world tour for the paper and was afterwards at Tel-el-Kebir, 1882, attended the Russian coronation in 1883 and saw action in Eastern Soudan, 1884, Khartoum, 1884, Bulgaria, 1886, Burma, 1887 and in the Graeco-Turkish War of 1897. Villiers was the earliest correspondent to be equipped with a cinematograph camera in the 1900s. He was present at the Siege of Port Arthur in 1904 and worked during the Great War, 1914-18. He was awarded twelve service medals. He died on 3 April 1922.

Publ: *Pictures of Many Wars [1902]; Port Arthur [1905]; Peaceful Personalities and Warriors Bold [1907]; Villiers, His Five Decades of Adventure [1921]*.
Contrib: *The English Illustrated Magazine [1883-84]; Black & White [1891]; The Idler; ILN [1900]*.
Exhib: M; RA; ROI.

**VILLIERS, H.**
Architectural draughtsman. He contributed to *The History of the Abbey Church of St. Peter's Westminster*, Ackermann, 1812.

**VILLIERS, Jean Francois Marie Huet**                      **1772-1813**
Miniature painter and draughtsman. He was born in Paris in 1772, the son of J.B. Huet and settled in London in 1801. He painted portraits and landscapes in oil and watercolours and was a member of the Sketching Society. He was appointed Miniature Painter to the Duke and Duchess of York and styled himself 'Miniature Painter to the King of France'. He died in London in 1813.

Illus: *Rudiments of Cattle [1805]; Rudiments and Characters of Trees [1806]*.
Contrib: *The History of the Abbey Church of St. Peter's Westminster [1812]*.
Exhib: BI; OWS; RA.
Colls: BM.

**VINE, W.**
Caricaturist. He contributed two cartoons to *Vanity Fair*, 1873. He signs 'WV' in monogram.

**VINYCOMB, John Knox    LRIBA**                            **fl.1894-1914**
Architect, heraldic draughtsman and illustrator. He was probably born in Belfast and became a member of the Royal Irish Academy and a Fellow of the Royal Society of Antiquaries of Ireland. He was an authority on and a designer of bookplates and became Vice-President of the Ex Libris Society.

Publ: *On the Processes For the Production of Ex Libris [1894]; Fictitious and Symbolic Creatures in Art [1906]*.
Colls: Newcastle.

**VIVIAN, George**                                          **1798-1873**
Amateur artist. He was born in 1798, one of the family of Vivian of Claverton Manor near Bath. He went to Eton and Christ Church,

Oxford, before travelling on the Continent and in the Near East where he met Lord Byron in 1824. He lived in Italy from 1844 to 1846 but contracted malaria from which he never fully recovered. He was a friend of J.D. Harding with whom his landscapes have some similarity. He died in 1873.

Illus: *Spanish Scenery [1838]; Scenery of Portugal and Spain; The Gardens of Rome [1848]*.

**VIZETELLY, Frank**                                        **1830-1883**
Special Artist and illustrator. He was born in London, the younger brother of Henry Vizetelly (q.v.). He was trained as a wood engraver and worked with his brother on *The Pictorial Times* and was Editor of *Monde Illustré* in Paris, 1857-59. In 1859 he was sent by *The Illustrated Times* to cover the Italian Campaign as Special Artist and was subsequently engaged by *The Illustrated London News* as their permanent War Artist. He was with Garibaldi in Sicily in 1860 and saw action on both sides in the American Civil War, 1861 and was present during the Prusso-Austrian War of 1866. He founded a society periodical called *Echoes of the Clubs* and in 1883 was sent by *The Graphic*, to accompany Hicks Pasha to the Soudan. He never returned and was believed to have been killed at El Obeid.

Colls: Witt Photo.
Bibl: H. Vizetelly, *Glances Back Through Seventy Years*, 1893.

**VIZETELLY, Henry**                                        **1820-1894**
Wood engraver, illustrator and editor. He was born in London on 30 July 1820, the elder brother of F. Vizetelly (q.v.). He was an engraver for *The Illustrated London News*, which he helped to found in 1842 and later established his own illustrated journals *The Pictorial Times*, 1843 and *The Illustrated Times*, 1855-65. In 1865 he became Paris correspondent of *The Illustrated London News* and lived there till 1872 when he settled in Berlin. He returned to London and worked on translations of Russian and French novels, dying at Fareham in 1894.

Publ: *Glances Back Through Seventy Years [1893]*.

**VOIGHT, Hans Henning    'Alastair'**                      **c.1889-1933**
Imaginative draughtsman and illustrator. He was born about 1889 of English, Spanish and Russian extraction. He was a self-taught artist and worked most of his life in Germany, interesting himself in decadence and transvestism. His black and white work is very sensuous and derivative from the work of Beardsley (q.v.), his colour illustrations have more the feel of the contemporary Russian school of ballet designers.

Illus: *Count Fanny's Nuptials [G.G. Hope Johnstone, 1907]; The Sphinx [Oscar Wilde, 1920]; Sebastian Van Storck [Walter Pater, 1927]; Manon Lescaut [Abbé Prevost, 1928]; Dangerous Acquaintances [Laclos, 1933 (Paris ed., 1929-30)]*.
Bibl: *Alastair: Forty-Four Drawings in Colour and Black and White With a Note of Exclamation by Robert Ross*, 1914; *Alastair: Fifty Drawings*, New York, 1925.

**VON HOLST, Theodore M.**                                  **1810-1844**
Genre painter. He was born in London on 3 September 1810, the son of a music teacher and after studying in the British Museum, attended the RA Schools under H. Fuseli. The latter's strong influence in seen in his work, which can be rather hard and Germanic in line. He died in London on 14 February 1844.

Illus: *The Rape of the Lock [c.1825]*.
Exhib: BI; RA; RBA.

**VOSPER, Sydney Carnow**                                   **1866-1942**
Watercolour painter, etcher and dry-point artist. He was born at Plymouth in 1866 and studied at Colarossi's in Paris, being elected ARWS in 1906 and RWS in 1914. He was working at Morbihan, France in 1904 and at Oxford from 1928. He died in 1942.

Contrib: *Punch [1902]*.
Exhib: B; L; M; RA; RI; RSW; RWS.

## WADDY, Frederick
fl.1878-1897

Ornamental artist and illustrator. He contributed initial letters to *The Illustrated London News*, 1883-84 and exhibited pencil drawings in London from 1878.

Illus: *For Faith and Freedom [Besant, 1897 (with Forestier)]*.

## WADE, Charles Paget   ARIBA
-1956

Architect, craftsman and illustrator. He was the son of a wealthy sugar planting family owning estates in the West Indies at St. Kitts and Nevis. He studied architecture and practised as an architect at Yoxford and Forest Gate, London before acquiring Snowshill Manor, Gloucestershire in 1925, which he totally restored and presented to the National Trust in 1951. He died in 1956.

Illus: *Bruges, A Record and Impression [Mary Stratton, 1914]; The Spirit of the House [G. Murray, 1915]*.
Exhib: RA.
Colls: Nat. Trust, Snowshill Manor.
Bibl: *Modern Book Illustrators and Their Work*, Studio, 1914.

## WADHAM, Percy
fl.1893-1907

Painter and illustrator. He was born at Adelaide, Australia and studied with T.S. Cooper and James Chapman. He was ARE from 1902-10.

Contrib: *The Pall Mall Magazine [1897]*.
Exhib: FAS; RA; RE.

## WAGEMAN, Thomas Charles   NWS
c.1787-1863

Portrait and landscape painter and illustrator. He was born about 1787 and was a founder member of the NWS in 1831 and became Portrait Painter to the King of Holland. He specialised in portraits of famous actors. He died in 1863.

Contrib: *Annals of Sporting [1827]*.
Exhib: BI; NWS; RA; RBA.

## WAIBLER, F.

German illustrator. He contributed to *The Illustrated London News*, 1872.

LOUIS WILLIAM WAIN 1860-1930. 'A quiet game at Nap'. Original drawing for illustration. Grisaille, signed and dated, 1st Dec '94. 17ins. x 22½ins. (43cm x 56.5cm).

**WAIN, Louis William**        **1860-1939**

Animal caricaturist and illustrator. He was born in London on 5 August 1860 of an English father and French mother. He was educated by the Christian Brothers and studied for a musical career until 1879. He then went to the West London School of Art, 1877-80 and was Assistant Master there, 1881-82. He joined the staff of *The Illustrated Sporting and Dramatic News* in 1882 and *The Illustrated London News*, 1886. From 1883, Wain began to draw cats as they had never been drawn before, cats in humorous guises in human situations but always beautifully handled. The titles speak for themselves, 'A Kittens Christmas Party', 'Nine Lives of a Cat' and 'Cats at Circus' although he was sometimes forced to draw dogs before he became well-known! His main success stemmed from his recognition by Sir William Ingram of *The 'News* who employed him regularly and included one picture of one hundred and fifty cats that took him eleven days to draw. Wain became popular in the United States and visited New York, 1907-10 where he was on the staff of the *New York American* for a time. He also turned his talents to the illustrating of short stories, published yearly gift books and was employed on postcards for Messrs Raphael Tuck. He was President of the National Cat Club and a member of many other committees connected with feline reform, but his obsession slowly turned to insanity and he died in poverty on 4 July 1939.

Illus: *Louis Wain's Annuals [1901-26]; Louis Wain's Summer Book [1906-7]; The Kitcats; 9 China Futurist Cats [1922]; Louis Wain Big Midget Book [1926-27].*
Contrib: *The Sporting & Dramatic News [1882]; ILN [1883-99]; The English Illustrated Magazine [1884-1900]; Moonshine [1893]; The Sketch; The Gentlewoman; Pall Mall Budget; The Boy's Own Paper; Judy [1898]; The Windsor Magazine; Lloyds Weekly News [1905].*
Exhib: RBA.
Colls: V & AM; Witt Photo.
Bibl: *The Idler*, Vol.8, pp.550-555; Rodney Dale, *LW The Man Who Drew Cats*, 1968, with bibliog. and chapter on Wain's illness by D.L. Davies.
See illustration (p.487).

**WAITE, Edward Wilkins**        **fl.1878-1920**

Watercolourist and illustrator. He worked at Blackheath and then at Dorking, 1892, Fittleworth, 1919 and Haslemere, 1920. He was elected RBA in 1893.

Illus: *The Story of My Heart [Richard Jefferies, 1912]; The Roadmender [1911].*
Exhib: B; G; L; M; New Gall; RA; RBA; RCA; RHA; ROI; RSA.
Colls: Bristol.

**WAKE, Richard**        **1865-1888**

Special Artist. He was born on 24 September 1865, the son of Hereward Crauford Wake, CB, Civil Magistrate of Arrah and a grandson of Sir George Sitwell. He was appointed artist for *The Graphic* at Suakim in 1888 and died there on 6 December after making his first drawings.

**WAKEFIELD, T.H.**

Amateur illustrator. Contributed design to *The Studio* competition, Vol. 8, 1896, p.252.

**WAKEMAN, William Frederick**        **1822-1900**

Landscape and topographical artist. He was born at Dublin in 1822 and was attached to the Ordnance Survey through the influence of G. Petrie (q.v.). He later worked as a drawing master in Dublin and taught at St. Columba's College, Stackallan and at the Royal School, Portora. He died in Coleraine in 1900.

Illus: *Ecclesiastical Antiquities [Petrie]; Ireland Its Scenery and Character [S.C. Hall]; Catalogue of Antiquities in the Royal Irish Academy [Wilde]; Lives of the Irish Saints [O'Hanlon].*
Contrib: *The Irish Penny Journal; Dublin Saturday Magazine; Hibernian Magazine.*
Exhib: RHA.
Colls: RIA.

**WALKER, Arthur George RA**        **1861-1939**

Sculptor, painter and designer in mosaics. He was born on 20 October 1861 and studied at the RA Schools and in Paris. He worked in Chelsea until 1914 and later at Parkstone, Dorset, he was elected ARA

in 1925 and RA in 1936. He died on 13 September 1939.

Illus: *The Lost Princess [G. Macdonald, 1895]; Stories From The Faerie Queen [Mary Macleod, 1897]; The Book of King Arthur [Mary Macleod, 1900].*
Exhib: G; L; RA; RI; RMS; ROI; RSA.
Bibl: R.E.D. Sketchley, *Eng. Bk. Illus.*, 1903, pp.116, 172.

**WALKER, E.J.**        **fl.1878-1886**

Domestic painter. He worked at Liverpool, 1878-79 and then at Regents Park, London. He contributed to *The Illustrated London News*, 1886, Christmas Number.

Exhib: L.

**WALKER, Francis S. RHA**        **1848-1916**

Landscape and genre painter, illustrator of social scenes and engraver. He was born in County Meath in 1848 and studied art at the Royal Dublin Society and at the RHA Schools. He obtained a scholarship there to study in London and came in 1868 to begin work with the Dalziel Brothers. He began to work for *The Graphic* in 1870 and *The Illustrated London News* in 1875. He was elected ARHA in 1878, RHA in 1879 and RE in 1897. He worked chiefly in North London and died at Mill Hill on 17 April 1916.

Illus: *Westminster [Walter Besant, 1897 (with others)].*
Contrib: *Cassell's Family Magazine [1868]; Good Words [1869]; The Sunday Magazine [1869]; Good Words For The Young [1869-72]; The Nobility of Life [1869]; London Society [1870]; Dalziel's Bible Gallery [1880]; Fun.*
Exhib: B; G; L; M; RA; RE; RHA; RI; ROI.
Colls: Witt Photo.

**WALKER, Frederick ARA**        **1840-1875**

Painter and illustrator. He was born in Marylebone on 24 May 1840 and began to study art at the British Museum before being apprenticed to an architect named Baker. He returned to the Museum after leaving the architect, sketched the Greek sculpture and attended Leigh's Life School in Newman Street. He attended the RA Schools and then went, in 1858, to work for J.W. Whymper (q.v.) who taught him to draw on the wood, where he met J.W. North (q.v.). He began to draw for the magazines in 1860 and that year through the influence of Thackeray (q.v.), he started to work for *The Cornhill Magazine*. It was the latter's admission of failure in illustrating his own story that gave Walker a wider public through its pages in 1862. In some ways Walker's art was an inheritance from Millais, but it was also an inheritance from his studies of sculpture and his studies of nature. All his illustrations whether contemporary in subject or costume pieces show a familiarity with the figure and with movement that is outstanding. Although his name is usually linked with George Pinwell (q.v.) their acquaintanceship was slight, and Walker is more of a narrative painter than either Pinwell or North with whom he went sketching, 1868. Walker visited Paris in 1867, Venice in 1868 and 1870 and visited the Highlands with Richard Ansdell, RA (q.v.). From book illustration Walker stepped into watercolours, proving himself an exquisite colourist and with a superb eye for detail. Such paintings as 'The Harbour of Refuge' show the second mood of Pre-Raphaelitism in the 1870s with an increased naturalism. Walker's failing health caused him to winter in Algiers in 1873-74 but he returned to this country and died at St Fillan's, Perthshire on 5 June 1875. He was elected AOWS in 1864, OWS in 1866 and ARA in 1871.

Contrib: *Everybody's Journal [1860]; Leisure House [1860]; Tom Cringle's Log [1861]; The Twins and Their Stepmother [1861]; Hard Times, Reprinted Pieces [Charles Dickens, 1861]; Good Words [1861-64]; The Cornhill Magazine [1861-66]; London Society [1862]; Willmott's Sacred Poetry [1862]; The Cornhill Gallery [1864]; English Sacred Poetry [1864]; Punch [1865, 1869]; A Round of Days [1866]; Ingoldsby Legends [Barham, 1866]; Touches of Nature by Eminent Artists [1866]; Wayside Poesies [1867]; Story of Elizabeth [1867]; Village on the Cliff [1867]; The Graphic [1869]; A Daughter of Heth [1872]; ILN [1875]; Thornbury's Legendary Ballads [1876].*
Exhib: OWS; RA.
Colls: Ashmolean; BM; Fitzwilliam; Manchester; V & AM; Witt Photo.
Bibl: J. Comyns Carr, *FW An Essay*, 1885; Claude Phillips, *The Portfolio*, June 1894; J.G. Marks, *Life and Letters of FW, RA*, 1896; The Brothers Dalziel, *A Record of Work*, 1840-90, 1901, pp.193-205; Gleeson White, *English Illustration*, 1906 pp.165-166; Forrest Reid, *Illustrators of the Sixties*, 1928 pp.134-152.

See illustration (p.489).

Drawn by F. Walker. (Engraved by J. Swain.

"IN THE NOVEMBER NIGHT."

Oswald Cray, page 371.

*FREDERICK WALKER ARA 1840-1875. 'In The November Night'. An illustration to the story* Oswald Cray, *in* Good Words, *1864. Wood engraving.*

**WALKER, Jessica (Mrs. Stephens)**                    fl.1904-1932
Painter, illustrator and writer. She was born in Arizona, USA and studied at the Liverpool School, winning the travelling scholarship to Italy and studying in Paris and Florence. She was for some years art critic of *The Studio.*
Contrib: *Women and Roses [Browning, 1905].*
Exhib: L; M; RCA.

**WALKER, John**
Topographer and illustrator. He is probably the same artist as the J. Walker exhibiting at the RA, 1796 to 1800.
Contrib: *The Copper Plate Magazine [1792-1802].*

**WALKER, Marcella**                    fl.1872-1917
Flower painter and illustrator. She worked at Haverstock Hill and contributed genre subjects to the magazines.
Contrib: *ILN [1885-94, 1903]; The Girl's Own Paper.*
Exhib: L; M; RA; RHA.

**WALKER, T. Dart**
Marine artist. He contributed illustrations of ships to *The Illustrated London News,* 1899.

**WALKER, W.H.**                    fl.1906-1926
Watercolourist and illustrator. He worked in pen with fresh colours in the style of Rackham and illustrated *Alice's Adventures in Wonderland* for Messrs Lane, in 1908. He was a member of the family who ran Walker's Galleries.
Exhib: L; RA.

**WALL, A.J.**                    fl.1889-1897
Illustrator specialising in animals and birds. He worked at Stratford-upon-Avon, but probably visited Australia in 1889-90 when he worked for *The Illustrated London News.*
Contrib: *The Sporting and Dramatic News [1891]; The Boy's Own Paper; The English Illustrated Magazine [1896-97].*
Exhib: B.

**WALL, Tony**
Figure artist. He contributed to *Punch,* 1902.

**WALLACE, Robert Bruce**                    -1893
Figure artist in watercolour and illustrator. He lived and worked in Manchester and assisted Ford Madox Brown (q.v.) with his Manchester frescoes. His illustrative work began with *Punch,* where he made contributions from 1875-78 after an introduction from Swain. He hoped to succeed Miss G. Bowers (q.v.) on the paper but when he failed to do so, he concentrated on serious illustration elsewhere. He was Secretary of the Manchester Academy of Fine Arts, a friend of Frederick Shields (q.v.) and died at Manchester in 1893.
Illus: *The Adventures of Phillip [W.M. Thackeray]; Catherine [W.M. Thackeray, Cheap Illustrated Edition, 1894].*
Contrib: *ILN [1898].*
Exhib: M; RBA.

**WALLACE-DUNLOP   See DUNLOP, Marion W.**

**WALLER, Pickford R.**                    1873-1927
Amateur illustrator and decorator. He worked in Pimlico, was a friend of J. McNeil Whistler (q.v.) and patronised many artists including S.H. Sime (q.v.). He practised the decoration of manuscript and extra illustrated books with his own initial letters. His sketchbooks, including some designs for Guthrie's Pear Tree Press, were sold at Sotheby's in April and November 1976.
Illus: *Songs and Verses by Edmund Waller [Pear Tree Press, 1902].*
Contrib: *The Studio [Vol.8, 1896 pp.252-253 illus.].*

**WALLER, Samuel Edmund**                    1850-1903
Genre and animal painter and illustrator. He was born at Gloucester on 16 June 1850 and studied with the Gloucester artist John Kemp. He was educated at Cheltenham and went to the RA Schools in 1869, beginning regular work for the magazines from about 1874. Waller was a good painter of horses and developed a style of sentimental genre picture in which they were usually involved, but he also made

489

zoological studies and painted landscapes. He married the portrait painter, Mary Lemon Waller, and was elected ROI in 1883. He died at Haverstock Hill on 9 June 1903.
Publ: *Six Week's in the Saddle; Sebastian's Secret.*
Illus: *Strange Adventures of a Phaeton [William Black, 1874].*
Contrib: *The Graphic [1874-81]; ILN [1895]; The Sporting and Dramatic News [1899].*
Exhib: B; FAS; G; L; M; RA; ROI.
Colls: Tate; Witt Photo.

### WALLIS, Henry   RWS                              1830-1916
Landscape and history painter and writer. He was born in London on 21 February 1830 and studied at Cary's Academy and then in Paris and at the RA Schools. He came under the influence of the Pre-Raphaelites at an early date and painted 'The Death of Chatterton', 1856 and 'The Stone-breaker'. His first flush of youthful talent did not last and he is included here for the academic illustrations that he made for his own books on ceramics. He was elected ARWS in 1878 and RWS in 1880. He died at Sutton, Surrey in December 1916.
Illus: *Egyptian Ceramic Art [1898]; Persian Lustre Vases [1899]; Nicola da Urbino at the Correr Museum [1905]; The Oriental Influence on Italian Ceramic Art [1900].*
Exhib: BI; G; L; M; RA; RBA; New Gall; RWS.
Colls: Birmingham; Tate; V & AM.
Bibl: J. Maas, *Victorian Painters,* 1970 pp.132-133 illus.

### WALSH, Captain Thomas
Army officer and amateur artist. He illustrated *Journal of the Late Campaign in Egypt*, 1803, AT 266.

### WALSHE, J.C.                                       fl.1889-1909
Genre painter and illustrator. He worked in Birmingham and contributed figure drawings to *Punch,* 1903-9, specialising in strong interiors.
Exhib: B.

### WALTERS, Thomas                                  fl.1856-1875
Domestic painter and illustrator. He worked in London and contributed to *Punch,* 1867-75.
Exhib: BI; RA; RBA.

### WALTON, Edward Arthur   RSA                       1860-1922
Landscape painter and genre artist. He was born in Glanderstone, Renfrewshire on 15 April 1860 and studied at the Glasgow School of Art and in Düsseldorf. He lived in London after 1894 but returned to Edinburgh in 1904. He was elected ARSA in 1889, RSA in 1905 and was President of the Royal Scottish Society of Painters in Watercolours, 1915. He died in Edinburgh on 18 March 1922.
Contrib: *The Yellow Book [1895-97].*
Exhib: G; L; M; NEA; New Gall; P; RA; RI; RSA; RSW; RWS.
Colls: Dundee; Glasgow; Leeds.

### WALTON, Elijah                                    1833-1880
Landscape and genre painter in watercolour and illustrator. He was born at Birmingham in 1833 and studied in Birmingham and at the RA Schools. He visited Switzerland and Egypt in 1860-62 and spent much of his time on the Continent or travelling in the Near East in the succeeding years. He is at his best when drawing mountainous landscape. He died at Bromsgrove in 1880. Fellow, Royal Geographical Society.
Publ: *The Camel its Anatomy, Proportions and Paces [1865]; Clouds and their Combinations [1869]; Peaks in Pen and Pencil [1872].*
Illus: *The Peaks and Valleys of the Alps [T.G. Bonney, 1867]; Flowers from the Upper Alps [T.G. Bonney, 1869]; The Coast of Norway [T.G. Bonney, 1871].*
Exhib: BI; RA; RBA.
Colls: BM; Birmingham.

### WALTON, George
Topographer. He contributed a view of Lichfield to *The Copper Plate Magazine,* 1792-1802.

### WALTON, T.
Contributor to *The Illustrated London News,* 1860.

### WARD, Charles D.                                  1872-
Landscape and portrait painter and illustrator. He was born at Taunton on 19 June 1872 and studied at the RCA. He married the portrait painter Charlotte Blakenay Ward and was elected ROI in 1915.
Contrib: *The Temple Magazine [1896-97]; The English Illustrated Magazine [1900-1].*
Exhib: D; G; L; NEA; RA; RBA; RI; ROI; RWA.
Colls: V & AM.

### WARD, Edward Matthew   RA                         1816-1879
Historical painter. He was born in Pimlico in 1816 and studied at the RA Schools and in Rome. He carried out extensive decorations for the new Houses of Parliament and was elected ARA in 1847 and RA in 1855. He was the father of Sir Leslie Ward (q.v.) and died at Slough in 1879.
Contrib: *The Traveller [Goldsmith, Art Union of London, 1851].*
Exhib: BI; NWS; RA; RBA.
Colls: BM; Witt Photo.

### WARD, Enoch                                       fl.1891-1921
Landscape and figure painter. He worked in the London area, was RBA 1898, and contributed genre subjects including social realism to the magazines.
Contrib: *ILN [1891]; Black & White [1891]; The Queen [1892]; The Ludgate Monthly [1897]; The Pall Mall Magazine.*
Exhib: RA; RBA; RI.

### WARD, Colonel Francis Swain                       c.1734-1805
Army officer and artist. He had two periods of service in India and retired as lieutenant-colonel in 1787. He died at Negapatam in 1805. Fellow of the Society of Antiquaries.
Contrib: *Twenty-Four Views in Hindustan [1805].*
Exhib: Society of Artists.

### WARD, Sir Leslie Matthew  'Spy'                   1851-1922
Portrait painter and caricaturist. He was born in London on 21 November 1851, the eldest son of E.M. Ward RA and the grandson of James Ward RA. He was educated at Eton and studied architecture with Sydney Smirke RA and at the RA Schools. He made caricature contributions to *The Graphic* from 1874, but is best remembered as the under-study and successor to Carlo Pellegrini (q.v.) on Vanity Fair, 1873-1909. Ward was the first English artist to develop the portrait chargé, but in a much gentler style than his predecessor. His likenesses are accurate and lively if lacking in insight, the watercolours are usually mixed with bodycolour and are often found on dove grey papers. Ward was a very popular artist and his range of characters from the turf, the army, the church, the stage and high life decorated the walls of many an Edwardian home. He was elected RP in 1891 and knighted in 1918. He died in London on 15 May 1922. Signs: *Spy*
Contrib: *Cassells Family Magazine.*
Exhib: G; P; RA; RE.
Colls: BM; Liverpool; NPG; V & AM; Garrick Club; Witt Photo.
Bibl: Leslie Ward, *Fifty Years of Spy,* c.1915; E. Harris & R. Ormond, *Vanity Fair,* NPG Cat. 1976.

See illustrations (p.491).

### WARD, Martin Theodore                             1799-1874
Animal painter. He was born in London in 1799, the son of William Ward and a pupil of Landseer. He worked in London at first and then in about 1840, moved to Yorkshire, dying there in poverty in 1874.
Contrib: *The Annals of Sporting [1826].*
Exhib: BI; RA; RBA.
Colls: Witt Photo.

*SIR LESLIE WARD 'SPY' 1851-1922. Caricature portrait of the writer and traveller, A.G. Hales, Original drawing for* Vanity Fair. *Watercolour. Signed. 21¼ins. x 15ins. (54cm x 38.1cm).* Author's Collection

## WARDLE, Arthur 1864-1949

Animal painter. He worked in London, where he was born and was elected RI in 1922. A painting of his was purchased by the Chantrey Bequest in 1904. He died in 1949.

Contrib: *The Queen.*
Exhib: B; FAS; G; L; M; RA; RBA; RHA; RI; ROI; RSA; RSW.

## WARING, John Burley 1823-1875

Landscape painter, watercolourist and architect. He was born at Lyme Regis on 29 June 1823 the son of a naval officer and was apprenticed to an architect and studied with Samuel Jackson. He travelled to Italy and wrote his autobiography, he died at Hastings on 23 March 1875.

Illus: *Architectural Art in Italy and Spain [1850, AT 42]; Studies in Burgos [1852, AT 157].*
Exhib: RA.
Colls; V & AM.

## WARREN, Henry PNWS 1794-1879

Landscape and genre painter and illustrator. He was born in London on 24 September 1794 and studied under Joseph Nollekens, the sculptor, and at the RA Schools, 1818. Warren began as an oil painter

but gradually turned his attention exclusively to watercolour, being elected NWS in 1835. He made many illustrations for the albums and annuals particularly those of a Spanish or Shakespearean flavour. He was also a musician and lithographer and was President of the NWS from 1839-73. He died in London in 1879.

Publ: *Hints upon Tints [1833]; On the Fine Arts [1849]; Artistic Anatomy [1852]; Painting in Watercolours [1856]; Warren's Drawing Book [1867]; A Text Book of Art Studies [1870]; A Treatise on Figure Drawing [1871]; Half-hour Lectures on Drawing and Painting [1874].*
Illus: *Sketches in Norway and Sweden [Rev. A. Smith, 1847].*
Contrib: *The Book of British Ballads [S.C. Hall, 1842]; The Book of Common Prayer [1845]; ILN [1848]; Lays of the Holy Land [1858]; The Welcome Guest [1860]; A Winters Tale; Lockhart's Spanish Ballads; Wordsworth's Pastoral Poems; Moore's Paradise and the Peri; The Children's Picture Book of Scripture Parables [1861].*
Exhib: BI; NWS; RA; RBA.
Colls: BM: V & AM; Witt Photo.

## WARRY, Daniel Robert fl.1855-1913

Architect and illustrator. He worked at Lewisham and Eltham and specialised in architectural and antiquarian drawings.

Contrib: *The Graphic [1881-82, 1884].*
Exhib: RA.

*SIR LESLIE WARD 'SPY' 1851-1922. Caricature portrait of A.G. Hales, as reproduced in* Vanity Fair.

491

**WATERS, David B.**  fl.1887-1910

Marine painter. He acted as Special Artist to the Fleet for *The Graphic*, in 1910. He worked in Edinburgh and London.

Contrib: *The Graphic [1901-10]; Punch [1906-7]*.
Exhib: RA; RSA.

**WATERFORD, Louise, Marchioness of**  1818-1891

Watercolourist and sculptress. She was born in Paris in 1818, the second daughter of Lord Stuart de Rothesay and inherited from him Highcliffe Castle in Hampshire. She married the 3rd Marquess of Waterford in 1841 and lived at Curraghmore in Ireland, becoming a friend and correspondent of John Ruskin (q.v.), Burne-Jones (q.v.) and G.F. Watts. She died at Ford Castle, Northumberland on 12 May 1891.

Contrib: *Story of Two Noble Lives [Augustus J.C. Hare]*.
Exhib: G; M; RHA; SWA.
Colls: V & AM; Tate; Witt Photo.

**WATERSON, David   RE**  1870-1954

Painter, etcher and engraver. He was born in 1870 and was elected ARE in 1901 and RE in 1910. He worked in Brechin, Scotland and undertook some illustration. He died on 12 April 1954.

Exhib: L; RE; RSA; RWA.
Bibl: *The Studio*, Vol.34, 1905 pp.346-348 illus.

**WATHEN, James**  c.1751-1828

Traveller and topographer. He was born at Hereford in about 1751 where he was a glover. He became famous as a pedestrian traveller under the name of 'Jemmy Sketch', making tours of Britain and Ireland from 1787. Wathen travelled to Italy to visit Byron in 1816 and made a tour of the East in 1811; he visited Heligoland in 1827. He died in Hereford in 1828.

Illus: *Journal of a Voyage to Madras and China [1814, AT 517]; Views Illustrative of the Island of St Helena [1821, AT 314]*.
Contrib: *The Copper Plate Magazine [n.d.]*.
Exhib: RA.
Colls: Witt Photo.

**WATKINS, Frank**  fl.1859-1894

Architectural illustrator. He was working at Feltham, 1875-76 and at Maida Hill, London, in 1890. He worked principally for *The Illustrated London News*, beginning in 1859, contributing in 1875, but featuring continously from 1884-94.

Exhib: M; RHA.

**WATSON, Edward Facon**  fl.1830-1864

Topographical and landscape painter. He was probably a pupil of J. Barber and collaborated with Cox in illustrating *Wanderings in Wales* by Radclyffe.

Exhib: RBA.

**WATSON, Harry**  1871-1936

Landscape and figure painter. He was born in Scarborough on 13 June 1871 and was educated at Scarborough and in Winnipeg. He studied at the Scarborough School of Art, the RCA and at the Lambeth School of Art. He was Life master at the Regent Street Polytechnic Art School and was elected ARWS in 1915 and RWS in 1920. He became ROI in 1932 and died in London on 17 September 1936.

Publ: *Figure Drawing [1930]*.
Contrib: *The Lady's Pictorial [1895]; The English Illustrated Magazine [1899]*.
Exhib: B; G; GG; L; M; NEA; RA; RBA; RI; ROI; RSA; RSW; RWS; RWA.
Colls: Maidstone; Tate; V & AM.

**WATSON, John Dawson**  1832-1892

Figure painter in oils and watercolour and illustrator. He was born at Sedbergh on 20 May 1832 and entered the Manchester School of Art in 1847. He attended the RA Schools in 1851 and returned to Manchester in 1852 where he exhibited at the Institution and made friends with Ford Madox Brown, 1856. He eventually left the North-West for London in 1860 and at once succeeded in obtaining important commissions particularly the illustrating of *Pilgrim's Progress* for Messrs Routledge in 1861. Watson began to do work for

the magazines and became one of the most popular of the 1860s illustrators with his dependable black and white figure work. He was clearly influenced by the Pre-Raphaelites and by the work of J.E. Millais (q.v.) in particular. His strongest subjects are those of rustic genre, where good penwork make up for his occasional lack of fire, his religious and historical drawings can be rather stiff. Watson's best work was done before 1865, after this he experimented more as a colourist and took up oil painting more vigorously. This move followed his election to the OWS in 1864 and full membership in 1869 and may be connected to his sister's marriage to Birket Foster (q.v.). He designed furniture and costumes for a production of Henry V at Manchester in 1872. He was elected RBA in 1882 and died at Conway, North Wales on 3 January 1892.

Watson's early illustrations and drawings are usually signed with one or other of his two monograms, the later work simply by his initials. A representative exhibition of his work was shown at Manchester in 1877. Signs: ⦊⦊  ⦊⦊  JDW

Illus: *Pilgrim's Progress [1861]; Eliza Cook's Poems [1861]; The Golden Thread [Dr. Norman Macleod, 1861]; Bennetts Poems [1862]; The Golden Harp [1864]; Robinson Crusoe [1864]; Old Friends and New [1867]; Wild Cat Tower [1877]; Princess Althea [1883]*.
Contrib: *Once a Week [1861]; Good Words [1861-63]; ILN [1861, 1872]; London Society [1862-67]; Willmott's Sacred Poetry [1862]; The Churchman's Family Magazine [1863]; The British Workman [1863]; The Arabian Nights [1863]; English Sacred Poetry of the Olden Time [1864]; Our Life Illustrated by Pen and Pencil [1865]; The Shilling Magazine [1865]; A Round of Days [1866]; Legends and Lyrics [1866]; Ellen Montgomery's Bookshelf [1866]; Ballad Stories of the Affections [1866]; Foxe's Book of Martyrs [1866]; The Sunday Magazine [1867]; Touches of Nature by Eminent Artists [1867]; The Savage Club Papers [1867]; The Illustrated Book of Sacred Poems [1867]; Cassell's Illustrated Readings [1867]; Cassell's Magazine [1868-69]; Tinsley's Magazine [1868-69]; The Nobility of Life [1869]; Pictures From English Literature [1870]; The Graphic [1870-77]; Leslie's Musical Annual [1870]; The Quiver [1873]; People's Magazine [1873]; Thornbury's Legendary Ballads [1876]*.
Exhib: BI; G; GG; L; M; RA; RBA; RCA; RWS.
Colls: Bedford; Manchester; Newcastle; V & AM; Worcester; Witt Photo.
Bibl: Chatto & Jackson, *Treatise on Wood Engraving*, 1861 p.600; The Brothers Dalziel, *A Record of Work 1840-1890*, pp.170-174; Forrest Reid, *Illustrators of the Sixties*, 1928 pp.166-171 illus.

**WATT, T.**

Illustrator and decorator supplying the head-pieces and initials to *The Pilgrim's Progress and The Holy War, Illuminated*, Lumsden Edition, c.1850.

**WATTS, Arthur George**  1883-1935

Artist and caricaturist. He was born in 1883 and was educated at Dulwich College and studied at Antwerp, Paris and the Slade School. He served in the First World War with the RNVR and won the DSO in 1918. He was a regular pen and ink contributor to the humorous magazines. He died on 20 July 1935. ARBA, 1923.

Contrib: *Punch; Life*.
Exhib: FAS; RA; RBA.
Colls: V & AM; Witt Photo.

**WATTS, Louisa Margaret**  fl.1890-d.1914
**(Mrs. J.T. Watts nee Hughes)**

Landscape painter. She worked in Liverpool and London and married James Thomas Watts, the Birmingham painter. She contributed an illustration to *The Quarto*, 1896, in a slight woodcut style.

Exhib: B; L; M; RA; RCA; RI; ROI; SWA.

**WATTS, William**  1752-1851

Topographer and engraver. He was born at Moorfields in 1752 and studied with Paul Sandby and Edward Rooker. He took over the publication of the latter's *Copper Plate Magazine* and during the years 1779 to 1788, issued one of the finest series of topographical views *Views of The Seats of the English Nobility and Gentry*. He lived in Camarthen, Bath and Bristol at various times and was in Paris during the Revolution. He eventually retired to Cobham and died there on 7 December 1851.

Contrib: *The Copper Plate Magazine [1792-1802]; Britton's Beauties of England and Wales [1802]*.
Colls: Witt Photo.

**WAUGH, F.J.** fl.1894-1906
Landscape painter. He worked in Sark, 1894 and London from 1899 and probably visited South Africa from 1901-4 where he contributed views of the Transvaal to *The Graphic*.
Exhib: L; RA.

**WAUGH, Ida**
Illustrator. She provided the drawings for *Twenty Little Maidens*, a child's book by Blanchard, 1894.

**WAY, Thomas Robert** 1861-1913
Landscape and portrait painter and lithographer. He worked in London and was a significant figure in the revival of lithography in Britain. He taught the medium to J. McNeil Whistler in 1878 and the artist became his intimate friend, working with Way on the printing of the Venice etchings for the Fine Art Society's exhibition in 1880. He was a regular exhibitor at London exhibitions and died there in 1913.
Publ: *The Art of James McNeil Whistler [1903]*.
Illus: *Reliques of Old London [H.B. Wheatley FSA, 1896]*.
Exhib: L; NEA; RA; RBA; RI; ROI.
Bibl: *The Studio*, Vol.34, 1905 pp.317-323 illus; E.R. and J. Pennell, *The Life of James McNeil Whistler*, 1908 p.157.

**WAYLETT, F.** fl.1895-1898
Painter and illustrator. He worked in Hampstead and contributed to *The Sketch*, 1898.
Exhib: NEA.

**WEBB, Ernest** fl.1907-1940
Sculptor and illustrator. He was working at Nottingham in 1923 and in London from 1927.
Contrib: *Punch [1906-7]*.
Exhib: G; L; RA.

**WEBB, Harry George** 1882-1914
Landscape painter, etcher and book decorator. He worked in London and specialised in architectural drawings and decorated *The Acorn*, 1905-6.
Exhib: L; M; RA; RBA; RE; ROI.

**WEBB, John** fl.1805-1816
Topographer. He contributed a view of Herefordshire to *Britton's Beauties of England and Wales*, 1805.
Exhib: RA, 1816.

**WEBB, William J.** fl.1853-1882
Animal and genre painter and illustrator. He studied in Düsseldorf and then worked at Niton, Isle of Wight, 1855-60, London, 1861-64 and Manchester, 1882. His work for magazines was mainly topography and travel, some influenced by the Pre-Raphaelites.
Illus: *The Great Hoggarty Diamond [Cheap Illustrated Edition, 1894]*.
Contrib: *ILN [1872-1874]*.
Exhib: BI; M; RA; RBA; Witt Photo.

**WEBER, H.**
Topographer. He contributed illustrations to *The Border Antiquities of England and Scotland*, Walter Scott, 1814-17. He may be synonymous with 'H. Webber' who exhibited scriptural subjects at the BI in 1830.

**WEBSTER, George** fl.1797-1832
Marine painter. He was based in London but travelled to Holland before 1816 and to Tripoli and the Gold Coast.
Publ: *Views of Various Sea-Ports [1831]*.
Exhib: BI; RA; RBA.
Colls: BM; V & AM.

**WEBSTER, Thomas   RA** 1800-1886
Genre painter. He was born in London on 20 March 1800 and was a chorister of St George's Chapel, Windsor. He entered the RA Schools in 1821 and made a speciality of children or as Chatto puts it 'Infantine Subjects'. The most famous of these is 'The Village Choir' and this and similar paintings were popularised by engravings. He was elected ARA in 1840 and RA in 1846. He died at Cranbrook on 23 September 1886.
Contrib: *The Deserted Village [Junior Etching Club, 1841]; Book of British Ballads [S.C. Hall, 1842]; Favourite English Poems [1859]*.
Exhib: BI; RA; RBA.
Colls: Bury; Preston; V & AM; Witt Photo.
Bibl: Chatto & Jackson, *Treatise on Wood Engraving*, 1861 p.599.

**WEBSTER, Tom** fl.1900-1930
Designer of music title covers, c.1900. Cartoonist for *The Daily Mail*.

**WEEDON, E.** fl.1848-1872
Marine painter and illustrator. This artist of whom nothing is known, was chief marine illustrator for *The Illustrated London News* from 1848-72. His work could be classified as ship portraiture and is usually accurate and spirited. He may be a relation of A.W. Weedon 1838-1908, the landscape painter.
Exhib: RA, 1850.

**WEEDON, J.F.**
Illustrator of sporting subjects. He contributed to *The Graphic*, 1888.

**WEEKES, William** fl.1856-1909
Animal and genre painter. He was the son of Henry Weekes 1807-1877, the sculptor. He lived at Primrose Hill, London and was a regular exhibitor.
Contrib: *ILN [1883]*.
Exhib: B; FAS; G; GG; L; M; RA; RBA; ROI.

**WEGUELIN, John Reinhard   RWS** 1849-1927
Painter and illustrator. He was born at South Stoke, Sussex on 23 June 1849, the son of a clergyman and was educated at Cardinal Newman's Oratory School, Edgbaston. He became a Lloyd's underwriter, 1870-73 and then entered the Slade School, where he studied under Poynter (q.v.) and Legros. He was a Victorian classicist and painted in the style of Alma-Tadema (q.v.), illustrating many books. He was elected ROI in 1888, ARWS in 1894 and RWS in 1897. He had worked in Sussex from 1900 and died at Hastings on 28 April 1927.
Illus: *Lays of Ancient Rome [Macaulay, 1881]; The Cat of Bubastes, A Tale of Ancient Egypt [G.A. Henty, 1889]; Anacreon [1892]; The Little Mermaid [Hans Andersen, 1893]; Catullus [1893]; The Wooing of Malkatoon [1898]*.
Contrib: *The Graphic [1888-1906]*.
Exhib: B; FAS; G; GG; L; M; New Gall; RA; RBA; RHA; ROI; RWS.
Bibl: R.E.D. Sketchley, *Eng. Bk. Illus.*, 1903 pp.29, 131; *The Connoisseur*, Vol.78, 1927.

**WEHNERT, Edward Henry** 1813-1868
Historical painter and illustrator. He was born in London in 1813, the son of a German tailor and was educated at Göttingen. He returned to England in 1837 after working in Paris and Jersey and settled in London where he made historical paintings and book illustrations. He was elected NWS in 1837 and was a competitor in the Westminster Hall Competition of 1845. Wehnert's art was strongly linear and Chatto describes it as 'essentially German'. He is known to have made one visit to Italy in 1858. He died at Kentish Town on 15 September 1868.
Illus: *History of the British Nation [Hutchinson, c.1835]; Grimm's Household Stories [1853]; Poe's Works [1853]; Longfellow's Poems [1854]; Eve of St Agnes [J. Keats, 1856]; Ancient Mariner [1856]; The Pilgrim's Progress [John Bunyan, 1858]; Grimm's Tales [1861]; Fairy Tales [Hans Andersen, 1861]; Robinson Crusoe [D. Defoe, 1862]*.
Contrib: *Art Union Annual [1845]; ILN [1848-49]; The Traveller [Art Union, 1851]; The Churchman's Family Magazine [1863]; Aunt Judy's Magazine*.
Exhib: BI; NWS; RA; RBA.
Colls: V & AM; Witt Photo.
Bibl: Chatto & Jackson *Treatise on Wood Engraving*, 1861 p.594.

**WEHRSCHMIDT, Daniel Albert    later Veresmith    1861-1932**

Portrait painter, engraver and lithographer. He was born at Cleveland, Ohio, USA on 24 November 1861 and studied at the Herkomer School, Bushey, Herts. He was Art Master at the Herkomer for 12 years, 1884-96, and was elected RP in 1915. He later lived at Doneraile, Co. Cork, 1921 and North Curry, Somerset, from 1927. He died on 22 February 1932.

Contrib: *The Graphic [1891]*. (Illustrations for Hardy's *Tess*.)
Exhib: B; FAS; G; L; M; New Gall; P; RA; RHA; RSA.

**WEIGALL, Charles Harvey    NWS    1794-1877**

Landscape and genre painter and illustrator. He was born in 1794 and was elected a member of the NWS in 1834 and was Treasurer of the Society from 1839-41. Weigall was interested in technique and wrote a number of exemplars, also modelling in wax and making intaglio gems. He was a proficient draughtsman of animals and birds. He died in 1877.

Publ: *The Art of Figure Drawing [1852]; A Manual of the First Principles of Drawing, with Rudiments of Perspective [1853]; The Projection of Shadows [1856]; Guide to Animal Drawing [1862]*.
Illus: *Juvenile Verse and Picture Book [1848]*.
Contrib: *ILN [1844-50]; The Illustrated London Magazine [1853]; The Graphic [1873]*.
Exhib: NWS; RA; RBA.
Colls: BM; Nat. Gall., Ireland; V & AM; Witt Photo.

**WEIR, Harrison William    1824-1906**

Animal painter and illustrator. He was born at Lewes, Sussex on 5 May 1824 and was educated at Camberwell before learning colour-printing under George Baxter. He preferred painting and from an early date devoted all his time to studies of birds and animals. Weir was an independant minded artist with an amazing capacity for work; he started to draw for *The Illustrated London News* in 1847 and was still working for them at the turn of the century, their longest serving artist. He was elected ANWS in 1849 and NWS in 1851, but retired in 1870 because he preferred working on commission. He numbered among his friends Charles Darwin and among his hobbies pigeon fancying and natural history; a further link with the animal painters was provided by his marriage to the daughter of J.F. Herring (q.v.). Weir is characterised by an extraordinary accuracy and life in his drawings, his poultry live in the farmyard and his birds in the wild, rare among Victorians. He designed some race cups for Messrs Garrard and among his less successful ventures were sentimental fancy pictures of cats and dogs which may have influenced Louis Wain. He died at Poplar Hall, Appledore, Kent on 3 January 1906.

Illus: *Domestic Pets [Mrs Loudon, 1851]; Cat and Dog Memories of Puss and Captain [1854]; The Farmer's Boy [Bloomfield, 1857]; Wild Sports of the World [J. Greenwood, 1862]; The History of the Robins [Mrs Trimmer, 1868]; Animals and Birds [1868]; The Tiny Natural Histories [1880]; Our Cats and All About Them [1889]; Sable and White [Stables, 1894]; Shireen [Stables, 1894]; Poultry and All About Them [1903]; Animal Stories Old and New; Bird Stories Old and New*.
Contrib: *ILN [1847-1900]; The Poetical Works of E.A. Poe [1853]; Punch [1854]; Poets of the Nineteenth Century [Willmott, 1857]; Gertrude of Wyoming [Scott, 1857]; Dramatic Scenes [Cornwall, 1857]; The Home Affections [Mackay, 1858]; Comus [1858]; Montgomery's Poems [1860]; The Welcome Guest [1860]; The Illustrated Times [1860]; Sacred Poetry [1862]; Parables From Nature [1867]; Episodes of Fiction [1870]; The British Workman; The Band of Hope Review; Chatterbox [1880]; Wood's Natural History; The Field; Black & White; The Poultry and Stock Keeper; The English Illustrated Magazine [1887]*.
Exhib: BI; NWS; RA; RBA.
Colls: V & AM; Witt Photo.
Bibl: Chatto & Jackson, *Treatise on Wood Engraving*, 1861 p.553; *AJ*, 1906.

**WEIRD, R. Jasper**

Probably a pseudonym of a figure artist contributing comic groups and animals to *Punch*, 1906.

**WEIRTER, Louis    1873-1932**

Artist, lithographer and illustrator. He was born in Edinburgh in 1873, the son of a Professor of Music and was apprenticed to a lithographer while studying at the RSA and the Board of Manufacturers Schools.

He was elected RBA in 1902 and worked in London, 1907 and Baldock, 1914, specialising in pictures of current events, the Diamond Jubilee and the War in the Air, 1914-18. He died 12 January 1932. He signs his paintings 'Louis Weirter' and his etchings 'Louis Whirter'.

Illus: *The Story of Edinburgh Castle; Stories and Legends of the Danube*.
Contrib: *The Evergreen*.
Exhib: RA; RBA; RSA.
Colls: V & AM.

**WELLS**

Topographer. Contributed drawings for *Knight's London*, 1841.

**WELLS, Joseph Robert    fl.1872-1895**

Marine artist. He was the principal marine artist of *The Illustrated London News* from 1873 to 1883, specialising in ship portraits. After this date he contributed occasional drawings till 1895, the figures usually by C.J. Staniland (q.v.).

Contrib: *The English Illustrated Magazine [1885]*.
Exhib: B; G; L; M; RA; RBA; RI; ROI.

**WELLS, Reginald Fairfax    1877-1951**

Sculptor and potter. He was born in Brazil in 1877 and studied at the RCA and under E. Lantieri. He was employed in the Chelsea Manufactory and acted as designer for Messrs Coldrum & Sons Pottery. He died in 1951.

Contrib: *The Sketch [1898]*.
Exhib: FAS; G; GG; L; RSA; RA.
Colls: V & AM.

**WEST, J.B.    fl.1804-1828**

Landscape painter and caricaturist. He published in 1804, *Design for Imperial Crown to be used at Coronation of the New Emperor*.

**WEST, J.C.**

Topographer. He contributed to *Griffiths' Cheltenham*, 1826.

**WEST, Joseph Walter    RWS    1860-1933**

Landscape and genre artist, illustrator and bookplate designer. He was born in Hull in 1860 and educated at Bootham School, York, by the Quakers and at the St Johns Wood and the RA Schools. He later studied in Paris and Italy and became proficient in many other mediums including tempera and lithography and practised mural painting. He used his Quaker background for many of his genre paintings, his illustrating is usually romatic. He was elected RBA in 1893, ANWS in 1901 and RWS in 1904. He worked at Northwood from 1902 and died there on 27 June 1933.

Illus: *Tryphena in Love [Walter Raymond, 1895]; Rosemary For Remembrance [Mary Brotherton, 1896 (title & cover); Ballads in Prose [Nora Hopper, 1896 (title & cover)]; Virgil's Georgics [frontis]*.
Contrib: *The English Illustrated Magazine [1887]; The Pall Mall Magazine*.
Exhib: B; FAS; G; L; M; New Gall; RA; RBA; RHA; RSW; RWS.
Colls: Hull; Tate; V & AM.
Bibl: *The Studio*, Winter No., 1900-1 pp.87-100 illus; Vol.37, 1906 pp.158-159 illus; Vol.40, 1907 pp.87-100 illus; *Pearson's Magazine*, 1907.

**WEST, Maud Astley    fl.1880-1916**

Flower painter. She was a student of the Bloomsbury School of Art and worked in London and Tunbridge Wells. She illustrated *Through Woodland and Meadow*, 1891, with M. Low.

Exhib: B; RA; SWA.

**WESTALL, Richard    RA    1765-1836**

Historical and figure painter and illustrator. He was born at Hertford in 1765 and apprenticed to a silver engraver in Cheapside, attending the RA Schools from 1785. He turned wholly to art on completing his apprenticeship in 1786 and became a popular and prolific book illustrator. He worked chiefly for publishers of poetry, decorating their pocket editions with vignettes and 'conversation piece' subjects within decorative borders. His drawings for these are firmly in the 18th century tradition, charming and delicate tinted drawings with highly finished faces. He collaborated with Alderman Boydell in painting five Milton subjects for his *Shakespeare Gallery* 1795-96 and illustrated the works of Crabbe, Moore and Gray. He was elected ARA in 1792 and RA in 1794 and gave lessons in drawing to the Princess Victoria. He died in London on 4 December 1836.

Publ: *A Day in Spring [1808].*
Illus: *Paradise Lost [Sharpe's Classics, 1822]; Boydell's Shakespeare [1802]; Elizabeth [Madame Cottin, 1817]; Illustrations from the Bible [1822]; Vicar of Wakefield [1828]; Illustrations of the Bible [1835-36]; Reflections on the Works of God.*
Contrib: *The Keepsake [1829]; Heath's Gallery [1836-38]; National Portrait Gallery of the 19th century.*
Exhib: BI; RA; RBA.
Colls: Ashmolean; BM; Eton College; Hertford; Nat. Gall., Scot; V & AM; Witt Photo.
Bibl: M. Hardie, *Watercol. Paint. in Brit.,* Vol.1, 1966 p.150 illus.
See illustrations (Colour Plate I p.19 and p.32)

**WESTALL, William    ARA**                                    **1781-1850**
Topographical illustrator. He was born at Hertford in 1785, the younger brother of Richard Westall (q.v.). He studied with his brother and at the RA Schools and was chosen by Benjamin West PRA to accompany the Flinders expedition to Australia as artist. On his return voyage he visited China and India, 1803-4 and was in Madeira and Jamaica in about 1808. He was elected AOWS in 1810 and resigned in 1812 when he was elected ARA. He spent the rest of his life painting English topography and died in London on 22 January 1850.
Illus: *Views of Scenery in Madeira, at the Cape, in China and India [1811]; Views of Australian Scenery [1814, AT 567]; Views of the Yorkshire Caves [1818]; Victories of the Duke of Wellington [1819, AL 381]; Britannia Delineata [1822]; Scenery, Costumes and Architecture of India [Grindlay, 1826-30, AT 422]; Picturesque Tour of the River Thames [1828].*
Contrib: *Ackermann's History of Rugby School [1816]; Ackermann's Repository [1825]; Illustrations of Warwickshire [1829]; Great Britain Illustrated [Thomas Moule, 1830]; Landscape Album [1832].*
Exhib: BI; OWS; RA; RBA.
Colls: Ashmolean; BM; Glasgow; Leeds; Manchester; Nottingham; Witt Photo.
Bibl: *AJ,* April 1850; Iolo Williams, *Early English Watercolours,* 1952 p.59 illus.

**WESTRUP, E. Kate**                                           **fl.1908-1927**
Sporting artist. She worked at New Milton, Hants, 1910 and in Cornwall, 1911-27. She was elected ASWA in 1923.

Illus: *The Rosebud Annual [1908].*
Contrib: *Punch [1914 (hunting)].*
Exhib: L; NEA; RA; SWA.

**WHARTON, S.**                                               **fl.1810-1816**
Architect. He was an honorary exhibitor at the RA, 1810-14 and showed drawings of London improvements. He published and illustrated *Waterloo,* 1816, AL 382.

**WHATLEY, Henry**                                            **1842-1901**
Landscape and genre painter. He was born in Bristol in 1842 and worked as a drawing-master there, teaching at Clifton College and other schools. He died at Clifton in 1901.

Illus: *Quiet War Scenes [J. Baker, 1879]; Pictures of Bohemia [J. Baker, 1894].*
Contrib: *ILN.*
Colls: Bristol.

**WHEELER, Dorothy Muriel**                                   **1891-1966**
Watercolour painter and illustrator. She worked in Plumstead, Kent and Esher, Surrey, in the 1900s and 1920s, producing pretty figure studies in a late Greenaway style with shepherdesses and architectural ornament.

Exhib: RA; SWA.

**WHEELER, Edward J.**                                        **fl.1872-1902**
Domestic painter and black and white artist. He began to work for *Punch* in 1880 and contributed figures for the theatrical pages, for the editorial and provided initial letters. He used an unusual sign-manual of a 'four-wheeler'.

Illus: *Tristram Shandy. [Smollett, 1894]; The Captains Room [W. Besant, 1897].*
Contrib: *Punch [1880-1902]; The Cornhill Magazine [1883].*

Exhib: London, 1872.
Bibl: M.H. Spielmann, *The History of Punch,* 1895 p.549.

**WHEELHOUSE, Mary V.**                                       **fl.1895-1933**
Painter and illustrator. She was probably a student at Scarborough School of Art, 1895 and lived in Chelsea from 1900.

Illus: *Cousin Phillis [Mrs Gaskell, Bells Queens Treasures Series, 1908]; Six to Sixteen [Mrs Ewing, 1908].*
Exhib: M; New Gall; RA; SWA.

**WHICHELO, C. John M.    AOWS**                              **1784-1865**
Watercolourist and topographer of marine and river subjects. He was born in 1784 and became a pupil successively of John Varley and J. Cristall. He became Marine and Landscape Painter to the Prince Regent in about 1812 and was elected AOWS in 1823. Whichelo drew mainly British subjects but travelled in the Low Countries, Germany and Switzerland.

Contrib: *Antiquarian and Topographical Cabinet [1806]; Britton's Beauties of England and Wales [1815].*
Exhib: BI; OWS; RA.
Colls: BM; Greenwich; V & AM; Witt Photo.

**WHISTLER, James Abbot McNeil**                              **1834-1903**
Painter, etcher, lithographer and caricaturist. He was born at Lowell, Massachusetts on 11 July 1834, the son of an army officer. He was brought up in Russia and England before entering West Point Military Academy, to begin an army career. He was later moved to the Navy as a cartographer, where he learned etching, but abandoned this for art and went to Paris in 1855 to study under Gleyre, where he met G. Du Maurier (q.v.), E.J. Poynter (q.v.) and was influenced by the work of Manet and Courbet. Whistler settled in London in 1859, remaining a leading figure in its art world but arrogant, temperamental and fiercely independant. His early years, particularly 1862, are the ones in which he undertook his few but very striking book illustrations for the magazines. They are very powerfully conceived and have a freedom of line which is unusual among the wood engravings of the 1860s, the finest is 'The Morning Before The Massacre of St Bartholomew', for *Once a Week.*
    Whistler's libel action with Ruskin in 1879 and his subsequent bankruptcy divides a spectacular career into two. His return to London in 1880 resulted in a triumphant exhibition of Venetian etchings and a series of fine lithographs. As Gleeson White commented 'one might as well praise June sunshine as Mr Whistler's etchings' and the whole force of his genius appears in the plates. His later polemical books have some decoration in their pages, but otherwise his contribution in this direction was small. His caricatures are witty and sharp, those of his adversary F.R. Leyland executed with an almost pathological savagery. Whistler was President of the SBA from 1886-88 but resigned due to controversy. He died in London in July 1903.

Contrib: *Once a Week [1862]; Good Words [1862]; Passages From Modern English Poets [1862]; Thornbury's Legendary Ballads [1876]; Scribner's Monthly and St Nicholas [1880-81].*
Exhib: FAS; G; GG; L; M; NEA; P; RA; RBA; RSA; RSW.
Colls: Ashmolean; Fitzwilliam; Glasgow; Manchester; V & AM.
Bibl: T.R. Way and G.R. Dennis, *The Art of JMcN W,* 1903; H.W. Singer, *JAMcN W,* 1904; J and E.R. Pennell, *The Life of JAMcN W,* 1908; B. Sickert, *W,* 1908; J and E.R. Pennell, *The W Journal,* 1921; J. Laver, *W,* 1930; H. Pearson, *The Man W,* 1952; D. Sutton, *Nocturne,* 1963; D. Sutton, *JMcN W,* 1966; R. McMullen, *Victorian Outsider,* 1973; S. Weintraub, *W,* 1974; *W The Graphic Work,* Walker Art Gall. Cat. 1976.

**WHITE, Edmund Richard**                                     **fl.1864-1908**
Landscape and genre painter in watercolour and illustrator. He worked in London and at Walham Green from 1880, and contributed comic genre subjects to *The Illustrated London News,* 1871.

Exhib: B; L; RA; RBA; RI; RSW.

**WHITE, George Francis**                    1808-1898

Professional soldier and watercolourist. He was born at Chatham in 1808 and served in India with the 31st Regiment until 1846 and sketched the landscape of the Himalayas. He was later a Chief Constable and DL of County Durham and died there in 1898.

Illus: *Views in India Chiefly Among The Himalaya Mountains . . . 1829-31-32*, Publ. in 2 pts., 1837.

**WHITE, Gleeson**                    1851-1898

Book decorator and editor. He was born at Christchurch on 8 March 1851 and was educated at Christchurch School before entering journalism. He was deeply involved with the arts and crafts movement and worked as Associate Editor on the New York magazine *Art-Amateur*, from 1891-92. He then became first Editor of *The Studio*, 1893-94, and was largely responsible for its international reputation and its encouragement of book illustration. Walter Crane recalled of White that his 'quick sympathy and recognition . . . extended to all young and promising designers in black and white.' He was himself a talented designer of book covers and the foremost historian of the art of the book of his period. He died in London on 19 October 1898.

Publ: *Ballads and Rondeaus, Canterbury Poets [1887]; Practical Designing [1893]; Salisbury Cathedral [1896]; English Illustration [1897]; Master Painters of Britain [4 Vols., 1897-98].*
Designed: *Hake, A Selection From His Poems [1894 (cover)]; Out of Egypt [P. Hemingway, 1895-96 (cover)].*
Bibl: *The Studio*, Vol. 15 1899 p.141 (obit.); *The Artist*, Nov. 1898 (obit.). *Apollo*, Vol. 108; October 1978, pp.256-261.

**WHITE, William Johnstone**                    fl.1804-1812

Illustrator. He worked in London and contributed drawings to Ackermann's *The History of the Abbey Church of St Peter's, Westminster*, 1812.

Exhib: RA.
Colls: BM; Nottingham.

**WHITEHEAD, Frances M.**                    fl.1887-1929

Landscape painter and etcher. She worked in the Birmingham area and illustrated a child's book *The Withy Wood*, Skeffington, 1903.

Exhib: B; RA; RI; SWA.

**WHITELAW, George**                    fl.1907-1930

Artist and illustrator. He worked in Glasgow, 1912 and London, 1920 and contributed cockney figure subjects to *Punch*, 1907.

Exhib: G; L.

**WHITING, Frederic or Fred**                    1873-1962

Portrait and figure painter and Special Artist. He was born at Hampstead in 1873 and was educated at Deal and St Mark's College, Chelsea and studied at the St John's Wood and RA Schools. He attended Julians, Paris, and was appointed artist on The Daily Graphic, 1890. He became Special Artist and War Correspondent on The Graphic in China, 1900-1 and during the Russo-Japanese War of 1904-5, he excelled in action subjects and equestrian scenes. He was elected RBA in 1911, ROI, 1915, RI, 1918 and RSW, 1921. Whiting was President of the Artists Society, 1919 and died on 1 August 1962.

Exhib: G; GG; L; P; RA; RBA; RHA; RI; ROI; RSA; RSW.
Colls: Brighton; Liverpool.

**WHITTOCK, Nathaniel**                    fl.1828-1851

Draughtsman and lithographer. He worked principally in London and Oxford and published drawing-books.

Illus: *The British Drawing Book [n.d.]; The Oxford Drawing-Book [1825]; History of the County of Yorks. [Allan, 1828]; The Art of Drawing and Colouring From Nature [1829]; A Topographical and Historical Description of Oxford [1829]; The Microcosm of Oxford [1830]; The Decorative Painter and Glaziers Guide [1837]; The Miniature Painters Manual [1844].*
Contrib: *Tallis's Illustrated London [1851 (frontis)].*
Colls: BM; Witt Photo.

**WHYMPER, Charles H.   RI**                    1853-1941

Landscape and animal painter and illustrator. He was born in London on 31 August 1853, the son of J.W. Whymper (q.v.) and studied at the RA Schools. He spent the whole of his working life illustrating books on travel, natural history and sport and had a one man show at the Walker Galleries in 1923. He was elected RI in 1909. He worked in London and then at Houghton, Hunts. from 1915 and died on 25 April 1941.

Illus: *Wild Sports in the Highlands [1878]; The Game-Keeper at Home [Jefferies, 1880]; Siberia in Europe [Seebohm, 1880]; Matabele Land [Oates, 1881]; Birds of Wave and Woodland [P. Robinson, 1894]; Big Game Shooting [1895]; The Pilgrim Fathers of New England [1895]; Off to Klondyke [1898]; Bird Life in a Southern County [C. Dixon, 1899]; Egyptian Birds [1909].*
Contrib: *ILN [1887-89]; Good Words [1891-]; The English Illustrated Magazine [1883-].*
Exhib: B; FAS; L; M; New Gall; RA; RBA; RI.
Colls: Witt Photo.

**WHYMPER, Edward J.**                    1840-1911

Alpinist and illustrator. He was born on 27 April 1840, the second son of J.W. Whymper (q.v.) and brother of Charles Whymper (q.v.). He joined the family wood engraving business and was responsible for engraving and illustrating many books in the 1860s, but his fame really rests on his pioneer work as an alpinist. He wrote *Peaks, Passes and Glaciers*, 1862 and was a medallist of the RGS. He died on 16 September 1911.

Illus: *Scrambles Among the Alps [1870]; Travels Among the Great Andes of the Equator [1892]; Chamonix and Mont Blanc [1896]; Zermatt and the Matterhorn [1897].*
Contrib: *The Sunday Magazine [1865]; The Leisure Hour [1867]; The Graphic [1870].*

**WHYMPER, F.**                    fl.1857-1869

Landscape painter. He was working in London, 1857-61 and contributed illustrations of Russian America to *The Illustrated London News*, 1868-69.

Exhib: RA; RBA.

**WHYMPER, Josiah Wood   RI**                    1813-1903

Landscape painter and engraver. He was born at Ipswich in 1813 and after being apprenticed to a stone mason, taught himself to draw. He settled in London in 1829 and studied with W.C. Smith, establishing himself as an illustrator after publishing an etching of London Bridge, 1831. Whymper's wood engraving business became one of the most thriving in London and did most of the work for Murrays, the publishers, and for the Religious Tract Society and the S.P.C.K., both at that time employing good artists. He had at various times Frederick Walker, Charles Keene, J.W. North, Charles Green, and G.J. Pinwell as pupils. He was elected ANWS in 1854 and NWS in 1857, and lived at Haslemere, where he died on 7 April 1903.

Illus: *The Child's History of Jerusalem [C.R. Conder, 1874]; Field Paths and Green Lanes [L.J. Jennings, 1877]; Tent Work in Palestine [C.R. Conder, 1878].*
Contrib: *Missionary Travels [David Livingstone, 1857].*
Exhib: L; M; RI; ROI.
Colls: V & AM.

**WIDGERY, Frederick John**                    1861-1942

Landscape and marine painter. He was born in 1861, the son of William Widgery, the Exeter painter, and studied at the Exeter School of Art and at South Kensington and Antwerp.

Illus: *A Perambulation of Dartmoor [S. Rowe, 1896]; Fair Devon Album [S. Rowe, 1902]; Devon [Lady R. Northcote, 1914]; Torquay [J. Presland, 1920].*
Exhib: L; RA; RI; ROI.
Colls: Exeter.

**WIEGAND, W.J.**                    fl.1869-1882

Figure artist. He worked in London and illustrated *Elliott's Nursery Rhymes* for Novello, 1870, and contributed to *Good Words For The Young*, 1869-73 and *The Sunday Magazine*, 1870.

**WIGHTWICK, George**     1802-1872

Architect and draughtsman. He was born at Mold, Flintshire on 26 August 1802 and was educated at Wolverhampton Grammar School. He failed to gain entrance to the RA Schools in 1818 but was given £100 by his stepfather to visit Italy, a tour he undertook from 1825-26. On his return he became an assistant to Sir John Soane and began illustrating and publishing, but success eluded him in London and he finally moved to Plymouth in 1829 and set up an architectural practice. He retired to Clifton in 1851 and to Portishead in 1855 and died there on 9 July 1872.

Illus: *Select Views of Roman Antiquities [1827]; Remarks on Theatres [1832]; Sketches of a Practising Architect [1837]; The Palace of Architecture [1840]; Hints to Young Architects [1846].*
Contrib: *Public Buildings of London [Britton]; Union of Architecture [Britton, 1827, AL 7].*
Exhib: RA.
Bibl: *Bentley's Miscellany,* Vol. 1852-54 pp.31-35; Vol. 1857-68 pp.42-43.

**WIGRAM, Sir Edgar Thomas Ainger, 6th Bart.**     1864-1935

Amateur artist and illustrator. He was born on 23 November 1864, and succeeded his cousin in the title 1920. He was educated at Kings School, Canterbury and Trinity Hall, Cambridge and was Mayor of St. Albans, 1926-27. He died on 15 March 1935.

Illus: *Northern Spain [1906]; The Cradle of Mankind [1914]; Spain [J. Lomas, 1925].*
Colls: Hertford.

**WILD, Charles**   OWS     1781-1835

Architectural and topographical illustrator. He was born in London in 1781 and was articled to the younger Thomas Malton. Wild was a careful delineator of Gothic cathedrals and colleges and was very influential through the engravings after his work in spreading the enthusiasm for Gothic art. He concentrated mainly on Britain but travelled abroad in the 1820s. He was elected AOWS in 1809 and OWS in 1812 and was Treasurer and Secretary in 1833. Increasing blindness caused his resignation in that year and he died in London on 4 August 1835.

Illus: *Twelve Views of Canterbury Cathedral [1807]; Twelve Views of York [1809]; An Illustration of Chester [1813]; An Illustration of Lichfield [1813]; An Illustration of Lincoln [1819]; An Illustration of Worcester [1823]; Foreign Cathedrals [1826, AT 93]; Select Examples . . . of Architecture . . . in England [1832]; Twelve Outlines . . . [1833]; Selected Examples of Architectural Grandeur [1837].*
Contrib: *History of the Western Division of the County of Sussex [Rev J. Dallaway, 1815-30]; Royal Residences [W.H. Pyne, 1819]; Oxford Almanac [1815, 1818, 1819, 1829, 1831, 1845].*
Exhib: BI; RA; OWS.
Colls: Ashmolean; BM; Chester; V & AM.
Bibl: M. Hardie, *Watercol. Paint. in Brit.,* Vol.3, 1968 pp.15-16 illus.
See illustration (Colour Plate II p.19).

**'WILDRAKE'**   see TATTERSALL, G.

**WILES, Frank E.**     fl.1899-1925

Portrait painter. He was working in Cambridge, 1899, when he entered for the South Kensington Competitions and in London, 1914-25.

Exhib: RA.
Bibl: *Modern Book Illustrators and Their Work,* Studio 1914.

**WILEY, H.W.**

Probably a student of the Birmingham School. Watercolour illustrations for a child's book in a Dutch whimsy style appear in *The Studio,* Vol.29, 1903 pp.69-70.

**WILKIE, Sir David**   RA     1785-1841

Genre and portrait painter and caricaturist. He was born at Cult, Fifeshire on 18 November 1785, the son of a Scottish minister. He studied at the Trustees Academy and at the RA Schools from 1805. Wilkie exhibited at the RA from 1806 and caused considerable interest with his domestic genre subjects which were based on Dutch genre paintings but had an obstinate Scottishness of their own. He was elected ARA in 1809 and RA in 1811, later being appointed King's Limner for Scotland, 1823, and Painter in Ordinary to the King,

1830. He travelled to Paris in 1814, to Scotland in 1817 and 1822 and ventured further afield for his health after 1825. He went on an extensive tour of the East in 1840, but died at sea on his return, 1 June 1840. He had been knighted in 1836.

Illus: *Old Mortality [Scott, 1830]; Sketches in Turkey, Syria and Egypt [1843, AT 379]; Sketches Spanish and Oriental [1846, AT 39].*
Contrib: *The Keepsake [1830]; Heath's Gallery [1836].*
Exhib: BI; RA.
Colls: Aberdeen; Bedford; BM; Fitzwilliam; V & AM; Witt Photo.
Bibl: D. Cunningham, *Life of DW,* 1843; A.L. Simpson, *The Story of Sir DW,* 1879; Lord G. Gower, *Sir DW,* 1902; W. Bayne, *Sir DW,* 1903; RA Exhibition Cat., 1958.

**WILKINS, Frank W.**     c.1800-1842

Portrait painter, miniaturist and engraver. He was born in about 1800 and was a pupil of Charles Wilkins. He died in London in 1842.

Contrib: *British Gallery of Contemporary Portraits [1822]; National Portrait Gallery of the Nineteenth Century [c.1830]; Burke's Female Portraits [1833].*
Exhib: BI; RA.
Colls: Witt Photo.

**WILKINSON, Charles A.**     fl.1881-1925

Painter of landscapes and ships. He worked in London from 1881 and at Farnborough, 1916.

Contrib: *Black & White [1891].*
Exhib: G; L; M; RA; RBA; RHA; RI; ROI; RSA.

**WILKINSON, G. Welby**     fl.1900-1925

Decorative artist. He worked at Haverstock Hill, London and contributed to *Fun,* 1900.

Exhib: London Sal.

**WILKINSON, Rev. Joseph**     1764-1831

Amateur landscape painter and illustrator. He was born at Carlisle in 1764 and educated at Corpus Christi, Cambridge, where he became a Fellow of the College. He became Rector of Wretham, Norfolk in 1803, having been a minor canon of Carlisle. He died at Thetford in 1831.

Illus: *Select Views in Cumberland [Wordsworth, 1810]; The Architectural Remains of Thetford [1822].*
Colls: V & AM.

**WILKINSON, Norman**   PRI     1878-1971

Marine painter and etcher. He was born in Cambridge on 24 November 1878 and was educated at Berkhampstead School and St. Paul's Cathedral Choir School. Wilkinson worked as an artist and illustrator on the magazines until 1914 when he entered the RNVR and invented camouflage for the shipping of the Allies, 1914-18, known as Dazzle painting. He was made OBE for this work in 1918. Wilkinson became Marine Painter to the Royal Yacht Squadron and was elected RBA in 1902 and ROI in 1908; he was RI from 1906 and President, 1937. He died in London in 1971.

Publ: *Virginibus Puerisque and other Papers [1913]; The Dardanelles: Colour Sketches from Gallipoli.*
Contrib: *ILN [1898-99]; The Graphic [1902-3]; The Idler.*
Exhib: FAS, 1907, 1915, 1953, 1958; G; GG; L; New Gall; RA; RBA; RI; ROI; RWA.

**WILKINSON, Tom**     fl.1895-1925

Black and white artist. He lived at Ipswich, 1914 to 1925, and drew figures in the style of Phil May (q.v.).

Contrib: *Judy [1895]; Fun [1895]; Punch [1897, 1903]; Illustrated Bits [1900].*

**WILKINSON, Tony**

Illustrator of children. He contributed to *Punch,* 1897-1902.

**WILLES, William**     -1851

Landscape painter. He was born in Cork and studied at the RA Schools, becoming Master at the Cork School of Design, 1849. He died there in 1851.

Contrib: *Ireland [S.C. Hall, 1841].*
Exhib: BI; RA.

*INGLIS SHELDON-WILLIAMS 1871-1940. 'The Coronation Durbar in Delhi, 1903.' Original drawing for illustration. Ink and watercolour. Signed and dated.*

**WILLIAMS, Captain    RA**
Army officer and amateur artist. He contributed illustrations of Canada to *The Illustrated London News*, 1860.

**WILLIAMS, Alexander    RHA**                                   **1846-1930**
Landscape painter in oil and watercolour. He was born in County Monaghan in 1846 and educated at Drogheda Grammar School and was in the choir of Trinity College, Dublin. He studied art at the RDS and was elected ARHA in 1883 and RHA in 1891. He wrote many articles on ornithology. He died in Dublin on 15 November 1930.
Illus: *Beautiful Ireland [S. Gwynn, 1911]*.
Exhib: B; RHA.

**WILLIAMS, Alfred SHELDON-**                                   **fl.1871-1875**
Farmer and illustrator. He lived and worked at Winchfield and specialised in equestrian subjects. He was the father of Inglis Sheldon-Williams (q.v.).
Illus: *The Book of The Horse [Cassell, 1875]*.
Contrib: *The Graphic [1871]; ILN [1874-75]*.
Exhib: RA; RBA.

**WILLIAMS, Alice Meredith see WILLIAMS, (Gertrude) Alice Meredith**

**WILLIAMS, Ann Mary**
Genre painter and illustrator. She was the sister and collaborator of Samuel Williams (q.v.).

**WILLIAMS, Charles**                                   **fl.1797-1830**
Illustrator and caricaturist. He was the chief caricaturist for Fores, the printseller and was a follower and copyist of James Gillray. His early work is published under the name 'Ansell' but the later is usually anonymous.
Illus: *Dr Syntax in Paris [1820, AT 109]*.
Colls: BM; Witt Photo.
Bibl: M.D. George, *Eng. Pol. Caricat.*, Vol.2 1959.

**WILLIAMS, Mrs Crawshay**                                   **fl.1890-1912**
Artist and illustrator. She was working in London in 1890 under her maiden name of Miss C. Crawshay.
Illus: *Oddle and Iddle [Lily Collier, 1912]*.
Exhib: L.

**WILLIAMS, F.A.**
Illustrator of comic animals. He contributed to *Punch*, 1903-7.

**WILLIAMS, (Gertrude) Alice Meredith**                                   **-1934**
Decorative painter and sculptor, stained glass artist. She was born at Liverpool and studied at the Liverpool School of Architecture and Applied Art, before going to Paris, 1904-7. She exhibited book illustrations at the Walker Art Gallery in 1900. She married the painter Morris Meredith Williams (q.v.) and died in 1934.
Exhib: G; L; RA; RSA; RSW.
Bibl: *The Studio*, Vol.20, 1900 p.196 illus.

498

**WILLIAMS, Hamilton**
Figure artist. He was working at Buckhurst Hill, Essex, 1913-14.
Contrib: *Punch [1909]; London Opinion [1913]*.
Exhib: RA; RSA.

**WILLIAMS, Hugh William 'Grecian'**     **1773-1829**
Landscape painter. He was born in 1773, the son of a sea captain and soon orphaned, being brought up at Edinburgh. He was a founder of the Associated Artists in 1808 and published engravings of Highland views. He made his reputation and earned his name from a Mediterranean tour he undertook through Italy and Greece in 1818. He retired to Edinburgh and died there on 23 June 1829.
Illus: *Travels in Italy, Greece and the Ionian Islands [1820]; Select Views in Greece [1827-29]*.
Contrib: *Scots Magazine; Britton's Beauties of England and Wales [1812]*.
Exhib: Edinburgh, 1808-9.
Colls: Aberdeen; BM; V & AM.

**WILLIAMS, Inglis SHELDON-**     **1871-1940**
Painter and Special Artist. He was born in 1871, the son of Alfred Sheldon-Williams (q.v.) and after the death of his father he emigrated to Canada where he farmed from 1887 to 1891. He returned to Europe and studied at the Slade, at the École des Beaux-Arts, Paris and with Sir Thomas Brock. He returned to Canada, 1895-96 and in 1899 after settling in London was appointed Special Artist to *The Sphere* to cover the Boer War in South Africa. The magazine sent him to cover the Russo-Japanese War in 1903 and the Fine Art Society commissioned him to make watercolours of the Delhi Durbar, 1902-3. He married in 1904, Ida Maud Thomson, the flower painter who had been a Slade student. Sheldon-Williams worked at Stroud, Gloucestershire in 1908 and later at Sharnbrook, Bedfordshire, 1934. A one man show was held at the Regina Art Gallery, in Canada in October 1969.
Illus: *After Pretoria, The Guerilla War [1902]*.
Contrib: *The Quest [1894-96]*.
Exhib: B; FAS, 1903; G; L; NEA; RA; RI; ROI.
Colls: BM.
Bibl: *The Studio*, Vol.41, 1907 pp.111-115; *Country Life*, 15 May 1975.
See illustration (p.498).

**WILLIAMS, J. Scott**     **fl.1909-1921**
Painter and illustrator. He worked in London, 1921 and contributed story illustrations to *The Illustrated London News*, 1909, with A.H. Buckland (q.v.).
Exhib: RA.

**WILLIAMS, Joseph Lionel**     **c.1815-1877**
Painter, watercolourist and engraver. He worked in London and drew architectural subjects and machinery for the magazines. He was an unsuccessful NWS candidate, and died in London in 1877.
Contrib: *ILN [1848-51]; The Art Journal*.
Exhib: BI; RA; RBA.
Colls: Sheffield.

**WILLIAMS, Morris Meredith**     **1881-**
Painter, illustrator and stained glass artist. He was born at Cowbridge, Glamorgan, in 1881 and studied at the Slade School and in Paris and Italy. He worked in Edinburgh, 1914-25 and afterwards at North Tawton, Devon. He married the decorative artist (Gertrude) Alice Meredith Williams (q.v.).
Contrib: *Punch [1906-7 (rustic)]*.
Exhib: G; L; P; RA; RSA; RSW.
Colls: Liverpool.

**WILLIAMS, Penry**     **1798-1885**
Landscape and view painter. He was born at Merthyr Tydfil in 1798 and studied at the RA Schools and won a Society of Arts silver medal in 1821. He settled in Rome in 1826 and remained there until his death painting pictures of the city for the tourist market. He was AOWS from 1828-33.
Publ: *Recollections of Malta, Sicily and the Continent [1847]*.

Contrib: *Britton's Union of Architecture [1827, AL 7]*.
Exhib: BI; OWS; RA; RBA.
Colls: BM; Fitzwilliam; V & AM.

**WILLIAMS, Richard James**     **1876-**
Painter and illustrator of children's books. He was born at Hereford in 1876 and studied at Cardiff University College, Birmingham and London, becoming Headmaster of the Worcester School of Arts and Crafts. He also worked as a wood engraver. ARCA.
Exhib: RCA; RI.

**WILLIAMS, Samuel**     **1788-1853**
Draughtsman, wood engraver and natural history illustrator. He was born on 23 February 1788 at Colchester and was apprenticed to a house-painter before learning the art of wood engraving. He settled in London in 1819 and became a popular and prolific illustrator, engraving much of his own work. He was assisted by his sister Ann Mary Williams (q.v.) and died in London in 1853.
Illus: *Robinson Crusoe [Daniel Defoe, 1822]; Natural History [Mrs Trimmer, 1823-24]; Hone's Everyday Book [1825]; British Forest Trees [Selby, 1842]; Pictures of Country Life [Miller, 1847]; The Poetical Works of John Milton [1854]; Wit Bought [Peter Parley, 1868 (reissue)]*.
Contrib: *Thomson's Seasons, The Castle of Indolence [1851]*.
Exhib: BI; RA.
Colls: BM.
Bibl: Chatto and Jackson, *Treatise on Wood Engraving*, 1861 p.572.

**WILLIAMS, Thomas H.**
Illustrator and engraver. He worked in Plymouth and Exeter and made topographical views of West Country subjects.
Illus: *Picturesque Tours in Devon and Cornwall [1801]; The Environs of Exeter [1815]; A Tour in the Isle of Wight [n.d.]; A Walk on the Coast of Devonshire [1828]*.
Exhib: NWS; RA; RBA.
Colls: Fitzwilliam.

**WILLIAMSON, F.M.**
Illustrator. He contributed comic animal drawings to *Punch*, 1903-6.

**WILLIAMSON, Isobel B.**
Illustrator. She may have been a Liverpool student and contributed drawings for *The Studio* competitions in 1897.
Bibl: *The Studio*, Vols.11 and 12, 1897 illus.

**WILLIAMSON, John**     **fl.1885-1896**
Portrait and figure painter and illustrator. He was working in Edinburgh, 1885-90 and in London from 1893, specialising in costume subjects.
Illus: *Kilgorman [Reed, 1894]*.
Contrib: *The English Illustrated Magazine [1895-96 (social)]*.
Exhib: RA; RBA; RSA.

**WILLIAMSON, Captain Thomas George**     **c.1758-1817**
Amateur artist. He contributed drawings which Howitt engraved for *Oriental Field Sports*, 1807.
Colls: Witt Photo.

**WILLIS, J.B.**
Amateur artist. He contributed figure subjects to *Punch*, 1908.

**WILLOUGHBY, Mrs. Vera**     **fl.1905-1927**
Watercolour painter, poster artist, book illustrator and decorator. She worked at Slindon, Sussex until 1913 and then in London. Her work is inspired by 18th century decoration, transformed by incipient art deco into pretty but stiff fantasies. Some of her soft pencil work dating from the 1920s is pleasantly cubist in feeling.
Illus: *The Humours of History [c.1914]; The Memoirs of a Lady of Quality, being Lady Vane's Memoirs [1925]; A Vision of Greece [1925]; Horati Carminum [1926]; A Sentimental Journey [1927]*.
Exhib: L; P; RI.
Colls: V & AM.

**WILLSON, Beckles**
Domestic painter. He contributed to *The Strand Magazine,* 1894.

**WILLSON, Harry**                    fl.1813-1852
Townscape painter. He worked in the style of Samuel Prout (q.v.).
Publ: *The Use of a Box of Colours [1842].*
Illus: *Willson's Fugitive Sketches in Rome, Venice etc. [1838].*
Colls: BM.

**WILLSON, John J.**                    fl.1875-1902
Landscape and sporting painter. He worked at Headingley, Leeds, and
was married to the painter E. Dorothy Willson.
Contrib: *The Graphic [1875].*
Exhib: L; RA.

**WILLYAMS, Rev. Cooper**                    1762-1816
Artist and topographer. He was born in Essex in 1762 and entered
Emmanuel College, Cambridge, 1780, being ordained in 1784. He held
the living of Exning, near Newmarket, 1788 and St. Peter, West Lynn,
1793. He became chaplain to Admiral Earl Jervis in 1793 and
accompanied him to the West Indies and with the Mediterranean
Fleet, 1798-1800, being present at the Battle of the Nile. He later held
livings at Kingston, Canterbury and Stourmouth. He died in London
in 1816.
Illus: *A History of Sudeley Castle [1791]; An Account of the Campaign in the
West Indies in 1794 [1796, AT 672]; Voyage up the Mediterranean [1802, AT
196]; A Selection of Views in Egypt, Palestine, Rhodes, Italy, Minorca and
Gibraltar [1822, AT 198].*
Contrib: *The Topographer.*
Colls: Witt Photo.

**WILMSHURST, George C.**                    fl.1897-1911
Portrait painter and illustrator. He worked in London and contributed
pen and ink drawings to magazines.
Illus: *The Cardinal's Snuff Box [Henry Havland, 1903].*
Contrib: *ILN [1905, 1908, 1911 (Christmas Nos.)].*
Exhib: M; RA.

**WILSON, Alexander**                    1766-1813
Ornithologist and engraver. He was born at Paisley on 6 July 1766 and
illustrated and engraved his own works, most notably *The American
Ornithology,* 1808-14. He died at Philadelphia on 23 August 1813.
Colls: Witt Photo.

**WILSON, Andrew**                    1780-1848
Landscape painter. He was born at Edinburgh in 1780 and studied
under Alexander Nasmyth (q.v.) and at the RA Schools. He made
several extensive tours of Italy, and on the second in 1803-5, he acted
as a dealer and brought a number of masterpieces back with him. He
was Professor of Drawing at the RMA, Sandhurst for ten years until
1818 and in 1826 he returned to Italy and settled there for twenty
years. He died in Edinburgh in 1848.
Contrib: *Britton's Beauties of England and Wales [1813-15 (Wales and
Oxford)].*
Exhib: BI.
Colls: BM; V & AM.

**WILSON, Charles Heath**                    1809-1882
Landscape painter and illustrator. He was born in London in 1809,
the son of the landscape painter Andrew Wilson (q.v.), with whom he
toured Italy, 1826. He went to live in Edinburgh in 1834, was elected
ARSA in 1835 and continued membership until 1858. He was Master
of the Trustees Academy, 1843-48, and he finally settled in Florence
in 1869. He died there in 1882.
Illus: *Viaggio Antiquario [P. Pifferi, 1832]; Voyage Round the Coasts of
Scotland [1842].*
Exhib: BI; RA.
Colls: Nat. Gall., Scotland.

**WILSON, David**                    fl.1895-1916
Draughtsman and caricaturist. He worked for various magazines
beginning with the *Daily Chronicle* in 1895. He was chief cartoonist
to *The Graphic,* 1910-16, specialising in full page drawings in chalk,
often strongly symbolic and fantastic.
Contrib: *Punch [1900-14]; Fun [1901]; The Graphic [1910-14]; The Sketch;
The Temple Magazine.*

**WILSON, Dower**                    fl.1875-1897
Domestic illustrator. He may be the same as 'D.R. Wilson' exhibiting
at the RA from Bushey, 1884-86.
Contrib: *ILN [1875]; Judy [1878-79]; Punch [1879, 1897]; Moonshine
[1891].*

**WILSON, E.**                    fl.1792-1802
Landscape painter and topographer. He contributed to *The Copper
Plate Magazine,* 1792-1802.
Exhib: RA.
Colls: Witt Photo.

**WILSON, Edgar W.**                    -1918
Painter and illustrator. He worked in London from 1886 and
specialised in the design of covers, initial letters and head and tail
pieces for books. He usually works in pen and ink or pen and wash
and is strongly influenced by Japanese art.
Contrib: *The Strand Magazine [1891]; Black & White [1891]; The Butterfly
[1893, 1899 (covers)]; St. Pauls [1894]; Madame [1895]; The Sketch;
Pick-Me-Up; Daily Chronicle [1895]; The English Illustrated Magazine [1896];
The Pall Mall Magazine [1897]; Pall Mall Gazette [1897]; The Windsor
Magazine; The Unicorn.*
Exhib: RA; RI.
Colls: V & AM; Witt Photo.

**WILSON, Godfrey**
Figure artist. He contributed to *Punch,* 1904.

**WILSON, H.P.**                    fl.1890-1895
Figure painter in watercolour, illustrator. He worked in London and
contributed to *The Sporting and Dramatic News,* 1890 and *Black and
White,* 1891.
Exhib: RA.

**WILSON, Helen Russell    RBA**
Painter and etcher. She studied at the Slade School and at the London
School under Frank Brangwyn (q.v.) and then went to Tokyo to learn
Japanese painting. She was elected RBA in 1911, settled at Tangier in
about 1913 and died there 22 October 1924.
Illus: *Angling and Art in Scotland [1908].*
Exhib: RA; RBA; RI.

**WILSON, John**
Amateur. He contributed illustrations of humorous insects to *Punch,*
1903.

**WILSON, Leslie**                    fl.1893-1934
Figure artist. He worked in London and contributed extensively to
magazines.
Contrib: *Judy [1886-93]; The English Illustrated Magazine [1893-94]; St. Pauls
[1894]; Madame [1895]; The Sketch; Pick-Me-Up; The Royal Magazine.*
Exhib: RBA.

**WILSON, Oscar**                    1867-1930
Portrait painter and illustrator. He was born in London in 1867 and
studied at South Kensington and Antwerp under Beaufaux and Verlat.
He was elected RMS in 1896 and ARBA in 1926, he died on 13 July
1930.
Contrib: *St. Pauls [1894]; The Sketch [1894-95]; Madame [1895]; ILN
[1897].*
Exhib. G; L; M; RABA; RCA; RI; RMS; ROI; RSA.

*PATTEN WILSON 1868-1928. 'So the wind drove us on to the cavern of gloom . . .' Illustration to* The Yellow Book, *Vol. 9, April 1896.*

**WILSON, Patten**                    **1868-1928**

Black and white artist and illustrator. He was born at Cleobury Mortimer in 1868 and studied under Fred Brown. Wilson was a very competent and original illustrator of fantastic subjects and a talented decorator of books. His talents led him to be employed by Messrs. Lane on book covers and title pages, and he completed the Keynote series for the firm after Beardsley's dismissal and was technical adviser for the later numbers of *The Yellow Book*, 1895-96. His greatest failing was over-invention and his drawings, which are rich in imagery and finely executed, lack a degree of clarity essential to textual illustration. He worked principally in London and died in 1928.

Illus: *Miracle Plays [1895]; Life in Arcadia [J.S. Fletcher, 1896]; A Houseful of Rebels [1897]; God's Failures [J.S. Fletcher, 1897]; Selections From Coleridge [1898]; King John [1899]; The Tremendous Twins [Ernest Ames, 1900]; A Child's History of England [1903].*
Contrib: *The Pall Mall Magazine.*
Exhib: L; RA.
Colls: V & AM.
Bibl: *The Artist*, Jan. 1898, pp.17-24 illus; *The Studio*, Winter No, 1900-1 p.51 illus; R.E.D. Sketchley, *Eng. Bk. Illus.*, 1903 pp.28, 131.
See illustration (above).

**WILSON, Thomas Harrington**                    **fl.1842-1886**

Landscape, genre and portrait painter and illustrator. He studied art at the National Gallery in company with Sir John Tenniel (q.v.) and

Charles Martin, later specialising in theatrical portraiture and being introduced to *Punch* by Swain, the engraver. He also made drawings of military subjects and contributed to *The Punch Pocket Books*, 1854-57.

Contrib: *Punch [1853]; ILN [1854-61 (theatre, 1855-60, objects 1876, 1890)]; The Illustrated London Magazine [1855]; The Graphic [1871].*
Exhib: BI; RA; RI; ROI.
Colls: Witt Photo.

**WILSON, Thomas Walter  RI**                    **1851-1912**

Landscape painter and illustrator. He was born in London on 7 November 1851, the son of T. Harrington Wilson (q.v.) and was educated in Chelsea, before studying at South Kensington Schools, 1868 and winning their scholarship, 1869. He was sent by the Department of Science and Art to study at Bayeux and then worked in Belgium and Holland. Wilson undertook a great deal of magazine work and as a *Graphic* artist was one of the finishers of drawings sent in by Fred Villers (q.v.), the Special Artist. He was elected ARI in 1877 and RI in 1879 and ROI in 1883. He died in 1912.

Contrib: *The Graphic [1880-85]; ILN [1888-99]; The English Illustrated Magazine [1895]; Good Words [1898-99]; The Sketch; The Minister; The Idler.*
Exhib: L; M; RI; ROI.
Colls: V & AM.

**WIMBUSH, Henry B.**                    **fl.1881-1908**

Landscape painter. He painted in Scotland and Wales and illustrated *The Channel Islands,* (E.F. Carey, 1904).

Exhib: B; FAS; L; M; RA; RI.

**WIMBUSH, John L.**                    **-1914**

Painter and illustrator. He was working in London from 1890 to 1902 and then at Dartmouth. He died in 1914.

Contrib: *The Strand Magazine [1891-]; The World Wide Magazine [1898]; The Idler; The Boy's Own Magazine.*
Exhib: B; L; M; RA; RBA.

**WIMPERIS, Edmund Morrison  VPRI**                    **1835-1900**

Landscape painter and illustrator. He was born at Chester on 6 February 1835 and after being put in a business there, he was apprenticed at the age of fourteen to Mason Jackson (q.v.), the London wood engraver. He studied with Birket Foster (q.v.) and did a great deal of work for *The Illustrated London News* and other publications before turning almost wholly to landscape watercolour. His best work is of Suffolk, Wales and the Home Counties, much of the work being drawn directly from nature. He was elected ANWS in 1873 and NWS in 1875, becoming Vice-President in 1895. He died on Christmas Day 1900.

Contrib: *The Book of South Wales [Mr. and Mrs. S.C. Hall, 1861]; Gray's Elegy [1869].*
Exhib: B; FAS; L; M; New Gall; RBA; RI; ROI.
Colls: BM; Bradford; Manchester; V & AM; Witt Photo.
Bibl: *Walker's Quarterly*, 4 1921.

**WINGFIELD, James Digman**                    **1800-1872**

Historical painter. He worked in London and specialised in costume subjects, often with Hampton Court Palace as their background. He made drawings of the 1851 Exhibition and was almost certainly an illustrator, two poetic works of his being engraved by Dalziel.

Colls: Nottingham; Witt Photo.

**WINZER, Charles Freegrove**                    **1886-**

Painter and illustrator. He was born at Warsaw on 1 December 1886 and worked in Morocco, Spain and Britain. He later travelled to India, Nepal and Ceylon, where he became Inspector of Fine Art. He contributed illustrations to a number of books in the 1920s and decorated the rhymesheets of Harold Monro's Poetry Bookshop.

Illus: *Sixteen Poems [J.E. Flecker]; The Chinese Drama [Johnson].*
Exhib: Toothe Gall.
Colls: Cambridge; Cardiff.

**WIRGMANN, Charles**                                         **1832-1891**

Figure artist and caricaturist. He was born in 1860, the brother of T.B. Wirgmann (q.v.). He worked in London before settling in Yokohama, Japan in 1860 and painting Japanese life. He contributed drawings of Manila, 1857 and China, 1860, to *The Illustrated London News*. He died in 1891 and an exhibition of his work was held in London in 1921.

Colls: BM.

**WIRGMANN, Theodore Blake**                                  **1848-1925**

Portrait painter and illustrator. He was born at Louvain, Belgium on 29 April 1848 into a Swedish family and entered the RA Schools, winning a silver medal there in 1865. He went to Paris to study with Hebert and on his return, worked extensively for *The Graphic* and as an assistant to Sir John Millais (q.v.). Perhaps his most notable achievement is the series of brilliant chalk portraits that he carried out for the magazine in 1884 to 1889, including politicians, writers and royalty. Wirgmann worked in London where he had an extensive practice, was elected RP in 1891 and died there on 16 January 1925.

Contrib: *Cassell's Family Magazine [1868]; The Graphic [1875-1901]; Daily Chronicle [1895]*.
Exhib: B; G; GG; L; M; New Gall; P; RA; RHA; RI; ROI.
Colls: Bradford; Middle Temple; NPG; Witt Photo.

**WITHERBY, Arthur George**                                   **fl.1894-1919**

Caricaturist. He was a painter, draughtsman and writer of Newton Grange, Newbury, who was a keen sportsman and for some time the proprietor of *Vanity Fair* to which he contributed illustrations, 1894-95 and 1899-1901.

Exhib: Walker's Gall.

**WITHERINGTON, William Frederick   RA**                      **1785-1865**

Landscape painter. He was born in Goswell Street, London on 26 May 1785 and studied at the RA Schools, 1805. Although he first exhibited landscapes, he gradually turned his attention to genre subjects and painted a scene from *The Rape of the Lock,* which may have been used for illustration, 1835. He was elected ARA in 1830 and RA in 1840. On account of ill health he spent many of his later years in the country, but died in London on 10 April 1865.

Exhib: BI; RA.
Colls: V & AM.

**WITHERS, Alfred   ROI**                                     **1856-1932**

Landscape painter, architectural painter and etcher. He was born on 15 October 1856 and worked in Kent and Surrey before settling in London in about 1903. He was elected ROI in 1897 and was a member of the Society of 25 Artists. He was also a member of the Pastel Society and received the Royal Order of Alfonso XII of Spain. He died on 8 August 1932.

Contrib: *ILN [1896]*.
Exhib: B; FAS; G; GG; L; M; New Gall; RA; RBA; RE; ROI; RSA.

**WITHERS, Augusta Innes**                                    **fl.1829-1865**

Botanical illustrator. She was a member of the RBA and of the Society of Lady Artists and contributed to *The Botanist,* c.1840.

Exhib: NWS; RA; RBA.

**WODDERSPOON, John**                                         **fl.1812-1862**

Landscape painter. He worked at Norwich, where he was sub-editor of *The Mercury.*

Publ: *Historic Sites of Suffolk [1841]; A New Guide to Ipswich [1842]; Picturesque Antiquities of Ipswich [1845]; Notes on the Grey and White Friars, Ipswich [1848]; Memorials of the Ancient Town of Ipswich [1850].*
Colls: Norwich.

**WOLF, Joseph   RI**                                         **1820-1899**

Animal and bird painter and illustrator. He was born at Mors, near Coblenz in 1820 and studied lithography and Darmstadt before entering the Antwerp Academy. He came to England in 1848 under the patronage of the Duke of Westminster and through the friendship of D.G. Rossetti and was employed at the BM on Gray's *The Genera*

*of Birds.* He illustrated extensively for the Zoological Society and visited Norway in 1849 and again in 1856 with John Gould, the ornithologist and illustrator. He was elected RI in 1874 and died in London on 20 April 1899.

Illus: *Life and Habits of Wild Animals [D.G. Elliott, 1873].*
Contrib: *ILN [1853-57, 1872]; Eliza Cook's Poems [1856]; Wordsworth's Selected Poems [1859]; Montgomery's Poems [1860]; Band of Hope Review [1861]; Good Words [1861-64]; Willmott's Sacred Poetry [1862]; Wood's Natural History [1862]; The Sunday Magazine [1866-68]; Once a Week [1866]; Poems by Jean Ingelow [1867]; North Coast and Other Poems [Buchanan, 1868]; Gould's Birds of Great Britain.*
Exhib: BI; RA; RI.
Colls: BM; V & AM; Sir John Witt.
Bibl: Chatto & Jackson, *Treatise on Wood Engraving,* 1861 p.573; *The Artist,* May 1899 pp.1-15 illus.

**WOLFE, Major W.S.M.**                                       **fl.1855-1862**

Amateur illustrator. Royal Artillery officer, who was promoted Captain in 1856 and Major of Artillery Brigade at Aldershot, 1862. He held the Crimean War medal and contributed drawings of the War to *The Illustrated London News,* 1855.

**WOLLEN, William Barnes   RI**                               **1857-1936**

Military painter and illustrator. He was born at Leipzig on 6 October 1857 and was educated at University College School and studied at the Slade. He was intended for an army career but took up painting as a professional and was sent as Special Artist for *The Graphic* to South Africa in 1900. He was elected RI in 1888, ROI in 1897 and HROI in 1934. He lived for most of his life in Bedford Park, West London and died there on 28 March 1936.

Illus: *Rex [L. Thompson, 1894].*
Contrib: *ILN [1882-99]; The Strand Magazine [1891-94]; Black & White [1891]; Chums [1892]; The Boy's Own Paper [1892-93]; Daily Chronicle [1895]; The Penny Illustrated Paper; Cassell's Family Magazine; The Wide World Magazine [1898]; The Graphic [1900-6].*
Exhib: B; G; L; M; RA; RHA; RI; ROI; RSA.
Colls: Witt Photo.

**WOMRATH, Andrew K**                                         **1869-**

Painter and illustrator. He was born at Frankfurt on 25 October 1869 and studied at the New York Academy and with L. O. Messon in Paris, before working at Mentone.

Contrib: *The Evergreen [1896]; The Savoy.*

**WOOD, F.W.**

Animal and bird illustrator. He contributed extensively to *The Illustrated London News,* 1855-58 and again in 1865-75.

**WOOD, Fane**

Figure artist. He contributed to *London Society,* 1868.

**WOOD, John George**                                         **fl.1793-1838**

Topographical illustrator. He contributed to Britton's *Beauties of England and Wales,* 1810.

Exhib: RA.

**WOOD, Lawson**                                              **1878-1957**

Black and white artist and illustrator. He was born at Highgate in 1878, the grandson of L.J. Wood, the landscape painter. He studied at the Slade School and at Heatherley's and was for six years the chief artist on the staff of C.A. Pearson Ltd. He served in the RFC during the First World War. Wood's work is usually in ink and watercolour and most of it is humorous in drawing and content, his repertoire of characters including peppery army officers, namby-pamby men and dominating old dames. The figures are heavily caricatured and he was one of the group of artists who made capital out of imaginary pre-historic scenes. He died in 1957.

Contrib: *Pearson's Magazine; The Royal Magazine; ILN [1905, 1908, 1912]; The Graphic [1907-11]; London Opinion [1913].*
Exhib: D; L; RA; RI.
Colls: V & AM; Witt Photo.
Bibl: *LW,* Brush, Pen and Pencil Series, Ed. by A.E. Johnson, c.1910.

See illustration (p.503).

*LAWSON WOOD 1878-1957. 'Remarkable Escapes'. Original drawing for illustration. Wash. Signed and dated 1903. 7½ins. x 13ins. (19.1cm x 33cm).*
Victoria and Albert Museum

**WOOD, Margery**
Amateur illustrator. She was a student at the Lambeth School and won a prize at the National Competition, 1904 for an illustration of Cranfordesque type.

Bibl: *The Studio*, Vol.32 p.327.

**WOOD, Olive**                                    **fl.1914-1933**
Miniature painter and illustrator of children's books. She studied at the Clapham and Camberwell Schools of Art and worked in Dulwich Village.

Exhib: RA.

**WOOD, Stanley L.**                                **1866-1928**
Military painter and illustrator. He was born in 1866 and worked in London for the leading magazines and was employed almost continuously by Messrs Chatto's as an illustrator of boys' adventure stories. He died in 1928.

Illus: *The Arabian Nights Entertainments [1890]; A Waif of the Plains [1890]; Maid Marian and Robin Hood [1892]; Romances of the Old Seraglio [1894]; Mr Sadler's Daughters [H.C. Davidson, 1894]; Rujub the Juggler [G. A. Henty, 1894]; A Protegée of Jack Hamlin [Brett Harte, 1894]; A Fair Colonist [1894]; The King's Assegai [B. Mitford, 1894]; A Ramble Round the Globe [T.R. Dewar, 1894]; The Lost Middy [G. Manville Fenn]; Rough Riders of the Pampas [Capt. F.S. Brereton, 1908]; In Empire's Cause [E. Protheroe, 1908].*
Contrib: *ILN [1889-90]; The Sporting and Dramatic News [1890]; Black & White [1891]; The Graphic [1903]; The Strand Magazine [1906]; Cassell's Family Magazine; The Idler; The Windsor Magazine; Pearson's Magazine; Wide World Magazine [1927].*
Exhib: L; M; RA; ROI.
Colls: Witt Photo; V & AM.

**WOOD, Starr**                                    **1870-1944**
Caricaturist and black and white artist. He was born in London on 1 February 1870 and was educated privately before being entered in a chartered accountant's office in 1887. He left in 1890 and began to draw for the magazines, having sufficient success to found his own magazine *The Windmill*, a quarterly, and later to run *Starr Wood's*

*Magazine,* from 1910 until at least 1935. The latter is filled entirely with his illustrations, à la May, à la Belcher and à la everyone else! Wood's humour is seldom above that of the seaside postcard but he can be a funny draughtsman, many of his works appear under the name of The Snark. He died on 2 September 1944.

Illus: *Rhymes of the Regiments [1896].*
Contrib: *Puck and Ariel [1890]; Fun [1892]; The Sketch [1893]; Judy [1895]; Pick-Me-Up [1895]; The Idler; Chums; The Parade [1897]; The English Illustrated Magazine [1898]; Punch [1900-2, 1908, 1914].*
Exhib: L.
Colls: V & AM; Witt Photo.

**WOOD, T.W., Jnr.**                                **fl.1867-1880**
Illustrator. He was the son of the animal artist Thomas W. Wood, and he illustrated *The Common Moths of England* by Rev. J.G. Wood, c.1880.

Contrib: *Punch [1865].*
Exhib: RA.

**WOOD, William**                                  **1774-1857**
Doctor and amateur topographer. He was born at Kendal in 1774 and practised in Calcutta. In 1833 he published *A Series of Twenty-eight Panoramic Views of Calcutta,* 1833.

Colls: BM.

**WOODHOUSE, F.W.**
Artist. He illustrated *Representation of the Brigade Field Day in Ware Park,* 1853, AL 383.

**WOODROFFE, Paul Vincent**                        **1875-1945**
Painter, illustrator and stained glass artist. He was born in Madras, India in 1875 and was educated at Stonyhurst and studied at the Slade School. Woodroffe specialised in book decoration, covers and end-papers as well as in illustration, he was also a poster artist. He settled in Campden, Gloucestershire in about 1904 and was associated

with the Arts and Crafts movement there and particularly in the design of stained glass. He was a member of the Art Workers Guild and of the Society of Master Glass Painters. He died in London in 1945.

Illus: *Ye Booke of Nursery Rhymes [1897]; Herrick's Hesperides [1897, 1907]; Shakespeare's Songs [1898]; The Little Flowers of St. Francis [1899]; The Confessions of St. Augustine [1900]; The Little Flowers of St. Benet [1901]; The Tempest [1908]; Alls Well [Robert Browning, 1913 (cover)].*
Contrib: *The Quarto [1896]; The Parade [1897]; ILN [1909].*
Exhib: FAS; G; NEA; RA; RHA; RMS.
Colls: V & AM; Witt Photo.
Bibl: R.E.D. Sketchley, *Eng. Bk. Illus.,* 1903 pp.13, 14, 131.

**WOODS, Henry  RA**                                    **1846-1921**
Genre and landscape painter and illustrator. He was born at Warrington on 22 April 1846 and studied at Warrington School of Art, winning a travelling scholarship. He attended the South Kensington Schools and joined *The Graphic* as an illustrator in 1870 with his brother-in-law, Sir Luke Fildes (q.v.). He did a considerable amount of work for the paper, often in collaboration with S.P. Hall (q.v.). He became ARA in 1882 and RA in 1893, having settled in Venice since 1876. He died there on 27 October 1921.

Illus: *Miss or Mrs? [Wilkie Collins, 1885 (with Fildes)].*
Exhib: B; FAS; L; M; RA; ROI.
Colls: Liverpool; Tate; Warrington; Witt Photo.

**WOODS, William**
Military illustrator. He contributed drawings to *The Illustrated London News,* 1860.

**WOODVILLE, Richard Caton, Snr.**                        **1825-1855**
Painter of battle scenes. He was born at Baltimore in 1825 and died in London in 1855. He contributed a drawing to *The Illustrated London News,* 1852.

Exhib: BI; RA.

**WOODVILLE, Richard Caton, Jnr.**                        **1856-1927**
Painter of battle scenes, Special Artist and illustrator. He was born in London on 7 January 1856, the son of R.C. Woodville Senior (q.v.). He studied art in Düsseldorf under Kamphussen after being brought up in St Petersburg, and lived in Paris before settling in London in 1875. He began to work almost at once for *The Illustrated London News* and went as artist to the Turkish War of 1878 and the Egyptian War of 1882, also serving in Albania and the Balkans. He turned increasingly to oil painting in the 1880s and finally abandoned black and white work altogether in 1897. Woodville's war drawings were always accurate and highly finished if somewhat lacking in the realities of action. The high gloss and glamour earned him comparisons with Meissonnier. He was elected RI in 1882 and ROI in 1883. He died in North London on 17 August 1927.

Illus: *Ravenstones [H. Kingsley, 1894].*
Contrib: *ILN [1876-1911]; The Cornhill Magazine [1883]; The Sketch; The Boy's Own Paper; The Windsor Magazine; The English Illustrated Magazine [1895-97]; Pearson's Magazine [1896].*
Exhib: FAS; G; L; M; New Gall; RA; RHA; RI; ROI.
Colls: Royal Coll., Windsor; BM; V & AM.
Bibl: R.C.W., *Random Recollections,* 1913; *The Idler,* 1897, Vol.10 pp.758-775; *The Illustrated London News,* 7 December 1895.

**WOODWARD, Alice Bolingbroke**                        **fl.1885-1920**
Illustrator of children's books. She worked principally in pen and watercolours but also in pencil, her designs have something of Rackham about them but lack his atmospheric and sinister elements. Her work was greatly admired by *The Studio.*

Illus: *Eric, Prince of Lorlonia [Lady Jersey, 1895]; Banbury Cross [1895]; To Tell The King The Sky is Falling [1896]; Bon Mots of the Eighteenth Century [1897]; Bon Mots of the Nineteenth Century [1897]; Brownie [1897]; Red Apple and Silver Bells [1897]; Adventures in Toyland [1897]; The Troubles of Tatters [1898]; The Princess of Hearts [1899]; The Cat and the Mouse [1899]; The Golden Ship [1900]; The House That Grew [Mrs. Molesworth, 1900]; Nebula to Man [H.R. Knipe, 1905]; The Pinafore Picture Book [W.S. Gilbert, 1908]; Alice's Adventures in Wonderland [n.d.]; Lost Legends of the Nursery Songs [M.S. Clark, 1920].*
Contrib: *ILN [1895]; Daily Chronicle [1895]; The Quarto [1896].*
Exhib: G; L; M; NEA; RA; RBA; RI; RSW.

Bibl: *The Studio,* Vo.9, 1897 p.216; Vol.10, 1897 p.232; Vol.15, 1899 p.214; Winter No. 1900-1 p.31 illus.; R.E.D. Sketchley, *Eng. Bk. Illus.,* 1903 pp.104, 172.

**WOODWARD, George Moutard**                        **1760-1809**
Amateur caricaturist. He was born in Derbyshire in 1760 and came to London about 1792. Between 1794 and 1800 he produced numerous political caricatures, some of them in strip form of his own innovation. His work is usually coarse and crude and was often etched by Rowlandson, Isaac Cruikshank, Roberts and Williams (qq.v.). He lived a dissolute life and died in a tavern in 1809.

Illus: *Elements of Bacchus [1792]; Familiar Verses from the Ghost of Willy Shakespeare to Sammy Ireland [1795]; The Olio of Good Breeding [1801]; The Musical Mania for 1802; The Bettyad [1805]; The Fugitive [1805]; Caricature Magazine [1807]; Eccentric Excursions [1807]; Chesterfield Travestie... [1808]; The Comic Works, in Prose and Poetry [1808].*
Colls: BM; Leeds; Witt Photo.

**WOODWARD, Mary**                                    **fl.1890-1914**
Miniaturist. She worked in London and designed invitation cards and may have illustrated books.

Exhib: B; G; L; RA; RBA; RHA; RI; RMS; RSA; SWA.

**WOOLEY, Harry**                                    **fl.1912-1920**
Figure artist. He worked in Bristol, 1912-13 and specialised in comic sketches in colour after the manner of Starr Wood (q.v.).

Exhib: L; RA; RMS.
Colls: Witt Photo.

**WOOLNER, Thomas**                                    **1826-1892**
Sculptor and draughtsman. He was born at Hadleigh, Suffolk on 17 December 1825 and after showing early promise he was apprenticed to the sculptor William Behnes. He entered the RA Schools in 1842 and won a silver medal of the Society of Arts in 1845, two years later meeting Rossetti and becoming a member of the Pre-Raphaelite Brotherhood. In the next few years Woolner concentrated on producing medallions, but in 1852, he set sail from Gravesend to try his fortune on the Australian goldfields, thus inspiring Ford Madox Brown's picture 'The Last of England'. He returned in 1854 and soon made a success of his portrait sculpture, being elected ARA in 1871 and RA in 1874. He died in London on 7 October 1892.

Contrib: *The Golden Treasury [1870]; Book of Praise [C.H. Seers].*
Exhib: M; RA.
Bibl: Amy Woolner, *TW, Life and Letters.*

**WOOLNOTH, Thomas**                                    **1785-c.1836**
Painter and engraver. He worked in London as a pupil of Charles Heath and contributed to *Heath's Gallery,* 1836.

Exhib: BI; NWS; RA; RBA.
Colls: NPG.

**WORMS, Jaspar von**                                    **1832-1924**
Painter, etcher and illustrator. He was born in Paris on 16 December 1832 and studied at the École des Beaux-Arts from 1849, exhibiting at the Salon from 1859. He specialised in Spanish genre subjects and died in 1924.

Contrib: *Cassell's Illustrated Family Paper [1853-57 (Crimea)].*

**WORTLEY, Mary Stuart (Countess of Lovelace)**            **-1941**
Portrait painter and illustrator. She was the daughter of the Rt. Hon. J.A. Stuart Wortley and married 2nd Earl of Lovelace in December 1880. She died on 18 April 1941.

Illus: *Zelinda and The Monster [1896].*
Exhib: B; G; M; New Gall.

**WRAY, A.W.**                                    **fl.1830-1840**
Figure artist and illustrator. He was a follower of George Cruikshank and 'Phiz' and made illustrations in their style for an unidentified novel.

Colls: Witt Photo.

**WRIGHT, Alan**  fl.1889-1925
Painter, illustrator and poet. He was working in Kensington in 1890 and at Burghfield Common, Berkshire after 1914. Wright was an illustrator of children's books and a book decorator of talent. Much of his work is in the style of the woodcut with strong Celtic and Gothic emphasis, he also made designs for eastern subjects. His book, *Climbing in the British Isles,* was illustrated by Ellis Carr (q.v.).
Illus: *Queen Victoria's Dolls [1894]; The Wallypug in London [G.E. Farrow, 1898]; Adventures in Wallypug Land [1898]; The Little Panjandrum's Dodo [1899]; The Mandarin's Kite [1900].*
Contrib: *The Girl's Own Paper [1890-1900]; The Strand Magazine [1891-94, 1906]; The Pall Mall Magazine; The Parade [1897]; The Dome [1897-99]; The Windmill [1899]; Punch [1905].*
Exhib: L; NEA; RA; RBA; ROI.
Bibl: R.E.D. Sketchley, *Eng. Bk. Illus.,* 1903 pp.107, 173.

**WRIGHT, Frank**  fl.1905-1911
Landscape painter. He worked in London and contributed illustrations of rustic figures to *Punch,* 1905.
Exhib: RA.

**WRIGHT, Gilbert S.**  fl.1900-1911
Figure painter. He worked in Forest Hill, South London and contributed drawings to *The Graphic,* 1910-11, Christmas numbers.
Exhib: RA.

**WRIGHT, Henry Charles Seppings**  1850-1937
Painter and Special Artist. He was born in Cornwall in 1850, where his father had a parish and after studying in Paris, worked for *The Pictorial World* from 1883. He joined the staff of *The Illustrated London News* in about 1888 and attended the Ashanti, Grecian, Spanish-American and Balkan wars on behalf of the paper. He was the representative of Armstrong-Whitworth in the Russo-Japanese War of 1904-5 and was on the Russian front in the First World War, 1915-16. He is believed to have contributed caricatures to *Vanity Fair,* 1891-1900 under the name of 'Stuff'. He died on 7 February 1937.
Publ: *The Soudan [1896]; With Togo [1906]; Two Years under The Crescent.*
Contrib: *ILN [1888-1900]; The Graphic [1887]; Black & White [1891]; The Boy's Own Paper [1892-93]; The Idler; Chums [1892]; The Pall Mall Magazine; The Sketch; The English Illustrated Magazine [1893-94]; The Sporting and Dramatic News [1896].*
Exhib: L; M; RA; RBA; RI.
Colls: V & AM; Witt Photo.
Bibl: *The Idler,* Vol.11, pp.89-101.

**WRIGHT, John Massey OWS**  1777-1866
Historical painter in watercolours. He was born at Pentonville on 14 October 1777, the son of an organ builder and worked as a piano tuner for Broadwoods. He was acquainted with Thomas Stothard (q.v.) and on settling in London he was introduced to a number of artists and was commissioned to paint scenery for the Strand Panorama and for Covent Garden. He was elected AOWS and OWS in 1824 and set up a fashionable drawing-master's practice in London, also working for the Annuals. He died on 13 May 1866.
Contrib: *The Literary Souvenir [1825-26]; The Amulet [1826-27]; Heath's Gallery [1836].*
Exhib: BI; OWS; RA; RBA.
Colls: Leeds; Manchester; V & AM; Witt Photo.
Bibl: Martin Hardie, *Watercol. Paint. in Brit.,* Vol.3, 1968 pp.87-88.

**WRIGHT, John William OWS**  1802-1848
Figure and portrait painter. He was born in London in 1802, the son of the miniature painter John Wright, and was apprenticed to Thomas Phillips, RA. His main work was in supplying historical portraits and scenes to the Annuals, he was elected AOWS in 1831 and OWS in 1841. He died in poor circumstances in 1848.
Contrib: *The National Gallery of Contemporary Portraits [1822]; Heath's Gallery [1836]; Finden's Gallery.*
Exhib: OWS; RA.
Colls: BM; Witt Photo.

**WRIGHT, Louise Mrs John W. Wright**  1875-
Fashion illustrator. She was born at Philadelphia, USA, in 1875 and married the watercolourist and etcher John Wright, 1857-1933. She also painted portraits, landscapes and still-lifes.

Exhib: Beaux Arts Gall; RA.
Bibl: *LW,* The Art of The Illustrator, ed. P.V. Bradshaw, 1916.

**WRIGHTSON, J.**  -1865
Engraver and illustrator. He worked at Boston and New York between 1854 and 1860 and drew three illustrations for Roscoe's *North Wales,* 1836.
Colls: Witt Photo.

**WYATT, Henry**  1794-1840
Portrait painter. He was born at Thickbroom, Lichfield, on 17 September 1794 and entered the RA Schools in 1812. He studied with Sir Thomas Lawrence before opening his own studio as a portrait painter in Birmingham, Manchester and finally London in 1825. He died at Prestwich on 27 February 1840.
Contrib: *Heath's Gallery [1836-38].*
Exhib: BI; RA; RBA.
Colls: V & AM; Witt Photo.

**WYATT, Thomas Henry FSA**  1807-1880
Architect. He was born in 1807, the brother of Sir Mathew Digby Wyatt. He was President of the RIBA, 1870-73 and Gold Medallist in 1873. He designed theatres and barracks and died in 1880.
Contrib: *Britton's Cathedrals [1832-36].*

**WYBURD, Francis John**  1826-
Genre painter. He was born in London in 1826 and was educated at Lille and studied with the lithographer, T. Fairland. He entered the RA Schools in 1848 and travelled in Italy in the 1850s. His only illustrations were the highly romantic and decorative ones for *The Poetry and Pictures of Thomas Moore,* c.1845. He died after 1893. RBA, 1879.
Exhib: BI; L; RA; RBA; ROI.
Colls: Witt Photo.

**WYLD, William RI**  1806-1889
Landscape painter. He was born in London in 1806 and became Secretary to the British Consul at Calais, where he took lessons in watercolours from F.L.T. Francia. He was a friend of Horace Vernet and travelled with him to Italy, Spain and Algiers, and settled in Paris. He was elected ANWS in 1849 and NWS in 1879. He died in Paris in 1889.
Illus: *Voyages Pittoresque dans La Région d'Alger [1833].*
Colls: BM; Fitzwilliam; Searight Coll; V & AM.

**WYLLIE, Charles William or Charlie RBA**  1859-1923
Marine painter and illustrator. He was born in London on 18 February 1859, the brother of W.L. Wyllie, RA (q.v.). He studied at Leigh's and the RA Schools and concentrated on coastal and genre subjects. He was elected RBA in 1886 and ROI in 1888. He worked in St John's Wood and died there on 28 July 1923.
Contrib: *The Graphic [1881-90]; The Picturesque Mediterranean [1891]; ILN [1893-96]; The Sunday Magazine [1894].*
Exhib: B; G; GG; L; M; New Gall; RA; RBA; ROI.
Colls: BM; V & AM; Witt Photo.

**WYLLIE, William Lionel RA**  1851-1931
Marine painter, illustrator and etcher. He was born in London in July 1851, the brother of C.W. Wyllie, RBA (q.v.) and half-brother of Lionel Percy Smythe (q.v.). He was brought up at Wimereux and studied at Heatherley's and the RA Schools and learnt the art of boat building. His pictures of the Thames Estuary and the shipping of Britain at the height of its Empire are among the most evocative and accurate existing. He was on the staff of *The Graphic* for some years as their marine illustrator and was sent to the United States by them in 1893. He was Marine Painter to the Royal Yacht Squadron, was elected NEA in 1887, ARA in 1889 and RA in 1907. He died on 6 April 1931.
Contrib: *The Graphic [1880-1904].*
Exhib: B; FAS, 1884, 1889, 1892, 1907; G; GG; L; M; NEA; RA; RBA; RE; RHA; RI; ROI.
Colls: BM; Fitzwilliam; Liverpool; Tate; Witt Photo.

Architectural painter and writer. He was born in Paris on 5 December 1832 and became a pupil of Constant-Dufeux. He died in 1898.

Contrib: *The Illustrated Times [1860 (Spain)]; ILN [1876 (Turkey)].*

### YEATS, Jack Butler    RHA      1871-1957

Painter, illustrator and caricaturist. He was born in Ireland in 1871, the son of J.B. Yeats, RHA and the brother of W.B. Yeats. He was educated in County Sligo and studied art at South Kensington and at the West London and Westminster Schools of Art. He lived in England from about 1890 to 1898 and concentrated on figure drawing for illustrations. His work at this period is highly inventive and free and among the best of it is the social realism of the East End of London captured magnificently in chalk or ink. His drawing was often criticised at the time for its lack of precision but its ruggedness looks forward to the 1920s and the humour of his sketches for *Fun,* 1901, is very modern in quality. Yeats returned to Ireland in about 1902-3 and concentrated for the remainder of his life on oil paintings. He was elected ARHA in 1915 and RHA in 1916. He sometimes illustrated under the name 'W. Bird'.

Illus: *The Life and Adventures of Captain Singleton [Defoe, 1895]; Romance and Narratives [Defoe, 1900]; Life in the West of Ireland [1912].*
Contrib: *Puck and Ariel [1890]; Chums [1892]; ILN [1892]; The Sketch [1894]; Judy [1895]; The New Budget [1895]; Lika Joko; Punch [1896-1914]; Cassell's Saturday Journal; The Quartier Latin [1898]; The Longbow [1898]; Fun [1901]; The Broadsheet [1902-3]; The Manchester Guardian [1905]; The Broadside [1908-15].*
Exhib: G; L; RA; RHA; ROI.
Colls: Bat. Gall., Ireland; V & AM; Witt Photo.
Bibl: *Modern Book Illustrators and Their Work,* Studio, 1914; C. Neve, *JY; Rider to The Sea,* Country Life, July 30, 1970; *The Dun Emer Press Later The Cuala Press,* 1973; Catalogue of *JBY, Early Drawings and Watercolours,* Victor Waddington Gallery, 26 Oct.-18 Nov. 1967.
See illustration (right).

### YENDIS, M.

Illustrator. He contributed to *Fun,* 1901.

### YOHN, Edmond Charles    or YON      1836-1910

French landscape painter. He was born in Paris on 2 February 1836 and became a pupil of Pouget and exhibited at the Salon from 1865. He was a talented wood engraver and worked on the illustrations for an edition of Victor Hugo. He died in Paris on 15 March 1897.

Contrib: *The Graphic [1905-6].*
Exhib: G.

### YORKE, Hon. Eliot Thomas      1805-1885

Landscape painter. He was the son of Admiral Sir J.S. Yorke and nephew of Elizabeth, Countess of Hardwicke (q.v.). He was taught watercolour by de Wint and sat as MP for Cambridgeshire, 1854-65.

Illus: *The Wanderer in Western France [G.T. Lowth, 1863].*

### 'YORRICK'

Pseudonym of illustrator of children's books. He illustrated *A Knowing Dog,* Greening, 1908 and contributed to *The Minster* and *The Idler,* 1895.

### YOUNG, Austin

Book decorator. He contributed the cover design and title page to *The Sonnet in England and Other Essays* by J.A. Noble for the Bodley Head, 1894.

### YOUNG, William Weston      fl.1797-1835

Topographer. He was originally a corn-merchant who settled at Neath in 1797, moving to Newton Nottage in 1806. He was also a coal owner and associated with the Swansea porcelain works.

Illus: *Guide to the Scenery of Glyn Neath [1835].*
Bibl: *The Connoisseur,* Vol.96, 1935 No.407.

*JACK BUTLER YEATS 1871-1957. Illustration to* Life in The West of Ireland, *1912.*

**ZANGWILL, Mark** fl.1890-1896

Rural and domestic illustrator. He may have been a relation of I. Zangwill, the Editor of *Puck and Ariel,* to which he contributed in 1890. He also made drawings for *The English Illustrated Magazine,* 1896.

**ZORNLIN, Georgiana Margaretta** 1800-1881

Portrait painter. She was born in 1800 and became a pupil of Benjamin Robert Haydon.

Contrib: *Dennis's Landscape Gardener [1835, AL 13 (liths)].*
Exhib: RA; RBA.
Colls: NPG.

**ZWECKER, Johann Baptist** 1814-1876

History painter, illustrator and etcher. He was born at Frankfurt on 18 September 1814 and became a student of the Institute Stadel and worked in Düsseldorf. He settled in London in about 1850 and made numerous illustrations for books and magazines, many of them of natural history subjects. He died in London on 10 January 1876.

Illus: *Wild Sports of the World [J. Greenwood, 1862]; Out on the Pampas [G.A. Henty, 1871]; The Child's Zoological Garden [1880]; The Rifle and The Hound in Ceylon [S.W. Baker, 1892].*
Contrib: *ILN [1860-66, 1872 (animals)]; Good Words [1861, 1868]; Wood's Natural History [1862]; The Churchman's Family Magazine [1863]; London Society [1864]; Krilof and His Fables [1867]; North Coast and Other Poems [Buchanan, 1868]; Good Words For The Young [1869-72]; The Graphic [1875].*
Exhib: BI; RA; RBA.
Bibl: Chatto and Jackson, *Treatise on Wood Engraving,* 1861 p.600.

*ARTHUR RACKHAM RWS 1867-1939. 'A Girl By a Pool.' Pen and ink. Signed and dated 1909. 3½ins. x 5⅜ins. (8.8cm x 13.6cm).*

# Appendix A
## Schools of Illustration*

### BIRMINGHAM

ARMOUR, Jessie Lamont
BATTEN, John Dixon
BRADLEY, Gertrude M.
BRISCOE, Arthur John Trevor
DAVIS, Louis
FAUX, F.W.
FRANCE, G. Cave (see A. Gaskin)
GASKIN, Arthur
GASKIN, Mrs. Arthur
GERE, Charles March

HOLDEN, Evelyn
HOLDEN, Violet M.
JONES, S.R.
LEVETUS, Celia
MASON, Fred
METEYARD, Sidney H.
MILLAR, Harold R.
MUCKLEY, L.F.

NEWILL, Mary J.
PAYNE, Henry A.
PEACOCK, Mildred A.
ROBINSON, F. Cayley
RUTLAND, Florence M.
SLEIGH, Bernard
SMITH, Winifred
SOUTHALL, J.E.
TARLING, G.T.
TREGLOWN, E.G.

### GLASGOW

CAMERON, Katharine
CARTER, D.B.
CHAMBERLAIN, D.
DUNCAN, J.A.
FRENCH, Annie

HAY, Helen
HORNEL, E.A.
KING, Jessie M.
MACBETH, Ann
MACDOUGALL, W.B.
ORR, Monro S.

ORR, Stewart
PARK, Carton Moore
PRYDE, James
SMYTH, Dorothy C.
URQUHART, Annie

### ARTISTS INFLUENCED BY AUBREY BEARDSLEY

BRADLEY, W.H.
CARMICHAEL, Stewart
CLARKE, Harry
FRENCH, Annie
HYLAND, Fred

JACKSON, F.E.
JAMES, Gilbert
KETTLEWELL, John
MACDOUGALL, W.B.

NIELSEN, Kay
ODLE, A.E.
PLANK, George
SPARE, Austin O.
VOIGHT, H.H.

### ARTISTS INFLUENCED BY GREENAWAY AND CALDECOTT

ANDRE, R.
ANGUS, Christine
EMERSON, H.H.

FARMILOE, Edith
GRAHAM, Winifred

HODGSON, William J.
HOUGHTON, Elizabeth Ellen
SOWERBY, J.G.

### ARTISTS INFLUENCED BY THE CHAP BOOK STYLE

ADAMS, W. Dacres
COLMAN-SMITH, Pamela
CRAIG, E. Gordon
CRAWHALL, Joseph

GAVIN, Jessie
HALKETT, George R.
HARDY, Dudley
KAPP, E.X.

NICHOLSON, William
PRYDE, James
ROBERTSON, W. Graham
SIMPSON, Joseph

*Artists listed may have been in-
fluenced by the Schools rather than
have attended them as students.

# Appendix B

## Specialist Illustration

ARMFIELD, Maxwell
BILLINGHURST, P.J.
BOYLE, The Hon. Mrs. E.V.
BROCK, H.M.
BRUNTON, W.S.
CALTHROP, Dion Clayton
COLLINGWOOD, W.G.
CRUIKSHANK, George
DEARMER, Mrs. Percy
DOYLE, Charles Altamont
DOYLE, Richard
DULAC, Edmund
EDWARDS, K. Ellen
FITZGERALD, J. Anster
FORD, Henry Justice
GANDY, Herbert
GASKIN, Arthur J.
GERE, Charles March

### FAIRY ARTISTS

GILBERT, William Schwenk
GOBLE, Warwick
GREENAWAY, Kate
HALSWELLE, Keeley
HILL, Vernon
HASSALL, John
HARRISON, Florence
HOLLOWAY, W. Herbert
HOPE, Mrs. Adrian C.
HUDSON, Gwynedd M.
HUGHES, Arthur
JAMES, Gilbert
KNOWLES, H.J.
KNOWLES, R.J.
LANDSEER, Thomas
MAYBANK, Thomas
MILLAR, Harold R.

MONSELL, J.R.
PATON, Sir J. Noel
RACKHAM, Arthur
RAILTON, Fanny
RIVINGTON, Reginald
ROBERTSON, W. Graham
ROBINSON, Charles
ROBINSON, Thomas
ROBINSON, W. Heath
ROUNTREE, Harry
SANDERSON, H.
SAVAGE, Reginald
SPEED, Lancelot
STEWART, Allan
STRATTON, Helen
TORRANCE, James
UPTON, Florence K.
WOODWARD, Alice B.

| | |
|---|---|
| ANDREWS, G.H. | ILN |
| BELL, Joseph | ILN |
| BULL, René | Black and White |
| CARMICHAEL, J.W. | ILN |
| CORBOULD, Chantrey | ILN |
| GOODMAN, A. Jules | |
| | Pall Mall Gazette |
| HALE, E.M. | ILN |
| HALL, Sidney | Graphic |
| HENTY, G.A. | Standard |
| HOUGHTON, A. Boyd | Graphic |
| LANDELLS, Ebenezer | ILN |
| LANDELLS, R.T. | ILN |
| LARSON, Axel | ILN |
| LARSEN, C.C. | ILN |
| MACPHERSON, Douglas | Sphere |
| MATANIA, F. | Sphere |
| MAUD, W.T. | Graphic |

### SPECIAL ARTISTS

| | |
|---|---|
| MAXWELL, Donald | Graphic |
| MENPES, Mortimer | |
| | Black and White |
| MONTAGU, Irving | ILN |
| MORGAN, Matt | Illus. Times |
| NAST, J. | Various |
| NORBURY, E.A. | Graphic |
| PAGET, H.M. | Sphere |
| PELCOQ, Jules | ILN |
| PELLEGRINI, Ricardo | Graphic |
| PORTCH, Julian | Illus. Times |
| PRATER, Ernest | Black and White |
| PRICE, Julius M. | ILN |
| PRIOR, Melton | ILN |
| READ, Samuel | ILN |
| RÉGAMEY, F.E. | ILN |

| | |
|---|---|
| SCHONBERG, John | ILN |
| SIMPSON, William | ILN |
| SHELDON, C.M. | Black and White |
| SKILL, F.J. | ILN |
| TEBBY, A.K. | Graphic |
| VALENTIN, Henry | Various |
| VIZETELLY, Frank | ILN |
| VIZETELLY, Henry | ILN |
| WAKE, R. | Graphic |
| WATERS, D.B. | Graphic |
| WHITING, Fred | Graphic |
| WILLIAMS, I. SHELDON- | |
| | Graphic and Sphere |
| WILSON, T. Harrington | ILN |
| WILSON, T.W. | ILN |
| WOLLEN, W.B. | Graphic |
| WOODVILLE, R.C. | ILN |
| WRIGHT, H.C. Seppings | ILN |

# Monograms

 CADENHEAD,
James

 HOUSMAN,
Laurence

 CLAXTON,
Marshall C.

 FORBES,
Elizabeth Adela
née Armstrong,
Mrs. Stanhope Forbes

 HUGES,
Arthur

 COODE,
Miss Helen Hoppner

 JALLAND,
G.H.

  AWC COOPER,
Alfred W.

 FURNISS,
Harry

 KEENE,
Charles Samuel

JOHNSON,
Alfred J.

 CORBOULD
Aster Chantrey

 GAVIN,
Miss Jessie

 KEENE,
Charles Samuel

LLOYD,
Arthur Wynell

 CROWQUILL,
Alfred

 GREGORY,
Margaret

 LOWINSKY,
Thomas Esmond

 DOYLE,
Richard

 'GRIP'
pseudonym of
Alfred BRICE

 PARSONS,
Alfred

SANDERCOCK,
Henry Ardmore

 EMANUEL,
Frank Lewis

 HASSALL,
John

 TENNANT,
Dorothy, Lady Stanley

 THOMSON,
Gordon

 NE ERICHSEN,
Nelly

 HOOD,
George Percy JACOMB-

 WARD,
Sir Leslie Matthew
'Spy'

 FAIRFIELD,
A.R.

 HOPKINS,
Everard

 WATSON,
John Dawson

510

# Bibliography

## GENERAL 1800-1850

Abbey, J.R.
*Scenery of Great Britain and Ireland In Aquatint And Lithography 1770-1860 . . . from the library of J.R. Abbey.* 1952.
*Life in England in Aquatint and Lithography 1770-1860 . . . from the library of J.R. Abbey,* 1953.
*Travel In Aquatint And Lithography 1770-1860 . . . from the library of J.R. Abbey,* 2 vols., 1956-57.

Beck, Hilary
*Victorian Engravings,* Victoria and Albert Museum, 1973.

Darton, F.J. Harvey
*Children's Books in England,* 1932.

Faxon, F.W.
*Literary Annuals and Gift Books, a Bibliography,* edited by E. Jamieson and I. Bain, Private Libraries Assoc., 1973.

Harvey, J.R.
*Victorian Novelists and Their Illustrators,* 1970.

Jerdan, W.
*An Autobiography,* 4 vols., 1853.

Kitton, F.G.
*Dickens and his Illustrators,* 1899.

Leslie, C.R.
*Autobiographical Recollections,* 2 vols., 1860.

Linton, W.J.
*Memories,* 1895.

Pye, John
*Patronage of British Art — An Historical Sketch,* 1845.

Raimbach, A.
*Memoirs and Recollections . . . ,* 1843.

Spielmann, M.H.
*The History of 'Punch',* 1895.

Vizetelly, Henry
*Glances Back Over Seventy Years,* 2 vols., 1893.

## GENERAL 1860-1875

Dalziel Brothers
*A Record of Work, 1840-1890,* 1901.

Freedmann, W.E.
*Pre-Raphaelitism A Bibliographical Study,* 1965.

Layard, G.S.
*Tennyson and His Pre-Raphaelite Illustrators,* 1894.

Reid, Forrest
*Illustrators of the Sixties,* 1928.

Sparrow, W.S.
*Book Illustration of the Sixties,* 1939.

Tinsley, W.
*Random Recollections,* 1900.

White, Gleeson
*English Illustration 'The Sixties' 1857-70,* 1897.

## GENERAL 1890s

Franklin, Colin
*Private Presses, A Bibliography,* 1969.

Hartrick, A.S.
*Painter's Pilgrimage Through Fifty Years,* 1939.

Jackson, Holbrook
*The Eighteen-Nineties, A Review of Art and Ideas At the Close of the Nineteenth Century,* 1913.

Krishnamurti, G.
*The Eighteen-Nineties — A Literary Exhibition,* National Book League, 1973.

Ludovici, A.
*An Artist's Life in London and Paris,* 1926.

Pennell, Joseph
*Pen Drawing and Pen Draughtsmen,* 1889.
*Modern Illustration,* 1895.
*The Illustration of Books,* 1896.

Sketchley, R.E.D.
*English Book Illustration of Today,* 1903.

Taylor, John Russell
*The Art Nouveau Book in Britain,* 1966.

Thorpe, James
*English Illustration of the Nineties,* 1935.

## CARICATURE

Ashbee, C.R.
*Caricature,* 1928.

Ashton, John
*English Caricature and Satire on Napoleon I,* 1888.

Brinton, Selwyn
*The 18th Century in English Caricature,* 1904.

Buss, R.W.
*English Graphic Satire,* 1874. Privately printed.

Davies, Randall
Editor. *Caricature of Today,* Studio, 1928.

Everitt, Graham
*English Caricaturists and Graphic Humorists of the Nineteenth century,* 1893.

George, M. Dorothy
    *British Museum Catalogue of Political and Personal Satires*, Vols. V-XI, 1935-1954.
    *English Political Caricature*, 2 vols., 1959.

Hofmann, Werner
    *Caricature from Leonardo to Picasso*, 1957.

Klingender, F.D.
    *Hogarth and English Caricature*, 1944.

Low, David
    *British Cartoonists, Caricaturists and Comic Artists*, 1942.

Lynch, Bohun
    *History of Caricature*, 1927.

Malcolm, J.P.
    *Historical Sketch of the Art of Caricaturing*, 1813.

Parton, James
    *Caricature and Other Comic Art*, 1878.

Paston, George
    *Social Caricature in the 18th Century*, 1905.

Veth, Cornelis
    *Comic Art in England*, 1930.

Wright, Thomas
    *Caricature History of the Georges*, 1867.

## TECHNICAL

Hardie, Martin
    *English Coloured Books*, 1906.

McLean, Ruari
    *Victorian Book Design and Colour Printing*, 1963.

Lewis, C.T.C.
    *The Story of Picture Printing in England during the Nineteenth Century*, 1928.

Sullivan, E.J.
    *Line An Art Study*, 1921.
    *The Art of Illustration*, 1922.

Wakeman, Geoffrey
    *Victorian Book Illustration — The Technical Revolution*, 1973.

## SURVEYS

Bland, David
    *A History of Book Illustration — The Illuminated Manuscript and The Printed Book*, 1958.

Bliss, D.P.
    *A History of Wood Engraving*, 1928.

Chatto, W.A. & Jackson
    *A Treatise On Wood Engraving*, 1839, enlarged 1861.

Crane, Walter
    *Of The Decorative Illustration of Books Old and New*, 1896.

Dyos H.J. & Wolff
    *The Victorian City*, 1973.

Du Maurier, G.
    *Social Pictorial Satire*, 1898.

Hogarth, Paul
    *The Artist As Reporter*, 1967.

Jackson, Mason
    *The Pictorial Press Its Origins and Progress*, 1885.

James, Philip
    *English Book Illustration 1800-1900*, 1947.

Muir, Percy
    *Victorian Illustrated Books*, 1971.

Peppin, B.
    *Fantasy Book Illustration*, 1975.

Price, R.G.G.
    *A History of 'Punch'*, 1957.

Ray, Gordon N.
    *The Illustrator And The Book in England From 1790 to 1914*. Pierpoint Morgan Library, 1976.

Slythe, R. Margaret
    *The Art of Illustration 1750-1900*, Library Association, 1970.

\*    Bibliographies of individual artists will be found in their Dictionary entries.

# Index

This index covers pages 13-212 but not the 'Dictionary'. It has been divided into two parts to facilitate use: an index of persons and an index of general subjects, including book titles.

## Index of Persons

# General Index

# THE COMIC ALMANACK

MAY JUNE JULY AUG APR SEP MAR OCT FEB NOV JAN DEC

EDITED BY HORACE MAYHEW

& Illustrated BY George Cruikshank

1848.
ONE SHILLING.

DAVID BOGUE, 86 FLEET STREET.

Vizetelly Brothers and Co. Printers and Engravers, 135 Fleet Street.